October 5–8, 2014
Honolulu, HI, USA

Association for
Computing Machinery

Advancing Computing as a Science & Profession

UIST'14

Proceedings of the 27th Annual ACM Symposium on User Interface Software and Technology

Sponsored by:

ACM SIGCHI & ACM SIGGRAPH

Supported by:

University of Toronto, AutoDesk, Microsoft, Marvell, Synaptics, Adobe, GRAND, WaCom, FXPal, Google, University of Hawaii, IBM Research, Tactual Labs, Yahoo! Labs, & Disney Research

Association for
Computing Machinery

Advancing Computing as a Science & Profession

The Association for Computing Machinery
2 Penn Plaza, Suite 701
New York, New York 10121-0701

ISBN: 978-1-4503-3069-5 (Digital)

ISBN: 978-1-4503-3370-2 (Print)

Additional copies may be ordered prepaid from:

ACM Order Department
PO Box 30777
New York, NY 10087-0777, USA

Phone: 1-800-342-6626 (USA and Canada)
+1-212-626-0500 (Global)
Fax: +1-212-944-1318
E-mail: acmhelp@acm.org
Hours of Operation: 8:30 am – 4:30 pm ET

Printed in the USA

Chairs' Welcome

It is our pleasure to welcome you to the 27th Annual ACM Symposium on User Interface Software and Technology (UIST), held from October 5-8th 2014, in Honolulu, Hawaii, USA.

UIST is the premier forum for the presentation of research innovations in the software and technology of human-computer interfaces. Sponsored by ACM's special interest groups on computer-human interaction (SIGCHI) and computer graphics (SIGGRAPH), UIST brings together researchers and practitioners from many areas, including web and graphical interfaces, input and output devices, information visualization, sensing technologies, interactive displays, tabletop and tangible computing, interaction techniques, augmented and virtual reality, ubiquitous computing, fabrication, wearable and mobile computing, and computer supported cooperative work.

UIST 2014 received a record 333 technical paper submissions from 34 countries. After a thorough review process, the 36-member program committee accepted 74 papers (22.2%). Each anonymous submission was first reviewed by three external reviewers, and a meta-review was provided by a program committee member. If any of the four reviewers deemed a submission to pass a rejection threshold, we asked the authors to submit a short rebuttal addressing the reviewers' concerns, and a second member of the program committee was asked to examine the paper, rebuttal, and reviews, and to provide their own meta-review. The program committee met in person in Toronto, Ontario, Canada on June 19th and 20th, 2014, to select which papers to invite for the program. Submissions were accepted only after the authors provided a final revision addressing the committee's comments.

In addition to papers submitted directly, the symposium program includes two papers from the ACM Transactions on Computer-Human Interaction journal (TOCHI), as well as 31 posters, 48 demonstrations, and 8 student presentations in the tenth annual Doctoral Symposium. Our program also features the sixth annual Student Innovation Contest. This year, there are 24 teams taking part in the contest, which is focused on household interfaces based on the *Kinoma Create* platform by Marvell. UIST 2014 will feature two keynote presentations. The opening keynote will be given by Mark Bolas (University of Southern California) on designing the user in the user interface. Bret Victor will deliver the closing keynote on the impact of dynamic media on representation of thought.

Our community has been growing tremendously both in the number of submissions as well as attendees. For the first time, this year's program will be held in two parallel tracks. We hope that you will find our program interesting and thought-provoking and that UIST 2014 will provide you with a valuable opportunity to exchange results at the cutting edge of user interfaces research, to meet friends and colleagues, and to forge future collaborations with other researchers and practitioners from institutions around the world.

Hrvoje Benko
UIST'14 General Chair
Microsoft Research, USA

Mira Dontcheva
UIST'14 Program Co-Chair
Adobe, USA

Daniel Wigdor
UIST'14 Program Co-Chair
University of Toronto, Canada

Table of Contents

Session 4: Novel Hardware I

Session 5: Modeling and Prediction

Session 6: Developer Tools I

Session 7: Fabrication

Session 8: Augmented Reality I

Session 9: Novel Hardware II

Session 10: Creative Tools

Session 11: Collaboration

Session 12: Touch & Gesture

Session 16: Developer Tools II

Closing Keynote Address

UIST 2014 Symposium Organization

General Chair:	Hrvoje Benko *(Microsoft Research, USA)*
Program Chairs:	Mira Dontcheva *(Adobe, USA)* Daniel Wigdor *(University of Toronto, USA)*
Poster Chairs:	Daniel Vogel *(University of Waterloo, Canada)* Gery Casiez *(University of Lille, France)*
Demonstration Chairs:	Per Ola Kristensson *(University of St. Andrews, UK)* Nicolai Marquardt *(University College London, UK)*
Doctoral Symposium Chair:	Patrick Baudisch *(Hasso Plattner Institute, Germany)*
Student Contest Chairs:	David Kim *(Newcastle University, UK)* Valkyrie Savage *(University of California Berkeley, USA)*
Video Previews Chairs:	Fanny Chevalier *(University of Toronto, Canada)* Stéphane Huot *(Université Paris-Sud, France)*
Registration Chairs:	Jakub Dostal *(University of St. Andrews, UK)* Siddharth Khullar *(Quanttus Inc., USA)*
Treasurer:	Kirstie Magness *(Microsoft Research, USA)*
Sponsorship:	Roel Vertegaal *(Queen's University, Canada)*
Proceedings Chair:	Clifton Forlines *(Tactual Labs, Canada)*
Local Arrangements Chair:	Scott Robertson *(University of Hawaii, USA)*
Student Volunteer Chairs:	Stefanie Mueller *(Hasso Plattner Institute, Germany)* Daniel Leithinger *(MIT Media Lab, USA)*
Web and Social Media Chair:	Florian Daiber *(DFKI, Germany)*
Publicity Chairs:	Chris Harrison *(Carnegie Mellon University, USA)* Kentaro Fukuchi *(Meiji University, Japan)*
Keynote Chair:	Otmar Hilliges *(ETH Zurich, Switzerland)*
Lasting Impact Award Chair:	Ken Hinckley *(Microsoft Research, USA)*
Interactive Program Guide Chairs:	Stephen Oney *(Carnegie Mellon University, USA)* Jason Wiese *(Carnegie Mellon University, USA)* Eiji Hayashi *(Carnegie Mellon University, USA)*
Design/Signage Chair:	Asta Roseway *(Microsoft Research, USA)*

Beach Chair: T. Scott Saponas *(Microsoft Research, USA)*

Program Committee: Maneesh Agrawala *(University of California Berkeley, USA)*
Saleema Amershi *(Microsoft Research, USA)*
Michael Bernstein *(Stanford University, USA)*
Floraine Berthouzoz *(Adobe Research, USA)*
Bernd Bickel *(Disney Research, USA)*
Jeff Bigham *(Carnegie Mellon University, USA)*
Joel Brandt *(Adobe Research, USA)*
Fanny Chevalier *(University of Toronto, Canada)*
Steven Drucker *(Microsoft Research, USA)*
Steve Feiner *(Columbia University, USA)*
Cliff Forlines *(Tactual Labs, Canada)*
Mark Gross *(University of Colorado Boulder, USA)*
Tovi Grossman *(Autodesk, Canada)*
Francois Guimbretiere *(Cornell University, USA)*
Otmar Hilliges *(ETH Zurich, Switzerland)*
Ken Hinckley *(Microsoft Research, USA)*
Eve Hoggan *(Helsinki Institute for Information Technology, Finland)*
Christian Holz *(Yahoo! Labs, USA)*
Pourang Irani *(University of Manitoba, Canada)*
Jun Kato *(AIST, Japan)*
Darren Leigh *(Tactual Labs, Canada)*
Yang Li *(Google Research, USA)*
Kent Lyons *(Yahoo! Labs, USA)*
Wendy MacKay *(INRIA, France)*
Meredith Ringel Morris *(Microsoft Research, USA)*
Tomer Moscovich *(Lab 126, USA)*
Brad Myers *(Carnegie Mellon University, USA)*
Jeff Nichols *(IBM Research, USA)*
Alex Olwal *(Google, USA)*
m.c. schraefel *(University of Southampton, UK)*
Sriram Subramanian *(University of Bristol, UK)*
Bruce Thomas *(University of South Australia, Australia)*
Gina Venolia *(Microsoft Research, USA)*
Daniel Vogel *(University of Waterloo, Canada)*
Jue Wang *(Adobe Research, USA)*
Andy Wilson *(Microsoft Research, USA)*

Doctoral Symposium Committee: Meredith Ringel Morris *(Microsoft Research, USA)*
m.c. schraefel *(University of Southampton, UK)*
Scott Hudson *(Carnegie Mellon University, USA)*

UIST 2014 Reviewers

Konstantin Aal
David Abraham
Mark Ackerman
Aseem Agarwala
Teemu Ahmaniemi
Imeh Akpan
Jason Alexander
Ahmad Aljadaan
Robert Allison
Fraser Anderson
Paul André
Michelle Annett
Alissa Antle
Caroline Appert
Bruno Araujo
Daniel Archambault
Ahmed Arif
Daniel Ashbrook
Ignacio Avellino
Daniel Avrahami
Magnus Axholt
Shiri Azenkot
Ron Azuma
Pierre Bénard
François Bérard
benjamin bach
Seok-Hyung Bae
Ronald Baecker
Brian Bailey
Gilles Bailly
Ravin Balakrishnan
Rafael Ballagas
Nikola Banovic
Jakob Bardram
Connelly Barnes
Sumit Basu
Olivier Bau
Thomas Baudel
Patrick Baudisch
Jean-Charles Bazin
Paul Beardsley
Michel Beaudouin-Lafon
Roman Bednarik
Serge Belongie
Steve Benford
Hrvoje Benko
Edward Benson
Marina Bers
Anastasia Bezerianos
Xiaojun Bi
Jacob Biehl
Eric Bier
Mark Billinghurst
Oliver Bimber
Renaud Blanch
Dan Bohus
David Bonnet
Kellogg Booth
Jan Borchers
Sebastian Boring
Sebastian Boring
Jonathan Botts
Patrick Bourdot
Adrien Bousseau
Doug Bowman
Jordan Boyd-Graber
Erin Brady
Andrew Bragdon
Stacy Branham
Helene Brashear
Karen Brennan
Stephen Brewster
Anke Brock
Eric Brockmeyer
Dave Brown
A.J. Brush
Nick Bryan-Kinns
Leah Buechley
Abdullah Bulbul
Andreas Bulling
Andrea Bunt
Margaret Burnett
D. Alex Butler
Andreas Butz
Bill Buxton
John Canny
Xiang Cao
Thomas Carter
Scott Carter
Géry Casiez
Steven Castellucci
Jessica Cauchard
Amira Chalbi
Liwei Chan
Remco Chang
Kerry Chang
Olivier Chapuis
Duen Horng (Polo) Chau
Siddhartha Chaudhuri
Ciprian Chelba
Alex Qiang Chen
Tao Chen
Nicholas Chen
Hsiang-Ting Chen
Jiawen Chen
Mike Chen
Xiang 'Anthony' Chen
Shiwei Cheng
Lung-Pan Cheng
Erin Cherry
Marshini Chetty
Fanny Chevalier
Pei-Yu Chi
Ed Chi
Lydia Chilton
Alvin Chin
Ming Ki Chong
Philip Chou
Tanzeem Choudhury
Michael Christel
James Clawson
Adrian Clear
Andy Cockburn
Michael Cohen
Gabe Cohn
Andrea Colaco
Sunny Consolvo
Stéphane Conversy
Jeremy Cooperstock
Nikolaus Correll
Dan Cosley
James Coughlan
Céline Coutrix
David Coyle
Michael Crabb
Jácome Cunha
Brian Curless
Allen Cypher
Tanja Döring
Marian Dörk
Laura Dabbish
Raimund Dachselt
Florian Daiber
Nicholas Dalton
Andreea Danielescu
Catalina Danis
Abe Davis
Nicholas Davis
Munmun De Choudhury
Alexander De Luca
David Dearman
Rob DeLine
Nick Demopoulos
Jia Deng
Anind Dey
Nicholas Diakopoulos
Paul Dietz
Danny Dig
Alan Dix
Morgan Dixon
Mingsong Dou
Paul Dourish
Steven Dow
Pierre Dragicevic
Nicolas Ducheneaut
Susan Dumais
Mark Dunlop
Paul Dunphy
Tim Dwyer
James Eagan
Florian Echtler
Keith Edwards
Serge Egelman
Michael Eisenberg
Jacob Eisenstein
Stephen Ellis
Alex Endert
Stephen Fairclough
Shelly Farnham
Ethan Fast
Jean-Daniel Fekete
Adrienne Felt
Ylva Fernaeus
Roland Fernandez

Jennifer Fernquist
Bruce Ferwerda
Rebecca Fiebrink
Leah Findlater
Andrew Fiore
Danyel Fisher
Stephen Fitchett
George Fitzmaurice
Geraldine Fitzpatrick
Morten Fjeld
Scott Fleming
James Fogarty
Sean Follmer
Adam Fourney
Euan Freeman
Dustin Freeman
Adrian Friday
Bernd Froehlich
Jon Froehlich
Hongbo Fu
Jun Fujima
Bill Fulton
Thomas Funkhouser
Krzysztof Gajos
Maribeth Gandy
Jizhou Gao
Jérémie Garcia
Henry Gardner
William Gaver
Hans Gellersen
Aaron Genest
Elizabeth Gerber
Kiel Gilleade
Yotam Gingold
Shiry Ginosar
Andreas Girgensohn
Mike Glaser
Michael Glueck
Mayank Goel
Dan Goldman
Richard Gomer
Liang Gou
Raphael Grasset
Keith Green
Mike Greenberg
Michael Greenberg
Saul Greenberg
Laurent Grisoni
Paul Gross
Jens Grubert
Jonathan Grudin
Jinwei Gu
Yves Guiard
Philip Guo
Sidhant Gupta
Ankit Gupta
Sean Gustafson
Carl Gutwin
Sinem Guven
Tobias Höllerer
Martin Hachet
Alaa Halawani
Michael Haller
Nur Al-huda Hamdan
Tracy Hammond
Jaehyun Han
Mark Hancock
richard harper
Chris Harrison
Björn Hartmann
Khalad Hasan
Jennifer Healey
Marti Hearst
Jeffrey Heer
Kurtis Heimerl
Robert Held
Florian Heller
Nathalie Henry Riche
Christin Henzen
Aaron Hertzmann
Otmar Hilliges
Serena Hillman
Juan David Hincapié-Ramos
Uta Hinrichs
Michitaka Hirose
Leanne Hirshfield
Shinsaku Hiura
Steve Hodges
Jeffery Hoehl
James Hollan
Jason Hong
M. Ehsan Hoque
Michael Horn
Kasper Hornbæ
Eva Hornecker
John Horton
Chang Hu
Jeff Huang
Yingdan Huang
Scott Hudson
Matt Huenerfauth
Julie Hui
Jessica Hullman
Seth Hunter
Stephane Huot
Amy Hurst
Takeo Igarashi
Masahiko Inami
Kori Inkpen
Stephen Intille
Shamsi Iqbal
Petra Isenberg
Tobias Isenberg
Edward Ishak
Yoshio Ishiguro
Hiroshi Ishii
Suguru Ishizaki
Poika Isokoski
Ali Israr
Howell Istance
Shahram Izadi
Melody Jackson
Robert Jacob
An Jacobs
Giulio Jacucci
Sushant Jain
Ghita Jalal
Jacek Jankowski
Yvonne Jansen
Alex Jansen
Kenneth Jay
Chandrika Jayant
Haojian Jin
Gabe Johnson
Brett Jones
Ricardo Jota
Wendy Ju
Sasa Junuzovic
Antti Jylhä
Yasuaki Kakehi
Evangelos Kalogerakis
Ece Kamar
Gila Kamhi
Eser Kandogan
Shaun Kane
Emre Karagozler
Karrie Karahalios
Maria Karam
David Karger
Abhijit Karnik
Hirokazu Kato
Danny Kaufman
Joseph 'Jofish' Kaye
Rubaiat Habib Kazi
Daniel Keefe
Caitlin Kelleher
Caitlin Kelleher
Sean Keller
Patrick Gage Kelley
Aisling Kelliher
Wendy Kellogg
Lyndon Kennedy
Andruid Kerne
Cem Keskin
Hamed Ketabdar
Azam Khan
Julie Kientz
Wolf Kienzle
Juho Kim
David Kim
Joy Kim
Jeeeun Kim
Kenrick Kin
Yoshifumi Kitamura
Kris Kitani
Kiyoshi Kiyokawa
Scott Klemmer
Gudrun Klinker
Eric Klopfer
Andrew Ko
Kenneth Koedinger
Jeffrey Tzu Kwan Valino Koh
Mark Kohler
Hideki Koike
Johannes Kopf
Jan-Peter Krämer
Antonio Krüger
Sven Kratz
Sivam Krish
Per Ola Kristensson

Ernst Kruijff
Todd Kulesza
Alexander Kulik
Chinmay Kulkarni
Ranjitha Kumar
Kai Kunze
Stacey Kuznetsov
Irwin Kwan
Hyo Sun Kwon
Anatole Lécuyer
Markus Löchtefeld
Ben Lafreniere
Shyong Lam
Heidi Lam
James Landay
Joel Lanir
Edward Lank
Gierad Laput
Eric Larson
Walter Lasecki
Celine Latulipe
Manfred Lau
Tessa Lau
Joseph LaViola Jr.
Edith Law
Matthew Lease
Eric Lecolinet
Bongshin Lee
Jinha Lee
Unseok Lee
Woohun Lee
Johnny Lee
Geehyuk Lee
Seungyon "Claire" Lee
Daniel Leithinger
Catherine Letondal
Golan Levin
Hao Li
Wilmot Li
Wei Li
Kevin Li
Thomas Lieber
Daniel Liebling
Jialiu Lin
Sharon Lin
Rhema Linder
David Lindlbauer
Agnes Lisowska Masson
Greg Little
Can Liu
Zhicheng Liu
Shixia Liu
Yen-Ting Liu
Mark Livingston
Corinna Loeckenhoff
Benjamin Lok
Pedro Lopes
Fabien Lotte
Danielle Lottridge
Hao Lu
Zhihan Lu
Andrés Lucero
Paul Lukowicz
Aran Lunzer
Kurt Luther
Christof Lutteroth
Kris Luyten
zhihan lv
Max Mühlhäuser
Jörg Müller
Blair MacIntyre
Scott MacKenzie
Pattie Maes
Jalal Mahmud
Andrew Maimone
Aditi Majumder
Lena Mamykina
Jennifer Mankoff
Gary Marchionini
Adam Marcus
Anders Markussen
Jennifer Marlow
Nicolai Marquardt
Kim Marriott
Diego Martinez Plasencia
Kenji Mase
Michael Massimi
Toshiyuki Masui
Justin Matejka
Justin Mathew
Noboru Matsuda
Tara Matthews
Kevin Matzen
Nolwenn Maudet
Walterio Mayol-Cuevas
James McCann
Jim McCann
Neil McCurdy
Sean McDirmid
David McGookin
William McGrath
Michael McGuffin
Andrew McPherson
Amir Meghdadi
David Mellis
Nemanja Memarovic
Sarah Mennicken
Paul Merrell
David Merrill
Ronald Metoyer
Natasa Milic-Frayling
Robert Miller
Nick Miller
Mark Mine
Niloy Mitra
Neema Moraveji
Dan Morris
Martez Mott
Bradford Mott
Stefanie Mueller
Florian Mueller
Sean Munson
Gail Murphy
Roderick Murray-Smith
Gautham Mysore
Mor Naaman
Miguel Nacenta
George Nagy
Naoto Nakazato
Mathieu Nancel
Michael Nebeling
Carman Neustaedter
Richard Newcombe
David Nguyen
Moira Norrie
Chris North
Frank Noz
Antti Nurminen
Ian Oakley
Marianna Obrist
Yoichi Ochiai
Peter O'Donovan
Lora Oehlberg
Hyunjoo Oh
Patrick Olivier
Inah Omoronyia
Stephen Oney
Carol O'Sullivan
Mai Otsuki
Antti Oulasvirta
Tom Ouyang
Sharon Oviatt
Neri Oxman
Tim Paek
Michel Pahud
Dinesh Pai
Aditya Pal
Leysia Palen
Xueni Pan
Tapan Parikh
Taiwoo Park
Andrea Parker
Amanda Parkes
Kurt Partridge
Kayur Patel
Shwetak Patel
Fabio Paternò
Donald Patterson
Neal Patwari
Reena Pau
Eric Paulos
Amy Pavel
Fabrizio Pece
Huaishu Peng
Alex Pentland
Lucas Pereira
Charles Perin
Trevor Pering
Annuska Perkins
Ken Perlin
Simon Perrault
Saverio Perugini
Jeffrey Pierce
James Pierce
Emmanuel Pietriga
Matthew Pike
Clément Pillias
Anne Marie Piper
Pol Pla
Henning Pohl
Franck Poirier
Suporn Pongnumkul

Erika Poole
Ivan Poupyrev
John Pruitt
Jie Qi
Yin Qu
John Quarles
John Quarles
Aaron Quigley
Stefan Rüger
Mashfiqui Rabbi
Emilee Rader
Hayes Raffle
Nitendra Rajput
Raf Ramakers
Gonzalo Ramos
Roberto Ranon
Jussi Rantala
Ramesh Raskar
Majken Kirkegaard Rasmussen
Kyle Rector
David Redmiles
Colorado Reed
Holger Regenbrecht
Derek Reilly
Steven Reiss
Jun Rekimoto
Xiangshi Ren
Philippe Renevier Gonin
Alexander Repenning
Mitchel Resnick
Penny Rheingans
Stephan Richter
Julie Rico
Alec Rivers
Tom Rodden
Daniel Roggen
Michael Rohs
Jannick Rolland
Ilya Rosenberg
Anne Roudaut
Thijs Roumen
Nicolas Roussel
Steve Rubin
Jaime Ruiz
Enrico Rukzio
Bryan Russell
Daniel Russell
Kimiko Ryokai
Jeffrey Rzeszotarski
Gábor Sörös
Daniel Saakes
Ramik Sadana
Adam Sadilek
Daisuke Sakamoto
Christian Sandor
T. Saponas
Sayan Sarcar
Arvind Satyanarayan
Greg Saul
Valkyrie Savage
Lauri Savioja
Manolis Savva
Christopher Scaffidi
Johannes Schöning
Florian Schaub
Dieter Schmalstieg
Chris Schmandt
Dominik Schmidt
Ryan Schmidt
Ryan Schubert
Julia Schwarz
James Scott
Stacey Scott
Sue Ann Seah
Julian Seifert
Kate Sellen
Abigail Sellen
Marcos Serrano
Peter Sestoft
Orit Shaer
Chirag Shah
Ariel Shamir
David Shamma
Ryan Benjamin Shapiro
Ehud Sharlin
Aaron Shaw
Eli Shechtman
Chia Shen
Karthik Sheshadri
Buntarou Shizuki
Ben Shneiderman
Garth Shoemaker
Mike Sinclair
Ronit Slyper
Mark Smith
Ross Smith
Brian Smith
Boris Smus
Noah Snavely
Kiley Sobel
Rajinder Sodhi
Erin Solovey
Jie Song
Hyunyoung Song
Alexander Sorkine-Hornung
Michiel Sovijärvi-Spape
Daniel Spelmezan
Robert St. Amant
Kay Stanney
Thad Starner
John Stasko
Anthony Steed
Jürgen Steimle
Frank Steinicke
Sophie Stellmach
Craig Stewart
James Stewart
Maureen Stone
Daniel Strazzulla
Daniel Strazzulla
Wolfgang Stuerzlinger
Simone Stumpf
Simon Stusak
Oezge Subasi
Ozge Subasi
Maki Sugimoto
Yuta Sugiura
Mengu Sukan
Sudeep Sundaram
Leila Takayama
Kentaro Takemura
Desney Tan
John Tang
Anthony Tang
Steven Tanimoto
Alex Taylor
Robert Teather
Jaime Teevan
Alexandru Telea
Michael Terry
Anuj Tewari
William Thies
James Tompkin
Cesar Torres
Melanie Tory
Caroline Traube
Adrien Treuille
Khai Truong
Theophanis Tsandilas
Nicolas Tsingos
Kathleen Tuite
Jayson Turner
George Tzanetakis
Brygg Ullmer
Marynel Vázquez
Kaisa Väänänen-Vainio-Mattila
Daniel Västfjäll
Rajan Vaish
Dimitar Valkov
Jan Van den Bergh
Kristof Van Laerhoven
Brad Vander Zanden
Lucy Vanderwende
Giovanni Vannucci
Aditya Vashistha
Radu-Daniel Vatavu
Ansh Verma
Arnold Vermeeren
Frederic Vernier
Roel Vertegaal
Chi Vi
Nicolas Villar
Simon Voelker
Juergen Vogel
Stephen Voida
Romain Vuillemot
Chat Wacharamanotham
Julie Wagner
Daniel Wagner
Ron Wakkary
James Wallace
Jagoda Walny
Yan Wang
Jingtao Wang
Feng Wang
Hao-Chuan Wang
Yi Wang
Roy Want
Jamie Ward

Peter Wardrip
Junji Watanabe
Martin Wattenberg
Jenny Waycott
Andrew Webb
Gerhard Weber
Carolyn Wei
Christian Weichel
Malte Weiss
Gregory Welch
Michael Weller
Stephan Wenger
Jonathan Westhues
reto wettach
Gordon Wetzstein
Sean White
Emily Whiting
Steve Whittaker
Alexander Wiethoff
Daniel Wigdor
Wesley Willett
John Williamson
Karl Willis
Graham Wilson
Max Wilson
Raphael Wimmer
Holger Winnemoeller
Jason Wither
Jacob Wobbrock
Kanit Wongsuphasawat
Woontack Woo
Allison Woodruff
Charles Woodward
Leslie Wu
Robert Xiao
Jianxiong Xiao
Cheng Xu
Xing-Dong Yang
Angela Yao
Lining Yao
Koji Yatani
Tom Yeh
William Yerazunis
Sai-Kit Yeung
Chuang-wen You
James Young
Massimo Zancanaro
Klaus-peter Zauner
Shumin Zhai
Haoqi Zhang
Hao (Richard) Zhang
Zhengyou Zhang
Yanxia Zhang
Haimo Zhang
Shengdong Zhao
Jian Zhao
Mianwei Zhou
Jamie Zigelbaum
John Zimmerman
Oleksandr Zinenko
Amit Zoran
Vinayak

UIST 2014 Sponsors & Supporters

UIST 2014 gratefully acknowledges our sponsoring SIGs and the support of the following organizations:

Sponsors

SIGCHI

ACM SIGGRAPH

Program Committee Meeting Sponsor

Computer Science
UNIVERSITY OF TORONTO

Platinum Supporters

AUTODESK.

Microsoft

Gold Supporters

MARVELL®

Synaptics®

Silver Supporters

Adobe®

GRAND

wacom®

Bronze Supporters

FXPAL
PALO ALTO LABORATORY

Google

HICHI
Hawaii
Computer-Human Interaction Lab
Information and Computer Sciences
University of Hawai'i at Mānoa

Bronze Supporters (Continued)

IBM Research

Tactual Labs

YAHOO! LABS

Friend of UIST

Disney Research

Designing the User in User Interfaces

Mark Bolas
Director for Mixed Reality Research
Institute for Creative Technologies
Associate Professor
USC School of Cinematic Arts Interactive Media Division

ABSTRACT
In the good old days, the human was here, the computer there, and a good living was to be made by designing ways to interface between the two. Now we find ourselves unthinkingly pinching to zoom in on a picture in a paper magazine. User interfaces are changing instinctual human behavior and instinctual human behavior is changing user interfaces. We point or look left in the "virtual" world just as we point or look left in the physical.

It is clear that nothing is clear anymore: the need for "interface" vanishes when the boundaries between the physical and the virtual disappear. We are at a watershed moment when to experience being human means to experience being machine. When there is not a user interface - it is just what you do. When instinct supplants mice and menus and the interface insinuates itself into the human psyche.

We are redefining and creating what it means to be human in this new physical/virtual integrated reality - we are not just designing user interfaces, we are designing users.

Author Keywords
user interace; virtual reality; posthuman factors; transhumanism; mixed reality

ACM Classification Keywords
H.5.2 User Interfaces (D.2.2, H.1.2, I.3.6): Prototyping

BIO
Mark Bolas is the Director of the Mixed Reality Lab at the USC Institute of Creative Technologies and an Associate Professor in the Interactive Media & Games division of the School of Cinematic Arts, where he directs the Mixed Reality Studio. His work focuses on researching perception, agency, and intelligence - creating virtual environments and transducers that fully engage one's perception and cognition to create a visceral memory of the experience.

Bolas leads research projects for the Army Research Office, the Office of Naval Research, and DARPA, as well as a variety of other clients, including content for the entertainment industry. He has led the development of a number of influential products including the open-source FOV2GO, which informed the design of the Oculus Rift; the Wide-5 HMD; Pinch interface gloves; and the Boom and Molly telepresence system. Bolas' 1988-89 thesis work "Design and Virtual Environments" was the first effort to map the breadth of virtual reality as a new medium.

In addition to USC, he has taught at Stanford University and Keio University, exploring tangible interfaces, augmented reality, and computational illumination. These projects have explored context-sensitive audio interfaces, socially interactive toys, augmented reality, confocal illumination, and mobile phone web logging.

Bolas co-founded Fakespace Labs, Inc. in 1988 and developed and sold VR hardware and systems for dozens of major research labs over the decades. He holds more than twenty patents and has been recognized with awards from the Consumer Electronics Association, Popular Science, SIGGRAPH Best Emerging Technology, IEEE's Industry Excellence, and IEEE's Virtual Reality Technical Achievement Award.

UIST'14, October 5-8, 2014, & *SUI'14,* October 4–5, 2014, Honolulu, HI, USA.
ACM 978-1-4503-3069-5/14/10.
http://dx.doi.org/10.1145/2642918.2642919

A Series of Tubes: Adding Interactivity to 3D Prints Using Internal Pipes

Valkyrie Savage †⋆
valkyrie@eecs.berkeley.edu

Ryan Schmidt †
ryan.schmidt@autodesk.com

Tovi Grossman †
tovi.grossman@autodesk.com

George Fitzmaurice †
george.fitzmaurice@autodesk.com

Björn Hartmann ⋆
bjoern@eecs.berkeley.edu

† Autodesk Research
⋆ UC Berkeley EECS

Figure 1. A collection of interactive objects designed using our tool. All have electronic sensing or actuation components routed through their *interior*. Left: a radio, haptic feedback rabbit, maze, and presence-aware pen holder. Center: touch-sensitive toys. Right: custom neon signs.

ABSTRACT

3D printers offer extraordinary flexibility for prototyping the shape and mechanical function of objects. We investigate how 3D models can be modified to facilitate the creation of *interactive* objects offering dynamic input and output. We introduce a general technique to support rapidly prototyping interactivity by removing interior material from 3D models to form internal pipes. We describe the design space of pipes for interaction design, where variables include openings, path constraints, topologies, and inserted media. We then present PipeDream, a tool for routing internal pipes through 3D models, integrated within a 3D modeling program. We use two distinct routing algorithms. The first has users define pipes' terminals and uses path routing and physics-based simulation to minimize pipe bending energy, allowing easy insertion of media post-print. The second lets users supply a desired internal shape to which it fits a pipe route: for this we describe a graph-routing algorithm. We present prototypes created using our tool showing its flexibility and potential.

Author Keywords

Fabrication; 3D Printing; Interactive Objects; Design Tools

ACM Classification Keywords

H.5.2 [User Interfaces (D.2.2, H.1.2, I.3.6)]: Prototyping.

UIST '14, Oct 05-08 2014, Honolulu, HI, USA
ACM 978-1-4503-3069-5/14/10.
http://dx.doi.org/10.1145/2642918.2647374

INTRODUCTION

Makers, researchers, and professional designers (jointly "makers" in this paper) increasingly leverage 3D printers as tools for design work. A wide array of objects, from toy figurines to video game controllers and jet engine blades, are now prototyped or even manufactured using these machines. Most models fabricated on 3D printers today are passive: they express the form, but not the interactivity, of an object.

Recently, human-computer interaction researchers have begun to explore adding interaction to 3D printed objects by creating appropriate structures inside those objects. They have introduced techniques such as printed light pipes [30] and printed hollow chambers for air pressure sensing [26]. These projects introduce point examples of particular techniques. In this paper we present a systematic design space of 3D printed pipes and cavities, and introduce a design tool enabling makers to add interactivity to their models using internal pipes.

This paper introduces a novel tool that provides path planning and other high-level functionality to support the design of interior pipes and cavities within 3D models. These pipes can be filled, post-print, with a variety of media to enable input, display, and tactile feedback. This *subtractive* approach is complementary to *additive* approaches that inject custom print materials, such as conductors, during the actual printing process [25]. While our approach requires some manual assembly after a print completes, it gives makers the opportunity to cheaply and rapidly prototype a range of interactive objects on 3D printers, including popular single-material fused-deposition modeling machines (colored objects in Figure 1). Our software contributions can also provide useful modeling capabilities for future multi-material printers, e.g., printers that that are able to deposit conductive materials directly, without manual assembly.

We describe a new design space of pipes for the purpose of interaction design, where variables include openings, path constraints, topologies, and inserted media. By exploring this design space, new opportunities for adding interactivity to 3D printed objects can be realized. For example, injecting conductive paint can turn pipes into conductors, which can in turn integrate electronic components into prints; electroluminescent (EL) wire can be threaded through pipes to create computer-controlled visual output; or air can be pumped through pipes to produce haptic effects. Existing sensing and actuation approaches, such as FlyEye [33], swept-frequency capacitive sensing [21], and Jamming User Interfaces [4], can be expanded to new contexts using pipes: makers utilizing such I/O strategies can locate input and output at arbitrary points on a printed 3D object's surface. We leverage these existing techniques for sensing and actuation while our work's novelty is in *internal modeling* for 3D printing and the *redirection* of I/O to or through arbitrary locations on a device.

Figure 1 shows a collection of interactive objects fabricated with the help of internal pipes. These objects can sense touch, detect object presence, generate haptic feedback, or show internal illumination. They could also contain other active and passive electronic components. However, manually modeling appropriate pipes for such functionality is not trivial. For one, many 3D modelling tools do not provide extensive tools for modelling the *interior* of 3D models. Furthermore, careful consideration needs to go into the design and routing of pipes when they are used to add interactivity. Pipes need maximum possible bend radius to ease the insertion of media post-print. Independent pipes cannot intersect, as this could lead to electrical shorting or other problems. Pipes should not pass too close to the surface: consumer-grade 3D printers do not guarantee air- or water-tightness of prints, so more than one printed layer may be required to prevent leakage. Pipes for applications like illuminated EL wire signs must allow a single pipe to follow a specific path (e.g., for writing text).

We contribute PipeDream, an interactive design tool for interior pipes. Our system addresses various challenges makers are likely to encounter, such as avoiding intersections and ensuring maximum bend angles. PipeDream offers 3D point-to-point routing of internal pipes based on physical simulation of flexible rods, and a graph algorithm-based path tracing technique for path-constrained pipes. We present a set of example objects, designed with the help of our tool, that demonstrate different interaction modalities. We conclude by discussing limitations and outlining areas for future exploration.

RELATED WORK

Our contributions relate to other efforts aiming to add interactivity to digitally fabricated objects and to techniques for routing and model modification.

Fabrication of Interactive Devices

Previous work has begun to investigate how to fabricate interactive objects using particular sensing and display technologies. Printed Optics [30] uses light pipes to create integrated displays and senses input optically through components added at print time, while Slyper et al., [26] fabricate flexible robot armatures capable of sensing interaction via changes in air pressure. Our work is inspired by these projects, and contributes a general design tool for modelling objects that can have such capabilities.

Sauron [22] tracks interactions with printed physical mechanisms by placing a camera inside hollow objects, where all components must be visible to it. Our technique instead can work with arbitrary, solid models and only carves pipes for interaction where needed. Midas [23] generates fabrication files for custom capacitive touch sensors. Their technique is limited to planar and unfoldable shapes, as it routes connections on the surface of objects. PipeDream can also be used for touch sensing, but routes conductors *through* objects.

Fabrication with Printed Electronics

Researchers are investigating how to print conductors and place electronic components as part of additive manufacturing. Sells, et al., [25] use a heated syringe to deposit metal in printed 2D circuitboard channels on objects' surfaces. Other experiments done by the RepRap project[1] use plastic filament blended with conductive materials, however the resistance is currently too high to be useful in circuitry. Sarik, et al., [20] use aerosol jetting of conductive material onto printed objects. Park, et al., [17] and Majidi, et al., [10] inject liquid metals, and Hudson [7] provides techniques for embedding conductive thread and other electronics within felted objects. Our approach does not deposit these materials automatically, but creates structures inside a model that make manual post-print injection of conductive ink possible.

Interaction for Fabrication vs. Fabrication for Interaction

HCI researchers are also developing novel interaction techniques for providing input to digital fabrication machines [13, 29, 32], new applications to extend machine capabilities [12, 7], and new hybrid hand tools that combine manual processes with digital fabrication [19, 36]. These projects are complementary as they target different aspects of the design process, though it is conceivable that our pipe design tools be added to AR modeling interfaces like MixFab [29].

Routing and Internal Modeling

Part of our contribution comprises algorithms and techniques for routing tubes through 3D objects. Circuitboard routing algorithms, such as Lee's maze router [8], assume 2D surfaces. Multi-layer boards consist of stacked 2D layers connected by vias. We compute true 3D point-to-point routing though the interior of solid models with flexible paths. This approach has been used in one-off designs [16] but we are not aware of design tools for this purpose.

Some prior work has also focused on modifying interior parts of 3D objects. In Make it Stand [18], material is removed from the interior of objects with the goal of changing their center of gravity. Infrastructs [31] encodes information using interior cavities that can be sensed using terahertz imaging. Bickel, et al., [1] enforced deformation behavior with multi-material blending inside objects. Modeling internal chambers

[1] `http://reprap.org`

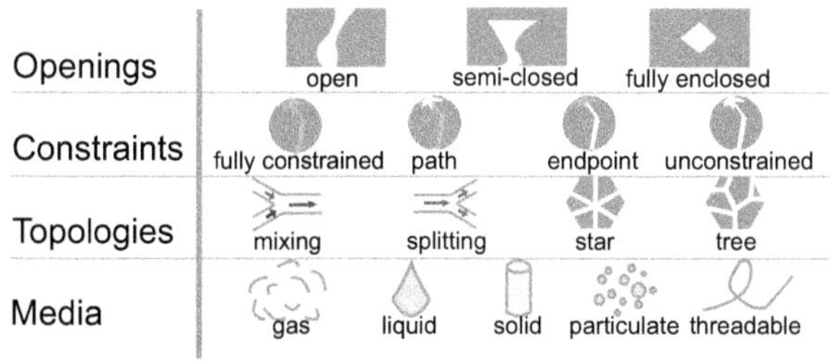

Figure 2. The design space of pipes. Pipe *openings*, *path constraints*, *topologies*, and inserted *media* give rise to unique input/output possibilities.

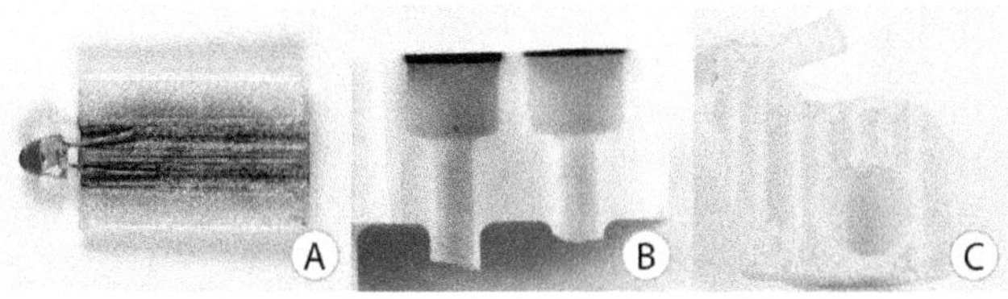

Figure 3. Pipe openings: a) shows a pair of *open* pipes filled with copper paint to power an LED. b) shows two *semi-closed* pipes capped by rubber membranes. In c), a rabbit has a *fully enclosed* chamber to modify its weight.

is one aspect of our work, however our focus is interaction rather than balance, identification, or deformation.

THE DESIGN SPACE OF PIPES

Our review of prior art indicates the potential benefits of using interior pipes for adding interactivity to 3D printed objects, although no general-purpose tools currently exist for this purpose. To guide the design of such a tool, we now provide a design space of the types of pipes that a maker may want to utilize. We have identified four relevant dimensions of pipe design: *openings*, *path constraints*, *topologies*, and inserted *media*. We describe the space in Figure ??.

Openings

Pipes inside solid objects can be either *open* to the outside on both ends, *semi-closed*, or *fully enclosed* (Figure ??). For interactive devices, openings can be either user-facing, where a user would, for example, touch a model; or system-facing, where sensors and actuators may be connected.

Open pipes may be used to create electronic circuitry. For example, an open pipe filled with conductive paint and connected to a battery can power an LED (Figure ??a). *Semi-closed* pipes are capped on one end and can be used to create tactile output. By fabricating a cap from a malleable material and attaching a pump to the open end, the flexible cap can be raised and depressed (Figure ??b). *Fully enclosed* pipes (cavities) are entirely internal. They may be used as weight modifiers [18] and for object identification [31] (Figure ??c). If printed in parts and assembled post-print, enclosed pipes could hold water or particles that would otherwise fall out.

Path Constraints

Depending on the purpose of the pipe, its geometry may be constrained to specific locations within the 3D model. An *endpoint-constrained* pipe requires specific start and end points, but the particular route of the internal path is irrelevant. This is the case for circuit schematics, where the electronic components have fixed locations, but many routing solutions are valid. In contrast, for a *path-constrained* pipe the shape of the path is important. For example, threading electroluminescent (EL) wire through a clear pipe enables makers to emulate neon art (Figure 1, right). A *fully constrained* pipe requires specific terminals as well as a specific path. If a maker wishes the EL wire to exit the rear of the sign to hide the electronics, she can use a fully-constrained path (Figure 1, right). Pipes may also be fully *unconstrained*, however in this paper we focus on contexts where designers deliberately place constraints on pipe endpoints or path.

Pipe Topologies

Pipe network topologies enable *splitting* or *mixing* of media (Figure ??). *Star* and *tree* topologies extend splitting and mixing primitives, encompassing multiple-in and multiple-out configurations; we use star topologies to create sensing locations for our touch-sensitive toys, with one terminal used for swept-frequency capacitive sensing (Figure 1, center).

Media in Pipes

After printing, different media can be inserted into pipes to change affordances and capabilities. We consider *gas*, *liquids*, *solids*, *particulates*, and *threadables*. Compressible fluids (*"gas"*) and incompressible fluids (*"liquids"*) inside semi-closed pipes can create haptic feedback; pressure can also be sensed to act as an input [27]. Gases can be used as carriers for scents or fog. Conductive liquids like copper paint, when dried, turn pipes into conductive paths and can also fix electronic components in place. Filling pipes with *solids* at print time enables designers to exploit the difference in material properties between pipe and contents. For example, in Printed Optics [30], different refractive indices between solid cladding material and transparent material inside pipes allow light transport along pipes for input and output. *Particulates*, either printed in-place or inserted, can be of varying densities and can contain particles of various and variable size. A single large particle can be used for display. Small particles agitated by air can generate sound. *Threadable* media, such as regular wire, electroluminescent wire, or commercial fiberoptic cables, can be threaded through pipes post-printing. Threading such media enables addition of conduction, illumination, or optical sensing using materials that can easily be procured, but cannot themselves be printed, e.g., on consumer printers with a single material.

In the next section we detail how different pipes within this design space space can be created with the help of our new design tool, PipeDream.

PipeDream - A TOOL FOR PIPE DESIGN

To allow makers to design novel objects with pipe-powered interfaces, we created a tool, PipeDream, to add pipe geometries to arbitrary 3D models. Pipe design is non-trivial. Independent pipes should not intersect inside an object lest their contents be unintentionally mixed. To permit easy insertion of media after printing, pipes should have smooth bends. Pipes, in general, need to avoid objects' surfaces to prevent fluid leakage when printed by hobbyist-grade machines. Finally, for designing path-constrained pipes that follow a user-specified path, we must ensure certain characteristics of that path (e.g., that it is connected).

PipeDream allows users to design pipes in two ways. In one, they select exterior anchor points on their objects; the tool then creates complete point-to-point routings using A* path search and physical rod simulation (Figure ??). In the other, users import vector art describing desired interior paths (Figure ??). PipeDream , using edge graph manipulation and Euler tour generation, creates a single path that follows the input shape. We thicken these routes to create pipes. The resultant pipes are subtracted from the user's mesh via voxelization and remeshing. Our tool is implemented in C++ as an extension to Meshmixer, a consumer 3D mesh editing tool [24].

Exterior Terminals

To create endpoint-constrained pipes, in which the location of exterior connection points matters, a brush tool is used to specify a pair of points on the mesh's surface (Figure ??a). The system automatically routes the pipe, and displays a preview. Using sliders, the user can independently adjust the starting and ending radii of the pipe. This is useful for, e.g, our breathing bunny (Figure ??b), whose pipes must fit a piece of hardware on one end, but on the other end should have as large an interactive surface as possible.

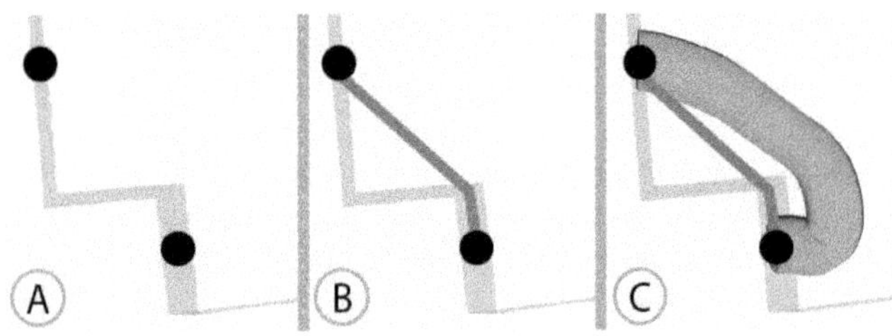

Figure 4. In a), an example mesh with exterior connection points selected. The smoothed A* routing (b) is drawn in red. In green is our physically-based rod after simulation (c).

Routing Algorithm and Physical Simulation

Given two points, we first find a path between them using the A* search algorithm on a voxel representation of the object [6]. A* finds a least-cost path through a graph of nodes given a cost function. Our graph comprises the grid of voxels as nodes, with edges between adjacent nodes; our path cost is based on the Euclidean distance to the selected end point. In this formulation, the routed path is naturally constrained to stay within the object boundaries (Figure ??b).

Our A* pathfinding produces the *shortest* path, but in many cases we require a smoother path to aid insertion of the desired medium, such as a threadable wire. In addition, the distance from the surface is not taken into account in the A* search and pipes may thus be routed along surface contours, which may cause leakage or structural deficiencies.

We solve this problem via physical simulation. We create a straight virtual wire (a 3D polyline or *discrete rod*), and then set its initial position as our A* path. Running the physical simulation allows the wire to attempt to return to a straight configuration, while satisfying the user-selected endpoint position constraints. In addition to user constraints, we require that the rod be perpendicular to the surface at its ends to prevent the terminals' shape from deforming (Figure ??c).

The wire is modelled as a *discrete rod*: a 3D poly-line with a bending constraint between adjacent segments. Our simulation is based on an implementation of Position-Based Dynamics (PBD) [14], with all constraints modelled as penalty forces. To keep the rod inside the mesh, we compute a discretized distance field, then constrain the rod to stay within our offset shell using a simple penalty force. This approach can successfully route pipes through complex geometries (Figure ??).

PBD simulations rarely converge to a steady state, so we simply halt after a fixed number of timesteps (250). Our voxel grid currently uses a resolution of 128x128x128 voxels, which enables interactive operations, but this parameter can be adjusted for different model requirements. The simulation takes about a second for our examples.

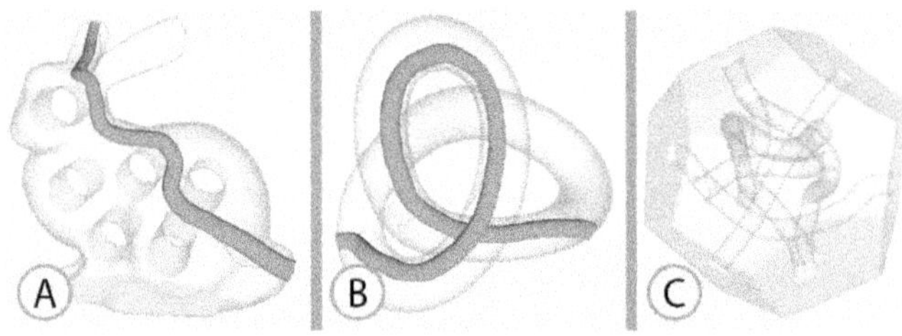

Figure 5. A set of example routings produced by our tool. Note that there is a tradeoff between bending and length of pipes: to reduce bending, pipes may be routed through longer paths around holes in genus > 0 meshes (a). Pipes successfully route through long, curving paths in knots (b), and multiple pipes placed in a single mesh in a tangled configuration successfully avoid each other (c).

Multiple Pipes

Pipes are routed and cut out of the mesh serially. This prevents pipe intersections: once a pipe has been cut out of the mesh, it cannot be part of valid routes in any future pipe routing operation (Figure ??c). After solving for a path, we add it as a constraint to the system, generating a penalty force that pushes additional paths away from it. However, we do not currently track all pipes for global optimization: we greedily select the best routing per pipe.

Pipes with Multiple Endpoints

To allow designers to create pipes with multiple endpoints (e.g., the star topologies as in Figure ??), we use one surface position per pipe and a central fixed endpoint that the user can interactively position (Figure ??). The user can connect several pipes, hitting a key to add each in sequence and positioning them with the mouse. The pipes route as normal.

Interior Paths

For path-constrained pipes, the route of the pipe must conform to a desired shape. A maker can import a vector graphics file (such as SVG) describing the path she wants for her pipes: all lines in this input file are interpreted as desired pipe components for the final artifact. Using sliders, she can change the pipes' radius (Figure ??). A preview is provided to show the radius and location of the cut, and the maker can align her model as appropriate.

In some cases, such as for the neon route in Figure ?? and resultant sign in Figure ??, a single path must pass through a set of disconnected path segments (i.e., all letters in the word "UIST"). PipeDream leverages graph theory algorithms to generate this single path, as described below. Without endpoint constraints, the path's exit(s) from the model are defined by the SVG: the maker can see where the path exits the model and translate the cut according to her desired outcome.

Routing

Our technique for routing this path is inspired by work in generating continuous line illustrations from images [2, 34]. Our routing problem is a version of the Chinese Postman Problem [11], in which we wish to traverse all edges of the graph described by the user's input, much as a postman needs to walk along every road at least once to deliver mail. In our relaxation, we allow the creation of new edges (i.e., the postman may jump from building to building in addition to using existing roads).

Setup: We first add a temporary edge that connects the user's desired start and end points, and create a full Eulerian graph. This edge is removed at the end to yield a semi-Eulerian graph that can be threaded after printing.

Connect disconnected components: To connect disconnected subgraphs, we find minimum Euclidean distance vertex pairs spanning two subgraphs, and greedily add edges to such pairs until all subgraphs are joined into a single graph.

Eulerization: In order to make our graph Eulerian, we consider all odd-degree vertices in the connected graph and make a clique of potential edges based on distance. We greedily add edges between odd nodes until no odd nodes remain. Finally, we remove our temporary edge, changing the graph from Eulerian to semi-Eulerian. This is a connected, semi-Eulerian graph that contains all edges in the input. A lower total weight matching is possible by connecting components and ensuring node evenness together in a global process, as well as by using minimum-weight matching rather than greedy selection, however this optimization is not crucial for our purposes.

Euler Tour: To find an Euler tour, we use Fleury's algorithm [3] with a modification to preserve continuity: at a given node, from multiple candidate edges, we prefer the edge(s) with the smallest angular deviation from the incoming edge (i.e., we prefer to pass straight through a node, if possible). This minimizes turns in the final artifact, which eases support

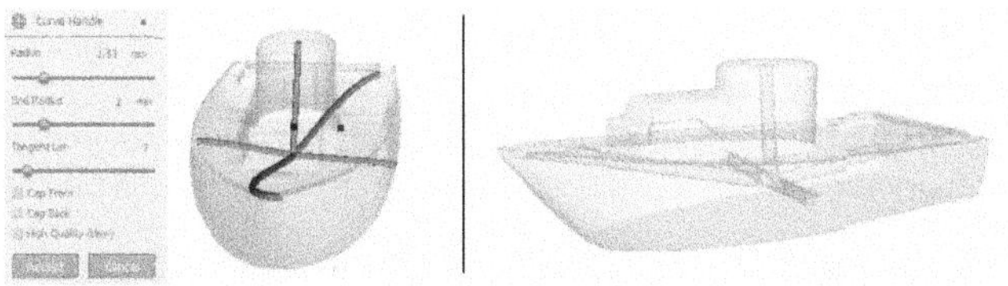

Figure 6. Left: Users can interactively position connection points for pipe topologies; they can also adjust pipe diameter and rod parameters. Right: Resulting model with cut pipes.

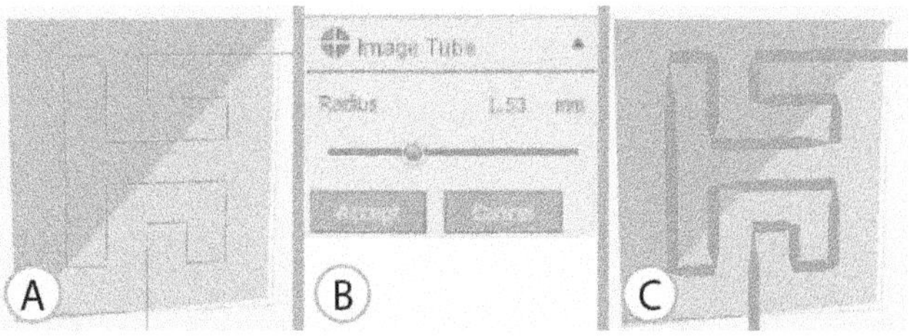

Figure 7. Users can interactively change the radius of their pipes using a slider (b). PipeDream's live preview shows the real size and location of the cut (a, c) before it is committed to the mesh.

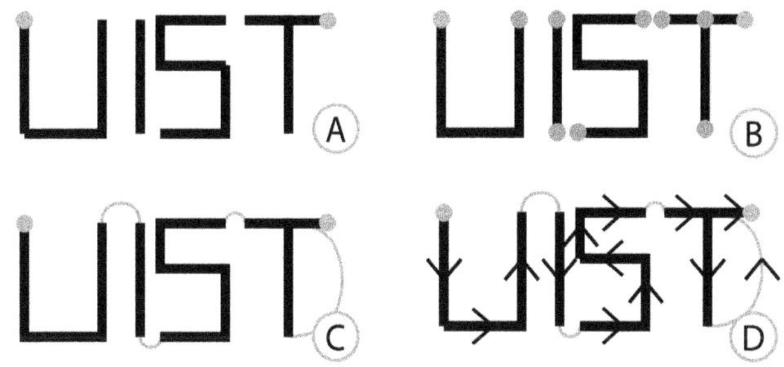

Figure 8. An input vector graphics file with the start and end points highlighted in gray (a) and the points which cannot be tubed as drawn highlighted in blue (b). The connected graph created by our software (c) and the resulting Euler tour (d) permit insertion of media post-print.

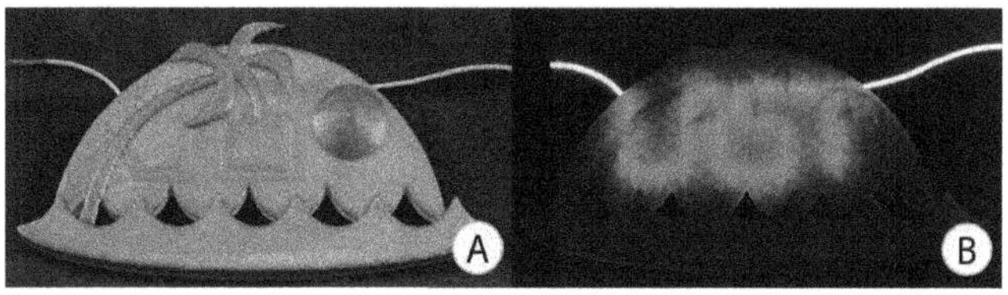

Figure 9. Our neon sign built using the process above. (a) shows the unlit sign, and (b) shows it lit.

material removal and assembly. Our EL wire in Figure ?? follows an Euler tour through the input nodes.

Edges that Intersect in the Plane

We do not currently redirect edges that intersect in the plane. Because we have a 3-dimensional canvas in which to work, it would be possible to push overlapping paths into the third dimension. However, we leave this to future work. For our specific applications so far, it has been unnecessary.

Separating at the Pipe Plane

We allow users the choice to separate their meshes at the pipe plane, which may be necessary for support material removal (discussed later) or insertion of media: e.g., EL wire can be bent much more sharply by hand in the plane than it can by pushing from one end into a pipe. To do this, we simply perform a plane cut after the mesh modification operation described below.

Mesh Modification

After the maker hits "Accept" on her preview, we must cut pipes out of the input mesh. At this stage, we verify whether the new pipe will intersect the surface or an existing pipe, and if so display a warning message suggesting that she should

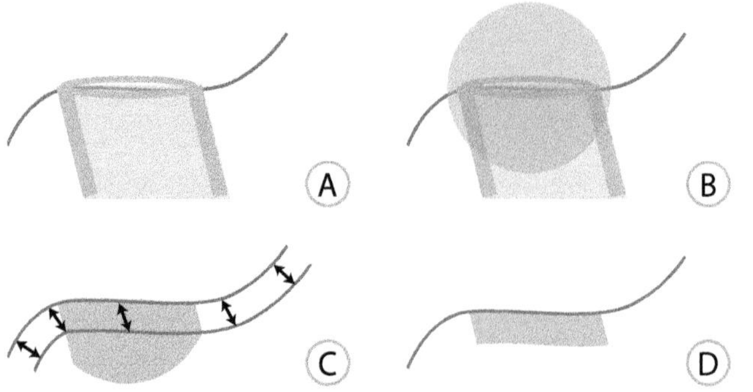

Figure 10. The process to "cap" the end of a pipe. In (a), a pipe end is placed on the surface of the mesh. In (b), we create a sphere whose radius is slightly larger than the radius of the pipe, centred at the pipe's endpoint. In (c), we consider the intersection of the sphere and the pipe, and create an offset surface of the mesh. Finally, in (d) we intersect with the offset surface. This is kept as a cap for the pipe in mesh subtraction.

consider a smaller radius. Our basic strategy for the cut is to create a polygonal tube by sweeping a profile polyline along the path, and subtract the tube from the mesh. We only use circular profiles in our examples, but clearly any other profile could be used. We allow different start and end radii, selected by the maker in the previous step, which are linearly interpolated along the path.

To avoid the complexities of direct mesh booleans and give us additional flexibility, we construct a discretized volumetric (i.e., voxel-based) representation of the original mesh and the tube mesh. Boolean subtraction is trivial in such representations. We specifically use narrow-band level sets [15], which represent the surface as the zero iso-contour of an approximate distance field. We then use marching cubes [9] to produce the final mesh for printing. This strategy does incur some resampling artifacts, however so does the 3D printing; compared to the print process, the time required to voxelize at high resolution is inconsequential. Since we have a distance field, we can easily introduce useful effects, such as the ability to add a thin membrane "cap" over the end of a tube. This is accomplished by applying a standard "thicken" operation to the level set version of the initial mesh, intersecting with a sphere placed at the tube endpoint, and then performing a boolean union with the initial shape-minus-tube result (Figure ??). A straightforward extension would be to add or subtract additional elements at the tube endpoints.

FABRICATION TECHNIQUES

Several pragmatic concerns arise when fabricating models with pipes and cavities. Pipes frequently lead to overhangs (where an underlying supporting layer has a smaller footprint than the subsequent layer). To allow overhangs, 3D printers may lay down support material that must be later removed from the model. The removal process can be time-intensive and challenging. The physical fabrication process used by different machines gives rise to differing strategies for avoiding support material or easing its removal. Techniques differ for fused deposition modeling (FDM) machines, such as the Makerbot[2], polyjet machines such as Stratasys Connex[3], powder-based machines (e.g., ZCorp[4]), and those that use stereolithography (e.g., Form 1[5]).

Support Types

The physical form of support material varies between printer types. On single-material hobbyist FDM machines, the support is created from the same type of material as the model, laid down in a different pattern to ease detachment. Multi-material FDM machines typically feature dissolvable support material: by submersing a part in lye, one can eventually remove support material while leaving the model material behind. Polyjet machines also use a secondary type of material for support: it can be melted out in some cases (e.g., ProJet wax material) or blasted out with high-pressure water. This blasting process requires fairly open access to the support material: the robot head and maze in Figure 1 were cut into two pieces along the plane of the pipes to give better access to the support. For powder-based and stereolithography machines, the material (powder or photo-cure liquid) that is not used for the model remains in the bed and forms the support structure — this is uniquely well-suited to removal, as it can simply be poured out after a print is completed. We hope to experiment with these types of printers more in the future.

Model Orientation and Pipe Geometries

The various types of printers permit different sorts of support-free prints. FDM allows approximately a 45° overhang before support is required. For polyjet machines, overhangs can be just 14°. Reorienting a part within the bed can lead to more or less support required. MeshMixer already has a built-in tool that reorients models to keep as much surface area as possible within the 45° constraint imposed by FDM printers, and alternative pipe cross-section geometries (e.g., teardrop) could alleviate the need for support material to bridge the tops of pipes. In the future, pipe routes could be optimized to minimize support material required.

Model Assembly

For especially complex geometries, models can be "cut up" into multiple pieces that can be assembled, avoiding support deposition or easing material removal; this can also ease insertion of the desired medium. This is somewhat undesirable as it means more time spent in assembly post-print, and additionally a cut pipe may no longer be fluid-tight. Our plane cut option offers a simple way to slice a model; more sophisticated techniques may be necessary for internal paths that are not constrained to a plane.

TOTALLY TUBULAR EXAMPLE OBJECTS

To evaluate and highlight our tool's capabilities, we fabricated a set of six prototype objects designed using PipeDream. To show that our approach is printer-independent, we fabricated some on a Makerbot Replicator

[2] `http://makerbot.com`
[3] `http://stratasys.com`
[4] `http://3dsystems.com`
[5] `http://formlabs.com`

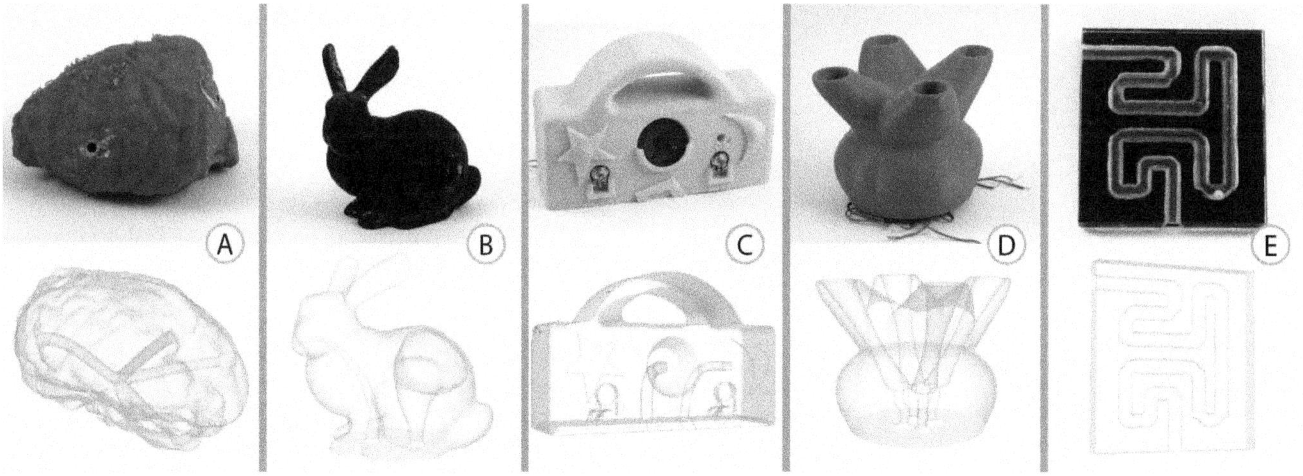

Figure 11. A series of example objects created using our system. (a) is a touch-sensitive brain toy. (b) is a rabbit which "breathes" using wind pipes we built. (c) shows a portable radio. (d) shows a presence-aware pen holder. (e) is a maze game.

2 and the rest on a Stratasys Connex 260. Each prototype object explores the expansion of an existing sensing or actuation technique to the surface of 3D printed objects.

Touch-sensitive Toys (open, endpoint, star, liquid)

To expand Touché [21] to 3D printed forms, we created a set of touch-sensitive toys and a companion app that identifies the objects as well as touched parts of the objects (inspired by the boat application in Acoustic Barcodes [5]). The objects — a brain and boat, in our example — can be set on a base, upon which the computer displays "brain" or "boat". Touching the brain model's front protrusion yields the announcement "olfactory bulb". The distinct touch points on each object are connected by an interior star topology, and touch sensing is performed via a single conductive connection to the base, using swept-frequency capacitive sensing (see Figure ??a). Since each toy and each gesture has a distinct capacitive signature, we use a simple classifier trained to detect both toy and gesture based on profile.

The model we used for the boat was downloaded from Thingiverse, while the brain model came from researchers at one of our instutions. We then used PipeDream to create the desired internal pipes. All components were fabricated on a Makerbot, support-free. After printing, we injected copper paint (CuPro-Cote) into the interior pipes using a craft syringe. This paint requires approximately 2 days to fully dry in this configuration (3mm diameter tubes, maximum tube length 10cm). The resistance of the paint with this cross-section is approximately $2\Omega/inch$. Our smart base is powered by an Arduino Uno running open-source SFCS code[6].

Breathing Bunny (semi-closed, endpoint, gas)

With inspiration from PneUIs [35] for using gases to both provide sensation to the user through openings and deform a model internally, we created a rabbit with a pair of tubes that can simulate breathing (see Figure ??b). When the rabbit inhales through its nose, its abdomen rises, and as it exhales its abdomen falls. For this, we used a combination air/vacuum pump (SparkFun ROB-10398): one terminal creates a vacuum while the other creates positive pressure. The rabbit model, the well-known Stanford Bunny[7], was downloaded from Thingiverse. We then used PipeDream to add two pipes: one open pipe exiting at its mouth, and one semi-closed pipe capped at its abdomen. We connected one pipe to each of our pump's terminals, and using a programmable power supply we mimic a rabbit's breathing pattern. This example was printed on the Connex using flexible material (100% TangoBlackPlus); support was flushed post-print.

Custom Radio (open, endpoint, threadable)

A custom radio (Figure ??c) shows how pipes can be used to integrate electronic components into the user-facing surface of an object. The radio includes a power and volume dial, and LED which goes on when the radio is on, and a tuner dial. An Arduino Uno microcontroller, Si4703 FM tuner, and 6V (4xAA) power supply are embedded in the base of the radio. The sound is played through a single .5 Watt speaker.

The radio shell was modelled in a commercial CAD tool. We included slots on the 3D model matching the shape of the electronic components that were to be embedded. The model was then imported into PipeDream, where we created a network of 8 individual open pipes (3 per potentiometer, 1 for the LED, 1 for the speaker) connecting the components to the radio's base. We fabricated the radio body on our Makerbot, support-free but cut in two pieces to allow the Arduino and battery pack to be inserted. We then threaded the pipes with wires to connect the components to the microcontroller contained in the base.

Presence-aware Pen Holder (open, endpoint, threadable)

Our presence-aware pen holder distinguishes which tool or tools a user has picked up (see Figure ??d). We use a modification of the FlyEye technique described by Wimmer [33] in which an IR camera senses a user's grasp on an object, getting data from light transmitted on fiber optic cables.

[6]`http://www.instructables.com/id/Touche-for-Arduino-Advanced-touch-sensing`

[7]`http://en.wikipedia.org/wiki/Stanford_bunny`

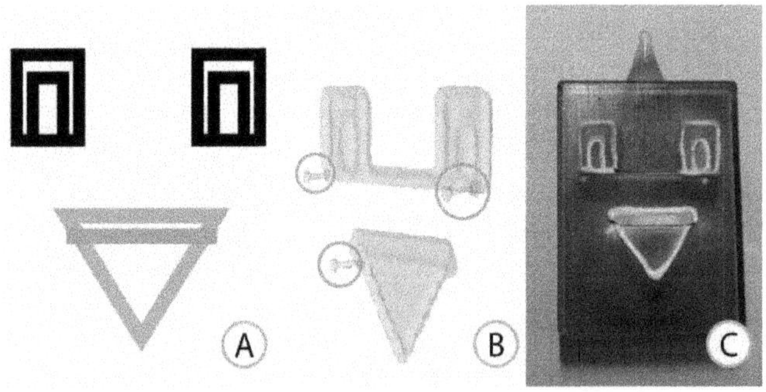

Figure 12. A two-state animated neon sign designed using our tool. (a) shows the input SVG files, with the eyes (non-animated) in black and the two states of the mouth in blue and gray. (b) shows the tubes we subtracted from the mesh, rear exit tubes circled in blue. In (c), we show the fabricated sign.

The penholder body was created in a commercial CAD tool. We used PipeDream to add four internal open pipes connecting each pen chamber to the base of the pen holder. This prototype was built on our Makerbot support-free. Each pipe was then threaded with Sparkfun clear core light pipe (PRT-10697), similar to fiber optic cable. We use a single cable per pipe; our 6mm diameter light pipe, in comparison to the fine fiber optics used in the original work, can emit and receive through the same cable because the cross-sectional area is large enough to accommodate both functions. At the base of each pipe is a QRE1113 line sensor breakout board, with integrated IR emitter and receiver. When a pen is in its appointed place, the emitted infrared light is reflected off its base and travels back to the receiver, where it appears bright.

Maze (fully enclosed, path, tree, particulate)

We created a maze game with a marble that can be navigated through a maze-like path, with exits on either side of the model (Figure ??e).

The maze is based on an SVG file we manually created and processed with our internal path routing tool. We printed the maze on the Connex using a transparent material (100% VeroClear) for the top and a black material (100% TangoBlackPlus) for the bottom. The final artifact was fabricated in two halves fastened together via glue, to allow removal of support material with a high-pressure water tool. We plugged the ends of the pipes post-print with additional material to ensure the ball does not escape.

Animated Neon Sign (open, fully constrained, threadable)

Neon art is traditionally made from hand-formed glass tubes containing neon gas. The tubes light up when a current is passed through them. For this type of art, the path of the tubes is of crucial importance, as it determines how the sign will look. We designed a custom neon robot head which can be animated to "talk". The external geometry of the model was imported into PipeDream, which created the associated pipes using its internal path routing tool. We added additional endpoint-constrained tubes as exits out the rear of the model to allow us to hide the controls (see Figure ??b). We then printed the model on the Connex using transparent material. The model was printed in two halves, cutting through the plane of the internal path, to facilitate assembly.

The pipes are threaded with electroluminescent wire which is lit in sequence, using a sequencer, to create the animation.

DISCUSSION

The promise of 3D printing is two-fold: it enables the manufacturing of complex objects at low volumes, and it allows for the manufacturing of geometries that are impossible to create using traditional techniques like injection molding. Printing pipes to prototype interactive objects exploits both advantages. Prototypes by definition are low-volume parts, and pipes require complex interior geometries that are very difficult or impossible to produce using other processes. Our work has focused on routing pipes that are manually filled after a print has completed. However, the fundamental operations of 3D path routing and topology specification that our tool offers will remain relevant as 3D printing technology advances. Multi-material printers are already available; as they advance and support the embedding of additional materials (e.g., conductors), PipeDream can enable designers to efficiently specify where different functional materials should be placed at design time.

Limitations and Future Work

While pipes provide a powerful mechanism for directing interaction to arbitrary locations on an object's surface, they do have shortcomings which warrant discussion. In particular, they cannot replace the active elements required for a functioning interactive device: they simply redirect sensing to different locations on an object's surface. All pipes need to, at some point, connect to a sensor, microcontroller, or pump.

Some media are difficult to insert in pipes, or may not be compatible with all types of pipes. Threadable materials in particular can provide challenges, as they can get stuck while being fed into pipes. Our system mitigates this by minimizing the bend energy of the interior pipes, but for complex pipe geometries threading could be a challenge.

Fluids also raise unique challenges. For example, the conductive paint we used in our designs can take multiple days to dry in long pipes. Liquids kept in the pipes can also cause discoloration due to seepage. Furthermore, not all printers guarantee watertightness of their prints, so leakage can occur.

As discussed, removal of support material can also be a challenge. Particularly on multi-jetting printers, printing support-free is not possible for most geometries, and detaching printed support is not always trivial. In some cases we printed our models in several pieces, to avoid this problem.

There are also areas for improvement and future work with our software tool. The design of PipeDream was based on our proposed design space of pipes. However, the design tool is not yet fully capable of realizing all possibilities in this design space. Specifically, we did not explicitly explore the mixing or splitting of pipes, and our path-constrained cuts are strictly 2D for now. A 2.5D SVG import using, e.g., line colors as height would be straightforward, and our described algorithm would continue to work properly. An extension to PipeDream could include detection of where the 2D path intersects itself; intersecting pipe components could be "pushed into 3D" using the discrete rods from our endpoint-constrained routing algorithm. Furthermore, since pipes are committed to the mesh one at a time, our tool does not currently optimize networks of multiple pipes. Instead, we utilize a greedy algorithm and route a single pipe at a time. This suggests the need for a better general 3D routing algorithm with multiple traces, which could take into account global bending energy, global pipe length, or other task-specific requirements. For integration with common electronic components, it would be possible to build a library of "footprints" which could be used for recessing them into printed objects' surfaces; such footprints could also be used for automatically generating connecting pipes based on an electrical connection graph, as in circuitboard routing tools like Eagle[8]. Future work should also include assisting makers in the fabrication process itself by automatically cutting objects to reduce support material removal issues.

The basic approach of using a discrete rod for physical simulation does have various limitations, in particular it cannot recover if the rod becomes tangled or unstable. However we have observed these problems only when attempting to break the system; they did not occur in any of the cases shown in our figures. Another issue is parameters, as the penalty forces used in PBD do not correspond to physical units. We avoided serious issues by uniformly scaling the initial mesh to a unit box, and tuning the parameters on several test cases.

We are also eager to test our tool with users and get feedback from makers who use it in the wild. Based on our own experiences, we believe our system could be readily utilized by makers and researchers, and serve as a useful tool for rapidly prototyping interactive 3D objects. We plan to release PipeDream as a part of Meshmixer later this year.

CONCLUSION

Pipe mediation opens new interactive device prototyping opportunities both for makers with consumer-grade 3D printers and research and industrial labs with higher-end machines. While today's 3D printers are not yet able to fabricate active components in-place, we suggest that 3D printed interactive devices can be created with redirection of active input and output via pipes. This amplifies and extends the utility of existing sensing and actuation approaches. In addition to describing the design space of pipes, we also presented PipeDream, a design tool for the creation of a series of tubes [28] inside arbitrary 3D models, and discussed many techniques that combine nicely with pipes. We fabricated several example objects using our tool to explore new points in the design space. We look forward to extending our software contribution into future multi-material 3D modelling tools.

ACKNOWLEDGEMENTS

The authors would like to thank Karl D. D. Willis for his incredibly broad knowledge of paper references and Tim Campbell for his assistance creating Instructables. This work is part of a line of research on digital fabrication that is supported in part by the NSF GRFP under grant DGE 1106400 and a Sloan Fellowship.

[8]`http://www.cadsoftusa.com`

REFERENCES

1. Bickel, B., Bächer, M., Otaduy, M. A., Lee, H. R., Pfister, H., Gross, M., and Matusik, W. Design and fabrication of materials with desired deformation behavior. In *SIGGRAPH 2010*, 63:1–63:10.
2. Bosch, R., and Herman, A. Continuous line drawings via the traveling salesman problem. *Operations Research Letters 32*, 4 (July 2004), 302–303.
3. Fleury, M. Deux problèmes de géométrie de situation. *Journal de mathématiques élémentaires 2*, 2 (1883), 257–261.
4. Follmer, S., Leithinger, D., Olwal, A., Cheng, N., and Ishii, H. Jamming user interfaces: Programmable particle stiffness and sensing for malleable and shape-changing devices. In *Proceedings of UIST 2012*, 519–528.
5. Harrison, C., Xiao, R., and Hudson, S. Acoustic barcodes: Passive, durable and inexpensive notched identification tags. In *Proceedings of UIST 2012*, 563–568.
6. Hart, P., Nilsson, N., and Raphael, B. A formal basis for the heuristic determination of minimum cost paths. *IEEE Transactions on Systems Science and Cybernetics 4*, 3 (July 1968), 100–107.
7. Hudson, S. E. Printing teddy bears: A technique for 3D printing of soft interactive objects. In *Proceedings of CHI 2014*, 459–468.
8. Lee, C. An algorithm for path connections and its applications. *IRE Transactions on Electronic Computers 10*, 2 (1961), 346–365.
9. Lorensen, W. E., and Cline, H. E. Marching cubes: A high resolution 3D surface construction algorithm. *Computer Graphics 21*, 4 (July 1987), 163–169.
10. Majidi, C., Kramer, R., and Wood, R. J. A non-differential elastomer curvature sensor for softer-than-skin electronics. *Smart Materials and Structures 20*, 10 (2011), 105017.
11. Mei-Ko, K. Graphic programming using odd or even points. *Chinese Mathematics 1* (1962), 273–277.
12. Mueller, S., Kruck, B., and Baudisch, P. LaserOrigami: Laser-cutting 3D objects. In *Proceedings of CHI 2013*, 2585–2592.
13. Mueller, S., Lopes, P., and Baudisch, P. Interactive construction: Interactive fabrication of functional mechanical devices. In *Proceedings of UIST 2012*, 599–606.
14. Müller, M., Heidelberger, B., Hennix, M., and Ratcliff, J. Position based dynamics. *Journal of Visual Communication and Image Representation 18*, 2 (Apr. 2007), 109–118.

15. Museth, K., Breen, D. E., Whitaker, R. T., Mauch, S., and Johnson, D. Algorithms for interactive editing of level set models. *Computer Graphics Forum 24*, 4 (2005), 821–841.

16. Navarrete, M., Lopes, A., Acuna, J., Estrada, R., MacDonald, E., Palmer, J., and Wicker, R. Integrated layered manufacturing of a novel wireless motion sensor system with GPS. *Technical Report, University of Texas at El Paso* (2007).

17. Park, Y.-L., Chen, B.-R., and Wood, R. J. Design and fabrication of soft artificial skin using embedded microchannels and liquid conductors. *IEEE Sensors Journal 12*, 8 (August 2012), 2711–2718.

18. Prévost, R., Whiting, E., Lefebvre, S., and Sorkine-Hornung, O. Make it stand: Balancing shapes for 3D fabrication. *ACM Transactions on Graphics 32*, 4 (July 2013), 81:1–81:10.

19. Rivers, A., Moyer, I. E., and Durand, F. Position-correcting tools for 2D digital fabrication. *ACM Transactions on Graphics 31*, 4 (2012), 88.

20. Sarik, J., Butler, A., Villar, N., Scott, J., and Hodges, S. Fabricating electronics with rapid prototyping tools. In *Adjunct Proceedings of TEI 2012*, 339–342.

21. Sato, M., Poupyrev, I., and Harrison, C. Touché: Enhancing touch interaction on humans, screens, liquids, and everyday objects. In *Proceedings of CHI 2012*, 483–492.

22. Savage, V., Chang, C., and Hartmann, B. Sauron: Embedded single-camera sensing of printed physical user interfaces. In *Proceedings of UIST 2013*, 447–456.

23. Savage, V., Zhang, X., and Hartmann, B. Midas: Fabricating custom capacitive touch sensors to prototype interactive objects. In *Proceedings of UIST 2012*, 579–588.

24. Schmidt, R., and Singh, K. Meshmixer: An interface for rapid mesh composition. In *SIGGRAPH 2010 Talks*, 6:1.

25. Sells, E. Rapid prototyped electronic circuits. `http://fennetic.net/irc/reprap_circuits.pdf`, 2004.

26. Slyper, R., and Hodgins, J. Prototyping robot appearance, movement, and interactions using flexible 3d printing and air pressure sensors. 6–11.

27. Slyper, R., Poupyrev, I., and Hodgins, J. Sensing through structure: Designing soft silicone sensors. In *Proceedings of TEI 2011*, 213–220.

28. Stevens, T. Full Committee Markup - Communications Reform Bill. `http://www.commerce.senate.gov`, June 2006.

29. Weichel, C., Lau, M., Kim, D., Villar, N., and Gellersen, H. Mixfab: A mixed-reality environment for personal fabrication. In *Proceedings of CHI 2014*, 3855–3864.

30. Willis, K. D. D., Brockmeyer, E., Hudson, S., and Poupyrev, I. Printed optics: 3D printing of embedded optical elements for interactive devices. In *Proceedings of UIST 2012*, 589–598.

31. Willis, K. D. D., and Wilson, A. D. InfraStructs: fabricating information inside physical objects for imaging in the terahertz region. *ACM Transactions on Graphics 32*, 4, 138:1–138:10.

32. Willis, K. D. D., Xu, C., Wu, K.-J., Levin, G., and Gross, M. D. Interactive fabrication: New interfaces for digital fabrication. In *Proceedings of TEI 2011*, 69–72.

33. Wimmer, R. FlyEye: Grasp-sensitive surfaces using optical fiber. In *Proceedings of TEI 2010*, 245–248.

34. Wong, F. J., and Takahashi, S. A graph-based approach to continuous line illustrations with variable levels of detail. *Computer Graphics Forum 30*, 7 (Nov. 2011), 1931–1939.

35. Yao, L., Niiyama, R., Ou, J., Follmer, S., Della Silva, C., and Ishii, H. PneUI: pneumatically actuated soft composite materials for shape changing interfaces. In *Proceedings of UIST 2013*, 13–22.

36. Zoran, A., and Paradiso, J. A. FreeD: a freehand digital sculpting tool. In *Proceedings of CHI 2013*, 2613–2616.

FlatFitFab: Interactive Modeling with Planar Sections

James McCrae
University of Toronto
mccrae@dgp.toronto.edu

Nobuyuki Umetani
University of Tokyo
n.umetani@gmail.com

Karan Singh
University of Toronto
karan@dgp.toronto.edu

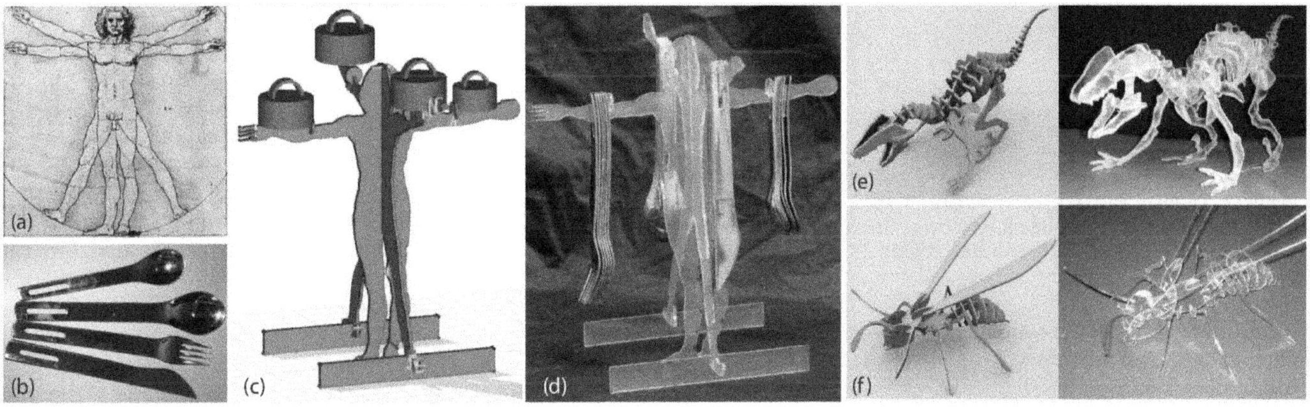

Figure 1. FlatFitFab is a comprehensive system for the interactive modeling, simulation and fabrication of planar section assemblies: Inspirational 3D models or images (the Vitruvian man) (a), and physical object parameters (cutlery weight and dimension) (b), feed into the interactive creation and composition of 3D planar sections (c) using a novel single-stroke workflow. Stress along planar sections (red and blue lines), subject to gravity and external forces (cutlery weight), is interactively simulated and visualized (c). Instant feedback on geometric stability, assembly and connectedness, further ensures that fabricated sections perform their intended function, e.g. a cutlery holder (d). A novel vocabulary of procedural operations designed for intersecting planar sections, e.g. vertebrae along the dinosaur spine (e), enables rapid and complex modeling by both experts (e) and amateurs (f).

ABSTRACT
We present a comprehensive system to author planar section structures, common in art and engineering. A study on how planar section assemblies are imagined and drawn guide our design principles: planar sections are best drawn in-situ, with little foreshortening, orthogonal to intersecting planar sections, exhibiting regularities between planes and contours. We capture these principles with a novel drawing workflow where a single fluid user stroke specifies a 3D plane and its contour in relation to existing planar sections. Regularity is supported by defining a vocabulary of procedural operations for intersecting planar sections. We exploit planar structure properties to provide real-time visual feedback on physically simulated stresses, and geometric verification that the structure is stable, connected and can be assembled. This feedback is validated by real-world fabrication and testing. As evaluation, we report on over 50 subjects who all used our system with minimal instruction to create unique models.

ACM Classification Keywords
H.5.2. User Interfaces: Graphical user interfaces; I.3.5 Computational Geometry and Object Modeling: Curve, surface, solid, and object representations.

Author Keywords
Interaction; fabrication; shape modeling; planar sections.

INTRODUCTION
Artists and sculptors effectively use minimal representations of shape to tease and inspire human perception. Planar section assemblies have been used for more than a century by artists such as Calder and Picasso to express both realistic forms and abstract ideas (Figure 2 (top row)). Such abstractions can be fabricated economically using a variety of machines and materials to create architectural forms, functional furnishings and decorative art (Figure 2 (bottom row)). The increasing popularity of 3D modeling software and digital manufacturing devices, aimed at hobbyists, has fueled a flurry of recent research on amalgamating stages of design and manufacturing. 3D planar section assemblies, compactly manufactured and packed as 2D sheets, form a unique junction of design, manufacturing and human perception (Figure 1) .

While the creation of manufacturable planar sections by slicing existing 3D objects (Figure 3 (right)) has received much attention in both research and industry (Autodesk 123D Make), artistic planar section structures rarely conform precisely to 3D models (Figure 3 (left, middle)). In fact, nearly all the structures shown in this paper cannot be created by simply slicing a 3D object using planes. In practice, like architecture [17], planar section assemblies are inspired by a mix of 2D images, 3D models, physical constraints and pure imagination. Fluid interfaces for creating such structures from scratch using a mixed bag of design inspirations, are relatively unexplored. We present such an interface, that

Figure 2. Outdoor planar section sculptures ©Alexander Calder (top row) . Planar section use (bottom row) in architecture (left), home furnishings (centre) and interior decoration (right).

incorporates images, 3D models and constraints into a single homogeneous workflow, to create intricate and physically sound planar section assemblies. Our system is a judicious combination of many novel and existing components, bigger than the sum of its parts and applicable to broader areas 3D modeling, deformation and scaffolding (for sketching [22] or animatronics [15, 31]). Specifically, the single stroke drawing workflow and magnetic cut deformation of 3D models are entirely novel components, and the overall physical simulation and corelated affine operations (the rib cage in Figure 9) are novel in the context of planar section structures.

Following a survey of *related work*, we present an *exploratory study* into planar section drawing. Conclusions from the study, and the simple observation that a planar section has one dimension less than a 3D model, motivate the design of our *interactive interface*, vocabulary of *procedural operations*, real-time *physical simulation* and *fabrication* constraints. As *evaluation*, we present the results of real-world fabrication and testing, and report on the usage of our system by over 50 high-school students and other users.

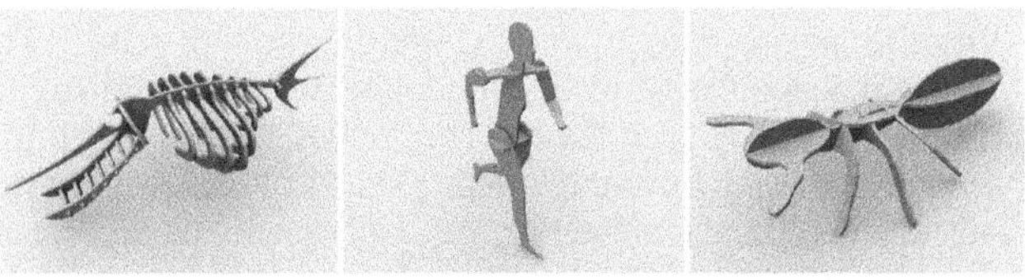

Figure 3. Planar sections can represent non-manifold scaffolds (left), conform partly (middle), or entirely (right) to 3D object contours.

RELATED WORK

Our system is informed by prior work on 3D shape abstraction, physical simulation, fabrication and interactive design.

3D shape abstraction for conceptual design: Much of sketch-based conceptual design [2, 22, 24] draws inspiration from traditional design drawing [5], to build sparse 3D curve representations of shape. A large percentage of these curves such as design cross-sections [24], are in fact planar and drawn to perceptually convey 3D shape. The planar contours created by our system are often logical completions of such design cross-sections. Planar contours drawn in 2D are fundamental to modeling systems from the seminal Sketchpad [25] to Teddy [8] and its successors [19]. Our single-stroke contour drawing workflow can streamline curve creation in these systems. Planar symmetry is also intrinsic to 3D shape and extensively used in interactive interfaces, both to infer and replicate 3D shape across symmetry planes [2], and such planar symmetry hierarchies can be readily authored using our system. The fact that most 3D objects can be satisfactorily abstracted by humans using a small number of planar sections [12], is a testament to the expressive power of planar section assemblies.

Physical simulation and analysis: Feedback on geometric constraints and physical simulation during interactive 3D modeling creates functionally improved models and reduces wasted iterations of real fabrication and testing [18, 27]. As general structural simulation using the Finite Element Method is still too slow for real-time feedback, reduced or approximate physical models for specific design problems have been developed. For example, interactive physical analysis has been shown to aid users in furniture design [27], to guide forms toward structurally sound masonry buildings [29], or to geometrically adapt 3D sculptures to stand once fabricated [18]. We similarly, propound a novel physics model based on cross-section samples [28], to compute stresses within and between connected planar sections in real-time.

Shape fabrication: A large body of recent research addresses problems on design and processing of 3D shapes for fabrication, by 3D printers [18], or using 2D routers such as laser cutters to create planar [9] or even LaserOrigami [13] bent sections, with a variety of joints and flexures [1]. Most work on planar sections is focused on automated processing of assemblies created by slicing existing 3D objects [4, 7, 12] (Figure 3 (right)), and formalizing geometric constraints necessary for the assembly of connected 3D planar sections [23]. We instead focus on the interactive creation of general planar section assemblies (a superset of sliced 3D models), combining elements of interaction, procedural modeling, geometric analysis and real-time simulation to produce structures that are both physically functional and aesthetically pleasing.

Interactive design: Within the interactive design space, planar sections have been used to make V-style pop-ups [11], or radial section lampshades by sketching volumes in 3D [30]. Planar sections have also been used in furniture design from rectilinear shapes [16] or extruded profiles [20], created using 2D interfaces, with regularity constraints [9]. We in contrast, enable planar section assembly creation in-situ, using procedural operations to facilitate regularity and complexity.

PLANAR SECTION EXPLORATORY STUDY

We performed an exploratory study to understand how users imagine and draw planar sections in 3D. We asked 6 users with varying artistic capability and 3D modelling experience to create planar section representations of both imagined objects and a set of reference 3D models (Figure 4). We developed an interactive system for this study that allowed planar curve sketching in 3D on a user manipulated planar canvas.

The system also logged user interaction details: strokes, canvas manipulation, camera motion and other geometric measurements. We analyzed the creations, log data and interviewed users to conclude the following design principles:

Design collateral: Users remarked that while their creations were often inspired by 2D images or 3D objects, the planar section assemblies they imagined would only partially conform to input boundaries, and connect expressively in the interior. Our proposed system allows users to meaningfully combine images, 3D models and blank canvas creation within a single modeless drawing workflow.

Plane orthogonality and regularity: We found drawing planes to be predominantly parallel or perpendicular to each another. Intersecting planes almost always met orthogonally. We also observed shape regularities between planar section contours, reflecting the connection between planes and symmetry in design [5]. We capture these regularities by procedural operations. Further, most cutting devices operate orthogonal to the planar contour, requiring intersecting sections to fit together orthogonally. We enforce and exploit this orthogonality property in our proposed interface.

Frontoparallel views: Sketching error, even for experts drawing on 3D planes, is clearly corelated to the degree of foreshortening of the plane [21]. We thus use frontoparallel views by default when drawing contours, since our own analysis confirmed that artists naturally tended to sketch from or near frontoparallel views, and sketching curves on oblique 3D planes consistently produced unpredictable results.

Single-view interface: We also experimented with a multi-view system such as [9], where users worked in disparate viewports to manipulate planes and contours. Artists overwhelmingly preferred a single 3D view for multiple reasons: maximal use of screen space, attention and drawing cursor is not shifted between views, and a single view provides a modeling context between new curves and the evolving design.

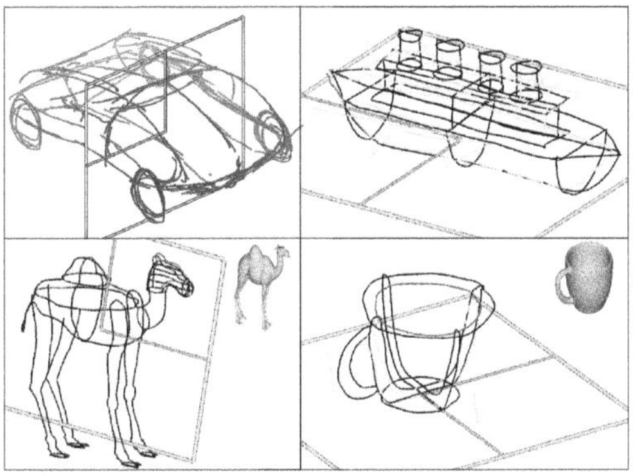

Figure 4. Pilot study artist creations: freeform objects (top row); reference objects with object shown inset (bottom row).

CREATING PLANAR SECTIONS

Our interface allows a mix of sketch-based drawing and CAD style control point editing of shape contours. Planar section structures may be exported in-situ in 3D (OBJ for visualization) or 2D (SVG for fabrication).

Single stroke planar section creation.

Central to our approach is the creation of a new planar section, accomplished using a single stroke, illustrated in Figure 5 and the accompanying video. This stroke entails:

Defining the slit: The stroke first defines the *slit*, where two orthogonal planar sections join. The stroke starts on the interior of an existing planar section, defining one endpoint for the slit axis, and defines a slit when the cursor exits the planar section interior. A new canvas plane containing the slit is defined orthogonal to the existing planar section.
View rotation and translation: The system rotates the view so the new canvas plane is viewed frontoparallel. Importantly, rotation is constrained so the slit endpoint remains fixed beneath the cursor. This rotation preserves drawing focus and view translation is used to ensure there is available screen space to draw the next planar section contour.
Deadzone: Using an earlier prototype, artists felt constrained being forced to start the planar section contour at the slit endpoint. The *deadzone*, a capsule shaped region in the viewport around the slit, addresses this issue. The deadzone prevents the planar section contour from being defined until the cursor exits the region, which has a fixed radius relative to the dimensions of the viewport. A planar section contour can thus begin near either slit endpoint, or anywhere in between.
Contour sketching: As the user sketches, our system fits a cubic Bézier spline, with a final Bézier segment to close the curve. When the stroke is completed, the planar section is created, completing the interaction. When there are no existing planar sections to start with, the contour is defined on a frontoparallel viewed plane that intersects a point at a fixed distance above the origin (default: 3.3 units).

A stroke principally on one side of the slit axis is effectively used to indicate symmetry across a planar section. If the ratio of maximal distances of the stroke on either side of the axis is sufficiently high (6.0 in our implementation), the stroke is mirrored across the axis and smoothly joined (Figure 6).

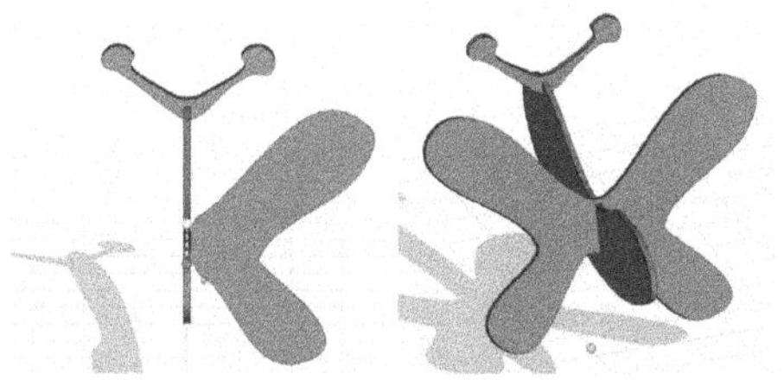

Figure 6. A planar section contour drawn principally on one side of the slit (left), is mirrored across slit and smoothly joined (right).

Template 3D objects

We typically use watertight 3D mesh templates, that produce closed planar section contours, but can also handle arbitrary meshes by smoothly joining open contours using cubic Bézier segments. The model is scaled (10 units) and centered in our interface to rest upon the ground plane (minimum Y vertex set to $Y = 0$). Precise ground contact is not essential as the planar sections are free to deviate from the template and are clipped to ensure proper ground contact. The model is rendered transparently so as not to obscure the planar sections

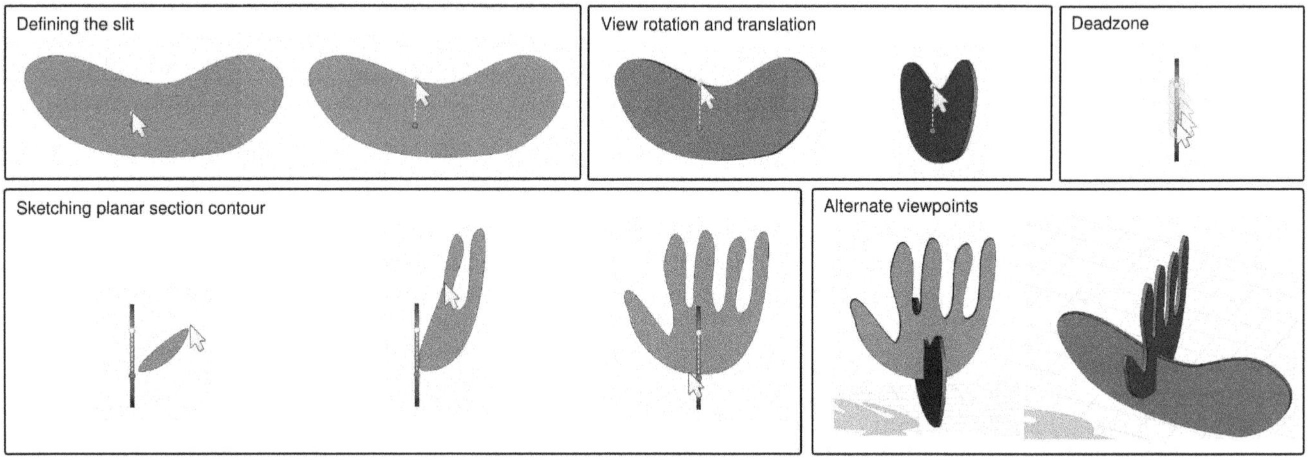

Figure 5. Single stroke planar section creation: once the user defines the slit connecting a new planar section to an existing section, the system rotates around the slit endpoint to a frontoparallel view (top row); the user moves outside the deadzone (top right) to begin sketching the contour (bottom row).

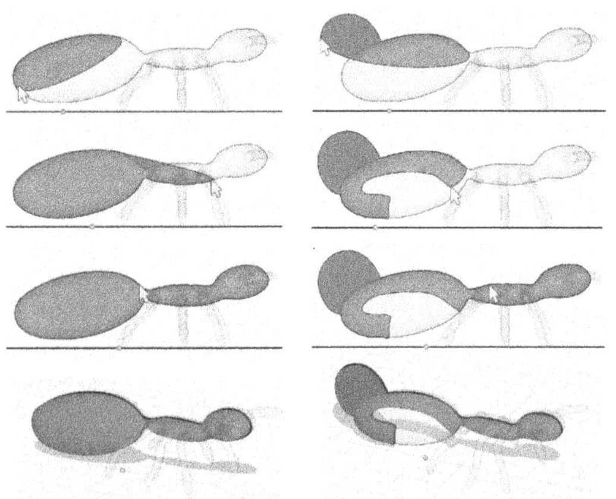

Figure 7. Snapping to a template object: a user sketches roughly along the guide curve to snap to the template object (left column) or deviate from it when desired (right column).

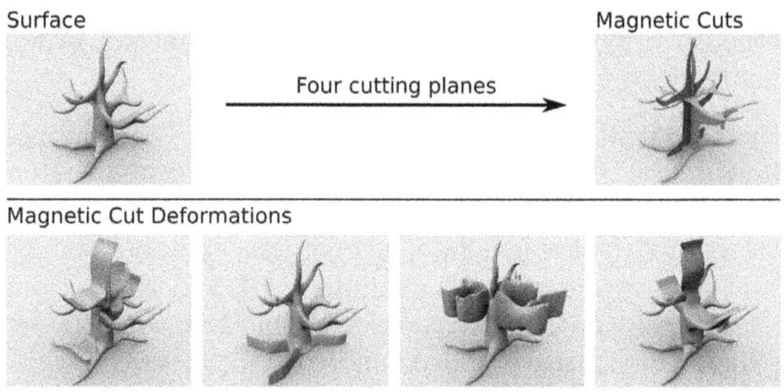

Figure 8. The template (top left) and 4 magnetic cut planar sections (top right). The deformation relative to each plane is shown (bottom row).

and serves as a guide for planar section creation ($\alpha = 0.25$ with back-face culling enabled in our implementation).

Ideal templates: Once the user draws the slit to define a new plane, guide curve(s) that are the intersection of plane and the template are shown. The user can then simply snap to desired parts of guide curves by over-tracing (distance to curve 0.5 units by default) or smoothly deviate from them (Figure 7).

Non-ideal templates: Objects with large articulations or highly non-planar curvature lines are inherently ill-suited to planar sections. Artists locally distort nearby surface features of such shapes so they lie on planar section contours. We propose a *magnetic cut* spatial deformation, that captures this behaviour. Points P within a distance r to the plane are attracted along the plane's normal N, towards the plane (Figure 8) to $P' = P + N\,[N \cdot (Q - P) + (N_P \cdot N)r]$, where Q is a point on the plane and N_P is the surface normal at P. The deformation moves the local shape silhouette viewed along N to lie along the planar section contour. In practice this works well for small deformations, and large articulations are best handled piece-wise, using multiple planar sections.

PROCEDURAL MODELLING

We are inspired by procedural modelling research [6, 10, 14], in defining a vocabulary of modeling operations that provide specific support for various inter-plane and contour shape regularities observed in artistic planar section structures.

Affine operations

We define a family of affinely transformed replicas of a *clone* planar section along a *root* planar section. The basic operation clones a planar section along one side of the root planar section, preserving the normal direction of the clone at a fixed offset. The replicated sections are also translated along the intersection axis, to ensure that the line of intersection between replica and root is of equal length for all replicas (Figure 9). Alternatively, sections can be replicated to conform to the root contour, by rotating the replicas using the tangent direction along the root. To keep the orientation of replicas consistent, the relative angle between the clone plane normal and root boundary tangent is maintained across all revolved replicas (Figure 11). We observe that often the scale of replicas naturally varies with the local thickness of the root contour, for example the ribs are larger where the spine is thicker and vice-versa (Figure 9). We can support this behaviour by uniformly scaling replicas based on local thickness of the root contour, computed as the contour girth along the line of intersection between replica and root (Figures 9 and 10).

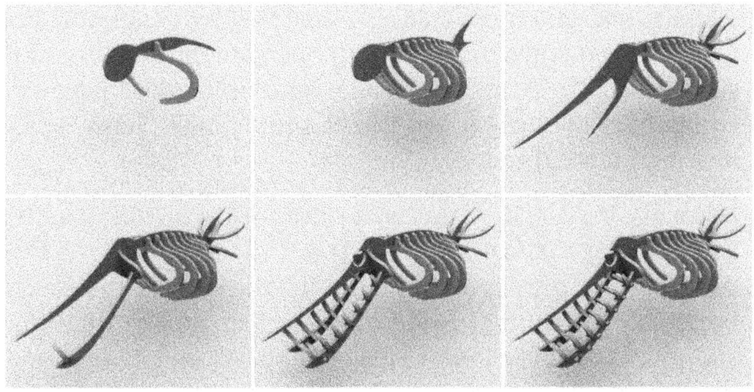

Figure 9. Fish skeleton created using affine operations, shaowing a variation in rib and tooth size with the local thickness of the spine and jaw.

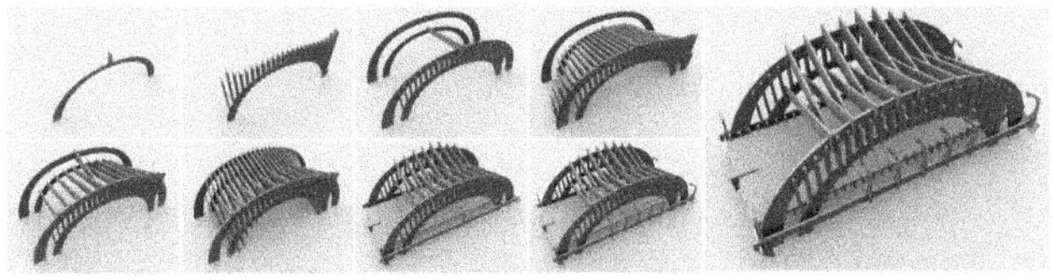

Figure 10. A bridge created using the range of affine operations.

Blend operation

The blend operation creates blended copies of two cloned planar sections P and Q along a root planar section, as simultaneously interpolated 2D contours and affinely transformed 3D planes, (Figure 12). We morph 2D contours by first finding a point-point correspondence between contours P and Q and then simply interpolate corresponding 2D point positions. The correspondence is computed by uniformly sampling both contours using n points (indexed p_i, q_i) and then finding an offset k that minimizes the sum of pairwise distances between points in P and Q (including a reversed point order), $\min_{k\in\{0,\ldots,n-1\}} \sum_{i=0}^{n-1} \left|\left|p_{((k+i) \bmod n)} - q_i\right|\right|_2$. The interpolated contours are then replicated in 3D, using an affine operation, where the relative angle between the clone plane normal and root tangent at P and Q is also interpolated.

Branching operation

The re-configurable nature of procedural planar sections also lends itself to hierarchical modeling. Given a planar section structure with a designated *root* section, connected to *child* sections, a branch operation replaces one or more of the children with replicas of the entire hierarchy. The slit on the root section where the replicated hierarchy is attached is interactively specified by the user. The children to be replicated and the scale of the replicated hierarchy can be randomized or user-controlled to rapidly produce complex and natural-looking planar section hierarchies (Figure 13).

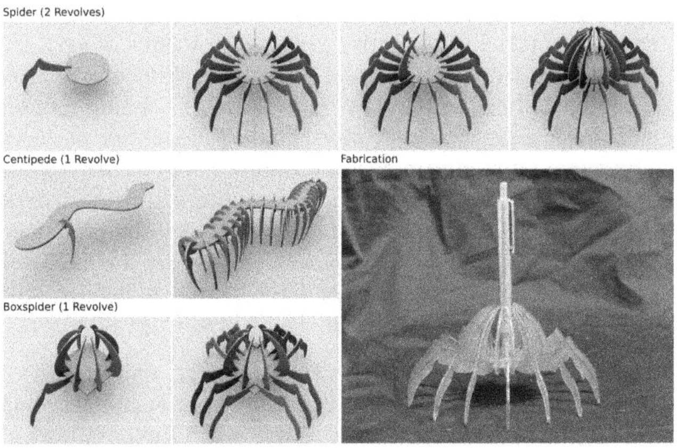

Figure 11. A number of insect-like examples, created using affine revolve operations. A fabricated spider holds a pen (bottom right).

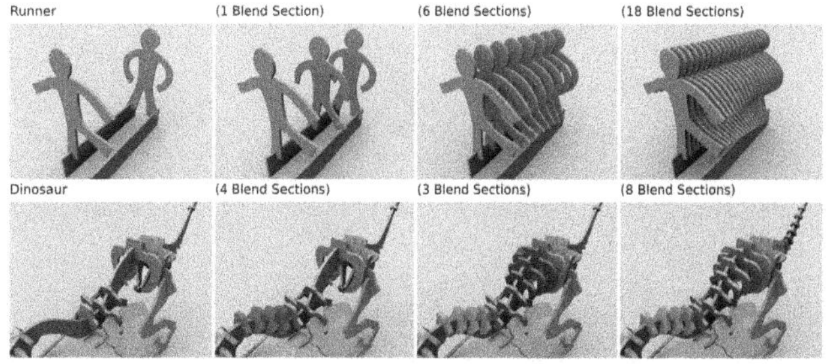

Figure 12. A figure in two different poses is blended using 1, 6 or 18 planar sections (top row). Three blend operations (rendered in blue) are used to create vertebrae and ribs along the dinosaur spine (bottom row).

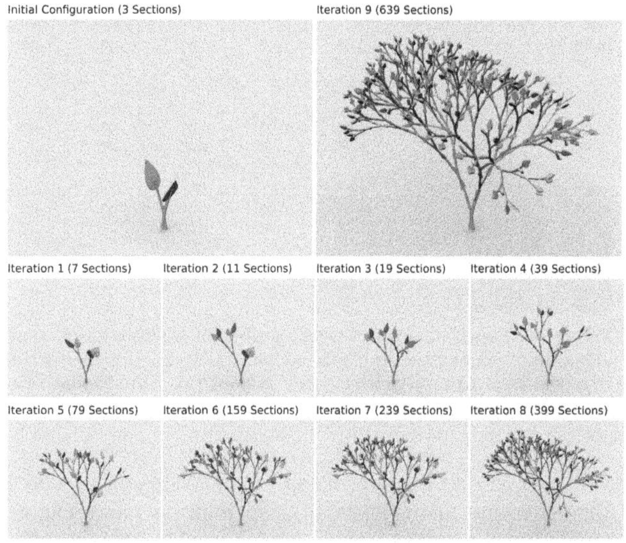

Figure 13. A Y-shaped root section and two leaf-shaped child sections (top left), produce a planar section tree structure (top right) after 9 iterations of branch operations (bottom rows) .

Grid operation

The physical dimensions of each planar section can be restricted by the size of the cutter-bed or material sheets used for fabrication. We address this using a grid operation that divides large sections into a collection of smaller sections

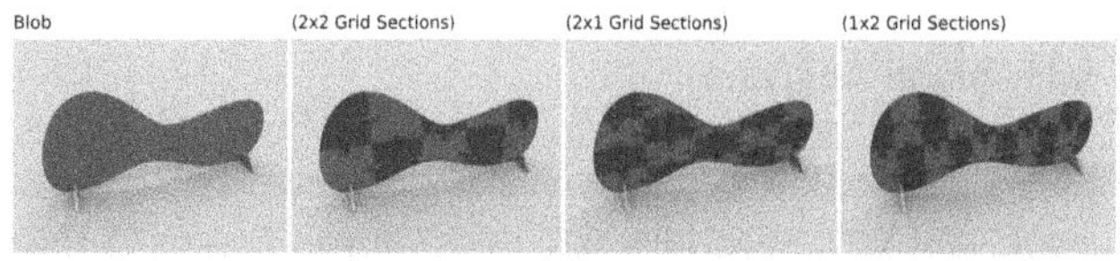

Figure 14. A planar section (left) is split into gridded sections (rendered in blue and green). H-shaped connecting sections (rendered in red) are automatically generated along grid edges.

Figure 15. Radial operations are used to control planar section contours, producing the discs, gears (top row) and holes (bottom row) shown in blue.

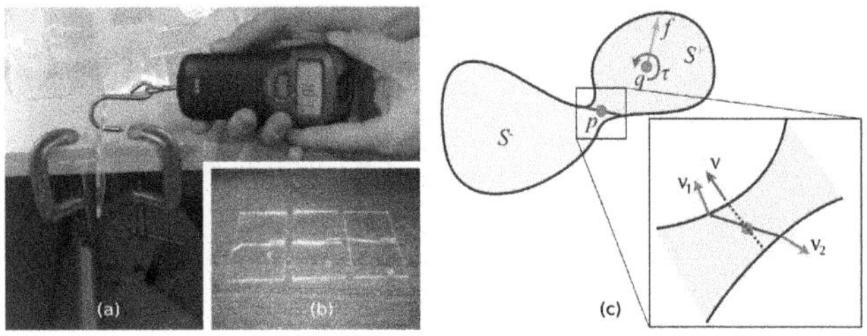

Figure 16. Experiment where force required for fracture was measured along three major axes on planar section joints (a). Fracture occured in a consistent pattern, across planar sections (b). Visualization of our cross-sectional structural analysis, based on beam theory (c).

which assemble together using automatically generated H-shaped connectors (Figure 14). Such an operation can also be used to create decorative jigsaw puzzle-like tiled sections.

Radial contour operation

As an example of procedural control over the contour shape of planar sections, we allow users to control the radial profile of a section to make circles, stars, holes or gear shapes with varying holes and teeth (Figure 15).

PHYSICAL SIMULATION

Our system is designed to produce functional objects from planar sections that friction fit together along slits, such as the cutlery holder in Figure 1 or glass holders in Figure 17. Users convey functional use in our system by interactively placing external weights at various points on the planar section assemblies (Figure 1c, 17). We exploit the structure of planar section assemblies to formulate a novel physical model that is able to conservatively compute stresses across planar sections in real-time, using a combination of *inter-plane* and *intra-plane* analysis, with the computation of cross-sectional bending moments for a planar section structure.

Inter-plane Analysis

We assume planar sections to be undeformable and unbreakable rigid bodies, across which we compute forces on slit joints and contact points. Planar sections, subject to forces from external loads, joints, ground contact points, and internal gravitational force, are analyzed in static equilibrium. Planes rotate and translate in response to gravity and placed weights and this movement is countered by computing contact and joint constraint forces to maintain the stability of the structure [27]. After the contact and joint forces have been computed, we analyze the stress within each planar section based on these forces.

Formally, a point $\mathbf{p} \in \mathbb{R}^3$ on a rigid planar section is moved as $\hat{\mathbf{p}}(\mathbf{R}, \mathbf{u}) = \mathbf{R}(\mathbf{p} - \mathbf{p}_{cg}) + \mathbf{p}_{cg} + \mathbf{u}$, where $\mathbf{p}_{cg} \in \mathbb{R}^3$ is the center of gravity of the section, $\mathbf{u} \in \mathbb{R}^3$ is the translation and $\mathbf{R} \in SO(3)$ is the rotation matrix. The translation and rotation for each section is obtained by energy minimization subject to joint constraints. The total energy of the rigid section structure is computed as the sum of potential energy as:

$$E = -\sum_{i \in S} m\mathbf{g} \cdot \mathbf{u}^i - \sum_{i \in F} \mathbf{d}_i^w \cdot \mathbf{f}_i^w, \tag{1}$$

where S is the set of planar sections, F is the set of weights, $\mathbf{d}^w$ is the displacement of the weight as a result of the sections' movement, and $\mathbf{f}^w$ is the force from the weight. At each joint, we apply a joint constraint that prohibits the relative displacement and rotation of connected sections. Let two rigid sections A and B be connected at a joint point $\mathbf{p}_J$ at the inner end of the slit. The joint point on section A for example after movement is $\mathbf{R}_A(\mathbf{p}_J - \mathbf{p}_{cg}) + \mathbf{p}_{cg} + \mathbf{u}_A$. The relative displacement constraint $(\mathbf{R}_A(\mathbf{p}_J - \mathbf{p}_{cg}) + \mathbf{p}_{cg} + \mathbf{u}_A) - (\mathbf{R}_B(\mathbf{p}_J - \mathbf{p}_{cg}) + \mathbf{p}_{cg} + \mathbf{u}_B) = 0$ thus implies that sections A and B remain connected at the joint point. A rotation constraint keeps the rotation of connected sections A and B the same, i.e. $(\mathbf{R}_A\mathbf{R}_B^T) = \mathbf{I}$,. Contact constraints keep the distance of points of contact from the ground plane at zero. We minimize the total energy in Equation 1, subject to the displacement, rotation and contact constraints, using Newton's method, and obtain the constraint forces at joint and ground contact points (detailed in [27]).

Intra-plane Analysis

Our intra-plane analysis uses the joint and contact forces from inter-plane analysis to compute the bending moment acting on cross-sections of a plane [28] and its consequent stress using beam theory [26]. The forces at contact points on either side of a planar cross-section (we assume the section is not an annulus) induce bending moments that are equal and opposite in equilibrium (Figure 16c). Classifying the sidedness of contact points relative to the cross-section of a plane is straightforward, allowing us to compute bending moments efficiently. In beam theory, the ratio between bending moment and stress along a cross-section is called the *section modulus*. The section modulus in turn is proportional to the rectangular dimensions of the cross-section, implying that the narrower the cross-section, the greater the stress. In our implementation, we display weak cross-sections, where the stress exceeds $1/5$ the maximum stress the material can handle, color coded from blue to red for 20%-100% of the maximum stress.

Formally, let the force points (joint, contact and weight) be $\mathbf{q}^i$ with linear force $\mathbf{f}^i$ and torque $\boldsymbol{\tau}^i$ (torque at contact points is zero), for $i \in K$, where K is the set of force points on a section (Figure 16c). In equilibrium, the linear forces sum to zero: $m\mathbf{g} + \sum_{i \in K} \mathbf{f}^i = 0$ where m is the mass of the section.

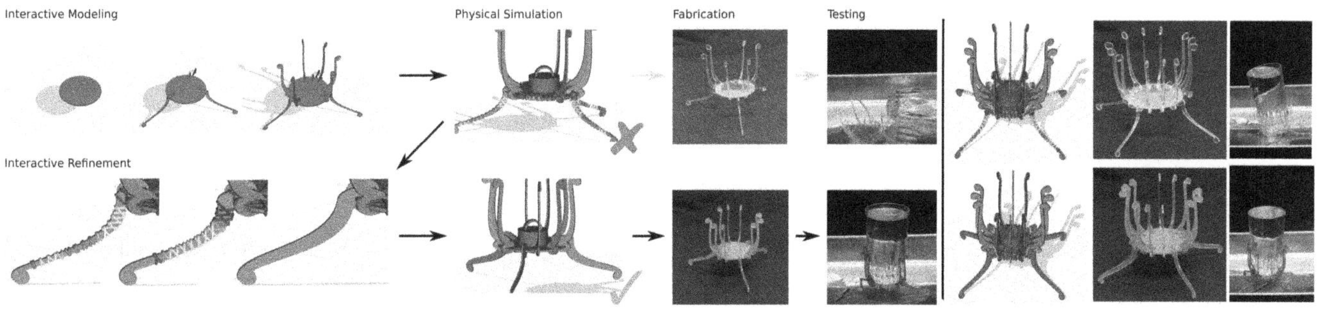

Figure 17. Our real-time physical simulation, interactively visualizes cross-sectional lines of stress along planar sections where fracture is likely (20%-100% maximum allowed stress rendered blue to red). Users interactively edit the model to satisfy both form and function. Physical fabrication of weak (top row) and strong (bottom row) variants of 3-legged (left) and 4-legged (right) glass holders validates predictions of fracture made by our system.

Moment equilibrium similarly, implies that the moment at the given point in the section $\mathbf{p}$ becomes zero:

$$m\mathbf{g} \times (\mathbf{p}_{cg} - \mathbf{p}) + \sum_{i \in K} \mathbf{f}^i \times (\mathbf{q}^i - \mathbf{p}) + \boldsymbol{\tau}^i = 0. \quad (2)$$

We compute the bending moment at the center of a cross-section $\mathbf{p}$ by partitioning Equation 2 into moments $\boldsymbol{\tau}^+$, $\boldsymbol{\tau}^-$ on either side of the cross-section S^+ and S^- (Figure 16c). $\boldsymbol{\tau}^+(\mathbf{p}) = m^+\mathbf{g} \times (\mathbf{p}^+_{cg} - \mathbf{p}) + \sum_{i \in K^+} \mathbf{f}^i \times (\mathbf{q}^i - \mathbf{p}) + \boldsymbol{\tau}^i$, where K^+ are force points on side S^+. $\boldsymbol{\tau}^- = -\boldsymbol{\tau}^+$ by Equation 2.

To model section fracture as the breaking of a beam, we define a medial axis passing through $\mathbf{p}$, with direction $\mathbf{v}$ making an equal angle to the two normals at the ends of the cross-section $\mathbf{v_1}$ and $\mathbf{v_2}$ (Figure 16c). The cross-section shape is rectangular with dimensions l and t, where l is the cross-section length projected on $\mathbf{v}$, and t is the thickness of the material. The section modulus (ratio of bending moment and maximum stress) for bending around $\mathbf{v}$ is $Z_v = \frac{1}{6}t^2 l$. The maximum stress for this bending direction is thus, $\sigma_v = |\boldsymbol{\tau}^+ \cdot \mathbf{v}|/Z_v$. We similarly compute bending around the normal direction $\mathbf{n}$ of the planar section, using section modulus $Z_n = \frac{1}{6}l^2 t$, and maximum bending stress $\sigma_n = |\boldsymbol{\tau}^+ \cdot \mathbf{n}|/Z_n$. Critical cross-sections have σ_v or σ_n in excess of the maximum material stress.

We performed a physical experiment (Figure 16a,b) to find that planar sections tend to fracture local to slits where sections join. We thus ensure that cross-section samples are selected aligned and local to each slit, in addition to uniformly sampling a cross-section grid over each planar section. We also note that while there is stress nonlinearity around slits, in practice we may compute a virtual stress assuming no slits and multiply it with a stress concentration factor (rarely above five). Our simulation is thus approximate but conservative, efficient and adequate for interactive modeling.

Verifying simulation predictions

We created various fabricated models that were consistent with the predictions of our physical simulation. Figure 1 shows a cutlery holder inspired by da Vinci's "Vitruvian Man". The two human forms were traced over the image on two orthogonal planes. The hands, contoured like the cutlery to be hung on each arm, deviated from the image. Weights were placed on the arms to simulate (viewed clockwise from above) 6 forks (376g), tablespoons (476g), teaspoons (185g) and knives (405g). The assembly was interactively scaled until the cutlery would hang clear of the ground, and the arms were strong enough to bear the cutlery weight. The values of the physical properties for the acrylic sheets were taken from catalogued values on a product website (density: 1190 kg/m^3, tensile strength: 60 MPa).

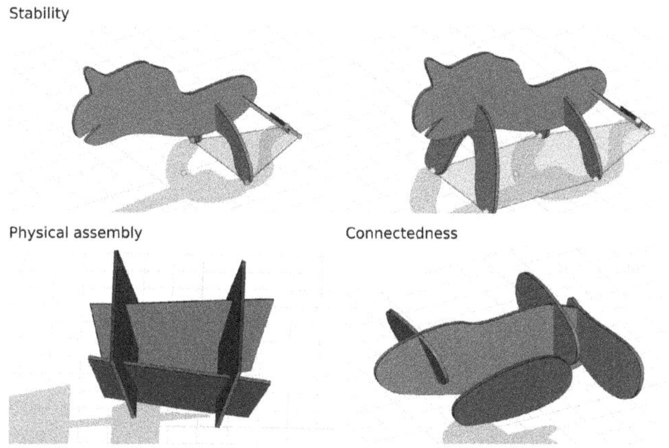

Figure 18. Our system performs various geometric feasibility tests and renders problems in red: a structure with center of mass outside the contact region will fall (top left); adding new ground contact points results in a geometrically stable model (top right); cycles of planar sections with non-parallel intersection lines cannot be physically assembled (bottom left); unconnected planar sections are flagged (bottom right).

Figure 17 shows four design variations of an object intended to hold a glass of water (275g, 350ml capacity). The first variation created had 3 thin legs, which fracture well before a glass can be filled (top row, left). Four thin legs are stronger but also fracture as predicted (top row, right). Three thicker legs just about support a full glass of water, and our system warns of a potential fracture where the legs and central disc meet (bottom row, left). A thicker 4 leg design (bottom row, right) is conservatively strong. Interactive physical feedback thus reduces wasteful real-world fabrication and testing.

FABRICATION

In addition to real-time physical simulation of the planar section structure, we perform geometric tests relating to stability, connectivity and the ability to assemble the planar sections.

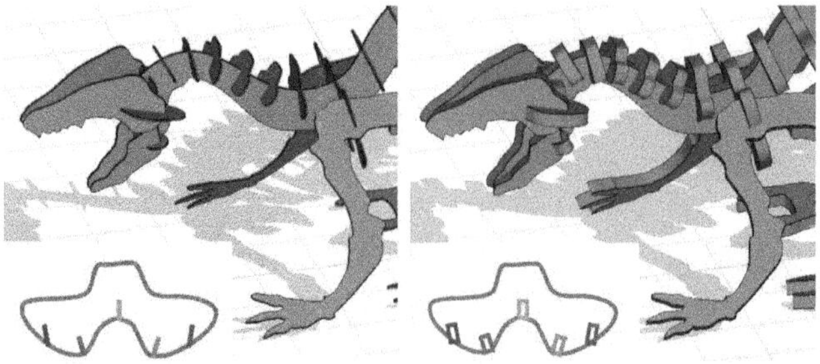

Figure 19. Adjusting planar section thickness (left: 0.02 units, right: 0.2 units). The material thickness value defines the slit width (inset).

Together, these tests ensure there are minimal issues during the fabrication process, while the model is still in digital form.

Feasibility tests

Geometric stability. Our system computes the center of mass of the model and the convex hull of any contact points with the ground plane. If the projected center of mass falls within the convex hull, the model is *geometrically stable* – it does not "fall over" when placed on a flat surface. Our system shows the convex hull of the extremal contact points and the center of mass on the ground plane (Figure 18 (top row)).

Our system also interactively translates the control points of planar section contours to remain on or above the ground plane, and visually emphasizes intersections of the current canvas plane with the ground plane. This ensures that manufactured models will have co-planar contact points.

Physical assembly. Not all planar section configurations can be physically assembled [23]. Planar sections which form cycles with non-parallel intersections make physical assembly impossible. Our system detects and reveals cycles that the user can resolve interactively (Figure 18 (bottom left)).

Connectedness. Planar sections which "float in space" cannot exist in the physical world, therefore we test *connectedness* throughout interaction. Planar sections are treated as vertices in a graph, and edges are defined by their intersections. Our system computes and reveals unconnected planar section components (Figure 18 (bottom right)).

Slits and section correspondence

Our system automatically computes the slits to cut into each planar section. For a given pair of planar sections, the axis of intersection of the planes is calculated. Then, the points on the planar section contours which intersect the axis are computed and sorted in order along the axis. When two adjacent contour points with index k and $k+1$ along the intersection axis belong to different planar sections, an intersection condition is detected and slit rectangles are made between points p_{k+1} and p_{k+2}. To locally approximate how the two planar sections slide together, we compute and compare the distances $d_1 = ||p_k - p_{k+1}||_2$, and $d_2 = ||p_{k+2} - p_{k+3}||_2$. Depending on the direction, one slit endpoint will be defined by the midpoint between p_{k+1} and p_{k+2}, and the other endpoint will be either p_{k+1} or p_{k+2}.

The slits are shaped as rectangles which follow the intersection axis, with a width equal to the thickness of the planar sections as they are shown during interaction. The planar section thickness can be adjusted interactively (Figure 19). Corresponding planar section slits are assigned specific colors (or numberic labels) when output as an SVG file to aid in assembly (Figure 19 (inset)).

EVALUATION

We comprehensively evaluated our system with two groups, comprising 38 high school students and 12 users with varying artistic experience.

High School Design Class

We provided our modelling software to students taking a design class at a local high school, along lines similar to [3]. On the first day, we instructed students at a higher level for 30 minutes on how to use the software, followed by 30 minutes of working with students individually, answering questions and offering suggestions. Students in three classes, with around 15 students in each, were given a design theme: creatures, architecture, or furnishings. The students were given one week to use the software (approximately 90 minutes of use everyday). On a follow-up visit we acquired the students' completed models (Figure 21), and had 38 students who used the software complete a questionnaire on the experience of using our software. Responses to each question were defined using a 5-point Likert scale (see Table 1).

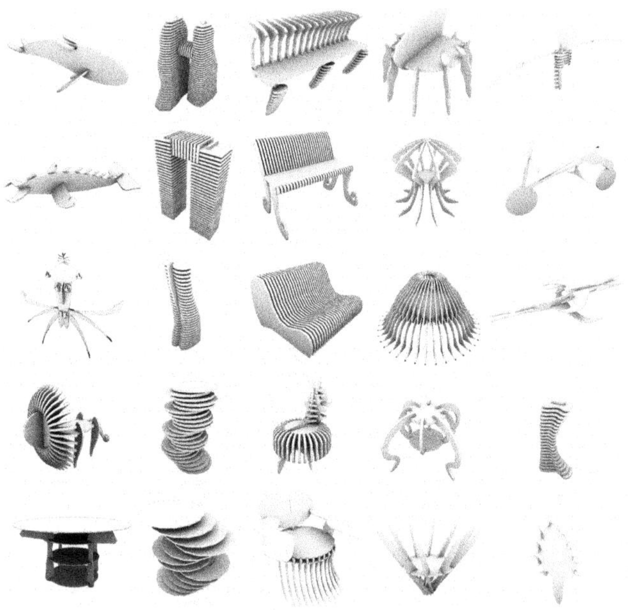

Figure 21. Models by 25 different students in a high school design class.

Other Users

We also provided our system to 12 users (with varying computer graphics experience), with a 15 minute tutorial video and a one-page instruction sheet. We show some of their creations in Figures 20 and 22. Users filled out an informal questionnaire, relating to modeling times, experience, and specific features. On average users reported: 5 to 30 minutes

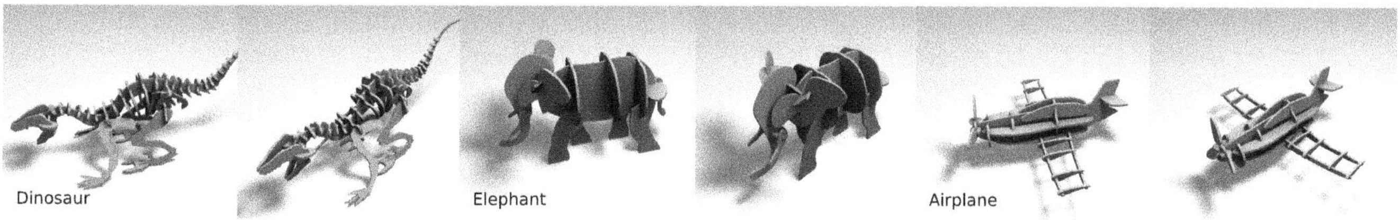

Figure 20. Planar section assemblies created using our system.

Shape modelling with planar sections?
Creation using a single continuous stroke?
Automatic view rotation?
Approach to 3D view manipulation?
The procedural modelling operations?
Dragging control points to edit a planar section?
Procedural modelling operations were ____ to use.
The program was ____ to learn.
The program was ____ to use.
The user interface of the program was ____.
Using the program was ____ to remember.
I am ____ to continue using the program.

Table 1. Evaluation by 38 high school students. Left-most values on the scale represent very negative responses and right-most values very positive responses.

Figure 22. A gallery of creations by the 12 other users.

for system familiarity, 2 to 8 hours modeling shapes, 2 to 6 objects modeled with creation times ranging from 15 to 30 minutes. The *single stroke* interface was considered by far the most "fun" and useful feature of the interface barring one user who said he would have preferred a split-view, engineering drawing based precision workflow. The *procedural operations* were easily understood and heavily used by all users. About half the users found the *physical feedback* very meaningful. The remainder (who were not fabricating the models) did not pay any heed to it. While we support local symmetry around a slit, some users found the lack of support for global symmetry problematic and time consuming. Such a feature is easily added given our graph structure for the planar sections.

CONCLUSION

We have presented a comprehensive system for the creation of planar section assemblies with real-time geometric and physical feedback, aimed at fabricating functional objects. Various components of our drawing workflow, magnetic cuts, some procedural operations (Figure 9) and physical simulation are novel, but we believe our biggest contribution is a carefully formulated overall system design. Our system has a few missing features, such as global symmetry support or testing for global collisions when assembling sections in a given order, which are subject to future work. More exciting though, are the possibilities of transcending planar sections to assemblies composed of interlocking curved surfaces using LaserOrigami [13] or height-field sections, milled using CNC routers or 3D printers. At the same time, we expect our system to positively impact the creativity of traditional cardboard and scissor hobbyists.

Perhaps the most interesting remark from one of our set of 12 users was, "I imagine in 3D but think and draw in 2D and this system allows me to do both seamlessly, in a way I find difficult with other 3D modeling software". We thus believe that our planar curve drawing technique will have application outside of planar section assemblies, as an overwhelming majority of 3D curves in design sketching are in fact planar [5].

REFERENCES

1. Cnc panel joinery notebook. `http://makezine.com/2012/04/13/cnc-panel-joinery-notebook/`. Accessed: 2014-07-03.

2. Bae, S., Balakrishnan, R., and Singh, K. ILoveSketch: as-natural-as-possible sketching system for creating 3d curve models. In *UIST* (2008).

3. Bae, S.-H., Balakrishnan, R., and Singh, K. Everybodylovessketch: 3d sketching for a broader audience. UIST '09, ACM (New York, NY, USA, 2009), 59–68.

4. Cignoni, P., Pietroni, N., Malomo, L., and Scopigno, R. Field-aligned mesh joinery. *ACM Trans. Graph. 33*, 1 (Feb. 2014), 11:1–11:12.

5. Eissen, K., and Steur, R. *Sketching: Drawing Techniques for Product Designers*. Bis Publishers, 2008.

6. Hart, G. W. Modular kirigami. *Journal of Mathematics and the Arts* (2007).

7. Hildebrand, K., Bickel, B., and Alexa, M. crdbrd : Shape Fabrication by Sliding Planar Slices. *Computer Graphics Forum (Eurographics 2012) 31*, 2 (2012).

8. Igarashi, T., Matsuoka, S., and Tanaka, H. Teddy: A sketching interface for 3d freeform design. SIGGRAPH '99, ACM Press/Addison-Wesley Publishing Co. (New York, NY, USA, 1999), 409–416.

9. Johnson, G., Gross, M., Do, E. Y.-L., and Hong, J. Sketch it, make it: sketching precise drawings for laser cutting. CHI EA '12, ACM (New York, NY, USA, 2012), 1079–1082.

10. Krecklau, L., and Kobbelt, L. Smi 2012: Full interactive modeling by procedural high-level primitives. *Comput. Graph. 36*, 5 (Aug. 2012), 376–386.

11. Li, X.-Y., Ju, T., Gu, Y., and Hu, S.-M. A geometric study of v-style pop-ups: theories and algorithms. In *SIGGRAPH* (2011), 98:1–98:10.

12. McCrae, J., Singh, K., and Mitra, N. J. Slices: a shape-proxy based on planar sections. *SIGGRAPH Asia 30*, 6 (2011), 168:1–168:12.

13. Mueller, S., Kruck, B., and Baudisch, P. Laserorigami: Laser-cutting 3d objects. In *Proceedings of the SIGCHI Conference on Human Factors in Computing Systems*, CHI '13, ACM (New York, NY, USA, 2013), 2585–2592.

14. Müller, P., Wonka, P., Haegler, S., Ulmer, A., and Van Gool, L. Procedural modeling of buildings. In *ACM SIGGRAPH 2006 Papers*, SIGGRAPH '06, ACM (New York, NY, USA, 2006), 614–623.

15. Oh, J.-H., Hanson, D., Kim, W.-S., Han, Y., Kim, J.-Y., and Park, I.-W. Design of android type humanoid robot albert hubo. In *IROS* (2006), 1428–1433.

16. OH, Y., JOHNSON, G., GROSS, M., and DO, E.-L. The designosaur and the furniture factory. In *Design Computing and Cognition 06*, J. GERO, Ed. Springer Netherlands, 2006, 123–140.

17. Paczkowski, P., Kim, M. H., Morvan, Y., Dorsey, J., Rushmeier, H., and O'Sullivan, C. Insitu: Sketching architectural designs in context. *ACM Transactions on Graphics 30*, 182 (12/2011 2011).

18. Prévost, R., Whiting, E., Lefebvre, S., and Sorkine-Hornung, O. Make It Stand: Balancing shapes for 3D fabrication. *ACM Transactions on Graphics (proceedings of ACM SIGGRAPH) 32*, 4 (2013), 81:1–81:10.

19. Rivers, A., Durand, F., and Igarashi, T. 3d modeling with silhouettes. In *ACM SIGGRAPH 2010 Papers*, SIGGRAPH '10, ACM (New York, NY, USA, 2010), 109:1–109:8.

20. Saul, G., Lau, M., Mitani, J., and Igarashi, T. Sketchchair: An all-in-one chair design system for end users. In *Tangible, Embedded, and Embodied Interaction*, TEI '11, ACM (2011), 73–80.

21. Schmidt, R., Khan, A., Kurtenbach, G., and Singh, K. On expert performance in 3D curve-drawing tasks. In *Proceedings of EUROGRAPHICS Symposium on Sketch-Based Interfaces and Modeling (SBIM)* (2009).

22. Schmidt, R., Khan, A., Singh, K., and Kurtenbach, G. Analytic drawing of 3d scaffolds. *ACM Transactions on Graphics 28*, 5 (2009), (to appear). Proceedings of SIGGRAPH ASIA 2009.

23. Schwartzburg, Y., and Pauly, M. Fabrication-aware design with intersecting planar pieces. *Computer Graphics Forum (Proceedings of Eurographics 2013) 32*, 2 (2013).

24. Shao, C., Bousseau, A., Sheffer, A., and Singh, K. Crossshade: shading concept sketches using cross-section curves. *SIGGRAPH 31*, 4 (2012), 45:1–45:11.

25. Sutherland, I. E. Sketch pad a man-machine graphical communication system. In *Proceedings of the SHARE Design Automation Workshop*, DAC '64, ACM (New York, NY, USA, 1964), 6.329–6.346.

26. Timoshenko, S. *Theory of Elasticity*, 3 ed. Mcgraw-Hill College, 6 1970.

27. Umetani, N., Igarashi, T., and Mitra, N. J. Guided exploration of physically valid shapes for furniture design. *ACM Trans. Graph. 31*, 4 (July 2012), 86:1–86:11.

28. Umetani, N., and Schmidt, R. Cross-sectional structural analysis for 3d printing optimization. In *SIGGRAPH Asia 2013 Technical Briefs*, SA '13, ACM (New York, NY, USA, 2013), 5:1–5:4.

29. Whiting, E., Shin, H., Wang, R., Ochsendorf, J., and Durand, F. Structural optimization of 3d masonry buildings. *ACM Transactions on Graphics 31*, 6 (2012), 159:1–159:11.

30. Willis, K. D., Lin, J., Mitani, J., and Igarashi, T. Spatial sketch: bridging between movement and fabrication. In *In Proc. Tangible, embedded, and embodied interaction* (2010), 5–12.

31. Zhu, K., and Zhao, S. Autogami: a low-cost rapid prototyping toolkit for automated movable paper craft. In *Proceedings of the SIGCHI Conference on Human Factors in Computing Systems*, CHI '13, ACM (New York, NY, USA, 2013), 661–670.

Paper3D: Bringing Casual 3D Modeling to a Multi-Touch Interface

Patrick Paczkowski* **Julie Dorsey*** **Holly Rushmeier*** **Min H. Kim†**
Yale University KAIST

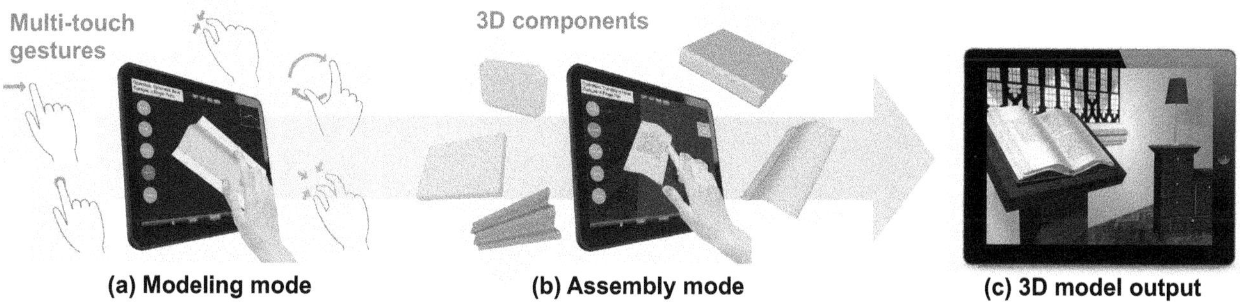

Figure 1. An overview of our novel 3D modeling technique, designed for a multi-touch interface to create 3D models on a tablet device. (a) Users fold 2D sheets of paper in the modeling mode, using gesture-based modeling tools such as folding, bending, extending, and cutting. (b) A set of modeled 3D components is assembled together through pinning and taping, resulting in (c) a complex 3D scene.

ABSTRACT
A 3D modeling system that provides all-inclusive functionality is generally too demanding for a casual 3D modeler to learn. In recent years, there has been a shift towards developing more approachable systems, with easy-to-learn, intuitive interfaces. However, most modeling systems still employ mouse and keyboard interfaces, despite the ubiquity of tablet devices, and the benefits of multi-touch interfaces applied to 3D modeling. In this paper, we introduce an alternative 3D modeling paradigm for creating developable surfaces, inspired by traditional papercrafting, and implemented as a system designed from the start for a multi-touch tablet. We demonstrate the process of assembling complex 3D scenes from a collection of simpler models, in turn shaped through operations applied to sheets of virtual paper. The modeling and assembling operations mimic familiar, real-world operations performed on paper, allowing users to quickly learn our system with very little guidance. We outline key design decisions made throughout the development process, based on feedback obtained through collaboration with target users. Finally, we include a range of models created in our system.

Author Keywords
3D Modeling; Multi-Touch Interface; Papercraft; Folding

ACM Classification Keywords
I.3.5 Computational Geometry and Object Modeling

UIST 2014, October 5–8, 2014, Honolulu, HI, USA.
Copyright © 2014 ACM 978-1-4503-3069-5/14/10 ...$15.00.
http://dx.doi.org/10.1145/2642918.2647416

INTRODUCTION
Creating shapes is an essential operation in 3D computer graphics. Packages such as Blender or Maya provide many modeling techniques, e.g., polygonal modeling, modeling with NURBS or subdivision surfaces. However, learning how to use the majority of existing 3D modeling packages is challenging, hindering widespread use. An additional difficulty commonly experienced by users is the communication of 3D modeling coordinates through the standard user interface. Typical input devices (such as mice) and displays provide 2D input and output. These devices are inadequate for specifying 6 degree-of-freedom (DoF) position and orientation. Conversely, haptic devices with a full 6-DoF (e.g., Geomagic Touch) are inaccurate and difficult for novice users to operate due to a lack of haptic feedback on the tip of the pointer.

Recently, motion sensing interfaces with higher DoF have been commercialized, such as LeapMotion and Microsoft's Kinect, but these still suffer from lack of accuracy, underconstrained input and lack of haptic feedback. By contrast, input devices with multi-touch interfaces have evolved in recent years, with products like the Apple iPad and the Samsung Galaxy Tab. Though each input touch is still two-dimensional, the combination of two or more touches has resulted in gestures with more information than the input of a traditional, single-point device. Due to their ubiquity and intuitiveness, these devices are particularly powerful for casual users.

In the field of 3D modeling, research problems such as 3D transformations on a multi-touch device have been recently studied, and there are domain-specific modeling systems for a multi-touch interface. However, systems specifically focused on casual 3D modeling by users with little modeling experience (e.g., sketch-based interfaces) are still fairly limited either in scope, learnability or modeling representation. This paper

* e-mail: {patrick.paczkowski;julie.dorsey;holly.rushmeier}@yale.edu
† e-mail (corresponding author): minhkim@kaist.ac.kr

presents a novel 3D modeling paradigm tailored for such use, and fully leverages the benefits of a multi-touch interface.

Inspired by traditional papercraft art forms such as origami, we devised a modeling technique in which deformations mimic physically-based operations commonly performed on sheets of paper, such as folding, bending, cutting, pinning and taping. We used the simple, yet powerful principles of these ancient art techniques as a foundation, and extended it into a broader, practical technique for modeling developable surfaces. We designed and integrated this technique from the ground up for a multi-touch device. We evolved the system design in collaboration with both casual and experienced users. Figure 2 demonstrates a range of 3D models created using our system. Our contributions are as follows:

- A new modeling paradigm inspired by papercrafting, and extended by operations related to other physical actions;
- An implementation of Paper3D, based on this new paradigm, designed from the ground up to use multi-touch gestures;
- A discussion of the user-guided design decisions made throughout the evolution of our system;
- A validation of the effectiveness and usability of our system through extensive user feedback;
- A demonstration of a range of models and scenes designed by users of our system.

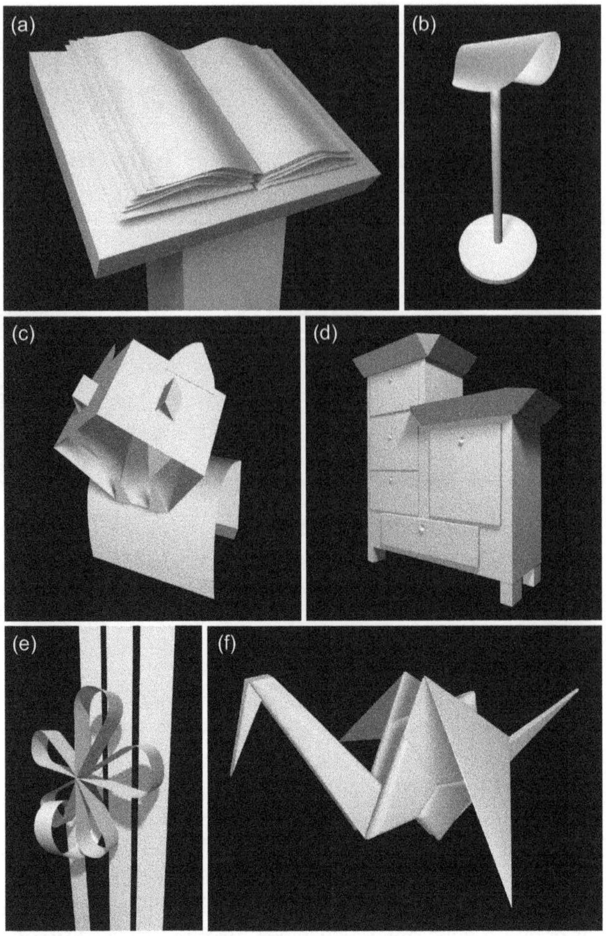

Figure 2. Six models created in our system (3D geometry shown only): (a) a book on a podium, (b) a lamp, (c) a papercraft tiger, (d) an armoire, (e) ribbons, and (f) an origami paper crane.

PREVIOUS WORK

This section surveys previous work in the fields of computing interfaces, 3D modeling and papercraft simulators.

Multi-Touch Interfaces

It is difficult to specify 3D coordinates using a 2D graphical interface (e.g., trackball, stylus, mouse), a limiting factor for intuitive graphical and modeling software. In recent years, indirect 3D graphical interfaces have gained popularity (e.g., Microsoft Kinect, LeapMotion, Geomagic Touch, etc.). Though these devices enable 6-DoF tracking, the lack of haptic feedback still limits their intuitiveness [9].

From their inception, it was clear that multi-touch interfaces, pioneered by Lee et al. [11], offer significant advantages with their wide range of natural inputs, such as pinch gestures. Multi-touch devices (Apple iPad, Microsoft Surface, etc.) are now widespread. In this work, we used a multi-touch graphical interface for a 3D modeling system. The *intuitiveness* of such devices does not fully eliminate the ambiguity of mapping 2D screen inputs into a 3D coordinate space, but we have found that users, particularly casual modelers, find these devices more natural.

3D Modeling Systems

This section surveys available 3D modeling alternatives.

Desktop Modeling Systems

Commercial desktop systems such as AutoCAD, Maya or SolidWorks provide extensive modeling capabilities suited for various industries. These tools are geared towards professionals who can go through extensive periods of training. More accessible, alternative modeling systems have gained in popularity, such as SketchUp (an easy to use system for architects) and ZBrush (a digital sculpting tool, relatable to traditional sculpting). It would be interesting to study how these systems might benefit from a multi-touch interface. For creating complex curved surfaces, desktop systems often rely on the specification of indirect control points (e.g., NURBS), which can take time to learn to use effectively.

Gesture-Based Modeling Systems

Most modeling techniques have one-point-based interaction – e.g., dragging a point or set of points to squash or stretch, grabbing something and moving it. There have been various papers describing and evaluating methods for transforming objects with multi-touch, e.g., [1, 3, 6, 12, 13]. However, this is just one small aspect of a modeling system. Some researchers have begun to explore how a multi-touch interface could be used to model primitive and abstract shapes [2, 8] or to interact with 3D objects [6]. De Araùjo et al. [4] introduced a semi-immersive environment for preliminary conceptual modeling without haptic feedback. While their experience was satisfactory, the modeling system itself proved insufficient for precise control of 3D geometry. Walther-Franks et al. [21]

performed a preliminary study by augmenting Blender, the 3D modeling tool, with a multi-touch interface. The multi-touch operations received positive feedback, but are mainly limited to object *animation* functions, rather than geometric modeling tools.

Recently, Autodesk launched a set of mobile products for modeling and design, including 123D Design and 123D Sculpt – notably simplified tools compared to their desktop counterparts. However, the modeling functions and interaction in these systems are still typical of *one-point-based* desktop modeling/sculpting systems – beyond view manipulation, little is done to take advantage of a multi-touch interface. Several domain-specific modeling systems have been created for multi-touch interfaces, such as Eden (for constructing organic sets) [10], Sun et al.'s system for architectural design [19], and Wilson et al.'s physics simulator [22]. However, these systems are not suitable for casual, general-purpose modeling, and are primarily targeted at domain-specific professional users.

Papercraft Simulators

Papercrafting is a set of art forms that use paper as an artistic medium to create physical 3D objects. In particular, origami, the traditional Japanese art of paper folding, has been extensively studied from a computer science and applied math perspective. Origami simulators have been implemented in various forms, including Maya plugins [17], stand-alone applications employing desktop interfaces [20], and others [14, 15]. Rather than producing a faithful simulation of origami, we use the time-honored principles of origami as a stepping stone to create a novel 3D modeling paradigm and system to design freeform 3D objects and scenes. Similar to the way sketching inspired the Teddy system by Igarashi et al. [7], we take inspiration from simple interactions with physical paper.

To summarize, our main goal is to propose a novel 3D modeling technique inspired by papercrafting and implemented as an intuitive system designed for a multi-touch interface. The following sections present details of Paper3D.

THE PAPER3D MODELING SYSTEM

To create an effective multi-touch modeling system, we observed that paper folding – a simple, physical process virtually anyone can identify with – has strong synergy with a multi-touch interface on a flat-surface device. We built on folding with additional physically inspired operations including cutting, bending, pinning and taping. We then further expanded the system to allow the assembly of sets of individually defined component objects into complex scenes. This form of inspiration allows us to focus purely on developable surfaces.

In the traditional papercraft art form of origami, a person begins with a single, square sheet of paper. Only three types of folds are permitted: mountain folds (forming a ridge), valley folds (forming a trough), and creases. Many combination folds exist (e.g., reverse, rabbit-ear, squash), but these are simply compositions of the three basic folds. Origami, and particularly the work of [15] inspired several initial modeling functions in our system. However, our work evolved into a modeling technique with broader functionality, extending far beyond the constraints of traditional origami or origami simulators. We give an overview of our modeling technique.

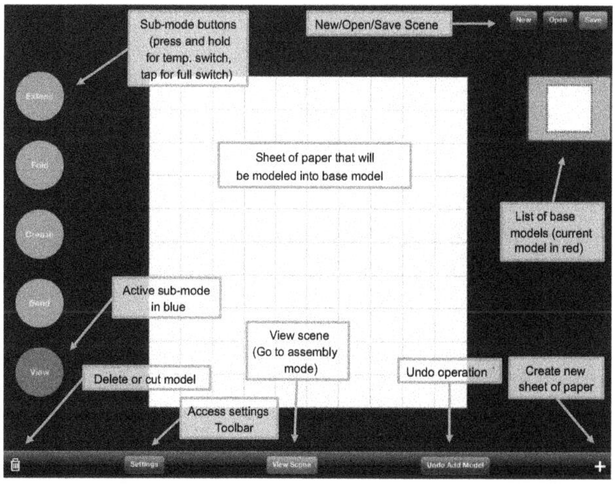

Figure 3. Interface for the *modeling* mode of Paper3D. Radio buttons (left) allow switching between submodes; the view submode is active. Model thumbnails (right) are used to select/edit a different model. The bottom toolbar offers additional functionality such as undoing. The *assembly* mode has different submodes but an otherwise similar interface.

This section gives a high-level overview of Paper3D (interface shown in Figure 3), followed by an in-depth description of the system's modeling and assembly tools in the next section.

Intuitive, Gesture-Based Interactions

Paper3D is created from the ground up for a tablet device with a multi-touch display (a third-gen. iPad). As such, the majority of user interaction with the system occurs through *intuitive* single- and multi-finger gestures. An intuitive interaction is one that has an easily understandable gesture mapping, is predictable and straightforward to replicate, and results in immediate visual feedback to the user. In the context of modeling, we focus on creating interactions that have a tangible, direct effect on a model. All user gestures requires a specific number of inputs – e.g., a 1-finger pan or a 2-finger pinch. We use the notation t_i to represent the normalized screen coordinate of the $(i+1)^{th}$ gesture input, and define t_{i_start} and t_{i_end} as the initial and new/final screen coordinates of the user's finger. The corresponding points projected along the camera view direction onto the plane of current face f are p_{i_start} and p_{i_end}. The primary gestures we used are illustrated in Figure 4.

Scene Objects

Similar to a standard polygonal mesh, each individual object, or *3D component* in our system consists of interconnected *faces*, *edges* and *vertices*. Each face is a convex, planar area of the component model; its closed outline is composed of n edges and vertices ($n \geq 3$). Every edge has exactly two

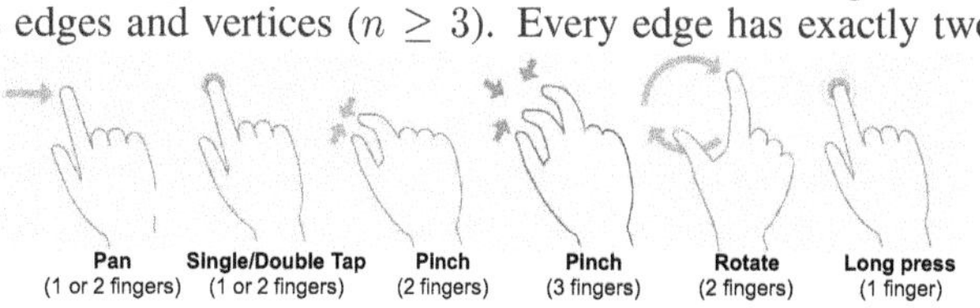

Figure 4. Examples of multi-touch gestures used in Paper3D.

vertices, and is classified as a *boundary edge* (belongs to a single face, or two folded-over faces), a *fold* (between two non-coplanar faces), or a *crease* (between two coplanar faces). Two or more edges can have the same vertex; we refer to a vertex belonging to two boundary edges as a *corner*.

System Modes

In Paper3D, there are two main stages of design (and corresponding modes): a *modeling* stage and an *assembly* stage. Figure 3 shows the interface of the modeling mode. Users can transition between the modes at any point. The *modeling mode* allows users to model sheets of source paper (one at a time) into 3D components through creasing, folding, bending, extending and cutting operations, as outlined in the previous section. In the assembly mode, users can insert models, transform them, and then intuitively group them together through pinning and taping operations.

Owing to the range of operations in each mode, certain functions require the same gesture. To remove ambiguity, the interface of each mode has five radio buttons to the left of the screen, grouping sets of operations into submodes. In the modeling mode, the five submodes are *extend, fold, bend, crease/cut*, and *view* (Figure 3). In the assembly mode, the submodes are *insert, transform, pin/tape, color*, and *view*. If desired, a user can rest a finger of their non-dominant hand on a submode button, activating the submode only for as long as they are holding the button. This can streamline operations – e.g., by allowing quick viewing of a model between modeling operations. In the modeling mode, thumbnails of existing models can be used to select a different model for editing. In the insert submode of assembly mode, these thumbnails can be used to drag in copies of each model into the scene.

3D MODELING AND ASSEMBLY TOOLS

This section describes user operations available to model paper in our system into 3D components, and subsequently assemble and texture them to create 3D scenes. Implementations of our modeling operations typically involve uses of functions $\text{SPLIT}(f, l)$ (divides a face f into two new faces along line l), $\text{ROTATE}(f, l, \theta)$ (rotates f about line l by an angle θ), and $\text{TRANSLATE}(f, l, d)$ (translates f a distance d along line l).

Gesture-Based 3D Modeling Tools

Creating a 3D component begins with an initially flat sheet of paper that can be resized and stretched using a pinch gesture,

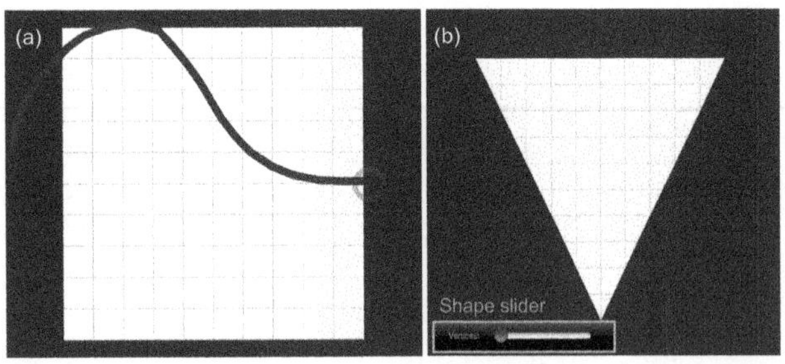

Figure 5. Creating a new sheet of virtual paper: (a) Users can define a freeform outline for the paper with a single finger pan. (b) Alternatively, a regular polygon can be selected using a shape slider to control the number of vertices (see inset).

which maps the two gesture inputs to the two opposite corners of the sheet. Its shape may also be defined with a freeform outline tool, or by choosing a predefined polygonal shape (e.g., triangle, circle). (See Figure 5.)

Planar Operations

Three fundamental operations available to the user are *creasing* (dividing one or more faces into two), *extending* (creating new, connected, coplanar faces), and *cutting* (dividing part of a model along a crease). The user defines a crease through two finger inputs p_0 and p_1, panning to adjust its position and orientation. (See Figure 6a.) Upon releasing, the face is divided through a $\text{SPLIT}()$ operation into two new faces connected along the crease. A outward pinch with fingers over a selected crease and one of its connected faces cuts that side of the model, either removing it or making it a separate component. (See Figure 6b.) To extend the current sheet, as seen in Figure 6c, the user can drag two fingers along the outward normal of any boundary edge, creating a new face. Two of its vertices are of the crossed boundary edge; the remaining ones are defined by the two projected gestural inputs p_0 and p_1.

Extending

In addition to planar extending, we provide additional extend tools. Users can bridge two edges using an *edge-to-edge extend*, by placing a finger over one edge and swiping the other edge towards the first (Figure 6d). A three-finger pinch on a face will extend the paper along all the boundary edges of a face simultaneously, along the normal to the original face. The distance the fingers are spread apart controls the width of the new faces, and the angle of the new faces can be subsequently adjusted (Figures 6e and 6f). A four-finger pinch performs an extend operation on all the faces of the component simultaneously, allowing users to quickly add thickness to their model. Any curved face is extended along its original normal prior to the added curvature.

Folding

A one-finger drag over one of the adjoining faces of a selected crease adjusts the angle of the crease (through a call to $\text{ROTATE}()$), turning it into a folded edge, with the angle defined by t_0 projected onto the normal of the edge. All faces connected to the rotating face (on the same side of the crease/fold) are rotated together with it. The angle of any existing crease or fold of the 3D component may be adjusted in this way. In a *corner fold* operation, a user's finger is dragged across the screen over a corner of a face (selecting it), and the user starts to fold over the face. (See Figure 6g.) The folding line l_{fold} is defined as the line perpendicular to $l(p_{start}, p_{end})$ and passing through the midpoint of p_{start} and p_{end}. The new, folded-over face f_{folded} is rotated 180° about l_{fold}. Similarly, *edge folding* lets the user fold over the paper by grabbing any boundary edge of the component (Figure 6h), with its final position unambiguously defined through a two-finger pan gesture. The midpoints of the two start and end touches, p_{0_mid} and p_{1_mid}, define the folding line l_{fold}, and the new face f_{folded} is rotated 180° about l_{fold}. (See Figure 7a and 7b.)

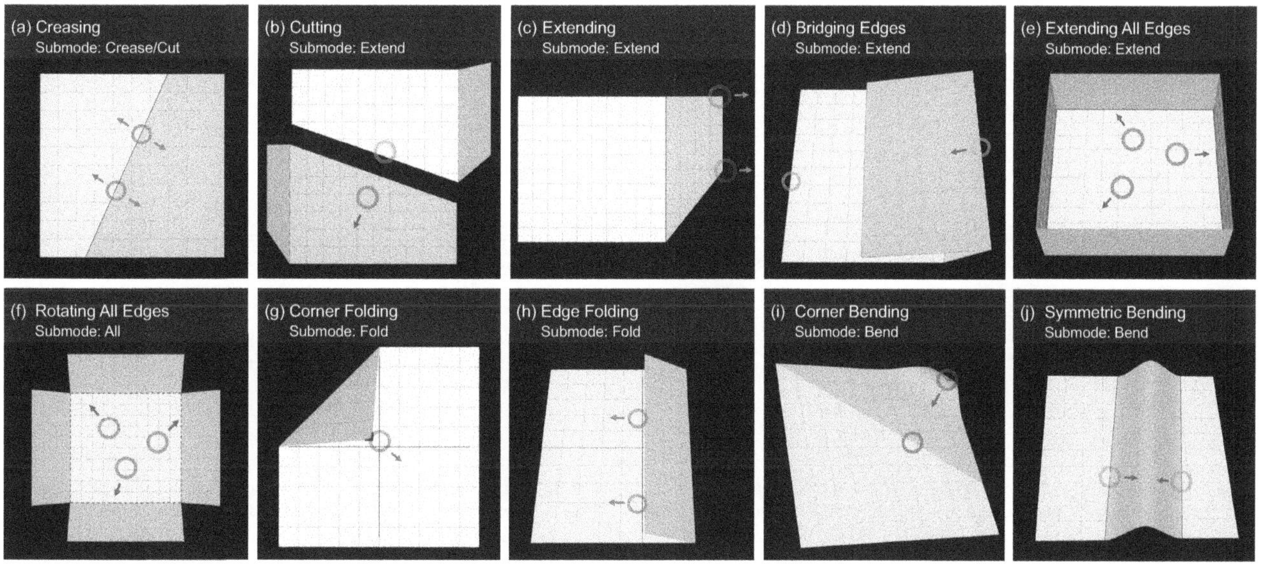

Figure 6. A selection of modeling tools in Paper3D: (a) creasing a sheet of paper, (b) cutting along an edge, (c) extending along an edge of a face, (d) bridging edges of two faces, (e) extending all edges of a face, (f) rotating all faces generated in (e), (g) corner folding, (h) edge folding, (i) corner bending, and (j) symmetric bending. Circles and arrows indicate the position and motion of user touches.

Algorithm 1 Corner bending

procedure $\text{CORNERBEND}(f_{orig}, t_0, t_1)$
    $p_{1\_end} \leftarrow \text{PROJ}(f_{orig}, t_1)$
    $w_{orig} \leftarrow \text{LENGTH}(p_{0\_start} - p_{1\_end})$
    $l_n \leftarrow \text{LINE}(p_{0\_start}, p_{1\_end})$
    $l_{fold} \leftarrow \text{LINE}(p_{1\_end}, \text{NORMAL}(l_n))$
    if $\text{ISBENDABLE}(f_{orig}, l_{fold})$ **then**
        $f_{fixed}, f_{folded} \leftarrow \text{SPLIT}(f_{orig}, l_{fold})$
        $f_{temp} \leftarrow \text{FACE}(\text{VECTOR}(l_n), \text{NORMAL}(f_{orig}), p_{1\_end})$
        $p_{0\_end} \leftarrow \text{PROJ}(f_{temp}, t_0)$
        $\text{BEND}(f_{folded}, p_{0\_end}, p_{1\_end}, w_{orig})$
    end if
end procedure

procedure $\text{BEND}(f, p_0, p_1, w_{orig})$
    $f_{bend\_prev} \leftarrow f$
    $l_{parts}, \theta_{folds} \leftarrow \text{COMPUTEBENDSTRIPS}(p_0, p_1, w_{orig})$
    for $i \leftarrow 0, n_{parts}$ **do**
        $f_{bend\_prev}, f_{bend\_curr} \leftarrow \text{SPLIT}(f_{bend\_prev}, l_{part\_i})$
        $\text{ROTATE}(f_{bend\_curr}, l_{part\_i}, \theta_{fold\_i})$
        $\text{ADDTOSUBFACES}(f, f_{bend\_curr})$
        $f_{bend\_prev} \leftarrow f_{bend\_curr}$
    end for
end procedure

Angled Folding and Bending

A pinch gesture on a multi-touch device lets us define an *angled corner folding* tool, allowing a user to simultaneously fold over a corner of the sheet of paper, while also controlling the folding angle between the fixed and folded-over parts. The folding line l_{fold} is defined as the line perpendicular to $\text{LINE}(p_{0\_start}, p_{1\_end})$ and passing through p_{1_end}. (See Figure 7c.) The angle of rotation of face f_{folded} is found using p_{0_end}, the 3D point found by projecting t_{0_end} onto the plane passing through p_{0_start} with normal parallel to l_{fold}. *Angled edge folding* is analogous, except it starts on a boundary edge instead of a corner. In *corner bending*, we extend angled folding to allow users to curve parts of their model (Figure 6i). The angled face f_{folded} is curved into n bend strips, through a recursive sequence of n SPLIT() and ROTATE() operations. Dividing lines l_1 to l_n are parallel to the initial dividing line l_{fold}. Following [15], we determine the line spacing and the angle of each rotation by minimizing the energy function

$$E = \alpha\Sigma_i(d_i - L)^2 + \beta\Sigma_i(a_i - a_{i+1})^2,$$

where L is a constant equal to $1/k$ multiplied by the distance between the line l and the selected corner at p_{0_start}, and d_i and a_i are the widths of and angles between the bend strips. Constants $\alpha = 0.6$ and $\beta = 0.4$ were determined experimentally. (See Figure 7d and Algorithm 1.) If the user's fingers are close together, the paper is curved into a cylindrical shape (instead of using the energy minimization function), connecting points p_{0_end} and p_{1_end}. *Edge bending* instead bends over an edge of the model, but is otherwise identical.

Symmetric Folding and Bending

A *symmetric bend* is activated when a user pinches an inner region of the paper. As the user's two fingers are drawn together, the paper bends upwards, forming a peak at the midpoint (Figure 6j). In the implementation, we define w_{orig} as half the original distance between the user's initial, projected contact points p_{0_start} and p_{1_start}. w_{bend} and h_{bend} are defined as the width and height of half the bent portion of the paper, computed based on the new/final contact points p_{0_end} and p_{1_end}. The original face f_{orig} is first divided along the line passing through the midpoint of p_{0_end} and p_{1_end}, and perpendicular to the line through those points. The two resulting faces are translated inwards by a distance equal to $w_{orig} - w_{bend}$, and then each is split into two new faces along the fold lines through points p_{0_end} and p_{1_end}. Finally, the inner two faces f_{0_folded} and f_{1_folded} are curved, such that they meet symmetrically at the peak of the bend p_{peak}, and maintain their original dimensions. (See Figure 7e and Algorithm 2.) The orientation of the bend and the thickness and height of the bend are readjusted in real-time in response to user input, until

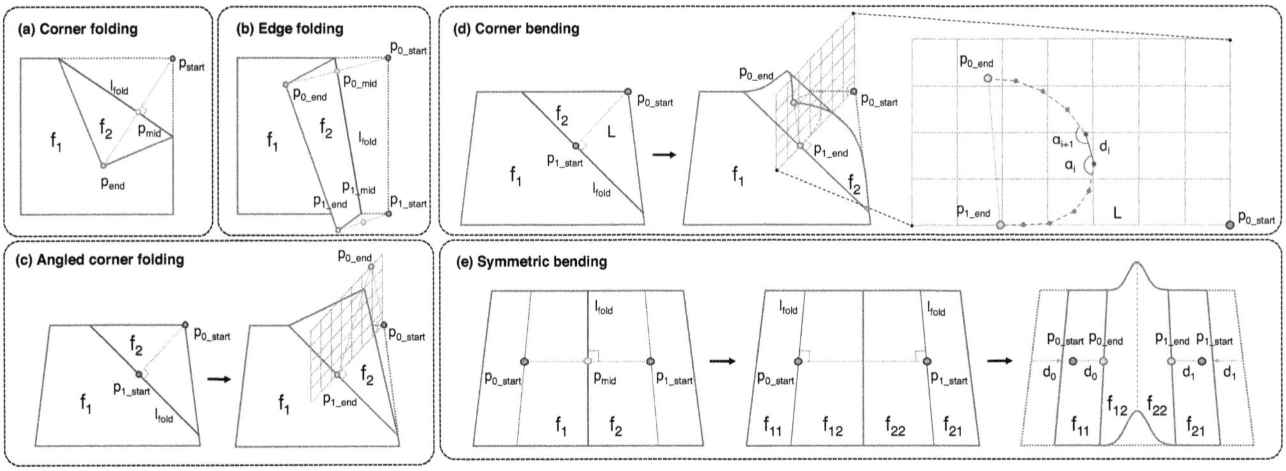

Figure 7. Technical details for a selection of tools in Paper3D. (a) and (b) show how the folding line l_{fold} is calculated for corner and edge folds. (c) illustrates how the two user inputs are projected onto a plane perpendicular to the current face, allowing the user to specify both the fold angle and orientation. (d) shows how a curve is fit between the two projected input points, resulting in the curved surface. (e) shows the effect a symmetric bend has on a face of the model, translating each half inwards as the bend is increased.

Algorithm 2 Symmetric bending

```
procedure SYMMETRICBEND(f_orig, t_0, t_1)
    w_orig ← 0.5 * LENGTH(p0_start − p1_start)
    w_bend ← MIN(0.5 * LENGTH(p0_end − p1_end), w_orig)
    h_bend ← SQRT(w_orig^2 − w_new^2)
    p0_end ← PROJ(f_orig, t_0)
    p1_end ← PROJ(f_orig, t_1)
    p_mid ← 0.5 * (p0_end + p1_end)
    p_peak ← p_mid + h_bend * NORMAL(f_orig)
    l_n ← LINE(p0_end, p1_end)
    l0_fold ← LINE(p0_end, NORMAL(l_n))
    l1_fold ← LINE(p1_end, NORMAL(l_n))
    l_mid_fold ← LINE(p_mid, NORMAL(l_n))
    if ISBENDABLEREGION(f_orig, l0_fold, l1_fold) then
        f_0, f_1 ← SPLIT(f_orig, l_mid_fold)
        d_trans ← (w_orig − w_bend)
        TRANSLATE(f_0, l_n, d_trans)
        TRANSLATE(f_1, l_n, −d_trans)
        f0_fixed, f0_folded ← SPLIT(f_0, l0_fold)
        f1_fixed, f1_folded ← SPLIT(f_1, l1_fold)
        BEND(f0_folded, p0_end, p_peak, w_orig)
        BEND(f1_folded, p1_end, p_peak, w_orig)
    end if
end procedure
```

the user's fingers are lifted off the screen. Subsequently, the position of the peak can be adjusted horizontally and vertically. Analogous to symmetric bending, a *symmetric fold* forms a peak at the midpoint of the two points of contact, where the portion of paper between the two pinched fingers is folded upwards, creating a folded peak in the middle.

Transforming, Grouping and Texturing Tools

Once a selection of single-sheet components has been constructed using our system's modeling operations and inserted into the scene, they can be transformed and assembled into more complex models using pinning and taping tools.

Pinning and Taping

A user pins two objects together by first tapping on a face f_0 of a model m_0. This creates a pin at projected location p_0, with normal equal to f_0's normal. A subsequent tap of face f_1 of a second model m_1 indicates a desired location and alignment of the first model. The two faces are pinned together; this is highlighted through animation. If m_0 has been pinned to the wrong side of f_1, it can be flipped over using a rotate gesture. Adjustments can subsequently be made by translating within the plane of f_1 or rotating about the pin axis. (See Figures 8a and 8b.) Taping is similar to pinning, except a user first taps an edge e_0 of m_0 (with two fingers, to distinguish from pinning), and then taps an edge e_1 of model m_1. The same transformation occurs as above, except now, e_1 is constrained to lie on e_0. The user can rotate m_0 about the axis of the tape (the line passing through e_1), or translate along this axis (Figures 8c and 8d).

Transforming and Duplicating

Individual and assembled models can both be transformed through uniform scaling (pinch gesture), translation within the plane of any face of the model (two-finger pan), and rotation about any edge of the model (one-finger pan). In addition, users can temporarily drop a pin or tape onto a model (without grouping), and translate and rotate about the pin/tape. Both individual models and groups can be duplicated using a one-finger drag operation.

Coloring and Texturing

As part of the assembly mode, we provide coloring and texturing tools to embellish the resulting models. In the coloring/texturing submode, a color picker allows users to select any desired color. Subsequently, a single one/two/three-finger tap on a face of a model will change the color of the face/model/group to the selected color. (See Figure 8e.) A long press over a model sets the current color to that of the indicated face. For texturing, the list of model thumbnails is replaced by a list of texture thumbnails. Once a texture is selected, it can be applied to a face/model/group in the same way as a color. The texture mapping can be adjusted using a pinch gesture. (See Figure 8f.)

IMPLEMENTATION DETAILS

Paper3D was implemented from the ground up for a tablet device with a multi-touch display (a third generation iPad). As

Figure 8. A selection of assembly operations. (a) The user adds a pin to the spine of the book. Tapping over the top of the bookstand attaches the two together at the pin location. (b) Users can then rotate the book about the pin, or translate the book in the plane of the stand. (c) The user has added tape to the edge of the loose book page; a two-finger tap over the spine of the book then attaches the page to the spine, aligning the two edges. (d) The alignment is adjusted. (e) The user can color an object using the color palette and a subsequent tap gesture. (f) Textures can be mapped onto any surface using a pinch gesture.

such, the majority of user interaction with the system occurs through single- and multi-finger gestures. Our system is implemented in a mix of C++ and Objective C, with OpenGL ES as the rendering API.

Object Storage

Each object instance in our system (i.e., vertices; edges; faces) is stored dynamically, and has a unique identifier. Standard map containers store pointers to these objects for easy access. Each model stores three separate maps for its faces, edges and vertices, respectively. As shown in Figure 9, each face stores a map of its edges and an ordered list of its vertices, while edges store pointers to their associated faces and vertices.

Modeling Updates

Figure 9 shows an example of how the internal data structures of the system are updated after a crease operation. Original face f_0 is divided into new faces, f_1 and f_2. The outline of f_0 is split: vertices v_0, v_5, v_6, v_2, and v_3 now make up the outline of f_1, while v_5, v_1 and v_6 comprise the outline of f_2. We maintain a history of operations performed on the models, as shown in the tree structures in the same figure. Each face has

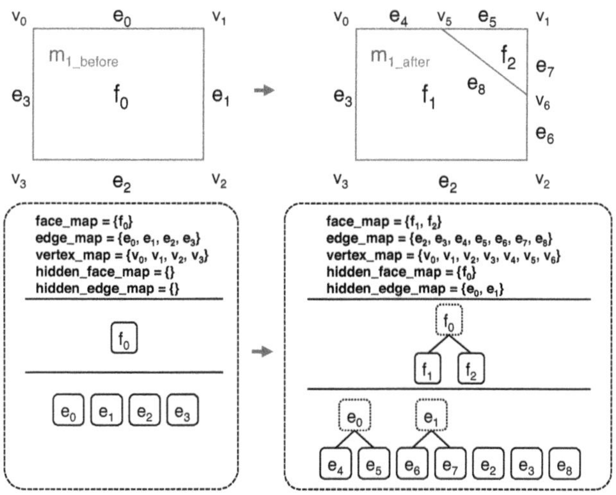

Figure 9. Overview of the object data structure in our system. The right-hand side shows how the data structure is updated when a face of the model is split (e.g., through folding).

a parent face and two children, all initially set to null. In this example, the parent face f_0 is labeled as hidden, and its left and right children are set to f_1 and f_2, respectively, while their parent is set to f_0. Edges are divided and updated similarly: e_0 is split into e_4 and e_5, e_1 is split into e_6 and e_7, while a new edge e_8 is created between f_1 and f_2. Parent and child edges are updated, as are edge map containers. If Figure 9 instead showed a corner bend operation, f_2 would subsequently be replaced by a curved surface, by recursively dividing it into a set of bend strips of near-equal length and parallel to edge e_8. Undoing an operation simply involves accessing the tree structures to determine the original objects.

RESULTS AND DISCUSSION

Paper3D went through a natural, user-guided evolution. Once we had a stable, preliminary version of our system, we showed our system to four modelers: three casual 3D modelers with only about three months of modeling experience, and a professional designer with extensive modeling experience. These four modelers learned to use our system (5–10 hours of practice), and each created a selection of 3D models using Paper3D, while providing us with feedback. This feedback resulted in subsequent modifications to the system.

3D Modeling Results

Figure 10 displays a selection of models and scenes created by the independent modelers using our system. Our best estimate is they spent an average of 4–5 hours conceptualizing and creating each scene. We attribute some of this to the fact that throughout the modelers' usage, we were making periodic changes to the system in response to user feedback. Figure 10a shows a papercraft-like jungle scene, with a collection of animals surrounded by plants and trees, easily created with the modeling operations of our system. The modern architectural interior in Figure 10b is composed of curved surfaces that would have been difficult to create in an existing modeling system. Figure 10c shows a more traditional interior of a library; again, note the nontrivial curvature of the lounge chair and the lamps. Figure 10d displays an artsy design made out of intertwined, twisting ribbons, and emphasizes

Figure 10. A selection of 3D models and scenes created by users of our system. (a) A papercraft-like jungle scene; (b) a modern architectural interior; (c) a library scene with a curved lounge chair; (d) an artsy design made out of intertwined, twisting ribbons; (e) a manuscript on a podium, with a lamp lighting an armoire in the background; (f) a modern, curved skyscraper; (g) a David Hockney inspired stage set; (h) a Queen Anne style house.

the simplicity with which natural forms of curvature can be modeled in Paper3D. Another such example is illustrated by the manuscript lying on the podium (Figure 10e), though the other elements of this scene were also created with little effort in Paper3D. The cross-section of the skyscraper in Figure 10f contains an array of curves which were easily modeled using the bending functions in our system. Figure 10g shows a David Hockney-like stage-set design; the paper-modeling operations of our system are ideally suited for a model like this one. Finally, though a system like SketchUp is tailored to creating models such as the Queen Anne style house (Figure 10h), we demonstrate that users of Paper3D can also successfully produce these types of models.

Discussion of System Evolution

We discuss a range of key design decisions that we made throughout development of the system, both a result of user feedback, and our own observations and insights.

Gesture Mapping

Though we used papercrafting as an inspiration, it was often not appropriate to directly simulate certain interactions, but rather to use gestures appropriate in the context of 3D modeling with a multitouch device. For example, the crease gesture in Paper3D uses a pinch gesture to define the orientation of the crease, even though this does not mimic physically creasing paper. Similarly, a corner fold uses a one finger pan – more natural on an iPad than grabbing the corner by pinching. Other operations, however, such as a symmetric bend, precisely mimic the physical interaction. In some cases, gestures with three or more fingers (and in some cases, only two fingers) led to significant screen occlusion, affecting our choices.

Curved Surfaces

Bending paper is not only a very natural, physically-realizable operation, but it can also be effectively simulated on a multitouch interface. Users can control two degrees of freedom simultaneously, streamlining the curve creation process. Paper3D is limited to creating developable surfaces, by virtue of using sheets of paper as a starting point – a conscious design decision, as doubly curved surfaces can be intimidating for inexperienced modelers. Instead, a strength of our system is making curved surface creation more accessible to casual 3D modelers.

Rendering Folded Edges

It was important to us to give users a visual sense that they are manipulating paper (as long as the rendering quality does not affect performance). Narain et al. [16] introduced a sophisticated simulation technique for rendering folded and crumpled paper; however, this algorithm could not run in realtime. Furuta et al. [5] provided a rendering algorithm, but only for flat, not curved edges. In Paper3D, we decided to render all folds as thin, curved areas between the two adjoined faces. The radius of the curve is determined in part by the relative ordering and computed offsets of layers of folded-over faces. Folding a face over itself multiple times results in increasingly thicker, more curved edges (Figure 11), giving models a more volumetric appearance.

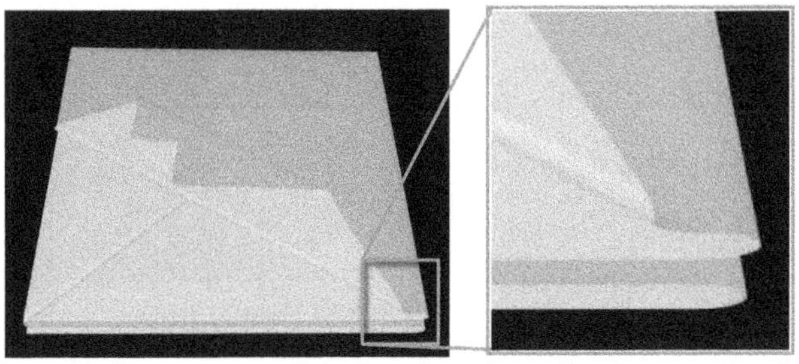

Figure 11. The representation of non-boundary edges in our system, i.e., creases, mountain folds and valley folds.

USER EVALUATION

The user-guided evolution of Paper3D afforded a running evaluation of our modeling system, following the long-term evaluation method of Shneiderman and Plaisant [18]. Once Paper3D evolved into its current form, we asked each of our testers for a summary review of the system, detailing both their experience with the tool, and how the system compares to previously used modeling systems. We present their overall impression of Paper3D, along with other notable feedback.

Overall Experience

All four modelers found their experience with the system to be very positive. One of the modelers thought Paper3D was more enjoyable than Autodesk Maya, since she was immediately able to learn all its functions and features, whereas she found Maya to be overcomplicated, with many features she had no idea how to use. The gesture-based system was singled out as more intuitive than using a mouse. The modelers found our system easier to learn, and objects within it easier to manipulate. All modelers thought Paper3D was enjoyable to use, and saw it as very accessible to people with little or no prior modeling experience. Users considered our system a competitive alternative to 3D modelers.

Mobility

The mobility of the iPad is an advantage over larger display devices (e.g., an Eizo Multitouch Radiforce device). The designer supported this, pointing out that Paper3D's mobility makes the modeling experience more enjoyable. Additionally, she observed that Paper3D could be useful as a casual, portable modeling tool for quick prototyping in the early phase of design.

Precision

Our users observed that using a mouse provides better precision than hand gestures, though in general, this did not negatively affect their modeling process. This agreed with our assumption that while the precision of a tablet device may not be sufficient for a professional modeler, it should suffice for a casual one. For enhanced precision, we provided a range of snapping features (e.g., corner-to-corner snapping during folding), and a secondary, orthogonal view for more complex operations. In the future, we plan to add guides for more accurate model selection, placement and grouping.

Number of Submodes

Though users did not mind having too many submodes, optimizing their number is an area of future work. Additionally, since more emphasis was placed on developing the system's gesture-based interface and modeling paradigm, improving the general button and toolbar layout of the present interface will be another future area of focus.

CONCLUSION AND FUTURE WORK

We have presented Paper3D, a novel 3D modeling system designed specifically for multi-touch interfaces. Our iPad application introduces a new style of modeling inspired by papercrafting, with intuitive, familiar operations, such as folding, bending, cutting, pinning, and taping. Our system is easily learned by experienced and casual modelers alike, allowing users to create a wide range of developable surfaces. We validated our claims by asking modelers to test Paper3D and use it to create a variety of models, while providing valuable feedback for iterative development. Their final reviews of the system were uniformly positive and encouraging. Several interesting future directions of Paper3D remain, such as improving input precision, experimenting with additional forms of curvature, improving rendering efficiency and quality, extensions to support animation, and hardcopy output.

ACKNOWLEDGMENTS

Julie Dorsey acknowledges support from the National Science Foundation under Award 1018470. Min H. Kim acknowledges partial support from Korea NRF grants (2013R1A1A10-10165 and 2013M3A6A6073718) and an ICT R&D program of MSIP/IITP (10041313). We thank Yumiko Nakamura, Victoria Nielsen, Marko Micic (Yale University), and Seijin Cha (KAIST) for their invaluable feedback and modeled designs.

REFERENCES

1. Au, O. K.-C., Tai, C.-L., and Fu, H. Multitouch gestures for constrained transformation of 3D objects. *Comput. Graph. Forum 31*, 2 (2012), 651–660.
2. Chang, S. H.-H., Stuart, L., Plimmer, B., and Wünsche, B. Origami simulator: a multi-touch experience. In *CHI Extended Abstracts*, ACM (2009), 3889–3894.
3. Cohé, A., and Hachet, M. Beyond the mouse: Understanding user gestures for manipulating 3d objects from touchscreen inputs. *Comput. Graph. 36*, 8 (Dec. 2012), 1119–1131.
4. De Araùjo, B. R., Casiez, G., and Jorge, J. A. Mockup Builder: Direct 3D modeling on and above the surface in a continuous interaction space. In *Proc. Graphics Interface* (2012), 173–180.
5. Furuta, Y., Mitani, J., and Fukui, Y. A rendering method for 3D origami models using face overlapping relations. In *Proc. Smart Graphics 2009*, vol. 5531, Springer (2009), 193–202.
6. Hancock, M. S., Carpendale, M. S. T., and Cockburn, A. Shallow-depth 3D interaction: design and evaluation of one-, two- and three-touch techniques. In *Proc. ACM CHI* (2007), 1147–1156.
7. Igarashi, T., Matsuoka, S., and Tanaka, H. Teddy: A sketching interface for 3D freeform design. In *Proc. SIGGRAPH* (1999), 409–416.
8. Joshi, A., Robertson, G., Wünsche, B., and Plimmer, B. Bubbleworld builder - 3D modeling using two-touch and sketch interaction. In *Proc. GRAPP* (2010), 116–122.
9. Keijser, J., Carpendale, S., Hancock, M., and Isenberg, T. Exploring 3D interaction in alternate control-display space mappings. In *Proc. Symp. on 3D User Interfaces* (2007), 526–531.
10. Kin, K., Miller, T., Bollensdorff, B., DeRose, T., Hartmann, B., and Agrawala, M. Eden: A professional multitouch tool for constructing virtual organic environments. In *Proc. ACM CHI*, ACM (New York, NY, USA, 2011), 1343–1352.
11. Lee, S. K., Buxton, W., and Smith, K. C. A multi-touch three dimensional touch-sensitive tablet. In *Proc. ACM CHI* (1985), 21–26.
12. Liu, J., Au, O. K.-C., Fu, H., and Tai, C.-L. Two-finger gestures for 6DOF manipulation of 3D objects. *Comput. Graph. Forum 31*, 7-1 (2012), 2047–2055.
13. Martinet, A., Casiez, G., and Grisoni, L. The design and evaluation of 3D positioning techniques for multi-touch displays. In *Proc. the Symposium on 3D User Interfaces* (2010), 115–118.
14. Mitani, J. The folded shape restoration and the rendering method of origami from the crease pattern. In *Proc. Int. Conf. on Geometry and Graphics* (2008), 1–7.
15. Miyazaki, S.-Y., Yasuda, T., Yokoi, S., and Toriwaki, J.-I. An origami playing simulator in the virtual space. *J. of Vision and Computer Animation 7*, 1 (1996), 25–42.
16. Narain, R., Pfaff, T., and O'Brien, J. F. Folding and crumpling adaptive sheets. *ACM Trans. on Graph. (TOG) 32*, 4 (2013), 51.
17. Nitsch, E. J. *When pigs fly: a study of computer generated paper folding*. M.S. thesis, Texas A&M University, 2008.
18. Shneiderman, B., and Plaisant, C. Strategies for evaluating information visualization tools: multidimensional in-depth long-term case studies. In *BELIV 06: Proc. the 2006 AVI workshop on Beyond* (2006).
19. Sun, Q., Lin, J., Fu, C.-W., Kaijima, S., and He, Y. A multi-touch interface for fast architectural sketching and massing. In *Proc. ACM CHI*, ACM (New York, NY, USA, 2013), 247–256.
20. Tachi, T. Rigid-foldable thick origami. *Origami 5* (2011), 253–264.
21. Walther-Franks, B., Herrlich, M., and Malaka, R. A multi-touch system for 3d modelling and animation. In *Proc. Smart Graphics*, Springer-Verlag (Berlin, Heidelberg, 2011), 48–59.
22. Wilson, A. D., Izadi, S., Hilliges, O., Garcia-Mendoza, A., and Kirk, D. S. Bringing physics to the surface. In *Proc. UIST 2008*, ACM (2008), 67–76.

Cheaper by the Dozen: Group Annotation of 3D Data

Aleksey Boyko
Princeton University
aboyko@cs.princeton.edu

Thomas Funkhouser
Princeton University
funk@cs.princeton.edu

ABSTRACT

This paper proposes a group annotation approach to interactive semantic labeling of data and demonstrates the idea in a system for labeling objects in 3D LiDAR scans of a city. In this approach, the system selects a group of objects, predicts a semantic label for it, and highlights it in an interactive display. In response, the user either confirms the predicted label, provides a different label, or indicates that no single label can be assigned to all objects in the group. This sequence of interactions repeats until a label has been confirmed for every object in the data set. The main advantage of this approach is that it provides faster interactive labeling rates than alternative approaches, especially in cases where all labels must be explicitly confirmed by a person. The main challenge is to provide an algorithm that selects groups with many objects all of the same label type arranged in patterns that are quick to recognize, which requires models for predicting object labels and for estimating times for people to recognize objects in groups. We address these challenges by defining an objective function that models the estimated time required to process all unlabeled objects and approximation algorithms to minimize it. Results of user studies suggest that group annotation can be used to label objects in LiDAR scans of cities significantly faster than one-by-one annotation with active learning.

ACM Classification Keywords

H.5.2. Information Interfaces and Presentation (e.g. HCI): User Interfaces; I.2.10. Artificial Intelligence: Vision and Scene Understanding; I.5.5 Pattern recognition: Applications

INTRODUCTION

There has recently been an explosion in the amount of 3D data collected in urban environments, as several companies (e.g., Google and Navteq) and government agencies (e.g., U.S. Geological Survey) are continuously collecting LiDAR data using scanners mounted on cars and/or airplanes flying overhead. For example, one such data set combining both types of data from Ottawa, Canada is shown in Figure 1.

While this LiDAR data provides immediate opportunities for visualization applications, its true value cannot be realized until semantic objects in the data have been segmented and labeled (colored points in Figure 1). If a semantically labeled 3D model of a city could be acquired, then applications such as urban planning, augmented reality maps, virtual tourism, and emergency response planning would be greatly enhanced. For example, identifying locations of stop signs, traffic lights, and street signs would augment electronic maps and help guide navigation of self-driving cars, and labeling fire hydrants, electrical power boxes, and fire escapes would help emergency response planning and disaster simulation.

Figure 1: Our goal is to label small objects in a 3D point cloud. This image shows a section of Ottawa, with the semantic labels of 1,224 small objects represented by colors.

With these applications in mind, a number of researchers have begun to develop systems aimed at automatic segmentation and labeling of 3D LiDAR point clouds. In particular, great progress has been made over the last several years on recognition of roads, buildings, trees and other large urban structures. Unfortunately, recognition of small objects (cars, signs, fire hydrants, etc.) is more difficult, and thus the accuracy of current labeling algorithms are relatively poor for those objects. For example, state-of-the-art labeling algorithms based on supervised learning [11, 19, 20, 33] achieve only 42%–82% accuracies depending on the number of categories and their generality, which is far lower than the 95+% that is required for consumer mapping, augmented reality, and urban simulation applications. Therefore, a person has to check and fix the predicted label for *every* object before a data set can be deployed to users (a practice common even for large urban structures at most companies that annotate electronic maps).

The goal of our project is to develop an interactive system for high-throughput and high-accuracy labeling of small objects in LiDAR scans of cities. This goal is a bit different than any previous system, and thus raises several interesting research opportunities. First, our goal is to produce a label for every object in a specific data set with as much com-

UIST 2014, October 5–8, 2014, Honolulu, HI, USA.

ACM 978-1-4503-3069-5/14/10 ...$15.00.
http://dx.doi.org/10.1145/2642918.2647418

puter assistance as possible, which is different than previous work in computer vision focusing on crowd-sourced creation of object recognition benchmarks where computer assistance is specifically avoided to ensure unbiased ground truth labels (e.g., [7, 39]). Second, our goal is to minimize the total time required to provide and/or confirm a label for every object in a data set, which is different than most previous work on interactive machine learning where the goal is mainly to maximize the accuracy of a classifier with the fewest training examples (e.g.,[28]). Finally, our goal is to label all objects residing in a single 3D environment (a city), and thus it is possible for our system to show multiple objects to a user in a single view and ask him/her to label them with a single command (e.g., if they all require the same label), which is different than almost all previous interactive labeling and classification systems where objects must be displayed and/or labeled separately.

This paper describes a system called IGRA (Intelligent Grouping for Rapid Annotation), which integrates ideas from human-computer interaction, active machine learning, and perceptual psychology to provide an interactive interface for labeling objects in LiDAR scans of cities quickly and accurately. The system starts from a point cloud acquired from LiDAR scans of a city and executes a number of preprocessing steps to segment the points into objects and compute geometric features for each object. It then executes an interactive labeling program that iteratively highlights groups of objects in the 3D point cloud and asks the user to perform one of three commands for each group: 1) confirm the predicted label for all objects in the group, 2) select a label for all objects in the group, or 3) decline to label the group, in which case a subset of the group will be highlighted in the next iteration. Each of these commands can be executed with a single key press (e.g., hitting the space bar confirms the predicted label for a group), and each command provides labels for multiple objects, and thus the system is very high-throughput. Moreover, the label for every object is explicitly confirmed by the user in at least one group, and thus the resulting set of labels is very high-accuracy.

The main research contribution of the paper is the introduction of an interactive labeling approach in which users are iteratively asked to label groups of objects. To investigate this approach, we developed: 1) an active learning algorithm to construct groups of objects that aims to maximize the expected labeling throughput (confirmed labels per unit time), 2) a perceptual model based on Gestalt principles to estimate the amount of time required for a user to recognize the label of a group or determine there is not one such label, and 3) an interactive system that incorporates visualization of 3D point clouds with interactive labeling in an interface that can be learned by novices in a few minutes. Experiments with this system suggest that our group annotation approach can label all small objects in a large city 1.7 times faster than a traditional one-by-one labeling approach.

RELATED WORK

Interactive annotation of multimedia data is an important problem with a long history of prior work.

Manual Annotation. There has been much work over the last decade on user-interfaces for manual annotation of visual data. For example, interactive methods have been proposed for labeling images by object category [7], segmenting and labeling scenes in images [26], and labeling 3D point clouds of indoor [30] and outdoor scenes [10]. These methods are directed mainly at producing ground-truth data sets for object recognition benchmarks and thus purposely limit the amount of computer-assistance provided to people when choosing object labels so as not to bias the results. In contrast, our paper is targeted at applications where the goal is to label a given 3D data set with as much computer assistance as possible.

Computer-Assisted Annotation. Other researchers have investigated interactive tools to annotate 3D data sets with algorithmic assistance [18]. For example, Nan et al. [21] and van de Hengel et al. [14] have proposed interactive tools for users to annotate primitives in 3D data and specify spatial relationships between them that allow an automatic algorithm to propagate annotations based on detected regular patterns. Other systems produce annotation hypotheses automatically and allow users to fix errors and/or refine them interactively [29, 38]. For example, Shao et al. propose a system of this type for segmentation and labeling of indoor RGBD scenes. While these systems share the same goal as ours, they require a much more taxing type of user interaction: the user must search for annotations to create/revise and then execute direct manipulation commands to apply them, which are difficult operations in complex 3D data sets. As a result, their interfaces require far greater skill and time than our approach.

Active Learning. Many systems provide assistance not only for specifying annotations, but also for finding which examples to annotate. For example, active learning systems use a utility function to choose examples for users to label when training a classifier [28]. This approach has been widely used to select frames to be annotated in images and videos [17], and it has been used to specify segmentations in 3D images interactively [32]. While these methods are related to ours, their goals and operations are quite different: they usually ask users about examples one-by-one with the goal of training a classifier with the highest accuracy in the fewest interactions. In contrast, we ask users about groups of objects for labeling a specific data set in the least amount of time.

Cost-Sensitive Active Learning. Others have made the observation that not all examples take the same amount of time for users to annotate, and thus the "cost" of an annotation should be considered when selecting examples for users to label (e.g., for training classifiers of images [34]). Other research have considered a value of information (*VOI*) framework that chooses the samples by balancing the risk of mislabeling a sample and the cost of annotation [23]. Our system leverages these ideas by introducing a model to estimate the accuracy and time for a user to annotate a group of objects in 3D, which is used to minimize the total time required for an interactive labeling session.

Multiple Instance Learning. Other systems have considered labeling data with multiple objects in a single query [2]. For example, in multiple-instance learning (MIL), labels are as-

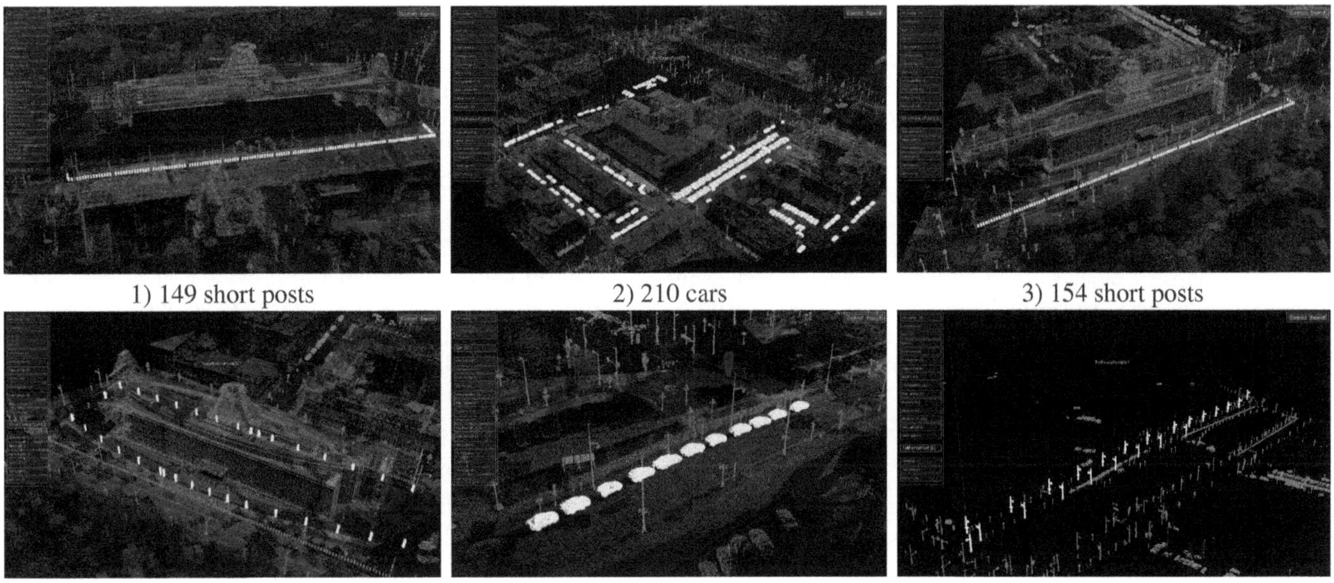

1) 149 short posts 2) 210 cars 3) 154 short posts

4) 33 tall posts 5) 11 cars 6) 23 street lights

Figure 2: Screenshots from an initial sequence of labeling operations in IGRA. The screenshots shows the objects (highlighted in yellow) labeled by a user in the first 6 group annotations, with the number of objects in each group listed below.

sociated with *bags*, which may contain multiple objects, and labels associated with a bag usually indicate that at least one object in the bag has the given label [8]. This MIL approach is best suited for data that inherently has multiple instances in a single data item that cannot be separated (e.g., multiple objects appearing in the same image). Since objects in 3D point clouds are relatively simple to separate with standard segmentation algorithms, we can easily construct arbitrary groups of objects to be labeled in our system.

OVERVIEW

This paper describes an interactive system for high-throughput and high-accuracy labeling of small objects in LiDAR scans of cities using group annotation. The input to the system is a set of segmented *objects*, each represented by a set of 3D points within a LiDAR scan of a city, and the output is a manually specified semantic label for each object.

At startup, the user is presented with an interface for viewing 3D point clouds, with which they can rotate, zoom, and pan a virtual camera and/or adjust how points and objects are displayed (e.g., turn on/off the display of points that are not parts of objects, turn on/off the display of current label names, etc.), much like many other 3D visualization systems.

The key new aspect of the system is that it iteratively selects groups of objects, shows them to the user (drawn in bright yellow from a spinning centered view as shown in Figure 2), predicts a single label for all objects in the group (shown in text above the group), and then asks the user to execute one of three actions: 1) confirm the predicted label (hit the space bar), 2) specify a new label (select a label from a menu on the left of the screen or hit an alphanumeric character associated with the label), or 3) ask the system to contract or expand the group (left-arrow or right-arrow key, respectively). If the user confirms or specifies a label for the group (actions 1 or 2), then all objects within the group are assigned that label and subsequently displayed in the color associated with the label. Otherwise, a new group is shown to the user. The system iterates this group labeling interaction until labels have been confirmed or specified for all objects in the data set (Figure 1).

This user interface was chosen for a number of reasons. First, it leverages a person's ability to recognize a semantic label for a group of related objects more quickly than a sequence of individual objects – e.g., it is possible to recognize that all the objects highlighted in first image of Figure 2 are short posts of a fence without carefully inspecting each one individually. Second, it automatically finds (groups of) objects that need labels and moves the virtual camera to view them automatically – e.g., avoiding the need for expensive visual search and interactive camera control. Third, it provides a rapid way for users to confirm the labels for all objects in the data set – e.g., if the labels predicted for a sequence of groups are correct, then the user must only hit the space bar to confirm them.

As an example, consider the sequence of screenshots in Figure 2 of the first six groups annotated by a novice user in an actual session in our user study. Each screenshot shows a group of objects (in yellow) labeled by a user with a single interaction (key click). From these screenshots, we can see that it is often possible to recognize the label for a large group of objects even without inspecting any single object closely – the pattern of objects helps us identify the appropriate label. We also observe that large numbers of objects can be labeled with just a few simple commands. The sequence shown in Figure 2 required a total of 7 key clicks (the fifth group was contracted before it was labeled) and provided confirmed labels for 578 objects in a total elapsed time of 137 seconds.

METHODS

The main research challenge in implementing our system is to develop effective methods for selecting groups to be annotated by a user at each step of an interactive labeling session.

Ideally, selected groups should contain very large number of objects, all of which require the same label, most of which have not been previously labeled, and all of which are arranged in patterns quickly recognizable by a person – then, large groups of objects could be labeled quickly and easily with our interface. However, building groups with these properties is non-trivial. Since the labels of objects are not known in advance, the system must predict them and model the probability that a group contains objects of the same type. Since different groups of objects require different amounts of time for a user to recognize their labels, the system must employ a model of human perception to estimate the cost of asking the user about a group. These considerations must be encoded into an objective function that models the benefit (time-savings) of labeling objects in a group.

Given such an objective function, we must develop an algorithm to search for the group with maximal benefit at every step of the labeling process. Our overall goal is to construct a sequence of groups that minimize the total time required by a user to label and/or confirm every object in the data set. Of course, achieving this goal is NP-Hard: choosing just one group is an instance of the optimal subset selection problem, which is NP-hard (e.g., [37]), let alone optimally choosing the entire sequence. In our interactive system, we select groups that approximately optimize this goal given current estimates of the object labels and annotation times.

Our solutions for these two main issues (defining an objective function and implementing a group selection algorithm) are discussed in the following sections.

OBJECTIVE FUNCTION

Our objective function, $B(G, L)$, estimates the expected benefit (time savings) of asking a user to select a label from a set L for a group of objects G (rather than annotating the objects one-by-one). Specifically, we define our objective function as:

$$B(G, L) = P_{\text{Label}}(G) T_{\text{1x1}}(G, L) - T_{\text{Group}}(G, L) \quad (1)$$

where $T_{\text{Group}}(G, L)$ is the expected time it will take a user to provide a response for a group G; $P_{\text{Label}}(G)$ is the expected probability that the user will provide a label for the group G (rather than contract or expand it); and $T_{\text{1x1}}(G, L)$ is the expected time it would take a user to label all objects in G one-by-one (without group annotation).

This benefit formulation reflects the fact that the total time for the annotation session is reduced by $T_{\text{1x1}}(G, L)$ time if the user provides a label for the group, which occurs with probability $P_{\text{Label}}(G)$. $T_{\text{Group}}(G, L)$ time is added to the session for the user to process the group, regardless of whether a label is provided or not. So, intuitively, $B(G, L)$ is higher if groups are larger ($T_{\text{1x1}}(G, L)$ is higher), more likely to contain objects of the same label ($P_{\text{Label}}(G)$ is higher), and faster for a person to recognize the label ($T_{\text{Group}}(G, L)$ is lower).

While this formulation is nice theoretically, it requires estimating three terms ($P_{\text{Label}}(G)$, $T_{\text{Group}}(G, L)$, and $T_{\text{1x1}}(G, L)$), all of which depend on unknowns (object labels, user behavior, etc.). The following paragraphs provide details for how we estimate values for those terms.

Estimating Probability that the User Provides a Label. Our first challenge is to estimate $P_{\text{Label}}(G)$, the probability that the user will provide a label for a given group G – i.e., confirm the predicted label or provide a new one explicitly. This can occur only if all objects in G belong to the same category (require the same label). Thus, we compute $P_{\text{Label}}(G)$ by estimating the joint probability that all objects $o_i \in G$ belong to the same category.

The challenge in estimating the joint probability is that we don't know which label will be assigned. In fact, it is possible that no instances of the correct label for a group have been previously entered by the user, or in fact that no labels have been entered at all, and therefore it is not always possible to simply train a classifier to estimate the probability of assigning any given label based on previous training data.

Our approach is to develop an estimator for the probability $P_{\text{Label}}(o_i, o_j)$ that any two objects o_i and o_j have the same label, and then combine those probabilities to estimate the joint probability of a single label for all objects in the group. To do this, we compute the product of $|G|-1$ pairwise probabilities, where the pairs are chosen to be the highest probability ones that span all objects in G. That is, if MST_{Label} is the minimum spanning tree of a fully-connected graph, where nodes represent objects and edges represent $1 - P_{\text{Label}}(o_i, o_j)$, then:

$$P_{\text{Label}}(G) = \prod_{(o_i, o_j) \in MST_{\text{Label}}} P_{\text{Label}}(o_i, o_j) \quad (2)$$

This method for combining the pairwise probabilities is based on two assumptions. First, the pairwise probabilities, $P_{\text{Label}}(o_i, o_j)$, are more reliable for high probability pairs than for any other (i.e., long-range distances in the feature space should not be trusted), and thus combining probabilities for pairs of objects connected in the MST is more reliable than using other pairs at all. Second, the pairwise probabilities for pairs of objects in the MST are independent, and thus they can be multiplied to estimate the joint probability.

While many ways could have been used to estimate $P_{\text{Label}}(G)$, this formulation was chosen because it leverages the latent structure of the data, even when labels have not yet been assigned for nearby examples (which is a common case in our system). This is a form of transductive learning [4, 9]. Like semi-supervised learning methods based on diffusion, we form groups of objects that are all likely to have the same label using transitivity through closely related objects.

Estimating Probability that a Pair Has Same Label. Motivated by this formulation for $P_{\text{Label}}(G)$, we must estimate $P_{\text{Label}}(o_i, o_j)$, the probability that any two objects o_i and o_j have the same label. To do this, we start by computing a feature vector for each object representing properties of its shape, such as height, width, etc.[1] Then, we model the dissimilarity of two objects based on the distance $D(o_i, o_j)$ between their feature vectors.

Instead of simply using the Euclidean distance in the feature space, we base our affinities on a density-sensitive distance metric using the formulation from [5] and algorithms from [40]. Density-sensitive distances capture cluster information about objects in the feature space and thus provide a better model for predicting which objects are in the same category. The way they do it is through analyzing the connectivity graph in shape space and computing distance as a weighted length of edges on the path between two objects in a fashion that reflects the changes in lengths of edges (variations of densities) along the way.

We follow the general density-based distance approach, but with several augmentations appropriate for our setting. First, to normalize for local densities, we shift distances down so that closest k nearest neighbors of every object are 0. This introduces asymmetry, and so we restore symmetry for every pair of objects o_i, o_j by taking the largest density-sensitive distance between $o_i \rightarrow o_j$ and $o_j \rightarrow o_i$.

Second, to account for objects that have already been assigned a label by the user (e.g., in a prior interaction within the same session), we define $D(o_i, o_j) = \infty$ if the nearest labeled neighbors of o_i and o_j are assigned different labels. Otherwise, we set it to be the minimum of $D(o_i, o_j)$ and $max(D(o_i, o_j^{NN}), D(o_j, o_i^{NN}))$, where o_i^{NN} and o_j^{NN} are the previously labeled objects (with the same label) that are closest in feature space to o_i and o_j, respectively. This adjustment creates zero-distance "wormholes" between separated clusters of objects that share the same label, a method derived from previous work on constrained clustering (e.g. [36]).

Third, we convert each distance $D(o_i, o_j)$ into an affinity $A_{\text{Label}}(o_i, o_j)$ by transforming into the range $[0, 1]$ by:

$$A_{\text{Label}}(o_i, o_j) = \frac{1}{1 + D(o_i, o_j)}$$

Finally, we estimate the probability that two objects will be assigned the same label by:

$$P_{\text{Label}}(o_i, o_j) = A_{\text{Label}}(o_i, o_j) C(o_i, o_j)$$

where $C(o_i, o_j)$ is a penalty term to account for pairs of objects that have appeared in groups of objects contracted by the user in previous interactions – i.e., if two objects were part of a group that the user declined to label in the past, they probably should not be grouped again. Initially, $C(o_i, o_j)$ for every pair of objects is one. Then, every time a group is contracted by the user all $C(o_i, o_j)$ where $o_{i,j} \in G$ are multiplied by $1 - 1/|G|$. This factor provides a soft penalty for showing poor groups of objects repeatedly.

[1] In our current implementation, we compute the following six shape properties for each feature vector: (1-3) the 5% trimmed spread, median, and median absolute deviation of Z-coordinates (Z is up), (4) the 5% trimmed maximum distance of a point from the centroid in the XY plane, and (5-6) the variances of points distribution in the two principle axis directions in the XY-plane.

Estimating Time for a User to Provide a Response. The next problem we must address is to develop a model for $T_{\text{Group}}(G, L)$, which estimates how long it will take a user to provide an annotation response when shown a selected group G for a given set of candidate labels L.

Such a model is difficult to estimate accurately, since it depends on the spatial reasoning aptitudes of individual users and complex factors related to perception of groups. However, we can apply basic principles of perceptual psychology to form a simple, approximate model that is adequate for our system. Our model is a sum of three terms:

$$T_{\text{Group}}(G, L) = T_{\text{Id}}(G, L) + T_{\text{Verify}}(G) + T_{\text{Cmd}}(L) \qquad (3)$$

where $T_{\text{Id}}(G, L)$ is the time required to identify a label for the group, $T_{\text{Verify}}(G)$ is the time to verify that all objects in the group require the same label, and $T_{\text{Cmd}}(L)$ is the time to convey the response to the system. Note that the second term is zero if there is only one object in G, and so

$$T_{\text{1x1}}(G, L) = (T_{\text{Id}}(G, L) + T_{\text{Cmd}}(L))|G|$$

Predicting the Time to Recognize a Label for a Group. The human visual system is capable of rapidly grasping the gist of images representing scenes. After exposure of as little 100ms [27], people can answer specific questions about what they saw [31]. The process of recognizing sets of similar objects is also fast [6] and robust [13]. Since a group of objects can be represented cognitively with summary statistics [3], recognition times for salient groups can be extremely rapid. Since items perceived as a group can "pop-out" from clutter [16, 25], they can often be recognized as a whole more quickly and accurately than as individuals [1, 24].

Accordingly, we model the time $T_{\text{Id}}(G, L)$ for a person to identify the label for a group as a function that is independent of the size of the group, but dependent on the numbers of labels to choose from. Specifically, we estimate it as the choice reaction time (CRT) of choosing among $|L|$ labels using Hick's law [15]:

$$T_{id}(G, L) = a_{\text{Id}} H_{eq}(|L|)$$

where $H_{eq}(n) = \log_2(n + 1)$ is the information-theoretic entropy of a decision among n equiprobable options, and a_{Id} is a processing speed constant factor.

Predicting the Time to Search for an Outlier. Although recognizing the label for a group of similar objects is extremely fast, the process of checking whether there is an outlier within a group can be much slower. In our system, we model the time $T_{\text{Verify}}(G)$ for a person to verify that the labels of all objects in the group are the same category using a sequence of binary decisions, where each binary decision determines whether two objects within G are in the same category or not. Under the assumption that a person considers best grouped perceptually pairs of objects available when making such a decision, we estimate the total time as a sum of binary decisions made for pairs of objects connected in a minimum spanning tree (MST_{Gest}):

$$T_{\text{Verify}}(G) = \Sigma_{(o_i, o_j) \in MST_{\text{Gest}}} T_{\text{Verify}}(o_i, o_j, G) \qquad (4)$$

where $T_{\text{Verify}}(o_i, o_j, G)$ is the time it takes a person to decide whether two objects within G have the same label, and MST_{Gest} is a minimum spanning tree constructed based on a cognitive measure of affinities between objects, A_{Gest}, which is defined below.

Predicting the Time to Check if Two Objects Have the Same Label. We model $T_{\text{Verify}}(o_i, o_j, G)$, the time it takes for a person to make a decision about whether two objects have the same label or not, as a choice reaction time (CRT) using Hick's law:

$$T_{\text{Verify}}(o_i, o_j, G) = a_{\text{Verify}}(o_i, o_j, G)H(P_{\text{Label}}(o_i, o_j))$$

where $a_{\text{Verify}}(o_i, o_j, G)$ is a task complexity function that depends on geometric properties of the object pair and $H(p) = p\log_2(\frac{1}{p}+1) + (1-p)\log_2(\frac{1}{1-p}+1)$ is the information-theoretic entropy of a binary decision, where p is the probability of each outcome, in our case modeled as the affinity between the two object shapes ($p = P_{\text{Label}}(o_i, o_j)$).

When estimating the task complexity function, $a_{\text{Verify}}(o_i, o_j, G)$, we expect people to recognize the match between labels of two objects more quickly if they are closer to one another and/or are arranged in a regular pattern governed by Gestalt rules [35]. We combine these factors as follows:

$$a_{\text{Verify}}(o_i, o_j, G) = T_{\text{Verify}}(A_{\text{Gest}}(o_i, o_j, G) + (1 - A_{\text{Gest}})d(o_i, o_j))$$

where T_{Verify} is the fastest possible time required to recognize whether two objects have the same labels, $A_{\text{Gest}}(o_i, o_j, G)$ is a measure [0-1] of how much the pair of objects participates in a group with strong Gestalt principles, and $d(o_i, o_j)$ is the distance between the objects in relative units ($d(o_i, o_j) = \frac{|o_i - o_j|_2}{max(|o_i|_\infty, |o_j|_\infty)}$). Intuitively, the value of $a_{\text{Verify}}(o_i, o_j, G)$ is equal to T_{Verify} for objects connected by strong Gestalt cues (when $A_{\text{Gest}}(o_i, o_j, G) = 1$), and otherwise is larger than T_{Verify} when Gestalt cues are weaker and/or the distance between objects is larger.

Estimating the Effects of Gestalt Cues. To estimate the affinity of two objects based on Gestalt cues, we detect regular patterns in the arrangements of objects in a group, and we model the proximities/sizes of objects:

$$A_{\text{Gest}}(o_i, o_j, G) = R(o_i, o_j, G)S(o_i, o_j) \quad (5)$$

where $R(o_i, o_j, G)$ is a value [0-1] representing how much o_i and o_j participate in a regular pattern within G, and $S(o_i, o_j)$ represents a measure of the proximity of two objects relative to their sizes.

When estimating $R(o_i, o_j, G)$, we consider objects as forming a regular pattern if they are situated along a line and share similar spacing between them. Hence the smallest size of the group that can exhibit such traits is three, and we set $R(o_i, o_j) = R(o_i) = 1$ for all pairs/objects in groups of less than three. To evaluate the regularity for any three objects $o_{i,j,k}$ we compute the translation between every two, replicate it and compute the distance to the third. Then we take the smallest of these distances $d_r(o_i, o_j, o_k)$ and compute regularity score as $R(o_i, o_j, o_k) = \exp(-d_r(o_i, o_j, o_k)/min(|o_i|_\infty, |o_k|_\infty, |o_k|_\infty))$. To define regularity available for two objects o_i and o_j within a group $R(o_i, o_j, G) = max_{o_k \in G}(R(o_i, o_j, o_k))$.

When estimating $S(o_i, o_j)$, we account for the effect that similarities of objects are harder to recognize when the objects are smaller on the screen. Since the virtual camera is positioned so that the entire group is within view, objects that are further apart relative to their sizes in world space appear smaller on the screen after perspective projection. So, we model the effects of object proximity and size as $S(o_i, o_j) = \frac{1}{1+max(0, d(o_i, o_j) - c)}$.

Estimating Time for User to Enter Label. Finally, we model the time $T_{\text{Cmd}}(L)$ for a person to provide a label to the system as another choice among $|L|$ labels using Hick's law [15]:

$$T_{\text{Cmd}}(L) = a_{\text{Cmd}}H_{eq}(|L|)$$

where a_{Cmd} is a processing speed constant factor.

In all, our model predicts that groups can be labeled more quickly if they have objects with more similar shapes, stronger regular patterns, closer proximities in 3D, larger sizes on the screen, and fewer potential labels.

GROUP SELECTION ALGORITHM

Given this objective function, our main algorithmic task is to select the best group of objects to present as a query to the user at each step of the interactive labeling process.

Finding the best group is a very difficult problem. Selecting an optimal subset is intractible even with simple objective functions [37], and ours is far from simple since the benefit of every group depends on a non-linear function of all objects in the group (e.g., to estimate Gestault cues).

To limit the search space, we first construct a hierarchical clustering tree $\mathfrak{T}$ of all objects in the data set $\mathfrak{D}$, with each node representing a group of objects in the leaf nodes of its subtree. Then, having constructed $\mathfrak{T}$, we search for the best group among its non-root nodes by evaluating $B(G, L)$. This limits the search space to a set of candidates that is linear in $\|\mathfrak{D}\|$. Additionally, it produces a hierarchical nesting of groups that naturally lends itself to implementation of the group contraction and expansion commands supported by our user interface.

Even with this reduced search space, building $\mathfrak{T}$ is non-trivial. In particular, hierarchical clustering based on $B(G, L)$ can lead to groups with poor regular patterns, since decisions made greedily in the early stages of the algorithm are based mainly on shape similarity and spatial proximity between objects (e.g., when just two objects are merged into a group) and therefore are likely to form small groups that cannot later be merged into large ones with good regular patterns. To avoid this, instead of joining groups according to $B(G, L)$, we join groups in the best-first order of $A_{\text{Gest}}(o_i, o_j, \mathfrak{D})$ - a version of $A_{\text{Gest}}(o_i, o_j, G)$ from eq. (5) that represents the best possible Gestalt score of a pair o_i, o_j with any third object from the entire $\mathfrak{D}$, not only from G. Specifically, our algorithm traverses pairs of objects $o_i \in G_i, o_j \in G_j, G_i \cap G_j = \emptyset$

in a descending order of $A_{\text{Gest}}(o_i, o_j, \mathfrak{D})$ until $B(G_{ij}, L) \geq \max(B(G_i, L), B(G_j, L))$; once such pair $(o_j, o_j)_k$ is discovered groups G_i and G_j are merged into G_{ij}. This enforces the priority of joining pairs of objects that are globally in stronger patterns.

Constructing $\mathfrak{T}$ in this way still requires evaluating $B(G, L)$ for $O(\|\mathfrak{D}\|^2)$ candidate groups. It is thus desirable to avoid having to recompute MST_{Label} (in eq. (2)) and MST_{Gest}(in eq. (4)) in every evaluation. Notice that when a decision to join groups G_i and G_j into G_{ij} is made, it is mandated by a pair of objects (o_j, o_j) in respective groups that appear in a globally strong pattern according to $A_{\text{Gest}}(o_i, o_j, \mathfrak{D})$. A set of all such edges $\{(o_j, o_j)_k\}$ that contributed to the appearance of a group G on $\mathfrak{T}$ thus forms a spanning tree $ST^{\sim}(G)$ over all objects in G with edges, chosen with the objective of the largest $A_{\text{Gest}}(o_i, o_j, \mathfrak{D})$ and non-decreasing benefit. $ST^{\sim}(G)$ is not exactly MST_{Gest} due to $A_{\text{Gest}}(o_i, o_j, \mathfrak{D}) \neq A_{\text{Gest}}(o_i, o_j, G)$, however $ST^{\sim}(G)$ is readily available without additional computations and allows for a recursive formulation of $T_{\text{Verify}}(G_{ij})$ from eq. (4)

$$T^{\sim}_{\text{Verify}}(G_{ij}) = T_{\text{Verify}}(o_i, o_j, \mathfrak{D}) + T^{\sim}_{\text{Verify}}(G_i) + T^{\sim}_{\text{Verify}}(G_j)$$

which reuses values previously computed for G_i and G_j. For the same reason of immediate availability we use $ST^{\sim}(G)$ instead of MST_{Label}, however, $ST^{\sim}(G)$ is built not directly considering $P_{\text{Label}}(o_i, o_j)$ at all. Using a product on $ST^{\sim}(G)$ as in eq. (2) is thus likely to over-constrain construction of $\mathfrak{T}$ and build only very small groups due to many elements of the product being much smaller than what they would have been if the actual MST_{Label} was used. To adjust, we replace the product with the minimum, which only estimates the group's density in the feature space instead of performing a likelihood computation, in the following fashion:

$$P^{\sim}_{\text{Label}}(G_{ij}) = \min(P_{\text{Label}}(o_i, o_j), P^{\sim}_{\text{Label}}(G_i), P^{\sim}_{\text{Label}}(G_j)).$$

which is also a recursive formulation allowing for reusing of values computed for subgroups during the tree construction.

These two approximations were made in the interest of constructing candidate groups (nodes of $\mathfrak{T}$) with large-scale regular patterns at interactive rates. They do not guarantee optimality of the candidate groups according to $B(G, L)$. However, we evaluate $B(G, L)$ for each group in the tree $\mathfrak{T}$ and choose the best one to show the user. Empirically, we observe that this approach produces groups with good $B(G, L)$ at interactive rates ($\sim$1 second per group).

RESULTS

We have performed a series of experiments to test how well group annotation works for labeling small objects in 3D points clouds with the IGRA system.

Data Set. For our experiments, we tested the proposed methods on a point cloud captured with 4 terrestrial (car-mounted) and 1 aerial (airplane-mounted) LiDAR scanners within a 6 km^2 section of downtown Ottawa, Canada [22] (see Figure 1).

The data set contains approximately 1 billion points, each of which is represented by a 3D position, RGB color, and scalar intensity, though the colors and intensities of terrestrial points are very noisy and thus not used by our system. It was chosen because it is has been used for evaluation by previous systems for recognition of small objects in LiDAR scans of cities. In particular it was first used by Golovinskiy et al. [12], who reported approximately 58% precision and 65% recall using fully automatic algorithms to recognize 1,063 objects amongst 17 semantic categories in a $0.3km^2$ "evaluation area." We executed our tests on similar set of 18 object categories (bush, fire hydrant, mailbox, newspaper box, parking meter, advertising kiosk, garbage can, recycle bin, phone booth, traffic sign, highway sign, A-frame sign, sidewalk light, street light, traffic ligth, short fence post, tall fence post, and car) in the same evaluation area of Ottawa, using a slightly expanded "ground-truth set" of 1,224 objects.

Data Segmentation. We segmented the LiDAR points into objects using the algorithms described in [11, 12]. Specifically, plane extraction algorithms were used to remove the points associated with major planar structures in the environment (ground and buildings), and then hierarchical clustering and graph cut algorithms were used to detect the locations of potential objects and cluster points into objects. The results of these automatic segmentations were improved interactively with a simple tool that allows a user to specify points inside and/or outside any object and then resolves the object segmentation boundary with a graph cut. These improved segmentations were used in our tests – the user only had to provide a label for each object.

We chose to create segmentations as a pre-process in our tests for several reasons. First, most small objects in a LiDAR scan of a city can be segmented automatically with high accuracy (90% in [12]), and so the segmentations in our tests are quite representative of those created with state-of-the-art algorithms. Second, segmentations can often be refined automatically after objects have been labeled – e.g., using an algorithm that aligns objects of the same type to form a consensus of the correct segmentation. So, precise pre-segmentations may not be necessary. Of course, there are complicated interplays between the accuracy of the segmentations with the effectiveness of the shape-based classifiers, the robustness of the consensus algorithms, the ability of people to recognize objects, the quality of the data, and so on. We defer investigation of these interplays to future work in order to focus on the main idea of the paper: group annotation. Finally, the proposed group annotation approach is not specific to labeling LiDAR data. It is a general idea for labeling any kind of data that can be shown in groups (perhaps cells in stained microscopic images, tumors in medical images, etc.). The segmentation challenges for each of those types of data is different. Hence, we avoid mixing our evaluation of the group annotation metaphor with the specific challenges of segmenting a particular data set.

User Study Design. To test whether group annotation is helpful for labeling objects in this data set, we ran a user study with 10 participants ranging in age from 20 to 40, including 4 women and 6 men.

We split the participants randomly into two sets of five. We asked one set of participants (GA) to label objects in the ground truth set using the group annotation interface described in this paper. We asked the other set (IA) to label the same objects with the same interface but with a classical least confidence active learning algorithm which suggests objects one-by-one. The order of assigning participants to one of these two conditions was random, and no participant was aware of which condition was the control.

Each participant was given written instructions and photographic examples of the types of objects to be labeled (copies are in the supplemental materials). Then, he/she executed a short interactive tutorial by labeling 163 objects covering all 18 object categories within a completely different area of Ottawa. During this tutorial, the participant was given immediate feedback if any label was assigned incorrectly and could proceed only after providing the correct label for every object.

Once the tutorial was completed, the participant proceeded to provide or confirm the label for all 1,224 objects in the evaluation area without any feedback or guidance using either the one-by-one or group annotation interface. Once done labeling all objects, he/she completed an exit questionnaire.

Experimental Results. During each user session, we logged all interactions and recorded times required to complete the task of providing/confirming labels for all objects in the evaluation set. Our hypothesis is that labeling all objects with the group annotation interface is faster.

Figure 3 shows a comparison of the results averaged across all five participants using each of the two interfaces. The horizontal axis represents the F-measure of the object labels predicted by the system with a nearest-neighbor classifier from the set of labels confirmed by the user, and the vertical axis indicates the earliest wall-clock time (in seconds) since the start of the test session for the system to achieve that F-measure. At the beginning, the system starts with no objects labeled, and so the curve starts at the origin. As it proceeds, the participant provides or confirms labels for more and more examples, which are fed into the training set, and so the nearest-neighbor classifier predicts larger numbers of objects correctly, and the F-measure rises. At the end (right side of the plot), every object has been confirmed by the participant explicitly, and so the F-measure is very close to 1.0 (deviations from 1.0 represent labeling mistakes by the participants).

We can make several interesting observations from this plot. First and foremost, they suggest that the group annotation interface (GA) provides faster times to task completion than the one-by-one interface (IA) – i.e., the group annotation curve is lower in the plot. In particular, the average time to completion is 2281+/-561 seconds with the group annotation interface and 3855+/-837 seconds with one-by-one labeling, a difference that is statistically significant at the 1% confidence level according to an independent two-sample two-tailed t-test. This result confirms our main hypothesis.

Second, the results suggest that the average number of labeling mistakes made by users of the group annotation interface (GA) is approximately the same as made with the one-by-one interface (IA). This can be seen by the fact that the f-measure

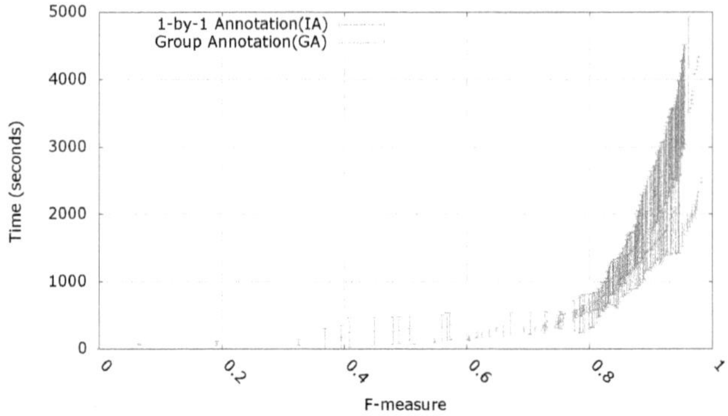

Figure 3: Comparison of average time to achieve F measure when labeling with group annotation (green) and 1-by-1 annotation (red) interfaces.

of the rightmost point in both curves is almost the same in both plots ($95\% +/- 1\%$ versus $95\% +/- 2\%$).

Finally, we see that it is possible for novice users to label 1,224 objects with 95% accuracy in approximately 40 minutes with group annotation – that's approximately one object every 2 seconds after a few minutes of training. This is much faster than alternative 3D labeling interfaces tested during pilot studies that require the user to interactively find and select mislabeled objects because the computer automatically moves the camera and selects objects, the operations that are very expensive for people to do.

Further Analysis. It is possible to analyze the activity logs and exit surveys to investigate further how people used the group annotation interface. For example, we can ask questions like: "how many groups were contracted by a user?," "what types of groups were contracted?," "were mistakes made more commonly in large groups of objects?," etc.

We first ask "how does the size of a group affect the probability that a person will provide a label for it?" Figure 4 addresses this question by showing a breakdown of what type of command users provided when presented groups of different sizes. The horizontal axis lists of the sizes of groups shown to the user. The vertical axis represents average numbers of objects in groups that were labeled/confirmed (green), contracted (red), or expanded (blue) for each group size. The plot shows that users labeled objects in groups as large as a few hundred objects at a time. For smaller groups the results show comparable frequencies of both labeling and contraction, and closer to the lower sizes of groups users prefer labeling to contraction. According to exit surveys, the main reasons for group contraction was impurity of the group, only 1 user mentioned that it was due to inability to see the entire group in the field of view. In the left-most bar, we see that ~20% of objects were labeled on their own, which is not surprising, since some object categories in this data set (e.g., mailboxes, garbage cans, fire hydrants, etc.) have instances scattered throughout the city, and thus are not conveniently labeled in a large group.

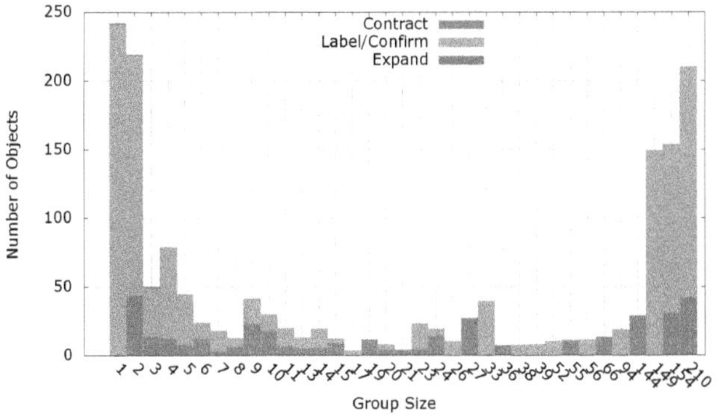

Figure 4: Average number of objects labeled (green), contracted (red), or expanded (blue) in groups of different sizes.

The second question we ask is "how does the size of a group affect the probability that a person will make a mistake when labeling it?" Figure 5 addresses this question by showing a breakdown of correct versus incorrect labels provided by users for groups of different sizes. Again, the horizontal axis lists of the sizes of groups shown to the user. The vertical axis represents average numbers of objects in groups that were labeled correctly (green) or incorrectly (red) for each group size. The plot indicates that the fraction of mistakes is larger for smaller groups. We have two explanations for this observation. First, some objects are very difficult to recognize – so the user probably contracts groups containing them before providing a label, and then sometimes still makes a mistake. Second, large groups appearing in regular patterns are easier to recognize than individual objects – the pattern provides context that aids recognition.

Overall, we conclude that the group annotation interface helps users label objects in less time and with as much accuracy as alternative interfaces based on one-by-one labeling.

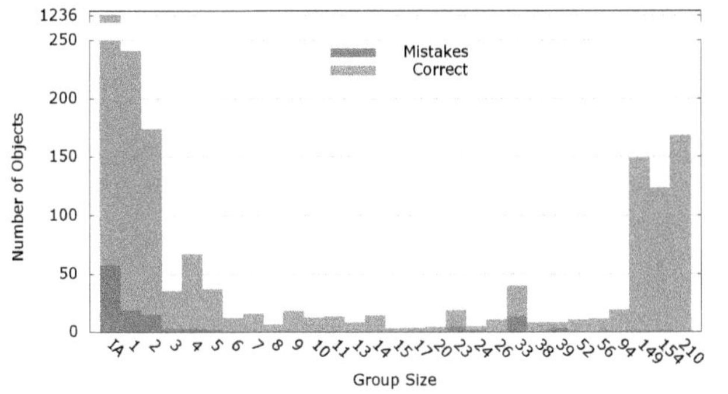

Figure 5: Average number of objects labeled correctly (green) or incorrectly (red) in groups of different sizes.

CONCLUSION AND FUTURE WORK

This paper investigates a group annotation approach to labeling 3D data. Besides the introduction of this idea, our research contributions include an active learning algorithm to construct groups of objects that minimize the expected time to label remaining objects, a perceptual model based on Gestalt principles to estimate the amount of time required for a user to recognize the label for a group of objects, and design of an interactive system that incorporates visualization of 3D point clouds with interactive labeling commands into an interface that can be learned by novices in a few minutes.

This paper provides an initial investigation and thus has many limitations. So far, we have focused only on pre-segmented data. This choice is appropriate for LiDAR scans of cities because automatic segmentation algorithms can achieve 90+% precision and recall for this type of data [12]. However, for other types of data (e.g., Kinect scans of interior environments), integration of segmentation into the labeling process provides an exta challenge that must be addressed. Second, we consider models of human recognition based only on shape similarities and spatial patterns, but of course other factors (e.g., color) are important as well and should be considered in further studies.

An interesting question for future work is to investigate "what other types of group annotation are most helpful?" We ask a user to provide a single label for *all* objects in a group or to indicate that none is possible. Previous work has asked users to provide a single label for *any* object in a group [8] or to explicitly select outliers before providing a label [7]. Different alternatives provide different levels of information and require different amounts of time for a user. We believe that the method proposed in this paper is one interesting point in this design space, but investigating other alternatives is an important topic for future work.

ACKNOWLEDGMENTS

We are grateful to Rebecca Fiebrink, David Mimno, Sean Gerrish, and Xiaofeng Ren for discussion and guidance. We thank Neptec, John Gilmore, and Wright State University for the 3D LiDAR dataset. We acknowledge NSF (IIS-1251217, CCF-0937139), Google, and Intel (ISTC-VC) for funding.

REFERENCES

1. Alvarez, G. A. Representing multiple objects as an ensemble enhances visual cognition. *Trends in cognitive sciences* (2011).

2. Amores, J. Multiple instance classification: Review, taxonomy and comparative study. *Artificial Intelligence 201* (2013), 81 – 105.

3. Ariely, D. Seeing sets: Representation by statistical properties. *Psychological Science 12*, 2 (2001), 157–162.

4. Chapelle, O., Vapnik, V., and Weston, J. Transductive inference for estimating values of functions. In *NIPS* (1999), 421–427.

5. Chapelle, O., and Zien, A. Semi-supervised classification by low density separation. In *Proc. 10th International Workshop on Artificial Intelligence and Statistics* (2005).

6. Chong, S. C., and Treisman, A. Representation of statistical properties. *Vision Research 43*, 4 (2003), 393–404.

7. Deng, J., Dong, W., Socher, R., Li, L.-J., Li, K., and Fei-Fei, L. Imagenet: A large-scale hierarchical image database. In *Proc. CVPR* (2009), 248–255.

8. Dietterich, T. G., Lathrop, R. H., and Lozano-Pérez, T. Solving the multiple instance problem with axis-parallel rectangles. *Artificial Intelligence 89*, 1-2 (1997), 31–71.

9. Gammerman, A., Vovk, V., and Vapnik, V. Learning by transduction. In *Fourteenth conference on Uncertainty in artificial intelligence* (1998).

10. Geiger, A., Lenz, P., Stiller, C., and Urtasun, R. Vision meets robotics: The kitti dataset. *International Journal of Robotics Research (IJRR)* (2013).

11. Golovinskiy, A., and Funkhouser, T. Min-cut based segmentation of point clouds. In *IEEE Workshop on Search in 3D and Video (S3DV) at ICCV* (2009).

12. Golovinskiy, A., Kim, V. G., and Funkhouser, T. Shape-based recognition of 3D point clouds in urban environments. *Proc. ICCV* (2009).

13. Haberman, J., and Whitney, D. The visual system discounts emotional deviants when extracting average expression. *Attention, Perception, & Psychophysics 72*, 7 (2010), 1825–1838.

14. Hengel, A. v. d., Dick, A., Thormaehlen, T., Torr, P., and Ward, B. Building models of regular scenes from structure and motion. In *Proc. BMVC* (2006).

15. Hick, W. E. On the rate of gain of information. *Quarterly Journal of Experimental Psychology 4*, 1 (1952), 11–26.

16. Itti, L., and Koch, C. Computational modelling of visual attention. *Nature Reviews Neuroscience 2*, 3 (2001), 194–203.

17. Kapoor, A., Grauman, K., Urtasun, R., and Darrell, T. Active learning with gaussian processes for object categorization. In *Proc. ICCV* (2007).

18. Kim, Y., Mitra, N., Huang, Q., and Guibas, L. J. Guided real-time scanning of indoor environments. *Computer Graphics Forum (Pacific Graphics) 32*, 7 (2013).

19. Lin, H., Gao, J., Zhou, Y., Lu, G., Ye, M., Zhang, C., Liu, L., and Yang, R. Semantic decomposition and reconstruction of residential scenes from lidar data. *ACM Trans. Graph. 32*, 4 (2013).

20. Musialski, P., Wonka, P., Aliaga, D. G., Wimmer, M., van Gool, L., and Purgathofer, W. A survey of urban reconstruction. In *EUROGRAPHICS 2012 State of the Art Reports*, Eurographics Association (2012), 1–28.

21. Nan, L., Sharf, A., Zhang, H., Cohen-Or, D., and Chen, B. Smartboxes for interactive urban reconstruction. In *Proc. SIGGRAPH*, ACM (2010), 93:1–93:10.

22. Neptec. Wright state 100, 2009. `http://www.ws-arc.org/applied-research-corporation/ottawa-data-files.html`. (Accessed April, 2014).

23. P. Welinder, P. P. Online crowdsourcing: rating annotators and obtaining cost-effective labels. In *Proc. CVPR* (2010).

24. Pelli, D., Majaj, N., Christian, C., Kim, E., and Palomares, M. Grouping in object recognition: the role of a Gestalt law in letter identification. *Cognitive Neuropsychology 26*, 1 (February 2009), 36–49.

25. Rosenholtz, R. A simple saliency model predicts a number of motion popout phenomena. *Vision Research 39*, 19 (1999), 3157 – 3163.

26. Russell, B. C., Torralba, A., Murphy, K. P., and Freeman, W. T. Labelme: A database and web-based tool for image annotation. *IJCV 77*, 1-3 (2008), 157–173.

27. Sanocki, T., and Epstein, W. Priming spatial layout of scenes. *Psychological Science 8*, 5 (1997), 374–378.

28. Settles, B. Active learning literature survey. Computer Sciences Technical Report 1648, University of Wisconsin–Madison, 2009.

29. Shao, T., Xu, W., Zhou, K., Wang, J., Li, D., and Guo, B. An interactive approach to semantic modeling of indoor scenes with an rgbd camera. *ACM Trans. Graph. 31*, 6 (2012), 136:1–136:11.

30. Silberman, N., Kohli, P., Hoiem, D., and Fergus, R. Indoor segmentation and support inference from RGBD images. In *European Conference on Computer Vision* (2012).

31. Thorpe, S., Fize, D., and Marlot, C. Speed of processing in the human visual system. *Nature 381* (1996), 520.

32. Top, A., Hamarneh, G., and Abugharbieh, R. Active learning for interactive 3D image segmentation. *Med Image Comput Comput Assist Interv 14*, 3 (2011), 603–610.

33. Velizhev, A., Shapovalov, R., and Schindler, K. Implicit shape models for object detection in 3D point clouds. *ISPRS Annals I-3*, 2012 (2012), 179–184.

34. Vijayanarasimhan, S., Jain, P., and Grauman, K. Far-sighted active learning on a budget for image and video recognition. In *Proc. CVPR* (2010), 3035–3042.

35. Wagemans, J., Elder, J. H., Kubovy, M., Palmer, S. E., Peterson, M. A., Singh, M., and von der Heydt, R. A century of gestalt psychology in visual perception: I. perceptual grouping and figure–ground organization. *Psychological bulletin 138*, 6 (2012), 1172.

36. Wang, Y., Asafi, S., van Kaick, O., Zhang, H., Cohen-Or, D., and Chen, B. Active co-analysis of a set of shapes. *ACM Trans. Graph. 31*, 6 (2012), 165:1–165:10.

37. Welch, W. J. Algorithmic complexity: Three NP-hard problems in computational statistics. *Journal of Statistical Computation and Simulation 15* (1982), 17–25.

38. Wong, Y.-S., Chu, H.-K., and Mitra, N. J. Smartannotator: An interactive tool for annotating rgbd indoor images. *CoRR abs/1403.5718* (2014). http://arxiv.org/pdf/1403.5718.pdf.

39. Xiao, J., Hays, J., Ehinger, K., Oliva, A., and Torralba, A. Sun database: Large-scale scene recognition from abbey to zoo. In *Proc. CVPR* (2010).

40. Zhu, Q., and Yang, P. Density sensitive based spectral clustering. In *Computer and Information Sciences*, vol. 62. 2010, 139–142.

Microtask Programming: Building Software with a Crowd

Thomas D. LaToza[1], W. Ben Towne[2], Christian M. Adriano[1], André van der Hoek[1]
[1]University of California, Irvine
Irvine, CA
{tlatoza, adrianoc, andre}@ics.uci.edu
[2]Carnegie Mellon University
5000 Forbes Ave, Pittsburgh, PA
wbt@cs.cmu.edu

ABSTRACT
Microtask crowdsourcing organizes complex work into workflows, decomposing large tasks into small, relatively independent microtasks. Applied to software development, this model might increase participation in open source software development by lowering the barriers to contribution and dramatically decrease time to market by increasing the parallelism in development work. To explore this idea, we have developed an approach to decomposing programming work into microtasks. Work is coordinated through tracking changes to a graph of artifacts, generating appropriate microtasks and propagating change notifications to artifacts with dependencies. We have implemented our approach in CrowdCode, a cloud IDE for crowd development. To evaluate the feasibility of microtask programming, we performed a small study and found that a small crowd of 12 workers was able to successfully write 480 lines of code and 61 unit tests in 14.25 person-hours of time.

Author Keywords
crowdsourcing; development environment; programming tools

ACM Classification Keywords
D.2.6 Programming environments: Interactive environments

INTRODUCTION
Microtask crowdsourcing systems enable crowds of workers of varying skill to complete large tasks quickly by decomposing work into short, self-contained microtasks, enabling mass contribution through low barriers to contribution and work to be completed quickly through extreme parallelism. This paradigm has a great potential appeal for software work: while open source development has brought open contribution to software work, joining an open source project is often a long and tedious process, discouraging contribution and reducing the pool of participants. Even in commercial development organizations, there is often a need to build software quickly, as time to market is often valuable. While microtasking may introduce overhead and thereby reduce the efficiency of the development process, there may be situations in which greatly broadening the pool of potential participants can lead work to be completed more quickly through larger scale and parallelization.

UIST 2014, October 5–8, 2014, Honolulu, HI, USA..

ACM 978-1-4503-3069-5/14/10...$15.00.
http://dx.doi.org/10.1145/2642918.2647349

Figure 1. An example of a microtask in CrowdCode.

Programming is an example of complex work, involving many interdependencies among components of the work produced. Recent crowdsourcing work has begun to explore approaches for microtasking complex work. For example, CrowdForge [12] introduces a Map-Reduce style paradigm in which the crowd first partitions a large problem into several smaller sub-problems, then solves the sub-problems (map), and finally merges the multiple results to a single result (reduce). However, an important limitation of existing workflows for complex work is that the decomposition structure is *static* and fixed by the requestor. For example, while a requestor might specify a workflow in which workers first partition work into sub-problems before workers then perform a map step, the workflow itself is fixed and cannot vary in response to the work done. For many creative tasks, this is an important limitation. For example, in programming, it is impossible to specify, a priori, the set of functions and tests necessary to implement a program. In the process of implementing functions, developers may discover new parts of the problem, requiring new functions to be written. Then, in the process of writing functions, developers may discover they must change their interface, requiring changes to be made to functions elsewhere.

Here, we present an approach for crowdsourcing problems using *dynamically* generated microtasks and illustrate this approach through the design of a system for microtask programming. Our key insight is to coordinate work through a graph of artifacts, generating microtasks in response to events that occur on artifacts rather than through a static workflow. Each microtask asks workers to perform a short well-defined task on a single artifact – a function or a test (e.g., Figure 1), allowing work to proceed on many artifacts in parallel. As workers complete microtasks, events are generated on the artifact, which may then trigger further microtasks to be generated. When an artifact changes, events are sent to artifacts that depend on it, allowing microtask structures to be dynamic and non-hierarchic. For example, when a function changes its signature (e.g., adding a parameter), artifacts that depend on it (callers and tests) are notified, generating microtasks to handle these changes. As artifacts may have many dependencies, artifacts may have multiple pending notifications of changes. To coordinate this work, each artifact has a microtask queue, allowing changes to be performed sequentially and preventing conflicts.

We implemented our approach in a prototype online IDE for microtask programming for Javascript: CrowdCode. Our approach has a number of important limitations: it does not support design tasks, does not crowdsource the design of data types, is limited to crowdsourcing small functional libraries, and requires the correctness of work to be evaluated solely through tests. Within this limited scope, we have explored an approach for microtasking writing code, writing tests, and debugging. To achieve this, we present a novel approach for the dynamic generation of microtasks through an artifact network, a microtask decomposition of programming, and self-contained microtasks for programming. To evaluate the possibility of a small crowd working on programming microtasks in parallel and to evaluate the basic feasibility of the approach, we performed a small user study in which 12 participants worked on a small programming task. We found that the participants were able to successfully program part of a library, completing 265 microtasks, writing 480 lines of code across 16 functions, and an additional 61 unit tests. We found that decontextualizing programming work had both strengths and weaknesses; but, overall, 11 of the 12 participants felt that a microtasking approach would make them more likely to contribute to an open source project.

RELATED WORK

Our research builds on work across several communities: open source software development, crowdsourcing complex work, and crowdsourcing software development. In open source, workers complete tasks to accrue status [4]. Yet this process differs fundamentally from microtasking, as tasks exist at a far larger granularity of hours or days. Workers face many barriers to contributing, including discovering ways to contribute, learning about tools, and tolerating harsh feedback from senior members [10][14][21]. Our approach is intended to reduce these barriers by decomposing work into microtasks, which take only minutes.

Complex work comprises interdependent tasks that require more cognitive effort than the typical tasks of labeling and transcribing data. Approaches to tackle interdependent and complex tasks rely on workflow mechanisms and crowd algorithms. For example, Soylent [2] enables a writer to partition work in smaller proof reading and editing tasks to be performed by a crowd. TurKit [16], provides a framework based on scripts to create and run tasks in Mechanical Turk. CrowdForge [12] expands those solutions by enabling the crowd to partition work. Our approach extends these models, supporting dynamic, non-hierarchic workflows.

Other work has begun to apply microtasking to programming at the level of individual development tasks such as testing or question answering. In Stack Overflow[1], developers ask questions, other developers answer them, and yet other developers evaluate the quality of the answers, concurrently curating a knowledge repository of frequent questions [11,17]. Other work has explored the use of crowdsourcing for recommending fixes to bugs [9,18] and compilation errors [22] and to checking and fixing unit test assertions [19]. In order to leverage larger pools of workers, some systems enable non-specialists to contribute. For instance, several systems have explored applying a gamification paradigm to verifying software models for correctness [15] or verifying for security vulnerabilities by playing with pipes [5].

One of the few systems to explore microtasking a programming process is Collabode [7,8]. In Collabode, an "original programmer" describes in prose short microtasks to be performed and workers then use a provided web IDE to complete the requested tasks. An evaluation of the system found that, while it was possible to microtask programming, there were several significant issues with the workflow used. As workers all worked with a global view of the entire codebase, it was sometimes distracting to see changes being made elsewhere. And there was a large overhead for the requestor in managing the crowd workers, as they needed to answer questions about the request and evaluate the work in detail. Moreover, code often had subtle bugs, which was difficult for the requestor to find through code inspection. Finally, workers were anonymous and thus sometimes did not take responsibility for their work. These considerations directly influenced our design choices in

[1] stackoverflow.com

Figure 2. The CrowdCode environment and the *Write Function* microtask.

CrowdCode, leading us to adopt a model with local, self-contained microtasks and test-based correctness evaluation.

EXAMPLE

To illustrate microtask programming in CrowdCode, we present an example. After logging in to CrowdCode and viewing a welcome screen, Alice is immediately presented with her first microtask. The microtask provides her with the description of a function in prose and asks her to enumerate test cases.

Not feeling in the mood for testing, she clicks the skip link at the bottom of the page. She's then presented a new microtask – *Write Function* (Figure 2) – and asked to write some code. Rather than completely implement the function, she sketches some pieces of it that come to mind, noting portions still to be done with pseudocode (yellow background). She thinks some of the functionality should really be implemented in other functions, and writes several pseudocalls describing what she thinks those functions should do. She submits the task.

She next receives a microtask to *Debug*, and is given some code and unit tests and sees that the unit test is failing. She edits the code, but the unit tests still are not passing. Looking at a list of inputs and outputs for function calls at the bottom, she sees that one of the functions is returning an erroneous value. After editing the output value, she reruns the tests, sees that they pass, and submits. She sees that her score has now increased to 20 points!

Alice next is assigned another microtask to edit a function, and sees that she has been reassigned the microtask for the function she started working on earlier. But it has now changed – some of the pseudocode she had written has now been replaced with code, and several of the pseudocalls have been replaced with actual calls. But she also sees that some of the new algorithm does not appear to work correctly, so she rewrites some of the code, adding new pseudocode and pseudocalls for some of the new portions.

DESIGN

The core of CrowdCode is a system for tracking work as a graph of artifacts, dynamically generating microtasks in response to state changes in artifacts and propagating events across dependencies. To enable workers to program using these microtasks, CrowdCode decomposes programming work into a set of microtasks, enabling workers to write code, reuse functions, test, and debug within self-contained microtasks. Finally, CrowdCode provides social features to motivate contributions including a simple point system. The following sections greater detail CrowdCode's design and concepts.

Generating Microtasks

In CrowdCode, all work performed by the crowd occurs in microtasks. A *microtask* is a short, independent, self-contained request for a piece of work to be completed. Each microtask focuses on a single *artifact* – a work product be-

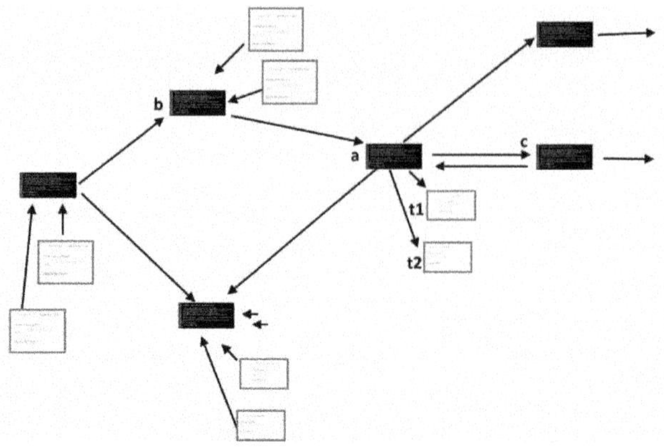

Figure 3. A graph of artifacts with functions (black background), tests (blue outline), and dependencies (arrows).

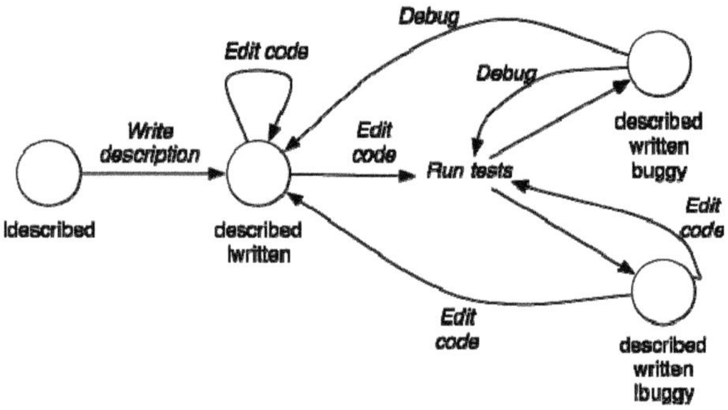

Figure 4. The function state machine.

ing produced by the crowd. After a crowd worker completes and submits a microtask, the microtask's corresponding artifact processes the work completed, updating its data and state accordingly.

In CrowdCode, the overall work product is maintained as a graph of artifacts (Figure 3). Each artifact – functions, tests, and the project – includes a set of attributes describing its *state*, describing the work which has been completed and the work which may be required. When a microtask is submitted, an artifact may change state, transitioning attributes as necessary. For example, when the *Write Function Description* microtask is submitted, a function changes state from *not described* to *described.* See Figure 4 for the function state machine.

Microtask submissions may also trigger an artifact to send an *event* to other artifacts that depends on it. For example, when a parameter is added to a function's signature, the function sends a signature change event to all functions that call it and all of the unit tests for the function, enabling these artifacts to generate microtasks in response. In Figure 3, adding a parameter to function *a* results in events being sent to functions *b* and *c* and tests *t1* and *t2*. In this way, changes to an artifact may propagate across the call graph, allowing related artifacts to be updated. CrowdCode currently implements two types of dependencies: function calls and tests that test a function.

CrowdCode also supports iterative workflows, where microtasks for the same work are repeatedly generated until work has been completed. If, after a microtask is submitted, the artifact's data is updated but it remains in the same state, it may generate a new microtask to continue the work. For example, developers editing a function can write *pseudocode*, leaving the state of the artifact in the *not written* state and iteratively generating microtasks until all of the pseudocode has been replaced with code.

Organizing work through explicit global tasks is challenging and fragile. As workers do work at scale throughout the system, in parallel throughout the system, this work must then be reassembled into a consistent whole. In our early work, we explored the use of *global* tasks, spanning multiple artifacts. For example, a debugging task might spawn a set of microtasks to be done on a set of functions, and would not be completed until the bug was definitively located in a function. However, as each function may be concurrently changing, a single function might concurrently participate in multiple debugging tasks all while other work is being done. Determining if a bug has been found, when the buggy function might have been concurrently changed as part of another task, was challenging.

As a result, we instead adopted a simpler, but powerful principle: each artifact may have a single microtask concurrently being performed and each microtask must act independently. When there are multiple microtasks to be done (e.g., a function fails a test and must also update a call to match a changed signature), each microtask is added to a queue. Each artifact ensures that it has only a single available microtask in the global queue at a time. Other microtasks are maintained in a separate per-artifact queue and released into the global queue as microtasks are completed. This design prevents merge conflicts, as only at most one microtask and worker have commit access to an artifact at any point in time. This poses the secondary issue that abandoned tasks could hold up development on an artifact, and timers that strictly or arbitrarily limit total microtask time might cause issues for e.g. function implementation tasks that a worker is spending more time on. Our implementation uses soft notices to submit after 8 minutes and includes inactivity timers, to help address this issue.

Workflow

CrowdCode crowdsources the implementation of libraries requested by a client developer. All work in CrowdCode begins with a client request specifying the API of a library to be implemented by the crowd. Clients describe an API through a set of functions, each containing a prose description of the functions purpose and its *signature*, including its name, return type, and list of parameters (including name, type, and text description/interpretation). Together, these functions describe the behavior of a library that can be incorporated by the client into a larger codebase. Clients also specify a set of data types, allowing each function to have a type describing the legal values that may be passed to and returned from the client and to be used internally within the library's implementation.

A central decision in the design of a crowdsourcing system is the granularity at which workers interact with the work products produced. A smaller granularity enables greater parallelism, as it increases the amount of crowd workers that can be working at the same time, in turn decreasing the time required to complete work. However, decomposing work into smaller pieces can also increase the amount of overhead, as more workers may need to understand some of the same aspects of the current status of the work to contribute.

CrowdCode attempts to balance these factors towards the smaller end of the granularity scale, using the function as the central unit of granularity. Functions are a natural and central boundary in programs, enabling a set of related statements to be organized into a coherent whole providing a single piece of functionality. Functions are a central unit of abstraction in programs, providing an interface through which clients may invoke the described functionality without seeing or reasoning about the code providing the function's implementation.

As workers work with code in CrowdCode, workers interact with a single function at a time. Through the function's description, workers can understand what callers expect of the function, enabling them to reason about and work on the function in isolation from the code of the other functions. Similarly, workers may request some functionality to be created (or reused) in the system. This request leads the crowd to find or create a function, which can then be called from the requesting function. In this way, functions and their interfaces provide boundaries establishing individual units of work that can each evolve separately.

Another central consideration in a crowdsourcing system is providing mechanisms to produce quality work. In CrowdCode, this is done through unit tests. Drawing inspiration from test-driven development [1], microtasks are separately created to write tests for each function. When all of the tests pass, the system is considered to be ready for acceptance testing by the client. If a test fails, a microtask is created to debug the function. By creating separate microtasks for writing code and testing, CrowdCode creates redundancy, ensuring that the code produced is correct enough that it passes its tests. If workers produce code that fails to pass the tests, more work will be created until the tests pass. Of course, the tests themselves may also be incorrect. When debugging, workers may report an issue with a test, generating a microtask to address the issue and correct the test.

As a result of requiring that bugs be able to be detected through tests, CrowdCode requires that code written is functional and neither mutates global state nor interacts

Microtask type	Description	Possible subsequent microtasks
Write Function	Sketch or implement a function using code, pseudocode, and pseudocalls.	*Write Function, Reuse Search, Machine Unit Test*
Reuse Search	Given a pseudocall and the surrounding code, determine if an existing function provides the functionality or that no function does.	*Write Call, Write Function Description*
Write Function Description	Given a pseudocall and the surrounding code, write a description and signature for a new function for this behavior.	*Write Call*
Write Call	Replace the specified pseudocall with a call to the specified function or edit the function to implement the behavior in an alternative way.	*Write Function, Reuse Search, Machine Unit Test*
Write Test Cases	Given a description of a function, list test cases.	*Write Test*
Write Test	Given a test case and the description of a function, implement the test case or report an issue in the test case.	*Machine Unit Test, Write Test Cases*
Machine Unit Test	Executes all implemented tests, notifying functions if they fail a test	*Debug*
Debug	Edit code to fix bug, report an issue in a test, or create stubs describing issues in function call	*Machine Unit Test, Write Function, Reuse Search*

Table 1. The microtasks in CrowdCode.

with the external environment (e.g., writing output to a screen). Functions must be able to be completely specified simply by evaluating the output they produce for each set of inputs. This enables functions to be evaluated for correctness simply by seeing if, for all tests, they produce the correct output. While this does not allow CrowdCode to write web apps with GUIs, CrowdCode can be used to write a library implementing key behavior as part of a larger application containing a GUI and other interactions with an environment.

Table 1 lists the microtasks in CrowdCode, which are discussed in detail in the following sections.

Writing code

Writing code involves a number of distinct tasks – writing descriptions for functions, envisioning and sketching a high-level outline or algorithm, implementing the sketch with code, locating existing functions to reuse or describing new functions to be created, adding function calls, and responding to changes in the interface of functions being called. In CrowdCode, each of these are separate microtasks performed by the crowd.

The first functions are initially requested and described by the client. The crowd begins contributing through a *Write Function* microtask (Figure 2). Workers are provided a description of the function and its signature and asked to begin implementing it. As workers begin writing the function, they may choose to simply sketch portions of the code using *pseudocode*. Workers may indicate that a portion of a line is pseudocode by the leading characters //#; pseudocode is indicated visually with a yellow background. Workers may submit incomplete functions with pseudocode, generating additional microtasks to iteratively continue the work [16].

Workers editing a function may also wish to reuse existing functionality or break up the work to be implemented into multiple functions. In CrowdCode, workers do not need to choose between these cases. Workers may write *pseudocalls,* indicated by a portion of a line beginning with //! and visually highlighted with a white background (against the black code editor background), to request that the crowd either locate an existing function with the specified behavior or to create a new function if no such function exists. This allows the worker editing the function to be oblivious to the other functions that may or may not currently exist – they simply request a function, and the crowd determines the most appropriate way to provide it.

CrowdCode also provides error checking. When a function has pseudocalls or pseudocode remaining, error checking of the function's body is suppressed. This allows workers to incorporate pseudocalls and pseudocode into lines of code in ways that makes the code itself syntactically invalid (e.g., branches and loops with some pseudocode components). In early pilot testing, we found that workers often wished to produce such code, and forcing them to always create syntactically valid code was a significant barrier. Whenever a function has no pseudocalls or pseudocode present, CrowdCode provides error checking, displaying an error panel below the code whenever code errors are present. CrowdCode provides basic syntax checking using JSHint[2].

In CrowdCode, workers can only create functions through the pseudocall mechanism. This prevents a single worker from writing a whole program in a single microtask and encourages workers to break the work to be done into additional microtasks, increasing the parallelism of the work

[2] www.jshint.com

process. To enforce this rule, CrowdCode displays an error message whenever the code editor contains more than one function.

Data types serve an important role in communicating the expected parameters of a function, signaling, for example, that the parameter *player* is expected to be a String in our example task described below. Defining good data types is often a central task of high-level design, requiring a global understanding of a code base. In a microtasking environment where no single worker has such a global view, this is challenging to achieve. Moreover, if a crowd were to iteratively create data types, every time the data types changed, all functions and tests with parameters using those data types might need to change, creating the potential for large amounts of work. Thus, in CrowdCode, all data types are defined by the client as part of the initial client request.

Clients specify data types with a name, list of fields, list of data types for each field, and a prose description (e.g., Board in Figure 2). CrowdCode supports nested data types and arrays of data types. Each parameter to a function and the return value must have a type, which is either a data structure or a primitive type (i.e., Number, Boolean, or String). Parameter types are specified in the comments of the function description (e.g., lines 15 – 17 in Figure 2). CrowdCode displays an error message when a provided type name is invalid. Descriptions of all data types in the system are listed above the code editor.

Reuse and creating functions

Whenever a worker submits code with a new pseudocall, a *Reuse Search* microtask is created. This microtask provides the text from the pseudocall and the code surrounding the pseudocall and asks the worker to search through existing function descriptions to determine if such a function already exists. When search text is entered, it is matched against existing descriptions, and a list of matches displayed. Workers can either select one of the functions or indicate that no existing function provides the requested functionality.

When a new function is required, a *Write Function Description* microtask is next generated (Figure 5). This again provides the pseudocall and the code surrounding the pseudocall and provides a structured editor for writing function descriptions. For each parameter, a textbox is provided for workers to provide the name, type, and description. Error checking is performed, checking for syntax errors, ensuring the function name is unique, and ensuring that the types provided are valid types.

After an existing function has been located or a new function has been described in *Write Function Description*, an *Add Call* microtask is generated (Figure 6). Workers are provided a code editor, functionally equivalent to the Edit a Function microtask, but more specific instructions to replace a specified pseudocall (also highlighted in the code) with a call to the described function or determine another

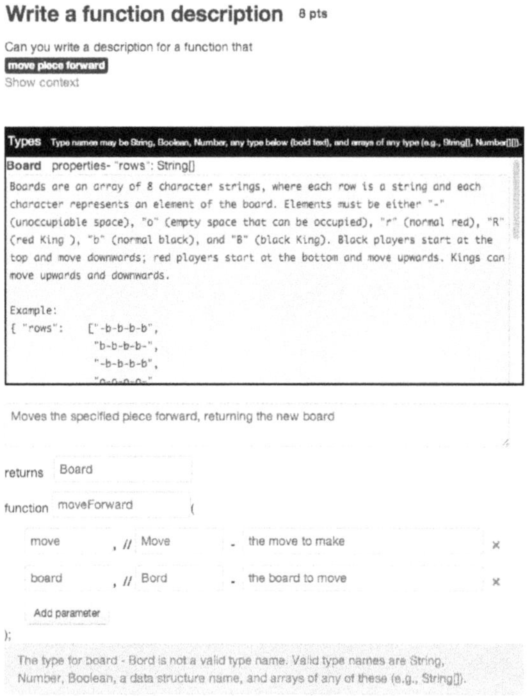

Figure 5. The *Write Function Description* microtask.

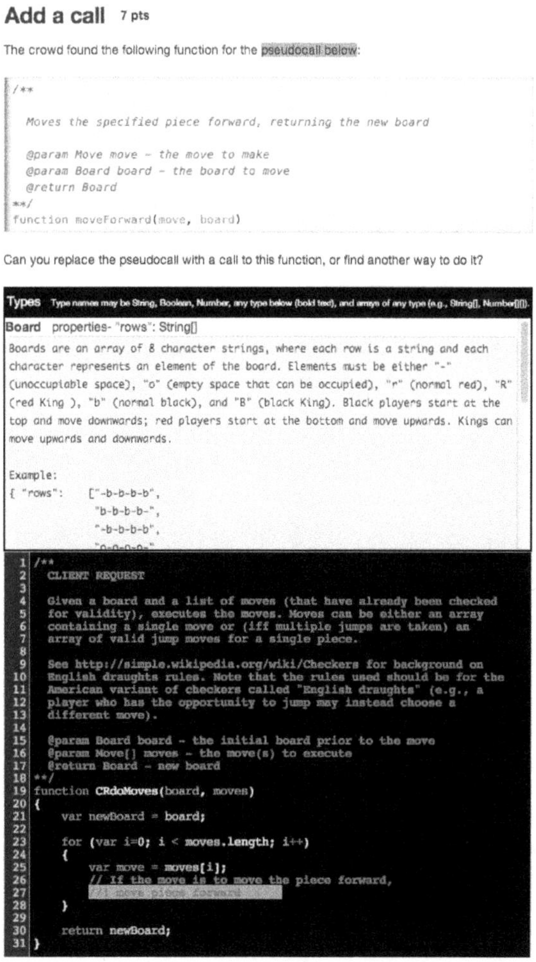

Figure 6. The *Add Call* microtask.

way to implement the specified behavior. Workers are free to edit whatever aspects of the code they wish, enabling them to make arbitrary changes in response to the new function or even to decide that a different way of implementing the requested behavior would be more effective. As in the *Write Function* microtask, adding pseudocode or pseudocalls generates the appropriate new microtasks. Whenever a function call is added, a dependency is created on the function by the function being called. As CrowdCode only permits direct calls to functions in the global scope (e.g., calls to functions on objects are not permitted), function calls can always be uniquely resolved to a single function, eliminating the possibility of any false positives or false negatives in creating dependencies.

When working in a function, workers may also decide to edit a function's description or signature. Workers may rename a function; add, remove, or rename parameters; and change the type of any parameter. Any of these changes signals a change in the function's interface. As a result, callers or tests of the function may need to change to reflect the function's new interface. Thus, CrowdCode generates microtasks signaling the description has changed for each caller and test. Each microtask includes a text-based diff of the old and new description and signature, describing the change to the function and allowing the worker to perform an appropriate edit, if necessary.

Testing

Tests are written in two-steps. As soon as a function has been described by a client or by the crowd, a microtask is generated to *Write Test Cases* (Figure 1). Workers are provided a description of the function and asked to enumerate short prose descriptions of test cases. Allowing a single worker to write all of the test cases helps ensure that test cases are not duplicative and have good coverage. To keep the microtask short, workers are asked to provide a prose description of test cases rather than a full implementation.

In the second step, each submitted test case generates a *Write Test* microtask. A worker is provided the function description and test case and asked to concretely specify the test case as a unit test. To make unit tests quicker and easier to write, CrowdCode provides an editor for simple unit tests, asking workers to specify appropriate values for each parameter and the return value (Figure 7). Test values are checked for syntax errors and that they are of the correct type.

If a worker feels that the prose description of a test case is incorrect for the function (e.g. testing an invalid input when the parameter is specified to have been validated), they may report an issue in the test case. This generates a new Write test cases microtask that prompts a different worker to consider the issue and edit, add, and remove the test cases to address the issue. Any changes to a test a case generate a new Write test microtask reporting the change to the test case and asking the worker to edit the test.

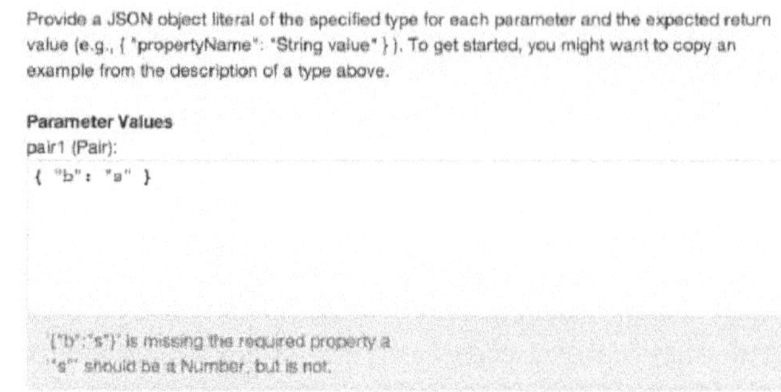

Figure 7. When implementing a unit test, workers are asked to write JSON literals for each parameter, which are checked for syntax and semantics errors.

Determining when tests should be run presents a potential need for global coordination. Generally, tests should be run whenever a function no longer contains pseudocode or pseudocalls (is written) and all of the functions it directly or indirectly calls are written. Global coordination such as this is again fragile: if a microtask is scheduled to run a test for a function and one of the functions it calls concurrently transitions to not written (e.g. by the addition of pseudocode in an editing task responding to a callee signature change), running the tests is no longer required. To prevent this need for global coordination, CrowdCode uses a simpler, local rule. Whenever (1) a function is edited which no longer contains any pseudocalls or pseudocode and (2) all of the functions' tests are currently implemented, the function notifies the project that it is ready to be tested. The project then generates a special *Machine Unit Test* microtask. This microtask requires no work by the worker; the worker simply briefly sees a microtask appear and a progress notification. The machine unit tests executes all implemented tests for all described functions, regardless of if they are written. The body of functions that are not yet written is replaced with an empty body that simply throws a *Not Implemented* exception. When running tests, if a *Not Implemented* exception is encountered, the test result is ignored. Otherwise, if a function fails its tests, the function is notified, transitions to the buggy state, and generates a Debug microtask.

Debugging

Whenever a function fails to pass a unit test, it transitions to the *buggy* state (Figure 4), and a *Debug* microtask is generated. Workers are provided a code editor and a list of unit tests, with passing unit tests listed in green and failing unit tests listed in red. To fix the bug, workers can edit the code, rerun the unit tests, and view the output. A worker may also decide that the issue is not in the code but in the test itself and instead submit a prose description of an issue for the unit test, generating a microtask to edit the test to address the issue.

In other cases, however, the bug may not be in the function under test but in one of the functions it calls. Indeed, much of the challenge of debugging often rests in the process of fault localization and determining the location within the program where the problem is located. Such a task is non-modular in that it requires developers to navigate the whole program, traversing function calls to determine the location of a fault.

How can workers debug such bugs through local microtasks which provide a view of a single function? Our solution is to allow workers to *edit* the return value of function calls, creating a *stub* overriding the function's return value for a specific set of inputs. For example, a worker might see that the call to the function add with the parameters -1 and 2 is returning -1 and edit the return value to be 1. Workers may then rerun the tests to determine if changing the callee's behavior fixes the bug, with the system automatically substituting the stubs for calls to the actual function through source rewriting. After the microtask is submitted, each stub then generates a test for the callee, which will be run and fail (assuming the callee has not been concurrently changed). A new worker can then continue debugging in the function being called.

Social features

To encourage workers to contribute, CrowdCode implements a simple point system. All microtasks are initially assigned a point value based on their type, approximately proportional to the anticipated difficulty of the task type. Each worker has a score and is awarded the microtask's points when the microtask is submitted. Workers can see the score of all workers in the system on a leaderboard (Figure 2), which is updated in real-time.

When a worker logs in to the system, they are automatically assigned a microtask by the system. Compared to manual task assignment in which workers themselves select microtasks, automatic task assignment has two key advantages. First, workers do not spend time searching for microtasks, increasing the time in which they can be working. Second, by using a queue to assign work to workers, the system can ensure that no microtasks *starve* because workers do not wish to attend to them, even initially. However, automatic task assignment reduces worker motivation, as workers no longer have a choice of work [13]. In order to provide the benefits of both automatic task assignment and choice, CrowdCode lets workers skip microtasks. Skipping a microtask adds the microtask back to the global queue, enabling it to be assigned to the next worker seeking work. To encourage workers to do microtasks that may be undesirable, skipping a microtask increases the points that will be awarded on successful completion of that microtask.

CrowdCode provides a number of features to help workers maintain awareness of the current state of the project. As workers complete microtasks, they are added to a personal activity feed (right side of Figure 2), letting workers track their work. Statistics on the current status of the project – the total lines of code, functions fully written, and microtasks completed (top of Figure 2) – let workers see a summary of overall progress in real-time.

In some cases, workers may require information that is not provided by the current microtask. In these cases, workers may choose to use a group chat with all currently logged in workers, a feature we termed *Ask the Crowd.* While global group chat is ultimately unscalable, we introduced the Ask the Crowd feature as a fail-safe measure to enable the crowd to still make progress in the face of unexpected information needs. It also enables workers to go off topic and forge closer relationships with other workers [13].

CrowdCode ultimately depends on workers in the system to work in ways that produce work for other workers to do, especially through writing code containing pseudocode and pseudocalls. In our early testing, we found that workers sometimes attempted to implement large portions of functionality in a single function rather than using pseudocalls to break the work up into separate functions. To address this issue, workers are explicitly encouraged to use pseudocalls and explicitly prompted after every 8 minutes of work on a microtask to submit, even if their work is incomplete, to create microtasks for other workers to do.

Implementation

CrowdCode is implemented as a web application on Google App Engine[3], providing an infrastructure for seamless technical scaling. All artifact and microtask state is stored server-side in AppEngine. When a worker logs into the system, the browser requests a microtask, transferring the necessary state to the browser. When a worker submits a microtask, the modified state is returned to the server and the state updated. All other information – points, the activity feed, leaderboard, chat – is synchronized across browsers in real-time using Firebase[4].

CrowdCode provides a project model. For each new client request, a project is created with its own artifacts, microtasks, and user statistics. Each project is associated with a unique URL, enabling workers to select a project by visiting its URL.

CrowdCode enables workers to write code in Javascript. This has several advantages. Javascript is currently a popular language whose syntax is well-known, making it more likely that workers can contribute without needing to learn a new language, and making it more likely they will easily be able to find answers to syntax questions on the Web. Moreover, Javascript can be executed client-side, enabling the unit tests to be run in the browser and quickly provide feedback for the debugging microtasks. However, a test that runs in the browser might also execute an infinite loop, causing the browser to hang and the worker to be unable to

[3] developers.google.com/appengine

[4] www.firebase.com

continue. To address this issue, all worker written code is executed on a separate thread using the HTML5 web worker API. Long running tests timeout and fail. The code editor is implemented using the CodeMirror editor[5] and the Esprima ECMAScript parsing infrastructure[6].

USER STUDY

To examine the possibility of a small crowd working on programming microtasks in parallel and to evaluate the basic feasibility of the approach, we performed a small user study. We used email distribution lists and personal contacts to recruit 12 participants from our university, all of whom had and/or were working on graduate degrees in computer science and/or related fields. All participants had prior experience programming in Javascript (average 0.6 years) and at least 6 months of experience in industry as a software developer (average 1.8 years). 11 participants were male and 1 female (P7). Participants were paid $60 for two hours of their time.

All participants participated in a single simultaneous session and were each given their own room to ensure that they were only able to communicate through CrowdCode. Participants were first provided a hands-on tutorial with the system and assigned to separate projects in which they each completed several representative microtasks for 10 – 20 minutes. After completing the tutorial, participants then entered a single project and worked on the primary task. Participants were asked to crowdsource game logic for checkers (i.e., English draughts). The experimenters seeded the project with a client request describing two functions to be written and several simple data types specific to checkers. Throughout the study, two experimenters circulated through participants' rooms and verbally answered questions about how to use CrowdCode (which we recognize as of limited scalability) but did not answer any questions about the work itself. Several participants were international students unfamiliar with the rules of Checkers and made use of the link to the rules we provided.

Midway through the Checkers task, participants were asked to complete a short mid-task survey, asking questions about their experiences and challenges. Fifteen minutes before the conclusion of the study session, all participants were stopped and asked to complete a more extensive post-task survey, containing items about their experiences and perceptions with working in CrowdCode.

Results

The twelve participants each worked for about 1.25 hours in CrowdCode (totaling exactly 14.25 person-hours). In total, participants completed 265 microtasks, wrote 480 lines of code across 16 functions, and an additional 61 unit tests

Microtask Type	Completed	Skipped	Mean completion time (minutes)
Debug	28	2	2.67
Machine Unit Test	16	0	0.17
Reuse Search	30	0	1.84
Add Call	8	1	3.81
Write Function	39	10	5.41
Write Test	99	25	2.84
Write Test Cases	36	7	1.85
Write Function Description	20	3	3.06

Table 2. Microtasks completed and skipped by participants.

(Table 2). Participants did not finish implementing checkers in the course of the study session.

One central characteristic of microtasking is a reduced context, enabling microtasks to be self-contained and independent. Participants differed in their reaction to this loss of context. Some found it to be freeing: "I had to keep less context in my head when writing functions, because I could not make assumptions [about] the rest of the program" (P6). Others found it burdensome and wanted other information about the current state of the system that the microtasks did not provide. One participant (P9) also reported that the mental context switching required by microtasks was a hindrance to usability.

A majority of participants agreed that the opportunity for communication beyond what was provided would help them to work more effectively. Participants cited a desire to share technical experience, clarify tasks, ask questions about material that others had written. This may partially reflect the patterns of work to which participants were accustomed. One participant stated that additional communication "might lead to conflicts in the case of disagreements. I thought guiding communication via the work and tasks itself was fairly productive" (P1). Participants used the global chat to socialize and clarify the rules of checkers.

Participants appreciated the ability to specialize in tasks they wanted to do and the ability to contribute according to their knowledge and abilities: "I think that CrowdCode would make me more likely to contribute as I could solve the tasks which I could do, and skip the others. I could take on tasks with higher difficulty as and when I feel comfortable. Hence, CrowdCode would be ideal in working in an open source project… [What I liked best was] collaborative coding - each person can effectively contribute according to his knowledge. For example, a testing person might con-

[5] codemirror.net

[6] esprima.org

tribute for test cases, and skip the code development parts if he feels so" (P11). P1 also reported that "I was willing to be imperfect with my work. It was more important for me to constantly push out new work." This suggests that the iteration process may have created an important "failure for free" condition ([20], Ch. 10) in which the cost of trying something and doing it is less than the cost of figuring out if it's OK to try. Participants found the social features of CrowdCode, especially the points and leaderboard, to be motivating and to "help building a productive vibe to coding" (P10).

11 of the 12 participants agreed that they would be more likely to contribute to an open source project using CrowdCode than with a traditional development process. Each cited the lower barrier to entry and ease of jumping in as opposed to the "taxing" "learning and involvement curve" (P7) of open source projects now, as well as the ability to specialize by skipping some tasks. P1 pointed out that the microtasks could be too constraining for seasoned developers but may be better for someone starting out and understanding a new system.

Work submitted with errors sometimes created issues in the microtasks that derived from the completed work. For example, workers sometimes entered incorrect parameter types in the *Write Function Description* microtask, such as indicating the type of a parameter or return value to be a String when it should be a client-defined data type. As a result, participants in the *Write Test* microtask were forced to write tests with the wrong data types, as they were unable to request a change in the function description.

The study also revealed several usability and platform robustness issues. Participants submitted syntactically invalid code that was not correctly flagged by the system. As a result, some participants were unable to successfully complete the *Debugging* microtask, as the test running infrastructure threw an exception and could not display the results of running the unit tests. Early in the session, some workers were forced to wait to receive microtasks. All of the microtasks were initially spawned in response to a client request for two functions, generating initial microtasks to write the functions and write test cases. Workers writing the functions initially spent a long time working, causing a delay in creating other microtasks for workers to perform.

DISCUSSION

We found that the workers in our study were successfully able to write code and tests within a dynamic microtasking workflow. Especially after the tutorial and early experience with the system, participants seemed to "get it" and found aspects of the system and microtask style that they enjoyed. We were surprised at the motivational power of the points system and leaderboard, especially because participants were well-paid and did not expect the points to have value after the conclusion of the study.

CrowdCode enables developers in a larger project to specify the behavior of a requested functionality as a library through an API (e.g., the API for executing checkers moves in our study), which can be implemented through CrowdCode and added to the project. However, this model imposes a significant burden on the requesting developer: they must precisely specify the behavior of the library, listing descriptions of functions and all necessary data structures. This model might be relaxed by enabling iterative communication between the crowd and requestors, allowing the API to evolve through the joint work of the requesting developer and crowd. Or, in some cases, it may be advantageous to allow requesting developers to play a larger role in the work itself, enabling them to see and direct a global view of the crowd's work.

Microtasking workflows clearly impose an overhead on a development process, and the total amount written per person-hour is likely lower with CrowdCode than with traditional approaches. However, if microtasking is able to successfully reduce the barriers to contribution and thereby harness value from the "long tail" of participation – the many willing to donate small amounts of time and effort – the benefits of tapping into a much larger available resource may still outweigh the overhead costs of using that "free" resource less efficiently.

Another important question is whether or not participants engaged in microtasked work feel that they are making an important and meaningful contribution. On the one hand, microtasked work decontextualizes contributions, which may make it more challenging for workers to understand the impact and significance of their work. On the other hand, by making work products more fine-grained and explicit, it may be possible to provide more information about the impact of work done. For example, a worker writing a function description might receive a notification in the newsfeed whenever the function is reused, letting them see how successfully they were able to craft a reusable API.

A fundamental challenge in crowdsourcing is that workers may produce bad work, even through good faith efforts. In CrowdCode, any of the information workers enter in microtasks may ultimately be wrong and need to be corrected. Unlike more traditional microtasking workflows in which redundant work or explicit reviews are used to ensure the quality of the work [6], CrowdCode embeds corrections into the workflow itself. CrowdCode provides two mechanisms to enable such corrections: workers may directly edit the artifact corresponding to the current microtask or may report an issue with related artifacts that are visible but not editable (e.g., a test case description in Write Test). Workers were often faced with a microtask resulting from bad work. The one area in which this was impossible – reporting an issue with a function signature when writing a test – caused significant problems. This highlights the importance of ensuring that all worker-produced data can be corrected.

Creative work done by large groups often has the structure of separate artifacts with dependencies, leading to corresponding challenges communicating about these dependencies (i.e., socio-technical congruence [3]). The general principles of our approach may apply to many of these domains. For example, in an engineering task, subcomponents may be spun off like pseudocalls, and automated test cases could include static and thermal analyses. In writing text, editing a paragraph in an article might be a microtask, enabling workers to create bullet points fleshed out by the crowd, requests for other related paragraphs to be written, and automatic tracking of dependencies to create microtasks to update work. Our approach may be most useful in contexts where parallelism-based speedups or broad participation through low barriers to entry are needed.

ACKNOWLEDGEMENTS

We thank Steven Morad, Patrick Nguyen, and Eric Chiquillo for their contributions to CrowdCode, we thank the participants in the study for their participation, and we thank Christoph Hannebauer and the anonymous reviewers for their helpful comments and suggestions on previous drafts. This work was supported in part by the National Science Foundation under grants NSF IIS-1111446, IIS-1302522, and CCF-1414197.

REFERENCES

1. Beck, K. *Test-Driven Development: By Example*. Addison-Wesley, Boston, 2003.
2. Bernstein, M.S., Little, G., Miller, R.C., et al. Soylent: A Word Processor with a Crowd Inside. *Proc. of UIST 2010*, 313–322.
3. Cataldo, M., Wagstrom, P. A., Herbsleb, J. D., and Carley, K. M. Identification of Coordination Requirements: Implications for the Design of Collaboration and Awareness Tools. *Proc. of CSCW 2006*, 353-362
4. Crowston, K., Wei, K., Howison, J., and Wiggins, A. Free/Libre Open-source Software Development: What We Know and What We Do Not Know. *ACM Comput. Surv.* 44, 2 (2012), 7:1–7:35.
5. Dietl, W., Dietzel, S., Ernst, M.D., et al. Verification Games: Making Verification Fun. *Proc. of FTfJP 2012*, 42–49.
6. Doan, A., Ramakrishnan, R., and Halevy, A. Y. Crowdsourcing Systems on the World-Wide Web. *Commun. of ACM* 54, 4 (2011), 86-96.
7. Goldman, M., Little, G., and Miller, R.C. Real-time Collaborative Coding in a Web IDE. *Proc. of UIST 2011*, 155–164.
8. Goldman, Max. *Software Development with Real-Time Collaborative Editing*. PhD Diss. Massachusetts Institute of Technology, 2012.
9. Hartmann, B., MacDougall, D., Brandt, J., and Klemmer, S.R. What Would Other Programmers Do: Suggesting Solutions to Error Messages. *Proc. of CHI 2010*, 1019–1028.
10. Jergensen, C., Sarma, A., and Wagstrom, P. The Onion Patch: Migration in Open Source Ecosystems. *Proc. of ESEC/FSE 2011*, 70–80.
11. Jiau, H.C. and Yang, F.-P. Facing Up to the Inequality of Crowdsourced API Documentation. *SIGSOFT Softw. Eng. Notes* 37, 1 (2012), 1–9.
12. Kittur, A., Smus, B., Khamkar, S., and Kraut, R.E. CrowdForge: Crowdsourcing Complex Work. *Proc. of UIST 2011*, 43–52.
13. Kraut, R.E. and Resnick, P. *Building Successful Online Communities: Evidence-Based Social Design*. MIT Press, 2012.
14. Krogh, G. v., Spaeth, S., and Lakhani, K. R. Community, Joining, and Specialization in Open Source Software Innovation: A Case Study. *Research Policy* 32, 7 (2003), 1217–1241.
15. Li, W., Seshia, S.A., and Jha, S. CrowdMine: Towards Crowdsourced Human-Assisted Verification. *Proc. of DAC 2012*, 1254–1255.
16. Little, G., Chilton, L.B., Goldman, M., and Miller, R.C. TurKit: Human Computation Algorithms on Mechanical Turk. *Proc of UIST 2010*, 57–66.
17. Mamykina, L., Manoim, B., Mittal, M., Hripcsak, G., and Hartmann, B. Design Lessons from the Fastest Q&A Site in the West. *Proc. of CHI 2011*, 2857–2866.
18. Mujumdar, D., Kallenbach, M., Liu, B., and Hartmann, B. Crowdsourcing Suggestions to Programming Problems for Dynamic Web Development Languages. *CHI '11 Extended Abstracts on Human Factors in Computing Systems*, ACM (2011), 1525–1530.
19. Pastore, F., Mariani, L., and Fraser, G. CrowdOracles: Can the Crowd Solve the Oracle Problem? *Proc. of ICST 2013*, 342–351.
20. Shirky, C. *Here Comes Everybody: the Power of Organizing Without Organizations*. Penguin, 2008.
21. Steinmacher, I., Silva, M. A. G., and Gerosa, M. A. Barriers Faced by Newcomers to Open Source Projects: A Systematic Review. *IFIP Adv. Inf. Commun. Technol.* 47 (2014), 153-163, Springer Berlin Heidelberg.
22. Watson, C., Li, F.W.B., and Godwin, J.L. BlueFix: Using Crowd-Sourced Feedback to Support Programming Students in Error Diagnosis and Repair. In E. Popescu, Q. Li, R. Klamma, H. Leung, and M. Specht, eds., *Advances in Web-Based Learning - ICWL 2012*. Springer Berlin Heidelberg, 2012, 228–239.

Situated Crowdsourcing Using a Market Model

Simo Hosio[1], Jorge Goncalves[1], Vili Lehdonvirta[2], Denzil Ferreira[1], Vassilis Kostakos[1]

[1] Department of Computer Science and Engineering
University of Oulu
Erkki Koiso-Kanttilan Katu 3, 90570 Oulu, Finland
firstname.lastname@ee.oulu.fi

[2] Oxford Internet Institute
University of Oxford
1 St Giles Oxford OX1 3JS United Kingdom
vili.lehdonvirta@oii.ox.ac.uk

ABSTRACT
Research is increasingly highlighting the potential for situated crowdsourcing to overcome some crucial limitations of online crowdsourcing. However, it remains unclear whether a situated crowdsourcing *market* can be sustained, and whether worker supply responds to price-setting in such a market. Our work is the first to systematically investigate workers' behaviour and response to economic incentives in a situated crowdsourcing market. We show that the market-based model is a sustainable approach to recruiting workers and obtaining situated crowdsourcing contributions. We also show that the price mechanism is a very effective tool for adjusting the supply of labour in a situated crowdsourcing market. Our work advances the body of work investigating situated crowdsourcing.

Author Keywords
Crowdsourcing; virtual currency; market; situated technologies.

ACM Classification Keywords
H.5.m. Information interfaces and presentation (e.g., HCI): Miscellaneous.

INTRODUCTION
An important limitation of existing crowdsourcing markets is the lack of domain-specific expertise in the workforce [11], and the difficulty in recruiting workers from particular geographic areas for tasks that require contextualised knowledge [8]. For instance, while the creation of newspaper articles [1] and the translation of documents [34] are appealing crowdsourcing applications, they require workers within a relevant context. Mobile-based crowdsourcing systems can address this limitation, but they introduce certain constraints: costs for workers (data plan), the installation of third-party software, and in some cases consent to being tracked [20].

Situated crowdsourcing technologies have emerged in an attempt to overcome these limitations of online and mobile crowdsourcing markets [7,11]. Goncalves et al.'s situated touchscreen prototype leveraged altruism and intrinsic motivation to recruit volunteers for medical image analysis [7], and Heimerl et al. used a touch-screen vending machine to attract workers and reward them with snacks [11]. These bespoke examples highlighted the potential benefits of crowdsourcing using situated technologies, but they fail to address an important question of scaling-up into a market: *can a situated crowdsourcing market be sustained*?

A second challenge for situated crowdsourcing is managing the influx of workers' contributions, and specifically the need for contributions at a particular geographic location or a time of day [9]. How can those be encouraged, given that altruism and intrinsic motivation are challenging to manipulate precisely [7]? Economic theory suggests that a market-like platform can use price-setting to adjust the supply of different types of labour [12]. Along these lines, Heimerl et al. used a market-based approach to situated crowdsourcing, but did not examine the feasibility of using the price mechanism for control [11]. Furthermore, their economic model was inconsistent between sessions, likely limiting its power to shape user behaviour. In addition, it has been noted that intrinsic, usability, and social factors may confound the effect of price-setting [18]. Thus, a second important question is: *can the price mechanism be used to control the supply of labour in situated crowdsourcing?*

We addressed both questions – regarding sustainability and price-setting – by building a situated crowdsourcing marketplace (Bazaar) and studying it experimentally over several weeks. Bazaar uses a grid of touch-screen kiosks scattered across campus, and rewards workers with a virtual currency (HexaCoins) for completing tasks. Workers can exchange HexaCoins for money, for other goods (e.g., movie tickets), or with other workers.

Our work is the first to systematically investigate workers' behaviour and response to economic incentives in a situated crowdsourcing market. Our findings indicate that the market-based model is a sustainable approach to recruiting workers and obtaining crowdsourcing contributions. We also show that the price mechanism is a very effective tool for adjusting the supply of labour from different locations, different times of the day, and different task categories. Finally, we found that the system's virtual economy encouraged some emergent user-to-user coordination, further boosting the labour supply.

RELATED WORK
Situated Crowdsourcing
Crowdsourcing with ubiquitous technologies is increasingly gaining researchers' attention [19,32], especially on mobile phones. This has allowed researchers to push tasks to workers anywhere and anytime. Most mobile platforms

UIST '14, October 05 - 08 2014, Honolulu, HI, USA

ACM 978-1-4503-3069-5/14/10…$15.00.
http://dx.doi.org/10.1145/2642918.2647362

have been deployed in developing countries targeting low-income workers and providing them with simple tasks (e.g., [10]). Recent advances in mobile technologies have also allowed for more intricate and creative tasks. For instance, location-based distribution of crowdsourcing tasks has allowed workers to perform highly context specific tasks for others. Some examples of this include giving location-aware recommendations for restaurants [1], providing instant weather reports [1] or authoring news articles by requesting photographs or videos of certain events from workers [31].

An active community has grown around the topic of crowdsourcing measurements and sensing [19]. This participatory sensing movement is part of the larger concept of "Citizen Science" [23] that relies on mobilizing large parts of the population to contribute to scientific challenges via crowdsourcing. Often this involves the use of smartphones for collecting data [5] or even donating computational resources while one's phone is idle [3].

Despite the appeal of mobile phones, using them for crowdsourcing requires workers' implicit deployment, configuration and use of the device. For example, in SMS-based crowdsourcing, participants need to explicitly sign up for the service, at the cost of a text message exchange. This makes worker recruitment challenging, as a number of steps are necessary before a worker can actually contribute using their device. An alternative approach is to embed input mechanisms (e.g., public displays, tablets) into a physical space and leverage users' serendipitous availability [22]. This means that, contrary to mobile crowdsourcing, situated crowdsourcing through embedded interfaces does not require any deployment effort from workers [7].

In such a deployment, Heimerl et al. reported Umati [11], which used a vending machine with a touch display for locally relevant tasks, albeit with certain limitations. For example, it was available at a single location only, and it lacked diverse tasks to keep users engaged for long. Goncalves et al.'s public display crowdsourcing deployment also suffered from the lack of diverse tasks [7]. These findings suggest that task diversity is key to sustaining a situated crowdsourcing market.

Digital Markets, Currencies, and Economies

It has become increasingly common to build digital markets, currencies, and entire "virtual economies" into multi-user computational systems, in order to coordinate and direct user attention and effort in desired ways [18]. One potential application area for this approach is crowdsourcing. Market as an abstract concept refers to the interaction of supply and demand for a particular good or service resulting in exchange [18]. A market can be implemented in a computational system by creating a marketplace. Crowdsourcing marketplaces, also known as online labour markets, are a prominent example [e.g. 10,11,12,15,21]. They are used as an alternative to other mechanisms (such as appeals to altruism [7]) to motivate user contributions and to allocate tasks to different users.

Theoretically, markets have certain properties that make them attractive for this purpose. First, markets encourage users to specialize in tasks where they have a comparative advantage and to develop their skills further. Second, the types and quantities of labour supplied through a market can be controlled and adjusted through price-setting. In comparison, altruism-based contributions are hard to control and adjust, as they depend on the person and the type of task at hand (e.g. editing a favourite article on Wikipedia vs. doing uninteresting microtasks). Third, markets are sustainable over time, as long as valuable rewards can be provided. In comparison, the sustainability of contributions based on altruism, social status and similar motivations is more idiosyncratic and unpredictable. Therefore, adopting a market model for general-purpose situated crowdsourcing can enhance the sustainability of such a platform.

Suppliers in a market must be naturally rewarded with something that is of value to them. For example, Heimerl et al. used snacks to reward workers in their vending machine-based situated task marketplace [11]. However, suppliers are not usually paid directly in goods; instead, they are paid with money, which can later be exchanged for goods. Economic literature suggests that money is used as an intermediary for three basic reasons [18]. First, money is a convenient medium of exchange, as it allows the holder to choose their most preferred set of final goods out of all the possible combinations. Second, money is a convenient way of storing value over time, until the most preferred moment of consumption or until sufficient value is accumulated. Third, money provides a convenient unit for measuring value accumulation in numerical terms. Any good or record used for these three purposes can be called money; the term "currency" emphasises the first purpose [18].

Heimerl et al.'s system implements a virtual currency that can be exchanged for snacks. However, it does not allow user-to-user credit transfers or the freedom that utilizing a national currency yields [11]. Many other task marketplaces reward workers in national currency [e.g. 12], which facilitates all three uses, and also has the advantage that the platform owner does not need to provide means for exchanging the currency to goods, as national currency can be exchanged elsewhere.

However, virtual currencies have one distinct advantage over national currencies in experimental systems: the cultural, regulatory, and security-related expectations relating to them are far more open, allowing for bold experimentation [18]. Virtual currencies can also be perceived as more playful [33], though this is not necessarily an advantage in serious task market. Thus, using a virtual currency affords all three traditional functions of money and to maximize the market's effectiveness in experimental settings, as long as the currency is redeemable for valuable goods.

Finally, some systems that feature a virtual currency also make it possible for users to transfer the currency between each other [18,33]. This has two potential advantages. First, it allows users to collaborate by e.g. pooling their efforts to reach high-value rewards, potentially creating social effects that increase the labour supply. Second, it allows users to potentially start using the currency to mediate transactions completely unrelated to the original platform, in the way national currency is used. For example, users of the Tencent QQ instant messaging platform began to use its "Q Coin" currency to trade everything from compact discs to online game items [18]. The advantage to the issuer is that this greatly increases demand for the currency, and in the case of a task market, the desirability of the tasks through which it is earned.

In summary, economic theory and practical experience highlight two important aspects for situated crowdsourcing: a market-driven model (rather than intrinsic motivation) can enhance its sustainability, and using a virtual currency (rather than directly goods) can provide enhancements to the market's operation, as long as it can be redeemed for goods. Taking these into account, we designed a market for situated crowdsourcing that uses a virtual currency, and has a redeeming mechanism to convert currency into goods. We call our market "Bazaar", and the virtual currency "HexaCoins".

SYSTEM DESCRIPTION

Bazaar is a grid of crowdsourcing kiosks (Figure 1) coordinated by an online server. Each kiosk contains an Android tablet with a 10.1" touch-screen, a charger, and uses WiFi to connect to the server. Our client software for the tablets was set to "kiosk mode" [29] to ensure that it was always visible on screen, it recovered from crashes, and unwanted OS functionality (notification bars, etc.) was disabled. The physical buttons of the tablet were physically obscured by the kiosk's enclosure.

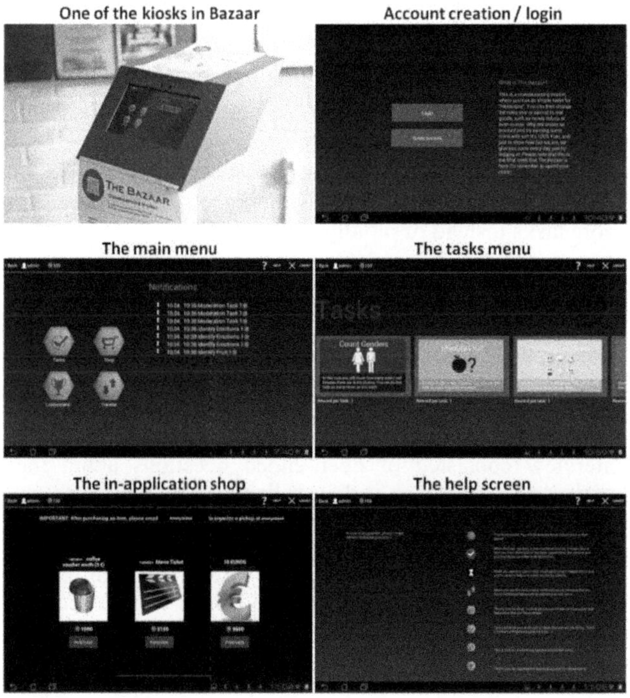

Figure 1. A close up photo of a crowdsourcing kiosk in Bazaar and screenshots of the application screens.

Kiosks

The welcome screen of the kiosks contained a brief description of the system, and prompted users to create an account or login. Registration required just a username and password because a lengthy process can reduce participation [4]. Upon login, users had to acknowledge a pop-up message that administrators can dynamically modify. Subsequently, users were shown the main screen:

- At all times the upper bar of the application displayed the HexaCoin balance of the user, and a link to the instructions window.
- Tasks allowed users to access the available crowdsourcing tasks and complete them.
- Leaderboard showed the nickname of users with most earnings to date.
- Shop allowed users to use HexaCoins to buy items.
- Transfer allowed users to send their HexaCoins to other users.
- Notifications showed confirmation that HexaCoins were credited to the account, or they were still pending moderation approval.

Participants could get money or goods in exchange for their HexaCoins by visiting the Shop page. It allowed them to purchase the desired items (cinema tickets, physical badges, tablet, money) using their HexaCoins. They subsequently had to email us to schedule the pickup from a physical shop we had setup in our laboratory premises. When visiting our lab, we asked them to verify their identity by logging into Bazaar on a dedicated computer. In addition, we used their visit as an opportunity to conduct interviews.

Tasks

We explicitly decided to provide a variety of crowdsourcing tasks to cater to the varying interests and skills of workers [15] and to keep them engaged longitudinally. Therefore we selected a diverse set of tasks with different stimuli and purposes. The workers always had the option to skip a particular task in case they did not know the answer. When a worker completed a task, the next one would automatically show up, chosen randomly from that task's repository. There were 6 different types of tasks available in Bazaar (Table 1 & Figure 2):

- **Data Categorisation**: Categorisation and labelling of photographs is a frequently offered crowdsourcing task due to its computational complexity. We provided one task where workers had to count the number of males and females in a photograph, and another where they had to type the name of the fruit shown in a photograph.
- **Sentiment Analysis**: Humans can identify at least six different emotional states (anger, happiness, sadness, fear, surprise and disgust) quite reliably [6], but the computational complexity makes this type of tasks frequent candidates for crowdsourcing. For this task we showed workers a looping 3-second video of a person's face, and asked them to identify the emotional state of the individual using six response buttons labelled with the above emotional states.
- **Content Creation**: Crowdsourcing content creation has been explored previously in the context of creating news articles [1], translating documents [34], and providing recommendations [31]. This type of task can greatly benefit from workers' local knowledge, which is key to in-situ crowdsourcing [8]. For this task, workers had to type a textual description of their surroundings. A worker could complete this task only once per Bazaar kiosk.
- **Content Moderation**: Quality control can be an overwhelming challenge for crowdsourcing [15], and one approach is to involve workers themselves to

"approve" each other's work [17]. For this task, workers had to review other workers' tasks and label them as "good" or "bad". This pool of tasks grew in real-time as workers completed tasks across all Bazaar kiosks.

- **Survey**: The survey was a one-off task that each worker could complete only once, and only after they had completed 30 other tasks. It contained a set of open-ended questions regarding how they found out about Bazaar, their motivations behind using it, any suggestions of improvements and a standardised System Usability Scale (SUS).

Task Category	Unique Tasks Available	Type	Stimulus	Worker Input	Reward (HexaCoins)
Counting Genders	373	Data categorisation (counting)	Static (images)	Text (numbers)	10
Identifying Fruits	370	Data categorisation (identification)	Static (images)	Text (short)	10
Identifying emotions	1350	Sentiment analysis	Dynamic (videos)	Multi-choice buttons (6)	5
Describing Location	4	Content Creation	Text	Text (long)	150
Moderation	Same as number of tasks approved	Content Moderation	Static, dynamic, text	Multi-choice buttons (2)	5
Survey	1	Survey	Text	Text and radio buttons	500

Table 1. Summary of number of unique tasks, types, stimuli, worker input and initial reward.

Figure 2. Examples of the tasks: identifying emotions and the in-application survey.

We chose to include both "typical" online crowdsourcing tasks and "situated" tasks. The "situated" tasks were the tasks in 3 categories: "Content Creation", "Survey", and "Moderation" (i.e. moderating the other situated tasks). Our decision aimed to enable the comparison of our results to those of online crowdsourcing studies, and at the same time to analyse how Bazaar performs with situated tasks. Platforms like Bazaar should not be built solely for situated tasks, but be regarded as complementary to already existing solutions. Thus, it is crucial to experiment with a rich variety of different tasks.

Rewards

Our rewards are HexaCoins, goods, and cash. When completing tasks, users receive HexaCoins. All completed tasks were subject to a 2-stage moderation. Administrators first rejected obviously flawed responses, and subsequently the crowd moderated the remaining responses. We decided that moderation and rewarding should be completed in chunks because per-task payment encourages gaming behaviour [15] and can reduce quality [16].

The HexaCoin value of different types of tasks varied, but we aimed to reward users with a baseline of approximately 3600 HexaCoins per hour of work. Furthermore, we rewarded users with 100 HexaCoins on the first login of each day, to motivate them to return daily and perform more tasks. Users could ultimately exchange HexaCoins for goods, using a rough exchange rate of 360 HexaCoins per 1€ (making the theoretical hourly wage 10€):

- Badges (i.e., insignia) that are popular decorations in students' ceremonial overalls (720 and 1080 HexaCoins)
- University cafeteria coffee vouchers of nominal value 3€ (1080 HexaCoins)
- Movie tickets to the local cinema (3150 HexaCoins)
- One 16Gb Android tablet (72000 HexaCoins)
- Money in the form of 10€ and 25€ packs (3600 and 9000 HexaCoins, respectively).

We avoided direct conversions between HexaCoins and money for simplicity and to encourage users to complete more tasks instead of rapidly cashing in.

Data Logging

Bazaar logged centrally all interactions on all kiosks: logins, logouts, starting and ending of performing tasks (time spent), answers for each task, HexaCoin transfers, responses to the survey. All users who bought goods from Bazaar were interviewed when they picked up their purchases from the shop set up at our laboratory. The interview consisted of open-ended questions about their motives to use Bazaar, if they collaborated with other users, why did they choose the particular rewards they purchased, would they continue to use the system if deployed for longer, how did they feel about having to perform tasks in such public spaces, and if they had prior experience with crowdsourcing in general.

STUDY

We designed a real-user experiment to investigate if Bazaar enabled the creation of a crowdsourcing market in the economic sense. Our experiment systematically manipulated the amounts of HexaCoins paid in reward at specific locations (week 1, 2); for specific tasks (week 2, 3); and during specific times of day (week 3), in an attempt to investigate if the labour supply responded accordingly.

We deployed four Bazaar kiosks across the University of Oulu (in Oulu, Finland) campus for 3 weeks. We did not actively promote Bazaar except by attaching an A3-sized poster on each of the kiosks. We specifically avoided the use of email lists, Facebook and Twitter, to minimise participation bias.

The locations where we deployed Bazaar were physically afar and at different faculty buildings (Figure 3):

- Location 1: a cafeteria visited mostly by technical students
- Location 2: next to the biggest on-campus restaurant
- Location 3: a lobby area with benches surrounding the kiosk
- Location 4: next to the main entrance of the main library

Figure 3. Bazaar deployment locations. Top row: cafeteria and next to the main restaurant. Bottom row: a lobby with benches and next to a library entrance.

During the study 194 accounts were created, 1067 logins, 75229 tasks completed (62602 approved) in 310114 seconds (86.1 hours) of crowdsourcing effort, and 832548 HexaCoins generated (Figure 5). The most popular task category was moderation (N=23986), followed by counting genders (N=14011), identifying emotions (N=13624) and identifying fruits (N=10765). On the other hand, the location description task was completed 138 times and the survey 78 times. A total of 25 transfers were registered (to 10 unique users) worth 14600 HexaCoins in total.

Of the 194 accounts created, 97 (50%) were returning users. Furthermore, 87% of the HexaCoins redeemed, while the remaining 13% (110014 HexaCoins) were simply unused. We also analysed how the HexaCoins generated within Bazaar were distributed amongst workers. Figure 4 depicts the relationship between HexaCoins and time spent working. It shows that workers enjoyed increasing returns on time spent working, suggesting that they developed their skills over time, just as in a conventional labour market.

"Happy Place" Manipulation of Rewards

Our experiment sought to investigate whether workers can be motivated to change their location, and complete tasks at particular kiosks on request. To test this manipulation we introduced a reward multiplier, applied to one of the kiosks at a time. For the duration of a whole day, a single kiosk (i.e. the "Happy Place") yielded twice (2x) the HexaCoins for each task completed, while all other kiosks operated as usual. We applied this manipulation on four sequential days (Mon-Thu), each day with a different Happy Place.

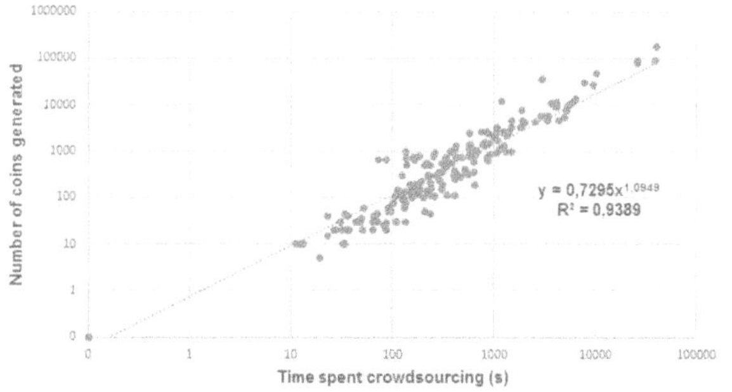

Figure 4. Scatterplot of how many HexaCoins (y-axis) and effort (x-axis) are attributed to each worker (data points). Both axes are in logarithmic scale.

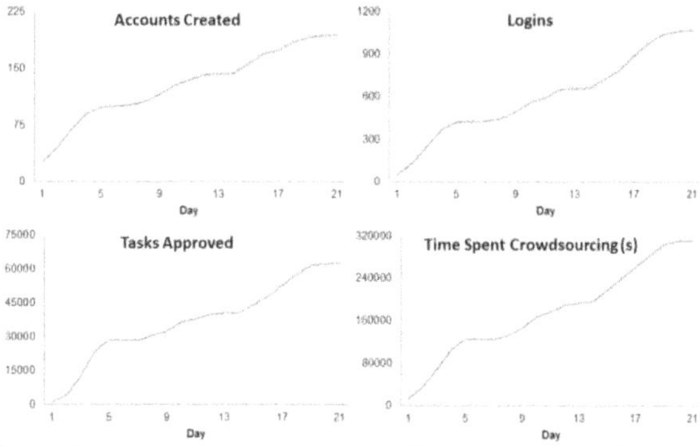

Figure 5. Cumulative progression of accounts created, logins, tasks approved and time spent crowdsourcing (s) throughout the deployment.

Figure 6 shows the breakdown of time spent by workers at each location when the Happy Place effect was active. For Monday-Thursday we observe that workers spent more time at the "Happy Place" than other locations by a factor of 4.02 on average. Friday did not have a happy place and is shown as a baseline assessment.

In the subsequent week we reduced the Happy Place multiplier from 2x to 1.5x, expecting to observe a reduced effect. In Figure 7 we show that, as expected, "Happy Places" were more popular than other locations by a factor of 3.77 on average. Thursday did not have a happy place and is shown as a baseline assessment.

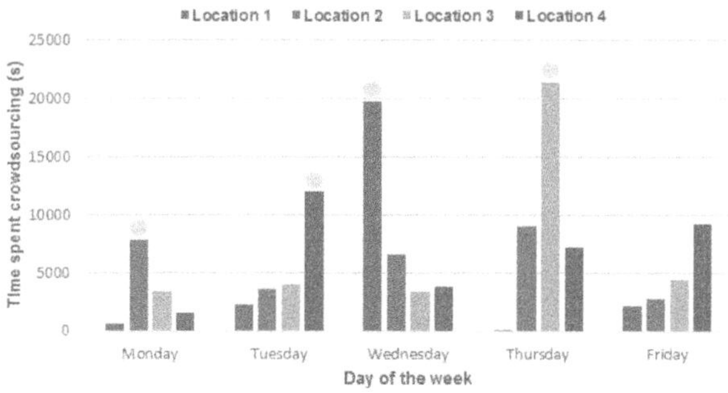

Figure 6. Crowdsourcing effort (seconds) at each location. "Happy Place" multiplier (2x) was used in locations with the yellow marker.

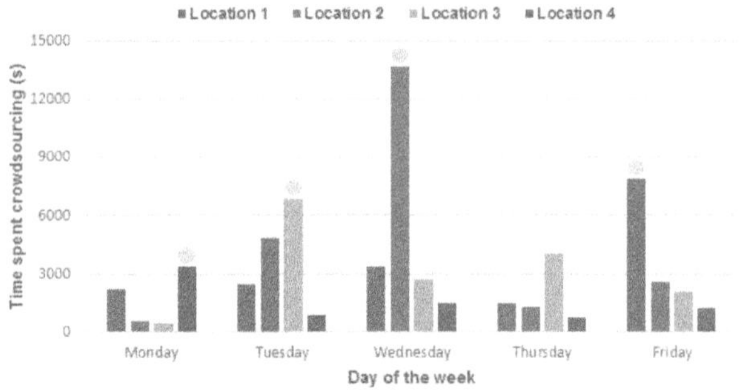

Figure 7. Crowdsourcing effort (seconds) at each location. "Happy Place" multiplier (1.5x) was used in locations with the yellow marker.

Manipulation of Task Rewards

During the first week of deployment the workers completed the tasks shown in Figure 8, indicating a strong preference for tasks in the Moderation category. We sought to investigate whether we can manipulate the popularity of tasks by manipulating their reward. Our manipulations had the expected result: an increase in HexaCoin reward yielded an increase in popularity, and vice versa.

During week 2 we modified the rewards per category (Table 1) as follows:

- The reward for tasks in the Moderation category was reduced from 5 to 2 HexaCoins. This yielded a 7-fold decrease in popularity during week 2.
- The reward for tasks in the Identifying Emotions category increased from 5 to 10 HexaCoins. This yielded a 3-fold increase in popularity during week 2.

During week 3 we made further manipulations to the rewards per category as follows:

- The reward for tasks in the Identifying Fruits category decreased from 10 to 5 HexaCoins. This yielded a 4-fold decrease in popularity during week 3.
- The reward for tasks in the Counting Genders category increased from 10 to 15 HexaCoins. This yielded a 10-fold increase in popularity during week 3.

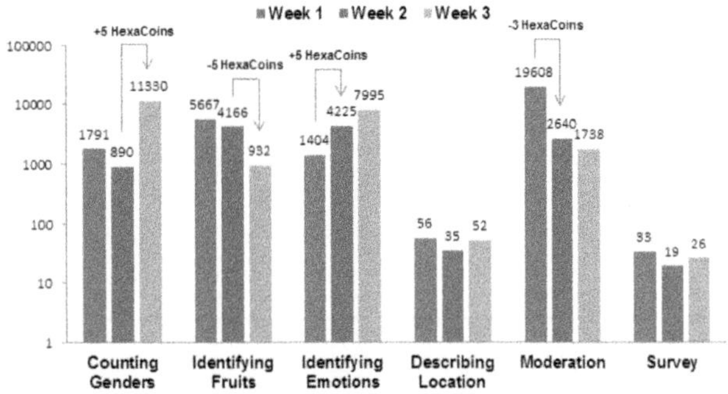

Figure 8. Number of tasks completed per category during each week of deployment (y-axis in logarithmic scale). The arrows indicate where a change in reward was done.

"Happy Hour" Manipulation of Rewards

During the first two weeks of deployment we observed that workers mostly completed tasks between 10am and 7pm (Figure 9). We investigated whether workers could be motivated to change the time when they perform tasks in Bazaar. To test this we introduced a "Happy Hour" reward multiplier (2x) applied to all kiosks simultaneously at certains times: 9-10am, and 8-9pm. These happy hours were chosen because they were relatively unpopular during the first two weeks. As expected, "Happy Hours" were significantly more popular during week 3 (Figure 9). Specifically, there was a 2-fold popularity increase between 9-10am, and an 8-fold popularity increase between 8-9pm.

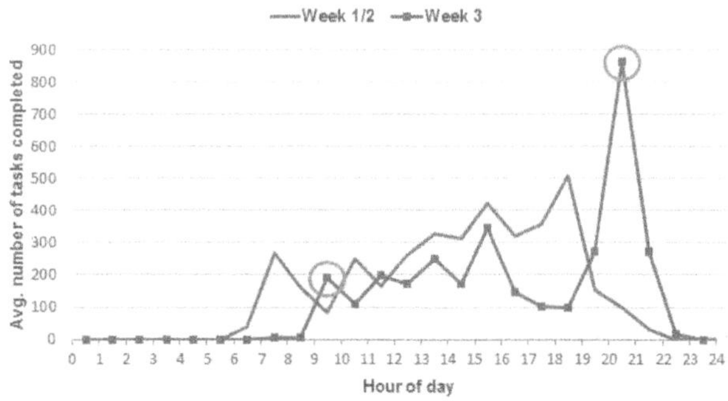

Figure 9. Average number of tasks complete per hour during the first 2 weeks (blue) and the third week (red). "Happy hours" are indicated with a circle.

Surveys and Interviews

In total 78 users completed the Bazaar survey task (51 male, 27 female). The average age was 23.8 (SD=4.1). The noted three key reasons for why they started using Bazaar: to get the rewards illustrated in the posters (N=22); they were recommended by a friend (N=14); or out of curiosity (N=41). One respondent did not answer. When asked where they learnt about it we identified two main responses: either the respondents indicated that they just stumbled upon the kiosks at the campus (N=55), or they were informed by their friends (N=23). The improvement suggestions we collected are summarised in the discussion.

Analysis of the SUS revealed a score of 81.3 (SD=10.8) on a scale from 0 to 100. The positive statement with the lowest value for positive was if users would like to use the system frequently (M=3.6, SD=1.2). Other values showed that users did not consider the system to be complex (M=1.8, SD=0.7), found that it was easy to use (M=4.4, SD=0.7), can quickly be learned (M=4.4, SD=0.7), and requires no technical support (M=1.2, SD=0.5). To provide a fairer grading assignment, we used percentiles like those calculated in [26] using a curved grading scale. This means that the SUS score for our system obtained an A grade (above 80.3%).

Finally, 45 workers (26 male, 19 female) of the 194 who created an account in Bazaar purchased prizes and were interviewed during their pick-up of the items. The average age was 23.9 (SD=3.8). The key findings from the interviews are used to support our discussion.

DISCUSSION

Situated crowdsourcing differs from online crowdsourcing substantially. Therefore, we do not consider it an alternative but a complementary means of enabling crowd work, which addresses certain limitations of online crowdsourcing [15].

Our study is the first in-depth investigation of how workers behave in a situated crowdsourcing market. Previous studies on situated crowdsourcing lacked task diversity, reward flexibility, and crucially the ability to track the behaviour of individual workers [7,11]. Our study addresses these limitations, and provides a holistic assessment of worker behaviour in a situated crowdsourcing market.

There are three criteria we use to judge the success of our study from a crowdsourcing perspective: attractiveness, speed, and quality. In addition, we assess the system's sustainability, the extent to which we were able to control the labour supply using the price mechanism, and the extent to which the virtual economy encouraged the emergence of advantageous user-to-user dynamics in the system.

We first highlight an important finding from our interviews: the majority of workers in Bazaar were completely new to crowdsourcing, and in interviews admitted to have never used any of the popular crowdsourcing markets such as Amazon's Mechanical Turk and Crowdflower. This strongly indicates the potential of situated crowdsourcing to reach untapped populations of workers.

Second, we point out that the number of tasks completed in Bazaar remained at a constantly high level: we approved 62602 tasks, or almost 3000 tasks per day. Task completion rate in situated crowdsourcing has been found generally greater than the completion rate of tasks on MTurk. For instance, Rogstadius et al. purchased labour from MTurk for a simple image analysis task, resulting in approximately 40 daily completed tasks [26]. Further, the performance of *Umati* was compared to MTurk, finding the situated approach with only a single deployed interface as capable of producing over 3x more daily labour at the rate of over 1000 tasks per day [11]. While MTurk studies with high task throughput exist [25], we feel that Bazaar with only four deployed kiosks achieved a workforce throughput that is at least comparable to MTurk and previous situated crowdsourcing studies.

Third, the quality of completed tasks was also high. We relied on crowd-based quality assurance, which has been reported as a viable mechanism [8,17]. In Bazaar, the moderation task resulted in 94% of positive votes, indicating high quality of the performed tasks. We also note that only a handful of workers abused the system by completing tasks in a negligent manner, which is expected when reward is per task rather than per hour [15]. However, our moderation and rejection of bad quality work did substantially curb Bazaar's abuse, and in fact we did notice abusive workers eventually produced high quality work.

Bootstrapping and Sustaining the Workforce

Worker acquisition is one of the key challenges for crowdsourcing [11]. Previous studies on situated crowdsourcing have highlighted its promising ability to rapidly attract capable workers [7,8]. Similarly in our study, Bazaar managed to quickly attract a large number of unique users (194) to create accounts and contribute work. The kiosks in four different appealed to a heterogeneous mixture or both males and females, students and staff, and from different faculties.

We note that the frequency of logins, time spent in performing tasks, and the number of tasks completed remained high until the end of the study (Figures 5-8). The surveys we deployed in Bazaar revealed the major role of curiosity in people's motives to start using the kiosks, and interview comments such as "*I use all new 'gizmos' around me out of pure interest, and then I realized that I can actually earn something using this!*" and "*I just happened to walk by during lectures and had free time to start exploring what it was*" do support this. This agrees with earlier research stating that public situated technologies are often initially used out of curiosity rather than with a clear motive in mind [22] and that they are thus capable of reaching broad audiences [13].

We also note that we did not actively promote Bazaar, and that many of the interviews and surveys noted that word-of-mouth was key in attracting new workers. In fact, the promotion of Bazaar was sustained by workers themselves. Many of the survey respondents indicated being recommended by their friends to start using it, and interviews further revealed that workers used Facebook, email and SMSs to inform their friends about Bazaar. This is crucial because public deployments often find it challenging to entice commitment from new users unless it clearly benefits them [4]. In our case, the value proposition to potential users was appealing and made credible by recommendations from friends. The promise of "real value" was constantly mentioned in the interviews, and especially when workers claimed rewards and informed (often bragged) about it to their friends, the appeal of Bazaar seemed to grow, leading into sustained use. Interview comments such as "I saw a friend claiming 20€ from it and wanted to try as well" or "One friend came with an overall patch and said that anyone can earn these things" illustrate how word-of-mouth promotion by the workers themselves was generating awareness about Bazaar.

An important factor in Bazaar's attractiveness was the diversity of offered tasks. Previous research has shown that the lack of task diversity can be detrimental [10,11]. Many mobile and ubiquitous crowdsourcing systems have been research-driven and have not involved stakeholders who are actually willing to pay for tasks to be completed. As a result, most systems involve rather unappealing tasks. As such, research has shown that workers lose interest quite rapidly [10], even when rewards are monetary. In Bazaar we attempted to provide a rich set of tasks so that workers would always have a diverse choice, even if that meant completed a task more than once. Some workers claimed in their interview to be annoyed by this, but most did not mind.

Controlling Labour Supply through Price-setting

One of the key aims of our experiment was to test whether price-setting can control labour supply. In small tasks such as those done in crowdsourcing, it is not obvious whether workers are motivated more by rewards or by intrinsic motivations such as altruism or the novelty of the system. In the latter case, increasing the rewards could fail to increase the contributions, or even decrease them [10]. A few studies have tested this in Mechanical Turk and found that in this context, higher rewards are indeed associated with more work delivered, but not necessarily of higher quality [26]. In the context of Bazaar the results could be different, because the contributors did not actively seek earnings opportunities, but instead the system was placed so as to capture contributors with the desired situated information. Thus it was important to test whether the price mechanism could be used to control the relative quantities of different types of contributions.

We systematically manipulated rewards to investigate if worker behaviour can be adjusted in terms of which tasks they perform, where they work, and when they work. Our results confirm that reward manipulation led to a predictable and proportional effect in terms workers preference of tasks (Figure 8), crowdsourcing location (Figures 6 and 7), and time of day when they worked (Figure 9). In economic terms, labour suppliers in the Bazaar marketplace exhibited high price elasticity, making it very feasible to control and adjust their contributions through the price mechanism.

When we asked the users whether they attempted to take advantage of the reward multipliers, 4 said no, while 40 claimed to have been motivated by them to adapt their working behaviour to earn Hexacoins faster: "*Yesterday I planned to. I had 30 minutes of free time, so I walked to a place with the multiplier [happy place], but it was occupied. I wanted to do the "survey" and "describe location" tasks somewhere with a higher multiplier, so I saved them for a later time*", "*Yes, I started randomly on whichever kiosk was close by and got lucky a few of times, starting immediately on correct one. Other times I tried to relocate, but they were occupied!*", or "*Yes, very much so. I moved to the locations with multipliers always when possible and when they were not occupied.*" Several quotes like this suggest that we could have scaled the system up by simply deploying more kiosks than just one per location. This behaviour can also be seen in our log data, but exact quantification is impossible as many users indicated that they used a kiosk with the multiplier multiple times by chance.

However, the price mechanism was not without limits. The interviews revealed that the morning "happy hour" was a somewhat misguided intervention because it coincided with lectures' schedule, or it was too early in the day for our workers. As a result, the yield of the morning "happy hour" was much less than from the evening one. This highlights the importance of understanding context when working with situated technology. In economic terms, opportunity costs created by prior commitments and contextual needs could in some cases be higher than the rewards offered by the market.

As expected, some interviewees also indicated that they were not motivated by the currency rewards as such, but by the goods that the currency could be exchanged for: "*I would never choose money. I rather have a more rewarding experience of getting something tangible...something that I will more likely remember in the future,*" "*I have exactly two movies that I want to see, and this way I know exactly where I will use the reward,*" or "*I love my student overalls and always want more patches for it. Money does not appeal to me.*" These statements also echo an important finding in economic sociology that all money is in fact not equal, as economic theory suggests [35]. People do mental accounting where they e.g. allocate money earned from a side job to an "entertainment budget", potentially making those earnings more desirable than the "boring money" earned from one's primary job.

Finally, at the end of the experiment 13% of the HexaCoins were not redeemed. In pre-paid value business (e.g. gift cards, calling cards), such unredeemed currency is known as "breakage". Breakage is seen as a natural phenomenon, and contributes significantly to profits. In a digital labour market such as Bazaar, breakage means free labour, but it might also indicate a problem with sustainability, especially if many workers leave their rewards unredeemed because they disappear from the system.

Emergent User-to-user Dynamics

Our assessment of workers' use of Bazaar involved a situated SUS survey. Previous research has shown that systems scoring above 80.3% (grade A) in SUS are more likely to be recommended by users to their friends [28]. Our analysis indicated that Bazaar scored 81.3%, just above the identified tipping point. This suggests that workers' use of Bazaar was enjoyable enough to promote to their friends. This is important because situated technologies are often used in groups, since the social pressure in public interaction [4] is lower when users are in groups [13].

Recent work has hypothesized that for crowdsourcing it might be beneficial to attract loners, i.e. individual users instead of groups, because the quality of their work is better than that of groups [7]. Our interviewees claimed that they used Bazaar practically always alone: it made no sense to perform tasks in groups given that only one would be rewarded. However, friends did form virtual groups, to work together towards a joint goal. For instance, the interviews revealed that a group of 4 workers decided to earn 2 movie tickets each to go see movies together. They collaborated very effectively and took advantage of happy places and hours: "*I even received SMS notifications from friends, saying where or when to go work today for maximum coins.*" 1 worker failed to notice the possibility to benefit from the multipliers.

Collaboration in the form of currency exchange, however, did not take place often. Based on our interviews the majority of the 25 recorded exchanges were motivated by curiosity, or workers quitting and transferring their HexaCoins to friends. Takayama & Lehdonvirta obtained similar results in an experimental virtual economy that allowed user-to-user transfers [30]. In contrast, user-to-user transfers have been extremely popular in some commercial virtual currency systems, and resulted in significant emergent behaviours [18]. These effects remain to be captured and exploited in a research setting.

Finally, many interviewees referred to Bazaar as a "game." This was surprising because it was not designed as such, but our interviews suggest that particularly the leaderboard influenced workers' perception: "*Yes, I guess it raised my competitive spirit, it's always nice to be #1, especially if there's not much to do to reach the position!*" and "*Yes, <another username> was right on my heels. Every morning when I came here she was ahead of me, which just motivated me to grind more. She eventually gave up, it seems (laughing).*" The leaderboard clearly motivated people to work more, as other studies on gamified crowdsourcing show [8], but at the same time it does shape people's perceptions.

Administering a Situated Crowdsourcing Market

In comparison to online crowdsourcing markets, situated markets have an additional key stakeholder: location managers [14]. These are the individuals who are involved in managing the physical location where a kiosk may be installed. While in developing countries Internet cafes are often a physical location where crowdsourcing work takes place, this aspect is amplified with situated markets. The commitment of location managers is crucial to the success of situated crowdsourcing. Therefore, the kiosks must provide value not only to workers, but also to the location managers who install them [14]. A straightforward way would be to give the managers a small percentage of the profits originating from the tasks performed at their location. This would also motivate the managers to maintain and advertise the opportunity to their audiences.

Our findings on manipulation can prove useful in a number of use cases benefiting location managers. For instance, an establishment that houses a crowdsourcing kiosk (e.g. pub or cafe) could willingly pay for the overhead in introducing reward multipliers to physically attract workers. In this sense, the platform could be used for attracting people to spaces and raising awareness of that space. Similarly, manipulating the rewards per different times of day can be used to avoid physical congestion at a particular kiosk by distributing workers' effort.

Further, the use of a virtual currency allows location managers to offer goods that their establishment actually provides (e.g. cake at a coffee house, beer at a pub) for the work performed at their premises. Utilizing a virtual currency for sustained engagement is key here, as it enables workers to work intermittently, and build towards their desired rewards. Given our findings on how money does not appeal to all workers, and the interviewees' feelings of getting "something for nothing" from Bazaar, this could benefit both the dwellers of an establishment as well as the managers.

Rewarding workers in situated crowdsourcing remains a relatively unexplored issue. On MTurk the average salary per hour is $5-7$. Therefore, in our case it is reasonable to question whether our hourly rate of roughly 10€ was too high. In Finland, where the experiment was conducted, 10€ is much lower than the average wage. The purchasing power of 10€ in our country is lower than a $7 hourly wage in cheap labour countries where workers on many online marketplaces come from. We suggest that it makes sense to adopt the price-setting in situated crowdsourcing to the contextual and cultural factors. Rewards in situated crowdsourcing cannot blindly follow online (e.g. MTurk prices) but should instead be influenced by the location of the kiosks.

We do not claim that the presented situated crowdsourcing deployment on our campus is a panacea. We argue that our crowdsourcing kiosks could be replicated at other locations that would be targeted for their potential workforce. We envision, for example, MTurk having an option to choose the types of locations where tasks are deployed.

Limitations

We acknowledge certain limitations in the presented study. We encountered run-time problems particularly with WiFi connectivity, leading to suboptimal user experience at times. This is however to be expected with any real-world deployment, and the outages usually lasted just a few minutes. The length and magnitude of the deployment, we feel, counterbalances the issue. Bazaar's current design is also not scalable, as there is only one centralized administrator view for moderating the tasks. Naturally all task providers should have their own accounts and views to the completed tasks. Similarly, we need to create facilities to input tasks runtime to the system. Finally, cultural issues were not investigated, which could affect the acceptability of situated crowdsourcing.

CONCLUSION

Bazaar is the first situated crowdsourcing platform using a market model. Over a period of three weeks, Bazaar attracted 194 workers who completed 75229 tasks in 86.1 hours of work. A clear majority of workers had no prior experience with obtaining rewards from online crowdsourcing. We demonstrate that if a platform is willing to make an effort to establish physical presence in certain locations, it will attract a populous workforce with comparable work quality to its online counterparts and a higher task uptake.

Our systematic manipulations show that Bazaar's price mechanism was capable of controlling the supply of different types of labour it produced. Specifically, we demonstrated that rewarding mechanism affected workers' preference on what kind of work to produce, where, and when to produce it. Moreover, a virtual currency was demonstrated as key enabler to sustaining workers' engagement and interest in Bazaar.

ACKNOWLEDGEMENTS

This work was supported by Microsoft Research through its PhD Scholarship Programme. Also the financial support of the Finnish Funding Agency for Technology and Innovation and Academy of Finland is gratefully acknowledged. This work is partly funded by EU grant agreement PCIG11-GA-2012-322138. We also thank Nemanja Vukota, Teemu Partanen, Miika Keisu, and Joonas Nikula for their technical contributions.

REFERENCES

1. Alt, F., Shirazi, A., Schmidt, A., Kramer, U. and Nawaz, Z. Location-based crowdsourcing: extending crowdsourcing to the real world. Proc. NordiCHI 2010, ACM (2010), 13-22.
2. Ariely, D. Predictably Irrational: The Hidden Forces That Shape Our Decisions. London: HarperCollins (2009).
3. Arslan, M.Y., Singh, I., Singh, S., Madhyastha, H.V., Sundaresan, K. and Krishnamurthy, S.V. Computing while charging: building a distributed computing infrastructure using smartphones. Proc. CoNEXT 2012, ACM (2012), 193-204.
4. Brignull, H. and Rogers, Y. Enticing people to interact with large public displays in public spaces. Proc. INTERACT, Vol. 3 (2003), 17-24.
5. Burke, J.A., Estrin, D., Hansen, M., Parker, A., Ramanathan, N., Reddy, S. and Srivastava, M.B. Participatory sensing. In Workshop on World-Sensor-

Web: Mobile Device Centric Sensory Networks and Applications at Sensys (2006).

6. Ekman, P. and Friesen, W.V. Constants across cultures in the face and emotion. Journal of Personality and Social Psychology 17, 2 (1971), 124-129.
7. Goncalves, J., Ferreira, D., Hosio, S., Liu, Y., Rogstadius, J., Kukka, H. and Kostakos, V. Crowdsourcing on the Spot: Altruistic use of Public Displays, Feasibility, Performance, and Behaviours. Proc. UbiComp 2013, ACM (2013), 753-762.
8. Goncalves, J., Hosio, S., Ferreira, D. and Kostakos, V. Game of Words: Tagging Places through Crowdsourcing on Public Displays. Proc. DIS 2014, ACM (2014), 705-714.
9. Goncalves, J., Pandab, P., Ferreira, D., Ghahramani, M., Zhao, G., Kostakos, V. Projective Testing of Diurnal Collective Emotion, Proc. Ubicomp 2014, ACM (2014).
10. Gupta, A., Thies, W., Cutrell, E. and Balakrishnan, R. mClerk: enabling mobile crowdsourcing in developing regions. Proc. CHI 2012, ACM (2012), 1843-1852.
11. Heimerl, K., Gawalt, B., Chen, K., Parikh, T. and Hartmann, B. CommunitySourcing: engaging local crowds to perform expert work via physical kiosks. Proc. CHI 2012, ACM (2012), 1539-1548.
12. Horton, J. J., and Chilton, L. The Labor Economics of Paid Crowdsourcing. Proc. ACM-EC 2010, ACM (2010), 209-218.
13. Hosio, S., Goncalves, J., Kostakos, V., Riekki, J. Exploring Civic Engagement on Public Displays. In S. Saeed (Ed.), User-Centric Technology Design for Nonprofit and Civic Engagements. Springer International Publishing (2014), 91-111.
14. Hosio, S., Goncalves, J., Kukka, H., Chamberlain, A., Malizia, A. What's in it for me: Exploring the Real-World Value Proposition of Pervasive Displays. Proc. PerDis'14, ACM (2014), 174-179.
15. Kittur, A., Nickerson, J.V., Bernstein, M., Gerber, E., Shaw, A., Zimmerman, J., Lease, M. and Horton, J. The future of crowd work. Proc. CSCW '13, ACM (2013), 1301-1318.
16. Kochhar, S., Mazzocchi, S. and Paritosh, P. The anatomy of a large-scale human computation engine. Proc. HCOMP 2010, ACM (2010), 10-17.
17. Lampe, C., Zube, P., Lee, J., Park, C.H. and Johnston, E. Crowdsourcing civility: A natural experiment examining the effects of distributed moderation in online forums. Government Information Quarterly 31, 2 (2014), 317-326.
18. Lehdonvirta, V. and Castronova, E. Virtual Economies: Design and Analysis. Cambridge, MA: MIT Press (2014).
19. Liu, Y., Lehdonvirta, V., Alexandrova, T. & Nakajima, T. (2012) Drawing on Mobile Crowds via Social Media. Case UbiAsk: Image Based Mobile Social Search Across Languages. Proc. Multimedia Systems 18, 1 (2012), 53-56.
20. LocalMind, URL: http://www.localmind.com/, cited 04/04/2014
21. Martin, D., Hanrahan, B.V., O'Neill, J. and Gupta, N. Being a turker. Proc. CSCW '14, ACM (2014), 224-235.
22. Müller, J., Alt, F., Michelis, D. and Schmidt, A. Requirements and design space for interactive public displays. Proc. Multimedia 2014, ACM (2010), 1285-1294.
23. Paulos, E., Honicky, R.J. and Hooker, B. Citizen science: Enabling participatory urbanism. In M. Foth (ed), Handbook of Research on Urban Informatics: The Practice and Promise of the Real-Time City. IGI Global (2008), 414-436.
24. Quinn, A.J. and Bederson, B.B. Human computation: a survey and taxonomy of a growing field. Proc. CHI 2011, ACM (2011), 1403-1412.
25. Rashtchian, C., Young, P., Hodosh, M. and Hockenmaier, J. Collecting image annotations using Amazon's Mechanical Turk. Proc. NAACL HLT 2010 Workshop CSLDAMT '10, ACL (2010), 139-147.
26. Rogstadius, J., Kostakos, V., Kittur, A., Smus, B., Laredo, J. and Vukovic, M. An Assessment of Intrinsic and Extrinsic Motivation on Task Performance in Crowdsourcing Markets. Proc. ICWSM 2011, AAAI (2011), 321-328.
27. Sauro, J. A Practical Guide to the System Usability Scale (SUS): Background, Benchmarks & Best Practices. Measuring Usability LLC, Denver, (2011)
28. Sauro, J. http://www.measuringusability.com/sus.php, cited: 08/04/2014
29. SureLock | Mobile Device Lockdown. http://www.42gears.com/surelock/, cited 04/04/2014
30. Takayama, C. & Lehdonvirta, V. EcoIsland: A System For Persuading Users To Reduce CO2 Emissions. In Pervasive Persuasive Technology and Environmental Sustainability Workshop, Proc. Pervasive 2008 Workshop Proceedings, Springer (2008), 113-119.
31. Väätäjä, H., Vainio, T., Sirkkunen, E. and Salo, K. Crowdsourced news reporting: supporting news content creation with mobile phones. Proc. MobileHCI 2011, ACM (2011), 435-444.
32. Vukovic, M. and Kumara, S. Second international workshop on ubiquitous crowdsourcing: towards a platform for crowd computing. Proc. UbiComp 2011, ACM (2011), 617-618.
33. Wang, Y. and Mainwaring, S. Human-Currency Interaction: Learning from Virtual Currency Use in China. Proc. CHI 2008, ACM (2008), 25-28
34. Zaidan, O.F. and Callison-Burch, C. Crowdsourcing translation: Professional quality from non-professionals. Proc. Annual Meeting of the Association for Computational Linguistics: Human Language Technologies-Volume 1, ACL (2011) 1220-1229.
35. Zelizer, V. A. The Social Meaning of Money, 2nd ed. Princeton: Princeton University Press (1994).

Crowd-Powered Parameter Analysis for Visual Design Exploration

Yuki Koyama Daisuke Sakamoto Takeo Igarashi
The University of Tokyo
7-3-1 Hongo, Bunkyo-ku, Tokyo, 113-0033, Japan
koyama@is.s.u-tokyo.ac.jp, {d.sakamoto, takeo}@acm.org

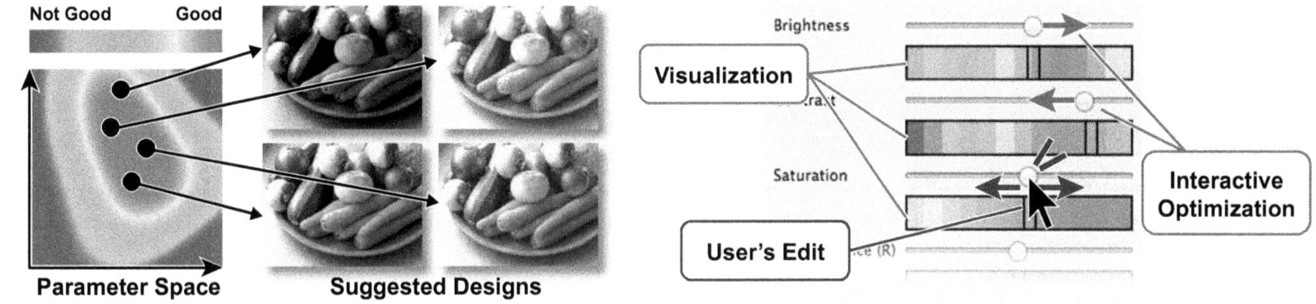

Figure 1. Two interfaces for visual design exploration that are realized by our analysis technique. (Left) *Smart Suggestion*: The user can obtain appropriate parameter sets as suggestions. (Right) *VisOpt Slider*: The user can adjust each parameter effectively by the visualization (*Vis*) near the slider and the optimization (*Opt*) that gently guides the current parameters to the optimal direction.

ABSTRACT

Parameter tweaking is one of the fundamental tasks in the editing of visual digital contents, such as correcting photo color or executing blendshape facial expression control. A problem with parameter tweaking is that it often requires much time and effort to explore a high-dimensional parameter space. We present a new technique to analyze such high-dimensional parameter space to obtain a distribution of human preference. Our method uses crowdsourcing to gather pairwise comparisons between various parameter sets. As a result of analysis, the user obtains a *goodness function* that computes the goodness value of a given parameter set. This goodness function enables two interfaces for exploration: *Smart Suggestion*, which provides suggestions of preferable parameter sets, and *VisOpt Slider*, which interactively visualizes the distribution of goodness values on sliders and gently optimizes slider values while the user is editing. We created four applications with different design parameter spaces. As a result, the system could facilitate the user's design exploration.

Author Keywords

Crowd-powered parameter analysis; parameter tweaking; design exploration; human computation;

UIST 2014, October 5–8, 2014, Honolulu, HI, USA.

ACM 978-1-4503-3069-5/14/10 ...$15.00.
http://dx.doi.org/10.1145/2642918.2647386

ACM Classification Keywords

H.5.2. Information Interfaces and Presentation (e.g. HCI): User Interfaces - Graphical user interfaces; I.3.6. Computer Graphics: Methodology and Techniques - Interaction techniques

INTRODUCTION

Exploring possible visual designs by tweaking parameters is a common practice when designing digital content. For example, if we want to clean up a photo for use at the top of a Web page, we first open the photo in Photoshop or GIMP, and then adjust the parameters—brightness, contrast, saturation, etc.—to explore which combination of parameters provides the best result. Similarly, when game developers create a 3D game scene, even for a simple scene, they have to adjust tens of hundreds of parameters—light positions, character positions, expressions, poses, colors of objects, values of shader parameters, etc.—that define the visual quality of the game.

These parameter-tweaking tasks can essentially be considered part of an iterative optimization process. In other words, we iteratively adjust the parameters of the visual design, and then evaluate the results. This process is often tedious and time-consuming, especially when there are a lot of parameters to adjust, and the high dimensionality of the space of the parameters makes it exponentially difficult to explore all possible ones. Moreover, unfamiliar parameters can be puzzling because we cannot predict their effect.

We present a method to facilitate parameter tweaking for visual design exploration. In the proposed approach, we use crowdsourcing to gather pairwise comparisons between various parameter sets. Users first specify an input parameter set and goodness criteria for a target application. The system then analyzes the parameter space using crowd workers and obtains a *goodness function*, which is a function that takes a parameter set as an input and computes how good it is. We then use the goodness function for two interfaces: *Smart Suggestion* and *VisOpt Slider*. Smart Suggestion is an interface that provides users with appropriate parameter set choices as suggestions. VisOpt Slider is an extension of the conventional slider component, in which the distribution of goodness values is directly visualized on sliders, and it can interactively update the visualization on the basis of the currently chosen slider values. The slider values are interactively and continuously optimized to a better direction as the user is editing. These two interfaces are complementary; e.g., a user can first obtain a reasonable starting point by Smart Suggestion, and then interactively tunes it up using VisOpt Slider.

In this work we offer two primary contributions:

- A method of assisting design exploration using a goodness function derived from analyzing design parameter space via on-demand crowdsourcing.
- Two specific user interfaces, Smart Suggestion and VisOpt Slider, which utilize the derived goodness function and enable users to effectively explore the parameter space.

To evaluate our method, we performed experiments with four applications: photo color correction (6 parameters), camera and light control in a 3D scene (8 parameters), shader (8 parameters), and blendshape facial expression (53 parameters). We checked the quality of analysis, and conducted an informal user study of our interfaces.

RELATED WORK

Crowd-Powered Analysis

Crowdsourcing is an emerging paradigm whereby we can stably employ a large number of temporary workers (crowd) through the Internet. From the viewpoint of *human computation* [15], we can consider this new platform a resource of *human processors* whereby we can easily obtain large amounts of human-processed data for analysis on demand, which previously had required temporally- and monetary-high cost.

One of the notable benefits of using crowds as human processors is that we can exploit popular human perception. Gingold et al. [6] introduced a technique for applying the perception of a crowd to the analysis of 2D images. Chaudhuri et al. [5] proposed AttribIt, an interface using semantic attributes for designing visual content, where they utilized crowds to learn the semantic attributes of design components. We also utilize crowds as human processors for analysis. Our goal is to analyze a design space that has been formed by continuous design parameters, and then use the results of the analysis for interfaces.

Secord et al. [19] analyzed the viewpoint preference when viewing 3D shapes, through a large perceptual user study conducted on a crowdsourcing platform. Their approach was to create a generalized model to predict the viewpoint preference of (even) unknown content while using domain-specific features. Reinecke et al. [17, 16] presented a perceptual model of aesthetics for web design learned by crowdsourced study, where they utilized the features specific to web design for their computational model. In contrast to these works, our goal is to deal with arbitrary design spaces and arbitrary criteria, and to provide a model tailored for specific content.

Visual Parameter Tweaking

Parameter tweaking is a common process in various design situations, and researchers have been tackling how to best facilitate it for a long time. One of the most successful approaches is inverse design [29, 13, 24], in which the system automatically computes the best-suited parameters from a user-specified final desired look, considering it as an inverse problem. However, this is not useful if the user does not have any clear goal and rather wants to explore a range of possible looks. Furthermore, this approach is often difficult to generalize because solving an inverse problem requires knowledge of the heuristics of each application. In contrast, our goals are to achieve an algorithm that can be used with many applications and to facilitate user's exploration.

Showing design options as suggestions or landmarks is an effective way to facilitate design exploration. Many previous works have investigated this approach [11, 12, 7, 20, 9], and several tools, such as Photoshop's Variations interface[1] and AfterEffects' BrainStorming interface[2], include this function. One of our own interfaces, Smart Suggestion, follows this concept. However, unlike the above works/tools, Smart Suggestion considers the goodness values estimated using crowd preferences when generating suggestions. In addition to showing suggestions, VisOpt Sliders provide informed exploration (guidance) around a selected sample.

Side Views [26] and Parallel Paths [27] enable fast "visits" of possible designs by showing visual designs along with GUI widgets such as sliders, then the user can efficiently evaluate which parameter is good or not good. In contrast, our approach enables users to avoid visits of meaningless designs by showing goodness values instead of "raw" designs. Scented Widgets [28] also shows "raw" data that the user should evaluate according to their situations. In contrast, our VisOpt Slider shows the distribution of explore-worthy parameters that directly guides user's exploration.

As an interface that utilizes the preferences of many people, Talton et al. [23] presented a parametric modeling tool that "knows" a good design space (called *collaborative design space*) thanks to the collaboration of many people. The main difference is that our work is designed for "on-demand crowdsourcing," or human computation, for specific target problem instance, while their work is designed for collaborative exploration. Their system collects final modeling results by dedicated users, so it takes time (e.g. a year). On the other hand, our system only requires the workers to "compare" instances as microtasks, so it is much easier to get many contributors (workers). Xu et al. [30] also proposed a design system using collective knowledge. Their purpose of using collective knowledge is to get feedback for a certain design, while ours is to analyze the entire design space.

[1] `http://www.adobe.com/products/photoshop/`
[2] `http://www.adobe.com/products/aftereffects/`

CROWD-POWERED PARAMETER ANALYSIS

Overview of the Process

Our approach employs a crowdsourcing platform to analyze parameters to support the tweaking of visual design parameters. The definition of a *parameter set* in this paper is an n-dimensional vector $\mathbf{x} \in \mathbb{R}^n$ that consists of n continuous parameters $x_i \in [0, 1]$ for $i = 1, \ldots, n$. Note that we do not deal with discrete parameters such as font or layout selection. We assume that the final form of a design task can be visualized as a 2D image I and that given a parameter set $\mathbf{x}$, the design software deterministically provides an image, which we describe as $I(\mathbf{x})$. In other words, our target design tasks can be completely parameterized by n parameters. This assumption is true in many cases, especially in the final steps of actual design processes. For example, when 3D game developers finish their implementation of game logic, the final step of the game creation could be the parameter tuning of the game scene visuals, such as the positions of game objects, the lighting conditions, the camera pose, and the shader parameters.

The goal of the analysis is to obtain a continuous scalar-valued function, or a goodness function, $f : \mathbb{R}^n \rightarrow \mathbb{R}$ that maps a parameter set to its estimated goodness; that is, to obtain a function f that takes a parameter set $\mathbf{x}$ as input and computes an estimated goodness value $y = f(\mathbf{x})$ as output. We define goodness as a continuous value from 0 to 1, where 1 is the most preferable and 0 is the least.

Our process to obtain a goodness function consists of four steps, as shown in Figure 2. First, the system generates sampling points on the high-dimensional parameter space (displayed here as 2-dimensional space). Second, using crowdsourcing, the system gathers pairwise comparisons of these sampling points. Third, on the basis of this comparisons, we analyze the goodness value for each (discrete) sampling point. Fourth, the system interpolates the goodness values and obtains a continuous scalar function, i.e., a goodness function, as a result of the analysis.

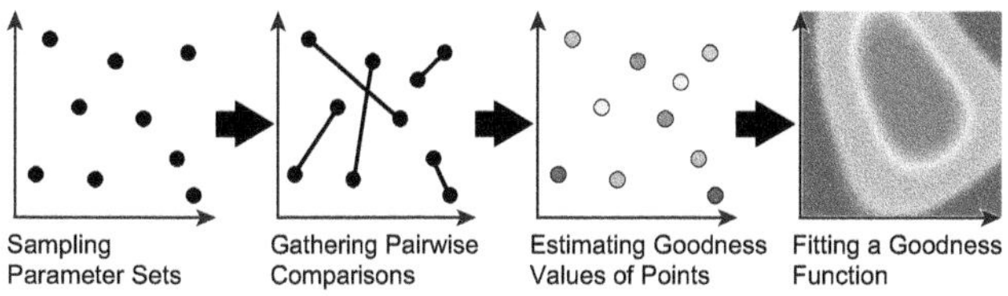

Figure 2. Overview of our algorithm of analysis.

Our method can be considered as one of the learning-from-crowd problems [25, 19, 5], but the problem we are addressing here requires some special treatments. First, the data that we deal with is a set of noisy relative scores between two sampling points, not absolute goodness values. In addition, the derived function is required to be very fast to compute its value for a given parameter set to realize our interaction techniques, and also required to be able to represent a highly nonlinear distribution to deal with various design spaces. In our understanding, any existing algorithm has not solved this specific problem yet, and cannot be applied to our problem without significant extensions.

Sampling Parameter Sets

First, the system samples M parameter sets $\mathbf{x}_1, \ldots, \mathbf{x}_M$ from the parameter space for the later process of crowdsourcing. To do this, we simply choose a random uniform sampling; the system randomly picks a parameter set up from the parameter space and then computes this process M times.

There might be smarter ways to sample parameter sets to achieve more effective crowdsourcing. For example, Secord et al. [19] took a *nearby sampling* approach, in which the system samples pairs of parameter sets that are located *near* to each other. However, nearby sampling requires empirical knowledge of the parameter space, which prohibits us from using it because we want to deal with various types of parameter spaces. Tamuz et al. [25] proposed a sophisticated adaptive sampling method for a crowd-powered analysis; however, their method cannot be directly applied for our problem because it is not designed to derive a continuous scalar function as output. It might be possible to further improve our results by using their adaptive sampling method, but the random sampling works sufficiently well for our requirements.

Gathering Pairwise Comparisons by Crowdsourcing

The next step is to gather information on the goodness of each sampling point. Because the goodness value is essentially evaluated by human preference, we use a human computation technique based on crowdsourcing. A possible naïve approach is to ask crowd workers to provide the absolute goodness values on sampling points directly; however, this is impractical because the concept of goodness is too abstract and the measure scale depends on the individual.

Thus, we take a *pairwise comparison* approach [19, 6, 5] in which crowd workers are shown a pair of designs and asked to choose the best one. As a result, relative scores instead of absolute ones are obtained. Unlike most of the previous approaches, we use the 5-pt Likert scale (1 to 5) to rate a design pair, where 1 means one design of the two is definitely better, 5 means the other design is definitely better, and 3 means neutral. Our algorithm welcomes the *neutral* score, as it is considered a constraint that the two parameter sets have the same or nearly the same goodness values.

Let P be a set of pairs of indices $\{(1, 2), \ldots, (M - 1, M)\}$. For each $(i, j) \in P$, the system generates two images $I(\mathbf{x}_i), I(\mathbf{x}_j)$, shows the pair side by side to a crowd worker, and asks him/her to rate its relative score. Eventually, it gathers $M/2$ scores, and each image is shown and rated once.

The instruction of the micro-task for crowd workers is important in terms of the quality of obtained data. Because the purposes and contexts of using our system differ depending on the situation, we prepare a template of instruction for users rather than providing a fixed instruction. The template that we used in our experimentation is:

> *Which of the two images of [noun] is more [adjective]? For example, [clause]. Please choose the most appropriate one from the 5 options below.*

In accordance with the purpose and the content, the user gives a noun, an adjective (such as "good" or "natural"), and a clause (which explains a concrete scenario to instruct crowd workers more effectively). After this instruction, two images and five options appear. These options are linked to the Likert scale; e.g., *"the left image is definitely more [adjective] than the right image"* is for option 1, and the complete opposite is option 5. Option 3 is *"these two images are equally [adjective], or are equally not [adjective]."* Figure 3 shows a screen capture of the micro task that was actually used in our experiments.

Figure 3. An example of the tasks used in our experiments. We took a pairwise comparison approach.

To control the quality of the data, we take the *duplicate* approach, as do several of the previous works [19, 6, 5]. We first asked 10 questions and then asked 10 more identical questions but with the arrangement of the two images flipped. If the answer of a question contradicted the duplicated correspondent, we simply discarded the answer. We also discarded all answers from a particular crowd worker if more than half the answers contradicted. This algorithm cannot detect if all 20 answers have been (lazily) rated as "3", and so the system checked such cases and discarded them if so.

In the remainder of this paper, we represent P' as a subset of P, each of which have passed the quality check, M' as the number of sampling points that have passed the quality check, and $Q = \{q_1, \dots, q_{M'}\}$ as a set of indices of sampling points that have passed the quality check.

Estimating Goodness Values of Sampling Points

Given the relative scores, the next goal is to compute the absolute goodness values $\mathbf{y} = (y_{q_1}, \dots, y_{q_{M'}})$ of the sampling points $\mathbf{x}_{q_1}, \dots, \mathbf{x}_{q_{M'}}$. Sýkora et al. [22] dealt with a similar problem where, given the relative orders of pairs of points, the system estimates the entire consistent orders of all points. The difference between their target problem and ours is the existence of inconsistent relative orders; in our case, the solution that satisfies all the relative orders does not generally exist because the data is from unreliable crowds and is based on human preference. Gingold et al. [6] presented a robust algorithm for this problem, but it can only handle relative orders of adjacent areas, and their 2D-based algorithm cannot be extended to high-dimensional parameter space due to its high computational cost.

Thus, we present a new formulation for this problem. We consider a constraint based on the relative scores as a cost function

$$E_{\text{relative}}(\mathbf{y}) = \sum_{(i,j)\in P'} \|y_i - y_j - d_{i,j}\|^2, \tag{1}$$

where $d_{i,j}$ is an offset distance between the i-th and j-th goodness values, defined as

$$d_{i,j} = \begin{cases} 1 & \text{(relative score} = 1) \\ 0.5 & \text{(relative score} = 2) \\ 0 & \text{(relative score} = 3) \\ -0.5 & \text{(relative score} = 4) \\ -1 & \text{(relative score} = 5) \end{cases}. \tag{2}$$

Considering only the relative constraint results in a disconnected, jagged distribution of goodness values (Figure 4, left). This is undesirable because we are handling continuous parameter space, and thus we expect the goodness function to also be continuous (Figure 4, right) and smooth in most cases. We therefore add a constraint based on the assumption of continuity:

$$E_{\text{continuous}}(\mathbf{y}) = \sum_{i\in Q} \left\| y_i - \frac{1}{N_i}\sum_{j\in N_i} y_j \right\|^2, \tag{3}$$

where N_i stands for the neighborhoods of the i-th sampling points, which are defined by 20-nearests in Euclidean distance. Note that this continuous constraint is popular in Laplacian-related techniques such as smoothing [21] and thus is beneficial for reducing data noise.

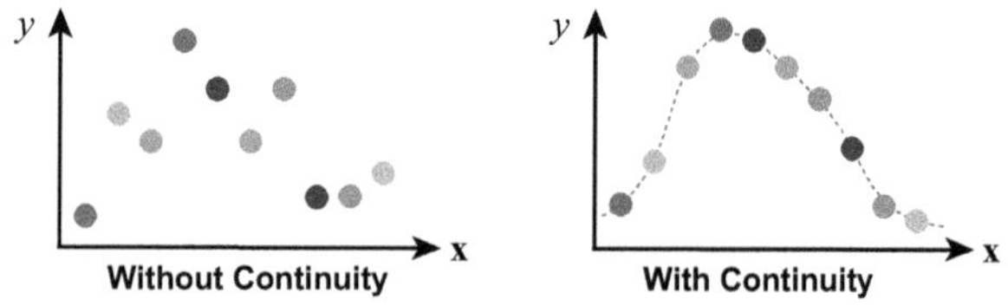

Figure 4. Constraint of continuity. This constraint ensures that the estimated goodness values are continuously distributed.

Taking these two constraints into consideration, the system solves the following minimization:

$$\min_{\mathbf{y}} \left(E_{\text{relative}}(\mathbf{y}) + \omega E_{\text{continuous}}(\mathbf{y}) \right), \tag{4}$$

where $\omega > 0$ is a parameter that defines the balance of these two constraints. In all experiments introduced in this paper, we set $\omega = 5.0$. We can solve this minimization problem as a simple linear algebraic equation. See the appendix for specific details. After solving this minimization problem, we linearly normalize the solution so that the maximum goodness value is 1 and the minimum is 0.

Fitting a Goodness Function

Our goal is now to obtain a continuous goodness function from the obtained goodness values of the sampling points. The fitted function needs to be efficient enough for use in real-time visualization and optimization for user interfaces, so we chose the Radial Basis Function (RBF) interpolation technique for fitting, which is often used to smoothly interpolate known values at various points (RBF centers) and thus create a continuous function [3]. We use the parameter sets $\mathbf{x}_{q_1}, \dots, \mathbf{x}_{q_{M'}}$ as the locations of the RBF centers and the obtained goodness values $y_{q_1}, \dots, y_{q_{M'}}$ as the target values. That is, we represent the goodness function f as $f(\mathbf{x}) = \sum_{i \in Q} w_i \phi(\|\mathbf{x} - \mathbf{x}_i\|)$, where $\phi(\cdot)$ is a radial basis function, and $\mathbf{w} = (w_{q_1}, \dots, w_{q_{M'}})$ are the RBF weights that we are going to compute. We used $\phi(r) = r$ as the basis function but found the Gaussian also works well and does not result in any significant differences.

The *exact* RBF interpolation scheme is not robust for dense, noisy data. We therefore add a regularization term when computing RBF weights [3]. Specifically, we solve the following minimization problem to obtain $\mathbf{w}$:

$$\min_{\mathbf{w}} \sum_{i \in Q} \left\| \sum_{j \in Q} w_j \phi\left(\|\mathbf{x}_i - \mathbf{x}_j\|\right) - y_i \right\|^2 + \lambda \|\mathbf{w}\|^2 \qquad (5)$$

where $\lambda \geq 0$ is the parameter for controlling regularization. We set $\lambda = 0.1$ in this work. We found that this regularization was able to avoid overfitting with our data. Optionally, we compute the reduction of RBF centers [4] to improve computational efficiency.

USER INTERFACE

We use the pararmeter analysis results to create two types of user interface to facilitate parameter tweaking tasks and design exploration.

Smart Suggestion

Smart Suggestion is a function that generates nine parameter sets having relatively high goodness values and displays the corresponding designs as suggestions. This interface facilitates design exploration by giving users a good starting point to find a better parameter set for the visual design.

Our current implementation takes a simple approach to generate quality suggestions: the system generates 2,000 parameter sets randomly and then selects the 9-best parameter sets according to their goodness values. This simple algorithm interactively provides suggestions of an adequate quality, which enables users to re-generate suggestions quickly enough for interactive use if none of the suggestions satisfy them. To generate higher-quality suggestions, other techniques such as *diversity optimization* [1] or the *dispersion* technique [11] could be useful. However, we feel that it is better to avoid spending too much time generating optimal suggestions, and instead focus on interactively providing suggestions of sufficient quality.

VisOpt Slider

The VisOpt Slider (Figure 1, left) displays bars with a "visualization" (*Vis*) of the results of parameter analysis. The distribution of goodness values is directly visualized on each slider using color mapping, which navigates the user to tweak parameters. When the "optimization" (*Opt*) is turned on, the parameters are automatically and interactively optimized while the user is dragging a slider. For example, a user drags a slider, and then the other sliders automatically move to better points corresponding to the user's operation.

A visual bar shows the distribution of goodness values along the line that passes the current parameter point and whose direction is the same as the parameter's axis (Figure 5). Note that when the user modifies a certain parameter, the visualizations of the other parameters will change dynamically. This visualization continuously tells the user which parameter should be modified and how much the parameter should be modified, thus achieving higher quality designs. This helps the user not only to find better parameter sets quickly but also to explore the design space effectively without visiting *bad* designs.

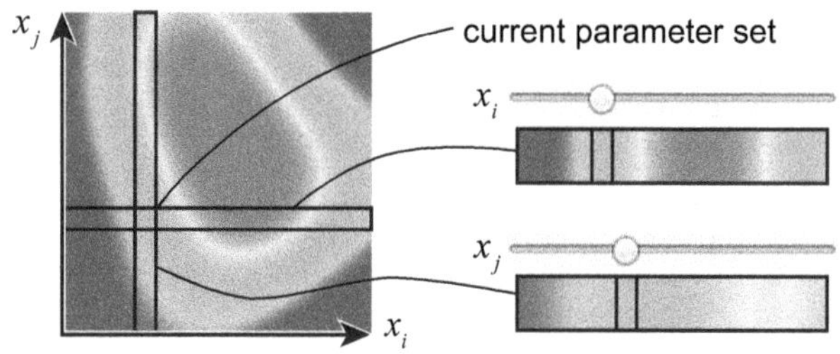

Figure 5. The bars visualize the distribution of the goodness values along each slider.

The purpose of the optimization is not to find the optimal parameter set automatically but rather to assist manual interactive exploration on the part of the user by gently guiding the current parameter set to a reasonable direction. To achieve this, we use the gradient descent method with a fixed number of iterations, following Prévost et al.'s work [14]. In this method, the system first computes the gradient of the goodness function at the current parameter set and then slightly modifies the set to move in the gradient direction instead of instantly jumping to the optimal solution. This enables the user to gradually approach to the optimal solution by continuously scribbling the slider knob back and forth. We numerically compute the gradient using forward differentiation. This process could be written as

$$\mathbf{x} \leftarrow \mathbf{x} + \alpha \nabla f(\mathbf{x}), \qquad (6)$$

where $\alpha > 0$ is a small value parameter that defines the strength of optimization. Note that, in order to avoid conflicting with the user's editing, the system does not update the currently edited parameter. This process is performed every time the system receives a slider-value-changed event. In our experimentations, we typically set $\alpha = 0.005$.

APPLICATIONS

We evaluated our method by using it with four example applications. All four applications are from different domains to demonstrate that the proposed method is suitable for general (not domain-specific) use. We chose CrowdFlower[3] as the platform of crowdsourcing. Table 1 lists a summary of the crowdsourcing statistics. We analyzed each parameter space using all the *valid* comparisons we obtained as a result of crowdsourcing.

Color Correction

When correcting digital photos, users have to tweak many parameters, including unintuitive ones such as saturation, which is sometimes quite difficult for novices. To facilitate this task, we selected six popular parameters for this application: brightness, contrast, saturation, and color balance (color of Red, Green, and Blue (RGB)). For this experiment, we chose a photo of vegetables (Figure 6, left) from a photo sharing service (morgueFile[4]) and asked crowd workers to choose which version would be better to use in a magazine or product advertisement.

Figure 6. (Left) The input image (goodness = 0.72). (Middle and Right) Typical suggested images (goodness = 0.98, 0.95).

Figure 6 (middle and right) shows typical images suggested by Smart Suggestion. Examples of VisOpt Slider visualizations with typical parameter sets are shown in Figure 7. These visualizations provide assorted useful information; for example, the photo at left needs to have a higher contrast, the center photo can be improved by making the brightness slightly higher and the red balance slightly lower, and the right photo is already good and does not require any dramatic improvements.

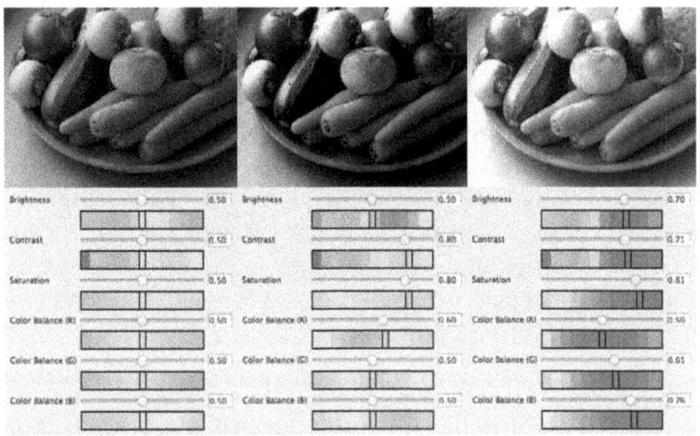

Figure 7. Visualizations for typical parameter sets in the application of color correction.

Camera and Light Control

Secord et al. [19] presented a general model of view direction goodness for 3D models; however, that model is limited to the view direction and does not consider any other factors. We feel that good views will change according to other conditions such as perspective and lighting. In this scenario, we chose a camera and light control task in a simple 3D scene containing a 3D model, a perspective camera, and a point light. There are eight parameters to tweak, including camera position $(-3.0 < xyz < 3.0)$, camera field of view, light position $(-3.0 < xyz < 3.0)$, and intensity of light. We used the dragon model (almost symmetric), and the bunny model (asymmetric). The rotation of the camera is automatically set so that it always looks at the center of the model. We asked crowd workers to choose the better one with the same instruction.

The results indicate a highly non-linear relationship between camera and light parameters. When the camera comes to the left side (camera.$z < 0.0$, Figure 8, middle) from the right side (camera.$z > 0.0$, Figure 8, left) of the dragon model, the visualization tells us that we should also move the light to the left side (light.$z < 0.0$) so that the model is adequately lit. Figure 8 right shows the views using the bunny model, where we applied exactly the same parameter sets as to the left one of Figure 8. We found that the visualizations between the case of the dragon and the bunny are quite different even when the parameter sets are equivalent, which indicates that different models have different goodness functions. This suggests that our approach of "final look-aware crowdsourcing" is key.

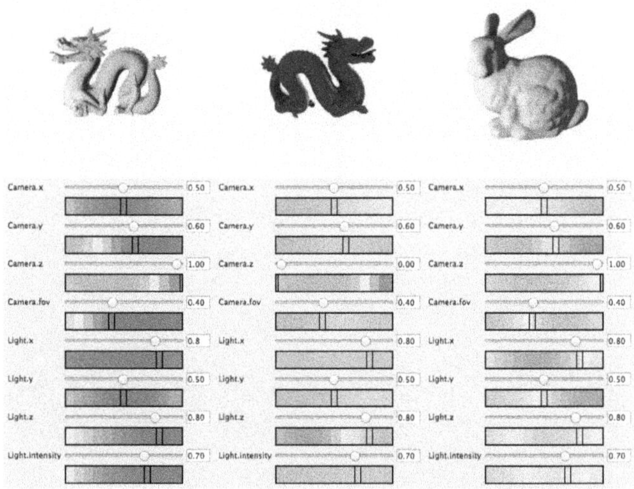

Figure 8. Designs and visualizations of the camera and light application. (Left) A parameter set is applied to the dragon scene, whose camera.z (the 3rd slider) is set to the maximum value. (Middle) Another parameter set whose values are the same as the left one except that camera.z is modified to the minimum value. (Right) The same parameter set as the left one is applied to the bunny scene.

Shader

As Talton et al. [23] discussed, shading is quite difficult for novices to understand and tweak and even game developers and computer graphics researchers struggle with it at times. The problem is that shaders often have unintuitive parameters that affect the final look in a way that is difficult for casual users to predict, such as "Fresnel Reflection" or "Metallics".

[3] `http://www.crowdflower.com`

[4] `http://www.morguefile.com`

Table 1. Statistics of crowdsourcing in our experiments. Adjective shows the words we used for the instructions. For each application, we ordered a fixed number of tasks at once, each of which contains 10 comparisons and 10 duplicated comparisons for quality control. We typically chose 200 for the number of tasks, but 600 for the facial expression application because the parameter space is quite high-dimensional. We paid a fixed amount of money for each task regardless of the quality; for example, in the case of the color correction, we paid $200 \times 0.02 = 4.00$ USD for workers in total. The number of valid comparisons indicates $|P'|$, which is the number of comparisons that passed quality check. We allowed crowd workers to perform two or more tasks if they want, so we also report the number of unique workers. Completion time denotes the passed time from the point when the first task is started to the point when the final task is finished.

	#Parameters	Adjective	#Tasks	Pay [USD / task]	#Valid comparisons	#Unique workers	Completion time [min]
Color Correction	6	good	200	0.02	1095	45	30
Camera and Light (Dragon)	8	good	200	0.02	1010	26	25
Camera and Light (Bunny)	8	good	200	0.02	922	35	40
Shader (Kitchen)	8	realistic	200	0.02	907	46	34
Shader (Window Seat)	8	realistic	200	0.02	875	47	24
Facial Expression	53	natural	600	0.02	1771	57	55

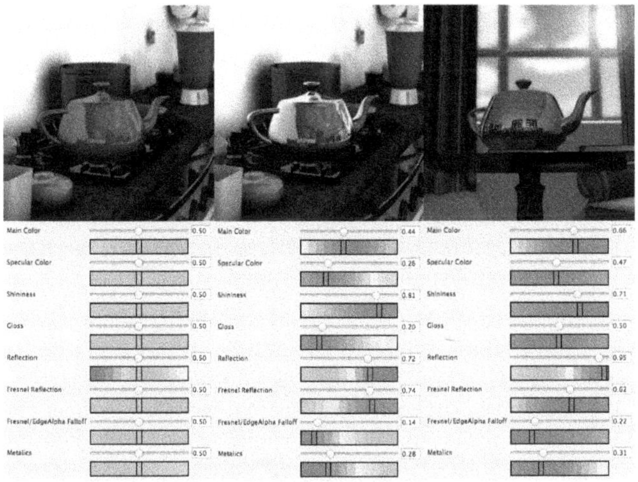

Figure 9. Typical designs and their parameter sets in the shader application. (Left and Middle) Kitchen scene. (Right) Window seat scene.

Furthermore, the final rendered images are different depending on many different factors such as lighting conditions and the geometric features of the 3D models. Thus, users have to explore the best parameters for each scene, which is time-consuming. For this experiment, we used a shader for photo-realistic metals provided in a popular shader package, Hard Surface Shaders Free[5] (Unity Asset Store). We applied this shader to a teapot model. We chose eight parameters from the shader parameters, and asked crowd workers to choose the one that was the most realistic as a stainless steel teapot. We experimented with two different scenes: a kitchen scene with standard lighting and a window seat scene with backlighting.

Figure 9 shows typical parameter sets with their visualizations. From these visualizations, we can learn, without any trial-and-error, that the "Reflection" parameter (the fifth parameter in Figure 9) performs the most important role in this application. We observed that the distributions of goodness values are different from each scene; for example, a parameter set whose goodness value was 0.67 in the kitchen scene had a goodness value of 0.93 in the window seat scene.

Blendshape Facial Expression

Blendshape is a standard approach to control the facial expressions of virtual characters [10], where a face model has a number of predefined continuous parameters and its expression is controlled by artists/designers by tweaking the parameters. Such direct control is made tedious because of the number of parameters. Furthermore, as discussed by Lewis et al. [10], the space of *valid* expressions is actually quite small in most cases, which means that extremely careful tweaking is required to ensure natural, unbroken expressions. In this scenario, we used a head model whose blendshape is defined with 53 parameters (48 based on FACS [18], and 5 for jaw control). To analyze the *validity* of this parameter space, we asked crowd workers to choose the better natural expression.

Figure 10 shows typical designs and their goodness values. We believe that the goodness function is successfully constructed and gives reasonable values for even this high-dimensional application. Unlike random suggestions (typical goodness values are 0.3–0.6), where most of expressions are broken, Smart Suggestion provides nice starting points (around 0.7) with a high enough quality to inspire users. The optimization also works well with this large number of parameters to avoid wasting time with *invalid* expressions. However, we found that the heatmap visualization was often useless because each visualization bar tends to show a similar color along its axis in this large parameter space.

EVALUATION

Quality of Analysis

Convergence with respect to Number of Comparisons

It is important to understand how many comparisons are necessary for each application. If there are too many comparisons, it takes extra time and money, and if there are too few, the obtained goodness function might be missing the important feature of the parameter space. Here, we discuss the convergence behavior graphs (Figure 11) of the shader and the facial expression applications, where the goodness values of 30 randomly selected parameter sets are plotted for each graph. Beginning with 20 comparisons, we computed the goodness function using the limited number of comparisons, and then repeatedly increased the number of used comparisons by 10. Invalid comparisons that did not pass the quality control were excluded.

As shown in the graph of the shader application, the curves are relatively stable with more than 400 comparisons (roughly more than 2 USD), though they do not converge completely. Since our goal is to assist users with interactive exploration

[5] `https://www.assetstore.unity3d.com/#/content/729`

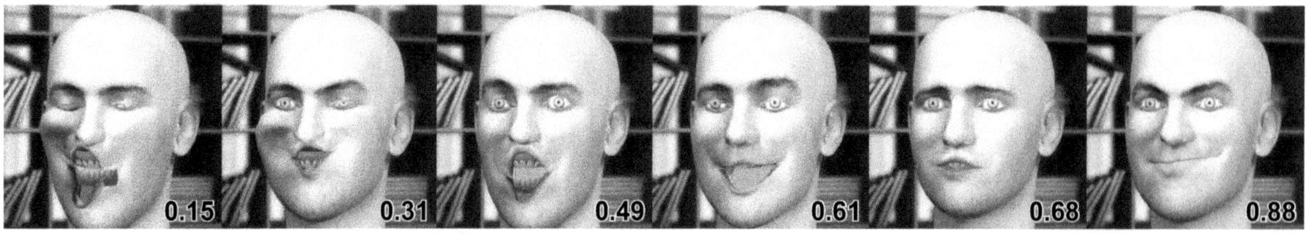

Figure 10. Typical designs of facial expressions controlled by 53 blendshape parameters. The values shown in each picture are the goodness values computed by our method.

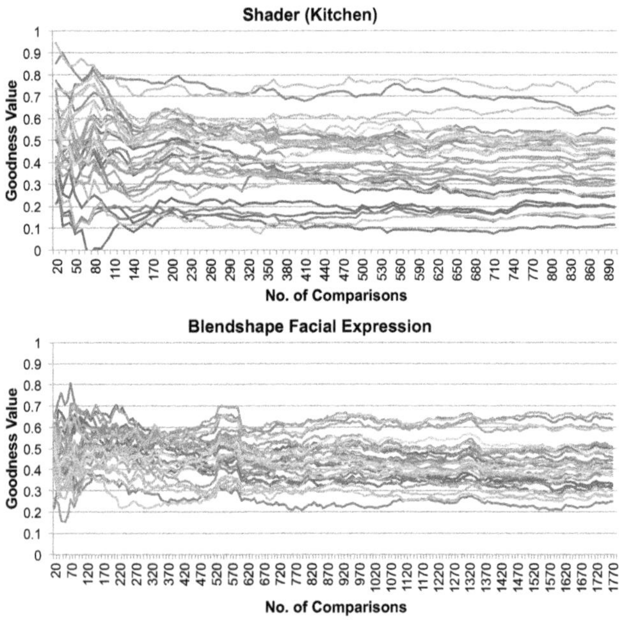

Figure 11. Convergence behavior with respect to the number of comparisons. Each curve shows the transition of the goodness value on a randomly selected parameter set.

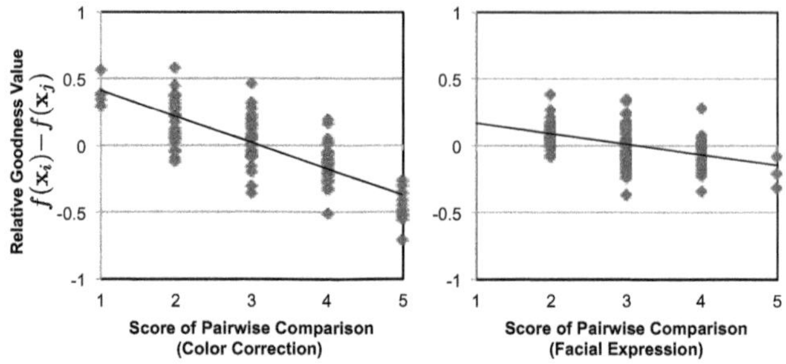

Figure 12. Relationship between the scores and their computed relative goodness values. Black lines are the fitted lines.

rather than to find the exact optimal parameter set automatically, we believe our analysis is convergent enough for the purpose. We observed similar convergence graphs in the other applications, and even, somewhat surprisingly, it is true in the facial expression with 53 parameters, where more than 900 comparisons are required to be stable.

Adequacy of Estimated Goodness Functions

To check the adequacy of the estimated goodness functions, we applied a cross-validation test to the acquired data set for the color correction and the facial expression applications. We randomly selected 100 samples from the valid comparisons P' obtained via crowdsourcing as a testing set, which we denote P'_{testing}. Then, we trained the goodness function f by using the rest of the valid comparisons $P'_{\text{training}} = P' - P'_{\text{testing}}$ as a training set (the size of training data set is 995 for the color correction and 1671 for the facial expression). If the estimated goodness function f obtained from P'_{training} is adequate, it should be able to predict the distribution of the scores of the comparisons in P'_{testing}. That is, as for a paired comparison in the testing set $(i, j) \in P'_{\text{testing}}$, the difference between the estimated goodness values $f(\mathbf{x}_i) - f(\mathbf{x}_j)$ should be correlated to the score (1–5) given to the pair by a crowd worker. We show such plots in Figure 12. Although the data shows large variance due to diversity of human preference and noise from careless workers, we can still observe a tendency that a crowd worker rated i higher than j when the goodness value for i ($f(\mathbf{x}_i)$) is higher than j ($f(\mathbf{x}_i)$). This indicates that the trained goodness function f successfully predicted the relative goodness values of paired comparisons that do not appear in the training set.

User Study of the Interfaces

We conducted an informal user study to determine whether Smart Suggestion and VisOpt Slider interfaces are useful for novice users or not. Four computer science students participated in this study. We asked them to explore the design spaces and find the best parameter sets on the four applications, where they can use both random suggestions/standard sliders and Smart Suggestion/VisOpt Slider. After the trial, we asked the participants to fill questionnaires.

We found all the participants could use our proposed interfaces effectively. The score of System Usability Scale (SUS) [2] was 77.5 on average ($SD = 11.6$), which could be considered as "good". All the participants preferred to use the Smart Suggestion rather than random suggestions (6.75 on average with 7-pt Likert scale; 7 is the best), and also preferred VisOpt Slider rather than standard sliders (6.25 on average). Overall, a combination of the Smart Suggestion and VisOpt Slider interfaces is preferable to use (6.25 on average).

DISCUSSION

The results of the user study suggests that the Smart Suggest and VisOpt Slider interfaces provide users with a good starting point for designing visuals. For examples, modeling a facial expression is usually quite difficult, but users successfully used Smart Suggestion to select a sample expression with which to start the precise control, thus reducing the amount of time needed to create a visual. In the case of the camera and lighting control application, the VisOpt slider helped users find better lighting parameters automatically simply by controlling one parameter for the camera. In another case of photo color correction, there are some automatic correction algorithms; however, such algorithms typically cannot consider the context of photos. For example, a user might want to make a photograph "sad" or "happy" by changing its color. This is not possible with the automatic method.

The facial expression application, for example, takes an hour and costs more than 10 USD for the crowdsourcing, which might reduce user motivation to use our interface. However, there are certain cases where the task is very critical (e.g. preparing a visual for a large-budget advertising campaign), and knowing general-public preference (customer opinion) via crowdsourcing is worth investing time and money. Another possible scenario for the facial expression application is that the 3D modeler can sell his/her 3D face model with the result of the parameter analysis. In this case, end users can use our user interface without running costly analysis by themselves.

Other Possible Representations of Goodness Function

In this work, we chose a non-parametric representation of RBF function as a representation of goodness function. The role of this function is similar to the ranking function proposed by Chaudhuri et al. [5], where they represented it as a simple weighted sum of the input vector. Secord et al. [19] proposed some representations for goodness function based on linear-K models and a quadratic model. We believe that simply applying their techniques to our problem cannot capture the non-linear distribution of goodness shown in our visualization, and also the non-linear relationships such as the relative positions of the camera and the light. Note that Secord et al. [19] also proposed a non-parametric representation based on the *K-nearest-neighbors* model in their paper. However, it cannot be used for our purpose since it cannot compute a goodness value for a single parameter set but only the preference in a pair of parameter sets; furthermore, it is computationally too expensive to use for interfaces.

Limitation

One of the most significant limitations of our approach is that the user has to make the instruction for crowdsourcing. This was not evaluated in the user study. Of course, we prepared an instruction template, but this cannot be automated.

At present, we cannot obtain the parameter analysis results in real-time because we use the crowdsourcing platform. From the statistics of the crowdsourcing we conducted, roughly half an hour seems required for around 8 dimensional design tasks and one hour for around 50 dimensional tasks. This might be a problem for users who cannot wait and want to obtain the results immediately. (Hopefully this process will become faster as the popularity of crowdsourcing expands.) In addition to the cost in terms of time, monetary cost is also a problem, as some users might feel the price of our analysis is too high. We paid 4 USD in total to crowd workers for the shader application, which we believe to be a reasonable price.

Design Implication

Learning the *personal* preference of the users (not the crowd) [20] could be an interesting future direction. Because human preferences differ depending upon the individual and the culture, considering clusters of crowds [8] could improve the quality of goodness functions. To lower the monetary and timing costs of crowdsourcing, it could be helpful to sample parameter sets in a progressive way and dynamically change the tasks [25]. Web design and presentation slide design contain many discrete parameters such as fonts so currently they are out of our scope, but considering such discrete parameters is an important direction to take in our future work. Similar to AttribIt [5], we feel that considering two or more types of goodness criteria for a design task could provide more useful interfaces. In our current approach, every different image task requires re-crowdsourcing, and this limits the scalability; to improve this, we are thinking of combining multiple crowdsourced results or reusing previous ones. Generating a small number of new sliders by using dimensionality reduction techniques is also a potential focus of our future work.

CONCLUSION

We presented a technique to analyze design parameter space via crowdsourcing. Analysis results are used to obtain a goodness function that maps a given parameter set to its goodness value. On the basis of this goodness function, we created two interfaces to facilitate design exploration: Smart Suggestion and VisOpt Slider. We applied our technique to various visual design tasks. As validation of our approach, we checked the quality of analysis and evaluated our interfaces through an informal user study.

ACKNOWLEDGMENTS

Yuki Koyama is funded by JSPS research fellowship. This work was supported by JSPS KAKENHI Grant Number 26·8574, 26240027. The face model is provided by faceshift AG under CC BY 3.0. The dragon and bunny models are provided by The Stanford 3D Scanning Repository.

REFERENCES

1. Agrawal, S., Shen, S., and van de Panne, M. Diverse motion variations for physics-based character animation. In *Proc. SCA '13*, ACM (2013), 37–44.
2. Bangor, A., Kortum, P. T., and Miller, J. T. An empirical evaluation of the system usability scale. *Int. J. Hum.-Comput. Int. 24*, 6 (2008), 574–594.
3. Bishop, C. M. *Neural Networks for Pattern Recognition.* Oxford University Press, Inc., 1995.
4. Carr, J. C., Beatson, R. K., Cherrie, J. B., Mitchell, T. J., Fright, W. R., McCallum, B. C., and Evans, T. R. Reconstruction and representation of 3d objects with radial basis functions. In *Proc. SIGGRAPH '01*, ACM (2001), 67–76.
5. Chaudhuri, S., Kalogerakis, E., Giguere, S., and Funkhouser, T. Attribit: Content creation with semantic attributes. In *Proc. UIST '13*, ACM (2013), 193–202.

6. Gingold, Y., Shamir, A., and Cohen-Or, D. Micro perceptual human computation for visual tasks. *ACM Trans. Graph. 31*, 5 (2012), 119:1–119:12.
7. Hartmann, B., Yu, L., Allison, A., Yang, Y., and Klemmer, S. R. Design as exploration: Creating interface alternatives through parallel authoring and runtime tuning. In *Proc. UIST '08*, ACM (2008), 91–100.
8. Kajino, H., Tsuboi, Y., and Kashima, H. Clustering crowds. In *Proc. AAAI '13* (2013).
9. Lee, B., Srivastava, S., Kumar, R., Brafman, R., and Klemmer, S. R. Designing with interactive example galleries. In *Proc. CHI '10*, ACM (2010), 2257–2266.
10. Lewis, J. P., Anjyo, K., Rhee, T., Zhang, M., Pighin, F., and Deng, Z. Practice and theory of blendshape facial models. In *EG 2014 - STARs*, Eurographics Association (2014), 199–218.
11. Marks, J., Andalman, B., Beardsley, P. A., Freeman, W., Gibson, S., Hodgins, J., Kang, T., Mirtich, B., Pfister, H., Ruml, W., Ryall, K., Seims, J., and Shieber, S. Design galleries: A general approach to setting parameters for computer graphics and animation. In *Proc. SIGGRAPH '97*, ACM Press/Addison-Wesley Publishing Co. (1997), 389–400.
12. Ngan, A., Durand, F., and Matusik, W. Image-driven navigation of analytical brdf models. In *Proc. EGSR '06*, Eurographics Association (2006), 399–407.
13. Okabe, M., Matsushita, Y., Shen, L., and Igarashi, T. Illumination brush: Interactive design of all-frequency lighting. In *Proc. Pacific Graphics '07* (2007), 171–180.
14. Prévost, R., Whiting, E., Lefebvre, S., and Sorkine-Hornung, O. Make it stand: Balancing shapes for 3d fabrication. *ACM Trans. Graph. 32*, 4 (2013), 81:1–81:10.
15. Quinn, A. J., and Bederson, B. B. Human computation: A survey and taxonomy of a growing field. In *Proc. CHI '11*, ACM (2011), 1403–1412.
16. Reinecke, K., and Gajos, K. Z. Quantifying visual preferences around the world. In *Proc. CHI '14*, ACM (2014), 11–20.
17. Reinecke, K., Yeh, T., Miratrix, L., Mardiko, R., Zhao, Y., Liu, J., and Gajos, K. Z. Predicting users' first impressions of website aesthetics with a quantification of perceived visual complexity and colorfulness. In *Proc. CHI '13*, ACM (2013), 2049–2058.
18. Sagar, M. Facial performance capture and expressive translation for king kong. In *ACM SIGGRAPH 2006 Sketches*, ACM (2006).
19. Secord, A., Lu, J., Finkelstein, A., Singh, M., and Nealen, A. Perceptual models of viewpoint preference. *ACM Trans. Graph. 30*, 5 (2011), 109:1–109:12.
20. Shapira, L., Shamir, A., and Cohen-Or, D. Image appearance exploration by model-based navigation. *Comput. Graph. Forum 28*, 2 (2009), 629–638.
21. Sorkine, O. Differential representations for mesh processing. *Comput. Graph. Forum 25*, 4 (2006), 789–807.
22. Sýkora, D., Sedlacek, D., Jinchao, S., Dingliana, J., and Collins, S. Adding depth to cartoons using sparse depth (in)equalities. *Comput. Graph. Forum 29*, 2 (2010), 615–623.
23. Talton, J. O., Gibson, D., Yang, L., Hanrahan, P., and Koltun, V. Exploratory modeling with collaborative design spaces. *ACM Trans. Graph. 28*, 5 (2009), 167:1–167:10.
24. Talton, J. O., Lou, Y., Lesser, S., Duke, J., Měch, R., and Koltun, V. Metropolis procedural modeling. *ACM Trans. Graph. 30*, 2 (Apr. 2011), 11:1–11:14.
25. Tamuz, O., Liu, C., Belongie, S., Shamir, O., and Kalai, A. Adaptively learning the crowd kernel. In *Proc. ICML '11*, ACM (2011), 673–680.
26. Terry, M., and Mynatt, E. D. Side views: Persistent, on-demand previews for open-ended tasks. In *Proc. UIST '02*, ACM (2002), 71–80.
27. Terry, M., Mynatt, E. D., Nakakoji, K., and Yamamoto, Y. Variation in element and action: Supporting simultaneous development of alternative solutions. In *Proc. CHI '04*, ACM (2004), 711–718.
28. Willett, W., Heer, J., and Agrawala, M. Scented widgets: Improving navigation cues with embedded visualizations. *IEEE Trans. Visual. Comput. Graphics 13*, 6 (2007), 1129–1136.
29. Witkin, A., and Kass, M. Spacetime constraints. *SIGGRAPH Comput. Graph. 22*, 4 (1988), 159–168.
30. Xu, A., Huang, S.-W., and Bailey, B. Voyant: Generating structured feedback on visual designs using a crowd of non-experts. In *Proc. CSCW '14*, ACM (2014), 1433–1444.

APPENDIX

Solving Minimization as a Linear Algebra

In our analysis, the system solves a minimization problem described in (4), which can be solved as a simple linear algebra. Using matrices, we can deform the formula into

$$\min_{\mathbf{y}} \left(\|\mathbf{A}\mathbf{y} - \mathbf{d}\|^2 + \omega \|\mathbf{L}\mathbf{y}\|^2 \right), \qquad (7)$$

where the first term corresponds to the relative constraint, and the second term corresponds to the continuous constraint. $\mathbf{A} \in \mathbb{R}^{M' \times M'}$ is defined as $A_{i,i} = 1, A_{i,j} = -1$ if $(i,j) \in P'$ and otherwise 0, $\mathbf{d} \in \mathbb{R}^{M'}$ is defined as $d_i = d_{i,j}$ if $(i,j) \in P'$ and otherwise 0, and $\mathbf{L}$ is the Laplacian matrix. By setting the derivative with respect to $\mathbf{y}$ to zero, we can obtain the following linear equation:

$$\left(\mathbf{A}^T \mathbf{A} + \omega \mathbf{L}^T \mathbf{L} \right) \mathbf{y} = \mathbf{A}^T \mathbf{d}. \qquad (8)$$

This provides the optimal solution of the minimization problem and could easily be solved by standard techniques such as Cholesky decomposition.

Expert Crowdsourcing with Flash Teams

Daniela Retelny, Sébastien Robaszkiewicz, Alexandra To, Walter Lasecki[*], Jay Patel, Negar Rahmati, Tulsee Doshi, Melissa Valentine, Michael S. Bernstein
Stanford University, University of Rochester[*]
{dretelny, robi, ato1120, jayhp9, negar, tdoshi, mav, msb}@cs.stanford.edu, wlasecki@cs.rochester.edu

ABSTRACT
We introduce *flash teams*, a framework for dynamically assembling and managing paid experts from the crowd. Flash teams advance a vision of expert crowd work that accomplishes complex, interdependent goals such as engineering and design. These teams consist of sequences of linked modular tasks and handoffs that can be computationally managed. Interactive systems reason about and manipulate these teams' structures: for example, flash teams can be recombined to form larger organizations and authored automatically in response to a user's request. Flash teams can also hire more people elastically in reaction to task needs, and pipeline intermediate output to accelerate completion times. To enable flash teams, we present Foundry, an end-user authoring platform and runtime manager. Foundry allows users to author modular tasks, then manages teams through handoffs of intermediate work. We demonstrate that Foundry and flash teams enable crowdsourcing of a broad class of goals including design prototyping, course development, and film animation, in half the work time of traditional self-managed teams.

Author Keywords
Crowdsourcing; expert crowd work; flash teams

ACM Classification Keywords
H.5.3 Information Interfaces and Presentation (e.g. HCI): Group and Organization Interfaces

INTRODUCTION
Crowdsourcing systems coordinate large groups of people to solve problems that a single individual could not achieve at the same scale. Microtasking systems typically use highly-controlled workflows to manage paid, non-expert workers toward expert-level results (e.g., [6, 28, 10, 25, 38]). While these crowdsourcing approaches are effective for simple independent tasks, many real-world tasks such as software development and design remain largely out of reach. Such tasks require deep domain knowledge that is difficult to decompose into independent microtasks anyone can complete [26, 42, 40]. Unlocking these capabilities is critical to the vision of universal, on-demand crowd support for end users. For example, could we enable anybody with a napkin sketch of a design idea to ask the crowd to follow the user-centered design process and create a user-tested, high-fidelity prototype of that idea within twenty-four hours?

UIST '14, October 5–8, 2014, Honolulu, HI, USA.

ACM 978-1-4503-3069-5/14/10$15.00.
http://dx.doi.org/10.1145/2642918.2647409

In this paper, we explore the feasibility of solving these complex, interdependent problems via *structured collaborations between experts from the crowd*. We aim to gather experts from online marketplaces such as oDesk [1] into small teams that can, for example, follow the user-centered design process to transform a napkin sketch into a fully user-tested prototype, create an animated movie from a prompt, or develop an entire online class platform complete with video content and quizzes — all in roughly one day.

Experts from the crowd, however, tend to work as isolated contractors, and microtask crowdsourcing techniques (e.g., [2, 30, 6, 25, 43]) cannot coordinate these experts because they do not effectively leverage participants' diverse skills and expertise. To enable end users to reliably crowdsource complex work, we take inspiration from organizational behavior research that suggests even temporary groups can coordinate complex work effectively, if they have an enabling team structure [41] to encode who is working together and who is responsible for which tasks [8, 5]. Our goal is to create such structures with far less manual effort and more scalable replicability than traditional organizations.

To achieve this goal, we frame expert crowd work around *sequences of linked tasks*. We hypothesize that these chains of focused work could maintain the coordinating strength of lightweight team structures while providing a representation that interactive systems can leverage to support collaboration, create new teams automatically, grow and shrink teams on demand, and combine teams into larger organizations.

We thus present *flash teams*, a framework for dynamically assembling and managing crowdsourced expert teams. Flash teams are a sequence of modular tasks that draw on paid experts from the crowd. Each task in a flash team requires an input (e.g., low-fidelity prototype) and produces an output of another type (e.g., heuristic evaluation). End users create workflows by linking these modular tasks together to pass each task's output as input to the next task. They then use a web application to launch and manage the team, monitoring the workflow if desired. For example, when creating a user-centered design flash team, the user might begin with a task where a UI designer creates a low-fidelity mockup of the

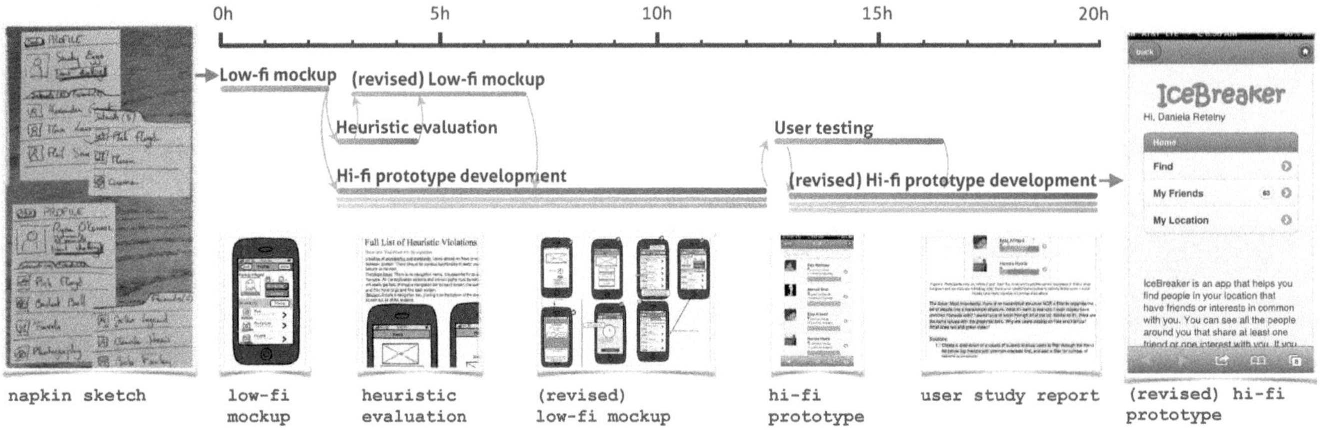

Figure 1: A flash team is a linked set of modular tasks that draw upon paid experts from the crowd, often three to six at a time, on demand. The napkin sketch design team follows the user-centered design process to create a series of prototypes and iterate based on feedback to produce a user-tested software prototype within a day. Multiple arrows indicate the beginning and end of pipelining; lighter bars indicate possible elastic growth.

user's idea. The designer would pass the mockup on to a UX researcher for a heuristic evaluation. Tasks would proceed through the chain of a revised mockup, a high-fidelity prototype, a user study and a revised software prototype, crossing diverse expertise from one or more UI designers, UX researchers, and software developers.

Flash teams' modular task structure is transparent to computational systems, enabling those systems to leverage the structure to orchestrate crowd dynamics. For example, teams can be *combined*: since teams are modular, their component tasks can be composed like Lego blocks to form larger organizations that persist only for a day or an afternoon. Moreover, by leveraging automated path search through the space of previous teams' intermediate inputs and outputs, end users can *assemble a flash team on-demand by providing only the desired input and output.* During runtime, flash teams are *elastic*: they grow and shrink to meet task demands by hiring additional members from the crowd. Finally, their work can be *pipelined*: when in-progress results are enough for downstream tasks to begin work, the system passes in-progress results along to accelerate completion times.

We embody this approach in *Foundry*, a platform for end users to create flash teams and a runtime environment to manage them. Foundry allows users to create flash teams by directly authoring each task or forking a team that other users authored and then recruit from the oDesk online labor marketplace [1]. For team members, Foundry takes on managerial responsibilities to walk team members through the workflow, notify them of any schedule shifts, scaffold the handoff process, and provide members with shared awareness [14]. For the end user, Foundry abstracts away low-level management effort while allowing for high-level oversight and guidance.

This research advances two important ideas. First, flash teams are the first to leverage the *scale of paid crowdsourcing for expert work.* This approach pushes beyond volunteer peer production systems with a vision of elastic and on-demand organizations that manage teams of paid experts from the crowd. Second, this paper offers a method of scaling expert crowd work through *computational management of an elastic workforce.* Flash teams enable complex work at crowd scale by automating the structures of traditional organizations. We introduce specific affordances such as structured handoffs, directly-responsible individuals (DRIs), and elastic growth, embedded within the Foundry platform. Empirical results from our field experiment demonstrate that flash teams can accomplish efficient and high-quality work.

RELATED WORK

In this section, we connect two threads of research: crowdsourcing and organizational behavior.

Crowdsourcing with experts

Crowdsourcing research aims to integrate large-scale, API-friendly labor marketplaces into software through open calls and task decomposition. Crowdsourcing has largely focused on tasks any individual can complete: many crowdsourcing platforms are built to accomplish tasks that require little training (e.g., Amazon Mechanical Turk) and recruit amateurs (e.g. FoldIt [10]). Consequently, most crowdsourcing workflows and algorithms [32] aim to structure non-expert contributions to produce expert-level performance. For example, MapReduce frameworks can guide crowds to write simple encyclopedia entries [25], and clustering workflows can produce expert-level taxonomies [9]. These workflows can even be authored by crowd members themselves [27]. Examples of microtask crowds pursuing expert performance include document editing [6], translation [21], and visual question answering [7]. AI techniques optimize these workflows [13]. Prior work that has gone beyond microtasks has still focused on recreating the performance of a single expert [29].

Prior work suggested that expertise might play a role in crowdsourcing [26]: flash teams instantiate a first step toward that goal. Other crowdsourcing campaigns already recruit experts, for example using workflow support tools [33] or helping solve planning problems [43]. Often these campaigns focus on a single expertise area such as math [12]. To date, these expert crowdsourcing efforts have been one-offs, needing to create an online presence to gather participants for each new goal. Our intent is to create a general approach and platform that can support a large number of tasks on demand. In doing so, we open the door to a range of higher-level workflows that can assume expert knowledge.

This work raises opportunities for platform design in expert crowdsourcing. Foundry draws inspiration from visual workflow tools [24, 27] and management tools such as Gantt charts to structure teams using a visual timeline language. It is possible to design for worker interest, honesty, and motivation (e.g., [3, 15]); Foundry thus aims to make collaborators visible and make the larger goal clear. Software concepts such as class hierarchies can integrate with business processes [34]: Foundry instantiates this vision with team structures.

Organizational behavior

Organizational behavior (OB) research has identified the obstacles to team coordination as well as the conditions and structures that enable effective team coordination. Obstacles to effective team coordination include geographic dispersion, technology-mediated communication, and fluid (or changing) team membership [39, 19, 11, 22]. These conditions impede team coordination because team members lack a shared understanding of their overall task, and each person's responsibilities within the task [36]. Because their communication is all electronically-mediated, teams also struggle to engage in the rich communication necessary to build a shared understanding [11]. Teams of experts who are pulled from the crowd will face these same obstacles in the extreme.

Foundry's design is inspired by specific OB studies that show how to support coordination under the challenging working conditions confronted by crowdsourced expert teams.

First, Foundry's composeable team structures are motivated by OB studies of the purpose and functioning of team structures. Team structures enable coordination by encoding who is responsible for what work and which team members are interdependent [8]. Even in the absence of ongoing relationships, lightweight team structures can help even relative strangers coordinate effectively, when the structures set up shared space and shared work around strictly defined work roles [41]. Second, Foundry's modular design is influenced by management modularity theory which shows how system components must be "loosely coupled" and have a standardized interface so that they can connect and interact in a variety of configurations [4]. Third, Foundry's design includes several integration mechanisms such as pipelining, structured handoffs and DRIs that address key points of coordination (which OB research shows are often neglected) [18].

We argue that for teams of crowdsourced experts to be most successful, they need to quickly understand their shared work, interdependencies and respective roles in completing that work [37]. Our aim is to provide the value of team structures, modularity, and coordinating mechanisms (as identified in OB research), but to do so in ways that leverage automation, computation, and the scale and flexibility of the crowd.

FLASH TEAMS

In this section we introduce *flash teams*, which are computationally-guided teams of crowd experts supported by lightweight, reproducible and scalable team structures. Flash teams aim to embed the techniques of high performing offline teams within a model that can take advantage of computation's ability to abstract, scale, and visualize progress. We take a position that expert crowd work can succeed via a linked set of modular tasks that interface with each other by publishing intermediate results. Each set of tasks is machine-understandable, which means that interactive systems can manage and manipulate the team structures so that flash teams can grow, adapt, and recombine into larger organizations.

Flash team composition

To structure expert crowd work, flash teams require small atomic actions called *blocks*. Each block represents one or more experts performing a task. It requires an input, instructions for what one or more members of the crowd should do, and specifies an output type (Figure 2). Blocks can then be connected to other blocks that can accept compatible inputs or outputs. Blocks aim to be self-contained so that they can be reused in other contexts. Inputs and outputs are represented as tags (e.g., `heuristic evaluation report`, `character art`, `voiceover script`, `voiceover audio files`), and any blocks that interface along the same input or output use the same tag. For example, suppose the user is building a team to execute the user-centered design process. Then, they might create a heuristic evaluation block to take `low fidelity prototype` as input and produce `heuristic evaluation report` as output. That user could then connect the heuristic evaluation block to any other block that takes `heuristic evaluation report` as input, for example a block that revises a mockup based on feedback.

Flash teams exhibit distributed leadership [33] where the user (requester) may be coordinating with different workers in each block. To avoid a diffusion of responsibility, for each block, the project requester specifies a *directly responsible individual* [31], or DRI, who takes on a temporary management position for the duration of that task. For example, if a task involves a collaboration between three software developers, one of those developers acts as the DRI and coordinates workers, brokers agreements, and ensures the task is completed on time and at high quality.

Users assemble and manage a flash team by chaining blocks like interlocking puzzle pieces to transform a starter input into a desired final output. Blocks can execute in parallel or in serial but they typically must wait on all their inputs to begin work. The complete set of blocks determines which crowd experts need to be recruited — for example, a UI designer,

Figure 2: The basic unit of a flash team is a *block*, which gathers one or more paid experts from the crowd to perform a focused task. Blocks can be connected via shared inputs and outputs.

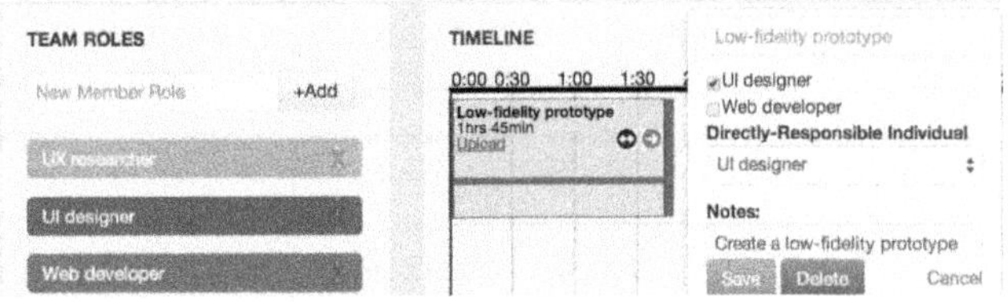

Figure 3: Foundry allows end users to author and manage flash teams. In authoring mode, the user can specify the expertise for each block and enter details about each block's requirements.

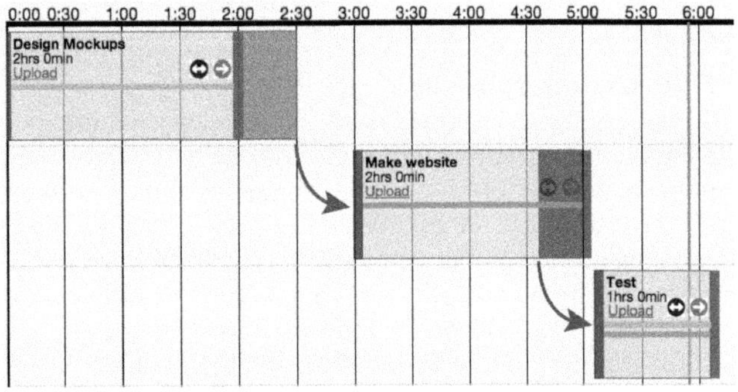

Figure 4: Foundry's runtime mode: the design mockups finished 30 minutes late but implementation finished early. The current user test block, marked by a red playhead, involves both (orange and green) experts.

UX researcher, and two software engineers — and when they are likely to be needed.

Foundry. Foundry (Figures 3–4) functions as both a flash team authoring environment with strongly typed handoffs and support for diverse expertise, and a runtime management platform. Users add blocks to the timeline as they would on a calendaring interface. Each block requires a title, a target length of time, input and output type tags, a description of the task (ideally with an example), and one or more of roughly 2,500 skills available on oDesk. To accelerate team creation, and based on an observation that many teams share some components, Foundry makes available a library of all blocks that previous teams have used for drag-and-drop. With Foundry, therefore, the requester can create new workflows from scratch using the library of task modules, fork a previously created workflow, or use Foundry's planner to formulate a workflow.

Most coordination between team members occurs via input/output handoffs. Foundry focuses the user on explicitly marking handoffs via arrows that connect tasks: this helps make dependencies visible. When each block is complete, worker(s) upload the output materials for their block to the team's shared folder, which Foundry automatically creates in Google Drive. When two blocks occur at the same time (e.g., a logo design block should be coordinating with the homepage layout block), users indicate that the blocks should be in synchronous collaboration.

Runtime and coordination

Users either author a team from scratch, or borrow from a list of existing teams and edit or run them. Workers are recruited from oDesk using the skills described in the blocks. oDesk provides a worker rating system that makes filtering relatively simple. We have recruited workers for teams in as little as fifteen minutes, and this number could decrease as such platforms become more popular and optimized. When the user is happy with their team, they launch the team by clicking "Start" in the Foundry interface. Foundry switches to runtime mode and adds a timer playhead that starts advancing along the timeline on the first block. Each worker receives a unique link that logs them in to the Foundry runtime with their tasks highlighted in the timeline.

Foundry embeds the basic affordances of computer-supported cooperative work systems for distributed teams. While the flash team is working, Foundry's goal is to remove the requester from as much management responsibility as possible by leveraging what it knows about the flash team's structure. Requesters can monitor progress, provide feedback, and answer questions through the chat. They can also pause the process, tweak the team structure and resume.

Foundry always displays the overall progress through the timeline, the currently active block details, and when the logged-in worker's next task begins. When a worker marks a block as complete, Foundry notifies workers for the next blocks that their task is active. Additionally, Foundry maintains awareness through a chat window that allows workers to coordinate out-of-band and the user to provide feedback on the process as it occurs.

It is not uncommon for teams to require tweaks as they go: for example, a task may finish early or run late. If a task finishes early, Foundry recalculates the starting times for all downstream tasks and emails all impacted workers with a new estimated start time for their next task. Likewise, if a task runs late, Foundry emails the DRI with a link to a form that requests the estimated time to completion. When the worker fills out the form, downstream tasks are again recalculated and workers are notified of the new start times.

Computationally-enhanced flash teams

Computation can leverage the machine-readable workflow representation of flash teams. For example, we can use a block's output tag to recommend a list of blocks that use the same tag as an input. In this section, we introduce mechanisms for Foundry to react, optimize and author flash teams on demand.

Modular combinations of teams

Because the blocks are modular and have clear boundaries, flash teams can be *combined* to create larger organizations. Entire teams can be abstracted into a block, much like one function in a computer program might contain many other function calls inside it. For example, to create a new platform for a massive open online course (MOOC), one flash team might combine several teams that can design and implement software with additional teams that can develop educational materials and animated videos. Each team might be forked from previously used teams in Foundry and tweaked for the particular needs of the project.

Through combination, users can create not just teams but the equivalent of entire small organizations for an afternoon or a day. These combinations draw on the elastic nature of the crowd by instantiating multiple copies of a flash team, and multiple types of teams, with little downtime.

Path search support for team authoring

So far, Foundry assumes that end users are fluent with creating teams (e.g., authoring tasks and handoffs). Most people, however, are neither natural programmers nor managers. Instead, they have a goal in mind that they want to accomplish, but may not have a strong idea of how it might get completed.

For example, suppose a user wanted to embed themselves as a character in their favorite video game. The user might have no experience with art or video game modding, but have a `photograph` of themselves and knows that they want a `3D model` to replace the default game avatar with. Using this, the system explores the set of existing teams and realizes that the `photograph` can be used as `source material` for a fashion designer from a theatre production task who creates a `clothing sketch` according to the world's style. The `photograph` and `clothing sketch` can then be passed to an illustrator from an eBook task, who in turn creates a `2D drawing` of character art. The `2D drawing` is then used by a 3D modeling expert originally from a product mock-up team to create a `3D model` which can be imported into the game.

By leveraging blocks' shared input/output tags, Foundry can search through the space of novel team combinations. If the user knows what they want, they can tell Foundry their starter input (e.g., `character sketch`) from the list of previously-observed tags and the output they want (e.g., `3D model`). If there is a path through the known blocks that can solve the user's problem, Foundry will find it using an AI planner. The resulting teams are not whole components of previous teams, but subsets of blocks from many other teams that come together to enable a new goal. The user can review the team to ensure that all team blocks make sense in this new context.

This team was automatically generated on demand to fill in details that the user may not have been able to specify themselves. The members of the team were not drawn from prior teams with a focus on video games, but Foundry identified that previous blocks shared an input/output vocabulary and could thus interface with each other. It brought them together to effectively complete the desired task.

Because of teams' modularity, the number of possible teams grows combinatorially with the number of teams seen by the system. Foundry thus uses a planning algorithm to find a set of blocks that connect from original input to final output, if such a path exists. We represent all known blocks in the STRIPS planning language [17]. Each block becomes a STRIPS action with all required inputs combined via a logical conjunction as the precondition, and all outputs listed as postconditions. An automated planner searches through transitions that connect a given starting state to a desired end state in order to find the shortest path. The general planning problem is NP-complete; however, boolean satisfiability solvers can scale these systems to thousands of actions [23].

Elasticity

Simple workflows cannot react to changing requirements: for example, a project may require additional help or a new skill. Because crowdsourcing platforms allow quick recruitment, the crowd can be an *elastic* resource, allowing teams to grow and shrink as needed. Elastic growth allows a single team abstraction to encompass a wide variety of actual runtime needs.

To enable elastic flash teams, the user specifies growth parameters for a block. The block may, for example, now allow up to two additional experts to join this task. If the user or the DRI feel that growth would be helpful, they can request the expansion and the user can approve it. One type of elasticity is replication: for example, the DRI for a software development task may ask for an additional developer to help accomplish the job on time. The second type of elasticity is specialization: if a team needs a specific skill, the DRI could recruit a team member with that skill (e.g., logo design). For instance, in one of the design teams, the team requested a Facebook API expert because the application required it. Users need to balance the temptation of growing a team against the increased coordination costs of larger groups.

Pipelining

Flash teams have been described as blocking operations: downstream tasks must wait for upstream tasks to complete before they can start. However, in many scenarios, early results may be enough for a downstream task to begin.

Flash teams can thus be *pipelined* by streaming intermediate results as they are ready, rather waiting for the entire task to complete. To pipeline a handoff, the user indicates that a block can stream its output — for example, that the heuristic evaluation block can stream each violation as the worker identifies them. The user also indicates that the downstream task can accept streamed results — for example, that the revision of the low-fidelity mockup can fix each violation as it arrives. The DRI for the upstream block uses Foundry to indicate when the task is ready to start streaming, and Foundry launches the downstream task.

Pipelining has two beneficial effects: less waiting and increased collaboration. There is a risk that downstream tasks might need to change course when they see more of the input, but in our experience pipelining scenarios allow team members to work productively in parallel. In addition, instead of communicating through a single handoff, pipelining encourages synchronous feedback between team members, reducing the risk of communication failures or misunderstandings.

EXAMPLE FLASH TEAMS

In this section, we present several flash teams and their results. We demonstrate how flash teams execute complex and creative tasks beyond the reach of paid microtasking and surpass the capabilities of traditional organizations via their scalable and flexible structure.

Napkin Sketch Design Team

Rapid iteration is a core tenet of the user-centered design process, and prototyping many ideas in parallel leads to improved design outcomes [16]. Flash teams could enable a designer to generate many ideas as sketches in a notebook, then get them prototyped in parallel — from low-fidelity prototypes, through a heuristic evaluation and live user testing, to

Task	Type of Team	Roles	Time [*hh:mm*]	Median Wage	Total Cost
Happily App	Napkin Sketch	UX, UI, Dev	31:30	$26.85	$744.48
Eventick App	Napkin Sketch	UX, UI, Dev1, Dev2, Dev3	18:00	$28.78	$1,270.28
Icebreaker App	Napkin Sketch	UI, UX1, UX2, Dev1, Dev2	23:10	$31.38	$1,200.97
Animation	Animation	Director, Voiceover, Animator, Illustrator, Scriptwriter	44:40	$56.94	$2,381.32
Diaphragm MOOC	Education Content, Animation	Education, Content, Director, Animator, Actor, Voiceover	19:20	$30.14	$1,597.32
Photography MOOC	Education Content, Animation	Education, Content, Director, Animator, Actor, Voiceover	19:00	$21.77	$741.58
Tower of Hanoi MOOC	Education Content, Animation	Education, Content, Director, Animator, Voiceover	11:30	$18.52	$446.49
MOOC Platform	Napkin Sketch 1, Napkin Sketch 2, Napkin Sketch 3	UX1, UI1, Dev1, UX2, UI2, Dev2, UX3, UI3, Dev3	13:00	$29.14	$1,015.80

Table 1: Eight flash teams created mobile web applications, video animations, and an online course platform with three courses.

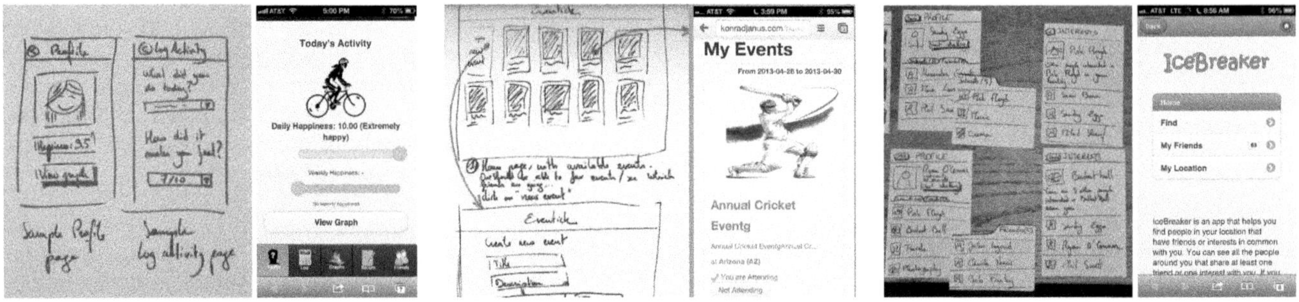

(a) Happily, an emotion-tracking site. (b) Eventick, a local event billboard site. (c) Icebreaker: a local social network site.

Figure 5: Sketched inputs and high-fidelity prototype results from the napkin sketch design teams. This team iterates from a sketch through low fidelity prototypes to produce a working, user-tested software prototype within a day.

an iterated high-fidelity prototype — in less than a day. This rapid, parallel cycle could allow end users to quickly iterate toward high-quality ideas.

The *napkin sketch design team* carries out the entire user-centered design process starting from a napkin sketch of the idea by combining techniques from HCI practice. Rather than acting as a turn-crank design solution or replacing designer insight, it enables designers to experiment and reflect on ideas quickly. The complete napkin sketch design team blocks are:

- *Low-fidelity prototype.* Produce a mockup of the sketched interface using a low-fidelity wireframing tool. Input: `napkin sketch`. Output: `low-fi mockup`. Role: UI designer. Target time: 2.5hr.
- *Heuristic evaluation.* Report the violations of Nielsen's heuristics for a design. Input: `low-fi mockup OR high-fi prototype`. Output: `heuristic evaluation`. Role: UX researcher. Target time: 2hr. Can pipeline output.
- *Revised low-fidelity prototype.* Iterate on a mockup based on usability feedback. Input: `low-fi mockup AND (heuristic evaluation OR user study report)`. Output: `low-fi mockup`. Role: UI designer. Target time: 4hr. Can pipeline input.
- *Software prototype.* Create a hosted, high-fidelity web prototype to instantiate a mockup design. Input: `low-fi mockup`. Output: `high-fi prototype`. Role: Web developer (elastic 1-3).
- *User study.* Run at least three users through a prototype and create a document that summarizes the results and recommendations. Input: `high-fi prototype OR low-fi mockup`. Output: `user study report`. Role: UX researcher. Can pipeline output.
- *Revised software prototype.* Fix problems with the prototype that were identified by the user study. Input: `high-fi prototype AND user study report`. Output: `high-fi prototype`. Role: Web developer (elastic 1-3). Can pipeline input.

Depending on whether the same workers participate in multiple blocks or new workers come online for each step, this team involves three to ten experts in UI design, UX research and web programming.

We ran the napkin sketch design team three times with inputs of varying complexity, all for prototypes of mobile web applications (Figure 5). We obtained the original application ideas and sketches from actual student projects in an Introduction to HCI course. The first design sketch was for Happily, a web application that helps users track their happiness throughout the day. The second was for Eventick, a mobile application where users can post local events and hear about events in their area. The third was for Icebreaker, a social networking site to help users find nearby individuals with common interests. These prototypes each contained roughly four working pages, a database backend, and content-specific requirements (e.g., Facebook API integration for Icebreaker).

Each flash team took advantage of more of flash teams' computational support than the previous iteration. Happily used a basic, sequential workflow, where one task occurred at a time and the next task could not begin until the previous one was completed. Eventick enabled pipelining: both heuristic evaluation and development began as soon as the first version of the mockup was complete. It also enabled elastic growth for replication, allowing the web development block to grow from one to three developers. Icebreaker was the most complex, enabling elastic growth for specialization: the DRI developer hired a developer specialized in Facebook API integration, and the team brought on a designer to create a logo for the homepage. Icebreaker also pipelined the user study results into the revised software prototype block.

These flash teams completed their prototypes in as little as eighteen hours of active work (Table 1). Workers were typically paid $25–$30 per hour, and costs ranged from roughly $750 to $1270 for up to five participants. The prototypes strongly reflected the designs articulated in the original napkin sketches, and many major design and usability problems had been ironed out through the heuristic evaluation and user study revisions. The initial napkin sketches and final prototypes are shown in Figure 5. We did not optimize the team to hand off across timezones, so actual wall clock time was often longer as team members needed to sleep and take breaks.

Animation Team

A quick review of YouTube videos is enough to realize that many people who have excellent ideas are not quite so excellent at communicating them. Unfortunately, for most of these people, hiring an expensive firm to bring their ideas to fruition is the only alternative. The animation flash team aims to make high quality video animations more broadly accessible. It also exercises flash teams in a creative, non-engineering domain. The animation team takes a high-level script outline as input and produces a short animated movie as output. The core blocks of the animation team (Figure 6) included:

- *Script.* Write the video script. Input: `script idea`. Output: `script`. Roles: director, scriptwriter. Target time: 2hr.
- *Storyboard.* Use the script to create a shot-by-shot storyboard for the video. Input: `script`. Output: `storyboard`. Roles: director, animator. Target time: 2hr.
- *Character design.* Design the characters' visual appearance and develop their art assets. Input: `script`. Output: `character assets`. Role: illustrator (elastic 1-3). Target time: 4hr. Can pipeline output (draft/final designs).
- *Character animation.* Import and animate character assets from the storyboard. Input: `storyboard AND character assets`. Output: `animation character layer`. Role: animator (elastic 1-3). Target time: 7hr. Can pipeline input.

To develop the flash team structure, we collaborated with a movie director from oDesk. The animation flash team consists of five roles: director, scriptwriter, illustrator, animator, and voiceover artist. Unlike the decentralized leadership of the napkin sketch team, the director role participates actively across the entire workflow. In the animation team we ran, the task was to create an animation that captures a memory from HCI researcher Terry Winograd's early life, where Terry builds a computer in his garage (Figure 7).

Education team

While many people step into the role of teacher at times, most do so without aid or feedback from trained educators. In addition, while the web can teach a wide variety of concepts, there are always concepts that are not well covered or not explained clearly where a user might want some explanation. The education flash team allows anyone to generate a short curriculum to learn a topic. It takes as input the educational goal (e.g., "teach the basic mechanics of singing from the diaphragm") and outputs a script that teaches the subject and multiple-choice test questions to self-test the content. The main blocks of the education team are:

- *Script.* Brainstorm and write out a script for the lesson. Input: `lesson idea`. Output: `lesson script`. Roles: educator, topic area expert. Target time: 3hr.
- *Quiz.* Generate a quiz based on the content of the lesson script. Input: `lesson script`. Output: `lesson quiz`. Roles: educator, topic area expert. Target time: 1hr.
- *Entertainment value script improvements.* Edit the script so it is as engaging as possible. Input: `lesson script`. Output: `edited script`. Role: director. Target time: 1hr.

The team draws together three sets of skills: expertise in the topic area of the lesson, curriculum development, and multimedia direction. The director takes a final pass over the script to ensure that it is as engaging as possible.

An example script snippet from a flash team generating a lesson on singing from the diaphragm: *"When you breathe in, or inhale, your back muscles engage and expand. At the same time, your diaphragm lowers so your lungs can expand."*

Composite team: online course platform

The napkin sketch, animation and education teams are relatively focused in their goals. Could flash teams enable users to pursue more ambitious goals that combine multiple domains of expertise? Flash teams' modularity promises to allow for organizations composed of many smaller teams.

We created a composite flash team that combined and replicated all three other teams. Its goal was to create a prototype platform for online education of long-tail skills such as photographing portraits, singing from the diaphragm and solving the Tower of Hanoi puzzle (Figure 8).

The composite team used abstracted versions of existing teams as single blocks, then tweaked their outputs and inputs. The blocks of the composite team included:

- *Homepage.* Design homepage for the site. Input: `napkin sketch`. Output: `high-fi prototype (homepage) AND design language`. Roles: napkin sketch team. Target time: 12hr. Can pipeline output (design language).
- *Class page.* Design the page to display a course. Input: `design language AND napkin sketch`. Output: `high-fi prototype (course)`. Roles: napkin sketch team. Target time: 12hr. Can pipeline input (design language).
- *Course content.* Write a script and quiz for the video. Input: `lesson idea`. Output: `multimedia-edited script`. Roles: education team. Target time: 4hr.
- *Course video.* Produce the video for the lesson. Input: `multimedia-edited script`. Output: `animation`. Roles: animation team. Target time: 16hr.

This team was composed of nine flash teams: three napkin sketch teams to create the three pages of the site, three education teams to write the video scripts and quizzes, and three animation teams to produce the videos. The first napkin sketch

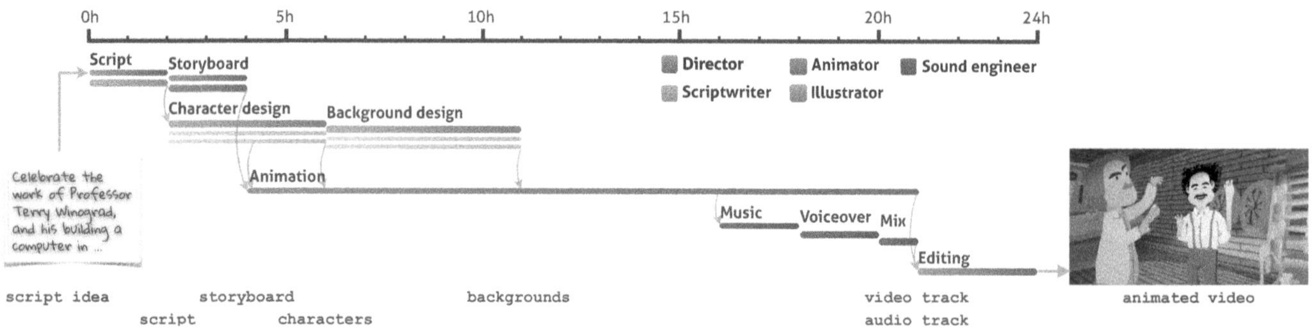

Figure 6: The workflow for the animation flash team, which takes a high-level script outline as input and produces a short animated movie as output.

Figure 7: The animation team produced a short movie of a young Terry Winograd building a computer in his garage.

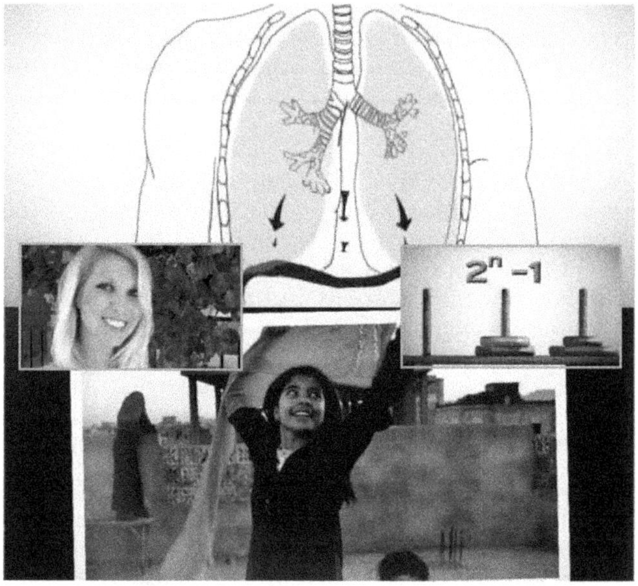

Figure 8: Course videos: singing from the diagram (top), portrait photography (left and bottom), and the Towers of Hanoi puzzle (right).

team pipelined the site design language. The nine teams created the platform and three interactive lessons in *19 hours and 20 minutes* of active work for a budget of $3,801.19 (Table 1). Wall clock time was longer because not all teams began simultaneously. The talent for the singing video included a professional singer from the Frankfurt Opera.

FIELD EXPERIMENT

This paper claims that flash teams enable expert crowd members to come together and complete complex, interdependent tasks in short periods of time. We conducted a controlled experiment to compare flash teams to a self-managed team approach where Foundry brings together the crowd experts and lets them choose their own path. To minimize costs, we focused on collecting data with a small number (3) of teams in each condition, totaling 22 crowd experts.

Method

We recruited six napkin sketch design teams from oDesk by requesting workers with expertise in UI design, UX research, and web application development. Teams were assigned to either the flash team or the control condition, resulting in a total of three teams in each condition. We used the same job postings on oDesk, recruitment process and task for the teams in both conditions. To keep conditions comparable, the same set of Foundry features was available, including a shared folder via Google Drive and a chat window.

To recruit the experts, we conducted brief filtering interviews and accepted applicants with high ratings. All workers were paid their profile's hourly wage. Members of each team had a median of at least 250 working hours on oDesk and ratings over 4.2 out of 5 stars (average 4.66/5). We randomized the 22 workers into teams and tasked them with creating a simple party planning task manager from an input sketch that would allow end users to add, edit and complete tasks. We asked all teams to follow the user-centered design process and requested that the final mobile web app be completed within 13 hours.

The main difference between the two conditions was the existence of the flash team workflow, whose presence indicated a path to the team members, and allowed Foundry to support coordination via handoffs and notifications. For the flash team condition, Foundry clearly specified each block and the details associated with it, including the duration, team member, DRI, input and output. This enabled Foundry's support for handoffs, task status, time until next task, and email noti-

Condition	Roles	Work Time [*hh:mm*]	Wall Clock [*hh:mm*]	Median Wage	Total Cost
Flash	UI, UX1, UX2, Dev	11:02	17:16	$18.00	$211.78
Flash	UI, UX, Dev	13:52	24:10	$22.22	$364.80
Flash	UI1, UI2, UX1, UX2, Dev	14:13	23:51	$14.45	$215.58
Control	UI, UX, Dev1, Dev2	14:30	37:03	$25.00	$322.22
Control	UI, UX, Dev	29:20	12:24	$16.67	$612.79
Control	UI, UX, Dev	27:30	37:01	$12.00	$430.59

Table 2: Time and cost comparison for the flash and control teams. On average, flash teams took half as many work hours than control teams.

fications. In contrast, for the control condition, the workflow on Foundry consisted of one long task and did not provide any details or information on how to complete it. This team was allowed to self-manage and make their own plan to complete the work in 13 hours.

Once each project started, we monitored the chat on Foundry to make sure the team was working and answer any questions that came up. We were equally responsive to the progress and questions of the experimental and control teams. If a team member left, we hired a replacement on oDesk immediately. Though we told teams to complete in 13 hours, we allowed teams as much time as they needed to complete the task.

Results

While all six of the teams completed the task and their applications were above-bar for quality, the flash teams took roughly *half as many work hours*, followed the iterative design process more closely, and required less coordination.

By active work time, even the *slowest* flash team completed the task faster than the *fastest* team in the control condition. As shown in Table 2, the cumulative number of hours worked for the flash teams ranged from 11hr2min to 14hr13min (mean = 13hr2min) and had little variance across teams (SD = 1hr45min). This small variance was consistent across all blocks: the average standard deviation across the six blocks' completion times was twelve minutes. In contrast, the cumulative number of hours worked for control teams ranged from 14hr30min to 29hr20min (mean = 23hr47min) and had tremendous variation (SD = 8hr5min). A one-tailed permutation test to compare the completion times in the two conditions was significant ($p = 0.05$), confirming that flash teams are significantly more efficient than self-managed teams of crowd experts. Wall clock time did not always align with total work time, since workers would sleep or take breaks.

The control teams took longer than the flash teams to finish each role's tasks (Table 3). The control teams spent 2.4x the time on UI Design, 1.9x the time on UX Research and 1.4x the time on Development, resulting in an additional 10hr44min in cumulative work. In observing the teams, we noted that team members would often invent work to do while waiting for a collaborator to finish a task. This overeager behavior, which we term *busy waiting*, particularly affected team members such as UI Design who had fewer hours of work that were officially required of them.

By following the sequence of modular tasks on Foundry, flash teams followed the iterative design process more closely than

Role	Flash Team [*hh:mm*]	Control Team [*hh:mm*]
UI Design	2:59 (σ=0:55)	7:20 (σ=3:39)
UX Research	3:42 (σ=0:33)	7:07 (σ=2:52)
Development	6:21 (σ=0:46)	9:20 (σ=2:01)
Total	**13:02 (σ=1:45)**	**23:47 (σ=8:05)**

Table 3: Average work time by role for the flash and control teams. The flash teams finished the tasks for each role faster than the control teams.

the control teams. In theory, since the self-managed teams weren't restricted to a precise workflow, they could have iterated more times than the flash teams. However, these teams produced fewer, if any, iterations on the mockups or developed web app. The control teams inefficiently decomposed the tasks, combining separate tasks into a single task (such as performing the heuristic evaluation and user testing on the same mockup) and in the wrong sequence (for example, the summative user testing was executed on the low-fidelity mockup, and the software prototype was never evaluated).

The flash teams required less coordination than the control teams and were more able to take advantage of on-demand recruiting from the crowd. The control teams' success was largely dependent on individuals' project management skills. For example, one of the control teams did not coordinate at all and found the experience extremely frustrating. Another control team adopted a fully interdependent workflow in which the experts treated Foundry as a collaborative war room environment [35] and established social and informational awareness to support their coordination efforts [37]; they all worked together to produce a high-quality outcome at great financial cost. When workers disappeared due to other commitments, flash teams were robust and could reach out to the crowd for a replacement quickly. In contrast, when members of one of the control teams quit (in multiple occurrences, they grew too frustrated with the experience and left), the entire team's performance suffered. When one of the developers was replaced, for example, the new developer had to start from scratch and was forced to work on his own since the other team members had disappeared by that point.

DISCUSSION AND FUTURE WORK

Flash teams enable users to gather and coordinate paid experts from the crowd to complete complex and interdependent tasks quickly and reliably. Rather than try to recreate the strengths of in-person expert teams, this approach suggests a "beyond being there" vision of expert crowd work [20]. In particular, flash teams afford dynamic recruitment and coordination of on-demand expertise that is extremely difficult in offline scenarios. Problems that might have plagued such teams, such as last minute dropouts, are relatively straightforward to solve in crowd work because another person can join on demand. Furthermore, flash teams can take advantage of timezone differences that could potentially allow them to carry on uninterruptedly for days or weeks.

Flash teams move beyond the typical conception of crowdsourcing as collecting multiple viewpoints on a single question. Rather than treating the crowd as redundant resources that cannot be fully trusted, flash teams view the crowd as an elastic, on-demand set of diverse and high-quality participants. The result is that flash teams often aim to gather experts with *different expertise* rather than redundant viewpoints. Even more ambitiously, flash teams can be combined to create new types of organizations with completely fluid boundaries — organizations that are composed of many smaller flash teams, each of which are spun up on demand, work in parallel, and disperse when complete.

Flash teams also have several important limits, which we intend to address in future work. While our controlled evaluation of flash teams was limited to napkin sketch design teams, in the future we plan to test other types of flash teams to better understand the types of tasks flash teams are well suited for. Furthermore, similar to traditional collocated and distributed teams, flash teams experience difficulties related to coordination and conflict. During informal interviews after the tasks were completed, flash team members indicated that they enjoyed working as a team, but wanted the opportunity to build more camaraderie — some members would finish their task and then just leave. One approach to improving team motivation would be to allow workers to find trusted colleagues and join into clusters that can be hired together.

It will be important for follow-on evaluations to compare flash teams to the same teams when led by project managers. Our current objective was to test flash teams against self-managing teams, which are the equally scalable alternative and therefore theoretically relevant for our paper. Research in organizational behavior has shown that self-managing teams are prevalent and effective. However, it is likely that many teams in future environments may want to consider human managers, which is a worthwhile tradeoff to understand.

Given that teams do not always go according to plan, future work should also explore issues related to runtime course correction and dispute resolution. When this happened in practice, the flash team tended to work within the existing task structure to resolve the issue. However, Foundry could provide more built-in support for veering off the path if the user allows it, or even algorithmic guides that allow for branching or looping. In addition, flash teams have disagreements like any other team. In one case, miscommunication and disagreement about artistic direction provoked a heated argument between experts on the animation team, causing the director to fire the illustrator and find a replacement.

Currently, the recruitment of each flash team requires a vetting process on oDesk to pre-clear a set of workers who are high-quality and available at the desired time. However, platforms such as oDesk are moving toward more automated hiring procedures. We envision a future where a user could request an expert for a given wage and quality, the platform mediates to provide one either algorithmically or through crowdsourcing consultants. In the meantime, Foundry could build up lists of trusted experts for each flash team structure in order to provide a quick and trusted recruiting experience.

In the future, the crowd scale of flash teams could enable end users to make more data-driven decisions about collaboration and work, and empower the scientific study of teams. As the same flash team gets run multiple times, Foundry could display estimates for how long tasks tend to take in practice. Likewise, Foundry raises the opportunity to randomly perturb team structures at scale to run field experiments and A/B test collaboration structures.

CONCLUSION

This paper offers a vision of how computation and crowdsourcing can shape the future of creative, engineering, and analytical work. We introduce flash teams, which are linked sequences of modular goals for crowd experts that can be represented and interpreted by interactive systems. Flash teams benefit from computational authoring: end users can combine modular team elements to create larger organizations and generate teams on request through automated path search. Flash teams also benefit from computational management: they can grow and shrink on demand via elastic recruitment and pipeline results to accelerate completion times. Offline organizations can embed similar techniques into traditional teams, but flash teams open the door to doing so at a much larger scale than previously.

Flash teams offer an opportunity to shift the paid crowdsourcing narrative in both research and practice. Rather than aiming for redundant, independent judgments, flash teams envision a future of crowdsourcing with dynamic collaborations of diverse and interdependent participants. This future would enable traditional organizations to become far more reactive: a few end users with an idea, for example, could temporarily augment their team on demand as the need for certain skills and expertise becomes apparent. Ultimately, we aim to enable experts and amateurs alike to contribute skills they enjoy, on a set of tasks that they find interesting, and at a scale we are just beginning to glimpse.

ACKNOWLEDGMENTS

Thank you to the oDesk workers who participated. This research was supported by the National Science Foundation under grant no. 1351131, the Hasso Plattner Design Thinking Research Program, the Precourt Energy Efficiency Center, and oDesk.

REFERENCES

1. oDesk. URL `www.odesk.com`.
2. Ahmad, S., Battle, A., Malkani, Z., and Kamvar, S. The jabberwocky programming environment for structured social computing. *Proc. UIST '11*, 2011.
3. Antin, J. and Shaw, A. Social desirability bias and self-reports of motivation: a cross-cultural study of Amazon Mechanical Turk in the US and India. *Proc. CHI '12*, 2012.
4. Baldwin, C.Y. and Clark, K.B. Managing in an age of modularity. *Harvard Business Review*, 75(5):84–93, 1997.
5. Bechky, B.A. Gaffers, gofers, and grips: role-based coordination in temporary organizations. *Organization Science*, 17(1):3–21, 2006.
6. Bernstein, M.S., et al. Soylent: a word processor with a crowd inside. *Proc. UIST '10*, 2010.

7. Bigham, J.P., et al. VizWiz: nearly real-time answers to visual questions. *Proc. UIST '10*, 2010.
8. Bunderson, J.S. and Boumgarden, P. Structure and learning in self-managed teams: why bureaucratic teams can be better learners. *Organization Science*, 21(3):609–624, 2010.
9. Chilton, L.B., et al. Cascade: crowdsourcing taxonomy creation. *Proc. CHI '13*, 2013.
10. Cooper, S., et al. Predicting protein structures with a multiplayer online game. *Nature*, 466(7307):756–760, 2010.
11. Cramton, C.D. The mutual knowledge problem and its consequences for dispersed collaboration. *Organization Science*, 12(3):346–371, 2001.
12. Cranshaw, J. and Kittur, A. The polymath project: lessons from a successful online collaboration in mathematics. *Proc. CHI '11*, 2011.
13. Dai, P., Mausam, and Weld, D. Decision-theoretic control of crowd-sourced workflows. *Proc. AAAI '10*, 2010.
14. Dourish, P. and Bellotti, V. Awareness and coordination in shared workspaces. *Proc. CSCW '92*, 1992.
15. Dow, S., Kulkarni, A., Klemmer, S., and Hartmann, B. Shepherding the crowd yields better work. *Proc. CSCW '12*, 2012.
16. Dow, S.P., et al. Parallel prototyping leads to better design results, more divergence, and increased self-efficacy. *TOCHI*, 17(4):18, 2010.
17. Fikes, R.E. and Nilsson, N.J. STRIPS: A new approach to the application of theorem proving to problem solving. *Artificial intelligence*, 2(3):189–208, 1972.
18. Heath, C. and Staudenmayer, N. Coordination neglect: how lay theories of organizing complicate coordination in organizations. *Research in Organizational Behavior*, 22:153–191, 2000.
19. Hinds, P., Liu, L., and Lyon, J. Putting the global in global work: an intercultural lens on the practice of cross-national collaboration. *The Academy of Management Annals*, 5(1):135–188, 2011.
20. Hollan, J. and Stornetta, S. Beyond being there. *Proc. CHI '92*, 1992.
21. Hu, C., Bederson, B.B., Resnik, P., and Kronrod, Y. Monotrans2: A new human computation system to support monolingual translation. *Proc. CHI '11*, 2011.
22. Huckman, R.S., Staats, B.R., and Upton, D.M. Team familiarity, role experience, and performance: evidence from Indian software services. *Management Science*, 55(1):85–100, 2009.
23. Kautz, H.A., Selman, B., and Others. Planning as satisfiability. *Proc. ECAI '92*, 1992.
24. Kittur, A., Khamkar, S., André, P., and Kraut, R.E. CrowdWeaver: visually managing complex crowd work. *Proc. CSCW '12*, 2012.
25. Kittur, A., Smus, B., Khamkar, S., and Kraut, R.E. Crowdforge: crowdsourcing complex work. *Proc. UIST '11*, 2011.
26. Kittur, A., et al. The future of crowd work. *Proc. CSCW '13*, 2013.
27. Kulkarni, A., Can, M., and Hartmann, B. Collaboratively crowdsourcing workflows with turkomatic. *Proc. CSCW '12*, 2011.
28. Lasecki, W., et al. Real-time captioning by groups of non-experts. *Proc. UIST '12*, 2012.
29. Lasecki, W.S., et al. Real-time crowd control of existing interfaces. *Proc. UIST '11*, 2011.
30. Lasecki, W.S., et al. Chorus: a crowd-powered conversational assistant. *Proc. UIST '13*, 2013.
31. Lashinsky, A. *Inside Apple*. Hachette Book Group, New York, 2012.
32. Little, G., Chilton, L., Goldman, M., and Miller, R.C. Exploring iterative and parallel human computation processes. *Proc. HCOMP '10*, 2010.
33. Luther, K., Fiesler, C., and Bruckman, A. Redistributing leadership in online creative collaboration. *Proc. CSCW '13*, 2013.
34. Malone, T.W., Crowston, K., and Herman, G.A. *Organizing Business Knowledge: The MIT Process Handbook*. MIT Press, Cambridge, MA, USA, 2003.
35. Mark, G. Extreme collaboration. *Communications of the ACM*, 45(6):89–93, 2002.
36. Mathieu, J.E., et al. The influence of shared mental models on team process and performance. *Journal of Applied Psychology*, 85(2):273–83, 2000.
37. Nardi, B.A. and Whittaker, S. The place of face-to-face communication in distributed work. In P.J. Hinds and S. Kiesler (editors), *Distributed Work*, pp. 83–113. MIT Press, Cambridge, 2002.
38. Noronha, J., Hysen, E., Zhang, H., and Gajos, K.Z. Platemate: crowdsourcing nutritional analysis from food photographs. *Proc. UIST '11*, 2011.
39. Olson, G. and Olson, J. Distance Matters. *Human-Computer Interaction*, 15(2):139–178, 2000.
40. Stol, K.J. and Fitzgerald, B. Researching crowdsourcing software development: perspectives and concerns. *ICSE '14 Workshop on Crowdsourcing in Software Engineering*, 2014.
41. Valentine, M. Team scaffolds: how minimal in-group structures support fast-paced teaming. *Academy of Management Proceedings*, 2012.
42. Yu, L. and Nickerson, J.V. Cooks or cobblers? Crowd creativity through combination. *Proc. CHI '11*, 2011.
43. Zhang, H., et al. Human computation tasks with global constraints. *Proc. CHI '12*, 2012.

Creating Interactive Web Data Applications with Spreadsheets

Kerry Shih-Ping Chang and Brad A. Myers
Human-Computer Interaction Institute
Carnegie Mellon University
Pittsburgh, PA 15213 USA
{kerrychang, bam}@cs.cmu.edu

ABSTRACT
While more and more data are available through web services, it remains difficult for end-users to create web applications that make use of these data without having to write complex code. We present Gneiss, a live programming environment that extends the spreadsheet metaphor to support creating interactive web applications that dynamically use local and web data from multiple sources. Gneiss closely integrates a spreadsheet editor with a web interface builder to let users demonstrate bindings between properties of web GUI elements and cells in the spreadsheet while working with real web service data. The spreadsheet editor provides two-way connections to web services, to both visualize and retrieve different data based on the user input in the web interface. Gneiss achieves rich interactivity without the need for event-based programming by extending the "pull model" of formulas that is familiar to the spreadsheet users. We use a series of examples to demonstrate Gneiss's ability to create a variety of interactive web data applications.

Author Keywords
Spreadsheets; web applications; web services; mashups; end-user programming; live programming

ACM Classification Keywords
D.2.2. Software engineering: Design tools and techniques – User interfaces; D.2.6. Software engineering: Programming environments – Graphical environments

INTRODUCTION
Many websites and mobile applications that people use daily are *web data applications* – applications that use backend data, supporting the searching, sorting, filtering and visualizing of the data based on the user input. For example, Yelp lets users search for restaurants and apply filters to show only the ones that accept credit cards. Expedia lets users search for hotels, sort the results by price, and plot the results on a map. Creating this kind of application requires a person to program a responsive web interface that can dynamically manipulate backend data and create a display based on the results. This usually involves writing complex code that has multiple nested callbacks to handle events and perform the appropriate actions such as firing web service requests, retrieving new data, and repopulating the interface.

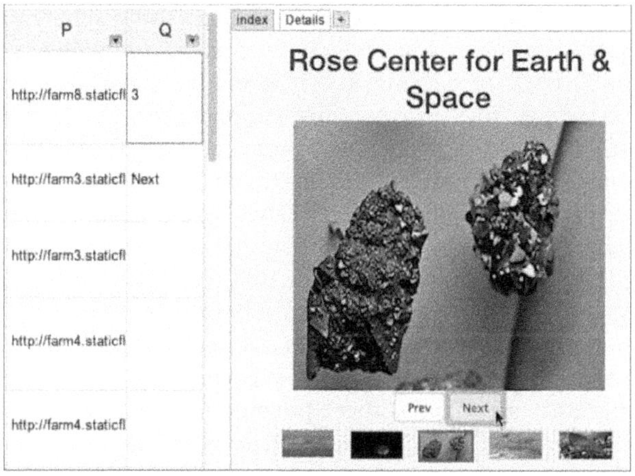

Figure 1: Gneiss lets people create interactive web applications in a spreadsheet editor. This is a screenshot of making a slideshow interface with photos from Flickr. At the left, column P stores a list of photo URLs, Q1 stores the current slideshow index (3), and Q2 stores the button that the user last clicked on ("Next"). At the right is the slideshow application. The thumbnails show the photos in column P. The large image is the photo at row 3 (the index value stored in Q1).

While most data sources provide a web interface and often a mobile application for accessing their data, the increasing demands of customized applications have led many companies to also provide web services that let people access the data programmatically. For example, Yelp and Expedia provide web services for restaurants and hotels. Flickr provides web services for photos (Figure 1). According to ProgrammableWeb.com, today there are over 10,000 web APIs available for use by the general public. Despite the popularity of web services, the programming skills required to incorporate them into a web application have limited their users to mostly professional programmers [24]. Prior studies found that end-users had the need to build web applications that access online databases but often failed to do so

UIST '14, October 05 - 08 2014, Honolulu, HI, USA

ACM 978-1-4503-3069-5/14/10..$15.00.
http://dx.doi.org/10.1145/2642918.2647371

[20]. Research on mashup tools has provided ways to let people extract and integrate web data from multiple sources without having to write conventional code [11,13,23], but it remains difficult for end-users to turn the collected data into anything more sophisticated than a table or a graph, let alone creating an interactive web application.

In this paper, we present Gneiss[1], a new tool that allows users to create interactive, data-driven web applications using the familiar spreadsheet language. Gneiss integrates a source panel for viewing and extracting web service data (Figure 2 at 1), a spreadsheet-like editor for manipulating the data and writing computational logic using spreadsheet formulas (Figure 2 at 2), and a web interface builder (Figure 2 at 3) for creating web interfaces. Like spreadsheets, Gneiss is a "live" programming environment, so new values are populated throughout the program and reflected in the output as soon as the user makes an edit. Gneiss uses a "programming-with-example" style [16], since example values are used while developing the program. These features allow Gneiss to achieve a different programming experience compared with conventional web programming tools where data are invisible and live changes are not supported. Gneiss is targeted at people who are already knowledgeable about spreadsheet programming and who know basic web design such as how to use an interactive editor.

A previous paper [6] presented how we extended conventional spreadsheets to work with web service data. In summary, the user can make a web API call and view the return data in the left panel (Figure 2 at 1), and use drag-and-drop to extract desired fields to the center spreadsheet (Figure 2 at 2). In the spreadsheet we use nested tables to preserve any structure in the extracted data. Data flow is two-way between the spreadsheet and the web service, as the user can bind parameters of the web API to spreadsheet cells.

This paper introduces how Gneiss allows users to create interactive web applications and graphical user interface (GUI) elements that visualize and control the data. By integrating with our previous work [6], data in the spreadsheet can be local data or web service data retrieved dynamically. Web application development with Gneiss utilizes the new right panel of the tool, which is a web interface builder where the user can drag a GUI element from the toolbar (Figure 2 at 4) and drop it to a desired location in the output pane (Figure 2 at 3). We introduce here two main extensions of the spreadsheet model to support interactive web applications. First, all GUI property values have all the capabilities of spreadsheet cells, and they can be referenced anywhere in Gneiss using a spreadsheet-like syntax. Similarly, the value of any GUI element property can be a constant or a value computed using a spreadsheet formula that depends on other cells. This enables data flow to be two-way between the web interface and the spreadsheet editor. The user's interactions with the web application could lead to changes in spreadsheet cells and further trigger different actions at run time such as to fire web service calls, retrieve new data, apply new sorting and filtering rules, and subsequently repopulate the web interface.

Second, while most spreadsheet tools do not allow circular references by default, our spreadsheet editor facilitates two-way communication by providing the "once-around" semantics of one-way constraint solvers, which has been shown to be useful in previous systems [14,15,18]. This, along with the dynamic properties of GUI elements that are triggered when the user interacts with the elements, and new formulas that control when a spreadsheet cell is re-evaluated, enable the user to program a wide range of interactive behaviors solely using a "pull model" that is consistent with the current spreadsheet formula evaluation paradigm. Gneiss eliminates the need for a conventional event-based model as is used by other GUI tools and toolkits. Some previous attempts to adapt spreadsheets for web programming have required an awkward hybrid of event-triggered (push) and formula-based (pull) execution [3,10], which Gneiss avoids.

Combining all these features, our work contributes a novel spreadsheet model for creating web applications that make interactive use of backend data. We evaluate Gneiss with a series of examples to demonstrate its ability to create a wide variety of web data applications without having to write anything more complicated than spreadsheet formulas.

In the rest of the paper, we first survey related work. We then describe Gneiss in detail and present the demonstrative examples. We conclude the paper with current limitations and future work.

RELATED WORK

Here we review related work on spreadsheets, mashups, and web programming tools for end-users.

Spreadsheet Tools and Programming Languages

Most conventional spreadsheet tools such as Google Spreadsheets and Microsoft Excel support one-way visualizations for spreadsheet data such as graphs and charts, but do not support building a web application where data flow between the web interface and the spreadsheet data is bi-directional. The idea of using the spreadsheet metaphor to support programming data-driven web applications was previously experimented in FAR [3]. FAR uses a table to present an e-commerce database and allows users to link a web interface to the database using spreadsheet syntax. Gneiss makes several novel contributions over FAR. First, while FAR only supports creating applications that connect to a single database, Gneiss allows users to create applications that use data from *multiple* local or online sources. Second, FAR uses special "query cells" to enable querying

[1] Gneiss (pronounced the same as "nice") is a kind of rock. Here it stands for Gathering Novel End-user Internet Services using Spreadsheets. Gneiss is available from http://www.cs.cmu.edu/~NatProg/gneiss

a database but did not support other kinds of data actions such as sorting and filtering. In contrast, Gneiss enables all spreadsheet cells and GUI element properties to be used in formulas to perform searching, sorting, and filtering data and other common actions just like in regular spreadsheet tools. Finally, FAR uses the mix of the spreadsheet "pull" model and conventional callback ("push") mechanisms to handle events. While convenient sometimes, this approach could potentially lead to bugs when the push and pull rules have conflicts and try to modify the same cell. In contrast, Gneiss's language uses solely the "pull" model and is able to support more types of interactive behaviors, such as animations and dynamic pages, than using the hybrid method in FAR. Quilt [1] is a recent system that lets users use HTML attributes to connect a web page to a spreadsheet that serves as a backend database to fetch and store data. Our work uses a different approach of letting users use the spreadsheet language to create two-way bindings between GUI element attributes and spreadsheet cells. Our tool also supports creating interactive behaviors, and has a focus on using web data sources.

Another category of related work describes research tools that extend the spreadsheet metaphor to support other kinds of programming activities. While some of these support programming graphical or UI objects, none of them support creating applications that make interactive use of backend data. For example, C32 [17] uses a spreadsheet-like visualization for specifying user interface constraints, but did not address handling events and did not deal with data sources. NoPumpG [22] and Forms/3 [2] extend spreadsheet languages to help with building graphical interfaces and support animations and events. However, both NoPumpG and Forms/3 have unconventional spreadsheet designs that may not be intuitive for end-users. They also do not handle data sources and do not have the notion of a backend database. A1 [10] is a spreadsheet environment for programming system administrator tasks such as monitoring network usage. A1's language is similar to conventional scripting languages and uses the callback mechanisms to handle events. It provides one-way graphical outputs such as graphs and charts, but does not support building arbitrary web interfaces with two-way connections to the spreadsheet editor.

End-user Mashup Tools

The majority of prior research on end-user mashup tools focuses on helping users extract or combine data from multiple web sources without writing conventional code. Many of these provide techniques to let users scrape web page data by demonstration such as novel ways to infer similar data using web page structure [9,21], or allowing users to automate the data scraping by recording a script [13]. Some tools support mashup data coming from a few web services hardwired into the tool (e.g., [11,23]). Gneiss currently supports *any* REST web service that returns JSON data but requires the user to show which parts of the data are desired using drag-and-drop [5]. In the future, we could extend Gneiss with graphical widgets for configuring some popular built-in web services such as those in [23], to assist users who do not have knowledge about how to use web services.

While most mashup tools provide tables (e.g., [13,21,23]) and visualizations such as charts and maps (e.g., [11,23]) to display the collected data, very few of them support building web applications that provide interactive use of the collected data. d.mix [8] lets users copy desired functionality from example applications and recompose them in a wiki page to create their own web applications. However, this approach is limited by the number of example applications because it requires each example to be manually annotated by professional programmers. Building a web application in a wiki page also requires knowledge of HTML syntax and does not support creating interactive behaviors. Data flow language tool such as Yahoo! Pipes [25] can let users create input objects and wire them to data manipulation modules to accept runtime values. However, studies have found that the data flow representation is often difficult for end-users to understand [4]. Our work here extends the spreadsheet model, with which many end-users are already familiar [2]. Debugging may also be easier in our tool, as the data being manipulated are exposed in a spreadsheet and the user can see live changes in the data as she programs the application, in contrast to dataflow languages where the data are usually hidden unless the user specifically looks for them.

End-User Web Programming Tools

Web interface builders and WYSIWYG web editors have been widely used in commercial products and research projects to help end-users make web interfaces. However, connecting a web page using a regular interface builder (like Adobe Dreamweaver or Microsoft Visual Studio) to a data source and presenting dynamic content still require writing extensive code. Some research tools help people use examples to create static styles [5,12] or interactive behaviors [19] of a web page. But they do not help users understand or reproduce how the example web pages use and interact with the backend data sources.

USAGE SCENARIO

Here we describe a scenario where Ted, a college student and a spreadsheet user, uses Gneiss to create a web application that helps him decide where to visit in a city. The application has a textbox that searches an online place database and shows the search results in a grid list. The user can choose to sort the results by rating or price using two radio buttons. Each item in the grid list contains the name, rating, price level of a place, and a checkbox that lets the user display the place on a map. Finally, the user can click on a place name to go to a "details" page that shows photos of the place retrieved from an online photo database. Figure 2 is a screenshot of part of the end result (with the created web application in the right panel at (3)). We use this scenario to give an overview of our tool.

Ted first enters Google's Place Text Search API in the URL box in the left panel (Figure 2 at 1). Hitting the refresh icon submits the query. The returned data, in JSON format, are

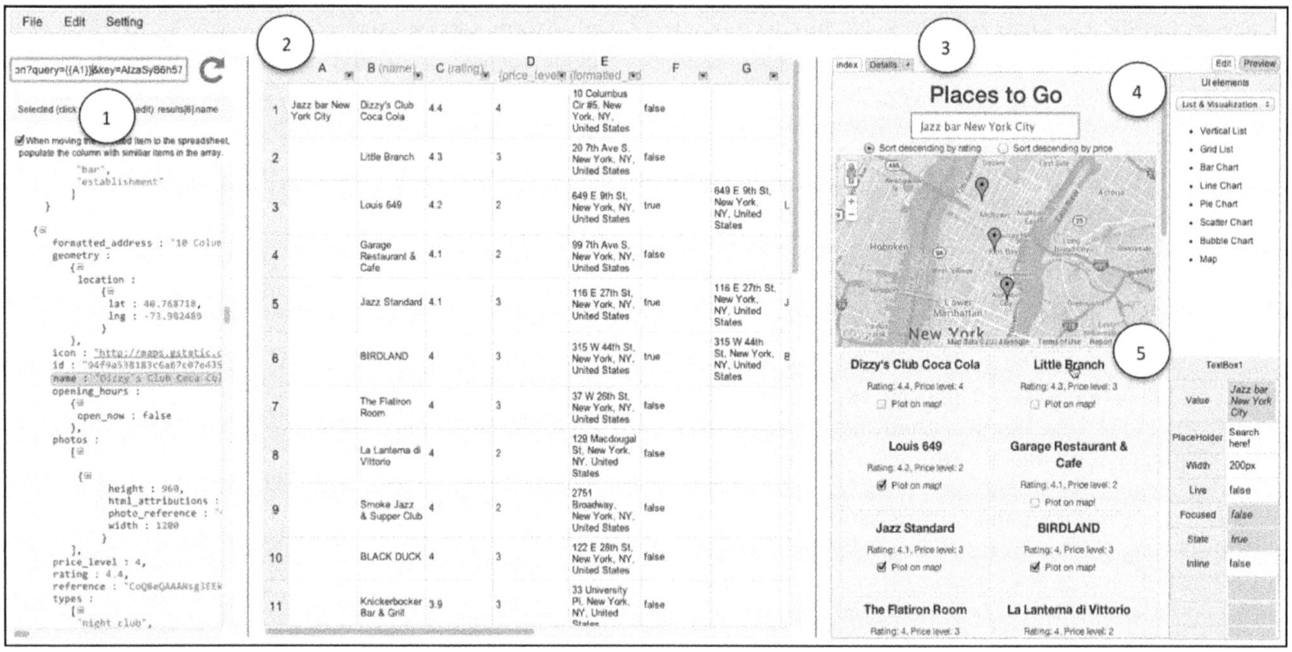

Figure 2. The Gneiss interface. (1) is the source panel where the user can load a web API in the URL box and extract desired fields from the return data to the spreadsheet editor through drag-and-drop. (2) is the spreadsheet editor that stores and manipulates the data to be used in the web application. (3) is the web interface builder where the user can create a web application by dragging-and-dropping GUI elements from the toolbar on the right (4) to the output page. The user can select a GUI element in the output page (the selected element is highlighted with a dark blue border, which currently is the textbox at the top of the page) and view its properties in (5). Property values are cells which can contain formulas and can be referenced by other cells.

shown below, and Ted can use this example data to demonstrate the next steps. After seeing that the API works with a constant string, Ted wants the value of the "query" parameter in the web API to be whatever the user types in the text box in the web application at runtime. To make the query string be dynamic, Ted first sets the value of the parameter to be the value of cell A1 in the spreadsheet, using the syntax `{{A1}}` (Figure 2 at 1, in the URL box). He then extracts the data he wants from the query result – the name, rating, price and address fields – to the spreadsheet in the center panel by drag-and-dropping each value into its own column (Figure 2 at 2, columns B-E). Because Ted has linked the query parameter in the web API to cell A1, every time cell A1's value changes, the system will make a new API request with the new query value and update the extracted data with the latest returned data. This, in turn, will refresh the spreadsheet columns.

Ted does a few queries by changing cell A1's value and makes sure everything works correctly. Because Gneiss is a "live" system, Ted can experiment with his code and view changes anytime. The spreadsheet shows data from Ted's latest query, which Ted can later use as example values to continue developing his program. This "programming-with-examples" style has been shown effective in helping users understand and test their program as it develops [7].

Ted now starts to create the web application, using the interface builder shown in Figure 2 at 3. He first drags a text label (for the header) and a text box (for the query string) from the tool bar at the right of the interface builder (Figure 2 at 4) to the output page. In the web interface builder, Ted can select any GUI element in the output page (which will then be highlighted using a blue border), and view and edit its properties, which are shown as a small one-column spreadsheet at the bottom right (Figure 2 at 5). Ted selects the heading text and changes its value to the constant "Places to Go". Ted then selects the text box. The "value" property of the text box is a dynamic property depending on what the user enters at runtime (currently "Jazz bar New York City"). Back in the spreadsheet, Ted types `=TextBox1!Value` in cell A1 to make it be the text box's value (we use this syntax to match current spreadsheets that use "!" when referencing cells in other worksheets or files). Now after Ted types in the text box and hits enter, cell A1 changes too and the system fires a new place search request based on A1's value (it would alternatively be possible for A1 to update character-by-character by changing the "Live" property of the text box from "false to "true", but that would not be appropriate for a web request).

Ted then drags in two radio buttons to control how the search results are sorted. Ted changes the label of the first radio button to "Sort descending by rating". Then he clicks on the small arrow icon at the top of column C, the column that stores the ratings, to open up a dialog box (Figure 3) that controls the sorting and filtering of that column. Ted sets the sorting rule to come from a computed value, and enters the formula `=IF (RadioButton1!Checked, "Descending", "None")` to sort the results descending by the rating column if the first radio button is checked. Ted uses the same method to set up the second radio button to control if the results are sorted by price (column D).

Ted continues to create the web application. He drags a grid list to the output page to show the search results. Ted drags two text labels and a checkbox to the first item of the grid list, and the system populates the rest of the grid items with corresponding UI objects. Ted wants the top text item in each grid item to be the name of the place. To do so, Ted selects the top text in the first grid item and changes its value to be `=B1`. The top text in each of the rest of the grid items automatically changes to be the value of the corresponding cell in column B. Ted uses the same method to change the second text to show the rating and the price level, and the label of the checkbox to be "Plot on map!".

Ted next needs to collect the addresses of all the checked items in order to tell the system to plot them on the map. To do so, Ted first enters `=CheckBox1!Checked` in cell F1 to get whether the checkbox in the first grid item is checked. Ted then selectes F1 and uses the standard spreadsheet mechanism to autofill down column F with the values of the "checked" property of each of the checkboxes. Now as Ted checks and unchecks a checkbox in the web interface, its corresponding cell in the spreadsheet column F changes its value too. In cell G1, Ted types in `=IF(F1, E1, "")` and autofills the rest of column G. This formula fills in the cell in column G with the address cell (column E) in the same row if the checkbox cell in that row (column F) is true. Finally, in the web interface panel, Ted drags a map visualization from the toolbar to the output page, and sets the "addresses" parameter of the map to be all cells in column G by typing in `=G:G` (the standard spreadsheet syntax to reference a whole column). Now Ted has an interactive map that dynamically displays the checked places.

The last step to finish this web application is to allow the place's name to be a hyperlink that goes to a new page that shows photos of the place from an online place database. This demonstrates how Ted can use Gneiss to combine data from *multiple* data sources. To do so, Ted creates a new page called "Details", and sets the "link" property of the place name text to be "Details". This causes the Details page to be brought to the front when a place name text is clicked. Ted then needs to use the latest clicked place name in order to fire a different API request to retrieve the photos for that place, and fill in the details page. In Gneiss, all UI objects have a "state" property that reflects how the mouse cursor interacts with it. For example, when the mouse moves over the text object and then the user clicks on the text, the state for the text changes from `"idle"` to `"hovered"` to momentarily be `"clicked"`. Ted autofills column I with the state property of the corresponding place name text. Then in J1 he types `=IF(COUNTIF(I:I, "clicked")>0,LOOKUP("clicked",I:I,B:B),J1)`, which uses the standard spreadsheet functions `COUNTIF` and `LOOKUP`. This formula will count how many cells in column I have value "clicked". If there are any, then J1 becomes the cell in column B (the name column) that is in the same row with the "clicked" cell in column I. Otherwise the formula does not change J1's value. This makes J1 become the name of the most recently clicked place. Ted then uses Flickr's Photo Search API and cell J1 as the query string to search for the photos of the clicked place, and uses similar methods as before to extract the photo data returned by Flickr and show the photos using a grid list in the web interface builder (Figure 1). Lastly, Ted adds a "Back" button to the Details page to let the user go back to the search page. Note that values are passed around and interactions are triggered using standard spreadsheet functions and formulas, without the need for any event-based programming.

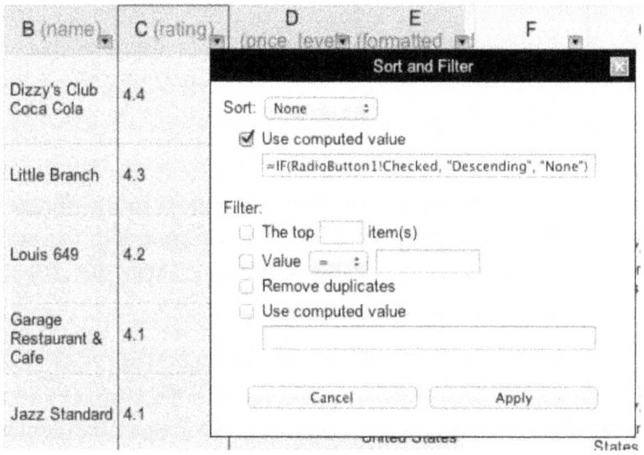

Figure 3. To sort and filter spreadsheet data by a column, the user can click on the arrow button at the top of the column to bring up a dialog box. Our tool allows sorting and filtering to be done by computed values that use other spreadsheet cells or GUI element properties. The system highlights the column it sorts and filters by with a blue border, and all columns sorted and filtered together in a purple background.

Ted now has finished creating the application! He plays with the application in preview mode, does a few test queries, and exports the application when done. Gneiss generates a URL that can be used to open this application anywhere in a browser from a laptop or a smartphone. Ted sends this URL to his friends to share the application.

KEY FEATURES

Here we described the key features of our system. We omit describing regular spreadsheet features and interface builder features since they are not the contribution of this work or were covered in [6].

Interacting with Web Services

The complete features and implementation details of how Gneiss allows users to interactively make web service requests and extract data were described in a previous paper [6]. Here we give a quick overview of some relevant features. Gneiss currently supports REST web services that return JSON data, the most popular type of web APIs today according to ProgrammableWeb.com. RESTful web APIs are HTTP URLs that contain a base URI and a set API parameters provided as name-value pairs. The user can enter a web API in the URL box in the source panel (Figure 2 at 1). The desired fields from the returned data can be copied to the spreadsheet editor for further manipulation by selecting a field (the selected field will be highlighted in a light blue background as in Figure 2) and dragging it to the spreadsheet editor. By default, if the value is from a list, the system will extract all of the corresponding fields and fill in the rest of the column (this can be turned off using the checkbox in Figure 2 at 1). For example, in the usage scenario, to extract the names of all of the places returned, Ted only needs to drag the first place name in the search results to cell B1. The system will automatically extract the names of all other places and put them in the rest of the cells in column B. The bottom of column B is grayed out to indicate that this column is automatically maintained and may change lengths (for example, if a future query returns a different number of values), so the user should not try to use any part of the column for other purposes.

Gneiss also allows data in the spreadsheet to flow back to the web service, by letting users replace any part of the web API with a reference to a spreadsheet cell wrapped in double braces. For example, in the usage scenario, Ted makes the value of the query parameter in web API be `{{A1}}` to let the value of cell A1 be sent to the web service as the query string. The double brackets syntax is adopted from JavaScript template libraries (such as [26]) to bind expressions to HTML templates. When the cell value changes, Gneiss will fire the API call again using the cell's computed value, and then any spreadsheet cells depending on the returned data will be updated in turn. For example, in the usage scenario, if A1 changes to "museums in D.C.", the system will send a new API request using "museums in D.C." as query string, and update columns B-E in the spreadsheet with the new returned data.

Other innovative data extraction features in Gneiss, such as using nested tables to preserve the structure of the extracted data and allowing independent data extractions to run in parallel, are described in detail elsewhere [6]. Our work in this paper focuses on creating interactive web applications that present and control the dynamic backend data.

Creating a Dynamic UI using Spreadsheet Data

As in many commercial web interface builders, our tool lets users create UI elements in a web page by drag-and-drop. Gneiss currently supports text and image objects, input elements (such as text boxes and buttons), lists, and visualizations, with the full set of HTML5 elements, properties and GUI controls planned for the future. In general, the properties of these elements include string properties (e.g., the text in a heading, the label of a button), styling properties (e.g., color and width), link properties, and interactive properties that change values as the user interacts with the element. String and styling properties let users style GUI elements using conventional mechanisms. A Link property turns a GUI element into a hyperlink that goes to the value of the property. The value can be a URL or the name of another page opened in the interface builder, allowing the user to create a multi-page application. The user can specify how the application transfers from one page to another, and how the contents of one page may depend on values from another, as described in the usage scenario.

In Gneiss, the user can edit a GUI element property just like editing a cell in the spreadsheet editor. A GUI element property can be a constant or a dynamic value computed from the spreadsheet data. Setting a property value to use spreadsheet cells will cause the property be recomputed every time that these cells change values. For example, if the user sets the "value" property of a text object to be `=CONCATENATE("Rating: ", C1))`, then each time that cell C1 in the spreadsheet editor changes, the text object will also change to show the latest value.

Dynamic Lists

Gneiss currently supports vertical lists and grid lists. Lists have a "Populate" property that if true will fill in all items of the list with the corresponding elements based on edits to the first item. For example, in the usage scenario, Ted only needs to drag two text labels and a checkbox into the first item of the grid list, and the rest of the items in the list are populated with the same objects as in the first item. Property values of a UI element in a list also populate in the same way, so changing the property of a UI element in the first item of the list will affect all of the corresponding UI elements in the rest of the items of the list. If the property value is a constant, all other UI elements are populated with the same value. If the property value is a formula that computes the value based on some cells in the spreadsheet, the system will populate other UI elements in the list with the corresponding cells in the same column but using the row based in the element's index. For example, in the usage scenario, Ted sets the value of the top text label in the first item of the grid list to be `=B1` (the name of the first place). The system automatically populates the top text label in the second list item to be `=B2`, and so on.

Items in a list can be shown and hidden dynamically at run time based on the spreadsheet data if the "NumberOfItems" property in the list object is set to "auto" (the default). The system will automatically adjust the number based on the number of non-empty rows in the column that the UI element's value depends on. For example, in the usage scenario, a different query can return a different number of places. The length of the grid list will dynamically adjust to fit the length of search results.

Alternative, the user can also set "NumberOfItems" to be a number and give the list a constant length or a length computed by a formula. The user can also set "Populate" to false. In this case, the list object becomes a pure layout object and the user can manually put different UI elements in different list items.

Two-way Data Flow

In Gneiss, user inputs into the user interface can also affect the spreadsheet data, making the data flow two-way. The user can reference any property of a UI element using the syntax `ElementID!PropertyName`, using a syntax similar to how a cell in another worksheet is referenced in conventional spreadsheets. References like this can be used not only in the spreadsheet editor but also in the GUI property sheets in the web interface builder as well. For example, the user can set `Text2`'s value property to be `=Text1!Value`, making the two text objects display the same content. We further added a convenient keyword `THIS` to let a GUI element property reference other properties in the same element using `THIS!PropertyName`.

"Autofilling" GUI Property Values

A common feature in spreadsheet tools is "autofilling" where the user selects one or multiple cells and drags a box in the lower right corner of the selection to fill in additional cells with corresponding values. We extend this feature to facilitate referencing properties of populated GUI elements in a list object. The user only needs to enter a reference in a cell for the desired property of the UI element in the first list item, and then select that cell and autofill down. For example, in the usage scenario, Ted types `Checkbox1!Checked` in cell F1, selects F1 and drags to F10. The system then fills in F2 to F10 with the "Checked" property of the checkboxes in the second to tenth items in the grid list.

Making Things Interactive

One of the most important innovations in Gneiss is the way that users can make their web applications interactive. Originally, we explored having Gneiss use a conventional event-based or callback architecture like Java and JavaScript, where UI elements would contain actions to be performed when operated. However, it is awkward to combine these "push" actions (where the action routine in a UI element would set other cells—*pushing* values to them) with the spreadsheet "pull" model (where cells compute their own values with formulas by *pulling* in the needed values). Therefore, we designed a novel way for the Gneiss user to define interactive behaviors without ever needing to write any callback or event procedures.

Instead, we designed interactive properties of GUI elements that change values at run time based on how the user interacts with them. Interactive properties can be used in the spreadsheet cells to compute different data based on the user's action. All GUI elements have an interactive property called "State" that shows how the mouse cursor interacts with them. Possible values for "State" include "idle", "hovered", "pressed" and "clicked". The "clicked" value stays for a few extra milliseconds after the click event so the user can notice that it happened. Other interactive properties are mostly for input elements, such as "Value" for text boxes and sliders, and "Checked" for radio buttons and checkboxes. Interactive properties are not editable from the property sheet since their values are controlled at runtime by the widgets, so their cells are shown using a grey background (Figure 2 at 5). In both the spreadsheet editor and the property sheet, values of interactive properties change dynamically in keeping with Gneiss's "programming-with-example" style.

To further enable more types of interactive effects to be created in our tool, we designed a timer formula `TIMER(ms, condition)` that starts a timer ticking every "ms" milliseconds if "condition" is true, and turns off the timer if "condition" is false. The formula returns true for one millisecond when the timer ticks, and false otherwise. The timer formula was designed specifically to follow Gneiss' "pull" programming paradigm and when used together with conventional spreadsheet formulas such as `IF` would enable timed transitions and animations in the spreadsheet, as demonstrated below.

Constraint Evaluation and Circular Constraints

By default when a spreadsheet cell's value changes, the cell will invalidate all other cells that directly depend on it. This causes the dependent cells to re-compute their values. If the value of that cell changes, then the cell continues to invalidate other cells that directly depend on it, and so on. Otherwise (if the value stays the same), the cell will not invalidate its dependent cells, and the propagation stops. This increases the system's performance and also ensures that web API requests are not run when a parameter value is updated to the same value as before. This tends to happen with constraints that contain `IF`s or other control structures, where the constraint must be re-evaluated, but ends up calculating the same value.

In rare cases, the user might want to re-evaluate the constraints that depend on a cell even if the cell's value does not change. For example, if the spreadsheet data are extracted from a news web service, the user might want to re-run the same query to get the latest news. We provide a formula `REFRESH(exp)` that when used in a cell will return the value of `exp` and invalidate all the children cells (causing them to be re-evaluated) even if `exp` is the same as before. So for instance, the user can set a cell that stores the query parameter to be `=IF(TIMER(600000, B1), REFRESH("world cup"),"world cup")` to get news about "world cup" every 10 minutes when B1 is set to true. Although the query cell's value is always "world cup", the `REFRESH` formula invalidates all constraints that depend on the cell, causing the web service request to be triggered and refresh the spreadsheet columns in turn.

Like some other one-way constraint solvers [14,15,18] our spreadsheet formula solver provides "once-around" semantics for circular constraints. We use an example to explain how this works. Suppose the user sets A1 to be 0 and A2 to be `A1+1`, which makes A2 be 1. The user then sets A1 to be `A2-1`, which creates a circular reference. Most spreadsheet tools will return errors in both A1 and A2. In contrast, our system allows circular references, and always evaluates any dependent cells exactly once when any cell in the cycle changes. Here, the system starts computing A1 by asking A2's value. Since A2 is `A1+1`, it goes back to A1 and finds that it has reached the beginning of the cycle. The system then stops the circular reference here and returns A1's old computed value, 0. That makes A2's value 1 (0+1), and A1's value stays 0 (1-1).

Supporting "once-around" circular constraints in the spreadsheet makes more types of expressions possible. For example, a spreadsheet cell can now reference itself. The system will return the cell's original value before it is recomputed. Combined with the `IF` statement, this allows the user to set a cell's value to something if a condition is true, otherwise having the cell *retain its original value*. This expression is useful to handle interactive behaviors as it allows the user to set a cell's value when a GUI element enters a certain state, but does not change the value back when the element enters another state. For example, suppose the user wants to change a hyperlink text to be another color once it is pressed. Even though the "State" of the text goes back to "idle" from "pressed" after the user releases the mouse button, using a self-reference, the text is able to stay the same color. Another use case of self-reference is that it allows a cell to compute its new value using its previous value. Used together with the `TIMER` formula, the user can set a cell to steadily increase or decrease its value, and bind the cell to a GUI element property to create an animation, such as expanding or shrinking the size of an element, or binding to a color property to create a fade-in/out effect. We provide more examples in the demonstrative examples section.

Dynamic Sorting and Filtering

An innovation in Gneiss is generalizing the sorting and filtering of the spreadsheet data to allow users to control this with a dynamic value computed using spreadsheet cells or GUI element properties. To sort or filter data in a column, the user can click on the small arrow button at the top of the column to open a dialog box (Figure 3). In the dialog box, the user can choose to apply constant rules for sorting and filtering as in conventional spreadsheets, or to apply a dynamic rule by checking the "Use computed value" checkbox and entering the rule in the corresponding textbox. This rule can use conventional spreadsheet functions, with which the user would already be familiar, and should return the same string values as shown in the popup menu. For example, for sorting, the computed value should be "Ascending", "Descending" or "None". Thus, entering `IF(A1>5, "Descending", "None")` as the rule will sort the column only when A1 is bigger than 5.

For filtering, the computed value should to be a comma-separated string with the first item being the filtering method ("FilterTop", "FilterValue" or "FilterDuplicates") and the second item being the argument required by the method (except for "FilterDuplicate", which has no argument). For example, entering `CONCATENATE("FilterValue, >=", A1)` as the rule will filter out cells that are less than A1.

Unlike regular spreadsheet tools where sorting and filtering data is a one-time action, our tool applies sorting and filtering rules to a column every time that a cell in the column changes its value. As described in depth in our previous paper [6] all of the columns corresponding to the same web query are grouped, so that sorting and filtering applies to all grouped columns equally. Thus, in the usage scenario, sorting on column C or D causes all of the columns B-E to be sorted together. If multiple columns in a group have sorting on, then the leftmost column is performed first, then any items that are identical are sorted by the next column, etc. (A more flexible approach with a user-defined order as in Excel is planned for the future.) When all columns in a group have sorting off, then the columns revert to the default order (as originally returned by the web service).

IMPLEMENTATION

The complete Gneiss system is implemented as a web application. We use ConstraintJS [18] to maintain the dependencies among the spreadsheet cells and GUI elements. We use Node.js as the backend server to send web service requests and host the user-created web applications.

DEMONSTRATIVE EXAMPLES

Here we use four more examples to demonstrate our system's ability to build elaborate interactive interfaces and support different types of web applications.

Photo Slideshow

Slideshow is a common UI design to show a list of photos. It usually contains a large photo at the center of the interface, a "previous" and "next" button that let the user change the photo displayed by going up and down the list, and thumbnails of all photos at the bottom of the interface. We will show here how the user can create a photo slideshow interface using our tool and regular spreadsheet formulas. The screenshot of the created application is in Figure 1.

First, the user would retrieve a list of URLs of photos using a photo web service (such as Flickr), in the same way as described in the usage scenario. Suppose the user filters the search results to see the first 5 photos and stores the photo URLs in cell B1 to B5. In the web interface builder, the user can drag an image object to the output page and two buttons before and after the image, changing the label of the buttons to be "Previous" and "Next". The previous and next buttons control the index of the photo being shown. The user decides to store the index of the current photo in cell A1. She types in "0" in A1 first. She then needs know if the "Previous" button or the "Next" button gets clicked. To do so, she types in A2:

```
=IF(Button1!State="clicked", "Previous",
IF(Button2!State="clicked", "Next", ""))
```

where Button1 is the previous button and Button2 the next button. This nested IF formula changes A2 to be set to either "Previous" or "Next" when a button is clicked. Now the user needs to add or subtract the index cell (A1) by one based on what button is clicked. She changes A1 to be:

```
=IF(AND(A2="Previous", A1>1), A1-1,
IF(AND(A2="Next", A1<10), A1+1, A1))
```

This nested `IF` formula not only updates A1's value based on what button is clicked, but also makes sure it stays between 1-10, as the photo URLs are in rows 1 to 10 of column B. (To alternatively make the buttons wrap around would be a simple change to this formula.) From the property sheet in the web interface builder, the user sets the "Source" property of the center image object to `=INDEX(B:B, A1)`. `INDEX` is a standard spreadsheet function that takes an array of cells (the first argument) and returns the cell at the given index (the second argument). The center image object now displays the photo at the index specified in A1, and will change when the user presses the previous or next buttons.

Lastly, the user has to create a list of thumbnails of all the photos. To do so, she drags a grid list to the bottom of the interface, drags an image object to the first item of the grid list, and set the "Source" property of that image object to be `=B1`. The system then populates the list to show photos from B2 to B5. The user wants the thumbnail displayed to as the center image to be highlighted with a blue border. To do so, the user enters the following formula in the "Border" property of the thumbnail image:

```
=IF(This!Source=Image1!Source, "solid blue
1px", "none")
```

where `Image1` is the center image. The formula sets the border of a thumbnail to be blue when the source of the thumbnail is the source of the center image. The user now has finished creating a web application that shows photos in a slideshow interface, using only four spreadsheet formulas!

Animations

Using the `TIMER` function, the user can create animations with our spreadsheet tool. Continuing the photo slideshow example, suppose the user wants the width of the image to slowly increase from 30 pixels to 60 pixels when the mouse enters, and to go back to 30 pixels when the mouse leaves. She first sets spreadsheet cell C1 to be 30 and sets the "Width" property of the thumbnail image to be C1. She then types the following formula in C1:

```
=IF(Image2!State="idle", IF(TIMER(15,
C1>30), C1-1, C1), IF(TIMER(15, C1<60),
C1+1, C1))
```

where `Image2` is the thumbnail image. When the image is in the `idle` state, this formula subtracts one from C1 every 15 milliseconds until it becomes less than or equal to 30. Otherwise, when not `idle`, the formula adds one to C1 every 15 milliseconds until it becomes more than or equal to 60. The user can then select C1 and drag it down to autofill C2 to C5, and apply this behavior to all five thumbnails in the output page.

Posting Data

We have shown our system's ability to create applications that pull data from a web data source. Our system can also create application that *posts* data back to a web data source using a POST web API. Suppose the user wants to create an application where she can type in a textbox and press a "Send" button to send the data to a web data source. The user starts by creating a text box and a button in the output page. Then in spreadsheet cell A1, she types: `=IF( Button1!State="clicked",TextBox1!Value, A1)` to fill A1 with the text box value when the button is clicked. She can then bind A1 to the value of the data parameter of the POST web API, which will send it to the data source.

Customized Personal Activity Visualization

The increased usage of personal wellness applications has made more personal information available on the cloud through web services. For example, Fitbit's web service lets a user access her recent food records, physical activities and sleeping hours programmatically. While these data sources might have their own interfaces to present the data, sometimes the user might want to create customized interfaces to show the data, or combine data from multiple sources. For example, Fitbit's mobile application shows the physical activities and sleeping hours in different tabs, but the user might want to compare them together to see if working out seems to help her sleep. Gneiss provides a set of popular charts and visualizations. For example, the standard spreadsheet formula `NOW()` can be used to get the current date, and the API can be used to retrieve her sleeping hours and exercising hours in the past seven days, which can be visualized using the built-in scatter plot.

LIMITATIONS

Gneiss targets users who are familiar with spreadsheet programming and know basic web programming. The examples above show that advanced spreadsheet knowledge may be needed to achieve some desired outcomes. If the user wants to connect an application to a web data source, she must also have basic knowledge about RESTful web APIs such as their format. Gneiss currently only supports REST web services that return JSON data, although we believe the same interaction techniques could be applied to other kinds of web data such as XML or CSV data. Gneiss currently does not support web services that require authentication. Currently, the value of an input element only changes when the application user interacts with it (such as typing something in the textbox). It cannot be edited programmatically from the spreadsheet or initialized based on data. In the future, we plan to make it possible for the developer to set the value of an input element using formulas, such as specifying the default text for a textbox. Gneiss currently supports basic GUI elements and mouse events. We plan to extend Gneiss to support more HTML5 elements, properties and events such as "drag" and "swipe" for touch devices. We believe that Gneiss's pull-based language could adapt to these new elements and events with minimum changes.

FUTURE WORK

In addition to the extensions mentioned above, we are interested in augmenting current spreadsheet interface to better support programming activities. We are also interested in extending spreadsheets to handle time-series data such as data from streaming web services or mobile sensors. We plan to run iterative usability evaluations to refine Gneiss's user interface, and a summative study to evaluate how well end-user programmers with various levels of programming ability can use Gneiss.

CONCLUSIONS

Gneiss provides a novel spreadsheet model for creating interactive web data applications. It allows properties of GUI elements to use spreadsheet data as their values and to be referenced by other cells. We designed new functions to support timers and to capture user events using dynamic GUI element properties that signal when the user interacts with them. Supporting once-around circular references in the spreadsheet editor enables a variety of interactive behaviors to be programmed using a "pull model" that is consistent with the current spreadsheet paradigm. As shown by the various examples, Gneiss can be used to program a wide variety of web applications using a wide variety of web service data sources.

ACKNOWLEDGEMENTS

We would like to thank the reviewers for their valuable comments. This research was funded in part by the NSF under grants IIS-1116724 and IIS-1314356. Any opinions, findings and conclusions or recommendations expressed in this material are those of the authors and do not necessarily reflect those of the NSF.

REFERENCES

1. Benson, E., Zhang, A., and Karger, D.R. Spreadsheet-Driven Web Applications. *Proc. UIST*, ACM (2014)
2. Burnett, M., Atwood, J., Walpole Djang, R., Reichwein, J., Gottfried, H., and Yang, S. Forms/3: A First-order Visual Language to Explore the Boundaries of the Spreadsheet Paradigm. *J. Funct. Program. 11*, 2, Cambridge University Press (2001), 155–206.
3. Burnett, M., Chekka, S.K., and Pandey, R. FAR: an end-user language to support cottage e-services. *Proc. HCC, IEEE* (2001), 195–202.
4. Cao, J., Rector, K., Park, T.H., Fleming, S.D., Burnett, M., and Wiedenbeck, S. A Debugging Perspective on End-User Mashup Programming. *Proc. VL/HCC*, IEEE (2010), 149–156.
5. Chang, K.S.-P. and Myers, B.A. WebCrystal: Understanding and Reusing Examples in Web Authoring. *Proc. CHI*, ACM (2012), 3205–3214.
6. Chang, K.S.-P. and Myers, B.A. A Spreadsheet Model For Using Web Service Data. *Proc. VL/HCC*, IEEE (2014).
7. Cypher, A., ed. *Watch What I Do: Programming by Demonstration*. The MIT Press, Cambridge, MA, 1993.
8. Hartmann, B., Wu, L., Collins, K., and Klemmer, S.R. Programming by a sample: rapidly creating web applications with d.mix. *Proc. UIST*, ACM (2007), 241–250.
9. Huynh, D.F., Miller, R.C., and Karger, D.R. Enabling Web Browsers to Augment Web Sites' Filtering and Sorting Functionalities. *Proc. UIST*, ACM (2006), 125–134.
10. Kandogan, E., Haber, E., Barrett, R., Cypher, A., Maglio, P., and Zhao, H. A1: End-user Programming for Web-based System Administration. *Proc. UIST*, ACM (2005), 211–220.
11. Van Kleek, M., Smith, D.A., Packer, H.S., Skinner, J., and Shadbolt, N.R. Carpe Data: Supporting Serendipitous Data Integration in Personal Information Management. *Proc. CHI*, ACM (2013), 2339–2348.
12. Kumar, R., Talton, J.O., Ahmad, S., and Klemmer, S.R. Bricolage: Example-based Retargeting for Web Design. *Proc. CHI*, ACM (2011), 2197–2206.
13. Lin, J., Wong, J., Nichols, J., Cypher, A., and Lau, T.A. End-user programming of mashups with vegemite. *Proc. IUI*, ACM (2009), 97–106.
14. Myers, B.A., Giuse, D.A., Dannenberg, R.B., et al. Garnet: Comprehensive Support for Graphical, Highly Interactive User Interfaces. *Computer 23*, 11, IEEE (1990), 71–85.
15. Myers, B.A., McDaniel, R.G., Miller, R.C., et al. The Amulet Environment: New Models for Effective User Interface Software Development. *Trans. Softw. Eng. 23*, 6 , IEEE (1997), 347–365.
16. Myers, B.A. Visual Programming, Programming by Example, and Program Visualization: A Taxonomy. *Proc. CHI*, ACM (1986), 59–66.
17. Myers, B.A. Graphical Techniques in a Spreadsheet for Specifying User Interfaces. *Proc. CHI*, ACM (1991), 243–249.
18. Oney, S., Myers, B., and Brandt, J. ConstraintJS: Programming Interactive Behaviors for the Web by Integrating Constraints and States. *Proc. UIST*, ACM (2012), 229–238.
19. Oney, S. and Myers, B. FireCrystal: Understanding Interactive Behaviors in Dynamic Web Pages. *Proc. VL/HCC*, IEEE (2009), 105–108.
20. Rosson, M.B., Ballin, J., and Rode, J. Who, what, and how: a survey of informal and professional Web developers. *Proc. VL/HCC*, IEEE (2005), 199–206.
21. Tuchinda, R., Szekely, P., and Knoblock, C.A. Building Mashups by example. *Proc. IUI*, ACM (2008), 139–148
22. Wilde, N. and Lewis, C. Spreadsheet-based Interactive Graphics: From Prototype to Tool. *Proc. CHI*, ACM (1990), 153–160.
23. Wong, J. and Hong, J.I. Making mashups with marmite: towards end-user programming for the web. *Proc. CHI*, ACM (2007), 1435–1444.
24. Zang, N., Rosson, M.B., and Nasser, V. Mashups: who? what? why? *CHI'08 Extended Abstracts*, ACM (2008), 3171–3176.
25. Yahoo Pipes. http://pipes.yahoo.com/.
26. Handlebar.js. http://handlebarsjs.com/.

Spreadsheet-Driven Web Applications

Edward Benson
MIT CSAIL
32 Vassar St., Cambridge MA
eob@csail.mit.edu

Amy X. Zhang
MIT CSAIL
32 Vassar St., Cambridge MA
axz@csail.mit.edu

David R. Karger
MIT CSAIL
32 Vassar St., Cambridge MA
karger@mit.edu

ABSTRACT

Creating and publishing read-write-compute web applications requires programming skills beyond what most end users possess. But many end users know how to make spreadsheets that act as simple information management applications, often with computation. We present a system for creating basic web applications using such spreadsheets in place of a server and using HTML to describe the client UI. Authors connect the two by placing spreadsheet references inside HTML attributes. Data computation is provided by spreadsheet formulas. The result is a reactive read-write-compute web page without a single line of Javascript code. Nearly all of the fifteen HTML novices we studied were able to connect HTML to spreadsheets using our method with minimal instruction. We draw conclusions from their experience and discuss future extensions to this programming model.

Author Keywords

Web design; Spreadsheets; End-user programming; Information architecture

ACM Classification Keywords

H.5.4. Information Interfaces and Presentation: Hypertext/Hypermedia - User Issues

INTRODUCTION

Spreadsheets are ubiquitous information management tools that cross technical and cultural divides. College students use them to plan parties, financial analysts use them to sway markets, and many companies use spreadsheets instead of databases to manage data [28]. According to the 2012 United States Census, over 55 million people in the United States "manipulate data with either spreadsheets or databases at work [26]." But while these authors use spreadsheets for a diversity of information management tasks, they have limited ability to view, edit, and share their data outside the grid-based interface spreadsheets provide. Showing a stylized schedule for an event planned with a spreadsheet, for example, typically requires copying and pasting raw data from the spreadsheet into the finalized design document.

UIST 2014, October 5–8, 2014, Honolulu, HI, USA.

ACM 978-1-4503-3069-5/14/10 ...$15.00.
http://dx.doi.org/10.1145/2642918.2647387

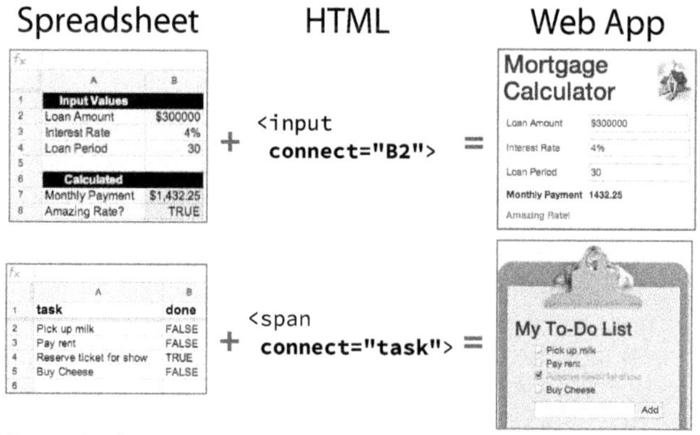

Figure 1: Our user study participants used Quilt to author the connective code to turn these HTML files and spreadsheets into reactive apps after a brief tutorial.

There is a separate overlapping community of people who know how to edit HTML. The size of this community is difficult to assess, but web literacy is undoubtedly growing. The ACM Computer Science Standards cite HTML and CSS authoring as basic components of computer literacy at the K-12 level [11]. Web authors build pages for a variety of purposes, ranging from personal to public to collaborative. Like spreadsheet authors, web authors face a steep hurdle once they try to move beyond the basic capabilities HTML offers. To create a web page with data storage and computation, an HTML author must learn to write client-server programs and possibly to design and administer databases.

In both cases, users have access to a tool that is specialized for one type of information-centric activity, such as data management or hypertext publishing, but does not natively support other activities. Past approaches to these two problems either focus heavily on providing pre-made widgets or templates [14] [27] or use new authoring and deployment environments that replace the user's existing ones [29] [22].

This paper stems from the intuition that spreadsheets and HTML are complimentary technologies waiting to be joined. Spreadsheet users enjoy structured data and computation but lack the ability to view and edit data in whatever flexible, stylized fashion suits them. HTML authors can create such styled displays, but studies show they both lack and greatly desire the ability to perform information management tasks such as data collection, storage, and retrieval [22] [24] [6], exactly what spreadsheets can step in to provide.

This paper presents and evaluates a system called Quilt[1].

[1] Source code is available at `treesheets.org` and a deployed version ready for use is at `cloudstitch.io`

Using Quilt, end users with basic spreadsheet and HTML-editing capabilities can skin their spreadsheets with a web page that serves as a more stylized alternative to the spreadsheet interface. From the web developer's perspective, Quilt enables rapid prototyping of reactive information management applications. Quilt uses relational annotations in HTML that do not require the author to understand dataflow. Using a tree synchronization algorithm, Quilt provides a reactive web experience based on these annotations. We show that simple information management applications, complete with sorting, searching, and table joins, can be crafted with Quilt, and demonstrate how inter-document formulas and spreadsheet scoping can support multi-user applications.

We then report results from a user study of 15 end users with basic HTML editing ability. After learning our method for fifteen minutes, they performed a series of authoring tasks: (1) connecting spreadsheets to web pages when provided both and (2) authoring (and then connecting) spreadsheets from scratch when provided only an HTML UI mockup. Participants were nearly all able to complete the tasks successfully in only a few minutes. We use videos, surveys, and interviews from this user study to evaluate Quilt's learnability and reflect on debugging with this method of authoring.

QUILT

We begin with a brief section to explain the Quilt language and operations. Assume a sample task of building a web interface to collaboratively plan a party with friends. The following spreadsheet contains a list of food items, their costs, the person responsible, and a computed cell for total cost:

	A	B	C	D
1	**Item**	**Cost**	**Person**	
2	Cheese	$15.00	Casey	total
3	Crackers	$5.00	?	$35.00
4	Wine	$15.00	?	

Quilt reactively connects an HTML web interface to the spreadsheet using four new HTML attributes: `connect`, `delete`, `show-if`, and `hide-if`. Depending on where they are used, these attributes can synchronize data between the web page and spreadsheet, add new rows, delete rows, and show/hide web elements depending on spreadsheet contents.

The following code snippet and output demonstrates how to connect HTML elements to spreadsheet cells. Cells can contain either plain text or computed values. In both cases, changes made on the spreadsheet flow automatically to the web page, replacing the element content. Changes to the web element content, through direct user action or Javascript manipulation, propagate automatically back to the spreadsheet.

```
<span connect="D3">cost</span>
```

→ $35.00

By placing the attribute `connect="rows"`, Quilt users can designate that an HTML element's contents should repeat once per row in the spreadsheet. Each repetition corresponds to the data in a row. Inside a repetition, one can `connect` HTML elements using the names of columns, or offer row deletion by placing `delete="row"` on a button. As before, runtime modifications, insertions, or deletions are synchronized between the web page and the spreadsheet.

```
<div connect="rows">
  <div class="party-item">
    <span connect="Item">item</span>
    <button delete="row">x</button>
  </div>
</div>
```

→ Cheese ⊗
Crackers ⊗
Wine ⊗

When a form carries the attribute `connect="rows"`, submitting that form appends a new row. Input elements connected to column names provide the new values for that row. When the new row is appended to the spreadsheet, data flows back to any connected elements on the web page.

```
<form connect="rows">
  Item: <input connect="Item">
  Cost: <input connect="Cost">
  <button>Add</button>
</form>
```

Item: [ ]
Cost: [ ]
[Add]

Finally, the commands `hide-if` and `show-if` hide and show a web element based on whether the connected cell is "Truthy," represented by anything other than an empty cell, the string 'FALSE', or the number 0. This example limits the output to show only food items with no assigned person:

```
<div connect="rows">
  <div class="party-item" hide-if="Person"> … </div>
</div>
```

Using these annotations, the Quilt engine can turn a static web mockup and a spreadsheet into a simple read-write web app, with the spreadsheet adding computation as well.

METHOD

Our design goals were to reuse existing HTML and spreadsheets as much as possible, while minimizing the introduction of "programming-like" concepts such as data-flow and ordered statements. Our hypothesis was that doing so would transform a task that today involves programming into one that feels like a natural extension of spreadsheet and HTML authoring. Our method consists of two components: web relations and the spreadsheet-view pattern.

Web Relations

Quilt's programming model, **web relations**, is a refinement of our work on the Cascading Tree Sheets project [5], which provides a language for merging data structures across the web. Web relations adhere to what we call the **CARB properties**—container-centric, annotational, relational, and bidirectional—which lets authors feel as if they are simply authoring HTML, but enable a runtime engine to transform that HTML into a reactive information management interface. To explain these properties, consider the following two code fragments, written in traditional web template style on the left and web relations on the right:

Web Template Style:

```
<ul>
 {for row in rows}
  <li>{{row.Item}}</li>
 {end for}
</ul>
```

Web Relation Style:

```
<ul connect="rows">
 <li connect="Item">Title</li>
</ul>
```

Container-centrism concerns language semantics. When traditional web templates are rendered, the template instructions are removed. The output of a web template is thus not a web template itself, and it lacks provenance information to trace back regions of dynamic data to their source. Web relations annotate HTML *containers* with statements about their *contents*. The UI can be rendered without removing relations, meaning that the output document in the browser is also a working template that can be reused and respond to new data.

Annotationality concerns the programming interface. Traditional web templates intermingle sequential instructions with the template output. Viewed in a web browser, these instructions render awkwardly alongside the HTML. Web relations occupy the attribute space, allowing for example data that is overwritten at runtime. This means the dynamic production template is also a static design artifact.

Relational templating is a contrast to imperative-style templates. Imperative templates provide instructions for a specific task, such as looping over an array and printing something. Relational templates simply represent relationships between data structures. Just like database relations, they can be exploited in different ways depending on context. In Quilt's case, context is the type of object participating in a relation and the data-change events on those objects. For example, consider three different ways the `connect` relation is interpreted based on context. If a `div` is connected to `rows`, its contents will be repeated once per row. If a `form` is connected to `rows`, it will instead append a new row when the form submit event occurs. If a `div` is connected to `A4`, it will mirror the value of cell A4. The `connect` attribute is a relation between structures, not an imperative command, enabling the runtime system to automate a variety of context-dependent tasks that otherwise would require custom code.

Bidirectionality concerns both language semantics and runtime engine design. Traditional web templates are interpreted as a one-way functions that accept data and produce an HTML fragment that is indistinguishable from a static HTML. Web relations define structural relationships that can be exploited in either direction, and container-centrism guarantees the durability of these relationships through the rendering process. A web relational engine can produce dynamic HTML from a data structure, but then also update either the HTML or data structure when the other changes at runtime.

Spreadsheets as "Models with Benefits"

The second part of our method is replacing the abstract model of the Model-View pattern with spreadsheet software. This means that all data and computation is visible, editable, and debugable in a well known environment, not hidden behind controller code and database APIs. Many bugs can be identified and resolved entirely as spreadsheet issues, independent of the HTML interface, or vice versa.

Web spreadsheet software (like Google Spreadsheets) also supports many database-like operations not supported by desktop spreadsheets. Formula-based filtering, sorting, and table-joining, as well as inter-document addressing and web API calls are all possible and can be parameterized by other cells. This open up real possibility for spreadsheets to provide a programming environment for non-trivial web applications. Figure 2 shows a portion of a multi-sheet wedding planning app we built to demonstrate this functionality. When the web user types into a search box on the web page, Quilt synchronizes that with a cell in a **Parameters** worksheet. This causes a column in the **RSVPs** sheet to recompute whether each row is a search result. Quilt synchronizes the new column data to the browser, where it toggles visibility of each list item.

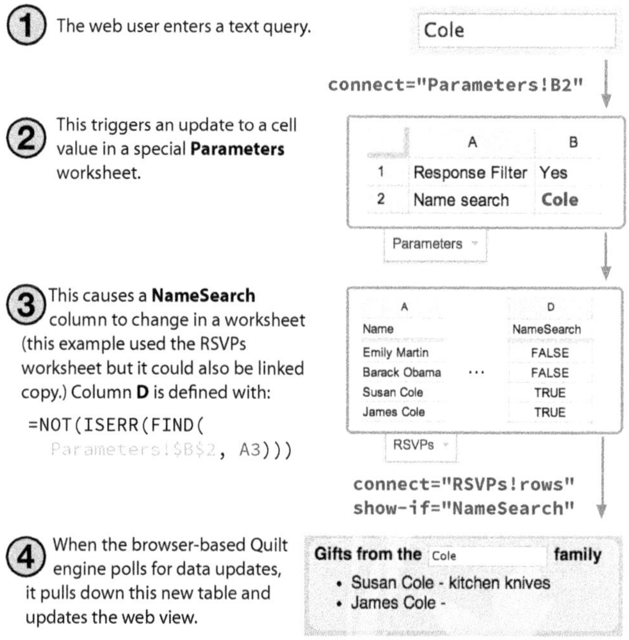

Figure 2: Demonstration of how Quilt's two-way data syncing enables data operations like reactive text search using web elements to parameterize spreadsheet functions.

The Discussion section delves into spreadsheet app design patterns, like partitioning different elements of the model and computation into separate sheets and handling multiple users.

SYSTEM ARCHITECTURE

Quilt is implemented as a Javascript library that integrates into a web page to simulate browser-native support for our extra HTML attributes. Figure 3 shows an annotated view of Quilt's internal architecture, along with the timeline of data operations Quilt performs. For re-implementors, the key point to extract from this figure is the way in which Quilt constructs **tree-shaped proxy representations** of all objects it is aware of. Each proxy tree listens to changes on the real object it represents (an HTML node or spreadsheet object) and triggers a synchronization process when a change occurs. This synchronization is enacted as manipulations of proxy tree nodes. A proxy tree is responsible for translating structural manipulations into changes in the root object it represents. While our implementation uses Google Spreadsheets, this proxy-tree design means any object (Excel, CSV, JSON, Database) could be integrated into Quilt's synchronization mechanism so long as it is wrapped in a proxy tree and provides a language to address nodes in that tree.

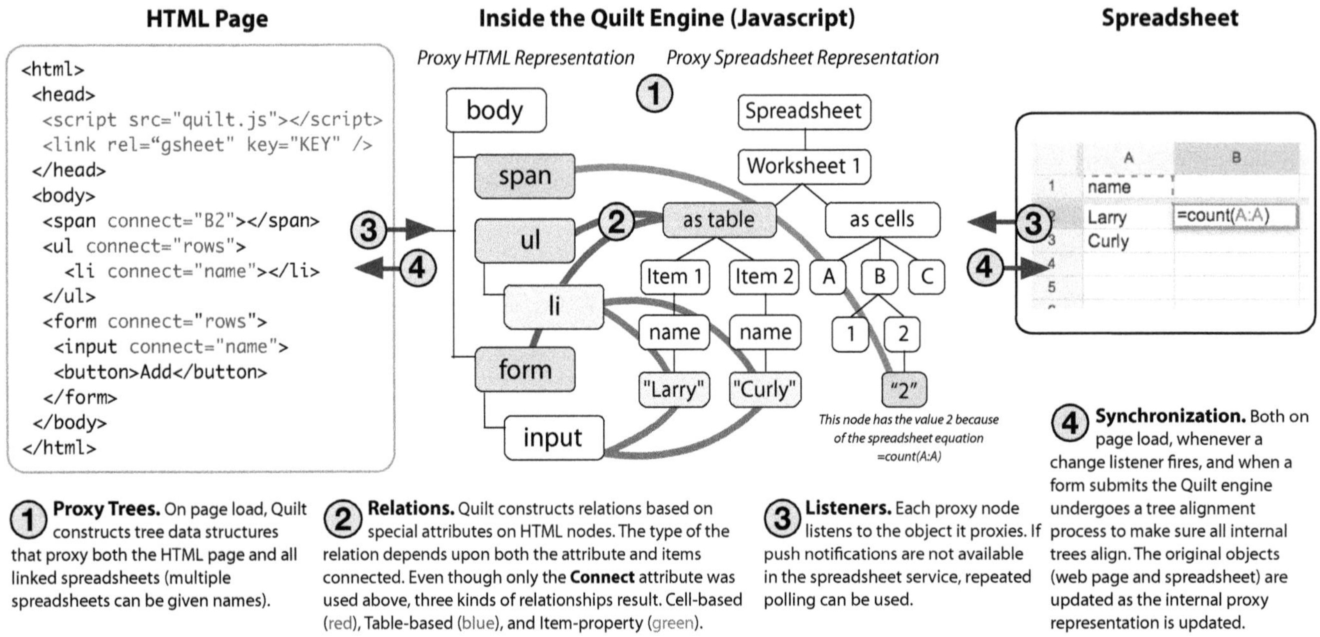

Figure 3: Quilt maintains mirrored, tree-shaped representations of the HTML and spreadsheet. It aligns these representations, rewriting the source objects whenever synchronization is appropriate, such as on web page load or user input.

EVALUATION

We performed user studies of 15 non-programmers to understand whether Quilt's approach can be learned and applied by individuals with only basic spreadsheet and HTML editing knowledge. Specifically, our study examines three questions: armed with a basic understanding of Quilt, can end users:

1. Connect an HTML interface mockup to a spreadsheet to create a web app?
2. Design and build a spreadsheet to support an HTML interface mockup provided to them, and then connect it?
3. Debug Quilt applications with only a browser and the spreadsheet?

Thirteen of the fifteen subjects were able to complete all tasks given to them. Combined with participant surveys and interviews, the data suggests Quilt's approach takes a step toward enabling this population to construct a class of simple interactive web applications they are otherwise unable to build.

Participants

We recruited 15 participants by visiting four local-area programming education organizations that provide introductory web page authoring classes. According to our survey, six participants had only been using HTML for "a few months" or less, nine for a year or less, and all but one for two years or less. Nine participants reported that they cannot write HTML without frequently referring to documentation, nine had never used the HTML `form` tag[2], and five had never used the `table` tag. All participants had used a spreadsheet, and all but one had used Google Spreadsheets. All but four had used a spreadsheet formula. Only four reported that they "understood the concepts" of programming. Of these four, only two had written a computer program before. Both had "about a year" of experience and self-rated as beginners.

Teaching Session

We provided each participant with a fifteen minute private teaching session that was scripted by a worksheet. Using examples, this three-page worksheet presented the main idea behind Quilt (2 minutes), explained the difference between "cell based" thinking—good for fixed inputs and outputs like a math equation—and "table based" thinking—good for lists of items with named properties (3 minutes), and introduced Quilt commands using an example weather report web site backed by a spreadsheet of forecasting data. Participants used this app to practice displaying data, accepting input, and showing/hiding HTML elements for both cell- and table-based addressing (10 minutes).

Tasks

We began the study with only two tasks, but expanded this to four half-way through because participants were completing the tasks with greater success and in less time than we anticipated. We wanted to both take advantage of the extra time and also proactively address the concern that our study was not targeted at the right level of difficulty. Eight subjects were only presented the first two tasks, and the final seven were given all four. Each task, as well as screenshots from participant sessions, is shown in Figure 4

For each task, we provided the participant with three windows: a web browser with a Google Spreadsheet, a text editor with an HTML page, and a web browser rendering that HTML page. The text editor was pre-loaded with an HTML mockup for an application we wanted them to finish. This

[2]That most participants had not used the `form` tag is indicative of how hard it is for this population to build read-write web pages, as `form` elements are only useful in conjunction with a server-side app.

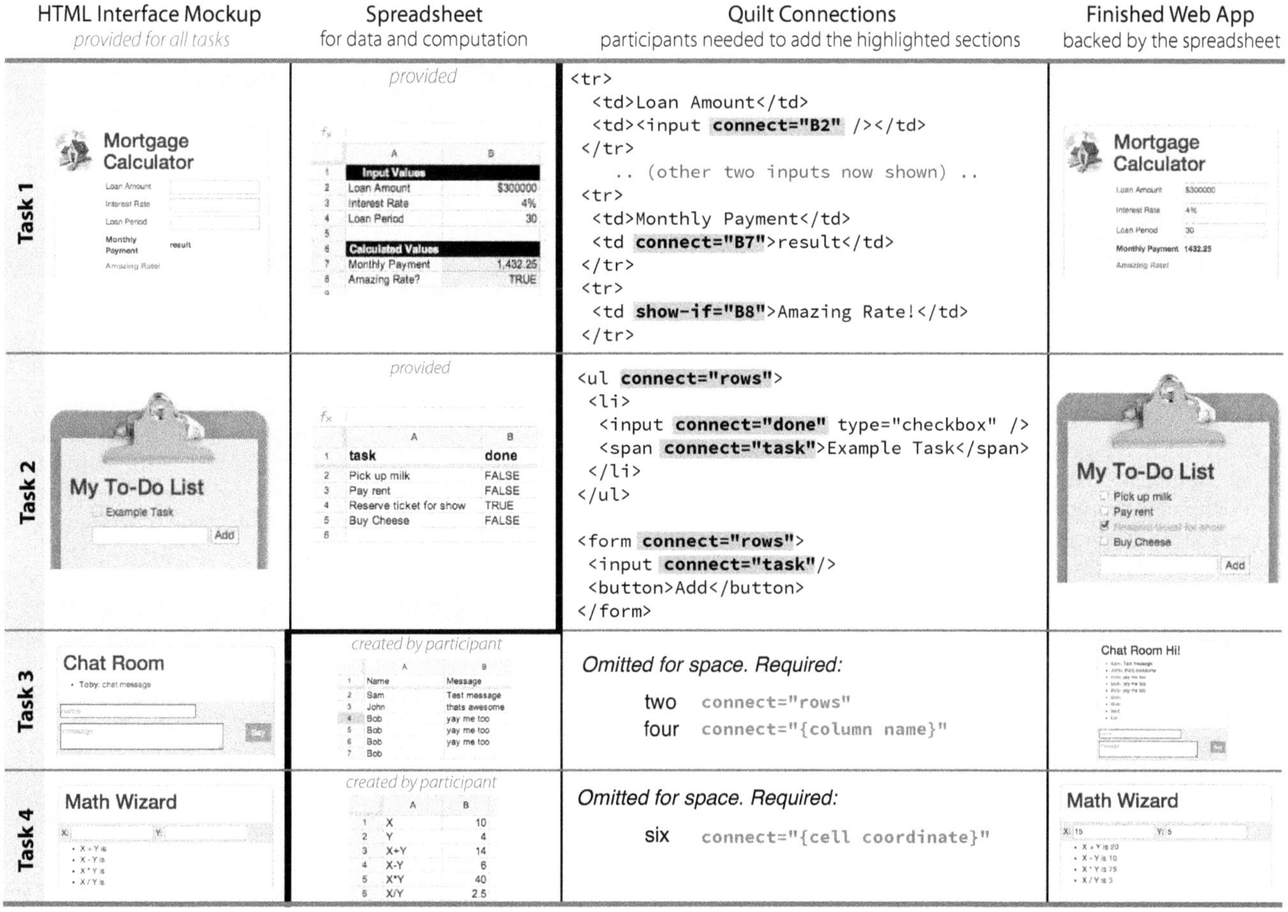

Figure 4: Tasks performed in our user study. For Tasks 1 and 2, participants were given an HTML interface mockup and a spreadsheet containing data. They were asked to author the necessary connections to connect the two documents as an application. The highlighted text in the HTML contains the necessary additions. For Tasks 3 and 4, participants were only given a user interface mockup and had to additionally design and implement the spreadsheet necessary to implement the mockup.

allowed us to study the participant's spreadsheet and Quilt activities without worrying about the separate task of web design, since in theory they all knew basic static HTML authoring. This UI mockup was pre-connected to the Spreadsheet (with a `script` and `link` tag in the `head`) but contained no other Quilt commands. The subject was briefed about the application purpose using a script and then asked to built it.

Tasks were always administered in the same order, and we recorded each task with a screen capture program. The participant was asked to work slowly and speak their thoughts aloud as they programmed. During each task the experimenter was silent except to notify the participant if they had made an undetected spelling error such as `conect` instead of `connect` (we informed them of the mistake's existence but not location).

Tasks 1 & 2 were designed to test whether the subject could learn Quilt and apply it without assistance. In these tasks, the user was provided a finished spreadsheet along with the HTML mockup. The activity required of them was to identify how this mockup should be connected to the spreadsheet to turn it into an application and to make those connections correctly. Task 1 was a mortgage calculator, requiring cell-based connections and the ability to perform output, input, and conditional visibility. Task 2 was a To-Do list, requiring table-based connections and the ability to perform enumeration, output, and row-appending operations.

Tasks 3 & 4 were designed to see if participants were capable of designing and implementing a spreadsheet-based data model to support a Quilt-based application. For these tasks, we provided them with only an HTML mockup and an empty spreadsheet. The activity required of them was to identify the data needs of the UI mockup, construct a spreadsheet to meet those data needs, and then use Quilt to connect the two. Task 3 was a chat website, in which users could post messages to a bulletin board. Task 4 was a math tutor that displayed various arithmetic functions of two input variables.

Result: Learning and Applying Quilt

Before learning Quilt, we showed each participant screenshots of Tasks 1 and 2 and asked how long it would take them to connect the finished web mockup, if provided, to a data source. Most estimated it would take many hours or workdays. Several provided time estimates but added that they had no idea how to actually go about the task, and two said they would not be able to complete the tasks at all ("not with all the time in the universe" said one). Inexperience likely drives much of the high estimate variance, but these estimates at least indicate perceptions of task difficulty.

After learning Quilt, fourteen of the fifteen participants completed Task 1 without any assistance, and thirteen of fifteen completed Task 2 without any assistance. The time it took to complete these tasks was four minutes or less for most participants, dramatically less than their estimates. Figure 5 shows timing information.

While the web apps in these tasks were simple, they required a set of skills these participants largely lacked using traditional methods: reading, writing, and modifying dynamic web data, appending new data items, and conditionally displaying user interface elements. That they could learn to accomplish these tasks with Quilt in only fifteen minutes indicates that Quilt's programming model translates these core data management operations into an approachable interface for non-programmers. One participant had neither written a computer program nor used HTML's `form` or `table` before. Before learning Quilt, she was unable to describe how one might build the Mortgage Calculator or To-Do List with current technologies. After learning Quilt and completing both tasks successfully, she remarked:

> It feels amazing. I thought it would take me three 8 hour days to do something like this. And then to be able to just do it with Google Docs which is something that I use so frequently, and for it to be so easy and to make so much sense, yeah, it's really cool.

The tasks were not all completed correctly on the first try, however. Twelve participants experienced a non-spelling error in at least one task, and five experienced an error in both tasks. In all cases where the participant ultimately completed the task correctly, they were able to identify and fix the error by reloading and sometimes experimenting with the web page and then altering the code they had written. More about this debugging behavior is in the Debugging section.

Designing Spreadsheets to Back Web Apps

Recall that Tasks 3 and 4 were added half way through the user study to see what would happen when participants were burdened with more of the work. These tasks, shown in Figure 4, only provided a web interface mockup. Participants had to create a spreadsheet to support that mockup themselves and then connect it to the HTML page.

We intended to offer seven participants Tasks 3 and 4, but two had to leave after completing Tasks 1 and 2 and could not be offered the tasks. Of the five that remained and were offered the tasks, all completed both tasks successfully. Their times are shown in Figure 5.

How difficult was this additional data modeling step? While we can not make strong conclusions from only five data points, timing information from the videos along with inter-

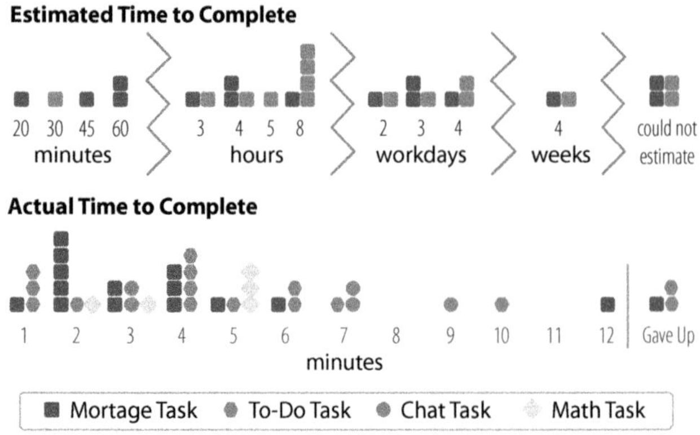

Figure 5: Estimated and Actual time to complete tasks in our study. Please take careful note of the x-axis units: most participants estimated that it would take them many hours or days to complete these tasks before learning Quilt. The actual time to complete these applications was a few minutes.

views was interesting. All five participants spent less than one-third of time working inside the spreadsheet for the Chat application—a table-based app. But four of five participants spent more than half of the time working inside the spreadsheet for the Math application—a cell based app.

Some of this difference is simply due to the fact that the math application required more spreadsheet work. But the recorded videos and audio make it clear that the lack of spatial coherence when addressing cells individually posed problems as well. All five users wrote the Chat spreadsheet (a table) correctly on their first attempt, but only two wrote a working Math Tutor spreadsheet without having to make structural changes. The common problem seems to have been that the HTML mockup contained a *list* of math functions, but the data model to support this list did not have any particular list structure to it. This left them unsure of the physical arrangement of data in the spreadsheet to support this interface.

One caught her mistake almost immediately, but the other two created finished tables of math functions, repeating X and Y once per row with a different math result in the third column. They caught their errors when trying to connect the spreadsheet to the web mockup. At this point, the modeling error was apparent because it was not clear how to make the connection. When asked what he was thinking the moment he revised the table, one replied, "Once I went through the process, used my hands instead of my brain, it started making more sense. Once I started trying to connect it to the HTML."

Debugging Behavior

Quilt does not offer any particular debugging assistance past that already in the browser and spreadsheet. One important question is how to best service the debugging needs of SV app authors who are unfamiliar with traditional programming and debugging concepts. To make progress toward answering this question, we coded all *successful* Task 1 and 2 videos to mark when non-spelling errors occurred and how long it took to fix them after being noticed. In these 27 videos, we found 19 errors across 12 (of 15) participants, all of which were identified and fixed by the participant without assistance. The time it took to fix these errors had high variance—the standard deviation ($77s$) was above the mean ($69s$)—likely due to different skill levels and error context.

While the data set is too small to make strong conclusions, the errors could be clustered into three categories. **Static errors** (13 recorded) were those immediately apparent upon viewing the web page, such as connecting and overwriting the wrong HTML element. No matter what the spreadsheet value, these are obvious. **Dynamic errors** (3 recorded) were those that might be immediately apparent, but might also require experimenting with different data inputs to surface, such as connecting a `show-if` to the wrong cell. If the right cell and the wrong cell had the same "truthiness" value, the error may not be apparent until data changes to reveal the inconsistency, tempting a novice to prematurely declare a correct implementation. **Omissive errors** (3 recorded) were those due to missing functionality or Quilt statements so mistyped that the page simply did not work but no visible clues were available to help diagnose, such as forgetting to connect the `form` element. These errors could be as easily fixed by "fiddling" with the HTML markup.

Figure 6 shows the most elaborate static error encountered: nearly the entire Mortgage web page was connected incorrectly, and the user went through a sequence of iterative modifications until figuring out the proper HTML nodes and spreadsheet cells to connect. At each step in Figure 6, the existence of the error was so clear that a nearest-neighbor walk toward correctness was possible. This participant recalled his thought process afterward, "I tested it out and it changed to the wrong thing so I'm like, 'OK. That's not right,' " Another participant who made an identical error said aloud while programming, "Alright so I put the `connect` in the wrong place. It needs to be connected to the input area."

While these categories may be useful in framing future work, other groupings may prove more appropriate with more data, e.g. connection, conditional, and form errors.

Overall Reactions

Overall reactions to our method were enthusiastic, as the population we studied appeared to be right in the middle of a demographic capable of quickly learning Quilt but not capable of building Quilt-style applications otherwise. Participants liked the immediate feedback and many saw it as a prototyping tool because of that. One participant cited the lack of needing to understand how to write sequential steps often required by programming as a benefit: "For somebody who is very familiar with spreadsheets it makes sense in my head. It doesn't require a lot of 'if this happens, this happens, if this happens this doesn't happen.' It just naturally makes sense,"

All reported that they would use a system like this if it was available to them. "As a beginning programmer, it feels incredible. I feel so much more empowered," one said. And another: "This is great because it lowers barrier to entry for someone who is never going to be a developer."

Figure 6: Most errors encountered could be identified and diagnosed by simply reloading the web page. This participant had the longest sequences of such activity. Other errors were harder to detect, requiring the user to experiment with different data values or manually inspect code to diagnose.

DISCUSSION

Low level end-user programming

Our approach is quite low-level compared to related work. Spreadsheet-backed visualizations using the Exhibit framework [14], for example, are built by invoking pre-made widgets from HTML tags. Quilt offers only the ability to connect raw HTML elements to spreadsheet entities. This puts the non-programming population in a position where they come very close to needing to think like programmers.

Concepts like our `show-if` command require understanding a bit about boolean logic. "`show-if` and `hide-if` were kind of confusing. `show-if`, show if what? It would make more sense if you called it 'show if true'," said one user. Others made mistakes concerning the notion of pointers, such as typing `connect="Loan Amount"` instead of `connect="B2"`. This suggests a more flexible addressing scheme that allows users to refence values by nearby cell lables may be useful.

There was also a physicality to some participant's understanding of the task at hand. Three users reported becoming confused when they realized they would need to connect a vertically organized UI element (e.g., Todo list) on the web page to the keyword `rows`, which they thought of as something horizontal. Despite these confusions, the fact that nearly all participants identified and corrected their bugs suggests that the web relations approach reduces the search space of possible programming statements to a set navigable by authors with only partial understanding of the concepts involved.

Participants did report having to adjust expectations to get used to the idea that one relation (e.g., `connect`) could provide so many different behaviors (output, append, modify, etc). One remarked, "I'm doing something totally different but it's the same wording," and this ran counter to her understanding of programming having many commands. Another commented "I have a sneaking suspicion this won't work," while typing `connect` into an `input` element after having just used it on a `span`. Ultimately, participants seemed to like this approach after getting used to it. "I felt like there were very few functions I needed to remember," one said when asked what she liked about Quilt, and another: "[I felt] overwhelmed, but then I knew I need to figure out where I will put my connects." The relational approach to templating offers the possibility that, in many cases, knowledge that two data objects should be "connected" is sufficient, without understanding the details of how to implement this connection.

In some cases, Quilt's compact programming language *induced errors* because participants got so used to typing `connect` they forgot other commands existed. One participant used `connect` for everything in Task 1, before realizing one of the elements required a `show-if`. She remarked, "I think it was just a matter of momentum. I was just connecting everything. It just seemed like `connect` would just work because everything else just worked with `connect`." Another who made the same mistake said, "I didn't think it through. It was just a natural reaction, because I was connecting a lot of things." One caught himself making this error and muttered, "It ends up being very repetitive. I must not get cocky."

Design Patterns

Because Spreadsheets are turing complete, the spreadsheet-view model can support arbitrarily complex application logic in theory. But the kinds of applications for which SV programming is a *practical approach* for end users will likely be impacted by design patterns developed to handle common scenarios. This is an interesting and fertile ground for future work. We provide two examples here.

Functional View Pattern

It is clear that information management applications have data models. But they also have view models, which represent a transformation of the data model that corresponds to what should be shown in the UI at any given time. In web applications, the view model is often left implicit, scattered across HTML, Javascript, and server-side state. This obfuscates a clear definition of view state in a way that complicate development and debugging.

SV applications provide an attractive way to make these concepts isolated, explicit, and functionally dependent by defining them as separate spreadsheets. Figure 7 shows this pattern, which is similar to the organization we used in the wedding planning app in Figure 2. Using inter-document formulas, the view model sheet is defined as a set of spreadsheet formulas that compute upon the data model sheet. These computations are parameterized by data in the parameters sheet.

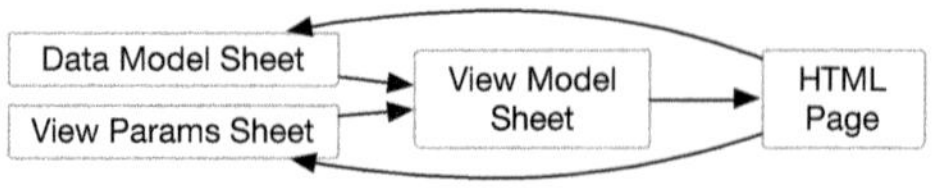

Figure 7: The Functional View Pattern, in which data for the HTML view is stored in a view model sheet. This sheet is a function of a data model sheet and view parameter sheet.

In this pattern, the HTML page displays data from the view model, but it writes data back into the data model and view parameter sheets. Google Spreadsheets natively causes these writes to propagate to changes in the view model, and Quilt causes changes in the view model to propagate forward into the web page. Quilt's spreadsheet addressing language is easily extended to specify which sheet, among many linked sheets on a page, is being referenced.

Quilt's current implementation supports this pattern, but exporting all view logic to a spreadsheet introduces UI latency. This is a problem of system implementation though, not one of end-user programming model design: related work [7] has shown it is possible to automatically rewrite portions a web app's data and computation and relocate it in the web browser for performance gain. The spreadsheet could thus serve as a useful authoring and debugging environment even if it is not the execution platform.

Introducing Multiple Users

Quilt supports multiple simultaneous users with a modification to the functional view pattern shown in Figure **??**. In this pattern, spreadsheets can be designated as either *shared* or *private* in the `link` element that identifies them in the web page's `head`. When a new user visits the web app, Quilt makes fresh duplicates of any sheets marked as private, creating a sandboxed data store for that user that can remain persistent through multiple visits. The private sheet may include both view parameters and user data, and the shared data sheet may aggregate values from many separate private user sheets. This pattern enables users to store private. It also avoids a problem in which simultaneous users might overwrite each other's view parameters (if they were sharing a global view parameter sheet).

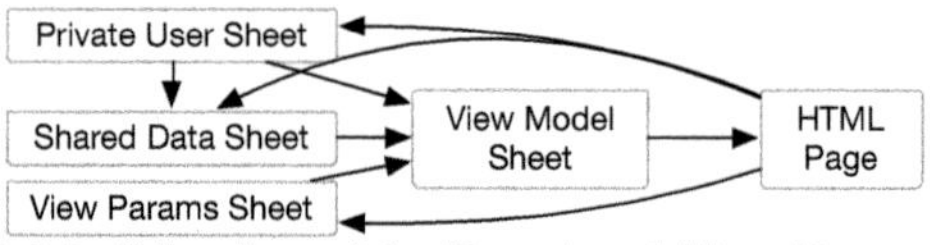

Figure 8: Modification of the Functional View Pattern to support multiple simultaneous users and private data.

UI Possibilities

Visual Programming

Many WYSIWYG environments for HTML authoring already exist, and spreadsheets themselves are a visual programming environment. By grounding Quilt in an HTML-based syntax and existing spreadsheet software, rather than creating a custom HTML+spreadsheet WYSIWYG application, we ensure that this method works independently of any WYSIWYG tools that may be layered on top. From an authoring UI perspective, Quilt only introduces the new step of crafting declarative relations between HTML elements and spreadsheet elements. Quilt could thus easily be made a visual programming environment by making this relation crafting step visual.

Such an environment might present the author with a split-screen view of their spreadsheet and their HTML UI. The author would then visually drag and drop spreadsheet entities (cells, rows, columns) onto the web page (or vice versa) to draw relations. After drawing a relation, the user selects what kind it is (`connect`, `delete`, `show-if`, or `hide-if`). Because web relations annotate ordinary web pages, this visual development environment could enable the user to interact with and debug the live page while editing it.

Web Worksheets embedded in Spreadsheets

Quilt demonstrates the potential of offering more flexibly designed spreadsheet UIs inside the spreadsheet application itself. Large spreadsheets with many worksheets for data and computation could include "web worksheets" written as HTML to provide a better user interface to the analyses than a tabular view provides. Applications built this way could contain rich UIs while relying upon a well-understood infrastructure that additionally permits users to view and edit the data and computation layers.

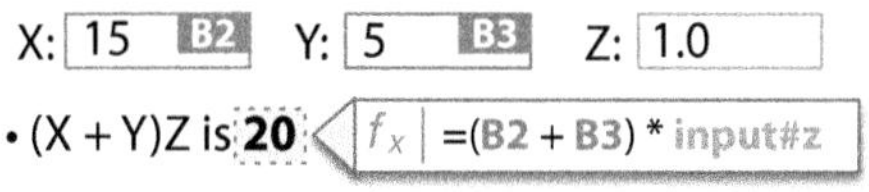

Figure 9: Mockup of what spreadsheet-style editing directly in a web page might look like, enabling spreadsheet elements (`B2` and `B3`) to be mixed with HTML elements (`input#z`).

These packaged web worksheets could even be editable in spreadsheet fashion, like the mockup in Figure 9. A user could select a web element, revealing a formula entry widget to bind the web element to a formula result. A user might even mix spreadsheet cell addresses with CSS selector addresses. The total amount for a restaurant bill might be the sum of column B, plus the Tip entered in a web input box, for example: `=sum(B:B, input#tip)`. A basic example would be re-implementing the spreadsheet UI as a `table` element, with each table cell representing a spreadsheet cell.

Future Work

In addition to performance and design pattern questions raised by our implementation, there are many intriguing questions to explore surrounding spreadsheet-view applications more generally. Understanding what class of applications can practically be authored using this approach, and the kind of user scaffolding required to create nontrivial applications is a key next step. Quilt's choice to use HTML and Spreadsheet software *as-is* enables it to work together with the many tools that already exist to support authoring in each respective medium. But there are also many benefits to be explored by taking a joint approach: modifying the spreadsheet software to embed awareness of the connected web page and explicit UI support for SV application authoring. Chang's work with Gneiss, done in pallel to our work on Quilt, explores this approach [9].

RELATED WORK

End User Web Programming. Building interactive web applications currently requires users to have some knowledge of programming. For the HTML author, this often means learning not only programming fundamentals but multiple new computer languages as well, considering most fully-featured web applications today combine five or more languages [23]. System-level design is also required to coordinate front-end and back-end systems, along with a data storage system such as a database. Research has found that novices struggle with these coordination and integration tasks [17] [16] [23].

The effects of this challenging environment can be seen in the difference between what is valued versus what gets built. Surveys of informal and professional web developers found there were considerable gaps between what web app features were deemed valuable and what got developed, and these gaps were wider for non-programmers [24]. Some of these features include login-based access, databases, online forms and surveys, member registration, and content management.

Mashup-based tools help end users create web applications that integrate data from multiple sources. These tools often require little or no programming, instead using direct manipulation [19] [4], graphical dialog boxes [29], or code samples [13]. Unlike Quilt, these applications only extract data from existing sources and have no interface for storing or managing the user's own data, unless the user can set up their own database. Other tools assist end users with modification and customization of their web experiences [8] [20] [2], but many of these require programming knowledge and also only have the ability to alter existing web pages.

More recently, industry frameworks such as Meteor [3] and Firebase [1] have pushed large parts of a web application into the browser. But both require heavy use of Javascript and learning a reactive data synchronization API. Firebase removes the need to write a back end but provides no support for computation and little support for editing raw data. Quilt also offers reactive data updates but requires no Javascript and leverages a spreadsheet for data editing and computation.

Web design tools for HTML and CSS do not offer support for bridging HTML documents with back-end databases, largely because there are no drop-in frameworks for animating a design. Indeed, a survey of professional web designers found an overwhelming desire for tools that can easily prototype data-driven interactions and provide database integration, even amongst users that knew a moderate to advanced level of programming [21]. In nearly all cases, designers found programming more difficult and time-consuming than web design.

Spreadsheets as End User Information Management Tools. Studies have shown that spreadsheets are an easily available and familiar information management tool for end users, but they present difficulties when scaling to many collaborators and across different physical locations [28]. Few end users convert their spreadsheets to more scalable enterprise database systems, though, because they are notoriously difficult to set up, modify, and query [15].

Much work has been directed at reducing the spreadsheet

errors that occur at larger scale. The Topes project helps end users define and perform data manipulation and validation tasks [25], and other recent work enables data cleaning by example [12]. Online services like Google Spreadsheets scale spreadsheets to many concurrent users, with operational transforms and UI indicators to support simultaneous edits. But because the spreadsheet UI is optimized for numeric calculations, text-heavy data editing remains a usability challenge for spreadsheets. Our method addresses this challenge by allowing spreadsheet data to be cast into HTML interfaces.

Spreadsheet-backed Visualizations. Several efforts have enabled better visualization of spreadsheet data outside the spreadsheet interface. Microsoft Excel has long supported APIs for interacting with spreadsheet data, and recent web-based spreadsheets such as Google Spreadsheets offer web-equivalent APIs as well. A focus of prior work in this area has been to develop ways to package and reuse widgets that make use of this data. The WebCharts [10] project and Google's Charting Widget API both provide a Javascript interface for authoring reusable visualization widgets that draw data from a spreadsheet. But these efforts require the user to learn Javascript and are read-only in nature—the goal is essentially to embed live charts rather than provide an alternate spreadsheet interface. Google Forms creates web-embedable information capture widgets, but they offer limited visual customization and can only append rows to a spreadsheet.

The FORWARD [18] project and Exhibit [14] offer web libraries of data visualization widgets. FORWARD widgets are read-write, but require learning a custom declarative programming language, writing SQL queries embedded in HTML, and using a full database. Exhibit widgets work with spreadsheets and can be invoked with a simple extension to HTML, but they are read-only. In both cases, the systems constrain users to building only those interfaces that can be constructed by snapping together the widgets provided.

Quilt's approach is read-write and widget-agnostic. Rather than provide a way to embed visualizations like charts and maps, Quilt targets the case in which a user seeks a better—or custom—interface to view, edit, and collect spreadsheet data. Because Quilt, like Exhibit, uses a small extension to HTML to provide these interfaces, Quilt apps inherit many attractive sharing and publishing qualities that web publishing provides.

CONCLUSION

This paper presents Quilt, a system that helps end users connect HTML pages to spreadsheets. Quilt authors learn only four new HTML attributes which mark ways in which HTML nodes are related to spreadsheet concepts. Quilt uses these "web relations" to turn an HTML UI mockup into a reactive data-backed user interface. Quilt enables a variety of simple information-management applications, with more complex ones requiring more complex spreadsheet design. Our user studies showed that HTML-savvy end users can quickly learn to use Quilt to connect HTML pages to spreadsheets and to design spreadsheets to support these pages.

REFERENCES

1. Firebase. `https://www.firebase.com`, 2014.
2. Greasemonkey. `http://greasemonkey.mozdev.org`, 2014.
3. Meteor. `https://www.meteor.com`, 2014.
4. Yahoo! pipes. `http://pipes.yahoo.com`, 2014.
5. Benson, E., and Karger, D. R. Cascading Treesheets and Recombinant HTML: Better Encapsulation and Retargeting of Web Content. In *WWW '13* (2013).
6. Benson, E., and Karger, D. R. End-Users Publishing Structured Information on the Web: An Observational Study of What, Why, and How. In *CHI* (2014).
7. Benson, E., Marcus, A., Karger, D., and Madden, S. Sync kit: a persistent client-side database caching toolkit for data intensive websites.
8. Bolin, M., Webber, M., Rha, P., Wilson, T., and Miller, R. C. Automation and customization of rendered web pages. In *UIST '05* (2005).
9. Chang, K. S.-P., and Myers, B. A. Creating Interactive Web Data Applications with Spreadsheets. In *UIST* (2014).
10. Fisher, D., Drucker, S. M., Fernandez, R., and Ruble, S. Visualizations everywhere: A multiplatform infrastructure for linked visualizations. In *IEEE Trans Vis and Comp Graphics* (2010).
11. Force, C. S. T. A. T. Csta k-12 computer science standards. ACM (2011).
12. Gulwani, S., Harris, W. R., and Singh, R. Spreadsheet data manipulation using examples. *Commun. ACM 55*, 8 (Aug. 2012).
13. Hartmann, B., Wu, L., Collins, K., and Klemmer, S. R. Programming by a sample: Rapidly creating web applications with d.mix. In *UIST '07* (2007).
14. Huynh, D. F., Karger, D. R., and Miller, R. C. Exhibit: Lightweight structured data publishing. In *WWW '07* (2007).
15. Jagadish, H. V., Chapman, A., Elkiss, A., Jayapandian, M., Li, Y., Nandi, A., and Yu, C. Making database systems usable. In *SIGMOD '07* (2007).
16. Ko, A. J., and Myers, B. A. Human factors affecting dependability in end-user programming. *SIGSOFT Softw. Eng. Notes 30*, 4 (May 2005).
17. Ko, A. J., Myers, B. A., and Aung, H. H. Six learning barriers in end-user programming systems. In *VLHCC '04* (2004).
18. Kowalczykowski, K., Ong, K. W., Zhao, K. K., Deutsch, A., Papakonstantinou, Y., and Petropoulos, M. Do-it-yourself custom forms-driven workflow applications. In *CIDR '09* (2009).
19. Lin, J., Wong, J., Nichols, J., Cypher, A., and Lau, T. A. End-user programming of mashups with vegemite. In *IUI '09* (2009).
20. Little, G., Lau, T. A., Cypher, A., Lin, J., Haber, E. M., and Kandogan, E. Koala: Capture, share, automate, personalize business processes on the web. In *CHI '07* (2007).
21. Myers, B., Park, S. Y., Nakano, Y., and Mueller, G. How designers design and program interactive behaviors. In *VLHCC '08* (2008).
22. Rode, J., Bhardwaj, Y., Pérez-Quiñones, M. A., Rosson, M. B., and Howarth, J. As easy as click: End-user web engineering. In *Web Engineering*. Springer, 2005, 478–488.
23. Rode, J., Rosson, M., and Pérez-Quiñones, M. The challenges of web engineering and requirements for better tool support. In *Virginia Tech Computer Science Tech Report TR-05-01* (2005).
24. Rosson, M. B., Ballin, J., and Rode, J. Who, what, and how: a survey of informal and professional web developers. In *VLHCC '05* (2005).
25. Scaffidi, C., Myers, B., and Shaw, M. Topes: Reusable abstractions for validating data. In *ICSE '08* (2008).
26. Scaffidi, C., Shaw, M., and Myers, B. Estimating the numbers of end users and end user programmers. In *VLHCC '05* (2005).
27. Valderas, P., Pelechano, V., and Pastor, O. Towards an end-user development approach for web engineering methods. In *Advanced Information Systems Engineering*, vol. 4001. 2006.
28. Voida, A., Harmon, E., and Al-Ani, B. Homebrew databases: Complexities of everyday information management in nonprofit organizations. In *CHI '11* (2011).
29. Wong, J., and Hong, J. I. Making mashups with marmite: Towards end-user programming for the web. In *CHI '07* (2007).

AttachMate: Highlight Extraction from Email Attachments

Joshua Hailpern
HP Labs
1501 Pagemill Road
Palo Alto, CA 94304
joshua.hailpern@hp.com

Sitaram Asur
HP Labs
1501 Pagemill Road
Palo Alto, CA 94304
sitaram.asur@hp.com

Kyle Rector
Comp. Sci. and Eng. Dept
University of Washington
Seattle, WA 98195
rectorky@cs.washington.edu

ABSTRACT
While email is a major conduit for information sharing in enterprise, there has been little work on exploring the files sent along with these messages – attachments. These accompanying documents can be large (multiple megabytes), lengthy (multiple pages), and not optimized for the smaller screen sizes, limited reading time, and expensive bandwidth of mobile users. Thus, attachments can increase data storage costs (for both end users and email servers), drain users' time when irrelevant, cause important information to be missed when ignored, and pose a serious access issue for mobile users. To address these problems we created AttachMate, a novel email attachment summarization system. AttachMate can summarize the content of email attachments and automatically insert the summary into the text of the email. AttachMate also stores all files in the cloud, reducing file storage costs and bandwidth consumption. In this paper, the primary contribution is the AttachMate client/server architecture. To ground, support and validate the AttachMate system we present two upfront studies (813 participants) to understand the state and limitations of attachments, a novel algorithm to extract representative concept sentences (tested through two validation studies), and a user study of AttachMate within an enterprise.

Author Keywords
email; attachment; summaries; attachment summaries

ACM Classification Keywords
H.5.3. Group and Organization Interfaces: Asynchronous interaction

INTRODUCTION
Email functions are the life-blood of enterprise communication, facilitating work-related activities from task management to personal archiving and asynchronous communication [30]. Enterprise workers are consistently overloaded with the volume of email, which has led to a large segment of HCI literature that focuses on improving the UI of and interacting with email messages [29]. However, one major aspect of email - attachments - has gone largely unexamined.

UIST'14, October 05 - 08 2014, Honolulu, HI, USA

http://dx.doi.org/10.1145/2642918.2647420

Attachments are files (documents, slides, etc) that are sent along with an email to supplement the email's content, or as the main/only informational content. These files can be large (multiple megabytes), lengthy (multiple pages), and not optimized for smaller screen sizes, limited reading time, or expensive bandwidth of mobile users. Thus, attachments can increase data storage costs (for both end users and email servers), drain users' time when irrelevant, cause important information to be missed if ignored, and pose a serious access issue for mobile users. In addition, users do not always describe the content of their attachments in detail (if at all).

In this paper, we address these attachment problems with a system called **AttachMate**. Our approach informs users of attachment content by extracting representative highlights from text documents (PDFs, plain text, and MS Word DOC and DOCX files) attached to an email, and injecting those summaries as plain text into the email body itself. This allows both desktop *and* mobile users to easily read the summary from each attachment, judge the value of the content, and make an informed decision about whether or not to read the attachment itself (or if the summary provides enough information). Further, while the summaries are sent with the emails, the attachment itself is securely stored on the AttachMate server, for user access upon request. By storing all attachments on a server (regardless of how many recipients a message is sent or forwarded to), the attachment is not replicated in every inbox and sent mail box (which are stored locally and on the server). Our approach is more accessible, more informative, and reduces data storage and network bandwidth consumption which is especially helpful for mobile phone users.

The **primary contribution** of this paper is the AttachMate client/server architecture. To support, ground and validate AttachMate itself, we have three secondary contributions; **First,** a novel algorithm to extract representative concept sentences from an attachment (which was tested and refined through two validation studies); **Second,** two upfront investigations (with 813 participants) to understand the current state and limitations of attachments (in an enterprise); and **Third,** a user study of AttachMate use within a corporate environment.

RELATED WORK
This paper spans literature from two distinct communities: document summarization and HCI research on email. Subsequently, this section will discuss each area in turn.

Email Interaction Research

HCI research on email systems has examined a wide variety of topics from email as information management[30] to predicting salient emails in universities [6] to studying semantics of communication [11]. Among this large volume of work, few researchers have examined the role of attachments within this email ecosystem, especially as pertaining to helping users identify the content of attachments.

The majority of attachment research focuses on email construction [28], or creating intelligent email systems that alert users if they fail to include an attachment [1, 7]. Hanqal's work on visualizing email databases included an attachment visualization akin to a museum wall[15]. In addition, some work outside of the HCI and IR community has examined the utility of attachment patterns to detect malicious email content [2]. However, none of this literature addresses the specific problems of attachment overload, or informs users about the content of email attachments.

Document Summarization

Automatic summarization is the process by which a description of a document or collections of documents is generated by a computer algorithm. Given the large and expansive literature, this paper's contribution can best be positioned by viewing automatic summarization along two axes: extraction vs. abstraction, and corpus vs single document.

Extraction summarization pulls sentence fragments or full sentences from the original text to create a summary[23], while abstraction summarization uses advanced natural langue processing (NLP) techniques to generate new sentences that describe the document(s)[10]. While abstraction summarization can be more descriptive, it is far more complex to implement and difficult to get 'right' due to the heavy reliance on complex and still imperfect NLP techniques.

Corpus summarization uses a large collection of documents to build a model of the topics being discussed (e.g. Topic Modeling [3, 5], SumBasic[13], KLSum[24]) or opinions rendered (e.g. Opinion Mining [14]). Single document summarization [20, 17] utilizes only one document to create a summary. Corpus summarization approaches rely upon a large body of documents from which patterns about the "whole" can be derived, and are generally easier and more powerful because they have more data from which to draw summaries. Through this power of large numbers, summarization of Twitter topics can be done [5]. Within single document summarization, most algorithms are designed to summarize long (e.g. book)[32], well structured (e.g. chapters or sections) text[8, 27, 31], thus maximizing the amount of text and structural cues from which to derive summaries.

This paper's context specifically requires an algorithm that can handle single documents since attachments are not guaranteed to have a related document corpus. In addition, the algorithm should assume the documents are unstructured (not all attachments exhibit structural elements that can be extracted), and of unknown length (attachments can be very short or very long). There are few unstructured, variable length, single document summarization algorithms (all of which are extraction based). The most notable in this domain are TextRank[23] and LexRank[9]. Both of these algorithms use a simple graph-based approach, treating each sentence as a node. The summary sentence of the document is calculated by finding the centroid of the graph based on a distance vector[1]. This general approach can be thought of as a baseline for novel algorithm development.

In commercial systems, Microsoft has created an Auto Summarize function within the Microsoft Word software[2]. While they do not officially document their algorithm, according to [12], Microsoft appears to use averaged term frequency within a sentence. We use the output of Microsoft's Auto Summarize functionality as another baseline for comparison.

SCOPE AND MOTIVATION

Given the limited research on attachment interaction and single unstructured document summarization, this work mainly contributes to both areas. Thus, the primary contribution of this work is **AttachMate**, a system that automatically summarizes email attachments, includes the summarization in the email, and stores the original attachments on a password protected server. This allows the user receiving the email to easily view the summary (even on mobile devices), as it is stored in plain text, and reduces the network bandwidth and data storage (local and server side) consumption by storing all attachments in the cloud and only sending links to end users. This system is validated through a real-world study.

In order to ground this work in additional motivation beyond existing research literature, we conduct two studies of email attachment usage in an enterprise setting: a survey of 777 enterprise employees' perception of email attachments, and an Outlook add-in that logged attachment usage for the daily workflow of 19 users from HP.

In order to facilitate attachment summarization this paper presents a secondary contribution, a novel approach to single unstructured document summarization through extraction. Multiple potential solutions are tested and compared to existing baselines via two Mechanical Turk studies.

While any of the above paper components could be expanded into a full paper, our goal was a single comprehensive AttachMate *system* publication. These components and studies were done to justify, create and test the systems impact.

ATTACHMENT PERCEPTION IN ENTERPRISE

Before building or designing any software system, we wanted to better understand the perception and challenges of attachments in an enterprise setting. A survey was distributed to the employees of HP located in Palo Alto, CA to which 777 employees responded (30.47% Male, 66.92% Female, 2.61% not reported) with a mean age of 39.37 years (σ=11.45 ). A broad and representative set of users responded,

[1]As a distance vector, TextRank uses words in common while LexRank uses TF-IDF and cosine similarity. Presumably LexRank would use term frequency for single documents.

[2]Part of Microsoft Office for Windows.

% of Total Attachments...	Mean (SD)	Median [IQ Range]	Histogram
...That You Read	0.73 (0.27)	0.80 [0.50,0.90]	
...That Have Value	0.53 (0.27)	0.50 [0.30,0.75]	

Table 1: Survey Quantitative Responses
percentage read refers to desktop access only

from multiple roles within the company[3] and educational attainment[4]. The survey asked basic demographic questions and some quantitative (Table 1) and short answer questions.

Overall, respondents reported reading a fairly high percentage of attachments (73%), though they found that only around half actually have any value. This suggests that many documents are read unnecessarily. Of those attached documents that are *not* opened, participants reported (short answer) that the primary reasons for not opening was: a perceived lack of relevance (25.51%), attachment length (18.69%), would take too much time to read (16.96%), lack of interest in the content (15.94%), assume most of the content is in the email body (12.32%), and 10.58% other reason. Though there are many reasons for people to not open an attachment, these study results explicitly showed that ~60% of the reasons were related to the length (making it too cumbersome or long to read) or unknown content.

Mobile attachment access was more pessimistically characterized, with 50.06% of respondents saying they never open attachments on mobile devices at all. In short answer responses, the primary issues with attachments on mobile devices were small screen/document length (22.17%), time to read/access (19.81%), difficulty in reading (18.73%), support for files on the mobile OS (12.06%), correct rendering/formatting of the attachment (11.95%), download time over cellular network (8.93%), and 20.78% other responses.

These responses indicate that almost half of all attachments have no value and yet, on desktop email systems, 27% of all attachments being opened are not important. In the respondents' own words, users are wasting time reading irrelevant, long documents. This problem is even worse on mobile devices, where half of all users don't bother to open attachments at all. For these mobile users, the top issues are not with content, rather the quality of the reading/access experience on the small devices. This suggests that solutions are needed to help both desktop *and* mobile users discriminate which attachments to read. For those on mobile devices, it is necessary to provide a minimal amount of access to attachment content without the burdens of attachment access itself.

ATTACHMENT USAGE IN ENTERPRISE

To further ground this work and understand how attachments are *actually* used in enterprise, we create an Outlook add-in (OAI) that logs email attachment usage on a secure server. We recruited 55 participants from the users who had completed the original survey, who filled out a demographic survey, and were sent instructions on how to get the OAI. Because we did not track which users actually participated (due to privacy), we can only report data from all 55 participants that signed up, though our final data set consisted of only 19 unique users (41% Female, with a mean age of 48.04, σ=11.11). As in the last study, participants spanned a large portion of an enterprise[5] with a wide variety of educational attainment[6].

Participants were asked to participate for 1-2 weeks (5-10 business days). However, the actual duration was up to each individual. Users participated on average for 8.68 days (σ=3.83) with a median participation length of 9 days [6,12].

During the experimental period, 7090 emails were logged[7]. Users received on average 42.27 emails (σ=24.88) per day, of those messages 25.32% (σ=11.46) contained attachments, and 32.84% (σ=15.24) of attachments are documents[8]. Roughly 8.79% of all emails (σ=6.73) contained documents as attachments. Of those emails with any type of attachment, on average 2.19 files were included (σ=1.20). When documents are sent, on average 1.34 (σ=0.35) documents are included. Documents averaged 0.58 MB (σ=0.48) in size, with the average largest document at 6.69 MB. Of those emails with documents as attachments, a large 65.5% of document attachments are opened.

From this real-world data, we can see that documents are fairly large, taking up a considerable amount of physical storage on local computers (and on exchange servers). In regard to attachment access, user data suggests that users are opening a large percentage of documents needlessly. A solution, like AttachMate, could therefore be used to improve access to, and reduce data footprint from, attachments.

ATTACHMATE: SYSTEM

Given the number of challenges highlighted in the above two studies we created **AttachMate**, a system that automatically summarizes email attachments. Summaries are injected as plain text in the body of the email, and the original attachments are stored on a server with a unique password for protection. AttachMate allows the user receiving an email to easily view the summary (even on mobile devices), reduces the network bandwidth consumed by the email (as the attachment only is transferred once, to the server), and greatly relieves the need for data storage (as attachments are only stored in one location, rather than every server and local mailbox). AttachMate was designed to be unobtrusive to users' daily routines. To this end, we built a server-client architecture with Microsoft Outlook[9] add-in (OAI) as our client. The OAI sends the emails and attachments to the **A**ttach**M**ate **S**erver (**AMS**) which performs the summarization, attachment storage, and email sending (with summaries included).

When the OAI is installed, if a user clicks the send button on an email with an attachment (PDF, MS Word or TXT file),

[3] 273 Management, 41 Research, 272 Engineering, 25 Finance, 8 Legal, 27 Administrative Assistant, 31 Business, 127 Other

[4] 71 PhD/JD/MFA, 237 MS/MA, 379 BS/BA, 85 AD, 32 HS

[5] 21 Management, 5 Business, 2 Marketing, 4 Legal, 6 IT, 12 Engineering, 2 Finance, 3 administrative assistant

[6] 3 PhD/MFA/JD, 19 MS/MA, 24 BS/BA, 5 AD, 5 HS

[7] Statistics reported are normalized on a per-user basis, and partial days (only containing data from the AM or PM) were thrown out so as to accurately report rates (per day) of usage.

[8] Examples of non-document attachments are images

[9] Outlook is the required mail client at HP

```
================ Highlights from "cloud media.docx" ================

This is particularly true in the case of Social Media where the data
sources are varied and no single tool can provide all the data required
for meaningful analytics.

Additional platforms and metric providers can also be integrated with
ExtractPro as and when they are identified.

These enhancements will make it a complete end-to-end social media
data extraction application.

To Download "cloud media.docx" please click (password: VCD70) -
http://11.222.333.44:80/attachmate/attachments/getAttachment/z2UghmvhaZlrreihKoIr

=====================================================================
```

Figure 1: Sample Summary Using AttachMate

AttachMate intercepts the email and asks the user (via pop-up) if they would like to use the AttachMate service[10]. If the user chooses to use AttachMate, the entire content, metadata, signature (as specified in the Outlook preferences), and the attachment(s) are sent to the AMS.

The AMS stores each attachment in the cloud. Every file stored is checked against any other files (via hash) to determine if the file is redundant (this reduces storage costs on the server end)[11]. The AMS then creates a unique URL for each file, and a randomly generated password to protect access. Distinct URLs and passwords are generated so each sent attachment appears to be unique. The content of each file is then extracted, and run through the summarization algorithm (described later).

The content of the summary is then inserted into the body of the email, before the sender's signature (if present)[12]. In addition to the summary sentences, AttachMate includes the URL to download the file, and the password for access. Visual delineation of the AttachMate summaries is included so that the reader can easily find the break points between the summary and body copy (Figure 1). The revised email content, and additional meta data are then sent via SMTP server to the recipient (spoofing the sender's address). AttachMate does not associate attachments with user names (senders or receivers), nor does it store the messages themselves.

Subsequently, the email recipient's mailbox (server or desktop) never receives the attachments themselves as the attachment(s) are only transferred once (sender to AMS). Downloads are therefore only executed by explicit user request[13]. Overall, this reduces storage costs, network costs, and access speeds as files are only ever stored once, and not replicated across multiple exchange server mailboxes or local Outlook caches. In addition, when emails are traditionally replied to or forwarded, attachments are also be included, thus increasing the proliferation of the file. With AttachMate, simply forwarding the links and passwords allows attachments to be shared (with summaries), but the files remain on the server (further reducing bandwidth and storage) across multiple mail service provides or on systems that do not have deduplications built in. Lastly, attachment storage on the server is further optimized by keeping only one copy of each unique file (though distinct URLs and passwords are generated so each sent attachment appears to be unique). Thus, redundant attachments are only stored once.

	Politics	Entertainment	Science	Sports	Technology
Grade Level[15]	11.81(2.76)	9.92(2.99)	14.27(4.06)	10.24(1.67)	12.49(3.10)
Reading Level[16]	49.23(14.47)	56.25(13.29)	36.58(17.74)	59.55(9.27)	46.25(11.91)
Fog Index[17]	8.79(1.37)	7.30(2.00)	9.92(2.61)	8.56(0.67)	9.22(2.35)
# Sentences	70.50(30.32)	57.25(6.75)	49.25(31.08)	52.75(14.77)	51.50(33.45)
Word Count	1481.00(523.88)	1020.25(208.36)	1068.50(415.81)	1117.50(306.86)	1053.75(497.70)

Table 2: Documents Source Statistics

Mean and Std Values Reported

SUMMARIZATION ALGORITHM: DESIGN AND TESTING

A major component in the creation of AttachMate is to define an *extraction* summarization algorithm to help summarize the content of a *single unstructured document.* As discussed above in the related work, summarizing single documents without any guaranteed length or structure is currently an open problem. We therefore set out to create a new extraction summarization algorithm to be used within the AttachMate system that could out-perform the existing techniques.

Rather than simply finding one sentence to summarize an entire attachment (e.g. centroid of a network), our goal was to design an algorithm that could find three "highlights" from a given document. By showing three[14], rather than one sentence, our aim is to provide users a broader view of an attachment's content and aid users in determining if the document should be read in full. This is especially necessary for mobile users where the time and effort required to read an attachment is much higher. In addition, not every document has one "perfect" sentence that covers all of its content. To this end, we designed, built and tested a series of algorithms to summarize an individual document. This section details the two rounds of development and testing. Testing was conducted using Amazon Mechanical Turk.

Documents

In order to test the comparative performance of any summarization algorithm, we collected a series of documents from 5 subject areas (Political Articles, Entertainment Reviews, Scientific Documents, Sports News, and Technology News). Within each subject area, 4 documents were selected from various sources and authors. Thus, each approach could be tested on a broad set of documents of various complexity, length and reading levels (Table 2).

[10]This ensures full transparency, requiring an explicit opt-in for any email using AttachMate.

[11]It should be noted that we do not claim that deduplication is a novel idea of this work, simply a technique to further optimize attachment server storage.

[12]If no signature is detected, the summary is injected either before (if the email is long) or after (for short messages) the body of the email.

[13]Given that only 65.5% of attached documents are opened, this would greatly reduce download bandwidth consumption

[14]We chose a "reasonable" number of sentences, as is standard practice in the Data Mining and IR community.

[15]Flesch-Kincaid grade level indicates that a student at that current U.S. school grade should be able to understand said document (e.g. 8.0 is eighth grade). 7.0 to 8.0 is "optimal."

[16]The Flesch reading ease rates text on a 100 point scale, with higher scores being easier to understand. 60-70 is "optimal."

[17]Years of education to understand a document in a single reading (e.g. 12.0 is a high school senior). 8.0 is considered "optimal."

	Algorithm	Mean (SD)	Median [IQR]	Histogram
Overall	Word	3.74 (1.69)	4 [2,5]	
	WDBC	**4.87 (1.27)**	**5 [4,6]**	
	Clus Cntr	4.11 (1.55)	4 [3,5]	
Politics	Word	3.87 (1.86)	4 [2,6]	
	WDBC	**5.00 (1.11)**	**5 [4,6]**	
	Clus Cntr	3.85 (1.46)	4 [3,5]	
Entmnt	Word	2.73 (1.37)	2 [2,4]	
	WDBC	**4.86 (1.18)**	**5 [4,6]**	
	Clus Cntr	4.14 (1.26)	4 [3,5]	
Science	Word	4.39 (1.80)	5 [3,6]	
	WDBC	4.58 (1.36)	5 [3,5]	
	Clus Cntr	**4.99 (1.45)**	**5 [5,6]**	
Sports	Word	3.54 (1.40)	3 [3,5]	
	WDBC	**4.91 (1.40)**	**5 [4,6]**	
	Clus Cntr	3.58 (1.57)	3 [2,5]	
Tech	Word	4.17 (1.49)	5 [3,5]	
	WDBC	**5.01 (1.29)**	**5 [4,6]**	
	Clus Cntr	3.99 (1.62)	4 [3,5]	

(a) Turk Study Summary Statistics - Round 1

	Algorithm	Mean (SD)	Median [IQR]	Histogram
Overall	**SBDC**	**4.76 (1.50)**	**5 [4,6]**	
	WDBC2	4.75 (1.50)	5 [4,6]	
	KSBT	4.63 (1.54)	5 [4,6]	
Politics	SBDC	4.61 (1.40)	5 [4,5]	
	WDBC2	**4.64 (1.54)**	**5 [3,6]**	
	KSBT	4.15 (1.53)	4 [3,5]	
Entmnt	**SBDC**	**4.84 (1.31)**	**5 [4,6]**	
	WDBC2	4.75 (1.51)	5 [4,6]	
	KSBT	4.33 (1.56)	5 [3,5]	
Science	SBDC	5.13 (1.38)	5 [4,6]	
	WDBC2	4.97 (1.27)	5 [4,6]	
	KSBT	**5.25 (1.31)**	**5 [5,6]**	
Sports	SBDC	4.51 (1.59)	4 [3,6]	
	WDBC2	4.39 (1.55)	5 [3,5]	
	KSBT	**5.04 (1.36)**	**5 [4,6]**	
Tech	SBDC	4.74 (1.74)	5 [4,6]	
	WDBC2	**5.02 (1.52)**	**5 [4,6]**	
	KSBT	4.42 (1.63)	5 [3,5]	

(b) Turk Study Summary Statistics - Round2

Table 3: Comparative User Study Results

Algorithm with largest mean score highlighted in bold — Overall refers to the combined dataset encompassing all 5 subject areas.

Round 1 – Algorithm Design

Our first approach, **Word Distance Based Clustering**, adapts the principles of summarization techniques for long, well-structured documents, to our problem space of single documents of unknown length and undefined, or nonexistent structure. As baselines for comparison, we use a commercially available summarization tool **MS Word** and our implementation of [23, 9] approaches for this context, **Cluster Center**.

Baseline - MS Word

To generate a summary using MS Word, we placed each document into an Office 2010 MS Word document. We then used the internal summarize feature to produce three sentences, which were used as that document's MS Word summary.

Baseline - Cluster Center

Following a parallel approach to that of TextRank[23] and LexRank[9], we created an approach that found the center of a cluster of documents (where each sentence was a node). However, TextRank and LexRank only produce one sentence as the center. In order to generate a fair comparison, we utilized k-means clustering to discover three cluster centers resulting from clustering sentences into three "topic" clusters.

We define a metric to measure sentence distance, analogous to LexRank's term frequency and TextRank's word co-occurence in TextRank. We use an information-theoretic definition of sentence distance [21] from the link clustering literature [16], and calculate the average of pairwise distance between words [22] for any two given sentences[18]. The pairwise distance between two words is calculated using [21], which uses WordNet (a graph of words linked by weighted edges based on semantic similarity) to find the semantic distance between the two concepts [19]. Thus, we can derive three cluster centers in a very similar approach to that of [23] and [9], which we refer to as Cluster Center.

[18]Only information heavy words (nouns and verbs) were used, and all words were lemmatized.

Word Distance Based Clustering (WDBC)

In order to create a new extraction-based, single document summarization algorithm we examined the types of features that other long-structured approaches have used. There are 4 main feature types that are used for the "selection of representative sentences" within long-structured documents [32]:

- **Thematic (semantic):** the meaning or content of the words
- **Location:** the relative or absolute location (physical placement) between words, sentences or paragraphs [20]
- **Headings/Structure:** using only elements that are explicitly providing sections or titles [8]
- **Cue Phrases:** probability of a sentence being relevant is determined by the presence of pragmatic words from a dictionary[19] *(e.g. above all, notably, unfortunately)* [8]

Using Location and Headings/Structure is not robust because attachments can be of variable length, variable structure, with/without headings and varied in content. We therefore focused on integrating the Thematic and Cue Phrases based approaches. Our algorithm, WDBC, specifically addresses the thematic features by building directly on TextRank[23] and LexRank[9] as follows:

1. *Extract document text from file and filter to include on information heavy words (nouns and verbs)*
2. *Lemmatize words to eliminate plurals, tense and conjugations*
3. *Remove extremely low frequency words[20] and low content sentences[21].*
4. *Compute similarity matrix between sentences and cluster using same technique as in Cluster Center*

[19]We utilized the Cue Phrase list from [18].

[20]A word is considered low frequency if it occurs less than 3 times or its frequency divided by total word count is less than 20%.

[21]At least 3 information heavy words.

	Algorithm Comparison	T-test
Round 1	Word vs WDBC	<0.001[§]
	Word vs Clus Cntr	0.001[†]
	WDBC vs Clus Cntr	<0.001[§]
Round 2	SBDC vs WDBC2	0.92
	SBDC vs KSBT	0.23
	WDBC2 vs KSBT	0.26
	WDBC vs WDBC2	0.23

Table 4: Turk Study Algorithm Comparisons

* *Less than 0.05,* † *Less than 0.01,* § *Less than 0.001*

5. *Within each cluster:*
   (a) *Remove sentences with less than 2 cue words (if no valid sentences, set threshold to 1, if still none, include all sentences)*[22]
   (b) *Take sentence with most unique words as representative sentence*
   (c) *If more than one sentence has the same number of unique words, take the one with the largest Inverse Term Frequency*

Mechanical Turk Study Design

Amazon Mechanical Turk (MT) HITs were constructed from each of the 20 documents. HITs were not grouped together so as to reduce order effects. A HIT consisted of the original source text, and the constructed summaries presented in random order. For each summary, participants were asked to respond to the statement *"The above three sentences give me a good overview of the article"* with a 7-point Likert scale (Strongly Disagree (1) to Strongly Agree (7))[23]. Each HIT was completed by 20 Turkers, yielding 400 measures of quality per summary (4 documents across 5 subject areas).

To ensure "legitimate" HIT completion, one "fake summary" was included with sentences extracted from other documents about different topics (e.g. a Science article having a summary from Sesame Street). These "fake summaries" were intended to be so outrageous that they would be ranked Strongly Disagree. If a Turker did not rate the "fake" summary as Strongly Disagree, then that response was thrown out and another HIT on the same document was posted to MT.

An ANOVA and Student's T-test are used to compare the algorithms' performance. While performing multiple comparisons may suggest statistical adjustment to a more conservative value (i.e., Bonferroni correction), we choose to highlight multiple thresholds of significance following [26]. **For transparency, we report t-test results and summary statistics broken down by subject area.** However, it is outside the scope of this paper to optimize for subject area.

Evaluation Limitations

Evaluating summarization presents a significant challenge, especially for large corpuses. This is mostly due to reviewers comparing the computer generated responses to their own mental images of an ideal human-generated summary. Therefore, receiving a perfect Strongly Agree is considered unlikely given the present standard of summarization tools.

Further, this study design is a controlled lab study, and like most lab studies has limited ecological validity in that these results do not account for the broader context of a document with a users workflow or email. In addition, we opted to use a human-centric evaluation technique rather than a gold standard based approach (e.g. ROUGE) due to the added complexity inherent in generating a high quality gold standard summary for each document. Our direct comparison technique finds the (statistically) best technique available to researchers, for integration within AttachMate.

Evaluation & Discussion - Round 1

Master level Turkers[24] were recruited to participate in the evaluation. Each completed HIT was paid 75 cents. 27 HITs were rejected for invalid responses to the "fake" summary. Results from this round are reported in Table 3a, which include mean, median and histograms of the distribution of MT responses. ANOVA comparing MS Word, WDBC and Cluster Center resulted in $p < 0.001$(F=56.15). Comparative t-test outputs between each algorithm are reported in first half of Table 4.

Overall WDBC performed quite well with a median score of 5, and a mean of 4.87. It is notable that WDBC statistically outperformed both MS Word and Cluster Center (the two baselines for comparison). In addition, when examining the histograms, inter quartile range and standard deviation, WDBC was much tighter as compared to the other existing techniques. While not a perfect score on the 7-point scale, which is challenging (as detailed earlier), WDBC is a stark and consistent improvement over alternative approaches.

Round 2 – Algorithm Design

Although high performing, WDBC has one major limitation – computing a similarity matrix between sentences (with average of pairwise distance between words) runs in $O(n^2 \log n)$ [22], and does not scale. While it runs in a matter of seconds on very short documents, it takes around 5 minutes on a 10 page CHI paper. We therefore wanted to determine if an alternative approach could be created that would run faster and perform as well as or better than WDBC. To this end, we created two new algorithms **Key Sentence By Thirds** (KSBT) and **SVD Based Distance and Clustering** (SBDC)[25]:

Key Sentence By Thirds (KSBT)

For KSBT, rather than clustering a document based on semantic distance of information heavy words (WDBC), we simplified our approach by dividing the document into thirds, based on the physical location of each sentence (first third, middle third, last third). This is an extremely fast method that leverages some sense of location [32]. Further, we streamline our representative selection process within each third using a

[22]While examining the raw text, few sentences had at least 2 or 3 cue words, and as the literature suggests, those sentences had high value.

[23]Ordered rank does not give relative distance/quality while individual assessment on an absolute scale does.

[24]Master level Turkers have 95% approval rate and a minimum of 1000 approve HITs

[25]Both approaches filter out non-information heavy words, and lemmatize remaining words.

proxy for semantic information, Singular Value Decomposition (SVD)[26], Cue Phrases, and location [32].

SVD is able to filter out the noise in relatively small or sparse data (often used as dimensionality reduction). SVD views each sentence as row in a sentence-word occurrence matrix (which can be calculated in O(n)), and its output can be used to calculate a weighted list of words, whose weight can be thought of as how "central" a word is to a document (a proxy for, though not exactly, semantic information [32]). We can then calculate the centrality of a sentence by summing the SVD output weights of the words in a given sentence. SVD values are calculated across the whole document.

The most representative sentence in each third is then selected by sorting all sentences (with an SVD score > 0 and Cue Phrases > 0) by the number of Cue Phrases present. Ties are broken by the sentence with the smallest distance (in number of sentences awry) to the start or end of the document (whichever is smaller). If there are no Cue Phrases > 0 or all are the same value, we select the most representative sentence by sorting all sentences by SVD score and taking the largest. Likewise, if all sentences have the same SVD score (or are all 0), we select the sentence with the highest Cue Phrase score.

SVD Based Distance and Clustering (SBDC)

At a conceptual level, KSBT's division of a document into three groups is extremely arbitrary. SBDC attempts to replace the document division by thirds with a clustering that is potentially more representative of distinct thematic parts. We begin by using SVD again to get a weighted list of words. Using the top 500 words from SVD, we create a similarity matrix of sentences, where the value in each cell is the cosine similarity between the vector representations of two given sentences. The vector representation of a sentence is the same as a row in the sentence-word occurrence matrix used in KSBT, except we use the weight of each word from SVD rather than just the number one, so that more "important" words get more impact[27].

Using this similarity matrix, we cluster sentences using k-means, into three thematic clusters. This approach has multiple benefits over the semantic approach in WDBC, the most notable being; the complexity is limited to the top 500 words, and; unlike the semantic distance calculation, SBDC does not need to calculate the distance of all pair-wise combinations of words in each sentence pair combination. Using the three clusters, we follow the same ranking approach used in KSBT.

Round 2 – Evaluation & Discussion

We conducted a second MT Study following the same protocol outlined earlier. This study compared KSBT and SBDC. In addition, we included the best performing algorithm from Round 1, WDBC, as a baseline for comparison (we refer to this in our tables as WDBC2). Turkers were recruited[28] with 95% approval rate and a minimum of 1000 approve HITs. Each completed HIT was paid 50 cents. 67 HITs were rejected for invalid responses to the "fake" summary. Results from this round are reported in Table 3b. ANOVA comparing WDBC2, KSBT and SBDC resulted in $p < 0.43$ (F=0.93). Comparative t-test output between each algorithm is reported in the second half of Table 4 to further highlight the lack of statistical difference found during the ANOVA.

In addition, we compared the performance of Word Distance Based Clustering in both experiments to see if the distribution of Turkers' responses are the same. The comparative T-test (Table 4) does not show statistical difference. However, because lack of statistical difference does not mean statistical similarity, we used Rita and Ekholm's measure of similarity [25][29]. This similarity metric utilizes a θ, or tolerance in the means between two data sets. We set a conservative θ to be one third a Likert interval (0.333). This represents $\frac{1}{18}$ (5.56%) of the possible answer range, and just 19.18% of the variance of Word Distance Based Clustering ($\sigma^2 = 1.74$) and 14.82% of the variance of WDBC2 ($\sigma^2 = 2.25$). The similarity test shows WDBC and WDBC2 are statistically similar ($p < 0.05$) as are WDBC2 vs. KSBT and WDBC2 vs. SBDC.

Summarization Algorithms Discussion – Overall

The Round 2 algorithms appear to have statistically equivalent performance to each other, and WDBC. However, both Round 2 approaches run faster, and scale better. Given that these Round 2 solutions run equally well (performance and quality), and perform better than existing standards (MS Word and Cluster Center), we need a metric by which to select the algorithm to use in AttachMate. Because KSBT's division is relatively arbitrary, we choose to use SBDC (which is more grounded) in the final version of AttachMate.

EXPERIMENT: ATTACHMATE DEPLOYMENT

In order to test the value and usage of AttachMate, we conducted a real-world, ecologically valid study in an enterprise setting. For experimental purposes, we instrumented the AMS to log attachment download access attempts as well as the number of senders and receivers of AttachMate email messages. Users' email addresses were not linked with the emails or attachments, and all activity was recorded using unique hashes of the sender (and receiver's) email addresses. This allows us to track individual users, while maintaining the required privacy and anonymity within HP.

AttachMate was deployed, and a broad invitation was sent out to all HP employees located in Palo Alto, CA to which 51 responded by filling out a demographic survey. Respondents were sent OAI download and install instructions. The OAI

[26]SVD is a more robust and semantically sensitive method for deriving word centrality as compared to raw word count as used in techniques like SumBasic[13].

[27]For example, a word with weight .6 that occurs 3 times in a sentence, would have a value of 1.8 in its bucket rather than 3.

[28]Master status was not required, however all were required to be living in the US, suggesting high familiarity with english.

[29]Rita and Ekholm's measure uses a similarity limit, θ such that the difference in the averages of the two data sets is smaller than θ in absolute value. This can be determined by examining the 95% confidence interval for the difference between the two data sets. If the θ is greater than the right 95% confidence interval and $-\theta$ is less than the left 95% confidence interval, 'there is a difference' with $p<0.05$.

		Mean (SD)	Median [IQ Range]	LN Histogram
Attachment	# Recipients	1.476 (0.722)	1.00 [1.00,2.00]	
	# Downloads (Unique IP)	0.314 (0.56)	0.00 [0.00,1.00]	
	Size (MB)	0.339 (1.01)	0.058 [0.018,0.223]	
	Traditional Footprint (MB)	1.60 (4.442)	0.262 [0.082,1.003]	
	AttachMate Footprint (MB)	1.216 (3.993)	0.196 [0.061,0.735]	
	Reduction %	70.897 (18.727)	75.00 [50.00,75.00]	
Document	# Recipients	1.356 (0.788)	1.00 [1.00,1.00]	
	# Downloads (Unique IP)	0.456 (0.633)	0.00 [0.00,1.00]	
	Size (MB)	0.415 (1.115)	0.084 [0.045,0.413]	
	Traditional Footprint (MB)	1.87 (4.544)	0.377 [0.216,1.672]	
	AttachMate Footprint (MB)	1.48 (4.41)	0.312 [0.164,1.333]	
	Reduction %	77.089 (18.057)	75.00 [75.00,90.00]	

Table 5: AttachMate Storage "Per File"

Data Normalized "Per User"— Traditional Footprint is with exchange infrastructure

Reduction Percentage is AttachMate/Traditional for each file

was downloaded 41 uniques times, with 28 unique AttachMate email senders during the study period. Due to privacy, we do not know which of the 51 respondents downloaded and used the OAI and all demographic information presented is from the full 51 respondents. As earlier, participation duration was left to the discretion of the individual, though we encouraged 5-10 business days of usage.

At the end of the study, a questionnaire was distributed to participants. This included Likert Scale, short answer, and SUS usability metric [4] questions. Due to the privacy limitations outline above, we were unable to directly followup with individual participants to ensure a high response rate. Subsequently, the survey was sent to all 51 initial respondents, resulting in only 6 survey completions (roughly 21% of unique senders). While this data may not be fully representative of all user experiences, we present results from the survey to help inform the observed behavior using AttachMate. In addition, due to the privacy concerns, we were unable to directly contact *recipients* of AttachMate emails to determine their reaction.

Demographics

Of the 51 individuals that responded to the survey, 54.9% were male. The average age was 40.99 (σ=10.43). As in prior studies, the educational attainment[30], subject area[31] and employment within HP[32] was highly variable, representing a broad cross-section of the company.

Results & Discussion: AttachMate Usage

On average, participants used AttachMate for 7.30 days each (median use length of six days). There were 28 unique senders, and 67 unique receivers of emails. Because each email can be sent to multiple recipients, it is important to examine AttachMate and the attachment usage from two distinct perspectives; those of the sender, and of the recipient. From the senders' perspective, 66 emails were sent using AttachMate, with a total of 105 attachments being sent (of which 73 were documents). Only 27.62% of the attachments and 38.36% of documents were downloaded. From the receivers' perspective, 93 emails were received, with a total of 155 attachments being received (99 of which were documents). Only 18.71% of attachments and 38.28% of documents were downloaded. These relatively low attachment download rates are well under the rate of 73% reported in the qualitative responses form users (Table 1) and real-world rate of 65.5% of documents in our enterprise logging study (presented earlier in the paper). This analysis strongly suggests a marked change in behavior when the only experimental intervention was AttachMate. This favorable change in user behavior suggests that AttachMate summaries were highly beneficial in information presentation *and* document discrimination, allowing users to discriminate which attachments to open and read.

Results & Discussion: AttachMate User Response

All participants mentioned the summarization of attachments to be the "best" feature of the AttachMate system. When presented with the statement *"Having Summaries is the key feature to AttachMate being successful"* and a 5-point Likert scale response, the average response was 4.6 (three participants marked 5 (strongly agree), two marked 4, and one marked 3). This is higher compared to other features such as Summary Quality (4.33), Saving Bandwidth (4.25), Mobile Access To Attachments (4.4). The only higher performing feature was Security of Files, to which all respondents reported 5 (Strongly Agree).

Mean users responses to the SUS usability metric was 70.00, which is considered slightly above average[4]. This was a surprisingly low score given the amount AttachMate was used, and the other responses on the survey. However, when we examined the short answer responses to *"What modifications are needed to make AttachMate Perfect?"*, participants universally mentioned two key features:

- Support for Microsoft PowerPoint and Excel files
- Preview Summaries Before Sending Emails

In short, the usability limitations stemmed from not supporting *all* file types and not presenting users with previews of the emails. Given that these two issues are the source of the slightly above average SUS score, we strongly believe with a large file type support[33] and a preview mode, the major issues of AttachMate can be addressed. Further, these issues do not appear to be intrinsic to or a reflection upon the summarization algorithm or the AttachMate system/infrastructure itself. This is codified in a short-answer response from one participant *"I really love the summarizer... What a cool job you have – inventing really valuable things."*

Results & Discussion: AttachMate Storage Benefits

While AttachMate's summarization system provides benefits for end users, its storage infrastructure provides financial benefits for their corporate employers. Table 5 shows the storage consumption for each file, normalized by user[34]. On average, documents are just under half a Megabyte in size. However, when we consider the multiple locations where the file is stored (sender's local sent folder, sender's exchange

[30] 49.02% BS/BA, 37.25% MS/MA, 5.88% PhD/MFA/JD, and 7.84% HS or HS Equivalent.

[31] 31.37% Business & Law, 21.57% CS, 15.69% Finance, 15.68% Science & Engineering 9.80% Humanities, 5.88% Communications

[32] 45.10% Management, 27.45% Engineering, IT and Research, 13.73% Business, 7.84 Admin % HR, 5.88% Finance

[33] Yet what a summary of an Excel or PowerPoint looks like is a question for future work.

[34] Data are normalized per user so that individuals who send more or less files have equal weight in the summary statistics.

sent folder, each receiver's server inbox, each receiver's local inbox), the average document footprint balloons to 1.87 megabytes. However, with AttachMate's improved storage this is reduced by 22.91% on a per file basis. Across all attachments, the reduction is larger, 29.10%. It should be noted, that this is without any redundant file optimization (only storing one copy of a duplicate file) enabled. This feature was not used during the study because it can only show impact over a large, ongoing dataset and the current experiment was too short and limited in participants.

DISCUSSION & FUTURE WORK

Overall, AttachMate successfully tackled the attachment file challenges uncovered earlier in this research. User responses, suggested that AttachMate is tackling a real problem, though the benefits of the AttachMate approach have not reached their full potential as additional types of files could benefit front the auto summarization process. This not only highlights the value of the summarization, but the success of our summarization technique (supporting the feedback from the MT studies). In addition, AttachMate reduces the data footprint of transferred documents by 22.91%, and 29.10% for all attachments. This is largely due to the provided summaries, which allow users to better triage which attachments need to be downloaded.

User feedback, and lessons learned through the development process, also suggest new directions for this work to expand. First, AttachMate should have a preview mode. When attachments need to be summarized, those summaries should be previewed by end-users. This additional mode could allow users to further refine and improve summaries by allowing users to see the "top N" highlights (as determined by the summarization algorithm). Subsequently, users could approve or replace sentences allowing for quick, but customized, summaries to be injected.

Another area of suggested feedback from our experiment is additional file types. While performance on PowerPoint slides may likely follow that of documents, determining what a "summary" of a spreadsheet looks like is unknown. This could be an open area of future work.

Lastly, if the AttachMate system is fully integrated with an exchange or other email service, attachments could be summarized if sent from non-AttachMate users. While this will not improve data storage costs, it will improve readability for end users, especially those on mobile devices. Further integration within a client can expand the "preview" mode, by visually showing users from where in the documents the summaries come from. This can allow users to keep summaries in context.

CONCLUSION

While much time and attention has been placed on the ubiquity of email within and beyond enterprise, little work has been done to address the growing problem of email attachments. These accompanying documents can be large (multiple megabytes), lengthy (multiple pages), and not optimized for the smaller screen sizes, limited reading time, or expensive bandwidth of mobile users. Thus, the triage of these overwhelming number of documents is left up to the end user, draining time, increasing storage/bandwidth costs, and if missed can cause important information to go unseen.

This paper presents the first system that directly addresses the problem of attachment overload, AttachMate. In addition to the system infrastructure itself, this research presents a novel single-unstructured document summarization algorithm that outperforms the existing approaches and commercial options. To better inform and ground this research, we present two upfront studies (813 participants) to understand the state and limitations of attachments, especially within enterprise. Lastly, a ecologically valid real-world deployment study of the entire AttachMate architecture was conducted with very encouraging results; reducing the data footprint, better informing users via summaries and helping users better discriminate which files to open.

While this research presents many contributions (study of attachments in enterprise, summarization algorithm, AttachMate system), and there are many exciting future directions this research can go, this work's primary contribution is the validation that email attachment overlaid is an important problem that can be addressed through grounded, robust and well tested solutions like AttachMate.

REFERENCES

1. Albakour, M.-D., Kruschwitz, U., and Lucas, S. Sentence-Level attachment prediction. In *IRFC'10*, Springer-Verlag (May 2010).
2. Bhattacharyya, M., Hershkop, S., and Eskin, E. MET: an experimental system for Malicious Email Tracking. In *NSPW '02: Proceedings of the 2002 workshop on New security paradigms*, ACM (Sept. 2002).
3. Blei, D. M., Ng, A. Y., and Jordan, M. I. Latent dirichlet allocation. *The Journal of Machine Learning Research 3* (Mar. 2003), 993–1022.
4. Brooke, J. SUS-A quick and dirty usability scale. *Usability evaluation in industry* (1996).
5. Chua, F., and Asur, S. Automatic Summarization of Events From Social Media. In *ICWSM* (2013).
6. Dabbish, L. A., Kraut, R. E., Fussell, S., and Kiesler, S. Understanding email use: predicting action on a message. In *CHI '05: Proceedings of the SIGCHI Conference on Human Factors in Computing Systems*, ACM Request Permissions (Apr. 2005).
7. Dredze, M., Lau, T., and Kushmerick, N. Automatically classifying emails into activities. In *IUI '06: Proceedings of the 11th international conference on Intelligent user interfaces*, ACM Request Permissions (Jan. 2006).
8. Edmundson, H. P. New Methods in Automatic Extracting. *Journal of the ACM (JACM 16*, 2 (Apr. 1969).
9. Erkan, G., and Radev, D. R. LexRank: Graph-based lexical centrality as salience in text summarization. *J Artif Intell Res(JAIR)* (2004).

10. Fiszman, M., Rindflesch, T. C., and Kilicoglu, H. Abstraction summarization for managing the biomedical research literature. In *Proceedings of the HLT-NAACL* ... (2004).
11. Gilbert, E. Phrases that signal workplace hierarchy. In *CSCW '12: Proceedings of the ACM 2012 conference on Computer Supported Cooperative Work*, ACM Request Permissions (Feb. 2012).
12. Gore, K. Cogito Auto Sum. *Slate.com Accessed 1/31/2013*, `http://www.slate.com/articles/briefing/articles/1997/02/cogito_auto_sum.html`.
13. Haghighi, A., and Vanderwende, L. Exploring content models for multi-document summarization. *NAACL 2009* (2009).
14. Hailpern, J., and Huberman, B. A. Echo: the editor's wisdom with the elegance of a magazine. In *EICS '13: Proceedings of the 5th ACM SIGCHI symposium on Engineering interactive computing systems*, ACM Request Permissions (June 2013).
15. Hangal, S., Lam, M. S., and Heer, J. MUSE: reviving memories using email archives. In *UIST '11: Proceedings of the 24th annual ACM symposium on User interface software and technology*, ACM Request Permissions (Oct. 2011).
16. Jain, A. K., Murty, M. N., and Flynn, P. J. Data clustering: a review. *Computing Surveys (CSUR 31*, 3 (Sept. 1999).
17. Katragadda, R., Pingali, P., and Varma, V. Sentence position revisited: a robust light-weight update summarization'baseline'algorithm. In *Proceedings of the Third* ... (2009).
18. Knott, A. *A Data-Driven Methodology for Motivating a Set of Coherence Relations*. PhD thesis, The University of Edinburgh: College of Science and Engineering: The School of Informatics, July 1996.
19. Leacock, C., Miller, G. A., and Chodorow, M. Using corpus statistics and WordNet relations for sense identification. *Computational Linguistics 24*, 1 (Mar. 1998), 147–165.
20. Lin, C.-Y., and Hovy, E. Identifying topics by position. In *ANLC '97: Proceedings of the fifth conference on Applied natural language processing*, Association for Computational Linguistics (Mar. 1997).
21. Lin, D. An information-theoretic definition of similarity. In *ICML* (1998).
22. Manning, C. D., Raghavan, P., and Schütze, H. *Introduction to Information Retrieval*. Cambridge University Press, July 2008.
23. Mihalcea, R., and Tarau, P. TextRank: Bringing order into texts. In *Proceedings of EMNLP* (2004).
24. Nenkova, A., and Vanderwende, L. The impact of frequency on summarization. Tech. Rep. MSR-TR-2005-101, Microsoft Research, 2005.
25. Rita, H., and Ekholm, P. Showing similarity of results given by two methods: A commentary. *Environmental pollution* (2007).
26. Savitz, D. A., and Olshan, A. F. Multiple comparisons and related issues in the interpretation of epidemiologic data. *American Journal of Epidemiology* (1995).
27. Seki, Y., Eguchi, K., and Kando, N. Compact summarization for mobile phones. *Mobile and ubiquitous information access* (2004).
28. Tang, J. C., Lin, J., Pierce, J., Whittaker, S., and Drews, C. Recent shortcuts: using recent interactions to support shared activities. In *CHI '07: Proceedings of the SIGCHI conference on Human factors in computing systems*, ACM Request Permissions (Apr. 2007).
29. Whittaker, S., Bellotti, V., and Moody, P. Introduction to this special issue on revisiting and reinventing e-mail. *Human-Computer Interaction 20*, 1 (June 2005).
30. Whittaker, S., and Sidner, C. Email overload: exploring personal information management of email. In *CHI '96: Proceedings of the SIGCHI Conference on Human Factors in Computing Systems*, ACM Request Permissions (Apr. 1996).
31. Yang, C. C., and Wang, F. L. Automatic summarization of financial news delivery on mobile devices. In *WWW'03* (2003).
32. Yang, C. C., and Wang, F. L. Hierarchical summarization of large documents. *Journal of the American Society for Information Science and Technology 59*, 6 (Apr. 2008).

Making the Web Easier to See with Opportunistic Accessibility Improvement

Jeffrey P. Bigham
Human-Computer Interaction and Language Technology Institutes
Carnegie Mellon University
jbigham@cs.cmu.edu

ABSTRACT
Many people would find the Web easier to use if content was a little bigger, even those who already find the Web possible to use now. This paper introduces the idea of *opportunistic accessibility improvement* in which improvements intended to make a web page easier to access, such as magnification, are automatically applied to the extent that they can be without causing negative side effects. We explore this idea with `oppaccess.js`, an easily-deployed system for magnifying web pages that iteratively increases magnification until it notices negative side effects, such as horizontal scrolling or overlapping text. We validate this approach by magnifying existing web pages $1.6x$ on average without introducing negative side effects. We believe this concept applies generally across a wide range of accessibility improvements designed to help people with diverse abilities.

Author Keywords
low vision; magnification; zoom; accessibility

ACM Classification Keywords
H.5.m. Information Interfaces and Presentation: Misc.

INTRODUCTION
In real life, what someone can do is a function of not only a static notion of their abilities, but also their dynamic context and the effort needed to complete a task. This is particularly true of people with visual impairments accessing web content. Some use screen magnifiers to make computer content larger, others sit closer to the screen, and some do both (Figure 1). It is difficult for content creators to anticipate and adapt to the various display needs that individuals may have, and so often content is not laid out in a way that fully leverages the available space.

This is important because a large number of people could benefit from content that is a little bigger. While 39 million people worldwide are blind, many more (246 million) have low vision [6]. Even more people do not consider themselves to have visual impairment and use no special software at all, but yet could benefit from improved accessibility, such as slightly larger content [3]. This is especially common among aging adults. Instead, these users may find their own solutions. For instance, they may prefer lower-resolution monitors on which content appears bigger, move their head closer to the screen when needed, or even prefer software programs or web sites that use larger fonts. Most are unaware that specialized software or features of their existing software exist, and many do not want (or would find it too complicated) to learn how to use it. As one example, we asked 50 Google Survey respondents over the age of 55 to tell us (without looking) how to make content in their web browser bigger. Only one wrote `ctrl+`, whereas the rest wrote some variant of "I don't know."

Figure 1. People with low vision use a combination of magnification software and physical accommodations like positioning themselves closer to the screen. *Opportunistic accessibility* is about improving accessibility when possible without adverse side effects, even if to a small degree.

In this paper, we explore the potential of automatically making the Web display a little bit larger when we can do so without causing negative side effects. We call the generalization of this idea *opportunistic accessibility improvement*. In the case of web magnification, the idea is to make content a little bigger on web pages that a user visits, but only so much as can be done without introducing problems that otherwise affect the page. Opportunistic accessibility provides a new way of thinking about the sort of "messy," dynamic, and adjustable accessibility needs that people have. It may open a space for access technology that does not provide a perfect solution to

http://dx.doi.org/10.1145/2642918.2647357

problems, but rather makes access easier for people when it can, recognizing that they often find a way to access content even when the tool is unable to help.

We introduce `oppaccess.js`, a system that helps to make the Web a little easier to see. `oppaccess.js` does not overhaul the Web —in most cases we suspect users won't even notice the changes made unless told. Instead, content is just a little bigger so it is easier to see and a little easier to use. It detects common problems that occur when magnifying web content, and automatically sets its magnification level to avoid those problems.

We make three contributions: *(i)* we introduce the idea of *opportunistic accessibility*, *(ii)* we demonstrate the opportunity for making the Web a little bigger while minimizing negative impacts on usability, and *(iii)* we introduce `oppaccess.js` to make many web pages a little bigger when it can.

MAGNIFICATION AND THE WEB

`oppaccess.js` builds on prior work on magnification. ZoomText[1] is a popular example of the magnification software used by people with low vision. It graphically zooms screen content, which applies across a wide variety of content but tends to introduce horizontal scrolling (Figure 2a). Web pages are generally designed for vertical but not horizontal scrolling, and so horizontal scrolling can cause usability problems, *e.g.* needing to scroll constantly from left to right while reading a block of text. Another approach is to allow users to apply standard magnification in layers —for instance, applying some level of base magnification to the entire content area, and then a higher level of magnification to content of interest [5]. This is the approach taken by *sitecues*[2], which allows users to magnify web page content in layers.

Web browser magnification features have the potential to do better than graphical zoom. As content is magnified, the Web browser's layout engine reflows content to better utilize available space. The effect of magnification on web page layout is similar to what happens if the width of the window is decreased proportionally. For instance, a $2x$ zoom produces a layout similar to what would result if the window's width was divided by 2. The Web is characterized by diversity in both content and displays, and web browsers have developed sophisticated layout engines to reflow content to adapt. One simple example is wrapping of inline elements, such as text and images, within containing block-level elements.

Designing web pages that adapt to different devices is difficult, which has caused many web pages to be developed inflexibly assuming minimum requirements, *e.g.* for some time it was common to create web page content that was 800px wide and much of this content still exists. Internally, web browsers implement zoom by simply multiplying any fixed dimensions by the zooming factor. A DIV element that has been assigned a width 800px will be a fixed 1200px if the zoom level is set to $1.5x$. When web pages designed in this way are magnified they quickly grow beyond the width of the web browser window and introduce horizontal scrolling.

[1]http://www.aisquared.com/zoomtext

[2]http://www.sitecues.com

Responsive design allows web content to flexibly adapt to constraints. One component is CSS media queries, which allow different stylesheets to be applied based on different characteristics of the media the page is being displayed on, *e.g.* apply a stylesheet that displays less content horizontally when the width of the media is small. Another component is using flexibly-sized container elements. For instance, instead of setting the width of a DIV to 400px, its width might be set to 40%. The element then takes up 40% of the window, regardless of the magnification level that is applied.

Pages that use responsive design well can be magnified to higher levels of zoom before introducing problems like horizontal scrolling. At high magnification levels, flexibly-sized elements can result in two other problems. The first is that elements assigned percentage dimensions eventually start to overlap (Figure 2b), and the second is that growing text sizes with word wrapping can cause very narrow lines (Figure 2c).

`oppaccess.js` detect the three problems outlined above: *(i)* introduction of horizontal scrolling, *(ii)* overlapping DOM elements, and *(iii)* lines that are too narrow. It magnifies web content until it either detects one of these problems or reaches a maximum (currently $3x$).

More intelligent magnification of content has generally been more complicated and not yet been successfully ported to the Web. For instance, Supple automatically personalizes an interface to make it better for people with visual and motor disabilities [4], but it requires a formal description of the interface as input. `oppaccess.js` is not meant as a replacement for these, but as a much simpler alternative that may be "good enough" for many people. The fact that some of the more complicated approaches are not yet widely used may be seen as partial validation for our simpler *opportunistic accessibility* approach, even if it isn't as powerful.

Past tools that do not fully replicate the functionality of existing solutions, yet are easy to access and transparent, have been successful. For instance, the WebAnywhere web-based screen reader has a subset of features available in screen readers and only works for the Web, but the fact that it can be accessed without installing new software has drawn hundreds of thousands of users [1]. `oppaccess.js` is similarly easy to install by injecting a single Javascript script via either a browser extension or by the web content developer.

MAKING THE WEB EASIER TO SEE

In this section, we describe `oppaccess.js`, our system for opportunistically magnifying web pages to make them easier to see. The system is implemented as a single cross-browser Javascript script (615 lines), not including jQuery. It can be delivered to web pages either by a web browser extension —we have implemented a Chrome extension —or by including the script directly in a web page. Thus, it can be used by either web developers to opportunistically improve the accessibility of their own web pages or by end users who want to apply it to all of the web pages they visit.

Magnifying web pages is surprisingly easy with Javascript. The base method is to programmatically set the value of the

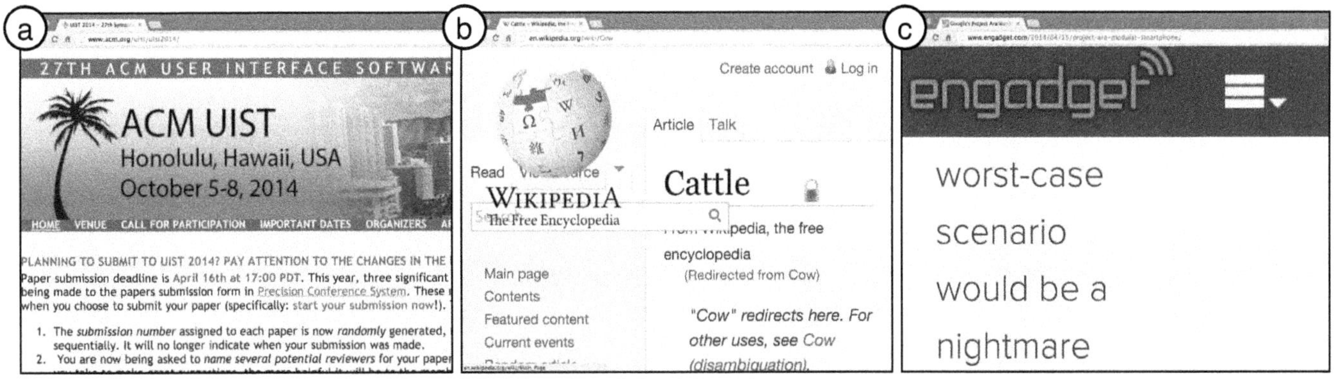

Figure 2. Illustrated examples of three of the most common problems introduced by web magnification: *(a)* graphical zoom introduces horizontal scrolling, *(b)* responsive design works well to adapt a web page to higher levels of magnification but often results in overlapping content as magnification grows too large, and *(c)* as the size of text grows too large relative to its container the lines of text become undesirably thin.

CSS property `document.body.style.zoom`. For instance, setting this property to 2.0 results in a doubling of the size of page elements. The effect is quite similar to what results when a user presses `ctrl` + or `cmd` + several times to manually magnify the page. Using the script, the magnification is optimally applied as soon as the page is loaded. The script uses a page-specific cookie to remember the optimal zoom level for the given web page, so that it can be magnified immediately next time.

Page Health

To determine the magnification level to apply, `oppaccess.js` iteratively increases magnification in steps of 0.1 and checks after each to see if it decreases what we call *page health*. The page health is currently defined as 1 minus the sum of the area of the page that *(i)* is horizontally scrolled out of the viewport, *(ii)* overlaps with another element, or *(iii)* contains narrow word-wrapped text. The area considers the full dimensions of the page, regardless of whether or not they are visible. The page health is calculated and recorded when the page loads because some pages exhibit these problems when they are first loaded. Iterative magnification is stopped whenever the page health decreases by more than 0.05. Modern web browsers are smart enough not to visually re-render the page in between iterations, and so it appears to happen all at once.

Horizontal Scrolling

Horizontal scrolling occurs when the width of the web page content is larger than the width of the viewport. Horizontal scrolling can be detected by comparing the width of a web page's `document` element to the width of the `window`. This is efficient and robust to check, and we have found it to be the first problem introduced when magnifying most web pages.

Overlapping Text

When elements are assigned CSS positioning other than the default, e.g. static, absolute, relative, there is potential for elements to overlap. The likelihood of this happening increases when web pages are magnified because usually the web page author has not carefully thought about or designed for this case. To detect area of the page that has overlapping text areas, `oppaccess.js` first finds all elements that contain text, records their location and dimension, and then runs an efficient line-scanning algorithm (also implemented in Javascript) to find overlapping area. It then returns the sum of the overlapped area.

Narrow Word Wrapping

A common problem encountered on web pages that use container elements with percentage widths is that as the text they contain grows larger with magnification, the number of words per line decreases (Figure 2c). `oppaccess.js` detects this sort of problem with word wrapping by checking each block-level element that contains text to ensure that enough words are able to be displayed per line (5 is currently used as the cut-off). It ignores elements that do not contain enough words ($2x$ the cut-off, so 10 in this example).

VALIDATING OUR APPROACH

In order to understand the diversity of the web in terms of what might be difficult for a person with low vision to see, we conducted a study with 50 Mechanical Turk workers. Each worker was instructed to enter the URL of a web page that they either currently had open in their browser or that they had recently visited (other than mturk.com). We also captured the width and height of each worker's window. The average window width was 1236px (SD=232.9), which was our primary concern since height does not influence page health. We then ran `oppaccess.js` on the URLs provided by each worker in a window with the width and height set to what the worker had provided. We recorded the magnification that `oppaccess.js` achieved, which component of page health prevented it from magnifying the page further, and the time required to do the calculation.

Overall, the web pages were magnified 1.6x (SD=0.9) without causing a significant decrease in page health (Figure 3). Magnification stopped on 41 of the web pages because of horizontal scrolling, on 6 because of narrow word wrapping, and on only 2 because of text overlap (Table 1). We also computed the achieved magnification level for web browsers with pixels widths from 500 to 2000. As expected, `oppaccess.js` is able to increase the magnification more as available width increases (Figure 4). Figure 5 shows the effect of `oppaccess.js` on the UIST 2014 homepage.

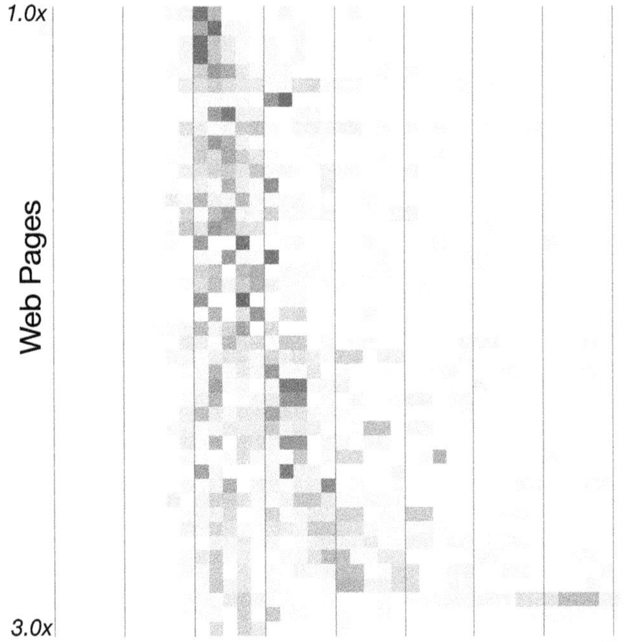

Figure 3. Font size distribution across 50 web pages (red) and the new spread when applying `oppaccess.js` (blue). Each row is a web page, and each column is a font size. Web pages are ordered by the level of magnification applied. The effect is to pull the font sizes higher.

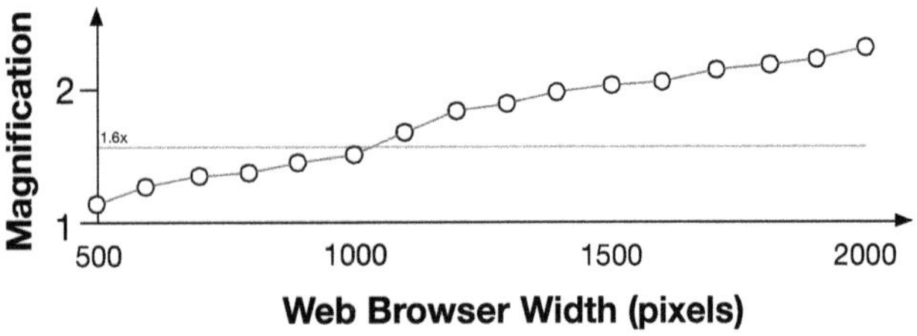

Figure 4. Achieved magnification level across different web browser widths. `oppaccess.js` is able to magnify content more when the window size is larger.

The time required to compute the magnification was 2.2 seconds (SD=3) on average, although this was dominated by the time required to check text overlap and word wrapping, *e.g.* those elements that result from responsive design. While web pages are likely to include these even more frequently in the future, we believe the performance of our implementation could be dramatically improved by either building it into the browser, using predictive methods, or by sharing the magnification levels that prior visitors with similar window sizes found useful. We conservatively increased magnification in an iterative fashion in case the browser rendered intermediate steps; in the future, a binary search approach may be used because modern browsers do not render the intermediate steps.

DISCUSSION & FUTURE WORK

This paper has introduced the idea of opportunistic accessibility improvement and validated the concept for web magnification by showing that `oppaccess.js` can magnify content by 60% without decreasing page health. We do not claim

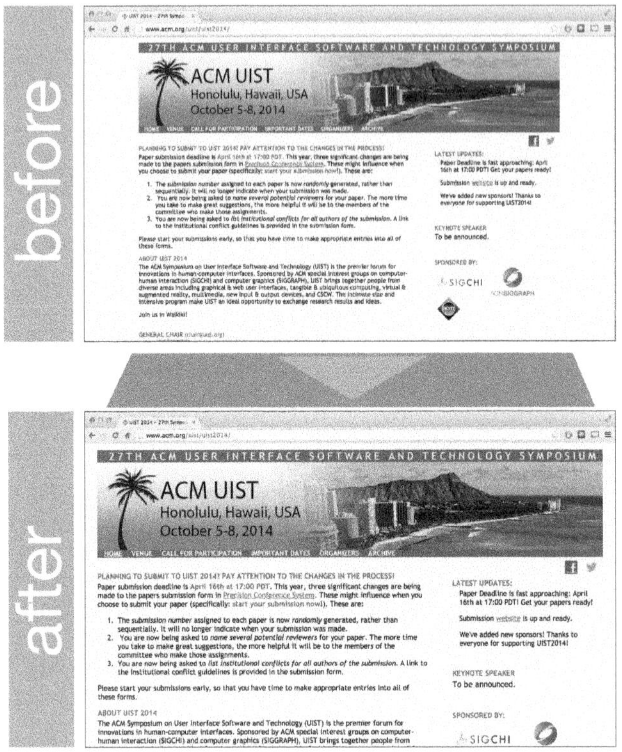

Figure 5. The observed result of applying *oppaccess.js* to the UIST 2014 web page. In the *after* screenshot the page is automatically magnified to 1.3x the original, while ensuring that negative effects (horizontal scrolling, overlapping elements, or narrow word-wrapping) are not introduced. This may seem like a small change, but can improve the realized accessibility of this web page for many people with low vision.

to have developed a robust solution to web access for people with visual impairments, only to have introduced a tool that will make web content slightly larger, which will benefit people who currently find it difficult to see. Future work may seek to better understand how much of a difference small improvements make.

Future work may also extend our approach for magnifying the Web. yIn particular, it may be possible to allow the user more direct control of how much magnification they would like to have. In the case that the desired magnification level has not been reached, we may involve the user in deciding how and to what extent they may be comfortable in reducing page health. Education about existing browser features, such as `ctrl +` are likely to be part of the solution. We might substitute other magnification strategies likely to affect the page in different ways or applied only to portions of the page that are not yet experiencing problems.

While the page health measures for text overlap and narrow word wrapping affected only 14% of web pages, it seems likely that this proportion will increase as responsive design becomes more popular. Elements of our methods for detecting when responsive design elements break down may find broader application. While the majority of the population may not use high levels of magnification, the duality between screen size and magnification means that these could be relevant for controlling responsiveness on small screen devices.

Many areas within accessibility could benefit from the idea of opportunistic accessibility improvement, especially those areas characterized by enormous variability. Problems for which people are currently "getting by" and could benefit from even small improvements seem most promising, such as those resulting from visual, motor, or cognitive impairments. The concept of opportunistic accessibility may open up the possibilty for tools to make targets a little easier to click or web interfaces a bit easier to understand.

To some extent, accessibility is already opportunistic. Assistive technology often only works correctly when content and software is produced in a way that allows it to work, which they often are not. As another example, the WebInSight system provided labels for images so that blind people could access them, but could provide labels for less than half of them [2]. Nevertheless, this technology is useful because of the increased access it provides when it does work, and so in some sense the idea is not new. Articulating the opportunistic nature of these tools may lead future work to embrace and leverage our inability to always make access perfect.

CONCLUSION

We have introduced *opportunistic accessibility improvement* and explored it through `oppaccess.js`, an easily-deployed Javascript system for magnifying web pages. We have shown that the Web could be on average 60% larger for people on the Web without introducing the most common negative effects of magnification. The approach of improving accessibility when possible without introducing negative side effects may make seemingly small improvements, but if broadly applied could improve experienced accessibility for a wide range of people.

ACKNOWLEDGEMENTS

This paper was developed under a grant from the Department of Education, NIDRR grant number H133A130057, National Science Foundation Award #IIS-1149709, and an Alfred P. Sloan Foundation Fellowship. We thank our anonymous reviewers for their many helpful comments.

REFERENCES

1. Bigham, J.P., Prince, C.M., and Ladner, R.E. WebAnywhere: A Screen Reader On-the-Go. W4A 2008. 73-82.
2. Bigham, J.P., Kaminsky, R.S., Ladner, R.E., Danielsson, O.M., and Hempton, G.L. WebInSight: making web images accessible. ASSETS 2006. 181-188.
3. Forrester Research. Accessible Technology in Computing —Examining Awareness, Use, and Future Potential. 2004.
4. Gajos, K.Z., Wobbrock, J.O., and Weld, D.S. Automatically generating user interfaces adapted to users' motor and vision capabilities. UIST 2007. 231-240.
5. Kline, R.L. and Glinert, E.P. Improving GUI accessibility for people with low vision. CHI 1995. 114-121.
6. World Health Organization. Visual impairment and blindness. 2013. http://www.who.int/mediacentre/factsheets/fs282/en/

URL	Magnification	Stopping Cause
http://www.espncricinfo.com/	1	scroll
http://www.oemcycle.com/Item/product/900076028/_Vid89455142n47	1	scroll
http://www.espncricinfo.com/	1	scroll
http://www.espncricinfo.com/ci/engine/current/match/scores/live.html	1	scroll
https://www.facebook.com/profile.php?id=XXXXXXXXXXX	1.1	scroll
http://www.imdb.com/title/tt1843866/reviews?ref=tt_urv	1.1	scroll
http://ibnlive.in.com/	1.1	scroll
http://bleacherreport.com/	1.1	scroll
http://torrage.com/	1.1	scroll
http://nav.sbilife.co.in/UI/DailyNavInputOutput.aspx	1.1	scroll
http://espn.go.com/nba/draft2014/story/_/id/10780763/	1.1	wrap
http://www.scribd.com/doc/61445642/Boolean-Expressions	1.2	scroll
http://www.goodbelly.com	1.2	scroll
https://www.facebook.com/fayiso77	1.2	scroll
http://hip2save.com	1.3	scroll
https://www.facebook.com/	1.3	scroll
http://www.hcrealms.com/index.php?page=units	1.3	scroll
http://radar.weather.gov/ridge/Conus/centgrtlakes_loop.php	1.3	scroll
https://www.mturk.com/mturk/findhits?match=true	1.3	scroll
http://www.limeroad.com/	1.3	scroll
http://www.pasadrexam2014.in/	1.3	scroll
http://oldnavy.gap.com/browse/category.do?cid=6825	1.3	scroll
https://www.google.com/	1.3	scroll
http://www.youtube.com/watch?v=jkNyC7FPJxc	1.3	scroll
http://slickdeals.net/	1.3	text
http://hw.reddit.com/r/sixwordstories/	1.4	scroll
http://www.mturkgrind.com/threads/15270-04-14-Happy-Black-Day-Monday!/page113	1.4	scroll
http://en.wikipedia.org/wiki/Tariq_Farid	1.4	wrap
http://translate.eu/	1.5	scroll
http://www.reddit.com/	1.5	scroll
https://tools.usps.com/go/ZipLookupAction_input	1.5	scroll
http://money.cnn.com/?hpt=sitenav	1.5	scroll
https://accounts.google.com/ServiceLogin?service=mail	1.5	scroll
http://en.wikipedia.org/wiki/Alexander_Mirtchev	1.5	wrap
http://www.noxxic.com/wow/pve/warlock/demonology/talent-build-and-glyphs	1.6	scroll
http://www.inboxdollars.com/search/...	1.6	scroll
https://hr.macys.net/iip/Login.aspx	1.6	scroll
http://www.oddee.com/	1.6	scroll
https://mail.google.com/mail/u/0/#inbox	1.7	scroll
https://www.cedarpoint.com/blog-article/online-fun/Winter-Scenes	1.7	scroll
http://foodomania.com/mor-kuzhambu/	1.7	scroll
https://us.battle.net/support/en/games/diablo3	1.7	scroll
https://chrome.google.com/webstore/category/apps?hl=en	1.8	wrap
http://www.twitch.tv/manvsgame	1.9	text
http://en.wikipedia.org/wiki/Italian_art	1.9	wrap
http://timesofindia.indiatimes.com/international-home	2.1	scroll
http://www.wral.com/severe-weather-freezing-temps-expected-tuesday/13567824/	2.8	scroll
http://www.pinterest.com/	3	none
https://www.flickr.com/photos/elisa_maza/12942331964/in/...	3	scroll
http://www.msnbc.com/rachel-maddow-show/the-bundy-crisis-nevada	3	wrap

Table 1. The web page URLs gathered during our Mechanical Turk study, ordered by the magnification `oppaccess.js` achieved on each and what caused magnification to stop —horizontal scrolling, text overlap, or narrow word wrapping.

Content-Aware Kinetic Scrolling for Supporting Web Page Navigation

Juho Kim[1] Amy X. Zhang[1] Jihee Kim[2] Robert C. Miller[1] Krzysztof Z. Gajos[3]
[1]MIT CSAIL {juhokim, axz, rcm}@mit.edu
[2]KAIST jiheekim@kaist.ac.kr
[3]Harvard SEAS kgajos@eecs.harvard.edu

ABSTRACT
Long documents are abundant on the web today, and are accessed in increasing numbers from touchscreen devices such as mobile phones and tablets. Navigating long documents with small screens can be challenging both physically and cognitively because they compel the user to scroll a great deal and to mentally filter for important content. To support navigation of long documents on touchscreen devices, we introduce *content-aware kinetic scrolling*, a novel scrolling technique that dynamically applies pseudo-haptic feedback in the form of friction around points of high interest within the page. This allows users to quickly find interesting content while exploring without further cluttering the limited visual space. To model degrees of interest (DOI) for a variety of existing web pages, we introduce *social wear*, a method for capturing DOI based on social signals that indicate collective user interest. Our preliminary evaluation shows that users pay attention to items with kinetic scrolling feedback during search, recognition, and skimming tasks.

Author Keywords
Kinetic scrolling; Pseudo-haptic feedback; Read wear; Social wear.

ACM Classification Keywords
H.5.2. User Interfaces: Input devices and strategies

INTRODUCTION
There are many examples of long pages on the web, including long-form articles, multi-level discussion forum threads, and social media and news feeds with infinite scrolling. These long documents raise problems for readers depending on the task at hand. When users are exploring a page and attempting to find relevant or interesting information, they must mentally engage in order to differentiate between different items. As a result, it takes greater time to sift through the content, and they still miss interesting information because interesting items are difficult to distinguish from less interesting ones. Poor page layout, noise, distraction, and eye fatigue may further weaken information scent [13] for items of interest.

ACM 978-1-4503-3069-5/14/10 $15.00.
http://dx.doi.org/10.1145/2642918.2647401

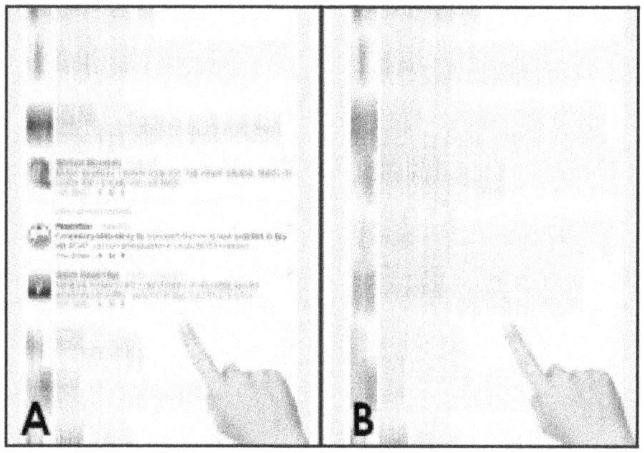

Figure 1. A) Content-aware kinetic scrolling applies friction in scrolling as the user passes over items of high interest. B) The user inadvertently passes over items of interest while scrolling.

Long documents also present problems for users trying to get a general overview of a page. For users without the time or inclination to slowly filter through the content, scrolling is often employed to capture some snapshots of different areas of the page. This type of navigation causes users to miss a great deal of potentially interesting content. Users might also access a skewed selection of the content because navigating to the end is time-consuming and physically demanding.

Navigating long documents on touchscreen devices such as mobile phones and tablets magnifies the challenges presented in these tasks. Limited screen real estate in touchscreen devices means that items are even smaller and harder to differentiate and may be competing with more visual cues per unit area for attention. Smaller screens also make scrolling more physically demanding and time-consuming because each scroll flick moves the user through less content.

Solutions for improving navigation of long documents should strive to draw people's **attention** to items with high degree of interest (DOI) to ease their cognitive load while exploring. At the same time, the solution must also support fluid **navigation** that maintains the overall context when users are looking to get a general understanding of a page. Drawing attention ensures that users notice items that are emphasized. Fluid navigation maintains the continuous flow and surrounding context of the content. Sometimes these goals conflict, and existing solutions address this challenge by semantically adapting to the content structure, visually manipulating the page layout, and dynamically responding to the user's scrolling behavior.

To address these challenges, we present **content-aware kinetic scrolling**, which applies pseudo-haptic feedback in the form of friction to high DOI items within a page. As the user scrolls on a touchscreen device, the scrolling speed decelerates around items with high DOI, as if a rubber band is pulling the item with force towards the center of the screen and the user's line of vision. This technique adds physical information scent to items with high DOI to help users discover interesting items. It is a generalizable technique that works with any DOI model. It is also easy to adapt to existing user interfaces because it is a purely input-based technique that does not require modification of existing content.

RELATED WORK

To estimate and visualize DOI in content, previous approaches captured user behavior on the page and extracted higher-level operations [5, 7]. Read wear [6] visualized usage history in the scrollbar, which has been extended by others who incorporated usage signals into graphical user interface widgets [17], or supported revisitation by capturing personal scrolling history [1]. Most existing approaches, however, rely on adding *visual* cues to represent DOI inside a document. While visual signals strongly draw users' attention, they have to compete against existing visual assets on the page for limited screen space. With web contents increasingly embedding visual media and widgets, purely visualizing DOI might distract users away from the main content.

Rather than adding visual signals, other scrolling techniques have focused on enhancing the scrolling behavior itself. Previous research modified non-positional dimensions of screen objects (e.g., transparency) upon scrolling [16], analyzed the document structure to vary scrolling direction, speed, and zoom [9], and applied dynamic zoom based on the scrolling speed [8]. Pseudo-haptic feedback [11] decouples visual feedback and device resistance to create an illusion of friction. Without dedicated hardware, similar effects can be achieved by applying acceleration to a mouse cursor [10], or more generally, altering the Control/Display ratio [3], defined as the ratio of the physical scrolling speed (control) to the display update speed. We extend this approach to touchscreen devices where no mouse cursor exists and natural deceleration with kinetic scrolling is already in effect.

Flicking is a throwing gesture that often triggers automatic scrolling with inertia and friction on touch devices. Flick-based interaction techniques include Superflick [15], which supported distant object placement on tabletops, and Flick-and-Brake [2], which supported fine-grained acceleration control with the finger after flicking. Our approach differs in that it automatically applies force to parts of content, based on signals that already exist on the page.

CONTENT-AWARE KINETIC SCROLLING

Kinetic scrolling [12] refers to the gradual deceleration of scrolling after the user lifts the finger from the screen. This technique has been implemented in most modern touchscreen devices. Flicking is a throwing-like gesture that invokes a transfer function [14], which turns kinetic scrolling into automatic scrolling with inertia. The inertial effect provides a natural and physical affordance for scrolling, and enables more precise scrolling control. The rate of deceleration is determined by the initial velocity at the time of finger release: the faster the initial velocity, the farther the scrolling destination is. Each time a function responsible for computing the current scrolling position is called, it updates the target position as a function of initial velocity, elapsed time since the finger release, and current scrolling offset from the top of the document. A default deceleration model used in our implementation is exponential decay, where the change in scrolling offset is computed as: $Ae^{-t/\tau}$. The amplitude (A) and time constant τ determine how stiff the initial effect is. This model is activated when no high DOI items are nearby.

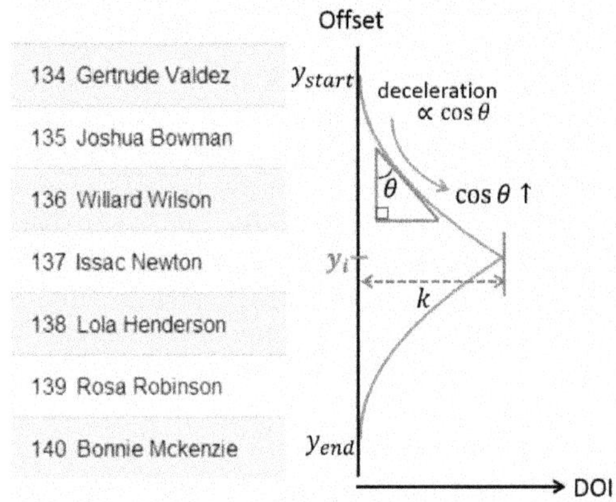

Figure 2. CAKS applies quadratic deceleration to a high DOI item ("Issac Newton") whose DOI value is k and vertical position of the midpoint is y_i. The deceleration is active between a range $[y_{start}, y_{end}]$.

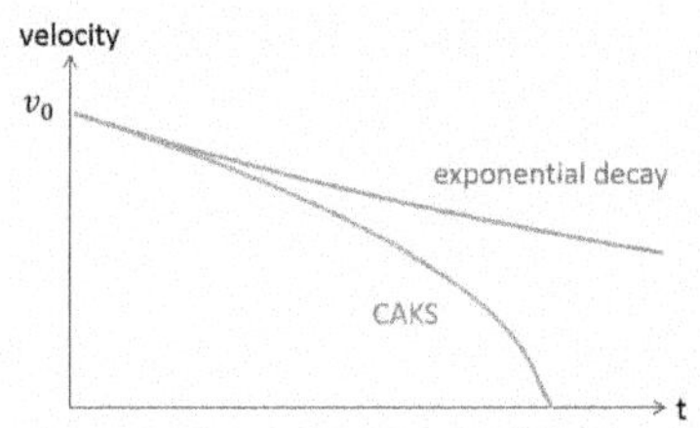

Figure 3. Scrolling velocity change over time (initial velocity: v_0), comparing exponential decay with normal scrolling against additional deceleration with CAKS.

Deceleration Model

Content-aware kinetic scrolling (CAKS) applies additional deceleration when there are items with high DOI on the scrolling path. It is analogous to adding a virtual hill that slows down the scroll head, whose deceleration is maximized at the peak of the hill. It creates a kinetic illusion that additional friction is applied, or some force is pulling the scroll. As a result, the user notices the additional deceleration and pays attention to the item that causes the pulling. Prototype testing with pilot users revealed that users are very sensitive when the scrolling speed change is abrupt. They feel that the scrolling is buggy and laggy when the speed model does not smoothly transition from the natural deceleration to additional deceleration. This is different from making the deceleration noticeable, which should not feel sluggish.

For a smooth transition from normal deceleration to additional deceleration, the deceleration model takes the current velocity and gradually increases deceleration when the current scroll position enters a DOI range. For an item i whose DOI value is k and offset position of the vertical midpoint is y_i, we apply the quadratic deceleration between a range $[y_{start}, y_{end}]$, whose midpoint is y_i. The range size can be optimized for each device and orientation mode. In practice, we find the screen height to be a reasonable choice for the range size (e.g., 1024px for the portrait mode in the iPad). Our deceleration model for high DOI items is a quadratic model, which computes the DOI in the current scrolling offset y as: $DOI_y = \frac{k}{(y_i - y_{start})^2} * (y - y_{start})^2$. Taking the first derivative of DOI_y gives the current slope of the virtual hill $\tan\theta$, where θ is the angle of elevation. Therefore, the magnitude of deceleration, modeling the force of gravity on a hill, is proportional to $\cos\theta$, computed as $\frac{1}{\sqrt{(\tan^2\theta+1)}}$.

While all visual items on the page can have DOI values, we apply kinetic scrolling to only select items. One of our prototypes applied continuous deceleration to all items on the page, but pilot users found it to be frustrating because it was harder to distinguish high DOI items from low DOI items. After we normalize all DOI values to a range between 10 and 100, we activate kinetic feedback to only the items above a threshold DOI value (default: 70). When multiple items have overlapping DOI ranges, we pick the maximum deceleration.

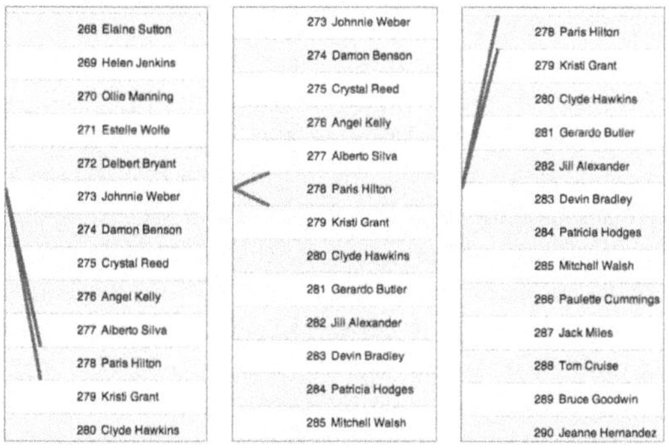

Figure 4. CAKS uses two bands to visually convey the deceleration for the item "Paris Hilton" in this list example. From left to right, the figures show how the rubber band-like visual feedback changes over time as the list scrolls downward when the user flicks their finger upward.

Visual Feedback

Although most pilot users were able to notice the kinetic deceleration without any visual feedback, visual feedback might be necessary in some cases, especially if the page contains many small items. For these pages, it is extremely difficult to precisely find which item in the current viewport is emphasized. We tried variants of visual feedback with the goals of 1) minimizing the modification of the content, 2) minimizing the space and time required to display the feedback, and 3) visualizing the deceleration behavior of CAKS.

Our solution emphasizes the target item with two bands connected to the left side of the screen (Figure 4). These bands are attached to the emphasized item, and their length and position are changed as if they were rubber bands pulling the item. This approach visually conveys the sense of deceleration. Also, this solution does not require applying styling to the DOM element of the content, and operates on another z-index layer. To minimize visual interruption, the bands disappear after 1.5 seconds if no further user interaction takes place.

Purpose-Aware Triggering

There are multiple scrolling patterns people use when using a touchscreen device. Users drag slowly to make small moves within the current viewport, which is useful for looking at nearby content at a slow speed. Finger flicking moves the scroll offset beyond the current viewport. Slow or weak flicking is useful when reviewing all content without missing anything, medium or moderate flicking is useful when skimming to get the general idea or to stumble upon interesting content, and fast or strong flicking is useful when skipping between content rapidly to reach a specific point in the document. We find CAKS to be effective when the user is applying slow and moderate flicking. With fast flicking, users continuously flick to quickly move to a target position, and in-between deceleration might not help them with their task.

Because a DOI model might not perfectly reflect a user's interest, CAKS makes it easy to ignore and cancel kinetic scrolling if the user wants to. A goal of CAKS is to draw attention to high DOI items, so if the user had already noticed the item, further deceleration might not be necessary. If the user initiates flick when the high DOI item is already within the viewport, we stop applying kinetic scrolling to that item.

Modeling Degree of Interest with Social Wear

CAKS requires the DOI model of a document as input. The technique is independent of the underlying DOI model or the method for constructing it. CAKS is compatible with any DOI model, as long as the DOI value and offset (y-position) information for each item are provided. Read wear [6] is one example of a DOI model CAKS can accept, which stores scrolling position data of all reading activity on the page.

A limitation of relying on scrolling data is that few websites collect this information. To address this issue, we introduce the concept of **social wear**, an alternative method for modeling user interest that does not require collecting DOI data a priori. Social wear reverse-engineers an existing web page to capture signals that may indicate user interest. Many web pages today contain potential DOI data to help users find what they are interested in, such as the number of shares, downloads, comments, or clicks. Social wear uses these signals to dynamically construct a DOI model that is the input for CAKS. We demonstrate examples of DOI models extracted from popular web services in the implementation section.

IMPLEMENTATION

CAKS is implemented as a Javascript library, which can be easily adopted by any web page by simply calling the initialization function with the DOI model. It is built on top of an open-source kinetic scrolling library [1]. It uses the `requestAnimationFrame` method for manipulating the scroll behavior, which is supported by most modern browsers today. Most settings and scrolling constants are configurable to provide a consistent experience across different form factors, touch sensitivity, and mobile operating systems.

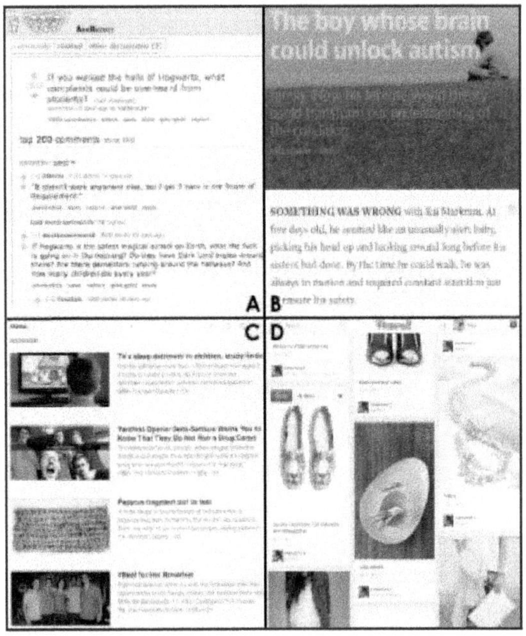

Figure 5. We applied CAKS to four examples above with social wear capturing DOI: A) Reddit discussion page (# of points), B) Medium article (# of per-paragraph comments), C) Feedly news reader (# of recommendations), D) Pinterest feed (# of re-pins).

We applied CAKS to a diverse set of web pages, some of which are shown in Figure 5. There are many types of websites that CAKS could potentially enhance and that we can construct a social wear DOI model from:

- Pages containing long lists, for instance a contact list containing rows of names or a publications page on a researcher's website, with DOI as the number of calls made or the click-through rate, respectively.
- Discussion forum threads, with comments growing into the thousands, that have a interest signal such as upvotes.
- Long-form text, such as long-form articles or online books, which support sentence or paragraph level annotations.
- News readers, such as applications like Feedly that surface the number of recommendations per article.
- Social media feeds, with infinitely scrolling content. The example shows a Pinterest feed using the number of repins as the DOI function, to highlight the capabilities of CAKS for purely visual content.

EVALUATION

We conducted a preliminary user study to understand how CAKS affects various content navigation tasks. Our goals were two-fold: 1) see if our technique successfully draws a user's attention when exploring for interesting or relevant content, and 2) see if our technique allows for fluid navigation when attempting to get a general summary of the content.

User Study Design

After a short trial session, participants were asked to perform three tasks: searching, recognition, and summarization. Each task was completed twice, once with CAKS and once with normal scrolling (NS), in a randomized order.

The **search** task was to find 10 names of famous people from a list of 500 names. In the CAKS condition, we removed visual feedback to see how participants perform only with physical feedback. Out of the 10 names to find, seven names were applied physical feedback while three were not, in order to simulate a content recommendation system with 70% accuracy. All names with feedback, however, were answers. The pages were 23,000 pixels long when rendered from the device used in the study. Figure 4 shows an example.

In the **recognition** task, we asked participants to spend three minutes reading comments interesting to them from a discussion forum thread on Reddit. We then presented them with 9 sentences and asked them to select the sentences that they remembered seeing on the discussion page. Each list included 3 sentences that were included in our DOI model, 3 that were not included in our DOI model, and 3 that were not present on the page. The DOI model leveraged the upvotes assigned to each comment on the Reddit platform by readers. The two threads used were 26,000 and 27,000 pixels long. Figure 5A shows an example thread.

The **summarization** task presented a long article on Medium.com and gave participants three minutes to skim and summarize the main points of the article on a sheet of paper. The DOI model was the number of comments attached to each paragraph, which did not reflect the importance of a paragraph. Thus, simply following high DOI items might not be useful for summarization. Our purpose was to see how a user reacts to items with feedback that do not support the task at hand. The pages were 53,000 and 41,000 pixels long. Figure 5B shows an example article.

After each task, participants completed the NASA TLX test [4] for measuring task load, in a 7-point scale. We had a debriefing session at the end, asking participants about their qualitative experience using both scrolling techniques.

Participants

We recruited 13 participants (6 male, 7 female) with ages between 18 and 43 (μ=24.2, σ=6.7) through a university mailing list. All participants self-reported that they used touch devices regularly. In all sessions, we used an iPad 2 in portrait mode, fixing the screen resolution to 768x1024 pixels.

Results

The post-task questionnaires and interviews indicated that CAKS drew attention to high DOI items for a majority of the users. When presented with the statement that the additional feedback affected their browsing in each task, 87% of responses responded with a rating of 4 or above out of 7. One participant commented, *"When it stopped me occasionally, I looked around to see if there's anything interesting going on."*

[1] https://github.com/ariya/kinetic/

Task completion times for the search task did not reveal any significant differences between CAKS (287s) and NS (312s), but did reveal a significant difference in the NASA TLX index measuring task load (χ^2=7, $p < 0.01$), with CAKS receiving 2.9 and NS receiving 3.4. For the recognition task, there was no significant difference in the overall recognition score between CAKS (5.9 correct) and NS (6.2 correct). For summarization tasks, we found evidence that users were able to ignore feedback from CAKS since the DOI model was not helping them. When asked how much the feedback affected their content scrolling, users rated this task 4.6, which is significantly different using a Friedman test from their rating of 6.4 for the recognition task (χ^2=7.4, $p < 0.01$).

DISCUSSION

Reduced Task Load While Searching

We found no significant difference in task load between CAKS and NS except for the search task. The lower task load may be due to the narrower search space caused by deceleration. When participants noticed deceleration, they knew that an answer was in their vicinity. One participant noted, *"Physical anchoring forces you to stop and look around. Almost adding physical load. This might unconsciously help people find things, even if they thought they didn't feel it."* We observed many users finding all items containing feedback first before going back for the three items without feedback. The time gained finding the items with feedback may have been offset by time lost in finding items without feedback.

Exploring Farther with Content-Aware Kinetic Scrolling

For the recognition task, users were given freedom to explore what they found interesting while still asked to try to traverse the entire page within 3 minutes. While users were not more likely to recall content with CAKS than NS, we found some indication that users with CAKS were more likely to notice items with DOI nearer to the bottom of the page. For instance, one item located around 70% (19,000 pixels) from the top of the document that contained feedback was recognized by four users with CAKS, compared to only one user with NS. This suggests that participants with CAKS navigated further down the content and were also paying attention to the items farther down the page that had feedback. We noticed that with NS, most users did not get through even half the content.

Ability to Disregard Feedback

In the summarization task, users were required to get a general understanding of a long text in a short amount of time, causing many to employ moderate scrolling. In this case, when the DOI model did not align with the task at hand, users successfully ignored CAKS without adding to their task load and fluidly navigate to their own points of interest. One participant noted *"[I] [b]arely noticed feedback, can't remember where I saw it."* during the summarization task.

CONCLUSION AND FUTURE WORK

We introduce content-aware kinetic scrolling, a novel scrolling technique that applies pseudo-haptic feedback to items with high DOI in a long document. To model DOI from a variety of existing web pages, we present the concept of social wear, which captures previous users' interest readily present on the document. Users noted that our technique drew their attention to high DOI items, even when no visual feedback was available.

For future work, we plan to experiment with more web pages that have new types of social wear signals. Another direction of research is expanding to 2D layouts instead of linear scrolling. For example, on a web-based map, places of interest can be applied kinetic feedback. We envision content-aware kinetic scrolling to be deployed publicly as a standalone library, providing a lightweight, versatile method for improving content navigation on touchscreen devices.

ACKNOWLEDGMENTS

The authors thank the members of the UID Group at MIT CSAIL for their feedback. This work was funded in part by Quanta Computer. Juho Kim is supported by the Samsung Fellowship.

REFERENCES

1. Alexander, J., Cockburn, A., Fitchett, S., Gutwin, C., and Greenberg, S. Revisiting read wear: Analysis, design, and evaluation of a footprints scrollbar. In *CHI '09* (2009), 1665–1674.
2. Baglioni, M., Malacria, S., Lecolinet, E., and Guiard, Y. Flick-and-brake: Finger control over inertial/sustained scroll motion. In *CHI EA '11* (2011), 2281–2286.
3. Blanch, R., Guiard, Y., and Beaudouin-Lafon, M. Semantic pointing: Improving target acquisition with control-display ratio adaptation. In *CHI '04*, ACM (2004), 519–526.
4. Hart, S. G., and Staveland, L. E. Development of nasa-tlx (task load index): Results of empirical and theoretical research. *Advances in psychology 52* (1988), 139–183.
5. Hijikata, Y. Estimating a user's degree of interest in a page during web browsing. In *IEEE SMC'99*, vol. 4 (1999), 105–110.
6. Hill, W. C., Hollan, J. D., Wroblewski, D., and McCandless, T. Edit wear and read wear. In *CHI '92* (1992), 3–9.
7. Holub, M., and Bielikova, M. Estimation of user interest in visited web page. In *WWW '10* (2010), 1111–1112.
8. Igarashi, T., and Hinckley, K. Speed-dependent automatic zooming for browsing large documents. In *UIST '00* (2000), 139–148.
9. Ishak, E. W., and Feiner, S. K. Content-aware scrolling. In *UIST '06* (2006), 155–158.
10. Lécuyer, A., Burkhardt, J.-M., and Etienne, L. Feeling bumps and holes without a haptic interface: The perception of pseudo-haptic textures. In *CHI '04* (2004), 239–246.
11. Lécuyer, A., Coquillart, S., Kheddar, A., Richard, P., and Coiffet, P. Pseudo-haptic feedback: can isometric input devices simulate force feedback? In *VR 2000. Proceedings. IEEE* (2000), 83–90.
12. Nokia. Qt Kinetic scrolling - from idea to implementation. `http://developer.nokia.com/community/wiki/Qt_Kinetic_scrolling_-_from_idea_to_implementation/`, 2010. [Online; accessed April-16-2014].
13. Pirolli, P., and Card, S. Information foraging. *Psychological review 106*, 4 (1999), 643.
14. Quinn, P., Malacria, S., and Cockburn, A. Touch scrolling transfer functions. In *UIST '13*, ACM (2013), 61–70.
15. Reetz, A., Gutwin, C., Stach, T., Nacenta, M., and Subramanian, S. Superflick: A natural and efficient technique for long-distance object placement on digital tables. In *GI '06* (2006), 163–170.
16. Smith, R. B., and Taivalsaari, A. Generalized and stationary scrolling. In *UIST '99* (1999), 1–9.
17. Willett, W., Heer, J., and Agrawala, M. Scented widgets: Improving navigation cues with embedded visualizations. *IEEE Transactions on Visualization and Computer Graphics 13*, 6 (Nov. 2007), 1129–1136.

FlexSense: A Transparent Self-Sensing Deformable Surface

Christian Rendl[1], David Kim[2], Sean Fanello[2], Patrick Parzer[1], Christoph Rhemann[2], Jonathan Taylor[2], Martin Zirkl[3], Gregor Scheipl[3], Thomas Rothländer[3], Michael Haller[1], Shahram Izadi[2]

[1]Media Interaction Lab, University of Applied Sciences Upper Austria
[2]Microsoft Research
[3]Institute of Surface Technologies and Photonics, Joanneum Research

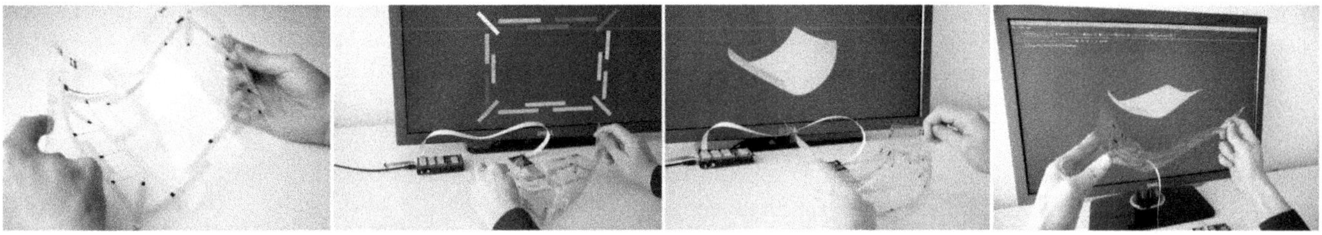

Figure 1: FlexSense is a fully flexible, transparent, thin-film surface, comprising of sparse printed piezoelectric sensors (left). Our main contribution is a new set of algorithms that takes these sparse sensor measurements (center), and reconstruct the dense 3D shape of the device and complex deformations in real-time (right).

ABSTRACT
We present FlexSense, a new thin-film, transparent sensing surface based on printed piezoelectric sensors, which can reconstruct complex deformations without the need for any external sensing, such as cameras. FlexSense provides a fully self-contained setup which improves mobility and is not affected from occlusions. Using only a sparse set of sensors, printed on the periphery of the surface substrate, we devise two new algorithms to fully reconstruct the complex deformations of the sheet, using only these sparse sensor measurements. An evaluation shows that both proposed algorithms are capable of reconstructing complex deformations accurately. We demonstrate how FlexSense can be used for a variety of 2.5D interactions, including as a transparent cover for tablets where bending can be performed alongside touch to enable magic lens style effects, layered input, and mode switching, as well as the ability to use our device as a high degree-of-freedom input controller for gaming and beyond.

Author Keywords
Flexible, transparent, sensor, deformation, reconstruction.

INTRODUCTION
There has been considerable interest in the area of flexible or deformable input/output (IO) digital surfaces, especially with recent advances in nano-technology, such as flexible transistors, eInk & OLED displays, as well as printed sensors. The promise of such devices is making digital interaction as simple as interacting with a sheet of paper. By bending, rolling or flexing areas of the device, a variety of interactions can be enabled, in a very physical and tangible manner.

Whilst the vision of flexible IO devices has existed for some time, there have been few self-contained devices that enable rich *continuous* user input. Researchers have either created devices with limited *discrete* bending gestures, or prototyped interaction techniques using *external* sensors, typically camera-based vision systems. Whilst demonstrating compelling results and applications for bending-based interactions, the systems suffer from practical and interactive limitations. For example, the bend sensors used in [7, 17] are limited to simple bending of device edges, rather than the complex deformations one expects when interacting naturally with a sheet of paper. In contrast, vision-based systems e.g. [31] are not self-contained, are more costly and bulky, and can suffer from occlusions, particularly when the hand is interacting with the surface.

In this paper, we present FlexSense, a transparent thin input surface that is capable of precisely reconstructing complex and continuous deformations, without any external sensing infrastructure (see Figure 1). We build on prior work with printed piezoelectric sensors (previously used for touch, gesture and pressure sensing, [23, 41]). Our new design uses only a sparse set of piezoelectric sensors printed on the periphery of the surface substrate. A novel set of algorithms fully reconstruct the surface geometry and detailed deformations being performed, purely by interpreting these sparse sensor measurements. This allows an entirely self-contained setup, free of external vision-based sensors and their inherent limitations. Such a device can be used for a variety of applications, including a transparent cover for tablets supporting complex 2.5D deformations for enhanced visualization, mode switching and input, alongside touch; or as a high degree-of-freedom (DoF) input controller.

In summary our contributions are as follows:

- We present a new sensor layout based on the prior PyzoFlex system [23], specifically for sensing precise and continuous surface deformations. This previous work demonstrated the use of printed piezoelectric sensors for touch and pressure sensing. In contrast, we present the idea of using these sensors to enable rich, bidirectional bending interactions. This includes the design of a new layout, associated sensor and driver electronics specifically for this purpose.
- Our main contribution are two algorithms that can take measurements from the sparse piezoelectric sensors and

UIST '14, Oct 5 – Oct 8 2014, Honolulu, HI, USA
Copyright 2014 ACM 978-1-4503-3069-5/14/10...$15.00.
http://dx.doi.org/10.1145/2642918.2647423

accurately reconstruct the 3D shape of the surface. This reconstructed shape can be used to detect a wide-range of flex gestures. The complexity of the deformations afforded by our reconstruction algorithms have yet to be seen with 'self-sensing' (i.e. self-contained) devices, and would typically require external cameras and infrastructure.
- We train and evaluate the different algorithms using a ground-truth multi-camera rig, and discuss the trade-offs between implementation complexity and reconstruction accuracy. We also compare to a single camera baseline.
- Finally, we demonstrate new interaction techniques and applications afforded by such a novel sensor design and reconstruction algorithms. In particular as a cover for tablets where IO is coupled, and as a high DoF input controller.

RELATED WORK

There is broad range of work on flexible sensing and displays. [31] distinguishes this work into two categories. The first are *external input devices* where the sensor is used to control a remote display and UI, and output is typically non-flexible. The second are *deformable handheld devices*, where input and output is coupled, and the display can also be deformable. We extend this categorization further, by identifying differences in sensing approaches. *Self-sensing* systems contain onboard sensors on the device, which can be used to directly estimate the deformation (e.g. devices based on embedded bend sensors). *External sensing* systems use sensors embedded in the environment rather than the device to estimate deformations (e.g. camera-based deformation systems). In this section we explore prior work on bendable and deformable surfaces, based on this broad taxonomy.

Perhaps the first example of a deformable *external input device* that supported *self-sensing* is the work by Balakrishnan et. al. [1] which used the ShapeTape sensor [3], and a NURBS (non-uniform rational basis spline) representation for 3D modeling. ShapeTape is a thin long rubber tape subdivided into a series of fiber optic bend sensors, each detecting bend and twist (inspired by the sensors used in data gloves e.g. [40]). This showed the potential for exploiting bimanual input for modeling 3D curves. [12] demonstrated the use of piezoelectric thin films to produce a device similar to ShapeTape. [2] use *external sensing* in the form of camera and vision techniques to reconstruct complex curves from long passive pieces of wire. The form-factor of these devices make them ideal for 3D curve drawing, but more complex 2D and 2.5D flexing and bending interactions are less natural.

The first conceptual *deformable handheld device* was the Gummi system [28]. The project was motivated by innovations in flexible displays and transistors. The prototype device could be considered *self-sensing* but used bend sensors placed behind a TFT display and a 2D trackpad at the rear. Only small discrete bending gestures were supported, but the work demonstrated some of the interactive possibilities that bending interfaces afford. [32] use a similar prototype setup to Gummi, for flicking through pages in an e-reader. Whilst IO is coupled in these systems, the display remains rigid.

PaperPhone was one of the first devices that coupled flexible IO into a single self-contained device [17]. A flexible PCB housed five bend sensors, and a kNN-based classifier was used to detect discrete bend gestures. A user study proposed a classification scheme that categorized bend gestures by location (top corner, side, or bottom corner) and direction (up or down). [36] also use a flexible PCB but with different bend sensor layout, to extend this classification scheme to include bend size and angle. The Kinectic Phone by Nokia [15] demonstrates a full color bendable phone, a manifestation of the early Gummi vision. Using this device, Kildal et al. [3] explore bending and twisting, and propose design guidelines for deformable devices. PaperTab [33] is a self-contained electronic-reader with two bidirectional FlexPoint sensors for input. The system demonstrates a progression of the digital desk concept [9, 38], which is a clear motivation for flexible, paper-like devices, but for the first time uses self-contained IO, as opposed to projectors and cameras.

Other *self-sensing* systems look purely at input sensing. Booksheet used two bend sensors on the back of acrylic sheets to create both a dual and single sheet flexible input device [37]. Bend gestures were coarsely categorized into four discrete classes, and mapped to turning pages in eBooks. FlexRemote [21] consists of 16 flex sensors on the periphery of a thin acrylic sheet which can recognize eight deformation gestures for remote input. Twend [8] uses eight fiber optic bend sensors embedded into a thicker substrate to detect 18 unique bends.

All these systems can be thought as *self-sensing* allowing for a great deal of mobility and compactness, and avoiding occlusions. These systems typically are not focused on accurate 3D reconstructions of surface shape, and most detect discrete bend gestures. This is partly because of the complexity of mapping from raw sensor readings to precise continuous deformations. An exploratory study by Lee et al. [20] captures data from users deforming a variety of non-digital substrates including paper, plastic as well as stretchable fabrics, demonstrating the richness and complexity of deformations afforded. These types of interactions can be difficult to capture purely using discrete gestures.

To enable such types of reconstructions, systems have employed *external sensors*, generally in the form of cameras. [6] use retro-reflective tags embedded into a deformable substrate to support flexing and folding gestures. [18] use the Vicon motion tracking system to reconstruct sparse 3D points and fit a mesh for simple 3D modeling. [16] use a magnetic tracker and spherical projection onto a deforming sheet of diffuse acrylic. [39] use a combination of external WiiMote sensor and projector, coupled with onboard pressure and bend sensors to create a hybrid deformable projected display. [31] use a Kinect and projector for advanced manipulations of a sheet of paper with coupled output. A 25×25 vertex plane is deformed to fit the observed Kinect data. Eight distinct poses can be linearly combined using a weighted interpolation scheme to form more complex shapes. Further, the system analyses the Kinect dot pattern to disambiguate the user's hand from the deformation surface.

Related to this area, is work on projector-vision based foldable [19, 13], rollable [14] and shape-changing displays [25]. Another related field is the shape sensing of malleable surfaces and materials. In Jamming User Interfaces [5], for example, the authors use two different techniques, namely structured light and electric field sensing for deriving shape information. DeforMe [22] projects images realistically onto deformed surfaces by tracking the deformation with an invisible infrared-based dot pattern on the material. In contrast,

PhotoelasticTouch [26] detects changing optical properties of a transparent deformable material, and Digital Foam [29] introduces a deformable device with embedded pressure sensors for 3D modeling.

Whilst interesting areas of research, our work is firmly focused on reconstructing the 3D shape and continuous deformations of a thin transparent surface. PrintSense demonstrates capacitive touch and proximity sensing on a flexible substrate, and allows for bend sensing using transmit and receive electrodes. Flexible touch and pressure sensors have been demonstrated, either using transparent piezoelectric sensors [23] or opaque IFSR sensors [24]. Murata have developed a high-transparency organic piezoelectric film for bend sensing on mobile devices[1] although details are currently limited.

Our work is inspired by and builds on these previous systems. We support rich, continuous and accurate 3D reconstructions of deformations of the surface, allowing high DoF input. Our system is fully self-sensing, enabling a compact, mobile form-factor, but without limiting the range of deformations. Our sensor is semi-transparent, allowing for unique capabilities, such as allowing placement at the front of a display rather than embedded in the back. Our sensor therefore supports both, the use as an external input device, or coupled closely with a display to support novel application scenarios.

DESIGNING FLEXSENSE

Our work builds on the flexible, transparent PyzoFlex sensor [23, 41]. In this section we provide a brief introduction to this work, which specifically relates to using these sensors for bending. We refer the reader to [23] for further technical details regarding the underlying piezoelectric sensor. Whereas in this prior work, the sensors were used for pressure sensing, our main goal in this paper is to exploit these sensors for precise 3D reconstruction of surface shape and bending to facilitate deformation-based interactions. This requires a rethinking of the existing sensor layout, as detailed in this section.

Piezoelectric bend sensors

Piezoelectric sensors work as follows: deformations of a piezo element causes a change in the surface charge density of the material resulting in a charge appearing between the electrodes. The amplitude and frequency of the signal is directly proportional to the applied mechanical stress. Since piezoelectricity reacts to mechanical stress, continuous bending is a well-suited application for such sensors. We propose an entirely printed, semi-transparent, and bidirectional bend sensor based on different functional inks (see Figure 2). The active sensor material is formed by a poled copolymer P(VDF-TrFE) which shows a large piezoelectric coefficient (32 pC/N) and can be printed as a 5μm thick transparent layer [41]. The screen printing process in general ensures low-cost and simple fabrication without cleanroom requirements or evaporation.

All components of the sensor have relatively good transparency values with low distracting absorbency ($\sim$ 85%). Note that the current sensors are optimized to provide a good trade-off between signal strength and transparency. If even higher transparency ($>$ 90%) is desired, metal nanowire inks can be used as electrode material instead of PEDOT:PSS. For reading sensor measurements printed, non-transparent conductive silver wires are used. In order to limit occlusions caused by silver

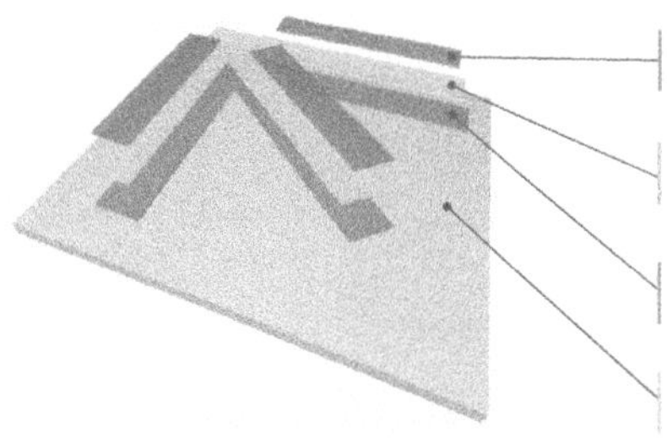

Figure 2: Our piezoelectric bend sensors consist of different, entirely printable functional inks. To have less (non-transparent) conductive silver lines all bend sensors printed on one substrate share one bottom electrode.

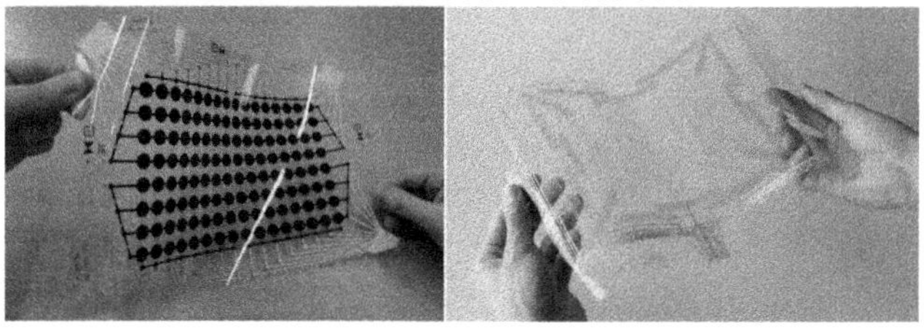

Figure 3: Layout of original PyzoFlex sensor (left) and our deformable sensor (right).

lines, all sensors on one substrate share one bottom electrode, which is separately wired to the driver electronics. The conductive traces can be placed freely across the surface, depending on application scenarios e.g. on the periphery or more central.

Sensor Layout

Multiple sensors must be combined together in order to be able to reconstruct the full deformations of the surface. We chose an A4 like form-factor because this matches commercially available flexible displays as well as common tablet screens, but is also big enough to be used as standalone input sensor.

Figure 3 (left) shows the original PyzoFlex sensor layout. As this layout was specifically designed for touch and pressure sensing, a dense grid of 16×8 sensors was employed in an active matrix arrangement. However, for bend sensing and shape reconstruction, this design is non-optimal. First, there is a large amount of sensor redundancy across the film. Second, the active matrix requires a large part of the outer film to be used for the printed silver wires. Finally, the active matrix scheme can suffer from ambiguities when many sensor measurements must be read at once, making such an arrangement problematic when bending (for more details see [23]).

Instead for FlexSense, we sought to use a sparse set of sensors, but placed in a more meaningful arrangement to optimize for a wide variety of continuous and smooth deformations, including extreme bends. The final design of our layout is shown in Figure 3 (right). In the remainder of this section, we provide more rationale for this sensor layout.

Existing Layouts in Related Work From related work, we identified the following, most essential requirements for our sensor layout: In order to track complex deformations an optimal bend sensor should consider properties such as location (where does the bend action happens), direction (upwards or downwards), size (involved surface area), angle (sharp or round angle), speed, and duration of bend actions [36].

To infer an optimal layout, we investigated arrangements used in prior work [7, 17, 36] in terms of the presented requirements and their sensor alignment. We recreated those layouts using

[1] `http://murata.com/new/news_release/2011/0921`

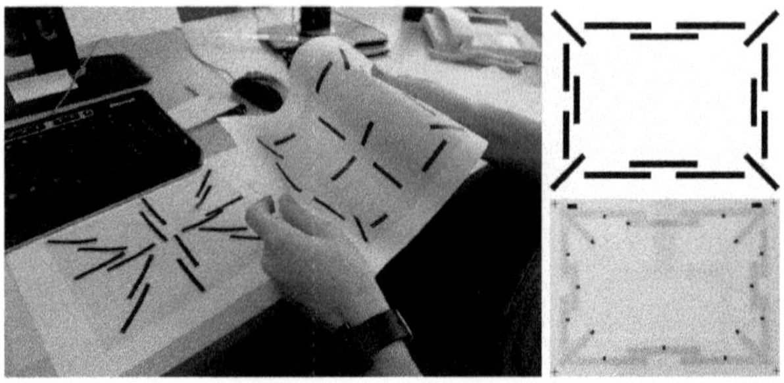

Figure 4: Paper prototyping to evaluate designs further (left). Our final layout (top right) and final printed clear surface (bottom right) is an optimal trade-off between limited amount of sensors and strong deformation sensing capabilities.

off-the-shelf bend sensor strips (as used in the papers) to be able to understand their strengths and weaknesses. Hence, we combined different concepts of existing sensor configurations into one solution, which is capable of tracking the identified requirements and therefore complex deformations.

Our Layout To create and evaluate several different sensor patterns, we used paper and Scotch tape for fast prototyping (see Figure 4, left). This enabled us to quickly evaluate different designs "hands-on". The flexibility of paper and tape allowed us to bend the prototypes into all directions revealing the pros and cons for each pattern, and a ruler was used to follow bend directions/orientations and to identify spots which are not covered by any sensors.

The final layout arranges 16 sensors at an outer ring of the sheet (see Figure 4, right). Since we use a plastic foil as substrate, it is not possible to deform the sheet only in the center. Therefore, every deformation changes the shape of the edges, which means that by tracking the edges accurately nearly every shape deformation can be reconstructed. Another strength of this layout is that each sensor overlaps with one or multiple other sensors resulting in additional information as to where a bend actually happens (as proposed in [36]). For example, the corner areas which are particularly interesting for bend interaction are covered by three sensors, one at a 45° angle and two at right angles. From this arrangement it is possible to accurately detect how the corner is bent (bend angle) as well as where the bend happens (bend position). Due to the permanent overlap of sensors nearly every deformation actuates multiple sensors, which enables the detection of a wide variety of possible deformations. Those complex patterns of sensor actuations allows for the reconstruction of complex and continuous deformations.

Driver Electronics

As mentioned earlier, every piezoelectric sensor creates a surface charge which correlates to the applied deformation. Since the total number of sensors in our layout is small, we can connect each individually using conductive silver ink to the driver board. This removes the issues associated with the active matrix described earlier. Each sensor is connected to a LMC6482 CMOS rail-to-rail amplifier. These are placed on a small PCB board that is connected to the foil. Before the amplification the signals run through a low pass filter, which protects it against electrostatic discharge. After the amplification a second low pass filter protects the signal from anti-aliasing issues. Each signal gets measured through a MAX127 12-bit data acquisition system which sends the data via a two-wire serial interface to a microcontroller board (Atmel SAM3X8E).

Signal Processing

The electric charges generated in a piezoelectric sensor decay with a time constant determined by the dielectric constant, the internal resistance of the active material and the input impedance of the readout electronics. Due to this fact, the raw signal of a piezoelectric sensor are not usable for *absolute* measurements. However, once the parameters of the exponential signal discharge of the piezoelectric sensors are known it is possible to predict the signal progression over time. Every deformation applied to the sensor will cause a deviation of this predicted signal, which is directly proportional to the applied mechanical stress. Integration over these deviations leads to absolute sensor measurements, which directly correlate with the strength of the applied deformations [23]. Note there is a trade-off with this approach, as integrated errors can persist over time and lead to sensor drift. This can be eliminated with a heuristic which resets the signal e.g. when there is no active interaction on the sensor. In the next section, we describe two reconstruction algorithms where one relies on the integrated signal and one is able to bypass the described issues working directly from the raw signal.

RECONSTRUCTING FLEXSENSE

Now that we have described the FlexSense hardware and sensor layout, we turn our attention to how these sparse (raw or integrated) sensor measurements can be used to accurately recover the 3D shape of the surface during deformation.

Main Pipeline

Reconstructing the full 3D surface shape from a sparse set of sensor measurements is clearly a challenging task. Each sensor reading from our foil is an amplified voltage measurement, and somehow we need to map these combined values to a real-world reconstruction of the surface. In this section we present two data-driven algorithms that tackle this problem. Both of our methods are first trained using pairs of sensor measurements and ground truth 3D shape measurements of the foil. This pre-processing training phase is what enables our algorithms to infer the shape of the foil from the sparse sensor data at runtime.

To collect ground truth measurements of the shape of the foil together with corresponding sensor measurements, we follow the approach illustrated in Figure 5. We print an array of markers on a sheet of paper covering our sensor foil. Then we use a custom-built multi-camera rig (described later) to track the 3D position of the markers with high accuracy. We leverage multiple cameras in order to track as many markers as possible despite occlusions due to the deforming foil and interacting hands. To estimate the positions of the remaining occluded markers (shown in red in Figure 5 and 7) we exploit the prior knowledge that the foil is locally rigid to extrapolate the reconstructed surface (described later).

We use this sequence of resulting ground truth shapes along with the corresponding sparse sensor measurements to train our two algorithms. In the upper left part of Figure 6 we show the training for our *linear interpolation* based approach. It clusters the training data into $K = 30$ common shapes. The mean shape of each cluster is called a blendshape and is stored together with its averaged corresponding sensor measurements. At runtime (see Figure 6, bottom left) the sensor data is used to retrieve the $K = 7$ blendshapes which match the input sensor data (based on a distance metric described later). The

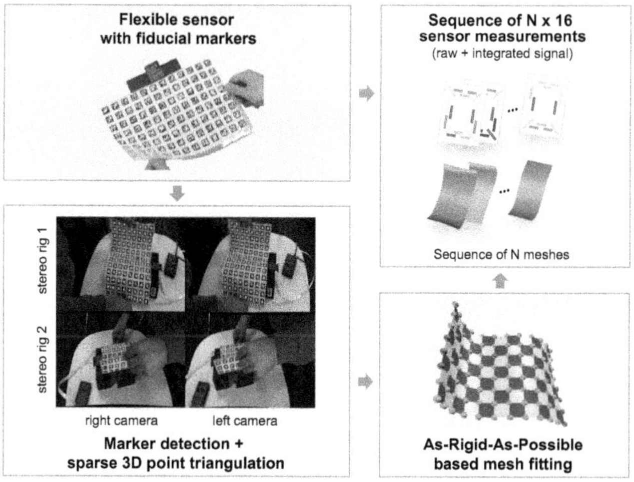

Figure 5: Processing pipeline for ground truth capture. We place fiducial markers on the front and backside of the foil and record their 3D position using a two stereo camera rig, together with the recorded sensor measurements (see text for more details).

final estimated shape is a weighted average of the retrieved blendshapes. This scheme is similar to the approach of [31] and its main benefit is that it is simple to implement, and can yield compelling results. However, a shortcoming of this approach is that it does not generalize well to large sensor signal variations. In practice, the measured sensor signal depends on many variables such as bending speed, temperature and whether the sensor is being grasped. In certain scenarios, this can result in inaccuracies and accumulation of error over time (see detailed discussion later).

To tackle these challenges we propose to use a more sophisticated *machine learning* algorithm. We train this method using the raw sensor data (see Figure 6, top right) to learn a (non-linear) mapping function from the raw sensor measurements to the mesh model. At runtime (see Figure 6, bottom right) it can efficiently infer the geometry given the learned mapping function and the sparse sensor data. This method generalizes well to unseen variations in the sensor signal and hence performs superior to the *linear interpolation* approach. However, it is more complex to implement. As shown later, there is value in each approach and we describe both in detail in the next section.

A tale of two algorithms

In this section we provide a deeper formulation of our two algorithms to aid replication.

Preliminaries Raw sensor measurements are represented as a vector $\mathbf{x} \in \mathbb{R}^F$ and integrated measurements as $\mathbf{z} \in \mathbb{R}^F$ ($F = 16$ for our sensor foil). Our goal is then to estimate the 3D "vertex" positions $\mathcal{V} = \{\mathbf{v}_1, ..., \mathbf{v}_N\} \subseteq \mathbb{R}^3$ of $N = 96$ canonical locations arranged in a 12×8 grid on the sheet. When the sheet is at rest, these vertices take on their known positions $\bar{\mathcal{V}} = \{\bar{\mathbf{v}}_1, ..., \bar{\mathbf{v}}_n\} \subseteq \mathbb{R}^3$.

In the following, it will sometimes be helpful to vectorize the vertex positions $\mathcal{V} = \{\mathbf{v}_n\}_{n=1}^N$ into a column vector $\mathbf{V} \in \mathbb{R}^{3N}$ that we wish to estimate given the raw or $\mathbf{x} \in \mathbb{R}^F$ or integrated signal $\mathbf{z} \in \mathbb{R}^F$. Further, when we are required to deal with a set of J instances of these variables, we will often label these variables as $\mathcal{V}_j = \{\mathbf{v}_n^j\}_{n=1}^N$, $\mathbf{V}_j$ and $\mathbf{x}_j$. In the case of a temporal sequence of length T we will instead use t to index these variable instances. We will, however, often leave off these indices when speaking of a single instance of these variables or when doing so makes equations more clear.

Ground Truth Capture As mentioned we take a data-driven approach for reconstructing the deformations of FlexSense and therefore require training data in order to correlate the sensor measurements of the flexible sensor with the 3D vertex positions. In this section, we therefore explain how to obtain ground truth for a variety of deformations.

In order to generate data of this form, we print an array of $N = 12 \times 8$ fiducial markers onto the front and backside of the flexible sensor foil as to coincide with the N vertex positions we wish to estimate (see Figure 5, top left). Although it is possible to directly estimate the position (and even orientation) of each marker with a single camera [11], this estimation is unreliable when the markers are considerably deformed as in our scenario. We therefore create a calibrated stereo rig (i.e., two cameras with known relative position and orientation) that we label A. In rig A, we are able to detect some subset $\mathcal{C}_A \subseteq \{1, ..., N\}$ of the N markers in both of the rig's cameras. For such a marker $n \in \mathcal{C}_A$, we use triangulation to estimate $\hat{\mathbf{v}}_n^A \in \mathbb{R}^3$ of vertex n.

Note that due to occlusions and strong deformations often only a small number of the marker positions can be estimated with stereo rig A. To increase the number of vertex positions that we can estimate, we use a second stereo rig that we label B to obtain estimates for a second set of markers $\mathcal{C}_B \subseteq \{1, ..., N\}$. The set of indices with estimations from both rigs $\mathcal{C}_A \cap \mathcal{C}_B$ defines two input point clouds in one-to-one correspondence. We obtain the optimal rigid transformation by using the Kabsch algorithm [10] to minimize

$$E_{\text{rigid}}(R, \tau) = \sum_{n \in \mathcal{C}_A \cap \mathcal{C}_B} \|\hat{\mathbf{v}}_n^A - (R\hat{\mathbf{v}}_n^B + \tau)\|^2 \quad (1)$$

where $R \in SO^3$ is a rotation matrix and $\tau \in \mathbb{R}^3$ is a translation. Using this transformation, we can obtain a set $\mathcal{C} = \mathcal{C}_A \cup \mathcal{C}_B$ in a common coordinate frame. To do this for $n \in \mathcal{C}$, we estimate the corresponding vertex as

$$\hat{\mathbf{v}}_n = \begin{cases} \frac{1}{2}(\hat{\mathbf{v}}_n^A + R\hat{\mathbf{v}}_n^B + \tau) & n \in \mathcal{C}_A \cap \mathcal{C}_B \\ \hat{\mathbf{v}}_n^A, & n \in \mathcal{C} - \mathcal{C}_B \\ R\hat{\mathbf{v}}_n^B + \tau & n \in \mathcal{C} - \mathcal{C}_A \end{cases} \quad (2)$$

As-Rigid-As-Possible Refinement Unfortunately, we are generally unable to estimate the locations of all N points even with two stereo rigs. Therefore, we exploit our prior knowledge that the sheet is locally rigid to extrapolate the reconstructed surface and provide estimates for the remaining points. To do this, we utilize the as-rigid-as-possible (ARAP) regularizer [30] which measures how locally non-rigid a point cloud with a neighborhood structure is. Here the local-rigidity for point n is measured in relation to the other points in a neighborhood $\mathcal{N}(n) \subseteq \{1, ..., N\}$, which in our case is simply the neighbors of n in the 12×8 grid. The ARAP measure of deformation with respect to the rest configuration $\bar{\mathcal{V}}$ is

$$E_{\text{ARAP}}(\mathcal{V}) = \sum_{n=1}^{N} \min_{R} \sum_{n' \in \mathcal{N}(n)} \|(\bar{\mathbf{v}}_{n'} - \bar{\mathbf{v}}_n) - R(\mathbf{v}_{n'} - \mathbf{v}_n)\|^2$$

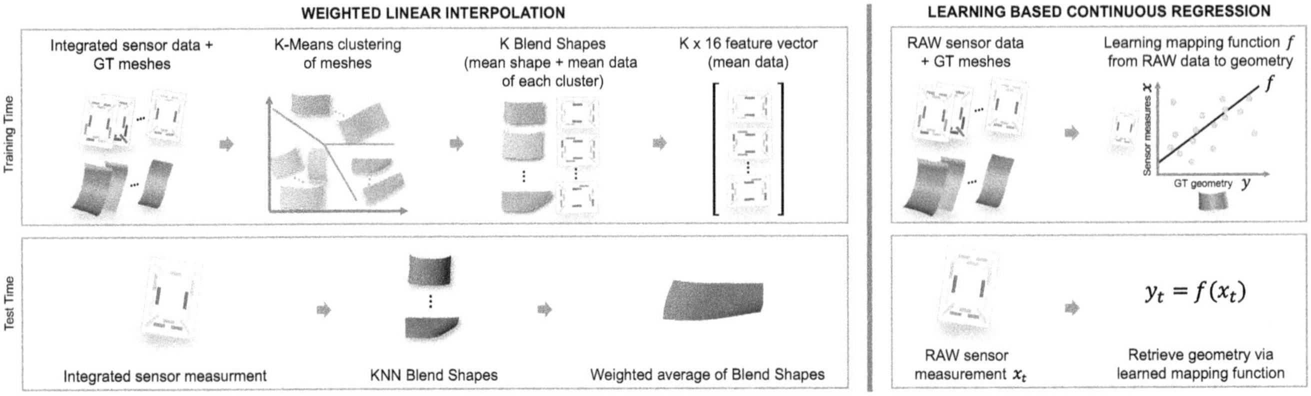

Figure 6: We present two reconstruction algorithms, both with different trade-offs. On the left: A weighted linear interpolation scheme using kNN. On the right: A machine learning based approach (see text for more details).

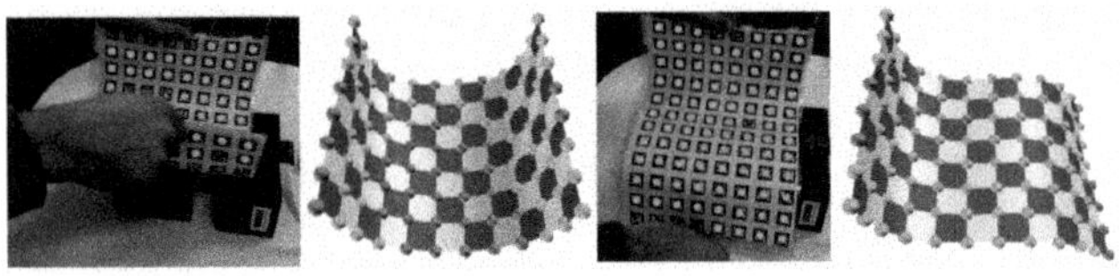

Figure 7: Ground truth capture. Markers are detected in each camera image (green and orange dots), and triangulated as a 3D point across each stereo pair (green dots in images and mesh). An ARAP refinement step regularizes for unseen or occluded vertices (red dots on mesh).

where $R \in SO^3$. This energy will be low for the smooth deformations that we expect (see Figure 4) as a rigid rotation can be used to approximate the deformation of the local deformation of each neighborhood. When this is impossible (e.g. sharp creases), however, the energy will be high. We therefore formulate the following energy

$$E(\mathcal{V}) = \sum_{n \in \mathcal{C}} \|\hat{\mathbf{v}}_n - \mathbf{v}_n\|^2 + \lambda_{\text{ARAP}} E_{\text{ARAP}}(\mathcal{V}) \quad (3)$$

defined over the vertex positions $\mathcal{V}$. By minimizing this energy, we are seeking to find a set of vertex positions $\mathcal{V}$ that approximately match the estimates $\{\hat{\mathbf{v}}_n : n \in \mathcal{C}\}$ while not substantially deforming (in the ARAP sense) from the rest configuration.

To minimize (3), we follow the lead of [34] and label each rotation matrix in (3) with latent variables $\mathcal{R} = \{R_n\}_{n=1}^N \subseteq SO^3$. This allows one to define

$$E'_{\text{ARAP}}(\mathcal{V}, \mathcal{R}) = \sum_{n=1}^{N} \sum_{n' \in \mathcal{N}(n)} \|(\bar{\mathbf{v}}_{n'} - \bar{\mathbf{v}}_n) - R_n(\mathbf{v}_{n'} - \mathbf{v}_n)\|^2$$

with the property that $E_{\text{ARAP}}(\mathcal{V}) = \min_{\mathcal{R}} E'_{\text{ARAP}}(\mathcal{V}, \mathcal{R})$. Plugging this into (3), we get that $E(\mathcal{V}) = \min_{\mathcal{R}} E'(\mathcal{V}, \mathcal{R})$ where

$$E'(\mathcal{V}, \mathcal{R}) = \sum_{n \in \mathcal{C}} \|\hat{\mathbf{v}}_n - \mathbf{v}_n\|^2 + \lambda_{\text{ARAP}} E'_{\text{ARAP}}(\mathcal{V}, \mathcal{R}) \,. \quad (4)$$

We thus minimize $E'(\mathcal{V}, \mathcal{R})$ using Levenberg-Marquardt[2]. We initialize this procedure by setting $\mathbf{v}_n = \bar{\mathbf{v}}_n$ and $R_n = I_3$ for each $n \in \{1, ..., N\}$. Finally, we parameterize the rotations using an axis-angle representation to enforce the constraint that each R_n remains a rotation matrix. In practice, this leads to a robust and real-time method for recovering the full mesh from a sparse set of vertices (see Figure 7).

[2] `https://code.google.com/p/ceres-solver/`

Dataset Construction We have shown how to capture ground truth vertex positions $\mathcal{V}$ to associate with a signal $\mathbf{x} \in F$. As we are capturing temporal sequences, in addition to the raw signal $\mathbf{x}_t$ and vertex positions $\mathcal{V}_t$ at time t, we will also record the integrated signal $\mathbf{z}_t \in \mathbb{R}^F$ up to time t and the instantaneous vertex displacements $\mathcal{D}_t = \{\mathbf{d}_1^t, ..., \mathbf{d}_N^t\} \subseteq \mathbb{R}^3$. The vertex displacement for vertex n is simply $\mathbf{v}_n^t - \mathbf{v}_n^{t-1}$. By capturing this information for a wide variety of sequences, we obtain a large fixed dataset $\{(\mathbf{x}_j, \mathbf{z}_j, \mathcal{V}_j, \mathcal{D}_j)\}_{j=1}^J$ that we will use for training.

Learning to Infer Shape and Deformation

In this section, we describe how to leverage this training set to predict the positions $\mathcal{V}$ of the vertices. In particular, as the rest pose $\bar{\mathcal{V}}$ is easily detected when $\mathbf{x} \approx \mathbf{0}$, we assume that we have seen a subsequent t time steps and attempt to predict $\mathcal{V}_t$. In order to estimate the 3D points $\mathcal{V}_t$ at time t, we propose two different approaches, both data-driven. The first uses a distance metric in the sensor input space (i.e. voltage measurements) to interpolate a set of key deformation modes. The second one uses machine learning techniques to directly regress the 3D vertex displacements.

Nearest Neighbor Lookup and Linear Interpolation Our first method assumes that the vertex position vector $\mathbf{V} \in \mathbb{R}^{3N}$ is a linear combination of a set of K blendshapes or deformation modes which we denote as $\{\mathbf{B}_1, ..., \mathbf{B}_K\} \subseteq \mathbb{R}^{3N}$. That is,

$$\mathbf{V} = \sum_{k}^{K} \alpha_k \mathbf{B}_k \quad (5)$$

where α_k defines the weight of the k'th deformation mode $\{v_{nk}\}_{n=1}^N \subseteq \mathbb{R}^3$. To find these K deformations we run K-means to extract K modes $\{\bar{\mathbf{v}}_k\}_{k=1}^K \subseteq$ from our set and which appear to cover all the common configurations we expect to use. For each k, we average the integrated signal

$$\bar{\mathbf{z}}_k = \frac{1}{|\zeta_k|} \sum_{j \in \zeta_k} \mathbf{z}_j \quad (6)$$

where $\zeta_k \subseteq \mathbb{R}^F$ is the set of integrated signals in the training set whose corresponding vertex positions were assigned to mode k in K-means. At runtime we see a new integrated signal $\mathbf{z}$ and compute α_k as

$$\alpha_k = \left(1 - \left(\frac{|\bar{\mathbf{z}}_k - \mathbf{z}_t|\frac{F}{f_k}}{\sum_j |\bar{\mathbf{z}}_j - \mathbf{z}_t|\frac{F}{f_j}}\right)\right)^\beta , \quad (7)$$

where $\frac{F}{f_k}$ weights the distances based on the number of sensors involved during the bending gesture. In particular F is the total number of sensors attached to the sheet and f_k are the activated sensors of the model k, those absolute values are greater than $\theta = 200$; β is a regularization term to ensure smoothness during the transition between different configurations. We then plug these weights into (5) to reconstruct the positions $\mathcal{V}$.

Learning-based Continuous Regression The basic method proposed in the previous section assumes that all the possible poses can be generated through a linear combination of K modes. Also, recall that the signal $\mathbf{z}$ comes from an integration process that could lead to drift effects over the time. Unfortunately, these properties can lead to inaccuracies in the final reconstruction.

To address these issues, we consider regression-based methods that directly estimate the vertex displacements $\mathcal{D}$ using the raw signal $\mathbf{x} \in \mathbb{R}^F$. In particular, we seek to leverage our large training set to directly learn a mapping

$$f_{in} : \mathbf{x} \rightarrow \mathbf{d}_{in} \quad \forall n = 1, \ldots, N \quad \forall i = 1, 2, 3 \tag{8}$$

from the raw signal $\mathbf{x}$ to the displacement $\mathbf{d}_{in}$ in coordinate i of vertex n. For coordinate i of vertex n, we extract from our training set the following set of tuples $\{(\mathbf{x}_j, \mathbf{d}^j_{in})\}_{j=1}^J$ of size J. We use this to learn a function f_{in} that minimizes the empirical risk

$$\frac{1}{J}\sum_{j=1}^{J}\mathcal{L}(f_{in}(\mathbf{x}_j, \mathbf{d}^j_{in})) + \mathcal{R}(f), \tag{9}$$

where $\mathcal{L}(\circ)$ is the loss function and $\mathcal{R}(\circ)$ is a regularization term that gives a tradeoff between the accuracy and the complexity of the model.

Linear Model. Since we want to predict the position of all the N vertices with real-time performance we use a linear regression model: $f_{in}(\mathbf{x}) = \mathbf{x}^\top \mathbf{w}_{in}$, with $\mathbf{w}_{in} \in \mathbb{R}^F$. Indeed, with a high sampling rate of the signal, it is reasonable to assume that the relation between the input and output can be approximated by such a linear function. Let $\mathbf{X} = [\mathbf{x}_1, \ldots, \mathbf{x}_J]^\top \in \mathbb{R}^{J\times F}$ be the matrix of all the examples J and given the groundtruth vertex displacements $\mathbf{Y} = [\mathbf{D}_1^\top, \ldots, \mathbf{D}_J^\top] \in \mathbb{R}^{J\times 3N}$ where $\mathbf{D}_j$ is just the set $\{\mathbf{d}^j_{in} : n \in \{1, ..., N\}, i \in \{1, 2, 3\}\}$ vectorized into a column vector. This allows us to rewrite (9) for all N vertices simultaneously as

$$\mathbf{W}^\star = \arg\min_{\mathbf{W}} \|\mathbf{Y} - \mathbf{X}\mathbf{W}\|_2^2 + \lambda\|\mathbf{W}\|^2 \tag{10}$$

where $\mathbf{W} \in \mathbb{R}^{F\times 3N}$ is the matrix of all the linear regressors, and $\| \circ \|^2$ is a regularizer that favors smaller norms (i.e. lower complexity). The above optimization problem is known as *Tikhonov regularization* or *Regularized Least Square (RLS)* [35, 4] and it has the close form solution:

$$\mathbf{W}^\star = (\mathbf{X}^\top\mathbf{X} + \lambda\mathbf{I})^{-1}\mathbf{X}^\top\mathbf{Y} \tag{11}$$

with $\mathbf{I} \in \mathbb{R}^{F\times F}$ being the identity matrix.

We also extended this approach to handle non-linear functions by using the Representer Theorem [27]. Both the linear and non-linear model are able to describe the relation between the sensor signal and vertices. However, due to the higher complexity of the non-linear model (linear growth with the number of examples T), our machine learning based approach relies on the linear model.

Run-Time. At run time, given the current signal $\mathbf{x}_t$ we compute the N vertex displacements as $\mathbf{D}_t = \mathbf{W}^\top\mathbf{x}_t$. The current position of the sheet is then computed as $\mathbf{V}_t = \mathbf{V}_{t-1} + \mathbf{D}_t$. The initial position $\mathbf{V}_0$ is assumed to be known (i.e. the resting pose). The learning method we propose ensures enough robustness against drift effects, which has little impact in the final reconstruction. However, it is always possible to accurately detect the resting pose when there is no activity on the sensor: by simply computing the standard deviation σ of the signal $\mathbf{x}_t$ and classify the current pose as initial position if $\sigma < \theta$.

RESULTS AND EXPERIMENTS

We now evaluate the proposed surface reconstruction methods, whereas the core question of the experiment is to measure our system accuracy with regard to the two proposed algorithms. For this we again use our ground truth rig. We acquire 10 sequences of bending gestures covering the most common deformations for interaction scenarios. Each sequence contains approximately 4,000 frames, in total, so our data-set is composed of 40,000 frames. We randomly split the data-set into training and validation set, where 30,000 examples are used for training and the remaining 10,000 for testing.

The error (in meters) is computed using the average Euclidean distances between the ground truth vertices and the predicted configuration.

Reconstruction Error

We first compare the reconstruction performances of the linear interpolation (blendshape model) and regularized least squares (RLS). In Figure 9 (left) the average error over 10,000 bending poses is reported, as a function of number of training examples. The learning methods achieve the best results with an average error of 0.015 ± 0.007m. Thanks to the strong correlation between the signal and the actual vertex displacement, the linear regressions are able to describe the relation between the sensor signal and the vertices. The blendshape approach, despite its simplicity also performs very well, with an average error of 0.018 ± 0.009m. Notice that around 10,000 training frames are enough for achieving the best results: this correspond roughly to a video sequence of 5 mins. A comparison of the running times shows, that both linear interpolation and RLS have a complexity equal to $\mathcal{O}(MN)$ where MN is the grid size. Qualitative examples of the shape reconstructions are shown in Figure 8 (left).

As a second experiment we evaluated which part of the flexible sheet obtains the highest error. We show the qualitative results in Figure 9 (right). As expected most of the errors are around the corners, where the interaction is mostly occurring. RLS has a maximum and minimum error of 0.021 ± 0.013m and 0.006 ± 0.001m respectively. Linear interpolation instead has a maximum error equal to 0.032 ± 0.024m and minimum of 0.007 ± 0.015m.

Comparisons with Marker-Based Vision Systems

Although camera-based systems have certain different constraints compared to our self-contained setup (i.e. spatial resolution of the camera, depth dependency, occlusions), we feel that existing camera-based systems (e.g. FlexPad [31]) offer the greatest degree of reconstruction quality currently. Therefore, being able to reconstruct our deformations without this

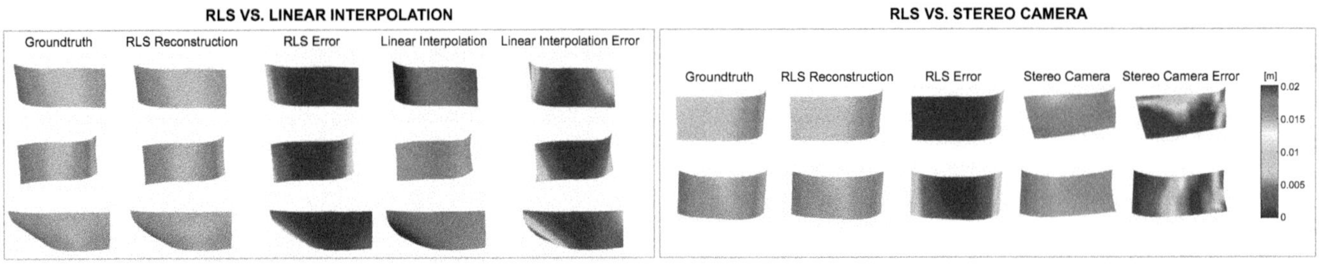

Figure 8: Left: Qualitative results showing the reconstruction performances of the linear interpolation (blendshapes) model versus the regularized linear regression of the vertex positions. Right: Reconstruction comparisons between RLS and a single stereo camera using markers. Most of the errors in the vision based system are due to occlusions.

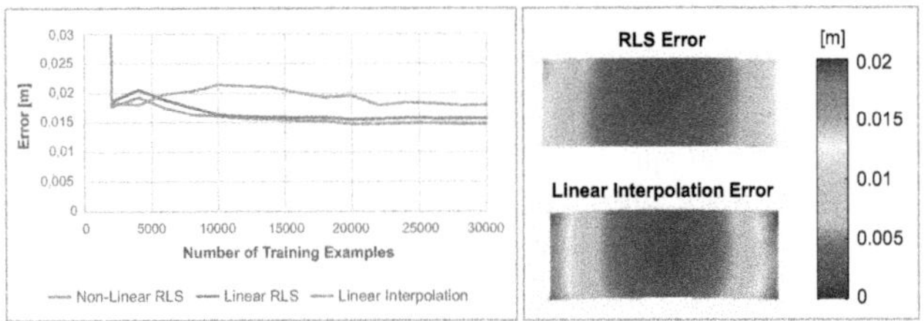

Figure 9: Left: Error [m] for the three reconstruction algorithms as a function of training samples. Right: Error maps of the linear interpolation and the regularized linear regressions with respect to the vertex positions. As expected, most of the error is located where the interactions often occurr.

type of sensing infrastructure felt like an important question to answer. For that reason, we compared our reconstructions with a single-view marker-based system. In Figure 8 (right) we show some examples where a single stereo camera is not able to reconstruct the surface of the sheet. This mainly occurs when the hands are occluding the markers and surface. On average, the single stereo marker-based system has an error of 0.023 ± 0.014m, whereas the machine learning approach achieves 0.011 ± 0.06m. This not only motivates our need for two stereo cameras for the ground truth capture, but also highlights that occlusions are a big challenge for systems that make use of single depth or regular cameras for surface tracking.

APPLICATIONS AND INTERACTION TECHNIQUES

In this section we cover some of the interactive affordances of FlexSense in two different application scenarios. These strongly highlight the benefit of the continuous, smooth and detailed level of reconstruction capabilities of our system, its transparency, and its compact and self-contained form-factor.

Transparent smart cover for tablets

In the first scenario, we used FlexSense as a replacement for existing tablet covers. By just adding a thin, transparent cover our sensor layout allows for paper-like interaction with rigid displays. Figure 10 depicts novel and natural usage examples, like switching between different layers in Photoshop or in online maps, performing rapid application switching to copy&paste content, comparing rendering enhancements for image or video filters, similar to tangible magic lens, or revealing on-demand solutions for games or education. Initial user feedback suggests that the *paper-like* feeling provides a completely novel, highly intuitive and natural interaction experience. The one-to-one mapping and directness of the input, as the user peels the foil back and forth, greatly utilizes the accuracy of the detailed reconstruction and lets the users accurately choose the area to reveal, providing direct immediate feedback.

One exciting use case for the transparent smart cover is in expanding traditional animation, where each frame is painstakingly drawn by hand. This work is mainly done with so-called 'animation desks', where animators sketch sequences on sheets of semi-transparent drafting film. These sheets are usually put on top of a light table and the animator is able to switch between the different frames by flipping the paper. Although, these light tables are being increasingly replaced by graphics tablets, many designers still use this "old style" of animation[3]. Our transparent sensor is thin enough to sense the stylus-input on the tablet. This allows the user to sketch directly on top of the transparent FlexSense and flip between different frames by bending the sensor, ushering this manual approach to animation back into digital domain.

With the use as cover of course certain practical implications arise, in particular general "wear and tear" issues of the foil, which are a general challenge of flexible devices. For later prototypes it will be necessary to think about other issues like durability, which we have not considered in this paper. However, we feel that new exciting possibilities are enabled through this configuration and inspire HCI researchers (including us) to work further in this space.

External high-DoF input device

As highlighted in related work, flexible sensors have also been used as external input devices [1]. What makes these types of sensors appealing is that they afford both 2.5D interactions, resting on a surface, as well as true in-air 3D interactions, while maintaining a level of tangible feedback (a problem for touchless interfaces in general). In Figure 10 (right) we demonstrate how the accurate reconstructions of the flexible sheet can be used in a 3D game. Continuous and discrete gestures are easily mapped to actions such as flying, steering, and firing a gun at varying rates. These gestures are simple to implement as we provide a fully tracked, temporally consistent mesh. A further example shown in Figure 10 (far right), is a physically realistic game where the reconstructions of shape and deformations, enable interactions with virtual objects (e.g. to catapult an object). The diversity of control in the examples would be difficult to achieve without the accuracy of our system and shows that continuous and precise reconstructions are crucial for these scenarios (as shown by prior work [1]). Whilst these are fun "toy" examples and exemplary show our system's capabilities, there are certain other scenarios, which could greatly benefit of the accurate reconstruction, such as 3D modeling and manipulations.

[3] `http://www.youtube.com/watch?v=fR3IDisAQwE` (from 4:50 mins)

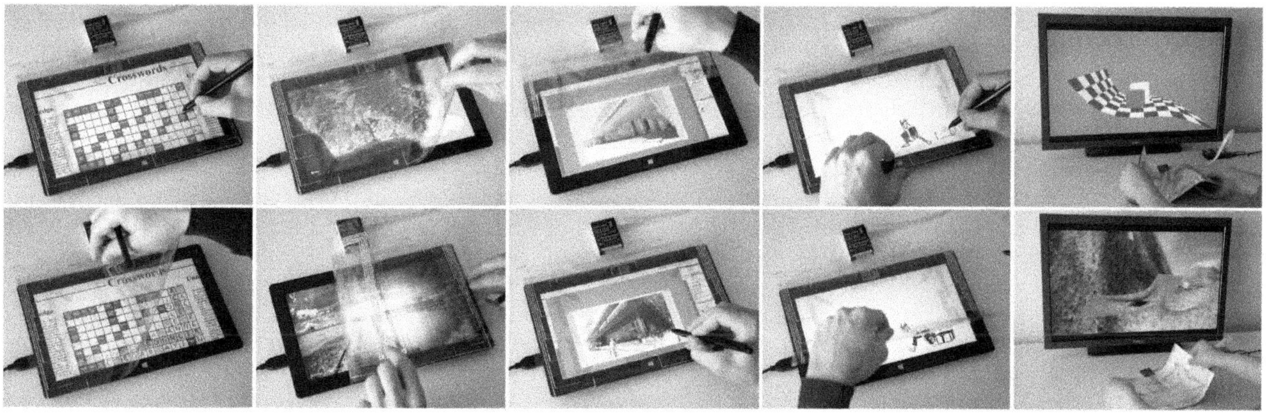

Figure 10: Example applications created using our sensor. A transparent tablet cover example, which acts as a magic lens revealing hidden metadata, applying rendering effects in photoshop, supporting window management, and allowing paper-like digital animation. Far right: using the foil as a high DoF 3D controller.

DISCUSSION & LIMITATIONS

We have discussed our sensor layout, reconstruction algorithms, and potential application scenarios. Our methods of reconstructing real-world shape and deformation from a sparse set of piezoelectric measurements are novel, and affords new interactive capabilities in self-contained lightweight form-factor. This combined with the transparent nature of the sensors creates many new application possibilities.

In describing our reconstruction algorithms, we have purposefully presented two methods, which have worked incredibly well in practice. Our linear interpolation model is relatively simple to implement, and works well even for complex models. Indeed some of the clear cover application scenarios were implemented with this model. The model can be trained and extended with new examples, in a relatively straightforward manner, and with limited samples can generate compelling results. The main need for an extended algorithm, however, comes in dealing with larger variations of shapes and deformations, and generalizing to unseen training data. For example, if we wanted to develop a 3D modeling tool using the precise surface deformation as input. However, given that the latter requires machine learning knowledge, we feel that both methods will have great value for practitioners. It is also worth noting, that our method should in theory generalize to other self sensing or external sensing setups, including other bend sensors. However, this remains future work. In terms of our algorithm, we have experimented with using ARAP during the prediction phase, at runtime. This type of regularization leads to over-smoothing, but another area of future investigation is to think about such a run-time regularizer particularly if more complex materials or geometries are to be modeled.

In terms of hardware, developing a new sensor is challenging and the FlexSense sensor does have limitations. The sensors deteriorate over prolonged periods when performing extreme gestures. Gestures such as folding are also problematic. The sensors are also not fully transparent, although indium tin oxide (ITO) used in traditional touch screens, has similar transmissive capabilities. Another limitation is, that the integrated sensor signal used in the linear interpolation approach can suffer from drift issues when performing rapid interactions.

Generally, however, the sensor is highly promising and has a lot of potentials for further projects. It will be interesting to conduct more profound user studies, particularly as new interaction techniques are developed further. Moreover, detailed comparisons of different existing sensor configurations with the FlexSense setup would be highly interesting. From a more general point of view, we would like to combine our input sensor with a flexible display (e.g. eInk / OLED). Smart watches are becoming more and more popular; especially, if they are combined with deformable shapes, we can imagine devices which have not been possible before. Another interesting area is that of touch/pressure sensing in combination with bend sensors. In particular the signal processing challenges of differentiating one from the other.

CONCLUSIONS

In this paper, we presented FlexSense, a new thin-film, transparent self-sensing surface, which can reconstruct complex deformations without the need for any external sensing, such as cameras. We have built on prior work to demonstrate a new piezoelectric bendable input device, with sensors printed on the periphery of the surface substrate. Our main contribution has been to devise a novel set of algorithms to fully reconstruct the complex deformations of the sheet, using only these sparse sensor measurements. We have demonstrated a number of new types of applications for such a device that exploit the accurate shape and deformations afforded.

ACKNOWLEDGEMENTS

We acknowledge Florian Perteneder, Cem Keskin and Barbara Stadlober for their invaluable input. The research leading to these results has received funding from the European Union, Seventh Framework Programme FP7/2007-2013 under grant agreement N° 611104.

REFERENCES

1. Balakrishnan, R., Fitzmaurice, G., Kurtenbach, G., and Singh, K. Exploring Interactive Curve and Surface Manipulation Using a Bend and Twist Sensitive Input Strip. In *I3D'99*, ACM, 1999, 111–118.
2. Caglioti, V., Giusti, A., Mureddu, L., and Taddei, P. A Manipulable Vision-Based 3D Input Device for Space Curves. In *Articulated Motion and Deformable Objects*. Springer, 2008, 309–318.
3. Danisch, L. A., Englehart, K., and Trivett, A. Spatially continuous six-degrees-of-freedom position and

orientation sensor. In *Photonics East*, International Society for Optics and Photonics, 1999, 48–56.
4. Evgeniou, T., Pontil, M., and Poggio, T. Regularization Networks and Support Vector Machines. In *Advances in Computational Mathematics*, 2000.
5. Follmer, S., Leithinger, D., Olwal, A., Cheng, N., and Ishii, H. Jamming User Interfaces: Programmable Particle Stiffness and Sensing for Malleable and Shape-changing Devices. In *UIST'12*, ACM, 2012, 519–528.
6. Gallant, D. T., Seniuk, A. G., and Vertegaal, R. Towards More Paper-like Input: Flexible Input Devices for Foldable Interaction Styles. In *UIST'08*, ACM, Oct. 2008, 283.
7. Gomes, A., Nesbitt, A., and Vertegaal, R. MorePhone: A Study of Actuated Shape Deformations for Flexible Thin-Film Smartphone Notifications. In *CHI'13*, ACM, Apr. 2013, 583.
8. Herkenrath, G., Karrer, T., and Borchers, J. TWEND: Twisting and Bending as new Interaction Gesture in Mobile Devices. In *CHI'08 EA*, ACM, Apr. 2008, 3819.
9. Holman, D., Vertegaal, R., Altosaar, M., Troje, N., and Johns, D. PaperWindows: Interaction Techniques for Digital Paper. In *CHI'05*, ACM, 2005, 591–599.
10. Kabsch, W. A solution for the best rotation to relate two sets of vectors. *Acta Crystallographica* (1976).
11. Kato, H., and Billinghurst, M. Marker Tracking and HMD Calibration for a Video-Based Augmented Reality Conferencing System. In *IWAR'99*, IEEE Computer Society, 1999.
12. Kato, T., Yamamoto, A., and Higuchi, T. Shape recognition using piezoelectric thin films. In *IEEE Industrial Technology*, vol. 1, IEEE, 2003, 112–116.
13. Khalilbeigi, M., Lissermann, R., Kleine, W., and Steimle, J. Foldme: Interacting with double-sided foldable displays. In *TEI'12*, ACM, 2012, 33–40.
14. Khalilbeigi, M., Lissermann, R., Mühlhäuser, M., and Steimle, J. Xpaaand: Interaction Techniques for Rollable Displays. In *CHI'11*, ACM, 2011, 2729–2732.
15. Kildal, J., Paasovaara, S., and Aaltonen, V. Kinetic Device: Designing Interactions with a Deformable Mobile Interface. In *CHI EA'12*, May 2012.
16. Konieczny, J., Shimizu, C., Meyer, G., and Colucci, D. A Handheld Flexible Display System, 2005.
17. Lahey, B., Girouard, A., Burleson, W., and Vertegaal, R. PaperPhone: Understanding the Use of Bend Gestures in Mobile Devices with Flexible Electronic Paper Displays. In *CHI'11*, ACM, May 2011, 1303.
18. Leal, A., Bowman, D., Schaefer, L., Quek, F., and Stiles, C. K. 3D Sketching Using Interactive Fabric for Tangible and Bimanual Input. In *GI'11*, Canadian Human-Computer Communications Society, 2011, 49–56.
19. Lee, J. C., Hudson, S. E., and Tse, E. Foldable interactive displays. In *UIST'08*, ACM, 2008, 287–290.
20. Lee, S.-S. et al. How Users Manipulate Deformable Displays as Input Devices. In *CHI'10*, ACM, Apr. 2010, 1647.
21. Lee, S.-S. et al. FlexRemote: Exploring the effectiveness of deformable user interface as an input device for TV. In *HCI International 2011–Posters' Extended Abstracts*. Springer, 2011, 62–65.
22. Punpongsanon, P., Iwai, D., and Sato, K. DeforMe: Projection-based Visualization of Deformable Surfaces Using Invisible Textures. In *ETech SA'13*, ACM, 2013.
23. Rendl, C. et al. PyzoFlex: Printed Piezoelectric Pressure Sensing Foil. In *UIST'12*, ACM, 2012.
24. Rosenberg, I., and Perlin, K. The UnMousePad: An Interpolating Multi-touch Force-sensing Input Pad. In *ACM Transactions on Graphics (TOG)*, vol. 28, ACM, 2009, 65.
25. Roudaut, A., Karnik, A., Löchtefeld, M., and Subramanian, S. Morphees: Toward High "Shape Resolution" in Self-Actuated Flexible Mobile Devices. In *CHI'13*, ACM, Apr. 2013, 593.
26. Sato, T., Mamiya, H., Koike, H., and Fukuchi, K. PhotoelasticTouch: Transparent Rubbery Tangible Interface Using an LCD and Photoelasticity. In *UIST'09*, ACM, 2009, 43–50.
27. Schölkopf, B., Herbrich, R., and Smola, A. A Generalized Representer Theorem. In *Conference on Computational Learning Theory*, 2001.
28. Schwesig, C., Poupyrev, I., and Mori, E. Gummi: A Bendable Computer. In *CHI'04*, ACM, Apr. 2004, 263–270.
29. Smith, R. T., Thomas, B. H., and Piekarski, W. Digital Foam Interaction Techniques for 3D Modeling. In *VRST'08*, ACM, 2008, 61–68.
30. Sorkine, O., and Alexa, M. As-rigid-as-possible surface modeling. In *SGP'07*, 2007.
31. Steimle, J., Jordt, A., and Maes, P. Flexpad: Highly Flexible Bending Interactions for Projected Handheld Displays. In *CHI'13*, ACM, Apr. 2013, 237.
32. Tajika, T., Yonezawa, T., and Mitsunaga, N. Intuitive Page-turning Interface of E-books on Flexible E-paper based on User Studies. In *MM'08*, ACM, Oct. 2008, 793.
33. Tarun, A. P. et al. PaperTab: An Electronic Paper Computer with Multiple Large Flexible Electrophoretic Displays. In *CHI EA'13*, ACM, 2013, 3131–3134.
34. Taylor, J. et al. User-specific hand modeling from monocular depth sequences. In *CVPR*, 2014.
35. Tikhonov, A., Leonov, A., and A.G., Y. Nonlinear Ill-Posed Problems. In *Kluwer Academic Publishers*, 1998.
36. Warren, K., Lo, J., Vadgama, V., and Girouard, A. Bending the Rules: Bend Gesture Classification for Flexible Displays. In *CHI'13*, ACM, Apr. 2013, 607.
37. Watanabe, J., Mochizuki, A., and Horry, Y. Bookisheet: Bendable Device for Browsing Content Using the Metaphor of Leafing Through the Pages. In *UbiComp'08*, ACM, Sept. 2008, 360.
38. Wellner, P. Interacting with paper on the DigitalDesk. *Communications of the ACM 36*, 7 (1993), 87–96.
39. Ye, Z., and Khalid, H. Cobra: Flexible Displays for Mobile Gaming Scenarios. In *CHI EA'10*, ACM, 2010, 4363–4368.
40. Zimmerman, T. G., Lanier, J., Blanchard, C., Bryson, S., and Harvill, Y. A Hand Gesture Interface Device. In *CHI'87*, ACM, 1987, 189–192.
41. Zirkl, M. et al. An All-Printed Ferroelectric Active Matrix Sensor Network Based on Only Five Functional Materials Forming a Touchless Control Interface. *Advanced Materials, Volume 23, Issue 18* (2011), 2069–2074.

Hover Pad: Interacting with Autonomous and Self-Actuated Displays in Space

Juilan Seifert[1], Sebastian Boring[2], Christian Winkler[1], Florian Schaub[3]
Fabian Schwab[1], Steffen Herrdum[1], Fabian Maier[1], Daniel Mayer[1], Enrico Rukzio[1]
[1]Institute of Media Informatics, Ulm University, Germany
[2]Department of Computer Science, University of Copenhagen, Denmark
[3]School of Computer Science, Carnegie Mellon University, USA
[1]{firstname.lastname}@uni-ulm.de, [2]sebastian.boring@di.ku.dk, [3]fschaub@cmu.edu

ABSTRACT
Handheld displays enable flexible spatial exploration of information spaces – users can physically navigate through three-dimensional space to access information at specific locations. Having users constantly hold the display, however, has several limitations: (1) inaccuracies due to natural hand tremors; (2) fatigue over time; and (3) limited exploration within arm's reach. We investigate *autonomous, self-actuated displays* that can freely move and hold their position and orientation in space without users having to hold them at all times. We illustrate various stages of such a display's autonomy ranging from *manual* to *fully autonomous*, which – depending on the tasks – facilitate the interaction. Further, we discuss possible motion control mechanisms for these displays and present several interaction techniques enabled by such displays. Our *Hover Pad* toolkit enables exploring five degrees of freedom of self-actuated and autonomous displays and the developed control and interaction techniques. We illustrate the utility of our toolkit with five prototype applications, such as a volumetric medical data explorer.

Author Keywords
Self-actuated displays; volumetric data sets; interaction.

ACM Classification Keywords
H.5.2 Information Interfaces and Presentation

General Terms
Design, Human Factors.

INTRODUCTION
With their mobility, handheld displays such as tablets suggest themselves for spatial exploration of information spaces. They can provide a digital window into a much larger three-dimensional information space (see Figure 1a). This approach can help users explore and understand complex volumetric data sets. Information spaces are typically either centered around the user's body [6, 33], or anchored to larger displays in the environment [11, 12, 27]. Previous research

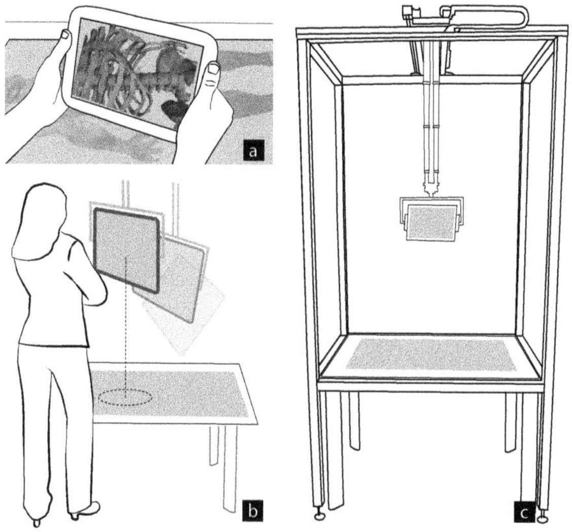

Figure 1. Handheld displays allow exploring volumetric data sets, yet users have to hold them in their hands at all times (*a*). Self-actuated and autonomous displays, on the other hand, jettison this requirement (*b*). Our prototype is a first realization of a self-actuated display that can autonomously move and hold its position (*c*).

has assumed that people move the display manually (may it be a tablet computer or a sheet of paper with projection) using their hands. While in motion, the display content changes continuously according to its position and orientation in space.

Manually controlling the display's position and orientation empowers users to navigate to a desired location in the information space. This approach, however, has its shortcomings: (1) users hold the device continuously (occupying at least one hand) which may increase fatigue; (2) exact positioning becomes difficult due to natural hand tremors [25]; and (3) users have to search for information within the information space which might be time-consuming and error-prone (i.e., missing important aspects in the data as users focus on finding a specific item instead). In summary, handheld displays are tied to the user's physical input (here: moving it in space) in order to change their content.

In this work, we set out to free handheld displays from the user's physical input constraints. That is, displays can autonomously move within the information space of a volumetric data set. Unlike previous systems (e.g., [11, 12, 27, 33]), users do not have to hold the display in their hands; instead

UIST '14, October 05 - 08 2014, Honolulu, HI, USA

http://dx.doi.org/10.1145/2642918.2647385

the display can move autonomously and maintain its position and orientation (see Figure 1b). This autonomous actuation can further be combined with manual input by users, e.g., a user moving the display to a position where it then remains. To investigate this new class of displays, we built *Hover Pad*– a self-actuated display system mounted to a crane. Our setup allows for controlling five degrees of freedom: moving the display along its *x*-, *y*-, and *z*-axes; and changing both *pitch* (i.e., the displays's horizontal axis) and *yaw* (i.e., the vertical axis) of the display.

With its self-actuated nature, our setup offers three advantages over displays held in hand that are positioned physically and manually by users: (1) the display can *move autonomously* in space without requiring a user's physical effort; (2) it allows for *hands-free interaction* as users do not have to hold the display in their hand continuously – thus reducing fatigue in arms and hands as well as using hands for parallel tasks; and (3), it offers enhanced *visual stability* compared to manually holding a still in a certain position and orientation (i.e., natural hand tremor).

In this paper, we investigate designing interactions with such displays based on our prototype. We focus on how their movement can be controlled either autonomously by the system or by users. We present techniques that, we believe, will benefit from *autonomous and self-actuated* displays. In summary, our work offers two main contributions:

1. A set of **interaction techniques** that allow for controlling the display position – either in a *semi-autonomous* fashion, where the display moves and orients itself on its own following a user's request, or in a *manual* fashion, where users explicitly control the display's motion.
2. A set of **example applications** that were built using our prototype setup of *Hover Pad*. These applications make use of the presented interaction techniques to demonstrate their utility in real-world scenarios.

Further, we present a prototyping toolkit that allows for rapid prototyping of such displays – including a detailed description of how such displays can be constructed. This toolkit enables developers to make use of the presented control mechanisms in a simplified way.

Note that our main contribution lies in the engineering domain to enable the exploration of *autonomous and self-actuated* displays. We do not present a user study of exploring volumetric data using tablet computers, as this has been explored already (e.g., [26, 24]).

RELATED WORK

Our work builds on (1) *spatial exploration of information spaces* with handheld devices, and (2) on *self-actuated objects* both on tabletops and in mid-air.

Spatial Exploration of Information with Handheld Devices

Our *Hover Pad* system combines a tablet and an interactive surface, emphasizing the importance of the spatial relationship between these devices. *Chameleon* and *Boom Chameleon* investigated manually controlled exploration of virtual reality in three-dimensional space [7, 28]. More recently, the combination of mobile devices and large displays has been explored. Schmidt et al.'s *PhoneTouch* locates where a mobile device (and which one) touched a surface [21]. Others explored tracking mobile devices in three dimensions in front of a display [2, 4].

Mobile devices have been used to explore three-dimensional information spaces. When the mobile device is used without another, larger display, these spaces are anchored around the device. In Yee's *Peephole Displays* users move the handheld display in mid-air to reveal content that is virtually located around the device [33]. With *Boom Chameleon*, users can navigate *around* an object in three-dimensional space [7, 28]. The display is attached to a boom, which allows for maintaining the displays's position and orientation after it has been changed *manually*. Unlike *Hover Pad*, its physical constraints prevent movement *through* virtual objects. Chen et al. constructed the information space around the user's body. The handheld display reveals different information based on its location relative to the user's body [6].

In many existing systems, the information space is anchored to a larger display in the environment with that display providing an overview (e.g., a bird's eye view) of the space, which is inspected in detail using a handheld display [26, 24]. Marquardt et al. demonstrate the use of a tablet computer to physically navigate through a pile of photographs [14]. Besides volumetric data, the interaction above or in front of a large display may also extend 2D visualizations. Izadi et al.'s *SecondLight* [11], for example, takes *Magic Lenses* [3] into the third dimension.

With the exception of *Boom Chameleon*, all of these approaches are based on handheld displays and thus require to constantly hold the display in-hand. Exploring the space out of arms' reach becomes impossible and it becomes increasingly difficult to hold the device still at a certain position. In addition, users have to move the device in very small steps in order to explore finer details within that space. This may slow down the interaction [25] and increasing fatigue as well as natural hand tremors make it difficult to examine fine-grained structures. Our design intends to overcome these limitations through self-actuated movement that allows precise positioning, hands-free interaction as well as reaching space out of the user's reach (e.g., exploring information spaces that extend beyond the user's immediate proximity).

Self-Actuated Objects on Interactive Surfaces

Self-actuated objects on interactive surfaces that allow, for instance, to physically animate application state changes (e.g., a slider value or position), have been studied previously. Most prominently, magnets embedded underneath the surface are used to move magnetic objects on top [8]. The *Actuated Workbench* provides feedback by moving tracked objects on an interactive surface [17]. *Pico* works similarly, but adds physical constraints to movable objects [18]. Weiss et al.'s *Madgets* further enable tangibles that can move vertically in a limited range [31]. In addition, they are able to simulate physical properties, such as friction, while people move the tangibles [30].

Others experimented with alternative approaches to self-actuated objects. Rosenfeld et al.'s *Planar Manipulator Display* [20] and Pedersen et al.'s *Tangible Bots* [19] create movable objects by attaching wheels to them. Ultra-sonic air waves [15] or vibration, as in *Touchbugs* [16], have also been explored to control autonomous movement of objects. However, both approaches are constraint in either the objects that are able to move (i.e., lightweight objects through sound) or the level of movement (i.e., one direction with vibration). Also, they can only move in one plane (directly on the top of the surface). Nevertheless, the aspect of physical feedback present in each of these systems also inspired our approach.

Movable Objects and Displays in Mid-Air

More recent work focused on moving objects and displays in three-dimensional space. Alrøe et al.'s *Aerial Tunes* [1] lets multiple balls hover over boxes using a controlled air stream in order to visualize an artistic sound installation. Lee et al.'s *ZeroN* [13] uses electromagnets to position a magnetic sphere in mid-air. When projected upon, this sphere is turned into a display. *ZeroN* can also provide force feedback by changing the magnetic field. In both systems, users are able to reposition objects as a form of input. Hörtner et al.'s *Spaxels* create a large scale volumetric display using small quadcopters, each representing one pixel in space [10]. *Hover Pad* is inspired by these diverse approaches. However, we chose a crane-based implementation for the self-actuated movement in order to achieve a high level of position accuracy and visual stability which allows to investigate diverse interaction techniques.

Besides objects, displays can also be moved in space (without requiring a user's physical effort). Wilson et al.'s *Beamatron* combines a steerable projector with a depth camera to empower users to move digital content in an environment through gestures [32]. In contrast to a projected display, Sinclair et al. mounted a touch-display onto a crane so that it can move forward and backward along one dimension when a user touches the display [23]. This motion allows for exploring physical attributes of virtual objects (e.g., weight). A display moving along one dimension was used by Hashimoto et al. to emphasize movement of a virtual game character moving through a virtual world [9]. With *RoCo*, Breazeal et al. present a robotic computer that features a self-actuated display that can respond to and influence its user's posture [5]. Our work allows for investigating (semi-)autonomous display motion control and interaction in a comparably large *three-dimensional* space.

MOVING SELF-ACTUATED DISPLAYS

The display in our setup can move fully *autonomously*. That is, it can follow predefined paths without requiring any user interaction. However, the setup also allows for two additional types of movement, each of which is triggered by user interaction: (1) the display can move *semi-autonomously* (e.g., in response to an alert or due to artificial intelligence in a game); and (2), its position and orientation can be controlled *manually* by the user. These options can also be combined in flexible ways. In the following we describe these two capabilities in more detail.

Semi-Autonomous Movement

The display can move to a location based on the user's request. However, it still moves to that location on its own without requiring the user to hold it in hand at any time. For example, the surface display could show a top-down view of a human body and the tablet shows the corresponding slice of a CT scan. The user could now request a specific location (say: a slice of the brain) by tapping on the location on the tabletop. This then triggers the display to move to that location in space. In contrast to existing systems, users do not have to physically search for a given area of interest in the information space. In particular, this enables two interaction techniques: *search & inspect* and *bookmark & recall.*

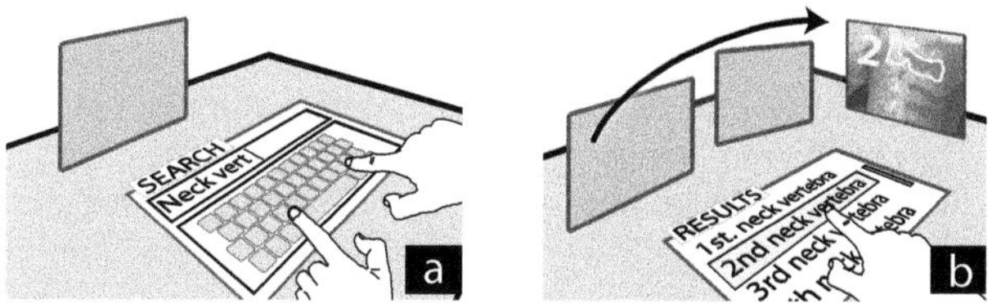

Figure 2. *Search & Inspect* for searching and selecting an item (a). The display then moves autonomously to that item in space (b).

Search & Inspect

Volumetric data sets are often structured and have specific, well-defined areas of interest (i.e., in a CT scan a specific density in a tissue area may indicate a tumor) the system is aware of these areas and knows their location. This allows users to *search* for specific locations and subsequently *inspect* data located there. Figure 2 shows the stages of this interaction technique in more detail: (a) users perform a search (i.e., by entering the name of the area of interest); (b) within the resulting list (neck vertebrae), users can now select the item of interest; (c) upon selection, the display transitions to that location in the volumetric data set for further inspection by the user. The surface display and the display's height can provide context information about this item's position in the volumetric dataset.

Bookmark & Recall

Similar to *Search & Inspect*, users can set *bookmarks* of a location within the volumetric data set – for example, when they come across a detail that they wish to inspect further at a later time. Figure 3 demonstrates the use of this interaction technique: (a) the user presses a button to bookmark a location. The display then stores the location (i.e., its position and orientation); (b) at a later point in time, the user can select a bookmark from a list of bookmarks. This triggers the display to return to the position associated with the bookmark.

Manually Controlling the Display's Motion

When a volumetric data set is more suited for users exploring data, the display's position has to be controlled manually. That is, users should be able to tell the display where to move to. We envision three basic types of interactions.

Directly Moving the Display

The most obvious way of controlling the display's position and orientation is by moving it manually in space. That is, users can grab it and move it directly to the desired location

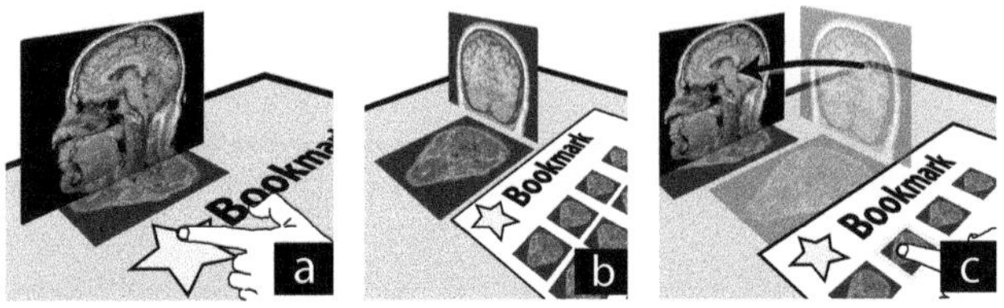

Figure 3. *Bookmark & Recall* allows users to create bookmarks of views (a). Later on, users can select one of these bookmarks from a list (b). This causes the mobile display to return to that bookmark's corresponding position and orientation (c).

(see Figure 4a). Once the display has been brought to the intended position, the user can let go of the display and it remains in that position, which frees the user's hands (e.g., for secondary tasks such as taking notes or switching between visualizations of the data). Note that – depending on the actual implementation – sensing of the user's input (i.e., force and direction) might be required (e.g., through touch sensors or pressure sensors) which is then translated to movement of the self-actuated display.

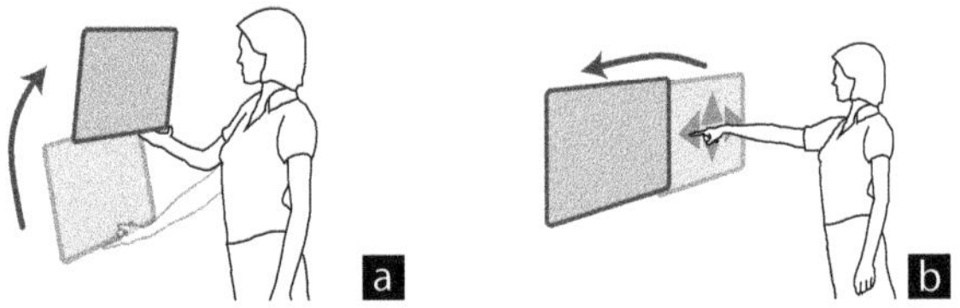

Figure 4. Directly moving the display allows users to directly grab and move the display to change its position and orientation (a). Widget-based interaction on the display's surface enables more fine-grained control of the same movement parameters (b).

Widget-based Motion Control

Widgets represent another opportunity to control a self-actuated display's position and orientation. These widgets can be displayed either on the display itself (see Figure 4b) or on another screen (e.g., the interactive surface below the display). One approach is to provide buttons that correspond to movement of each supported DoF. That is, each possible motion attribute can be manipulated in two directions: *'increase'* and *'decrease.'* A mapping function then determines the granularity of movement – either fine-grained for *slow* or coarse for *fast* movements.

Controlling Motion through Gestures

Another way to control a self-actuated display in space is the use of gestures. We envision that users can apply gestures either (1) in mid-air or (2) on the connected interactive surface. Mid-air gestures allow for controlling the display position while the display is out of reach. Figure 5 shows one possible gesture: (a) the user applies a *picking* gesture to activate motion control; (b) the hand's motion is then mapped either with a *zero order mapping* (i.e., the hand's motion controls the display's position) or with a *first order mapping* (i.e., the hand's motion controls the display's speed).

On the context providing interactive surface, users can perform multi-touch gestures on that device to control the display's motion. For instance, *pinch* gestures for controlling

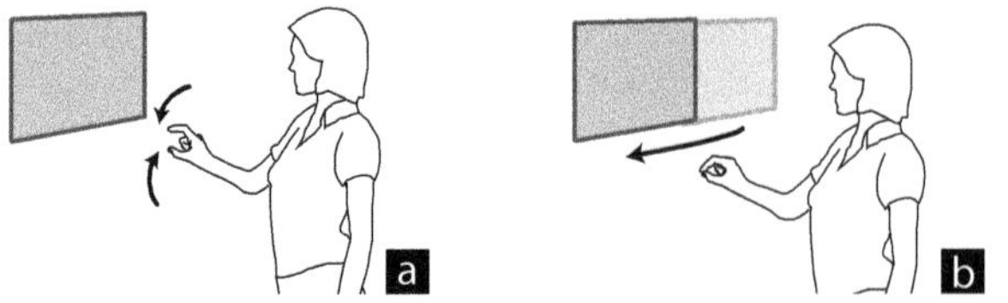

Figure 5. With gesture control, the user first performs a *pinch* gesture (a) to bind the hand's movement to the display's motion. This then allows for continuously controlling the display's position and orientation (b).

the height, and *swipe* gestures for controlling the *x*- and *y*-position of the tablet.

IMPLEMENTATION

To explore the aforementioned aspects in more detail, we built *Hover Pad* – a prototype that resembles a *self-actuated and autonomous* display. We further designed a toolkit that implements all the aforementioned motion controls. In this section, we highlight both hardware and software of our prototype. Note that *Hover Pad*'s blueprints as well as the software toolkit are available as open source.[1]

Hardware Setup

The prototype uses a Nexus 10 tablet as *self-actuated display* as well as a Microsoft Surface 2 (Samsung SUR40), which is situated underneath and acts as a secondary display in the environment to provide contextual information. Figure 6a shows the overall setup. To allow for self-actuated movement of a display in three-dimensional space, we designed and built a custom overhead gantry crane. One sliding carriage moves the tablet along the *x*-axis. This carriage holds a second sliding carriage that moves the display along the *y*-axis (see Figure 6b). Sliding carriages are moved by separate step motors (1.8° step angle; 0.5 Nm holding torque; 12V operating voltage) connected to drive belts. The motors driving the carriages as well as the motor controlling vertical movement are connected to a controller unit. This unit provides command messages and power for these motors.

Two parallel telescope bars are connected to the carriage responsible for movement along the *z*-axis (see Figure 6c). Each of these custom engineered telescope bars consists of six elements (made of aluminum; supported through integrated brass rings as gliding means) with one element being 22 cm long.

Attached to them is a mount holding the tablet (see Figure 6d). This mount enables self-actuated rotation along two axes: *pitch* and *yaw*. Accordingly, two motors are integrated in the mount (see Figure 6d-*i* and *iv*). The motors are controlled via an Ioio OTG board (6d-*v*) which is connected to the tablet via Bluetooth. The frame further includes a battery (see 6d-*iii*) for powering the motors and the Ioio OTG board. The frame is equipped with 16 capacitive buttons located on the frame's rim front, side, and back (e.g., 6d-*ii*). These buttons can be mapped freely (by registering event listeners) to user-defined actions or steering commands in order to implement *direct movement of the display* as described in the previous section.

[1] `http://www.uni-ulm.de/?hover-pad`

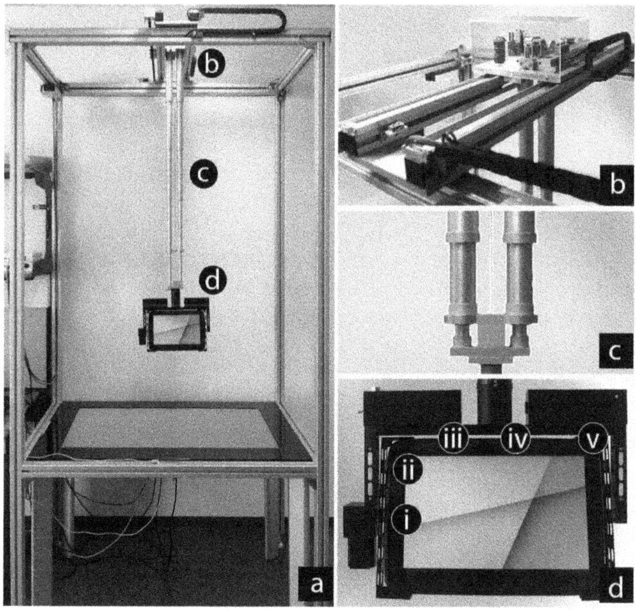

Figure 6. Overview and details of the *Hover Pad* hardware setup (a) with details regarding the sliding carriages for *x,y*-motion (b), the telescope bars for vertical motion (c), and the display's frame for rotation (d), comprising two motors (i, iv), a controller board (iii), a battery pack (v), and 16 capacitive buttons (ii).

The overall setup allows for an operational range of 90 × 50 × 107 cm (*width / x* × *length / y* × *height / z*). The base of the operational range is aligned with the interactive surface. In order to limit the movement of the carriages and to prevent them from running out of bounds, five limit switches are installed (two on the *x*- and *y*-axes; one on the *z*-axis). With our current settings on the motor controller unit, the display needs about one second per 10 cm moving distance. Along the *z* and *y*-axis, the smallest possible movement step is about 0.05 mm. The display mount allows for continuous rotation around the *z*-axis (yaw) with a speed of 2.0 sec. per rotation (360°). Due to the mechanical construction, which includes a motor with a very low holding torque, the angle can be determined only with a tolerance of ±10°.

Software Toolkit

To enable rapid prototyping of applications that make use of *Hover Pad*'s capabilities, we created a software toolkit. This toolkit consists of four main components: the mobile client, the surface server, the crane motion, as well as the control component (see Figure 7).

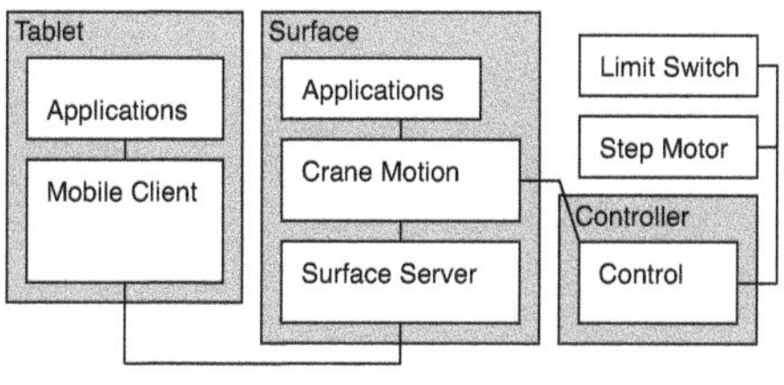

Figure 7. Overview of the *Hover Pad* software toolkit components.

The mobile client is implemented as an Android service running on the tablet and is responsible for managing communication with the surface server which runs on the interactive surface (here: SUR40). The mobile client and the surface server constantly exchange the tablet's position data via *JSON* objects (through HTTP via WiFi). The user's manual rotation of the tablet is sensed by an X-IMU sensor-box that is mounted on the display's back and connected via Bluetooth to the tablet. Also, when the crane motion component is called (i.e., by an application or a user's interaction) the updated position data is sent to the mobile client.

The crane motion component provides an application programming interface (API) that provides simplified methods allowing applications to request position changes of the tablet. Application developers can do so by either providing absolute positions (which requires an initial calibration of the system) or relative position changes. In both cases, it is sufficient to provide a vector with *x*, *y*, and *z* values (all in mm). The crane motion component then determines the number of steps each step motor has to perform in order to reach the requested position. The control component runs on an Arduino board (here: Mega 2560) integrated into the controller unit. It receives calls from the crane motion component (via USB) and sends these commands to the step motors.

In the following, we briefly illustrate how the *Hover Pad* toolkit supports rapid prototyping of applications. In particular, we highlight basic motion control options. Please note, a detailed documentation is available alongside the toolkit sources. Applications for *Hover Pad* are generally distributed, including a component running on the surface side and another component running on the tablet side.

Motion Control Options

Motion control calls can be performed by placing a request to move the tablet to an absolute or relative coordinate (see Listing 1). First, a coordinate is defined (by defining millimeter values, which correspond to exact physical distance). When requesting an absolute position, the tablet moves to this position in relation to the setup coordinate system. In case of relative movement, the given coordinate is used for movement in relation to the current position.

```
coordinate = new Point3D(23, 42, 5); //in cm
_mController.sendAbsolutePoint3D(coordinate);
// alternative relative movement
_mController.sendRelativePoint3D(coordinate);
```

Listing 1. Starting motion to an absolute or relative position.

In order to rotate the tablet in a specific orientation, the movement can be controlled through activating the rotation motors for a desired period of time (e.g., 50 ms). For convenience, a target angle can be set (see Listing 2): First, the auto rotation is activated and a tolerance value is defined. Finally, the angle is defined which triggers the movement instantly.

```
_mController.activateAutomaticOrientation();
_mController.setDeltaAngel(10); //degree
_mController.setYaw2be(90); // degree
```

Listing 2. Automatic rotation management of the tablet.

Connecting Interaction Controllers

On an application level, toolkit users can connect controls that enable interaction options, by simply adding a motion request call to the corresponding callback function. For instance, we used a Leap Motion controller to track mid-air gestures in front of the *Hover Pad* setup. These gestures can be mapped easily to *Hover Pad* movement, as shown in Listing 3.

```
_gestureTracker.gestureChange += new EventHandler<
    GestureEventArgs>(gestureDetected);
void gestureDetected(object sender,
    GestureEventArgs e) {/*trigger movement*/}
```

Listing 3. Mapping a gesture tracker *Hover Pad* movment.

EXAMPLE APPLICATIONS

We envision the usage of self-actuated and autonomous displays in various contexts that involve spatial relations and volumetric data such as education (e.g., in schools or museums), medical application, engineering and mining, surveillance of buildings, or production lines. We realized five example applications for *Hover Pad* that demonstrate how the key advantages support interaction, i.e., *autonomous movement*, *hands free interaction*, and *visual stability*. Examples were selected to showcase how *Hover Pad*'s key characteristics enable novel interaction. Table 1 gives an overview of which aspects are highlighted by the examples. The video figure illustrates the interactions of each of these examples.

	Phys. Object	Map Explorer	Volume Explorer	Anatomy Explorer	Game
Autonomous Movement	+	+	-	+	+
Hands Free Interaction	+	+	-	-	+
Visual Stability	+	-	+	+	+

Table 1. Example applications benefit from *Hover Pad* characteristics.

Physical Object Augmentation and Exploration

The first application allows users to explore a physical object (i.e., a model of the Empire State Building) that is placed on a map (of New York) shown on the interactive surface. The mobile display augments the physical object with virtual annotations (see Figure 8a). On the surface, the user can select points of interest from a list (e.g., a *bookmark* pointing to the 102nd floor), which triggers the tablet to move and show this point (see Figure 8b).

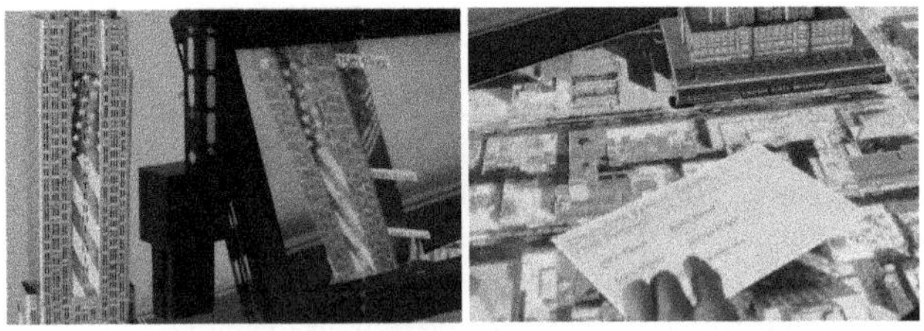

Figure 8. Augmenting physical objects with spatially registered annotations (a) allows users to select and explore diverse points of interest (b) that are than presented through the tablet.

With *Hover Pad* moving autonomously to selected targets, the interaction is predominantly *hands-free*. That is, users do not have to hold and maintain the tablet in one distinct position. This further allows users to interact with the augmented physical objects (e.g., rotate them while the augmentation follows). Through *self-actuated movement*, *Hover Pad* provides the unique possibility to guide users to specific views (based on *Bookmark&Recall*). Physical objects of arbitrary complexity can be augmented through *Hover Pad* with labels, explanations, or hints such as alerts. For instance, an unknown workpiece (e.g., an engine) could be explored by workers where *Hover Pad* would provide a list of changes that could be visited and examined one by one.

As users can freely move physical objects in relation to the *Hover Pad* setup, this example application required the usage of camera based object tracking[2] in addition to the *Hover Pad* framework. This allowed precise spatial correlation between the physical object and the rendered view on the tablet.

Map Explorer

The map explorer application allows users to view a focused 3D visualization of buildings on the tablet (similar to the *Tangible Geospace* by Ullmer and Ishii [29]). The interactive surface below provides context by displaying the surrounding environment (see Figure 9a) and allows users to control the tablet through *widgets-based* position control provided on the surface. The tablet acts as a *magic lens* and allows to switch between different views such as map or satellite view (see Figure 9b). The hight of the tablet is mapped to the zoom level of the provided view.

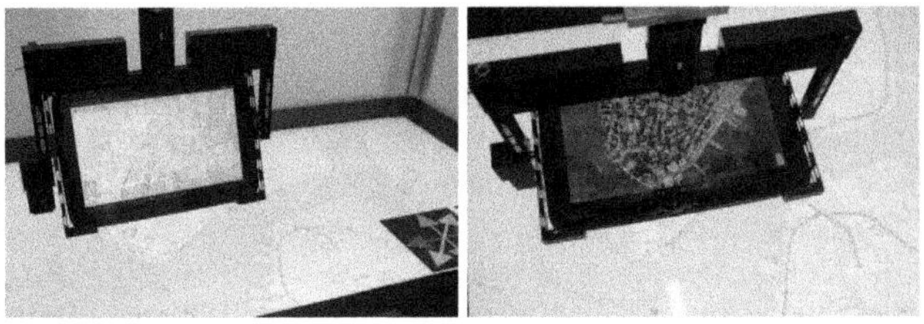

Figure 9. *Hover Pad* supports exploring maps by providing context on the surface and different spatially registered views such as a 3D view (a) or an alternative satelitte view (b).

The spatially registered displays (tablet and surface) allow users to simultaneously observe a focused view and context without any required transitions. Further, the *self-actuated* motion control allows uniquely logging and saving coordinates in a motion history that can be revisited automatically when desired (see *Bookmark&Recall*). Also, the view provided by the tablet enables autonomously controlled tracking shots that could, for instance, visualize flight route of a plane.

Medical Volumetric Data Explorer

A volumetric data viewer allows users to explore volumes such as computer tomography data sets. On the tablet a slice cut of the volume is displayed (see Figure 10a). On the surface the slice position is visualized on a schematic outline in order to support orientation (see Figure 10b).

Users can control the position of the tablet in a *direct and explicit* way by using the touch buttons on the rim of the tablet

[2] Based on Vuforia `http://www.vuforia.com/`

Figure 10. The anatomy explorer allows users to explore, for instance, the human skeleton (a) by selecting bookmarked bones from a list (b) which triggers the tablet to move to that position.

frame. This creates an experience similar to moving the tablet manually (i.e., touching a button on the right to push the tablet to the left). However, the user does not carry the weight of the tablet thus preventing fatigue. Also, the user can release the tablet which remains in its current position (*visual stability*) in order to have time to study and discuss e.g., a complex structure. Requiring explicit input to trigger movement has the advantage over gesture control that positioning can be finely controlled without the risk of accidentally causing the display to move while gesturing towards the point of interest. This application demonstrates how *Hover Pad* allows uniquely to transition *through* a volumetric data set while keeping *visual stability* as the user can release the tablet at any time which remains at this position.

Educational Anatomy Explorer

An anatomy explorer[3] allows users to view a virtual skeleton through the tablet computer (see Figure 11a). On the surface, the user can select, for instance, bookmarked bones that are revealed by the tablet upon selecting a target from a list (see Figure 11b). Alternatively, the user can explicitly move the tablet through space to explore the data set.

Figure 11. The anatomy explorer allows users to explore, for instance, the human skeleton (a) by selecting bookmarked bones from a list (b) which triggers the tablet to move to that position.

Using the *Bookmark&Recall* technique, users can explore human anatomy as *Hover Pad* shows specific body parts in spatial relation upon selecting a bookmark. For instance, in an anatomy class, the application helps users to find specific otherwise unknown details, which is only possible through *self-actuated* movement.

Mixed-Reality Gaming

A mixed-reality game for *Hover Pad* combines *autonomous behavior* and movement in space and interaction with tangible objects on the interactive surface. On the tablet, a virtual character is displayed that follows a virtual path. Accordingly, the tablet moves autonomously to follow the character

[3]Based on 4D Anatomy Explorer; **`http://daqri.com/`**.

Figure 12. A mixed reality game based on *Hover Pad* requires users to support an autonomously moving virtual character displayed on the tablet (a). The user places physical wall pieces on the surface to prevent the character from falling (b).

in order to keep it in view (see Figure 12a). The user is required to arrange tangible items on the interactive surface below. These objects serve as bridges or staircases, for example, and ensure that the virtual character does not fall down (see Figure 12b).

This application leverages the unique characteristic of *Hover Pad* to combine autonomous behavior with *self-actuated* movement, which cannot be achieved by manually moving spatial displays. This application shows that *direct interaction* can be implemented in various ways: here, tangible objects (tracked through markers attached to their bottom) allow users to react quickly to *Hover Pad*'s autonomous behavior and movement in space.

DISCUSSION

Our example applications implemented with *Hover Pad* highlight possible scenarios in which *autonomous and self-actuated* displays provide advantages over existing, manual systems proposed in related work. *Hover Pad*'s *autonomous and semi-autonomous movement* capabilities enable search & inspect interaction, e.g., in the physical object augmentation application and the educational anatomy explorer, as well as bookmark & recall, e.g., in the medical volumetric data explorer and the map explorer. In contrast to existing systems, users can focus on the information associated with respective points of interest, instead of having to navigate the tablet to those data points manually. Such physical self-actuated movement of a display is in particular of advantage, if an application includes an overview (e.g., a large display or a physical object) that is to be inspected in detail (i.e., using a spatial display). Furthermore, *Hover Pad* provides *hands-free interaction*. In contrast to related work on handheld displays, our *Hover Pad* hardware ensures that the display remains at the desired position and orientation, which enables users to study the displayed content and interact with it (e.g., on the primary display), or with augmented physical objects with both hands and without having to hold the display for prolonged periods of time. This hands-free interaction further has the advantage of providing visual stability, as *Hover Pad* fixates the display's five degrees of freedom when needed. These aspects also result in more fine-grained control of the position of the display, which is particularly important in high resolution data, such as volumetric medical data.

While tablets that are physically moved through an information space by users could theoretically support six *degrees of freedom* (DoF), these 6 DoF would need to be supported by tracking methods as well. Thus, even systems that combine top-projection with paper surfaces (e.g., [27]) likely only support 5.5 DoF, because projection from underneath is hard to achieve. Yet, conceptually, these systems have been shown to be sufficient for exploring the information space. Our current hardware setup provides 5 DoF (i.e., *roll* is not supported), but provides the advantages of hands-free interaction and visual stability noted before. Considering the number of available degrees of freedom of supported movement, it appears that it depends heavily on the supported application how many degrees of freedom are required. For instance, Touch Mover [23] supports movement only along one dimension, yet it allows tactile exploring of volumetric objects. Additional degrees of freedom could even be a disadvantage for some applications. *Hover Pad* however, allowing for max. five degrees of freedom provides a high level of flexibility as all five degrees of freedom can be individually utilized or disabled depending on an application's requirements. This is not possible for approaches that require the user to manually control a handheld display.

Accordingly, accuracy of positioning a display is limited by the operating user in the case of handheld display based approaches. In contrast, systems such as *Hover Pad* that provide self-actuated position control are not limited in their positioning accuracy, as long as the employed hardware components can provide the required movement resolution. An analog coherence exists for the operational space: handheld and user operated approaches cannot be upscaled to larger screen and projection sizes as easily as it is theoretically possible for approaches based on self-actuated movement, because movement in user-operated approaches is restricted by users' body height and arm length. Self-actuated movement also constitutes a fundamental advantage over user-operated approaches: such a system can lead users to points of interest without discarding the spatial relations. For instance, as illustrated with the *physical object augmentation and exploration* application, users can be guided through an information space, which can reduce search time and increase an understanding of spatial relations. In addition to self-actuated movement, system-driven and autonomous position control, for instance, used in games, allows users to interact with *Hover Pad* in a novel way that is a clear distinctive feature regarding user-operated approaches found in related work.

Considering the information fidelity provided, *Hover Pad* provides a high definition display as a spatial display. This level of fidelity has not been achieved by previous approaches in connection with self-actuated movement in space.

The presented implementation of *Hover Pad* constitutes an initial step towards truly *hovering* displays. Our approach enables investigation of relevant interaction patterns, as well as prototyping of applications for such displays. Our prototype has a number of limitations, which we plan to address in future work.

When using a spatial display that is self-actuated, the movement of the display is limited the hardware capabilities (motor speed, stability etc.). Hence, by using handheld spatial displays, users can enjoy a more *responsive* and *immediate* display position control as there is no delay. On the other hand, when using such powerful hardware that is capable in terms of speed to mimic a handheld display, safety aspects have to be considered which is not necessary for *Hover Pad* as the mechanical forces applied by the currently used motors are too weak to be considered dangerous.

In the current prototype, the display swings slightly for a short moment after reaching a desired 3D coordinate with autonomous movement, which is caused by the tension forces acting on the telescope bar. For future iterations, we plan to enhance the rigidness of the telescope bar with advanced materials (e.g., carbon composites) and reduce the weight of the display unit to address this issue. Another approach would be the utilization of a robot arm.

The current prototype, due to its static crane construction, cannot support mobility, e.g., a display device that would follow a user while walking through a museum. Recently, drone- and quadcopter-based displays have been proposed (e.g., [22]). While those approaches may facilitate mobility, they would raise other challenges, e.g., in terms of accuracy and viewing stability. *Hover Pad* could serve as a versatile prototyping platform for applications for such mobile displays, while associated challenges are being addressed.

CONCLUSIONS & FUTURE WORK

We introduced our vision of displays that can move autonomously and semi-autonomously in mid-air to navigate through three-dimensional information spaces. We discussed the potential of this new class of devices and identified relevant interaction patterns enabled by them. We presented *Hover Pad* as a prototype system and framework to explore *hovering* self-actuated and autonomous displays. Our approach enables semi-autonomous control of hovering displays, including hands-free interaction and visual stability.

With our *Hover Pad* system providing rich and diverse interaction and application possibilities, we were interested in understanding how different ways of interaction support diverse classes of tasks. For this purpose, we realized a diverse set of example applications highlighting *Hover Pad*'s capabilities. In future work, we plan to further assess the different interaction techniques and motion control options of *Hover Pad*. Further, we are planning to investigate the potential and impact of *multiple* autonomous and self-actuated displays in an environment on user interaction. Finally, we plan to explore the effect of the presence of additional screens (e.g., the interactive surface) in the vicinity of the self-actuated display on the users' understanding of spatial relations in volumetric data and information spaces.

ACKNOWLEDGMENTS

We would like to thank Alexander Vogel, Johannes Augsburger, and all involved members of the scientific workshop at Ulm University for their support. This work was conducted within the Emmy Noether research group "Mobile Interaction with Pervasive User Interface" and the Transregional Collaborative Research Centre SFB/TRR 62 "Companion-Technology for Cognitive Technical Systems" both funded by the German Research Foundation (DFG).

REFERENCES

1. Alrøe, T., Grann, J., Grönvall, E., Petersen, M. G., and Rasmussen, J. L. Aerial tunes: exploring interaction qualities of mid-air displays. In *NordiCHI '12*, ACM (2012).
2. Baur, D., Boring, S., and Feiner, S. Virtual projection: exploring optical projection as a metaphor for multi-device interaction. In *CHI '12*, ACM (2012).
3. Bier, E. A., Stone, M. C., Pier, K., Buxton, W., and DeRose, T. D. Toolglass and magic lenses: the see-through interface. In *SIGGRAPH '93*, ACM (1993).
4. Boring, S., Baur, D., Butz, A., Gustafson, S., and Baudisch, P. Touch projector: mobile interaction through video. In *CHI '10*, ACM (2010).
5. Breazeal, C., Wang, A., and Picard, R. Experiments with a robotic computer: Body, affect and cognition interactions. In *HRI '07*, ACM (2007), 153–160.
6. Chen, X. A., Marquardt, N., Tang, A., Boring, S., and Greenberg, S. Extending a mobile device's interaction space through body-centric interaction. In *MobileHCI '12*, ACM (2012).
7. Fitzmaurice, G. W. Situated information spaces and spatially aware palmtop computers. *Commun. ACM 36*, 7 (July 1993).
8. Fitzmaurice, G. W. *Graspable User Interfaces*. PhD thesis, Graduate Department of Computer Science, University of Toronto, 1996.
9. Hashimoto, S., Suzuki, R., Kamiyama, Y., Inami, M., and Igarashi, T. World locomotion. `http://s-hashimoto.org/?page_id=73&lang=en`, 2013. (Last access: 2014/06/30).
10. Hörtner, H., Gardiner, M., Haring, R., Lindinger, C., and Berger, F. Spaxels, pixels in space. `http://www.aec.at/futurelab/files/2012/07/spaxels_revision_final_20120615.pdf`. (Last access: 2014/04/16).
11. Izadi, S., Hodges, S., Taylor, S., Rosenfeld, D., Villar, N., Butler, A., and Westhues, J. Going beyond the display: a surface technology with an electronically switchable diffuser. In *UIST '08*, ACM (2008).
12. Konieczny, J., Shimizu, C., Meyer, G., and Colucci, D. A handheld flexible display system. In *Visualization, 2005. VIS 05. IEEE* (2005).
13. Lee, J., Post, R., and Ishii, H. ZeroN: mid-air tangible interaction enabled by computer controlled magnetic levitation. In *UIST '11*, ACM (2011).
14. Marquardt, N., Jota, R., Greenberg, S., and Jorge, J. A. The continuous interaction space: interaction techniques unifying touch and gesture on and above a digital surface. In *INTERACT'11* (2011).
15. Marshall, M., Carter, T., Alexander, J., and Subramanian, S. Ultra-tangibles: creating movable tangible objects on interactive tables. In *CHI '12*, ACM (2012).
16. Nowacka, D., Ladha, K., Hammerla, N. Y., Jackson, D., Ladha, C., Rukzio, E., and Olivier, P. Touchbugs: actuated tangibles on multi-touch tables. In *CHI '13*, ACM (2013).
17. Pangaro, G., Maynes-Aminzade, D., and Ishii, H. The actuated workbench: computer-controlled actuation in tabletop tangible interfaces. In *UIST '02*, ACM (2002).
18. Patten, J., and Ishii, H. Mechanical constraints as computational constraints in tabletop tangible interfaces. In *CHI '07*, ACM (2007).
19. Pedersen, E. W., and Hornbaek, K. Tangible bots: interaction with active tangibles in tabletop interfaces. In *CHI '11*, ACM (2011).
20. Rosenfeld, D., Zawadzki, M., Sudol, J., and Perlin, K. Physical objects as bidirectional user interface elements. *Computer Graphics and Applications* (2004).
21. Schmidt, D., Seifert, J., Rukzio, E., and Gellersen, H. A cross-device interaction style for mobiles and surfaces. In *DIS '12*, ACM (2012).
22. Schneegaß, S., Alt, F., Scheible, J., Schmidt, A., and Su, H. Midair displays: Exploring the concept of free-floating public displays. In *CHI '14 Extended Abstracts* (2014).
23. Sinclair, M., Pahud, M., and Benko, H. TouchMover: Actuated 3D Touchscreen with Haptic Feedback. In *ITS '13*, ACM (2013).
24. Spindler, M., Büschel, W., and Dachselt, R. Use your head: tangible windows for 3D information spaces in a tabletop environment. In *ITS '12*, ACM (2012).
25. Spindler, M., Martsch, M., and Dachselt, R. Going beyond the surface: studying multi-layer interaction above the tabletop. In *CHI '12*, ACM (2012).
26. Spindler, M., Tominski, C., Schumann, H., and Dachselt, R. Tangible views for information visualization. In *ITS '10*, ACM (2010).
27. Steimle, J., Jordt, A., and Maes, P. Flexpad: highly flexible bending interactions for projected handheld displays. In *CHI '13*, ACM (2013).
28. Tsang, M., Fitzmaurice, G. W., Kurtenbach, G., Khan, A., and Buxton, B. Boom chameleon: simultaneous capture of 3d viewpoint, voice and gesture annotations on a spatially-aware display. In *UIST '02*, ACM (2002).
29. Ullmer, B., and Ishii, H. The metadesk: Models and prototypes for tangible user interfaces. In *UIST '97*, ACM (1997), 223–232.
30. Weiss, M., Remy, C., and Borchers, J. Rendering physical effects in tabletop controls. In *CHI '11*, ACM (2011).
31. Weiss, M., Schwarz, F., Jakubowski, S., and Borchers, J. Madgets: actuating widgets on interactive tabletops. In *UIST '10*, ACM (2010).
32. Wilson, A., Benko, H., Izadi, S., and Hilliges, O. Steerable augmented reality with the beamatron. In *UIST '12*, ACM (2012).
33. Yee, K.-P. Peephole displays: pen interaction on spatially aware handheld computers. In *CHI '03*, ACM (2003).

Graffiti Fur: Turning Your Carpet into a Computer Display

Yuta Sugiura[1], Koki Toda[1], Takayuki Hoshi[2], Youichi Kamiyama[1], Takeo Igarashi[3] and Masahiko Inami[1]

[1] Graduate School of Media Design, Keio University, 4-1-1 Hiyoshi, Kohoku, Yokohama, 223-8526 Japan

[2] Center for Innovative Young Researchers, Nagoya Institute of Technology, Gokiso, Showa, Nagoya, 466-8555 Japan

[3] Department of Computer Science, The University of Tokyo, 7-3-1 Hongo, Bunkyo, Tokyo, 113-0033 Japan

{y-sugiura | kmd-std.8979 | kamiyama | inami}@kmd.keio.ac.jp, star@nitech.ac.jp, takeo@acm.org

ABSTRACT

We devised a display technology that utilizes the phenomenon whereby the shading properties of fur change as the fibers are raised or flattened. One can erase drawings by first flattening the fibers by sweeping the surface by hand in the fiber's growth direction, and then draw lines by raising the fibers by moving the finger in the opposite direction. These material properties can be found in various items such as carpets in our living environments. We have developed three different devices to draw patterns on a "fur display" utilizing this phenomenon: a roller device, a pen device and pressure projection device. Our technology can turn ordinary objects in our environment into rewritable displays without requiring or creating any non-reversible modifications to them. In addition, it can be used to present large-scale image without glare, and the images it creates require no running costs to maintain.

Author Keywords

Fur Display; BRDF; Living Environment;

ACM Classification Keywords

H.5.m. Information interfaces and presentation (e.g., HCI): Miscellaneous.

INTRODUCTION

Computer displays play an important role in connecting the information world and the real world. In the era of ubiquitous computing, it is essential to be able to access information in a fluid way and non-obstructive integration of displays into our living environment is a basic requirement to achieve it. However, common displays such as LCDs are not ideal for continuous use in living environments; they occupy considerable space, emit glaring light that disturbs human vision and consume electric power.

UIST 2014, October 5–8, 2014, Honolulu, HI, USA.
Copyright © 2014 ACM 978-1-4503-3069-5/14/10...$15.00.
http://dx.doi.org/10.1145/2642918.2647370

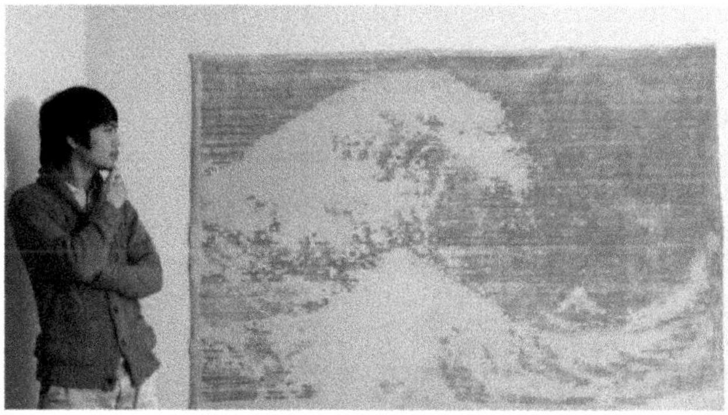

Figure 1: The devices convert your carpet into a computer display.

On the other hand, projection-type displays are suitable for ubiquitous environments because they can project images onto any surface in the living environment [4, 12, 24]. Accordingly, the environment does not require large-scale modifications. In addition, it is possible to switch the projection rapidly and project colorful images. However, projectors have disadvantages. For example, the projected images cause glare and are hard to see in a bright room. In addition, the electricity costs of continuously projecting images are quite high.

There have been many proposals and implementations of non-emissive displays that can easily be integrated into living environments without causing any glare, such as E-ink [1] and wooden displays [18]. They do not require electricity except when rewriting. However, all pixels are integrated in the device as hardware, and they require a large device to be installed in the environment in order to show large images.

Instead of placing a display device, information can be displayed on an object or the environment itself by using

[1] http://www.eink.com/

passive ink. Traditional inkjet printers are immobile, but hand-held printers are now available, making it possible to print on objects or areas in the environment [7, 16]. An ink surface can also be made remotely rewritable by using a projector and thermo chromic ink [19]. For these ink-type displays, as electronic components are not needed on the surface, the system itself can be miniaturized. However, they modify the environment non-reversibly by applying ink materials onto the object surface, which limits their applicability in living environments.

In order to solve the problems mentioned above, we propose a display technology that utilizes the phenomenon whereby the shading properties of fur change as the fibers are raised or flattened. The property is in accordance with Bidirectional Reflectance Distribution Function (BRDF). One can erase drawings by first flattening the fibers by sweeping the surface by hand in the fiber's growth direction and then draw lines by raising the fibers by moving a finger in the opposite direction. These material properties can be found in various items such as carpets and plush toy in our living environment. Our technology can turn these ordinary objects into computer displays without requiring or creating any non-reversible modifications to the objects. In addition, it can be used to make a large-scale display and the drawings it creates have no running costs.

We have developed three different devices to draw patterns on a "fur display" utilizing this phenomenon: a roller device, pen device and pressure projection device. The roller device has an array of rods under it. These rods move up and down independently as the user moves the device on the fur. Lowered rods selectively raise the fibers, leaving a pattern on the surface. The pen device is used for freehand drawing by the user. A small continuously rotating rubber wheel is attached to the pen tip and it raises the fibers when in contact. The pen device is also equipped with a gyro sensor, and it continuously adjusts the orientation of the wheel so that the wheel can raises the fur regardless of the holding posture. The pressure projection device uses focused ultrasound to remotely raise or flatten fur.

Our contributions are summarized as follows:

- We present a new display technology leveraging the natural properties of fur.
- We developed three devices to draw patterns on the display.
- We assessed the capability of using the fur display as a computer display in various experiments.

RERATED WORK

There have been many proposals for non-emissive displays that can be easily integrated into our living environment without causing any glare effects. In particular, many recent studies have attempted to construct displays from natural materials that can be easily integrated into the living space or easily attract users. Wakita and Shibutani developed a display that consists of threads dyed in liquid crystal ink and conductive fiber, knitted into a square textile [23]. Many researchers proposed hairy displays to give the ambient information by moving hairs which is placed in grid layout [1, 8, 13, 15]. Furukawa et al. proposed Fur Display, a soft material interface for creating an organic bristling effect with a vibration motor embedded in animal fur [2]. However, in all of these studies, electronic devices are required to control each pixel actively on the display's surface, so a large-scale system is needed to create drawings on larger surfaces.

Ink is a powerful means to put patterns onto the materials. Kawana developed a stamp with electronically controllable pattern [7]. Pixelroller is a performance tool that allows user to draw characters or pictures on the wall by emitting ink from a nozzle [16]. Saakes et al. developed a system in which user can draw rewritable pattern freely on soft material by projecting laser light to object coated by thermochromic ink [19]. However, inking causes non-reversible modification to the environment, which is problematic for the living environment.

The BRDF displays have been proposed in computer graphics and art fields [6, 9, 11, 14, 18]. Hullin et al. proposed a method to change the reflection of an object on a water surface by creating and controlling waves on the surface at high speed [6]. Ochiai et al. proposed a method to project images on the back of a vibrating soap bubble to create a membrane screen [14]. Wooden Mirror is an artwork that is drawn from reflected light by controlling an array of wooden blocks [18]. Our method is advantageous because it is possible to use existing objects in the environment (e.g. standard carpet) as BRDF displays without making any permanent modifications to them.

We are not the first to display information by manipulating the shape of "existing" physical materials or controlling their reflectance. Rice paddy art[2] is an attempt to create large-scale drawings in a farm space over a long period of time, by planting seeds that have buds of various colors. Karesansui[3] is a Japanese traditional culture method of drawing patterns in a garden with stones. A modern version of this art form, Lazy man Zen garden, is able to draw a pattern automatically in sand [10]. Large patterns can also be drawn by walking on the snow[4]. Hanna's Water Calligraphy device is attached to a bicycle and dispenses water from hose array to draw Chinese characters on the streets over [3]. A lawn mower can be used to draw striped and circular patterns on grass fields.

Our work is inspired by recent attempts to expand the functions of existing soft objects in the living environment

[2] http://www.cbc.ca/strombo/news/living-artworks-in-japans-rice-paddys.htm

[3] http://en.wikipedia.org/wiki/Japanese_rock_garden

[4] http://www.viralnova.com/simon-beck-snow-art/

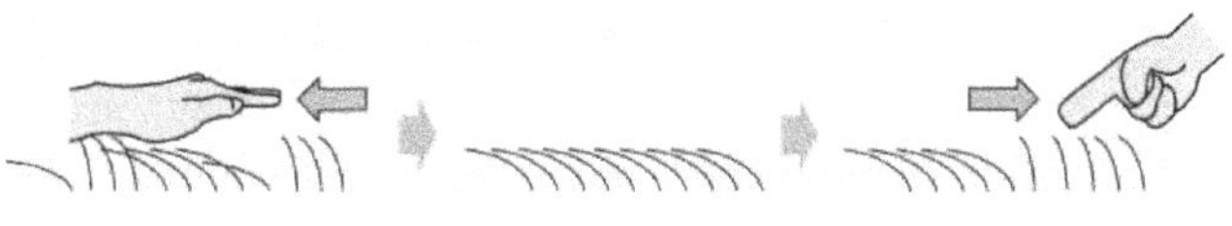

Figure 2: Principle of drawing on fur. Sweeping the fur surface in its growth direction flattens it, and sweeping it in the opposite direction raises it.

by using the power of computing. Sugiura et al. proposed a ring-type device that can be attached to plush toys to move its limbs [21]. Sugiura et al. also developed FuwaFuwa, a sensor module placed inside a cushion to measure the contact position or change in pressure when a user touches the cushion [20]. Our goal is to enable displays of information on these soft objects without the need to modify them.

Our work is also inspired by hybrid fabrication methods that combine human operation and computer control. Rivers et al. proposed a way to precisely position a cutting tool with a combination of manual and automatic positioning, thereby allowing the system to be used to cut out arbitrary patterns [17]. FreeD is a hand-held, digitally controlled milling device, which matches the user's hand-craft work, to allow user without any sculpture knowledge to create 3D models [25].

PRINCIPLE

We leverage the phenomenon that raised fur looks different from flattened fur. Fur fibers have a natural growth direction, and one can flatten the fur by sweeping the surface in that direction and raise it by sweeping the surface in the opposite direction. Since raised and flattened regions of fur have different reflectance properties, one can visually distinguish them. In general, flattened fur reflects more light and looks brighter than raised fur. Figure 2 shows how the phenomenon works.

Shading Property of Fur Display

The appearance of fur dynamically changes according to

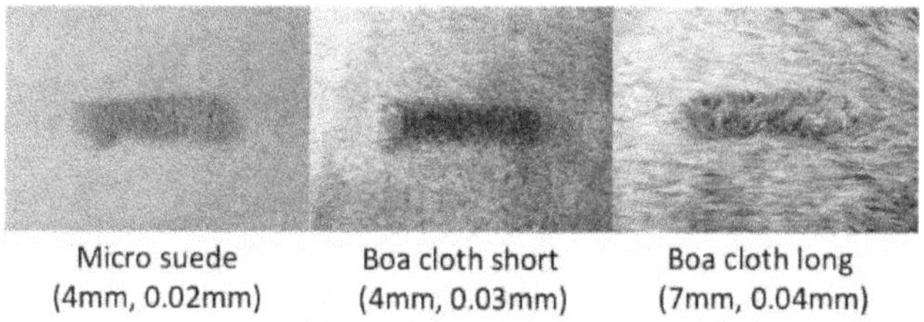

Figure 3: Materials used in the experiment. Numbers indicate fiber length and diameter.

Figure 4: Experiment tool.

the incoming light and viewing direction. We ran a simple experiment to measure this appearance change in order to obtain an insight for deciding where to put the light source and from where to view the fur display to maximize contrast. We used three different materials shown in Figure 3. These three materials were selected as representative materials among those available at local stores. For each material, we first prepared flattened surfaces and surfaces in which the fibers were raised by hand. We then illuminated the two surfaces from various light positions and measured the appearance from various viewing positions. Figure 4 shows the experimental set-up. We rotated the light and measurement device positions from −60° to +60° on planes parallel and orthogonal to the fur growth direction (both

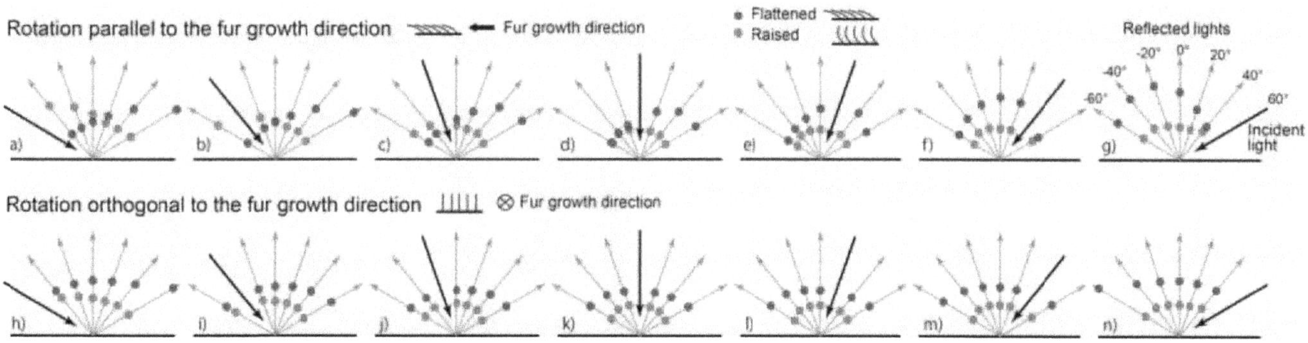

Figure 5: Radial plot of the measured radiances of micro suede. The top row and bottom row respectively show the results of rotating the light and viewing position in planes parallel and orthogonal to the fur growth direction. Each graph (a-n) plots measured radiance values for six reflected light directions and a fixed incident light direction. The incident light direction and reflected light direction cannot be the same because we cannot put the measurement device and light at the same location.

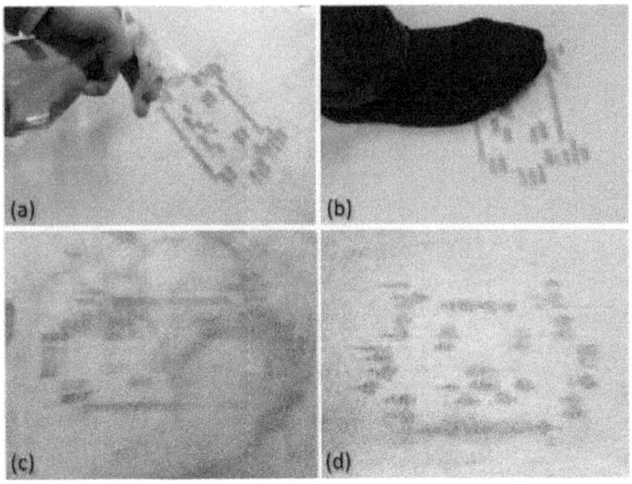

Figure 6: Fixing a pattern with laundry starch, (a) Fixing a pattern on a carpet by spraying laundry starch, (b) walking on the pattern ten times, (c) result without laundry starch, and (d) result with laundry starch.

planes orthogonal to the fur surface). The radiance was measured using a commercial goniophotometer and goniospectrophotometric color measurement system.

Figure 5 shows the measured radiances of micro suede material. All three materials show similar characteristics. The results show strong anisotropy. Both flattened and raised surfaces show strong specularity when the light and viewing position rotated parallel to the fur growth direction (a-g). The plot implies that the surface normal of the flattened fibers is somewhere around +20° and that of the raised one is around −60°. In contrast, the diffuse component seems to be more dominant when the light and the viewing position rotate orthogonal to the fur growth direction (h-n) with slight specularity on the flattened surface.

We calculated the contrast by dividing the radiance of the flattened surfaces by that of the raised surfaces. The maximum contrast (2.57) was obtained when the surface was illuminated against the fur growth direction (−40°) and viewed from the opposite side (+60°) (b). However, this configuration is not very stable; the contrast vanishes when the viewer is in front of the surface (0°) and even flips when the viewer and light are on the same side (−60°). In order to obtain stable results when the viewer position changes, it is recommended to illuminate along the fur grown direction (g), or rotate the light position orthogonally to the fur growth direction (h-n). The maximum contrast of the other materials were 8.21 (boa cloth short) and 34.72 (boa cloth long).

Fixing the Pattern with Laundry Starch

An advantage of our method is that the user can easily erase the pattern by sweeping the fur surface if the result is not satisfactory or the pattern is no longer necessary. However, this feature can be a problem when the user wants to have the pattern stay on the fur surface for a while. In such a case, the user can fix the pattern by spraying a mixture of laundry starch and water onto the fur after drawing a pattern. To check the ability of fixing a pattern with laundry starch, we fixed a pattern drawn by spraying it with 100 g of laundry starch mixed with 200 ml of water. We then walked on the fixed pattern and an untreated pattern ten times respectively (Figure 6 (a-b)). The pattern in the carpet without laundry starch disappeared (Figure 6 (c)). However, the pattern in carpet sprayed with laundry starch remained unchanged after people walked on it (Figure 6 (d)). As laundry starch is water-soluble, the carpet can be restored to its original form by washing it with water.

IMPLEMENTATION

We developed three different devices to draw figures on fur by exploiting this phenomenon. One is a roller device which raises fur by using an array of rods underneath the device, another is a pen device which raises fur with a rotating robbing wheel attached to the tip, and the other is a pressure projection device which raises/flattens fur without physical contact. The remainder of this section describes these devices.

Roller Drawing Device

The hardware consists of 16 fur-raising components attached to the bottom of the roller as shown in Figure 7. Each component consists of a rod and a servomotor that lowers and lifts the rod. When the rod is lowered, it raises the fiber as the user moves the roller (Figure 7 top). In addition, a rotary encoder is mounted on the wheel shaft to measure the horizontal movement of the roller. The rotary encoder and servomotors are controlled by an Arduino Mega ADK microcontroller. The system lowers and raises the rods according to the measurements of the rotary encoder to leave patterns on the fur.

Drawing with the device proceeds as follows. The user first measures the size of the canvas and prepares a binary dot

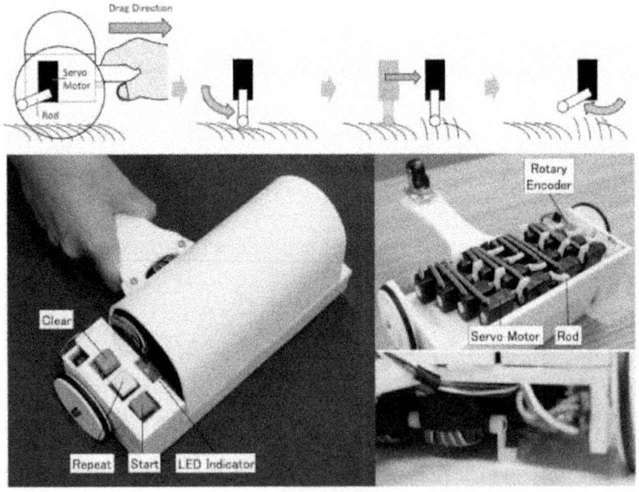

Figure 7: Roller device. Principle (top) and composition (bottom).

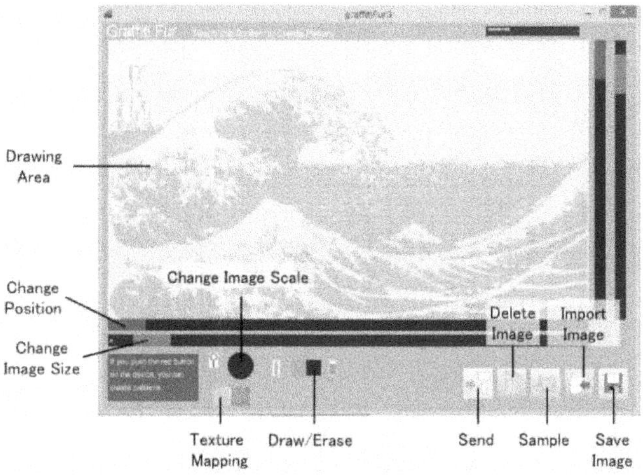

Figure 8: Application UI.

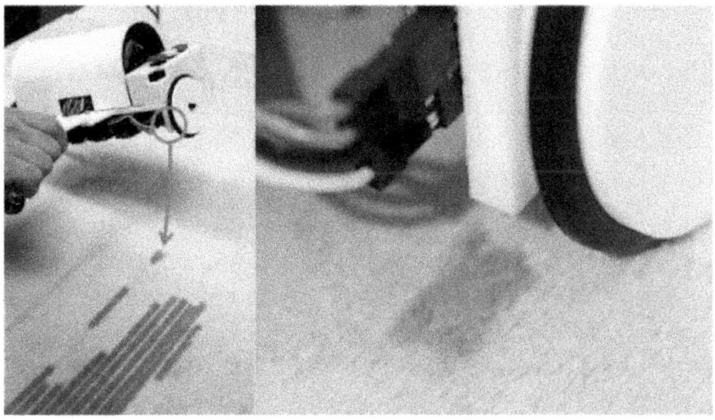

Figure 9: Marker for making multiple drawings.

matrix of appropriate size using an application program. Our current application program provides four methods to prepare the dot matrix (Figure 8): (1) drawing freely using a finger or pen, (2) reading a monochrome picture or illustration, (3) taking a picture with a camera, or (4) typing text. The system provides a preview image of raised and flattened fur.

Second, the user transmits the dot matrix data to the device and starts drawing the pattern on the fur surface by moving the device over its surface in the direction opposite to the fur growth direction. The surface needs to be fully flattened by hand prior to drawing. The user presses the red button on the device to initiate drawing. If the dot matrix consists of a single row, the drawing finishes after a single sweep. If the user continues the sweep, the pattern will be repeated. When the dot matrix consists of multiple rows, the user needs to repeat sweeps multiple times. The system indicates the end of a sweep with an LED mounted on it, and the user starts the next sweep by pressing the red button. To assist the user in aligning the starting point of the sweeps, the system leaves a tick mark at the beginning of each sweep. The user aligns the starting point by pressing the red button and placing the roller so that the mark on the roller aligns with the tick mark (Figure 9). Pressing the yellow button lets the user repeat the same row. The user can move the roller backwards to erase an already-drawn pattern. In this case, all the rods are lowered automatically. The blue button clears the drawing data.

The horizontal and vertical extents of a dot are 12 mm and 8 mm, respectively, assuming that the roller moves horizontally. This means that the display resolution of a pattern drawn by the device is approximately 2.12 dpi. The main limiting factor is the size of the servo motors and capability of the rotary encoder. The drawing speed is constrained by the speed of the servomotors. In our current implementation, the maximum speed of the roller sweep is 15 cm/sec, and the device fails to generate an appropriate pattern if the user sweeps the device faster than this limit. It requires approximately 20 minutes to draw a large picture such as shown in Figure 1 right (size: 2×1.2 m) with all the lines carefully matched together.

Pen Drawing Device

The user can draw an arbitrary pattern using his or her bare fingers, raising the fiber selectively after flattening the fur. It is relatively easy to draw a line in the opposite direction of the fur growth because the user can simply move his or her fingers across the fur in that direction once. However, it is very tedious to draw lines in the orthogonal or opposite

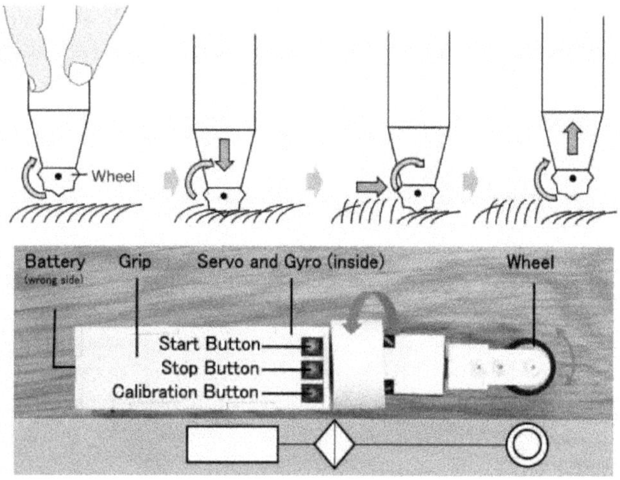

Figure 10: Pen device. Principle (top) and composition with kinematic diagram (bottom).

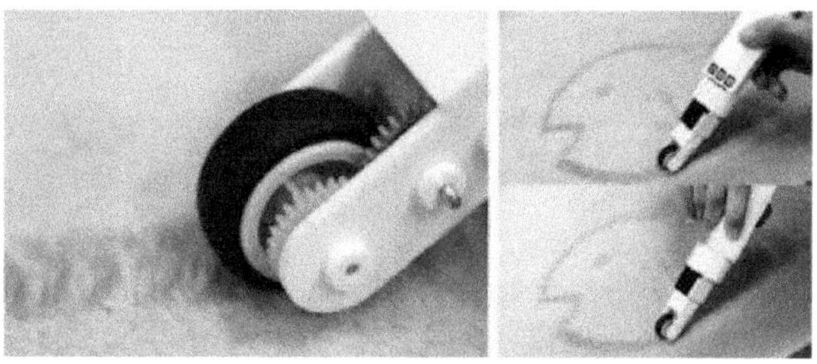

Figure 11: Tip of the pen device (Left): the system always keeps the wheel orientation parallel to the fur growth direction and adjusts the direction of wheel rotation (Right).

Figure 12: Difference between drawing with a finger and pen device: using own finger (left), using pen device (Right).

direction because the user needs to make many short scratches. We therefore developed a pen device to save this effort by raising the fibers using a continuously rotating wheel which is always oriented parallel to the growth direction of the fur. (Figure 10 top).

The device consists of a grip, control buttons, a wheel, servo motor, and gyro (Figure 10 bottom). The gyro measures the global orientation of the pen grip, and the servomotor twists the pen tip according to the measurement from the gyro. The user first calibrates the system by pressing the calibration button while holding the pen in the canonical posture facing toward the fur growth direction. The other button is used for starting and stopping. Afterwards, in whatever orientation the user holds the pen grip, the system always keeps the wheel orientation parallel to the fur growth and adjusts the direction of the wheel rotation so that the wheel continuously raises the fibers (Figure 11).

We did a comparison to observe the differences between drawing with a finger and drawing with a pen-device. When the user drew with his finger, if the drawing direction is aligned with the direction of the fur growth, it was difficult to draw (Figure 12). It is also difficult to draw a line orthogonal to the fur growth direction. On the other hand, using the pen device, the user was able to draw pictures without paying attention to the direction of the fur. However, as the smoothness of the pen-device movement is limited by the power generated by the motor rotation, we found that the user was required to get used to the device before drawing fluently.

Pressure Projection Drawing Device

It is known that a high-amplitude ultrasound can be used to push objects in the direction of propagation (acoustic radiation pressure). The Airborne Ultrasound Focusing Devices (AUFD) developed in [5] generate high-amplitude ultrasound based on the phased-array focusing technique. This focused ultrasound can be used to raise/flatten the fur fiber without the device making physical contact (Figure 13 (a)). The diameter of the ultrasonic focal point is a few centimeters and its position can be controlled three-dimensionally.

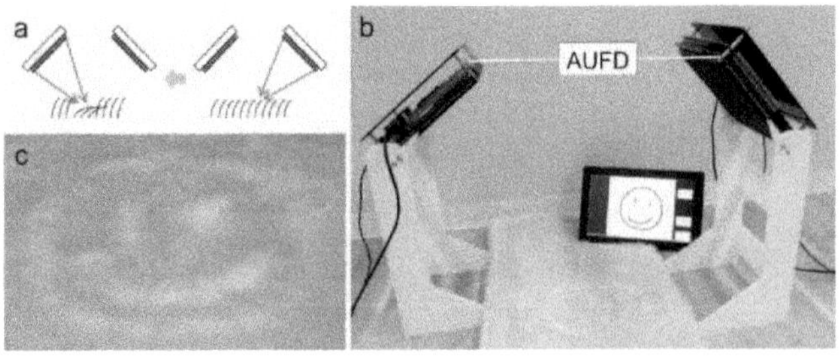

Figure 13: Pressure projection device; (a) principle, (b) composition and (c) result.

The specifications of the AUFD are as follows. 285 ultrasound transducers (10 mm diameter, T4010A1, Nippon Ceramic Co. Ltd.) are arranged in a rectangular area whose side length D is 17 cm. The resonant frequency of the transducers is 40 kHz (i.e. $\lambda = 8.5$ mm). The diameter w of the focal point is determined by D, λ, and the focal length R (the distance between the AUFD and the surface of fur): $w = 2\lambda R/D$. For example, w is 20 mm when R is set at 20 cm. The maximum output force is 16 mN (measured). The spatial resolution of the position of the focal point is 0.5 mm. The position can be updated at the rate of 1 kHz.

Two AUFD are placed face to face in the drawing system (Figure 13 (b)). Before drawing, fur fibers should be in the ordinal raised state. One AUFD is used to raise the fur fibers by projecting pressure. The other AUFD is used to flatten the fur fibers by projecting pressure from the opposite direction. Because the AUFD units have been placed at a tilt, the focal lengths are controlled depending on the projecting point. The display resolution of a pattern is approximately 1.2 dpi in the current implementation. The drawing speed is constrained by the time to raise the fur fibers and pressure level. In our current implementation, the maximum drawing speed of the line is 30 cm/sec on boa cloth (18 mm fur length, 0.02 mm diameter). The material that can be controlled by current pressure level is limited. Fur fiber length should be more than 18 mm in our simple trial. The pattern (size: 20×20 cm) in Figure 13 (c) was drawn by the system in 4 seconds. Erasing the drawing takes around quadruple the time because fur fiber has the tendency to retain shape.

EXAMPLES

Our display can be used in a number of daily living contexts, in particular, on large spaces such as floors or walls and on objects such as toys, clothes, and curtains. Figure 14 (a) to (e) illustrate the usage of the display in a large space. Users can draw special pictures for their loved ones on their birthday or write messages for visitors (Figure 14 (a)). Children can play storytelling games with others using the drawings they have drawn (Figure 14 (b)). Here, the display is used to make line drawings of train tracks for train toys to move along. Children can easily modify their drawings according to the story or game they are playing. Carpets with various patterns can be used to decorate the

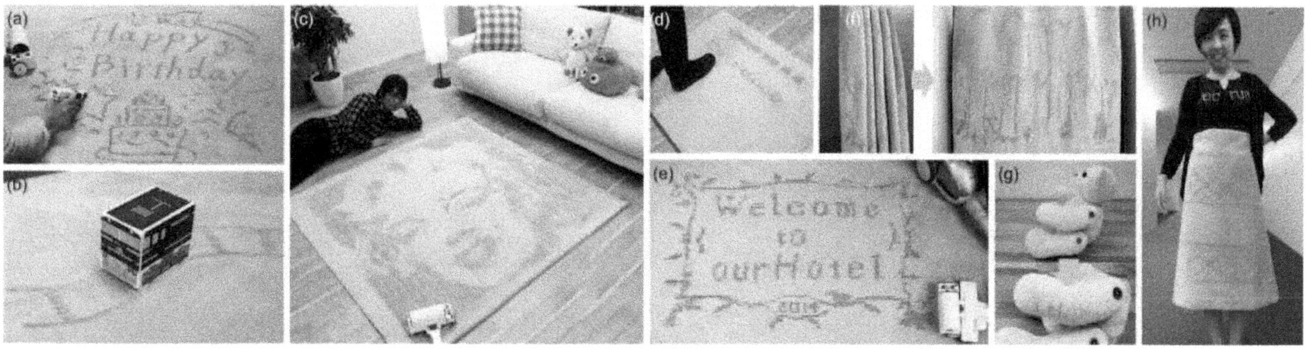

Figure 14: Application examples: (a) birthday party, (b) having a toy follow a drawn path, (c) drawing art on the floor, (d) visitor navigation guides, (e) greetings on a carpet, (f) changing patterns, (g) Pattern on plush toy, (h) temporary drawing on clothing.

living space, and users can change the drawings according to their mood (Figure 14 (c)). A hotel can use our devices to display information for guests on their welcome mats. An example would be a mat showing the direction of the entrance (Figure 14 (d)). It is also possible to implicitly tell that a carpet is cleaned by leaving a message (Figure 14 (e)).

Figure 14 (f) to (h) illustrate various usages on everyday objects. On a soft, foldable object, one can reveal different images by folding and opening the object. For example, users can draw on a curtain and fold the curtain to show a different illustration (Figure 14 (f)). Many people like to dress up their soft toys as well, to give them their own individuality. Using our system, users can easily draw patterns on their soft toys without needing to modify them (Figure 14 (g)). Finally, our system allows users to draw different patterns on their clothing everyday (Figure 14 (h)).

USER STUDY

We prepared an environment resembling a living area and conducted an informal observational study to see how people use the roller and pen devices and what kind of drawings they draw. We invited 18 people among visitors to a local science museum to the study, consisting of six parent-child pairs and six children. We placed various fur objects as drawing canvases, including a sofa, mat, cushion, plush toys, carpet, and tapestry in the environment. A couple of roller and pen devices and a Tablet PC were provided for the users to use freely.

Figure 15 shows some snapshots taken in the study. Overall, participants were able to understand how to use the device and the application within five minutes and were able to draw their own drawings in the environment. One child created a story integrating a picture drawn using the device with plush toys. We also observed an unexpected creative use of the technology in which a participant raised all fur fibers first and then draw a pattern by flattening selected fibers using the devices, that is, drawing bright strokes on a dark canvas (this is the reverse of our initial intention). Not only the proposed devices but also users can draw pattern with their fingers. In the user study, we observed participants could interactively modify the pattern drawn by the devices. The study also revealed some problems with the method. Participants commented that the device was too heavy for young participants to draw on a wall. They also found it difficult to draw patterns on a sofa when users pressed the device strongly because it may sink into it.

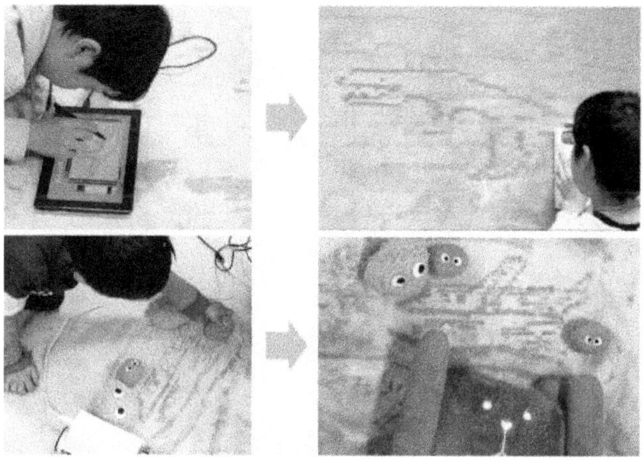

Figure 15: Drawing a dinosaur using the multiple layer function (top), Making up a story with common household objects (bottom).

LIMITATION

There are several limitations to our current devices, which we plan to address in the future. The current roller device doesn't have a sensor to detect its own position in the environment, so the users have to fix the device on the floor and carefully drag the device. In the future, by mounting a sensor that can measure the absolute position of the device, we plan to allow user to draw pattern by moving the device more freely. We also plan to combine the roller device with a mobile robot to implement fully autonomous drawing device. As for the pen device, the wheel stops rotating when the user presses the pen tip to the fur surface too hard. Durability of the fur material is another concern. When one draws on the same spot too many times, the fur will be slowly worn off, making it difficult to observe the pattern. To prevent this, the carpet has to have certain durability. We plan to improve the device to reduce the wear it causes. Finally, our current method cannot draw patterns in multiple colors. One possible solution is to create a special carpet consisting of fur strands with multiple colors and then raise and flatten these colored strands selectively. This is an interesting prospect.

CONCLUSION

We presented a display technology that utilizes the phenomenon whereby the shading properties of fur change as the fur fibers are raised or flattened. We developed three devices, roller, pen and pressure projection device, to draw patterns on fur display. We assessed the capability of the fur display and discussed various applications in daily living contexts. Our technology can turn ordinary objects into computer displays without requiring or creating any non-reversible modifications to them. It is also free from glare and requires virtually no cost to maintain.

ACKNOWLEDGMENTS

We are grateful to Norimichi Tsumura for their significant contributions in investigating property of fur display. This work was supported by JSPS KAKENHI Grant Number 26700017.

REFERENCES

1. Coelho, M. and Maes, P. Sprout I/O: a texturally rich interface. In *Proc. TEI '08*. ACM, pp. 221-222.
2. Furukawa, M., Uema, Y., Sugimoto, M., and Inami, M. Fur interface with bristling effect induced by vibration. In *Proc. AH '10*, ACM, Article 17, 6 pages.
3. Hanna, N. Water Calligraphy Device. http://www.nicholashanna.net/.
4. Harrison, C., Benko, H., and Wilson, A.D. OmniTouch: wearable multitouch interaction everywhere. In *Proc. UIST '11*. ACM, pp. 441-450.
5. Hoshi, T. Compact ultrasound device for noncontact interaction. In *Proc. ACE '12*, ACM, pp. 502-505.
6. Hullin, M.B., Lensch, H, Raskar, R., Seidel, H., and Ihrke, I. Dynamic display of BRDFs. In *Computer Graphics Forum (Proc. EG)*, pp. 475-483.
7. Kawana, H. dotanco, http://gekitetz.com/dotanco/.
8. Kushiyama, K., Ikei, R., and Sasada, S. Tactile grass landscape. In *ACM SIGGRAPH 2008 posters*. ACM, Article 39, 1 pages.
9. Malzbender, T., Samadani, R., Scher, S., Crume, A., Dunn, D., and Davis, J. Printing reflectance functions. *ACM Trans. Graph.* 31, 3, Article 20 (June 2012), 11 pages.
10. Master, B. Lazy man Zen garden, http://youtu.be/rNGPErdIqZA.
11. Matusik, W., Ajdin, B., Gu, J., Lawrence, J., Lensch, H. P. A, Pellacini, F., and Rusinkiewicz, S. Printing spatially-varying reflectance. *ACM Trans. Graph. 28*, 5, Article 128 (December 2009), 9 pages.
12. Mistry, P., Maes, P., and Chang, L. WUW - wear Ur world: a wearable gestural interface. In *Ext. Abst. CHI '09*. ACM, pp, 4111-4116.
13. Nojima, T., Ooide Y., and Kawaguchi, H. Hairlytop interface: An interactive surface display comprised of hair-like soft actuators, In *Proc. WHC '13*, IEEE, pp. 431 - 435.
14. Ochiai, Y., Oyama, A., Hoshi, T., and Rekimoto, J. Theory and Application of the Colloidal Display: Programmable Bubble Screen for Computer Entertainment. In *Proc. ACE '13*, Springer, pp. 198-214.
15. Raffle, H. Joachim, M.W., and Tichenor, J. Super cilia skin: an interactive membrane. In *Ext. Abst. CHI '03*. ACM, pp. 808-809.
16. rAndom International. PIXELROLLER. http://random-international.com/work/pixelroller/.
17. Rivers, A., Moyer, I.E., and Durand, F. Position-correcting tools for 2D digital fabrication. *ACM Trans. Graph. 31*, 4, Article 88 (July 2012), 7 pages.
18. Rozin, D. Wooden Mirror. http://www.smoothware.com/danny/woodenmirror.html
19. Saakes, D., Inami, M., Igarashi, T., Koziumi, N., and Raskar, R. Shader printer. In *ACM SIGGRAPH 2012 Emerging Technologies*, ACM, Article 18, 1 pages.
20. Sugiura, Y., Kakehi, G., Withana, A., Lee, C., Sakamoto, D., Sugimoto, M., Inami, M., and Igarashi, T. Detecting shape deformation of soft objects using directional photoreflectivity measurement. *In Proc UIST '11*. ACM, pp. 509-516.
21. Sugiura, Y., Lee, C., Ogata, M., Withana, A., Makino, Y., Sakamoto, D., Inami, M., and Igarashi, T. PINOKY: a ring that animates your plush toys. In *Proc. CHI '12*, ACM, pp. 725-734.
22. Sugiura, Y., Toda, K., Hoshi, T., Inami, M. and Igarashi, T. Graffiti Fur: Turning Your Carpet Into a Computer Display. In *ACM SIGGRAPH 2014 Emerging Technologies*, ACM, 1 pages.
23. Wakita, A., and Shibutani, M. Mosaic Textile: Wearable Ambient Display with Non-emissive Color-changing Modules, In *Proc. ACE '06*, ACM, Article 48.
24. Xiao, R., Harrison, C., and Hudson, S. E. WorldKit: Rapid and Easy Creation of Ad-hoc Interactive Applications on Everyday Surfaces. In *Proc. CHI '13*. ACM, pp. 879-888.
25. Zoran, A., and Paradiso, J.A. FreeD: a freehand digital sculpting tool. In *Proc. CHI '13*. ACM, pp. 2613-2616.

LightRing: Always-Available 2D Input on Any Surface

Wolf Kienzle, Ken Hinckley
Microsoft Research
One Microsoft Way, Redmond, WA 98052
{wkienzle,kenh}@microsoft.com

ABSTRACT
We present *LightRing*, a wearable sensor in a ring form factor that senses the 2d location of a fingertip on any surface, independent of orientation or material. The device consists of an infrared proximity sensor for measuring finger flexion and a 1-axis gyroscope for measuring finger rotation. Notably, *LightRing* tracks subtle fingertip movements from the finger *base* without requiring instrumentation of other body parts or the environment. This keeps the normal hand function intact and allows for a socially acceptable appearance. We evaluate *LightRing* in a 2d pointing experiment in two scenarios: on a desk while sitting down, and on the leg while standing. Our results indicate that the device has potential to enable a variety of rich mobile input scenarios.

Author Keywords
mobile; input; sensors; wearable; finger; ring

ACM Classification Keywords
H.5.2. [Information interfaces and presentation]: User Interfaces—Graphical user interfaces; Input devices and strategies

INTRODUCTION
The increasing ubiquity of computing devices has created a demand for data input techniques that are *always-available* [9]. Wearable devices naturally meet this requirement and are gaining popularity for simple control tasks, for example, to skip tracks or change volume on a music player. Unfortunately, always-available input remains a largely unsolved problem for richer applications, such as text entry or web browsing, which typically require accurate 2d pointing or stroke input.

In this paper we propose *LightRing* (*Fig. 1*), a small input device that is worn on the finger and tracks 2d fingertip movements while the hand rests on any surface, regardless of orientation or material.

UIST '14, October 05 - 08 2014, Honolulu, HI, USA
Copyright is held by the owner/author(s). Publication rights licensed to ACM. ACM 978-1-4503-3069-5/14/10...$15.00.
http://dx.doi.org/10.1145/2642918.2647376

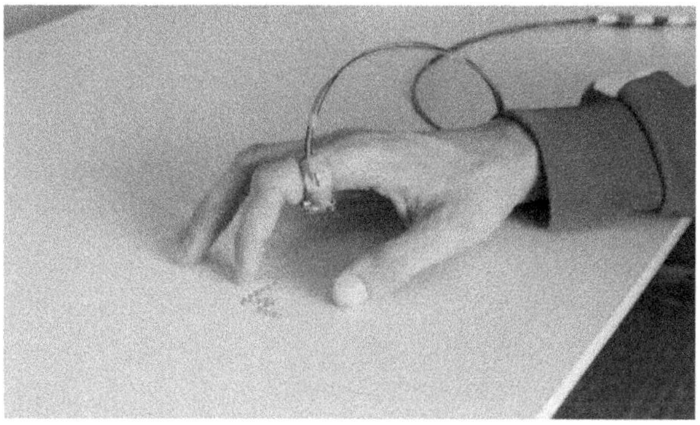

Figure 1. ***LightRing*** **tracks the 2d position of a fingertip on any surface.**

Previous finger-worn devices for 2d input include *MIDS* [7], which tracks the fingertip with accelerometers on the finger. *MagicFinger* [13] uses an optical flow sensor (as used in optical mice) attached to the finger for 2d tracking. *FingerPad* [2] and *uTrack* [3] instrument the fingertip with a small (passive) magnet, and a second finger with an active device that tracks the finger by magnetic field changes.

Unfortunately, these solutions cannot be worn at the finger *base* but require instrumentation of a lower finger segment. Compared to an ordinary ring (e.g. a wedding band) such devices have a higher risk of interfering with the normal hand function, and are therefore facing a hurdle for wide adoption and social acceptance.

The key contribution of *LightRing* is a solution to the fundamental problem of sensing fine-grained, subtle fingertip motion *from the finger base* with a very simple and small device that looks and feels like an ordinary ring.

HARDWARE
Our hardware prototype (*Fig. 2, left*) consists of a plastic ring and two simple sensors. The first sensor is a 1-axis gyroscope. We use a *Sparkfun* board with an *IvenSense ITG-3200* gyroscope that has three axes, but we only use the rotation rate $d\Phi$ in the plane of the red circuit board as illustrated in Fig. 2 (left). Note that the board also has an accelerometer on it, which we currently do *not* use.

The second sensor consists of an infrared emitter (*Osram SFH4550*) and detector (*Honeywell SD5410*). Together, these serve as a proximity sensor: the amount of IR light seen by the detector relates to the distance between the ring and the middle segment (*middle phalanx*) of the instrumented finger. Assuming Lambertian reflectance of the skin, the light intensity should fall off quadratically with distance (*inverse square law*). This distance changes when the finger is flexed or extended. The emitter and detector parts were chosen to have a narrow viewing angle (6° and 12°, respectively) to prevent spurious reflections from other fingers or the input surface. To suppress ambient lighting changes we measure distance by first registering the detector output with the LED *off*, and then subtracting this value from the output with the LED *on* (after 1 millisecond). We refer to the measured value as **d**.

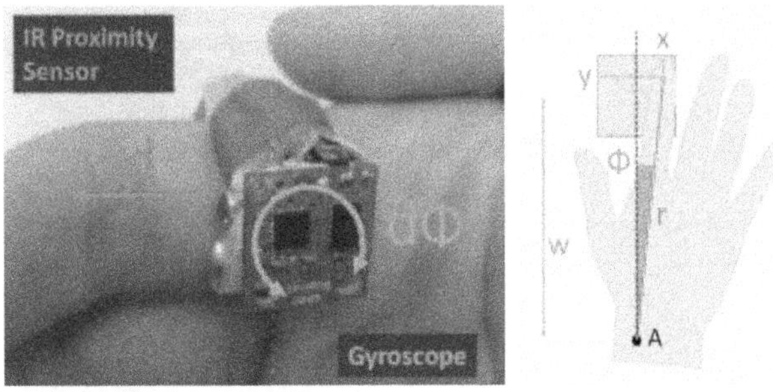

Figure 2. *(Left)* Sensor hardware. The "blue" light from the IR emitter is invisible to the human eye. *(Right)* Fingertip position (x, y) in wrist coordinates (blue square) and its corresponding angle Φ and radius *r*. The dashed black line denotes x = Φ = 0, the current "up" direction.

The ring is wired to an Arduino UNO board. The sensors run at 50Hz which we found sufficient for our application. The sampling resolution of the gyroscope part is 14bit, the proximity values are read by the analog input on the Arduino UNO, which uses a 10bit ADC.

This setup suffices for evaluating 2d pointing precision and speed in a user experiment. Real-world applications will likely require adding a button to the ring, for example, on the side where it can be tapped with the thumb. Also, the simple hardware design should lend itself well to making the ring battery-powered and wireless.

It should be noted that optical sensors have been proposed for measuring finger flexion in wrist-worn devices as well [1][5][6][10]. Those systems typically offer more degrees of freedom (e.g. recover full hand pose [6]), much like to glove-based input devices [12], but are also more complex.

INPUT METHOD

The sensor hardware described above can track subtle fingertip locations on any surface as follows. First, the user rests the wrist (*carpus*) the surface (*Fig. 1*). Then, the tip of the instrumented finger is moved within an *imaginary 2d coordinate system* [4], using two basic movements:

1) rotate the hand around the wrist ("left/right")
2) flex the instrumented finger ("up/down")

Resting the wrist and finger on the surface has two important effects: first, it prevents fatigue of the arm and hand during the interaction. Second, it limits the variety of hand movements and promotes those that can be measured with our sensors. In fact, we have only seen a small number of ways in which users can move their finger so that the system fails. These are enumerated in the Discussion below.

The concept of *imaginary coordinates* is borrowed from [4]. We use the term loosely since the main application studied in this paper (pointing) is not screen-less but includes visual feedback. However, our design does not preclude screen-less operation, for example, for gestures.

We refer to our imaginary coordinate system as *wrist coordinates*. At the beginning of the interaction the wrist coordinate system (**x**, **y**) is established on the surface such that its origin is at a fixed distance **w** to the wrist, and the finger points in the **y** ("up") direction (*Fig. 2, right*). The physical size of the unit square in wrist coordinates is defined by the user's comfortable motion range. Both the physical size and the origin's distance to the wrist **w** are defined during the calibration procedure described below.

MODEL

To recover fingertip positions from the sensor readings we use the model illustrated in Fig. 2 (right). We assume that the center of the wrist is fixed in space, creating an anchor point **A** around which the user rotates the hand during the interaction. A left/right rotation of the hand will move the fingertip along a circle with radius **r** and change the angle Φ. Flexing and extending the finger will move the fingertip further and closer to the wrist, changing **r**.

Clearly, if we know Φ and **r**, we can recover the fingertip position in wrist coordinates **x** and **y**. By design, determining Φ amounts to integrating the gyroscope output dΦ over time. Specifically, we integrate dΦ from the beginning of interaction, when Φ = 0. For the short interactions tested in this paper (less than 20 seconds) gyro drift was not a problem, but it may be necessary to correct for drift with a magnetometer for other longer interactions. Determining **r** involves an additional step. In general, the mapping between the measured quantity **d** and the fingertip radius **r** is determined by several nonlinear effects, including kinematics of the flexing movement, the IR brightness falloff, and nonlinearities in the IR detector. The mapping can be estimated with a calibration procedure, e.g. by letting the user move their finger along a set of known radii **r**, and recording the corresponding **d** values.

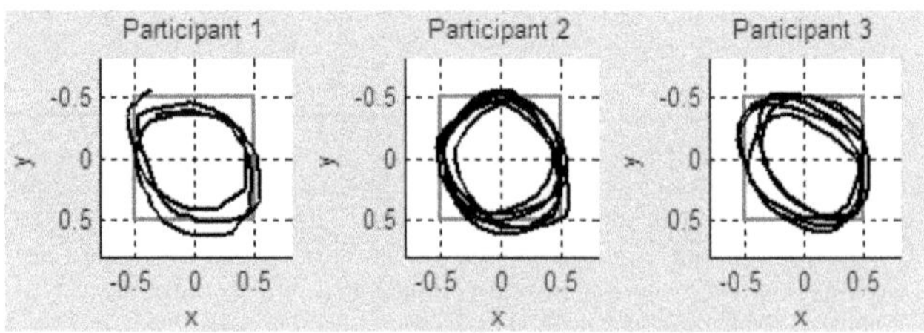

Figure 3. Calibration data (black line) from three users mapped to wrist coordinates (blue square).

By experimenting with different calibration schemes we found that the mapping between **d** and **r** can be approximated by a linear model without losing much accuracy. For the scope of this paper the added value of a simpler and more robust calibration procedure seemed to outweigh the small distortions coming from the linear approximation. Moreover, we noticed that the range of wrist angles Φ is typically small, which lets us approximate **x** ~ Φ. Overall, our model for mapping sensor readings to wrist coordinates is simply linear: **x** = **a***Φ and **y** = **b*****d** - **w**.

CALIBRATION

With the linear model the calibration process reduces to finding the sensor values **d** and Φ that correspond to the center and physical size of the wrist coordinate system. To calibrate the system the user continuously traces a freehand circle on a flat surface (many shapes would suffice, but we found users could produce circles consistently and comfortably). No visual guide or feedback is provided. The user is instructed to choose the vertical position and size of the circle such that the motion covers most of the comfortable range, but does not require full extension of the finger (which would be outside the proximity sensor range).

Once the user finds a comfortable circle location and diameter (typically 3-5cm), five seconds of sensor data are recorded and the calibration parameters are computed as: **a** = 0.35/SD(Φ), **b** = 0.35/SD(**d**), and **w** = **b***mean(**d**). Here, SD means standard deviation and the 0.35 factor (≈1/2√2) is the inverse SD of a sine wave signal with peak-to-peak amplitude 1. The rationale is that since the user traces a circle, Φ and **b** will be sine waves, and so this scale factor maps the user's circle to the unit square (the physical size) of the wrist coordinate system. The mapped calibration circles of three users are shown in Fig. 3. The fact that these shapes are recognizable as circles supports the validity of our linear approximation.

EVALUATION

We tested the pointing performance of *LightRing* in a reciprocal pointing task [8]. We showed black circular targets in a white 22x22cm square (mapped to the wrist coordinate system) on a 23" LCD display at 60cm distance. Participants used their non-dominant hand to select targets by pressing a hardware push button. We tested four angles (0°, 45°, 90°, 135°), two distances (9.6cm, 19.2cm), three widths (1.1cm, 2.2cm, 4.4cm), overall: 3x2x3=24 trials. Each trial consisted of 10 repetitions. We further tested two conditions: using *LightRing* on a desk while sitting down, and using it on the side of the leg while standing. For standing, the display was elevated to eye level. We ran two blocks of 24 trials for each condition. The condition order was counterbalanced between subjects. This yielded 960 data points per subject.

Average movement times (*MT*) were 1.2s (SD 0.20s) for desk and 1.1s (SD 0.12s) for leg. Error rates (% clicks outside target) were 5.9% (SD 2.4%) for desk and 7.6% (SD 4.8%) for leg. We also computed throughput as *TP* = *IDe*/*MT*, where *IDe* = log2(*D*/*We* + 1) (in bits) is the effective index of difficulty, *D* is the target distance, and *We* is 4.133 times the standard deviation of participants selection coordinates [8]. Throughput was 2.9 bps (bits/second) (SD 0.31) for desk and 2.8 bps (SD 0.36) for leg. Neither of these differences was significant. Fig. 4 (top row) shows *MT* and Error rates per *ID* = log2(*D*/*W*) (*W*=actual target width). The correlation coefficient was ρ=0.86 for the desk condition and ρ=0.91 for the leg condition, indicating reasonable agreement with Fitts' law.

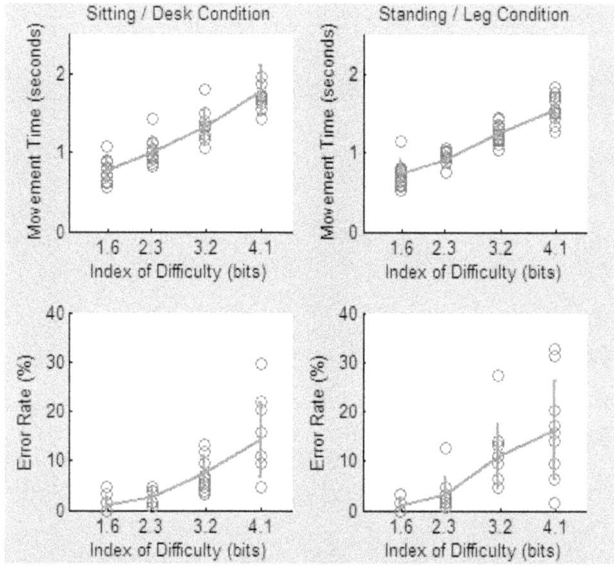

Figure 4. Pointing performance vs. Index of Difficulty (ID), while sitting *(left column)* and standing *(right column)*. *Top row:* movement time, *bottom row:* Error rate. A blue circle denotes average performance for one participant. The red line shows the average over participants with one SD error bars.

A perhaps surprising result was that participants achieved similar performance for leg and desk. We expected lower performance in the leg condition due to the uneven surface of the clothing and due to a higher cognitive demand caused by performing the input with the hand pointing down to the floor. Instead, some subjects reported that the leg condition was "easier" due to less friction compared to the tabletop.

We also analyzed learning effects. There were no significant differences in *MT*, Error rate, or *TP* between the first and second block of either condition. However, over the course of all four blocks (both conditions, counterbalanced for order), *MT* changed significantly ($F(3,9)=5.2$, $p<0.01$). A post-hoc Tukey's test ($p<0.05$) revealed that MT was higher during the first block (1.3s) than during the following three blocks (1.1s). Similarly, *TP* changed significantly between blocks ($F(3,9)=5.05$, $p<0.01$), with *TP* lower during the first block (2.6 bps) than following blocks (2.9-3.0 bps). Error rates did not change significantly between blocks ($F(3,9)=0.83$, $p=0.48$).

DISCUSSION

The current sensor design is based on the assumption that there is a monotonic relationship between **r** and **d**: the closer the fingertip to the wrist, the higher the IR detector output **d**. However, **d** merely reflects the angle of the *proximal interphalangeal* (*PIP*) joint, which is not the only joint that can move during finger flexion. In practice, we have seen two cases where this causes our system to fail: first, if pressure is applied the *distal interphalangeal* (*DIP*) joint can "snap" back and forth, changing **d**, but not **r** (Figure 5, left). Second, if the fingertip is moved by fully extending the finger and rotating it around the *meta-carpophalangeal* joint (*MCP*) (Figure 5, right), **r** changes, but **d** does not (besides **d** being out of range of the IR sensor if the finger is fully extended).

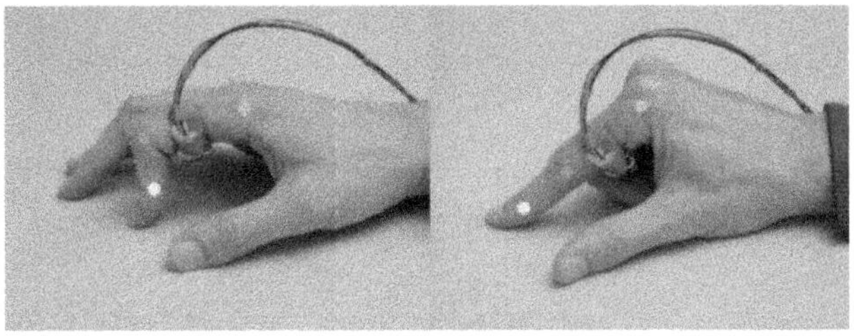

Figure 5. Failure cases and the finger joints involved (green=MCP, red=PIP, yellow=DIP): *(Left)* applying pressure. *(Right)* keeping the finger fully extended.

Interestingly, once users are instructed to avoid 1) pressure, and 2) fully extending their finger, the system appears to work fine. A possible explanation can be found in the *Digits* system [6], a wrist-worn that is sensor able to reconstruct the full 3d hand pose. *Digits* assumes that during *natural finger flexion* PIP, DIP, and MCP not only work in concert, but their angles are *related by fixed ratios at all time*, a motion that would satisfy our monotonicity assumption as well. Thus, although natural flexion occurs in mid-air, not on a surface, we conjecture that as soon as users avoid pressure and full extension, they switch to a gentler motion, closer to natural flexion, which has the above properties and thus makes *LightRing* work.

We also observed that in order to move the fingertip left and right some users rotated the finger around the MCP joint instead of rotating the hand around the wrist. Please note that this does not violate our modelling assumptions: it merely shifts the "wrist" anchor point **A** (*Fig. 2, right)* to the actual point of rotation, i.e. the MCP joint. The same argument holds for the elbow as rotation anchor.

The linear calibration model turned out to be very robust. Once calibrated, *LightRing* can be slightly rotated around the finger, even taken off and on again, without requiring recalibration. Larger accidental rotations would have to be addressed explicitly, however, e.g. by giving the ring an asymmetric shape (like an engagement or class ring) so that the user can feel the orientation. Or, multiple proximity sensors could be placed around the ring to recover the signal in any orientation (using techniques like *iRing* [9] to determine absolute rotation angle).

In this note we have not provided a solution for initiating or "unlocking" the interaction. One way would be to use a button on the ring. Alternatively, the calibration procedure itself could be used as an unlocking mechanism: the user could simply trace, say, three circles on the surface. This would also allow for the size the wrist coordinate system to adapt to different applications or body poses (which may differ in terms of comfortable motion ranges). In systems with visual feedback (i.e. a cursor), another possibility is to keep the interaction "always on" by clamping the cursor position at the screen edges, so that when the user moves towards a screen edge, any further movement in that direction will simply drag the wrist coordinates along.

CONCLUSION AND FURTHER WORK

We have introduced *LightRing*, a novel finger-worn sensor for digitizing subtle, fine-grained fingertip movements on any surface. User data indicates that the system is accurate and fast enough—about 3 bits/second pointing throughput after minimal practice—to enable real-world applications on the go that would traditionally require a mouse or touchpad. For example, *LightRing* could enable mobile text entry with smart glasses, or browsing the web on a distant display. To explore these scenarios in an ecologically valid manner we are planning to make *LightRing* wireless and add a capacitive button for selecting targets. Moreover, we are interested in investigating applications without visual feedback (and potentially eyes-free), such as recognition of 2d gestures.

ACKNOWLEDGMENTS

We would like to thank Scott Saponas, Desney Tan, and Mike Sinclair for insightful discussions.

REFERENCES

1. Ahmad, F. and Musilek, P. UbiHand: a wearable input device for 3D interaction, SIGGRAPH 2006 (poster)
2. Chan, L., et al. FingerPad: private and subtle interaction using fingertips. UIST 2013.
3. Chen, K., et al. uTrack: 3D input using two magnetic sensors. UIST 2013.
4. Gustafson, S., et al. Imaginary interfaces: spatial interaction with empty hands and without visual feedback. UIST 2010.
5. Howard, B. and Howard, S. Lightglove: Wrist-worn virtual typing and pointing. IEEE ISWC 2001
6. Kim, D., et al. Digits: freehand 3D interactions anywhere using a wrist-worn gloveless sensor. UIST 2012.
7. Lam, A., et al. MIDS: micro input devices system using MEMS sensors. IEEE Intelligent Robots and Systems 2002.
8. MacKenzie, I. S. Fitts' law as a research and design tool in human-computer interaction. *Hum.-Comp. Interact.* 7(1) 1992.
9. Morris, D., et al. Emerging Input Technologies for Always-Available Mobile Interaction. Foundations and Trends in Human–Computer Interaction 4 (4) 2011.
10. Niikura, T. et al. Anywhere surface touch: utilizing any surface as an input area. AH 2014.
11. Ogata, M., et al. iRing: intelligent ring using infrared reflection. UIST 2012.
12. Sturman, D. J., and Zeltzer, D. A survey of glove-based input. Computer Graphics and Applications 1994.
13. Yang, X., et al. Magic finger: always-available input through finger instrumentation. UIST 2012.

WristFlex: Low-Power Gesture Input with Wrist-Worn Pressure Sensors

Artem Dementyev **Joseph A. Paradiso**
Media Lab, Massachusetts Institute of Technology
75 Amherst Street, Cambridge, MA, USA
{artemd, joep}@media.mit.edu

ABSTRACT
In this paper we present WristFlex, an always-available on-body gestural interface. Using an array of force sensitive resistors (FSRs) worn around the wrist, the interface can distinguish subtle finger pinch gestures with high accuracy (>80%) and speed. The system is trained to classify gestures from subtle tendon movements on the wrist. We demonstrate that WristFlex is a complete system that works wirelessly in real-time. The system is simple and light-weight in terms of power consumption and computational overhead. WristFlex's sensor power consumption is 60.7 μW, allowing the prototype to potentially last more then a week on a small lithium polymer battery. Also, WristFlex is small and non-obtrusive, and can be integrated into a wristwatch or a bracelet. We perform user studies to evaluate the accuracy, speed, and repeatability. We demonstrate that the number of gestures can be extended with orientation data from an accelerometer. We conclude by showing example applications.

Author Keywords
Gesture recognition; wrist interface; machine learning; FSR

ACM Classification Keywords
H.5.2. Information Interfaces and Presentation: User Interfaces

INTRODUCTION
We envision a future where users have an ability to seamlessly control wearable devices and facilities in the environment. For that purpose, always-available on-body gestural interfaces will need to be developed. Such interfaces would be seamlessly worn on the body and ready to work at any moment, and in any situation.

To have better usability, the always-available gestural interface needs to satisfy four main criteria: First, such an interface should be *subtle*. The user should be able to use the interface in any scenario, without physical discomfort or embarrassment. The device should be small enough to be comfortably worn on the body without interfering with natural hand movements. Second, the interface should be *natural*. The gestures should be simple and intuitive, to avoid cognitive interference and fatigue. Third, the interface should be *low-power*. Users should not have to worry about constantly recharging the battery or carrying a large battery. There is a tradeoff between the power consumption and the complexity of the system; a low power interface will be light-weight and simple. Fourth, the interface should be *easily accessible*. It should be on-body, so users do not need to pull out a device from their pocket. The device should have one-hand input, so it can be used when the other hand can not be accessed.

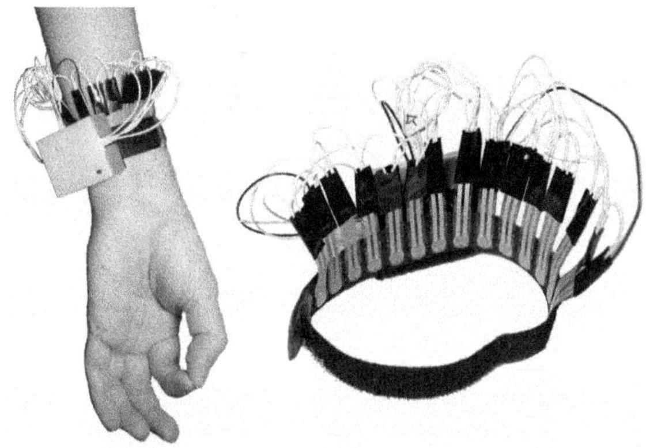

Figure 1: WristFlex prototype. Left image: device worn on the wrist, while performing a finger pinch gesture. Right image: the side of the device that contacts the skin, exposing an array of force sensitive resistors (FSRs).

There is no existing device that can satisfy all the criteria of a seamless interface. So, the motivation of this paper is to satisfy those criteria. We present a gesture recognition system that uses pressure distribution around the wrist to discern finger movements. We find the wrist to be an attractive location for a future always-available interface. We are used to wearing wrist watches and bracelets, and the wrist is already used for a number of smart-phone-connected accessories such as the Galaxy Gear watch and the Fitbit activity monitor. The wrist is connected to the hand and fingers, therefore it could be used as a proxy for finger gestures. By putting sensors

UIST 2014, October 5–8, 2014, Honolulu, HI, USA.

http://dx.doi.org/10.1145/2642918.2647396

on the wrist, your hand remains completely free for natural interactions.

The contributions of this paper are the following:

1. We present a novel, simple and low-cost gesture input system that can detect individual finger pinches from the pressure distribution around the wrist.

2. Using our wireless and real-time capable prototype, we perform user studies to assess its performance.

3. We optimize the power consumption of the device, so it can potentially last for a week on a single battery charge.

4. We explore broader interactions with the addition of an accelerometer and different usage scenarios.

RELATED WORK

In this section we will review the literature on always-available on-body input methods. On-body machine vision systems use wearable cameras to detect gestures. For example, Digits uses a wrist-worn 3D infrared camera to recognize finger gestures [10]. Another system used a time-of-flight camera [16]. Camera-based systems can not satisfy all the criteria of an always-available gesture system because of fundamental limitations. Cameras suffer from line-of-sight occlusions and have large power consumption and heavy computation requirements. Furthermore, privacy concerns might prevent a vision based approach from being always available.

Inertial based systems use accelerometer and gyro sensors to discern gestures. Some systems use off-body sensors such as Nintendo Wii remote [15]. Other systems use on-body sensors such as a glove [12] or rings [3] with accelerometer. Inertial sensors are low-power but have caveats e.g., they have to be worn on the fingers to sense finger movement. Such complications can reduce dexterity of the hands, therefore limiting physical interactions.

Brain-computer and muscle-computer interfaces detect neuronal electrical potentials and map them to gestures. A number of research projects explored electromyography (EMG), where electrodes are placed below the elbow to detect hand gestures [14]. Recently, a commercial product named Myo appeared that uses EMG for gesture detection [11]. Myo might have problems detecting finer finger gestures, because it uses less sensitive dry electrodes. EMG systems require the user to wear a bulky array of electrodes below the elbow, so they cannot be integrated with a wristwatch or a bracelet. Furthermore, EMG requires a high data rate and extensive signal processing, therefore it has high power consumption.

Bio-acoustic methods include detecting taps on different places on the skin [8], tapping fingers on surfaces [1], and performing hand motions [4]. Those methods might have problems with external noise and mapping of intuitive gestures to specific inputs.

Previous research showed some success with muscle activity recognition using arm-worn pressure sensors [2]. However, we are not aware of any projects that explored finger gesture recognition from wrist-worn pressure sensors and developed a real-time system. Several projects focused on inferring finger and hand gestures from the wrist, and were inspirational for our work. Gesturewrist project looked at sensing capacitive changes around the wrist to detect gestures [13]. This method can be low power, but it was tested with two hand gestures, and did not distinguish individual finger movements. Similarly, another study placed photodiodes and infrared LEDs around the wrist to infer gestures from infrared reflectance [5]. This approach worked for classifying 8 hand gestures, but reflectance can be affected by sweat and dirt, and might not be energy efficient since it requires pulsing of high power infrared LEDs.

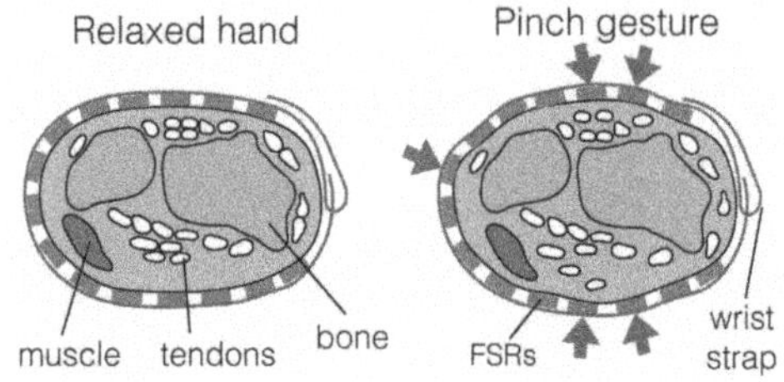

Figure 2: Sketch of the wrist cross section anatomy during two gestures. Individual FSRs are shown as green rectangles. The FSRs with the blue arrows are detecting higher pressures caused by the movements of tendons during a pinch gesture.

PRINCIPLE OF OPERATION

Pressure Sensing

We used force sensitive resistors (FSRs) for sensing pressure. Specifically, we chose the FSR400 (Interlink Electronics), because of small size and off-the-shelf availability. It is made from two copper traces that contact a sheet of conductive polymer. The resistance of the polymer decreases when pressure is applied, thus changing the resistance between the two copper traces. When no pressure is applied the polymer acts as an insulator. We chose to use FSRs because they have low power consumption, do not need complex interfacing and signal processing, are inexpensive, and small enough to fit the wrist.

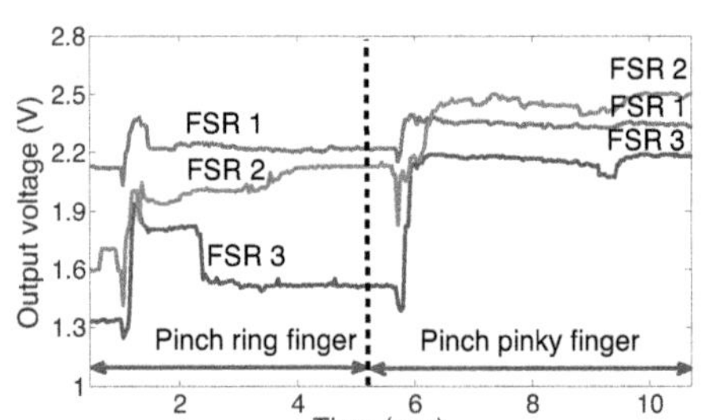

Figure 3: Differences in raw FSR readings at the wristband when pinching ring finger, and later pinky finger.

Gesture Recognition

The muscles that move the fingers and the hand are located mostly in the forearm. Fingers are connected through tendons to those muscles. As sketched in Figure 2, the movement of tendons on the wrist slightly changes the shape of the wrist. Those changes can be detected with an array of pressure sensors. There is a unique pressure signature for each gesture. For example, Figure 3 shows raw data from three pressure sensors on the wrist when first pinching thumb and ring finger, and later thumb and pinky. These pressure distributions can be learned and used to classify new gestures. We pose this as a supervised machine learning task.

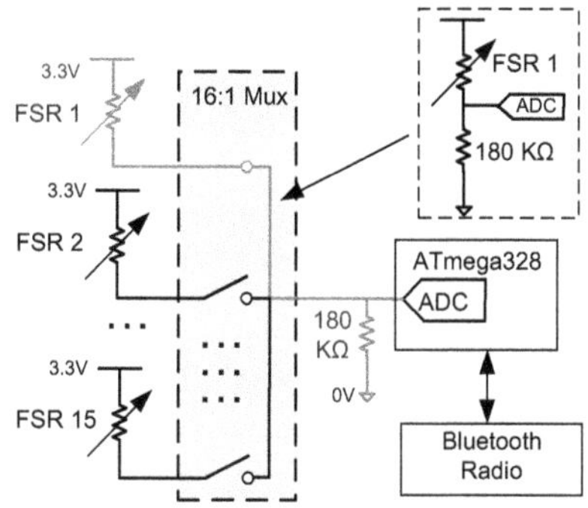

Figure 4: System diagram, showing sampling of FSR 1. The parts in red show the active circuit. This circuit can be simplified into a voltage divider, as shown in the right top corner. The gray rectangle is the multiplexer, showing 3 of 15 FSRs.

PROTOTYPE DESIGN

Hardware

As shown in Figure 1, we constructed a prototype that can be worn on the wrist. We made a custom Velcro wrist-strap to hold pressure sensors in place and to provide a tight contact between the pressure sensors and the wrist. As shown in Figure 5, a custom circuit board was made to fit the electronics.

An ATmega328 (Atmel) microcontroller was used to sample pressure sensors. The samples were transmitted to a laptop using a Bluetooth module (RN-42 Roving Networks). To allow real-time feedback to the user, data was sent at a 30 Hz rate. A 110 mAh lithium polymer battery was used for power. For more functionality, a 3-axis accelerometer ADXL335 (Analog Devices) was added.

We used 15 FSRs to densely cover as much of the circumference of a wrist as possible. As seen in Figure 4, FSR sensors were selected via a 16 to 1 multiplexer (CD74HC4067, Texas Instruments). The system is scalable to more or fewer sensors; they are read sequentially, so only one sensor is electrically connected at a time. Once active, the sensor became part of the voltage divider with a 180 KOhm resistor. Using one voltage divider for all sensors reduced power consumption by 15 times. The microcontroller's analog-to-digital converter (ADC) was connected to the output of the voltage divider.

We found that a 180 kOhm resistor provides enough range to sense gestures, while minimizing energy consumption. With a smaller resistors the range is bigger, but energy consumption is higher. An op-amp circuit should be added between the voltage divider and the ADC if using high sampling rate and a dynamic adjustment of the sensor's gain and range.

It was important to avoid mechanical strain and twisting of FSRs, since that can cause false pressure readings. We used long and flexible wires for connecting the sensors to provide strain relief. Also, we used wireless communications and a battery to avoid external communications and power cables.

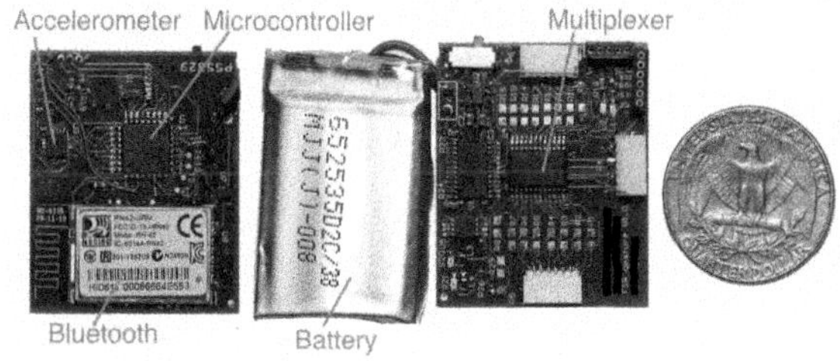

Figure 5: Circuit board: front and back. A U.S. Quarter is added for size comparison.

Machine Learning and Software

A Support Vector Machine (SVM) with a polynomial kernel was used for training and classification. We used Sequential Minimal Optimization (SMO) from the WEKA library [7], which is an optimized version of SVM. Instantaneous pressure readings were used as features. To exclude redundant and irrelevant sensors, correlation feature selection (CFS) was used. The classifier ran in real-time at 30 Hz. In this paper, the classifier ran on a laptop, but it can be adapted to a mobile device such as an Android phone.

As indicated in pilot studies, linear classification algorithms such as linear SVM and linear regression had low accuracy (about 30 to 50%) due to nonlinear output of FSRs and the voltage divider. A non-linear classifier, such as the polynomial SVM used here, was able to fit data better.

EVALUATION OF FINGER PINCH GESTURES

Setup

We recruited 10 participants (4 female, 6 male) to test 5 gestures. Ages ranged from 25 to 30 (mean: 27). As shown in Figure 6, gestures 1 to 4 involved pinching the thumb and one of the other fingers. Gesture 5 was hand in a relaxed position.

We picked this gesture set because pinching two fingers is subtle and involves only minor hand movements, hence the gesture set does not fatigue the user's hand. Also, pinch gestures are not socially obtrusive, they can be performed with hand-at-side, without drawing attention, and the finger pinch gestures are difficult to distinguish by other techniques such as EMG and vision-based techniques. We picked five gestures for this experiment, because it becomes difficult for the user to remember more. In the later section, we show how to increase the number of gestures.

Initially, each gesture was trained 3 times. To capture some pressure variations, each gesture was sampled 20 times for 2 sec interval. The training time was about 1 minute. After training, the participant was asked to practice gestures for about 2 minute to familiarize themselves with the system.

For the evaluation, participants were asked to do specific gestures from on-screen instructions. Each gesture was done 12 times, for a total of 60 gestures. Participants had to do each gesture for a 5-second period to make sure there was enough time to read and follow directions. The gestures were presented in a randomized order. Real-time feedback was provided for the first 30 gestures; the computer displayed what gesture it classified. No feedback was given for the last 30 gestures. The evaluation was done on the last 10 pressure readings in each 5 second period, which equates to an approximately 300 millisecond window.

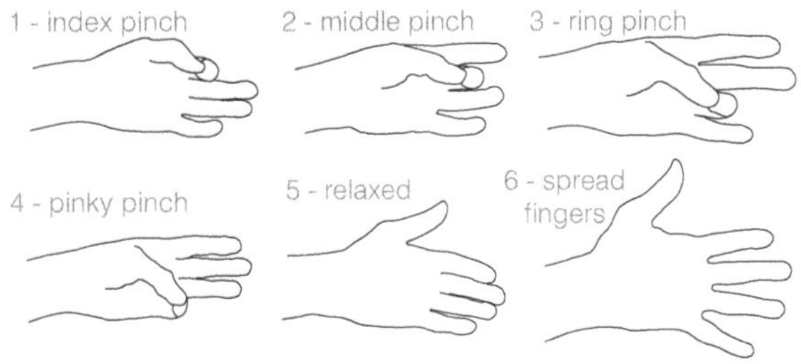

Figure 6: Gestures 1 to 5 were used in the finger-pinch experiment. Gesture 6 was used as a wake-up gesture.

Results and Discussion

Accuracy: Accuracy is defined as the number of correctly classified samples divided by the total number of samples. The accuracy due to chance was 20%. Off-line accuracy was computed using 10-fold cross-validation of the evaluation data. The mean accuracy across all participants was 96.3% (SD: ±2.7%). Cross-validation represents the upper bound of accuracy. Also, we computed accuracy using the initial training data only, which reflects the real-time performance of the system. In this case, the accuracy was 80.5% (SD: ±8.7%). With no feedback accuracy decreased to 69.3% when using training data, and remained the same with cross-validation (96.3%). As seen in Figure 8, misclassification occurred most often in the index finger pinch, likely because tendons connected to the index finger were not fully covered by the sensors. As shown shown in Figure 7, that area was covered by the band's fastening strap. The relaxed hand position and pinky pinch was rarely misclassified.

Sensor contributions: Correlation feature selection showed that the number of relevant FSR sensors varied from 4 to 11 (mean: 7.1). As shown in Figure 7, sensors on top of the wrist were more relevant than on the bottom; tendons on the top are near the skin, while tendons on the bottom are bundled together and are deeper. Also, sensors located near muscles were relevant, thus likely contributed to high classification rate of pinky pinch.

Pinch force: The force between fingers during pinch gestures was measured to be between 20 and 169 grams. The measurement was done by calibrated FSR located between the two fingertips. We were concerned that wearing the system can cause discomfort, since FSRs need to be in tight contact with the skin, but none of the participants reported discomfort during the short studies. But, sweating under the band could be uncomfortable during prolonged wear (>2hours).

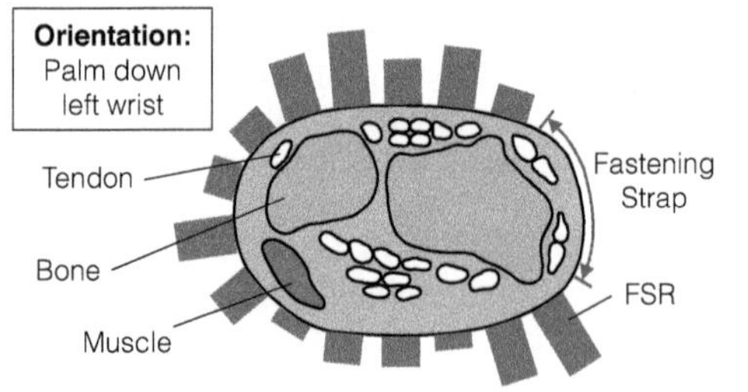

Figure 7: Cross section of the wrist. FSRs are shown in their approximate locations, with heights proportional to the number of times particular FSR was selected as a feature by CFS.

Speed: An important consideration is how fast gestures can be performed. In practice gestures could be performed faster than the allocated 5 seconds. It took a mean of 1.60 sec (SD: ±0.28 sec) to classify a new gesture from the time the command to do the gesture was given to stable classification of gesture by the real-time classifier. The main limitation is the settling time of FSRs, because movements between gestures create large pressure variations that are picked up by FSRs.

Reproducibility: The user should be able to remove the device from the wrist and put it back, without the need to retrain the classifier. We tested reproducibility by removing and putting the device back 3 times for 3 participants, and performing finger pinch experiment during each trial. Participant was provided with immediate feedback. The same initial training data was used in 3 trials. Mean accuracy decreased as trials progressed: 83.2%, 73.3%, and lastly 67.5%. Our results show the low end of accuracy as there was no guidance or calibration mechanisms. Also, applying consistent tightness using Velco strap was especially problematic. The decrease of accuracy was mostly due to completely losing 1 or 2 gestures; as the training data was too rigid to account for tightness. With a calibration mechanics and an automated way to guide sensor placement, no retraining should be needed.

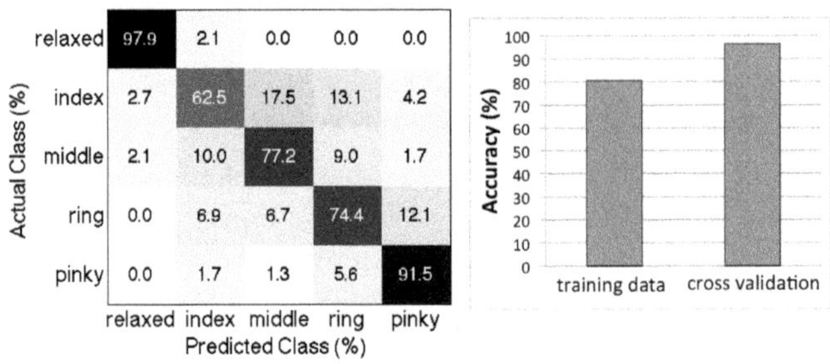

Figure 8: Finger-pinch experiment results. Left: confusion matrix for accuracies using training data. Right: accuracy using training data and cross-validation.

ADDITIONAL GESTURES WITH ACCELEROMETER

The same set of gestures could be identified differently by rotating the hand. In this experiment by using two different hand orientations, we increase the number of gestures from 5 to 10. The advantage of an accelerometer is low power; it adds only 72.6μW to the system's power consumption.

We created an assembly of three SVM classifiers: one for the accelerometer and two for the pressure. The accelerometer classifier used 3 features: accelerations in the X, Y, and Z axis. The pressure classifier was the same as before. Based on the orientation (accelerometer) classifier, one of the two pressure classifiers is activated. We used 3 separate classifiers to avoid the problem of uneven feature sizes: accelerometer had only 3 features, while pressure has up to 15 features.

We recruited 3 participants (1 female, 2 males, age 27-30) for the experiment. A set of 10 gestures was tested. We used the same pinch gestures as before. One set was performed with palm facing the hip, so the palm is parallel to the hip. In the second set the hand was rotated 45 degrees, to be perpendicular to the hip. Each gesture was performed 12 times. Feedback was provided. The accuracy with 10-fold cross-validation was 94.4% (SD: $\pm$ 13.14%), and 73.9% (SD: $\pm$ 17.5%) when using training data only. Accuracy due to chance was 10 %.

LOW POWER OPERATION

Power consumption is an important parameter for on-body and always-available devices. Lower power consumption allows for smaller size and longer operation. Because of the multiplexer, only one FSR is active at any moment. As a result, the voltage divider consumes 60.4μW in a worst case scenario, when the FSR resistance is zero. The multiplexer consumes a maximum of 0.33μW. Therefore, the total power consumption of analog circuitry and sensors is 60.7μW. In comparison, in a state-of-the-art wrist-worn camera-based gesture system [10] the camera itself consumes 60mW, which is at least 3 orders of magnitude higher.

Increasing microcontroller clock speed greatly increases the power consumption. We run the clock at a low speed of 1 MHz, which is sufficient here, because the microcontroller does not need to do any math operations such as filtering. It is only used to sample and send the data. This shows how a light-weight sensing system can save energy. At that speed, microcontroller consumes 2.9mW. The Bluetooth module is the most energy intensive part, requiring a transmission rate of 30 Hz for a real-time operation. At that rate, the Bluetooth consumes 93.1mW. The total power consumption of 96.0mW, allows for 4 hours of continuous wireless operation. A lighter-weight radio (e.g., Bluetooth Low Energy) could reduce the power consumption further.

In a real-world application, the device would be used only occasionally, and should be asleep most of the time. We used a spread-finger gesture, shown in Figure 6, to wake up the device. Once awake, the device will operate continuously and transmit data through the Bluetooth. If no new gestures are detected the device will go back to sleep. During sleep, the system wakes up every 2 seconds to check the pressure readings, and decide to continue sleep or to wake up. The classification of the wake up gesture is done locally on the microcontroller, so data is not send to a laptop for processing. The total energy consumption during sleep mode is 185.0μW. If the device is used for 30 minutes a day, the operation time could be increased to 7 days.

FALSE POSITIVES

If the interface is worn in everyday life, it will be important to avoid false positives; accidental recognition of gestures. Besides reducing energy consumption, wake up gesture has a purpose of unlocking the device; the device would only work once intentionally unlocked. The wake up gesture has higher mean FSR value, than all gestures and hand movements we tested. The wake up gesture was tested during the finger-pinch experiment, and could be detected with a 100% accuracy by thresholding of mean value of all FSRs. Also, as previously proposed in [4], a possible way to prevent false positives is to activate gestures only in specific hand orientation, such as when hand is pointing down.

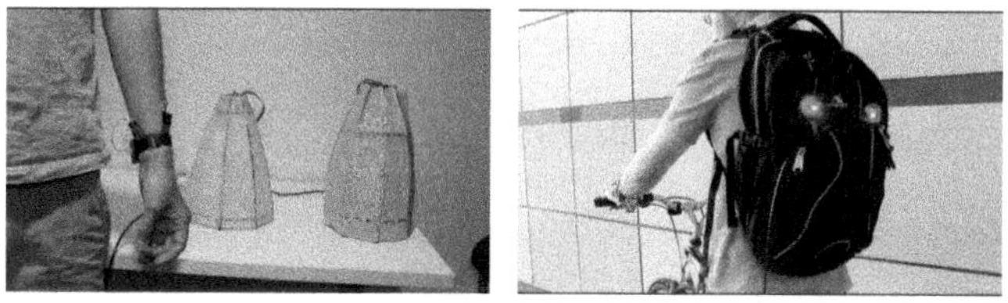

Figure 9: Example applications. Left: controlling two red-green-blue (RGB) lamps. Right: controlling bicycle lights.

EXAMPLE APPLICATIONS AND GESTURE SPACE

To illustrate the real-time performance and to understand the gesture space we developed two applications. The applications are shown in Figure 9, and in the accompanying video.

1. Remote controller application: The 4 pinch gestures can be used as 4 virtual buttons for interaction with external devices, such as a phone or an appliance. Running on the top of the classifier, we developed software that translates finger pinch gestures into button presses. To settle pressure variability, software outputs a button press only if the classifier outputs 10 same gestures in a row. We developed an application to address and control two RGB lamps. The activation gesture is used to connect to the lamps. Using the index and the middle finger pinch gestures, the user cycles and selects which lamp to modify. The selected lamp provides feedback by flashing, and final selection is confirmed with the pinky pinch. Once selected, 3 pinch gestures are used to switch between red, green or blue colors. Finally, with a pinky pinch, the function of the buttons changes and pinches adjust the brightness and turn on/off the lamp.

2. Context awareness app: The system can be trained to detect natural gestures (e.g, hand postures during actions), and infer context. We developed an application for bicycle riders, where wearable lights are controlled by the device. Such app as can enhance safety for riders at night by dynamically controlling the lights. When the rider's hand engages the break handle, the stop light turns on. Also, when the user is gripping handlebars, the lights turn on automatically. Finally, left or right blinkers can be turned on by lifting the middle or pinky fingers.

2. Continuous gestures: As our explorations indicate, the device can track the rotations of the hand. This could provide a 2D input similar to a computer mouse. Also, in the pinch gesture, it is possible to discern how hard two fingers are pressed, therefore adding continuous gestures to pinches. This could add another dimension to pinch gestures, which would be useful in, e.g., controlling volume or zoom.

LIMITATIONS AND FUTURE WORK

Gestures: As mentioned above, the rotation of the hand and pressure variations in pinch gestures could be used as continuous gestures. However, they will cause misclassifications in the discrete pinch gestures. It is part of our future work to develop a mechanism to reliably transition between the continuous and discrete gestures.

Machine learning: We found that each participant needed unique training data; the classifier can not yet generalize the pinch gestures. Also, if gestures are trained using one hand orientation and position, they might not work in a different hand position. To alleviate those issues the classifier should take into account the biomechanics of the hand, and use an inertial measurement unit (IMU) to sense and compensate for different hand positions. Furthermore, in real-life the device might rotate during wear, thus the classifier should be rotation-invariant.

Sensors: We used off-the-shelf FSRs that were not designed for this wearable application. They are relatively large, require assembly into an array, and are affected by sweat and humidity. Using custom-made dense matrix of small pressure sensors would result in higher accuracies, since it will pick up finer pressure variations and cover larger area. Currently, such a matrix can be commercially printed with the FSR ink (e.g., [6]), but the cost and prototyping time is high. Alternatively, FSR arrays can be prototyped using conductive ink-jet technology [9] and Velostat as a pressure-sensitive semiconductor. To prevent effects from sweat and humidity FSRs can be sealed in a waterproof material. Also, a calibration mechanism could be added to compensate for those effects, such as with a skin conductance or temperature sensors. We plan to develop custom FSRs for quick and inexpensive prototyping.

CONCLUSION

In this paper we presented WristFlex, a novel gesture recognition device that uses wrist-worn pressure sensors. We show that the system can detect finger pinch gestures in real-time with high accuracy (>80%) and speed (1.6 sec). Also, we demonstrated the addition of an accelerometer to greatly extend the number of gestures. Furthermore, we explored interaction scenarios such as using of the system to control lighting and context sensing for bicycle riders. The system is attractive for always-available one-hand gesture input. The system has low power consumption; the current prototype can potentially last for a week on a single charge. The device is unobtrusive; it can be made into a small wrist-worm bracelet. Custom pressure sensor arrays can be prototyped with an off-the-shelf printer and conductive ink or commercially with FSR ink. WristFlex is a viable alternative to EMG and camera-based approaches.

ACKNOWLEDGMENTS

This project is partially supported by National Science Foundation award 1256082. We thank B. Knox, C. Kao, N.W. Gong, M. Feldmeier, and G. Dublon for help and advice.

REFERENCES

1. Amento, B., Hill, W., and Terveen, L. The sound of one hand: a wrist-mounted bio-acoustic fingertip gesture interface. In *Proc. CHI '02*, 724–725.
2. Amft, O., Junker, H., Lukowicz, P., Troster, G., and Schuster, C. Sensing muscle activities with body-worn sensors. In *BSN '06*, 4–pp.
3. Bainbridge, R., and Paradiso, J. A. Wireless hand gesture capture through wearable passive tag sensing. In *BSN '11*, 200–204.
4. Deyle, T., Palinko, S., Poole, E. S., and Starner, T. Hambone: A bio-acoustic gesture interface. In *ISWC '07*, 3–10.
5. Fukui, R., Watanabe, M., Gyota, T., Shimosaka, M., and Sato, T. Hand shape classification with a wrist contour sensor: development of a prototype device. In *Proc. Ubicomp '11*, 311–314.
6. Grau, A. M., Hendee, C., Rizzo, J.-R., and Perlin, K. Mechanical force redistribution: enabling seamless, large-format, high-accuracy surface interaction. In *Proc. CHI '14*, 4137–4146.
7. Hall, M., Frank, E., Holmes, G., Pfahringer, B., Reutemann, P., and Witten, I. H. The weka data mining software: an update. *ACM SIGKDD Explorations Newsletter 11*, 1 (2009), 10–18.
8. Harrison, C., Tan, D., and Morris, D. Skinput: appropriating the body as an input surface. In *Proc. CHI '10*, ACM (2010), 453–462.
9. Kawahara, Y., Hodges, S., Cook, B. S., Zhang, C., and Abowd, G. D. Instant inkjet circuits: lab-based inkjet printing to support rapid prototyping of ubicomp devices. In *Proc. Ubicomp '13*, 363–372.
10. Kim, D., Hilliges, O., Izadi, S., Butler, A. D., Chen, J., Oikonomidis, I., and Olivier, P. Digits: freehand 3d interactions anywhere using a wrist-worn gloveless sensor. In *Proc. UIST '12*, 167–176.
11. Nuwer, R. Armband adds a twitch to gesture control. *New Scientist 217*, 2906 (2013), 21.
12. Perng, J. K., Pister, K. S., Fisher, B., and Hollar, S. Acceleration sensing glove. In *ISWC '09*, 178–178.
13. Rekimoto, J. Gesturewrist and gesturepad: Unobtrusive wearable interaction devices. In *ISWC '01*, 21–27.
14. Saponas, T. S., Tan, D. S., Morris, D., Balakrishnan, R., Turner, J., and Landay, J. A. Enabling always-available input with muscle-computer interfaces. In *Proc. UIST '09*, 167–176.
15. Schlömer, T., Poppinga, B., Henze, N., and Boll, S. Gesture recognition with a wii controller. In *Proc. TEI '08*, 11–14.
16. Way, D., and Paradiso, J. A usability user study concerning free-hand microgesture and wrist-worn sensors. In *Proc. BSN '14*,

CommandSpace: Modeling the Relationships between Tasks, Descriptions and Features

Eytan Adar
University of Michigan
Ann Arbor, MI
eadar@umich.edu

Mira Dontcheva
Adobe Research
San Francisco, CA
mirad@adobe.com

Gierad Laput
Carnegie Mellon University
Pittsburgh, PA
gierad.laput@cs.cmu.edu

ABSTRACT
Users often describe what they want to accomplish with an application in a language that is very different from the application's domain language. To address this gap between system and human language, we propose modeling an application's domain language by mining a large corpus of Web documents about the application using deep learning techniques. A high dimensional vector space representation can model the relationships between user tasks, system commands, and natural language descriptions and supports mapping operations, such as identifying likely system commands given natural language queries and identifying user tasks given a trace of user operations. We demonstrate the feasibility of this approach with a system, COMMANDSPACE, for the popular photo editing application Adobe Photoshop. We build and evaluate several applications enabled by our model showing the power and flexibility of this approach.

Author Keywords
Deep-learning, application language domain, natural language interfaces

ACM Classification Keywords
H.5.2 [Information interfaces and presentation]: User Interfaces. - Natural language

INTRODUCTION
There is a fundamental, and well-recognized, gap between the language of an application and the language people use to describe what they want to accomplish [22]. In large and complex applications, such as Adobe Photoshop and GIMP, new features are constantly added, and the number of ways to put these features together into new workflows grows even more rapidly. End users—even experts—find it increasingly difficult to identify the right set of application commands to fulfill a task, find alternative workflows, or learn how to retarget a familiar workflow to an unfamiliar problem.

To accomplish a task, an end user will often respond in the same way: by searching for Web pages—be they manuals, tutorials, forums, or question answering sites. Unfortunately, leveraging this collective knowledge is hampered by restrictive tools. Conventional search engines allow an end-user to express a query, refine that query when the results are not suitable, dig through the results to find the right information, and repeat the process again—an inefficient and limited solution to the problem. Query-Feature Graphs (QF-Graphs) [7] attempt to solve this problem by directly tying popular user queries to system features, but they still rely on the underlying bipartite structure of the Web where natural language and system features are held distinct from each other.

In this work, we approach the problem from the perspective of jointly modeling system features and natural language in the same continuous vector space (i.e., each "token"—a word, phrase, or system feature—is represented by an n-dimensional vector). Specifically, we apply a "deep-learning" approach to embed natural language words and phrases (e.g., "orange" or "comic books") as well as system features (e.g., "Filter > Render > Clouds" or "Edit > Transform Warp") in the same vector space. As we demonstrate, this approach supports a number of use cases directly. The simplest, and most natural, calculates the distance from "queries" to commands (e.g., finding all commands related to creating a comic book effect). Similarly, using a command as a query can obtain related commands or even a ranked list of tasks that often use the command.

The appeal of this approach, however, extends beyond these simple mappings. As both syntactic *and* semantic relationships are preserved in this vector space, many other possible applications emerge. For example, a workflow can be retargeted by similarity (e.g., identifying that functions useful for scar removal in a portrait are also applicable to removing a scratch on a car), or even by analogy (e.g., barrel distortion *is to* filter>lens correction *as* mustache distortion *is to* ?). Because these spaces model relationships at a low-level, answers to questions can be provided even if no exact match was ever described on a specific Web page (e.g., while a specific page on removing scratches from cars may not exist, the model will have learned that scars on portraits and scratches on cars are analogous). All of these applications are supported through simple vector algebra.

In this paper we describe COMMANDSPACE, a system to create and query this joint model as well as a set of demonstration applications that make use of the model. We apply COMMANDSPACE to the domain of the image editing software Adobe Photoshop by collecting and processing a corpus of

UIST '14, October 05 - 08 2014, Honolulu, HI, USA
Copyright 2014 ACM 978-1-4503-3069-5/14/10$15.00.
http://dx.doi.org/10.1145/2642918.2647395

Web pages and PDF documents. Unlike prior work, this approach does not require query logs, thesauri or supervise the training in any way. Additionally, by utilizing a deep-learning model, COMMANDSPACE offers a number of desirable features: (a) it works efficiently on extremely large text datasets (we train on nearly 200 million words in a few hours), (b) it is unsupervised and requires no ground truth, (c) it supports a large vocabulary, (d) it is robust to syntactic and semantic transformations, and (e) it offers a flexible mapping between many different constituents (e.g., system features, tasks, common verbs) of an application's domain that can be easily embedded in a variety of applications.

Our contribution in this work is a mechanism for modeling an application's domain language using a deep-learning approach. We demonstrate how system features and other tasks can all be mapped into the same vector space, which preserves syntactic and semantic relations. We identify key properties of this space, demonstrating how to achieve complex tasks using simple vector operations. Finally, we build and evaluate a number of applications using the vector space. These include the standard task-to-tool mapping, which achieves a high level of precision, as well as applications to map commands to tasks, and a mechanism for identifying alternative workflows. Because the system relies on little more than a collection of text related to a domain, we believe that COMMANDSPACE can be readily applied to a variety of applications and APIs.

RELATED WORK

Tasks to commands

To bridge the language gap between user task and system features many modern applications build extensive search features directly into the applications. These can be viewed as a form of "search-driven interactions" where natural language can be used to identify relevant commands. Some companies (e.g., Adobe) couple their help systems with a broader corpus of pages created by people outside the company and offer an in-application shortcut to a Web-search engine that more rapidly ties the query to possible solutions. Others (e.g., Microsoft Office) have sought to enhance their help offering by supporting "show-me" features. Examples include highlighting matching commands in the menu, or controlling the mouse and demonstrating the action.

There are a number of natural-language interfaces that seek to simply bridge the language gap by using natural language as the system language. Commercial systems such as Apple's Siri, Android's Google Now, and Microsoft's Cortana all attempt to directly interpret a user's speech to execute system commands. Others have tried to provide natural language interfaces to applications such as databases [2], image editing tools [14], and the operating system [4]. Such systems are rapidly improving and are becoming more flexible and more powerful. Nonetheless, they are carefully engineered to support mapping human language to system language.

One approach to mapping user tasks to system commands is to use a standard search engine (e.g., search for task on a search engine and extract matching commands from retrieved documents). However, such an approach requires an extensive thesaurus to work effectively as many task variants will never be observed in the corpus. Even approaches with extensive thesauri [25] still can not easily account for the domain specific terms or other syntactic or semantic relationships. Similarly, traditional techniques that use query-log mining [27] to find associations between queries (e.g., identifying instances of refinement or expansion) are not feasible as they require data that is difficult to obtain.

The most similar approach to our own is the work on QF-Graphs [7]. QF-Graphs are built by identifying common tasks by search log mining and connecting those to system features. A bi-partite graph with common tasks on one side and features on the other is constructed by linking tasks with commands through text mining. Fourney et al. suggest a number of applications for this model including search driven interactions (e.g., search for a task and get back a list of commands), dynamic tooltips (mapping back from feature to task to display in a tooltip), and app-to-app analogy (mapping a feature in one application to a feature in another). While powerful, this technique is limited in that it does not attempt to jointly model features and tasks. Each "translation" step potentially accumulates errors. For example, to find similar commands using the QF abstraction, one needs to map commands to tasks and back to commands (with no indication about the type of relationship between the two commands). In COMMANDSPACE, commands exist in the same space and their relationship (angle and magnitude in vector space) reflect specific relationships (e.g., "alternative" or "inverse"). Furthermore, QF-graphs are focused on terms that are present in the search query logs. With our approach, we can use semantic relationships to offer suggestions for tasks that were never explicitly described in a document. For example, there may not be a tutorial for removing silverware out of a scene, but there may be tutorials showing how to mask silverware and tutorials how to remove objects. COMMANDSPACE models the relationship between these tasks using system features and can make appropriate recommendations for a task where it does not have a repository of content. Finally, QF-Graphs rely on search-engine APIs, which offer little information as to how the result list is generated or how synonyms are used.

Commands to commands

The CommunityCommands system [17] builds models of commands by utilizing ideas from collaborative filtering. Namely, the space is modeled by using a user-item representation where each end-user has a vector representation of command usage. This allows the system to identify similar users (those that utilize similar commands) and to propose non-overlapping commands to each other user. This approach effectively provides users with suggestions to unfamiliar tools. However, CommunityCommands is not designed to offer alternatives to a particular tool because these relationships are not explicitly modeled.

Commands to tasks

The Lumiere Project [10], the basis of Microsoft's Clippy, was the first system to model user behavior and make in-app suggestions. However, this approach was not intended

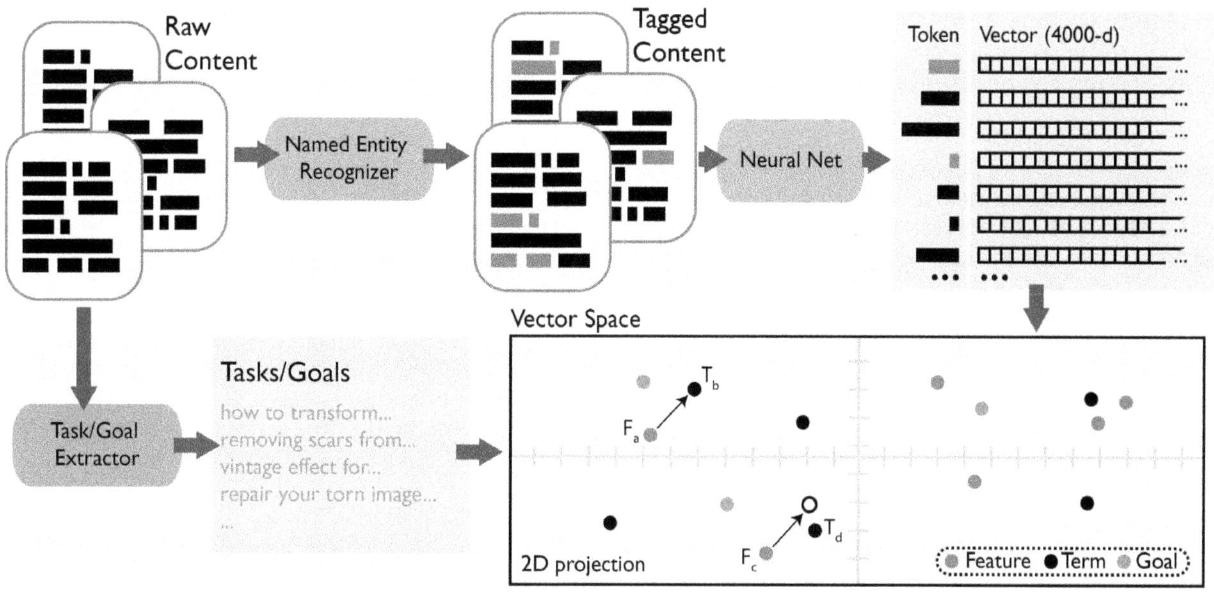

Figure 1. Here is the general architecture for COMMANDSPACE. Raw content crawled from the Web is analyzed by a CRF-based Named-Entity Recognizer (NER) and tagged. The Neural Network transforms all terms (including identified system features) into a n-dimensional vector space representation (n=4000). Simultaneously a task/goal extractor component pulls possible task descriptions from the raw content. A linear vector space allows us to compare generic terms (T), goals (G), and system features (F) in the same space, thus supporting our mapping function.

to scale to the whole of the application's language (or the end user's) but focused on narrow task prediction. While there has been some effort to identify common repeated subsequences (extensively reviewed in [8]), or to predict next commands (e.g., [6, 15]), these are fundamentally different tasks. They often rely on collected logs or traces to identify patterns and produce predictions. Our goal is to be able to support related (and next) commands by mining "found" text.

In the software engineering community a few solutions have tried to bridge API elements and error language (e.g., compiler errors) to explanatory material (e.g., [12, 9]). This material may be produced by crowd-workers or simply be highly ranked pages in a search result. This task is fundamentally different in that it is intended to support the end user in their developer role by finding relevant documentation (rather than automatically "explaining" what they are doing). That said, errors are part of the application's language domain and may lead to interesting connections between features, tasks, and errors. While our dataset includes information about errors, we did not explicitly tag errors in COMMANDSPACE. This remains an interesting direction for future work.

Distributed vector representations

Recent work on "deep-learning" has focused on expanding the techniques to text [20, 19]. Specifically, this research has utilized neural networks to learn continuous language models through large text collections. The techniques offer a mechanism for projecting text into a lower dimensional representation that preserves semantic and syntactic relationships. Conventionally, such models are trained on a text collection where tokens are single words or simple phrases. The models themselves are based on a number of "architectures," including continuous-bags-of-words (CBOW) and skip-grams. CBOW architectures predict a word given the observed words immediately before and immediately after the term (e.g., predict w_n given w_{n-1} and w_{n+1}). Skip-grams (or n-grams in which skipping words is allowable) predict the words immediately before and immediately after the observed term (e.g., predict w_{n-1} and w_{n+1} given w_n). The probabilities associated with each term are learned and represented in a lower-dimensional vector space. In our work we use these techniques to model the space of commands and text. By identifying references to commands in the original text and converting these to special tokens, command "objects" and natural language words and phrases can be simultaneously projected into the same space, thus supporting simultaneous vector transformations.

SYSTEM OVERVIEW

Figure 1 illustrates the COMMANDSPACE architecture. To train the system, we crawl text documents on the Web including step-by-step tutorials, question-and-answer websites, and discussion forums. Such documents capture both the general function of system features (e.g., "*Filter > Blur* averages adjacent pixel values to smooth the image") as well as contextualized use (e.g., "*Filter > Blur* can be used to achieve a tilt-shift effect"). A Named-Entity Recognizer (NER) based on a trained Conditional Random Field (CRF) extractor identifies system features in the raw text and replaces those with unique identifiers. The labeled data then goes into a neural-network, which models the application's domain language using a distributed vector representation. To do this modeling we leverage the *word2vec* implementation [18]. Finally, we use simple vector transformations to map natural language to system features and vice versa.

COMMANDSPACE also identifies phrases describing "goals" or "tasks" from the raw content using a simple, heuristic-based extractor. The extracted goals can be projected into our vector space (Figure 1, labeled in blue) by summing the vectors for the constituent terms and normalizing. Thus, we can calculate similarities and find the features that are most similar to specific goals.

COLLECTING THE DATA

To create our collection of Photoshop-related text documents, we issued queries to the Yahoo! search engine through the Yahoo! BOSS API [26] for each of 1339 known "features" (these were semi-automatically extracted from localization strings for Photoshop with some manual cleaning and annotation). Features include tools (e.g., *Line Tool*), menus (e.g., *"Layer > Layer Style > Global Light"*), and panels (e.g., *Channel Select*). Because some tools can appear in multiple applications, we included the term 'photoshop' in each query to restrict results from the search engine (e.g., *photoshop 'Line Tool'*). We retrieved up to 1000 matching results for each query yielding 187346 unique URLs that mentioned both Photoshop and at least one menu or command. Using the Nutch Web crawler [3], we crawled outward through the links of each webpage to collect 1.4M Web pages. In addition, we introduced the full text of approximately two dozen books related to Photoshop.

Identifying and labeling system features

First, we used Boilerpipe [11] to strip page template information and retain only page text. Next, we tagged tool or menu references in the text using either direct string matching for known strings (the 1339 known features) or a trained Conditional Random Field (CRF) extractor. We trained the CRF on a small set of tutorial pages using the features described in [13]. The CRF learned contextual cues indicating the presence of a string representing a system feature. For example, a button is often preceded by the phrase "click on." The CRF identified the *Clouds Filter* in both sentences: (1) "Click the Filter > Render > Clouds ...," and (2) "Click the Clouds option from the Filter > Render ...." In the first sentence the tagged phrase is "Filter > Render > Clouds" and in the second the CRF tags "Clouds option from the Filter > Render."

We compared tagged phrases to all known commands using Jaccard distance, which measures text overlap, and selected the one with the highest score. While more sophisticated variants of this are possible [23], we found that this simple approach worked well enough. We replaced each matched phrase with a unique feature ID in the raw text. In the example above, both sentences became: "Click the filter_render_clouds ..." This unique ID was treated as a single token in the neural network, which creates a vector for each token representing a system feature.

Despite crawling 1.4M webpages, we were only able to find roughly 50% of the 1339 system features in those webpages. Qualitatively, we found that tagging was not nearly as accurate as described in [13] (largely due to the extreme diversity of language in the "wild"). While we believe we are able to capture the more popular system features, we can increase system feature coverage by dynamically creating vectors for any missing features without loss in performance. We describe this in more detail below.

Adding common natural language phrases

In addition to tagging system features, we also tag common natural language phrases. For example, we replace all occurrences of "comic books" with *comic_books*, "album cover" with *album_cover*, and "brightly colored" with *brightly_colored*. To do this tagging, we use the *word2phrase* program (part of the *word2vec* suite [20, 19]) and identify common n-grams that have been observed a significant number of times (in our case, 30).

Final tagged content

In a final step, we filtered the 1.4M set of webpages to English text pages that contained at least one system feature. We define English text pages as pages that contain at least 60% English words. The result set includes 173,567 pages with over 173M words.

MODELING THE SPACE

To perform the vector space modeling we make use of the *word2vec* implementation [18]. We experimented with a number of configurations (see Evaluation) to determine the training parameters. We resolved on a vectors size of 4000, a window of 10 words, an occurrence threshold of .001, using hierarchical softmax, and a minimum number of word occurrence of 30. Once trained, the neural network produces a set of vectors that can support a variety of mapping functions. Because both system features and natural-language text are mapped to the same space–they are both treated as "tokens"–we are able to measure distances between the vector forms of those terms to identify the best match.

Mapping terms, features and goals

Given goal statements, G (e.g., "give this image a comic book effect" or simply "comic book") we would like to identify those system features F (e.g., "halftone effect filter") that can be used to support it: $S(g_i \in G) \rightarrow F$, where S is our search function. Conversely, we would like to identify possible goals given a set of utilized features: $S(f_i \in F) \rightarrow G$. In the former case, the end users are expressing a need or goal in descriptive natural language, and we would like to isolate those system features that could support them in their task. In the latter case, we may have a partial trace of the user actions within the application, and we would like to identify the most likely goals they are pursuing. While this second type of mapping is less conventional, there are a number of compelling applications. For example, a developer could leverage this technique to label collected log traces of user behavior to understand not just which features are being used but *why*.

The vector space representation allows us to use conventional vector-based distance measures (e.g., euclidean, Manhattan distance, and cosine similarity). We have experimented with a few techniques and qualitatively found cosine distance to work well both in providing good results and being highly performant. Thus, our mapping function S is calculated as:

$$S(t_i \in T) = max_k(cosine(t_i, t_j), t_j \in T, t_i \neq t_j)$$

Where T are all tokens, max_k are the top-k most similar tokens to our input token, t_i. The cosine distance is simply the normalized dot product: $(A \cdot B)/(||A|| \times ||B||)$ where A and

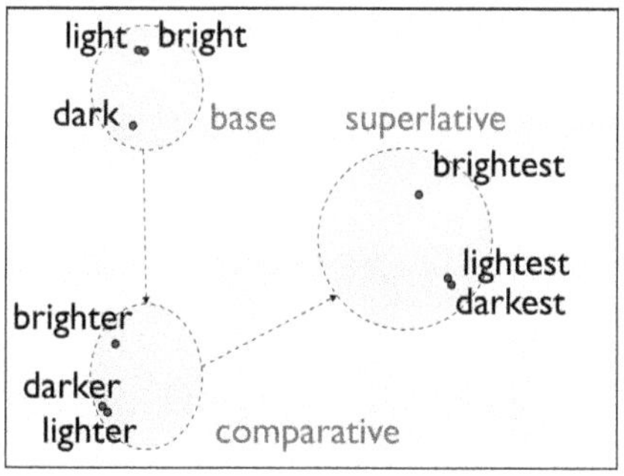

Figure 2. Mappings of term vectors (using PCA) for comparative terms.

B are vectors. If the input to S are multiple tokens we generate a new vector by summing the vectors for all tokens and re-normalizing (e.g., $V(\text{"A B"}) = V(A) + V(B)$).

As a simple demonstration of the function in practical use, we query for the string "shrink nose." (i.e., $S(shrink\ nose) \rightarrow F?$). Internally, we sum the vectors for "shrink" and "nose" to generate a new vector. This vector is compared to the vector of each system feature. The 10 most related features returned are: (1) *filter > liquify* (distance = 0.20); (2) *edit > transform > skew* (0.18); (3) *layer > arrange > send to back* (0.18); (4) *layer > new layer > via cut* (0.17); (5) *select > transform selection* (0.17); (6) *select > grow* (0.16) ; (7) *view > zoom in* (0.16) ; (8) *edit > transform warp* (0.16); (9) *edit > transform > distort* (0.15); (10) *view > show selection edges* (0.15).

The "shrink nose" example shows the power and downside of this approach. While all the results are reasonable, they confound different tasks. For example, the intent may be to literally shrink the nose. The results returned, however, capture both the idea of shrinking the nose (through layers, transforms, and the liquify filter) but also the idea of zooming in and out of the canvas to "shrink." We consider this challenge later when building our applications.

Syntactic and semantic regularities

As described earlier, vectors generated by the neural network maintain a number of regularities. While it is more evident that synonyms should be near each other, distributed vectors also preserve other relationships that are significantly more complex. The common example in the literature [20, 19] is that the vector for King, $V(King)$, minus the vector for Man, plus the vector for Woman is equal to the vector for Queen ($V(King) - V(Man) + V(Woman) = V(Queen)$). We refer the interested reader to this literature for further examples of semantic relationships.

Figure 2 illustrates one such relationship. The visualization is the 2D Principle-Component Analysis (PCA) projection of the tokens in each of the diagrams. The Figure maps base adjectives (light, dark, bright) with their comparative forms (lighter, darker, brighter) and superlative forms (lightest, darkest, brightest). Note that the forms cluster and that pairs (e.g., base:comparative, base:superlative, comparative:superlative) have roughly the same magnitude and direction of transformation (e.g., getting from light to lighter is the same transform as dark to darker). This regularity may be used, for example, to identify different spectrums of actions and associated commands (e.g., which commands produce *light* $\rightarrow$ *lighter* $\rightarrow$ *lightest*). Other relationships that are preserved include pluralization and part-to-whole semantics (e.g., tree to leaf and eye to mouth).

These regularities can be leveraged using the "analogy" transformation. That is, if we select a pair of vectors, $V(F_a)$ and $V(T_b)$, where we know the relationship we want to maintain (e.g., plural, base:comparative, part:whole, etc.) we can find other pairs by picking a new token, F_c and transforming it in the same magnitude/direction. That is, if $F_a : T_b :: F_c : T_d$ then $V(T_d) \approx V(F_a) - V(T_b) + V(F_c)$.

Phrases from strings

While any specific phrase (e.g., "create a grungy album cover") may not occur frequently enough in the corpus for the system to identify it as a token (e.g., *create_a_grungy_album_cover*), we nonetheless want to construct a vector representation for this string so that comparisons are possible (e.g., how close is this goal to a specific system feature?). We find that it is often appropriate to simply sum the constituent tokens into a new vector. In this case, $V(create\_a\_grungy\_album\_cover = V(create) + V(a) + \cdots + V(cover)$. While we would rather have actual instances of the entire phrase, we demonstrate that this works well enough for many applications.

Interestingly, one can weight specific terms by adding extra vectors into the sum. For example, to emphasize "grungy" we can add an extra $V(grungy)$ to the sum. Conversely, one can de-emphasize specific terms tokens by subtracting them out. For example (see Table 1), when identifying commands related to the query "erase," the system returns a combination of eraser tools (e.g., *Eraser Tool* or *Background Eraser Tool*) as well as operations related to masking (e.g., *Layer > Layer Mask > Apply* and *Layer > Layer Mask > Delete*). All these commands are highly similar to the *erase* vector (and are in fact different ways to erase content in Photoshop). By adding or subtracting vectors, the set of operations can be focused. For example, $V(erase) + V(mask)$ biases the recommendations to those commands that are close to both by moving the erase vector in the direction of the mask vector. On the other hand, $V(erase) - V(mask)$ will eliminate masking related commands by subtracting out the mask vector from erase. As Table 1 shows, the results can be radically different.

Returning to our previous nose-shrinking example, instead of adding the vector for the command $V(filter\_liquify)$ to the query string, we may simply remove zoom: $V(shrink\ nose) - V(zoom)$. All returned commands now correctly target distortion related operations. We believe that this technique can be used to refine suggestions dynamically based on either behavioral input (the user said 'erase' and then clicked on a mask tool) or explicitly expressed in language (e.g., 'erase without masking').

Growing the vector space

In some situations we would like to "permanently" add novel tokens into our vector space. For example by adding system features that we were unable to detect in the text or creating representative "goal" vectors.

V_1, erase	V_2, erase + mask	V_3, erase - mask
eraser tool	eraser tool	eraser tool
background eraser tool	layer > layer mask > delete	background eraser tool
brush tool	layer > layer mask > reveal all	pencil tool
layer > layer mask > reveal all	layer > layer mask > hide all	dodge tool
layer > layer mask > delete	layer layer mask from transparency	3d > progressive render selection
pencil tool	layer > vector mask > reveal all	view > clear guides
layer> layer mask > from transparency	brush tool	edit > transform warp
layer > layer mask > apply	layer > layer mask > apply	edit > step backward
select inverse	layer > layer mask hide selection	smudge tool
edit clear	background erase tool	select brush

Table 1. Top 10 most similar commands to 3 vectors: $V_1 = V(erase)$; $V_2 = V(erase) + V(mask)$; **and** $V_3 = V(erase) - V(mask)$

Improving system feature coverage

The limitation of the CRF-driven feature extraction is that some system features are never found. Nearly 500 unique system features (roughly 50%) are not observed in a significant enough quantity to be included in the model. Though these are often less-popular system features, there are applications in which their applications might be useful.

To recover their vector forms, we can use the summation trick to create a new vector. For all commands that we were unable to find a match, we take their human-readable name and calculate a new vector. This allows us to create new "tokens" even when we have never observed them in the raw text. For example, the *filter > sketch > conté crayon* is not found in a significant number of our crawled pages (often because it is mislabeled as "conte crayon"). We generate a vector by summing $V(filter) + V(sketch) + V(conté) + V(crayon)$ and add this new vector into our space of commands.

Goal construction

Once generated, the vector space largely contains tokens representing words and simple phrases (e.g., grungy or "comic book"). However, we often would like to make use of higher-level goal descriptions. The challenge is finding high quality descriptions and then projecting them into the vector space. QF-Graphs [7] address this by finding common search query suggestions. However, while this may identify common tasks the approach does not capture the long-tail of workflows.

Instead, we leverage our crawled datasets to find natural-language task descriptions. As a first step, we simply extract all page titles and section headings from the crawled documents. We filter common strings that are not task related (e.g., "privacy policy" or "responses to ...") and remove non-English strings. From each string we also remove text such as "step 1:" that precedes the actual descriptive text (e.g., "step 1: create a new layer"). This process generates over 200k unique strings. These can be further refined by finding phrases that start with common verbs related to Photoshop actions (e.g., create, remove, restore, etc.) or statements that start with "How to..." For the experiment reported in the next section we selected the 20.4k goal statements that included the phrase "how to."

Given the task statements, we can generate vectors for them as before (summing constituent vectors). However, because task descriptions often build on previously identified sub-

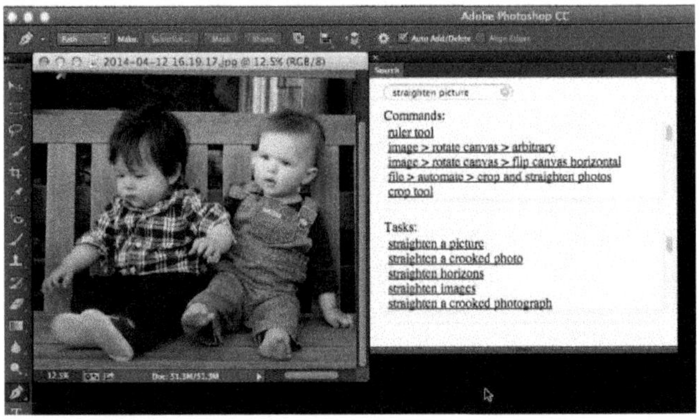

Figure 3. We built a in-app task and command recommender prototype for Adobe Photoshop. In this application of COMMANDSPACE, recommendations are calculated using simple distance metrics (e.g., cosine distance) since tasks and commands are modeled into a single vector representation.

phrases, we pre-process the data to find multi-word tokens. For example, a task description could be "create a graphic novel effect." While we could sum the $V(graphic)$ with $V(novel)$, COMMANDSPACE has already learned a vector for graphic_novel which is preferable (it is more specific). We therefore implement a simple, greedy, phrase matching algorithm that identifies these tokens. Using a suffix-tree we greedily match phrases in the string into their token form (e.g., graphic novel becomes graphic_novel).

APPLICATIONS

We briefly describe a number of applications created using the underlying COMMANDSPACE vector space. We believe that this is but a small sample of what can be constructed.

Keyword search

While users can already use natural language to search the Web for learning materials, COMMANDSPACE enables a task-specific search engine similar to what Brandt et al. built for programmers [5]. Figure 3 shows such an interface inside of Adobe Photoshop. The user can simply type a keyword query to see relevant commands. Additionally, COMMANDSPACE shows tasks that correspond to the query in case the user needs step-by-step guidance. To show relevant commands, COMMANDSPACE maps natural language to Photoshop commands (finding the 5 most similar). To show relevant tasks, COMMANDSPACE maps natural language to the high-level tasks extracted from our corpus. Both commands and tasks are interactive. Clicking on a command invokes it in the software. Clicking on a task, opens the webpage or document corresponding to that task (but can also be used to query back into COMMANDSPACE as a form of query refinement).

Figure 3 shows the results for the query *straighten picture*. Note that COMMANDSPACE returns not just one tool for straightening but four different ones (*ruler tool*, *image > rotate canvas > arbitrary*, *crop tool*, *file > automate > crop and straighten photos*), which can all be used to rotate a photo that may be slightly crooked. If we use a traditional search engine and look for documents that describe how to straighten photos, we find plenty of step-by-step tutorials, but each one focuses on a specific technique rather than giving an overview of all the different tools for straightening. This list of alternatives is not only useful for novices who are still learning about all the available tools, it is also very useful for advanced users who may not know about new features that make their workflows easier. For example, the *image > rotate canvas > arbitrary* feature predates the ruler tool and is much more difficult to use than the *ruler tool*.

query: *remove blur*

Commands	*Tasks*
1) filter > blur > shape blur	1) remove gaussian blur
2) blur tool	2) remove blur without disturbing the other area
3) filter > sharpen > sharpen edges	3) remove facial blemishes
4) layer > smart filter > delete filter mask	4) remove freckles
5) filter > blur > blur	5) reduce blur

COMMANDSPACE can implicitly incorporate user feedback for result optimization. For instance, when the user queries for *remove blur*, many of the command suggestions cause blur rather than remove it. The user selects the sharpen edges filter since that one seems most appropriate. COMMANDSPACE keeps track of the user's choice and offers a new list of commands and tasks to reflect the user's selection. In this case, it offers sharpening tools and features. To support this functionality, we create a new mapping function that takes as input the user's goal (remove blur) and a command feature (the sharpen edges filter). In vector space, we simply add the two vectors together before computing similarity to the space of features and tasks.

While monitoring actions and refining the list can be implicit feedback, an application could also support explicit feedback. In this case, a user can opt to include or exclude selected tasks or commands (e.g., include "reduce blur" but exclude "remove freckles"), and the new query into the system would be a simple linear combination (i.e., $V(reduce\_blur) - V(remove\_freckles)$). This can be used as a form of classical relevance feedback [24] or active learning [1]. However, in an in-application interface, this may be too complex for an end user to understand the semantics, so we opted not to expose those features in the current prototype.

Tool and task recommendations

Previous work has shown that offering recommendations for application commands can be effective in helping users discover new parts of an application [17]. With COMMANDSPACE, we can build a recommender system that maps commands to other commands using natural language words. Rather than using collaborative filtering to base recommendations on how others use the application, we can make recommendations based on how people talk about specific tools and which tools they discuss with the same semantics. For example, when the user is working on a comic book effect and using the ink outlines filter, COMMANDSPACE can recommend relevant subsequent tools or alternative tasks.

query: *filter_brush_strokes_ink_outlines*

Commands	*Task*
1) filter > brush strokes > sumi-e	1) use ink outlines filter to get a cool ink sketch look
2) filter > sketch > charcoal	2) use the oil paint filter
3) filter > artistic > fresco	3) create a graduated and filter effect
4) filter > brush strokes	4) sharpen using high pass filter
5) filter > brush strokes > dark strokes	5) filter snakeskin textures

Similarly, when the user removes an object using the content-aware fill tool, COMMANDSPACE suggests other ways to use the fill tool, such as creating background patterns.

query: *edit_fill*

Commands	*Task*
1) layer > layer style > pattern overlay	1) create seamless background pattern
2) layer > new fill layer > pattern	2) create checkered chess pattern
3) filter > artistic > rough pastels	3) create damask scrapbook paper or pattern repeat background
4) filter > stylize > tiles	4) add gradient fill layer
5) edit > preset manager > patterns > delete pattern	5) create zig zag pattern

As described above, the user can give the system feedback by the tools they use or by giving more information about their intent by selecting a task. COMMANDSPACE can flexibly take as input a trace including any number of commands and task descriptions. We simply sum the respective vectors and calculate new closest commands and tasks.

Connecting commands

COMMANDSPACE can connect commands at the semantic level. Though we can calculate the distances between commands in vector space, it is often unclear why these tools are linked. Are they often used together? Do they act on the same kinds of objects? Do they create similar effects? One of the benefits of our representation is that we can begin to answer these questions by leveraging the human language that is embedded in the space. We achieve this by identifying parts-of-speech tokens (e.g., verbs, nouns, adjectives, etc.) that are similar to the system feature vectors. That is, we identify triads of strongly connected (high similarity) tokens where two of them are commands and the third is a word or phrase.

For example, we see that *File > Automate > Photomerge* and *Image > Adjustments > HDR Toning* are connected, but not why. A Photoshop expert might recognize that to achieve a High Dynamic Range effect (HDR), one often imports multiple images that were exposed at different levels, combines them, and then makes adjustments to specify how to integrate this. If we took the noun "HDR" we would find that it is close to both the *file_automate_photomerge* and *image_adjustments_hdr_toning* system features. This acts to "explain" the relationship between the two commands. Or

Tutorial	Commands (subset)
Retro Comic Book Effect	film_grain, filter_pixelate_color_halftone
Tilt Shift Photograph	gradient_tool, image_adjustments_hue_saturation, filter_blur_lens_blur
Straighten Crooked Photos	ruler_tool, image_rotate_canvas_arbitrary, crop_tool
Content Aware Editing	edit_fill, spot_healing_brush_tool, lasso_tool
Black And White High Key Effect	layer_new_adjustment_layer_gradient_map, filter_blur_gaussian_blur
Sepia	layer_layer_style_blending_options, layer_new_adjustment_layer_photo_filter
Enlarging An Image	image_image_size
Vintage Photo Effect	layer_new_adjustment_layer_curves, image_adjustments_curves

Table 2. A subset of the tutorials used in our COMMANDSPACE evaluation

we might note that the *Sponge Tool* is connected to the *Dodge Tool* but not understand why (the expert would know that both tools are used to change lightness/darkness in different ways). However, by looking at verbs that connect the two, we identify the common verb "brighten" and "whiten."

To do this at a large scale, we tagged the 20k task descriptions we mined from the Web using a conventional part-of-speech tagger [21], and built lists based on their labels (e.g., verbs, nouns, adjectives, adverbs, etc.). The top-100 most frequently appearing words in each category were then used as candidate "explanations." For each word we retrieved the most similar commands (cosine similarity > 0.2) and compute similarity between all of the system features. The edge between those features is labeled with the explanation terms. Note that this map does not include all features, just the ones that are relevant for the most common tasks. Diagrams showing these maps are available as supplementary materials.

The labels we generate can be pushed to the interface to explain recommended commands. For example, if the user chooses the *Crop Tool*, the system can suggest (1) the *Recompose Tool* because both are used to "straighten," and (2) the *Image > Crop* command because both features are used to "crop." Similarly, *Edit > Copy* and the *Magic Wand Tool* are related since both are used to act on a "selection."

EVALUATION

In order to test the various mappings provided by COMMANDSPACE, we created a test set of 40 workflows described in online tutorials. These were selected based on common workflow categories (e.g., turning an image to black and white, dimension adjustments, filters and effects, spot correction). Since some tasks can be completed through many different techniques, we made sure our tutorials covered a range of techniques (e.g., we had three different tutorials describing how to turn an image into black and white). For each tutorial, we performed the steps described and captured all commands used, a subset of which are shown in Table 2. We further categorized all of the commands as task-specific or general-purpose. Task-specific commands are discriminative of a task (e.g., content-aware fill for removing objects), while general purpose commands are task independent (e.g., selecting a layer or moving an object). For the subsequent analysis, we only used task-specific commands since they allow us to better evaluate the effectiveness of COMMANDSPACE.

System commands to user tasks

To assess how well COMMANDSPACE can map a list of system commands to a high-level user task, we performed two analyses—first, at the command level, and then at the workflow level. In the first analysis, we looked at how well COMMANDSPACE predicts the natural language descriptions that correspond to each command. In the workflow-level analysis, we evaluate whether using all commands in a workflow would allow us to predict the title of the tutorial. While ideally our system would be able to identify the correct tutorial as a "top hit" (for direct end-user applications), it is still valuable for us to have a probability distribution over all tutorials.

Command-level descriptions

For each of the 40 tutorials, we generated a vector representation based on the tutorial name. We took the 152 commands that were used in these tutorials and issued them as queries to find the top ranked tutorial (i.e., which tutorial vector was most similar to the command). In all, we found the mean rank to be 16.3 (median: 15, stdev: 12). While this would appear discouraging, it is worth noting that many of the commands are used broadly across many tasks (e.g., *Lasso Tool* or *Gradient Tool*). Thus, the discriminative power of most commands is fairly low. On the other hand, if we took the command that was most discriminative for each tutorial (i.e., the one that resulted in the highest ranking), we found a mean rank of 5.5 (median: 3.5; std: 5.8). Note that a random ordering would deliver an expected rank of 20 for each tool.

In a user application, one would likely want to eliminate these non-discriminative system features. One could identify these non-discriminative features by polling for highly ranked goals or task vectors that are returned for each tool. If this number is low, the tool is not particularly discriminative and may be removed from consideration.

Task-level descriptions

In addition to the test above, we were curious if the union of all features used in a tutorial would be a good signal for what the tutorial was about. We created a summative vector for all the commands in each tutorial, and used this new vector to query into the tutorial space. Again, we identified the rank of the matched result. Here we found a mean of 12.6 (Median: 9, and stdev: 11.4). While the union appears to be more discriminative than each system feature individually, the performance may still be too low for a user-facing application. Again, by weighting those features that are discriminative, this number can likely be improved significantly.

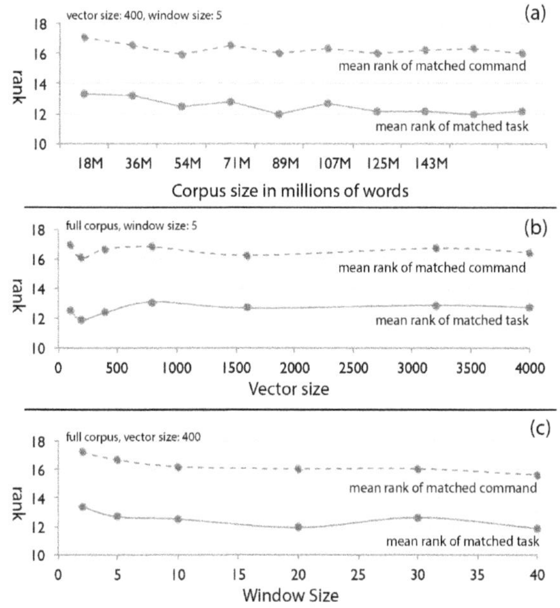

Figure 4. Model performance on command and task evaluations with varying word2vec configurations: (a) varying corpus size; (b) varying vector length; (c) varying window size.

User tasks to system commands

To evaluate whether a natural language query returns the correct set of commands, we query COMMANDSPACE with the titles of our test tutorials. For each command that COMMANDSPACE returns, we match it with all the commands in a given tutorial. We find that on average, COMMANDSPACE returns 23.9% of the commands required by the tutorial in the top 20 results. Qualitatively, we find that the commands that are returned constitute the "key" pieces to a task.

While these results may not make our deep-learning approach useful for all tasks, we believe that our numbers reflect a conservative baseline that can be significantly improved even for conventional search tasks. A great deal of optimization can be achieved by leveraging conventional information retrieval techniques to weight queries and rank responses (e.g., weighting query terms, including models of likelihood of tool use, etc.). Google, as an example, includes 100s of features in page ranking (ranging from document features to click behaviors). Finally, "deep learning" in the context of text is rapidly developing. For example, a recent paper [16] demonstrated vector representations on sentences and paragraphs rather than just words. Given enough data, incorporating such an approach could also improve performance.

Parameter sensitivity

To determine if our results were sensitive to corpus size and training parameter, we constructed a number of different models using *word2vec*. Figure 4 illustrates the effect of using different corpus sizes (a), vector sizes (b), and windows (c). Performance increased (rank of results goes down) with increasing amounts of data. However, even a modest corpus of 17M words (about 35K pages) produced good results. Performance on the specific tasks above appeared to be best with a vector length of 400. Nonetheless, we qualitatively found that longer vectors encoded more semantic relationships. Additional work would be necessary to confirm the optimal size given specific tasks. As the model file size and memory requirements are dramatically reduced with fewer dimensions, tasks that are less demanding in modeling relationships may prefer to use smaller vectors. Finally, we observed some performance gain with increasing window size, but given increased computational costs, the benefit may not justify the time costs.

Comparison to query-feature graphs

To evaluate the Web-mined dataset in isolation, we utilized the set of 20 queries used to test Query-Feature Graphs [7]. These commands were used to test the accuracy of queries related to the GIMP photo-editing software, and were largely (though not entirely) applicable to Photoshop. We modified the commands to their general form and eliminated one which did not apply to Photoshop because they manipulated the UI. Similar to Fourney et al., we used mean precision at 1, 5, and 10 to measure the proportion of test queries whose top-ranking result is judged to be relevant. Table 3 shows our results. Note that we do not view this as an entirely fair comparison, as we crawled a larger corpus. Also, it is possible that Photoshop-related pages are of different and possibly better quality than GIMP pages. Nonetheless, we report these results for completeness.

	P@1	P@5	P@10
COMMANDSPACE	100%	96.6%	85.0%
Query Feature Graphs	80%	66%	43%

Table 3. Comparison between QF-Graphs and COMMANDSPACE

Performance

CRF-Tagging was by far the most costly operation in our chain (approximately 20 pages per minute per core on an Intel Quad Core Q9550 @2.38GhZ with 8Gb of RAM). We believe that this can be significantly optimized by only running the CRF on sentences that are likely to contain matches (as identified by a significantly "cheaper" classifier).

Training the neural network took under 16 hours on 11 cores of a 12 core server (2 Six-Core AMD Opteron(tm) Processor 2431 2.4GHz with 48Gb of RAM). The resulting model could be loaded into approximately 1Gb of memory and held approximately 65k tokens and their corresponding vectors (words, phrases, commands, etc.). Calculating cosine similarities against *all* tokens took under 4 seconds using a naive Python implementation (approximately 60 microseconds per calculation). However, as most applications only compare the "query" against a smaller set, many achieve a real-time feel ($< 100ms$ response times) even in a desktop environment.

CONCLUSIONS

We present COMMANDSPACE, a novel system tying natural language descriptions and low-level application commands. By combining the application's language and the end-user's language together, we are able to create a model that incorporates the syntactic and semantic relationships between terms, goals, and system features. The advantage of the distributed vector representation is that it can be trained in an unsupervised fashion on fairly large corpora. The output is a model that is robust to many transformations and offers flexible mapping between different elements of an application's domain, ranging from natural language to system commands.

New innovations in deep-learning techniques are opening many avenues for integrating these models with user interfaces. We are eager to apply this approach to other domains and to embed the vector models in new tools and existing applications (e.g., desktop applications such as Excel and PowerPoint). We also think that a similar approach may make programming APIs such as jQuery or D3 more accessible. These libraries have a similar vocabulary gap between user goals and specific APIs. Given their popularity and the wealth of available documentation, we believe we can effectively model these domain spaces and support new interactions.

Additional materials and examples are available at http://cond.org/commandspace.html.

REFERENCES

1. Amershi, S., Fogarty, J., and Weld, D. Regroup: interactive machine learning for on-demand group creation in social networks. In *CHI'12* (2012), 21–30.
2. Androutsopoulos, I., Ritchie, G. D., and Thanisch, P. Natural language interfaces to databases-an introduction. *arXiv preprint cmp-lg/9503016* (1995).
3. Apache. Nutch. `https://nutch.apache.org/`. Accessed: 2014-04-15.
4. Branavan, S., Zettlemoyer, L. S., and Barzilay, R. Reading between the lines: Learning to map high-level instructions to commands. In *ACL'10* (2010), 1268–1277.
5. Brandt, J., Dontcheva, M., Weskamp, M., and Klemmer, S. R. Example-centric programming: Integrating web search into the development environment. In *CHI'10* (2010), 513–522.
6. Davison, B. D., and Hirsh, H. Predicting sequences of user actions. In *AAAI/ICML Workshop on Predicting the Future* (1998), 5–12.
7. Fourney, A., Mann, R., and Terry, M. Query-feature graphs: bridging user vocabulary and system functionality. In *UIST'11*, ACM (2011), 207–216.
8. Han, J., Cheng, H., Xin, D., and Yan, X. Frequent pattern mining: current status and future directions. *Data Mining and Knowledge Discovery 15*, 1 (2007), 55–86.
9. Hartmann, B., MacDougall, D., Brandt, J., and Klemmer, S. R. What would other programmers do: suggesting solutions to error messages. In *CHI'10*, ACM (2010), 1019–1028.
10. Horvitz, E., Breese, J., Heckerman, D., Hovel, D., and Rommelse, K. The lumiere project: Bayesian user modeling for inferring the goals and needs of software users. In *Uncertainty in Artificial Intelligence*, Morgan Kaufmann Publishers Inc. (1998), 256–265.
11. Kohlschütter, C., Fankhauser, P., and Nejdl, W. Boilerplate detection using shallow text features. In *WSDM'10*, ACM (2010), 441–450.
12. Kononenko, O., Dietrich, D., Sharma, R., and Holmes, R. Automatically locating relevant programming help online. In *VL/HCC'12*, IEEE (2012), 127–134.
13. Laput, G., Adar, E., Dontcheva, M., and Li, W. Tutorial-based interfaces for cloud-enabled applications. In *UIST'12*, ACM (2012), 113–122.
14. Laput, G. P., Dontcheva, M., Wilensky, G., Chang, W., Agarwala, A., Linder, J., and Adar, E. Pixeltone: a multimodal interface for image editing. In *CHI'13*, ACM (2013), 2185–2194.
15. Lau, T., Bergman, L., Castelli, V., and Oblinger, D. Sheepdog: learning procedures for technical support. In *IUI'04*, ACM (2004), 109–116.
16. Le, Q. V., and Mikolov, T. Distributed representations of sentences and documents. *CoRR abs/1405.4053* (2014).
17. Li, W., Matejka, J., Grossman, T., Konstan, J. A., and Fitzmaurice, G. Design and evaluation of a command recommendation system for software applications. *TOCHI 18*, 2 (2011), 6.
18. Mikolov, T. word2vec, accessed 2014-04-15. `https://code.google.com/p/word2vec/`.
19. Mikolov, T., Chen, K., Corrado, G., and Dean, J. Efficient estimation of word representations in vector space. *arXiv preprint arXiv:1301.3781* (2013).
20. Mikolov, T., Yih, W.-t., and Zweig, G. Linguistic regularities in continuous space word representations. In *NAACL-HLT'13* (2013), 746–751.
21. NLTK. Natural language toolkit. `http://www.nltk.org/`. Accessed: 2014-04-15.
22. Norman, D. A. Cognitive engineering. *User centered system design* (1986), 31–61.
23. Ratinov, L., Roth, D., Downey, D., and Anderson, M. Local and global algorithms for disambiguation to wikipedia. In *NAACL-HLT'11*, ACL (2011), 1375–1384.
24. Rocchio, J. J. Relevance feedback in information retrieval. In *The SMART Retrieval System: Experiments in Automatic Document Processing*, G. Salton, Ed. Prentice-Hall, Englewood Cliffs NJ, 1971.
25. Varelas, G., Voutsakis, E., Raftopoulou, P., Petrakis, E. G., and Milios, E. E. Semantic similarity methods in wordnet and their application to information retrieval on the web. In *International Workshop on Web Information and Data Management*, ACM (2005), 10–16.
26. Yahoo! Search BOSS. `https://boss.yahoo.com/`. Accessed: 2014-04-15.
27. Zhang, Z., and Nasraoui, O. Mining search engine query logs for query recommendation. In *WWW'06*, ACM (2006), 1039–1040.

Predictive Translation Memory: A Mixed-Initiative System for Human Language Translation

Spence Green*, **Jason Chuang**†, **Jeffrey Heer**†, and **Christopher D. Manning***
*Computer Science Department
Stanford University
{spenceg, manning}@stanford.edu
†Computer Science Department
University of Washington
{jcchuang, jheer}@uw.edu

ABSTRACT
The standard approach to computer-aided language translation is post-editing: a machine generates a single translation that a human translator corrects. Recent studies have shown this simple technique to be surprisingly effective, yet it underutilizes the complementary strengths of precision-oriented humans and recall-oriented machines. We present Predictive Translation Memory, an interactive, mixed-initiative system for human language translation. Translators build translations incrementally by considering machine suggestions that update according to the user's current partial translation. In a large-scale study, we find that professional translators are slightly slower in the interactive mode yet produce slightly higher quality translations despite significant prior experience with the baseline post-editing condition. Our analysis identifies significant predictors of time and quality, and also characterizes interactive aid usage. Subjects entered over 99% of characters via interactive aids, a significantly higher fraction than that shown in previous work.

Author Keywords
Language translation; interface design; mixed-initiative; empirical study.

ACM Classification Keywords
H.5.2 Information Interfaces: User Interfaces; I.2.7 Natural Language Processing: Machine Translation

Language translation has all the makings of a mixed-initiative task [11]. Some translations are straightforward and can be routinized while others require linguistic and world knowledge that is difficult to represent. Consider the French word *interprète*, which can mean 'interpreter', 'artist', 'performer', 'spokesperson', or even the pejorative 'mouthpiece.' Whether one is a spokesperson or a mouthpiece depends greatly on context. Recall-oriented machines can instantly generate all of these translations, but humans, equipped with world knowledge, may be needed to select the appropriate one. *Interactive machine translation*—in which humans and machines collaborate—has thus intrigued the research community for decades [8], yet has largely failed in user studies. We hypothesize that classic traps in mixed-initiative design [24], in addition to machine translation (MT) quality, are to blame and are partially responsible for slow commercial uptake.

UIST 2014, October 5–8, 2014, Honolulu, HI, USA.

ACM 978-1-4503-3069-5/14/10 ...$15.00.
http://dx.doi.org/10.1145/2642918.2647408

Figure 1: Example of three interactive aids in PTM. The system predicts which French input words have been translated and shades them in blue. The gray text in the typing box shows the best system prediction for the rest of the translation. The user can accept parts of the system suggestion from the dropdown.

We present *Predictive Translation Memory* (PTM), an interactive, mixed-initiative system for language translation. *Translation memory* is a standard term that refers to a set of bilingual string-string mappings usually consulted via text queries. Our system can be seen as an intelligent translation memory that interactively suggests translations based on user activity. The interface provides *source* (input language) term lookups, local *target* (output language) suggestions at the point of text entry (Figure 1), and full translation suggestions to support gisting of meaning. All suggestions update in real-time according to the user-specified partial translation, yet this updating is discreet to minimize distractions. We focus on the interface design, which minimizes gaze shift and maximizes legibility by interleaving source and target text. In contrast, nearly all translator workbenches use a two-column format, much like a spreadsheet. Qualitative feedback from users supports our design choices.

If a principal problem in the design of interactive knowledge-based systems is the transfer of expertise from human to machine [46], then the system should also enable adaptive MT updating, or *human-assisted machine translation* [44]. Because PTM observes user behavior, the machine is able to refine its suggestions in real-time. Contrast this model with post-editing where the MT system has just one opportunity to produce a suggestion. Our analysis shows that PTM leads to final translations that are significantly different from the initial MT suggestion, but have higher quality according to automatic quality metrics. Crucially, the last machine suggestion is both of high quality and relatively close to the final user translation. This by-product should be useful for future work on automatic MT model updating.

To test the system we conducted the largest published interactive MT user study to date. We hired 32 professional French-English and English-German translators, all of whom were regular users of existing computer-aided translation (CAT) tools. We compared our system to *post-editing*, which is a strong baseline [29, 21], and is also the most common commercial use of MT. We investigated three questions: (1) Is PTM faster than post-edit?, (2) Does PTM enable higher quality translation relative to standard translation quality metrics?, (3) Which interactive aids are most effective? We find that while users are slightly slower in the interactive mode—they must read suggestions in addition to translating—they produce higher quality translations. Translators also use the suggestions to a far greater degree than was observed in the largest previous study of interactive MT [37]. Qualitative feedback shows that most users believe that they would be more productive in the interactive mode with practice.

RELATED WORK

The idea of a "human-machine" partnership for language translation—a mixed-initiative design—was proposed as early as 1960 [4]. Interactive machine translation was first investigated in the 1970s [8] as research funding for fully automatic MT, which was deemed infeasible, was discontinued [44]. Here we review both theorized and implemented systems in both the NLP and HCI literature. We also describe how collaborative translation—recently investigated in HCI—can be seen as interactive translation.

Theorized Interactive MT Systems

Bisbey and Kay [8] proposed a system in which pre-editors would annotate the input with linguistic and semantic information, and then target-language post-editors would select from among ranked machine translations. Although it was never implemented,[1] this system became a template for most subsequent work on interactive MT.

In a survey of qualitative studies, Church and Hovy [14] concluded that users regarded post-editing as "an extremely boring, tedious, and unrewarding chore." They proposed a "superfast typewriter" with an autocomplete key that could fill in the remainder of a word or phrase. Our system draws heavily on their idea of interactive MT as target-text completion.

Evaluated Interactive MT Systems

Early interactive MT systems focused on source pre-editing rather than target generation. Loh and Kong [35] presented a Chinese-to-English system in which human translators annotate the input extensively (phrase boundaries, word senses, etc.). Unpublished results showed greatly reduced post-editing effort to achieve human quality [44]. Whitelock et al. [46] evaluated an English-to-Japanese system in which the machine would query human users about linguistic properties of the English input.

To our knowledge, TransType was the first interactive system [17] that incorporated a modern, statistical MT backend. TransType eschewed source pre-editing in favor of target-text generation aids. The basic unit of translation was the character, whereas our system translates at the word level (however, it provides character-level completions via string-matching in the interface). The TransType UI [18] included an autocomplete dropdown with variable length suggestions selected by an empirical user preference model [19]. Our system instead uses source syntactic constraints to set the prediction length. Their user study [32] found that translation time increased 17% relative to translation from scratch, and that users often typed translations even when the right suggestion was displayed.

TransType2 [16] added a playback mechanism for reviewing user sessions [38] and the ability to accept a full MT suggestion. Additional user studies [36] showed that translators would often accept a full translation and then edit it rather than progressively working through a translation. Our interface explicitly permits this usage via a hot-key, although we most users preferred the interactive aids.

Caitra [30] also included an autocomplete function, and allowed the user to query translations for individual words and phrases. The system could refine its suggestions, but not in real-time: search graphs were pre-computed offline. A user study [29] showed that interactive assistance offered no improvement in terms of time or quality over simple post-editing. In contrast, our system generates new translations each time the user input changes, fully utilizing the search space.

Casmacat [2] is the successor of Caitra. It shares the same back-end MT engine, but has a new UI [1] that supports post-editing, text completion, and term lookup. However, the interface is the standard two-column layout and the full MT suggestion is not always available for gisting, a feature that users have found useful in previous studies [21]. Casmacat still uses pre-computed search graphs. A pilot user study [3] showed a slight improvement in automatic quality relative to post-editing.

The system of Barrachina et al. [6] is exceptional in that it provided interactive post-editing. The MT system proposed a partial suggestion that the user would correct and accept. Then the system would recompute its suggestion and the process would repeat. An analysis of keystroke ratio found a reduction relative to translation from scratch. In contrast, our system recomputes suggestions in real-time and passively tracks what the user is doing; the user can ignore the suggestions.

Collaborative Translation

Collaborative translation can be seen as an alternate mode of interactive assistance, albeit a slow one. Morita and Ishida [40, 41] partitioned a translation job between source pre-editors and target post-editors who iteratively refine a translation. The process is seeded by MT. This design hearkens back to the earliest conceptions of interactive translation [28]. A quality evaluation showed that collaborative translation could improve the raw MT output.

Hu et al. [25, 26] proposed a similar process, but added a richer interface and language-independent annotations for collaboration. Collaborative translations were consistently rated higher than the original MT output. However, this method was very slow, requiring days to post-edit fewer than 100 sentences.

[1]Personal communication with M. Kay.

Mixed-Initiative Interaction Principles

We believe that the failure of previous interactive MT systems (in user studies) may result from known pitfalls of mixed-initiative design. For example, consider Horvitz's [24] principle #2: *considering uncertainty about a user's goals*. Most previous systems violate this principle by assuming that users need either source or target aids, but not both, or neither. Early interactive systems assumed that pre-editing (source) was most useful [35, 46], whereas later systems like TransType and that of Barrachina et al. [6] focused on the target, sometimes forcing the user to accept portions of the target before proceeding. PTM conceals most aids until the user initiates them, and even allows the user to drop into basic text-editing mode if desired.

Also relevant is Horvitz's principle #8: *minimizing the cost of poor guesses about action and timing*. Later systems like Caitra expose portions of the MT system such as translation rules and associated scores directly on the interface. Confidence is usually coded with color. However, MT systems almost certainly contain a very different internal representation of the translation process than humans. Human translators may not understand why, for example, MT systems can propose non-grammatical and incorrect translations like *avec⇒them with* with high confidence. The translation model is full of these noisy rules that can be very useful to the machine, but uninterpretable to the human. Our interface applies rules to aggregated k-best predictions to select human-interpretable, high-confidence suggestions.

The design of PTM draws on additional principles of mixed-initiative design. As a baseline, generating automatic machine translations follows Horvitz's principle #1: *developing significant value-added automation*. PTM users can also select alternate translations from a drop-down menu or simply type the desired target text, both in keeping with principle #5: *employing dialog to resolve key uncertainties*. Following principle #6: *allowing efficient direct invocation and termination*, interactive translation aids are easily toggled on and off with the Escape key, and source word lookups are invoked only upon mouse hover of source text. Real-time updates of machine translations in response to user input enact principle #9: *providing mechanisms for efficient agent-user collaboration to refine results*. Finally, visualizing source coverage of translated words supports principle #11: *maintaining working memory of recent interactions*.

PREDICTIVE TRANSLATION MEMORY

The Predictive Translation Memory system is designed for expert, bilingual translators. Previous studies have shown that professional translators work quickly—they are paid by source words translated—and are usually touch typists [12]. Therefore, the interface is designed to be very responsive, and to be primarily operated by the keyboard. Most aids can be accessed via typing or one of the two hot keys. The current design focuses on the point of text entry and does not include conventional translator workbench features such as workflow management, spell checking, and text formatting.

The system has three components. The *client UI* is written in JavaScript and runs entirely in a web browser. The UI communicates via a RESTful API with the *web service*, which is written in Python and backed by a SQL database. The web service manages translation sessions, serving source documents and recording user actions. The web service also forwards translation requests to the *MT service*, which is a Java servlet running in a J2EE web server. The MT service runs the open source Phrasal MT system, which we heavily modified to support PTM [20]. All UI events are logged to enable analysis and playback. Any translation session can be loaded from the database and replayed in its entirety on the client UI.

In this section, we focus on the UI design decisions. We applied an iterative design process using paper prototyping, rapid prototyping of the client UI connected to the live MT service, a small-scale pilot study, and finally the large-scale user study described in this paper.

Many UI design decisions required significant backend engineering which, in turn, enabled novel interactions. For example, real-time suggestion updating requires the MT service to generate translations at nearly human typing speed.

UI Overview and Walkthrough

We categorized interactions into three groups: source comprehension, target gisting, and target generation. The following outline summarizes the interactions, which are detailed in the following sections. Although the specific design of each feature is novel, those in **bold** have, to our knowledge, never appeared in a translation workbench:

1. Source comprehension
   (a) Word lookups
   (b) **Source coverage**: highlight translated words
2. Target gisting
   (a) Full best translation
   (b) **Real-time updating**: full translation generation
3. Target generation
   (a) Real-time autocomplete dropdown
   (b) **Target reordering**
   (c) Insert complete translation

Human and machine translations appear together in the target text box. During prototyping we found that users were very sensitive to updates in the text box. They wanted to edit the machine suggestions using conventional text manipulation (cut/paste, etc.) rather than the autocomplete interactions. To clarify ownership of regions of the textbox, we adopted the following target text convention:

Black text belongs to the human translator and is never modified by the machine. Gray text belongs to the machine and is never modified by the human translator.

Interactions allow the user to accept portions of the gray text, which becomes black. Subsequent tests showed that users learned to trust that black text is inviolate, and that gray text is only accessible through certain interactions.

Suppose Joe Translator wants to translate a document from French to English. He opens the document in PTM and sees the

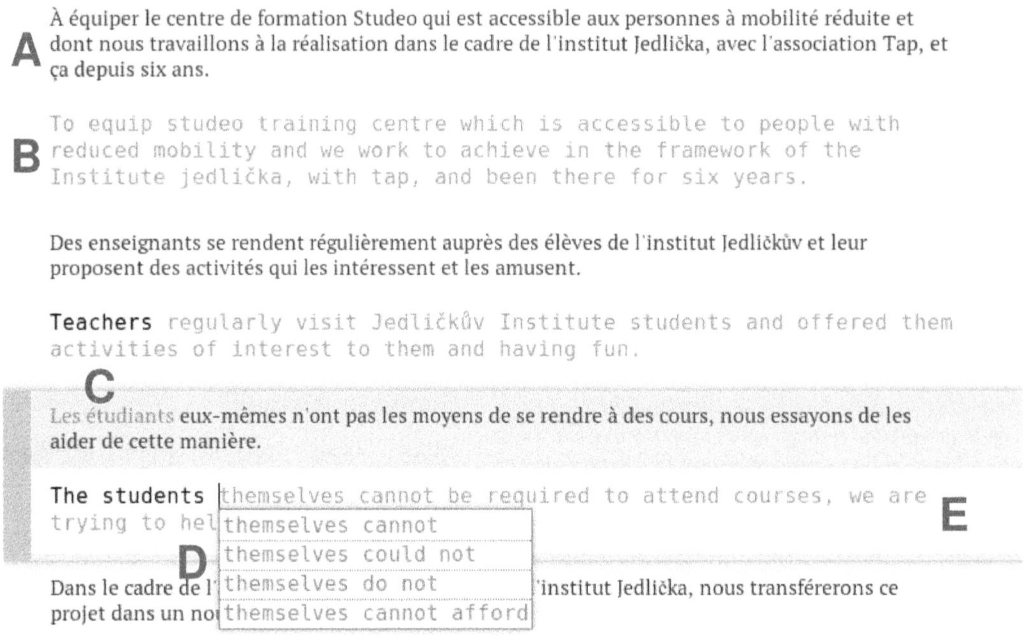

Figure 2: Main translation interface. The interface shows the full document context, with English source inputs (A) interleaved with suggested target translations (B). The sentence in focus is indicated by the blue rectangle, with translated source words shaded (C). The user can navigate between sentences via hot keys. The user can also hide/unhide the autocomplete dropdown (D) and full translation suggestions (E) by toggling the Escape key.

screen in Figure 2. The French sentences (A) are interleaved with English suggested translations (B). Joe must then finalize the translations. When an English translation is finalized, the text becomes black. The following sections describe the interactive aids available to Joe.

Source Comprehension

Word Lookup

Users often trace the source with the mouse cursor while reading [21]. When Joe hovers over source words in the main UI (Figure 2), a menu of up to four ranked translation suggestions appears (Figure 3). We previously proposed [21] showing suggestions proactively for certain parts of speech, but prototyping revealed that this design distracted users. Consequently, we chose a direct-invocation design following Horvitz's principle #6: *allowing efficient direct invocation and termination.* The menu is populated with individual translation rules from the MT translation model. This query does not depend on source context, so it does not require full MT and is very fast, usually returning in under 50ms. The width of the horizontal bars indicates confidence, with the most confident suggestion placed at the bottom, nearest to the cursor. The user can insert a translation suggestion by clicking.

Source Coverage

The interface predicts which source words have already been translated and shades them in blue (Figure 2, C). Joe can quickly find untranslated words in the source. The source coverage is a record of translation interactions consistent with Horvitz's principle #11: *maintaining working memory of recent interactions.* The interaction is based on the word alignments between source and target generated by the MT system. In pilot experiments we found that the raw alignments were too noisy to show to users. We thus developed MT rule-level heuristics that filter the alignments returned to the interface.

Target Gisting

The most common use of MT output is *gisting* [31, p.21]. A rough translation is often sufficient to convey meaning. Translators find MT useful as an initial draft [21].

Full Best Translation

The gray text below each black source input shows the best MT system output (Figure 2, B). As Joe works on the focus translation, the gray text adjusts in the target textbox to show the best suggested completion (Figure 2, E).

Real-time Updating

When Joe starts working on a source sentence, the gray text will update to the most probable completion (Figure 2, E) for his partial translation (black text). The update always appears as a gray completion following the black translation prefix. The human and machine refine the translation collaboratively (Horvitz's principle #9: *providing mechanisms for efficient agent-user collaboration to refine results*) with the machine in a strictly responsive role.

Target Generation

The target textbox shows both the user and machine state simultaneously. This allows Joe to accept parts of the machine suggestion without touching the mouse. The black portion is a text editor: Joe can cut, copy, paste, or otherwise manipulate the black text. However, the gray text is immutable. It cannot be highlighted with the cursor or changed. Joe accesses it through three interactions.

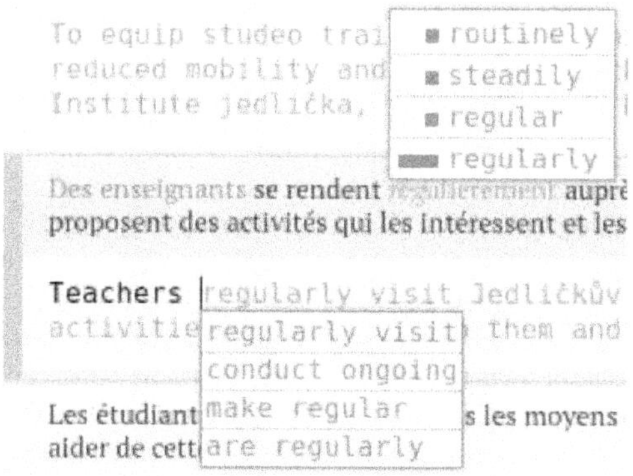

Figure 3: Source word lookup menu (top), which only appears with the autocomplete dropdown (bottom) when the user hovers over a source token. The word lookup suggestions do not depend on the partial translation *Teachers*, so the list of suggestions is different from those shown in the autocomplete dropdown for the same term.

Autocomplete Dropdown

The autocomplete dropdown at the point of text entry is the main translation aid (Figure 2, D). Each time Joe enters a target word or otherwise edits the black prefix, the MT service returns a list of completions conditioned on the accepted prefix. Up to four unique suggestions appear in the target dropdown. The top suggestion can be selected via either the Tab or Enter keys. The dropdown can be navigated with the arrow keys, the mouse, or by beginning to type the desired suggestion. Suggestions that do not match the partial word are filtered until the desired suggestion is at the top of the list. Then the Tab or Enter keys can be used to select it.

The suggestion length is based on the syntax of the source language. As an offline, pre-processing step, we create syntactic parses of the source input with Stanford CoreNLP [39]. The UI combines those parses with word alignments from the full translation suggestions to project syntactic constituents to the target. Syntactic projection is a very old idea that underlies many MT systems (see: [27]). Here we make novel use of it for suggestion prediction filtering. Presently, we project noun phrases, verb phrases (minus the verbal arguments), and prepositional phrases. If no constituents can be projected, then the UI backs off to single-word suggestions.

Target Reordering

So far we have assumed a left-to-right generation scheme, but that design fails for long-distance reordering. For example, in English-to-German translation, some verbs will need to be moved to the very end of a sentence. To that end, the UI supports keyboard-based reordering.

Suppose that Joe sees the (partially correct) suggestion *Wirtschaftliche Offences* 'economic offences' in the gray text (Figure 4) and wants to move that suggestion to the insertion position. Joe can begin typing that string, and the UI will update the autocomplete dropdown with matching strings from the gray text. Consequently, sometimes the autocomplete dropdown will contain suggestions from several positions in the full suggested translation. The user can insert the suggestion from the dropdown in the usual ways.

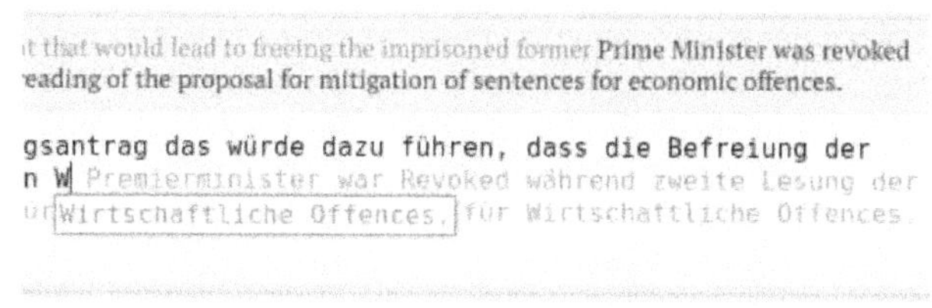

Figure 4: Target reordering feature. The user can move a suggestion to the current editing position by typing the prefix. The system predicts the suggestion length.

Insert Complete Translation

At any time, Joe can accept the full completion by pressing the Control+Enter hot key. Notice that if the user presses this hot key immediately, the full suggestion is inserted, and the interface is effectively a post-editor. This feature greatly accelerates translation when the MT is mostly correct, and the user only wants to make a few changes.

Layout and Typographical Design

Carl [12, p.11] showed that translators spend up to 20% of any translation session reading source text and revising target text, and that harder translations can significantly increase this fraction. However, we noticed that most translator workbenches are optimized for typing, and conform to a tabular, two-column spreadsheet layout—source and target are aligned by row. A spreadsheet design may not be optimal for reading text passages.

Our UI is based on a single-column layout so that the text appears as it would in a document. Sentences are offset from one another primarily because current MT systems process input at the sentence-level. We interleave target-text typing boxes with the source input to minimize gaze shift between source and target. Contrast this with a two-column layout in which the source and target focus positions are nearly always separated by the width of a column.

The compact, single-column layout can obscure the boundaries between source and target, especially for languages with similar writing systems. We found that rendering source and target in different typefaces restored legibility. In our UI, source is rendered in a serifed font, which is commonly used for body text [45]. The target text appears in a monospaced, sans-serif font. Monospaced fonts are conventional for text entry forms. We chose the Paratype[2] font family, which features a large x-height for more readable type [45].

Summary of MT Service

Statistical MT systems come in two general flavors: phrase-based and hierarchical/syntactic. Phrase-based systems *decode* input (i.e., search for translations) left-to-right and can run in $O(n)$ time. Hierarchical/syntactic systems are not restricted to left-to-right processing, but decode with the slower $O(n^3)$ CKY parsing algorithm. Although the left-to-right constraint may not necessarily correspond to the human translation process, we found in pilot studies that users tended to value speed and responsiveness, hence we chose a phrase-based system.

[2] `http://www.paratype.com/public/`

Both types of MT systems are trained in a sequential pipeline: word alignment, translation rule extraction, model parameter learning, and finally decoding of source input. A deployed system like ours must also perform pre- and post-processing of inputs and outputs since the MT system typically expects and generates lowercased, tokenized (e.g., punctuation is separated from words) text that should not be shown to the user. Our system is trained offline prior to usage, but performs pre- and post-processing online inside the MT service.

The UI design required considerable backend engineering to support real-time suggestion updating [20]. Here we summarize a few of the more interesting details.

First, to support suggestions that match a user prefix, we implemented a novel variant of forced decoding. Forced decoding constrains an MT system to produce a specific translation and is sometimes used for parameter learning or diagnostics. Our variant is called *prefix decoding*: we force the system to match the user prefix, and then allow it to translate freely the remainder of the source input. The challenge is that the user prefix may contain words that the system has never seen before, and forced decoding ordinarily fails in this scenario. To solve this problem, we generate synthetic translations from each source word to each unseen target word on-the-fly, and allow the MT system to guess which rules to use.

Second, in pilot experiments we found that unless the MT service could return translations in less than about 300ms, users deemed the UI as "sluggish." The phrase-based decoding algorithm is an instance of *beam search*, an approximate procedure that maintains a ranked list of candidates. Reducing the list (*beam*) size at decoding time increases search speed but usually reduces translation quality, a classic tradeoff. However, we found that if we reduced the beam size during parameter learning, and ran the learning procedure longer, we could mostly recover these losses.

Finally, although we made the MT system considerably faster, it is nonetheless slow relative to conventional AJAX requests (e.g., database queries). Since requests arrive at approximately typing speed while the translator works, the MT service can exhaust its request handling threads waiting on the MT system, and new requests cannot be processed. To solve this problem, we implemented asynchronous request handling via the Java Servlet 3.0 suspend API. Requests can be suspended while waiting for the MT system so that new requests can be queued. This architecture is critical to making the UI responsive.

EXPERIMENTAL DESIGN

We conducted a language translation experiment with a 2 (translation conditions) x n (source sentences) mixed design, where n depended on the language pair (Table 1). Translation conditions (post-edit and PTM/interactive) and source sentences were the independent variables (factors). Experimental subjects saw all factor levels, but not all combinations, since one exposure to a sentence would certainly influence another.

We randomized the assignment of sentences to translation conditions and the order in which the translation conditions appeared to subjects. At most five sentences appeared per screen, and those sentences appeared in the source document order. Subjects received untimed breaks both between translation conditions and after about every five screens within a translation condition.

Subjects completed the experiment remotely on their own hardware. They received personalized login credentials for the web service, which administered the experiment. Upon login, subjects were assured that no identifying personal information would be recorded, and were asked to consent to having translation session information recorded for playback and analysis. Subjects then completed a demographic questionnaire that included information such as prior experience with CAT and self-reported language proficiency. Next, subjects completed a training module that included a 4-minute tutorial video and a practice "sandbox" for developing proficiency with the two translation UIs. Then subjects completed the translation experiment. Subjects could move among sentences within a screen, but could not go back to previous screens to make corrections. Finally, they completed an exit questionnaire. Most of the questions asked users to rate parts of the experiment and the interfaces according to a 5-point Likert scale. Free-form responses to several questions were also solicited.

To minimize the number of learned interactions, we replaced the document navigation hot keys with mouse navigation. To force a contrast with post-edit, we also disabled the Escape key so that subjects could always see at least the full target translation (gray text) and the autocomplete drop-down.

Subjects completed the experiment under time pressure. We used an idle timer identical to that of Green et al. [21], and asked subjects to complete the experiment in a single day.

Linguistic Materials

We chose two language pairs: French-English (Fr-En) and English-German (En-De). French and English are typologically similar, whereas English and German can have different canonical word orders. Anecdotally, French-English is a very easy language pair for MT, whereas English-German is very hard due to long-distance reordering and complex German morphology (e.g., case, gender agreement, etc.).

We chose three text genres: software, medical, and informal news. These genres differ significantly from the majority of the data used to train the MT system, thus replicating the domain mismatch commonly occurring in the translation/localization industry. The software data came from the graphical interfaces of Autodesk AutoCAD and Adobe Photoshop. The medical data was a drug review from the European Medicines Agency. These data came from the TAUS data repository[3] and contained professional human reference translations. The informal news data came from the Workshop on Machine Translation (WMT) 2013 shared task test set [9].

We expected that the software would be hardest, the medical data would be moderately difficult, and the newswire would be easiest. The exit survey confirmed that the software data was indeed hardest, but that the newswire was more challenging than the medical data. Despite the presence of jargon in the

[3] `http://www.tausdata.org/`

	Fr-En	En-De
#subjects	16	16
male/female	7/9	4/12
#source tokens	3,003	3,002
#source sentences	150	173
$ / subject	$265.26	$265.18
Total	$4,244.16	$4,242.88
Grand Total	$8,487.04	

Table 1: Full user study summary. We also conducted a pilot study with four professional Fr-En translators that cost $981.52.

drug review, the sentences were formulaic, and the translators apparently did not need medical expertise to translate them.

The Fr-En dataset contained 3,003 source tokens; the En-De dataset contained 3,002. Average human translators process about 2,700 source tokens per day [43, p.36], so the experiment was designed to replicate a slightly demanding work day.

Selection of Subjects

We recruited professional, freelance translators on Proz, which is the largest online translation community.[4] We posted ads for both language pairs at $0.085 per source word, an average rate in the industry. In addition, we paid $10 to each translator for completing the training module. Table 1 summarizes the experimental subjects and data.

All subjects had significant prior post-editing experience with commercial CAT workbenches. We tried to balance the subject pool by gender, but could not find enough male participants.

MT System

We trained large-scale Fr-En and En-De translation systems on all of the constrained data from the WMT 2013 shared task.[5] For coverage, we also added 61k parallel segments of TAUS data to the En-De bitext, and 26k TAUS segments to the Fr-En bitext. We aligned the parallel data with the Berkeley aligner [33] and built 5-gram language models with lmplz [23]. The MT model contained 18 baseline features [22]. We set the beam size to 800 for both parameter learning and decoding. The held-out parameter tuning set contained a third medical data, a third software, and a third newswire.

Evaluation Metrics

We analyze PTM and post-edit in terms of the two sentence-level response variables: *time* and *quality*. We also measure interactive aid usage by UI event gross statistics.

For quality, we choose BLEU+1 [34], which is the sentence-level variant of the corpus-level BLEU metric [42]. Both variants are computed relative to a reference translation, and combine measures of string and length similarity. To maximize BLEU, a system must produce a translation that contains similar n-grams and is of similar length to the reference. Values are conventionally reported as pseudo-percentages, with 100 indicating an exact match with the reference. BLEU has numerous well-known limitations like invariance to permutations [10]. Nevertheless, it correlates surprisingly well with human judgment [13] and is thus the standard in MT research.

More importantly, BLEU is an MT-tunable metric. Horvitz's principle #12 is *continuing to learn by observing*: a true mixed-initiative MT system will improve with use. Human assessment is the final arbiter when evaluating MT systems, yet it is slow and expensive, preventing its practical application for tuning to human feedback. Therefore we focus on automatic quality assessment, leaving a human evaluation to future work.

We excluded one Fr-En subject and two En-De subjects from the models. One subject misunderstood the instructions of the experiment and proceeded without clarification; another skipped the training module entirely. The third subject encountered a technical problem that prevented session logging.

TIME RESULTS AND ANALYSIS

Our analysis uses linear mixed effects models (LMEM) built with the `lme4` [7] R package. LMEMs are more robust to type II errors than ANOVA when factors represent samples from larger populations. In our case, both subjects and source sentences are small samples from the human and linguistic populations, respectively.

The log of time (in seconds) is the response and the independent variable of interest is translation condition. We also found several other significant covariates and added them to the model. The maximal random effects structure [5] includes random intercepts and slopes for subject, source sentence, and text genre.

Table 2 shows the results. PTM is slightly slower for both language pairs. For Fr-En, the LMEM predicts a mean time (intercept) of 46.0 sec/sentence in post-edit vs. 54.6 sec/sentence in PTM, or 18.7% slower. For En-De, the mean is 51.8 sec/sentence vs. 63.3 sec/sentence in PTM, or 22.1% slower.

The other significant effects reveal more about translator behavior and differences between the two language pairs. Translators were consistently slower for longer sentences (*log source length*) and when suggestions required more editing (*normalized edit distance*). Females were slower, but only at a statistically significant level in En-De. The unbalanced En-De subject pool (Table 1) may be the cause.

The significance and coefficient of *ui order* shows that subjects improved in both conditions with practice. Subjects were significantly slower in En-De, but there is also a significant interaction between interface condition and ui order, meaning that subjects were significantly faster in PTM as the experiment progressed. Figure 5 shows visual evidence.

The high significance level of *no edit* shows that accurate initial MT provided significant acceleration.

Qualitative Time Analysis

The time models show that users were initially slower with PTM, but that they improved over the course of the session. Many users believed that with more practice they could translate faster with PTM. However, this optimism came with the

[4] `http://www.proz.com`

[5] We ended up excluding the noisy CommonCrawl Fr-En data.

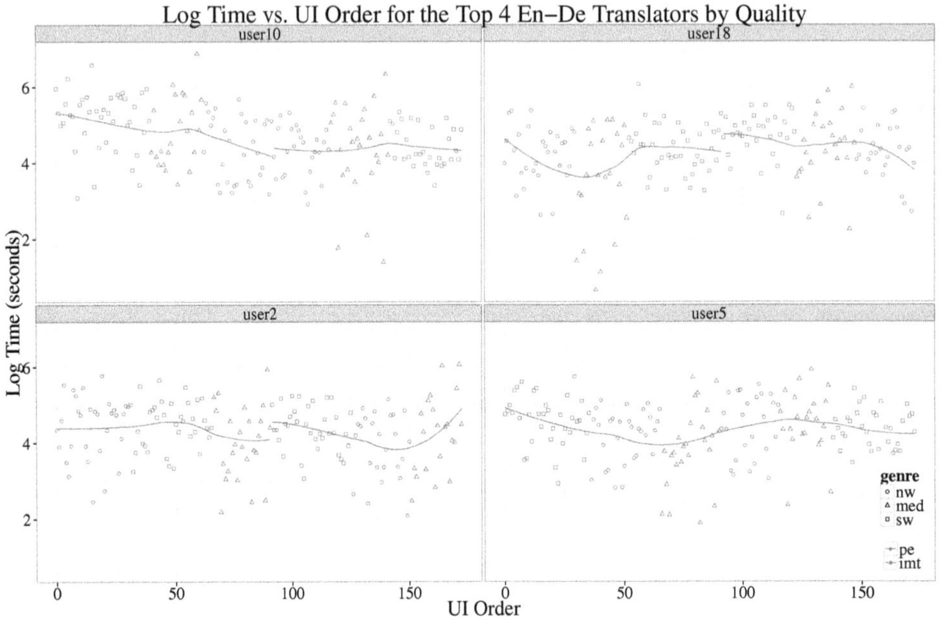

Figure 5: Log time vs. ui order for the top four En-De subjects (according to quality) with loess trend lines. In the post-edit condition (red), three of the four subjects maintain a relatively steady level of performance, whereas in the PTM condition (blue) all four subjects improve with practice. Recall that the order of translation conditions and documents were randomized.

	Fr-En		En-De	
	sign	p	sign	p
ui (PTM)	+	∘	+	••
ui order	−	•	−	••
normalized edit distance	+	•••	+	•••
no edit (True)	−	•••	−	•••
gender (Female)	+		+	•
log source length	+	•••	+	•••
ui (PTM) : ui order	+		−	•

Table 2: LMEM time results for each fixed effect with contrast conditions for binary predictors in (). *normalized edit distance* is computed with respect to the initial MT suggestion, and is normalized by the source length. *ui order* is the order of the source sentence in each ui condition for each subject. The sign of the coefficients can be interpreted as in ordinary linear regression. Statistical significance was computed with a likelihood ratio test: ••• $p < 0.001$; •• $p < 0.01$; • $p < 0.05$; ∘ $p < 0.1$.

caveat that the interactive mode was necessarily more labor intensive. There are more aids to operate and more information to read and analyze:

> Because you spend more time on each word, you have opportunity to see alternative translations.

Subjects noticed that MT quality greatly affected the usefulness of the interactive aids:

> If drop-down suggestions are not of a good quality, reading (without selecting them) may consume extra time.

When asked, "In which interface did you feel most productive?", subjects were almost evenly divided, with 15 selecting post-edit and 14 choosing PTM. When asked, "In general, which interface did you prefer?", the proportions were the same; all but two subjects chose the same interface for both questions. The slight preference for post-edit may result from prior familiarity with that mode. When asked to respond to the statement, "I would use interactive translation features if they were integrated into a CAT product", 11 subjects chose "Strongly Agree" and nine responded "Agree"; only four disagreed with the statement. More encouragingly, when presented with the statement, "I got better at using the interactive interface with practice/experience," 25 subjects agreed or strongly agreed, and none of the subjects disagreed. Free-form responses elaborated on this theme:

> The post-edit mode was easier at first, but in the end the interactive mode was better once I got used to it.

> I felt that if I had time to use the interactive tool and grow accustomed to its way of functioning, it would be quite useful...

> I am used to this [post-edit], this is how Trados [the preeminent CAT tool] works.

TRANSLATION QUALITY RESULTS AND ANALYSIS

We build LMEMs with the same random effects structure but with the log of BLEU+1 as the dependent variable. Table 3 shows the results. For Fr-En, the LMEM predicts a mean (intercept) BLEU+1 score of 33.7 for post-edit and 34.6 for PTM. For En-De, the mean is 25.4 for post-edit and 26.3 for PTM. For both language pairs there is a significant main effect for interface condition.

The inclusion and significance of *log time*—the dependent variable in the previous section—merits discussion. We hy-

	Fr-En		En-De	
	sign	p	sign	p
ui (PTM)	+	∘	+	•
no edit (True)	+	•••	+	∘
gender (Female)	−		+	
log time	−	•••	−	•••

Table 3: LMEM sentence-level quality (BLEU+1) results for each fixed effect with contrast conditions for binary predictors in ().

	Fr-En		En-De	
	BLEU	HBLEU	BLEU	HBLEU
post-edit	38.1	63.7	29.4	44.1
PTM	38.4	62.6	29.5	41.0

Table 4: Corpus-level quality for the two translation conditions. BLEU is the human translations with respect to the independent references; HBLEU is the initial MT suggestion with respect to the human translations. For both metrics a higher score indicates greater similarity.

pothesize some correlation between time and quality. Consider a subject who simply submits the initial MT immediately without any editing. Absent perfect MT this strategy optimizes time at the expense of quality. The time analysis also showed that translation with PTM tends to be slower than post-edit. We have two options: a multivariate model for time and quality, or inclusion of time as a independent variable.

Here we include time as an independent variable since it also captures an important property of BLEU+1. Time is positively correlated with source length ($\rho = 0.53$ for Fr-En and $\rho = 0.43$ for En-De): longer sentences take longer to translate.[6] It is *negatively correlated* with BLEU+1 ($\rho = -0.21$ for Fr-En and $\rho = -0.24$ for En-De). This is a common property of automatic metrics. Since a longer sentence has many more possibilities for translation, the overlap between any single translation and any single reference tends to decrease with length. The models reflect this tendency: for both language pairs *log time* has a negative coefficient.

The significant predictor *no edit* has a positive coefficient for Fr-En. We found that the baseline Fr-En MT system produced a higher corpus-level BLEU score than *any* human subject.[7] This result corroborates previous work [15][31, p.229] on the inability of BLEU to discriminate among accurate translations.

We also computed corpus-level BLEU and HBLEU (Table 4). BLEU is a measure of similarity with the independently generated references. Overall, users produced slightly higher BLEU scores with PTM.[8] HBLEU is measure of similarity with the initial MT suggestions. In post-edit subjects tended to deviate less from the initial MT than in the interactive mode.

We hypothesize two explanations for the results in Table 4. First, our previous work on unaided vs. post-edit [21] showed that MT suggestions prime translators. PTM exposes translators to many more alternatives, encouraging them to deviate further from the initial MT suggestion (lower HBLEU). Second, we do not know the conditions under which the independent references were generated. For example, the En-De references contain English transliterations or loan words for many medical terms, whereas the subjects in our study tended to seek faithful target-language translations. The automatic metrics are sensitive to lexical differences possibly making independent references less useful for general CAT evaluation. A human quality assessment between PTM and post-edit is needed for a final verdict.

[6] Consequently, we remove *log source length* and *normalized edit distance* from the quality model.

[7] Conversely, *all* humans exceeded the baseline En-De MT system.

[8] It is not possible to compute statistical significance because the translations in each condition are unbalanced. Recall that we filtered three subjects completely, and also removed individual translations for which the idle timer expired.

Qualitative Quality Analysis

Subjects perceived our baseline MT systems to be unusually effective. They often submitted lightly edited translations in the post-edit condition. The baseline MT systems were trained on a small amount of in-domain TAUS data, which probably increased accuracy relative to a generic MT system. This may have benefitted the post-edit condition more than PTM:

> I found the machine translations (texts in gray) were of a much better quality than texts generated by Google Translate

> The translations generally did not need too much editing, which is not always the case with machine translations.

Some users articulated aesthetic critiques about MT in general. MT systems tend to produce more literal translations. When users wanted to render more stylistic translations, they believed that PTM was less useful:

> ...choosing a very different translation approach (choice of words, idioms with no equivalent in English...) would be like going against the current—but may have provided a better quality.

> ...distracts from own original translation process by putting words in head that confuse [my] initial translation vision

> ...the translator is less susceptible to be creative

Some users noticed and seemed to resist priming by MT suggestions, even if priming can lead to better translations [21].

INTERACTIVE AID RESULTS AND ANALYSIS

We analyzed the methods subjects used to enter text by aggregating UI events into five modes of target generation: autocomplete-best, source suggestion, autocomplete-alternative, interactive typing, and non-interactive typing.

Autocomplete-best refers to users accepting the best machine translation, turning a block of gray text to black either incrementally (via tabbing) or completely (via the *Insert Complete Translation* interaction). *Source suggestion* refers to users looking up the translation of a source word, and inserting it into the text box via a mouse click. *Autocomplete-alternative* refers

	Fr-En	En-De	Overall
autocomplete-best	17.46	7.85	12.03
interactive typing	45.58	43.06	44.16
non-interactive typing	36.94	49.06	43.79
source suggestion	0.01	0.01	0.01
autocomplete-alternative	0.01	0.01	0.01

Table 5: Percentage (%) of editing events corresponding to the five modes of target generation using the PTM system.

	Fr-En	En-De	Overall
autocomplete-best	71.09	60.46	65.61
interactive typing	15.92	18.37	17.18
non-interactive typing	12.90	20.93	17.04
source suggestion	0.04	0.06	0.05
autocomplete-alternative	0.05	0.19	0.12

Table 6: Percentage (%) of text entered (measured by the number of characters modified) via the five PTM modes of target generation.

to users selecting (using the mouse or down arrow) and accepting a translation from the drop-down menu. *Interactive typing* refers to users typing and modifying the last word in the partial translation, triggering real-time updates to the machine translation. *Non-interactive typing* refers to users modifying any other word in the partial translation.

We recorded over 1.1 million UI events across all translation sessions. Focusing on only PTM sessions, we identified a subset of 258,000 editing events corresponding to the five modes. We exclude non-editing events, such as hovering over the source text for word lookup without insertion. We thus measure the direct means by which the translators entered their translations. A notable shortcoming of previous systems is that users tended to eschew interactive aids in favor often typing.

Table 5 shows the proportions of editing events. Table 6 shows the total amount of text modified, measured by the number of characters entered or deleted by the users. We find that nearly two thirds (65.61%) of the text generated came from autocomplete-best at an average of 14.01 characters per keystroke. Over 88% of the editing events came from typing, but such actions accounted for only 34.22% of the text generated. While a direct comparison with previous systems is not possible, we point out the following contrasts. In the TransType system, the authors commented that their users often "[accepted] predictions in [their] entirety and then edited to ensure its correctness" and reported that 52% of target characters were typed [36]. In the "prediction+options" experiment conducted by Koehn et al. [29], the authors reported that 36% of the final translations were typed, 36% entered via a mouse click, and 27% entered via the tab key to accept machine translations. When working in our PTM system, users directly utilized machine translations to a greater degree than previously reported.

As many professional translators are touch typists, one of our design goals is was retain user focus at the point of text entry and optimize text entry via the keyboard. Tables 5 and 6 show success: 99.98% of the editing events (corresponding to 99.83% of the text entered) were performed using the keyboard via autocomplete-best, interactive, or non-interactive typing.

Qualitative Analysis

We asked the subjects to select the least and most useful interactive aids. Target aids were deemed most useful. The target full translation (gray text) received the most votes (11) followed closely by autocomplete (8). Surprisingly, source aids were deemed least useful, with subjects equally ambivalent about the source coverage aid (11) and the word lookup feature (11).

We also asked subjects to rate each aid on a 5-point Likert scale. Aggregating these ratings leads to a global ranking over aids. Here subjects rated autocomplete highest, the target full translation second, and word lookup third. We also asked subjects to rate the usefulness of the suggestion reordering and length prediction features. The majority of users (20) either agreed or strongly agreed that the length prediction was useful, validating our syntactic projection technique. Subjects were less enthusiastic about reordering, with half disagreeing that it is useful. However, this feature is admittedly the most complex interaction in the UI, so it probably takes the longest to learn and master. Additional development might focus on simplifying or improving the reordering feature.

CONCLUSION

We presented *Predictive Translation Memory*, a new interactive, mixed-initiative language translation system. A large-scale evaluation on two language pairs showed that subjects approach the speed of simple post-editing but with an improvement in automatically evaluated translation quality. The baseline post-edit condition was very strong since all subjects were regular users of post-editing software. Qualitative analysis showed that users liked the interactive aids, and many believed that with more practice, PTM could increase their productivity. Future work should focus on the potential for PTM to improve quality according to a human assessment.

Log analysis revealed that users engaged interactive aids to a greater degree than in previous work on interactive MT. We hope to exploit the rich interaction logs generated by these aids to create an MT system that learns and adapts to each user. The automatic quality results augur well for this research direction. Comparison of French-English and English-German strongly suggested that MT accuracy does affect user behavior. An adaptive system could further increase productivity, especially for language pairs with poor baseline MT.

ACKNOWLEDGEMENTS

We thank TAUS for access to their data repository. The first author is supported by a National Science Foundation Graduate Research Fellowship. This work was also supported by the Defense Advanced Research Projects Agency (DARPA) Broad Operational Language Translation (BOLT) program through IBM. Any opinions, findings, and conclusions or recommendations expressed are those of the author(s) and do not necessarily reflect the view of either DARPA or the US government.

REFERENCES

1. Alabau, V., Bonk, R., Buck, C., Carl, M., Casacuberta, F., García-Martínez, M., et al. Advanced computer aided translation with a web-based workbench. In *2nd Workshop on Post-Editing Technologies and Practice (WPTP)* (2013).
2. Alabau, V., González-Rubio, J., Leiva, L., Ortiz-Martínez, D., Sanchis-Trilles, G., Casacuberta, F., et al. User evaluation of advanced interaction features for a computer-assisted translation workbench. In *MT Summit XIV* (2013).
3. Alabau, V., Leiva, L. A., Ortiz-Martínez, D., and Casacuberta, F. User evaluation of interactive machine translation systems. In *EAMT* (2012).
4. Bar-Hillel, Y. The present status of automatic translation of languages. *Advances in Computers 1* (1960), 91–163.
5. Barr, D. J., Levy, R., Scheepers, C., and Tily, H. J. Random effects structure for confirmatory hypothesis testing: Keep it maximal. *Journal of Memory and Language 68*, 3 (2013), 255–278.
6. Barrachina, S., Bender, O., Casacuberta, F., Civera, J., Cubel, E., Khadivi, S., et al. Statistical approaches to computer-assisted translation. *Computational Linguistics 35*, 1 (2009), 3–28.
7. Bates, D. M. `lme4`: Linear mixed-effects models using S4 classes. Tech. rep., R package version 1.1-5, **`http://cran.r-project.org/package=lme4`**, 2007.
8. Bisbey, R., and Kay, M. The MIND translation system: a study in man-machine collaboration. Tech. Rep. P-4786, Rand Corp., March 1972.
9. Bojar, O., Buck, C., Callison-Burch, C., Federmann, C., Haddow, B., Koehn, P., et al. Findings of the 2013 Workshop on Statistical Machine Translation. In *WMT* (2013).
10. Callison-Burch, C., Osborne, M., and Koehn, P. Re-evaluation the role of BLEU in machine translation research. In *EACL* (2006).
11. Carbonell, J. AI in CAI: An artificial-intelligence approach to computer-assisted instruction. *IEEE Transactions on Man-Machine Systems 11*, 4 (1970), 190–202.
12. Carl, M. A computational framework for a cognitive model of human translation processes. In *Aslib Translating and the Computer Conference* (2010).
13. Cer, D., Manning, C. D., and Jurafsky, D. The best lexical metric for phrase-based statistical MT system optimization. In *NAACL* (2010).
14. Church, K. W., and Hovy, E. Good applications for crummy machine translation. *Machine Translation 8* (1993), 239–258.
15. Culy, C., and Riehemann, S. Z. The limits of n-gram translation evaluation metrics. In *MT Summit IX* (2003).
16. Esteban, J., Lorenzo, J., Valderrábanos, A. S., and Lapalme, G. TransType2: An innovative computer-assisted translation system. In *ACL 2004, Demonstration Session* (2004).
17. Foster, G., Isabelle, P., and Plamondon, P. Target-text mediated interactive machine translation. *Machine Translation 12*, 1/2 (1997), 175–194.
18. Foster, G., Langlais, P., and Lapalme, G. TransType: text prediction for translators. In *HLT* (2002).
19. Foster, G., Langlais, P., and Lapalme, G. User-friendly text prediction for translators. In *EMNLP* (2002).
20. Green, S., Cer, D., and Manning, C. D. Phrasal: A toolkit for new directions in statistical machine translation. In *WMT* (2014).
21. Green, S., Heer, J., and Manning, C. D. The efficacy of human post-editing for language translation. In *CHI* (2013).
22. Green, S., Wang, S., Cer, D., and Manning, C. D. Fast and adaptive online training of feature-rich translation models. In *ACL* (2013).
23. Heafield, K., Pouzyrevsky, I., Clark, J. H., and Koehn, P. Scalable modified Kneser-Ney language model estimation. In *ACL, Short Papers* (2013).
24. Horvitz, E. Principles of mixed-initiative user interfaces. In *CHI* (1999).
25. Hu, C., Bederson, B., and Resnik, P. Translation by iterative collaboration between monolingual users. In *Graphics Interface (GI)* (2010).
26. Hu, C., Resnik, P., Kronrod, Y., and Bederson, B. Deploying MonoTrans widgets in the wild. In *CHI* (2012).
27. Hwa, R., Resnik, P., Weinberg, A., and Kolak, O. Evaluating translational correspondence using annotation projection. In *ACL* (2002).
28. Kay, M. The proper place of men and machines in language translation. Tech. Rep. CSL-80-11, Xerox Palo Alto Research Center (PARC), 1980.
29. Koehn, P. A process study of computer-aided translation. *Machine Translation 23* (2009), 241–263.
30. Koehn, P. A web-based interactive computer aided translation tool. In *ACL-IJCNLP, Software Demonstrations* (2009).
31. Koehn, P. *Statistical Machine Translation*. Cambridge University Press, 2010.
32. Langlais, P., and Lapalme, G. TransType: Development-evaluation cycles to boost translator's productivity. *Machine Translation 17*, 2 (2002), 77–98.
33. Liang, P., Taskar, B., and Klein, D. Alignment by agreement. In *NAACL* (2006).
34. Lin, C.-Y., and Och, F. J. ORANGE: a method for evaluating automatic evaluation metrics for machine translation. In *COLING* (2004).
35. Loh, S.-C., and Kong, L. An interactive online machine translation system (Chinese into English). In *Translating and the computer : proceedings of a seminar, London, 14th November, 1978*. North Holland, 1979.
36. Macklovitch, E. The contribution of end-users to the TransType2 project. In *Machine Translation: From Real Users to Research*, vol. 3265 of *Lecture Notes in Computer Science*. Springer Berlin Heidelberg, 2004, 197–207.
37. Macklovitch, E. TransType2: The last word. In *LREC* (2006).
38. Macklovitch, E., Nguyen, N. T., and La, G. Tracing translations in the making. In *MT Summit X* (2005).
39. Manning, C., Surdeanu, M., Bauer, J., Finkel, J., Bethard, S., and McClosky, D. The Stanford CoreNLP natural language processing toolkit. In *ACL, System Demonstrations* (2014).
40. Morita, D., and Ishida, T. Collaborative translation by monolinguals with machine translators. In *IUI* (2009).
41. Morita, D., and Ishida, T. Designing protocols for collaborative translation. In *Principles of Practice in Multi-Agent Systems* (2009).
42. Papineni, K., Roukos, S., Ward, T., and Zhu, W. BLEU: a method for automatic evaluation of machine translation. In *ACL* (2002).
43. Ray, R. Ten essential research findings for 2013. In *2013 Resource Directory & Index*. Multilingual, 2013.
44. Slocum, J. A survey of machine translation: Its history, current status, and future prospects. *Computational Linguistics 11*, 1 (1985), 1–17.
45. Tinkel, K. Taking it in: What makes type easy to read and why. Tech. rep., Adobe, 1996.
46. Whitelock, P. J., Wood, M. M., Ch, B. J., Holden, N., and Horsfall, H. J. Strategies for interactive machine translation: the experience and implications of the UMIST Japanese project. In *COLING* (1986), 329–334.

Tohme: Detecting Curb Ramps in Google Street View Using Crowdsourcing, Computer Vision, and Machine Learning

Kotaro Hara[1,2], Jin Sun, Robert Moore[1,2], David Jacobs, Jon E. Froehlich[1,2]
[1]Makeability Lab | [2]Human Computer Interaction Lab (HCIL)
Computer Science Department, University of Maryland, College Park
{kotaro, jinsun, dwj, jonf}@cs.umd.edu; rmoore15@umd.edu

Figure 1: In this paper, we present *Tohme*, a scalable system for semi-automatically finding curb ramps in Google Streetview (GSV) panoramic imagery using computer vision, machine learning, and crowdsourcing. The images above show an actual result from our evaluation.

ABSTRACT
Building on recent prior work that combines Google Street View (GSV) and crowdsourcing to remotely collect information on physical world accessibility, we present the first "smart" system, *Tohme*, that combines machine learning, computer vision (CV), and custom crowd interfaces to find curb ramps remotely in GSV scenes. Tohme consists of two workflows, a human labeling pipeline and a CV pipeline with human verification, which are scheduled dynamically based on predicted performance. Using 1,086 GSV scenes (street intersections) from four North American cities and data from 403 crowd workers, we show that Tohme performs similarly in detecting curb ramps compared to a manual labeling approach alone (F-measure: 84% *vs.* 86% baseline) but at a 13% reduction in time cost. Our work contributes the first CV-based curb ramp detection system, a custom machine-learning based workflow controller, a validation of GSV as a viable curb ramp data source, and a detailed examination of why curb ramp detection is a hard problem along with steps forward.

UIST '14, October 05 - 08 2014, Honolulu, HI, USA

http://dx.doi.org/10.1145/2642918.2647403

Author Keywords
Crowdsourcing accessibility; computer vision; Google Street View; Amazon Mechanical Turk

ACM Classification Keywords
H.5.m Information interfaces and presentation; I.4.m Image processing and computer vision; K.4.2 Social Issues

INTRODUCTION
Recent work has examined how to leverage massive online map datasets such as Google Street View (GSV) along with crowdsourcing to collect information about the accessibility of the built environment [21–25]. Early results have been promising; for example, using a manually curated set of static GSV images, Hara *et al.* [23] found that minimally trained crowd workers in Amazon Mechanical Turk (turkers) could find four types of street-level accessibility problems with 81% accuracy. However, the sole reliance on *human* labor limits scalability.

In this paper, we present Tohme[1], a scalable system for remotely collecting geo-located curb ramp data using a combination of crowdsourcing, Computer Vision (CV), machine learning, and online map data. Tohme lowers the overall human time cost of finding accessibility problems in GSV while maintaining result quality (Figure 1). As the first work in this area, we limit ourselves to sidewalk curb

[1] Tohme is a Japanese word that roughly translates to "remote eye."

ramps (sometimes called "curb cuts"), which we selected because of their visual salience, geospatial properties (*e.g.*, often located on corners), and significance to accessibility. For example, in a precedent-setting US court case in 1993, the court ruled that the "*lack of curb cuts is a primary obstacle to the smooth integration of those with disabilities into the commerce of daily life*" and that "*without curb cuts, people with ambulatory disabilities simply cannot navigate the city*" [2].

While some cities maintain a public database of curb ramp information (*e.g.*, [1, 12]), this data can be outdated, erroneous, and expensive to collect. Moreover, it is not integrated into modern mapping tools. In a recent report, the National Council on Disability noted that they could not find comprehensive information on the "*degree to which sidewalks are accessible*" across the US [37]. In addition, the quality of data available in government systems is contingent on the specific policies and technical infrastructure of that particular local administration (*e.g.*, at the city and/or county level). While federal US legislation passed in 1990 mandates the use of ADA-compliant curb ramps in all new road construction and renovation [44], this is not the case across the globe. Our overarching goal is to design a scalable system that can remotely collect accessibility information for any city across the world that has streetscape imagery, which is now broadly available in GSV, Microsoft Bing Maps, and Nokia City Scene.

Tohme is comprised of four custom parts: (i) a web scraper for downloading street intersection data; (ii) two crowd worker interfaces for finding, labeling, and verifying the presence of curb ramps; (iii) state-of-the-art CV algorithms for automatic curb ramp detection; and (iv) a machine learning-based workflow controller, which predicts CV performance and dynamically allocates work to either a human labeling pipeline or a CV + human verification pipeline. While Tohme is purely a data collection system, we envision future work that integrates Tohme's output into accessibility-aware map tools (*e.g.*, a heatmap visualization of a city's accessibility or a smart navigation system that recommends accessible routes).

To evaluate Tohme, we conducted two studies using data we collected from 1,086 intersections across four North American cities. First, to validate the use of GSV imagery as a reliable source of curb ramp knowledge, we conducted physical audits in two of these cities and compared our results to GSV-based audit data. As with previous work exploring the concordance between GSV and the physical world [4, 9, 21, 25, 40], we found high correspondence between the virtual and physical audit data. Second, we evaluated Tohme's performance in detecting curb ramps across our entire dataset with 403 turkers. Alone, the computer vision sub-system currently finds 67% of the curb ramps in the GSV scenes. However, by dynamically allocating work to the CV module or to the slower but more accurate human workers, Tohme performs similarly in detecting curb ramps compared to a manual labeling approach alone (F-measure: 84% *vs.* 86% baseline) but at a 13% reduction in human time cost.

In summary, the primary contribution of this paper is the design and evaluation of the Tohme system as a whole, with secondary contributions being: (i) the first design and evaluation of a computer vision system for automatically detecting curb ramps in images; (ii) the design and study of a "smart" workflow controller that dynamically allocates work based on predicted scene complexity from GIS data and CV output; (iii) a comparative physical *vs.* virtual curb ramp audit study (Study 1), which establishes that GSV is a viable data source for collecting curb ramp data; and (iv) a detailed examination of why curb ramp detection is a hard problem and opportunities for future work in this domain.

RELATED WORK

We describe work in sidewalk assessment, crowdsourcing, computer vision, and dynamic workflow allocation.

Sidewalk Assessment

Traditionally, sidewalk assessment has been conducted via in-person street audits [41, 46] which are labor intensive and costly [40], or via citizen call-in reports, which are done on a reactive basis. Recent mobile apps such as *seeclickfix.com* or NYC311 allow citizens to report street infrastructure problems including damaged or missing curb ramps. However, these systems require *in situ* observation and thus do not scale as well as remote, virtual inquiry.

Crowdsourcing

Recently, Bigham *et al.* argued that current technological infrastructure provides unprecedented access to large sources of human power that can be harnessed to address accessibility challenges [6] (*e.g.*, via crowdsourcing). Examples include VizWiz [5] and Legion:Scribe [34]. Most relevant to this paper is the recent exploration of combining GSV and crowdsourcing for collecting street-level accessibility data including sidewalks [23], bus stops [25], and intersections [21]. Though this prior work demonstrates GSV as a potential accessibility data source, the studies do not examine semi-automatic methods (*e.g.*, using machine learning or CV) as we do here.

Tohme's performance is contingent on crowd workers' speed and accuracy in processing GSV imagery. Prior work exists in studying how to efficiently collect image labels (*e.g.*, [13, 42]). Su *et al.* investigated cost-performance tradeoff between majority vote based labeling and verification based data collection [42], finding quality control via verification improves cost-effectiveness. Recent work by Deng [13] explores methods of efficiently collecting multiclass image annotations by incorporating heuristics such as correlation, hierarchy, and sparsity (*e.g.*, the presence of a keyboard in an image also suggests the presence of correlated objects such as mouse and monitor); however, to our knowledge, no prior work exists on efficiently collecting image labels from crowd workers on large panoramic imagery.

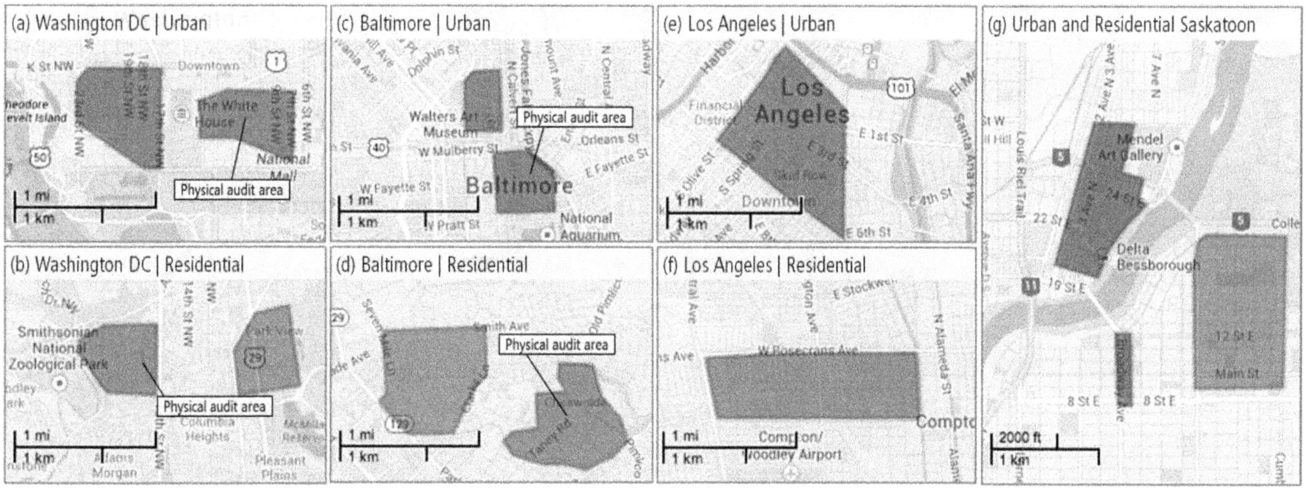

Figure 2: The eight urban (blue) and residential (red) audit areas used in our studies from Washington DC, Baltimore, LA, and Saskatoon. This includes 1,086 intersections across a total area of 11.3km^2. Among these areas, we physically surveyed 273 intersections (see annotations in a-d).

	WASHINGTON DC		BALTIMORE		LOS ANGELES		SASKATOON		OVERALL
Region Type	Downtown	Residential	Downtown	Residential	Downtown	Residential	Downtown	Residential	
Total Area (km²)	1.52	1.13	0.73	2.24	1.91	1.89	0.74	1.13	11.28
# of Intersections	140	124	132	139	132	132	141	146	1,086
# of Curb Ramps*	818	352	476	229	358	186	321	137	2877
# of Missing Curb Ramps*	8	35	32	69	43	214	24	222	647
Avg. GSV Data Age (SD)	1.9 yrs (0.77)	1.6 yrs (0.63)	2.1 yrs (0.75)	0.4 yrs (0.65)	2.0 yrs (0.31)	0.9 yrs (0.24)	4.0 yrs (0.0)	4.0 yrs (0.0)	2.2 (1.3)

Table 1: A breakdown of our eight audit areas. Age calculated from summer 2013. *These counts are based on ground truth data.

Computer Vision

There is a growing body of research applying CV techniques to GSV [48–52]. For example, Xiao *et al.* introduced automatic approaches to model 3D structures of streetscape and building façades using GSV [48, 49]. Zamir *et al.* showed that large-scale image localization, tracking, and commercial entity identification are possible [50–52]. This work demonstrates the potential of combining CV with GSV; however, automatically detecting curb ramps or other accessibility features has not been studied.

Tohme builds on top of existing object detection algorithms from the CV community [11, 16, 45]. For example, we use *Deformable Part Models* (DPMs) [16, 17], one of the top-performing approaches in the PASCAL Visual Object Classes (VOC) challenge, a major object detection and recognition competition [16]. Despite a decade-long effort, however, object detection remains an open problem [7, 47]. For example, even the DPM, which won the "Lifetime Achievement" Prize at the aforementioned PASCAL VOC challenge, has reached 30% precision and 70% recall in 'car' detection [16]. Due to their variation in size, shape, and appearance, curb ramps are similarly difficult to detect. Consequently, we incorporate a "smart" workflow algorithm that attempts to predict poor CV performance and, in those instances, route work to human labelers.

Dynamic Workflow Allocation

Tohme uses machine learning to control its workflow for efficiently collecting data from GSV. Typical workflow adaptions include: varying the number of workers to recruit for a task [30, 47], assigning stronger workers to harder versions of a task [10], and/or fundamentally changing the task an individual worker is given [29, 35] These workflow decisions are made automatically by workflow controllers often by analyzing worker performance history, inferring task difficulty, or estimating cost.

Most relevant to our work is workflow adaptation research in crowdsourcing systems [30, 35, 47]. For example, Lin *et al.* and Welinder *et al.* rely on worker performance histories to either assign different tasks [35] or recruit different numbers of workers [47]. More similar to our work is [29, 30] who infer task difficulty via automated methods and adapt work accordingly. For example, Kamar *et al.* [30] analyzed image features with CV algorithms to predict worker behaviors *a priori* on image annotation tasks and used this to dynamically decide the number of workers to recruit.

Though similar, our work is different both in problem domain (finding curb ramps) as well as in approach. Rather than vary the number of workers per task, our workflow controller infers CV performance and decides whether to use crowd worker labor for verifications or labeling. In addition, we do not simply rely on image features or CV output to determine workflow but also contextual information such as intersection complexity and 3D-point cloud data.

DATASET

Because sidewalk infrastructure can vary in quality, design, and appearance across geographic areas, our study sites include a range of neighborhoods from four North American cities: Washington DC, Baltimore, Los Angeles, and Saskatoon, Saskatchewan (Figure 2; Table 1). For each

Figure 3: Example curb ramps (top two rows) and missing curb ramps (bottom row) from our GSV dataset.

city, we collected data from dense urban cores (shown in blue) and semi-urban residential areas (shown in red). We emphasized neighborhoods with potential high demand for sidewalk accessibility (*e.g.*, areas with schools, shopping centers, libraries, and medical clinics).

We used two data collection approaches: (i) an automated web scraper tool that we developed called *svCrawl*, which downloads GIS-based intersection data, including GSV images, within a geographically defined region; and (ii) a physical survey of a subset of our study sites (four neighborhoods totaling 273 intersections), which was used to validate curb ramp infrastructure found in the GSV images. In all, we used *svCrawl* to download data from 1,086 intersections across 11.3km^2 (Table 1).

To create a ground truth dataset, two members of our research team independently labeled all 1,086 scenes using our custom labeling tool (svLabel). Label disagreements were resolved by consensus. From the ground truth data, we discovered 2,877 curb ramps and 647 missing curb ramps (Figure 3). Of the 1,086 scenes, 218 GSV scenes did *not* require marking a curb ramp or missing curb ramp because the location was not a traditional intersection (*e.g.*, an alleyway with no vertical drop from the sidewalk). These 218 scenes are useful for exploring false positive labeling behavior and were kept in our dataset. The remaining 868 intersections had on average 3.3 curb ramps (*SD*=2.3) and 0.75 missing curb ramps (*SD*=1.3) per intersection. A total of 603/868 intersections were marked as *not* missing any curb ramps. We use the ground truth labels for training and testing our machine learning and CV algorithms and to evaluate crowd worker performance.

At download time (summer 2013), the average age of the GSV images was 2.2 years (*SD*=1.3). As image age is one potential limitation in our approach, it is necessary to first show that GSV is a reasonable data source for deriving curb ramp information, which we do next.

STUDY 1: ASSESSING GSV AS A DATA SOURCE

To establish GSV as a viable curb ramp data source, we must show: (i) that it presents unoccluded views of curb ramps, (ii) that the curb ramps can be reliably found by humans and, potentially, machines, and (iii) that the curb ramps found in GSV adequately reflect the state of the physical world. This study addresses each of these points. Multiple studies have previously demonstrated high concordance between GSV-based audits and audits conducted in the physical world [4, 9, 21, 25]; however, prior work has not examined curb ramps specifically. Though this audit study was labor intensive, it is important to establish GSV as a reliable data source for curb ramp information, as it is the crux of our system's approach.

We conducted physical audits in the summer of 2013 across a subset of our GSV dataset: 273 intersections spanning urban and residential areas in Washington DC and Baltimore (Figure 2). We followed a physical audit process similar to Hara *et al.* [25]. Research team members physically visited each intersection, capturing geo-timestamped pictures (*Mean*=15 per intersection; *SD*=5). These images were analyzed *post hoc* for the actual audit. Surveying the 273 intersections took approximately 25 hours as calculated by image capture timestamps.

Auditing Methodology.

For the auditing process itself, two additional research assistants (different from the above) independently counted the number of *curb ramps* and *missing curb ramps* at each intersection in both the physical and GSV image datasets. An initial visual codebook was composed based on US government standards for sidewalk accessibility [31, 44]. Following the iterative coding method prescribed by Hruschka *et al.* [28], a small subset of the data was individually coded first (five intersections from each area). The coders then met, compared their count data, and updated the codebook appropriately to help reduce ambiguity in edge cases. Both datasets were then coded in entirety (including the original subset, which was recoded). This process was iterated until high agreement was reached.

Calculating Inter-Rater Reliability between Auditors

Before comparing the physical audit data to the GSV audit data, which is the primary goal of Study 1, we first calculated inter-rater reliability between the two coders for each dataset. We applied the Krippendorff's Alpha (α) statistical measure, which is used for calculating inter-rater reliability of count data (see [33]). Results after each of the three coding passes using the iterative scheme from [28] are shown in Table 2. Agreement was consistently high, with the 3rd pass representing the reliability of codes in the final code set. There was initially greater inconsistency in coding *missing* curb ramps *vs.* coding existing curb ramps, perhaps because identifying a missing ramp requires a deeper understanding of the intersection and proper ramp placement.

	PHYSICAL AUDIT IMAGE DATASET			GSV AUDIT IMAGE DATASET		
	1st Pass (α)	2nd Pass (α)	3rd Pass (α)	1st Pass (α)	2nd Pass (α)	3rd Pass (α)
Curb Ramp	0.959	0.960	0.989	0.927	0.928	0.989
Missing C. Ramp	0.647	0.802	0.999	0.631	0.788	0.999
Overall	0.897	0.931	0.996	0.883	0.917	0.996

Table 2: Krippendorff's alpha inter-rater agreement scores between two researchers on both the physical audit and GSV audit image datasets. Following Hruschka *et al.'s* iterative coding methodology, a 3rd audit pass was conducted with an updated codebook to achieve high-agreement scores—in our case, α > 0.996.

Comparing Physical vs. GSV Audit Data

With high agreement verified within each dataset, we can now compare the count scores *between* the datasets. Similar to [25, 40], we calculate a Spearman rank correlation between the two count sets (physical and GSV). This was done for both the curb ramp and missing curb ramp counts. To enable this calculation, however, we first merged the two auditor's counts by taking the average of their counts for missing curb ramps and the average for present curb ramps at each intersection. Using these average counts, a Spearman rank correlation was computed, which shows high correspondence *between* datasets: ρ=0.996 for curb ramps and ρ=0.977 for missing curb ramps ($p < 0.001$). Overall, 1,008 curb ramps were identified in the virtual audit compared to 1,002 with the physical audit; differences were due to construction. The number of missing curb ramps was exactly the same for both datasets (89).

Study 1 Summary

Though the age of images in GSV remains a concern, Study 1 demonstrates that there is remarkably high concordance between curb ramp infrastructure in GSV and the physical world, even though the average image age of our dataset was 2.2 years. With GSV established as a curb ramp dataset source, we now move on to describing Tohme.

A SCALABLE SYSTEM FOR CURB RAMP DETECTION

Tohme is a custom-designed tool for remotely collecting geo-located curb ramp information using a combination of crowdsourcing, CV, machine learning, and online map data. It is comprised of four parts depicted in Figure 4: (i) a web scraper, *Street View Crawl (svCrawl)*, for downloading street intersection data; (ii) two crowd worker interfaces for finding, labeling, and verifying the presence of curb ramps called *svLabel* and *svVerify*; (iii) state-of-the-art CV algorithms for automatically detecting curb ramps (*svDetect*); and (iv) a machine learning-based workflow, called *svControl*, which predicts CV performance on a scenes and allocates work accordingly.

We designed Tohme iteratively with small, informal pilot studies in our laboratory to test early interface ideas. We also performed larger experiments on Amazon Mechanical Turk (MTurk) with a subset of our data to understand how different interfaces affected crowd performance and, more generally, how well crowds could perform our tasks. The CV sub-system, svDetect, also evolved across multiple iterations, and was trained and evaluated using the aforementioned ground truth labels. While our ultimate goal is to deploy Tohme publicly on the web, the current prototype and experiments were deployed on MTurk. Below, we describe each Tohme sub-system.

svCrawl: Automatic Intersection Scraping

svCrawl is a custom web scraper tool written in Python that downloads GIS-related intersection data over a predefined geographic region (Figure 2). It uses the Google Maps API (GMaps API) to enumerate and extract street intersection

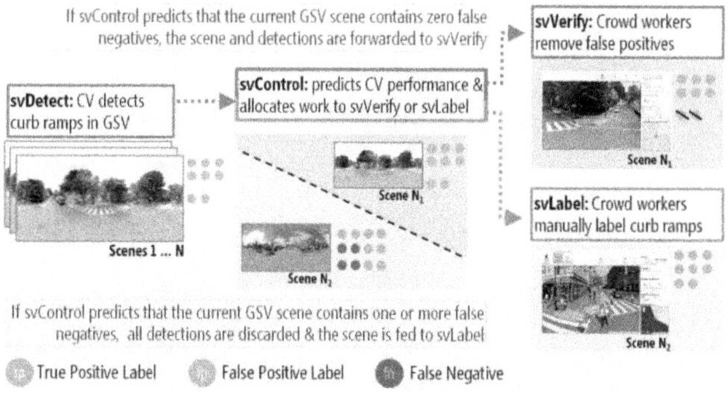

Figure 4: A workflow diagram depicting Tohme's four main sub-systems. In summary, *svDetect* processes every GSV scene producing curb ramp detections with confidence scores. *svControl* predicts whether the scene/detections contain a false negative. If so, the detections are discarded and the scene is fed to *svLabel* for manual labeling. If not, the scene/detections are forwarded to *svVerify* for verification. The workflow attempts to optimize accuracy and speed.

points within selected boundaries. For each intersection, svCrawl downloads four types of data:

1. **A GSV panoramic image** at its source resolution (13,312 x 6,656px). This is our primary data element (*e.g.,* Figure 1).
2. **A 3D-point cloud**, which is captured by the GSV car using LiDAR [3]. The depth data overlays the GSV panorama but at a coarser resolution (512 x 256px; Figure 10). This is used by svDetect to automatically cull the visual search space and by svControl as an intersection complexity input feature.
3. **A top-down abstract map image** of the intersection obtained from the GMaps API (Figure 13), which is used as a training feature in our work scheduler, svControl, to infer intersection complexity (like the depth data).
4. **Associated intersection GIS metadata**, also provided by the GMaps API, such as latitude/longitude, GSV image age, street and city names, and intersection topology.

svLabel: Human-Powered GSV Image Labeling

In Tohme, intersections are labeled either manually, via svLabel, or automatically via svDetect. svLabel is a fully interactive online tool written in Javascript and PHP for finding and labeling curb ramps and missing curb ramps in GSV images (Figures 5-7). Unlike much previous crowd-sourcing GSV work, which uses static imagery to collect labels [21–23], our labeling tool builds on *Bus Stop CSI* [25] to provide a fully interactive 360 degree view of the GSV panoramic image. While this freedom increases user-interaction complexity, it allows the user to more naturally explore the intersection and maintain spatial context while searching for curb ramps. For example, the user can pan

Figure 5: Example curb ramp and missing curb ramp labels from our turk studies. The green/pink outline points denote presence/absence.

Figure 6: The svLabel interface. Crowd workers use the *Explorer Mode* to interactively explore the intersection (via pan and zoom) and switch to the *Labeling Mode* to label curb ramps and missing curb ramps. Clicking the *Submit* button uploads the target labels. The turker is then transported to a new location unless the HIT is complete.

(a) After labeling one corner, the user pans to the right. (b) The user then zooms to get a closer look (c) The user begins labeling the new corner in the zoomed view

Figure 7: svLabel automatically tracks the camera angle and repositions any applied labels in their correct location as the view changes. When the turker pans the scene, the overlay on the map view is updated and the green "explored" area increases (bottom right of interface). Turkers can zoom in up to two levels to inspect distant corners. Labels can be applied at any zoom level and are scaled appropriately.

around the virtual 3D-space from one corner to the next within an intersection.

Using svLabel. When a turker accepts our HIT, they are immediately greeted by a three-stage interactive tutorial (see supplementary video included with paper). The stages progressively teach the turker about the interface (*e.g.*, the location of buttons and other widgets), user interactions (*e.g.*, how to label, zoom, and pan), and task concepts (*e.g.*, the definition of a curb ramp). If mistakes are made, our tutorial tool automatically provides corrective guidance. Turkers must successfully complete one tutorial stage before moving on to the next.

Once the tutorials are completed, we automatically position the turker in one of the audit area intersections and the labeling task begins in earnest. Similar to Bus Stop CSI [25], svLabel has two primary modes of interaction: *Explorer Mode* and *Labeling Mode* (Figure 6). When the user first drops into a scene, s/he defaults into Explorer Mode, which allows for exploration using Street View's native controls. Users are instructed to pan around to explore the 360 degree view of the intersection and visual feedback is provided to track their progress (bottom-right corner of Figure 6). Note: users' movement is restricted to the drop location.

When the user clicks on either the *Curb Ramp* or *Missing Curb Ramp* buttons, the interface switches automatically to Labeling Mode. Here, mouse interactions no longer control the camera view. Instead, the cursor changes to a pen, allowing the user to draw an outline around the visual target—a curb ramp or lack thereof (Figure 5). We chose to have users outline the area rather than simply clicking or drawing a bounding box because the detailed outlines provide a higher degree of granularity for developing and experimenting with our CV algorithms. Once an outline is drawn, the user continues to search the intersection. Our tool automatically tracks the camera angle and repositions any applied labels in their correct location as the intersection view changes. In this way, the labels appear to "stick" to their associated targets. Once the user has surveyed the entire intersection by panning 360 degrees, s/he can submit the task and move on to the next task in the HIT, until all tasks are complete.

Ground Truth Seeding. A single HIT is comprised of either five or six intersections depending on whether it contains a ground truth scene (a scene is just an intersection). This "ground truth seeding" [39] approach is commonly used to dynamically examine, provide feedback about, and improve worker performance. In our case, if a user makes a mistake at a ground truth scene, after hitting the submit button, we provide visual feedback about the error and show the proper corrective action (see video). The user must correct all mistakes before submitting a ground truth task. If no mistakes are detected, the user is congratulated for their good performance. In our current system, there is a 50% chance that a HIT will contain one ground truth scene. The user is not able to tell whether they are working on a ground truth scene until after they submit their work.

svVerify: Human-Powered GSV Label Verification

In addition to providing "curb ramp" and "missing curb ramp" labels, we rely on crowd workers to examine and verify the correctness of previously entered labels. This verification step is common in crowdsourcing systems to increase result quality (*e.g.,* [23, 42]). svVerify (Figure 8) is similar to svLabel in appearance and general workflow but has a simplified interaction (clicking and panning only) and is for an easier task (clicking on incorrect labels).

While we designed both svLabel and svVerify to maximize worker efficiency and accuracy, our expectation was that the verification task would be significantly faster than initially providing manual labels [42]. For verification, users need not perform a time-consuming visual search looking for curb ramps to label but rather can quickly scan for incorrect labels (false positives) to delete. And, unlike labeling, which requires drawing polygonal outlines, the delete interaction is a single click over the offending label (similar to [45]). This enables users to rapidly eliminate *false positive* labels in a scene.

To maintain verification efficiency, however, we did not allow the user to spatially locate *false negatives*. This would essentially turn the verification task into a labeling task, by asking users to apply new "curb ramp" or "curb ramp missing" labels when they noticed a valid location that had not been labeled. Instead, svVerify gathers information on false negatives at a coarser-grained level by asking the user if the current scene was missing any labels after s/he clicks the submit button. Thus, svVerify can detect the presence of

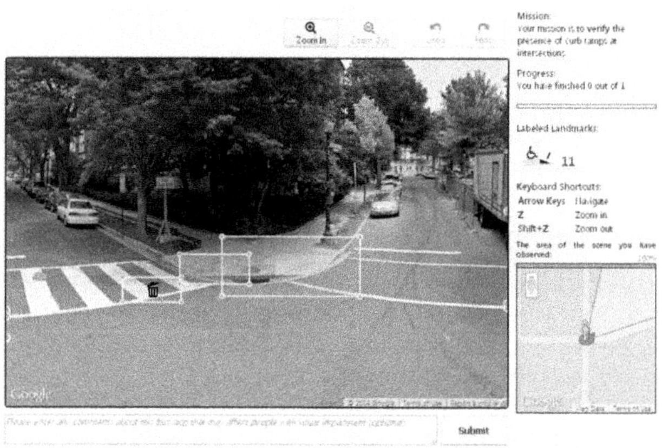

Figure 8: The svVerify interface is similar to svLabel but is designed for verifying rather than labeling. When the mouse hovers over a label, the cursor changes to a garbage can and a click removes the label. The user must pan 360 degrees before submitting the task.

false negatives in an intersection but not their specific location or quantity.

Similar to svLabel, svVerify requires turkers to complete an interactive tutorial before beginning a HIT, which includes instructions about the task, the interface itself, and successfully verifying one intersection. Because verifications are faster than providing labels, we included 10 scenes in each HIT (*vs.* the 5 or 6 in svLabel). In addition, we inserted one ground truth scene into *every* svVerify HIT rather than with 50% probability as was done with svLabel. Note that not all scenes are sent to svVerify for verification, as discussed in the svControl section below. We move now to describing the two more technical parts of Tohme: svDetect and svControl.

svDetect: Detecting Curb Ramps Automatically

While svLabel relies on manual labeling for finding curb ramps, svDetect attempts to do this automatically using CV. Because CV-based object detection is still an open problem—even for well-studied targets such as cars [17] and people [11]—our goal is to create a system that functions well enough to reduce the cost of curb ramp detection *vs.* a manual approach alone.

svDetect uses a three-stage detection process. First, we train a *Deformable Part Model (DPM)* [17], one of the most successful recent approaches in object detection (*e.g.,* [14]), as a first-pass curb ramp detector. Second, we post-process the resulting bounding boxes using non-maximum suppression [36] and 3D-point cloud data to eliminate detector redundancies and false positives. Finally, the remaining bounding boxes are classified using a Support Vector Machine (SVM) [8], which uses features not leveraged by the DPM, further eliminating false positives.

svDetect was designed and tested iteratively. We attempted multiple algorithmic approaches and used preliminary experiments to guide and refine our approach. For example, we previously used a linear SVM with a Histograms of Oriented Gradients (HOG) feature descriptor [26] but found

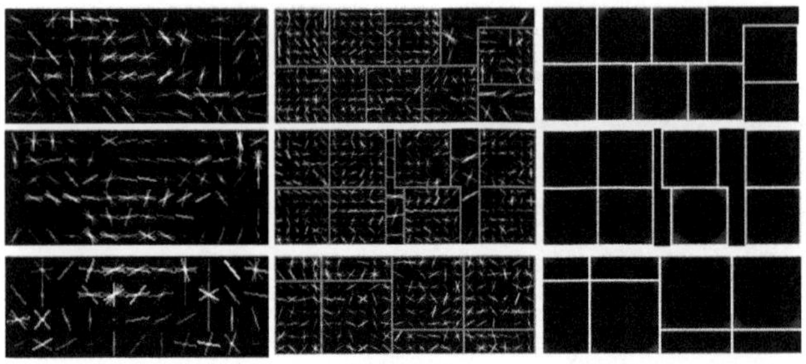

(a) Root filter (b) Parts filter (c) Displacement costs

Figure 9: The trained curb ramp DPM model. Each row represents an automatically learned viewpoint variation. The root and parts filter visualize learned weights for the gradient features. The displacement costs for parts are shown in (c).

that the DPM was able to recognize curb ramps with larger variations. In addition, we found that though the raw GSV image size is 13,312 x 6,656 pixels, there were no detection performance benefits beyond 4,096 x 2,048px (the resolution used throughout this paper). Because it helps explain our design rationale for Tohme, we include our evaluation experiments for svDetect in this section rather than later in the paper.

First Stage: The Curb Ramp Deformable Part Model (DPM)

DPMs are comprised of two parts: a coarse-grained model, called a root filter, and a higher resolution parts model, called a parts filter. DPMs are commonly applied to human detection in images, which provides a useful example. For human detection, the root filter captures the whole human body while part filters are for individual body parts such as the head, hand, and legs (see [16]). The individual parts are learned automatically by the DPM—that is, they are not explicitly defined *a priori*. In addition, how these parts can be positioned around the body (the root filter) is also learned and modeled via displacement costs. This allows a DPM to recognize different configurations of the human body (*e.g.,* sitting *vs.* standing).

In our case, the root filter describes the general appearance of a curb ramp while part filters account for individual components (*e.g.,* edges of the ramp and transitions to the road). DPM creates multiple *components* for a single model (Figure 9) based on bounding box aspect ratios. We suspect that each component implicitly captures different viewpoints of a curb ramp. For our DPM, we used code provided by [19].

Second Stage: Post-Processing DPM Output

In the second stage, we post-process the DPM output in two ways. First, similar to [36], we use non-maximum suppression (NMS) to eliminate redundant bounding boxes. NMS is common in CV and works by greedily selecting bounding boxes with high confidence values and removing overlapping boxes with lower scores. Overlap is defined as the ratio of intersection of the two bounding boxes over the union of those boxes. Based on the criteria established by the PASCAL Visual Object Classes challenge [15], we set our NMS overlap threshold to 50%.

Figure 10: Using code from [38], we download GSV's 3D-point cloud data and use this to create a ground plane mask to post-process DPM output. The 3D depth data is coarse: 512 x 256px.

Our second post-processing step uses the 3D-point cloud data to eliminate curb ramp detections that occur above the ground plane (*e.g.,* bounding boxes in the sky are removed). To do so, the 512 x 256px depth image is resized to the GSV image size (4096 x 2048px) using bilinear interpolation. For each pixel, we calculate a normal vector and generate a mask for those pixels with a strong vertical component. These pixels correspond to the ground plane. Bounding boxes outside of this pixel mask are eliminated (Figure 10 and 11).

Third Stage: SVM-Based Classification

Finally, in the third stage, the remaining bounding boxes are fed into an additional classifier: an SVM. Because the DPM relies solely on gradient features in an image, it does not utilize other important discriminable information such as color or position of the bounding box. Given that street intersections have highly constrained geometrical configurations, curb ramps tend to occur in similar locations—so detection position is important. Thus, for each bounding box, we create a feature vector that includes: RGB color histograms, the top-left and bottom-right corner coordinates of the bounding box in the GSV image along with its width and height, and the detection confidence score from the DPM detector. We use the SVM as a binary classifier to keep or discard detection results from the second stage.

svDetect Training and Results

Two of the three svDetect stages require training: the DPM in Stage 1 and the SVM in Stage 3. For training and testing, we used two-fold cross validation across the 1,086 GSV scenes and 2,877 ground truth curb ramp labels. The GSV scenes were randomly split in half (543 scenes per fold) with one fold initially assigned for training and the other for testing. This process was then repeated with the training and testing folds switched.

To train the DPM (Stage 1), we transform the polygonal ground truth labels into rectangular bounding boxes, which are used as positive training examples. DPM uses a sliding window approach, so the rest of the GSV scene is treated as negative examples (*i.e.,* comprised of negative windows). For each image in the training set, the DPM produces a set of bounding boxes with associated confidence scores. The number of bounding boxes produced per scene is contingent on a minimum score threshold. This threshold is often learned empirically (*e.g.,* [1]). A high threshold would

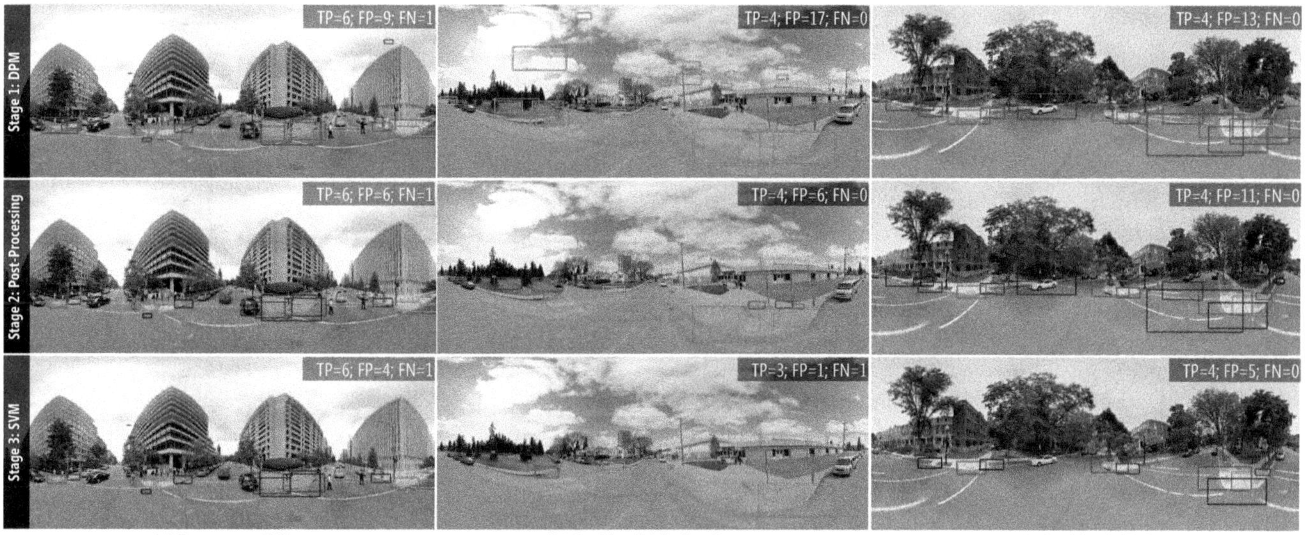

(a) Downtown DC (b) Residential Saskatchewan (c) Residential DC

Figure 11: Example results from svDetect's three-stage curb ramp detection framework. Bounding boxes are colored by confidence score (lighter is higher confidence). As this figure illustrates, setting the detection threshold to -0.99 results in a relatively low false negative rate at a cost of a high false positive rate (false negatives are more expensive to correct). Many false positives are eliminated in Stages 2 and 3. The effect of Stage 2's ground plane mask is evident in (b). Acronyms: TP=true positive; FP=false positive; FN=false negative.

produce a small number of bounding boxes, which would likely result in high precision and low recall; a low threshold would likely lead to low precision and high recall.

To train the SVM (Stage 3), we use the post-processed DPM bounding boxes from Stage 2. The bounding boxes are partitioned into positive and negative samples by calculating area overlap with the ground truth labels. Though there is no universal standard for evaluating "good area overlap" in object detection research, we use 20% overlap (from [18]). Prior work suggests that even 10-15% overlap agreement at the pixel level would be sufficient to confidently localize accessibility problems in images [23]. Thus, positive samples are boxes that overlap with ground truth by more than 20%; negative samples are all other boxes. We extract the aforementioned training features from both the positive and negative bounding boxes. Note that SVM parameters (*e.g.*, coefficient for slack variables) are automatically selected by grid search during training.

Results. To analyze svDetect's overall performance and to determine an appropriate confidence score cutoff for svDetect, we stepped through various DPM detection thresholds (from -3-to-3 with a 0.01 step) and measured the results. For each threshold, we calculated true positive, false positive, and false negative detections for each scene. True positives were assessed as bounding boxes that had 20% overlap with ground truth labels and that had a detection score higher than the currently set threshold. The results are graphed on a precision-recall curve in Figure 12. To balance the number of true positive detections and false positives in our system, we selected a DPM detection threshold of -0.99. At this threshold, svDetect generates an average of 7.0 bounding boxes per intersection (SD=3.7); see Figure 11 for examples. Note: svDetect failed to generate a bounding box for 15 of the 1,086 intersections. These are still included in our performance comparison.

In the ideal, our three-stage detection framework would have both high precision and high recall. As can be observed in Figure 12, this is obviously not the case as ~20% of the curb ramps are never detected (*i.e.*, the recall metric never breaches 80%). With that said, automatically finding curb ramps using CV is a hard problem due to viewpoint variation, illumination, and within/between class variation. This is why Tohme combines automation with manual labor using svControl.

svControl: Scheduling Work via Performance Prediction

svControl is a machine-learning module for predicting CV performance and assigning work to either a manual labor

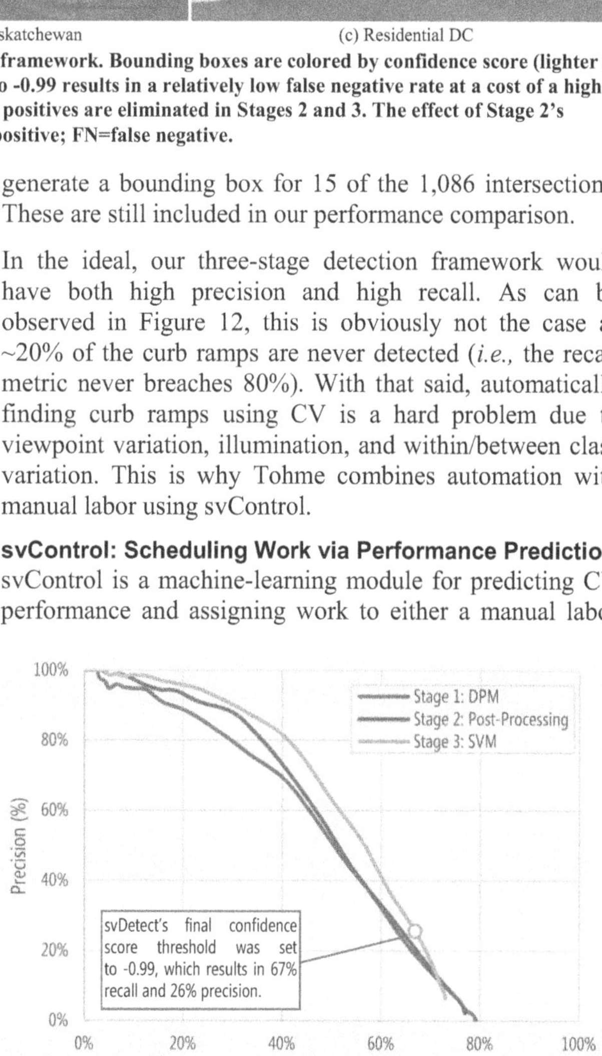

Figure 12: The precision-recall curve of the three-stage curb ramp detection process constructed by stepping through various DPM detection thresholds (from -3-to-3 with a 0.01 step). For the final svDetect module, we selected a DPM detection threshold of -0.99, which balances true positive detections with false positives.

pipeline (svLabel) or an automated pipeline with human verification (svDetect + svVerify)—see Figure 4. We designed svControl based on three principles: first, that human-based verifications are fast and relatively low-cost compared to human-based labeling; second, CV is fast and inexpensive but error prone both in producing high false positives and false negatives; third, false negatives are more expensive to correct than false positives.

From these principles, we derived two overarching design questions: first, given the high cost of human labeling and relative low-cost of human verification, could we optimize CV performance with a bias towards a low false negative rate (even if it meant an increase in false positives)? Second, given that false negatives cannot be eliminated completely from svDetect, can we predict their occurrence based on features of an intersection and use this to divert work to svLabel instead for human labeling?

Towards the first question, biasing CV performance towards a certain rate of false negatives is trivial. It is simply a matter of selecting the appropriate threshold on the precision/recall curve (recall that the threshold that we selected was -0.99). The second question is more complex. We iterated over a number of prediction techniques and intersection features before settling on a linear SVM and Lasso regression model [43] with the following three types of input features:

- **svDetect results (16 features):** For each GSV image, we include the raw number of bounding boxes output from svDetect, the average, median, standard deviation, and range of confidence scores of all bounding boxes in the image, and descriptive statistics for their XY-coordinates. Importantly, we did not use the *correctness* of the bounding box as a feature since this would be unknown during testing.
- **Intersection complexity (2 features):** We calculate intersection complexity via two measures: *cardinality* (*i.e.*, how many streets are connected to the target intersection) and an *indirect measure* of complexity, for which we count the number of street pixels in a stylized top-down Google Map. We found that high pixel counts correlate to high intersection complexity (Figure 13).
- **3D-point cloud data (5 features)**: svDetect struggles to detect curb ramps that are distant in a scene—*e.g.*, because the intersection is large or because the GSV car is in a sub-optimal position to photograph the intersection. Thus, we include descriptive statistics of depth information of each scene (*e.g.*, average, median, variance).

We combine the above features into a single 23-dimensional feature vector for training and classification.

svControl Training and Test Results

We train and test svControl with two-fold cross validation using the same train and test data as used for svDetect. Given that the goal of svControl is to predict svDetect performance, namely the occurrence of false negatives, we define a svDetect *failure* as a GSV scene with at least one false negative curb ramp detection. The SVM model is trained to make a binary failure prediction with the aforementioned features. Similarly, the Lasso regression model is trained to predict the *raw number* of false negatives of svDetect (regression value > 0.5 is failure).

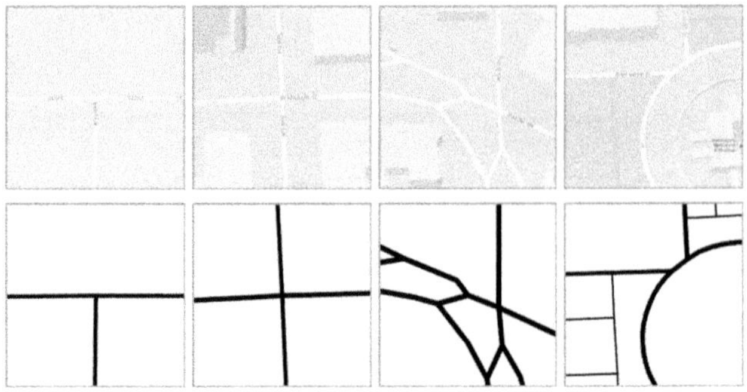

Figure 13: We use top-down stylized Google Maps (bottom row) to infer intersection complexity by counting black pixels (streets) in each scene. A higher count correlates to higher complexity.

To help better understand the important features in our models, we present the top three correlation coefficients for both. For the SVM, the top coefficients were the label's x-coordinate variance (0.91), the mean confidence score of automatically detected labels (0.69), and the minimum scene depth (0.67). For the Lasso model, the top three were mean scene depth (0.69), median scene depth (-0.28), and, similar to the SVM, the mean confidence score of the automatically detected labels (0.21). If either the SVM or the Lasso model predicts failure on a particular GSV scene, svControl routes that scene to svLabel instead of svVerify.

svControl Results. We assessed svControl's prediction performance across the 1,086 scenes. While not perfect, our results show that svControl is capable of identifying svDetect failures with high probability—we correctly predicted 397 of the 439 svDetect failures (86.3%); however, this high recall comes at a cost of precision: 404 of the total 801 scenes (50.4%) marked as failures were false positives. Given that we designed svControl to be conservative (*i.e.*, pass more work to svLabel if in doubt about svDetect), this accuracy balance is reasonable. Below, we examine whether this is sufficient to provide performance benefits for Tohme.

STUDY 2: EVALUATING TOHME

To examine the effectiveness of Tohme for finding curb ramps in GSV images and to compare its performance to a baseline approach, we performed an online study with MTurk in spring 2014. Our goal here is threefold: first, and most importantly, to investigate whether Tohme provides performance benefits over manual labeling alone (baseline); second, to understand the effectiveness of each of Tohme's sub-systems (svLabel, svVerify, svDetect, and svControl); and third, to uncover directions for future work in preparation for a public deployment.

Tohme Study Method

Similar to Hara *et al.* [23], we collected more data than necessary in practice so that we could simulate performance with different workflow configurations *post hoc*. To allow

	Turkers	GSV Scenes	HITs	Tasks	Avg. Turkers / Intersection	Label Stats	Avg. Task Time
SVLABEL	242	1,046	1,270	6,350	6.1 (0.6)	20,789 labels (17,327CRs, 3,462MCRs)	94.1s (144.4s)
SVVERIFY	161	1,046	582	5,820	5.6 (0.6)	42,226 verified labels (28,801RLs, 13,425KLs)	43.2 (48.7s)

Table 3: An overview of the MTurk svLabel and svVerify HITs. While Tohme's svControl system would, in practice, split work between the svLabel and svDetect+svVerify pipelines, we fed every GSV scene to both to perform our analyses. Acronyms above include CRs=Curb Ramps; MCRs=Missing Curb Ramps; RLs=Removed Labels; KLs=Kept Labels. svVerify was 2.2x faster than svLabel.

us to compare Tohme *vs.* feeding all scenes to either workflow on their own (svLabel and svDetect+svVerify), we ran *all* GSV scenes through both. To avoid interaction effects, turkers hired for one workflow (labeling) could not work on the other (verifying) and vice versa.

Second, to more rigorously assess Tohme and to reduce the influence of any one turker on our results, we hired at least three turkers per scene for each workflow and used this data to perform Monte Carlo simulations. More specifically, for both workflows, we randomly sampled one turker from each scene, calculated performance statistics (*e.g.*, precision), and repeated this process 1,000 times. Admittedly, this is a more complex evaluation than simply hiring one turker per scene and computing the results; however, the Monte Carlo simulation allows us to derive a more robust indicator of Tohme's expected future performance.

Of the 1,086 GSV scenes (street intersections) in our dataset, we reserved 40 for ground truth seeding, which were randomly selected from the eight geographic areas (5 scenes from each). We calculated HIT payment rates based on MTurk pilot studies: $0.80 for svLabel HITs (five intersections; $0.16 per intersection) and $0.80 for svVerify (ten intersections; $0.08 per intersection). As noted in our system description, turkers had to successfully complete interactive tutorials before beginning the tasks.

Analysis Metrics

To assess Tohme, we used the following measures:

- **Label overlap compared to ground truth:** as described in the svDetect section, we use 20% overlap as our correctness threshold (from [23]).
- **We calculate standard object detection performance metrics** including precision, recall, and F-measure based on this 20% area overlap—the same overlap used by svDetect.
- **Human time cost**: cost is calculated by measuring completion times for each intersection in svLabel and svVerify.

Tohme Study Results

We first present high-level descriptive statistics of the MTurk HITs before focusing on the comparison between Tohme *vs.* our baseline approach (pure manual labeling with svLabel). We provide additional analyses that help explain the underlying trends in our results.

Descriptive Statistics of MTurk Work

To gather data for our analyses, we hired 242 distinct turkers for the svLabel pipeline and 161 turkers for the

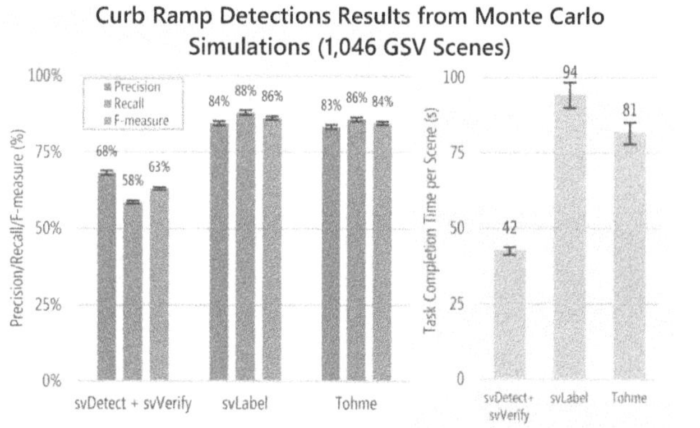

Figure 14: Tohme achieves comparable results to a manual labeling approach alone but with a 13% reduction in time cost. Error bars are standard deviation.

svVerify pipeline (Table 3). As noted previously, all 1,046 GSV scenes were fed through both workflows. For svLabel, turkers completed 1,270 HITs (6,350 labeling tasks) providing 17,327 curb ramp labels and 3,462 missing curb ramp labels. For svVerify, turkers completed 582 HITs (5,820 verification tasks) and verified a total of 42,226 curb ramp labels. On average, turkers eliminated 4.9 labels per intersection (*SD*=2.9). We hired an average of 6.1 (*SD*=0.6) turkers per intersection for svLabel and 5.6 (*SD*=0.6) for svVerify.

Evaluating Tohme's Performance

To evaluate Tohme's overall performance, we first examined how well each pipeline would perform on its own across the entire dataset (1,046 scenes). This provides two baselines for comparison: (i) the *svDetect + svVerify* results show how well Tohme would perform if the svControl module passed *all* work to this pipeline and, similarly, (ii) the *svLabel* results show what would happen if we only relied on manual labor for finding and labeling curb ramps.

We found that Tohme achieved similar but slightly lower curb ramp detection results compared to the manual approach alone (F-measure: 84% *vs.* 86%) but with a much lower time cost (13% reduction); see Figure 14. As

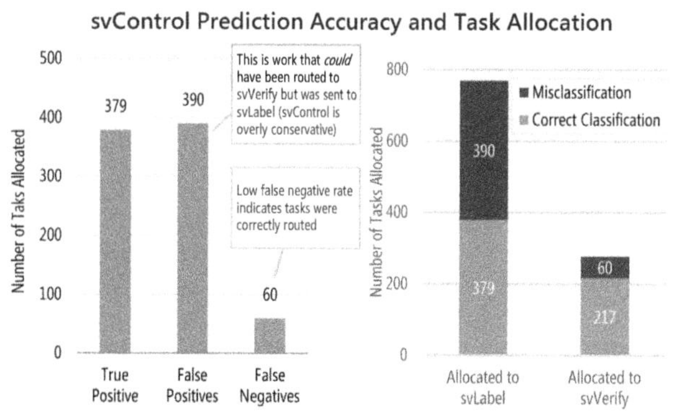

Figure 15: svControl allocated 769 scenes to svLabel and 277 scenes to svVerify. 379 out of 439 scenes (86.3%) where svDetect failed were allocated "correctly" to svLabel. Recall that svControl is conservative in routing work to svVerify because false negative labels are expensive to correct; thus, the 86.3% comes at a high false positive cost (390).

Figure 16: Finding curb ramps in GSV imagery can be difficult. Common problems include occlusion, illumination, scale differences because of distance, viewpoint variation (side, front, back), between class similarity, and within class variation. For between class similarity, many structures exist in the physical world that appear similar to curb ramps but are not. For within class variation, there are a wide variety of curb ramp designs that vary in appearance. White arrows are used in some images to draw attention to curb ramps. Some images contain multiple problems.

expected, while the svDetect + svVerify pipeline is relatively inexpensive, it performed the worst (F-measure: 63%). These findings show that the svControl module routed work appropriately to maintain high accuracy but at a reduced cost. Tohme reduces the average per-scene processing time by 12 seconds compared to svLabel alone. The overall task completion times were 12.3, 27.3, and 23.7 hours for svDetect + svVerify, svLabel, and Tohme respectively.

The above results were calculated using the aforementioned Monte Carlo method. If we, instead, use only the *first* turker to arrive and complete the task, our results are largely the same. The F-measures are 63%, 86%, and 85% respectively for svDetect + svVerify, svLabel, and Tohme with a 10% drop in cost for Tohme (rather than 13%). This includes 65 distinct turkers for svDetect + svVerify, 97 for svLabel, and 149 for Tohme.

Task Allocation by svControl

As the workflow scheduler, the svControl module is a critical component of Tohme. Because the svVerify interface does not allow for labeling (*e.g.,* correcting false negatives), the svControl system is conservative—it routes most of the work to svLabel otherwise many curb ramps would possibly remain undetected. Of the 1,046 scenes, svControl predicted svDetect to fail on 769 scenes (these results are the same as presented in the svControl section but with the 40 ground truth scenes removed). Thus, 73.5% of all scenes were routed to svLabel for manual work and the rest (277) were fed to svVerify for human verification (Figure 15). Again, svControl's true positive rate is high: 86%. However, if svControl worked as a perfect classifier, 439 scenes would have been forwarded to svLabel and 607 to svVerify. In this idealized case, Tohme's cost drops to 27.7% compared to a manual labeling approach with the same F-measure as before (84%). Thus, assuming limited improvements in CV-based curb ramp detections in the near future, a key area for future work will be improving the workflow control system.

Where Humans and Computers Struggle

The key to improving both CV and human labeling performance is to understand *where* and *why* each sub-system makes mistakes. To assess the detection accuracy of human labelers, we calculated the average F-measure score per scene based on the average number of true positives (TP), false positives (FP), and false negatives (FN). For example, if the average for a scene was (TP, FP, FN) = (1, 1, 2), then (Precision, Recall, F-measure) = (0.5, 0.3, 0.4). For CV, we simply used the F-measure score for each scene based on our svDetect results. We sorted the two F-measure lists and visually inspected the best and worst performing scenes for each. For the top and bottom 10, the average F-measure scores were 99% and 0% for CV and 100% and 25% for human labeling respectively. Common problems are summarized in Figure 16.

Crowd workers struggled with labeling distant curb ramps (scale) or due to placement and angle (viewpoint variation). To mitigate this, future labeling interfaces could allow the worker to "walk" around the intersection to select better viewpoints (similar to [25]); however, this will increase user-interaction complexity and labeling time. Perhaps as should be expected, crowd workers were much more adept at dealing with occlusion than CV—even if a majority of a curb ramp was occluded, a worker could infer its location and shape (*e.g.,* middle occlusion picture). CV struggled for all the reasons noted in Figure 16. Given the tremendous variation in curb ramp design and capture angles, a larger training set may have improved our results. Moreover, because multiple views of a single intersection are available

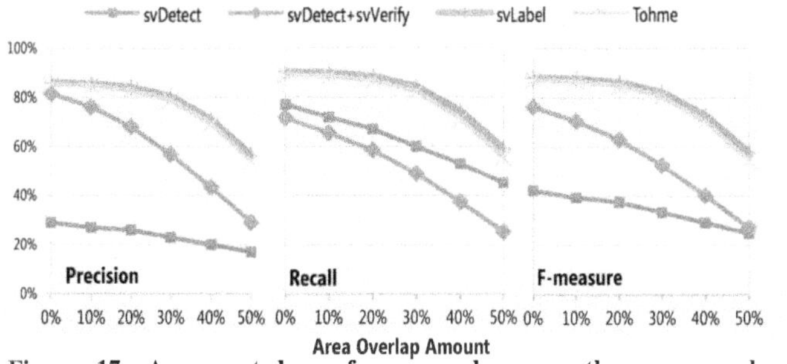

Figure 17: As expected, performance drops as the area overlap threshold increases; however, the relative difference between Tohme and baseline (svLabel) remains consistent.

in GSV via neighboring panoramas, these additional perspectives could be combined to potentially improve scene structure understanding and mitigate issues with occlusion, illumination, scale, and viewpoint variation. The semantic issues—*e.g.,* confusing structures similar to curb ramps—are obviously much more difficult for CV than humans. We describe other areas for improvement in the Discussion.

Effect of Area Overlap Threshold on Performance

As noted previously, there is no universal standard for selecting an area overlap threshold in CV; this decision is often domain dependent. To investigate the effect of changing the overlap threshold on performance, we measured precision, recall, and F-measure at different values from 0-50% at a step size of 10% (Figure 17). For *overlap=0%,* at least 1px of a detected bounding must overlap with a ground truth label to be considered correct.

A few observations: first, as expected, performance decreases as the overlap threshold increases; however, the relative performance difference between Tohme and baseline (svLabel) stays roughly the same. For example, at 0% overlap, the (Precision, Recall, F-measure) of Tohme is (85%, 89%, 87%) and (86%, 90%, 88%) for svLabel and at 50% overlap, (54%, 55%, 55%) *vs.* (57%, 59%, 58%). Thus, Tohme's relative performance is consistent regardless of overlap threshold (*i.e.,* slightly poorer performance but cheaper). Second, there appears to be a more substantial performance drop starting at ~30%, which suggests that obtaining curb ramp label agreement at the pixel level between human labelers and ground truth after this point is difficult. Finally, though svDetect + svVerify has much greater precision than svDetect alone, this increase comes at a cost of recall—a gap which widens as the overlap threshold becomes more aggressive. So, though human verifiers help increase precision, they are imperfect and sometimes delete true positive labels.

DISCUSSION

Our research advances recent work using GSV and crowdsourcing to remotely collect data on accessibility features of the physical world (*e.g.,* [21–23, 25]) by integrating CV and a machine learning-based workflow scheduler. We showed that a trained CV-based curb ramp detector (svDetect) found 63% of curb ramps in GSV scenes and fast, human-based verifications further improved the overall results. We also demonstrated that a novel machine-learning based workflow controller, svControl, could predict CV performance and route work accordingly. Below, we discuss limitations and opportunities for future work.

Improving Human Interfaces

How much context is necessary for verification? We were surprised that verification tasks were only 2.2x faster than labeling tasks. Though we attempted to design both interfaces for rapid user interaction, there is some basic overhead incurred by panning and searching in the 360-degree GSV view. In an attempt to eliminate this overhead, we have designed a completely new type of verification interface, *quickVerify*, that simply presents detected bounding boxes in a grid view (Figure 18). Similar to the facial recognition verifier in Google Picasa, these boxes can be rapidly confirmed or rejected with a single-click and a new bounding box appears in its place. In a preliminary experiment using 160 GSV scenes and 59 distinct turkers, however, we found that accuracy with quickVerify dropped significantly. Unlike faces, we believe that curb ramps require some level of surrounding context to accurately perceive their existence. More work is needed to determine the appropriate amount of surrounding view context to balance speed and accuracy.

Improving human labeling. Human labeling time could be reduced if point-and-click interactions were used for labeling targets rather than outlining; however, as demonstrated in Figure 16, curb ramps vary dramatically in size, scale, and shape. Clicking alone would be insufficient for CV training. Moreover, labeling will *always* be more costly than verification because it is a more difficult task (*i.e.,* finding elements in an image requires visual search and a higher mental load). With that said, we currently discard *all* svDetect bounding boxes—even those with a high confidence score—when a scene is routed to svLabel. Future work should explore how to, instead, best utilize this CV data to improve worker performance (*e.g.,* by showing

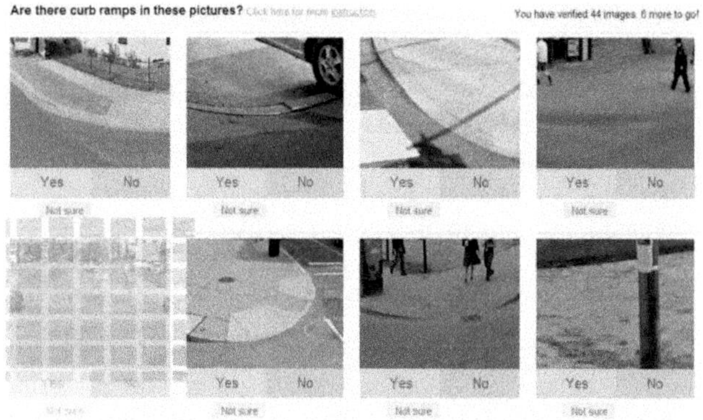

Figure 18: In the *quickVerify* interface, workers could randomly verify CV curb ramp detection patches. After providing an answer for a given detection, the patch would "explode" (bottom left) and a new one would load in its place. Though fast, verification accuracies went down in an experiment of 160 GSV scenes and 59 turkers.

detected bounding boxes with high scores to the user or as a way to help *verify* human labels). Finally, similar to quickVerify, future work could explore GSV panorama labeling that is not projected onto a 3D-sphere but is instead flattened into a 2D zoomable interface (*e.g.,* [32]) or specially rendered to increase focus on intersection corners.

Improving Automated Approaches

As the first work in automatically detecting curb ramps using CV, there are no prior systems with which to directly compare our performance. Having said that, there is much room for improvement and advances in CV will only increase the overall efficacy of our system.

Improving CV-based curb ramp detection. We are currently exploring three areas of future work: (i) *Context integration.* While we use some context information in Tohme (*e.g.,* 3D-depth data, intersection complexity inference), we are exploring methods to include broader contextual cues about buildings, traffic signal poles, crosswalks, and pedestrians as well as the precise location of corners from top-down map imagery. (ii) *3D-data integration.* Due to low-resolution and noise, we currently use 3D-point cloud data as a ground plane mask rather than as a feature to our CV algorithms. We plan to explore approaches that combine the 3D and 2D imagery to increase scene structure understanding (*e.g.,* [27]). If higher resolution depth data becomes available, this may be useful to directly detect the presence of a curb or corner, which would likely improve our results. (iii) *Training.* Our CV algorithms are currently trained using GSV scenes from all eight city regions in our dataset. Given the variation in curb ramp appearance across geographic areas, we expect that performance could be improved if we trained and tested per city. However, in preliminary experiments, we found no difference in performance. We suspect that this is due to the decreased training set size. In the future, we would like to perform training experiments to study the effects of per-city training and to identify minimal training set size. Relatedly, we plan to explore active learning approaches where crowd labels train the system over time.

Improving the workflow controller. While our current workflow controller focuses on predicting CV performance, future systems should explore modeling and predicting human worker performance and adapting work assignments accordingly. For example, struggling workers could be fed scenes that are predicted to be easy, or hard scenes can be assigned to more than one worker to take majority vote [10, 30]. Similar to CV detection, per-city training and active learning should also be explored.

Who pays? The question of who will pay for data collection (or if payment is even necessary) in the future is an important, unresolved one. Our immediate plans are to build an open website where anyone can contribute voluntarily. From conversations with motor impaired (MI) persons and the accessibility community as a whole (*e.g.,* non-profit organizations, families of those with MI), we believe there is a strong demand for this system. For example, with a public version of Tohme, a concerned, motivated father could easily label over 100 intersections in his neighborhood in a few hours. A website akin to walkscore.com could then visualize the accessibility of that neighborhood using heatmaps and also calculate accessible pedestrian routes.

Limitations

There are two primary limitations to our work. First, there is a workload imbalance between svLabel and svDetect. svLabel gathers explicit data on both curb ramps *and* missing curb ramps while svDetect only detects the former. It is likely that if the svLabel task involved only labeling curb ramps, the labeling task completion time would go down, which would affect our primary results. And, while the *lack* of a detected curb ramp could be equated to a missing curb ramp label for svDetect, we have not yet performed this analysis. Clearly, more explorations are needed here but we believe our initial examinations are sufficient to show the potential of Tohme.

Second, there is no assessment of how our curb ramp detection results compare to traditional auditing approaches (*e.g.,* performed by city governments). Anecdotally, we have found many errors in the DC government curb ramp dataset [12]; however, more research is necessary to uncover whether our approach is faster, cheaper, and/or more accurate. Ultimately, Tohme must produce sufficiently good data to enable new types of accessibility-aware GIS applications (*e.g.,* pedestrian directions routed through an accessible sidewalk path).

CONCLUSION

This paper contributes the design and evaluation of a new tool, Tohme, for semi-automatically detecting curb ramps in GSV images using crowdsourcing, computer vision, and machine learning. To our knowledge, we are the first work to design and investigate CV algorithms for curb ramp detection, an important sidewalk accessibility attribute. We are also the first to combine crowdsourcing with automated methods for collecting accessibility information about the physical world in GSV scenes. Tohme's custom workflow controller predicts CV performance and routes work accordingly to balance accuracy and human labor. Through an MTurk study of 1,086 intersections across four North American cities, we showed that Tohme could provide comparable curb ramp detection accuracy at a 13% reduction in cost. As computer vision and machine learning algorithms continue to improve, Tohme should only become more efficient.

While this paper focuses specifically on curb ramps, we believe a similar approach could be applied to analyze the accessibility of external building facades (*e.g.,* the presence of stairways), the safety of intersections (*e.g.,* the presence of painted cross walks), or even the accessibility of store aisles as mapping companies increasingly focus on the indoors (*e.g.,* [20]).

ACKNOWLEDGMENTS
Thanks to Victoria Le for help with physical audits, Ruofei Du and Zachary Lawrence for some data analysis and software development, and Leah Findlater for feedback on earlier drafts of this paper. This work was supported by an NSF grant (IIS-1302338), a Google Faculty Research Award, and an IBM Ph.D. Fellowship.

REFERENCES
[1] 311 Online http://311.dc.gov/

[2] 3rd Circuit, C. of A. 1993. *Kinney v. Yerusalim, 1993 No. 93-1168.*

[3] Anguelov, D., Dulong, C., Filip, D., Frueh, C., Lafon, S., Lyon, R., Ogale, A., Vincent, L. and Weaver, J. 2010. Google Street View: Capturing the World at Street Level. *Computer.* 43, 6 (Jun. 2010), 32–38.

[4] Badland, H.M., Opit, S., Witten, K., Kearns, R.A. and Mavoa, S. 2010. Can virtual streetscape audits reliably replace physical streetscape audits? *Journal of urban health : bulletin of the New York Academy of Medicine.* 87, 6 (Dec. 2010), 1007–16.

[5] Bigham, J.P., Jayant, C., Ji, H., Little, G., Miller, A., Miller, R.C., Miller, R., Tatarowicz, A., White, B., White, S. and Yeh, T. 2010. VizWiz: nearly real-time answers to visual questions. *Proceedings of the 23nd annual ACM symposium on User interface software and technology* (New York, NY, USA, 2010), 333–342.

[6] Bigham, J.P., Ladner, R.E. and Borodin, Y. 2011. The design of human-powered access technology. *The proceedings of the 13th international ACM SIGACCESS conference on Computers and accessibility (ASSETS '11)* (New York, NY, USA, 2011), 3–10.

[7] Branson, S., Wah, C., Babenko, B., Schroff, F., Welinder, P., Perona, P. and Belongie, S. 2010. Visual Recognition with Humans in the Loop. *European Conference on Computer Vision (ECCV)* (Heraklion, Crete, 2010).

[8] Burges, C.C. 1998. A Tutorial on Support Vector Machines for Pattern Recognition. *Data Mining and Knowledge Discovery.* 2, 2 (1998), 121–167.

[9] Clarke, P., Ailshire, J., Melendez, R., Bader, M. and Morenoff, J. 2010. Using Google Earth to conduct a neighborhood audit: reliability of a virtual audit instrument. *Health & place.* 16, 6 (Nov. 2010), 1224–9.

[10] Dai, P., Mausam and Weld, D.S. 2011. Artificial Intelligence for Artificial Artificial Intelligence. *AAAI* (2011).

[11] Dalal, N. and Triggs, B. 2005. Histograms of oriented gradients for human detection. *IEEE Computer Society Conference on Computer Vision and Pattern Recognition, 2005. CVPR 2005.* (2005), 886–893 vol. 1.

[12] Data Catalog http://data.dc.gov/

[13] Deng, J., Russakovsky, O., Krause, J., Bernstein, M., Berg, A. and Fei-Fei, L. 2014. Scalable Multi-label Annotation. *Proceedings of the SIGCHI Conference on Human Factors in Computing Systems (CHI '14)* (2014), 3099–3102.

[14] Everingham, M., Van~Gool, L., Williams, C.K.I., Winn, J. and Zisserman, A. The PASCAL Visual Object Classes Challenge 2012 VOC2012 Results.

[15] Everingham, M., Van~Gool, L., Williams, C.K.I., Winn, J. and Zisserman, A. 2010. The Pascal Visual Object Classes (VOC) Challenge. *International Journal of Computer Vision.* 88, 2 (Jun. 2010), 303–338.

[16] Felzenszwalb, P., McAllester, D. and Ramaman, D. 2008. A Discriminatively Trained, Multiscale, Deformable Part Model. *CVPR* (2008).

[17] Felzenszwalb, P.F., Girshick, R.B., McAllester, D. and Ramanan, D. 2010. Object Detection with Discriminatively Trained Part-Based Models. *Pattern Analysis and Machine Intelligence, IEEE Transactions on.* 32, 9 (Sep. 2010), 1627–1645.

[18] Ferrari, V., Fevrier, L., Jurie, F. and Schmid, C. 2008. Groups of Adjacent Contour Segments for Object Detection. *Pattern Analysis and Machine Intelligence, IEEE Transactions on.* 30, 1 (Jan. 2008), 36–51.

[19] Girshick, R.B., Felzenszwalb, P.F. and McAllester, D. Discriminatively Trained Deformable Part Models, Release 5.

[20] Google Maps Business View: *http://www.google.com/maps/about/partners/businessview/.* Accessed: 2014-04-15.

[21] Guy, R. and Truong, K. 2012. CrossingGuard: exploring information content in navigation aids for visually impaired pedestrians. *Proceedings of the SIGCHI Conference on Human Factors in Computing Systems (CHI '12)* (New York, NY, USA, 2012), 405–414.

[22] Hara, K., Le, V. and Froehlich, J. 2012. A Feasibility Study of Crowdsourcing and Google Street View to Determine Sidewalk Accessibility. *Proceedings of the 14th international ACM SIGACCESS conference on Computers and accessibility (ASSETS '12), Poster Session* (New York, NY, USA, 2012), 273–274.

[23] Hara, K., Le, V. and Froehlich, J. 2013. Combining Crowdsourcing and Google Street View to Identify Street-level Accessibility Problems. *Proceedings of the SIGCHI Conference on Human Factors in Computing Systems (CHI '13)* (New York, NY, USA, May 2013), 631–640.

[24] Hara, K., Le, V., Sun, J., Jacobs, D. and Froehlich, J. 2013. Exploring Early Solutions for Automatically Identifying Inaccessible Sidewalks in the Physical World Using Google Street View. *Human Computer Interaction Consortium* (2013).

[25] Hara, K., Shiri, A., Campbell, M., Cynthia, B., Le, V., Pannella, S., Moore, R., Minckler, K., Ng, R. and Froehlich, J. 2013. Improving Public Transit Accessibility for Blind Riders by Crowdsourcing Bus Stop Landmark Locations with Google Street View. *Proceedings of the 15th International ACM SIGACCESS Conference on Computers and Accessibility Technology* (2013), 16:1–16:8.

[26] Hara, K., Sun, J., Chazan, J., Jacobs, D. and Froehlich, J. 2013. An Initial Study of Automatic Curb Ramp Detection with Crowdsourced Verification using Google Street View Images. *Proceedings of the 1st Conference on Human Computation and Crowdsourcing (HCOMP'13), Work-in-Progress* (2013).

[27] Hoiem, D., Efros, A. and Hebert, M. 2008. Putting Objects in Perspective. *International Journal of Computer Vision*. 80, 1 (2008), 3–15.

[28] Hruschka, D.J., Schwartz, D., St.John, D.C., Picone-Decaro, E., Jenkins, R.A. and Carey, J.W. 2004. Reliability in Coding Open-Ended Data: Lessons Learned from HIV Behavioral Research. *Field Methods* . 16 , 3 (Aug. 2004), 307–331.

[29] Jain, S.D. and Grauman, K. 2013. Predicting Sufficient Annotation Strength for Interactive Foreground Segmentation. *ICCV* (2013), 1313–1320.

[30] Kamar, E., Hacker, S. and Horvitz, E. 2012. Combining Human and Machine Intelligence in Large-scale Crowdsourcing. *Proceedings of the 11th International Conference on Autonomous Agents and Multiagent Systems - Volume 1* (Richland, SC, 2012), 467–474.

[31] Kirschbaum, J.B., Axelson, P.W., Longmuir, P.E., Mispagel, K.M., Stein, J.A. and Yamada, D.A. 2001. *Designing Sidewalks and Trails for Access, Part II of II: Best Practices Design Guide, Chapter 7.*

[32] Kopf, J., Chen, B., Szeliski, R. and Cohen, M. 2010. Street Slide: Browsing Street Level Imagery. *ACM Transactions on Graphics (Proceedings of SIGGRAPH 2010)*. 29, 4 (2010), 96:1 – 96:8.

[33] Krippendorff, K.H. 2003. *Content Analysis: An Introduction to Its Methodology*. Sage Publications, Inc.

[34] Lasecki, W., Miller, C., Sadilek, A., Abumoussa, A., Borrello, D., Kushalnagar, R. and Bigham, J. 2012. Real-time captioning by groups of non-experts. *Proceedings of the 25th annual ACM symposium on User interface software and technology* (New York, NY, USA, 2012), 23–34.

[35] Lin, C.H., Daniel, M. and Weld, S. 2012. Dynamically switching between synergistic workflows for crowdsourcing. *In Proceedings of the 26th AAAI Conference on Artificial Intelligence, AAAI '12* (2012).

[36] Malisiewicz, T., Gupta, A. and Efros, A.A. 2011. Ensemble of Exemplar-SVMs for Object Detection and Beyond. *ICCV* (2011).

[37] National Council on Disability 2007. *The Impact of the Americans with Disabilities Act: Assessing the Progress Toward Achieving the Goals of the ADA.*

[38] Princeton Vision Toolkit: *http://vision.princeton.edu/code.html*. Accessed: 2014-04-07.

[39] Quinn, A.J. and Bederson, B.B. 2011. Human Computation: A Survey and Taxonomy of a Growing Field. *Proceedings of the SIGCHI Conference on Human Factors in Computing Systems* (New York, NY, USA, 2011), 1403–1412.

[40] Rundle, A.G., Bader, M.D.M., Richards, C.A., Neckerman, K.M. and Teitler, J.O. 2011. Using Google Street View to audit neighborhood environments. *American journal of preventive medicine*. 40, 1 (Jan. 2011), 94–100.

[41] Stollof, E.R. and Barlow, J.M. 2008. *Pedestrian Mobility and Safety Audit Guide.*

[42] Su, H., Deng, J. and Fei-Fei, L. 2012. Crowdsourcing Annotations for Visual Object Detection. *AAAI Technical Report, 4th Human Computation Workshop* (2012).

[43] Tibshirani, R. 1994. Regression Shrinkage and Selection Via the Lasso. *Journal of the Royal Statistical Society, Series B*. 58, (1994), 267–288.

[44] United States Department of Justice, C.R.D. 1990. *Americans with Disabilities Act of 1990, Pub. L. No. 101-336, 104 Stat. 328.*

[45] Viola, P. and Jones, M. 2001. Rapid Object Detection using a Boosted Cascade of Simple Features. *Computer Vision and Pattern Recognition, IEEE Computer Society Conference on*. 1, (2001), 511.

[46] Walk Audit: *http://streetswiki.wikispaces.com/Walk+Audit*. Accessed: 2014-04-15.

[47] Welinder, P. and Perona, P. 2010. Online crowdsourcing: rating annotators and obtaining cost-effective labels. *In W. on Advancing Computer Vision with Humans in the Loop* (2010).

[48] Xiao, J., Fang, T., Tan, P., Zhao, P., Ofek, E. and Quan, L. 2008. Image-based Fa\ÇAde Modeling. *ACM Trans. Graph.* 27, 5 (Dec. 2008), 161:1–161:10.

[49] Xiao, J., Fang, T., Zhao, P., Lhuillier, M. and Quan, L. 2009. Image-based Street-side City Modeling. *ACM Trans. Graph.* 28, 5 (Dec. 2009), 114:1–114:12.

[50] Zamir, A.R., Darino, A. and Shah, M. 2011. Street View Challenge: Identification of Commercial Entities in Street View Imagery. *ICMLA (2)* (2011), 380–383.

[51] Zamir, A.R., Dehghan, A. and Shah, M. 2012. GMCP-Tracker: Global Multi-object Tracking Using Generalized Minimum Clique Graphs. *ECCV (2)* (2012), 343–356.

[52] Zamir, A.R. and Shah, M. 2010. Accurate Image Localization Based on Google Maps Street View. *Proceedings of the European Conference on Computer Vision (ECCV)* (2010).

Zero-Latency Tapping: Using Hover Information to Predict Touch Locations and Eliminate Touchdown Latency

Haijun Xia[1], Ricardo Jota[1,2], Benjamin McCanny[1], Zhe Yu[1], Clifton Forlines[1,2], Karan Singh[1], Daniel Wigdor[1]
[1]University of Toronto [2]Tactual Labs
{haijunxia | jotacosta | bmccanny | zheyu | cforlines | karan | daniel}@dgp.toronto.edu

ABSTRACT
A method of reducing the perceived latency of touch input by employing a model to predict touch events before the finger reaches the touch surface is proposed. A corpus of 3D finger movement data was collected, and used to develop a model capable of three granularities at different phases of movement: initial direction, final touch location, time of touchdown. The model is validated for target distances >= 25.5cm, and demonstrated to have a mean accuracy of 1.05cm 128ms before the user touches the screen. A user study of different levels of latency reveals a strong preference for unperceivable latency touchdown feedback. A form of 'soft' feedback is proposed, as well as other performance-enhancing uses for this prediction model.

INTRODUCTION
The time delay between user input and corresponding graphical feedback, here classified as interaction latency, has long been studied in computer science. Early latency research indicated that the visual "response to input should be immediate and perceived as part of the mechanical action induced by the operator. Time delay: No more than 0.1 second (100ms)" [25]. More recent work has found that this threshold is, in fact, too high, as humans are able to perceive even lower levels of latency - for direct touch systems, it has been measured as low as 24ms when tapping the screen [20], and 6ms when dragging [27]. Furthermore, input latencies well below 100ms have been shown to impair a user's ability to perform basic tasks [20, 27].

While the touchdown latency of current commercial touch devices can be as low as 75ms, this latency is still perceptible to users. Eliminating latency, or at least reducing it beyond the limits of human perception and performance impairment, is highly desirable. Both Leigh *et al.* and Ng *et al.* demonstrated direct-touch systems capable of less than 1ms of latency [22, 27]. While compelling, these are not commercially viable for most applications: an FPGA replaced a general-purpose processor and software, they employ a high-speed projector rather than a display panel, and each is capable of displaying only simple geometry.

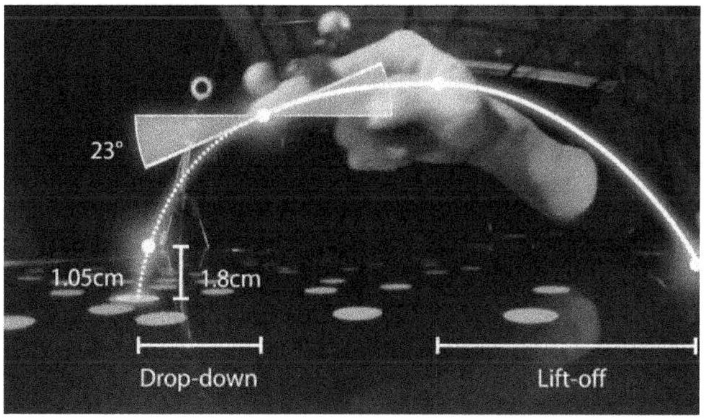

Figure 1: The model predicts the location and time of a touch. Parameters of the model are tuned to the latency of the device to maximize accuracy while guaranteeing performance.

While completely eliminating latency from traditional form factors may ultimately prove to be impossible, we believe that it *is* possible to reduce the *apparent* latency of an interactive system. We define apparent latency as the time between an input and the system's *soft* feedback to that input, which serves only to show a quick response to the user (e.g.: pointer movement, UI buttons being depressed), as distinct from the time required to show the *hard* feedback of an application actually responding to that same input.

This paper investigates methods for eliminating the apparent latency of tapping actions on a large touchscreen through the development and use of a model of finger movement. We track the path of a user's finger as it approaches the display and predict the location and time of its landing. We then signal the application of the impending touch so that it can pre-buffer its response to the touchdown event. In our demonstration system, we trigger a visual response to the touch at the predicted point *before* the finger lands on the screen. The timing of the trigger is tuned to the system's processing and display latency, so the feedback is shown to the user at the moment they touch the display. The result is an improvement in the apparent latency as touch and feedback occur simultaneously.

In order to predict the user's landing point, we must first understand the 3D spatial dynamics of how users perform touch actions. To this end, we augmented a Samsung SUR40 tabletop with a high fidelity 3D tracking system to

UIST '14, October 05 - 08 2014, Honolulu, HI, USA

ACM 978-1-4503-3069-5/14/10...$15.00.
http://dx.doi.org/10.1145/2642918.2647348

record the paths of user finger movements through space as they performed basic touchscreen tasks. We collected data on input paths by asking 15 participants to perform repeated tapping tasks. We then analyzed this data using various numerical and qualitative observations to develop a prediction model of 3D finger motion for touch-table device interaction. This model, which was validated by a subsequent study for targets at least 25.5cm distant, enables us to predict the movement direction, touch location, and touch time prior to finger-device contact. Using our model, we can achieve a touch-point prediction accuracy of 1.05cm on average 128ms before the user touches the display. This accuracy and prediction time horizon is sufficient to reduce the time between the finger touch down and the system's apparent response to beneath the 24ms lower bound of human perception, described by Jota *et al* [20].

In this paper, we first describe relevant prior art in the areas of hover sensing, input latency, and touch prediction. We then describe a pair of studies that we used to formulate and then validate our predictive model. Next, we describe a third study in which participants' preferences for low-latency touch input were investigated. Finally, we describe a number of uses for our model beyond simple feedback and outline future work that continues the exploration of touch prediction.

RELATED WORK

We draw from several areas of related work in our present research: the detection and use of hovering information in HCI, the psychophysics of latency, the use of predictive models in HCI, and the modeling of human motion in three dimensions.

Hover Sensing

A number of sensing techniques have been employed to detect the position of the user prior to touching a display. In HCI research, hover sensing is often simulated using optical tracking tools such as the Vicon motion capture system, as we have done in this work. The user is required to wear or hold objects augmented with markers, as well as the need to deploy stationary cameras. A more practical approach for commercial products, markerless hover sensing has been demonstrated using optical techniques, including through the use of an array of time-of-flight based range finders [3] as well as stereo and optical cameras [35].

Non-optical tracking has also been demonstrated using a number of technologies. One example is the use of acoustic-based sensors, such as the "Flock of Birds" tracking employed by Fitzmaurice *et al.* [8], which enables six degrees of freedom (DOF) position and orientation sensing of physical handheld objects. Although popular in research applications, widespread application of this sensor has been elusive. More common are 5-DOF tools using electro-magnetic resonance (EMR). EMR is commonly used to track the position and orientation of styli in relation to a digitizer, and employed in creating pen-based user input. Although typically limited to a small range beyond the digitizer in commercial applications, tracking with EMR has been used in much larger volumes [12].

Most touch sensors employed today are based on projective capacitance. Fundamentally, the technique is capable of sensing the user's presence centimeters away from the digitizer, as is done with the Theremin [31]. Such sensors employed today are augmented with a ground plane, purposefully added to eliminate their ability to detect a user's finger prior to touch [6]. More recently, sensors have been further augmented to include the ability to not only detect the user's finger above the device, but also to detect its *distance* from the digitizer [2, 14, 18, 34].

Use of Hover

Prior work has explored the use of sensing hover to enable intentional user input. Our work, in contrast, effectively hides the system's ability to detect hover from the user, using it only for prediction of touch location and timing, and elimination of apparent latency.

Hover has long been the domain of pen-operated devices [9, 19]. Subramanian *et al.* suggest that the 3D position of a pointing device affects the interaction on the surface [30]. The authors propose a multi-layer application, with an active usage of the space above the display, where users purposefully distance the pen from the display to activate actions. Grossman *et al.* present a technique that utilizes the hover state of pen-based systems to navigate through a hover-only command layer [15]. Spindler *et al.* [28] propose that the space above the surface be divided into stacked layers, with layer specific interactions – this is echoed by Grossman *et al.* [16], who divided the space around a volumetric display into two spherical 'layers' with subtly differentiated interaction. This is distinct from Wigdor *et al.*, who argued for the use of the hover area as a 'preview' space for touch gestures [33], similar to Yang *et al.* who used hover sensing to zoom on-screen targets [37]. In contrast, Marquadt *et al.* recommend that the space above the touch surface and the touch surface be considered one continuous space, and not separate interaction spaces [24].

These projects focused on differentiating the space around the display, and using it as an explicit interaction volume. Our approach is more similar to that taken by Hachisu and Kajimoto [17], who demonstrate the use of a pair of photo-sensing layers to measure finger velocity and predict the time of contact with the touch surface. We build on this work through the addition of a model of motion that allows the prediction of not only time, but also early indication of direction, as well as later prediction of the location of the user's touch, enabling low-latency visual feedback in addition to the audio feedback they provide.

Latency

Ng *et al.* studied the user perception of latency for touch input. For dragging actions with a direct touch device, users were able to detect latency levels as low as 6ms [27]. Jota *et al.* studied the user performance of latency for touch input and found that dragging task performance is affected if latency levels are above 25ms [20]. In the present work, we focus on eliminating latency of the touchdown moment when the user first touches the screen. Jota *et al.* found that users are unable to perceive latency of responses to tapping that occur in less than 24ms [20] – we use prediction of touch location to provide soft touchdown feedback within this critical time, effectively eliminating perceptible latency.

Predicting Input

Predicting users' actions has been an active area of research in the field of HCI. Mackenzie proposes the application of Fitts's Law to predict movement time for standard touch interfaces [23]. By building a Fitts's model for a particular device, the movement time can be predicted given a known target and cursor position. Wobbrock *et al.* complements this approach with a model to predict pointing accuracy [36]. Instead of predicting movement time, a given movement time is used to predict error. In many pointing experiments, the input device is manipulated by in-air gestures, including Fitts's original stylus-based apparatus [7]. Murata proposes a method for predicting the intended target based on the current mouse cursor trajectory [26]. The author reports movement time reductions when using the predictive algorithm, but notes limited returns for dense target regions. Baudisch *et al.* adopted this approach: instead of jumping the cursor close to the target, this technique wraps eligible targets around the cursor [4].

We sought to build on these projects by developing a model of hand motion while performing touch-input tapping tasks, and apply this model to reducing apparent latency.

Models of Hand Motion

Biomechanists [32] and neuroscientists [10, 13] are actively engaged in the capture and analysis of 3D human hand motion. Their interest lies primarily in the understanding of various kinematic features, such as muscle actuation and joint torques, as well as cognitive planning during the hand movement. Flash [10] modeled the unconstrained point-to-point arm movement by defining an objective function and running an optimization algorithm. They found that the minimization of hand jerk movements generates an acceptable trajectory. Following the same approach, Uno [32] optimizes for another kinematic feature, torque, to generate the hand trajectory. While informative, these models are unsuitable to our goal of reducing latency, as they are computationally intensive and cannot be computed in real-time (for our purposes, as in little as 30ms).

We propose a generic model focusing on the prediction of landing location and touch time based on the pre-touch movement to reduce the time between the finger landing on the screen and the system's apparent response.

Having examined this related work, we turned our attention to the development of our predictive model of hand motion when performing pointing tasks on a touchscreen display. To that end, we first performed a data collection experiment. The data from this experiment was then used to develop our model.

DATA COLLECTION

To form our predictive model of tap time and location, we began by collecting data of tap actions on a touchscreen display. Participants performed tap gestures with varying target distance and direction of gesture. The data were then used to build our model, which we subsequently validated with a study we will later describe.

Participants

We recruited 15 right-handed participants (6 female) aged 22-30 from the local community. Participants reported owning 2 (mean) touch devices and spend 2-4 hours a day using them. Participants were paid $20 for a half-hour session.

Apparatus

The study was implemented using two different sensors: to sense touch, a Microsoft Surface table 2.0 was used (Samsung SUR40 with PixelSense). Pre-touch data was captured using a Vicon tracking system. Participants wore a motion capture marker-instrumented ring on their index fingertip, which was tracked in 3D at 120Hz.

The flow of the experiment was controlled by a separate PC, which received sensing information from both the Surface touch system and the Vicon tracking system, while triggering visual feedback on the Surface display. The experiment was implemented in python and shown to the user on the Surface table. It was designed to (1) present instructions and apparatus to the participant, (2) record the position and rotation of the tracked finger, (3) receive current touch events from the Surface, (4) issue commands to the display, and (5) log all of the data.

Task

Participants performed a series of target selection tasks, modeled after traditional pointing experiments, with some modifications made to ensure they knew their target before beginning the gesture, thus avoiding contamination of collected data with corrective movements. Target location was randomized, rather than performed in sequential-circle. Further, to begin each trial, participants were required to touch and hold a visible starting point (r=2.3cm), immediately after the target location was shown. They were required to hold the starting point until an audio cue was played (randomly between 0.7 and 1.0 seconds after touch). If the participant anticipated the beginning of the trial and moved their finger early, the trial would be marked as an error.

Immediately after the participants touched the starting point, at the opposite side of the circular arrangement a target point would appear for participants to tap. The target size of 2.3cm was selected as a trade-off between our need to specify end-position while minimizing corrective movements. Once a successful trial was completed, participants were instructed to return to another starting point for the next trial. Erroneous tasks were indicated with feedback on the Surface display and repeated.

Procedure

Participants were asked to complete a consent form and a questionnaire to collect demographic information. They then received instruction on how to interact with the apparatus and successfully completed 30 training trials. After the execution of each trial, a text block at the top right corner of the screen would update the cumulative error rate (shown as %). Participants were instructed to slow down if the error rate was above 5%, but were not given any instructions regarding their *pre-touch* movement.

Design

Tasks were designed according to two independent variables: target *direction* (8 cardinal directions) and target *distance* (20.8cm and 30.1cm). The combination of these two variables produces 16 unique gestures. There were four repetitions for each combination of direction and distance. Therefore, a session included a total of 64 actions. The ordering of the trials was randomized within each session. Participants completed 3 sessions and were given a 5-minute break between sessions.

In summary, 15 participants performed 192 trials each, for a total of 2880 trials.

Measures and Analysis Methodology

For each successful trial we captured the total completion time; finger position, rotation, and timestamp for every point in the finger trajectory; as well as the time participants touched the screen. Tracking data was analyzed for significant tracking errors, with less than 0.3% of the trials removed due to excessive noise in tracking data. Based on the frequency of the tracking system (120Hz) and the speed of the gestures, any tracking event that was more than 3.5cm away from its previous neighbor was considered an outlier and filtered (0.6%). The raw data (including outliers) for a particular target location are shown in Figure 2.

After removing 8 trials due to tracking noise, we had 2872 trials available for the development of our predictive model.

ANALYSIS & PREDICTING TOUCH

Having collected these tapping gestures, we turned our attention to modeling the trajectories with the primary goal of predicting the time and location of the final finger touch. Here we describe our approach, beginning with a discussion of the attributes of the touch trajectories, followed by the model we derived to describe them.

Note that our three-dimensional coordinate system is right-handed: x and y representing the Surface screen; the origin at the bottom-left corner of the Surface display; and z, the normal to the display.

Numerical and Qualitative Observations

Time & Goals: participants completed each trial with an mean movement time of 416ms (std.: 121ms). Our system had an average end-to-end latency of 80ms: 70ms from the Vicon system, 8ms from the display, and 2ms of processing. Thus, to drop touch-down latency below the 24ms threshold, our goal was to remove at least ~56ms via prediction. Applying our work to other systems will require additional tuning.

Movement phases: Figure 3 shows that all the trajectories have one peak, with a constant climb before, and a constant decline after. However, we did not find the peak to be at the same place in-between trajectories. Instead the majority of trajectories are asymmetrical, 2.2% have a peak before 30% of the total path, 47.9% have a peak between 30-50% of the total path, 47.1% have a peak between 50-70% of the total path, and 2.8% have a peak after 80% of the trajectory completed path.

We have found it useful to divide the movement into three phases: *lift-off*, which is characterized by a positive change in height, *continuation*, which begins as the user's finger starts to dip vertically, and *drop-down*, the final plunge towards the screen. Each of the lift-off and drop-down phases has interesting characteristics, which we will examine.

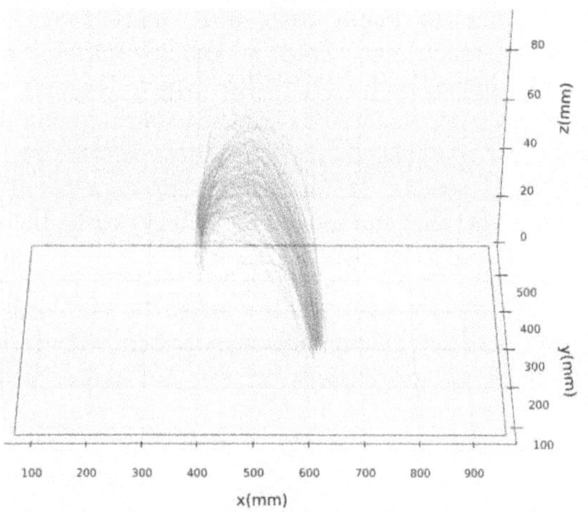

Figure 2: Overlay of all the pre-touch approaches to a northwest target. The blue rectangle represents the interactive surface used in the study.

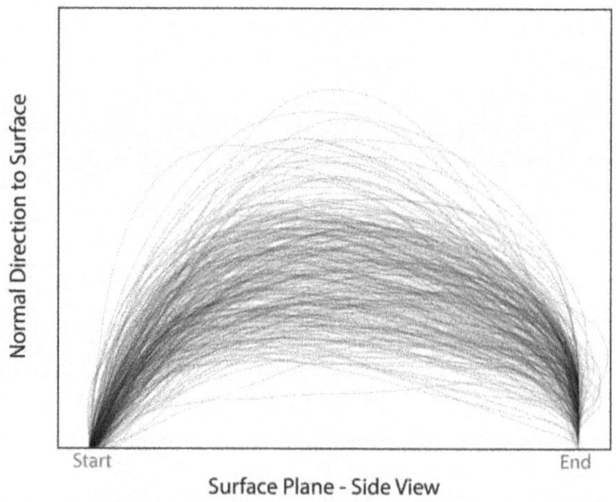

Figure 3: Side view overlay of all trials, normalized to start and end positions.

Figure 4: Trajectory for the eight directions of movement, normalized to start at the same location (center). The blue lines represent the straight-line approach to each target.

Lift-off direction: As might be expected, the direction of movement of the user's hand above the plane of the screen is roughly co-linear to the target direction, as shown in Figure 4. Fitting a straight line to this movement, the angle of that line to a straight line from starting point to the target is, on average, 4.78°, with a standard deviation of 4.51°. Depending on the desired degree of certainty, this information alone is sufficient to eliminate several potential touch targets.

Drop-down direction: Figure 5 and Figure 7 show the trajectory of final approach towards the screen. As can be seen, the direction of movement in the drop-down phase roughly fits a vertical drop to the screen. We also note that, as can be seen in Figure 7, the final approach when viewed from the side is roughly parabolic. It is clear when examining Figure 7 that a curve, constrained to intersect on a normal to the plane, will provide a rough fit. We examined several options, shown in Figure 6, and found that a parabola, constrained to intersect the screen at a normal, and fit to the hover path, would provide the best fit.

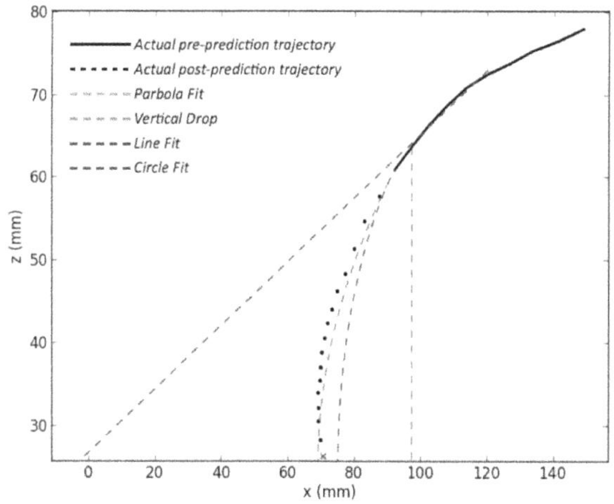

Figure 6: Trajectory prediction for line, parabola, circle and vertical fits. Future points of the actual trajectory (black dots) fit a parabola best.

Predictive Touch Model

Based on these observations, we present a prediction model, which makes three different predictions at three different stages in the user's gesture. They are initial direction, final touch location, and final touch time. Making predictions at three different moments allows our model to provide progressively more accurate information, allowing the UI to react as early as possible.

Prediction 1: Direction of Movement

Lift-off begins with a user lifting a finger off the touch surface and ends at the highest point of the trajectory (peak). As we discussed, above, this often ends before the user has reached the halfway point towards their desired target. As is also described, the direction of movement along the plane of the screen can be used to coarsely predict a line along which their intended target is likely to fall. At this early stage, our model provides this line, allowing elimination of targets outside of its bounds.

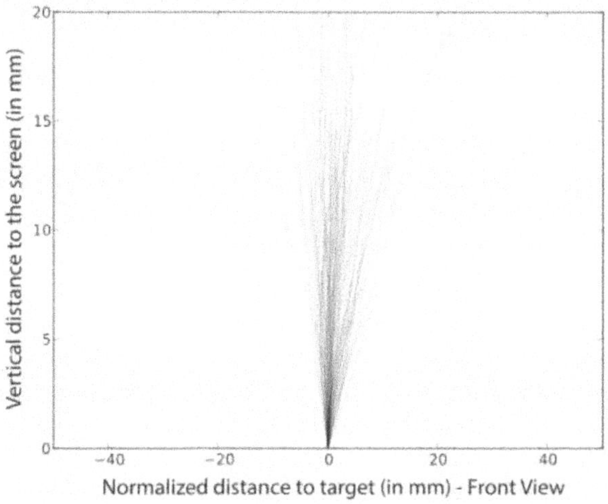

Figure 5: Final finger approach, as seen from the approaching direction

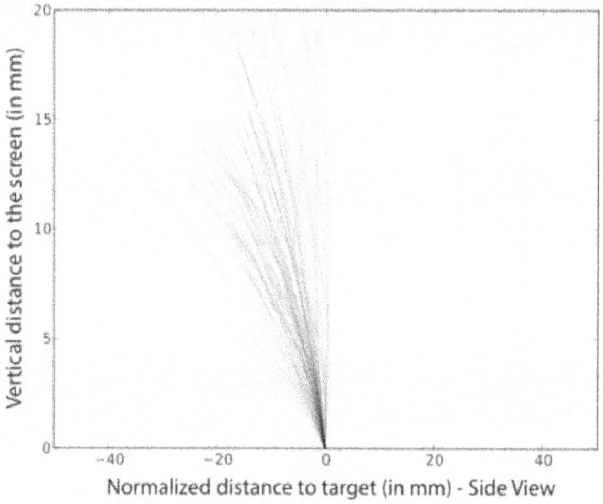

Figure 7: Final finger approach, as seem from the side of the approaching direction

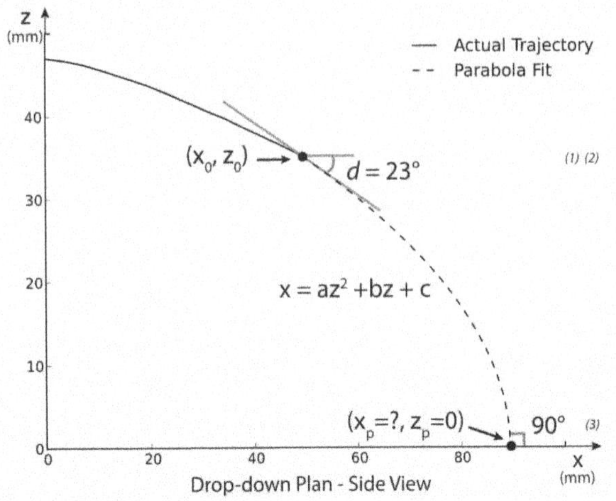

Figure 8: The parabola is fitted in the drop-down plane with (1) an initial point, (2) the angle of movement, (3) and the intersection is orthogonal with the display

Prediction 2: Final Touch Location

A prediction of the final location of the touch, represented as an x/y point, is computed by fitting a parabola to the approach trajectory. This parabola (Figure 8) is constrained as follows: (1) the plane is fit to the (nearly planar) drop-down trajectory of the touch; (2) the position of the finger at the time of the fit is on the parabola; (3) the angle of movement at the time of the fit is made a tangent to the parabola; (4) the angle of intersection with the display is orthogonal. Once the parabola is fit to the data, and constrained by these parameters, its intersection with the display comprises the predicted touch point. The fit is made when the drop-down phase begins. This is characterized by two conditions: (1) the finger's proximity to the screen; and (2) the angle to xy plane is higher than a threshold.

For each new point *i*, when the conditions are satisfied, the tapping location is predicted. To calculate the tapping location, we first fit a vertical plane to the trajectory. Given the angle *d and* (x_0, z_0), we predict the landing point, (x_p, z_p), by fitting a parabola:

$$x = az^2 + bz + c$$

Based on the derivatives at (x_0, z_0) and (x_p, z_p):

$$x_0' = \frac{-1}{tan(d)} \quad x_p' = 0$$

we calculate *a, b,* and *c* as follows:

$$a = \frac{x_p' - x_0'}{2(z_p - z_0)} \quad b = x_0' - 2az_0$$

$$c = x_0 - az_0^2 - bz_0$$

The landing point in this plane is defined as:

$$(x_p, z_p) = (c, 0)$$

Converting (x_p, z_p) back to the original 3D Vicon tracking coordinate system yields the landing position.

The timing of this phase is tuned based on the overall latency of the system, including that of the hover sensor: the later the prediction is made, the more accurate it will be, but the less time will be available for the system to respond. The goal is to tune the system so that the prediction arrives at the application so that it can respond immediately, and have its response shown on the screen at the precise moment the user touches. Through iterative testing, we found that, for the latency of our system (display + Vicon, approximately 80ms) setting thresholds of 4cm (distance to display) and 23° (angle to plane) yielded the best results. Given these unusually high latencies values, a more typical system would see even better results.

With these thresholds, our model predicts a touchdown location with an average error (distance to actual touch point) of 1.18cm and standard deviation of 1.09cm, on average, 91 milliseconds (std.: 72ms) before touchdown and at an average distance of 3.22cm (std.: 1.30cm) above the display. For the same set of trials, the errors for other curves (see Figure 6): circular fit (avg.: 1.72cm, std.: 1.62cm), vertical drop (avg.: 2.43cm, std.: 2.04cm) and a linear fit (avg.: 9.3cm, std.: 4.83cm) are larger than the parabolic fit.

The visual results and statistics indicate that pre-touch data has the potential to predict touch location long before the user touches the display. We validate the parabolic prediction model in a secondary study by using it to predict touch location in real time.

Prediction 3: Final Touch Time

Given that the timing of the prediction of final touch location is tuned to the latency of the system on which it is running, the time that it is delivered ahead of the actual touch is reliable. The goal of this final step is to provide a highly-accurate prediction of the time the user will touch, which necessitates waiting until the final approach to the display. We observed that the final 'drop' action, beyond the final 1.8cm of a touch gesture, experiences almost no deceleration. Thus, when the finger reaches 1.8cm from the display, a simple linear extrapolation is applied assuming a constant velocity.

We are able to predict within 2.0ms (mean; std.: 19.5ms), 51ms (mean; std.: 42ms) before touchdown. Note that, due to the 80ms latency of our Vicon sensor, this prediction is typically generated *after* the user has actually touched. We include it here for use with systems not based on computer vision and subject to network latency.

MODEL EVALUATION

Having developed our model using the collected data, we sought to validate the model outside the condition of the first study. We recruited 15 new right-handed participants from the local community (7 female) that had not participated in the first study with ages ranging from 20 to 30. On average, our participants own two touch devices and spend two to four hours a day using them. Participants were paid $10 for a half-hour session.

From the first study we observed that arm joint movement skews the trajectory. The longer the distance, the more skewed the trajectory becomes. Secondly, people dynamically correct the trajectory. The smaller the target, the more corrections were observed. To further study these effects, we included target distance and size as independent variables. Therefore, our validation study was designed according to three different independent variables: *target direction* (8 cardinal directions), *target distance* (25.5cm, 32.4cm, and 39.4cm), and *target size* (1.6cm, 2.1cm, and 2.6cm). The combination of these three variables produces 72 unique tasks. The order of target size and distance was randomized, with target direction always starting with the south position, and going clockwise for each combination of target size and distance. Participants completed 3 sessions and were given a break after each session.

The procedure and apparatus were identical to the first study, with the exception of the prediction model running in the background in real time. The prediction model did not provide any feedback to the participants. For each trial we captured the trajectories and logged the prediction results.

Results

Prediction 1: On average, the final touch point was within 4.25° of the straight-line prediction provided by our model (std.: 4.61°). On average, this was made available 186ms (mean; std.: 77ms) before the user touched the display. We found no significant effect for target size, direction, or distance on prediction accuracy.

Prediction 2: On average, our model predicted a touch location with an accuracy of 1.05cm (std.: 0.81cm). The finger was, on average, 2.87cm (std.: 1.37cm) away from the display when the prediction was made. The model is able to predict, on average, 128ms (std.: 63ms) before touching the display, allowing us to significantly reduce latency. We found no significant effect for target size, direction, or distance on prediction accuracy.

Prediction 3: On average, our model predicted the time of the touch within 1.6ms (std.: 20.7ms). This prediction was made, on average, 49ms before the touch was made (std.: 38ms). We found no significant effect for target size, direction, or distance on prediction accuracy.

These results indicate that our prediction model can be generalized to different target distances, sizes, and directions, with an average drift from the touchdown location of 1.05cm, 128ms prior to the finger touching the device. To provide context, given that our mean trial completion time for the experiment was approximately 447ms, this means that we were able to predict the location of the final touch before 29% of the approach action was completed.

PREFERRED LATENCY LEVEL

Armed with our prediction model, we are able to provide tapping feedback with a latency range from -100ms to 100ms. From previous work, we know that latencies below 24ms are unperceivable by humans [20], however we have no understanding if unperceivable latency UI is, indeed, preferred by users. Using our predictive model, we generated widgets with different levels of latency and evaluated what amount of latency participants prefer. We were particularly curious about participants' responses to *negative* latency – that is, having a UI element respond *before* they finish reaching for it.

Participants

We recruited 16 right-handed participants from the local community (8 male, 8 female) with ages ranging from 20 to 31. On average, our participants own two touch devices and spend three to four hours a day using them. We paid participants $10 for a half-hour session.

Task

The participants were shown a screen with two buttons, each with different response latency. Before tapping each button once, they were asked to touch and hold a visible starting point until audio feedback, which would occur randomly between 0.7 and 1.0 seconds later, was given. They then were asked to indicate which button they preferred.

Design

Tasks were designed with one independent variable, response latency. To limit combinatorial explosion, we decided to provide widget feedback under five different conditions: immediately as a finger prediction is made (0ms after prediction) and then artificially added latencies of 40, 80, 120, and 160ms to the predicted time, resulting in 10 unique pairs of latency. To remove the possible preference for buttons placed to the left or right, we also flipped the order of the buttons, resulting in 20 total pairs. The ordering of the 20 pairs was randomized within each session. Latency level was also randomly generated. Participants completed 7 sessions of 20 pairs and were given a 1-minute break between sessions, for a total of 2240 total trials.

Methodology

To calculate the effective latency we first calculate the response time and the touch time. The response time is calculated by artificially adding to the time of prediction some latency (between 0 and 160ms). For touch time, we consider when the Surface detected the touch and subtract a known Surface latency of 137ms, measured using the methodology described in [27]. The effective latency is the difference between the response time and the touch time.

Results

After pressing both buttons in one trial, participants indicated which button they preferred. Each trial resulted in 2 points (not shown) in Figure 9; one at (L1, 1) for the preferred latency L1, and one at (L2, 0) for the other latency L2. For each participant, a curve is fit to 280 data points. Three possible curves emerged, increasing, decreasing, and peaked. During debriefing, we questioned participants regarding how they select the preferred latency, and identified three strategies (Faster is Always Better, On Touch, Visible Latency), aligned with the curve of each participant. Three corresponding curves in Figure 9 were

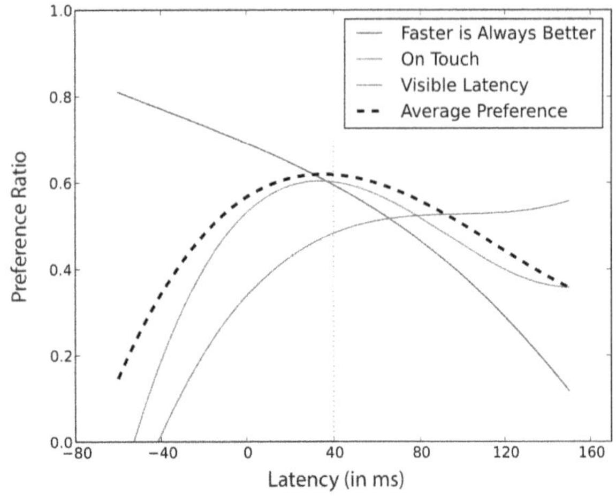

Figure 9: Preference curve for each observed trend and average latency preference for all participants.

generated from the participants in each of these three groups. The dotted line is a curve fit to all data points, indicating that overall participants preferred latencies around 40ms.

Faster is Always Better. Four participants that preferred negative latency were aware that the system was providing feedback before the actual touch, but are confident that the prediction is always accurate and therefore, the system should respond as soon as a prediction is possible.

On Touch. Eight participants preferred a system where effective latency is between 0ms and 40ms. Participants commented that they liked that the system reacted exactly when their finger touched, but not before. When asked why they did not prefer negative latency, participants mentioned loss of control and lack of trust regarding the predictive accuracy of the system as reasons for this preference.

Visible Latency. Four participants preferred visible latency. When asked about the feeling of immediate response, they expressed that they were not yet confident regarding the predictive model and felt that an immediate response wasn't indicative of a successful recognition. Visible latency gave them a feeling of being in control of the system and, therefore, they preferred it to immediate response. This was true even for trials where prediction was employed.

Our results show that there is a strong preference for latencies that are only achievable through the use of prediction. Overall, our participants indicated that they preferred the lower-latency button in 62% of the study's trials. We ran a Wilcoxon Signed-Rank test comparing the percent of trials where the lower latency was preferred to the percent of trials where the higher latency was preferred, and found a significant difference between the two percentages ($Z = 2.78$ $p = 0.003$). 12 out of 16 participants preferred effective latencies below 40ms, which was concluded to be unperceivable for 85% of the participants [20].

NEW OPPORTUNITIES AND CONSIDERATIONS

In this section, we detail a number of new interaction opportunities that our prediction model provides and discuss some of the considerations that system designers must address when employing these techniques.

Reducing Apparent Latency

Our motivating use case is the reduction of visual latency in order to provide the user with a more reactive touch-input experience. Based on our validation study, our model can predict touch location accurately enough at a sufficient time horizon to support simultaneous touch and visual response. A prediction 128ms prior to the finger touching the device is sufficient to pre-buffer and display the visual response to the input action. We believe that this work validates the assertion that computer systems can be made to provide immediate, real-world-like responses to touch input.

Beyond accelerating traditional visual feedback, our approach enables a new model of feedback based on predicted and actual input. With the prediction data from this model, soft feedback can be designed to provide an immediate response to tapping, eliminating the perception of latency. After the touch sensor captures the touch event, a transition from the previous soft feedback to the next user interface (UI) state can be designed to provide a responsive and fluent experience, instead of showing the corresponding UI state directly.

Reducing Programmatic Latency

Beyond changes to the visual appearance of GUI elements, touch-controlled applications execute arbitrary application logic in response to input. A 128-200ms prediction horizon provides system designers with the intriguing possibility of kicking-off time consuming programmatic responses to input *before the input occurs*.

As an example, consider the widely adopted practice of pre-caching web content based on the hyperlinks present in the page being currently viewed. Pre-caching has been shown to significantly reduce page-loading times. However, it comes at the expense of increasing both bandwidth usage and the loads on the web servers themselves, as content is often cached but not always consumed. Additionally, with the potential for many referenced URLs on any one page, it is not always clear to algorithm designers which links to pre-fetch, meaning that clicked-on links may not have already been cached.

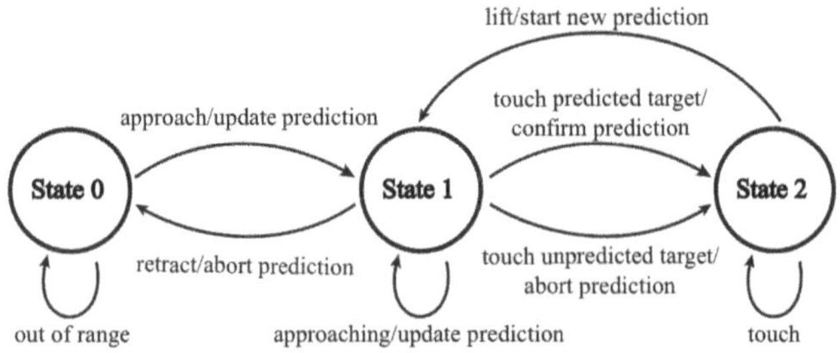

Figure 10: Transitions between 3 states of touch input that model the starting and stopping of actions, based on prediction input.

A web-browser coupled with our input prediction model would gain a 128-200ms head-start on loading linked pages. Recent analysis has suggested that the median web-page loading time for desktop systems is 2.45s [1]. As such, a head-start could represent a 5-8% improvement in page loading time, without increasing bandwidth usage or server burden. Similar examples include the loading of launched applications and the caching of the contents of a directory.

To fully take advantage of predicted input, we propose a modification to the traditional 3-state model of graphical input, proposed by Buxton [5], that allows for programmatic responses to be started and aborted as appropriate as the input system updates its understanding of the user's intent. Figure 10 shows this model: in State 1, related actions can be issued by the input system as predictions (direction, location, and time) of a possible action are received. When no actual input is being performed (e.g. the user retracts hand), the input system will stop all actions. When the actual touch target turns out not to be the predicted one, the system may also stop all actions but this will not add extra latency compared to the traditional 3-state model. On the other hand, if the touch sensor confirms the predicted action, the latency of the touch sensor, network, rendering, and all the procedure related parts will be reduced.

Recognizing unintended input

Another possible application of our prediction model is the reduction of accidental input by masking unintended areas. Based on our data analysis, the lift-off itself affords a coarse prediction of target direction, as the majority of touches we recorded were roughly planar. In addition, as the prediction target is updated, the potential area for touchdown will shrink. Therefore, the input system can label the touch events in the areas where touchdown is not likely as accidental events and ignore them.

DISCUSSION

Our results indicate that solving the problem of latency has clear implications about how users perceive system performance. If the predicted touchdown point is not accurate users can detect the difference, not always favorably, especially when presented with negative latency. On the other hand, it seems that if we are capable of eliminating perceived latency, with time, users will adapt and expect an immediate response out of their interactive systems.

Our prediction model is not constrained to only solving latency. The approach is rich in motion data and can be used to enrich many UIs. For example, the velocity of a finger can be mapped to pressure, or the approach direction can be mapped to different gestures. Equally important, perhaps, is the possibility to predict when a finger is leaving a display but not landing again inside the interaction surface, effectively indicating that the user is stopping interaction. This can be useful, for example, to remove UI elements from a video application when the user is leaving the interaction region.

The model relies on a high fidelity 3D tracking system, currently unavailable for most commercial products. Here we provide a detailed discussion about how to enable it in everyday life. We used a Vicon tracking system, running at 120Hz, to capture the pre-touch data. As this high frequency tracking is not realistic for most commercial products, we tested the model at 60Hz, slower than most commercial sensors. Although prediction is delayed 8ms on average, the later fit has the benefit of increasing prediction accuracy, because the finger is closer to the display.

Some commercial products already include accurate hover sensing technique, such as Wacom Intuos with EMR-based sensor and Leap Motion with vision-based sensor; both are able to run at 200Hz, with sub-millimeter accuracy. Moreover, the model predicts tapping location when the finger is 2.87cm and 3.22cm away from the screen in our studies; these results are within capabilities of EMR [12] and vision. Additionally, a number of plausible technologies for achieving hover sensing appeared recently in HCI research. HACHIStack [17] has a sensing height of 1.05cm above a screen with 31μs latency. Retrodepth [21] can track hand motion in a large 3D physical input space of 30x30x30cm. Therefore, we believe an accurate, low-latency hover sensing is on its way soon. We also envision that, when faster touch sensor and CPU finally bring the nearly zero tapping latency, this model will remain useful for achieving negative latency, impossible even for a zero-latency touch sensor.

In this paper, we built a prediction model and evaluate long ballistic pointing tasks. However, in realistic tasks, the finger motion will be much more complex, with pauses, hesitation, and short tracking distances. To make the model robust to these changes, we propose the fine-tuning of two variables that determine when the system starts predicting: the vertical distance, tuned at 4cm (in Z) to avoid direction changes normal to touch approaches, and approach angle tuned at 23° (for our system) to confirm that the finger entered a drop down phase. With this tuning, the model predicts location and time in the last 29% of the entire trajectory. Other kinematic features, such as the approaching velocity and direction can also be integrated into the model to make it more robust. Still, there is no doubt that the model would benefit from evaluation with real tasks, and we encourage the effort to make the model work perfectly in the real world.

CONCLUSION

We present a prediction model for direction, location, and contact time of a tapping action on touch devices. With this model, the feedback is shown to the user at the moment they touch the display, eliminating the touchdown latency. Results from the user study reveal a strong preference for unperceived latency feedback. Also, predicting the touch input long before the actual touch brings the opportunity to reduce not only the visual latency but also latency of various parts of a system that are involved in the response to the predicted touch input.

ACKNOWLEDGEMENTS
We would like to thank members of DGP and Tactual Labs for their support of the project. We also thank Kate Dowd for her writing assistance.

REFERENCES

1. http://news.softpedia.com/news/The-Average-Web-Page-Loads-in-2-45-Seconds-Google-Reveals-265446.shtml
2. http://www.samsung.com/global/microsite/galaxys5/ Samsung Galaxy S5
3. Annett, M., *et al.* 2011. Medusa: a proximity-aware multi-touch tabletop. *UIST '11*, 337-346.
4. Baudisch, P., *et al.* 2003. Drag-and-Pop and Drag-and-Pick: techniques for accessing remote screen content on touch- and pen-operated systems. INTERACT '03, 57-64.
5. Buxton, W. 1990. A Three-State Model of Graphical Input. *INTERACT '11*, 449-456.
6. Dietz, P., and Leigh, D.. 2001. DiamondTouch: a multi-user touch technology. *UIST '01*, 219-226.
7. Fitts M.. 1954. The information capacity of the human motor system in controlling the amplitude of movement. J. of Experimental Psychology, Vol 47, N6,. 381–391.
8. Fitzmaurice, G., Ishii, H., and Buxton, W. 1995.. Bricks: laying the foundations for graspable user interfaces. *CHI'95*, 442-449.
9. Fitzmaurice, G., Khan, A., Pieké, R., Buxton, B., Kurtenbach, G..2003. Tracking Menus. *UIST '03,* 71-79.
10. Flash T., and Hogan N.. 1985. The Coordination of Arm Movements: An Experimentally Confirmed Mathematical Model. *Journal of Neurosciences*. Vol 5. N7, 1688-1703.
11. Forlines, C. and Balakrishnan, R.. 2008. Evaluating tactile feedback and direct vs. indirect stylus input in pointing and crossing selection tasks. *CHI '08*. 1563-1572.
12. Funahashi, T., Toshiaki S., and Tsuguya Y.. 1989. Position detecting apparatus. U.S. Patent No. 4,878,553.
13. Galloway, J. & Koshland, G.. 2002. General coordination of shoulder, elbow and wrist dynamics during multijoint arm movements. *Exp. Brain Rsch*, Vol 142,163-180.
14. Grosse-Puppendahl, T. *et al.* 2013. Swiss-cheese extended: an object recognition method for ubiquitous interfaces based on capacitive proximity sensing. *CHI '13*.
15. Grossman, T., Hinckley, K., Baudisch, P., Agrawala, N., and Balakrishnan, R.. 2006. Hover widgets: using the tracking state to extend the capabilities of pen-operated devices. *CHI '06*, 861-870.
16. Grossman, T., Wigdor, D., and Balakrishnan, R. 2004 Multi finger gestural interaction with 3D volumetric displays. *UIST '04*, 61-70.
17. Hachisu, T. and Kajimoto, H.. 2013. HACHIStack: dual-layer photo touch sensing for haptic and auditory tapping interaction. *CHI '13,* 1411-1420.
18. Hilliges O. *et al.* 2009. Interactions in the air: adding further depth to interactive tabletops. *UIST '09*, 139-148.
19. Hinckley, K. *et al.*1998. Interaction and modeling techniques for desktop two-handed input. *UIST '98*, 49-58.
20. Jota R. *et al.* 2013. How fast is fast enough? A study of the effects of latency in direct-touch pointing tasks. *CHI '13*.
21. Kim D. *et al.* 2014. RetroDepth: 3D silhouette sensing for high-precision input on and above physical surfaces. *CHI '13*, 1377-1386.
22. Leigh, D. *et al.* 2014. High-rate, low-Latency multi-touch sensing with simultaneous orthogonal multiplexing. *UIST '14*
23. MacKenzie, I. S.. 1995. Movement time prediction in human-computer interfaces. *Readings in HCI*, 483-493.
24. Marquardt N. *et al.* 2011. The continuous interaction space: interaction techniques unifying touch and gesture on and above a digital surface. *INTERACT '11*, 461-476.
25. Miller, R. B.. 1968. Response time in man-computer conversational transactions. *Joint Comp.* 1968, 267-277.
26. Murata, A.. 1998. Improvement of pointing time by predicting targets in pointing with a PC mouse. *IJHCI '98*. 10, 1, 23–32.
27. Ng, A., Lepinski, J., Wigdor, D., Sanders, S., and Dietz, P.. 2012. Designing for Low-Latency Direct-Touch Input. *UIST '12*, 453-464.
28. Spindler, M., Martsch, M., and Dachselt, R.. 2012 Going Beyond the Surface: Studying Multi-Layer Interaction Above the Tabletop. *CHI '12*, 1277-1286.
29. Steed, A. 2008. A simple method for estimating the latency of interactive, real-time graphics simulations. *VRST '08*,123-129.
30. Subramanian, S., *et al.* 2006. Multi-layer interaction for digital tables. *UIST '06*, 269-272.
31. Theremin, L.. 1928. Method of and apparatus for the generation of sounds. U.S. Patent No. 1,661,058..
32. Uno, Y., Mitsuo, K., and Rika S., 1989. Formation and control of optimal trajectory in human multijoint arm movement. *Biological Cybernetics*, 61, 89-101.
33. Wigdor, D., and Wixon, D.. *Brave NUI World: Designing Natural User Interfaces for Touch and Gesture*, 1 ed. Morgan Kaufmann, Apr. 2011.
34. Wilson A.. 2010. Using a depth camera as a touch sensor. *ITS '10*, 69-72.
35. Wilson, A.. 2004. TouchLight: An imaging touch screen and display for gesture-based interaction. *ICMI '04*,69-76.
36. Wobbrock, J., Cutrell, E., Harada, S., and MacKenzie, S.. 2008. An error model for pointing based on Fitts' law. *CHI '08*, 1613-1622.
37. Yang, X., Grossman, T., Irani, P., and Fitzmaurice,G.2011. TouchCuts and TouchZoom: Enhanced Target Selection for Touch Displays using Finger Proximity Sensing. *CHI '11*, 2585-2594.

Detecting Tapping Motion on the Side of Mobile Devices By Probabilistically Combining Hand Postures

William McGrath*
Stanford University
wmcgrath@stanford.edu

Yang Li
Google Research
yangli@acm.org

ABSTRACT
We contribute a novel method for detecting finger taps on the different sides of a smartphone, using the built-in motion sensors of the device. In particular, we discuss new features and algorithms that infer side taps by probabilistically combining estimates of tap location and the hand pose—the hand holding the device. Based on a dataset collected from 9 participants, our method achieved 97.3% precision and 98.4% recall on tap event detection against ambient motion. For detecting single-tap locations, our method outperformed an approach that uses inferred hand postures deterministically by 3% and an approach that does not use hand posture inference by 17%. For inferring the location of two consecutive side taps from the same direction, our method outperformed the two baseline approaches by 6% and 17% respectively. We discuss our insights into designing the detection algorithm and the implication on side tap-based interaction behaviors.

Author Keywords
Mobile interaction; motion gestures; machine learning.

INTRODUCTION
The capacitive touchscreen, as the major input medium of mobile devices, has been overloaded with interaction behaviors. To access rich functionalities and data items on a mobile device, a user often needs to navigate deep hierarchies of interfaces and deal with mode-switching issues, which can be frustrating, time consuming and error-prone. Thus, it is important to enable new input events to expand the bandwidth of mobile interaction.

Previous work has explored a variety of techniques for enhancing existing touchscreen behaviors (e.g., [1, 2]) or expanding the input vocabulary of mobile devices (e.g., [5, 9, 11]). In particular, side taps—tapping on the side of the physical frame of a mobile device—has shown promise. As a natural extension of tapping actions beyond the touchscreen, side taps can be performed eyes-free and do not cause the user to block the screen with their fingers.

Previously, Ronkainen et al. investigated the feasibility and usability of tap input using custom sensors and platforms [8], which revealed the usefulness of side taps and the challenges for detecting them reliably. Recently, Samsung Galaxy S III smartphones allowed a user to double tap the top of the phone as a shortcut for moving to the top of a list [10]. We intend to develop methods to not only detect the occurrence of a side tap event but also the side of the phone that is tapped, which provides additional parameters for activating tap location-specific functionality (see Figure 1).

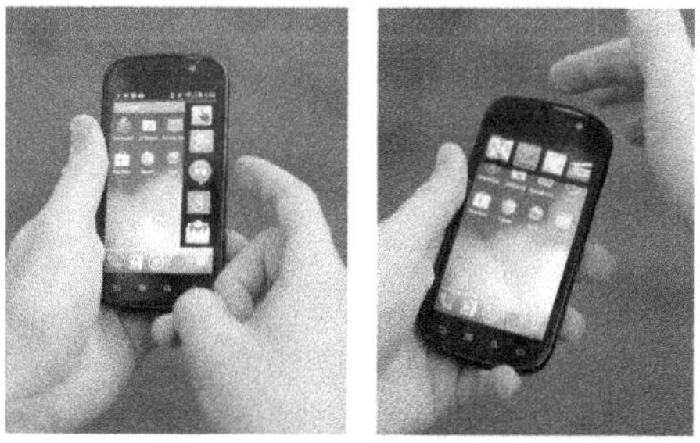

Figure 1. The user taps the right and the top side of a phone that bring out different sets of shortcuts.

In this paper, we devised a novel method for detecting finger-tapping motion on the sides of a smartphone using the built-in inertial sensors of the phone, with no additional hardware. To predict which side of the device the user has tapped, our method uses the hand pose—which hand is holding the device—as a hidden variable and then probabilistically combines estimates of the hand pose and tap location, which effectively reduces the complexity for classification and improves the accuracy compared to previous methods. This approach can potentially be applied to other handheld motion inference situations. We elaborate on the design of our detection method and its performance in comparison to other baseline methods. We also discuss its implication in designing side tap-based interaction.

RELATED WORK
Previous work has explored a variety of enhancements for mobile devices for detecting new interaction events, such as using acoustic sensors [5], custom capacitive touchscreens [1, 11], pressure sensors [13], or even building custom smartphones [8]. Although these methods demonstrated

UIST '14, October 05 - 08 2014, Honolulu, HI, USA

ACM 978-1-4503-3069-5/14/10...$15.00.
http://dx.doi.org/10.1145/2642918.2647363

* The work was done during an internship with Google Research.

potential for detecting new events, they rely on custom sensors or platforms, which limits their practicality.

In contrast, on-board sensors such as accelerometers and gyroscopes are widely available on commodity devices. However, these sensors are often less expressive or precise than custom ones for capturing specific behaviors. As a result, prior work has mostly employed on-board sensors for detecting easily distinguishable motion events [9, 10] or used them as auxiliary channels for inferring or disambiguating touchscreen input [2, 6, 7, 12]. For example, previous work investigated the feasibility of inferring tap location on the touchscreen, using motion sensors, as the user types on a soft keyboard on the touchscreen [6, 7]. Prior work also developed methods for improving touchscreen text entry by compensating for extraneous movement due to the user walking [2], or dynamically adapting for detected hand postures [3, 4].

Compared to the prior art, we focused on detecting tap events on the side of a device. Although early work has investigated the usefulness of side taps [8], little work in the literature has discussed the methods for detecting the occurrence and location of these events, especially using on-board sensors on commodity mobile devices. BezelTap combines a tap on the tablet bezel and a successive tap on the touchscreen for fast activation [12], rather using the tap on the bezel as a standalone event. Spelmezan et al. augmented an iPod touch device with continuous pressure sensors on its side for easy navigation [13]. Ronkainen et al. investigated the usability of tap input using custom sensors and platforms [8] and revealed the challenges for detecting them reliably. Recently, Samsung Galaxy S III smartphones enabled double tapping on the top of the phone as a shortcut event [10]. However, none of the previous work provides a viable solution for detecting side tap events (especially single taps) and tap locations using built-in mobile sensors. In addition, the previous work lacks technical details and empirical analyses, which makes it difficult for comparison and improvements for further research.

Because mobile devices are often handheld while used, it is natural to consider the hand posture in detecting motion.

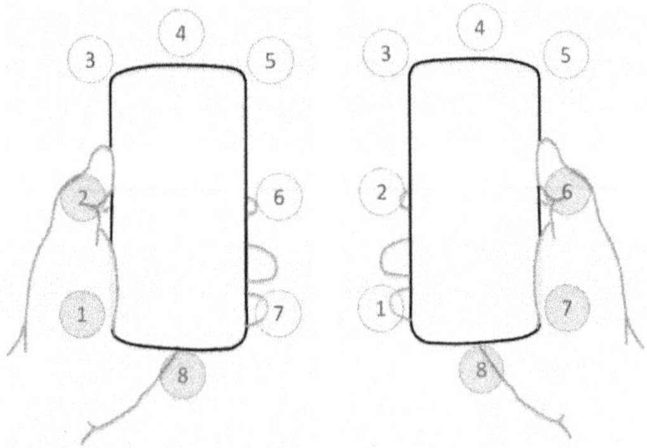

Figure 2. The side tap targets that we sampled for each holding hand during data collection. The locations labeled red in shaded circles are excluded for that holding hand.

Prior work has demonstrated the usefulness of using hand postures to improve interaction and inference [1, 3, 4]. Compared to previous work, our method probabilistically combines the estimate of the hand posture and tap location, rather than deterministically using the best guess of the holding hand for further inference as the prior work does. Our method is theoretically sound and it outperformed the deterministic use of hand postures.

THE DESIGN OF SIDE TAP DETECTION METHODS

To scope our exploration, we focus on detecting side taps when the mobile device is in use, rather than enabling an always-active motion gesture such as what PocketTouch does [11]. We also aim at detecting which side of the device is being tapped to allow location-specific behaviors.

Data Collection

To reliably detect side taps and their locations, we collected side tap samples—positive samples—and several hours of ambient data—negative samples—from 10 participants (6 female, 4 male). They ranged in age from 20 to 32 years old. 9 were right-handed and one was left-handed. All but one were regular smartphone users.

Procedures & Tasks. Participants were asked to complete tasks in two situations: *seated* versus *walking*. In the seated condition, participants were seated comfortably in an office chair. In the walking situation, participants were asked to walk at a natural pace following a square path roughly 20 feet on a side. We focus on the posture where the user is holding the smartphone with one hand and interacting with the device using their other hand. We asked participants to alternate the holding and interaction hands during the study.

To collect the motion data produced during everyday smartphone usage, we asked participants to perform a list of typical smartphone tasks, such as writing messages and browsing the Internet. We also asked participants to press hard buttons on the side of the device such as the volume buttons since they might generate similar motion to side taps. We then asked participants to execute a series of side taps on the device. Although we ultimately only classify a tap as top, left, or right, we instructed the participants to tap the side of the phone at five of the eight compass directions with the index finger of their hand that was not holding the device (see Figure 2), a common interaction scenario. The order that the directions were presented was randomized. Three locations, marked as red labels in the shaded circles, for either hand position were excluded because they were either awkward to reach or often blocked by the holding hand. Since each participant was instructed to perform 5 sets of 10 taps under each condition (2 use situations x 2 holding hands), the process collected 2000 side tap samples. However, issues during one trial reduced the useful number of samples to 1800 across 9 users.

Data Processing. Our data collection was conducted using a Samsung Galaxy S phone running Android. Our data collection tool instructed the participants to hold the device with a specific hand and tap on a target location in a 2-

second window. A side tap typically lasts from 100ms to 300ms, but a 2-second window allows the participant time to react to the tool's prompt. Our tool recorded the phone's accelerometer and gyroscope data as it was used. Ambient data was collected continuously whenever the tool was not expecting a tap, i.e., outside of the tap window.

Because using the entire 2-second window of a sample can introduce additional noise and might incorrectly capture consecutive side taps at runtime, we extracted a 300ms positive sample containing the largest absolute acceleration value from each original tap sample based on the observation that a side tap tends to co-occur with the largest absolute acceleration value. For the ambient motion data, we extracted negative samples by segmenting the ambient motion stream of each participant using a 300ms-sliding window, which generated 26000 negative samples in total.

Featurization

To effectively detect side taps, we need to design features that can characterize side tap motion. In particular, we hypothesize that a side tap motion consists of two physical stages: the *impact* motion that is generated when a side tap impacts the device towards a specific direction and then the opposite *return* motion that is when the user's arm brings the device back to its original position after the impact. Based on the collected side tap samples, we found that some side tap samples are consistent with our hypothesis (see Figure 3). We can easily calculate the impact direction of a side tap using the magnitude of acceleration on the X and Y axes at the first spike—*atan2*(y, x).

However, we found many other side tap samples missed either the impact or the return acceleration spike. One important reason for this phenomenon is that a side tap happens too fast for the accelerometers in our experimental smartphone (sampling at 50HZ) to reliably capture these spikes. To make our approach robust to low acceleration sampling rates, we only attempt to capture one spike in a side tap and calculate a direction angle feature based on the acceleration along the sensor's X and Y axes when either records the largest absolute magnitude of acceleration during the tap. However, without knowing if the spike is from the impact or the return motion, we cannot reliably determine which side the tap comes from. Instead, the direction angle feature is a good discriminator for determining the holding hand (see Figure 4). Since the holding hand serves as a pivot, side tapping causes the device moves diagonally rather than along perfect horizontal or vertical directions.

In addition, to capture the characteristics of a side tap that are less obvious, we added brute force features that are frequently used by previous work for motion detection, such as the mean, the standard deviation, skewness and kurtosis of each sensor axis. We also implemented correlation features between the axes of the same sensor, such as the 1-norm, Infinity norm and Frobenius norm by treating each axis as a matrix column [6], and between sensors, such as Pearson correlation coefficients. For the

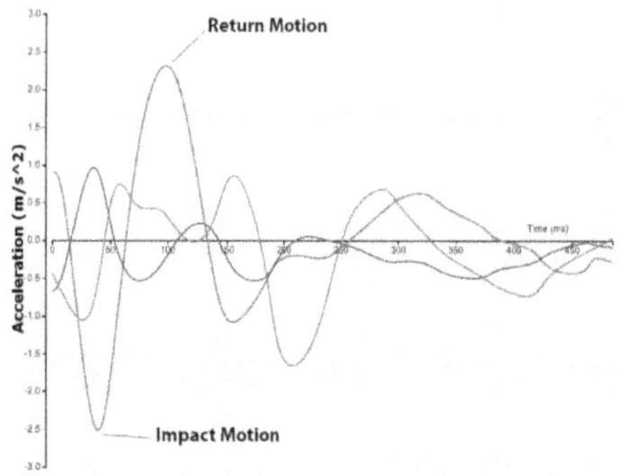

Figure 3. The interpolated acceleration plot of a side tap sample on the X (red), Y (green) and Z (blue) axes when holding the phone with the left hand and tapping the right side of the phone with the index finger of the right hand.

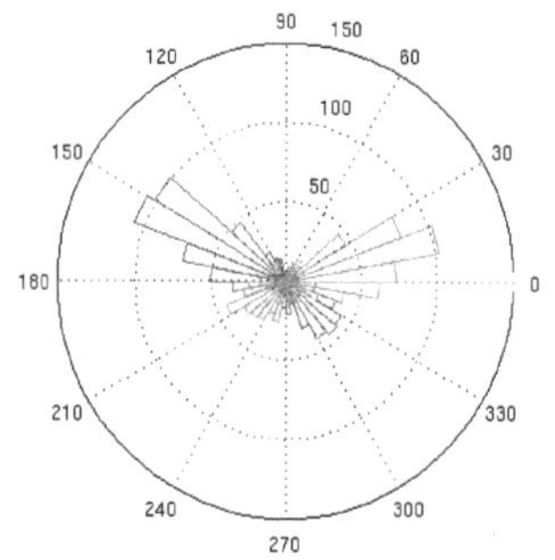

Figure 4. An angle histogram of side taps from all sampled directions while holding the smartphone with the left hand (blue) vs. the right hand (red).

following training and prediction stages, the feature values of each sample are standardized based on the mean and variance of each feature of training samples. We also normalized each feature vector with its L2 norm.

Recognizing Side Taps

There are two steps in recognizing side taps. We first need to detect the occurrence of a side tap event from the continuous sensor streams. Once detected, we need to determine which side of the device the user has tapped.

Detecting Side Tap Occurrences. We trained a Linear SVM classifier based on the side tap data (the positive samples) and the ambient data (the negative samples). Because this classifier needs to continuously run, we decided not to use the matrix features for detection to save computation, as the results were acceptable without their inclusion. Because the ambient data has significantly more samples, we balanced the training data set of positive and negative samples to avoid negatively skewing our classification model. Based on a 9-fold cross validation splitting on participants—8 participants' data for training and 1 participant's for testing, our tap detection classifier achieves high accuracy 97.9% with mean precision of 97.3% and recall 98.4%. In particular, we found side taps were rarely confused with physical side-button presses (such as the volume buttons), because side taps are generally more swift and forceful, which generate an acceleration of much larger magnitude in a short period of time than button presses.

Inferring Side Tap Locations. We infer which side of the device the user has tapped, $Side_{tap}$, as the side, L, that has the highest probability based on sensor readings, s.

$$Side_{tap} = \underset{L \in \{Left, Top, Right\}}{\operatorname{argmax}} P(L|s) \quad (1)$$

As mentioned in the previous section, there are three target sides, i.e., the left, top and right side. The bottom side is excluded because it is ergonomically difficult to use. Previous work has shown that knowing the hand posture can improve the efficiency of follow-up predictions [3]. This insight is important in our context—there are only two of the three sides usable in each holding hand condition. As a result, we decide to leverage the holding hand information in our tap location inference by introducing a hidden variable H (see Equation 2).

$$P(L|s) = \sum_{H \in \{Left, Right\}} P(L|Hs)P(H|s) \quad (2)$$

H represents the hand holding the device—left or right. Notice that in contrast to prior work that uses the best guess of the holding hand deterministically and switches its follow-up prediction model, we probabilistically combine the outcome of the holding hand prediction and the tap location recognition, conditioned on a given holding hand. We hypothesize that our probabilistic approach could outperform the deterministic approach due to imperfect holding hand detection.

Equation 2 uses two types of classifiers: one infers the holding hand and the other infers tap locations given each holding hand—that includes two separate classifiers, one for each holding hand. We trained the holding hand binary Linear SVM classifier based on the tap samples. It operates on the full feature vector that includes the matrix features, since it will only be invoked once a tap is detected. Based on a 9-fold cross validation on participants, the classifier achieves 89% mean accuracy (SD=6%), which is encouraging but not perfect, as we speculated.

We then trained a tap location classifier (also using a Linear SVM) for each of the holding hand conditions. Because our side tap samples were collected for specific locations on the side, there are several ways to train the classifier. We can train a binary classifier for the two target sides in each holding hand condition, by merging the data belonging to each side, e.g., location 6 and 7 belong to the right side and location 3 and 4 belong to the top (see Figure 2). The corner locations such as location 5 can be considered as a part of either side, so their data can be left out or shared by both the sides. Alternatively, we can train a multi-class classifier that infers 5 locations in each holding hand condition and then combine their probabilities according to the side to which they belong. Empirically we found the second strategy that combines probabilities outperforms the first approach that merges the training data.

One important detail in calculating Equation 2 is that we need to transform SVMs scores to probabilities before they can be combined. This is important to make the impact of each component in Equation 2 probabilistically proportional on the final outcome. We achieved this by fitting a probability density function (using a Gaussian mixture model) over the output scores of each classifier in Eq. 2 based on the training data.

To find out how our approach performs, we compared it with two baseline approaches: directly predicting the tapped side without using holding hand information or using the holding hand information deterministically—that resembles the previous work [3]. We used Linear SVMs based on the same dataset for these baseline methods. Based on a 9-fold cross validation, our probabilistic combination approach achieved 83% mean accuracy (SD=8%), which outperforms the two baseline approaches: 80% (SD=8%) with deterministic use of holding hand information and 66% (SD=9%) with no holding hand used (see Figure 5), χ^2_2 =102.48, p<.01. The difference between the Probabilistic and Deterministic methods is not significant, χ^2_1 =3.04, p=0.08, due to the high variance across participants. However, after we remove the two lowest performers (participant 6 and 7) from analysis, the difference between the two methods becomes significant, χ^2_1 =4.1025, p=0.04.

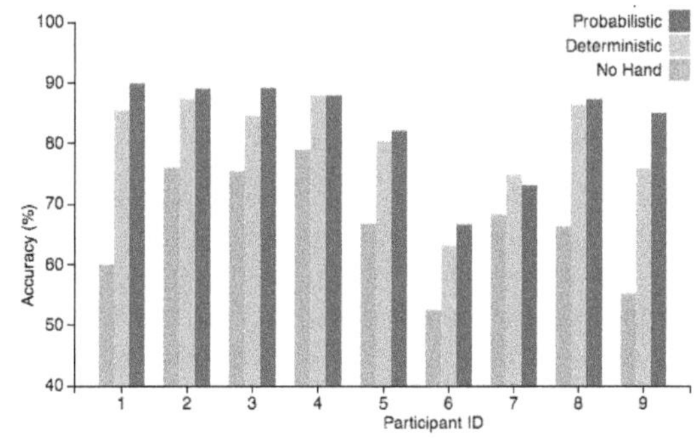

Figure 5. The accuracy for inferring the location of single side taps for each round in a 9-fold cross validation, under three conditions: probabilistically combining hand postures (Blue), deterministically using the best guess of hand postures (Green), and directly inferring tapping location without hand posture inference (Red).

Using single side taps as a building block, we can construct a variety of compound interaction events by combining side taps from the same or different locations. We analyzed how well our method can detect the location of two consecutive single taps from the same direction using the same feature set, based on data samples synthesized from our single tap data. We found the accuracy of our method achieved 90% (SD=8%) accuracy, which again outperformed the baseline methods: 84% (SD=10%) of the deterministic use of hand postures and 73% (SD=12%) when no hand posture inference is involved (see Figure 6), χ^2_2 =127.32, p<0.01. The pairwise difference between Probabilistic and Deterministic methods is significant, χ^2_1 =13.32, p<0.001, even when all the participants are included. This analysis indicated that higher accuracy can be acquired for detecting the locations of a side tap sequence.

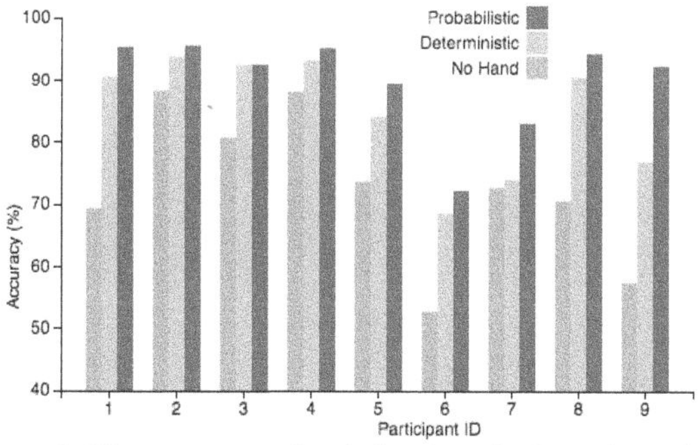

Figure 6. The accuracy for inferring the location of two consecutive single taps from the same side of the device.

DISCUSSIONS

The experiments showed that our method can reliably detect the occurrences of single side tap events using smartphones' built-in motion sensors. This presents substantial progress beyond prior work in the literature [8] as well as existing commercial products [10] that only detect double side tap occurrences. In addition, while prior work only discerns one tap direction, our method infers more details about a side tap event—which of the three sides of the device the user has tapped—to enable invoking tap location-specific actions (see Figure 1).

Our method demonstrated an accuracy advantage over two baseline methods in detecting side tap locations. But, the mean accuracy of our method for inferring single tap locations is still less than ideal for a fundamental interaction event. Because our method is data-driven, its performance is largely determined by the quality of training data we collected. Excluding low quality data, such as Participant 6's, from both training and testing can tremendously improve the reported accuracy. In addition, the motion sensors of our data collection phone are less sensitive than latest smartphones. Using a motion-sensitive device is crucial as a single tap event occurs extremely fast (<300ms). With the latest models, we expect better accuracy from our method.

Our method has only been trained and tested in a two-handed interaction scenario. There does not seem to be a fundamental reason that our method should have trouble with other scenarios such as tapping with the holding hand provided that it has been trained with sufficient data from those scenarios. However, there could be subtleties in feature analysis for these scenarios, e.g., we might see more motion along the Z-axis in the one-handed situation.

Lastly, an important consideration in designing side tap interaction is how to surface feedback to the user about side tap's activation status. For instance, a weak single tap could show a visual indication that certain functionality is associated with a side of the device, without activating it. A stronger single tap could skip the preview stage and activate the functionality immediately. We can easily enable this interaction scenario using a dual threshold mechanism, i.e., a lower threshold for tap detection for weak taps and a higher threshold for stronger taps—a higher precision but a lower recall.

CONCLUSIONS

We contributed a novel method for detecting side taps and their location as input events for button-less mobile interaction. The experiments indicated that our method can reliably detect side tap occurrences and outperformed two baseline approaches in detecting tap locations. Our concept of factoring hand postures probabilistically into further motion inference can be generalized and potentially benefit other handheld motion inference problems.

REFERENCES

1. Cheng, L.-P., Liang, H.-S., Wu, C.-Y., and Chen, M.Y. iGrasp: grasp-based adaptive keyboard for mobile devices. CHI'13. 3037-3046.
2. Goel, M., Findlater, L., and Wobbrock, J. WalkType: using accelerometer data to accomodate situational impairments in mobile touch screen text entry. CHI'12. 2687-2696.
3. Goel, M., Jansen, A., Mandel, T., Patel, S.N., and Wobbrock, J.O. ContextType: using hand posture information to improve mobile touch screen text entry. CHI'13. 2795-2798.
4. Goel, M., Wobbrock, J., and Patel, S. GripSense: using built-in sensors to detect hand posture and pressure on commodity mobile phones. UIST'12. 545-554.
5. Harrison, C., Schwarz, J., and Hudson, S.E. TapSense: enhancing finger interaction on touch surfaces. UIST'11. 627-636.
6. Miluzzo, E., Varshavsky, A., Balakrishnan, S., and Choudhury, R.R. Tapprints: your finger taps have fingerprints. MobiSys'12. 323-336.
7. Owusu, E., Han, J., Das, S., Perrig, A., and Zhang, J. ACCessory: password inference using accelerometers on smartphones. HotMobile'12. 1-6.
8. Ronkainen, S., Häkkilä, J., Kaleva, S., Colley, A., and Linjama, J. Tap input as an embedded interaction method for mobile devices. TEI'07. 263-270.
9. Ruiz, J. and Li, Y. DoubleFlip: A Motion Gesture Delimiter for Mobile Interaction. CHI'11. 2717-2720.
10. Samsung. *Galaxy SIII,* http://www.samsung.com/us/support/owners/product/SPH-L710RWPSPR.
11. Saponas, T.S., Harrison, C., and Benko, H. PocketTouch: through-fabric capacitive touch input. UIST'11. 303-308.
12. Serrano, M., Lecolinet, E., and Guiard, Y. Bezel-Tap gestures: quick activation of commands from sleep mode on tablets. CHI'13. 3027-3036.
13. Spelmezan, D., Appert, C., Chapuis, O., and Pietriga, E. Side pressure for bidirectional navigation on small devices. MobileHCI'13. 11-20.

Prefab Layers and Prefab Annotations: Extensible Pixel-Based Interpretation of Graphical Interfaces

Morgan Dixon, Conrad Nied, and James Fogarty
Computer Science & Engineering
DUB Group, University of Washington
{mdixon,anied,jfogarty}@cs.washington.edu

ABSTRACT
Pixel-based methods have the potential to fundamentally change how we build graphical interfaces, but remain difficult to implement. We introduce a new toolkit for pixel-based enhancements, focused on two areas of support. *Prefab Layers* helps developers write interpretation logic that can be composed, reused, and shared to manage the multi-faceted nature of pixel-based interpretation. *Prefab Annotations* supports robustly annotating interface elements with metadata needed to enable runtime enhancements. Together, these help developers overcome subtle but critical dependencies between code and data. We validate our toolkit with (1) demonstrative applications and (2) a lab study that compares how developers build an enhancement using our toolkit versus state-of-the art methods. Our toolkit addresses core challenges faced by developers when building pixel-based enhancements, potentially opening up pixel-based systems to broader adoption.

Author Keywords
Prefab; layers; annotations; pixel-based reverse engineering.

ACM Classification Keywords
H.5.m. Information interfaces and presentation (e.g., HCI).

INTRODUCTION AND MOTIVATION
Pixel-based methods can enable modification of interfaces without their code, independent of their implementation. For example, the applications in Figure 1 use pixel-based methods to enhance the entire desktop. The first is an implementation of the Bubble Cursor [5,12], which dynamically resizes to always select the nearest target. The next is an implementation of sliding widgets [7,18], which replaces mouse-based interface elements with touchscreen widgets. The third translates the language of interfaces for improved localization [8]. Other examples include accessibility enhancements, testing frameworks, automation tools, and help systems [6,8,30,31]. These enhancements modify interfaces in a variety ways, but they are all enabled by methods that use pixels as a universal representation.

UIST '14, October 05 - 08 2014, Honolulu, HI, USA.

http://dx.doi.org/10.1145/2642918.2647412

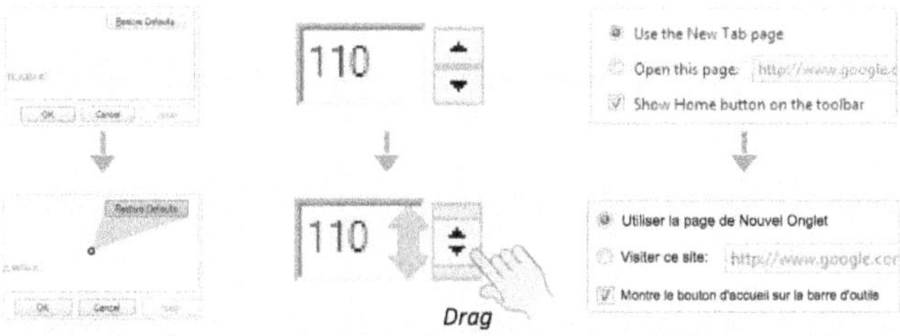

Figure 1: We present a toolkit that streamlines the implementation of pixel-based enhancements. Three examples supported by our toolkit include the Bubble Cursor [5,12], sliding widgets [7,18], and interface language translation [8].

Unfortunately, enhancements like these are difficult to implement, and so relatively few are available. There are at least two major reasons for this. First, interpreting an interface from its raw pixel values is a large and multi-faceted problem. For example, the translation enhancement requires mechanisms to identify interface elements, recover text, and perform higher-level analysis of that text. Requiring all of this functionality in a single application quickly leads to monolithic code that is difficult to develop and maintain. This problem is magnified by the fact that different enhancements require different interpretations. For example, in contrast to the translation enhancement, the Bubble Cursor is agnostic to text values and only needs to identify clickable targets. When enhancements do require similar methods that could potentially be reused, the current lack of structured support leads developers to re-implement large portions of code.

Second, writing sophisticated code is not enough to successfully interpret most interfaces. This is because some information is not obtainable through raw pixel analysis. For example, Dixon et al. report that clickable "targets" are often ambiguous and cannot be reverse engineered without human intervention [5]. This ambiguity is pervasive in pixel-based methods and causes unavoidable errors. Developers then patch their code by mixing in their own outside knowledge about an interface. This results in fragile and monolithic code that is difficult to broadly deploy.

We address these two problems in a new toolkit for pixel-based reverse engineering of graphical interfaces. First, *Prefab Layers* helps developers write interpretation logic that can be composed, reused, and shared to manage the multi-faceted nature of pixel-based methods. Second, *Prefab Annotations* supports robust annotation of interface elements with metadata that has been inferred, provided by a developer, or collected from end-users of pixel-based enhancements. Together, Prefab Layers and Prefab Annotations help developers focus on the high-level functionality of their enhancements instead of the low-level challenges of pixel-based analysis.

Contributions of this work to pixel-based methods include:

- Prefab Layers, which offer a set of techniques to simplify the development of interpretation code while encouraging composition and reuse.
- Prefab Annotations, which offer a set of techniques for managing portable and robust interface metadata.
- Demonstration of reusable interpretations implemented using our methods. These range from low-level reusable components to high-level pixel-based enhancements.
- A comparison of how developers use our methods versus state-of-the-art tools. We show that our methods speed up development time, enable code reuse, require less data management, and help developers focus on the high-level behavior of their enhancement.

RELATED WORK

We focus on pixel-based interpretation of graphical interfaces, as applied to runtime modification of existing interfaces. This section overviews prior runtime modification work, and then looks more specifically at the current strengths and limitations of pixel-based methods.

Runtime Modification

Runtime modification has broad applications in accelerating innovation and facilitating adoption. In classic work, Edwards et al. [10] and Olsen et al. [22] modify existing interfaces by replacing the toolkit drawing object and intercepting commands (e.g., draw_string). They use this to update old interfaces with new functionality, such as search and bookmark widgets. More recent examples of runtime modification leverage the open nature of a website's Document Object Model (DOM) to access and modify existing interfaces. Web-based modifications include creating mash-ups between existing applications [11,14,28], re-authoring web applications for mobile interfaces [20,21], and automating repetitious interactions [2,28].

Although websites expose a DOM, traditional approaches to modifying desktop applications are based in accessibility APIs [28] or injecting into an interface toolkit [9,10,22]. Accessibility APIs expose interface state, but unfortunately are frequently incomplete because application developers fail to implement the API. For example, Hurst et al. found 25% of elements are completely missing [15]. Injection techniques insert custom logic into an interface via the toolkit or other runtime system. However, injection must be carefully crafted for each interface and underlying toolkit. This limits the utility of injection for general-purpose enhancements, as people typically use a variety of applications implemented with several toolkits.

In contrast, pixel-based methods do not require cooperation from the developers of an interface and circumvent fragmentation of interfaces and toolkits. Leveraging these advantages, researchers have explored a variety of pixel-based approaches to recover and modify the structure of an interface. St. Amant's Segman uses hand-crafted code to identify specific types of interface elements [27]. Sikuli uses template matching and voting on local features for image-based identification of interface elements [30]. Savva uses more sophisticated computer vision techniques for automated visualization retargeting [26]. Finally, PAX presents a hybrid approach, supplementing the accessibility API with pixel-based processing [3].

Flexibility and Robustness of Pixel-Based Methods

Prior pixel-based methods enable a variety of modifications to existing interfaces, including contextual and video-based tutorials [1,25,31], interface testing frameworks [4], new window managers [29], note-taking overlays [23], and systems for exploring document workflow histories [13]. Although these begin to demonstrate the potential of pixel-based methods, most of this initial success is based on a low-level understanding of existing interfaces (e.g., the locations of salient regions in an image, the position of a single element that matches a specific template). There are few enhancements based on higher-level interpretations, as current tools are not flexible or robust enough to support multiple levels of interpretation.

Althought it is difficult to recover high-level information from pixels, the Bubble Cursor and sliding widgets enhancements in Figure 1 require relatively sophisticated interpretation. Their success is due to their combination of interpretation code and human annotation of identified elements. Specifically, their systems heuristically infer semantic information about interface elements and then use human-provided corrections to override erroneous inferences. The goal of our toolkit is to support these and other complex enhancements. Our validation demonstrates that developers can build the same methods used by the state-of-the-art Bubble Cursor implementation, and we also show how our methods allow developers to easily extend the cursor to support more advanced behaviors. We describe the details of other enhancements enabled by our toolkit, and we also describe how annotations and code can be shared among multiple enhancements.

We build on Prefab's methods for reverse engineering interface structure [6,8]. Prefab identifies interface elements from pixels and organizes them into a hierarchy. The root corresponds to the processed image, and identified elements are added as children to elements in which they are spatially contained. This spatial hierarchy is not the same as an interface's logical hierarchy, but represents visible containment (e.g., buttons, group boxes, tab panes).

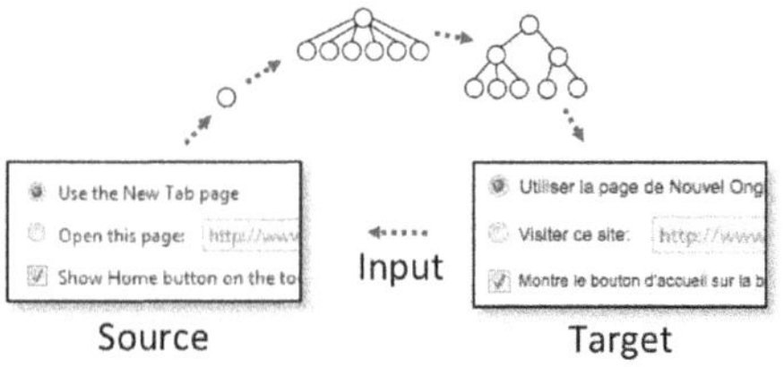

Figure 2: We present a new toolkit that structures pixel-based interpretation as a series of tree transformations.

Importantly, this tree only provides identified elements and does not include metadata about elements (e.g., whether they are targets, their widget type). The following sections describe how developers use our methods to build high-level interpretations on Prefab's low-level hierarchy.

OVERVIEW AND SCENARIO WALKTHROUGH

We now introduce our toolkit with a brief overview. To clarify how developers use our toolkit, this section also presents a scenario that walks through the development of the interface language translation enhancement in Figure 1.

Toolkit Overview

As in prior work [5,6,7,8], our methods are designed to be combined with input and output redirection. Figure 2 illustrates: (1) a source window bitmap is captured, (2) the source image is interpreted, (3) a modified interface is presented in a target window, (4) input in the target window is mapped back to the source, which then (5) generates new output that is captured to update the target. Runtime modification is realized by rapidly and repeatedly executing this cycle. Implementing this cycle is hard because of the lack of support for interpreting the source image in step (2).

To address this challenge, our toolkit decomposes interpretation into a series of tree transformations, as shown at the top of Figure 2. Interfaces are hierarchies and can be reverse engineered by iteratively working from raw pixels to a detailed interpretation. Developers implement custom interpretations for their enhancement using a combination of **layers**, **layer chains**, **interface metadata** (specifically **tags** and **annotations**), and **annotation libraries**.

A **layer** is a script that performs a specific set of tree transformations using the current structure and properties of the interface hierarchy, the pixel values of the captured screenshot, and any interface metadata.

A **layer chain** is a group of layers that execute in sequence. An interface is interpreted by passing the raw image into the first layer as a single root node, then passing the output of each layer into the next. Developers reuse and compose existing functionality by concatenating layer chains. Alternatively, they modify or enhance a chain by adding or replacing layers. As mentioned, Prefab recovers a spatial hierarchy from pixels, and so we include this functionality as the default set of layers at the beginning of a chain. Developers typically append their own custom layers to infer higher-level semantics on top of Prefab's hierarchy.

Interface metadata stores information about a specific node in a hierarchy (e.g., whether a node is a target, a corrected translation for a given node). A critical distinction is the intended persistence of the metadata representation. A **tag** is interface metadata stored on a node in the hierarchy created by a particular layer chain's interpretation of a source image. An **annotation** is interface metadata described in terms of the source image, which can be persistently stored and used with different layer chains.

An **annotation library** is a set of related annotations, and a developer will typically create a library for each type of annotation used by an enhancement. Before a layer chain executes, each layer can *import* annotations to be used at runtime. The details of how these are robustly stored and imported are challenging and discussed in a later section.

Enhancements are therefore implemented by creating and composing combinations of layers and annotation libraries. An enhancement might use several instances of a layer, but point each at a different annotation library. Alternatively, an enhancement might contain several layers that work together and share a single annotation library.

Our toolkit is implemented in C#, with annotation libraries implemented as CouchDB databases. We selected CouchDB in part because its replication support allows easy sharing and synchronization of annotation libraries. As a convenience, we also provide an interpreter that uses Iron Python to allow layers to be defined in short Python scripts. For clarity, this paper presents its example layers in Python.

Scenario: Runtime Interface Translation

To better understand how developers use our toolkit, let us follow Emily as she implements the interface translation enhancement from Figure 1. Emily has found many applications do not support her native language, or their translations are erroneous and incomplete. Instead of being stuck hoping application developers will add or fix their translations, she decides to develop an enhancement to recover text from the pixels of an interface, translate that text, and re-render interfaces incorporating the translations. Figure 3 illustrates her implementation. Emily primarily composes and parameterizes existing layers, writing only a small amount of custom behavior (as shown here in red).

Emily starts by creating an input and output redirection loop as shown in Figure 2, within which a layer chain executes upon receiving a screenshot. She then imports a layer providing Prefab's base recovery capabilities. This outputs a tree representing the elements of an interface, as recovered from its pixels. Emily finds the base layer does not recover text (an optimization based on the fact that text recovery is expensive and many enhancements do not require textual content). Emily will obviously need the interface text, so she adds a standard text recovery layer.

```
# main.py
import prefab_layers
chain = prefab_layers.new_chain()
chain.import_layer('prefab_identification')
chain.import_layer('text_recovery')
```

Emily is unable to find a layer implementing translation, so she authors a custom layer. Within her layer, she walks the tree recovered by previous layers. For each node containing recovered text, she runs the text through a web translation service and tags the node with the resulting translation.

```
# translate_text.py
from microsoft_translator import Translator
translator = Translator('client id', 'client secret')

def interpret(interpret_data):
    ''' This method is called by the Prefab Layers
        toolkit when it needs this layer
        to perform its transformations '''
    root = interpret_data.tree
    recursively_translate (root, interpret_data)

def recursively_translate(currnode, interpret_data):
    ''' This method recursively visits each node
        and translates its text value to French '''
    if currnode.get_tag('is_text'):
        text = currnode.get_tag('text_value')
        french = translator.translate(text, 'fr')
        interpret_data.add_tag(text,'translation',french)

    for child in currnode.get_children():
        recursively_translate(child, interpret_data)
```

With her core layers built, Emily now focuses on the behavior of her enhancement. For each node tagged with a translation, she uses Prefab's pixel-level methods to overlay a mask that removes the element's original text. She then renders the translated text within the same bounds.

With her enhancement now working, Emily finds many of the translations are erroneous and decides to add interactive correction. She builds an interface that allows a person who observes an erroneous translation to view the original text and provide a correction. She wants these corrections to be persistent, so she stores them as an annotation library. She then imports a layer that uses the annotations at runtime to tag elements with their corresponding corrections.

```
# main.py
params = { 'library' : 'translation_corrections' }
prefab_layers.import_layer('apply_annotations', params)
```

Emily also notices she is translating text that should not be modified, such as system paths in file widgets. Emily adds an annotation library for a "do not translate" flag, updates her interface to allow toggling this flag for any element, adds a layer to tags nodes according to this annotation, and updates her machine translation layer to respect the flag.

Emily is satisfied her enhancement gives control over whether to translate each element, but wants to minimize the need to tag elements. She therefore uses a layer that trains a classifier using collected annotations as training data. Emily does not need to implement this functionality, she just imports an existing layer and parameterizes it to use her annotation library for training. It then learns a classifier based on the annotations and at runtime tags any nodes that the classifier determines should not be translated.

With her enhancement implemented, Emily uses it in a variety of applications. She can also share her enhancement and its annotation libraries with other people. Eventually, she might decide to parameterize her layers to allow people to choose a target language. This would require adjustments to how she invokes machine translation and would probably introduce different annotation libraries to store corrections in different languages. Importantly, her layers and annotations continue to work together, so she is not burdened with migrating data or code as she iterates.

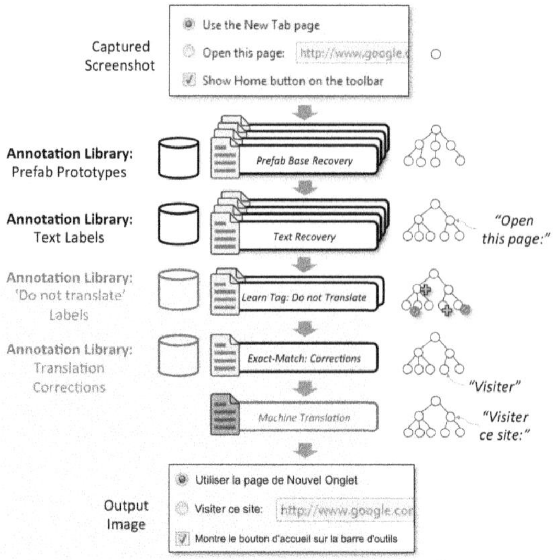

Figure 3: Our toolkit simplifies runtime interface translation. It uses layers that recover interface text, decide what text should be translated, and then present translations obtained using both machine translation and human correction.

PREFAB LAYERS

In defining pixel-based interpretation as a series of tree transformations, the primary challenge is ensuring layers have the power and flexibility to construct arbitrary interpretations while also preserving simplicity in each layer (i.e., obtaining a high *ceiling* and low *threshold* [19]). The naïve approach of simply allowing layers to arbitrarily mutate a hierarchy falls short for at least two reasons. First, it could be expected to easily regress to monolithic layers, undermining our goals for reuse and composition. Second, we have found it difficult to reason about the entire structure of a 2D interface, especially when in-progress mutations mean the current hierarchy represents neither the input nor the output of a layer. It is difficult to even traverse a hierarchy while also mutating it, and we found more complex transformations near impossible to reason about.

Prefab Layers therefore gives each layer an *immutable* view on its input. We provide a set of tree transformation operations, and layers can request any number of operations be applied to nodes in the hierarchy. All operations are then applied in batch after the layer terminates (i.e., the hierarchy is mutated *between* layers in a layer chain). This guarantees layers always observe trees that are in a stable state, making it easier to reason about a hierarchy. It also limits the scale of transformation that can be accomplished in a single layer, encouraging developers to think of interpretation in discrete steps. In the terminology of Myers et al. [19], we create a *path of least resistance* toward reuse and composition by leading developers to create layers that each implement a single piece of well-defined functionality.

Our specific operations are *tagging* a node, *setting an ancestor* for a node, and *deleting* a node. We chose these operations for simplicity and completeness. Each operates on a single element or a pair of elements, and they can be combined to create any hierarchy.

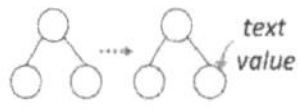

Tagging. Layers can add interface metadata at runtime by tagging nodes. Subsequent layers can read that metadata to inform their own execution.

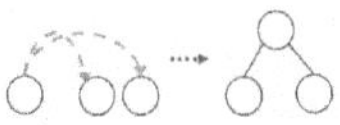

Setting an Ancestor. Layers can require a hierarchy be modified to ensure a given node is an ancestor of another given node. This can be set for two existing nodes (i.e. set one as the parent of the other), for an existing ancestor node (i.e., inserting a new child), or for an existing child (i.e., inserting a new parent).

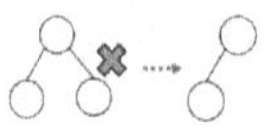

Deleting. Layers can delete nodes from a hierarchy. Any children of a deleted node are attached to the deleted node's parent.

After a layer requests a set of operations, we efficiently apply all operations to its input hierarchy. Tag operations are trivial, but are executed in batch as part of encouraging layers that perform a single step of interpretation. For each delete operation, we remove the node and attach its children to the deleted node's parent. We apply ancestry requests by adding an edge from each ancestor to its descendent and pruning any redundant edges. Finally, we raise an exception if these requests do not produce a valid tree (e.g., if operations create cycles or multiple paths between nodes).

PREFAB ANNOTATIONS

The goal of Prefab Annotations is to store metadata about specific interface elements, such that the metadata can be accessed and shared by arbitrary layers. Storing metadata is trivial, but robustly storing the interface element itself is challenging. This is because different layer chains represent the element differently (i.e., the tree structure recovered from a screenshot depends on the specific layer chain used). For example, the sliding widgets enhancement requires a tree with related buttons grouped (so they can be replaced with a single slider, as in Figure 1). In contrast, language translation can leave these buttons separate, but needs to group related text. As a result, annotations cannot be stored in an encoding that depends on the structure of one specific layer chain. Otherwise it would be difficult to share libraries of annotations among enhancements. Even within a single enhancement, a developer would not be able to iteratively build and test a layer chain because its tree representations would change throughout development.

Prefab Annotations address this challenge by storing annotations using a *pixel-level* representation. Specifically, an annotation library contains a set of image annotations, each stored as an image of an interface, a region within that image to be annotated, and associated metadata. When a layer imports an annotation library at runtime, the pixel-level representations are converted to trees consistent with the current layer chain. Therefore, the sliding widget enhancement views an annotated element as a node in a tree where related buttons are grouped together. Similarly, the translation enhancement views that same annotated element in a different tree where text is grouped together.

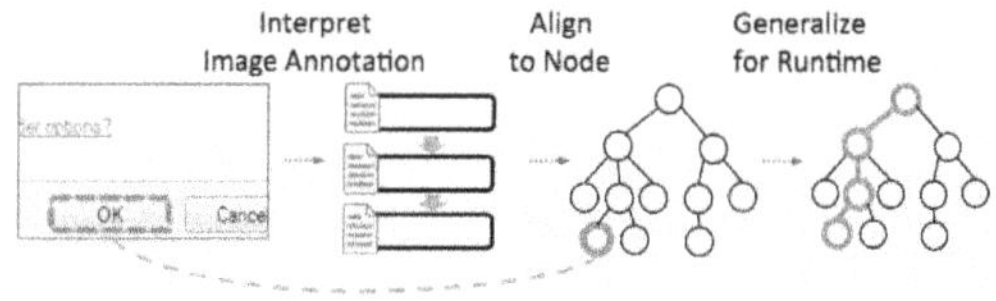

Figure 4: When a layer imports an annotation library, we provide a tree representation for each annotated element. Image annotations are interpreted by preceding layers, aligned to nodes in the resulting hierarchies, and then handed to the layer, where it computes information it will need at runtime.

Figure 4 illustrates this process. First, images in the library are interpreted by the *preceding* layers in the current chain. This creates hierarchies consistent with the current runtime. We then use region information in each annotation to identify the corresponding hierarchy node. We pass these matched pairs of image annotations and aligned tree nodes to the layer (together with a list of image annotations that do not match any nodes). Using these matched pairs, the layer computes and stores any information it will need at runtime (e.g., path descriptors, a learned classifier).

For clarity, Figure 5 presents the entire script for a simple layer that uses annotations. This layer tags elements at runtime that were previously annotated with metadata. The layer indexes each annotation using a unique reference that can be matched against nodes at runtime. Specifically, it computes an XPath-like *path descriptor* based on properties of the annotated node and its ancestors. Importantly, this layer does not attempt to generalize the annotation. At runtime it visits each node in the input tree and checks if the node's path matches any of descriptors it has stored. If there is a matching descriptor, it tags that node with the corresponding metadata. Importantly, these path descriptors always represent a valid path that can be retrieved at runtime because they are computed from hierarchies consistent with the current layer chain. For example, the sliding widgets layer can import this layer and use it with an annotation library of "replace this widget" Boolean flags. The language translation enhancement can similarly import this layer with a library of translation corrections.

This simple tagging layer is one of several *exact-match* layers in our toolkit, each performing one of the tree operations in our toolkit. An exact-match deletion layer similarly deletes any node that matches a path descriptor. These layers are designed to be simple building blocks for more advanced layer chains, and the next section introduces several additional strategies that go beyond exact-matching of path descriptors to more sophisticated generalizations.

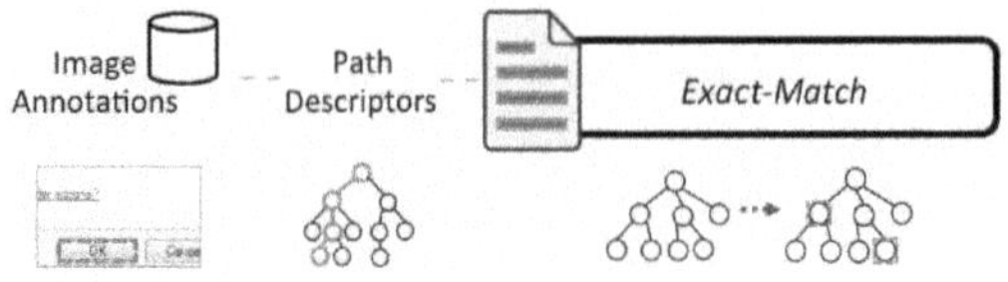


```
def import_annotations(annotation_data):
    ''' This method indexes annotations using
        path descriptors, so it can tag these
        annotated elements at runtime.'''
    runtime_storage = annotation_data.runtime_storage
    annotated_nodes = annotation_data.annotated_nodes
    for annotation in annotated_nodes:
        path = get_path(annotation.node, annotaion.root)
        runtime_storage[path] = annotation.metadata

def interpret(interpret_data):
    ''' This method tags nodes with annotation metadata
        by matching path descriptors against each node '''
    currnode = interpret_data.node
    path = get_path(currnode, interpret_data.tree)
    if path in interpret_data.runtime_storage:
        metadata = interpret_data.runtime_storage[path]
        for key in metadata:
          interpret_data.add_tag(currnode, key, metadata[key])
    #recurse on children
    for child in currnode.get_children():
        interpret(interpret_data, child)
```

Figure 5: Layers import annotations for use at runtime. Here an *exact-match* creates a path descriptor from each annotation and uses those descriptors to tag nodes at runtime.

VALIDATION THROUGH EXAMPLE LAYER CHAINS

Our toolkit is designed to support diverse pixel-based methods. In this half of our validation, we demonstrate and give insight into our toolkit by implementing and discussing several example layer chains. In the terminology established by Olsen [24], these examples demonstrate an *inductive combination* of functionality. Specifically, we select examples to illustrate how interpretation code can be composed, reused, and shared, and also how annotations can be used and shared among enhancements. We start with examples of low-level reusable interpretations and then move to high-level composition in full enhancements.

Reusable Low-Level Layer Chains

This section expands upon the previous section's reusable exact-match layer. Specifically, we present two more example layer chains: (1) a reusable chain that learns to automatically generalize Boolean annotations, and (2) a text recovery chain that applies multiple techniques to recover text from an interface. Like the exact-match layer, these are reusable building blocks that can be parameterized with an annotation library to obtain a desired capability. Decoupling the code layers from the data annotations thus creates building blocks for developers to create complex behaviors.

Learning-Based Annotation

Exact-match annotations are sufficient and even preferable for many applications, but others benefit from expediting annotation through generalization. We support such inference with a layer chain that learns to tag nodes based on positive and negative example annotations. For example, Figure 2's demonstration uses this chain to generalize its "do not translate" annotation. We implement learning as two layers sharing a library of Boolean annotations. The first is an exact-match layer, tagging nodes that are explicitly annotated as either positive or negative. The second applies a classifier to generalize tags onto nodes that are not explicitly tagged. Annotations are thus treated as ground truth and always override the classifier. Sharing the annotation library means a single annotation both tags a specific element and contributes to training the classifier.

Our learning layer uses a decision tree, with features computed from an element's spatial properties, its location in a hierarchy, and tags applied by preceding layers. It imports annotations by using them as training examples to create a classifier. During interpretation, it applies the classifier to nodes not tagged by the exact-match layer. Our current classification algorithm was designed and evaluated in the context of the applications described in this paper, so its performance is optimized for our explorations. However, our goal in implementing this example is to illustrate how any learning algorithm could be deployed in our toolkit. Developers could swap in layers that implement custom classification algorithms tailored for their application, or could use general-purpose classifiers they customize by populating an annotation library of training data.

Text Recovery

The exact-match and learning-based chains are relatively simple, with their power coming from how they can be composed. But it is also possible to implement complex layer chains providing sophisticated reusable functionality. One example is our current chain to recover textual content. Prior work has found the extremely low resolution of interface text makes it difficult to implement text recovery with off-the-shelf character recognition, instead turning to human transcription [8]. Other work explores incorporating text from the accessibility API [3]. Failures are inevitable in both approaches, so we leverage the flexibility of our toolkit to combine recovery from the accessibility API with human transcription. Figure 6 presents an overview of the layer chain, which consists of four main components: text classification, grouping related text, human transcription, and accessibility recovery.

The first layer tags each interface element with a Boolean indication of whether the node represents text. The chain is a parameterization of the learning-based annotation chain, trained with positive and negative examples of text elements. Prefab's background differencing discovers many types of elements (e.g., text, icons, widgets), but does not indicate the types of those discovered elements. This layer therefore identifies which should be processed as text.

The second and third layers are used to group related text. Low-level methods often naturally group text within a parent. For example, a button with a two-word label will group the two text elements. But text rendered without a visible container may need explicit grouping (e.g., a checkbox may have a multi-word label with no visible enclosure). We implement grouping in two layers. A first learns to tag each element with a Boolean flag indicating whether it should be grouped with the next sibling in reading order. A second then performs the actual grouping.

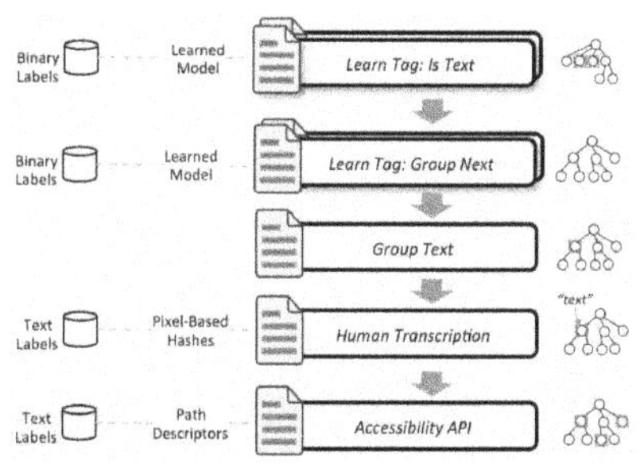

Figure 6: Layer chains can implement sophisticated reusable interpretation logic. Our text recovery chain combines human transcription with text recovered from the accessibility API.

The final two layers tag elements with text values. The first obtains these from human transcriptions. It works similar to an exact-match layer, but generalizes the annotations differently. It uses a hash of the pixel-level appearance of annotated text to apply that same annotation whenever it finds the same pixels (e.g., it matches multiple buttons with the same "OK" label). The second layer obtains text values from the accessibility API hierarchy corresponding to the captured interface. It finds the set of corresponding nodes in the pixel-based hierarchy by testing for spatial containment, and tags the parent node with the textual labels.

Full Layer Chains for Enhancements

Our final examples demonstrate how our toolkit can be used to compose full layer chains used by enhancements. Specifically, we examine interface translation, target-aware pointing, and sliding widgets. Our toolkit both: (1) lowers the *threshold* to developing enhancements, and (2) raises the *ceiling* to enable new pixel-based enhancements.

Language Translation

We previously presented pixel-based language translation [8], but the implementation in that initial work is fragile. Lacking explicit support for modular and reusable code, most of that work focuses on text recovery methods and ignores important aspects of translation. For example, that work ignores interactive correction (e.g., incorrect machine translations, elements that should not be translated at all). Figure 2 and our introductory scenario present a new and more extensible implementation addressing these issues. Our new solution builds directly on reusable low-level layer chains, so there is a minimal new work required (as illustrated by Figure 3's red highlights of that new work).

Target-Aware Pointing

Our prior Bubble Cursor implementation is an example of the state-of-the-art in pixel-based enhancements [5,12]. It enables target-aware pointing across the entire desktop, identifying targets using Prefab and human annotations. Specifically, it: (1) uses Prefab to identify a hierarchy of elements, (2) uses path descriptors to store annotations about whether to target an element (e.g., target a button, do not target an icon), and (3) expedites annotation with two heuristics, one that targets leaf nodes and one that generalizes annotations across identical subtrees.

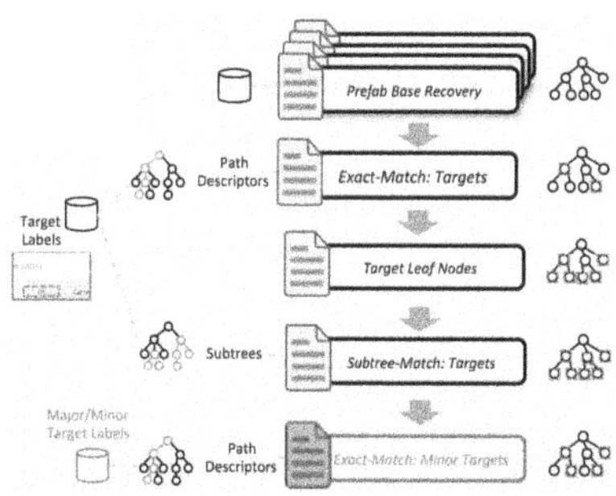

Figure 7: We streamline and expand our Bubble Cursor enhancement [5], resolving important limitations of our previous implementation.

Our new toolkit dramatically streamlines this enhancement. Figure 7 shows our new implementation, where we first instantiate a base Prefab layer and then an exact-match layer for target annotations. We then add two custom layers, one for each of the target heuristics. Importantly, the subtree matching layer shares the same annotation library as the exact-match layer, but generalizes those annotations. Alternatively, we could replace these lightweight layers with our learning-based chain from the previous subsection.

We also expand upon our prior work by differentiating *major* and *minor* targets. In our prior work we identified that some targets are infrequently used and act as distractors to more important targets. We suggested it would be valuable to distinguish major versus minor targets, but our prior monolithic implementation did not allow exploration of this idea. Figure 7 shows that our new toolkit makes it trivial to add a layer and annotation library to support exploration of this distinction. Existing target annotations can continue to be used, and a new annotation is added to indicate which of those are minor targets. This example shows our new abstractions raising the ceiling relative to what we could accomplish with the prior state-of-the-art.

Sliding Widgets

The two previous layer chains highlight re-implementations of prior systems, but we have also used our toolkit to implement an entirely new enhancement. As shown in Figure 1, sliding widgets are touchscreen widgets activated by sliding a moveable element [7,18]. In the course of developing our toolkit, we implemented an enhancement that replaces mouse-based widgets with sliding widgets. A detailed presentation is presented in our recent work [7].

The sliding widgets enhancement would have been tedious or impractical to develop without our toolkit. Developing a new enhancement like this requires iteratively refining code and exploring different approaches. But that code also requires annotations, and prior approaches to storing such annotations are brittle to code changes and would need to constantly be migrated. Our toolkit also provides a clear conceptual model for reasoning about and describing our sliding widgets enhancement. Using figures similar to the layer chain illustrations throughout this paper, that paper is able to succinctly overview the code and data used in the enhancement [7]. Our current contribution is therefore not

Study Outline for Each Condition

Hello World
1) Tag leaves as text
2) Correct text labels using annotations
3) Group related text

Bubble Cursor
4) Tag leaves as targets
5) Correct targets using annotations
6) Identify, group, and target text
7) Tag major and minor targets

Figure 8: Participants were given 7 tasks in each condition. The first three implement a *Hello World* enhancement. The next four implement and expand upon the *Bubble Cursor*.

only code, but also a set of abstractions that allow effective description of pixel-based interpretation.

VALIDATION WITH DEVELOPERS IN THE LAB

The previous section explored examples implemented using our toolkit. We also conducted a lab study that compared how developers used our toolkit versus a baseline toolset.

The baseline tools were designed to reflect state-of-the-art methods presented in our prior implementation of the Bubble Cursor [5]. Specifically, there were two main differences between our toolkit and prior methods. First, the baseline interpretation logic is implemented as a single method, where developers manually organize any code invoked in that method. Second, the baseline stores annotations using path descriptors, as used in our prior work and in a wide variety of DOM-based enhancements.

To the best of our knowledge, Prefab's prior methods provide the most extensive support for combining code and data in real-time modifications. Yeh et al.'s Sikuli offers robust scripting tools [30], but less support for annotating arbitrary interface elements. In addition, their pixel-based methods require a reported 200msec to identify all occurrences of a *single* target. Our toolkit is designed to support enhancements that need to more quickly identify and annotate all occurrences of *many* elements, so Prefab's prior methods are a more meaningful comparison.

We recruited six experienced developers to participate in our study. They were all male, with ages ranging from 24 to 28 years. Although all currently develop software, their backgrounds included applied natural science, computer vision, software engineering, and programming languages. All were familiar with Python and at least one other programming language. None of the participants had experience with pixel-based reverse engineering.

Study Protocol

Study sessions took approximately three hours. Participants were asked to implement interpretation logic for two enhancements: *Hello World* and *Bubble Cursor*. Both were implemented twice, once with our toolkit and once with the baseline. Participants were allotted 90 minutes for each task. To control for learning effects or fatigue, we counterbalanced the order in which we presented each condition. The *Hello World* enhancement was designed to familiarize participants with the condition. It replaces identified text with the string "hello world", using the masking technique described in our scenario walkthrough. In both enhancements, participants were asked to reverse engineer screenshots captured from an Apple iTunes dialog and a Microsoft Word settings dialog.

The experiment was conducted using a standard desktop computer running Windows 7. Developers authored code using an off-the-shelf text editor. We also equipped participants with a debugging tool that worked similarly to a webpage DOM inspector. Using the tool, participants could load screenshots, compile and execute their code, navigate and inspect the hierarchy output by their code, add or delete annotations, and browse through their annotations.

Both conditions consisted of seven tasks, as in Figure 8. The first three were to identify text for the *Hello World* enhancement. Participants implemented a simplified version of text recovery, where (1) leaves are heuristically classified as text, (2) erroneous tags are corrected with annotations, and (3) related text is grouped. For the grouping task, we wanted to examine how developers make use of existing code, so we gave participants access to grouping logic originally developed for an enhancement that classified widget types. In our toolkit, the functionality could be imported as a layer chain. In the baseline, it could be obtained using Python's standard mechanism for importing modules. Developers were also free to copy and paste any code from the existing enhancement.

The next four tasks were to classify targets for the *Bubble Cursor*. In these tasks, participants were able to reuse any functionality from their *Hello World* enhancement. Two tasks directly correspond to our original implementation: (4) leaf nodes are tagged as targets, and (5) erroneous tags are corrected with annotations. The next then improved upon that implementation by (6) identifying and grouping related text so that it can be targeted. We have noticed that groups of text are often clickable targets, such as URLs and the text adjacent to checkboxes, but our original implementation only targeted individual glyphs of text. Finally, in the seventh task (7) minor targets are tagged based on annotation. These tasks were designed to follow the natural progression of an implementation, simulating how a developer might build an enhancement in the wild.

Successes

When using our toolkit, participants took an average of 43 minutes to complete all tasks. No participants completed the baseline. Figure 9 presents a breakdown of completion times for each task. Most importantly, our toolkit enabled participants to implement core logic for a state-of-the-art enhancement and address unexplored shortcomings of that enhancement all within a relatively short study session.

To better understand of the difference in completion times, we conducted a semi-structured interview at the end of the study and examined the code authored by participants. We identified important differences between the conditions pertaining to code reuse and organization, data management, and the relationship between code and data.

Code Reuse and Organization

Participants wrote less code and reused a higher percentage of their code when using our toolkit. Specifically, they wrote an average of 36 lines using our toolkit versus 75 in the baseline. This difference was mostly due to our decomposition of code into layer chains. With our toolkit, participants would often reuse a layer several times in their chain, each parameterized with a different annotation library. In contrast, most of the code in the baseline was a result of participants copying from another enhancement, then editing that code to fit their enhancement. Participants reflected on these differences during the interview: P4 stated that *"the modular approach is good for code reusability"*, and P3 said our toolkit *"is the great Unix way - piping inputs and outputs, reusing small methods"*.

Participants also noted that our toolkit yielded more clear and understandable solutions. For example, when asked to compare the two conditions, P4 mentioned that *"the pipeline was easier to reason about"* with our toolkit, and P6 stated that *"my organization was bad, mainly because I was copy-pasting stuff around"* in the baseline condition.

Participants also viewed our framework as more extensible. We asked them to explain which tools they would use for developing enhancements that are more sophisticated than the *Bubble Cursor*. P2 responded, *"I definitely would use [Prefab Layers and Prefab Annotations] because it would be easy to package up layers and give them to someone, and when I add new layers they don't break my code."* P1 stated, *"it would be easy to extend my code with some machine learning, because of the two-step process for importing and then using annotations."*

These successes demonstrate the value of decomposing code into layers. Participants were not required to write large amounts of code, but our toolkit still created a path of least resistance towards clear, extensible, and reusable code.

Understanding Annotations

Participants found our toolkit made it easy to understand the contents of their annotation libraries. In comparison, it was challenging to understand the path descriptors used in the baseline condition. This is partially because our toolkit provides the entire hierarchy containing an annotated element. Thus when debugging their code, participants were able to print the annotation node to the console, inspect its properties, and view its location in the image. In contrast, the path descriptors were cryptic because they only revealed the minimal details of an element's path needed to provide a unique reference. P6 mentioned this problem in the interview, stating, *"I liked the tree view a lot, as a way of navigating and examining elements"*. This suggests Prefab Annotations are a better *expressive match* [24].

Relationship between Code and Data

Participants using our toolkit worked through each task as Emily did in our scenario walkthrough. In contrast,

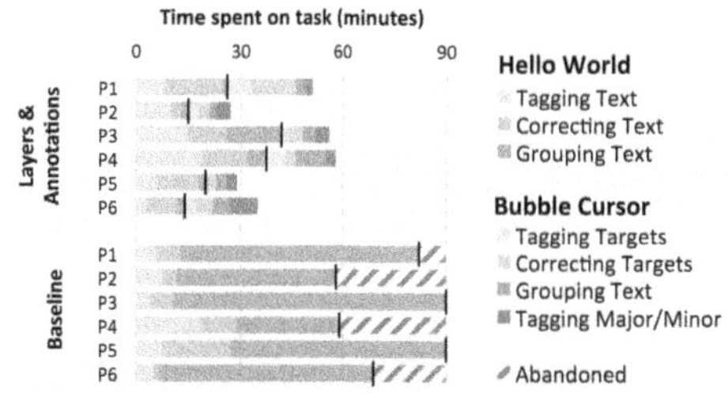

Figure 9: This graph presents each participant's completion times for each task. None of the participants were able to complete the baseline condition.

participants faced a critical roadblock in the baseline condition. This was to address subtle dependencies between annotations and code. This was exemplified in P2's session when implementing *Hello World*. The next paragraph steps through this as a comparison to our scenario walkthrough.

P2 successfully implemented functionality for task (1) that tagged leaf nodes as text. P2 then wrote code to correct erroneous tags using annotations and added a few corrections using the debugging tool. With the annotations working, P2 imported functionality for grouping text and added a few more corrections. However, these annotations did not cause any change in the output hierarchy. Confused, P2 spent several minutes inspecting code while adding and removing annotations. P2 then discovered the problem: they were storing path descriptors computed from the final hierarchy, which was different from the hierarchy in which corrections were applied before grouping. P2 thus rearranged their code such that the text corrections were applied after the grouping. However, this did not work either because the grouping code relied on those corrections to robustly determine which elements were text. At this point, P2 realized they would need to restructure the path descriptors to be consistent with the tree as it exists before grouping. P2 spent the remainder of their time developing this migration. Prefab Annotations removes the need for developers to migrate annotations between representations.

Challenges for Future Work and Conclusion

We also discovered challenges our participants faced when using our toolkit. Unanimously, participants found our toolkit to have a steeper learning curve than the baseline. Most of this difficulty was regarding the method for importing annotations. Specifically, participants initially did not see the benefit of writing explicit code to generalize annotations. This suggests that it might be useful for layers to generalize annotations by default, then allow developers to override the default with their own logic. Importantly, developers understood the point of defining their own generalizations, and reported that this added flexibility to implement more sophisticated enhancements.

Participants also noted that modularity introduced by layers would sometimes make it difficult to know when a piece of code would execute. Similarly, they wanted each layer to document its dependencies on any other layers, as they felt it was easy to lose track of how a single layer worked in the context of a larger chain. Ultimately, we see this overhead as a pervasive problem in modular programs and view this as a rich area for future work.

Participants in both conditions found it difficult to understand the computed path descriptors because they were based on the low-level pixel hierarchy recovered by Prefab. This raised a larger issue that elements in the hierarchy did not have human-readable names. Thus, it might be useful to include a default set of layers that tag Prefab's pixel-identified elements with such names.

Finally, participants requested the ability to more easily inspect the hierarchy at any point in a layer chain execution. This highlights a need for improvements in debugging tools, within which developers might toggle layers on and off or set breakpoints to view output at specific layers. We also believe there is an opportunity to explore IDEs for pixel-based methods, perhaps drawing on ideas from runtime modification or computer vision [16,17].

Prefab Layers and Prefab Annotations dramatically streamline the implementation of pixel-based runtime enhancements. Specifically, they help developers overcome subtle but critical dependencies between code and data. This toolkit is available at https://github.com/prefab, and we ultimately see this work as a step towards enabling the adoption of pixel-based methods in research and practice.

ACKNOWLEDGMENTS

We thank Jeffrey Heer, Dan Weld, and Jacob Wobbrock for discussions related to this work. This work was supported by the National Science Foundation under award IIS-1053868.

REFERENCES

1. Banovic, N., Grossman, T., Matejka, J., and Fitzmaurice, G. Waken: Reverse Engineering Usage Information and Interface Structure from Software Videos. *UIST 2012*. 83–92.
2. Bolin, M., Webber, M., Rha, P., Wilson, T., and Miller, R.C. Automation and Customization of Rendered Web Pages. *UIST 2005*. 163–172.
3. Chang, T.-H., Yeh, T., and Miller, R. Associating the Visual Representation of User Interfaces with Their Internal Structures and Metadata. *UIST 2011*. 245–254.
4. Chang, T.-H., Yeh, T., and Miller, R.C. GUI Testing Using Computer Vision. *CHI 2010*. 1535–1544.
5. Dixon, M., Fogarty, J., and Wobbrock, J. A General-Purpose Target-Aware Pointing Enhancement Using Pixel-Level Analysis of Graphical Interfaces. *CHI 2012*. 3167–3176.
6. Dixon, M. and Fogarty, J. Prefab : Implementing Advanced Behaviors Using Pixel-Based Reverse Engineering of Interface Structure. *CHI 2010*. 1525–1534.
7. Dixon, M., Laput, G., and Fogarty, J. Pixel-Based Methods for Widget State and Style in a Runtime Implementation of Sliding Widgets. *CHI 2014*. 2231-2240.
8. Dixon, M., Leventhal, D., and Fogarty, J. Content and Hierarchy in Pixel-Based Methods for Reverse Engineering Interface Structure. *CHI 2011*. 969–978.
9. Eagan, J.R., Beaudouin-Lafon, M., and Mackay, W.E. Cracking the Cocoa Nut: User Interface Programming at Runtime. *UIST 2011*. 225–234.
10. Edwards, W.K., Hudson, S.E., Marinacci, J., Rodenstein, R., Rodriguez, T., and Smith, I. Systematic Output Modification in a 2D User Interface Toolkit. *UIST 1997*. 151–158.
11. Fujima, J., Lunzer, A., Hornbæk, K., and Tanaka, Y. Clip, Connect, Clone: Combining Application Elements to Build Custom Interfaces for Information Access. *UIST 2004*. 175-184.
12. Grossman, T. and Balakrishnan, R. The Bubble Cursor : Enhancing Target Acquisition by Dynamic Resizing of the Cursor's Activation Area. *CHI 2005*. 281–290.
13. Grossman, T., Matejka, J., and Fitzmaurice, G. Chronicle: Capture, Exploration, and Playback of Document Workflow Histories. *UIST 2010*. 143–152.
14. Hartmann, B., Wu, L., Collins, K., and Klemmer, S.R. Programming by a Sample: Rapidly Creating Web Applications with d.mix. *UIST 2007*. 241–250.
15. Hurst, A., Hudson, S.E., and Mankoff, J. Automatically Identifying Targets Users Interact with During Real World Tasks. *IUI 2010*. 11–20.
16. Kato, J., Mcdirmid, S., and Cao, X. DejaVu : Integrated Support for Developing Interactive Camera-Based Programs. *UIST 2012*. 189–196.
17. Meng, X., Zhao, S., Huang, Y., Zhang, Z., and Eagan, J.R. WADE : Simplified GUI Add-on Development for Third-party Software. *CHI 2014*. 2221–2230.
18. Moscovich, T. Contact Area Interaction with Sliding Widgets. *UIST 2009*. 13–22.
19. Myers, B., Hudson, S.E., and Pausch, R. Past, Present, and Future of User Interface Software Tools. *TOCHI 7 (1)*. 3–28.
20. Nichols, J., Hua, Z., and Barton, J. Highlight: A System for Creating and Deploying Mobile Web Applications. *UIST 2008*. 249–258.
21. Nichols, J. and Lau, T. Mobilization by Demonstration: Using Traces to Re-author Existing Web Sites. *IUI 2008*. 149–160.
22. Olsen, D.R., Hudson, S.E., Verratti, T., Heiner, J.M., and Phelps, M. Implementing Interface Attachments Based on Surface Representations. *CHI 1999*. 191–198.
23. Olsen, D.R., Taufer, T., and Fails, J.A. ScreenCrayons: Annotating Anything. *UIST 2004*. 165–174.
24. Olsen, D.R. Evaluating User Interface Systems Research. *UIST 2007*. 251–258.
25. Pongnumkul, S., Dontcheva, M., Li, W., Wang, J., Bourdev, L., Avidan, S., and Cohen, M. Pause-and-Play: Automatically Linking Screencast Video Tutorials with Applications. *UIST 2011*. 135–144.
26. Savva, M., Kong, N., Chhajta, A., Fei-fei, L., Agrawala, M., and Heer, J. ReVision: Automated Classification, Analysis and Redesign of Chart Images. *UIST 2011*. 393–402.
27. St Amant, R., Riedl, R., Ritter, F.E., and Reifers, A. Image Processing in Cognitive Models with SegMan. *HCII 2005*.
28. Stuerzlinger, W., Chapuis, O., Phillips, D., and Roussel, N. User Interface Façades: Towards Fully Adaptable User Interfaces. *UIST 2006*. 309–318.
29. Waldner, M., Steinberger, M., Grasset, R., and Schmalstieg, D. Importance-Driven Compositing Window Management: CHI 2011. 959–968.
30. Yeh, T., Chang, T.-H., and Miller, R.C. Sikuli: Using GUI Screenshots for Search and Automation. *UIST 2009*. 183–194.
31. Yeh, T., Chang, T.-H., Xie, B.,Walsh, G., Watkins, I., Wongsuphasawat, K., Huan, M., Davis, L.S., Bederson, B. Creating Contextual Help for GUIs Using Screenshots. *UIST 2011*. 145–154.

Programming by Manipulation for Layout

Thibaud Hottelier
UC Berkeley
tbh@cs.berkeley.edu

Ras Bodik
UC Berkeley
bodik@cs.berkeley.edu

Kimiko Ryokai
UC Berkeley
kimiko@ischool.berkeley.edu

ABSTRACT
We present Programming by Manipulation, a new programming methodology for specifying the layout of data visualizations, targeted at non-programmers. We address the two central sources of bugs that arise when programming with constraints: ambiguities and conflicts (inconsistencies). We rule out conflicts by design and exploit ambiguity to explore possible layout designs. Our users design layouts by highlighting undesirable aspects of a current design, effectively breaking spurious constraints and introducing ambiguity by giving some elements freedom to move or resize. Subsequently, the tool indicates how the ambiguity can be removed, by computing how the free elements can be fixed with available constraints. To support this workflow, our tool computes the ambiguity and summarizes it visually. We evaluate our work with two user-studies demonstrating that both non-programmers and programmers can effectively use our prototype. Our results suggest that our tool is 5-times more productive than direct programming with constraints.

Author Keywords
Programming by demonstration; layout editing; constraint-based layout

ACM Classification Keywords
H.5.m. Information Interfaces and Presentation (e.g. HCI): Miscellaneous; D.2.1. Requirements/Specifications: Tools

INTRODUCTION
Visual layout is the art of arranging visual elements in a pleasing manner. Layout spans multiple application domains, including the layout of documents; the layout of GUIs; the layout of websites, which is a hybrid of document and GUI layouts; and the layout of data visualizations. Both non-technical users and expert programmers design layouts, by using WYSIWYG editors or by writing code that customizes an existing layout library. Either way, creating a layout entails fixing the sizes and positions of some visual elements and specifying, in some manner, the rules for computing sizes and positions of the remaining elements.

Over the years, many alternative ways of specifying layout have been proposed. (See Hurst *et al.* [9] for a recent overview of the field.) Constraints are arguably the most widespread and successful programming technique. For example, the foundations of TEX are laid upon constraints. CSS, the ubiquitous web template language, also relies on constraints, although in a more restricted and indirect manner [9].

UIST 2014, October 5–8, 2014, Honolulu, HI, USA.

ACM 978-1-4503-3069-5/14/10 ...$15.00.
http://dx.doi.org/10.1145/2642918.2647378

Data visualizations are among the hardest layout problems, in part because the data may have a recursive (tree) structure and/or the visual layout is not "boxy." Today, the task of building data visualizations consists of crafting a tailored layout engine for a dataset. The current state-of-the-art, general purpose frameworks [6, 4, 7]—*e.g.*, Protovis and its successor D3—require the advanced technical expertise of seasoned programmers. As such, they are inaccessible to many potential users, such as non-programmer scientists.

Our solution, *Programming by Manipulation (PBM)*, streamlines layout specification by allying user demonstrations with guided exploration of the layout design space. Targeted toward non-programmers, PBM is designed to prevent users from getting stuck in either ambiguities or conflicts (contradictions), the two symptoms of bugs when programming layouts with constraints. Before we detail our solution, we summarize the programmability challenges posed by constraints.

Programming with Constraints
Constraint-based layouts are powerful and versatile (see Related Work). By stating properties of the layout directly, constraints promise to yield a precise and predictable layout specification. However, manipulating constraints directly can be tedious and error-prone. Specifically, programmers must carefully navigate between two hazards: ambiguities and conflicts. Ambiguities arise when we do not state enough constraints of the goal layout (under-specification) allowing multiple distinct layouts to satisfy the constraint system. The first solution found by the solver is unlikely to be the intended one. Worse, the selected solution might be different each run, causing non-determinism. As such, ambiguities make the resulting layout unpredictable for users. However, by stating too much (over-specification) we risk introducing conflicts, *i.e.*, inconsistencies among constraints. When a conflict occurs, there exists no layout satisfying all constraints. Our user-study shows that resolving such conflicts can be challenging, even for experienced programmers. In practice, the solver is often allowed to drop some constraints, sometimes based on a priority hierarchy, until the system admits one or more solutions [2, 26].

Ambiguities are commonly alleviated by casting layout as an optimization problem. If at most one layout maximizes the utility metric, the ambiguity is removed. Leaving aside the difficulty of capturing layout esthetics with a mathematical metric, optimization does not fully address the problem. For instance, it is well known that optimization-induced "spring-effects" result in unexpected layouts [26], forcing designers to twiddle with constant parameters by trial and error. Furthermore, ambiguities are reintroduced when conflicts are handled by dropping constraints, because there may be alternative ways to drop constraints, each leading to a distinct layout. This choice falls back upon the solver, which does not have adequate information to make an educated guess, even with priorities attached to constraints[1].

Ultimately, ambiguities and conflicts have the same consequences for users: the resulting layout may be unpredictable and may appear to be chosen arbitrarily. The only certain method for determining the effects of constraints is to run the solver and examine its output. This limitation motivated the programming of constraints by demonstration.

Programming by Demonstration

The advent of Programming by Demonstration (PBD) gave rise to GUI builders. They enable users to express layout by example, from which the necessary layout constraints are inferred automatically. By lowering the level of discourse to concrete visual entities (widgets), away from abstract positioning rules, demonstrations make layout programming accessible to a wider audience. For visual domains such as layout, a natural form of demonstration is a paper and pencil sketch. However, users' drawings contain small errors and imprecisions: they cannot be interpreted literally by PBD systems. For this reason, GUI builders adopted a constructive approach: instead of drawing the entire layout at once, users demonstrate step by step, by progressively adding widgets onto a canvas. However, even with demonstrations, the central issue remains: ambiguities and conflicts creep in during demonstrations, for example when a new widget cannot be inserted without breaking a constraint on existing widgets[2]. When a conflict or ambiguity occurs, users have no other recourse than diving into the constraints to resolve them manually, it may be a challenging task for someone who does not program.

We conjecture that the root causes behind the difficulty of programming with constraints—ambiguities and conflicts—have not been fully addressed. There has been exciting recent work in this area [25]. Most notably, ALE has introduced a language fragment (ALE excluding manual constraints) that is free of both ambiguities and conflicts. In terms of programmability, this is an ideal language. However, some layouts can be difficult to express. For instance, to center a widget globally, users need to manually add constraints from outside this fragment, which may reintroduce conflicts.

[1]With CSS, text overflowing the borders of a container is a classic illustration of conflict resolution not matching the designer's intent [15]. This phenomenon occurs with only two boxes: Box A containing the text with a preferred width of 300px, and its decoration, box B, set to half as wide as the window. The designer would like A to be contained inside B. In CSS, this is expressed indirectly by making A a child of B. When the user resizes the window to 500px, CSS will overflow the text of A out of B. If B has a visible border, the resulting layout is unlikely to please.

[2]We illustrate this problem with an example inspired by ALE [12, 25]. Using a GUI builder, we add two text boxes next to each other and horizontally justified on a window 240px wide. We set the width of each text-box to 100px. By adding a third widget to the same row whose width must be at least 50px to be displayed properly, a combo-box for instance, we create a conflict. The sum of width of our three widgets is over 240px. When faced with this situation, XCode silently drops the width constraint of the text-boxes. ALE extracts the relevant conflicting constraints to help the designer understand and eventually repair the constraints manually.

Layout for Visualizations

With the understanding that ambiguities and conflicts are the central programmability issues, let us now look at the specific needs of data visualization layout. Consider a biologist (a non-programmer) trying to define a phylogenetic tree. Precise control over positions and alignment is crucial, because the layer in which each node is drawn has biological meaning: it determines when two species branch off. The number of possible tree layouts is very large: by considering only positional aspects of tree layouts such as the overall architecture (flat, radial, flower-like); the layering strategies; the space allocation strategies between both parent/children and siblings, we count over a hundred possible designs. It is unlikely that our biologist will find the required layout in a library of prepackaged visualizations, such as ManyEyes [22]. Therefore, we propose to steer the exploration of designs by manipulating the layout of the sample document.

Finally, data visualization has requirements distinct from GUI: layouts are non-boxy and recursive, and datasets inevitably change and grow. Therefore, layout engines must be generic enough to be reusable for new, updated data. Moreover, scientific datasets can be massive; users must be able to demonstrate the layout semantics on a small subset of the data and then run the resulting layout engine on the full dataset.

We summarize our design principles in the following four points:

1. The language of constraints must be rich enough to capture a wide class of data visualizations, including recursive and non-boxy ones.

2. The system must be resistant to the small imprecisions present in drawing-based demonstrations.

3. Ambiguities and conflicts must either be ruled out or be explained at a level of discourse understandable by non-programmers.

4. Users must be able to demonstrate the desired layout on a small subset of their data. The demonstration must generalize to other datasets.

Programming by Manipulation (PBM)

We propose Programming by Manipulation (PBM), a new example-driven programming paradigm, based on guided exploration of the space of layout configurations. We cast layout as a *satisfaction* problem, avoiding the reliance on an optimization utility function. To help our designer select constraints just sufficient to yield a single solution, we develop a manipulation methodology that guarantees the absence of conflicts and actively steers the user away from ambiguities by explaining them visually and proposing potential resolutions. Our manipulation explores a design point opposite to ALE, which rules out ambiguities and explains conflicts.

Creating a data-visualization with PBM proceeds in two main stages (Figure 1a). First, the user selects the broad class of the layout, *e.g.*, a tree, by building a sample document. This document is constructed by instantiating building blocks from a library. Each block is flexible, in that it encapsulates a large set of constraints that are individually activated based on configuration switches. For instance, most blocks provide one constraint per alignment strategy, and a switch controls which strategy the block should use. By choosing which blocks to use, the user already defines the principal characteristics of the layout: is the layout flow-based (*e.g.*, a tree) or guillotine-based (*e.g.*, a treemap); is it radial or Cartesian? The sample document is a partial specification of the layout; it is partial because the configuration switches have not yet been set. This configuration process happens in the second step, where the user *browses* through possible configurations, each yielding a different layout. The user does not toggle switches directly. Instead, she steers the exploration by manipulating the layout of the sample document by dragging blocks.

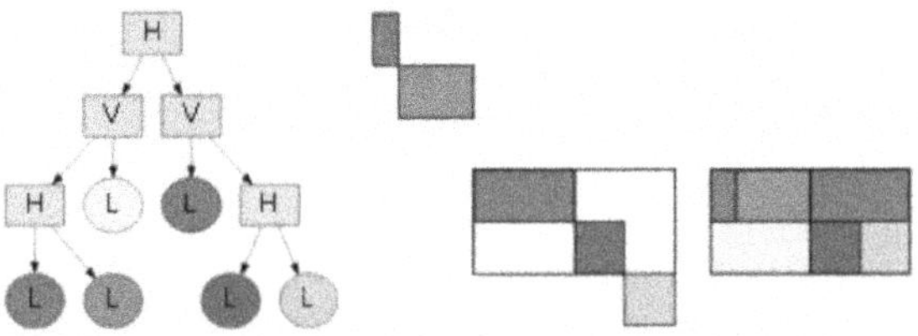

(a) First the user create a sample document, a tree of blocks (left). Then, starting from an arbitrary initial configuration (middle), she manipulates the layout (of the sample document) until obtaining the final (desired) configuration (right).

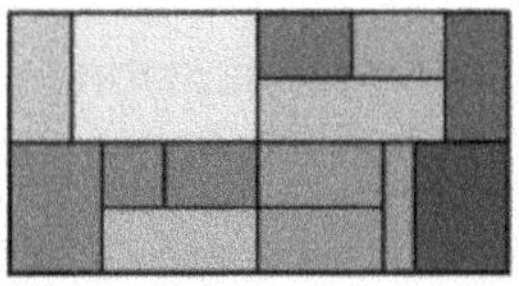

(b) The final configuration can now be applied to larger datasets (documents).

Figure 1. Creating a treemap with PBM. The 3 stages (a) to establish a layout specification, which is reusable (b).

Our tool—the PBM manipulator (PBMM)—allows the user to perform two moves: (i) *generalizing* the layout by disabling some constraints, thereby introducing ambiguities; or (ii) *specializing* the layout by enabling new constraints, effectively resolving ambiguities. Generalizations are expressed with a new type of demonstration which tolerates imprecisions in manual demonstrations, so-called *what is wrong (WiW)* manipulations (Figure 2a). Like StopThat interactions [14], WiW manipulations are negative demonstrations. Instead of indicating what the desired layout should be, the user points out one incorrect aspect of the current layout by dragging a block away from its constrained position. To interpret such manipulations, PBMM only considers the "direction" of the WiW manipulation as opposed to the final locations of the displaced blocks. Behind the scenes, PBMM determines which constraints to toggle off to allow the block to move in the demonstrated direction (Figure 2b). It does so by choosing the ones for which the newly introduced ambiguities best align with the direction of the WiW manipulation. We have essentially sidestepped the interferences originating from the inherent imprecisions of user drawings. Specializations are expressed by letting the user choose one layout feature among a range of options (Figure 2c). Only safe specializations (conflict-free) are proposed.

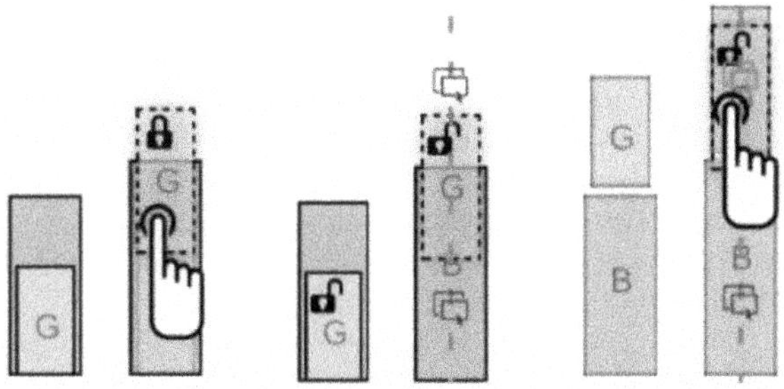

(a) WiW manip. (b) Generalization (c) Specialization

Figure 2. Three steps to modify a barchart from overlapping bars to stacked bars: By dragging the green box upward, past its snapping radius (a), we break its vertical positioning constraint. To explore alternative layouts, freedom is introduced in response to our WiW manipulation by the PBM system (b). Both green boxes, two instances of the same block, are now vertically free. Finally, by dropping one of the green boxes onto the topmost specialization site (red icon), we fix the vertical position of both green bars at once by adding a new constraint to the configuration (c).

Unfortunately, we cannot shield users from both ambiguities and conflicts: starting from a deterministic layout of the sample document, to hop to the next deterministic layout, we must toggle switches to both disable (generalize) and enable (specialize) constraints. Depending on which operation is performed first, the user will be confronted at the intermediate point with either an ambiguous or conflicting layout. We argue that conflicts are more difficult to explain than ambiguities. Ambiguities can be conveyed by examples, by showing a range of possible layouts. Whereas, to explain conflicts, one must spell out why something is impossible, a task intrinsically more difficult to visualize. For this reason, we chose to prevent users from ever creating conflicts and to have them tolerate ambiguities by explaining them with visual cues. We condense all ambiguities into a few "axes of freedom" which convey not only which blocks are unconstrained, but also which layout aspects of those blocks remain to be specified. For instance, a block might have a fixed horizontal position while being unconstrained vertically.

Once the layout has been configured, we know which constraints to use: we have established the complete specification of the layout. We can finally turn the configuration into a layout engine (*i.e.*, an executable layout template) which takes the document as a runtime input and lays it out (Figure 1b).

Contributions

Programming by Manipulation brings the following benefits: First, conflicts can no longer arise; specialization only lets users enable constraints which resolve ambiguities previously introduced via generalizations. At worst, users browse back to a previously seen layout. Second, we explain ambiguities with a visual summary understandable at a glance. Finally, our exploration-centric approach enables users to discover for themselves which layouts are feasible given the language of constraints and settle for a close enough approximation if necessary [11].

This paper makes the following contributions:

1. The Programming by Manipulation[3] paradigm targeted toward non-programmers for visual domains such as data-visualization.

2. A new type of demonstration—What is wrong (WiW) manipulations—which is resistant to users' imprecisions, inherent in drawing. Instead of sketching the desired layout, users steer the exploration by pointing out what they would like to change on a given layout. Only the direction of the manipulation is interpreted by PBMM.

3. Two user-studies, the first one showing that non-programmers can design interesting visualizations using our PBM tool. 10 out of 11 participants completed all five visualization tasks. The second study demonstrates that proficient programmers are more productive with PBM than with conventional constraint programming. With PBM, programmers needed on average one fifth of the time and three times fewer attempts to complete the same tasks.

RELATED WORK

Programming by Manipulation builds on the foundations laid by constraint-based layout systems, GUI builders, and the recent work on fully automatic layout inference.

Constraint-based Layout

Constraints have been used in many languages to specify layout [5, 19, 13, 18, 1, 12, 10, 9]. Much work has focused on expressibility and solving efficiency. (In contrast, we are concerned primarily with programmability, by preventing conflicts and explaining ambiguities.) Typically, layout has been phrased as an optimization problem by either maximizing a utility metric or satisfying as many constraints as possible. We chose to cast layout as a satisfaction problem, with the following trade-offs: satisfiability is a simpler problem in term of computability; rich constraints such as polynomials, which are common in visualizations, become tractable. Satisfaction also enables a deeper level of analysis: we leverage the power of SMT-solvers to prevent conflicts, summarize ambiguities, and efficiently compute both generalizations and specializations.

GUI Builders

With GUI builders, users can construct user interfaces graphically by progressively adding widgets to a canvas [17, 18, 20, 23]. Each time a widget is added, new layout constraints fixing its position are inferred, sometimes with the help of semantic snapping [8]. More advanced systems produce flexible GUIs which adaptively resize to occupy the space available [25]. Naturally, GUI builders are tailored toward UI boxy or tab-stop layout [12]; it is unclear whether these techniques can be adapted to recursive layouts common in data visualizations, such as a radial tree.

Most GUI builders delegate the resolution of conflicts and ambiguities to users. Our user-study suggests that this is a challenging task. Recent work has focused on this programmability challenge: ALE [25] is a layout editor which guarantees that the layout is well-defined (non-ambiguous) and explains conflicts by computing the maximum satisfiable set of constraints. ALE also defines a safe, conflict-free fragment of the layout language (one without manual constraints). This comes at the cost of some expressiveness; for instance, centering globally is not possible. We took the opposite approach and chose to rule out conflicts but tolerate ambiguities. We believe that ambiguities (and their resolution) are easier to convey to users than conflicts. We condense all ambiguities into a summary: a set of "axes of freedom" understandable at a glance by non-programmers. ALE and PBM have orthogonal approaches to how a layout is constructed. We start from a full, complete but incorrect specification, and progressively adjust it by enabling and disabling constraints. In contrast, ALE starts with an empty specification and progressively fleshes it out by inferring more constraints as widgets are added to the layout.

Automatic Layout Inference

Fully automatic methods for layout generation have been studied as well. Layout can be inferred from topological descriptions [24], or directly from user-drawn mock-ups [21]. In the latter work, a subdivision of the space expressed as a tree of vertical and horizontal dividers is extracted from a single demonstration, a mock-up. This hierarchy is then encoded with CSS rules which can be laid out by a web browser. Since a single mock-up may not be a sufficient specification of the layout, user guidance is invoked to deal with the ambiguity. This user guidance takes the form of configuration options which include manually fixing some of the subdivision steps.

PROGRAMMING BY MANIPULATION

This section provides a detailed overview of layout by manipulation, using a phylogenetic tree as a running example (Figure 3). The goal for our user is to establish the core aspects of layout, such as position, size, alignment, and margins. In the next paragraph, we take a step back to explain why we think our exploration-centric workflow is a crucial feature for PBD systems such as this one.

Our early prototypes performed rather poorly. With neither exploration nor manipulation, users were asked to sketch the desired layout by repositioning all layout elements in one comprehensive demonstration. The combination of constraints inferred rarely produced the desired layout. In our informal observations, we saw that users were left perplexed, knowing neither what they did wrong nor how to improve their demonstration. This direct approach failed because users are unaware of which layouts are expressible with the constraints embedded in the sample document. This is a common flaw of PBD systems [11]. The target program, as represented in a user's mind, is often not expressible. Interestingly, there often exists an equivalent program or a close approximation which is expressible and for which users would settle if they could discover it [11]. This observation led us to our exploration-centric approach.

To create any visualization, we first need to construct a sample document. In a second step, we will configure this document by directly manipulating its layout. Concretely, since we cast

[3]Try our online demo at `http://pbm.cs.berkeley.edu`.

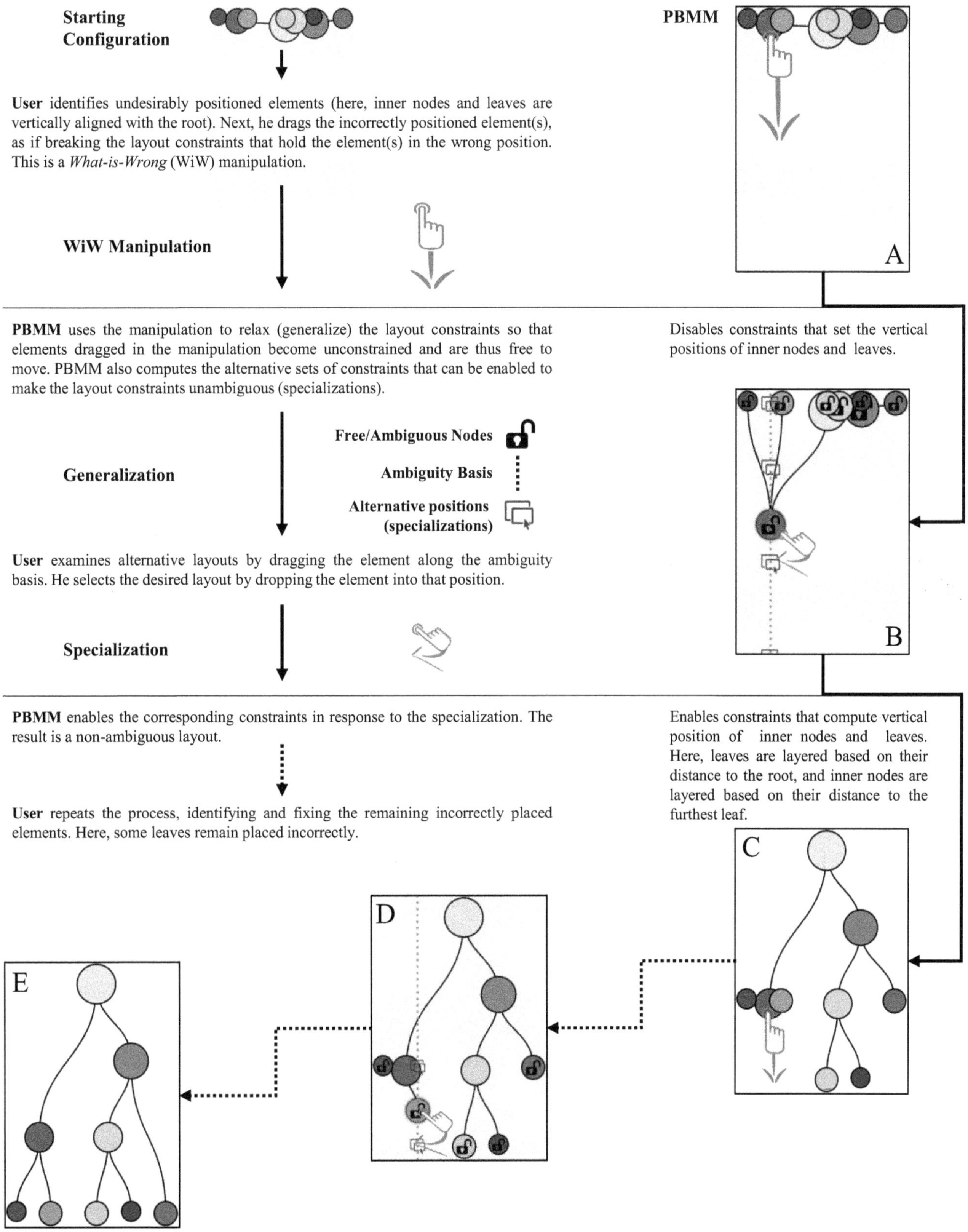

Figure 3. The five configurations explored to establish the node layering of a tree. The hand icon illustrates the manipulation performed by the user. Configurations B&D are ambiguous; their axes of freedom are shown only for the selected node.

layout specification as a satisfaction problem, we must find a combination of constraints leading to a single, unique layout. This combination of constraints constitutes our "layout configuration". Once established, we can reuse the same configuration to create other documents which will share the same layout properties. In CSS terminology, a layout configuration would be called a template.

Creating a sample (unconfigured) document

To create a sample document, the (layout) designer selects blocks from a library and nests them: a *document* is a tree of instances of blocks. By choosing which blocks to use, the designer is already painting the broad strokes of the layout: a barchart and a tree are built from radically different blocks. For our phylogenetic tree, we nest instances of three blocks: *TreeRoot* is the root of our sample document, inner nodes are instances of *TreeNode*, and the leaves are *TreeLeaf*. The sample document must be representative of the type of documents to be supported by the layout configuration. In practice, we found that documents with about 10 to 20 nodes are most useful. A tree with a single node does not provide enough information. However, our biologist's full dataset of over one hundred nodes for a phylogenetic tree has too many entities, making manipulation difficult.

Blocks

Blocks are crafted from constraints by an expert programmer. They have flexible layout behavior controlled by configuration switches that enable or disable individual constraints. It is the role of manipulation to configure these switches. Each block contains both attributes (*e.g.*, sizes and positions) and constraints. Some attributes are known constants, for instance the size of an image, while others need to be computed at runtime. The constraints defining a block range not only over its own attributes but also over those of its neighbors in the document hierarchy.

Since blocks are reusable across many visualizations, we collect them in a library. Each block also bundles an English description of its function for designers. Other frequently used blocks include horizontal/vertical dividers for guillotine layouts (*H/VDiv*), grouping boxes (*HBox, VBox, HVBox*) for box-based layouts, floating elements for flow-layouts (*FloatBox*), as well as various containers. We describe the language constraints behind blocks in the next section.

Layout

Under the hood, a document is a constraint system composed as a conjunction of all enabled constraints. As such, each *configuration* (of switches) yields a different constraint system. The set of all possible configurations forms the *configuration space*. Given a configuration, the *layout* of a document is a solution to its constraint system. In other words, a layout is an assignment of values for each document's attributes, such that all enabled constraints are satisfied. Depending on how many layouts exist for a document, we distinguish three kinds of documents: (i) a document is *deterministic* if it admits exactly one layout; (ii) a document for which there exists no layout is inconsistent: some of its constraints are *conflicting*; and (iii) a document which admits more than one layout is *ambiguous*. We compute the layout of a configured document by solving the corresponding constraint system. Modern solvers [16] can handle documents with hundreds of blocks in less than a second. Finally, once the document is laid out, it can be passed to a renderer for display.

Demonstrating the layout configuration

To establish the finer aspects of the visualization, the designer explores the configuration space in search of the configuration which yields the best layout of the sample document. We built a tool supporting this exploration-centric workflow: the PBM manipulator (PBMM), devised to help designers finding an interesting layout quickly, even in huge configuration spaces. PBM turns conventional demonstrations upside down: Instead of directly demonstrating the goal, designers highlight one layout aspect (*e.g.*, horizontal alignment) they would like to change by dragging one block away from its constrained position. We call such manipulations "what is wrong" (WiW) manipulations.

PBMM presents the layout of the sample document according to the currently active configuration. Figure 4a shows the user interface. The exploration always starts from an arbitrary configuration that yields a deterministic document. Then, by manipulating the layout itself, the designer can make a step in the direction of his choosing, which enables him to hop from configuration to configuration. To steer the exploration, the designer either (i) points out an incorrect layout feature; or (ii) chooses an alternative layout from among a range of options. Figure 3 illustrates the exploration process on our phylogenetic tree. In four manipulations, we establish the desired tree layering.

The designer's manipulations are translated into two types of "moves" through the configuration space. One move *introduces* ambiguities and the other one *resolves* them:

- *Generalizations* introduce ambiguities by switching off one[4] constraint currently enabled, effectively weakening the constraint system of the sample document. By toggling off one constraint, we move to a new configuration which admits a superset of the layouts of the current configuration. Generalizations are expressed with WiW manipulations: the designer highlights incorrect aspects of the layout by dragging blocks to displace them from the position constrained by the current configuration. Generalizations are triggered by the "Break Rules" button (Figure 4a).
- *Specializations* resolve ambiguities by strengthening the constraint system of the current configuration. To do so, we switch on one disabled constraint, which brings us to a new configuration admitting a subset of the current configuration layouts. To specialize a layout, designers choose one layout from a list of alternatives.

To browse configurations effectively, designers need to understand the nature of the configuration space: they need to know both "where they are" and "where they can go". While removing constraints (generalization) is always possible, adding constraints (specialization) can create conflicts. As such, PBMM

[4]Constraints are actually switched on or off in groups to handle interdependencies and subsumption. To simplify the presentation, we assume that only one constraint is toggled after each step.

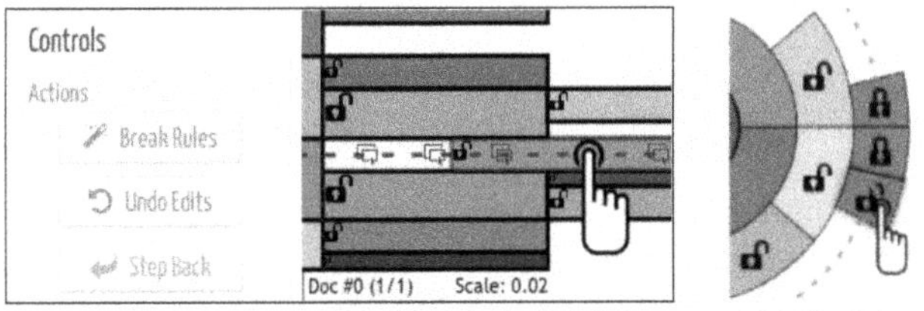

(a) A flat ambiguity base in PBMM 's GUI (b) Radial

Figure 4. Two examples of ambiguity bases. Ambiguous (free) blocks are indicated with unlocked icons. PBMM displays the ambiguity base of the selected block with axes of freedom (dashed-lines). Here, the bases of each selected block are constituted of a single axis. To enable users to "feel" constraints, each block moves freely along its axes of freedom, but resists displacement in other directions by snapping to its axes. We also show PBMM's user interface (a). The "Break Rules" button triggers generalizations.

must also convey which constraints can be added safely to specialize the current configuration. This translates into two responsibilities for PBMM: explaining ambiguities and proposing potential resolutions.

Introducing Ambiguities by Breaking Constraints

To control the introduction and resolution of ambiguities, designers need to know not only which blocks are free (*i.e.*, not fully constrained) but also which aspects (*e.g.*, height or horizontal position) of the blocks are free. A naive solution would be to display each and every possible layout of the sample document. Unfortunately, this is impractical: an ambiguous configuration may admit a very large, sometimes even unbounded, number of layouts. For example, in the barchart illustrated in Figure 2, we remove the vertical stacking constraint of the green bars through a generalization step. As a result, their vertical positions become completely unconstrained, yielding an unbounded number of ways to lay out the green bars. This example illustrates the need to synthesize all ambiguities present in a document into a brief summary, understandable by designers at a glance.

We visualize the ambiguity of a layout with dashed lines, which show which blocks are free and how they are free to move. We call these dashed lines *axes of freedom*. More technically, we summarize the ambiguity with an *ambiguity base*, which is an algebraic base of the space of all admissible layouts of the sample document. The ambiguity base is the same concept as the base of the solution space of a system of equations in linear algebra. In essence, we condense all admissible layouts into the set of independent dimensions. To translate this base into a graphical summary understandable by designers, we display one admissible layout, augmented with axes of freedom, one per dimension of the ambiguity base. PBMM highlights free blocks with unlocked icons. When the designer selects a free block, PBMM displays its axes of freedom. For ambiguity dimensions related to positional attributes, we represent each with a dashed line. Similarly, for attributes related to sizes of elements, we overlay a double arrow mimicking familiar resizing icons. To do so, PBMM understands the visual semantics of common block attributes. Figures 4a and 4b show two ambiguous configurations and their respective axes of freedom, both on Cartesian and polar layouts.

As a bonus, we can use the ambiguity base to make browsing more intuitive through semantic snapping [8]. For instance, blocks which are dragged beyond the layouts admissible by current configuration should resists the designer's action by snapping back to a legal position. As a result, designers can "feel" constraints by manipulating blocks. This also enables us to explain generalizations with the following UI metaphor: by dragging a block past its snapping radius, the designer is "breaking" constraints.

It remains for us to discuss how we compute the ambiguity base. Since our constraints can be both non-linear and non-equational, computing the ambiguity base precisely by cylindrical algebraic decomposition would be prohibitively expensive. Instead, we compute an over-approximation: we determine the subset of the document attributes which can take more than one value under the current configuration. Each such attribute becomes one independent dimension of the ambiguity base. Our over-approximation ignores all relationships between attributes forming the ambiguity base: some of these attributes can be interdependent. For instance, the size of an image might be unconstrained with the exception of its aspect ratio: $4 * \text{height} = 3 * \text{width}$. Such relationships are lost by our approximation: we will consider both height and width to be independent dimensions. In essence, we over-approximate the precise ambiguity base with an enveloping base of higher dimensionality.

Proposing Resolutions (Specializations)

After the designer breaks some constraints, she proceeds to remove the ambiguity by introducing other constraints. Our tool proposes safe resolutions by computing which constraints can be enabled without creating a conflict. Each of these constraint yields a safe specialization of the current configuration

To communicate available specializations to the designer, we represent each of them as a point in the ambiguity space. Given a free block, we mark the points on its axes of freedom where the block would be positioned if that specialization were chosen. Our interface uses semantic snapping to emphasize these specialization points [8]. The designer chooses one of them by drag&dropping a free block onto one of its specialization points. For example, in Figure 2b, the green bars are vertically free. The underlying block behind both green bars embeds multiple vertical alignment constraints. In this simple case, each green bar could be positioned, relative to its respective blue bar, below, above, or vertically aligned along its bottom edge. Each of these positions is marked on the axis of freedom of each green bar, providing a visual enumeration of the potential resolutions. Behind the scenes, each of these positions constitute a specialization of the current configuration. To select one, the designer drags and drops one green bar onto a marked site, as illustrated in Figure 2c.

IMPLEMENTATION

First, we present an overview of the language of constraints used by the expert programmer to construct blocks. Then, we explain how we architected PBMM to be independent of the constraints used and to support new blocks without modifications. Finally, we detail our technique to compute generalizations and explain how we select which ambiguity to introduce based on the WiW manipulation.

Language of Constraints

To capture a wide class of layouts, we support rich constraints including non-linear ones. For instance, polynomials are frequently used to capture ratios of relative sizes. Under the hood, we rely on the SMT bit-vectors theory [3] which provides an expressive set of primitive constructs from which we build our constraints. Figure 5 illustrates the versatility of our blocks with an example of flow-layout with justification.

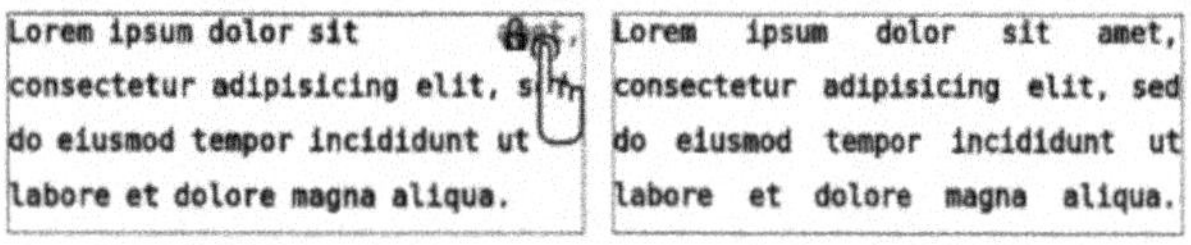

(a) Left justification (b) Full justification

Figure 5. We illustrate the expressibility of our constraints by capturing text-layout. Both line-break insertions and word-spacing are specified and computed as part of the layout. On the left figure, the user is making a WiW manipulation to go from left justification to full justification.

Our constraints are non-directional (also called bi-directional), they leave the flow of computation unspecified. Non directionality enables greater flexibility and reuse: for example, the expert programmer can fix aspect ratio of an image while leaving open whether the height is computed from the width or vice-versa. The flow of values will be indirectly decided by the designer when she chooses a configuration.

The same constraints are reused across many blocks: for instance, all boxy blocks implement the CSS box model which defines margins, borders and padding. To avoid duplicating such concepts in every block, the library supports composable modules of constraints called *traits*. Beside box models, we have traits for concepts such as horizontal/vertical alignment, grouping, spacing, justification, guillotine dividers, etc. We show below one trait setting up a polar coordinate system. It is used by all our radial layouts (*e.g.*, Figure 4b).

```
mandatory
trait Polar2Cart(x, y, angle, radius) {
    x = radius * cos(angle)
    y = radius * sin(angle)
}
```

While most constraints are enabled by configuration switches, there exists a few mandatory ones for essential features such as coordinate systems, as shown above.

To give the flavor of our language, we present some of the constraints available to control the horizontal alignment of the first child of a box.

```
optional trait HAlignFirstChild(width) {
    children[0].left = 0
    children[0].right = width
    children[0].right = children[1].left
    children[0].left = children[1].right
    children[0].right = 0
    ...
}
```

The configuration switches are implicit. Equal symbols signify equality, not assignment, since our constraints are non-directional. The first pair of constraints aligns the left/right edge of the (first) child with the corresponding edge of its parent. The next pair places the child to the left/right of its sibling. The last pair of constraints place the child just outside its parent, on the left/right of it.

PBM Manipulator (PBMM)

PBMM has to function out-of-the-box with any blocks written by the expert programmer, and do so without requiring any modification. In essence, PBMM must be constraint-agnostic. The responsibilities of PBMM can be summarized in three computational tasks: Given a sample document together with a configuration, PBMM must (i) compute the layout and the ambiguity base; (ii) compute which specializations are safe (*i.e.*, conflict-free); and (iii) generalize the current configuration given a WiW manipulation.

We accomplish these three tasks by encoding the entire configuration space as defined by the sample document in the SMT bit-vector theory. We used Z3 [16] as our solver. PBMM always starts from a deterministic configuration. We iteratively query the solver for stronger (more switches toggled on) configurations until we find a deterministic one. After that, all computations are performed on-demand, in response to manipulations. Conveniently, our satisfiability approach to layout lets us cast all three PBMM tasks as satisfiability queries. The encoding of the first two tasks are straightforward and have been omitted for space reasons. However, we detail our technique to select which ambiguities to introduce when generalizing configurations.

First, we enumerate all configurations with one less switch toggled on than the current one. This is our set of candidate generalizations, from which we will select the configuration whose ambiguities are most in line with the WiW manipulation. For the sake of explanation, we assume that only one block was displaced by the designer. Consequently, we abstract the WiW manipulation into one vector, capturing the direction of displacement. Then, we rank candidates by counting how many dimensions of their ambiguity base align with the direction vector. Intuitively, we are selecting the principal components of the direction vector expressed in terms of the ambiguity base. More technically, we compute the dot-product between the direction vector and each dimension of the ambiguity base, both normalized to unit length. We consider that the direction vector aligns with an ambiguous dimension if their dot-product is greater than $\frac{1}{\sqrt{n}}$, where n is the dimensionality of the ambiguity base.

EVALUATION

We evaluate our new methodology—PBM—for designing data-visualizations, together with our prototype implementation along the following two axes:

1. Can non-programmers successfully use PBMM to design data visualizations?
2. Can proficient programmers also benefit from PBM by increasing their productivity with the help of PBMM?

Task	Completion		Time [s]	Steps
Barchart A	11	(100%)	17 ± 19	3.6
Barchart B	11	(100%)	64 ± 30	8.4
Icicles	10	(91%)	60 ± 88	8.5
Treemap	11	(100%)	137 ± 55	14.8
Tree	11	(100%)	64 ± 28	5.4

Table 1. Non-programmer results. The columns indicate the number of participants who successfully completed the task; the median time taken in seconds with the standard deviation; and the average number of steps to the goal.

To investigate these two questions, we conducted two user-studies. In the first, we asked non-programmers to configure five data visualizations using PBMM. To answer the second question, we performed a within-subject study on seasoned programmers. We asked them to complete the same five visualization tasks both with PBMM and with an interface mimicking standard constraint programming.

Non-Programmers

We recruited 11 participants (3 males, 8 females, ages 22 to 39) either students or staff from outside the engineering disciplines, largely from the Biology and Linguistics departments. Participants were selected for their lack of formal training in programming. When shown a picture of an icicle graph and asked whether they could program a layout template producing this type of visualization, all participants answered no.

Each session proceeded as follows: Participants were first introduced to PBMM by a 10 minute long, written tutorial, culminating in a simple exercise. Each participant was tasked with creating five visualizations: two barcharts, one icicle layout (Figure 4a), one treemap (Figure 1), and a custom tree layout (Figure 3). These tasks were chosen to showcase the applicability of our method to a variety of layouts, while offering a gradual increase in complexity. Each task consisted of a short introduction motivating the visualization, followed by an illustration of the goal layout. To complete each task, candidates had to produce the goal layout in 10 minutes or less using PBMM.

All participants but one solved each of the five tasks within the time limit. One participant was not able to complete the icicle graph. Results are summarized in Table 1. The treemap is a particularly interesting case: Participants found creative, unexpected ways to complete the task with 8 unique paths through the design space to the goal layout. The shortest path goes through 7 configurations, whereas the longest explores 19, indicating that PBM supports a range of ways to configure a template and accommodates many different thinking processes.

Programmers

To make a fair comparison with manual constraints programming, we focus on the significant aspects of programming, such as resolving ambiguities and conflicts, while abstracting away irrelevant factors like language syntax. To do so, we built a second programming tool which mimics the relevant part of programming with constraints. Instead of typing code, participants toggled GUI switches to enable/disable constraints. In essence, we have reduced the task of constraint programming to finding a set of constraints leading to the desirable layout. We refer to the mock-up tool as the "button" tool.

The interface of the button tool is divided in two: The top half displays the current layout. Users can scroll and zoom in/out, but no other interaction such as dragging an element is possible. The second half is a table of toggle switches controlling constraints. The table has one row per block. Each row contains all the constraints pertaining to one layout element. Columns organize constraints by category, such as "horizontal alignment" or "height computation." Within each cell, each switch is labeled with simplified pseudo-code of the constraint it toggles. If a conflicting set of constraints is enabled, the button tool reports that the selected constraints cannot be satisfied, and no layout is displayed in the top half. The button tool does not provide a debugging aid for identifying conflicting constraints such as the maximum satisfiable subset or the unsat core. However, to explain ambiguous layouts, the button tool does provide the same visual aids as PBMM: the tool shows one possible layout augmented with axes of freedom representing the base of ambiguity for each partially constrained block.

We recruited 16 participants (13 male, 3 female, of ages between 22 and 30), students and staff from engineering departments, mainly Computer Science. All participants had taken at least one CS class and had been programming for at least 3 years. When shown an illustration of an icicle graph, all participants but one claimed they could write a layout template producing this type of visualization.

The programmer study is a within-subject experiment: every participants used both the button tool and PBMM to solve the set of five layout tasks twice. We reused the same five tasks from the non-programmer study. To compensate for learning effects, half of the participants started with the button tool, and half with PBMM. The setup for this study was similar to the non-programmer setup. Participants first read a written, 10 minute long tutorial introducing the first tool, then did a warm-up exercise, and then solved the five layout tasks using the first tool. They then repeated this process (both tutorial and tasks) with the second tool. Finally, we interviewed participants for 10 minutes about which tool they found to be more effective and improvements they would make to either of the tools.

To compare the productivity of participants with each tool, we measured the following indirect indicators: time taken and the length of the path in the design space from the start layout to the goal. Each step in the path corresponds to a configuration which was reached, either by demonstrations or by toggling constraints with switches.

All tasks but two were completed within the 10 minute time limit. One participant could not complete the treemap, and another did not finish the tree, both while using the button tool. We performed an ANOVA of completion times with task and tool as independent factors. The times were log-transformed to make the distribution closer to a Gaussian. We observed a strong main effect of the tool ($F = 345$, $p \ll 0.001$), and significant effect of the task ($F = 72$, $p \ll 0.001$). Since the tasks were specifically chosen to be gradually increasing in

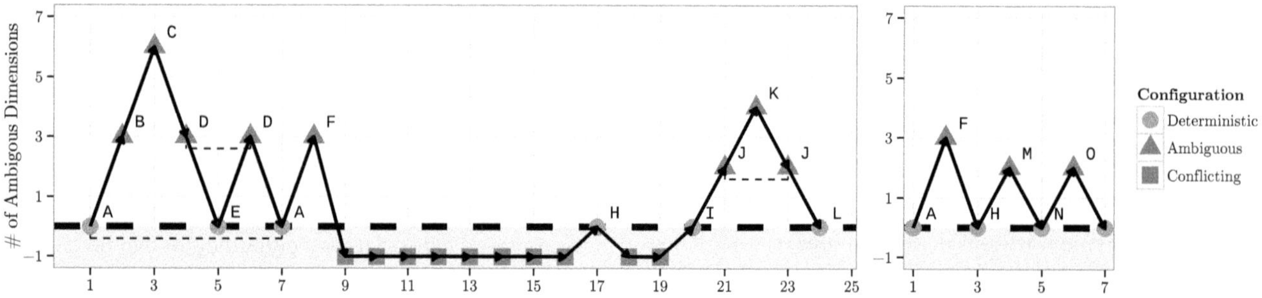

(a) Button tool (b) PBM Manipulator

Figure 6. Paths through the configuration space on the icicles task from the same participant using both tools. Each configuration is uniquely identified by a capital letter. A thin dashed-line highlights configurations explored twice due to backtracking. Configurations along the x axis (0 ambiguous dimension) are deterministic. Conflicting configurations are represented with a negative number of ambiguous dimensions.

difficulty, this was expected. PBMM increased the speed of programmers by a factor ranging from 2.5 (Barchart A) to 10.6 (Barchart B). Across all tasks, the median speed-up was 5.3. To analyse the effect of the tool on path lengths, we used a Wilcoxon signed-rank test. We found that the manipulation tool required fewer steps through the design space than the button tool, with strong confidence ($V = 3236$, $p \ll 0.001$). Here again, we observed that paths are approximately 3.6 times shorter on average across all tasks with PBMM.

Discussion

Our first user-study demonstrates that non-programmers can successfully design data visualizations using PBMM, while the second study shows that programmers would also be more productive with PBMM when programming constraints. It is important to note that, in our experiments, the button tool provided instantaneous feedback. The consequences of toggling constraints were immediately visible. In practice, the situation is often worse; programmers must wait for the compilation-execution cycle to finish before seeing the results of their modifications, thereby increasing the time cost of making changes. Consequently, in practice, longer paths to the goal layout are more detrimental to productivity, and the ability of PBM to quickly converge on the goal becomes more relevant.

We have combined the results from both studies to compare the difference in productivity between programmers and non-programmers using PBMM. Non-programmers took on average 53% longer than the subset of programmers who started with PBMM. This is to be expected, since programmers are more familiar with concepts such as constraints: they are able to build a mental model of the inner workings of our tool faster than non-programmers. We argue that a 53% increase in time spent is a small price to pay to enable non-programmers to accomplish tasks which were previously out of reach.

To further understand how participants used each tool; which actions led to dead ends, where users spent time thinking; and where they got stuck; we have examined in detail the traces from programmers with each tool. Figure 6 shows two such traces, one per tool, taken by one participant on the moderately difficult icicle chart. The two traces we have chosen are typical of what we have observed on this task. Note that this particular participant started with PBMM. Let us start with the trace from the button tool. At the beginning, this participant got lost in highly ambiguous layouts and backtracked twice (steps 6 and 7), in effect revisiting the same configurations again. To recover, he eventually backtracked all the way back to the starting point. Then, he started exploring layouts in another direction but got stuck on a conflict (steps 9–16) shortly afterward. It took him eight attempts and a large amount of time—more than two thirds of the total time—to resolve the conflict. Toward the end of the trace (step 23), this participant was deceived one more time by ambiguities, causing him to backtrack again before finally reaching the goal.

Let us now look at the second trace, from PBMM. Interestingly, our participant took a completely distinct path through the design space: Only the start and goal layout engines are common to both traces. Not only did PBMM prevent our participant from creating conflicting configurations, but it also kept our participant in a portion of the configuration space with lower degrees of ambiguity. Recall that the same visual cues (axes of freedom) are used by both tools to explain ambiguities. But even with those aids, understanding what is and is not constrained in layouts with high degrees of ambiguities remains difficult. Highly ambiguous layouts tend to overwhelm users with too much information. Consequently, users are more likely to add an undesirable constraint by mistake in resolving ambiguities. When such mistakes are corrected, the same configuration is explored twice, thereby creating a backtracking step. This "lost in ambiguities" phenomenon highlights the importance of steering users towards layouts with few ambiguities. By proposing possible resolutions for each dimension of ambiguities, PBMM encourages users to settle ambiguities immediately after their introduction. Our participant dealt with at most three degrees of ambiguity, versus six with the button tool. As a result, he never had to backtrack from an erroneous specialization.

In the interviews concluding each session of the programmer study, all but one participant stated they would use PBMM rather than the button tool if given the choice. The one participant who preferred the button tool stated that "the button tool was more challenging thus more fun". Participants expressed frustration with debugging conflicts with the button tool. A common request was to disable (grey out) buttons which would trigger a conflict if toggled. These comments reinforce our belief that addressing ambiguities and conflicts is essential to making constraint programming more accessible.

On the negative side, participants from the programmers study reported feeling a "lack of control": they would have liked to see how layout engines are modified by their manipulations and which constraints are added or removed. We designed the user interface of PBMM with non-programmers in mind: constraints are completely hidden beneath the UI. For technically-literate audiences, we are considering optionally displaying the layout engine code and using animations to highlight the changes created by each manipulation.

CONCLUSION

We presented Programming by Manipulation, a new methodology for specifying layout with constraints targeted at non-programmers. With PBM, users steer the exploration of layout designs by directly displacing blocks of a sample document. With such manipulations, users can break constraints and subsequently introduce new ones. PBM focuses on programmability and addresses the two principal sources of bugs with constraints: conflicts can no longer arise and ambiguities are explained with a visual summary.

Participants from our user-study seem interested in combining PBM with document authoring so that the sample document can be edited while specifying layout. Our participants were also very enthusiastic about using PBMM to customize CSS templates. This boils down to expressing CSS with constraints, which has been partially done [1]. If one could capture all of CSS, a manipulation-based layout system for the web becomes possible, opening PBM to a very large audience.

ACKNOWLEDGMENTS

This work was supported in part by awards from the National Science Foundation (CCF–0916351, CCF–1139138, and CCF–1337415), as well as gifts from Google, Intel, Mozilla, Nokia, and Samsung.

REFERENCES

1. Badros, G. J., Borning, A., Marriott, K., and Stuckey, P. Constraint cascading style sheets for the web. UIST (1999), 73–82.
2. Badros, G. J., Borning, A., and Stuckey, P. J. The cassowary linear arithmetic constraint solving algorithm. CHI (2001), 267–306.
3. Barrett, C., Stump, A., and Tinelli, C. The Satisfiability Modulo Theories Library. `www.SMT-LIB.org`, 2010.
4. Bostock, M., Ogievetsky, V., and Heer, J. D3 data-driven documents. *IEEE Trans. on Visualization and Computer Graphics* (2011), 2301–2309.
5. Freeman-Benson, B. N. Converting an existing user interface to use constraints. In *UIST* (1993), 207–215.
6. Heer, J., and Bostock, M. Declarative language design for interactive visualization. *InfoVis* (2010), 1149–1156.
7. Heydon, A., and Nelson, G. The juno-2 constraint-based drawing editor. In *Digital Systems TR131a* (1994).
8. Hudson, S. E., and Yeatts, A. K. Smoothly integrating rule-based techniques into a direct manipulation interface builder. UIST (1991), 145–153.
9. Hurst, N., Li, W., and Marriott, K. Review of automatic document formatting. DocEng (2009), 99–108.
10. Jacobs, C., Li, W., Schrier, E., Bargeron, D., and Salesin, D. Adaptive grid-based document layout. *ACM Trans. Graph. 22*, 3 (2003), 838–847.
11. Lau, T. Why pbd systems fail: Lessons learned for usable ai. *AI Magazine* (2009), 65–67.
12. Lutteroth, C., Strandh, R., and Weber, G. Domain specific high-level constraints for user interface layout. *Constraints 13*, 3 (2008), 307–342.
13. Maloney, J. H. *Using constraints for user interface construction*. PhD thesis, Univ. of Washington, 1992.
14. McDaniel, R. G., and Myers, B. A. Getting more out of programming-by-demonstration. CHI (1999), 442–449.
15. Meyerovich, L. personal communication, 2012.
16. Moura, L. D., and Bjørner, N. Z3: An efficient smt solver. TACAS'08/ETAPS'08 (2008), 337–340.
17. Myers, B. A., and Buxton, W. Creating highly-interactive and graphical user interfaces by demonstration. SIGGRAPH (1986), 249–258.
18. Myers, B. A., Zanden, B. V., and Dannenberg, R. B. Creating graphical interactive application objects by demonstration. UIST (1989), 95–104.
19. Sannella, M. Skyblue: a multi-way local propagation constraint solver for user interface construction. UIST (1994), 137–146.
20. Singh, G., Kok, C. H., and Ngan, T. Y. Druid: A system for demonstrational rapid user interface development. UIST (1990), 167–177.
21. Sinha, N., and Karim, R. Compiling mockups to flexible uis. ESEC/FSE (2013), 312–322.
22. Viegas, F. B., Wattenberg, M., van Ham, F., Kriss, J., and McKeon, M. Manyeyes: A site for visualization at internet scale. *IEEE Trans. on Visualization and Computer Graphics* (2007), 1121–1128.
23. Vlissides, J. M., and Tang, S. A unidraw-based user interface builder. UIST (1991), 201–210.
24. Weitzman, L., and Wittenburg, K. Automatic presentation of multimedia documents using relational grammars. MULTIMEDIA (1994), 443–451.
25. Zeidler, C., Lutteroth, C., Sturzlinger, W., and Weber, G. The auckland layout editor: An improved gui layout specification process. UIST (2013), 343–352.
26. Zeidler, C., Lutteroth, C., and Weber, G. Constraint solving for beautiful user interfaces: How solving strategies support layout aesthetics. CHINZ (2012), 72–79.

Global Beautification of Layouts with Interactive Ambiguity Resolution

Pengfei Xu[1] Hongbo Fu[2] Takeo Igarashi[3] Chiew-Lan Tai[1]
[1]HKUST [2]City University of Hong Kong [3]The University of Tokyo

ABSTRACT
Automatic global beautification methods have been proposed for sketch-based interfaces, but they can lead to undesired results due to ambiguity in the user's input. To facilitate ambiguity resolution in layout beautification, we present a novel user interface for visualizing and editing inferred relationships. First, our interface provides a preview of the beautified layout with inferred constraints, without directly modifying the input layout. In this way, the user can easily keep refining beautification results by interactively repositioning and/or resizing elements in the input layout. Second, we present a gestural interface for editing automatically inferred constraints by directly interacting with the visualized constraints via simple gestures. Our efficient implementation of the beautification system provides the user instant feedback. Our user studies validate that our tool is capable of creating, editing and refining layouts of graphic elements and is significantly faster than the standard snap-dragging and command-based alignment tools.

Author Keywords
Global beautification; layout editing; snapping; alignment; ambiguity resolution; gestural interface

ACM Classification Keywords
H.5.2 Information Interfaces and Presentation (e.g. HCI): User Interfaces – Graphical user interfaces (GUI)

INTRODUCTION
Specifying precise relationships, such as alignment and equal-spacing between graphic elements, might be one of the most fundamental operations when creating or editing diagrams and other graphical documents. This is commonly achieved in commercial software packages, like Adobe Illustrator and Microsoft PowerPoint, by using command-based arrangement tools (e.g., issuing a command to equally space the selected elements horizontally) and/or direct positioning aided by snapping.

Snapping might be the simplest beautification technique. It first infers spatial relationships between an element being manipulated and each of the existing elements, and then provides snapping suggestions to interactively achieve desired relationships [5]. We classify snapping as a *local beautification* technique, since each time only a current element is being beautified while all existing elements are kept fixed, leading to an *element-by-element* beautification process. Due to its local nature, snapping itself is not very effective for designing constrained global patterns (e.g., equal-spacing patterns with the ending elements aligned, as shown in Figure 1). Therefore, snapping-based alignment tools are often used together with command-based tools. As we will discuss shortly, such traditional tools are rather tedious and require a carefully ordered set of manual operations to achieve a desired layout.

http://dx.doi.org/10.1145/2642918.2647398

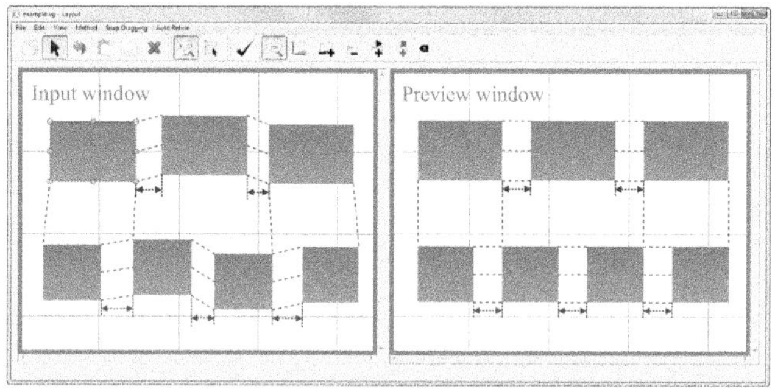

Figure 1. Our novel interface for global beautification of layouts of graphic elements with the power of interactive ambiguity resolution. Grids are visualized for reference purpose only but not for editing.

On the other hand, humans are able to unambiguously tell the desired layouts of graphic elements by viewing all elements as a whole. This motivates us to design a tool for *global beautification* of layouts of graphic elements, i.e., to first infer perceptually meaningful relationships among a set of roughly placed graphic elements and then refine their positions and sizes to get a well-aligned layout that involves only small changes to the input layout. While similar concepts of global beautification have been proposed for sketch-based user interfaces, the existing methods (e.g., [12, 22]) simply apply global beautification results directly to elements being edited, as often done for local beautification interfaces. Early beautification of elements being edited would prevent the user from placing them freely to form a global pattern, thus disturbing the process of layout design.

We present a novel user interface for addressing a commonly known ambiguity problem in global layout beautification. As shown in Figure 1, our interface shows a preview of the beautification, without immediately modifying any input element. In our prototype, this preview is displayed in a separated window. While this interface is simple, it has the following benefits. First, the user can focus on the layout design by manipulating individual elements in the input window. Second, the user might refine the beautification results by slightly modifying the input elements. To facilitate a more direct con-

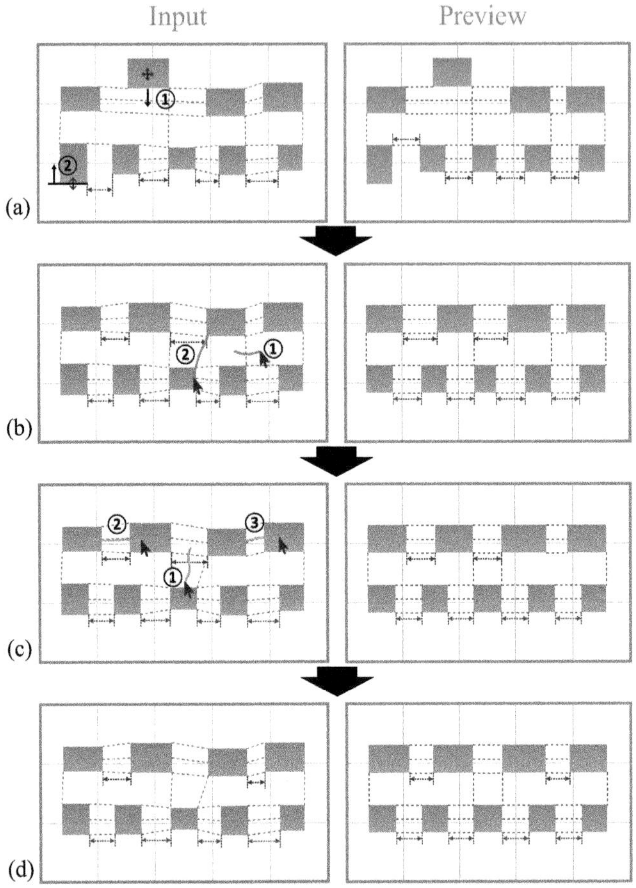

Figure 2. To refine a beautified layout, as previewed in the right column, the user may directly reposition (a-1) or resize (a-2) individual elements, or remove inferred (b-1) or add new (b-2) edge-alignment relationships, or remove inferred (c-1) or add new (c-2 and c-3) equal-spacing relationships.

trol of the beautification results, we also present a gestural interface, which allows easy editing of automatically inferred constraints, i.e., desired relationships between elements in the input window. See Figure 2 and the accompanying video for live demos.

We present an efficient and effective implementation of the proposed global layout beautification interface. Our tool allows interactive refinement of graphic elements and/or constraints, with instant beautification feedback. We conduct two studies to verify the effectiveness of our interface. First we run a study to evaluate the effectiveness of beautification preview. Second, we run a study to evaluate whether our tool could replace the standard snapping and alignment commands, omitting other layout helper features (e.g., equal-sizing, auto-align) which can peacefully coexist with our tool. Our results are promising and show that our tool provides a faster way for creating, editing, and refining the test layouts. The intuitiveness and ease-of-use of our interface are also confirmed by the user study participants.

RELATED WORK

It is hard to track down the history of shape alignment tools. Command-based alignment tools might be one of the most common ways to align objects [24]. They adopt a two-step procedure: first select a group of objects to be aligned and then issue a certain arrangement command (e.g., left-align or equally space the selected objects). Snapping is another widely used technique [4, 5]. It provides aligned positions by snapping an object to either the background grids, manually created guides, or other objects [11]. Snapping supports direct manipulation and is thus more intuitive to use, while command-based tools are more effective in aligning multiple objects simultaneously and have a better control of global alignment. Given their unique advantages, these traditional tools collectively are capable of creating very complex well-aligned layouts of graphic elements. However, even a simple arrangement task as shown in Figure 1 already demands a series of operations with the traditional alignment tools. The repeated use of operations like snapping, element selection, and command selection, is tedious and error-prone, especially for complex layouts. In addition, since different ordering of such operations might lead to different results, a user has to plan a series of operations beforehand and pay special attention to their order during editing. This somewhat diverts the user from the tasks of layout design and creation.

Beyond the basic snapping and alignment commands, there exist many layout helper features, some of which have already been integrated into commercial editors. For example, many algorithms have been proposed for automatic or semi-automatic graph layout generation [25, 26, 29], e.g., the *auto-align* and *auto-space* tools in Microsoft Visio. However, they often significantly change the layout of the input elements, without attempting to infer and maintain the underlying patterns in the input layout. The equal-sizing feature in Microsoft Visio allows easy size-adjustment of selected elements. Several editors such as OmniGraffle and PowerPoint support easy creation of equally spaced elements when duplicating an element multiple times. These helper features are very efficient for only specific tasks and are orthogonal to our tool.

Our work is inspired by the previous efforts on beautification, which also aims to bring as little change as possible when improving content aesthetics. There are plenty of beautification techniques mainly developed for sketch-based user interfaces to tolerate errors from freehand input sketches. These existing techniques can be largely categorized into two groups [23]: *local beautification* and *global beautification*. Similar to snap-dragging [5], local beautification of freehand sketches beautifies a current input stroke based on either itself (often through sketch recognition [1, 2, 14, 21]) or its geometric relationship(s) to the existing elements (e.g., [18, 33, 34]). A typical user interface for local beautification achieves beautification progressively, stroke by stroke. Each stroke is replaced with its beautified version and kept fixed during the beautification of subsequent strokes. Due to the local nature, such interfaces are often easy to control. However, unfortunately, local beautification is not suitable for the beautification of layouts, which should be treated globally.

Compared to local beautification, global beautification has been insufficiently explored. Pavlidis and Van Wyk [22] present the first automatic beautifier for drawings and illustrations. Their algorithm focuses on inferring and enforcing relations among points and lines, and thus can be extended for our layout beautification problem by considering special requirements like how to preserve aspect ratios of elements. However, they do not give details about the user interface of their system. Bolz [6] presents for the first time a user interface for global beautification of drawings. It concentrates on how to deal with parameter settings (e.g., via a parameter menu). Due to possibly frequent parameter changes, the beautifier by default is manually activated each time, though it is discussed that automatic activation of the beautifier (like ours) is a desired feature. Bolz's system overlays the beautified drawing with an outline of the unmodified version for some seconds. A similar visualization of the original and beautified versions is adopted in [12], which however deliberately defers the beautifier's feedback. Otherwise, the user may easily get disturbed by beautification results. In contrast, our user interface allows instant feedback with minimal disturbance. Cheema et al. [7] present a novel sketch beautification algorithm but adopt a simple interface similar to Bolz's. None of the above methods has explored an interface for editing constraints.

Our optimization strategy for determining valid constraints bears some resemblance to the previous solutions for identifying geometric features towards sketch recognition. For example, Veselova and Davis [30] employ studies of human perception to determine which geometric features are the most important for symbol recognition. Hammond and Davis [15] present a graphical debugging tool for learning structural descriptions from automatically generated near-miss examples. Similar to earlier work [18, 22], we adopt an automatic, iterative approach to avoid dramatic changes to the input layout.

It is not always possible to infer desired relationships among roughly placed elements, especially when there are ambiguities. A possible solution for ambiguity resolution is to provide multiple alternatives as suggestions from which the user can then choose [17, 18, 20]. The effectiveness of such suggestion-based interfaces has been demonstrated for progressive beautification [18, 20]. It is unclear whether suggestions can be used to effectively resolve the ambiguity from global beautification, since a handful of ambiguous relationships may easily lead to a large set of suggestions. Instead of attempting to select the best suggestions from a big pool, we design a gestural interface for directly editing a limited number of constraints.

Constraint-based systems have been extensively studied and a detailed review is beyond the scope of this paper. Most constraint-based systems require the user to specify constraints explicitly (e.g., [9, 13, 28]). Instead, our beautification interface focuses on automatic inference of geometric constraints, and thus only very few edits on constraints (after roughly placing elements) are needed to achieve a desired layout. Note that our current system performs once-off alignment only and does not maintain inferred constraints during subsequent editing [31]. Recently Zeidler et al. [32] introduce a novel layout preview but focus on the resizing behavior of a constraint-based layout during the design phase. Since constraint-based systems often need to deal with various linear and nonlinear constraints, possibly with complex interactions among them, significant effort has been devoted to the topic of constraint solving (e.g., [3, 16, 19, 27]). Such solvers can be potentially used for our beautification optimization problem.

USER INTERFACE

In this section we first describe our main interface for global beautification and then present our gestural interface for editing constraints. To make it simple, we first assume that the beautifier is already activated and applied to all input elements, and will discuss how our beautifier can coexist with other tools at the end of this section.

Global Beautifier Interface

Our global beautifier takes a set of roughly placed elements as input and returns a well-aligned layout as output. Since the desired relationships might not be immediately clear during editing, even to a human viewer, we design a user interface that does not directly change the location and size of elements in the input layout, but rather gives a preview of the refined layout in another window (Figure 1). In this way the user can focus on layout design itself by placing elements roughly, without being disturbed by the beautifier's feedback.

Since the input layout is not immediately replaced with the beautified version, the user may keep editing the current layout by translating or resizing individual elements, and our beautifier gives instant feedback in the preview window. This simple interface is suitable for creating, editing or refining layouts. At any point the user may confirm to apply the beautified layout to the input one.

Gestural Interface for Editing Constraints

Automatically inferring underlying relationships among elements plays a vital role in layout beautification. Since relationships are formulated as constraints in the beautification optimization, we will use the terms relationships and constraints interchangeably in the following discussion.

Automatically inferred relationships might not always be wholly desirable. This problem might be *indirectly* solved by interactive refinement of certain elements' position and/or size. Alternatively the user may *directly* add or remove relationships using a gestural interface as shown in Figure 2 (b) and (c). Our implemented beautifier currently supports two types of geometric relationships: edge alignment and equal-spacing.

At any time the user may edit constraints in the input window, where he or she may edit elements for interactive refinement. To facilitate the editing of constraints, we display all automatically inferred relationships using dashed lines and arrows in both the input and preview windows (Figure 1). The visualized constraints in the input window are editable via the gestural interface while those in the preview window are read-only for examining the currently achieved relationships. In real-world applications, constraints may be displayed on demand to avoid visual clutter, since in many cases only very few constraint edits often suffice.

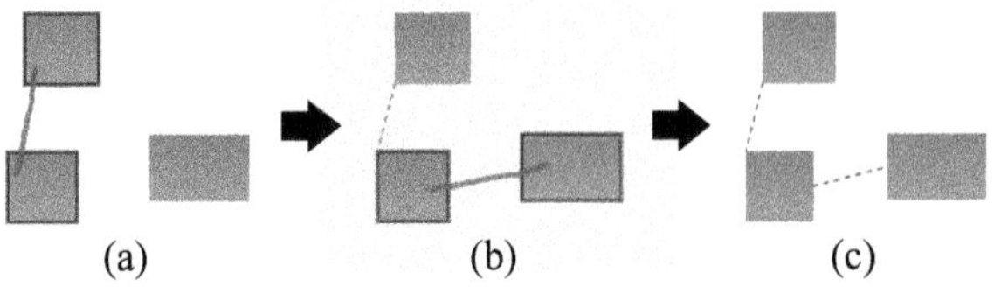

Figure 3. Two examples of our gestural interface for adding alignment constraints. An appropriate constraint is automatically determined by examining the relative location of two involved elements and the position of the stroke's ending points relative to the elements.

The user enters the mode for editing edge alignment constraints by clicking an "alignment constraint editing" button, which might be replaced with a gesture in the future implementation. In this mode, repositioning and resizing of individual elements are disabled. To remove an existing alignment constraint, the user performs a cutting gesture on a constraint of interest (Figure 2 (b-1)), i.e., drawing a stroke roughly perpendicular to the dashed line corresponding to the constraint. To add a new alignment constraint, the user simply draws a stroke connecting a pair of elements of interest (Figure 2 (b-2)). Our interface automatically determines whether a horizontal or vertical alignment constraint is needed by examining the relative location of the two elements. For example, the stroke in Figure 3 (a) is interpreted as an intention for vertical alignment while the stroke in Figure 3 (b) is for horizontal alignment. For horizontal alignment, the user may indicate the preference for top-, middle- or bottom-align by placing the ending points of the stroke into the respective parts of the elements. For this reason, the stroke in Figure 3 (b) is recognized for achieving middle alignment. A similar control exists for vertical alignment (see an example in Figure 3 (a)). To make the interface more user-friendly, we may put three control handles (e.g., small translucent circles) on each side of an element, indicating that the user can drag from one handle to another in order to set alignments. The mode for editing alignment constraints is deactivated when the user switches to other editing modes.

For simplicity, the activation and deactivation of our gestural tool for editing equal-spacing constraints are achieved via mode-switching buttons. To remove an equal-spacing constraint the user performs a cutting gesture (Figure 2 (c-1)). To add a new equal-spacing constraint, the user invokes multiple (at least two) strokes, with each of them connecting a pair of elements (Figure 2 (c-2 and c-3)). Constraints for equal-spacing between the specified pairs of elements will then be added. Horizontal or vertical equal-spacing is automatically determined by looking into the relative position of pairs of elements.

Not all automatically inferred constraints can be enforced at the same time. Our interface only visualizes the constraints that can coexist. However, the user may introduce constraints that conflict with the existing ones. To capture the user's latest intention, any constraint that is in conflict with the newly added constraint will be removed. Thus in some cases the user may see one or more existing constraints removed due to the new constraints.

IMPLEMENTATION

Now we describe how we implement the proposed beautifier interface. Our implementation essentially follows the general beautification framework proposed by Pavlidis and Van Wyk [22]. We describe our implementation details for completeness.

Pattern Detection

We focus only on axis-aligned edge alignment and equal-spacing relationships, since they already enable all the functions of snapping and alignment commands. For illustration, we always use rectangles to represent graphic elements, since element alignment is often achieved at the bounding box level.

Inferring edge-alignment relationships. We will explain only the implementation for horizontal alignment. Detecting relationships for vertical alignment is done similarly. Following the snapping tools in existing editors like Microsoft Visio, we allow horizontal edge-alignment to happen only at the top edge denoted as s_t, bottom edge s_b and middle edge s_m (i.e., a horizontal segment passing through the center) of the bounding box of an element. Given a group of n graphic elements (Figure 4 (a)), we thus have $3n$ edges (Figure 4 (b)), from which our beautifier will infer desired alignment relationships (Figure 4 (d)), i.e., detect a set of horizontal lines along which the relevant elements get aligned (Figure 4 (c)). This is essentially a 1D clustering problem. Although there exist many general techniques for such clustering problems, most of them require indicating the scale of the cluster by parameters, which in most techniques are global. However, the alignment lines in a given layout may have different qualities. Some of them would be invalid if all alignment lines are detected under the same configuration. Therefore, the clustering algorithm should be adaptive to each alignment line.

Our solution is a variant of the classic *RANSAC* algorithm [10]. Since the number of edges is usually not big (from dozens to hundreds), it is possible to find globally optimal lines without randomness. Specifically, for every edge, we use the following iterative procedure to find a candidate alignment line: 1) the current edge as an initial inlier gives an initial fitted line. 2) All other edges are tested against the fitted line to find an updated set of inliers. 3) Refit the line to the updated set of inliers. Steps 2 and 3 are repeated till convergence. Each edge as the initial inlier gives a candidate alignment line, and we pick the best line as the determinate alignment line. The inliers (edges) of the picked line are then removed from the current set of edges (initially, $3n$ edges) and we repeat the above iterative procedure to find the next alignment line till no more lines can be found. See the appendix for more details of Steps 2 and 3.

Once we find a candidate alignment line for each edge, we select the best alignment line $\mathcal{P}_a$. Generally we prefer an alignment line with a larger group of inliers and a lower variance of the vertical coordinate among the inliers. All the inlier edges corresponding to the selected alignment line have edge-alignment relationships between each other (Figure 4 (d)).

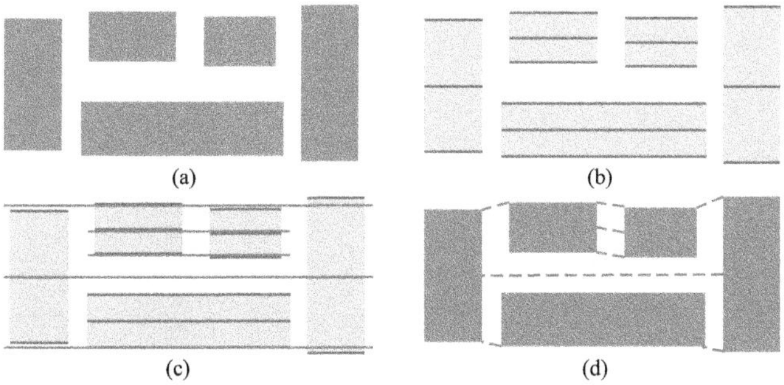

Figure 4. Illustration for inferring relationships (dashed lines) for horizontal alignment.

Inferring equal-spacing relationships. In our implementation we allow the existence of equal-spacing relationships only in a group of graphic elements that have edge-alignment relationships. We use an iterative bottom-up clustering approach to detect equal-spacing relationships. The spacing is defined as the distance between every pair of *adjacent* elements. Initially, each spacing cluster consists of only one spacing. Each iteration groups two clusters with the smallest distance. The distance between two spacings d_1 and d_2 is defined as $|d_1 - d_2|/(d_1 + d_2)$. For two spacing clusters, it is defined as the difference of the average spacing between two clusters. The clustering process continues until the distance of the best pair of spacing groups is larger than a predefined threshold (we set as 0.15). Note that our gestural interface allows interactively adding equal-spacing constraints to non-adjacent pairs of elements (see an example in Figure 2 (c)).

Layout Refinement by Optimization

Following the previous beautification works [22], we use an optimization-based approach to refine the layout to satisfy the inferred relationships while retaining as much as possible the original layout, in terms of both the position and size of each graphic element.

Objective. Let s_t, s_b, s_m, s_l, s_r, s_c denote the top, bottom, (horizontal) middle, left, right, (vertical) center edges of a graphic element. The objective of bringing the least change to the original layout can be achieved by preserving the coordinates $p(\cdot)$ of the edges s_* of each graphic element $g \in \mathcal{G}$, where $\mathcal{G}$ is the set of input graphic elements. Specifically, for vertical edges, s_l, s_c and s_r, $p(\cdot)$ are their horizontal coordinates, and for horizontal edges, s_t, s_m and s_b, $p(\cdot)$ are their vertical coordinates. To retain the original layout we minimize the following objective function:

$$E = \sum_{g \in \mathcal{G}} \sum_{*} (p'(s_*^g) - p(s_*^g))^2, \quad (1)$$

where $p'(\cdot)$ denotes the changed coordinates of the edges after refinement.

Constraints. The above minimization is subject to a set of constraints. We first identify the intrinsic constraints of each graphic element g, which are $p'(s_l^g) + p'(s_r^g) = 2p'(s_c^g)$ and $p'(s_t^g) + p'(s_b^g) = 2p'(s_m^g)$. If the aspect ratio a^g needs to be retained during the refinement (e.g., for images), an extra constraint is added: $p'(s_r^g) - p'(s_l^g) = a^g(p'(s_t^g) - p'(s_b^g))$.

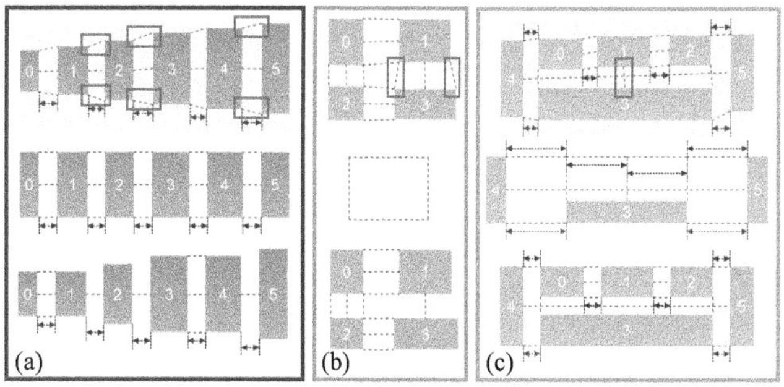

Figure 5. Top: input layouts. Middle: results by simultaneously enforcing all detected constraints, leading to degenerating cases in (b) and (c). Bottom: our results, by automatically rejecting the highlighted constraints. Note that the constraint of keeping the aspect ratios of elements is enforced in (b) and (c) but not (a).

These three constraints hold for every graphic element and must be satisfied by the optimal solution.

The rest of the constraints are derived from the detected relationships. Let $\mathcal{S}_a$ denote a set of inliers that will be aligned to the same line $\mathcal{P}_a$. If the edges s_i and s_j have edge-alignment relationships between them, we have $p'(s_i) = p'(s_j)$. Each pair of neighboring graphic elements in $\mathcal{P}_a$ gives rise to one such equality constraint, resulting in a total of $|\mathcal{S}_a| - 1$ constraints, where $|\mathcal{S}_a|$ is the cardinality of $\mathcal{S}_a$. Let $\mathcal{S}_s$ be a set of element pairs with the equal-spacing relationship detected for every element pair. Similarly, this introduces another $|\mathcal{S}_s| - 1$ equality constraints.

Optimization. In general, only a subset of the constraints can be enforced during the optimization. This is because simultaneously enforcing some constraints may cause the refined layout to deviate too much from the original layout (Figure 5 (a)). Worse, the layout may become degenerate in that the sizes of some graphic elements may become zero or negative (Figure 5 (b) and (c)).

Similar to [18, 22], we use an iterative approach to determine valid constraints. Specifically, we iteratively check the validity of each of our alignment and spacing equality constraints by examining the optimized layout. After adding each constraint to the system, we check the current optimal solution and drop the constraint if the layout becomes degenerate or changes too much. Since all the constraints are in the linear equality form, and the constraints are added incrementally, this strategy works efficiently. The alignment constraints are added in the order in which the corresponding alignment lines are detected, i.e., the constraints are preserved in a higher priority if the corresponding alignment line is detected earlier. Within the $|\mathcal{P}_a| - 1$ edge-alignment constraints corresponding to a specific alignment line, we rank them by their alignment error. This means that a constraint $p'(s_i) = p'(s_j)$ has a higher priority if $||p(s_i) - p(s_j)||$ is smaller. After considering all the constraints of an edge-alignment pattern, we add the detected equal-spacing relationships from this alignment pattern. All constraints of an equal-spacing pattern are simultaneously added, and they are all rejected if the new layout becomes degenerate or deviates too much from the original layout, since equal-spacing often exists as a global pattern. We use the CHOLMOD sparse linear system solver [8] to in-

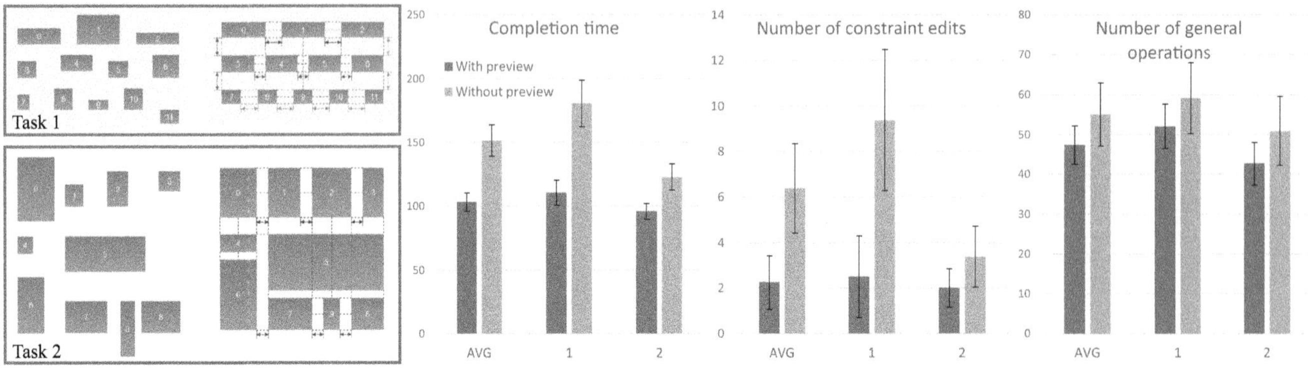

Figure 6. Two layout refinement tasks used in study 1 and the resulting statistics. Error bars represent standard error of the mean.

crementally solve the resulting constraint optimization problem after each constraint is added. It provides fast update for the linear system, without repeatedly solving it from scratch, and thus is able to solve the incremental constraint optimization problem efficiently.

While our simple strategy generally works well and efficiently, we are aware of another possible solution which determines constraints by adding linear inequality constraints to restrict the solution domain. For example, the refined size of a graphic element should be within a certain range. We can then incrementally add a constraint and retain it only if the feasible region of this constraint problem is not empty. For this solution, we may resort to existing constraint solvers like QOCA [19] and Gecode [27].

USER STUDIES

We have extensively tested our technique on layouts of various patterns, most of which are time consuming to produce when snapping and alignment commands are used. See some of the tested layouts in Figures 5–8. Our tool is also applicable to layouts with nested elements (See Figure 7). Note that a fixed set of parameter values were always used throughout our experimentation. Two user studies were conducted to evaluate the effectiveness of our our technique.

Study 1: Evaluation of Beautification Preview

We first evaluated the performance of the beautifier with and without a preview window. Eight university students helped with the evaluation. All of them had extensive experience in using the traditional alignment tools, e.g., in Microsoft PowerPoint.

Apparatus. The study was conducted on an ordinary PC (DELL Optiplex 960), with 3.00 GHz Intel Core 2 Duo CPU and 4.00 GB RAM. Two LCD display monitors (20-inch and 17-inch) were connected, one for the beautifier interface (with the preview window if used), and the other only for displaying a static target layout. Our beautifier achieved real-time performance for moderately complex layouts. For example, for a typical layout containing a dozen of elements like those shown in Figure 8, it took our technique less than 0.01 seconds for alignment relationships inference and less than 0.02 seconds for layout refinement.

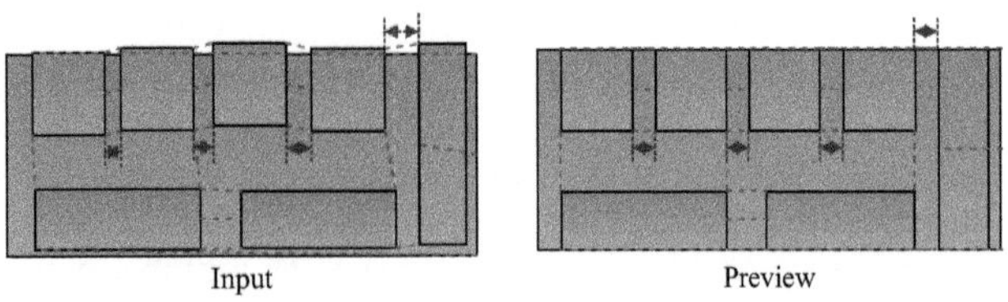

Figure 7. The application of our tool to layouts with nested elements.

Tasks. We asked participants to perform layout refinement. For each task, each participant was asked to refine a source layout, which already resembled a target layout with visualized alignment and equal-spacing relationships (Figure 6), displayed on a separate monitor. The source and target layouts were consistently numbered so that the participants knew the correspondence between the elements. Common operations, such as element translation, resizing and selection (by single click or rectangle selection tool), were allowed. But we disabled element creation and removal.

Two tasks (Figure 6) were tested and had different layout complexity. Task 1 was more challenging, since it involved more potential ambiguities during refinement. Each participant was required to complete each of the two tasks, with two tools: our beautifier with and without a preview window. For the latter, the beautified result was instantly applied to the input layout, as similarly done in the previous works [6, 12]. See the accompanying video for such an interface in action. In total we had 8 (participants) $\times$ 2 (tools) $\times$ 2 (tasks) = 32 trials.

With each of the two tools (i.e., the beautifier with and without a preview), the participants were asked to quickly reproduce each of the two target layouts by achieving as many visualized target relationships as possible. However, they were allowed to proceed to the next task without fully reproducing the target layout of the current task. To help the participants better track their progress, the alignment and equal-spacing relationships of the layout were visualized and shown in the preview window or the input window in the case of no preview window. The order of the tasks and the tools in each task were counter-balanced across participants. Before the study, the participants were introduced to these two tools, and they practiced in a short warm-up session until they felt comfortable. The whole study lasted less than 20 minutes on average for each participant.

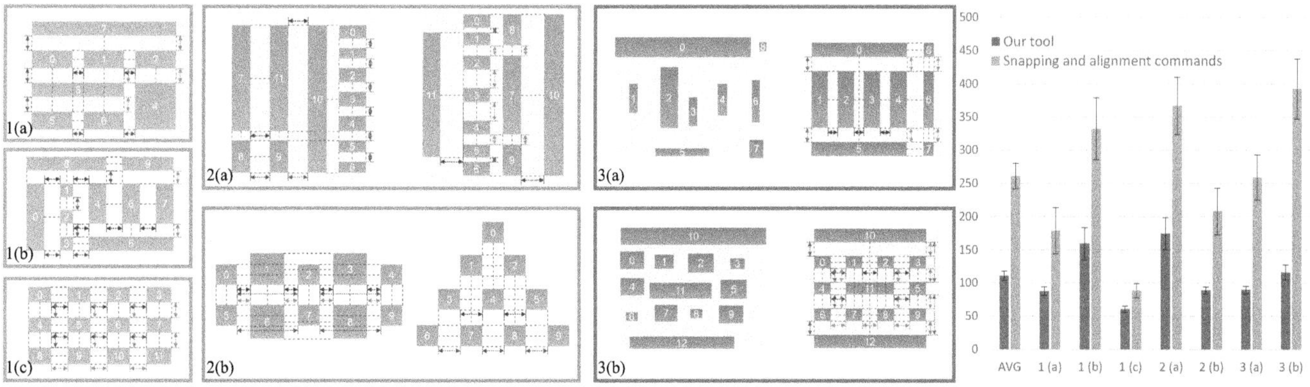

Figure 8. From left to right: 1(a)-(c): target layouts used in the layout creation scenario; 2(a)&(b): source layouts (left) and target layouts (right) in the layout editing scenario; 3(a)&(b): source (left) and target layouts (right) in the layout refinement scenario; average completion time (in seconds) of each task. Error bars represent standard error of the mean.

Performance measures. During the study, the following information was recorded for quantitative analysis: the completion time of individual trials, the time spent on element editing (selection, moving, resizing), the number of general operations (moving, resizing, duplicate, removal, undo), and the number of edits for edge-alignment constraints and equal-spacing constraints.

Results. Figure 6 plots the statistics of the core information captured in Study 1. The preview window significantly shortened the average completion time per task among the participants, from 151.7 seconds to 103.2 seconds. A significant difference was confirmed by repeated measures analysis of variance (repeated measures ANOVA): $F = 57.77$ and $p = 0.000126$. The benefit of our interface with the preview window was even clearer for Task 1, a more challenging task. The average completion time of Task 1 was 110.5 seconds with our interface, compared to 180.6 seconds without the preview window ($F = 41.59$, $p = 0.000351$).

Figure 6 also shows the average number of operations for editing constraints and the average number of general operations (moving, resizing, etc). While on average the number of general operations was less with our interface, the difference was not statistically significant. Repeated measures ANOVA confirmed a significant difference in the average of constraint edits for Task 1 ($F = 17.78$, $p = 0.003954$) but not for Task 2 ($F = 2.951$, $p = 0.12951$) between the beautifier with and without the preview window. For the more challenging Task 1, without the preview window, the users easily got distracted by intermediate beautification results, making them difficult to achieve desired layouts simply by direct repositioning and resizing of elements. Thus they had to resort to the tools for editing constraints more often. It is interesting to note that the standard errors here were relatively large, indicating that different participants might have difference preferences for the interface for editing constraints.

Study 2: Comparing to Snapping & Alignment Commands

We conducted a user study to evaluate the effectiveness of our technique, compared to snapping and alignment commands, which are arguably the most popular tools available in almost all commercial graphic editors like OmniGraffle, Visio, and InDesign. We implemented these standard tools in a way like in PowerPoint 2013. Specifically, snapping was activated only for the element being dragged. This element could be snapped to achieve edge/center alignment or equal spacing with other elements. The compared system supported 8 commands: align top/middle/bottom/left/center/right, and distribute horizontally/vertically. We chose the lead object for alignment similar to PowerPoint, e.g., the topmost element for top-align, and the outermost elements for even distribution. We deliberately excluded layout helper features beyond the standard snapping and alignment commands, since it is expected that such extra functions would similarly benefit our tool and the compared system.

Apparatus and participants. We used the same set of instruments as those in Study 1. Another 11 university students were recruited for the user study. Again all of them had used traditional alignment tools extensively. A handful of them were even good at vector graphics editing and were familiar with professional software like Adobe Illustrator.

Tasks. Besides layout refinement, we evaluated the performance of the traditional tools and ours in another two scenarios, i.e., creating and editing layouts. In the creation scenario, three tasks were tested. For each task, each participant was asked to create a layout from scratch towards a reference target layout (Figure 8 1(a)-(c)). The participants were allowed to draw, duplicate, or remove elements. The layout editing scenario comprises two tasks, each of which required the participants to significantly change an input layout towards a target layout (Figure 8 2(a)-(b)). Element creation and removal were disabled. Like Study 1, the participants were asked to complete two layout refinement tasks (Figure 8 3(a)-(b)). But this time we locked the aspect ratios of the elements, controlled by a toggle button. For the editing and refining scenarios, consistent correspondence numbers were provided.

In total there were seven tasks under the three scenarios. Each participant was asked to complete each of them twice, one with our tool and the other with the set of traditional alignment tools. That is, our experiment involved 11 (participants) $\times$ 2 (tools) $\times$ 7 (tasks) $=$ 154 trials. The tools in each task were (almost) counter-balanced and the order of the tasks in each scenario was random. The participants took breaks between different scenarios so that they were briefed on the newly enabled or disabled operations before each scenario. For simplicity no break was allowed between tasks in each scenario.

Performance measures. Besides the measures used in Study 1, the following information was also recorded: the time spent on drawing the elements (for the creation scenario only), and the number of specific operations with the traditional tools (commands like edge alignment and equal spacing).

Results. Figure 8 shows the target layouts in each task, and the corresponding average completion times. Repeated measures ANOVA found a significant difference in the average completion time per task among the participants between our tool and the traditional tools ($F = 78.8$, $p < 4 \times 10^{-6}$). On average, significantly less time was needed to accomplish each task using our tool (110.7 seconds) compared to the traditional tools (260.7 seconds).

Our tool performed much better than the traditional tools for target layouts involving complex relationships such as Tasks 1(b) and 2(a). For easier tasks, such as Tasks 1(a) and 1(c), our tool was still faster. For the tasks in the refinement scenario, due to the locked aspect ratios of the elements, the editing freedom was seriously restricted, making such tasks more challenging to complete for the traditional tools. The performance of the traditional tools was severely affected by this restriction on editing freedom. More than half of the participants failed to reproduce the target layouts with the traditional tools, while all of them had no difficulty with our tool.

In Figure 9 we show more statistics from the user study. There was no statistically significant difference in the drawing time between the two tools ($p = 0.465$), though we observed that our tool was still slightly faster. Our tool required significantly fewer general operations ($p < 5 \times 10^{-5}$). The task success rates also reflects the effectiveness of our tool. For almost all the tasks, each participant could successfully reproduce the target layouts with our tool. In contrast, the completion rates for the traditional tools were much lower, despite they had been used by all the participants on a regular basis. This confirms the ease of use of our tool, even for the first-time users.

Figure 9 also shows the average number of edits on edge alignment and equal-spacing constraints for individual tasks. While the number of edits was small, constraint editing was performed for 5 out of 7 tasks. We speculate that the number of constraint edits needed is correlated with layout complexity, which is somewhat reflected by the (average) completion time. For example, the number of constraint edits used for Task 1(b) was much bigger than that for Task 1(a) and Task 1(c). A similar conclusion on the average completion time of these tasks could be reached.

It can be seen that the standard error of the mean (shown as error bars in Figures 8 and 9) of the completion time, editing time, and editing number is much larger with the traditional tools. This means that the performance of our tool was more consistent across all participants. In other words our

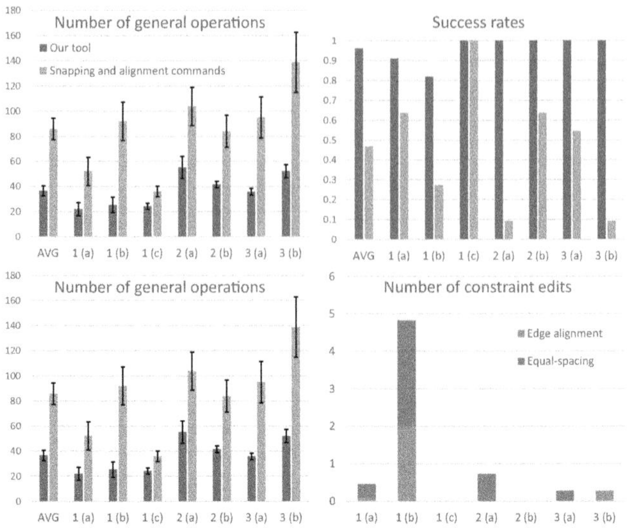

Figure 9. More statistics. The timings are in seconds. Error bars represent standard error of the mean.

tool was less dependent on the experience of the individual participants.

Our statistics show that on average each participant performed 0.97 edge-alignment commands and 1.90 equal-spacing commands per task. This is mainly because equal-spacing commands were more indispensable, while edge-alignment commands could be replaced with more intuitive snapping operations. This reiterates the fact that snapping has to be used together with command-based alignment tools in many cases.

We also got some interesting observations from the user study. With our tool, some participants tended to draw or edit elements carefully at the beginning despite being told that our tool can tolerate rough inputs. However, they quickly get used to our tool and performed the creation and editing operations more casually. Another observation was that, in the refining scenario, when using the traditional tools, some participants moved all the elements away before editing, though most of the input elements were already located very close to the target positions. Such behavior was never observed with our tool. This behavior was largely due to the not-aligned elements triggering often excessive and distracting suggestions from snap-dragging.

After completing the tasks, we asked each participant to provide feedback on the two tools in terms of their ease of use. All participants except one preferred our tool. They expressed that our tool enables them to disregard the order of specific operations and focus on the layout design. One participant who preferred the traditional tools liked the full user control and disliked rough inputs. This concern could be addressed by integrating snap-dragging into our framework.

DISCUSSIONS

To use our tool in existing graphic editors like PowerPoint, the user may first select a set of target elements and then enter a "layout beautification mode", for example, via an activation button, menu or gesture. Similar to the interface described in our prototype, we may pop up a dialog to edit elements and/or constraints while previewing the beautified layout in the input panel. In the mode of element editing, our interface is completely compatible with existing layout helper features. All edits are confirmed after the user hits the "apply" button; otherwise they are canceled.

While the results of Study 1 imply the usefulness of having a preview of the refined layout in the experimental condition, rendering the original and refined layouts in separate windows might cause the problem of divided attention. To alleviate this problem we might use a smaller preview window instead of a full-scale copy of the design. We believe that it is not necessary to always activate the preview window especially when the input layout is undergoing dramatic changes, e.g., at the beginning of layout editing and creation tasks in Study 2.

To further solve the problem of divided attention and to save space required by an extra preview window, we could show the preview in place. For example we might overlay the beautified layout as a translucent layer on top of the original layout. Since this solution easily results in visual clutter, it might work well for only relatively simple layouts with fewer elements, but would likely not be able to scale to very complex diagrams. In the future it is worth evaluating whether such alternative solutions would be more effective than a simple preview window in our current prototype.

Since our main goal in this work is to find a better alternative to snapping and alignment commands, we focused only on a limited set of simple constraints, i.e., alignment and equal spacing. However, it is easy to incorporate new constraints, such as symmetry and length equality into our framework, as already suggested by Pavlidis and Van Wyk [22]. Similarly, although our current prototype concentrated on grid-like layouts, it is possible to handle more general layouts by introducing advanced pattern detectors, e.g., to detect elements distributed roughly along an arbitrary line, circle etc.

CONCLUSION AND FUTURE WORK

We presented a novel user interface for layout beautification. Our user studies confirmed that our technique is very effective and can even be used as a better replacement of the standard snapping and command-based alignment tools, given its faster performance and better ease of use. We speculate that the advantages of our tool would be even clearer to novice users who have little or no experience in creating precise layouts. It would be interesting to apply our tool to real-world examples like posters and to really integrate it with existing graphic editors to examine the interplay between our tool and other layout helper features. Our current implementation requires explicit mode switching to activate or deactivate the gesture interface for editing geometric constraints. In the future we will explore a modeless interface where the user could use the editing operations of both element and constraint without explicit mode switching. We are also interested in extending the proposed interface to 3D layout design, where the traditional tools are even more cumbersome.

Acknowledgements

We thank the reviewers for their constructive comments and the user study participants for their time. This work was partially supported by grants from the Research Grants Council of HKSAR, China (Project No. 113513, 619611, and 11204014) and the City University of Hong Kong (Project No. 7003058).

REFERENCES

1. Alvarado, C. Sketch recognition user interfaces: Guidelines for design and development. In *Proceedings of AAAI Fall Symposium on Intelligent Pen-based Interfaces*, vol. 1 (2004).
2. Arvo, J., and Novins, K. Fluid sketches: continuous recognition and morphing of simple hand-drawn shapes. In *UIST '00* (2000), 73–80.
3. Badros, G. J., Borning, A., and Stuckey, P. J. The cassowary linear arithmetic constraint solving algorithm. *ACM Transactions on Computer-Human Interaction (TOCHI) 8*, 4 (2001), 267–306.
4. Baudisch, P., Cutrell, E., Hinckley, K., and Eversole, A. Snap-and-go: helping users align objects without the modality of traditional snapping. In *CHI* (2005), 301–310.
5. Bier, E. A., and Stone, M. C. Snap-dragging. In *ACM SIGGRAPH Computer Graphics*, vol. 20 (1986), 233–240.
6. Bolz, D. Some aspects of the user interface of a knowledge based beautifier for drawings. In *IUI '93* (1993), 45–52.
7. Cheema, S., Gulwani, S., and LaViola, J. Quickdraw: Improving drawing experience for geometric diagrams. In *CHI '12* (2012), 1037–1064.
8. Davis, T. Cholmod: a sparse supernodal cholesky factorization package., version 2.1.2, 2013. University of Florida, Available online at http://www.cise.ufl.edu/research/sparse/cholmod/.
9. Dwyer, T., Marriott, K., and Wybrow, M. Dunnart: A constraint-based network diagram authoring tool. In *Graph Drawing* (2009), 420–431.
10. Fischler, M. A., and Bolles, R. C. Random sample consensus: a paradigm for model fitting with applications to image analysis and automated cartography. *Commun. ACM 24*, 6 (1981), 381–395.
11. Frisch, M., Kleinau, S., Langner, R., and Dachselt, R. Grids & guides: multi-touch layout and alignment tools. In *CHI '11* (2011), 1615–1618.
12. Galindo, D., and Faure, C. Perceptually-based representation of network diagrams. In *International Conference on Document Analysis and Recognition*, vol. 1 (1997), 352–356.
13. Gleicher, M., and Witkin, A. Drawing with constraints. *The Visual Computer 11*, 1 (1994), 39–51.

14. Hammond, T., and Davis, R. Automatically transforming symbolic shape descriptions for use in sketch recognition. In *AAAI '04*, AAAI'04, AAAI Press (2004), 450–456.

15. Hammond, T., and Davis, R. Interactive learning of structural shape descriptions from automatically generated near-miss examples. In *IUI '06* (2006), 210–217.

16. Hosobe, H. A modular geometric constraint solver for user interface applications. In *UIST '01* (2001), 91–100.

17. Igarashi, T., and Hughes, J. F. A suggestive interface for 3D drawing. In *UIST '01* (2001), 173–181.

18. Igarashi, T., Matsuoka, S., Kawachiya, S., and Tanaka, H. Interactive beautification: a technique for rapid geometric design. In *UIST '97* (1997), 105–114.

19. Marriott, K., and Chok, S. S. Qoca: A constraint solving toolkit for interactive graphical applications. *Constraints 7*, 3-4 (2002), 229–254.

20. Murugappan, S., Sellamani, S., and Ramani, K. Towards beautification of freehand sketches using suggestions. In *6th Eurographics Symposium on Sketch-Based Interfaces and Modeling* (2009), 69–76.

21. Paulson, B., and Hammond, T. PaleoSketch: accurate primitive sketch recognition and beautification. In *IUI '08* (2008), 1–10.

22. Pavlidis, T., and Van Wyk, C. J. An automatic beautifier for drawings and illustrations. In *ACM SIGGRAPH Computer Graphics*, vol. 19 (1985), 225–234.

23. Plimmer, B., and Grundy, J. Beautifying sketching-based design tool content: issues and experiences. In *Proceedings of the Sixth Australasian conference on User interface-Volume 40* (2005), 31–38.

24. Raisamo, R., and Räihä, K.-J. A new direct manipulation technique for aligning objects in drawing programs. In *UIST* (1996), 157–164.

25. Reinert, B., Ritschel, T., and Seidel, H.-P. Interactive by-example design of artistic packing layouts. *ACM Trans. Graph. 31*, 6 (2013).

26. Ryall, K., Marks, J., and Shieber, S. An interactive constraint-based system for drawing graphs. In *UIST '97* (1997), 97–104.

27. Schulte, C., Lagerkvist, M., and Tack, G. Gecode. *Software download and online material at the website: http://www. gecode. org* (2006).

28. Sutherland, I. E. Sketch pad a man-machine graphical communication system. In *Proceedings of the SHARE design automation workshop* (1964), 6–329.

29. Tollis, I., Eades, P., Di Battista, G., and Tollis, L. *Graph drawing: algorithms for the visualization of graphs*, vol. 1. Prentice Hall New York, 1998.

30. Veselova, O., and Davis, R. Perceptually based learning of shape descriptions for sketch recognition. In *AAAI '04* (2004).

31. Wybrow, M., Marriott, K., Mciver, L., and Stuckey, P. J. Comparing usability of one-way and multi-way constraints for diagram editing. *ACM Transactions on Computer-Human Interaction (TOCHI) 14*, 4 (2008), 19.

32. Zeidler, C., Lutteroth, C., Sturzlinger, W., and Weber, G. The auckland layout editor: an improved gui layout specification process. In *UIST '13* (2013), 343–352.

33. Zeleznik, R. C., Bragdon, A., Liu, C.-C., and Forsberg, A. Lineogrammer: creating diagrams by drawing. In *UIST '08* (2008), 161–170.

34. Zitnick, C. L. Handwriting beautification using token means. *ACM Trans. Graph. 32*, 4 (2013), 53:1–53:8.

APPENDIX

We first describe how we estimate a (horizontal) line $\mathcal{P}_i$ from a set of inliers $\mathcal{S}_i$ at iteration i (Step 3). We estimate the vertical coordinate of $\mathcal{P}_i$ as the weighted mean of the vertical coordinates of all inliers in $\mathcal{S}_i$. Specifically, the weight of each inlier $s \in \mathcal{S}_i$ is defined as $w(s) = e^{-(y(\mathcal{P}_{i-1})-y(s))^2/l(s)^2}$, where $l(s)$ is the length of the inlier edge s, $y(s)$ and $y(\mathcal{P}_{i-1})$ are the vertical coordinates of s and the line estimated in the previous iteration $\mathcal{P}_{i-1}$, respectively. This Gaussian weighting scheme indicates that the contribution of an inlier to the new line is higher if the inlier is longer or closer to the previous line. The vertical coordinate of the new estimated line $\mathcal{P}_i$ is then computed as $\sum_{s\in\mathcal{S}_i} \hat{w}(s)y(s)$, where $\hat{w}(s)$ is the normalized weight.

Now we give the details of Step 2: how to get an updated set of inliers $\mathcal{S}_{i+1}$ given the line $\mathcal{P}_i$. We introduce an adaptive inlier range for robust inliers detection. Specifically, an edge t is added into $\mathcal{S}_{i+1}$ if and only if $y(t) \in [y(\mathcal{P}_i)-r, y(\mathcal{P}_i)+r]$, where $r = \min(\overline{r}(1+\sigma)h(t), 2\overline{r})$ is adaptively determined. $\overline{r}$ is fixed as the average size of the input elements, multiplied by a fixed factor (0.125 in our implementation). $\sigma = \sqrt{\sum_{s\in\mathcal{S}_i} \hat{w}(s)(y(\mathcal{P}_i) - y(s))^2}$ measures the variance of the vertical coordinate among the inliers in $\mathcal{S}_i$. This changes the range adaptively with respect to the degree of alignment of the previous set of inliers. The term $h(t)$ is motivated by the Gestalt law of proximity: objects that are near to one another are perceived as belonging together as a unit. We thus define $h(t) = e^{-\hat{d}_t^2}$, where $\hat{d}_t$ measures the *horizontal* distance between t and the inliers in $\mathcal{S}_i$, normalized by the average horizontal and vertical distance between neighboring elements in the input layout. When t is away from the previous set of inliers, it is less likely to be detected as an inlier.

Deconstructing and Restyling D3 Visualizations

Jonathan Harper
University of California, Berkeley
jharper@eecs.berkeley.edu

Maneesh Agrawala
University of California, Berkeley
maneesh@cs.berkeley.edu

ABSTRACT

The D3 JavaScript library has become a ubiquitous tool for developing visualizations on the Web. Yet, once a D3 visualization is published online its visual style is difficult to change. We present a pair of tools for deconstructing and restyling existing D3 visualizations. Our deconstruction tool analyzes a D3 visualization to extract the data, the marks and the mappings between them. Our restyling tool lets users modify the visual attributes of the marks as well as the mappings from the data to these attributes. Together our tools allow users to easily modify D3 visualizations without examining the underlying code and we show how they can be used to deconstruct and restyle a variety of D3 visualizations.

Author Keywords

Visualization, chart understanding, restyling, D3

ACM Classification Keywords

H.5.2. Information Interfaces and Presentation (e.g. HCI): User Interfaces – Graphical User Interfaces

INTRODUCTION

The D3 library [7] has emerged as one of the most popular tools for producing visualizations on the Web. News and media websites such as the New York Times [22], MTV [21] and the Boston Globe [8] regularly publish D3 visualizations that reach hundreds of thousands of viewers. Beyond these high-traffic sites, a large community of Web developers has posted thousands of example D3 visualizations online [33, 25, 2].

Because D3 is built using Web standards (e.g. HTML, SVG, JavaScript) skilled developers can modify the visual style of an existing visualization by copying and editing the code. Yet, such modification requires significant coding expertise in the Web standards and an interest in understanding how the visualization code works. So for most viewers, once a D3 visualization is published its visual style is effectively fixed.

Nevertheless, there are many reasons a viewer may want to modify the style of a visualization. For instance, a colorblind viewer may need to shift the red and green marks in a chart to colors that are easier to distinguish. A blogger might wish to embed a scatterplot in her blog, but change the color, shape and size encodings of the marks to match the overall design of her webpage. A viewer might prefer to view a pie chart in the form of a bar chart so that it is easier to compare the data values. But, without understanding the underlying code and how it maps data to marks, making such stylistic changes to a D3 visualization is out of reach for most viewers.

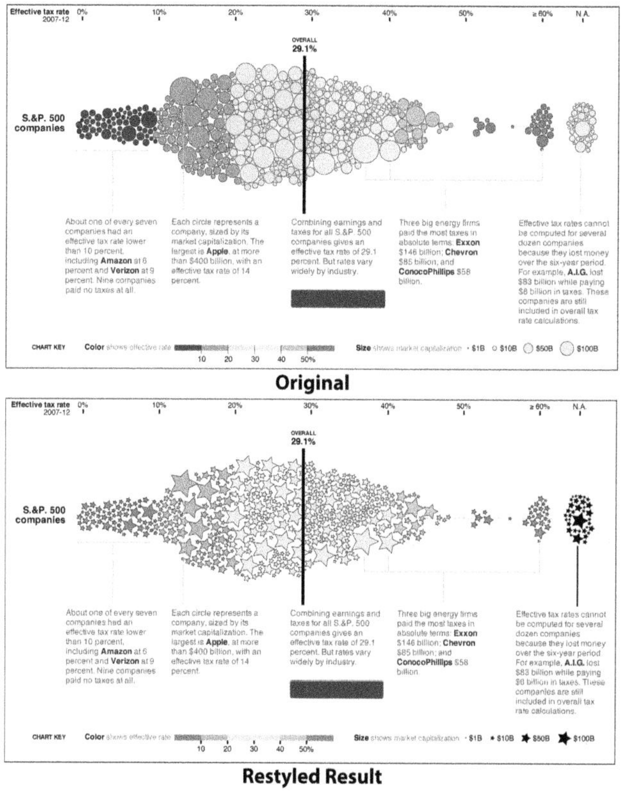

Figure 1. Our deconstruction and restyling tools allow a viewer to modify the shape and color encodings of a D3 visualization published by the New York Times. The restyled result changes the circles to stars and re-maps the tax rate data field to a new color scale.

We introduce a tool that can automatically deconstruct existing D3 visualizations, to extract the data, the marks, and the mappings between them. We also provide a graphical restyling tool that lets users modify the visual attributes of the marks as well as the mappings from the data to these attributes. Our tool warns users when such modifications break an existing mapping so that users can make sure the restyled visualization conveys all of the data shown in the original visualization. Together our tools allow users to easily restyle existing D3 visualizations without examining the underlying code (Figure 1). We demonstrate the versatility of our tools by deconstructing and restyling a number of different types of D3 visualizations including bar charts, scatterplots, donut charts, choropleth maps and line charts.

UIST'14, October 05–08, 2014, Honolulu, HI, USA.

http://dx.doi.org/10.1145/2642918.2647411

RELATED WORK

Visualizations convey information by mapping data to the visual attributes of graphical marks. Bertin first described this mapping process in his seminal work *Semiology of Graphics* [1]. Visualization design tools like Excel, Google Spreadsheets, Polaris/Tableau [28], and Lyra [26] let users directly specify how data maps to mark attributes through a graphical user interface. Programmatic toolkits and libraries such as Infovis Toolkit [14], Prefuse [16], ProtoVis [6], ggplot2 [34], D3 [7] and Vega [32], let programmers specify these mappings in code at different levels of abstraction. While these tools facilitate the process of constructing visualizations, our work addresses the inverse problem; we deconstruct an input visualization to recover its data and marks as well as the mappings relating them. We focus on D3 visualizations because they are ubiquitous and are based on open Web standards (HTML, CSS, SVG, etc.) that allow inspection.

Bitmap images of charts are even more commonly available online than D3 visualizations. Researchers have applied computer vision techniques for recognizing the chart type (e.g. bar chart, pie chart, etc.) of such images. These techniques first extract high-level shape descriptors from the image and then classify the image based on these features [18, 23] Others have developed specialized image processing methods to extract the data-encoding marks from such chart images [36, 19, 18, 17, 35]. These methods analyze the edges in the image and apply heuristics based on knowledge of the chart type to identify the bars, pie slices, etc.

Savva et al.'s ReVision [27] combines such chart type classification with mark extraction and then further analyzes the marks to semi-automatically extract the underlying data from an input chart image. However, their complete pipeline is only designed to work for bar and pie charts, and the overall accuracy of their recovered data (38-53% depending on chart type) is limited by image resolution, noise, compression artifacts and classification errors. In contrast, because we focus on deconstructing D3 visualizations, we can directly access the data bound to each mark and our recovered data is always 100% accurate. Unlike ReVision, our approach also extracts mappings between the data and mark attributes.

Our restyling tool is inspired by recent work on transforming images of visualizations to explore new visual forms [10] or aid chart reading [20]. However, because these techniques operate on bitmap images of visualizations, they are limited to warping the entire image or adding graphical overlays onto the image. Because our restyling tool operates on D3 visualizations, it can directly modify mark attributes and thereby provide far more restyling control than the earlier techniques.

D3 PRELIMINARIES

D3 is a JavaScript library for building visualizations by manipulating the Document Object Model (DOM) of a webpage. The DOM is a hierarchical representation in which each node is a tagged element such as `<body>` or `<img>` from HTML or `<rect>`, `<circle>` or `<polygon>` from Scalable Vector Graphics (SVG). Most D3 visualizations are built using SVG because it provides a complete scene graph representation for 2D vector graphics. Therefore, we focus on SVG-based D3 visualizations in this work

SVG includes several types of nodes, including a root node `<svg>` that creates a viewport for the graphics, group nodes `<g>` that allow hierarchical grouping of sub-nodes to form an SVG tree, and mark generating nodes such as `<rect>`, `<circle>`, or `<polygon>`, which produce marks on-screen. Each SVG node establishes its own local coordinate system and provides a tranformation matrix from the parent space to the local space. The mark generating nodes also include a set of visual attributes such as *position, width, height, fill-color* and *stroke-width*, that define the appearance of the mark when it is rendered. D3 developers have shown that this set of SVG primitive nodes is expressive enough to represent a wide variety of visualizations.

A key feature of D3 is that it allows developers to bind input data to SVG elements as they construct and modify a visualization. This binding lets developers specify functional relationships between the data and visual attributes of the SVG elements. Consider the bar chart example in Figure 2a-b. Lines 4-6 of the code fragment create a set of `<rect>` nodes, each bound to one entry in the `items[]` data array. Line 7 appends each `<rect>` node as a child of the root `<svg>` node to form the SVG tree (Figure 2c). Lines 8-16 apply data-dependent functions to assign the *x-position, height* and *fill-color* visual attributes of the `<rect>` nodes, while lines 17-18 set the *width* and *stroke-width* of these nodes to constants. Thus, each fully specified `<rect>` node includes a `__data__` property holding the bound data as well as a set of visual attributes (Figure 2d).

OVERVIEW

Our system includes two main tools; one for *deconstructing* a D3 visualization and one for *restyling* the visualization. The deconstruction tool analyzes the SVG representation of the visualization to recover its constituent data and marks, and to infer the mappings between them. The restyling tool uses the deconstructed information to help users change the style of a visualization while warning them when such style changes conflict with the data-encodings in the original visualization.

The data D3 binds to DOM elements is only accessible from within the JavaScript environment in which the visualization was constructed. So, in order to analyze a D3 visualization our tools require access to its environment. We built our tools as an extension for Google Chrome browser [11] because such extensions are allowed to inject code into the JavaScript environment of an existing webpage and can thereby access the bound data.

DECONSTRUCTION

To initiate deconstruction, users must right click anywhere within a D3 visualization. Our deconstruction tool listens for such click events, finds the DOM node containing the click and then walks up the DOM tree to find the root `<svg>` node of the visualization The resulting DOM sub-tree contains all of the SVG elements comprising the visualization and we analyze this sub-tree to deconstruct the visualization.

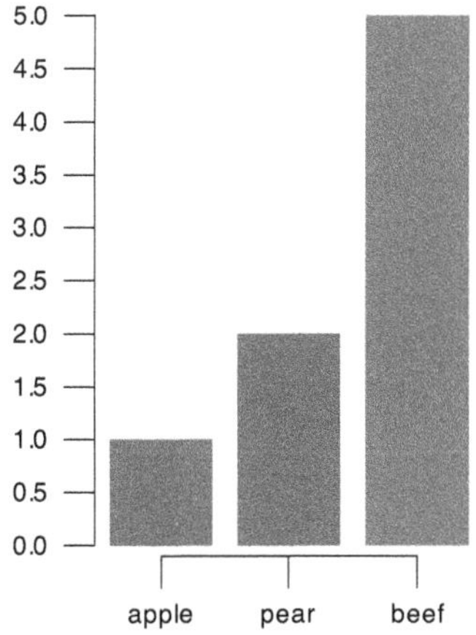

(a) Bar Chart

```
1 items = [{name: "apple",type: "fruit", cost: 1.00},
2          {name: "pear", type: "fruit", cost: 2.00},
3          {name: "beef", type: "meat",  cost: 5.00}]
4 var bars = svg.selectAll("rect")
5                 .data(items)
6                 .enter()
7                 .append("rect");
8 bars.attr("x", function(d, i)
9         {return i * 25;})
10     .attr("y", function(d)
11       {return h - d.price * 10;})
12     .attr("height", function(d)
13       {return d.price * 10;})
14     .attr("fill", function(d, i)
15       {if(d.type == "fruit"){return "green";}
16        else if (d.type == "meat"){return "red";}})
17     .attr("width", "20px")
18     .attr("stroke-width", 0);
```

(b) D3 Code Fragment Generating Colored Bars

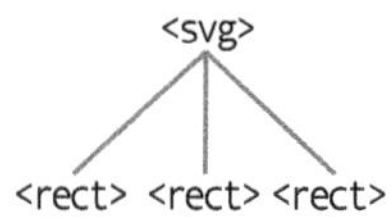

(c) SVG Tree

```
tagName: rect
__data__:
          name: pear
          type: fruit
          cost: 2.00
attributes:
          x: 25
          y: 50
          width: 20
          height: 100
          fill: green
          stroke-width: 0
```

(d) SVG Element

Figure 2. Example bar chart visualization (a) and D3 code fragment generating the rectangular marks representing the bars in the chart (b). The code creates three <rect> nodes and binds one data point to each of them (lines 4-7). It then sets the visual attributes of each using a combination of data-dependent functions and constants (lines 8-18). The code for generating the axes and labels is not shown. The resulting SVG tree (d) contains a single parent <svg> node and three children <rect> nodes (c). Each <rect> node includes a __data__ property holding the data that is bound to it as well as a set of visual attributes (d).

Extracting Data and Marks

To extract the data and marks from the selected visualization, we traverse the SVG sub-tree in pre-order and enumerate all nodes that meet two conditions; (1) the node generates a graphical mark[1] and (2) the node is bound to data. These two conditions ensure that the resulting list of nodes captures all of the data-encoding marks in the visualization. In the case of our bar chart example, we enumerate a sequence of three <rect> nodes that form the bars of the chart.

Data extraction. Most D3 visualizations bind one data item to one mark generating SVG node. In such cases we extract the data by retrieving the `__data__` property from each node in our enumerated list. The retrieved data may consist of a simple typed value (e.g. a number, a string, etc.) or a more complex JavaScript object containing one or more data fields and a value for each field. In our bar chart example (Figure 2), each <rect> node is bound to a data object which contains the fields *name*, *type* and *cost*, and a value for each one. We refer to the set of data fields associated with a data object as its data *schema*. If the data consists of a simple value rather than an object, we treat its data type as the schema.

D3 visualizations can include multiple data schemas. For example, a grouped bar chart may contain one set of bars bound to a data schema for movie box office revenue, while another set of bars is bound to a schema for DVD revenue. In such cases, we group the data by schema as we extract it and generate one data table per schema. We extract 3 data tables for our bar chart example (Figure 3). The first table represents the `item[]` data bound to the <rect> nodes. The other two tables represent the string label data (e.g. "apple", "pear", "beef") bound to the *x*-axis and the numeric label data (e.g. 0.0, 0.5, ... 5.0) bound to the *y*-axis. When D3 generates axes, it binds such label data to <line> nodes forming tick marks and <text> nodes for graphically displaying the labels. Note that Figure 3 does not show the third table.

Some visualizations use the ordering in which data is bound to the elements to assign the visual attributes of the marks. For example, in line 13 our example bar chart sets the *x*-position of the bar based on the ordering index *i* in which the bar is constructed. As we extract the data we recover this ordering index by saving the pre-order tree-traversal index for each node as an additional *deconID* field in the data table. Although the pre-order traversal index may not exactly match the original data binding order *i*, there is usually a linear relationship between them. We exploit this linear relationship when we construct mappings between the data fields and visual mark attributes (see next Section on Mappings). Finally we keep a reference to the original SVG node in the visualization so that we can later modify and re-style the element.

Mark extraction. Next we extract a set of mark attributes from each SVG node in our enumerated list. These attributes fall into two categories:

- ***Appearance attributes*** determine the the visual look of the mark. Examples include *shape*, *fill-color*, *stroke-color*, *stroke-width*, *font-style* and *font-size*.
- ***Geometric attributes*** determine the spatial properties of the mark. Examples include *x-position*, *y-position*, *width*, *height*, and *area*.

The primary appearance attribute is *shape* as it defines the visual form of the mark. In the deconstruction stage we treat the tag name of the mark generating SVG node (e.g. <rect>, <circle>, etc.) as the *shape* attribute. Note that although some nodes such as <polygon> and <path> may represent many different shapes, since we only extract the tag name as the *shape* attribute our deconstruction tool can not differentiate between the different shapes that a <polygon> could encode (e.g. triangle, pentagon, hexagon, etc.). However, our restyling tool does allow users to map data to specific types of polygons (see Restyling Section).

[1]We consider any SVG node that produces visible marks on-screen as a mark generating node (e.g. <rect>, <circle>, <line>, <polygon>, <path>, <text>). In contrast nodes like <svg> and <g> set up and transform the view but do not produce marks.

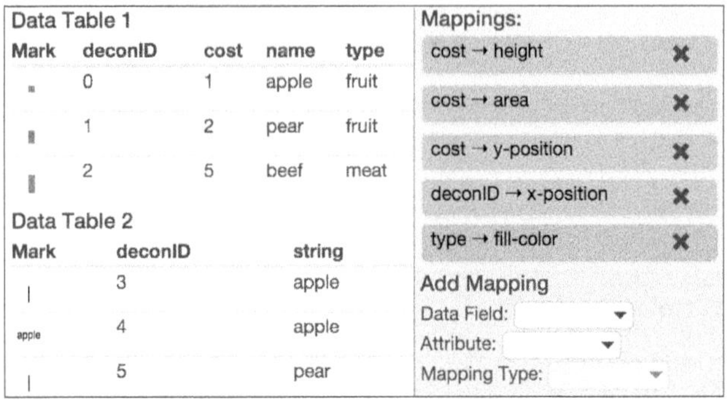

Figure 3. Deconstructed data and restyling interface for the bar chart from Figure 2. Data Table 1 contains the data and marks for the bars. while Data Table 2 constains the data and marks for the x-axis tick marks and text labels. The Mappings Panel shows mappings extracted from the chart for Data Table 1, with linear mappings shown in purple and nominal mappings shown in green. Users can remove, change and add mappings through the Mappings and Add Mappings Panels.

All other appearance attributes directly correspond to visual attributes of the SVG node. Some of these attributes such as *fill-color*, *stroke-color*, and *stroke-width*, are defined for every mark generating node in SVG, while others such as *font-style* and *font-size* attributes are only defined for a subset of SVG nodes—e.g. the `<text>` node. As we analyze each SVG node we retrieve all of the appearance attributes that exist for it and leave the other appearance attributes as undefined.

In SVG, the representation of geometric information such as position, width, height and area can differ depending on the type of the node. For example the *position* of a `<circle>` node represents the location of its center while the *position* of a `<rect>` node represents the location of its upper left corner. However, SVG also provides access to a bounding box representation for every type of mark generating node. The geometric attributes of the bounding box are the same regardless of node type and there is usually a linear relationship between the geometric attributes of the bounding box and the corresponding geometric attributes of the underlying mark (e.g. the area/width/height of an ellipse is linearly related to the area/width/height of its bounding box). Therefore we treat the geometric attributes of the bounding box as the geometric attributes of the mark.

We use the center of the bounding box as the position of the mark and apply transformations with respect to this center point. We also transform the bounding boxes into the coordinate space of the root SVG node before extracting the geometric attributes so that the geometric information for every mark in the visualization is in the same global coordinate space. As we extract the mark attributes for each SVG node we store them with the corresponding row of the data table.

Handling line charts. While most D3 visualizations bind one data item to one mark generating SVG node, line charts typically bind an array of data to a single mark generating SVG `<path>` node which produces a polyline on screen. Conceptually each data item in the array is bound to the corresponding point in the polyline. To deconstruct such line charts, we split the data array into a sequence of individual data items and add each one to the data table. For each data item we also add a *line-id* field to the data table which stores the index of the item within the array. Similarly, we split the polyline into individual geometric points and set the *position* mark attribute of the corresponding data item to the coordinates of the point. We set the other geometric mark attributes, *width*, *height*, and *area*, to 0. Finally we set the remaining mark appearance attributes for each of these data items based on the attributes of the `<path>` node.

Extracting Mappings

Visualizations encode information by mapping data values to visual mark attributes. For example, our bar chart (Figure 2), sets the *x-position*, *height*, and *fill-color* of each bar based on functions of the underlying ordering index *i*, and the data fields *cost* and *type*. The first two functions (lines 8-13) are *linear mappings* between numeric data and numeric mark attributes (ordering index $i \rightarrow$ *x-position*, *cost* $\rightarrow$ *height*). The third function (lines 14-16) is a *categorical mapping* in which all data items of the same value map to the same mark attribute value (*type* $\rightarrow$ *fill-color*). Unlike a linear mapping, a categorical mapping does not require either the data field or mark attribute to be a numeric type. We recover both kinds of data-dependent mappings for each data table.

We first test for linear mappings between the numeric data fields and each numeric mark attribute by fitting a linear model using linear regression. If the resulting R^2 value for the model is equal to 1, the data fields are linearly mapped to the mark attribute and we save the line parameters (slopes and intercept) of the fitted model.

In visualizations, a single mark attribute sometimes represents a linear combination of multiple data fields. However, if any of the data fields in such a mapping are themselves linearly related, there is a simpler set of mappings each of which includes exactly one of these linearly related data fields. We recover this *parsimonious* set of linear mappings which use the fewest data fields necessary to explain the relationship between the data and a mark attribute using an iterative approach. We first check for mappings between single data fields and each mark attribute. If we find mappings for an attribute we remove it from further consideration. If we do not find a mapping for an attribute, we check for mappings between pairs of data fields and that attribute. We continue to iteratively add data fields in this manner until we find one or more mappings for the attribute or we exhaust the set of data fields in the data table. The resulting set of mappings for each attibute is its parsimonious set.

If we do not find any linear mapping for an attribute or the attribute is non-numeric, we test for categorical mappings between each data field and the attribute. Specifically, we check whether whether there is a bijective, one-to-one correspondence between the data field values and the mark attribute values by testing whether each unique data value corresponds to a unique mark attribute value.

Our approach often finds multiple mappings between different data fields and the same mark attribute. For example, if a data table includes two or more data fields that are linearly related to each other, and any of these fields is mapped to a mark attribute, our tool recovers a mapping between each of these fields and the attribute. Similarly, our tool may find multiple categorical mappings between different data fields and a single mark attribute. In both of these cases all of the extracted mappings are equally valid and can reveal unexpected correlations or structure in the data. Thus, we show all of these mappings to the user.

However our deconstruction tool may also find both a linear and a categorical mapping to the same mark attribute. Because linear mappings offer a simpler model of the relationship between a data field and a mark attribute, we automatically filter out categorical mappings in such cases. In the bar chart example, we initially recover a linear mapping *cost* $\rightarrow$ *y-position* as well as a categorical mapping *deconID* $\rightarrow$ *y-position*, but then filter out the more complex categorical mapping.

Figure 3 shows the mappings we recover for our bar chart example. Note that although our extracted data table does not recover the original ordering index *i*, it does find a linear mapping between the pre-order traversal index *deconID* and *x-position*. Clicking on a linear mapping shows two data values and their corresponding attribute values. Since linear mappings are fully specified by any two such correspondences, we show the minimum and maximum data values to reveal the full range of the correspondence. Clicking on a categorical mapping shows each unique data value and the corresponding attribute value.

Handling color attributes. Color attributes are special cases for the mapping process because they may be mapped either linearly or categorically to the underlying data in several different color spaces (e.g. RGB, HSL, LAB, etc.). For color mark attributes we test for linear mappings to each color channel independently in RGB space and in HSL space. For categorical mappings we consider the color triplet in RGB space as a single complex-typed value.

Splitting data tables. Users may sometimes wish to operate on a subset of rows in the data table. Our interface allows users to select a set of rows in a deconstructed table and generate a new table from the selection. For example, a D3 axis typically binds the same data to both the `<line>` node representing a tick mark and the `<text>` node representing a label. In order to compute mappings for these sets of nodes independently, the user can select all of the `<text>` nodes and place them in a separate data table.

RESTYLING

Our restyling tool lets users change the look of a visualization by manipulating mark attributes using three kinds of operations; (1) remove mapping, (2) change mapping, and (3) add mapping. These operations are accessible by clicking on different parts of the Mappings Panel in our interface (Figure 3). Each operation first updates the data table with new attribute values for the marks and then propagates the changes to the visualization by updating the SVG nodes corresponding to the mark. Figure 4 shows an example of how we can apply these three operations in a sequence of steps to convert our example bar chart from Figure 2 into a colored dot plot.

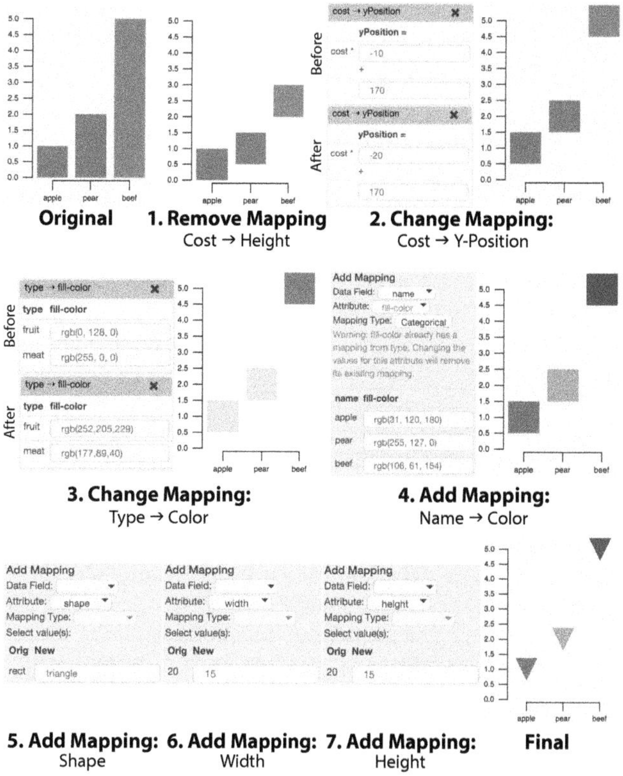

Figure 4. Restyling the example bar chart from Figure 2 using a sequence of 7 restyling operations. Step 1 removes the *cost* $\rightarrow$*height* mapping. Step 2 changes the *cost* $\rightarrow$*y-position* to raise the marks. Step 3 changes the *type* $\rightarrow$*fill-color* mapping to modify color or marks. Step 4 adds a mapping from *name* $\rightarrow$*fill-color* and to replace the mapping from step 4 despite warnings. Steps 5-7 add mappings that are not based on data values to modify the *shape, width* and *height* attributes of the marks.

Remove Mapping

Users can remove a mapping by clicking the 'X' button next to it in the Mappings Panel (Figure 3). Upon removal our tool updates the value of the mapped attribute to a constant value for every item in the data table. For linear mappings, our tool sets the constant to the attribute value of the mark with the minimum data value. For categorical mappings our tool sets it to the attribute value of the mark with the lowest *deconID*. In step 1 of our restyling example (Figure 4) we remove the *cost* $\rightarrow$ *height* mapping, and our tool scales the height of each bar to that of the bar with the lowest cost. Since our system transforms marks about the center of their bounding boxes, the two largest bars no longer touch the *x*-axis.

Change Mapping

Users can change any existing mapping by clicking on it in the Mappings Panel (Figure 3). For linear mappings users can specify new line parameters (slopes and intercept) for the mapping, which our restyling tool then applies to update the attribute values of every item in the data table. For categorical mappings users can specify the attribute value corresponding to any unique data value. Our tool then updates the attributes values for all data items that share this data value.

In step 2 of our restyling example (Figure 3) we change the linear *cost* $\rightarrow$ *y-position* mapping to re-position the rectangular marks so that their centers align with their corresponding costs on the *y*-axis. In step 3 we change the categorical *type* → *fill-color* mapping so that 'fruit' maps to 'pink' and 'meat' maps to 'brown'.

Add Mapping

Users can add a new mapping by selecting three mapping properties – one or more data fields, a mark attribute and a mapping type – via drop-down menus in the Add Mapping Panel (Figure 3). The data field menu includes each of the extracted fields in the data schema as well as an option to choose 'none'. The mark attribute menu includes all of the extracted appearance and geometric attributes. The mapping type menu includes linear and categorical types as well as an option to choose 'none'. As a user selects from these menus our interface further constrains the available options to ensure that the resulting mapping is valid. Specifically, it checks that linear mappings always map numeric data fields to a numeric mark attribute. For instance, if the user selects linear as the mapping type, our interface grays out and disables selection for all non-numeric data fields and mark attributes. Conversely, if the user selects a non-numeric data field or mark attribute, our interface disables the linear mapping type.

A key feature of the interface is that it warns users if they try to add a mapping to an attribute that already encodes a different data field. In such cases it is likely that the new mapping conflicts with the existing mapping and would change the information conveyed by the visualization. We warn users of such conflicts in two ways. First, in the mark attributes drop-down menu we highlight in red all attributes that are already part of an existing mapping. Second, if the user selects one of these red attributes we display a text warning explaining that adding the new mapping will invalidate the existing mapping. If the user proceeds to add the new mapping despite the warnings, our restyling tool removes the existing mapping before creating the new one.

After selecting the three mapping properties, users can specify how data values map to attribute values using the same interface as for the change mapping operation. Finally the newly created mapping is added to the list of mappings in the Mappings Panel.

In step 4 of our restyling example (Figure 4) we decide to re-color the marks using the *name* data field instead of *type*. To make this change we add a categorical *name* → *fill-color* mapping. But because the *type* → *fill-color* mapping already maps a data field to the *fill-color* attribute, our interface highlights *fill-color* in red in the drop-down menu and displays warning text as soon as we select it from the menu. Despite the warnings we continue to build the new mapping by specifying that 'apple' maps to 'blue', 'pear' maps to 'orange' and 'beef' maps to 'purple'. Our tool then removes *type* → *fill-color* and adds *name* → *fill-color* to the Mappings Panel.

The data-encoding marks in a visualization often include some attributes that do not encode data but significantly effect the look of the visualization. In our restyling example, the *shape* attribute of the marks does not encode data. Users can modify such attributes values by selecting the attribute and setting the data field to 'none' in the Add Mapping Panel. Our interface then displays the set of unique attribute values that appear in the visualization and users can interactively specify new values for them. In step 5 of our restyling example (Figure 4) we change the shape of the marks from 'rect' to 'triangle'. Similarly in steps 6 and 7 we change the widths and heights of the marks from 20 to 15.

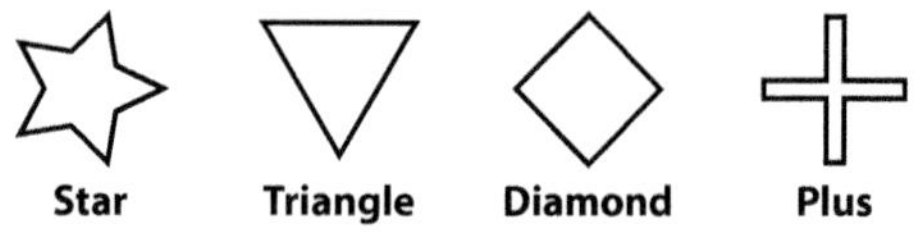

Figure 5. Symbolic shapes supported by our restyling tool.

Updating Marks in the Visualization

As users perform restyling operations our tool updates mark attributes in the data table and then updates corresponding SVG nodes in the DOM of the original visualization. For each updated mark the restyling tool creates a new SVG node with its type specified by the *shape* attribute. Although the *shape* attribute is usually an SVG node type, our restyling tool also supports a set of symbolic shapes (star, diamond, triangle, plus) that are all represented as SVG `<polygon>` nodes with pre-defined geometry (Figure 5). If the *shape* attribute is one of these symbolic shapes our tool converts it into the corresponding pre-defined `<polygon>` node.

Our restyling tool also transforms all geometric attributes from the global coordinate space into the local space of the original SVG node representing mark. It then converts these bounding box based geometric attributes into attributes appropriate for the node type (e.g. *position* is upper-left corner for `<rect>` nodes, but center for `<circle>` nodes). Our tool then sets the geometric and appearance attributes of the new SVG node and binds data as well as event handlers from the original node to the new node. Finally, our tool replaces the original SVG node with the newly created node.

RESULTS

As shown in Figures 1, 6 and 7 we have used our system to deconstruct and restyle a number of D3 visualizations from a variety of sources. These examples incorporate modifications of many different mark attributes including *fill-color* (Figures 1, 6a–c, 6e, 6f, 7g–i), *stroke-color* (Figure 6b, 6e, 6f, 7g), *stroke-width* (Figures 6e, 6f), *font-style* (Figure 6a, 6b, 6f, 7g), *shape* (Figures 1, 6a, 6c, 6d, 6f, 7g, 7i), *position* (Figures 6a, 6d, 7g-i), as well as *width* and *height* (Figures 6a, 6b, 6d, 6f, 7g-i). All of our restyled examples represent the same data as the original visualization, but some examples re-map data fields to different mark attributes (Figures 6c, 6e–f, 7g, 7i), while other examples change the parameters of the existing mappings (Figures 1, 6a, 6b,6d–f, 7g, 7h). Many examples also modify mark attributes that do not encode data but affect the look of the visualization (Figures 1, 6a, 6b, 6e, 6f, 7g, 7i.

New York Times Chart (Figure 1). In the original visualization U.S. companies are represented by circles that show each company's effective tax rate using the *fill-color* and *x-position* attributes. Each company's market capitalization is mapped to the *area* attribute. In our restyled result we change the *fill-color* attribute to color marks using a red to blue diverging color scale [9]. We also change each mark's *shape*

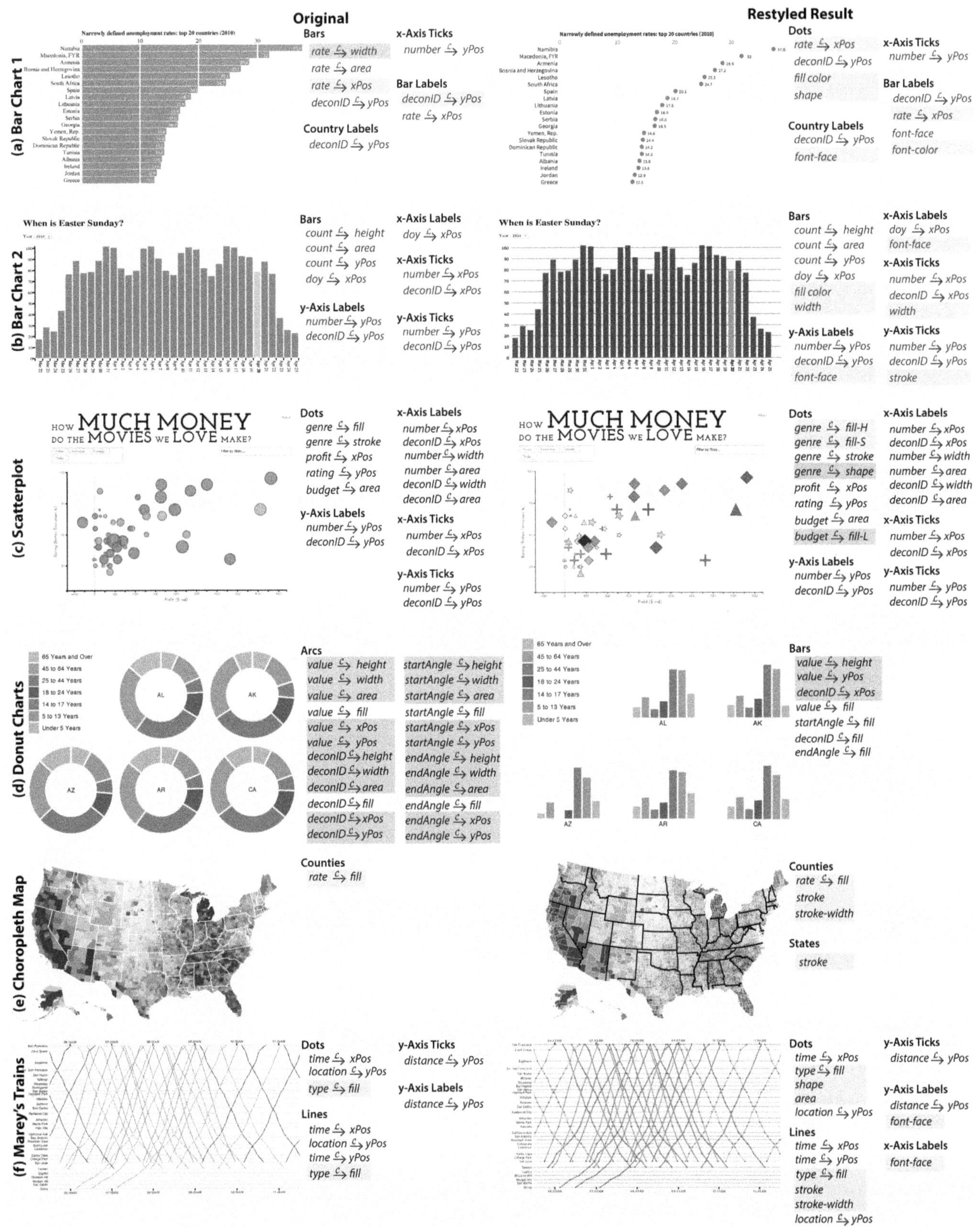

Figure 6. A variety of D3 visualizations collected from the Web, before (left column) and after (right column) deconstruction and restyling with our tools. Deconstructed mappings are shown to the right of the original visualization, and the mappings after restyling are shown to the right of the restyled result along with any unmapped attributes that were changed in the restyling. We use the $\xrightarrow{L}$ and $\xrightarrow{C}$ notation to indicate linear and categorical mappings respectively. Mappings removed and added during restyling are highlighted in red and and green respectively. Changed mappings and attributes are highlighted in blue.

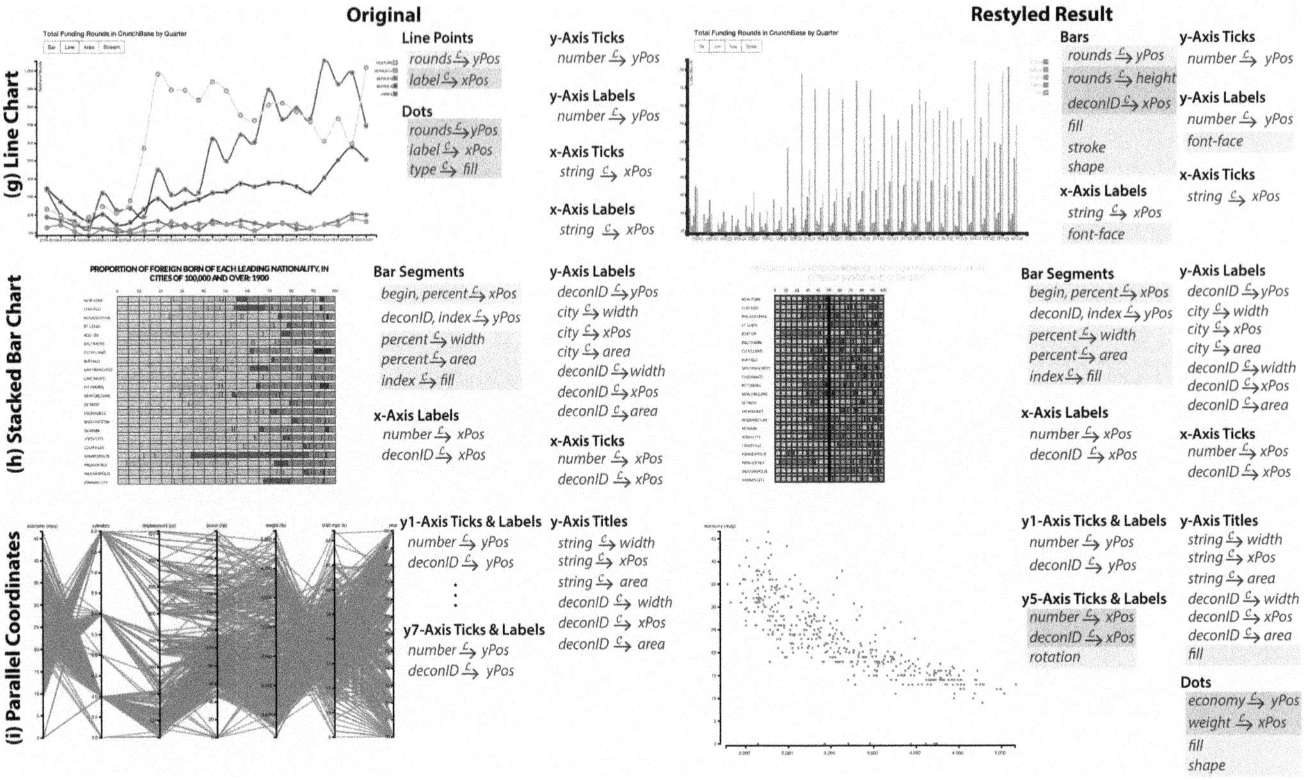

Figure 7. A variety of D3 visualizations collected from the Web, before (left column) and after (right column) deconstruction and restyling with our tools. Deconstructed mappings are shown to the right of the original visualization, and the mappings after restyling are shown to the right of the restyled result along with any unmapped attributes that were changed in the restyling. We use the $\xrightarrow{L}$ and $\xrightarrow{C}$ notation to indicate linear and categorical mappings respectively. Mappings removed and added during restyling are highlighted in red and and green respectively. Changed mappings and attributes are highlighted in blue.

attribute to represent the companies using stars but we leave the *market capitalization* $\rightarrow$ *area* mapping unchanged. Original visualization from the New York Times [29].

Bar Chart 1 (Figure 6a). The original bar chart shows the 20 countries with the highest unemployment rates sorted by unemployment rate along the *y*-axis. We restyle the chart into a dot plot using the approach outlined in Figure 4. Original visualization by Leon du Toit [13].

Bar Chart 2 (Figure 6b). The original chart shows the dates Easter Sunday falls on with frequency of each day represented by bar height. The chart highlights one bar in light blue representing the date for Easter on the year selected in a drop-down menu. We restyle the bar chart to resemble the visual design of charts published by the Economist by changing the values of several unmapped mark attributes. Original visualization by Chris Pudney [24].

Scatterplot (Figure 6c). The original scatterplot depicts the Rotten Tomatoes data including the *rating, profit, genre,* and *budget* for popular movies using several different mark attributes. We restyle the chart by adding a redundant categorical mapping *genre* $\rightarrow$ *shape* to visually differentiate the genres. We also add a redundant linear mapping *budget* $\rightarrow$ *fill-color-L* so that the lightness channel of each mark's color depicts the movie budget while the original mapping of *genre* to the hue and saturation of the *fill-color* is unchanged. Original visualization by Jim Vallandingham [30].

Donut Charts (Figure 6d). Each donut chart in the original visualization represents the percentage of the population of a U.S. state by age group. We restyle each donut chart into a bar chart by removing the mappings to the attributes of the arcs and then changing the *shape* attribute of each arc to a rectangle. Finally we create new mappings for the *height*, *x-position* and *y-position* of each bar. Original visualization by Michael Bostock [4].

Choropleth Map (Figure 6e). The original choropleth map shows U.S. unemployment by county using the fill-color of each map region. We restyle the coloring of the map by changing the *rate* $\rightarrow$ *fill-color* mapping for counties to a multi-hue yellow to red scale [9]. We also update the *stroke-color* and *stroke-width* attributes for map regions to emphasize the borders between states and counties. Original is a modified version of a visualization by Michael Bostock [3].

Marey's Trains (Figure 6f). The original visualization is a recreation of Marey's train schedule chart. Each line represents a train and the original visualization maps the *time*, *location* and *train type* (regular, limited service, baby bullet) data fields for each train to the *x-position*, *y-position* and *fill-color* attributes respectively. We restyle the visualization, changing the mappings to *fill-color* and as well as the values of several unmapped attributes in order to emphasize the different types of trains as well as their stops times and locations. Original visualization by Michael Bostock [5].

Line Chart (Figure 7g) The original line chart shows the number of tech company funding rounds by quarter, with each line representing a different type of investment. We change the line chart into a grouped bar chart by first changing the points deconstructed from each line into rectangle shapes. We then add mappings from the *funding rounds* data field to the *height* and *y-position* attributes of the bars. We arrange the bars into groups using a *deconID* $\rightarrow$ *x-position* mapping. We change the mapping *investment type* $\rightarrow$ *fill-color* to change the coloring of the bars. Finally, we modify the unmapped *font-face* attribute. Original visualization by Steven Hall [15].

Stacked Bar Chart (Figure 7h). The original visualization shows the proportion of immigrants by nationality in large U.S. cities around 1900. We restyle the visualization to a narrower aspect ratio by modifying the *begin, percent* $\rightarrow$ *x-position* and *percent* $\rightarrow$ *width* mappings. The original bar colors are not colorblind safe, so we also change the *nationality* $\rightarrow$ *fill-color* mapping to a qualitative color scale that is perceptually distinguishable for protanopes – red-green colorblind individuals [9]. Original visualization by Jim Vallandingham [31].

Parallel Coordinates (Figure 7i). The original parallel coordinates chart depicts seven properties (*economy*, number of *cylinders*, *displacement*, *power*, *weight*, *acceleration*, and *year* of release) of different kinds of cars. We restyle the chart into a scatterplot that shows the relationship between two of these properties – *economy* and *weight*. Specifically we change the *shape* attribute of each line mark to a circular dot. We then add *economy* $\rightarrow$ *y-position* and *weight* $\rightarrow$ *x-position* mappings for each dot. Finally, we remove all axes except the first and fifth which represent weight and economy. We then generate a new x-axis by changing the *rotation* attribute of the weight axis (fifth y-axis) marks. Original visualization by Jason Davies [12].

Our deconstruction and restyling tools allow rapid iteration on the visual design of a D3 visualization without having to understand its implementation. While our tools do assume that users understand that charts are comprised of mappings between data and mark attributes, users do not need experience with D3 or JavaScript to use our tools effectively. In practice we have found that even experienced D3 developers in our lab prefer to use our tools to explore the design space of a visualization to avoid the overhead of modifying code.

Limitations

While our tools can successfully deconstruct and restyle many different types of D3 visualizations, they have some limitations. Our deconstruction tool currently focuses on extracting linear and categorical mappings because they are most common. However, visualizations can include more complex functional mappings. For example, some D3 visualizations map numeric data fields to colors using a piecewise linear mapping that interpolates between pairs of colors in a sequential color scale [9]. Similarly, logarithmic, exponential and polynomial transforms are sometimes used to map data to positions of marks (e.g. log scale in a scatterplot). Our tool cannot deconstruct such non-linear functional mappings.

Our tools parameterize the geometric attributes of marks using their bounding boxes. While this approach provides control over the position, size and area of marks independent of their shape, it prevents our tools from manipulating the vertices and angles of shapes. In donut charts such as the one in Figure 6d, our deconstruction tool cannot recover the mapping from data to arc angle. However, our tool does recover the data bound to each mark and we can therefore create a new mapping from the data to rectangular marks to convert the donut chart into a bar chart.

Our restyling tool is also unable to add new SVG nodes to the visualization, which limits the kinds of visual redesigns it can produce. For example, in Figure 6d our tool cannot add text labels to the bar charts indicating the value of each bar, because no such `<text>` node existed in the original visualization. With the ability to add new SVG nodes bound to an existing data schema, our restyling tool could generate text labels displaying the percentage represented by each bar.

After restyling a visualization using our tools, the interaction and animation effects of the original may no longer be functional in the restyled version. Although we attach event listeners and data from the original SVG nodes in the to new nodes in the restyled visualization, these listeners often contain D3 code that depends on specific attributes values of the original node (e.g. shape, width or height). As we modify these attributes the interaction and animation code may no longer function correctly.

CONCLUSION AND FUTURE WORK

We have presented a pair of tools for deconstructing and restyling D3 visualizations. Our tools empower viewers to modify the visual look of existing D3 visualizations without having to understand or examine the underlying code. We believe there are several open directions for future work.

Handling a wider range of functional mappings. While linear and categorical mappings between data and mark attributes are most common, some visualizations include more complex mappings (e.g. logarithmic, polynomial, piecewise linear). It may be possible to automatically discover such mappings using data mining techniques. Similarly it should be possible to extend our restyling tool to let users define complex mappings between the data and mark attributes.

Visualization style transfer. Style transfer is the problem of applying the visual style of an exemplar visualization to a target visualization. The challenge is to ensure that the target visualization conveys the same data it conveyed before the style transfer. By analyzing the deconstructed mappings in the original exemplar and target visualizations it may be possible to perform the style transfer while preserving informational content of the original target.

Acknowledgments

This work was partially supported by the NSF Graduate Research Fellowship DGE 1106400.

REFERENCES

1. Bertin, J. *Semiology of graphics: Diagrams, networks, maps*. University of Wisconsin press, 1983.

2. Bostock, M. D3 Gallery. https://github.com/mbostock/d3/wiki/Gallery. Retrieved April 2014.
3. Bostock, M. Choropleth. http://bl.ocks.org/mbostock/4060606/, Nov. 2012. Retrieved April 2014.
4. Bostock, M. Donut Multiples. http://bl.ocks.org/mbostock/3888852/, Oct. 2012. Retrieved April 2014.
5. Bostock, M. Marey's Trains. http://bl.ocks.org/mbostock/5544008/, May 2013. Retrieved April 2014.
6. Bostock, M., and Heer, J. Protovis: A graphical toolkit for visualization. *IEEE TVCG 15*, 6 (2009), 1121–1128.
7. Bostock, M., Ogievetsky, V., and Heer, J. D^3 data-driven documents. *IEEE TVCG 17*, 12 (2011), 2301–2309.
8. Boston Globe. 'Women' a central theme in Menino's speech. http://www.bostonglobe.com/2013/01/30/mai/yWQCjhK7lyBaqgqFrakrlM/story.html, May 2013. Retrieved April 2014.
9. Brewer, C. ColorBrewer: Color Advice for Maps. http://colorbrewer2.org/. Retrieved April 2014.
10. Brosz, J., Nacenta, M. A., Pusch, R., Carpendale, S., and Hurter, C. Transmogrification: Causal manipulation of visualizations. In *Proc. of UIST*, ACM (2013), 97–106.
11. Chromium. https://developer.chrome.com/extensions/getstarted. Retrieved April 2014.
12. Davies, J. Parallel Coordinates. http://bl.ocks.org/jasondavies/1341281, Nov. 2011. Retrieved July 2014.
13. du Toit, L. Unemployment ranked with horizontal bars. http://bl.ocks.org/leondutoit/6436923/, Sept. 2013. Retrieved April 2014.
14. Fekete, J. The infovis toolkit. In *INFOVIS* (2004), 167–174.
15. Hall, S. Multi Chart — delimited. http://projects.delimited.io/experiments/multi-series/multi-chart.html. Retrieved April 2014.
16. Heer, J., Card, S. K., and Landay, J. A. Prefuse: A toolkit for interactive information visualization. In *Proc. of SIGCHI* (2005), 421–430.
17. Huang, W., Liu, R., and Tan, C. L. Extraction of vectorized graphical information from scientific chart images. In *Proc. of ICDAR*, vol. 1, IEEE (2007), 521–525.
18. Huang, W., and Tan, C. L. A system for understanding imaged infographics and its applications. In *Proc. of DocEng*, ACM (2007), 9–18.
19. Huang, W., Tan, C. L., and Leow, W. K. Model-based chart image recognition. In *Graphics Recognition*. Springer, 2004, 87–99.
20. Kong, N., and Agrawala, M. Graphical overlays: Using layered elements to aid chart reading. *IEEE TVCG 18*, 12 (2012), 2631–2638.
21. MTV. http://vma-twittertracker.mtv.com/live/. Retrieved April 2014.
22. New York Times. Across U.S. Companies, Tax Rates Vary Greatly. http://www.nytimes.com/interactive/2013/05/25/sunday-review/corporate-taxes.html, May 2013. Retrieved April 2014.
23. Prasad, V. S. N., Siddiquie, B., Golbeck, J., and Davis, L. Classifying computer generated charts. In *Proc. of CBMI*, IEEE (2007), 85–92.
24. Pudney, C. Easter Sunday. http://bl.ocks.org/cpudney/2248382/, Mar. 2012. Retrieved April 2014.
25. Ros, I. https://bl.ocksplorer.org. Retrieved April 2014.
26. Satyanarayan, A., and Heer, J. Lyra: An interactive visualization design environment. In *EuroVis* (2014), To appear.
27. Savva, M., Kong, N., Chhajta, A., Fei-Fei, L., Agrawala, M., and Heer, J. Revision: A utomated classification, analysis and redesign of chart images. In *Proc. of UIST* (2011), 393–402.
28. Stolte, C., Tang, D., and Hanrahan, P. Polaris: A system for query, analysis, and visualization of multidimensional relational databases. *IEEE TVCG 8*, 1 (2002), 52–65.
29. Times, T. N. Y. Across u.s. companies, tax varies greatly. http://www.nytimes.com/interactive/2013/05/25/sunday-review/corporate-taxes.html/, May 2013. Retrieved April 2014.
30. Vallandingham, J. How Much Money Do The Movies We Love Make? http://vallandingham.me/vis/movie/. Retrieved April 2014.
31. Vallandingham, J. Nationality by City. http://vallandingham.me/vis/nationality_by_city.html. Retrieved April 2014.
32. Vega. http://trifacta.github.io/vega/. Retrieved April 2014.
33. Viau, C. The Big List of D3.js Examples. http://christopheviau.com/d3list/. Retrieved April 2014.
34. Wickham, H. *ggplot2: elegant graphics for data analysis*. Springer, 2009.
35. Yang, L., Huang, W., and Tan, C. L. Semi-automatic ground truth generation for chart image recognition. In *Document Analysis Systems VII*. Springer, 2006, 324–335.
36. Zhou, Y. P., and Tan, C. L. Hough technique for bar charts detection and recognition in document images. In *Proc. of ICIP*, vol. 2, IEEE (2000), 605–608.

InterState: A Language and Environment for Expressing Interface Behavior

Stephen Oney[1,2], **Brad Myers**[1]
[1]Carnegie Mellon University
{soney, bam}@cs.cmu.edu

Joel Brandt[2]
[2]Adobe Research
joel.brandt@adobe.com

ABSTRACT
InterState is a new programming language and environment that addresses the challenges of writing and reusing user interface code. InterState represents interactive behaviors clearly and concisely using a combination of novel forms of *state machines* and *constraints*. It also introduces new language features that allow programmers to easily modularize and reuse behaviors. InterState uses a new visual notation that allows programmers to better understand and navigate their code. InterState also includes a *live* editor that immediately updates the running application in response to changes in the editor and vice versa to help programmers understand the state of their program. Finally, InterState can interface with code and widgets written in other languages, for example to create a user interface in InterState that communicates with a database. We evaluated the understandability of InterState's programming primitives in a comparative laboratory study. We found that participants were twice as fast at understanding and modifying GUI components when they were implemented with InterState than when they were implemented in a conventional textual event-callback style. We evaluated InterState's scalability with a series of benchmarks and example applications and found that it can scale to implement complex behaviors involving thousands of objects and constraints.

Author Keywords
GUI Programming; Constraints; State Machines; Visual Editors; Live Programming

ACM Classification Keywords
D.2.6 Programming Environments

INTRODUCTION
User interface development is notoriously difficult [22]. The event-callback model used by nearly all widely-deployed user interface frameworks tends to produce error-prone "spaghetti" code by splitting the implementation of a single behavior across many locations [21,26]. Researchers and practitioners have tried to address this problem by augmenting traditional programming languages with programming paradigms more suitable for expressing user interfaces. Two of the common difficulties these libraries address are managing *states*—an interface's status, which often controls its appearance and behavior [1,33]—and expressing *constraints*—relationships among interface components and underlying data models [21,26,30]. However, it is still difficult to integrate constraints or state models into imperative languages, in part because most development tools are designed for presenting, navigating, and debugging sequential code [22]. Further, the mechanisms for code reuse and modularization in imperative languages often do not match the needs of user interface programmers [18].

UIST '14, October 05 - 08 2014, Honolulu, HI, USA

http://dx.doi.org/10.1145/2642918.2647358

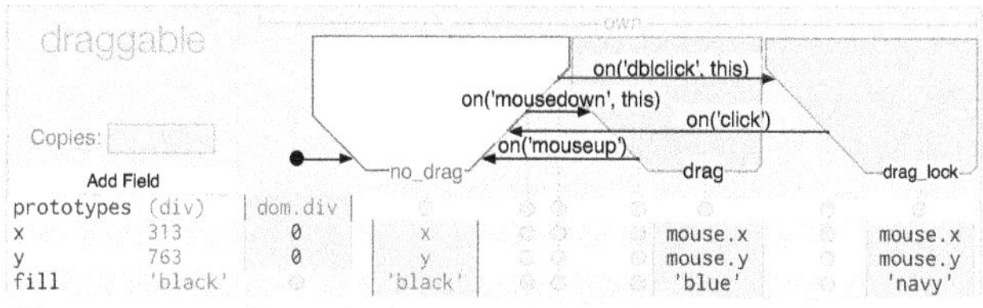

Figure 1: A basic InterState object, named `draggable`, which implements draggable and drag lock behaviors. Properties that control `draggable`'s display are represented as rows (e.g. `x`, `y`, and `fill`). States and transitions are represented as columns (e.g. `no_drag` and `drag`). An entry in a property's row for a particular state specifies a constraint that controls that property's value in that state. Here, while `draggable` is in the `drag` state, `x` and `y` will be constrained to `mouse.x` and `mouse.y` respectively, meaning `draggable` will follow the mouse.

InterState Overview and Contributions
We created *InterState* with the insight that we can improve user interface development tools by redesigning the language and runtime features in concert. InterState contributes to the state of the art for user interface development tools by introducing a novel computational model, a visual notation, an inheritance mechanism, and a live editor for its visual notation. Further, InterState demonstrates how designing these features to work well together improves both the individual components and the usability of the system as an integrated whole.

Computational Model — The state of a user interface often controls its appearance and behavior, which in turn are defined by relationships among objects. In event-callback code, it is difficult to manage, maintain, debug, and understand these states and relationships [26,30]. InterState introduces a computational model that addresses these challenges by including state machines and constraints as fundamental language constructs. This model expresses interactive behaviors as constraints that are enforced only in particular states [30]. It also removes much of the boilerplate that is required to express constraints in other systems [21,23,24,30], allowing programmers to express constraints with simple equations—like those in spreadsheets—rather than with a complex syntax.

Visual Notation — In most languages, understanding what user events affect a particular property or, conversely, what properties are affected by a particular user event, can be difficult because event-callback code is usually spread throughout multiple locations [26]. InterState introduces a visual notation that concisely represents interactive behaviors as a table whose rows are properties and columns are states. Combined with its computational model, the visual notation allows programmers to see which events affect a property by scanning the property's row and which properties an event affects by looking at that event's column. Further, InterState's visual notation helps overcome some well-known issues with constraints, such as that they can be hard to understand and control [22].

Behavior Reuse — Programmers often want to reuse, combine, and inherit behaviors, but nearly every widely-used programming language only allows properties and methods to be inherited. InterState introduces a style of inheritance that extends traditional prototype-instance inheritance mechanisms to allow *behaviors* to be inherited. This is possible in InterState because its computational model defines behaviors using state machines whose structure can be inherited. Because interactive behaviors are often combined, InterState supports multiple inheritance by combining property values across states. The table-based representation of property values offers an intuitive way to resolve the ambiguities inherent in multiple inheritance in other systems: potential conflicts use left-most precedence, which is readily visible due to the clear visual notation. InterState also introduces a mechanism for *templates* that allows items in a list of interactive components to be dynamically created and updated to reflect changes in an underlying data model.

Live Development — Quick experimentation and parameter tuning are crucial parts of the design process that are not well supported by today's programming environments [5,6]. InterState introduces a live editor for its visual notation, where edits are immediately reflected in the running application (runtime) and changes in runtime state and property values are highlighted in the editor. This helps bridge the "gulf of evaluation" in determining the effects of a change [28], which has been shown to be a significant barrier for experienced and new programmers [16] alike.

Complimentary Features — In addition to innovations in the aforementioned areas, a significant contribution of InterState is in designing these features and concepts to complement each other in a cohesive programming environment. We start this paper with a motivating example and sample applications before detailing the design of InterState's programming primitives and editor. We conclude with an evaluation of InterState's usability and scalability for complex behaviors.

```
var isDragLocked = false,
    mm_listener  = function(mm_event) {
        draggable.attr({ x: mm_ev.x, y: mm_ev.y });
    },
    mu_listener  = function(mu_event) {
        removeEventListener("mousemove", mm_listener);
        removeEventListener("mouseup",   mu_listener);
    };
draggable.mousedown(function(md_ev) {
    draggable.attr({ x: md_ev.x, y: md_ev.y });
    addEventListener("mousemove", mm_listener);
    addEventListener("mouseup",   mu_listener);
}).dblclick(function(md_event) {
    if(isDragLocked) {
        removeEventListener("mousemove", mm_listener);
    } else {
        addEventListener    ("mousemove", mm_listener);
    }
    isDragLocked = !isDragLocked;
});
```

Figure 2: A representative JavaScript snippet that implements draggable and drag lock for an object named `draggable`.

MOTIVATING EXAMPLE

Drag-lock is an example of a common interactive behavior. Drag-lock is a standard accessibility feature that augments "drag and drop" to allow users to double click an object and drag it until they double click again. Suppose we want to implement drag-lock on an object named `draggable` which we will later reuse throughout a user interface. We asked an expert programmer to implement this behavior in JavaScript and refactored their code for clarity by adding more descriptive variable names and removing unnecessary lines. The resulting code is shown in Figure 2. At 20 lines, it is compact but difficult to follow and even more difficult to write correctly. When a user double clicks on `draggable` to initiate a drag lock, five different snippets of code are executed in an order that is difficult to predict (`mousedown`, `mu_listener`, `mousedown`, `mu_listener`, then `dblclick`). Some of these listeners also activate and deactivate other listeners, making it even more difficult to understand the snippet's state at a given time.

Compare this with InterState's implementation of the same behavior, shown in Figure 1. With InterState, the execution flow is clearly illustrated, as are the different possible values for `x` and `y`. Further, InterState makes it easy to follow which state the `draggable` object is in by highlighting the active state and relevant values, and by animating transitions as they fire. In the evaluation described later in this paper, we found that these features were effective in helping programmers implement this behavior over twice as fast with InterState than with JavaScript.

Further, suppose we want to extend this example to add some common usability features that users expect: keyboard accessibility and a visual indication of the current state. Specifically, in our example, pressing `ESC` should terminate dragging, and the color of `draggable` should change when it is "locked". In JavaScript, adding keyboard accessibility requires at least eight more lines of code, including modifications to the previous code. In InterState, it simply requires the addition of two new transitions (from the `drag` and `drag_lock` states) and no modifications of the existing states or transitions. In JavaScript, adding a visual state indication to `draggable` (e.g. so it is black by default, blue while dragging, and navy when drag-locked) requires five more carefully placed lines that, again, would modify the original code. In InterState, this simply requires specifying the color in three existing states (see Figure 1). Finally, modifying the behavior to use a single click to escape drag-lock rather than a double click, which is seemingly trivial, requires nearly a complete rewrite of the JavaScript code (to work with the original `mouseup` and `dblclick` listeners) but only requires modifying one transition in InterState. Figure 1 shows the InterState code after all of these modifications have been made, but the JavaScript code would be about twice as long as Figure 2.

Now, suppose we want to reuse our drag-lock behavior in other contexts (e.g. a drag-lock slider). In JavaScript, we would need to carefully abstract and package this behavior to be reusable in a way that does not interfere with other behaviors. In InterState, this is supported by default since other objects can simply inherit from `draggable`. Frameworks that include a notion of state [1,3,30,36] would allow drag-lock to be declared in a more natural way than plain JavaScript. However, they lack InterState's visual notation, which makes understanding and debugging this behavior relatively easy. Further, none of these other frameworks address the challenge of behavior reuse.

Applications

To illustrate InterState's expressiveness, we implemented a number of example applications. We will briefly describe three of these example applications and link to their working implementations. We will refer back to these examples in subsequent sections.

Music Player & Playlist Editor http://istate.co/music

This music player includes a playlist manager that allows users to create and edit playlists. It takes advantage of InterState's ability to call JavaScript functions to play music with the HTML5 audio API.

Breakout http://istate.co/breakout

Our version of the classic game "breakout" includes bonuses and power-ups. It also interfaces with Box2D, a third-party physics engine, for collision detection and reactions.

Touchscreen Maps http://istate.co/touch_map

This application allows users to pan and zoom a map image using touch and accelerometer events on touchscreen devices. It illustrates InterState's ability to express behaviors using multiple input modalities.

INTERSTATE'S COMPUTATIONAL MODEL

InterState starts with a computational model that builds on the idea of defining interactive behaviors using constraints that apply in specific states, as used in ConstraintJS [30]. This combination of state machines and constraints allows programmers to express interactive behaviors by tracking UI state and declaring nuanced relationships between elements that depend on its state. Moving this computational model from an imperative context (ConstraintJS in JavaScript) to a declarative model (InterState) required two fundamental additions to increase its expressiveness.

First, property values can be set either on states (as usual) but also on *transitions*, in which case they are evaluated *once* when the transition executed, so the value stays fixed even if dependencies change. In contrast, constraints on *states* are continuously updated whenever dependencies change while in that state. Setting on transitions allows programs to store the value of an expression at specific points in time, for example, to calculate offsets for dragging an object based on the initial mouse point and peg it to its last location when it finishes dragging. Second, InterState carefully controls the order in which property values are evaluated on transitions by determining the appropriate property evaluation order when two separate transitions fire simultaneously based on internal dependencies.

Constraint Expressions

Constraints are a built-in primitive in InterState, which allows many other InterState features to benefit from their expressiveness; state machine transitions can use constraints to express mutable targets and events, objects can dynamically vary their prototypes using constraints, and constraints can express a dynamic list of items to be displayed with a given template. InterState allows programmers to express constraints with simple equations—like those in spreadsheets—rather than with a complex syntax, as required in previous work [21,23,24,30]. These equations are still capable of concisely expressing many complex constraints. For instance, constraints may contain indirection (the target object can itself be calculated by a constraint) [23,24,37] such as:

```
this.currentlyPlayingSong.title
```

It is also often useful to express operations on *groups* of objects [31]. InterState includes a function called `find` for making such queries with a chaining syntax inspired by other query languages, including EET [8] and HANDS [31]. For example, in Breakout, players reach the next level by destroying all of the blocks in the current level. This can be expressed in a transition as:

```
find(blocks).in_state('alive').is_empty()
```

Every InterState object exists in a containment hierarchy. References and scoping across a large containment hierarchy can be challenging, sometimes requiring specialized query languages—e.g. XQuery or Sizzle (sizzlejs.com). In other frameworks, referencing objects elsewhere in the containment hierarchy requires long chains of "parent" expressions that are brittle with respect to changes to the program's structure [23]. InterState makes referencing fields in constraints easier by naming every field, unlike the DOM and other XML-based containment hierarchies. This allows references to jump up the containment hierarchy by using unique field names in a manner analogous to scoping rules in textual languages. Although this requires an effort on the part of the programmer to name every field and provide unique names for important fields, it makes the resulting code more readable and robust to structural changes.

State Machines

Including state machines as a built-in primitive allows InterState to handle the stateful nature of user interface behaviors [33]. While some previous systems have included state as a separate primitive [1,3,17,29], including state as a fundamental part of objects is crucial to InterState's support of behavior inheritance and reuse. This is because an object's state machines and fields define its behavior; so allowing both to be inherited makes it possible for other objects to reuse its behaviors.

InterState objects contain one or more state machines and any number of named properties, which map every state and transition of its state machine to a value. This value can be empty (represented as a grey circle in the editor) in which case the property's last value remains in use. Otherwise, the value can be a constant or a constraint. Thus, a property's value in a state might depend upon which transition was fired to arrive at that state.

Starting State

As we will discuss in the "scalability" section below, scalability is a multifaceted issue in programming tools. Most of this paper focuses on ways that InterState can scale *up* to express complex behaviors. However, it is also important to consider how programming frameworks scale *down* to concisely express simple behaviors. The difficulty of expressing a behavior should rise linearly with the complexity of the behavior [22].

In InterState, creating static interfaces (no interactivity) is straightforward. InterState objects start with one state to match the simplicity of property sheets [34], which allow programmers to easily see and modify an object's settable properties. However, whereas property sheets can only specify the *look* of an application, InterState's state machines scale to allow programmers to specify its *behavior*.

This is in contrast to previous systems that have integrated state machines as a layer [27,36] where interface behavior code goes *inside* of states. Consequently, these systems scale down to static interfaces only as well as their underlying imperative languages. Further, by relying on side-effects to define behavior, these systems can still be subject to the "spaghetti" code problem that makes it difficult to determine how an interactive behavior works [26].

Combining State Machines

Behaviors often combine multiple state machines; an object might, for instance, be draggable *and* selectable. In order to avoid the *state explosion* problem [29] where programmers would have to create combinatorial numbers of states (e.g. `draggingAndSelected`, `idleAndSelected`, etc.), InterState borrows two ideas from StateCharts [12]: concurrent and nested states. As discussed below, objects can contain *multiple* state machines that operate independently. When multiple states are active, InterState uses left-to-right precedence to choose which active value the properties should use in the event of conflicts, a convention that is easy to understand in InterState's visual notation.

Transition Events

InterState's event model is input agnostic. Any event exposed by the runtime environment (usually the browser) can be used. For instance, when the runtime is running on a mobile touchscreen device, InterState transitions can be triggered by touch and accelerometer events.

To allow programmers to concisely and declaratively express complex events, event targets can be computed by dynamic constraints, e.g. `on('click', currentlyPlayingSong)`. Such dynamic targets have been tried in previous systems [8] but were hampered by performance and implementation challenges. In InterState's runtime implementation, we optimized performance for dynamic event targets by using JavaScript's native event listener mechanism, rather than distributing events in the runtime. This required modifying our constraint solver, which is normally lazy (pull-based), so that constraints used to calculate the active event listeners are updated whenever an event's target is changed (push-based).

Constraint Events

Another innovative way that InterState allows events to be dynamically calculated is to support events that refer to changes in constraint values. For instance, in our Breakout example, the player should lose a life when the ball goes past the paddle. In imperative languages, this usually requires passing property changes through a setter method, which then triggers the corresponding state change. InterState simplifies this by introducing *constraint events*—Boolean expressions like `(ball.cy > paddle.y)`—that fire any time the value of the expression switches from `false` to `true`. While constraint events have technically been possible in other constraint systems [21], InterState reduces the syntactic burden of expressing them by allowing constraint events to be expressed using the same syntax as constraints. Further, the efficient eager evaluation mechanism discussed in the previous section makes these constraint events practical.

Manipulating Visual Objects

InterState is output-agnostic and can be made to work with any output supporting a structured graphics model (sometimes called a "retained object model"). We have fully implemented output mechanisms for HTML DOM objects and Scalable Vector Graphics (SVG) objects. We have also created a prototype to confirm the feasibility of using WebGL as an output mechanism for creating 3D interfaces.

New outputs can be added by writing a JavaScript wrapper that maps changes in InterState objects' fields and containment hierarchy to operations in the output mechanism. Depending on the specific output mechanism, additional code might also be needed to detect input events. In total, our wrapper for the SVG output mechanism only requires about 300 lines of JavaScript.

To make an SVG graphical object appear on the screen in InterState, programmers can make that object inherit from one of seven types of SVG objects: `circle`, `ellipse`, `image`, `rectangle`, `text`, `group`, and `path`. (Programming with HTML DOM or other output models works similarly.) All of these prototypes provide *default* values for their display properties (for example, `rectangle` has a `width` attribute with a default value of `150` and `image` has a `src` attribute with a default URI that points to the InterState logo). InterState also includes attributes that allow programmers to specify how display properties should animate between values, using CSS transitions. Finally, to enable a dynamic DOM hierarchy despite the static containment hierarchy of InterState objects, InterState DOM objects include a property that allows programmers to express a node's DOM children as a dynamic constraint.

BEHAVIOR REUSE IN INTERSTATE

User interfaces often re-use and combine behaviors. InterState supports this by introducing an inheritance mechanism that allows behaviors to be re-used as easily as fields and methods are in traditional inheritance.

Inheritance

Other toolkits have achieved behavior inheritance by requiring that programmers create separate *interactor* objects that describe specific built-in behaviors and can be attached to graphical objects [15,23,24]. Rather than requiring such specialized mechanisms, InterState's inheritance model extends traditional prototype-instance inheritance [23] by adding several features to support behavior inheritance.

First, when one InterState object inherits from another, it also inherits an *instance* of that object's state machine. For example, in Figure 4, `my_selectable_draggable` gets an instance of the state machines for both `selectable` and `draggable`. The fact that an *instance* of the state machine is inherited, rather than the state machine itself, is important; we usually do not want all of the objects that inherit from a particular object to be in the same state. For example, we do *not* want every object that inherits from `draggable` to enter the `dragging` state when one of them does. When the structure (not current state) of a prototype's state machine is changed, that change is instantly reflected in the structure of all objects that inherit from it. This allows programmers to quickly modify the behavior of objects in their interface to explore behavior variations. For example, in an interface with a number of draggable elements, drag-lock could be implemented for every element by modifying the definition of one "draggable" prototype.

Second, rather than inheriting a property's *value,* InterState inherits the property's *constraint.* Further, the values of the of references in the constraint expression are computed based on the context of the instance, not the prototype. By inheriting the constraint's definition and redetermining ref-

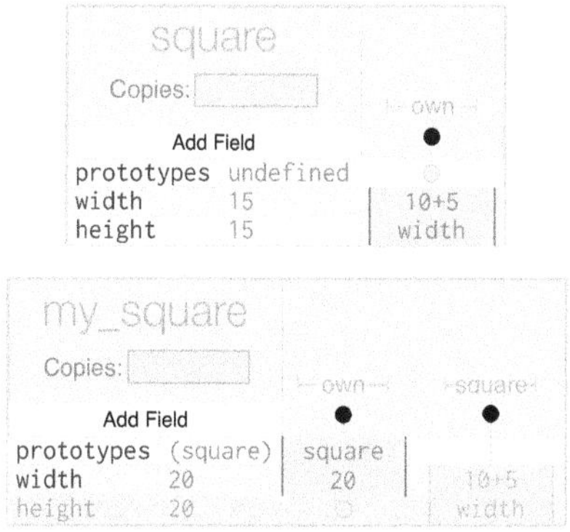

Figure 3: InterState uses a prototype-instance inheritance model with multiple inheritance. Prototypes are simply specified in the `prototypes` property. Here, `my_square` inherits from `square`. Because `my_square` does not define a value for `height`, it inherits the definition of `square.height`, as indicated by the greyed out text in the columns on the right. Note that `my_square` inherits the *definition* of `height`, not the value. Thus, its `width` property evaluates to a different value (`20`) than it does in `square` (`15`).

erents, InterState allows prototypes to define behaviors that reference the state and property values of the objects that inherit from them. This is illustrated in Figure 3, where `my_square` inherits the definition of `height`, rather than its value, and the value computed for `my_square.height` depends on **`my_square`**`.width`, not **`square`**`.width`. Amulet and Garnet included a similar mechanism [23,24], but using a more verbose syntax.

Third, unlike most prototype-instance inheritance models, InterState allows multiple inheritance. A handful of other prototype-instance frameworks have included multiple inheritance, but only for fields [24,35]. In InterState, multiple inheritance is crucial because interface components often combine multiple inherited behaviors. InterState objects may inherit from any number of other objects. InterState then *combines* inherited values across states. If an object's property is not defined for a state but it is in one of the object's prototypes, that prototype's definition is used for the state. This allows multiple behaviors to control the same property simultaneously. For example, in Figure 4, `selectable` and `draggable` define `color`. `my_selectable_draggable` combines the definitions of both of these prototypes. In the `selected` state, it will be `'blue'`; otherwise, it will be `'black'` or `'red'`, depending on the dragging state. For conflicting values, the leftmost value is used; a convention that is easy to control and understand in concert with the visual notation.

Previous multiple inheritance frameworks have been hampered by the "diamond problem", which occurs when objects `B` and `C` both inherit from `A` and object `D` inherits from both `B` and `C`, leading previous systems to inherit `A` twice [19]. InterState addresses the diamond problem by detecting duplicate prototypes and only inheriting them once. If there are conflicts among prototypes (i.e. two prototypes set the same field for the same state), InterState gives precedence to the first (leftmost) prototype.

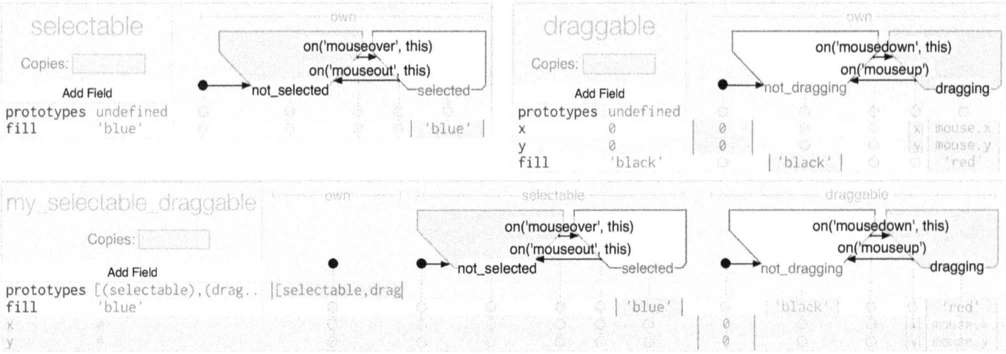

Figure 4: An object that inherits from both `draggable` and `selectable` behaviors. Note that the definitions for the `color` property are inherited from `draggable('red')` and `selectable('blue')`.

Finally, `prototypes`, like every other property, can have different values in different states, and can even be computed by constraints, allowing the prototypes of any given object to depend on its current state. This dynamic inheritance provides a declarative way for interface elements to modify their behavior based on the interface state [35]. For instance, programmers can declaratively change an SVG object from a rectangle to a circle by changing its prototype, rather than imperatively removing and creating objects.

Copies and Templates

User interfaces often contain lists of items that behave similarly. Programmers should not have to declare a display for every item in such a list, because it is too tedious and because that list of items may be computed at runtime. In imperative languages, this functionality has been implemented as list views in data-binding libraries, or as special groups [23] that allow programmers to specify a template display and to specify the number of instances they want. Most template mechanisms, however, require separate template objects and a special template syntax [30]. InterState's template mechanism improves on this by enabling the features of templates without requiring a special syntax or special form for template objects.

InterState adds an optional `copies` field to all objects. Like other fields, `copies` can be dynamic and can reference other fields or JavaScript objects. When `copies` is set to an array or a number, its parent object then creates an array of objects. The editor visually signals this by displaying a stack under the object's display (see Figure 5). For every copy, InterState sets two properties: `my_copy`, which carries the corresponding value from the `copies` array (e.g. `'Jane'`, `'Sue'`) and `copy_num`, which carries an item's index (e.g. `0`, `1`). When the value of `copies` changes (dynamically due to a constraint or by edits at design time), the list is efficiently updated with respect to added, moved, and removed items instead of recreating the entire list.

In our music player application, for instance, the list of playlists is stored in the `playlists` property. A playlist display will be automatically created for every item in `playlists` by setting `copies` of `playlistsView`. We then create a list of songs per-playlist by setting `copies` of `currentPlaylistView` to `currentPlaylist.songs`. When the user modifies either the list of songs in a playlist or the list of playlists themselves, new elements are added and removed automatically.

This feature integrates well with InterState's dynamic inheritance model, since copies can vary their displays. For instance, a directory viewer application might set `copies` of `itemView` to the current directory's contents. Copies could inherit from `folderView` if `my_copy` is a folder or from `fileView` if it is a file. This example could create a recursive tree structure by making `itemView` a child of `folderView` with a copy for every item in its folder.

INTERSTATE VISUAL NOTATION AND EDITOR

In event-callback code, property values can be modified in any callback [21,26]. InterState's computational model, by contrast, allows property values to change in two ways: either a constraint in that property is recomputed (e.g. `mouse.x` changes when the mouse moves) or the property's specified value changes (e.g. a state change or the programmer edits the property's value). This design trades some flexibility—losing the ability to set properties anywhere—for readability by ensuring all of a property's possible values are visible in its row.

To achieve a tabular layout with every state and transition represented in a column, InterState's visual notation "flattens" its state machines to allocate horizontal space for all local and inherited states. The trapezoidal shape of states is designed to allocate a column for every transition, horizontally centered where the transition's arrow begins.

InterState Live Editor

Previous research has shown how live programming can improve the experience of both novice and professional programmers [11,20]. The declarative nature of InterState's computational model reduces many of the technical challenges of creating live editors in imperative languages [6].

InterState's editor is displayed in a separate window that

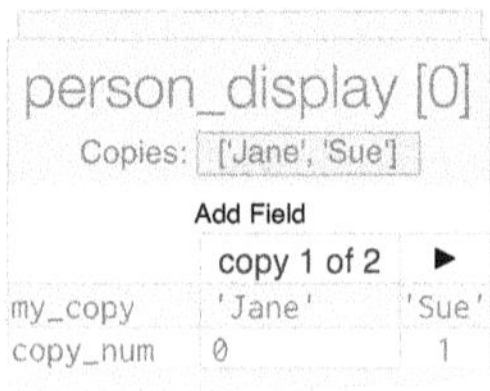

Figure 5: An object with multiple copies; `copies` is set to `['Jane', 'Sue']`. Every copy has two properties: `my_copy`, which is set to that copy's item (here, either `'Jane'` or `'Sue'`) and `copy_num`, which is set to that copy's index. Here, we are looking at the first copy.

communicates with the runtime. The editor displays current field values and highlights and animates state changes to inform programmers of the current state of their program. When developing non-desktop applications (e.g. for a touchscreen phone or tablet), the editor can alternatively be displayed on a separate computer connected via a network. This allows the programmer to interact with their running program while editing its behavior.

Space Efficiency and Navigation

Navigability is an important consideration in live editors [6]. Programmers should be able to navigate between objects in the editor and their representations in the runtime. InterState's editor was built to enable quick exploration and navigation. The runtime allows users to inspect objects in the runtime display pane to open those objects in the editor window. Conversely, objects in the runtime display pane are highlighted whenever the mouse is hovered over the corresponding representation in the editor. When properties reference other objects in the containment hierarchy, programmers can click the name of the object to navigate to it.

By default, the InterState editor displays a single object at a time. To show every field immediately referenceable by the current object, the editor displays the names of every parent in the containment hierarchy, along with field names and a compact summary of their current value. The editor also allows programmers to "pin" objects so their display stays on the screen so they can be referenced while editing another object. InterState's editor includes an inline text editor useful for quickly editing of short constraint values and a full multi-line text editor useful for editing longer values, like method definitions.

Error Reporting & Debugging

One of the barriers to the adoption of constraint systems has been the difficulty of understanding and fixing bugs in constraint specifications [22]. When there is a bug in a constraint method, many constraint systems will halt program execution and present a cryptic error message [23,24].

InterState's runtime was designed to enable programmers to always have a running application, like in spreadsheet programming, where constraint errors do not halt updates of other constraints [7,22]. InterState achieves this by "localizing" errors: constraints with errors only prevent the parts of the program from running that depend on those constraints. In the editor, errors are displayed next to the problematic constraint expression (see Figure 6).

Constraints are also challenging to debug in imperative languages because of their declarative nature [22]. Breakpoints in imperative languages are of limited use because they can freeze the program while the constraint solver is in an inconsistent state (i.e. in the middle of code maintaining a dependency). InterState's editor makes constraint debugging easier by allowing programmers to always see the current values calculated by constraints, and to set breakpoints that halt its constraint solver in a consistent state just before a constraint is reevaluated. Breakpoints can also be set on transitions or states so programmers can see what relationships are being maintained at any point in their program.

Figure 6: Syntax and runtime errors are highlighted in the editor but do not prevent the program from running.

EVALUATIONS OF INTERSTATE

To understand the efficacy and limitations of InterState, we evaluated it in three ways. First, implementing the example applications described earlier allowed us to evaluate the expressiveness of InterState's model. Second, a comparative laboratory study helped us understand InterState's learnability. Finally, performance benchmarks measured our runtime's scalability.

Comparative Laboratory Study

Given the design goals of InterState, we hypothesized that programmers could more easily understand and modify user interface code with InterState than in event-callback code.

Method

To evaluate this hypothesis, we conducted a comparative laboratory study with 20 experienced programmers (ages 19-41). There were two different study tasks and two systems with which to implement them (regular JavaScript or InterState), all counterbalanced to control for learning effects and differences in task difficulty. Participants were given the same task description regardless of implementation language. For each behavior, we asked participants to make modifications to evaluate their ability to understand the implemented behavior and express a new behavior.

For one behavior, participants were given code for a standard drag and drop behavior and were asked to implement the drag-lock behavior described earlier. For the other behavior, participants were given code for an image carousel that displayed a large "featured" image and a series of thumbnails. The featured image changes when a thumbnail is clicked or auto-advanced after a timeout. We asked participants to change display features of the thumbnails, the auto-advance interval, and to add a progress bar below the featured thumbnail to indicate the auto-advance interval.

To make our comparison as fair as possible, we started with third-party code for the JavaScript implementations and simplified them by reducing boilerplate and adding descriptive variable names that were consistent with those used in the InterState implementations. We also used a "live" JavaScript editor (JSBin) that immediately re-evaluates JavaScript snippets when their source changes. Finally, participants were given tutorials and reference sheets for JavaScript and InterState.

Results

Participants were able to implement the drag lock task significantly faster with InterState—taking less than half the time (JavaScript: 19.5±13.6 min, InterState: 8.0±6.8 min, two-tailed heteroscedastic Student's t-test $p < 0.05$). Although relatively few lines of code were required, reasoning about callbacks' timing in the JavaScript task proved challenging for many users, and many participants used console logs to help them understand their interface's state.

Participants also completed the image carousel task significantly faster with InterState, again in about half the time (JavaScript: 28.3±7.6 min, InterState: 14.7±5.5 min, $p < 0.01$). For this task, participants added a timer indicator. Participants in both implementations used one of two strategies for this: either creating an indicator for each thumbnail or creating one indicator that follows the featured thumbnail. Both implementations already had a property that tracked the number of milliseconds before the featured image auto-advanced, which the programmers could utilize. Most JavaScript participants missed this variable while most InterState participants found it, apparently by observing how its value changed over time.

Discussion

Most participants felt comfortable with InterState's visual notation, calling it "intuitive" and "clean". Nearly every user cited InterState's ability to display the current application state and live property values as one of the most useful aspects of the editor. This helped many users quickly debug and deduce the meaning and roles of properties.

Our evaluation also pointed to several ways to improve InterState, some of which are already reflected in the design described above. For example, we added the ability to jump from an on-screen object in the runtime to its representation in the editor as a result of observing the difficulty several participants had finding objects. Additionally, the ability to "pin" objects in the editor was suggested by a participant. Both of these features were added after this study.

The most common mistakes made in InterState were the result of a few conceptual barriers that we plan on improving. For example, some participants were not sure whether edits to an object with multiple copies changed every copy or just one, a distinction that the editor could make clearer. Some participants also had difficulty reasoning about the interaction between state machines in different copies. In the image carousel example, when the user clicks a thumbnail, that thumbnail should become selected and the previously selected thumbnail should become deselected. This is a breakdown of the visibility principle—by only showing one copy at a time, InterState's representation of state machines does not make it clear how user events can affect multiple state machines.

Scalability

We designed InterState to be "scalable" in three senses of the word. *Application* scalability refers to InterState's ability to scale to implement even complex GUIs. *Performance* scalability refers to InterState's ability to deal with large numbers of components. *Editor* scalability concerns the ability of the InterState editor to keep source code readable, understandable, and navigable even as applications become more complex.

Application Complexity

To scale in terms of application complexity, InterState includes a number of features. First, behavior inheritance and templating enable code re-use, which makes writing complex applications more practical.

Second, InterState includes a number of pre-built widgets, such as sliders and radio buttons that programmers can easily include in their application. Unlike many widget libraries, however, these widgets are not black-boxes, but can be inspected and modified if users want variations.

Finally, many applications require complexity in back-end code. For instance, a mailbox application might need to communicate with a server over IMAP to retrieve e-mail messages. Thus, InterState includes mechanisms for communicating with back-end code written in other languages, allowing programmers to connect a front-end written in InterState with a back-end written in another language.

Performance

We conducted a series of performance tests to evaluate InterState's ability to scale for behaviors involving large numbers of objects. These tests were performed in Safari 7.0 on a 2.3 GHz Intel i7 Macintosh with 16 GB of RAM. We ran three tests and measured the delay between changing an attribute value in InterState's runtime model and when that change was reflected in the runtime output.

In the first test, we created an object named `obj` whose prototype chain is N objects long, as in:

```
obj.prototypes = proto1
proto1.prototypes = proto2
...
proto(N-1).prototypes = protoN
```

We then measured the latency between changing `protoN` and the runtime updating its DOM output for `obj`. In the second test, we measured the same latency for an object with N prototypes, as in: `obj.prototypes = [proto1, ..., protoN]`. In the third test, we created an object with N copies and measured the time it took for a change to affect the runtime's DOM output for every copy.

For each test, we measured the highest value of N for which a change was perceived to be instantaneous (100 milliseconds). We found that performance scaled linearly in all tests. The first test indicated that a prototype chain of 58 objects could be handled instantaneously. By contrast, the longest prototype chain in the implementation of the Eclipse IDE is only nine classes long. The second test indicated that an object could have about 2,400 prototypes before changes have any visible delay. This is far more than necessary in real-world interfaces. The third test indicated that 1,200 simultaneous changes to DOM attributes would appear instantaneous. By contrast, InterState's constraint solver, ConstraintJS [30], could handle about 2,000 simultaneous changes in the same testing environment, which indicates that the InterState runtime only adds a 40% overhead. Much of this overhead comes from parsing and interpreting constraints, which is done in the runtime (rather than natively) to enable InterState's dynamic scoping. As our results indicate, InterState can scale up to real-world interfaces with respect to performance. It is also important to note that a developer can implement any performance-critical operations natively and reference them in InterState.

Editor Scalability

InterState's editor includes a number of features to allow programmers to navigate and understand complex behaviors. We described some of these techniques—such as pinning, and links to navigate between InterState objects—in the "InterState Visual Notation and Editor" section above.

Additionally, InterState's visual notation for state machines is able to convey behaviors using less space than textual code. For instance, the image carousel from the user study required about 60 lines of JavaScript. In InterState, the same behavior required two objects (with three states and six transitions total) and 33 constraints across 22 properties. With the same font size, the InterState implementation required 30% *less* display space despite conveying *more* information (e.g. inherited properties and current property values). This is primarily because InterState's visual notation reduces the verbosity needed to express states and establish constraints.

RELATED WORK

InterState is influenced by work in multiple domains, some of which we have described in previous sections.

Spreadsheet and Visual Programming

Many researchers consider spreadsheets to be the most popular form of "programming" [22]. InterState leverages several spreadsheet conventions, such as localizing errors only to problematic cells. Several other systems have used spreadsheet-like ideas to make it easier to create graphical-interfaces. For example, Forms/3 [7] demonstrated that procedural and data abstractions and graphical output were viable with spreadsheets. InterState builds on these spreadsheet-like concepts by combining them with state machines. These state machine are represented graphically, an idea explored by a number of visual programming systems—see [14,25,38] for surveys.

Constraint Libraries for Imperative Languages

A number of constraint libraries for imperative languages have tried to simplify the development of interactive behaviors [4,9,21,23,24,30]. These systems have explored ways to make constraints more expressive, including with multi-way constraints and constraint hierarchies. Of these, the most relevant to InterState is ConstraintJS (CJS), a JavaScript library on which InterState is built [30]. While InterState and CJS both define interactive behaviors by combining states and constraints, CJS was built specifically to fit into the context of imperative JavaScript code, whereas InterState introduces a novel visual notation to allow programmers to express interactive applications with little or no imperative code. Achieving this goal went beyond simply adding a visual notation on top of CJS; it also required designing many new language features, as discussed above.

Finite State Machine Libraries

A number of libraries have also added support for finite-state machines in textual languages to address the challenge of tracking GUI state [29]. TKZink, IntuiKit [17], and HsmTk [3] use state machines to allow interface designers to specify different application appearances in different states. Similarly, SwingStates [1] integrates finite state machines with the Java Swing toolkit. By adding constraints to its notion of state, InterState's programming model makes it easier to specify how an interface reacts to state changes.

Event Languages and Models

Many commercial and research systems have used and augmented the event-action framework. Early event models, like Sassafras [13] and the University of Alberta User Interface Management System [10] inspired the features of future commercial systems [22]. One interesting extension of the standard event model is the elements, events, & transitions (EET) model, which allows programmers to more concisely express how user interfaces should respond to user events [8]. We built on some of the ideas introduced in these systems, such as dynamic event targets in transitions, to increase the expressiveness of InterState's state machines.

UIDLs and Frameworks for Interactive Systems

User Interface Description Languages (UIDLs) have been created to explore alternate ways to represent GUI behavior and appearance. ICOs [27] combines petri nets with fragments of imperative code and also provides a visual editor. Despite addressing a related problem, InterState's design is conceptually different. For instance, by placing state machines *inside* of objects (as opposed to treating petri-nets as top-level), InterState's allows behaviors to be inherited in the same fashion as properties. Other frameworks have explored alternative ways to declare GUI behaviors. Loa [2], for instance, combines data bindings, templates, and interactors. However, Loa's feature set, like ConstraintJS, was built to fit in with existing imperative languages.

CONCLUSION & FUTURE WORK

Currently, we have only tested InterState with experienced programmers, but we believe the ideas behind InterState will also allow end-user programmers who are familiar with spreadsheets to create custom behaviors. Although the current syntax for InterState constraints seems somewhat natural for mathematical expressions (e.g. `width*2`), it could be improved for more complex expressions, which currently use JavaScript syntax (e.g. `other_obj[this.prop_name]`). We plan on investigating ways of making the constraint syntax more beginner-friendly, guided by commonalities in how users naturally describe behaviors [32].

InterState's primary goal is to simplify the specification of GUI behaviors, so it is best for *interactive* user interfaces (the *feel*). Tools like Adobe Photoshop or Illustrator are still better for specifying the *look* of non-interactive interfaces or components. We plan on investigating ways to allow designers to design the look of components in Photoshop and the behavior of those components in InterState.

InterState shows how innovations in the execution model, combined with a visual notation and live editor, can work together to enable programmers to express interactive behaviors concisely and naturally. InterState also addresses many of the previously identified issues of programming with state machines and constraints and shows the value of putting these ideas together into a single cohesive programming framework. The InterState editor and an InterState tutorial are available online at http://istate.co.

ACKNOWLEDGEMENTS

Funding for this research comes from Adobe and from NSF grant IIS-1116724. Any opinions, findings, and conclusions or recommendations are those of the authors and do not necessarily reflect those of any of the sponsors.

REFERENCES

1. Appert, C. and Beaudouin-Lafon, M. SwingStates: Adding state machines to Java and the Swing toolkit. *Software: Practice and Experience 38*, 11 (2008), 1149–1182.
2. Beaudoux, O., Clavreul, M., Blouin, A., et al. Specifying and Running Rich Graphical Components with Loa. *EICS*, (2012), 169–178.
3. Blanch, R., Beaudouin-lafon, M., and Futurs, I. Programming Rich Interactions using the Hierarchical State Machine Toolkit. *AVI*, (2006), 51–58.
4. Bostock, M., Ogievetsky, V., and Heer, J. D^3: Data-Driven Documents. *Visualization and Computer Graphics 17*, 12 (2011), 2301–2309.
5. Brandt, J., Guo, P.J., Lewenstein, J., and Klemmer, S.R. Opportunistic Programming: Writing Code to Prototype, Ideate, and Discover. *IEEE Software 26*, 5 (2009), 18–24.
6. Burckhardt, S., Fahndrich, M., de Halleux, P., et al. It's Alive! Continuous Feedback in UI Programming. *SIGPLAN 48*, 6 (2013), 95–104.
7. Burnett, M., Atwood, J., Djang, R.W., Gottfried, H., Reichwein, J., and Yang, S. Forms/3: A First-Order Visual Language to Explore the Boundaries of the Spreadsheet Paradigm. *Functional Programming 11*, 2 (2001), 155–206.
8. Frank, M.R. Model-Based User Interface Design By Demonstration and By Interview. *GT PhD Thesis*, (1995).
9. Freeman-Benson, B. Kaleidoscope: Mixing Objects, Constraints, and Imperative Programming. *OOPSLA*, (1990), 77–88.
10. Green, M. A Survey of Three Dialogue Models. *ACM Transactions on Graphics 5*, 3 (1987), 244–275.
11. Hancock, C.M. Real-Time Programming and the Big Ideas of Computational Literacy. *MIT PhD Thesis*, (2003).
12. Harel, D. Statecharts: A Visual Formalism for Complex Systems. *Science of Computer Programming 8*, 3 (1987), 231–274.
13. Hill, R.D. Supporting Concurrency, Communication, and Synchronization in Human-Computer Sassafras UIMS. *Graphics 5*, 3 (1987), 179–210.
14. Hils, D.D. Visual languages and computing survey: Data flow visual programming languages. *JVLC 3*, 1 (1992), 69–101.
15. Hudson, S.E. and Mankoff, J. Extensible Input Handling in the subArctic Toolkit. *CHI*, (2005), 381–390.
16. Ko, A.J., Myers, B.A., and Aung, H.H. Six Learning Barriers in End-User Programming. *VL/HCC*, (2004), 199–206.
17. Lecoanet, P., Lemort, A., Mertz, C., et al. Revisiting Visual Interface Programming: Creating GUI Tools for Designers and Programmers. *UIST*, (2004), 267–276.
18. Letondal, C., Chatty, S., Phillips, W.G., and André, F. Usability requirements for interaction-oriented development tools. *PPIG*, (2010), 12–26.
19. Malayeri, D. and Aldrich, J. CZ : Multiple Inheritance Without Diamonds. *OOPSLA*, (2009).
20. Maloney, J.H., Loop, I., and Smith, R.B. Directness and Liveness in the Morphic User Interface Construction Environment. (1995), 21–28.
21. Meyerovich, L., Guha, A., and Baskin, J. Flapjax: A Programming Language for Ajax Applications. *OOPSLA*, (2009), 1–20.
22. Myers, B., Hudson, S., and Pausch, R. Past, Present, and Future of User Interface Software Tools. *TOCHI 7*, 1 (2000), 3–28.
23. Myers, B.A., Mcdaniel, R., Miller, R., et al. The Amulet Environment: New Models for Effective User Interface Software Development. *TOSE 23*, 6 (1997), 347–365.
24. Myers, B.A. Garnet: Comprehensive Support for Graphical, Highly Interactive User Interfaces. *Computer 23*, 11 (1990), 71 – 85.
25. Myers, B.A. Taxonomies of Visual Programming and P rogram Visualization. *Visual Languages and Computing 1*, 1 (1990), 97–123.
26. Myers, B.A. Separating Application Code from Toolkits: Eliminating the Spaghetti of Callbacks. *UIST*, (1991), 211–220.
27. Navarre, D., Palanque, P., Ladry, J.-F., and Barboni, E. ICOs: A Model-Based User Interface Description Technique dedicated to Interactive Systems Addressing Usability, Reliability and Scalability. *TOCHI 16*, 4 (2009), 1–56.
28. Norman, D. *The Design of Everyday Things*. Doubleday, New York, New York, USA, 1988.
29. Olsen, D.R. *User Interface Management Systems: Models and Algorithms*. Morgan Kaufmann, San Mateo, CA, 1992.
30. Oney, S., Myers, B., and Brandt, J. ConstraintJS: Programming Interactive Behaviors for the Web by Integrating Constraints and States. *UIST*, (2012), 229–238.
31. Pane, J.F., Myers, B.A., and Miller, L.B. Using HCI Techniques to Design a More Usable Programming System. *HCC*, (2002), 198–206.
32. Park, S.Y., Myers, B., and Ko, A.J. Designers' Natural Descriptions of Interactive Behaviors. *VL/HCC*, (2008), 185–188.
33. Samek, M. Who Moved My State? *Dr. Dobb's Journal*, 2003.
34. Travers, M. Recursive Interfaces for Reactive Objects. *CHI*, (1986), 379–385.
35. Ungar, D., Chambers, C., Chang, B.-W., and Hölzle, U. Organizing programs without classes. *Lisp and Symbolic Computation 4*, 3 (1991), 223–242.
36. Wingrave, C.A. and Bowman, D.A. Tiered developer-centric representations for 3D interfaces: Concept-Oriented design in Chasm. *VR*, IEEE (2008), 193–200.
37. Vander Zanden, B.T., Myers, B.A., Giuse, D.A., and Szekely, P. Integrating Pointer Variables into One-Way Constraint Models. *TOCHI l*, 2 (1994), 161–213.
38. Zhang, K. *Visual Languages and Applications*. Springer, 2007.

WirePrint: 3D Printed Previews for Fast Prototyping

Stefanie Mueller[1], Sangha Im[2], Serafima Gurevich[1], Alexander Teibrich[1], Lisa Pfisterer[1], François Guimbretière[2], Patrick Baudisch[1]

[1]Hasso Plattner Institute
Potsdam, Germany
{firstname.lastname}@hpi.uni-potsdam.de

[2]Cornell University, Information Science
Ithaca, NY 14850
{si237,francois}@cs.cornell.edu

ABSTRACT
Even though considered a *rapid* prototyping tool, 3D printing is so slow that a reasonably sized object requires printing overnight. This slows designers down to a single iteration per day. In this paper, we propose to instead print low-fidelity *wireframe previews* in the early stages of the design process. Wireframe previews are 3D prints in which surfaces have been replaced with a wireframe mesh. Since wireframe previews are to scale and represent the overall shape of the 3D object, they allow users to quickly verify key aspects of their 3D design, such as the ergonomic fit.

To maximize the speed-up, we instruct 3D printers to extrude filament not layer-by-layer, but directly in 3D-space, allowing them to create the edges of the wireframe model directly one stroke at a time. This allows us to achieve speed-ups of up to a factor of 10 compared to traditional layer-based printing. We demonstrate how to achieve wireframe previews on standard FDM 3D printers, such as the *PrintrBot* or the *Kossel mini*. Users only need to install the WirePrint software, making our approach applicable to many 3D printers already in use today. Finally, wireframe previews use only a fraction of material required for a regular print, making it even more affordable to iterate.

Author Keywords: rapid prototyping; 3D printing.

ACM Classification Keywords: H5.2 [Information interfaces and presentation]: User Interfaces.

INTRODUCTION
The recent development in rapid prototyping tools, such as 3D printers [5] allows users to prototype one-off objects and to iterate over designs. Unfortunately, 3D printers are inherently slow, because they fabricate objects voxel-by-voxel and layer-by-layer. A reasonably sized object thus tends to print overnight, slowing designers down to a single iteration per day [15].

We therefore argue that the process of how 3D printers are used for quick design iteration is not yet optimal. In other disciplines, such as in user interface design, designers achieve a fast and efficient process by iterating from low-fidelity prototyping techniques to high-fidelity techniques.

UIST '14, October 05 - 08 2014, Honolulu, HI, USA
Copyright 2014 ACM 978-1-4503-3069-5/14/10...$15.00.
http://dx.doi.org/10.1145/2642918.2647359

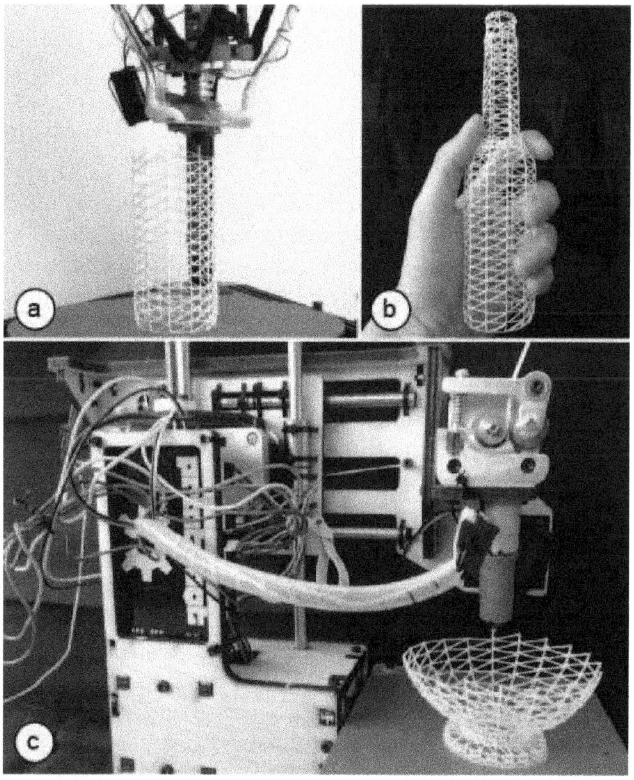

Figure 1: WirePrint prints 3D objects as wireframe previews. By extruding filament directly into 3D space instead of printing layer-wise, it achieves a speed-up of up to a factor of 10, allowing designers to iterate more quickly in the early stages of design. WirePrint achieves its maximum speed-up on (a) 3D printers based on the delta design, but also works on traditional Cartesian-based printers such as the PrintrBot shown in (c).

In order to allow designers to iterate quickly, low-fidelity techniques, such as sketching and paper prototyping, give priority to speed over functionality. This trade-off pays off in the early phases of design because it encourages the quick exploration of several versions before committing further resources, eventually leading to a better design [2].

We argue that the same principle should apply to 3D printing – a concept we call *low-fi fabrication.* In contrast to the traditional workflow, in which the 3D model is always fabricated as slow hi-fidelity print, *low-fi fabrication* fabricates all intermediate versions as fast low-fidelity previews. Only at the end, when the design is finished, the complete 3D model is printed as hi-fidelity (Figure 2).

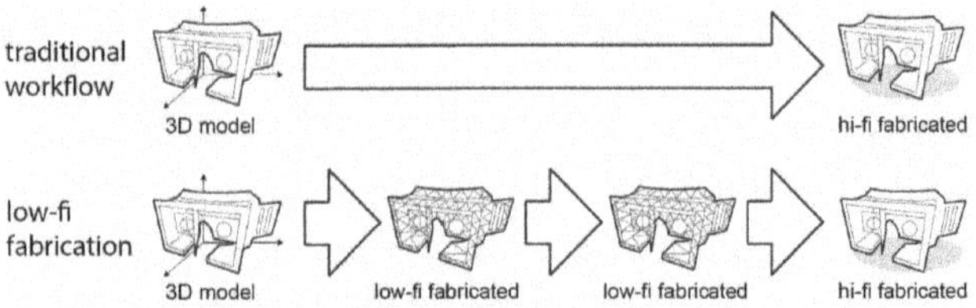

Figure 2: Low-fi fabrication: all intermediate versions are fabricated as fast low-fidelity prints. Only the final version is fabricated as hi-fidelity.

One *low-fi fabrication* approach is faBrickation [15]—a system that achieves speed-up by substituting less crucial parts of a 3D model with Lego bricks. Unfortunately, faBrickation requires users to manually assemble the bricks, so is effectively trading in printing time for manual effort.

In this paper, we present a *low-fi fabrication* approach that is not only fast, but also fully automated. The key idea is to print the 3D object as a wireframe preview, i.e. a 3D print in which surfaces have been replaced with a wireframe mesh. Our approach runs on standard FDM 3D printers, such as the *PrintrBot* or the *Kossel mini* (rather than on a 5 axis robot arm [12])—users only need to install the WirePrint software. Additional cooling around the print head helps to maximize the printing speed.

RELATED WORK

The work presented in this paper builds on personal fabrication, fast fabrication of three-dimensional objects, and wireframe structures.

Personal Fabrication

Personal fabrication devices such as 3D printers and laser cutters allow users to rapidly fabricate one-off physical objects [5]. Recently, HCI researchers proposed interfaces for a wide variety of applications: *Printed Optics* [23] shows how to prototype optical sensors and display elements, *Printing Teddy Bears* [9] how to fabricate soft objects for wearable technology, *interactive speakers* [10] how to print freeform audio technology, and *Sauron* [18] how to create interactive controllers using a single camera.

Interactive Fabrication

The traditional workflow in personal fabrication requires users to first create a digital model in a CAD program. In contrast, *interactive fabrication systems* [24] offer an alternation between user and system control. For instance, *ModelCraft* [20] allows users to modify physical paper models by annotating directly on the model, *CopyCAD* [4] allows users to copy geometry from existing objects using a milling machine, and *constructable* [13] allows users to directly draw on the work-piece inside a laser cutter using a handheld laser pointer. Other systems allow users to fabricate around a digital model: *Position-correcting router* [16] automatically corrects the user's path according to a digital model. Similar, *FreeD* [25] is a milling machine that can stop its spindle to prevent users from making mistakes.

Fast Fabrication of Three-Dimensional Objects

Different approaches try to reduce 3D printing time by either massively parallelizing the printing process using multiple heads [5] or by assembling objects layer-wise from prefabricated voxels of equal size [8]. faBrickation [15] uses a different approach by limiting 3D printing to regions where the high-resolution is required, and by using standard building blocks everywhere else.

Wireframes

To save material costs, Wang et al. [22] use wireframe support structures printed layer-wise underneath the object's surface instead of using a solid infill as support. To allow users to quickly create 3D printable wireframe meshes for layer-wise printing, Srivivasan et al. [21] designed a custom 3D editor. Gramazio et al. [5] demonstrated how to build architectural structures as wireframes by using a 5 axis robotic arm. Finally, artist Lia uses varying extrusion parameters to create *Filament Sculptures* [11].

Recently, two devices demonstrated the possibility to extrude material in 3D space: the 3Doodler [1] is a handheld pen that allows the user to sketch into 3D space using ABS plastic. Material [10] is a 5-axis robotic arm that uses a two-component material, which sets immediately after extrusion.

WIREPRINT

Figure 1a shows the 3D wireframe of a bottle in the process of being printed using WirePrint. WirePrint takes 14 minutes to 3D print the bottle (on our *Kossel mini* 3D printer [3]). This is 8.5 times faster than a traditional full-detail 3D print on the same 3D printer.

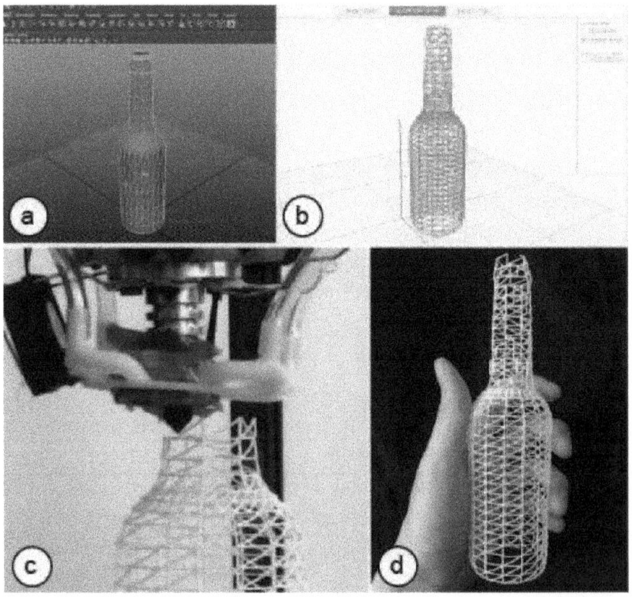

Figure 3: Iterating a design using WirePrint: (a) adjusting the model in a 3D editor, (b) converting it in the WirePrint software, (c) reprinting, (d) testing.

3D wireframes created with WirePrint allow designers to quickly validate the high-level design of a 3D object, such as its ergonomic fit. After examining the bottle shown in Figure 1b, the designer notices that the bottle does not yet rest comfortably in the hand—the designer thus decides to change the model. Figure 3 illustrates the typical workflow when iterating over a design using WirePrint. (a) The designer adjusts the thickness of the bottle in a 3D modeling program, (b) converts the model in the WirePrint software, (c) reprints it, and (d) tests its fit in the hand again. The designer may repeat the process until the bottle fits well. At this point, the designer moves on to the details of the design, until finally 3D printing the bottle (1:59 hours). WirePrint allows this design process, including its iterations, to be completed within only a couple of hours.

How WirePrint works

WirePrint converts a 3D object into a wireframe representation by (1) slicing the 3D model along its vertical axis into horizontal slices and (2) extracting the contours. It then (3) fills the space between slices with a zigzag pattern.

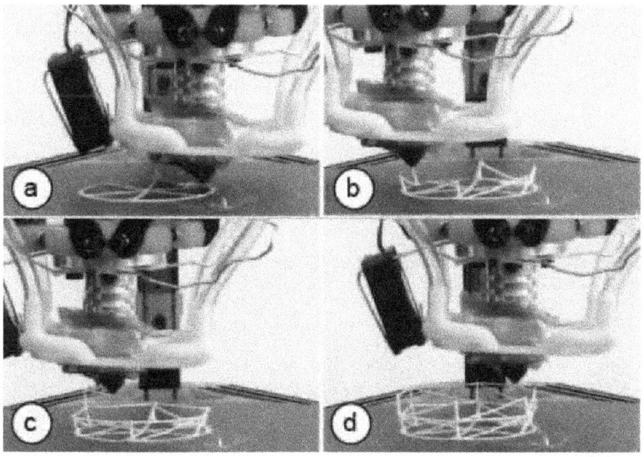

Figure 4: WirePrint's layouts consist of an alternation between (a) contour and (b) zigzag.

As illustrated by Figure 4, WirePrint fabricates objects by alternating between (a) printing a contour and (b) creating one layer of the zigzag pattern on top of the contour. Unlike traditional 3D printers that stack filament on filament, WirePrint creates its layers by moving the print head up and down repeatedly.

If a slice contains multiple disconnected contours, such as the telephone receiver shown in Figure 5, WirePrint prints all contours located on the same slice first (i.e. the contour of the left ear cap, then the contour of the right ear cap), before moving up to the next slice.

Figure 6 illustrates why WirePrint uses this particular contour-plus-zigzag approach. The main challenge in printing wireframes is that the print head has to respect already printed material in order to prevent collisions. Each bit of printed material results in additional volume becoming inaccessible.

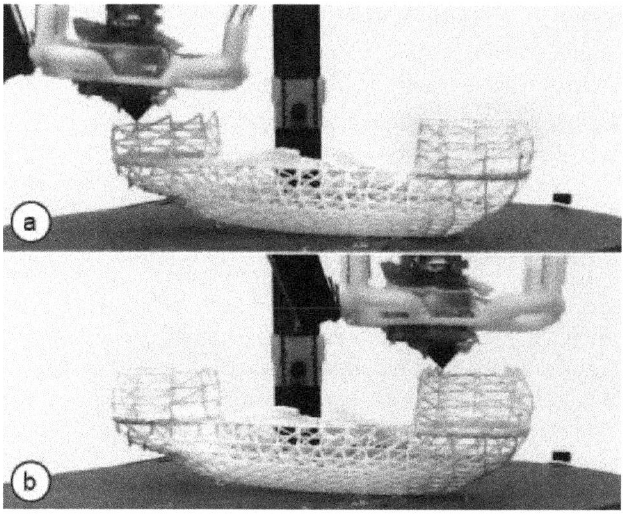

Figure 5: Multiple contours are printed one at a time.

Figure 6 describes the consequences that result from volume becoming inaccessible: (a) Two vertical edges, for example, need to be spaced at least one print head diameter apart. (b) While it is always possible to print upwards, we cannot print downwards steeper than the slant of the print head itself, as steeper edges can cause the slanted tip of the print head to collide with what is just being printed. In the case of our 3D printer (a *Kossel Mini* [3]), for example, this threshold angle is 32 degrees.

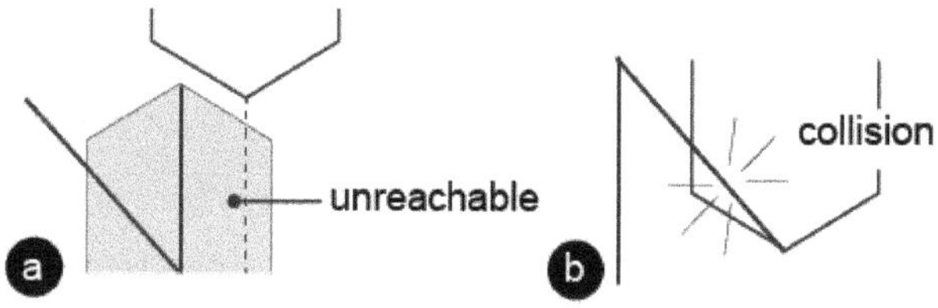

Figure 6: To prevent collisions, (a) the print head can neither print next to already printed material, (b) nor descend more steeply than the threshold angle.

These constraints still allow for several different approaches to convert a 3D model into a printable wireframe. Figure 7c shows another approach that leaves out the contour and uses a different pattern. While this approach respects the constraints stated above, it leads to less sturdier results.

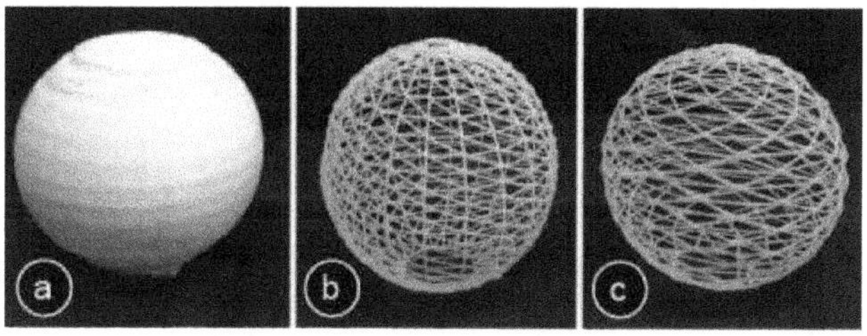

Figure 7: (a) Solid sphere. (b,c) Different ways of printing the sphere as a wireframe.

EXTENDING WIREPRINT

In this section, we present extensions to our basic approach that allow us to handle additional scenarios.

Additional detail by mixing in layer-wise printing

WirePrint also allows designers to preview detailed parts using layer-wise printing while the rest is printed as a wireframe. For instance, in the case of the bunny head shown in Figure 8, the designer wants to preview the details of the face, such as the eyes and the nose, in the context of the face. This hybrid mix of both techniques allows for quick iteration while ensuring enough detail in those regions where it is required. To mark a region for layer-wise printing, the user simply uses the *fill-brush* in the WirePrint software and brushes the sections of the zigzag pattern that should be printed in additional detail.

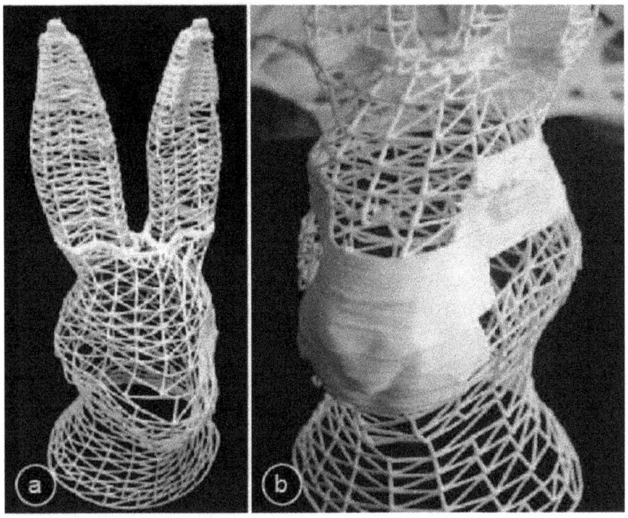

Figure 8: Mixing in layer-wise printing: (a) after checking the shape of the bunny head, the designer decides to (b) print additional detail in the next iteration.

As shown in Figure 9, WirePrint prints hybrid models slice-by-slice. (a) It starts each slice by printing the contour, which is shared between the traditionally printed part and the wireframe printed part. It then prints the wireframe zigzag, while it is still able to place the slanted starting point. It finally prints the layer-wise printing part. (b) Afterwards, WirePrint continues with the procedure on the next slice.

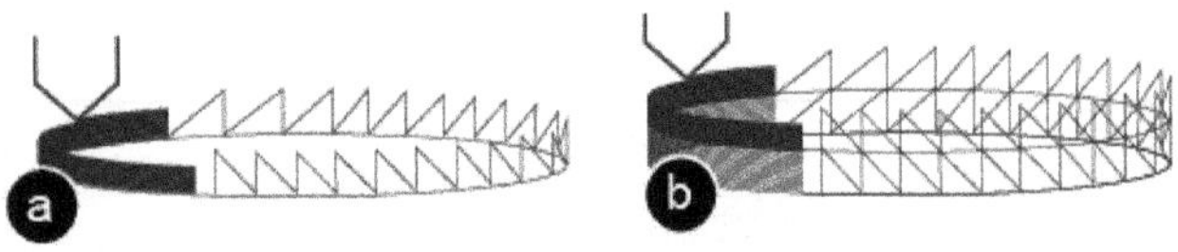

Figure 9: Order of printing edges for hybrid printing when wireframe and traditional printing are mixed.

Objects with filled surfaces

Some 3D models, including the bottle mentioned in the previous section, require closed surfaces. To close the surface, we dip the wireframe print into glue (see Figure 10). An added advantage of this approach is that it strengthens the model.

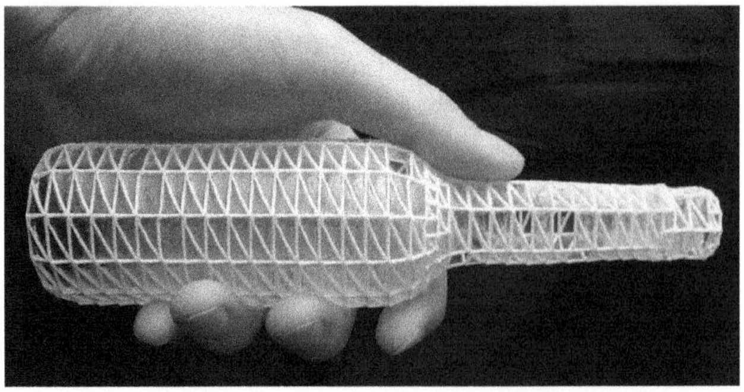

Figure 10: Filling surfaces, here the walls of the bottle, by dipping the wireframe into glue (e.g. Mod Podge).

CONTRIBUTION, BENEFITS, AND LIMITATIONS

In this paper, we make three contributions. (1) We propose 3D printing *wireframe representations* of 3D models as an approach to faster iteration in the early stages of 3D design. (2) To maximize the speed-up, we print edges directly into 3D space, i.e., we instruct 3D printers to extrude filament not layer-by-layer, but along actual strokes in 3-space. This approach allows us to achieve speed-ups of up to a factor of 10 compared to traditional layer-wise 3D printing (factors range from 2.5-10 depending on the model geometry).

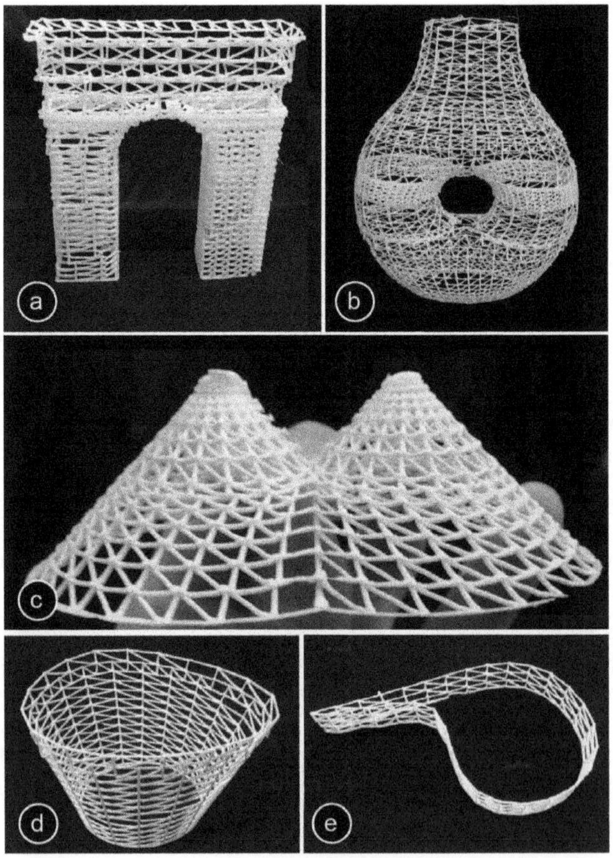

Figure 11: A selection of objects we have 3D printed using WirePrint.

Given that only a fraction of material is extruded, our approach is also substantially cheaper, making it even more affordable for designers to iterate. (3) To make our approach applicable to a wide range of users, we demonstrate how to create wireframe previews with existing FDM 3D printers—users only need to install the WirePrint software.

On the flipside, our approach is less suitable for the later stages of design, i.e., stages where users want to test the actual physical strength of their design, when details and textures matter, or if objects have to perform mechanical functions (e.g., a screw).

In addition, WirePrint is limited to model geometries that take the print head constraints into account (see section *How WirePrint works).*

WirePrint is especially designed to speed up *fused deposition modeling* (FDM) 3D printing (e.g. *PrintrBot, Kossel mini, MakerBot).* It does not speed up 3D printers that print layers as raster images (e.g. Polyjet, ZCorp) and only small speed ups might be achieved on selective laser sintering or stereo lithography approaches.

THE MECHANICAL ASPECTS BEHIND WIREPRINT

The main objective of the mechanical design behind WirePrint is to maximize the stability of the produced objects while minimizing printing time.

Delta Printer

All of the wireframe models shown in this paper were printed on *Kossel mini* 3D printer (Figure 12), i.e., a small volume printer that actuates the print head using six vertically actuated arms (a so-called *delta* design).

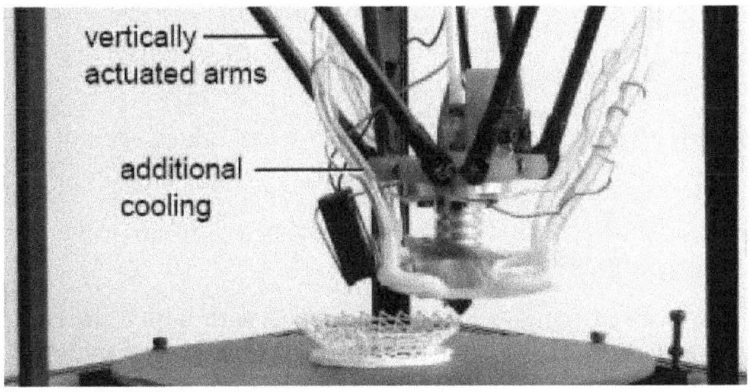

Figure 12: We use a Kossel mini delta printer. For additional speed we improved the fan cooling system.

WirePrint is particularly fast on the delta design, because delta printers allow the print head to move up and down quickly. 3D printers following the more traditional Cartesian design tend to be slower along the vertical axis since layer-wise printing does not require high speeds in this direction. However, since the axis speed in the z-direction is simply a design decision of the manufacturers, WirePrint can be made equally fast on Cartesian printers with the proper hardware design, i.e. by changing both the movement/turn ratio and the stepper motor speed in the z-direction.

Optimizing the filament for fast wireframe printing

Since WirePrint requires frequent transitions between compliant and solid, we found materials that have a quick transition time to work best. From the two currently most common 3D printing materials PLA and ABS, the latter one works best. The reason is that ABS has a smaller temperature range, in which it changes its viscosity from compliant to solid (230–250° C) than PLA (180–250° C).

Extrusion thickness

A larger opening in the extrusion nozzle leads to thicker and thus sturdier edges and thus to sturdier objects. On the flipside, thicker edges require more time to cool down, which slows down the printing process. For our purposes, we found a 0.7mm extrusion nozzle to lead to the best results, i.e. sturdy and fast to print.

Cooling

We attached two air jets that are controlled by a solenoid valve to our print head (Figure 12). WirePrint controls the airflow by opening and closing the valve using g-code (command M42). The additional cooling causes the filament to solidify faster after extrusion, which allows WirePrint to move on even faster. In cases where WirePrint needs the filament to stick to another part of the model, it turns the cooling off. In cases where no additional cooling can be added to the 3D printer, WirePrint can either make use of the weaker built-in fan or can add an additional pause to wait for material to solidify.

Support structures

One interesting aspect of our technique is that WirePrint requires less support material than regular layer-wise 3D printing because it can print overhangs of up to 90°. An example of a small 90° overhang can be seen in Figure 1c at the bottom part of the model (the maximum length we tested was 6.5cm length). WirePrint can print these overhangs because the string of extruded material is put under tension until it is completely sturdy.

Yet other geometry, such as a human figure extending the arms downwards, can only be printed with support. As in the layer-wise FDM approach, the need of support will reduce the overall print speed. However, one can think of using WirePrint to print support structures—again saving time compared to the currently existing approach.

IMPLEMENTATION

To help readers replicate our results, we use the following two sections to explain the details of our software implementation, as well as the mechanical aspects behind our approach.

The WirePrint system

Our system WirePrint loads 3D models in STL format and generates custom g-code (i.e., the instruction language used by 3D printers). The user can then export the g-code and load it into the standard 3D printing software for printing (we use Repetier Host [16]). The custom g-code moves the print head along the desired path and controls how much material is extruded at which points.

WirePrint is written in *CoffeeScript* and uses the *constructive solid geometry* library for its geometry operations.

#1 Slicing the model

After loading the 3D model, WirePrint slices the model into a set of slices. The locations of the slices is determined by (1) important features on the model geometry, and (2) the minimum and maximum height of the zigzag between two subsequent slices (we use a 0.7mm extrusion nozzle, which leads to 1.4mm minimal height, and our print head is 6mm high which leads to 6mm maximum height). To generate a slice, WirePrint cuts the 3D model against a horizontal slice (width and length of the object's bounding box) at a specific height using a Boolean intersect operation.

#2 Extracting the contour of a slice

From each slice, WirePrint extracts the top contour by converting it to a high-resolution bitmap and then applying OpenCV's findContour algorithm. If there are multiple contours on one slice, OpenCV's findContour algorithm also returns their relationship to each other, i.e. whether they are located next to each other or contained in each other. We use this information to determine the printing order.

#3 Generating the zigzag pattern

When generating the zigzag pattern, WirePrint maximizes the object's physical stability by aligning all vertical lines across slices. Simply using the points from the slice below does not work, because subsequent slices might: (1) have a different contour length, which can lead to insufficient space between two subsequent points (print head collision), and (2) slices might have different heights, which can lead to invalid printing angles. We therefore use a mixed approach: First we calculate the optimal even spacing of points for each contour. Then we calculate the minimum distance from a point on the bottom slice to the top slice. We then use the average of both, which leads to good stability and a comparably homogeneous spacing. In the case that two vertical lines are still too close to each other, we ignore one of them.

#4 Compensating for mechanical aspects

After generating the wireframe according to the model geometry, WirePrint applies all geometrical modifications that are required due to the mechanical properties of filament and print head e.g. removing the last diagonal edge of the zigzag from the list of edges to avoid print head collision.

#5 Exporting g-code

In the last step, WirePrint converts the geometry information into g-code. For this, it traverses the list of edges (all contours and zigzag patterns) to export them in the right order for printing. It uses the start and end point coordinates of each edge to generate the movement commands for the print head and the length of the edge to determine how much extrusion is required (e.g. G1 X10 Y 10 Z10 E5 means: move to those coordinates and extrude 5 units of filament on the way). Our g-code exporter also generates the commands for turning the fan on and off to properly cool the wireframe edges. The g-code exporter writes these g-code commands into a .gcode file that the user can then execute on the 3D printer.

#6 Detecting geometry splits in the geometry

In cases where a slice has a single contour and its subsequent slice has two (and vice versa), we print them on top of each other without the intermediate zigzag pattern. We use this particular approach to ensure that the zigzag of each new slice has filament printed underneath it.

#7 Combining with layer-wise printing

For mixing in layer-wise 3D printing, WirePrint generates additional slices between two subsequent wireframe slices. The number of additional slices depends on the printing resolution (e.g. if two wireframe slices are 3.5mm apart and the extrusion nozzle is 0.7mm, WirePrint will generate 3.5mm/0.7mm = 5 additional layers).

After generating the slices and extracting their contours, WirePrint analyzes which part has been selected for layer-wise printing. It then cuts the contours at the start and end point of the selected part. The remaining part is filled with the zigzag pattern.

EXPERIMENTATION TO OPTIMIZE PRINTING SPEED

To create accurate and sturdy wireframes, WirePrint needs to take into account the edge deformation that appears when filament is not yet solidified (see Figure 13).

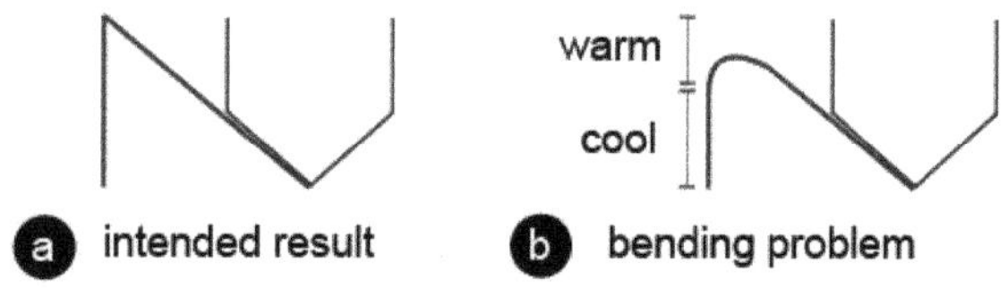

Figure 13: Deformation problem when edges are not yet solidified.

We identified three potential approaches to improve the quality of a WirePrint:

1. WirePrint reduces the overall speed with which the print head moves, allowing the filament to solidify as it's being printed;
2. WirePrint moves the print head quickly, but pauses at the end of each vertical edge to let the edge solidify;
3. WirePrint prints full speed, but anticipates the deformation by extending the vertical movement of the print head (see Figure 14).

Through experimentation, we discovered that the fastest way to print is to add a delay at the end of each floating edge. Although a pause at the end of each vertical edge initially seemed unattractive, it lead to the most accurate results because the edges solidify under tension. Anticipating the deformation during printing was attractive at first, but the extra traveling time of the print head quickly undermined the benefit of a faster printing speed, and in general the results where less appealing.

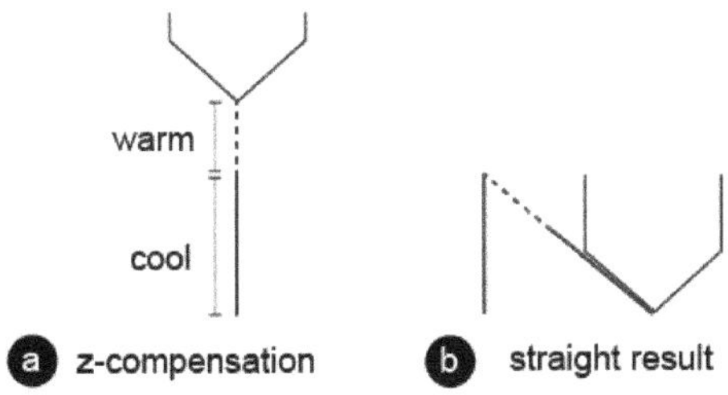

Figure 14: Approach #3: compensating for material transition time.

To better understand the interactions between speed and delay, we performed a series of test prints with a sphere (radius=3.9cm), which are shown in Figure 15. During our tests, we found that the best solution is to move with the maximum extrusion speed of the printer (30mm/s) combined with a 1s pause at the end of each vertical line.

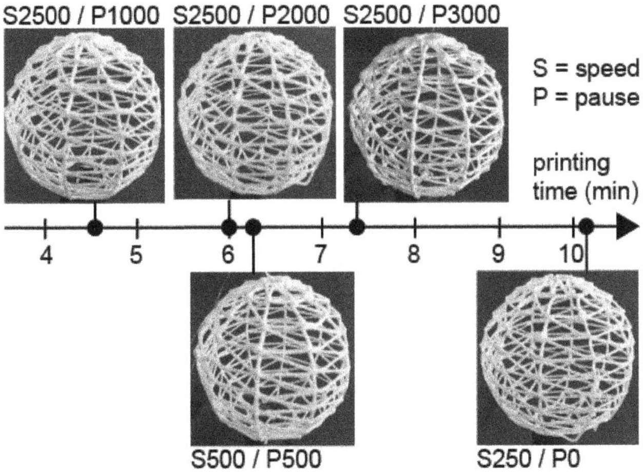

Figure 15: Print head speed/pause trade-off.

VALIDATION

The main strength of WirePrint is that it produces a substantial speed-up of up to a factor of 10. To validate that this speed-up results from extruding filament into 3D space, we also implemented wireframe printing based on traditional layer-wise 3D printing as a control condition.

We implemented layer-wise wireframe printing as follows: (1) print only the edges of a model, and (2) minimize the use of support material, as this adds to the printing volume (support material is required for all overhangs larger than 45 degree). We wrote a piece of software that converts a 3D model into a wireframe mesh and that adds additional 45 degree edges as support structures where needed. For instance, a cube processed with our software has support edges for the horizontal edges at the top (see Figure 16b).

We compared the three conditions using the simple example of a 28mm cube. Figure 16 shows the printing times for (a) traditional layer-wise 3D printing (solid with 10% infill), (b) traditional layer-wise 3D printing (wireframe, edges have 10% infill), and (c) WirePrint.

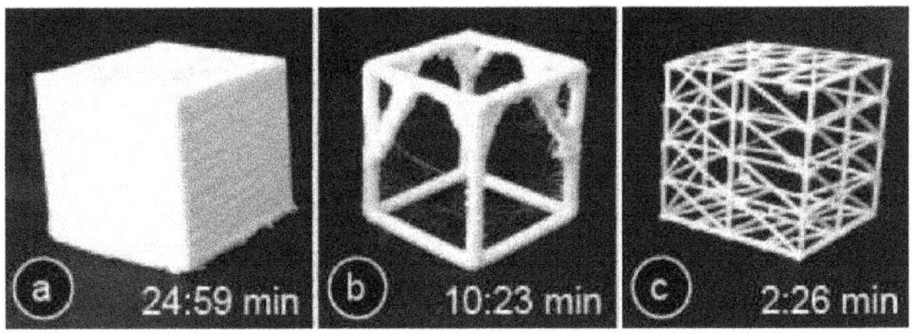

Figure 16: Printing times: (a) layer-wise 3D printing with 10% infill, (b) layer-wise 3D printing of a wireframe (reduced volume, 10% infill), (c) WirePrint.

Although printing a wireframe layer-wise substantially reduces the volume, there is only modest improvement in printing time (factor 2x, 24:59 minutes for layer-wise solid printing vs. 10:23 minutes for layer-wise wireframe printing). The layer-wise printed wireframe was also substantially slower than the model generated by WirePrint (10:23 minutes for layer-wise printing vs. 2:26 minutes for WirePrint).

Surprisingly, the layer-wise printed wireframe model only provided a 2x speed up compared to the regular printed model with faces and more infill material. We found that the main reason for this is that the path for the print head remains almost the same. Figure 17 illustrates this: Since the material is printed layer-wise, the print head still has to traverse the entire cube outline as it moves from corner to corner, bottom-up.

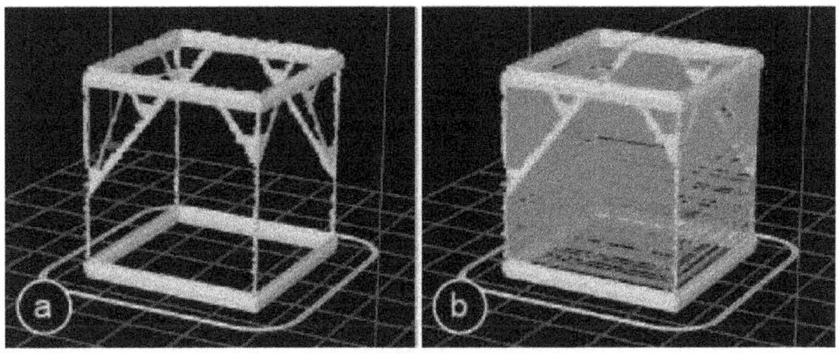

Figure 17: The print path simulation (gray lines) shows that for layer-wise printing, the print head has to move along the entire cube outline.

Our quick validation shows that the performance benefits of WirePrint indeed result from implementing the ability to extrude strokes in 3D space, rather than printing them layer-wise.

CONCLUSION

In this paper, we proposed a novel approach to 3D prototyping, i.e. to print wireframe representations instead of a filled model and to extrude filament directly into 3D space instead of printing layer-wise. Our validation shows that in combination, these two approaches indeed lead to a substantial speed up of up to a factor of 10 and thus allow designers to iterate more often.

For future work, we plan to explore how fast 3D printing allows for novel types of interfaces that close the feedback loop between digital editing and physical fabrication.

ACKNOWLEDGEMENTS

This work was made possible in part by a gift from Microsoft Research. We would like to thank Steve Marshner for suggesting the simplified layer setting shown Figure 7c. We thank Johannes Frohnhofen, Kai-Adrian Rollmann, Dustin Beyer, Tobias Mohr, and Sven Koehler for their help.

REFERENCES

1. 3Doodler, http://the3doodler.com/
2. Buxton, B. *Sketching User Experiences: Getting the Design Right and the Right Design.* Morgan Kaufman, 2007.
3. Delta Printer, Kossel Mini Kit, blomker.com
4. Follmer, S., Carr, D., Lovell, E., Hiroshi, I. CopyCAD: remixing physical objects with copy and paste from the real world. *Adjunct Proceedings UIST '10,* 381-382.
5. Gershenfeld, N. *Fab:* The Coming Revolution on Your Desktop--From Personal Computers to Personal Fabrication. *Basic Books,* '07.
6. Gramazio, F., Kohler, M., Langenberg, S. Fabricate: Negotiating Design and Making. *gta Verlag,* '14.
7. Hansen, C. J., et al. High-Throughput Printing via Microvascular Multinozzle Arrays. *Advanced Materials'12.*
8. Hiller, J., Lipson, H. Methods of Parallel Voxel Manipulation for 3D Digital Printing. *Proc. Solid Freeform Fabrication Symposium'07,* 200-211.
9. Hudson, S. Printing Teddy Bears: A Technique for 3D Printing of Soft Interactive Objects. *Proc. CHI'14*, 459-468.
10. Ishiguro, Y., Poupyrev, I. 3D Printed Interactive Speakers. *Proc. CHI'14,* 1733-1742.
11. Lia. Filament Sculptures. 2014. http://www.liaworks.com/theprojects/filament-sculptures/
12. Mataerial, http://www.mataerial.com/
13. Mueller, S., Lopes, P., Baudisch, P. Interactive Construction: Interactive Fabrication of Functional Mechanical Devices. *Proc. UIST '12,* 599-606.
14. Mueller, S., Kruck, B., Baudisch, P. LaserOrigami: Laser-Cutting 3D Objects. *Proc. CHI'13*, 2585-2592.
15. Mueller, S., Mohr, T., Guenther, K., Frohnhofen, J. faBrickation: Fast 3D printing of Functional Objects by Integrating Construction Kit Building Blocks. *Proc. CHI'14,* 3827-3834.
16. Repetier Host, http://www.repetier.com/
17. Rivers, A., Moyer, I.E., Durand, F. Position-correcting tools for 2D digital fabrication. *Proc. SIGGRAPH'12 (TOG),* Vol 31, Issue 4, No. 88.
18. Savage, V., Chang, C., Hartmann, B. Sauron: Embedded Single-Camera Sensing of Printed Physical User Interfaces. *Proc. UIST'13*, 447-456.
19. Schwartzburg, Y., Pauly, M. Fabrication-aware Design with Intersecting Planar Pieces. *Proc. Eurographics'13,* Vol.32, No.2.
20. Song, H., Guimbretière, F., Lipson, H., Hu, C. ModelCraft: Capturing Freehand Annotations and Edits on Physical 3D Models. *Proc. UIST '06*, 13-22.
21. Srinivasan, V., Ozener, O., Mandal, E., Akleman, E. Solidfying Frames For Architecture. *CAAD FUTURES '05.*
22. Wang, W., Wang, T. Y., Yang, Z., Liu, L., Tong, X., Tong, W., Deng, J., Chen, F., Lia, X. Cost-effective printing of 3D objects with skin-frame structures. *ACM Trans. Graph.* 32, 6, Article 177, '13.
23. Willis, K.D.D., Brockmeyer, E., Hudson, S.E., Poupyrev, I. Printed Optics: 3D Printing of Embedded Optical Elements for Interactive Devices. *Proc. UIST '12,* 589-598.
24. Willis, K.D.D., Xu, C., Wu, J.K., Levin, G., Gross, M.D. Interactive fabrication: new interfaces for digital fabrication. *Proc. TEI '11*, 69-72.
25. Zoran, A., Paradiso, J.A. FreeD: a freehand digital sculpting tool. *Proc. CHI'13,* 2613-2616.

PrintScreen: Fabricating Highly Customizable Thin-film Touch-Displays

Simon Olberding, Michael Wessely, Jürgen Steimle

Max Planck Institute for Informatics and Saarland University
Campus E1.7, 66123 Saarbrücken, Germany
{solberdi, mwessely, jsteimle}@mpi-inf.mpg.de

Figure 1. PrintScreen contributes a digital fabrication approach to enable non-experts to print custom flexible displays. They can be fully folded or rolled and enable manifold applications in ubiquitous, mobile and wearable computing.

ABSTRACT

PrintScreen is an enabling technology for digital fabrication of customized flexible displays using thin-film electroluminescence (TFEL). It enables inexpensive and rapid fabrication of highly customized displays in low volume, in a simple lab environment, print shop or even at home. We show how to print ultra-thin (120 μm) segmented and passive matrix displays in greyscale or multi-color on a variety of deformable and rigid substrate materials, including PET film, office paper, leather, metal, stone, and wood. The displays can have custom, unconventional 2D shapes and can be bent, rolled and folded to create 3D shapes. We contribute a systematic overview of graphical display primitives for customized displays and show how to integrate them with static print and printed electronics. Furthermore, we contribute a sensing framework, which leverages the display itself for touch sensing. To demonstrate the wide applicability of PrintScreen, we present application examples from ubiquitous, mobile and wearable computing.

Author Keywords

Flexible display; Thin-film display; TFEL; Electroluminescence; Printed electronics; Digital fabrication; Rapid prototyping; Touch input; Ubiquitous Computing.

UIST '14, October 05 - 08 2014, Honolulu, HI, USA

ACM 978-1-4503-3069-5/14/10...$15.00.
http://dx.doi.org/10.1145/2642918.2647413

INTRODUCTION

Printed electronics is becoming a powerful and affordable enabling technology for fabricating functional devices and HCI prototypes that have very thin and deformable form factors. For many years already, printing has been a powerful means allowing end-users to produce customized *static* print products rapidly, inexpensively and in high quality. Recent work has contributed methods for easily printing custom *interactive* components on thin and flexible substrates. While sensing of user *input* has been successfully demonstrated [7, 13], it has not been possible so far to print customized flexible *displays* rapidly and inexpensively. Printing flexible displays, such as OLEDs or Electronic Paper, required a high-end print lab, complex machinery and expert skills, making it prohibitive to fabricate custom displays in low volume.

We present PrintScreen, a versatile platform that enables non-expert users to design and fabricate highly customized flexible interactive displays. The displays are technically based on thin-film electroluminescence (TFEL).

The platform proposes a novel perspective on displays: instead of buying an off-the-shelf display, the designer can create a custom digital design, which meets the specific demands of the application, and then simply print the display. Printing customized flexible displays empowers makers and designers to create customized interactive print products, digital signage, smart objects, personalized computing devices and crafts with embedded display. For HCI researchers and practitioners, this is a powerful enabling technology for mobile, wearable and ubiquitous computing interfaces. It enables rapid and high-fidelity prototyping of functional HCI devices with embedded displays of highly custom shapes, on deformable and on unconventional materials.

Based on a holistic five-dimensional view on customized displays, we present the following main contributions:

1) We present *two methods for non-expert printing* of customized thin-film displays, using either screen printing or conductive inkjet printing. The approach is rapid, inexpensive, and does not require much hardware nor technical knowledge. Despite the restrictions stemming from manual fabrication, the display features a high luminance, is only 120 µm thick, bendable, fully rollable, and even foldable at arbitrary positions. It can contain custom-defined high-resolution segments (resolution of contours comparable to 250 dpi laser print) and/or a low-resolution passive matrix (up to 30 pixels per inch). Each segment or pixel can have a color defined at design-time from a wide palette of possible colors. At run-time, it has adjustable brightness intensity. We show that the display can be printed on a *large variety of substrates*, such as paper, plastic, leather or wood, making it ideal for mobile, embedded and wearable applications. PrintScreen can be used to fabricate displays of *irregular and unconventional shapes,* including 2D shapes, folded 3D shapes and adaptable shapes.

2) We propose a digital design approach for displays, which is based on conventional 2D vector graphics. We contribute the first systematic overview of *display primitives* for user-printed displays, which act as basic building blocks in the graphical design. Moreover we show how to integrate printed display primitives with static printed artwork and with printed electronics.

3) We contribute a *sensing framework*, which allows using the printed TFEL display itself for a variety of input sensing. We demonstrate this principle for integrated touch sensing.

To demonstrate how PrintScreen can be used and to show its wide applicability, we present five *example applications* from ubiquitous, mobile and wearable computing. Results from a technical evaluation show that the displays are bright and very robust to bending and folding. We conclude by discussing benefits and limitations of PrintScreen.

RELATED WORK

Digital Fabrication of Electronics

An emerging body of related work is demonstrating the potential of printed electronics for applications in Human-Computer Interaction. Midas [30] introduced a platform for fabricating custom circuits to sense touch input, based on vinyl cutting. Kawahara et al. [13, 14] introduced conductive inkjet printing with an off-the-shelf printer as an instant means for printing customized sensors and antennae. This approach was also used for flexible multi-touch sensor sheets [7, 14]. Pyzoflex [27] leverages printed piezoelectric elements to capture pressure and temperature on a thin sheet. Poupyrev et al. [12] have shown how printed conductors can capture user-generated energy. This body of previous work did not address visual output.

Thin-film Display Technologies

Organic light emitting diodes (OLEDs) and electrophoretic displays (electronic paper) can be printed on flexible substrates. Both technologies enable high-resolution displays, in addition OLED displays support a wide color spectrum. However, they are still complicated to produce. For instance, an OLED display typically requires six layers [15]; moreover it is very sensitive to oxygen during fabrication and requires proper permanent sealing during use. Therefore, a high-end print lab environment is required. While rollable and fully foldable OLED and electronic paper displays have been demonstrated as prototypes, they are not commercially available yet.

Thermochromic [19] and electrochromic [3] displays are less complicated to manufacture. However, they have very long switching intervals and precise control of thermochromic displays is challenging, as the ink is influenced by the ambient temperature.

Electroluminescent (EL) displays are very robust, have fast switching times and a long lifetime of up to 50,000 hours [6]. Therefore the technology is often used for lighting applications [4, 21]. Inspired by [4, 35], we propose electroluminescence for custom-printed displays. The technology, a simple form of OLED, is based on phosphoric inks, which act as luminescent material. The print process requires only 4 layers [15]. Recent chemical advancement allow for inks that can be easily processed and need low curing temperatures. EL displays require higher AC voltages but very little current to operate. Previous work proposed creating simple EL displays by cutting out segments from an EL film [2]; in contrast, our approach relies on high-resolution printing and therefore enables fabrication of a much wider spectrum of displays.

A substantially different approach is based on 3D printed optics [36]. Printed light pipes transmit light from a conventional rigid display to custom points on the surface of a 3D printed object. This allows for easily designing 3D shaped displays of custom shapes, supporting full color and a high resolution. However, designed for 3D printing the approach is not compatible with thin-film form factors, since the printed optical elements need some volume.

Applications of Deformable and Custom-shaped Displays

A body of work demonstrates the need for objects that are augmented with interactive displays of different size and shape [10, 16, 23, 24, 34, 37], resolution [9, 24] and substrate [24]. One stream of research proposes deformable displays of various shapes and sizes for use in mobile and wearable contexts [5, 17, 20, 25, 31, 33, 37, 29]. Another stream investigated projection-augmented paper prints [16, 18, 34], even in large poster sizes [36]. Work on interactive paper origami proposes manually attached LEDs as active output on folded paper objects [24]. Prototypes from previous work use projection, tiled rigid displays or rectangular flexible displays on plastic substrates. The PrintScreen plat-

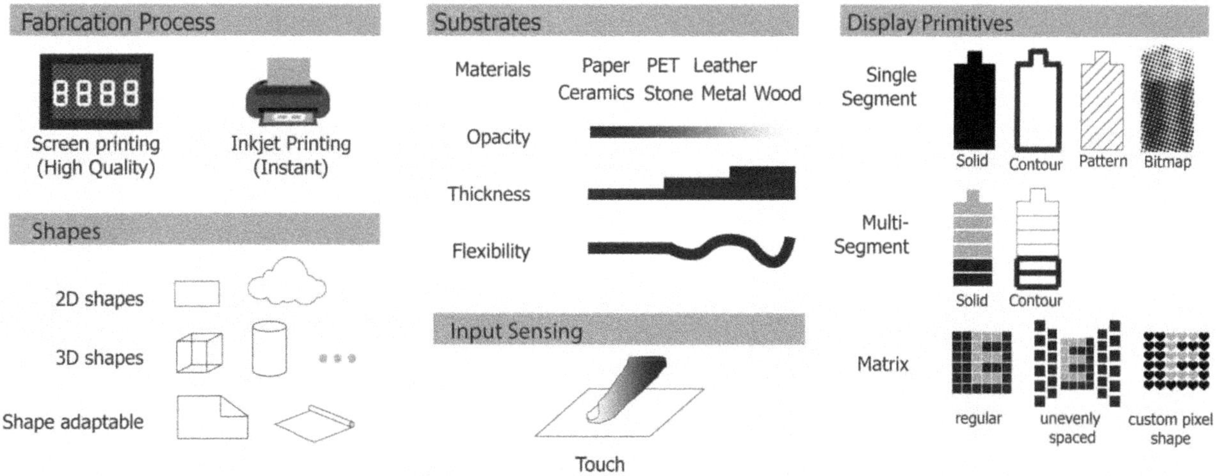

Figure 2. Five-dimensional design space for digital fabrication of customized displays.

form opens up substantially more degrees of freedom in designing custom displays for HCI prototypes.

DESIGN SPACE OF CUSTOMIZED DISPLAYS

Custom-made displays open up considerably more degrees of freedom for the design than off-the-shelf displays. We identified five key dimensions for digital fabrication of customized displays, which systematize the design options. This section provides an overview of these dimensions, which form the foundation of the PrintScreen platform. The design space is illustrated in Fig. 2.

Fabrication Process: How to print

We propose a digital fabrication approach for production of customized displays. The designer generates a digital model of the display and then prints this model. Ideally, printing is as instant and easy as sending a document to an office printer. This would enable prototyping with rapid and many design iterations. We introduce an instant fabrication process based on conductive inkjet printing, which comes close to this ease of fabrication. Moreover, we propose a second fabrication approach, which requires screen-printing on a beginner's level. While it takes longer to fabricate a display, it is of higher quality and supports the full set of substrate materials, display primitives and sensing modes presented in this paper.

Substrate Materials: On what to print

Customized displays may be printed on various materials that vary in thickness, flexibility, texture and opacity. PrintScreen supports many substrate materials, including highly deformable and foldable office paper, transparent or nontransparent PET film, leather, wood, ceramics, stone (marble) and metal (steel). The display adds only 110 µm of thickness to the base substrate.

Display Primitives: What to print

Customized displays offer a large variety of design options regarding the display contents, far more than the regular matrix which one would intuitively think of. If contents are known at design time, segmented and multi-segmented displays are a compelling option. They feature very sharp contours and homogeneous fill, even if printed in large sizes, while nevertheless being easy to control. In addition, we introduce segments that feature an arbitrary bitmap pattern which is defined at design-time. For very dynamic applications, matrix displays are the preferred option. PrintScreen allows for printing conventional matrices in a custom resolution, but adds options for customization by offering unevenly spaced matrices and pixels in custom shapes.

Display Shapes: What form factors are possible

A key question for any application is the size and shape of the display. With off-the-shelf displays, the designer has relatively little choice. Non-rectangular outlines, extreme aspect ratios, curved or 3D shapes are typically not available. However, such non-standard shapes are important to make an embedded display fit within an object or the physical environment. PrintScreen offers the designer a much higher degree of design flexibility. It supports custom 2D outlines; moreover it enables custom 3D shapes, which are created by bending and folding. Moreover, displays can be made shape-adaptable and resizable, using bending, folding or rolling, but are not stretchable.

Integrated Input Sensing: How to interact

User input is a key property of interactive display surfaces. We contribute a generic platform for sensing of user input, which is directly integrated with the printed display. As examples we demonstrate touch input.

In the following main part of the paper, we will discuss each of these dimensions.

FABRICATION PROCESS

We contribute two approaches to allow non-experts to fabricate customized thin-film electroluminescent displays: a high-quality and an instant process. Both are easy to learn and perform for non-experts and require only off-the-shelf tools and consumables.

Printed Electroluminescent Displays

Thin-film electroluminescent displays actively emit light. A segment of a TFEL display consists of two overlaid electrodes, which act as a capacitor. Inside the capacitor is a

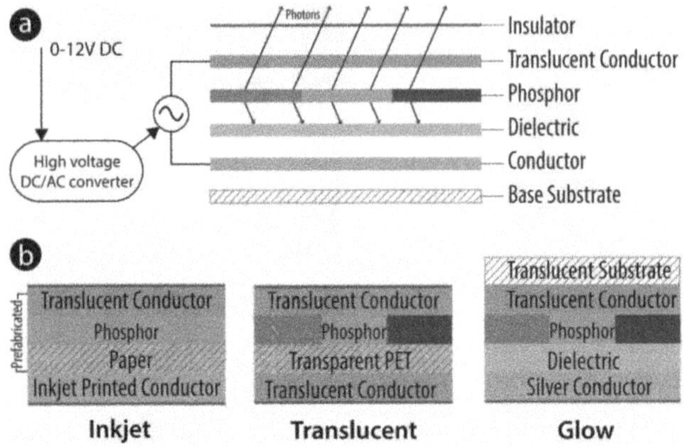

Figure 3. a) Composition of the printed layers of an electroluminescent display: Silver Conductor (C2131014D3, 100mΩ/sq), a barium titanate based dielectric (D2070209P6), phosphor (e.g. C2101125P4) and a PEDOT based translucent conductor (D2070209P6, 500-700 Ω/sq). b) Variations of the standard structure to create translucent displays, display glowing through materials or inkjet-printable displays.

layer made of phosphor and a dielectric layer. If a high voltage, low current AC signal is applied, the phosphor emits photons (see Fig. 3 a). TFEL displays are used in many commercial products, e.g., as backlight for car dashboards.

Digital Design

The designer of the display first creates a digital design in a standard 2D vector graphics editor, such as Adobe Illustrator. Each segment or pixel is created as if it was ordinary visual artwork, using the application's tools for creating lines, polygons, text, fills, etc. Hence, designing an interactive display is pretty much comparable to designing conventional 2D graphics.

For screen printing, the designer generates four adjacent identical copies of the design – one for each print layer (see Fig 3). If segments and pixels shall be printed in more than one color, one more layer is added for each additional color. Laying out the copies adjacently allows to create one single print mask that contains all print layers, making screen printing cheaper and faster. For inkjet printing, only one copy is required. Next, the designer lays out the wires that are required for controlling the segments. The minimum width is 300 µm. On the first copy (bottom electrode), each segment is connected with an individual input pin. For screen printing, all segments on the fourth copy (top electrode) are connected to a shared ground pin. Alternatively a grid of segments or pixels can be wired as a matrix.

Screen Printing for High Quality

For screen printing, we used off-the-shelf equipment for hobbyists (approx. 200 €). We follow a standard multi-layer screen-printing process [22], which is commonly used for printing on paper or on fabrics and can be easily learned by non-experts. Each layer of the display stack is printed successively, from bottom to top. Details on the inks, available

Figure 4. Dual sided print on office paper

colors, mesh density of the screen and the instructions of use can be found in [8]. For multi-color displays, two or more layers of differently-colored phosphor are printed. Finally, the top layer is insulated with acrylic insulating spray (dielectric strength 80kV/mm). Overall, the display adds 110 µm to the substrate. We successfully printed a display on a 10 µm thick PET film (Gwent, F2111117D1), resulting in 120 µm as the minimal thickness of the final printed display. To create a dual-sided display (see Fig. 4), the same process can be repeated on the reverse side of the substrate.

Segments can be printed in a resolution of up to 30 lines per inch (lpi). As a rule of thumb, this corresponds approximately to 60 pixels per inch (ppi). For comparison, a conventional office laser printer has between 35 ppi (300 dpi) and 75 ppi (600 dpi). We use printed guidelines to improve inter-layer alignment. However, the manual printing process introduces an offset between individual layers. We analyzed 10 display samples and measured the maximum offset between individual layers. We found the designer can ensure the full segment be functional by enlarging the top and bottom electrodes as well as the dielectric by 300 µm to each side.

Printing of the application examples presented in this paper took one person between two and four hours. The time depends not on the complexity of the display contents, but on the display size and the number of different colors. The cost

Figure 5. Instant inkjet printing. A printed electrode (left, upper right) is illuminated (lower right).

of consumables for printing a completely covered A4-sized display is approx. 2 € for the screen mesh and 19 € for the inks. Many applications require segments only on some locations on the substrate, which can further reduce cost quite considerably.

Conductive Inkjet Printing for Instant Fabrication

The second fabrication process ensures instant fabrication, which is important for design iterations in rapid prototyping. No screen print equipment is required. However, it offers fewer design options.

The designer uses a prefabricated display film (Fig. 3b and Fig. 5). This film contains all printed layers except the bottom electrode. It consists of a sheet of coated paper (Mitsubishi NB-WF-3GF100), which acts as substrate and dielectric. On top of it, a fully filled layer of phosphor (in one color) and a fully filled layer of transparent conductor is printed. This film can be fabricated in bulk using screen printing, as describe above; in the future a paper manufacturer could make it commercially available for purchase.

The designer uses conductive inkjet printing [14] to print the digital design (aka. the bottom electrode layer) on the reverse side of the prefabricated display film. We use an off-the-shelf, consumer-grade inkjet printer (Canon IP-100) with Mitsubishi NBSIJ-MU10 silver ink. Finally, to seal the bottom electrodes, insulating spray is applied, or a thin layer of dielectric (e.g. office paper) is glued or laminated onto the reverse side of the display.

In the prefabricated film, the top electrode, phosphor and dielectric cover the entire surface. This restricts what types of display can be realized. In particular, the display is unicolored. Only segments, but no matrix can be designed. Segments always have a solid fill, and wires used for tethering the electrodes with the controller light up on the display. Touch sensing is restricted to a single touch contact on the entire display. However, contours and surface patterns can have a high resolution, which is defined by the resolution of the inkjet printer (600 dpi).

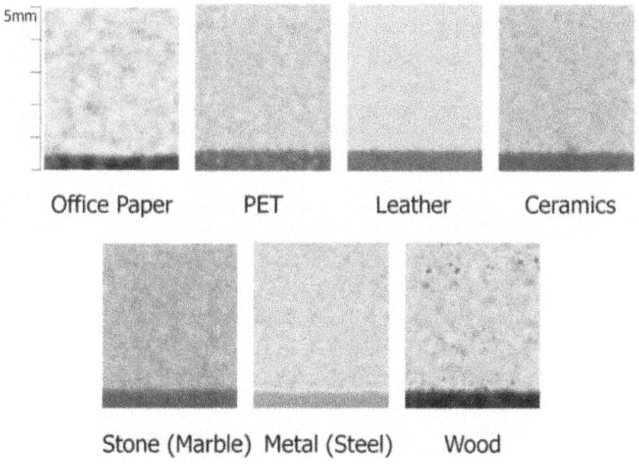

Figure 6. Enlarged view of an illuminated segment and its contour, printed on various substrates.

Controller

To light up a display segment, the controller applies a high-voltage, low current AC signal between the upper and lower electrodes. The luminance of a display segment or pixel is controlled using pulse-width modulation, a standard method for controlling the luminance of LEDs.

For mobile applications, our prototypical controller uses a small driver IC (Model Durel D356B, sine wave, 220 Vpp, 230Hz to 390Hz). This driver IC generates the high-voltage AC signal from a 1.0-7.0V DC power source. If a higher luminance is required, a stronger 0-12.0V driver IC with a slightly bigger footprint can be used (Model Sparkfun DC12V10M, sine wave, 220Vpp, 800Hz to 3.5KHz). A microcontroller (ATmega2560) triggers optocouplers (MOC3063) for multiplexing the high-voltage signal between display pins.

The TFEL-specific ghosting effect in passive matrix displays can be significantly reduced by using a slightly modified controller design [11], thus further increasing the contrast of the matrix. To interface the display with the controller, we solder copper wires onto printed pin areas. For a larger number of pins, a flat-ribbon cable and 3M Electrically Conductive Adhesive Transfer Tape 9703 can be used.

The number of output pins of the internal microcontroller restricts our controller to up to 40 separate segments or a 20x20 matrix with passive matrix time-division multiplexing. However, the number of segments or pixels can be substantially increased by using multiplexers to increase the number of output pins of the microcontroller and additional optocouplers to switch high voltages. To keep the size of the controller (currently 5x7cm) small, small optocouplers (TLP266J) can be used.

Despite high voltages, the approach is safe and energy efficient, and even usable for fully mobile applications, because the current is very low and the TFEL display is very energy efficient (2.6 mW/cm^2 in highest luminance, using DC12V10M). The inkjet method uses a thicker dielectric; therefore power consumption increases to 38 mW/cm^2.

SUBSTRATE MATERIALS

For applications in ubiquitous, embedded and wearable interaction, it is of high importance that the display can be integrated with a variety of materials. Our screen printing approach allows for printing the display right onto the substrate material, integrating it fully with the object and making additional carrier materials and lamination obsolete.

We successfully printed displays on a wide variety of materials, including highly flexible, translucent and transparent materials (see. Fig. 6). Among them was office paper, PET, leather, ceramics, marble, steel and untreated wood. Figure 6 shows that the surface structure, contours and color saturation of an illuminated display segment varies depending on the material; the contours of the printed segment are more or less crisp.

We experienced that successful prints largely depend on the (ideally high) smoothness of the material's surface, leading to a homogenous display surface and crisp contours. We could not print on extremely uneven surfaces, such as cotton fabrics or suede leather. But we could successfully print on quite porous materials, such as office paper and untreated wood, with some decrease in homogeneity and crisp contours. In our experience the absorbency of the material is not decisive: we could print even on steel and stone in a very high quality.

Since the phosphor inks are not transparent, printing on the material inherently changes its visual properties. To fully hide the display components, the display can be printed on the reverse side of translucent materials. We also successfully printed the display on the backside of translucent materials, such as PET (see Fig. 8), paper (see Fig. 9), and wood veneer (see Fig. 6 lower right).

DISPLAY PRIMITIVES

Custom displays come in a large variety, ranging from easy to control segmented displays to highly generic matrix displays. In this section, we contribute a systematic overview of display primitives, structuring known primitives and contributing new ones. This acts as a graphical inventory from which the designer can combine elements to design the visual contents of the display. As PrintScreen applies principles from 2D vector graphics for the digital fabrication approach, the designer has extensive design flexibility and can make use of the powerful tools of modern vector graphics editors.

Single Segment

A single segment features an area or a contour, or a combination of both. A TFEL display homogeneously lights up the element, even over a large surface area. A segment features sharp contours, even if printed in large size. A segment can be printed with a high resolution of 60 ppi with screen print and 75 ppi with conductive inkjet print.

We contribute over previous work on display segments by allowing the designer to very flexibly vary the shape, the fill and the contour of the segment in the digital design. This is illustrated in Figure 7. The fill can be either *empty* (not lighting, fully transparent), *solid* (lighting homogeneously in one color), can contain *line art or line patterns* as a visible structure, or can show a predefined greyscale *bitmap image*. For bitmap images, we use half-toning, a method that produces greyscale with one color by printing dots of different density and size on the substrate.

A non-solid fill is realized as follows: like for a solid fill, the top and bottom electrodes and the dielectric are kept solid, covering the entire area of the segment. In contrast, phosphor is printed only at locations that should light up, i.e. lines for line patterns or dots for half-toning. In our experience modifying the phosphor layer is preferable to modifying one of the electrode layers, as the former approach ensures that the full electrode remains conductive, independently of the pattern.

Figure 7. Display segments: (a) contour, (b) solid fill, (c) line pattern fill, (d) bitmap fill.

The contour of a segment can be solid or made of a dashed pattern. If realized as two separate electrodes, contour and filled area can be separately controlled. Displayed dots should have a minimum diameter of 300 microns.

Multi-Segment

A multi-segment splits a single segment up into several sub-segments that can be independently controlled. Examples include a seven-segment display for numerical values or a progress bar. The principles introduced for single segments fully apply to multi-segments.

Matrix

PrintScreen supports printing a regular matrix display (Fig. 8a). We print the rows of the matrix as the bottom electrode and the columns of the matrix as the top electrodes. The phosphor layer and dielectric are continuous. Time-multiplexing between rows and columns allows for addressing individual pixels. The designer can define the size of the matrix and the pixel density. The maximum density is defined by the resolution of the screen printing equipment,

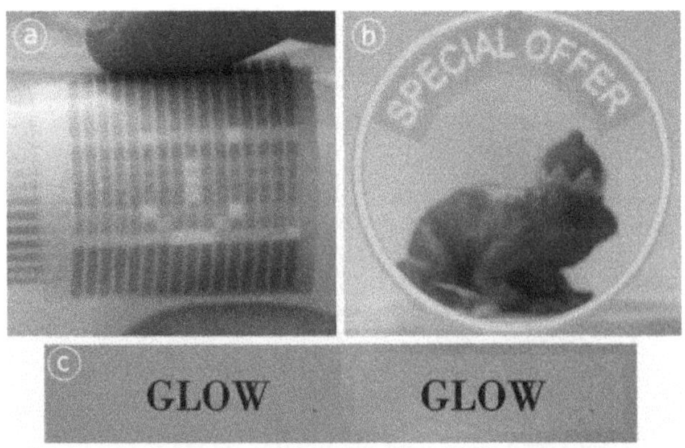

Figure 8. a) Passive Matrix Display. b) Translucent displayed on transparent PET film, in front of an object. c) Integration with laser-printed static visuals.

in our case 30 parallel lines per inch, leading to 30 pixels per inch.

We extend the design possibilities for matrix displays in two ways: (1) *Unevenly-spaced and -sized pixels* allow for varying the information density, e.g. higher resolution in the center and lower resolution in the periphery of a display. (2) *Custom-shaped pixels* allow for creating a unique visual appearance of the display, e.g. for digital signage or artistic installations. Both these options come at virtually no extra cost, as it is very easy to modify these parameters in the digital design.

Translucent Display Segments

To fabricate translucent display segments, the back electrode is printed with translucent conductive ink on the reverse side of a transparent PET film (see Fig. 3b). The film itself acts as the dielectric, eliminating the need for non-transparent dielectric ink. The phosphor and top electrode layers are printed on the front side. The conductor and phosphor inks are translucent, leading to a translucency of 32% at positions where segments are printed. Note that the display is fully transparent at locations without segments. Fig. 8b shows an application example for a shop window showcase.

Integration with Static Visual Print

A display can be printed alongside and integrated with static visual print. The designer uses an office laser or inkjet printer to print static visuals onto the paper or PET substrate. Next, display primitives are printed with screen printing onto the same substrate. This enables the following functionality:

Adjacent: Display primitives can be adjacent to printed visuals, for instance allowing for underlines or pop-out elements that light up on demand.

Contour: They can be more directly integrated. For instance, a static printed headline can be augmented by a luminescent contour. As long as the segment is not filled, visual print inside the segment remains fully visible.

Highlight: If the display primitive is printed at the reverse side of a slightly translucent substrate (see Fig. 3b), it can glow though static print on the front side and act as a dynamic highlight. The example in Fig. 8c demonstrates a highlight printed on the reverse side of office paper.

Integration with Printed Electronics

PrintScreen enables integrating display primitives with additional printed electronic applications on a single substrate. The bottom electrode layer can be used for designing additional electronics next to display primitives. Using silver ink for the bottom electrode, users can design printed traces and components. The principles for silver-ink printed components from previous work directly transfer to this case, e.g. for printing sensors [7, 9, 13]. Moreover, additional surface-mount components can be soldered onto the substrate.

DISPLAY SHAPES

PrintScreen offers the designer a high degree of design flexibility, supporting custom 2D and 3D shapes as well as reshapeable displays.

2D Shapes

Virtually any (rectangular, circular, irregular) 2D contour of the display can be realized in the digital design and then cut out of the fabricated display substrate. The only restriction is that each segment must be connected with the controller. The size of a display can range from only a few square centimeters up to large sizes. Screen printing of up to A2 size is feasible with hobbyist's toolkits.

3D Shapes

Screen printing does not allow for printing on curved objects. However, it supports printing on flexible substrates. Once printed the substrate can be deformed to create curved or folded 3D surfaces (see the examples in Fig. 1 and Fig. 10.

Shape adaptable

The flexibility of the substrate even allows for resizable and deformable displays. In technical experiments, we could demonstrate that the printed display can be folded anywhere on its surface and remains fully functional. It can also be rolled up on a scroll with a radius of 3 mm; this enables for applications for rollout displays. A technical evaluation shows that the displays are very robust to repeated bending or folding.

INTEGRATED SENSING OF USER INPUT

Sensing of user input is a key requirement for interactive display surfaces. We contribute an approach for integrating different modalities of input sensing with a printed TFEL display, using the same set of electrodes both for display and for sensing. It is *not* necessary to print additional sensing elements on top or behind the display, as it would be necessary for LCD screens. We demonstrate the principle with capacitive touch sensing.

The approach is based on the key insight that the phosphor layer only lights up when a high AC voltage is applied on one electrode while the electrode on the other layer is grounded. It does not light up when DC or a low voltage AC (we identified < 14 V) is applied, or when one electrode is set to high impedance. Many sensing approaches fulfill these requirements, e.g. for sensing of touch [6, 7, 26], hover [7] or deformation [7], to give only a few examples.

By time-multiplexing between a display and a sensing cycle, the electrodes on one, or even on both layers, can be used for sensing. In case of DC sensing, the driver IC is turned off during the sensing cycle. The time for discharging depends on the charge of the internal capacitors. In our implementation, we measured a maximum discharging time of 1.7ms.

As an example instantiation, we implemented capacitive touch sensing using projected capacitance [26]. During the sensing cycle, we leave the high voltage AC signal on the lower electrode, set the higher electrode to high impedance and measure the transmitted signal. When touching the electrode, the signal amplitude drops (see Fig. 9). The amplitude of the signal is used for recognizing touch contact, as introduced in [26].

If display and sensing cycles alternate quickly and the display cycle is sufficiently long, there is no perceivable decrease in display quality. We identified the following cycle durations to not add flickering: a display cycle of 5ms is followed by a sensing cycle of 2ms. This results in a frame rate of 140 Hz. The sensing cycle decreases the luminance of the display by 24%, which however can be fully compensated for by increasing the AC voltage. If used in a passive matrix display, the frame rate is divided by the number of lines of the display.

The spatial resolution of sensing depends on the number, size and arrangement of display electrodes. If required, additional electrodes used exclusively for purposes of sensing can be printed in-between display segments. It is also possible to enlarge the top and lower electrodes of a display segment for sensing, without increasing the segment on the phosphor layer.

APPLICATION EXAMPLES

We present five application examples of custom-printed displays. They instantiate various dimensions of the design space and demonstrate the potential for applications in ubiquitous, mobile and wearable computing. The applications are illustrated in Fig. 10

Interactive Paper Postcard

Interactive display segments can be integrated with static visual print. We printed a paper postcard that features on-demand visual information on a historical car. Two printed touch areas capture user input. The display segments are printed on the reverse side of the postcard. This application shows the high resolution of very custom-shaped segments and demonstrates the applicability for augmented paper and smart signage applications.

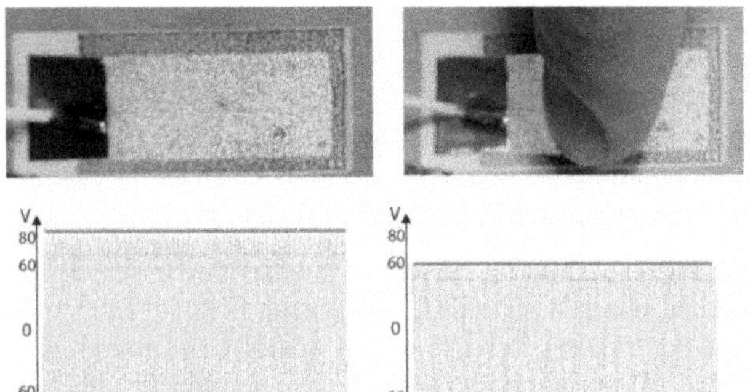

Figure 9. Touch sensing. The amplitude of the AC signal drops when the segment is touched.

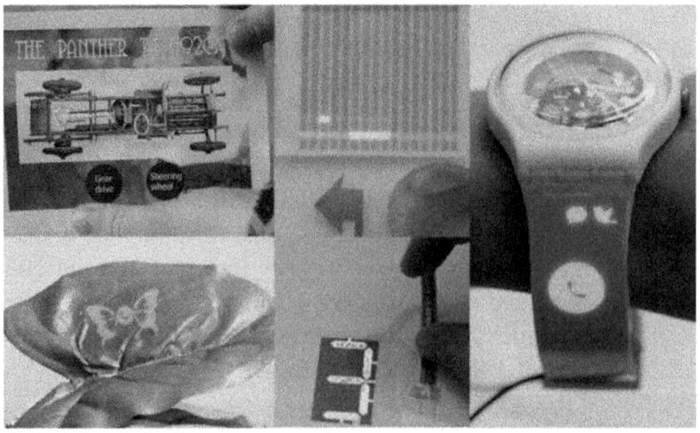

Figure 10. Application examples

Interactive Watchstrap

PrintScreen enables customized wearable displays. In this application, a notification display is integrated in a watchstrap of a traditional wristwatch. It is printed on the backside of a thin white PET film, which is laminated onto the watchstrap. The display can be customized to fit the individual shape of the watchstrap. This smartwatch concept has the benefit to maintain the esthetics of a traditional watch.

Printed Pong

To demonstrate interaction with a printed matrix display and its responsiveness, we implemented an instantiation of the Pong game. The 16x16 matrix display features two capacitive touch buttons to control the paddle. Technical Evaluation.

Awareness Flower

We augmented an artificial plant with displays on the backside of its flexible leafs, to provide awareness information. If an update (e.g. a new e-mail) arrives, the segment lights up. This application demonstrates how PrintScreen enables ubiquitous displays that seamlessly integrate with the underlying object and fade into the background when not needed.

Integration with Electronics

This application demonstrates that PrintScreen can be used for creating flexible circuit boards with integrated display elements. The bottom electrode layer contains additional printed circuitry for wiring of additional electronic components. A physical bend sensor allows the user to modify the number on a seven-segment display.

TECHNICAL EVALUATION

Luminance

The light intensity of the display can be controlled by varying the AC voltage (amplitude and frequency). We analyzed the maximum light intensity of the displays. It depends on several factors: the substrate, the AC voltage and the strength of the inverter. When driven with the DC12V10M inverter at its maximum input voltage of 12V DC, the luminance of the display varies between 120 and 280 cd/m^2. On paper, PET, ceramics and leather, we measured a maximum luminance of approx. 170 cd/m^2. On very smooth materials (steel and marble), 280 and 250 cd/m^2 are reached. On wood, a quite porous material, we measured only 120 cd/m^2. In our experience, the strength of the inverter is the main limiting factor. In experiments with a stronger inverter, we measured intensities between 270 and 570 cd/m^2 at 18V DC. When using the mobile driver IC chip [28] with 7V DC, the displays are less bright, ranging between 15 and 35 cd/m^2. This is comparable to a super bright white LED.

Bending and Folding

To analyze how robust the display is when repeatedly bent or folded, we used an automated test setup. We used a display sample with a 6x1.5cm single segment, printed on office paper. A simple robotic apparatus bent or folded the display repeatedly, returning each time to a completely flattened state. A light sensor, placed 10 cm above the display surface when in flat state, automatically measured the luminosity after each deformation.

In a first test, the apparatus bent the display successively 10,000 times to a radius of 1.5 cm. After the test, the display was still functional and did not show any decrease in luminance. We tested this high number of repetitions to account for continuous deformations occurring when the display is used in wearable applications.

In a second test, the apparatus fully folded (with a sharp folding crease) and unfolded a different display sample a total of 3,411 times before parts of the segment ceased to emit light. During the test, the display did not show any decrease in luminance.

DISCUSSION AND LIMITATIONS

Ease of Fabrication

All display samples presented in this paper were printed by two persons who both were not familiar with screen printing before joining this project. They used online tutorials and videos on the Web to learn the process. It took them between 3 to 5 hours to get familiar with the theory and another day to get practical experience. They did not encounter any real difficulties. One of the persons first had problems with homogeneously applying the UV-sensitive emulsion onto the mesh for UV lithography, but had learned doing it correctly after a few trials. Fine prints with thin lines require a steady hand. Despite the imprecision of the manual process, our non-experts could robustly print conductive lines and lighting dots of 300 μm width and diameter. Printing of the displays for our example applications took between 2 and 4 hours. This demonstrates the practical feasibility of the approach.

Display Color

Our process requires for each segment or pixel to choose the color at design time. For our display samples, we used only one color. A full color display could be realized by printing three red, green and blue sub-pixels for each pixel [15]. Given the maximum pixel density in manual print, this is a viable approach only for displays that are looked at from some distance.

Safety

All substances used for fabrication of the displays are non-toxic.

Safety for production: Users should read the health and safety guidelines in the material data sheets of the inks. It is recommended that the printing process take place in a well-aired room especially when curing the inks. Users should wear rubber gloves and goggles to protect eyes and hands. The display should be sealed properly.

Safety after production: After the inks are cured, the display is safe to interact with. A current of max. 10mA is considered being physiologically safe [31]. For example, the EL driver IC can provide a maximum output current of 1.0 mA at 220 Vpp [28]. This driver IC can drive a segment area of 4 sq. inches. If we assume 10 driver ICs are connected in a parallel circuit (driving a surface of 40 sq. inch, a reasonable size for most mobile/wearable applications) the overall current is max. 10mA.. If stronger inverters are used or if the display is exposed to mechanical stress or scratching, we recommend lamination with an insulating film.

Comparison with OLED Displays and Electronic Paper

In applications where a high-resolution matrix display or use of a full-color display is a prime requirement, off-the-shelf OLED or electrophoretic displays are still the solution of choice. However, if very strong bendability or even foldability is required for functional interface prototypes, our approach is without competitors, as to our knowledge such displays are neither commercially available nor can they be produced using a different approach. Likewise, PrintScreen is to our knowledge the only solution for designers, makers and HCI experts that allows direct integration of displays with various base substrates, very thin dual-sided and translucent displays and custom shapes.

CONCLUSION

PrintScreen is an enabling technology for digital fabrication of customized thin-film displays. We presented a systematic overview of graphical display primitives that act as buildings blocks for the digital design of the display. In order to instantiate the design, PrintScreen contributes two methods for rapid and inexpensive fabrication of the display, in a lab environment, print shop or even at home. The displays are deformable (even fully foldable and rollable) and can be highly customized by the user in several dimensions: their 2D and 3D shape, the material they are printed on, and the way contents are displayed. We further presented a framework that integrates sensing of user input (e.g., touch input) right into the display. Due to its versatility, PrintScreen opens up a wide space of new applications in ubiquitous, mobile and wearable computing.

Acknowledgement
This work has partially been funded by the Cluster of Excellence "Multimodal Computing and Interaction" within the German Federal Excellence Initiative. We thank Sergio Soto for his valuable technical advice.

REFERENCES

1. Alexander, J., Lucero, A., and Subramanian, S.: Tilt displays: designing display surfaces with multi-axis tilting and actuation. *Proc. MobileHCI '12.*
2. Amiraslanov, O., Cheng, J.; Chabrecek, P.; Lukowicz, P.: Electroluminescent based Flexible Screen for Interaction with Smart Objects and Environment. Workshop on Interacting with Smart Objects. *Proc. IUI'14.*
3. Andersson, P., Forchheimer, R., Tehrani, P. and Berggren, M.: Printable All-Organic Electrochromic Active-Matrix Displays. *Advanced Functional Materials*. 2007.
4. Franzke, L: Decay: Designing Ephemeral Interactive Devices. Master Thesis. 2013.
5. Girouard, A., Tarun, A., and Vertegaal R.: DisplayStacks: interaction techniques for stacks of flexible thin-film displays. *Proc.* CHI '12.
6. Gong, N., Hodges, S., and Paradiso, J. A.: Leveraging conductive inkjet technology to build a scalable and versatile surface for ubiquitous sensing. *Proc. UbiComp'11.*
7. Gong, N., Steimle, J., Olberding S., Hodges, S., Gillian, N., Kawahara, Y., Paradiso, J. A.: PrintSense: A Versatile Sensing Technique to Support Multimodal Flexible Surface Interaction. *Proc. CHI'14.*
8. Gwent Group: http://www.gwent.org. Last accessed: April 2014.
9. Hodges, S., Villar, N., Chen, N., Chugh, T., Qi, J., Nowacka, D., and Kawahara, Y. Circuit Stickers: Peel-and-Stick Construction of Interactive Electronic Prototypes. *Proc. CHI'14.*
10. Holman, D. and Vertegaal, R.: Organic user interfaces: designing computers in any way, shape, or form. *Commun. ACM 51.* 2008.
11. Johnston, D., Barnardo, C. and Fryer, C.: Passive multiplexing of printed electroluminescent displays. *Journal of the Society for Information Display*. 2005.
12. Karagozler, M. E., Poupyrev I., Fedder G. K., and Suzuki, Y.: Paper generators: harvesting energy from touching, rubbing and sliding. *Proc. UIST '13.*
13. Kawahara, Y., Hodges S., Cook B., Zhang, C. Abowd G. Instant Inkjet Circuits: Lab-based Inkjet Printing to Support Rapid Prototyping of UbiComp Devices. *UbiComp'13.*
14. Kawahara, Y., Hodges, S., Gong N., Olberding S. and Steimle, J: Building Functional Pervasive Computing Prototypes using Conductive Inkjet Printing. In *IEEE Pervasive Computing,* 13 (3), p. 30-38, IEEE Press, 2014.
15. Kitai, A: Luminescent Materials and Applications. ISBN: 978-0-470-05818-3. *Wiley*. 2008.
16. Khalilbeigi, M., Lissermann, R., Mühlhäuser, M., and Steimle, J.: Xpaaand: interaction techniques for rollable displays. *Proc. CHI '11.*
17. Lahey, B., Girouard, A., Burleson, W., and Vertegaal, R.: PaperPhone: Understanding the use of bend gestures in mobile devices with flexible electronic paper displays. *Proc. CHI '11.*
18. Liao, C., Liu, Q., Liew, B., and Wilcox, L. Pacer: fine-grained interactive paper via camera-touch hybrid gestures on a cell phone. *Proc. CHI '10.*
19. Liu, L., and Peng, S., Wen, W., and Ping, S.: Paperlike thermochromic display. *Applied Physics Letters*. 2007.
20. Lyons, K., Nguyen, D., Ashbrook, D., and White, S.: Facet: a multi-segment wrist worn system. In *Proc. UIST '12.*
21. Oryon Tech: http://www.oryontech.com. Last accessed: June 2014.
22. Paparone, N., Dillon, J.: Print Liberation: The Screen Printing Primer. *North Light Books*. 2008.
23. Pla, P. and Maes, P.: Display blocks: a set of cubic displays for tangible, multi-perspective data exploration. *Proc.* TEI '13.
24. Qi, J. and Buechley, L. Electronic Popables: Exploring paper-based computing through an interactive pop-up book. *Proc. TEI '10.*
25. Ramakers, R., Schöning, J. and Luyten, K.: Paddle: Highly Deformable Mobile Devices with Physical Controls. *Proc. CHI '14.*
26. Rekimoto, J.:SmartSkin: an infrastructure for freehand manipulation on interactive surfaces. *Proc. CHI'02.*
27. Rendl C., Greindl, P, Haller, M, Zirkl, M, Stadlober, B, and Hartmann. PyzoFlex: Printed piezoelectric pressure sensing foil. *Proc. UIST '12.*
28. RogersCorp, Electroluminescent Driver IC.: http://www.rogerscorp.com/durel/producttypes/2/DUREL-EL-Driver-ICs.aspx. Last Accessed: April 2014.
29. Roudaut, A., Karnik, A., Löchtefeld, M., and Subramanian, S.: Morphees: toward high "shape resolution" in self-actuated flexible mobile devices. *Proc. CHI '13.*
30. Savage, V., Zhang, X., and Hartmann, B. Midas: fabricating custom capacitive touch sensors to prototype interactive objects. *Proc. UIST '12.*
31. Scherz, P., Monk, S.: Practical Electronics for Inventors. Third edition. Tab Books, 2013.
32. Schwesig, C., Poupyrev, I., and Mori, E.: Gummi: a bendable computer. *Proc. CHI '04.*
33. Steimle, J., Jordt, A., and Maes P.: Flexpad: Highly flexible bending interactions for projected handheld displays. *Proc. CHI '13.*
34. Song, H., Grossman, T., Fitzmaurice, G., Guimbretiere, F., Khan, A., Attar, R. and Kurtenbach, G. PenLight: combining a mobile projector and a digital pen for dynamic visual overlay. *Proc. CHI '09.*
35. Telhan, Orkan: http://gizmodo.com/this-silk-screened-art-glows-with-electroluminescent-in-589610692. Last accessed June 2014.
36. Willis, K., Brockmeyer. E., Hudson, S., and Poupyrev, I.: Printed optics: 3D printing of embedded optical elements for interactive devices. *Proc. UIST '12.*
37. Yeh, R. B., Brandt, J., Klemmer, S. R., Boli, J., Su, E., Paepcke, A.: Interactive Gigapixel Prints: Large Paper Interfaces for Visual Context, Mobility, and Collaboration. *Technical Report*. 2006.

ShrinkyCircuits: Sketching, Shrinking, and Formgiving for Electronic Circuits

Joanne Lo, Eric Paulos
Electrical Engineering and Computer Sciences
University of California, Berkeley
{jlo, paulos}@berkeley.edu

ABSTRACT
In this paper we describe the development of ShrinkyCircuits, a novel electronic prototyping technique that captures the flexibility of sketching and leverages properties of a common everyday plastic polymer to enable low-cost, miniature, planar, and curved, multi-layer circuit designs in minutes. ShrinkyCircuits take advantage of inexpensive prestressed polymer film that shrinks to its original size when exposed to heat. This enables improved electrical characteristics though sintering of the conductive electrical layer, partial self-assembly of the circuit and components, and mechanically robust custom shapes - including curves and non-planar form factors. We demonstrate the range and adaptability of ShrinkyCircuits designs from simple hand drawn circuits with through-hole components to complex multilayer, printed circuit boards (PCB), with curved and irregular shaped electronic layouts and surface mount components. Our approach enables users to create extremely customized circuit boards with dense circuit layouts while avoiding messy chemical etching, expensive board milling machines, or time consuming delays in using outside PCB production houses.

Author Keywords
Creativity support tools; DIY; Prototyping; Sketching; Electronics; Fabrication; Sustainability design; Education

ACM Classification Keywords
H.5.m. Information interfaces and presentation (e.g., HCI): Miscellaneous

INTRODUCTION
The ability to envision, prototype, and construct electronic and computational interfaces using low-cost and accessible materials has been transformative to not only professional practitioners within HCI and Design and K-12 students as an educational tool but more recently as a catalyst within the emerging online maker communities. This "maker movement", as it is often called, is radically transformative — affecting a broad range of fundamental and critical cultural themes such as education, manufacturing, healthcare, and the economy, to name just a few [1-6]. One primary new element of this movement has been its ability to empower individuals and communities to imagine, design, collage, make, and share new, often interactive, physical artifacts and objects [7, 8]. It is the promise of this new opportunity for creative innovation that continues to inspire and proliferate this movement. We have already observed the impact of how these sharing resources and tools can inspire learning and empower personal creativity. However, there remains a rich landscape of opportunities to bring the benefits of tangibility and playfulness to elaborate and robust hardware design. In this paper we describe the development of ShrinkyCircuits, a techniuqe that captures the flexibility of sketching and leverages properties of a common everyday plastic polymer to enable prototyping circuits of differing complexity and diverse design (Figure 1).

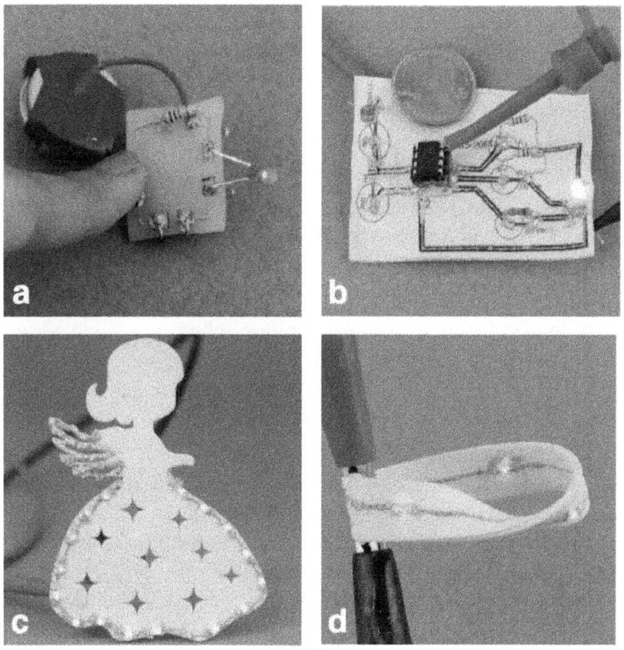

Figure 1. Different types of ShrinkyCircuits. a) A LED circuit with a physical switch and through-hold electronic components. b) An Eagle generated design with a microcontroller and through-hole components. c) A LED circuit board with fine cutout details made with a low-cost vinyl cutter. d) A Möbius strip LED circuit.

UIST 2014, October 5–8, 2014, Honolulu, HI, USA.
Copyright 2014 ACM 978-1-60558-246-7/09/04...$10.00.
http://dx.doi.org/10.1145/2642918.2647421

MOTIVATION

Drawing and sketching have played a critical role within the development of user interface design [9, 10]. In particular, we have seen sketching bringing interesting elements to hardware prototyping, sparking creative innovations within the maker community[9, 11-20]. The familiar form factor and the ease of use of the conductive pen have made it the predominant circuit-sketching tool. While the existing conductive pen methods are sufficient for simple designs, their delicate and often unreliable nature severely limit the complexity and application-base procedure [8, 21]. The final designs of such conductive pen and paper-based approaches are far from robust, as the paper folding and creasing often break the electrical connections. Lacking any rigid structure, most sketched paper circuits cannot be used in any real system even as a rough prototype.

Inspired by a rich body of prior work, our goal is to maintain the affordance of sketched circuits while addressing the limitations commonly encountered by circuit design, fabrication, assembly, and deployment. This paper presents a low-cost, flexible approach to physical prototyping that affords a sketch-like rapid iteration method that:

(1) Enables more complex structural designs (i.e. multi-sided and multi-layered circuits)

(2) Manifests a wide range of form factors including non-planar, irregular, and curved

(3) Provides a mechanism for miniaturization,

(4) Improves the electrical conductivity of the overall circuit sketched with a conductive pen

(5) Enables partial self-mounting of circuit components, thus decreasing prototyping time

(6) Creates a robust final product that can be deployed and evaluated in everyday contexts outside of the typical fragile laboratory setting (i.e. allows for testing such systems in situ)

Our solution uses a novel technique where users can draw circuit designs free form with a conductive pen on a large piece of prestressed polymer film. The prestressed polymer film will relax and shrink to its original size when exposed to heat. There are numerous advantages to this approach including achieving the six goals we detailed above and providing additional benefits that we will describe. In this paper, we detail our approach to sketching, designing, making, and deploying a wide variety of working circuits using this technique through a series of examples.

RELATED WORK

Crafting and Sketching Electronics

Injecting craft in electronic making is an important element in DIY practice and hacking. Projects such as Kit-of-No-Parts and Scrapyard Challenge encourages participants to explore circuit making by combing everyday objects in creative ways [19, 22]. Makers of any electronic skill level can learn to build circuits in a tangible and engaging manner using commercially available electronic Tookits such as LittleBits and Snap Circuits. Hudson et al. investigated created physical interfaces from cardboard, thumbtacks, tin foil, and masking tape [23]. Jacoby et al. set up a storytelling platform for children by providing them to paint with conductive ink [8]. Saul et al. designed various functional electronic products by printing electronic connections on paper, folding them into desired shapes, and incorporating electronic component into the products [13]. Commercial products such as the Lilypad Arduino allow users to easily integrate electronics into their craft projects [24]. Inspired by this body of work, our fabrication method maintains the tangible and playful manner of electronic crafting, but also aims to create circuits that are more robust and reliable.

Prototyping Electronics

Prototyping circuits is a major element in electronic prototyping. PCB's are often the preferred electronics platform for integrating into hardware products due to their compact size and robustness. However, prototyping circuit boards is not an easy task, and it is often one of the major bottlenecks in creating the final electronic product[25, 26]. If the user does not have access to expensive PCB printing machines or the time and funds to send the design to a vendor, they commonly resort to a method involving DIY chemical etched PCB. Although this DIY PCB method enables users to have the freedom to customize their PCB's, the process is lengthy and potentially unsafe[27]. Electronic products such as Arduino serve as a platform that allow users to customize a more robust circuit board according to their applications, but the predefined trace lines still take away the creative freedom. To address the difficulties in prototyping electronics, our ShrinkyCircuits utilize an easy, safe, streamlined fabrication method to customize and prototype more reliable circuits that can be easily integrated with larger systems.

Applications of Prestretched Polymers Films

Prestressed polymer films have been used to realize many engineering and scientific applications. In 3M Research, engineers use shrink film polymer substrate to create conductive traces smaller than 50μm [28]. In microfluidics, prestressed polymer enables researchers to create channels that are tens of microns by first etching wider channels into the polymer sheet with inexpensive lithographic equipment, and then shrinking them [29, 30]. Using a similar method, Odom et al created large arrays of 200nm-features by shrinking the master template [31]. These arrays of nanofeatures have huge implications in various areas such as nanophotonic single-particle sensors, long-range optical communications, and high-density solar cells [31]. The malleable and shape shifting nature of polymer also enables makers to create customized products by applying moderate amounts of heat or light [32]. Our ShrinkyCircuits process utilizes the technology enablement and crafting nature of prestreched polymers to provide an innovative way for sketching and prototyping complex circuit designs (i.e. multi-sided and non-planar) with robust electrical and mechanical properties.

SYSTEM DETAILS AND FABRICATION PROCESS

We selected prestressed thermoplastic polymer sheet as our dielectric substrate to take advantage of its interesting mechanical properties. Prestressed thermoplastic polymers, such as polyolefin and polystyrene, will shrink to a predetermined size when they are exposed to heat. In this paper, we chose to demonstrate our novel fabrication process using a commercially available, inexpensive ($0.55-$1.90/sheet), readily available prestressed thermoplastic polymer more commonly known as Shrinky Dinks™. There are three major benefits to using a shrinkable polymer as the dielectric substrate for prototyping electronic circuit boards.

First, circuit boards with small features and footprints can be created while by sketching at the larger scale prior to shrinking. This is due to the fact that all features drawn on the dielectric will shrink to 40% (+/- 2%) of their original size once heated. This is particularly beneficial to applications such as wearable or mobile electronics, where PCB real estate is a precious resource.

Second, the traces are more conductive and reliable via two mechanisms. First, the conductive ink is sintered when the Shrinky Dink is heated and thus forms a solid conductive trace, which is a well-known technique for improving the conductivity of traces created by conductive pens. In addition, the metallic particles in the conductive ink condense as the substrate shrinks to 40% of its original size, thus ensuring a higher metal-to-metal contact ratio within the trace volume. Due to these two factors, traces that are conductive and reliable can be created simply by drawing a line with only a single pass on the substrate.

Finally, the electronic components can be easily and securely loaded on the circuit board to enable partial component assembly. Prior to the shrinking process, holes are cut or punched into the substrate and through-hole components are loaded into the holes. The holes in which the electronic components are inserted then decrease in size during the heating process, and tighten around the leads of the components. Because of the shrinking substrate, the conductive ink surrounding the electronic components forms mounds that envelop the leads. These mounds act as solder on a PCB, and they provide a reliable conductive and mechanical connection.

Mechanical and Electrical Properties

Shrinky Dinks™ are made of thermoplastic polymer sheets of polystyrene that have been preheated and stretched. When they are heated up to their glass transition temperature again (approximately 100°C), they relax and shrink back to their original size. This results in a dramatic in-plane uniform reduction in size, which ranges from 50%-60% depending on the prestressed strength.

For this study, we used Shrinky Dinks™ for Inkjet Printers, and we observe a 60% +/- 2% shrinkage in these particular Shrinky Dinks™ polystyrene sheets. Although there is no observable difference within one sheet of polymer [31], there were minor variations (+/- 2%) between different sheets. The sheet-to-sheet variation did not pose major problems in the circuit fabrication in this study.

The glass transition temperature that is required for shrinkage is easily achieved with a range of household appliances, such as toaster ovens, craft heat guns, incandescent and infrared lights [32]. The relatively safe and easy usage of Shrinky Dinks™ has made it a popular children's toy as well as a novel and reliable tool for scientific discovery[29-31].

We also performed studies on the increase in conductivity by cutting out five long, thin polymer strips (uniform in size, 28cm x 0.5cm) and coating them with one layer of the conductive ink. Prior to heating, the samples have an average resistance of 11.48Ω, which equates to a resistivity of 0.205/square. After heating the five samples at 100°C for five minutes, the strips shrunk to 11cm x 0.2cm and the resistance reduced to an average of 1.4Ω (0.0255/square). The net result is an increased conductivity of 800%. In contrast, a 22-gauge wire of the same length (11cm) has a resistivity of 0.4Ω. This demonstrates that heating the polymer substrate resulted in an 8 times reduction in resistivity, but the traces are not as conductive as a piece of wire (in this example our final trace is 29% conductive as a 22-gauge wire of equal length). If higher conductivity is needed for the circuit, user can deposit more conductive ink on the traces prior to heating. However, a thin line drawn with a conductive pen on the polymer substrate was sufficiently conductive for most DIY electronic applications and provided the necessary mechanical structure to maintain these electrical characteristics. To examine the physical effect of heating have on the silver conductive ink, we took scanning electron micrograph (SEM) pictures of the silver-ink-coated polymer strips before and after heating. Figure 2a shows that the silver ink patches were not well connected prior to heating. Figure 2b shows that the silver ink was well connected after heating, thus forming a better conductive path.

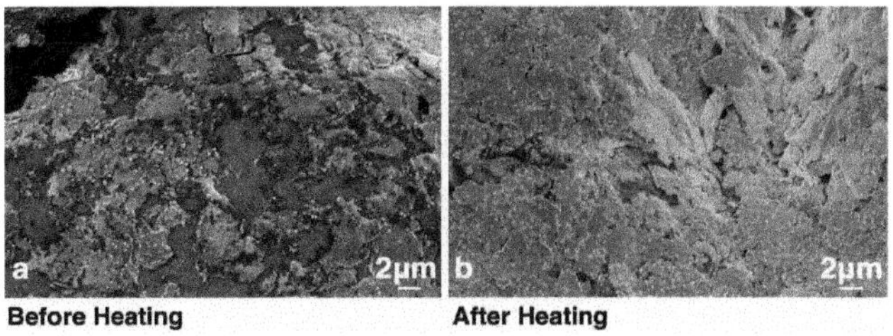

Figure 2: Scanning electron microscopy (SEM) pictures of the conductive silver ink on a polymer substrate. a) Before the silver ink and the substrate are heated. b) After the silver ink and the substrate are heated.

Fabricating with ShrinkyCircuits

The following three basic steps serve as building blocks for many variations of ShrinkyCircuits:

1. **Sketch**: Sketch the desired circuit on a piece of ShrinkyDinks™ polystyrene sheet (Shrinky Dinks for Inkjet Printers, amazon.com) with a regular pen and determine the placement of the electronic components. If through-hole components are used, cut holes on the polymer sheet so that the components can be inserted later.
2. **Trace**: Trace the circuit with a conductive pen (CircuitWriter™ Precision Pen, $21.25). Simply draw a thin line for traces and pads (in any shape) for the electronic components. The lines drawn with conductive pens with only one pass often appear to be too thin or not uniformly filled. With the ShrinkyCircuit fabrication technique, the traces do not need to by refilled the conductive ink will connect in the shrinking process The circuit can be drawn on both front of back of the polymer sheet. The two sides can be connected by drawing a dot on the edge if needed.
3. **Heat**: Heat up the assembly with a toaster oven set to approximately 100°C or with a crafting heat gun (PaperSource Embossing Heat Tool was used in this study, $23.95). Remove the assembly from the heat once the substrate has shrunk (usually after 3-5min).

The resulting ShrinkyCircuit is ~40% of its original footprint and nine times thicker. This increased thickness provides increased structural support making the assembly more durable and easier to handle. The electronic component mounting steps are slightly different for each type of component, and they will be discussed in following sections.

When sketching the circuits in Step 1, the user should calculate the size of the original circuit from the desired size of the end product. Based on our measurements, a user would sketch the circuit 2.5 times the desired final size. We will later show an automated process to achieve the desired size by simply scaling a circuit layout prior to tracing using common image scaling techniques.

DESIGNING WITH SHRINKYCIRCUITS

ShrinkyCircuit is an extremely versatile circuit prototyping method and can be used to create circuits of many difference shapes and form. The aforementioned fabrication procedure can be easily extended to create a plethora of different circuit types. In the following sections we describe six simple variations to the basic fabrication procedure and discuss the benefits and limitations through a series of examples.

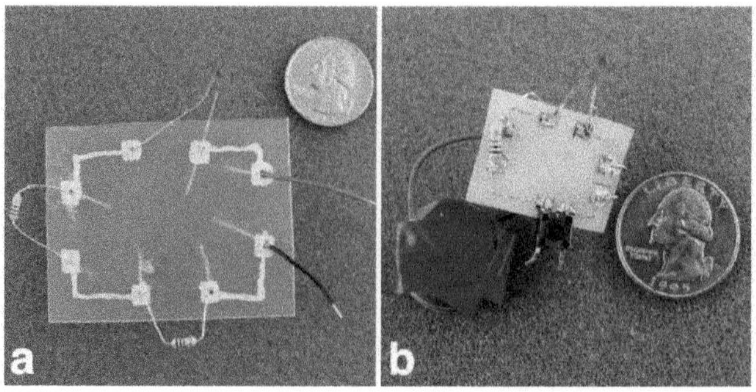

Figure 3: ShrinkyCircuit with through-hole components. a) Components are loosely held in place prior to shrinking. b) Components are "self-soldered" onto circuit board after the substrate shrinks.

Through-hole Components

Clearly, most circuits will require additional through-hole components to be added. This can be done using the same basic fabrication procedure mentioned previously with an added hole-cutting and component mounting step. Before drawing the circuit onto the polymer substrate, cut or drill holes that are slightly bigger then the component leads on where they are to be inserted. After the circuit is drawn on, insert the components leads into the holes (Figure 3a). Subsequent to heating, the through-hole electronic components would all be securely loaded on the board as the conductive ink wraps and the substrate around the leads during the shrinking process - therefore, no additional soldering is necessary (Figure 3b). Please note that components with no flexible leads would not shrink conformably with the circuit and therefore should be inserted after the heating step.

For even a moderately complex circuit (i.e. 4 thorough-hole components), the entire process from sketching, tracing, and loading electronic components, to shrinking the polymer substrate, can be completed in 10 minutes or less. Except for the 5-7 minutes of waiting time during the final heating process, the time required to build a through-hole ShrinkyCircuit is comparable to circuit breadboarding. However, unlike breadboarding, the result of this process is a robust circuit board with "self-soldered" electrical components.

ShrinkyCircuit can also support rapid changes to a circuit design. While rerouting traces with ShrinkyCircuits requires crafting jumpers and breaking traces, ShrinkyCircuits do enable individual components to be easily swapped. Replacing damaged LEDs, changing resistor values, capacitors and similar electronic components can be done by simply pulling the component with a moderate force and inserting a new component back into the holes. This component swapping is possible because the holes created by the conductive ink melt and compress around the original leads, and therefore the holes are of the perfect size for a snug fit around the same component. Throughout our studies with ShrinkyCircuits, we observed consistently snug and secure electrical connections over several component swaps without any physical deformation to the holes. Even after repeated swaps when we encountered loosening in the electrical connection, it was straightforward to simply apply a small amount of additional conductive ink around the connection.

Surface Mount Components

One important feature of PCBs is their compactness, which is often achieved by using small surface mount components. Surface-mount components can be loaded into ShrinkyCircuits by slightly modifying the basic procedure described earlier. When using surface mount components, the circuit is again directly sketched on the polymer substrate, but this time without cutting any holes for through-hole components. To prepare for the loading of surface-mount components, appropriately sized gaps are drawn to accounting for the shrinkage that will occur. After the design is sketched, the polymer substrate is heated and shrunk without the surface mount components loaded. The surface mount components are then simply glued on with conductive epoxy (i.e. MG Chemicals 8331 Two-part Silver Conductive Epoxy, $42.95). This adhesive process is similar to traditional surface-mount component soldering processes and yield remarkable similar results. To swap out components, the old component could be pried out with a razor blade and another component can be reloaded using the conductive paste. Although the number of step of the surface-mount ShrinkyCircuit is same as soldering on a PCB, the ShrinkyCircuit board is quicker to make and significantly safer due to the absence of dangerous chemical handling in the process.

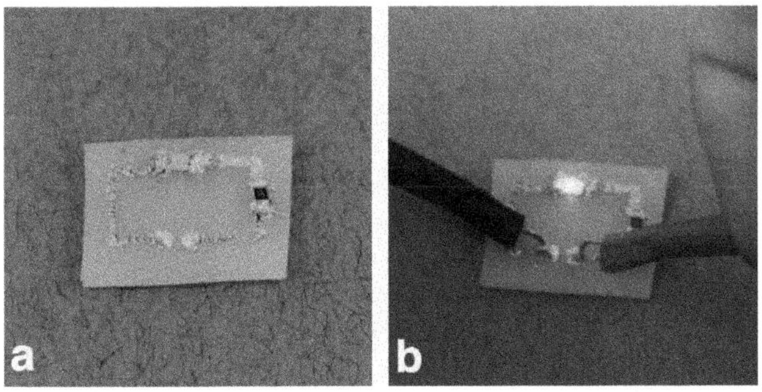

Figure 4: ShrinkyCircuit with surface-mount components. a) Circuit board after the components are loaded with conductive epoxy. b) The ShrinkyCircuit under operation.

Using PCB Layout Software Tools

Sketching ciruits is fast and flexible. However, as circuit designs become more complex, it is often more convenient to use a PCB layout software, such as Eagle as a design tool. Designs in Eagle can be easily and quickly prototyped with ShrinkyCircuits. First, the Eagle layout is printed onto the polystyrene polymer sheet with an inkjet printer (HP PhotoSmart C4780 was used in this study). Next, holes are cut out for inserting any through-hole components. The printed trace markings (red lines in Figure 5) are then traced over with a conductive pen, and the through-hole components with flexible leads are inserted (Figure 5a). After the assembly is heated and shrunk, IC holders can be inserted to house the IC of choice (Figure 5b).

To demonstrate this process, an RGB LED circuit with a photodiode and DIP footprint ATtiny85 Microcontroller was fabricated. For demonstration purposes, this circuit is designed to blink red, blue and green when the photocell detects light (Figure 5c).

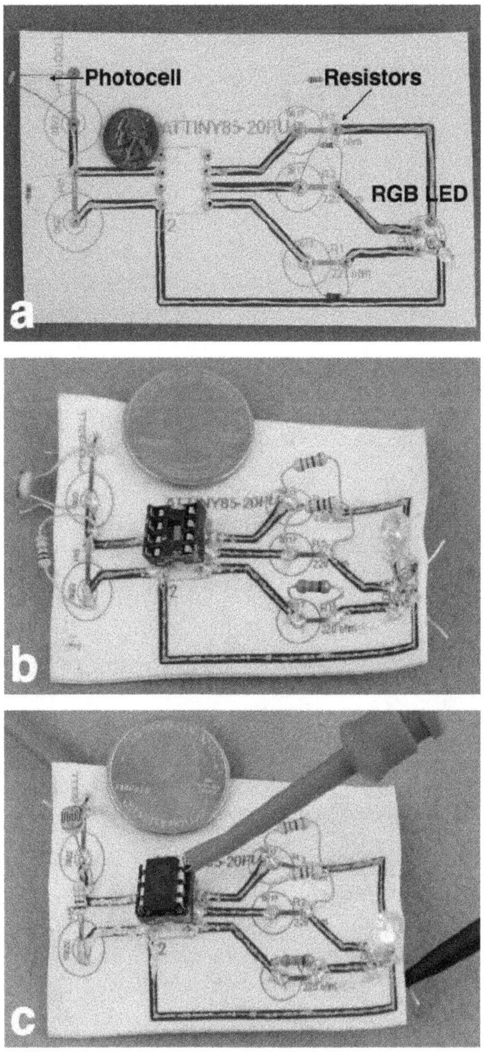

Figure 5: A ShrinkyCircuit designed using Eagle PCB software. a) Electronic components loaded on a circuit printed on polymer sheet with inkjet printer. The electrical connections are traced with a connective pen. c) IC holder is inserted into the shrunk circuit after the polymer substrate is heated. d) The ShrinkyCircuit under operation.

Crafting Uniquely Shaped ShrinkyCircuits

In addition to providing benefits similar to that of a PCB, the cardstock-like nature of the prebaked polymer sheet also brings an element of craft to ShrinkyCircuit. It is often very expensive to purchase PCBs of non-rectangular shapes from vendors and very labor-intensive to mill out special shapes with a 2D CNC mill. This is a problem that cannot be easily solved by making homemade DIY PCBs since most purchasable boards are rectangular. These thick and rigid boards can be cut into different shapes with a saw, but creating fine features is nearly impossible. This poses a problem for designs that often need circuit boards with small and irregular form factors, such as wearable or mobile applications.

ShrinkyCircuit can easily overcome this difficulty since it can be cut into the desired shape easily with a pair of scissors in its preheated state. For small features or complicated shapes, a low-cost craft vinyl cutter (i.e. Silhouette Cameo Electronic Cutting Tool, $259.38) can be used to cut the polymer sheet. In our study, we demonstrate this by cutting out an angel figure with fine features on its wings and skirt (Figure 6a). We then sketched an LED circuit on the cutout, heated up the substrate, and loaded the surface-mount LEDs (Figure 6b). The electrical power pads are drawn on the back of the angel to reduce clutter on the front. The versatility of this fabrication method not only brings a playful quality to advanced circuit making, it also provide makers the freedom of creating any board shapes that fit their products.

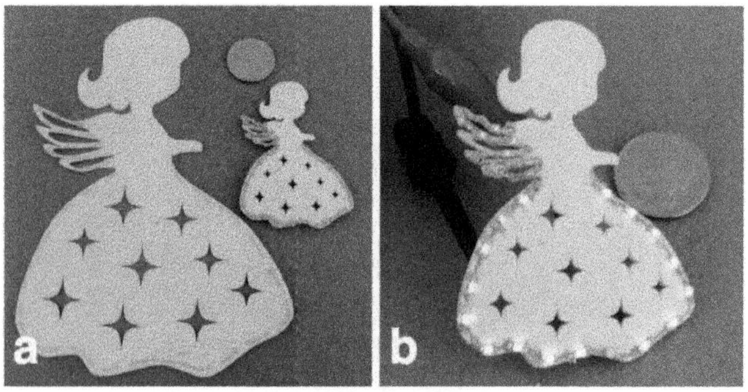

Figure 6: ShrinkyCircuit cut with a low-cost vinyl cutter. a) Polymer substrate prior to shrinking. b) ShrinkyCircuit under operation.

Multi-layer Circuits

Multi-layer circuits are essential in applications where horizontal space is precious. In PCBs, multiple layers of circuit board can be stacked up vertically and connected using vias. Multi-layer ShrinkyCircuits can be made using a similar process. By inserting a conductive material (i.e. wire, resistor leads) into multiple layers of polymer sheets, the layers will be guided to shrink together during the heating process. In this study, a two-layer ShrinkyCircuit was created to demonstrate this concept. Two striped wires were inserted into two polymer sheets with pre-cut holes (Figure 7a). The circuit design was drawn on with a conductive pen, with pads drawn around the wires on s both layers. The whole assembly was then heated up in an oven to shrink the substrates. The two layers were automatically connected electrically in the resulting circuit as both layers connected securely to the wires with conductive ink forming mounds around the wires. The resulting circuit is shown in Figure 7b.

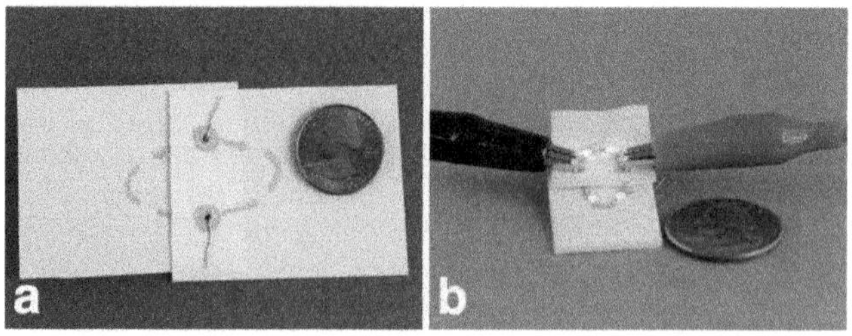

Figure 7: Dual-layer ShrinkyCircuits. a) Two polymer sheets are connected by inserting wires into precut holes. b) The daul-layer circuit can be powered by connecting to the exposed leads.

Non-planar Board Shapes

Perhaps one of the most powerful aspects of ShrinkyCircuits is the ability to easily explore the design space of non-planar, curved, and three-dimensional board shapes. This invites a rich landscape of possible new circuit designs that are better adapted for their final application, can be more densely packed, can be embedded into complex product form factors, or allow for new sensor and actuator placement strategies. The flexibility of the prestressed polymer sheet prior to heating enables the fabrication of non-planar, 3D circuits - something that cannot be accomplished using traditional PCBs. The fabrication process of non-planar circuits is also very craft-like, and affords rapid exploration of many possibilities with even a few simple, creative manipulations. To demonstrate the concept, three methods for making non-planar circuits are shown in this paper.

Angular ShrinkyCiruits

To make structures with angular connections, slots can be cut out from each polymer sheet. Figures 8 a) and b) illustrate this concept by showing two possible circuit configurations. For the structure in Figure 8a, the polymer sheets with the slot cutouts were first assembled, and then flattened temporarily to draw on the circuit. After the circuit was traced onto the sheet, the assembly was put back into its three-dimensional shape and heated up in the oven. The final step employed the standard approach for attaching the surface mount LEDs.

ShrinkyCiruits Frame

For the structure in Figure 8b, the circuit was drawn separately on four polymer strips, with connection pads drawn around the slot cutouts. The strips were then assembled and heated up. Again, the surface-mount LEDs were loaded after the heating process (i.e. when the structures were in their final three-dimensional shapes).

Folded ShrinkyCiruits

Non-planar ShrinkyCircuits can also be made by taking advantage of other conductive materials. Figure 8c shows a bow-shaped ShrinkyCircuit powered by the integrated conductive threads connected to a power supply. This structure was created by first drawing the circuit and cutting holes for inserting the through-hole components. The ends of the strip were then sewn together using conductive threads, thus forming the bow shape. After the electronic components were loaded, the assembly was heated up. The result was a rigid bow-shaped circuit that could be powered by connecting to the conductive threads.

Möbius ShrinkyCiruits

The Möbius strip LED circuit was fabricated by twisting a polymer strip and connecting the end with glue (Gorilla Glue All-Purpose Adhesive was used in this study). After the glue dried, a single line was drawn around the Möbius strip, leaving gaps for loading the LEDs. The Möbius strip was then heated up and the LEDs loaded onto the finished structure (Figure 8d).

Sculptable ShrinkyCircuits

The polystyrene substrate is somewhat malleable before it fully cools down from the baking process. By taking advantage of this property, functional objects with integrated ShrinkyCircuits can be molded. The flower-shaped tealight was made by first coloring a cutout using colored pencils, and then carefully folding up the petals as the shrunk substrate was taken out of the oven (Figure 8e). The nightlight was fabricated by first printing the desired pattern onto the substrate, and then loading the through-hole components into the precut holes. The curved lampshade-shape was created by bending the entire substrate before it fully cooled down (Figure 8f).

There are many different ways that ShrinkyCircuits can be made into interesting non-planar structures, and we only show a few of the possible examples with mechanical structures, conductive threads, and glue, in this paper. We envision a variety of additional ways users can potentially connect the polymer sheets by incorporating more materials and adhesives to create even more complex and novel designs and structures.

LIMITATIONS

Although ShrinkyCircuits provides tremendous new features and benefits to prototyping circuits, there are several limitations. With the self-soldered through-hole component process, heat sensitive components sometimes get damaged when the temperature of the oven gets over the storage temperature of the electronic component. This problem can be remedied by using components with higher temperature tolerance or heating the substrate with a heat gun. When using the heat gun to shrink the substrate, the user can control the amount of time and the direction (i.e. focus the heat onto the substrate but not the component) heat is applied to the heat sensitive components, thus avoiding damage to the components.

Another limitation with the through-hole component process is substrate warping in shrunk circuit boards. In addition to being an aesthetic and mechanical fit problem, the warping also distorts the alignment of the circuit. This is not ideal especially when it comes to loading tight tolerant parts such as DIP and SIP components. We believe that this problem is caused by the protruding leads of the electrical components that prevent the substrate from relaxing and conforming to the oven tray. A specially designed weighted "shrinking guide" may ameliorate this problem and help the substrate flatten evenly when it relaxes.

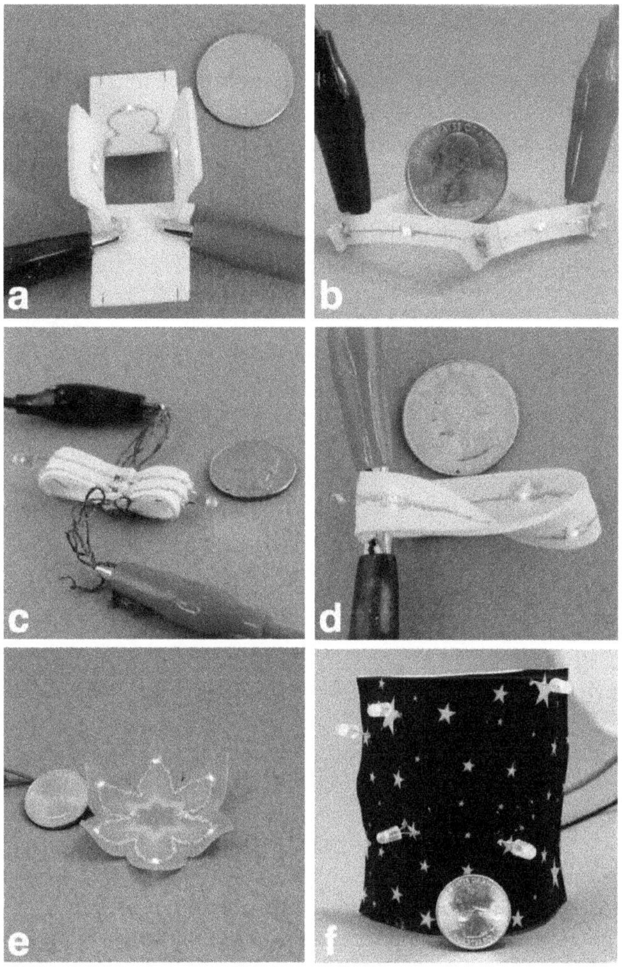

Figure 8: Non-planar ShrinkyCircuits. a) A box-like circuit held together by slot cutouts. b) A square frame held together with slot cutouts. c) A bow-tie circuit connected with conductive threads. d) A Möbius strip LED circuit. e) A flower-shaped tealight decorated with color pencils. f) A night light with patterns printed with an inkjet printer.

DISCUSSION AND FUTURE APPLICATIONS

The development of ShrinkyCircuit has big impact potential in multiple fields, including prototyping, education, scientific research, and electronic crafting. Schoolchilrdren and expert makers alike could utilize this fabrication process to create structurally complex circuits due to it safe (i.e. requires no toxic chemicals) and tangible nature. We would like to continue to investigate ways to improve the process to create more reliable circuits in new forms and at lower cost. Beyond shrinking the whole substrate, we plan to study methods for localized heating of the substrate in order to fold and shrink the circuit in a highly controllable manner. We believe that our technique can contribute to a wide array of engineering fields, including wireless communications with three-dimensional antennas, sensing-circuit-integrated microfluidic platform, and wearable devices. We would also like to explore the usage of ShrinkyCircuits for educational purposes by breaking down common circuits into stampable design elements, which would allow younger children to explore circuit making without drawing fine lines by hand for traces. We envision ShrinkyCircuit to be useful both in introductory science and art classes, where teachers can pique students' interest in circuits by exploring creative ways to incorporate electronics into multidimensional designs. With the exception of the bake step, every step is an opportunity for interactive learning and creativity for students of all ages. While older students could perform all the steps independent of their teacher's input, younger students could be supervised and assisted by their teachers where needed while still learning valuable lessons and skills.

CONCLUSION

In this paper, we have described our work on ShrinkyCircuit, a novel circuit prototyping technique that creates robust and reliable circuits. The ShrinkyCircuit process enables the self-soldering of through-hole component during the heating step, which further speeds up the circuit prototyping process. Moreover, non-planar ShrinkyCircuit can be crafted by mixing various construction methods and conductive mediums. The ShrinkyCircuit enables makes of all levels to freely construct functional, durable, and fully customizable circuits of various shapes, while reaping the benefits of a fun and tangible craft-like fabrication process.

ACKNOWLEDGMENTS

We would like to thank the anonymous reviewers for their valuable feedback on this work as well as generous financial support provided through NSF IIS-1211047.

REFERENCES

1. Anderson, C.: Makers: The New Industrial Revolution. Crown Business (2012).
2. Frauenfelder, M.: Make: Technology on Your Time. Maker Media, Inc (2005).
3. Frauenfelder, M.: Made by Hand: Searching for Meaning in a Throwaway World. Portfolio Hardcover (2010).
4. Gershenfeld, N.: Fab: The Coming Revolution on Your Desktop--from Personal Computers to Personal Fabrication. Basic Books (2007).
5. Kuznetsov, S., Paulos, E.: Rise of the Expert Amateur:DIY Projects, Communities, and Cultures. Presented at the NordiCHI 2010, Reykjavik, Iceland October 16 (2010).
6. Buechley, L., Rosner, D., Paulos, E., Williams, A.: DIY for CHI: Methods, Communities, and Values of Reuse and Customization. Presented at the CHI 2009, Boston, MA, USA April 3 (2009).
7. Jacobs, J., Buechley, L.: Codeable Objects: Computational Design and Digital Fabrication for Novice Programmers. CHI 2013. 1–10 (2013).
8. Jacoby, S., Buechley, L.: Drawing the Electric: Storytelling with Conductive Ink. 1–4 (2013).
9. Scott R Klemmer, J.L.J.L.J.A.L.: Papier-Mâché: Toolkit Support for Tangible Input. 1–8 (2004).
10. Landay, J., Myers, B.: Sketching Interfaces: TowardMore Human Interface Design. 1–9 (2001).
11. Spiessl, W., Villar, N., Gellersen, H., Schmidt, A.: VoodooFlash: Authoring across Physical and Digital Form. Presented at the TEI'07 February 16 (2007).
12. Zamora, S., Eyjólfsdóttir, E.A.: CircuitBoard: Sketch-Based Circuit Design and Analysis. 1–9 (2009).
13. Saul, G., Xu, C.: Interactive Paper Devices: End-user Design & Fabrication. 1–8 (2009).
14. Olberding, S., Gong, N.-W., Tiab, J., Paradiso, J.A., Steimle, J.: A Cuttable Multi-touch Sensor. Presented at the UIST'13, St. Andrews, United Kingdom August 8 (2013).
15. Mellis, D.A., Jacoby, S., Buechley, L., Perner-Wilson, H., Qi, J.: Microcontrollers as Material: Crafting Circuits with Paper, Conductive Ink, Electronic Components, and an "Untoolkit." TEI 2013. 1–8 (2012).
16. zoran, A., Paradiso, J.A.: *FreeD* – A Freehand Digital Sculpting Tool. CHI 2013. Session: Fabrication, 1–4 (2013).
17. Greenberg, S., Fitchett, C.: Phidgets: Easy Development of Physical Interfaces through Physical Widgets. Presented at the CM UIST 2001 Symposium on User Interface Software and Technology, Orlando, Florida November 11 (2001).
18. Karagozler, M.E., Poupyrev, I., Fedder, G.K., Suzuki, Y.: Paper generators. Presented at the the 26th annual ACM symposium, New York, New York, USA (2013).
19. Perner-Wilson, H., Buechley, L., Satomi, M.: Handcrafting Textile Interfaces from A Kit-of-No-Parts. Presented at the TEI'11, Funchal, Portugal January 22 (2011).
20. Mueller, S., Kruck, B., Baudisch, P.: LaserOrigami: Laser-cutting 3D Objects. Presented at the Proceedings of the SIGCHI Conference on Human Factors in Computing Systems, New York, NY, USA (2013).
21. Russo, A., Ahn, B.Y., Adams, J.J., Duoss, E.B., Bernhard, J.T., Lewis, J.A.: Pen-on-Paper Flexible Electronics. Adv. Mater. 23, 3426–3430 (2011).
22. Brucker-Cohen, J., Moriwaki, K.: Scrapyard Challenge Workshops, http://www.scrapyardchallenge.com/about/.

23. Hudson, S., Mankoff, J.: Rapid Construction of Functioning Physical Interfaces from Cardboard, Thumbtacks, Tin Foil and Masking Tape. UIST. 1–9 (2006).
24. Buechley, L., Eisenberg, M., Catchen, J., Crockett, A.: The LilyPad Arduino: Using Computational Textiles to Investigate Engagement, Aesthetics, and Diversity in Computer Science Education. Presented at the CHI 2008, Florence, Italy April 5 (2008).
25. ASCAS: DIY Customized Circuit Board (PCB Making), http://www.instructables.com/id/Making-A-Customized-Circuit-Board-Made-Easy/?ALLSTEPS.
26. VC, M., P, J., Hadley, C.: How to Create Printed Circuit Boards, http://www.wikihow.com/Create-Printed-Circuit-Boards.
27. Iron(III) Chloride MSDS. Sigma-Aldrich, 3050 Spruce Street, Saint Loius, MO 63103.
28. Voss-Kehl, J., Halverson, K., Ylitalo, C., Lehmann, M., Botzet, S.: Printed circuits on shrink film, (2005).
29. Chen, C.-S., Breslauer, D.N., Luna, J.I., Grimes, A., Chin, W.-C., Lee, L.P., Khine, M.: Shrinky-Dink microfluidics: 3D polystyrene chips. Lab Chip. 8, 622 (2008).
30. Grimes, A., Breslauer, D.N., Long, M., Pegan, J., Lee, L.P., Khine, M.: Shrinky-Dink microfluidics: rapid generation of deep and rounded patterns. Lab Chip. 8, 170 (2007).
31. Lee, M.H., Huntington, M.D., Zhou, W., Yang, J.-C., Odom, T.W.: Programmable Soft Lithography: Solvent-Assisted Nanoscale Embossing. Nano letters. 11, 311–315 (2011).
32. Liu, Y., Boyles, J.K., Genzer, J., Dickey, M.D.: Self-folding of polymer sheets using local light absorption. Soft Matter. 8, 1764 (2012).

Teegi: Tangible EEG Interface

Jérémy Frey* Univ. Bordeaux jeremy.frey@inria.fr
Renaud Gervais* Inria renaud.gervais@inria.fr
Stéphanie Fleck Univ. Lorraine stephanie.fleck@univ-lorraine.fr
Fabien Lotte Inria fabien.lotte@inria.fr
Martin Hachet Inria martin.hachet@inria.fr

*Co-first authorship, both authors contributed equally to this work.

ABSTRACT
We introduce Teegi, a Tangible ElectroEncephaloGraphy (EEG) Interface that enables novice users to get to know more about something as complex as brain signals, in an easy, engaging and informative way. To this end, we have designed a new system based on a unique combination of spatial augmented reality, tangible interaction and real-time neurotechnologies. With Teegi, a user can visualize and analyze his or her own brain activity in real-time, on a tangible character that can be easily manipulated, and with which it is possible to interact. An explorative study has shown that interacting with Teegi seems to be easy, motivating, reliable and informative. Overall, this suggests that Teegi is a promising and relevant training and mediation tool for the general public.

Author Keywords
Tangible Interaction; EEG; Spatial Augmented Reality; Learning

ACM Classification Keywords
H.5.1 Multimedia Information Systems: Artificial, augmented, and virtual realities; H.5.2 User Interfaces: Interaction styles; H.1.2 User/Machine Systems: Human information processing; I.2.6 Learning: Knowledge acquisition

INTRODUCTION
Electroencephalography (EEG) measures the brain activity of participants under the form of electrical currents, through use of a set of electrodes connected to amplifiers and placed on the scalp [17]. This technology is widely used in medicine for diagnostic purposes. It is also increasingly explored in the field of Brain-Computer Interfaces (BCI), the goal of which is to enable a user to send input commands to interactive systems without any physical motor activities, by using brain activity alone [35]. BCI is an emerging research area in Human-Computer Interaction (HCI) that offers new opportunities for interaction, beyond standard input devices [28]. These emerging technologies are becoming increasingly more popular. It feeds into fears and dreams in the general public where many fantasies are linked to a misunderstanding of the strengths and weaknesses of such new technologies. *No, it is not possible to read thoughts!* But what can be done exactly? Our motivation is to provide a tool that allows one to better learn how EEG works, and to better understand the kinds of brain activity that can be detected in EEG signals. Beyond the knowledge of the brain that a user can acquire, we believe that a dedicated tool may help demystify BCI, and consequently, it may favor the development of such a promising field.

ACM 978-1-4503-3069-5/14/10 ...$15.00.
http://dx.doi.org/10.1145/2642918.2647368

Figure 1. Teegi (Tangible EEG Interface) is a friendly interactive character that users can manipulate to observe and analyze their own brain activity in real-time.

We followed a multidisciplinary approach, combining Human-Computer Interaction (Spatial Augmented Reality, Tangible User Interfaces), Neurotechnologies (EEG, brain signal processing) and Psychology/Human sciences (Human Learning and Representations, Scientific Mediation) to design an interactive multimedia system that enables novice users to get to know more about something as complex as EEG signals and the brain, in an easy, engaging and informative way. Our final goal is to enhance learning efficiency and knowledge acquisition by letting users actively and individually manipulate and investigate the concept to be learned [31], i.e. EEG signals.

This gave birth to Teegi (Tangible EEG Interface), a physical character that users can manipulate in a natural way to observe and analyze their own brain activity projected in real-time on the character's head (see Figure 1). Beyond the technical description of Teegi, this paper depicts an explorative study we conducted, which provides an experimental basis for discussions and future works. Our major contribution for this paper is the design of the first system to make EEG signals and brain activity easily accessible, interactive and understandable. This work is based on theoretical foundations, technical developments, and preliminary investigations.

NEUROIMAGING AND EEG

EEG signals are small electrical currents (in the μV range) that can be measured on the surface of the scalp [17]. They reflect the synchronous activity of millions of neurons from the brain cortex (i.e., the outer layer of the brain). Compared to alternative neuroimaging techniques, such as MagnetoEncephaloGraphy or functional Magnetic Resonance Imaging, EEG is simultaneously cheap, portable and provides good time resolution. Because of these advantages, EEG has been used for many years in medicine, e.g., for the diagnosis of sleep disorders or epilepsy [17]. More recently, with the advance of computer processing performance, it became possible to measure and analyze in real-time the content of these EEG signals. This paved the way for the rise of BCI which uses real-time analysis and decoding of EEG signals in order to identify the mental state of the user and translate it into a command for an application [35].

The currently available tools used to visualize and analyze such signals are tailored for experts with a deep understanding of the brain, EEG principles and EEG signal processing [17]. Figure 2 (left and center) shows some typical visualizations of EEG signals used by experts, i.e., EEG signal traces and a 2D topographic map. More complex visualizations have been proposed, such as 3D topographic maps (Figure 2, right), but they require many mouse inputs to be observed from all angles, which make them inconvenient to use in practice.

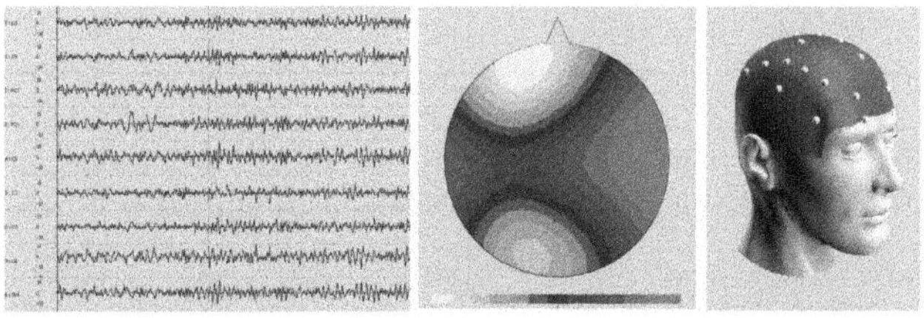

Figure 2. (Left) A trace of EEG signals collected from multiple sensors. 2D (center) and 3D (right) topographic maps. (Screenshots from OpenViBE [23]). The first two views are traditionally used by experts.

Although EEG visualizations are intended for experts only, the general public is often compelled by how the brain works and how its activity is measured. Anyone wondering about brain injuries, epilepsy, sleep or learning disorders, aging, etc. may want to seek further knowledge about how the brain works. Currently, the public is increasingly exposed to neurotechnologies due to the availability of consumer grade EEG devices, such as the Emotiv EPOC or the Neurosky MindWave. Consequently, it has become necessary to design tools and user interfaces which will allow the general public to visualize, understand and interact with EEG signals. For instance, Mullen *et al.* proposed a software solution to process EEG signals collected using wearable EEG devices and visualize them in 3D [16]. This software enables the user to estimate brain activity sources and connectivity but is still mainly designed for brain signal and neuroscience experts, and not so public-friendly. Another recent work, more suited to lay persons, is the "Portable Brain Scanner" [26]. This system makes use of a consumer-grade EEG device (the Emotiv EPOC) and a smartphone to provide a cheap and portable solution enabling anyone to visualize the sources of their brain activity on their smartphone in 3D. Another more attractive work, which is the most closely related to our Teegi system, is the "Mind-Mirror" system [15]. This system combines Augmented Reality (AR), 3D Visualization, and EEG to enable users to visualize their own brain activity in real-time superimposed to their own head, thanks to a semi-transparent mirror-based AR setup.

This short review of the existing literature about making EEG accessible to the general public revealed that this is still a vastly unexplored area. Moreover, these solutions do not take into account any representation that the general public may have regarding the brain and EEG signals – many lay people do not even know what EEG signals are – in order to provide suitable visualizations and interaction devices to better understand these concepts. Some rare studies have indicated that misconceptions about brain functions prevail in general public [7, 10, 25]. These works stress the importance of popular scientific communication and indicate that communication efforts should be focused on increasing public awareness. It is important to note that the existing works mentioned above are mostly centered on visualization, with little or no interaction possibilities to manipulate and understand the EEG signals in real-time and in a friendly way. This further deters the general public from understanding brain activity [30]. Therefore, with the aim to enhance general public awareness, our work associates technical innovation and user-centered design.

INTRODUCING TEEGI

Founding principles

Design choices were made according to pedagogical principles. It has long been recognized that learner-centered education is much more effective than transmission-based education, even in informal situations [33]. According to the constructivist paradigm, people create unique personal meanings by reflecting on interactive learning experiences. Therefore, people/learners should investigate and manipulate in order to become conscious of complex phenomena, change their misconceptions and construct scientific knowledge [31]. In association, meaningful models play an important role in this type of learning processes [9]. This motivated the design of an anthropomorphic interface that can be freely manipulated.

Our user-centered interactive media uses Spatial Augmented Reality (SAR) and tangible interaction. SAR, introduced by Raskar *et al.* [22], adds dynamic graphics to real-world surfaces by the means of projected light. Many systems were designed using projectors to add "painted" surface [22] or to give the illusion of virtual elements actually being there [34, 2]. A related approach is Tangible User Interface (TUI). TUI is concerned with providing tangible (i.e. physical) representations to digital information and controls [24]. One of the strengths of tangibles is their situatedness: the interaction takes place in a real-world environment that often hides most of the technological aspects to expose physical interaction components only. They are particularly well suited for mediation purposes as they tend to be more inviting compared to mouse-screen based interfaces [12].

SAR and TUIs are often found together [29, 21]. They are very complementary in that they both take place in the real world, in a common canvas. The tangible interaction allows for a hands-on approach by offering different input affordances (as well as physical constraints) to the user while the SAR technology allows for a flexible and situated way to give feedback. SAR can also be used as an affordable way to embed dynamic graphics on a physical surface that would otherwise require curved displays [4] or rear projection [3].

There are examples of systems that use either tangible or AR principles to interact or review physiological data. Hinckley *et al.* [11] designed a system which used tangible props to do neurosurgical planning. A small tangible head was used in conjunction with a plastic plane to select the cutting planes to be visualized on a screen. Also mentioned above, the "Mind-Mirror" [15] is the work closest to Teegi. However, with Teegi, the data is not co-localized with the data source. It provides flexibility and easier visualization as the users can change viewpoints by tangible interactions instead of rotating their head while keeping their eyes on the mirror. This "out-of-body" visualization also enables collaboration where multiple users can explore the data.

General description

Teegi is a tangible interface that enables users to visualize and analyze a representation of their own brain activity recorded via an EEG system in real-time and displayed on a physical character. After some processing of the raw signals, a dedicated visualization is projected directly on top of the character. This character is tracked, which allows us to co-locate the projection with the character's head, at any time. Hence, the user can easily visualize a realistic modeling of the EEG signals in any part of the scalp by manipulating the character, while maintaining a good spatial topology of the observed data. Teegi was purposely given a child-like appearance, as well as animated eyes (also projected) that blink at the same time as the users do, in order to breathe life to the character and enhance attractiveness. Indeed blinking can be easily detected in electrodes neighboring the eyes.

Three different filters can be applied to the raw data (see the technical section for details) enabling users to investigate influences of motor motions, visual activities or meditation, on their brain activity in real-time. To remain consistent with the tangible philosophy of this project, we decided to control the filters by way of small tangible characters (mini-Teegis) that can be moved on a "filter area", which is highlighted on the table by a projected halo (see Figure 3). For example, if a user wants to apply a filter that will allow her to better see what happens when moving her hand, she just needs to take the dedicated mini-Teegi, i.e. the one with the colored hands, and to move it to the filter area. Then, by moving her right hand, she should see changes in EEG amplitude on the left hemisphere of Teegi's head, as illustrated in Figure 4. The manipulation of Teegi requires a motor activity. Therefore, when the motor filter is on, manipulating Teegi will obviously lead to observable changes in brain activity.

Figure 3. Three mini-Teegis can be used to apply high-level EEG filters to highlight brain processes associated to *Motor*, *Vision* and *Meditation* activities. To do so, the user simply needs to move the desired mini-Teegi into a specific zone projected on the table (green circle).

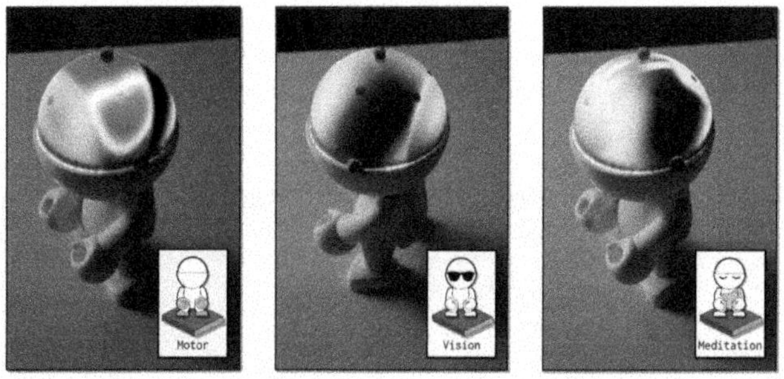

Figure 4. Examples of the displayed visualizations on Teegi for each of the provided filters. Once a filter is active, the brain area corresponding to the selected and processed activity is highlighted in colors while the remaining EEG signals are displayed in grayscale.

At the end of this paper, we present an explorative study we conducted to obtain feedback about the main features of Teegi. However, Teegi is not limited to these first features. In the next section, we describe additional interaction metaphors we have explored, and that may benefit more advanced users. These advanced features were not evaluated during the study.

Advanced features

Visualizing the raw signal recorded on each electrode of the EEG is not very informative for the general public. However, this can be instructive for students who are learning EEG signal processing and analysis. In our approach, we can display on the table these raw data, as shown in Figure 5 (left). This creates a visual link between what is recorded with the EEG system, and the visualization that is provided on Teegi's head. This is possible because we know the rough position of the user, and the exact position of Teegi. When applying a filter, as described in the previous section, the user can see the effect of his or her action on the signal (see Figure 5, right). Compared to a standard approach where everything takes place on a screen, we believe that such a spatial and tangible approach might ease the understanding of the filters' effect.

Figure 5. (Left) The raw EEG readings are displayed going from the user to the filter area and then rerouted towards Teegi. (Right) When a mini-Teegi (*i.e.* a filter) is active, the corresponding filtered signals are displayed between the filter area and Teegi instead.

Another dimension we explored is the use of tangible actions to control some parameters of the EEG signal processing. As an example, we have implemented a technique where the user can control the amplitude of the visualization color map by moving a tangible object on the table (figure 6). This could be useful to reveal tiny fluctuations of EEG signals. With such interaction techniques, the whole analysis could be conducted without the use of a screen or a mouse, which remains consistent with the tangible philosophy of the project.

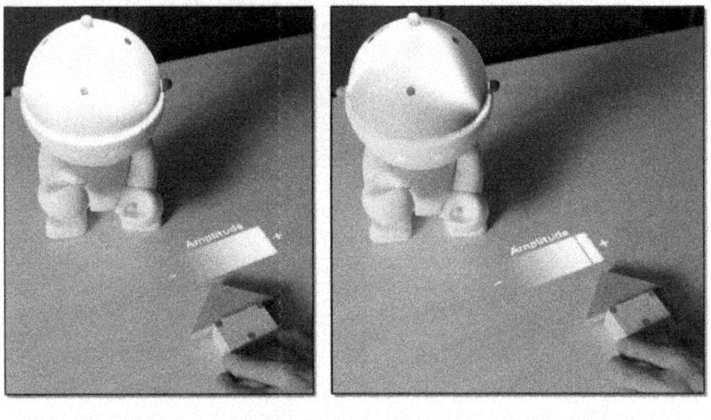

Figure 6. A moving tangible cursor is controlling the amplitude of the visualization color map.

Finally, we developed a solution that highlights the relationship between EEG signals and localized cortical sources, that is where the signals come from *inside* the brain. Using sLORETA inverse modeling [19] and Brainstorm to compute the kernel matrix [27], we obtained a model of the cortex containing 2002 voxels linked to the 32 EEG electrodes we used. We can then project in real time the activity which arises from the outer regions of the cortex on an object representing the brain, alongside with Teegi (Figure 7). Since both Teegi and the brain proxy are tracked, it becomes possible to manipulate two synchronized representations of the same brain activity (the source at the surface of the brain and the measures on the scalp). This opens way to mediation activities that are more advanced all the while keeping the simplicity and ease of use brought forth by using SAR and tangible interaction.

Figure 7. Using an inverse model, the cortical activity and EEG measures are presented together to users.

TECHNICAL DESCRIPTION

EEG

We designed different EEG signal processing pipelines that each create a specific visualization tailored to identify specific elements in the signal. The details of these pipelines are transparent to the user. Each pipeline corresponds to a mini-Teegi filter. In particular, we set up the following EEG signal processing pipelines:

1. Wide-band EEG activity: EEG signals were band-pass filtered between 3 Hz and 26 Hz, in order to filter DC drift and part of the artifacts (e.g., facial muscle activity [8]) that may pollute them. Their power is then computed before being displayed. This corresponds to unspecific brain signals, hence they were labeled as "raw" signals.
2. Sensorimotor activity: EEG signals were first band-pass filtered in the β band (16-24Hz), a brain rhythm highly involved in sensorimotor tasks [20]. Then, they were spatially filtered, i.e., the signals from several neighboring EEG sensors were combined in order to enhance the signal of interest. In particular, we used and displayed Laplacian spatial filters around electrodes C3, C4 and Cz. This enabled the users to visualize EEG activity changes due to movements of the left hand, right hand and feet. Indeed, it is known that the power of EEG signals in the β rhythm decreases in electrodes C3/Cz/C4 during right hand/feet/left hand movements respectively, and increases just after the end of this movement [20].
3. Visual activity: EEG signals were band-pass filtered in the α band (8-12 Hz), then only electrodes P3, Pz, P4, PO3, POz, PO4, O1, Oz and O2 (located on the back of the head, above the neck) were selected and displayed. These electrodes are indeed located over the visual cortex of the brain, i.e., the brain area in charge of visual information processing. The amplitude of the α rhythm is actually known to increase while the user is closing his/her eyes and is thus

not processing any visual information [17]. To ensure that the user could perceive this increase after he/she reopened his/her eyes, the visualization was delayed by 0.5s.

4. Meditation: on a more exploratory note, we used the synchronization between the signals from the anterior and posterior cortex (AFz/Pz), which was measured in a 7-28 Hz band with instantaneous phase locking value [13]. There are different outcomes (increase/decrease in synchronization) depending on meditation type. Mindfulness and body focus practices decrease the synchronization while transcendental practice increases it [14].

EEG signals were acquired with a 32-channels EEG device (made of two g.tec g.USBAmp EEG amplifiers). This professional-grade system ensured that our prototype had a good signal-to-noise ratio and accurate electrode location, avoiding unneeded uncertainties. Signals were processed in real-time using OpenViBE [23]. For pipelines 1 to 3, the displayed colors correspond to signal power strength; for pipeline 4 they correspond to the degree of synchronization.

Spatial Augmented Reality

In order to create an augmented character, we have designed a tabletop augmentation setup (see Figure 8). Teegi itself is a 25cm high Trexi DIY toy. The mini-Teegis are also 10cm high Trexis. The main program handling the whole installation was created with vvvv [1]. The primary projected content (Teegi augmentation and GUI display) is handled with a single wide lens projector ProjectionDesign F20SX of resolution 1024x768 located over the table in a top-down orientation. The tracking of Teegi is achieved with an OptiTrack V120:Trio. It runs at 120 FPS with an overall latency of 8.3ms and a precision of 0.8mm. The OptiTrack is located in the same configuration as the main projector and both devices are calibrated together manually. The tracking data is sent to vvvv using OptiTrack's NatNet protocol. Teegi's eyes are projected using a second projector (Vivitek Qumi Q2) that is located on the side of the table.

The filter selection is done using a Sony PSEye web camera pointed at the position of the program selection GUI. Each mini-teegi representing a filter has a fiducial marker attached to it. The library ARToolkitPlus [32] is used to detect which marker is currently selected.

The EEG signals are processed by the OpenViBE software [23] that also generates a grayscale texture of the scalp signals. This texture is then exported to a local shared samba folder which is then fetched and remapped to an appropriate color scale in vvvv before being mapped to Teegi's head. In addition, the raw EEG signals are sent to vvvv over VRPN for display purposes (see Figure 5).

EXPLORATIVE STUDY AND DISCUSSIONS

Protocol

We conducted an explorative study where participants had to manipulate Teegi following a given scenario. The objectives of this study were to i) evaluate the general usability of the interface and ii) obtain initial feedback about the relevance of the approach to help users understand EEG signals and the brain. Ten participants (6 males, 4 females, mean age 28.6 (SD=9.7)) took part in this study. Pre-tests confirmed they were rather naive on the subject. They manipulated the version of Teegi described in the General Description section (no advanced features). The general procedure was as follows:

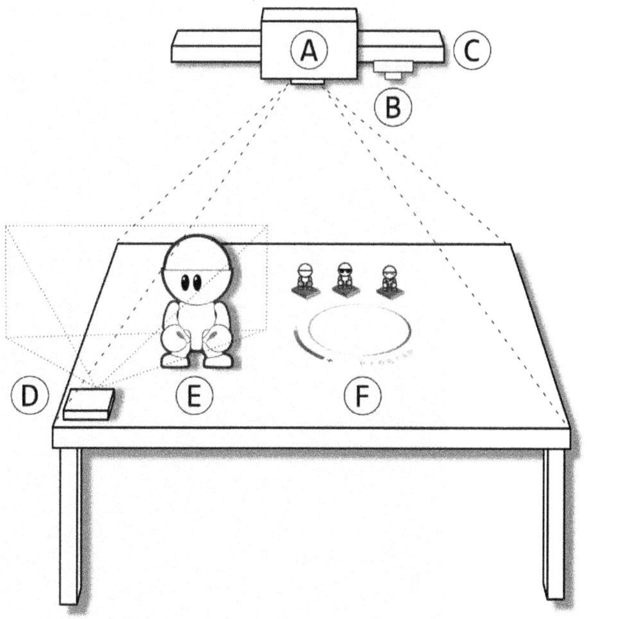

Figure 8. Diagram of the installation. (A) ProjectionDesign F20SX projector (B) Sony PSEye web camera (C) OptiTrack V120:Trio (D) Vivitek Qumi Q2 projector (E) Teegi (F) Program selection zone and mini-Teegis.

1. Pre-tests: The participant answered a first questionnaire assessing his or her representation of the brain. The participant then filled in different forms to measure his or her previous knowledge; one form per studied brain process (motor, vision and meditation).
2. Setting-up: The experimenter positioned the EEG cap on the participant's head. In parallel, the participant, guided by the experimenter, was made aware of the four didactic "cards" explaining the different filters *i.e.*, *Motor*, *Vision*, *Meditation* and *Raw*. Each card was comprised of an image of the mini-Teegi associated with the filter along with basic instructions to follow (e.g. the *Motor* card indicated to the participants to move their hands or feet while staying relaxed). There were also two cards describing the two types of visualization participants could face, *signal strength* and *synchronization*. Once the participant was equipped, a quick calibration phase occurred. While Teegi was still inactive, participants were asked to close their eyes for a few seconds, and to move their hands and feet in order to identify the baseline activity for visualization.
3. Personal Investigation: The participant was asked to freely manipulate Teegi as well as the filters to be able to answer the following questions:
   - What happens when you move your hands or feet?
   - What happens when you close your eyes?
   - What happens when you meditate?

During the whole study the participant sat comfortably in a chair. To avoid the occurrence of muscle artifacts that may pollute the signals, the user was instructed to stay relaxed and to refrain from making strong head movements.

4. Post-tests: The participant answered the questions above on dedicated forms, the same that were given at the beginning of step 1. Finally, he or she filled in a user survey questionnaire based on a 7-point Likert scale.

The whole session lasted approximately 1.5 hours per participant, with 15 to 20 minutes of hands-on time with Teegi. Each session was video-recorded. Video segments were separately visualized and labeled with the corresponding behavior (i.e. tangible and visual interactions, emotional expressions, and investigation strategies) using The Observer XT® 11.5 (Noldus, Info Tech, Wageninen, The Netherlands). After the session, the experimenter had an informal talk with the participant. He corrected the answers, making sure the participant was not leaving with false knowledge, and explained in more detail some aspects of the system (e.g. relationship between visual filter and attentional states, the various effects of meditation, ...). This phase lasted from 30 min to 1 hour depending on the participant's curiosity.

Results and discussions

To better understand the inherent strengths of Teegi towards learning, we assessed three main aspects of Teegi: its technical reliability, its relevance to ease understanding for non-experts, and the User eXperience (UX) it provides. This evaluation is based on 1) the results of the questionnaire that are summarized in Figure 9, 2) the analysis of the video recordings, and 3) the analysis of the forms the participants filled in to assess their pre and post-knowledge of the brain and EEG.

Technical reliability

Participants unanimously reported that the whole system worked properly. The quality of the SAR display is valued by the participants. In particular, they reported that the resolution was appropriate, and they did not report problems of offset between the display and the physical character. Participants declared that they were not disturbed by occlusion problems. The mild temporal delay between their action and their consequences seems not to be an issue.

Manipulations of Teegi were numerous and frequent. Teegi was touched or moved on average 25% of the session's duration, twice per minute. These manipulations consisted mostly of rotations, and to a lesser extent of lifting Teegi to enhance visual perception. Two participants reported difficulties in grasping Teegi while the remaining 8 were comfortable with the form of the character. Video analyses did not show difficulties for the manipulation of Teegi. Similarly, applying filters by manipulating the mini-Teegis seemed easy for the participants.

Relevance of the interface to ease understanding

The participants reported that they understood the visualization associated with the filters. Video analyses indicated that they systematically used all filters several times (3 times per session on average) for a similar duration (Raw filter : 30.4% (SD 13.3) of session duration; Motor filter: 26.0% (8.3); visual filter: 16.9% (5.5); meditation filter: 26.6% (8.7)). Interestingly, the visual activity filter seemed slightly easier to understand than the other filters. Moreover, video analyses indicated that the participants did not have difficulty observing the signals on Teegi's head, as soon as they found the right location to observe. Overall, participants reported that they were able to use Teegi without any difficulties.

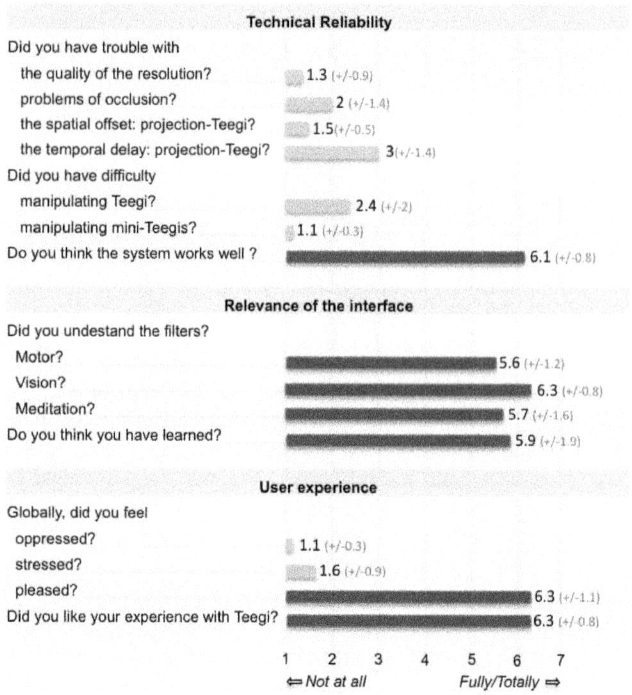

Figure 9. Results of the questionnaire (selected questions). Note that purple (resp. orange) bars indicate questions measuring Teegi's qualities (resp. limitations).

All participants completed the required tasks. They used instruction cards 5 times per session on average. They reported that they could focus on the tasks rather than on the mechanisms used to achieve them. This suggests that Teegi is a rather transparent interface. Regarding learning of brain processes and EEG, participants reported that they believed they had learned while doing the study. This was confirmed by the results of the pre- and post-test assessments (see Figure 10). These assessments focused on the recognition and the understanding of brain activation during Motor activities, Visual activities and Meditation. Understanding was marked as acquired if 1) the activated areas were correctly localized and 2) the explanations of the brain process were correct. It was marked as under way if only 1) or 2) was satisfied but not both; and as not acquired if neither 1) nor 2) were satisfied. The marks obtained by the participants improved after using Teegi. Overall, this suggests that Teegi offers many interesting features to ease learning and mediation.

All our results indicate that Teegi clearly promotes real-time tangible interactions, which contributes to enhancing awareness. Constructivism and inquiry-based science education principles indicate that, to become conscious of complex phe-

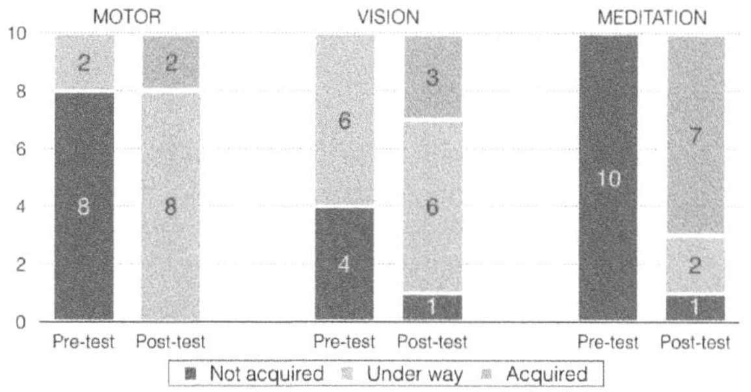

Figure 10. Marks obtained by the participants during the pre- and post-test assessments. See text for details.

nomena and construct scientific knowledge, people/learners have to experiment by interacting with and physically manipulating the content [30]. This is particularly true for brain activity that is difficult to understand because it cannot be sensed [6], contrary to other activities (e.g. respiratory) that are perceived through sensory-motor mechanisms. Hence, brain activities need to be conceptualized, and the success of learning processes strongly depends on the interface. Teegi, which has been largely promoted by the participants, seems to fulfill this function.

User eXperience

The general experience with Teegi was rated as pleasant, attractive and stimulating, and participants did not feel stressed or oppressed. Overall, participants reported that they liked interacting with Teegi. The emotion expression analyses confirmed those statements. They showed that on average participants expressed curiosity and questioning about Teegi feedback during almost 20% (20.1% SD=9.1) of the manipulation duration. Other emotion expressions observed for all participants were joy and pleasure (e.g. smile, laugh, joyful verbal expression...). They occurred during almost 10% (9.8% SD= 6.7) of the interaction duration with Teegi. Surprise emotions were observed but less frequently. Interestingly, boredom, weariness expressions occurred rarely (only for 2 users) and only at the end of the manipulation time. We did not observe any occurrence of exasperation or irritation. These results suggest a high level of acceptance for Teegi. This is a fundamental requirement for a tool aiming at improving access to knowledge.

Behavior observations indicated that the majority of participants spoke with Teegi and used morphological zones specific to human interactions while manipulating it. For example, they held its hands and held it up by the waist as one would do with a child. Some users spoke in the first person when they observed changes on the character's scalp for example "so, when I move my hands, I light up on the sides"; many said aloud that Teegi was their own image, for example "so, Teegi is me!". This identification suggests that an activation of associations between the perceived character's personality and self-perception may have occurred [18]. It is known that identification can be associated with increasing loss of self-awareness, and its temporary replacement with elements of the perceived character's personality [5]. Therefore a human shaped, child-like character, made lifelike by animated projected eyes, could enhance both empathy and implicit self-perception of one's own brain activity, as provided by our interactive media. The anthropomorphic appearance of Teegi could explain the motivation and positive UX reported by the users. All these hypotheses would be the aim of a more extensive UX study.

Regarding visual attention, the participants were apparently paying attention to Teegi most of the time (83.3%, SD 7.6). This supports the fact that Teegi mobilized user attention. It also indicates a cognitive user engagement. Personal investigations were permanent (only 1.9% of inactivity was measured during the session duration; SD=1.7). Behavior analyses indicate that participants made predictions, hypotheses and tested them by conducting experiments. Numerous trial and error strategies were frequently used. This clearly indicates personal active control of the task and inquiry processes. Overall, Teegi stimulates investigations and encourages persistence in task completion.

CONCLUSIONS

In this paper, we presented Teegi, a tangible interface that makes EEG understandable to non-expert users. Our main contribution is the interface itself, which is built from both theoretical foundations, notably from human learning and scientific mediation and technical developments, including spatial augmented reality, tangible interaction and real-time neurotechnologies. We also demonstrated that this interface was well accepted by a first pool of users. In the future, we plan to make a more in-depth investigation into how well users are able to learn about EEG and brain activity with Teegi. To this end, we will conduct dedicated experiments with students and/or visitors in scientific museums. We would also like to precisely evaluate how Teegi benefits learning compared to standard approaches. For more advanced users, ad-hoc tangible filter creation could prove to be of great interest, adding flexibility to the overall system. Finally, it is known that BCI requires the user to learn to control his/her own brain activity to input computer commands [35], which is a long and tedious task. We expect Teegi to be a motivating and informative way to support this training in the future.

REFERENCES

1. VVVV. `http://vvvv.org`.
2. Benko, H., Jota, R., and Wilson, A. Miragetable: freehand interaction on a projected augmented reality tabletop. In *CHI '12*, ACM (2012), 199–208.
3. Benko, H., Wilson, A. D., and Balakrishnan, R. Sphere: multi-touch interactions on a spherical display. In *UIST '08*, ACM (2008), 77–86.
4. Brockmeyer, E., Poupyrev, I., and Hudson, S. PAPILLON: Designing Curved Display Surfaces with Printed Optics. In *UIST '13*, ACM (2013), 457–462.
5. Cohen, J. Defining Identification: A Theoretical Look at the Identification of Audiences With Media Characters. *Mass Communication and Society 4*, 3 (2001), 245–264.
6. Damasio, A. R. *Descartes' error: emotion, reason, and the human brain*. 1994.

7. Dekker, S., Lee, N. C., Howard-Jones, P., and Jolles, J. Neuromyths in education: Prevalence and predictors of misconceptions among teachers. *Front. Psychol. 3* (2012).
8. Fatourechi, M., Bashashati, A., Ward, R., and Birch, G. EMG and EOG artifacts in brain computer interface systems: A survey. *Clin Neurophysiol 118*, 3 (2007), 480–494.
9. Fleck, S., and Simon, G. An Augmented Reality Environment for Astronomy Learning in Elementary Grades: An Exploratory Study. In *IHM '13* (2013), 9.
10. Herculano-Houzel, S. Do you know your brain? A survey on public neuroscience literacy at the closing of the decade of the brain. *The Neuroscientist 8*, 2 (2002), 98–110.
11. Hinckley, K., Pausch, R., Goble, J. C., and Kassell, N. F. Passive real-world interface props for neurosurgical visualization. In *CHI '94*, ACM (1994), 452–458.
12. Horn, M. S., Solovey, E. T., Crouser, R. J., and Jacob, R. J. Comparing the use of tangible and graphical programming languages for informal science education. In *CHI '09*, ACM (2009), 975–984.
13. Lachaux, J.-P., Rodriguez, E., Le Van Quyen, M., Lutz, A., Martinerie, J., and Varela, F. J. Studying single-trials of phase synchronous activity in the brain. *Int. J. Bifurcation Chaos 10*, 10 (oct 2000), 2429–2439.
14. Lehmann, D., Faber, P. L., Tei, S., Pascual-Marqui, R. D., Milz, P., and Kochi, K. Reduced functional connectivity between cortical sources in five meditation traditions detected with lagged coherence using EEG tomography. *NeuroImage 60*, 2 (apr 2012), 1574–86.
15. Mercier-Ganady, J., Lotte, F., Loup-escande, E., Marchal, M., and Lécuyer, A. The Mind-Mirror: See Your Brain in Action in Your Head Using EEG and Augmented Reality. In *VR*, IEEE (2014).
16. Mullen, T., Kothe, C., Chi, Y. M., Ojeda, A., Kerth, T., Makeig, S., Cauwenberghs, G., and Tzyy-Ping, J. Real-time modeling and 3D visualization of source dynamics and connectivity using wearable EEG. In *IEEE Eng Med Biol Soc*, vol. 2013 (2013), 2184–2187.
17. Niedermeyer, E., and da Silva, F. L. *Electroencephalography: basic principles, clinical applications, and related fields*. Lippincott Williams & Wilkins, 2005.
18. Paiva, A., Dias, J., Sobral, D., Aylett, R., Woods, S., Hall, L., and Zoll, C. Learning by Feeling: Evoking Empathy with Synthetic Characters. *Applied Artificial Intelligence 19*, 3-4 (2005), 235–266.
19. Pascual-Marqui, R. Standardized low resolution brain electromagnetic tomography (sLORETA): technical details. *Methods Find Exp Clin Pharmacol 24D* (2002), 5–12.
20. Pfurtscheller, G., and da Silva, F. H. L. Event-related EEG/MEG synchronization and desynchronization: basic principles. *Clin Neurophysiol 110*, 11 (1999), 1842–1857.
21. Piper, B., Ratti, C., and Ishii, H. Illuminating clay: a 3-D tangible interface for landscape analysis. In *CHI '02*, ACM (2002), 355–362.
22. Raskar, R., Welch, G., Low, K.-L., and Deepak, B. Shader Lamps: Animating Real Objects With Image-Based Illumination. In *Rendering Techniques 2001*, S. Gortler and K. Myszkowski, Eds., Eurographics. Springer Vienna, 2001, 89–102.
23. Renard, Y., Lotte, F., Gibert, G., Congedo, M., Maby, E., Delannoy, V., Bertrand, O., and Lécuyer, A. OpenViBE: An Open-Source Software Platform to Design, Test and Use Brain-Computer Interfaces in Real and Virtual Environments. *Presence-Teleop Virt 19*, 1 (2010), 35–53.
24. Shaer, O. Tangible User Interfaces: Past, Present, and Future Directions. *Foundations and Trends in Human-Computer Interaction 3*, 1-2 (2009), 1–137.
25. Simons, D. J., and Chabris, C. F. What people believe about how memory works: A representative survey of the US population. *PloS one 6*, 8 (2011), e22757.
26. Stopczynski, A., Stahlhut, C., Larsen, J. E., Petersen, M. K., and Hansen, L. K. The Smartphone Brain Scanner: A Portable Real-Time Neuroimaging System. *PloS one 9*, 2 (2014), e86733.
27. Tadel, F., Baillet, S., Mosher, J. C., Pantazis, D., and Leahy, R. M. Brainstorm: a user-friendly application for MEG/EEG analysis. *Comput Intell Neurosci 2011* (Jan. 2011), 879716.
28. Tan, D., and Nijholt, A. *Brain-Computer Interaction: Applying our Minds to Human-Computer Interaction*. Springer-Verlag: London., 2010.
29. Underkoffler, J., and Ishii, H. Urp: a luminous-tangible workbench for urban planning and design. In *CHI '99*, ACM (1999), 386–393.
30. Vosniadou, S. Knowledge Acquisition and Conceptual Change. *Applied Psychology 41*, 4 (1992), 347–357.
31. Vosniadou, S., Ioannides, C., Dimitrakopoulou, A., and Papademetriou, E. Designing learning environments to promote conceptual change in science. *Learn Instr*, 11 (2001), 381–419.
32. Wagner, D., and Schmalstieg, D. Artoolkitplus for pose tracking on mobile devices. In *CVWW '07* (2007), 139–146.
33. Wellington, J. Formal and informal learning in science: The role of the interactive science centres. *Physics Education 25*, 5 (1990), 247.
34. Wilson, A., Benko, H., Izadi, S., and Hilliges, O. Steerable augmented reality with the beamatron. In *UIST '12*, ACM (2012), 413–422.
35. Wolpaw, J. R., and Wolpaw, E. W. *BCI: Principles and Practice*. Oxford University Press, 2012.

Individual Variation in Susceptibility to Cybersickness

Lisa Rebenitsch
Michigan State University
428 South Shaw Rd
East Lansing, MI 48824
rebenits@msu.edu

Charles Owen
Michigan State University
428 South Shaw Rd
East Lansing, MI 48824
cbowen@msu.edu

ABSTRACT
We examined background characteristics of virtual reality participants in order to determine correlations to cybersickness. As 3D media and new VR display technologies from companies such as Occulus and Sony become more popular, the incidence of cybersickness is likely to increase. Understanding the impact of individual backgrounds on susceptibility can help shed light on which individuals are more likely to be impacted. Past history of motion sickness and video game play have the best predictive power of cybersickness of the factors studied. A model to estimate the likelihood of cybersickness using background characteristics is posed.

Author Keywords
Cybersickness; individual variation; virtual reality; habituation.

ACM Classification Keywords
H.5.2 **[User Interfaces]:** Evaluation/methodology; H.5.1 **[Multimedia Information Systems]:** Artificial, augmented, and virtual realities.

INTRODUCTION
Virtual reality systems and 3D displays are rapidly becoming mainstream, but general usage guidelines are still lacking. A significant issue with these systems is the onset of motion sickness-like symptoms, a phenomenon referred to as *cybersickness*. One difficulty we have encountered when studying this effect is high individual variability, with factors such as video game play and habituation due to previous exposure. Including individual histories when testing for cybersickness has been proposed, but it is not in wide use. We examine possible background characteristics that correlate to cybersickness.

There are time considerations when determining a participant's susceptibility. There is also uncertainty in appropriate selection of individual characteristics that may affect cybersickness. Ideally, these characteristics should be objective, fast to determine, and explain the majority of the individual variation. The most common measurement of individual susceptibility is a questionnaire on past history of motion sickness. These questionnaires are simple to administer, but are subjective and are usually long, consisting of two or more pages. Another hazard is assuming that motion sickness in one condition or mode of transport will result in the same symptoms in a different condition. Sharples et al. demonstrated a change in symptoms when changing the display [20]. Another potential issue is assuming that the same characteristics associated with increased motion sickness will have the same effect in cybersickness. Arns and Cerne recommend that this assumption should be applied cautiously [1]. In their pilot study, the impact of age on susceptibility differed substantially between motion sickness and cybersickness.

We performed an exploratory study of individual sources and variation of susceptibility to cybersickness with the intent of determining possible background characteristics that affect the individual susceptibility beyond past history. Identifying the largest sources of susceptibility will allow shorter susceptibility tests, and better explain cybersickness due to individual, application, and hardware characteristics. This is beneficial when developing shorter pre-immersive surveys that can be used to better advise participants and researchers. *Habituation* is the decrease in impact of a stimulus due to repeated exposure. Potential sources of habituation other than a virtual reality display itself are relatively unexplored. Video games and 3D movies can provide similar stimuli. Given the past correlations reported with motion sickness history, we employed the motion sickness susceptibility questionnaire [8] and a usability survey to test for additional sources of habituation.

Since different virtual reality systems can have different effects on cybersickness [20], participants were tested with two similar systems. One issue that arose was that since the questionnaire is subjective, participants could forget past instances of motion sickness or not wish to admit unpleasant or embarrassing past experiences. In the instance of those not wishing to admit illness, participants were likely to not admit the onset of cybersickness during a session. In the instance of participants mentioning that they forgot past instances of motion sickness, the history survey failed to provide accurate values.

UIST 2014, October 5–8, 2014, Honolulu, HI, USA.

ACM 978-1-4503-3069-5/14/10...$15.00.
http://dx.doi.org/10.1145/2642918.2647394

We administered background and symptoms surveys following virtual reality use, and then tested for correlation between symptoms and background characteristics. We found several trends and significant correlations in participant background characteristics. We found correlation with vision correction, past history of motion sickness, and carnival ride sickness. We found trends in video game play and motion sickness when riding trains. Linear regression using background characteristics explained 43% to 58% of the variance of cybersickness scores. The background characteristics required can be attained quickly for future normalization purposes.

BACKGROUND

Cybersickness is the malfunction of the visual-vestibular system that results in developing oculomotor disruptions, disorientation, and/or nausea symptoms when viewing virtual environments. Cybersickness has been studied for several decades in the context of head mounted displays, CAVE automated virtual environments (CAVE), and simulators. The most common measure of symptoms in cybersickness is the simulator sickness questionnaire (SSQ) by Kennedy et al. [17]. The SSQ requests the severity of 16 symptoms on a 0-3 scale (i.e. none, mild, moderate, and severe). The symptoms can be grouped as a whole or into 3 subcategories of nausea (e.g. nausea, stomach awareness), oculomotor (e.g. eye strain, blurred vision), and disorientation (e.g. dizziness, vertigo), each with their own weighting. The total score ranges from 0-224, with a score of less than 10 considered to be normal.

Systemic elements that have been shown to influence the likelihood onset of symptoms consistent with cybersickness can be grouped into three categories: hardware, software, and individual. Hardware and software have had greater attention as they are easier to control, with the possible exception of interpupillary distance (IPD) or the distance between the eyes, and are regularly considered independently of individual susceptibility.

Two known hardware characteristics that affect cybersickness are display type (e.g. monitor, head mounted display (HMD), projection screen, etc.) and field of view (FOV). Sharples et al. showed a change in susceptibility among HMDs, large screen displays, and desktop applications [20]. Dizio and Lackner reported that doubling the FOV nearly doubled the SSQ total [6]. With these large effects, the display and FOV should be included in any general model of cybersickness.

Software may have a larger effect on cybersickness than hardware. The choice of navigation mode has been shown to impact symptomatology. Jaeger and Mourant indicated that the choice of input device can have an effect by demonstrating lower cybersickness score when using a treadmill than when using a mouse [14]. Increasing forward movement speed has also been shown to have an impact [23]. The visual stimuli themselves can also have an effect. So, Ho, and Lo showed the radial, vertical, and horizontal luminosity frequency can have an effect [22]. The application characteristics vary more than hardware, but both must be included for a complete model of cybersickness.

Researchers have proposed models to include multiple sources of variation. Chen, Yuen, and So proposed the cybersickness dose value [4]. This model uses luminosity frequency and velocity of the scene to predict cybersickness. Luminosity frequency is the luminance variation over a spatial frequency power spectral density function. This is typically found using the fast Fourier transform on the luminance of the pixels along a line in a frame. Bos proposed modeling the stimuli as the discrepancy of what the vestibular and visual systems feel in a virtual environment compared to true gravity[2]. Jones et al. proposed using the average effect of a particular characteristic to increase or decrease expected values [15]. None of these models include individual susceptibility, and only Jones et al. includes hardware differences.

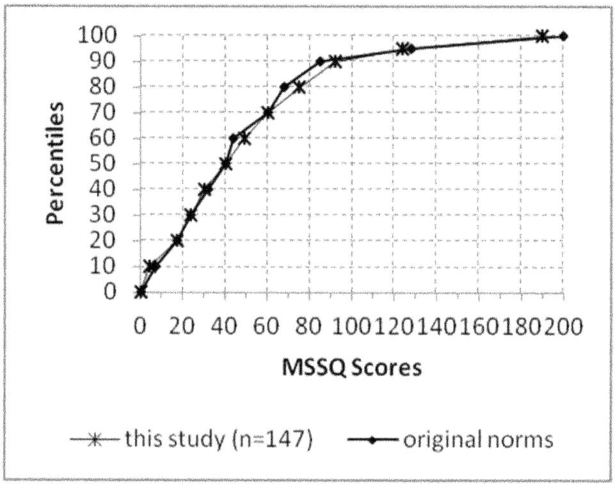

Figure 1. MSSQ Percentiles from [8]

Individual susceptibility is the hidden aspect in that it is not directly observable in a system. Individual susceptibility may vary widely, but recognizing the sources will help better advise participants with general use of virtual environments, and to improve performance with these systems. Past studies have suggested gender, past history of motion sickness, age, weight/height, vision acuity, and familiarity to estimate susceptibility.

Gender is one of the most studied aspects. Females regularly display more symptoms than males [14,18,26]. However, some studies have seen no significant difference between genders [10,25]. One theory for this disparity is that males are less willing to report feelings of illness. Another theory is from a study by Harm et al. [12]. In this study, women became ill sooner, but also recovered faster. This suggests that women will better tolerate short, but frequent sessions, while males would be better able to tolerate a single, longer session. The lack of understanding of effect of gender makes it difficult to include in a general model of susceptibility. We originally intended to include gender in our analysis to provide additional support and clarity to this variable.

Past history of motion sickness likely has the most predictive power of cybersickness [26]. There are multiple available questionnaires including Golding's motion sickness susceptibility questionnaire (MSSQ) [8], Gianaros et al. motion sickness assessment questionnaire (MSAQ) [7], and Kennedy and Graybiel's Motion History Questionnaire (MHQ) [16]. The MHQ reviews the history of motion sickness in various modes of travel including trains, airplanes, carnival rides, cars, and others. It then combines the scores from each mode of travel weighted by the severity and frequency of the symptoms. Stanney et al. found a correlation of low and high susceptible groups with the full MHQ and carnival ride motion sickness [26]. The MSSQ is very similar to the MHQ. It also asks for the frequency of motion sickness in the last ten years and during childhood, but it is somewhat more compact. The scores range from 0 to 200, with a 50 percentile of 45 as shown in Figure 1. It has shown good correlation with other forms of motion sickness. This makes it a good candidate to identify individual variation of cybersickness scores. We use this questionnaire in our studies and further consider which portions of the MSSQ best correlate to cybersickness.

Age is a relatively new aspect as it has been assumed that cybersickness would follow the same pattern as motion sickness. Motion sickness is more prevalent in younger individuals, but Arns and Cern demonstrated the opposite for cybersickness [1]. They reported visitors to their virtual reality facility under the age of 15 had noticeably less cybersickness than adult visitors. Park et al. also reported substantially fewer early withdrawals with younger participants than older participants (13.7% and 37.3%, respectively) [18]. Given that age is an easily determined characteristic, it can be included in a general model of cybersickness when its pattern of effect is well established. Unfortunately, recruiting older participants can be difficult. Studies that include age regularly focus on age or have a virtual system open to the public over a long period of time [1,18].

Height and body mass index (BMI) have shown correlation with cybersickness. Taha et al. reported that taller participants had fewer symptoms [29]. They caution that results are preliminary due to small sample sizes (10 participants, 1 per height). While Taha et al. did not find an effect of raw weight, Stanney et al. did find a correlation of a participant's body mass index (BMI) and oculomotor symptoms [26]. A participant's BMI may not be willingly given, which makes it difficult to include in a general estimate. Given the preliminary results, height was not included in our analysis.

How well a participant may view a display may have an effect on cybersickness. This is both a hardware and individual attribute. In hardware, the resolution can be altered. In individuals, stereo acuity, IPD, and the need for vision correction vary. Since many virtual environments are stereoscopic, a participant's stereo acuity could have an effect on cybersickness. Research suggests that it has little effect. Hale and Stanney reported no statistical difference in symptoms between low and high stereo acuity groups [11]. Studies may require participants to have proper vision correction, but have not tested whether the need for vision correction could affect cybersickness. Since glasses can shift the optics of HMDs and add another layer of refraction, we include this in our study.

Habituation has a demonstrated effect on symptoms. Participants who reuse a system show a decreasing severity of symptoms over time [13,19,27]. Howarth and Hodder demonstrate that session frequencies of 2-7 days will allow most people to adjust to a system [13]. Since habituation so highly impacts susceptibility, it can make within-subject studies over time difficult. The length of time required between exposures to avoid habituation is unknown. Unfortunately, session frequencies of over a week can result in a number of participants not returning for all sessions.

Similar stimuli could also form habituation. We include video game use, 3D display use, and frequency of hat/caps usage as additional potential sources. Video games and 3D displays provide similar visuals. The inclusion of hats is due to the use of a HMD for the virtual reality system. Those who wear hats may be more comfortable and familiar with items being placed on their heads.

PROCEDURE

20 participants were recruited through local advertising. The only restriction for attending was that the participants must be over 18 years old and currently not ill when arriving for their session. Participants were requested to test two similar HMD-based virtual environments a minimum of one week apart. During their first visit, participants signed a consent form and were given a tutorial on the system and controls.

The participants were monitored during a session via a verbal one-point scale, or "immersion rating." The maximum time spent in an environment was 24 minutes. The SSQ was administered immediately following the session. A usability survey was given after the first session and the MSSQ following the second session. The full text of the survey is available in the Appendix. The surveys were given separately to avoid survey fatigue. No SSQ pretest was given to minimize the possibility of demand characteristics, or the effect of increasing results due to anticipating them, as mentioned by Young et al.[30].

Of the 20 participants there were 3 females and 17 males recruited for the study. Participants' ages ranged from 18 to 31, with all except one under 22. While gender and age were originally intended to be included in the analysis, we felt it was inappropriate to include in the analysis due to possible bias in the data pool. This bias could not be remedied with our available volunteer pool. Therefore, the results are likely more accurate for young adult, males. Four withdrew before the second session due to scheduling difficulties. This resulted in 20 participants who completed the usability study and 16 who completed the MSSQ survey.

Measurements Employed

There were four sources of information during the study: the MSSQ, the SSQ, the usability survey, and the immersion ratings. The MSSQ provided a standardized measurement of the past history of motion sickness. The SSQ provided a standardized cybersickness score. The usability survey examined additional sources of individual variation and proper design of virtual environments. The questions on the usability survey are included in the Appendix.

The immersion rating was included to monitor participants during immersion for safety. Participants were asked every three minutes, "*On a scale of 0-10, 0 being how you felt coming in, 10 is that you want to stop, where you are now?*" The question was phrased to permit withdrawal for any reason rather than only nausea. Out of 37 sessions, we had 3 early withdrawals from a session, all male. Missing values from participants who withdrew early were replaced by the maximum rating of 10. Single question verbal scales are in wide use, but no single scale is currently used across the majority of labs. Bos et al. [3] and Griffin and Newman's [9] scales correlate to the SSQ, and Dahlman's [5] correlates to a longer motion sickness questionnaire. However, all three of these scales focus on symptoms of nausea and had young adult populations. Given that using nausea in the question can cause demand characteristics, an undesirable effect, any verbal score that used nausea in the question or response was not viable. We derived our question with no reference to nausea with a 0-10 range as it is common range in the literature and is familiar to participants. As Bos et al. had a similar population, a requested the same number of sessions and range, we were expected good correlation with our scale [3].

The effect of our choice to permit exiting for any reason was seen in the cited reasons of our dropouts. Only one cited nausea as their reason for leaving. Of the remaining two, one cited eyestrain and dizziness and the other cited fatigue.

Given the good correlation with carnival motion sickness Stanney et al. reported [26], the MSSQ subcategories were calculated independently for analysis. The original calculation was a weighted sum of childhood and adult frequency of being ill in various modes of transport. Motion sickness and vomiting frequency were each indicated on a 0-4 scale (i.e. never, rarely, sometimes, frequently, always), and travel frequency was calculated on a 0-3 scale (i.e. never, 1-4 trips, 5-10 trips, 11 or more trips) Each individual mode of transport was calculated as follows:

$$MSSQ_c = 2.64 * \frac{Child(m_c + v_c) + Adult(m_c + v_c)}{Child(t_c) + Adult(t_c)} \quad [1]$$

In this equation, m_c is the motion sickness frequency of the subcategory, v_c is the vomiting frequency of the subcategory, and t_c is if the participant has used that mode of travel (1) or has never used that mode of travel (0).

Usability Survey

The usability survey in the Appendix was administered to learn a participant's past experience with similar devices and includes general question regarding display comfort and usability. Questions 2-5 address prior experience with HMDs and 3D displays. Questions 1, 6, and 7 address potential habituation characteristics. Video games provide similar visual stimuli and may aid in habituation. Hat usage may affect comfort of the head mounted display. Vision correction may be correlated with cybersickness, and was split into four categories: none, contacts, glasses, and both. Vision correction results in additional refraction of light and may make a participant more sensitive to virtual reality discrepancies. Also, since virtual reality displays are often designed for wearing without glasses, the glasses may affect the proper position of the display.

Question 8 and 9 asked for the comfort of the virtual reality display. Although participants could withdraw early if they gave an immersion rating of 10, it was reasonable to assume that a participant may choose to avoid virtual reality with fewer symptoms. This value is called the *self-limiting immersion rating*. Question 10 was to determine where virtual reality may be used in non-academic settings, if the technology was readily available.

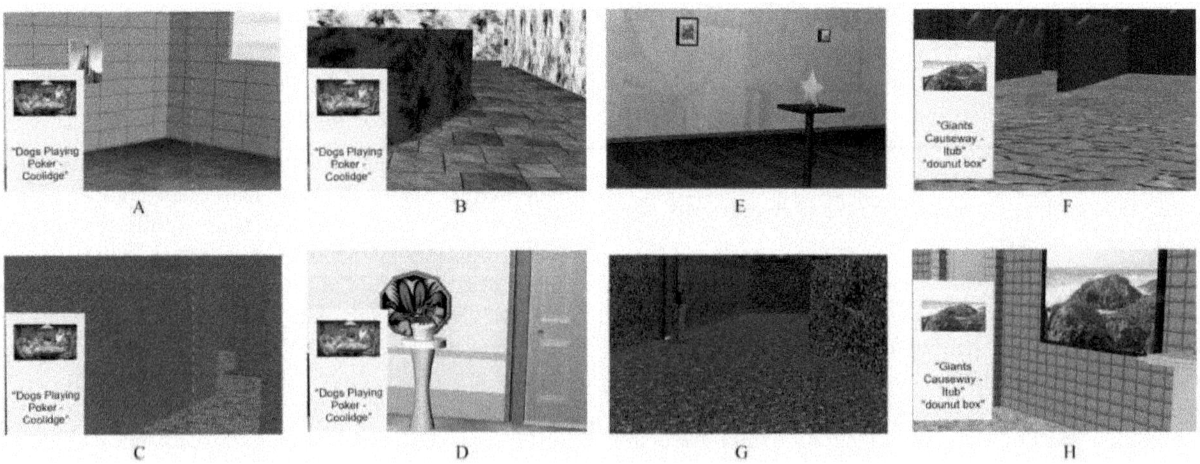

Figure 2. Environment Screenshots (A-D from world 1, and D-H from world 2)

ENVIRONMENT

The intent of the environment was to provide a realistically available application. This was to provide symptom ratings similar to what would be seen in general settings. Virtual reality is used in design, training, entertainment, and historical (e.g. archeology, museum) contexts. Most of these settings require a full environment and do not have explicit intent to induce cybersickness.

From the above the following criteria were applied:

- Head tracking
- Full world (e.g. ground, walls, sky)
- No intentional cybersickness inducing elements

We choose a mixture of museum and entertainment contexts for the system. Participants were given a set of connected picture rooms and mazes. Since participants had two sessions, two sets of rooms were made (Figure 2). The room sets were presented in a random order. To assure consistency, there was always one rectangular maze and one curved wall maze and 3-4 picture rooms. One of the mazes had a low-orientation cue texture (Figure 2, C and G) and one had textures with orientation cues (Figure 2, D and H).Participants were given a menu with a list of items to locate. They then tried to locate all items as quickly as possible. The participant with the fastest time was given a $15 prize, and second place participant was given $5.

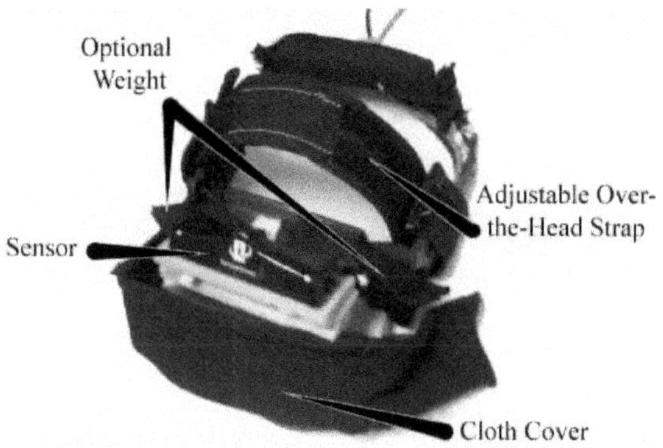

Figure 3. Head Mounted Display Used

Participants used a modified Sony Glasstron HMD when exploring the environment as shown in Figure 3. The HMD's original behind-the-head strap was replaced with a padded strap. It also had an optional weight pouch and an additional over-the-head band added to decrease tightness of the strap. The added weight was to mimic the feel of heavier displays. The application was rendered in stereo and was head tracked with 6-degrees of freedom. Participants were given the HMD with or without the additional weight in random order.

Participants were informed they could move up to one step in each direction from the starting position. Longer distance movement required use of an XBox controller. The joysticks permitted forward-back motions and yaw (left-right) rotation. Joystick navigation was independent of head tracking, with the head position and orientation added onto the joystick's location. The joystick's forward walking speed was a maximum of 2 m/s and rotation was a maximum of $\pi/3$ radians/s. A run and float button was included which increased the forward speed by a factor of 2. A float button which rose to viewpoint to 2.5 meters was added to aid in navigation (no forward movement was permitted when floating).

HARDWARE AND SOFTWARE SPECIFICATIONS

The system was run using Vizard 3.0 with 3-sample antialiasing and in stereo with a software interpupillary distance of 6cm. The computer had a 2.5GHz dual core, 4GB RAM, and a Quadro FX 3700 graphics card. The application frame refresh rate was an average of 60 Hz. The HMD was a Sony Glasstron LDI-D100B, with an 800X600 resolution, non adjustable interpupillary distance, and a 35 degree diagonal FOV. The application was rendered with a 33.3 degree diagonal FOV. Tracking was done with an Intersense IS900 which has a specification latency of 4ms. Formal tracker-to-display latency calculations were not performed.

ANALYSIS

The SSQ and MSSQ values were tested for correlations with background information, and the variance attributable to background variables was determined. The SSQ and MSSQ values failed to meet the Shapiro test for normality. The MSSQ values were transformed by a square root to achieve normality. The full SSQ did not achieve normality under normal transformations so non-parametric tests were employed. The Kendall non-parametric test was used to test for correlations with non-normalized data, and the Spearman test was used with ordered data (e.g. frequency of 3D exposure).

Participant's background characteristics from the usability survey were used to identify variables that correlated with susceptibility in addition to their motion sickens history. Game Play, 3D Display Exposure, and Hat Usage were reported as continuous values. Game Play and Hat Usage were binned into weekly averages. Game Play was binned into rarely (0-2 hours), sometimes (2.5-6), and regularly (6.5 and over hours). 3D Display Exposure was binned into never, monthly, and yearly. Hat Usage was binned into rarely (less than 6 hours), sometimes (6-15 hours), and frequently (over 15 hours).

To better predict symptoms in participants, their background characteristic were fitted to a linear model. This linear model can be used to estimate a participant's symptom severity by summing the contribution from multiple characteristics, and how much the symptoms vary from participant to participant. Through linear regression we estimated the variance due to background characteristics, or how much a set of characteristics contributes to susceptibility. The independent variables were initially tested separately to identify the best characteristic for predicting susceptibility. Characteristics that explained greater variation were then merged to develop better models.

By determining which characteristics correlate best to the SSQ and contribute to most to variance, we can create a shorter susceptibility survey for cybersickness. Also, by normalizing cybersickness results with respect to individual variance, we can better determine the effect of hardware and software in later studies.

RESULTS

We found a few significant correlations with the SSQ total and past motion sickness history and vision correction. There were trends between the SSQ and binned Game Play and train motion sickness. The largest source of variance was with Vision Correction. Most participants confirmed that they would use virtual reality in some settings.

The MSSQ scores were substantially below average with a mean of 16.7 (before square root transformation). We had 4 participants who gave an MSSQ of 0. A true MSSQ score of 0 means that the participant is incapable of becoming motion sick, and, therefore, may be incapable of becoming cybersick. According to the percentiles put forth by Golding, less than 2% of the population should have a MSSQ of 0 [8]. Two of the individuals who gave an MSSQ score of 0 also had an immersion rating greater than the minimum and non-negligible SSQ nausea scores, indicating susceptibility in spite of the reported MSSQ score.

Usability and Usage Survey Reponses

Participants had minimal to moderate experience with virtual reality related displays before the experiment. 30% had prior head-tracked virtual reality experience, but only one participant had prior experience with an HMD. Due to this, past display experience was removed from analysis. Five participants had never seen a 3D movie or used a 3D television. Only three used 3D displays on a monthly basis

Six participants mentioned symptoms during previous 3D display use. Most of the write-in responses related to eye strain and dizziness, though one mentioned nausea and one mentioned glasses discomfort.

Table I lists the percentages of participants who preferred TV or virtual reality for certain activities, and the write-in responses. In the open ended section of Question 10, we had two participants mentioning uncertainty of use and one wishing it was available for education. The range of self-limiting immersion ratings varied widely. We had one participant who would avoid the system if there were any symptoms at all, and one who would continue to use the system to maximum tolerance. The mean was 5.6 with a standard deviation of 2.71.

	Watching TV	*Movies*	*Video games*	*Landmark exploration*
TV	90%	90%	25%	20%
VR	10%	10%	70%	70%
Write In	0%	0%	1) *Depends on the game*	1) *Real life* 2) *Depends*

Table I. Preferences

Game Play ranged from 0 to 10 hours per week. 30% played 0-2 hours, 35% played 2-6, and 35% played 6-10 hours per week. The experiment was run during the winter so more participants were wearing caps during this time. 40% did not wear hats during this time. 30% wore hats 1-6 hours per week. 20% wore hats 6-15 hours per week, and 10% wore hats over 15 hours per week. 55% did not require vision correction. 45% did require vision correction with 25% using contacts, 10% using glasses, and 10% using both.

Sources of Habituation Correlations

We found a significant correlation with the SSQ scores and the MSSQ, MSSQ carnival subcategory, Vision Correction, and maximum immersion ratings. There were trends between the SSQ and binned Game Play and the MSSQ train subcategory. The correlation and p values are available in Table II. The self-limiting immersion rating MSSQ was significant ($p<0.05$) with a correlation of $r= -0.53$. Since the correlation is negative, the more frequently a participant became motion sick in the past, the fewer symptoms they will tolerate in virtual reality.

	Max Immersion Rating and SSQ	**Past VR Experience and SSQ**	**Vision Correction and SSQ**	**Past 3D Screen Discomfort and SSQ**	**Binned 3D Display Exposure and SSQ**
Correlation	0.52	-0.218	.37	-0.13	0.205
P -value	0**	0.13	0.01**	0.35	0.23
Test	Kendall	Kendall	Kendall	Kendall	Spearman

	Binned Game Play and SSQ	**Binned Hats and SSQ**	**Self-Limiting Immersion Rating and MSSQ**	**MSSQ and SSQ**	**MSSQ Airplane and SSQ**	**MSSQ Train and SSQ**
Correlation	0.297	-0.17	-0.53	0.297	0.23	0.283
P -value	0.08·	0.33	0.03*	0.03*	0.13	0.055·
Test	Spearman	Spearman	Pearson	Kendall	Kendall	Kendall

	MSSQ Playground and SSQ	**MSSQ Small Boat and SSQ**	**MSSQ Carnival and SSQ**	**MSSQ Big Boat and SSQ**	**MSSQ Cars and SSQ**	**MSSQ Playground and SSQ**
Correlation	0.0237	-0.247	0.395	0.193	0.129	0.0237
P -value	0.87	0.11	0.004**	0.2	0.37	0.87
Test	Kendall	Kendall	Kendall	Kendall	Kendall	Kendall

Table II. Cybersickness Rating Correlations (p <0.01, * p<0.05, · p <0.1)**

Our immersion ratings from 37 sessions were significantly correlated ($p<0.01$) with the SSQ, meaning that our 0-10 scale is likely viable to monitor symptoms during immersion. Game Play and train motion sickness had a trend with the SSQ scores ($p < 0.1$). Previous experience with virtual reality, hats, and other subcategories of the MSSQ lacked significance.

Variation due to Measured Sources

Since linear models are more accurate when data meets the normality condition, we used the averaged SSQ total value per participant. This averaged value did not meet normality according to the Shapiro test. The averaged values were transformed by a square root to meet normality. The difference between sessions rarely exceeded 20 on the SSQ 224 point scale.

	Variance Contribution
MSSQ	10.8%
Video Games	9.2%
Hats	-3.8%
Past 3D Discomfort	-5.7%
VR Experience	-5.4%
Vision	17.9%
3D Exposure	0.3%

Table III. Variance due to Characteristics

The variation attributable to each individual measurement ranged from -5.7% to 17.9% and are shown in Table III. Vision Correction explained the greatest variation at 17.9%. The MSSQ and Game Play also explain over 5% of the variance, while frequency of 3D screens was surprisingly negligible. The remainder display negative variance which means the inclusion of the variables was detrimental when explaining SSQ total scores

Since individual characteristic only explained 17.9% of the variance at best, we combined two or more characteristics to seek a more thorough explanation of the variance. Vision Correction, MSSQ, and Game Play were used in linear regression to develop a more complete model. 3D Exposure was removed due to its negligible contribution to variance.

Initially, only a combination of the MSSQ, Game Play and Vision Correction were used in the analysis. The following model yielded the highest contribution to variance:

$$Individual = 0.32\,MSSQ - 1.89\,Vision.Contacts + 2.47 Vision.Glasses + 1.05 Vision.Both + 2.6230 \quad [2]$$

This model explained 24% of the variance, but none of the coefficient estimates reached significance, representing a poor model. Given that adding Game Play decreased variance, we hypothesized that Game Play may be affecting the susceptibility scores. To include this in our model, we changed to a weighted linear model. A weighted linear model places additional importance to specific data points according to the weighting variable. It is used when two or more independent variables may be correlated. We used the original values of Game Play rather than the binned values for the weighting. This resulted in the following improved linear model:

$$Individual = 2.53 MSSQ + 0.60\,(Weighted\ by\ Game\ Play) \quad [3]$$

This model explained 29% of the variance, with both the intercept and MSSQ coefficient reaching significance.

The above model used the full MSSQ score. Similar to Stanney et al. [26], we found the MSSQ carnival subcategory was also correlated to the SSQ. We reran the best models using the MSSQ carnival score in place of the full score. This resulted in better models. The two best being:

$$Individual = 0.76\,MSSQ\ Carnival + 3.14\,(Weighted\ by\ Game\ Play)) \quad [4]$$

$$Individual = 0.65\,MSSQ\ Carnival - 2.10\,Vision.Contacts + 3.48\,Vision.Glasses + 1.79\,Vision.Both + 1.8708 \quad [5]$$

Which explained 43% and 58% of the variance, respectively. However, the weighted model had significance with the estimated values representing a better fit despite having a lower variance.

DISCUSSION

Cybersickness remains a prevalent issue with virtual environments, and as of yet we do not have a good predictive models of cybersickness. This is due to both the widely varying displays and application configurations and the highly individualistic aspect of the symptoms of cybersickness.

We learned of multiple characteristics that affect cybersickness. Past history of motion sickness does correlate to cybersickness, and carnival motion sickness alone correlated better with cybersickness than a general MSSQ score. Although, video game play only displayed a trend correlating with cybersickness, it proved useful with developing better models that predict susceptibility. We also discovered that participants with a greater history of motion sickness are less likely to tolerate symptoms in virtual environments. Our best models, Equations 4 and 5, explain 43%-58% of the variance in the cybersickness scores. The most highly associated when considered separately were the MSSQ and Vision Correction explaining 10.8% and 17.8% of the variance, respectively.

	MSSQ + Game Play + Vision	MSSQ + Game Play	MSSQ + Vision	MSSQ (Weighted by Game Play)	MSSQ + Vision (Weighted by Game Play)	Vision + GamePlay
Variance Contribution	17%	11%	24%	29%	27%	14%

	MSSQ Carnival	MSSQ Carnival + Vision	MSSQ Carnival + Game Play	MSSQ Carnival + Vision	MSSQ Carnival (Weighted by Game Play)
Variance Contribution	18%	58%	22%	58%	43%

Table IV. Variance with Linear Model

By defining the individual component of the SSQ scores, we can normalize result with respect to individual variation. This still leaves a large percentage of variation that is not explained. The display, application, and individual susceptibly are likely to contribute the overall variance.

Vision correction requires further study. Although there was good correlation with the SSQ, which categories have an effect is uncertain. With our sample only two participants used glasses exclusively and two participants used glasses and contacts. When removing the participants who exclusively used glasses, and only considering if a participant required vision correction, the linear regression with the MSSQ carnival and Vision Correction weighted by Game Play increased to explain 65% with all coefficients reaching significance.

Video game use also requires further study. Although it only showed a trend correlating with the SSQ, the improvement in the linear regression when weighting the MSSQ values by Game Play suggests that Game Play is correlated with motion sickness history scores.

Three likely additional characteristics are age, gender and past history of headache and migraines. Studies show cybersickness may increase with age [1]. Although we did not include gender due to the limited number of females in our sample, gender may be affected by the duration and frequency of breaks [12]. More recently, studies into 3D movies have found a correlation with past history of headaches and migraines [21]. This was not included in our usability study as it would have required a change in procedure midway through data collection as we were unaware of this study beforehand. Our future susceptibility survey will include this variable.

By better understanding the background characteristic that affect susceptibility to cybersickness, we can better advise users as to how to use virtual environments. We also can suggest better means to habituate participants to virtual environments that may be required for training. Although the results are preliminary, if console games do decrease motion sickness and therefore cybersickness, it will provide an entertaining means of habituating to virtual environments for those that must use them. This is particularly beneficial for participants with a past history of motion sickness as we found they are more likely to avoid virtual reality with fewer symptoms. Better prediction of a individual's characteristics contribution to the SSQ scores allows for shorter susceptibility surveys and normalizing SSQ scores with respect to individual variance to better determine the effect of hardware and software in future studies.

REFERENCES

1. Arns, L.L. and Cerne, MM., "The Relationship Between Age and Incidence of Cybersickness Among Immersive Environment Users," in Proc.of the IEEE VR 2005, Bonn, Germany, 2005, pp. 267-268.
2. Bos, JE., "Why Cybersickness?," in Proc. of the 1st International Symposium on VIMS, Hong Kong, 2007.
3. Bos, J.E., de Vries, SC., van Emmerik, ML., and Groen, EL., "The Effect of Internal and External Fields of View on Visually Induced Motion Sickness," Applied Ergonomics, vol. 41, no. 4, pp. 516-521, July 2010.
4. Chen, W., Yuen, SL, and So, RHY, "A Progress Report on the Quest to Establish a Cybersickness Dose Value," Proc. of the HFES, vol. 46, no. 26, pp. 2119-2123, September 2002.
5. Dahlman, J., "Psychophysiological and performance aspects on motion sickness," Linköping University, Linköping, Sweden, Thesis 2009.
6. Dizio, P. and Lackner, JR., "Circumventing Side Effects of Immersive Virtual Environments," in International Conference on HCI, San Francisco, 1997.
7. Gianaros, P.J., Muth, ER., Mordkoff, JT., Levine, ME., and Stern, RM., "A Questionnaire for the Assessment of the Multiple Dimensions of Motion Sickness," ASEM, vol. 72, no. 2, pp. 115–119, 2001.
8. Golding, J.F., "Motion Sickness Susceptibility Questionnaire Revised and Its Relationship to Other Forms of Sickness," Brain Research Bulletin, vol. 47, no. 8, pp. 507–516, November 1998.
9. Griffin, M.J. and Newman, MM., "Visual Field Effects on Motion Sickness in Cars," ASEM, vol. 75, no. 9, pp. 739-748, September 2004.
10. Hakkinen, J., Vuori, T, and Paakka, M, "Postural stability and sickness symptoms after HMD use," in IEEE SMC, October 2002, pp. 147-152.
11. Hale, K.S. and Stanney, KM., "Effects of Low Stereo Acuity on Performance, Presence and Sickness within a Virtual Environment," Applied Ergonomics, vol. 37, no. 3, pp. 329–339, May 2006.
12. Harm, D.L., Taylor, LC., and Bloomberg, JJ., "Adaptive Changes in Sensorimotor Coordination and Motion Sickness Following Repeated Exposures to Virtual Environments," NASA Human Research Program Investigators' Meeting, League City, Technical report 2007.
13. Howarth, P.A. and Hodder, SG., "Characteristics of habituation to motion in a virtual environment," Displays, vol. 29, no. 2, pp. 117-123, March 2008.
14. Jaeger, B.K. and Mourant, RR., "Comparison of simulator sickness using static and dynamic walking simulators," in Proc. of the HFES, Santa Monica, 2001.
15. Jones, M.B., Kennedy, RS., and Stanney, KM., "Toward Systematic Control of Cybersickness," Presence, vol. 13, no. 5, pp. 589-600, October 2004.

16. Kennedy, R.S. and Graybiel, A, "The Dial Test: A Standardized Procedure for the Experimental Production of Canal Sickness Symptomatology in a Rotating Environemnt," Naval School of Aviation Medicine, Pensacoloa FL, Joint Report MSAM-930, 1965.
17. Kennedy, R.S., Lane, NE., Berbaum, KS., and Lilienthal, MG., "Simulator Sickness Questionnaire: An Enhanced Method for Quantifying Simulator Sickness," International Journal of Aviation Psychology, vol. 3, no. 3, pp. 203-220, 1993.
18. Park, G.D., Allen, RW., Fiorentino, D, Rosenthal, TJ., and Cook, ML., "Simulator Sickness Scores According to Symptom Susceptibility, Age, and Gender for an Older Driver Assessment Study," in Proc. of the HFES, San Francisco, USA, 2006, pp. 2702-2706.
19. Regan, C., "An investigation into nausea and other side-effects of head-coupled immersive virtual reality," Virtual Reality , vol. 1, no. 1, pp. 17-31, 1995.
20. Sharples, S., Cobb, S, Moody, A, and Wilson, JR., "Virtual Reality Induced Symptoms and Effects (VRISE): Comparison of Head Mounted Display (HMD), Desktop and Projection Display Systems," Displays, vol. 29, no. 2, pp. 58–69, march 2008.
21. Solimini, A.G., Mannocci, A, Domitilla, DT., and La Torre, G, "A survey of visually induced symptoms and associated factors in spectators of three dimensional stereoscopic movies," BMC Public Health , vol. 12, no. 1, pp. 1-11, September 2012.
22. So, RHY.HATK. and Lo, WT, "A Metric to Quantify Virtual Scene Movement for the Study of Cybersickness: Definition, Implementation and Verification," Presence, vol. 10, no. 2, pp. 193-215, April 2001.
23. So, R.HY., Lo, WT., and Ho, ATK., "Effects of Navigation Speed on Motion Sickness Caused by an Immersive Virtual Environment," Human Factors, vol. 43, no. 3, pp. 452-461, Fall 2001b.
25. So, R.HY. and Yuen, SL., "Comparing Symptoms of Visually Induced Motion Sickness Among Viewers of Four Similar Virtual Environments with Different Color," Proc. of the 2nd International Conference on VR, pp. 386-391, 2007.
26. Stanney, K.M., Hale, KS., Nahmens, I, and Kennedy, RS., "What to Expect from Immersive Virtual Environment Exposure: Influences of Gender, Body Mass Index, and Past Experience," Human Factors, vol. 45, no. 3, pp. 504-520, Fall 2003.
27. Stanney, K.M. and Kennedy, RS., "The Psychometrics of Cybersickness," Communications of the ACM, vol. 40, no. 8, pp. 66-68, Aug. 1997.
29. Taha, Z., Hartomo, , Jen, YH., Gadzila, RAR., and Chai, APT., "The Effect of Body Weight and Height on Incidence of Cyber sickness Among Immersive Environment Malaysian Users," in 17th World Congress on Ergonomics, Beijing, China, 2009.
30. Young, SD., Adelstein, BD, and Ellis, SR, "Demand Characteristics of a Questionnaire Used to Assess Motion Sickness in a Virtual Environment," in VR, Alexandria, 2007.

APPENDIX: USABILITY SURVEY

1. How many hours per week on average do you play console video games?
2. Have you ever used virtual reality before (e.g. head-mounted displays, large screen where your viewpoint is tracked, or moving platform rides, not games such as "Second Life" where the virtual reality is only experienced on a conventional computer screen)? **Y / N**
3. Have you ever used virtual reality with the type of device you just used? **Y / N**
4. How frequently do you view 3D movies or 3D TV?
5. Have you had any discomfort with viewing 3D movies, if so what?
6. How many hours per week on average do you wear hats or headbands?
7. Do you use glasses? Contacts? Neither? (circle)
8. Was there anything in particular about this virtual reality system that was causing any discomfort?
9. On a scale from 1 to 10, 1 being how you felt upon arrival and 10 being, 'I want to stop,' at what score would you choose to avoid using this virtual reality system?
10. Would you prefer a regular TV/monitor or this virtual reality system (if money was not an issue) for the following (please circle):
    a. Watching TV **TV** **VR**
    b. Movies **TV** **VR**
    c. Video games **TV** **VR**
    d. Landmark exploration (e.g. Maps, museums, archeological sites) **TV** **VR**
    e. Other (please list)

In-air Gestures Around Unmodified Mobile Devices

Jie Song[1], Gábor Sörös[1], Fabrizio Pece[1], Sean Ryan Fanello[2], Shahram Izadi[2], Cem Keskin[2], Otmar Hilliges[1]

[1]Department of Computer Science, ETH Zurich, Switzerland
[2]Microsoft Research, Cambridge, UK

{jsong|gabor.soros|fabrizio.pece|otmar.hilliges}@inf.ethz.ch {seanfa|shahrami|cemke}@microsoft.com

Figure 1: Touch input is expressive but can occlude large parts of the screen (A). We propose a machine learning based algorithm for gesture recognition expanding the interaction space *around* the mobile device (B), adding in-air gestures and hand-part tracking (D) to commodity off-the-shelf mobile devices, relying only on the device's camera (and no hardware modifications). We demonstrate a number of compelling interactive scenarios including bi-manual input to mapping and gaming applications (C+D). The algorithm runs in real time and can even be used on ultra-mobile devices such as smartwatches (E).

ABSTRACT

We present a novel machine learning based algorithm extending the interaction space around mobile devices. The technique uses *only* the RGB camera now commonplace on off-the-shelf mobile devices. Our algorithm robustly recognizes a wide range of in-air gestures, supporting user variation, and varying lighting conditions. We demonstrate that our algorithm runs in real-time on unmodified mobile devices, including resource-constrained smartphones and smartwatches. Our goal is not to replace the touchscreen as primary input device, but rather to augment and enrich the existing interaction vocabulary using gestures. While touch input works well for many scenarios, we demonstrate numerous interaction tasks such as mode switches, application and task management, menu selection and certain types of navigation, where such input can be either complemented or better served by in-air gestures. This removes screen real-estate issues on small touchscreens, and allows input to be expanded to the 3D space around the device. We present results for recognition accuracy (93% test and 98% train), impact of memory footprint and other model parameters. Finally, we report results from preliminary user evaluations, discuss advantages and limitations and conclude with directions for future work.

Author Keywords

HCI; mobile interaction; mobile gestures; gesture recognition; mobile computing; random forests

UIST 2014, October 5–8, 2014, Honolulu, HI, USA.
Copyright © 2014 ACM 978-1-4503-3069-5/14/10 ...$15.00.
http://dx.doi.org/10.1145/2642918.2647373

ACM Classification Keywords

H.5.2 User Interfaces: Input devices and strategies, Interaction styles; I.3.6 Methodology and Techniques: Interaction techniques; I.4.8 Scene Analysis: Object recognition

INTRODUCTION

Today's mobile devices have realized the vision of ubiquitous access to information. Data is now literally at our fingertips no matter where we are. It is clear that these devices have already changed the way how we consume and produce information. However, the question of how best to interact with mobile content is far from solved. While direct touch interaction is clearly intuitive and popular, it also comes with drawbacks. In particular, as mobile devices continue to be miniaturized, touchscreen real-estate becomes increasingly limited, leading to smaller on-screen targets and fingers causing occlusions of displayed content. This can be an issue during prolonged interaction, for example, while reading on a mobile device or when attempting to perform complex manipulations that require many on-screen controls.

Not surprisingly, many HCI researchers have attempted to extend the interaction space around the device. For example using infrared (IR) proximity sensors [3, 23] or handheld magnetic tags [20]. Others have attempted to address the input scarcity issue by leveraging the human body [11] or surfaces in the environment [10, 34] as interactive platforms. However, all of these require hardware modifications of the device and/or user instrumentation. This can be a major barrier to adoption, and limits seamless unencumbered user interaction.

Our work builds upon and extends this body of research, in so doing, we leverage the fact that almost all mobile devices contain RGB cameras for video and image capture. We propose a novel machine learning based algorithm to extend the interaction space around mobile devices by detecting rich gestures performed behind or in front of the screen. The technique uses *only* the built-in RGB camera, and recognizes a wide range of gestures robustly, copes with user variation, and varying lighting conditions. Furthermore, the algorithm runs in real time entirely on off-the-shelf, unmodified mobile devices, including compute-limited smartphones and smartwatches.

Our goal is not to replace the touchscreen as primary input device but to complement it and to enrich the interaction vocabulary. While touch input works well in many scenarios, there are numerous interaction tasks such as mode switches, application and task management, menu selection and certain types of navigation, where touch input can be cumbersome and the size of mobile devices, and hence that of on-screen controls, becomes problematic. While multi-touch gestures are a feasible way to increase the expressiveness of touch interaction, they cover even more screen real-estate and worsen the occlusion issue.

We argue that such tasks and interactions can be complemented well by sporadic, low-effort gesturing behind or in front of the device. For example, while sitting comfortably on a couch a quick flick of the wrist behind the phone may be used to advance the page in an e-book. Similarly, while using touch to pan a map, symbolic gestures could be used to adjust the map-viewing mode, to adjust the zoom level or to enable additional data views such as traffic information. Furthermore, we present a number of compelling interaction scenarios that would be difficult to achieve with a touchscreen only. For example, the non-dominant hand can be used to invoke and control a fish-eye lens while the touch screen may be used to select targets in the magnified region.

Contributions and overview of the paper

Our proposed gesture recognition algorithm is based on random forests (RF) [2], which have proved to be powerful for prediction of static hand gestures, hand pose [19] and body pose [33], but using PCs and depth sensing cameras. However, these classifiers trade discriminative power and run-time performance against memory consumption. Given a complex enough problem and large enough training set, memory requirement will grow exponentially with tree depth. This is of course a strong limitation for application on resource constrained mobile platforms.

To our knowledge, we present the first real-time implementation of RFs for mobile devices for a pixel labelling task. Furthermore, the algorithm does not rely on highly discriminative depth features but works using only 2D images. We describe a method to robustly and efficiently classify hand states (i.e., gestures) and salient features (i.e., fingertips) using only binary segmentation masks. We also describe techniques to make the classifier robust to in-plane rotation (i.e., wrist articulation or rotating the device itself) and to variations in depth of the hand. We introduce different techniques, specifically designed for mobile devices, to compactify the forests and to reduce memory consumption drastically, while maintaining classification accuracy. These techniques are necessary to reduce the memory footprint of the classifier for mobile phones but generalize to any computing device.

The remainder of the paper is structured as follows: we discuss the relevant literature in the areas of augmented mobile devices, touch and in-air gesture recognition. We then introduce a number of compelling interaction techniques and application scenarios. This is followed by an in-depth discussion of the gesture recognition method and several techniques to reduce the memory footprint of the RF classifier. The algorithm is simple enough to be replicated quickly. In this regard, we provide pseudo-code detailing the classification pipeline alongside training data in order to enable the community to replicate and extend our algorithm. We present our initial results in terms of recognition accuracy, impact of tree depth and other parameters. Finally, we report results from preliminary user evaluations, discuss advantages and limitations and conclude with directions for future work.

RELATED WORK

Advances in processing, sensing and display technologies have enabled rich, powerful computational platforms to fit into our hands and pockets . The current generation of mobile computing relies on touch for interaction but this limits the expressiveness of input. Here we review the literature that expands the input space from the touchscreen to the areas immediately above, behind and around it.

A number of systems have used *cameras* to *extend* the interaction space beyond the display of mobile devices. LucidTouch uses a rear-mounted, protruding 2D camera to detect multi-touch input on the back of mobile devices [40]. Niikuura et al. [28] leverage IR LEDs and a 2D camera to recognize a single fingertip for in-air typing. Samsung has shipped several basic in-air swipe and hover gestures with their Galaxy S4* using a single IR proximity sensor. Others have proposed using body-worn cameras and diffuse IR illumination [9, 36] or RGB cameras [26, 37], demonstrating simple 2D pinch gestures [9] or detecting fingers using markers [26]. [36, 37] classify a wider set of discrete hand postures e.g. for sign language but require a desktop PC for processing. Jones et al. find, in a study of around the device interaction, that in-air gestures can perform as well as touch and define comfort zones for interaction [17].

Researchers have also explored handheld [16, 27] and shoulder-worn [10] depth cameras, focusing on sensing touch interaction with planar [10] or more complex physical surfaces [16, 27]. Others have attempted to leverage the human body directly as input source either sensing muscle or tendon activity to recognize a small set of discrete hand gestures [31, 32], leveraging acoustics to coarsely localize touch on the body [11], or using wristbands of IR proximity sensors for detecting coarse gestures performed on the forearm [29]. Wrist-worn camera based sensors have also been demonstrated to reconstruct full 3D hand pose [21].

The approaches above require new (or augmented) mobile hardware, body-worn cameras, user instrumentation or external tracking, and oftentimes off-board processing. These issues pose serious barriers for user adoption. We propose a real-time system that runs on unmodified mobile devices and recognizes a rich set of gestures alongside accurate fingertip detection for pointing and stroke-based interaction.

The challenges of camera based systems have led researchers to experiment with *non-camera based sensing* around mobile devices. For example, using simple IR proximity sensors fac-

*`http://www.samsung.com/global/microsite/galaxys4/`

ing outwards [3] or upwards [23, 24]. *Magnetic field sensing* has been used to track rigid motion around a device by pairing permanent magnets and magnetometers either by wearing both [4] or by using the device's built-in IMU (inertial measurement unit) [1, 15, 20]. Just like optical sensing solutions, magnetic field sensing can suffer from coarse sensing fidelity and input is limited to tracking a restricted number of discrete points and often with limited degrees-of-freedom (DoF). More recently, a transparent *electric field sensing* antenna has been demonstrated that enables sensing of 3D hand and fingertip locations [7]. While more compact than external camera augmentations, these approaches still require device or user augmentation. Our technique allows for richer gestures that go beyond tracking of discrete points and does not require any augmentation of the device nor the user.

A particularly important aspect of our work is that we aim to complement touch input with gestures. In this sense we share commonality with prior work combining pen+touch input [14], motion+touch [13], in-air and on-body gestures [25], or input from multiple devices [5]. We explore new interaction techniques and application scenarios that combine touch input on and gestural interaction around a mobile device.

Our work clearly relates to the vast body of literature on computer vision methods for hand gesture recognition. Early work focused on hand tracking from 2D cameras. However, recognizing complex hand gestures is clearly challenging from such 2D input [6]. The recent advancements in processing power and the emergence of consumer grade depth cameras, however, have enabled a number of high fidelity gestural interactive systems in HCI [10, 12, 21] and fine-grained 3D hand-pose estimation in real-time [19, 30, 35]. The current state-of-the art can be broken down into methods relying on model-fitting and temporal tracking [30, 35], and those leveraging per-pixel hand part classification [19, 38].

Our algorithm is designed for the recognition of rich and varied gestures and detection of salient hand parts (i.e., fingertips) rather than full hand pose estimation. It is important to note though, that our algorithm works without relying on highly discriminative depth data and rich computational resources of a high-end desktop machine. To our knowledge we present the first implementation of a RF-based gesture recognition algorithm that i) runs in real-time on off-the-shelf mobile devices ii) relies only on the built-in RGB camera(s) and iii) makes no strong assumptions about the user's environment and iv) is reasonably robust to rotation and depth variation.

IN-AIR GESTURES ON THE MOVE

Our system opens up the input space around a mobile device. In doing so, our aim is to couple regular touchscreen input with gestures performed around the device. Rather than replace one modality with the other, we believe that it is this combination that is powerful.

Before detailing the technical gesture recognition approach, we illustrate a number of compelling interaction scenarios, enabled by in-air gestures around mobile devices, in particular bi-manual, multi-modal input. We highlight scenarios where the user tries to perform complex operations that require mode-switching or simultaneous input on different screen locations. Such interactions are typically mapped to multi-touch gestures, which can cause occlusion issues and decrease pointing performance, especially on very small screens.

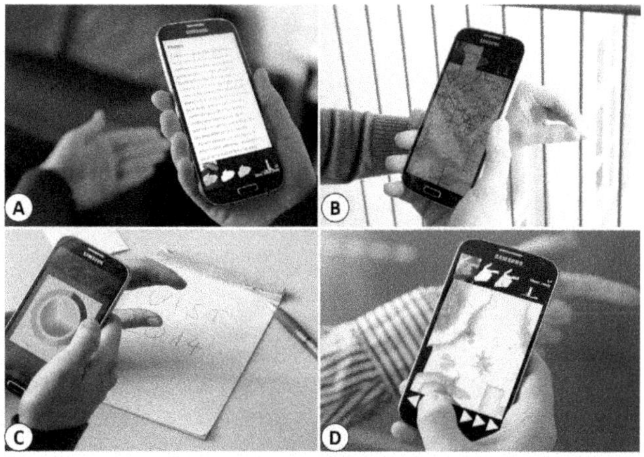

Figure 2: Usage scenarios: (A) Panning and zooming a document. (B) Bimanual map browsing with a magnifier lens (C) Using gestures to control mode-switches and tool parametrization in a drawing app. (D) Shooting in a scrolling shooter game.

Fig. 2 summarizes a selection of interactive scenarios enabled by our approach. In its most basic form, our algorithm can enable *division of labor* bimanual input [8]. For example, a user sitting on a couch can use touch input to continuously navigate a map or document while the non-dominant hand can be used to occasionally adjust the zoom level of the document, without occluding the screen, or interrupting the touch-based navigation (see Fig. 2 (A)).

The two hands can also work in a more tightly integrated fashion, where an in-air pinch gesture invokes a magnifier lens to magnify a particular area of interest on the document (e.g., an underground map). The magnifier lens can then be positioned by moving the hand behind the device. This illustrates the usefulness of jointly recognizing gestures and fingertips. The magnification factor can be adjusted by opening or closing the pinch gesture. Touch input can then be used to highlight text in a document, place a positional marker on a map or to otherwise interact with the magnified content (see Fig. 2 (B)). Combining touch and gestures makes interactions that simultaneously modify multiple parameters more integrated than what would be possible with touch input alone.

Similarly, gestures around the device can be used to streamline interaction with more complex user-interfaces that require explicit mode changes and allow the user to parametrize tools and functionalities. We have implemented a simple drawing application to illustrate this (Fig. 2 (C)). Here the user can draw using touch input, while a pinch gesture will invoke a brush-selection menu directly at the current touch location. The menu selection can then be performed using touch, without requiring the user's finger to travel to a menu. Analogously, the open pinch (a C-shaped hand) can invoke an in-place color picker. A final, compelling interaction scenario is mobile gaming. We interface our gesture recognition engine with an open-source 2D scroller game†. Touch input is used to control the helicopter position, whereas gestures are used to shoot weapons (see Fig. 2 (D)).

† `https://code.google.com/p/orange-grass`

Interacting with other mobile devices

One of the main contributions of our work is supporting a classifier that is efficient enough to run in real time on very resource-constrained platforms. The fact that cameras are now ubiquitous on many mobile platforms, makes our system applicable to a wide range of mobile computing scenarios, including mobile phones, tablets but also smartwatches.

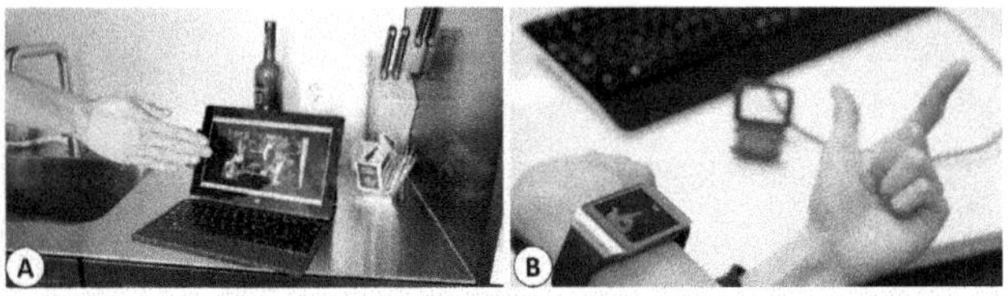

Figure 3: Our algorithm runs on a variety of mobile form factors and enables different interaction scenarios. (A) A tablet media player in the kitchen can be controlled using simple, effortless gestures without touching the screen with wet hands. (B) In-air pointing gesture in front of the smartwatch triggers a photo sharing application.

Fig. 3 (A), shows our system running on an off-the-shelf tablet. Here we leverage the front-facing camera for gesture recognition. The user controls a media application where a flat, closed hand pauses the playback of a video and the flat, splayed hand resumes playback. The user may also control other applications such as advancing a photo slideshow using swipe gestures, or controlling (semantic) zoom in a PDF reader. We argue that this type of low-effort, casual gestures can complement touch in certain scenarios for example when the tablet is rested on the user's lap or on a table.

Ultra-mobile devices such as smartwatches are clearly becoming important mobile platforms. However, their input expressiveness is severely limited by the small size of the touchscreens, making typical multi-touch gestures cumbersome or infeasible. Not surprisingly, multiple efforts have been undertaken to enable gestural interaction with such devices (e.g., [23, 31]). However, these typically require modification of the watch and suffer from limited input fidelity. We enable recognition of the same rich gestures as on tablets and phones (e.g., static gestures and fingertip detection) on a smartwatch[‡]. For example, to take pictures and navigate the photo stream without occluding the screen (see Fig. 3 (B)).

Data-driven gesture recognition

The application scenarios discussed here give a flavor for the types of interactions enabled by our system. While already enabling new scenarios, we do not claim that the gestures currently implemented constitute the best possible or even final gesture set. Quite contrary, the proposed algorithms are data driven and therefore it is a matter of capturing new training data, and retraining the classifier, to redefine the gesture set – not a matter of rewriting any code. We highlight two further aspects of this work:

First, due to power and size constraints, currently no readily procurable mobile devices exist with integrated depth sensors. However, state-of-the art gesture and hand-pose estimation algorithms rely on depth data. Robustly detecting hand gestures from a monocular, moving camera, in uncontrolled lighting conditions and with arbitrary backgrounds remains a challenging and difficult task - in particular on mobile devices. At the same time, our main design goal is to support unmodified mobile devices to lower the barrier of use.

Second, the initial gesture set is what we consider to be a useful but also a challenging gesture set. The gestures are different enough from each other that it would be difficult to conceive a single, non-probabilistic algorithm (for example based on geometric heuristics) that could detect them all. Moreover, there is sufficient similarity between the pairs of gestures (e.g., flat hand, splayed-hand) that distinguishing these from each other (heuristically) is an even more challenging task. Moreover, in many interaction scenarios we are not only interested in hand states (i.e., gestures) but also salient hand parts such as fingertips or the wrist, further complicating the detection problem.

These two aspects suggest that recognizing this gesture set or a similar set alongside hand parts would be challenging using heuristics-based approaches only. We therefore explore a novel recognition architecture that combines very simple and computationally efficient image processing techniques with powerful machine learning classification techniques for robust and extensible gesture recognition.

SOFTWARE PIPELINE

So far we have concentrated on describing our system at a high-level and discussing interactive possibilities it affords. We now provide an overview of the software pipeline before detailing the gesture classification algorithm. The pipeline consists of fairly easy and established image processing steps interwoven with a new, staged gesture and part classification pipeline. All components of the pipeline have been carefully chosen and designed with runtime and memory efficiency in mind, in order to achieve real-time performance even on ultra-mobile and resource restricted devices.

Segmentation and Pre-processing

Our gesture recognition algorithm relies on binary masks of the hand, segmented from the background. Therefore, the first step of our pipeline is foreground extraction via skin color detection. Despite much research this problem remains a challenging task under arbitrary lighting conditions. A good summary of various techniques is provided by [18]. We have experimented with many techniques, including HSV and GMM-based adaptive thresholding. However, due to the large variation in skin color and the influence of lighting and background, currently none of these methods provide high enough accuracy of segmentation under arbitrary conditions.

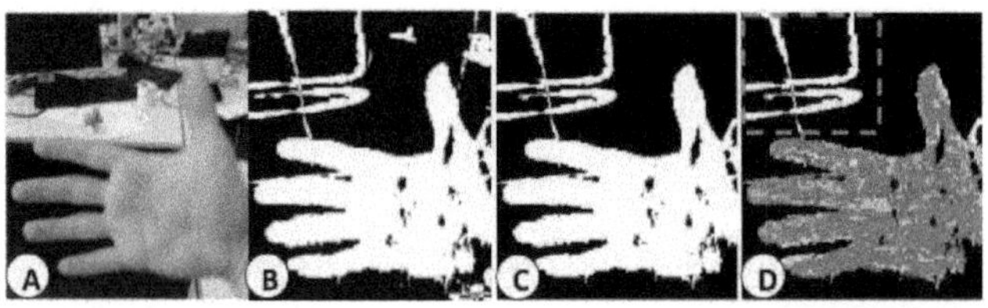

Figure 4: Segmentation by classification. A) Input frame. B) Foreground mask after color thresholding. C) Salt'n'pepper noise is cleaned up by connected component analysis; larger connected non-hand regions remain. D) Result after classification. Colored pixels indicate class label, white pixels indicate noise (red box).

‡ `http://www.samsung.com/global/microsite/galaxynote3-gear/`.

Therefore we opted for a very simple thresholding technique that is i) easy to implement ii) computationally cheap and iii) provides a good compromise between true positives and false negatives. We segment the hand from the background by:

$$S_t(u) = \begin{cases} 1, if min(R_t(u) - G_t(u), R_t(u) - B_t(u)) > \tau_t \\ 0, otherwise \end{cases} \tag{1}$$

where R_t, G_t and B_t denote the RGB-components at frame t and image pixel u, τ_t is a threshold value and S_t the segmentation. This technique provides reasonable segmentation but suffers from *false positives*, that noise outside the hand region (see Fig. 4 (B)). Some of this noise can be suppressed using connected component analysis but regions of noise will remain if connected to the hand (see Fig. 4 (C)). However, the proposed hand state classification algorithm can be made robust to this particular type of noise as detailed below. At this stage it is important to attain a segmentation that does not suffer from too many false negatives, in particular we wish to persist the contour of the hand for accurate classification results. Please note that the technique only relies on a single parameter τ that can be tuned at runtime (via an on-screen slider), and hence it can be quickly adapted to work under many different illumination conditions.

Hand State Classification Method

Our gesture recognizer is based on random forests (RF) [2] which have been used successfully for a number of vision problems, including body pose estimation [33] and hand pose and state estimation [19, 38] using depth cameras, but also in HCI using different sensing modalities [7, 22, 39].

A RF is an ensemble of decision trees, each tree in the ensemble produces a noisy classification result. However, accurate classification results can be attained by averaging the results from multiple, non-biased classifiers together. Each tree consists of split nodes and leaf nodes; the split nodes themselves can be seen as very primitive classifiers. Each node will evaluate a simple and computationally inexpensive function and as a result forward the currently evaluated datum (in our case a pixel) to its left or right child until the datum reaches one of the leaf nodes. The split functions can be seen as simple questions where each answer adds a little more information, or in other words reduces the uncertainty about the correct class label for the particular pixel. The leaf nodes contain probability distributions describing the likelihood with which a pixel belongs to any of the classes in the label space.

Recent work based on RFs (e.g., [19, 33, 38]) leverages highly descriptive depth images and complementary depth-invariant features for classification. These approaches use continuous valued features (typically simple depth differences), and the split functions compare the feature response against a continuous valued threshold. Our approach cannot rely on depth. Furthermore, we cannot rely on color, as the variation in appearance of different hands under arbitrary lighting conditions is too large to cover all variations. Hence, our method relies only on shape (i.e., binary masks cf. Eq. (1)) to infer hand states and features. We use split criteria of the form:

$$C_j^L(w, v, \Gamma_j) = \{(S, u) | F_{w,v}(S, u) = \Gamma_j\} \tag{2}$$

$$C_j^R(w, v, \Gamma_j) = \{(S, u) | F_{w,v}(S, u) \neq \Gamma_j\} \tag{3}$$

where F_j is the feature response and Γ_j is a selector value stored at each split node j. Here C_j^L and C_j^R are the mutually exclusive sets of pixels assigned to the left and right children of the split node. For a given segmented image S we define the feature response at the pixel location u as

$$F_{w,v}(u) = [S(u + w), S(u + v)] \tag{4}$$

this is a 1×2 vector where w and v are random offsets and $S(u)$ is the binary pixel value at that location. The feature response is discrete and each element of it can take on only two values; 1 for foreground and 0 for background pixels. At evaluation time we simply compare this vector with $\Gamma_j \in \{[0, 0], [1, 0], [0, 1], [1, 1]\}$.

An important aspect is that the order in which the split functions are concatenated (the tree structure) and that the final probability distributions are learned from annotated training data. In the case of RF this is done by randomly selecting multiple split candidates and choosing the one that splits the data best. The quality metric for the split thereby is typically defined by the information gain I_j at node j:

$$I_j = H(C_j) - \sum_{i \in L,R} \frac{|C_j^i|}{|C_j|} H(C_j^i) \tag{5}$$

where H is the Shannon entropy of C. Decrease in entropy, denoted by I_j, means increase in information, or in other words that the uncertainty about the decision boundary goes down. At training time we exhaustively enumerate all possible splits (w, v, Γ_j) and select the one maximizing I_j (for more details see [2, 33]). We provide pseudo-code for forest evaluation, for others to easily extend our results (cf. appendix).

The binary features employed in our method allow training of a complex data-set while keeping the computational time and memory footprint low. This, however, does not impact precision. Conceptually, the binary and shift values encode the hand shape information and hence the probability that a given pixel belongs to the hand and to which gesture. As the classifier is trained and operates only on such data, the amount of variance in the learning data that needs to be modelled is drastically reduced compared to training directly on color images. Ideally, we could use a larger number of offsets to increase the discriminative power of our classification technique. However, this would strongly affect the training time as the number of offset combinations increases exponentially.

Multi-stage Classification

Now that we have characterized how we leverage the RF framework for per-pixel classification of binary images, we next detail how this can be utilized to recognize a rich set of gestures and hand-parts, highlighting aspects that are specific to computationally restricted mobile devices.

Given the interactive scenarios outlined earlier, our classifier has to infer much from binary images alone. First, the gestures themselves are challenging, due to the similarity between pairs of gestures. Second, we are not only interested in hand states (i.e., whole image classification) but also more fine-grained part information, in particular the location of fingertips. Third, the classifier has to work with hands of different shapes and sizes. Fourth, due to the complexity of skin

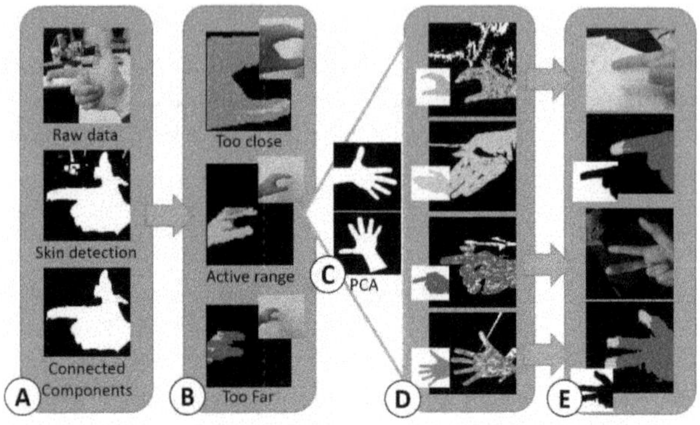

Figure 5: Multi-stage classification. A) Pre-processing segments hands from background. B) DCF coarsely estimates the depth of hand and in-range frames are forwarded. Effective range is between 15-50 cm. C) PCA is used to find in-plane rotation of hands. D) SCF classifies foreground pixel into 6 gesture classes + plus noise. E) PCF classifies location of fingertips for pointing-like gestures.

appearance the classifier has to operate on noisy segmentation data, in particular with regions of noise that are connected to and are indistinguishable from fingers (cf. Fig. 4 (C)). Fifth, natural gestures display a lot of variation in gesture execution (across users but also within), in particular, in terms of rotations of the hand relative to the camera and of course distance between the mobile device and the user's hand. Our goal was to produce a classification scheme that would be able to deal with all of these challenges to a high degree and in real-time.

One approach to achieve this goal is to amass a training database that covers all the expected variations and train a single, potentially very deep forest on this data. The classification step is very efficient so that even deep trees can be evaluated on modern hardware in only a few milliseconds. However, the size of the forest can quickly become an issue as the memory footprint of the trees grows exponentially with tree depth. A further issue is that the different objectives of the classifier are not necessarily aligned with each other. For example, we experimentally confirmed that gesture classification accuracy tremendously benefits from near perfect segmentation. Hence, jointly classifying noise and hand state might not be the optimal approach. A final concern is that of overfitting. With very deep trees the danger exists that a forest learns how to precisely separate the data in the training set but does not have the model capacity to generalize well on unseen test data.

A different approach is that of multi-stage or multi-layered forests [19]. This is a configuration where expert forests are trained for a particular task (e.g., finding hand parts after first determining the overall hand shape) and only those images corresponding to a particular class are forwarded to a second forest, trained only on examples from this class. Each of the forests then needs to model less variation and hence can be comparatively shallow. We propose an algorithm similar to [19]. Ours differs in that it combines forests trained on completely separate tasks and combines forests that modify the image before forwarding it to the next stage (e.g., removing noise). This can be thought of as a pipeline of independent but inter-related classifiers as illustrated in Fig. 5.

Stage 1: Coarse Depth Classification The segmented but noisy foreground mask $S(u)$ is classified into three levels of depth (see Fig. 6 (A)). The depth classification forest (DCF) serves a dual purpose. By coarsely estimating the depth of the hand and by rejecting frames where the hand is either too close or too far from the device, the DCF greatly reduces the variation in depth that the downstream pipeline has to deal with. Equally important, at this stage, the system can detect whether it will be able to correctly classify a gesture with sufficient probability, information that can be fed back to the user. Currently the system is trained to accept gestures performed in an interval of 15-50cm, corresponding to a comfortable arm pose (see Fig. 6 (A)).

Stage 2: Shape Classification On the foreground masks that passes the DCF we run principal component analysis (PCA). The angle of the hand is computed from the major axis (see Fig. 5, C). Instead of rotating the image, which would be costly on mobile hardware, we pass this angle to the next classifier and during evaluation, we rotate the features. This makes the features pseudo-rotation invariant and allows us to reduce the number of images necessary in the training data (and consequently to train shallower forests), while not sacrificing runtime performance. The shape classification forest (SCF) classifies the images into (currently) six gesture classes, one additional *no-gesture* class, and a per-pixel noise class (i.e. eight classes in total). The latter is necessary to deal with remaining false positives from the segmentation, and the former to robustly reject *non-gesture* motion in front of the camera. Fig. 6 illustrates typical classification results with colored pixels indicating the class label and white pixels being classified as noise.

Stage 3: Part Classification Images containing pointing like gestures (i.e., 'point', 'gun', 'splayed hand') are processed by a part classification forest (PCF, see Fig. 5, E), performing per-pixel hand part classification. Due to the lack of depth information we do not attempt to classify all hand parts (cf. [19]), but only select parts of interest for interaction. Concretely we detect the location of fingertips and the wrist which can then be used to implement more fine-grained, localized in-air gestures. The PCF benefits from the previous steps, as practically all noise is cleaned up and only images with visible fingertips will be forwarded to it (see Fig. 6 (C)). Hence, the forest is fairly accurate at a very shallow depth of 10 levels.

Training Data

The RF relies on good training data for high classification accuracy. To train a classifier, robust to the large amount of

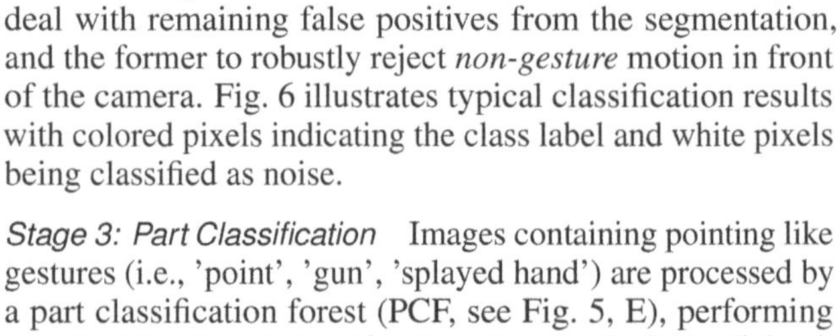

Figure 6: Multistage classification: (A) First hand is classified into three different coarse depth bins. (B) Next hand shape is classified into 6 classes. (C) Finally, fingertip parts are detected by PCF.

variation in hand shapes, sizes and distances to the camera and gesture execution, we need a large and balanced training data set.

We asked 20 subjects from our institution to perform the seven gestures under natural variation and recorded short sequences of each gesture. This included one 'no-gesture' where participants were instructed to just casually move their hands and fingers. This was performed per participant and at different distances away from the phone (see Fig. 7 inset). We recorded $\sim 50K$ images covering enough variation in rotation, depth and appearance for training the SCF.

We collected additional $8K$ images to train the DCF, covering a larger depth range, selected $35K$ images from the original data set to train the SCF, and collected additional $5K$ images to train the PCF. The raw training data was processed using the runtime pre-processing pipeline. However, we have to attain clean segmentation masks and label false positives as such. This was achieved by first acquiring the gesture sequences in front of a uniform (typically black) background with carefully tuned threshold τ (see Fig. 7 (A+B)). We then capture empty scenes of arbitrary backgrounds, which are segmented with the same τ, producing some realistic noise signal (Fig. 7 (C+D)). The hand segmentation is then superimposed over the noise and the resulting image is cleaned up using connected component analysis. Finally, to attain a labeled image we subtract the clean hand from the noisy image to separate the hand region from connected false positives (Fig. 7 (E-G)).

This semi-automatic method is reasonably fast in producing training data that contains both clean hand segmentations as well as realistic, labeled noise.

SYSTEM EVALUATION

So far we have presented what we believe is the first real-time implementation of RFs for pixel-labelling tasks on mobile devices. The algorithm does not rely on highly discriminative depth features but works using only 2D images. We detail experiments to characterize the performance of our recognizer. Please note that we report accuracy figures from a single SCF, trained on the entire dataset. As evident from Fig. 10 this serves as lower bound, and as we show later, the pipelined version performs as well or better. The SCF is the best testbed to access the pure discriminative power of the algorithm.

Fig. 8 demonstrates qualitative results of our system classifying different hand gestures. Note the variation we see in the distance to the camera, orientation, of the hand, and the different backgrounds and lighting conditions, as well as the robustness of the segmentation step (labeled white).

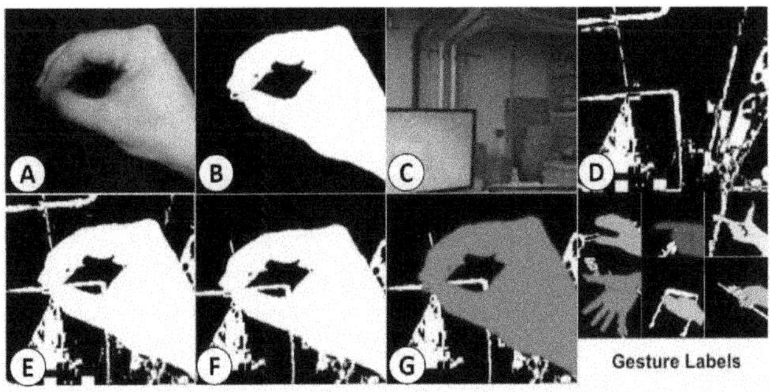

Figure 7: Training data generation and labels used for training.

Test Data and Forest Parameters

The forest size (number of trees) and the depth of the trees are the two main parameters affecting classifier performance. Increasing the number of trees can enhance accuracy in certain cases, but always increases computational cost and memory footprint linearly. To ensure that recognition is fast enough for real-time interaction at 30 Hz, we use three trees.

For test data, we instructed participants to gesture roughly at a range of $15 - 50$ cm, which is a comfortable range of operation, and well represented in the training data.

Gesture Recognition Accuracy

We report results using both leave–one–subject–out cross–validation and by using half of the gesture samples in the set for training and the remaining half for validation. Table 1 summarizes overall classification accuracy for a single SCF, averaged over all recognized gestures.

	15	16	17	18	19	20
Tr PPCR	0.79	0.82	0.85	0.87	0.89	0.92
Tr SCR	0.88	0.92	0.94	0.96	0.97	0.98
Ts PPCR	0.75	0.77	0.78	0.79	0.80	0.80
Ts SCR	0.86	0.89	0.92	0.92	0.92	0.93

Table 1: Per-frame accuracy for half–training / half–test (Tr) and leave–one–subject–out (Ts) cross validation of SCF. PPCR stands for per-pixel classification rate and SCR for state classification rate. Columns report accuracy for different depths.

Users have their own preferences for natural gestures, and the way gestures are performed may vary considerably. Hence, the accuracy of the leave–one–subject–out technique directly depends on the inter-personal variation in the dataset. As the number of subjects increases, so does the variation covered in the training set, and the model's capacity to generalize to previously unseen subjects. This accuracy (avg. 93%) can therefore be viewed as a lower bound and a good estimate of (unfiltered) real-world performance.

The half training–half test scheme is provided to give a better estimate of the power of the proposed method, independent of the quality and make-up of the training data. Overall, recognition performance is very good even with shallow trees (cf. Table 1). Fig. 9 summarizes classification accuracy as a confusion matrix for the entire gesture set, using both validation methods. Our technique achieves generally near perfect classification accuracies with a mean per-class, per-frame accuracy (mean of the confusion matrix's diagonal) of 98% and 93% respectively. In practice this translates to a very robust gesture recognizer with very little temporal filtering necessary (currently we use a 3 frame box filter), as evident by the video.

Increasing tree depth improves classification accuracy but also increases training time and memory footprint. On our data no overfitting effect was observed, indicating that we could increase mean accuracy even further by training deeper trees. However, beyond 20 levels we hit the memory limits of mobile devices. This issue of memory footprint for mobile uses reaffirms our need for multi-staged forests, which we evaluate in the next section.

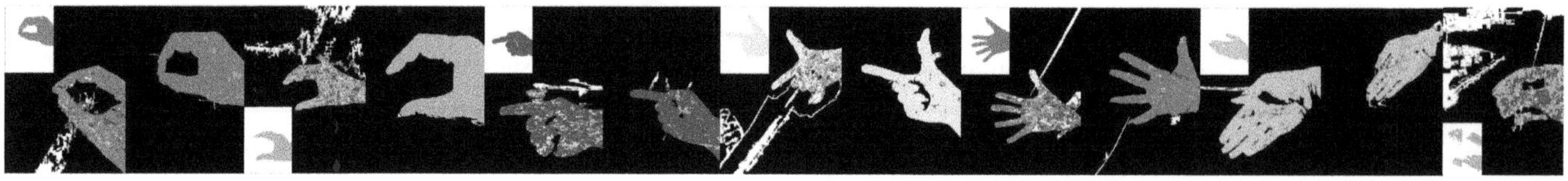

Figure 8: The current gesture set recognized by our classifier. Training data samples insets. Note the variation in scale and rotation as well as robustness to false positives from the segmentation step. the right-most image represents the background noise class.

PinchOpen	0.98	0	0	0	0	0	0.01	0.88	0.03	0	0	0	0	0.02
PinchClose	0	1	0	0	0	0	0.01	0	0.93	0.05	0	0	0	0.01
Pointing	0.02	0	0.99	0	0	0	0	0.02	0.01	0.9	0.04	0	0	0.01
Gun	0	0	0	1	0	0	0	0	0	0.02	0.95	0	0	0
SplayedHand	0	0	0	0	0.99	0	0	0	0	0	0.01	0.99	0	0
FlatHand	0	0	0	0	0.01	0.99	0.07	0.05	0	0	0	0.01	0.99	0.11
No-Gesture	0	0	0.01	0	0	0.01	0.91	0.05	0.03	0.03	0	0	0.01	0.85

Figure 9: Confusion matrix; data from 20 users. Left: half–test / half–train cross-validation; avg. accuracy 98% Right: leave–one–subject–out; avg. per-frame accuracy 93%.

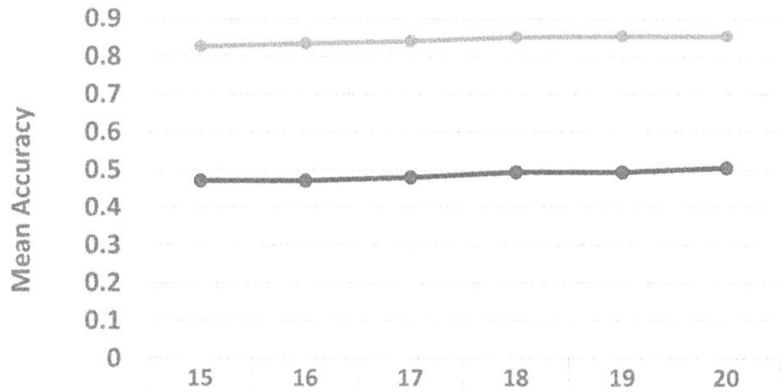

	15	16	17	18	19	20
SCF	0.471	0.471	0.48	0.494	0.494	0.506
DCF+SCF	0.826	0.834	0.84	0.851	0.854	0.854

Figure 10: Comparison of classification accuracy as function of tree depth when extreme gesture depth variations occur. DCF+SCF (orange) outperforms single SCF (blue) in terms of accuracy averaged over all classes.

Multi-staged Forests: Accuracy vs. Memory Footprint

In this section we quantify why splitting forests into separate specialized classifiers improves memory consumption, whilst greatly improving accuracy. For this experiment, we assessed both the performance of the pipelined classifier (DCF+SCF) and the standalone forest (SCF). We chose a far more challenging test dataset, where six users performed an extreme set of gestures at different ranges from $2-90$cm, which is far beyond the expected range of interaction. This was intentional as we wanted to stress-test both classifiers.

Fig. 10 shows the comparison of the two classifiers. The drop in performance of SCF in this experiment is explained by the extreme hand poses and distances that we captured in this test set. SCF was not able to cope with this large variation, and could not exceed an accuracy much greater than 50%. Our DCF+SCF multi-stage classifier was able to continuously outperform the SCF producing an average accuracy of $\sim 85\%$. What is perhaps most compelling about this approach is the memory footprint of DCF+SCFs compared to SCFs. The combination of a DCF+SCF with depths 10 and 15 consumes only 4.5MB, versus 110MB for the SCF at depth 20 but performs $\sim 30\%$ better. At level 18 the DCF+SCF still saves 81MB and outperforms the single SCF by 35%. All memory figures are for a single tree and have to be multiplied by the number of trees in the forest.

MOBILE PLATFORM IMPLEMENTATION

The details of our implementation including pseudo-code for the forest evaluation can be found in the appendix. Here, we briefly summarize the most important aspects.

Our recognition pipeline is written in native C++ and handles the camera access, performs background segmentation, random forest evaluation, gesture filtering and visualization of the different stages. At runtime we read images from the camera directly into an OpenGL ES texture and perform skin detection and bilinear downsampling on the GPU. Next, we download the segmentation mask to the CPU and perform connected component analysis (CC) on the binary image, and we compensate for transformations via principal component analysis (PCA). The resulting binary mask is then classified by the DCF, SCF and, if applicable, by the PCF. Each forest updates a label image as well as the input mask. After classification we upload the gesture labels and the cleaned segmentation mask back to the GPU for display. The per-pixel label probabilities are pooled across the image $c^* = \underset{c}{\operatorname{argmax}} \frac{1}{|u|} \sum_0^{|u|} p(c|S, u)$, where c^* is the final output mode or class label. Finally, a low-pass filter stabilizes the class labels temporally and a Kalman filter stabilizes the part labels spatially. The filtered gestures are injected as events to the Java-based Android apps. Camera capture, GPU computations, CPU computations, and user interaction run in four different synchronized threads.

PRELIMINARY USER EVALUATION

So far we have concentrated on evaluating the gesture recognition accuracy and the impact of *pipelining the classifier*, which we deem one of our main contributions. However, the main goal is to enable new forms of interaction and to enhance user experience on mobile devices. Hence, we gathered quantitative and qualitative data from a small pilot user study.

Bi-manual interaction One of the most compelling interaction scenarios for our technique is the use of touch and gestures in concert, freeing up display real-estate but allowing for complex bimanual interactions. To assess this hypothesis we ran a baseline experiment comparing multi-touch input with the combination of touch plus gestures in a comparative experiment. Participants had to repeatedly switch mode in a finger drawing application either using traditional menus in the touch condition or gestures in the bi-manual condition.

Experimental design We asked 9 subjects (6 male, 3 female) from our institution to trace a given figure using the *touch+gesture* interface or *touch only*. In both cases users had to repeatedly switch brush size and brush color. In the *touch only* condition both functionalities are controlled via a standard Android radial menu (see Fig. 11, left). In the *touch+gesture* condition the color chooser was invoked using the "C" gesture and the brush-size was toggled using the closed pinch gesture. Presentation order of the conditions is counterbalanced. Each user is asked to trace a total of 10 drawings requiring a total of 6 mode changes each.

Our results, summarized in Fig. 11 right, indicate that the *touch+gesture* condition is faster on average (mean=80.66s, SD=17.62) than the pure *touch* condition (65.22s, SD=15.06). A student's t-test shows that this difference is statistically significant($p < 0.007$). This is inline with our observation that most users instantaneously picked up on how to effectively leverage the gestures in this task. Only one user in our sample was faster with touch (104 versus 111 sec) and this user reported issues with remembering which gesture was mapped to which function.

Qualitative Feedback

While the quantitative results are promising, not all aspects of our system lend themselves to a formal evaluation. To attain a more holistic impression on the perceived user experience we conducted informal sessions with 8 participants (5 male, 3 female) again recruited from our lab. We gave users the opportunity to experiment with the applications we have built and discussed in the section "In-Air Gestures On The Move". This was followed with informal interviews.

Overall the feedback was very positive and users were impressed by the robustness of the gesture recognition engine. Scenarios that tightly couple touch input and gestures, for example the gaming scenario, were particularly well received. Furthermore, most users commented on the usefulness of the 'back of device' zoom and 'page flip' functionality in the Reader app. However, the participants were split in their opinion about the zoom functionality on the map application; with those not liking it saying *'I'm simply too well trained on touch and pinch–to–zoom on mobile phones'*. Finally, the magnifier functionality was generally received positively, with many users highlighting that this could be very useful, remarking that current mobile OS do not allow for simultaneous positioning of the magnifier and interaction with magnified content. The lack of dwell-time for lens invocation was also appreciated.

Of course, these observations are only preliminary. Our gesture set was in part designed to evaluate the range of variation our recognizer can cope with. Nonetheless, the current gestures illustrate the utility of the bi-manual touch+gestures interaction style. Furthermore, only two participants thought that more gestures would have been useful, whereas the rest of the participants found the overall gesture set useful and easy to remember. One user commented on the compelling

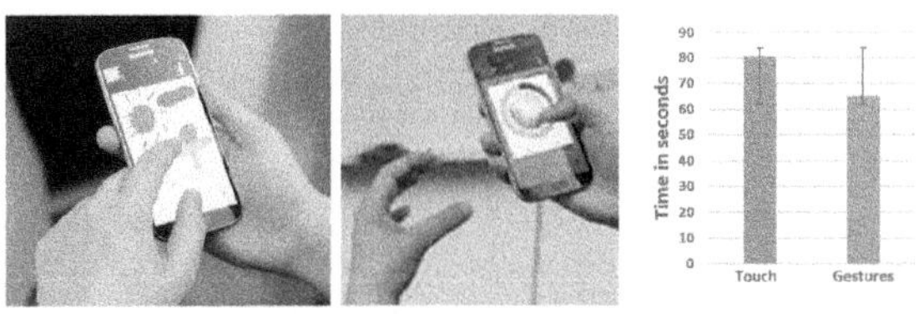

Figure 11: Tracing experiment. A) *Touch* condition B) *Touch+gestures* condition. C) Time to completion results in secs per drawing. Error bars signify standard deviation.

possibility to train different forests for different apps (*'for example, each game could come with it's own gestures'*). While the classification engine could be built into the OS, the specific trained forest could be shipped as middleware for each application. Finally, users commented that the absence of an explicit mode switch is very compelling. This can be seen as partial confirmation of our initial design goal of low-effort gestures, leveraging touch as primary input channel, complemented by smooth transitions to in-air gesturing then back.

DISCUSSION AND FUTURE WORK

The initial quantitative and qualitative results of our system are promising. Classification results performed by a variety of users in different lighting conditions and with changing backgrounds illustrates that even our initial prototype can be used for a diverse set of gestures, on off–the–shelf mobile phones, tablets and even smartwatches. To our knowledge this is the first time that a real-time implementation of the RFs has been demonstrated on such devices, especially with this level of robustness for gesture recognition. One important aspect to note is that given our recognition engine is machine learning based, new gestures can be added simply by providing new examples, and retraining our system. There are also clearly many areas of improvement, which we discuss in this section, outlining limitations and future work.

More Gestures, Better Features To demonstrate the extendability of our system we have trained the recognizer on a gesture set compiled from the American Sign Language alphabet but taking only gestures that have a unique contour (see supplementary material). The resulting set contains 12 classes and on leave–one–subject out validation achieves an avg. accuracy of 83%. However this demonstrates that our approach is limited to recognizing and discriminating gestures that provide a unique shape or contour, and therefore can miss subtle differences in gestures. For future work we will explore the feasibility of using more discriminative features and going beyond classifying binary images. For example, a feature that captures texture information may be able to differentiate between a flat hand facing down and one facing up.

Dynamic Gestures While we already detect a number of continuous interactions such as tracking fingertips or computing the ratio between open and close pinch (cf. supplementary material), our recognizer is *static* in nature. For future work we want to explore means to extend this to be able to capture dynamic gestures such as flicks and swipes directly. We plan to built upon recent work demonstrating the usage of RFs for motion gestures [39].

Lighting conditions As with all vision systems, ambient light is an issue. We have demonstrated that the system can cope with a variety of natural lighting as can be found in many indoors and outdoors locations. However, sudden changes in lighting such as entering or leaving a building or switching on strong direct light sources are still an issue. In particular, our technique is sensitive to segmentation failure – primarily false negatives as these impact the shape of the hand. To some degree this is counteracted by using a skin detection scheme with a single parameter and keeping the user in the loop to tune this setting. However, ultimately more sophisticated and reliable detection mechanisms would be desirable. Inspired by the promising results we achieved on classifying false positives we will explore the possibility of pushing the entire segmentation into the random forest.

CONCLUSIONS

We have presented, for the first time, a random forest based gesture recognizer, running in real-time on off–the-shelf mobile devices, including tablets, mobile phones and smartwatches. The algorithm avoids any hardware modifications, requiring only images from a regular RGB camera which are now commonplace on such devices. This makes natural gestures on mobile devices accessible to a large user base. We have also proposed a number of compelling interaction scenarios, allowing users to seamlessly transition between touch and gestural interaction, and allowing for bi-manual, simultaneous touch+gesture interaction. To achieve maximum accuracy for minimal memory footprint we have introduced multi-stage classification forests. Our hope is to provide a compelling new platform for researchers and practitioners alike to create new gestural interfaces on mobile devices.

ACKNOWLEDGMENTS

We thank Jibin Ou for writing the mobile phone apps used in the user study and the logging software for the experiments. Furthermore, we thank Emily Whiting and Alec Jacobson for providing the voice-over for the video. Finally, we thank the study participants for their valuable time and feedback.

REFERENCES

1. Ashbrook, D., Baudisch, P., and White, S. Nenya : Subtle and Eyes-Free Mobile Input with a Magnetically-tracked Finger Ring. In *Proc. ACM SIGCHI* (2011), 2043–2046.
2. Breiman, L. Random Forests. *Mach. Learn. 45*, 1 (Oct. 2001), 5–32.
3. Butler, A., Izadi, S., and Hodges, S. SideSight: multi-touch interaction around small devices. In *Proc. ACM UIST*, UIST '08 (2008), 201–204.
4. Chen, K.-Y., Lyons, K., White, S., and Patel, S. uTrack: 3D input using two magnetic sensors. In *Proc. ACM UIST* (2013).
5. Chen, X. A., Grossman, T., Wigdor, D., and Fitzmaurice, G. Duet: Exploring Joint Interactions on a Smart Phone and a Smart Watch. In *Proc. ACM CHI'14* (2014).
6. Erol, A., Bebis, G., Nicolescu, M., Boyle, R. D., and Twombly, X. Vision-based hand pose estimation: A review. *Comput. Vis. Image Underst.* (2007).
7. Goc, M. L., Taylor, S., Izadi, S., and Keskin, C. A Low-cost Transparent EF Sensor for 3D Interaction on Mobile Devices. In *Proc. ACM CHI* (2014).
8. Guiard, Y. Asymmetric Division of Labor in Human Skilled Bimanual Action. *J. Mot. Behav. 19*, 4 (1987).
9. Gustafson, S., Bierwirth, D., and Baudisch, P. Imaginary interfaces. In *Proc. ACM UIST* (2010), 3–12.
10. Harrison, C., Benko, H., and Wilson, A. D. OmniTouch: Wearable Multitouch Interaction Everywhere. In *Proc. ACM UIST*, ACM (2011), 441–450.
11. Harrison, C., Tan, D., and Morris, D. Skinput: Appropriating the Body As an Input Surface. In *Proc. ACM CHI* (2010), 453–462.
12. Hilliges, O., Kim, D., Izadi, S., and Weiss, M. HoloDesk: Direct 3D Interactions with a Situated See-Through Display. In *Proc. ACM CHI* (2012).
13. Hinckley, K., and Song, H. Sensor synaesthesia: touch in motion, and motion in touch. In *Proc. ACM CHI* (2011).
14. Hinckley, K., Yatani, K., Pahud, M., Coddington, N., Rodenhouse, J., Wilson, A., Benko, H., and Buxton, B. Pen + touch = new tools. In *Proc. ACM UIST* (2010).
15. Hwang, S., Ahn, M., and Wohn, K.-y. MagGetz: customizable passive tangible controllers on and around mobile devices. In *Proc. ACM UIST* (2013).
16. Izadi, S., Kim, D., Hilliges, O., Molyneaux, D., Newcombe, R., Kohli, P., Shotton, J., Hodges, S., Freeman, D., Davison, A., and Fitzgibbon, A. KinectFusion: Real-time 3D Reconstruction and Interaction Using a Moving Depth Camera. In *Proc. ACM UIST* (2011), 559–568.
17. Jones, B., Sodhi, R., Forsyth, D., Bailey, B., and Maciocci, G. Around device interaction for multiscale navigation. In *Proc. of MobileHCI* (2012).
18. Kakumanu, P., Makrogiannis, S., and Bourbakis, N. A survey of skin-color modeling and detection methods. *Pattern Recognit. 40*, 3 (2007), 1106–1122.
19. Keskin, C., Kirac, F., Kara, Y. E., Akarun, L., and Kiraç, F. Hand Pose Estimation and Hand Shape Classification Using Multi-layered Randomized Decision Forests. In *Proc. ECCV* (Berlin, Heidelberg, 2012).
20. Ketabdar, H., Roshandel, M., and Yüksel, K. A. Towards using embedded magnetic field sensor for around mobile device 3D interaction. In *Proc. MobileHCI* (2010).
21. Kim, D., Hilliges, O., Izadi, S., Butler, A. D., Chen, J., Oikonomidis, I., and Olivier, P. Digits: Freehand 3D interactions anywhere using a wrist-worn gloveless sensor. In *Proc. ACM UIST* (2012).
22. Kim, D., Izadi, S., Dostal, J., Rhemann, C., Keskin, C., Zach, C., Shotton, J., Large, T., Bathiche, S., Nieß ner, M., Butler, A., Fanello, S., and Pradeep, V. RetroDepth: 3D Silhouette Sensing for High-Precision Input On and Above Physical Surfaces. In *Proc. ACM CHI* (2014).
23. Kim, J., He, J., Lyons, K., and Starner, T. The Gesture Watch: A Wireless Contact-free Gesture based Wrist Interface. In *IEEE ISWC* (2007), 1–8.
24. Kratz, S., and Rohs, M. HoverFlow: expanding the design space of around-device interaction. In *Proc. MobileHCI*, ACM (2009), 4.
25. Lee, S. C., Li, B., and Starner, T. AirTouch: Synchronizing In-air Hand Gesture and On-body Tactile Feedback. In *IEEE ISWC* (2011), 3–10.
26. Mistry, P., and Maes, P. SixthSense: a wearable gestural interface. In *ACM SIGGRAPH ASIA Sketches* (2009).
27. Molyneaux, D., Izadi, S., Kim, D., Hilliges, O., Hodges, S., Cao, X., Butler, A., and Gellersen, H. Interactive environment-aware handheld projectors for pervasive computing spaces. In *Pervasive Comput.* (2012).
28. Niikura, T., Hirobe, Y., Cassinelli, A., Watanabe, Y., Komuro, T., and Ishikawa, M. In-air typing interface for mobile devices with vibration feedback. In *ACM SIGGRAPH Emerg. Technol.* (2010).
29. Ogata, M., Sugiura, Y., Makino, Y., Inami, M., and Imai, M. SenSkin: adapting skin as a soft interface. In *Proc. ACM UIST* (New York, New York, USA, 2013).
30. Oikonomidis, I., Kyriazis, N., and Argyros, A. A. Tracking the Articulated Motion of Two Strongly Interacting Hands. In *IEEE CVPR* (Providence, 2012).

31. Rekimoto, J. GestureWrist and GesturePad: unobtrusive wearable interaction devices. In *IEEE ISWC* (2001).
32. Saponas, S., Tan, D., Morris, D., Balakrishnan, R., Turner, J., and Landay, J. Enabling always-available input with muscle-computer interfaces. In *Proc. ACM UIST* (2009).
33. Shotton, J., Fitzgibbon, A. W., Cook, M., Sharp, T., Finocchio, M., Moore, R., Kipman, A., and Blake, A. Real-time human pose recognition in parts from single depth images. *Commun. ACM 56*, 1 (2013), 116–124.
34. Song, H., Guimbretiere, F., Grossman, T., and Fitzmaurice, G. MouseLight: Bimanual Interactions on Digital Paper Using a Pen and a Spatially-aware Mobile Projector. In *Proc. ACM CHI* (2010).
35. Sridhar, S., Oulasvirta, A., and Theobalt, C. Interactive Markerless Articulated Hand Motion Tracking Using RGB and Depth Data. In *IEEE ICCV* (2013).
36. Starner, T., Auxier, J., Ashbrook, D., and Gandy, M. The gesture pendant: a self-illuminating, wearable, infrared computer vision system for home automation control and medical monitoring. In *IEEE ISWC* (2000), 87–94.
37. Starner, T., Weaver, J., and Pentland, A. A wearable computer based American sign language recognizer. In *IEEE ISWC*, ISWC '97 (1997).
38. Tang, D., Yu, T., and Kim, T. Real-time Articulated Hand Pose Estimation using Semi-supervised Transductive Regression Forests. In *IEEE ICCV* (2013).
39. Taylor, S., Keskin, C., Hilliges, O., Izadi, S., and Helmes, J. Type-Hover-Swipe in 96 Bytes: A Motion Sensing Mechanical Keyboard. In *Proc. ACM CHI* (2014).
40. Wigdor, D., Forlines, C., Baudisch, P., Barnwell, J., and Shen, C. LucidTouch: A See-Through Mobile Device. In *Proc. ACM UIST*, ACM Press (2007).

APPENDIX

Extended gesture set

The main body of the paper demonstrates a gesture set consisting of only six gestures. In order to demonstrate the scalability and discriminative power of the approach, we have conducted further experiments with a larger gesture set. We selected 12 gestures from the American Sign Language alphabet (ASL) based on the uniqueness of their shape. As our algorithm relies only on binary images, differences in appearance that are fully contained within the silhouette of a hand pose are difficult to discriminate using the binary features. For example, the letters A, M, N, S, and T produce near identical outlines. Furthermore, we excluded signs with dynamics (i.e., motion) as we currently only recognize static gestures.

Fig. 12 shows the confusion matrix for the 12 gestures selected from the ASL alphabet. On this gesture set we achieved similar performance to our original gestures. The overall average per-class accuracy is of 83% for leave–one–out validation. This additional experiment further demonstrates the power of the classification algorithm and we believe that even more complex gesture sets could be handled. However, the feature we chose limits the type of gestures to those that produce visually discernible contours. In our future work we will investigate different types of features to overcome this limitation and to exploit the additional information that is present in the data (e.g., texture, edges).

O	0.776	0	0	0	0	0	0	0	0	0	0	0
C	0.029	0.904	0.044	0.032	0.04	0.074	0.184	0	0	0.002	0	0.012
D	0	0.024	0.887	0.143	0	0.011	0	0	0.012	0.068	0	0.058
L	0	0	0	0.431	0	0	0	0	0	0	0	0.12
Five	0	0	0	0	0.849	0	0	0	0	0.013	0	0
B	0.018	0.016	0.015	0.028	0.001	0.856	0	0	0	0.03	0	0
E	0	0	0	0	0	0	0.761	0	0	0	0	0
Y	0.006	0	0	0.128	0.064	0	0	0.92	0	0.033	0	0
P	0.13	0.051	0.054	0.092	0.046	0.041	0.045	0.076	0.988	0.08	0.001	0.05
Three	0	0	0	0.046	0	0	0	0.002	0	0.774	0	0
I	0.031	0.005	0	0	0	0.018	0	0.002	0	0	0.999	0
X	0.01	0	0	0.1	0	0	0.012	0	0	0	0	0.76

Figure 12: Confusion matrix for 12 gestures selected from American Sign Language.

Continuous gesture switching

Currently our algorithm can only handle static gestures. However, in many situations application programmers are interested in continuous valued input. For example, one might want to implement a gesture to control the volume of an audio player dynamically. One possibility to do so based on our approach is to exploit the per-pixel nature of the classifier. We have observed that the probabilities of symmetric gesture pairs (e.g., open and closed pinch) increase and decrease smoothly during the transition between the two gestures. Fig. 13 plots the raw, unfiltered relative probability ratio between the pair of gestures (*PinchOpen* and *PinchClose*). The ratio between these two values can be mapped to continuous inputs.

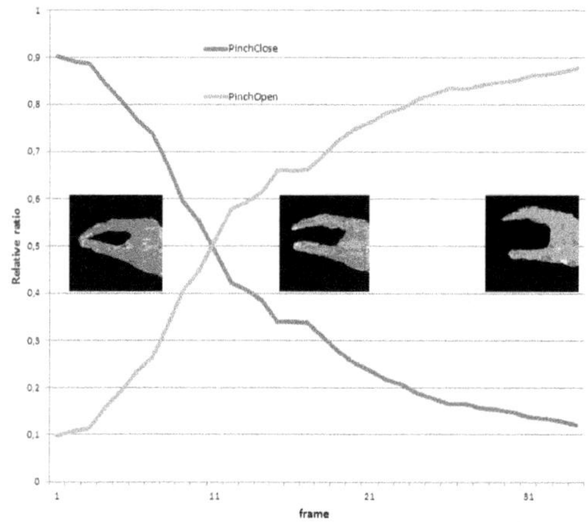

Figure 13: Continuous gesture input can be implemented by looking at the ratio of the first two modes in the per-pixel class probability distribution.

For instance, we have implemented a mapping application in which a fisheye lens can be invoked using the *PinchOpen* gesture. Subsequently, the size (and hence magnification factor) of the fisheye lens can be controlled by opening and closing the pinch gesture. The location of the lens can then be controlled via the fingertip locations (see Fig. 14).

Figure 14: The size of magnifier on the map can be adjusted continuously by the transitions between *PinchOpen* and *PinchClose* gesture pair.

ParaFrustum: Visualization Techniques for Guiding a User to a Constrained Set of Viewing Positions and Orientations

Mengu Sukan Carmine Elvezio Ohan Oda Steven Feiner
Dept. of Computer Science
Columbia University
New York, NY 10027
{ms3774, ce2236, oo2116, skf1}@columbia.edu

Barbara Tversky
Dept. of Human Development
Teachers College
Columbia University
New York, NY 10027
btversky@stanford.edu

Figure 1. (a) ParaFrustum defining a range of acceptable viewing positions and orientations, as visualized by the ParaFrustum-InSitu visualization. (b) Unsatisfied ParaFrustum-InSitu visualization, as seen from inside. (c) ParaFrustum-HUD visualization.

ABSTRACT
Many tasks in real or virtual environments require users to view a target object or location from one of a set of strategic viewpoints to see it in context, avoid occlusions, or view it at an appropriate angle or distance. We introduce ParaFrustum, a geometric construct that represents this set of strategic viewpoints and viewing directions. ParaFrustum is inspired by the look-from and look-at points of a computer graphics camera specification, which precisely delineate a location for the camera and a direction in which it looks. We generalize this approach by defining a ParaFrustum in terms of a look-from volume and a look-at volume, which establish constraints on a range of acceptable locations for the user's eyes and a range of acceptable angles in which the user's head can be oriented. Providing tolerance in the allowable viewing positions and directions avoids burdening the user with the need to assume a tightly constrained 6DoF pose when it is not required by the task.

We describe two visualization techniques for virtual or augmented reality that guide a user to assume one of the poses defined by a ParaFrustum, and present the results of a user study measuring the performance of these techniques. The study shows that the constraints of a tightly constrained ParaFrustum (e.g., approximating a conventional camera frustum) require significantly more time to satisfy than those of a loosely constrained one. The study also reveals interesting differences in participant trajectories in response to the two techniques.

UIST '14, October 05–08 2014, Honolulu, HI, USA

http://dx.doi.org/10.1145/2642918.2647417

Author Keywords
Augmented reality; virtual reality; view frustum; viewing specification.

ACM Classification Keywords
H.5.1 [Information Interfaces and Presentation]: Multimedia information systems—Artificial, augmented, and virtual realities; H.5.2 [Information Interfaces and Presentation]: User interfaces—Input interaction styles

INTRODUCTION
When coordinating action with something or someone in the world, such as repairing equipment or sighting a distant object, it can be important to be in the right place and to orient one's body and head in the correct direction. Some tasks require that users view a domain object or location from a precise position and orientation, while others are more flexible, allowing many possible positions and orientations. Using language to communicate spatial location is

not straightforward, as everyday spatial language is not precise (e.g., [5,14]). Demonstrating a correct position and orientation may also be problematic, as the user and the helper cannot occupy the same 6DoF pose at the same time. In addition, these solutions require colocation of both participants.

How might this range of possible head poses be represented and communicated to a user? Choosing just one allowable head pose from the set may suffice in some cases. However, requiring the user to assume an overly specific head pose—when others may be just as good—may take longer and be more difficult than necessary. Furthermore, there are tasks in which the most comfortable head position and orientation will differ depending upon the user's height, which may not be known in advance. Therefore, it is important to determine how to effectively encode a parameterized set of acceptable head poses and how to present them to a user.

To address the problem of encoding a set of head poses, we introduce the *ParaFrustum*, which loosens the constraints imposed by a conventional computer graphics camera specification. We use the prefix "para" to mean "going beyond" a frustum. A virtual camera in 3D computer graphics can be defined in part by using a look-from point (center of projection) and a look-at point to determine the precise position and orientation (not counting roll) of a camera frustum. In contrast, a ParaFrustum generalizes the concept of a single position and orientation to a set of acceptable positions and orientations (not counting roll) for a frustum. It does this by replacing the look-from point with a look-from volume (the *head volume*) and the look-at point with a look-at volume (the *tail volume*). The user must place their eyes within the head volume, and orient their head to look in a direction determined by the tail volume. (While the head and tail volumes may, in general, be of arbitrary shape, we use ellipsoids in our implementation.)

We assume that the user is ultimately viewing the task domain within which a ParaFrustum resides through one (monoscopic) or two (stereoscopic) display frusta. Each *display frustum* corresponds to a virtual or real camera frustum—a truncated pyramid whose position and orientation are controlled by the user (e.g., by head motion or hand motion for a head-worn or hand-held display). We define a set of rules that express how the display frusta should be positioned and oriented relative to the ParaFrustum to satisfy its constraints.

To address the problem of communicating the valid poses allowed by a ParaFrustum and assist a user in assuming one of them, we created two visualization techniques intended for use in augmented reality (AR) or virtual reality (VR). One visualization, *ParaFrustum-InSitu*, interactively superimposes in the world coordinate system the head and tail volumes, wrapped by a convex hull, as shown in Figure 1(a). It signals position, orientation, and height information to the user, encompassing the user's eyes (Figure 1b), in the process of achieving an acceptable position, orientation, and height. The other visualization, *ParaFrustum-HUD*, superimposes in the coordinate system of the user's head a HUD (head up display) composed of a set of three dials that signal the user's position and orientation relative to the poses encoded by the ParaFrustum, providing continuous feedback to users to guide them as they approach the target (Figure 1c). Thus, ParaFrustum-InSitu is part of the viewer's 3D world, whereas ParaFrustum-HUD is analogous to a set of 2D dials in a cockpit. ParaFrustum-InSitu integrates the information needed to assume an appropriate head pose, yet presents an unfamiliar way of navigating. ParaFrustum-HUD separates the needed information, allowing users to satisfy constraints in sequence, with some of the familiarity of a videogame HUD.

To test the effectiveness of the ParaFrustum and its visualizations, we designed and performed a user study that explores visualizations of different shaped ParaFrusta, measuring the speed and accuracy with which participants can assume an acceptable pose associated with the ParaFrustum being visualized. The study shows that the constraints of a tightly constrained ParaFrustum (e.g., approximating a conventional camera frustum) require significantly more time to satisfy than those of a loosely constrained one. The study also reveals interesting differences in participant speed and trajectories in response to the two techniques; these differences are most likely due to the strategies that participants adopt.

Thus, this paper makes three contributions: (1) We introduce the ParaFrustum, which generalizes the specification of a permissible head pose by using two volumes of points that together constrain the sets of acceptable 3D viewing positions and orientations. (2) We describe two different visualization techniques that communicate information about the acceptable positions and orientations, and are designed to interactively guide a user to assume a position and orientation satisfying those constraints. (3) We present a user study that explores the time and trajectories that users take to reach an acceptable position and orientation using examples of these visualizations that express varying levels of tightness in position and orientation.

In the remainder of this paper, we first provide an overview of related work. Next, we describe in detail the ParaFrustum, and the ParaFrustum-InSitu and ParaFrustum-HUD visualizations, including how they are defined, used, and implemented. Then, we present a user study that measures the performance of these visualizations in guiding users to an acceptable head position and orientation, comparing the effects of different size head and tail volumes on time, effectiveness, and trajectory. Finally, we present our conclusions and directions for future work.

RELATED WORK

Calling Attention to a 3D Target

There has been much previous work on how to call a user's attention to a target in a 3D environment, whether real or virtual, when viewed with a 6DoF-tracked display. Perhaps the simplest is highlighting. However, highlighting by itself does not work when the target is occluded or offscreen. One approach to signaling objects that are hard to see uses a leader line anchored onscreen on one end, with the other end terminating on an onscreen target; in the case of an offscreen target, the line is clipped at the screen edge in the direction of the target [7]. The user can then "follow the leader," turning the tracked display toward the clipped portion of the line to bring the target onscreen.

An alternative approach minimizes the portion of the screen devoted to directing the user's attention by using a small conical pointer anchored at its base in the bottom portion of the screen of a head-worn display [6]. Its tip points directly toward an onscreen object, left or right to offscreen objects in front of the user, and down to offscreen objects behind the user. The attention funnel [2] replaces the simple geometry used in these techniques with a carefully designed set of components that attract the user's attention toward the target, using a high-frequency pattern of lines to mark the path toward the object.

There is also a class of visualizations intended to provide situational awareness, such as so-called "radar views" that are often used in the "heads-up displays" overlaid on a first-person view in games. These "radar views" often feature a small circle representing an area around the user located at the center, as seen in an overhead plan view, overlaid by a shaded sector of the circle representing the user's field of view. If a representation of the target is shown in the circle (or marked on the circumference for targets outside the circle), the radar view can guide the user toward the target, by showing the change in position to reach it and orientation to see it. If the altitude of the target is also important, a second radar view can show a side elevation view centered about the user.

Specifying Position and Orientation Relative to a 3D Target

While the techniques mentioned above direct the user's attention to a target, they do not specify how the user should be positioned and oriented relative to that target. One way to do this uses the familiar geometric representation of a camera as a pyramidal frustum, with a center of projection at the pyramid apex (the look-from point) and a base delineating the target, with a look-at point at the center of the base. Snavely et al. [21] visualize a set of such pyramids, each representing a photograph from which the frustum is derived by the system. The set is displayed at their positions and orientations in a 3D desktop UI, from which the user can choose one to view its photograph.

Güven and Feiner [13] describe an outdoor AR system in which a line-drawn pyramid view volume is erected over a photograph texture-mapped onto its base and located at the approximate position and orientation from which the photograph was taken, derived from an analysis of the photograph. When users position their heads at the pyramid apex, they can view the image registered with the real world.

Bae et al. [1] use an alternative approach to guide the user to a desired position and orientation for rephotography (the process of taking a photograph at the same location and orientation as a previous reference photograph). Their system interactively analyzes the current view seen by a camera and, if the camera captures a view sufficiently similar to the reference photograph, the system determines how the camera should be translated to bring it to the correct location. They present the photographer with an interface showing two views of a camera: An overhead plan view of the camera facing forward is overlaid with a 2D arrow showing the direction parallel to the ground in which to move the camera. This is complemented with a rear elevation of the camera as seen from the back, overlaid with a 2D arrow showing the direction in the plane of the camera back in which to move the camera. Finally, the view seen by the camera is overlaid with the edges of the reference view to allow the user to adjust the camera orientation.

Specifying a Constrained Set of Positions and Orientations in 3D

The problem we address here differs from that of the work discussed above, in that we do not want to restrict the user to a specific position and orientation, but instead allow a range of possible positions and orientations. Research on automated cinematography (e.g., [10][4]) has addressed ways of expressing and resolving general constraints on camera specifications; however, this work was not directed toward helping a user to physically realize an acceptable camera pose. The most relevant previous work that we know of is by Shingu et al. [20], who created an AR visualization to assist with a rephotography task in an industrial setting for inspecting an item before and after a process. A red sphere is positioned around a target of interest and a cone whose apex is at the center of the sphere protrudes from the sphere. The sphere encloses what must be visible and the cone constrains the angle from which it must be viewed. The cone disappears when the camera's viewpoint is inside, and the sphere turns green when it is fully inside the camera frustum, together indicating that an acceptable camera position and orientation have been achieved.

ParaFrustum provides a significant advance over this previous work. ParaFrustum supports a much wider range of shapes and relative sizes of the volumes containing the look-from and look-at points, makes it possible to constrain the maximum distance the camera can be from the target, and is complemented by a set of visualizations to assist in realizing an acceptable pose that are better suited to the more general geometry of ParaFrustum. ParaFrustum makes a clear distinction between look-from and look-at volumes, allowing the look-at volume to constrain only orientation. In contrast, the Shingu et al. sphere serves double duty: a look-at volume and an implicit bound on how close the user can get to the sphere. While Shingu et al. do

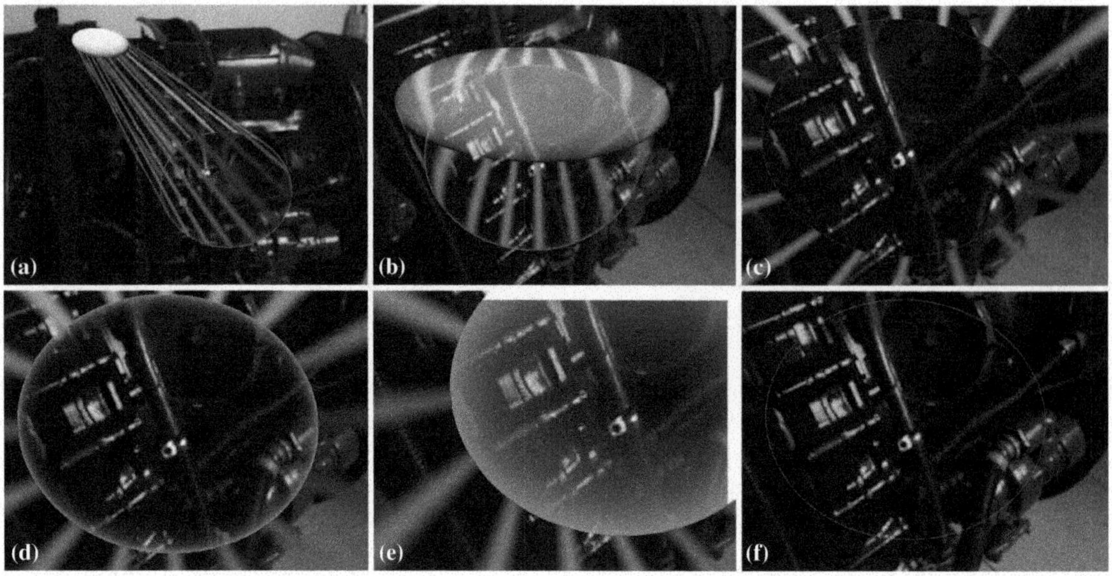

Figure 2. ParaFrustum-InSitu visualization. (a) Viewed from a distance, head volume is opaque. (b) Head volume becomes more transparent as user approaches. (c) Looking toward tail volume with eyes inside head volume, red ring and ribs are visible. (d) Eyes have exited rear of head volume, and red ring becomes thicker. (e) Eyes continue further forward and tail volume starts becoming opaque. Tail volume extends beyond top and right edges of view volume, causing them to be highlighted in white. (f) Eyes return back into head volume and orientation is correct, so only faint red ring remains.

not impose a bound on how far the user can get, providing one by putting a base on the cone would still not produce ParaFrustum's explicit visible head volume, which we use in our visualizations as a target at which users can aim. Because ParaFrustum's tail volume can be asymmetric, it better supports situations in which more leeway is needed in one axis than another. ParaFrustum's rules also allow partial visibility of the tail volume, and explicitly support stereo. Furthermore, the performance of ParaFrustum and its visualizations has been validated in a formal user study investigating a range of sizes and shapes for the head and tail volumes.

PARAFRUSTUM

The ParaFrustum head volume defines the set of acceptable viewing positions, while the ParaFrustum tail volume defines the set of endpoints for a bundle of viewing vectors that originate in the head end. The head and tail volumes can be thought of as being wrapped by a convex hull that includes all directed lines between any point in the head volume and any point in the tail volume.

We define the set of acceptable viewing locations for the ParaFrustum to require that the center(s) of projection of the display device's camera frusta (one for mono, two for stereo) be fully contained by the head volume. In addition to defining the set of allowable eye positions, the head volume presents a target toward which the user can travel when first approaching the ParaFrustum, as we will describe later.

To define the set of acceptable viewing orientations, we have developed a set of rules that attempt to maximize the portion of the tail volume that is visible to the user. We determine this relative to the intersection of the two display/camera frusta for stereo (the single display/camera frustum for mono), which we will call the *view volume*. As seen from a location within the head volume, the tail volume may either fit fully within the view volume or may exceed it. If the tail volume is able to fit fully, then the head orientation will be considered to be correct. On the other hand, the tail volume may extend past one or more of the left, right, top, or bottom of the view volume. If the tail volume extends past only one of the left and right sides, and/or only one of the top and bottom, the orientation will not be considered correct. The rationale is that in these cases, the user should change their orientation so that the tail volume is fully contained by or extends past both of the top and bottom sides and both of the left and right sides, to maximize the visible portion of the tail volume.

We note that it is possible to choose pathological combinations of head and tail volumes that make it impossible to establish an acceptable viewing position or orientation under these criteria; however, we have found it easy in practice to select head and tail volumes that establish constraints that are satisfiable and make sense for realistic viewing tasks.

It is easy to understand that, in general, smaller head volumes impose tighter constraints on viewing location, while larger head volumes impose looser constraints. The impact of tail volume size is less obvious. Under the criteria for acceptable viewing orientations that we use, the tightest constraint on orientation would be imposed by a tail volume that just fits the view volume; for example, this could be an ellipsoid whose projection is circumscribed by the outline

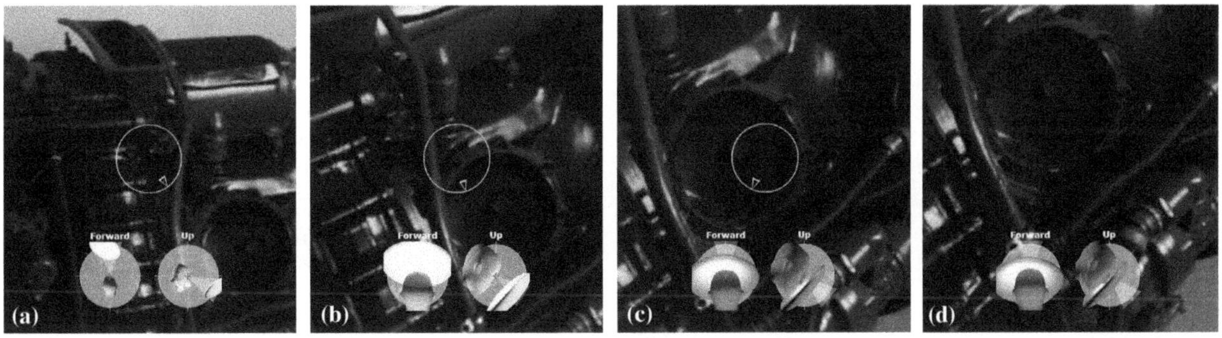

Figure 3. ParaFrustum-HUD visualization. (a) Two radar views and orientation-offset indicator are combined in one visualization. (b) User has approached head shape, which has become larger in Forward and Up radar views. (c) User intersects head shape in both Forward and Up radar views. (d) User is looking in correct direction and is inside head volume.

of the view volume, or whose projection circumscribes the outline of the view volume. As a tail volume that can be contained by the view volume shrinks in size, the orientation constraint it imposes becomes looser, until the tail volume becomes a point, providing horizontal and vertical leeway corresponding to the horizontal and vertical field of view of the view volume. In contrast, as a tail volume whose projection circumscribes the outline of the volume grows in size, it also provides successively more leeway, which can range beyond the horizontal and vertical field of view of the view volume. Note that alternatives to these rules are possible. For example, the tail volume could define a set of points that need only intersect with the view volume or with the view volume's center axis, so that larger tail volumes always result in looser orientation constraints.

ParaFrustum-InSitu Visualization

ParaFrustum-InSitu (InSitu) includes a number of visual aids to assist the user in assuming an acceptable pose. As shown in Figure 2(a), the head volume is visible only from outside the shape and the tail volume is rendered as a thin red outline. The head and tail volumes are wrapped by a convex hull that is displayed as a series of ribs extending from the head to the tail. As the user approaches the head volume, it becomes more transparent (Figure 2b), until a maximum transparency value is reached. Since the head volume is completely invisible from within, we limit the maximum transparency on approach in order to display a discrete jump in color to full transparency when breaching the shell of the head volume (Figure 2c). The tail now appears as a faint red ring (defined by the contour of the tail volume, as viewed from the current perspective).

Using a technique inspired by the silk cursor [23], if the user continues to move forward from inside the head volume, exiting the head volume and entering the hull proper, the tail shape quickly transitions to a thicker elliptical ring around the limb of the volume (Figure 2d), to a nearly opaque ellipsoid (Figure 2e). This is done to warn the user that they have exited the head volume, (which cannot be seen from inside the ParaFrustum, when looking in the correct general direction). If the user returns back into the head volume, the tail volume returns to its shading. Once the user assumes an acceptable pose, the ribs will shrink until they are completely invisible, and only the light red ring around the tail volume is visible (Figure 2f).

Recall that if the tail volume extends past only one of the left and right sides, and/or only one of the top and bottom of the view volume, the user might be able to change their head orientation to make the tail volume fit. In this case, the system highlights the offending side(s) of the view volume with a thick white line, as shown at the top and right of Figure 2(e). If that happens, the user can turn their head in the direction of the line(s) to try to make the tail volume fit completely inside the view volume. If it does not fit, then the tail shape will be cut by both the left and right sides, or both the top and bottom. When this occurs, the thick white line(s) and ribs connecting the ellipsoids disappear, meaning that an acceptable head pose has been achieved.

Implementation

The InSitu hulls are generated by passing the head and tail volumes to a convex hull library [19] to generate a convex hull wrapping the two end shapes. Once the hull is generated, the two end shapes are subtracted from it using Constructive Solid Geometry (CSG) [17]. The two original end shapes are then placed back in the visualization and attached to the hull.

In our current implementation, ParaFrusta are built with ellipsoid head and tail volumes. The ribs of the hull are rendered with a shader that applies a sinusoidal function to the alpha value of the hull material's diffuse property.

While InSitu uses each visible component for the purpose of visualizing some element of the user's current deviation from an acceptable pose, it can potentially obstruct important physical objects in the real world. We have attempted to mitigate this by making the visualization somewhat transparent at all times. However, there is always some indication of its presence when the user is not in an acceptable pose. The benefit here is that the user is always made aware of the constraints on pose, allowing refinements to be made immediately.

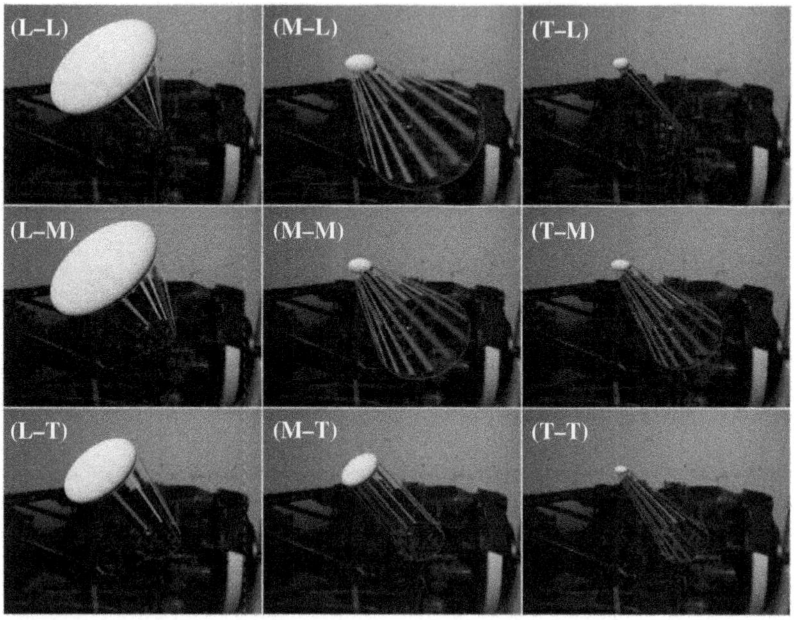

Figure 4. ParaFrusta, visualized using ParaFrustum-InSitu. Labels specify levels of tolerance, and are of form "PositionTolerance–OrientationTolerance", where PositionTolerance and OrientationTolerance are one of "L" (Loose), "M" (Medium), and "T" (Tight).

In each row, position tolerance decreases left to right, corresponding to decreasing head volume size.

In each column, orientation tolerance decreases top to bottom. Relationship of tail volume size to orientation tolerance is more complex than head volume size to position tolerance. In left column, tail volume size increases top to bottom, fitting within frustum; in middle column, tail volume size decreases top to bottom (top two larger than frustum, bottom smaller); in right column, tail volume size increases top (smaller than frustum) to center (larger than frustum), and decreases center to bottom (slightly smaller than frustum).

ParaFrustum-HUD Visualization

ParaFrustum-HUD (HUD) uses a system of multiple 2D circular dials, similar to those used in game head-up displays. Three dials were displayed in the user's field of view, as seen in Figure 3(a). The lower left dial (the "Forward" radar view) indicates the user's position and heading by a top-down orthographic plan view of a mannequin head model and the ParaFrustum head volume, showing the disparity between the heading of the operator and the desired heading. The lower right dial (the "Up" radar view) shows an orthographic side elevation view indicating the vertical height of the user's head and the ParaFrustum head volume, information that was not needed in some cases. The middle dial shows the user's offset from the final orientation in yaw and pitch, displaying an arrowhead in the direction in which the user must look.

As the user moves closer to the head volume, the scale enlarges (Figure 3b). The correct position has been achieved when the projected head volume surrounds the centers of both the Forward and Up radar views, causing the mannequin heads and projected head volumes to turn red (Figure 3c). When the user is looking in an acceptable direction, the middle dial disappears (Figure 3d) and will become visible again only if the user's orientation is no longer acceptable.

Unlike InSitu, HUD also works when the head is tracked, but the display is not (e.g., handheld). Although the user could attempt to integrate the information from all three dials in moving toward the target, tracking three changing objects is challenging (e.g., [9]). Another strategy that users could apply is to follow each dial in a natural sequence, adjusting to each one in turn. The lower left dial could guide users to the right position, simply by walking along a path that aligned the nose with the desired orientation. Once in position, users could orient their heads, following the direction indicated in the upper dial. Applying this strategy predicts that users would walk a straight line, then turn and walk straight again.

Comparison

The dials in HUD are essentially a changing diagram or visualization of the parts of the environment relevant to navigation and orientation, superimposed on the user's field of view, rather than an integral part of the environment. In contrast, InSitu is part of the user's environment. It is a 3D enclosure that the operator/user must enter. This is similar to entering a doorway, a task that people accomplish with exquisite accuracy (e.g., [8]). In addition, InSitu combines and integrates the information that is presented in three separate dials for HUD. Using InSitu, users can anticipate the entire sequence of movements needed, the trajectory from the start point to the viewing point and the viewing angle and height. Considerable research has shown that people make anticipatory movements of the body, head, and eyes; that is, they are preparing the next set of movements as they enact the current set (e.g., [3,11,12,15]). Due to anticipation, walkers using InSitu are expected to take a curved path toward a target. In the present case, walking a curved path toward the position outside the target position would keep the expected position quite central in users' fields of view, as well as allow users to anticipate the position, orientation, and height of the body and head as they reach the viewing point.

In contrast, the straight/turn path that seems optimal for HUD would not keep the expected viewing position in the users' field of view on many occasions. However, because users' movements are guided wholly by the dials, keeping the expected viewing point in the field of view would not necessarily be helpful.

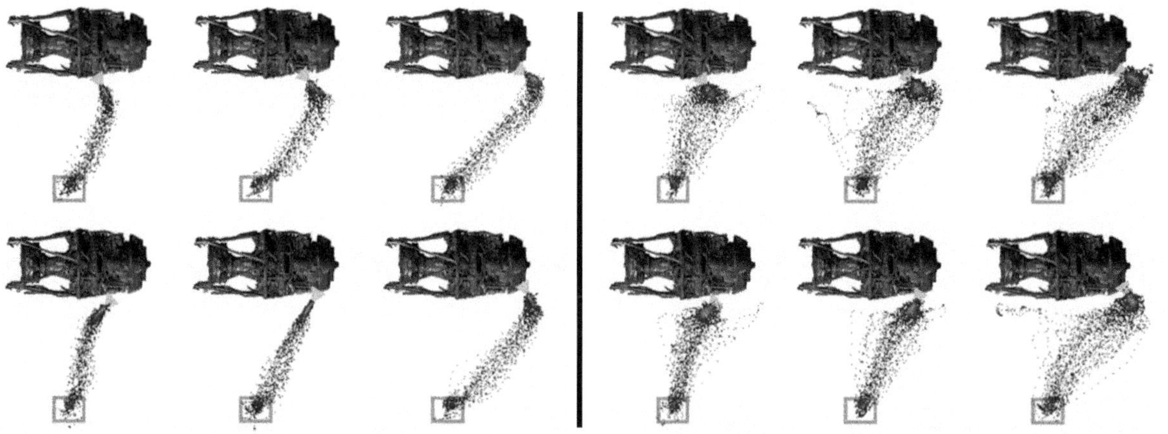

Figure 5. Heatmap showing plan views of participants' paths to six of the possible twelve targets. (a) InSitu. (b) HUD. Target positions and orientations are shown symbolically as green triangles. Home location is shown as a blue square.

USER STUDY

Pilot Study

Prior to conducting the formal user study, we performed an informal pilot study with our lab members and four compensated students. We defined a set of seven ParaFrusta, representing a combination of the basic ParaFrustum position and orientation tolerances (roughly categorized as loose, medium, and tight). Based on the results, we decided on a single length of ParaFrustum to use in the formal study, increased the number of trials for the formal study, and changed the placement of targets to ease analysis. Additionally, we increased the number of combinations from seven to nine, as shown in Figure 4, adding two new combinations: tight position and loose orientation (T–L), and loose position and loose orientation (L–L).

Hypotheses

Several predictions follow from our analysis and pilot study.

H1. The InSitu condition should lead to faster accomplishment of the task than HUD, because the InSitu visualization is embedded in the surrounding world and integrates the needed information, allowing the anticipatory actions that people perform well naturally [8].

H2. Due to the difficulty of integrating information from multiple indicators, participants in the HUD condition are expected to follow one indicator at a time sequentially, leading to increased time and variability in position and orientation, because following a single indicator at a time may lead to misalignment on the other indicators. On the other hand, InSitu's integrated display allows participants to enact an anticipatory curved trajectory.

H3. Both InSitu and HUD conditions should take longer for tighter constraints than looser ones; in general, this would predict that it should be faster to assume a pose specified by a less constrained ParaFrustum than by a precise frustum.

H4. Participants will prefer InSitu over HUD, for the same reasons provided for H1.

Methods

Participants

The participants were 18 students (3 female), 19–33 years old (average 24), at our institution. They were recruited from mailing lists and email, and each was paid $15 for their participation. All participants used computers on a daily basis and two had experience with AR, though not with this project. The experiment took approximately 1 hr.

Equipment

Participants wore a Canon HM-A1 stereo video–see-through Head Worn Display (HWD), tracked by a 12-camera NaturalPoint Optitrack S250E tracking system, and interacted with an application written using Goblin XNA [16], running on a computer powered by an Intel i7-3770k with 16GB of RAM and using a Nvidia GeForce GTX 780. We positioned the target poses (volumes) around an aircraft engine, looking at various portions of the engine. Participants held a Nintendo Wii remote in their hand and pressed its *A* button to interact with the system.

To minimize the stress placed on the user during the study, and simplify study analysis, we automatically adjusted the height of each target so it would match the user's recorded height. While real world tasks will often require that users assume potentially uncomfortable poses, we decided to eliminate this potential confound.

Design

There were two within-subject visualization conditions (InSitu and HUD) × six target positions per condition × nine head–tail shape combinations per target position = 108 timed trials. Trials were blocked by visualization and randomized by position and shape combination. Each block also included an initial nine practice trials. Half the participants experienced InSitu first and half HUD.

In each block, visualizations were placed at three distances from the home location. Each distance was represented by two possible left–right symmetric positions around the engine, and each position had two unique orientations, yielding 12 possible targets. Figure 5 uses a plan view of the

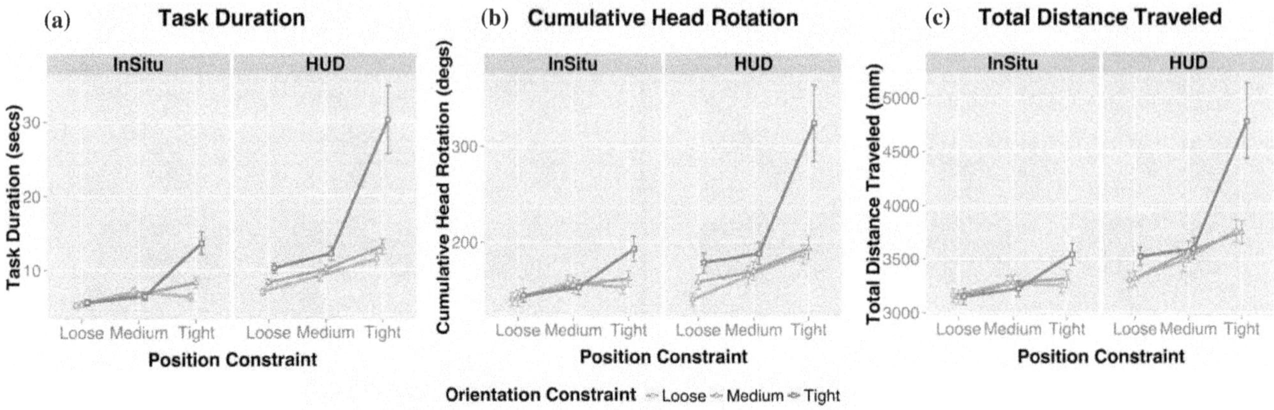

Figure 6. User study results by Position Constraint, Orientation Constraint, and Technique.

layout to show for both visualization conditions the three target positions on the right side of the engine in each row, with their two unique orientations (shown as green triangles) in each column. The nine head–tail shape combinations were all utilized for each visualization. Each of the nine head–tail combinations was placed at all six target positions, and randomly set at one of two possible orientations for each position.

Procedure

Participants were welcomed by the study coordinator and given the Stereo Optical Co. Inc. Stereo Fly Test to screen for stereo vision. All participants successfully completed the test. They were then introduced to the study, and given instructions for playing the part of a technician taking virtual snapshots of the engine. At the beginning of each block, the participants received a detailed explanation of the visualization condition, and were allowed to explore the position and orientation tolerances they were expected to encounter in a series of practice trials. Participants were given a small break between blocks.

At the start of each trial, the participant was asked to enter a "home" zone marked on the floor and to look towards the engine. The participant was then presented with a ParaFrustum visualization and asked to assume a pose that it allowed. Once the participant found a pose they believed to satisfy the visualization, they pressed the *A* button on the Wii remote to "take a photo" and lock in their answer. Head position and orientation were recorded continuously throughout each trial, and the offset in head position and orientation were also recorded when the *A* button was pressed.

Participants completed a four-part questionnaire during and after the study, asking them to assess both InSitu (represented as "X") and HUD (represented as "Y"). The questionnaire included both an unweighted NASA TLX and questions asking participants to assess the ease, accuracy, and speed of the techniques using seven-point Likert scales (1 = worst, 7 = best).

Results

Outliers in the data were first eliminated. Several participants took as many as three minutes on trials where median completion times were 6.08 and 9.51 seconds for InSitu and HUD, respectively). Scrutinizing the data revealed that these were a small number of cases where users were so

Visualization	Position Accuracy	Orientation Accuracy
InSitu	96.85%	99.10%
HUD	97.51%	97.28%

Table 1. Accuracy by Visualization.

tightly constrained that it was nearly impossible for them to get their head into an acceptable pose even after the height adjustment. We labeled records outliers using a conservative version of Tukey's outlier filter—the "outside fence" [22], using 3 times the interquartile range to determine the cutoff points per 2 (Visualization Condition) × 9 (Constraint Type) conditions, which we expected to have significant effect on completion time. These outliers, which accounted for 3.14% (3.09% InSitu, 3.19% HUD) of all users across 2 visualization conditions × 54 trials, were removed from further analyses. Hypotheses were then evaluated for significance with an α of .05.

We performed a 2 (Visualization Condition) × 9 (Constraint Type) × 6 (Target position) repeated-measures ANOVA on completion times, with participants as the random variable using the R Statistical Package [18]. Results from the ANOVA showed that Visualization Condition was a significant main effect, $F(1,3) = 40.509$, $p < .008$, at $\alpha = .05$. Participants found an acceptable viewpoint significantly faster using InSitu (7.20 secs) than HUD (12.50 secs), validating H1. Mean completion times for each condition are depicted in Figure 6(a). The greater cumulative head rotation and total distance traveled for HUD over InSitu (Figure 6b–c), and the increased positional variability for HUD over InSitu, along with the more uniformly curved trajectories of InSitu relative to HUD (Figure 5) support H2.

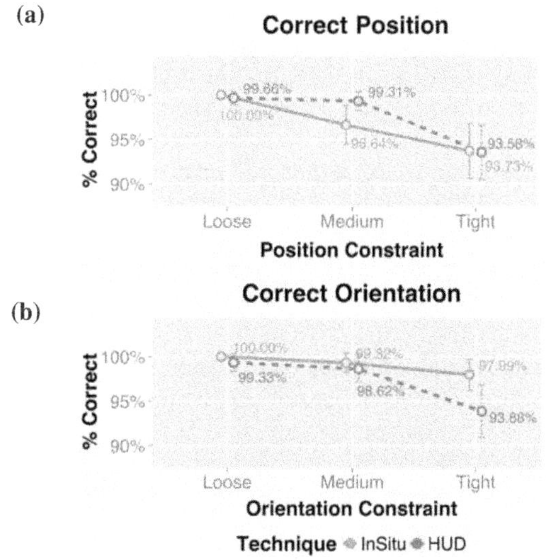

Figure 7. Position accuracy by Position Constraint and orientation accuracy by Orientation Constraint.

The effect of Constraint Type, was also significant, $F(8,24) = 32.044$, $p < .001$, at $\alpha = .05$, as shown in Figure 6(a). The most constrained shape (T–T), which provides a good approximation of the tightly constrained position and orientation of a frustum, took significantly longer on average (21.93 secs) than the rest of the constraints, which have a combined mean time of (8.34 secs), validating H3.

There were no effects of target position, nor of any 2-way or 3-way interactions. We performed binary accuracy checks for the user's head position and orientation at the time they indicated that they had satisfied the constraints for each trial. Overall, users performed very well in terms of both position and orientation accuracy across visualization conditions (Table 1).

A Pearson's Chi-squared test revealed that there was no significant difference between visualizations for position $\left(\chi^2_{(1,N=1{,}876)} = 1.629, p = 0.2018\right)$, but InSitu was significantly more accurate for orientation $\left(\chi^2_{(1,N=1{,}876)} = 7.2472, p < 0.01\right)$. Not surprisingly, constraint type had a significant impact on accuracy; that is, users made more mistakes when the constraints were tighter both for position $\left(\chi^2_{(1,N=1{,}876)} = 40.1464, p < 0.001\right)$ and for orientation $\left(\chi^2_{(2,N=1{,}876)} = 26.114, p < 0.001\right)$ (Figure 7).

The results of the unweighted NASA TLX survey showed that participants found InSitu less demanding than HUD, both mentally and physically, while perceiving it to be easier and faster (Figure 8). Fourteen out of 18 participants preferred InSitu over HUD, supporting H4.

Discussion

Participants successfully navigated using both visualizations. However, InSitu led to faster performance with shorter and less variable trajectories, and less head rotation. The advantages were especially evident in tight cases. Participants also preferred InSitu. Thus, although InSitu's visualization may initially appear unfamiliar compared to the dials of HUD, this was more than compensated for by the benefits of InSitu being embedded in the user's 3D world.

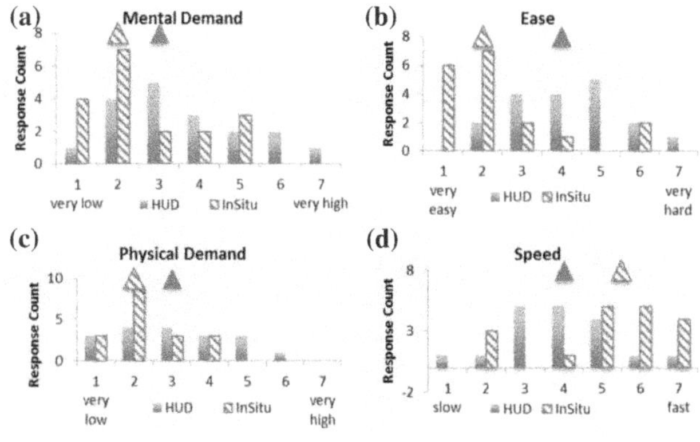

Figure 8. Questionnaire results.

CONCLUSIONS AND FUTURE WORK

We have presented ParaFrustum, a geometric construct that generalizes a computer graphics camera frustum to make it possible to represent a range of positions and orientations associated with acceptable views of a task. We developed two visualizations that can communicate to a user how to achieve one of the views encoded by a ParaFrustum. A user study showed that visualizations of more loosely constrained ParaFrusta can guide a user to an acceptable pose significantly more quickly than visualizations of more tightly constrained ParaFrusta, providing a potential advantage for tasks that can be performed from a range of acceptable positions and orientations. The study showed faster performance with less head rotation and shorter and more direct trajectories with InSitu. Participants also preferred InSitu. Thus, all four hypotheses were supported.

The significant increase in cumulative motion and orientation for HUD, especially in tightly constrained situations (Figure 6b–c), suggests increased cognitive load from following three dials, as predicted by Franconeri et. al. [9]. We speculate that the increased variability and unnecessary motion is due to HUD requiring users to (1) transform the mediated information into their own frame of reference and (2) integrate information from multiple sources, whereas InSitu presents an integrated visualization embedded directly in the environment. Notably, users corroborated this increased load in the questionnaire.

Authoring is an important area for future work. Authoring for a specific user and task could be accomplished pragmatically by collecting and processing 6DoF head pose data while the user assumes good (and bad) views for the task. An alternative approach could involve automated analysis of the task and environment to determine head poses that meet constraints on visibility and legibility, as well as user-specific constraints on height, reach, grasp, and general comfort (e.g., as computed by tools such as Siemens PLM Jack). In some cases, a ParaFrustum could be parameterized on user height by pivoting a head volume about a tail volume or changing the ParaFrustum's height. A generalized ParaFrustum might also be constructed using the union of the head volumes of more specific ParaFrusta, when the increased size does not cause problems (e.g., when the larger head volume accommodates taller users, but can be ignored by shorter ones).

While our current implementation handles convex head and tail volumes, concave volumes would provide better support for complex viewing constraints (e.g., to rule out points from which important objects are obscured). Concave volumes could be wrapped by a ParaFrustum's convex hull; however, the containment evaluation and user feedback employed in our visualizations would need to change. For example, after exiting a concave head volume, additional portions of it might still lie between the user's head and the tail volume. Therefore, the visualization would need to determine which way to guide the user to reenter the head volume, while minimizing obscuration of the tail volume.

Finally, we acknowledge that ParaFrustum is not fully general. For example, it does not independently constrain head roll independent of head position and does not account for eye gaze in addition to head orientation. Furthermore, it does not account for situations in which different points within a single head volume should be associated with different tail volumes, or situations in which pose must change as the task is performed. However, we believe that ParaFrustum represents a large family of useful viewing constraints, making it possible to communicate to a user how to assume an acceptable pose more quickly than existing approaches, potentially speeding up a number of tasks.

ACKNOWLEDGMENTS

This research was funded in part by NSF Grants IIS-0905569 and IIS-0905417. Canon U.S.A. Inc. generously lent the HM-A1 HWD. Goblin XNA was developed in part through funding from Microsoft Research and NSF. We thank Steve Henderson for refurbishing the aircraft engine used in the study.

REFERENCES

1. Bae, S., Agarwala, A., & Durand, F. Computational rephotography. *ACM Trans. Graph. 29*, 3 (2010), 24:1–24:15.
2. Biocca, F., Tang, A., Owen, C., & Xiao, F. Attention funnel: Omnidirectional 3D cursor for mobile augmented reality platforms. *Proc. ACM CHI*, (2006), 1115–1122.
3. Bouisset, S. & Zattara, M. A sequence of postural movements precedes voluntary movement. *Neuroscience Letters 22*, 3 (1981), 263–270.
4. Burtnyk, N., Khan, A., Fitzmaurice, G., Balakrishnan, R., & Kurtenbach, G. Stylecam: Interactive stylized 3d navigation using integrated spatial & temporal controls. *Proc. ACM UIST*, (2002), 101–110.
5. Clark, H.H. *Using Language*. Cambridge University Press, 1996.
6. Feiner, S., MacIntyre, B., Höllerer, T., & Webster, A. A touring machine: Prototyping 3D mobile augmented reality systems for exploring the urban environment. *Proc. IEEE ISWC*, (1997), 74–81.
7. Feiner, S., Macintyre, B., & Seligmann, D. Knowledge-based augmented reality. *Commun. ACM 36*, 7 (1993), 53–62.
8. Franchak, J.M., Celano, E.C., & Adolph, K.E. Perception of passage through openings depends on the size of the body in motion. *Experimental Brain Research 223*, 2 (2012), 301–310.
9. Franconeri, S., Jonathan, S., & Scimeca, J. Tracking multiple objects is limited only by object spacing, not by speed, time, or capacity. *Psychological Science 21*, 7 (2010), 920–925.
10. Friedman, D. & Feldman, Y.A. Automated cinematic reasoning about camera behavior. *Expert Systems with Applications 30*, 4 (2006), 694–704.
11. Grasso, R., Glasauer, S., Takei, Y., & Berthoz, A. The predictive brain: Anticipatory control of head direction for the steering of locomotion. *Neuroreport 7*, 6 (1996), 1170–1174.
12. Grasso, R., Prévost, P., Ivanenko, Y.P., & Berthoz, A. Eye-head coordination for the steering of locomotion in humans: An anticipatory synergy. *Neuroscience Letters 253*, 2 (1998), 115–118.
13. Güven, S. & Feiner, S. Interaction techniques for exploring historic sites through situated media. *Proc. IEEE 3DUI*, (2006), 111–118.
14. Levelt, W.J.M. *Speaking: From Intention to Articulation*. MIT Press, 1989.
15. Mennie, N., Hayhoe, M., & Sullivan, B. Look-ahead fixations: Anticipatory eye movements in natural tasks. *Experimental Brain Research 179*, 3 (2007), 427–442.
16. Oda, O. & Feiner, S. Goblin XNA Framework. http://goblinxna.codeplex.com/.
17. Perry, A. & Wallace, E. Constructive Solid Geometry (CSG) for Unity in C#. https://github.com/omgwtfgames/csg.cs.
18. R Core Team. *R: A Language and Environment for Statistical Computing*. R Foundation for Statistical Computing, 2014.
19. Sehnal, D. & Campbell, M. MIConvexHull Library. http://miconvexhull.codeplex.com/.
20. Shingu, J., Rieffel, E., Kimber, D., Vaughan, J., Qvarfordt, P., & Tuite, K. Camera pose navigation using augmented reality. *Proc. IEEE ISMAR*, (2010), 271–272.
21. Snavely, N., Seitz, S.M., & Szeliski, R. Photo tourism: Exploring photo collections in 3D. *ACM TOG 25*, 3 (2006), 835–846.
22. Tukey, J.W. *Exploratory Data Analysis*. Addison-Wesley, 1977.
23. Zhai, S., Buxton, W., & Milgram, P. The "Silk Cursor": investigating transparency for 3D target acquisition. *Proc. ACM CHI*, (1994), 459–464.

Through the Combining Glass

Diego Martinez Plasencia[1], Florent Berthaut[1], Abhijit Karnik[2], Sriram Subramanian[1]
[1]Department of Computer Science, University of Bristol, UK
[2]School of Computing and Communications, Lancaster University, UK
{diego.martinez-plasencia, sriram.subramanian}@bristol.ac.uk, a.karnik@lancs.ac.uk

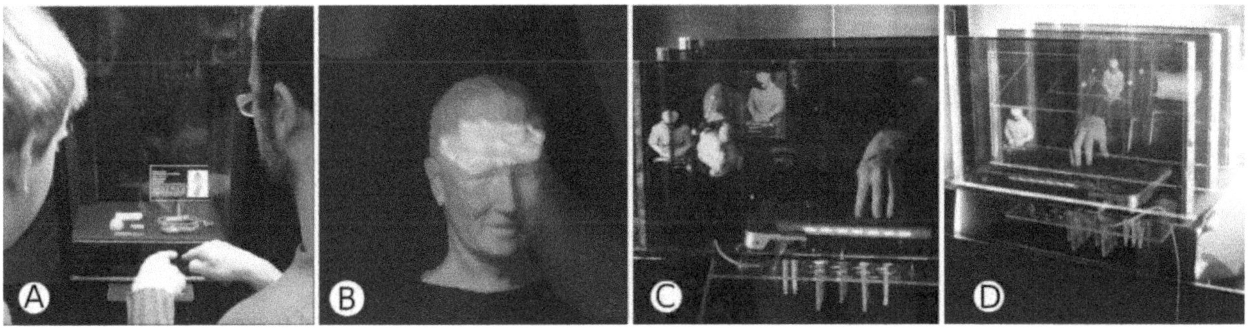

Figure 1: Interaction opportunities of our design space: (A) Reflections allow users to interact with artifacts inside a museum cabinet. (B) Reflections can reveal internal details of real objects. (C) A Digital Musical Instrument augmented with projection mapping and a volumetric display. (D) This augmentation is visible from any point of view and from both sides of the mirror.

ABSTRACT

Reflective optical combiners like beam splitters and two way mirrors are used in AR to overlap digital contents on the users' hands or bodies. Augmentations are usually unidirectional, either reflecting virtual contents on the user's body (Situated Augmented Reality) or augmenting user's reflections with digital contents (AR mirrors). But many other novel possibilities remain unexplored. For example, users' hands, reflected inside a museum AR cabinet, can allow visitors to interact with the artifacts exhibited. Projecting on the user's hands as their reflection cuts through the objects can be used to reveal objects' internals. Augmentations from both sides are blended by the combiner, so they are consistently seen by any number of users, independently of their location or, even, the side of the combiner through which they are looking. This paper explores the potential of optical combiners to merge the space in front and behind them. We present this design space, identify novel augmentations/interaction opportunities and explore the design space using three prototypes.

Author Keywords

Optical Combiners; Augmented Reality; Multi-user

ACM Classification Keywords

H.5.m. Information interfaces and presentation (e.g., HCI):

UIST '14, October 05 - 08 2014, Honolulu, HI, USA
Copyright 2014 ACM 978-1-4503-3069-5/14/10 $15.00.
http://dx.doi.org/10.1145/2642918.2647351

INTRODUCTION

Reflective transparent surfaces (beam splitters, half-silvered mirrors, shopping windows or, more formally, *planar reflective optical combiners*), show our reflection overlapped with the objects behind them. The planar nature of the surface ensures that each point of the reflection produces a *stigmatic pair* [19]. The reflection of any point is seen at a unique 3D position behind the combiner, independent of the observer position and reflections are perceptibly indistinguishable from a real object behind the mirror [3]. Also, the partially transparent nature of the combiner implies that the objects behind the combiner are merged with the reflections of the objects in front of it.

Augmented mirrors [1, 9, 11, 21, 27] use reflections as high fidelity avatars that can be augmented with virtual clothes or visual effects. Situated AR [13, 14, 24] exploits planar reflections by overlapping 3D virtual objects with the physical space and enabling direct interaction with those objects. In all these applications, augmentations remain unidirectional – either augmenting our real self or reflected body with virtual contents.

However, *planar reflective optical combiners* have a bigger potential. They visually merge the physical spaces in front and behind them, which enables many more novel augmentations and interaction possibilities.

Firstly, users' reflections can overlap unreachable content placed behind the combiner, enabling interaction with this content. For instance, when looking at objects inside a museum cabinet (as in Figure 1.A) we can use the fingers' reflection to create a 3D cursor that is visible inside a museum cabinet, to any number of users without specialised eyewear. In the *Augmented Musical Instrument* prototype the user can interact with content inside a

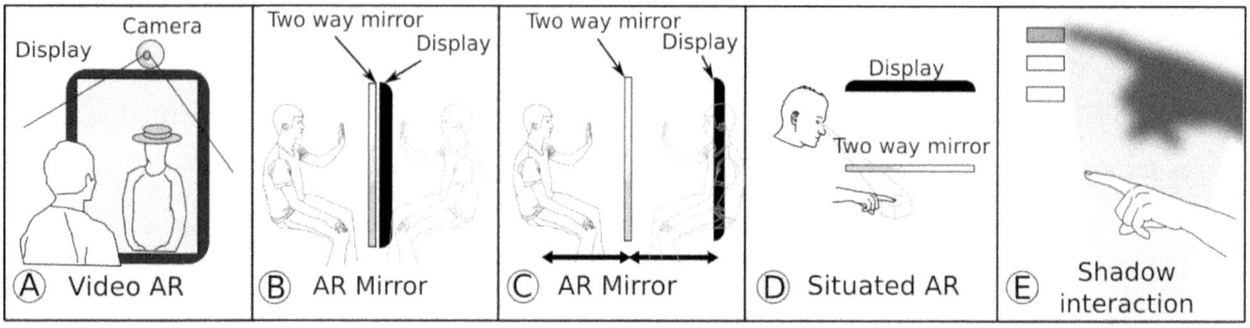

Figure 2: Approaches related to interacting through the mirror: (A) Video see-through augmented mirrors, (B and C) different implementations of augmented mirrors. (D) Situated Augmented Reality. (E) Shadow-based interaction.

volumetric display, which in most cases cannot be reached into (Figure 1.C).

Secondly, augmentations can be bidirectional. As both spaces are blended, both can contribute to create a unified experience. Simple projection mapping on the artifacts inside the museum cabinet can easily augment their surface. However, as illustrated in Figure 1.B, by projecting on users' hands in front of the combiner we can allow the user to slice through the museum artifacts to reveal their internal structure. The reflection is actually mapped inside the object and this augmentation is visible from any viewpoint.

Thirdly, the combination of spaces achieved by placing a planar optical combiner and looking through it can be consistently seen by any number of users, independent of their location or the side of the combiner through which they are looking. This for example, allows spectators of our *Augmented Musical Instrument* to freely move around the two-way mirror, and yet always see the musician immersed with the digital contents (Figure 1.C and . Figure 1.D)

This paper takes a new perspective on *planar reflective optical combiners*, focusing on their ability to merge the spaces in front and behind them. We describe the design space, identify novel interaction and augmentation possibilities. We describe relevant features that designers need to address and demonstrate/exemplify them using three prototype systems. We also report interviews with practitioners, which illustrate the potential of our approach and suggest even more examples of how our techniques can be used in practice.

RELATED WORK

Reflections have captivated our imagination and drawn the attention of many pieces of literary and cinematographic fiction. Their ability to create a reflected version of the real world has been used to portray them as portals to alternative realities (e.g. Through the looking glass[1]). Other stories use mirrors that not only reflect the visible world, but also show other elements beyond our perception. In the Never Ending Story[2], Atreyu faces a mirror that reflects the viewer's true self, which becomes one of the most revealing points in the story. The Mirror of Erised[3] reveals Harry Potter's deepest desires. Exploiting this aura of mystery, magicians and theatre performances have used mirrors to create different special effects, such as the well known Pepper's ghost[4].

This idea of augmenting reflections with non-real (virtual) elements has been explored in practice. Approaches like *i-Mirror* [12], *augmented mirror box* [26] or the virtual mirrors by Adidas [9] and Bloomingdale's[5] use video see-through AR (see Figure 2.A), recording the user and adding virtual elements to the digital image. These approaches lose the affordances of real mirrors, replacing volumetric reflections with digitized 2D images of the users, having a fixed perspective (i.e. the actual position of the camera) and inhibiting mutual eye contact between two observers.

Other systems combine a planar optical combiner with 2D displays. In some of them, the image of the augmentations is formed on the combiner's surface (Figure 2.B), either because a flat display is right in contact with it [11, 12, 21, 27] or they use projectors pointing at the back of the mirror [1]. Given the limited depth of field (DOF) of human eye, in most of these systems (with the exception of *YouMove* [1]), users will be able to focus on either their reflections or the augmentations, but not both.

Acknowledging this constraint, systems like *i-Mirror* [12], *Holoflector*[6] and *Holocubtile* [8] place the display at a distance from the optical combiner. This allows the augmentations to appear at the correct depth (Figure 2.C). The user's eye is able to correctly focus on both the reflection and the augmentations. It also allows the augmentations to correctly map to the location of the user's body (*Holoflector*) or around/inside the *Holocubtile*. Also several observers can see virtual contents correctly aligned to the real ones. Disney's Haunted Mansion[7] uses a similar

[1] http://en.wikipedia.org/wiki/Through_the_Looking-Glass
[2] http://en.wikipedia.org/wiki/The_NeverEnding_Story_(film)

[3] http://harrypotter.wikia.com/wiki/Mirror_of_Erised
[4] http://en.wikipedia.org/wiki/Pepper%27s_ghost
[5] http://gizmodo.com/245716/interactive-mirror-debuting-at-bloomingdale
[6] http://research.microsoft.com/apps/video/default.aspx?id=159487&l=i
[7] https://disneyworld.disney.go.com/attractions/magic-kingdom/haunted-mansion/

approach to enable interaction of virtual ghosts with users' reflections (e.g. swapping visitor's heads). However, the resulting systems have a large footprint; the contents are flat and can only be presented at a fixed depth.

Situated Augmented Reality systems [5], like the *Virtual Workbench* [24], *Toucheo* [13] and *HoloDesk* [14] use the same principle in an inverse manner. These systems reflect virtual contents that seem to overlap a user's real hands (see Figure 2.D). In these devices, the display's reflection appears at the approximate depth where the user's hands will be located. The smaller working area decreases the footprint and active or passive stereo can be used to display 3D contents. However, they usually support only one user and place constraints on the location of the user's eyes and hands. *Vermeer* [6] and *RePro3D* [37] combine other arrangements (parabolic mirrors and two-way mirrors with retro-reflective materials, respectively) with a volumetric display to collocate the user's finger into the 3D volume. No eyewear is required in this situation, but the footprint limitations and constraints on observer locations still apply.

A 2D approach with some resemblance to our approach is shadow-based interaction (Figure 2.E) as demonstrated by Myron Kreuger's *VideoPlace* [20] or Benko and Wilson [2]. In these examples, the users' shadows become 2D embodiments that allow them to interact in a remote 2D surface (i.e. to play games or explore the night sky). In the case of *VideoPlace*, these "shadow embodiments" can also be augmented/modified, but the reverse possibility (shadows to augment projected contents) was not considered.

COMBINED SPACES THROUGH THE GLASS

Planar reflective surfaces create *stigmatic pairs* [19]. This means that they create a bijective mapping, where each point in front of the mirror is reflected as exactly one point behind the mirror ($f(x,y,z)=(x,y,-z)$, assuming the mirror plane as $z=0$). This mapping is independent of the optical path (observer location). If thin optical combiners are used (to minimize the effects of refraction), this results in reflections: a) that are exactly similar to the original object; b) whose location is consistently overlapping a unique point behind the combiner and c) are visible at that location independent of the observer position.

The ability of optical combiners to also transmit a part of the light incident on them allows reflections to overlap the objects behind it. A second benefit is that the bijective mapping is also effective from the other side of the mirror. As a result, any observer looking through the combiner will see the spaces in front and behind the mirror blended, irrespective of his/her position or the side of the mirror he/she is looking through. It is even possible for users to establish mutual eye contact (reinforcing agency and immersion). However, this illusion of two collocated spaces only happens while users look through the combining glass.

A common theme within previous approaches using *planar reflective optical combiners* is that these systems aim to augment our real or reflected body with virtual contents. One space contains the virtual contents only (displayed through some display technology), while the user is constrained to the other side.

We acknowledge the potential of such an approach, but consider it as a limited use-case of the ability of planar optical combiners to merge the space in front and behind the mirror. In the following subsections we describe novel interaction/augmentation possibilities that result from applying our perspective: a) merging our (real or reflected) body with elements on the other side of the combiner; b) the potential of objects in any of these spaces to augment the other space (bidirectional augmentations); or c) the possibility to experience them from both sides of the combiner.

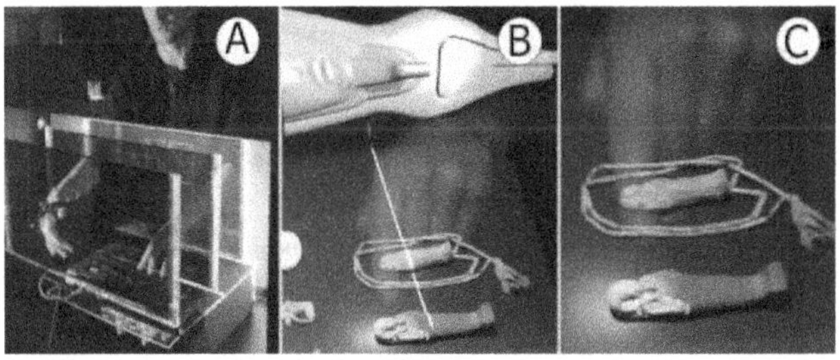

Figure 3: A. Musician's reflection can reach through the panels of our volumetric display. (B and C) Reflected hands serve as multiuser 3D pointers inside the cabinet.

Using reflections as interactive avatars

The combiner enables an environment where the user's reflection can co-habit a physical space behind the combiner. Such a reflection can act as a high-resolution and responsive virtual avatar that can interact with objects on the other side of the combiner. This has obvious benefits when the objects need to be beyond our reach, such as in a museum or a jewellery shop.

While the user perceives the reflected avatar as a physical embodiment collocated with objects behind the mirror, the avatar has no corporeal form. Thus it can pass through solid objects and is not affected by toxic or dangerous objects. In an operating theatre scenario, an instructing surgeon's reflection can be mapped by the operating table without affecting the sterile environment. As discussed later in our Musical Instrument example, the combiner allows the reflection of the musician to reach into a volumetric display (Figure 3.A) which is inaccessible in many cases.

The reflected avatar can also solve technical constraints that cannot be solved by using real physical objects. For example, it would be very difficult to create a 3D cursor that was visible inside a museum cabinet, to any number of users without specialised eyewear. However, our reflected fingertip can easily act as a 3D cursor floating inside the cabinet. For instance, we use the reflection as a virtual camera to explore 3D reconstructions of museum exhibits. This can reveal close details of the artifacts that are hardly visible from outside the cabinet (Figure 3.B). We also use it as a little lamp, to illuminate the artifacts and facilitate inspection (Figure 3.C).

It is important to note that interacting using your reflection can raise challenges. While moving in the plane parallel to the mirror is simple, others interactions might be more difficult. We discuss these issues later in this paper.

Bidirectional augmentation

For any user looking through the combiner, both spaces appear blended together. Augmentations can be used on either side to create a unified space. For example, we can place a volumetric display like DepthCube [34] on one side of a planar optical combiner overlapping it with musical controller itself augmented through projection mappings. The volumetric display at the other side of the mirror shows augmentations that seem to float over the controller, together with the augmentation on the controller's side (see Figure 4.C).

In addition to augmenting reflections with virtual contents, optical combiners can allow our reflection to slice through solid objects placed behind them. Using projection mapping on a handheld physical prop, one can see it overlapped inside the object (Figure 4.B). The projected image is reflected off the planar combiner and aligned with the intersection of the slicer and the object when viewed through the combiner. This can be consistently perceived by any number of observers when seen through the optical combiner. An example scenario where this is useful is airport security checks, where the screening agent can visually reveal where the passenger may be hiding something while both of them are separated by a glass wall.

DESIGNING WITH REFLECTED SPACES

This section describes relevant aspects that designers need to take into account when creating systems that merge the spaces in front and behind the mirror. The prototypes, described later in this paper, are used here to explore the design space, demonstrating each of its aspects (e.g. materials, illumination, display technologies). They are also used to illustrate interesting uses of our concepts, such as the ability to use our reflection to overcome constraints that apply behind the combiner, using augmentations on either side to build a common interactive experience or the possibility to see them from any point around the mirror.

Controlled combination of spaces

Pepper's ghost[4] is one of the earliest techniques exploiting the combination of contents in front of and behind the mirror. In this theatre technique, a half silvered mirror located at 45 degrees to the stage maps a dark, hidden room on top of the visible stage. By increasing the lighting of the hidden room, the objects within seemed to appear, like ghosts, in the middle of the stage. This is a very powerful

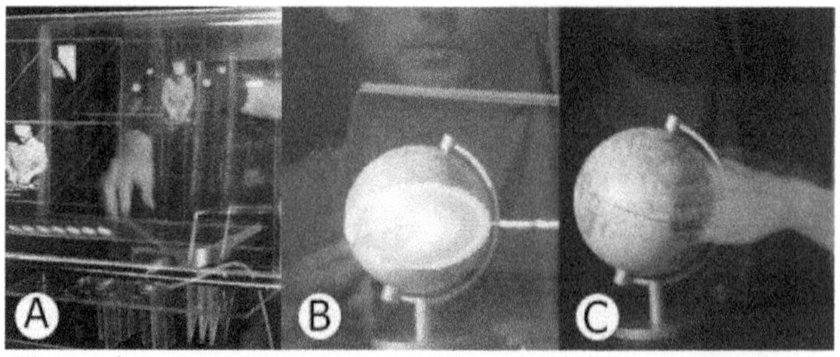

Figure 4 A. Augmentations on either side of the combiner are merged. (B and C) Projector based illumination allows interactions between objects (i.e. internals and intersection).

feature that designers need to consider when creating interactive experiences through a combiner. The perceived visibility of each space depends on two factors: the Transmission to Reflectance (TR) ratio of the reflecting surface and the illumination of each space.

Mirror fabrication techniques allow optical combiners with a wide range of TR ratios. The TR ratio determines the static visibility/blending of both spaces and its choice will be influenced by the requirements of the system being designed. For instance, our museum cabinet uses a low reflectance surface, as users are more interested in seeing the objects within the cabinet than their own reflection. In the *Augmented Musical Instrument (AMI)* and *AR mirrors*, we use a 50% TR two way mirror, as the goal is to equally merge both the user/musician and the virtual contents in a common 3D space.

The second relevant factor is illumination, which allows us to control the dynamic visibility of both spaces. Apart from a global control, like the used in Pepper's ghost, the use of projector based illumination [25] and advanced sensing technologies allows us to exert a fine grained control over the visibility of elements.

Reproducing effects such as consistent occlusions requires observer tracking and a different optical combiner for each user [5], which would break our unified combined space. However, other viewpoint independent effects, like intersections (hiding the parts of the objects inside other objects), can be reproduced consistently. Figure 4.A shows how only the parts of the hand that are outside the earth are illuminated. Non-illuminated parts seem to disappear inside the objects.

Reflections, depth of focus and display technologies

One can use a wide range of technologies to create the virtual 3D contents that augment the combined space. Many taxonomies have been proposed to classify these 3D capable displays, for e.g. Holliman et al. [17]. The classification is primarily based on the depth perception cues that they afford, identifying two broad categories *true depth 3D displays* and *flat panel 3D displays*.

As mentioned earlier, reflections in a mirror provide all perception cues and are indistinguishable from a real object placed behind the mirror (although occlusions of objects

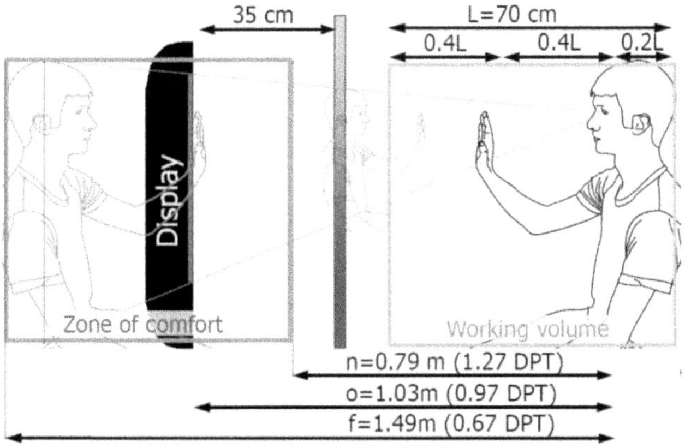

Figure 5: Parameters to consider to assure reflections fall within the zone of comfort of the planar display.

behind the mirror will be missing). This allows reflections to be naturally blended with contents in *true depth 3D* displays. The museum cabinet and *AMI* exemplify the usage of projection mapping and volumetric displays (two broad categories of true depth 3D displays).

Flat panel 3D displays (e.g. parallax barriers or multi-view displays), on the other hand, can suffer from vergence-accommodation (VA) conflicts. This conflict arises when these displays show an object that appears at a different depth than the plane of the display. The user's eyes verge towards the location where the object is supposed to be, but they still need to focus on the display screen. There exists a "zone of comfort" where the conflict causes less severe symptoms (see [29] and [16] for an interesting discussion). Several estimations have been proposed [22, 28], and it is commonly assumed that human eye has an average *depth of field* (DOF) of ±0.3 dioptres (DPT), allowing objects at that distance from the display to remain in focus [7].

The AR mirrors following the approach in Fig 2.C. (i.e. the display is located right behind the mirror) can illustrate the relevant role that DOF plays in our systems. In these systems, our reflection is located behind the mirror, but augmentations appear on the mirror's surface. If we focus on our reflected face, the screen can fall outside the depth of focus of our eyes, so we cannot fixate on the virtual content. If we focus on the screen, we might not be able to fixate on the reflection. Both our reflection and the augmentations should fall inside the DOF of our eye, but in this approach (i.e. the display is located right behind the mirror) this only happens when the observer is further apart than 1.66 meters of the mirror (i.e. the display depth is 1/1.66m = 0.60 DPT and the reflection 1/3.33 = 0.30 DPT; the difference matches the average human DOF, so both remain in focus).

Thus, some consideration is needed when placing the display, so that its contents are merged with the observer's reflection. We describe four steps required to avoid these issues and we will use our prototype of AR mirror as an example to illustrate these steps (Figure 5).

Determine size of the interactive space around the user
Determine the space that will be mapped behind the mirror and immersed with the contents shown in the display (working volume). In our AR mirror the user's arm length (L) is used as the baseline for our design. Users must be able to use their reflection to interact comfortably. While fully stretching the arms can be uncomfortable, a distance between 0.4L and 0.8L allows for comfortable interaction [35]. We also wanted to be able to modify the user's facial appearance. The size L=70 cm (average arm's length in a male adult) was found enough to accommodate the user's arms during interaction and his face/body, as to augment his appearance.

Determine location of the planar 3D display
The size of the zone of comfort of a planar display is determined by the distance between the observer and each point of the display, which results in a parabolic shape. However, from a design point of view it is usually more practical to identify the closest point and approximate the shape by a parallelepiped.

Considering the observer distance to the display (o), the limits of the region (i.e. near (n) and far (f) planes) need to satisfy some conditions. First, their distances to the display in dioptries must equal the estimated DOF used (R=0.3 DPT). Also, they must accommodate the size of the working volume (Eq 3).

$$\frac{1}{o}-\frac{1}{n}=R \ (1); \quad \frac{1}{f}-\frac{1}{o}=R \ (2); \quad f-n=L \ (3)$$

Solving this set of equations, one can determine the required observer distance (Eq 4) and the distances of the near and far planes (Eq5 and Eq3). Given the size of the working volume in our example (L=70 cm), this means that the display must be located at o=1.03 m, to provide a zone of comfort of the desired size (*n=0.79 m (1.27 DPT); f=1.49 m (0.67 DPT)*).

$$o=\sqrt{\frac{L}{(2+R\cdot L)\cdot R}} \ (4); \quad n=\frac{o}{1+R\cdot o} \ (5);$$

Determine location of the mirror
Once we determined the space around the user (working volume) and the display's zone of comfort, the designer needs to position the mirror to make sure that the working volume is mapped within the display's zone of comfort.

The working volume in our example covers 56cm in front of the observer's eyes (space for user to interact with objects) and 14 cm behind (to include the rest of the head and back). The plane at 56cm in front of the observer will be mapped to the near plane of the zone of comfort, at 78cm in front of the observer. As a result (assuming negligible refraction), the mirror needs to be located at *(56+78)/2=67* cm in front of the user (almost at the limit of his reach). The display is located *103-67 ~ 35 cm* behind

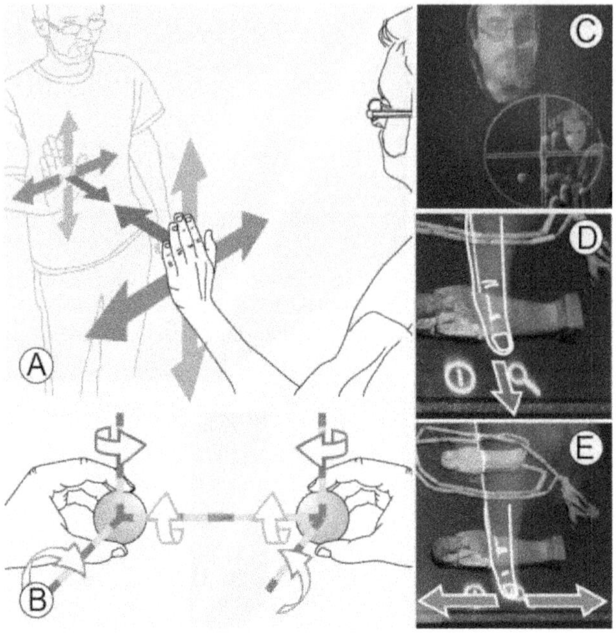

Figure 6: Analysis of translations (A) and rotations (B) through the mirror. Example interactions that streamline natural and non natural translations in the museum cabinet (C and D) and the AR Mirror (E).

the mirror. This allows us to allocate real objects between the mirror and the display, as explained later in the description of the AR mirror.

Determine the size of the display

Given that the mirror lays in the exact midpoint between us and our reflection, the size of our reflection when projected on the mirror is always, exactly, half our size [3]. Once the location of the mirror and the display technology has been determined, the interaction designer should use this feature to work out the required size of the planar display, so that the whole reflection overlaps the display, making it possible to augment the reflection. In our AR mirror example, the required size of the panels was 61x38 cm to actually cover the whole of the user's head and torso (80x50 cm).

Manipulation through a mirror

A particular property of the systems proposed in this paper is that users need to look through the optical combiner to experience the blended spaces. This implies that they will always interact with their reflected image.

Mirrors have been used to explore our ability to interact using reflected images, or even totally different mappings. Mirror tracing tasks [30] reveal that even though performance is initially significantly lower, subjects learn quickly over time [30].

George M. Stratton explored a variety of more complex mappings. For several days he wore contraptions that allowed him to only see the world upside-down [32], left-right inverted [33] or even observing his own body from above [31]. These experiments revealed that, even though proprioceptive conflicts were initially very strong, these disappeared after three days of usage. These experiments give evidence of the ability of human brain to learn and adapt to this kind of interaction, and are encouraging as they indicate that, should mirror interaction become widespread, users could easily learn and adapt to it.

However, we still need to manage the interaction to support walk-up and use interactions where the user will not have the opportunity to learn through repeated use. As shown in Figure 6.A, translations along the mid-frontal plane remain natural (movements parallel to the mirror are mapped to similar actions in the other side of the mirror) but, translations along the Z axis are inverted.

The opposite situation arises with rotations (Figure 6.B). Rotations around the Z axis are natural, but those involving the other two axes are inverted. Our initial observations revealed that manipulations were easily understandable as far as they remained in one of these two categories (i.e. translations parallel to the mirror or purely perpendicular to them). However, trajectories involving both (i.e. movements in a horizontal plane) were more confusing.

The interaction designer should take these limitations into consideration when creating the interactive dialogue [10] with the system. Even if the task has three degrees of freedom (e.g. translation), and the finger/hand can provide them, it seems preferable to decompose it in steps that do not mix natural and inverted interactions, whenever possible.

The menus in our AR mirror follow this rationale. When the user raises his hand in front of him, a ring like menu appears. He can select a specific category using natural translations in the plane parallel to the mirror (Figure 6.C).

The museum cabinet poses a more challenging scenario. Users first select artifacts with their finger. This is a coarse selection, and actually needs to mix natural and inverted translations, as artifacts are laid horizontally on the cabinet. When the options menu is shown, users need to perform a translation along the Z axis (inverted) to select it, which corresponds to a mid-grained interaction (Figure 6.D). Users can then select specific options (fine grained interaction) using natural translations (Figure 6.E).

CASE STUDIES

We used our prototypes to exemplify the different aspects discussed in our design space and to give examples of how our techniques can be used. This section provides technical details related to their implementations but, more importantly, it describes the feedback we obtained while presenting them to different practitioners (musicians, museum staff). This feedback highlights the usefulness of different elements in our prototypes, but also proposes new ways in which our techniques can be applied.

Interactive Museum Cabinet

Our AR cabinet is designed to be included in the archaeological exhibition of the Bristol Museum and Art Gallery museum. The exhibit currently involves an exhibition coordinator, a digital manager and a content curator of archeological content. We report the implementation of our AR cabinet and relevant impressions/conclusions, relative to the use of reflections, gathered from the museum staff.

Current museum cabinets contain the exhibition artifacts, but users need to refer to touch panels by the cabinet to receive information about them. This forces them to divert their attention from the actual artifacts and interaction is often described as boring and not engaging enough. At the same time, when several visitors are discussing about the artifacts, they need to point at them through the glass, which can lead to misunderstandings (e.g. "which artifact are you talking about?"). Also, users can accidentally touch the cabinet, making it dirty or, even, triggering security alarms.

Our prototype allows users to select artifacts by using the reflection of their hands. Several users can mutually see these reflections, which facilitate understanding and discussion. We also emulate a little spotlight attached to the user's fingers. This allows users to illuminate parts of the artifacts to see them better. Our preliminary impressions seem to indicate that the spotlight facilitates the discoverability of our technique. When users move their hands in front of the cabinet, they soon realize that the spotlight moves in a mirrored way, which facilitates them to realize that it is actually their reflection which allows them to interact. By touching the artifacts, users can get short overviews (name and picture) about the artifacts. They can also get additional content related to the artifact (textual information, explore 3D reconstructions) by touching buttons projected close to the artifact.

The current prototype only contains replicas of actual artifacts. Some of them are modeling clay reproductions, textured using projection mapping. We use a Leap motion to track the users' fingers and compute the position of the finger reflection inside the cabinet, a projector in the top to project augmentations and a TFT panel in the back to display textual information. The cabinet's combiner has low reflectivity, which allows reflections to be marginally visible but maximizes the visibility of the objects within. Illumination outside the cabinet only affects the users' hands, so these are reflected (i.e. but not their faces). Also, the short user distance to the back display (60cm) creates a zone of comfort of only 10 cm in front of it. As a result, a user reading information will not be able to fixate on the hand reflections, avoiding distractions. The dotted connecting line between the artifacts and the dialogues allows progressive adaptation of the focus, when users transition between the dialogues and the actual artifacts.

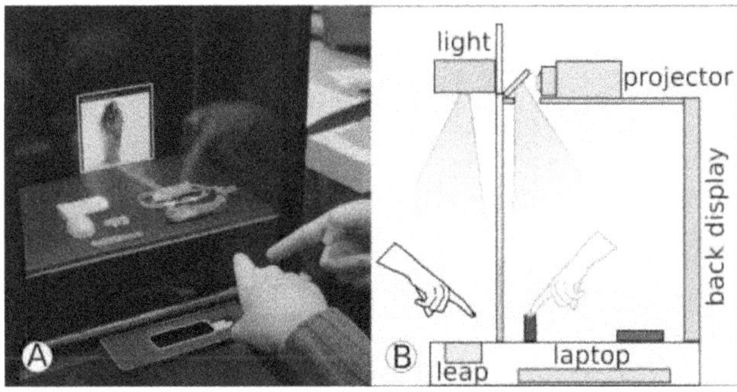

Figure 7: (A) Our AR museum cabinet allows users to interact with artifacts inside it, keeping track of the actions of other users in front of the cabinet. (B) Design of the cabinet.

We presented the prototype to the museum staff, guiding them through its various features. Besides comments related to adapting cabinets for other sizes and formats (e.g. portrait mode, more non-textual information for kids), they had a very positive reaction to the capability of directly interacting with the artifacts and the fact that several visitors could understand each other's actions.

They found that the interaction with the menus around the artifacts was initially confusing, but agreed that it was easy to learn after some minutes. They proposed placing a cabinet with reduced functionality in the entrance hall (that displays overviews when users touched the artifacts) to allow users understand the technique, and cabinets with complete functionality inside the exhibition, to get full benefit of their potential.

They found the spotlight especially interesting, as it allows the cabinet to remain almost dark, only illuminating the artifacts when someone is looking at them. This can be useful for delicate artifacts (i.e. sensitive to light radiation) being even possible to dynamically dim the light when users illuminate sensitive parts.

They also proposed an unexpected use for the two sided feature of planar combiners discussed in this paper. A wide angle camera could be placed inside the cabinet, facing towards the users. This would record the user's actions, but the artifacts' reflections would also be visible as users interact with them. This image could be displayed in a bigger screen, by the cabinet in the entrance hall, so incoming visitors would see and learn how cabinets work.

The possibility to reveal object's internals by projecting on the users was found especially attractive for younger audiences and some specific exhibition artifacts (e.g. rich people were buried in nested coffins, which could be revealed with our technique).

AR mirror

This prototype was also the result from our interviews with the museum staff. During one of them, they realized the back panel in our cabinet was placed at approximately the same distance from the combiner as the user's face. As a

Figure 8: (A) Our AR mirror uses a two way mirror, an LC sandwich, to support several autostereoscopic techniques and allocate real objects. (B) Augmentations overlaid on a user.

result, it would be possible to display augmentations that seemed to overlap their faces (e.g. a pharaoh mask for younger audiences), mimicking the behavior of *Holoflector*.

In order to minimize footprint and allow users to move in front of the mirror, we use a modified LC sandwich arrangement, similar to *MUSTARD* [18]. It allows us to use a variety of 3D techniques for planar displays: perspective corrected *FishTank VR* [36], parallax barriers [23] and multiuser random hole masks [18]. This development also led us to realize the special considerations that need to be considered when mixing planar displays and reflections, and allowed us to solve the limitations in previous approaches to AR mirrors (i.e. simultaneous fixation on reflection and virtual imagery (see Figure 2.C and D)).

The system (Figure 8.A) uses a Kinect to track the user's eyes, required to provide motion parallax and perspective correction, but also to recomputed the masks in the LC panels. The Kinect tracks the user's arms and body, which allows us to map augmentations such as hats, glasses or avatars (Fig 8.B).

Using the four steps described earlier and an average adult's arm length $L=70$ *cm*, we determined that the display needs to be located 35 cm behind the mirror, and the observer at 67 cm. This gap would still be enough to fit medium size exhibits. Also, the mirror is still in the limits of the users reach, so touch interactions with the surface of the mirror would also be possible.

Digital Musical Instrument

In collaboration with local artists, we used a planar optical combiner to augment a Digital Musical Instrument, with the aim of creating new musical performance experiences and exploring new musical interaction possibilities. The original instrument features a hardware controller with pressure sensors alongside linear and angular potentiometers. Sounds are triggered by hitting the sensors and modulated by applying pressure to them. These manipulations can be recorded and played as loops afterwards. These complex and subtle interactions of the musician with the instrument sometimes make it hard to understand the connections between his actions and the music [4].

Our prototype uses a two way mirror to combine both spaces, so that they are approximately equally visible. The musician and augmented controller are on one side, and a low fidelity implementation of *DepthCube* [34] is on the other. This volumetric display is built using three modified LG IPS2321P 23", 1980x1080 LCD monitors. We dismounted them from their frames and removed their front and back polarizers. Then we installed them in a transparent mounting frame, and this one inside a box containing a backlighting, front and back polarizers. The box is purposely bigger, as to allow bigger viewing angles for the spectators.

The controller is augmented with light diffusing acrylic and a projector in order to amplify musical gestures. A Kinect records the musician as she creates the loops. These point clouds are shown inside the volumetric display, at the other side of the mirror as if they floated above the controller. This allows spectators to visualize the musicians' actions that produced the sound in the loop. At the same time, it extends the manipulation of loops into the volumetric space above the controller. Loops can be placed over different sensors to control them in different ways.

The mirror combines the augmentations from both sides, showing the musician, the extensions under the controller and the loops above, all inside a common space. Regardless of where the spectators stand, they will always see the combined space (musician and augmentations) through the mirror.

Musicians we worked with really appreciated the augmentation possibilities offered by the combined space. They were enthusiastic about the additional interaction capabilities created by the mirror. They also believed that it could dramatically improve spectators' perception and understanding of digital performances. In particular, they pointed out three main aspects of the system that enhanced audience engagement.

They felt that the augmentations could be used to improve the connections between the elements of the instrument such as sensors with the visual representations of the loops. For example, links could be projected between them in both the real and virtual spaces. They were extremely positive about the visibility of the virtual content and wished for dynamic visibility control of both the virtual content displayed on our DepthCube and of the musician. A solution would be to increase the brightness of our display by using more transparent LC panels or to switch to greyscale panels to prevent colour filters from interfering. Along with this we can also provide projection mapping on the musician. Finally, in addition to the Depth Cube they were really enthusiastic about the possibility of using their own reflection or the audience's reflection as a way to reveal and play with augmentations that could be placed anywhere in the combined space. Instead of revealing the internals of an object as shown in Figure 4B, spectators could reveal the components of the instrument through more active interaction with the optical combiners; for example, by moving parts of their body/ reflection through the combined space.

THROUGH THE DISTRIBUTED GLASS

One of the implicit limitations of the design space explored in this paper is the fact that the mirror can only overlap the spaces immediately in front and behind it. While this lends itself to a variety of applications (surgery rooms, security checks, museums, etc.); it does not allow collaboration with remote participants.

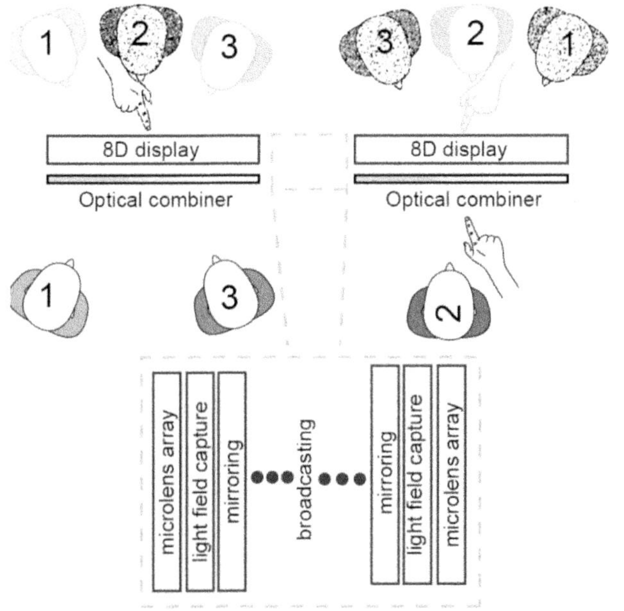

Figure 9: A schematic of how a distributed combining glass could be implemented.

Advances in display technology seem to indicate that such scenarios would be possible. Lightfield cameras that capture a low angular resolution lightfield are commercially available[8] and Hirsch et al. [15] proposed a display that captured an approximately 7x7 lightfield in front of it, to illuminate a virtual scene inside the display.

Instead of projecting the captured lightfield forward, one could reflect it, mimicking the behavior of a mirror. This would create a digitized version of the reflection, which could then be then broadcasted to enable collaborations like the ones proposed in this paper in a distributed environment. Users would stand in front of the optical combiner, seeing their own reflections and the digitized reflections of other remote users (see Figure 9).

Unlike computational holography displays, the lightfield is not computed, but could directly be captured and retransmitted. Advances in camera sensor integration and appropriate lenses to increase angular resolution of the lightfield would allow the complete lightfield to be digitized. Improvements in broadband connections would also be necessary as to retransmit such lightfields. Such a scenario would provide exciting possibilities, such as telemedical assistance, interaction with people in restricted environments like nuclear power-plants, hard-to-reach areas and military combat environments. Challenges such as bandwidth and angular range of the captured lightfield need to be overcome before such future scenarios can be realised.

CONCLUSIONS

In this paper, we have explored the design potential of planar optical combiners as a means to merge physical spaces in front and behind the combiners with interactive virtual display spaces. The merged space offers a wide range of interactive capabilities. We discuss the design considerations pertinent for a designer using such optical combiner setups. In addition to this, we implemented three independent prototypes that leverage different aspects of the interactive capabilities. We demonstrated two of the prototypes to the museum staff and gathered initial impressions from the curators of the museum. The third prototype (AMI) was deployed for a musical performance for musicians. Finally we discuss how the optical combiner approach can be further extended to operate in a distributed setup allowing remote collaboration and natural telepresence. We believe that our exploration of the design space adds to the existing work and extends it into new and exciting directions.

ACKNOWLEDGEMENTS

We thank Alex Jones, Nick Janaway and the personal of the Bristol Museum and Art Gallery for their advice in designing and evaluating our prototypes. We thank Matt Sutton for taking the images and the video. This work is supported by the European Research Council (Starting Grant Agreement 278576) and the EU Marie Curie Action (IEF 2012 Number 330770) both under the Seventh Framework Programme.

REFERENCES

1. Anderson, F., Grossman, T., Matejka, J., and Fitzmaurice, G. YouMove: enhancing movement training with an augmented reality mirror. In Proc. of UIST'13. 2013. ACM.
2. Benko, H. and Wilson, A.D. Pinch-the-sky dome: freehand multi-point interactions with immersive omni-directional data. In Proc. of CHI'10 Extended Abstracts. 2010. ACM.

[8] https://www.lytro.com/camera/

3. Bertalini, M., Mirrors and the mind. The Psychologist, 2010. 23(2): p. 112.
4. Berthaut, F., Marshall, M., Subramanian, S., and Hachet, M. Rouages: Revealing the Mechanisms of Digital Musical Instruments to the Audience. In Proc. of NIME. 2013.
5. Bimber, O. and Raskar, R., Spatial Augmented Reality: Merging Real and Virtual Worlds. 2005.
6. Butler, A., Hilliges, O., Izadi, S., Hodges, S., Molyneaux, D., Kim, D., and Kong, D. Vermeer: direct interaction with a 360 degree viewable 3D display. In Proc. of UIST'11. 2011. ACM.
7. Campbell, F.W., The depth of field of the human eye. Journal of Modern Optics, 1957. 4: p. 157.
8. De la Riviere, J.B., Dittlo, N., Emmanuel, O., Kervegant, C., and Courtois, M. Holocubtile: 3D multitouch brings the virtual world into the user's hands. In Proc. of ITS'10. 2010. ACM.
9. Eisert, P., Rurainsky, J., and Fechteler, P. Virtual Mirror: Real-Time Tracking of Shoes in Augmented Reality Environments. In Proc. of ICIP'07. 2007. IEEE.
10. Foley, J.D., van Dam, A., Feiner, S.K., and Hughes, J.F., Computer graphics: principles and practice (2nd ed.). 1990: Addison-Wesley Publishing Co., Inc. 1174.
11. Fujinami, K., Kawsar, F., and Nakajima, T. AwareMirror: a personalized display using a mirror. In Proc. of 3rd international conference on Pervasive Computing. 2005. Springer-Verlag.
12. Fujinami, K., Ushida, K., Tanaka, Y., Naemura, T., and Harahima, H. i-mirror: An Interaction/Information Environment Based on a Mirror Metaphor Aiming to Install into Our Life Space. In Proc. of ICAT. 2002.
13. Hachet, M., Bossavit, B., Cohe, A., and Riviere, J.P. Toucheo: multitouch and stereo combined in a seamless workspace. In Proc. of UIST'11. 2011. ACM.
14. Hilliges, O., Kim, D., Izadi, S., Weiss, M., and Wilson, A.D. HoloDesk: direct 3d interactions with a situated see-through display. In Proc. of CHI'12. 2012. ACM.
15. Hirsch, M., Izadi, S., Holtzman, H., and Raskar, R. 8D display: a relightable glasses-free 3D display. In Proc. of SIGGRAPH'12 Posters. 2012. ACM.
16. Hoffman, D.M., Girshick, A.R., Akeley, K., and Banks, M.S., Vergence-accommodation conflicts hinder visual performance and cause visual fatigue. Journal of Vision, 2008. 8(3): p. 33.
17. Holliman, N.S., Dodgson, N.A., Favalora, G.E., and Pockett, L., Three-Dimensional Displays: A Review and Applications Analysis. IEEE Trans. on Broadcasting, 2011. 57(2): p. 362-371.
18. Karnik, A., Mayol-Cuevas, W., and Subramanian, S. MUSTARD: a multi user see through AR display. In Proc. of CHI'12. 2012. ACM.
19. Korsch, D., Reflective Optics. 1991: Academic Press.
20. Krueger, M., Artifitial Reality II. 1991: Addison Wesley
21. Li, W.H.A. and Fu, H. Augmented reflection of reality. In Proc. of SIGGRAPH'12 ETech. 2012. ACM.
22. Percival, A.S., The prescribing of spectacles. 1920: J. Wright.
23. Perlin, K., Paxia, S., and Kollin, J.S. An autostereoscopic display. In Proc. of SIGGRAPH'00. 2000. ACM.
24. Poston, T. and Serra, L. The virtual workbench: dextrous VR. In Proc. of VRST'64. 1994. World Scientific Publishing Co., Inc.
25. Raskar, R., Welch, G., Low, K.-L., and Bandyopadhyay, D. Shader Lamps: Animating Real Objects With Image-Based Illumination. In Proc. of 12th Eurographics Workshop on Rendering Techniques. 2001.
26. Regenbrecht, H.T., Franz, E.A., McGregor, G., Dixon, B.G., and Hoermann, S., Beyond the looking glass: Fooling the brain with the augmented mirror box. Presence: Teleoper. Virtual Environ., 2011. 20(6).
27. Sato, H., Kitahara, I., and Ohta, Y., MR-Mirror: A Complex of Real and Virtual Mirrors, in Virtual and Mixed Reality, Shumaker, R., Editor. 2009, Springer Berlin Heidelberg. p. 482-491.
28. Sheard, C., The prescription of prisms. American Journal of Optometry, 1934. 11: p. 364.
29. Shibata, T., Kim, J., Hoffman, D.M., and Banks, M.S., The zone of comfort: Predicting visual discomfort with stereo displays. Journal of Vision, 2011. 8(11): p. 11.
30. Starch, D.A., Demonstration of the trial and error methid of learning. The Psychological Bulletin, 1910. 5.
31. Stratton, G.M., A mirror pseudoscope and the limit of visible depth. Psychological Review, 1898. 5(6): p. 632.
32. Stratton, G.M., Upright Vision and the Retinal Image. Psychological Review, 1897. 4(2): p. 182.
33. Stratton, G.M., Vision without inversion of the retinal image. Psychological Review, 1897. 4(5): p. 463.
34. Sullivan, A. DepthCube solid-state 3D volumetric display. In Proc. of SPIE. 2004.
35. Valkov, D., Steinicke, F., Bruder, G., and Hinrichs, K. 2d touching of 3d stereoscopic objects. In Proc. of CHI'11. 2011. ACM.
36. Ware, C., Arthur, K., and Booth, K.S. Fish tank virtual reality. In Proc. of CHI '93 1993. ACM.
37. Yoshida, T., Shimizu, K., Kurogi, T., Kamuro, S., Minamizawa, K., Nii, H., and Tachi, S. RePro3D: full-parallax 3D display with haptic feedback using retro-reflective projection technology. In Proc. of ISVRI'11. 2011. IEEE

Loupe: A Handheld Near-Eye Display

Kent Lyons
Yahoo Labs
701 First Ave.
Sunnyvale CA 94089
klyons@yahoo-inc.com

Seung Wook Kim, Shigeyuki Seko, David Nguyen
Nokia
200 S. Mathilda Ave, Sunnyvale, CA 94086
seungwook.k@gmail.com, shigeyuki.seko@nokia.com,
david.h.nguyen@nokia.com

Audrey Dejardins
Simon Fraser University
Surrey, BC, Canada
adesjard@sfu.ca

Mélodie Vidal
Lancaster University
Lancaster, UK
m.vidal@lancaster.ac.uk

David Dobbelstein
Ulm University
Ulm, Germany
david.dobbelstein@uni-ulm.de

Jeremy Rubin
MIT
Cambridge, MA
jlrubin@mit.edu

ABSTRACT
Loupe is a novel interactive device with a near-eye virtual display similar to head-up display glasses that retains a handheld form factor. We present our hardware implementation and discuss our user interface that leverages Loupe's unique combination of properties. In particular, we present our input capabilities, spatial metaphor, opportunities for using the round aspect of Loupe, and our use of focal depth. We demonstrate how those capabilities come together in an example application designed to allow quick access to information feeds.

Author Keywords
virtual displays; near-eye display; handheld

ACM Classification Keywords
H.5.2 [Information interfaces and presentation]: User Interfaces. - Graphical user interfaces.

INTRODUCTION
Near-eye displays use small high resolution micro-displays placed in close proximity to the eye. Given the closeness to the eye and small size of the pixels, the user can not focus directly on the display. Instead, optics are used to create a virtual image at a distance that the user can see. These displays are used in the electronic view finders of digital cameras to show the picture and emulate an optical view finder. Near-eye displays are also used in devices such as Google Glass and the Epson Moverio where the display and optics are incorporated into a device worn somewhat like glasses. While head-up displays offer their users some unique capabilities such as providing a virtual display, they also suffer from some limitations. For example, creating compact high quality optics is technically challenging leading to larger form-factors [7]. These devices are worn on the user's face and can have negative social implications which are critical to consider [9].

UIST 2014, October 5–8, 2014, Honolulu, HI, USA.

ACM 978-1-4503-3069-5/14/10...$15.00.
http://dx.doi.org/10.1145/2642918.2647361

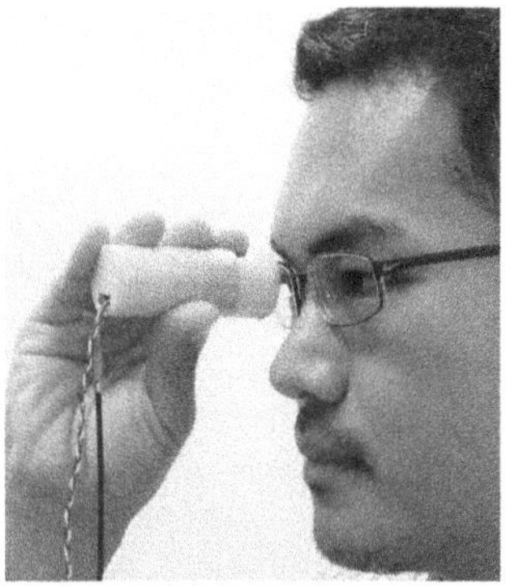
(a)

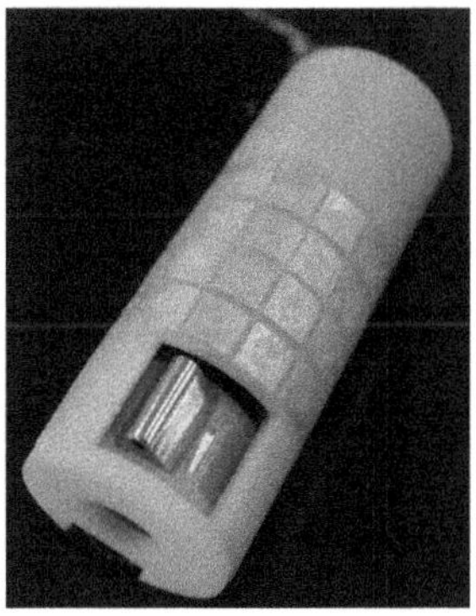
(b)

Figure 1: a) The user looks into the end of Loupe to see a virtual image. b) Our prototype showing touch electrodes and focus mechanism.

We conducted this work seeking to gain some of the unique advantages associated with head-mounted displays, but not their associated drawbacks. In particular, Loupe is a handheld near-eye display (Figure 1). The user brings the device in front of the eye and looks into it much like a jeweler's loupe, spyglass, or medical scope to see a virtual image. The handheld form enables the user to manipulate the device in numerous ways. When not in use, Loupe can be worn like a pendant or placed in a shirt pocket for easy access. In this paper, we situate Loupe in the context of other mobile devices and discuss its unique combination of features as a novel platform. Next, we present our use of sensing and the interaction opportunities afforded by this device. Finally, we present an example application demonstrating the capabilities of Loupe.

RELATED WORK
While there has not been much research into handheld near-eye displays, it is not completely without precedent. A decade ago, Nokia released the short lived Kaleidoscope pocket image viewer[1]. It had a 266x225 pixel display and the user looked into the end of the device to view an image. This device offered very minimal interaction allowing a user to

[1] `http://nds1.nokia.com/phones/files/guides/Nokia_Kaleidoscope_I_UG_en.pdf`

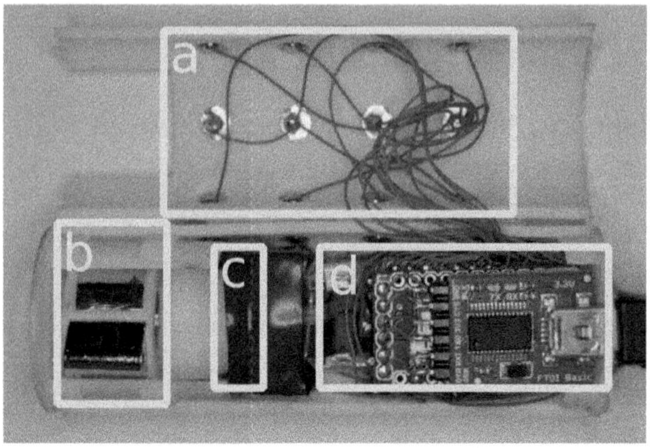

Figure 2: Inside Loupe: a) inside of capacitive pads. b) optics from jeweler's loupe, c) Epson micro-display (under tape), and d) circuit broads for sensing, Arduino & display driver. The optic's microswitch & IR sensor are not visible.

press buttons to switch between pictures. In the intervening decade, we have seen tremendous advancements in technology. Micro-displays have much higher resolutions and we see fully integrated solutions with display, on-board computation and sensing in compact forms. Given these advancements, we are revisiting a handheld form factor and explore how it might be used in an interactive device.

More broadly, it is useful to situate Loupe as a platform relative to other mobile devices. Head-mounted displays have a lot of technical similarity using micro-displays and optics to create a virtual image at a distance from a user [7]. The ability to create such an image means these devices are unaffected by presbyopia (becoming farsighted with age), a common source of frustration with smartphones [6]. Another advantage is that one can engineer the perceived field of view and create a compact device with a display that appears large. In contrast, if one wants a larger field of view with a phone or a watch, the display must be made physically larger or the user needs to bring it closer to their eyes. Near-eye displays are also very personal and private because the optics make it so the virtual image is only viewable when the device is in exactly the right relationship to the eye [7]. Finally, there is a social signaling component of using wearable displays [9]. Determining if a user is looking at or looking through a head-up display can be more nuanced than understanding use of a phone or watch. While Loupe has a virtual display, the handheld nature provides the benefit of a strong indication of use to onlookers.

Input is an important consideration for near-eye displays. There is no way to directly manipulate the visual content like on a phone or smartwatch since there is no physical display to touch. Devices like Google Glass, for example, offer a relatively small surface for touch input. The handheld cylindrical nature of Loupe provides a convenient location for touch sensing similar to [11] and other work using touch off the device's display [4, 12]. We also incorporated a variety of sensors for user input [3, 5].

We also surveyed the form factor of existing (non-computing) ocular devices as we considered the shape of Loupe. There are many devices in this space including kaleidoscopes, handheld telescopes, binoculars, medical scopes, range finders, opera glasses, Stan Hope rings, and our namesake, jeweler's loupes. We decided to implement a long cylindrical shape with a monocular display. This form relates to many of the objects surveyed, provides an opportunity to explore a round design, and affords a surface for input. Finally, we designed Loupe to be worn and quickly moved into position for rapid access and to enable micro-interactions [1, 2].

DEVICE IMPLEMENTATION

Our Loupe prototype is composed of several components and Figure 2 shows the device opened into two halves. At the heart of Loupe is the micro-display obtained from an Epson Moverio BT-100 binocular head-up display. We disassembled the Epson glasses, discarded the glasses' optics and housing, and extracted one of the LCDs and associated LED backlight. The LCD is a 0.52 inch color display with a resolution of 960x540. We also retained the electronics so the display is still driven by the Epson Android computer.

In front of the display, we use simple magnifying optics. Here, we use a jeweler's loupe to provide the needed magnification. This loupe has a diameter of 13mm and a nominal magnification of 20x[2]. These are not ideal optics as they create visible aberrations in the displayed image; however, for our prototype, the image quality was sufficient and allowed us to explore different magnifications and physical forms.

We provide a mechanism allowing the optics to move and change the perceived distance to the virtual display. This movement changes the focal depth from approximately one meter to tens of meters. The focal depth determines where in space the user must focus to see the virtual content. When the focus is set to the close state, the user must refocus their eyes and look near. Likewise, when it is set to far, the user must look far away. Focal depth is a property of most near-eye displays, however many choose a single focal depth (typically far). We added a microswitch inside Loupe so it is depressed when set to the far focal depth. In this work, we leverage the ability to sense the focal depth state (near or far) as part of the user interface. In a different prototype, we explored setting focal depth programmatically by displacing the LCD with a shape memory alloy wire. This approach showed promise but we did not use it in Loupe to reduce mechanical complexity.

Loupe has numerous sensors for input. We use an Arduino Pro Mini to collect and preprocess sensor data which is then forwarded to the Android control box of the Epson Moverio. We have 9 DOF motion sensing with a 3-axis accelerometer, magnetometer, and gyroscope (Sparkfun SEN-10724). Using a sensor fusion algorithm, this data provides the orientation of the device and we use relative changes for continuous input. An infrared proximity sensor (Vishay VCNL4000) is placed on the end next to the optics to determine when the device is placed in front of the user's eye.

[2] `http://www.amazon.com/gp/product/B001C9LG60`

Figure 3: As the user rotates the device, both icons and central content reorient to counteract the user's movement. The background color changes to match the selected icon.

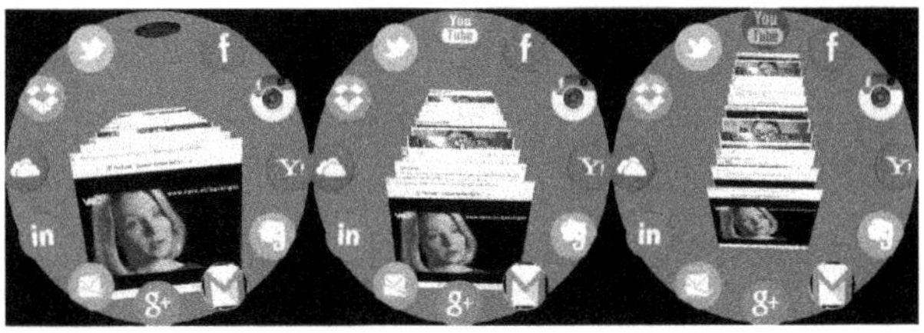

Figure 4: Pivoting down transitions from a 2D rendering of a single piece of content, to a 3D array of multiple elements.

Loupe has four Freescale MPR121 capacitive touch sensor controllers to sense an array of 48 touch points. We use pieces of copper foil as electrodes in a circular array around the circumference of Loupe. Each electrode has an area of 7.9x7.9 mm and has an adhesive back we used to attach them to the outer shell of Loupe. The shell has small holes where we solder on leads to the electrodes and connected them to the touch controller (Figure 2). We configured the touch controllers to report binary touch points. We also perform simple gesture detection to determine when the user swipes their thumb or a finger against the device in one of four cardinal directions. Loupe has provisions for bimanual use. The user can apply their second hand to twist on the surface of the device similar to using the focus ring on an SLR camera. After detecting a region being held, we look for two new touch points which we assume to be a pinch by the second hand. We then track movement around the circumference and emit clockwise or counterclockwise movement events as appropriate. Finally, we track the touch points and determine when the user is rolling the Loupe in their hand.

All of these electronics are assembled into a custom 3D printed shell to house the optics and electronics. We built multiple generations of Loupe each time shrinking the device and adding more capabilities. Our final version is 3 cm in diameter and 8 cm long, and a set of cables exits the rear of device tethering it to the Epson computer and Arduino.

LOUPE INTERACTIONS AND APPLICATION

Based on the form factor and input capabilities, we created a set of interactions for Loupe and an example application to demonstrate how all of these concepts come together as part of an overall platform. Our prototype was built using Unity3D and runs on the original Epson Android device.

The general model of this application is to allow quick access to notifications and numerous feeds of information the user might be interested in throughout the day. This could be updates from various social media sites, news, or updates from friends and family. The user interface provides a central detailed area surrounded by icons representing different applications with different feeds (Figure 3). To indicate the active application, its icon spins in place. The three-dimensional motion helps the user distinguish it from the central content and reinforces our use of depth throughout the user interface.

We assume one would wear Loupe around the neck or store it in a shirt pocket. In this storage position, the display is within view if the user looks down but it is not legible because of the nature of the optics. When a new piece of content comes into Loupe while not in use, the display starts blinking as a notification. This is implemented by rendering two contrasting solid colors (e.g., red and cyan) alternatively on the entire micro-display. The user can notice this visual indication by glancing through the optical opening. If desired, they pick up the device which is sensed by the IMU and IR proximity sensor and in turn launches the related application feed. Additionally, the eye proximity sensor allows us to detect more subtle changes in pose. If the user rapidly moves the device away and returns it, we can use that as a signal to advance in the application. In contrast, if the device is in the non-use state for awhile, we reset to the home screen.

We accentuate the roundness of Loupe with the physical form and user interface. To overcome the lack of a natural upright orientation, we use the inertial sensors to determine the gravity vector and rotate the user interface so it appears upright to the user. We also use this rotation for explicit user input. As the user rotates the device around its main axis, Loupe switches between applications and the background color gradually changes to match the color of the next application thus notifying the user of the new selection. Figure 3 shows images from the computer's perspective as the user physically rotates the display.

We also take advantage of the inertial sensors to enable two-dimensional panning. The small size, the way the device is held, and its proximity to the eye, all combine to allow the user to make movements to pan through a two-dimensional environment by pivoting the device in front of the eye. In each application, a number of pieces of content are laid out in a one-dimensional array away from the user toward the screen depth. The user can see additional content by gradually making a downward panning motion (Figure 4) and then swiping on the touch area moves through the content array.

Finally, our device has the ability to change the focal depth of the virtual image. We leverage this ability to incorporate additional depth cues in the user interface. As discussed above, we are using two states: near and far. The user has to focus their eyes at the appropriate focal depth to see the image, otherwise it is out of focus and blurry. We use the two focal depths in the user interface to render two different but related views of content. The near focal distance is used as a metaphor for personalized content, whereas generic content is displayed at the far focal depth. For example, when viewing Twitter posts in the default far mode, the system

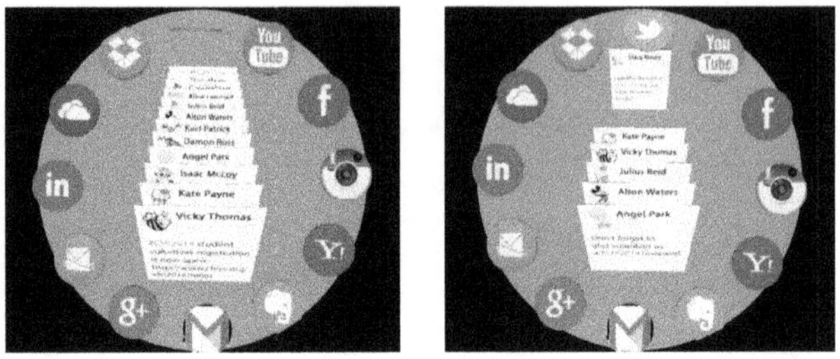

Figure 5: We use the shift in focal depth as a metaphor. The left is far focus showing all Twitter feeds and the right is the near focal depth showing close friends' feeds.

shows feeds from all users (Figure 5, left). When the focus is switched to the close mode, the user needs to look nearby and the interface only shows feeds from the user's close friends (Figure 5, right). Thus, as part of our interaction design, we change depths both physically with focal length and semantically with different information.

DISCUSSION AND FUTURE WORK

A novel aspect of Loupe is the ability to detect the focal depth state and to incorporate this information in the user interface. In this work, we tied together the focal depth to the semantics of content. Exploring other design options for focal depth is a clear area for future work. Also, we explicitly picked only two different focal depths as re-accommodating to the virtual image can be a challenge for novice users. Selecting which and how many focal depths the device could support should be informed by additional near-eye display research.

We believe the interaction elements we proposed are well supported by Loupe and its form, but other design choices can be made. For instance, we embraced roundness in Loupe using it in the form, touch array, and user interface. Alternatively, it would be straightforward to design a rectangular device to match the display aspect ratio. For a different prototype, we used a half-silvered mirror to create an optical see through device that could be used for an augmented reality interface. It had a vertical orientation and more closely resembles a medical scope. We also briefly explored much flatter, and wider shapes using optics similar to the waveguide in the Epson Moverio glasses, Saarikko's exit-pupil expander [10], or Light Field Displays [8]. This shape would enable forms similar to a pocket watch or magnifying lens. Loupe's current form was chosen for its relative simplicity as a starting point for exploring this design space. However, all of these forms show promise and could offer different affodances.

Our demonstration application enables quick access to notifications and information feeds similar to some applications on Google Glass or smartwatches. Loupe's resolution (even with a 540 pixel diameter) compares favorably relative to these devices. And while this type of use is plausible, there needs to be research to uncover possible applications similar to other explorations being conducted on smartwatches and glasses.

Many current near-eye displays are always worn and can confuse onlookers as to if one is looking at the virtual content or the physical world. We believe this is an artifact of the form factor and not of near-eye display technology. Loupe provides an alternative in a handheld form. It would be interesting to explore the social implications of near-eye displays and Loupe might serve as a foil to glasses-based approaches.

CONCLUSION

We presented Loupe, a novel near-eye display in a handheld form factor. It offers a wearable form that can be quickly moved into position like a smartwatch and uses a virtual image presented at a distance like a head-up display. Using these capabilities, we presented our Loupe application showing how to use this device to gain access to information feeds. We also discuss how our set of sensing capabilities, virtual image, and two focal depths combine to form an interesting and novel mobile computer.

REFERENCES

1. Ashbrook, D. *Supporting Mobile Microinteractions.* PhD thesis, Georgia Institute of Technology, 2010.
2. Ashbrook, D. L., Clawson, J. R., Lyons, K., Starner, T. E., and Patel, N. Quickdraw: the impact of mobility and on-body placement on device access time. In *Proceedings of CHI* (2008), 219–222.
3. Bartlett, J. F. Rock'n'scroll is here to stay. *Computer Graphics and Applications, IEEE 20*, 3 (2000), 40–45.
4. Baudisch, P., and Chu, G. Back-of-device interaction allows creating very small touch devices. In *Proceedings of CHI* (2009), 1923–1932.
5. Harrison, B. L., Fishkin, K. P., Gujar, A., Mochon, C., and Want, R. Squeeze me, hold me, tilt me! an exploration of manipulative user interfaces. In *Proceedings of CHI* (1998), 17–24.
6. Hasegawa, S., Fujikake, K., Omori, M., and Miyao, M. Readability of characters on mobile phone liquid crystal displays. *International Journal of Occupational Safety and Ergonomics (JOSE) 14*, 3 (2008), 293–304.
7. Kress, B., and Starner, T. A review of head-mounted displays (hmd) technologies and applications for consumer electronics. In *SPIE Defense, Security, and Sensing*, International Society for Optics and Photonics (2013), 87200A–87200A.
8. Lanman, D., and Luebke, D. Near-eye light field displays. *ACM Trans. Graph. 32*, 6 (Nov. 2013), 220:1–220:10.
9. McAtamney, G., and Parker, C. An examination of the effects of a wearable display on informal face-to-face communication. In *Proceedings of CHI* (2006), 45–54.
10. Saarikko, P. Diffractive exit-pupil expander with a large field of view. In *Proceedings of SPIE*, vol. 7001 (2008).
11. Song, H., Benko, H., Guimbretiere, F., Izadi, S., Cao, X., and Hinckley, K. Grips and gestures on a multi-touch pen. In *Proceedings of CHI '11* (2011), 1323–1332.
12. Sugimoto, M., and Hiroki, K. Hybridtouch: an intuitive manipulation technique for pdas using their front and rear surfaces. In *Proc. of Mobile HCI* (2006), 137–140.

High Rate, Low-Latency Multi-Touch Sensing with Simultaneous Orthogonal Multiplexing

Darren Leigh[1], Clifton Forlines[1], Ricardo Jota[1,2], Steven Sanders[1], Daniel Wigdor[2]

Tactual Labs[1]
New York, NY
USA
{first.last}@tactuallabs.com

Department of Computer Science[2]
University of Toronto
Toronto, ON, Canada
daniel@dgp.toronto.edu

ABSTRACT

We present "Fast Multi-Touch" (FMT), an extremely high frame rate and low-latency multi-touch sensor based on a novel projected capacitive architecture that employs simultaneous orthogonal signals. The sensor has a frame rate of 4000 Hz and a touch-to-data output latency of only 40 microseconds, providing unprecedented responsiveness. FMT is demonstrated with a high-speed DLP projector yielding a touch-to-light latency of 110 microseconds.

INTRODUCTION

Touch sensors in commercial use today typically operate at 60-85 frames per second. Such frame rates imply a "best" worst-case latency of at least 16 milliseconds, from the time a user's finger touches the sensor until the moment that information is made available to the system bus. Recent work from Microsoft and the University of Toronto has demonstrated that as little as 25 milliseconds of latency can impair performance [1], and that two milliseconds can be noticed by users of direct-touch systems [2]. Thus, it is the first goal of the present research to build a sensor capable of supporting an overall end-to-end latency of less than two milliseconds.

Ng *et al.* describe the results of analysis that suggest typical mobile devices have "end-to-end" latency, that is, a time between an input and the result being shown on the display, in the range of 75-125 milliseconds [2]. Other sources provide different measures of latency [3]. This variability is expected given that end-to-end latency includes performance characteristics of user-space software. As Ng *et al.* further describe, there are three broad sources of latency: the touch sensor, the software stack, and the display controller along with its refresh rate. The latency in these components is additive: while introducing a fast sensor will not, on its own, enable sub-2 millisecond responses, it is necessary to achieve this goal. Further, as Jota *et al.* describe, the impairment of user input to direct touch displays caused by latency is a continuous function – therefore any reduction of latency is expected to improve input performance [1].

UIST '14, October 05-08 2014, Honolulu, HI, USA

ACM 978-1-4503-3069-5/14/10...$15.00.
http://dx.doi.org/10.1145/2642918.2647353

Traditional projected capacitive (PCAP) sensors utilize a time-division multiplexing (TDM) approach to sensing: the controller continuously monitors sense traces, shown as columns in Figure 1 (top). Each drive trace, shown as a row, is then sequentially activated. If no touching object is present, an expected crosstalk signal is transferred from the active drive trace to all sense traces, and no touch is recorded. If, however, the user's finger is present on the sensor, a different amount of signal is transferred. The (x,y) coordinates of a touch are determined as follows: in the example in the figure, the x coordinate is the identity of the sense trace at which the signal change is detected, and the y coordinate corresponds to the drive trace that is active at the time of the change.

PCAP sensors offer a number of advantages over resistance-based sensors; durability and rigidity among them. Even more important in today's commercial market is their ability to detect multiple simultaneous touches on a transparent surface. Thus, their inherent limitation in sensor throughput has been tolerated.

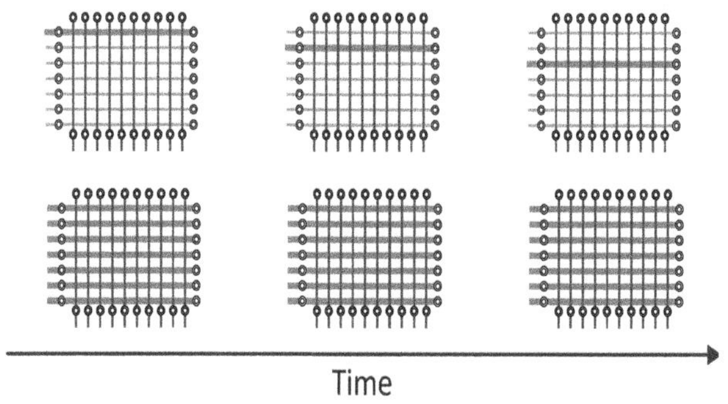

Figure 1: Top row: Traditional TDM-based projected capacitive sensors scan each row sequentially, which takes time. Bottom row: FMT sensors scan all rows simultaneously.

Our goal was to build a projected capacitive sensor, complete with all of these advantages, which is also able to perform at a significantly higher rate. To achieve this, we eliminate the sequential scanning inherent in a TDM approach by instead activating all drive traces simultaneously using orthogonal signals: instead of looking for a signal strength change at a given sense trace, the controller examines each sense trace for the strength of every orthogonal signal transmitted on the set of drive traces. This is shown in Figure 1 (bottom).

RELATED WORK

A thorough review of the literature examining interaction latency is provided in [1], and so we omit it here. Instead, we briefly review alternative methods for sensing touch: traditional PCAP, optical techniques, and resistive methods.

The use of capacitive sensing of touch input dates to at least the mid-1960's [4], and for multi-touch to the mid 1980's [5]. More recently, SmartSkin [6] was a PCAP system that used a TDM scheme, transmitting bursts of 400 kHz square wave on each row, in turn, and looking for the response at the columns. SmartSkin had a 30 Hz frame rate, and therefore a "best" worst-case latency of about 33 milliseconds. Westerman *et al.* also demonstrated a similar method [7], and illustrated its use to compose complex multi-touch gestures on an opaque touchpad. That work formed the basis of the FingerWorks product line.

DiamondTouch [8] was a multi-user touch system, though not fully multi-touch: it could sense multiple touches, but only as projections along the rows and columns. It employed the rows and columns identically as transmitters, with receivers in contact with the users' bodies for identification purposes. It was, therefore, not PCAP, but a close cousin.

DiamondTouch used a TDM scheme, transmitting a 100 kHz square wave burst on each row/column in turn. Several versions of this system were produced, with frame rates ranging from 20 to 40 Hz, implying "best" worst-case latencies from 25 to 50 milliseconds.

PCAP forms the basis of most multi-touch screens used to date. In contrast, alternative sensing techniques for touch have also been demonstrated.

A number of optical techniques have been demonstrated for touch input. As early as 1982, optical methods were employed for multitouch input using a camera for imaging and diffuse illumination for lighting [9]. More recently, frustrated total internal reflection (FTIR) systems use cameras to detect where light leaks from a sheet of plastic due to touches frustrating the total internal reflection of light that is propagating within [10]. Camera-based optical techniques are difficult to implement in thin form factors, such as mobile devices, because of the standoff necessary for the sensor – this is manifest as a large volume behind the display, or as a bezel surrounding the screen. Further, for techniques that employ 2D cameras, the latency is limited by processing time, as well as the frame rate of the sensor: standard 60 frame-per-second cameras would imply a "best" worst-case latency of 17 milliseconds, similar to traditional PCAP techniques. Bezel-mounted optical sensors enable sensing of touch [11], and do not require 2D image processing. However, they too suffer from the need for a bezel. A detailed overview of many different optical techniques is provided in [12].

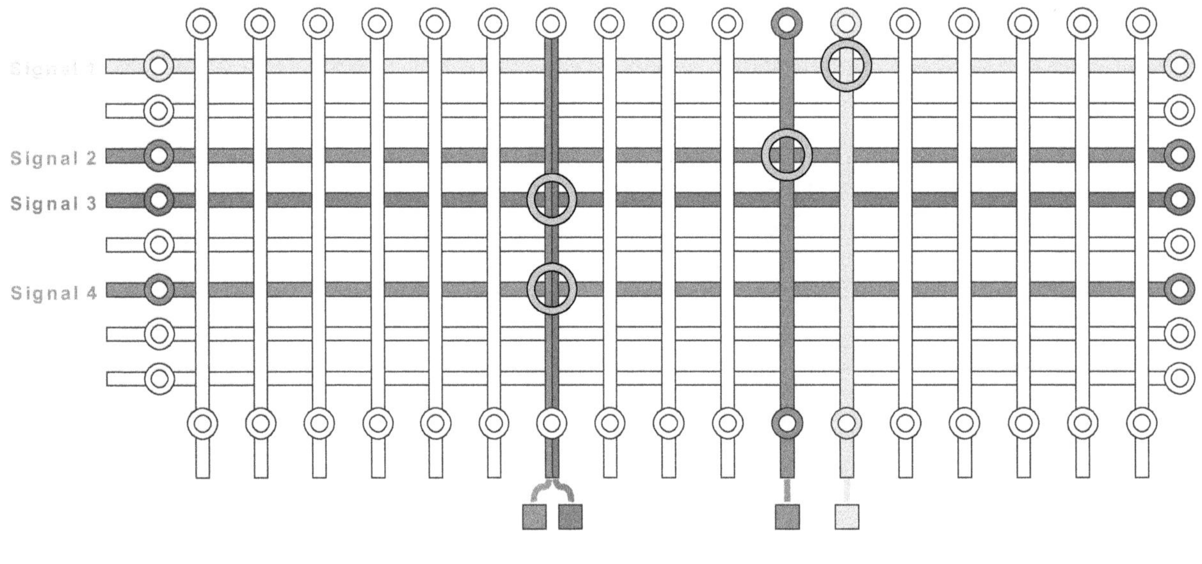

Figure 2: Orthogonal signals are simultaneously transmitted on each row. Where touches occur (the pink rings in the figure), signals from the affected rows are coupled into the affected columns. Column receivers determine the amount of each row signal present on that column to determine the affected row/column intersections.

Ng *et al.* developed a very fast multi-touch system based on a resistive technique, and used it to study and characterize low-latency touch interaction [2]. They demonstrated an end-to-end latency of about one millisecond. Unfortunately, the design and technique of their touch system is proprietary and has never been publically disclosed, beyond a cursory mention of its "resistive" nature. Because of limitations in durability and requirements of application of active pressure, resistive techniques methods have largely been supplanted by PCAP. From Ng we draw the method for enabling fast visual of output of sensor data, completing the quick round trip. We utilize the same projector, and similar FPGA-based approach to generating the imagery.

ORTHOGONAL SIGNAL CAPACITIVE TOUCH SENSING

Our goal is to detect touch events from human fingers, or other capacitive objects, on a two-dimensional manifold such as a planar surface. It is important that multiple simultaneous touch events be detected and distinguished from each other. For the reasons we have described, it is also important that the touch events be detected, processed and supplied to downstream computational processes with very low latency, i.e. on the order of one millisecond or less.

To accomplish this goal, we have developed a projected capacitive method that has been enhanced for a high update rate and low latency measurement of touch events. Our technique employs parallel processing and higher frequency waveforms to gain the above advantages. We have also developed methods to make the measurements sensitive and robust, allowing the technique to be used on transparent display surfaces and permit the economical manufacture of products that employ it.

BASIC TECHNOLOGY

The touch surface is comprised of a series of rows and columns[1], along which signals can propagate. The rows and columns are designed so that, when not being touched, a negligible amount of signal is coupled between them.

A different signal is transmitted onto each of the surface's rows. These signals are designed to be "orthogonal" in the mathematical sense, *i.e.*

$$\int f_i(x)\, f_j(x)\, dx = 0\,, \quad i \neq j \qquad \text{Equation 1}$$

so that a linear combination of them can be separated and the individual signals distinguished from one another. The use of orthogonal signals allows us to take advantage of matched-filter receiver techniques, which can be optimal under real-world conditions.

When a row and column are touched simultaneously, a small amount of the signal that is present on the row is coupled into the corresponding column. A receiver, attached to each column, is designed to receive any of the transmitted signals, or an arbitrary combination of them, and to individually measure the quantity of each of the orthogonal transmitted signals that is present on that column.

Touch events correspond to the received signals on the columns. For each column, the different signals received there indicate which of the corresponding rows is being touched simultaneously with that column. The quantity of each signal received is related to the amount of coupling between the corresponding row and column and may indicate the area of the surface covered by the touch, the pressure of the touch, etc. A touch is detected for a particular row / column intersection when that intersection's row signal is detected (above a threshold) by the intersection's column receiver.

Signal Pathway

The basic architecture of FMT is shown in Figure 2. The row signals, transmitted with amplitude V, pass through the rows, fingers and columns and then into the column receivers, where they are detected with a matched filter. The matched filter (one for each expected row signal) integrates over a time period τ, producing a measured level for that row signal on that column. That level can be expressed by the formula:

$$\text{received signal level} = \alpha A V \tau \qquad \text{Equation 2}$$

where A is the area touched by the finger and α is a scale factor that is a function of signal attenuation along the rows and columns, coupling between the finger and the touch surface, and various other gain parameters. To get the best system performance, it is important that we maximize the received signal level by making good design choices.

Choosing a Set of Orthogonal Signals

There are an infinite number of orthogonal signal sets that could be used to implement our fast touch sensor and, in theory, they are all equivalent. In practice, the specific details of each signal type have advantages and disadvantages that will cause us to choose one that is optimal for our needs. Some of these factors include:

- Ease and expense of implementation
- Dynamic range, or the ability to distinguish simultaneous weak touch signals from strong ones
- Immunity to noise and interference

A good signal set will be easy and inexpensive to implement, have high dynamic range and be relatively immune to noise and interference. A real-world implementation will require some tradeoffs between these.

[1] The nature of the rows and columns is arbitrary and the particular orientation is irrelevant. In fact, it is not even necessary that the rows and columns be in a square grid.

The choice of signal sets is similar to those used for multiplexing in communication systems, and includes:

Time Division Multiplexing (TDM), in which the measurement period is divided into segments and each channel is assigned one of those segments in which to transmit.

Frequency Division Multiplexing (FDM), in which each channel is assigned a separate frequency band.

Code Division Multiplexing (CDM), in which each channel is a assigned a separate "spreading code": a random-looking waveform that is statistically uncorrelated with the others.

Time division multiplexing, as described in the introduction, is the technique used by SmartSkin [6] and most other PCAP touch systems today. It has the advantage of being simple to implement, with a minimum of hardware. However, the inherent delays from time-slot to time-slot add latency to the system. Removing this latency is possible by decreasing the duration of the time slots, but this would lower the integration period τ of the receivers, decreasing the received signal strength (per Equation 2).A designer can compensate for the shorter integration period by increasing the transmit amplitude V – and commercial products often do this – but there are practical limits. Increasing the amplitude to achieve very low latencies might require the transmitter to put out hundreds of volts.

Frequency division multiplexing and code division multiplexing both allow the entire frame time to be used for the receiver integration period, because the orthogonal signals are transmitted *simultaneously* and there is no need to divide the frame into separate time slots.

CDM has the advantage of being easy to generate and receive (because the modulation time reference is local), and is more immune to external noise and interference due to the "random" nature of its signals. Unfortunately, CDM suffers from dynamic range problems, making it difficult to receive weak signals in the presence of strong ones.

Even worse, CDM signals are broadband and can suffer degradation if the communication channel's frequency response is not "flat" (the same at all frequencies). A PCAP system being touched at multiple points at random times by uncharacterized appendages is unlikely to present a flat frequency response. This problem will be exacerbated if the sensor's rows and columns are made from a material that is less conductive than would be desired, which is the case with transparent conductors such as indium-tin-oxide (ITO).

Frequency division multiplexing can be very robust under bad channel conditions because a channel tends to be well-behaved over the narrow bandwidth occupied by its individual frequency band. For this reason, variants of it, such as orthogonal frequency division multiplexing (OFDM), are widely used in communication systems with poorly-behaved channels, including WiFi, digital TV broadcasting and power-line communication. FDM can be more prone to external noise and interference, but there are mitigation techniques that can be employed to lessen the effects.

The dynamic range of FDM depends strongly on the receiver architecture, but it is possible to achieve results almost as good as TDM.

For these reasons, we chose to use frequency division multiplexing for FMT. In the simplest implementation, the orthogonal signals being transmitted onto the rows are unmodulated sinusoids, each of which has a different frequency. The frequencies are chosen so that they can be easily distinguished from each other in the receiver.

We use a "comb" of frequencies, where the spacing between adjacent frequencies is constant, to allow easy detection using a discrete Fourier transform (DFT). Due to the Fourier relationship between time and frequency, the spacing between frequencies, Δf, must be at least the reciprocal of the integration period τ. Otherwise the signals will not be "orthogonal" and will be confused with each other in the receiver. For example, if we desire to determine which row signals are present at a column receiver, and we wish to do so once per millisecond, then the frequency spacing $\Delta f > 1/\tau$ or greater than one kilohertz. In reality, the frequency spacing should be greater than the minimum to permit a simpler, more robust design.

We also ensure that the highest transmitted frequency is less than twice the lowest, in order to avoid any problems with harmonics. Harmonics are integer multiplies of a fundamental frequency that are created by non-linearities and other problematic physical processes. If our highest frequency is greater than twice the lowest, then it is possible that a harmonic of a low frequency will be interpreted as a legitimately transmitted signal, causing false readings. By constraining our transmitted frequencies so that none of their harmonics would overlap any of our deliberately generated signals, we can avoid this problem.

The Fourier and harmonic conditions described above combine to constrain the minimum signal frequencies that we can successfully implement. If an FMT touch sensor has n rows and a latency of L, then we must transmit n frequencies that are at least $1/L$ apart, yielding a minimum frequency bandwidth of n/L. Because the highest frequency can be no more than twice the lowest, the minimum signal we can transmit must be no lower than n/L. Therefore, for a forty row touch sensor with a latency of one millisecond, the lowest possibly frequency that can be used is 40 kHz.

Our FMT demonstrator has thirty rows and therefore requires thirty separate frequencies — one per row. In its fastest mode, the system has a frame update period of 40 microseconds, which means that our frequency spacing must be at least $1/40$ µsec or 25 kHz. We use an actual spacing of about 163 kHz, with our lowest frequency being 5.371 MHz and our highest 10.091 MHz.

Modulated sinusoids
The use of unmodulated sinusoids has two problems. First, the sinusoids might cause radiofrequency interference to other devices near the touch surface, and a device employing such might have problems passing regulatory testing (e.g. FCC, CE). Second, sinusoids in the environment, whether from deliberate transmitters or from other interfering devices (perhaps even another identical touch surface), might cause false or degraded touch measurements on our device.

An effective technique for minimizing such interference is to modulate or "stir" the signals we are transmitting in a manner such that we can demodulate ("unstir") or otherwise compensate for the modulation of the signals when they reach the receiver. Signals emitted or received under such a technique are highly uncorrelated with anything else, and so act as mere noise instead of appearing to be similar to other signals present in the environment.

Two straightforward ways of doing this are frequency modulation and direct-sequence spread spectrum modulation. FMT was built to do the latter, and includes bi-phase modulators (multiplied by +1 or -1, i.e. selective inversion) in both the row transmitters and the column receivers. These modulators share a control signal so that all of the signals, at both the transmitters and receivers, flip polarity at the same time. The control signal is pseudo-random, causing the transmitted signal to spread in a wider bandwidth on the touch surface, and then be unspread in the receiver before we attempt to detect the sinusoids.

Care must be taken not to spread the signals too much, or we will run into the channel problems described above for CDM. A good rule of thumb is to spread on the order of the row frequency spacing.

Signal Detection
To determine which rows and columns are being simultaneously touched, we need to receive any signals present on the columns and determine which of the transmitted frequencies appear. This can be done with common frequency analysis techniques, such as a Fourier transform or filter bank.

From each column's signal, we determine the strength of each of the transmitted frequencies that it contains. If the strength of a frequency is greater than some threshold, then we have determined that there is a touch event between the column and the row corresponding to that frequency. Signal strength information can be used to determine the area of the touch event, which may correspond to various physical phenomena including the size of the finger, the pressure with which it is pressing down, the fraction of row/column intersection that is being touched, etc.

Once we calculate the signals strengths for each frequency (corresponding to a row) for each column, we can create a two-dimensional "heat map" of these, with the signal strength being the value of the map at that row/column intersection.

The heat map can be thresholded to determine touch events, or can be used to infer information about the shape, orientation, etc. of the object touching the surface.

Our FMT demonstrator implements a complete radio receiver with a Fast Fourier Transform (FFT) detection scheme for every column. This digitizes the RF waveform, detects the sinusoids and performs digital signal processing on them.

POST PROCESSING
After the signal strengths from each row in each column are calculated, the system does some post-processing to convert this 2-D "heat map" into usable touch events. The process includes "field flattening", touch point detection, interpolation and touch point matching between frames.

Because we requireme very low latency, the processing steps are as optimized and parallelized as possible.

Field Flattening
Due to signal attenuation across rows and columns and other systematic error sources that affect signal strengths, we first perform field flattening by normalizing these strengths across the whole touch surface. This can be done with a known calibration object, measuring the signal strength response that it causes for every row/column intersection, and computing both an additive and multiplicative offset for that intersection. When the offsets are applied, the responses are normalized across the entire touch surface.

Our FMT demonstrator does not require much field flattening, because its touch surface uses copper rows and columns, which are very conductive. Field flattening is much more important when compromise conductors, such as transparent ITO, are used.

Touch Point Detection
Once the heat map is generated and "field flattened", we determine the coarse touch points. This is done by finding local maxima in the normalized signal strengths. We use a fast and parallelizable method for finding these, by comparing each element of the normalized heat map to its neighbors and labeling it a local maximum if it is strictly greater than all of them, and above a given threshold.

We can define the set of neighbors in various ways, but the two most useful sets will probably be the Von Neumann neighborhood and the Moore neighborhood (see Figure 3). The Von Neumann neighborhood consists of the four elements that are vertically and horizontally adjacent to the element in the center (i.e. the elements to the north, south, east and west of it). This is also called the "four-connected" neighborhood. The Moore neighborhood consists of the eight elements that are vertically, horizontally and diagonally adjacent to the element in the center (i.e. the elements to the north, south, east, west, northeast, northwest, southeast and southwest of it). This is also called the "eight-connected" neighborhood.

The neighborhood we choose will depend on the interpolation scheme we use to calculate the fine touch points.

Interpolation

Once the coarse touch points are determined, we compute the fine touch points using interpolation. A straightforward way to do this is to model the capacitive contact of a distributed touch as a second-order function in two dimensions, fitting it to a paraboloid.

For a Von Neumann neighborhood, the relevant points look like Figure 3 (left) with the central blue element being the local maximum and the subscripts being the coordinates of a particular element relative to it. The positions and signal strengths of the five elements allow us to fit them to the following equation:

$$Ax^2 + Cy^2 + Dx + Ey + F = z \qquad \text{Equation 3}$$

where x and y are the position of an element, z is the signal strength of the element, and A, C, D, E and F are the coefficients of the second-order polynomial. Relative to the central point, all of the element x, y positions are constant. The z values are the measured signal strengths at each element, and thus are known. The five polynomial co-efficients are the only unknowns, so we need five simultaneous equations to solve for them. Each equation represents one of the five points, including the central point and its four neighbors.

We solve for the polynomial coefficients by inverting a Vandermonde-like matrix, which yields:

$$\begin{bmatrix} A \\ C \\ D \\ E \\ F \end{bmatrix} = \frac{1}{2} \begin{bmatrix} 0 & 1 & -2 & 1 & 0 \\ 1 & 0 & -2 & 0 & 1 \\ 0 & -1 & 0 & 1 & 0 \\ 1 & 0 & 0 & 0 & -1 \\ 0 & 0 & 2 & 0 & 0 \end{bmatrix} \begin{bmatrix} z_{0,1} \\ z_{-1,0} \\ z_{0,0} \\ z_{1,0} \\ z_{0,-1} \end{bmatrix} \qquad \text{Equation 4}$$

Note that the polynomial coefficients are a linear combination of the signal strengths and that only simple multiplications, involving negation and a single shift, are required to calculate them. This means that they can be efficiently computed in an FPGA or ASIC. By fitting our data to a paraboloid, we are assuming that the fine touch point is at its maximum, which occurs at the point x_f, y_f where:

$$x_f = -\frac{D}{2A} \quad \text{and} \quad y_f = -\frac{E}{2C}$$

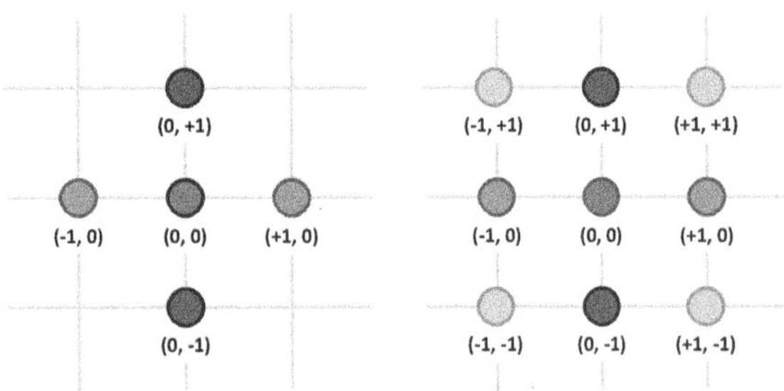

Figure 3: On the left is a Von Neumann neighborhood. On the right is a Moore neighborhood.

The values x_f and y_f are independent of each other, with x_f depending only on the signal strengths of the elements to the left and right of the center point, and y_f depending only on the signal strengths of the elements above and below it.

For the Moore neighborhood, the relevant points look like Figure 3 (right). The positions and signal strengths of the nine elements can be fit to the following second-order equation:

$$Ax^2 + Bxy + Cy^2 + Dx + Ey + F = z \qquad \text{Equation 5}$$

which is similar to the previous case, but with an added xy cross term. This is an over-determined system with nine simultaneous equations (one per element), so we must employ a least-squares technique to solve it. This yields:

$$\begin{bmatrix} A \\ B \\ C \\ D \\ E \\ F \end{bmatrix} = \frac{1}{36} \begin{bmatrix} 6 & -12 & 6 & 6 & -12 & 6 & 6 & -12 & 6 \\ -9 & 0 & 9 & 0 & 0 & 0 & 9 & 0 & -9 \\ 6 & 6 & 6 & -12 & -12 & -12 & 6 & 6 & 6 \\ -6 & 0 & 6 & -6 & 0 & 6 & -6 & 0 & 6 \\ 6 & 6 & 6 & 0 & 0 & 0 & -6 & -6 & -6 \\ -4 & 8 & -4 & 8 & 20 & 8 & -4 & 8 & -4 \end{bmatrix} \begin{bmatrix} z_{-1,1} \\ z_{0,1} \\ z_{1,1} \\ z_{-1,0} \\ z_{0,0} \\ z_{1,0} \\ z_{-1,-1} \\ z_{0,-1} \\ z_{1,-1} \end{bmatrix}$$

Equation 6

Note again that the polynomial coefficients are a linear combination of the signal strengths. The multiplications are slightly more complicated, but many of the multiplicands can be factored out and applied a single time near the end of the calculation to make the computation more efficient. Because we are interested in the maximum of the paraboloid – meaning that overall scale factors are irrelevant and we are only concerned with relative values and the arguments which maximize the function – we may be able to cancel out many of them altogether.

The fine touch point is at the maximum of the paraboloid, which occurs at the point x_f, y_f where:

$$x_f = (BE - 2CD)/(4AC - B^2)$$

and

$$y_f = (DB - 2AE)/(4AC - B^2)$$

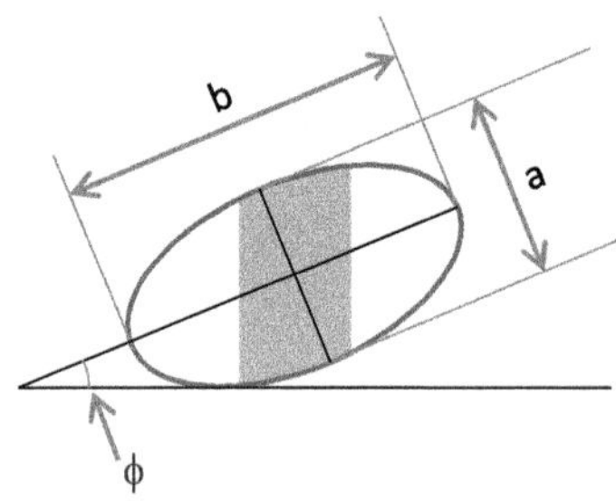

Figure 4: An elliptical fit to an asymmetric touch point. The aspect ratio and tilt angle can provide useful information about the touching object.

For the eight-connected neighborhood, the values x_f and y_f are not independent of each other. Both depend on the signal strengths of all eight neighbors. This might seem like a disadvantage because of the increased computational burden, and the possibility that certain combinations of signal strengths will produce singular values for the fine touch points. However, there are advantages as well. Because of the least-squares nature of the eight-connected calculation, it is more robust against noisy signal strength values. Small errors in one signal strength will be compensated for by the increased amount of data used in the calculation, and the self-consistency of that data.

Another advantage of the eight-connected neighborhood is that it provides an extra piece of information that might prove useful as part of a user interface. The B coefficient of the xy cross-term can be used to characterize asymmetry in the fitted paraboloid and, along with the aspect ratio information inherent in the A and C coefficients, can allow software to determine the angle at which the touch is occurring.

Figure 4 shows a notional touch point with an elliptical cross section, which can be obtained by truncating the paraboloid at a particular z value. The values of a and b can be obtained from the A and C coefficients of the polynomial, and they give us information about the aspect ratio of the object touching the surface. For example, a finger or stylus would not necessarily be circularly symmetric, and the ratio of a to b can tell us about its shape.

Knowledge of the angle ϕ can tell us how the ellipse is oriented, which might indicate which way the finger or stylus is pointing or at what angle it is tilted with respect to the touch surface. We can calculate ϕ from the eigenvalues and eignevectors of the 2 x 2 matrix M given in Equation 7:

$$M = \begin{bmatrix} A & B/2 \\ B/2 & C \end{bmatrix} \qquad \text{Equation 7}$$

Blob Detection

The above post-processing steps work for isolated touches, like single fingers, but don't handle extended "blob"-like touches. The FMT demonstrator currently does not do blob detection and, instead, responds to an extended touch with a swarm of single touches. We are currently investigating highly-parallel, low-latency algorithms for detecting and representing extended touches.

Frame Matching

To properly track objects moving on the touch surface over time, it is important to match the calculated touch points with each other between frames. While this is a fundamentally hard problem – and insoluble in the general case – we are aided by geometry and physics. Because the items that are in contact with the touch surface are of finite size, and move according to certain physical principles, we will not experience the worst cases.

Fingers and styluses have a minimum size and are unlikely to approach each other closely enough to cause an ambiguous case. They also travel at speeds characteristic of the motion of a human arm, which bounds the problem.

Because the our touch system has such a high update rate – well over a kilohertz – fingers and styluses touching the surface cannot move arbitrarily far or at extreme angles from one frame to the next. This makes the problem much easier, allowing us to do frame matching mostly by choosing the closest point in adjacent frames. Another useful heuristic for matching touch points between frames is the use of dynamics, calculating the time derivatives of touch point positions and using them to predict the likely position in the next frame. We can also use the signal strengths and shapes of previous touch points to distinguish between touch points and to infer likely candidates for matches. Both the Moore neighborhood calculation and extended blob matching would be useful.

A robust frame matching system would likely combine all of the above techniques, performing simple matching in most cases and more complicated matching in ambiguous ones.

IMPLEMENTATION

Our demonstration system appears in Figure 5. It was built around circuit boards and development kits that were intended for radio astronomy use. We designed the FMT demonstrator to be extremely flexible and adaptable so that we could experiment with parameters and new use cases. We can control the transmit signal strengths, independently set the transmit frequencies on a per-row basis, control the receive timing and FFT spacing, turn the CDM modulation of the sinusoids on and off, mask the analog-to-digital converter outputs to simulate different ENoBs (effective numbers of bits), etc. This flexibility is very useful in exploring ways that the system can be optimized, trying new touch substrate materials, etc.

The Touch Surface

The touch surface itself was created from a two-layer printed circuit board. It approximates a 25 centimeter diagonal screen, similar to an Apple iPad, and contains 30 rows and 40 columns. The top layer contains the rows and columns, and the bottom layer contains the ground plane (and jumpers for the columns). The row and column pattern consists of interlocking diamond shapes, similar to those used by DiamondTouch and in many commercial PCAP touch sensors. This geometry provides the maximum capacitive coupling between the touching finger and the rows and columns, while minimizing cross talk between those. The row and column pitch is 5 millimeters, which we have found is well matched to the size of human fingers.

Need for a Ground Plane

Not all PCAP touch systems use a ground plane under the rows and columns. The ground plane helps with several issues. First, it ensures that all capacitive interactions occur very close to the physical surface, eliminating "hover" and producing a very satisfying touch experience. Without the ground plane, the touch detection occurs more gradually as a finger approaches the surface, producing a "mushy" feel.

Figure 5: The FMT demonstrator. Note the dot of light on the finger, emanating from the high-speed projector.

Second, the large capacitance between the ground plane and the rows and columns dominates the smaller capacitance between them and the environment. This means that, when a row/column intersection is touched, the amount of row signal transferred onto the column increases. Without the closely coupled ground plane, the signal would actually decrease. Most commercial PCAP systems do not use a ground plane.

Signal generation hardware

Our row signal generators consist of a bank of forty Analog Devices AD9834 direct digital synthesizers that are set up to generate sinusoids in the range from DC to about 12 MHz. They are individually programmable and contain a phase selection input that can be used for bi-phase modulation. They are followed by an amplifier that lets us transmit row signals with amplitudes up to five volts peak-to-peak.

Receiver hardware

Our receiver front ends consist of forty Texas Instruments VCA8613 programmable gain amplifiers with a gain of up to 40 dB and a 12 MHz low-pass filter. These feed a bank of analog-to-digital converters, based on the TI ADS5272, which sample at a rate of 50 Msps. The ADCs have high-speed serial outputs that feed the touch processing unit.

Processing

The processing unit is a "mini-ROACH" (**R**econfigurable **O**pen **A**rchitecture **C**ompute **H**ardware) field programmable gate array (FPGA) board that was developed as part of the CASPER (Collaboration for Astronomical Signal Processing and Electronics Research) effort [13]. The mini-ROACH is based on a Xilinx Virtex-5 FPGA and includes Ethernet and a large amount of digital I/O. It performs both the row signal detection for each column receiver and also post-processing to turn the "heat map" into useful, interpolated touch events.

Our processing does not use any "tricks", such as assuming a limited number of touch points or where the touches might be. There are no fundamental limits on the number of touch points that can be detected or tracked. For convenience of implementation, the firmware is currently limited to sixteen simultaneous touches, but this can easily be changed by recompiling with new parameters.

Outputs

The FMT processor board has two outputs, including a fast, low-latency parallel port that sends processed touch events to the high-speed display, and an Ethernet port. The Ethernet port is used for control and monitoring, including being able to upload raw "heat maps" to a computer for visualization and debugging. The low-latency parallel port includes a "dial a latency" feature, allowing us to add calibrated amounts of delay to the demonstrator for testing purposes.

Display

We required an extremely fast video display to demonstrate FMT's capabilities without adding its own excessive latency. The DLP Discovery 4100 kit from Texas Instruments, which uses their digital micro-mirror technology to modulate light at a 32 kHz rate, was able to provide the necessary speed and low latency. This is the same display used by Ng *et al* [2].

PERFORMANCE

The touch sensor operates with an update rate of 4 kHz and each of those frames has a latency of 40 microseconds. The mismatch was done for implementation convenience and, during the remaining 210 microseconds of a 4 kHz frame, the processor is basically idle. A more optimized system could use the extra time to provide a 25 kHz frame rate, or to perform a longer integration (from 40 microseconds to 250 microseconds), increasing the system's signal-to-noise ratio by 8 decibels.

We have calculated the touch sensor's inherent latency from our FPGA code, and also directly measured the entire system's end-to-end (touch instant to display output) latency. We used a piezo transducer as a fast impact sensor to detect the instant of touch by attaching it to a fingertip and tapping the sensor quickly. The piezo transducer generates a voltage when it is mechanically strained, which is easily seen on oscilloscope when the transducer is tapped on a hard surface. Its metal construction registers a touch point on the surface as well as a finger alone does. We also used a photodiode sensor to measure the light level being projected onto the tapping finger. Using an oscilloscope, we measured the time difference between the tap and the displayed response. Our system's end-to-end latency, from touch to light, is approximately 110 microseconds.

Because FMT makes no prior assumptions about the number and kinds of touches, and merely reports high-speed samples of where it has been touched, measuring the latency of a single finger tap is sufficient to know he latency of any other kind of touch operation, such as dragging.

High speed video, taken at 400 fps and 1200 fps, confirms these figures and shows a dot of light keeping up with and tracking the finger very smoothly. There is no noticeable lag.

Variable Latency "Pong"

To see how changes in latency affect video game play, we implemented a version of the classic "Pong", but with one player experiencing no perceptible latency and the other burdened with 150 milliseconds of lag. While we did not do a formal user study, there was anecdotal consensus that the "zero" latency side was much easier to play. The high latency side required some getting used to, but even so, was significantly disadvantaged.

IMPLICATIONS

An extremely low-latency touch system opens up many new application areas. Opaque FMT can be used to implement highly-responsive track pads and game controls, providing unprecedented, immersive gaming experiences.

FMT is not limited to flat surfaces, and could be implemented on any two-dimensional manifold. Sports equipment, such as golf clubs and tennis rackets, could be instrumented to show where the player's grip is, and how it changes over the course of a swing.

Automobile dashboards, steering wheels and entertainment systems could take advantage of high-resolution, low latency touch to permit the driver to control the cabin environment in an intuitive, almost subconscious manner; because latency makes a user interface harder to use and causes distraction, removing that latency could keep more of the driver's attention on the road and increase traffic safety.

Transparent versions of FMT can be designed into tablets, phones and other mobile devices. Although these will not achieve the strikingly low end-to-end latencies described here, due to the delays added by their software and display, about 15-20 milliseconds of latency will be removed in a stroke, which will incrementally improve the user experience. And as latency is removed from other parts of these devices, we will approach our goal of user interfaces that have "zero" perceptible lag.

CONCLUSIONS

Our system works well and has a very good feel. It's scalable to both large and small sizes, due to PCAP's need to connect only rows and columns (which scale linearly), while the touch surface area scales as thee square.

When designing such a fast, low-latency system, we found it useful to think in terms of radio frequency design (transmission lines, signal strength, cross-talk, modulation) instead of slower, precision electronic design (capacitors, charge, electric field). Although both terminologies can be used to describe the same physical implementation, we believe that the former mindset helped to influence our design decisions to meet our goals more rapidly and with a better final outcome. FMT's rows and columns, above a ground plane, are in effect leaky transmission lines between which a finger can induce cross-talk.

FUTURE WORK

Although our demonstration surface is opaque and uses front-projection, we realize that many practical commercial products will require a transparent touch surface on top of an LCD or OLED display, as might be found on a mobile computing device. We are currently working toward a transparent version that will provide one-millisecond class performance with existing (or perhaps optimized) ITO and metal mesh touch sensors, despite their lower conductivity.

If multiple users are touching the surface at the same time, it would be useful to disambiguate one user's set of touches from the others'. This would allow proper recognition of multi-finger gestures by each user. We believe that it would be possible to implement such a capability by taking advantage of residual row signals that travel through a user's body, from each of their touching fingers to the others. We are actively investigating this area.

We are also researching the possibility of including an active stylus capability, in which the stylus transmits its own compatible set of orthogonal signals to the touch surface. We believe that this might be a method of providing a very rich, multimodal input experience, including extremely low latency.

The current FMT demonstrator is bulky and power hungry, consuming nine watts (not including the high-speed projector). We are working to move the technology onto an ASIC, which would permit ultra-low latency touch capability in a much smaller form factor that consumes much less energy. We are also investigating power saving features that would allow FMT to be used on even highly constrained battery-powered devices.

One of our goals for future work is attempting to determine if virtual interaction, implemented with a low-latency touch sensor and display, can sufficiently imitate a real-world physical interaction to fool an observer. We call this the "Touch Turing Test", because it is analogous to Alan Turing's famous thought experiment on how to determine if a computer can be considered "intelligent" [14]. In our case, we wish to test how closely virtual interactions can come to their real world counterparts. We believe that this is important because the human mind evolved with the constraints of the physical world and is more accustomed to these natural types of interaction. User interfaces designed with this in mind may behave in better and more interesting ways.

ACKNOWLEDGMENTS

We would like to acknowledge and thank Rick Raffanti of Techne Instruments, who put together the FMT sensor demonstrator, and Alex Rodionov of the University of Toronto, who programmed the high speed DLP projector to visualize the output of our sensor.

REFERENCES

[1] R. Jota, A. Ng, P. Dietz and D. Wigdor, "How fast is fast enough?: a study of the effects of latency in direct-touch pointing tasks" in *Proceedings of the SIGCHI Conference on Human Factors in Computing Systems (CHI '13)*, 2013.

[2] A. Ng, J. Lepinski, D. Wigdor, S. Sanders and P. Dietz, "Designing for Low-Latency Direct-Touch Input" in *Proceedings of UIST 2012*, Boston, MA, 2012.

[3] F. Bérard and R. Blanch, "Two touch system latency estimators: high accuracy and low overhead" in *Proceedings of the 2013 ACM international conference on Interactive tabletops and surfaces (ITS '13)*, New York, NY, 2013.

[4] E. Johnson, "Touch display–a novel input/output device for comuters" *Electronic Letters,* vol. 1, no. 8, pp. 219-220, 1965.

[5] S. Lee, W. Buxton and K. Smith, "A Multi-Touch Three Dimensional Touch-Sensitive Tablet" in *ACM CHI*, 1985.

[6] J. Rekimoto, "SmartSkin: an infrastructure for freehand manipulation on interactive surfaces" in *Proceedings of the SIGCHI Conference on Human Factors in Computing Systems (CHI '02)*, 2002.

[7] W. Westerman, Hand Tracking, Finger Identification, and Chrodic Manipulation on a Multi-Touch Surface, University of Delaware, 1999.

[8] P. Dietz and D. Leigh, "DiamondTouch: a multi-user touch technology" in *Proceedings of the 14th annual ACM symposium on User interface software and technology (UIST '01)*, 2001.

[9] N. Mehta, Flexible Machine Interface, Toronto: University of Toronto, 1982.

[10] J. Han, "Low-cost multi-touch sensing through frustrated total internal reflection" in *Proceedings of the 18th annual ACM symposium on User interface software and technology (UIST '05)*, 2005.

[11] P. McAvinney, The Sensor Frame - A Gesture-Based Device for the Manipulation of Graphic Objects., Carnegie-Mellon University, 1985.

[12] J. Moeller and A. Kerne, "ZeroTouch: an optical multi-touch and free-air interaction architecture" in *ACMCHI*, 2012.

[13] CASPER: "Collaboration for Astronomy Signal Processing and Electronics Research" [Online]. Available: `https://casper.berkeley.edu/`.

[14] A. Turing, "Computing Machinery and Intelligence" in *Mind, 59*, 1950, pp. 433-460.

GaussStones: Shielded Magnetic Tangibles for Multi-Token Interactions on Portable Displays

Rong-Hao Liang*† Han-Chih Kuo* Liwei Chan‡ De-Nian Yang§ Bing-Yu Chen‡
*‡National Taiwan University †§Academia Sinica
*{howieliang,andikan}@cmlab.csie.ntu.edu.tw
‡{liweichan,robin}@ntu.edu.tw §dnyang@iis.sinica.edu.tw

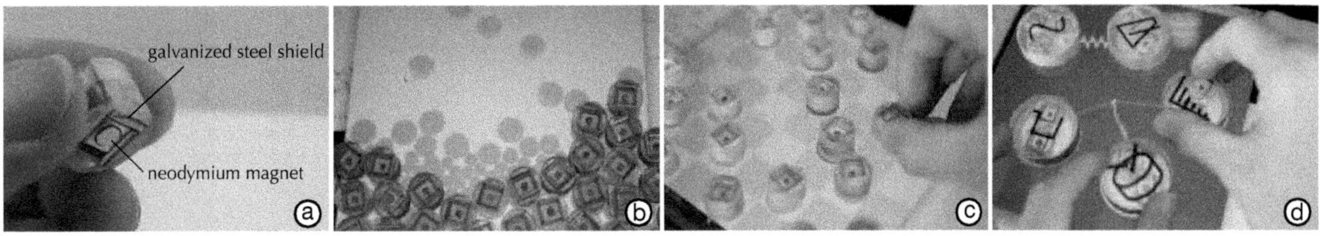

Figure 1. (a) GaussStones are magnetic tangibles with magnetic shielding that eliminates interference between magnetic tangibles and enables various multi-token applications on portable displays, including (b) sculpting and simulation, (c) board gaming, and (d) live music performance.

ABSTRACT
This work presents *GaussStones*, a system of shielded magnetic tangibles design for supporting multi-token interactions on portable displays. Unlike prior works in sensing magnetic tangibles on portable displays, the proposed tangible design applies magnetic shielding by using an inexpensive galvanized steel case, which eliminates interference between magnetic tangibles. An analog Hall-sensor grid can recognize the identity of each shielded magnetic unit since each unit generates a magnetic field with a specific intensity distribution and/or polarization. Combining multiple units as a knob further allows for resolving additional identities and their orientations. Enabling these features improves support for applications involving multiple tokens. Thus, using prevalent portable displays provides generic platforms for tangible interaction design.

Author Keywords
Magnetism; Tangible Interactions; Portable Display; GaussSense; Analog Hall-Sensor Grid

ACM Classification Keywords
H.5.2. [Information Interfaces and Presentation (e.g. HCI)]: User Interfaces

INTRODUCTION
Prevalent portable displays provide tangible interaction experiences for users by tracking physical objects. In addition to traditional vision- and capacitive-based object tracking methods, researchers have begun exploiting magnetic object tracking in tangible interaction designs for several reasons. First, since magnetics can provide signals for 3D tracking without batteries and micro-controllers, magnetic tracking sensors are easily maintained and constantly available. Moreover, magnetic tracking sensors such as magnetometers [8] and analog Hall sensor grids [15] are highly portable and easily retrofitted to existing devices without hardware modifications. Object tracking mechanisms can track multiple objects on, above, and around devices with high robustness and high responsiveness [8, 14]. These promising features enhance the potential applications of tangibles in interactive surfaces.

However, since nearby magnetics naturally repel or attract each other, a general limitation of magnetic tangibles is the shortage of supporting applications that involve multiple tokens. To compensate, additional mechanisms may be needed to fix them to the surface, e.g., by using glue [8], adding weight [14], attaching friction pad to the bottom of token [14], or attracting the magnetic token to a ferro-surface [12]. Adding these mechanism on the tokens not only reduces freedom of control, but also constrains the tangible interaction design.

GaussStones: Shielded Magnetic Tangibles
This work presents GaussStones (Figure 1), a system of shielded magnetic tangibles, which solves the above problems in analog Hall-sensor grid tracking and in portable display object tracking. Unlike prior works [14], each GaussStone is shielded with a case made of inexpensive but highly permeable metals (e.g., galvanized steel), which isolates its magnetic field and prevents interference with others on the surface. Each GaussStone provides a sufficiently strong magnetic field as a signal source that the sensor grid can use to identify its position and orientation. Each GaussStone can be

UIST 2014, October 5–8, 2014, Honolulu, HI, USA.

http://dx.doi.org/10.1145/2642918.2647384

differentiated by its magnetic polarity and/or intensity distributions. Therefore, the system can support multi-token applications in portable displays, including sculpting and simulation, board gaming, and live music performance.

The proposed shielded magnetic tangible design uses numerous small but easily identifiable tokens in portable displays to facilitate space-multiplexed input. Moreover, the small token size allows users to perform embodied gestures such as gathering the particles (tokens) on the portable displays in haptic-rich ways that can be detected precisely by the system. The tokens have the same benefits of magnetic tangibles, i.e., they can be robustly sensed without contact, even when occluded or in darkness. Thus, they can provide continuous and satisfiable user experiences.

The rest of the paper is organized as follows. First, related work is discussed. Magnetic shielding principles are then explained, and the design space of this technique is explored. The proposed design for magnetic tangibles and its applications are then introduced. Finally, possible generalizations and limitations of this technique are discussed.

RELATED WORK

Tabletop tangible user interfaces enable simultaneous two-handed and multi-user by providing multiple tangibles in the interactive surface applications [9], such as board gaming [2], music editing [11], and particle-based simulations [18]. In these applications, users can rapidly access binding information and computational models by grasping and manipulating physical tokens [21], which provide immediate and realistic haptic feedback for users on the afforded 3D gestures.

Recent studies have attempted to apply advanced object tracking capability in prevalent portable platforms. The primary object tracking method uses a capacitive multitouch panel for object tracking [19, 5]. TUIC [24] presented capacitance tag designs for identifying different tangibles by passive 2D patterns or by active 1D frequency patterns. A method of disambiguating the capacitance tag and user finger touch was also proposed for each tag type. In Capstones [4], combinations of stacked tangibles can be identified by mapping the combinations to different 2D marker. The PUCs [22] further demonstrated the feasibility of detecting capacitive tangibles without touch. Transparency is achieved by applying indium tin oxide (ITO) coatings. These works demonstrated the successful use of capacitance tags for identifying multiple objects or individual objects. However, since most current portable platforms are mainly used for sensing finger touch and regard touch as a binary event, they cannot effectively discriminate touch and objects by single touch point. Therefore, they have additional space requirements (passive 2D pattern) or power requirements (active frequency tag) [24] for disambiguating different tags and finger touches. These additional requirements hamper the multi-token interactions on small portable displays.

Methods other than capacitive tracking include SenseTable [17], which was implemented in a tangible workbench by using an electromagnetic resonance (EMR)[1] sensor. EMR sensor has recently been embedded mobile devices to detect a passive stylus[2]. The PICO [16] further uses LC-Tag tracking technologies to simplify puck designs for multi-token tracking. However, since most conventional portable displays do not support EMR- and LC-tag sensing, these systems are difficult to implement in portable displays. Since most of portable displays have a built-in magnetometer, Magnetic Appcessories [3] and MagGetz [8] used the magnetometer to identify and sense multiple magnetic widgets on and around the display. Although magnetometers are highly portable, widgets requires calibration before use, and the positions of tangibles must be fixed, which reduces the degree of freedom.

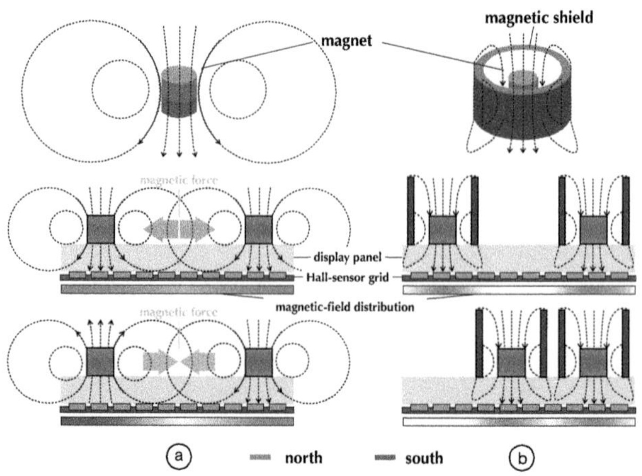

Figure 2. Visualization of magnetic forces and magnetic fields (a) without magnetic shield and (b) with magnetic shield.

Imaging sensors such as optical cameras or analog Hall-sensor grids can also be used to enhance the object tracking capability of portable displays and do not require hardware modifications. Portico [1] mounted two cameras above a display to track visual markers on a screen and on the surrounding surface. Top-down detection methods were sensitive to environmental light and hand occlusion, which limited the form factors of the token and degraded the user experience. Although the occlusion and lighting issues can be mitigated by back-of-device or in-cell optical sensing methods, e.g., ThinSight [10] and MightyTrace [7], which can track multiple on-screen tangibles attached to reflexive markers on its bottom, e.g., SLAP [23], these technologies require considerable hardware modifications.

The GaussSense [15] analog Hall-sensor grid is a portable and occlusion-free imaging sensor that enables monitoring of multiple magnetic tangibles on and above a portable display [14]. It resolves the geometry of a construction of multiple magnetic building blocks in real-time [13] and can be easily attached to the back of a portable display. However, magnetic forces raise issues of interference and identification in multi-token applications. Figure 2a shows that several magnetic tangibles placed on a display surface tend to attract or repel each other, which impedes user interactions. The magnetic fields also merge with or counteract each other,

[1] http://www.wacom.com/

[2] http://www.samsung.com/

which invalidates the sensing of position, orientation, and ID information. Proposed solutions such as using non-ferrous constraints or adding weight and friction pads on the bottom of tangibles to separate the magnets from each other [14] increase the size and weight of the tokens, which is inappropriate for small portable displays and multi-token applications. Hence, multi-token applications must be composed of a new material.

UNDERSTANDING MAGNETIC SHIELDING

Principles of Magnetic Shielding

Multi-token interactions are facilitated by using magnetic shielding to mitigate interference between magnetic tangibles. Magnetic shielding is widely used to protect electronic components from electromagnetic (EM) interference. However, thin magnetic shields cannot effectively block magnetostatic fields, which have stronger penetrability. Therefore, the most effective way to shield magnetostatic fields is by *redirecting* them rather than by blocking them.

Eliminating this interference required a case composed of highly permeable material, such as galvanized steel, mu-metal, etc. In this study, the magnet was affixed to the inside of the case as shown in Figure 2b. The case absorbed magnetic fields by attracting nearby magnetic flux, which allowed the flux to flow through the surface of the case and prevented the magnetic flux from penetrating. The magnetic shield enabled magnetic objects to be placed close to each other without affecting the signal quality or the physical state.

In addition to using highly permeable materials, another important factor is the geometry design of the shields. An inappropriate geometric design may fail to eliminate interference and may even block signals and make them invisible to magnetic field sensors. To understand how to provide a shielding mechanism that effectively maintains the quality of the signal source, a series of formal measurements were performed to establish parameters for an effective shielded magnetic tangible design.

Explorative Study

Apparatus

According to the definition of shielding factor in [20], shielding capability depends on the dimensions of the shield. Figure 3a shows the nine different shielded magnetic token types that were measured. The tokens were 1.5cm(W)×1.5cm(H) acrylic cuboids, each of which contained a N35-class neodymium magnet (radius, 2.5mm; height, 1cm). The magnets were fixed to the acrylic cases. Several 1.5mm(W)×1.5mm(H) galvanized steel chips were cut from 1.2mm-, 2mm-, or 3mm-thick galvanized steel sheets and attached to the tokens to provide shielding. Since only two of the six faces were shielded, the shapes of the magnetic fields could be observed on the unshielded faces.

Figure 3b shows the 32×32 = 1024 Winson[3] WSH138 analog Hall sensors with a 16(W)×16(H) cm^2 sensing area, which were mounted as a grid to capture the magnetic-field image of the shielded magnetic tokens. Each sensor element detects

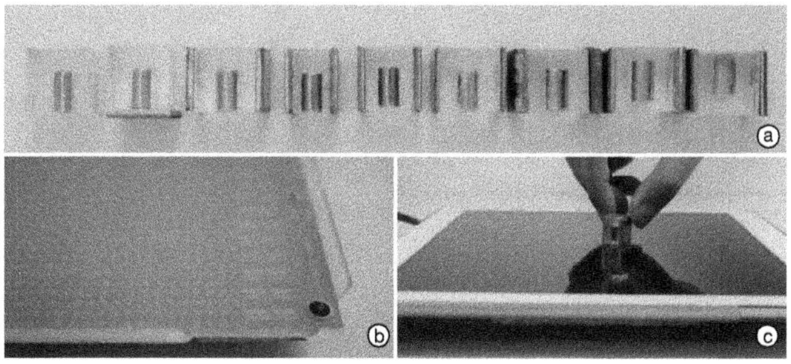

Figure 3. (a) Shielded tokens for testing. (b) Analog Hall-sensor grid. (c) Measurement platform.

both N- and S-polar magnetic field intensities in a range from 0 to 200 gauss on a 256-point scale and at a sampling rate consistently higher than 40 fps. The N- and S-polar magnetic fields at each sample point are mapped to a red or blue color intensity of the corresponding pixel on a 310 px×310 px bitmap, respectively. The sensitivity of the Hall-sensor grid is calibrated using the method presented in [13]. The analog Hall-sensor grid is attached to the back of a 7.9mm-thick iPad Air tablet (Figure 3c). Alternatively, a 3mm-thick acrylic sheet can be used as the measurement platform.

Task and Procedures

The measurement was performed in two parts. The first part measures the magnetic fields horizontal to the magnetic dipole vector. After the shielded tokens were laid down, the tokens on the 3mm-thick acrylic sheet are measured. The second part was measuring the magnetic fields vertical to the magnetic dipole vector. After the shielded magnetic tokens were erected, the tokens on the iPad Air were measured. Each unit was measured by arbitrarily moving it on the surface of the 16×16 cm^2 sensing area. For each unit measured, 1000 samples were captured. The analysis included 2 (parts) × 9 (units) × 1000 (samples) = 18000 bitmaps of magnetic-field images.

Data Processing

The distribution of the magnetic fields was observed by using several thresholds of magnetic field intensity for N(orth) and S(outh) fields, $T_{N,i}$ and $T_{S,i}$, where $T_{x,i} = T_{x,i-1}+10$ gauss for all $i > 0$ and $x \in \{N,S\}$, to extract the corresponding N-pole and S-pole blobs from the magnetic field image. For each sample, the blob size and maximum N-field and S-field intensities were recorded.

Results and Findings

Figure 4 to Figure 7 show the complete results. For all samples, the x-y plane plots the mean values and ranges for two standard deviations of blob sizes. The horizontal axis plots the means and the range of two standard deviations of N-field and S-field intensity. This format is used to visualize the implementation throughout the following discussion. In addition to the statistical data are the sample raw data, which are aligned and visualized underneath the token, to illustrate further information that is not shown in the statistics. Based on the results, the four main findings of the study and guidelines for designing shielded magnetic tangibles are summarized.

[3]http://www.winson.com.tw/

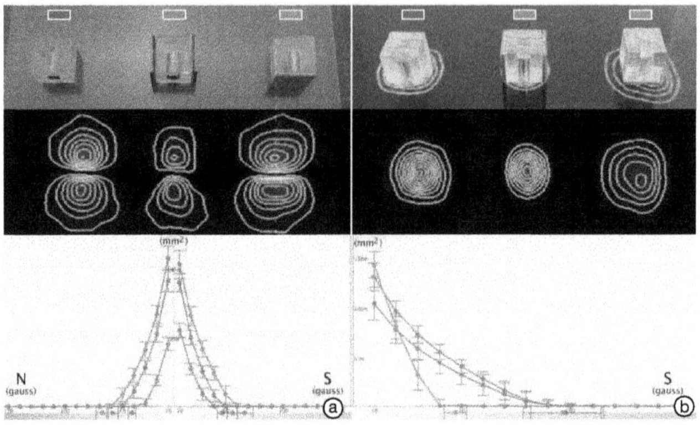

Figure 4. Experimental results for different shielding methods. (Blue) Un-shielded. (Orange) Shielded on the side. (Green) Shielded on the bottom. The distributions of magnetic fields as sensed and visualized from (a) the sides of the tokens, and (b) the bottoms of the tokens.

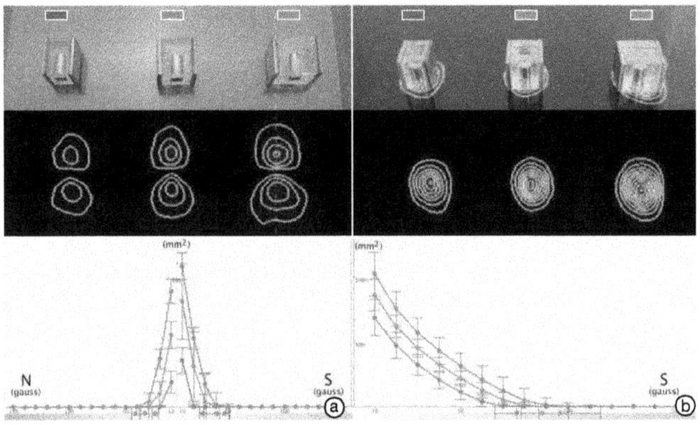

Figure 5. Experimental results of different gap distances between the magnet and the shield. (Blue) 2mm (Green) 3.5mm (Orange) 5mm. Distributions of magnetic fields] sensed and visualized from (a) the sides of the tokens, and (b) the bottoms of the tokens.

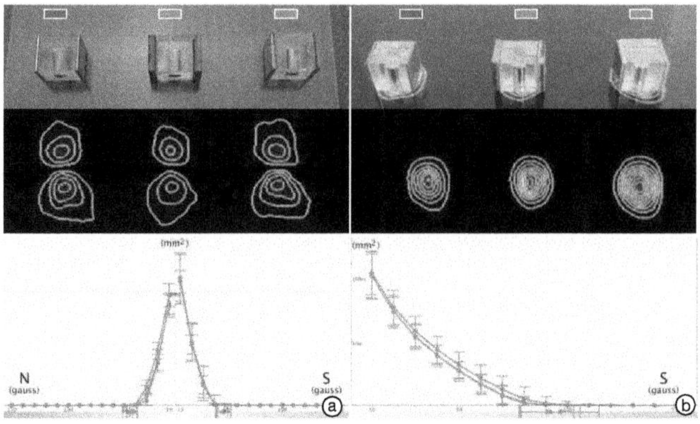

Figure 6. Experimental results for different shield thicknesses (Blue) 1.2mm-thick. (Green) 3mm-thick. (Orange) 2mm-thick. The distribution of magnetic fields as sensed and visualized from (a) the sides of the tokens, and (b) the bottoms of the tokens.

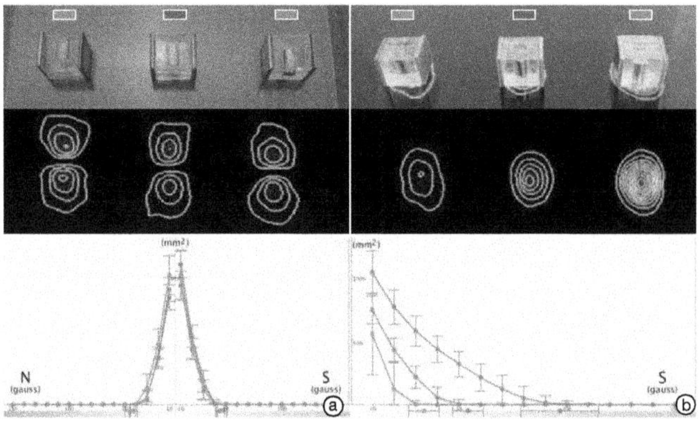

Figure 7. Experimental results for different vertical distances between the magnet and the sensor: (Green) 5mm, (Blue) 2.5mm and (Orange) 0mm from the bottom. The distributions of magnetic fields as sensed and visualized from (a) the sides of the tokens, and (b) the bottoms of the tokens.

1. The shield should be in parallel to the magnetic dipole. Figure 4 shows that the shielding is highly effective when it is parallel to the dipole vector of the magnet, and signal strength is unaffected if the shield is an adequate distance with the magnet. In contrast, the shielding is ineffective when the shield is directly attracted by the dipole of the magnet, which also reduces signal strength.

2. Decreasing the gap between the magnet and the shield reduces signal strength. Figure 5 shows that decreasing the gap significantly reduces the blob sizes in both measurements, which confirms the effectiveness of the mechanism. The experimental results show that a user can make smaller shielded magnetic tokens by using smaller shields. The results also imply that the magnet should be positioned horizontal to the center of a token to ensure the similar capability of shielding in all directions. Nonetheless, as the gap distance decreased, the signal strengths significantly decreased as well. Consequently, stronger or larger magnets may be needed to compensate for the loss of signal strength.

3. Increasing the shield thickness improves shielding quality without affecting the signal strength. Figure 6 shows that the shield thickness does not significantly affect the blob size or signal strength. However, the raw data indicate that a thicker shield is better in terms of locking the magnetic fields even though the blob size does not decrease in statistics. The experimental results suggest that, if the shielded tokens must be placed very close to strong magnets in the shield, thicker shields are preferable.

4. Stuffing magnets deep inside the shield does not affect shielding but reduces the signal strength. Figure 7 shows that stuffing magnets deep inside the shield does not affect shielding strength. However, since it substantially reduces signal strength, larger or stronger magnets may be needed. Therefore, rather than increasing the depth of the magnets, positioning a small magnet as close as possible to the surface would be more effective way to control token size as well as the signal strength.

Summary

This study explored several possible design parameters, excluded several inefficient parameters, and identified shield dimension, shield thickness, and magnet strength as efficient parameters when designing shielded magnetic tangibles. Small shielded magnetic tangibles require both stronger

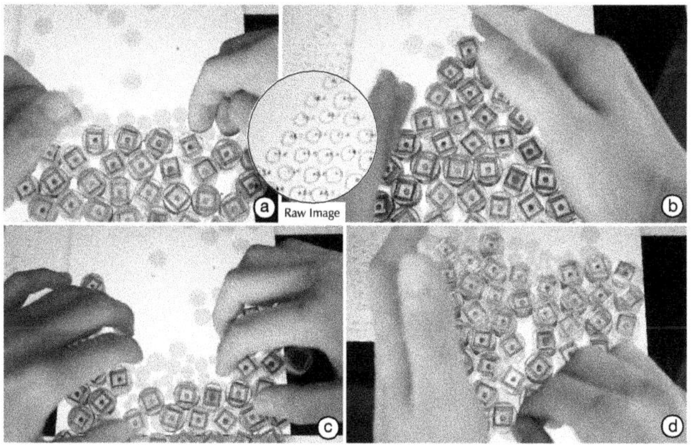

Figure 8. (a) For sculpting and simulation applications, users can shape the particles by 3D hand gestures such as (b) building a mountain, (c) digging a valley, or (d) making favorable shape. Simulation results respond to the shape in real time.

magnets and thicker shields to keep both shielding and signal valid. This requirement is a design constraint in shielded magnetic tokens. In contrast, large shielded magnetic tokens have relatively few constraints and allow for adjustment of the relationships between shield dimensions and thicknesses to create different magnetic field distributions or intensities for advanced sensing. The next section introduces the design and application of the smallest token design and then gradually relaxes the size constraint to provide a larger design space.

DESIGNING GAUSSSTONES IN DIFFERENT SIZES

This section introduces designs for different-size GaussStones to fit the requirements of different applications. The three categories of GaussStone designs are 1) particles, 2) tokens, and 3) knobs. An iPad Air and a macbook pro display with a 2mm-thick analog Hall-sensor grid attached to the back are used for presentation.

Designing GaussStones as Particles

Small particles can support applications that requires fine manipulation, such as sculpting [6] or geographic simulation [18]. Figure 1a shows the smallest shielded magnetic particle obtained for the presentation platform (radius, 7.8mm; height, 10mm; weight, 6g). Inside the particle is a 1cm×1cm cuboid shield composed of 4 pieces of 2mm-thick rectangular galvanized steel sheet. Inside the shield is a 2mm-radius(W)×5mm-radius(H) cylindrical neodymium magnet, which is fixed to the center bottom of the shield by a laser-cut acrylic case. The shielded magnet is encapsulated in a 7.8mm-radius×1cm-height acrylic cylinder, which functions not only as a safety gap to ensure reliable detection, but also as a favorable shape for manipulation.

Sensing the particle position

The system tracks the on-screen position of the particles by analyzing the obtained bi-polar magnetic field image. A noise intensity threshold is first used to separate all connected components and remove the unwanted noises. All connected components are then extracted from the magnetic field image regardless of the polarization. The centroid of each component is used to represent a particle position.

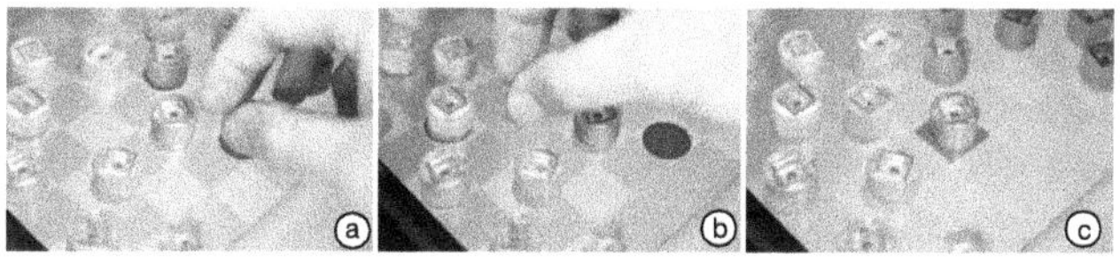

Figure 9. (a) In a checkers game, two types of tokens, S-type (blue) and N-type (red), are clearly distinguishable. (b) When the token is lifted, the display provides hints for the possible landing position and the possible threats from the opponent. (c) Visual hint for removing the defeated piece.

Application: Sculpting and Simulation

The sculpting and simulation application (Figure 8) allows a user to place a maximum of 100 particles in the sensing and display area. In the display area, users gather bunches of particles and use their hands to shape the particles into terrain features such as mountains or valleys. Then, users can activate the raining simulation, letting the raindrops fall into the built terrain. As the user changes the terrain, such as separating the valley to let the rain drain away, the simulation responds in real time. Since the particles are physical, sculpting with tangible particles provides useful haptic feedback. Users can perform the task naturally or freely improvise as they would in the physical world.

Designing GaussStones as Tokens

The two polarities of each magnet have the same intensity. Hence, simply flipping the magnet within the particle creates a paired set of data, which requires no modification on the geometry design of the shield. The token position is sensed using the same method used to sense particles, but the polarization, North and South, is now used to recognize the tokens as N- and S-type, respectively.

Application: Board Gaming

In a checkers game (Figure 9), 12 S-type tokens and 12 N-type tokens are placed on each side of the checker board. In each round, the player grasps the tokens to move diagonally from one square to another square. When a token is lifted from the display, the system gives a visual hint for the possible positions and possible threats of opposing pieces on the display. If the opponent places a piece in the wrong position, the system ignores the move and continues waiting for the right player to put his/her piece on it. When a player jumps over an opposing piece, the system recognizes the move and prompts the user to remove the defeated piece to move the game forward. The same concept is applicable to board games that use only two token types, e.g., Othello, Abalon, Gomoku, etc.

Identification Using Magnetic Field Intensity Distribution

For applications that require tokens that contain or represent information, the tokens require features for identifying themselves. Small field shapes and intensities of particles are too weak to carry additional ID information. Using stronger magnets or using thinner shields can increase the magnetic field intensity, but also reduces the effectiveness of the shielding. Hence, another finding of the exploratory study is that a larger token is needed.

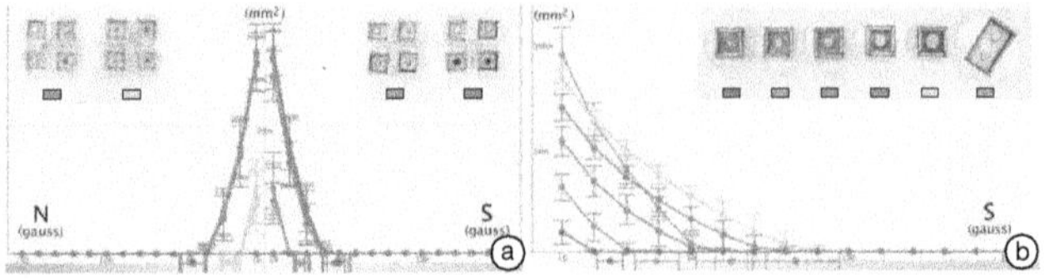

Figure 10. Area-intensity profiles of the two sets of ID. (a) Sixteen 8.6mm-radius tokens are clearly classified into four IDs. The area-intensity profiles of tokens in the same ID are very similar. (b) Five S-type 12mm-radius tokens and one 15mm-radius token are clearly differentiated into six IDs.

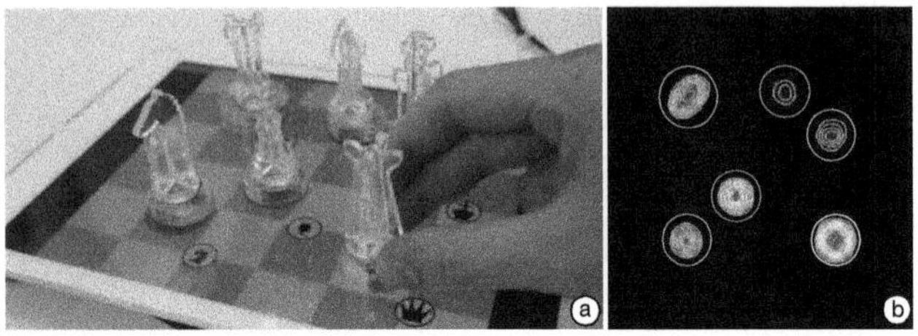

Figure 11. Chess game. (a) All chess types of a player are represented by six S-type tokens. (b) Image of corresponding magnetic field, which is locked inside each token.

Therefore, two sets of GaussStone designs were implemented to test the concept of coding additional IDs by using magnetic field intensity and shape. Figure 10a shows the first set, which has a 8.6mm-radius and consists of a 1.1cm×1.1cm cuboid shield made of 1.2mm-thick rectangular galvanized steel sheet. Two types of cylindrical magnets (height, 5mm with radius, 1.5 and 2mm) are stuffed to provide 2 intensities. The application of this token type is discussed in the next section (Figure 13a). The second set, which has a radius of 12 mm, consists of a 1.4cm×1.4cm cuboid shield made of 2mm-thick rectangular galvanized steel sheet. Five types of magnets can be stuffed (height, 5mm and radius, 1.5,2,2.5,3,3.5mm) to provide five distinguishable blob sizes (note that the intensities of the five types are not fully distinguishable), as shown in Figure 10b. The cylinders in both GaussStone types are 1cm-high. By building the token in two polarities, the two token types can provide 4 and 10 IDs.

Beside magnetic-field intensity, the magnetic field shape is another potential dimension of ID design. The rectangular shield in Figure 10b fixed two nearby magnets in it creates a magnetic field with a new shape and a unique distribution of blob areas, which are easily differentiated from the tokens consisting of only one magnet. This unique *area-intensity profile* allows the system to classify and identify tokens. (Figure 11) shows that six IDs for both N- and S-type are sufficient for playing a chess game.

Identifying Tokens Using Area-Intensity Profile

Figure 10a shows that magnetic tokens with the same specifications have similar distributions of magnetic field intensity, thus are regarded as the same class. After selecting one token from each class, the same data collection and processing method introduced in EXPLORATIVE STUDY was applied to obtain 1000 samples. In each sample, several different thresholds were used to extract the blobs, and the sizes of the blobs were calculated. For each threshold, the mean blob size and standard deviation were calculated for all samples. Figure 10 shows the area-intensity profiles for the classes of ID, which were based on the obtained mean and standard deviations.

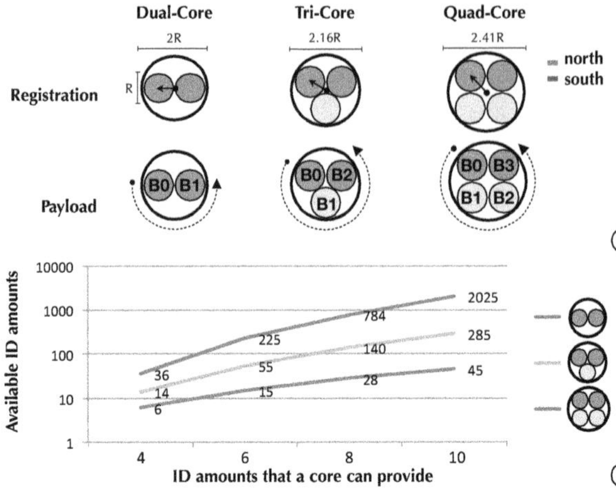

Figure 12. (a) The ID methods for the dual-, tri-, and quad-cores knobs. (b) Available number of IDs according to number of cores and number of IDs provided by a core.

After a token is placed on the display platform and the sensed intensity value stabilizes, the system finds the profile most similar to that of the current token and assigns the ID of the profile to the token. Once the token is identified, it allows for near-surface interactions such as hover [14]. The ID is kept until the token is removed away from the display surface. Based on the simple classification mechanism used herein, all tokens presented in the applications were reliably recognized with near-zero false recognition rate.

Designing GaussStones as Knobs

In addition to 1D and 2D translation, tokens that support 1D rotation can function as knobs to provide an additional 1 degree of control. The knob was easily built by combining shielded magnetic cores as shown in Figure 12a.

Since the magnetic cores inside the knob do not affect each other, each of them can function as an unique payload bit. Combining at least two payload bits provides a feature for registering the location and orientation of the ID. The location is defined by the centroid O of the inscribed circle of the combination. After that, the representative target B_0, for example, the magnetic core which has the smallest value $v = I_N - I_S$, where I_N and I_S are the maximum intensities in N- and S-fields, respectively, is used to define the orientation of the knob as $\vec{OB_0}$.

The magnetic cores also provide information used to identify the token. When the cores are identified, the system can extract the payload bits of the knob in a numerical series from B_0 to B_{k-1} in a k-core knob, as shown in Figure 12a. Each bit is reported as $n-1$ if the core has n-th largest value v. The ID of a k-core knob ID_{knob} then is decoded as:

$$ID_{knob} = \sum_{i=0}^{k-1} B_i * (N_{core})^i, \quad (1)$$

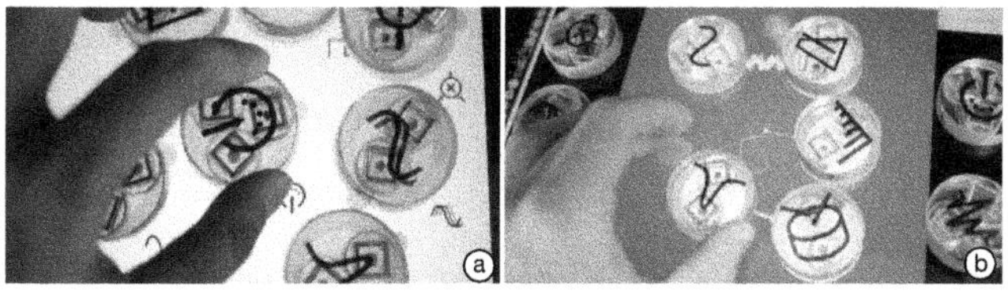

Figure 13. (a) Each dual-core and tri-core token provides its ID, position, and orientation information. (b) Live music performance application.

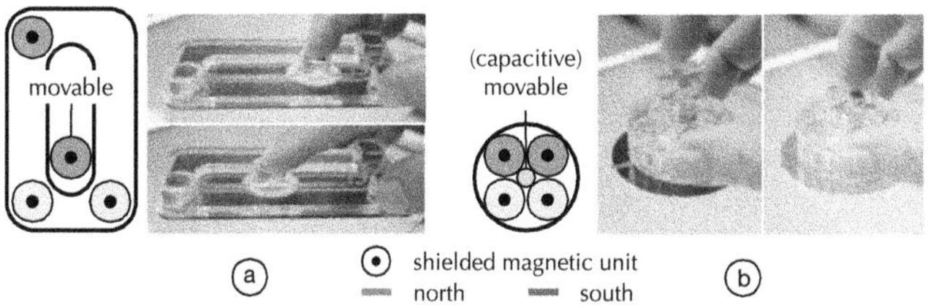

Figure 14. Two sample multi-part widget designs. (a) Slider. (b) Knob with a button.

where N_{core} denotes the number of IDs that a core can provide. However, since an asymmetric ID is needed to provide orientation information, the available ID amount N_k of k-core knobs can be derived as:

$$N_k = \sum_{i=1}^{N_{core}-1} (N_{core} - i)^{k-1}, \quad (2)$$

where N_{core} denotes the number of IDs that a core can provide. Notably, knobs with different numbers of cores have different ID spaces. Thus, they can be used simultaneously. Figure 12b shows that increasing the number of cores and the number of IDs that a core can provide both increase the ID space. Nevertheless, either increase would result in an increased token size. Designers can choose the suitable design based on the number of IDs required by the application.

Application: Live Music Performance

Figure 13 shows the music performance workbench, which was similar to ReacTable [11]. Twelve dual-core or tri-core knobs on the display represent different tools that can be used for controlling or synthesizing music. To add a patch, a music clip, or an effector into the show, the user can place the corresponding knob on the portable display, arrange the geometric relationships with other tokens, and rotate the knob to adjust the parameter. Multiple users can also stand near the portable display to jam and collaborate with each other.

DISCUSSION

Possible Generalizations

Designing GaussStones as Multi-Part Widgets

As in SLAP widgets [23], it is feasible to design GaussStones with multiple parts and with larger widgets that contain both ID and movable parts. Multi-part widget designs require shielded magnetic units in both ID and movable parts to avoid interactions between the two parts, as the slider design shown in Figure 14a. In capacitive multitouch displays, it is also feasible to make movable parts conductive and the ID part magnetic since the two sensing methods do not interact, as the knob with a button design shown in Figure 14b. Fusing conductive and magnetic parts for multi-part widget designs can further reduce the required widget size so that more widgets can be kept on the small display surface.

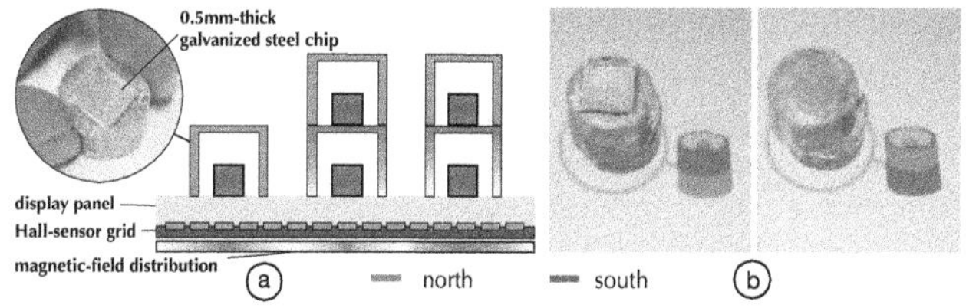

Figure 15. Stackable token design that allows for resolving stacking structures. (a) Visualization of magnetic fields. (b) Results.

Stacking GaussStones

Stackable GaussStones can also be built as GaussBricks [13] since stacked tokens with the varied magnetic-field strength can be used to identify stack operations. In stackable token design, the geometry alignment should be considered. Since the ferrous shielding may attract the magnetic core, and the magnets in different polarities can not attract to each other and cause unexpected results, users can add a thin (0.5mm-thick) galvanized steel chip (Figure 15a) on the top of the token to force the alignment. The stacking token magnetize the underlying token's galvanized steel chip and shield, strengthen or weaken its magnetic field strength according to the polarity. The increase or decrease of the sensed magnetic field strength thus can be used to identify the stacking token, as shown in Figure 15b. The system recognizes stacked structures by up to two layers. Similar to the knobs, combining multiple stackable cores as a unit allows for resolving additional identities while stacking.

Scalability and Limitation

The two main factors in the scalability of the proposed system are particle size and display platform thickness. Regarding particle size, given the fixed resolution of the Hall-sensor grid (26dpi before 10x up-sampling), a particle with a 7.8mm (0.3inch)-radius was the smallest valid particle for both shielding and sensing on the tested platform, 7.9mm-thick iPad Air. Using higher density sensor grids or thinner displays can obtain smaller particles by enabling use of smaller magnets and thinner shields. Regarding the thickness of presentation platform, the system effectively identified the particles and knobs on displays with thickness ranges of 0.3 - 1.0cm with calibration. Displays outside this range of thickness may require sensors with different sensitivities and/or magnets with different strengths. However, since using stronger magnets requires a stronger shielding mechanism, which increases the size and weight of tokens, the proposed technique should be applied in thin-form displays.

CONCLUSION

This work presented *GaussStones*, a system of shielded magnetic tangibles that improves support of multi-token applications by portable displays. The findings of this exploratory study showed that the range of design space of the shielded magnetic tangibles is relevant to the size of token. The use of different token sizes on portable displays was then discussed, including using GaussStones as particles for sculpting and simulation, using the identifiable GaussStones for board-gaming, and using rollable GaussStones for live music performances. These proposed applications are fundamental and essential to demonstrate the potential use of the proposed new magnetic-composite material, which unlocks new applications of tangible interaction design on portable displays.

ACKNOWLEGEMENTS

We sincerely acknowledge the helpful comments of the Associate Chairs and the anonymous reviewers. We also thank Fan Wang, Wei-Tse Lee, Shun-Yao Yang, and Li-Ming Yang for their assistances on implementation. This paper was partially supported by Ministry of Science and Technology, National Taiwan University and Intel Corporation under Grants MOST103-2221-E-002-158-MY3, NSC102-2911-I-002-001, and NTU103R7501.

REFERENCES

1. Avrahami, D., Wobbrock, J. O., and Izadi, S. Portico: tangible interaction on and around a tablet. In *Proc. UIST '11* (2011), 347–356.
2. Baudisch, P., Becker, T., and Rudeck, F. Lumino: tangible blocks for tabletop computers based on glass fiber bundles. In *Proc. CHI '10* (2010), 1165–1174.
3. Bianchi, A., and Oakley, I. Designing tangible magnetic appcessories. In *Proc. TEI '13* (2013), 255–258.
4. Chan, L., Müller, S., Roudaut, A., and Baudisch, P. CapStones and ZebraWidgets: sensing stacks of building blocks, dials and sliders on capacitive touch screens. In *Proc. CHI '12* (2012), 2189–2192.
5. Dietz, P., and Leigh, D. DiamondTouch: a multi-user touch technology. In *Proc. UIST '01* (2001), 219–226.
6. Follmer, S., Leithinger, D., Olwal, A., Cheng, N., and Ishii, H. Jamming user interfaces: Programmable particle stiffness and sensing for malleable and shape-changing devices. In *Proc. UIST '12* (2012), 519–528.
7. Hofer, R., Kaplan, P., and Kunz, A. Mightytrace: Multiuser tracking technology on lc-displays. In *Proc. CHI '08* (2008), 215–218.
8. Hwang, S., Ahn, M., and Wohn, K.-y. MagGetz: Customizable passive tangible controllers on and around conventional mobile devices. In *Proc. UIST '13* (2013), 411–416.
9. Ishii, H. Tangible bits: beyond pixels. In *Proc. TEI '08* (2008), xv–xxv.
10. Izadi, S., Hodges, S., Butler, A., Rrustemi, A., and Buxton, B. ThinSight: versatile multi-touch sensing for thin form-factor displays. In *Proc. UIST '07* (2007), 259–268.
11. Jordà, S., Geiger, G., Alonso, M., and Kaltenbrunner, M. The reactable: Exploring the synergy between live music performance and tabletop tangible interfaces. In *Proc. TEI '07* (2007), 139–146.
12. Leitner, J., and Haller, M. Geckos: combining magnets and pressure images to enable new tangible-object design and interaction. In *Proc. CHI '11* (2011), 2985–2994.
13. Liang, R.-H., Chan, L., Tseng, H.-Y., Kuo, H.-C., Huang, D.-Y., Yang, D.-N., and Chen, B.-Y. GaussBricks: Magnetic building blocks for constructive tangible interactions on portable displays. In *Proc. CHI '14* (2014), 3153–3162.
14. Liang, R.-H., Cheng, K.-Y., Chan, L., Peng, C.-X., Chen, M. Y., Liang, R.-H., Yang, D.-N., and Chen, B.-Y. GaussBits: Magnetic tangible bits for portable and occlusion-free near-surface tangible interactions. In *Proc. CHI '13* (2013), 1391–1400.
15. Liang, R.-H., Cheng, K.-Y., Su, C.-H., Weng, C.-T., Chen, B.-Y., and Yang, D.-N. GaussSense: Attachable stylus sensing using magnetic sensor grid. In *Proc. UIST '12* (2012), 319–326.
16. Patten, J., and Ishii, H. Mechanical constraints as computational constraints in tabletop tangible interfaces. In *Proc. CHI '07* (2007), 809–818.
17. Patten, J., Ishii, H., Hines, J., and Pangaro, G. Sensetable: A wireless object tracking platform for tangible user interfaces. In *Proc. CHI '01* (2001), 253–260.
18. Piper, B., Ratti, C., and Ishii, H. Illuminating clay: a 3-d tangible interface for landscape analysis. In *Proc. CHI '02* (2002), 355–362.
19. Rekimoto, J. SmartSkin: an infrastructure for freehand manipulation on interactive surfaces. In *Proc. CHI '02* (2002), 113–120.
20. Rikitake, T. *Magnetic and Electromagnetic Shielding*. Springer, 1987.
21. Tuddenham, P., Kirk, D., and Izadi, S. Graspables revisited: Multi-touch vs. tangible input for tabletop displays in acquisition and manipulation tasks. In *Proc. CHI '10* (2010), 2223–2232.
22. Voelker, S., Nakajima, K., Thoresen, C., Itoh, Y., Øvergård, K. I., and Borchers, J. PUCs: Detecting transparent, passive untouched capacitive widgets on unmodified multi-touch displays. In *Proc. ITS '13* (2013), 101–104.
23. Weiss, M., Wagner, J., Jansen, Y., Jennings, R., Khoshabeh, R., Hollan, J. D., and Borchers, J. SLAP widgets: bridging the gap between virtual and physical controls on tabletops. In *Proc. CHI '09* (2009), 481–490.
24. Yu, N.-H., Chan, L.-W., Lau, S. Y., Tsai, S.-S., Hsiao, I.-C., Tsai, D.-J., Hsiao, F.-I., Cheng, L.-P., Chen, M., Huang, P., and Hung, Y.-P. TUIC: enabling tangible interaction on capacitive multi-touch displays. In *Proc. CHI '11* (2011), 2995–3004.

Tag System with Low-Powered Tag and Depth Sensing Camera

Hiroyuki Manabe, Wataru Yamada, Hiroshi Inamura
Research Labs, NTT DOCOMO
3-6, Hikarinooka, Yokosuka, Kanagawa, Japan
{manabehiroyuki, wataruyamada}@acm.org, inamura@nttdocomo.com

ABSTRACT
A tag system is proposed that offers a practical approach to ubiquitous computing. It provides small and low-power tags that are easy to distribute; does not need a special device to read the tags (in the future), thus enabling their use anytime, anywhere; and has a wide reading range in angle and distance that extends the design space of tag-based applications. The tag consists of a kind of liquid crystal (LC) and a retroreflector, and it sends its ID by switching the LC. A depth sensing camera that emits infrared (IR) is used as the tag reader; we assume that it will be part of the user's everyday devices, such as a smartphone. Experiments were conducted to confirm its potential, and a regular IR camera was also tested for comparison. The results show that the tag system has a wide readable range in terms of both distance (up to 8m) and viewing angle offset. Several applications were also developed to explore the design space. Finally, limitations of the current setup and possible improvements are discussed.

Author Keywords
Tag; liquid crystal; PDLC; depth sensing camera; AR

ACM Classification Keywords
H.5.2. Information Interfaces and Presentation (e.g. HCI): User Interfaces

INTRODUCTION
Linking real objects to on-line information is one of the key functions of ubiquitous computing. It is essential in various applications such as augmented reality (AR) and location or posture estimation from object(s) that have information. Many studies have tackled marker-less object and scene recognition [8, 15, 23], but tags are still the best approach for linking objects to their information because they offer low cost, robustness, and quick recognition. The priority of tag specifications (such as physical size, information size, cost, readable distance, visibility, and directionality) strongly depends on the application. For example, barcodes attached to low-cost products should be extremely cheap, tags used to prevent object loss should be able to determine distances precisely, and tags used for AR should have acceptable readable distances and accurate directionality.

UIST '14, October 05 - 08 2014, Honolulu, HI, USA
Copyright is held by the owner/author(s). Publication rights licensed to ACM.
ACM 978-1-4503-3069-5/14/10...$15.00.
http://dx.doi.org/10.1145/2642918.2647404

Since users can now easily access displays anytime, anywhere in the form of smartphones and head mounted displays (HMDs), the impact of AR applications is increasing in everyday life. As one example, consider a user searching for a specific book from among many on a bookshelf. Ubiquitous technologies should shorten the search time, but current technologies give only limited benefits. For example, visual tags require the camera to be placed near them, but the user has to move the camera to scan all books. An RFID tag on a book offers identification even if the tag is several meters from the reader, but directionality is poor and the user still needs to search visually. Light-based tags, such as LED or LC-based tags, are another candidate. LED-based tags, unfortunately, require large batteries, making it impractical to attach a tag to each book. LC-based tags with retroreflectors require little power to operate, but they also require a special reader with a light emitter. Due to such technical limitations, no current ubiquitous technology can effectively support book search applications. Clearly the design space of ubiquitous applications will be expanded by overcoming the existing limitations and realizing tiny tags that can be attached to the widest range of objects and provide readable distances of up to several meters with excellent directionality.

It is also essential that the tag reading system can be based on any of the user's everyday devices rather than dedicated devices. Since the launch of Kinect [3], the cost and size of depth sensing cameras have been decreasing dramatically. This tendency will continue, and depth sensing capability will come to be offered by many devices. Assuming that the user's everyday devices, such as smartphones, have depth sensing cameras, the tag system proposed here offers a practical approach to linking objects to their information by using the cameras and LC-based tags.

RELATED WORK

Tags
Many visual tags already surround us; for example, barcodes on product packages and 2D codes, such as QR codes [6], can transmit information. These printed codes are low cost, easy to implement, and do not require any power supply, which are all highly desirable attributes. They are used in various interaction applications, such as AR [13, 29, 31] and indoor mapping [22]. Since the information is encoded spatially in

such tags, it has to occupy several tens of pixels in the captured image. This makes it difficult to recognize tags at long distances. Moreover, regular visual tags cannot be read in dark environments. Printed tags tend to be visually disruptive since they are clearly artificial. Invisible tags [22] ease these concerns, but others remain.

Wireless tag systems including RFID, Bluetooth, and WiFi tags offer many advantages such as small size and robustness against visible occlusion and are readily implemented because many smartphones can already read them. They are being used for not only interaction [26, 32] but also localization [16, 30]. Although several methods can estimate the spatial relationship between the tag and reader, directionality is limited, which does not satisfy our assumed applications such as book searching.

Light communication is a different approach, and LED-based tagging techniques have been proposed [18, 19]. While a regular visual tag encodes information spatially, light communication uses temporal encoding, so that the LED works even if it occupies only one pixel on the captured image, which greatly extends readable distance and practicality. While RFID tags have poor directionality, light communication offers accurate directionality. These characteristics suit AR applications. Unfortunately however, active light sources consume too much power, which increases tag size. Moreover, readable angular range is limited due to the narrow beam angle of LEDs. The power consumption can be reduced by high-speed switching, but this requires a high-speed camera as a reader. Several techniques use photosensitive tags and encode the light emitted by the external light source [17, 26, 27]. However, these tags require some power to record and decode the light and send the result instead of emitting light, making the tag difficult to miniaturize. LC shutters with retroreflectors can be used instead of LEDs [21, 24, 34]. Thanks to their low power consumption, the LC shutters can be driven by a photovoltaic (PV) module [21] or the energy supplied by a RFID reader [24]. While a regular LC attenuates light by more than 50% even when it is transparent, polymer dispersed liquid crystal (PDLC), which normally scatters light and becomes transparent when proper voltage is applied, improves the efficiency (Figure 1). It is often used as an electrically controlled screen [11] or privacy glass and has been applied as a programmable window [28]. PDLC can be applied as a shutter [9, 25], and an investigation of several types of switchable retroreflector including a PDLC with a retroreflector has been reported [33].

Bokode is a unique tag that embeds information spatially but appears as a point light source to the human eye [20]. It is suitable when the tags are sparsely distributed, but overlaps occur when many tags lie in the camera's viewing angle and angular offset is limited to 20°.

Depth sensing

Depth sensing provides an additional dimension to the 2D images captured by regular cameras and enhances the interactions. For example, it enables regular surfaces to support multi-touch interaction in combination with projectors [10] and rapid detailed 3D reconstruction of indoor environments

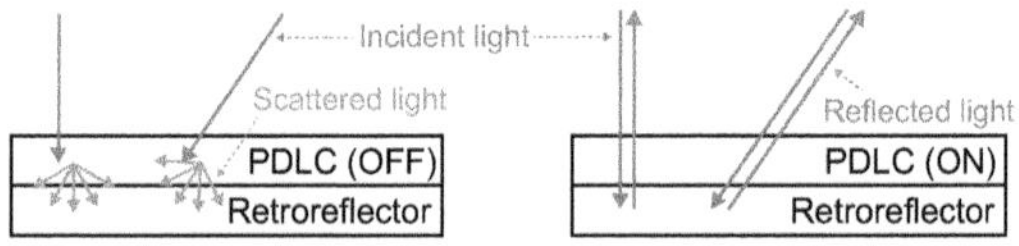

Figure 1. The combination of PDLC and retroreflector. When PDLC is OFF, the incident light is scattered within the PDLC, reflected at retroreflector, and scattered again at PDLC. Very little incident light returns to the light source. When PDLC is ON and transparent, most light returns to the light source.

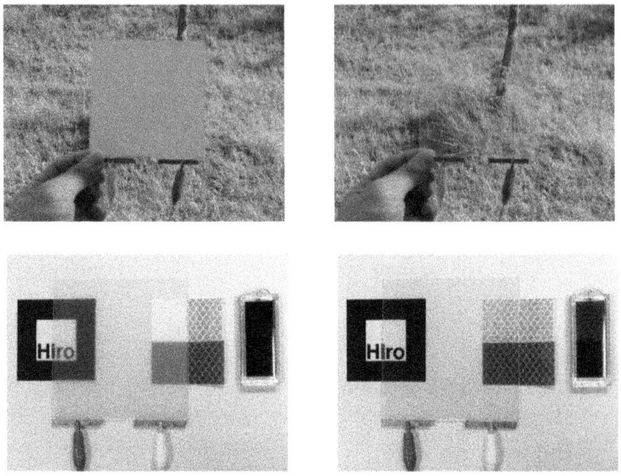

Figure 2. PDLC operation. The left photos were taken when the PDLC was OFF (scattering), and the right photos when it was ON (transparent). In the lower photos, the PDLC lies right above both a printed visual marker and colored retroreflectors. While the color changes and the light becomes weak with normal LC (shown as reference), the PDLC offers less visual obstruction and strong reflection levels.

[12]. Conventional depth sensing is performed by stereo cameras, but novel vision-based technologies have been proposed, such as those that use moving cameras [8, 15, 23]. Another approach uses IR-based depth sensing cameras. Kinect [3] is based on structured light, while SoftKinetic's DS325 [5] is based on time-of-flight (ToF). Work continues on improving the depth sensing camera itself, for example integrating RGB and depth sensing cameras [14], which will hopefully result in many future cameras with depth sensing capability. A prototype smartphone has already been announced that will have a depth sensor embedded [1]. This work will yield ubiquitous depth sensing cameras. While such cameras are generally deemed to be attractive due to their depth sensing capability, the proposed technique focuses on their continuous light emitting function in addition to depth sensing.

PROPOSED SYSTEM

Our proposed system provides a practical solution for tag-based ubiquitous applications assuming the ubiquity of depth sensing cameras. Since a depth sensing camera emits IR, LC-based tags can be used without additional light sources, so no special device is needed for tag reading. Our tag is designed for use everywhere, so it is small enough to be attached to various objects, be visually unobtrusive, and offer low maintenance cost. Moreover, experiments reveal that the combination of a reader and a tag provides wide readable ranges,

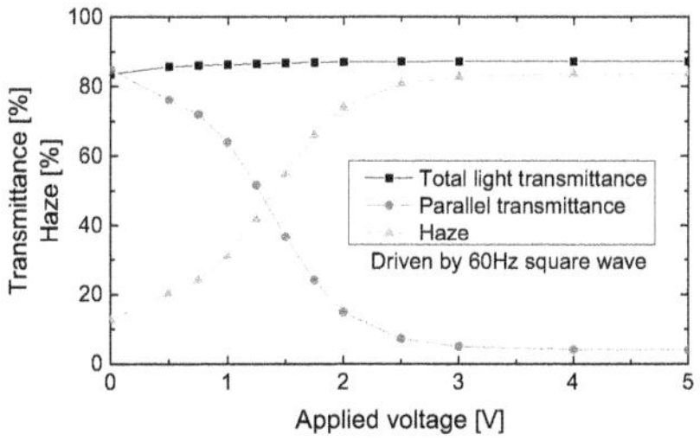

Figure 3. Optical characteristics of the PDLC implemented in the tag. When square wave over 3V (6V peak-to-peak) is applied, the characteristic is almost saturated.

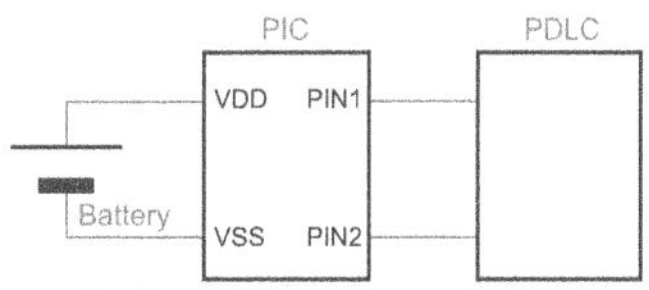

Figure 4. Simplified schematic for battery prototype. A PIC microcontroller driven by a 3V lithium battery controls the PDLC directly.

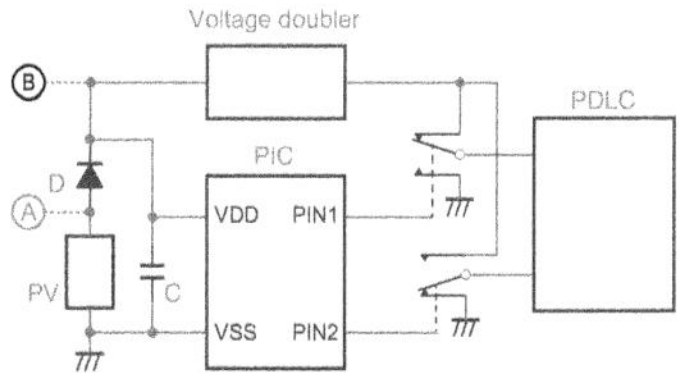

Figure 5. Simplified schematic for PV powered prototypes. Since the voltage supplied by the PV is too low to operate the PDLC, a voltage doubler is added and the PDLC is controlled via analog switches.

which expands not only distance but also the design space of applications.

PDLC-based Tag

The tag used in the proposed system consists of a PDLC, a retroreflector, a microcontroller, and a power source. It sends ID continuously via the PDLC switching pattern. The power is supplied by a battery or PV module. Light communication based on a LC shutter has advantages over that based on a LED: a wider readable angular range and power consumption low enough to allow miniaturization. Though the system can work when a normal LC replaces the PDLC, there are several advantages to using the PDLC. For example, a PDLC achieves a high transmittance rate (over 80%) and so is far superior to normal LCs, which offer less than 50%. This means that its reflected light is stronger and that its readable range is expanded for the same depth sensing camera. While the tag color changes if a normal LC is used, PDLC has little impact on the object underneath it, so the human-visible information remains usable, and it also suits our everyday environment. Figure 2 shows PDLC operation, while the lower photos also show a normal LC with colored retroreflectors. Note that the normal LC is visually taxing. The LC operation can be hidden by covering the LC with an IR transparent but visible light absorbing filter, which makes it easy to install in regular environments. Unfortunately however, the filter degrades performance.

Depth sensing camera as a tag reader

For a tag reader, we assume the use of a readily available IR-based depth sensing camera. Since the tag modulates the IR emitted from the depth sensing camera, the ID is observed as time sequential change in the intensity of the received light, which is basically independent of depth. The flashing of the tag is found on the IR intensity map. In addition to decoding the ID, the tag's location on the 2D image can be exactly determined. The depth sensing capability of the camera provides the distance to the tag when it is within the camera's depth sensing range. In short, the tag's 3D location and its ID can be detected by using a depth sensing camera as a tag reader. The combination of such benefits has encouraged us to create several attractive applications as described later. Since regular depth sensing cameras capture at less than 60fps and are unlikely to improve in the near future, the bit rate for ID transmittance is quite low, which is a major disadvantage for the proposed system.

IMPLEMENTATION

Developed tags

Many PDLCs operate at high voltages, e.g. 50 or 100V AC. Since the major application of PDLC is switchable privacy glass installed in buildings or rooms, the operating voltage is not a concern. Since our PDLC will have to be very small, a regular one is difficult to use. PDLCs with low operating voltages are already in use for special purposes [2]. Our embedded 22 x 12mm PDLC (9 x 9mm for LC effective area) was specially designed for low operating voltages by Seiko Electric [4]. The characteristics of the PDLC are shown in Figure 3. Note that the characteristics were captured under 60Hz square wave and that the voltage shown in the figure represents only positive voltage (the peak-to-peak value is twice that shown in the figure). The optical characteristics become saturated over 3V, which corresponds to the potential of lithium coin batteries. The reaction time of the PDLC is slow and asymmetric, about 20ms to change to transparent and 170ms to scattering (these values correspond to a change from 10% to 90%). This slow and asymmetric reaction of the PDLC negatively affects the quality of encoding. The 8 x 8mm retroreflector was attached to the center of the PDLC. The ID consists of five bits (including one start bit), uses Manchester encoding, and is sent two seconds after completion of previous ID sending. To match the camera frame rate and slow PDLC operation used in the experiments, the bit rate of the ID was preset to 2.4bps (2.1s for 5bit). Due to the asymmetric response time, the durations for activating and deactivating the PDLC were adjusted: shorter for activation and longer for deactivation. A PIC microcontroller, 12LF1840, was embedded to control the tag. It works at 31kHz when activated and sleeps when the state of PDLC does not need to be changed to reduce the power consumption.

Two types of power source were examined: a lithium coin battery CR1025 and a PV module. Simplified schematics are shown in Figures 4 and 5. With battery power, the PIC controls the PDLC directly by switching the voltage of the output pins (for example, PIN1 is HIGH/LOW and PIN2 is LOW/HIGH) for activating PDLC, and both PIN1 and PIN2 are set LOW to scatter the light. When a PV is used, the PIC drives analog switches because the voltages used for driving the PIC and for the PDLC differ. A PV module with only a few cells generates only low voltage, and a diode that drops the voltage is necessary to prevent energy loss in the capacitor. A voltage doubler controlled by the PIC raises the voltage to suit PDLC operation. Since the voltage the PV module generates depends on the environmental light level, this voltage is monitored, and the PIC activates peripheral devices (just to consume the energy) when it exceeds the preset range and stops operation when it is lower than the range. The ID is sent only when the voltage is within the range. Two types of PV modules were examined: Panasonic's amorton AM-1456, which consists of four series-connected PV cells, and a six-series array of Sphelar Power Corporation's Sphelar One(s), which looks like a regular LED. The former and latter are made of amorphous silicon and single-crystal silicon, and the resulting prototypes are labeled amorphous prototype and single-crystal prototype, respectively. The battery driven prototype is labeled battery prototype. The three prototypes are shown in Figure 6.

Tested cameras

A depth sensing camera, SoftKinetic's DS325 [5], was used as the reader because it provides both an RGB image and IR image, simultaneously. It uses a diffused laser as an IR emitter and captures depth at a resolution of 320 x 240pixel, 74 x 58° in the depth field of view at 60fps; its nominal operating range is 0.15 - 1.0m. The image provided by the depth sensing camera is not the same as that captured by a regular IR camera. It outputs a depth map, confidence map, and phase map as IR related images. Of these, the confidence map, which consists of confidence values for depth sensing, is comparable with the image captured by a regular IR camera. Roughly speaking, when the intensity of reflected light is low, indicating the object is far away or PDLC is OFF, the confidence value becomes low, and vice versa.

Since the depth sensing camera can be replaced by an IR camera with an IR emitter, it is important to evaluate and compare their performances and highlight the benefits of the former. In the following experiments described below, a cheap IR-sensitive camera with IR LEDs was used: Hanwha Japan's DC-NCR13U with a viewing angle of 78° and a frame rate of up to 30fps. When the IR camera was used, an IR pass filter was placed in front of the lens, its multiple IR LEDs were turned on, and resolution was set to 640 x 480pixels. The captured images were converted into eight-bit gray scale equivalents. One of the major differences between the two cameras is that the IR camera requires many parameters to be automatically or manually set, such as exposure and focus, both of which affect the image quality, while the depth sensing camera has only a few parameters to be set. A regular IR camera outputs captured IR intensity and so includes the reflection of the camera's IR output and ambient IR. The depth sensing camera records values when the emitter is on and off and outputs the confidence value, which is based on the difference between the on and off values.

Tag reading setup

The captured image is processed by a laptop computer. Since here we focus on evaluating the basic performance rather than developing practical applications, a quite simple scheme was used to read the tag under restricted conditions. In the evaluations, both the camera and tag were fixed and the tag location on the image was manually set. On the other hand,

Figure 6. Developed tags. From left to right: battery prototype, amorphous prototype and single-crystal prototype. They differ in their energy sources.

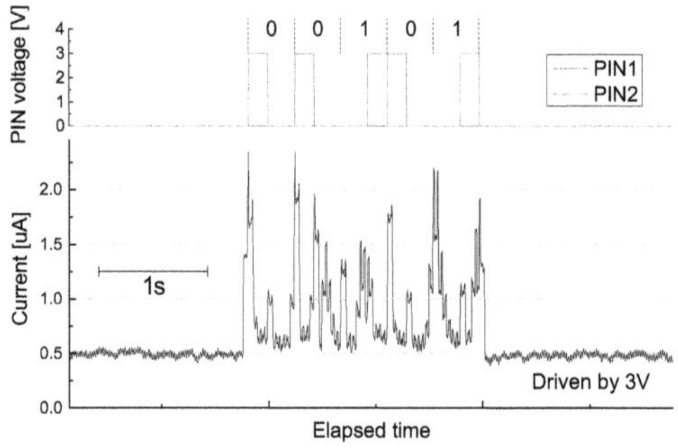

Figure 7. Current flowing to the tag driven by 3V during ID sending. The average current during ID sending was about 0.9μA, and that during PIC's sleep was about 0.5μA.

in the developed applications, the tag location was detected automatically by calculating the difference between current and previous frames. If the difference at a pixel exceeded the threshold, it was estimated as a tag candidate. Then, the maximum pixel value in the area around the location (the search area) was used as the tag's value. If the time sequential values were successfully decoded without error recovery, the system output the ID. Some slight movement of the tag is acceptable if the tag remains within the search area, but larger movements are not supported.

EVALUATION

Experiments were conducted to evaluate system performance. The developed tag itself was evaluated, followed by the combination of the tag and both a regular IR and a depth sensing camera.

Evaluation of the tag

Power consumption

Power consumption was measured using the battery prototype working at 3.0V. Current measured during ID sending is shown in Figure 7. Note that the recorded current data was subjected to a 50ms moving average because current changes dynamically with PIC operation. During ID sending, about 0.9μA current flowed on average, while during sleep, it was about 0.5μA. The overall average was about 0.7μA. Since the capacity of the battery is 50mAh, it is calculated that the tag would operate for eight years in theory. Such low power consumption allows PV powered prototypes to work in dark environments. It was confirmed that the amorphous prototype worked at 60lx and the single-crystal prototype at 320lx in an indoor environment. Note that since much more current

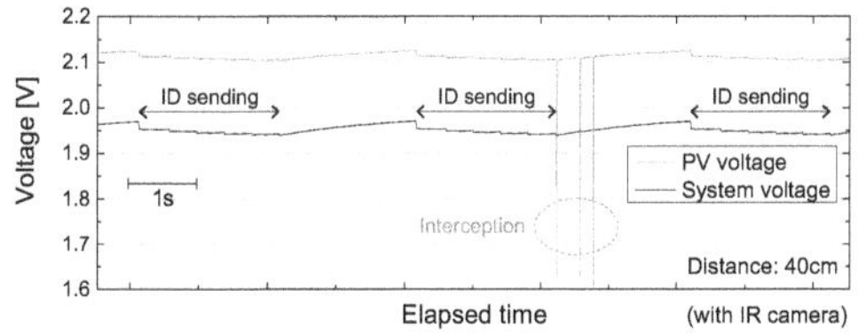

Figure 8. PV and system voltages of single-crystal prototype driven by only IR emitted from the IR camera in a quite dark environment. The graph shows performance at 40cm distance. The three drastic drops in PV voltage correspond to the blocking of the IR beam by a swinging bar used to replicate LED deactivation. These drops show the potential for reverse communication, from the reader to tag.

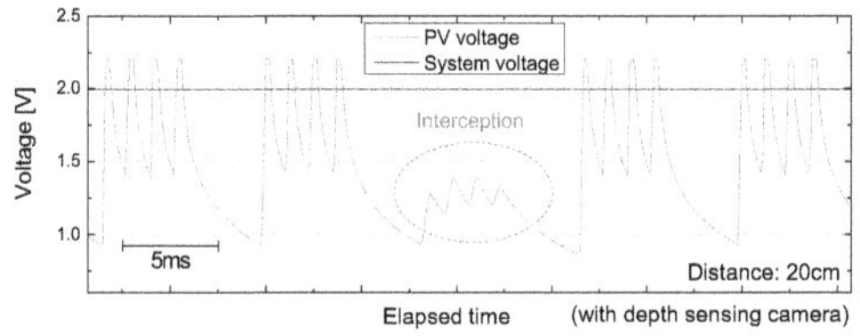

Figure 9. PV and system voltages of single-crystal prototype driven by only IR emitted from the depth sensing camera at a distance of 20cm. Since the depth sensing camera emitted IR as pulses, the PV voltage reflects the pulses, which differs from the IR camera. This pulsation and blocking (the same as in Figure 8) caused low PV voltage and offers the possibility of reverse communication.

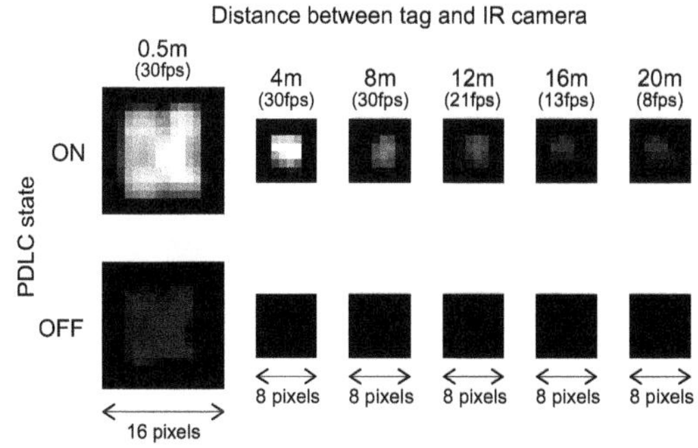

Figure 10. Images captured with the IR camera from various distances. The tag occupies about one pixel on the camera's sensor at 5m. When the distance becomes longer and the tag corresponds to less than one pixel, several pixels represent PDLC operation.

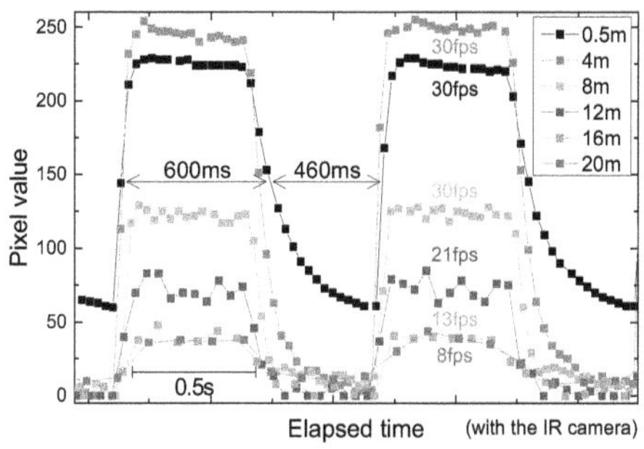

Figure 11. Pixel value with the IR camera (PDLC was switched ON and OFF every 530ms). From short distance to long distance, PDLC operation was detected when the camera parameters were set properly. Due to the asymmetric response time of the PDLC, the duration corresponding to OFF was shorter (460ms) than that to ON (600ms).

is required at startup, the tag was started manually after the voltage of the capacitor became high enough.

Boosting energy generation with IR

The single-crystal silicon PV cells have higher sensitivity to IR than visible light. This means the IR emitted by the camera boosts the energy generated by the PV. Two interesting effects are expected. One is that if the distance is short enough, the tag can work using only the IR emitted by the camera, i.e. extremely dark environments. The other is interactive communication.

In a less than 0.5lx environment, the single-crystal prototype using only the IR of the IR camera could operate at a 45cm distance at most, while the depth sensing camera could operate at a 20cm distance at most. Two voltages (PV and system voltages, corresponding to A and B in Figure 5) were measured with the IR camera when the distance was 40cm (Figure 8). The PV voltage always exceeded the system voltage by about 0.15V, reflecting the voltage drop due to the Schottky diode. Both PV and system voltages repeated cycles: drop, decrease slightly for 2.1s, and increase slowly. The decrease corresponds to ID sending, and the increase corresponds to sleep. The drop was caused by the peripherals (digital-to-analog module and comparator module) used to check whether the voltage was high enough for sending ID. Three drastic drops in PV voltage were found due to the swinging bar used to replicate LED deactivation. Figure 9 shows the voltages measured with the depth sensing camera at 20cm. Unlike the IR camera, the depth sensing camera emitted pulsed IR, to which the low PV voltage corresponds. Additionally, interruption of the camera's IR probe light by a swinging bar also affects the PV voltage in the same way as the IR camera. The pulsed IR and interruption reduce the PV voltage but do not affect the system voltage. This offers the possibility of reverse data transfer, from the camera to the tag.

Captured image and its value

The tag was symmetrically switched ON and OFF every 530ms and located at the center of the captured image. The captured images and their values were recorded.

Capture by the IR camera

Figure 10 shows the captured images. Note that the camera parameters (including gain, exposure, and brightness) were set manually, and that the exposure affects the frame rate. Tag operation could not be clearly observed when improper parameters were used. The IR camera was manually focused to about 4m. The tag corresponds to less than one pixel on the image at distances over 5m in theory, but several pixels reflect PDLC operation due to blurring and lens flare. This implies that the physical size of the tag is not restricted by the camera's resolution and that the tag can be further miniaturized. The pixel values during tag operation are shown in Figure 11. When the distance was moderate, such as 4m, a high dynamic range was available. As the distance became longer, the dynamic range decreased. Due to the asymmetric response time of the PDLC, the duration corresponding to OFF was shorter (460ms) than that corresponding to ON (600ms), and the decrease in pixel value is slower than the increase.

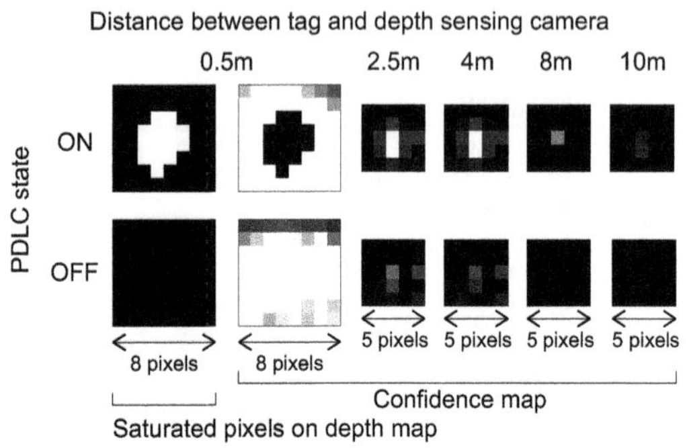

Figure 12. Examples of the images (maps) output by the depth sensing camera at various distances. Even when the tag occupied less than one pixel (over 2m), its operation was detectable. In close conditions, the response on the confidence map reversed.

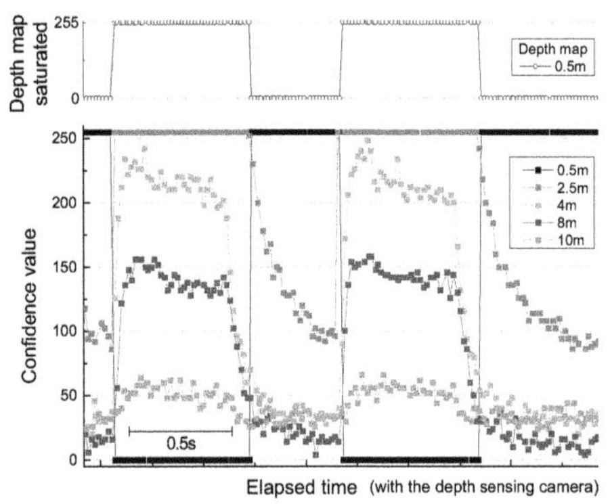

Figure 13. Confidence value of the depth sensing camera while the tag was cycled between ON and OFF. In close conditions (0.5m), the response reversed. The upper graph shows whether the pixel was saturated on the depth map (255 corresponds to saturated), which is almost the same as the confidence map for the longer distances.

Capture by the depth sensing camera

The confidence maps captured by the depth sensing camera are shown in Figure 12. Note that the physical size of the tag corresponds to less than one pixel at distances over 2m and 1/16th of a pixel at 8m. The pixel value of the confidence map is expected to be high/low when the PDLC is ON/OFF. Unfortunately, the pixel value of the confidence map stays high even if the PDLC is OFF when the distance is short (about less than 2m). This is reasonable because it reflects the confidence in sensing the depth to the surface of PDLC when it is near or within the depth sensing range (0.15 - 1.0m). If the distance is shorter than the range, the pixel value of the confidence map becomes zero, especially when PDLC is ON, because the reflected light is too strong. At distances such as 0.5m, the response of the confidence map is inverted: low/high when the PDLC is ON/OFF. The camera outputs a special value on the depth map when the pixel is saturated and can be used to read the tag at very short distances. The saturated pixels on the depth map were replaced by 255, otherwise 0, as is shown for 0.5m. Figure 13 shows the confidence values during tag operation (lower). At 0.5m, both the confidence and whether the value on the depth map was saturated (upper) are also shown. The confidence and depth maps were converted into eight-bit values. At long distances, the confidence value reflects the tag's operation, while at short

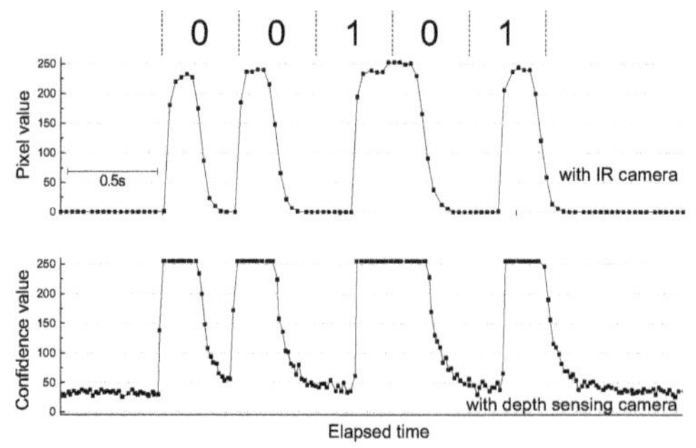

Figure 14. Examples of tag reading with the IR camera (upper) and depth sensing camera (lower) at 4m. Since the duration corresponding to one bit was already known, the ID was decoded simply from the captured pixel value.

distances, whether the pixel was saturated or not on the depth map is an effective metric. Compared with the IR camera, the depth sensing camera detects the tag at various distances without parameters being manually adjusted.

Readable range

The readable range is a major concern of the tag system. The tag, battery prototype, was set to send a continuous series of IDs from 0 to 15 with a 2s interval between IDs, which was defined as one set. Since the recognition accuracy was measured for two sets, 32 IDs in total were decoded for one condition. Examples of reading the tag are shown in Figure 14. Recognition accuracy was measured under various conditions including distances between the camera and the tag and tag offset angle ϕ, (see Figure 15). In this evaluation, the finding process was omitted by manually centering the tag on the image.

Range with the IR camera

The camera parameters were first manually adjusted when the angle ϕ was set at 0° for the tested distance. Then the angle increased along with the same camera parameters (constant setting). After the recognition accuracy dropped under 50%, the parameters were adaptively changed (adaptive setting). Figure 15 shows the results. When the accuracy was less than 50%, it was plotted as 0%. Tag reading failed at 20m but succeeded at significant distances such as 16m. The acceptable offset angle ϕ increases as the distance decreases. Especially when very close (0.5m), the acceptable offset angle was quite large, up to 70°.

Range with the depth sensing camera

Both confidence and depth maps were used to decode the tag when using the depth sensing camera. The confidence map was used to cover all distances, and the depth map only for a short distance (0.5m). Figure 16 shows the recognition accuracy. The readable angular range from the confidence map generally increases as the distance decreases, except for 0.5m. At 0.5m, the confidence map was effective only for large angles, over 70°, since the reflected light was too strong at smaller angles. The decrease in accuracy at 2.5m and 0° was also caused by excessively strong light reflection. By using the depth map instead of the confidence map for the 0.5m distance, the tag was decoded for angular offsets of up

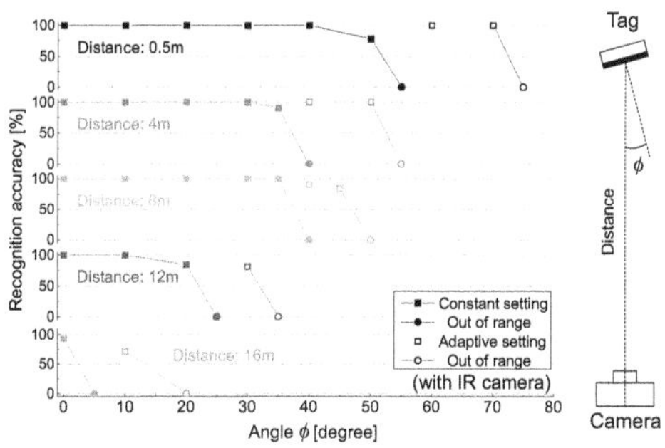

Figure 15. Recognition accuracy with the IR camera. Camera parameters were adjusted to suit the distance, and decoding was conducted at various angles ϕ using the constant setting. The accuracy indicated by adaptive setting means the parameters were tuned to suit the specific condition.

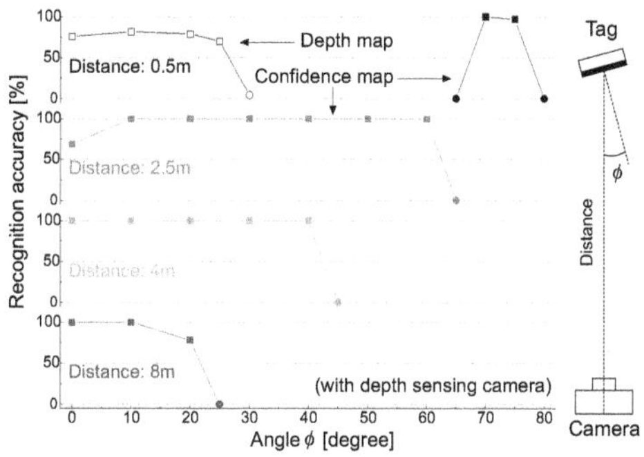

Figure 16. Readable range with the depth sensing camera. The depth sensing camera provided a wide readable range, up to 8m. Many of the results were obtained from the confidence map, except for 0.5m. Due to the reversed response of the confidence map at close distances, two types of accuracy were obtained at 0.5m: that from the depth map and that from the confidence map.

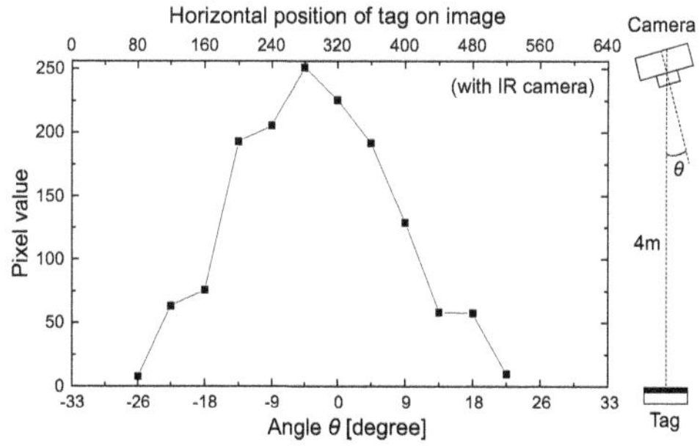

Figure 17. Pixel value with the IR camera according to the angle θ (tag's horizontal positions). Since the LEDs on the camera have strong directionality, the intensity of reflected light decreases with the offset angle θ.

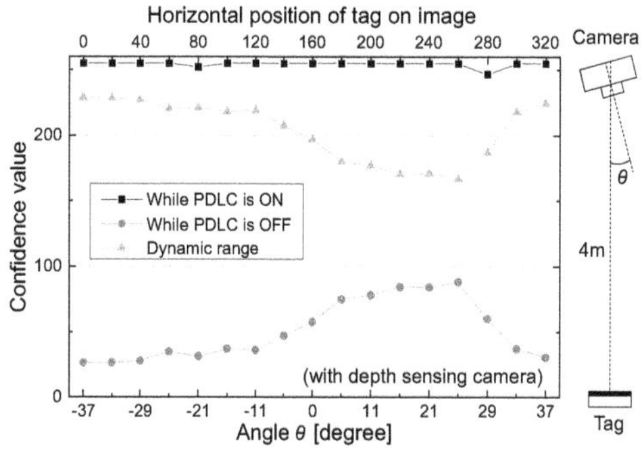

Figure 18. Confidence value with the depth sensing camera according to the angle θ. Even though the value was saturated while the PDLC was ON, high dynamic range was obtained for all positions. This offered a wide range in offset angle, unlike the IR camera.

to 25°. However, recognition failed at medium angular offsets. Though this non-linearity of the confidence map is more discriminative than the output of the IR camera, a seamless, long, and wide angular readable range will be made possible if the non-linearity can be resolved.

Dependency of performance on illumination angle

All light sources, including those on the cameras, are directional to some extent. To assess the impact of oblique illumination, the distance between the reader and tag was fixed to 4m and the camera was rotated θ degrees as shown in Figure 17. This moved the tag away from the center of the image. The angle θ was calculated from the tag's location on the image.

Dependency with the IR camera

Figure 17 shows the pixel values with the IR camera when the PDLC was ON. Since the values were low when the PDLC was OFF, the dynamic range for PDLC operation is basically equal to the values when the PDLC was ON. The camera parameters were manually adjusted once when the angle θ was 0° then kept for other angles. The values are greatly affected by the angle. The range at which high pixel values were observed (over 190) corresponds to a viewing angle of 18°. This means that adequate reading performance is achieved only within a limited range of angles. Note that high values are observed when "adaptive setting" is applied.

Dependency with the depth sensing camera

Figure 18 shows the confidence values of the depth sensing camera according to the angle θ. Since the confidence values were saturated (255) in almost all cases when the PDLC was ON, the value captured when the PDLC was OFF determined the dynamic range. Unlike the IR camera, the dynamic range of the depth sensing camera for capturing PDLC operation was high regardless of the angle, which means the depth sensing camera offers a quite wide angular range. Note that the value itself may change with the environment; for example, the value at 4m in Figure 13 is lower than that in Figure 18. However, the fact that the depth sensing camera offers a high dynamic range and a wide angular range does not change. This wide acceptable angle is important for practical use and is one reason to select the depth sensing camera over the regular IR camera.

DEVELOPED APPLICATIONS

The experiments confirmed that the tag system has a readable range wide enough to cover most of the spatial volume within which we interact with objects in everyday life. Moreover, its special features such as depth sensing capability, can be used to develop attractive new applications. Indeed, several applications have been developed. In addition, further possible applications are discussed later to explore the design space.

Figure 19. An example of simple tag reading from several meters away. The figure includes a larger tag (left) that shows human-visible information formed by a colored retroreflector; the application demonstrates the simultaneous use of multiple tags.

Figure 20. Combination with QR code. The tag covered with IR pass filter replaces a black part of a QR code. Basic information is provided by the tag at long distances, while more detailed information is given by the QR code at short distances.

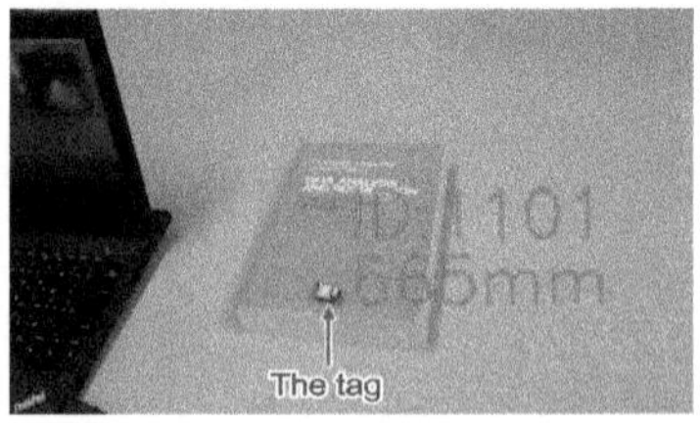

Figure 21. Screen capture of a depth enhanced application. The information of an object with the tag is provided together with its 3D location (2D location on the image and the distance).

Simple tag reading
An application that simply reads the tag and overlays the decoded ID on the RGB image was developed as a basic form of AR. Tag reading was successful at distances of several meters. It also supports multiple tags: two tags could be read as shown in Figure 19. A larger tag, 4 x 3cm, which has human-visible information formed by a colored retroreflector was also tested (left in the figure). Since the PDLC has little visual impact on the object underneath it, the information is always visible regardless of the PDLC operation. Though the information can be printed by ink, the colored retroreflector provides better reading performance than mere ink would. Note that reading distance for the larger tag exceeded 13m and that sometimes its reflection on a window was misrecognized as a tag due to the strength of the reflection.

Combination with visual tag
It is easy to combine our proposal with other visual tags. Since IR is used for sending ID, not visible light, the tag can be camouflaged with an IR transparent filter. For example, Figure 20 shows a tag with a black IR-pass filter that replaces a part of the black region of a QR code. The information provided by this combined tag changes with the distance: a brief message related to tag ID at long distances, and more details via the QR code at short distances.

Tag reading with depth information
Depth information is available in addition to the ID, which offers a 3D location of the tag. Since the camera used offers depth information for quite close distances (less than 1m), the combination offers usage within arm's reach. For example, the system can inform the user that, "the book is 60cm to your right", which is especially effective in assisting the visibly impaired and people searching for an object on a cluttered desk. An example is shown in Figure 21.

DISCUSSION
Since the experiments examined the basic performance of the proposed tag system, further evaluations are required for practical use. This section first addresses the limitations of the proposal and then discusses possible solutions. Finally, further applications yielded by the proposed tag system are mentioned.

Limitations of current setup
The most significant limitation for practical use is the low bit rate of ID sending, 2.4bps. The low bit rate delays any subsequent interaction and limits the amount of information transmitted and the maximum number of co-sited tags. It also makes it difficult to support tag/camera movement (all evaluations were made without movement). Though it offers a wide readable range, the permissible offset angle at long distances needs to be widened further. The experiments showed the differences between the regular IR and depth sensing camera, and imply that the depth sensing camera is very suitable for tag reading. However, drawbacks were also found. The tag was developed as a prototype, and several improvements are possible such as further miniaturization. Several drawbacks were noted during the experiments, such as recognition errors and the capture of quasi-tags on windows, which indicates the need for some error recovery mechanism in practical use. Moreover, since the experiment was conducted in a lab environment, further research is required to apply the tag in everyday environments that contain several noise sources such as IR-based remote controllers and sunlight.

Potential improvements in tag reading performance
The required performance varies among applications, and the current prototypes already satisfy certain applications such as surveillance of contents in a shop or a museum. However, other applications require better performance. Therefore, it is important to improve performance including bit rate and readable range.

Bit rate
In the current setting, the bit rate was adjusted to achieve robust recognition at 30fps or less. Since the depth sensing camera offers 60fps, it supports higher bit rates. More sophisticated decoders would strengthen recognition performance. However, two factors limit the bit rate in principle: the camera's frame rate and the PDLC's response time. It is assumed that the cameras installed in personal devices such as smartphones or HMDs will likely continue to work at up to 60fps. Thus, further improvement of the PDLC is hoped for. A PDLC that reacts in about 1ms has already been developed [7], but it requires high voltage to operate. Therefore, a PDLC must be developed that offers both low operating voltage and quick response.

The difficulty of finding and reading moving tags is another negative consequence of the low bit rate. Though this technique is not suitable for AR applications in which tags and/or camera are aggressively moved, movement should be supported to some extent. Our current idea is to apply image processing techniques and object tracking on the RGB image such as [8, 15]. Robustness can be improved by feeding the result back to the confidence map.

Readable range

Simply increasing the intensity of the reflected light received by one imaging cell results in widening the readable range in terms of distance and angle. Approach 1 is to boost the IR light emitted by the camera. Approach 2, the most effective solution, is to increase the size of the retroreflector. Approach 3 is to improve the transmittance of the PDLC and reflection performance of the retroreflector, which will also expand the range. Considering practical use, it seems important to improve the angular range at long distances. We can extend the permissible offset angle ϕ (see Figure 16) by using tags that have round or polyhedral form factors, which will, combined with the results shown in Figure 18, offer extremely wide readable range.

Camera selection for tag reading

The experiments showed the differences between the IR and depth sensing camera. The advantages of the depth sensing camera include wide angular range and no need to adjust camera parameters. Depth sensing capability is, of course, another advantage. On the other hand, several drawbacks were found such as short readable distance and non-linearity of the confidence map with the intensity. The former is mainly caused by low spatial resolution and is likely to be addressed in the future. The latter should be effectively addressed by designing a depth sensing camera that also suits tag reading (for example, outputting differential values instead of confidence maps). Since the intensity of reflected light from the retroreflector can be strong enough to detect the distance to the tag even if it is located outside the depth sensing range, depth sensing should be performed even for pixels that normally would be thought of as characteristic of noise and thus ignored. These improvements would make the depth sensing camera a stronger tool for ubiquitous applications with tag reading functionality.

Miniaturization of the tag

The tag can be further miniaturized. For example, its power source can be replaced with a smaller battery or smaller PV module. It is also possible to replace the PDLC with a smaller one. Note that the power consumption of the PDLC and the power capacity of the battery and PV module are linear to size, so the power consumption must be reduced, especially during sleep, for miniaturization. Reducing the power consumed by the microcontroller is particularly important. Approaches include decreasing the operating voltage, exploring extremely low power driving techniques, and using a more power efficient microcontroller. Various researchers have addressed reductions in current consumption and also PV inefficiencies, and further improvements seem possible.

Possible applications

First, it should be mentioned that the technique is not suitable to some tag-based applications in which the tag is aggressively moved, due to its low bit rate. The technique works effectively for applications in which both the tags and camera are almost fixed or the tags can be stabilized using some kind of image processing. Usage situations include relaxing in a living room, walking in a museum, and searching for a book. Several applications have been developed, and more are possible.

For example, if the depth sensing range is long and tags are attached to doors, the technique can be used for indoor navigation, giving information such as "the exit is 4m ahead". The bi-camera configuration (RGB and depth sensing camera) will help to improve the depth sensing capability by stereo vision. It can easily provide location specific meta information for 3D reconstruction of the environment such as Kinect-Fusion [12]. The proposed tag system can also be applied for indoor localization without depth sensing, which is one of the key functions for ubiquitous computing. When multiple tags are captured and the tag locations can be recovered from the server using the IDs, the 3D location of the camera can be estimated. The long readable range allows the tags to be placed sparsely, for example every 5m, to estimate the camera's location. The combination of human-visible information (see Figure 19) is applicable to traffic signs with retroreflectors. Some cars already have a kind of depth sensing camera to detect danger, and the proposed technique will offer safer driving. While legacy visual tags offer one-way communication, the single-crystal prototype enables interactive communication if the camera emits encoded IR light. Such interactive communication allows, for example, a flashlight-based application [18], and also easy modification of the tag setting.

CONCLUSION

A tag system was proposed that offers a practical step towards ubiquitous computing. It consists of small tags consisting of a PDLC, a retroreflector, and a power source. Each tag sends its ID by switching the PDLC. A ToF-based depth sensing camera, which is assumed to be installed on a user's everyday devices, is used as the reader. Since the tag requires quite low power ($0.7\mu A$ on average), it works with a small coin battery or small PV module and can be miniaturized. Experiments confirmed that the readable range reached 8m and that the depth sensing camera offered several advantages over the regular IR camera such as wide angular range. Several applications were developed to explore the design space, and the proposed tag system was confirmed to expand the design space. Finally, limitations of the current setup and possible improvements were discussed.

REFERENCES

1. Google, Project Tango. `https://www.google.com/atap/projecttango/`.
2. Masunaga Glasses, Wink Glasses 2013. (in Japanese). `http://www.e-meganeya.com/wink2013/`.
3. Microsoft, Kinect for Windows. `http://www.microsoft.com/en-us/kinectforwindows/`.
4. Seiko Electric, SILF. `http://foreign.seiko-denki.co.jp/product/component/component05/`.
5. SoftKinetic, DS325. `http://www.softkinetic.com/products/depthsensecameras.aspx`.

6. QR code 2005 bar code symbology specification. ISO/IEC 18004:2006, (2006).
7. Date, M., Hisaki, T., Naito, N., Nakadaira, A., Suyama, S., Tanaka, H., Uehira, K., and Koshiishi, Y. 52.3: Direct-viewing display using alignment-controlled PDLC and holographic PDLC. *SID Symposium Digest of Technical Papers 31*, 1 (2000), 1184–1187.
8. Davison, A. Real-time simultaneous localisation and mapping with a single camera. In *Proc. IEEE Conf. Computer Vision '03*, vol. 2 (2003), 1403–1410.
9. Drzaic, P. S. Polymer dispersed nematic liquid crystal for large area displays and light valves. *Applied Physics 60*, 6 (1986), 2142–2148.
10. Harrison, C., Benko, H., and Wilson, A. D. OmniTouch: wearable multitouch interaction everywhere. In *Proc. UIST '11* (2011), 441–450.
11. Izadi, S., Hodges, S., Taylor, S., Rosenfeld, D., Villar, N., Butler, A., and Westhues, J. Going beyond the display: a surface technology with an electronically switchable diffuser. In *Proc. UIST '08* (2008), 269–278.
12. Izadi, S., Kim, D., Hilliges, O., Molyneaux, D., Newcombe, R., Kohli, P., Shotton, J., Hodges, S., Freeman, D., Davison, A., and Fitzgibbon, A. KinectFusion: real-time 3d reconstruction and interaction using a moving depth camera. In *Proc. UIST '11* (2011), 559–568.
13. Kato, H., and Billinghurst, M. Marker tracking and HMD calibration for a video-based augmented reality conferencing system. In *Proc. IWAR '99* (1999), 85–94.
14. Kim, S.-J., Kang, B., Kim, J. D. K., Lee, K., Kim, C.-Y., and Kim, K. A 1920x 1080 3.65 μm-pixel 2D/3D image sensor with split and binning pixel structure in 0.11μm standard CMOS. In *Proc. IEEE Solid-State Circuits Conference Digest of Technical Papers* (2012), 396–398.
15. Klein, G., and Murray, D. Parallel tracking and mapping for small ar workspaces. In *Proc. ISMAR '07* (2007), 225–234.
16. Kulyukin, V., Gharpure, C., Nicholson, J., and Pavithran, S. RFID in robot-assisted indoor navigation for the visually impaired. In *Proc. IROS '04*, vol. 2 (2004), 1979–1984 vol.2.
17. Lee, J. C., Dietz, P. H., Maynes-Aminzade, D., Raskar, R., and Hudson, S. E. Automatic projector calibration with embedded light sensors. In *Proc. UIST '04* (2004), 123–126.
18. Ma, H., and Paradiso, J. The FindIT Flashlight: responsive tagging based on optically triggered microprocessor wakeup. In *Proc. UbiComp '02*. Springer Berlin Heidelberg, 2002, 160–167.
19. Matsushita, N., Hihara, D., Ushiro, T., Yoshimura, S., Rekimoto, J., and Yamamoto, Y. ID CAM: A smart camera for scene capturing and ID recognition. In *Proc. ISMAR '03* (2003), 227–236.
20. Mohan, A., Woo, G., Hiura, S., Smithwick, Q., and Raskar, R. Bokode: imperceptible visual tags for camera based interaction from a distance. *ACM Trans. Graph. 28*, 3 (2009), 98:1–98:8.
21. Nakamura, Y., Nishimura, T., Itoh, H., and Nakashima, H. ID-CoBIT: a battery-less information terminal with data upload capability. In *Proc. IEEE IECON '03*, vol. 3 (2003), 2511–2516.
22. Nakazato, Y., Kanbara, M., and Yokoya, N. Localization system for large indoor environments using invisible markers. In *Proc. VRST '08* (2008), 295–296.
23. Newcombe, R. A., and Davison, A. Live dense reconstruction with a single moving camera. In *Proc. IEEE CVPR '10* (2010), 1498–1505.
24. Noonpakdee, W., Liu, J., Hyun, K. D., and Shimamoto, S. Hybrid RFID employing optical wireless communication. In *Proc. IEEE ICWITS '10* (2010), 1–4.
25. Petti, L., Mormile, P., and Blau, W. Fast electro-optical switching and high contrast ratio in epoxy-based polymer dispersed liquid crystals. *Optics and Lasers in Engineering 39*, 3 (2003), 369 – 377.
26. Raskar, R., Beardsley, P., van Baar, J., Wang, Y., Dietz, P., Lee, J., Leigh, D., and Willwacher, T. RFIG Lamps: interacting with a self-describing world via photosensing wireless tags and projectors. *ACM Trans. Graph. 23*, 3 (2004), 406–415.
27. Raskar, R., Nii, H., deDecker, B., Hashimoto, Y., Summet, J., Moore, D., Zhao, Y., Westhues, J., Dietz, P., Barnwell, J., Nayar, S., Inami, M., Bekaert, P., Noland, M., Branzoi, V., and Bruns, E. Prakash: lighting aware motion capture using photosensing markers and multiplexed illuminators. *ACM Trans. Graph. 26*, 3 (2007).
28. Rekimoto, J. Squama: modular visibility control of walls and windows for programmable physical architectures. In *Proc. AVI '12* (2012), 168–171.
29. Rekimoto, J., and Ayatsuka, Y. CyberCode: designing augmented reality environments with visual tags. In *Proc. DARE '00* (2000), 1–10.
30. Rekimoto, J., Miyaki, T., and Ishizawa, T. LifeTag: WiFi-based continuous location logging for life pattern analysis. In *Proc. LoCA '07* (2007), 35–49.
31. Rekimoto, J., and Nagao, K. The world through the computer: computer augmented interaction with real world environments. In *Proc. UIST '95* (1995), 29–36.
32. Rekimoto, J., Ullmer, B., and Oba, H. DataTiles: a modular platform for mixed physical and graphical interactions. In *Proc. CHI '01* (2001), 269–276.
33. Schultz, P., Cumby, B., and Heikenfeld, J. Investigation of five types of switchable retroreflector films for enhanced visible and infrared conspicuity applications. *Applied Physics 51*, 17 (2012), 3744–3754.
34. Swenson, C. M., Steed, C. A., De La Rue, I. A., and Fugate, R. Q. Low-power FLC-based retromodulator communications system. In *Proc. SPIE*, vol. 2990 (1997), 296–310.

Trampoline: A Double-sided Elastic Touch Device to Create Reliefs

Jaehyun Han **Jiseong Gu** **Geehyuk Lee**
HCI Lab, KAIST,
291 Daehak-ro, Yuseong-gu, Daejeon, Rep. of Korea
jay.jaehyun@gmail.com jiseong.gu@kaist.ac.kr geehyuk@gmail.com

ABSTRACT
Although reliefs are frequently used to add patterns to product surfaces, there is a lack of interaction techniques to model reliefs on the surface of virtual objects. We adopted the repoussé and chasing artwork techniques in an alternative interaction technique to model relief on virtual surfaces. To support this interaction technique, we developed the double-sided touchpad Trampoline that can detect the position and force of a finger touch on both sides. Additionally, Trampoline provides users with elastic feedback, as its surface consists of a stretchable fabric. We implemented a relief application with this device and the developed interaction technique. An informal user study showed that the proposed system can be a promising solution to create reliefs.

Author Keywords
Repoussé and Chasing; Trampoline; Double-sided Touchpad; Elastic Touchpad; 3D Modeling.

ACM Classification Keywords
H.5.2 [User Interfaces]: Input devices and strategies (e.g., mouse, touchscreen).

INTRODUCTION
Relief is a traditional sculpting technique that has been applied in many artworks. Recently, it has also been used to add patterns to product surfaces (Figure 1a). Automatic relief mapping is a popular method to create a relief on the surface of a virtual object and uses an image to produce a surface volume on the virtual model. However, this method fails to provide designers with the freedom to directly modify the virtual surface. Additionally, interaction techniques from traditional computer-aided design (CAD) applications and studies [1, 4, 7, 11, 14, 15] focus primarily on modeling the three-dimensional (3D) shapes of virtual objects and do not support intuitive interactions to create reliefs. Previous studies introduced software to support adding depth to a two-dimensional (2D) plane [8, 17].

UIST 2014, October 5–8, 2014, Honolulu, HI, USA.
Copyright © 2014 ACM 978-1-4503-3069-5/14/10...$15.00.
http://dx.doi.org/10.1145/2642918.2647381

Figure 1: Products with reliefs (a) and an artwork by using the repoussé and chasing techniques (b, Wikipedia).

Interaction techniques in these studies were designed with a 2D input device, such as a mouse or a stylus. There is therefore enough possibility to develop intuitive interaction techniques to create reliefs with a new input device. We aimed to develop an interaction technique and an input device that is specialized for relief modeling of a virtual surface.

There are many relief modeling techniques, such as repoussé, chasing, casting, and carving. From these techniques, we chose the metaphors of repoussé and chasing for a new modeling technique. Artists can model a relief using repoussé and chasing by working on both sides of a surface (Figure 1b). We believe that users can easily learn the new modeling technique, as many are already familiar with the concepts of repoussé and chasing from their real world experiences.

In a preliminary study, Han et al. [5] introduced Trampoline, a double-sided elastic touch device that supports repoussé and chasing techniques. To support the proposed interaction technique, the touchpad could estimate the touch position as well as the force applied on both sides of the touch surface. However, the early version of Trampoline had limitations, such as a small interaction space, a not so intuitive method for mode switching, and a lack of haptic feedback for the manipulation state. In this paper, we introduce an improved Trampoline device with a refined design of interaction techniques. Additionally, we conducted a user study with the implemented relief application to find usability issues with this new type of touch device and verify the proper working of both the interaction design and the device.

RELATED WORK

We summarize previous studies on modeling techniques for virtual models, as well as sensing techniques for a bi-directional touch device and a malleable device.

Modeling technique

Joshi and Carr introduced a method that applied the concept of repoussé to add depth information to a 2D plane [8]. This study mainly focused on an interpolation method to inflate the 2D surface from the input curves. Unlike this study, we focused on bringing the metaphors of the repoussé and the chasing techniques from the real world to the interaction techniques to create relief on virtual surfaces.

There are many interaction techniques to support 3D modeling processes by non-CAD users [1, 4, 7, 11]. Bae et al. proposed a technique that used strokes as an input parameter to draw 3D stroke models [1]. Igarashi et al. also introduced a technique that builds 3D models from 2D strokes [7]. This technique provided intuitive usage of 2D strokes to create 3D models. Galyean and Hughes proposed a modeling system that used a 3D isotonic device with elastic feedback [4]. McDonnell et al. proposed a system that used Phantom haptic device to track finger movements [11]. These studies provided intuitive mapping of the input device with the interaction technique and the users' real world experience. However, the primary focus of these studies was to model the shapes of 3D virtual objects. In contrast to these studies, this paper focuses on an interaction technique for relief modeling, for which few research examples exist [13, 17]. *Relievos* is a rare example that demonstrates an interaction technique to create a relief on a touch phone [13]. Ventura et al. introduced a sketch-based tool to model the 3D mark-up of a photograph using a pen interface [17]. However, these techniques failed to relate their interaction techniques to real-world user experiences of modeling reliefs.

To seek intuitive modeling techniques, studies have also been conducted on 3D modeling with physical proxies to represent virtual objects [14, 15]. To implement such a system, Sheng et al. used a Vicon tracking system that captured the relative positions of fingers and a physical proxy [14]. In comparison, Smith et al. used a custom sensor system that comprised of a matrix of resistive sensors [15]. Modeling 3D models with these systems can be applicable to relief modeling. However, prototypes from these studies cannot sense raises of the device surface. Thus, in these studies the embossing (or extrusion) operation required an additional mode, whereas our device supports concurrent embossing and engraving operations.

Sensing technique

To concurrently support bi-directional deformation of a surface, an input device must sense the manipulation on both sides of the input surface. A common approach used in double-sided touch interactions is combining two capacitive touch devices [19, 20]. Wigdor et al. introduced a mobile device that could sense bi-directional touch by adding an additional touch panel on the back of a touch screen [19]. A similar approach was used to make a tabletop device that was capable of sensing bi-directional touch [20]. However, the rigid surfaces of such a combination cannot provide the appropriate elastic and compliant haptic feedback to support the users' repoussé and chasing skills.

Many techniques have been introduced to sense the deformation of a physical surface [2, 12, 18]. These techniques use a camera to capture the surface deformation. Follmer et al. proposed a system to sense 2.5D surface deformations by objects and touching fingers. The surface of this system consisted of a malleable material and three sinusoidal fringe patterns that were projected onto the surface [2]. Noguchi et al. built a soft-surfaced multi-touch table by placing an elastic material on the surface of a frustrated total internal reflection tabletop [12]. Vlack et al. introduced a technique to sense deformations of an elastic body that contained two spherical layers [18]. The back side of these devices had to be kept clear in order to capture images of the deformed patterns or touch images. Therefore, these techniques were limited in supporting interaction techniques on both sides of the surface.

There are techniques to sense the deformation of a physical surface that do not use a camera [3, 6, 9, 16]. Follmer et al. introduced a method that measured the capacitance of a dielectric material between two electrodes covered by a malleable material [3]. Hoshi and Shinoda used a 3D accelerometer to capture the shape change of a sheet that was composed of a lattice matrix. Each accelerometer was placed on the lattice and had its orientation information [6]. *Sinkpad* consisted of a pressure sensor matrix. The matrix was placed under an elastic material and the deformation of the elastic material changed the sensor's output [9]. These techniques can have a thin form factor. However, they consist of complex sensor structures to achieve a high resolution, and have limitations in sensing the direction of the touched surface. Sugiura et al. proposed a method to measure a tangential force on a stoking using the change of transmissivity of IR light through the stocking [16]. The method can be used for measuring tangential forces, but its use for 2D position sensing needs further development.

The contributions of this paper are two-fold considering the aforementioned prior work. First, we adopted repoussé and chasing in an interaction technique for relief modeling on virtual surfaces. Second, we proposed a new input device that supported an interaction technique based on estimating the 2D touch position and the force applied on both sides of an elastic surface.

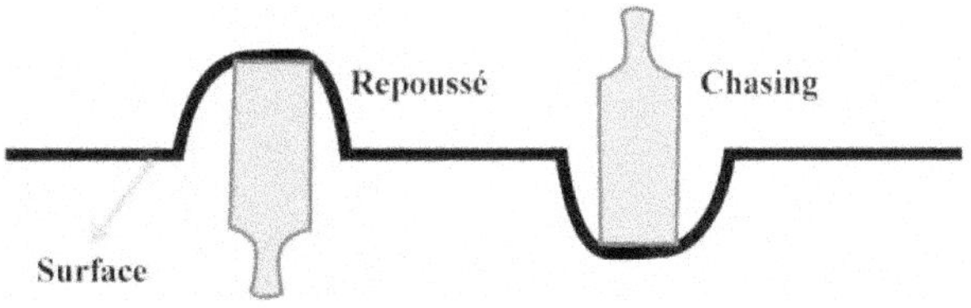

Figure 2: Concepts of repoussé and chasing.

REPOUSSÉ AND CHASING

Repoussé and chasing are metalworking techniques that are used for relief modeling. The concept of repoussé is easy and straightforward: the surface is raised as a person presses on the back side of a surface as shown in Figure 2. The surface is stretched, but remains continuous and the amount of stretching is proportional to the applied force. Accordingly, the person will feel the resistance of the surface deformation proportionally to the applied force. Hammering and pressing are two formative actions that are used in repoussé. Hammering the surface causes it to stretch extensively in a small area. By pressing the surface, a person can control the amount of deformation and change the position of the deformation while moving their tool on the surface. Chasing is the opposite of repoussé as shown in Figure 2. It has the same formative action, but the force is applied on the front side of the surface.

Using both techniques, a person can concurrently emboss and engrave the surface. The magnitude of the force on the surface determines the amount of surface deformation. The resistance to the deformation helps the person control their hand to achieve the intended deformation. Users may be familiar with the deformation resistance, because of their experience from the physical world. Thus, users can create reliefs more intuitively when both the input device and the interaction techniques support this concept.

TRAMPOLINE

In order to support the repoussé and chasing techniques, we imposed three design requirements on the input device. First, the device should be a 2D touchpad with the ability to sense the touch position on both the front and back sides of the device surface. Second, the amount of deformation on the virtual surface should be controlled by the applied forces on the touch surface for a realistic user experience. Lastly, the device should provide elastic feedback, because in the real world resistance increases with increasing deformation. We anticipated that the elastic feedback would provide the users with a feeling of resistance caused by the surface deformation.

Hardware specification

To our knowledge, no device in existing studies satisfied our design requirements. As a result, we decided to develop a new touch device called *Trampoline*. The device consists of four linear hall sensors (A1362, Allegro MicroSystems Inc.), four permanent magnets, and an elastic fabric, i.e. general spandex. One side of each magnet is attached to a corner of the elastic surface and the opposite side of the magnet is attached near the hall sensor as illustrated in Figure 3. The tilting angle of the magnet with respect to the xy-plane can range over approximately ± 45 degrees. The linear hall sensors has a 4.5 mV/G sensitivity, which was sufficient for the required position and force accuracy of *Trampoline*. The size of the device is 175 x 175 mm and that of the elastic surface is 100 x 100 mm with 15 mm thickness. A handle is placed on the left side of the device to provide a stable grip. Two linear resonance actuators are placed on the top of the handle to provide additional haptic feedback for the applied force on the surface.

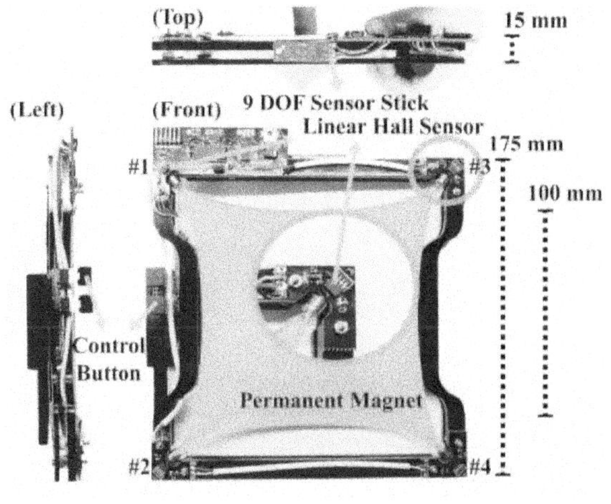

Figure 3: *Trampoline* prototype.

To support additional interactions, *Trampoline* has two buttons on the left side and a nine-degree-of-freedom (9-DOF) sensor stick (SEN-10724, Sparkfun) on the top. The four analog signals from the hall sensors are converted into digital values. In addition to these values, the states of the two buttons and the output from the 9-DOF sensor stick are sent to tracking software at 15 ms intervals.

Working principle

The device estimates the touch position and the force on the surface based on the output of the hall sensors. The strength of the magnetic field at each hall sensor is determined by the orientation of the magnet and the sensor (θ and ρ in Figure 4) when the distance between them is constant. Therefore, one can approximate the orientation of a magnet by measuring the sensor output. When two magnets are attached to the end of an elastic material as shown in Figure 4, the ratio of the outputs from the two sensors represents the approximate location where the force is applied (Figures 4a and 4b). The sum of the two outputs can be used for pseudo force estimation (Figures 4a and 4c), because the displacement of a finger is mapped to the applied force on the surface. As shown in Figures 4a, 4b, and 4c, the sensor output is positive when the direction of the magnetic field and the sensing direction of a hall sensor are the same. The output becomes negative in the opposite case (Figure 4d). Thus, one can predict the touch direction by observing the sign of a sensor's output.

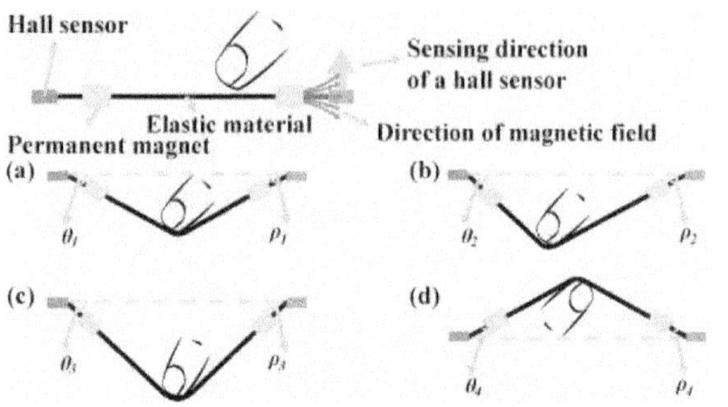

Figure 4: Working principle of *Trampoline*.

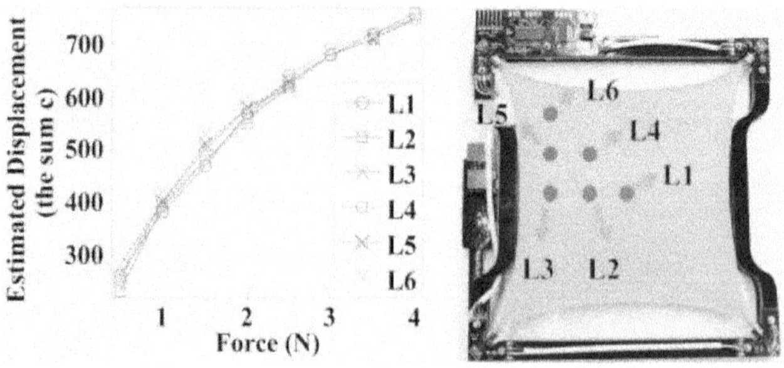

Figure 5: Applied force on the surface versus the estimated displacement.

Signal processing

The tracking software has four signal processing steps to estimate the touch position, the side touched, and the displacement along the z-axis. First, the software stabilizes the raw sensor values using a low-pass filter. Second, to cope with the individual difference of the sensors, the stabilized values s_n (with n the index to the four sensors, marked as # in Figure 3) from the previous step are calibrated by multiplying them with constants A_n, i.e. $c_n = A_n \times s_n$. Third, the software estimates a touch position, a direction, and a displacement using the calibrated values c_n. The horizontal and vertical positions, p_x and p_y, of a touch point are estimated by the following equations:

$$p_x = (c_1 + c_2) / c \text{ and } p_y = (c_1 + c_3) / c, \text{ where } c = \sum c_n$$

The sign of the sum c indicates the side that is touched. The estimated displacement of the finger along the z-axis is estimated by the sum c. The sum c is ignored when it falls below a certain threshold, because it always contains some amount of noise. This threshold is also useful to reduce the oscillation effect of the elastic fabric. Oscillation occurs when users release the fabric quickly, causing false touch events. This threshold also means that a very light touch is ignored, but the threshold is small enough not to affect the usability of *Trampoline*. Finally, a speed-dependent low-pass filter [10] is applied to the estimated touch position to reduce jitter without causing noticeable latency.

After applying these signal processing steps, we verified that *Trampoline* had enough functionality to support the desired interaction techniques. We measured the resolution and accuracy of the 2D position sensing of the current prototype. When the force on the device surface was 0.5 N, the resolution was around 0.2 mm and the accuracy was around 0.7 mm. The estimation of 2D position was stable enough to make an intended movement, but we observed a small shift at the beginning of a movement. We also measured the mapping between the force applied to the surface and the estimated displacement c at six different positions as shown in Figure 5. The mapping is slightly nonlinear, but does not depend much on measurement positions. We did not try to compensate the nonlinearity with a calibration step because *Trampoline* interaction would depend more on visual feedback on the screen than on proprioceptive feedback.

RELIEF APPLICATION

We implemented a relief modeling application to demonstrate the feasibility of our prototype and modeling techniques. The application is written in C# and uses the OpenTK library and the OpenGL shading language. The size of the application screen is 1,500 x 1,000 pixels. As shown in Figure 6, a control panel is placed on the left-top side of the application screen, which has eight buttons to select the current operation tool and a deformation shape, as well as undo and redo buttons. The remaining screen area shows the surface where the deformation occurred. An interaction window is located on the surface, represented by a black wire square. The surface in the interaction window is mapped to the surface of *Trampoline* through an absolute mapping; pushing the same position on the device's surface causes the deformation of the virtual surface at the same position.

Interaction techniques

We designed two basic operations analogous to their physical-world counterpart operations. The first operation is pressing. In this operational mode, users can choose one out of three deformation shapes: a fingertip, a pen-tip, or a brush-tip. The surface is deformed smoothly with the fingertip and sharply with the pen-tip. The brush-tip deforms a wide area of the surface. The diameter and depth of the deformation is proportional to the force applied to the surface. The other operation, smoothing, applies a bi-cubic interpolation to the vertices in the cursor area, thereby reducing discontinuity in the surface. During a smoothing operation, interpolation is repeatedly applied to the surface.

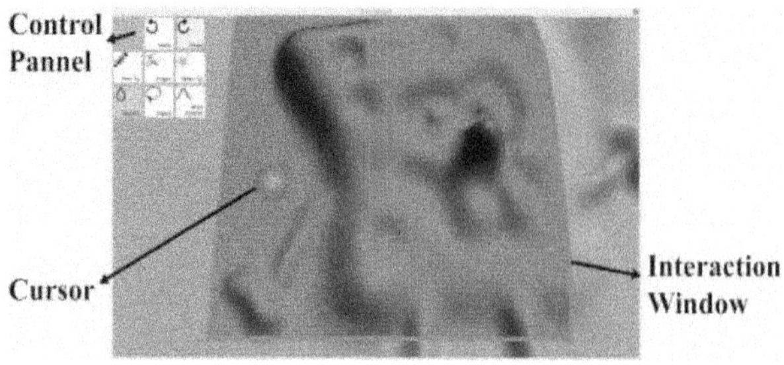

Figure 6: Application screen, consisting of the modeling surface, the control panel, and the interaction window.

In addition to these two basic operations, we implemented operations such as area selection, area modification, and undo/redo operations. Area selection is achieved by dragging. The selected area is colored yellow. After selection, one can modify the selected area by using the area manipulation operation. The depth of the modification of each vertex in the selected area is proportional to the distance between the vertex and the cursor. This operation can be used to create a continuous deformation over the selected area. This operation is, for example, useful in making the face and body of an animal.

There are two touch states, which depend on the amount of force applied: the light-touch and the heavy-touch state. In the light-touch state only the feedback of the current position is given, whereas the current operation is performed in the heavy-touch state. In the heavy-touch state, the amount of deformation or the cursor size is proportional to the applied force on the device surface.

The application has three input modes to support seamless integration of these operations: 1) modeling reliefs, 2) choosing the current operation tool, and 3) manipulating the target interaction window. Users can select one of these modes by pushing one of two physical buttons on the left side of the device. The default mode is for modeling reliefs. In this mode, users can deform the virtual surface with the currently selected operation tool. In the second mode, users can change the current operation tool. Pushing the upper physical button toggles between these two modes. In this mode, all visual feedback, like the cursor and the interaction window, disappears, and the whole device surface, divided into 3 x 3 areas, is mapped to the 3 x 3 buttons of the control panel. For example, users can select the redo button by pushing the right upper side of the device surface.

The last mode is for interaction window manipulation. This mode is activated temporarily while the lower physical button is held down. In this mode, users can control the position of the window by tilting the device along the x- and y-axes. Users can also control the size of the window by pushing or pulling the device's elastic surface. The window becomes smaller when users pushes the device surface, and larger with the opposite touch direction. The viewing angle changes depending on the position and size of the window. This enabled seamless deformation operations at various resolutions without distracting from the working context.

USER FEEDBACK

We conducted an informal user study with the relief application and *Trampoline*. The purpose of the user study was to see if they would consider the interaction metaphor natural and intuitive and if they could learn to use the interface with a minimal instruction.

Six people who were not familiar with 3D modeling (right handed, one female, and mean age 28.7) participated in this study and created one or two relief models after a short tutorial. The tutorial session was held in order to explain the concept of the device and the interaction techniques of the relief application. We showed the participants the example models made by an expert user. This session took about 10 min. After the tutorial, the participants had a practice session to familiarize themselves with the various operation tools and input modes. During the main session, we asked the participants to create relief models as shown in Figure 7. We gave them sufficient time to finish the relief models to their satisfaction. This usually took about half an hour, but took about an hour for two of them. After finishing the relief models, the participants were interviewed about their experience of using *Trampoline*.

All participants agreed that the absolute mapping between the cursor and the finger position was easy to understand. One participant mentioned that this mapping was conflicting with the experience of using a touchpad, but he could get used to this mapping soon. Some participants complained about the sensitivity of the 2D position mapping, which was rather high for novice users. We think that an accompanying elastic force was one possible reason for their difficulty. They had to use different tangential forces for different normal forces to move the same distance on the surface because friction on the surface is proportional to the normal force. In addition, the angle of the finger was not usually perpendicular to the surface, which caused a slight cursor movement when the applied force increased.

Participants also agreed that the amount of the surface deformation and the applied force on the device surface was mapped intuitively. Some participants mentioned that the cursor was important for them to perceive an applied force on the surface. The combination of the elastic feeling of the device surface and the cursor on the virtual surface seemed helpful during the modeling process. One participants mentioned that the mapping from the force applied to the surface to both the diameter and depth of a surface deformation seemed to make interaction difficult. The separate control of the diameter and the depth of the deformation could have been a better design choice. One

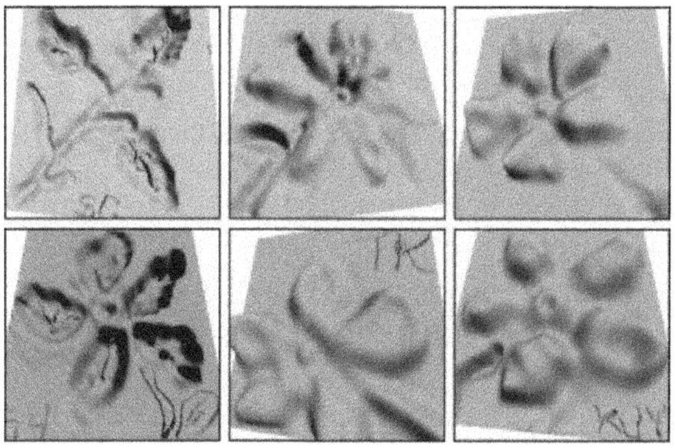

Figure 7: Relief models from six participants (colors were applied after the modeling process).

participant commented that the elastic feeing of the device was similar to making a physical model out of clay.

Regarding the bi-directional manipulation of the device, all participants preferred manipulating the upper side of the device surface. Two participants mentioned that they had to change the hand grip depending on the touch direction and this reduced the comfort of using *Trampoline*.

Overall, the participants felt that the current system was easy to use and enjoyed using *Trampoline*, especially because of the elastic feeling of the device surface. Two participants mentioned that using *Trampoline* was like playing with a toy.

CONCLUSION

We adopted the metaphors of repoussé and chasing as an interaction technique to model relief on virtual surfaces. In order to support the interaction technique, we implemented *Trampoline*, which could estimate the position and force of a finger touch on both sides of an elastic surface. We then designed a relief modeling application for *Trampoline* and could show that the new interaction technique with *Trampoline* was indeed effective to create reliefs on a virtual surface, especially due to the absolute mapping and the elastic feedback properties of *Trampoline*. Immediate future work will seek more general uses of *Trampoline* that can utilize its novel characteristics.

ACKNOWLEDGMENTS

This work was supported by the IT R&D program of MKE/KEIT. [KI10041244, SmartTV 2.0 Software Platform]

REFERENCES

1. Bae, S., Balakrishnan, R., and Singh, K. ILoveSketch: As-Natural-As-Possible Sketching System for Creating 3D Curve Models. In Proc. UIST, ACM Press (2008), 151-160.
2. Follmer, S., Johnson, M., Adelson, E., and Ishii. H., deForm: An Interactive Malleable Surface for Capturing 2.5D Arbitrary Objects, Tools and Touch. In Proc. UIST, ACM Press (2011), 527-536.
3. Follmer, S., Leithinger, D., Olwal, A., Cheng, N., and Ishii, H. Jamming User Interfaces: Programmable Particle Stiffness and Sensing for Malleable and Shape-Changing Devices. In Proc. UIST, ACM Press, (2012), 519-528.
4. Galyean, T. A., and Hughes, J. F. Sculpting: An Interactive Volumetric Modeling Technique. In Proc. SIGGRAPH, ACM Press (1991), 267–274.
5. Han, J., Heo, S., Gu, J., and Lee, G. Trampoline: A Double-sided Elastic Touch Device for Repoussé and Chasing Techniques, In Proc. CHI EA, ACM Press (2014).
6. Hoshi, T. and Shinoda, H. Gravity-based 3D Shape Measuring Sheet. In Proc. SICE, IEEE, (2007), 2126-2131.
7. Igarashi, T., Matsuoka, S., and Tanaka, H. Teddy: a Sketching Interface for 3D Freeform Design. In ACM SIGGRAPH courses, ACM Press (2007).
8. Joshi, P. and Carr, N. A. Repoussé: Automatic Inflation of 2D Artwork. In Sketch-Based interfaces and Modeling, Eurographics Association (2008)
9. Kuribara, T., Shizuki, B., and Tanaka, J. Sinkpad: A Malleable Mouse Pad Consisted of an Elastic Material. In Proc. CHI EA, ACM Press, (2013), 1251-1256.
10. Lee, G., Lee, S., Bang, W.-C., and Kim, Y. A TV Pointing Device Using LED Directivity. In Proc. ICCE, IEEE (2011), 619–620.
11. McDonnell, K. T., Qin, H., and Wlodarczyk, R. A. Virtual Clay: A Real-time Sculpting System with Haptic Toolkits. In Proc. Interactive 3D graphics, ACM Press (2001), 179–190.
12. Noguchi, A., Kurosawa, T., Suzuki, A., Sakamoto, Y., Oe, T., Yoshikawa, T., Shizuki, B., and Tanaka, J. Evaluation of a soft-surfaced multi-touch interface. In Human-Computer Interaction. Interaction Modalities and Techniques. Springer Berlin Heidelberg, (2013), 469-478.
13. Relievos, Apple App Store, https://itunes.apple.com/us/app/relievos/id429120513?mt=8
14. Sheng, J., Balakrishnan, R., and Singh, K. An Interface for Virtual 3D Sculpting via Physical Proxy. In Proc. GRAPHITE, ACM Press (2006), 213–220.
15. Smith, R. T., Thomas, B. H., and Piekarski, W. Digital Foam Interaction Techniques for 3D Modeling. In Proc. VRST, ACM Press (2008), 61–68.
16. Sugiura, Y., Inami, M., and Igarashi, T., A Thin Stretchable Interface for Tangential Force Measurement. In Proc. of UIST, ACM Press, (2012), 529-536.
17. Ventura, J., DiVerdi, S., and Hollerer, T. A Sketch-based Interface for Photo Pop-up, In Sketch-Based interfaces and Modeling, Eurographics Association (2009)
18. Vlack, K., Mizota, T., Kawakami, N., Kamiyama, K., Kajimoto, H., and Tachi, S., GelForce: A Vision-based Traction Field Computer Interface. In Proc. CHI EA, ACM Press (2005), 1154-1155.
19. Wigdor, D., Forlines, C., Baudisch, P., Barnwell, J., and Shen. C. Lucid touch: a See-Through Mobile Device. In Proc. UIST, ACM Press, (2007), 269-278.
20. Wigdor, D., Leigh, D., Forlines, C., Shipman, S., Barnwell, J., Balakrishnan, R., and Shen, C. Under the Table Interaction. In Proc. UIST, ACM Press (2006).

Skin Buttons: Cheap, Small, Low-Power and Clickable Fixed-Icon Laser Projections

Gierad Laput Robert Xiao Xiang 'Anthony' Chen Scott E. Hudson Chris Harrison

Human-Computer Interaction Institute
Carnegie Mellon University, 5000 Forbes Avenue, Pittsburgh PA 15213
{gierad.laput, brx, xiangchen, scott.hudson, chris.harrison}@cs.cmu.edu

ABSTRACT

Smartwatches are a promising new interactive platform, but their small size makes even basic actions cumbersome. Hence, there is a great need for approaches that expand the interactive envelope around smartwatches, allowing human input to escape the small physical confines of the device. We propose using tiny projectors integrated into the smartwatch to render icons on the user's skin. These icons can be made touch sensitive, significantly expanding the interactive region without increasing device size. Through a series of experiments, we show that these "skin buttons" can have high touch accuracy and recognizability, while being low cost and power-efficient.

ACM Classification: H.5.2 [Information interfaces and presentation]: User Interfaces - Input devices and strategies.

Author Keywords: Wearable devices; around device interaction; sensors; ADI; on-body computing; mobile computing; interaction techniques; touch input; smartwatch.

INTRODUCTION

Smartwatches are an emerging computational form factor, made commercially viable by recent advances in miniaturization and battery technology. However, because they are small and our fingers are relatively large, their interfaces tend to be simplistic. Touchscreen smartwatches allow the watch face to be used for a multitude of interfaces, providing flexibility that physical buttons cannot, but suffer from lack of tactile feedback and finger occlusion. These issues would be partially mitigated if we could simply provide more space for interaction. However, simply making smartwatches larger is not an option, as this would make them more obtrusive. Thus one possible approach is to appropriate surface area around the watch for interaction.

To achieve this, we propose using tiny projectors that can be integrated into a smartwatch. These render icons onto the user's skin – for example, notification icons could be projected for missed calls or new messages (Figure 1). Infrared (IR) proximity sensors complement these projectors to enable touch sensitivity. For example, tapping a pulsating text message icon could allow users to quickly jump to that message. In addition to providing a projection surface, the skin also provides useful tactile feedback.

Figure 1. Skin Buttons are touch-sensitive projected icons. Here, application-centric buttons are projected: email, notification, music player and heart. Tapping an icon launches the corresponding application.

We make the following contributions: (1) an approach providing around-device, on-body input with projected, graphical feedback, which augments a smartwatch's small screen with lightweight peripheral icons; (2) the design and implementation of the prototype hardware system and icon set; (3) an evaluation of the system's feasibility: power consumption, size, and cost; and (4) a user study of its usability: recognizability, visibility, and accuracy.

RELATED WORK

Enabling rich interactions on small devices has been a stubborn HCI problem, leading to a wide variety of approaches being considered. One strategy is to make better use of limited screen real estate through better software and interaction techniques (e.g., [8]). Alternatively, other parts of the watch itself can be used for input, such as the bezel [2,20], band [19,24], underside [3], and face [29].

More related to this work are approaches that provide input beyond the physical confines of the device. For example, Nenya [1] and iRing [22] proposed using rings as an interactive accessory, capturing input such as rotation on the finger. Abracadabra [9] used a finger-worn magnet and magnetometer for in-air finger tracking and gesturing. GestureWatch [15] use IR proximity sensors to sense gestures above the display. SideSight [4] used IR proximity sensors along the sides of the device to detect the position of one or more proximate fingers, enabling peripheral multitouch

UIST '14, October 05 – 08, 2014, Honolulu, HI, USA.

ACM 978-1-4503-3069-5/14/10 $15.00.
http://dx.doi.org/10.1145/2642918.2647356

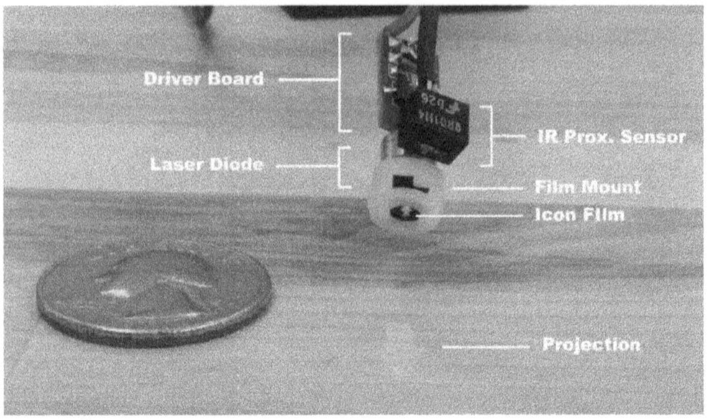

Figure 2. Close-up of a single Skin Button projector.

Figure 3. Internal view of our prototype. Note the projectors fitted into 20° angled ports on the sides of the enclosure. Also, note the extent of the projected light (no films inserted).

actions, such as pan, zoom and rotate. These free-space interactions often fall under the category of "around device" interaction, which has evolved into a significant area of study (see e.g., [13]).

Lastly, our work was also inspired by research into wearable and "on-body" systems. A wide variety of sensing techniques have been evaluated, from bioacoustics [11] and electromyography (EMG) [25], to computer vision [7,14, 30] and ultrasound. Of note, SonarWatch [17] and PUB [18] used oblique ultrasonic rangefinders to localize finger inputs on the forearm. SenSkin [21] measures shear forces using two armbands to enable trackpad-like interactions on the skin. Another approach entirely is for interfaces to be implanted under the skin [12]. Finally, there is a growing body of literature that looks at how to design touch interfaces and gestures for the skin [26,27].

IMPLEMENTATION

Our prototype smartwatch contains four fixed-icon laser projectors, described subsequently, with accompanying infrared proximity sensors. These are connected to a Femtoduino board, which communicates over USB with a host computer. Similarly, a 1.5-inch, 280x220 TFT LCD display is driven from the host computer. We used an external computer to facilitate prototyping, though a commercial implementation would be self-contained.

Fixed-Icon Laser Projectors

We chose 5 mW red laser diodes (650 nm) for our projectors (Figure 2). We removed the collimating lens, enabling the diodes to output a cone of light (Figure 3). By using lasers (i.e., coherent light), we achieve focus-free projection, which is crucial as the oblique angle of the emitter produces widely variable distances to the skin surface. Further, this eliminated the need for lenses, which reduced size, cost and complexity. The laser diodes were driven by standard automatic power control (APC) circuitry, with brightness controlled using pulse width modulation (PWM). This allows for a wide range of expressive light behaviors [10].

To create static image projections, we rendered icons to photographic film at 5780 DPI (an "8K process"). The best results were achieved by using black-and-white film stock (Figure 4). These films are placed 3mm in front of the laser emitter aperture (Figure 2). Our 3D printed enclosure contains precise openings for our emitters and icon films, ensuring correct and stable projection geometry (Figure 3). The resulting field of view is 62° horizontally and 17° vertically, which is ideal for short range, oblique projection.

Surface Calibration

The projectors are mounted in the smartwatch chassis at 20° from horizontal. The light from the laser diode first passes through a circular aperture 4 mm in diameter (Figure 2). This circle of light expands broadly across the skin surface, resulting in a parabolic cone of light (Figure 3). The film, placed between the diode and the aperture, must be carefully designed so that the projected icon will appear correct on the skin surface, taking into account the oblique projection angle and the curvature of the arm (Figures 4 and 5).

To generate the perspective-corrected images on our film, we performed a calibration procedure to establish the projector pose relative to the skin. We used a mannequin arm (Figure 5) to model a human arm and provide a fixed calibration target. We repeated the procedure for all four projectors, producing films specific to each.

The calibration process models the appearance of the icon onto the skin as a projective transformation. Rays are imagined casting out from the projector, through the film, and onto a resulting point on the skin. To establish the initial correspondence between skin points and film points, we printed a film containing an evenly spaced 5x5 grid of points. The resulting pattern projection was measured to derive "skin coordinates" corresponding to the film's grid points. These coordinate pairs were fed into OpenCV's camera calibration routine, which provided the pose, focal and nonlinear distortion parameters of the projector. Finally, we used these parameters to transform the icon images from skin coordinates to film coordinates. A comparison of calibrated and uncalibrated icons is shown in Figures 4 and 5.

Luminance Correction

Our current films are binary in nature, in that they are either clear or opaque to the laser light. Because our laser light is not collimated, it diminishes in intensity as the square of the distance, producing widely variable luminance across the skin. We therefore experimented with gradated (grayscale)

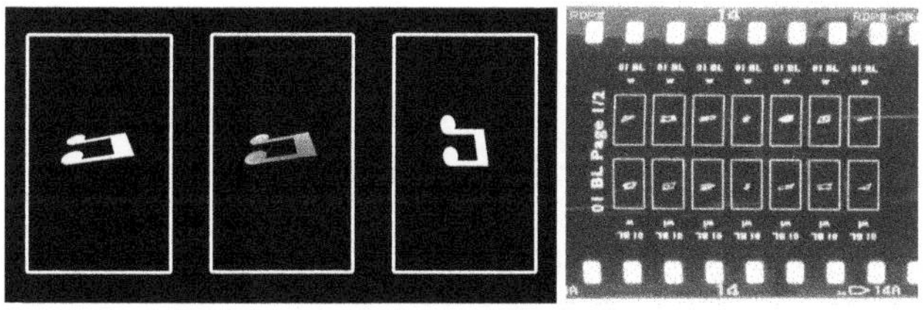

Figure 4. Left: Example icons: perspective-corrected, perspective- and luminance-corrected, and uncorrected. Right: icons rendered onto film (bottom row luminance corrected).

films, in which we selectively darken regions of the film to produce a more even luminance distribution. We measured the approximate visual intensity of the laser light at each point on the skin using a camera, and then darkened the film correspondingly to balance the intensity. The resulting icons from this process can be seen in Figure 4, bottom-right.

Unfortunately, we found the results to be suboptimal. The icons were substantially dimmer, as the light was attenuated over the majority of the icon. This made icons less visible, requiring more power output to achieve equivalent brightness. Additionally, from a visual perception standpoint, humans are generally less sensitive to smooth changes in luminance [28]. Instead, the hard edges between lit and unlit areas (i.e., icon edges) are most noticeable, and so we found it more desirable to exaggerate this difference by employing maximum illumination, regardless of luminance regularity.

Touch Sensing

To capture touch events, we use a Fairchild QRD1114 phototransistor/emitter (Figure 2), which measures the intensity of reflected infrared light from proximate surfaces up to 3 cm away. Infrared proximity sensing of this type has been used in many applications, including input devices (see e.g. [4,15]). For our purposes, these sensors are paired with a laser projector and oriented obliquely to the skin. To compensate for ambient infrared light, we capture two sensor values, once with the IR emitter active and once without. These values are then subtracted to get a better estimate of proximate reflections. Additionally, to help reject false positives, we also use an accelerometer, which disables touch sensing while the arms are in significant motion.

Although this infrared sensing approach is not novel, we are not aware of any work that uses such sensors on the skin in this fashion. SideSight [4] is most similar from a configuration perspective, using oblique infrared proximity sensing to detect fingers on either side of a device when situated on a table. Also related is Digits [14], which used an oblique infrared line laser and 2D camera to estimate 3D hand pose.

Compared with mechanical buttons, skin buttons could be made very small (potentially a single IC), yet still provide large, comfortable input. Conversely, mechanical buttons cannot provide notifications (no output), are not solid state (durability issues), and must be large enough for fingers.

Size, Weight and Cost

We built our Skin Button projectors from off-the-shelf components costing roughly $5 each. In volume, we anticipate the price to be $1 or less. Our prototype projector, seen in Figure 2, is approximately 8x10x19 mm, occupies less than 0.4 cm^3 of space, and weighs less than 3 g. With tighter integration, we do not foresee significant obstacles to shrinking this by a factor of two or more. The biggest gains to be made are by moving the laser driver onto the smartwatch mainboard PCB, sharing some components, and switching to surface mount components. In the future, a single dedicated IC could handle all of the sensors.

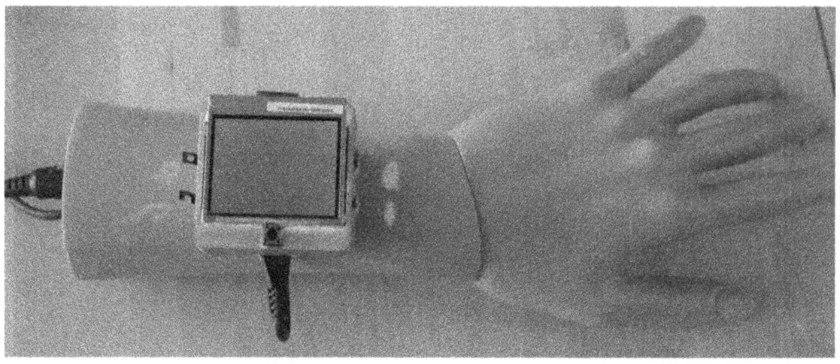

Figure 5. A mannequin was used for rapid prototyping. Note that the top-left icon ("music") is perspective-corrected while the bottom-left icon is not, leading to distortion.

ICON SET DESIGN STRATEGIES

Over the course of several months of ideation, development and user testing, it became clear that skin button icon sets fell into one of three primary use strategies. In the next section, we offer an example application for each approach.

Application Centric – This approach dedicates Skin Buttons for key applications or actions, such as launching the phone app or triggering a voice search (example set in Figure 1).

Navigation Centric - Skin Buttons could also be used primarily for navigation. For example: up, down, select, and back (Figure 6). This is also the (physical) button set used in the Pebble Smartwatch. The general nature of these buttons means they could be used for input across a wide variety of applications, from music players to contact lists.

Screen-Coupled – It is also possible to associate Skin Buttons with on-screen labels (Figure 7), enabling flexible and fully generalized use, more akin to a touchscreen. Actions could range from app launching on the home screen to playback controls in a music app. Importantly, these labels could be much smaller than an equivalent on-screen touch button, allowing more of the screen to be used for content.

EXAMPLE APPLICATIONS

To demonstrate the immediate potential of our approach, we created three proof-of-concept applications, seen in Figures 1, 6 and 7 (see also Video Figure). These illustrate the three strategies described in the previous section.

Today's smartwatches are used extensively for notifications. Additionally, most devices have a "home" screen, from which to access key functionality. *Application-centric* Skin Buttons could augment both of these features by offering easily accessible application icons. As an example, we fitted our prototype with four application icons: email, notifications, music player, and favorites (Figure 1). These

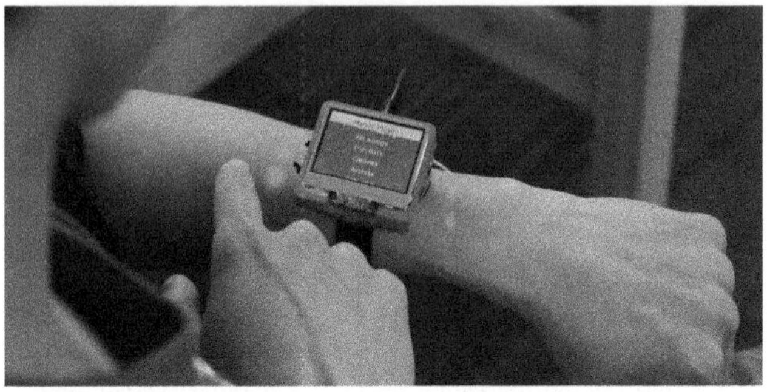

Figure 6. Music Player application features a navigation-centric icon set. Clockwise from top right: up arrow, down arrow, circle (select), back arrow.

Figure 7. In our clock app, users can set an alarm and change watch faces. In stopwatch mode, seen here, users can start, resume/pause, reset, or return to the clock.

icons can be tapped to quickly launch the corresponding application. Additionally, icons can pulse, flash or have other light behaviors [10] to indicate that e.g., a missed phone call, or that a text message has been received.

We also created a music player that used our *navigation-centric* icon set (Figure 6). 'Up' and 'down' buttons are used to scroll, the 'select' button enters a sub-list (e.g., playlist or album) or activates an item (e.g., play a song), and 'back' traverses up through the hierarchical interface.

Finally, as a demonstration of application-specific, *screen-coupled* Skin Buttons, we created a clock application. When in the clock mode, buttons allow the user to customize the 'watchface', toggle the 'alarm', set the 'alarm time', and enter 'stopwatch' mode (Figure 7). When in stopwatch mode, there are buttons to 'start', 'pause/resume', 'reset', and go 'back' to clock mode.

EVALUATION

To assess the performance of Skin Buttons, we ran a series of small, targeted experiments, which took approximately 30 minutes in total. We recruited 20 participants (7 female, mean age 24), who were given $10 for their involvement in the study. To assess if posture had an effect on use, ten participants completed the study standing, while the other ten were seated. The experiment was performed under normal office ambient lighting conditions. For the experiment, we used email, up-arrow, music, and heart icons.

As our prototype was calibrated assuming the watch was worn on the left wrist, only participants who reported they would wear a watch in this fashion were recruited. In addition to standard demographics information, participants also completed the Fitzpatrick Scale questionnaire [6], which provides a schema for skin color (types I to VI, ranging from lightest to darkest skin color). We had the following breakdown: Type II, III, IV, V and VI had 4, 4, 7, 2, and 3 participants respectively, representing almost the entire spectrum of skin tones. The experimenter also recorded hairiness and any other notable skin features (e.g., wrinkliness, freckle density) for later analysis.

Projected Icon Recognizability

Our first experiment sought to assess if icons had enough *fidelity* to be recognizable when projected on the skin. After participants put on our smartwatch prototype, all four Skin Buttons were illuminated at an intensity determined to be comfortable in piloting. The experimenter then announced the icon names (e.g. "the email icon") in random order, asking the participant to point out each icon as it was announced. For the arrow icon, the experimenter additionally asked the participant to identify the direction it was facing.

Out of 80 recognition trials, participants pointed to the wrong target two times, yielding an overall recognition accuracy of 98%. All participants correctly identified the arrow icon, but two misidentified the direction. We believe these results suggest our prototype icon design and projection fidelity is reasonably robust. Following the recognition trials, we asked participants two Likert-scale questions: "I could easily recognize the different projected icons" and "After a few days of use, I believe I could easily recognize the different projected icons" (1–Strongly disagree, 5–Strongly agree). These elicited average scores of 3.7 and 4.6 respectively (SD=1.0 and 0.49).

Projection Visibility

Next, we wished to investigate the more general question of *visibility*. Put simply: at what level of brightness can the projection be seen and what level is sufficient to enable reliable use in typical lighting conditions? To answers these questions, we allowed participants to adjust the brightness of the Skin Buttons using arrow keys on a laptop. Participants were asked to find three levels of brightness:

- "I can just barely see that the icons are active at this level of brightness" (*barely*)
- "I can comfortably see that the icons are active at this level of brightness" (*comfortable*)
- "I would generally never need an icon to be stronger than this level of brightness" (*high*)

Participants were able to adjust and revisit the three questions until they were satisfied with their selected levels of brightness. When participants indicated they were done, our software recorded the corresponding duty cycles of the laser projectors. We found that barely visible icons required an average duty cycle of 10.0% (SD=3.6%), comfortable visibility required 17.3% (SD=6.2%), and high visibility required 27.9% (SD=10.7%).

Touch Sensing Accuracy

To assess the touch sensing accuracy of our approach, we had our participants "click" our four Skin Buttons 25 times each in a random order. Participants were told to simply "click the icon" without any further guidance. Before performing the trials, participants practiced with the system for two minutes. There were two possible error modes: 1) another skin button was inadvertently triggered or 2) the click was not detected. In the latter case, the experimenter recorded the false negative and the participant clicked again. In total, our 20 participants provided 2000 click trials, of which 2.8% (56 trials) had false negatives. When a finger tap was detected, the system was 96.9% accurate in triggering the intended button. Anecdotally, 99%+ accuracy appears achievable if people can use the device for a longer period than the study permitted.

Power Consumption

Our approach has to two distinct processes that consume power: touch sensing and projection. For reference, the Samsung Galaxy Gear (2013) contains a 1200 mWh battery.

As noted previously, the touch-sensing scheme we employ takes two samples, one with and one without IR illumination. This process takes approximately 40 µs. Our prototype smartwatch polls these sensors at 50 Hz, resulting in 1.0 mW of power draw per sensor. Even if active continually for 24 hours, this would drain less than 2% of the battery.

The power draw of our projectors depends on their intensity, which we vary using pulse width modulation (PWM). In our projection visibility experiment, we found that 17.3% was the mean duty cycle (SD=6.2%) needed to achieve a "comfortable" level of brightness. This equates to a power consumption of 19.9 mW when active, including both the laser diode and driver circuitry. In other words, each hour, a projected icon would consume roughly 1.7% of a Galaxy Gear's battery. Icons that are "barely" visible require roughly half the power, only 11.5 mW. Pulsing or flashing an icon could cut power consumption in half or more.

Importantly, if Skin Buttons allow interactions to proceed without turning on the main display (e.g., by flashing the phone icon to convey a "missed call" instead of activating the LCD), they have the potential to extend battery life. It should also be noted that these numbers should be treated as an upper bound, as tighter integration and further refinement would undoubtedly reduce power consumption.

Skin Color and Other Effects

There were no statistically significant effects regarding gender, age, hairiness, skin color, or standing vs. sitting. As such, the above experimental results were combined.

Interview

At the end of the study, we conducted an open-ended interview with participants to elicit their feedback. Overall, we found that participants found the concept compelling and useful. Seven had tried smartwatches in the past; all but two had discontinued use due to a poor user experience. With respect to touching the skin for interaction, users generally thought Skin Buttons were "cool" and "satisfyingly responsive." One participant mentioned that "touching buttons on her skin" made the smartwatch experience "more intimate." Several participants commented on the visual appearance of icons, suggesting the recognizability was affected by "negative space", "simplicity of shape", "exaggerated features", "brightness", and good "reuse [of] symbolic conventions."

Figure 8. By substituting film for a very small liquid crystal display, it is possible to project primitive dynamic icons, including characters, symbols and system icons (e.g. a battery). Far right: the LCD we used, which contains four LCD blocks, each 3x5 pixels in resolution.

LIMITATIONS AND FUTURE WORK

The major limitation of our current prototype is the use of fixed projected icons. Dynamic projection is certainly more desirable, and so we performed an early experiment to explore this approach. We repurposed a small LCD module with an active area consisting of four 1.8x2.2 mm 3x5 pixel arrays (Figure 8). Using an LED as a light source, we were able to project various icons. Due to the limited resolution, these are not perspective-corrected. Small, high-resolution LCDs (e.g. 32x32) could allow for perspective-corrected, high-resolution, dynamic icons in the near future.

Diffraction gratings are another option for static icon projection. We experimented with these early on, but found the output to be poor at short throw distances. We hope to design our own diffraction gratings in the future – these have high setup costs, but are very low cost to manufacture in volume. Additionally, our current prototype is monochromatic (red); moving to full color is interesting, but comes at the cost of increased size. Regarding size, we believe further miniaturization is possible (see "implementation").

The use of fixed icons also means that projection calibrations must be "one-size-fits-all". We noted during our experiments that the icon appearances were primarily affected by the projection angle, rather than the curvature of the arm. Nevertheless, there may well be incompatible arm geometries; e.g. icon sets would have to be modified for watches that are worn on the right arm.

There are also challenges in achieving high fidelity projected output on the skin. Foremost, light hitting the skin causes subdermal light scattering [16], which increases local illumination, thus decreasing contrast. Additionally, at the scales at which we are operating, the fine details in our icons can produce light interference effects. Moreover, laser light tends to produce a speckle pattern, which can make the icons appear to "sparkle", reducing the visibility and identifiability of the icon [5]. Despeckling methods exist that can reduce this effect (see e.g., [23]), but future work is needed to see if these techniques are compatible with small devices.

Finally, the IR proximity sensors we use can be inadvertently triggered by movement or flexing of the arm and wrist, and also by proximate clothing and jewelry. We attempt to mitigate the former by using an accelerometer to reject touch input while in motion, but outside of the lab, this will be a greater challenge. Sensor fusion, e.g., by combining IR touch sensing with bio-acoustics, may be the best way forward, and we plan to explore this in future work.

ACKNOWLEDGEMENTS

This work was generously supported by grants from Yahoo! InMind, Google and NSF (IIS-1217929), as well as fellowships from Qualcomm, Disney and NSERC of Canada.

CONCLUSION

Skin Buttons are low cost, very small projectors that can render a fixed image onto the skin at an oblique angle. These properties make them suitable for inclusion into smartwatches, where they can extend the interactive area beyond the small screen. We further added touch sensitivity through infrared proximity sensing, enabling interactive touch functionality. We described our proof-of-concept implementation and results from our study, which show that the projections are easily recognized, easily clicked, and have power requirements approaching commercial feasibility.

REFERENCES

1. Ashbrook, D., Baudisch, P. and White, S. Nenya: subtle and eyes-free mobile input with a magnetically-tracked finger ring. In *Proc. CHI '11*, 2043-2046.
2. Ashbrook, D., Lyons, K. and Starner, T. An investigation into round touchscreen wristwatch interaction. In *Proc. MobileHCI '08*, 311-314.
3. Baudisch, P. and Chu, G. Back-of-device interaction allows creating very small touch devices. *Proc. CHI '09*, 1923-1932.
4. Butler, A., Izadi, S. and Hodges, S. SideSight: multi-"touch" interaction around small devices. In *Proc. UIST '08*, 201-204.
5. Dainty, C. (Ed). Laser Speckle and Related Phenomena. *Topics in Applied Physics*, Vol. 9, 1975, Springer.
6. Fitzpatrick, T. B. Soleil et peau. *Journal de Médecine Esthétique*, Vol. 2, 1975, pp. 33–34.
7. Gustafson, S., Holz, C. and Baudisch, P. Imaginary phone: learning imaginary interfaces by transferring spatial memory from a familiar device. In *Proc. UIST '11*, 283-292.
8. Gutwin, C. and Fedak, C. Interacting with big interfaces on small screens: a comparison of fisheye, zoom, and panning techniques. In *Proc. GI '04*, 145-152.
9. Harrison, C. and Hudson, S. Abracadabra: wireless, high-precision, and unpowered finger input for very small mobile devices. In *Proc. UIST '09*, 121-124.
10. Harrison, C., Horstman, J., Hsieh, G. and Hudson, S. E. Unlocking the Expressivity of Point Lights. In *Proc. CHI '12*, 1683-1692.
11. Harrison, C., Tan, D. and Morris, D. Skinput: appropriating the body as an input surface. In *Proc. CHI '10*, 453-462.
12. Holz, C., Grossman, T., Fitzmaurice, G. and Agur, A. Implanted user interfaces. In *Proc. CHI '12*, 503-512.
13. Jones, B., Sodhi, R., Forsyth, D., Bailey, B. and Maciocci, G. Around device interaction for multiscale navigation. In *Proc. MobileHCI '12*, 83-92.
14. Kim, D., Hilliges, O., Izadi, S., Butler, A., Chen, J., Oikonomidis, I. and Olivier, P. Digits: freehand 3D interactions anywhere using a wrist-worn gloveless sensor. In *Proc. UIST '12*, 167-176.
15. Kim, J., He, J., Lyons, K. and Starner, T. The Gesture Watch: A Wireless Contact-free Gesture based Wrist Interface. In *Proc. ISWC '07*, 1-8.
16. Krishnaswamy, A. and Baranoski, G. A Biophysically-Based Spectral Model of Light Interaction with Human Skin. *Computer Graphics Forum*, 22(6), 2004, pp. 331-340.
17. Liang, R., Lin, S., Su, C., Cheng, K., Chen, B. and Yang, D. SonarWatch: appropriating the forearm as a slider bar. In *SIGGRAPH Asia 2011*, Emerging Technologies, Article 5.
18. Lin, S., Su, C., Cheng, K., Liang, R., Kuo, T. and Chen, B. PUB - point upon body: exploring eyes-free interaction and methods on an arm. In *Proc. UIST '11*, 481-488.
19. Lyons, K., Nguyen, D., Ashbrook, D. and White, S. Facet: a multi-segment wrist worn system. In *Proc. UIST '12*, 123-130.
20. Oakley, I. and Lee, D. Interaction on the edge: offset sensing for small devices. In *Proc. CHI '14*, 169-178.
21. Ogata, M., Sugiura, Y., Makino, Y., Inami, M. and Imai, M. SenSkin: adapting skin as a soft interface. In *Proc. UIST '13*, 539-544.
22. Ogata, M., Sugiura, Y., Osawa, H. and Imai, M. iRing: intelligent ring using infrared reflection. In *Proc. UIST '12*, 131-136.
23. Pan, J. and Shih, C. Speckle reduction and maintaining contrast in a LASER pico-projector using a vibrating symmetric diffuser. *Optics Express,* 22(6), 2014, 6464-6477.
24. Perrault, S., Lecolinet, E., Eagan, J. and Guiard, Y. WatchIt: simple gestures and eyes-free interaction for wristwatches and bracelets. In *Proc. CHI '13*, 1451-1460.
25. Saponas, D., Tan, D., Morris, D., Balakrishnan, R., Turner, J. and Landay, J. Enabling always-available input with muscle-computer interfaces. In *Proc. UIST '09*, 167-176.
26. Wagner, J., Nancel, M., Gustafson, S., Huot, S. and Mackay, W. Body-centric design space for multi-surface interaction. In *Proc. CHI '13*, 1299-1308.
27. Weigel, M., Mehta, V. and Steimle, J. More Than Touch: Understanding How People Use Skin as an Input Surface for Mobile Computing. In *Proc. CHI '14.*
28. Wolfe, J.M., Kluender, K.R., Levi, D.M., Bartoshuk, L.M, Herz, R.S., Klatzky, R.L. and Lederman, S.J. (2006). *Sensation and Perception.* Sinauer Associates, Sunderland, MA.
29. Xiao, R., Laput, G., and Harrison, C. Expanding the input expressivity of smartwatches with mechanical pan, twist, tilt and click. In *Proc. CHI '14*, 193-196.
30. Yamamoto, G. and Sato, K. PALMbit: A Body Interface utilizing Light Projection onto Palms. *Jour. of The Inst. of Image Info. and Tele. Eng.*, 61(6), 2007, pp. 797-804.

Kitty: Sketching Dynamic and Interactive Illustrations

Rubaiat Habib Kazi[1], Fanny Chevalier[2], Tovi Grossman[1], George Fitzmaurice[1]
[1]Autodesk Research [2]INRIA
rubaiat.habib@gmail.com, fanny.chevalier@inria.com, {tovi.grossman, george.fitzmaurice}@autodesk.com

Figure 1: Example of a dynamic interactive illustration authored with Kitty. (a) Objects in the scene are interactive: the egg held by the cook can be dragged down, as if falling into the pot, triggering subsequent animations, such as soup splashes (b) and closing of the cat's eyelids (c). Turning the knob increases the fire and steam (d). The resulting dynamic illustration captures the living nature of the scene, where the gas stove flames burn and steam emits from the pot.

ABSTRACT
We present Kitty, a sketch-based tool for authoring dynamic and interactive illustrations. Artists can sketch animated drawings and textures to convey the living phenomena, and specify the functional relationship between its entities to characterize the dynamic behavior of systems and environments. An underlying graph model, customizable through sketching, captures the functional relationships between the visual, spatial, temporal or quantitative parameters of its entities. As the viewer interacts with the resulting dynamic interactive illustration, the parameters of the drawing change accordingly, depicting the dynamics and chain of causal effects within a scene. The generality of this framework makes our tool applicable for a variety of purposes, including technical illustrations, scientific explanation, infographics, medical illustrations, children's e-books, cartoon strips and beyond. A user study demonstrates the ease of usage, variety of applications, artistic expressiveness and creative possibilities of our tool.

Author Keywords
Sketching; interactive illustrations; causal animation.

ACM Classification Keywords
H.5.2. Information interfaces and presentation: User Interfaces – Graphical Interface.

UIST '14, October 05 - 08 2014, Honolulu, HI, USA

http://dx.doi.org/10.1145/2642918.2647375

"Dynamic pictures will someday be the primary medium for visual art and visual explanations" – Bret Victor [24]

INTRODUCTION
Due to the recent advances in mobile devices and web technologies, there is a growing demand for interactive illustrations to enrich the content found on mediums such as websites, e-books, and teaching materials. In contrast to static pictures and videos that are consumed by a passive observer, interactive illustrations respond to a user's input, providing a more playful or informative experience. For example, an interactive illustration of a mechanical system invites exploration through interaction as users investigate hypotheses, which may help develop insights about significant relationships and causal patterns [11].

Traditionally, crafting such interactive illustrations is achieved through programming or scripting. This requires the artist to work with abstract textual representations of visual entities, their interactive behavior, and their relationships to other entities. To alleviate these prerequisite programming skills, researchers and practitioners have developed notable tools for authoring interactive illustrations, relying on techniques such as drag-and-drop interaction [18], sketching [14] or visual programming [24]. While powerful, these tools are usually tailored for special purpose applications (e.g. simulating blood flow [25]).

In this paper, we present Kitty, a sketch-based tool for authoring a wide range of interactive dynamic illustrations (Figure 1). Kitty builds upon Draco [7], a recent system that allows users to create dynamic illustrations – timeless, continuous animated textures that capture the living quality of a scene. Dynamic illustrations are driven by parameters, encoding *visual*, *spatial*, *temporal* and *quantitative* information of the entities. Kitty extends Draco to incorporate interactivity and functional relationships between these parameters into the illustrations.

Kitty supports both an authoring and presentation mode. An artist (*author*) can produce illustrations to be interacted with, while a viewer (*user*) can directly manipulate an entity's' parameters (*e.g.* turn the knob in Figure 1) which causes subsequent changes of the parameters of the related entities and animations (*e.g.* flames burn more intensely).

To specify the interactive behavior of entities, Kitty relies on an underlying *relational graph* structure, where nodes correspond to the entities and edges represent the functional correspondence between the entities' parameters. Kitty displays this graph in the context of the illustration, and authors can specify edges and their associated functions through freeform sketching. This enables an intuitive interaction, without requiring any programming or scripting.

Before presenting the Kitty user interface, we describe a general framework that can support the authoring of interactive dynamic illustrations. The generality of this framework makes our tool applicable for a variety of purposes, including technical and medical illustrations, scientific explanation, infographics, children's e-books, cartoon strips and beyond. A user study demonstrates the ease of usage, variety of applications, artistic expressiveness and creative possibilities of our tool. We conclude by discussing limitations and future opportunities.

RELATED WORK

The breadth of related works in crafting dynamic illustrations is large. Here, we focus our review on prior representative tools for authoring animated illustrations, explanatory illustrations, and sketch-based user interfaces.

Crafting Dynamic Illustrations

Many tools for crafting various types of dynamic graphics have been proposed, including tools for creating animations (e.g., Flash, Maya, 3D Studio Max), presentations (e.g., PowerPoint, Keynote), and visualizations (e.g., [2,5]). Of particular relevance are tools that provide support to specify relationships between entities and interactivity.

Support for Relational Dynamics

In Flash and visualization toolkits [2,5], entities' parameters can be accessed as variables in scripts that enable coordination between them. Other professional animation tools allow users to specify procedural relationships between the attributes of visual entities by scripting 'Expressions' with equations. Other systems enable constrained deformation of shapes using an underlying model [16] or mesh [14]. While powerful, these tools' lack of interactive graphical support to ease the manipulation of the relationships between entities, and require users to deal with abstract textual representations. Scratch [18] is another system relying on visual programming for children to create their own animations with programmable constructs. Rather than relying on pre-defined models or programming, Kitty provides an interface where relationships can be defined by directly manipulating the underlying relational graph, displayed in the context of the illustration.

Support for Interactivity

Flash and SLIGHTY [26] enable the creation of interactive media, but again, this is achieved through programming like in visualization toolkits [2,5]. Traditional presentation tools (e.g. PowerPoint) also support interactivity, though they are typically limited to triggers which progress an animation through a linear global timeline. Kitty capitalizes on freeform sketching, and allows artists to directly sketch the correspondence function between visual parameters. Such an approach not only facilitates the authoring of expressive relational patterns, the entities in the resulting interactive dynamic illustrations can also be directly manipulated.

Systems for Explanatory Illustrations

Static explanatory illustrations (*i.e.* diagrams) are effective for communicating design ideas, technical assembly and scientific concepts [21]. Tools have been proposed to manually [25] or automatically [13] generate such diagrams. To depict dynamics, they rely on arrows and text, which do not convert timing and manner of movements and require users to *infer* relations rather than *perceive* them.

When carefully designed, animated diagrams can yield benefits beyond their static counterparts [22]. Most of the tools to create dynamic diagrams rely on physical modeling [20] or are designed for special-purpose applications, such as explaining medical phenomena [23] and illustrating dynamic fluid systems [25], which limits variety of usage.

These tools often employ a graph model to represent the dynamics of a system [13,25], an effective conceptual representation to encode relationships. Kitty uses a similar model, which the artist can directly manipulate through sketching. The generality of this approach makes our tool expressive, and applicable to diverse application domains.

Sketch-Based User Interfaces

Sketching is a powerful tool for rapid design and visual thinking, and many sketch-based applications have been explored for domains such as interface prototyping [8, 15], mathematical expressions [9] and data storytelling [10]. Sketching for animation has first been introduced by Baeker [1], and several subsequent tools have been developed since [3,7,14]. Most relevant to our work, K-Sketch [3] and Draco [7] are tools designed to ease animation authoring through freeform sketching. While Draco allows users to create rich animation effects, the resulting artifacts are not interactive and do not capture the functional relationship between the visuals, whereas in K-Sketch, the relationship of (non interactive) animated entities are manually authored through synchronization along a global linear timeline.

Kitty builds on and extends Draco to depict the dynamic relationships and make them interactive. Kitty relies on the sketch-based paradigm, and provides a general framework for the creation of a variety of types of interactive dynamic illustrations. To our knowledge, this is the first system that allows authoring of interactive illustrations and functional relationships between objects through direct manipulation.

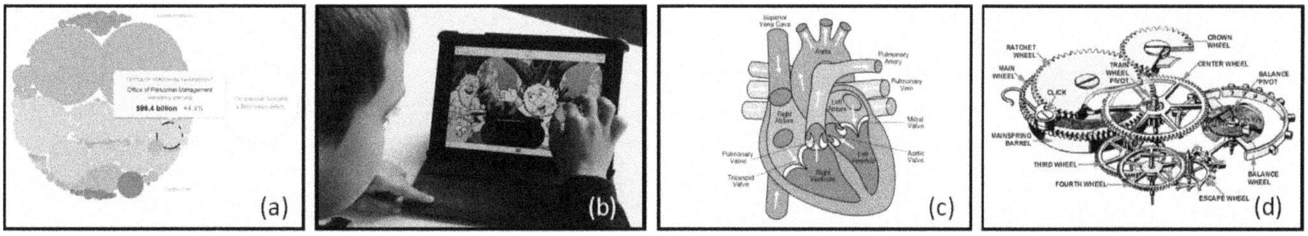

Figure 2: Example domains that could benefit from dynamic and interactive illustrations. (a) An infographics with a bubble set depicting the US budget allocation, in New York Times, (b) a children's e-book illustration of a monster scene, (c) a medical illustration explaining blood circulation of the heart, and (d) a technical illustration showing how a mechanical watch works.

MOTIVATION: APPLICATIONS AND PRINCIPLES

With the current growth and advancement of multimedia devices and web technologies, there are a number of domains where dynamic and interactive illustrations could be valuable or are already being deployed, such as interactive infographics and children's e-books (Figure 2). Dynamic illustrations have numerous advantages over static representations. They can be more compelling and more engaging, and they can also help depict situational dynamics of phenomena [22]. The associated authoring tools, however, often come with a complex interface and typically require programming skills, which greatly limits the targeted audience and require a tedious process that may discourage even the most experienced users. We aim to alleviate this challenge, by providing an easy-to-use, yet expressive tool for authoring interactive dynamic illustrations through freeform sketching and direct manipulation.

A dynamic illustration consists of visual entities, driven by parameters representing *information* that changes over time. This information is consumed and assimilated by observers to build *knowledge*. In order to provide an effective tool for authoring dynamic illustrations, we need to understand how our brain processes a visual scene and what types of information is absorbed. This understanding is imperative to provide effective support to construct the visual entities, parameterize the visuals and capture the dynamics.

The Visual Thinking Process

In his influential work *The Back of the Napkin* [19], Roam illustrates a simple perceptual framework depicting how our brain processes information, based upon prior neurological findings [17]. Roam breaks down the visual thinking process into the "six W's" as follows:

- *Object* Who and What
- *Quantity* How many and how much
- *Position in Space* Where
- *Position in Time* When
- *Relations* How
- *Interpretation* Why

When processing a visual scene, we first identify the *objects* – visually distinguishable entities, *e.g.* a dog, a doorknob – involved, and in which *quantity* they appear. Each of these objects and collections of objects occupies a specific location in the scene, *e.g.* the dog on the right, the trees in the background. Given a spatial referential, objects configuration can be characterized by transformations with regard to the origin (*i.e.* translation, rotation and scale). In a dynamic representation, the objects themselves and their position can change over time. Our vision system also tracks these *temporal* variations, *e.g.* the dog walks to the left. Such changes are usually depicted using simple animation. All three above components (what, where and when) can effectively define a dynamic visual scene. But there is much more that the human brain processes than the individual behavior of objects: we also extract functional relations between objects, including coordination and cause-and-effect (*e.g.* throwing a pebble in a pond results in water splashes and ripples).

The last two points of Roam's framework refer to such *relations* (how) and subsequent knowledge we construct through *interpretation* (why). In other words, when a particular event occurs and triggers a chain effect, we infer functional relationships and the impact of one thing upon another, resulting in new knowledge about causal patterns.

Interactivity

Prior literature on education and learning suggests that correlations and cause-and-effect relationships are best apprehended when the observer is given control over the pace of the animation [11, 22]. Thus, not only is it important for dynamic illustrations to accurately convey information, this information will also be best assimilated if the observer can manipulate the entities directly.

To summarize, a dynamic visual scene consists of *visual entities* with *spatial* and *temporal* properties. Most research efforts have been devoted to facilitating the authoring of such parameters at the individual level of objects and object collections, while editing functional relations between them – though critical to the understanding of a dynamic scene – has not been directly addressed. In traditional animation tools, the artist is required to manually coordinate temporal events on a linear global timeline, a tedious process that leaves little opportunities for interactive exploration of individual relations. Kitty rather focuses on the importance of depicting and presenting functional relationships between visuals entities and depicting knowledge in an interactive fashion. In the following, we describe the framework that we designed to meet these goals.

BACKGROUND: DRACO KINETIC TEXTURES

Before describing our new framework, we first provide necessary background information on the Draco system [7] which Kitty is built upon. Draco introduced *kinetic textures*, an animation component that encodes collections of objects and their motion. This section recalls these concepts.

A kinetic texture consists of a *patch* and *motion properties*. The patch is a set of representative objects for the collection. The motion properties – *global motion* and *granular motion* – define an object's movement. Draco introduced two types of kinetic textures: *emitting textures* and *oscillating textures* (Figure 3).

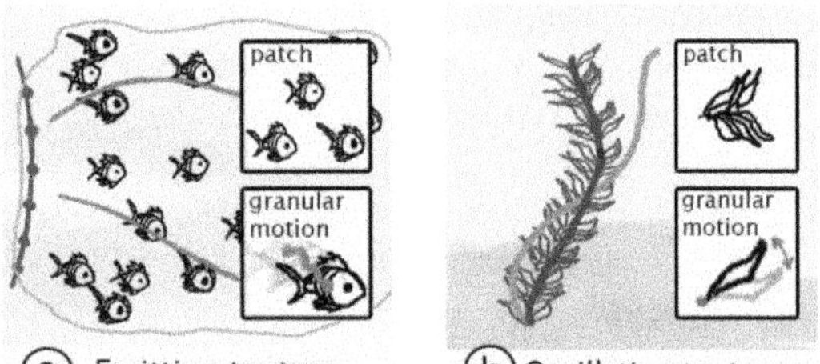

Figure 3: Kinetic textures: (a) Emitting texture, defined by a source patch, emitter (blue), global motion paths (red) and granular motion, and (b) oscillating texture, defined by a source patch, brush skeleton (brown), oscillating skeleton (orange), and granular motion. Figure taken from [7].

Emitting Textures

Emitting textures continuously emit a stream of objects, following a global motion trajectory guided by motion path(s) (*e.g.* fish swimming) (Figure 3a). The objects emanate from an *emitter*, and follow a global motion trajectory, which is guided by an underlying motion vectors field. This field is computed from a set of *motion path(s)*. Additional emitting texture attributes include a *texture outline* and *mask(s)*. Objects are removed when they cross the outline, and hide as they pass through a mask. *Emission velocity* controls velocity of the objects and the *emission frequency* controls the frequency of emissions.

Oscillating Textures

Oscillating textures consist of a duplicated collection of elements from the patch along a *brush skeleton* (*e.g.* leaves along the stem of a plant) (Figure 3b). The global motion of an oscillating texture is defined by the oscillatory movement between the initial brush skeleton and a target *oscillating skeleton*. Oscillating textures can also have a *texture outline* and *mask(s)*. Additionally, an oscillating texture has a velocity attribute which defines the speed of the global oscillations.

Granular Motion

Granular motions can also be applied to individual objects of the collection: translation defines a two-dimensional path that the individual objects move within (Figure 3a) and rotation defines a pivot point and path that the objects rotate about (Figure 3b). The final trajectory and orientation of individual objects in the collection results from the combination of the global and granular motions.

DYNAMIC INTERACTIVE ILLUSTRATIONS: FRAMEWORK

With respect to our motivation, Draco's kinetic textures satisfy a subset of the visual thinking process, but provide no interactivity. Based on these remaining open challenges, we designed a framework to further support the visual thinking process and also provide interactivity. Our framework consists of 1) the *objects and collections* which serve as the visual entities in a scene, 2) the *parameters* defining the visual properties of these entities, 3) a *relational graph* structure which defines the functional relationships between the entities, and 4) *interactivity* of the elements in the dynamic illustration. The key innovations beyond Draco lie in visualizing and defining the relational graph and associated correspondence function, configuring interactivity, and the interactive presentation mode.

Objects and Collections (What and How Much)

A visual scene comprises one or multiple identifiable visual entities characterized by *attributes* that define their visual (*e.g.* color, shape) and spatial (*e.g.* location, scale) properties. In dynamic illustrations, visual entities can be animated, which adds a set of *temporal attributes* (*e.g.* motion). In our framework, we refer to individual animated entities as *objects*, defined by a set of strokes and their attributes. An individual animated object can have a continuous ambient motion, *e.g.* a boat rocking on the sea, and also global motion, *e.g.* the same boat moving forward.

Our framework supports collections of objects using *kinetic textures* [7] as described above. Both emitting textures and oscillating can possess both global and granular motion.

Objects and kinetic textures form the base components in dynamic illustrations. They are characterized by attributes that define their visual and temporal properties. We also use a subset of these attributes as *parameters* in functional relations and for input control.

Parameters (Where, When, and How Much)

We refer to an attribute as a *parameter* if its value can be changed in response to user interaction, or based on other visual entities' behaviors. Parameters are used as the basis of our system to create a dependency mapping between the visual entities. While any attribute could possibly be considered as a parameter, we discuss here only the subset of attributes that we will use for our implementation. Our choices were guided by informal pilot studies and usage scenarios curated from various sources such as "how it works" textbooks, interactive infographics and storybooks, This helped us identify the type of content and effects to be supported and subsequently, the attributes that would be the most useful to have control upon in our framework.

The parameters of individual objects are: *translation* (along a trajectory), *rotation* (about a pivot), *scale, opacity* and *ambient speed* of the object's continuous ambient motion.

The global parameters for the kinetic textures include *opacity*, *emission frequency*, and *emission speed* for emitting textures and *opacity* and *skeleton length* for oscillating textures. The skeleton length defines how long the brush skeleton extends. The *granular velocity* serves as a single local parameter.

Relational Graph (How and Why)

In a dynamic scene, visual entities can interact with one another, depicting the coordination and cause-and-effect relations between them. Similar to prior work on explanatory illustrations [13, 25], we use an underlying *relational graph* to capture such information, where nodes correspond to visual entities and edges encode the functional relations between entities' parameters (Figure 4).

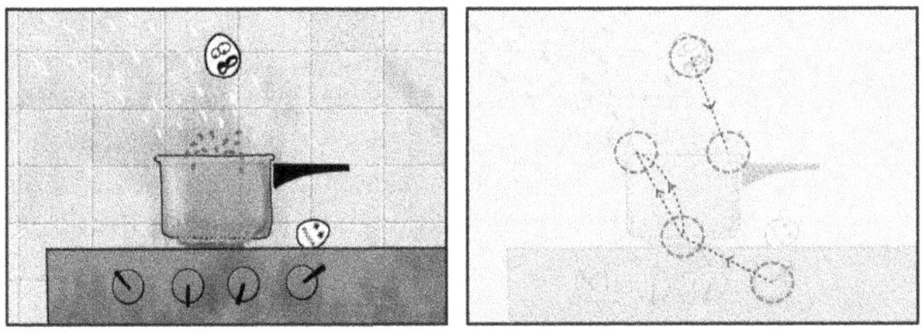

Figure 4: A simplified version of Figure 1 (left) and its associated relational graph (right).

Nodes

Nodes in the relational graph represent the visual entities – objects and kinetic textures. The graph of Figure 4 has five nodes, corresponding to two objects (green nodes), two emitting textures (blue) and one oscillating texture (orange). Each node has an associated set of parameters that can be used to create a functional dependency with other nodes.

Edges

Edges in the relational graph capture the functional relationship between the parameters of a source node and a target node. Each edge is directed, and has an associated *functional mapping* – a correspondence function that encodes the dependent behavior from a specific parameter of the target node to a specific parameter of the source node. For example, in Figure 4 the steam intensity (emission frequency parameter) is a function of the rotation of the knob (global rotation parameter): the more the knob is turned, the higher the emission frequency will be.

Two types of events could cause a source parameter to change. If the source entity is *interactive*, then the associated parameter could be directly manipulated. Alternatively, the source parameter itself could be the target of another relation, making it an intermediary parameter in a *chain effect*. In both cases, the target parameter will also change, as defined by the edge's functional mapping.

Functional Mapping

To specify the dependent behavior of a target parameter based on the status of a source parameter, we rely on a one-dimensional function as follows:

$$t_p = f(s_p)$$

where s_p and t_p denote the value of the source and the target parameters of the linked visual entities.

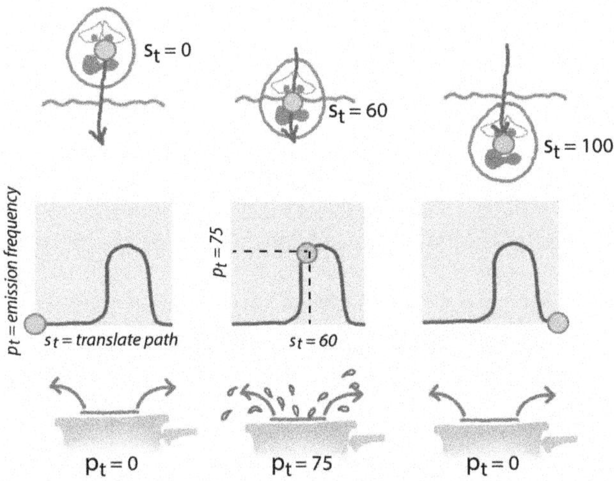

Figure 5: Functional relationship between the translation path of the egg and the emitting frequency of soup splashes.

For example, in Figure 4 the egg is interactive. Moving the egg into the pot causes the soup to splash. Here, the relation involves the translation of the egg as the source parameter s_p, and the emission frequency of the soup splashes as the target parameter t_p. The associated mapping function f is such that emission frequency is highest when the egg hits the surface (Figure 5).

Chain Effects

Multiple edges can be combined in sequence, resulting in a chain of relations across the parameters. In Figure 4, the global rotation parameter of the knob (object) impacts the scale parameter of the fire (oscillating texture), which in turn impacts the emission frequency of the steam (emitting texture). The resulting chain effect is such that when turning the knob, the fire increases in intensity, which causes more intense steam from the pot.

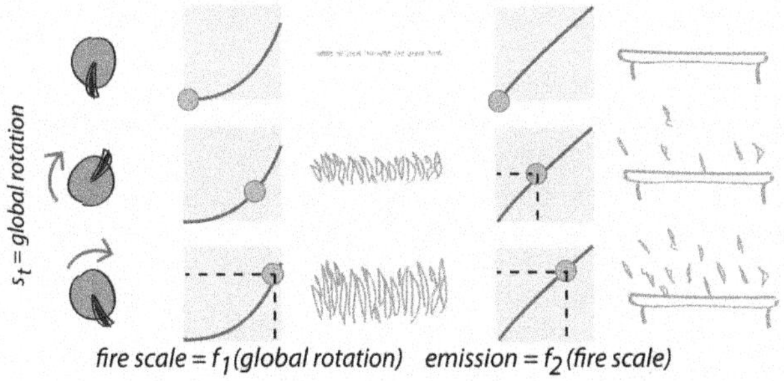

Figure 6: Chain effect with functional relationships.

Interactivity (How and Why)

The interactivity of a visual entity is defined at the node level. Each node can have one of its parameters assigned for input control, to enable manipulation. For example, in Figure 4, the egg's global translation parameter, and the knob's global rotation parameter are both interactive. Note that a visual entity does not necessarily have to be involved in a relation to be interactive.

KITTY: IMPLEMENTATION

We designed and implemented Kitty, a sketching tool to author interactive dynamic illustrations. Artists can create animated objects and textures and specify how the parameters of an illustration's visual entities are related and respond to each other. Artists can also define how these objects respond to user interaction. Figure 7 shows the Kitty user interface, consisting of a main canvas, as well as global and contextual toolbars. In addition to supporting authoring, Kitty also provides a presentation mode for both authors and subsequent viewers to interact with the illustrations.

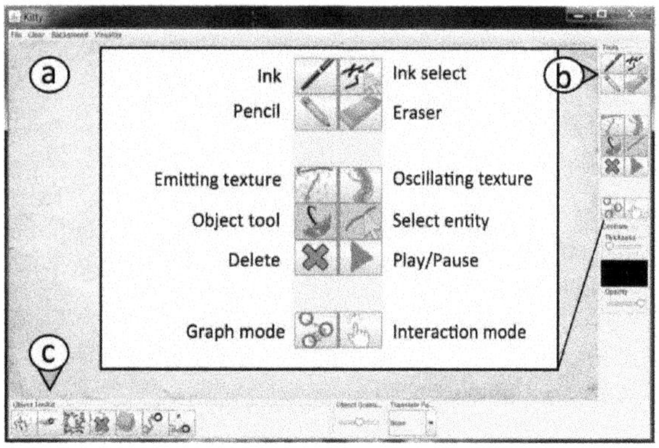

Figure 7. Kitty user interface comprising: (a) the main canvas, (b) the global toolbar and (c) contextual toolbar.

Global Toolbar

The global toolbar is comprised of the main drawing tools and tools for creating animated objects (Figure 7b). It also provides access to a graph mode, where the artist can define the underlying relational graph, and to an interaction mode.

The *ink* tool is the primary drawing tool, and has an associated color widget, brush thickness slider, and opacity slider. Artists can select a group of ink strokes with the lasso *stroke selection* tool to move or delete them. A *pencil* tool is also available to draw a rough outline of an illustration, which can be deleted with the *eraser* tool.

Dynamic and interactive entities are created using the *object* tool, *emitting texture* tool, and *oscillating texture* tool. The artist can also select an existing visual entity with the *entity select* tool and subsequently edit its properties using the tools in the contextual toolbar (Figure 7c).

Creating Visual Entities

Kitty supports three types of animated visual entities: objects, emitting textures and oscillating textures.

Creating and Editing Objects

To create an object, the artist starts by sketching the set of strokes defining the object using the *ink* tool (Figure 8a). She then defines these strokes as components of a new object, by clicking on the *object* tool in the global toolbar and selecting the strokes with a lasso (Figure 8b).

The object contextual toolbar allows the artist to further configure the created object: the *translation path* tool is used to sketch a global translation path; the *mask* tool is used to draw a mask region where the object is hidden; and the *ambient rotation* and *ambient translation* tools allow the artist to define continuous motion. For ambient rotation, a pivot point can first be dragged to set the origin of rotation (Figure 8c). Specifying ambient rotation and translation is done through direct manipulation of the associated object (Figure 8d).

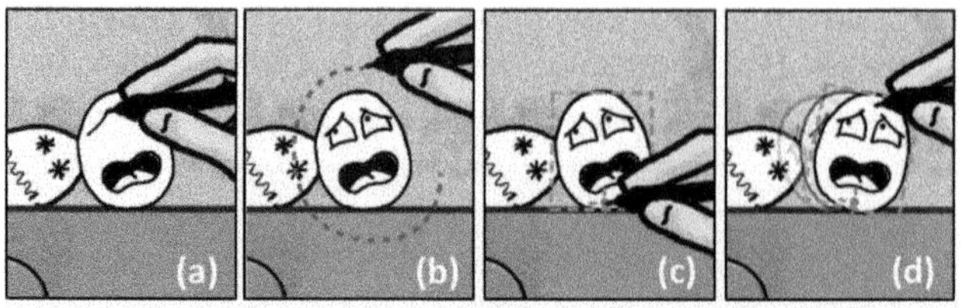

Figure 8: Creating and editing objects. (a) The artist sketches an egg with the *ink tool* and (b) defines the strokes as a new object. (c) Upon creation, the bounding box (green outline) and default pivot point (in red) are displayed. The artist drags the pivot point to a new location, and (d) specifies a continuous motion through direct manipulation using the *ambient rotation tool.*

Creating and Editing Emitting and Oscillating Textures

We used similar interactions to Draco's for authoring kinetic textures. We refer the reader to the Draco system for a complete description of the interactions [7]. Sketching the example strokes and an emitter creates an *emitting texture*, while sketching example strokes and a brush skeleton creates an *oscillating texture*. The example strokes are also displayed in a small patch widget which can be used to add granular motions.

Similar to objects, the artist can edit the components of the currently selected texture through the contextual toolbar. For an emitting texture, she can edit the *motion paths* and *emitter*. For an oscillating texture, she can define or edit the *oscillating skeletons*. In addition, for both types of kinetic textures, the artist can define a *mask* and *outline,* and induce granular motion to the texture by directly manipulating the strokes in the example patch widget.

Defining Functional Relationships

To create functional relationships between the visual entities, the artist is required to enter the *graph mode* from the global toolbar. The system animates to an abstract graph view of the visual entities and their relations, displayed in the context of the illustration canvas (*e.g.* Figure 4). Each entity in the illustration is automatically associated to a node in the relational graph.

We use a force-directed layout algorithm [3] to guarantee minimal distance between nodes, facilitating their selection. The nodes are also color-coded to distinguish between objects (green nodes), emitting textures (in blue), and oscillating textures (in orange). When exiting the graph mode, visual entities snap back to their original location in the illustration. Creating a functional relationship between two visual entities follows a three-step process.

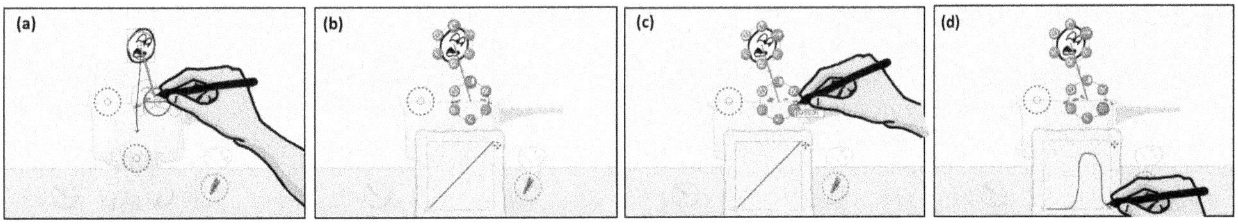

Figure 9: (a) Sketching a path between the source object node (the egg) and the target emitting texture node (soup splash), creates a relation between the two visual entities. (b) Upon creation, the relation control widget (radial menus and mapping function widget) are made visible. (c) The artist selects the parameters for the relation, then (d) directly sketches the mapping function.

Step 1: Specify the source and target nodes.

To connect two nodes in the graph, the artist simply sketches a stroke from the source to the destination node (Figure 9a), creating an edge between them. All edges are directed, but if desired, bi-directional edges can be created by specifying two separate edges in opposite directions.

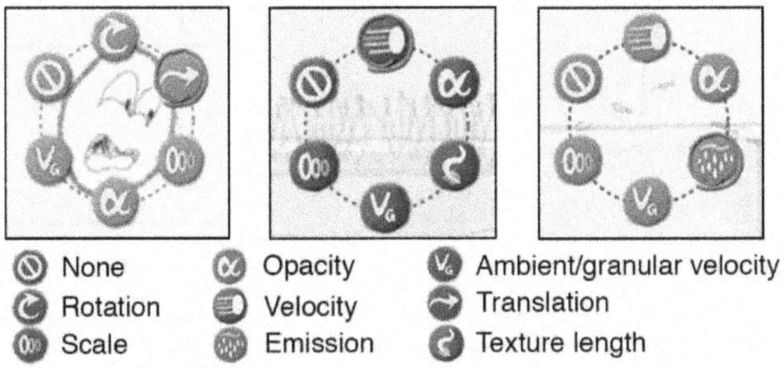

Figure 10: The parameter radial menus for an object (left), an oscillating texture (middle) and an emitting texture (right).

Step 2: Select parameters.

Upon creation of an edge, Kitty displays all candidate parameters of the source and target nodes in radial menus (Figure 9b). Figure 10 illustrates the radial menus and parameters associated which each of the three node types. The artist can select the pair of particular parameters for the functional mapping by clicking on the corresponding icons on the menus (Figure 9c). Each edge is associated to one source parameters s_p and one target parameter t_p. Creating multiple edges between the same nodes allows an author to define mappings for additional pairs of parameters.

Step 3: Specify the functional mapping.

When an edge is created or selected, a function mapping widget visualizes the functional correspondence between the associated source parameter s_p (x axis) and the target parameter t_p (y axis). By default, this function is set to identity ($t_p = s_p$), which the artist can overwrite by directly sketching a new curve within the widget (Figure 9d). The widget is equipped with an *exploration cursor* that the artist can drag within the mapping space to help identify relevant mapping points: when moving this cursor, the visual entities are automatically updated to preview the corresponding source and target parameter values.

Kitty also allows an artist to load a mapping function from an external quantitative data file (csv format), enabling precise functional relationships between visual entities. This can be particularly useful in infographics.

Editing Edges and Nodes

Existing edges and nodes can be selected to adjust their associated parameters and mapping functions. A selected edge (and associated functional relations) can also be deleted using the *delete* tool in the global toolbar.

Setting Interactivity

The interactivity of objects can also be specified in the graph mode by tapping on a node and selecting the desired interaction parameter in the radial menu (or the *none* icon for no interactivity). In the resulting interactive illustration, all visual entities with a defined interaction parameter are considered to be interactive and can be manipulated.

Presentation Mode

The artist can switch to the *presentation mode* to test the interactive dynamic illustration. The presentation mode is also used by subsequent viewers of a saved illustration.

Figure 11: Interaction guides as the user hovers over the canvas. a) Direct manipulation is used for spatial parameters, such as rotating the windmill. b) Swiping gestures are used for non-spatial parameters, such as increasing the wind speed.

Kitty displays red visual cues when the user hovers over an interactive visual entity with a mouse or stylus, or when the user taps the screen when using direct touch. These guides indicate the possible interactive gestures (Figure 11). For spatial parameters (*e.g.* rotation and translation), the expected direct manipulations are used, such as directly rotating the windmill (Figure 11a). For other parameters, such as emission frequencies, a swiping gesture towards and away from the entity will decrease and increase the parameter value respectively. Figure 11b shows an example of increasing the wind emission speed.

As the user performs a gesture, the corresponding parameter's value changes, and all subsequent dependent parameters in the illustration are updated in real-time

Chain effects are carried out by traversing the relational graph, starting at the node of interaction. Any edge which would induce a cycle is not traversed. This prevents infinite loops while still allowing for bi-directional relationships.

Resulting Interactive Dynamic Illustrations

Inspired from the examples that motivated us to develop Kitty (Figure 2), we authored several interactive dynamic illustrations using our tool (featured in Figure 13-Figure 15 and in the accompanying video): a weather infographics, a technical illustration without kinetic textures showing how car steering operates, a comic-style animation illustrating the passing of time, and a children's illustration. These results help demonstrate the creative capabilities and expressive power of Kitty.

USER EVALUATION

We conducted a user evaluation with both professional and amateur animators and illustrators, to gain insights about the capabilities and potential applications, and identify any limitations or opportunities for future advancements. This study was also used to gather feedback on how our system compares to existing approaches, although we do not perform any sort of formal comparison to existing commercial tools.

Participants

We recruited eight participants (2 female) aged 24-45 for our study. Participants completed a questionnaire about their background before the study began: all participants have moderate to good experience with sketching and illustration and are proficient with sketch-based digital painting tools. Two were professional animators (*P5, P8*), and the six other participants had little to moderate experience with animations.

Study Protocol

The study was conducted using the Wacom CINTIQ 21ux tablet display at our laboratory or at the professional animators' studios. The evaluation lasted for approximately 60 minutes, consisting of the three following steps.

Overview and training (20-25 minutes). Participants completed five training tasks designed to familiarize them with the system's drawing tools, kinetic textures, visual entities functional relationships, and interaction modes. The facilitator provided light guidance during these tasks.

Exercise task (15-25 minutes). At the end of the training, participants were given an exercise task (Figure 4) to reproduce with Kitty. The exercise task required participants to author five visual entities, including two objects (egg, knob), two emitting textures (soup splash, emitting smoke) and one oscillating or emitting texture (fire) on top of a provided background image. Participants were also required to coordinate and create the four functional relationships between the entities. A video of the target scene was prompted in a separate display to facilitate the task. The facilitator recorded observations but did not intervene during the exercise task.

Freeform usage (20-25 minutes). After completing the exercise task, participants were free to explore the tool on their own to craft illustrations. Participants then completed a questionnaire about the system.

Results

In general, participants responded positively to the user interface and functionality of Kitty. Participants commented that crafting visual entities and specifying their functionalities was easy to learn and use. On a 5-point Likert scale (1=very difficult to 5=very easy), participants rated 4.4 on average for the ease of crafting visual entities (min: 4) and also 4.4 for the ease of specifying functional relationships (min: 4).

All participants commented that specifying and sketching the functional relationship was simple to comprehend and easy to use. We were encouraged to see that all of them were very quick at picking up the mechanisms behind the graph structure and the mapping function. The visualization in the graph mode (color coded nodes, radial menus, edges) facilitated the association between the graph elements and their corresponding visual entities (objects and textures).

Participants commented that crafting interactive illustrations using the conceptual relational graph in Kitty would be tedious and time consuming with other tools. Our participants were proficient with Flash (all but *P1* and *P2*), ToonBoom Harmony (*P8*) Maya (*P2, P5*), PowerPoint (*P1, P6, P7*), After Effects (*P4*) and Lightroom (*P5*) to create animated and interactive contents.

> *P1*: "*Very nice to use, fluid interaction; can create results that I cannot imagine doing any other way.*"

> *P6*: "*Just four tools to do anything, I cannot get myself lost! For the use I have of animation [Note: presentations], it's more than enough and give me finer control than timeline.*"

> *P8 [pro]: "I only bothered adding interactivity to animations for my website. I know how to make them with Flash, but programming the most basic interactions takes me forever. I'm really impressed I made this [exercise task] so quickly."*

P1 pointed out that functional relations in Kitty provide an elegant alternative way to coordinate animations, conceptually easier to create and manipulate in contrast to timeline based 2D animation systems that require planning. *P5* and *P7* also found that the timeless nature of Kitty alleviates planning requisites, enabling a more spontaneous and playful authoring.

> *P1*: "*I use PowerPoint to create animated technical diagrams, having a timeline with relative events starting one after another. So, if I have to change anything, I have to re-order all the transitions [...] this [system] is much more flexible to co-ordinate between the animations.*"

> *P3: "I like the ability to create functional animated graphics in a matter of minutes... It's almost like being able to do Flash stuff without learning ActionScript and being bothered by timeline... I have to prepare a day to figure out how to do this (exercise task) with Flash."*

> *P6*: "*If I had this tool in PowerPoint, I would put interactive illustrations everywhere in my presentations. For now, I merely create very basic animations, because it takes me too much time to craft something satisfying.*"

Exercise Task Performance

All the participants were able to complete the exercise task without assistance. On average, the participants took 22 minutes (min 9:30, max 34:00) to complete the exercise task. This is encouraging to us, indicating that after only a short training period, participants could accomplish realistic tasks is reasonable time duration. During the studies, our eight participants encountered 10 errors in total. Errors include drawing an edge in wrong direction (twice by one participant), tool mix-up when participants created an emitting texture when the intended effect was an oscillating texture (twice), and choosing the wrong parameter (three times, the task required to select emission, but the participant chose velocity). A common mistake was that participants did not initially specify the interactivity of the nodes (8 times). This was easily resolved in all cases, but participants had assumed that interactivity was automatically specified. Several participants accidently added ambient rotation to the knob, causing the knob to rotate continuously.

Observed strategies

Participants used different strategies to author the entire illustration. Three participants broke down the process into three phases, first drawing all of the visual entities involved in the illustration, then setting interactivity for all of them, and finally specifying the relationship with repeated switches between the graph mode and the presentation mode for fine tuning. The other five participants broke down the process by relations instead. For each of the three relations, they started with the creation of the source and the target nodes, then directly entered the graph mode to specify the relation before checking the result in the presentation mode. Almost all the participants used control points to coordinate the animations and the functional relationships, which they commented was a useful addition for quick exploration of the mapping space.

Overall, the strategies used demonstrate that Kitty requires little planning: we observed the participants complete the subtasks as they came to mind. This suggests that the underlying graph abstraction was a suitable design.

Follow-Up Usage

Two of the participants volunteered to continue to use the tool after the study and sent us sample illustrations which they created (Figure 16 and Figure 17).

DISCUSSION

Our evaluation indicates that users are able to quickly grasp the concepts of the Kitty system and author their own illustrations after only a short training period. Our observations of user strategies demonstrated that the system is flexible to a variety of effective workflows. The sample content created by two of our participants, in addition to the samples which we have created, demonstrates that Kitty successfully provides a sketch-based interface for authoring a variety of rich interactive and animated effects.

While these are all encouraging results, there are also a number of limitations and opportunities for future improvements that warrant discussion.

Limitations

Grouping of Visual Entities

Currently, Kitty does not support the definition of groups of visual entities. Objects and kinetic textures are the atomic components of our system and cannot be grouped into collections. Such hierarchal groupings would allow for richer animation expression, and could also speed up repetitive operations. In particular, grouping visual entities into hierarchal-objects would allow the coordinated movement of multiple animated elements that together form some higher level object (*P5, P6*).

Grouping objects or relations would also allow authors to apply common parameters to a set of visual entities in a single interaction. Participants said it would be helpful if they could replicate the same mapping function across relations (*P7, P8*). One participant wanted a smoke emitting texture to follow the global motion of a car (*P5*), which is not currently supported.

Time-varying parameters

Kitty occupies an interesting space between the timeless dynamic illustrations composed of looping animated textures, and traditional animations based on a global timeline. The timeless nature of Kitty's visual entities is at the root of the underlying conceptual framework. However, some participants mentioned that they would like to have controls for more sophisticated storytelling, such as deformations over time, or the redefinition of the motion paths and masks of visual entities according to an another entity's parameter (P2, P7, P8).

Sophisticated effects

Kitty does not support sophisticated effects such as inter-object interactions, temporal relationships and underlying physics (momentum, gravity), which would enable to create substantially complex scenes with natural dynamics. In the future, it would be interesting to explore the combination of sketch-based and physics-based animation effects.

While designing Kitty, we chose expressiveness and simplicity over sophistication, offering an alternative to complex professional tools. We feel the existing system supports sufficient complexity to allow for a wide range of content. New features would make it more powerful, but at the detriment of ease of usage.

Scalability

Our system has an upper bound on the number of nodes, depending on the screen size. As the number of nodes and edges increases, the graph gets complicated. Grouping objects as discussed above could partly address these scalability limitations. Layers and storyboarding are other traditional ways of decomposing complex (spatio-temporal) visual content into sub-components that are more manageable for manipulation.

Applications

Participants pointed out a number of potential application scenarios apart from artistic use cases, including technical and scientific diagrams, presentations, education material, interactive comics, e-books, prototyping, data journalism, point-and-click games, and more broadly, visual media for the web. Currently, we use our own file format to store interactive illustration authored with Kitty. The ability to export dynamic illustrations in an HTML5 format (*P8*) would certainly contribute to the adoption of Kitty.

CONCLUSION

We have presented Kitty, a sketching tool to author animated and interactive illustrations driven by parameters. Kitty enables artists to create functional correspondence between visual entities with freeform sketching, offering a new way to author dynamic systems. Kitty is particularly beneficial in that dynamic and interactive illustrations can be authored in the matter of minutes, without any scripting or programming prerequisites. Overall, participants found the associated framework to be simple, yet expressive. We believe tools like Kitty requiring no programming language might place crafting high quality interactive and dynamic contents in the hands of a broader audience.

ACKNOWLEDGEMENTS

We thank Guia Gali and Mathieu Nancel for their illustrations. The cat in Figure 1 is drawn in likeness of Simon's Cat, used with permission of Simon's Cat Ltd. Copyright © 2009-2014.

REFERENCES

1. Baecker, R.M. (1969) Picture-Driven Animation. *AFIPS Spring Joint Computer Conference*, 273-288.
2. Bostock, M., Ogievetsky, V., & Heer, J. (2011). D³ data-driven documents. Visualization and Computer Graphics, IEEE Transactions on, 17(12), 2301-2309.
3. Davis, R. C., Colwell, B., & Landay, J. A. (2008). K-sketch: a 'kinetic' sketch pad for novice animators. ACM CHI, 413-422.
4. Fruchterman, T. M., & Reingold, E. M. (1991). Graph drawing by force-directed placement. *Software: Practice and experience*, 21(11), 1129-1164.
5. Heer, J., Card, S.K., Landay, J.A. (2005). prefuse: a toolkit for interactive information visualization. *ACM CHI*, 421-430.
6. Igarashi, T., Moscovich, T., & Hughes, J. F. (2005). As-rigid-as-possible shape manipulation. *ACM Trans. on Graphics* 24(3): 1134-1141.
7. Kazi, R. H., Chevalier, F., Grossman, T., Zhao, S. & Fitzmaurice, G. (2014) Draco: Bringing Life to Illustrations with Kinetic Textures. *ACM CHI*, 351-360.
8. Landay, J. A. & Myers, B.A. (2001).Sketching Interfaces: Toward More Human Interface Design.*Computer* 34(3):56-64.
9. LaViola, J. J., & Zeleznik, R. C. (2007). MathPad 2: a system for the creation and exploration of mathematical sketches. *SIGGRAPH courses*.
10. Lee, B., Kazi, R. H., & Smith, G. (2013). SketchStory: Telling more engaging stories with data through freeform sketching. *IEEE TVCG*, 19(12), 2416-2425.
11. Lowe, R. (2003). Animation and learning: selective processing of information in dynamic graphics. *Learning and instruction*, 13(2), 157-176.
12. Miller, T., & Stasko, J. (2001). The InfoCanvas: information conveyance through personalized, expressive art. *ACM CHI Extended Abstracts*. 305-306.
13. Mitra, N. J., Yang, Y. L., Yan, D. M., Li, W., & Agrawala, M. (2010). Illustrating how mechanical assemblies work. *ACM Trans, on Graphics*, 29(4), 58.
14. Moscovich, T. (2001). Animation sketching: An approach to accessible animation. *Master's Thesis*, CS Department, Brown University.
15. Newman, M. W., Lin, J., Hong, J. I., & Landay, J. A. (2003). DENIM: An informal web site design tool inspired by observations of practice. *Human-Computer Interaction*, 18(3), 259-324.
16. Ngo, T., Cutrell, D., Dana, J., Donald, B., Loeb, L., & Zhu, S. (2000). Accessible animation and customizable graphics via simplicial configuration modeling. *ACM SIGGRAPH*, 403-410.
17. Ramachandran, V.S., & Blakeslee, S. (1998). Phantoms of the brain: Probing the mysteries of the human mind.
18. Resnick, M., Maloney, J., Monroy-Hernández, A., Rusk, N., Eastmond, E., Brennan, K., & Kafai, Y. (2009). Scratch: programming for all. *Communications of the ACM*, 52(11), 60-67.
19. Roam, D. (2008). The back of the napkin.
20. Scott, J., & Davis, R. (2013, October). Physink: sketching physical behavior. *ACM UIST adjunct*. 9-10.
21. Suwa, M., & Tversky, B. (2002). External representations contribute to the dynamic construction of ideas. *Diagrammatic representation and inference*. 341-343.
22. Tversky, B., Heiser, J., Mackenzie, R., Lozano, S., & Morrison, J. (2008). Enriching animations. *Learning with animation*, 304-356.
23. Vainio, T., Hakkarainen, K., & Levonen, J. (2005). Visualizing complex medical phenomena for medical students. *ACM CHI*. 1857-1860.
24. Victor, B. (2009). Drawing Dynamic Visualizations. *CUSE*.
25. Zhu, B., Iwata, M., Haraguchi, R., Ashihara, T., Umetani, N., Igarashi, T., & Nakazawa, K. (2011). Sketch-based dynamic illustration of fluid systems. *ACM Trans. on Graphics*, 30(6), 134.
26. Zongker, D.E., & Salesin, D. (2003). On creating animated presentations. ACM SIGGRAPH, 298-308.

APPENDIX: AUTHOR AND PARTICIPANT GENERATED EXAMPLES

Figure 12 [author generated]: Animated weather infographics which updates dynamically as the user slides the calendar marker.

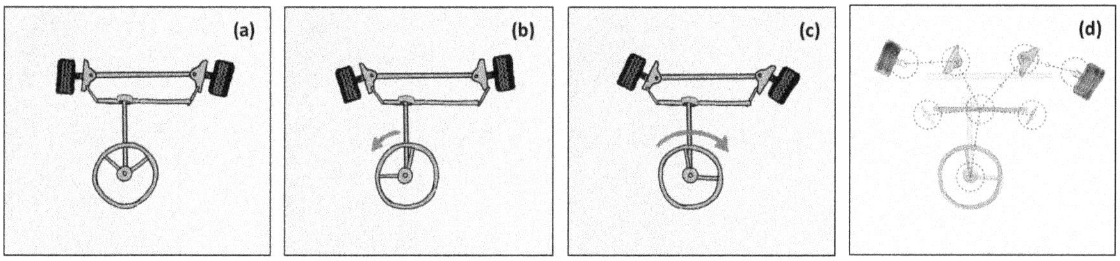

Figure 13 [author generated]: An interactive mechanical diagram illustrating how car steering operates.

Figure 14 [author generated]: An interactive comic-style animation. Time passes as the user drags the plant or the clock hand.

Figure 15 [author generated]: An interactive children's illustration. Animations respond to user interactions.

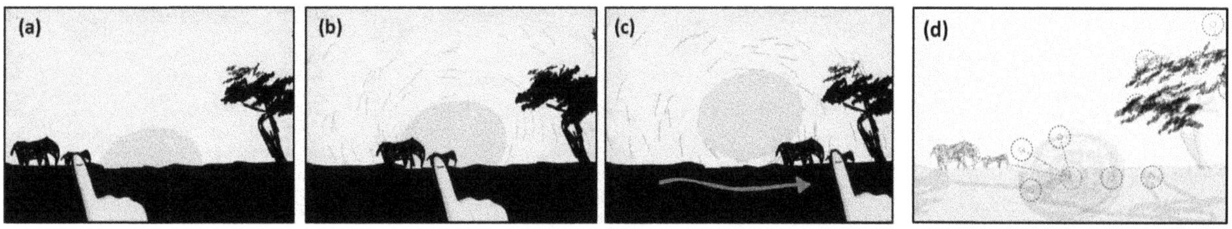

Figure 16 [participant generated]: A user drags the elephant across the horizon, and the sun rises.

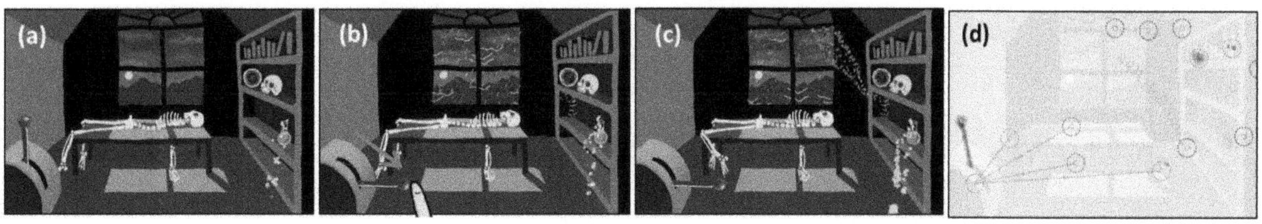

Figure 17 [participant generated]: Dr. Frankenstein's Laboratory comes to life when the user pulls the lever.

PortraitSketch: Face Sketching Assistance for Novices

Jun Xie
Univ. of Washington

Aaron Hertzmann
Adobe Research

Wilmot Li
Adobe Research

Holger Winnemöller
Adobe Research

(a) Source 1 (b) Unassisted sketch (c) Auto adjusted (d) Source 2 (e) Assisted sketch

Figure 1: Results generated with PortraitSketch. Starting from image (a), a novice user created sketch (b) using our system without automated assistance. The same user created sketch (e) with automated assistance. For direct comparison, we post-adjusted (b) to generate (c). The assisted results (c and e) exhibit cleaner, more accurate outlines and more evenly distributed shading, compared to the unassisted drawing (b). All nine of our independent judges voted that (c) is a better drawing than (b). *Image credits: (a) and (d): Levy Carneiro Jr and chris zerbes, under a Creative Commons license.*

ABSTRACT

We present PortraitSketch, an interactive drawing system that helps novices create pleasing, recognizable face sketches without requiring prior artistic training. As the user traces over a source portrait photograph, PortraitSketch automatically adjusts the geometry and stroke parameters (thickness, opacity, etc.) to improve the aesthetic quality of the sketch. We present algorithms for adjusting both outlines and shading strokes based on important features of the underlying source image. In contrast to automatic stylization systems, PortraitSketch is designed to encourage a sense of ownership and accomplishment in the user. To this end, all adjustments are performed in real-time, and the user ends up directly drawing all strokes on the canvas. The findings from our user study suggest that users prefer drawing with some automatic assistance, thereby producing better drawings, and that assistance does not decrease the perceived level of involvement in the creative process.

Author Keywords

Sketching; Portraits; Novices; Creativity Support Tool

ACM Classification Keywords

H.5.2 HCI: User Interfaces

UIST 2014, October 5–8, 2014, Honolulu, HI, USA.

http://dx.doi.org/10.1145/2642918.2647399

INTRODUCTION

Drawing/sketching is arguably one of the most accessible art forms, requiring only a drawing tool, some paper, and the willingness to engage in a creative task. However, many people feel that they lack the ability to draw well and end up creating primitive, iconic sketches [8]. According to many art books, a high-level problem is that non-artists tend to draw "*what they know*," instead of "*what they see*." In other words, non-artists draw objects based on their knowledge of the object geometry whereas artists choose which lines to draw based on the pose and lighting of the scene they are trying to depict. Furthermore, non-artists often lack low-level technical skills that can affect drawing quality, such as the ability to produce accurate, clean outlines or shaded regions with even tone. Art books and courses can help novices improve their drawing ability, but most people do not have the time to attend classes and hone their skills through dedicated practice.

The goal of our work is to develop a digital drawing system for novices, which they can use to create better sketches without requiring formal artistic training. There are several important requirements for such a system. Since novices are the target audience, the system should be ***easy to learn*** and ***robust*** to input from users with poor drawing skills, while still producing good results. The system should also promote the users' sense of ***ownership*** over their drawings. If a user feels he significantly contributed to the creation of a drawing that is of sufficient aesthetic quality, he might perceive the process as a rewarding experience of creative expression. Additionally, every user draws lines slightly differently, which results in a unique style. Ideally, the system should ***preserve style***.

There clearly is tension between these requirements. A completely automatic system that generates drawings at the push of a button is easy to learn and robust to unskilled input, but does not preserve a user's style or encourage ownership over the results. Conversely, a completely manual drawing system preserves style but is not robust. In our view, resolving this tension is the main challenge in designing a successful drawing system for novices. In essence, our goal is a system that assists with the low-level mechanics of drawing, such as ensuring that lines align well with the image, but where all high-level decisions are made by the user.

In this paper, we present PortraitSketch, an interactive drawing system that helps users create drawings of faces.

Faces have clear social importance but are very difficult to draw. In our recruiting survey (59 respondents), 85% said they would like to draw Portraits (vs. Landscape 70%, Abstract 61%, Still Life 56%, Other 3%). The main drawing interaction of PortraitSketch involves users tracing over a transparent version of a source portrait photograph. The system has three key features that address the requirements described above:

Automatic outline adjustment. PortraitSketch automatically adjusts the shape, position, thickness and opacity of outline strokes based on important visual features in the source image, such as strong gradients and facial landmarks. In this, we build on the work of Limpaecher et al. [16], while making a number of improvements.

Automatic shading adjustment. The system adjusts shading strokes to produce more even tones that match the shading variations in the source portrait.

Shading guidance. PortraitSketch provides an interactive shading visualization, suggesting where users might add additional shading strokes to better match the source image.

These features make the system robust to novice input by improving the accuracy and quality of the outline and shading strokes, and by helping users visualize where to add shading. At the same time, the fact that PortraitSketch allows users to add every stroke in the final image themselves keeps them highly involved in the creative process and gives them significant control over the style of the output. Figures 1 and 7 show results generated using our system, both with and without automatic assistance. Note that our system makes very subtle changes, but with a substantial effect on the quality of the resulting drawing. In general, the assisted drawings are more aesthetically pleasing and show a range of interesting stylistic variations.

To evaluate our system, we recruited 24 novices to create drawings using PortraitSketch, with different levels of assistance. We collected self-rating data about the drawing behavior, drawing results, and subjective ownership experienced across the assistance conditions. We also asked independent judges to evaluate the resulting drawings. Our findings suggest that users prefer drawing with some amount of assistance over no assistance, and that assistance does improve the quality of the drawings. There is no evidence that assistance diminishes the perceived involvement of users in the creative task, and visual inspection of the drawings indicates that many unique stylistic qualities of individual users are preserved across all levels of assistance.

RELATED WORK

There exists extensive work on producing artistic renderings of portraits (see Zhao and Zhu [22] for an overview). However, these techniques are designed to work automatically, while we aim to provide an interactive drawing experience where the user actively engages in the creative process. Our work does share some technical details with recent work by Berger et al. [3], who adopt a data-driven method for generating face images in a range of different styles. Our face feature analysis and edge detection model is similar to theirs, and a measure related to their importance estimation of edges for level-of-detail abstraction is heuristically encoded in our parametric adjustments for facial outlines. Still, their high-level goal remains the automatic synthesis of images rather than interactive assistance. Furthermore, their model does not address shading, which is a key component of our system.

A related topic is sketch refinement or beautification [1, 2, 17]. These systems aggressively modify the user's drawing to produce results that meet specific critiera and in the process significantly change the style of input strokes, often combining or removing them entirely. Moreover, beautification systems typically do not provide assistance during the drawing process. Our method also modifies strokes, but it does so in an interactive manner that is designed to both assist novice users and preserve their unique drawing style. We note that Zitnick [23] does present a real-time sketch beautification system that aims to preserve style, but the approach focuses on handwriting (or other repetitive symbols) rather than faces.

Some previous work on drawing has focused on teaching traditional skills. Dixon et al. [7] help users learn to draw faces by providing step-by-step instructions, analyzing a user's performance, and giving feedback about inaccuracies. Cummings et al. [6] apply the same approach to eyes. While such systems help users improve their drawing ability, this process takes time. Our aim is to enable novices to create compelling results at their current skill level. Although users may eventually learn some transferable skills after creating drawings with PortraitSketch, this is not our primary goal. In addition, most teaching systems require manual curation or preparation of the learning content, which makes it difficult scale to new content (e.g., arbitrary source photographs). One exception is the work of Iarussi et al. [12], who analyze a source image and propose construction lines used in traditional drawing to guide the user and help them learn how to perceive and transfer shape and proportions to the page. While we also use image analysis to assist novice users as they draw, we adopt different techniques that are designed to work well with faces.

The most relevant previous efforts are those that focus specifically on real-time assistance for creative drawing tasks. Fernquist et al. [9] allow users to follow tutorials that are automatically generated from artists recorded performances and provide corrective feedback of the tutorial. However, this process still requires manual, expert curation. Lee et al. [14]

compare user strokes to edges in a database of images to suggest possible future lines using a blended-average shadow visualization. Their system is geared toward serendipitous exploration of the database content, whereas our focus is on assisting users in drawing a specific portrait. Flagg et al. [10] propose a multi-projector display to offer visual painting guidance for real-world painting. We would like to offer a simple solution without complex hardware requirements.The DrawAFriend system [16] for tracing portrait photographs is most closely related to PortraitSketch. However, rather than using image analysis and computer vision to assist the user, they rely on crowd-sourcing. While this approach works well for common, popular images (e.g. photos of celebrities), DrawAFriend does not help an individual user draw a specific personal photo. In addition, since the consensus for determining an ideal sketch in DrawAFriend is deduced from many novice peers, it is possible that common novice mistakes (e.g., drawing eyes as simplified almond shapes) may result in sub-optimal drawing corrections. Additionally, we use facial landmarks to ensure that any single outline stroke is only mapped to a single facial feature (e.g., eye or mouth). Finally, we also aim to help users create hatched shading regions. While Salisbury et al. [18] provide high-level tools for creating hatching in user-specified regions, our system allows users to participate more actively in the drawing process by directly drawing their own shading strokes.

SYSTEM

PortraitSketch is designed for ease-of-use. The user simply loads a facial portrait photograph, and starts tracing over the image with a drawing tool. The system is used with a Wacom stylus and tablet, though a mouse or touch interface could be used instead. The tracing is shown on a white background with the portrait faded, and opacity controlled by a slider.

Only two tools are available to the user: The *outline* tool, to depict the shapes of an image, and the *shading* tool, optionally used to apply different types of shading, such as hatching, cross-hatching, scumbling, or "fill." Using two tools, instead of one, has several advantages. We find that users obtain better results when starting with at least a basic outline of a face before shading it, and using two tools encourages this workflow. Outlines and shading are often drawn in different styles (line thickness etc.) and the two tools can be conceptualized as presets for these styles. Finally, the system can give more targeted assistance if it knows the type of line being drawn.

To help users overcome their artistic and technical challenges, PortraitSketch offers several forms of assistance: (1) *Stroke beautification*, which makes strokes look better; (2) *Geometric corrections*, which improves shape depiction; (3) *Semantic corrections*, which de-emphasizes strokes that a skilled artist would be unlikely to draw; and (4) *Visualization*, which guides users in where to draw next.

To foster a user's sense of ownership over the results, we adhere to the following guidelines when providing assistance: each stroke shown by the system is drawn by the user; no strokes are generated automatically. Adjustments are kept "small;" strokes may not be dramatically altered, and, even when altered, we aim to preserve the user's style.

OUTLINE TOOL

The outline tool assists in drawing outlines and contours. The user draws strokes, represented initially as polylines, and the system applies several types of adjustments to the strokes. These adjustments are based on the typical problems with strokes drawn by novices. In particular, strokes may be uncertain and jittery, they may lack dynamics (skillful pressure variations of an artist's pen), they may represent "incorrect" lines due to semantic bias, and even correct lines may be misplaced due to poor hand-eye-coordination. The latter issue can also arise for trained artists when using a low-fidelity input device, such as a touch-screen ("fat finger problem").

Beautification

The raw polyline input for each stroke must be resampled and smoothed, to reduce data-size and jitter. To avoid discarding intentional curvature variations, smoothing is performed in a curvature-adapted manner, similar to Zitnick [23], in which we sequentially re-sample the input stroke based both on the amount of curvature and the distance of samples. The resampled points are fitted with cubic B-splines, which are rendered as thick triangle strips, with optional tapering or brush textures for increased realism. This approach is simple to implement, yet supports a variety of styles.

Geometric Adjustment: Outline

The geometric adjustment stage modifies stroke positions to better align with image contours, while still preserving the user's stroke style. This helps when a user has difficulty following the shape of curves in the reference image.

Guidance Map and Face Part Labeling — Geometric adjustment requires the system to have a best guess as to where strokes should be drawn. Prior to the drawing process, we produce a binary Guidance Map, where black pixels represent suggested locations for strokes (Figure 2). We also identify facial landmark positions, corresponding to facial parts, such as eyes, nose, etc. Additionally, each black pixel in the Guidance Map is labeled with the closest facial part.

Previous findings have shown that many artist-drawn strokes can be explained in terms of image intensity gradients [4]. Motivated by this, we had two artists draw outlines and shading of several faces. We then evaluated various edge-detection filters before settling on the eXtended Difference-of-Gaussians (XDoG) [21] filter, which produces a binary image resembling a line drawing. As shown in Figure 2, the XDoG yields a reasonable approximation not only of the outlines an artist might draw, but also indicates shading regions well. The XDoG filter produces an image curvature (κ) value for each pixel, which we use to compute pixelwise correspondences, since pixels with similar curvatures are more likely to correspond.

Facial landmarks (Figure 2(f)) are located using an existing labeling algorithm [19] that identifies points on the face corresponding to the eyes, eyebrows, nose, mouth and contour. We also manually add eye iris and forehead landmarks, though the labeling algorithm could easily be trained to detect

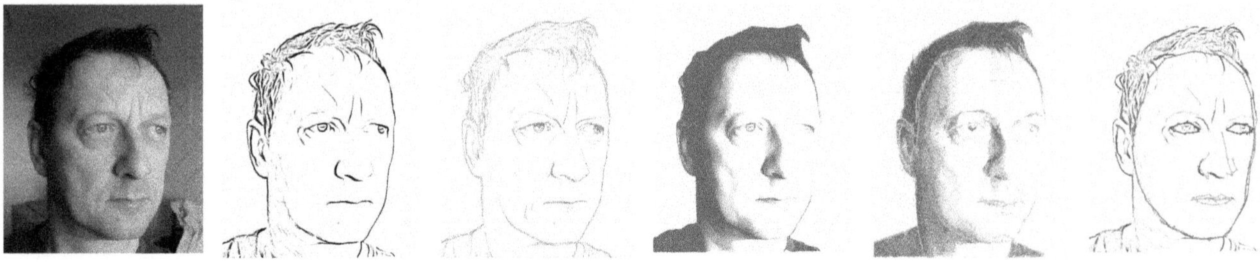

Figure 2: Guidance map. (a) Source portrait. (b) Output of original XDoG algorithm. (c) Overlay of outline sketch by a trained artist over the XDoG response. (d) Output of XDoG algorithm with settings for shading. (e) Overlay of artist's shading sketch and XDoG response. (f) Facial landmarks. Each landmark is a point on the face. Landmarks are connected by line segments, for visualization (and curvature computation.). *Image credits: Erich Ferdinand, under a Creative Commons license.*

them automatically. The landmarks are connected by predetermined polylines, and per-landmark curvatures (κ) are computed from the angles of the polyline.

We also precompute a part labeling of each pixel in the Guidance Map. Each black pixel in the Guidance Map is assigned the label of the nearest landmark in (x, y, κ) space. Non-face pixels are labeled as *background*.

Optimization — Given the input stroke and the precomputed maps, our goal is to correct a user's input stroke toward the closest guidance feature, while retaining as much of the input stroke's stylistic variations as possible. We formulate an energy function comprised of a Guidance Map energy, face landmark energy, and user input variation:

$$E = \alpha E_{guide} + \beta E_{land} + \gamma E_{var} \tag{1}$$

The weights α, β, γ adjust the contribution of each component. For our study, we experimentally choose their values to be 4, 2, and 1, respectively. The input stroke is described by a list of N points in 2D: $\mathbf{p}_{1:N} = [\mathbf{p}_1, ..., \mathbf{p}_N]$, and the optimization produces a new list of points $\mathbf{q}_{1:N} = [\mathbf{q}_1, ..., \mathbf{q}_N]$.

Prior to optimization, the algorithm assigns a face-part label for the stroke, to determine correspondence between the stroke and the Guidance Map. Assuming that users typically draw a stroke for one face feature at a time, we disambiguate conflicting labels of a stroke's control points by majority voting. Namely, each control point is assigned the nearest label from the nearest landmark. Thus, unlike the DrawAFriend system [16], our system effectively prevents a single stroke from being aligned to multiple facial features (e.g., the eye and eyebrow). This gives N votes, and the majority label is assigned to the stroke. Ties are broken in favor of the label with the smallest average distance to nearest neighbors.

The objective terms are as follows. For alignment with *Guidance Map edges*, we define

$$E_{guide}(\mathbf{q}_{1:N}) = \sum_{i=1}^{N} \frac{\|\mathbf{q}_i - \mathbf{g}_i\|^2}{\|\mathbf{p}_i - \mathbf{g}_i\|} \tag{2}$$

where $\mathbf{g}_i$ is the position of the closest Guidance Map pixel to $\mathbf{p}_i$ with the same part label as the stroke. The denominator is used to downweight this term for distant pixels that are less likely to represent a correct guidance match.

Similarly, for *face landmark alignment*, we define

$$E_{land}(\mathbf{q}_{1:N}) = \sum_{i=1}^{N} \frac{\|\mathbf{q}_i - \mathbf{f}_i\|^2}{\|\mathbf{p}_i - \mathbf{f}_i\|} \tag{3}$$

where $\mathbf{f}_i$ is the facial feature closest to $\mathbf{p}_i$ with the same label as the stroke. To preserve *stylistic input variations*, we minimize changes to the curve tangents, similar to [16]:

$$E_{var}(\mathbf{q}_{1:N}) = \sum_{i=2}^{n} \|(\mathbf{q}_i - \mathbf{q}_{i-1}) - (\mathbf{p}_i - \mathbf{p}_{i-1})\|^2 \tag{4}$$

Subfigures 3(b,c,d) show an example of an outline sketch before and after geometric correction. The optimization in Equation 1 is solved by a least squares solver.

We also provide a level-of-assistance parameter $\lambda \in [0 \ldots 1]$. Given the optimized stroke $\mathbf{q}^*$, the final output stroke is a linear interpolation of the input stroke and the optimized stroke:

$$\mathbf{q}_i^{\text{out}} = \lambda \mathbf{q}_i^* + (1 - \lambda)\mathbf{p}_i \tag{5}$$

Semantic Correction: Outline

Even when tracing, a novice may draw lines that a trained artist would not. This is typically caused by a semantic bias, where knowledge of object properties bias a novice to depict lines that are either weak or merely imagined. To mitigate this problem, our system emphasizes lines that are deemed to be "correctly" drawn, whereas de-emphasizing lines that are drawn "incorrectly".

For each point on an outline stroke, the algorithm computes the distance from the point to the nearest Guidance Map pixel. This distance is smoothed along the stroke, and then used to adjust the width and opacity of the stroke. Emphasized strokes are wider and/or more opaque while de-emphasis uses the opposite mechanism. Figure 3(e) shows the sketch result after semantic correction.

(a) (b) (c) (d) (e)

Figure 3: Outline Adjustment Comparison. (a) Source portrait. (b) No assistance. (c) Geometric correction. (d) Overlay of no assistance (red) and geometric correction (black). (e) Semantic correction. Note the geometric correction of the lower eyelid and semantic correction of the teeth and right bridge of the nose. Here, we use opacity for stroke emphasis.

Freehand Strokes

Outline strokes are left unadjusted in 2 situations, as follows.

First, input strokes too far from guidance features are left unadjusted. This case is detecting by checking if

$$\frac{1}{N}\sum_{i=1}^{N}\max\left(\|\mathbf{p}_i - \mathbf{g}_i\|, \|\mathbf{p}_i - \mathbf{f}_i\|\right) \quad (6)$$

passes above a preset threshold. In this case, λ is set to zero.

Second, strokes drawn in "*fill*" regions are uncorrected. We define *fill* regions as dense XDoG regions whose response is close to the shading response (see below). For example, hair regions often exhibit too many edges to meaningfully align user strokes. We detect such regions by comparison with shading regions and locally set $\lambda = 0$.

SHADING TOOL

Shading gives visual cues about lighting, 3D shape of a depicted object, and can indicate material properties and texture such as hair. Shading is a more advanced skill than outline drawing, and is particularly challenging and tedious for novices. We now describe a novel tool for assisting in the drawing of shading strokes.

Shading Region Detection

The shading tool takes as input a Shading Map, indicating parts of the image requiring shading. This is used in the interactive system both for shading visualization and assistance.

The Shading Map is generated by first defining the total face area (using face feature data) minus eyes and mouth regions, as these should not be shaded. The color histogram of the remaining face pixels typically exhibits two peaks, intuitively corresponding to skin color and shadow. These regions are clustered by fitting a Gaussian Mixture Model with two clusters as $\mathcal{N}(\mu_1, \sigma_1)$ and $\mathcal{N}(\mu_2, \sigma_2)$. XDoG is run twice on the image with two different threshold parameter settings: $\epsilon_1 = \mu_1 - 3\sigma_1$ and $\epsilon_2 = \mu_2 - 3\sigma_2$. The difference of the filter responses defines the shading region. We also run the Mean Shift algorithm [5] to extract shadable skin regions outside the face (e.g., neck, shoulders). The final shading region is shown in Figure 4(a).

Shading Guidance Visualization

The suggested shading regions are overlaid on the reference image in transparent red with opacity corresponding to shading intensity. An optional feedback mode fades the shading guidance according to the amount of shading strokes already applied by the user.

Shading Strokes Correction

As soon as they are drawn, shading strokes are re-sampled and smoothed in the same way outlines are. Then, the system adjusts the spacing of shading strokes to distribute them more evenly to produce an even tone [18].

Our hatching stroke correction uses an energy minimization inspired by the streamline placement method of Turk and Banks [20]. When the user places a new shading stroke, we optimize *all* strokes in a local neighborhood of the new stroke, including the input stroke. Let k index this set of K strokes, so that $\mathbf{P}^{(k)} = [\mathbf{p}_1^{(k)}, ...\mathbf{p}_{N_k}^{(k)}]$ is the k-th stroke. Our goal is to produce updated positions $\mathbf{Q}^{(k)}$. We minimize an energy over all control points of all neighboring strokes:

$$E(\mathbf{Q}^{(1:K)}) = E_{tone}(\mathbf{Q}^{(1:K)}) + E_{var}(\mathbf{Q}^{(1:K)}) \quad (7)$$

The first term E_{tone}, encourages strokes to be evenly distributed while matching the target tone. Let S be a binary image of all strokes, and $G * S$ be a Gaussian-blurred version of this image, and let the target (suggested) shading map from preprocessing be T. The energy is:

$$E_{tone}(\mathbf{Q}^{(1:K)}) = \|G * S(\mathbf{Q}^{(1:K)}) - T\|^2 \quad (8)$$

This energy is summed over all pixels in the image, though in implementation only pixels nearby the control points being optimized need to be considered.

As in (Equation 4), E_{var} preserves input stroke tangents:

$$E_{var} = \sum_{k=1}^{K}\sum_{j=2}^{N_k} w_j \,\|(\mathbf{q}_j^{(k)} - \mathbf{q}_{j-1}^{(k)}) - (\mathbf{p}_j^{(k)} - \mathbf{p}_{j-1}^{(k)})\|^2 \quad (9)$$

where w downweights strokes that are perpendicular to the input stroke to allow for cross-hatching. In particular, let $\mathbf{d}^{(k)} = \mathbf{q}_{N_k}^{(k)} - \mathbf{q}_1^{(k)}$ be the average direction of a stroke. We

Figure 4: Shading Adjustment Comparison. (a) Source portrait with visual shading guidance. (b) No assistance. (c) Geometric correction. (d) Semantic correction.

set w inversely proportional to $\mathbf{d}^{(k)} \cdot \mathbf{d}^{(\text{in})}$. When the angle between these directions is greater than $> 30°$, the weight is set to zero, which typically corresponds to cross-hatches.

The level of assistance is adjusted by the λ parameter as in Eq. 5. We solve the above optimization as follows. The algorithm computes the blur map $G * S$. Then, each control point is separately updated by a few gradient descent steps, and the process repeats. Image gradients are computed by finite differences. The algorithm runs about 10-30 iterations to convergence, requiring about 1-2 ms per iteration.

Multi-stroke Support

Fine hatching can be tedious and difficult. To make it easier, the hatching tool draws multiple parallel stroke for each user stroke (similar to [13]). The number of strokes reduces locally in areas with little shading to allow for finer shading control. The multi-stroke feature naturally creates evenly spaced lines, thereby enhancing overall stroke distribution.

Semantic Correction: Shading

Semantic adjustment is used to de-emphasize strokes in regions that need no shading. We use the previous shading map T and the stroke map S as guidance sources. We first lower the dynamic range of T to prevent excessive variations in shading appearance. For each new shading stroke $\mathbf{Q}$, the shading error is computed at each control point as:

$$\epsilon_{shading}(\mathbf{q}_i) = k \cdot \lambda(T(\mathbf{q}_i) - \min(G * S(x_i), \delta_s)) \quad (10)$$

where k is a constant and the level-of-assistance λ is used to modulate this correction. The shading density parameter δ_s can be adjusted via the UI. As in the outline tool, this value is used to de-emphasize strokes by making them smaller and more transparent when the value of ϵ is large. As more shading strokes are added to a region, new strokes become thinner and lighter, to prevent the region from darkening too much.

Figure 4 shows a shading sketch before and after adding assistance. In the zoomed-in window, shading strokes are placed in a more regular pattern compared to the original input. After the semantic adjustment, the shading also has a better interpretation of the face's structure and luminance variations.

EVALUATION

To evaluate how well PortraitSketch achieves our stated goals, we consider the following three questions:

1. Do novices prefer the assisted behavior of PortraitSketch over unassisted drawing?
2. Do novices create better drawings with assistance?
3. Do novices feel ownernship over their assisted drawings?

The remainder of this section describes the methodology of the user study we designed to help answer these questions.

Methodology

Our evaluation consists of two phases. First, we asked novice participants to create drawings using four versions of PortraitSketch with different levels of assistance. After completing the drawings, subjects answered several questions about the drawing behavior, drawing results and their perceived level of involvement in the creative process across the four conditions. In the second phase, we asked independent judges to evaluate the novice drawings.

Novice Drawing Study

For our novice drawing study, we recruited 24 participants who self-rated their drawing skills at 2 or lower (on a scale from 1–Novice to 5–Expert), who draw infrequently (monthly or less), and are interesting in drawing more. To evaluate how well our system works for different drawing styles, we also asked potential participants to rate their level of interest in creating drawings in one of three target styles (Figure 5). We picked styles that resemble many example portrait sketches that we found online and have visual characteristics that are distinct from one another (e.g., width, length

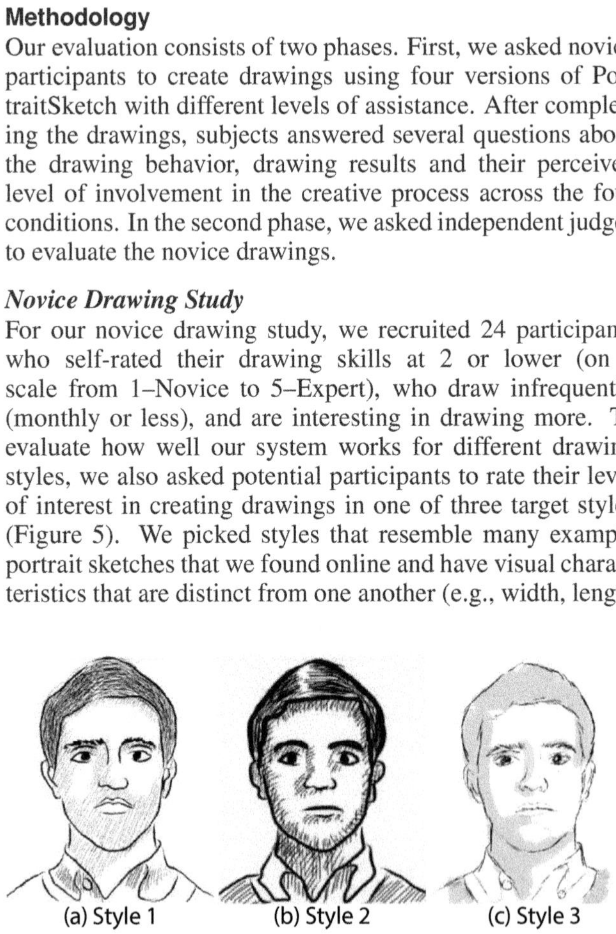

Figure 5: Target styles for user study.

and "cleanness" of outlines, type of shading, etc.) Based on their responses, we assigned participants to draw in one of the three target styles such that each style had eight participants and all subjects were assigned their (co-)favourite style.

For the study itself, we used a within-subjects design, where each subject created drawings of four different source images using four different levels of assistance: *None* ($\lambda = 0$), *Low* ($\lambda = \frac{1}{3}$), *Med* ($\lambda = \frac{2}{3}$), and *High* ($\lambda = 1$). We modified the UI to show an example sketch in the target style (as a reference image) to the right of the drawing canvas (please refer to the submission video). For the source images, we selected an equal number of male and female portrait photos with (approximately) fronto-parallel viewing angles. Three of our source images are from the DrawAFriend dataset of celebrity photos [16]. For each target style, we counterbalanced the order of assistance conditions and the pairings between conditions and source images based on a Greco-Latin Square design that accounts for both immediate ordering effects and condition-stimulus pairing effects [15].

At the beginning of each study session, we played a brief video introducing the key features of the PortraitSketch UI. We then allowed users to practice with the unassisted version of PortraitSketch for up to ten minutes to get comfortable with the setup (a Wacom tablet and stylus in front of a 24" display) and to clarify any questions about the UI. After the practice session, we asked subjects to create four drawings. We explained that some system parameters affecting drawing behavior would change between each drawing, but we deliberately said nothing about the nature of the changes. This was done to alert subjects to behavior changes without biasing their experience. For each task, we asked users to do their best to draw the given source image in the target style in eight minutes or less.

After completing the tasks, subjects filled out an exit questionnaire. To determine whether users could identify the different types of drawing assistance, we asked subjects to explain what differences they noticed (if any) about the drawing behavior. We also asked subjects to rate how much they liked the drawing behaviors and their actual drawing results across the four conditions on a scale from 1 (strongly dislike) to 5 (strongly like) and to explain these ratings by describing what they liked and disliked about the behavior and results. Finally, to assess ownership, we asked users to rate on a scale from 1 (strongly disagree) to 5 (strongly agree) the following two statements: "I created the image by myself," and "The system helped me with creating the image."

Independent Judges

To gain more insight into the quality of the assisted versus unassisted drawings, we asked independent judges to evaluate the drawings. We recruited two experts, who are both professional designers with extensive formal training and experience in drawing. We also recruited seven non-artists to act as peer judges. We asked the experts to give absolute rankings for each set of four drawings created by the same user on a scale from 1 (Worst) to 4 (Best) based on two different criteria: 1) the artistic quality of the drawings and 2) the artistic quality of the drawings *as a likeness of the subject of the portrait.* While we expected these two rankings to be correlated, we felt there might be some cases where one drawing was artistically superior but a worse likeness and vice versa. To help keep the two rankings independent, we first asked the judges to rank all 24 sets of images using the first criterion, before adding the source images and asking the judges to rank all 24 sets of images again based on the second criterion.

The ranking tasks described above require judges to evaluate drawings from four different source images. For more direct comparisons, we took each *None* (no assistance) drawing created by a novice participant and generated an auto adjusted version *AutoMed* by playing back the recorded strokes in PortraitSketch with the *Med* assistance settings. We chose this assistance level because it typically produces noticeable differences, and as reported below, the *Med* condition received the highest mean drawing behavior rating. These auto adjusted drawings represent a worst-case version of the assisted output from PortraitSketch since users tends to adjust their drawing behavior based on visual feedback from the system during real drawing sessions. After generating the assisted images, we asked both our expert and peer judges to select the better result from each pair of *None* and *AutoMed* drawings. (We added peer judges for this evaluation as it required less expertise to compare.)

For all ranking tasks, we randomized the order in which the image quadruples/pairs were presented, and for each individual ranking task, we also randomized the layout of the drawings, which were arranged in a horizontal row.

RESULTS

To summarize the data from our study, we present boxplots that show the median and interquartile ranges for each set of ratings/rankings, with upper and lower quartiles computed using the method of Freund and Perles [11]. For brevity, we aggregate ratings across the three target styles.

Do novices enjoy the assisted drawing behavior?

Figure 6a summarizes the drawing behavior ratings for all 24 participants. Both the *Low* and *Med* conditions are rated more favorably than the *None* condition. Interestingly, the *High* condition received very similar ratings to the *None* condition. Looking more closely at the explanations of these ratings from the exit questionnaire, the relative lack of enthusiasm for *High* was likely due to the perception that the automated assistance was overly aggressive in this condition, which several participants noted. This highlights the tradeoff between user control and assistance; even when the *High* setting produced the best results, some users were frustrated by the system not following their input.

Do novices create better drawings with assistance?

Overall, the drawing result ratings increase with increasing levels of assistance (Figure 6b), which suggests that participants generally preferred the drawings they created with more assistance. The rankings from expert judges also show a preference for the assisted drawings over the *None* condition (Figures 6e–f) . Finally, the comparisons between the *None* and *AutoMed* (auto adjusted) image pairs produced the clearest results; judges preferred the assisted drawings 70% of the

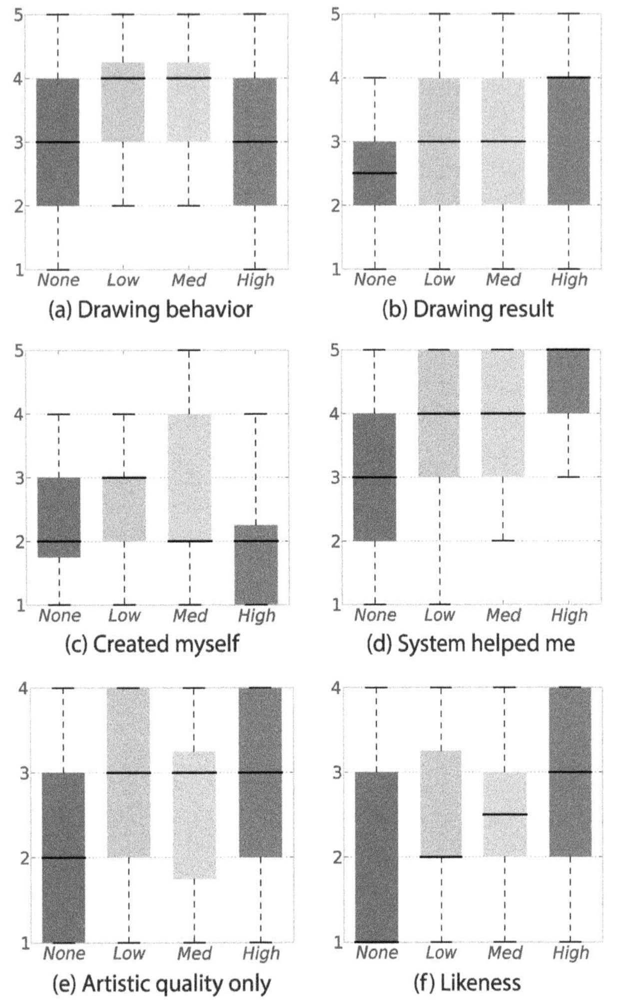

Figure 6: Results from user study. Boxplots a–d show aggregated self-rating results from our exit questionnaire (1: strongly dislike . . . 5: strongly like). Boxplots e–f show expert ranking results (1: Worst . . . 4: Best). Overall, the results suggest that users prefer drawing with some assistance over no assistance (a) and that assistance results in better drawings (b, e, f). The responses also suggest that while users clearly notice the system helping more at higher assistance levels (d), this may not impact their feelings of involvement in the creative process (c). The thick black line in each colored box indicates the median.

time, with only five of the 24 *None* drawings receiving more than four out of nine possible votes. In general, both the outlines and shading contribute to the improved quality of the assisted drawings. As shown in Figure 7, more accurate outlines tend to make the sketch more similar to the source image, and more even shading increases the technical quality of the result.

Do novices feel ownernship over assisted drawings?

While this is a difficult question to answer conclusively, the ratings for the statements "*I created the image by myself*" and "*The system helped me with creating the image*" provide some insight. For the first statement, there is no obvious trend across the four conditions. *None* and *Low* have a similar distribution of ratings, with *Med* rated somewhat higher and *High* somewhat lower (Figure 6c). However, the ratings for the second statement clearly increase with increasing assistance (Figure 6d). Thus, while participants notice the increasing levels of assistance, this does not seem to diminish their sense of involvement in the creative process, at least up until the *Med* condition. We consider this a desirable result.

Moreover, the ability of the system to preserve characteristics of individual users' drawing style may also contribute to a sense of ownership. While we did not evalute style preservation explicitly in our study, almost all of the drawings from different users exhibit clear stylistic differences (even the drawings in the same target style). For example, Figure 8 shows four sets of drawings in two different target styles with various levels of assistance. In the top row, subject 129 uses very loose, messy outlines and shading, while subject 136 has a much tighter, more controlled style with lots of structured, parallel shading lines. In the bottom row, subject 144 uses fairly clean outlines and focuses on details around the eyes, while subject 138 draws with long, wavy outlines and relatively little detail, which gives the drawings a more abstract look. These types of differences suggest that, even with assistance, PortraitSketch users are still able to create drawings in their own unique styles.

Free-form responses

We asked users to describe the *drawing behavior* changes they noticed. Only 2 users noticed no difference and most users correctly identified *assistance* as the behavior change. We analyzed the given descriptions and grouped them into three connotation categories: Positive (e.g. help, assistance), Neutral (e.g. snapping, correction), and Negative (e.g. restrictive). If a description used words from multiple categories, we counted the less favorable one. 5 users made positive mention, 8 users were neutral, and 3 users made negative comments about the assistance. Several users noticed behavior changes that were not real, and might reflect a subjective learning experience. This evaluation mirrors the quantitative data in that most users seemed comfortable with the given assistance, or even appreciated it.

For *positive feedback*, 8 users specifically mentioned liking the *assistance*; 5 users thought that *tracing* made the task fun and manageable; 6 users mentioned the *shading visualization*; and 9 users commented on the usefulness of adjusting the *opacity* of the reference image.

Suggested *system improvements* include: An eraser tool to delete arbitrary lines (12 users); manual adjustment of outline and shading thickness (11 users); additional shading styles (3 users); and ability to adjust assistance (3 users).

Interesting feedback from a *general comments* question include: (146) "[. . .] I found when I tried to use the shading system I was more focused on the guide than the image itself which had some bad results."; (132) "i can create wonderful sketch with this software"; (120) "Fun factor [. . .] I think that will help in freehand drawing"; (110) "It was surpris-

Figure 7: Some results from user study. We show unassisted (b), auto adjusted (c), and assisted (e) drawings by three different novice users (organized by row) in our study. PortraitSketch's automatic adjustments produce more accurate outlines (compare the face contours and eyes in columns (b) and (c)) and more even shading (e.g., the hair and neck in top row drawings). While some differences are subtle, several small adjustments often produce noticeable improvements in the overall drawing. The blue numbers in column (c) indicate the fraction of independent judges who preferred the auto adjusted images over the unassisted drawings in column (b). All three users produced the assisted drawing (e) *before* the unassisted one (b) in their study sessions. *Image credits: (a) top to bottom: Levy Carneiro Jr, Edgar Meritano and chris zerbes. (d) top to bottom: chris zerbes, chris zerbes and Pete Souza. All are under a Creative Commons license.*

ingly fast and easy to use and understand. I also feel like I could quickly draw something, if tasked"; (166) "I lack creativity, so I like that there was a 'tracing' aspect to help me draw"; (127) "Overall, I was very impressed when I saw the outcome. Can't wait to try out more drawings, it's addictive :-)"; (138) "[An exercise] that gave me hope that maybe I actually could produce something worth looking at! :)"; (121) "It gave me hope that I could actually learn to draw".

DISCUSSION & FUTURE WORK

Our system assists novices in creating sketches by making subtle adjustments to technical qualities of their drawings. Two situations may lead to sub-optimal assistance conditions: 1) Facial feature detection and XDoG edge extraction may fail (due to low contrast, facial occlusion, etc.) 2) The user creates drawings with little correspondence to the source image. Our study gives preliminary evidence that this kind of assistance enhances the resulting drawings, enhances user's enjoyment and pride in their work, while maintaining the sense of ownership they would feel in a conventional interface. The

Figure 8: Preserving stylistic differences. Each set of three drawings was created by one of our study participants using three different levels of assistance. The drawings by each user exhibit unique characteristics that distinguish them from the drawings by other users. These stylistic differences are present even when comparing drawings in the same target style; for example, (a–b) are in target style 1, and (c–d) are in target style 3.

behavior and drawing result ratings suggest that there may be a sweet spot around the *Med* level of assistance, which provides enough help to noticeably improve drawing quality but does not modify user outlines and shading too aggressively. We chose not to explain the nature of the assistance to participants, but we observed that some users who figured out our system produced better results.

We observed several potential sources of noise in our study, including unfamiliarity with the Wacom tablet, learning effects, and variation between the different types of source images. Although we counterbalanced for each of these effects, they did reduce the observed effect sizes.

Many novices are interested in creative expression but lack the confidence and skills to partake in art projects. Indeed, several study participants initially apologized for their lack of drawing skills, but, at the end, were thrilled with their results. One user even captured her drawings with her phone to immediately share with her friends. We think that additional guidance for difficult drawing elements, such as hair or clothing could be useful. While we focus on novices, even professional artists, who quickly have to produce a rough sketch, might benefit from image-based drawing assistance. We see the encouraging results from our user study as evidence that building creative assistance tools for novices is an important goal and we intend to apply our assistance approach to other artistic domains in the future.

REFERENCES

1. Arvo, J., and Novins, K. Fluid Sketches: Continuous Recognition and Morphing of Simple Hand-drawn Shapes. In *Proc. UIST* (2000), 73–80.
2. Barla, P., Thollot, J., and Sillion, F. Geometric Clustering for Line Drawing Simplification. In *Proc. EGSR* (2005).
3. Berger, I., Shamir, A., Mahler, M., Carter, E., and Hodgins, J. Style and Abstraction in Portrait Sketching. *ACM Trans. Graph. 32*, 4 (July 2013).
4. Cole, F., Golovinskiy, A., Limpaecher, A., Barros, H. S., Finkelstein, A., Funkhouser, T., and Rusinkiewicz, S. Where Do People Draw Lines? *ACM Trans. Graph. 27*, 3 (Aug. 2008).
5. Comaniciu, D., and Meer, P. Mean Shift: A Robust Approach Toward Feature Space Analysis. *IEEE Trans. PAMI 24*, 5 (May 2002), 603–619.
6. Cummmings, D., Vides, F., and Hammond, T. I Don't Believe My Eyes!: Geometric Sketch Recognition for a Computer Art Tutorial. In *Proc. SBIM* (2012).
7. Dixon, D., Prasad, M., and Hammond, T. iCanDraw: Using Sketch Recognition and Corrective Feedback to Assist a User in Drawing Human Faces. In *Proc. CHI* (2010).
8. Eitz, M., Hays, J., and Alexa, M. How Do Humans Sketch Objects? *ACM Trans. Graph. 31*, 4 (July 2012).

9. Fernquist, J., Grossman, T., and Fitzmaurice, G. Sketch-sketch Revolution: An Engaging Tutorial System for Guided Sketching and Application Learning. In *Proc. UIST* (2011).
10. Flagg, M., and Rehg, J. M. Projector-guided painting. In *Proc. UIST* (2006).
11. Freund, J., and Perles, B. A new look at quartiles of ungrouped data. *American Stat 41* (1987), 200–203.
12. Iarussi, E., Bousseau, A., and Tsandilas, T. The Drawing Assistant: Automated Drawing Guidance and Feedback from Photographs. In *Proc. UIST* (2013).
13. Kazi, R. H., Igarashi, T., Zhao, S., and Davis, R. Vignette: Interactive texture design and manipulation with freeform gestures for pen-and-ink illustration. In *Proc. CHI* (2012).
14. Lee, Y. J., Zitnick, C. L., and Cohen, M. F. ShadowDraw: Real-time User Guidance for Freehand Drawing. *ACM Trans. Graph. 30*, 4 (July 2011).
15. Lewis, J. R. Pairs of latin squares to counterbalance sequential effects and pairing of conditions and stimuli. In *Proc. Human Factors and Ergonomics* (1989).
16. Limpaecher, A., Feltman, N., Treuille, A., and Cohen, M. Real-time Drawing Assistance Through Crowdsourcing. *ACM Trans. Graph. 32*, 4 (July 2013).
17. Pusch, R., Samavati, F., Nasri, A., and Wyvill, B. Improving the sketch-based interface. *The Visual Computer 23*, 9-11 (2007), 955–962.
18. Salisbury, M. P., Anderson, S. E., Barzel, R., and Salesin, D. H. Interactive pen-and-ink illustration. In *Proc. SIGGRAPH* (1994).
19. Saragih, J. M., Lucey, S., and Cohn, J. F. Deformable Model Fitting by Regularized Landmark Mean-Shift. *Int. J. Comput. Vision 91*, 2 (Jan. 2011), 200–215.
20. Turk, G., and Banks, D. Image-guided Streamline Placement. In *Proc. SIGGRAPH* (1996), 453–460.
21. Winnemöller, H., Kyprianidis, J. E., and Olsen, S. C. XDoG: An eXtended difference-of-Gaussians compendium including advanced image stylization . *Computers & Graphics 36*, 6 (2012), 740–753.
22. Zhao, M., and Zhu, S.-C. Artistic Rendering of Portraits. In *Image and Video-Based Artistic Stylisation*, P. Rosin and J. Collomosse, Eds. Springer, London, 2013.
23. Zitnick, C. L. Handwriting Beautification Using Token Means. *ACM Trans. Graph. 32*, 4 (July 2013).

Painting with Bob: Assisted Creativity for Novices

Luca Benedetti
ISTI-CNR and
University of Bath
Bath, U.K.
l.benedetti@bath.ac.uk

Holger Winnemöller
Adobe Systems, Inc.
Seattle, U.S.A.
hwinnemo@adobe.com

Massimiliano Corsini
ISTI-CNR
Pisa, Italy
m.corsini@isti.cnr.it

Roberto Scopigno
ISTI-CNR
Pisa, Italy
r.scopigno@isti.cnr.it

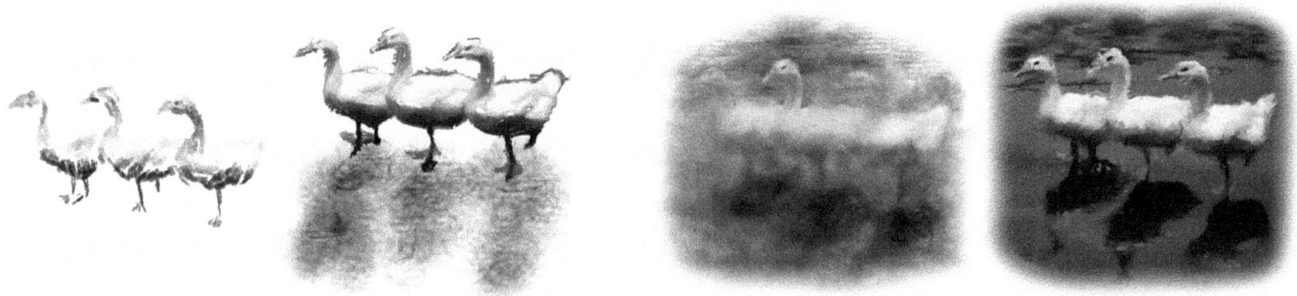

Figure 1. Several examples of geese painted by novice users with *Painting with Bob* in under ten minutes.

ABSTRACT

Current digital painting tools are primarily targeted at professionals and are often overwhelmingly complex for use by novices. At the same time, simpler tools may not invoke the user creatively, or are limited to plain styles that lack visual sophistication. There are many people who are not art professionals, yet would like to partake in digital creative expression. Challenges and rewards for novices differ greatly from those for professionals. In this paper, we leverage existing works in Creativity and Creativity Support Tools (CST) to formulate design goals specifically for digital art creation tools for novices. We implemented these goals within a digital painting system, called *Painting with Bob*. We evaluate the efficacy of the design and our prototype with a user study, and we find that users are highly satisfied with the user experience, as well as the paintings created with our system.

Author Keywords

Painting; novices; creativity;

ACM Classification Keywords

I.3.4 Graphics Utilities: Paint systems; J.5 ARTS AND HUMANITIES: Fine arts; I.3.3 Picture/Image Generation

INTRODUCTION

> *"Every child is an artist, the problem is staying an artist when you grow up"* – Pablo Picasso

UIST 2014, October 5–8, 2014, Honolulu, HI, USA.

http://dx.doi.org/10.1145/2642918.2647415

Most children readily engage in many forms of creative expression, including play, pretending, and art projects such as painting and drawing [14, 15]. But as we grow older, many adults disengage from creative expression, with explanations such as *"I cannot draw"*, *"I am not creative"*, or *"I do not know what to draw"*. Various factors affect creativity and may explain this different approach between children and adults. Amabile [1] differentiates between self-motivated (pleasure) versus extrinsic (reward) motivations for the respective groups, and states that extrinsic motivations are often associated with anxieties that inhibit creativity. Time constraints in our busy daily lives may also adversely affect creativity [2]. Yet, despite all these obstacles, the benefits of (adult) creative expression are well documented [12].

Painting is a good example of this rift between childhood and adult creativity. Finger painting is accessible even to a young toddler, while the "proper" mastery of brushes and paints takes years of training. In this paper, we design a creativity support tool (CST) for digital painting for the vast majority of adults who rarely or never engage in fine arts. Artistic challenges and rewards are different for novices and professionals [9, 26]. The average novice does not seek the approval of an art critic or a paying customer, but rather seeks the enjoyment of the task and the approval of his (novice) peers. Novices face various challenges: They are unfamiliar with tools and techniques, they are intimidated by the blank page, they are unwilling to invest a lot of time, and they are easily frustrated or discouraged [9, 30]. We therefore seek to create a *safe* playground for novices to experiment with painting, where safe means "controlled to guarantee a minimum degree of quality". Controlling the user's environment necessarily limits their creative choices, so a balance must be struck between the two. The type of creativity we enable in this paper is that of a 'cooking challenge', where the ingredients and preparation techniques are pre-determined to maximize the likelihood of a pleasant-tasting dish, while the user is free to experiment within the constraints of the challenge.

Our painting system, affectionately dubbed "*Painting with Bob*" (PwB) is specifically designed to overcome the above artistic, technical, and creative challenges. We start by formulating a set of system design guidelines for creative support tools for novices. We then describe the implementation of PwB to fulfill the design requirements. We propose a practical user study to demonstrate the efficacy of our system design and report on its results. We see the main contributions of our paper as the design guidelines for a fine art CST for novices, along with a detailed case study of creating and evaluating a CST based on these guidelines. While we are clear that the results we obtained are specific to our digital painting tool (PwB), we argue that many of the design decisions and evaluation methods make no limiting reference to digital painting, and could be applied to other digital fine arts for novices, such as drawing, sketching, cartooning, etc.

RELATED WORK

Creativity is a complex phenomenon with varying definitions, depending on the context in which it is discussed. Using Beghetto and Kauffman's [21] taxonomy, we focus on little-c and mini-c (personal level) creativity, rather than Big-C or Pro-c (domain level) creativity. Davis et al. [9] discuss the challenges of CSTs for novices. They distinguish two types of novices: The *tool* novice already has skills applicable to a given domain (e.g. a traditional painter), but an appropriate CST may increase their productivity (e.g. acquiring digital painting skills). In contrast, a *domain* novice is unfamiliar with both the domain as well as the CSTs used in that domain. Davis et al. illustrate this concept with a *skill-threshold* that needs to be overcome by the domain novice to even participate in that domain. The authors argue that since novices are often unwilling to invest sufficient time in learning, they are underrepresented within the CST community, yet require significantly different strategies to support their creativity [9]. Designing CSTs that artificially (through the help of computer assistance) lift the novice above the skill threshold can enable them to immediately participate in creative exploration, and that is the approach taken in this paper.

Much of research into Creativity Support Tools [30] focuses on professionals, as these most commonly engage in creative endeavors [26]. Creative professionals are exposed to significant external pressures (time, money, novelty, recognition), whereas novices are generally motivated by aspects of play [15, 28] and what Csikszentmihalyi calls "*flow*" [7], defined as "a mental state of complete immersion and energized focus". While flow is not a prerequisite for creativity, people often experience flow during phases of extreme productivity or creativity. Specifically, flow is associated with the following subjective experiences: 1) There are clear goals every step of the way; 2) There is immediate feedback to one's actions; 3) There is a balance between challenges and skills; 4) Action and awareness are merged; 5) Distractions are excluded from consciousness; 6) There is no worry of failure; 7) Self-consciousness disappears; 8) The sense of time becomes distorted; 9) The activity becomes autotelic (the purpose of the activity is within itself). Within these concepts, our goals for a CST for novice art creation focus primarily on designing a user experience that supports all elements of flow, thereby maximizing the likelihood of such an experience for the user. That is, we define success in terms of a subjectively rewarding experience for the novice user, rather than some more objective measures of artistic mastery, novelty, or critical praise that might be applied to professionals. Our approach to CST design and evaluation is therefore different from those supporting professional or domain expert creativity [24].

Of those CSTs designed for novices, many focus on educational goals [29, 32]. iCanDraw [10] guides users through a series of steps to draw faces, providing automatic user feedback about the accuracy of their efforts. Iarussi et al. [19] presented an educational tool to practice traditional drawing-by-observation techniques. Cummings et al. [8] developed a tutorial system to draw eyes. While those works demonstrated skill improvement in their user studies, the actual tutorials are highly specific and do not scale to different artistic skills or motifs. Sketch-Sketch Revolution by Fernquist et al. [11] addressed the scalability issue by basing their tutorials on recorded sessions of real artists. In contrast to these works, our goal is *not* to teach users traditional skills, as this is necessarily time consuming and delays gratification, thereby creating an impedance for engagement. Instead, we aim to enable novices to partake in the artistic process immediately, even if this means that initially they can only be successful within the constraints of the CST. If an individual feels encouraged by their experience to acquire the necessary skills to substitute for the CST, we consider that an added bonus, but we do not see it as a requirement of our approach.

Non-educational CSTs can be classified as supporting *tool* or *domain* novices [9]. Kazi et al. [22]'s *Vignette* system helps with the design and manipulation of textures in pen-and-ink illustration. Their approach simplifies an artist's workflow but still requires significant skills and must thus be considered a *tool novice* CST. A notable example of a *domain novice* CST, much aligned with our own motivations, is the *ShadowDraw* system by by Lee et al. [23]. Here, a database of images is analyzed for strong contours, matched to user input, and blended to create "shadows" of many possible forms, allowing for serendipitous exploration of the objects in the database. While the authors demonstrate interesting artworks by novices, the paper focuses on the technical aspects of the system and omits user-centric aspects such as subjective satisfaction, ownership, personal style, etc., all of which we believe to be important design goals for domain novice CSTs.

Several commercial systems bear superficial similarities to PwB. *PsykoPaint* is a web application that allows the user to upload an image and paint over it. Painting tools are grouped in "styles" with many free parameters for each style and the associated usability and discoverability issues. *GMX PhotoPainter* uses image analysis to create smart tools (similar to PwB), however their analysis seems limited, requiring a large number of free parameters. *Studio Artist* replaces many free parameters with "thousands of presets", which can only be discovered through exhaustive experimentation. We argue that thousands of presets are just as unmanageable for novices as dozens of parameters. Microsoft's *Freshpaint*, implements recent oilpaint techniques [5] and provides a paint-by-number mode for novices, but apart from visual tracing lines the user still has to paint mostly unassisted. *Artrage* is a media simulation system only offering automatic color selection, similar to the "simple" assistance mode we present in this paper. *Photoshop* is a well-known CST. Its standard brushing model contains no assistive mode and many dozens of parameters. Photoshop's *Art History Brush* tool allows a user to paint stylized strokes based on image content. This tool itself is less sophisticated than the above systems in terms of visual quality, automated assistance, and ease of use. For these reasons, and to give a better comparison between varying degrees of assistance in CSTs for novices, we compare PwB with a simplified version of itself, rather than with existing commercial systems.

For rendering, our paper takes inspiration from earlier efforts on digital painting based on stroke libraries and orientation fields [27]. However, in those works the user interaction is limited to parameter selection (e.g. [17]) or semantic disambiguation of the image components (e.g. [35]).

SYSTEM DESIGN

In this section, we review several creativity frameworks, and we distill design goals from these theories that pertain to our specific problem domain of art creation CSTs for novices.

Schneiderman [30] suggests four design principles for general CSTs: S1) support exploratory research; S2) enable collaboration; S3) provide rich history-keeping; and S4) design with "*low thresholds, high ceilings*, and *wide walls*". Of these, we find only S4 to be relevant in our context. Specifically, *Low thresholds* suggests a minimal training requirement, while *High ceilings* represent support for levels of sophistication (e.g. from first-timer to casual enthusiast). Finally, *Wide walls* describes the breadth of expression of a CST (e.g. personal style).

Read et al. [25] propose three dimensions of *fun*. R1) The perceived experience is better than the predicted one; R2) The user feels engrossed in the experience; and R3) A willingness exists to continue or repeat an activity.

Rubin et al. [28] suggest six factors of *play*, many of which overlap the nine elements of *flow* [7], listed again in shortened form: F1) Clear goals; F2) Immediate feedback; F3) Balanced challenges; F4) Merged action and awareness; F5) No distractions; F6) No fear; F7) No self-consciousness; F8) Ignorance of time; F9) Autolectic activity.

In selecting our design goals for art CSTs for novices we draw from several of the aforementioned theories (listed in parentheses), but we also add novel goals that are specific to our intended domain and audience:

N1) Kickstart Novices often do not know what to create ("blank page problem"). The CST should offer a simple and obvious starting point.

N2) Easy to learn Effectively needing little or no training, thereby reducing the time investment necessary to engage in the creative process (S4,F3).

N3) Easy to use The UI should be simple and intuitive. The user should easily find the right tool, and the tool's response to user actions should be predictable (F4).

N4) WYSIWYG The user should be given immediate and accurate visual feedback about the results of their interactions with the system (F2).

N5) Guaranteed success Aesthetically pleasing results (to the user) should be attainable in a short amount of time, with possible improvements for greater time investment (S4,F6).

N6) Ownership & Achievement Despite any technological assistance, users should identify with having created the final artifact. Ideally, they should feel proud of their creation (F7).

N7) Enjoyment The user should find enjoyment in the act of working with the system (R1,R2,R3,F9)

N8) Creative flexibility User guidance and free-form flexibility are opposing goals. Within the confines of the assistive technology, the user should feel as much freedom for creative expression as possible (F3).

N9) Individual results Different users should be able to create different results. Allowing users to develop a personal *style* is a vital aspect of creative expression.

The above design goals are useful for a variety of art creation CSTs for novices. However, the act of *painting* that we have chosen for our case study, carries some domain-specific challenges in support of the general goals, above:

P1) Brushes Common digital brushing systems have an overwhelming number of free parameters that are difficult for the novice to adjust → PwB brushes should be simple to configure, yet be visually appealing with a range of natural media appearances, such as watercolor or acrylic (N2,N3,N5,N8).

P2) Technique A typical painting consists of hundreds or thousands of individual brush strokes. The domain novice does not have the knowledge or skill to apply individual strokes for the desired effect → PwB should offer the user control at a higher level than individual strokes, thus reducing the task from painting each stroke to painting more or less "detail" (N2,N3,N8,N9).

P3) Fidelity Skilled artists perform brushes strokes that, in aggregate, suggest texture, materials, etc. → PwB must use image analysis techniques to automatically choose and configure brushes to reproduce accurate local detail (N3,N5).

Other domain-specific techniques exist, such as *Dark-to-light*, *Coarse-to-fine*, and *Back-to-front* (see Results section). A question arises as to which of these techniques should be addressed by the CST. Our approach is minimalistic: We want to empower novices without restricting them too much by overly constraining the user experience (N8). Referring to Davis et al.'s [9] "*skill-threshold*", we choose to include the techniques that we deem necessary to lift a user above the threshold, whereas we purposely exclude techniques which merely increase productivity beyond that level. That is, we offer the user enough support to engage with a creative domain (e.g. P1-P3), but we leave it to the user to acquire any additional high-level skills (Dark-to-light, etc.)

IMPLEMENTATION

Fundamentally, PwB is a simple system, related to Haeberli's [16] original work. PwB offers the user a virtual canvas and a set of tools to paint on it. The user starts by loading a source image. The system analyzes the image and computes various metrics. The tools may query any metric to augment the user interactions, thereby producing "*smart*" tool behavior. The user interface (Fig. 2, Left) and experience are kept minimalistic (N2, N3, N4). The user can choose between four tools and use these to paint over a faded version of the source image. Using an existing image to paint on addresses goal N1. The only user-specified tool parameters are tool-size and brush-alpha. Additionally, the user can pan/zoom the painting, adjust the visibility of the reference image and undo/redo actions. The system is a multi-threaded C++ application, uses Lua scripting for tool behavior, OpenCV for image analysis, and OpenGL for rendering.

Brushes – Paint marks are chosen from a brush library of 56 post-processed scans of real brush strokes. First, we painted several dozen paint strokes (long/round, straight/wavy, dab/smear, dry/wet) with green acrylic paint on white paper. We scanned the marks and separated them in Photoshop into two channels: a texture channel representing bristle details, and an alpha channel representing the shape and opacity of paint (Fig. 2, Right). A paint mark can be rendered as-is, or be deformed along a Beziér path. A global brush alpha value can be increased to create a watercolor-like appearance, or decreased to simulate thicker paint. A fragment shader, based on the brush's texture channel, adds shadows and specular highlights. PwB's brushing system is fast, flexible, and produces realistic looking brush strokes, thereby addressing (by design) goals N2, N3, N5, P1, P2, and P3.

Analysis – To drive smart tool behavior (N3,N5,P3), we compute the following analysis measures: *Meanshift* filtering [6] simplifies the source image's color palette for sampling by tools. Successive Gaussian filter passes are applied for sampling by larger tool radii. *Edge Tangent Flow (ETF)* [20] computes a set of progressively smoothed orientation fields. The *Laplacian response* of the grayscale image, indicates regions of high frequency content. *CIE Y variance* approximates local saliency. *Oriented Gabor filter* responses [13] indicate local isotropy and orientation histograms. Image analysis is performed on downsampled ($\sim$1Mpix) source images at load-time, takes $\sim$20 seconds (unoptimized code), and is cached for future sessions.

User Actions – As the user brushes over the canvas, the cursor coordinates are regularized by fitting them to a spline which is then sampled according to tool size. Each resampled position holds coordinates and input data, such as screen-space speed, and pressure, tilt & rotation, where available.

A tool's Lua script uses this data, along with any data queried from the analysis metrics, to issue paint commands to the rendering system. Each command consists of: texture-id, position, orientation, size, color, transparency, texture highlights and shadows, and optional deformation along a spline. A tool script can be viewed as a mapping of user input and image metrics, onto rendering commands. Interactivity is maintained by multi-threaded computation of tool scripts and rendering, thereby addressing N4, and facilitating N6-N9.

Tool Design – To avoid confusing the user with too many tools, we empirically determined a minimal set of tools. We first created a large number of brush behaviors based on physical brushes and painting tutorials. We then painted many images in the subject categories that we wanted PwB to support: portraits, rural landscapes, cityscapes, and nature. We compared notes on which brushes were useful in creating the visual aspects of each motif. The foliage and noisy textures of rural landscapes and nature scenes suggested a brush that quickly fills large areas with many paint marks. The regular structure of hair, fur, and architecture suggested a brush with long strokes along such structures, etc. Based on our observations, we distilled a set of four tools: (1) The *Single* tool paints a sequence of individual paint marks; (2) The *Fill* tool covers an area with a number of marks; (3) The *Structure* tool paints long, possibly curved paint strokes; and (4) the *Eraser* tool removes paint.

Simple & Smart Tools – To test the effect that painting assistance would have on the quality of images produced with PwB (N5) and user experience (N6-N9) we created two versions of the four tools, a *simple* version with little assistance, and a *smart* version with more assistance (Fig. 3).

The *simple toolset* automatically chooses a (size-dependent) color and contrast values (highlights & shadows) for each brush mark. Additionally: (1) The *Simple Single* tool paints a sequence of paint marks following the input path. The user's speed controls the brush's aspect ratio and spacing along the path; (2) The *Simple Fill* fills the area under the cursor with a number of simple single instances; (3) The *Simple Structure* creates a single long stroke along the user's path with the color of the path's starting point; and (4) The *Simple Eraser* deletes all paint within the cursor area.

The *smart toolset* enables higher-level user control by adding assistance beyond the simple toolset: (1) The *Smart Single* tool aligns paint marks along the (size-dependent) ETF orientation field and uses local Gabor responses to adjust brush rendering: In low contrast, isotropic regions, brush textures near unit aspect-ratio are chosen and rendered large and more transparent, with low brush contrast. Paint marks in high-contrast and anisotropic regions are chosen to be small, oblong, more opaque, with high brush contrast; (2) The *Smart Fill* applies many smart single instances within the cursor area. The tool implements a local coarse-to-fine technique by sorting selected paint marks by aspect ratio, rendering them in order of increasing value; (3) The *Smart Structure* tool generates a series of splined brushes, each following local ETF orientations. Splines are sub-divided at significant color discontinuities. Brush transparency and contrast are modulated as above; (4) The *Smart Eraser* deletes only areas that have a color similar to the starting point of the user path.

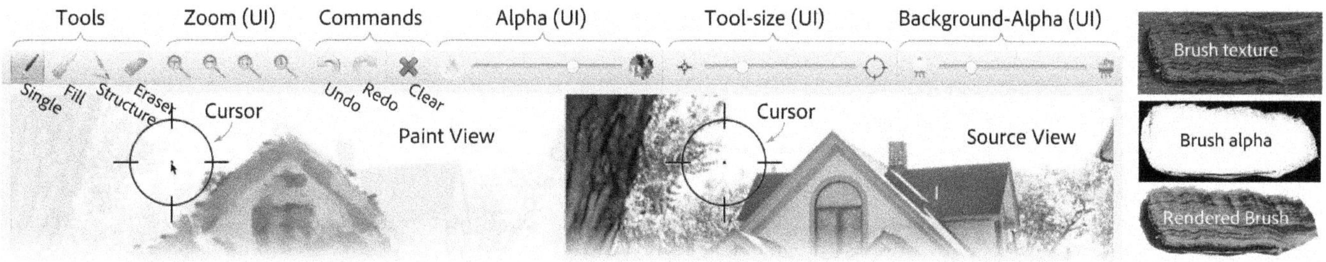

Figure 2. (Left) The user interface, showing tools, commands, UI elements (zoom and sliders), views, and dual-cursor. (Right) Brush components.

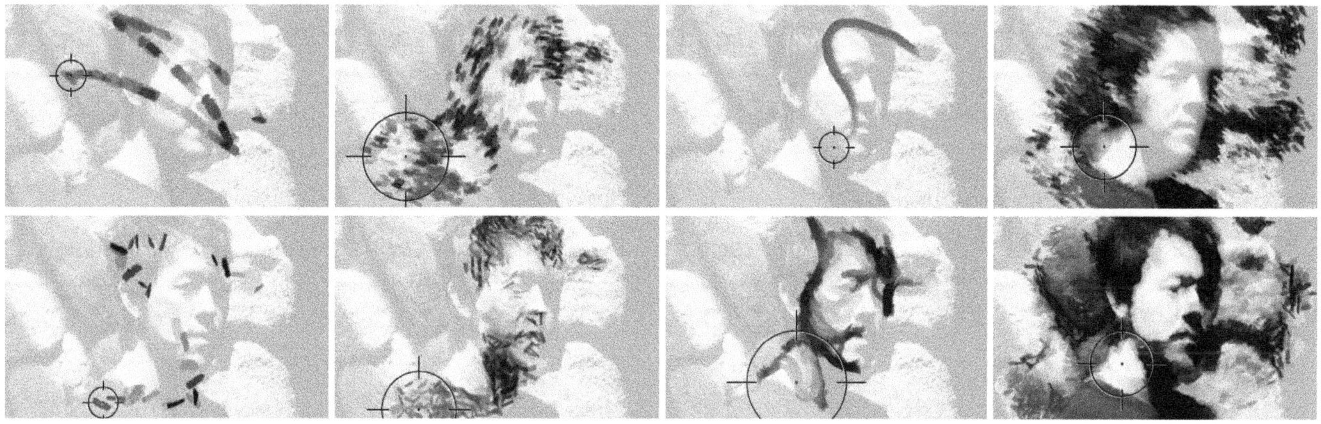

Figure 3. Examples of a single user interaction. Top: Simple tools. Bottom: Smart tools. From left-to-right: Single, Fill, Structure, and Eraser

EVALUATION

To demonstrate the efficacy of our PwB implementation in supporting the general goals for art creation for novices (N1-N9) and specifically for digital painting (P1-P3) we propose a targeted user study. Specifically, we are interested in two main questions: (1) *Is the design of PwB successful in achieving the aforementioned goals?* (2) *Is there a substantial impact of user assistance through smart brushes on these goals?*

Verification and analysis of CSTs is a complex topic, partly due to the complex nature of creativity itself. Sternberg [31] argues that different types of creativity may be used in acts of drawing versus writing versus problem solving, and that different strategies are needed to measure each type. Carroll et al. [3] list three basic approaches to measuring creativity used by the community, along with caveats and benefits: (1) *Self-reporting* is a cheap and easy analysis tool, commonly taking the form of a survey. However, problems with self-evaluation for task-performance and other objective quantities are widely acknowledged within the community [18]. (2) *Psychophysical Measures* include biometrics like EEG, fMRI, galvanic skin response, etc. They provide the most objective data, but are expensive and difficult to procure, calibrate, and operate. (3) *External Judges* may be able to offer a reasonably objective opinion about the quality of a given work. Challenges include the cost and time-requirements of such domain experts. Hocevar [18] also cautions that judges may not be able to distinguish between technical skills, aesthetics, and creativity.

Due to the shortcomings of each method, Carroll et al. [3] perform all three methods, and triangulate the results to improve overall confidence of the findings. While the authors observed interesting correlations between pairs of the three methods, they acknowledged that the setup and analysis costs are prohibitive and only increased confidence slightly.

Our own study design is driven by three main goals: (1) *Relevance*: As discussed above we are not interested in traditional aspects of creativity for professionals. Rather, we want to promote creative experiences for novices. Hocevar [18] asserts that most practical experiments measure creativity *correlates*, rather than creativity itself. The correlates we are interested in are related to *flow*; (2) *Reproducibility*: We see our work as a first step in a more general framework for CSTs for novice art creation. Thus, we want our methodology to apply to similar CSTs, and be affordable to implement and evaluate; (3) *Reliability*: Despite the above constraints, we want the results of our user study to make quantifiable statements about the success and failure of a specific CST.

Like Carroll et al. [3] we propose a multi-pronged approach to measure the multitude of facets affecting creativity. We instrumented PwB to record all UI interactions, allowing us to create usage statistics for the application, and representing a de facto screen recording of each user session, which could then be coded and analyzed. Unlike a screen recording, our usage logs can be queried and analyzed electronically. As several of our design goals are highly subjective (e.g. N6,N7), we employed self-reporting to obtain relevant data. Finally, we used external judges to rate paintings created with PwB. Since our ultimate goal is not high art, and the most likely audience of novice paintings are personal social circles, we recruited peer judges instead of domain experts.

Assistance Levels – In our user study, we compare tools with two levels of painting assistance (*simple* vs. *smart*) to measure the effect of assistance on our design goals. We specifically do not compare with commercial tools to limit biases due to UI, overall software complexity, and brush quality.

Protocol – We selected 20 volunteers from over 50 candidates, to balance gender, favor minimal digital painting experience, non-computer scientists, and a broad age range. Participants were offered a voucher for their efforts.

Each user took part in two sessions of about one hour each. We randomly assigned users to two groups to control for mode sequence: Group A used *simple* tools in the first session and *smart* tools in the second session. Group B did the reverse. To minimize painting strategies from the first session influencing the second session, we spaced the sessions 1-4 days apart (depending on subject availability). Each session was subdivided in the following phases: Introduction→Learning→Painting→Feedback.

The *Introduction* phase of the *first* session began by explaining the aim of the study and its phases. Then an intake questionnaire was administered (Q1).

The *learning* phase was sub-divided into three steps: learning of the UI and tools (by showing a 5 minute video), and practical training (5–7 minutes). Volunteers were encouraged to ask questions during this step, as no feedback would be given during the painting phase (to prevent experimenter bias).

In the *painting* phase, users were asked to perform 3 paintings, with a maximum time of 10 minutes for each one. To allow for a variety of painting results while minimizing total session durations, the 3 input images were chosen by rotation from the 4 images shown in Fig. 5, which in turn were selected to represent the 4 supported subject categories (landscape, portrait, city, nature). Participants were encouraged to share their thoughts with the experimenter. Users could stop the painting once they were satisfied with the result.

The *final* phase consisted of a feedback questionnaire (Q2).

For the *introduction* phase of the *second* session, subjects were given the same introductions as before, without the questionnaire. The *learning* and *painting* phases were administered as before with the same 3 source images, in the same order, but with a new tool set.

In the *feedback* phase, subjects filled out questionnaire Q3. Finally, participants ranked the 6 paintings produced in both session with a visual sorting program. The initial sequencing of images was randomized and no meta-data from the images was shown.

Questionnaires – For brevity, the questionnaires are summarized here. Full versions are available online.

Intake questionnaire (Q1) gathers demographic (gender, age, normal/corrected vision), as well as experience and skill assessments (computer, traditional art, digital art).

Questionnaire (Q2), presented after each user session, asks questions related to design goals (N1-N9) and domain challenges (P1-P3). The questions are partially derived from the Creativity Support Index (CSI) [4], but adapted to a domain novice CST. For example questions, see Table 1.

Questionnaire Q3, consists of two parts. The first part is identical to Q2 (for the latest session). Part two asks about personal preferences between the two tool sets used, the amount of control over the tools, the perceived creativity, and the subjective quality of the produced paintings.

Logs – All user sessions were recorded with detailed event logs and 5-second-interval screenshots. The logs captured all paint events, UI adjustments (alpha, tool size, zoom, etc.) as well as command usage (undo, redo, clear), so that exact statistics could be computed about usage patterns.

One researcher (not physically involved with the user study) coded usage behavior, as follows: Scanning all session recordings in random order, common vs. distinct usage patterns (features) were identified. In a second pass, again randomized, feature occurrences were noted for each session.

Peer Evaluation – We argue that peer judges (social circles) are the most likely critics of novice artwork and that they might use different evaluation criteria compared to expert judges. We thus asked 30 volunteers (not overlapping with those of the main study) to evaluate the quality of paintings produced with PwB. This allowed us to compute a relative ranking of images, users, and sessions.

RESULTS

Data of the three questionnaires was aggregated following the ITU-T Rec. P. 910 [33] by modeling scores with gain and bias (per subject) plus noise to identify systematic and random errors. An ANOVA analysis indicated that a gain and bias normalization was not required. A Kurtosis analysis (Annex 2 of [34]) was used to calculate range values to identify outliers, resulting in the removal of 2 of 20 subjects.

Data was aggregated by calculating the average (s_j) and standard deviations (σ_j) for each question, reported here as $s_j \pm \sigma_j$. For multiple choices questions, the data was aggregated by computing a histogram of the respective answers.

Population – Questionnaire Q1 tells us basic information about the demographic that participated in the user study. Subjects are divided almost equally between males (44%) and females (56%), and ages are distributed with 28% in the 15–30 range, 33% in the 30–40 range, and 39% in the 40 and above range. Most subjects had never taken art lessons (78%), and only 56% had decorated or painted something. While many subjects had prior experience with creative software (78% photo-editing, 61% drawing, 44% video-editing), they rated their skills in using such software as mediocre (photo editing:5.0 ± 1.42, drawing software:4.0 ± 2.26, all out of 10). As such, our average study subject was not entirely naïve in digital art creation, but could certainly be considered novice (non-professional), as per our intent.

Aggregate Data – Table 1 lists the results for feedback questions of Q2 and part one of Q3, regarding the subjective goals N5–N9. Average scores are high for many of the factors un-

Feedback (FB1-FB6)	Scores (10)
1-I like to play with this software (N7)	8.69 ± 1.15
2-I like the paintings I created (N5, N6, N7)	6.94 ± 1.52
3-I would share the paintings on my social network (N6, N9)	6.04 ± 2.74
4-This software makes me feel creative (N6, N9)	6.83 ± 2.17
5-This software is able to increase my creativity (N6, N9)	7.06 ± 1.84
6-I cannot realize these images without this software (N5)	8.64 ± 1.62

Table 1. Selected questions with associated goals and survey scores

der examination such as enjoyment, guaranteed success, creative flexibility etc. Two very high values include 8.7 ± 1.15 for FB1, and 8.6 ± 1.62 for FB6. The only score lower than we hoped for, with 6.0 ± 2.74, is for FB3, aimed at judging ownership & achievement. However, while answering the questionnaire, most users spontaneously commented that this is because they could not choose the source image, and that they were pleased with their paintings. Feedback was quite uniform with two exceptions. Users felt more creative in their second session (7.2 ± 1.9) compared with the first (6.5 ± 2.3). This may be a sign that users were successfully lifted above the *skill-threshold* of creative engagement [9] during the first session. Users also liked paintings created with smart tools significantly more (7.2 ± 1.4) than those created with simple tools (6.6 ± 1.5). Additionally, 94.4% of users stated that they would like to have this software on their PC/smartphone, while 72.2% of subjects would pay 5 euros for a print of one of their paintings. Overall, the survey responses indicate a high degree of enjoyment and personal satisfaction with the user experience and artworks created. Note that similar results could be obtained with other CSTs. In fact, it is our hope that our paper might inspire comparative studies between multiple novice CSTs.

Simple vs. Smart tools – An important aspect of our user study was the degree to which user assistance (*simple* or *smart*) had an effect on the goals of our system design, particularly the interplay between assistance and creative freedom and perceived control.

As stated above, numerical ratings per image indicated that users preferred *smart tool* paintings. We obtain similar results when looking at user preference by session: 50% preferred paintings produced in smart tool sessions, vs. 39% who preferred paintings from simple tool sessions (11% stated no preference). In contrast, most people preferred the simple tool sessions compared to the smart sessions (50% vs. 33%), they experienced more control over the system (50% vs. 33%), and felt more creative (50% vs. 39%). As expected, there exists a strong correlation between control, and perceived flexibility and creativity. So while increased assistance leads to a higher level of satisfaction with the final paintings, this needs to be weighed against the need of users to feel "in charge". Given the overall high feedback scores, it seems that PwB managed to strike a reasonable balance.

Log Analysis

While we instructed users in the use of the UI, we did not advise them on any painting related strategies. Consequently, when coding the users' log files we observed a number of common painting technique challenges, along with techniques that users naturally (without guidance) developed to overcome these challenges.

Figure 4. (Left): Foreground elements (geese) drawn first; (Right): Attempts to fill in background (space between geese) results in irregular background and noticeable seams between foreground and background.

Painter's algorithm – The painter's algorithm refers to a technique that draws background (BG) elements first, followed by foreground (FG) elements. This approach is beneficial as it naturally deals with the occlusions of BG elements by FG elements. This strategy seems unnatural to novices, as they tend to first paint what interests them most (generally FG elements). The users then have trouble painting a coherent BG without affecting FG elements. This often leads to notable seams between FG & BG areas (Fig. 4). While only one user demonstrated a proper back-to-front approach in the first image, about half the users developed this skill by the last painting of the second session.

Coarse-to-fine – This technique refers to directing the viewer's attention by the amount of detail that is painted in different parts of the image. That is, a viewer looks where there is more amount of detail. This effect is commonly achieved by painting most of the image with coarse settings, and then refining areas that are semantically important. Our coding finds this technique to be discovered (not evident in early paintings, but present in later ones) by at least 6 users.

Content aware vs. Content agnostic vs. Novel content – Particularly for simple tools there were different approaches to brush movement over the image (N6,N8,N9). These approaches can be categorized as: (*Content aware*) User brushes emulating image content. E.g. swirly for clouds or wavy for water; (*Content agnostic*) User brushes unrelated to content, often in back-and-forth motions to quickly fill an area. Smart tools tend to produce better results for such behavior; (*Novel content*) User brushes in patterns unrelated to image content, but with an intent to create elements not part of the original image (add path to barn, smiley in the sky, etc.), a sign of playfulness and creativity (N7,N8,N9). We observed half the users paint content aware and half content agnostic in the beginning. At least 4 content agnostic users developed content aware skills by their last image. Notably, at least 7 users showed signs of novel content painting.

Preconceived notions

Just as most users lacked knowledge of proper painting techniques, some users' strategies were clearly influenced by prior experiences in different media or other assumptions.

Sketcher's technique – At least 7 users started by drawing thin outlines of objects and then filled these outlines with a larger tool. We assume that novices more commonly sketch than paint, and thus try to transfer this skill. About half of the sketchers developed strategies more suitable to painting, while others were reasonably successful with their technique.

Paint on white assumption – We observed many users erasing a region before re-painting, whereas in most observed cases it would have been simpler to just layer new paint over old paint, without erasing. This reluctance to paint over existing paint might explain the challenges in discovering back-to-front or coarse-to-fine painting, which are best achieved by painting over existing paint.

Peer Judgments

Each of the 30 peer judges ranked the 4 best and worst paintings for each of the 4 source images. Despite not being expert judges, rankings were quite consistent: Votes for best images (by user) were 3.3 standard deviations from the mean, while votes for the worst paintings were 2.8 deviations from the mean. Of the best ranked images over all judges, 227 paintings were created with smart tools vs. 253 painted with simple tools, a slight but insignificant difference. However, for the worst paintings 175 were created with smart tools vs. 305 with simple tools. We interpret this finding to indicate that our smart tools do not help people create the best paintings at the high end, but they seem to create a minimum level of quality at the low end, compared with manual tools. This satisfies our goal N5 (*Guaranteed success*).

Additionally, we observe a definite learning effect: While 196 preferred paintings come from the first user session, 284 paintings come from the second one. Even within each session, the last paintings are rated higher on average than the first paintings, with most improvement noticed during the first session. While some of this learning effect could be increasing familiarity with handling of a stylus, it should be noted that PwB requires very little precision (e.g. compared to sketching). We also found evidence of skill improvements through the log analysis and therefore conclude that goal N2 (*Easy to learn*) is satisfied within PwB.

In retrospect, using the 4 best and worst pictures instead of a complete image ranking may introduce a potential bias due to outliers. A frequency analysis of our data shows that this bias it not present in our results, but we underline that a more reliable analysis should be based on a full rank.

DISCUSSION & FUTURE WORK

In this paper we proposed 9 general design goals for novice art CSTs (N1–N9), and 3 goals domain-specific to digital painting (P1–P3). The latter (P1–P3), N1 (Kickstart), and N4 (WYWISYG) were addressed by the technical implementation of PwB. The basic usage of PwB was *easy to use* (N3) and *easy to learn* (N2), as almost all users were able to produce pleasing looking paintings in under 10 minutes (low threshold). The average user improved their drawing skills dramatically within the first user session, with some slighter improvements in the second session, as rated by objective third party judges. More surprisingly, a number of users developed basic painting techniques (coarse-to-fine, back-to-front, level-of-detail, etc.) without instructions, by mere experimentation (high ceiling). The goal of *guaranteed success* (N5) was achieved by multiple standards. The example images in this paper (e.g. Fig. 7) and the accompanying video demonstrate the visual quality of paintings produced with PwB. Of course, not every user was successful in obtaining high-quality images, as shown in Fig. 8. Satisfaction scores of users for their paintings were high, and most users stated that they would be unable to produce similar results without PwB. Responses to our *ownership and achievement* (N6) question in Q3 were lower than hoped, but partially explained by the lack of choice for the source images. *Enjoyment* (N7) ratings from the questionnaires were very high. One of our fears was that users would choose a default setting, fill the image carelessly and thus all generating a similar look. This was not the case. Each user was able to achieve *individual results* (N9), as demonstrated in Figs. 1 and 6. Finally, the assistance of the painting program should not unduly impede *creative flexibility* (N8). We were astonished by the unexpected and innovative paintings and techniques demonstrated by our users (e.g. Fig. 9), indicating that creative expression is possible even within a controlled system like PwB. An even higher level of creativity (compositional) could be achieved by allowing users to paint elements from different source images into a single painting.

One surprising result is that while *smart tools* increased subjective painting quality, the *simple tools* were still much appreciated for their sense of control. We believe that merely providing high-quality, yet simple-to-use brushes (auto-color; only 2 parameters, identical for every tool) could be sufficient to lift domain novices over the *skill-threshold*. In such case, future work might investigate more closely how this threshold is defined in terms of techniques or skill sets. Another surprise was the degree to which individuals naturally acquired various painting skills, with only minimal exposure to PwB (2 hours). We are interested in investigating how incidental learning could be maximized in novice art CSTs without negatively impacting our design goals. Finally, we would like to apply our design goals and evaluation techniques to other fine arts, such as sketching, cartooning, etc.

REFERENCES

1. Amabile, T. M. Motivation and creativity: Effects of motivational orientation on creative writers. *J. of Personality and Social Psych. 48*, 2 (1985), 393–399.
2. Amabile, T. M., Hadley, C. N., and Kramer, S. J. Creativity under the gun. *Harvard business review 80*, 8 (2002), 52.
3. Carroll, E. A., and Latulipe, C. Triangulating the Personal Creative Experience: Self-report, External Judgments, and Physiology. In *Proc. of Graphics Iterfaces 2012* (2012), 53–60.
4. Carroll, E. A., Latulipe, C., Fung, R., and Terry, M. Creativity factor evaluation: Towards a standardized survey metric for creativity support. In *Proc. Creativity and Cognition '09*, ACM (2009), 127–136.

Figure 5. The four input images[1] for the user study. Each user painted three of these images.

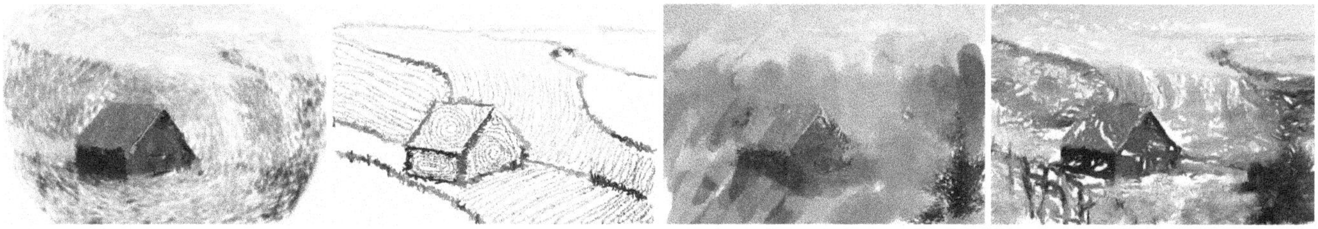

Figure 6. An example of the diversity of final results obtained by different users from the same reference image.

Figure 7. Four "successful" results, where the system clearly allowed the user to express a well-defined style.

Figure 8. Four "failure" results, where the user was not able to exploit the system to reach the intended completion of the painting.

Figure 9. Four "creative" interesting results, where the user has been able to express a unique personal style.

5. Chu, N., Baxter, W., Wei, L.-Y., and Govindaraju, N. Detail-preserving paint modeling for 3D brushes. In *NPAR '10*, ACM (2010), 27–34.

6. Comaniciu, D., and Meer, P. Mean shift: a robust approach toward feature space analysis. *IEEE PAMI 24*, 5 (2002), 603–619.

7. Csikszentmihalyi, M. *Creativity: Invention, Flow and the psychology of discovery and Invention*. Perennial & Harper, 1997.

8. Cummmings, D., Vides, F., and Hammond, T. I Don't Believe My Eyes!: Geometric Sketch Recognition for a Computer Art Tutorial. In *Proc. of SBIM'12* (2012), 97–106.

9. Davis, N., Winnemöller, H., Dontcheva, M., and Do, E. Y.-l. Toward a cognitive theory of creativity support. In *Proc. Creativity & Cognition '13* (2013), 13–22.

10. Dixon, D., Prasad, M., and Hammond, T. iCanDraw: Using Sketch Recognition and Corrective Feedback to Assist a User in Drawing Human Faces. In *Proc. SIGCHI '10*, ACM (2010), 897–906.

11. Fernquist, J., Grossman, T., and Fitzmaurice, G. Sketch-sketch revolution: an engaging tutorial system for guided sketching and application learning. In *UIST '11*, ACM (2011), 373–382.

12. Flood, M., and Phillips, K. D. Creativity in older adults: A plethora of possibilities. *Issues in Mental Health Nursing 28*, 4 (2007), 389–411.

13. Gabor, D. Theory of communication. part 1: The analysis of information. *Electrical Engineers-Part III: Radio and Communication Engineering, Journal of the Institution of 93*, 26 (1946), 429–441.

14. Gardner, H. *Art, Mind, And Brain: A Cognitive Approach To Creativity*. Basic Books, New York, NY, USA, 1982.

15. Goncu, A., and Gaskins, S. *Play and Development: Evolutionary, Sociocultural, and Functional Perspectives*. The Jean Piaget Symposium series. Taylor & Francis, New York, NY, USA, 2007.

16. Haeberli, P. Paint by numbers: Abstract image representations. *SIGGRAPH Comput. Graph. 24*, 4 (Sept. 1990), 207–214.

17. Hertzmann, A. Painterly rendering with curved brush strokes of multiple sizes. In *SIGGRAPH '98*, ACM (New York, NY, USA, 1998), 453–460.

18. Hocevar, D. Measurement of creativity: Review and critique. *Journal of Personality assessment 45*, 5 (1981), 450–464.

19. Iarussi, E., Bousseau, A., and Tsandilas, T. The drawing assistant: Automated drawing guidance and feedback from photographs. In *Proc. UIST '13*, ACM (New York, NY, USA, 2013), 183–192.

20. Kang, H., Lee, S., and Chui, C. K. Coherent line drawing. In *Proc. NPAR '07*, ACM (2007), 43–50.

21. Kaufman, J. C., and Beghetto, R. A. Beyond big and little: The four c model of creativity., 2009.

22. Kazi, R. H., Igarashi, T., Zhao, S., and Davis, R. Vignette: Interactive texture design and manipulation with freeform gestures for pen-and-ink illustration. In *Proc. CHI '12*, ACM (2012), 1727–1736.

23. Lee, Y. J., Zitnick, C. L., and Cohen, M. F. Shadowdraw: real-time user guidance for freehand drawing. *ACM Trans. Graph. 30*, 4 (July 2011), 27:1–27:10.

24. Obrenovic, v., and Martens, J.-B. Sketching interactive systems with sketchify. *ACM Trans. Comput.-Hum. Interact. 18*, 1 (May 2011), 4:1–4:38.

25. Read, J., MacFarlane, S., and Casey, C. Endurability, engagement and expectations: Measuring children's fun. *Interaction Design and Children 2* (2002), 1–23.

26. Reilly, R. C. Is expertise a necessary precondition for creativity?: A case of four novice learning group facilitators. *Thinking Skills and Creativity 3*, 1 (2008), 59–76.

27. Rosin, P., and Collomosse, J. *Image and Video-Based Artistic Stylisation*. Computational imaging and vision. Springer London, Limited, London, United Kingdom, 2013.

28. Rubin, K., Fein, G., and Vandenberg, B. Play. In *Handbook of Child Psychology*, Wiley (New York, New York, USA, 1983), 693—-774.

29. Ryokai, K., Marti, S., and Ishii, H. I/O Brush: Drawing with Everyday Objects As Ink. In *Proc. CHI '04* (2004), 303–310.

30. Shneiderman, B. Creativity support tools: accelerating discovery and innovation. *Communications of the ACM 50*, 12 (Dec. 2007), 20–32.

31. Sternberg, R. J. *Handbook of creativity*. Cambridge University Press, Cambridge, UK, 1999.

32. Takagi, S., Matsuda, N., Soga, M., Taki, H., Shima, T., and Yoshimoto, F. A learning support system for beginners in pencil drawing. In *Proc. GRAPHITE '03* (2003), 281–282.

33. Union, I. T. ITU-T Rec. P.910: Subjective video quality assessment methods for multimedia applications, 1996.

34. Union, I. T. ITU-T Rec. BT.500-11: Methodology for subjective assessment of the quality of television pictures, 2002.

35. Zeng, K., Zhao, M., Xiong, C., and Zhu, S.-C. From image parsing to painterly rendering. *ACM Trans. Graph. 29*, 1 (Dec. 2009), 2:1–2:11.

[1] The first three images of Fig. 5 are from Flickr users "swainboat", "Martino Pizzol", and "Vinoth Chandar" (from left to right), they are released under a Creative Commons Attribution 2.0 licence (**https://creativecommons.org/licenses/by/2.0/legalcode**).

InterTwine: Creating Interapplication Information Scent to Support Coordinated Use of Software

Adam Fourney[1] **Ben Lafreniere**[1] **Parmit Chilana**[2] **Michael Terry**[1]

[1]Cheriton School of Computer Science, [2]Management Sciences
Univeristy of Waterloo, Waterloo, ON, Canada
{ afourney, bjlafren, pchilana, mterry }@uwaterloo.ca

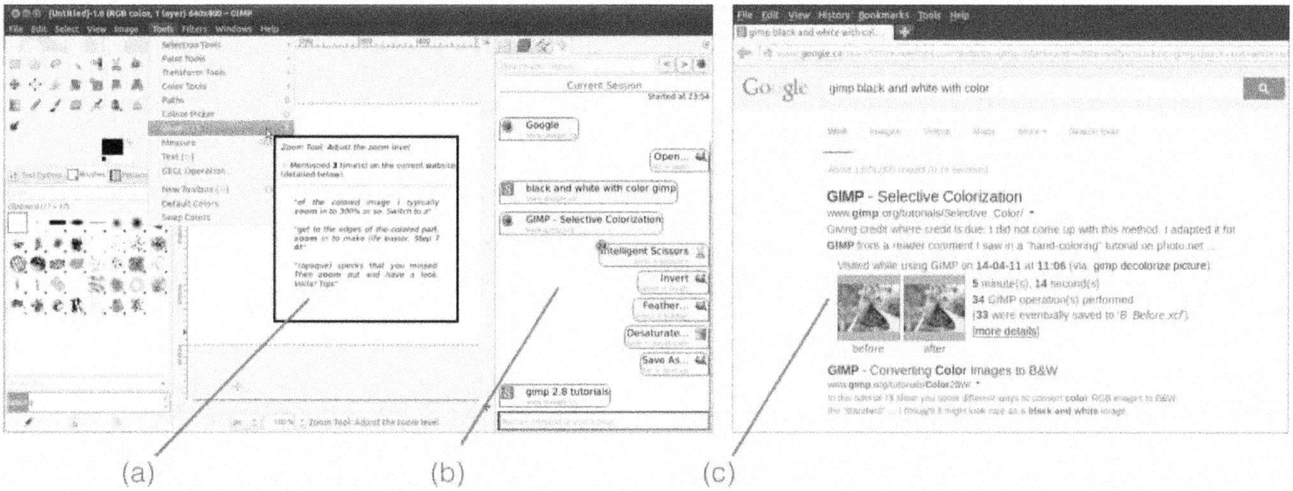

Figure 1. InterTwine links web browsers with feature-rich software applications to create *interapplication information scent*. Specifically, InterTwine modifies application tooltips to describe how they are mentioned on the web page currently open in the browser (a). Likewise, InterTwine extends web search snippets with details of how work documents evolved when that web page was last accessed (c). Finally, InterTwine maintains an interactive interapplication event history to facilitate re-finding past actions and relevant web pages (b).

ABSTRACT
Users often make continued and sustained use of online resources to complement use of a desktop application. For example, users may reference online tutorials to recall how to perform a particular task. While often used in a coordinated fashion, the browser and desktop application provide separate, independent mechanisms for helping users find and re-find task-relevant information. In this paper, we describe *InterTwine*, a system that links information in the web browser with relevant elements in the desktop application to create *interapplication information scent*. This explicit link produces a shared *interapplication history* to assist in re-finding information in both applications. As an example, InterTwine marks all menu items in the desktop application that are currently mentioned in the front-most web page. This paper introduces the notion of interapplication information scent, demonstrates the concept in InterTwine, and describes results from a formative study suggesting the utility of the concept.

UIST 2014, October 5–8, 2014, Honolulu, HI, USA.

http://dx.doi.org/10.1145/2642918.2647420

Author Keywords
interapplication information scent; finding & re-finding

ACM Classification Keywords
H.5.m. Information Interfaces and Presentation (e.g. HCI): Miscellaneous

INTRODUCTION
When using desktop software, users frequently rely on the web to access tutorials, troubleshoot problems, or learn how to use specific software features [5, 6]. As users gain experience with the application, they often continue to rely on these external resources, learning *where* to retrieve relevant task-specific information, rather than committing specific operational details to memory [3, 14, 25]. In all cases, online materials provide information that is useful for the successful completion of a given task. This tightly coupled use of web-based information with desktop software suggests that it is worthwhile to consider these separate systems—the web browser and desktop application—as parts of a *single system* for performing work [2].

In this paper, we are concerned with the processes of finding and re-finding task-specific information when using desktop software. In this context, the theory of information foraging provides a useful framework for considering these practices [22]. Information foraging posits that people make use of *information scent* to guide their selection and use of information resources within "patches," or collections, of information [4]. When using the web, information scent is provided by elements such as a search engine's autocomplete service, the short page snippets shown in search results, or previously visited links rendered in a different color. In desktop software, menu hierarchies, command names, tool icons, and tooltips all provide affordances that can be considered forms of information scent that assist users in finding relevant functionality.

While these separate systems each provide useful forms of information scent to guide the pursuit of desired information, they largely function independently of one another: the activities in one application have no effect on the presentation of information in the other, forcing the user to manually link information patches between the two applications. For example, desktop software generally has no awareness of when the user turns to the web to learn how to complete a task with the software. Thus, when the user finds relevant information on the web, they must manually connect that information with the affordances and cues provided by the desktop software. In this research, we are motivated to develop mechanisms that more effectively link these distinct systems, to ease the processes of finding and re-finding information within and across applications.

This paper describes *InterTwine*, a system that introduces the concept of *interapplication information scent*. Interapplication information scent links the separate information patches of the web browser and desktop software, injecting novel forms of information scent into both applications to facilitate the finding and re-finding of information. For example, InterTwine embellishes a desktop application's menus with markers (what we call "beacons") for menu items described in the currently open, front-most browser window or tab (Figure 1a). Our current implementation explores these concepts in the context of the Firefox web browser and the GNU Image Manipulation Program (GIMP).

InterTwine is composed of three conceptual entities: 1) a shared, interapplication history produced by recording actions in the web browser and desktop application, 2) mechanisms to identify information likely to be of relevance from this shared history, and 3) novel interface mechanisms that introduce context-aware, interapplication information scent synthesized from this shared history.

Within this system, we demonstrate three different classes of interapplication information scent: application bridges, history snippets, and history digests.

Application bridges are information scent cues that link information in the currently open web page with the relevant features of the desktop application. The previously mentioned menu beacons are an example of application bridges. InterTwine also bridges applications by injecting relevant snippets from the open web document into the tooltips of the desktop application. Together, these bridges help users establish and maintain a shared information context *across* application spaces, easing the process of locating information referenced in one application in the other application.

History snippets are a form of information scent that communicate the context surrounding the past use of a command or web page. InterTwine provides history snippets by embellishing tooltips with a paged display that lists the commands and web pages leading up to, and following, previous invocations of the command. This context helps people re-trace past steps at a glance, and re-access relevant web content.

History digests provide context-dependent summaries of how the desktop application was used with respect to a given web page. InterTwine presents these history digests by augmenting Google search results with summaries that include before and after screenshots of the related application document, and the commands invoked in the desktop application when that web page was open. Warnings are presented to the user for pages in which operations were performed but later abandoned (suggesting the page may not have been that useful for the task). This shared information scent helps users more effectively locate web pages previously found to be useful.

Collectively, this paper makes the following contributions:

1. We present results from a formative study that informed the need for, and design of, mechanisms that provide interapplication information scent
2. We introduce the concepts of a shared, interapplication history and interapplication information scent, and demonstrate three types of interapplication information scent: application bridges, history snippets, and history digests
3. We demonstrate these concepts within InterTwine, a system that ties together the separate information spaces of Firefox and GIMP
4. We validate these concepts via the results obtained from our formative study

In the remainder of this paper we review related work, then present the details of our formative study. We describe the InterTwine prototype, and the types and instances of interapplication information scents it provides, then describe our strategy for constructing interapplication history. Finally, we report how participants of the formative study and iterative design process responded to the final version of the software, and discuss future directions for research.

BACKGROUND

The central premise of this work is that web browsers, online materials, and feature rich applications are often used together as a single productivity system. This perspective is strongly supported by recent research that examines how web search and access to online resources affects work practices [3, 8, 14]. In particular, past work has observed that people are more likely to be able to recall how to re-access helpful material than the actual steps necessary to complete a task. This effect is especially prevalent in the field of software development, where programmers make extensive use of online resources when writing code [3], or when answering technical questions in online forums [8]. More generally, Sparrow et al., describe this phenomena as "*an adaptive use of memory – to include the computer and online search engines as an external memory system that can be accessed at will*" [25].

When users rely on online materials as an external memory store, they are counting on their ability to re-access those materials as needed at a later date. However, people rarely take proactive measures to ensure their ability to return to important information (e.g., bookmarks are underutilized) [12]. Instead, people trust their ability to re-find information using strategies such as web search. Unfortunately, this re-finding strategy is imperfect: users often express frustration in recreating their search sessions [21], and fail to accurately remember up to 30% of previously issued searches after only a few hours [26]. These breakdowns motivated the development of systems such as SearchBar [20] and ActionShot [17], which are both designed to help users more effectively retrace their browsing sessions using data automatically collected in the browser. InterTwine functions similarly to these systems, but is differentiated by two important details: (1) InterTwine focuses on *interapplication* history, and (2) InterTwine actively modifies existing interfaces to enhance and create information scent. We discuss these two details next.

Shared, Interapplication Context

InterTwine maintains a shared interapplication history between the application and the browser. Other projects arrange for applications to share their immediate state or *context*, without maintaining historical details. For example, Pongnumkul et al.'s *Pause and Play* system [23] demonstrates how a 3D modeling application can work together with a video player to more effectively manage video playback when users are following video demonstrations. Likewise, Ekstrand et al. explored how search engines might leverage contextual cues provided by a vector graphics drawing application in order to return more relevant search results for a given task [5]. InterTwine is differentiated from both projects by its focus on injecting novel forms of information scent, and by its use of historical data to help users re-find pages, or to retrace their previously performed steps.

Hartmann's HyperSource [10], and Goldman's Codetrail [9] are systems that also share context between a browser and a given application. More specifically, HyperSource helps developers document and track the origin of code copied and pasted from websites [10]. Codetrail is similar to HyperSource, but forms these associations automatically by comparing recently written code to the text of pages in the web browsing history [9]. InterTwine builds on these concepts, extending them to end-user applications which require different forms of shared context and information.

Scented Widgets and Snippets

InterTwine creates interapplication information scent through embellishments to application widgets and search snippets. In the literature, there are a number of projects that also embellish widgets to enhance their information scent. Notably, Willett et al. present guidelines and a Java framework for embellishing standard interface widgets with small visualizations to enhance navigation of information spaces [27]. Likewise, Matejka et al. demonstrate how interfaces can be overlaid with heat maps describing past use of the software by the user, and by his or her community [18]. InterTwine draws upon these projects for motivation, but differs from these projects by its focus on building and maintaining contextually aware *interapplication* scent trails. For example, InterTwine embellishes widgets only if they are mentioned in the website that is open in the user's browser.

Finally, there are a number of projects that modify or extend search result snippets to enhance their information scent. Ekstrand's system [5], discussed previously, embellishes Google search result snippets for Inkscape tutorials by listing the Inkscape commands listed therein. Likewise, Schwarz and Morris extend search result pages with badges, bar charts and other visualizations, designed to help users judge the credibility of a particular search result [24]. InterTwine's embellishments differ in that they are personalized using interapplication history.

In summary, users of complex software leverage online resources as a form of external memory, but rarely take proactive measures to ensure their ability to re-access this information in the future. Instead, users attempt to re-find materials using search—a strategy that often fails. InterTwine addresses this issue by maintaining a shared interapplication history. It then uses this history to create interapplication information scent, embellishing search results and interface widgets to support finding and re-finding information. While past work has separately explored many of these issues, InterTwine unites these ideas into a single system.

FORMATIVE STUDY

To guide development of InterTwine, we conducted a formative study to: 1) understand the breakdowns that occur when online resources are used to support work in feature-rich applications, and 2) collect feedback on early designs of InterTwine. Eleven individuals (six male, five female, mean age of 26), with varying levels of experience with image editing software, participated in this study. Participants received a $10 Amazon gift card as remuneration for participating in the formative study.

Each session was divided into two parts. In the first part of the session, we asked participants to perform a pair of tasks (described below) using unmodified versions of GIMP 2.8 and Firefox 26. This afforded an opportunity to observe, first-hand, how people find, follow, and re-find online materials when performing tasks in a feature-rich application.

In the second half of each session, participants performed the exact same tasks again, but using our experimental interface designs. These designs ranged from sketches to fully implemented prototypes. For non-functional prototypes, we explained how they functioned and asked users for feedback on their utility to complete the tasks they just performed. For functional prototypes, participants were asked to think aloud as they used the prototypes to complete the same tasks again. Whenever possible, our prototypes were populated with data generated in the first half of each session, thus giving participants a chance to evaluate designs with "live" data. Designs were iterated after each interview, to continually evolve the prototype.

We chose two tasks whose solution is non-trivial in GIMP. One task was to place a thick black border around a sample of large text (i.e., outlining the text). The other task was to modify a color photo so that the background was black and white (i.e., selective desaturation). In all cases, tasks were presented as pairs of before and after pictures without any descriptive text. The order of presentation of tasks was counterbalanced across participants. Prior to performing the first task, participants were strongly advised to seek online materials for assistance.

Participants' actions were captured by event logging software, screen capture software, and an audio recording device.

Summary of Study Results and Implications for Design

In our study, we found that participants initially experienced trouble locating commands mentioned in the web-based tutorials when switching back to GIMP. Participants also had difficulty recalling their previous actions, both online (e.g., search queries, as in [26]), as well as in the application (e.g., commands and procedures).

While we expected participants would encounter some of these issues, they occurred more frequently and with greater severity than expected. For example, we observed participants identify promising commands mentioned in tutorials, and then almost immediately forget the identity, location, and details of those commands when switching into the desktop application. This difficulty was observed even when tutorials explicitly and unambiguously mentioned the locations of commands in the interface. In all of these situations, participants typically adopted a strategy of systematically exploring an application's menus and tooltips in the hope of recognizing their target.

These results suggest there is value in linking the separate information spaces of the web browser and desktop application, to make finding information presented in one application easier to locate in the other application. The difficulty in recalling past actions also suggests the value of mechanisms that assist in re-finding task-specific information at a later time. These results directly led to the development of application bridges and history snippets in InterTwine.

Our iterative design process also revealed that participants were enthusiastic about seeing previously edited GIMP work documents associated with relevant web pages in web search result snippets. However, they expressed disinterest when presented with fine-grained details of errors, dead-ends, or unsuccessful sequences. Accordingly, we developed history digests that summarize past activities, while indicating which web pages appear to have had no effect on advancing the solution.

We also asked participants how they would feel if non-relevant web pages were wrongly associated with GIMP work documents (e.g., linking a work document to a news article that was coincidentally open in the web browser). Participants commented that such errors were easy to spot from the snippets provided, and could be safely ignored, but posited that a high frequency of errors would quickly eliminate any such system's advantages over the status quo. As such, InterTwine takes several measures to ensure the relevance of any associations made between web pages and GIMP documents.

Finally, when presented with a shared history depicting the use of both applications, our participants expressed a desire to see the full history, without omissions. Early designs revealed only the most important commands or web pages, and were generally disliked, as were designs that presented browsing and procedural details in separate locations. Accordingly, InterTwine includes a shared history that shows *all* activity in both applications.

We now describe InterTwine's design in detail.

INTERTWINE

InterTwine is composed of three conceptual parts: a shared interapplication history, mechanisms to identify potentially relevant information from that history, and interapplication information scent that helps users link the separate information spaces of the web browser and desktop application.

We implemented these individual parts via a plugin-in for the Firefox web browser, a modified version of the GIMP image manipulation system, and a shared datastore and associated shared history service that mediates communication between Firefox and GIMP.

While the shared history service serves a key role in the system, it operates automatically in the background, and is not directly accessed by the user; users access its capabilities through the various interface components described below.

InterTwine modifies GIMP by adding an *interapplication history transcript*, by embellishing its menu items with *beacons*, and by adding *history snippets* to tooltips. In Firefox, InterTwine augments Google search result pages with *history digests*. We describe each of these components in turn.

Interapplication History Transcript

The foundation of the InterTwine system is an interapplication interaction history. While these data are used to derive many of InterTwine's other features, users can also directly view and interact with this history.

Our current implementation depicts this shared history in a pane that adopts the metaphor of a chat program. When an action is performed in an application, a "speech bubble" is produced representing that action (Figure 2). Entries contributed by GIMP appear on the right. Entries contributed by Firefox appear on the left. We chose this metaphor to make it easier to visually parse the histories, and to establish a common visual design that can be used in other parts of the interface.

All items displayed in the transcript are interactive. Clicking on a GIMP command bubble causes the command to be invoked, and clicking on a web page bubble causes the web page to open in Firefox and the web browser to come to the foreground.

The transcript can also be searched. InterTwine's transcripts are indexed by command names, command tooltips, file names, web page titles, internet search queries, web page body text, dates, and times. This extensive coverage is designed to allow users to index into the transcript using almost any detail recalled about a previous session, and addresses the goal of helping users re-find information.

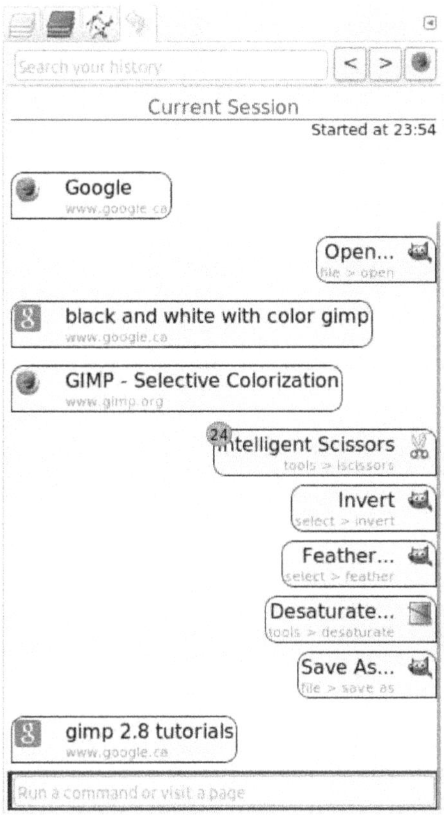

Figure 2. InterTwine adopts the metaphor of a chat program to communicate interapplication event history. When users issue commands in GIMP, the commands appear as speech bubbles on the right-hand side. When users visit pages in Firefox, the pages appear as speech bubbles on the left-hand size.

Finally, embracing the notion of a chat system, users can directly add to this transcript by typing at the chat prompt (Figure 3). When users begin typing at the prompt, their input is automatically completed with the names of GIMP commands, as well as the titles of web pages in the browsing history. Selecting an item from the list of suggestions causes the command to be performed, or the website to be opened and brought to the foreground. This capability draws some inspiration from Hendy et al.'s graphical enhanced keyboard accelerators [11].

As with all InterTwine features, autocompletion makes extensive use of the interapplication history and the current state of both applications when determining what suggestions to provide, as well as their order. As an example, if a web page is open in the user's browser, then the suggested commands are embellished with one style of beacon (i.e., marker) if they are mentioned in that web page, and another style of beacon if they were previously used the last time that web page was open (as seen in Figure 3).

Interapplication Information Scent in Menus and Tooltips

InterTwine modifies the presentation of GIMP menus and tooltips to provide interapplication information scent. This information scent is informed by the shared history and the currently visible web page.

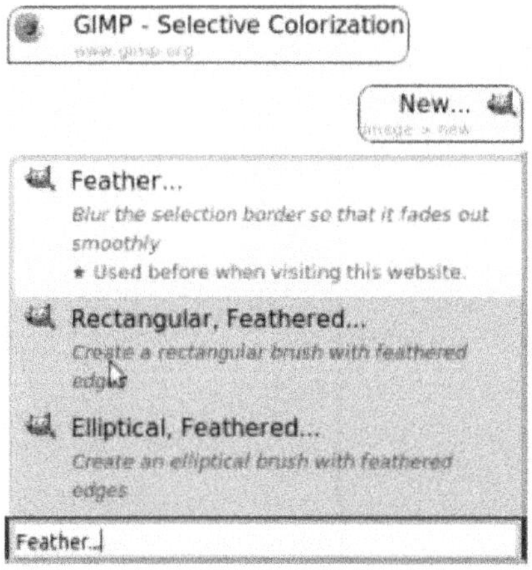

Figure 3. A "chat prompt" is located directly below the transcript. From this prompt, users can execute GIMP operations or visit web pages by typing commands. The prompt autocompletes the input, allowing users to issue commands with only a few key presses.

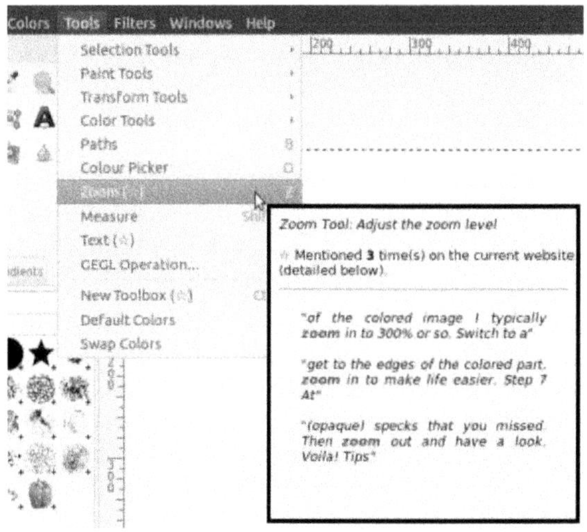

Figure 4. InterTwine embellishes menu items with beacons (star icons) when those items are mentioned by name in the currently visible web page. Likewise, menu tooltips gain snippets describing the context in which each menu item is mentioned in the web page.

InterTwine embellishes menu items with a hollow star icon (a beacon), to communicate that a given menu item is mentioned on the web page the user currently has open in the browser (Figure 4). These menu items' tooltips are also augmented to present web page excerpts that mention the given menu item. These beacons and excerpts are designed to increase the information scent of relevant menu items, and help bridge the separate information spaces of the web page and the desktop software.

InterTwine's menu items are further enhanced based on their history of use. Specifically, if users have previously visited a web page and issued a command with that page open, then InterTwine displays a filled star icon next to the menu item to indicate past relevance. Furthermore, the item's tooltip contains excerpts of the interapplication history transcript detailing its context of use (Figure 5). In cases where the menu item has been used in multiple contexts, users can page through

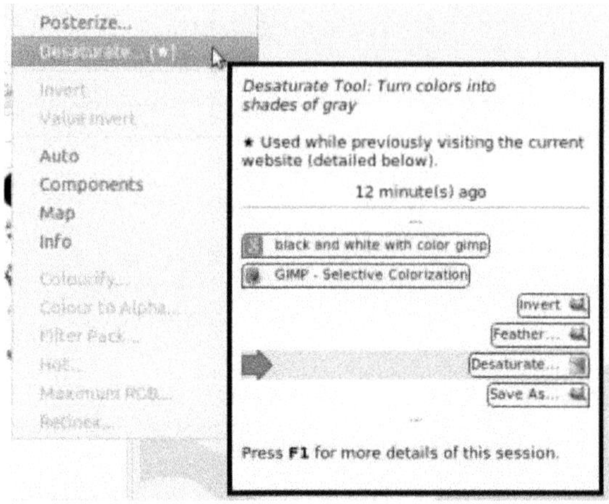

Figure 5. When revisiting a web page, InterTwine places additional beacons (filled-stars) next to commands that were used before in the context of the web page. In these cases, the tooltips gain excerpts from the interapplication history, describing their earlier context of use.

a slideshow of these excerpts using the left and right arrow keys. Finally, at any time, users can press the *F1* key to scroll the full interapplication history (described above) to the corresponding time when the command was used.

Interapplication Information Scent in Web Search Results

In Firefox, InterTwine modifies the Google search results page by enriching the standard search result snippets with details extracted from the interapplication history.

In situations where a search result item has been previously visited, InterTwine retrieves details of the past visit, and generates a summary (or digest) of this information for review (Figure 6). These digests include two screenshots of GIMP's canvas: one taken when the user first accessed the search result, the other taken when leaving the target web page. These images serve as a visual summary of the work that was done when previously visiting the page.

The snippet also details how long the page was previously open, as well as the number of GIMP operations performed while the page was focused in the browser. Two different counts are presented: the total number of operations performed, and the number of operations ultimately saved to the work document. These counts differ when commands are undone, or when the user closes a document without saving or exporting a result. In extreme cases where all commands are abandoned, the snippets instead present a warning (Figure 7).

Finally, users can optionally click a hyperlink in the snippet to reveal the context in which the page was previously accessed. As with tooltips, these details are presented as excerpts from the interapplication history.

IMPLEMENTATION

InterTwine's implementation consists of three components that interoperate on a user's local machine: a modified version of the GIMP image manipulation system, a plugin-in for the Firefox web browser, and a local coordination service that mediates communication between Firefox and GIMP. We describe each of these in turn.

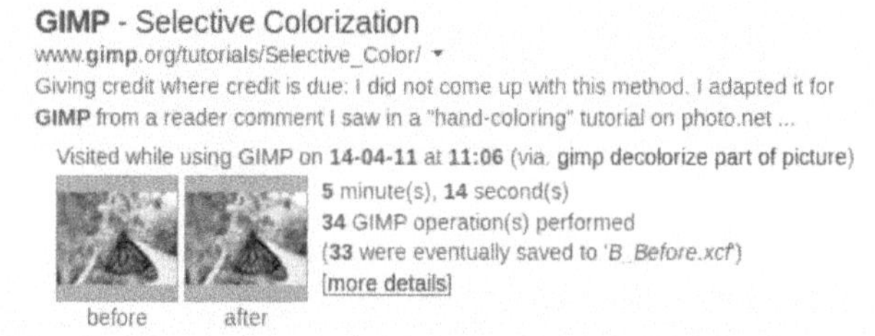

Figure 6. InterTwine modifies Google search result snippets when web pages have been previously visited. Here, InterTwine presents history summaries, which include screenshots of how the user's document evolved when previously reading the page. Additionally, the summaries present statistics describing the time spent, and the number of commands issued.

Figure 7. InterTwine's history summaries present warnings to the user in cases where earlier page visits resulted only in commands that were later abandoned (e.g., commands that were undone or unsaved).

InterTwine requires two distinct sets of modifications to GIMP. First, GIMP must be instrumented to record a user's low-level interactions with the software, as well as to record screenshots of the user's work document as it involves over time. GIMP must also be modified to display the interapplication history transcript, as well as custom menu items and tooltips. InterTwine implements the transcript and the custom tooltips by embedding a Webkit browser directly into the GIMP application. As such, InterTwine's tooltips and transcripts are themselves implemented in HTML and JavaScript. This architecture was especially useful during the formative study, allowing us to quickly iterate InterTwine's designs.

As with the modifications to GIMP, InterTwine's Firefox plug-in serves two roles. First, it instruments the browser to track a user's actions online. Second, it modifies the presentation of the interface (i.e., Google search results). In both cases, these actions are achieved by injecting custom JavaScript code into the pages a user visits online. Instrumentation is achieved by coercing visited web pages to signal interface events (e.g., page loads, scrolling, etc.) by making an asynchronous request to InterTwine's local service.

Finally, InterTwine's local coordination service consists of a lightweight web server running in the background of the user's machine. This service both collects instrumentation data from GIMP and Firefox, and generates content for GIMP transcript and tooltips, as well as the Google search result snippets. Additionally, this service processes the instrumentation data to generate the interapplication history. Next, we describe our method of generating and refining the interapplication history.

Creating and Refining Shared Histories

In our formative study, users made extensive use of tabbed browsing, and followed hyperlinks by opening each in a new tab. Once opened, tabs were rarely closed before the end of each session. Instead, participants returned to earlier pages by switching tabs rather than by relying on the browser's backward and forward buttons.

We also observed two users adopting a strategy of "pre-fetching" search results by opening promising links in new tabs prior to visiting any individual result. In these cases, it was common to retrieve pages that were never actually consulted.

Finally, when participants leveraged online resources to perform unfamiliar tasks, they often continued to explore and experiment with the application's interface, sampling the application's capabilities and undoing many commands.

All of these practices complicate the process of producing a meaningful, shared interapplication history: By the time users complete a task, the histories and interactions logs are extremely noisy, with relevant commands and web pages hidden in a sea of dead-ends and failed experiments. Accordingly, we found it necessary to process and filter the shared interapplication history.

In an effort to improve upon the naïve approach to creating a shared history, InterTwine gathers additional interaction details not present in standard browsing histories. In particular, InterTwine records which browser tabs are visible at any given moment, providing an indication of relevance for each tab. Likewise, InterTwine records interaction events that occur on web pages (e.g., page scroll events), and uses these events to estimate the degree to which a page is being utilized. Specifically, application commands are attributed to web pages only if the web pages mention the name of the application ("GIMP") in their body text, and if the application commands occur within 5 minutes of a web page interaction event.

Additionally, InterTwine tracks the outcome of each command, noting if the command is ever undone, and if not, whether the application document is ever saved (indicating that the work in that document was deemed useful). These data are then reflected in the history digests shown with Google search results: digests display whether a visited web page previously contributed any commands that were still intact when the work document was saved.

FEEDBACK ON FINAL DESIGN

To evaluate the final design of InterTwine, we invited participants from our initial formative study to return 15 days after their initial session. In addition to collecting feedback on how the design had improved (or regressed), this final session afforded an opportunity to observe breakdowns that occur when people repeat tasks several weeks apart, providing a way to validate the system's core purpose (i.e., to assist in re-finding information). Five participants responded to our invitation, and returning participants received an additional $10 Amazon gift card as remuneration.

In this return session, participants were asked to perform one of the original tasks. Since each participant experienced a different prototype in the formative study, and because early prototypes were not always functional, we could not carry forward a participant's earlier interapplication history. Instead, participants were greeted with a fresh installation of GIMP, Firefox, and InterTwine. As with the formative study, minimal instructions were provided. Tasks were presented as pairs of before and after pictures without descriptive text, and participants were advised to seek online materials. InterTwine's features were discussed as they were discovered, and participants were asked for their interpretations before correct use was demonstrated.

Results

At the onset of this final session, all five participants felt they remembered enough about the task to complete it without consulting the web. However, when the time came to actually perform the task, none were able to complete the task without consulting web resources. When asked about this discrepancy, one participant explained:

> *"I think my dependence on the Internet is pretty high. I'm sure I could have [completed the task], but sometimes I doubt myself and think I'll do this faster with Google"* **P2**

After participants visited a few web pages, we called attention to InterTwine's interapplication history, and provided a brief overview of InterTwine's other features. Participants were then asked to continue the task, and to provide feedback as they worked.

Participants were generally positive about InterTwine's individual features. For example, P1, P3 and P5 were very enthusiastic about InterTwine's menu and tooltip enhancements. P3 had the following to say about these features:

> *"You don't have to guess anymore. When you read something and you think yeah, OK, and [then]... I mean, I was powering through this pretty quick, because I thought I knew how to do it. But if you are on a web page and you go up there and... [in] the two seconds you actually read something versus going to do it, you forget what's going on, and then boom, it's right there [referring to InterTwine's beacons] "* **P3**

Likewise, participants P2, P3 and P4 explicitly mentioned finding the shared history to be a useful tool. P2 reported this feature as the single most significant improvement from the prototypes discussed in the formative design process. P3 was especially enthusiastic about the shared history's command prompt, stating:

> *"I'm just thinking like for an advanced user, someone who has been using it for a while, just having the quick keys [command prompt] down here rather than going through all that, that's kind of nice... Yeah, so once you get handy with that I can see it being really, really powerful."* **P3**

All five participants felt that the historical digests, added to Google search results, were especially useful. This was not unexpected, as 10 of the 11 original formative design participants responded enthusiastically to prototypes with this feature. On this topic, P5 noted:

> *"I like where it says how long you've been on the web page and what [you] did. It will tell me I saw this web page quickly and I didn't like it so I X'ed out of there."* **P5**

Finally, P2 noted that InterTwine's features were compelling enough to switch image editors:

> *"My image editor of choice is Paint because it's really simple... I do have Paint.NET on my computer, but I don't use it. But with this sort of input, I would be more likely to use GIMP, because it would help me do some more advanced things that would be difficult to figure out otherwise."* **P2**

Areas for Improvement

While participant feedback was very positive, participants offered suggestions for improvements. For example, despite being very enthusiastic about the menu beacons, P3 initially failed to notice them at all. When the beacons were pointed out by the researcher, the participant explained that the beacons looked like menu text, and he was not sufficiently familiar with GIMP to know if they were something new. This suggests the need to refine the presentation of these markers, so that their designs better communicate their purpose.

Likewise, P5 noted that she found the features of InterTwine's shared history (e.g., search and auto-complete) to be complex, and worried that she would not "use it to its full potential." However, P5 felt that the excerpts of the history, presented in the tooltips and search results page, were acceptable.

Finally, both P1 and P2 requested a mechanism for manually managing the history. In particular, they expressed interest in the ability to rate pages and command sequences, as well as the ability to hide or delete items with poor ratings. We feel that these are excellent feature requests, and that manual management of interapplication history is a compelling design dimension to explore in the future.

A final encouraging sign that InterTwine is offering features that are generalizable, and of value, is that participants offered numerous suggestions for other applications that could benefit from the same interactions. For instance, P5 suggested InterTwine could be applied to SPSS, Minitab, and other statistics packages to help users recall how to perform various statistical tests. Likewise, P1 commented that an InterTwine-like system would be useful when using geographic information systems. Finally, P2 stated:

> *"I'm just thinking like, even writing an essay, like if you had your documents up like in Mendeley or whatever, you can know you wrote this with this document open, and you know what to cite. I'm just thinking of other applications. It seems... I'm just astounded, this is really cool."* **P2**

DISCUSSION & FUTURE WORK

InterTwine represents one targeted exploration of the notion of interapplication information scent. The types of interaction mechanisms chosen in this research were largely determined by following the most salient leads uncovered in the formative study. In this section, we discuss other promising research trajectories, and other possible application domains.

Community Aggregation

InterTwine operates entirely on one's own personal computer, leveraging only personal browsing history and interaction logs. One noteworthy finding from our formative study was that participants were almost entirely unconcerned with sharing their interaction details with a central service like Google (10 of 11 participants had few or no concerns). Given this, one could imagine aggregating a community's interapplication histories, enabling a number of additional applications.

One compelling use of this aggregated data would be to improve indexing of web-based tutorials. For example, a search engine could use this information to influence the ranking of search results, steering users away from tutorials that frequently result in abandoned commands. Likewise, since interapplication history does not depend on page text, these data could be used to index non-textual tutorials such as screencasts and video demonstrations. For example, a search engine could index tutorial videos using the names of the application commands and tools that users typically invoke while visiting each video. Users could then search for video demonstrations by naming commands of interest. With additional instrumentation of the web browser, video timestamps could be extracted and synchronized with application command invocations, allowing search engines to index *into* videos, and enabling capabilities similar to those described in [13, 15, 16]. Beyond indexing web documents and videos, aggregate data could also be applied to command recommendation systems (e.g., [19]), and related projects (e.g.,[7, 18]).

Interapplication Information Scent in Other Domains

InterTwine creates interapplication information scent between a web browser and a feature-rich raster graphics application. Other application pairings are possible—including ones that do not involve a web browser. As an example, a video editing application might notice coordinated use of audio editing software, and could adapt by highlighting the menu commands necessary to insert a new audio track into the video. Likewise, an operating system's file browser might visually modify folder icons in cases where the user has a terminal open in those directories, presenting a persistent visual trail as the user navigates the command shell through the file system. Finally, after using graphical user interface design software, such as QT Creator, programming environments could highlight lines of code related to objects recently worked with in the interface designer.

Fading Information Scent

In our current implementation, interapplication information scent is generated from the past history and current context of both applications. These information scents persist as long as the relevant context is present. However, it is possible that this context (especially from the shared history) could result in too much information scent accumulating, reducing the effectiveness of the concept.

To deal with this problem, interapplication information scent could fade out over time, similar in spirit to Baudisch et. al's [1] phosphor effects in the interface. For example, menu beacons could begin to fade after a web page has been open for 20 minutes. In general, we have not considered the possibility of incorporating hysteresis into our relevance models, but this capability may be especially useful for some of the mechanisms proposed above (such as the trails left through the file system as the user browses directories).

CONCLUSION

Online resources play an integral role in people's strategies for dealing with the complexities of feature-rich applications. However, applications and web browsers currently function as separate isolated entities, unaware of how activities in one application may relate to activities in the other.

In this paper, we introduced InterTwine, a system that bridges these two application domains through the constructs of *interapplication history* and *interapplication information scent*. We demonstrate three classes of tools to provide interapplication information scent: application bridges, history snippets, and history digests. Together, these mechanisms help users find and re-find task-relevant commands and resources.

A formative study spanning two sessions reveals that InterTwine's features resonate with users and suggest their overall utility. Though InterTwine's current implementation is tied to GIMP and the Firefox web browser, we believe the ideas presented in this paper can be generalized to other feature-rich applications. This sentiment is shared by many of those who took part in the participatory design process, as evidenced by their many enthusiastic suggestions for which applications to work on next.

REFERENCES

1. Baudisch, P., Tan, D., Collomb, M., Robbins, D., Hinckley, K., Agrawala, M., Zhao, S., and Ramos, G. Phosphor: Explaining transitions in the user interface using afterglow effects. In *Proceedings of the 19th Annual ACM Symposium on User Interface Software and Technology*, UIST '06, ACM (New York, NY, USA, 2006), 169–178.
2. Brandt, J., Dontcheva, M., Weskamp, M., and Klemmer, S. R. Example-centric programming: integrating web search into the development environment. In *Proc. CHI '10*, ACM (New York, NY, USA, 2010), 513–522.
3. Brandt, J., Guo, P. J., Lewenstein, J., Dontcheva, M., and Klemmer, S. R. Two studies of opportunistic programming: interleaving web foraging, learning, and writing code. In *Proc CHI '09*, ACM (New York, NY, USA, 2009), 1589–1598.
4. Chi, E. H., Pirolli, P., Chen, K., and Pitkow, J. Using information scent to model user information needs and actions and the web. In *Proc CHI '01*, ACM (New York, NY, USA, 2001).
5. Ekstrand, M., Li, W., Grossman, T., Matejka, J., and Fitzmaurice, G. Searching for software learning resources using application context. In *Proc. UIST '11*, ACM (New York, NY, USA, 2011), 195–204.
6. Fourney, A., Mann, R., and Terry, M. Characterizing the usability of interactive applications through query log analysis. In *Proc. CHI '11*, ACM (New York, NY, USA, 2011), 1817–1826.
7. Fourney, A., Mann, R., and Terry, M. Query-feature graphs: Bridging user vocabulary and system functionality. In *Proc. UIST '11*, ACM (New York, NY, USA, 2011), 207–216.
8. Fourney, A., and Ringle Morris, M. Enhancing technical Q&A forums with CiteHistory. In *Proc. ICWSM '13* (2013).
9. Goldman, M., and Miller, R. C. Codetrail: Connecting source code and web resources. *J. Vis. Lang. Comput. 20*, 4 (Aug. 2009), 223–235.
10. Hartmann, B., Dhillon, M., and Chan, M. K. HyperSource: bridging the gap between source and code-related web sites. In *Proc. CHI '11*, ACM (New York, NY, USA, 2011).
11. Hendy, J., Booth, K. S., and McGrenere, J. Graphically enhanced keyboard accelerators for GUIs. In *Proc. GI '10*, Canadian Information Processing Society (Toronto, Ont., Canada, 2010), 3–10.
12. Jones, W., Bruce, H., and Dumais, S. How do people get back to information on the web? how can they do it better. In *Proc. INTERACT '03* (2003), 793–796.
13. Kim, J., Nguyen, P. T., Weir, S., Guo, P. J., Miller, R. C., and Gajos, K. Z. Crowdsourcing step-by-step information extraction to enhance existing how-to videos. In *CHI '14*, CHI '14, ACM (New York, NY, USA, 2014), 4017–4026.
14. Lafreniere, B. *Task-Centric User Interfaces*. PhD, University of Waterloo, Waterloo, ON, Canada, Apr. 2014.
15. Lafreniere, B., Grossman, T., and Fitzmaurice, G. Community enhanced tutorials: Improving tutorials with multiple demonstrations. In *CHI '13*, CHI '13, ACM (New York, NY, USA, 2013), 1779–1788.
16. Lafreniere, B., Grossman, T., Matejka, J., and Fitzmaurice, G. Investigating the feasibility of extracting tool demonstrations from in-situ video content. In *CHI '14*, CHI '14, ACM (New York, NY, USA, 2014), 4007–4016.
17. Li, I., Nichols, J., Lau, T., Drews, C., and Cypher, A. Here's what i did: Sharing and reusing web activity with ActionShot. In *Proc. CHI '10*, ACM (New York, NY, USA, 2010), 723–732.

18. Matejka, J., Grossman, T., and Fitzmaurice, G. Patina: Dynamic heatmaps for visualizing application usage. In *Proc CHI '13*, ACM (New York, NY, USA, 2013), 3227–3236.
19. Matejka, J., Li, W., Grossman, T., and Fitzmaurice, G. CommunityCommands: command recommendations for software applications. In *Proc. UIST '09*, ACM (New York, NY, USA, 2009), 193–202.
20. Morris, D., Ringel Morris, M., and Venolia, G. SearchBar: a search-centric web history for task resumption and information re-finding. In *Proc. CHI '08*, ACM (New York, NY, USA, 2008).
21. Obendorf, H., Weinreich, H., Herder, E., and Mayer, M. Web page revisitation revisited: implications of a long-term click-stream study of browser usage. In *Proc. CHI '07*, ACM (New York, NY, USA, 2007), 597–606.
22. Pirolli, P., and Card, S. Information foraging. *Psychological Review 106*, 4 (1999), 643–675.
23. Pongnumkul, S., Dontcheva, M., Li, W., Wang, J., Bourdev, L., Avidan, S., and Cohen, M. F. Pause-and-play: Automatically linking screencast video tutorials with applications. In *Proc. UIST '11*, ACM (New York, NY, USA, 2011), 135–144.
24. Schwarz, J., and Morris, M. Augmenting web pages and search results to support credibility assessment. In *Proc. CHI '11*, ACM (New York, NY, USA, 2011).
25. Sparrow, B., Liu, J., and Wegner, D. M. Google effects on memory: Cognitive consequences of having information at our fingertips. *Science 333*, 6043 (2011), 776–778.
26. Teevan, J., Adar, E., Jones, R., and Potts, M. A. S. Information re-retrieval: repeat queries in yahoo's logs. In *Proc. SIGIR '07*, ACM (New York, NY, USA, 2007), 151–158.
27. Willett, W., Heer, J., and Agrawala, M. Scented widgets: Improving navigation cues with embedded visualizations. *IEEE Transactions on Visualization and Computer Graphics 13*, 6 (Nov. 2007), 1129–1136.

Generating Emotionally Relevant Musical Scores for Audio Stories

Steve Rubin
University of California, Berkeley
srubin@cs.berkeley.edu

Maneesh Agrawala
University of California, Berkeley
maneesh@cs.berkeley.edu

ABSTRACT
Highly-produced audio stories often include musical scores that reflect the emotions of the speech. Yet, creating effective musical scores requires deep expertise in sound production and is time-consuming even for experts. We present a system and algorithm for re-sequencing music tracks to generate emotionally relevant music scores for audio stories. The user provides a speech track and music tracks and our system gathers emotion labels on the speech through hand-labeling, crowdsourcing, and automatic methods. We develop a constraint-based dynamic programming algorithm that uses these emotion labels to generate emotionally relevant musical scores. We demonstrate the effectiveness of our algorithm by generating 20 musical scores for audio stories and showing that crowd workers rank their overall quality significantly higher than stories without music.

Author Keywords
Audio stories, storytelling, musical scores, music retargeting

ACM Classification Keywords
H.5.m. Information Interfaces and Presentation (e.g. HCI): Miscellaneous

INTRODUCTION
The tradition of oral storytelling is thousands of years old and still endures today through digital recordings like audiobooks and podcasts. At audiobook sites like Audible [2] and LibriVox [13], these recordings number in the hundreds of thousands. In 2013, users downloaded over 500 million hours of audiobooks from Audible alone [2], nearly 15% of Americans listened to an audiobook [37], and 14% of Americans listened to podcasts every month [32].

Highly-produced audiobooks, podcasts, and children's stories combine a speech recording, which vocally conveys the story, with a musical score that serves to emphasize and add nuance to the emotions of the speech. Yet, crafting such a musical score involves smoothly re-sequencing, looping and timing the music to match the emotions in the story as they change over the course of the narrative. This process requires significant audio production expertise and is challenging even for expert producers. As a result, most of the recorded stories available today focus on providing the speech track and do not contain a musical score.

UIST 2014, October 5-8, 2014, Honolulu, HI, USA.
ACM 978-1-4503-3069-5/14/10.
http://dx.doi.org/10.1145/2642918.2647406

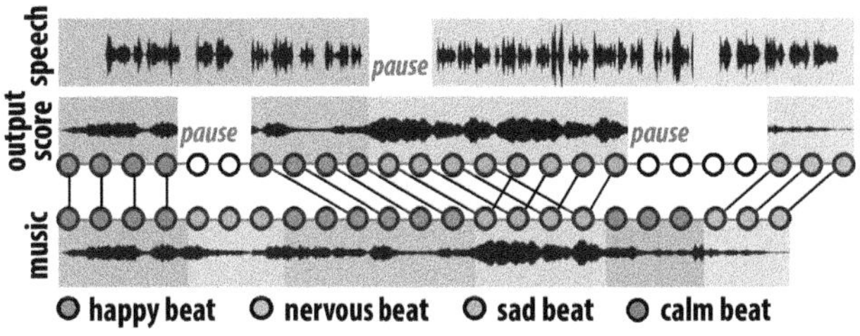

Figure 1. Our algorithm re-sequences the beats (circles) of the input music (bottom row) to match the emotions of the speech (top row). Our algorithm inserts pauses in speech and music, and makes musical transitions that were not in the original music in order to meet these constraints.

In this paper we present a system that allows users with no audio editing expertise to generate high-quality, emotionally relevant music scores for audio stories. To generate a score, our system requires a speech track with associated emotion labels, and one or more music tracks with associated emotion labels. Our system uses a dynamic programming optimization approach to re-sequence the input music tracks so that the emotions of the output score match those of the speech (Figure 1). We studied how expert producers use music in audio stories and incorporate additional constraints into the optimization that correspond to structural and stylistic design decisions in their scores.

We investigate three techniques for labeling the speech and music. We provide a manual interface for hand-labeling speech emotion by annotating a text transcript, and for labeling music emotion by listening to and annotating segments of the music. We also provide a crowdsourcing method for generating the labels, where crowd workers use the labeling interface and our system combines their responses. Finally, our system includes a fully automatic method for computing the emotion labels for the speech and music using sentiment analysis techniques. These three approaches offer different trade-offs in time and label quality that affect the overall quality of the music scores that our system generates.

We demonstrate the effectiveness of our score generation tools by generating a total of 20 musical scores including examples using each of our three labeling methods. We ask listeners to rank the overall quality of these results. Surprisingly, listeners rank the results generated with our crowd-labeling technique as high or higher than the hand-labeled results, which are in turn better than results using our automatic approach and no music. Our system generates scores that are preferable to no musical score for all of the speech tracks. We also investigate the inter-labeler reliability of agreement and find that human-produced labelings tend to agree more with each other than with our automatic labelings.

RELATED WORK

Automatically scoring audio and video stories is a longstanding problem in multimedia research. Foote et al. [9] automatically create music videos by editing video clips to match a piece of music. Their method finds suitable locations to cut video and then splices video to match points in music where audio features change. Our work instead edits the music to create a soundtrack tailored to the speech by matching emotions rather than low-level audio/video features. Monteith et al. [18, 17] generate new music MIDIs to match automatically-labeled emotions in stories. They learn generative models of different music emotions and then sample new music from these models. However, because their algorithm only considers local matching of speech and music, the soundtracks they generate may not contain story-level structure or cohesion. Our algorithm uses the emotion labels across an entire story to generate a globally coherent musical score. We generate emotionally relevant musical scores by re-sequencing existing, high quality music tracks instead of MIDIs, and we provide more options for emotion labeling.

Rubin et al. [22] focus on the process of editing speech and adding music to audio stories. Their system offers a high-level editing workflow and requires a user-in-the-loop to refine speech and music edits. Our system asks for even higher-level input and does not require a user to specify or refine edits directly. Earlier work from Rubin et al. [21] allows producers to generate a musical score for a short section of speech, while our system creates an optimal musical score for an entire story. Neither of these systems deal directly with matching the emotions of speech and music. Our system allows novices to create emotionally relevant musical scores for audio stories.

Dynamic programming is a common strategy for concatenative music synthesis, where short music clips are re-sequenced from a database to create new music that mimics existing music, or to create music that follows certain note patterns [28, 27] Our work follows this general approach, but we offer constraints that generate emotionally relevant music scores rather than music that imitates other music. Wenner et al. [34] and Rubin et al. [22] present methods for music retargeting to find optimal paths through music that match constraints of videos or audio stories. Our work builds on these algorithms and describes new constraints to match emotions of the speech and music, add pauses with flexible length, bound music segment lengths, and create scores from multiple music tracks. Other work applies belief propagation [29] and genetic algorithms [33] to music re-sequencing, but we use dynamic programming instead to efficiently find optimal solutions. Algorithms for video synthesis often apply dynamic programming techniques as well, as in Schödl et al.'s [26] video textures, and Arikan et al.'s [1] annotation-based character motion synthesis.

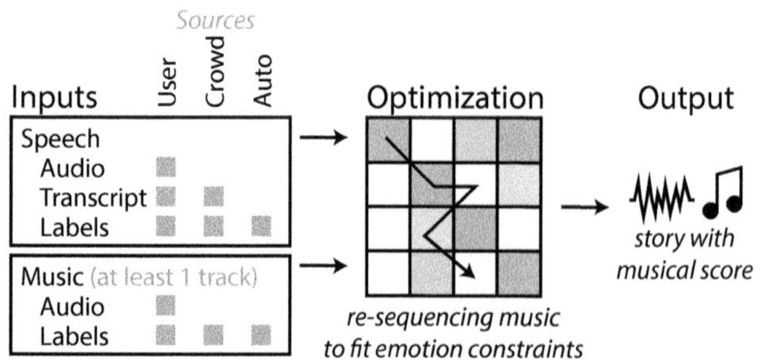

Figure 2. Our automated musical score generation system requires a speech track and music tracks, and emotion labels on those tracks. Our algorithm re-sequences the music tracks to create an output musical score that matches the emotions of the speech. The green boxes denote the sources—user, crowd, and fully automatic—that our system provides for obtaining each input. Our system also requires a speech transcript so users and crowd workers can more quickly label the emotions by reading the text instead of listening to the speech.

Affect prediction is a well-studied problem for speech [6], text [4], and music [11]. We draw on these techniques to provide automatic emotion labeling tools in our system. Our work concentrates on the application of affect labeling and understanding rather than on its prediction.

LABELING EMOTIONS

Figure 2 shows our pipeline for generating emotionally relevant musical scores. A user begins by selecting a speech track such as an audiobook, and one or more instrumental music tracks (i.e., music without lyrics). Our system then gathers emotion labels for each of the speech and music tracks. After collecting these labels, our system constructs a musical score by re-sequencing the input music tracks so the emotion labels of the output music match the emotion labels of the speech.

Our system offers three methods for obtaining the required emotion labels: hand-labeling, crowd-labeling, and automatic labeling. These three methods offer trade-offs in time, effort, and personalization. Hand-labeling produces emotions that reflect the user's emotions and may result in the most personal musical score, but it takes the most time for the user. The crowd-labeling method requires no extra work on the user's part and incorporates human ratings. However, this method takes more time than hand-labeling to acquire emotion labels. Finally, the fully automatic method produces labels immediately, but they may not accurately reflect the personal emotions that the user—or any human—feels about the story and the music. As we will show, all of these methods require a speech transcript, which may cost money to obtain. The crowd-labeling method has the added cost of paying workers.

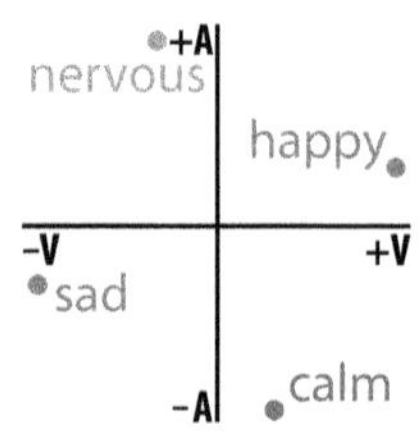

Affect researchers have found Russell's circumplex model [23] of quantifying emotion with 'valence' and 'arousal' to be highly consistent with behavioral and cognitive neuroscience study results [20]. The valence dimension indicates whether an emotion is positive or negative, whereas arousal indicates the intensity of the emotion. A user does not need to learn the circumplex model. Instead, we focus on four emotions, *happy, nervous, sad,* and *calm*, because they almost evenly span the circumplex [23]. As shown in the inset, we set their coordinates to $(.95, .31)$, $(-.31, .95)$, $(-.95, -.31)$, and $(-.95, .31)$, respectively, an equal distribution near their original locations [20].

Speech Emotion Labels

Our goal is to break the speech into segments of similar emotions. Segmenting a speech track into emotionally similar segments based solely on the raw waveform requires careful listening and can be difficult. In text, however, paragraphs usually represent topically-coherent segments that convey one predominant emotion. Therefore, we obtain a text transcript of the speech and use its paragraph boundaries to segment the speech.

Audiobooks and even some podcasts often have readily available transcripts, but if not, the user can obtain one a from crowdsourced transcription site like CastingWords [5] for \$1.00 per minute of audio. We time-align the text transcript and the speech using a variant of the Penn Phonetics Lab Forced Aligner [36] from Rubin et al [22]. The time-alignment allows our system to find the segment of speech that corresponds to each paragraph of the text.

The user chooses one of the three labeling methods to get emotion labels for each speech segment.

Hand-labeling the speech. If users wish to personalize the emotion labels of the speech, they can label the emotion of each paragraph of the text transcript by hand (Figure 3).

Crowd-labeling the speech. To crowd-label the emotions of the speech, our system posts tasks to Amazon's Mechanical Turk. These tasks are identical to the hand-labeling interface (Figure 3).

Crowd workers often try to complete tasks as quickly as possible so they can maximize their hourly rate. Such workers may not fully engage with the speech or its emotions and produce inaccurate emotion labels. Yet, emotions labels can be subjective, and there is no way to test the accuracy of a worker's labeling. Our approach is to obtain emotion labels from multiple workers and then select the labeling of a single worker that best represents all of the workers.

We interpret each worker's complete speech labeling as a sample from the distribution of possible speech labelings, first assigning each paragraph i a distribution p_i where $p_i(l)$ is the probability that a worker labeled paragraph i with emotion l in all of the labelings we have collected. For example, if we have ten workers total and 7 label paragraph 1 as 'sad' and 3 label it as 'calm'—then $p_1(sad) = 7/10$, $p_1(calm) = 3/10$, and $p_1(happy)$ and $p_1(nervous)$ are both zero. We then find the worker that gave the most probable labeling according to this distribution. Suppose $\ell = \{l_1, \ldots, l_k\}$ is a worker's labeling of the sequence of paragraphs in the speech. We compute the probability of this labeling as

$$P(\ell) = \prod_{i=1}^{k} p_i(l_i).$$

Our system computes this probability for each worker's labeling and assigns the labeling with the highest probability to the speech. An alternative to our *most probable worker labeling* approach is to choose the most frequently labeled emotion for each paragraph independently. However, such a voting scheme can yield emotion transitions between paragraphs that did not appear in any of the individual worker's labelings. In contrast, our approach yields a labeling that is guaranteed to be consistent with at least one worker's labeling. This strategy of picking one representative rather than averaging or aggregating worker results has been used in recent work to ensure self-consistent results [12, 35].

Automatically labeling the speech. To automatically label the speech, our system estimates the emotion of each paragraph based on the emotion conveyed by each word. Warriner et al. [31] have collected a corpus of crowdsourced valence and arousal ratings for nearly 14,000 English words. We normalize these scores by the global valence/arousal mean and standard deviation. We then compute the average of the normalized valence/arousal scores of all words in a paragraph. Our system projects those averages to the nearest of our four labels to obtain an emotion label for each paragraph.

Music Emotion Labels

Our system provides techniques for music emotion labeling similar to our speech labeling methods. As in speech labeling, we first break the music into segments. Structural segments of music often contain one predominant emotion because the features that differentiate structure—timbre, pitch, volume, and self-similarity—are also indicative of music emotion. Following McFee and Ellis [15], our system segments music by computing a hierarchical clustering of self-similarities in a track and finding an optimal pruning of the cluster tree.

The user selects one of the three labeling methods to get emotion labels for each music segment.

Hand-labeling the music. If users wish to personalize the emotion labels of the speech, they can listen to and assign labels for each music segment (Figure 3) As in hand-labeling the speech, this method is preferable for users that have time and desire a personalized musical score.

Crowd-labeling the music. To crowd-label the emotions of the music, our system asks workers on Mechanical Turk to listen to and label the emotions of the music segments for an entire track (Figure 3). Our system then selects a final emotion labeling by finding the worker's labeling that best represents all of the worker labelings (see earlier section on *Crowd-labeling the speech*).

Automatically labeling the music. Schmidt et al. [24, 25] have developed methods for automatically predicting the valence and arousal of music. Their MoodSwings Turk dataset consists of a large set of crowd-generated, per-second valence/arousal labels and accompanying audio signal processing features (MFCCs [14], spectral contrast [10], and chroma [7]). Our goal is to automatically predict the emotion of each music segment, but the dataset contains per-second labels and no notion of segments. We follow Schmidt et

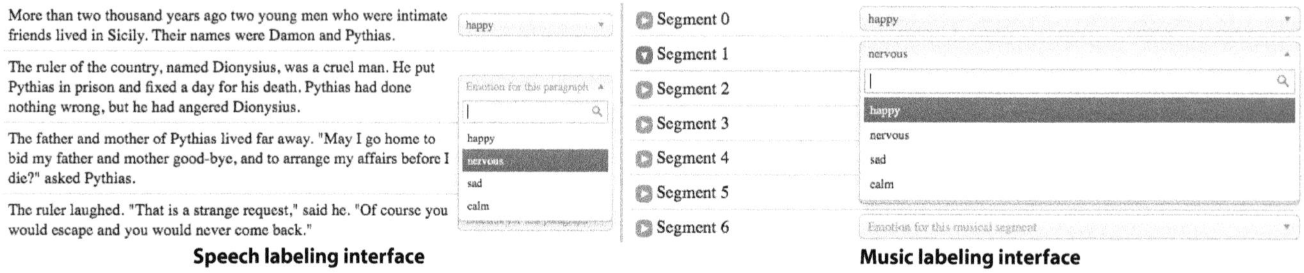

Figure 3. Our interface for labeling speech emotion (left) asks the labeler to annotate each paragraph with an emotion. Our interface for labeling music emotion (right) asks the labeler to label each music segment with an emotion.

al. [24] and train a multiple linear regression model on the MoodSwings Turk dataset to predict per-second emotions.

Emotion in music has a time dependency. That is, emotions at times before time t influence the emotion at time t. To account for this dependency, our model uses ten seconds (times $t-9,\ldots,t$) of per-second MFCC features to predict the valence and arousal at time t [24]. Our system predicts the valence/arousal at each second of each music segment and then finds the average of the predictions. Because of a limited corpus of music in the training set, this model often reports that all segments of a track have the same emotion whereas human labelers give more varied labelings. We subtract the overall segment average from each music segment's average to get a new, more varied prediction. Then, we project each prediction to the nearest of our four emotion labels to get a label for each segment.

SCORE GENERATION ALGORITHM

We designed our score generation algorithm to generate musical scores that match the emotion of the speech while also following other characteristics of high quality musical scores. We identified these characteristics by listening to hours of expertly-produced audio stories, noting structural and stylistic patterns in their musical scores. We further studied books and online sources on audio story production to refine these characteristics. Figure 1 shows an example of how our algorithm re-sequences input music to match the emotions of the speech. To generate an emotionally relevant score, our algorithm translates emotion matching and our other constraints into numeric costs. The two primary costs are *matching costs*—costs of how well the music emotions match the speech emotions—and *transition costs*—costs for beat-to-beat transitions in the music. Once our algorithm computes these costs, it searches for the lowest cost musical score using dynamic programming.

We specify our optimization and constraints on beats, which are short, structural units of time in music. Formally, we consider a piece of music as a set of n beats $\mathbb{B} = \{b_1, b_2, \ldots, b_n\}$ where $b_1, b_2, \ldots, b_n$ is the natural order of beats in the music. To detect the beats in a piece of music we apply Ellis' beat tracking algorithm [7]. Beats lengths within a song vary because tempo often shifts within a music track, so we use the average beat length as our unit of time throughout the algorithm. Next we compute m, the number of music beats required to score the speech. We set m to the duration of the

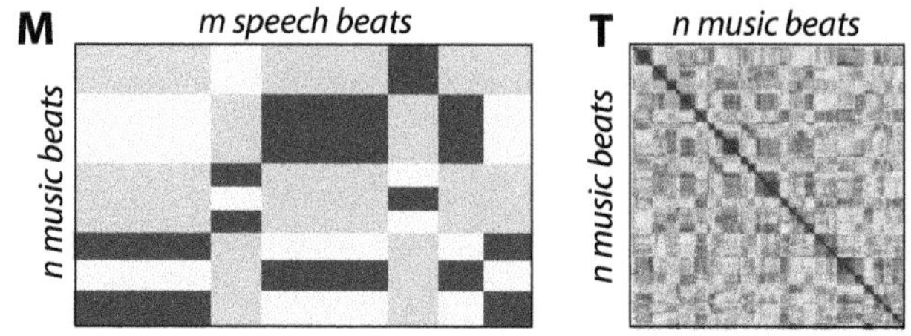

Figure 4. The matching cost table M (left) has lower cost when music beat b_i and speech beat k have the same emotion. The transition cost table T (right) gives the cost of moving between beat b_i and beat b_j. These examples show transition and matching cost tables with only the transition and matching constraints. Darker colors imply cheaper costs.

speech track divided by the average beat length of the music. Our algorithm searches for a sequence $\boldsymbol{s}$ of m beats that minimizes the matching and transition costs; it then generates the output musical score by re-sequencing the original beats according to $\boldsymbol{s}$. Figure 1 shows an example of re-sequencing music beats (bottom row of beats) to match story emotions and duration (top row of beats).

Tables M with size $n \times m$ and T with size $n \times n$ store the transition and matching costs, respectively (Figure 4). Entry $M_{i,k}$ is the cost for playing beat b_i at speech beat k in the output score. The matching cost encodes how well the music emotion fits the speech emotion. Entry $T_{i,j}$ is the cost for moving from beat b_i to beat b_j and is independent of the location in the output score. The transition cost encodes whether the music could make a seamless-sounding jump from b_i to b_j. Our algorithm searches for the sequence of beat indices $\boldsymbol{s} = [s_1, \ldots, s_m \mid s_i \in \{1, \ldots, n\}]$ of m beats that minimizes

$$cost(\boldsymbol{s}) = \sum_{k=1}^{m} M_{s_k,k} + \sum_{k=1}^{m-1} T_{s_k,s_{k+1}} \quad (1)$$

where k is the speech beat index in the output score. A recursive form of this equation enables us to apply dynamic programming to find the optimal beat sequence. So, the recursive minimum cost of a length-m sequence $\boldsymbol{s}$ ending with beat b_j is

$$c(j, m) = \min_{i \in \{1,\ldots,n\}} \left(c(i, m-1) + M_{j,m} + T_{i,j}\right).$$

The right-hand side is a minimum over three terms. The first term, $c(i, m-1)$ is the minimum cost $(m-1)$-length sequence that ends in beat b_i. The second and third terms, $M_{j,m} + T_{i,j}$ are the matching and transition costs for the last beat b_j. The optimal sequence s with any ending beat then has cost

$$\min_{j \in \{1,\ldots,n\}} c(j, m).$$

Because we have expressed the minimum cost sequence recursively, in terms of its subproblems, we can apply dynamic programming to find the optimal beat sequence.

Matching costs

The main purpose of our system is to create music that matches the emotions of the accompanying speech. The speech and music contain emotion tags (happy, nervous, sad, and calm) and their respective numerical values in valence/arousal space. We set matching costs in table M so the valence and arousal of the optimal output score matches the valence and arousal of the speech as closely as possible.

To encode this constraint in our optimization, we compute the ℓ_2 distance $D_{va}(i, k)$ between speech valence/arousal and music valence/arousal at each music beat b_i and speech beat k. We set matching cost $M_{i,k} = w_{va} D_{va}(i, k)$, where w_{va} is a constant that controls the importance of the matching cost in our optimization.

Transition costs

A transition from beat b_i to another beat b_j sounds natural when the timbre, pitch, and volume of b_j are similar to the timbre, pitch, and volume of b_{i+1}, the next beat in the original beat sequence. We compute the transition cost table T by combining timbre, pitch, and volume distances (D_t, D_p, and D_v) for each pair of beats:

$$T_{i,j} = w_t D_t(i+1, j) + w_p D_p(i+1, j) + w_v D_v(i+1, j)$$

Our algorithm estimates timbre differences by computing MFCCs [14] for each beat, and then computing the cosine distance $D_t(i, j)$ between MFCCs for pairs of beats b_i and b_j. We similarly estimate pitch differences by computing chroma features [7] for each beat, and then computing the cosine distances $D_p(i, j)$ between beat pairs.

Two beats that are similar in pitch and timbre may not be similar in volume. A large volume difference between beats can create a jarring listening experience. We compute the RMS energy, a measure of volume, of each beat and then take the absolute energy difference between all beat pairs (b_i, b_j) to get $D_v(i, j)$.

The weights w_t, w_p, and w_v allows us to control the acceptable range of timbre, pitch, and volume differences in beat transitions. These transition cost constraints ensure that the original beat progression—a natural sounding progression—has zero transition cost (i.e., $T_{i,i+1} = 0$).

Structural constraints

Our algorithm can generate musical scores that match the emotions of speech using only the basic matching cost and transition cost constraints. However, high-quality scores contain additional structure by using pauses and limiting music segment lengths.

Pauses. In most high-quality audio stories, the music is not constantly playing. Instead, music occasionally fades in and out to create sections of the story without music. These pauses call attention to the fact that the musical score exists, forcing listeners to think about the music and its emotions.

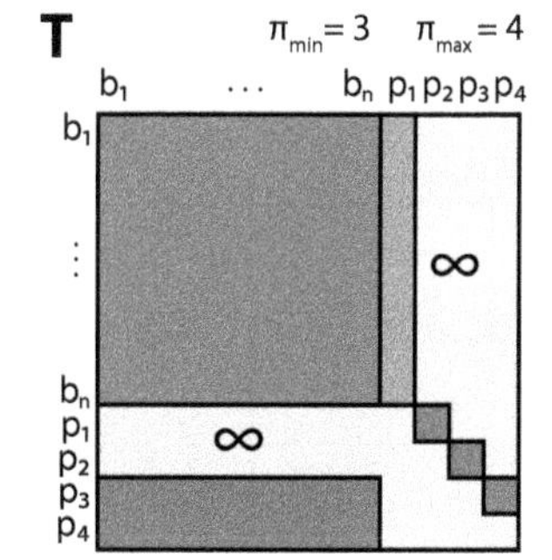

Figure 5. Our algorithm enables pauses in the musical score by extending the transition cost table T with pause beats.

Figure 5 shows how we adjust our transition cost table T to accomodate pauses in a musical score. We first define π_{min} and π_{max}, the minimum and maximum beat lengths of pauses, respectively. We concatenate π_{max} rows and columns to the original T (the blue block in Figure 5 is the original T). The π_{max} new beats are pause beats. Each of these added beats p_i represents the ith beat of a pause.

Every pause in music starts at the first pause beat; any beat in music can transition to beat p_1 but no other pause beats (green rectangle in Figure 5). To maintain the invariant that p_i is the ith beat of a pause, we only allow p_i to transition to p_{i+1} (purple squares). Any pause beat at or above the minimum pause length π_{min} has a free cost transition back to any music beat (red rectangle). In practice, we assign a cost κ_{start} to entering a pause (green rectangle) that is greater than the cost of a natural-sounding music transition (see *Setting Parameters*, below). This cost ensures that our score does not add pauses when it can play good-sounding music. We also add a small cost of κ_{intra} to transitions between p_i and p_{i+1} if $i > \pi_{min}$. Without this cost, most pauses would have length π_{max} because the intra-pause transitions would be free while optimal sequences in music often contain non-free transitions.

Music segments. High-quality audio stories tend not to play overly short or long segments of music. Short segments do not give the music time to integrate with the speech and its emotions, while overly long segments can cause the listener to "tune out," or ignore the music. Our algorithm constrains the length of music segments in the output score.

Figure 6 shows how we constrain the length of a music segment to at least δ_{min} beats and at most δ_{max} beats. In order to keep track of the lengths of music segments, we create a new transition cost table T'. Each index in the table represents a (beat, segment-length) pair (b_i, d_k) where segment length d_k represents the kth beat in the current music segment. We construct this new table by copying blocks from the existing transition cost table (the colored blocks from Figure 5 correspond to the colored blocks in T' in Figure 6).

To maintain the invariant that a beat a segment length d_k is the kth beat of the music segment, we only allow (b_i, d_k) to transition to (b_j, d_{k+1}) for any beats b_i and b_j (blue squares in Figure 6). Once the music has been playing for δ_{min} beats, a pause can begin. Any (beat, segment-length) pair that is at or above the minimum segment length δ_{min} can transition to

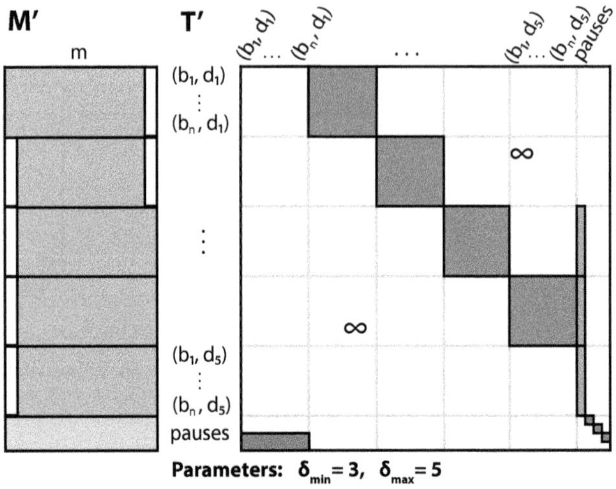

Figure 6. We provide constraints on the length of music segments by creating a new matching cost table M' and transition cost table T'. The indices of the new tables are (beat, segment-length) pairs rather than just beats. We build the M' table from δ_{max} copies of M, except that the music must start at beat-length d_1 and end at beat-length greater than δ_{min}. We copy blocks of table T in Figure 5, indicated by colors, to create table T'.

the first pause beat p_1 (green rectangles). We copy the intra-pause transitions directly from T (purple squares). Finally, a pause must transition back to a (beat, segment-length) pair at segment length d_1, because all music segments start with length 1 (red rectangle).

We also create a new M' with constraints for music segment lengths. The first (beat, segment-length) pair of the output score must be at music segment length 1. Otherwise, we could not enforce the minimum length on the first music segment in the output score. The last (beat, segment-length) pair of the output score must be at music segment length at least δ_{min}, so the last segment of the score is longer than the minimum segment length. We set the matching costs to infinity where these conditions do not hold (see M' in Figure 6).

Stylistic constraints

Expertly created scores employ specific stylistic techniques in order to improve the overall score quality. We have designed constraints to imitate these techniques.

Minimum loop constraint. High-quality musical scores often contain loops to allow a short section of music to score a longer section of speech, but if these loops are too short, the music can sound unnaturally repetitive. We introduce a minimum loop constraint to prevent the score from looping sections of music that are less than eight beats long by setting $T_{i,j} = \infty$ if $i - 8 < j \leq i$.

Musical underlays. Expert producers often add *musical underlays* to audio stories, aligning changes in structure, timbre, and volume of music with important points of emphasis in speech. After the music change, the speech pauses for a short period of time and the music plays solo. Rubin et al. [21] describe the benefits of adding musical underlays to audio stories.

To generate musical underlays in our optimization, we first preprocess the input speech, adding 6 second pauses at all emotion changes—emphasis points often occur at emotional changes in the speech, so these are the candidate locations for musical underlays.

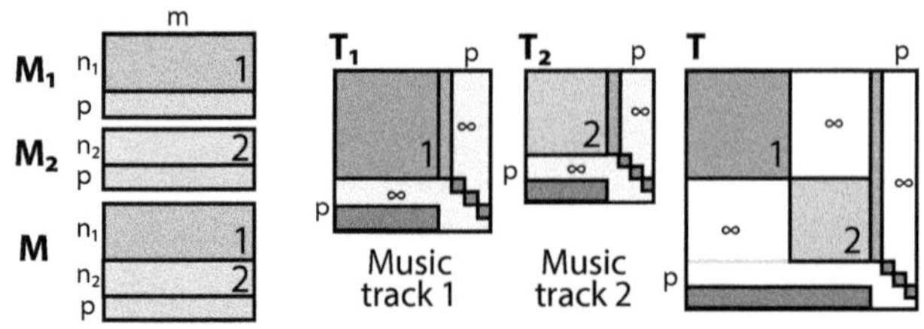

Figure 7. Our algorithm generates scores composed of multiple music tracks. It first computes tables M (left) and T (right) for each music track using a consistent speech beat unit, and then combines the tables to form the final M and T. This construction of T does not allow inter-song transitions, but does allow for efficient optimization.

We then modify the matching table M to align music change points with the speech emphasis points we added in the preprocessing step. To do this, our algorithm first finds the set of change point beats in the music using a novelty-based change point detection algorithm [8, 22]. This algorithm computes a similarity matrix of per-beat music features, and then identifies large changes on the diagonal, which indicate significant differences in the music features. We examine the music segment on either side of each change point to identify change points that correspond with transitions in emotion labels. Our transition cost table gives a large preference to playing music change points in the output score when emotion changes in music match emotion changes at speech emphasis points. If b_i is a change point whose emotion change matches the emotion change at speech beat k, we increase $M_{j,k}$ by constant $\kappa_{changepoint}$ for all $j \neq i$. This effectively penalizes all other music beats when a change point music beat matches the speech emotion change.

Another strategy expert producers use to emphasize points in the speech is to start or stop the music at those points. To apply this strategy, we penalize music stopping and starting at points other than emotion change boundaries. If speech beat k is not an emotion change boundary, we add cost κ_{exit} to $M_{p_1,k}$ and κ_{enter} to $M_{p_i,k}$ for $i \geq \pi_{min}$. This approach lowers the relative cost for starting and stopping music at emotion changes in the story.

After the algorithm has generated the optimal score, some of the 6 second speech pauses we added in preprocessing may align with pauses in the musical score. Rather than playing six seconds of silence, our algorithm contracts the final audio, deleting regions where a pause in speech aligns with a pause in the music.

Multiple music tracks. Musical scores often contain segments from multiple music tracks, especially for longer stories. Moreover, most music tracks do not contain every emotion, so using multiple tracks increases the likelihood of matching the output score to the speech emotions.

Figure 7 shows how our algorithm combines transition and matching cost tables from two songs. We insert the music beat transition costs from each music track's T along the diagonal (blue squares in Figure 7. Music beats can only tran-

Speech tracks					Generated musical scores		
Speech name	Author	Narrator	Dur.	Source	Hand labeled	Crowd Labeled	Auto Labeled
Damon and Pythias	Ella Lyman Cabot	Ginger Cuculo	1:38	LibriVox	**alice**	**alice**, 2815ad, highschool, tub, learn	**alice**
Not That I Care	Molly Reid	James Wood	2:38	NPR	**2815ad**	**2815ad**, alice+timemachine	**2815ad**
Roosts	Zach Brockhouse	Michael Cunningham	3:12	NPR	**tub+highschool**	**tub+highschool**, intriguing+alice	**tub+highschool**
Goldilocks		LearnEnglish Kids	2:10	YouTube	**learn**	**learn**, timemachine	**learn**
The Story of an Hour	Kate Chopin	Matt Bohnhoff	7:20	LibriVox		intriguing+learn	

Table 1. We generated 20 scores spanning five different audio stories. The short names on the right correspond to music in Table 2. Crowd listeners evaluated the musical scores in bold. A '+' represents a musical score generated with two tracks using our multiple tracks constraint.

Short name	Music track	Artist
alice	Alice Returns	Danny Elfman
2815ad	2815 A.D.	Thomas Newman
highschool	Highschool Lover	Air
learn	You Learn	Jon Brion
tub	The Bathtub	Dan Romer
timemachine	Time Machine	Ryan Miller
intriguing	Intriguing Possibilities	Trent Reznor & Atticus Ross

Table 2. We used seven different instrumental music tracks in the musical scores we generated.

sition to other beats within the same music track or to pause beats.

After a pause ends, either music track can play (red rectangle, Figure 7). We stack the two matching cost tables to create a new matching cost table that covers all possible beats in the musical score (orange rectangles, Figure 7). The running time of our algorithm increases linearly in the duration of music added, instead of quadratically, because it does not need to consider inter-music-track transitions.

Setting parameters

We set the main structural parameters based on listening to audio stories: π_{min} of 20 seconds, π_{max} of 35 seconds, δ_{min} of 20 seconds, and δ_{max} of 90 seconds.

Next, we set the distance weights in our optimization empirically, based on the importance of the constraints. We set the acoustic distance parameters $w_t = 1.5, w_p = 1.5$, and $w_v = 5$—volume differences are small in magnitude relative to timbre and chroma cosine distance. We set the emotion matching distance parameter $w_{va} = 1$.

Finally, we set the cost parameters: the cost for entering a pause $\kappa_{pause} = 1.4$, empirically less than an audibly "bad" music transition; the intrapause penalty $\kappa_{intra} = .05$, cheaper than all but perfect music transitions; the music start and stop costs—which penalize otherwise free transitions—to small $\kappa_{enter} = \kappa_{exit} = .125$. Lastly, $\kappa_{changepoint} = 1$, which strongly favors inserting musical underlays whenever possible.

Score synthesis

The dynamic programming returns a sequence s of beat and pause indices. We then synthesize the final output score from s by concatenating the audio data for each beat and pause. We ensure smooth-sounding music transitions by inserting crossfades between beats s_i and s_{i+1} if they are not consecutive beats in the original music. In some cases, the musical score becomes out of alignment with the speech because music beats have variable length and we assume a fixed beat length on the speech. Our system corrects this problem every time the music pauses. If a pause segment ends at speech beat k, we start the music again exactly at speech beat k times the average beat duration regardless of the current time in the output. This re-aligns the score with the speech after every pause.

Our system adjusts the volume of the musical score so it is always audible but never overpowers the speech. We control the volume of the output score in two steps. First, we add volume curves for the score to follow: music fades in for three seconds after music pauses to a low level, increases exponentially to a high-level at speech emphasis points, decreases rapidly to a low level after music solos, and fades out for three seconds as music pauses begin. The second step adjusts these volumes relative to the speech volume. For every segment of the final output where both speech and music are playing, we adjust the decibel level of the music to lie 12 dB below the decibel level of the speech. Finally, we notch the 2.76 kHz and 5.63 kHz music frequencies by 6 dB because those frequencies contain important acoustic information for decoding consonants and vowels in speech [16].

RESULTS

We have generated 20 musical scores spanning seven music tracks and five speech tracks. We used all three of our emotion labeling techniques: hand-labeling, crowd-labeling, and automatic labeling. Table 1 shows our input speech tracks and summarizes the results we have generated, and Table 2 details our music tracks. Our supplemental material[1] includes all of these audio results. The first author of this paper labeled the emotions of each story by hand and we had an average of 17.5 crowd workers label each story at an average cost of $4.38 per story. The first author hand-labeled the music segments for all tracks, and we had an average of 18.5 crowd workers label the segments ($4.63 per track). Our algorithm computes the music track distance tables as a preprocess. On a 2.7 GHz Intel Core i7 processor with 8 GB of RAM, our system takes less than 1 second to find and generate the optimal musical score for a three minute story and two three minute music tracks. If we add music segment length constraints with d_{min} of 20 seconds and d_{max} of 90 seconds, the optimization takes 3 minutes. We generated all of our results with d_{min} of 20 seconds and d_{max} of 90 seconds except for "The Story of an Hour" musical score, which we use to demonstrate a longer story with a higher d_{min} (see supplemental material). We also include a basic example of a musical score that we generated for a children's book video.

[1] http://vis.berkeley.edu/papers/emotionscores

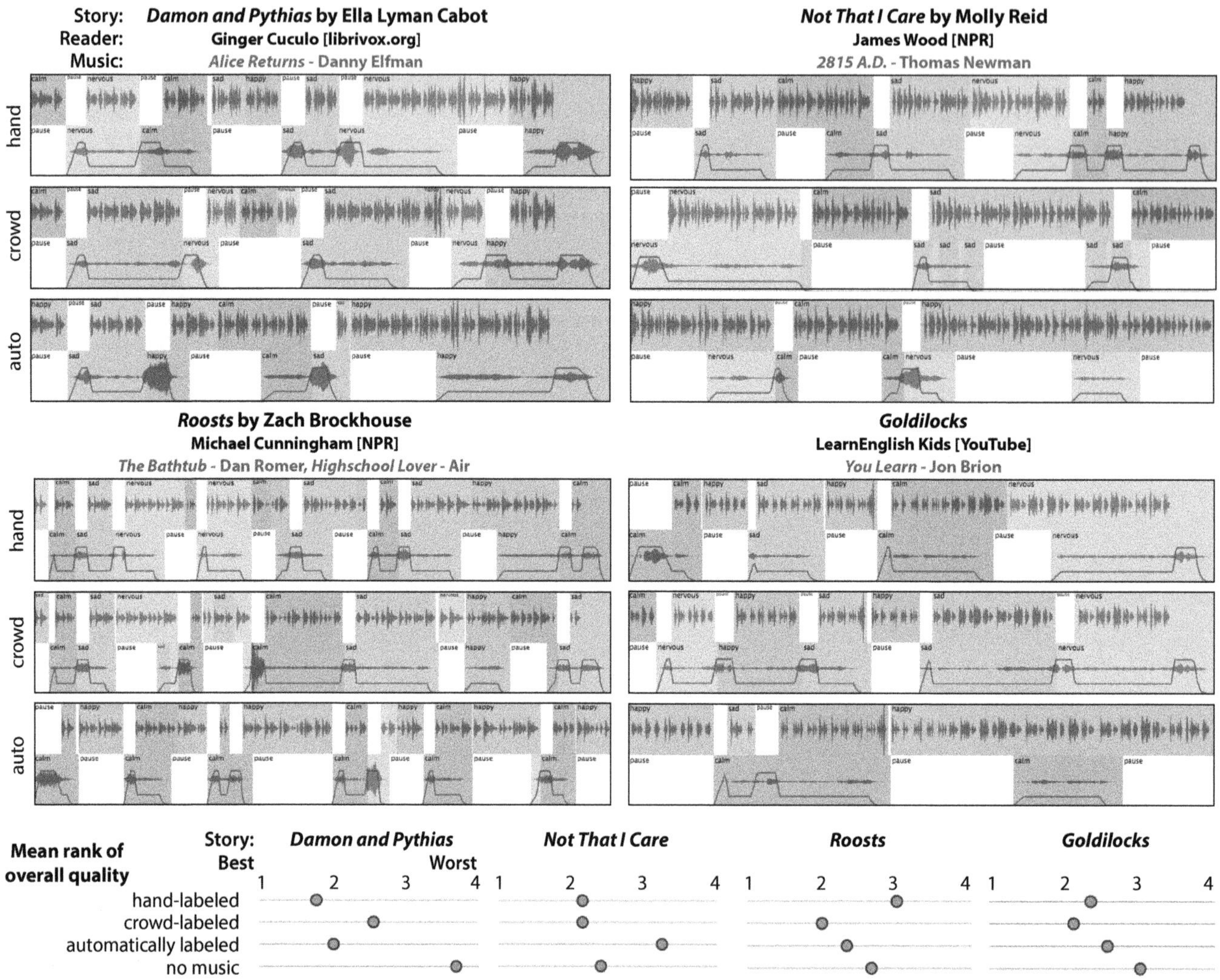

Figure 8. We visualize twelve of our generated results above. Each speech/music pair was generated using all three of our labeling methods. Evaluators on Mechanical Turk listened to three different scores for a speech track and the original speech without music. These charts show the average ranking in overall quality of the four clips among the evaluators.

Figure 8 shows a visualization of the twelve of our results—four speech/music combinations with each of the three labeling methods—which correspond to the bold-faced results in Table 1. The emotions in the speech and music consistently match in the hand- and crowd-labeled results. In two instances ("Roosts"/crowd and "Not That I Care"/crowd), an incorrect emotion plays in the music for a small number of beats, but neither is audibly noticeable. The automatic results do not match emotions as strongly. In "Not That I Care"/auto and "Goldilocks"/auto, the automatic approach matches large sections of "happy" speech with other music emotions. This happened because the automatic music labeling did not predict any "happy" segments of music, while the automatic speech labeling predicted spans of "happy" that are longer than the maximum length pause π_{max}.

Evaluation. To evaluate our results, we asked crowd workers to listen to and rank four versions of a story—*hand-labeled*, *crowd-labeled*, *automatically labeled*, and *no music*—in terms of overall quality. For each story, twelve US workers, each with over 95% approval rates on Mechanical Turk, evaluated the results. We rejected evaluation tasks if a worker did not spend enough time on the task to listen to all of the audio stories; we removed 24.6% of the ratings based on this test. Figure 8 shows the average ranking for each of the four versions for each speech track. Surprisingly, listeners ranked the results generated using crowd labels (average rank over the four stories of 2.21) as high as hand-labels (average of 2.3). Both methods generated higher quality results than automatic labels (average of 2.52) and the stories with no music (average of 2.95). We find the differences in rankings to be significant ($\chi^2(3) = 9.02$, $p < .05$) using Friedman's nonparameteric test for differences in ranks. Subsequent pairwise comparisons using the Wilcoxon signed rank test find a significant preference for crowd results over no music ($p < .005$) and hand-labeled results over no music ($p < .05$). This result suggests that the "wisdom of crowds" might apply to affective tasks. Our results also show that for all of the speech tracks, our system generates musical scores that improve in overall quality versus the speech without music.

To evaluate the consistency of the emotion labels, we compute Fleiss' and Cohen's kappa values. The average Fleiss' kappa is 0.271 between workers for the speech labels and 0.2 for the music labels. The average Cohen's kappa between our hand-labeled emotions and the most probable crowd labeling is 0.189 for speech and 0.437 for music, which suggests a large difference between the typical crowd-labeling and our expert hand-labeling. Finally, the reliability between our hand-labels and the automatic labels is nearly zero, at kappa of 0.0484 for speech and 0.136 for music. This discrepancy between human and automatic labels is a likely cause of the automatic method's low ranking in our listening evaluation.

CONCLUSION AND FUTURE WORK

Emotionally relevant musical scores can improve the quality and engagement of an audio story, but they are challenging and time-consuming to produce. We have presented a system for collecting emotion labels on speech and music, and an algorithm for generating an optimal score that matches emotions of music to speech. With this system, novice producers can generate high-quality musical scores for entire stories without needing audio editing expertise.

We believe there are promising directions in automatically editing multimedia based on emotion. However, applying our general method to scoring, for example, video and slideshows raises new challenges. An algorithm to generate musical scores for a visual medium must be able to insert pauses in the visuals to enable techniques like musical underlays. One approach may be to add video textures [26] that match the start and end frames in these pauses, as in Berthouzoz et al.'s [3] work on editing interview videos.

One bottleneck in applying our approach to more complex domains is in optimally setting the constraint parameters as we add new constraints to the optimization. We currently set these parameters by hand, but if the constraints become more complicated in the video and slideshow applications, we could apply Nonlinear Inverse Optimization (NIO) to learn a parameter assignment from example musical scores, following work from O'Donovan et al. [19] and Vollick et al. [30] in visual layout optimization.

Our system does not account for some characteristics of voice. In future work, we hope to study how the properties of voice, e.g., loud and rhythmic vs. soft and timid, impact the creation of relevant musical scores. Additionally, while our system uses emotion labels to match the music to speech, we plan to explore other labeling vocabularies that may provide new insight in linking music, speech, and visuals.

ACKNOWLEDGMENTS

This work is supported in part by a Google Faculty Research Award and the Intel Science and Technology Center for Visual Computing.

REFERENCES

1. Arikan, O., Forsyth, D. A., and O'Brien, J. F. Motion synthesis from annotations. *ACM Transactions on Graphics (TOG) 22*, 3 (2003), 402–408.
2. Audible. http://audible.com, Apr. 2014.
3. Berthouzoz, F., Li, W., and Agrawala, M. Tools for placing cuts and transitions in interview video. *ACM Transactions on Graphics (TOG) 31*, 4 (2012), 67.
4. Calvo, R. A., and D'Mello, S. Affect detection: An interdisciplinary review of models, methods, and their applications. *Affective Computing, IEEE Transactions on 1*, 1 (2010), 18–37.
5. CastingWords. https://castingwords.com, Apr. 2014.
6. El Ayadi, M., Kamel, M. S., and Karray, F. Survey on speech emotion recognition: Features, classification schemes, and databases. *Pattern Recognition 44*, 3 (2011), 572–587.
7. Ellis, D. P., and Poliner, G. E. Identifying cover songs with chroma features and dynamic programming beat tracking. In *Acoustics, Speech and Signal Processing, 2007. ICASSP 2007. IEEE International Conference on*, vol. 4, IEEE (2007), IV–1429–IV–1432.
8. Foote, J. Automatic audio segmentation using a measure of audio novelty. In *Multimedia and Expo, 2000. ICME 2000. 2000 IEEE International Conference on*, vol. 1, IEEE (2000), 452–455.
9. Foote, J., Cooper, M., and Girgensohn, A. Creating music videos using automatic media analysis. In *Proceedings of the tenth ACM international conference on Multimedia*, ACM (2002), 553–560.
10. Jiang, D.-N., Lu, L., Zhang, H.-J., Tao, J.-H., and Cai, L.-H. Music type classification by spectral contrast feature. In *Multimedia and Expo, 2002. ICME'02. Proceedings. 2002 IEEE International Conference on*, vol. 1, IEEE (2002), 113–116.
11. Kim, Y. E., Schmidt, E. M., Migneco, R., Morton, B. G., Richardson, P., Scott, J., Speck, J. A., and Turnbull, D. Music emotion recognition: A state of the art review. In *Proc. ISMIR* (2010), 255–266.
12. Lasecki, W. S., Murray, K. I., White, S., Miller, R. C., and Bigham, J. P. Real-time crowd control of existing interfaces. In *Proceedings of the 24th annual ACM symposium on User interface software and technology*, ACM (2011), 23–32.
13. Librivox. https://librivox.org, Apr. 2014.
14. Logan, B. Mel frequency cepstral coefficients for music modeling. In *ISMIR* (2000).
15. McFee, B., and Ellis, D. P. Learning to segment songs with ordinal linear discriminant analysis. In *Acoustics, Speech, and Signal Processing, 2014. ICASSP'14. Proceedings. 2014 IEEE International Conference on*, IEEE (2014).
16. McKee, J. Using music: The kitchen sisters. http://transom.org/2014/using-music-the-kitchen-sisters/, Feb. 2014.

17. Monteith, K., Francisco, V., Martinez, T., Gervas, P., and Ventura, D. Automatic generation of emotionally-targeted soundtracks. In *Proceedings of the Second International Conference on Computational Creativity* (2011), 60–62.

18. Monteith, K., Martinez, T. R., and Ventura, D. Automatic generation of music for inducing emotive response. In *Proceedings of the First International Conference on Computational Creativity* (2010), 140–149.

19. O'Donovan, P., Agarwala, A., and Hertzmann, A. Learning layouts for single-page graphic designs.

20. Posner, J., Russell, J. A., and Peterson, B. S. The circumplex model of affect: An integrative approach to affective neuroscience, cognitive development, and psychopathology. *Development and psychopathology 17*, 03 (2005), 715–734.

21. Rubin, S., Berthouzoz, F., Mysore, G., Li, W., and Agrawala, M. Underscore: musical underlays for audio stories. In *Proceedings of the 25th annual ACM symposium on User interface software and technology*, ACM (2012), 359–366.

22. Rubin, S., Berthouzoz, F., Mysore, G. J., Li, W., and Agrawala, M. Content-based tools for editing audio stories. In *Proceedings of the 26th annual ACM symposium on User interface software and technology*, ACM (2013), 113–122.

23. Russell, J. A. A circumplex model of affect. *Journal of personality and social psychology 39*, 6 (1980), 1161.

24. Schmidt, E. M., and Kim, Y. E. Prediction of time-varying musical mood distributions from audio. In *ISMIR* (2010), 465–470.

25. Schmidt, E. M., and Kim, Y. E. Modeling musical emotion dynamics with conditional random fields. In *ISMIR* (2011), 777–782.

26. Schödl, A., Szeliski, R., Salesin, D. H., and Essa, I. Video textures. In *Proceedings of the 27th annual conference on Computer graphics and interactive techniques*, ACM Press/Addison-Wesley Publishing Co. (2000), 489–498.

27. Schwarz, D. The caterpillar system for data-driven concatenative sound synthesis. In *Proceedings of the COST-G6 Conference on Digital Audio Effects (DAFx)* (2003), 135–140.

28. Schwarz, D., et al. A system for data-driven concatenative sound synthesis. In *Digital Audio Effects (DAFx)* (2000), 97–102.

29. Tauscher, J.-P., Wenger, S., and Magnor, M. A. Audio resynthesis on the dancefloor: A music structural approach. In *VMV*, M. M. Bronstein, J. Favre, and K. Hormann, Eds., Eurographics Association (2013), 41–48.

30. Vollick, I., Vogel, D., Agrawala, M., and Hertzmann, A. Specifying label layout style by example. In *Proceedings of the 20th annual ACM symposium on User interface software and technology*, ACM (2007), 221–230.

31. Warriner, A. B., Kuperman, V., and Brysbaert, M. Norms of valence, arousal, and dominance for 13,915 english lemmas. *Behavior research methods 45*, 4 (2013), 1191–1207.

32. Webster, T. The podcast consumer 2012. http://www.edisonresearch.com/home/archives/2012/05/the-podcast-consumer-2012.php, May 2012.

33. Wenger, S., and Magnor, M. A genetic algorithm for audio retargeting. In *Proceedings of the 20th ACM international conference on Multimedia*, ACM (2012), 705–708.

34. Wenner, S., Bazin, J.-C., Sorkine-Hornung, A., Kim, C., and Gross, M. Scalable music: Automatic music retargeting and synthesis. In *Computer Graphics Forum*, vol. 32, Wiley Online Library (2013), 345–354.

35. Willett, W., Ginosar, S., Steinitz, A., Hartmann, B., and Agrawala, M. Identifying redundancy and exposing provenance in crowdsourced data analysis. *Visualization and Computer Graphics, IEEE Transactions on 19*, 12 (2013), 2198–2206.

36. Yuan, J., and Liberman, M. Speaker identification on the scotus corpus. *Journal of the Acoustical Society of America 123*, 5 (2008), 3878.

37. Zickuhr, K., and Rainie, L. A snapshot of reading in america in 2013. http://www.pewinternet.org/2014/01/16/a-snapshot-of-reading-in-america-in-2013/, Jan. 2014.

APPENDIX - EFFICIENT OPTIMIZATION

Because our m and n are small (roughly $n = 500$ beats in a song, and roughly $m = 1000$ beats in the desired output), the entire table can fit in memory and we can use a dynamic programming algorithm to efficiently find this sequence of beats. However, music segment length constraints increase the size of this search space.

If we apply music segment length constraints, our goal is to find the lowest cost sequence of (beat, segment-length) pairs $\boldsymbol{s'}$, using T' and M' in place of T and M in Equation 1. The search space at each step has grown from size $(n + \pi_{max})^m$ to size $(n\delta_{max} + \pi_{max})^m$ because we need to consider the state space of all (beat, segment-length) pairs. The running time of a normal dynamic programming algorithm increases quadratically with δ_{max}. However, most of the entries in T' are infinity and are never in an optimal sequence of beats.

We take advantage of these hard constraints to implement an efficient version of this dynamic programming optimization whose runtime increases linearly with δ_{max}. We never explicitly compute T', which can grow prohibitively large. We define our new table T' in terms of blocks from T (see Figure 6), so we only store T. We then take advantage of the block structure of T' to limit our search space. For example, if the previous (beat, segment-length) pair in a path is (b_i, d_j), and segment length d_j is less than δ_{min}, our algorithm only needs to minimize over (beat, segment-length) pairs at length d_{j+1} instead of all possible (beat, segment-length) pairs.

Likewise, we do not construct the full table M'. Instead, we have a condition in our algorithm to check if speech bear $t = 1$, which forces the output beat/length pair to have length 1. In other cases, we tile δ_{max} copies of a column in M when our algorithm requires a column of M' during the optimization.

World-Stabilized Annotations and Virtual Scene Navigation for Remote Collaboration

Steffen Gauglitz **Benjamin Nuernberger** **Matthew Turk** **Tobias Höllerer**
Department of Computer Sciene, University of California, Santa Barbara
Santa Barbara, CA 93106, USA
{sgauglitz, bnuernberger, mturk, holl}@cs.ucsb.edu

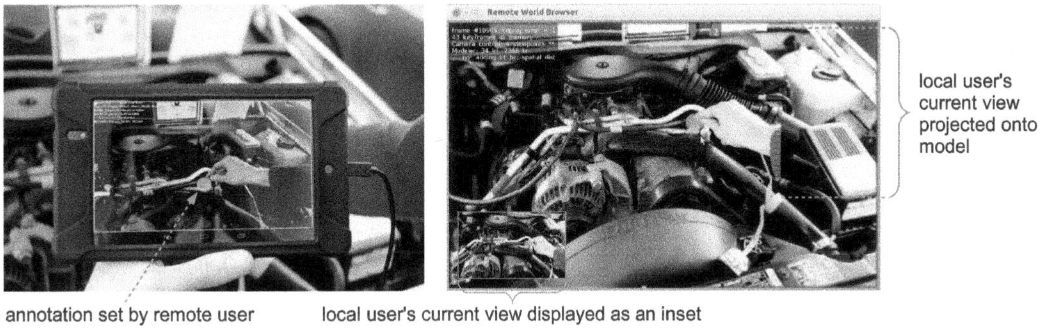

Figure 1. Live AR-based remote collaboration with our prototype. Left: the local user in front of a car engine, identifying a particular element which the remote user has marked with the yellow dot. Right: the remote user's view onto the scene, which (at this moment) shows more context than the local user's current view. The latter is shown as an inset on the bottom left as well as being projected onto the model. The remote user can browse this environment independently of the local user's camera and can set annotations, which are immediately visible to the local user in AR.

ABSTRACT
We present a system that supports an augmented shared visual space for live mobile remote collaboration on physical tasks. The remote user can explore the scene independently of the local user's current camera position and can communicate via spatial annotations that are immediately visible to the local user in augmented reality. Our system operates on off-the-shelf hardware and uses real-time visual tracking and modeling, thus not requiring any preparation or instrumentation of the environment. It creates a synergy between video conferencing and remote scene exploration under a unique coherent interface. To evaluate the collaboration with our system, we conducted an extensive outdoor user study with 60 participants comparing our system with two baseline interfaces. Our results indicate an overwhelming user preference (80%) for our system, a high level of usability, as well as performance benefits compared with one of the two baselines.

Author Keywords
CSCW; video-mediated communication; augmented reality; telepresence

UIST 2014, October 5–8, 2014, Honolulu, HI, USA.

ACM 978-1-4503-3069-5/14/10 ...$15.00.
http://dx.doi.org/10.1145/2642918.2647372

ACM Classification Keywords
H.5.1 [Information interfaces and presentation] Multimedia information systems: Artificial, augmented, and virtual realities; H.5.3 [Information interfaces and presentation] Group and organization interfaces: Computer-supported cooperative work

INTRODUCTION
In recent years, the use of video conferencing has become ubiquitous. However, with current technology, users are limited to passively watching disjoint video feeds which provide no means for interaction with the remote physical environment. As effective collaboration often involves sharing, exploring, referencing, or even manipulating the physical environment, tools for remote collaboration should provide support for these interactions. Researchers have explored various means to do so; however, two of the most common limitations in existing work are that the remote user's view onto the scene is constrained to the typically small field of view of the local user's camera, and that any support for spatially referencing the scene is contingent upon a stationary camera.

In this work, we leverage computer vision and the paradigm of augmented reality (AR) to facilitate more immersive interaction with the remote environment in general, and to address the aforementioned limitations in particular. We describe a fully functional system for mobile remote collaboration, running on off-the-shelf hardware, in which the remote user can (a) control a virtual camera and thus explore the live scene independently of the local user's current camera position, and (b) communicate via spatial annotations that are immediately visible to the local user in AR (cf. Figure 1). Our system does not require any preparation or instrumentation of the environment. Instead, the physical scene is tracked and modeled incrementally in real time and in 3D, using monocular vision-based simultaneous localization and mapping (SLAM) and subsequent surface modeling. The emerging model then supports anchoring of annotations, virtual navigation, and synthesis of novel views.

We further present an extensive outdoor user study with 60 participants (30 teams) comparing our system with two baselines. Both user ratings and task performance are discussed in detail. To our knowledge, our study is among the first user studies overall to rely purely on visual SLAM technology as an enabling technology (rather than as the subject of interest) in an outdoor environment.

RELATED WORK

Research on remote collaboration and telepresence is multifaceted; for example, several systems focus on creating fully immersive, three-dimensional telepresence experiences with increasingly lower instrumentation barriers (e.g., [28, 37]).

Support for spatial references to the remote scene in video-mediated collaboration or telepresence has been an active research topic. Notable early works include "VideoDraw" [41] and the "DoubleDigitalDesk" [44]. Modalities that have been investigated include remote pointers [2, 5, 11, 21], drawing onto a live video stream [7, 11, 14, 21, 22, 34], and transferring videos of hand gestures [17, 22, 33]. These annotations are then displayed to the collaborator on a separate screen in a third-person perspective [11, 18], on a head-worn display [2, 17, 33], or via projectors [14].

However, in order to support spatially referencing physical objects, all of these systems either assume a stationary camera (at least during the relevant interaction), since otherwise the virtual annotations lose their referents [2, 7, 11, 14, 17, 21–23], or require extensive equipment and prepared environments to track and thus maintain the locations of the annotations [5, 33]. Further, the remote user's view onto the physical scene is either restricted to a stationary camera [11, 22] or tightly coupled to the local user's head or body movement [2, 5, 17, 21, 23], thus forcing the remote user to constantly re-orient and ask the local user to hold still (or, in the case of [2], enforcing this by freezing both users' views) when referencing an object.

One alternative is to use a robot which can be controlled by the remote user [14, 24]; however, this requires specialized hardware and limits the range of operation.

In our work, we leverage computer vision-based tracking and modeling and the paradigm of collaborative AR [3] to support world-stabilized annotations and virtual camera movements. Early implementations of both concepts for the purpose of collaboration are reported by Mayol et al. [29] and Lee and Höllerer [26].

Our system follows the conceptual framework for an AR-based collaboration system proposed in Gauglitz et al. [12], and our user study follows a similar pattern. However, while the prototype described therein works in planar environments only and offers only a camera "freeze" feature without any further navigation or view synthesis, our system operates in environments of arbitrary geometric complexity (which has implications for almost all components of the system), and provides a feature-rich virtual navigation that allows the remote user to explore the environment independently of the local user's current camera position. (Conceptually, this has been described as a possibility in Gauglitz et al. [12].) Further, our system consists of two stand-alone off-the-shelf hardware entities that communicate via wireless network.

Sodhi et al. [39] present a system with a similar vision. They use a customized setup with a mobile device and two active depth sensors mounted onto a monopod which gives the ability to reconstruct the environment (on the local user's side) and to reconstruct and transfer hand gestures (from the remote user's side) in 3D. In contrast, our system needs only an off-the-shelf tablet, but uses simpler annotations. Another difference worth noting is the method of scene navigation by the remote user: Sodhi et al. equip the remote user with a mobile device as well and use the device's physical movement to navigate the remote (virtual) environment, while we use virtual navigation. We contrast the two approaches in more detail below. They conducted a usability study reporting results with respect to ease of use, etc., but no comparative or performance-based evaluation was reported.

The system by Adcock et al. [1] also reconstructs the environment via active depth sensors and allows the remote user to control the viewpoint (via a touch interface) and draw annotations, which are displayed using a statically mounted projector.

Further, Jo and Hwang [20] presented an interactive, fully mobile system which allows for world-stabilized drawings, albeit only for panoramas (i.e., rotation movements). Two particular interesting aspects of this work are the physical navigation of the panorama by the remote user and switching between front and back cameras (upon permission by the local user).

With respect to reconstructing a physical scene from image data and navigating it based on this reconstruction, our work bears similarity in particular with Snavely et al.'s "Photo tourism" [38] and similar works. However, while Photo tourism deals with a (potentially large) set of photos in a batch manner and offers offline navigation, we process a live video in real time and offer live viewing of the evolving model. Further, we extract a detailed 3D surface rather than using planar surface proxies for the rendering.

With respect to individual features, our system bears similarity with further works: Tatzgern et al. [42] very recently presented an AR system which allows the user to switch between a live video ("AR view") and synthesized views of a reconstructed environment ("VR view"). Lastly, Sukan et al. [40] presented a study comparing physical navigation with virtual navigation via saving and revisiting virtual snapshots. Here, we employ similar techniques for the interaction with a remote environment.

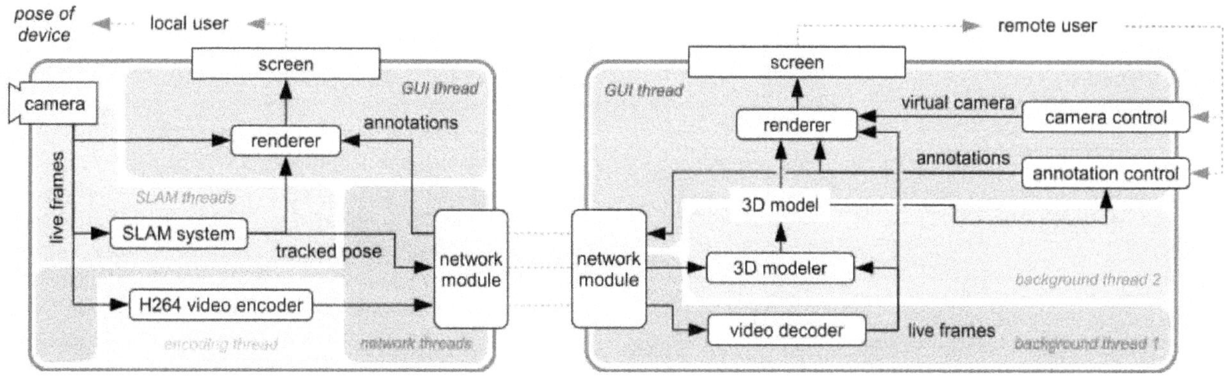

Figure 2. System architecture of both the local user's system (left; running on an Android-based lightweight tablet or smartphone) and the remote user's system (right; running on a commodity PC with Ubuntu). The main components are described in the text in detail.

SYSTEM OVERVIEW

Figure 2 shows an overview of the system architecture of both the local user's and the remote user's system. Since device hardware (camera and display), network communication, real-time processing, and background tasks are involved, both systems employ a host of components and threads.

LOCAL USER'S SYSTEM

The local user's interface, running on a lightweight tablet, is intentionally simple. From the user's perspective, it behaves exactly like a live video of the user's own view plus AR annotations, i.e., a classic magic lens. (We emphasize that the local user's view is not affected by remote user's camera control.) The only control the user exerts during its operation is by manipulating the position and orientation of the device. We note that the system could equally be used with other AR displays such as a head-worn or projective display.

Under the hood, the system runs a SLAM system and sends the tracked camera pose along with the encoded live video stream to the remote system. The local user's system receives information about annotations from the remote system and uses this information together with the live video to render the augmented view.

The system is implemented as an Android app, running on several state-of-the-art Android devices. For the user study, we used a Google Nexus 7 2013, a 7" tablet powered by a Qualcomm Snapdragon S4 Pro with 1500 MHz Krait quad core CPU. The core SLAM implementation, including access to the live camera frames and support for rendering for them, has been provided to us by Qualcomm. Communication with the SLAM system, handling of the raw image data, and rendering are implemented in C/C++, while higher-level app structure, user interface, and network communication are implemented in Java, with data exchange between the two layers via JNI. The live frames are encoded as a H.264 video stream. A minimal HTTP server streams the data (encoded video, tracked camera pose, and other meta-data) upon request from a remote connection, and manages remote requests for insertion/deletion of annotations (encoded as HTTP requests).

The system operates at 30 frames per second. We measured system latencies using a camera with 1000 fps which observed a change in the physical world (a falling object passing a certain height) as well as its image on the respective screen. The latency between physical effect and the local user's tablet display — including image formation on the sensor, retrieval, processing by the SLAM system, rendering of the image, and display on the screen — was measured as 205 ± 22.6 ms.

REMOTE USER'S SYSTEM

The remote user's interface, running on a commodity PC (without high-end GPUs or such), starts off as a live video stream, but is augmented by two controls, the *camera control* and *annotation control*.

The system consists of five main modules — network module, 3D modeler, camera control, annotation control, renderer — and the framework to hold them together. Due to this modular framework, different implementations for each module can be readily swapped in and out upon the start of the program via command line arguments. For example, for comparing our prototype against two baseline interfaces in our user study, we simply replaced the respective modules with simpler ones. In a similar fashion, we also implemented modules that load virtual 3D models (instead of modeling from live video) and allow for other types of camera control.

The latency between physical effect and the remote user's display — including image formation on the local user's sensor, retrieval, processing by the SLAM system, video encoding, transmission via wireless network, video decoding, rendering, and display — was measured as 251 ± 22.2 ms; i.e., less than 50 ms between the local and the remote user's display.

Network module

The network module receives the data stream from the local user's device, sends the incoming video data on to the decoder, and finally notifies the main module when a new frame (decoded image data + meta-data) is available.

3D modeler

From the live video stream and associated camera poses, we construct a 3D surface model on the fly as follows. We select keyframes based on a set of heuristics (good tracking quality, low device movement, minimum time interval & translational distance between keyframes), then detect and describe features in the new frame using SIFT [27]. We then choose the four closest existing keyframes, match against their features

# of keyframes in model	1–10	11–25	> 25
Keypoint detection	32 ± 2	32 ± 3	34 ± 2
Keypoint description	904 ± 124	868 ± 144	795 ± 167
Stereo matching	121 ± 59	166 ± 38	153 ± 45
Merging & filtering of vertices	$<1 \pm 1$	5 ± 1	9 ± 2
Updating tetrahedralization	$<1 \pm 1$	2 ± 2	3 ± 3
Calculating graph costs	10 ± 6	51 ± 14	128 ± 28
Solving graph cut	$<1 \pm <1$	$1 \pm <1$	1 ± 1
Extracting & smoothing surface	4 ± 8	9 ± 21	21 ± 9
Total time	1082 ± 140	1159 ± 175	1201 ± 208

Table 1. Average timings of the 3D modeler to process and integrate one new keyframe into the model, running on a single core of a 3 GHz Intel i7 CPU with 4 GB RAM. All times are given in milliseconds, with associated standard deviations. Incorporating all logs from the user study to be discussed below, the data in the three columns are based on 300, 429, and 481 keyframe integrations, respectively.

(one frame at a time) via an approximate nearest neighbor algorithm [30] and collect matches that satisfy the epipolar constraint (which is known due to the received camera poses) within some tolerance as tentative 3D points. If a feature has previously been matched to features from other frames, we check for mutual epipolar consistency of all observations and merge them into a single 3D point if possible; otherwise, the two 3D points remain as competing hypotheses.

Next, all tentative 3D points are sorted by the number of supporting observations and are accepted one by one unless one of their observations has been previously "claimed" by an already accepted 3D point (which, by construction, had more support). We require at least four observations for a point to be accepted, and we further remove a fraction of points with the largest 3D distances to their two nearest neighbors. The algorithm is thus robust to even large fractions of mismatches from the stereo matching stage.

To obtain a surface model from the 3D point cloud, we implemented the algorithm by Hoppe et al. [16]: First, a Delaunay tetrahedralization of the point cloud is created. Each tetrahedron is then labeled as "free" or "occupied," and the interface between free and occupied tetrahedra is extracted as the scene's surface. The labeling of the tetrahedra works as follows: A graph structure is created in which each tetrahedron is represented by a node, and nodes of neighboring tetrahedra are linked by edges. Each node is further linked to a "free" (sink) node and an "occupied" (source) node. The weights of all edges depend on the observations that formed each vertex; for example, an observation ray that cuts through a cell indicates that this cell is free, while a ray ending in front of a cell indicates that the cell is occupied. Finally, the labels for all tetrahedra are determined by solving a dynamic graph cut problem. For details on how the edge weights are computed we refer the reader to [16].

We refined Hoppe et al. [16]'s algorithm by taking the orientation of observation rays to cell interfaces into account, which reduces the number of "weak" links and thus the risk that the graph cut finds a minimum that does not correspond to a true surface.

As Hoppe et al. describe, both updating the graph costs and solving the graph cut can be implemented in a incremental manner, with cost almost independent of the overall model size. As these steps were found to take up a negligible amount of time in our application (cf. Table 1), for simplicity we did not even implement the incremental algorithm. Nonetheless, the entire processing of a new keyframe and updating of the 3D surface model is completed within 1-1.5 seconds (cf. Table 1), which is easily fast enough for our purposes, as it is smaller than the interval at which keyframes are added on average. Currently, the vast majority of the time is taken up by the keypoint description, which is independent of the model size. If necessary, the computation could be significantly sped up by using a more efficient descriptor implementation or algorithm and/or implementing the incremental graph update. Thus, the overall modeling algorithm is highly scalable to environments much larger than demonstrated here.

Camera control (virtual navigation)

The remote user's ability to navigate the remote world via a virtual camera, independent of the local user's current location, is one of the key contributions of our work.

As mentioned earlier, Sodhi et al. [39] provide a similar feature, but use physical device movement for navigation. While this is arguably very intuitive, using physical navigation has two disadvantages; one being generally true for physical navigation and the other one being specific to the application of live collaboration: First, the remote user needs to be able to physically move and track his/her movements in a space corresponding in size to the remote environment of interest[1], and "supernatural" movements or viewpoints (e.g., quickly covering large distances or adopting a bird's-eye view) are impossible. We refer to Bowman et al. [4] for a more detailed discussion of physical vs. virtual travel, and Sukan et al. [40] for a comparison on a particular task in the context of AR. Second, it does not allow coupling of the remote user's view to the local user's view (and thus have the local user control the viewpoint) without breaking the frame of reference in which the remote user navigates. Lanir et al. [25] presented a study on the issue of control of viewpoint with mixed results, suggesting that it may be dependent on the particular task.

We thus decided to use virtual navigation, and we deem it important that our navigation gives the remote user the option of coupling his/her view to that of the local user.

Within virtual navigation, we decided to use a keyframe-based navigation as explained in the following for several reasons: first, mapping unconstrained 3D navigation to 2D controls requires relatively complex interfaces [19]; second, our model is inherently constrained by what has been observed by the local user's camera, and a keyframe-based approach offers a natural way to constrain the navigation accordingly; third, a keyframe-based approach allows for image-based rendering with high levels of fidelity.

Therefore, the camera control module continually stores new keyframes with their associated camera poses from the live video stream if the tracking quality is good enough. (These

[1] In fully immersive virtual reality, "redirected walking" [36] can be used to "fit" a virtual environment into a smaller physical space under certain conditions.

keyframes are independent of the ones used by the modeler; they serve a different purpose and are maintained separately.) Keyframes that have become obsolete because they are close to a newer keyframe are automatically discarded.

The individual controls were designed to be as intuitive as possible and resemble controls familiar from other exploration tools such as Google Street View and Photo tourism [38]. Viewpoint transitions are implemented by smoothly interpolating between the camera poses and are rendered as visually seamlessly as possible (cf. the description below).

Freeze & back to live

The application starts with the remote view coupled to the local user's live view. With a single right-click, the remote user "freezes" his/her camera at the current pose, for example in order to precisely set annotations, or as a starting point for further navigation. Whenever the remote user's view is not coupled to the local user's view, the latter is displayed to the remote user as an inset (cf. Figure 3). A click onto this inset or pressing 0 immediately transitions back to the live view. (This feature, resembling the "Frame & Freeze" technique by Güven et al. [15], is the only camera control feature implemented in the prototype in [12].)

Panning & zooming

By moving the mouse while its right button is pressed, the user can pan the view in a panorama-like fashion (rotate around the current camera position). To prevent the user from getting lost in unmapped areas, we constrain the panning to the angular extent of the modeled environment. To ensure that the system does not appear unresponsive to the user's input while enforcing this constraint, we allow a certain amount of "overshoot" beyond the allowed extent. In this range, further mouse movement away from the modeled environment causes an exponentially declining increase in rotation and visual feedback in the form of an increasingly intense blue gradient along the respective screen border (Figure 3). Once the mouse button is released, the panning quickly snaps back to the allowed range. Thus, the movement appears to be constrained by a (nonlinear) spring rather a hard wall.

The user can also zoom into and out of the view with the scroll wheel. Zooming is implemented as a change of the virtual camera's field of view (rather than dollying) to avoid having to deal with corrections for parallax or occlusions from objects behind the original camera position.

Click to change viewpoint

When the user right-clicks into the view, we compute the 3D hit point, and subsequently find the camera whose optical axis is closest to this point (which may be the current camera as well). We then transition to this camera and adapt yaw and pitch such that the new view centers around the clicked-upon point. This allows the user to quickly center on a nearby point as well as quickly travel to a far away point with a single click.

Saving & revisiting viewpoints

Further, the user can actively save a particular viewpoint to revisit it later (similar to the navigation investigated by Sukan et al. [40]). Pressing `Alt` plus any number key saves the current viewpoint; pressing the respective number key alone revisits

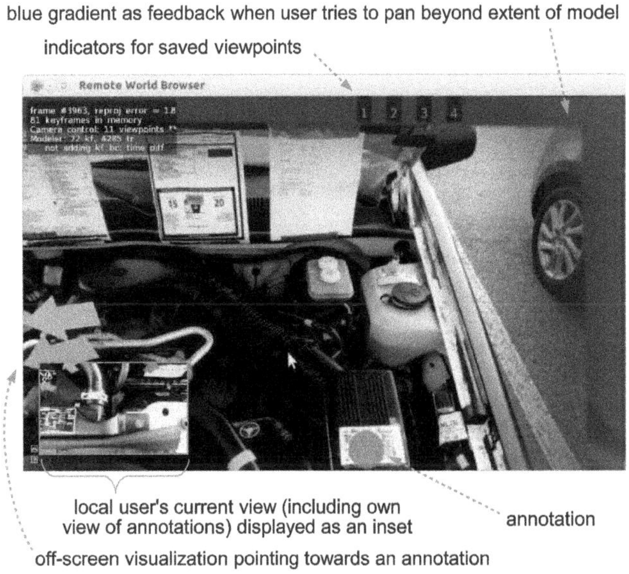

Figure 3. Screenshot of the remote user's interface.

this view later. Small numbers along the top of the screen indicate which numbers are currently in use (see Figure 3).

We postulate that this keyframe-based navigation is simple and intuitive and allows for flexible exploration of a scene. However, there are situations in which it is limited: it does not allow navigation to a never-visited viewpoint, or control over each degree of freedom individually, as may be desired by advanced users for fine-grained maneuvering [4, 19].

Annotation Control

In addition to being able to control the viewpoint, the remote user can set and remove virtual annotations. Annotations are saved in 3D world coordinates, are shared with the local user's mobile device via the network, and immediately appear in all views of the world correctly anchored to their 3D world position (cf. Figures 1 and 3).

For this prototype, we implemented only simple, animated spherical markers. If annotations are outside the user's current field of view, an arrow appears along the border of the screen pointing towards the annotation (see Figure 3; also cf. [12]). Annotations are "pulsing" with 1 Hz and 15% amplitude to increase their visual saliency. Together with the independent viewpoint control as described above, the remote user can thus effectively direct the local user to elements outside the local user's current field of view.

The remote user sets a marker by simply left-clicking into the view (irrespective if "live" or "decoupled"). The depth of the marker is derived from the 3D model, presuming that the user wants to mark things on physical surfaces rather than in mid-air. Pressing the space bar removes all annotations. More complex and/or automatic erasure management [11, 20] could be integrated as desired.

These annotations were sufficient for our task (cf. user study tasks below), but other tasks may require more complex annotations. As discussed earlier, other works have experimented with 2D drawings [14, 22, 34] or transfer of hand gestures [17, 18, 22], which are undoubtedly more expressive but thus far have been used mostly with stationary cameras. More complex annotations like this could be integrated (now world-stabilized as well) as needed.

Renderer

Finally, the renderer renders the scene using the 3D model, the continually updated keyframes, the incoming live camera frame (including live camera pose), the virtual camera pose, and the annotations. In addition to a generally desirable high level of realism, a particular challenge rather unique to our application is the seamless transition to and from the live video (also cf. [42]). That is, as the virtual camera approaches the physical camera, the views should become identical, with no noticeable transition from "model view" to "live view." We achieve this by using image-based rendering as follows.

The 3D model is rendered as a polygonal model, upon which the images of the live frame and closest keyframes are projected using projective texture mapping. As the virtual camera moves, the different textures are faded in and out by adapting their opacity. In areas which are modeled accurately, transitions are thus completely seamless, with lighting effects naturally blending in. More sophisticated image-based rendering techniques (e.g., [6]) could be integrated as appropriate.

We note that the live view may extend beyond the area currently modeled in 3D. To ensure that these areas do not suddenly "disappear" immediately after transitioning away from the live view, we extend the model with a proxy plane (at the model's average distance to the camera) on which textures can be projected. To soften artifacts, we blur the parts of the projective textures that fall onto this part.

In effect, when the remote user's virtual camera pose is identical (coupled) to the local user's current physical camera pose, the rendered image is identical to the live video, and transitions to and away from it are seamless.

Due to the nature of our camera control, the camera is often at the location of a previously cached keyframe (albeit with possibly modified yaw, pitch, or field-of-view), which enables image-based rendering with high levels of fidelity. The 3D model is rarely visible as a polygonal model, thus modeling artifacts are rarely apparent. However, the more accurate the model, the better the transitions can be rendered, and the more precisely annotations can be anchored.

We encourage the reader to inspect the virtual navigation and the rendering in the supplemental video.

SYSTEM LIMITATIONS & DISCUSSION

While our prototype delivers a robust, real-time AR experience, there are some assumptions and system limitations.

Level of detail of model

Building upon a tetrahedralization of a sparse point cloud, the modeling approach taken here is very fast (as demonstrated above), but results in a model that does not exhibit the level of detail as achievable, for example, with dense volumetric fusion [9, 32, 35]. While the existence of the 3D model is quintessential for anchoring of annotations and rendering, a relatively coarse level of detail is, arguably, acceptable, as the keyframe-based navigation and rendering de-emphasize modeling artifacts.

However, techniques to create a more detailed model exist, and since our system is modular — none of the other components depend on this particular modeling algorithm — other algorithms could be plugged in as needed. This includes algorithms to densify the point cloud [10] while keeping the overall approach the same, using other, computationally more intensive, vision-based algorithms [35], or (where permissible by the application) active depth sensor-based modeling [32].

Static scene

Our system generally assumes that the scene is static. While the SLAM system on the local user's side is quite robust to partial and/or gradual changes in the scene, adapting the modeling, navigation and rendering would require an active detection and invalidation of changed regions.

Stereo initialization

Like any monocular SLAM system, our system requires a stereo initialization (i.e., a distinct camera movement) before it tracks robustly. This is done quickly and thus not a problem if the user is aware of the requirement; however, we feel that it stands in the way for truly transparent and user-friendly operation. The research community is investigating ways to reduce this burden [13, 31].

Occlusion of annotations on local side

Currently, the 3D model is available only on the remote user's side. Thus, annotations can be correctly occluded by the physical scene by the remote user's renderer, but not by the local user's renderer. While other depth cues (most notably, parallax) still indicate the annotation's location, it would be desirable to enable occlusion. The remote system could send either the model geometry or alternatively some sort of local visibility information per annotation back to the local device. Designing an elegant, bandwidth-efficient solution for either approach is an interesting aspect for future work.

One-way annotations

Our system currently limits creation of annotations to the remote user. The rationale is that the local user can spatially refer to the environment with his/her hands (as seen in Figure 1 and the supplemental video) — it is the remote user who needs additional means (cf. related work using one-way annotations [11, 22, 25]). However, if deemed appropriate, it would be straightforward to also allow the local user to create annotations, for example by tapping onto his/her screen.

USER STUDY: DESIGN & METHOD

To evaluate our system, we conducted a remote expert–local worker user study comparing our system with two baselines: a video+audio only interface and an interface with static annotations (also called "markers" throughout the study). Both the local and the remote users were study participants.

We first conducted several pilot study trials with a total of 20 users (10 teams), during which we refined study parameters, overall procedure, and training procedure.

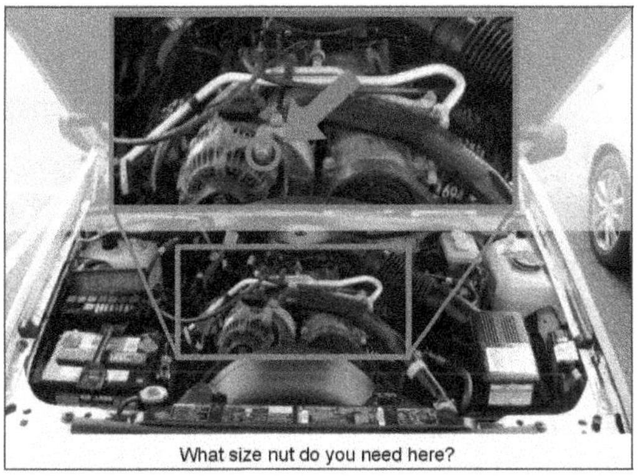

Figure 4. One example out of 80 individual tasks. These instructions were provided to the remote user, who then needed to communicate the information to the local user.

Task & Physical setup

We chose a "car repair" task for the study. The local user stood in front of a car, hood open, and received help from the remote user in "identifying the problem" (cf. [7] for a similar scenario). The study took place outdoors, and while we used a relatively isolated location with no direct sunlight, several environment factors were beyond our control, including weather, light conditions, passers-by, and noise from a nearby street and a nearby airport. The study's external conditions were thus close to a real scenario. Network infrastructure and the remote user's PC were mounted onto a cart and positioned adjacent to the car such that the participants could communicate verbally, but not see each other.

To make sure that the individual tasks were roughly equivalent, quick enough to perform, independent of the individual user's dexterity, and not dangerous in any way, we used proxy tasks that would require similar communication between the users but little or no physical labor, such as locating individual elements and finding pieces of information. For example, instead of unscrewing a bolt, we asked the users to identify its size by testing it with a set of provided nuts, which requires the same communication between the users in order to identify the correct element but little physical labor. For each individual task, the remote user was given simulated expert knowledge in the form of a specific question (e.g., size of a particular screw or cable, rating of a particular fuse, serial number of a part) and a diagram indicating where the answer could be located (see Figure 4). The remote user then had to communicate this information to the local user, who had to locate the requested information and write it down.

Conditions

In all conditions, the two users were able to talk to each other without restrictions.

- **Interface A: video only.** The live video from the local user's camera is streamed to the remote user; the remote user does not have any means of interacting with the video or providing visual/spatial feedback. This is similar to using today's standard video conferencing tools.
- **Interface B: video + static markers.** In addition to the features in condition A, the remote user can click into the video to create a marker visible to both users. However, the marker's position is stored in *screen* coordinates and thus moves with the camera rather than "sticking" to the world object. This condition is effectively similar to related works that assume a stationary camera [11].
- **Interface C: our prototype as presented above.**

As in Gauglitz et al. [12], conditions B and C both allowed up to five concurrent markers in different colors, with further clicks re-setting the oldest marker.

Experimental Design

We used a within-subjects design with one independent variable (interface type) and one dependent variable (task completion time). We also recorded the number of errors and obtained several user ratings via questionnaires. The order of the interfaces was completely balanced, with each of the six possible orderings traversed by five of the 30 teams. For each team, three lists with 15 tasks were created at random, with the remaining tasks reserved for training.

Our hypotheses about the study's outcome were as follows:

H1 Users will complete the task faster with interfaces B and C than with interface A.

H2 Users will complete the task faster with C than with B.

H3 Users will prefer interface C over both A and B.

Participants

60 users (18–30 years (mean 20.8), 29 female, 31 male) participated in the main study, working together in 30 teams (8 female/female, 7 female/male, 6 male/female, 9 male/male (local/remote user)). Each user received a compensation of USD 10; all teams additionally competed for a bonus of USD 10 / 20 / 40 per person for the top 5 / second fastest / fastest error-free task performances for all three conditions combined.

In two teams not included in the numbers above, one user was color blind. It remains unclear whether this affected the task performance. However, we used color extensively (markers, labels in the car, etc.), and at least one of the users was unable to disambiguate a few of the elements. We thus decided not to include the data from these two trials in the analysis.

Procedure & Training

Each participant completed a color blind test and a pre-study questionnaire with background information. The general setup and task were then explained in detail.

For each session, the study administrator explained the respective interface features in detail, then the users conducted several training tasks with the respective interface. Each user completed a minimum of five training tasks for each new feature and was asked explicitly if they were comfortable using the interface before proceeding to the timed session. After each session, the users filled out an intermediate questionnaire rating this interface. Lastly, each user filled out a post-study questionnaire and received their compensation.

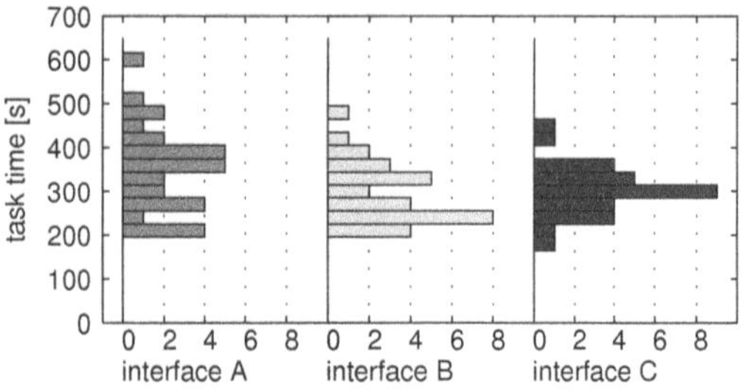

Figure 5. Histogram of task times per interface.

During the pilot study trials, it quickly became clear that not all of the camera control features that our prototype (interface C) featured were necessary for this particular environment and task, and that the limited amount of time prohibited explaining and training the user on each of them. We thus concentrated the training on a subset of features that appeared to be most useful in this context, namely, the freezing of the camera, and the saving/revisiting of viewpoints. However, the other features (panning, zooming, change viewpoint via click) were still available and were occasionally discovered and used by participants.

To ensure a consistently high quality of the required stereo initialization, the study administrator conducted the initialization step (until the modeler had started to extract 3D surface) before handing the device to the local user.

USER STUDY: RESULTS & DISCUSSION

Task performance

Overall, 98.5% of the tasks were answered correctly (21 errors at a total of 30×3×15 tasks). Analyzing the number of errors, Mauchly's test indicated that the assumption of sphericity against interface had not been violated ($W(2)=0.95$, $p=0.50$), and no significant effect of interface on the number of errors was found using a one-way repeated measures ANOVA ($F(2,58)=0.47$, $p=0.63$, and $\eta^2_{\text{partial}}=0.016$). Additionally, we note that 5 of the 21 errors were made on two particular subtasks in which the expert knowledge diagram may have been confusing. We conclude that all users worked meticulously and thus that the comparison of the task times is meaningful.

Analyzing the task times, Mauchly's test indicated that the assumption of sphericity had not been violated ($W(2)=0.99$, $p=0.93$). With a one-way repeated measures ANOVA, we found a significant effect of interface on task completion time with $F(2,58)=6.94$, $p=0.0020$, and $\eta^2_{\text{partial}}=0.19$. Post hoc comparisons using Tukey's HSD test indicated that users were significantly faster with both interfaces B ($M=313.6$, $SD=69.6$) and C ($M=317.5$, $SD=57.6$) than with interface A ($M=364.7$, $SD=96.7$), thus supporting hypothesis H1. No significant difference was found between B and C; hence, hypothesis H2 was not supported.

Questionnaires

In the intermediate questionnaires filled out immediately after each session (i.e., before the next interface was introduced), the users were asked to rate their level of agreement on a 7-point scale to the statements, "This interface helped me to solve the task," "This interface made me feel confident that I was doing the task correctly," and "I had difficulties using this interface." The responses are aggregated in Figure 6.

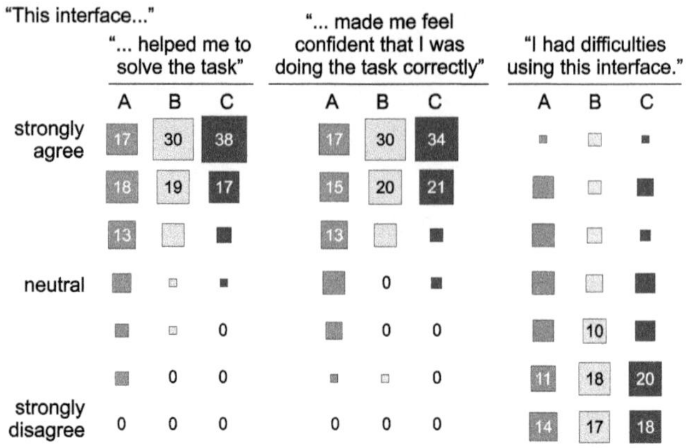

Figure 6. Results from intermediate questionnaires: interface ratings.

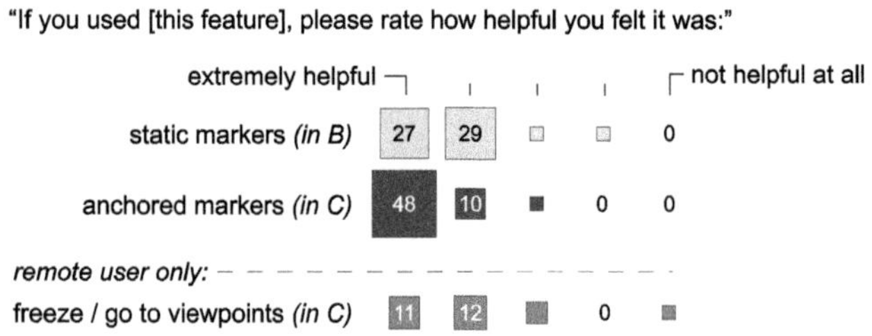

Figure 7. Results from intermediate questionnaires: individual features.

For these ratings, we decided to use a non-parametric test for the analysis to avoid the assumptions of interval data, normality and spherecity.

According to Friedman's test, the ratings in response to the first two statements differ significantly among the interfaces ($\chi^2(2)=34.5$, $p < 10^{-7}$, and $\chi^2(2)=37.8$, $p < 10^{-7}$, respectively). Pairwise comparisons with Bonferroni's correction applied indicated that both B and C were rated better than A. For the third question ("I had difficulties..."), Friedman's test also indicated a significant difference ($\chi^2(2)=8.1$, $p=0.017$), but pairwise comparisons with Bonferroni's correction applied only revealed a possible borderline significant difference between A and C at $p = 0.019$ (compared to the corrected threshold of 0.017).

Users were further asked to rate the helpfulness of individual features on a 5-point scale from "extremely helpful" to "not helpful at all" (Figure 7). Wilcoxon's paired signed rank test ($V=25$, $p < 10^{-4}$) showed that the anchored markers (in interface C) were perceived as more helpful than the static markers (in interface B), with 80% of the users perceiving the former as "extremely helpful." The camera control features were perceived as "extremely" or "very" helpful by 77% of the remote users.

In the post-study questionnaire, users were asked to rank the three interfaces ("Which interface did you like best /

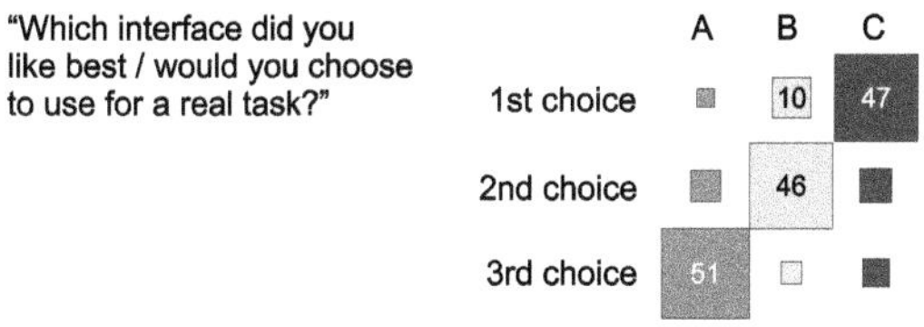

Figure 8. Results from post-study questionnaire: interface preference.

would you choose to use for a real task?"). There is a significant difference in ranking according to Friedman's test ($\chi^2(2) = 71.42$, $p < 10^{-15}$). Pairwise comparisons (with Bonferroni's correction applied) indicated that all pairwise differences are significant. 80% of the users selected interface C as their first choice (cf. Figure 8), supporting H3. The preference for C is 83% among tablet users and 77% among PC users, but this difference was not significant according to Wilcoxon's paired signed rank test ($V = 29$, $p = 0.45$).

Open-ended questions on the questionnaires revealed several interesting details, most notably an inadvertent side effect of the world-stabilization of markers: Since the markers in interface C had a constant world size, they ended up being quite large when the user got very close to the object, and were thus too large for some tasks, as described by this user: *"Overall, the markers and viewpoints were extremely helpful. However, [...] for the tasks where text needed to be located, the marker was much bigger than the words."* Having constant screen size, the markers in B did not have this side effect.

Several users expressed their preference for interface C, but commented that too many keys had to be memorized: *"[C] was more useful [...] but it was sometimes difficult to remember which buttons would navigate to which screen shots, what to press to unfreeze the pane, and so on. However, I imagine it would get much easier with additional practice"*; *"[C] was by far the most helpful user interface, but it was a bit difficult to use due to the [number of] buttons."*

Discussion

To summarize the results, an overwhelming majority of the participants (in both roles) preferred our system over both baselines (H3 supported); users performed significantly faster with it than with a video-only baseline (H1 supported); but no significant difference in task performance was found in comparison with a static marker condition (H2 not supported).

Differences in task performance

We note two particular artifacts of the study design that may have reduced the differences in task performance between the interfaces in general and counteracted potential benefits of interface C in particular:

First, as users started, the difficulty of verbally giving spatial and directional instructions — including confusion regarding "left" and "right" (relative to the car's driving direction or the user's perspective?) and "up" and "down" (in world or screen coordinates?), as well as misidentification of elements — was very apparent, which supports the need for spatial annotations. However, as an artifact of the training, the within-subjects design, and the small task environment, users quickly became experts in giving and understanding directions for this particular task, possibly more so than becoming experts in using the interfaces. Oftentimes, users came up with names for different parts of the engine, which did not have to be technically accurate in order to be effective (the most creative moniker may have been "rainbow keyboard" for the fuse box). As one user commented when asked about the usefulness of the camera control: *"[It] wasn't very useful since I already knew the layout of the engine from previous tasks."* For real applications, we might assume the opposite: users become familiar with the interfaces available to them and communicate with new partners in new environments. To account for this, different environments could be used for each training and interface session, which however poses a challenge in terms of practicality and ensuring fair conditions across all sessions.

Second, because of the increasingly familiar environment, and additionally motivated by the incentives, the tasks became very fast-paced. Thus, the remote user's mental load of understanding the next instructions (cf. Figure 4), aligning them with his/her mental model of the engine, and then with his/her view of the scene, was oftentimes slower than the actual task execution, which required little physical labor and could thus be completed very quickly. As the time-critical path shifted from the local to the remote user, a potential benefit of the virtual camera control — namely, that the remote user could browse and familiarize him/herself with the environment (e.g., for the next task) — became less relevant, while a potential downside (increased complexity) became more relevant. One user commented: *"Using the multiple views was a little more hectic on the 'expert's' side, but only because we were trying to complete the tasks as quickly as possible. In a situation in which this technology would be used, this feature would no doubt be very helpful for quality and efficiency of task completion."* We note that this is also an artifact of the study setup: in a real application, no simulated expert knowledge has to be understood, and the local user's task may require more physical labor or travel.

Other factors that may have played a role are: While the users' ratings suggest that they did not perceive interface C as more difficult to use, it may require more training for optimal use (cf. comments on the number of keys above). Lastly, with C, some users took extra time to carefully position the camera to save viewpoints for later use, but the amortization of this time investment was limited by the short task duration.

Type of task

In this work, in order to validate our system design and establish its usefulness, we chose a relatively simple task with clearly defined roles, as commonly used in this context (e.g., [2, 5, 11, 12, 34]). Looking forward, it would be important to study more complex collaborative tasks. As the features that the system provides are very general in nature, we are confident that they provide benefits in a variety of contexts.

CONCLUSIONS

In this paper, we described a system for mobile remote collaboration that uses real-time computer vision-based tracking and modeling of the environment to facilitate live, remote controlled AR annotations and remote virtual scene navigation. We believe that these features add promising new dimensions to remote collaboration. We further presented an extensive comparative user study.

Our system was overwhelmingly preferred by users. With regard to task performance time, our study showed a significant benefit compared with only one of the two baseline interfaces. We discussed several artifacts which may have contributed to this outcome. Some of these are common to many studies of collaboration, such as small environments, proxy tasks, and simulated expert knowledge. Thus, we hope that our study also informs the design of future studies in this area. Altogether, our results demonstrate the maturity and usability of our system, as well as producing insights into which aspects of the interface can be further improved. Limitations of the system which future work might target have also been discussed above.

While the system is complex under the hood, we feel that one important advantage of our approach is that it seamlessly extends the ubiquitous videoconferencing paradigm; it adds to it, but it does not take anything away. If desired, the user can fall back to simply watching the live video feed.

In the bigger picture, our work bridges and creates a synergy between video conferencing (Skype, Apple FaceTime, Google Hangouts, etc.) and remote world exploration (Microsoft Photosynth, Quicktime VR [8], Google StreetView, [43], etc.) in a unique coherent interface via live collaborative AR. However, our prototype has only started to tap into the significant potential of this synergy. Areas to explore include the integration of more complex annotations such as gestures or gaze [29] in a world-stabilized manner and the integration of cloud-based data (e.g., maps/larger models of the environments). The live navigation of remote worlds — both within virtual navigation as well as in comparison with physical navigation [20, 39] — also warrants further investigation.

This synergy could further be explored beyond the two-user remote expert–local worker scenario, with respect to both roles and numbers of users: We note that the presented paradigm is equally applicable to scenarios with shared expertise or a local expert (e.g., in an educational context), and naturally extends to more than one local user and/or more than one remote user. Here, the environment model is to integrate video streams and annotations from all users.

ACKNOWLEDGMENTS

We thank Qualcomm, and in particular Serafin Diaz, Daniel Wagner and Alessandro Mulloni, for making their SLAM implementation available to us for this project. We thank Susan Fussell for advice concerning the design of the user study, and Yuqi Chen for her help with the statistical analysis. Further, we thank Jhon Faghih-Nassiri and Krithika Chandrasekar for looking into multimedia streaming, Lukas Gruber and Domagoj Baričević for OpenGL tricks, John O'Donovan letting us borrow the car for the study, Michael Liebling and Kevin Chan for letting us use their high-speed camera, and Mock Suwannatat and Julia Gauglitz for their help recording the video.

This work was supported by NSF grants IIS-1219261 and IIS-0747520, ONR grant N00014-14-1-0133, and a Chancellor's fellowship for S.G. from UCSB.

REFERENCES

1. Adcock, M., Anderson, S., and Thomas, B. RemoteFusion: Real time depth camera fusion for remote collaboration on physical tasks. In *Proc. ACM SIGGRAPH VRCAI* (2013), 235–242.
2. Bauer, M., Kortuem, G., and Segall, Z. "Where are you pointing at?" a study of remote collaboration in a wearable videoconference system. In *Proc. IEEE ISWC* (1999), 151 –158.
3. Billinghurst, M., and Kato, H. Collaborative augmented reality. *Commun. ACM 45* (July 2002), 64–70.
4. Bowman, D. A., Kruijff, E., LaViola, J., and Poupyrev, I. *3D User Interfaces: Theory and Practice*. Addison-Wesley, Boston, 2005.
5. Chastine, J., Nagel, K., Zhu, Y., and Hudachek-Buswell, M. Studies on the effectiveness of virtual pointers in collaborative augmented reality. In *Proc. IEEE 3DUI* (March 2008), 117 –124.
6. Chaurasia, G., Duchene, S., Sorkine-Hornung, O., and Drettakis, G. Depth synthesis and local warps for plausible image-based navigation. *ACM Trans. Graph. 32*, 3 (2013), 30:1–30:12.
7. Chen, S., Chen, M., Kunz, A., Yantaç, A. E., Bergmark, M., Sundin, A., and Fjeld, M. SEMarbeta: mobile sketch-gesture-video remote support for car drivers. In *Proc. Augmented Human Int'l Conf.* (2013), 69–76.
8. Chen, S. E. QuickTime VR: an image-based approach to virtual environment navigation. In *Proc. ACM SIGGRAPH* (1995), 29–38.
9. Curless, B., and Levoy, M. A volumetric method for building complex models from range images. In *Proc. ACM SIGGRPAPH* (1996), 303–312.
10. Furukawa, Y., and Ponce, J. Accurate, dense, and robust multiview stereopsis. *IEEE Trans. Pattern Anal. Mach. Intell. 32*, 8 (2010), 1362–1376.
11. Fussell, S. R., Setlock, L. D., Yang, J., Ou, J., Mauer, E., and Kramer, A. D. I. Gestures over video streams to support remote collaboration on physical tasks. *Hum.-Comput. Interact. 19* (2004), 273–309.
12. Gauglitz, S., Lee, C., Turk, M., and Höllerer, T. Integrating the physical environment into mobile remote collaboration. In *Proc. ACM MobileHCI* (2012).
13. Gauglitz, S., Sweeney, C., Ventura, J., Turk, M., and Höllerer, T. Model estimation and selection towards unconstrained real-time tracking and mapping. *IEEE Trans. Vis. Comput. Graphics 20*, 6 (2014), 825–838.
14. Gurevich, P., Lanir, J., Cohen, B., and Stone, R. TeleAdvisor: A versatile augmented reality tool for remote assistance. In *Proc. ACM CHI* (2012), 619–622.

15. Güven, S., Feiner, S., and Oda, O. Mobile augmented reality interaction techniques for authoring situated media on-site. In *Proc. IEEE and ACM ISMAR* (Washington, DC, USA, 2006), 235–236.
16. Hoppe, C., Klopschitz, M., Donoser, M., and Bischof, H. Incremental surface extraction from sparse structure-from-motion point clouds. In *Proc. BMVC* (Bristol, UK, 2013).
17. Huang, W., and Alem, L. HandsinAir: A wearable system for remote collaboration on physical tasks. In *Proc. ACM CSCW* (2013), 153–156.
18. Huang, W., Alem, L., and Tecchia, F. HandsIn3D: Augmenting the shared 3D visual space with unmediated hand gestures. In *SIGGRAPH Asia 2013 Emerging Technologies* (2013), 10:1–10:3.
19. Jankowski, J., and Hachet, M. A survey of interaction techniques for interactive 3D environments. In *Eurographics – STAR* (2013), 65–93.
20. Jo, H., and Hwang, S. Chili: Viewpoint control and on-video drawing for mobile video calls. In *ACM CHI Extended Abstracts* (2013), 1425–1430.
21. Kim, S., Lee, G. A., Sakata, N., Vartiainen, E., and Billinghurst, M. Comparing pointing and drawing for remote collaboration. In *Proc. IEEE ISMAR Extended Abstracts* (2013), 1–6.
22. Kirk, D., and Stanton Fraser, D. Comparing remote gesture technologies for supporting collaborative physical tasks. In *Proc. ACM CHI* (2006), 1191–1200.
23. Kurata, T., Sakata, N., Kourogi, M., Kuzuoka, H., and Billinghurst, M. Remote collaboration using a shoulder-worn active camera/laser. In *Proc. ISWC* (2004), 62–69.
24. Kuzuoka, H., Oyama, S., Yamazaki, K., Suzuki, K., and Mitsuishi, M. GestureMan: A mobile robot that embodies a remote instructor's actions. In *Proc. ACM CSCW* (2000), 155–162.
25. Lanir, J., Stone, R., Cohen, B., and Gurevich, P. Ownership and control of point of view in remote assistance. In *Proc. ACM CHI* (2013), 2243–2252.
26. Lee, T., and Höllerer, T. Viewpoint stabilization for live collaborative video augmentations. In *Proc. IEEE and ACM ISMAR* (Washington, DC, USA, 2006), 241–242.
27. Lowe, D. G. Distinctive image features from scale-invariant keypoints. *Int'l Journal of Computer Vision 60*, 2 (2004), 91–110.
28. Maimone, A., Yang, X., Dierk, N., State, A., Dou, M., and Fuchs, H. General-purpose telepresence with head-worn optical see-through displays and projector-based lighting. In *Proc. IEEE Virtual Reality 2013* (Orlando, USA, March 2013).
29. Mayol, W. W., Davison, A. J., Tordoff, B. J., Molton, N. D., and Murray, D. W. Interaction between hand and wearable camera in 2d and 3d environments. In *Proc. BMVC* (Sept. 2004).
30. Muja, M., and Lowe, D. G. Fast approximate nearest neighbors with automatic algorithm configuration. In *Proc. VISSAPP* (2009), 331–340.
31. Mulloni, A., Ramachandran, M., Reitmayr, G., Wagner, D., Grasset, R., and Diaz, S. User friendly SLAM initialization. In *Proc. IEEE ISMAR* (2013), 153–162.
32. Newcombe, R. A., Izadi, S., Hilliges, O., Molyneaux, D., Kim, D., Davison, A. J., Kohli, P., Shotton, J., Hodges, S., and Fitzgibbon, A. KinectFusion: Real-time dense surface mapping and tracking. In *Proceedings of the IEEE International Symposium on Mixed and Augmented Reality (ISMAR)* (2011).
33. Oda, O., Sukan, M., Feiner, S., and Tversky, B. Poster: 3D referencing for remote task assistance in augmented reality. In *Proc. IEEE 3DUI* (March 2013), 179–180.
34. Ou, J., Fussell, S. R., Chen, X., Setlock, L. D., and Yang, J. Gestural communication over video stream: supporting multimodal interaction for remote collaborative physical tasks. In *Proc. ICMI* (2003), 242–249.
35. Pradeep, V., Rhemann, C., Izadi, S., Zach, C., Bleyer, M., and Bathiche, S. Monofusion: Real-time 3D reconstruction of small scenes with a single web camera. In *IEEE ISMAR* (2013), 83–88.
36. Razzaque, S. *Redirected Walking*. PhD thesis, University of North Carolina at Chapel Hill, 2005.
37. Sadagic, A., Towles, H., Holden, L., Daniilidis, K., and Zeleznik, B. Tele-immersion portal: Towards an ultimate systhesis. In *Proc. 4th Annual Intl. Workshop on Presence of Computer Graphics and Computer Vision Systems* (2001).
38. Snavely, N., Seitz, S., and Szeliski, R. Photo tourism: exploring photo collections in 3D. *ACM Trans. on Graphics 25*, 3 (2006), 835–846.
39. Sodhi, R. S., Jones, B. R., Forsyth, D., Bailey, B. P., and Maciocci, G. BeThere: 3D mobile collaboration with spatial input. In *Proc. ACM CHI* (2013), 179–188.
40. Sukan, M., Feiner, S., Tversky, B., and Energin, S. Quick viewpoint switching for manipulating virtual objects in hand-held augmented reality using stored snapshots. In *Proc. IEEE ISMAR* (2012).
41. Tang, J. C., and Minneman, S. L. VideoDraw: a video interface for collaborative drawing. *ACM Trans. Inf. Syst. 9* (1991), 170–184.
42. Tatzgern, M., Grasset, R., Kalkofen, D., and Schmalstieg, D. Transitional augmented reality navigation for live captured scenes. In *Proc. IEEE Virtual Reality* (Minnesota, USA, 2014).
43. Uyttendaele, M., Criminisi, A., Kang, S. B., Winder, S., Szeliski, R., and Hartley, R. Image-based interactive exploration of real-world environments. *IEEE Comput. Graph. Appl. 24*, 3 (May 2004), 52–63.
44. Wellner, P., and Freeman, S. The DoubleDigitalDesk: Shared editing of paper documents. Tech. Rep. EPC-93-108, EuroPARC, 1993.

Physical Telepresence: Shape Capture and Display for Embodied, Computer-mediated Remote Collaboration

Daniel Leithinger* Sean Follmer* Alex Olwal† Hiroshi Ishii
MIT Media Lab
Cambridge, MA, USA
{daniell, sean, olwal, ishii}@media.mit.edu

ABSTRACT
We propose a new approach to Physical Telepresence, based on shared workspaces with the ability to capture and remotely render the shapes of people and objects. In this paper, we describe the concept of shape transmission, and propose interaction techniques to manipulate remote physical objects and physical renderings of shared digital content. We investigate how the representation of user's body parts can be altered to amplify their capabilities for teleoperation. We also describe the details of building and testing prototype Physical Telepresence workspaces based on shape displays. A preliminary evaluation shows how users are able to manipulate remote objects, and we report on our observations of several different manipulation techniques that highlight the expressive nature of our system.

Categories and Subject Descriptors: H.5.2 User Interfaces: Haptic I/O, Interaction Styles

General Terms: Design, Human Factors

Keywords: Shape-Changing User Interfaces; Shape Displays; Actuated Tangible Interfaces; Teleoperation; Physical Telepresence

INTRODUCTION
As the world becomes increasingly connected, collaborative work is often distributed across multiple locations. A large number of commercial products are available to support video-mediated communication and shared digital documents, but many limitations for telepresence and telecollaboration remain. Much co-located collaborative work focuses on physical objects, surfaces, spaces and interpersonal relationships that rely on physical interaction with other participants, such as a handshake. The affordances of the physical environment and presence of co-located collaborators are often missing in screen-based remote collaboration.

*The first two authors contributed equally to this work.
†Secondary affiliations: KTH – Royal Institute of Technology (Stockholm, Sweden); Google [x] (Mountain View, CA)

UIST '14, October 05 - 08 2014, Honolulu, HI, USA.

ACM 978-1-4503-3069-5/14/10$15.00.
http://dx.doi.org/10.1145/2642918.2647377

Figure 1. Physical Telepresence provides physical embodiment, remote manipulation and new capabilities through computer-mediated teleoperation. Here, local and remote users physically interact with a 3D car model.

Researchers in distributed computer-supported collaborative work (CSCW) propose improving video-mediated collaboration by situating it in the physical world through the use of shared media spaces [30] and projected Augmented Reality (AR) [33]. However, these interfaces still lack many physical aspects of collaboration, as remote participants are only visually present on the screen, which limits their ability to collaborate through physical objects. To overcome these challenges, telepresence robots have been proposed to embody remote participants for social presence and to manipulate the physical world from a distance [13].

A different approach to physical remote collaboration is presented by remote Tangible User Interfaces (TUIs), which focus on *synchronized distributed physical objects* [2]. These physical objects, or tokens, are synchronized with a remote counterpart to represent shared content, rather than embodying collaborators.

By introducing *Physical Telepresence*, one of our goals is to extend the physical embodiment of remote participants, which is common in telepresence robotics, and combine it with the physical embodiment of shared content, common in remote TUIs. An example of such a system is shown in Figure 1, where the hands of a remote collaborator along with a shared digital model are materialized on a shape display.

In this paper, we investigate different ways in which shape displays [23, 7] can physically embody remote people and objects to enable communication and collaboration. The flexibility of shape rendering also allows us to loosen the direct 1:1 link between remote shapes, both in terms of rendering users and data. We introduce computer-mediation for physical telepresence and explore how shape displays enable new forms of interactions that overcome the user's physical limitations. We can, for example, replace a remote user's arm with custom end effectors that are rendered on demand, as opposed to being limited to the static, prebuilt end effectors of a telepresence robot. We also propose interaction techniques that allow users to manipulate remote objects through gestures, mediating objects, tools, and direct touch. Finally, we report on a preliminary evaluation to explore potential use patterns in telemanipulation scenarios.

CONTRIBUTIONS

- An exploration of physical telepresence for shared workspaces, using shape capture and rendering for rich, real-time physical embodiment and manipulation.
- Interaction techniques for manipulation of remote physical objects and shared, physically rendered, digital models.
- Interaction techniques that leverage physical computer-mediation to amplify user capabilities in remote operation.
- A technical software and hardware platform, which enables synchronous physical interaction for remote users, physical objects, and shape deformation.

RELATED WORK

Video-Mediated Communication

Several early research projects investigate video-mediated collaboration for shared workspaces [31, 30, 11]. More recently, these techniques have been applied to applications, such as collaborative website development [4], remote board games [33] and family communications [34].

Mixed Reality

Collaborative tools can also leverage more spatial interaction and mixed reality displays. TelePointer [17] allows an expert to point in a remote user's real environment through a user-worn laser pointer, while more advanced Spatial AR techniques have been proposed for future collaborative workspaces [24, 1]. Handheld AR can support mobile scenarios [28] whereas larger, situated displays have other benefits, such as immersion [9].

Telerobotics

A body of research focuses on representing remote people with telepresence robots (e.g., [32] [21]). The Personal Roving Presence concept [21] was an early exploration into tele-embodiment using, e.g., screen-based robots and flying blimps. Research has also explored such devices' role in the workplace, and their influence on the sense of social presence [13]. Our approach of rendering captured geometry without semantic knowledge of user input, is quite different from common telepresence robots. Our interactions focus on leveraging the shape display for a rich, shared workspace, with less emphasis on mobility.

Another related domain of telerobotics is telemanipulation. Early master-slave manipulators used mechanical linkages, and now robotics arms and end effectors, to remotely handle hazardous materials or other objects at a distance [20]. A more specific example is that of telesurgery robots, which not only allow for remote operation, but give surgeons more precise control and remove tremors [29]. In contrast to prior work on telemanipulation, we focus on supporting collaborative work and the ability to switch between arbitrary end effectors on demand.

Tangible Remote Collaboration

TUIs can also be beneficial for remote collaboration. PsyBench [2] actuated a tangible object to mirror the movement of a remote physical token. Actuated Workbench [19] added more advanced control over multiple tokens, and represented remote user's presence through projected digital shadows and haptic feedback. Researchers have also explored small tabletop robots for remote TUI collaboration [26, 27]. Video portals have been used to play games over a distance, where physical pucks appearing from underneath the video create the illusion of a single shared object [18]. TUIs for remote collaboration often utilize actuated physical objects to represent content, rather than collaborators [2, 19, 26, 27]. However, as remote actors themselves are not physically embodied, object movement can result in a disconnected experience, since graphics can only partially simulate the presence of a co-located collaborator.

Shape Displays for Remote Collaboration

Since Project Feelex [12], various form factors for 2.5D shape displays have been developed for co-located collaboration and interaction [15, 23, 7, 22]. While Lumen discussed the potential for remote presence and demonstrates an example application [23], remote collaboration has been less of a focus for past shape display research [25].

PHYSICAL TELEPRESENCE FOR SHARED SPACES

We introduce the concept of Physical Telepresence for shared workspaces, where capturing and rendering shapes has the potential to increase the sense of presence, expand the interaction bandwidth, and to extend human capabilities with computer-mediated interaction techniques.

Physical Telepresence is especially relevant for domains where physical presence, spatial information display and rich interaction is required. We primarily emphasize the potential in interactions with shared digital models of arbitrary shapes, linked physical objects, and manipulation of remote objects through direct gesture.

We explore these interactions through three implemented systems:

- Bi-directional interaction through deformation on two linked shape displays (see Figure 15).
- Bi-directional interaction through shape capture and rendering: split-view on a single shape display (see Figure 3).
- Asymmetric teleoperation: A shape display linked to a video-mediated environment with shape capture (see Figure 14).

Figure 2. A user manipulating a sphere through his remote physical embodiment.

Example Scenario: Remote 3D design collaboration

Bill and Jean are two designers working on a new car body design at different locations using their respective Physical Telepresence systems. Bill sees Jean's face on a vertical screen and her hands physically rendered on a horizontal shape display; Jean has a similar view of Bill. As Jean moves her hands, Bill's shape display adapts to update the hands' physical form.

Bill opens their shared car design model, which appears as a physical rendering. To bring the headlights in view, Jean gestures above it on her shape display, rotating and scaling the car, which updates the car model in real-time for Bill. When Bill deforms the headlights with his hands, these changes in the shared model are propagated to Jean's display.

After discussing the changes, Bill moves the car to the side, and reaches for a headlamp that he 3D printed earlier. When placing it on the surface, a physical rendering appears on Jean's display. Jean rotates the rendering, which also rotates the 3D print on Bill's side. They make some digital annotations, which are projected over the physical part and the physical rendering. After reviewing necessary changes, they part ways, and Bill 3D prints the updated model.

Remote Physical Embodiment

The ability to provide relevant and adequate representations of remote participants and environments, which otherwise would have been co-located, is one of the grand challenges of telepresence systems. This embodiment has a great influence on realism, interaction capabilities and sense of presence.

In a shape-display-mediated telepresence scenario, we identify four primary types of content to represent:

Users. Tracked remote and local users, with their representation transmitted to support interaction and telepresence.

Environment. The static or dynamic physical environment at each location, where the interaction takes place. We introduce a number of novel possibilities for computational control and actuation of the local and remote environment.

Figure 3. Top: Two linked tangible tokens at two locations, with synchronized position. Bottom: A tangible token rendered with the shape display at a remote location.

Objects and Tools. Tangible artifacts can be sensed in the environment, allowing them both to be manipulated by the system, or by a remote user through the shape display, in addition to direct manipulation by a local user.

Shared Digital Models. We can use a shape display to represent shared objects in multiple locations. Changes are updated in the computational model and propagated to remote locations. Shared Digital Models may have different viewports in different locations.

Representations: Physical and Virtual

Various techniques exist to capture the appearance, geometry and interactions from local participants and objects, which the system can use to form a representation that can be transmitted and materialized at a remote location.

Physical Shape Rendering. The physical shape of remote users, objects, and environment can be dynamically rendered through actuation on a shape display.

Linked Tangible Objects. Passive tangible objects, or tokens, placed on the surface of the table can represent remote objects. These passive objects can be manipulated through shape actuation [7]. This makes it possible to go beyond the limited degrees-of-freedom of the shape display by using external objects on its surface (see Figure 3, top, right).

2D Graphics. Different displays can be used to add graphics to the physical output. Previous work has explored integrating LED lights for color and illumination into shape display pins [23]. To overcome the low resolution of shape displays, high-resolution visual content can also be projected onto the shape rendering. This makes it possible to synchronize the 3D capture of geometry with a video stream that is projection-mapped onto a dynamic, physical surface topology.

Augmented Reality. With Sublimate, we showed how AR can add registered virtual content that extends beyond the range of the shape display [14]. This allows content that is floating in mid-air, has variable opacity, uses complex shapes, or has other properties that are not physically feasible or practical using current shape display technology.

Complimentary Displays. Other communication tools can be added to complement shape rendering, such as a vertical screen that give users face-to-face video. The video can, e.g.,

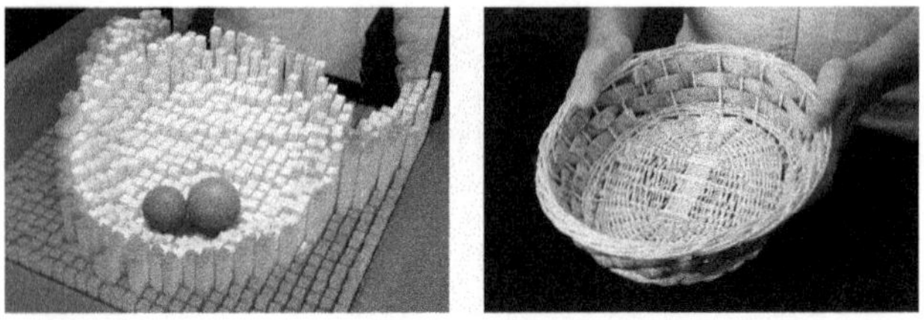

Figure 4. Improvising with physical objects: Using a basket to scoop up remote balls.

be aligned with the shape rendering to provide the illusion that the physical hands are coming out of the screen.

Switching between Representations. It may be advantageous to switch between these representations. A tangible token, e.g., could be represented by a remote tangible object, but if the remote user does not have enough tokens a physical rendering can be used instead (see Figure 3). Hands can be represented as physical renderings when manipulating an object, or as a virtual rendering when pointing or annotating (see Figure 7). These state transitions are in part inspired by our Sublimate concept [14].

PHYSICALLY MANIPULATING REMOTE OBJECTS

Prior work [7, 5] has shown how shape displays can be used to manipulate physical objects, e.g., using translation and rotation. Here, we explore different control schemes to allow a user to manipulate remote objects. Using shape capture and display, users can reach through the network and pick up a remote physical object. These interaction techniques were developed through iterative prototyping with our inFORM system. Hundreds of visitors to our lab tried different techniques to manipulate objects remotely, and their comments and our observations lead us to develop and improve the following techniques.

Gesture Control

Direct Gesture Control allows a user to interact directly with a remote tangible object through transmitted physical embodiment, which is rendered on the remote shape display. The rendered shape of the user directly applies a force to objects placed on the surface. For example, if the user forms a cup with the hands and raises them, this will be rendered and the pins could move a ball upwards. By observing the reaction of the physical object to their transmitted gestures, users can improvise to expressively manipulate a variety of objects. While our shape displays currently apply vertical forces, objects can still be translated laterally by tilting and sliding [7]. In addition to users' hands and arms, any object that is placed in the shape capture area can be transmitted and used to manipulate remote objects (see Figure 4). Because our shape display, based on inFORM [7], can only render shapes 0-100 mm in height, there is a question of how to render the remote environment, which most likely extends beyond 100 mm in height. We explored two mappings: Scaled and 1:1 with gesture zones. The scaled mapping takes all depth data and maps its height values to the shape display's maximum extent. The second mapping, 1:1 with gesture zones, take some portion of the input space that is the same height as the maximum height travel and renders it on the shape display. This can be directly

Figure 5. Pushing against the side of a shape-rendered objects with the brush tool moves it.

above the surface, or mid air, allowing users to touch the pin array without manipulating remote objects. In our teleoperation scenario we use a 1:1 mapping, with the gesture zone of physical rendering starting right above the horizontal screen.

Mediated Gesture Control exploits that the remote object's pose is tracked and can be updated and moved to keep it synchronized with its underlying digital model [7]. *Physics-based Gestures* detect the user's collisions with the model, to update and move it, using a physics library. The updated model then causes the remote object to be physically moved. This is similar to the proxy-based approach in HoloDesk [10], but with actuated physical output. *Iconic Gestures* provide users with more abstract control. The user can pinch over the representation of the remote object to grab it, move their arm to another location, and open the pinch gesture to release it. The remote object is then actuated by the system to move to that location.

Interface Elements

Interface elements, such as virtual menus, can be projected around the rendering of a remote object to provide access to different operations. *Dynamically rendered physical affordances* [7], such as buttons or handles, that appear around the remote objects can be used for control. The user could press, push or pull such affordances to move the object.

Tangibles and Physical Tools

Tangible Tokens can be used to control a remote object. As the user moves the token, the model of the remote object is updated, and the remote object is moved to reflect the changed state. Two tangible tokens can be linked such that moving one causes the other to move, and vice versa, allowing for bi-directional control [19].

Tools allow users to manipulate remote objects by interacting with the local physical rendering. Tools can provide additional degrees of freedom (DOFs) of input, when interacting with the rendering. Our brush tool, for example, allows users to push remote objects (see Figure 5). The bristles of the brush serve two purposes. First, they decrease the friction between the tool and the pins, which may get stuck when a lateral force is applied. Second, they smooth the haptic feedback resulting from the discrete, jerky motion when a physically rendered object is translated on a limited resolution shape display. To determine the direction in which to move the object, the brush tool's pose is tracked by an overhead camera, while a mechanical switch senses pressure.

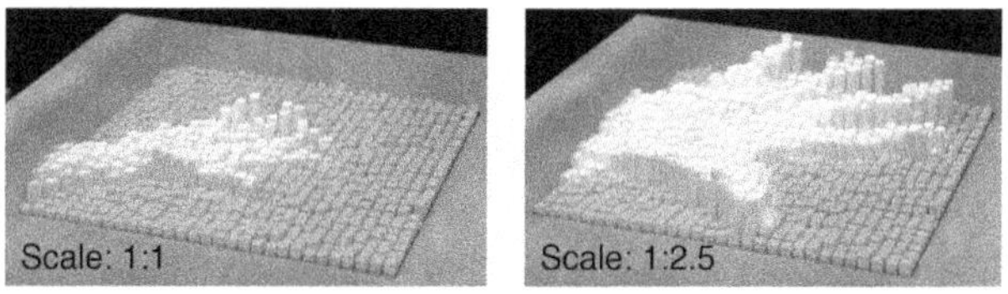

Figure 6. Scaling a users hand to interact with larger objects.

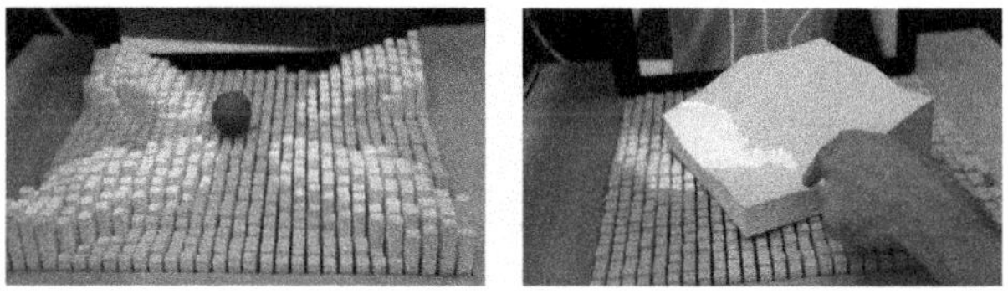

Figure 7. Copying and rendering multiple hands simultaneously (left) and switching to a virtual, non-physical, representation (right).

COMPUTER-MEDIATED SHAPE I/O

While shape capture and output literally adds a physical dimension to telecommunication, we find it interesting to go beyond representations that are symmetric in time and space. How can we create interfaces that enable remote participants to go beyond physically being there? The relaxation of 1:1 capture/output mapping opens up significant potential for new interaction techniques. Consider, e.g., an audio system with real-time translation of a speaker's voice to the listener's language. Here, the mediation emphasizes the relevant and simplifies the interaction. The introduction of shape output allows us to apply similar transformation concepts to the physical domain. We explore shape mediation, such as transformation of physical form, altered representation, data filtering and replication, changing motion dynamics and time-domain manipulations.

Transformation of Physical Form: Bending Body Limits

In our system, users can apply transformations to their activity in the remote environment, for example with scaling, translation, rotation, shearing, stretching and other distortions. Translation offsets geometry and can extend reach, with potential ergonomic benefits. Scaling can make a hand larger or smaller for manipulation of objects of varying sizes (see Figure 6). A small hand could avoid undesirable collisions in dense topologies, while an enlarged hand could carry multiple items. The transformations allow continuous real-time changes during the interaction, e.g., enabling smooth changes in size or position while holding an object. Examples of other transformations include replication or mirroring, e.g., to approach objects from multiple angles.

Altered Representation: Becoming Something Else

With user and object tracking, there are benefits to switching representation for new capabilities. A system that captures geometry does not need to propagate all of it. It may be useful to just send a user's hand and not the arm. As we are only limited by what the shape display can render, we can also morph into other tools that are optimal for the task, while controlled by the user. Examples include grippers, bowls, ramps, and claws — tools with specific properties that facilitate or constrain the interactions (see Figure 8 and 9). The tools could

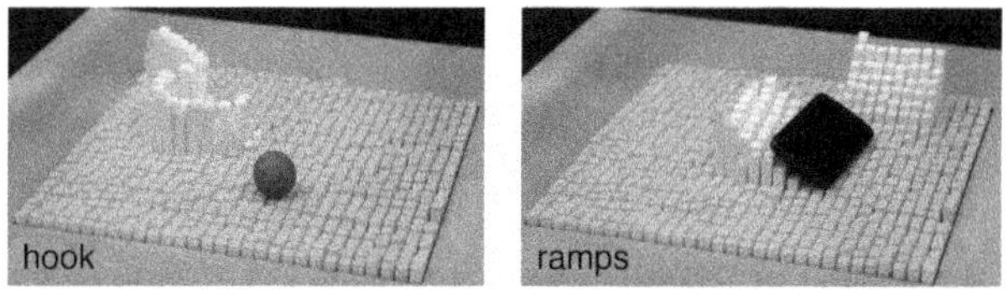

Figure 8. Replacing hands with a hook to reach or ramps to slide objects.

Figure 9. The claw tool open and closed to enclose and move an object.

also be animated or semi-autonomously use the sensed geometry on the remote side to influence their behavior. Switching to a purely graphical representation to avoid collisions, is another example (see Figure 7).

Filtering: Adding and Removing Motion

Signal processing can be applied to refine propagated motion, e.g., using smoothing or low-pass/high-pass filters. Such approaches are in use, e.g., in surgical robotics where hand tremors can be suppressed. Our system could also prevent fast motion or access to protected areas to avoid involuntary movements. In addition to reducing human noise, it may also alleviate system limitations, such as sampling resolution, speed, range and vibrations.

Motion Dynamics: Warping Time

Non-linear mapping of the propagated motion is interesting for many interactions. The properties of certain remote artifacts might, e.g., require slower or faster mapped motion, or require brief freezing or slow-down to emphasize an effect or make it legible. Such manipulations of time need, however, to be designed with great care, as they break the temporal link between the remote locations.

PROTOTYPE APPLICATIONS

Telepresence Workspace

When discussing a physical design over distance, it is important for both parties to have an understanding of a shared model. We propose to render physical models on shape displays during remote collaboration meetings. The shape output is combined with video for viewing the upper body and face of remote collaborators. By aligning the tabletop shape display with the vertical screen, the two collaborators perceive a shared physical workspace, where the remote person can reach out of the vertical screen to physically point at a model. We support collaboration through shape rendering in several ways:

Shared Digital Model. The model is mirrored on the remote shape displays and provides a shared frame of reference.

Transmitted Physical Model. When a user places a physical model onto the surface, its shape and texture is transmitted to the remote site.

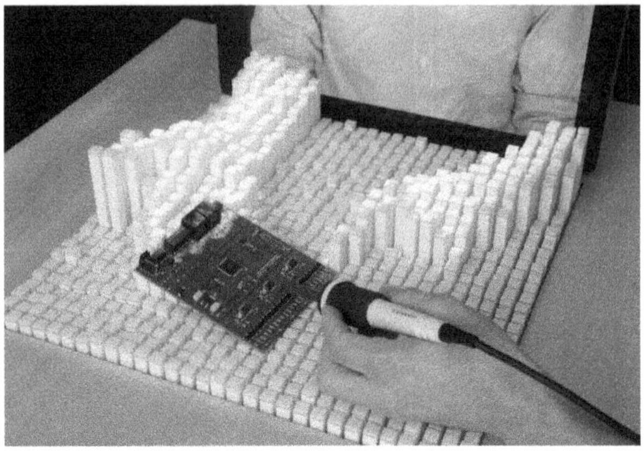

Figure 10. Remote assistance: A remote expert helps a local user by supporting the workpiece with one hand and pointing with the other.

Physically-rendered Remote Collaborators. When a user reaches out and places a hand on the table, its shape is physically rendered at the remote site. This conveys presence and enables remote pointing and manipulation. Figure 10 shows an example application, where a remote expert supports a local user.

Unidirectional Shape Output

The shape output link described in the above scenarios can be uni- or bidirectional. An ideal bidirectional configuration, where both sites have a shape display, may not always be feasible due to size, cost and required infrastructure. A unidirectional link is still advantageous, as it allows remote participants to be more present with physically rendered body representations. It makes it possible to also capture and transmit physical objects to the remote site.

Collaborative 3D Modeling

A specific example of a telepresence workspace with a shared digital model is collaborative 3D modeling. In this case, users can deform the model, with any change reflected through the model on the connected site (see Figure 11). However, rendering the remote person's hands may obstruct the changes to the model. Therefore, our application allows switching to rendering the model geometry without the user's hands.

Another consideration is the potential conflict that may occur when two users try to simultaneously deform a model. We therefore use a turn-taking protocol for manipulation. When the system detects deformation, control is passed to the active user. The changes will be reflected on the remote connected model, while concurrent remote input is ignored. When the user stops modifying the model, the collaborator at the remote site may take control by starting a new deformation. Passing control between users can be applied to the whole model or to each pin individually.

Shared Presence: Connected Membranes

This application conveys the presence of remote participants through a shared digital membrane that uses two connected shape displays, each rendering the inverse shape of the other (see Figure 12). When a users pushes down a pin, the corresponding remote pin pops out. This is conceptually similar to a physical link between the pins. We implemented two modes:

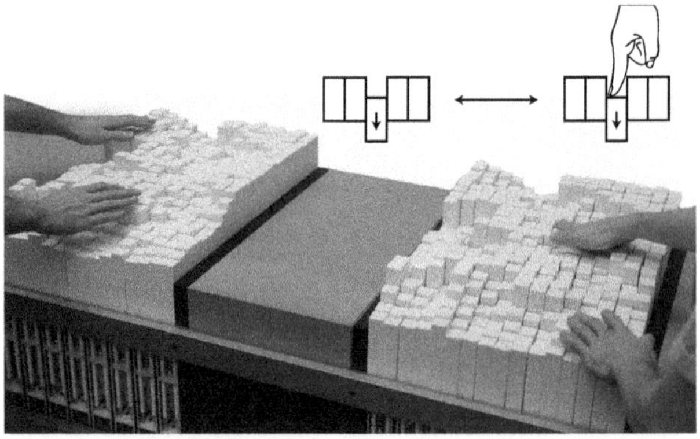

Figure 11. Collaborative 3D modeling of two linked landscape models.

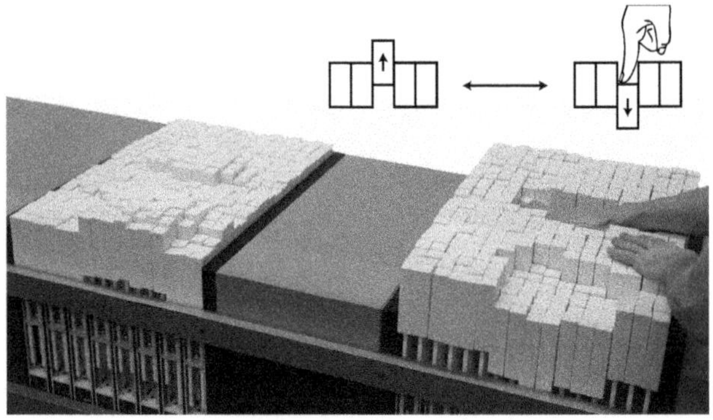

Figure 12. Connected Membrane: When a user pushes into the membrane on one site, the inverse shape appears at the other.

Pin screen. Pins remain in their position after users push or pull them. This leaves behind a trace of past deformations, until it is erased.

Elastic. Pins always spring back to a neutral flat state when they are not being deformed. This mode conveys whether someone on the other end is pushing at that very moment.

TECHNICAL IMPLEMENTATION

Shape Output

Our proposed systems utilize 2.5D shape displays, which consist of arrays of linear actuators.

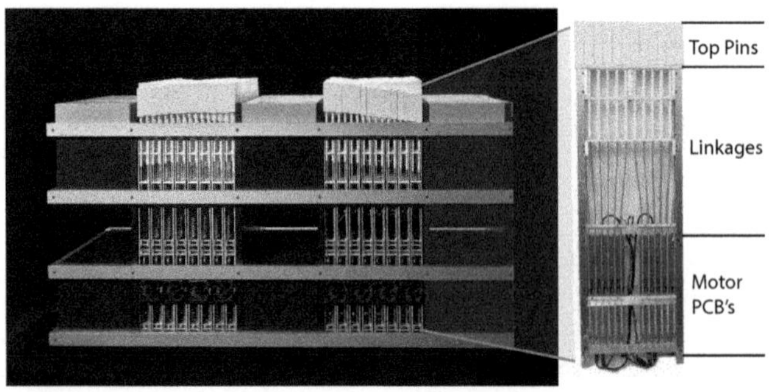

Figure 13. Side view of the TRANSFORM system with a single 12x2 actuation module.

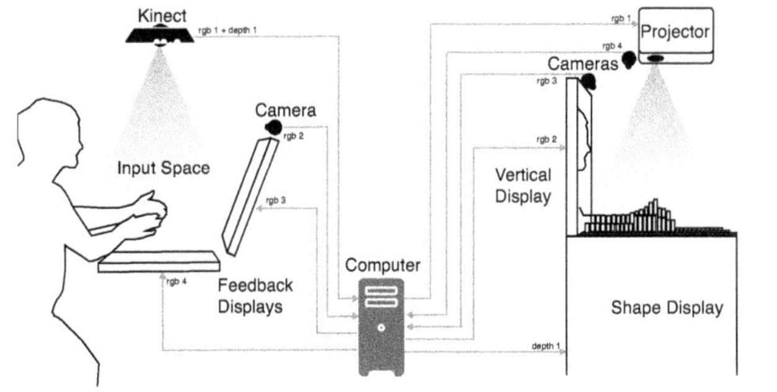

Figure 14. System diagram of the telemanipulation system using shape capture and remore shape display.

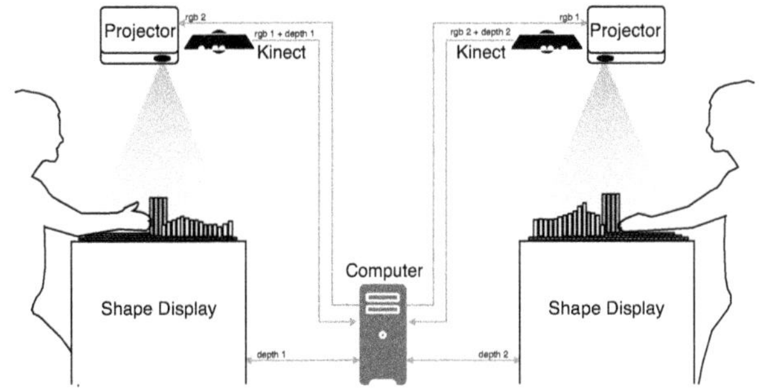

Figure 15. System diagram of connected workspaces with bidirectional shape capture and shape rendering.

The *inFORM* platform [7] consists of 30×30 individually actuated, plastic pins, built into a tabletop. The pins cover an area of 381×381 mm with each pin measuring 9.5×9.5 mm with 3.175 mm spacing between pins, and they can extend up to 100 mm in height. Actuation speed is 0.644 m/s and each pin can exert up to 1.08 Newtons.

TRANSFORM is a platform based on actuator modules with 2×12 styrene pins on an area of 305×50.8 mm, which extend up to 100 mm from the surface (see Figure 13). The individual actuators and control boards are the same as used by inFORM. The modules can be seamlessly combined to form a larger shape display surface. We created two shape displays, 16×24 pins each, covering an area of 406.4×610 mm.

The shape display hardware uses custom Arduino boards that run a PID controller to sense and move the positions of 6 connected styrene pins through motorized slide potentiometers. Our applications are written in C++/OpenFrameworks and support 3D models (OBJ) and grayscale images as contents. The application renders a depth image, which is sent to the shape display over USB to RS485. Graphics from OpenGL are projected onto the white shape display pins through a calibrated ceiling-mounted projector (see [7] for details).

Sensing Shape Deformation Input

The pin positions that are reported from the shape display to the computer can be used to detect when a person deforms the surface. By comparing the shape image sent to the display and the position image received from the display, any deformation will be visible as a discrepancy. As the physical shape rendering contains some noise and the motors require a certain time to reach their target position, our detection algorithm thresholds the deformation image and compensates for the time delay. This filtering is critical when sharing the depth information with a connected system, as the network delay and added noise can result in a feedback loop that results in false deformation detection.

Tracking People and Objects With a Depth Camera

We track objects and gestures with a depth camera (first-generation Microsoft Kinect, 640×480@30 Hz). The 8-bit depth image is cropped, scaled and thresholded to fit to the size of the interaction area. The values are then normalized to match the range of the shape display. Our algorithm analyses the depth image to differentiate between the users' hands, shared tangible objects and arbitrary geometry. Hands are detected contours that touch the image boundary. After detecting the tip of the hand, its shape can be replaced by a tool. Shared tangible objects are colored spheres, which are tracked through their size and color.

Latency and Manipulating Objects

The latency of our telemanipulation system, see Figure 14, is between 150 and 200 ms, depending on the amount and direction of travel for the pins. This is inline with latency used for other types of telemanipulation systems [16] and its impact is lessened by the lack of haptic feedback to the remote user. The latency is caused by a number of factors, such as the latency of the depth camera, depth image processing, communication bus, motor speed, and the camera and video latency for displaying to the remote user. Latency causes problems for keeping remote connected objects in sync, as shown in Figure 3. In order to adress this, we track the current position of the local object and move it at a controlled rate to the updated target position (dictated by the remote object).

PRELIMINARY EVALUATION

Demonstrations at our lab of the teleoperation system to hundreds of users provided us with many interesting informal insights. Although the limited degrees of freedom of the system do not perfectly map to operations such as real-world grasping, lifting, and moving of objects, it does still provide meaningful interaction due to its real-world physics. We wished to examine this further in a controlled, qualitative study, to get a more nuanced picture of remote object manipulation strategies and interaction techniques.

In this preliminary evaluation we focus on teleoperation, since we believe that our techniques for remote physical manipulation introduce and enable significant new capabilities. We were particularely interested in the gestures that participants would use.

Apparatus

We used our telemanipulation setup (see Figure 14), where participants were in the same room as the shape display, but visually separated by a divider (see Figure 16). The remote environment is shown with an orthographic 1:1 top-down view on a horizontal display, and a perspective view on a

Figure 16. Setup of the telemanipulation study. Left: The participant's gestures are captured and two screens provide visual feedback. Right: Shape output moves the target ball.

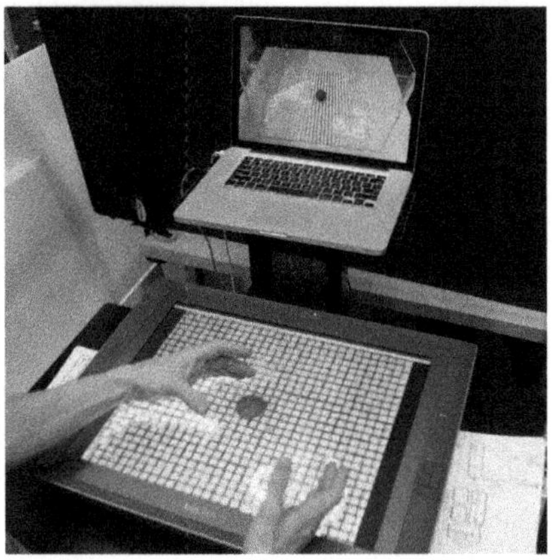

Figure 17. Participant's view of the remote scene, with a top down 1:1 view on the horizontal screen, and a perspective view on the vertical.

vertical display. An overhead, depth-sensing camera tracks gestures above the horizontal display (see Figure 17).

Participants

We recruited 8 participants (2 female), ages 21–37 years old from our institution, who were compensated with 15 USD. All were daily computer users, 5 were monthly users of depth-sensing devices (e.g., Microsoft Kinect). Sessions lasted 45–60 min.

Task, Conditions and Procedure

The three tasks required the participant to move a remote wooden sphere (⌀4 cm) to a target location (⌀5 cm). Users were not required to hold the ball in the target, only to touch (overlap greater than 50%) or cross it.

1. *2D docking*. Randomized target position projected on the remote surface, and 30 cm away from previous target for consistent task difficulty.
2. *3D docking*. Randomized target position as before, but at a height between 40–80 mm.
3. *Obstacle*. Participants were instructed to not knock over the obstacle (water bottle, ⌀7 cm, 20 cm in height) that was placed at the center of the surface, in a variation of the 2D docking task.

There were four interaction technique conditions:

1. *Dominant hand*.

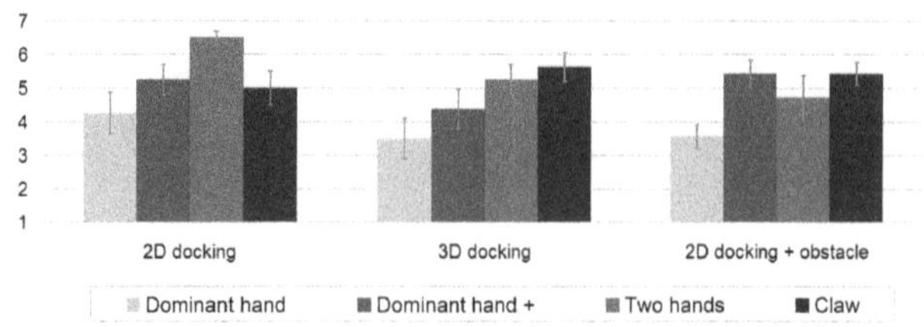

Figure 18. Averages of users' ratings of task difficulty for 4 different input conditions in each task. (7-point likert scale, 7 is best/easiest). Error Bars are standard error of the mean (SEM).

2. *Dominant hand+*, which could be scaled, rotated or switched to virtual-only, by button press with the non-dominant hand.
3. *Two hands*.
4. *Claw* representation of dominant hand. Non-dominant hand could press a button to open and close the claw.

Participants had 5–10 minutes to familiarize themselves with the 4 different interaction techniques. Conditions were randomized and counterbalanced across participants. After each task, participants rated task difficulty in each condition and provided explanations. A post-test questionnaire had the participants provide additional comments. Video was recorded and reviewed for interaction patterns.

Results and Discussion

All users successfully completed all tasks. While some users noticed the system latency of 200 ms, they did not comment that it impeded them. However, we observed that all users adjusted their gesture speed when moving objects to compensate for latency effects. Because of our interest in emerging use patterns and a small sample size, we focus on reporting qualitative data and feedback.

The ratings (1–7, 7 is best/easiest) indicate that different techniques were preferred in different scenarios (Figure 18). Participants preferred using two hands in 2D docking, using the claw for 3D docking, and using one hand that could be transformed or the claw in the third, obstacle-avoiding task. The scores matched our observations and post-test interviews.

Qualitative user feedback

Two hands for the *2D task* was intuitive and similar to how one would move a real ball. *"Moving the ball with two hands was a much more natural interaction for me"* Participants also used hand gestures similar to how they would in real life. *"When I had to claw the ball, I could psychologically and physiologically feel the pressure of grabbing it, although it was virtual."*

Using two hands was the most effective strategy in 2D, since participants could better enclose the ball, stop it, or move it. There were, however, other strategies: *"The biggest challenge was whether the cupping object (hand or claw) would sufficiently enclose the ball to prevent it from rolling away while moving it. The claw, scaled hand, and two hands were all large enough to easily move the ball, but the scale control was the only mode that allowed for tuning the size."*

In the *3D docking task*, raising the ball without having it fall out of the remote hands, was a challenge for many participants. The claw tool was more popular here, as it constrained the ball well during 3D movement.

Real-world collaborative workspaces tend to have many objects in use. We were interested in how users would handle additional obstacles, without haptic feedback. As expected, participants found the *obstacle task* the most challenging, while also the most realistic. *"Two hands were surprisingly frustrating in comparison to the prior tasks because they take up more space"*. But participants were able to use a variety of different representations to more easily complete the tasks.

The claw's small footprint simplified navigation around objects. *"It enabled me to move the ball without having my arm get in the way. Rotating the view while using one hand also worked fairly well because it enabled me to adjust my trajectory to avoid the obstacle"*

Other participants preferred the invisible hand for obstacle avoidance. *"...most useful to go around the obstacles."* But in general this technique was harder for people to discover. *"It took me a while to get a hang of the transparent feature, but it was good because it made my interaction faster, and give it a mouse like feel where I could hover and not click as when you use a mouse."* Participants also commented on picking up objects: *"I also found myself wanting a way to come from below an object – and didnt realize until much later that this is what the ghost/invisible mode enables."*

Observed patterns of use

A number of techniques were used to manipulate the remote object and we outline the most prevalent. To avoid bias, we had not given any instructions on gestures.

- *Push:* Hand (sideways like paddle), back of the hand, index finger, back of the arm, V-shape with fingers (thumb + index).
- *Hook:* Hook shape with hand (bring object closer).
- *Flicking:* Flick object with index finger.
- *Ghost:* Switch to virtual, move inside object, switch to shape to pick up.
- Scoop: Cup hands, scoop and move around. *"Two hands were easier to use when I had my palms close together. "*
- Capture: Approach with two opposing V-shaped hands.

Our overall observation on the gestures emerging during the study was that participants adapted quickly to the degrees of freedom supported by the system and did not try to grasp the object. Instead, everyone interacted as if the remote sphere was a slippery object; pushing it sideways to translate on the surface, and scooping it with cupped hands to move in 3D.

LIMITATIONS AND FUTURE WORK

Many of the limitations of Physical Telepresence are related to the hardware used to implement it.

2.5D rendering using physical pins limits our system's DOFs to rendering reliefs and prevents overhangs. This is especially important for telemanipulation, since it only allows application of vertical forces to surface objects. The system can thus not grasp objects [3], only lift them or translate them by tilting and sliding. Robotic grippers could, however, be combined with shape displays to provide more dexterous manipulation. Shape displays with more DOFs of output can also be explored to allow lateral forces with more intricate control. Latency, as discussed, is another parameter that limits remote manipulation, and further improvements in hardware and interaction techniques could address this.

Limited resolution of current shape displays affect what content can be represented. Due to sampling requirements we need to have a resolution twice that of the smallest feature to be able to clearly display it. We observed this issue when rendering fingers (2 cm wide) on our shape display with 2.54 cm spacing. Increasing the resolution and pin travel will allow for more complex content and more realistic representation of remote users.

Collisions between remote and local objects can affect the possible physical rendering. We implement techniques to address this, such as not physically rendering geometry where users' hands are on the local surface. More compliant shape displays could be built using soft actuators [6, 8]. In addition, users cannot reach inside a rendered object, as is possible with virtual graphics [10]. Our previously introduced Sublimate system, however, provides an approach that combines AR and shape rendering [14].

Network latency was not investigated with our current systems, as these were not deployed as distributed setups. However, the effect of latency is a critical factor for effective remote manipulation, and further studies are required to investigate how it will affect operator performance.

In addition to the limitations of shape display hardware, further work and evaluation is needed to explore new types of interaction techniques to control these different renderings of remote participants.

Beyond these improvements to the system, we would also like to further explore other application domains, such as education, medical, and industrial. We envision that teachers could show remote students how to play instruments, and slow down the playback of their hands so pupils could see more clearly, while doctors could use Physical Telepresence for telepalpation of remote patients.

CONCLUSIONS

We have introduced the space of Physical Telepresence enabled by shape capture and shape display in a shared workspace context. Physical Telepresence allows for the physical embodiment and manipulation of remote users, environments, objects, and shared digital models. By loosening the 1:1 link in shape capture and remote shape output, we have begun to explore how remote users can go beyond physically being there. In addition, we highlighted a number of application domains and example applications that show how Physical Telepresence can be put to use for shared work on 3D models, remote assistance, or communication.

ACKNOWLEDGMENTS

We thank Philipp Schoessler, Mark Feldmeier, James Patten, Jen Lusker, David Doan, Melinda Cross, Clara Rhee and the members of the Tangible Media Group. This research was supported in part by the National Science Foundation Graduate Research Fellowship under Grant No. 1122374 and the Swedish Research Council.

REFERENCES

1. Benko, H., Jota, R., and Wilson, A. MirageTable: freehand interaction on a projected augmented reality tabletop. In *ACM CHI '12* (2012), 199–208.
2. Brave, S., Ishii, H., and Dahley, A. Tangible interfaces for remote collaboration and communication. In *ACM CSCW '98* (Nov. 1998), 169–178.
3. Cutkosky, M., and Howe, R. Human grasp choice and robotic grasp analysis. In *Dextrous Robot Hands*, S. Venkataraman and T. Iberall, Eds. Springer New York, 1990, 5–31.
4. Everitt, K. M., Klemmer, S. R., Lee, R., and Landay, J. A. Two worlds apart: bridging the gap between physical and virtual media for distributed design collaboration. In *ACM CHI '03* (Apr. 2003), 553–560.
5. Festo. WaveHandling:Transporting and sorting in one. In *http://www.festo.com/cms/en_corp/13136.htm* (2013).
6. Follmer, S., Leithinger, D., Olwal, A., Cheng, N., and Ishii, H. Jamming user interfaces: programmable particle stiffness and sensing for malleable and shape-changing devices. In *ACM UIST '12* (Oct. 2012), 519–528.
7. Follmer, S., Leithinger, D., Olwal, A., Hogge, A., and Ishii, H. inFORM: dynamic physical affordances and constraints through shape and object actuation. In *ACM UIST '13* (Oct. 2013), 417–426.
8. Genecov, A. M., Stanley, A. A., and Okamura, A. M. Perception of a Haptic Jamming display: Just noticeable differences in stiffness and geometry. In *2014 IEEE Haptics Symposium (HAPTICS)*, IEEE (Feb. 2014), 333–338.
9. Gross, M., Lang, S., Strehlke, K., Moere, A. V., Staadt, O., Würmlin, S., Naef, M., Lamboray, E., Spagno, C., Kunz, A., Koller-Meier, E., Svoboda, T., and Van Gool, L. blue-c: a spatially immersive display and 3D video portal for telepresence. *ACM Transactions on Graphics 22*, 3 (July 2003), 819–827.
10. Hilliges, O., Kim, D., Izadi, S., Weiss, M., and Wilson, A. HoloDesk: direct 3d interactions with a situated see-through display. In *ACM CHI '12* (May 2012), 2421–2430.
11. Ishii, H., and Kobayashi, M. ClearBoard: a seamless medium for shared drawing and conversation with eye contact. In *ACM CHI '92* (June 1992), 525–532.
12. Iwata, H., Yano, H., Nakaizumi, F., and Kawamura, R. Project FEELEX: adding haptic surface to graphics. In *ACM SIGGRAPH '01* (Aug. 2001), 469–476.
13. Lee, M. K., and Takayama, L. "Now, i have a body": uses and social norms for mobile remote presence in the workplace. In *ACM CHI '11* (May 2011), 33–42.
14. Leithinger, D., Follmer, S., Olwal, A., Luescher, S., Hogge, A., Lee, J., and Ishii, H. Sublimate: state-changing virtual and physical rendering to augment interaction with shape displays. In *ACM CHI '13* (Apr. 2013), 1441–1450.
15. Leithinger, D., Lakatos, D., DeVincenzi, A., Blackshaw, M., and Ishii, H. Direct and gestural interaction with relief: a 2.5D shape display. In *ACM UIST '11* (Oct. 2011), 541–548.
16. Lum, M. J., Rosen, J., Lendvay, T. S., Sinanan, M. N., and Hannaford, B. Effect of time delay on telesurgical performance. In *IEEE ICRA'09* (2009), 4246–4252.
17. Mann, S. Telepointer: Hands-Free Completely Self Contained Wearable Visual Augmented Reality without Headwear and without any Infrastructural Reliance. In *2012 16th International Symposium on Wearable Computers* (Oct. 2000), 177–178.
18. Mueller, F. F., Cole, L., O'Brien, S., and Walmink, W. Airhockey over a distance. In *CHI '06 extended abstracts* (Apr. 2006), 1133–1138.
19. Pangaro, G., Maynes-Aminzade, D., and Ishii, H. The actuated workbench: computer-controlled actuation in tabletop tangible interfaces. In *ACM UIST '02* (Oct. 2002), 181–190.
20. Paul, R. P. *Robot manipulators: mathematics, programming, and control: the computer control of robot manipulators.* Richard Paul, 1981.
21. Paulos, E., and Canny, J. PRoP: personal roving presence. In *ACM CHI '98* (Jan. 1998), 296–303.
22. Piper, B., and Ishii, H. PegBlocks: a learning aid for the elementary classroom. In *ACM CHI '02 extended abstracts* (Apr. 2002), 686–687.
23. Poupyrev, I., Nashida, T., and Okabe, M. Actuation and Tangible User Interfaces: the Vaucanson Duck, Robots, and Shape Displays. In *ACM TEI '07* (Feb. 2007), 205–212.
24. Raskar, R., Welch, G., Cutts, M., Lake, A., Stesin, L., and Fuchs, H. The office of the future: a unified approach to image-based modeling and spatially immersive displays. In *ACM SIGGRAPH '98* (July 1998), 179–188.
25. Rasmussen, M. K., Pedersen, E. W., Petersen, M. G., and Hornbæ k, K. Shape-changing interfaces: a review of the design space and open research questions. In *ACM CHI '12* (May 2012), 735–744.
26. Richter, J., Thomas, B. H., Sugimoto, M., and Inami, M. Remote active tangible interactions. In *ACM TEI '07* (Feb. 2007), 39–42.
27. Riedenklau, E., Hermann, T., and Ritter, H. An integrated multi-modal actuated tangible user interface for distributed collaborative planning. In *ACM TEI '12* (Feb. 2012), 169–174.
28. Sodhi, R. S., Jones, B. R., Forsyth, D., Bailey, B. P., and Maciocci, G. BeThere: 3D mobile collaboration with spatial input. In *ACM CHI '13* (Apr. 2013), 179–188.
29. Staub, C., Ono, K., Mayer, H., Knoll, A., Ulbrich, H., and Bauernschmitt, R. Remote minimally invasive surgery –haptic feedback and selective automation in medical robotics. *Applied Bionics and Biomechanics 8*, 2 (Apr. 2011), 221–236.
30. Tang, J. C., and Minneman, S. VideoWhiteboard: video shadows to support remote collaboration. In *ACM CHI '91* (Mar. 1991), 315–322.
31. Tang, J. C., and Minneman, S. L. Videodraw: a video interface for collaborative drawing. *ACM Transactions on Information Systems 9*, 2 (Apr. 1991), 170–184.
32. Tsui, K. M., Desai, M., Yanco, H. A., and Uhlik, C. Exploring use cases for telepresence robots. In *ACM/IEEE HRI '11* (Mar. 2011), 11–18.
33. Wilson, A. D., and Robbins, D. C. Playtogether: Playing games across multiple interactive tabletops. In *IUI Workshop on Tangible Play: Research and Design for Tangible and Tabletop Games* (2007).
34. Yarosh, S., Tang, A., Mokashi, S., and Abowd, G. D. "almost touching": parent-child remote communication using the sharetable system. In *ACM CSCW '13* (Feb. 2013), 181–192.

3D-Board: A Whole-body Remote Collaborative Whiteboard

Jakob Zillner[1], Christoph Rhemann[2], Shahram Izadi[2], Michael Haller[1]

[1]Media Interaction Lab, University of Applied Sciences Upper Austria
[2]Microsoft Research

ABSTRACT

This paper presents *3D-Board*, a digital whiteboard capable of capturing life-sized virtual embodiments of geographically distributed users. When using large-scale screens for remote collaboration, awareness for the distributed users' gestures and actions is of particular importance. Our work adds to the literature on remote collaborative workspaces, it facilitates intuitive remote collaboration on large scale interactive whiteboards by preserving awareness of the full-body pose and gestures of the remote collaborator. By blending the front-facing 3D embodiment of a remote collaborator with the shared workspace, an illusion is created as if the observer was looking through the transparent whiteboard into the remote user's room. The system was tested and verified in a usability assessment, showing that *3D-Board* significantly improves the effectiveness of remote collaboration on a large interactive surface.

Author Keywords

Remote Collaboration, Shared workspace, Teleconferencing, Interactive Whiteboard, Reconstruction

Figure 1: The virtual 3D embodiment of a remote user superimposed on top of the digital content of the interactive whiteboard.

INTRODUCTION

Interactive whiteboards in combination with video conferencing systems are becoming evermore popular. In current solutions, the video image of a geographically distributed user and the shared workspace are separated resulting in a cumbersome collaboration. Systems such as [20, 12] demonstrate that superimposing the life-sized video of a remote user on top of the shared content can improve the cooperation. These related solutions mainly focus on 2D video images, showing a rear-view of the distributed participants. This paper presents *3D-Board*, a whiteboard featuring a novel visualization of the collaborator enhancing the experience of working remotely.

With *3D-Board*, we facilitate social presence in a shared working environment by blending a front-facing 3D embodiment of the remote user with the digital content of the interactive whiteboard (cf. Figure 1). Our solution creates the impression as if the remote collaborator would stand behind the shared, interactive whiteboard. Summarizing, the main contributions of this paper are:

- Enabling remote face-to-face collaboration on a large, interactive surface without the need for a holographic screen or half-silvered mirror, with a simple and new front-facing visualization technique.
- A study that demonstrates the benefits of our visualization technique that supports full body 3D virtual embodiment of the remote user. Our study shows that the 3D front facing approach improves the user awareness and provides additional features that makes remote collaboration tasks more efficient.
- Robustly segmenting the remote user from the background scene to avoid occlusion when superimposing the transparent, virtual embodiment on top of any digital content.
- And finally, our hardware setup is a self-contained unit, since all cameras can be easily mounted on the edges of a whiteboard and do not have to be behind or in front of the screen.

UIST '14, Oct 5 – Oct 8 2014, Honolulu, HI, USA
Copyright 2014 ACM 978-1-4503-3069-5/14/10...$15.00.
http://dx.doi.org/10.1145/2642918.2647393

The design and results of this study are discussed after setting the context in the related work section and presenting our implementation. Finally, the overall findings are discussed alongside future work.

RELATED WORK

Facilitating awareness for the remote user is one of the most important challenges in computer supported cooperative working environments. Distributed tabletop and whiteboard applications often provide user embodiments to improve the awareness among collaborators [2]. Therefore, deictic gestures and gestures in general are highly essential for a distributed conversation [9, 14, 8].

Although the video image is serving as the connection between the distributed users [3], the video has to fuse with the actual shared content into a single, common workspace [21, 18, 25, 16, 26]. ClearBoard [15] is one of the most inspiring setups that combines face-to-face conversation and shared drawing activities into one screen. Based on the ideas of ClearBoard, Gumienny et al. developed Tele-Board [12]. Tele-Board features video- and data-conferencing by overlaying the transparent content of an interactive whiteboard over the full-screen rear or side video view of the remote collaborators. Similarly, CollaBoard [20] separates the user from the background to superimpose the full-sized back-view of the upper body on top of the digital data. While this approach provides accurate deictic gestures, natural interaction is limited since the face-to-face communication is restricted.

Our work is also inspired by Onespace [21], which utilizes a depth-sensing camera to segment users from the background and to get their position in 3D space. Therefore, a 2D representation can be placed in a virtual environment and the distributed partners can collaboratively interact with their digital surroundings. The front-view makes gaze-awareness and gestures possible, but the depth-sensing cameras force users to keep a certain distance to the screen. In addition, a mirrored representation of the co-located person needs to be displayed in order to raise the awareness of one's position in 3D space.

Maimone et al. [22] use multiple depth-sensing cameras to capture a scene in 3D. The reconstructed scene can then be viewed by utilizing a head-tracking system and an auto stereoscopic display. Similarly, Beck et al. present an immersive group-to-group telepresence setup by using multiple Kinect sensors [1]. TeleHuman [19] is a videoconferencing system that uses a cylindrical 3D display portal to feature a 360° view of a geographically distributed user. By supporting stereoscopic 3D and motion parallax, the system is capable of conveying accurate hand pointing gestures and body poses. Edelmann et al. focus on the interaction with digital content [7]. The system features a stereo camera setup behind a semi-transparent holographic multi-touch screen to capture the remote scene. This allows for a natural face-to-face collaboration on the interactive surface. However, the need for shutter glasses and the opaque holographic screen disrupt the telepresence experience. In addition, the remote user is not separated from the background, thus the video occludes much of the workspace.

The visualization and presentation of the virtual embodiment has a vast influence on the workspace awareness. Different possibilities have mostly been evaluated in the context of tabletops [6, 10, 27, 23]. Doucette et al. [6], for instance, used different levels of abstraction for arm embodiments while interacting with the tabletop. The remote collaborator therefore sees the local user's arms as either just a thin line, a colorized arm, or as a real picture. In the context of a tabletop setup, the results clearly show that almost all digital arm embodiments, regardless of the level of abstraction, do not significantly raise the awareness for the remote user. However, when dealing with interactive whiteboards, the presence of a virtual embodiment is highly relevant since the full body of the collaborator is visible. Gaze awareness [28], facial expressions, and hand pointing [17] play an important role while interacting with another person on such devices. By utilizing a large see-through display and face detection, Tan et al. [24] developed a system supporting eye contact and gaze by offsetting the video stream based on the viewer's position.

In contrast to the related work, our system is encumbrance free, featuring a 3D view of the remote collaborator without the need for shutter glasses. Utilizing the full size of the screen, the virtual embodiment can be placed over any digital content. Moreover, *3D-Board* features a natural face-to-face visualization of the remote user, without having to place a camera behind an opaque screen.

3D-BOARD

Creating the impression of looking through an interactive whiteboard into the remote collaborator's room requires capturing every pose and gesture of a person directly in front of the whiteboard. The recorded scene is then reconstructed and rendered in 3D at the local user's screen. In the following sections, we highlight the key system components and discuss in detail the implementation of our approach.

Prototype Setup and Hardware

Currently, our setup consists of two interactive whiteboards: one for capturing the remote user in front of the screen and the other for observing the virtual embodiment. Both boards have a size of $1.6m \times 1.2m$ with a resolution of 1280×800 pixels and were operated by a Vivitek D795WT short throw projectors, with input through Anoto digital pens (ADP 601) [13]. To avoid networking issues, both whiteboards are driven by the same PC with an Intel Core i7-3770 CPU, 8GB of RAM and a Nvidia Quadro K2000, 2GB GDDR5.

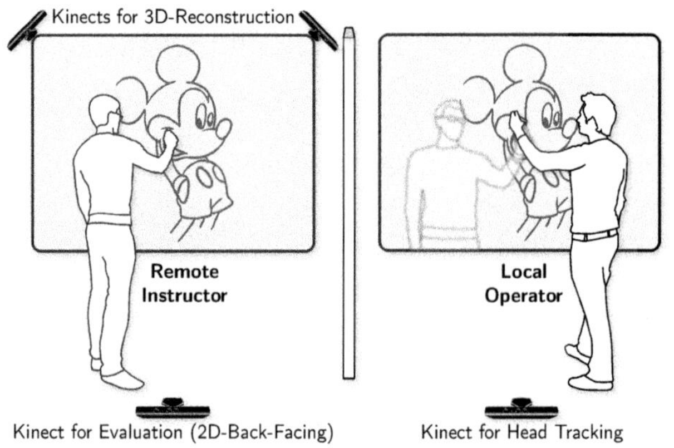

Figure 2: The prototype of *3D-Board*. The two upper Kinects capture the interaction of the *instructor* with the whiteboard (left). The *operator* (right) can observe the *instructor's* virtual embodiment in 3D by utilizing a third Kinect for head tracked motion parallax. A fourth Kinect, placed behind the *instructor*, was solely used for another technique (*2D-Back-Facing*) during the evaluation and is not part of *3D-Board*.

In total, four Microsoft Kinect (v1) cameras are used (cf. Figure 2). Two are attached to the top left and top right corner of the remote user's whiteboard. The data acquired from these depth sensors are used to reconstruct a 3D virtual embodiment of the geographically distributed person. Rotated downwards at a 45° angle, the two Kinects capture the user's actions from directly on the whiteboard's surface up to $1.2m$ away from the screen. Both sensors are operating in near-mode in order to cover the whole width and height of the board with only a minimal loss of about $10cm$ in the upper corner regions of the whiteboard. At the other (local) workspace, another Kinect sensor is capturing the full size of the second whiteboard from the back of the room. This camera tracks the head of the local observer to support motion parallax by changing the viewpoint of the rendering accordingly. The fourth Kinect is not part of the *3D-Board* setup. It was solely used to capture a 2D view of the back of the remote user for the second technique, discussed later in the evaluation section of this paper. With all

Kinects operated at a color and depth resolution of 640×480 pixels, the setup is running with approximately 30 Hz.

Camera Calibration

In order to merge the output of the two Kinect sensors attached to the upper corners of the remote user's whiteboard, the cameras need to be calibrated. The calibration is done using OpenCV's[1] implementation of the method of Zhang [29]. At first, multiple images of a checkerboard calibration target are taken from the RGB-camera in order to compute the camera intrinsics (focal length, principal point, distortion coefficients). Then the relative translation and rotation of the two cameras towards each other are determined using stereo camera calibration (by imaging the same calibration target simultaneously from both viewpoints). By computing the intrinsic and extrinsic camera parameters, the point clouds from the Kinect sensors can be transformed into a common coordinate space and rendered as a merged output.

Novel View Synthesis

Given the color and depth streams from multiple Kinect cameras located around the whiteboard, our goal is to render the user that is interacting with the board from a viewpoint of a virtual camera located behind the screen. This requires fusing the live color and depth data from all Kinect sensors in real time and rendering of the merged foreground data from a novel viewpoint. For accessing the Kinect's data, the official driver and SDK are used. The output is rendered in *DirectX* and displayed in a *Windows Presentation Foundation* (WPF) window.

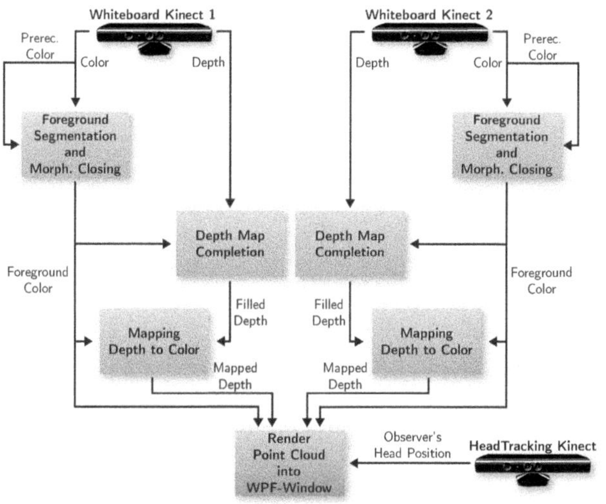

Figure 3: The rendering pipeline of *3D-Board*.

The data processing and rendering pipeline (cf. Figure 3) of *3D-Board* comprises of three subsequent steps:

1. *Segmentation*: In order to separate the user from the background, a foreground mask is computed from the viewpoint of each Kinect camera.

2. *Depth Map Completion*: Since the depth output is often incomplete, we estimate the geometry (depth) for all foreground masks to fill small holes.

3. *Depth Map Fusion & Rendering*: The foreground geometry from the two sensors is fused into a single, complete 3D point cloud that can be rendered from a virtual viewpoint by utilizing the previously discussed camera parameters.

Segmentation Given the color image C from the Kinect sensor, we aim to separate the dynamic foreground regions from the static background via frame differencing. To this end, we pre-record an image C_{clean} that shows the scene without foreground objects. Every pixel i in the live color image C that differs more than a threshold θ from C_{clean} in color space is added to the set of foreground pixels Ω_F. We fill small holes in the foreground mask Ω_F by applying a morphological closing operation.

Depth Map Completion Next, we infer the geometry (i.e. depth) for each pixel inside the foreground mask Ω_F. Each Kinect sensor provides a depth map D that can be rendered from the viewpoint of the color camera of the Kinect. However, depth maps are usually incomplete due to errors in triangulation as well as due to interference of multiple sensors. Since the overlap between the two Kinect cameras in the *3D-Board* setup is very small, interference can be handled by our geodesic depth map filling algorithm and does not require an additional hardware solution [5].

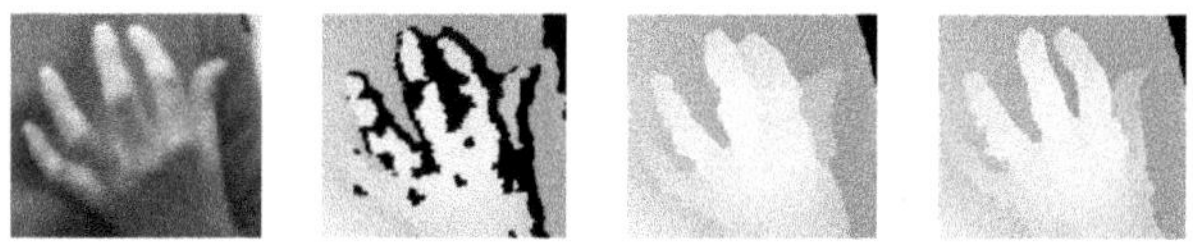

(a) (b) (c) (d)

Figure 4: Geodesic depth map filling: (a) RGB input image (b) Depth map from Kinect (c) Euclidean NN filling (d) Geodesic NN filling

We denote the set of pixels with valid depth as Ω_D and the set of foreground pixels with valid depth as $\Omega_{FD} = \Omega_F \cap \Omega_D$. For pixel i inside the foreground region without a valid depth, we find the geodesic nearest neighbor NN_{geo} in Ω_{FD}. We then copy the depth from the nearest neighbor to pixel i: $D(i) = D(NN_{geo}(i))$. The geodesic nearest neighbor NN_{geo} in set Ω_{FD} is defined as:

$$NN_{geo}(i) = \arg \min_{j \in \Omega_{FD}} d(j, i), \tag{1}$$

where

$$d(j, i) = \min_{P_{j,i}} \sum_{k \in P_{j,i}} W(k). \tag{2}$$

$P_{j,i}$ is a path connecting pixels i and j and the weight $W(k)$ is defined by the image gradient at pixel k. Intuitively, the nearest geodesic neighbor is found along a path along which the color in the RGB image varies only slightly. This is in contrast to the euclidean nearest neighbor that is found along a straight line. Since the geodesic nearest neighbor takes the color image data into account, a better completion of the depth map can be achieved. An example of depth map filling using geodesic distances is shown in Figure 4 which depicts a hand in front of a person's chest (cf. Figure 4 (a)). The corresponding depth map from the Kinect sensor (cf. Figure 4 (b)) shows missing depth values between the fingers (shown in black in Figure 4 (b)). Filling the missing values with the nearest neighbor in

[1]`http://opencv.org/`

euclidean space (cf. Figure 4 (c)) leads to wrong depth values between the fingers. Filling with the closest pixel in geodesic space yields superior results (cf. Figure 4 (d)). We use the approximate algorithm of [4] to compute the geodesic nearest neighbor efficiently.

Depth Map Fusion & Rendering The registration of the filled depth image to the color image is done by the Kinect SDK. The resulting mapped depth texture and the foreground color texture can then be visualized as a colored point cloud in the shader pipeline.

The point cloud is constructed by projecting each pixel of the filled and mapped depth texture into 3D space by multiplying the depth pixels with the inverse of the camera intrinsics matrix. The resulting 3D point is expanded into a fixed sized quad in the geometry shader. The color of the quad is sampled from the foreground color texture. To keep the RGB values consistent across all cameras we set the exposure time and the color temperature for each Kinect sensor to the same fixed value. In addition, the size of each billboard is enlarged with increasing depth to avoid gaps in the visualization.

This efficient point-based rendering technique allows us to visualize multiple point clouds on top of each other without having to merge their surfaces. The point clouds of both Kinects are fused by projecting them into the same coordinate space. Therefore each point is multiplied with the inverse of the extrinsic camera matrix.

The merged point cloud is then rendered from a virtual camera located at the observer's point of view. The viewpoint of the observer is computed for each frame by tracking the user's head with the third Kinect sensor that is mounted at the back side of the local user's room. The final output is rendered into a transparent (75%) WPF window that does not capture any input events from the mouse, the keyboard or the digital Anoto pens. Thus, the virtual 3D embodiment of the remote user can be superimposed on top of any content and is independent of the underlying application.

EVALUATION

Two empirical studies were conducted to explore the benefits and limitations of our proposed *3D-Board* technique. Both experiments were carried out with the same techniques, participants, and apparatus.

Apparatus

The studies were conducted in a quiet room with two interactive whiteboards, as illustrated in the implementation section (cf. Figure 2). Each of the whiteboards was dedicated for one of the two participants. The workplaces were separated from each other by a metal frame with blinds for visual cover. Thus, participants were unable to see the other whiteboard, but could communicate via voice commands and the technique in use.

Participants

In total, 12 paid volunteers (6 female, 6 male) from the local university participated. Their age ranged from 20 to 29 years ($M = 24.08$, $SD = 2.53$). Participants performed both studies in pairs of two. One was acting as an *instructor*, giving commands to the *operator*. The *operator* on the other hand, had to interpret the given instructions and acted accordingly. An important aspect of both experiments was to investigate the impact of a certain technique on the users' perception of their personal space. Thus, to increase the effects on the physical and social distance between users, we made sure that the paired up participants had never met before.

While 75% of the participants reported not being familiar with interactive whiteboards, 6 out of 12 had more experience with pen-based interfaces. Finally, 67% of the participants were using voice-over-IP application on a daily/weekly basis.

Techniques

Three different techniques were tested to compare the performance as well as the accuracy of our proposed technique:

- *3D-Board*: When using the *3D-Board* technique a front-facing 3D embodiment of the remote user was displayed, as described in the implementation section.
- *2D-Back-Facing*: This technique was chosen as a comparison with the recent related work of *CollaBoard* [20]. We maintain the same physical setup, with the camera placed behind the *instructor* (cf. Figure 2) to highlight the limitations of a 2D back-facing approach. The 2D image of the back of the user is captured and projected onto the remote whiteboard. Therefore, the body of the user can occlude the arms, forcing the users to find a good posture with their arms visible to the camera.
- *Co-located*: In the baseline condition, both participants were collaboratively working in front of the same whiteboard, thus simulating a co-located, face-to-face situation. This reflected best the everyday usage of a situated interactive display as used in both experiments.

EXPERIMENT 1: ABSTRACTED ENVIRONMENT

The first experiment investigated the performance of the techniques in an abstracted pointing task.

Task

Our task environment, based on the experiment of Grossman et al. [11], consisted of a grid of targets with the highlighted target objects being candidates for selection (cf. Figure 5).

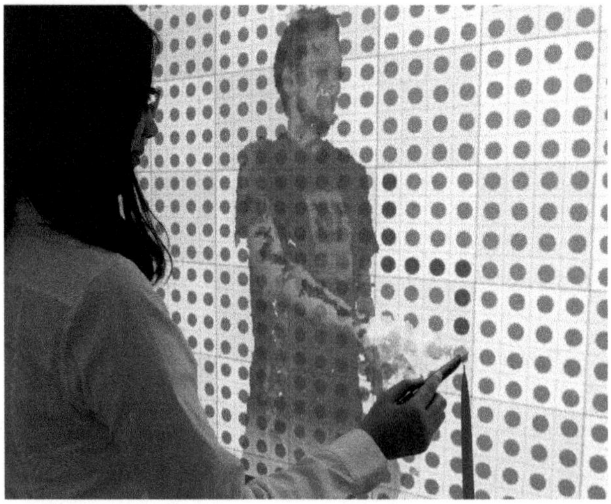

Figure 5: In the first experiment, the *instructor* pointed at target structures of different complexity levels. The *operator* had to mark the target points accordingly.

At the beginning of each trial, all targets were inactive (black). Next, a set of targets turned red, only visible for the *instructor*. Now the *instructor* had to point to all highlighted (red) targets as quickly as possible using finger/hand gestures. Following these instructions, the *operator* on the other side had to find out which of the targets to select. During the first experiment, the participants were not allowed to talk or correct each other. Targets were marked by tapping the corresponding objects once with the pen. The set of targets varied in terms of complexity. Two different levels of complexity (*Simple* and *Complex*) for the target shapes were tested. Simple targets were single line-chains, while complex objects consisted of three chains connected over two corners. The diameter of the target at the interactive whiteboard under the simple condition was $3.5cm$ and $2cm$ under the complex condition. Both participants were told to complete each trial as fast as possible. Trial times were measured between pressing the start button (on the *instructor* side) and the end button (on the *operator* side).

Design

A repeated measures within-subject design was used. Technique *3D-Board*, *2D-Back-Facing*, *Co-Located* and Complexity (simple, complex) were used as independent variables. The presentation order for the techniques was counterbalanced. For each turn, a total of three trials had to be completed. Summarizing, each group completed a total of 36 trials (3 techniques $\times$ 2 complexities $\times$ 3 trials $\times$ 2 users). In addition, qualitative feedback was collected after each technique using user experience questionnaires. Participants had to rate each technique on a 5-point Likert scale using the criteria: easy-to-use, accuracy and pointing awareness. Task load ratings were collected with NASA TLX questionnaires. After completing one full cycle of trials, participants were also asked to switch from the *instructor* to the *operator* role and vice versa. The whole test, including training sessions and questionnaires, lasted for approximately 40 minutes for each group.

Hypotheses

The experiment was designed and conducted with the following hypotheses in mind:

- *Hypothesis 1*: *3D-Board* is at least equally fast as the Co-Located technique.
- *Hypothesis 2*: *2D-Back-Facing* is the slowest technique.
- *Hypothesis 3*: *3D-Board* is more accurate than *2D-Back-Facing*.

Quantitative Results

Error rates and trial completion times were analyzed using a repeated measures ANOVA ($\alpha = 0.05$) separately for each level of complexity. The Greenhouse-Geisser correction was used if the assumption of sphericity was violated. Post-hoc analyses on the main effects were conducted in order to confirm/reject the formulated hypotheses. These consisted of paired-samples t-tests with family wise error rate controlled across the test using Holms sequential Bonferroni approach. For all bar charts, the error bars indicate the range of two standard errors of the mean (above and below the mean).

Trial Completion Time & Hit rate A repeated measures analysis of variance showed main effects for the *Technique* ($F_{2,10} = 20.057, p < 0.0001$) as well as for the *Complexity* ($F_{1,11} = 82.227, p < 0.0001$). Figure 6 depicts the overall mean time for each technique. Post-hoc analyses showed that the *3D-Board* technique was significantly faster ($M = 13.5s, SD = 3.3s$) than *2D-Back-Facing* ($M = 20.98s, SD = 6.97s$) with $p < 0.001$ for the complex task. One reason was that *operators* could instantly recognize the pointing gesture since *instructors* were not occluding the projected target with their bodies. On the other side, participants performed slightly faster in the *Co-Located* scenario than in the *3D-Board* setup. A pairwise comparison, however, showed no statistical significance ($p = .596$). This confirms *Hypothesis 1* since *3D-Board* can be considered as fast as the *Co-Located* technique. With *2D-Back-Facing* being the slowest technique, *Hypothesis 2* is confirmed as well. The same results were found for the simple task (cf. Figure 6).

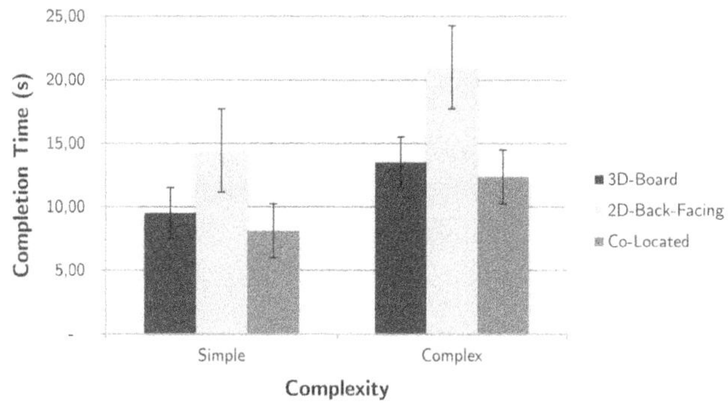

Figure 6: Overall completion time by Techniques and Complexity (Simple vs. Complex).

In addition to the trial times the number of errors were counted. On average 7.44 points were candidates for selection per trial for the complex target structures. 7.22 ($SD = 1.08$) targets have been selected correctly using the *3D-Board* technique compared to 7.25 ($SD = 1.01$) targets using the *Co-Located* technique, and 7.06 ($SD = 1.47$) using the *2D-Back-Facing* technique respectively. Given such small error rates, no significant difference could be found for selecting the correct targets. Thus, *Hypothesis 3* needs to be rejected since all three techniques appear to be very accurate.

Qualitative Results

After each technique block, participants were asked to rate the different techniques. The rating was based on a 5-point Likert scale (1 = strongly agree; 5 = strongly disagree).

Overall, 91.67% of the participants found the *3D-Front-Facing* technique either very easy or easy to use. In contrast, 75.0% of the participants rated the *2D-Back-Facing* to be difficult or very difficult to be used. Most of the participants found *3D-Board* to feel as natural as the *Co-Located* setup. The *instructor* could directly point onto the whiteboard and the *operator* would immediately understand. When using the *2D-Back-Facing* technique, we noticed that the *instructors* often tended to move sidewise with their body to avoid occluding their arms with the torso. 8 out of 12 participants also had the impression to know exactly where their partner was pointing under the *3D-Board* condition. This was in contrast to the *2D-Back-Facing* technique, where 11 out of 12 disagreed to know where their partner was pointing to.

Figure 7 depicts the task load ratings (1 = very low; 5 = very high) for all techniques, focusing on Physical Demand, Performance, Effort, and Frustration, where significant differences have been found. No significant main effects could be found for both Mental and Temporal Demand.

Interviews and Observations

According to the participants, the main advantages of *3D-Board* was the direct connection between the digital content and the superimposed 3D embodiment. This created the im-

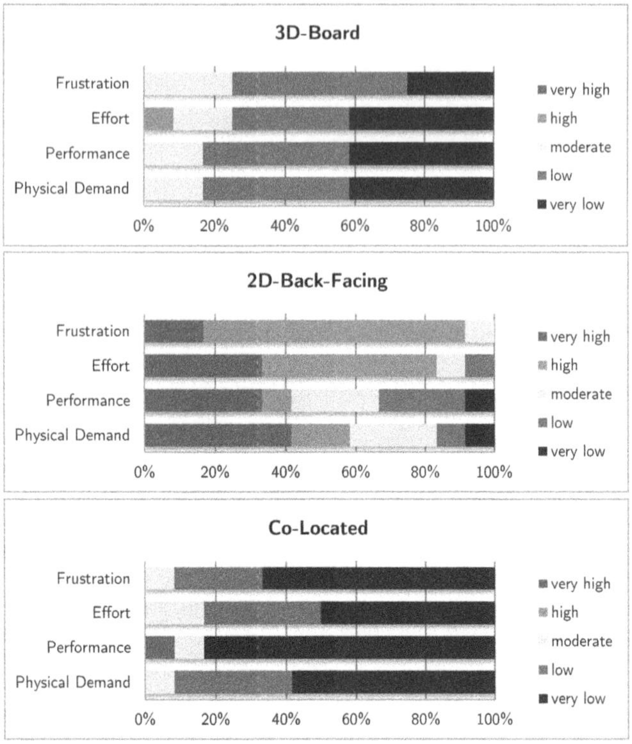

Figure 7: Task load ratings of the first experiment with significant differences for *3D-Board*, *2D-Back-Facing*, and *Co-Located*.

pression of working face-to-face with the remote user only separated by a glass window.

> *While using the 3D-Board technique, it was easy to see where the* instructor *was pointing to, because it gave me the impression that my partner was behind the wall. The interaction with someone who is behind the wall is exciting. –Participant 2A*

A lot of participants stated the *2D-Back-Facing* technique *needs a lot of practice*. One participant stated that acting as an *instructor* was a lot more mentally demanding and they had to hold the fingers in an ideal position to point to the target correctly.

The most convincing argument for the *3D-Board* was to work face-to-face with the other user.

> *I liked the feeling of communication in the 3D-Board condition, because the other person was looking at me, which made me feel more in contact with him. –Participant 5B*

Finally, they also appreciated it to see the other person in full size.

> *It was strange and at the same time felt good to see the other partner in full size. –Participant 6A*

We noticed increased interaction between users under the *3D-Board* condition. In addition, users tended to use more gestures and acted as if the remote participant was physically present.

EXPERIMENT 2: INTERIOR DESIGN

While in the first experiment we were mainly focusing on pointing gestures, in the second experiment, we investigated the performance of the *3D-Board* technique in a realistic scenario to test the natural interaction between users.

Task

In the second task, the *instructor* was presented a floor plan and adequate furniture, which had to be selected, scaled, rotated, and translated accordingly by the *operator* based on the instructions provided. In addition to rearranging the furniture, the *operator* had to draw three inner walls by sketching them on the surface (cf. Figure 8). Thus, the *instructor* had to use a big variety of gestures in order to give the *operator* precise guidelines. The *instructor* was also allowed to use voice commands, creating a realistic scenario of collaboration. The task was finished once the *instructor* was satisfied with the floor-plan.

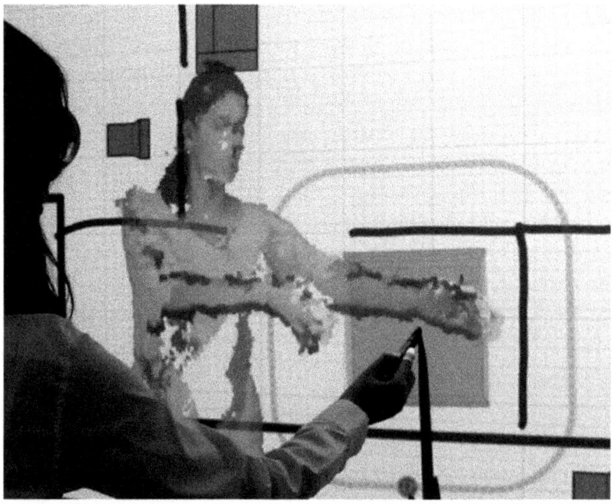

Figure 8: In the second experiment both participants had to work simultaneously while drawing and rearranging furniture on a floor plan.

Design

A within-subject design was used. The presentation order for the three techniques was counterbalanced. Per technique one unique floor plan had to be completed. The participants could familiarize themselves with the application before the trials began. After completing the trials for all techniques the *instructor* and *operator* switched roles. It took one group about 20 minutes to complete all trials. User satisfaction, ease-of-use, and engagement were gathered through interviews and questionnaires. Task load ratings were collected using the NASA TLX questionnaires.

Hypotheses

With the user experience in mind these additional hypotheses were formulated for the second experiment:

- *Hypothesis 4*: *Co-Located* is the preferred technique.
- *Hypothesis 5*: *3D-Board* raises workspace awareness.
- *Hypothesis 6*: The *3D-Board* embodiment does not violate the collaborator's personal space.

Qualitative Results

Qualitative user feedback showed that participants were highly positive about the concept of *3D-Board*. Half of all participants preferred *3D-Board* over all other techniques, and no one of them mentioned *3D-Board* as their least favorite. Thus, *Hypothesis 4* has to be rejected since *3D-Board* and *Co-Located* were equally popular.

On a five-point Likert scale (1 = very easy/strongly agree; 5 = very difficult/strongly disagree), participants found *3D-Board* easy to use ($ME = 1.5$) and easy to learn ($ME = 1.0$). In contrast, the *2D-Back-Facing* technique was rated as being moderate to use ($ME = 3.0$) and moderate to learn ($ME = 2.5$). In addition to that, 66.67% of the participants also felt a high or very high personal engagement when using *3D-Board*. The *Co-Located* scenario achieved better results with 83.33% while only 58.33% felt high or very high engagement when using *2D-Back-Facing*. A Wilcoxon signed-rank test showed significant differences for both usability ($z = 2.375, p = 0.018$) and learnability ($z = 2.326, p = 0.020$), for the comparison of *3D-Board* and *2D-Back-Facing*.

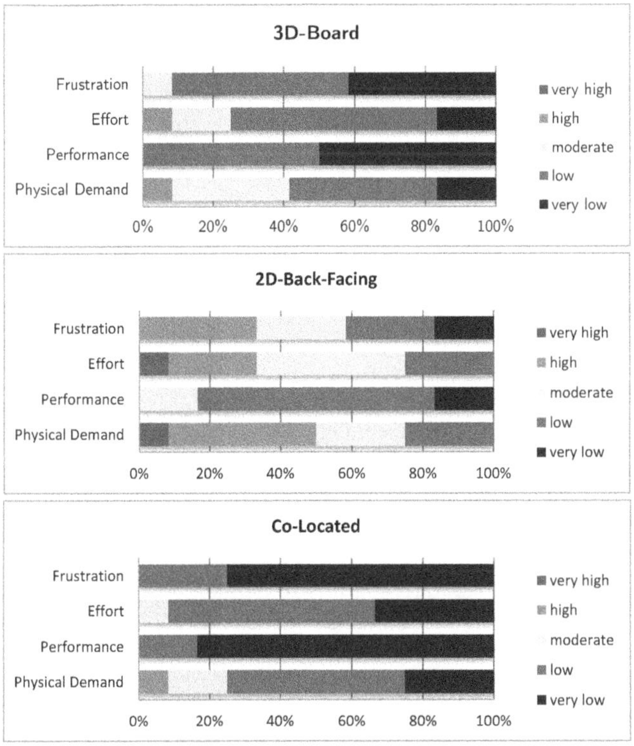

Figure 9: Task load ratings of the second experiment with significant differences for *3D-Board*, *2D-Back-Facing*, and *Co-Located*.

Figure 9 depicts the task load ratings for all techniques, focusing on Physical Demand, Performance, Effort, and Frustration, where significant differences have been found. As in the first experiment, no significant main effects could be found for both Mental and Temporal Demand. The post-condition questionnaire data (1 = very low; 5 = very high) were analyzed using two related samples Wilcoxon signed-rank tests. Overall, participants found *3D-Board* ($ME = 2.0$) less physically challenging than the 2D technique ($ME = 3.5$), $z = -2.414, p = 0.016$. In addition, most of the participants also felt the performance was better when using *3D-Board* ($ME = 4.5$) than with *2D-Back-Facing* ($ME = 4.0$), $z = -2.449, p = 0.014$. Also the effort was rated lower for *3D-Board* ($ME = 2.0$) than for *2D-Back-Facing* ($ME = 3.0$), with $z = -2.972, p = 0.003$. Finally, participants felt less frustration using the 3D technique ($ME = 2.0$) than using the 2D technique ($ME = 3.0$), $z = -2.739, p = 0.006$.

Awareness Once asked about how easy it was to make oneself well understood as an *instructor*, the majority of the participants voted in favor of the front-facing *3D-Board* technique ($ME = 1.0$) compared to the back-facing technique ($ME = 2.0$), $z = 2.714, p = 0.007$. When acting as the *operator*, the majority of the participants knew better what the *instructor* was doing when using *3D-Board* ($ME = 1.5$) compared to *2D-Back-Facing* ($ME = 2.0$), $z = 2.810, p = 0.005$. However, the *Co-Located* technique outperformed *3D-Board* ($ME = 1.0$) in terms of awareness with $z = -2.236, p = 0.025$. Thus, although *3D-Board* can raise the workspace awareness better than *2D-Back-Facing*, *Hypothesis 5* needs to be rejected, since *Co-Located* is still the preferred technique in this case.

Territoriality Similar to [6], we asked the participants to rate their agreement with the statements, "I often had the feeling that my personal space was invaded by my partner", and "I often had the feeling of invading my partner's personal space". While approximately 75% of the participants disagreed or strongly disagreed with the first statement of their personal space being invaded by the partner under the *3D-Board* condition, only 58.33% of all participants disagreed under the *Co-Located* condition. Similar results were observed with the second question. Again, 75% of the participants disagreed in the *3D-Board* setup, while 66.67% of all participants disagreed in the *Co-Located* setup. A Wilcoxon signed-rank test showed no main effects. In our experiment, participants had complete freedom to choose where to stay and how to interact with their remote partner. We noticed that the *operator* and *instructor* often stood face-to-face and made use of working simultaneously on the same spot of the whiteboard when using *3D-Board*.

Interviews and Observations

At the end of the study, participants were asked about the advantages *3D-Board* has compared to the *Co-Located* condition and what they liked best about it.

Two participants found that the technique provides more space, which would also *allow more people to work on the whiteboard simultaneously*. In addition to that, a user will automatically have more private space. It was interesting to see that even though the remote collaborator was directly in front of a person, the *instructor* was not noticed as a disturbance as it would be the case in a *Co-Located* setup, where people would step on each other's toes.

> *The collaboration was easier once you see the remote person in front of you - it gives you the feeling to work really face-to-face. And this, without treading on someone's foot –Participant 5A*

Participants appreciated the front-facing approach a lot, which provided a better gestural interaction, while working on the same content.

> *The facial expression was highly relevant for the interaction and although the remote participant was superimposed, I could clearly see the* instructor's *gestures. –Participant 4B*

On the other side, three participants found no advantages using the *2D-Back-Facing* technique. One participant found that the *2D-Back-Facing* technique was *exhausting* and lacked facial expression. Similarly, another participant also missed the gestural interaction. Overall, most of the participants found it more difficult to interact without seeing the remote worker face-to-face. Summarizing, these observations confirm *Hypothesis 6* since users showed a tendency of acting more confident when using *3D-Board*.

APPLICATION SCENARIOS

We have tested *3D-Board* in two scenarios (cf. Figure 10). In the first scenario, we superimpose the entire video image

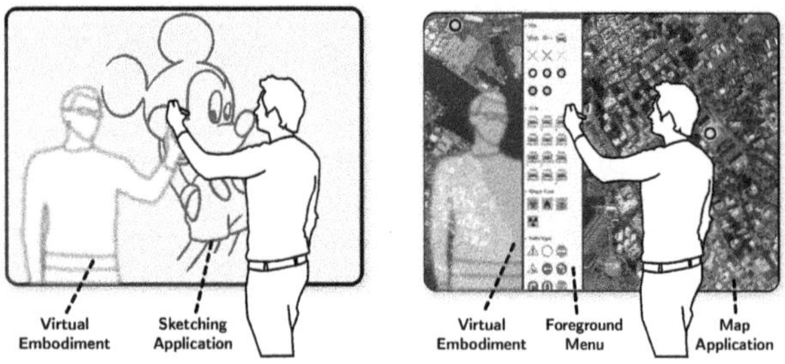

(a) (b)

Figure 10: While in the first demo application the entire data screen is occluded by the video image (a), specific content (e.g. menus) is not superimposed by the video image in the second demo application (b).

on top of a full-screen application. In the second scenario, important content, such as on-screen menus, are rendered as the topmost element to avoid occlusion and keep them visible at all time.

Remote sketching application

For the first demonstrator, we implemented a simple sketching tool. As depicted in Figure 11, the superimposed remote

Figure 11: In the remote sketching application, the entire working space is occluded by the transparent (75%) video image.

collaborator is occluding parts of the underlying application. However, because of the size of the surface, the transparency of the virtual embodiment and the nature of the content the users never felt that the virtual embodiments was distracting from the actual content.

Remote Map Surveillance

The main idea for 3D Board came from a close collaboration with the local police. The police needed an intuitive and easy-to-use remote Common Operational Picture (COP) based on an interactive whiteboards. Larger operations often require additional support from other groups situated in geographically distributed control rooms. To provide an effective operational picture, it is important that all data is merged in a single view as quickly as possible without overwhelming the officers.

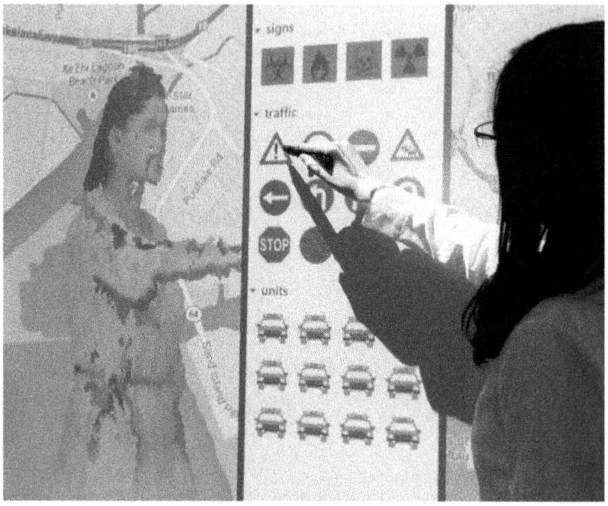

Figure 12: In the Common Operational Picture application, police vehicles had to be placed accordingly. Important windows (e.g. dialogs) are always on top and not occluded by the video image.

In our scenario, police officers utilize an interactive wall to monitor a large city map. The map is augmented with GPS-tracked police vehicles that had to be coordinated by multiple co-located and remotely located police officers.

While the main COP environment is again superimposed by the remote collaborator (similar to the sketching application), it was important avoid occlusion for important items. Thus, menus for icon selection are rendered as the topmost elements to avoid occlusion.

CONCLUSION & FUTURE WORK

In this paper we have presented *3D-Board*, a digital whiteboard featuring life-sized 3D virtual embodiments of geographically distributed users. By blending the front-facing 3D embodiment of a remote collaborator with the shared workspace, an illusion is created as if the observer is looking through the transparent whiteboard into the remote user's room. Our approach is characterized by a simple setup and front-facing rendering technique, providing an easy-to-understand and easy-to-learn face-to-face experience for remote collaboration.

The system was tested and verified in a usability assessment, showing that *3D-Board* significantly improves the effectiveness of remote collaboration on a large interactive surface (especially compared with a *2D-Back-Facing* setup). We also noticed that participants explicitly appreciated the face-to-face communication. It was interesting to see participants working in the same area of the shared workspace simultaneously, since they experienced the remote collaborator as standing behind the screen. During the study we could also observe that the participants were more involved and a lot more activity happened. In contrast, participants would keep a certain distance to each other in the *Co-Located* setup.

There are several areas that we would like to improve. The current image quality is inferior and should be further enhanced. Although the study results were highly promising and participants did not mention the rendering to be have negative effects for our approach, the noisy look has to be improved with more advanced depth data processing techniques. Moreover, we would like to improve the frame rate and implement more rendering stages on the GPU. In addition, we would like to test the setup using newer depth sensors and try alternative setups with the overall goal to embed the sensors in the frame of the interactive whiteboard.

Acknowledgments

The research leading to these results has received funding from the Austrian Research Promotion Agency (FFG) within the research program KIRAS under grant agreement #29335581 (ERiC).

REFERENCES

1. Beck, S., Kunert, A., Kulik, A., and Froehlich, B. Immersive group-to-group telepresence. *IEEE Trans. Vis. Comput. Graph. 19*, 4 (2013), 616–625.
2. Benford, S., Bowers, J., Fahlén, L. E., Greenhalgh, C., and Snowdon, D. User embodiment in collaborative virtual environments. In *CHI '95*, ACM Press/Addison-Wesley Publishing Co., 1995, 242–249.
3. Bly, S. A., Harrison, S. R., and Irwin, S. Media spaces: Bringing people together in a video, audio and computing environment. *Commun. ACM 36*, 1 (Jan. 1993), 28–46.
4. Borgefors, G. Distance transformations in digital images. *Comput. Vision Graph. Image Process. 34*, 3 (June 1986), 344–371.
5. Butler, D. A. et al. Shake'n'sense: Reducing interference for overlapping structured light depth cameras. In *CHI'12*, ACM, 2012, 1933–1936.
6. Doucette, A., Gutwin, C., Mandryk, R. L., Nacenta, M., and Sharma, S. Sometimes when we touch: How arm embodiments change reaching and collaboration on digital tables. In *CSCW '13*, ACM, 2013, 193–202.
7. Edelmann, J., Peter, G., Mock, P., Schilling, A., and Strasser, W. Face2Face - a system for multi-touch collaboration with telepresence. In *ESPA'12*, IEEE, 2012, 159–162.
8. Fussell, S. R. et al. Gestures over video streams to support remote collaboration on physical tasks. *Hum.-Comput. Interact. 19*, 3 (Sept. 2004), 273–309.
9. Genest, A., and Gutwin, C. Characterizing deixis over surfaces to improve remote embodiments. In *ECSCW'11*, Springer, 2011, 253–272.
10. Genest, A. M., Gutwin, C., Tang, A., Kalyn, M., and Ivkovic, Z. Kinectarms: A toolkit for capturing and displaying arm embodiments in distributed tabletop groupware. In *CSCW '13*, ACM, 2013, 157–166.
11. Grossman, T., Baudisch, P., and Hinckley, K. Handle flags: Efficient and flexible selections for inking applications. In *GI'09*, 2009, 167–174.
12. Gumienny, R., Gericke, L., Quasthoff, M., Willems, C., and Meinel, C. Tele-Board: Enabling efficient collaboration in digital design spaces. In *CSCWD'11*, IEEE, 2011, 47–54.
13. Haller, M. et al. The nice discussion room: Integrating paper and digital media to support co-located group meetings. In *CHI '10*, ACM, 2010, 609–618.
14. Hauber, J., Regenbrecht, H., Billinghurst, M., and Cockburn, A. Spatiality in videoconferencing: Trade-offs between efficiency and social presence. In *CSCW'06*, ACM, 2006, 413–422.
15. Ishii, H., and Kobayashi, M. Clearboard: A seamless medium for shared drawing and conversation with eye contact. In *CHI'92*, ACM, 1992, 525–532.
16. Izadi, S. et al. C-slate: A multi-touch and object recognition system for remote collaboration using horizontal surfaces. In *Tabletop*, IEEE, 2007, 3–10.
17. Jota, R., Nacenta, M. A., Jorge, J. A., Carpendale, S., and Greenberg, S. A comparison of ray pointing techniques for very large displays. In *GI'10*, Canadian Information Processing Society, 2010, 269–276.
18. Junuzovic, S., Inkpen, K., Blank, T., and Gupta, A. Illumishare: Sharing any surface. In *CHI '12*, ACM, 2012, 1919–1928.
19. Kim, K., Bolton, J., Girouard, A., Cooperstock, J., and Vertegaal, R. Telehuman: Effects of 3d perspective on gaze and pose estimation with a life-size cylindrical telepresence pod. In *CHI'12*, ACM, 2012, 2531–2540.
20. Kunz, A., Nescher, T., and Küchler, M. Collaboard: A novel interactive electronic whiteboard for remote collaboration with people on content. In *CW'10*, IEEE, 2010, 430–437.
21. Ledo, D., Aseniero, B. A., Greenberg, S., Boring, S., and Tang, A. Onespace: Shared depth-corrected video interaction. In *CHI '13 Extended Abstracts*, ACM, 2013.
22. Maimone, A., and Fuchs, H. Encumbrance-free telepresence system with real-time 3d capture and display using commodity depth cameras. In *ISMAR*, IEEE, 2011, 137–146.
23. Pinelle, D., Nacenta, M., Gutwin, C., and Stach, T. The effects of co-present embodiments on awareness and collaboration in tabletop groupware. In *GI'08*, Canadian Information Processing Society, 2008, 1–8.
24. Tan, K.-H., Robinson, I. N., Culbertson, W. B., and Apostolopoulos, J. G. Connectboard: Enabling genuine eye contact and accurate gaze in remote collaboration. *IEEE Trans. on Multimedia 13*, 3 (2011), 466–473.
25. Tang, J. C., and Minneman, S. Videowhiteboard: Video shadows to support remote collaboration. In *CHI '91*, ACM, 1991, 315–322.
26. Tuddenham, P., and Robinson, P. Remote review meetings on a tabletop interface. *CSCW'06* (2006).
27. Tuddenham, P., and Robinson, P. Territorial coordination and workspace awareness in remote tabletop collaboration. In *CHI '09*, ACM, 2009, 2139–2148.
28. van Eijk, R., Kuijsters, A., Dijkstra, K., and IJsselsteijn, W. Human sensitivity to eye contact in 2D and 3D videoconferencing. In *QoMEX'10*, IEEE, 2010 2010, 76 – 81.
29. Zhang, Z. A flexible new technique for camera calibration. *IEEE Trans. Pattern Anal. Mach. Intell. 22*, 11 (2000), 1330–1334.

RichReview: Blending Ink, Speech, and Gesture to Support Collaborative Document Review

Dongwook Yoon[1, 2] dy252@cornell.edu
Nicholas Chen[1] nchen@microsoft.com
François Guimbretière[2] francois@cs.cornell.edu
Abigail Sellen[1] asellen@microsoft.com
[1]Microsoft Research
21 Station Road, Cambridge CB1 2FB, UK
[2]Cornell University, Information Science
Ithaca, NY 14850

ABSTRACT
This paper introduces a novel document annotation system that aims to enable the kinds of rich communication that usually only occur in face-to-face meetings. Our system, RichReview, lets users create annotations on top of digital documents using three main modalities: freeform inking, voice for narration, and deictic gestures in support of voice. RichReview uses novel visual representations and time-synchronization between modalities to simplify annotation access and navigation. Moreover, RichReview's versatile support for multi-modal annotations enables users to mix and interweave different modalities in threaded conversations. A formative evaluation demonstrates early promise for the system finding support for voice, pointing, and the combination of both to be especially valuable. In addition, initial findings point to the ways in which both content and social context affect modality choice.

Author Keywords
Annotation; multi-modal input; voice; speech; pointing gesture; pen interaction; collaborative authoring; asynchronous communication.

ACM Classification Keywords
H.5.2. Information interfaces and presentation (e.g., HCI): User Interfaces.

INTRODUCTION
The production of documents where collaborators iteratively review and exchange feedback is fundamental to many workplace and academic practices. Effective communication of edits, questions and comments is central to the evolution of a document [27] as well as playing a role in maintaining group dynamics [2].

Working face-to-face (F2F) has many advantages for these kinds of collaborative processes. F2F collaborators enjoy a shared context in which they can verbally explain details and gesture over documents with each other, often taking notes as they do so. These different ways of communicating are interleaved seamlessly and often support each other. It is therefore no surprise that many of the most important discussions about documents occur in face-to-face meetings [8,20].

UIST '14, October 05 - 08 2014, Honolulu, HI, USA

http://dx.doi.org/10.1145/2642918.2647390

Figure 1. RichReview running on tablet. Hovering the pen over screen leaves traces of gesture (blue blob on top). Inking can be done on expansion space (middle). Voice recording is shown as waveform (bottom).

One challenge of F2F meetings (and related techniques like video conferencing) is that they constrain collaborators to be co-present (temporally), which may not always be possible or desirable. In response, people often collaborate asynchronously over communication channels such as ink markup, textual annotations, and email. These techniques, compared to F2F interactions, undermine the production of an implicit shared context and largely restrict communications to a single modality.

In this paper, we describe RichReview, a document annotation system that brings some of the richness and expressivity of F2F discussion to asynchronous collaboration scenarios. RichReview allows collaborators to quickly produce and consume annotations consisting of voice, ink, and pointing gestures on top of ordinary PDF documents.

On the creation side, RichReview introduces a unified, fast, and minimally intrusive set of interactions for creating multi-modal annotations on text. The three different modalities that are supported can be freely interleaved and combined. RichReview additionally leverages automatic speech recognition (ASR) to segment audio recordings at the word level to simplify the process of trimming or cleaning up audio.

On the consumption side, RichReview's interface streamlines navigation and access to the contents of these rich annotations. Any visual representations of RichReview annotations are recorded with time-stamps to support quick navigation. For instance, voice annotations are rendered as waveforms annotated with an ASR-generated transcript. This provides an interface to easily browse and access any point in the audio stream. RichReview also leverages the time-synchronization between voice, ink, and gesture streams by providing users the ability to use one modality to index into another.

We conducted a formative study investigating how people use (and do not use) RichReview features when discussing documents. RichReview's support for ink, voice and pointing gestures was widely used. Users also took advantage of the freedom and flexibility that RichReview afforded by structuring and responding to annotations in a variety of ways. Based on our results, we discuss design implications for future implementations, including enhancing time indexing and making the system more practical at scale.

RELATED WORK

RichReview has its roots in the Wang Freestyle system [10] which pioneered the use of a combination of speech and ink to annotate a document. It also builds on research that shows that combining modalities allows people to communicate more efficiently and with more depth [19]. However, RichReview's support for annotation production goes beyond existing work by capturing pointing gestures in addition to speech and ink. RichReview also provides improved support for consuming annotations in the form of new visualizations and interactions. The contribution of this work, therefore, is to build on the work of others as we shall outline below. At the same time we wish to broaden the flexibility and expressiveness with which annotations can be made without added complexity for the user.

Ink

Freeform ink annotations are pervasive and used extensively for document work because they are fast to create, can be interleaved with the reading process [20], and are highly flexible in the information they represent [11]. As a result, several annotation systems in the literature have employed ink as a primary modality. The collaborative editor MATE [7] supported the use of ink both for low-level editing commands as well as serving as a general medium for communication. Similarly, the XLibris reading device, which supported pen input, was used to explore various use scenarios of collaborative ink annotations [12]. Unlike these previous systems, ink is not the exclusive annotating modality of RichReview. Rather, it is used in conjunction with gestural and speech-based annotations. Moreover, RichReview employs contemporary techniques such as TextTearing [26] to alleviate issues with limited writing space on digital documents.

Gestures

People often use gestures in a deictic role (i.e. pointing to areas of interest) to streamline discussion around a document [1]. Gestures help people establish a common understanding and offer a shortcut to verbose verbal descriptions [4]. As such, they are an integral complement to spoken language [13]. BoomChameleon [22] is one of the first systems to explore pointing gestures in the form of the Flashlight tool which allowed users to refer to regions of interest in 3D environments. RichReview employs a Spotlight tool to achieve similar functionality in textual documents. A key difference between Spotlight and Flashlight is that Spotlight traces can be used as an index to rapidly jump into the middle of an annotation.

Speech

Speech has been shown to be a uniquely strong medium for identifying high-level problems with a document. Because speaking is faster than writing or typing, it is an efficient way to display complex concepts. Chalfonte and Kraut have also shown that spoken annotation's expressiveness and richness are more suitable for describing structural or semantic issues in comparison with written annotation [3,8]. Furthermore, Neuwirth et al. found that speaking, when compared with writing, generates more detailed explanations and nuance that can lead to better perceptions of comments at the receiving end [16].

Despite these advantages, speech-based annotation is rarely employed. Ethnographic studies of writing [18] make no mention of the use of audio commenting features available in word processing packages. One reasons may be that, as Grudin has noted, speech is slower and more difficult to access than text, which can undermine its use in collaborative applications [6].

One way voice annotation systems have dealt with this accessibility problem is by using ink strokes as navigational indices into an audio stream [21,24,25]. This approach is also used in commercial applications such as the LiveScribe Pulse SmartPen and Microsoft OneNote. Another strategy is to use automatic speech recognition to produce a textual transcript to enable faster browsing and access to the underlying audio [23]. Given the diversity of annotation strategies, RichReview includes both techniques to maximize navigational flexibility: either ink or text can be used to browse and navigate through speech annotations. This combined approach for accessing speech content is similar to what is used in the NoteVideo [14] online lecture browser. It bears noting that all annotation elements, regardless of whether they are voice, ink strokes or Spotlight, can participate in cross-indexing operations.

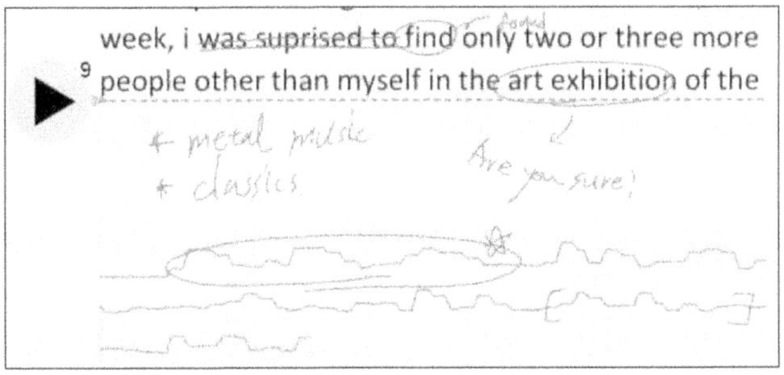

Figure 2. A mixture of static ink annotations along with the playback control for a multi-modal annotation.

RICHREVIEW DESIGN PHILSOPHY

Based on our analysis of previous work, it was apparent that a successful, fully functional, multi-modal annotation tool has yet to be developed. However, equally apparent was that such a system needed to be sensitive to the way that people create and use annotations. With that in mind, we proposed the following goals:

- ***Limiting System Complexity*** Introducing multiple annotation modalities runs the risk of bringing in additional complexity and overhead. The added overhead could then affect all annotation activities. Therefore a significant part of the design of our system was focused on ensuring that annotations are created and consumed in ways that are lightweight and fluid. Satisfying this design goal argued against locking the user into interaction modes or adding additional interaction steps. RichReview employs a simple and consistent set of interactions for creating any kind of annotation.
- ***Versatility and Choice*** The literature provides many examples showing that the optimal modality for communicating varies by its content and purpose. For example, inking is popular for lightweight copyediting, and a combination of voice and pointing can be useful to describe structural issues of a writing. For this reason, a second design goal is to allow users to employ a flexible mix of annotation modalities.
- ***Balancing Emphasis on Production and Consumption*** The success of groupware is contingent on the balance of benefits to different stakeholders [6]. Thus an annotation system that supports collaborative tasks must focus as much on improving the ability of recipients to skim, access, and revisit annotations as it does on supporting the creation of them in the first place. Given that non-textual content can be difficult to access and skim, we place an emphasis on techniques that assist users in consuming rich annotations.

RichReview was expressly designed for use with tablet devices, since tablets are a preferred form factor for active reading activities [15]. Moreover, current tablet devices contain the necessary hardware to capture the three input modalities we are interested in.

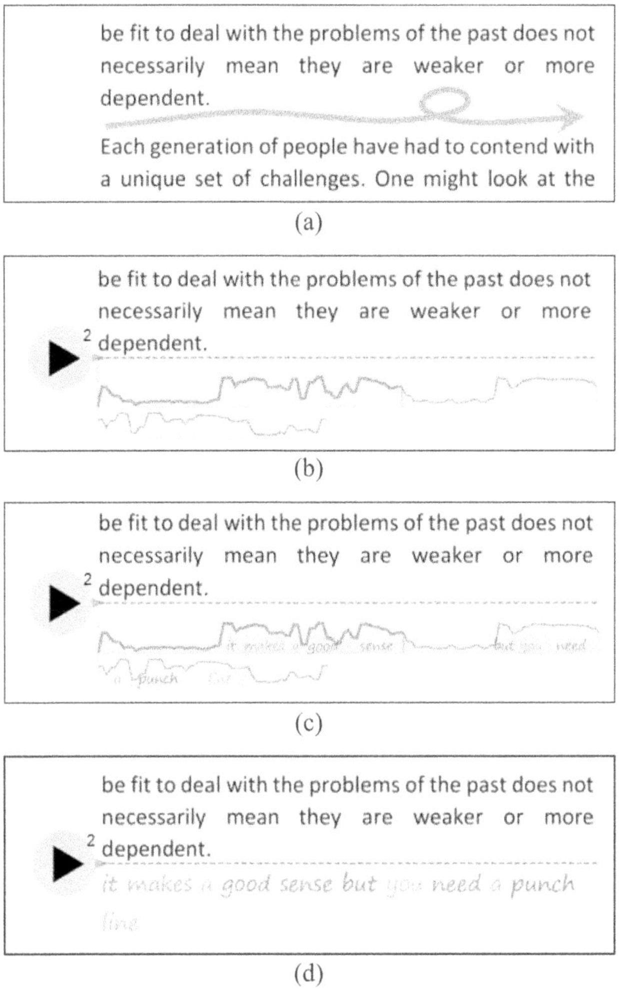

Figure 3. Recording and visualizing speech: (a) Pigtail gesture to begin and anchor recording (b) Waveform during replay (c) Waveform with word overlays (d) Transcription with varying opacities based on recognition confidence.

CREATING ANNOTATIONS IN RICHREVIEW

Ink Annotations

RichReview retains the paper metaphor in which inking can be performed anytime without entering a special mode. When there is insufficient space for writing, TextTearing interactions [26] can be used to create additional writing space in between lines of text. Users can execute this by drawing a horizontal line at the approximate place, followed by a pigtail in the *vertical* direction. All annotations (including the multi-modal ones described later) are anchored to the nearest line of text, graphic, or expansion region on the page (Figure 2). When the position of these elements shift in response to re-layout, the anchored annotation also moves. Annotations created in this way can also be collapsed so that the original layout of the document is preserved.

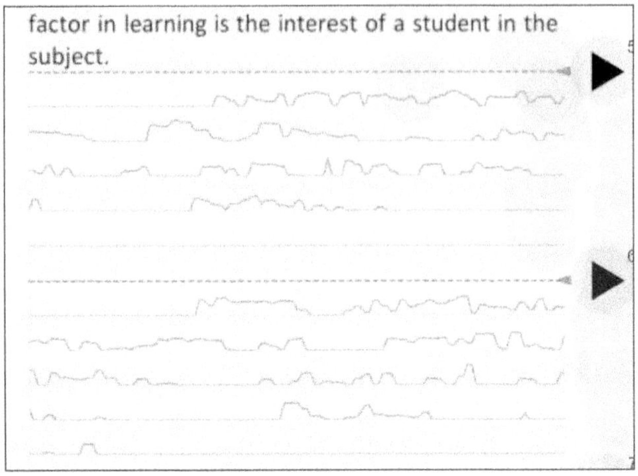

Figure 4. List of recording structures voice annotation by topic (footage from the real-user data, P7).

Multi-Modal Annotations

RichReview's multi-modal annotation recordings capture voice in conjunction with ink and pointing gestures. RichReview requires users to explicitly start and stop the recordings to dispel privacy concerns associated with a system that is always-on. A recording session is started using an underline followed by a pigtail that extends in the *horizontal* direction (Figure 3 (a)). This gesture was selected due to its similarity to the gesture for TextTearing in order to reinforce the idea that annotation activities commence with an underline followed by a pigtail. The location of the underline specifies the anchor point of the annotation and creates a small playback control icon in the margins at the same vertical position on the page. The icon doubles as a marking menu containing commands for working with the annotation.

Capturing Voice

When the recording session begins, a small amount of extra space is inserted between the lines of text where the initial underline gesture is drawn. Inside this space, a waveform representation of the captured audio grows from left to right. Upon reaching the end of the line, the space expands slightly downward and the waveform continues into the new space.

RichReview also includes features to help users add structure to their speech annotations. Similar to Audio Notebook [21], users can structure their voice annotations by creating time-indexed ink notes that the recipient can later use to jump into import parts of the annotation. Also, performing an annotation creation gesture while a recording session is active ends the active recording and immediately starts a new one. This is useful when the annotation moves to a different topic; the interaction saves the user from the interruption incurred from stopping the recording and creating a new one. Performing the annotation creation gesture over an existing annotation appends a new recording to the existing one (Figure 4).

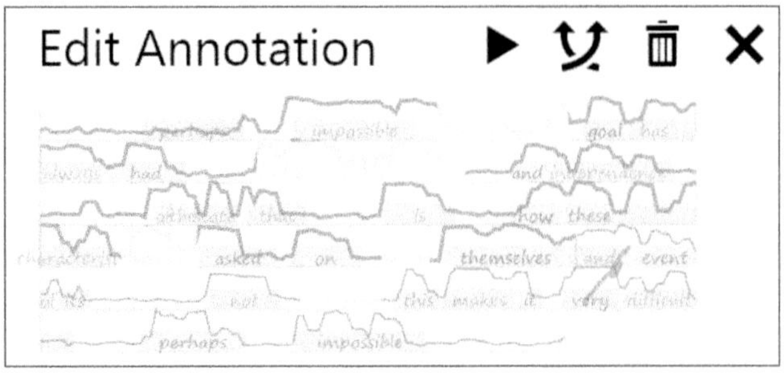

Figure 5. Voice editing user interface presented with waveform. Editing symbol in red deletes a word from the voice recording.

Capturing Pointing Gesture

Pointing at a location in a document is a fast and lightweight way of supporting discussion with reference to specific parts of a document [1]. RichReview provides the *Spotlight* interaction to reproduce this capability. With the Spotlight interaction, hovering the pen over the page while recording creates a circular translucent region at the pen's position (Figure 1). When recording ends, translucent trails of where the Spotlight has been are shown on the document.

Another way that a user can communicate the location of the region of interest is through the creator's viewpoint (i.e. what the creator was looking at during the recording). Similar cues are used in F2F collaboration by observing a collaborator's gaze. To convey this information to recipients, RichReview records viewpoint adjustment operations such as panning and pinch-to-zoom gestures for later playback.

Audio Post-Processing

When a recording is complete, the captured audio is passed to an automatic speech recognizer running in the background. When the transcription is complete, the words in the transcript are shown over the portion of the waveforms corresponding to when they were spoken (Figure 3 (c)). Displaying words over the existing waveform maintains visual continuity with unadorned waveform representation. However, when improved readability of the transcript is desirable, users can display the transcription on its own (Figure 3 (d)) by selecting an option from the marking menu.

The transcribed audio can be used to trim or tidy up the audio in the audio editing tool (Figure 5). In the editing tool, crossing through words or portions of the waveform or transcript grays out those sections of the recording and removes them from the recording. Crossing through a deleted section reverses the deletion. Edits made with the tool are automatically snapped to word boundaries so that the result does not slice the audio in the middle of a word.

CONSUMING ANNOTATIONS IN RICHREVIEW

The ink, gesture, and audio (and transcript) within a recording share the same timebase. RichReview leverages

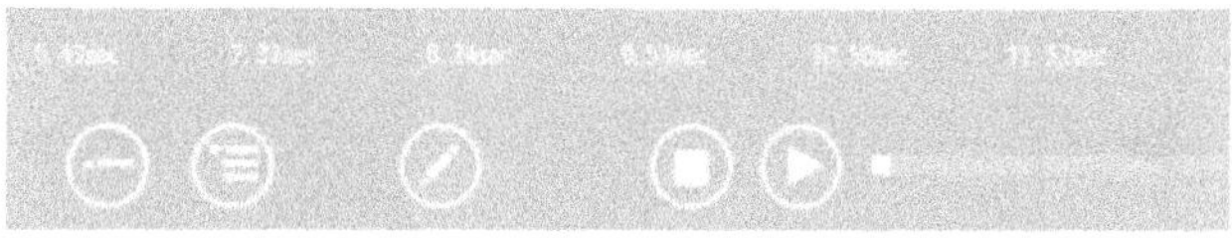

Figure 6. Recording list and media control. A list of annotations, sorted in order of creation, runs across the top. Buttons are used to collapse, expand, edit, stop and play annotations, respectively.

time synchronization to provide a rich rendering of the way the original annotation was created and lets users quickly jump to a specific parts of the annotation stream.

Basic Playback

Basic access to annotation recordings is through the play icon at the annotation anchor or media control at the bottom of the screen (Figure 6). During playback, ink is rendered in a grayed out form if playback has not reached the point where it was created (Figure 7) and then drawn with a colored stroke afterwards. Spotlight traces are rendered as an animated, translucent circle.

Enhanced Navigation of Rich Annotations

Although the basic playback controls are sufficient for the linear consumption of annotation content, they can be inadequate for random access. For example, users may wish to skim through annotations or visit a specific part of an annotation. RichReview offers several features that support these more complex navigation tasks.

Cross-Modal Indexing

For example, users can tap on a point in the waveform or transcript to skip to the corresponding point in the annotation recording. The waveform can be useful for finding gaps in the audio, which often delimit sections within an annotation stream. For finer-grained navigation, the transcript (Figure 3 (d)) can be used to visit parts of an annotation based on words of interest. The need for random-access to audio is critical in light of the fact that speech-to-text technology can still be quite error-prone; generally it is not possible to use the transcript on its own to consume speech content. Therefore, it is imperative that users have a way to quickly jump to and listen to the actual audio.

Ink strokes and Spotlight trails can similarly be used to index into an annotation. One important design decision we made was to show the entirety of the ink and Spotlight traces at all times, so that they can be promptly accessed when needed. On the one hand, this choice does not preserve the exact appearance of the page during annotation creation. However, we believed that giving the ability to skip forwards into an annotation outweighed this concern. We distinguish between strokes that have been made and those that have yet to appear by rendering strokes in different colors.

We also explored other ways of leveraging the links between different modalities that were not as useful. For example, in early prototypes, we highlighted portions of the waveform if they corresponded to times when inking or Spotlight was active. We found that these highlights were not very useful because the highlights provided few cues about the specific objects on the page to which they referred.

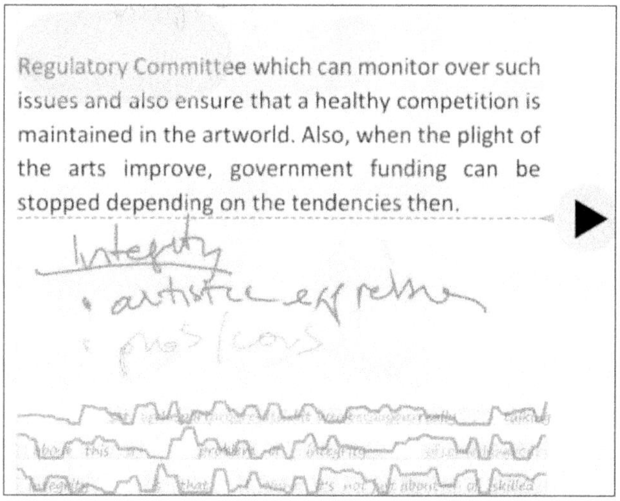

Figure 7. Spotlight trails along with dynamic ink. Recorded strokes are dynamically replayed as playback advances. Grayed out strokes will come in the future. The speech annotation here is structured by writing keywords while speaking.

Viewpoint Control Options

Users can control whether their viewpoint is locked to match the creator's viewpoint during playback. When locked, the recipient sees what the creator sees. Otherwise, the extent of the creator's viewport is shown as a box.

Thumbnail View

Finally, RichReview provides a high-level overview of all annotations using a space-filling thumbnail (SFT) [5] layout. Pinching more than four fingers zooms the document view out to SFT view. The overview gives a sense of the busiest pages and paragraphs and annotations can be quickly accessed by tapping on one of the page thumbnails.

RESPONDING TO ANNOTATIONS

Given the iterative nature of collaborative writing tasks, RichReview provides collaborative annotation features that allow users to respond to existing annotations made by peers. These features help "close the loop" when people collaborate on a document. In RichReview, annotation entities, such as waveforms, ink, playback controls, and Spotlight traces are color-coded by user identity. However, tracking and showing user identity is only a small part of providing multi-user support.

RichReview differs from other collaborative annotation systems in that it is possible to respond to an annotation using a different modality. The way RichReview enables

Figure 8. Red user inserted a voice annotation in the middle of existing Blue user's voice transcript (footage from the real-user data, P7). Red user's Spotlight is anchored on the transcript.

this is to treat ink and audio annotations in the same way as the underlying body text of the document. There are two benefits of this design decision.

First, mark-up operations that could be applied to the original document can also be applied to annotation entities. For example, ink can be used to circle portions of a waveform (Figure 9) and the Spotlight can be used to bring attention to a part of the transcript (Figure 8).

Second, treating annotations like the underlying text provides multi-modal support for discussions between collaborators conducted through threaded comments. For instance, users can create an expansion space in the middle of an audio waveform and insert a comment using ink (Figure 9). Inserting a voice comment under an existing inking space is also possible (Figure 10, top).

In some cases, interleaving annotations with the body text can break the flow of reading due to annotations having a large visual footprint. In these situations, RichReview allows users to collapse or expand annotations. An option in the marking menu accessed through the play icon allows this to be done on a per-annotation basis. Collapse-all and expand-all buttons in the bottom toolbar can also be used to switch back and forth between the original document layout and the fluid layout.

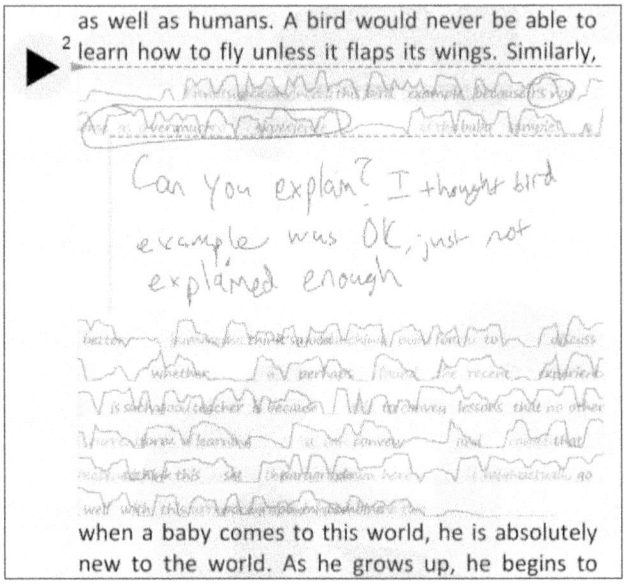

Figure 9. Circling on waveform to designate a part of the voice (footage from the real-user data, P10)

These multi-user features that allow users to converse and engage in discussion through annotations are illustrative of how our initial design goals of interactional consistency and flexibility pervade the entirety of our system.

IMPLEMENTATION

RichReview is a C++ Windows Store app. We use the MuPDF library to extract the location of graphical elements for anchoring annotations as well as to rasterize the PDF document itself. The graphics are performed using a mix of DirectX (Direct3D and Direct2D) and XAML UI elements. Speech recognition is performed using the built in Speech Services in Microsoft Windows. We primarily tested RichReview on a Lenovo Thinkpad Tablet 2 tablet, which has a 10.1'' display screen, an inductive pen digitizer and 5-points multi-touch. However, we have also used RichReview successfully on a range of other pen-enabled tablet devices. We generally prefer to use a Bluetooth headset supporting 16 KHz wideband audio for the audio capture since writing can introduce undesirable rattling noises when recording using the built-in microphone on the tablet.

EVALUATION

We wished to determine whether users could successfully employ the features of RichReview to make comments on a document. Moreover, we wanted to investigate how these features were actually used. Therefore, we conducted a qualitative, formative user study using our prototype system.

Study Design

To prompt realistic feedback from participants, we designed a task based on a representative classroom situation. We asked the participants to assume that they were working as

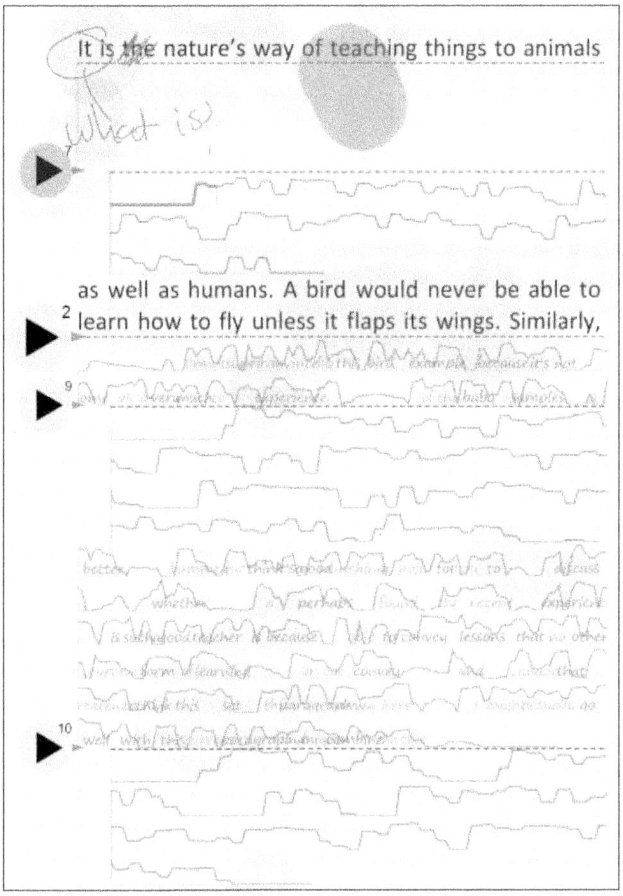

Figure 10. New annotations can be inserted under existing expansion space or in the middle of existing waveform (footage from the real-user data, P2); here the red user has replied to the blue user's existing voice comment.

a teaching assistant (TA) for an introductory, undergraduate writing class, commenting on a student's essay assignment.

Operating under the assumption that the social relationship between collaborators may influence annotation behavior, we told half of our participants that their annotations would be shared with the instructor of the course. We told the other half that their comments would be shared with a peer grader. Note, the point of splitting our participants into two groups was to expand our coverage of possible usage scenarios rather than to carry out a controlled comparison or test a hypothesis.

Procedure

Our study consisted of a practice session that helped participants familiarize themselves with RichReview interactions followed by an open-ended session with full-fledged tasks. During the practice session, we introduced each feature of the system to each participant by demonstrating a specific use case, and then letting them try out the features first hand. For example, the Spotlight feature was introduced in the context of referring to a location of document while recording. Next, we gave each participant a set of practice tasks to carry out. We ended the practice session by having participants use the audio editing functionality: participants were asked to pick one of the most problematic recordings amongst the ones they had created, and edit it so that could be better understood. The practice session took less than 40 minutes.

The open-ended annotation session consisted of two parts. Participants started with the production part where they gave constructive feedback on an essay for 15 minutes. They were asked to create at least 6 comments on an essay concerning any kind of writing issue. Then, participants performed the consumption part, which looked at how rich annotations are consumed and discussed. We asked participants to listen to a set of pre-made annotations, and then respond with constructive feedback for 20 minutes. In both tasks, participants were not required to use any specific interaction techniques. We concluded the evaluation with a 10 minute of semi-structured interview session. In total, the study tasks required approximately 90 minutes to complete.

Materials

The materials used in the study were sample essays to the "Analyze an Issue" portion of the Graduate Record Exam used in the United States for entrance to graduate school. These essays tend to be around 500 to 650 words long (approximately 1 page) and of moderate writing quality. We picked two different essays, counter balanced across participants to rule out text dependencies. Each participant used the same essay across the production and consumption tasks, in order to save reading time.

The pre-made annotations in the consumption task were composed of various discussion topics and consisted of diverse modality combinations. These were based on real annotation data captured in earlier pilot tests of our system.

Participants

We recruited 12 participants from student mailing lists at a large university. The average age of our participants was 21.3 years old. All but one participant was a native English speaker and all had experience with collaborative writing tools. The most frequent discussion channel for their writing tasks was e-mail (5.33 hours/week), followed by F2F meeting (3.67 hours/week). The participants received $15 for taking part in the study.

RESULTS

Broadly speaking, the results of our study demonstrated that participants could successfully employ RichReview to communicate complex ideas about a document. Voice and Spotlight introduced additional expressiveness and efficiency on top of the communication capability of the legacy collaboration tools that were based on textual means. Moreover, cross-modal commentaries and indexing features helped users achieve fluid modality combination and lightweight annotation access.

Experience of Using RichReview

Users compared the overall experience of using RichReview to having a collaborator virtually present. P3, when talking about the Spotlight feature remarked, "It (Spotlight) was like I was talking to someone in person when I point to an area." Further evidence of this was the fact that in annotations, participants often used the pronoun "you" reinforcing the sense that they were talking *through* the computer rather than talking *to* the computer.

Annotation Production

Ink Annotations

Direct inking without additional forms of recording was the most widely used form of annotation. All of the participants used ink for simple mark-up such as circling, underlining, question marks, brackets, proofreading symbols, connecting lines, and personal notes that they wanted to revisit. This highlights the importance of static inking for lightweight interaction.

Voice Annotations

Voice recording was used by all participants when they wanted to make a comment that was longer or more detailed. Participants praised voice's speed and expressiveness. As P4 said, "Now I can hear someone's voice and understand completely what they're trying to say versus just seeing their note and trying to interpret." All participants except P1 and P8 used voice in conjunction with writing and the Spotlight. These two users used voice on its own.

Participants structured their voice annotation in many different ways. One way was to write ink as a visual guidance for the verbal description. For example, participants first made underlines on body-texts or wrote down key points in white space while reading, and then used voice or Spotlight to refer to these points while recording. Another way was to write keywords *during* the recording session to allow their hypothetical recipient navigate to a certain topic in the recording by tapping on a corresponding keyword. Additionally, P3, P5, P8, P9, P11 used the feature where additional annotations could be appended onto an existing one; they used this feature when they had multiple points to talk about in a single paragraph.

Another interesting observation was that participants tended to use voice when they disagreed with an idea and ink when they agreed with it. The reason for this was because when they disagreed, they would use voice to provide a detailed explanation for their disagreement (P6, P7, P10, and P11). This suggests that support for voice annotations could be the best method for achieving group maintenance goals [2].

Spotlight Annotations

Participants frequently used Spotlight when speaking. The Spotlight feature was used to refer not just to the underlying text, but also to other people's ink marks and a part of waveform or transcripts. Annotations about paragraph structure or logical inconsistencies were often accompanied by the spatial cues that Spotlight conveyed. Overall, the feature was seen to be a powerful deictic tool: As P3 said, "I liked that feature (Spotlight) a lot, because it could direct somebody while recording to the specific spot that they are talking about."

Participants did raise some implementation issues, however. P1, P9, and P10 reported that Spotlight was sometimes recorded inadvertently when the pen hovered over the screen for other reasons. P1 complained that the Spotlight trail was too thick to point to a specific line of text or word. In future iterations of the system, these issues could be addressed by filtering out spurious hovering gestures and by changing the blob size.

Socially-Driven Modality Choices

Besides the annotation content and purpose, we found that the social factors affected which communication modalities participants felt comfortable employing. For example, P2 and P8 regarded simple scribbles, such as circling or checkmarks, as an impolite or casual form of annotation, choosing instead to leave voice comments. Similarly, P1 and P8 thought that writing a complete message was more polite than voice. In this case, they claimed written comments were easy to understand and that voice is a "lazy form (P8)". While we cannot draw any conclusions on this basis, this does raise some interesting research questions for future research on annotation and target users.

Editing Audio

Most participants found the voice editing interface easy to use and efficient especially for removing long pauses or utterances such as "Um". This suggests that automatic detection and trimming of the pauses might be useful. However, considering that some users depend on long pauses as a navigation cue for time indexing operations, removing these also might be problematic. Ultimately the long term usefulness of these features would need to be assessed in real practice.

Annotations Use and Organization: Annotation Positioning

Most annotations were placed immediately under the relevant text. If it was about a sentence or keyword, participants would position the annotation under a line in the middle of a paragraph. However, P1 and P8 were reluctant to break the paragraph structure, instead placing the recording below the paragraph and making a reference to the targets using inking or the Spotlight. Some annotations do not have an obvious anchor point such as when they are about multiple paragraphs or global writing issues. In these cases, participants usually placed the recordings below the end of the right column, making them hard to distinguish from those relating to the last paragraph. This observation suggests that a distinct space to anchor meta-commentary [27], possibly close to the bottom of the page, might be useful.

Consuming Annotations

Navigation via the visual representation of the audio was actively used to jump into or revisit a voice annotation. Participants were able to use the waveform as a navigation cue effectively when there were salient features they could focus on, such stretches of silence. Other participants sometimes used the words in the transcript as a way to navigate (P7, P9, and P12).

However, most of participants preferred using the waveform over transcription because of the detrimental effect of transcription errors. For instance, P11 recounted one instance where the phrase "kind of this" was recognized as "Kennedy." Although P11 was aware it was a transcription error, the participant found it very hard to ignore.

Participants found Spotlight trails useful for getting a sense of what an annotation was about. However, participants did not use ink or Spotlight trails to index into annotations. We believe there were two reasons for this: First, Spotlight traces became too cluttered; second, users were not familiar enough with the style of annotation to know how the ink or Spotlight element was structured in relation to the audio.

Creating Responses and Discussion Threads

The ability to create rich annotations about existing ones was well adopted by all participants. In general, most responses tended to be placed immediately below the annotation to which it responded. For instance, P2 inserted a voice annotation in the middle of an existing audio stream (Figure 10). P10 made a written reply below a part of existing spoken annotation making use of cross-modal commentary features (Figure 9). They used cross-modal mark-up features for referring to parts of spoken or written annotations. For instance, P7 used the Spotlight to point to the visual representation of the audio (Figure 8), and P10 marked it up with ink (Figure 9).

DISCUSSION AND FUTURE WORK

Taken together, the results of our study show that supporting multiple modalities within an annotation tool can indeed enable creative and expressive ways for users to comment on and discuss documents with others. Our participants sometimes drew on one modality at a time, and other times intertwined their use of ink, speech and gesture. Indeed, the majority of our participants ended up using a mixture of modalities for a variety of purposes. Further, the reasons participants gave for employing specific modalities, such as speech being a better mode for conveying explanations when there was disagreement, were in line with what previous work has identified as specific strengths of non-textual comments and annotations.

Efficacy of RichReview

Of course, determining whether RichReview is in fact *useful* rather than simply *usable* will depend on its deployment in a naturalistic setting, assessed alongside other collaborative tools. In order to prepare the RichReview system for deployment, a number of issues must be addressed. First, ASR accuracy needs to be improved. One possible solution of this issue is to offer a tiered approach using a more sophisticated system in the cloud or even transcribed via crowd sourcing if extra accuracy is desired. Second, the visual clutter from Spotlight traces can be resolved by employing a filtering feature that renders a part of relevant data only. Finally, tighter integration of RichReview and authoring environments (e.g. LaTeX, Microsoft Word) to support the full write-revise-review workflow is critical.

Additional Application Domains

Looking further, we believe that the ideas behind RichReview can be extended to other application domains. For example, making the system practical for larger groups can be a useful extension. One possible application of the RichReview system at scale is to support discussion in large distributed courses such as MOOCs. There are challenges to tackle in doing this, however. For instance, the current presentation of Spotlight turned out to be cluttered when there are many annotations on the page. Another issue was that participants were concerned about fluid document layout and that introducing too many gaps for annotations would adversely affect the readability of the main body text.

RichReview can also be used to discuss other types of documents. For instance, engineering documents like electronic schematics or architectural drawings, or source code are often created through collaborative processes. These types of documents can similarly benefit from the expressiveness that the RichReview system brings. The general obstacles that needs to be resolved when extending RichReview to these other domains is to make it compatible with the unique discussion requirements and structure of the documents used in these other domains.

CONCLUSION

We have shown a system for rich annotation that offers users flexibility, versatility and expressivity, not only in terms of the creation of annotations, but also in consuming them. The core innovation is our design decisions to support commentaries and indexing across different annotation modalities. The fact that early users felt that they could communicate through and around the document using this tool, even achieving a sense of remote presence, shows promise. At the same time, the design, implementation and evaluation of the system so far has raised a number of interesting research questions for further work including improving navigation of dynamic annotations, making the system scalable, and expanding application areas. The possibilities opened up through multi-modal annotation systems are undoubtedly both diverse and compelling.

ACKNOWLEDGEMENTS

Yoon gratefully acknowledges support from the Kwanjeong Educational Foundation. This work was supported in part by a gift from FXPAL. We would also like to thank Robert Corish and Bill Buxton for their design input.

REFERENCES

1. Bickmore, T., Pfeifer, L., and Yin, L. The role of gesture in document explanation by embodied conversational agents. *International Journal of Semantic Computing*, (2008).
2. Birnholtz, J., Steinhardt, S., and Pavese, A. Write here, write now! *Proceedings of the SIGCHI Conference on Human Factors in Computing Systems - CHI '13*, ACM Press (2013), 961.
3. Chalfonte, B.L., Fish, R.S., and Kraut, R.E. Expressive richness. *Proceedings of the SIGCHI conference on Human factors in computing systems Reaching through technology - CHI '91*, ACM Press (1991), 21–26.
4. Clark, H. and Brennan, S. Grounding in communication. *Perspectives on socially shared cognition*, (1991).
5. Cockburn, A., Gutwin, C., and Alexander, J. Faster document navigation with space-filling thumbnails. *Proceedings of the SIGCHI conference on Human Factors in computing systems - CHI '06*, (2006).
6. Grudin, J. Why CSCW applications fail: problems in the design and evaluationof organizational interfaces. *Proceedings of the 1988 ACM conference on Computer-supported cooperative work - CSCW '88*, ACM Press (1988), 85–93.
7. Hardock, G., Kurtenbach, G., and Buxton, W. A marking based interface for collaborative writing. *Proceedings of the 6th annual ACM symposium on User interface software and technology - UIST '93*, ACM Press (1993), 259–266.
8. Kraut, R., Galegher, J., Fish, R., and Chalfonte, B. Task Requirements and Media Choice in Collaborative Writing. *Human-Computer Interaction 7*, 4 (1992), 375–407.
9. Kraut, R.E., Gergle, D., and Fussell, S.R. The use of visual information in shared visual spaces. *Proceedings of the 2002 ACM conference on Computer supported cooperative work - CSCW '02*, ACM Press (2002), 31.
10. Levine, S. and Ehrlich, S. The Freestyle System. *Human-Machine Interactive Systems*, (1991).
11. Marshall, C.C. and Brush, A.J.B. Exploring the relationship between personal and public annotations. 2004, 349–357.
12. Marshall, C.C., Price, M.N., Golovchinsky, G., and Schilit, B.N. Collaborating over portable reading appliances. *Personal Technologies 3*, 1-2 (1999), 43.
13. McNeill, D. *Language and gesture*. 2000.
14. Monserrat, T.-J.K.P., Zhao, S., McGee, K., and Pandey, A.V. NoteVideo. *Proceedings of the SIGCHI Conference on Human Factors in Computing Systems - CHI '13*, ACM Press (2013), 1139.
15. Morris;, M.R., Brush;, A.J.B., and Meyers, B.R. Reading revisited: Evaluating the usability of digital display surfaces for active reading tasks. *Horizontal Interactive Human-Computer System*, (2007), 79 – 86.
16. Neuwirth, C.M., Chandhok, R., Charney, D., Wojahn, P., and Kim, L. Distributed collaborative writing. *Proceedings of the SIGCHI conference on Human factors in computing systems celebrating interdependence - CHI '94*, ACM Press (1994), 51–57.
17. Nicholson, R.T. Usage patterns in an integrated voice and data communications system. *ACM Transactions on Information Systems 3*, 3 (1985), 307–314.
18. Noël, S. and Robert, J.-M. Empirical Study on Collaborative Writing: What Do Co-authors Do, Use, and Like? *Computer Supported Cooperative Work (CSCW) 13*, 1 (2004), 63–89.
19. Oviatt, S. Ten myths of multimodal interaction. *Communications of the ACM 42*, 11 (1999), 74–81.
20. Sellen, A. and Harper, R. The Myth of the Paperless Office. *MIT Press*, .
21. Stifelman, L., Arons, B., and Schmandt, C. The audio notebook: paper and pen interaction with structured speech. *of the SIGCHI conference on*, (2001), 182–189.
22. Tsang, M. and Fitzmaurice, G. Boom chameleon: simultaneous capture of 3D viewpoint, voice and gesture annotations on a spatially-aware display. *Proceedings of the 15th annual ACM symposium on User interface software and technology*, (2002), 111–120.
23. Whittaker, S., Hirschberg, J., Amento, B., et al. SCANMail. *Proceedings of the SIGCHI conference on Human factors in computing systems Changing our world, changing ourselves - CHI '02*, ACM Press (2002), 275.
24. Whittaker, S., Hyland, P., and Wiley, M. FILOCHAT. *Proceedings of the SIGCHI conference on Human factors in computing systems celebrating interdependence - CHI '94*, ACM Press (1994), 271.
25. Wilcox, L.D., Schilit, B.N., and Sawhney, N. Dynomite. *Proceedings of the SIGCHI conference on Human factors in computing systems - CHI '97*, ACM Press (1997), 186–193.
26. Yoon, D., Chen, N., and Guimbretière, F. TextTearing. *Proceedings of the 26th annual ACM symposium on User interface software and technology - UIST '13*, ACM Press (2013), 107–112.
27. Zheng, Q., Booth, K., and McGrenere, J. Co-authoring with structured annotations. *Proceedings of the SIGCHI conference on Human Factors in computing systems - CHI '06*, ACM Press (2006), 131.

Sensory Triptych: Here, Near, Out There

Eric Paulos, Rundong Tian, Chris Myers
Electrical Engineering and Computer Sciences
University of California, Berkeley
{paulos, rutian, chrismyers}@berkeley.edu

Paxton Paulos
Berkeley Arts Magnet
Berkeley Unified School District
paxton@paulos.net

ABSTRACT
Sensory Triptych is a set of exploratory, interactive sensors designed for children that invite "new ways of seeing" our world from the perspective of the *here* (the earth, air, and water around us), *near* (things just out of sight), and *out there* (orbiting satellites and space junk) using familiar and novel interfaces, affordances, and narratives. We present a series of novel physical design prototypes that reframe sensing technologies for children that foster an early adoption of technology usage for exploring, understanding, communicating, sharing, and changing our world. Finally, we discuss how such designs expand the potential opportunities and landscapes for our future interactive systems and experiences within the UIST community.

Author Keywords
children; sensors; toys; education; citizen science; citizen exploration; critical design

ACM Classification Keywords
H5.m. Information interfaces and presentation (e.g., HCI): Miscellaneous.

INTRODUCTION
Sensory Triptych explores new form factors, interaction models, experiences, and sensing technologies for children that foster an early adoption of technology usage for exploring, understanding, communicating, sharing, and changing our world. Presenting technologies that promote curiosity, collaboration, and wonderment rather than computer games and mobile apps, Sensory Triptych operates across three themes. *Here* — By integrating soil sensors into common sandbox toys with light, vibration, sound, and e-ink displays for facial expressions, **Earth Explorers** encourage children to approach sensing and technology as tools for exploring, interrogating, and investigating their world in creative and playful ways. **Air Explorers** measure air quality with low-cost air particle sensors embedded into toy airplanes and skateboards while **Water Explorers** embed flexible total dissolved solids (TDS) water sensors into toy boats to explore water quality in baths, sinks, lakes, streams, pools, and gutters. *Near* — **Adventure Watch** is a watch that provides real-time "nearness" for a narrow set of "interesting" kid specific places just beyond their field of view — parks with cool slides, junkyards, toy stores, skate parks, trains, earthquake fault-lines, etc. It invites a sense of adventure and discovery in seeking out and finding nearby places. As a car passenger, it encourages kids to imagine the world of adventures just beyond their vantage as it enables a "new way of seeing" the world around them. *Out There* — **Overhead** is a personal domestic object that continuously senses the world above us, outer-space, by tracking and reporting the flyovers of the more than 17,000 currently tracked orbiting objects as they passes overhead.

UIST '14, October 05 - 08 2014, Honolulu, HI, USA
Copyright 2014 ACM 978-1-4503-3069-5/14/10...$15.00.
http://dx.doi.org/10.1145/2642918.2647410

Figure 1. Examples of the three themes. *Here*: Earth Explorer, *Near*: Adventure Watch, and *Out There*: Overhead

RELATED WORK
Over the past few years, researchers have developed a range of sensing systems to measure our local environment [1-8]. Personal, mobile devices coupled with novel sensors have empowered users to monitor factors such as air pollution, water flow in creeks [9], noise pollution [10], and metal content in soil [11]. Compelling visualizations of this citizen-collected data using graphs and maps have provided powerful tools for informing communities and expert analysis [12]. Many of these phone based citizen science platforms have enabled a new practice of public participation around data collection and analysis. Similarly, there has been a growing body of work into the interaction design of children's toys and technologies [13-17]. Finally, we have also seen a series of exciting projects exploring sensor legibility through critical design artifacts and ambiguity [18-19].

Figure 2. Examples of e-ink based facial expressions on the Earth Explorer: Sleeping, waking up, waiting for a sample, measuring a sample, and expressing a final result using a wink.

Our work leverages this impressive collection of important work to present a series of technologies that explore sensing, citizen science, sensor legibility, sensor epistemology, and learning through novel form factors, contexts, and interactions.

FROM CITIZEN SCIENCE TO CITIZEN EXPLORATION

While citizen science has been an emerging and important theme in the research community, it may overly foreground a scientific agenda within the work. We argue that the primary value of these projects is in rekindling a curiosity in our world by promoting and engaging individuals to look, feel, interact with, and explore the world around them. A more appropriate term is "Citizen Explorer" rather than Citizen Science. This paper explicitly focuses on foregrounding the design elements of such "exploratory" technologies through a series of physical prototypes and examples.

DESIGN MOTIVATION

The motivation for this work is at the conflux of childhood curiosity and citizen exploration technologies. From the latter, many of our technologies focus on providing universal interfaces to services and systems such as social media, email, online banking, weather, games, mapping, etc. While the ubiquity of our mobile tools makes them arguably strong candidates for embedding citizen exploration applications, we wanted to explore form factors and designs that avoided this interface overloading. To sufficiently vary the range of "seeing", we used *proximity* as a sensing differentiator. This led to looking at sensing things that are very close (i.e. here), close by not visible (i.e. near), and very far (i.e. out there). One could imagine other ways to discretize this distance parameter. For us the main factor was to provide a design landscape that avoided solely focusing on most common type of sensing, here. This distance design constraint parameter worked well in showcasing alternative sensing approaches and opportunities.

The second motivation came through the authors' observations and conversations with young elementary school children, boys and girls, aged 4-8. To be clear, we have not yet conducted user studies of these designs, and issues of usability, how well these objects promoted curiosity, and even gender issues have not yet been measured sufficiently to document in this paper. We can report that the children that have serendipitously encountered the technologies have expressed overwhelming excitement, enthusiasm, and desire to have one themselves. Similarly, we can describe the observations and interactions with children that motivated this work. For example, when looking for design opportunities for environmental sensing, we studied and brainstormed starting with toys commonly played with by children outside. This led to the set of Earth Explorers designs. We also observed first hand examples of children questioning the visual "nearby" places that scrolled by peripherally on GPS car navigation systems. This childhood curiosity and in some cases genuine emotions of disappointment at missing out on seeing or visiting a nearby park or train track led to our more focused brainstorm that led to the Adventure Watch design. Finally, in discussions with children about far away things we found satellites, rockets, and planets to be a common theme. We intentionally ignored planets to avoid any overt "planet education" messaging and instead focused on the lesser explored experience of satellites. We were also drawn to satellites because, similar to other environmental issues such as air pollution and water quality, satellites are a product of and directly influenced by the actions of our industrialized society. However, to be clear the goal of these projects was not to produce a set of digital eco-toys. Rather, we wanted to explore new designs for seeing and exploring our world beyond mobile apps and overt sensing technologies.

HERE

The first theme within Sensory Triptych is *here* which is focused on developing new interfaces to sensing the immediate present place of play for children. We do this by integrating a range of sensing into familiar toys and playful affordances. The interaction design of these objects is not intended to deliver exact numerical values or signal ecological fear in children. Rather, these interactive environmental sensing toys provide signals to children about the soil, water, and air variations to promote curiosity and reflection. The feedback of the system through facial expressions, lights, sounds, and vibration, provide playful elements for children to develop into their own narrative. The *here* theme is manifest in three novel exploratory forms as described below.

Earth Explorers

We have integrated off the shelf soil moisture and pH sensors into a series of common sandbox toys such as a toy dump tuck and bulldozer. Within each of these land based explorers are an array of sensors and output mechanisms such as lights, sounds, and vibration. The Earth Explorers also use e-ink for expressive facial output on these technologies. While the measurements and outputs are accurate, the goal is not to output literal values but rather to develop experiences around the sensors that invite curiosity and child driven narrative into play.

Initially the Earth Explorer is asleep as represented by closed eyes on the e-ink display. Shaking the toy causes it to wake up and begin looking around curiously. When the bulldozer or dump truck is filled with dirt, as detected by a photodiode, the eyes on the toy look towards the loaded dirt and a light inside the cab of the toy flashes briefly to indicate a measurement has been taken. The sensed value, soil moisture for example, is mapped into four discrete ranges and output through a vibratory motor that can be felt when holding the toy. We combine high and low motor speeds with long and short pulse times to represent the four sensor value ranges.

Air Explorers

Similar architecturally to the Earth Explorers, Air Explorers integrate a newly designed laser particle sensor we have developed call *MyPart* to provide low-cost, low-power, air particle sensing into a toy airplane. Air Explorers express a similar range of output modalities including light, sound, and vibration for expressing measured air particle counts in real time which relates directly to air quality and health. The main difference in output modality from Earth Explores is that readings are taken continuously every few seconds rather than triggered by an event such as loading dirt. This means that as the toy airplane is being "flown" around several seconds of particle data are collected, mapped into four discrete ranges, and then output through vibrations similar to the Earth Explores.

Water Explorers

Integrating our recently developed low-cost, flexible total dissolved solids (TDS) water sensor called *MyWater* into a toy boat, Water Explorers invite children to explore water quality in their bath, sink, lakes, streams, pools, and gutters. The Water Explorers interaction functions similarly to the Air Explorer by taken readings every few seconds and outputting the results through a set of discrete vibration pulses.

Hardware and Sensor Details

All of the *here* theme artifacts (Earth, Air, and Water Explorers), leverage our existing body of work in citizen science, low-cost sensing, and critical design. As mentioned, we developed two low-cost, low-power sensors, namely *MyWater* and *MyPart*, that are integrated into the Sensory Triptych project and we describe them below.

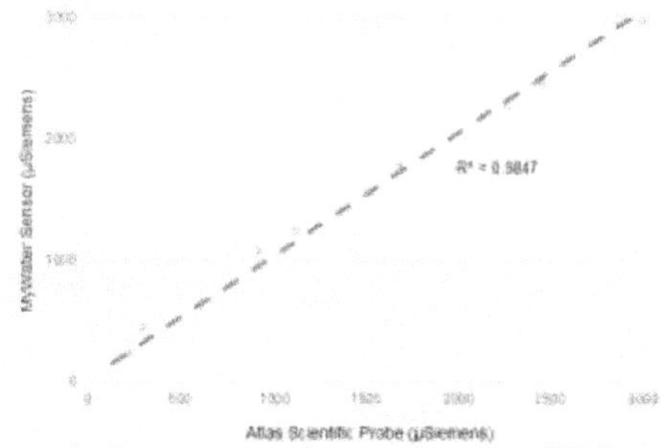

Figure 3. Data comparing our low-cost TDS sensor with a calibrated Atlas Scientific Conductivity Probe.

Total Dissolved Solids (TDS)

Total Dissolved Solids (TDS) is a measure of the combined content of all inorganic and organic substances contained in a liquid (in our case water). While TDS is not generally considered a primary pollutant, it is often used as an indication of chemical or other contaminates in drinking water. Using an small microprocessor, a handful of passive components, and nickel chromium wire, we have developed a low-cost, low-power, flexible TDS sensor for a fraction of the cost and size of off the shelf sensors that performs respectably against much more expensive scientific grade circuits and probes.

The *MyWater* sensor in the Water Explorers uses a TDS sensor we designed to measure the amount of total dissolved solids in water through electrical conductance. To detect changes in conductance, we used a standard Wheatstone bridge with the water of interest as the unknown resistor. The probes that contact the liquid are made of Nickel Chromium, a highly unreactive alloy. To prevent electroplating the probes, the direction of voltage through the Wheatstone bridge is alternated every second. The voltage between the two midpoints of the bridge is measured with a ten bit ADC onboard the AtTiny85 microcontroller. Tests were conducted against the Atlas Scientific Conductivity Probe (a $150 sensor), and our sensor exhibited comparable performance across a range of 3000 microsiemens. The total cost of all components of our sensor was under $10 (see Figure 3).

Laser Air Quality Particle Counter

Low-cost air quality sensing often consists of some form of gas sensor. These are typically a thermal conductivity based detector tuned to respond to carbon monoxide, ozone, nitrogen oxides, or other gases. However, these devices do a poor job of accurately measuring the actual gas concentrations due to sensor response selectivity and gas interaction problems. Furthermore, these gas sensors are high-power due to their thermal heating requirements. Most importantly, these gas sensors do not measure the primary air pollutant in regards to human health which is airborne particles. To address this problem, we have engineered a

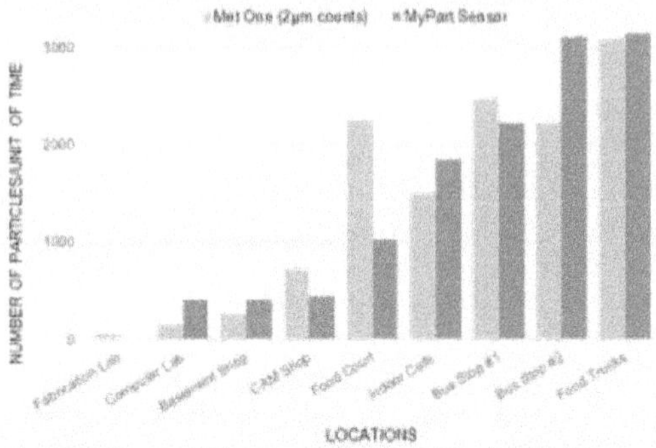

Figure 4. Data comparing our low-cost air particle sensor with a calibrated MET-ONE particle count sensor.

novel, functional, low-cost laser air particle counter. Our device demonstrates a signal response consistent with highly calibrated particle sensors in our lab. Again, because of the smaller, flexible form factor, and low-power usage, we are able to explore a wide variety of embedded applications, data logging, and wireless possibilities for this sensor.

The *MyPart* sensor in the Air Explorers uses a laser and photodiode arranged orthogonally such that the focal point of the laser is located directly above the photodiode. Air is drawn through the system across the photodiode using a small computer fan. Particles in the air stream that intersect the path of the laser scatter light onto the photodiode, and the resulting voltage signal is amplified by an op-amp circuit and sampled by a microcontroller with a ten bit ADC. The data is analyzed for peaks, which indicate that a particle has been detected. Preliminary tests were conducted against a MET-ONE HPPC-6 (a highly calibrated $2000 particle counter used in cleanroom applications) at different locations of varying ambient light intensity and air quality. The results show promising correlation between the *MyPart* sensor and the MET-ONE (see Figure 4).

NEAR

The *near* theme presents a new form of mapping constrained to near "places" just slightly out of sight. For example, while driving a car, adults focus on the the desired route and traffic as presented by most navigation GPS systems. However, for the backseat child, it is the objects "on screen" but just out of sight that draw their curiosity - the park on the next street over, the train tracks just beyond the visible trees, or the junkyard behind the adjacent buildings.

The Adventure Watch

The near theme delivers a highly constrained, curated experience of specifically chosen near places through a watch form factor. Tuned to only "slightly out of view", nearby places, it foregrounds those sites of specific child fascination beyond 50 meters but within 500 meters. The watch uses GPS, a digital compass, and a small screen to signal when sites of childhood curiosity are nearby along with heading and distance information. The Adventure Watch is designed for a child but equally fascinating for sparking even a childhood curiosity in adults (Figure 5).

Figure 5. Adventure Watch indicating nearby train tracks.

Unlike a traditional GSP units, the Adventure Watch is a GPS device that provides an abstracted proximity indication to an intentionally limited and selectable set of "places" of interest to children - parks with cool slides, junkyards full of a day's adventure, toy stores, skate parks, etc. The Adventure Watch invites a sense of adventure and discovery as an exploratory tool for children to seek out and find nearby places of extreme personal interest and delight. When the child is a passenger is in a car or walking, the watch encourages them to reflect, imagine, and wonder about the world of adventures just beyond their vantage as it enables a "new way of seeing" the world around them. The directional heading and compass aid in the final navigation if the child sets of to actually discover the "landmark".

OUT THERE

Finally, the *out there* theme provides a mechanism to sense objects permanently far away. So far away in fact that it is nearly impossible to travel to them or view them directly. In fact the sensed data must be believed at face value since direct measurements are often impossible.

Overhead

The *out there* theme of exploratory sensors is represented by Overhead (Figure 6) which presents a new level of curiosity and degree of trust reporting on the flyovers of overhead satellites and space junk in real-time with corresponding facts and data. It lives comfortably in a child's bedroom. Overhead is an personal domestic object that senses the world above us, outer-space, by tracking and reporting the flyovers of Earth orbiting objects as they passes overhead. Decades of launches have left Earth surrounded by a halo of space junk with more than 17,000 trackable objects larger than a coffee cup and less than 7% of those as operational satellites. Based on its GPS location and orientation, Overhead uses real-time data to signal and report on each orbiting object — from the International Space Station to military spy satellites, discarded rocket engines, astronaut tools, and space junk. Overhead points out each orbiting object by swinging towards its actual position, projecting a small icon on the ceiling to track its transit in real-time, while it communicates data about the satellite through a set of three integrated clear screens embedded within each of its solar panels. Data includes, satellite name, country of origin, date launched, satellite type (i.e. communications, reconnaissance, weather, debris, etc), and a scrolling list of mission facts. An image of the satellite is also displayed with a human for scale.

This work is thematic with the Plane Tracker Project [19] which invites a similar curiosity around visible airplanes as they fly by. However, the work we present in the *out there* theme is specifically focused on exploring sensors that deliver information concerning mostly un-viewable objects. That is, while one can plan and observe a limited set of major satellites such as the International Space Station or Hubble Space Telescope near dawn and dusk, this represents only a tiny fraction of the over 17,000 tracked objects that orbit the earth and are invisible to the naked eye.

DISCUSSION

We present these prototypes as critical designs that demonstrate how reframing the landscape of sensing and interaction can afford new design opportunities for HCI practitioners. This Sensory Triptych demonstrates the value of designs that present sensor data in incomplete narratives or stripped of meta data and measured context. Instead these designs develop early childhood expectations of roles for technology away the limited framings found in many of today's devices which often overemphasize a focus on improving efficiency, productivity, and accuracy.

Epistemology and Sensor Legibility

This series of objects reference epistemological issues around knowledge and truth in the manner in which it invites "new ways of seeing" our world. It questions ideas of "what is real" as it provides a mediated mapping of our world through digital sensing. It invites questions on the limits and consequences of sensors, values, and truth in what we see and cannot observe directly. It also draws out a separate debate around sensor legibility as it positions itself within a landscape of the literal and abstract. The project is a mix of juxtaposing narratives from the exactness, seriousness, and problem solving professionalism of overt sensing performed by experts to the embedding of casual sensors collaged within the playful curiosity of children and toys. It also inverts the idea of expert itself by framing children as the ultimate experts, storytellers, and explores of our world through their well developed craft of play, curiosity, and narrative. Finally, it argues for a children as activists and participants both within their own world and the larger context of Dewey's framing of the "public" [20].

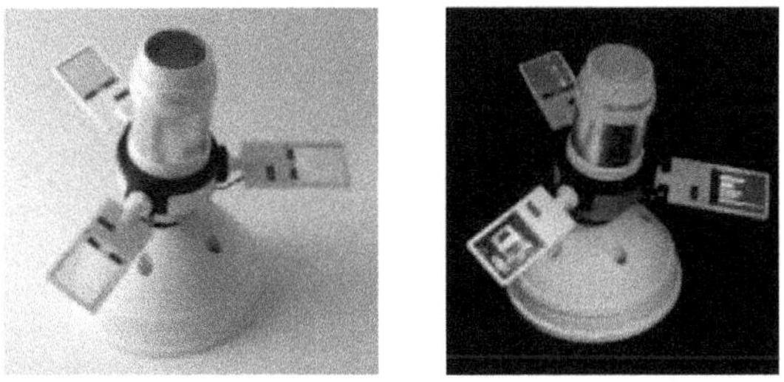

Figure 6. Overhead (illuminated and in darkness) communicating location by pan/tilt and displaying detailed satellite facts on its clear screens during each orbital flyover.

Critical Design: Curious Toys and Curious Technologies

All of these objects critique current trend in technology and its adoption through critical design. There are several issues at play. First, the pervasive nature of electronics and technology embedded within children's toys have led to a series of distracting sounds, flashing lights, voices, and gyrating motions for toys. Worse, these toys often strive to complete narratives rather than encourage and foster the rich natural curiosity in children. Similarly, most current discussions of technologies for kids almost always gravitate towards mobile apps, computer games, and screen based experiences. But future innovation will come in a variety of forms and experiences beyond today's touch screens. Getting dirty with crowd-sourced sandbox sensing, playground curiosities, and real-time orbiting satellites generates a narrative essential to this debate of technologies for children and our future devices.

Finally, this work focuses around reframing technologies to avoid the constant push to find friends, download hip music, and locate great restaurants and instead provide incomplete information, inviting individuals to engage more directly with the co-creation with technology and fostering of narratives and storytelling. How can our technologies celebrate these seams? That is, rather than viewing the edges of technological limitations or lack of connectivity as problems, how can they be explored as opportunities for engagement, curiosity, and wonderment?

CONCLUSION

We have presented a set of exploratory, interactive devices that invite "new ways of seeing" our world from the perspective of the *here*, *near*, and *out there* through sensing technologies design for children that foster an early adoption of technology usage for exploring, understanding, communicating, sharing, and changing our world. We used this series of examples to identify and highlight how reframing the interface and experience away from expected standard practices can reveal a wealth of important and valuable potential interaction opportunities and new design landscapes.

ACKNOWLEDGMENTS

We would like to thank all of the children that inspired our thinking with their contagious curiosity and creativity, the anonymous reviewers, and support from NSF IIS-1211047.

REFERENCES

1. Burke, J., Estrin, D., Hansen, M., Parker, A., Ramanathan, N., Reddy, S., and Srivastava, M. 2006. Participatory sensing. In World Sensor Web Workshop. ACM, New York, 1-5.
2. Bales, E., Nikzad, N., Quick, N., Ziftci, C., Patrick, K., and Griswold, W. 2012. Citisense: Mobile air quality sensing for individuals and communities. *Pervasive Health*, 155-158.
3. Henriques, J. J., Bojarski, B., Byrd, K. W., and Von Wald, M. 2013. Crowd-sourcing urban air-quality in developing countries through open source technologies, *Global Humanitarian Technology Conference*, 447-451.
4. Aoki, P. M., Honicky, R. J., Mainwaring, A., Myers, C., Paulos, E., Subramanian, S., Woodruff, A. 2009. A vehicle for research: using street sweepers to explore the landscape of environmental community action. *SIGCHI,* 375-384.
5. Paulos, E., Honicky, R. J., and Hooker, B. 2008. Citizen Science: Enabling Participatory Urbanism. *Handbook of Research on Urban Informatics: The Practice and Promise of the Real-time City*. 414-436.
6. Kuznetsov, S., Davis, G. N., Cheung, J. C., and Paulos, E. 2011. Ceci N'est Pas Une Pipe Bombe: Challenges to Urban Authoring and Participatory Sensing. *SIGCHI* 2375-2384.
7. Kim, S. and Paulos, E. 2010. inAir: Sharing Indoor Air Quality Measurements and Visualizations. *SIGCHI*, 1861-1870.
8. Kim, S., Paulos, E., and Gross, M. 2010. WearAir: Expressive T-Shirts for Air Quality Sensing. *ACM TEI*, 295-296.
9. Kim, S., Robson, C., Zimmerman, T., Pierce, J., and Haber, E. M. 2011. Creek watch: pairing usefulness and usability for successful citizen science. *SIGCHI*, 2125-2134.
10. Maisonneuve, N., Stevens, M., Niessen, M. E., Hanappe, P., Steels, L. 2009. Citizen noise pollution monitoring. *Digital Government Research*, 96-103.
11. Kuznetsov, S., Harrigan-Anderson, W., Faste, H., Hudson, S. E., and Paulos, E. 2013. Community Engagements with Living Sensing Systems, *ACM C&C*, 213-222.
12. Willett, W., Heer, J., Hellerstein, J., and Agrawala, M. 2011. CommentSpace: structured support for collaborative visual analysis. *SIGCHI*, 313-3140.
13. Westeyn, T., Kientz, J., Starner, T., Abowd, G. 2008. Designing toys with automatic play characterization for supporting the assessment of a child's development. *Interaction design and children*, 89-92.
14. Eisenberg, M. 2003. Mindstuff educational technology beyond the computer. *Convergence: International Journal of Research into New Media Technologies*. 9(2), 29-53.
15. Druin, A. 2009 *Mobile technology for children: designing for interaction and learning*. Morgan Kaufmann.
16. Grufberg, K. and Jonsson, M. 2012. Sciensations: making sense of science by designing with sensors. *Interaction Design and Children*, 116-124.
17. Ryokai, K., Su, P., Kim, E., Rollins, B. 2014. EnergyBugs: energy harvesting for children. *SIGCHI*, 1039-1048.
18. Gaver, W., Bowers, J., Boehner, K., Boucher, A., Cameron, D., Hauenstein, M., Jarvis, N., and Pennington, S. 2013. Indoor weather stations: investigating a ludic approach to environmental HCI through batch prototyping. *SIGCHI*, 3451-3460.
19. Gaver, W., Boucher, A., Law, A., Pennington, S., Bowers, J., Beaver, J., Humble, J., Kerridge, T., Villar, N., Wilkie, A. 2008. Threshold Devices: Looking out from the Home. *SIGCHI*, 1429-1438.
20. Dewey, J. 1954 *The Public and Its Problems*. Swallow Press.

Going to the Dogs:

Towards an Interactive Touchscreen Interface for Working Dogs

Clint Zeagler
Georgia Institute of Technology
clintzeagler@gatech.edu

Scott Gilliland
Georgia Institute of Technology
scott.gilliland@gatech.edu

Larry Freil
Georgia Institute of Technology
larry.freil@gatech.edu

Thad Starner
Georgia Institute of Technology
thad@gatech.edu

Melody Moore Jackson
Georgia Institute of Technology
melody@cc.gatech.edu

ABSTRACT
Computer-mediated interaction for working dogs is an important new domain for interaction research. In domestic settings, touchscreens could provide a way for dogs to communicate critical information to humans. In this paper we explore how a dog might interact with a touchscreen interface. We observe dogs' touchscreen interactions and record difficulties against what is expected of humans' touchscreen interactions. We also solve hardware issues through screen adaptations and projection styles to make a touchscreen usable for a canine's nose touch interactions. We also compare our canine touch data to humans' touch data on the same system. Our goal is to understand the affordances needed to make touchscreen interfaces usable for canines and help the future design of touchscreen interfaces for assistive dogs in the home.

Author Keywords
Animal Computer Interaction; Assistance Dog Interface Design; Touchscreen Interactions; Fitts' Law

ACM Classification Keywords
H.5.2 [Information interfaces and presentation]: User Interfaces---user-centered design

INTRODUCTION
Touchscreens surround all of us. Just as Weiser envisioned they are now ubiquitous in many domains [35]. We interact with our touchscreen phones and tablets constantly throughout the day. We see touchscreen futures promoted in Corning and Samsung videos [5,7] where everything around us becomes an interactive surface. Touchscreens and interactive surfaces work so well and seem so promising because of the research that has gone into creating good touchscreen interactions. A whole segment of HCI research is dedicated to predictive models and human factors associated with on-screen and touchscreen interactions. However, extending this research to working dogs could significantly impact the effectiveness of assistance dog communication.

Recent work has shown that assistance dogs can interact with wearable sensors on their vests to provide important, potentially life-saving, information to their handlers [13]. In the home, however, most assistance dogs do not wear their vests, for comfort reasons. Touchscreens could provide a viable alternative to wearable sensors for assistance dog communication.

Assistance Dog Communication
Since formal guide dog training began around 1918, assistance dogs have improved the lives of many thousands of people with disabilities [3, 30]. Dogs can work in many ways: guide dogs serve people with visual impairments; service dogs aid people with physical disabilities; and hearing dogs alert people with auditory disabilities to sounds (Figure 1). These highly trained canines can provide independence from human assistants and significantly enhance quality of life. However, communication between human and canine partners is limited. Handlers give verbal or hand signal commands, and dogs respond with trained behaviors, which can sometimes have ambiguous meanings to the handlers and to others around the handler.

For example, imagine that Sam, who has epilepsy, is hosting a dinner party for his colleagues, most of whom do not know that Sam is epileptic. Sam's medical alert dog, Gilbert, is loose in the house, helping Sam to greet his guests. A short time into the party, Gilbert detects that a seizure is imminent, before Sam or his or dinner guests can know what is happening. Gilbert nudges Sam to alert him, but Sam is so intent on greeting his guests he does not

UIST 2014, October 5–8, 2014, Honolulu, HI, USA.

ACM 978-1-4503-3069-5/14/10...$15.00.
http://dx.doi.org/10.1145/2642918.2647364

realize he is about to have a seizure. If Gilbert could walk to a touchscreen mounted on the wall in the living room, and touch a sequence of icons with his nose, he could send a clear and direct message to Sam's cell phone, as well as Sam's wife's cell phone, and possibly even call 911. Sam could get the help he needs before the situation becomes life-threatening.

Hearing assistance dogs alert their handlers to sounds by physical contact, such as nudging with a nose or paw, and then leading their handler to the source of the sound [3]. However, if a dog could tell his handler immediately whether the source of the sound was the doorbell or the tornado siren, the handler could make better decisions about how to respond. Improving dog-to-handler communication could have profound implications for assistance dog teams.

Figure 1. (Left) Guide dog and handler [30]; (Right) Hearing dog and handler [3]

Our previous work [13] shows that dogs can operate sensors based on their natural abilities of biting, tugging, and nose touching [10, 16]. These on-dog-body interactions are appropriate for typical service dogs accompanying their handlers outside the home, but service dogs often do not wear their vests in their home environments. However, if an assistance dog was at home without his communication-enabled vest on, he could still easily walk up to a touchscreen interface and make a selection combination sending the *Tornado Alarm* text to his handler's smart phone. These life saving use scenarios indicate why it might be important to extend touchscreen interfaces to working dogs.

This study explores the research question of whether dogs can effectively make selections using touchscreens, and proposes some possible design guidelines for canine touchscreen interfaces. Does a dog have the ***ability*** to interact with his/her own touchscreen computer in the house? If a dog had a touchscreen at his level and was trained to use the touchscreen to make selections, what would those interactions look like? What ***distances*** and selection ***target sizes*** should the interface have to conform to a dog's needs? How long will a dog interact with a touchscreen before becoming ***fatigued*** and what ***other insights*** might we gain from the data collected by touchscreen interactions from the dogs interacting with them? Do the prevalent predictive models, which designers use to create touchscreen interfaces for humans have any correlation when designing for dogs? Basic foundation theory is needed to help ground this field of dog-computer-interaction, based on previous work in human-computer interaction.

BACKGROUND AND RELATED WORK

Animals have operated machines since the time of Skinner in scientific experiments [31]. However, here we wish focus on improving the affordances of devices for Animal Computer Interaction (ACI), as opposed to focusing primarily on animals using machines in an aid to understanding animal cognition [6, 26, 29]. Amundin et al. [2] explain a very interesting system for dolphins to interact with using echolocation, like our system it is a type of touchscreen. Amundin's was built to work with dolphins, and tested to provide insight into how dolphin might best use a touchscreen system.. In Mankoff *et al* [18], researchers describe a "Fitts' Law" test consisting of throwing a tennis ball to a particular location to gauge speed of access; however it does not report results for this study, but does start to think about canines using computer interfaces. Other researchers have explored novel approaches to animal interactions. Games such as "Cat Cat Revolution" [20] and "Feline Fun Park" [37] allow humans to play with cats mediated by computing. The "Canine Amusement and Training" (CAT) system focuses on games as a way to teach humans to train and interact with dogs [36]. Remote interaction systems allow a human to monitor, care for, and play with their pets at home when they are away [12, 15, 18]. Researchers have trained an assistance dog to take commands from a speaker worn on his body [28]. While some of these studies support handler-to-dog communication or monitoring, they have not fully addressed dogs activating interface devices.

DOG TOUCHSCREEN INTERACTION ABILIITY

To be able to understand a dog's ***ability*** to interact with a touchscreen interface, we designed a touchscreen system and application for dogs which we also hoped we could compare to human interactions.

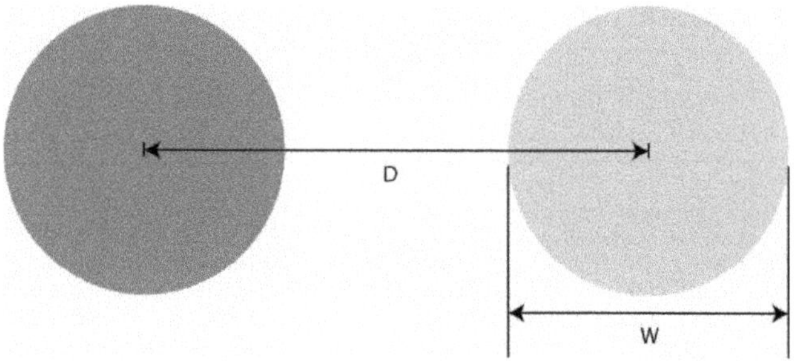

Figure 2. Tapping targets were chosen to be circles, both the distance between the centers of the target and the width of the targets are important.

We modeled our dog touchscreen interaction system and study after a Soukoreff and MacKenzie's *multidirectional tapping task* [32]. Circles were chosen as our tapping targets to ease the target selection analysis; with oblong or irregular shapes it becomes more difficult to understand the dog's selection intention. By using this type of study we are able to compare a set of dogs' interactions to a set of humans' interactions more effectively.

We wrote a Java program to display the targets in a series of sizes and distances. The sizes and distance selections can be controlled and changed by the dog handler before administering the interaction test to the dog (Figure 4). The program can also change the angle of targets displayed.

One circle-tapping target is blue and the other circle is yellow. Dogs are not completely colorblind as many people believe, but they do have difficulty seeing the difference between red and green [19]. Yellow and blue are the colors they can most easily differentiate. On a spacebar keystroke, both the blue and yellow circle targets are displayed to the dog at the same time on a large touch surface. We measure the time for the dog to touch the blue and then the yellow circle target with his nose. We also measure where on the screen the dog touches, even if the dog misses the target. In this way we can collect the target distance, target time, target selection speed, and location of selection.

Figure 3. Dog user selecting the yellow dot after first touching the blue dot with his nose.

The location of selection is important to record because humans, through the years of target selection studies, have been found to 'optimize' when targets are large and close together. We touch the inside of the closest edge of tapping targets.

The reason for training the dogs to perform a color picking order is so we can also test for directional effect on interface difficulty. It is important that as the targets move around the screen the dog knows which target to choose first and which to choose second.

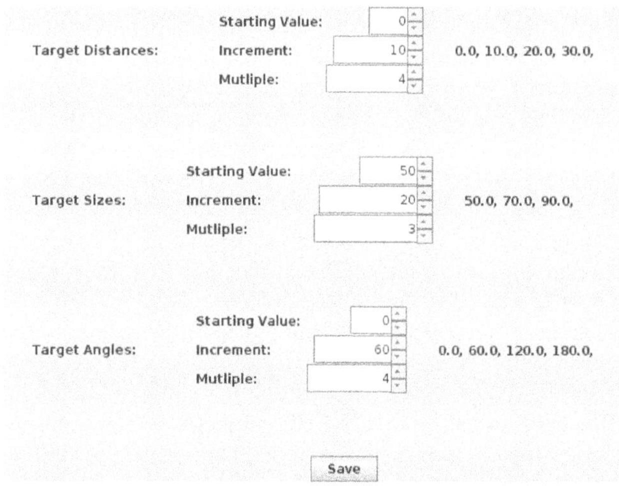

Figure 4. The configuration screen allows the test administrator to choose which target distance variations, target size variations, and target angle variations to cycle through and what multiple to cycle through.

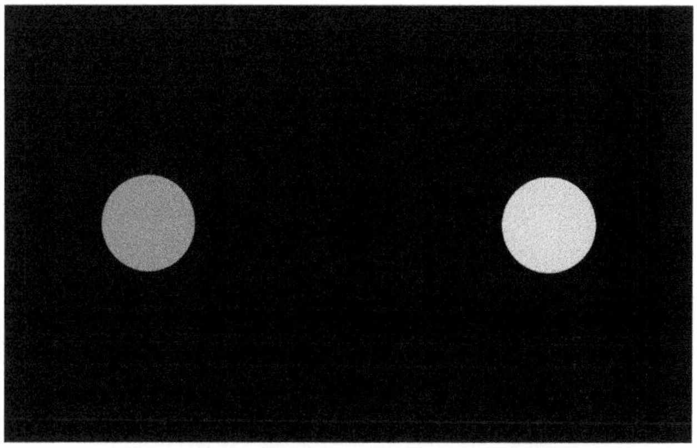

Figure 5. The dog is presented with a blue and yellow dot on a black background. The dog first selects the blue then yellow target with his nose.

Touch Surface, and Projector / Display Selection

The hardware used in building a touchscreen interface for canines has great influence on the dog's ***ability*** to operate the system effectively. Dog saliva and nose moisture matter. The first touchscreen we selected, like most current touchscreens, was a capacitive touchscreen. Moisture from the dog's nose or mouth that remained on the screen from the tapping task also has a capacitive change effect on the screen, thus holding the mouse cursor in the location of the dog saliva. Because of this effect it was not possible to use a capacitive touchscreen for our study. The next touchscreen we attempted was an ultrasonic touch screen, which also had the same issue. Finally we were able to find and use an infrared touch surface. The dog was able to leave moisture on the infrared touch surface without altering his ability to make selections.

To run our study we used the infrared touch sensor mounted to a surface made from glass. We began by using rear projection to produce the visual image the dog was selecting (Figure 3). When selecting a projector we first selected a color wheel style projector. This type of projector creates colors by flashing RGB (or other colors) in series through a grey-scale LCD faster than the human eye can detect. Thanks to the persistence of vision in the human eye, these images blend together to form a single color image. The dogs that interacted with this projector seemed to have difficulty finding the yellow tapping target consistently. We believe this is because the dogs may have seen the red/green flashing instead of a solid yellow target. We then switched to a 3-LCD projector with a constant color projection over time, and the dogs seemed to find the yellow target much easier. While we never pinpointed any problems to this display, we were concerned that the wavelength of the light coming from the projector's gas-discharge lamp might be perceived differently by the dog's eye, as dog's color vision is more or less sensitive at different wavelengths than humans.

As a result, our final system included a 60" LED flat screen television for the display. (Figure 6) The television works much better and the brightness of the tapping targets are now much easier to view in a lighted room. Additionally, we confirmed that the backlight is a smooth curve across all wavelengths, so the dogs should perceive the colors equally well. We began our study after building a rugged secure frame and stand to hold the touch surface with the television.

Figure 6. Infrared touchscreen held within robust mounting in front of 60" LED television.

TOUCHSCREEN INTERACTIONS

Much HCI research has been done in how humans interact with touchscreens. Potter, Weldon, and Shneiderman describe three main ways interfaces can be designed to accept touch interaction. [23]

Land-on, where the curser is under the touch, and only the first impact point counts. [23]

First-Contact, where the cursor is under the touch, but the first contact with the target counts even if its not the first impact with the surface. [23]

Take-off, cursor is offset, and selections are made by where the touch lifts off the surface. [23]

We chose to use a *first-contact* model for this round of dog touchscreen interaction experiments. To be able to train the dogs efficiently we believed the *land-on* type of interaction might initially be too strict and difficult for the dogs to be able to offer. We also did chose to initially stay away from the *take-off* interaction style because it would be hard to use other predictive models to compare this interaction type to humans.

To be able to compare our findings with canines to humans we decided to look at the data we collected from our testing apparatus through the lens of Fitts' law.

Soukoreff and MacKenzie [32] state:

"Fitts' law (1954) describes the relationship between movement time, distance, and accuracy for people engaged in rapid aimed movements. It has been verified over a wide range of conditions. Of interest to HCI researchers is that the law applies to pointing and dragging using a mouse, trackball, stylus, joystick, and touchscreen. Fitts' law has been applied by HCI researchers as a predictive model."

Computer interface designers use Fitts' law when developing interfaces for human interactions. Understanding and predicting the load and difficulty of using certain aspects of an interface can help a designer lay out the interface to be used more quickly and easily.

$$MT = a + b * ID_e$$

The Fitts' law equation is parameterized by the effective index of difficulty as well as the intercept and slope parameters of a line. The effective index of difficulty can be calculated from movement data collected during an experiment. An interface's parameters can be estimated using linear regression as described by Soukoreff and MacKenzie [32].

$$ID_e = log_2(\frac{D_e}{W_e} + 1)$$

The effective index of difficulty is a log ratio of effective distance between centers of the targets and the effective width of the target. Again, we use Fitts' law as a framework for comparing the dogs' interactions with a set of humans' interactions, and not as a definitive statement about how dog interactions should be measured.

Dog Training method

Although we initially trained several dogs, we selected three subjects to completely train for testing. All the subjects have had previous training in targeting (touching the handler's hand or a specified target with his nose). Dogl and Dog2 are agility dogs, and Dog3 has been previously trained as an assistance dog. The dogs have already been trained with operant conditioning techniques [31], specifically *shaping*, which is building new behaviors by selectively reinforcing behaviors the dog offers [24]. For the experiment, we only used positive reinforcement (R+); we did not employ any type of correction or punishment.

We classically conditioned [22] the dogs with high-value reinforcement (food) to a tone generated by a computer. This tone became a "reward marker" that allowed the dog to know when he had accomplished the dog interaction test task. By marking desired behaviors with the tone at the moment of execution, we shaped the dog towards the final interaction goal.

This dog touchscreen interaction task is a complex series of behaviors, so initially we subdivided the task, teaching the dog to touch the blue dot (reward was given when the tone sounded) and the yellow dot separately. Canines sense objects with sight, touch of their whiskers, and scent. As the virtual "objects" on the touch screen can only be sensed with sight, we needed to teach the dog to interact with only sight. The dog was rewarded for first touching the screen with his nose, then for seeking out the dot shape to touch with his nose. The dots on the screen sometimes cannot be easily seen at close proximity, so the dog started his task sitting on a mat (Figure 3 & 7) approximately two feet from the screen to help him locate his targets.

Once the dog understood the task of touching a dot with his nose, we trained him to touch the dots in sequence with *backchaining* [24]. Backchaining is a shaping method that teaches the dog to perform a complex task ("behavior chain") with multiple behaviors by training the last behavior first, then adding the next-to-last behavior, and so forth. We began with teaching the dog to place himself in the correct position on the mat. Then we added touching the yellow dot with his nose. When the dog was proficient with that simple behavior chain, we taught him to go to his mat, then touch the blue dot, then the yellow dot, and return to his mat for reward. Through a *variable reinforcement schedule*, we increased the dog's speed by rewarding only when he touched the blue then yellow dots quickly and in sequence.

When the behavior chain was confirmed, we began the dog interaction testing sessions, varying the size and distance of the dots. The dogs understood the new requirements of the task without additional training, locating each of the dots as quickly as possible. We tested the dog in sessions of no longer than 15 minutes, with at least 30 minutes rest in between sessions.

EXPERIMENT

For this initial exploration we tested three dogs. Two were border collies previously trained as agility dogs and one was a labrador retriever trained as an assistance dog. We try to avoid making claims with this limited dataset but feel that the observations and challenges to date are of sufficient value to report.

Figure 7: Dog 3 waiting for the handler to turn on the interface.

The dogs completed 15 runs. ***Runs*** were defined as a set of 16 tapping target size and distance combinations. Each individual ***tapping task trial*** was defined as selecting the blue then yellow target. So each run contained each of the 16 tapping task trials, which were displayed to the dog in a random order. A ***session*** was defined as any number of runs performed at the same sitting or general time period. Most dogs could complete 3-5 runs in one session before becoming tired of the task. At the end of 15 runs the dogs have completed each of the 16 tapping task trials 15 times. Every session was video recorded to be able to compare anomalies in the data with what happened in the actual session.

Target Distance Between Circle Edges	
20 pixels	½" (~13 mm)
120 pixels	3 ¼" (~82.5 mm)
220 pixels	6" (~152.5 mm)
320 pixel	8 ¾" (~222.25 mm)

Table 1: Actual Target Distances as measured from the 60" LED touchscreen.

Each tapping task trial consists of one nose press on the blue target, zero or more erroneous touches, followed by one touch on the yellow. When the dog makes a correct selection, first hitting the blue target, a lower frequency tone is played to signify to the dog he/she has made the blue selection. After selecting the blue target if the dog selects the yellow target a higher frequency tone is played, and the targets disappear from the screen upon lift off of the successful yellow target touch, signifying that the dog has completed the task. For each touch, we record the time that the dog nose first contacted the touchscreen and the time the dog nose leaves the touchscreen. For the purposes of comparing to Fitts' law, we consider the ***task time*** between touches to be the time between the dog's noses first correctly contacting the two targets, ignoring erroneous touches.

Target Diameter	
100 pixels	2 ½" (~63.5 mm)
200 pixels	5 ½" (~140 mm)
300 pixels	8" (~203 mm)
400 pixels	10 ¾" (~273 mm)

Table 2: Actual Target Sizes as measured from the 60" LED touchscreen.

The times and distances are measured by the software displaying the targets to the dog, and actual distance and target size are automatically recorded with the timing data. We measure target distance as the distance between the target centers, and we measure the target width as the diameter of the targets. The program developed to display the targets uses the inside edges of the circle targets to determine distances. Therefore, if the program is asked to display four different distances, it will display these as the distance between the circle edges. Once the different sizes and distances are selected the program will display them in a random order. Our distances were originally collected in units of screen pixels. For the purpose of reproducing the study the converted sizes and distances used can be seen in Tables 1 and 2. During training sessions we have seen that at least one dog has the ability to follow the changing angle and learned to select blue then yellow, but for the purposes of this study we decided to start with just researching a horizontal dog interaction.

To be able to compare a dog's interactions with a human's interactions we also asked three people to complete the same tapping task trials in the same way on the same system. We asked the humans to complete the tapping tasks as fast as possible.

RECORDED AND OBSERVED INTERACTIONS

We recorded the locations and timing of all interactions on the touchscreen while the tapping task targets were displayed. Figure 8 shows a human's interaction with the touch screen. All 15 tapping task trials' touch interactions for distance 120 pixels and size 300 pixels are shown on one diagram. The blue and yellow circles are representative of the tapping targets that were on the screen when the touches were performed. The green dots represent where a successful first touch was made to select the blue target. The red dots represent where a successful second touch was made to select the yellow target. Green lines passing through green dots (as in Figure 9) indicate drags on the touch screen, which triggered a successful blue target selection, whereas lines intersecting red dots indicate drags taking place after a successful yellow target selection. Orange lines indicate a drag, which left the blue target and continued dragging until successfully selecting the yellow target. Grey X's indicate erroneous touches, which did not activate any targets.

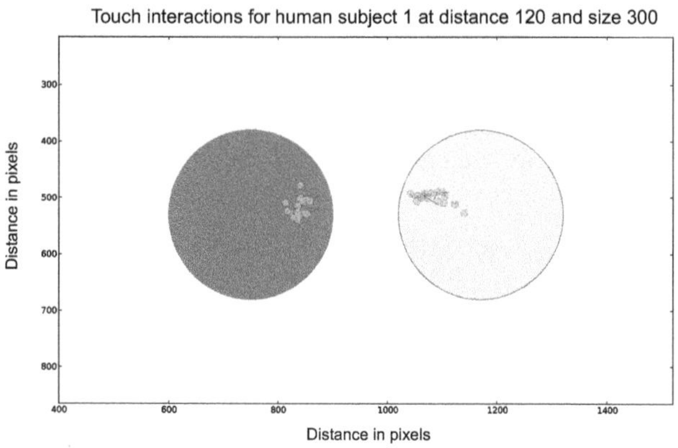

Figure 8. Example diagram of recorded touchscreen interactions from Human 1. Green dots are the first successful touch; red dots are the second successful touch.

Notice in Figure 8 when asked to perform the "tapping task" the human tapped and lifted his finger without any intentional dragging. We can also see the human intentionally touched the inside edges of the targets to be able to select them as quickly as possible.

Each dog participant developed different strategies to be able to select the targets as quickly as possible. Two of our canine participants (both the agility trained dogs) commonly selected the blue target and then dragged into the yellow target. As can be seen in the example in Figure 9, Dog1 and Dog 2 (not shown) selected the inside edge of the blue target and then dragged directly into the inside edge of the yellow target. This strategy was particularly common when the target separation distance was small. The dragging selection was made possible because we chose the *first-contact* interaction model [23].

This dragging significantly changed the type of interaction the dogs had, and occurred because of the way we presented the task to the dogs. To them, any interaction that got the software to 'beep' was good enough, as the 'beep' was their reward marker. Since our software allowed drags into, out of, and between the targets, the dogs had no incentive to perform very precisely.

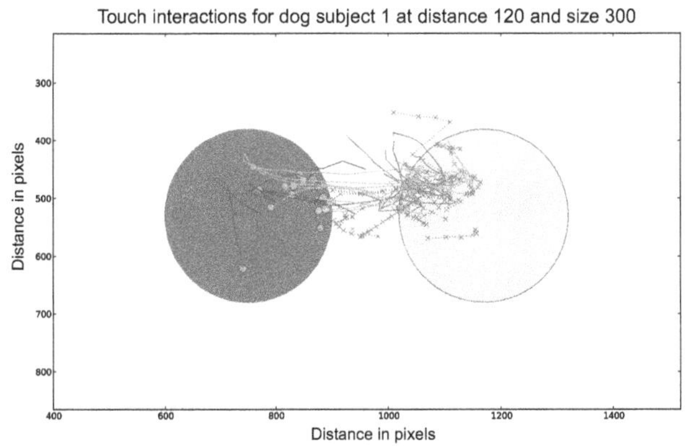

Figure 9. Example diagram of recorded touchscreen interactions from Dog 1. Green dots are the first successful touch, red dots are the second successful touch. Green lines are drags from the first touch, and orange lines are drags from the second touch.

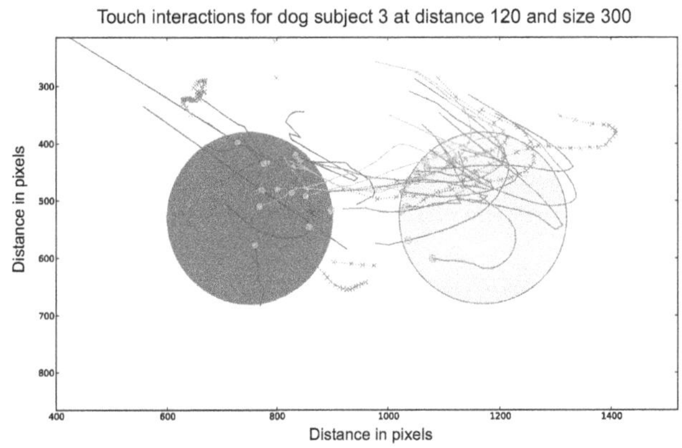

Figure 10. Example diagram of recorded touchscreen interactions from Dog 3.

Accordingly, the interactions the dogs performed in these cases were closer to the discrete orthogonal goal-crossing or continuous orthogonal goal-crossing task as defined by Accot and Zhai [1]. It would certainly make for a more accurate system to use the *take-off* model of interaction [23], but this approach would also make it harder to use our Fitts' Law comparison.

Dog3 was trained as a wheelchair assistance dog. He had a much more methodical approach to selection. Figure 10 shows he did not drag to select nearly as much as his agility dog counterparts. He also lingered longer on the screen after the selection. After his yellow selection he always looked back up slowly to the trainer for approval, and this behavior can be seen in the red trails following the orange selection circles on the yellow target.

The dogs' selections are not as consistent as the humans' selections, and there are many more erroneous touches. Some of these extra or mistaken touches can be explained by the dog's fur. As the dog nears the touch screen, the infrared detectors pick up anything that passes through its detection plane, about 1/8" (3mm) from the surface of the glass, including the dogs' fur. Using a capacitive screen could solve this problem, but we have already ruled out capacitive screens due to selection problems associated with dog saliva. There are ways to design for the addition of some erroneous touches, and we will cover these in our design guidelines for canine touchscreen section.

RESULTS

The results shown are from the three dogs that participated in our study. Outliers have been removed from the data to make the data easier to read and also more understandable. We removed the outliers by first looking at the data and then comparing anomalies in the data with the recorded video of the sessions. On more than one occasion, the monitor displaying the targets accidentally lost video synchronization and turned off, and this failure accounted for some erroneous task times of up to 96 seconds. These very large task times skewed the results of the data tremendously and were removed. We had a total of 721 tapping task trials of which we pruned out 35 that had more than five seconds between touching the blue target and touching the yellow target. We omitted another 50 tapping task trials that had more than three touches in the trial. In total we excluded 11.8% of the dogs' trial data.

In other trials, the dogs made an initial attempt, missed one of the two targets, and then got distracted or confused by the failure. For example, they might activate the blue target, then miss the yellow, and then try the entire task again, beginning with blue. These instances were obviously not clean blue-yellow interactions, and we felt confident in a decision to remove any dog tapping task which exceeded three touches between activation of blue and activation of yellow, or which had a task time of greater than five seconds.

All of the dogs at some point dragged their noses from the blue target to the yellow target to make a selection; such events are shown as one touch in Figure 11. These one-touch drag interactions create the fastest task times. We have found that our system records a multi-touch press1+press2+liftoff1+liftoff2 interaction as one single press+drag+liftoff. When the distance is very small between the two targets, as it is in our 20-pixel condition, a single dog nose could accidentally trigger such a multi-touch interaction. These multi-touch interactions account for the very short single touch task times.

Figure 12 shows a seemingly improbable finding. Dog2's approximate 200-millisecond interaction at a separation distance of 320 seems suspect, and we determined the cause upon viewing the video. Dog2 began using his nose and paw at the same time to select both tapping targets at once. This agility trained Border Collie (Dog2) found it most effective (quicker) at larger distance target tasks to lunge at the screen with his nose and right paw up. This behavior was hard to extinguish because the system responded by giving him reward beeps, and unlike a human we could not explain to the dog to only use one hand (or his nose) to complete the task. Because we wanted to view the data with instances of quick interaction time and we could not tell the dogs not to drag or use multi-touch interactions, we decided to leave this data in the dataset we used for calculations.

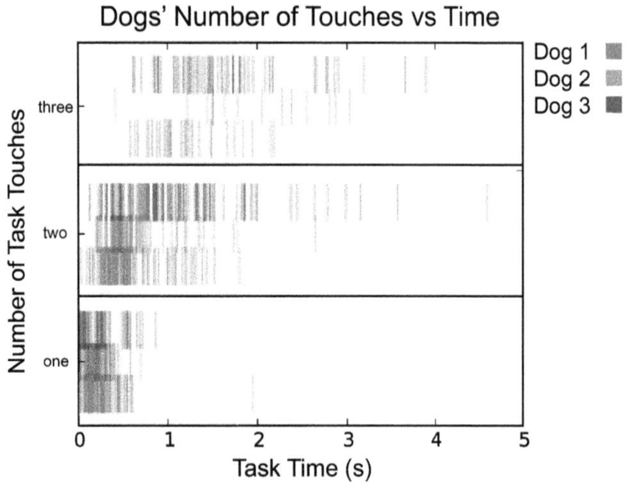

Figure 11 The number of dog touches to complete each tapping task trial versus the time it took the dog to complete each tapping task trial. Each line represents a single tapping task trial colored coded by the dog performing the trial.

When determining effective width for our Fitts' law comparison calculations we chose to use the point where the yellow target (second target) was first activated. It is important to note that on tapping trials where dogs dragged into the circle, this point shows up as an edge or near edge condition. We chose to include these conditions because most of the drags seemed intentional by the dogs as the quickest and shortest way to get from blue to yellow.

To be able to compare the dogs' interactions against a humans' interactions we decided to analyze both the dogs' dataset and the human dataset using Fitts' Law. We are not claiming here that dogs follow the same predictive models as humans, but it is an interesting comparison. Fitts' Law would expect that the graph in Figure 14 and 15 to have linear regressions intercepting the y-axis (time) at zero [32]. However, Soukoreff and MacKenzie [32] expect a good model to fit with an intercept of the time axis between -200ms and 400ms. Our results from our dog trials are only slightly outside this range

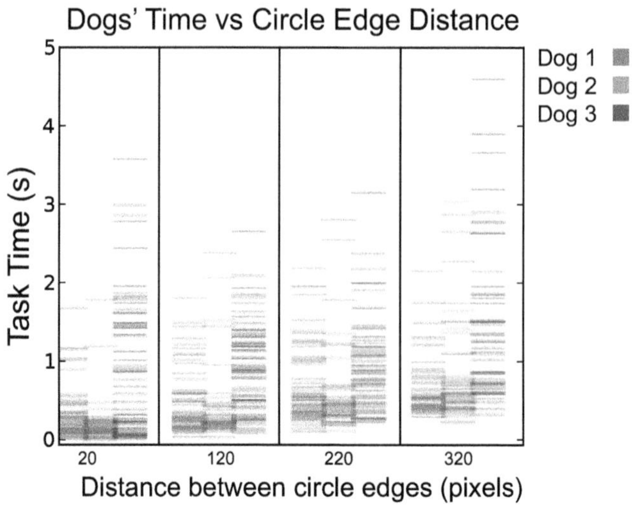

Figure 12 The dog's task time compared to the distance between the inside edges of the tapping targets. Each line represents a single tapping task trial colored by the dog performing the trial.

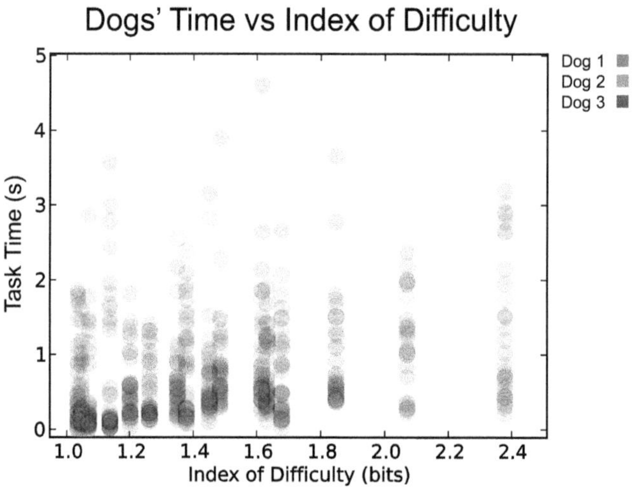

Figure 13 The dog's task time as compared to the displayed target-width's Fitts' Law Index of Difficulty. Each dot indicates a single tapping task trial colored by the dog performing the trial.

By looking at looking at Figure 14 we also see an interesting correlation of the graphed data to the dogs' drive, or eagerness. The dogs' drive levels were described a priori by their owners who train/compete at a national level. "Drive" is a common feature described when seeking appropriate dogs for particular tasks. Unlike with humans who can understand that the task must be performed as fast as possible, with dogs we have to use a motivating factor, such as praise or dog treats. Dog3 who shows the highest times was trained to be an assistance dog and has much lower drive than the other dogs, who are trained as agility dogs. It seems to be possible to view this temperament difference in the graph, although it is very hard to make any claims with only three dogs and no quantifiable way to describe dog drive. If dogs can be trained to perform this task, it might be used in the future as a good indicator of dog temperament and drive.

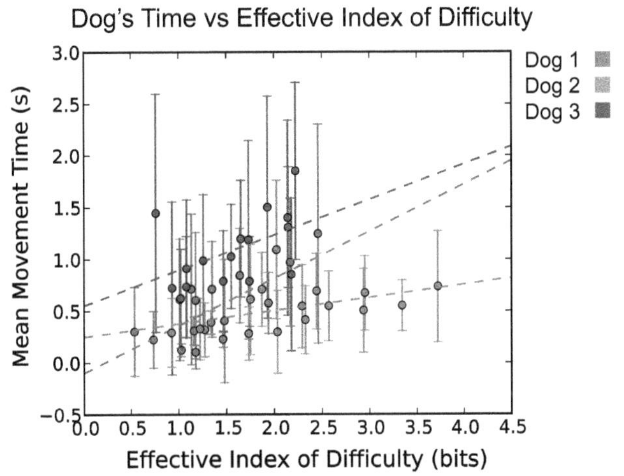

Figure 14 The dog's task time as compared with Fitts' Law Effective Index of Difficulty. Each dot represents an individual participant's average performance for each tapping task trial size/distance.

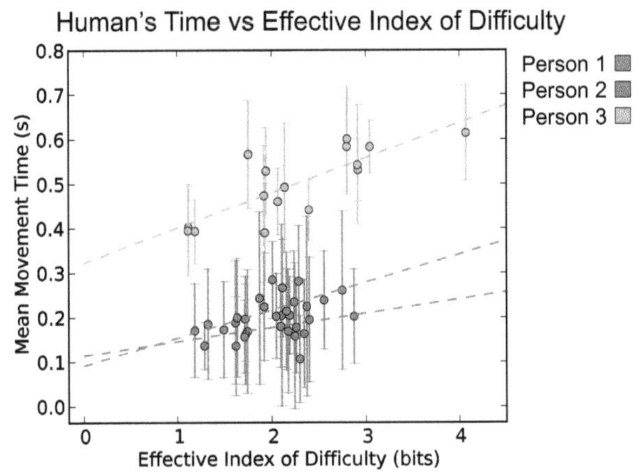

Figure 15 Human's task time as compared with Fitts' Law Effective Index of Difficulty. Each dot represents an individual participant's average performance for each tapping task trial size/distance.

DISCUSSION AND POSSIBLE DESIGN GUIDELINES FOR CANINE TOUCHSCREEN INTERFACES.

We summarize the key points from our preliminary efforts below.

Ability – Dogs have the ability to be trained to perform touches on a screen in response to virtual/displayed shapes. The selection interactions can be somewhat complex. We have seen dogs learn to select first one, then another target. We have observed that dog can devise multi-touch techniques such as near simultaneous nose and paw touches of their own accord. We have also seen all three dogs in our study decide to drag from one selection point to another on the touch surface.

Distance – We found when the distance between selection points is very short, in our case 20 pixels apart, our dog participants had a tendency to select both targets at the same time. This result could be due to the width of a dog's nose, and that dogs, like humans, aim for the inside edge of tapping targets. It seems advisable to place targets, or selection points in an interface further apart so that dogs can make more accurate distinctions between intended selections. Intention here is key; if a dog was trying to call emergency services (911), designers should create interfaces which will account for a large nose or furry face by providing adequate distance between selection points.

Target Size – We noticed that target size was important for our dog participants. Obviously it is harder to hit a smaller target, but in the dogs' case they are also selecting the targets with their noses. We chose this method of selection because dogs tend to use their face and nose as the first method of physical investigation. When a dog gets close enough to make a selection of the 100 pixels (or smaller) target the dog can no longer see the target. With a larger size target (200 pixels or larger) the dog can still see the target in his field of view if he misses and can adjust quickly to make the correct selection. It seems that targets or selection points for dog touchscreen interfaces should be larger than 2 ½", and probably should be 3 ½" or larger. There might be some future work allowing for offset cursor selection with dogs as seen in the work by Cockburn et al. done with humans [4]. The concept of an offset cursor might be outside the understanding of a dog, and harder to train.

Fatigue – From our observation our dog participants were only able to complete at most five runs of 16 tapping task trials in a single session. Towards the end of the last run in each session the dog was less responsive to prompts and seemed slower at the tasks. Dog2 seemed to actually become less patient with the system and would bark at the screen and the handler if he was unable to quickly make a correct choice. The consensus among the handlers and Dog2's owner was that Dog2 was not just physically tired after five runs, but was also emotionally tired and frustrated.

Other Insights – Because we have video of the dogs that performed the tapping tasks and have worked with these dogs before in other studies, we can glean the general temperament of the dogs within this study. It is interesting to compare handlers' observations of the dogs' temperaments with the findings in Figure 14. The lower drive of Dog3 can be seen in his interactions with the touchscreen. Dog1, on the other hand, is highly driven and motivated to complete tasks as fast as possible, and his task times are much lower. Drive is an important indicator for a good assistance dog. Dog 3 (Figure 7) was actually trained, but released as an assistance dog because of low drive. It costs on average $25K to train assistance dogs [3], and if a test could be developed to help predict suitability it could be of great help in saving money for non-profit assistance dog training programs.

Another interesting finding involving dog saliva came during the training sessions for the dogs to use the touch surface. As the dogs were given treats as food rewards for completing portions of the tapping task, the screen started to smell of the treats from saliva left on the screen from the tasks. Some dogs found this stimulus distracting when interacting with the screen. When moving across the screen if they passed over a previous selection spot with strong smelling saliva, the dog would pause to sniff before completing the tapping task. This pause in between taps greatly influences the outcome of the data and produced some of the outliers we have seen in our data. We learned it is important to wipe the touch surface with water between every round of 16 tapping task trials to lessen the saliva sniffing effect.

FUTURE WORK

One obvious next step in our work is to train other dogs and collect more data. It would be interesting to reprogram the system to only allow selection on touch lift-off; this modification would eliminate drag interactions and would more closely match Potter's *Take-off* style of touchscreen interaction [23]. Changing the system in this way might also have drawbacks in that where the dog lifts off the target might not be where he was aiming originally. These types of lift off selections might produce data, which will be inconsistent when trying to fit to Fitts' law, but might be the correct interactions for designing a canine touchscreen. We also would like to collect data on how the angle change of the tapping task affects the dogs' ability to perform the task.

Assuredly dogs of different breeds will perform differently on the tapping tasks, but will they perform in scale and relation to other dogs or does each breed have its own logarithmic scale of performance? We have already seen a difference between a labrador retriever and a border collie. Would we be able to test other dogs in the future to find out which breeds work best with touchscreens? There may be more variables than just intelligence involved; the amount of dog saliva and the length of a dog's fur/hair seems to also affect a dogs ability to interact with a touchscreen. Would a pug with a flat face be able to make selections with its nose as easily as a long snouted dog?

We would also like to create a more realistic interface. A product prototype of a touchscreen selection interface ready to test will make a great case study of our findings here. With dogs now already trained to interact with the touchscreen we can easily produce a system ready for use. We might even be able to place the system within the Georgia Tech Aware Home for a more real world venue our observations [14].

Eventually our research team would also like to look at other classic HCI standards and laws and see if they apply to interfaces that are used by dogs. For example, we might compare dog data to human data with respect to the power law of practice. In this way we can continue to aid and inform the design process of dog computer interfaces.

ACKNOWLEDGEMENTS

This material is based upon work supported by the National Science Foundation under Grant No. 1320690.

REFERENCES

1. Accot, J., and Zhai, S. (2002, April). More than dotting the i's---foundations for crossing-based interfaces. In *Proceedings of the SIGCHI conference on Human factors in computing systems* (pp. 73-80). ACM.
2. Amundin, M., Starkhammar, J., Evander, M., Almqvist, M., Lindström, K., & Persson, H. W. (2008). An echolocation visualization and interface system for dolphin research. *The Journal of the Acoustical Society of America*, *123*(2), 1188-1194.
3. Canine Companions for Independence. www.cci.org (last accessed 4/16/14)
4. Cockburn, A., Ahlström, D., and Gutwin, C. "Understanding performance in touch selections: Tap, drag and radial pointing drag with finger, stylus and mouse." *International Journal of Human-Computer Studies* 70.3 (2012): 218-233.
5. A Day Made of Glass... Made possible by Corning. https://www.youtube.com/watch?v=6Cf7IL_eZ38 (last accessed 4/16/14)
6. Delfour, F., & Marten, K. (2005). Inter-modal learning task in bottlenosed dolphins (Tursiops truncatus): A preliminary study showed that social factors might influence learning strategies. *Acta Ethologica*, *8*(1), 57-64.
7. Display Centric World by Samsung: Future. https://www.youtube.com/watch?v=ZSn0lnjgFag (last accessed 4/16/14)
8. Fitts, P.M., The information capacity of the human motor system in controlling the amplitude of movement. *Journal of Experimental Psychology*, 47 (6) (1954), pp. 381–39
9. Forlines, C., Wigdor, D., Shen, C., And Balakrishnan, R. (2007, April). Direct-touch vs. mouse input for tabletop displays. In *Proceedings of the SIGCHI conference on Human factors in computing systems* (pp. 647-656). ACM.
10. FSR 400 Data Sheet: FSR 400 Series Round Force Sensing Resistor.

http://dlnmh9ip6v2uc.cloudfront.net/datasheets/Sensors/ForceFlex/2010-10-26-DataSheet-FSR400-Layout2.pdf (last accessed 4/16/14)
11. History of Guide Dogs International Guide Dog Federation. www.igdf.org.uk/about-us/facts-and-figures/history-of-guide-dogs/ (last accessed 4/16/14)
12. Hu, F., Silver, D. and Trudel, A. "Lonely Dog@Home", *Proc of the Conf on Web Intelligence and Intelligent Agent Technology Workshops*, 2007, pp. 333-337.
13. Jackson, M., Zeagler, C., Valentin, G., Martin, A., Martin, V., Delawalla, A., Blount, W., Eiring, S., Hollis, R., Kshirsagar, Y., And Starner, T., "FIDO – Facilitating Interactions for Dogs with Occupations: wearable dog-activated interfaces." *Proceedings of International Symposium on Wearable Computers ISWC*, Sept 2013, pages 81-88.
14. Kidd, C. D., Orr, R., Abowd, G. D., Atkeson, C. G., Essa, I. A., MacIntyre, B., and Newstetter, W. (1999). The aware home: A living laboratory for ubiquitous computing research. In *Cooperative buildings. Integrating information, organizations, and architecture* (pp. 191-198).
15. Lee, S. P., Cheok, A. D., And James, T. K. S. "A mobile pet wearable computer and mixed reality system for human-poultry interaction through the internet", *Personal and Ubiquitous Computing*, v.10, 2006, pp.301-317
16. LilyPad Arduino. http://arduino.cc/en/Main/ArduinoBoardLilyPad
17. Mancini, C., van der Linden, J., Bryan, J., & Stuart, A. (2012, September). Exploring interspecies sensemaking: dog tracking semiotics and multispecies ethnography. *In Proceedings of the 2012 ACM Conference on Ubiquitous Computing* (pp. 143-152).
18. Mankoff, D.; Dey, A.; Mankoff J.; and Mankoff, K. Supporting interspecies social awareness: using peripheral displays for distributed pack awareness, in *Proc of UIST*, ACM Press, 2005.
19. Neitz, J., Geist, T., & Jacobs, G., Color Vision in the Dog, in *Visual Neuroscience* (1989), 3, pages 119-125.
20. Noz F. and An, J. Cat cat revolution: an interspecies gaming experience, in *Proceedings of CHI '11*, ACM Press, 2011.
21. Paldanius, M., Karkkainen, T., Vaananen-Vainio-Mattila, K., Juhlin, O., and Hakkila, J. . (2011). Communication Technology for Human-Dog Interaction: Exploration of Dog Owners' Experiences and Expectations. *Proc. CHI 2011.*
22. Pavlov, I.P. *Conditional Reflexes*. New York: Dover Pubs, 1927.
23. Potter, R. L., Weldon L.J., and Shneiderman B. Improving the accuracy of touch screens: an experimental evaluation of three strategies. *Proceedings of the SIGCHI conference on Human factors in computing systems*. ACM, 1988.
24. Pryor, K. *Reaching the Animal Mind*: Scribner, Simon & Schuster, Inc., 2009.
25. Resner, B. I. *Rover@home: Computer Mediated Remote Interaction Between Humans and Dogs.* (Master's Thesis), Massachusetts Institute of Technology, 2001.
26. Reiss, D., & McCowan, B. (1993). Spontaneous vocal mimicry and production by bottlenose dolphins (Tursiops truncatus): Evidence for vocal learning. *Journal of Comparative Psychology*, *107*(3), 301.
27. Sasangohar, F., MacKenzie, I. S., And Scott, S. D. (2009, October). Evaluation of mouse and touch input for a tabletop display using Fitts' reciprocal tapping task. In *Proceedings of the Human Factors and Ergonomics Society Annual Meeting* (Vol. 53, No. 12, pp. 839-843). SAGE Publications.
28. Savage, J., Sanchez-Guzman, R. A., Mayol-Cuevas, W., Arce, L., Hernandez, A., Brier, L., . . . Lopez, G. Animal-machine interfaces. *Proc. The 4th Intl Symp on Wearable Computing*, IEEE. (2000)
29. Savage-Rumbaugh, E. S. (1986). *Ape language: From conditioned response to symbol*. Columbia University Press.
30. The Seeing Eye. http://www.seeingeye.org/
31. Skinner, B.F. *The behavior of organisms: an experimental analysis*. Oxford, England: Appleton-Century, 1938.
32. Soukoreff, W., And MacKenzie, S., Towards a standard for pointing device evaluation, perspectives on 27 years of Fitts' law research in HCI. *International Journal of Human-Computer Studies*, Volume 61, Issue 6, December 2004, Pages 751-789
33. Teensy USB Development Board. http://www.pjrc.com/teensy/
34. Weilenmann, Alexandra, & Juhlin, Oskar. "Understanding people and animals: the use of a positioning system in ordinary human-canine interaction." *Proc. SIGCHI Conference on Human Factors in Computing Systems*, 2011.
35. Weiser, Mark. The computer for the 21st century. *Scientific American* 265.3 (1991): 94-104.
36. Wingrave, C.A.; Rose, J.; Langston, T.; And LaViola, J.J. "Early Explorations of CAT: Canine Amusement and Training", in *Extended Abstracts of CHI '10*, ACM Press, 2010, pp.2661-2670.
37. Young, J.; Young, N.; Greenberg, S.; and Sharlin, E. Feline Fun Park: A Distributed Tangible Interface for Pets and Owners, in *Video Proceedings of Pervasive*, 2007.

Gaze-touch: Combining Gaze with Multi-touch for Interaction on the Same Surface

Ken Pfeuffer, Jason Alexander, Ming Ki Chong, Hans Gellersen
Lancaster University
Lancaster, United Kingdom
{k.pfeuffer, j.alexander, m.chong, h.gellersen}@lancaster.ac.uk

Figure 1: Users select by gaze, and manipulate with multi-touch from anywhere (a). This can enable seamless switching between indirect (a) and direct manipulation (b), implicit mode switching during direct-touch tasks (c), zooming into map locations the user looks at (d), and dragging multiple targets that are out of the hand's reach (e). The gray cursor indicates the user's gaze.

ABSTRACT
Gaze has the potential to complement multi-touch for interaction on the same surface. We present gaze-touch, a technique that combines the two modalities based on the principle of "gaze selects, touch manipulates". Gaze is used to select a target, and coupled with multi-touch gestures that the user can perform anywhere on the surface. Gaze-touch enables users to manipulate any target from the same touch position, for whole-surface reachability and rapid context switching. Conversely, gaze-touch enables manipulation of the same target from any touch position on the surface, for example to avoid occlusion. Gaze-touch is designed to complement direct-touch as the default interaction on multi-touch surfaces. We provide a design space analysis of the properties of gaze-touch versus direct-touch, and present four applications that explore how gaze-touch can be used alongside direct-touch. The applications demonstrate use cases for interchangeable, complementary and alternative use of the two modes of interaction, and introduce novel techniques arising from the combination of gaze-touch and conventional multi-touch.

Author Keywords
Gaze input; multi-touch; multimodal UI; interactive surface

ACM Classification Keywords
H.5.2. Information interfaces and presentation: User Interfaces: Input devices and strategies

http://dx.doi.org/10.1145/2642918.2647397

INTRODUCTION
As eye tracking is maturing, gaze input can become as widely available for interaction with surfaces as multi-touch is presently. In past HCI research, gaze has often been considered as an alternative to default modalities [6, 10, 14, 16] although it has also been argued that gaze might have greater potential as an addition to other modalities [25]. In this work, we explore how gaze can complement multi-touch to advance interaction on the same surface.

We present gaze-touch, a technique that integrates the gaze and touch modalities with a clear division of labour: *gaze selects, touch manipulates*. Gaze-touch is best explained in comparison with direct-touch interaction, which normally involves: (i) moving the hand to the target, (ii) touching down on the target to select it, and (iii) direct manipulation with the fingers on the surface. Gaze-touch, in contrast, is based on (i) looking at the target, (ii) touching down anywhere on the surface to select it, and (iii) manipulation with the fingers on the surface (but displaced from the target, Figure 1a).

Gaze-touch spatially separates the hand from the target. The potential utility of this separation can be considered from two viewpoints:

- More expressive input from the same touch position (Fig. 2): finger touches in the same position can resolve to selection of any point on the surface. Without moving their hands out of position, users can reach and select any position on the surface, and rapidly switch context using their gaze.
- More expressive input to the same target (Fig. 3): the same target can be manipulated from different positions on the surface. Users can move their hands off an object but continue to manipulate it with their hands "out of the way". This can help address occlusion, and also enable novel in-

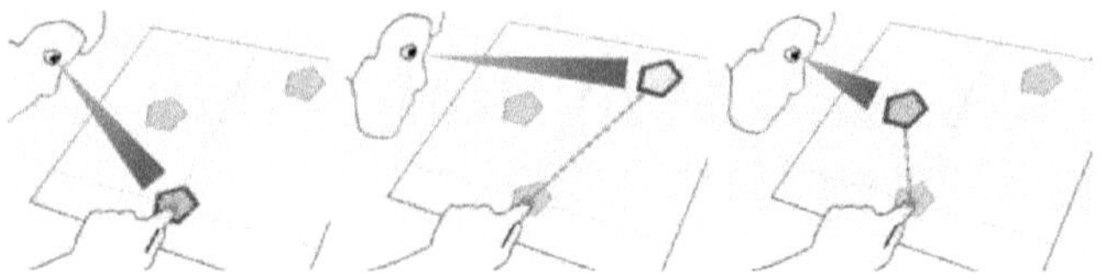

Figure 2: More expressive input from the same touch position: three examples of users touch on the same touch position, but each time manipulate a different target.

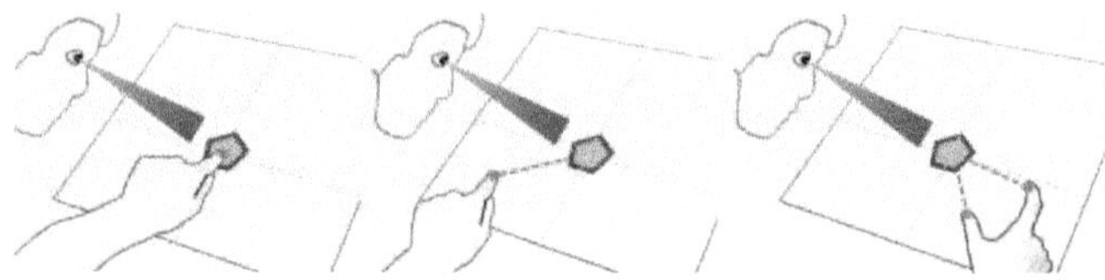

Figure 3: More expressive input to the same target: three examples of manipulating the same target that the user sees, but each time with different touches on the surface.

direct manipulation techniques, for instance with variable control-display gains to adjust precision of input.

The idea of gaze-touch is to complement direct-touch. Our focus in this work is therefore to understand how these two modes of interaction compare, and how gaze-touch can be employed alongside direct-touch. For this reason, we first characterize gaze-touch in comparison to direct-touch input through an analytical discussion of their interaction properties. The second part of the paper demonstrates four different applications that explore how gaze-touch can be used in relation to direct-touch:

1. Gaze-touch *or* direct-touch. The Image Gallery application allows users to manipulate the same image indirectly by gaze-touch (gaze and touch are separate (Figure 1a)), or directly with direct-touch (users look and touch at the same target (b)).
2. Gaze-touch *and* direct-touch. The Paint application allows users to draw and manipulate primitive shapes with direct-touch on the main canvas, and switch e.g. colour mode on the menu through gaze-touch (Figure 1c).
3. Gaze-touch *instead of* direct-touch. The Map Navigation application allows users to zoom into their gaze location instead of where they touch (Figure 1d).
4. Gaze-touch *extends* direct-touch. The Multiple Objects application allows users to quickly select and drag multiple targets anywhere on the surface (Figure 1e).

Our work makes four contributions. First, we introduce gaze-touch as a novel mode of interaction to complement direct interaction on the same interactive surface. Second, we analyse the design space of gaze-touch in comparison to default direct-touch interaction. Third, we demonstrate how gaze-touch complements direct-touch in four application examples. Fourth, we present nine interaction techniques that are based on gaze-touch and introduced with the applications.

RELATED WORK

Related work of gaze-touch can be regarded from three perspectives: multimodal gaze based interaction, gaze and touch based interaction, and indirect multi-touch interaction.

Although gaze has shown efficient pointing speed faster than any other input device [11, 16], it suffers from not having a natural mechanism to confirm a selection ('Midas Touch', [10]). To approach this issue, gaze is often complemented with a second modality in order to add selection confirmation. The second modality can be, for example, voice [12], mouse and keyboard (e.g., [10, 25]), hand gestures [12, 15], or touch [19, 20, 21, 22]. Notably, Zhai et al.'s gaze and mouse hybrid presented work where gaze was firstly used to improve performance of manual pointing, in essence making the point that gaze may have a better part to play in advancing other modalities than in replacing them [25]. Our approach follows in the same spirit: looking to enhance multi-touch with gaze, rather than pursuing gaze as an alternative.

While multi-touch has emerged as a new dominant paradigm on a wide range of devices from phones and tablets to tabletops and interactive walls, there has been little work on integration with gaze. Stellmach and Dachselt employed touch on a handheld device to assist with gaze acquisition and manipulation of targets on a remote screen [19, 20]. Turner et al. studied the same combination of devices, and combined gaze selection on remote screens with touch gestures on the handheld device to support transfer of content [21, 22]. Our work is distinct from these prior works on gaze and touch in four aspects. First, we use gaze to advance established direct interaction, e.g. by providing solutions for occlusion or fatigue issues. Prior work focused on interaction over distance where these issues do not occur. Second, we present techniques that leverage gaze and multi-touch on one large surface, that affords flexible multi-touch input with both hands, and seamless transitions between gaze-touch and direct-touch modes of interaction. In contrast, prior work was based on separated input (handheld) and output (remote display) where touch was constrained to single-point and two-point input (two thumbs, [20]). Third, our techniques consistently use the division of *gaze selects, touch manipulates*, while prior work applied gaze for positioning of targets. Forth, our techniques are grounded in a design space analysis of gaze-touch in comparison to conventional direct interaction.

Previous research on multi-touch surfaces has contributed techniques that complement the default direct-touch with means for providing indirect input in order to address problems of reach and occlusion. For example, Albinsson and Zhai, and Benko et al. proposed dual finger techniques to select targets more precisely [2, 4]. These techniques can improve the acquisition of small targets, and increase the precision of their manipulation. Banerjee et al. used in-air pointing above the surface to reach remote targets on tabletops [3]. Further research suggested widgets that are specifically designed for remote selection with touch, such as The Vacuum [5], or I-Grabber [1]. In Rock & Rails, proxies to the target were created where the first hand as a fist selects the proxy's position, and the second hand selects the target [23]. In general, these approaches require management of these indirect handles, augment the user interface, or require multi-finger or bimanual input for single target selections. Conse-

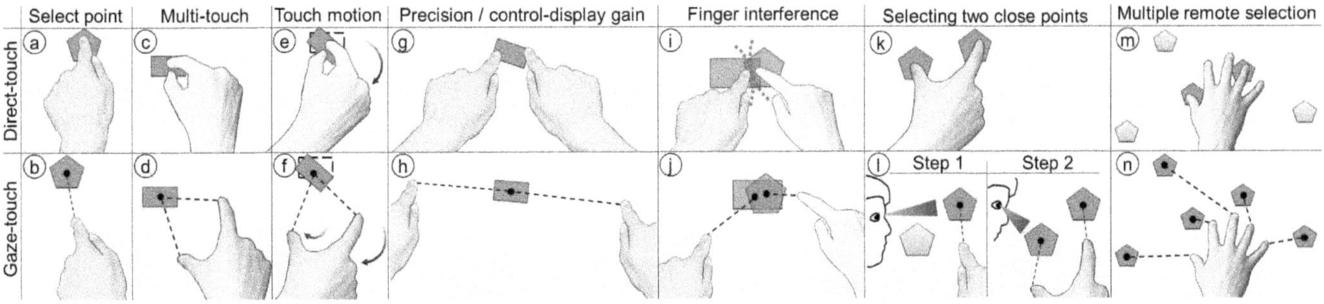

Figure 4: Illustrated differences between gaze-touch and direct-touch.

PROPERTY	DIRECT-TOUCH		GAZE-TOUCH	
Manipulation start time	**Direct** (manipulate the moment of touch down)			
Manipulation location	**Direct**	(touch point is point of manipulation)	**Indirect**	(point of manipulation is remote from touch)
Manipulation motion	**Similar** (manipulate with similar hand motion)			
Remote targets	**Low**	(only targets in physical reach)	**High**	(reach any target by look)
Occlusion	**Moderate**	('fat-finger') to **Large** (palm, pinch, hand)	**Low**	(object separate from touch)
Precision of selection	**Moderate**	(precise, but 'fat-finger')	**Moderate**	(no 'fat-finger', but gaze imprecision)
Precision of manipulation	**Moderate**	(usually control-display ratio of 1)	**High**	(control-display ratio through finger distance, that user can adjust)
Physical feedback	**High**	(finger/hand indicate current manipulation)	**Low**	(finger/hand separate from manipulation point)
Physical fatigue	**Moderate**	(move hand / arm)	**Low**	(look, and little hand / arm movement)
Physical interference	**High**	(multiple fingers/hands in same location)	**Low**	(fingers/users can be remote)
Acquisition time	**Moderate**	(move finger to position then touch down)	**Low**	(look and touch down anywhere)
Speed of selection of multiple objects within hand's reach	**High**	(select multiple objects at once)	**Low**	(Must sequentially select each object by gaze & touch)
Selection of multiple objects out of hand's reach	—	(needs two hands or other indirect method)	**High**	(multiple remote targets can be selected with sequential gaze & touch)
Degrees of freedom per point	**Low**	(1 touch per point)	**High**	(multiple touches can map to one gaze point)

Table 1: Summary of the differences of direct-touch to gaze-touch.

quently the point in time when manipulation starts is delayed, and effort increased. In comparison to these indirect methods, gaze-touch is also spatially indirect as the touch is separated from the object position. However, gaze-touch is different as manipulation can start directly at touch down, similar to direct-touch input. This enables the speed of direct-touch selection, while at the same time gaining indirect properties such as minimizing hand movement, enabling remote manipulation, or avoiding occlusion.

DESIGN SPACE: DIRECT-TOUCH VS. GAZE-TOUCH

To gain a deeper understanding of the conceptual differences between direct-touch and gaze-touch, we analyse the two techniques. We provide a design space analysis under the following headings, without claiming completeness: *similarities*, *occlusion*, *precision of selection*, *precision of manipulation*, *physical aspects*, *multiple object selection*, and *multi-touch to one point*. Table 1 provides a summary of the comparison and Figure 4 illustrates the conceptual differences.

Similarities. Both gaze-touch and direct-touch are temporally direct, as manipulation of an object starts as soon as users touch the surface. Both techniques accept a single touch point for 'clicking' an object (see Figure 4a & 4b), and two touch points for manipulating an object (Figure 4c & 4d). Gaze-touch uses the same hand motion for object manipulation; e.g. rotating two touch points to rotate a selected object (see Figure 4e & 4f), and pinch gestures to scale (Figure 4g & 4h). These similarities enable ease of learning and preserve consistency, as users can transfer their knowledge of direct-touch for operation of gaze-touch.

Occlusion. A direct-touch gesture causes surface occlusion, because users place their hands on top of an object for selection. As users place more fingers on an object, the area of occlusion increases (see Figure 4c). Researchers have suggested indirect methods that avoid occlusion, like creating proxies to the objects [23]. However, these methods can lead to additional effort for users, and can delay the manipulation task. Gaze-touch prevents occlusions by enabling spatially indirect manipulation (Figure 4d). Since touch actions are disjoint from the gaze-selected object, users can touch down on any surface location while looking at the object.

Precision of selection. Using direct-touch for target selection can be problematic when the target's size is smaller than the user's finger [9]; known as the 'fat-finger' problem. Although researchers suggested techniques to alleviate this problem by using multiple touch points (e.g. [2, 4]), the use of multiple fingers or hands hinders the selection process. Using gaze for selection in principle can overcome this issue. However, our eyes naturally jitter, and inaccuracy of eye trackers can cause imprecision [26]. Touch is still more precise for single-finger taps on large objects, but gaze-touch is potentially more suitable when the interaction requires placement of multiple fingers on an object (see Figure 4c & 4d).

Precision of manipulation. The precision of manipulation differs between gaze-touch and direct-touch. The standard direct-touch model is based on a 1:1 control-display ratio, so fine-grained manipulations can become difficult as they require tiny and precise movements. In practice, the size of objects has a limit; an object becomes difficult to manipulate if its size is too small to be selected or manipulated with fingers (Figure 4g). The standard touch technique could be improved by having users first select a target and then put their fingers elsewhere to manipulate (like the Rock&Rails technique [23]). The necessity to select and deselect the object complicates the interaction and delays the manipulation. In contrast, gaze-touch allows users to draw their fingers as far apart as the screen allows, and to immediately start manipulation at the moment of touch down (see Figure 4h).

Physical aspects. In gaze-touch, the finger touch positions are detached from the gaze position. Users only see digital *feedback* in their sight radius, i.e. on the selected object. However, the fingers are probably out of the users' sight. This contrasts direct-touch, where users can see physical feedback to the selected objects, because their fingers are placed on the object. Further, detaching the touch and gaze reduces muscle *fatigue*. Users' can keep their hands within their comfortable regions and still able to manipulate gaze-selected objects. On the other hand, the active use of gaze to select targets could lead to eye fatigue, as the eyes, a channel to perceive visual content, should not be overloaded with motor tasks [25]. Another benefit of detaching gaze and touch is that it avoids finger interference. Interference can occur when multiple fingers or hands collide within the same location, which interrupts the task (Figure 4i). With gaze-touch, the objects can be separate from the finger's position, so physical collision is prevented (Figure 4j).

Multiple object selection. Gaze is a single-point input, while multi-touch supports simultaneous input from multiple points (Figure 4k). With gaze, users must select multiple targets by looking at each object and placing a touch down (Figure 4l). Although conceptually gaze selection of multiple targets is slower than direct-touch, gaze-touch yields a benefit that users can select scattered objects on a surface. Selection of multiple objects with direct-touch is limited by the distance that a hand can reach and users can only select multiple objects that are near by each other (Figure 4m). Gaze-touch in contrast eliminates this restriction (Figure 4n).

Multi-touch to one point. Gaze-touch can map multiple touch points to a single gaze point (Figure 4d). This contrasts with direct-touch where one finger can be physically mapped to one point on the screen (Figure 4a & 4k). Furthermore, a gaze-touch is invariant of the hand's posture. In a rotation gesture with direct-touch, a user fits their hand to the object's shape to then perform the rotation from this hand posture (Figure 4c & 4e). Prior work has shown that there are several occasions where rotation or scaling postures and motions can be difficult [7, 8]. Using a gaze-touch, target acquisition is more comfortable as users only look at the object and touch down remotely with any hand posture (Figure 4d & 4f).

APPLICATIONS

In the following we describe four applications that each demonstrate a specific use of gaze-touch. Each application is described in its own section. Within each application, we describe concept, interaction techniques, and implementational details. The first three applications were also part of a preliminary user study which design and setup are described once, and which task and results are described within each application section. Notably, the gray circle indicates the user's current gaze point in all figures.

APPLICATION: IMAGE GALLERY

This application demonstrates that gaze-touch *or* direct-touch can be used for the same task. Users can browse through their set of images. They can scale them up for a detailed view, rotate the images to correct the aspect ratio, and drag images across the surface for sorting, grouping, or other object manipulation tasks. In essence, users can perform two types of touch gestures: single-touch dragging, and multi-touch rotate, scale, and translate (RST). Multiples of these gestures can be performed at the same time, when using multi-finger and bimanual input.

Switching between Gaze-Touch or Direct-Touch

The switching between direct-touch and gaze-touch is accomplished through using the user's coordination between gaze and touch position. When a user looks at an image and at the same time touches on it, direct-touch is enabled. This means the touch point is used as input, and not the gaze point (Figure 5a). However, when the user looks at a target but touches down somewhere else, gaze-touch is enabled (b, c).

Interaction Techniques

In addition to standard direct-touch translate, rotate, and scale gestures, the user can perform the following gaze-touch techniques:

Accelerated-Object-Dragging

When users look at an image and touch down once remotely, they can drag the image with their finger. While the selection is similar to previous techniques for interaction over distance [20, 21, 22], this technique only uses touch dragging for positioning. This dragging of images uses a dynamic control-display gain. We implemented a dragging acceleration similar to windows XP mouse acceleration, which amplifies the speed of the dragging finger. This enables to overcome larger distances with shorter movement, and be more precise when moving the finger slowly.

Indirect-Rotate-Scale-Translate (RST)

This technique is the gaze-touch counterpart for the RST gesture. Users touch down two fingers while looking at the same image (similar to [20], however without mode-switching). It has some characteristics that are distinct to direct-touch. Users only need the gaze point to be on the image, enabling manipulation of images that are too small to directly lay multiple fingers on it (Figure 5b), and when high precision is required (c). The further the user draws apart their fingers at touch down, the more precise is the manipulation. This provides the user with a choice of how precise they want to manipulate the image: users can place their fingers very close for fast manipulation (b), or very far apart for high precision (c).

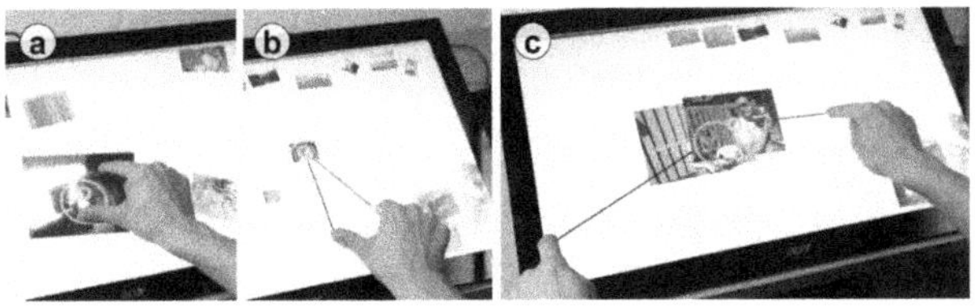

Figure 5: Indirect-RST: in addition to direct image manipulation (a), users can indirectly manipulate images for easy acquisition of small targets (b), or more precision (c).

Multi-Image-Dragging

While users can sequentially drag multiple images with the *Accelerated-Object-Dragging* technique, they can also drag multiple objects at once (Figure 6). The user first selects each image by looking at each image and each time touching down, to then perform one drag gesture. This is particularly interesting as, in contrast to direct-touch, users can simultaneously drag objects that would be out of the hand's reach.

Figure 6: Multi-Image-Dragging: after multiple gaze-touch selections, users can drag them out of the pile using a single dragging gesture. Through a dynamic control-display gain, small movements can overcome large distances.

Implementational Details

The moment the user touched down, the system decides if it is a gaze-touch or a direct-touch. If the user touches on an image and does not look at another image, direct-touch is triggered. Else, gaze-touch is active. The gaze point is set as the target of manipulation of a touch input session until the user lifts their finger. Intermediately received touch events of this session (touch_update) are executed on the point of gaze that was received at the moment of touch_down (for gaze-touch, respectively). To counter inaccurate gaze data, we used target-assistance. The image is highlighted as 'looked', when the system's gaze estimate is close to the image.

An interesting case is the control-display gain for multi-touch gestures, such as two-finger scaling. In direct-touch, this case is clear as the distance between the two fingers can be mapped to the same distance on the screen, thus an absolute 1:1 control-display gain. RST with gaze-touch relates two-touch input to one gaze point, and therefore it is unclear to what display-distance it should be mapped to. In our application instance, the distance between the fingers of a two-touch gesture is mapped to the radius of the target's size.

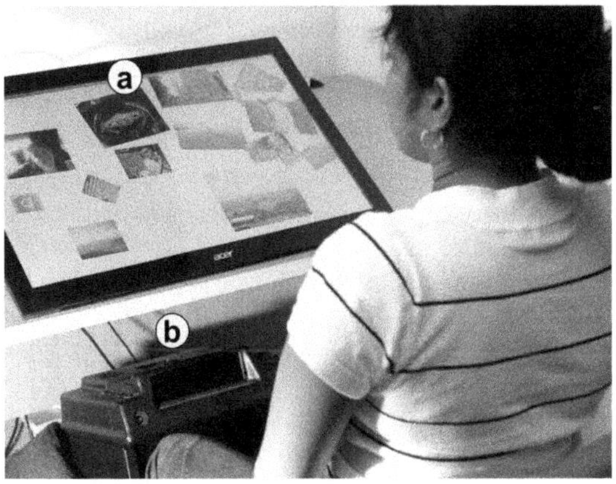

Figure 7: The system consists of a 27" 1080p multi-touch sensitive surface (a), and the 120hz Eye Follower eye tracking device (b).

Study Design

We conducted a preliminary user study to demonstrate the feasibility of and to gather user opinions about the applications. 13 volunteers between 22 and 33 years took part in the study (M=27.9, SD=3.73, 4 female). On a scale between 1 (no experience) to 5 (very experienced), users perceived themselves as well experienced with multi-touch (M=4.3, SD=0.9), and as less experienced with eye based interaction (M=2.5, SD=1.4). After a brief introduction, users were once calibrated to the eye tracking system. Users then interacted with the applications (counterbalanced). Each application began with a short training session where the experimenter explained the interaction techniques, and ended with an interview session. Each application test and interview lasted approximately 5-10 minutes. Users were not bound to a specific performance goal of the tasks to keep it to natural usage of the interactions.

Apparatus

We use an LC Technology Eye Follower with a touchscreen that is tilted 30° toward the user to enable convenient touch reaching (Figure 7). The user's eyes were approximately 50cm in front of the screen's center. Occlusion of the eye tracking camera could occur during the use. In practice, however, mostly users bend their arms around the tracking camera's view because of the close proximity of the touchscreen. As touchscreen we used an Acer t272 27" 1080p display that allows up to 10-finger multi-touch input. The system is running at a frame rate of 60hz, on a quadcore i7 2.3GHz CPU computer. The applications are written in Java using the Multitouch For Java library[1]).

User Feedback

Users were provided with ten images and were trained using both direct-touch and gaze-touch techniques. They performed two tasks of sorting images into groups (e.g. indoor/outdoor), and two tasks of searching for an image with a specific element in it (e.g. a bus). Before each task, the images were randomly placed, rotated, and sized. Users could scale the images between 50 and 750px.

[1] Used library available at http://www.mt4j.org (16/04/2014)

All users got quickly used to the techniques in this applications. Users did not have difficulties to switch between the direct and indirect counterpart. The study showed that most users stick to one technique for each particular task:

Single-Touch Dragging. Twelve users kept on using gaze-touch after the training. Interviews revealed that their reasons were speed, ease, and less physical effort. This was considered important with multiple images, where moving back and forth for each image is avoided, as one user stated: *"you do not always have to go back with your hand, but [you] keep it [the hand] stationary while your gaze goes back to the imagepool"*. Users emphasized that gaze-touch has less physical fatigue (*"You just move your arms, not your whole body"*). Users also liked the speed of dragging (*"It is effortless to move, as you can accomplish more with less movement"*). Some users were also positive about less occlusion through their fingers (*"My fingers sometimes obscure the pictures [with direct-touch]."*).

Two-Touch RST. Seven users kept on using direct-touch and four users gaze-touch. The user who preferred direct-touch found it to be easier and more intuitive (*"It is more intuitive, the movement"*). They also stated prior knowledge of direct-touch (*"I prefer on the picture [...] based on how I use my phone"*). An interesting case occurred when these users wanted to acquire small images with two fingers. They tried to put their fingers directly on it, yet in a failed attempt they put their fingers only close to the image as it was too small. This triggered gaze-touch on the very image (users looked and touched close to it) with which users scaled it up, without being aware of a gaze-touch.

Errors. Three users stated some difficulties with overlapping images. Inaccurate gaze tracking by the hardware we used lead to false positive image selections (*"When pictures overlapped sometimes, it did not jump at the picture that I wanted"*). Another issue occurred when selecting an image to drag. The user already looked away to the dragging destination during touch down, which lead to a wrong selection (*"I already looked at where I wanted to move it before I touched, so it moved something else"*).

Specific Findings. Two users stated they used direct in front (user's comfort zone), and gaze-touch in the remaining area. They intuitively use direct-touch in close proximity, however to avoid reaching out, gaze-touch became convenient (*"When it is far from me, then I can drag it from distance. If it is close to me, I can use the picture itself"*). One user emphasized an interesting feature of gaze-touch: users can manipulate an image, even though touching on another (*"If I look at a picture, I can go anywhere with my fingers. Even if I have my fingers on another picture"*).

Summary
Our evaluation showed that having direct and indirect manipulation within the same application is feasible. The majority of users kept using gaze-touch for single-touch dragging, and direct-touch for two-touch scaling and rotation. Users acknowledged the speed, reachability, reduced movement and reduced fatigue of gaze-touch in comparison to direct-touch. However, many users preferred using direct-touch for RST gestures. They perceived it easier to perform this gesture directly on the image.

APPLICATION: PAINT
This application demonstrates how gaze-touch *and* direct-touch are used. The user is provided with standard tools of a drawing application. With direct-touch, users can draw on the main canvas of the interface. In the menu, users can create three types of primitive shape (rectangle, circle, triangle), that initially have a size of 100x100px. After creation, they can be dragged and scaled using direct-touch input. Thus the user can create figures based on individually drawn lines and these primitive shapes.

The menu is completely gaze-touch enabled (but can also be directly touched). The menu provides the functions select colour, create primitive, and copy existing primitive. To trigger a menu mode, users look at a menu icon, and select it by touching down anywhere on the surface. We believe this can have an advantage for drawing tasks, as users do not need to remove hands from their current target. And after a mode is switched on the menu with gaze-touch, users do not need to relocate the previous position of the hand to continue the task. Users can keep their hand at the drawing position, and from there perform gaze-touches to the remote menu. This concept can be applied to many applications that involve a main interactive area and remotely positioned menus, such as ribbon menus in office tools, tabs in browsing, etc.

Interaction Techniques
Remote-Colour-Select
Most actions of the user are around the main canvas, where the figure is drawn directly. From here, users can quickly change the colour through gaze-touch (Figure 8). The user looks up at the colour (a), and touches down at their current position to confirm (b). Once done, the user can continue the drawing task (c). This technique can be easily extended to multiple finger use. Users can touch down many fingers, and each time look at a different colour, to simultaneously draw with several colours. In direct-touch, the user would have to reach out to the canvas or use a second hand to apply different colours to each fingers.

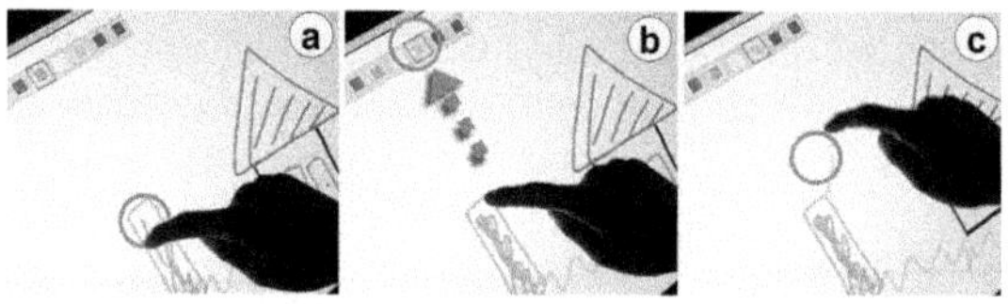

Figure 8: Remote-Colour-Select: a user draws the tree stem directly (a). The user then changes to the 'green' colour by a look at the corresponding menu icon, and a tap (b). The user directly continues drawing (c).

Create-Object
Contrary to mode changes, this technique creates a new element into the canvas. When users perform a gaze-touch on a graphical primitive icon of the menu, the primitive is created at the position of the user's touch. From here, the user can directly drag it to a more precise position, or perform direct

RST manipulation. The operation of this technique is similar to drawing (Figure 8), but instead of a colour it adds an object.

Copy-Paste-Object
Graphical primitives are direct-touch enabled in our application, thus users can drag them with single-touch on it. However, a single-touch can also be used for copy-paste of the primitive. The system switches to this special mode when users touch on the object, while they look at the copy-paste icon in the menu (Figure 9). This creates a copy directly under the user's finger, that can then be dragged elsewhere. This technique is distinct as the user is required to coordinate both the touch and gaze point. This requires more mental effort. However, this technique allows the user to perform two different tasks (dragging or copying) with a single-touch on the object, that are distinguished by where the user looks at. The technique also scales to multi-touch. Users can instead touch down two fingers to create two copies simultaneously.

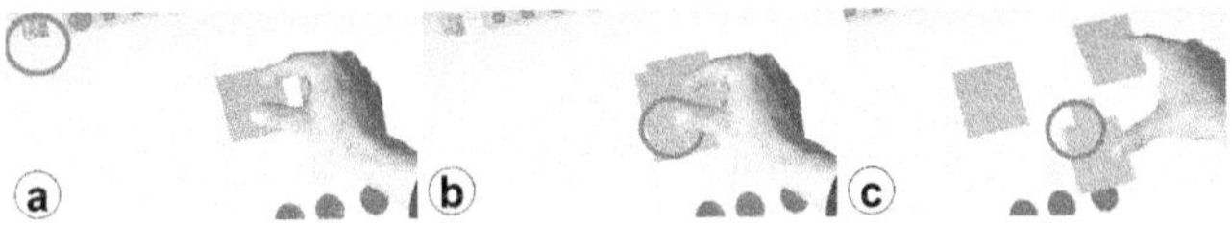

Figure 9: Copy-Paste-Object: the user can copy an existing object with a single-touch. Usually, a touch on the object leads to dragging. However, when the user looks at the copy icon in the menu (a), and then touches down on the object, the user obtains a copy of the touched object under her finger (b). Then, the user can directly drag the new copy to a desired position (c).

Implementational Details
The moment the user touched down, the system determines whether the gaze position is on one of the icons of the menu. If true, a gaze-touch is triggered, otherwise direct-touch is kept. To aid a potential inaccurate gaze position, we used target-assistance for the icons. If the gaze cursor is close to the menu, it attaches to the closest icon. No gaze cursor is shown, but the icons in the menu are highlighted when the user looks at them.

User Feedback
For the purpose of this study that investigates the switching between direct-touch and gaze-touch, we limited the interactions to direct-touch drawing on the canvas, and gaze-touch selection of colours in the menu. The task of the users was to draw a house, a tree, a car, a sun, and their name with various colours. All users were able to perform the drawing tasks.

The interviews revealed that seven users were positive, three users negative, and the other participants had mixed opinion about the application. Most users commented that the gaze-touch menu is easy to use, fast, and convenient (*"It goes quicker to select the colour [...] than by hand"*). Also it was noticed that it helps to focus on the main drawing task (*"It indirectly saves interaction, you can focus on the draw surface"*), and that it reduces mental effort (*"There is less thinking involved"*).

Negative user comments were mainly based on false positive colour selections. This had two reasons: (1) inaccuracy of eye tracking hardware, and (2) eye-hand coordination of the system. Often, users looked at a colour, but already moved on before touch down. It occurred that users passed close to other colours when looking back to the canvas, which the target-assistance wrongly interpreted as the colour of choice. This has been reported as 'Late-Trigger errors' and can be addressed by delayed selection [13].

Two users stated that they disliked the gaze-touch menu, because of mental demand (*"I feel like I have to focus"*) and non-normal behaviour (*"Often your eyes move without you knowing [that] they are moving"*).

Summary
The evaluation showed users can use direct-touch in conjunction with gaze-touch. Both techniques are used for separate areas on the screen, and therefore give the user a clear separation of input. Users recognized that gaze-touch is useful for menus that are often out of reach. They also confirmed that it is easy to use, comfortable, and contributes to better focus on the main drawing task. On the downside, our implementation led to false positive colour selections for some users (further discussed by Kumar et al. [13]).

APPLICATION: MAP NAVIGATION
This application demonstrates where gaze-touch can be used *instead of* direct-touch. The application begins with a world map, that the user can then explore with direct single-touch dragging gestures to pan the whole map, and gaze-touch based zooming to zoom in locations. To complement previous work that used gaze for interaction on maps [18], we use gaze implicitly as the target of a two-finger zooming gesture.

Gaze-Focused-Zooming
To perform zooming, the user looks at the location of interest, and then performs a pinching gesture anywhere on the surface. This triggers zooming into the user's gaze point. This yields several benefits over the direct counterpart. First, users can keep their hand on the same position for multiple zooms that reduces hand movement, occlusion, and fatigue, as only the user's gaze is used for target selection (Figure 10). Second, the user's gaze is faster than the hand for the selection of a zooming target. Third, users are able to change the zooming target during the gesture. With direct-touch, the target is fixed to the touch position once touched down. With gaze-touch, users can change the position by a glance. This becomes useful for corrective zooming: if a user zoomed into the wrong area, the user can zoom out, look at a different location, and zoom in again; all within a single pinch gesture.

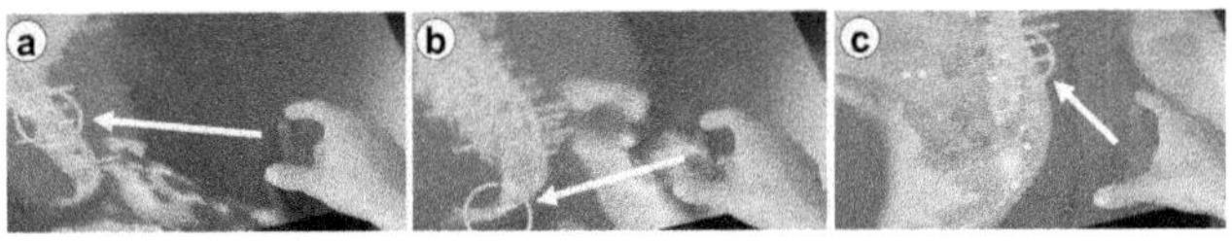

Figure 10: Gaze-Focused-Zooming: users can change their zoom-in position during several zooms without changing the pinching position.

Implementational Details

Within the touch input manager, we changed the zooming target from the touch center position to the gaze position. During zooming gestures, the system receives gaze events on-line to enable dynamic changing of the zooming focus. We also added a gaze cursor for this application. To avoid distracting behavior and gaze jittery, the cursor is set large (width=250px) and we average jittering gaze samples for 150 ms when only short eye movements occur.

User Feedback

In this part of the study we let user compare direct-touch against gaze-touch zooming. Users performed both conditions (counterbalanced). In each condition, users searched for five capital cities starting from a world view. Users did not have any difficulties finding the cities. Four users stated they had to get used to the gaze-based approach within the first or first two city tasks.

Preferences. Nine users favored map navigation with gaze-touch, two users thought they were equal, and the remaining two preferred direct-touch zooming. Users preferred gaze-touch zooming because of ease, speed, less physical effort, precision, and reachability. Users commented that it is more precise and reliable, as with direct-touch *"You often zoom in a bit too close, [...] and you have to zoom out again to correct"*. Interaction with gaze-touch was perceived as easy and intuitive, since users already look where they want to zoom anyway (*"I always look at the area where I expect the city"*). A user mentioned that it is much less fatiguing in comparison to her own touch-enabled device: *"Because sometimes with the IPad you always use your hands, you get tired"*. In addition, users were positive about no occlusion through hands and less body movement (e.g. *"[With direct-touch] I cover what I see with my hand and when the area is further away I have to lean forward to zoom in with the hand"*). Two users favored direct-touch zooming. The first user thought it was more precise with direct-touch (*"It is a little vague with the eyes"*). The other user stated the gaze-cursor that is used is confusing, as it moved constantly with the user's gaze.

Gaze-Touch Experience. While some users did not notice any difference, other users perceived a different map experience with gaze-touch. For example, users stated that gaze-touch helps map navigation (*"It helps you on what you are searching, you are not distracted"*). Another user mentioned increased zooming awareness (*"I was more aware of where I zoom"*) and another user perceived it as being guided (*"It is like you are guided"*).

Summary

The majority of users preferred gaze-touch over direct-touch for zooming. Reasons were speed, less effort, precision, and reachability. Further discussions with users showed that the map navigation experience is altered; users felt it is more helpful, and increases location-awareness.

APPLICATION: MULTIPLE OBJECTS

This application demonstrates how gaze-touch *extends* direct-touch interactions. The application allows users to manipulate a large number of objects spread across the surface. It is configurable with regards to number, shape, size, and colour of objects. Users can quickly select multiple objects, and reposition them by dragging gestures. Users can touch down with up to ten fingers, that would lead to 10 object selections. This allows us to experiment with gaze-touch's capability of fast and simultaneous manipulation of objects. To overcome the physical friction of the screen and gain fluent and reliable multi-touch, we used multi-touch gloves in our demonstrations. Because of its experimental state, this application was not included in the user study. These techniques can be useful, for example, in visual analytics that commonly involve sorting, searching, or grouping of many objects [24, 17].

Implementational Details

Our goal was to optimize object dragging. Therefore a touch down will always map to the target that is closest to the user's gaze point on the screen. Further, one touch will only map to a single target. This allows to quickly select multiple objects, e.g. when touching down two fingers at once, the two objects closest to the user's gaze are selected. In addition, the dragging acceleration from the Image Gallery application is integrated.

Interaction Techniques

Instant-Multi-Object-Dragging

Users can instantly select up to five objects to a hand (Figure 11). When the user touches down, the system binds the closest object to the finger. If multiple fingers are downed, each finger will get one object associated (a). This can be useful, for example, when sorting a large amount of objects. The user can sort out all selected objects at once by a single dragging gesture (b, c). Immediately after this, the user can continue to sort out the next objects as the user only needs to look at the next objects.

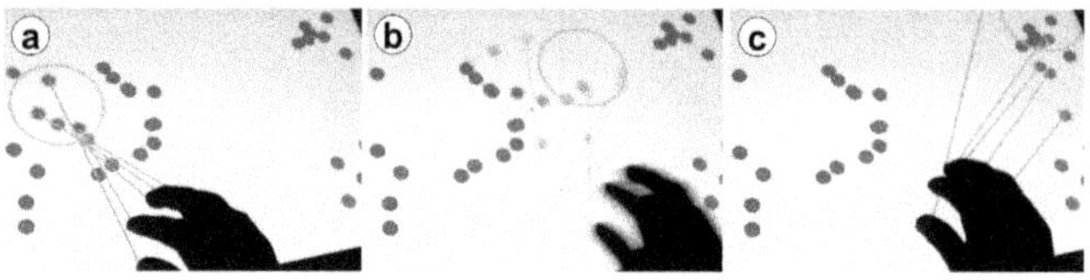

Figure 11: Multi-Finger-Dragging: users can select the five closest objects to their gaze by touching down five fingers (a). Users can then sort them out at once with a single dragging gesture (b, c).

Multi-Object-Pinching

We implemented a variant of this application where pinching leads to relative movement of objects toward the user's hand. When the user selects multiple objects as explained above, the user can perform a pinching gesture to move all objects to the hand's position (Figure 12). The distance between each finger and the center of all fingers is mapped to the distance between the object and the fingers' center. Thus this technique allows continuous movement of objects toward the hand, but moreover, it can also be used for positioning anywhere on the screen. To move close objects far apart, the user can start with a small distance between the fingers. By expanding the fingers (pinch-out), the objects would be drawn away (Figure 12, from (b) to (a)).

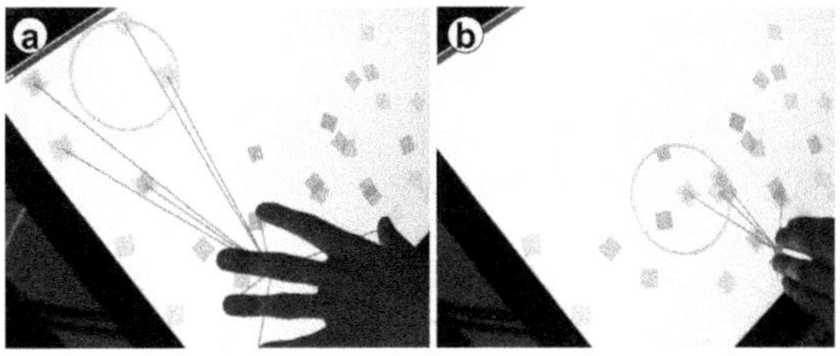

Figure 12: Multi-Object-Pinching: when multiple objects were selected (a), a pinching gesture moves the objects to the hand's position (b).

DISCUSSION

Starting from our conceptual analysis we outlined the differences between gaze-touch and direct-touch. The beneficial differences that we identified, such as reachability, no occlusion, speed, less fatigue, and less physical movement, were confirmed in our user study. Besides differences, a key characteristic of gaze-touch is its similarities to direct-touch. Users can manipulate objects at the moment they place a touch down, they can perform the same multi-touch gestures to manipulate content, and they look at the target before they initiate manipulation. These similarities greatly reduce learning effort as users are already familiar with touch-based interaction, so that they can apply the established knowledge to gaze-touch. This was further shown in our user study. Our participants required little training, and were able to get used to gaze-touch interaction very quickly.

The similarities between gaze-touch and direct-touch enable users to switch seamlessly between the techniques. Users can use direct-touch to interact with objects that are within their immediate comfort zone, while they can seamlessly switch to gaze-touch for reaching distant objects or mode switching as illustrated in our paint application. Furthermore, direct-touch enables single target manipulation by simply touching an object, and users can employ gaze-touch for multi-target operations. Our images application allows the use of both techniques; which led many participants to choose direct for single-target scaling and rotation, and gaze-touch for multi-target dragging. Our participants confirmed that these kind of divisions improve the interaction within the applications.

Our work shows many and varied potentials and examples of using gaze and touch for interactive surfaces of combined input and output. While we can confirm prior work that this combination allows to efficient reaching of remote targets [19, 20, 21, 22], we discovered additional benefits for surface interaction. A single-touch is now more expressive as it can have many different meanings – users can drag an object like in direct-touch, but also copy, delete, add, or any other task depending on which mode the user looks at. Users can perform the same task either directly or indirectly with gaze-touch, in essence providing more expressive input to the same target. Techniques can take advantage of both gaze and touch point, e.g. drag objects to the close touch position, or copy the object that is under the touch. Multiple target manipulations are more efficient. Users look at each target and perform manipulation on the same position, such as zooming into different locations, or manipulate all targets in sight at once, such as sorting of multiple images across the surface.

Limitations

Eye Tracking

In our setup, the position of the eye tracker is non-trivial because users can occlude the camera's view. When users positioned their arms in front of the eye tracker, the action can block the tracking of the users' eyes. Another problem is eye tracking inaccuracy by hardware limits and natural eye jittering, that can increase with a larger surface space [11]. We approached this issue individually for each application: e.g. target assistance when objects were involved (e.g. the menu of Paint application), or by filtering gaze noise (Map Navigation application), however further improvements can allow a smoother gaze-touch experience.

Inappropriate Tasks

A conceptual limitation of gaze-touch is that it requires the user to look at a target of interest. For many tasks the user's gaze is already at the target of interest, but there are cases where users do not need to look at the target. For example, when users are familiar with the input position, they simply use their muscle memory for input (e.g. PIN entry). This example, however, only applies to input targets that are fixed in location, and in this case gaze-touch can simply be disabled. In other cases however, where content is dynamic e.g. image aligning, video editing, or multi-view interfaces, the use of gaze-touch might become difficult. In these cases gaze-touch is more of benefit when used complementary to direct-touch, e.g. as shown in our Paint application (gaze-touch for mode switching, direct-touch for primary task).

Eye-Hand Coordination

Eye-hand coordination plays a relevant role in gaze-touch. Often users already gaze away from the target before acquisition. Known as the 'Late-Trigger errors' [13], it can be approached by selection delay or intelligent eye fixation detection, however a deeper understanding might be needed.

Multiple Selection and Eye Overload

A gaze-touch selection is completely based on the single-channel gaze modality. This principally disallows simultaneous selection of multiple targets. One approach is selecting as many objects close to the user's gaze as the user touches down fingers (c.f. our 'Multiple Objects' application). However, when sequences of tasks require users to visually fixate many points over time, the users' cognitive or visual abilities might get overloaded. While our principle 'gaze selects, touch manipulates', reduces gaze usage to the moment when users touch down, it is yet unknown how much it affects the user's mental and physical abilities. In this context, it has to be considered that the utility of gaze-touch is its complementary nature, in cases direct-touch is limited.

CONCLUSION

In this paper we introduced gaze-touch as a novel interaction technique that faciliates gaze and multi-touch on the same surface. The technique makes existing direct interactions more flexible, as it allows for implicit mode switching by a glance, and manipulation of many targets without directly touching them. This leads to novel application designs where gaze-touch can be used complementary or alternately to existing direct manipulation, and even can replace or extend tasks that previously belonged to the territory of direct input. Gaze-touch enhances touch interactions with seamless and efficient interaction techniques, as reachability, physical movement and fatigue are overcome, while the speed and familiarity with common multi-touch gestures prevail. Gaze-touch is simple in its core technique, but lends itself to extend surface interactions with dynamic and effortless capabilities.

REFERENCES

1. Abednego, M., Lee, J.-H., Moon, W., and Park, J.-H. I-grabber: Expanding physical reach in a large-display tabletop environment through the use of a virtual grabber. In *ITS '09*, ACM (2009), 61–64.
2. Albinsson, P.-A., and Zhai, S. High precision touch screen interaction. In *CHI '03*, ACM (2003), 105–112.
3. Banerjee, A., Burstyn, J., Girouard, A., and Vertegaal, R. Pointable: an in-air pointing technique to manipulate out-of-reach targets on tabletops. In *ITS '11*, ACM (2011), 11–20.
4. Benko, H., Wilson, A. D., and Baudisch, P. Precise selection techniques for multi-touch screens. In *CHI '06*, ACM (2006), 1263–1272.
5. Bezerianos, A., and Balakrishnan, R. The vacuum: facilitating the manipulation distant objects. In *CHI '05*, ACM (2005), 361–370.
6. Hansen, J. P., Tørning, K., Johansen, A. S., Itoh, K., and Aoki, H. Gaze typing compared with input by head and hand. In *ETRA '04*, ACM (2004), 131–138.
7. Hoggan, E., Nacenta, M., Kristensson, P. O., Williamson, J., Oulasvirta, A., and Lehtiö, A. Multi-touch pinch gestures: Performance and ergonomics. In *ITS '13*, ACM (2013), 219–222.
8. Hoggan, E., Williamson, J., Oulasvirta, A., Nacenta, M., Kristensson, P. O., and Lehtiö, A. Multi-touch rotation gestures: Performance and ergonomics. In *CHI '13*, ACM (2013), 3047–3050.
9. Holz, C., and Baudisch, P. The generalized perceived input point model and how to double touch accuracy by extracting fingerprints. In *CHI '10*, ACM (2010), 581–590.
10. Jacob, R. J. K. What you look at is what you get: eye movement-based interaction techniques. In *CHI '90*, ACM (1990), 11–18.
11. Jacob, R. J. K. Eye movement-based human-computer interaction techniques: Toward non-command interfaces. In *Advances in Human-Computer Interaction*, Vol. 4, Ablex Publishing (1993), 151–190.
12. Koons, D. B., Sparrell, C. J., and Thorisson, K. R. Intelligent multimedia interfaces. American Association for Artificial Intelligence, Menlo Park, CA, USA, 1993, ch. Integrating Simultaneous Input from Speech, Gaze, and Hand Gestures, 257–276.
13. Kumar, M., Klingner, J., Puranik, R., Winograd, T., and Paepcke, A. Improving the accuracy of gaze input for interaction. In *ETRA '08*, ACM (2008), 65–68.
14. Mateo, J. C., San Agustin, J., and Hansen, J. P. Gaze beats mouse: Hands-free selection by combining gaze and emg. In *CHI EA '08*, ACM (2008), 3039–3044.
15. Pouke, M., Karhu, A., Hickey, S., and Arhippainen, L. Gaze tracking and non-touch gesture based interaction method for mobile 3d virtual spaces. In *OzCHI '12*, ACM (2012), 505–512.
16. Sibert, L. E., and Jacob, R. J. K. Evaluation of eye gaze interaction. In *CHI '00*, ACM (2000), 281–288.
17. Stasko, J., Görg, C., and Liu, Z. Jigsaw: Supporting investigative analysis through interactive visualization. *Information Visualization 7*, 2 (Apr. 2008), 118–132.
18. Stellmach, S., and Dachselt, R. Investigating gaze-supported multimodal pan and zoom. In *ETRA '12*, ACM (2012), 357–360.
19. Stellmach, S., and Dachselt, R. Look & touch: gaze-supported target acquisition. In *CHI '12*, ACM (2012), 2981–2990.
20. Stellmach, S., and Dachselt, R. Still looking: investigating seamless gaze-supported selection, positioning, and manipulation of distant targets. In *CHI '13*, ACM (2013), 285–294.
21. Turner, J., Alexander, J., Bulling, A., Schmidt, D., and Gellersen, H. Eye pull, eye push: Moving objects between large screens and personal devices with gaze & touch. In *INTERACT '13*, Springer (2013), 170–186.
22. Turner, J., Bulling, A., Alexander, J., and Gellersen, H. Cross-device gaze-supported point-to-point content transfer. In *ETRA '14*, ACM (2014), 19–26.
23. Wigdor, D., Benko, H., Pella, J., Lombardo, J., and Williams, S. Rock & rails: Extending multi-touch interactions with shape gestures to enable precise spatial manipulations. In *CHI '11*, ACM (2011), 1581–1590.
24. Wise, J. A., Thomas, J. J., Pennock, K., Lantrip, D., Pottier, M., Schur, A., and Crow, V. Visualizing the non-visual: Spatial analysis and interaction with information from text documents. In *INFOVIS '95*, IEEE (1995), 51–58.
25. Zhai, S., Morimoto, C., and Ihde, S. Manual and gaze input cascaded (magic) pointing. In *CHI '99*, ACM (1999), 246–253.
26. Zhang, X., Ren, X., and Zha, H. Improving eye cursor's stability for eye pointing tasks. In *CHI '08*, ACM (2008), 525–534.

Air+Touch: Interweaving Touch & In-Air Gestures

Xiang 'Anthony' Chen, Julia Schwarz, Chris Harrison, Jennifer Mankoff, Scott E. Hudson
Human-Computer Interaction Institute, Carnegie Mellon University
{xiangche, julia.schwarz, chris.harrison, jmankoff, scott.hudson}@cs.cmu.edu

ABSTRACT
We present Air+Touch, a new class of interactions that interweave touch events with in-air gestures, offering a unified input modality with expressiveness greater than each input modality alone. We demonstrate how *air* and *touch* are highly complementary: touch is used to designate targets and segment in-air gestures, while in-air gestures add expressivity to touch events. For example, a user can draw a circle in the air and tap to trigger a context menu, do a finger 'high jump' between two touches to select a region of text, or drag and in-air 'pigtail' to copy text to the clipboard. Through an observational study, we devised a basic taxonomy of Air+Touch interactions, based on whether the in-air component occurs before, between or after touches. To illustrate the potential of our approach, we built four applications that showcase seven exemplar Air+Touch interactions we created.

ACM Classification
H5.2 [Information interfaces and presentation]: User Interfaces - Input devices and strategies, Graphical user interfaces.

Keywords
Touch input; free space gestures; interaction techniques; input sensing; around device interaction.

INTRODUCTION
A generation of mobile devices has relied on touch as the primary input modality. However, poking with a fingertip lacks immediate expressivity. In order to support richer actions, touch must be overloaded in time (e.g., long press), space (e.g., drawing an 's' to silence the phone) or configuration (two-finger tap is 'alt click'). These approaches suffer from one or more of the following issues: scalability of gesture set, time consuming to perform, "Midas" touch, and significant finger occlusion on small screens. Thus, there is an ongoing challenge to expand the envelope of touch interactions by combining it with new input dimensions that increases richness.

Recently, devices such as the Samsung S4 smart phone [22] have emerged with hover sensing capability. In-air (or "free-space") gesturing is an area of intense research (see e.g., [7, 17]). These interactions are attractive as they can utilize a space many times larger than a device's physical boundaries, allowing for more comfortable and potentially richer interactions. However, in-air gestures are typically treated as a separate input modality, rather than integrated with existing touch-based techniques. Further, in-air gestures suffer from the challenge of segmentation: little literature has discussed how to systematically separate intentional gestures from accidental finger movements.

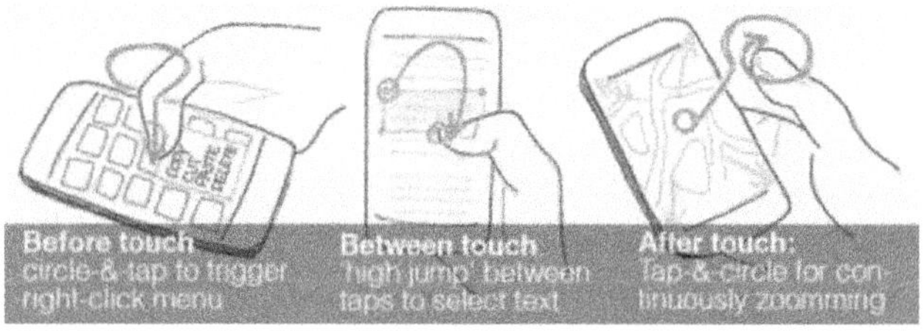

Figure 1. We propose that touch and in-air gestures be interwoven to create fluid and expressive interactions.

In this paper, we reconsider touch and in-air gestures beyond their individual domains. We propose a synthesis of these two input modalities, achieving interaction richness and robustness that neither can provide alone. Indeed, we found in-air and touch inputs to be highly complementary: touch is used to designate targets and segment in-air gestures, while in-air gestures add expressivity and modality to touch events. This Air+Touch modality outlines a class of interactions that enable fluid use of a device's screen and the space above it.

To explore this possibility, we start with a focus on the scenario of single-finger interaction, where a person uses his or her thumb or index finger to gesture in the air and also touch the screen. Through an observational study, we devised a simple taxonomy of Air+Touch interactions. We propose that in-air gestures can augment interactions *before*, *between* and *after* touch events. And in turn, touch events are used to segment in-air gestures and can also specify an on-screen target (e.g., a photo or map location). In-air gestures can be parameterized based on shape, velocity and/or time of a finger's movement. Figure 1 offers three examples, from left to right: 1) circle-in-air and tap an icon to trigger a context menu, 2) do a finger 'high jump' between two taps to select a region of text, or 3) tap and cycle the finger in air to continuously zoom a map.

RELATED WORK
Our work extends the input area from the touch screen to the space immediately above it, which is related to research that situates *interactions beside, behind & above* digital surfaces. For example, *SideSight* [3] uses infrared sensors to

UIST '14, October 05 - 08 2014, Honolulu, HI, USA

http://dx.doi.org/10.1145/2642918.2647354

track finger movements from the sides of a mobile device. Magnetic sensors have also been used to enable similar interaction styles in *Abracadabra* [6] and *MagiTact* [14]. Wigdor et al. explore the design space of a two-sided interactive tabletop surface [25]. *NanoTouch* [2] and *LucidTouch* [24] demonstrated that the back surface of a device can be used to increase the interactive area.

A number of research projects have focused on the space above interactive tabletops, such as Hilliges *et al.*'s *Interactions in the Air* [7], Marquardt et al.'s *Continuous Interaction Space* [17], and Banerjee et al.'s *Pointerable* [1]. In the realm of mobile devices, *HoverFlow* uses infrared sensors [16] and Niikura et al. use a high frame rate camera [18] to track hand/finger gestures above a mobile device. Marquardt et al. propose blending a digital surface and the space above it into a *continuum* wherein touch, gesture and tangibles can equally take place [17]. However, there is no discussion of mechanisms for segmenting in-air gestures (i.e., rejecting unintended finger movements). Further, the free-space and touch gestures generally co-exist, rather than being interwoven as we propose.

A natural next step is for researchers to explore in-air gestures in the space surrounding a device. Kratz et al. show that gestures above, beside and behind a mobile device yield better performance, compared to a virtual trackball, in manipulating 3D objects [15]. Jones et al. find that around-device free-space interaction can be as good as touch [13]. This work also defines 'comfort zones' around a device, which has strong implications for applying different sensor orientations. Samsung has shipped several basic in-air gestures with their Galaxy S4 [22]: A hand hovering on a lock screen shows time and notifications, and swiping left or right above a screen navigates a photo album.

Air+Touch also builds off of previous work that synthesized multiple inputs to create new interaction possibilities. *Pen+Touch* [11] synthesized pen and touch inputs to create new tools, such as using touch to hold a photo and pen to drag off and create a copy. *Motion+Touch* [10] combined touch with the motion sensing capability of a mobile device to yield touch-enhanced motion gestures and motion-enhanced touch. *Pen+Motion* [9] combined pen input with pen motions, enabling new gestural input abilities. Our work synthesizes touch and in-air gesture in several new ways. First, we provide an input structure to segment in-air gesture using touch, and to augment touch using in-air gesture. Second, air and touch interleave each other, yielding a permutation of input sequences than can richly parameterize interactions.

DESIGN FINDINGS FROM OBSERVATONAL STUDY

To ground and guide our initial exploration of Air+Touch interactions, we conducted a study to observe finger behavior above mobile screens when users are engaged in interactive tasks. We recruited 12 participants (5 female, ages 24-36). One participant was left-handed, one was ambidextrous, and all were regular smartphones users.

We asked each participant to perform a set of common tasks on a smartphone (e.g., compose a text message, navigate on a map). We videotaped the sessions and looked for patterns in how fingers hovered or moved in the space immediately above the screen. From this, we distilled a set of features that could translate into gestural input, while avoiding collisions (i.e., reducing confusion) with natural finger movements. Next, we discuss how these features can contribute to the design of in-air gestures, and further, how touches can be used as natural delimiters to segment these actions.

Air: Properties of Above-Screen Finger Movements

Participants in our study exhibited a wide range of in-air, above-screen finger behaviors. This included hovering over the screen between touches, retracting to the bezels when the screen needed to be read, and wiggling fingers when uncertain about what to do (such as while searching for a button). When discussing the contents of the screen, people also used their fingers to point and wave at content, or to gesture as they spoke, similar to how hand gestures are used in conversation. In particular, we focused on three main categories of finger movement behavior 1) path – the trajectory of fingers' movement, 2) position – fingers' particular positions above the screen, and 3) repetition –how users repeat certain finger movement.

These observations informed Air+Touch design in two ways. Foremost, they illuminated the kinds of above-screen finger movements users can comfortably reproduce, which we then adopted as part of our vocabulary of in-air movements. Secondly, it allowed us to craft a vocabulary of gestures that can be easily disambiguated from natural finger movements. Below are some exemplar findings that later informed our design of Air+Touch gestures:

Elliptical paths: Few of the finger motions we observed followed smooth, elliptical paths. This suggested that a circling action could be distinctive.

Rectangular paths: Similar to what Grossman et al. found in [5], few participants exhibited right angles in their finger trajectories. This suggested that paths with corners, such as an L-shaped gesture, could also be robustly recognized.

Leveraging height: Most users' finger movements occurred close to the screen. This suggested that in-air gestures with atypical height components could be disambiguated from typical interactions.

Using framing gestures: Whack Gestures [12] demonstrated that simple gestures (e.g., a *whack*) can yield expressive input when used as a framing feature (i.e., *<frame_gesture> primary_gesture </frame_gesture>*). Matched framing gestures can dramatically decrease the probability of false positives, even when the underlying gesture has a high error rate. In our study, we observed that users seldom touched the same location twice, except when scrolling, and in this case, rarely performed any finger movement of interest in the intervening time. This suggested that in-air gestures could be performed between framing touches. Another possibility is to include framing within the air gesture, such as using the first in-air circle as the signal that triggers recognition for subsequent finger circling (similar to using consective "whacks" in [12]).

Touch: Delimiting In-Air Gestures

Even with a carefully designed in-air gesture set, the uncertain nature of free space gestures demands a more explicit way to signal when an interaction is actually taking place. Our observations suggested that touch events could serve as a powerful and intuitive delimiter.

In a typical interactive task, touch interleaves 'air' by bringing an in-air finger movement to a *closure* when the finger touches the screen or by *introducing* a new chunk of in-air movement as the finger disengages itself from the screen. Thus touch naturally segments in-air gestures into three possible categories: *before*, *between* or *after* touches. This allows the in-air gesture recognition engine to search only a small window of time for applicable in-air finger movements (i.e., instead of constant monitoring). In the remainder of the paper, these temporal categories serve as the organizing principle for the example Air+Touch interactions we created.

Air+Touch: A Gesture Vocabulary

Our observations also helped us to craft an initial vocabulary of in-air gestures, which can be delimited by touch events in three ways as described in the previous section. To further explore this space, we looked at existing applications and considered whether any of the Air+Touch gestures could be adopted to enhance the present interaction. This helped us come up with four applications covering a set of seven Air+Touch gestures (Figure 2, in red) that are representative (but not inclusive) of the entire design space.

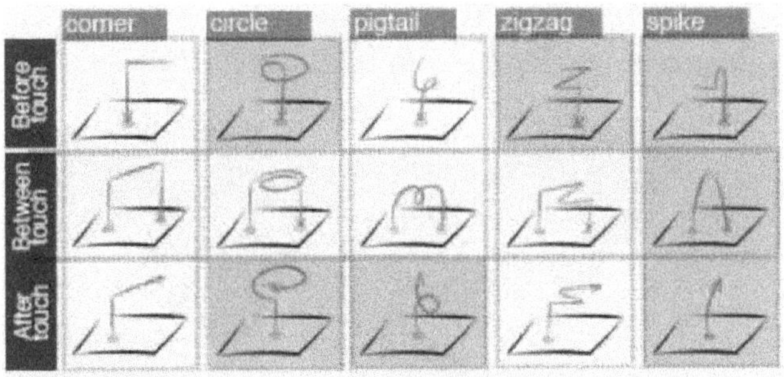

Figure 2. A proof-of-concept design space of Air+Touch gestures. We implemented seven of these techniques (red shading).

- *Corner*: the finger contains a 90-degree angle in air (on a plane perpendicular to the screen);
- *Circle*: the finger draws smooth, cyclical paths in the air.
- *Pigtail*: the finger draws a small loop along its in-air trajectory.
- *Zigzag*: the finger makes sharp 'turns' in air (on a plane parallel to the screen), e.g., drawing an 'L' or 'Z';
- *Spike*: the finger reaches a 'special' air position during its movement, e.g., reaching a position higher than the usual hover range, or a position outside the screen boundary.

AIR+TOUCH PROTOTYPE

There are an increasing number of devices featuring capacitive touchscreens able to track fingers in the air (i.e., hover sensing). At CES 2014, Synaptics demonstrated a prototype touchpad able to track fingers at up to 4cm away [23]. All indications suggest this technology will continue to improve and become more pervasive. Unfortunately, the sensing range on today's consumer devices is limited. For example, the Samsung Galaxy S4 has a tracking range of approximately 1.5cm.

Thus, in order to explore the full range of Air+Touch interactions that might be possible in a few years, it was necessary to build our own prototype. Although bulky today, our prototype served as a useful vehicle for exploration and investigation. We also used this platform to build seven demonstrations of Air+Touch interactions (Figures 2 and 6-12), which span our outlined design space and demonstrate the viability of our approach.

Hardware

Our prototype finger tracking system consists of a commercial smart phone and a PMD Camboard Nano [19] depth camera obliquely mounted to a common chassis (Figure 3). The Camboard Nano has a 90°×68° field of view and senses a 160×120px depth and infrared image from 5 to 50 cm at up to 90 fps. Finger tracking is performed on an external PC, and finger positions are sent to a mobile client via a wireless network. This setup allowed us to rapidly prototype ideas without having to instrument any customized hardware into the smart phone.

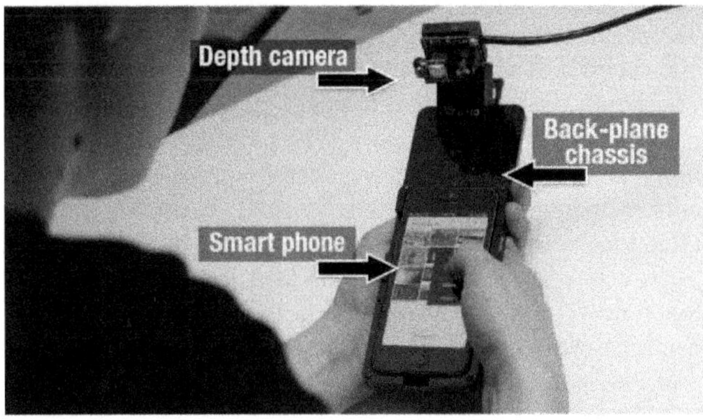

Figure 3. Our prototype smart phone uses a depth camera to simulate future, more advanced hover-capable devices. We used this setup as a vehicle for exploration and also as a platform to develop several Air+Touch augmented applications.

Finger Tracking

Our finger-tracking software is written in C++ and uses the OpenCV library. Since the geometry of the phone is known, we can perform simple volume-based background subtraction (Figure 4b). We also remove noise due to infrared reflection from the phone's screen (Figure 4c). Using this image, we identify the largest blob in the scene and perform contour analysis. We assume the fingertip to be the farthest contour point from the blob centroid (Figure 4d). To help reject false positives, we only look at contours situated along the fingers' major orientation.

In cases when the finger is pointing towards the depth camera, the fingertip will not lie along a contour, but will rather lie inside the finger boundary. We detect this case by using our camera's infrared image; due to skin's high infrared reflectance (and the infrared emitter our depth camera employs), the fingertip will appear as a bright, roughly Gaussian spot. In this instance, we use the brightest spot as the fingertip position.

This process yields a camera-space, fingertip X/Y/Z position representing the point of interest during an Air+Touch gesture. We then transform this raw 3D coordinate to X/Y screen coordinates (in pixels), along with a Z value (distance perpendicular from the screen). This transformation matrix is computed using three known points on the phone's screen, selected in 3D camera space during a one-time calibration procedure (Figure 4, hollow dots). Finally, fingertip position is lightly smoothed with an exponentially weighted moving average.

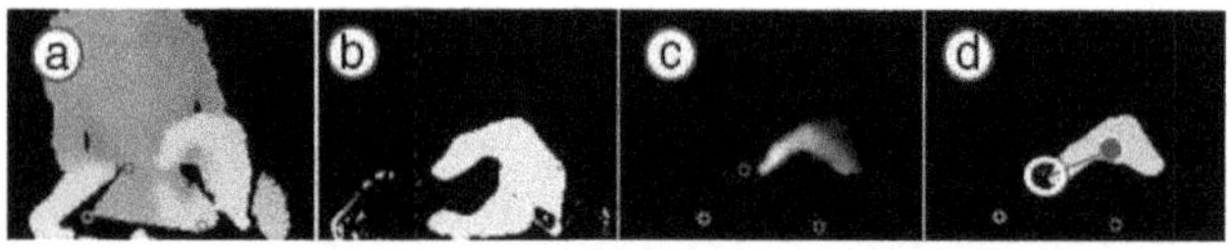

Figure 4. Finger tracking pipeline: a) raw image, b) background removal, c) noise removal & blob tracking, and d) fingertip localization.

In-Air Gesture Classification

Our system records 3D finger position at 20 frames per second and maintains a positional history of approximately one second. When a touch down event occurs, we run the $1 gesture recognizer [26] on the X and Y coordinates (as projected onto screen space) of the buffered finger positions. If a good shape match is found with sufficient size, a corresponding interactive event is fired. For in-air gestures after touch, we run the recognizer on the buffer after approximately one second following the touch up event. In the touch-down case, we also check to see if a reciprocal touch event happened within the last one second, and if so, interpret this as an in-air gesture being performed *between* two touch events.

To support in-air gestures that utilize Z distance (and not shape), we use a virtual plane situated 4cm above the screen as a threshold, providing something akin to a 3D crossing gesture. Each time this plane is crossed, a timestamp is recorded. If a touch event occurred within ±500ms, an interactive event is fired.

EXAMPLE AIR+TOUCH INTERACTIONS TECHNIQUES

Based on our design findings from the observational study, we developed a set of example Air+Touch interactions (Figure 5). To provide a use context for these interaction techniques, we created four host applications: photo viewer, drawing app, document reader, and map. Please also see our Video Figure.

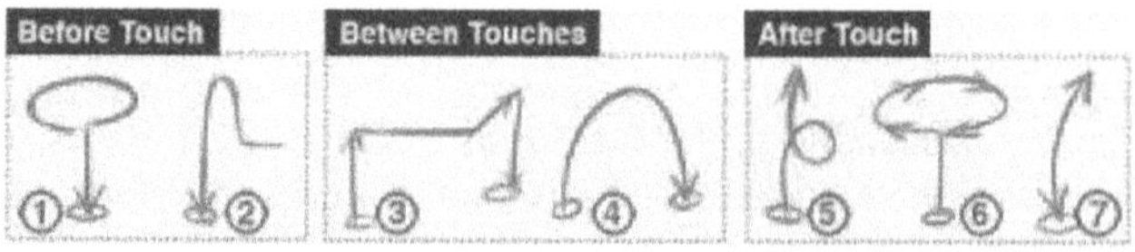

Figure 5. Air+Touch interactions can be characterized as air before touch (e.g., 1 - circle-in-air and tap, 2 - high-up and tap) air between touches: (e.g., 3 - draw an 'L', 4 - finger 'high jump') and air after touch (e.g., 5 - draw a 'pig tail', 6 - cycling in air, 7 - hovering.).

Air Before Touch

Unlike a mouse, touch (generally) only has one 'button'. This has led to a persistent need for additional modal mechanisms, such as touch-and-hold to invoke e.g., a context menu. Toolbars are also popular, but consume valuable screen real estate. To mitigate this problem, Air+Touch allows users to perform in-air gestures before or en route to touching the screen, as a way to parameterize the touch event. We offer two example interactions for this technique.

Circle-in-Air and Tap

In our photo viewer application (Figure 6), a user can trigger an image's context menu by performing an in-air circling motion (Figure 6a-c) immediately before tapping on a desired image (Figure 6d-e). The in-air gesture specifies the command (in this case, trigger context menu), while the touch specifies the item of interest (e.g., a photo). These two motions are combined into a single, fluid finger motion: circle-and-tap.

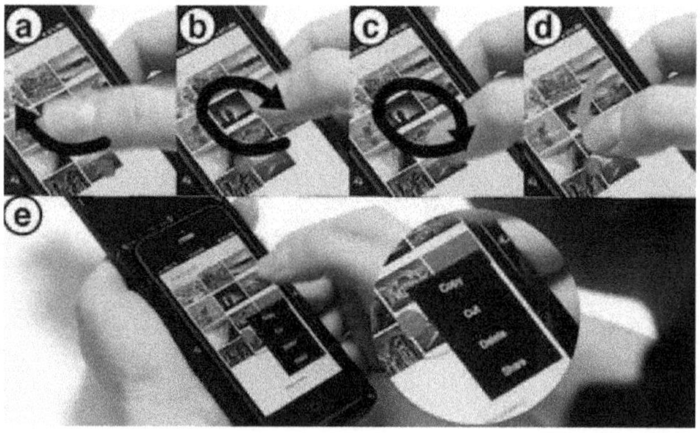

Figure 6. In our photo viewer, a circle-in-air (a,b,c) and tap (d) brings up a context menu (e).

High-up and Tap for Mode Switching

One-handed map navigation is difficult on a mobile handheld device when only the thumb is available for interaction. Our map application demonstrates how Air+Touch allows users to switch between panning and zooming modes simply by raising the thumb 'high-up' before a tap (Figure 7). The person can then scroll on the screen to pan the map (Figure 7ab), or to zoom in/out of it as if using a virtual slider (Figure 7cd).

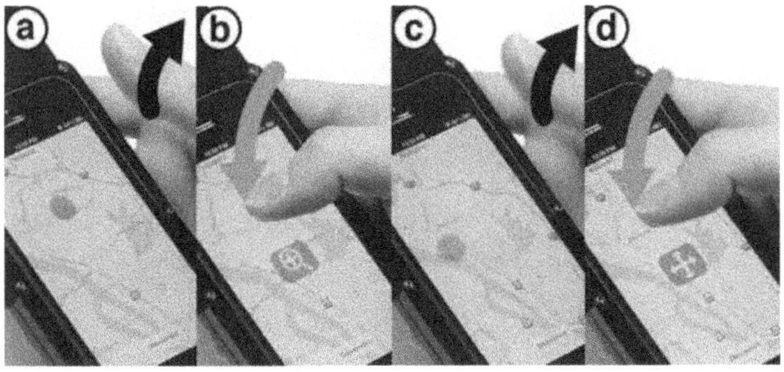

Figure 7. In our map app, raising the finger 'high-up' (a, c) before touch down switches between pan/zoom modes (b, d).

Air Between Touch

Performing an in-air gesture in between consecutive touch events offers the opportunity to parameterize two-point or even multi-point actions.

Finger 'High Jump' Between Touches to Select Text

Because there is no immediate way to disambiguate between scrolling and selection in touch interfaces, routine actions such as copy and paste are unwieldy. Air+Touch can streamline this process with a solution that takes two taps (Figure 8). A user can select a region of text by 1) tapping the beginning of the desired selected region, 2) raising the finger up high, and then 3) touching the end of the selected region. In sequence, these three steps can be executed in a single finger movement. Further touches can provide fine-grained adjustment if needed (d). This creates a gestural shortcut that chunks [4] the specification of text area and the intention to select it into a single finger 'high-jump'.

Drawing an 'L' Between Touches for Marquee-Selection

Similarly, cropping or selecting a sub-region of an image typically requires first interrupting the current interaction and then specifying a special application mode (e.g., through toolbar buttons). However, with Air+Touch, this can be achieved in a more fluid manner, by performing an 'L' gesture in-between two touches. The first and second touches specify the opposite corners of a rectangular marquee. In piloting, we found that drawing an 'L' was a succinct and natural way of expressing the intention of selecting a rectangular area.

Air After Touch

In this category, a person performs in-air gesture as the fingers leave the surface. Air augments touch by mapping touch to a specific function (similar to air before touch) or by allowing touch to continue the interaction unconstrained

Figure 8. In our reader app, a finger 'high jump' (b) between two touches (a,c) defines and selects a region of text. The user then can also use touch to adjust the selection (d).

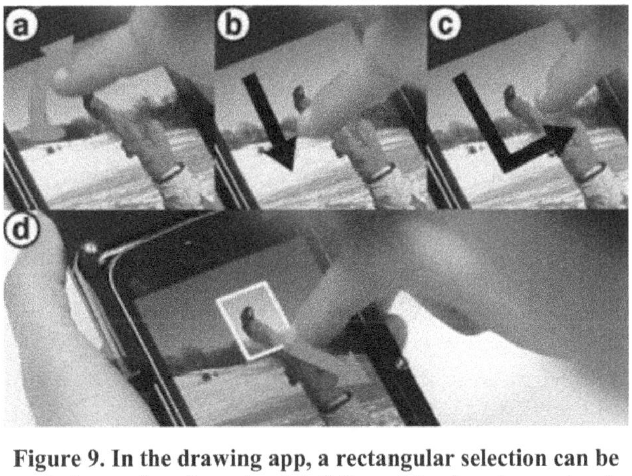

Figure 9. In the drawing app, a rectangular selection can be made by performing a tap (a), followed by drawing an in-air 'L' gesture (b.c), and finally closed by another tap (d).

by screen size, e.g., clutch-free scrolling and zooming.

Drawing a 'Pigtail' After Touch for Free-form Selection

In our drawing application, dragging a finger on the screen is used to draw. However, this path can be parameterized with a post-touch, in-air gesture. For example, by lifting the finger and performing a pigtail motion in the air (Figure 10), the last drawn path is converted into a clipped region that can be e.g., moved, scaled or copied to the clipboard.

Cycling In-Air After Touch to Zoom on a Map

We previously described an air before touch technique that enables quick mode switching between pan and zoom. Another solution is to 'divide the labor' – touch can be used to pan, while in-air cycling zooms.

More specifically, a person starts by tapping on e.g., a map to specify the zoom center (a). As she releases her finger from the screen, a 'zoom mode' may be triggered by drawing a circle high in the air (Figure 11b). Once in 'zoom mode', continuously cycling the finger in the air zooms in or out (depending on cyclical direction) at the tapped location (Figure 11cde). Tapping on the screen, or a short period of non-cyclical finger motion exits the zoom mode. This

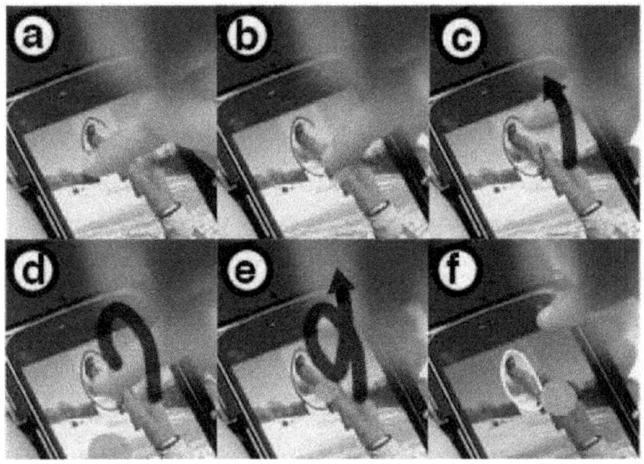

Figure 10. In our drawing app, a user can specify a clipping region by using touch to draw an arbitrary path (a,b), lifting her finger (c), and drawing a pigtail in the air (d,e,f).

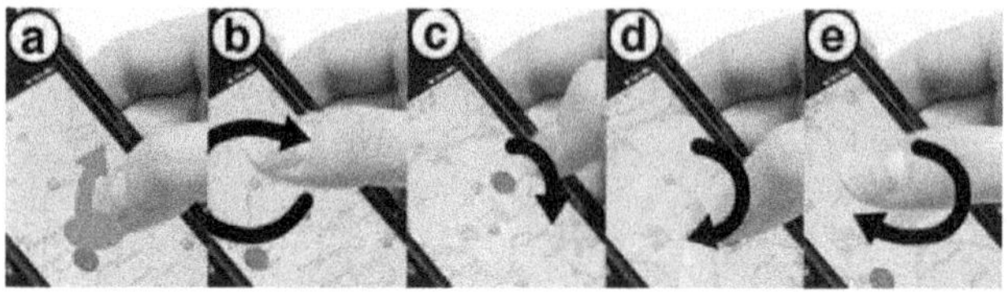

Figure 11. In our map app, a tap (a) followed by a 'circle' high above the screen (b) allows one to continuously zoom at the map by cycling the finger (c,d,e).

technique leverages the concept of a repeated gesture; even if the finger accidentally draws a circle in-air after touch, it will at worst turn on the zooming mode but not cause any actual zooming.

Hovering After Touch to Change Scroll Speed

On a touch screen, clutching is inevitable as touch is constrained by the screen's physical surface. For example, scrolling through a long page requires repetitive finger flicking [20, 21]. Our reader application enables fine control of page scrolling for long lists. When a user triggers inertial scrolling via a flick (a), he can use the hover height of the finger to control the scrolling speed – higher finger position maps to faster scrolling (Figure 12b-d). This is similar to Zliding and Zoofing techniques [20, 21], but uses Z-distance instead of pressure. Touching the screen stops scrolling. Two height thresholds are used to differentiate this 'hover scroll' from a normal scrolling, which is unaffected.

DISCUSSION

The example techniques we have presented above are only a small subset of the possible interactions, yet we believe demonstrate the expressiveness and promise of Air+Touch. Importantly, Air+Touch actions can work in concert with conventional touch gestures, such as one finger pan and click, pinch to zoom, and various chorded swipes. As highlighted by our observational study and implemented in our example applications, Air+Touch techniques can weave in-air gestures before, between, and after touch events. Through extensive use and piloting, it become apparent that these categorization have different strengths and can support a variety of interactive tasks:

- Both *air before* and *after touch* enable quick mode switching connected to a touch down/up (e.g., Figure 6). They can also specify an action specific to a set of touch points (e.g., Figure 10);
- *Air after touch* further allows a user to continue a touch-initiated operation with in-air, continuous motions (e.g., Figure 11);
- *Air between touches* is good for tasks that by nature require specifying multiple screen positions. An air-gesture command can be embedded in between the touch events, saving the overhead of tool or mode switching (e.g., Figure 9).

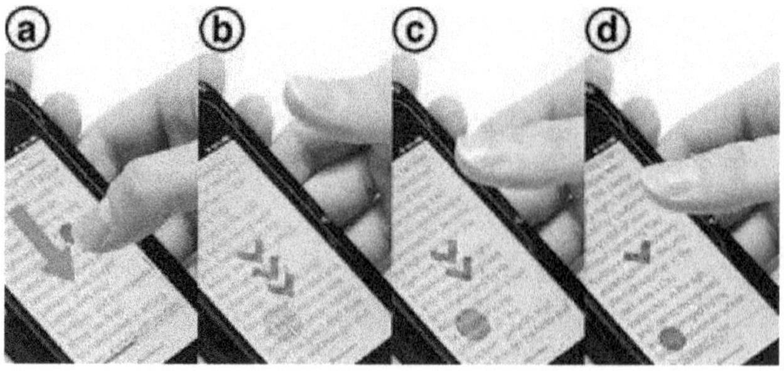

Figure 12. In our reader app, one can use the finger's hover height to control the auto-scrolling speed.

Chunking Air and Touch into Fluid Interactions

Table 1 provides a comparison of how Air+Touch techniques approach the design for six interactive tasks in comparison with existing touch-only interaction. While the elements of these tasks remain the same (e.g., text selection consists of specifying the selection mode and the region to select), a touch-only design presents them as discrete steps. Air+Touch, however, chunks these elements into fluid interactions [4]. For expert users, Air+Touch could become integrated into their interactions as *a single flow* of movement, whereas touch-only actions are inherently sequential.

Choosing Air Gestures based on Accompanying Touch

Our initial concept to trigger a context menu (Figure 6e) was by drawing a 'pigtail' and tapping on an target (similar to [8]'s design). However, we found it difficult to perform, because as the finger drew the 'pigtail', it strayed from its original target, requiring the user to retarget at the end of the gesture. In contrast, a full 'circle' gesture was easier, as the finger could complete a full loop, naturally returning to its starting point, from which the user could simply tap down onto the target. Conversely, when designing after-

	Touch Only	Air + Touch
Open context menu	**Tap** to open image → **tap** menu button (or **tap** and hold)	Circle in air → **tap** on image
Zoom on map	**Pan** to center zoom area → **tap** buttons to zoom in or out	**Tap** on zoom center → cycle finger in air to zoom
Marquee select	**Tap** to bring up toolbar → **tap** 'marquee selection' → **tap** and drag to specify selection	**Tap** start point → draw 'L' in air → **tap** end point
Text selection	**Tap** to specify cursor location → **tap** and hold → **tap** and drag to specify selection	**Tap** starting point → finger high jump → **tap** end point
Free form selection	**Tap** to bring up toolbar → **tap** 'free-form selection' button → **tap** and drag to specify selection	**Tap** and drag to specify selection region → draw pig tail in air
Scrolling	**Tap** and scroll (repeat as needed)	**Tap** to scroll → hover continues to scroll

Table 1. Air+Touch techniques for six interactive tasks (right) in comparison with existing touch-only approach (left). Air+Touch is able chunk steps of interaction into fluid movement of the finger on and above the device's screen.

touch in-air gestures, we found that 'pigtails' became easy to perform, as there was no ending targeting constraint. This suggests that the choice of in-air gesture should consider whether it affects the touch that precedes or follows it.

Segmenting Air Gestures Before and After Touch

For air before and after touch, touches only segment air's start or end points, leaving the developer to decide when to start/stop processing the finger's remaining movement. This translates to the implementation level question of setting the size of the buffer that keeps a history of the finger's 3D positions. In prototyping, we visualized the finger's trajectory as a projection onto the screen. We chose buffer sizes that neither gave an incomplete gesture (too few points), nor overshot it (too many points). An alternate approach would be to analyze different buffer sizes, choosing gestures that yield highest recognition confidences.

CONCLUSION

The prevalence of hover technologies at CES 2014 and the continued inclusion of hover in flagship devices (such as the soon-to-be-released Galaxy S5) suggests in-air technologies will continue to mature and could play an increased role in touch devices. Today, a scant few 'air' gestures are supported and are fundamentally compartmentalized from touch interactions. Our work helps point the way to more powerful interactions, by synergistically interweaving touch and air modalities, where air augments touch, adding expressivity, and touch segments in-air gestures to resolve segmentation ambiguity. With good design, these actions can blend into single, fluid movements, offering a level of expressivity rarely achieved by each modality in isolation. Nonetheless, there is much future work to consider, including expanding the gesture vocabulary, capturing not just 3DOF position, but also 3DOF rotation of the fingers, as well as utilizing several fingers at once.

REFERENCES

1. Banerjee, A., Burstyn, J., Girouard, A., and Vertegaal, R. Pointable: an in-air pointing technique to manipulate out-of-reach targets on tabletops. In *Proc. ITS '11*, 11-20.
2. Baudisch, P. and Chu, G. Back-of-device interaction allows creating very small touch devices. In *Proc. CHI '09*, 1923-1932
3. Butler, A., Izadi, S., and Hodges, S. SideSight: multi-"touch" interaction around small devices. In *Proc. UIST* '08, 201-204.
4. Buxton W. Chunking and phrasing and the design of human-computer dialogues. In *Human-Computer Interaction*. Morgan Kaufmann, San Francisco, CA, USA 494-499.
5. Grossman, T., Hinckley, K., Baudisch, P., Agrawala, M., and Balakrishnan, R. Hover widgets: using the tracking state to extend the capabilities of pen-operated devices. In *Proc. CHI '06*, 861-870.
6. Harrison, C. and Hudson, S.E. Abracadabra: wireless, high-precision, and unpowered finger input for very small mobile devices. In *Proc. UIST '09*, 121-124.
7. Hilliges, O., Izadi, S., Wilson, A.D., Hodges, S., Garcia-Mendoza, A. and Butz, A. Interactions in the air: adding further depth to interactive tabletops. In *Proc. UIST '09*, 139-148.
8. Hinckley, K., Baudisch, P., Ramos, G. and Guimbretiere, F. Design and analysis of delimiters for selection-action pen gesture phrases in Scriboli. In *Proc. CHI '05*, 451-460.
9. Hinckley, K., Chen, X. and Benko, H. Motion and context sensing techniques for pen Computing. In *Proc. GI* '13.
10. Hinckley, K. and Song, H. Sensor synaesthesia: touch in motion, and motion in touch. In *Proc. CHI '11*, 801-810.
11. Hinckley, K., Yatani, K., Pahud, M, Coddington, N., Rodenhouse, J., Wilson, A., Benko, H. and Buxton, B. Pen + touch = new tools. In *Proc. UIST '10*, 27-36.
12. Hudson, S.E., Harrison, C., Harrison, B.L., and LaMarca, A. Whack gestures: inexact and inattentive interaction with mobile devices. In *Proc. TEI '10*, 109-113.
13. Jones, B., Sodhi, R., Forsyth, D., Bailey, B., and Maciocci, G. Around device interaction for multiscale navigation. In *Proc. MobileHCI '12*, 83-92.
14. Ketabdar, H., Yüksel, K.A., and Roshandel, M. MagiTact: Interaction with Mobile Devices Based on Compass (Magnetic) Sensor. In *Proc. IUI '10*, 413-414.
15. Kratz, S., Rohs, M., Guse, D., Müller, J., Bailly, G. and Nischt, M. PalmSpace: continuous around-device gestures vs. multitouch for 3D rotation tasks on mobile devices. In *Proc. AVI '12*, 181-188.
16. Kratz, S. and Rohs, M. HoverFlow: expanding the design space of around-device interaction. In *Proc. MobileHCI '09*, 1-8.
17. Marquardt, N., Jota, R., Greenberg, S. and Jorge, J.A. The continuous interaction space. In *Proc. INTERACT '11*, 461–476.
18. Niikura, T., Hirobe, Y., Cassinelli, A., Watanabe, Y., Komuro, T. and Ishikawa, M. In-air typing interface for mobile devices with vibration feedback. In *Proc. SIGGRAPH* '10, 1–1.
19. PMD Technologies. Camboard Nano camera. http://pmdtec.com/products_services/reference_design.php
20. Quinn, P. and Cockburn, A. Zoofing!: faster list selections with pressure-zoom-flick-scrolling. In *Proc. OZCHI '09*. 185-192.
21. Ramos, G. and Balakrishnan, R. Zliding: fluid zooming and sliding for high precision parameter manipulation. In *Proc. UIST '05*. 143-152.
22. Samsung. Galaxy S4. http://www.samsung.com/galaxys4
23. Synaptics. 3D Touch. http://blog.synaptics.com/?p=401
24. Wigdor, D., Forlines, C., Baudisch, P., Barnwell, J. and Shen, C. Lucid touch: a see-through mobile device. In Proc. UIST '07, 269-278.
25. Wigdor, D., Leigh, D., Forlines, C., Shipman, S., Barnwell, J., Balakrishnan, R. and Shen, C. Under the table interaction. In *Proc. UIST '06*, 259-268.
26. Wobbrock, J.O., Wilson, A.D. and Li, Y. Gestures without libraries, toolkits or training. In *Proc. UIST '07*, 159-168.

SideSwipe: Detecting In-air Gestures Around Mobile Devices Using Actual GSM Signals

Chen Zhao[1], Ke-Yu Chen[1], Md Tanvir Islam Aumi[2], Shwetak Patel[1,2], Matthew S. Reynolds[1,2]

[1]Electrical Engineering, [2]Computer Science & Engineering, UbiComp Lab, DUB Group
University of Washington
Seattle, WA 98195 USA
{chzhao, kychen, tanvir, shwetak}@uw.edu, matt.reynolds@ee.washington.edu

ABSTRACT

Current smartphone inputs are limited to physical buttons, touchscreens, cameras or built-in sensors. These approaches either require a dedicated surface or line-of-sight for interaction. We introduce SideSwipe, a novel system that enables in-air gestures both above and around a mobile device. Our system leverages the *actual (unmodified)* GSM signal to detect hand gestures around the device. We developed an algorithm to convert the bursty reflected GSM pulses to a continuous signal that can be used for gesture recognition. Specifically, when a user waves their hand near the phone, the hand movement disturbs the signal propagation between the phone's transmitter and added receiving antennas. Our system captures this variation and uses it for gesture recognition. To evaluate our system, we conduct a study with 10 participants and present robust gesture recognition with an average accuracy of 87.2% across 14 hand gestures.

ACM Classification: H.5.2 [Information interfaces and presentation]: User Interfaces. - Graphical user interfaces.

Keywords: GSM, antenna, in-air hand gesture

INTRODUCTION AND MOTIVATION

Despite an exponential increase in the computation and storage capabilities of mobile devices, the space available for touch interaction will continue to be limited by what users are willing to carry. Although capacitive touch displays have effectively made the entire front face of most mobile devices interactive, occlusion remains an inherent problem. Researchers have proposed many ways to extend interaction on small mobile devices. This includes leveraging the backs of devices [20] or the space directly in front and behind the device using cameras and microphones [8,19]. Other works utilized the space directly above the screen using Electric-field sensing like GestIC[4], the surface on which a device may reside [9], and even the human body [10].

Figure 1. The SideSwipe system. Our system leverages the unmodified GSM signal to enable in-air hand gestures both above and on the side of the phone.

The spaces that currently remain "blind" from existing sensors are the areas surrounding the mobile device (*i.e.,* the sides, top, and bottom). These areas are out of the view of the front and back facing cameras and microphones. In addition, placing proximity sensors on the sides of a mobile device [2] would largely be occluded when a user holds it. An alternative method explored in the past uses magnetic-field sensing for inputs [3,11,17]. However, these techniques require the user's finger to be instrumented with a permanent magnet. Other researchers have explored RF signals radiated from the ambient environment to detect 1D hand gestures using a low-power analog receiver [12]. This work has been limited to simple 1D gestures and requires either a continuous signal source, such as an RFID emitter or a constant envelope ambient signal, like that from a digital TV tower. Our approach is similar to [12]; however, we leverage the GSM signal that already exists on a mobile phone and is modulated as a result of human motion. Instead of filtering these modulations out, we show that they can be used for enhancing user experience.

In this paper, we introduce SideSwipe, a new system that enables in-air gestures around a mobile device using the existing GSM signal (Figure 1). Specifically, when the hand moves around the phone, the reflected GSM signal is amplitude-modulated as a result of induced multipath propagation. Our system captures such variations from the re-

UIST '14, October 05 - 08 2014, Honolulu, HI, USA
Copyright 2014 ACM 978-1-4503-3069-5/14/10...$15.00.
http://dx.doi.org/10.1145/2642918.2647380

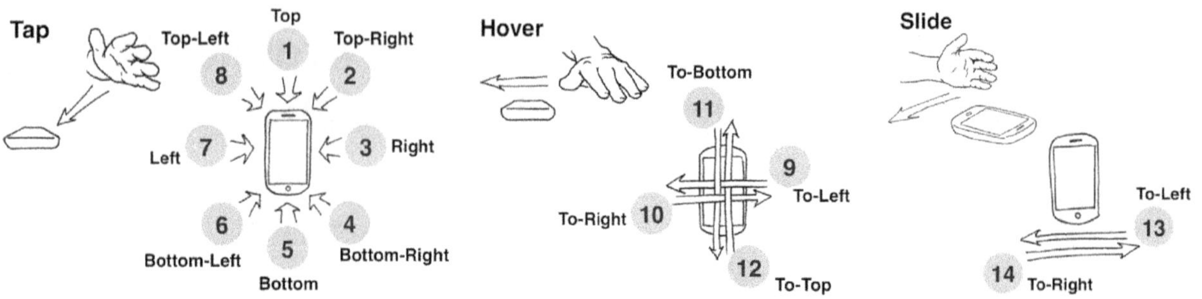

Figure 2. The gestures performed in the user study, including eight tapping gestures (**left**), four hover gestures (**middle**) and two sliding gestures (**right**). The sliding gestures (13 and 14) were performed at the bottom of the phone.

flected GSM pulses and uses them to extract hand gestures. That is, unlike prior work, we do not require a custom transmitter or an external signal source. Our approach requires little modification to the mobile device and could easily be adopted by mobile phone manufacturers. We demonstrate the robust recognition of 14 gestures: tapping at corners, tapping on the four sides of the phone, swipes over the face, and swipes at the bottom of the phone (Figure 2).

Specifically, our contributions include:

1. A technique using the *unmodified* GSM signal, which is bursty in nature, for in-air gesture sensing.
2. A simple antenna array that captures amplitude-modulated GSM signals to enable hand gesture detection around the phone.
3. A set of interaction techniques that leverage this capability.

RELATED WORK

Because of the increasing popularity of Natural User Interfaces (NUI), gesture recognition has become a very promising approach to enhance human-computer interaction. Kim *et al.* instrumented IR cameras on the wrist to capture finger gestures [13]. Commercial products, such as Kinect [18] and Leap Motion[1], use computer vision to detect in-air gestures for laptops and desktops. For mobile devices, PointGrab[2] and CrunchFish[3] are also popular commercial solutions using computer-vision based technologies for gesture recognition. Recently, the Samsung Galaxy S4 introduced in-air gestures using a front-facing IR camera. While these systems are able to detect hand or finger gestures, they require direct line-of-sight (LoS) between the device and may be brittle due to varying lighting conditions. SideSwipe, on the other hand, does not require LoS and works in various scenarios, even when the phone is in the pocket or when the gesture occurs outside camera's field-of-view.

Apart from these vision-based techniques, there are other interesting approaches that use electric field (E-fields), Doppler effect, and inertial sensing. GestIC[4] is a promising E-field based sensing technique, but it requires a comparatively larger surface area to act as an antenna (~10cm^2) and restricts hand gestures to the front and back surfaces. SoundWave [8] is an ultrasonic-based Doppler shift detection technique, but it only enables 1D gestures. Finally, there are some on-body sensing solutions using inertial sensing, but they require instrumenting the human body [6,7]. Our system addresses all these limitations, as it does not require any instrumentation on the human body.

Over the past decades, wireless signals have proven to be a promising approach in detecting a moving object [1,4]. Researchers have also used various wireless signals for localization [5,15,21]. Recently, researchers have started using wireless signals to recognize gestures. Pu *et al.* extract gestures from wireless signals like Wi-Fi at a whole-home range [16]. While these solutions are promising, they require a dedicated, continuous signal source, a fundamental limitation that inhibits their ubiquity in practical scenarios. In contrast, our system utilizes the unmodified GSM signal inherently radiated from mobile devices for gesture recognition and classification.

BACKGROUND AND THEORY OF OPERATION

The SideSwipe system leverages GSM signals to detect hand gestures. GSM networks operate in several carrier frequency bands (e.g., AT&T uses 850MHz/1900MHz, while T-Mobile uses 1900MHz). GSM is a frequency-modulated signal that uses two different frequency components to transmit logical 1's and 0's, a technique called Gaussian Filtered Minimum Shift Keying (GMSK). Comparing to amplitude-shift keying and on-off keying signals, GMSK signal maintains a nearly constant envelope. As a minimum shift modulation, GMSK encodes each bit as a half sinusoid, which reduces the power fluctuation caused by non-linear distortion. The envelope of the GMSK signal is independent of the transmitted data; that is, we can measure the magnitude of the fading propagation channel without knowing the content or encryption status of transmitted data.

[1] https://www.leapmotion.com/

[2] http://www.pointgrab.com/

[3] http://crunchfish.com/

[4] http://www.microchip.com/pagehandler/en_us/technology/gestic

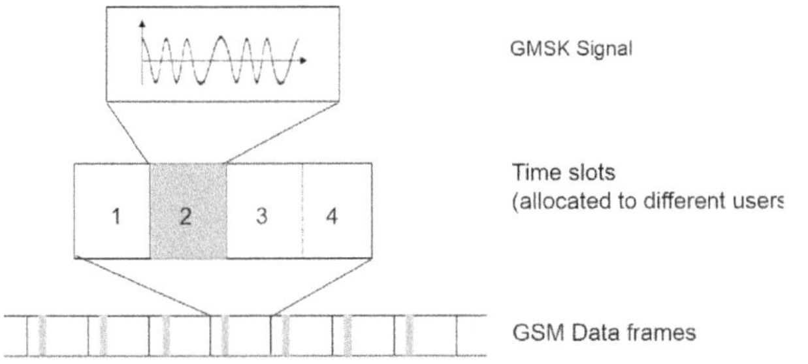

Figure 3. Time Division Multiple Access (TDMA) in the GSM system. The bandwidth is divided into frames for multiplexing. The GSM signal appears as a sequence of random bursts.

In order to allow multiple users to share the same frequency channel, GSM uses Time Division Multiple Access (TDMA), which divides the bandwidth into different slots (Figure 3). In turn, the phone's transmitted GSM signal is a sequence of bursts in certain time slots. Without knowing the modulation details, the distribution of slots appears as the outcome of a random process. In addition, the cellphone signal is normally mixed with other communication signals (e.g. WiFi, Bluetooth and even LTE). To leverage these random signal bursts for gesture recognition, our system filters out unnecessary signals and leverages the GSM pulses to sample the continuous motion of the user's hand.

Detecting Hand Gestures

When the user is making a call, the phone transmits GSM pulses to communicate with the cellular station. Around the mobile phone, there are a number of propagation paths. Such paths start from the transmitting antenna of the mobile phone and end up at each of our receiving loop antennas. When the user moves their hand around the mobile phone, their skin, muscle, and bones affect the character of the propagation path by absorbing or reflecting part of the signal. The absorption reduces the signal intensity, while the reflection generates Doppler shift. As a combination of the signals from all propagation paths, the envelope of the receiving signal will be changed by the absorption and Doppler shift. The outcome of these effects is an amplitude-modulated envelope. Our system captures this envelope modulation and uses it for gesture recognition. We will detail our algorithm in the following section.

The GSM pulses non-uniformly sample the propagation channels at staccato time intervals. Since the average frequency of the pulse is nearly 80 Hz, which is more than twice the rate of hand gestures (on the order of 10 Hz), we can reconstruct the propagation channel variation by the received GSM pulses [14].

IMPLEMENTATION DETAILS AND ALGORITHM

In this section, we describe the SideSwipe system in detail, including the hardware design and gesture detection algorithm.

Hardware Design

To build a system for detecting hand gestures, we designed a circuit board with four antennas (Figure 4). These four antennas (i.e., top, down, left, and right) allow the system to capture the signal fluctuations caused by hand movements from all directions around the phone. Each of these 4 receiving channels has a loop antenna and a RF power detector (Analog Devices AD8361). We designed four directional loop antennas pointing to distinct directions. The receiving antenna array is attached to the back of the phone and close to the transmitting antenna. The radius of the loop antennas is 1 cm and its circumference is close to a quarter of the GSM wavelength. It should be noted that we chose to design a custom antenna array to allow for hand gestures from all directions around the devices; however, the technique presented here applies to existing antenna systems in current mobile devices as well, with the limitation that they will allow only 1-D gesture recognition.

In our prototype, we put four antennas on the four edges of the PCB board and separately connect them to RF power detectors located at the center of the PCB. Since every antenna has a unique radiation pattern, we are able to get different signal intensity fluctuations from distinct antennas when the user is performing gestures. In addition, we placed a ground plane on the back of the PCB to enhance the difference in radiation patterns of the antennas.

Antenna Simulation

We use CST Microwave Studio to simulate our antennas and PCB board as well as calculate the radiation patterns (Figure 5). The simulation is done at 850MHz (*i.e.,* the same frequency in AT&T's GSM network). These figures show distinct radiation patterns for each of the four antennas. Because the sensitivity range of each antenna is determined by the direction and gain of the main lobe, each antenna is able to receive the signal through a unique propagation path. In our simulation, we only consider parameters from the PCB board such as antenna size and distance. Although modeling an accurate radiation pattern requires thorough consideration of all environmental factors, including

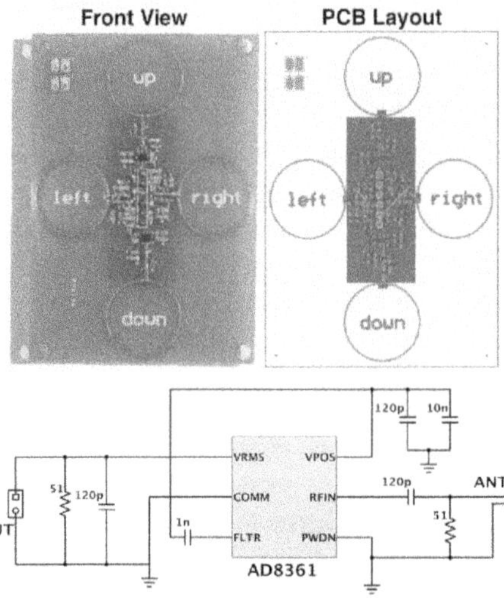

Figure 4. The PCB design of SideSwipe, including the front view of circuitry **(left)**, the layout **(right)** and the schematic view of the up antenna **(bottom)**.

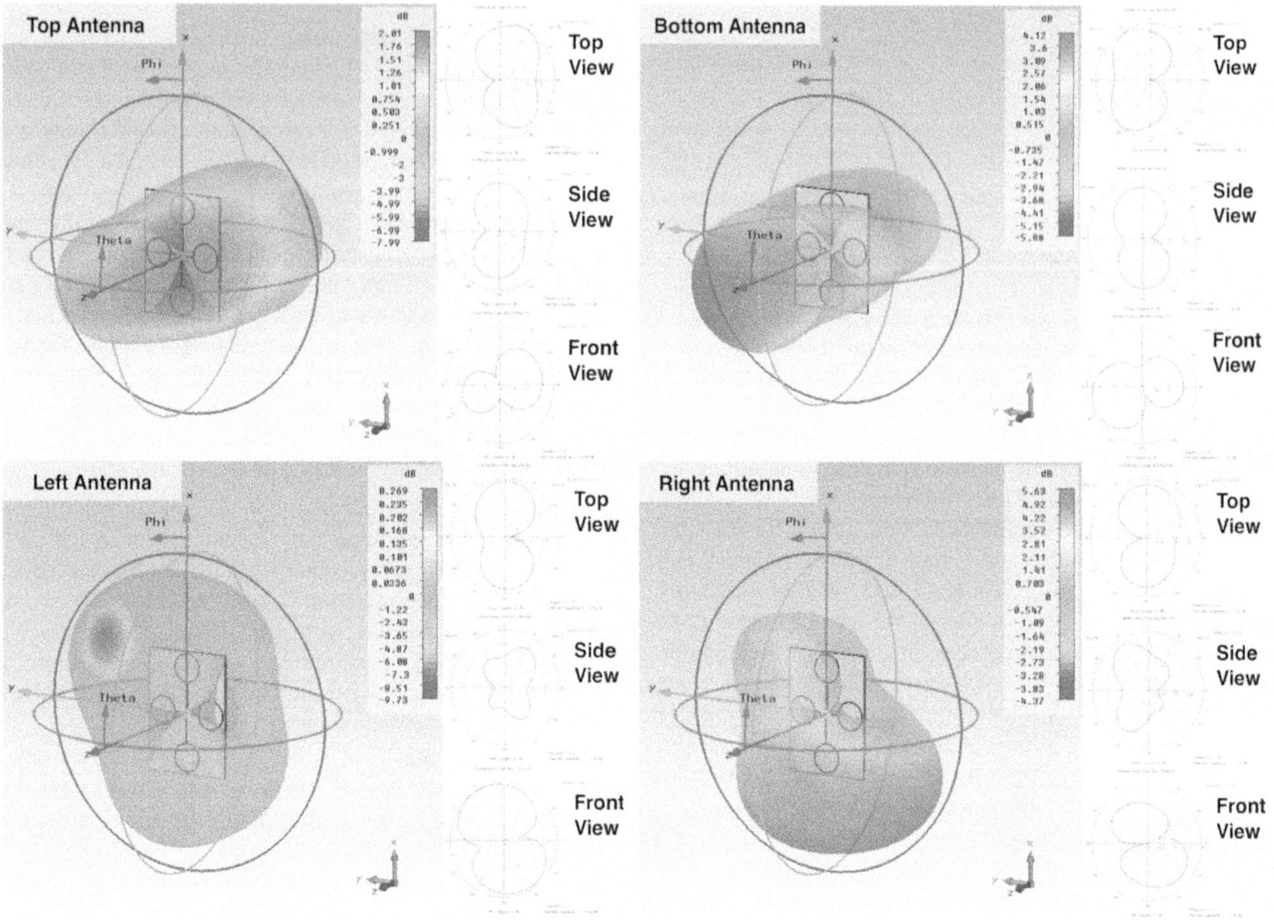

Figure 5. Simulation results for the top, bottom, left and right antenna. Each antenna has a distinct sensitive range and is able to perceive signals through their respective propagation path. The received signals from the four antennas yield unique signal patterns that can be used for gesture detection and classification.

the human body, clothes, and cellphone, the simulation provides guidance for the antenna design. Given this simulation, we are able to understand the sensitivity of sensing a gesture from all directions around the board and the best instrumentation of this board to a mobile device. That is, it describes the *interaction space* and provides guidance in designing a new gesture.

Gesture Recognition Algorithm

SideSwipe leverages unmodified GSM bursts that inherently exist when the user is using GSM communication (*e.g.*, making a call). When one performs a hand gesture, the antennas pick up the fluctuation in their respective propagation paths. By combining the signals from four antennas, we are able to identify a unique pattern for different gestures. In our prototype, we used a sliding window of 2.5 seconds to capture a hand gesture. Figure 6 shows the block diagram of our gesture recognition algorithm, including four major steps: (1) Bursts to Continuous Wave interpolation, (2) Smoothing and Segmentation, (3) Feature Extraction and (4) Gesture Recognition.

Bursts to Continuous Wave interpolation

As described earlier, the unmodified GSM signal appears as random bursts in communication. We need to first convert these bursts to a continuous signal before they can be used to extract any features for gesture recognition. To do this, we developed an algorithm to detect GSM pulses. Intuitively, we identify the GSM pulses by suppressing undesired wireless signals (*e.g.*, WiFi or Bluetooth) and interpolating these pulses to a continuous wave. Based on our observation, the duration length of each GSM pulse is approximately 0.67 ms (*i.e.*, 12 samples at our system's sampling rate of 18 KHz) and WiFi and Bluetooth signal both have relatively shorter pulse widths (*i.e.*, less than 8 samples). Therefore, we apply a threshold on the pulse width at 8 samples to filter these undesired signals. Furthermore, we use a fixed threshold (80 mV for our hardware design) to determine the rising and falling edges of the pulses.

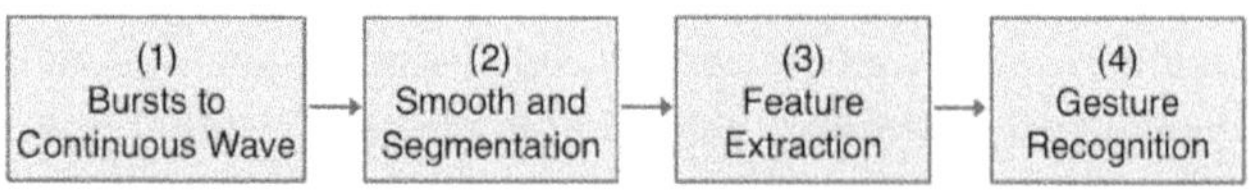

Figure 6. The gesture recognition algorithm. The system converts the actual GSM bursts to a continuous wave, which can be used for gesture recognition.

Output voltage of receiving channels (V)				V_{det} (V)
Top	Down	Left	Right	
3.22	3.22	3.22	3.22	**1.49**
3.22	3.22	3.22	3.22	**1.26**
3.25	3.22	3.22	3.22	**0.99**
2.11	3.22	3.22	3.22	**0.78**
1.56	3.22	2.81	3.22	**0.60**
1.57	3.22	2.80	3.22	**0.49**
1.32	2.66	2.24	2.91	**0.38**
0.99	2.09	1.75	2.23	**0.31**
0.58	1.47	0.95	1.74	**0.25**
0.47	1.18	0.77	1.41	**0.21**
0.37	0.94	0.62	1.12	**0.18**
0.30	0.75	0.49	0.89	**0.15**
0.32	0.64	0.51	0.69	**0.13**
0.24	0.49	0.39	0.52	**0.12**
0.20	0.41	0.32	0.44	**0.11**
0.16	0.35	0.25	0.36	**0.10**

Table 1. The profile of the five channels on an NI DAQ (see Fig 10). V_{det} is the voltage referring to the phone's transmitting power. By normalizing the receiving signals, our system eliminates the undesired fluctuation due to varying transmitting power.

The GSM system usually adjusts its transmitting power to maintain a stable gain in a fluctuating environment and in turn affects the receiving power density perceived by our antenna array (Figure 7). Such fluctuation is undesirable in gesture recognition, as two signal patterns of the same gestures may appear completely different. To adapt to this fluctuation, we normalize the received data corresponding to the transmitting power. For this, we recorded 20 minutes of data without any gestures being performed and saved the transmitting power and receiving gain in a table (Table 1). When receiving a GSM pulse, the system measures the transmit power from the phone and uses it to find the corresponding receiver gain in Table 1. Next, we divide the mean voltage of the GSM pulse with this gain. This approach eliminates possible power variations caused by fluctuating transmitting power. It is noted that there are only 16 different levels of transmitting power, so maintaining such a table in the memory will be low-cost. Although we built this signal profile manually, this calibration can be easily done using an automatic scanning process.

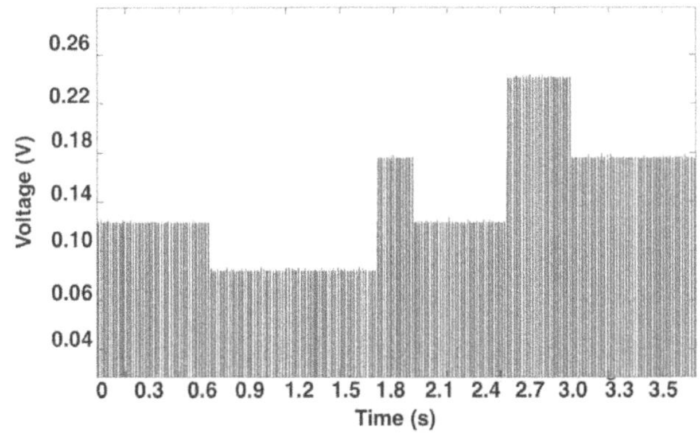

Figure 7. The fluctuation of the transmitting power.

After a GSM pulse is recognized, we calculate the mean of the middle six points and use the mean to represent the received magnitude in the respective antenna. Finally, we interpolate this discrete sequence to construct the continuous wave. Figure 8 shows our approximated continuous signal using actual GSM pulses.

Smoothing and Segmentation

We next identify and segment the hand gesture from this continuous wave. The reconstructed wave is noisy and difficult to be used for gesture detection and therefore, we apply signal processing techniques to extract the gesture segment. Figure 9 demonstrates the process of gesture detection. For each of the four antennas' data, we first apply a Savitzky-Golay (SG) filter with a window size of 301 to smooth the curve (red line, Figure 9 (1)). The SG filter is able to de-noise the signal while maintaining the shape of its original curve. Next, we take the 1st derivative of the smoothed curve to capture the significant signal variations caused by a hand gesture.

Since a gesture may cause signal changes in any of the four receiving antennas, we sum up the absolute value of the derivative curves from all of the channels (Figure 9 (2)). In turn, we are able to find an observable peak, which represents a possible hand gesture. Finally, we take another 1st derivative on the cumulative-derivative curve and use a global threshold to identify a hand gesture (Figure 9 (3)). The threshold was selected to be the equal error rate using all of the data from our user study. The green circles in Figure 9 denote the starting and end point of a hand gesture segment.

Feature Extraction

After recognizing a hand gesture, we extract features from gesture segmentations for classification. The system calculates the midpoint of the start and end of a gesture segment and truncates a window of 4500 data points (*i.e.*, 2.5 sec) centered at the midpoint. We use these data points as the feature set, which describes the shape of the receiving signal. These data points are further demeaned to decrease possible environmental influences, such as putting the

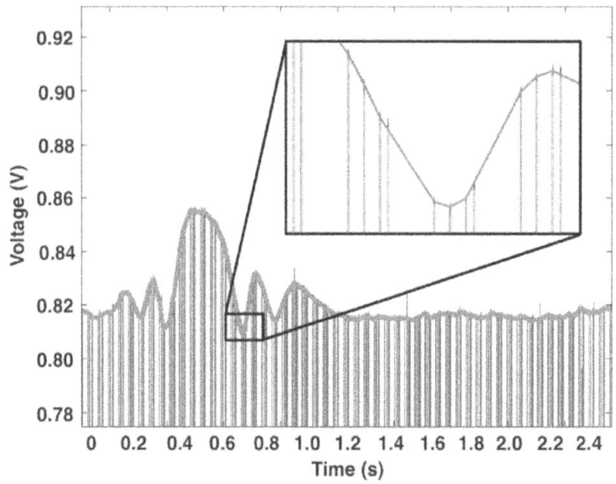

Figure 8. Converting actual GSM bursts (blue stems) to a continuous wave (red curve).

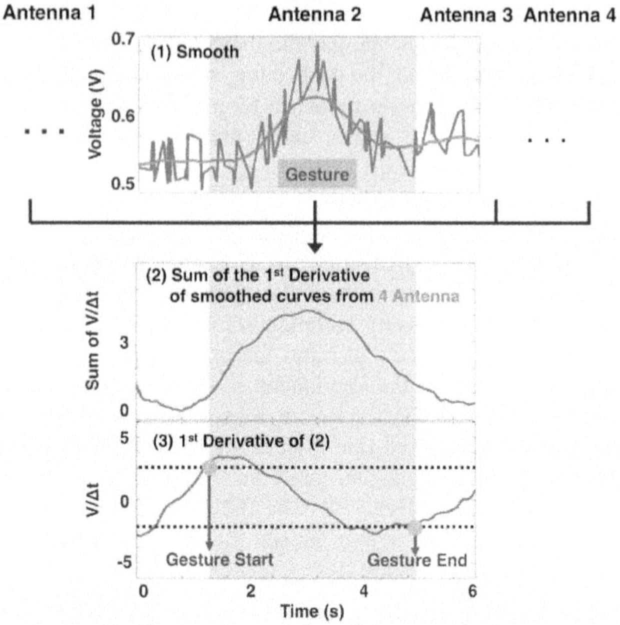

Figure 9. Gesture detection algorithm. In step (2), we sum up the absolute value of 1st derivative of the smoothed curve (**red** line in (1)) from four antennas. This captures significant energy variation in any of our four antennas. In (3), we used a global threshold to identify the start and end of a gesture (**green circles**).

phone in the pocket or on different surfaces. Combining the data points from the four antennas, we generate a feature vector with 18,000 elements. This feature vector represents a unique pattern for different gestures. We further reduce the feature space by down-sampling the feature vector to 80 elements (*i.e.*, 20 elements per channel). In this study, we evaluate 14 hand gestures (Figure 2) performed at a natural speed. These gestures have no high frequency components, and therefore, it is sufficient to describe the signal pattern using only the time domain data.

Gesture Recognition

We next feed the data set into Weka for gesture classification. In Weka, we perform 14-fold cross validation using a Support Vector Machine with PUK kernel. The PUK kernel has the flexibility to vary among Gaussian, Lorentzian, and other shapes, and therefore can be used as a universal kernel in our case. Since the signal pattern of a gesture may vary from person to person (*e.g.*, waving the hand at different speeds), this PUK kernel is able to better adapt to signals that have various shapes.

EVALUATIONS

To evaluate the performance of our system, we setup an experiment in a lab-controlled environment and conducted a 10-user study (3 females). The data collected from all participants are used to empirically decide a global threshold in our gesture recognition algorithm. The analysis shows the optimal threshold of 2.5 V, yielding a perfect event detection rate.

Experimental Setup

Figure 10 shows the experimental setup for data collection. The PCB antenna array was attached on the back of the mobile phone (Samsung Nexus S). To extract the magnitude of transmitting power, we connect a wire to the output pin of the power detector on the TX Front-End module of the Nexus S ("V_{det}" in Figure 10). It is noted that the power information could also be retrieved by tweaking the device driver without modifying any hardware when the driver's source code is accessible. To record the GSM bursts, we utilized a National Instruments USB 6259 ("NI DAQ" in Figure 10) data acquisition unit. The unit takes 16-bit voltage samples at 18 KS/s and streams the 5-channel data to the computer through a USB cable. To get ground truth, we installed proximity sensors on four sides of the phone.

Gesture sets

Figure 2 shows 14 gestures performed in this study, within three categories: **Tap**: top tap (TT), top-right tap (TRT), right tap (RT), bottom-right tap (BRT), bottom tap (BT), bottom-left tap (BLT), left tap (LT) and top-left tap (TLT); **Hover**: hover-to-left (H2L), hover-to-right (H2R), hover-to-bottom (H2B) and hover-to-top (H2T); **Slide**: slide-to-left (S2L) and slide-to-right (S2R). This gesture set covers both gestures being performed above and around the mobile phone. We regard these gestures as the basic building blocks that can be easily combined to form a more complicated vocabulary.

User Study Design

In the beginning of the study, we introduce the gestures to our participants and inform the appropriate speed in performing each gesture. All participants can practice the gestures for three to five times. Although we controlled the gesture speed to avoid unnecessary false detections, participants were still allowed to perform gestures at arbitrarily fast or slow speeds. During data collection, they were required to perform each gesture 13 to 15 times and in total, 1746 gestures were collected. All gestures were performed at a distance within 30cm.

Results

Using a global threshold and the hand gesture detection algorithm described earlier, we obtained 100% detection rate across all of our user data. Using the same global threshold, we only detect 3 false positives over 10 minutes

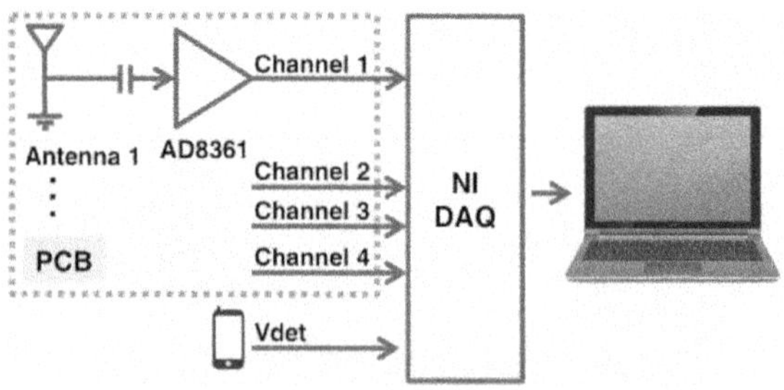

Figure 10. Partial schematic of the PCB board and experimental setup for data collection. National Instruments USB 6259 (NI DAQ) records the GSM bursts and streams the data to a laptop.

	1	2	3	4	5	6	7	8	9	10	11	12	13	14
Top Tap - 1	66.9	23.0	0.7	0.0	0.0	0.0	0.7	8.6	0.0	0.0	0.0	0.0	0.0	0.0
Top-Right Tap - 2	3.4	81.2	0.9	0.0	0.0	0.0	0.0	13.7	0.0	0.0	0.0	0.0	0.0	0.9
Right Tap - 3	0.8	1.5	86.2	9.2	0.0	0.8	0.8	0.8	0.0	0.0	0.0	0.0	0.0	0.0
Bottom-Right Tap - 4	0.0	0.0	8.0	90.6	0.7	0.0	0.0	0.0	0.0	0.0	0.0	0.0	0.0	0.7
Bottom Tap - 5	2.1	0.0	0.0	4.2	90.9	0.0	0.7	1.4	0.0	0.0	0.0	0.0	0.7	0.0
Bottom-Left Tap - 6	5.8	0.7	0.0	0.0	0.0	87.1	0.0	2.9	1.4	1.4	0.7	0.0	0.0	0.0
Left Tap - 7	0.7	0.0	0.0	0.0	0.0	1.5	90.3	6.7	0.0	0.0	0.0	0.0	0.0	0.7
Top-Left Tap - 8	2.8	1.8	0.0	0.0	0.0	0.9	0.0	94.5	0.0	0.0	0.0	0.0	0.0	0.0
Hover-to-Left - 9	2.2	0.0	0.0	0.0	0.0	2.2	0.0	0.0	91.4	2.9	0.7	0.7	0.0	0.0
Hover-to-Right - 10	0.0	0.0	0.0	1.7	0.0	0.0	0.0	0.0	5.8	88.4	0.0	4.1	0.0	0.0
Hover-to-Bottom - 11	0.0	0.0	0.0	0.7	1.4	0.0	2.1	0.0	2.9	0.7	86.4	5.7	0.0	0.0
Hover-to-Top - 12	0.0	0.0	0.0	0.0	0.0	0.0	0.0	0.0	1.7	0.0	3.5	94.8	0.0	0.0
Slide-to-Left - 13	0.0	0.0	0.0	0.8	0.0	0.8	0.0	0.8	0.0	0.0	0.0	3.9	88.4	5.4
Slide-to-Right - 14	0.8	0.0	0.0	0.0	0.0	0.8	0.0	0.8	1.7	0.0	0.0	2.5	7.6	85.7

Figure 11. Confusion matrix for 14 gestures.

of data where no gestures were performed. It shows that our algorithm is able to reliably detect all hand gestures while maintaining low false alarms.

For gesture classification, we trained a 14-class (*i.e.*, representing the 14 hand gestures) SVM classifier and tested the model by 14-fold cross validation using all user data, as shown in Figure 11. We obtained an average accuracy of 87.2% (chance=7.14%). The results show that our algorithm is able to robustly differentiate in-air hand gestures using the actual GSM signal. In addition, although we randomly chose the folding number of 14, we did not see significant difference in accuracy when using other folding numbers (86.77% for 10-fold and 85.69% for 5-fold).

From Figure 11, it can be seen that there is confusion between the top-right tapping (TRT), top tapping (TT) and top-left tapping (TLT). These gestures are relatively further from the transmitting antenna and therefore have weaker signals. Also, our simulation results (see Figure 5) show that the top-right corner of PCB has a null between lobes, and therefore there is a bigger confusion between top-right (TR) and top tapping (TT). Furthermore, the confusion between bottom-right tapping (BRT) and right tapping (RT) resulted from the fact that participants tend to use their right hand to perform BR tapping and R tapping. In such case, the whole arm causes much stronger fluctuations than that caused by the palm. Such user behaviors resulted in similar signal patters of these two gestures and cause confusion. As shown earlier, we are able to classify all 14 gestures with 87.2% accuracy; however, using a reduced gesture set of 13 gestures (i.e., removing top tap) yields 90% (chance=7.7%).

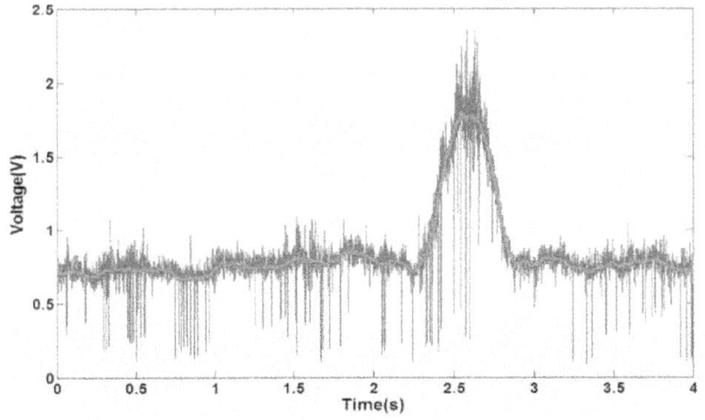

Figure 12. Fluctuation of LTE signals (**blue**) when user performs a bottom-tap gesture. The similarity in observed signals shows that our algorithm can easily adapt to future network standards.

POTENTIAL INTERACTION AND APPLICATIONS

Incoming Call Management

Our system can be beneficial when user receives phone call in a non-appropriate situation (*e.g.,* during a meeting). Instead of taking the phone out of her pocket, she can just use hand gesture to respond to the incoming call. We envision three gestures to control the three modes: enable silent mode with a downward gesture towards the phone, send predefined text with a right swipe gesture, and decline incoming calls by tapping on the phone.

Phone Navigation from Distance

In some situations, it becomes difficult for the user to touch the screen in order to navigate through the phone. To accommodate user inputs in such cases, a user can perform an upward gesture to enable scrolling while following a recipe. In addition, a user can perform in-air gestures to control their music listening experience in a variety of touch unfriendly situations. Besides accommodating touch unfriendly situation, this navigation system can also accommodate user's need in different situational impaired scenarios such as driving. The user can easily switch between map, music, and messaging app with simple left and right swipe gestures without having to touch specific location of her phone ever. Once selected, any app specific feature (e.g., map zoom in/out, turn GPS on/off) can then be navigated using inward or outward swipe gestures. These eyes-free gestures could reduce users' secondary task burden and allow them to focus more on primary driving task.

DISCUSSION AND FUTURE WORK

Our current prototype uses reflected GSM pulses to sample the gesture induced variation in propagation channels and hence, the rate of GSM pulses may limit the detectable hand gestures. As described earlier, the hand gesture usually occurs on the order of tens of Hz, which is smaller than the rate of GSM pulses (i.e., 80 Hz). However, for faster gestures like quick flicking, the high frequency components of the gesture may not be reconstructed using GSM pulses.

In our prototype, we take advantage of using GSM bursts when the user is making (or during) a phone call. It is possible to tweak the built-in GSM module to activate the GSM communication, generating a low gain-level, always-existing signal for sensing gestures. Furthermore, our approach, unlike prior Doppler-effect-based approaches, does not require high-speed ADC and FFT computation, and thus reduces the power consumption.

To explore the compatibility of our system with more modern wireless standards, we use the same experimental setup as shown in Figure 10, to capture LTE data uplink signal on an Apple iPhone 5s (AT&T version). Figure 12 shows the signal variation caused by a bottom-tap gesture. As shown in Fig 12, the duty cycle of LTE signal is much higher than that of GSM and therefore, the first step in Figure 6 is unnecessary. In addition, as the smoothed signal in Fig 12 (red line) is similar to the continuous signal in Fig 8, we believe that our methods could be easily adapted to future 4G standards such as LTE, which uses OFDMA / SC-FDMA in the uplink. We will further explore this in the future.

We also consider a couple of alternatives to improve our system. As shown in Fig 5, the right antenna has obvious null at the top-right corner, which reduces the accuracy of gesture classification. To enhance the performance, we could modify of the design of the antenna array to change the radiation patterns. Also, instead of using AD8361, it is possible to use different RF power detectors such as Analog Device's ADL5903 to retrieve the gestures from CDMA, WCDMA, TD-SCDMA and LTE signal.

CONCLUSION

In this work, we present SideSwipe, a system that enables in-air gestures for mobile devices using unmodified GSM signals. Our novel algorithm is able to interpolate the reflected GSM pulses into a continuous waveform and use it for gesture detection. In our prototype, we designed and built a receiver with four antenna elements. Since each antenna has a unique propagation path, hand movements around the phone perturb the GSM signal and these propagation paths. By combing the received signals from the four antennas, our system is able to build a unique pattern for various gestures. In our evaluation, we present 100% gesture detection and are able to recognize 14 gestures with 87.2% accuracy. Lastly, we show that SideSwipe can be easily adapted to future standards such as the LTE network.

REFERENCES

1. Adib, F. and Katabi, D., See Through Walls with Wi-Fi!. In *Proc SIGCOMM 2013*
2. Butler, A., Izadi, S., and Hodges, S. SideSight: multi-touch interaction around small devices., In *Proc UIST 2013*, pp. 201-204.
3. Chen, K., Lyons, K., White, S., and Patel, S. uTrack: 3D input using two magnetic sensors. In *Proc UIST 2013*, pp. 237–244.
4. Chetty, K., Smith, G., Guo, H., and Woodbridge, K. Target detection in high clutter using passive bistatic WiFi radar. *2009 IEEE Radar Conference*, pp. 1–5.
5. Chintalapudi, K., Padmanabha Iyer, A., and Padmanabhan, V.N. Indoor localization without the pain. In *Proc MobiCom 2010*, 173.
6. Cohn, G., Morris, D., Patel, S., and Tan, D. Your noise is my command: sensing gestures using the body as an antenna. In *Proc CHI 2011*, pp. 791–800.
7. Cohn, G., Morris, D., Patel, S., and Tan, D. Humantenna: using the body as an antenna for real-time whole-body interaction, In *Proc CHI 2012*, pp. 1901-1910
8. Gupta, S., Morris, D., Patel, S., and Tan, D. Soundwave: using the doppler effect to sense gestures. In *Proc CHI 2012*, pp. 1911-1914.
9. Harrison, C. and Hudson, S. Scratch input: creating large, inexpensive, unpowered and mobile finger input surfaces, . In *Proc UIST 2008*, pp. 205-208
10. Harrison, C., Tan, D., and Morris, D. Skinput: appropriating the body as an input surface, In *Proc CHI 2010*,, pp. 453-462
11. Hudson, S.E. Abracadabra : Wireless , High-Precision , and Unpowered Finger Input for Very Small Mobile Devices, In *Proc UIST 2009*, pp. 121-124.
12. Kellogg, B., Talla, V., and Gollakota, S. Bringing Gesture Recognition To All Devices. In *Proc NSDI 2014*,
13. Kim, D., Hilliges, O., Izadi, S., and Butler, A. Digits: freehand 3D interactions anywhere using a wrist-worn gloveless sensor, In *Proc UIST 2012*, pp. 167-172
14. Marvasti, F. *Nonuniform sampling: theory and practice*. Springer, 2001.
15. Minka, T. and Choudhury, R.R. Spot, Precise Localization using PHY Layer Information, In *Proc HotNets-X 2012*
16. Pu, Q., Gupta, S., Gollakota, S., and Patel, S. Whole-Home Gesture Recognition Using Wireless Signals, In *Proc MobiCom 2013*, pp. 27-38.
17. Ring, M.F., Ashbrook, D., Baudisch, P., and White, S. Nenya : Subtle and Eyes-Free Mobile Input with a magnetically-tracked finger ring, In *Proc CHI 2011*, pp. 2043–2046.
18. Shotton, J., Fitzgibbon, A., Cook, M., et al. Real-time human pose recognition in parts from single depth images. In *Proc CVPR 2011*, pp. 297–1304.
19. Starner, T., Auxier, J., Ashbrook, D., and Gandy, M. The gesture pendant: a self-illuminating, wearable, infrared computer vision system for home automation control and medical monitoring. In *Proc ISWC 2000*, pp. 87–94.
20. Wigdor, D., Forlines, C., Baudisch, P., Barnwell, J., and Shen, C. LucidTouch : A See-Through Mobile Device, In *Proc UIST 2007*, pp. 269-278.
21. Xiong, J. and Jamieson, K. Towards Fine-Grained Radio-Based Indoor Location Categories and Subject Descriptors, In *Proc HotMobile 2012*.

Vibkinesis: Notification by Direct Tap and 'Dying Message' Using Vibronic Movement Controllable Smartphones

Shota Yamanaka
Meiji University
Nakano, Tokyo, Japan
stymnk@meiji.ac.jp

Homei Miyashita
Meiji University and JST CREST
Nakano, Tokyo, Japan
homei@homei.com

ABSTRACT
We propose Vibkinesis, a smartphone that can control its angle and directions of movement and rotation. By separately controlling the vibration motors attached to it, the smartphone can move on a table in the direction it chooses. Vibkinesis can inform a user of a message received when the user is away from the smartphone by changing its orientation, e.g., the smartphone has rotated 90° to the left before the user returns to the smartphone. With this capability, Vibkinesis can notify the user of a message even if the battery is discharged. We also extend the sensing area of Vibkinesis by using an omni-directional lens so that the smartphone tracks the surrounding objects. This allows Vibkinesis to tap the user's hand. These novel interactions expand the mobile device's movement area, notification channels, and notification time span.

Author Keywords
Smartphone; mobile device; notification; vibration; mobile sensing.

ACM Classification Keywords
H.5.m. Information interfaces and presentation: Miscellaneous.

INTRODUCTION
Smartphones can notify users of different events, such as phone calls and received emails, through screen alerts, sounds, or vibrations. Recently, several novel methods have been proposed to enrich information output using new materials and devices, e.g., by bending the body of a smartphone [9], moving its surface [23], and expanding its body [14]. These technologies augment the information channels available between mobile devices and users.

There are other methods that do not require the physical appearance of the smartphone to change. inFORM [8] demonstrates an application that transports a mobile phone to a user when the mobile phone receives an incoming call. In the commercial field, several types of robots that transport smartphones are sold [1, 3]. These mechanical fields and robot methods rely on a fixed table or floor because of issues with their mobility. In other words, such methods satisfy a different goal from ours in this paper because they do not involve self-contained mobile devices.

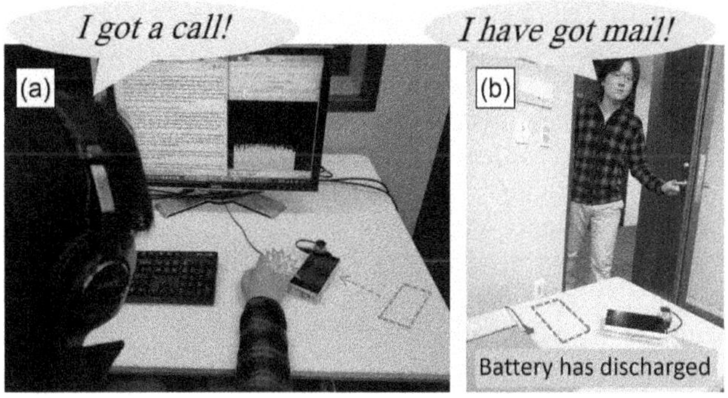

Figure 1. Vibkinesis concept of self-moving smartphone. The user notices by Vibkinesis (a) direct tap, and (b) changed orientation.

We propose Vibkinesis, a self-contained smartphone that can move on a tabletop by vibrating. The smartphone controls four pairs of attached vibrating motors that allow it to slide on a flat surface. Vibkinesis changes its orientation by rotating and relocating, as shown in Figure 1. Furthermore, Vibkinesis can directly contact a user. Obviously, such a method of freely moving smartphones can be achieved through robots [1, 3], or by attaching several tires, motors, servo-motors, and a microcontroller to the phone. However, from the perspective of mobility and compatibility, we believe Vibkinesis is satisfactory implementation because it requires only eight small vibrators and a microcontroller. This setup does not negatively affect the smartphone's mobility. Moreover, the peculiarity of the system's entire appearance is important in daily use, especially for mobile systems, because such systems are used in public. Vibkinesis looks like a smartphone with a small thick case. Thus, it is different from robotic phones or smartphones with tires.

By allowing smartphones to move freely on a tabletop,

* The term "Dying Message" in the title is the last message written by a dying character in Japanese mystery novels and comics.

UIST '14, October 05 – 08, 2014, Honolulu, HI, USA.
Copyright 2014 ACM 978-1-4503-3069-5/14/10...$15.00.
http://dx.doi.org/10.1145/2642918.2647365

users can obtain information through a new channel. For example, if a user is working while listening to music through headphones (thereby losing the smartphone's aural channel), he/she can become aware of an incoming phone call through a *direct tap* from the smartphone (using the haptic channel). Moreover, and to the best of our knowledge, previous methods proposing self-contained mobile devices have not addressed situations where the battery of a mobile device is discharged and the device is not able to notify the user of messages or other events. We could not find studies that addressed such a limitation, although all mobile devices have a battery limit. We propose a solution to this issue through a novel capability of Vibkinesis: the smartphone persists in a rotated orientation even after the battery has discharged, as though it had written a last message.

It is well known that mobile devices move due to the embedded vibrators. Cycloramic [2] uses this effect to rotate a phone 360° in order to capture panoramic images. However, there is no method to control the angle of rotation of the phone, or its direction of movement and rotation. In this paper, we propose several practical notifications through two-dimensional movement and rotation methods by using eight vibration motors. Another contribution of Vibkinesis is a new focal point for mobile devices and a solution: notification using its orientation even after the battery has discharged.

RELATED WORK

Notification Methods of Mobile Devices

Traditional sound and haptic notifications are well reviewed in [10]. Recently, several other notification methods have been proposed for mobile devices in addition to screen displays, sounds, and vibrations. MorePhone [9] bends the phone's surface such that the user is aware of the device's change, even when wearing headphones. Surflex [6] also changes its shape by bending. Shape-changing Mobiles [14] change their protuberance such that users can notice whether devices are leaning to the front or back. Take Me By The Hand [13] changes the shape and weight gravity point of a mobile phone for eyes-free navigation.

Several methods use vibrators to obtain more complete information, especially as feedback. Ambient Touch [19] produces complicated vibrating patterns so that the user can obtain more information than from simple vibrations. Haptic-emoticon [18] provides a continuous two-dimensional haptic feedback using nine discrete vibrators located at the bottom of the phone. Sahami has proposed embedding six vibrators for navigation [24]. Brown et al. propose sending messages to the user through vibrators attached to his/her arm [4]. SemFeel [29] provides feedback with regard to the user's operation through multiple vibrators attached to the bottom of the device. Users can thus sense the part of the display that they touch without looking at it. These navigation or feedback methods are used when a user holds the device. On the contrary, the vibration motors of Vibkinesis are activated when the device is on a surface (not held by a user). Thus, Vibkinesis does not focus on direct vibrotactile stimuli.

Changing Device Shape

Shape-changing devices in the field of Human-computer Interaction have been developed to alter the functions and affordances. The mechanisms and categories of shape-changing interfaces are well documented in [7, 21]. As in MorePhone [9], a shape-memory alloy is used to change the shape of a device [12, 20]. Morphees [22] also use shape-memory alloys but focus on functions related to usability, such as changing into a prehensile shape. The aforementioned devices are able to shape-change provided they receive electrical power. This includes shape-memory alloys, which can bend only when powered by electricity. Therefore, shape-changing mobile devices can notify users only if they are charged.

Sensing Methods of Mobile Devices

Sensing the environment is necessary for mobile interfaces to perform appropriate actions. Hinckley et al. propose rotating the displayed image depending on the tilt of the device [15]. SideSight [5] allows the user multi-touch interactions around the device using two arrays of infrared (IR) proximity sensors. PaperPhone [17] recognizes bending gestures using a flexible electronic paper display. Harrison et al. propose using a small RGB light and sensor to detect the material on which a mobile device is resting for placement-aware mobile computing [11]. Surround-see [28] uses an omni-directional lens to view the surrounding environment, such as the user's proximity or hand gestures. Vibkinesis employs the same setup as that of Surround-see for the smartphone to move toward a user's hand to notify him/her about an event.

There also exist sensing techniques that only use the default sensors in a device. TinyMotion [27] senses the user's actions using a camera image. Accelerometers are used to detect touch and tap gestures [25, 30], including foot gestures [26], when the phone is in a user's pocket. VibroTactor [16] determines the location of the smartphone using vibrations and sound echoes. For most of these methods, sensing technologies are used to detect the user's actions. The exception is VibroTactor, which can determine the location when the smartphone is placed on a surface.

IMPLEMENTATION

Vibration-controlling Hardware and Software

Our Vibkinesis prototype is implemented using a Sony Xperia Z with three plastic cases, eight Tokyo Parts Industrial vibration motors FM34F, and a microcontroller ATmega328P on an Arduino Nano. The four pairs of vibrators are attached to a base case using double-sided tape, and an Arduino Nano is attached in a similar manner (Figure 2, middle). Another cover case is attached to the base case in an inverted position using tape, and the smartphone is placed on top of the mount case (Figure 2, right). The smartphone and the Arduino Nano are connected by a USB host cable for power and serial communication. Applications that run on Android OS are programmed using Processing for Android with libraries for serial communication and camera image processing. In this setup, the measured energy supplied by Arduino Nano is approximately 3.1 V × 60 mA = 0.18 W for each vibrator. Each pair behaves independently, and thus the maximum electrical requirement at one time is 0.18 W × 2 = 0.36 W.

The combinations of vibrators and movements for the current Vibkinesis setup are shown in Figure 2 (left). In any implementation, it is difficult to move the device exactly in a straight line. However, this issue is not critical because the software can correct the direction of movement of the device by rotating it.

We assume that the rotation and direction of movement of Vibkinesis depend on the turning directions of the eccentric wheel motors in the attached vibrators. The applied power from the weights in the motors alters depending on their positions. When a weight goes through the inside of the device, the effect of this applied power is slightly weakened; when going through outside, the power remains. In this way, when the motors at the top turn to the left, the device rotates to the left; the device rotates to the right when the bottom motors turn to the right. We also assume the left and right motor pairs' power lean to one side, and then the device moves roughly in the opposite directions.

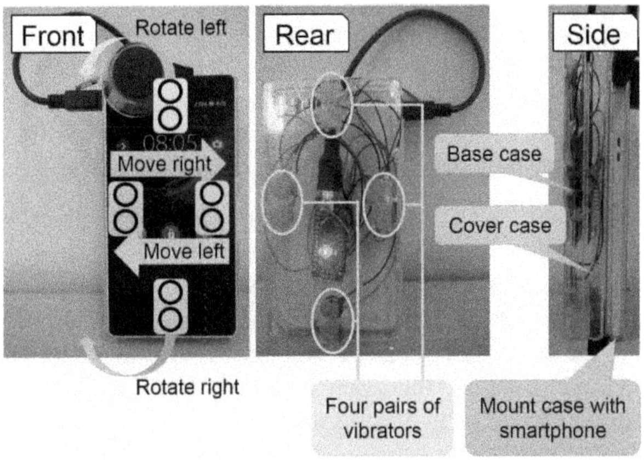

Figure 2. Vibkinesis hardware setup. *Front* view shows combinations of each activated two-vibrator set and movement/rotation directions.

For our first prototype, we mounted a vibrator on each edge of the base case (for a total of four motors). However, the power of the vibrations was not sufficient to move the smartphone. We then used two vibrators for each direction, following which the system moved as intended for Vibkinesis. The entire system, including the weight of the smartphone (146 g), weighs 231 g, and its thickness is 31 mm (including the smartphone's thickness of 7.9 mm). Technically, this setup will be implemented in a smartphone because vibrators are commonly embedded in smartphones; the smartphone typically acts as the microcontroller in such setups. Our prototype is sufficient to exemplify the idea underlying Vibkinesis. However, a light-weight setup is recommended.

Other options for implementing vibration control are as follows:

1) Wi-Fi using XBee instead of a USB host cable for data communication with the microcontroller: a clear limitation of our current prototype is the USB cable connection. XBee eliminates the physical connection between the smartphone and the Arduino Nano; however, an additional battery is required for the microcontroller. A USB host cable can be used for both power supply and data communication. If we use XBee and an additional battery, the total weight of the system increases and its mobility consequently decreases. Moreover, we would then be required to separately charge the smartphone and the additional battery. For these reasons, and for mobility and simplicity of daily use, we chose the USB host cable for our proof-of-concept prototype.

2) Stronger vibrators can reduce the number of motors needed. However, the fewer motors in this case require higher voltage, due to which it becomes necessary to add another battery. This means that the system requires a more complicated circuit using field-effect transistors (FETs) with resistances. The vibration motors we use for the current prototype require 2.5 to 3.5 V, which is supplied by the USB host cable; therefore, the system is lighter. Obviously, stronger motors can carry a heavier system, but its mobility suffers. Consequently, we chose light motors.

Sensing Rotation Angle

In order for the smartphone to stop vibrating when it rotates to a certain degree, e.g., 90°, it is necessary to measure the extent to which the smartphone turns after it starts vibrating. We had some options for sensors, such as the three-dimensional accelerometer, a magnetic field sensor (compass), and a camera. Moreover, if we develop Vibkinesis as a tabletop interface, we can use external sensors, such as Kinect. However, our concept of Vibkinesis is as a self-contained mobile system; thus, we selected embedded sensors. We chose to use a compass because it would simply return the direction that the smartphone is facing.

Our prototype exhibits robustness with regard to the angle of rotation. Even if the smartphone accidentally rotates to an excessive degree when, for example, someone strikes the table when the smartphone is vibrating, Vibkinesis detects the exceedance, and then rotates accordingly in the opposite direction. In this manner, a different notification can be avoided.

A limitation of the compass is that it is influenced by surrounding magnetic objects, including magnets from the mounted vibration motors. However, we experimentally confirmed that the magnetic force of the eight small vibrators is not sufficiently strong to considerably alter the compass direction. Furthermore, and for practical purposes, the smartphone's compass function can be used without trouble in the presence of some magnetic forces, such as audio speakers or the TV. Therefore, using the compass to detect the angle of rotation is of no consequence for incremental rotations of 45° or 90°.

More sophisticated sensing methods can be used, for example, the optical flow processing of camera images. In use cases of Vibkinesis, the smartphone always rests on a surface; its front camera thus faces the ceiling and the rear camera faces the surface (this requires clear cases). Thus, the smartphone can calculate the angle at which it rotates by observing the ceiling or the surface. Our current prototype uses the compass only because it is sufficient to show our concept of rotation notification. However, integration with other smart methods can help improve its angle precision.

Sensing Direction of User's Hand

Vibkinesis can move to tap a user's hand on a table by detecting the direction of the hand. Following the detection technique of Surround-see [28], we attached an omni-directional lens, Kogeto, which enhances the field-of-view to 360° in the horizontal plane, to the front camera of the smartphone using double-sided tape. Of course, more sophisticated methods are available. However, simple RGB thresholds are sufficient to detect skin color for the proof-of-concept of Vibkinesis. When a user is working at a table, e.g., performing paperwork or conducting tasks using a PC, his/her hands are located at the lower position of sensed images. We can avoid the user's face/neck region by using only the lower two-thirds of the images. Vibkinesis senses 1280 × 720 pixel images at 10 fps, and then verifies skin color per 10 pixels. Vibkinesis assumes that the gravity point of the skin-colored pixels is the direction of the user's hand. In the *direct tap* application, Vibkinesis controls the vibrators' ON/OFF function until it reaches the hand.

This sensing method has limitations in accordance with those of common computer vision, e.g., light effect, the skin color of naked forearms, individual skin color, and surrounding objects that have a color parameter close to that of the human skin. There are several solutions that use additional items, for instance, wearing a tracking marker on a wrist or a finger, using a depth sensor, or attaching a non-contact thermometer. An omni-directional lens can detect the user's hand without problem for the purpose of exhibiting our Vibkinesis concept. However, the aforementioned alternatives might improve detection accuracy.

Measurement

We tested two types of measurements – rotating times and moving times – on three types of surfaces – wood, glass, and plastic. The rotation time for each surface is calculated as the average of rotating the proposed device by 45° on that surface five times to the right and to the left, for a total of 30 times. The movement time is measured similarly, as the average of moving the device 5 cm five times to the right and to the left, on each surface. We test the flatness of each surface using a spirit level. The smoothest surface is glass, followed by plastic.

Figure 3 shows that the rotation time is shortest on the wood surface. This means that a certain level of grip helps the rotation of Vibkinesis. On the contrary, the time taken to move is not significantly different for other surfaces. These data show that Vibkinesis can work on surfaces that we commonly use. Moreover, we confirmed that only an extremely strong frictional force, e.g., that on a carpet, can prevent movement.

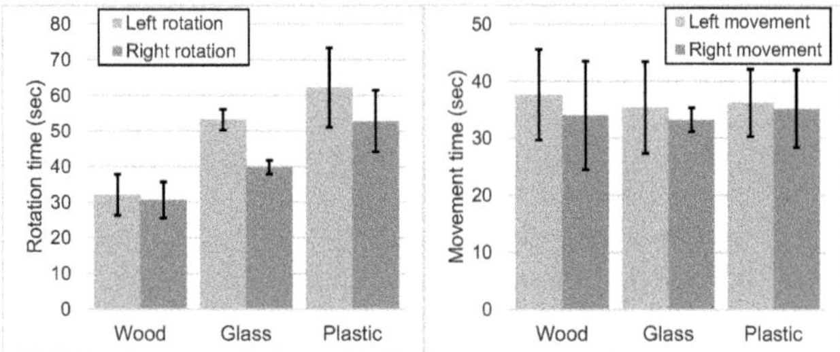

Figure 3. (Left) Rotation times and (Right) movement times on each type of surface.

SAMPLE APPLICATIONS AND CAPABILITIES

We developed applications for different scenarios to show the capabilities of Vibkinesis.

Informing by Tapping (Direct Tap)

Sometimes, users might not notice smartphone alarms even when in close proximity to the phone. Vibkinesis informs the user of notifications by tapping the user's hand, in the same manner as being tapped by another person.

A simple direct tap, which constitutes moving to the user's hand then continuing to vibrate, is effective for a user wearing headphones. Moreover, Vibkinesis can move away from the user, and thus provides a repeat of tapping and moving away. An irregular tapping pattern might be more effective because the user is more likely to notice an irregular stimulus than a regular one.

Hand detection and movement to the user's hand are ineffective in case of obstacles (e.g., objects between the user's hand and the phone, or when the phone rests on an object, such as a book, placed on the surface). Moreover, if the phone and the user's hand are on the same surface, normal vibration transfers through the surface to the hand. However, this detection is influenced by parameters, such as how efficiently the table transfers vibrations, or the extent to which the user's hands move. Thus, tapping the hand is more *direct* for the user's tactile perception, under the condition that the phone can reach the hand.

Notification by Rotation (Dying Message)
When users are away from their smartphones, they obviously cannot observe any notifications, such as messages. Thus, once they return, they have to actively check their phones to see if they have a pending notification; otherwise, they risk missing it. Commonly, several solutions are adopted, such as displaying the message until the user can verify missed messages, or providing a notification at regular time intervals.

Vibkinesis adds a new notification channel: changing its orientation by rotating. If the smartphone has rotated, say, by 90° to the left when the user returns, the user might notice its abnormal appearance. In this application, the user can configure the combination of messages and rotation (direction and angle). For example, rotating 45° to the right per email received, or rotating 180° when a call from a designated person is received.

Vibkinesis can notify the user even after the smartphone's battery has been discharged. This is the capability of our proposal most distinct from other related work. For example, users should recharge the battery of their device if they expect important communication, such as an email. However, users sometimes do not notice that the battery has discharged. This is especially true when the user is away from the device. In such situations, displaying a message, such as "Remaining battery: X%," or using other alerts, is useless. Previous methods, including using shape-memory alloys, did not address and solve this problem. Obviously, alert-forever methods (displaying, alarming, and vibrating) cannot be used in this situation. Vibkinesis proposes another solution: informing the user of messages missed by its orientation change, even after the battery has discharged.

Vibkinesis also provides multiple data: that the battery is discharged, and there are (or there are not) important messages pending perusal. For example, if the battery was discharged and no messages were received, Vibkinesis rotates by a certain degree (e.g., 90° to the right); if the battery was discharged after receiving a call from a person identified by the user as important, Vibkinesis rotates by a certain additional degree (e.g., plus 45°, for a total of 135°). In this way, users can determine whether they have to recharge the battery as soon as possible.

DISCUSSION

Rotation Noticeability
We demonstrated our current prototype to several people at our university. Almost all individuals responded positively to our basic idea: if the smartphone had rotated 90° in their absence, they would have noticed the abnormal orientation. On the other hand, one of the people said that he would not be aware of the rotation because he always placed his smartphone in random orientations. However, he also indicated that he might notice if the device had rotated 180° because there is no reason to place a device on a table in an entirely inverted orientation. As this person mentioned, the rotating resolution is important to notice. Attaching different messages to high resolutions, e.g., at every 5° rotations, the messages are difficult to distinguish. On the contrary, significantly low resolutions, e.g., 180° as the person suggested, can only be attached to few different messages. Therefore, it is necessary to investigate the best resolution for Vibkinesis.

Battery Life
The battery discharges faster with Vibkinesis because of the USB host power supply, the image processing, and the magnetic sensing. The problem of battery life cannot be considered independently of mobile systems. However, application designs help solve such problems, similar to Vibkinesis' dying message. With Vibkinesis, the user does not have to worry about remaining battery even if there is an important message.

Physical Limitations
Physical conditions, such as leaning and surface friction, influence the movement of Vibkinesis. In our operational verification of the prototype, the smartphone was not able to move along a steep slope that we intentionally created. Further, surfaces with very high or very low friction disturb its movement. Not all surfaces are suitable for Vibkinesis, but it can be used on flat surfaces made of wood, glass, and plastic, such as those used for daily work.

CONCLUSION AND FUTURE WORK
In this paper, we proposed Vibkinesis, a smartphone that notifies users by changing its orientation and by direct tapping. We built a proof-of-concept prototype by controlling vibronic movement. We introduced the capabilities of Vibkinesis in certain situations: when the user is away from the smartphone, after the battery is discharged, and when the user cannot hear the smartphone's alarm.

For our future work, we will investigate the rotation angle resolution most suited for Vibkinesis applications. Moreover, surface conditions should be tested more extensively. We will also look to develop other capabilities in Vibkinesis. For example, another approach to solve the problem of the battery being nearly discharged is to move to a wireless charging sheet. Further, we plan to test the usability of Vibkinesis in daily use after developing a more sophisticated, light-weight, and powerful version. The power of the current prototype is not sufficiently strong to move objects around it. If Vibkinesis had more power available, it can make its appearance more abnormal to inform the user of an important notification. For example, if stationery, cups, or other objects on the table have fallen to the floor while Vibkinesis is still on the table, the user would very likely notice the extraordinary circumstances. Vibkinesis will be able to create such notifications by interacting with the real world, which cannot be performed through screen displays, sounds, or simple vibrations.

REFERENCES

1. Cotbots. http://cotsbots.wordpress.com/
2. Cycloramic. http://www.cycloramic.com/
3. ROMO. http://www.romotive.com/
4. Brown, L.M., Brewster, S.A., and Purchase, H.C. Multidimensional Tactons for Non-Visual Information Presentation in Mobile Devices. In *Proc. of MobileHCI 2006*, 231-238.
5. Butler, A., Izadi, S. and Hodges. S. SideSight: multi-"touch" interaction around small devices. In *Proc. of UIST 2008*, 201-204.
6. Coelho, M., Ishii, H., and Maes. P. Surflex: a programmable surface for the design of tangible interfaces. In *Proc. of CHI 2008 Extended Abstracts*, 3429-3434.
7. Coelho, M. and J. Zigelbaum. Shape-changing interfaces. *Personal and Ubiquitous Computing,* Volume 15, Issue 2 (2011), 161-173.
8. Follmer, S., Leithinger, D., Olwal, A., Hogge, A. and Ishii, H. inFORM: Dynamic Physical Affordances and Constraints through Shape and Object Actuation. In *Proc. of UIST 2013*, 417-426.
9. Gomes, A., Nesbitt, A. and Vertegaal, R. MorePhone: A Study of Actuated Shape Deformations for Flexible Thin-Film Smartphone Notifications. In *Proc. of CHI 2013*, 583-592.
10. Hansson, R., Ljungstrand, P. and J. Redström. Subtle and public notification cues for mobile devices. In *Proc. of UbiComp 2001*, 240-246.
11. Harrison, C. and Hudson, S.E. Lightweight Material Detection for Placement-aware Mobile Computing. In *Proc. of UIST 2008*, 279-282.
12. Hawkes, E., An, B., Benbernou, N., Tanaka, H., Kim, S., Demaine, E.D., Rus, D. and Wood, R.J. Programmable matter by folding. In *Proc. Nat. Acad. Sci.*, Volume 107, Issue 28 (2010), 12441-12445.
13. Hemmert, F., Hamann, S., Löwe, M., Wohlauf, A., Zeipelt, J. and Joost, G. Take me by the hand: haptic compasses in mobile devices through shape change and weight shift. In *Proc. of NordiCHI 2010*, 671-674.
14. Hemmert, F., Hamann, S., Löwe, M., Wohlauf, A. and Joost, G. Shape-changing mobiles: tapering in one-dimensional deformational displays in mobile phones. In *Proc TEI 2010*, 249-252.
15. Hinckley, K., Pierce, J., Sinclair, M. and Horvitz, E. Sensing Techniques for Mobile Interaction. In *Proc. of UIST 2000*, 91-100.
16. Hwang, S., Wohn, K-y. VibroTactor: low-cost placement-aware technique using vibration echoes on mobile devices. In *Proc. of IUI 2013 Companion*, 73-74.
17. Lahey, B., Girouard, A., Burleson, W. and Vertegaal, R. PaperPhone: Understanding the use of bend gestures in mobile devices with flexible electronic paper displays. In *Proc. of CHI 2011*, 1303-1312.
18. Nakatsuma, K., Hoshi, T. and Torigoe, I. Haptic-Emoticon: Haptic Content Creation and Sharing System to Enhancing Text-Based Communication, In *Proc. of SICE 2013*, 218-222.
19. Poupyrev, I., Maruyama, S. and Rekimoto, J. Ambient Touch: Designing tactile interfaces for handheld devices. In *Proc. of UIST 2002*, 51-60.
20. Probst, K., Seifried, T., Haller, M., Kentaro, Y. and Sugimoto, M. and Inami, M. Move-It: Interactive Sticky Notes Actuated by Shape Memory Alloys. In *Proc. of CHI 2011 Extended Abstracts*, 1393-1398.
21. Rasmussen, M., Pedersen, E., Petersen, M.G., Hornbæk, K. Shape-Changing interfaces: A review of the design space and open research questions. In *Proc. of CHI 2012*, 735-744.
22. Roudaut A., Karnik A., Löchtefeld, M. and Subramanian, S. Morphees: toward high "shape resolution" in self-actuated flexible mobile devices. In *Proc. of CHI 2013,* 593-602.
23. Roudaut, A., Rau, A., Sterz, C., Plauth, M., Lopes, P. and Baudisch, B. Gesture output: eyes-free output using a force feedback touch surface. In *Proc. of CHI 2013*, 2547-2556.
24. Sahami, A., Holleis, P., Schmidt, A. and J. Häkkilä. Rich tactile output on mobile devices. In *Proc. of AmI 2008*, 210-221.
25. Saponas, T. S., Harrison, C. and Benko, H. PocketTouch: Through-Pocket Capacitive Touch Input. In *Proc. of UIST 2011*, 303-308.
26. Scott, J., Dearman, D., Yatani, K. and Truong, K.N. Sensing Foot Gestures from the Pocket. In *Proc. of UIST 2010,* 199-208.
27. Wang, J., Zhai, S. and Canny, J. Camera Phone Based Motion Sensing: Interaction Techniques, Applications and Performance Study. In *Proc. of UIST 2006*, 101-110.
28. Yang, X-D., Hasan, K., Bruce, N. and Irani, P. Surround-see: enabling peripheral vision on smartphones during active use. In *Proc. of UIST 2013*, 291-300.
29. Yatani, K. and Truong, K.N. SemFeel: A User Interface with Semantic Tactile Feedback for Mobile Touch-screen Devices. In *Proc. of UIST 2009*, 111-120.
30. Zhang, C., Parnami, A., Southern, C., Thomaz, E., Reyes, G., Arriaga, R.I. and Abowd, G.D. BackTap: Robust Four-Point Tapping on the Back of an Off-the-Shelf Smartphone. In *Proc. of UIST 2013 Adjunct*, 111-112.

Video Lens: Rapid Playback and Exploration of Large Video Collections and Associated Metadata

Justin Matejka, Tovi Grossman, and George Fitzmaurice
Autodesk Research, Toronto, Canada
{*firstname.lastname*}@Autodesk.com

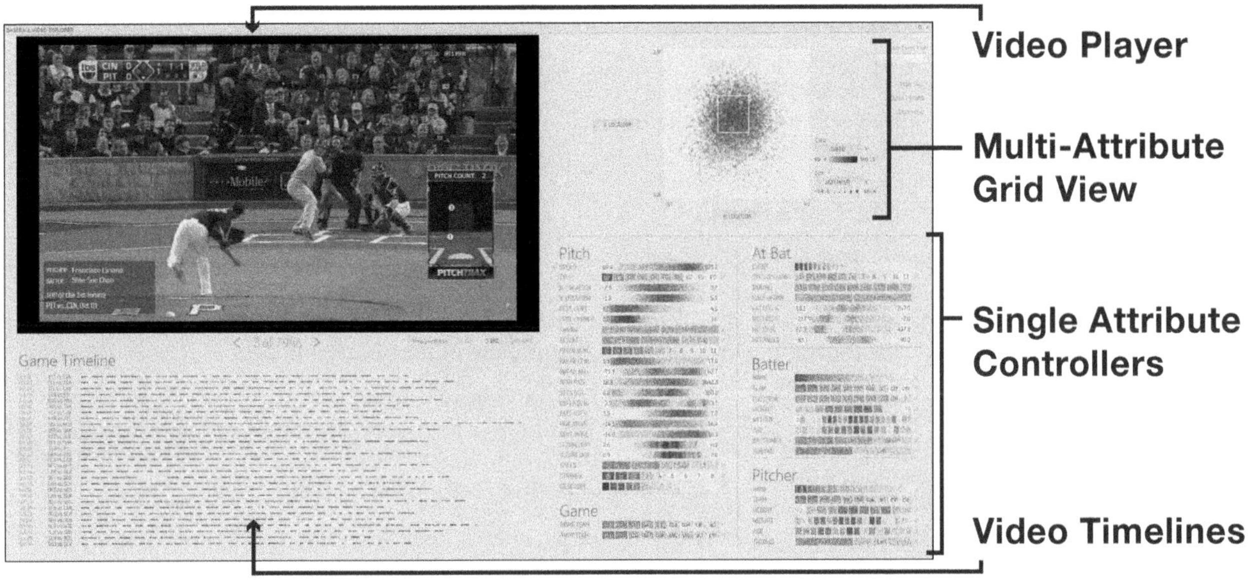

Figure 1. Overview of the Video Lens interface consisting of a video player in the top left surrounded by the Multi-Attribute Grid, Single Attribute Controllers, and Video Timelines which support the faceted search and selection of video events based on a multi-dimensional set of timeline-based metadata.

ABSTRACT
We present *Video Lens*, a framework which allows users to visualize and interactively explore large collections of videos and associated metadata. The primary goal of the framework is to let users quickly find relevant sections within the videos and play them back in rapid succession. The individual UI elements are linked and highly interactive, supporting a faceted search paradigm and encouraging exploration of the data set. We demonstrate the capabilities and specific scenarios of *Video Lens* within the domain of professional baseball videos. A user study with 12 participants indicates that *Video Lens* efficiently supports a diverse range of powerful yet desirable video query tasks, while a series of interviews with professionals in the field demonstrates the framework's benefits and future potential.

INTRODUCTION
In the last 10 years, the trend of storing large collections of online videos has exploded. YouTube and Netflix alone account for a significant percentage of all internet traffic[1], while domain specific systems such as sports video streaming [27, 37] and software video capture [7] are active commercial and research areas.

UIST '14, October 05 - 08 2014, Honolulu, HI, USA
Copyright 2014 ACM 978-1-4503-3069-5/14/10...$15.00.
http://dx.doi.org/10.1145/2642918.2647366

As a result, there has been a recent surge in interest looking at ways to allow users to efficiently locate and navigate to scenes of interest within videos [9, 15, 16]. However, finding a specific scene or event within a *large collection* of videos remains an open challenge. Furthermore, if multiple results match a query of interest, there are few known techniques that would allow the user to efficiently play back all of the results. Status quo solutions, such as playlists, work when interested in a collection of entire videos, but do not suffice if only a small part of each video is of interest.

For example, consider a baseball fan who wishes to watch all home runs hit by their favorite player during the 2013 baseball season. Even if the user manages to create a playlist of all videos (games) where the events of interest (home runs) occurred, it would still be laborious to find the event of interest within each of these videos.

Learning from data exploration techniques, a faceted search paradigm [33] could be of use. Faceted search is commonly employed by users working with collections with many dimensions of metadata, allowing them to filter the data set into small subsets that are of direct interest [8]. Indeed, many

[1] http://www.cnet.com/news/netflix-youtube-gobble-up-half-of-internet-traffic/

forms of video collections do have associated timeline metadata, such as the plays that occur during a sporting event [6], the commands that occur during a software tutorial [7], or the faces that appear in a TV show [38]. However, the possibility of using such meta-data to support the faceted search of large video libraries has been under-explored.

In this paper, we present *Video Lens*, a framework which allows users to visualize and interactively explore large collections of videos and associated meta-data. The interface of *Video Lens* is comprised of four main components: Video timelines, which show each individual video in the library with its associated event locations; single-attribute controllers, which provide support for faceted search; a multi-attribute grid, which visualizes the current data set across a user-specified set of attributes; and a video player, which supports rapid playback of query results (Figure 1).

We describe the design goals of the *Video Lens* system and its framework in detail, and discuss some of the specific challenges that arise when aligning large collections of video with metadata. We then demonstrate the capabilities and specific usage scenarios of *Video Lens* within the domain of professional baseball videos, known to be a rich source of data and analysis [22]. A user study with 12 participants indicates that *Video Lens* efficiently supports a diverse range of powerful yet desirable video query tasks, while a series of interviews with professionals in the field demonstrates the framework's benefits and future potential.

RELATED WORK

Finding/Watching Sections of Video

With the increase in the quantity and length of digital videos available a number of projects [9, 15, 16, 23] have explored ways to improve the process of manually finding a particular section of a video file. However, these techniques do not consider searching through a library of videos, and they do not use any metadata about the video content to assist in the search task. Chronicle [7] uses metadata about the events in a software tutorial video to facilitate searching and jumping to relevant sections. Pause-and-Play [21] similarly uses metadata to link the playback of a tutorial video to the progress of a workflow. However, both of these operate on a single video at a time.

The Ambient Help [14] system looks at a collection of software tutorial videos along with metadata describing which commands occur at which times in each video, and automatically plays back video segments which might be relevant to the user. This is similar to *Video Lens* in that it uses a collection of videos with timeline metadata, but the metadata in Ambient Help only has only one dimension (command name), and the user does not have any control over which video clips are presented.

Some work has looked at generating metadata for video files by automatically analyzing audio and video streams [1, 5, 14, 17, 25, 26], as well as through crowdsourcing [10]. The *Video Lens* system assumes that videos already have a set of rich timeline metadata, but a system to automatically extract time stamped metadata would be a useful companion.

Faceted Search

The idea of using faceted search techniques to filter though a multi-dimensional set of data has been well explored [8, 11, 28, 30, 33] and applied to finding items in many domains including research publications [13], webpages [4], e-commerce [29], image search [32, 34], and to a lesser extent, video collections [5, 31].

The interfaces for faceted search systems typically consist of a list of attributes, or facets, and a set of valid options or ranges for each. Similar to *Video Lens*, the Selfiecity Project [36] displays the distribution of values for each attribute within the individual facet control. The main differences being that Selfiecity uses area charts to represent the distribution while *Video Lens* uses an array of individual dots, and the Selficity controls are manually crafted to represent the underlying data, while the *Video Lens* attribute controls are meant to be generic and automatically adapt to the structure of the underlying data.

Sports Video Systems

The topics of analyzing, searching, and viewing sports videos have received significant attention recently, both in the literature and as deployed systems.

Olsen *et al.*'s Time Warp Sports [18] presented a customized interface for watching videos of sporting events, making use of event markers to support operations such as jumping to the next or previous play. The *Video Lens* system can support a similar workflow by selecting all of the events in a single video, and then moving to the next and previous events in the resulting set.

Major League Baseball (MLB) has an online video presence in the form of MLB.tv [27] which gives viewers access to an entire season's worth of baseball games and highlights. The video player has some advanced browsing features such as jumping to a specific inning by clicking on the corresponding cell in the box score. The Baseball Savant website [39] has a comprehensive tool to query the same advanced PITCHf/x event metadata [6] we use in the *Baseball Video Lens* example, however, the search interface is more traditional in the sense that it does not allow for iterative refinement of a query, and video clips are available for only a small set of "highlight" plays, such as home runs. Professional (and some amateur) baseball teams often make use of proprietary software for video analysis. Our interviews with professional teams indicated that the BATS package from Sydex Software [40] is the most frequently used package, however, it does use a faceted search paradigm.

The National Basketball Association (NBA) recently released a compelling Stats Video feature on their website [37]. By clicking on a stat in a game timeline or on a player's individual stat page, a custom playlist is created to show all of the plays where those events happened. The system however does not allow for the combining of multiple search criteria into a single query, limiting the expressiveness of the resulting clip collections.

THE VIDEO LENS FRAMEWORK

There are many usage domains where a user may want to view multiple clips from a collection of video files, such as sports [41], entertainment [42, 43], and learning [12, 14]. Typically, the process of finding and viewing the relevant clips is a manual and time-consuming process.

To support the process of finding and viewing relevant clips within a collection of videos, we created the *Video Lens* framework (Figure 1). The primary goal of the framework is to allow interactive exploration of a collection of videos with associated metadata information. Besides being useful for purposeful, directed tasks, the interface also encourages free-form exploration through the use of highly-interactive controls and immediate viewing of results.

Design Goals

The design of the *Video Lens* framework was directed by a set of four design goals.

D1: Maximize Information Density

One design goal for the *Video Lens* framework is to maximize information density to reveal as much about the underlying data as possible. When considering a large collection of videos, each with a rich set of metadata, there are lots of data points to be displayed. We want *Video Lens* to display as much of that information as possible.

D2: Treat Events as the Primary Entity

Even though *Video Lens* works with a collection of videos, the primary entity of interest are individual "events" within those videos. To preserve as much information as possible, the aggregation of the event data should be avoided.

D3: Support Rapid Playback of Video Results

Playing back the selected video clips should be both immediate to start, and then advance quickly through the clips. Only the relevant parts of a clip should be played, and the next clip should begin without any noticeable delay. This design goal allows for a user to watch as many relevant events as possible in the shortest amount of time.

D4: Encourage Exploration of the Data

Video Lens should work for users who have predefined, predetermined queries they need to perform, but perhaps more importantly, it should also encourage users to freely explore the data. The system can accomplish this goal by exposing as many unique attributes/data points as possible, employing highly responsive and interactive data controls, and minimizing the "cost" of trying something out.

Metadata Requirements and Processing

We assume that each of the videos in a corpus already has an associated set of metadata pertaining to individual "events" occurring within the video. For example, in a software tutorial video, the relevant "events" might be command invocations [7], and for TV shows or movies the events could be individual scenes [38]. Our implementation requires each event to have a timestamp indicating where in the video it occurs, plus some number of descriptive attributes about the event. The event data is stored in a database.

Individual attributes are classified as *discreet* or *continuous*. *Discreet* attributes have a finite number of possible values, while *continuous* attributes can have any value between a maximum and minimum value. If the discreet values are numerical, the attribute is considered to be *ordered discreet*, otherwise it is *unordered discreet*. These attributes form the basis of how specific events within a video are selected for playback, and how the events are visually represented throughout the interface.

Interface Elements

The *Video Lens* interface consists of four main components: three data viewing/filtering components, and the video playback window.

The UI elements in each data viewing/filtering component are tightly linked to each other so that hovering over events in one view highlights them in the other views, and selections in one view are immediately represented in the others. In response to our desire to treat events as the primary entity (*D2*), a constant mapping of "1 dot = 1 event" is followed. That is, a single dot in any of the viewing/filtering UI elements always represents a single event. Additionally, a red dot is universally used to highlight the event currently being played.

Single-Attribute Controller (SAC)

Each attribute from the metadata is represented by a single-attribute controller (*SAC*). Each *SAC* has a relatively short height (20 pixels) to allow for many to be stacked vertically on the display and help maximize information density (*D1*). Each *SAC* has a label with the attribute's name on the left, and a value strip showing the attribute values on the right (Figure 2).

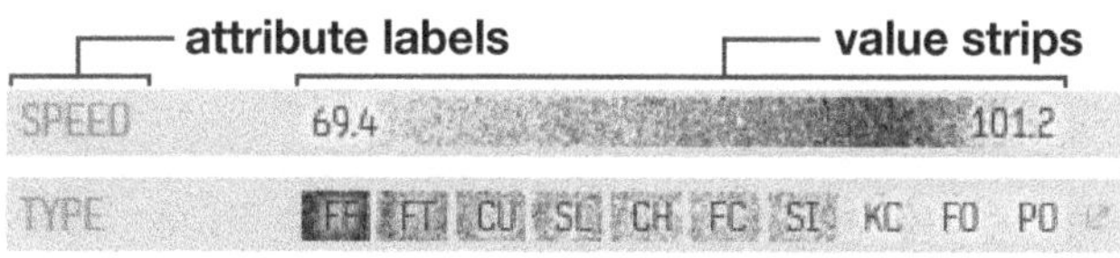

Figure 2. Two example Single-Attribute Controllers. On top, "Speed" is a *continuous* attribute, and on the bottom, "Type" is a *discreet* attribute.

In the value strip, each event is represented by one point. To improve legibility, the opacity of each dot is dynamically lowered as the number of data points increases. The horizontal position of each point is based on the value of the variable for each event. For *continuous* variables the horizontal position is based on the value's relative position between the minimum and maximum values of the attribute, and for *discreet* variables, the value strip is divided into discreet buckets, with the point placed randomly within the width of the proper bucket. With *ordered discreet* variables the buckets are sorted numerically, while *unordered discreet* variables are sorted from highest to lowest by the number of events in each category. For all variable types, the vertical position of each dot is randomly chosen.

Real-Time Brushing

As the cursor moves over a value strip, the events at the cursor position are placed into a "hovered" state. For *discreet* variables, all events within the same bucket as the cursor are considered hovered. While the cursor is moving over one *SAC*, the value strips on all other *SACs* are faded, and the hovered events are highlighted (Figure 3).

This "linking" behavior between multiple plots [2, 3] is typically done in combination with "brushing" or selecting data in one data view, and then applying the highlighting effect to the selected points in the other views. Our real-time hover based approach can expose the user to interactions between the attributes that they may not have even been looking for, thereby encouraging exploration of the dataset (*D4*).

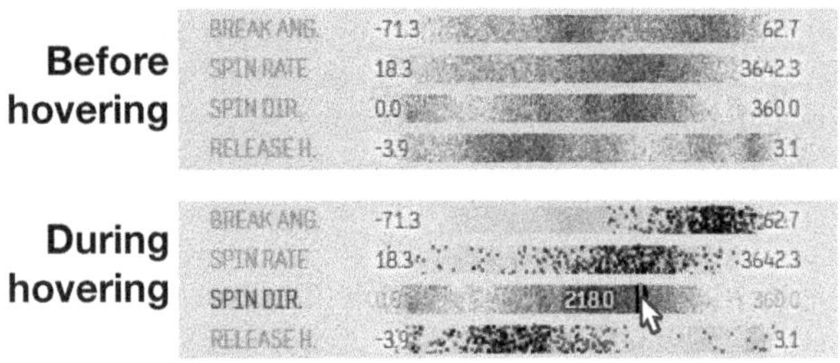

Figure 3. A collection of SACs before and during a hover operation.

Filtering

Filtering the events based on a single attribute is primarily accomplished through clicking or dragging within the value strip. In a *continuous SAC*, clicking selects a very narrow slice of the data range (Figure 4, top), and click-dragging selects a broader region (Figure 4, middle). In a *discreet SAC*, clicking selects all the points in a discreet bucket, and dragging in *discreet SACs* is only supported when the data is *ordered. Discreet* attributes have an icon to the right of the value track which launches a dialog allowing for multiple selections (Figure 4, bottom). Once a selection has been made in a SAC, the areas which have been filtered out are indicated with a hatched background pattern. Additionally, a "clear" icon appears to the left of the attribute label to clear the selection from this attribute (Figure 4).

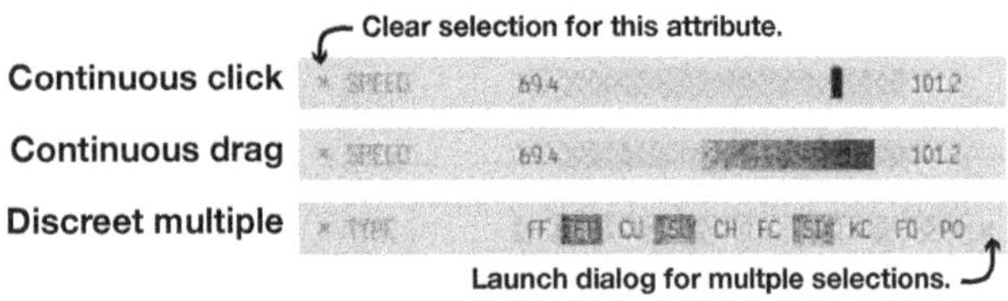

Figure 4. Example selections made in *continuous* and *discreet* Single-attribute Controllers.

Search and Highlight

Since the *Video Lens* framework supports and encourages the inclusion of many attributes (*D1)*, finding a particular event type may be difficult. A real-time search field allows for searching within the attribute names, tooltips, and discreet value labels. As text is entered in the search box, the label or "launch selection dialog" button for any matching *SAC* is highlighted as are any matching entries in the variable selection dialog (Figure 5).

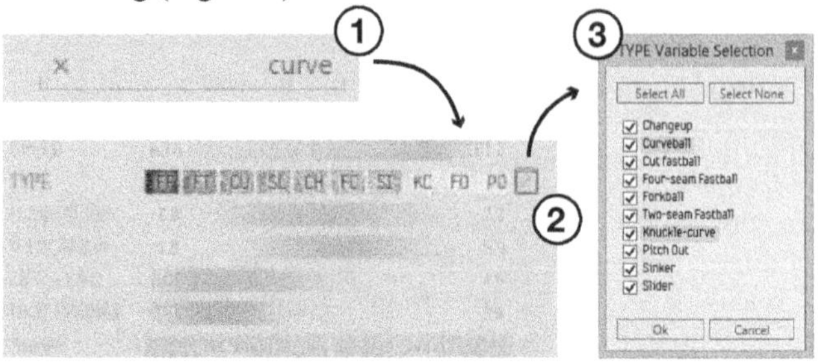

Figure 5. Workflow of the search/highlight feature.

Multi-Attribute Grid (MAG)

The top-right corner of the interface contains a Multi-Attribute Grid (*MAG*) component (Figure 6). The main area of the *MAG* is a two-dimensional grid with an attribute mapped to each of the horizontal and vertical axes. Within the grid are points mapped to each of the events in the active collection (Figure 6B,C). Besides the horizontal and vertical axes, attributes can also be mapped to the color and size of the individual points (Figure 6D,E). These mappings are set by dragging an attribute label from a *Single Attribute Controller* onto one of the four variable dimensions on the *Multi Attribute Grid* (horizontal axis, vertical axis, color, size). The simple interaction of dragging *SAC* labels onto dimensions of the *MAG* encourages exploration of the data (*D4*). The *MAG* also contains controls to clear the current selection, reset the application state, and to save/load specific views (Figure 6H).

For continuous attributes the grid is scaled so the minimum and maximum values span the entire length of the axis. When one axis is mapped to a discreet variable, the axis is split into a set of groups with a small gap between categories (Figure 7, bottom left, bottom right). With both axes mapped to discreet variables, the plot is divided into a number of equal sized cells (Figure 7, top right). Within the grid, events are selected with a lasso (Figure 6F). As with the *SACs*, while hovering the cursor over the *MAG*, the events under the area around the cursor are highlighted in the other event visualizing UI components.

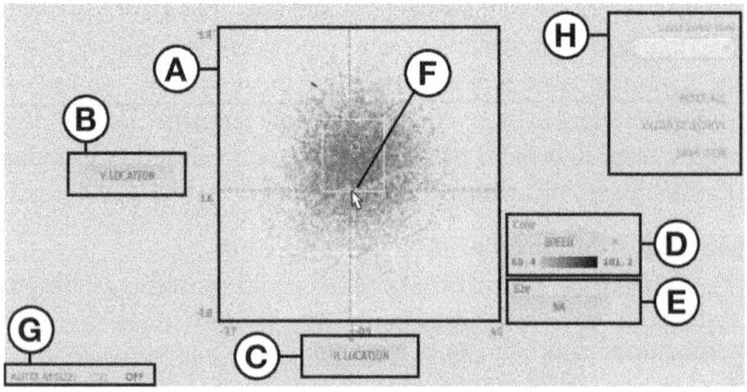

Figure 6. Elements within the Multi-Attribute Grid (MAG) area of the interface.

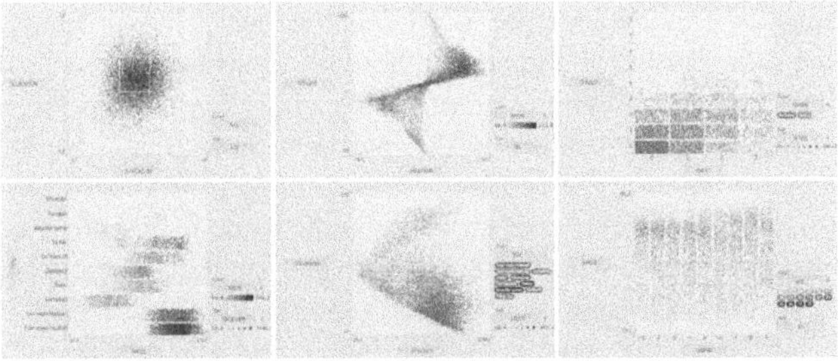

Figure 7. Examples of Multi-Attribute Grid with different combinations of attributes mapped to the dimensions.

The color dimension will accept any facet type, and colors each dot using a coloring scheme based on the variable type (Figure 8). When a discreet variable is used for the color dimensions, small 'pill' buttons show only the values of the attribute which are present in the currently set of events. Hovering over an individual value highlights those events in the grid (and other UI components), and clicking on one filters the selection down to only those matching events. The size dimension is only available for continuous variables.

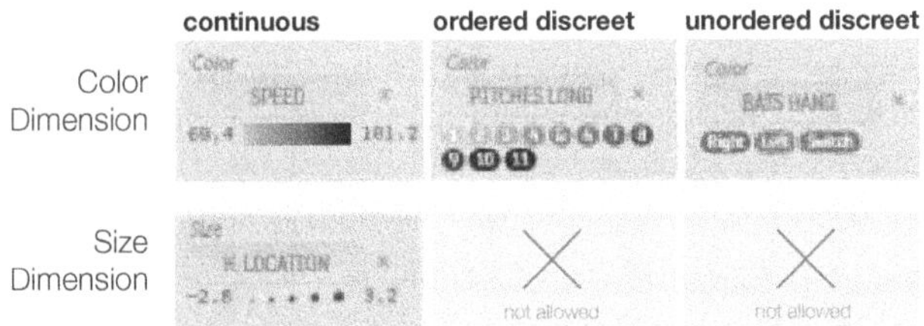

Figure 8. Color and Size dimension appearances for each of the attribute variable types.

Video Timelines

The final set of UI components displaying the events are a set of *video timelines*. There is one timeline for each video in the collection. The events are placed along the timeline based on their timestamp (Figure 9). A scroll bar is used if there are more videos in the collection than will fit on the screen. Hovering, clicking, and dragging operations on the timeline work much the same way as they do for the *SACs*; they highlight and select a set of events. Clicking on the video description label selects all events in the video, and an 'x' icon clears the selection made in the video timeline.

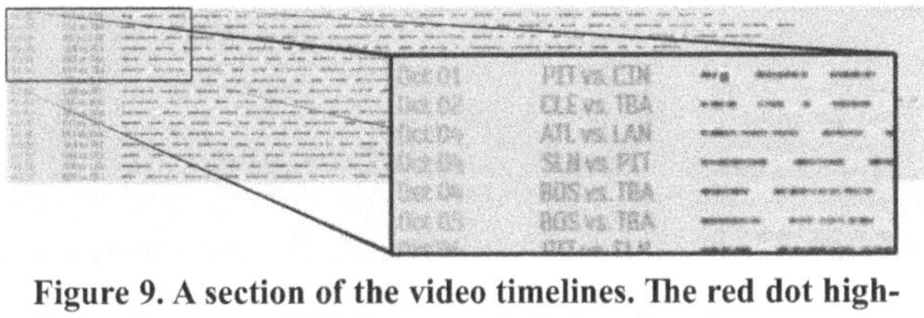

Figure 9. A section of the video timelines. The red dot highlights the event which is currently being played.

Video Playback

The relevant video segments are played in the top-left corner of the interface (Figure 10). Clicking on the video will pause and resume playback. Controls below the video allow the user to manually move forward and back through the collection of clips (Figure 10A). Semi-transparent overlays shows general information about the currently playing clip (Figure 10B), and specific values for the attributes which have filters applied to them (Figure 10C).

By default, the selected events are played back automatically, advancing from one segment to the next once the first event has finished. This is referred to as the *variable* auto-advance setting, since each event is played for a variable amount of time depending on the length of the event. Options are also available to display 1 second or 3 seconds from the start of the event for cases where only the beginning of an event is of interest. Auto-advance can also be disabled completely giving the viewer control over when to view the next clip.

Figure 10. Video Playback section of the interface.

When initializing playback of a video at a specific location, the video decoder requires some amount of time to load the video, and queue playback to the desired start location. To support rapid playback of the results (*D3*), it is important to eliminate the delay between clips. Video Lens uses two video players (*Player$_1$*, *Player$_2$*) overlaid at the same location on the screen. To the viewer there appears to be only one video player. While *Player$_1$* is in the foreground playing video clip C_n which has a duration of D_n, *Player$_2$* is in the background loading the next video clip C_{n+1} and beginning playback D_n seconds before the actual start time of C_{n+1}. This way, once C_n is complete, C_{n+1} is already loaded and playing at the start time of the next event. The video players seamlessly swap, with *Player$_1$* going to the background and preloading the next clip, C_{n+2} (Figure 11).

To accommodate delays in the loading of the background video, either due to network latency or vide decoding, a timer fires every .25s to check the playback position of the background video player against where playback should be, and the playhead position is adjusted if needed.

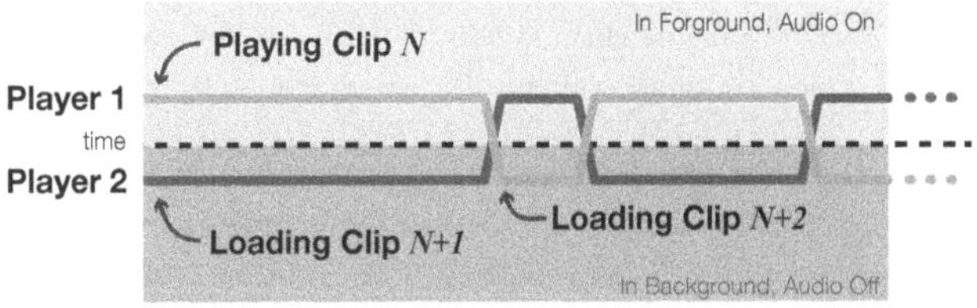

Figure 11. The next video clip in a sequence is always being preloaded by a second background video player.

BVL: BASEBALL VIDEO LENS

Conceptually, the *Video Lens* framework is general enough to accommodate any large set of videos with metadata. In practice however, an implementation for any specific usage domain may impose unique design challenges.

As a test case for the *Video Lens* framework we created *BVL*, or *Baseball Video Lens*. In general, sports are a popular test bed for visualization systems [19, 20, 22], and we chose baseball as the target domain due to the large amounts of professional baseball video produced each year and the depth of event-based metadata which has become available for these games in recent years.

The *BVL* system is designed with two main usage types in mind: *casual* usage by serious baseball fans, and *professional* use by baseball teams, broadcaster organizations, or journalists. While each of these user groups have different goals (Table 1), they all have a need/desire to find collections of clips within a large set of baseball videos.

CASUAL	SERIOUS BASEBALL FANS Find clips they like; *Watch all the times their favorite player hit a homerun.* Quickly watch a game; *Watch the events from game, but skip downtime between pitches.*
PROFESSIONAL USERS	BASEBALL TEAMS/FRONT OFFICE Advanced scouting on next opponent; *Where does tomorrow's pitcher usually throw his curveball?* Self assessment; *Why is our player having trouble hitting inside fastballs?*
	BROADCAST ORGANIZATIONS Find the clip of the last time a particular circumstance occurred. *Show the clip of the last time somebody hit a ball over 400 feet but only got a single.*
	JOURNALISTS/BLOGGERS Collect all the occurrences of an interesting event for a story; *Look at all the pitches that bounced before the plate yet resulted in a hit. Watch the lowest pitches hit for a homerun last year.*

Table 1. Sample use cases of the Baseball Video Lens system for each of the target user groups.

Implementation

The Video Lens framework is a C# Microsoft WPF application. The metadata is stored on the Amazon AWS cloud, and to simplify implementation, all videos are stored locally.

Data Collection

For this initial prototype version of *BVL*, we use a collection of 29 baseball games from the 2013 MLB playoffs. The "pitch" is considered the primary even type in the data, so throughout the interface the visual convention is "1 dot = 1 pitch". The total length of video in the corpus is 105 hours, and a total of 7983 pitches were thrown. The metadata for these events were obtained from the "PITCHf/x" system [6] and the MLB Advanced Media department XML files [24], both freely available for download. Together these data sources provide a wealth of pitch and game-based metadata. We downloaded and imported these files into a database with the structure shown in Figure 12. We chose to expose a large subset (43) of attributes in the interface, as well as three attributes which were dynamically computed from other fields (distance from center of strike zone, distance from corner of strike zone, and whether or not the batter swung at the pitch). A specific implementation could tune the number of visible attributes to the expertise level of the target user group.

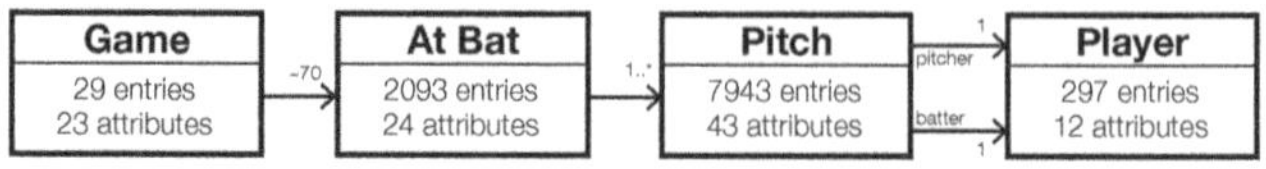

Figure 12. Object classes and relationships from the baseball dataset.

The metadata contains a timestamp for the beginning of each pitch, but no indication of the length of each event. To support rapid playback (*D3*), we need at least an estimate of how long a viewer would like to watch each play. Ideally we could manually determine an "end time" for each event, but even for a small set of events this is not practical. To estimate event lengths at a higher level, two authors independently watched a number of clips for each *at bat* type (home run, strikeout, etc.). For each play, they recorded when they considered the play to be "over". Based on these timings, nominal event lengths for each *at bat* type were determined.

Timeline Alignment/Audio Analysis

To synchronize the events with the video, we need timestamps of each event. Unfortunately our meta-data only provides the time-of-day for each event (8:32:12PM, for example). One method to coordinate the times is to manually mark the time of the first event relative to the beginning of the video. This offset could then be applied to all remaining events. However, even for a small collection of videos this is a time consuming and error prone process.

To develop an automatic process, we leveraged the audio track of the videos. Within the audio there is a noticeable spike from the "crack of the bat" when a pitch is hit, as well as when the ball hits the catcher's glove (Figure 13).

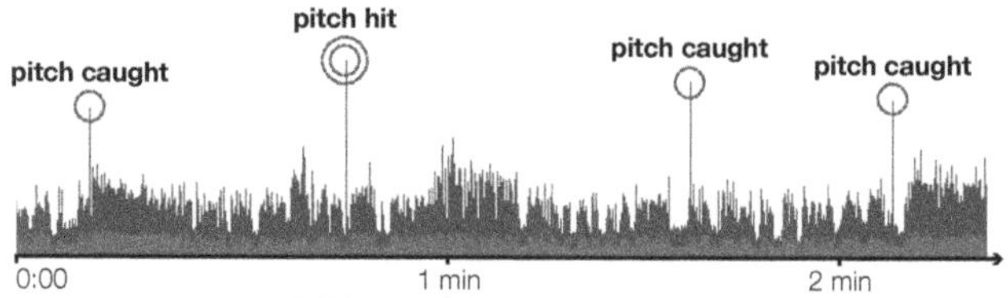

Figure 13. Audio waveform from a 2:15 long section of a baseball game showing the spikes during pitch events.

To detect these spikes we perform a sweep over the audio track at a resolution of 20ms, looking for peaks greater than 2 times the average amplitude of the previous 3 seconds. This gives a collection of "probable pitch events". The system then looks at possible offsets for the metadata file ranging between 0 and 45 minutes, in steps of 1/24th of a second (equivalent to one frame of video). At each step a simple fitness function calculates how well the metadata timing fits to the "probable pitch event" data. The fitness function looks at the time of each pitch in the metadata plus the current offset. If the set of probable pitch times contains an entry within 0.5 seconds of that time, the fitness score is incremented. At the end of each iteration, the fitness score indicates how many pitches in the metadata found a "match" in the probable pitches extracted from the audio, and the time with the highest score is used as the offset for the game (Figure 14).

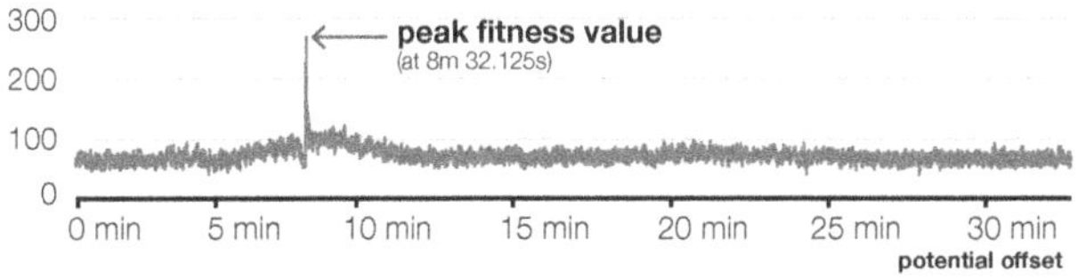

Figure 14. Graph of fitness values for a single game over a range of possible metadata offset times, with the maximum fitness value and time highlighted.

This technique worked to automatically align all 29 game videos with their metadata. The calculations took less than a second per game on a workstation computer.

Timing Micro Adjustments

Another limitation in our timing metadata is that time is rounded to the nearest second. In casual viewing situations one could start playback 2 or 3 seconds before the actual pitch event to ensure the pitch is seen. However, since one of the goals for *Video Lens* is to watch as many events as possible in the shortest amount of time (*D3*), we desired a more accurate solution.

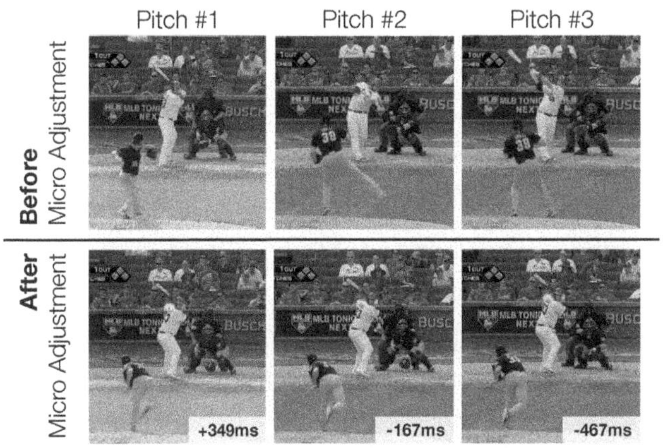

Figure 15. Frame 0.5 sec into clip for using the *one second* auto-advance mode for three pitches *before* and *after* the audio-based timing micro adjustments are applied. (Note the varied position of the pitcher and batter in the *before* row, and the consistent positions *after*.)

We again used the detection of probable pitches through the audio track to calculate the exact pitch times at a finer resolution. For example, if the metadata reports the pitch occurred 38 seconds after the first pitch, but a spike is detected at 38.375 seconds, we adjust time of the pitch in the metadata to 38.375. When using the *one second* auto-advance setting, the video begins playback 0.7 seconds before the pitch reaches the plate and continues for 0.3 seconds afterwards. Figure 15 shows the frame 0.5 seconds into the clip for three consecutive pitches before, and after, the micro adjustments are applied.

The algorithm was able to successfully find a "probable pitch event" within the appropriate time window and apply the timing micro adjustment to 94% of the pitch events in the database.

Sample Tasks

To demonstrate several ways in which the *BVL* system can be used, we now provide a walkthrough of how to complete three representative tasks.

Task 1: Watch the lowest pitches hit for a homerun

First, the user filters the "at bat event type" to only show the homeruns (Figure 16, Step 1). Then the user makes a lasso selection around the lowest points in the Multi-Attribute Grid (Figure 16, Step 2), which is by default mapped to the horizontal and vertical location of the pitch. Alternatively, the user could select the lowest values in the "V. Location" *single-attribute controller* (Figure 16, Step 2 alternate). The three homerun clips immediately play in the video player.

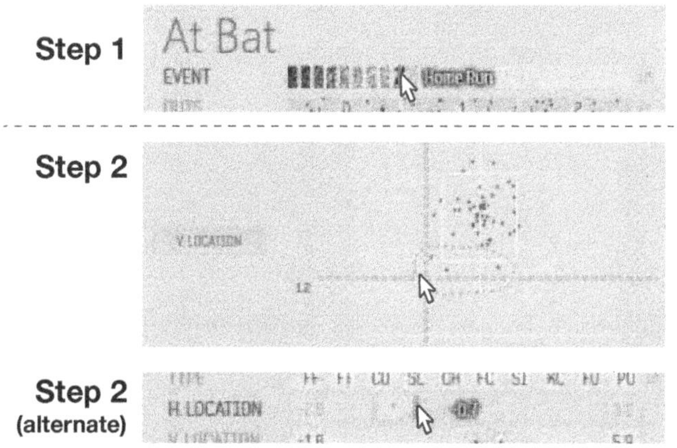

Figure 16. Watching the lowest pitches hit for a homerun.

Task 2: Watch all strikeouts in a particular game

For this task we are going to watch all strikeouts in the October 2nd game between the Tampa Bay Rays and the Cleveland Indians. The user could first click on the video timeline label for the "OCT 2 CLE vs TBA" game (Figure 17, Step 1). At this point the video player displays all pitches from this game, and using the *variable* timing auto-advance mode, would give the viewer a quick way to watch the recap of an entire game. To watch only the strikeouts, the user would filter the "at bat event type" to show only strikeouts (Figure 17, Step 2). Due to the faceted nature of the filtering interface, these two steps could be done in either order.

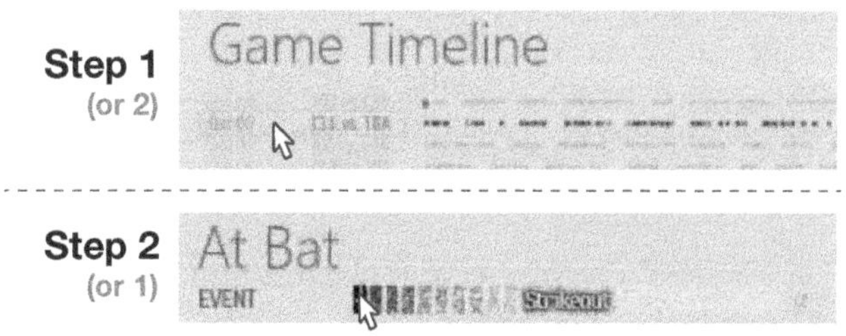

Figure 17. Watching all strikeouts in a particular game.

Task 3: Analyze the release points of Jon Lester's pitches
This is the type of task baseball teams often do for "advance scouting" of their opponent. In this case we imagine that we are playing against Jon Lester tomorrow and want to see what we can learn about how he pitches.

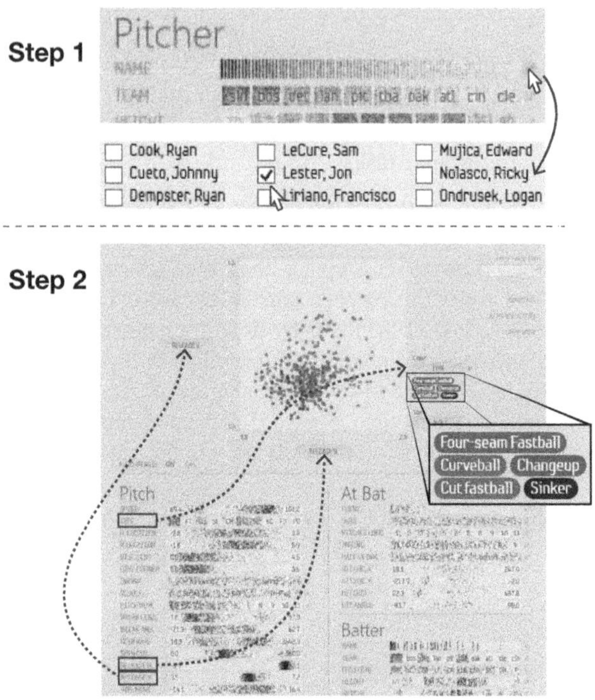

Figure 18. Analyzing the pitches thrown by Jon Lester.

The first step is to filter the "pitcher name" attribute to "Lester, Jon" (Figure 18, Step 1). Then, we drag the "Release H." and "Release V." attributes, representing the horizontal and vertical position of the ball as it leaves the pitcher's hand, up to the *MAG*. At this point we see the location where all of the pitches were released. To look for patterns, we drag the "pitch type" attribute to the *color* dimension (Figure 18, Step 2). Now we can see that the pitcher releases his curveballs from a higher position than his other pitches. This information can increase the batters chance of getting a hit [44]. At this point the clips of all Jon Lester pitches are playing, so we can watch the video and verify these visual tells.

EVALUATION

To evaluate the *BVL* system, we recruited members from each of the four target user groups (Table 1).

Qualitative User Study

We first wanted to get feedback on the *BVL* system for recreational use by serious baseball fans. We recruited 12 paid volunteers (2 women) between the ages of 27-50 (mean 32) who classified themselves as "baseball fanatics". Participants reported watching an average of 15 hours of baseball-related programming per week, and 11 of the 12 watch baseball videos on a secondary device such as a tablet or phone. Additionally, 8 of the 12 participants subscribe to MLB.TV, a paid service which provides access to all games and highlights throughout the MLB season.

The study took approximately 45 minutes and was conducted on a desktop computer driving a 42" LCD. For the first 10 minutes the proctor demonstrated the features of the system, followed by 5 minutes for the participant to explore the system and ask the proctor questions. For the final 30 minutes the participants worked through a series of 18 tasks (including the three described in the previous section) (Figure 19). Some tasks were adapted from a series of posts on a popular blog for analytics-minded baseball fans. The collection of tasks was designed to utilize the full set of functionality available in the system. Participants were timed from when they began the task until the system was set up to view the resulting clips. After the study tasks, participants were given 5 minutes to experiment with the system before completing a post-study questionnaire.

Participants were able to complete 7 of the 18 tasks in a median time less than 30 seconds, and 16 of the 18 tasks in a median completion time less than 1 minute (Figure 19). The two most difficult tasks used attributes the participants were not necessarily familiar with. The increased time for these tasks was mostly due to the participants thinking through the task and coming up with an optimal strategy.

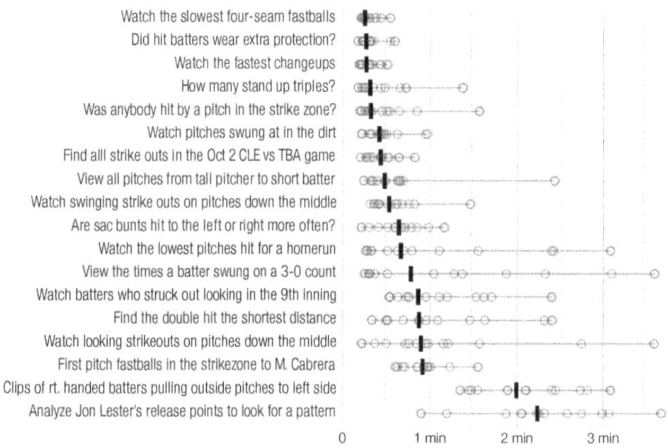

Figure 19. Completion times for each of the study tasks. Median time shown with black bar.

The subjective results are shown in Figure 20. Participants were positive about the system, all saying they found the system enjoyable to use, and 11 out of 12 said that they would use the system if it were available to them; *"This is amazing! If I had this I would lose entire days using it.* (P2)*"*.

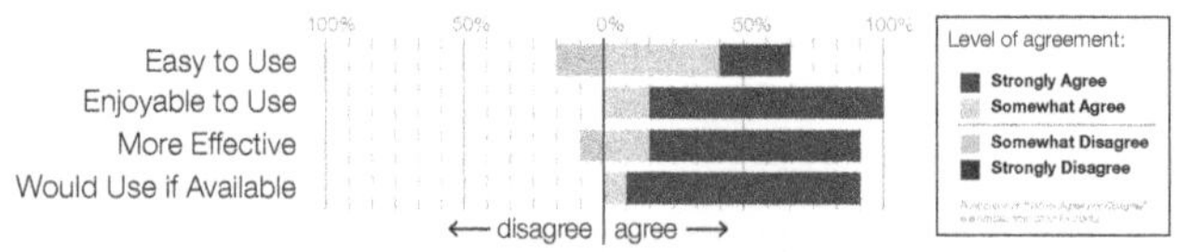

Figure 20. Subjective results from participant survey.

Participants were generally impressed with the set of video-browsing tasks which were made possible by our system, with one participant saying he *"...would have no idea how to even begin finding these clips without this system* (P6)*"*.

Despite the large number of UI elements in the interface, participants found the interface generally easy to use: *"It is remarkable how easy it is to go from the huge collection of pitches down to the couple of things you want* (P3)*"*. They were also genuinely interested viewing the clips they found during the study, even though they were free to move on to the next task once the query was set up. In fact, 4 of the 12 participants asked in the middle of the study if they could try a query of their own, sparked by one of the study tasks. While they were asked to wait until the study was over, this reinforces the idea that they really would like to have access to such a system.

Professional User Feedback

To get feedback on the suitability of the *BVL* system from users in a professional context, we recruited members from the three identified professional user groups. We recruited baseball analysts from two MLB teams (MLB1, MLB2), a writer/editor from a popular baseball analytics website (WR1), and a researcher from a major sports broadcasting organization (BR1). We sent each a copy of the system to experiment with on their own time, and a short video and document explaining how the system worked. After they had a chance to use the system, feedback was provided to us through a phone interview or written questionnaire.

Overall, the response from the professional users was encouraging. After seeing a two minute video of the system in action, WR1's initial response was *"holy god damn that's incredible."* Given the chance to use the program, WR1 appreciated the ease of which he could try new things, *"The tool essentially lets me play. I can go exploring, like you would through the woods. It would prompt questions I might not have ever even thought of asking."* Many of WR1's articles contain animated .gifs for a collection of events. His current workflow involves finding the events from a database, loading up MLB.tv, playing the appropriate game, and manually finding the event. WR1 stated that *BVL* could *"conceivably save [me] hours a week."*

From a broadcasting perspective, BR1 said that finding video clips based on event metadata is something that he currently needs to do, and that he could see the *BVL* system being useful for broadcasting organizations. His organization currently uses a custom-made, internally-designed tool for these sorts of tasks, but he liked the speed in which *BVL* was able to access and display the clips. He suggested that in broadcasting the key is to get to the clips quickly (rather than exploring the data), and that a version of *BVL* with less attributes might be more suitable in a broadcasting scenario.

From the perspective of professional baseball teams, both MLB1 and MLB2 felt the *BVL* system was something that would be useful for MLB teams, and without any hands-on training, were comfortable using the system within a couple of minutes. Both organizations have existing proprietary solutions they currently use for these types of tasks.

In particular, MLB1 liked the *"flow"* of the *BVL* system and mentioned *"The UI is really nice. Visualizing the ranges of the variables makes it easy to eliminate the things I don't want."* MLB1 also liked the immediacy in which he could get results, as the system his team currently uses requires him to set up the entire query up front, and then wait up to a minute before the results are presented to him. MLB2 suggested that for maximum utility for MLB teams, it would need to be integrated with existing scouting and statistical databases.

DISCUSSION AND FUTURE WORK

The main function of the *Video Lens* is to allow users to find and view relevant video clips. Visualizing the attribute values in the various UI components are primarily meant to aid in the workflow of selecting a set of events to watch. However, several participants saw on opportunity to extend the system to also answer more analytical questions (e.g. "What percentage of curve balls are hit for home runs?").

Another common request was the ability to see "what happens next". For example, P1 wanted to see all the pitches Clayton Kershaw threw *after* he threw a curveball. This type of functionality, along with options for sorting the clip order during playback would be useful additions.

To represent the distribution of values within the *Single Attribute Controllers* we looked at several other visual encodings besides the overplotted dots, including area charts, line graphs, and 1D colored histograms. Besides the benefit of maintaining continuity with the dot/event representation of the *Video Timelines* and *Multi Attribute Grid* components, the dots also provided the clearest representation of outlying data values, which are often the most interesting ones to watch. We would like to continue exploring the benefits of this style of visual representation.

Our implementation of the baseball video lens raised several interesting domain specific challenges. We believe *Video Lens* could be adapted to other usage domains, but similar domain-specific issues should be expected. For example, we addressed the timing discrepancies using audio information specific to baseball. It would be interesting to explore what audio/visual clues could be used to perform the task of aligning metadata in other domains. Perhaps for soccer we could use the increased volume of the fans and announcers [35], or for software tutorials we could analyze the position and appearance of the cursor and buttons [1].

Overall, we believe the *Video Lens* framework represents a valuable solution for exploring a large collection of metadata rich video content, and the *Baseball Video Lens* system can serve as a baseline example for future work in this area.

REFERENCES

1. Banovic, N., Grossman, T., Matejka, J., and Fitzmaurice, G. Waken: Reverse Engineering Usage Information and Interface Structure from Software Videos. *ACM UIST*, (2012), 83–92.
2. Becker, R.A. and Cleveland, W.S. Brushing Scatterplots. *Technometrics 29*, 2 (1987), 127–142.
3. Buja, A., McDonald, J.A., Michalak, J., and Stuetzle, W. Interactive Data Visualization Using Focusing and Linking. *IEEE VIS*, (1991), 156–163.

4. Capra, R.G. and Marchionini, G. The Relation Browser Tool for Faceted Exploratory Search. *ACM JCDL '08*, (2008), 420–420.
5. Derthick, M. Interactive Visualization of Video Metadata. *ACM JCDL '01*, (2001), 453–.
6. Fast, M. What the heck is PITCHf/x. *The Hardball Times Annual*, (2010), 153–8.
7. Grossman, T., Matejka, J., and Fitzmaurice, G. Chronicle: Capture, Exploration, and Playback of Document Workflow Histories. *ACM UIST '10*, (2010), 143–152.
8. Hearst, M. UIs for Faceted Navigation: Recent Advances and Remaining Open Problems. *Int. Journal of Machine Learning and Computing*, (2008), 337–343.
9. Jackson, D., Nicholson, J., Stoeckigt, G., Wrobel, R., Thieme, A., and Olivier, P. Panopticon: A Parallel Video Overview System. *ACM UIST '13*, (2013), 123–130.
10. Kim, J., Nguyen, P., Weir, S., Guo, P.J., Miller, R.C., and Gajos, K.Z. Crowdsourcing step-by-step information extraction to enhance existing how-to videos. *CHI*, (2014).
11. Koren, J., Zhang, Y., and Liu, X. Personalized Interactive Faceted Search. *ACM WWW '08*, (2008), 477–486.
12. Lafreniere, B., Grossman, T., Matejka, J., and Fitzmaurice, G. Investigating the Feasibility of Extracting Tool Demonstrations from In-Situ Video Content. *CHI, 2014*.
13. Lee, B., Smith, G., Robertson, G.G., Czerwinski, M., and Tan, D.S. FacetLens: Exposing Trends and Relationships to Support Sensemaking Within Faceted Datasets. *ACM CHI*, (2009), 1293–1302.
14. Matejka, J., Grossman, T., and Fitzmaurice, G. Ambient Help. *ACM CHI*, (2011), 2751–2760.
15. Matejka, J., Grossman, T., and Fitzmaurice, G. Swift: Reducing the Effects of Latency in Online Video Scrubbing. *ACM CHI*, (2012), 637–646.
16. Matejka, J., Grossman, T., and Fitzmaurice, G. Swifter: Improved Online Video Scrubbing. *CHI*, (2013).
17. Monserrat, T.-J.K.P., Zhao, S., McGee, K., and Pandey, A.V. NoteVideo: Facilitating Navigation of Blackboard-style Lecture Videos. *ACM CHI*, (2013), 1139–1148.
18. Olsen, D.R., Partridge, B., and Lynn, S. Time Warp Sports for Internet Television. *ACM Trans. Comput.-Hum. Interact. 17*, 4 (2010), 16:1–16:37.
19. Perin, C., Vuillemot, R., and Fekete, J.-D. SoccerStories: A Kick-off for Visual Soccer Analysis. *IEEE Trans. on Vis. and Computer Graphics 19*, 12 (2013), 2506–2515.
20. Pileggi, H., Stolper, C.D., Boyle, J.M., Stasko, J.T., and Member, S. SnapShot: Visualization to Propel Ice Hockey Analytics. *IEEE Vis* (2012).
21. Pongnumkul, S., Dontcheva, M., Li, W., et al. Pause-and-play: Automatically Linking Screencast Video Tutorials with Applications. *ACM UIST*, (2011), 135–144.
22. Rao, R. and Card, S.K. The Table Lens: Merging Graphical and Symbolic Representations in an Interactive Focus + Context Visualization for Tabular Information. *ACM CHI '94*, (1994), 318–322.
23. Schoeffmann, K., Taschwer, M., and Boeszoermenyi, L. The Video Explorer: A Tool for Navigation and Searching Within a Single Video Based on Fast Content Analysis. *ACM MMSys '10*, (2010), 247–258.
24. Schumaker, R.P., Solieman, O.K., and Chen, H. Web Sports Data Extraction and Visualization. In *Sports Data Mining*. Springer, 2010, 71–87.
25. Smeaton, A.F., Over, P., and Kraaij, W. Evaluation campaigns and TRECVid. *MIR '06:* (2006), 321–330.
26. Song, Y., Hua, X.-S., Dai, L.-R., and Wang, M. Semi-automatic Video Annotation Based on Active Learning with Multiple Complementary Predictors. *MIR* (2005).
27. Stone, B. MLB.TV Adds Enhanced Video and User-Selected Replays. *The New York Times*, 2009. http://www.nytimes.com/2009/02/09/technology/internet/09mlb.html.
28. Stuart-Moore, J., Evans, M., and Jacobs, P. Interface Design for Browsing Faceted Metadata. *JCDL* , (2006).
29. Vandic, D., Frasincar, F., and Kaymak, U. Facet Selection Algorithms for Web Product Search. *CIKM*, (2013).
30. Voigt, M., Werstler, A., Polowinski, J., and Meißner, K. Weighted Faceted Browsing for Characteristics-based Visualization Selection Through End Users. *EICS*, 2012.
31. Worring, M., Nguyen, G.P., Hollink, L., Van Gemert, J.C., and Koelma, D.C. Accessing video archives using interactive search. *ICME*, (2004), 297–300 Vol.1.
32. Yee, K.P., Swearingen, K., Li, K., & Hearst, M. Faceted metadata for image search and browsing. *CHI*, 2003.
33. Ben-Yitzhak, O., Yogev, S., Golbandi, N., et al. Beyond basic faceted search. *WSDM*, (2008).
34. Van Zwol, R., Ng, P., Ramani, A., et al. Faceted exploration of image search results. *WWW*, (2010).
35. Efficient Multimodal Features for Automatic Soccer Highlight Generation. *IEEE ICPR*, (2004), 973–976.
36. selfiecity. *selfiecity*, 2014. http://selfiecity.net/.
37. NBA Stats - Stats Video. http://stats.nba.com/statsVideo.html.
38. TVplus | Synced Metadata. http://www.tvplus.com/#!synced-metadata/c11fw.
39. Baseball Savant: Your Source For Advanced MLB Statistics. http://baseballsavant.com/pitchfx_search.php.
40. BATS, Sydex Software. http://www.sydexsports.com/html/baseball.html.
41. College Football 2012-2013 Season Highlights (Part 1) | Catches, Hits, Fails, Amazing Plays Etc. - YouTube. https://www.youtube.com/watch?v=PlDtqO1hR3k.
42. Kramer's Entrance - YouTube. https://www.youtube.com/watch?v=XXSGV5wEv1o.
43. David Letterman: "Are Those Your Drums?" - YouTube. https://www.youtube.com/watch?v=M65Dx0STe2M.
44. Interpreting PITCHf/x Charts | FanGraphs Sabermetrics Library. http://www.fangraphs.com/library/interpreting-pitchfx-charts/.

Glance: Rapidly Coding Behavioral Video with the Crowd

Walter S. Lasecki
Computer Science Department
University of Rochester
wlasecki@cs.rochester.edu

Mitchell Gordon
Computer Science Department
University of Rochester
m.gordon@rochester.edu

Danai Koutra
Computer Science Department
Carnegie Mellon University
danai@cs.cmu.edu

Malte F. Jung
Information Science
Cornell University
mfj28@cornell.edu

Steven P. Dow
HCI Institute
Carnegie Mellon University
spdow@cs.cmu.edu

Jeffrey P. Bigham
HCI and LT Institutes
Carnegie Mellon University
jbigham@cs.cmu.edu

ABSTRACT
Behavioral researchers spend considerable amount of time coding video data to systematically extract meaning from subtle human actions and emotions. In this paper, we present Glance, a tool that allows researchers to rapidly query, sample, and analyze large video datasets for behavioral events that are hard to detect automatically. Glance takes advantage of the parallelism available in paid online crowds to interpret natural language queries and then aggregates responses in a summary view of the video data. Glance provides analysts with rapid responses when initially exploring a dataset, and reliable codings when refining an analysis. Our experiments show that Glance can code nearly 50 minutes of video in 5 minutes by recruiting over 60 workers simultaneously, and can get initial feedback to analysts in under 10 seconds for most clips. We present and compare new methods for accurately aggregating the input of multiple workers marking the spans of events in video data, and for measuring the quality of their coding in real-time before a baseline is established by measuring the variance between workers. Glance's rapid responses to natural language queries, feedback regarding question ambiguity and anomalies in the data, and ability to build on prior context in followup queries allow users to have a conversation-like interaction with their data – opening up new possibilities for naturally exploring video data.

Author Keywords
Data analysis; subjective coding; crowdsourcing; video

ACM Classification Keywords
H.5.m. Information Interfaces and Presentation: Misc.

INTRODUCTION
Behavioral video coding provides researchers in the social sciences a lens for studying human interactions [3]. In the domain of HCI, for example, researchers use video analysis to

UIST '14, October 05 - 08 2014, Honolulu, HI, USA

ACM 978-1-4503-3069-5/14/10. $15.00.
http://dx.doi.org/10.1145/2642918.2647367

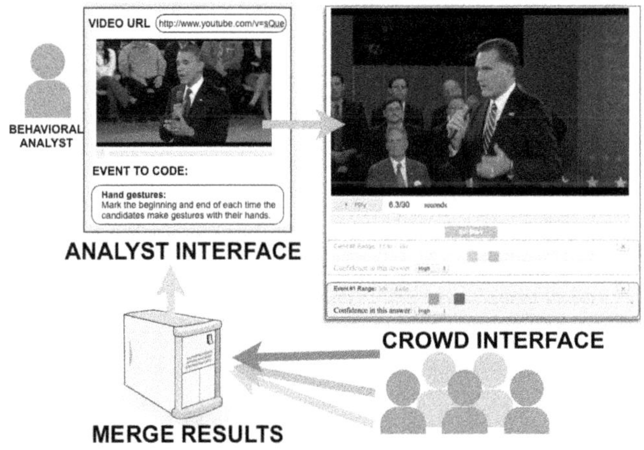

Figure 1. Glance codes behavioral events in video quickly and accurately. When a question is asked, small clips from the video are sent to crowd workers who label events in parallel. The judgments are then quickly merged together and displayed. In this example, we use Glance to count the frequency and duration of eye contact between presidential candidates during a 2012 debate.

study how users interact with computational systems [21, 19] and to develop theories that explain those interactions (e.g., [3, 4]). While video coding affords a systematic measure of behavior, it is notoriously time-consuming. By some accounts, video coding analysis takes 5-10x longer than the play time of video [20]. This does not include the time to develop a reliable coding scheme, to train coders, or to check for inter-rater reliability. Given the high cost and lengthy turnaround required to test a hypothesis, researchers may exhibit sunk-cost reasoning and resist changes to their coding scheme.

Ideally —and maybe eventually —computational approaches will mature to the point of being able to automatically label segments of behavior. However, due to the diverse contexts and subtly interpretive nature of video coding, automated analysis of human behavior currently yields poor results. While commercial video coding tools make this process easier for a research team, they do not eliminate the bottleneck of sequentially viewing all the video [22, 1].

In this paper, we introduce *Glance*, a system that allows researchers to analyze and code events in large video datasets by parallelizing the process across a crowd of online workers (Figure 1). This approach significantly reduces the amount of time required to test a coding hypothesis within video data. Video data can be coded in a fraction of the actual time depending on the size of the available crowd. By distributing the same video segments among multiple workers, Glance can calculate the variance to provide quick feedback result reliability. Glance provides a front-end interface for analysts to enter natural-language queries and to visualize coding results as they arrive.

To evaluate Glance, we coded multiple behavioral events in several different types of video data, including a publicly broadcast political debate and lab-based social science experiment. To investigate the speed of the approach, we coded occurrences of a single type of behavioral event in an hour-long video. Glance produced judgments on a 12 minute-long video in 2 minutes (6× speedup), and coded 48 minutes of video in just 5 minutes (a nearly 10× speedup).

To evaluate accuracy, we coded for the occurrence and time window of variable-length behavioral events and compared them to a gold standard. Using 10 simultaneous workers for each video segment, Glance was able to accurately identify on average over 99% of the event occurrences and estimated the time window of these events within a 1-second margin of error, in terms of both when they occur and for how long.

By dramatically reducing the speed and increasing the reliability of video coding, researchers have the opportunity to interact more "opportunistically" with their data. Glance's interface visualizes coding results in real-time, allowing an analyst to issue new queries, and cancel or re-frame their original one after seeing initial results. The resulting conversational style of interaction allows video analysts to more quickly explore, develop and refine research hypotheses in ways that are not feasible today.

Our contributions can be summarized as follows:

- We propose a conversational interaction paradigm for video coding that leverages crowd workers with minimal expertise to provide rapid judgments on natural language queries about behavioral events in video data.
- We introduce Glance, a video coding tool for researchers that *(i)* recruits and coordinates an online crowd for behavioral coding, *(ii)* segments video data and distributes video coding tasks to individual crowd workers, and *(iii)* collects and visualizes individual judgments and aggregate statistics in real-time.
- We provide experimental evidence via a large study with Amazon Mechanical Turk workers that the crowd can quickly and accurately identify events in video on-demand.
- We demonstrate an end-to-end interaction using Glance to explore real-world data, and show that the results are quick, accurate, and allow analysts to make informed decisions about subsequent steps in their data exploration process.

ENVISIONED INTERACTION

In this section, we overview an envisioned interaction with a video coding system, which inspired Glance, the system that we introduce in this paper.

Alice is a human-computer interaction researcher who wants to analyze 18 hours of video of computer game play sessions to determine if the system she has built improves players' engagement with one another. She begins by opening her behavioral coding software package and loading the video she recorded during her experiments. Once loaded, she asks the system to find all of the times when at least one person was talking in the video. Instantly, indicators appear below the play bar that mark the 75% of her videos that contain someone talking. She then asks the system to find "when two players are engaged with one another". The system responds with several instances as well as a message indicating that the question is too vague and there is low confidence in the reported results. Realizing that she has underspecified the problem, Alice researches the literature for behavioral cues to look for when measuring engagement, and asks the system to find instances of eight such cues. The system returns separate event logs for all eight behaviors, and from this visualization, Alice is able to see that only five of the behaviors occur more than once in her data.

Given the few returned instances, Alice suspects that those might be only a small part of the two-person interactions in the video. For this reason, she asks the system to find all times where two people talk directly to one another, as a subset of the times when people are talking. The system realizes that this is a follow-up query and only checks sections of the video that it knows has someone talking in them. After seeing the results, Alice realizes her suspicions were correct – only about 60% of conversations were coded for the target engagement metrics. Looking at her initial coding scheme, she realizes that she was only coding for positive engagement cues. After doing another search, she tries asking the system to mark a few negative engagement cues during periods where other cues were not found, but that had two players talking to one another. The system returns a number of examples, and Alice is able to see that, at some points, players are fighting with one another about in-game decisions. In further interactions with the system, she is able to make a number of other corrections to her initial assumptions and develop a well-informed coding scheme that other analysts can be trained on to get reportable data for her research.

Alice's interaction with the behavioral coding tool demonstrates a best-case scenario: the system understands natural language queries, replies instantly, gives feedback on the clarity and expected accuracy of queries even when no ground truth is available, and allows follow-up queries as subsets of previous queries – similar to a Q&A conversation.

In this paper, we present a system, Glance, that attempts to bring analysts closer to this type of ideal interaction by using the crowd to provide highly parallelizable on-demand human intelligence when answering queries. But, before we introduce the tool, we review related work and empirically evaluate to what extent the speed and accuracy of crowd-based video coding could support the interaction we envision.

RELATED WORK

Glance is a crowd-powered system that allows users to rapidly iterate on a video coding task. It draws from prior work in both behavioral coding and crowd-powered systems. Prior research in behavioral coding illustrates what would need to be done to approach the envisioned interaction presented in the last section, and work on crowd-powered systems suggests a path for achieving it.

Behavioral Observation and Coding

Observing and coding behavioral events in video is a common research practice in the social sciences, used in fields as diverse as human-computer interaction, linguistics, anthropology, psychotherapy, and child psychology [11, 20]. Systematic observation through video focuses on creating a precise measurement of behavioral streams. To demonstrate rigor, researchers often use "properly trained observers to produce identical protocols, given that they observed the same stream of behavior" [3]. In practice these are often undergraduate students who are given training that may range from a day to multiple weeks for complex events.

Bakeman and Gottman [3] provide a comprehensive introduction into this technique that is largely performed in three steps. First a coding scheme, which defines the set of behavioral categories, has to be developed. This can be done in a bottom-up, top-down approach [34], or, more often, a hybrid approach. In a bottom-up approach the coding scheme is constructed from behavioral features observed during careful viewing and re-viewing of the video, while in a top-down approach it is derived from theory.

The second step is then to train coders. The amount of training required largely depends on the complexity of the coding scheme, and can take up to several weeks or require detailed training curriculum.Training is often seen as a continuous process even after the actual coding has started. For example, Coan and Gottman [11] describe a practice in which coders collectively watch practice videos in order to clarify confusions. We integrate a similar (but shorter) form of training into our tasks to prepare crowd workers.

The final step is then to categorize or "code" the video data according to the coding scheme. At least one independent observer should code some of the videos for a second time to test reliability. Researchers often selectively test inter-rater agreement [12] throughout the process to refine the coding scheme. Practitioners recommend that analysts make several passes through the video data and *code one event type at a time*, in order to avoid missing occurrences [20]. This increases reliability, but also greatly increases the amount of time required to code a video.

Video Coding Tools

Several tools have been developed to support the video coding process, particularly steps two and three described above. For example, ANVIL, Datavyu [1], VACA [9], and VCode [18] all provide an interface for easily annotating audio and video with event tags, and some allow for testing of inter-rater agreement, *but only* for the *overlap* of observed events. Tools such as GSEQ [4] calculate agreement statistics and provide visual feedback for coders.

Despite this growing availability of video coding tools, there is a lack of support for the highly iterative process of developing, testing, and re-visiting a coding scheme . This process can take several times longer than the length of the video content itself, and as a result, researchers invest considerable time in each iteration of their coding scheme. This makes it challenging for researchers to reanalyze video based on initial findings, to thoroughly explore the different types of events, or to modify a coding scheme based on preliminary analysis. In this paper we address these shortcomings by providing tool-support for a process of rapidly iterating and testing coding schemes via the inherent parallelism of the crowd.

Measuring Agreement

Observer agreement describes the degree to which two or more observers agree with each other [3]. This is different from observer reliability that describes the degree to which an observation aligns with an established "truth", such as a baseline observation protocol. Most observational research only assesses agreement, while reliability is assumed given sufficient agreement. Measuring agreement can: (i) indicate the trustworthiness of observations in the data, and (ii) provide feedback to calibrate observers against each other or against baseline observations. If one assumes the baseline to be "true", then observer agreement can be used to assess reliability. A commonplace statistic to assess observer agreement is Cohens Kappa [12] which corrects for chance agreement between two workers.

Crowdsourcing Video Annotations

Crowdsourcing leverages human computation [32] in the form of open calls to paid online workers from platforms such as Amazon's Mechanical Turk. Crowdsourcing has been used on tasks that rely on human judgment and that are difficult for automated systems. For example, Soylent [7] uses the crowd to edit or shorten writing, VizWiz [8] answers questions about photographs quickly, and Legion [24] follows natural language commands to intelligently control a GUI.

The crowd has also been leveraged in the context of activity recognition systems. For instance, VATIC [33] allows crowd workers to tag where objects appear in a scene. While the crowd provides these annotations, it is not designed to respond quickly to the end-user. Similarly, Legion:AR [25, 28] explores crowd labeling of *low-level* actions in video for assistive home monitoring: workers are asked to watch a video stream as it happens live, and then an automated system labels activities soon after they occur. Unlike our approach, Legion:AR does not process video any faster than an individual can, and is designed for use *not* by a human analyst, but by a Hidden Markov Model-based system.Di Salvo et al. [14] added game elements to an annotation task to get the crowd to mark where an object appears. With Glance, workers identify complex or subtle events, and to accurately identify the range over which they occurred.

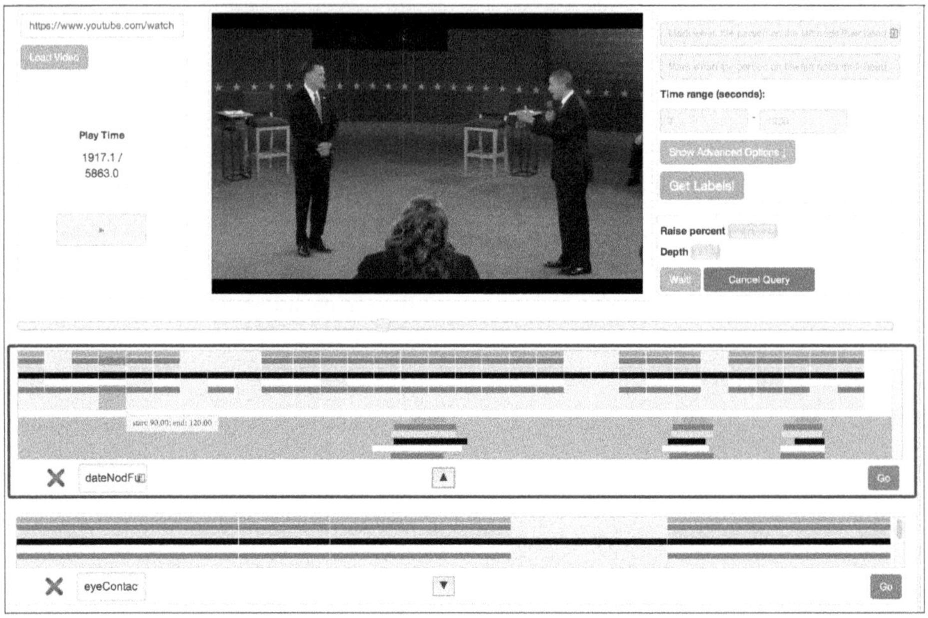

Figure 2. The Glance analyst user interface (AUI). Analysts can load a video from YouTube, ask if or when an event occurs in the video in natural language, and set parameters to control cost and speed. Crowd workers then process this query and return results in a fraction of the playtime of the video. These results are aggregated to simplify the answer for the analyst, and make it more reliable than a single worker's answer.

GLANCE

Glance is a video coding tool that leverages online crowds to produce rapid analyses of video data (Figure 1). To reach envisioned conversation-like interaction with data, Glance allows analysts to ask questions about events in natural language, provides nearly-immediate responses, and supports query refinement by building on known context. We describe the user experience here, then detail the novel technical components in the next sections.

Recruiting a Crowd

When an analyst arrives to Glance's analyst user interface (AUI), shown in Figure 2, the system begins recruiting workers into a retainer using the LegionTools toolkit (http://rochci.github.io/LegionTools/). This retainer allows workers to be available within a matter of seconds of posing a query [8, 6]. To load a video, the analyst provides the system a YouTube link, a link to a video on their own server, or directly uploads a file. The video is immediately loaded into the embedded player, and the query creation tool becomes active.

Posing Queries

When the analyst wants to ask Glance a question about the video, they enter a name for the query and a natural language description of the hypothesized behavioral event. To more clearly specify the sought-after event, the analyst has the option to select one or more parts of the video to serve as examples. These example video segments will then be shown to workers during a short training session.

When a query is posted, Glance sends tasks to multiple crowd workers in parallel and retrieves answers as soon as possible. In order to reduce the cost of these queries, especially during early exploration where complete coverage of the video might not be necessary, Glance lets analysts select a portion of video to focus on. The system also allows analysts to adjust the following parameters:

- **Redundancy.** Glance lets the user control the size of the crowd being used (and thus the cost of the query) in part by selecting a level of redundancy for each query. This defines the number of workers who will label each video clip. If the analyst wants to increase the reliability of the response later in the process, Glance lets them increase the level of redundancy – building upon already completed work.
- **Playback Rate.** For some queries, costs can be reduced by increasing the playback rate of the video. While this is also common practice for current video coding systems, combining it with the parallelism of the crowd can lead to even quicker responses. As increasing playback speed is not practical with all types of data and events, we leave it to analysts to know when it is appropriate to use.
- **Sampling Rate.** To get an initial idea of what types of events occur in a video, Glance lets analysts select a video clip sampling rate. This allows analysts to see how frequently their events arise, without needing to hire workers for a complete run. Glance selects this percentage of clips uniformly across the analyst-specified range. If analysts want to take a closer look at their data later, Glance lets them increase the sampling rate without repeating work that has already been done.
- **"Gist" Mode.** In "gist" mode, the system asks workers to simply mark if any instance of the event occurs within a the clip, rather than asking them to mark the exact range in which it occurs. This option provides a means for quickly illustrating the high-level frequency of pertinent events.

Each of these parameters lets the analyst fully specify the limitations and behavior of the system for a specific query. Note that this additional complexity is entirely voluntary – analysts

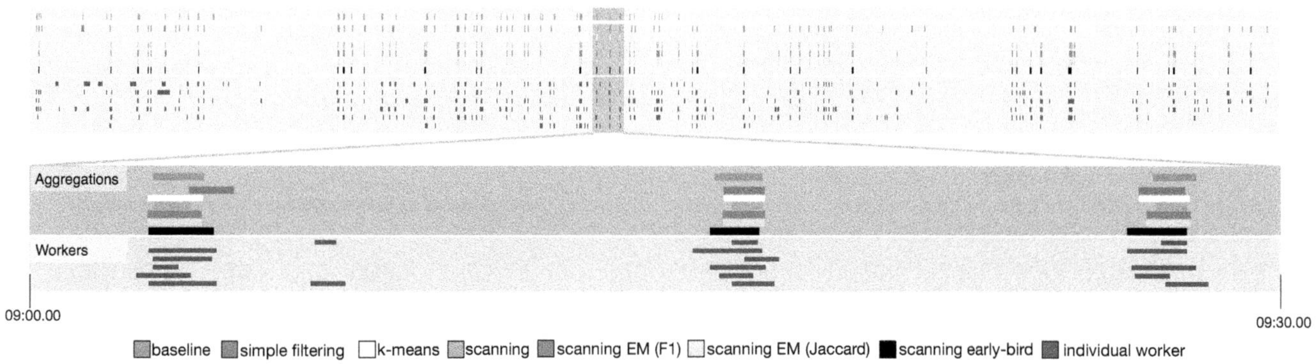

Figure 3. A visualization of crowd worker responses when coding "head nodding" events in a 20-minute video. Colored lines denote the marked span of an instance of the event. The top half of the figure shows the results for all 20 minutes, and the bottom half shows a zoomed-in version of one 30-second clip. Worker inputs are shown at the bottom of the zoomed clip, while the aggregated spans produced by our 6 schemes are shown above.

may use the built-in defaults for any or all of these settings if they so choose.

Visualizing Results

Once a worker codes a video clip, the judgement gets displayed in the video coding UI. Glance visualizes partial results to show analysts the work-in-progress results. In order to reduce the complexity inherent in multiple worker judgements, Glance aggregates the answers. Analysts may choose to use one or more aggregation algorithms, and may choose to see raw worker input as well. Figure 3 shows an example visualization and the next section provides details on the aggregation algorithms.

The problem of visualizing results that come in over time is one that has been studied in data analytics as well (e.g., [5]). There, the bound is the speed of machine computation over large datasets, which parallels the human computation delay seen in Glance, or any crowd-powered system.

Receiving Feedback on the Query

The reliability of the resulting worker judgements is understandably tied to the description given by the analyst. To help guide analysts, Glance provides feedback about a query's clarity and likelihood of convergence. The system analyzes variance between workers and predicts the quality of results, even before a query is finished, and even when there is no baseline data for comparison.

Glance can also highlight when individual clips may contain an exception to an otherwise stable rule (e.g., highlighting when one worker may have either made an error or noticed something the rest of the crowd did not). The next section details how Glance facilitates this feedback by observing agreement levels between workers.

Refining a Query with Followup Questions

To further support conversation-like interaction with video data, Glance supports followup queries that use prior responses as filters to reduce the number of video clips under consideration. For example, an analyst can search for the existence of a broad category of behavior, and then — only within clips that have this behavior — ask for more specific variations of that behavior. To select a filter query, the analyst can select one or more previously completed queries, and the new query will only be run over positive instances of the returned clips. Conversely, the 'inverse' selection tells the system to only run a query in selected clips where a previously coded event was *not* found.

In sum, Glance supports conversation-like interaction with video data by accepting natural language queries, responding quickly, providing feedback when queries are too vague or when anomalies occur, and supporting a "layering" approach to queries that build on prior coding results. The next section describes three empirical studies that demonstrate the technical innovations in Glance.

FEASIBILITY EVALUATIONS

To further describe and validate the core features of Glance, we ran a series of feasibility experiments. The following three sections provide empirical studies for three core aspects of the Glance system: *(i)* the time required to respond to natural language queries, *(ii)* the accuracy of multiple workers in aggregate, and *(iii)* the feedback provided to analysts to improve their natural language queries based on incoming coder agreement. First, we describe the sample data, participants, and procedures used for these experiments.

Method

Sample Data

We evaluated the core components of Glance using video clips from two different data sets:

- **2012 presidential debates.** We leverage the first hour of video from the presidential town hall debate between Barack Obama and Mitt Romney. Presidential debates have long been subject to scientific analysis, examining aspects such as visual camera treatment [31], gesture analysis [10], and social media reactions to debate dynamics [30, 15]. The video shows the two candidates interacting with each other, audience members, and the moderator.
  Across our studies, Glance coded for five different types of behavioral events. Workers were instructed to mark the spans of time when the candidates: 1) made eye contact with each other, 2) argued with each other, 3) transitioned from sitting to standing or vice versa, 4) exhibited rapid

changes in mood, and 5) used hand gestures. To establish a baseline for the purposes of quality comparisons, 2 researchers from our team independently hand-coded a portion of the overall video (5-minute clips for the first 4 events, and a 10-minute clip for the 5th event), then came to a consensus on each event.

- **Design team interactions.** We selected a second data set from a human-subjects experiment where two people worked together on a design task and provide feedback to each other on their designs [16]. The data comprise 30 seconds of interaction with 10 different pairs of people; all participants provided written permission to be included in this study. We kept these clips short, similar to Gottman's 'thin-slice' studies of married couples [2]. Across our studies, Glance coded for four different behavior events: Workers marked segments of video when the designers 1) made eye contact, 2) shifted their focus between different designs, 3) provided positive feedback, and 4) displayed a burst of excitement. To establish a baseline for quality comparisons, our research team independently coded these same four events in all ten clips.

These two data sets are representative of data typically analyzed using video coding. They are sufficiently large and complex to allow us to confidently evaluate our approach.

Setup and procedures

Participants: Across the various studies, we recruited a total of 493 unique workers from Mechanical Turk. In total, these workers marked 2593 clips.

Training: When a worker arrives to the task, she is first shown a brief tutorial on the general coding task she will be asked to perform, and then asked to complete an interactive tutorial that confirms she understands what to do, or provides feedback until she completes the sample task correctly. At this point, the worker remains in the retainer model until a query gets posted.

Task: When an analyst posts a query, workers in the retainer pool first see a brief description of the event to be coded, and an example, if the analyst specified one. Then they proceed to Glance's worker UI (Figure 4) where they see a video clip and a button that lets them mark the beginning and end of behavioral events. As they watch the video, they can press this button and then a new slider will appear below the video that marks the beginning of the event and follows the current position in the video until they click the button again to mark the end of a behavioral event. Workers can then go back and adjust times if corrections are needed. Workers can also mark as many or as few event spans as they see fit.

In 'gist' mode, the worker UI is simplified to elicit only whether the event has occurred or not. As soon as a worker marks the presence of an event and hits submit, the worker gets a new clip and the data gets recorded and displayed in the analyst's UI.

Study 1: Eliciting Rapid Results

The first of three feasibility studies focuses on how rapidly Glance can respond to natural language queries. For this evaluation, we ran several preliminary time trials, as well as, a live real-time experiment at scale.

Figure 4. Glance's worker interface. Workers are asked to press a button when they see an event start or end to get an initial estimate of the time range of the event. Workers can then correct the marked range if needed by sliding the start or end marker. In "gist" mode, workers are only asked to mark whether or not they saw the event occur at all.

Time trials

We measured the average time that it took workers to view and mark events in 30-second clips from the debate video. In this trial, we had ten workers per clip code one of four different behavioral events (eye contact, arguments, sit/stand transitions, and mode shifts. It took an average of 60.05 seconds ($\sigma = 12.29$) per clip to mark the start and end times of all events. On average, there were 0.93 events per clip.

We also tested the "gist" mode where workers provide a binary answer — instead of a time span – as soon as they perceive a behavioral event. This *drastically* reduced the coding time — by nearly 10× — by removing the need to watch the entire clip and to fine-tune the event markers. The same 30-second clips of the debate videos took ten workers an average of 8.7 seconds ($p < .01$).

To get even faster results, we can increase the video playback rate. When we increase the playback rate ten-fold, we get a significant improvement from 8.7 to 4.4 seconds ($p < .05$). We further explored how playback speed and worker redundancy affected the time to detect an event (Figure 5). In general, increasing the playback speed reduces the time to return coded events, but sees diminishing value above 2x speed. Similarly, if an analyst wants to increase confidence by hiring multiple workers per clip, this increases the coding time.

Increasing playback speed is also a common technique in traditional video coding. Other traditional approaches for reducing latency can also apply to crowd video coding, although some may require more training.

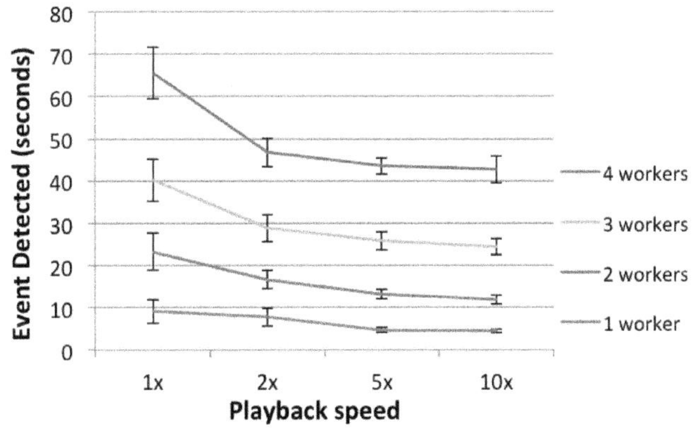

Figure 5. As playback speed is increased, there is a non-linear decrease in the response rate of the first N workers (gist mode).

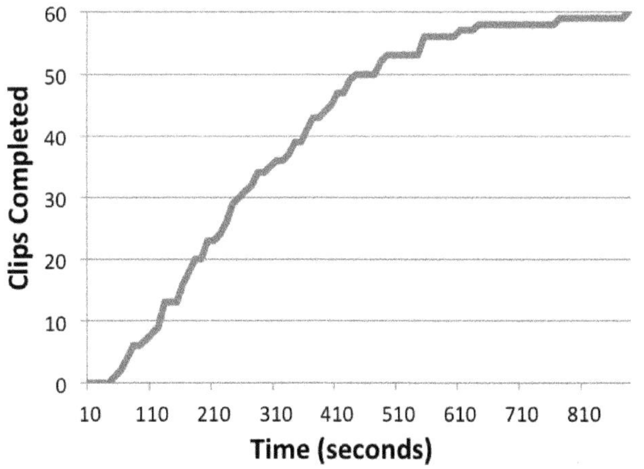

Figure 6. A plot of the number of 1-minute clips from an hour-long video being completed by crowd workers in real-time as part of our live trial. In two minutes, 20% of the content was labeled. In five minutes, 80% of the 60 clips were labeled. This demonstrates that large groups of workers (> 50 people in all in this case) can be recruited simultaneously to complete our coding task quickly.

Coding an hour of video in real-time

To understand how Glance performs on a real video coding task, we coded an entire hour of video from the presidential debate as sixty one-minute clips. We set the playback rate to 2× speed and performed a full coding of the start and end times for all occurrences of eye contact between the two candidates. To optimize for speed, we recruited roughly 50 workers into a retainer. Recruiting workers using a retainer model [8, 6] allows Glance to get workers started on a task in as little as a second.

Figure 6 shows the amount of time required to complete all 60 clips. After about 60 seconds, while the first workers view the video and mark events, answers begin to arrive. In the first 5 minutes after submitting the query, 48 minutes of the video (80%) had been fully coded. As the task nears completion, we see a decrease in the completion rate, in part due to having fewer workers in the retainer at that point. These results confirm that it is possible to code large amounts of video very quickly, especially if enough workers are recruited (in this case, we had just under 50 workers for the first 48 clips).

Study 2: Aggregating Results

The second feasibility study focuses on the accuracy of multiple workers when aggregated. Through crowdsourcing and massive parallelism, Glance can quickly produce answers to queries. However, with multiple workers coding the single clip, we observe different levels of agreement, due to the specificity/ambiguity of queries and worker differences (Figure 9). Individual crowd workers could miss events or misunderstand the query. Some workers put no effort into tasks. To conceal these details and give analysts a clear indication of the occurrences of behavioral events, Glance aggregates worker responses using an *input mediator*.

Glance uses a variety of input mediators to fit the needs of analysts (e.g., favoring recall over precision, or visa versa). To explore the space of mediation strategies, we implemented six input mediators for illustrating the consensus opinion on each clip:

1. **Simple Filtering.** Our first approach uses a set of heuristic filters to disambiguate worker input by removing outliers (mid-points or spans more than 2 standard deviations from the mean), then determines the mode of the numbers of segments marked in a clip and averages the start and end points of responses from workers that match the correct number of segments marked. To avoid discarding input from workers who saw the same basic events, but marked them slightly differently (e.g., as two sequential events instead of a single continuous one) we also look at input where segments are subsumed by the majority of other workers with the correct number of inputs.
2. **k-means Clustering.** To move beyond basic overlap detection, we implemented a k-means clustering algorithm that groups the start and end times of k clusters. To select k, we use the mode number of events marked by workers, after combining all majority-subsumed events into single spans (as described for filtering). Once worker segments are clustered, the final answer is generated by averaging all of the spans in each cluster and defining an equivalent range around the cluster's centroid.
3. **Scanning.** As opposed to trying to aggregate their marked spans directly, this approach uses a "scanning" pass to determine if the majority of workers agreed that an event occurred at that point in time. To calculate this, we discretize the clip into 10-millisecond bins and check for agreement within each bin. To prevent small coincidental gaps in majority agreement from fracturing events into multiple instances, we set a 0.5 second minimum bound for how small the gap can be between two events for them to be considered distinct.
4. **Scanning with E-M on the F1 Score.** The Scanning approach tended to produce a bias for shorter spans (the core parts of a behavioral event where most workers agree), and often single events were split into multiple because of coincidental gaps in coverage that caused the agreement to fall below majority during a small span of time. To counteract this, we implemented a new mediator that uses the initial scanning pass as a starting point, and then runs a version of Expectation-Maximization proposed by Dawid and Skene [13] to improve the initial guess for the seg-

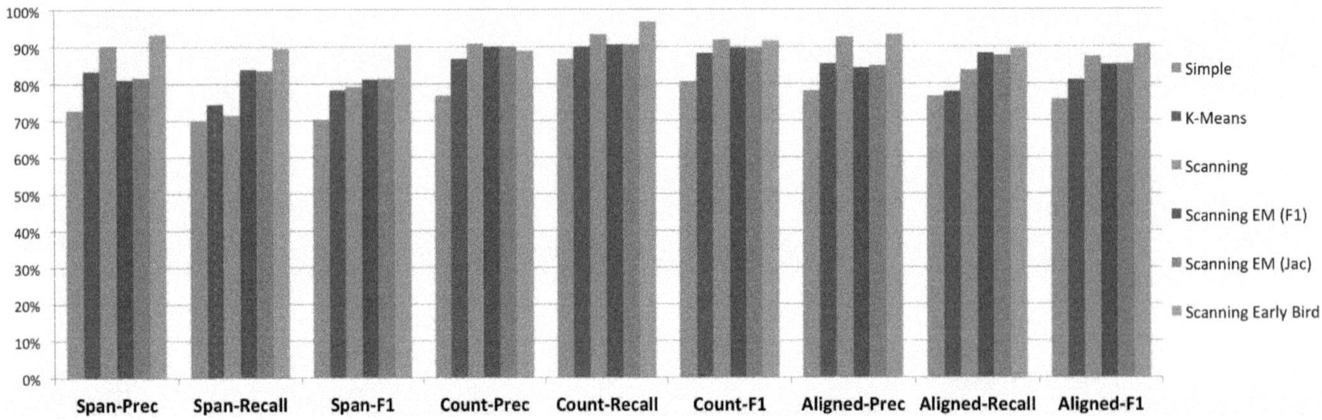

Figure 7. Precision, recall, and F1 score results for all 6 of the worker aggregation schemes we explore. Using our "scanning" approach with additional filtering and adjustments proves the most effective overall, and is significantly better than simple filtering or k-means clustering ($p < .05$).

ment with multiple observers. Specifically, the following two steps occur iteratively: (a) the workers are assigned weights that correspond to our *confidence* in their answers and (b) the start and end point of the best-guess segment are updated by computing the weighted average of the workers' start and end points, respectively. Our confidence in a worker corresponds to the agreement between her individual answer and the current best guess for the segment. In this approach, we use the F1 score[1], where the answer of a worker is tested against the current best guess for the segment. We repeat these two steps until the method converges —when the weights (confidence) of the workers do not change, or equivalently, the best guess for the segment remains the same.

5. **Scanning with E-M on the Jaccard Index.** This approach is similar to the one above, but runs Expectation-Maximization using the Jaccard index between the worker's answer and the current best guess as the confidence level in a worker.
6. **Scanning with Filtering and Early-Bird Bias.** We found that both of the EM modifications to scanning typically resulted in over-sized spans for events. The recall improved, but at the cost of precision. As a result, we looked at other potential improvements to the basic scanning method. Due to a natural latency in human response, the scanning methods tend to mark the onset of behavioral events a bit late (the observed start time was often behind the true time). To counteract this, we created a mediator that uses scanning to find the bins where a majority agreed, but then it shifts the start time earlier. We calculate a time shift using the average of the earliest start time reported by a worker and the aggregate start time across all workers. We use the midpoint because the earliest worker often observed subtle cues that let them anticipate the event early. To prevent this use of a single response from adding potentially far-fetched answers to the final response, we remove all starting times that are outliers from this selection process.

To compare our input mediators, we calculated precision, recall, and F1 score using three different strategies: 1) agreement of the occurrence time and *span*, 2) agreement in the number of behavioral occurrences *count*, and 3) agreement of the span after running multiple sequence alignment to correct for any slight misalignment that may have otherwise produced low precision and recall (*aligned*). As Figure 7 shows, our modified scanning approach was the most effective overall. It was significantly better than the simple filtering and k-means approaches ($p < .01$), and borderline significantly better than the basic scanning approach ($p = .05$). Basic scanning did not perform significantly better than the scanning with EM approaches.

[1]We also tried using the precision and recall individually to define the confidence in each worker, but the F1 score —which appropriately combines the two metrics —works better.

Study 3: Giving Feedback by Measuring Agreement

The third feasibility study focuses on how Glance provides feedback to help analysts improve their natural language queries based on emerging coder agreement and potential edge cases in the data. This feature stems from the realization that not all queries are created equal. Since analysts specify their queries to Glance in natural language, their descriptions could be vague or underspecified. Queries are "ambiguous" when their lack of specificity leaves them open to multiple interpretations by workers. In contrast, we refer to well-defined queries as "concrete". Of course, every query falls on a continuum between these two classifications, and generally speaking, as analysts develop a coding scheme, their queries will become less ambiguous.

In this section, we explore how we can give analysts feedback on the clarity of their query, detect edge cases in descriptions, and even predict the quality of crowd responses without requiring baseline values.

Detecting Agreement

To give analysts feedback on how well workers understand their query, and how good the resulting responses are likely to be, we measure the level of agreement between workers. As a preliminary trial, we compared the total count occurrence between workers when coding two different descriptions within the same clip, concrete ("the person is leaning forward") versus ambiguous ("the person is engaged"). From this trial, we find that the ambiguous description led to significantly more disagreement among workers in the total count of behavioral events ($p < .01$). Further, we see an obvious difference in

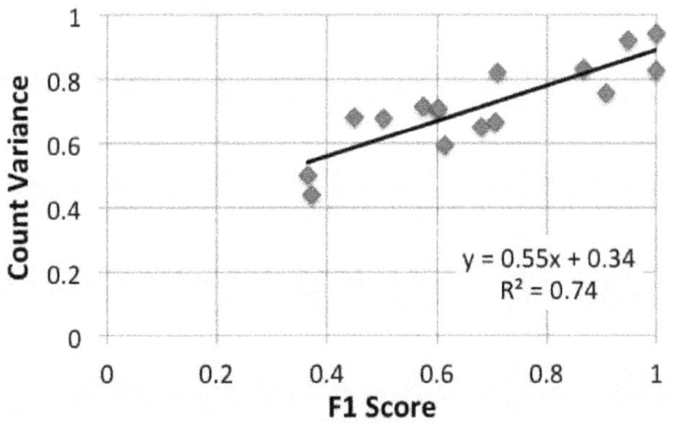

Figure 8. Correlation between our agreement score (variance in the number of segments marked by workers in a single clip) and the aligned F1 score ($R^2 = .74$). This suggests that the level of agreement between workers can be used as a predictor of the overall answer quality even when no baseline is available to compare to.

the variance of concrete events ($\sigma^2 = 0.014$) versus more ambiguous events ($\sigma^2 = 0.884$) (Figure 9). Intuitively, this makes sense – when subjectively coding an ambiguous event, different workers may have different interpretations. This can be avoided if analysts provide clear descriptions of events, and one (or more) examples to workers.

To turn this insight into a means of providing feedback to analysts, we created two different agreement metrics. We look at how well each agreement measure predicts the F1 score of the aligned metric described in the previous section. The aligned metric provides a good measure of overall fitness due to the fact that it tolerates small time shifts in the marked segments.

- **Fleiss' Kappa:** A common way to measure agreement level is to use a kappa score to measure inter-rater reliability [17]. When more than two coders are present, Fleiss' kappa can be used. However, Fleiss' kappa assumes that fixed, discrete information is being coded (such as whether a paragraph of text is written in a hostile tone or not). To adapt this measure to our continuous domain, we again bin time into $10ms$ units, then determine if each worker is implicitly contributing a 'yes' or 'no' vote for the event occurring in that bin (i.e., 'yes' if they marked that bin in one of their event spans, and 'no' otherwise). Despite its roots in existing inter-rater reliability settings, it is not a strong predictor of the final accuracy of a given set of inputs. Comparing to the aligned F1 score[2], we find $R^2 = .24$.
- **Count Variance:** Another important way to measure agreement is the overall variance of the different worker inputs. We explored using the variance in the number of events workers marked in a segment (count), total duration of the segments they marked (span), and area of each segment marked (area), as well as combinations of the three. Most combinations scored between $R^2 = .3$ and $R^2 = .5$. In the end, measuring the count variance was the most predictive of the F1 score of the whole clip, with a Pearson correlation of 0.86, $R^2 = .74$ (Figure 8).

[2]We use the aligned F1 score because it is most indicative of the overall quality of the final answer.

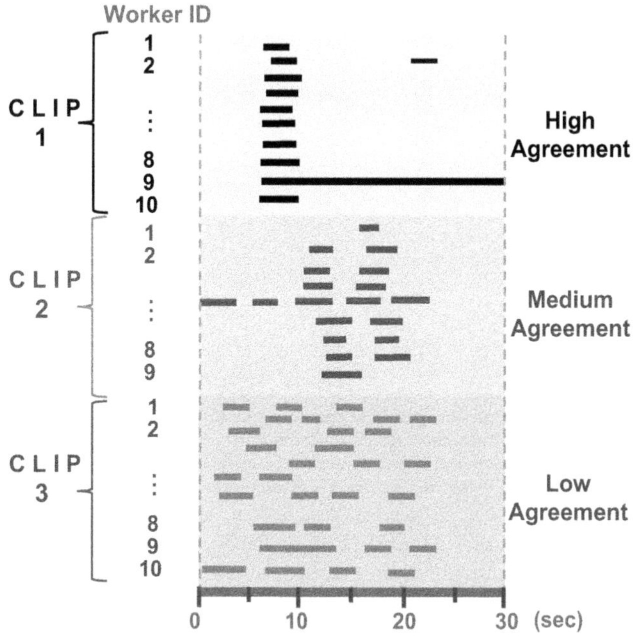

Figure 9. Visualization of the agreement levels between workers for three 30-second clips (in black, blue, red, respectively). The Y-axis is the worker ID and the X-axis is time (position). Each bar (segment) represents an event marked in the video clip.

While different in their predictive power, the two measures did support one another's findings. The count variance tightly correlates with the Fleiss' kappa, with a Pearson correlation of 0.87, and $R^2 = 0.76$ (Figure 10).

Threshold Pruning

Our ultimate goal in measuring agreement is to use it as a proxy for performance that can be calculated immediately, without the need for a baseline to be calculated (which would defeat the point of having a rapid-response tool!) The trend observed when plotting F1 score against agreement score (Figure 8) indicates that the count variance is a good predictor. But does it really work?

The results shown in Figure 7 have been filtered by removing low-agreement clips. To compare the clips in terms of workers' agreement level (response), we performed ANOVA analysis with the clip ID as a single factor with 10 levels. We found that at least one clip had a significantly different mean agreement level from the other sample means ($F_{9,55} = 4.4555, p < .001$). To understand how the mean agreement levels differ, we performed multiple pairwise comparisons using Tukey-Kramer HSD, to correct for Type I errors. At the 95% confidence level, we found that the highest mean agreement value was statistically significantly different from the mean agreement values of four other sessions. We used this as a threshold value (an agreement level of 0.72) and filtered out the three significantly lower trials. This resulted in a 7.8% to 11.1% average increase in the performance of each aggregation method.

In practice, we will not have such a wide range of results to draw from when selecting a cutoff. Thus, we won't be able to predict an exact threshold a priori. However, our goal

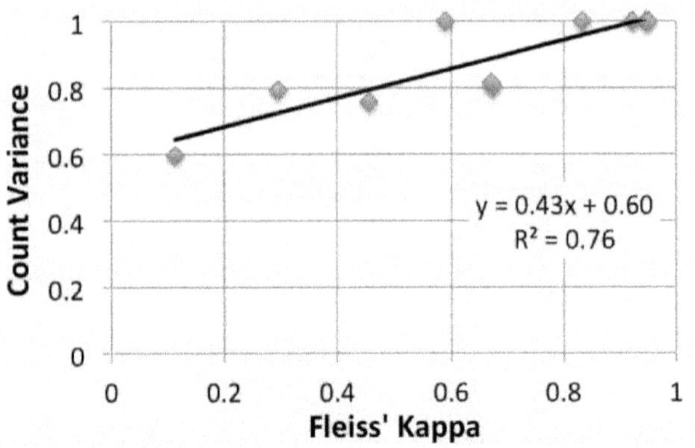

Figure 10. While the count variance is much more predictive of the final F1 score of a response ($R^2 = .74$ versus $R^2 = .24$ for Fleiss' kappa), the count variance still tightly correlates with Fleiss' kappa, suggesting they are measuring similar aspects of agreement.

when providing agreement as feedback to analysts is to provide some signal that they can use to determine how confident they can expect to be in Glance's results. In high-agreement cases, Glance's precision and recall exceeded 99%.

Giving Feedback

The correlation and corresponding effectiveness of filtering based on differences in agreement levels denote it is an effective indicator of the final quality of the answers to a query. This in turn suggests that we can provide this measure to analysts to allow them to judge how consistently workers are agreeing with one another, and thus how accurate they can expect their results to be. For particularly low values of responses for a query (we use below 0.50 in practice), Glance can even alert users to the potential issues with their query. Most commonly, low values will occur when very subjective descriptions are provided because each worker will interpret the event they are looking for slightly differently. As results arrive, this measure can instantly be applied, potentially allowing analysts to retract their query before it is completed in the event that it is unclear to workers – something not possible using current approaches where results are typically not seen until after they are completed.

Even when the overall agreement score is acceptably high, Glance can detect when a subsection of the video (even a single clip) falls below the expected norm. In this case, it is likely true that something in that video is causing confusion for workers (e.g., an edge case that the analyst did not think or know to clarify for in the initial description). In these cases, the clip can be highlighted and shown to analysts who can choose to skip the clip, redefine the query, or continue.

EXAMPLE SCENARIO AND EVALUATION

To demonstrate Glance and the AUI, we present an example interaction between an analyst and Glance. Throughout this example, we report *real* data coded by the crowd. This data came from a third video dataset showing a couple on a date, which is 20 minutes long and includes baseline data for 4 events for the entire video, resulting in 80 minutes of video content. This video is separate from the one used in the evaluations of the individual approaches above.

Our imaginary analyst is a relationship researcher interested in quickly coding a video of a couple dating. Since our analyst initially does not even know what she is most interested in or if the data is valid, she decides to run a rapid-response task with no redundancy but 100% coverage to determine when the two people are talking to one another. This query takes an average of 9.6 seconds to return results, and correctly identifies 100% of the 35 segments in the video that have conversation. The same query with a redundancy level of three would have still only taken 20.6 seconds on average.

Once our analyst sees that there are enough instances of conversation between the two partners to make the video potentially interesting, she decides to ask a follow-up question: "when are the people in the video engaged?" This question is asked about only the 35 clips that contain interaction between the two people in the video since it is a follow-up. After just 5 clips are completed, the system alerts our analyst that worker agreement on the answer is potentially very low. She sees that the agreement score is just 0.57 (recall that our threshold value was 0.72 before), so she decides to stop the query early and rephrase her question to be more clear.

In an attempt to make her query less ambiguous, she asks workers to code specific actions instead of broad interaction properties. For her first query, she asks "when is the person on the right laughing?", of which the crowd finds 71.0% of the 53 instances with 99.9% precision. For her second query, she asks "when is the person on the left nodding?", of which the crowd finds 64.6% of the 87 instances with 99.2% precision.

To check for negative signs during the interaction, she then asks the crowd to find any instances where someone is checking their phone during the date. Because she is mainly interested to find out if this happens a notable number of times, she turns on the gist mode for a quick response. She soon finds that Glance correctly identified 100% of the 13 instances of someone checking their phone. Based on the high amount of direct interaction, our researcher begins to create a final coding scheme that best fits her data.

DISCUSSION

Glance's quick, conversation-style interaction goes beyond the paradigm adhered to by prior work, which assumed that making coding faster, even for data exploration, was something that must be done while focusing on a single human in the loop. Glance uses the parallelism available via the crowd to not only greatly improve the speed at which video data can be explored by analysts while effectively compensating for the added complexity of getting multiple results, but actually uses the presence of multiple overlapping contributors to predict the effectiveness of the codes based on their agreement. But there are many challenges involved in robustly supporting analysis of behavioral video.

Query Ambiguity

Our results suggest that the quality of worker responses is highly dependent on the level of ambiguity in analysts' queries. While this is a drawback, it is a bias shared with existing approaches that involve human coders. However, with shorter training times and more exploratory coding schemes compared to the well-evaluated ones used in traditional approaches, where getting coding data is very time consuming and expensive, Glance may help analysts better understand the ambiguity of their queries and refine their coding scheme and instructions to compensate.

Context

Maintaining context for workers, who may need to know information from prior clips to accurately understand an event's context within a task, is also a key issue when splitting tasks among multiple people. The general case of this problem, where information from any previous point in the video may provide the necessary context for workers, requires novel techniques and is beyond the scope of this paper. However, the current version of Glance does try to ensure that individual events are captured in their entirety in a single video. To do this, we can look at workers who label events that continue to the end of a clip or begin immediately, allowing for some small ϵ of error. In our experiments, less than a second was enough to capture all instances where an event was split, but this type of division happened so little in our experiments that no generalizable rule could be devised. Situations where information from more than one clip away was needed to code and event never arose, largely due to the types of questions we were asking in our examples.

Worker Training

We do not claim that Glance can code every type of event. For coding systems that are highly granular, and that capture very subtle events coders would normally be trained for periods up to weeks to be proficient enough to complete their task reliably. Crowd based coding has the potential to reduce training efforts, particularly for complex coding schemes, as each worker only has to learn a subset of the codes rather than the entire coding system.

We currently use two forms of on-the-spot training to prepare workers for tasks: (i) a general interactive tutorial that gives workers feedback on an example task until they can complete it successfully (given before workers are sent to the retainer pool), and (ii) a dynamically created tutorial for the specific event being coded that consists of a text description and one or more video examples, if provided by the analyst. However, this does not fully leverage prior work that has shown workers remember task details from one session to the next [29], potentially facilitating long-term learning, but instead presents a tool for using crowd workers' common knowledge to code events now, while future work will explore how to train interested crowd workers over time to allow them to handle increasingly complex tasks.

Cost

Workers were paid $0.15 USD per task to code 30 seconds of video, which took them one minute on average. This equates to a $9/hour effective rate, which is comparable to a work study student. In some scenarios, video is coded redundantly. At a depth of 5 workers, which we do not believe to be necessary in practice, the cost per minute could be as high as $2 \times 5 \times \$0.15 = \$1.50$/minute. The potential advantage of Glance comes from the ability to get feedback more quickly, which means that money is less likely to be wasted on coding that is not used or that has to be changed later. Therefore, total coding costs could be less.

FUTURE WORK

Glance is still only the first step towards allowing analysts to truly have a "conversation with their data". Latency can be further improved by integrating automated coding where possible. By using the crowd to make it possible to handle these natural language requests now, realistic data on how users pose and refine questions can be collected and used to train automated systems to both elicit clear queries and recognize events more accurately.

For longer, more in-depth tasks, context can be maintained more robustly through crowd curation of a shared "memory", and a richer interaction with the system is possible by allowing workers to respond to queries (individually or as a collective) when something is unclear [23, 27]. This is similar to other types of message passing that has been observed as an effective way to boost problem-solving abilities in crowdsourcing before [35]. This might also lead to cases of serendipitous discovery of new information, as has been observed with crowd-powered conversational search tasks [23].

We will be releasing this tool for open use to both allow analysts access to the coding tool to advance their own work, as well as to collect data on how our conversational interaction paradigm is used in real settings to code video. Ongoing work will explore how the potential for privacy threats (see [26]) might be mitigated using video filtering techniques that allow for recognition of the queried events, without revealing the identity of people in the video.

CONCLUSION

In this paper, we have presented the motivation, design, and evaluation of Glance, a crowd-powered system for rapidly coding video. We have shown that by incorporating the effort of many human workers, the system is able to analyze video very quickly, making possible a conversation-like interaction with data that was not previously feasible. To further support iterative refinement and validation of hypotheses on video data sets, we have introduced methods that use variance in crowd responses to support iterative improvement of coding schemes, and introduced aggregation strategies that help produce reliable codes over time span inputs. Glance dramatically reduces the time required for the arduous and slow task of video coding, and in the process may change how social scientists do their work.

ACKNOWLEDGEMENTS

This work was supported by National Science Foundation awards #IIS-1149709, #IIS-1218209, #IIS-1208382, #IIS-1217096, and #IIS-1217559, a Sloan Foundation Fellowship, a Google Research Grant, and a Microsoft Research Ph.D. Fellowship. The authors would also like to thank Stephanie O'Keefe for her input on this work.

REFERENCES

1. Datavyu. http://datavyu.org/.
2. Ambady, N., and Rosenthal, R. Thin slices of expressive behavior as predictors of interpersonal consequences: A meta-analysis. *Psychol bull 111*, 2 (1992), 256.
3. Bakeman, R., and Gottman, J. M. *Observing interaction: An introduction to sequential analysis*. Cambridge University Press, 1986.
4. Bakeman, R., and Quera, V. *Sequential Analysis and Observational Methods for the Behavioral Sciences*. Cambridge University Press, 2011.
5. Barnett, M., Chandramouli, B., DeLine, R., Drucker, S., Fisher, D., Goldstein, J., Morrison, P., and Platt, J. Stat!: An interactive analytics environment for big data. In *SIGMOD 2013* (2013), 1013–1016.
6. Bernstein, M. S., Brandt, J. R., Miller, R. C., and Karger, D. R. Crowds in two seconds: Enabling realtime crowd-powered interfaces. In *UIST* (2011), 33–42.
7. Bernstein, M. S., Little, G., Miller, R. C., Hartmann, B., Ackerman, M. S., Karger, D. R., Crowell, D., and Panovich, K. Soylent: a word processor with a crowd inside. In *UIST* (2010), 313–322.
8. Bigham, J. P., Jayant, C., Ji, H., Little, G., Miller, A., Miller, R. C., Miller, R., Tatarowicz, A., White, B., White, S., and Yeh, T. Vizwiz: nearly real-time answers to visual questions. In *UIST* (2010), 333–342.
9. Burr, B. Vaca: A tool for qualitative video analysis. In *SIGCHI EA* (2006), 622–627.
10. Casasanto, D., and Jasmin, K. Good and bad in the hands of politicians: Spontaneous gestures during positive and negative speech. *PLoS One 5*, 7 (2010), e11805.
11. Coan, J. A., and Gottman, J. M. *Handbook of Emotion Elicitation and Assessment*. Series in Affective Science. Oxford University Press, 2007, ch. The Specific Affect Coding System (SPAFF).
12. Cohen, J. A Coefficient of Agreement for Nominal Scales. *Educ Psychol Meas 20*, 1 (1960), 37.
13. Dawid, A. P., and Skene, A. M. Maximum likelihood estimation of observer error-rates using the em algorithm. In *Appl Stat - J Roy St C* (1979), 20–28.
14. Di Salvo, R., Giordano, D., and Kavasidis, I. A crowdsourcing approach to support video annotation. In *VIGTA* (2013), 8:1–8:6.
15. Diakopoulos, N. A., and Shamma, D. A. Characterizing debate performance via aggregated twitter sentiment. In *SIGCHI* (2010), 1195–1198.
16. Dow, S., Fortuna, J., Schwartz, D., Altringer, B., Schwartz, D., and Klemmer, S. Prototyping dynamics: Sharing multiple designs improves exploration, group rapport, and results. In *SIGCHI* (2011), 2807–2816.
17. Fleiss, J. L. Measuring nominal scale agreement among many raters. *Psychol Bull 76*, 5 (1971), 378–382.
18. Hagedorn, J., Hailpern, J., and Karahalios, K. G. Vcode and vdata: Illustrating a new framework for supporting the video annotation workflow. In *AVI* (2008), 317–321.
19. Hailpern, J., Karahalios, K., Halle, J., DeThorne, L., and Coletto, M.-K. A3: A coding guideline for hci+autism research using video annotation. In *ASSETS* (2008), 11–18.
20. Heyman, R. E., Lorber, M. F., Eddy, J. M., West, T., Reis, E. H. T., and Judd, C. M. *Handbook of Research Methods in Social and Personality Psychology*. Pending, 2014, ch. Behavioral observation and coding.
21. Jordan, B., and Henderson, A. Interaction analysis: Foundations and practice. *J Learn Sci 4*, 1 (1995), 39–103.
22. Kipp, M. ANVIL- a generic annotation tool for multimodal dialogue. *Eurospeech* (2001), 1367–1370.
23. Lasecki, W., Wesley, R., Nichols, J., Kulkarni, A., Allen, J., and Bigham, J. Chorus: A crowd-powered conversational assistant. In *UIST* (2013).
24. Lasecki, W. S., Murray, K. I., White, S., Miller, R. C., and Bigham, J. P. Real-time crowd control of existing interfaces. In *UIST* (2011), 23–32.
25. Lasecki, W. S., Song, Y. C., Kautz, H., and Bigham, J. P. Real-time crowd labeling for deployable activity recognition. In *CSCW* (2013).
26. Lasecki, W. S., Teevan, J., and Kamar, E. Information extraction and manipulation threats in crowd-powered systems. In *CSCW* (2014).
27. Lasecki, W. S., Thiha, P., Zhong, Y., Brady, E., and Bigham, J. P. Answering visual questions with conversational crowd assistants. In *ASSETS* (2013).
28. Lasecki, W. S., Weingard, L., Ferguson, G., and Bigham, J. P. Finding dependencies between actions using the crowd. In *SIGCHI* (2014), 3095–3098.
29. Lasecki, W. S., White, S., Murray, K. I., and Bigham, J. P. Crowd memory: Learning in the collective. In *CI* (2012).
30. Shamma, D. A., Kennedy, L., and Churchill, E. F. Tweet the debates: understanding community annotation of uncollected sources. In *SIGMM* (2009), 3–10.
31. Tiemens, R. K. Television's portrayal of the 1976 presidential debates: An analysis of visual content.
32. von Ahn, L. *Human Computation*. PhD thesis, Carnegie Mellon University, 2005.
33. Vondrick, C., Patterson, D., and Ramanan, D. Efficiently scaling up crowdsourced video annotation. *Int J of Comput Vision* (2012), 1–21.
34. Weingart, L. R., Olekalns, M., and Smith, P. L. Quantitative coding of negotiation behavior. *Int Negotiation 3*, 9 (2005), 441–456.
35. Zhang, H., Horvitz, E., Miller, R. C., and Parkes, D. C. Crowdsourcing general computation. In *SIGCHI Workshop on Human Compuation* (2011), 622–627.

Data-Driven Interaction Techniques for Improving Navigation of Educational Videos

Juho Kim[1] Philip J. Guo[1,2] Carrie J. Cai[1] Shang-Wen (Daniel) Li[1]
Krzysztof Z. Gajos[3] Robert C. Miller[1]

[1]MIT CSAIL
Cambridge, MA USA
{juhokim, cjcai, swli, rcm}@mit.edu

[2]University of Rochester
Rochester, NY USA
pg@cs.rochester.edu

[3]Harvard SEAS
Cambridge, MA USA
kgajos@eecs.harvard.edu

ABSTRACT
With an unprecedented scale of learners watching educational videos on online platforms such as MOOCs and YouTube, there is an opportunity to incorporate data generated from their interactions into the design of novel video interaction techniques. Interaction data has the potential to help not only instructors to improve their videos, but also to enrich the learning experience of educational video watchers. This paper explores the design space of data-driven interaction techniques for educational video navigation. We introduce a set of techniques that augment existing video interface widgets, including: a 2D video timeline with an embedded visualization of collective navigation traces; dynamic and non-linear timeline scrubbing; data-enhanced transcript search and keyword summary; automatic display of relevant still frames next to the video; and a visual summary representing points with high learner activity. To evaluate the feasibility of the techniques, we ran a laboratory user study with simulated learning tasks. Participants rated watching lecture videos with interaction data to be efficient and useful in completing the tasks. However, no significant differences were found in task performance, suggesting that interaction data may not always align with moment-by-moment information needs during the tasks.

Author Keywords
Video learning; Interaction peaks; Video summarization; MOOCs; Multimedia learning; Video content analysis.

ACM Classification Keywords
H.5.1. Multimedia Information Systems: Video

INTRODUCTION
Millions of people watch free educational videos online on platforms such as Khan Academy, Coursera, edX, Udacity, MIT OpenCourseWare, and YouTube. For example, the "Education" channel on YouTube currently has over 10.5 million subscribers, and a typical MOOC has thousands of video-watching learners. In addition, learners also take paid video-centric courses on commercial platforms such as Lynda, Udemy, and numerous university e-learning initiatives.

The server logs of these platforms contain fine-grained, second-by-second data of learners' interactions with videos, which we refer to as *interaction traces*. This data is now being used for real-time analytics to optimize business metrics such as viewer engagement time. Researchers have also used this data to perform retrospective empirical analyses. For example, video analytics studies on MOOCs have compared the effects of video production methods on learner engagement [13] and identified common causes of peaks in learner activity within videos [20].

Interaction data provides a unique opportunity to understand collective video watching patterns, which might indicate points of learner interest, confusion, or boredom in videos. However, to our knowledge, researchers have not yet attempted to feed these patterns back into the video navigation interface to support learners. While learners might have diverse goals in navigating through a video, existing video interfaces do not provide customized navigation support beyond scrubbing on a linear timeline slider with thumbnail previews and synchronizing with a textual transcript. Adapting to collective video watching patterns can lead to richer social navigation support [10].

This paper explores the design space of navigation techniques for educational videos that leverage interaction data. We introduce novel data-driven interaction techniques that process, visualize, and summarize interaction data generated by many learners watching the same video. For instance, in a typical MOOC, at least a few thousand learners watch each video. Based on prior findings about learner intent and typical formats of educational videos [13, 20], we have designed these techniques to support fluid and diverse video navigation patterns. Typical video watching scenarios include:

- Rewatch: "Although I understand the high-level motivation, I didn't quite get the formal definition of 'admissible heuristic' the first time I watched this lecture. So I want to rewatch the section explaining the formal definition."
- Textual search: "I want to jump to where the instructor first mentioned the phrase 'alpha-beta pruning.'"

UIST'14, October 5–8, 2014, Honolulu, HI, USA.

ACM 978-1-4503-3069-5/14/10 $15.00.
http://dx.doi.org/10.1145/2642918.2647389

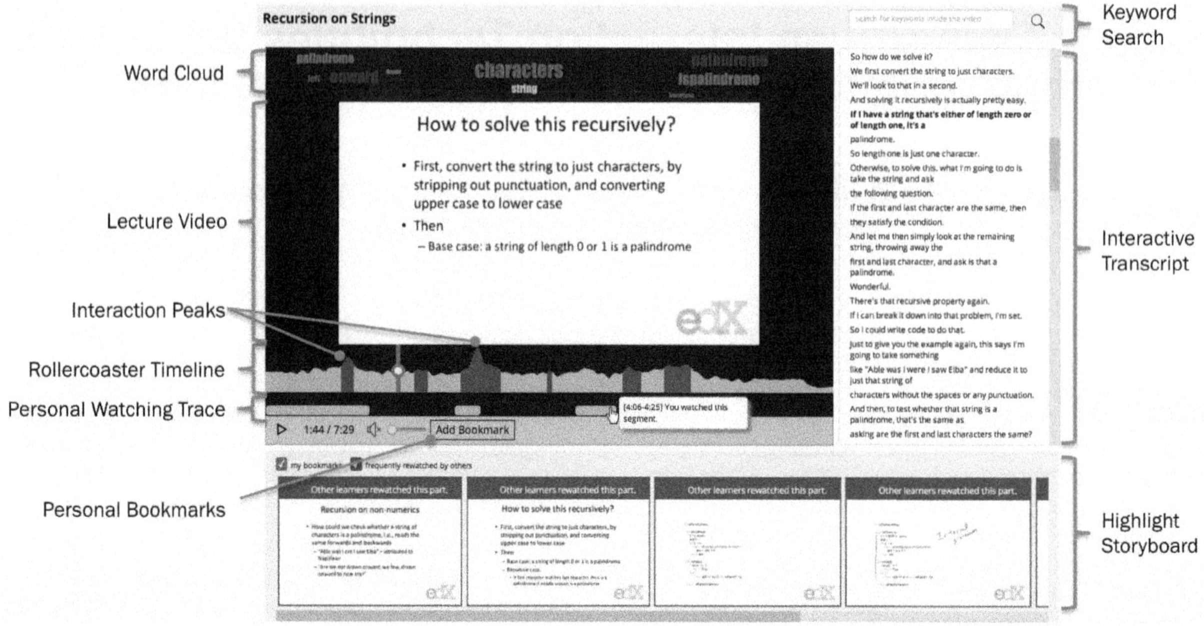

Figure 1. This paper presents three sets of novel interaction techniques to improve navigation of educational videos. 1) Dynamic timelines (Rollercoaster Timeline, Interaction Peaks, and Personal Watching Trace), 2) Enhanced in-video search (Keyword Search and Interactive Transcript), 3) Highlights (Word Cloud, Personal Bookmarks, Highlight Storyboard). All techniques are powered by interaction data aggregated over all video watchers.

- Visual search: "I remember seeing this code example in a diagram somewhere in the video. I want to find it again."
- Return: "Hey, that was annoying! I don't want to see the instructor's talking head. I'm not done looking at this PowerPoint slide yet. I want the slide back!"
- Skim: "This lecture seems somewhat trivial. I'll skim to see if there's something I probably shouldn't miss."

Specifically, we developed interaction techniques to augment a traditional Web video player with 1) a Rollercoaster timeline that expands the video timeline to a 2D space, visualizes collective interaction traces of all learners, and dynamically applies non-linear scrolling to emphasize interaction peaks, 2) enhanced in-video search that visualizes and ranks occurrences on the timeline and recommends salient keywords for each video section, and 3) a video summarization method that captures frames that are frequently viewed by other learners. These techniques combine learners' collective interaction traces with text and visual content analysis.

We package all of these techniques together in LectureScape, a prototype Web-based video interface shown in Figure 1. In a laboratory study with simulated search and skimming tasks, we observed that participants employ diverse video navigation patterns enabled by our techniques. Specifically, they noted that LectureScape helped them to quickly scan the video and efficiently narrow down to parts to direct their focus. They also found interaction data to be useful in identifying important or confusing pedagogical points within videos. However, no significant differences were found in task performance, suggesting that interaction data may not always align with moment-by-moment information needs participants had for the study tasks.

This paper makes the following contributions:

- a conceptual design approach for interaction techniques that leverages information about other learners' behavior to improve the video learning experience,
- a set of novel video interaction techniques powered by real log data from learners in a MOOC platform, introducing 1) a 2D, non-linear timeline, 2) enhanced in-video search, and 3) a data-driven video summarization method,
- and an empirical evaluation of the techniques with learners, which enabled fluid and diverse video navigation.

RELATED WORK

We review previous research in leveraging interaction history to improve user interfaces and video navigation.

Leveraging Interaction History

There is a rich thread of research in using interaction history data to analyze usage patterns and improve users' task performance. Interaction history data is automatically collected by applications during normal usage. Examples include Web browsers logging Web page visit history, search engines capturing query history, and video players storing video interaction clickstreams such as play and pause events. Read Wear [14] presented a visionary idea in this space to visualize users' read and edit history data in the scrollbar. Chronicle [12] captured and provided playback for rich, contextual user interaction history inside a graphical application. Dirty Desktops [16] applied magnetic forces to each interaction trace, which improved target selection for commonly used widgets. Patina [26] separated individual and collective history and added overlays on top of the GUI, to help people find commonly used menu items and discover new ways of completing desktop-related tasks. Causality [30] introduced an application-independent conceptual model for working with interaction history. This paper uses video interaction history to support common navigation tasks in video-based learning.

To model user interest in video watching, researchers have proposed features such as viewership [38], scrubbing [39], zooming and panning [7], and replaying and skipping [9] activities. SocialSkip [9] applied signal processing to replaying activity data in order to infer interesting video segments. Other researchers have used more explicit input from video watchers, including user ratings [33], annotations [38], and the "this part is important" button [36]. Most existing approaches introduce a modeling technique or data visualization. We take this data further to build new interaction techniques for video navigation, which prior work has not done. Also, we combine both implicit user history data and explicit user bookmarks to support diverse learning tasks, which extends prior work on supporting social navigation for lecture videos [28].

Video Navigation Techniques

To improve video navigation with interaction data, we designed novel techniques to 1) add richer interactions to the video timeline, 2) support enhanced in-video search, and 3) automatically summarize video content. We now review related work for each of the three techniques.

To improve video scrubbing, YouTube displays thumbnail previews for quickly skimming local frames, and Swift [25] overlays low-resolution thumbnails to avoid network latency delays. The content-aware timeline [34] extracts keyframes with content analysis and plays a video snippet around these points when the user scrubs the timeline. Elastic interfaces [24] use the rubber band analogy to control scrubbing speed and support precise navigation, as seen in the PV Slider [35] and Apple's iOS video interface. We extend this line of research by asking: "What if the scrubbing behavior adapts to learners' watching patterns, as collected from interaction history data?" To our knowledge, no video scrubbing technique has leveraged interaction history data.

Another thread of research introduced techniques to support navigation of how-to videos, a sub-genre of educational video that includes procedural, step-by-step instructions about completing a specific task. Existing systems reveal step-by-step structure by adding rich signals to the video timeline, such as tool usage and intermediate results in graphical applications [8, 21]. Classroom lecture videos tend to be less structured than how-to videos, which makes capturing clear structural signals harder. We instead turn to interaction data that is automatically logged for learners as they watch the video.

Popular GUI applications such as Web browsers and text editors have incremental search features where the scrollbar and text visually highlight locations of search term occurrences. Also, video players on educational platforms such as edX show a synchronized transcript alongside the currently playing video. Learners can search for text in the transcript and then click to jump to the corresponding spot in the video. We improve these interfaces by augmenting search results with interaction data and visualizing them on the video timeline.

Existing video summarization techniques use video content analysis to extract keyframes [3], shot boundaries [22], and visual saliency [15]. To provide an overview of the entire clip at a glance and support rapid navigation, recent research has used a grid layout to display pre-cached thumbnails [27], short snippets [18] in a single clip, personal watching history for multiple clips [1], a conceptual hierarchy visualization [19], or a 3D space-time cube display [31]. For educational lecture videos, Panopticon [18] has been shown to shorten task completion time in seeking information inside videos [32]. For blackboard-style lecture videos, NoteVideo [29] reverse-engineers a rendered video to create a summary image and support spatial and temporal navigation. This paper introduces a new summarization technique that uses *interaction peaks*, points in a video with significantly high play button click activity, to generate highlight frames of a clip.

DESIGN GOALS

This work focuses on supporting video navigation patterns common in online education, which differ from watching, say, a movie or TV show in a sequential, linear manner. Our designs are informed by quantitative and qualitative findings from analyses of educational videos, which suggest that learners often re-watch and find specific information from videos. Prior work in video clickstream analysis on four edX MOOCs found many *interaction peaks*, i.e., concentrated bursts in play/pause button clicks during certain segments of a video [20]. 70% of automatically-detected peaks coincided with visual transitions (e.g., switching between an instructor's head and a slide) and topic transitions [20]. A challenge in using interaction data to support learning is that the meaning of an interaction peak can be ambiguous (e.g., interest, confusion, or importance). In this paper, we do not assume a specific meaning behind interaction peaks, but do assume they are worth emphasizing regardless of the real cause. If a peak indicates importance, it would make sense to highlight it for future learners. If it indicates confusion, it may still make sense to emphasize so that learners would pay more attention.

To discover unsupported needs in lecture video navigation, we also conducted multiple rounds of feedback sessions with learners using our initial prototypes. The data analysis and interviews led to three high-level goals that informed our design of data-driven video interaction techniques.

Provide easy access to what other learners frequently watched. Our observations suggest that learners find it hard to identify and navigate to important parts of information-dense educational videos. To help a learner make more informed decisions about which part of the video to review, we leverage other learners' interaction traces, especially interaction peaks. We designed navigation techniques to emphasize these points of interest while the learner visually scans the video or physically scrubs the timeline.

Support both personal and collective video summaries. To prepare for homework assignments or exams, learners often take notes and watch videos multiple times to create a meaningful summary. Since there are often thousands of learners watching each video, we explore ways to present collective interaction traces as an alternative summary to complement each learner's personal summary. We extend prior work on social navigation in videos [28], history visualization, and revisitation mechanisms by supporting both manual bookmarking and automatic personal and collective watching traces.

Support diverse ways to search inside of a video. In our formative studies, learners described different ways they look for specific information inside a video. They would rely on both textual cues (e.g., topic and concept names) and visual cues (e.g., an image or a slide layout) to remember parts of the video. A more challenging case is when they cannot remember what the cue was for their particular information need. This observation inspired us to support both active search (e.g., when the learner has a clear search term), and ambient recommendations (e.g., when the learner does not know exactly what to search for). We designed techniques to enhance existing search mechanisms with interaction data, which provide social cues to serve both search scenarios.

DATA-DRIVEN VIDEO NAVIGATION TECHNIQUES

We introduce three interaction techniques to improve navigation of educational videos: an alternative timeline, search interface, and summarization method. Our main insight is to use the non-uniform distribution of learner activity within a video to better support common navigation patterns. Although the prototypes shown in this paper use videos on edX, a MOOC (Massive Open Online Course) platform, the techniques can be implemented for other video platforms such as YouTube because they use only standard Web technologies.

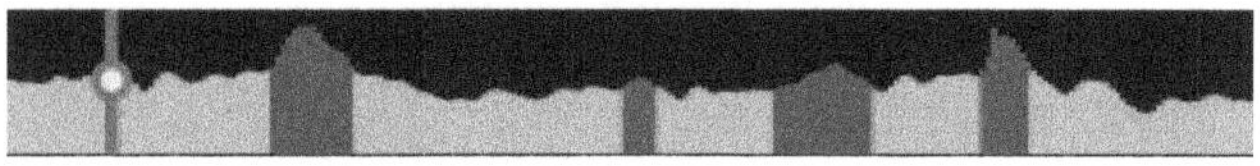

Figure 2. The 2D Rollercoaster timeline that appears below each video instead of a traditional 1D timeline. The height of the timeline at each point shows the amount of navigation activity by learners at that point. The magenta sections are automatically-detected interaction peaks.

The Rollercoaster Timeline: 2D, Non-Linear Timeline

To help learners identify and navigate to important parts of the video, we introduce the rollercoaster timeline. Unlike a traditional 1D timeline, the rollercoaster timeline is 2D with an embedded visualization of second-by-second learner interaction data (Figure 2). It visualizes the navigation frequency as a proxy of importance, as revealed by the behavior of other learners, and modifies the timeline scrubbing behavior to make precise navigation in important regions easier.

Navigation events are logged when the learner pauses and resumes the video, or navigates to a specific point. The Rollercoaster timeline uses navigation event counts as the vertical dimension. This visualization can also show other kinds of interaction events, including the number of viewers, rewatchers, unique viewers, or play or pause button clicks.

2D timeline

If the learner wants to jump to a specific point in the video, he can click on any point in the 2D timeline, which will capture the x coordinate of the click and update the playhead. The embedded peak visualization shows the intensity and range of each peak, and the overall distribution of the peaks within a video. Since interaction peaks are highlighted in magenta and span a wider region than other points, the learner can visually review and navigate to the commonly revisited parts in the video. We use the Twitinfo [23] peak detection algorithm to detect peaks in the server log data.

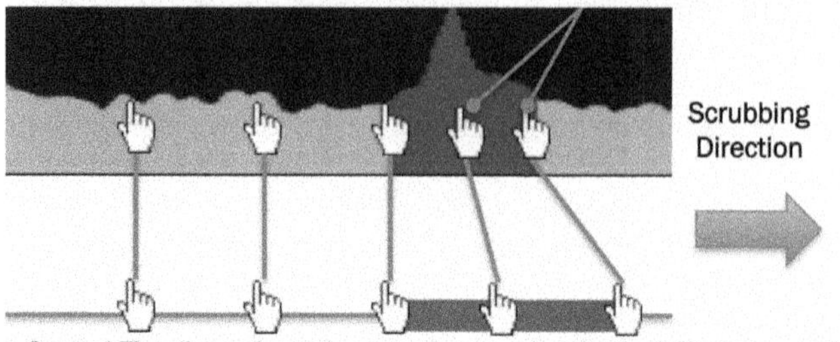

Figure 3. Non-linear scrubbing in the Rollercoaster timeline. To draw the learner's attention to content around interaction peaks, the phantom cursor decelerates scrubbing speed when the cursor enters a peak range.

Non-linear scrubbing with the phantom cursor

This timeline also enables dynamic, non-linear scrubbing, which takes advantage of interaction peaks. The basic idea is to apply friction while scrubbing around peaks, which leads to prolonged exposure so that learners can get a more comprehensive view of the frames near the peaks even when scrubbing quickly. Friction also makes it easier to precisely select specific frames within the range, since it lowers the frame update rate. It is an example of control-display ratio adaptation [5, 16, 37], dynamically changing the ratio between physical cursor movement and on-screen cursor movement.

Previous techniques have applied elastic, rubber band-like interactions to scrubbing [17, 24, 34, 35]. Our technique differs in that 1) it uses interaction data instead of content-driven keyframes, 2) elasticity is selectively applied to parts of the timeline, and 3) the playhead and the cursor are always synchronized, which reduced user confusion in our pilot studies.

When the mouse cursor enters a peak region while dragging, the dragging speed slows down relative to the dragging force, creating the sense of friction. The faster the dragging, the weaker the friction. We achieve this effect by temporarily hiding the real cursor, and replacing it with a *phantom cursor* that moves slower than the real cursor within peak ranges (Figure 3). The idea of enlarging the motor space around targets is inspired by Snap-and-Go [4].

Figure 4. The real-time personal watching traces visualize segments of the video that the learner has watched.

Personal watching trace visualization

When we observed pilot study users navigating videos with our timeline, a common desire was to keep track of which parts of the video they personally watched, which might not align with the aggregate interaction peaks collected over all learners. Thus, we added another stream under the timeline to visualize each learner's personal watching traces. Previous research has separated personal and collective history traces to support GUI command selection [26], and added history indicators to a document scrollbar [2], which improved task performance in information finding. We extend these approaches to video navigation by using personal watching traces to support revisitation. Once the learner pauses the video or jumps to a new point, the current watching segment is visualized on a separate track below the timeline (Figure 4). Clicking on a generated segment replays the segment. More recent segments are displayed with higher opacity to further emphasize them over older ones. These traces can be stored on a per-user basis to help learners quickly find points of interest when they return to re-watch a video at a later date.

Keyword Search and Visualization

To better support searching for relevant information inside of a video, we use interaction data to power keyword search and transcript analysis. Instead of weighing all occurrences equally, our search technique rewards results in sections of the video where more learners watched. Since key concepts often appear dozens of times in a video, this feature helps the learner prioritize which parts of the video to review. Furthermore, to support novice learners who do not necessarily have the vocabulary to translate their information needs into a direct search query, we suggest major topics discussed in each section of the video in a word cloud. These topics serve as a keyword summary that can help learners recognize and remember the main topics discussed in each video.

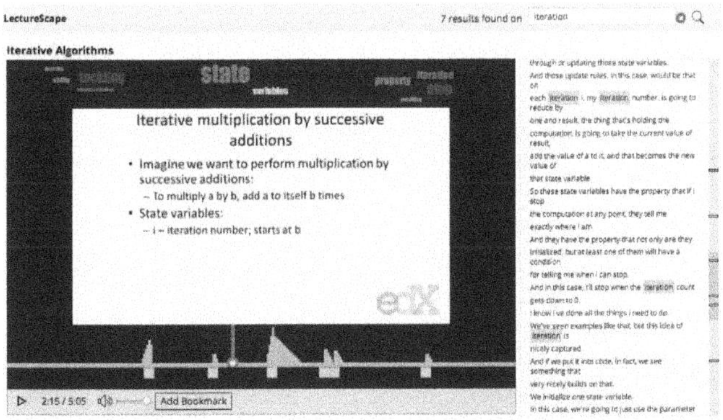

Figure 5. Our interaction data-driven keyword search brings in more context for the learner to decide where to focus on when searching for a keyword. For instance, the learner can visually check the distribution of when the lecturer said the keyword in the current video, which is useful in seeing where it was heavily discussed versus simply introduced.

Keyword search

If the learner has a keyword to search for, she can type it in the search field (top right in Figure 5), which searches over the full transcript of a video clip, and displays results both on the timeline and in the transcript. When the learner enters a search query, the timeline dynamically displays the search results instead of the default interaction visualization (see Figure 6). In this way, the timeline serves as a dynamic space for supporting different learner tasks by changing the peak points it emphasizes. Each result renders as a pyramid-shaped distribution, whose range is the duration of the sentence the word belongs to and whose peak is where the term is spoken. Figure 7 shows how hovering over the result displays a tooltip, and clicking on the result plays the video from the beginning of the sentence that includes the search term. This sentence-level playback provides the learner with more context surrounding the term.

Figure 6. The search timeline appears below the video after each search. It visualizes the positions of search results, as well as the relative importance of each. Here the high peak in the middle indicates both that it contains the search term and that lots of learners watched that part.

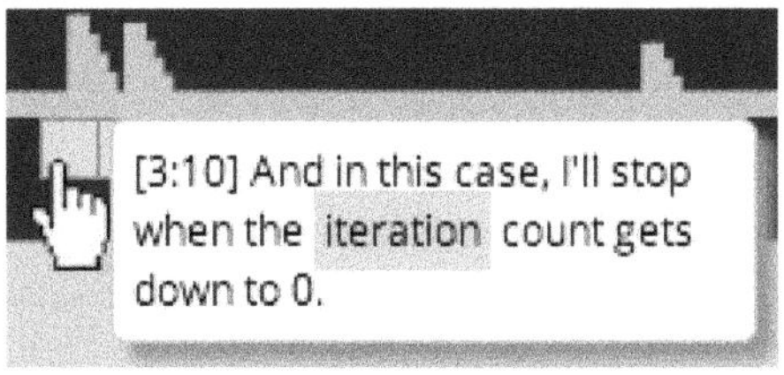

Figure 7. Hovering on a search result displays a tooltip with the transcript sentence that contains the search term. Clicking on the result plays the video starting at the beginning of the sentence to assist the learner with comprehending the surrounding context.

Because key terms are repeated many times even during a short video, it can be hard for the learner to locate the most important search result. For example, in a 5-minute edX video on iterative algorithms, "variable" is mentioned 13 times, and "state" 12 times. We use interaction data to rank search results, with the assumption that parts of the video more frequently watched by previous learners are likely to reflect the current learner's interest. Our ranking algorithm analyzes learner activity around a search result and assigns a weight to the result, giving higher weights to sentences that were viewed by more learners. It then computes the relevance score by combining this weight with term frequency within the sentence. To support quick visual inspection of search results, we represent the computed score as the height on the timeline (gray peaks in Figure 6). If the term was mentioned multiple times in a sentence, we convolve the distributions for all occurrences and assign the maximum score to it.

Figure 8. The word cloud displays automatically-extracted topics for the currently visible section of the video, providing a keyword-based summarization of the video. Clicking on any word triggers a search for it.

Word cloud: topic summarization and visualization

To address the low visual variation between frames in many videos and to help learners recognize and remember major topics in the clip, we use word clouds to dynamically display keywords in different segments of the video. We use TF-IDF (term frequency-inverse document frequency) scores for extracting keywords and weighing their importance. To compute the TF-IDF scores for the keywords in a transcript, we define a document as the transcription sentences between two consecutive interaction peaks, and the background corpus as the collection of all video transcripts in the entire course. This user activity-driven mechanism extracts self-contained segments from each video.

The visualization is positioned directly above the video as a panel consisting of three word clouds (see Figure 8), and gets updated at every interaction peak. The center cloud corresponds to the present segment being viewed, and two additional clouds represent the previous and upcoming segments, respectively. These displays are intended to give a sense of how lecture content in the current segment compares to that of surrounding segments. To bring focus to the current word cloud, we de-emphasize the previous and next word clouds by decreasing their opacity and word size relative to the current cloud. Clicking on any keyword in the cloud triggers a search using that term, visualizing the occurrences in the transcript as well as on the timeline.

Video Summarization with Highlights

To enable a quick overview of important points, we present a strip of visual highlights of selected video frames. Consistent with our design goal of providing access to both personal and collective interaction traces in the timeline, we support both collective and personal highlights. Collective highlights are captured by interaction peaks, while personal highlights are captured by the learner bookmarking a frame of interest.

Interaction peak highlights

We capture interaction peaks and provide one-click access to them to support common watching patterns such as jumping directly to these points. The storyboard-style display of the peak frames allows the learner to visually scan the video's progress (Figure 1). These highlights are visually-oriented, while the word cloud of Figure 8 is text-oriented.

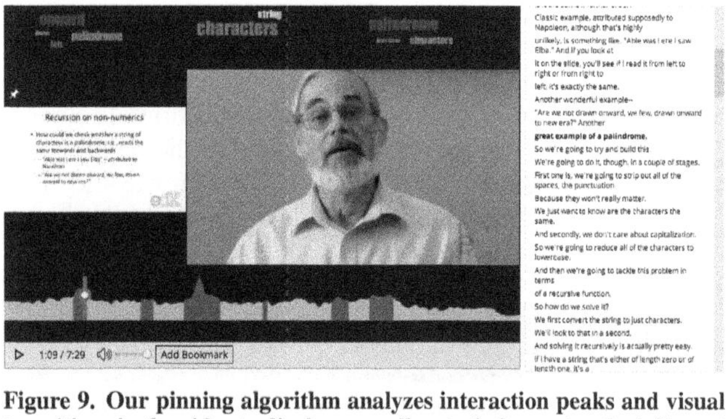

Figure 9. Our pinning algorithm analyzes interaction peaks and visual transitions in the video to display a smaller static frame (on the left) next to the video (on the right). Learners can manually pin any frame as well.

Pinning video frames

Most existing video players display only one frame at a time. This ubiquitous interface is sensible for the narrative structure of general-purpose videos such as TV shows, where a sequential flow is natural. However, educational videos are information-heavy, and active learning involves skimming and scrubbing [20]. For example, an instructor might verbally refer to the formula she described in the previous PowerPoint slide, but the formula might no longer be available on screen. A learner who wants to refer to that formula has to scrub the video timeline to go back to a frame with the relevant formula slide. To support watching patterns that are not easily supported by existing players, our video player pins a relevant frame next to the video stream for easy reference (Figure 9).

Our video player automatically determines a frame to pin. A relevant pinned frame should 1) not be identical to what is currently shown in the video, 2) include important content that is worth referencing, and 3) contain readable content such a textual slide or technical diagram, not merely a static frame of the instructor's face or students sitting in a classroom. Otherwise, juxtaposing a static frame next to the video might cause distraction and visual clutter. To meet these requirements, our pinning algorithm uses both interaction peaks and visual transitions. It automatically pins an interaction peak frame if there is a visual transition shortly after the peak. Checking for a visual transition ensures that the pinned frame is not visually identical to the frames right after the transition. Also, pinning an interaction peak frame ensures that the frame at least includes content viewed by many others.

The learner can also manually pin a frame by clicking the pin icon attached to each peak frame, which replaces the current pinned frame with the learner's. While the system attempts its best effort to show the most relevant frame at a given time, the learner also has the flexibility to control what gets displayed.

Figure 10. The learner can add a labeled bookmark, which is added to the highlights stream below the video for visual preview and revisitation.

Personal bookmarks

While peak frames might be a reasonable summary of a video, individual learners might have summarization needs that are not captured by the collective traces. The learner can add personal bookmarks by clicking on the "Add Bookmark" button. The learner can see the captured frame at the point of click and add their own label for future reference (Figure 10). Once a bookmark is saved, it is added to the highlights stream, chronologically ordered along with other bookmarks and interaction peak highlights. This view allows the learner to choose between naturally-formed interaction peaks by other learners as well as self-generated bookmarks.

LECTURESCAPE: WEB-BASED PROTOTYPE

This section introduces LectureScape, a prototype lecture video player that combines all of the techniques in a unified interface (see Figure 1). The main goal of LectureScape is to give learners more control and flexibility in deciding how to navigate educational videos. LectureScape features the video player in the main view, along with the Rollercoaster timeline below the video and the word cloud above it. The interactive transcript is in the right sidebar, and the highlights are positioned at the bottom of the screen. The search box at the top enables keyword search. The widgets are all collapsible to reduce visual clutter and to hide unused features.

We implemented LectureScape using standard Web technologies: HTML5, CSS3, and JavaScript. The word cloud and Rollercoaster timeline are rendered with D3 [6]. Our customized HTML5 video player does not require additional re-encoding or streaming, and is independent of the encoding or streaming method used. It only requires interaction data for each video to activate the data-driven interaction techniques. Our data processing pipeline formats interaction traces and generates visual assets from an existing video.

First, three data streams are stored for each video: interaction data, TF-IDF results on the transcript, and visual transition data. Our peak detection algorithm runs on page load, which allows dynamic parameter tuning. Peak detection is run on both the interaction data and visual transition data, which returns interaction peaks and shot boundaries, respectively.

Second, the system generates thumbnail images for each second of a video. Because many of our interactions require displaying a thumbnail of a video frame on demand, low latency in image loading is crucial in supporting seamless interactions. It is especially important for educational videos whose visual changes are more subtle than in movies or TV shows, and whose on-screen information matters for learners to read and comprehend. Upon a page load, the system preloads all thumbnails for a video. When a learner drags the timeline, instead of loading the video each time a dragging event is triggered, our player pauses the video and displays an overlay screenshot. This results in much less latency and smoother dragging, similar to the benefits reported by Swift [25].

EVALUATION

To assess the feasibility of using interaction data to enhance video navigation, we conducted a user study comparing video players with and without our data-driven interaction techniques. We explored three research questions:

- **RQ1.** How do learners navigate lecture videos with LectureScape in typical kinds of learning tasks such as search and summarization?
- **RQ2.** How do learners interpret interaction data presented in LectureScape?
- **RQ3.** Are LectureScape's features useful and learnable?

Study Design

The study was a within-subjects design, where each learner used both LectureScape and a baseline interface that stripped off all interaction data-related features from LectureScape. The baseline interface still included the interactive transcript and preview thumbnails on hover, to emulate what is available in platforms such as edX or YouTube. To maintain uniformity in look and feel for our comparative study, the baseline interface had the same layout and visual design as LectureScape.

Learners performed three types of learning tasks for lecture videos: visual search, problem search, and summarization. These tasks represent realistic video watching scenarios from our observations, and match common evaluation tasks used in the literature on video navigation interfaces [11, 32].

- **Visual search** tasks involved finding a specific piece of visual content in a video. These tasks emulated situations when a learner remembers something visually and wants to find where it appeared in a video. For example, for a video about tuples in Python, a visual search task asked: *"Find a slide where the instructor displays on screen examples of the singleton operation."* Targets were slides that appeared briefly (less than 20 seconds) in the video. We mixed tasks that had targets around interaction peaks and non-peaks to investigate how LectureScape fares even when the target is not near a peak. For all visual search tasks, we provided learners with only the video timeline (linear timeline in baseline, 2D timeline in LectureScape) and removed all other features (e.g., transcript, word cloud) to restrict video navigation to timelines only. Learners were told to pause the video as soon as they navigated to the answer.
- **Problem search** tasks involved finding an answer to a given problem. These tasks emulated a learner rewatching a relevant video to answer a discussion forum question or to solve a homework problem. For example, for a video about approximation methods, a problem search task asked: *"If the step size in an approximation method decreases, does the code run faster or slower?"* Learners were asked to find the part in the video that discussed the answer, and then state their answer.
- **Summarization** tasks required learners to write down the main points of a video while skimming through it. We gave learners only three minutes to summarize videos that were seven to eight minutes long, with the intent of motivating learners to be selective about what parts to watch.

All videos used in the study were from an introductory computer science course on edX. Interaction data was collected from server logs during the first offering of the course in fall 2012. The course has been recurring every semester since then. Each of the eight tasks in the study used different videos to minimize learning effects. We also chose videos of similar length, difficulty, and style within each task type to control for differences across videos.

Participants

We recruited 12 participants (5 male, mean age 25.6, stdev=11.0, max=49, min=18) via a recruitment flyer on the course discussion forum on edX and the on-campus course website, both with consent from instructors. We recruited only learners who were currently enrolled in the introductory CS course (either on edX or on campus) to which the videos belong. The on-campus version of the course shares the same curriculum but is taught by different instructors. Furthermore, we picked videos for lessons given earlier in the semester, so that participants were likely to have already been exposed to that material before coming to our study, as is often the case in video re-watching scenarios. Four participants were enrolled in a current or previous edX offering of the course, while six were taking the on-campus version. Two had previously registered in the online offering but were currently taking the on-campus course. Participants received $30 for their time.

Procedure

A 75-minute study session started with 15-minute tutorials on both interfaces. Next, participants performed eight learning tasks: four visual search tasks, two problem search tasks, and two summarization tasks. After each task, they answered questions about confidence in their answer and prior exposure to the video. After each task type, we interviewed them about their task strategy. For each task type, we counterbalanced the order of the interfaces and the assignment of videos to tasks. After completing all the tasks, participants completed a questionnaire on the usability of each interface and their experience and opinions about interaction data. All click-level interactions were logged by the server for analysis.

Results

RQ1. Navigation Patterns for Search and Summarization

In **visual search**, most participants in the baseline 1D timeline sequentially scanned the video using thumbnail previews or dragging. In contrast, participants using the 2D Rollercoaster timeline often jumped between interaction peaks to reach the general area of the answer. But the latter strategy did not help in many cases because interaction data represents collective interests in a video, not results for a search query.

For the two out of four tasks where the search targets were located near interaction peaks, it took participants in both conditions similar amounts of time (LectureScape: μ=85 seconds, σ=51, baseline: μ=80, σ=73). This difference was not statistically significant with the Mann-Whitney U (MWU) test ($p>0.4$, Z=-0.9). For the other two tasks where the search targets were outside of an interaction peak range, it took participants in the LectureScape condition longer to complete (μ=117, σ=44) than in the baseline condition (μ=90, σ=50), although the MWU test showed no statistical significance ($p>0.1$, Z=-1.5) The longer time might be due to the fact that many participants navigated by clicking on the peaks to see if the answer existed around peaks. Nonetheless, results show that LectureScape did not adversely affect task completion times even when the answer was not in peak ranges.

Because **problem search** tasks required some understanding of the context to provide an answer, participants often tackled the problem by narrowing down to a section of the video that mentioned relevant concepts and then watching the section until they found the answer. In the process of narrowing down to a video section, most participants in the baseline condition relied on searching for keywords (10 out of 12) and clicking on transcript text (11 / 12), while participants with LectureScape used search (6 / 12) and clicking on transcript text (6 / 12) less frequently, and additionally clicked on interaction peaks on the timeline (6 / 12) or highlights below the video (6 / 12). Over all problem search tasks, participants in the LectureScape condition completed them slightly faster (μ=96, σ=58) than participants in the baseline condition (μ=106, σ=58), although the difference was not significant (MWU test, p=0.8, Z=0.3).

In comparison to the other tasks, participants in **summarization** tasks did not rely on keyword search (1 / 12 in both conditions), because the task required them to quickly scan the entire video for the main points. Many participants with LectureScape scanned the peak visualization, word cloud, and highlights for an overview, and clicked on interaction peaks (9 / 12) or highlights (6 / 12) for a detailed review. In one video, all six participants with LectureScape visited an interaction peak almost at the end of the video (located at 6:35 in the 7:00 clip). This slide summarized main ideas of variable binding, which was the topic of the video. In contrast, in the baseline condition, only one learner navigated to this section of the video. Most participants spent majority of their time in the earlier part of the video in the baseline condition.

Despite inconclusive evidence on quantitative differences in task completion time, participants believed that they were able to complete the tasks faster and more efficiently with LectureScape than with the baseline interface. Answers to 7-point Likert scale questions on the overall task experience revealed significant differences between the two interfaces in participants' belief in speed (LectureScape: μ=5.8, Baseline: μ=4.8) and efficiency (LectureScape: μ=6.1, Baseline: μ=4.8). The MWU test shows that both differences were significant at $p<0.05$ for these questions.

RQ2. Perception of Interaction Data

Generally, participants' comments about watching videos augmented by others' interaction data were positive. Participants noted that *"It's not like cold-watching. It feels like watching with other students."*, and *"[interaction data] makes it seem more classroom-y, as in you can compare yourself to what how other students are learning and what they need to repeat."*

In response to 7-point Likert scale questions about the experience of seeing interaction data, participants indicated that they found such data to be "easy to understand" (μ=5.9), "useful" (5.3), "enjoyable" (5.2), that interaction peaks affected their navigation (5), and that interaction peaks matched their personal points of interest in the video (4.4).

In an open-ended question, we asked participants why they thought interaction peaks occurred. Common reasons provided were that these parts were "confusing" (mentioned by 8 / 12), "important" (6 / 12), and "complex" (4 / 12). Identifying the cause of a peak might be useful because they can enable more customized navigation support. While most participants mentioned that highlighting confusing and important parts would be useful, some noted that personal context may not match the collective patterns. One said, *"If it were a topic where I was not very confident in my own knowledge, I would find it very helpful to emphasize where others have re-watched the video. If however it was a topic I was comfortable with and was watching just to review, I would find it frustrating to have the physical scrolling be slowed down due to others' behavior while watching the video."*

RQ3. Perceived Usability of LectureScape

Many participants preferred having more options in navigating lecture videos. As one learner noted, *"I like all the extra features! I was sad when they got taken away [for the baseline condition]."* Also, when asked if the interface had all the functions and capabilities they expected, participants rated LectureScape (6.4) significantly higher than the baseline interface (4.3) ($p<0.001$, Z=-3.2 with the MWU test).

However, some expressed that LectureScape was visually complex, and that they would have liked to hide some widgets not in use at the moment. They found it more difficult to use than the baseline (ease of use: 4.7 vs. 6.3, $p<0.001$, $Z=2.7$ with the MWU test). This perception leaves room for improvement in the learnability of the system. A participant commented: *"[LectureScape] is fairly complex and has a lot of different elements so I think it may take a bit of time for users to fully adjust to using the interface to its full potential."* These comments are consistent with our design decision to support collapsible widgets to reduce visual clutter, although the version of LectureScape used in the study had all features activated for the purpose of usability testing.

Due to the limitations of a single-session lab study, few participants actively used personal bookmarks or personal history traces. A longitudinal deployment might be required to evaluate the usefulness of these features.

Navigation Pattern Analysis

Now we provide a detailed analysis of how participants navigated videos during the study. In all tasks, most participants' strategy was to start with an overview, and then focus on some parts in detail. Participants alternated between the overview and focus stages until they found what they were looking for, or covered all major points in the video for summarization.

While the high-level strategy was similar in the two video interfaces, participants' navigation patterns within each of the two stages differed noticeably. With LectureScape, participants used more diverse options for overview and focused navigation, making more directed jumps to important points in the video. With the baseline interface, most participants sequentially scanned the video for overview and clicked on the timeline or transcript for focusing. Another common pattern in the baseline condition was to make short and conservative jumps on the timeline from the beginning of the video, in order not to miss anything important while moving quickly.

In the **overview** stage, most participants tried to scan the video to grasp the general flow and select a few points to review further. One learner described her strategy with LectureScape in this stage: *"having this idea of 'here's where other people have gone back and rewatched, being able to visually skim through very quickly and see titles, main bullet points, and following along with the transcript a little bit as well was definitely helpful."* Although visual scanning did not result in click log entries, our interviews with participants confirm that it was a common pattern. They pointed out three main features in LectureScape that supported overview:

- the 2D timeline with an overall learner activity visualization: *"I could use the 2D overlay to scroll through... I think I took a quick scan through and saw the general overview of what was on the slides."*
- highlight summaries with a strip of screenshots: *"They would get me close to the information I needed. They also made it easier to quickly summarize."*
- the word cloud with main keywords for sections in the video: *"I just looked at the top keywords, then I watched the video to see how [the instructor] uses those keywords."*

After scanning for an overview, participants chose a point in the video to watch further. All of the methods described above provide a single-click mechanism to directly jump to an "important" part of the video. Participants reviewed data-driven suggestions from LectureScape to make informed decisions. The log analysis reveals that participants using LectureScape made direct jumps such as clicking on a specific point in the timeline or a highlight 8.4 times on average per task, in contrast to 5.6 times in the baseline condition.

In the **focus** stage, participants watched a segment in the video and reviewed if content is relevant to the task at hand. In this stage they relied on methods for precise navigation: scrubbing the timeline a few pixels for a second-by-second review, and re-watching video snippets multiple times until they fully comprehend the content. With LectureScape, participants had options to use the slowed-down scrubbing around peaks in the rollercoaster timeline, automatic pinning of the previous slide, and sentence-level playback in search. To navigate back to the previously examined point, participants frequently used timestamped anchors attached to search results, interaction peaks, and highlights.

In summary, with LectureScape, participants used more navigation options in both the overview and focus stages. A learner commented that *"[LectureScape] gives you more options. It personalizes the strategy I can use in the task."* They had more control in which part of the video to watch, which might have led them to believe that they completed the tasks faster and more efficiently.

DISCUSSION AND FUTURE WORK

Availability of interaction data: Discussion throughout this paper assumes the availability of large-scale interaction data. With modern Web technologies, clickstream logging can be easily added with APIs for video event handling.

There remain unanswered questions around interaction data, such as "Will using the data-driven techniques bias the data so that it reinforces premature peak signals and ignores other potentially important ones?", and "How many data points are required until salient peaks and patterns emerge?" Our future work will address these questions through a live deployment on a MOOC platform such as edX. We will also explore other types of interaction data such as active bookmarking and content streams such as voice to enrich video-based learning.

Adaptive video UI: The data-driven techniques introduced in this paper open opportunities for more adaptive and personalized video learning experiences. In this paper, we demonstrated how collective viewership data can change the video interface dynamically, influencing the physical scrubbing behavior, search ranking algorithm, and side-by-side frame display. We envision future video UIs that adapt to collective usage. Also, incorporating interaction data can lead to personalized video learning. Because interaction data is likely to represent an average learner, comparing personal history traces against collective traces may help model the current user more accurately and improve personalization.

Beyond MOOC-style lecture videos: While this paper used MOOC-style lecture videos for demonstration, we believe our techniques can generalize to other types of educational videos such as programming tutorial screencasts, how-to demonstration videos, and health education videos. We expect to apply the techniques introduced in this paper to these videos.

CONCLUSION

This paper introduces a novel concept of designing video interaction techniques by leveraging large-scale interaction data. We present three sets of data-driven techniques to demonstrate the capability of the concept: 2D, non-linear timeline, enhanced in-video search, and a visual summarization method. In a lab study, participants found interaction data to draw attention to points of importance and confusion, and navigated lecture videos with more control and flexibility.

Ultimately, the design techniques we have presented provide enriched alternatives to conventional video navigation. We envision engaging a community of learners in creating a social, interactive, and collaborative video learning environment powered by rich community data.

ACKNOWLEDGMENTS

The authors thank the members of the UID Group at MIT CSAIL for their feedback, and the 6.01x course staff for study advertisement. This work was funded in part by Quanta Computer. The Samsung Fellowship has supported Juho Kim.

REFERENCES

1. Al-Hajri, A., Miller, G., Fong, M., and Fels, S. S. Visualization of personal history for video navigation. In *CHI '14* (2014).
2. Alexander, J., Cockburn, A., Fitchett, S., Gutwin, C., and Greenberg, S. Revisiting read wear: Analysis, design, and evaluation of a footprints scrollbar. In *CHI '09* (2009), 1665–1674.
3. Arman, F., Depommier, R., Hsu, A., and Chiu, M.-Y. Content-based browsing of video sequences. In *MULTIMEDIA '94* (1994), 97–103.
4. Baudisch, P., Cutrell, E., Hinckley, K., and Eversole, A. Snap-and-go: Helping users align objects without the modality of traditional snapping. In *CHI '05* (2005), 301–310.
5. Blanch, R., Guiard, Y., and Beaudouin-Lafon, M. Semantic pointing: Improving target acquisition with control-display ratio adaptation. In *CHI '04* (2004), 519–526.
6. Bostock, M., Ogievetsky, V., and Heer, J. D^3 data-driven documents. *Visualization and Computer Graphics, IEEE Transactions on 17*, 12 (2011), 2301–2309.
7. Carlier, A., Charvillat, V., Ooi, W. T., Grigoras, R., and Morin, G. Crowdsourced automatic zoom and scroll for video retargeting. In *Multimedia '10* (2010), 201–210.
8. Chi, P.-Y. P., Liu, J., Linder, J., Dontcheva, M., Li, W., and Hartmann, B. Democut: generating concise instructional videos for physical demonstrations. In *UIST '13*, ACM (2013).
9. Chorianopoulos, K. Collective intelligence within web video. *Human-centric Computing and Information Sciences 3*, 1 (2013), 10.
10. Dieberger, A., Dourish, P., Höök, K., Resnick, P., and Wexelblat, A. Social navigation: Techniques for building more usable systems. *Interactions 7*, 6 (Nov. 2000), 36–45.
11. Ding, W., and Marchionini, G. A study on video browsing strategies. Tech. rep., College Park, MD, USA, 1997.
12. Grossman, T., Matejka, J., and Fitzmaurice, G. Chronicle: capture, exploration, and playback of document workflow histories. In *UIST '10* (2010).
13. Guo, P. J., Kim, J., and Rubin, R. How video production affects student engagement: An empirical study of mooc videos. In *L@S '14* (2014), 41–50.
14. Hill, W. C., Hollan, J. D., Wroblewski, D., and McCandless, T. Edit wear and read wear. In *CHI '92* (1992), 3–9.
15. Hou, X., and Zhang, L. Saliency detection: A spectral residual approach. In *CVPR '07* (2007), 1–8.
16. Hurst, A., Mankoff, J., Dey, A. K., and Hudson, S. E. Dirty desktops: Using a patina of magnetic mouse dust to make common interactor targets easier to select. In *UIST '07* (2007), 183–186.
17. Hürst, W., Götz, G., and Jarvers, P. Advanced user interfaces for dynamic video browsing. In *MULTIMEDIA '04* (2004), 742–743.
18. Jackson, D., Nicholson, J., Stoeckigt, G., Wrobel, R., Thieme, A., and Olivier, P. Panopticon: A parallel video overview system. In *UIST '13* (2013), 123–130.
19. Jansen, M., Heeren, W., and van Dijk, B. Videotrees: Improving video surrogate presentation using hierarchy. In *CBMI 2008*, IEEE (June 2008), 560–567.
20. Kim, J., Guo, P. J., Seaton, D. T., Mitros, P., Gajos, K. Z., and Miller, R. C. Understanding in-video dropouts and interaction peaks in online lecture videos. In *L@S '14* (2014), 31–40.
21. Kim, J., Nguyen, P., Weir, S., Guo, P., Gajos, K., and Miller, R. Crowdsourcing step-by-step information extraction to enhance existing how-to videos. In *CHI '14* (2014).
22. Li, F. C., Gupta, A., Sanocki, E., He, L.-w., and Rui, Y. Browsing digital video. In *CHI '00* (2000), 169–176.
23. Marcus, A., Bernstein, M. S., Badar, O., Karger, D. R., Madden, S., and Miller, R. C. Twitinfo: aggregating and visualizing microblogs for event exploration. In *CHI '11* (2011), 227–236.
24. Masui, T., Kashiwagi, K., and Borden, IV, G. R. Elastic graphical interfaces to precise data manipulation. In *CHI '95* (1995), 143–144.
25. Matejka, J., Grossman, T., and Fitzmaurice, G. Swift: Reducing the effects of latency in online video scrubbing. In *CHI '12* (2012), 637–646.
26. Matejka, J., Grossman, T., and Fitzmaurice, G. Patina: Dynamic heatmaps for visualizing application usage. In *CHI '13* (2013), 3227–3236.
27. Matejka, J., Grossman, T., and Fitzmaurice, G. Swifter: Improved online video scrubbing. In *CHI '13* (2013), 1159–1168.
28. Mertens, R., Farzan, R., and Brusilovsky, P. Social navigation in web lectures. In *HYPERTEXT '06* (2006), 41–44.
29. Monserrat, T.-J. K. P., Zhao, S., McGee, K., and Pandey, A. V. Notevideo: Facilitating navigation of blackboard-style lecture videos. In *CHI '13* (2013), 1139–1148.
30. Nancel, M., and Cockburn, A. Causality: A conceptual model of interaction history. In *CHI '14* (2014).
31. Nguyen, C., Niu, Y., and Liu, F. Video summagator: An interface for video summarization and navigation. In *CHI '12* (2012), 647–650.
32. Nicholson, J., Huber, M., Jackson, D., and Olivier, P. Panopticon as an elearning support search tool. In *CHI '14* (2014).
33. Olsen, D. R., and Moon, B. Video summarization based on user interaction. In *EuroITV '11* (2011), 115–122.
34. Pongnumkul, S., Wang, J., Ramos, G., and Cohen, M. Content-aware dynamic timeline for video browsing. In *UIST '10* (2010), 139–142.
35. Ramos, G., and Balakrishnan, R. Fluid interaction techniques for the control and annotation of digital video. In *UIST '03* (2003), 105–114.
36. Risko, E., Foulsham, T., Dawson, S., and Kingstone, A. The collaborative lecture annotation system (clas): A new tool for distributed learning. *Learning Technologies, IEEE Transactions on 6*, 1 (2013), 4–13.
37. Scott MacKenzie, I., and Riddersma, S. Effects of output display and control–display gain on human performance in interactive systems. *Behaviour & Information Technology 13*, 5 (1994), 328–337.
38. Shaw, R., and Davis, M. Toward emergent representations for video. In *Multimedia '05* (2005), 431–434.
39. Yew, J., Shamma, D. A., and Churchill, E. F. Knowing funny: genre perception and categorization in social video sharing. In *CHI '11* (2011), 297–306.

Video Digests: A Browsable, Skimmable Format for Informational Lecture Videos

Amy Pavel, Colorado Reed, Björn Hartmann, Maneesh Agrawala
University of California, Berkeley
{amypavel, cjrd, bjoern, maneesh}@cs.berkeley.edu

ABSTRACT
Increasingly, authors are publishing long informational talks, lectures, and distance-learning videos online. However, it is difficult to browse and skim the content of such videos using current timeline-based video players. Video digests are a new format for informational videos that afford browsing and skimming by segmenting videos into a chapter/section structure and providing short text summaries and thumbnails for each section. Viewers can navigate by reading the summaries and clicking on sections to access the corresponding point in the video. We present a set of tools to help authors create such digests using transcript-based interactions. With our tools, authors can manually create a video digest from scratch, or they can automatically generate a digest by applying a combination of algorithmic and crowdsourcing techniques and then manually refine it as needed. Feedback from first-time users suggests that our transcript-based authoring tools and automated techniques greatly facilitate video digest creation. In an evaluative crowdsourced study we find that given a short viewing time, video digests support browsing and skimming better than timeline-based or transcript-based video players.

Author Keywords
video digests; education; video presentation interfaces

ACM Classification Keywords
H.5.m. Information Interfaces and Presentation (e.g. HCI): Miscellaneous

INTRODUCTION
Informative videos such as classroom lectures, seminar talks, and distance-learning presentations are increasingly published online. For instance, websites such as edX [1], Khan Academy [2], and TED [3], offer thousands of informative video presentation on a wide variety of topics. Unlike live presentations, viewers can pause, replay, navigate, and alter playback speed to change the pace and structure of the video. The permanency of video also provides a referencable resource for later review.

Yet, one problem with video as a medium for informative presentations, is that it is difficult for viewers to browse and skim the underlying content. Viewers must scrub back-and-forth through a video to gain an overview of the presented topics or locate content of interest. Some platforms, such as edX and TED, let users search and navigate videos via a transcript; clicking a word in the transcript plays the video at that location. While transcripts do expose the content of the video, transcripts of informational videos often consist of long blocks of text and usually contain disfluencies and redundancies typical of speech. This makes the transcripts time-consuming to read and difficult to skim. Moreover, without a structured organization to the text, it can be difficult for viewers to browse the topics covered in the video or get a high-level overview of the content.

Recently, Bret Victor introduced a format for informational video presentations that is explicitly designed to helps viewer browse and skim a video presentation [41]. As shown in Figure 1, this format uses a textbook-inspired chapter/section structure to explicitly display the major themes in a presentation (the "chapters") as well as lower-level summaries of these themes (the "sections"). Specifically, each chapter corresponds to a topically-coherent segment of the video and consists of an embedded video player, a description (title) of the major theme in the segment, and a sequence of section elements. Each section element provides a short text summary and representative keyframe for a video segment within the chapter-level segment. We call this format a *video digest*.

The visual design of such video digests directly exposes the content of a video at a topical level: viewers can browse the chapter titles to obtain an understanding of the major themes in the presentation and skim the short summaries and keyframes to gain a finer-grained understanding of the presented content. This format encourages dividing informative presentations into short, topically-coherent video segments which, as indicated by prior work, aids knowledge transfer and decreases dropouts for educational videos [32, 20, 26]. However, creating a video digest is a time-consuming process: authors must segment the videos at multiple granularities (chapter/section), compose section summaries, select representative keyframes, and create the final output display.

In this paper, we present a set of tools to help authors create video digests by efficiently segmenting and summarizing the video through *transcript-based interactions*. The key insight of our approach is that much of the information in lecture videos is conveyed through speech. Therefore, our interface allows authors to navigate, segment and summarize the video using a time-aligned transcript of the speech. We also provide algorithmic tools for automatically segmenting the video

UIST 2014, October 5–8, 2014, Honolulu, HI, USA.
ACM 978-1-4503-3069-5/14/10.
http://dx.doi.org/10.1145/2642918.2647400

Figure 1. A video digest affords browsing and skimming through a textbook-inspired chapter/section organization of the video content. The chapters are topically coherent segments of the video that contain major themes in the presentation. Each chapter is further subdivided into a set of sections, that each provide a brief text summary of the corresponding video segment as well as a representative keyframe image. Clicking within a section plays the video starting at the beginning of corresponding video segment.

and a crowdsourcing pipeline for summarizing the resulting segments. Authors can further refine these auto-generated digests in the authoring interface if necessary.

We use our tools to generate video digests for several kinds of informational videos, ranging from a TED talk to an online MOOC lecture. We compare manually authored digests to auto-generated digests and find that they both distill the informational content to the most important topics. However, the auto-generated digests are more verbose than the manually authored digests. Feedback from first-time authors suggests that our transcript-based authoring tools combined with the automatic seeding greatly facilitate digest creation. We also conduct a crowdsourced study comparing video digests to timeline-based and transcript-based video player. We find that given 2 minutes to view lecture videos that are about 15 minutes long, viewers can recall up to twice as many of the key topics of the video using the digest format. At 8 minutes of viewing time, the differences between formats recedes. These results suggest that video digests support browsing and skimming of lecture videos better than the standard formats.

RELATED WORK

Our video digest format is inspired by Bret Victor's hand-crafted presentation design that he created for his talk *Media for Thinking the Unthinkable* [41]. Similarly, our work also draws from Jonathan Corum's slide-based presentation format that juxtaposes an image of each presentation slide with a transcript of the corresponding speech [15]. These examples were hand-crafted using a collection of off-the-shelf video editing, image retouching and HTML/Javascript coding tools. In contrast, our authoring tools combine techniques from prior work in video summarization, text summarization and media editing to facilitate the creation of video digests.

Video Summarization

Automatically summarizing a video to include only the most salient content is a long-standing research problem. Truong and Venkatesh's [39] survey of work on this problem divides video summarization methods into two main approaches; *keyframe methods* identify a sequence of static frames that together represent the salient video content [40, 8, 4, 22], while *video skim methods* shorten the input video by removing non-essential content [36, 23, 38, 14]. Keyframe methods primarily focus on conveying the visual content of a video in static form and are not designed to expose any of the information content contained in the vocal audio track. Video skims concatenate important segments of a video into a shorter video, but still rely on opaque, timeline-based navigation of the video's content. In contrast, our work focuses on presenting the informational content of a video in a hierarchically organized chapter/section structure that supports browsing and skimming.

An alternative to algorithmic video summarization is to crowdsource the summarization task. Adrenaline [5] uses a crowdsourcing pipeline to extract representative keyframes from video segments. EpicPlay [37] uses viewers' interactions on social media to identify important moments in sports video. Lasecki et al. [29, 30] use non-expert crowds to transcribe videos and to describe activities in videos. Most related to our technique is the work by Kim et al. [26] which annotates steps in how-to videos. They use a Find-Verify-Expand technique to label steps in a how-to video and associates before and after images of each actionable step. Our work similarly relies on crowdsourced judgments to extract information from a lecture video.

Text Summarization

Text summarization can be divided into two alternative approaches [33]: *extractive* summaries concatenate existing text fragments from the document, while *abstractive* summaries generate new language to convey the main topics of the text. As lecture transcripts often contain disfluencies and redundancies typical of speech, directly concatenating portions of the transcript into an extractive summary often generates incoherent results. Therefore we focus on generating abstractive summaries for video digests, but because current algorithmic techniques cannot produce human quality abstractive summaries [21], we use crowdsourcing to generate them.

Our work builds on several previous crowdsourcing techniques for abstractive summarization of text. Soylent [6] employs human language understanding to generate abstractive summaries to shorten text: different sets of crowd workers identify lengthy sentences, rewrite to shorten these sentences, and vote on the best edits. However, edits are limited to single sentences and the resulting summaries are not always coherent across different edits. Burrows et al. [9] develop a crowdsourcing pipeline for summarizing text documents that includes an automatic classifier designed to filter out poor summaries. Researchers have also presented techniques for using crowdsourced summaries of text documents to improve machine translation pipelines [10, 16]. We are inspired by these prior techniques and introduce a new crowdsourcing method to generate high-quality abstractive summaries based on text and video information.

Media Editing Tools

Our tools for generating video digests also build upon prior work on transcript-based video and audio editors. Several systems have used time-aligned transcripts to support audio/video editing through text manipulation operations [43, 11, 7, 35]. Such tools provide, for example, clip segmentation through editing markers in the transcript. Other metadata, such as annotations of actions and steps, can facilitate automatic shortening of how-to videos [12]. Drawing from this body of work, we have focused the video digest editing interface on transcript-based interactions.

CREATING A VIDEO DIGEST

A video digest uses a textbook-inspired chapter/section structure to make the video easier to browse and skim (Figure 1). The chapter elements correspond to topically-coherent segments of the video that present a major theme, and the section elements segment the chapter into lower-level topic shifts.

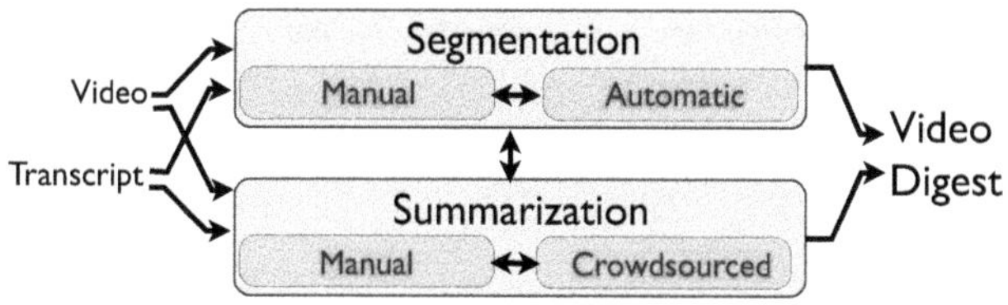

Figure 2. Given an input video and transcript, our authoring interface provides users with the ability to manually segment/summarize the content, automatically segment the content and crowdsource the summaries, or apply any combination of these two approaches.

Each section provides a brief summary and representative keyframe for its corresponding video segment (Figure 1).

To produce such a digest, an author must complete the following tasks: (1) segment the video into chapters, (2) title the chapters, (3) segment the video into short sections, (4) compose a text summary for each section and (5) select a keyframe for each section. Although most of these tasks can be interleaved, in practice we have found that video digest authors sometimes work bottom-up and create sections first (tasks 3-5), before grouping them into chapters (tasks 1-2), while at other times they work top-down creating chapter segments first (tasks 1-2), and then breaking them further into sections (tasks 3-5). Cycling between these two strategies is common [42].

Regardless of the strategy, each of the five tasks is time-consuming with current tools. Segmenting a video by topic often involves watching the video several times and scrubbing back-and-forth to find topic boundaries. Composing section summaries also typically requires re-watching a segment multiple times to make sure the main points are fully captured in the summary.

We have developed a set of tools to facilitate video digest creation (Figure 2). Our tools take a video and a corresponding transcript as input and lets users segment and summarize the video using a combination of manual, automatic, and crowdsourcing techniques. Users can interleave segmentation and summarization steps in any order. We first describe our video digest authoring interface and then present the algorithmic methods underlying this interface.

VIDEO DIGEST AUTHORING INTERFACE

As shown in Figure 3, our video-digest authoring interface consists of two main panes: an *Aligned Transcript pane* (right) lets authors read the speech content, click on a word to navigate to the corresponding point in the video player, and mark chapter/section start points, while a *WYSIWYG Editor pane* (left) lets authors specify chapter titles, sections summaries and keyframes.

To support transcript-based navigation, segmentation and summarization, our interface relies on a time-aligned text transcript of the input video. When possible we obtain transcripts from the video source. For example, edX and TED provide transcripts of their talks online. Otherwise we use the crowdsourcing transcription service `rev.com` which accepts an audio file as input and returns a verbatim transcript for $1.25 per minute. We then time-align the transcript to the

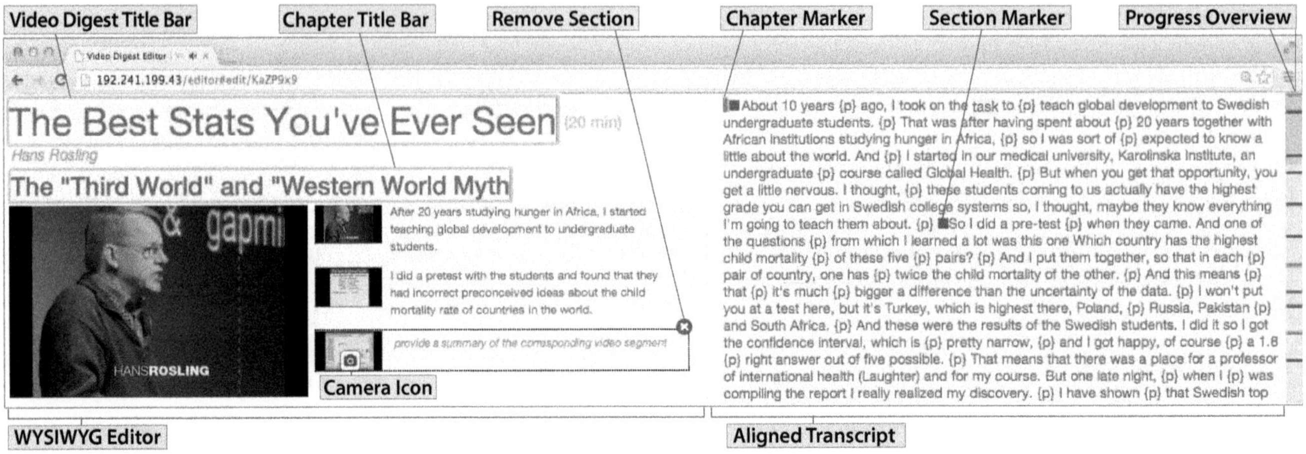

Figure 3. Our interface facilitates creating and editing video digests. The interface consists of two main panes: (1) An Aligned Transcript pane for navigating, segmenting and summarizing the talk and (2) a WYSIWYG Editor pane for adding chapter titles, summaries and keyframes for each section. Additionally, a Progress Overview scrollbar allows authors to view their segmentation progress and return to areas for refinement.

audio track of the video using the phoneme estimation and mapping technique of Rubin et al. [35, 44].

Chapter and Section Segmentation

To segment the video into topically-coherent chapters and sections, authors place chapter markers (red) and section markers (blue) in the Aligned Transcript pane using mouse clicks with modifier keys ('ctrl+alt' for chapter, 'ctrl' for section). Chapter markers denote the start of a major theme in the presentation while section markers denote less-significant topic changes within each chapter. Dragging these markers to different locations in the transcript changes the starting point of the chapter/section. In addition, clicking a section marker with the chapter modifier key creates a new chapter at that location, and the clicked section as well as all remaining sections in the original chapter are automatically moved into the new chapter. This operation splits the original chapter into two chapters at the clicked section marker. Conversely, clicking a chapter marker with the section modifier key removes the original chapter and appends all of its sections to the preceding chapter. This operation merges the clicked chapter with the preceding chapter. The Progress-Overview scrollbar on the right side of the Aligned Transcript pane represents the entire length of the video as a vertical bar. It shows the locations of all chapter/section markers and allows the author to quickly assess areas that need segmentation or refinement.

When the author places a new chapter marker in the transcript, our interface generates a new chapter in the WYSIWYG Editor with its video element cued to the location of the chapter marker. Similarly, when the author places a new section marker, our interface generates a new section keyframe and summary box in the WYSIWYG Editor pane at the appropriate location. By default, it fills the keyframe with the first frame of the corresponding video segment and places the cursor in an empty adjoining summary box. The WYSIWYG Editor automatically updates when the author drags a section/chapter start point to a different location or splits/merges chapters by clicking on chapter or section markers with the opposite modifier keys. Authors can delete sections by clicking the "Remove Section" button that appears when hovering over or modifying a section. Removing all sections from a chapter deletes the chapter.

In addition to these manual segmentation operations, the author can select a portion of the transcript and then invoke our automatic segmentation algorithm (see Algorithmic Methods Section) on the selected text, using a right-click menu.

Section Summaries and Keyframes

Authors compose section summaries directly in the summary boxes of the WYSIWYG Editor. Clicking on a summary box scrolls the transcript view to the corresponding text segment for quick reference. The author can replace the default keyframe by navigating the chapter's video player to the desired location and clicking a camera icon beneath the desired keyframe. Alternatively, an author can right-click on the summary box to invoke our crowdsourcing summarization pipeline (see Algorithmic Methods Section). The pipeline returns a crowd generated section summary and keyframe which the author can then refine if necessary. Finally, the author can set the video digest title and chapter-level titles by directly editing the text in the respective title bars.

ALGORITHMIC METHODS

Our system provides automated techniques for segmenting a video into topically-coherent units and obtaining summaries of such segments via a crowdsourcing pipeline.

Algorithmic Segmentation

Automatic text segmentation is a well-studied problem in natural language processing [24, 13, 17]. Eisenstein et al.'s [18] Bayesian topic segmentation (BSeg) algorithm is one of the leading techniques for segmenting speech-based text. BSeg is designed to group sequences of lexically cohesive text fragments into a segment – the text fragments can be any user-defined sequence of words in the text such as phrases, sentences or paragraphs.

The strength of BSeg is its ability to incorporate a variety of features such as cue phrases (e.g. "in conclusion", "therefore", "so", etc.) that might signal topic transitions. In pilot experiments[1] we found BSeg to outperform several other modern text segmentation algorithms [24, 31]. As a result, we use BSeg to automatically obtain both section- and chapter-level segments in our system.

BSeg produces a *linear* segmentation of the input text rather than the *hierarchical* chapter/section segmentation needed by our system. To obtain a hierarchical segmentation, we apply BSeg twice. First, we use the sentences from the original transcript as the input text fragments and BSeg returns a sequential grouping of these sentences into section-level elements. Next, we apply BSeg again, but we treat the output section-level elements from the first application as the input fragments to the second BSeg application. If summaries of the sections are available, we instead use these summaries as the input fragments to the second BSeg application. In either case this second application of BSeg groups the section-level segments into topically-coherent units that form the chapters of our digest.

Crowdsourced Section Summaries

We have developed a crowdsourcing pipeline for obtaining section summaries. In our pipeline, one set of crowdworkers compose a summary and select a representative keyframe for each of the input sections. A second set of crowdworkers rank the summaries and keyframes based on quality. We then return the top-ranked summary for each section to the authoring interface.

In order to create browsable and skimmable video digests, each summary must concisely summarize the main topic of the corresponding section and use the same grammatical person and tense as the surrounding sections. We emphasize these goals in a set of guidelines we provide to the crowdworkers. We tell them that the summary should: (1) convey the main point(s) of the section, (2) omit non-essential details, (3) use the same tense (e.g. past, future) and grammatical person (e.g. first person, third person) as the section transcript, and (4) use concise wording, free of grammatical errors. In early experiments with the task, we found that workers often generated overly-detailed summaries. Based on these experiments, we added the guideline that (5) the summary should be less than three sentences in length.

For each summary task, we provide workers with the video and the aligned transcript cued to the section start point (Figure 4). We give workers access to the complete video and transcript so that they can build additional context when needed (e.g. to resolve ambiguous pronoun references in the section). We ask at least three crowdworkers to provide summaries and keyframes for each section. To ensure high-quality summaries, we then pipe these summaries into a ranking stage, where a different set of crowdworkers rank the quality of the summary-keyframe pair from the set of such pairs for each section. We ask these crowdworkers to base their rankings on the summary writing guidelines and to provide a short justification for their top-ranked selection. To reduce the cognitive load required to understand each section, we ask each crowdworker to summarize or ranks three consecutive sections.

[1] See supplementary material for details on these experiments and our technique for setting BSeg's parameters.

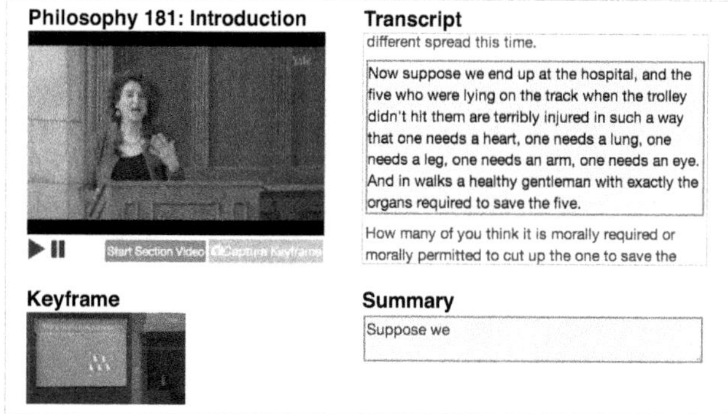

Figure 4. Crowdworker task for summarizing a section of the video. Workers can navigate the video using the timeline-based player (left) or the aligned transcript (right). The video is initially cued to the beginning of the section that must be summarized and the corresponding portion of the transcript is highlighted in red. Workers can select a keyframes by clicking on the *capture keyframe* button area, and they can write a text summary in the *summary* textbox.

We pay crowdworkers $0.60 to write three section summaries and select the corresponding keyframes. To incentivize high-quality work we offer $0.10 bonuses to the worker who writes the top-ranked summary for each section. Similarly we pay crowdworkers $0.60 to rank the summary-keyframe pairs for three sections.

RESULTS

Figure 5 shows manual and auto-generated video digests produced using our tools. The complete interactive results can be viewed at `http://vis.berkeley.edu/papers/videodigests`. These results were generated using the following set of input videos (Table 1):

- *Philosophy 181: Introduction* by Tamar Gendler [19]: a 13.3 minute recording of an in-class philosophy lecture at Yale University (Figure 5A,B)
- *The Power of Prototyping* by Scott Klemmer [28]: a 13.8 minute introductory lecture from Coursera that uses a slide-based presentation (Figure 5C,D)
- *US History Overview: Jamestown to the Civil War* by Salman Khan [25]: a 18.5 minute overview of U.S. history from Khan Academy that uses a pen-based screencast presentation (Figure 5E,F)
- *The Best Statistics You've Ever Seen* by Hans Rosling [34]: a 19.9 minute high-production-quality, stage-based presentation (Figure 5G,H)

One of the paper authors created the manual video digests, and we created the auto-generated digests by combining our automatic segmentation algorithm on the entire transcript with our crowdsourced summarization pipeline. Table 1 shows the total time and cost required to create the manual

Figure 5. Manual and auto-generated video digests for four lecture videos Gendler (A,B), Klemmer (C,D), Khan (E,F) and Rosling (G,H). Differences between the manual and auto-generated results are highlighted below (I-M). Example (I) and (J) show differences in segmentation where two sections in the manual digest are combined into one section in the auto-generated digest and vice-versa. Example (K) shows how sections summaries can be very similar between the manual and auto-generated digests. However, examples (L) and (M) show that the manual digests often include more succinct summaries than the corredponding auto-generated digests.

(M) and auto-generated (A) digests respectively. We instrumented our authoring tools to record the time spent performing each subtask involved in digest creation. In the manual case, we spent 48% of the total time reviewing the transcript and lecture video, 42% of the time composing section summaries, 6% of the time writing chapter titles, and the remaining 4% of time performing all other operations including placing segments. Overall, the time to create the digests manually was about 3-4 times the length of the input lecture. In the auto-generated case we recruited three unique crowdworkers to generate summaries and keyframes for each section and three more to rank each summary-keyframe pair. The total crowdsourcing cost was between about $0.50 and $1.00 per minute of the input lecture.

	Gendler		Klemmer		Khan		Rosling	
	M	A	M	A	M	A	M	A
Time to create	40m	–	34m	–	41m	–	62m	–
Crowdwork cost	–	$19	–	$23	–	$35	–	$54
Num. of chapters	2	3	3	4	6	6	4	8
Num. of sections	20	26	14	13	17	16	20	40
Compression ratio	4.8	3.7	10.0	6.3	7.7	4.6	7.1	3.3

Table 1. Creating manual (M) and an auto-generated (A) video digests for four lecture videos required either authoring time (M) or payments to crowdworkers (A). We report the number of chapters, sections and compression ratios for each of the resulting digests.

	User 1		User 2	
	M	E	M	E
Lecture	Klemmer	Gendler	Gendler	Klemmer
Time to create	54m	37m	30m	20m
Num. of sections	19	13	14	16
Num. of sections edited	–	6	–	4
Summary-edit keystrokes	3812	1355	1011	317

Table 2. In an informal evaluation two users created a manual video digest (M) and edited an auto-generated digest (E). We report the number of sections created for both (M) and (E), but only include the number of sections each user edited in the latter case.

Table 1 also shows that the manual and auto-generated digests contain similar chapter and section counts for all of the lectures except Rosling. The Rosling lecture contains many short anecdotes that each use different vocabulary. In the auto-generated digest, BSeg segments the lecture based on the frequent vocabulary changes and produces twice as many chapters and sections as in the manual digest. Unlike BSeg, the manual digest author grouped together the anecdotes into higher-level concepts. Despite the differences in chapter/section counts, Figures 5G and 5H show that the two Rosling digests cover the same topics, but at different granularities. Other differences in the section-level segementations are shown in Figures 5I and 5J.

Finally we note that the manual digests usually contain less summary text overall than the auto-generated digests. Table 1 reports the compression ratio – the number of words in the original transcript divided by the number of words in the digest – for the lectures. Although the manual digests achieve higher compression ratios than the auto-generated digests, both condense the information compared to the transcript. The examples in Figures 5L and 5M suggest that crowdworkers tend to put more context into their section summaries which makes them longer than manually authored summaries. Because crowdworkers only summarize a small part of the lecture and cannot see the surrounding summaries, they may be compensating by repeating contextual information. In contrast, the author of a manual digest has access to all of the summaries and can eliminate such redundancies. Nevertheless, as demonstrated in Figure 5, the crowdsourced summaries do capture the the main concepts of each section similar to the manual summaries.

INFORMAL USER FEEDBACK

To gauge the utility of our video digest creation tools, we conducted an informal evaluation with two users (U1 and U2). We asked them to manually create a video digest and also to refine an auto-generated digest using our authoring tools. We examined the time they spent editing the digests and the number/type of edits they made. We also conducted a post-evaluation interview to gather qualitative feedback.

In the evaluation, U1 manually created a digest for Scott Klemmer's *Power of Prototyping* lecture and refined an auto-generated digest for Tamar Gendler's *Philosophy 181* lecture. U2 completed the opposite tasks for these two lectures. Both of these input videos are approximately the same length. Before starting the tasks, we presented each user with an example of a video digest, explained the chapter/section structure, and demonstrated the authoring interface. For the refinement task, we instructed the users to refine the digest so that it matched the quality of their manually created digest.

Table 2 shows that both users spent less time refining the auto-generated digest than creating the manual digest and edited fewer than half of the auto-generated section summaries. Both users performed fewer keystrokes when editing the auto-generated summaries, than when creating the summaries manually from scratch. When editing the auto-generated digests, modifying the sections was the dominant form of interaction. U1 focused on improving the flow between section summaries, while U2 mainly adjusted section boundaries. They rarely modified default keyframes or adjusted chapter boundaries when they were refining the auto-generated result. Although both users did edit the auto-generated summary text, they also provided positive feedback on the auto-generated summaries: U1 stated that the auto-generated summaries were "summarized in a way that I wouldn't think of myself, and I think what they did was correct and great." U2 noted that the auto-generated summaries were "on-target." U1 noted encountering a single incorrect summary, while U2 found one unnecessary segment boundary.

STUDY: DO DIGESTS SUPPORT BROWSING/SKIMMING?

We performed a comparative study to test the hypothesis that video digests afford browsing and skimming better than alternative formats. In our experiment we asked crowdworkers to watch one of four lectures (Gendler, Klemmer, Khan, Rosling) using one of the following formats:

- ***Manual:*** a manually created video digest using our tools.
- ***Auto:*** an auto-generated video digest.
- ***Video:*** a timeline-based video player.
- ***Script:*** a transcript-based video player.

We gave the crowdworkers a fixed length of viewing time (either 2, 5 or 8 minutes) and asked them to "quickly browse and skim" the content of the lecture. We then hid the lecture and asked them to provide "an approximately 5 sentence summary" of the main points covered in the lecture. We purposely did not give the crowdworkers enough time to watch the entire lecture so that they had to browse and skim its content to write a complete summary.

We asked 4 unique crowdworkers to summarize each combination of independent variables (lecture, format, viewing time) yielding 192 total summaries (4 lectures $\times$ 4 formats $\times$ 3 viewing time $\times$ 4 crowdworkers). We paid each crowdworkers \$0.90 for the summary plus a \$1.00 bonus if the

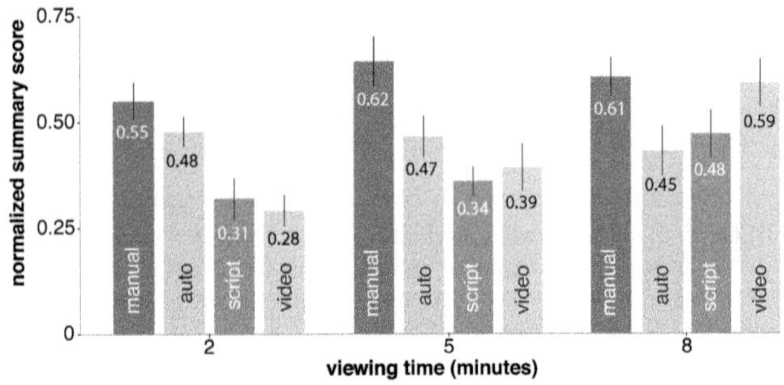

Figure 6. Crowdworkers viewed a video lecture in one of four formats (manual, auto, script, video) for 2, 5 or 8 minutes and then wrote a summary of the presentation. We scored these summaries using a gold standard topic list. Each bar shows the mean and standard error of the scores for each condition.

worker obtained the highest summary score for the (lecture, format, viewing time) condition.

To evaluate the five sentence crowdworker summaries the first two authors of this paper worked together to manually build a *gold standard* list of key topics discussed in each of the four lectures. We then used these lists to score the number of topics covered in each crowdworker summary. Finally, we normalized the scores based on the total number of gold standard topics for each lecture.

Figure 6 shows the normalized scores for each format and viewing time aggregated across the four lectures. Using a Kruskal-Wallis test, we found significant difference in these scores when compared across viewing times (2 minutes: $\mu = 0.408$; 5 minutes: $\mu = 0.457$; 8 minutes: $\mu = 0.530$. $\chi^2(2) = 9.92$, $p = 0.007$). Further analyzing each viewing time, we found a significant difference in scores when comparing across the formats for 2 minutes ($\chi^2(3) = 18.31$, $p < 0.001$) and 5 minutes ($\chi^2(3) = 16.23$, $p = 0.001$) , but not for 8 minutes ($\chi^2(3) = 6.77$, $p = 0.080$). Pairwise Mann-Whitney tests with Holm-Bonferroni correction indicated significant differences in the following format pairs: At 2 minutes of viewing time, manual-video ($U(15) = 32$, $p = 0.002$), manual-script ($U(15) = 44.5$, $p = 0.009$), and auto-video ($U(15) = 58.5$, $p = 0.037$) are significantly different. At 5 minutes of viewing time, the manual-video ($U(15) = 56.5$, $p = 0.03$) and manual-script ($U(15) = 33.5$, $p = 0.002$) were significantly different.

Further analyzing the formats, we found a significant increase in scores when comparing across the viewing times for only the video format ($\chi^2(2) = 13.26$, $p = 0.001$). Pairwise Mann-Whitney tests with Holm-Bonferroni correction find significant differences in the following viewing time pairs: 2 minute-8 minute ($U(15) = 34.5$, $p = 0.001$) and 5 minute-8 minute ($U(15) = 67.5$, $p = 0.047$).

In short, at viewing times of 2 and 5 minutes, the video digest formats (manual and auto) allowed viewers to recall up to twice as many of the key topics than the video player formats (script and video). However, this effect diminished for the longest viewing time of 8 minutes. For the roughly 15 minute long lecture videos we tests, viewers could successfully recall many key topics after only 2 minutes of viewing time using the video digest; giving extra viewing time yielded little improvement that was not statistically significant. In contrast, with the standard timeline-based video player, summarization performance was low when viewers were given only 2 minutes, and gradually improved with additional time. Together these results suggest that both of the video digest formats – manually authored and auto-generated – facilitate browsing and skimming of informational lecture videos.

CONCLUSION AND FUTURE WORK

We have presented a set of tools for creating video digests; a new format for informational talks that exposes the structure of the content via section-level summaries and chapter-based grouping. We provide a transcript-based authoring interface and explore techniques for automatically segmenting and summarizing an input video. An informal evaluation suggests that our tools make it much easier for authors to create video digests, and a crowdsourced experiment indicates that the video digest format affords browsing and skimming better than alternative video presentation interfaces. As more and more informational videos are published online, we believe these tools will make it easier for people to browse and skim the underlying content and identify topics of interest. We see several promising directions for future work.

Ensuring consistency across crowdsourced summaries. Our current crowdsourcing pipeline does not ensure consistency between section summaries produced by different workers. Separate workers may include redundant information or use pronouns that are ambiguous given previous summaries. One solution might be to include an additional stage in the crowdsourcing pipeline where new crowdworkers check multiple consecutive summaries for overall consistency. These crowdworkers could also provide titles for the video digest chapters as our current system does not produce such titles automatically.

Support for highly-technical content. We tested our automatic pipeline on four lectures that are accessible to a broad, well-educated audience. However, we have not tested our tools with lectures that require specialized knowledge, or highly-technical content where crowdworkers may not have the necessary background to write summaries. One fruitful direction for MOOC style lectures may be to ask students who choose to watch a lecture to write the summaries, e.g. students in a graduate-level quantum mechanics course. Creating summaries may help the students learn the material and also generate high-quality summaries for technical material.

Use video data in algorithmic segmentation. Our segmentation algorithm only uses the transcript to segment the video. Future work could incorporate visual and audio information to improve video segmentation. It may also be possible to use viewer interaction data to automatically infer segmentation points in the video in the manner of Kim et. al [27].

ACKNOWLEDGMENTS

We thank Bret Victor for showing us how he manually created his video digest and helping us think through the interface design for creating video digests. This work was partially supported by a SanDisk fellowship, an NDSEG fellowship and NSF grants IIS-1210836 and IIS-1252819.

REFERENCES

1. edX. `http://www.edx.org`.
2. Khan Academy. `http://khanacademy.org`.
3. TED. `http://www.ted.com/`.
4. Barnes, C., Goldman, D. B., Shechtman, E., and Finkelstein, A. Video tapestries with continuous temporal zoom. *ACM Trans. Graph. 29*, 4 (July 2010), 89:1–89:9.
5. Bernstein, M. S., Brandt, J., Miller, R. C., and Karger, D. R. Crowds in two seconds: Enabling realtime crowd-powered interfaces. In *UIST*, ACM (2011), 33–42.
6. Bernstein, M. S., Little, G., Miller, R. C., Hartmann, B., Ackerman, M. S., Karger, D. R., Crowell, D., and Panovich, K. Soylent: a word processor with a crowd inside. In *Proc. of the 23nd annual*, ACM (2010), 313–322.
7. Berthouzoz, F., Li, W., and Agrawala, M. Tools for placing cuts and transitions in interview video. *ACM Trans.Graph. 31*, 4 (2012), 67.
8. Boreczky, J., Girgensohn, A., Golovchinsky, G., and Uchihashi, S. An interactive comic book presentation for exploring video. In *Proceedings of the SIGCHI Conference on Human Factors in Computing Systems*, CHI '00, ACM (New York, NY, USA, 2000), 185–192.
9. Burrows, S., Potthast, M., and Stein, B. Paraphrase acquisition via crowdsourcing and machine learning. *ACM Transactions on Intelligent Systems and Technology (TIST) 4*, 3 (2013), 43.
10. Buzek, O., Resnik, P., and Bederson, B. B. Error driven paraphrase annotation using mechanical turk. In *Proceedings of the NAACL HLT 2010 Workshop on Creating Speech and Language Data with Amazon's Mechanical Turk*, Association for Computational Linguistics (2010), 217–221.
11. Casares, J., Long, A. C., Myers, B. A., Bhatnagar, R., Stevens, S. M., Dabbish, L., Yocum, D., and Corbett, A. Simplifying video editing using metadata. In *Proceedings of the 4th conference on Designing interactive systems: processes, practices, methods, and techniques*, ACM (2002), 157–166.
12. Chi, P.-Y., Liu, J., Linder, J., Dontcheva, M., Li, W., and Hartmann, B. Democut: generating concise instructional videos for physical demonstrations. In *UIST*, ACM (2013), 141–150.
13. Choi, F. Y. Advances in domain independent linear text segmentation. In *Proceedings of the 1st North American chapter of the Association for Computational Linguistics conference*, Association for Computational Linguistics (2000), 26–33.
14. Christel, M. G., Smith, M. A., Taylor, C. R., and Winkler, D. B. Evolving video skims into useful multimedia abstractions. In *Proceedings of the SIGCHI conference on Human factors in computing systems*, ACM Press/Addison-Wesley Publishing Co. (1998), 171–178.
15. Corum, J. Storytelling with Data. `http://style.org/tapestry/`, February 2014.
16. Denkowski, M., Al-Haj, H., and Lavie, A. Turker-assisted paraphrasing for english-arabic machine translation. In *Proceedings of the NAACL HLT 2010 Workshop on Creating Speech and Language Data with Amazon's Mechanical Turk*, Association for Computational Linguistics (2010), 66–70.
17. Du, L., Buntine, W., and Johnson, M. Topic segmentation with a structured topic model. In *Proceedings of NAACL-HLT* (2013), 190–200.
18. Eisenstein, J., and Barzilay, R. Bayesian unsupervised topic segmentation. In *Proceedings of the Conference on Empirical Methods in Natural Language Processing*, Association for Computational Linguistics (2008), 334–343.
19. Gendler, T. Philosophy 181: Introduction. `http://oyc.yale.edu/philosophy/phil-181/lecture-1`, Spring 2011.
20. Guo, P. J., Kim, J., and Rubin, R. How video production affects student engagement: An empirical study of mooc videos. In *Proceedings of the first ACM Learning@ scale conference*, ACM (2014), 41–50.
21. Gupta, V., and Lehal, G. S. A survey of text summarization extractive techniques. *Journal of Emerging Technologies in Web Intelligence 2*, 3 (2010), 258–268.
22. Haubold, A., and Kender, J. R. Augmented segmentation and visualization for presentation videos. In *Proceedings of the 13th annual ACM international conference on Multimedia*, ACM (2005), 51–60.
23. He, L., Sanocki, E., Gupta, A., and Grudin, J. Auto-summarization of audio-video presentations. In *Proceedings of the seventh ACM international conference on Multimedia (Part 1)*, ACM (1999), 489–498.
24. Hearst, M. A. Texttiling: Segmenting text into multi-paragraph subtopic passages. *Computational linguistics 23*, 1 (1997), 33–64.
25. Khan, S. Us history overview: Jamestown to the civil war. `https://www.khanacademy.org/humanities/history/history-survey/us-history/v/us-history-overview-1--jamestown-to-the-civil-war`, April 2011.
26. Kim, J., Nguyen, P., Weir, S., Guo, P. J., Miller, R. C., and Gajos, K. Z. Crowdsourcing step-by-step information extraction to enhance existing how-to videos. In *Proceedings of the 2014 ACM annual conference on Human factors in computing systems*, ACM (2014).

27. Kim, J., Shang-Wen, L. D., Cai, C. J., Gajos, K. Z., and Miller, R. C. Leveraging video interaction data and content analysis to improve video learning. In *CHI'14 Extended Abstracts on Human Factors in Computing Systems*, ACM (2014).

28. Klemmer, S. The power of prototyping. `https://class.coursera.org/hci/lecture`, 2012.

29. Lasecki, W., Miller, C., Sadilek, A., Abumoussa, A., Borrello, D., Kushalnagar, R., and Bigham, J. Real-time captioning by groups of non-experts. In *UIST*, ACM (2012), 23–34.

30. Lasecki, W. S., Song, Y. C., Kautz, H., and Bigham, J. P. Real-time crowd labeling for deployable activity recognition. In *Proceedings of the 2013 conference on Computer supported cooperative work*, ACM (2013), 1203–1212.

31. Malioutov, I., and Barzilay, R. Minimum cut model for spoken lecture segmentation. In *Proceedings of the 21st International Conference on Computational Linguistics and the 44th annual meeting of the Association for Computational Linguistics*, Association for Computational Linguistics (2006), 25–32.

32. Mayer, R. E., and Moreno, R. Nine ways to reduce cognitive load in multimedia learning. *Educational psychologist 38*, 1 (2003), 43–52.

33. Nenkova, A., Maskey, S., and Liu, Y. Automatic summarization. In *Proceedings of the 49th Annual Meeting of the Association for Computational Linguistics: Tutorial Abstracts of ACL 2011*, Association for Computational Linguistics (2011), 3.

34. Rosling, H. The best statistics you've ever seen. `http://www.ted.com/talks/hans_rosling_shows_the_best_stats_you_ve_ever_seen`, February 2006.

35. Rubin, S., Berthouzoz, F., Mysore, G. J., Li, W., and Agrawala, M. Content based tools for editing audio stories. In *UIST*, ACM Press (2013), 113–122.

36. Smith, M. A., and Kanade, T. Video skimming and characterization through the combination of image and language understanding. In *Content-Based Access of Image and Video Database, 1998. Proceedings., 1998 IEEE International Workshop on*, IEEE (1998), 61–70.

37. Tang, A., and Boring, S. # epicplay: crowd-sourcing sports video highlights. In *Proceedings of the SIGCHI Conference on Human Factors in Computing Systems*, ACM (2012), 1569–1572.

38. Taskiran, C. M., Pizlo, Z., Amir, A., Ponceleon, D., and Delp, E. J. Automated video program summarization using speech transcripts. *Multimedia, IEEE Transactions on 8*, 4 (2006), 775–791.

39. Truong, B. T., and Venkatesh, S. Video abstraction: A systematic review and classification. *ACM Transactions on Multimedia Computing, Communications, and Applications (TOMCCAP) 3*, 1 (2007), 3.

40. Uchihashi, S., Foote, J., Girgensohn, A., and Boreczky, J. Video manga: generating semantically meaningful video summaries. In *Proceedings of the seventh ACM international conference on Multimedia (Part 1)*, ACM (1999), 383–392.

41. Victor, B. Media for thinking the unthinkable. `http://worrydream.com/MediaForThinkingTheUnthinkable`, April 2013.

42. Victor, B. Personal communication, December 2013.

43. Whittaker, S., and Amento, B. Semantic speech editing. In *Proceedings of the SIGCHI conference on Human factors in computing systems*, ACM (2004), 527–534.

44. Yuan, J., and Liberman, M. Speaker identification on the scotus corpus. *Journal of the Acoustical Society of America 123*, 5 (2008), 3878.

Brain-Based Target Expansion

Daniel Afergan, Tomoki Shibata, Samuel W. Hincks, Evan M. Peck, Beste F. Yuksel, Remco Chang, Robert J.K. Jacob
Tufts University
Medford, MA USA
{afergan,tshibata,shincks,epeck02,byukse01,remco,jacob}@cs.tufts.edu

ABSTRACT
The bubble cursor is a promising cursor expansion technique, improving a user's movement time and accuracy in pointing tasks. We introduce a brain-based target expansion system, which improves the efficacy of bubble cursor by increasing the expansion of high importance targets at the optimal time based on brain measurements correlated to a particular type of multitasking. We demonstrate through controlled experiments that brain-based target expansion can deliver a graded and continuous level of assistance to a user according to their cognitive state, thereby improving task and speed-accuracy metrics, even without explicit visual changes to the system. Such an adaptation is ideal for use in complex systems to steer users toward higher priority goals during times of increased demand.

Author Keywords
brain-computer interface; BCI; fNIRS; adaptive interface; bubble cursor.

ACM Classification Keywords
H.5.m. Information Interfaces and Presentation (e.g. HCI): Miscellaneous

INTRODUCTION
In most graphical user interfaces (GUIs), navigating and pointing to an interface element is a necessary prerequisite to select it. A nearly incessant exchange between computer and user, clicking on graphical elements is a problem for which slight optimization can be extraordinarily impactful over longer sessions [6]. Consequently, considerable research has focused on improving users' speed and accuracy in basic point-and-click tasks [27, 50]. Small differences in interaction technique times can make much bigger differences in cognitive strategies and thus in high-level task performance beyond just the change in interaction time [18]. Because a system receives no extra information while a cursor travels through empty space [20], Grossman and Balakrishnan's bubble cursor creates an area cursor that always selects the closest target to the cursor [19]. Bubble cursor improves overall performance compared to a standard cursor in these types of GUIs, and we introduce an augmentation which further enhances the technique's usability by integrating passive brain input as well as a ranking of the target's importance. While bubble cursor decreases movement time by always selecting the closest target, we can increase the effective width of high-importance targets with a variable parameter, making it easier to select these targets with no extra effort from the user. The variable parameter essentially gives us a flexible parameter that can be set in real time instead of defining it as a constant. Specifically, we propose a target expansion technique that aids the user in focusing on high importance objectives when necessary by monitoring the user's cognitive state and increasing the effective width of high-priority targets whenever we detect a state of multitasking.

In a pointing task, performance tends to suffer while the user is simultaneously completing multiple tasks with high cognitive workload [22]. It might be appropriate, therefore, to modify a user interface so that it facilitates the user's capacity to engage the essential on-screen elements. But the user's goals and capacity to meet those goals may change on a moment-to-moment basis, and an interface that emphasizes high-priority targets at all times comes at the expense of interaction with lower priority elements. Ideally, the interface should be sensitive to the user's context as it changes over time, dynamically and unobtrusively adapting to meet the user's needs. Unfortunately, standard cursor adaptations are limited to direct user input and by the transmission capacity between the user and the input device.

We propose to address this problem by incorporating *physiological computing*, which "has the potential to extend the communication bandwidth of HCI and enable a dynamic, individualised dialogue between user and system" [15] without any effort on the part of the user. By monitoring user cognitive state, we can tell when the user may be multitasking and aid the user in selecting targets of higher priority by increasing the width in bubble cursor calculations. Using this state information, we may be able to make higher priority targets easier to select at the expense of lower priority ones at critical moments, improving movement time and accuracy. In this paper, we propose a brain-computer interface (BCI) using functional near-infrared spectroscopy (fNIRS) as real-time input to influence target width in a pointing task.

In contrast to systems which use physiological data to determine when to turn on and off system automation, we use a more graded, continuous level of target adjustment, which

http://dx.doi.org/10.1145/2642918.2647414

aids the user without committing entirely. The system applies this assistance without any visual feedback to the user to avoid suggesting that the user has been deemed in need of help and spawning a feedback loop.

Small improvements to interface navigation systems can have a measurable impact on user performance in the long run [18]. These benefits may be particularly useful in high intensity interaction scenarios where a primary task demands the user's finite cognitive resources, leaving little for control of the interface. In some of these scenarios, the user must engage and hold in mind audio content while navigating a GUI. For example, an air traffic controller may be directing pilots while simultaneously interacting with graphical depictions of planes on the screen or an emergency response dispatcher may be communicating with units while selecting medical resources. Unmanned aerial vehicle operators speak to each other while monitoring vessels and financial traders may communicate while placing orders. These situations, which pose high and variable demands on the user's workload, call for seamless and adaptive interfaces. In performance-critical situations, we posit that an interface should sacrifice the ease of completing incidental goals in favor of more urgent goals.

We base our experiment on previous literature that shows the capability to detect cognitive multitasking signals in the anterior prefrontal cortex [29, 45, 46] using brain-sensing technologies and these patterns translate to dual verbal-spatial working memory tasks [33]. We use fNIRS, which shines near-infrared light at different wavelengths into the scalp and detects the amount of light that is reflected back. From this, we can infer changes in blood flow and oxygenated and deoxygenated hemoglobin levels in the prefrontal cortex, which correlate well to cognitive activities. The fNIRS sensors are comfortable, easy, and quick to setup, and they are non-intrusive so that a user can still perform tasks normally while wearing the sensor. Thus, it is ideal for passive physiological sensing because it can directly access brain signals without significantly disturbing the user, and it has been shown to measure working memory and multitasking [11, 29, 39]. In addition, recent research by McKendrick et al. [33] has shown that we can measure activation patterns during a dual verbal-spatial working memory task. Recent fNIRS literature has shown that we can continuously model fNIRS data and measure workload in real time [1, 23, 31, 38].

In this paper, we prototype and evaluate an area cursor system with brain-based dynamically expanding targets. To make the transition of expanding targets seem fluid, the user only witnesses the effect of the area cursor and does not see a visual increase in target size. In an interface with targets of variable importance, we increase the reach of bubble cursor to be more attracted to high-priority elements when we detect brain signals correlated to a cognitive multitasking signal (called *branching*). To demonstrate its efficacy and to configure adaptation and expansion parameters, we run a controlled experiment that modulates workload during a visual search and pointing task. We show that the time and accuracy savings by predicting user state correctly and helping the user easily navigate to high-priority targets outweighs the slight cost of the user having to move closer to a lower priority target when we guess incorrectly. In addition, we show that a constant expansion of high-priority targets actually leads to an overall decrease in performance, highlighting the importance of accurately and continuously measuring the user's need for this assistance and applying it only at the appropriate times.

This paper makes three primary contributions:

- We show that we can use fNIRS brain input to improve performance in a target selection task by dynamically updating a target's activation area.
- We demonstrate that adjusting the activation function, rather than the visual form of targets, can improve user performance without disrupting the user's mental model of the visual interface.
- We highlight a physiological interface that treats user input as a continuous measure, as opposed to binary or discrete user classification.

BACKGROUND AND RELATED WORK

Target acquisition tasks are often measured in terms of speed (movement time) and accuracy (error rate). We use the fundamental concepts of this field to design ways in which we can leverage human physical input with passive brain input.

Movement Time and Bubble Cursor

The general principle that accounts for the effectiveness of area cursors is a familiar and accepted one in HCI. *Fitts' law* measures the speed and accuracy of pointing performance, and as Kelso explains, "the relation between amplitude, movement time, and precision (or tolerance)" [28]. Although the formula has been altered for many purposes, a stable and widely used version is MacKenzie's 1992 formula, describing movement time (MT) as:

$$MT = a + b\, log_2(\frac{A}{W} + 1) \quad (1)$$

where A is the amplitude (distance) of the movement and W is the target width [30], *a* and *b* are interface constants, referring to the start/stop time of the device and device speed, respectively. The logarithmic portion of this equation is also known as the index of difficulty, and refers to the amount of work needed to reach a target. This implies that either increasing target size (W) or decreasing distance (A) on a pointing task will decrease movement time. Manipulating these variables allows the opportunity to improve performance in target selection tasks and lays the foundation for area cursors.

In 2005, Grossman and Balakrishnan first introduced the bubble cursor, a target acquisition technique that resized the activation area of a cursor to automatically select the closest target and provide the user visual feedback about the target selected [19]. In the Fitts' law equation, this mechanism increases *effective target width*, the size of a targets activation boundaries [19], and thus reduces movement time in a target acquisition scenario that includes surrounding distractor targets. Bubble cursor has shown consistently large performance improvements over a standard cursor, and custom tweaks can further enhance performance. Mott and Wobbrock's *Bubble Lens* augmentation of bubble cursor with an additional lens is the fastest pointing technique to date [36].

Other techniques focus on increasing target size by expanding clusters of targets [6], creating cascading menus with enlarged activation areas [9], or expanding targets once the cursor comes close [5]. These techniques expand the boundary of each target based on a *Voronoi tessellation* so that each target encompasses its maximum effective size without interfering with other targets. Zhai et. al showed that users performed better even when they did not anticipate an increase in target size [52]. Finally, McGuffin showed that pointing in these tasks is still dictated by Fitts' law and that "performance is governed by the target's final size, not its initial one" [32], even if the target only increases in size once the user has navigated the cursor close to the target. This indicates that users can take advantage of larger targets even if they were not expecting this increase.

While most of these variants have proven efficient in decreasing movement time by changing the width parameter in Fitts' law, they assume that the user is focused on the pointing task and do not consider situations where the user may be doing other work. In addition, these area cursors often entail an extra layer of visual distraction since they provide additional graphical feedback and stray from the traditional cursor model. Our goal is to add to the efficiency of the bubble cursor by subtly and dynamically adapting the size of the high-priority targets based on the user's cognitive state. In our custom version, we change the motor space of the uppercase targets, having the width increase and take up part of the motor space for lowercase letters (without visual indication).

Brain-Computer Interfaces

Since optimal target width may vary depending on the user's context or cognitive state, we monitor relevant cues in the user's changing physiology. We build off the field of *passive brain-computer interfaces* - systems that use input from brain sensors to covertly adapt their function, controls, or display automatically in response to changes in the users state. Passive systems stand in contrast to *active BCIs*, where neural correlates of the user's intention map directly to system inputs [51]. In target-selection-based active BCIs, the system responds explicitly based on user thought, directing the cursor and clicking by monitoring the brain's unique response when it imagines mouse navigation movements and activating a target [14, 43]. While these projects are invaluable for people with limited motor function, the usability of brain-controlled navigation systems pales in comparison to an ordinary mouse. Instead, using passive BCI, our goal is to identify and leverage naturally-occurring user states to subtly enhance interaction target selection within the general population.

Cutrell and Tan suggest that the implicit commands inferred from a users changing brain activity may be the most promising, universal application of BCI [12]. The model must be very cautious since users are often in a different mental state during offline calibration and online feedback [47]. Researchers have recently begun exploring new types of passive, realtime BCI systems using fNIRS. Girouard et. al built an application which altered music based on task predictions from an fNIRS processing algorithm [17]. Solovey et al.'s Brainput system adapted in real-time to a scenario where an interactive human-robot system changed its state of autonomy based on whether it detected a particular state of multitasking [46] and Peck et al. demonstrated a passive adaptive movie recommendation system [37]. In these systems, the brain processing algorithms typically predict the user's mental activity on a discrete, often binary scale (e.g., high vs. low workload), which then maps one-to-one with a system adaptation. In the present experiment, we explore a more continuously adaptive scheme, where measures of classification confidence provide a proxy for differentiating the degree of multitasking.

Brain Sensing with fNIRS

Functional near-infrared spectroscopy (fNIRS) is an optical brain sensing technique that observes similar physiological parameters to functional magnetic resonance imaging (fMRI). Near-infrared light is sent into the forehead at frequencies of 690 nm and 830 nm which enters the tissue at depths of 1-3cm [48]. Critically, light penetrates biological tissue and bone at these wavelengths but is absorbed by oxygenated (oxy-Hb) and deoxygenated hemoglobin (deoxy-Hb) in the bloodstream [26]. Since active neurons summon and consume oxygen, a sharp increase of blood flow [13] coupled with decreased levels of deoxy-Hb and increased levels of oxy-Hb tends to signify that a neural region at large is at work performing meaningful computation. Because the optical properties of deoxy-Hb and oxy-Hb differ, the attenuation of the near-infrared light at different wavelengths returning to the sensors on the forehead describes localized brain activation.

FNIRS signals have shown resliency against head movement, facial movement, ambient noise, heartbeat, and muscle movement [44]. Relying on simple and cheap fundamental technology, fNIRS is safe, comfortable, easy-to-setup, and has the potential for portability. The data from the device has been used to differentiate between levels of workload [3, 25, 37, 42], verbal and spatial working memory [24], game difficulty levels [16], and cognitive multitasking. Putting this data to practical use, predictive models have been applied in real time to adapt user interfaces to these physiological states [45, 46].

Multitasking and Cognitive Workload

Working memory has been defined as the "temporary storage and manipulation of the information necessary for such complex tasks such as language comprehension, learning and reasoning" [4]. Repovš and Baddeley's [41] multicomponent model and Wickens' four-dimensional multiple resource model [49] both regard working memory as a limited pool of cognitive resources. Even if two different tasks, such as auditory and visual, do not interfere with each other, they are still competing for common resources. There is no perfect allocation of resources, and a strain on the auditory components of working memory affect the resources available to visual and motor components, and vice versa.

Specifically, visual search is not efficient while humans are manipulating information held in working memory. This was demonstrated in an experiment by Han and Kim [22] in which participants performed a visual search task while simultaneously performing other tasks (counting backwards from a digit or reordering alphabet letters). These conditions reduced speeds in the visual search task when compared to the search-alone condition [22]. The authors concluded that the extra load of the additional tasks affected the working memory's executive processes and hindered performance in a branching scenario.

Speed and error rate suffer when the amount of effort available for a point-and-click task is limited. Balancing accuracy and speed, the user's "two concurrent minimization efforts draw from a *common pool of resources*, and this pool is *limited*" [21]. In general, multitasking refers to the act of performing multiple tasks simultaneously in pursuit of various independent goals. This planning strategy requires cognitive resources located in different parts of the prefrontal cortex [7].

However, certain types of multitasking have different neural signatures and their activations can be distinguished. Koechlin et al. showed that although keeping a goal in mind over time or alternating between goals did not lead to an increased activation in the prefrontal cortex, this area of the brain is responsible for the "ability to hold in mind goals while exploring and processing secondary goals." [29] Koechlin et al. [29] describe a particular state of multitasking, *branching*, where the user must remember one or more primary goals, while simultaneously processing and shifting between secondary goals. In Koechlin's study, the participants' fMRI data exhibited significant activation in the anterior prefrontal cortex when the user was branching compared to other states of multitasking [29], and Solovey et al. demonstrated that this branching signal is distinguishable via fNIRS [45] and can be used to power an adaptive real-time system [46].

Because branching indicates that the user is focused on a primary task while working on a secondary goal, it is the ideal opportunity to adapt a system to guide the user's focus toward the essential parts of a secondary goal and reduce the total working memory load.

Based on the working memory and search task literature, we explore if we can aid the user in working memory tasks by adapting interaction with visual elements in a secondary task. When the user enters a state of branching, they will not be as efficient on the visual search task. In this circumstance, it benefits the user to focus attention on the main elements of the visual search. Therefore, when the fNIRS device detects evidence of this neurophysiological signal, the GUI should aid the user and focus on higher priority targets, increasing their effective width at the expense of the lower priority targets.

FNIRS AS AN INPUT FOR MULTIMODAL TASK ADAPTATIONS

In this paper, we explore the possibility of using fNIRS to provide useful changes to the backend of a visual interface. The main questions we sought to answer are:

- Can we use brain input to detect when a user is multitasking in a challenging multimodal task?
- Can we improve user performance in an on-screen task by using brain state without changing the visual interface?

Adaptation Mechanism: Target Expansion

We propose dynamically manipulating the size of high-priority targets as a function of the user's current state. During periods of difficult multitasking, the target size of high-priority targets expand, making them easier to click and the lower priority targets, in effect, comparatively evasive. Under less mentally strenuous circumstances, the size of high-priority targets returns to default settings. This manipulation allows the user to focus on high-priority targets during critical moments, without forfeiting access to low-priority targets during less demanding periods of work.

We introduce two important design features of adaptive target expansion. First, unlike traditional bubble cursors, as targets change in size, there are **no changes to the visual representation of the targets**. We make this design decision based on long-standing research on the sensitivity of our perceptual system to movement in the visual field. Frequent, unpredictable changes to the visual representation of the target could disrupt the user and renders the system more sensitive to inaccurate user classifications.

Second, we use a **continuous adaptation mechanism**. Rather than modifying target size between two system states (default target size and maximum target size) that directly correspond with two user states, the target size may also be anywhere between the default and maximum size, depending on output from the user model. We believe that this design creates a gentle, less obtrusive adaptation that is (again) less sensitive to potential misclassifications of the user model. We discuss the mapping of user state to target size in more detail in our system description.

EXPERIMENT SCENARIO

In this section, we explain how we control our adaptive simulation with brain-sensing, and provide evidence of its efficacy with a user study. Using fNIRS while the user is performing a calibration task, we build a machine learning model of what the user's brain activation looks like during a particular multitasking state, contrasting it against different forms of multitasking. When we detect branching multitasking during the simultaneous tasks, we modify the bubble cursor to aid the user in focusing on high-priority targets.

In order to test the efficacy of a system that dynamically adjusts target size based on passive brain input, we designed a highly-controlled multitasking scenario that involves both audio and visual interface tasks. The user's goal is to maximize performance in the primary task while also completing

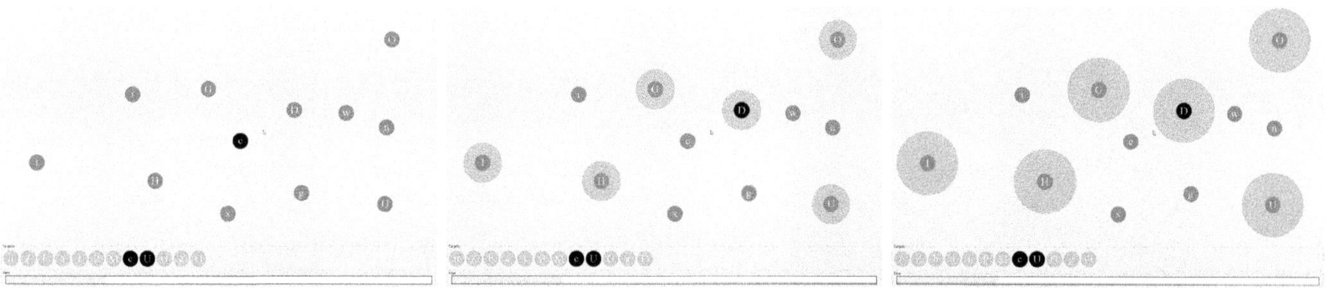

Figure 1. Simulated screen captures of our three target expansion conditions, with visual indications of expanded target widths. The letters on the bottom are the list of letters for the user to select, while the top is the visual search canvas. Although users never saw the expanded widths (indicated by light pink outer circles), these increased widths were used to make it easier for users to select the high-priority targets in the *adaptive* and *static* conditions. With *no expansion*(left), all targets have the same width. Although the users did not see these changes, we show the effects of target expansion in the *adaptive expansion* condition (center), where uppercase target expansion varied according to brain measures, and *static expansion* (right), where uppercase target widths were expanded by 300%.

as much of the secondary task as possible. Because there is a performance tradeoff, we developed an adaptation with the goal of helping the user.

The users complete a known multitasking task, the "tablet" task, and we use a machine learning model of their cognitive activity during this task to predict their cognitive state and adapt the cursor while simultaneously performing n-back and visual search tasks.

Primary Audio Task: N-Back

In order to test our system, we chose a highly controlled task that is grounded in the psychology literature for our experimental testbed. We believe this work generalizes to real-world audio tasks that people typically engage in – communicating to pilots, emergency dispatchers talking to callers, and financial traders communicating during transactions.

A well-validated method to manipulate workload [34, 35, 40], the *n-back task* served as the primary task in this experiment. Participants performed an audio recall n-back task, which has been shown in multiple studies to increase task demand on a user as *n* increases "without requiring direct conflict with manual control or visual processing demands" [35]. In the audio n-back, participants listened to a list of single-digit numbers and after each number, repeated out loud the number that they just heard (0-back), the previous number (1-back), or the number that they heard two numbers ago (2-back). Each n-back set consisted of 16 individual trials, with each digit (0-9) being represented as one of the first ten digits, followed by a sequence of six non-repeating digits.

Secondary Interface Task: Visual Search

In order to construct a controlled task that mimics time-sensitive interface selection activity, we designed an experimental secondary task based on visual search. Visual search tasks require a combination of visual and motor skills in order for users to find and select targets. In our task, users were presented with a canvas containing both uppercase and lowercase letters scattered randomly across the screen, as seen in Figure 1. At the bottom of the screen was a list of 12 letters (6 uppercase and 6 lowercase) as well as a timer.

Participants were instructed to click on letters from the list in sequential order. We consider the uppercase letters to be high-priority targets that may be modified given our adaptive strategy and the lowercase letters as low-priority targets. We show Figure 1 as a demonstration of the target expansions, but there was no visual indication of these changes. The width of the lowercase letters was never explicitly affected in any of the conditions, but occasionally decreased if they were bordered by expanded uppercase targets. Participants were informed that they could skip lowercase letters without penalty, but that they must click on all uppercase letters. However, they could not go back once they advanced in the list and skipped letters.

Scoring

Participants performed this visual search task concurrently with the audio n-back, and were instructed that n-back responses were worth 20 points, uppercase letters were worth ten points, and lowercase letters were worth five points. Their goal was to earn as many points as possible in the time allowed. They were told to go as quickly and accurately as possible and to click once the desired letter was highlighted. After each click on a correct target, the canvas reset and shuffled the locations of all the letters.

SYSTEM DESIGN

The user performs the simultaneous audio n-back and visual search task. During this, we use machine learning to predict the user's multitasking state. At each screen refresh (once the user selects a target), we use the confidence value of the model for the last five seconds as an expansion coefficient to increase the effective width of the uppercase letter targets. We compare the performance in this condition to two other controls: never expanding the target, and always completely expanding the target.

Equipment

We used a multichannel frequency domain Imagent fNIRS device from ISS Inc. (Champaign, IL) for data acquisition. Two probes were placed on each participant's forehead, as shown in Figure 2. Each probe had four light sources, each emitting light at 690 nm and 830 nm, and one detector. The

Figure 2. A user with two fNIRS probes held on with a headband.

source-detector distances ranged from 1.5 to 3.5 cm and the sensor sampling rate was 11.79 Hz.

Multitasking Calibration Task

In order to induce branching in our subjects, we replicated Koechlin et al.'s multitasking experiment, which has been shown to produce neurophysiological changes during the branching condition measurable by both fMRI and fNIRS [29, 45, 46]. Participants were shown a series of uppercase and lowercase letters from the word "TABLET" and had to respond according to different rules for the *delay*, *dual-task*, and *branching* conditions.

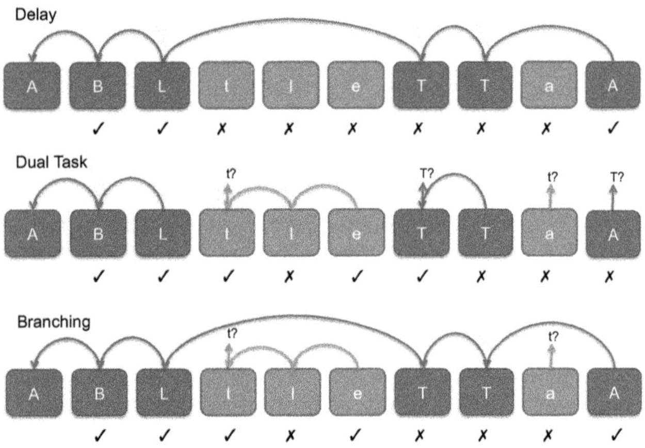

Figure 3. Conditions of the tablet task. Stimuli were uppercase (red) or lowercase (blue) letters, and participants responded according to rules for each task.

- In the *Delay* condition, the user must ignore the stimuli of a secondary task that is interrupting a primary task. Participants ignored lowercase letters and responded if two consecutively presented uppercase stimuli were in succession in the word "tablet."
- In the *Dual-task* condition, the user switches tasks without retaining any information about the previous task. Participants had to respond if two consecutive stimuli of the same case were in immediate succession in the word "tablet." However, if the two stimuli were of different cases, participants had to respond if the second stimulus was a 'T' or 't.'
- In the *Branching* condition, participants had to keep information about one goal in mind while working on another. Participants had to respond to the uppercase letters the same as the delay condition, always remembering the last uppercase letter. For lowercase letters, they responded the same as the dual-task condition, answering if the two consecutive stimuli were in immediate succession in "tablet" if they were both lowercase, but responding if stimulus was a 't' for a change of case.

For each trial of the "tablet" task, participants viewed 11 letter stimuli, each presented for 500 ms, with a 2500 ms period to respond between stimuli. Participants completed 32 trials of the "tablet" task, 16 *branching* and eight of both the delay and dual-task in order to ensure that the machine learning model had the same number of *branching* and *non-branching* trials. We kept the timing of stimuli and probability of a match identical to Koechlin et al., and ran the trials in random order. Although each trial was 33 seconds, we classified brain data on the first 15 seconds of brain data. A pilot study (n=8) using the same task suggested that we could achieve similar or better accuracy using a short period for classification. There was a 15 second rest period between trials in order to allow the brain to return to its resting state, and participants were allowed to take a break after every ten trials. Although each participant had an individual model, the overall trends are shown in Figure 4. Our data logs, as well as Koechlin and Solovey's studies [29, 45], show strong similarities between the performance metrics for branching and dual-task conditions (while the control task is much easier), but the brain activation patterns for the branching task are differentiable from the dual-task and control task (which are similar). Therefore, for our machine learning model, we distinguish branching from non-branching signals (delay + dual-task).

FNIRS Signal

During the tablet task, raw fNIRS data was collected by Boxy (software from ISS, Inc.) and sent to a specialized analysis system which was built in-lab using MATLAB. There, the system calculated the time series of change in fNIRS data over individual trials for each information channel (2 probes x 4 light sources x 2 wavelengths), labeling them as examples of either *branching* or *non-branching*. The signals were filtered for heart rate, respiration, and movement artifacts using a third-degree polynomial filter and low-pass elliptical filter. In the past, this process has been used to support other real-time fNIRS adaptive systems [1, 2, 37, 46].

Machine Learning Model

We constructed a model for the user multitasking states *branching* vs. non-branching (*delay* and *dual-task*), as Solovey et al. 2012 had also done. In order to determine user state, we built a machine learning model based on prefrontal cortex activation signals during the calibration task.

For each of the 32 "tablet" task trials, we calculated the mean and slope of the change in the light intensities for each of the 8 source-detector pairs at two different wavelengths. Thus, each trial consisted of 32 features.

We labeled each of these examples as *branching* or *non-branching* and fed them to LIBSVM, a support vector machine classification system [8]. Per the recommendation of

Cui et al. [10], we used a linear kernel to prevent overfitting the data and did a parameter search to find the best combination of C and γ parameters for each user.

We used ten-fold cross-validation to ensure that the model was accurate, and we did not use data from two participants that could not be accurately modeled (cross-validation accuracy of less than 50%).

For testing, the LIBSVM model received an input example and provided both a classification and a confidence measure (probability estimate) between 50% and 100%. This allows us to receive predictions of intermediate states instead of just 0% and 100%.

Change in Oxy-Hb during Branching vs. Non-Branching Trials

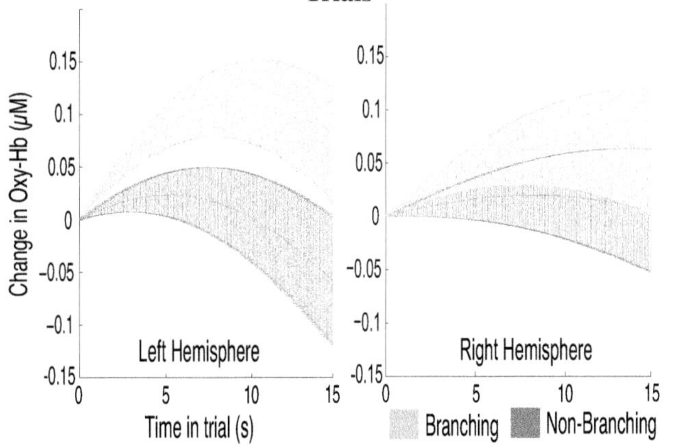

Figure 4. Although we model each participant individually, the fNIRS signal exhibited general trends as participants interacted with the branching and non-branching task. Plotting the mean change in oxy-Hb across all training trials and all participants (16 trials * 12 participants) shows that higher levels oxy-Hb correlate with the branching task. The standard error of the mean is shown with the width of the plots.

Adaptation Trigger and Design

The machine learning classifier provided a prediction every .5 seconds based on the last 15 seconds. We merged predictions from an overlapping sliding window of five seconds (with 4.5 seconds of overlap), computing the average certainty levels of the *branching* state. This means that the system used the average of the last ten classifications, discarding the oldest classification every time it received a new one. This measure directly controlled the uppercase letter target expansion: from no expansion up to three times the original target radius. The expansion radius changed only after each user click to avoid inconsistent cursor behavior.

EXPERIMENT DESIGN AND PROCEDURE

We ran 12 participants (five female) between the ages of 19 and 31. All participants were right-handed, native English speakers with no history of brain damage or disease and had normal or corrected-to-normal vision. Participants were paid for their time and incentivized with a performance bonus for their overall score. All participants were trained to proficiency on the tasks before testing.

Participants were tasked with simultaneously completing audio n-back and visual search tasks. Because of incentives in the point system, they considered the audio n-back their primary task and the visual search task their secondary task. We expected that the completely expanded targets would aid them to click during times of multitasking but would hinder the user in clicking in other situations.

Although we manipulated n-back difficulty level, the primary independent variable under investigation was the level of adaptation of system:

- *no expansion:* we use a standard area bubble cursor and no expansion of the uppercase letters. The cursor always selects the nearest target.
- *static expansion:* we expand the uppercase (priority) targets by three times the original radius and fix its size for the entire trial.
- *adaptive expansion:* the size of the uppercase targets increases and decreases as a function of the classifier's confidence that the user was in a branching state.

We expect that a brain-based target expansion will aid the user in clicking uppercase letters compared to the control condition of *no adaptation*, but the target expansion techniques leave less activation area for the lowercase letters, so the mean time to select lowercase letters will increase. We expect that these results will be extreme for the *static condition*, where users will be able to select uppercase targets the most quickly, but take the most time to select lowercase letters.

We also modified the difficulty of the primary task (the audio n-back) between 0-back (easy), 1-back (medium), and 2-back (hard). Thus for each adaptive condition, participants simultaneously performed nine consecutive audio n-back trials (three 0-back, 1-back, and 2-back trials) and fourteen visual search trials. Each audio n-back lasted 40 seconds with a three second break, totaling 6 minutes and 27 seconds. Participants were given 25 seconds for each visual search task with a three second break, totaling 6 minutes and 32 seconds. Participants were told that the mouse cursor might sometimes be more attracted to uppercase letters in order to help them focus on the higher priority visual targets.

Before experimentation, a set of stimuli for the audio n-back and visual search tasks were randomly generated. This set was used for each participant and the order that tasks were presented was counterbalanced. In addition, the visual search tasks were designed so that there would be no overlap between targets, regardless of expansion.

Dependent Measures

In order to evaluate the interaction between adaptive techniques and multitasking condition, we recorded the following dependent measures:

- *N-back accuracy rate:* the percentage of correct answers in the primary audio n-back task. Participants gave 135 n-back responses per condition.
- *Number of targets selected:* the average number of targets that the user selected, out of 168 targets (84 uppercase, 84 lowercase).

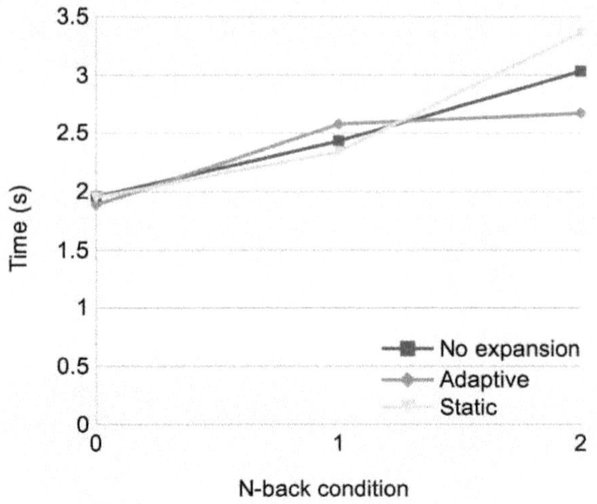

Figure 5. Movement time for uppercase letters by expansion condition.

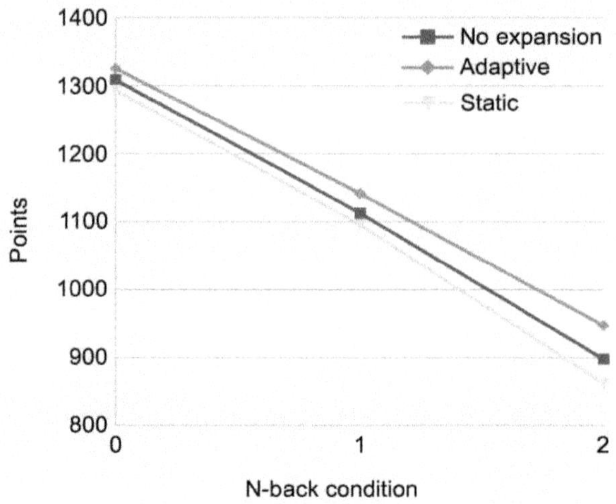

Figure 6. Points by expansion condition. Participants earned 20 points for each correct audio n-back response, while simultaneously earning ten points for each uppercase letter they clicked on and five points for each lowercase letter.

- *Combined score:* the average score the user achieved, as measured with the weighted points system. The maximum total score was 3960 points.
- *Movement Time:* the average amount of time it took between target selection.
- *Target acquisition error rate:* the percentage of clicks that missed the target.

We hypothesize that if we can improve performance on the visual task by improving target selection and focusing on only high-priority targets when the user is busy, the audio n-back accuracy rate should remain constant or improve since the user will have extra cognitive resources.

RESULTS

Task Performance Results

A Kolmogorov-Smirnov test showed that there was a normal distribution of the data. We found that users performed better on both tasks with the adaptive condition compared to the other two conditions. With a two-way ANOVA, there were significant main effects of target expansion condition, $F(2,10) = 4.24, p < .05$, and n-back condition, $F(2,10) = 49.14, p < 0.001$ on the total number of correct n-back responses. A Tukey's pairwise comparison revealed that the *adaptive* condition significantly outperformed the *static* condition ($p < .001$). We also found significant main effects of target condition, $F(2,10) = 5.62, p = 0.001$ and n-back condition, $F(2,10) = 165, p < 0.01$ on the total number of correct target clicks, and a Tukey's pairwise comparison analysis showed that the *adaptive* condition significantly outperformed both *no expansion* ($p < .05$) and *static* ($p < .05$). This also yielded a significant total difference on total score ($p < .005$), with *adaptive* again outperforming *no expansion* ($p < .05$) and *static* ($p < .05$) conditions.

Users performed better on both tasks when we adaptively throttled the expansion of targets, but actually performed worst when they received the expansion for the entire trial.

Speed and Accuracy Results

We found significant differences between conditions for average movement time across trials. Mauchly's test showed a violation of sphericity against Group ($W(2) = 0.26, p < 0.01$). We ran a one-way repeated-measure ANOVA and made Greenhouse-Geisser correction ($\varepsilon = 0.57$). It revealed a significant effect of target condition on movement time (in seconds), $F(2,10) = 6.99, p < 0.005$. A Tukey's pairwise comparison revealed significant differences between the *adaptive* and *static* conditions ($p < 0.01$) movement times as well as between the *no expansion* and *static* adaptation tasks ($p < 0.1$). We also used a two-way repeated-measure ANOVA and found a significant effect of n-back condition ($p < .001$) on movement time and a significant target expansion X n-back interaction on time ($p < .05$), with all three n-back conditions having significant differences ($p < .001$).

A further analysis of movement time revealed that there was a significant difference across expansion ($F(2,10) = 2.24, p < .05$) and n-back conditions ($F(2,10) = 25.45, p < .001$) in movement time for uppercase letters, as shown in Figure 5. The Tukey's pairwise comparison showed that *adaptive* expansion outperformed the *no expansion* ($p < .05$) and *static* expansion conditions. In addition, movement time in the *no expansion* condition was significantly better than the *static* condition. There was no significant difference in expansion condition across lowercase letter movement times.

These results indicate that movement time actually becomes worse when we uniformly apply target expansion to the uppercase letters, but improves if we only do it when the user is in a state of branching.

Because bubble cursor ensures that a user always clicks on a target, we found the hit rate for all three conditions extremely high. There was no significant difference between expansion conditions in the 0-back and 1-back task, but we used a one-way ANOVA and found that in the 2-back, there was a signif-

Measure	No Expansion	Adaptive Expansion	Static Expansion
N-back accuracy rate	90.4%	91.7%	87.97%
Number of targets selected (uppercase)	116.5 (66.9)	122 (67.7)	114.58 (66.2)
Combined score (points)	3358.75	3423.33	3278.75
Movement time - total (s)	2.55	2.49	2.63
Movement time - uppercase (s)	2.47	2.37	2.55
Movement time - lowercase (s)	2.60	2.59	2.70
Target acquisition error rate	1.63%	1.52%	2.80%

Table 1. Average results by expansion condition. All of these measures were significant ($p < .05$) across expansion condition and n-back condition except for movement time for lowercase targets and target acquisition error rate.

icant effect of condition ($F(2, 10) = 2.24, p < .05$). Similar to Grossman and Balakrishnan, we choose not to do a full speed-accuracy analysis because our hit rates were well below the standard 4% error rate used to calculate target effective width in other target acquisition studies.

The index of difficulty across conditions was insignificant across target and n-back conditions, showing that participants performed roughly the same difficulty of task across conditions. We also looked at distance traveled, throughput (the ratio of index of difficulty to movement time), and path metrics, but did not find any differences across conditions. In addition, we found no learning effect either within trials of a condition or across conditions.

DISCUSSION

These results suggest that participants were able to perform more critical work with a higher accuracy rate in a brain-based target *adaptive expansion* system than in a standard bubble cursor interface. Our results show that we could create a continuous level of adaptation with only implicit, non-visible assistance.

Although bubble cursor already shows large improvements over standard point cursors, we found additional performance increments using brain input to control target expansion for bubble cursor. Using expansion at the correct times helps users by an average of 60 milliseconds per click (100 milliseconds for high-priority targets). As expected, we find that performance increases when the user is selecting a high-priority target, but we are able to do this without a negative impact on low-priority targets. Although these slight increases are not dramatic, in a repeated task such as target acquisition, over time they can yield powerful changes in user capabilities. In addition, the user does slightly better in the primary audio task, which may indicate that the user is devoting less resources to the visual interface. Because of these gains, we see that the user is able to select an extra 5.5 targets on average. This means that the user is able to take advantage of the pointing performance increases and select more targets.

Although a calculated level of expansion helps the user, a constant maximum expansion actually impedes performance in both tasks. While we expected the *static* expansion condition to aid in acquisition of uppercase targets, we see that it only helps during low workload conditions and actually performs worst of all three conditions in the 2-back condition. We hypothesize this is due to the user spending extra cognitive and visual resources trying to figure out the limits of the target. In addition, although there is almost no difference between the other two conditions in selecting lowercase letters, the *static* expansion fares far worse in selecting lowercase letters.

From our results, it is clear that target adaptation alone is not enough to incite task improvements, but this adaptation must be judiciously applied, taking effect only when the user is dividing mental focus.

ACKNOWLEDGEMENTS

We thank Alvitta Ottley, Eli Brown, Fumeng Yang, Lane Harrison, Sergio Fantini, and Angelo Sassaroli from Tufts University, Erin Solovey from Drexel University, and R. Jordan Crouser from MIT Lincoln Laboratory. We also thank Google Inc. and the NSF for support of this research (NSF Grants Nos. IIS-1065154 and IIS-1218170). Any opinions, findings, conclusions, or recommendations expressed in this paper are those of the authors and do not necessarily reflect the views of Google Inc. or the National Science Foundation.

REFERENCES

1. Afergan, D., Peck, E. M., Solovey, E. T., Jenkins, A., Hincks, S. W., Brown, E. T., Chang, R., and Jacob, R. J. K. Dynamic Difficulty Using Brain Metrics of Workload. In *Proc. ACM CHI 2014*, ACM Press (2014).
2. Ayaz, H., Onaral, B., Izzetoglu, K., Shewokis, P. A., McKendrick, R., and Parasuraman, R. Continuous monitoring of brain dynamics with functional near infrared spectroscopy as a tool for neuroergonomic research: empirical examples and a technological development. *Frontiers in Human Neuroscience 7* (2013).
3. Ayaz, H., and Willems, B. Cognitive workload assessment of air traffic controllers using optical brain imaging sensors. In *Advances in Understanding Human Performance: Neuroergonomics, Human Factors Design, and Special Populations*. CRC Press, 2010, 21–32.
4. Baddeley, A. Working memory. *Science* (1992).
5. Balakrishnan, R. Beating fitts' law: virtual enhancements for pointing facilitation. *International Journal of Human-Computer Studies 61*, 6 (2004), 857–874.
6. Baudisch, P., Zotov, A., Cutrell, E., and Hinckley, K. Starburst: a target expansion algorithm for non-uniform

target distributions. *Proceedings Working Conference on Advanced Visual Interfaces* (2008).

7. Burgess, P. W., Veitch, E., de Lacy Costello, A., and Shallice, T. The cognitive and neuroanatomical correlates of multitasking. *Neuropsychologia 38*, 6 (2000), 848–63.
8. Chang, C., and Lin, C. LIBSVM: a library for support vector machines. *ACM Transactions on Intelligent Systems and Technology* (2011), 1–39.
9. Cockburn, A., and Gin, A. Faster cascading menu selections with enlarged activation areas. In *Proc. Graphics interface 2006*, Canadian Information Processing Society (2006).
10. Cui, X., Bray, S., and Reiss, A. L. Speeded near infrared spectroscopy (NIRS) response detection. *PLoS one 5*, 11 (2010).
11. Curtis, C. E., and D'Esposito, M. Persistent activity in the prefrontal cortex during working memory. *Trends in Cognitive Sciences 7*, 9 (2003), 415–423.
12. Cutrell, E., and Tan, D. BCI for passive input in HCI. In *Proc. CHI 2008*, ACM Press (2008).
13. D'Esposito, M., Zarahn, E., and Aguirre, G. K. Event-related functional MRI: implications for cognitive psychology. *Psychological Bulletin 125*, 1 (1999), 155.
14. Fabiani, G., and McFarland, D. Conversion of EEG activity into cursor movement by a brain-computer interface (BCI). *IEEE Transactions on Neural Systems and Rehabilitation Engineering 12*, 3 (2004).
15. Fairclough, S. H. Fundamentals of physiological computing. *Interacting with Computers 21*, 1-2 (2009), 133–145.
16. Girouard, A., and Solovey, E. Distinguishing Difficulty Levels with Non-invasive Brain Measurements. *INTERACT 2009*, Figure 1 (2009), 440–452.
17. Girouard, A., Solovey, E. T., and Jacob, R. J. K. Designing a passive brain computer interface using real time classification of functional nearinfrared spectroscopy. *International Journal of Autonomous and Adaptive Communications Systems 6*, 1 (2013), 26–44.
18. Gray, W. D., and Boehm-Davis, D. A. Milliseconds matter: An introduction to microstrategies and to their use in describing and predicting interactive behavior. *Journal of Experimental Psychology: Applied 6*, 4 (2000), 322.
19. Grossman, T., and Balakrishnan, R. The bubble cursor: enhancing target acquisition by dynamic resizing of the cursor's activation area. In *Proc. CHI 2005*, ACM Press (2005).
20. Guiard, Y., Blanch, R., and Beaudouin-Lafon, M. Object pointing: a complement to bitmap pointing in GUIs. In *Proc. Graphics Interface 2004* (2004), 9–16.
21. Guiard, Y., Olafsdottir, H. B., and Perrault, S. T. Fitts' Law as an Explicit Time/Error Trade-Off. In *Proc. CHI 2011*, ACM Press (2011).
22. Han, S.-H., and Kim, M.-S. Visual search does not remain efficient when executive working memory is working. *Psychological Science 15*, 9 (2004), 623–8.
23. Harrison, J., Izzetoglu, K., and Ayaz, H. Human Performance Assessment Study in Aviation Using Functional Near Infrared Spectroscopy. *Foundations of Augmented Cognition* (2013), 433–442.
24. Hirshfield, L., Gulotta, R., and Hirshfield, S. This is your brain on interfaces: enhancing usability testing with functional near-infrared spectroscopy. In *Proc. CHI 2011*, ACM Press (2011).
25. Hirshfield, L. M., Solovey, E. T., Girouard, A., Kebinger, J., Jacob, R. J. K., Sassaroli, A., and Fantini, S. Brain Measurement for Usability Testing and Adaptive Interfaces: An Example of Uncovering Syntactic Workload with Functional Near Infrared Spectroscopy. In *Proc. CHI 2009*, ACM Press (2009).
26. Huppert, T., and Hoge, R. A temporal comparison of BOLD, ASL, and NIRS hemodynamic responses to motor stimuli in adult humans. *Neuroimage 29*, 2 (2006), 368–382.
27. Kabbash, P., and Buxton, W. The "Prince" Technique : Fitts' Law and Selection Using Area Cursors. In *Proc. CHI 1995*, ACM Press (1995).
28. Kelso, J. Theoretical concepts and strategies for understanding perceptual-motor skill: From information capacity in closed systems to self-organization in open, nonequilibrium. *Journal of Experimental Psychology: General* (1992).
29. Koechlin, E., Basso, G., Pietrini, P., Panzer, S., and Grafman, J. The role of the anterior prefrontal cortex in human cognition. *Nature 399*, 6732 (1999), 148–51.
30. MacKenzie, I. S. Fitts' law as a research and design tool in human-computer interaction. *Human-computer interaction* (1992).
31. Maior, H. A., and Pike, M. Continuous Detection of Workload Overload: An fNIRS Approach. In *Proc. International Conference on Ergonomics & Human Factors 2014*, CRC Press (2014).
32. McGuffin, M., and Balakrishnan, R. Fitts' law and expanding targets: Experimental studies and designs for user interfaces. *Transactions on Computer-Human Interaction 12*, 4 (2005), 388–422.
33. McKendrick, R., Ayaz, H., Olmstead, R., and Parasuraman, R. Enhancing dual-task performance with verbal and spatial working memory training: continuous monitoring of cerebral hemodynamics with NIRS. *Neuroimage 85* (2014), 1014–1026.

34. Mehler, B., Reimer, B., and Coughlin, J. F. Sensitivity of Physiological Measures for Detecting Systematic Variations in Cognitive Demand From a Working Memory Task: An On-Road Study Across Three Age Groups. *Human Factors: The Journal of the Human Factors and Ergonomics Society 54*, 3 (2012), 396–412.

35. Mehler, B., Reimer, B., Coughlin, J. F., and Dusek, J. A. Impact of Incremental Increases in Cognitive Workload on Physiological Arousal and Performance in Young Adult Drivers. *Transportation Research Record: Journal of the Transportation Research Board 2138*, 2 (2009), 6–12.

36. Mott, M. E., and Wobbrock, J. O. Beating the bubble: using kinematic triggering in the bubble lens for acquiring small, dense targets. In *Proc. CHI 2014*, ACM Press (2014).

37. Peck, E. M., Afergan, D., and Jacob, R. J. K. Investigation of fNIRS brain sensing as input to information filtering systems. In *Proc. Augmented Human International*, ACM Press (2013).

38. Peck, E. M., Afergan, D., Yuksel, B. F., Lalooses, F., and Jacob, R. J. Using fNIRS to measure mental workload in the real world. In *Advances in Physiological Computing*. Springer, 2014, 117–139.

39. Pike, M. F., Maior, H. A., Porcheron, M., Sharples, S. C., and Wilson, M. L. Measuring the effect of think aloud protocols on workload using fNIRS. In *Proc. CHI 2014*, ACM Press (2014).

40. Reimer, B., Mehler, B., Coughlin, J. F., Godfrey, K. M., and Tan, C. An on-road assessment of the impact of cognitive workload on physiological arousal in young adult drivers. *Proc. AutomotiveUI 2009* (2009).

41. Repovš, G., and Baddeley, A. The multi-component model of working memory: explorations in experimental cognitive psychology. *Neuroscience 139*, 1 (2006), 5–21.

42. Sassaroli, A., Zheng, F., Hirshfield, L. M., Girouard, A., Solovey, E. T., Jacob, R. J. K., and Fantini, S. Discrimination of Mental Workload Levels in Human Subjects with Functional Near-Infrared Spectroscopy. *Journal of Innovative Optical Health Sciences 1*, 2 (2008), 227–237.

43. Schalk, G., McFarland, D. J., Hinterberger, T., Birbaumer, N., and Wolpaw, J. R. BCI2000: a general-purpose brain-computer interface (BCI) system. *IEEE Transactions on Biomedical Engineering 51*, 6 (2004), 1034.

44. Solovey, E. T., Girouard, A., Chauncey, K., Hirshfield, L. M., Sassaroli, A., Zheng, F., Fantini, S., and Jacob, R. J. K. Using fNIRS Brain Sensing in Realistic HCI Settings: Experiments and Guidelines. In *Proc. UIST 2009*, ACM Press (2009).

45. Solovey, E. T., Girouard, A., Jacob, R. J., Lalooses, F., Chauncey, K., Weaver, D., Parasi, M., Scheutz, M., Sassaroli, A., Fantini, S., and Schermerhorn, P. Sensing cognitive multitasking for a brain-based adaptive user interface. *Proc. CHI 2011* (2011).

46. Solovey, E. T., Schermerhorn, P., Scheutz, M., Sassaroli, A., Fantini, S., and Jacob, R. Brainput: Enhancing Interactive Systems with Streaming fNIRS Brain Input. In *Proc. CHI 2012*, ACM Press (2012).

47. Vidaurre, C., Kawanabe, M., von Bünau, P., Blankertz, B., and Müller, K. R. Toward unsupervised adaptation of LDA for brain-computer interfaces. *IEEE Transactions on Biomedical Engineering 58*, 3 (2011), 587–97.

48. Villringer, A., and Chance, B. Non-invasive optical spectroscopy and imaging of human brain function. *Trends in neurosciences 20*, 10 (1997), 435–42.

49. Wickens, C. Multiple resources and mental workload. *Human Factors: The Journal of the Human Factors and Ergonomics Society 50*, 3 (2008), 449–455.

50. Worden, A., Walker, N., Bharat, K., and Hudson, S. Making computers easier for older adults to use: area cursors and sticky icons. In *Proc. CHI 1997*, ACM Press (1997).

51. Zander, T. O., Kothe, C., Welke, S., and Rötting, M. Utilizing secondary input from passive brain-computer interfaces for enhancing human-machine interaction. In *Foundations of Augmented Cognition, Neuroergonomics and Operational Neuroscience*, Springer Berlin Heidelberg (2009), 759–771.

52. Zhai, S., and Conversy, S. Human on-line response to target expansion. In *Proc. CHI 2003*, ACM Press (2003).

Pinch-to-Zoom-Plus: An Enhanced Pinch-to-Zoom That Reduces Clutching and Panning

Jeff Avery, Mark Choi, Daniel Vogel, Edward Lank
Cheriton School of Computer Science
University of Waterloo
Waterloo, ON, Canada N2L 3G1
{j2avery, hichoi, dvogel, lank}@uwaterloo.ca

ABSTRACT
Despite its popularity, the classic pinch-to-zoom gesture used in modern multi-touch interfaces has drawbacks: specifically, the need to support an extended range of scales and the need to keep content within the view window on the display can result in the need to clutch and pan. In two formative studies of unimanual and bimanual pinch-to-zoom, we found patterns: zooming actions follows a predictable ballistic velocity curve, and users tend to pan the point-of-interest towards the center of the screen. We apply these results to design an enhanced zooming technique called Pinch-to-Zoom-Plus (PZP) that reduces clutching and panning operations compared to standard pinch-to-zoom behaviour.

Author Keywords
mobile; multi-touch; interaction.

ACM Classification Keywords
H5.2 Information interfaces and presentation: User Interfaces - Input devices and strategies.

INTRODUCTION
Increasing or decreasing the document zoom level (i.e. scale or magnification) according to the distance between two simultaneous touch points [9,18] is a standard gesture on virtually all multi-touch devices. This "pinch-to-zoom" interaction technique is direct, simple, and intuitive, but not perfect. To reach distant zoom levels, frequent clutching is needed (where both fingers are lifted to reset the distance between touch points to continue zooming). Specifying the optimum zoom origin is difficult and often requires panning to keep the location of interest from moving off the screen. These problems are exacerbated by extreme focus+context tasks which require frequent zooming in-and-out between a close-up view to perform an action, and an overview of the entire document [12,13,15]. Past work has proposed replacing pinch-to-zoom with new multi-touch zoom techniques to eliminate clutching [6,7,14] and switch between an overview and close-up [4]. As of yet, none of these techniques have reduced pinch-to-zoom's dominance.

Rather than replacing pinch-to-zoom, we designed Pinch-to-Zoom-Plus (PZP), and enhancement of the standard pinch-to-zoom technique that reduces clutching and panning. It is fully compatible with current pinch-to-zoom and it works regardless of device size, handedness, or whether under bimanual or unimanual control.

The design parameters in PZP are based on results of two formative studies investigating kinematic and clutching characteristics of standard pinch-to-zoom. We found the velocity of pinch and spread behaviours follows a ballistic pattern, and used this to justify and parameterize pan and zoom acceleration to reduce clutching. We also observed a tendency to pan targets towards the center of the screen, and used this to justify automatic pan-to-centre while zooming. Our results complement recent work on pinch-to-zoom performance and ergonomics [10,17] and provides new insights and practical applications for results.

Our contributions are twofold: a detailed analysis of clutching and panning behaviour with current pinch-to-zoom technique; and the design and evaluation of PZP, an enhanced pinch-to-zoom technique shaped by that analysis. Our PZP technique reduces clutching and panning operations compared to standard pinch-to-zoom and can be implemented on all current multi-touch devices.

RELATED WORK
Buxton [2] traces the history of pinch-to-zoom to the early 1980s based on a demonstration of two-finger pinch and pan interaction in Wellner's Digital Desk video [19]. Hinckley et al. also describe the Pinch gesture [9] which allows users to zoom and pan around the center of two contact points. Pinch-to-zoom has since become the standard zooming gesture on multi-touch devices.

Despite its popularity, there are obvious problems with pinch-to-zoom for a certain subset of interactions: precision-pointing and occlusion problems are well known [16], but there are also specific issues with focus+context tasks [12]. While the pinch gesture allows users to zoom

UIST 2014, October 5–8, 2014, Honolulu, HI, USA.

http://dx.doi.org/10.1145/2642918.2647352

in to see detail, users also need to zoom back out to see high-level context. Interacting at multiple zoom scales requires frequent interaction to continually zoom the document in and out [12,13,15]. These operations often require frequent clutching, which can be slow. It can also be difficult to accurately specify the zoom origin due to finger occlusion. As a result, the location of interest can move unpredictably while zooming, even off the screen forcing users to pan to correct the position. When frequently zooming in and out during focus+context tasks, these problems are exacerbated.

To address these shortcomings, techniques other than pinch-to-zoom have been proposed. Albinsson and Zhai's Zoom-Pointing [1] is a bimanual technique in which the user draws a bounding box to define a persistent zoom area. Zoom-Pointing thus allows a user to specifically delineate the content they wish to see on-screen. This overcomes the need to pan after zooming to accurately position zoomed content. Forlines and Shen's DTLens [6] is similar, but adds controls for minimizing, closing or annotating the enlarged viewport. It also allows users to save and restore zoom levels. However, both techniques require an explicit zoom-out to return to overall context.

Other techniques have a transient zoom mode. Käser et al.'s Fingerglass [12] allows users to specify a zoom-target using a non-dominant hand, then interact with the zoomed-in area using their dominant hand. When the non-dominant hand is released, the view returns to the default zoom level. Fingerglass does not support clutching, so only a limited range of zoom scales is possible. Negulescu et al.'s two handed Offset technique moves the zoom origin out from under one finger into the user's view [15] and is transient by snapping back to the default zoom level when both fingers are lifted. Like Fingerglass, clutching is not supported limiting the range of zoom scales.

These techniques all attempt to address excessive clutching and panning by replacing pinch-to-zoom. However, pinch-to-zoom is already ubiquitous, and a technique that enhances pinch-to-zoom rather than replacing it, may be more approachable. For that reason, researchers have begun looking more closely at pinch-to-zoom. Hoggan et al. [9] examine the ergonomics of pinch-to-zoom, identifying factors that contribute to performance, such as direction, distance, angle and position. Tran et al. [15] build a quantitative model of pinch-to-zoom performance. We extend this work with a complementary analysis of pinch-to-zoom with focus+context tasks. However, we go beyond examining current behaviour, and our results to motivate and provide design parameters for an improved pinch-to-zoom technique.

ANALYZING PINCH-TO-ZOOM

We conducted two formative studies to study pinch-to-zoom scale adjustment with and without panning to alter translation. This is based on pilot studies, where we observed users performing both sequential and separate zoom and pan actions and simultaneous zoom and pan actions. The first study centered all targets requiring zoom actions, but not panning, so that we could examine zoom clutching in isolation. The second study placed targets around a perimeter to encourage panning along with zooming. The pilot studies also revealed people perform pinch-to-zoom on a tablet with one or two hands: using one finger from each hand (bimanual) or two fingers from one hand (unimanual). We control for these two variants in both studies.

Apparatus

Both studies were performed on a Toshiba AT200 1.2 GHz Dual Core tablet with a 1280 by 800 pixel display (218 by 136 mm, 5.88 px-per-mm). Custom software was implemented in Android 4.03, and tuned to duplicate standard Android pinch-to-zoom behaviour. Observed lag was minimal, and events were logged at a device sample rate of 60Hz. The tablet was placed flat on a standard desk in landscape mode, and anchored to the surface using rubber pads to prevent movement. An overhead video camera recorded the session.

Study 1: Only Zoom Required

The goal of the first study was to examine clutching in pinch-to-zoom gestures using a simple docking task with the target and dock centered on the display (see Figure 1). The target was a blue opaque square and the docking area was a semi-transparent blue rectangle with a border thickness representing the fit tolerance. The background was textured to provide context and simulate a document task, like map navigation. At the start of the task, the dock was placed mid-screen with the target centered over it. Panning could be used to move the target, but the dock did not move from the center. Thus, panning was allowed, but was not required to complete the task. The dock highlighted when the target fit correctly, and the task was completed when both fingers were released in that state. Note that all trials were ultimately successful, but intermediate errors caused by tighter fit tolerance increased the difficulty of the task.

Twenty right-handed participants (3 female), with an average age of 27 (SD 5.44) participated in our first study. All participants had prior experience with multi-touch tablets or smartphones. $10 remuneration was provided.

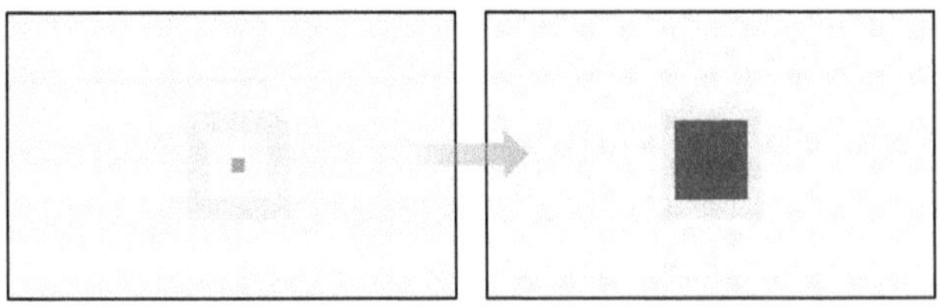

(i) (ii)

Figure 1: Study 1 docking task. Participants were asked to zoom the target (i) to make it fit within the docking area (ii). Targets turn bright blue when properly scaled to the docking area, indicating that the operation was successful.

The design is within-subjects with independent variables for hand condition (unimanual/bimanual), tolerance of docking region (4 mm, 7 mm, 10 mm tolerances), zoom direction (zoom-in, zoom-out), and zoom level (4, 7, 10, 13, 16, 19x for zoom-in, and multiplicative inverse levels for zoom-out). The zoom-out direction required participants to scale a large target down, and zoom-in required the opposite. The six zoom levels were chosen to cover typical pinch-to-zoom scenarios; for example, the maximum zoom level of 19x is roughly equivalent to zooming from a map of a large city (10 km per cm) down to a city block (525 m per cm). Hand condition (unimanual/bimanual) was counterbalanced between participants, and all tolerances, zoom levels, and zoom directions were fully crossed and presented in a random ordered block of trials, to balance potential learning effects. Five blocks were presented creating five repetitions.

An initial practice block of 12 trials presented a subset of tolerances {7 mm, 10 mm} and zoom levels {4, 7, 15, 0.25, 0.14, 0.06}. Not counting these practice trials, the experiment had 360 trials per participant. The experiment time was approximately 45 minutes.

Pre-Processing

We define an *action* as the sequence of two finger dragging movements occurring between touch down and touch up events. Note that a clutch occurs between actions. We classify each action as either a *zoom* or *pan* using thresholds determined in our pilot study:

- *Pan actions* are defined as actions where fingers spread less than 5 px (0.85 mm). Pans of less than 2 px (0.34 mm) were discarded as unintentional movements.
- *Zoom actions* are defined as actions where fingers spread more than 5 px (0.85 mm). We differentiate between zoom-in and out based on spread direction.

For each trial, we calculated the completion time and number of zoom-in, zoom-out, and pan actions. One participant was an outlier with all completion times more than two standard deviations from the overall mean, and was excluded from analysis. Learning effects of block on elapsed time were observed ($F_{2,18}$ = 7.79, p < .01), so block 1 was excluded. Excluding practice blocks and block 1 tasks, the remaining 19 participants performed a total of 4104 tasks.

Results

Mean task completion time was 5.65 s (SD 2.71). Handedness had no significant effect on elapsed time ($F_{1,18}$ = 0.418, ns). As expected, tolerance had an effect on the elapsed time, with smaller targets taking significantly longer to complete ($F_{2,18}$ = 210.85, p < .01). Zoom level also had a significant impact on time ($F_{2,18}$ = 32.83, p < .01), with the completion time increasing as greater zoom levels were required to achieve the target.

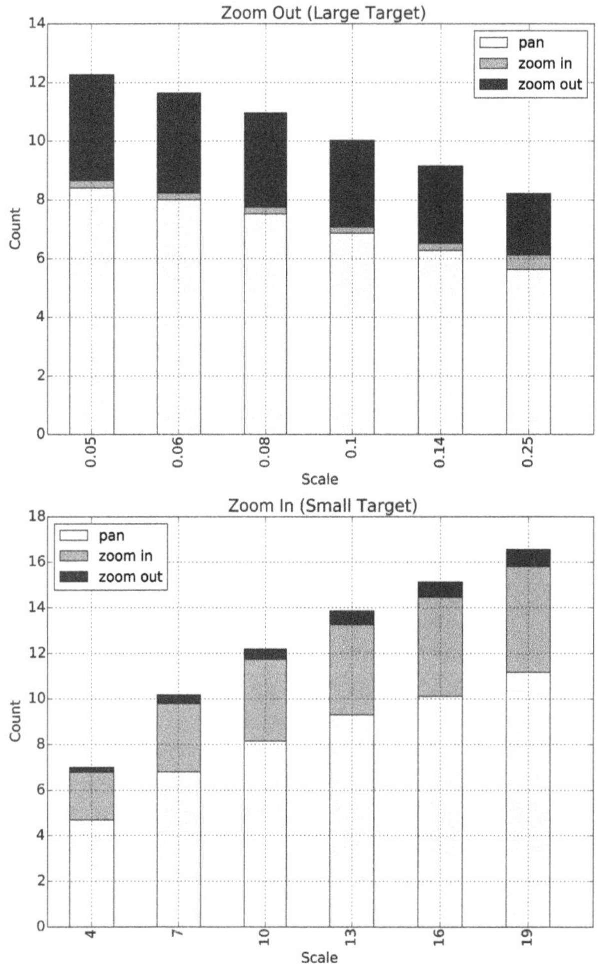

Figure 2: Count of zoom and pan actions by zoom level. More than 1 zoom or pan action requires a clutch (i.e. 1 action has 0 clutches, 2 actions require 1 clutch, etc.)

Mean counts of actions per task were 1.94 zoom-in actions (SD 2.33), 1.75 zoom-out actions (SD 1.86) and 7.76 pan actions (SD 4.66). Zoom-in count was not significantly affected by handedness ($F_{2,18}$ = 2.096, ns), but was affected by tolerance ($F_{2,18}$ = 41.94, p < 0.01) and scale ($F_{2,18}$ = 125.66, p < 0.01). Zoom-out count was not significantly affected by handedness ($F_{2,18}$ = 0.374, ns) but was affected by tolerance ($F_{2,18}$ = 199.792, ns) and zoom-out ($F_{2,18}$ = 125.148, ns). Pan count was not significantly affected by handedness ($F_{2,18}$ = 0, ns) but was affected by tolerance ($F_{2,18}$ = 89.49, p < 0.01) and scale ($F_{2,18}$ = 41.65, p < 0.01). Smaller or larger targets, and low-tolerance targets, require more zoom and pan actions to acquire.

The pattern indicates that even a small change in zoom-level requires clutching: 1.94 clutches for zoom-in (4x had a mean of 2.1 zoom-in actions) and 1.75 clutches for zoom-out (0.25x had a mean of 2.1 clutches). Exceeding 10x or 0.01x zoom level required more than three clutches on average (Figure 2). The mean clutch time (between two successive zoom actions) was 180.5 ms (SD 250.7).

We were somewhat surprised by the number of pan operations. Note that target and dock were located in the center of the display and the dock was initially positioned over the target. Thus, panning was not a required operation during our study. Even if one assumes that zooming in (i.e. enlarging content) would require pan operations to ensure that content did not migrate off the screen, the similarity in frequency of pan actions when zooming out is not explained by this. Even a small change in resolution, 4x for zoom-in and 0.25 for zoom out, was associated with a significant number of pan actions: averages of 4.69 and 5.62 pan actions, respectively. The prevalence of pan actions when a target was optimally positioned in the center of the display raises the question of how and why participants chose to reposition content.

Study 2: Zoom and Pan

This goal of the second study is to expand the scope of the first study by placing the dock and target around the perimeter of the screen. In addition to the docking task from study 1, we add a drawing task that required a simple drawing to be performed after docking.

As in our first study, the docking task is to zoom a target in or out until it fits in a docking area, within a certain tolerance (Figure 3). Unlike our first study, targets are placed at one of 8 locations around the perimeter of the display. Panning caused both the target and dock to move together, so panning was not required to complete the task – successful docking only required zooming. However, based on the voluntary panning of study 1, we believed participants would use pan as part of the zoom operation and/or to optimize the placement of the target.

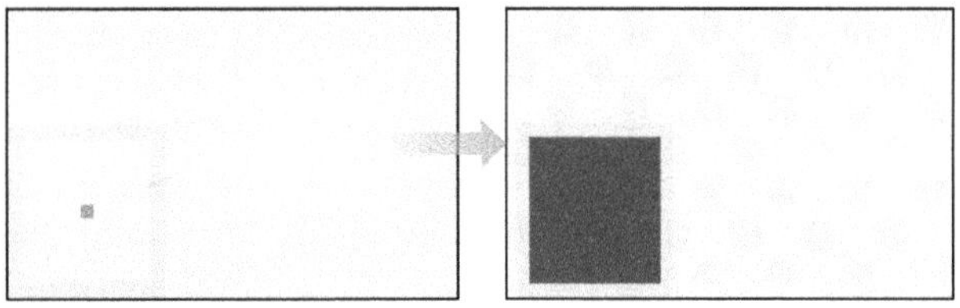

(i) (ii)

Figure 3: Study 2 docking task with targets positioned around the edge of the screen. Participants are asked to zoom the square (i) until it falls within the docking area (ii). Targets turn bright blue when properly scaled within the docking area, indicating that the operation was successful.

The second task simulates editing tasks like annotating maps or editing photographs. The presentation is the same as the docking task, except that the target and dock are circular. After reaching the required zoom level with the target fit inside the dock, participants also had to draw a circle within a confined region of the target (Figure 4). This was done to encourage participants to interact with the target, making it difficult to complete the task unless the target remained visible on the screen. For brevity, we label this second task a *drawing* task. Drawing tasks did not include a zoom-out condition, because the nature of the task required a large target in which to draw.

The screen was divided into a 3 x 3 grid of 9 regions, which were used to determine initial target position (the middle was excluded, so 8 regions were available). At the start of each task, a region was chosen randomly, and the dock and target were centered within that region. All tasks were performed with a 7 mm tolerance, the median tolerance from the first study. We used 2 zoom levels for the docking task, 13x for zoom-in, and the multiplicative inverse for zoom-out, and one zoom level for the drawing task, 13x. The decision to use a single tolerance and zoom level was motivated by the observation that any scale factor required clutch and pan actions, so fully varying across all tolerances and scales was not necessary and allowed us to limit our study to a reasonable length or time for our participants.

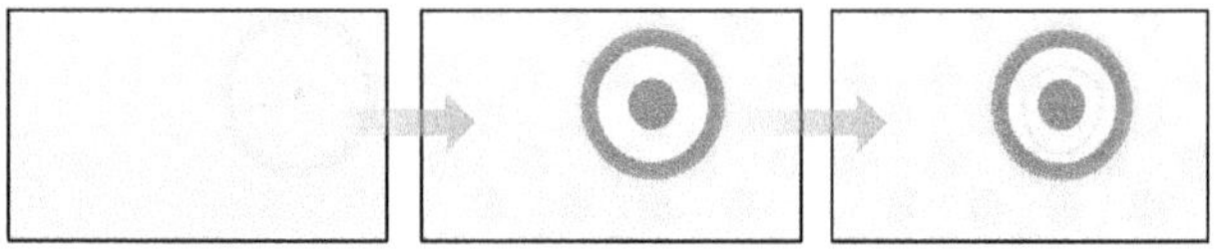

(i) (ii) (iii)

Figure 4: Study 2 drawing task. Participants are asked to zoom until the circular target (i) falls within the docking area (ii), and then draw a line along the inside path (iii).

We recruited 17 right-handed participants (4 female), and 3 left-handed participants (all male) with an average age of 27.7 (SD 4.98). All participants had prior experience with multi-touch tablets or smartphones. A $10 voucher was offered as remuneration.

Participants performed docking tasks first, then after a 3 min break, performed all drawing tasks. Each task was repeated for bimanual and unimanual hand conditions, with the order counterbalanced across participants. In the docking task, a practice block of 6 trials was presented at the beginning of each condition (24 trials in total). Drawing tasks included 8 trials per block, representing the 8 positions. Not counting practice trials, the experiment had 384 trials per participant (256 docking tasks plus 128 drawing tasks). The total time for the experiment was 60 minutes.

Pre-Processing

A learning effect existed across four blocks, for both docking tasks ($F_{1,19} = 18.52$, $p < .01$) and drawing tasks ($F_{1,19} = 13.75$, $p < .01$). To minimize this effect, the first block was excluded, resulting in a total of 5780 experimental tasks performed (3860 docking and 1920 drawing tasks). Actions were classified using the same tolerance as study 1 into pan actions (movement without significant zoom), zoom-in actions (scale increasing) and zoom-out actions (scale decreasing).

Results

Two-factor ANOVA and Bonferroni-Dunn correction were used for pairwise comparisons including the effects of target position, and hand condition.

Docking tasks had a mean task completion time of 4.84 s (SD 2.16). Handedness had no significant effect on time ($F_{1,19}$ = 1.005, ns). Starting target position had an effect on task time in docking tasks, both for zoom-in ($F_{1,19}$ = 4.934, $p < .01$) and zoom-out ($F_{1,19}$ = 2.752, $p < .01$), although post hoc analysis did not find which position was significant (likely due to the number of tests required).

Drawing task completion time was defined as the time required to zoom to the desired zoom-level, and excluded drawing time. Mean task completion time was 7.64 s (SD 2.10). Since users had to interact with the content after zooming in the drawing task, users appeared to spend more time positioning the target before proceeding. As with the docking task, handedness had no effect on task time $F_{1,19}$ = 4.11, ns. Starting target position had an effect on task time in drawing tasks as well ($F_{1,19}$ = 4.88, $p < .01$). As with docking tasks, post hoc analysis was unable to indicate which position was significant.

Docking tasks had a mean count of 3.5 zoom-in actions (SD 4.17), 5.67 zoom-out actions (SD 5.87), and 10.94 pan actions (SD 8.98) per task. Drawing tasks had a mean count of 7.03 zoom-in actions (SD 4.72), a mean count of 1.37 zoom-out actions, and a mean count of 14.43 pan actions (SD 9.68). These are higher than study 1.

For both docking and drawing tasks, hand condition (bimanual/unimanual) had no significant effect on zoom-in count ($F_{1,19}$ = 1.33, ns; $F_{1,19}$ = 4.16, ns) or zoom-out count ($F_{1,19}$ = 0.24, ns; $F_{1,19}$ = 4.22, ns). Handedness did have a significant effect on pan count for the docking task ($F_{1,19}$ = 67.39, $p < 0.01$), but not on the drawing task ($F_{1,19}$ = 0.19, ns). Position had no effect on zoom-in count ($F_{1,19}$ = 0.98, ns) or zoom-out count ($F_{1,19}$ = 0.97, ns) but did have an effect on pan count ($F_{1,19}$ = 22.39, $p < .01$) with targets on the left-hand side requiring more pans than targets positioned to the center or right-hand side. We observed participants panning targets towards their dominant hand when the target is further away, which is consistent with this data. For drawing, position affects zoom-in count ($F_{1,19}$ = 5.25, $p < .01$), zoom-out counts ($F_{1,19}$ = 6.00, $p < .01$), and pan counts ($F_{1,19}$ = 3.61, $p < .01$). Targets at the horizontal midpoints of the display (top-center and bottom-center) appear to require fewer zoom actions.

Synthesis and Further Analysis

Multiple clutch and pan actions were observed in both of our studies, regardless of hand condition, location, or zoom direction. In this section, we further analyze zoom and pan gestures to explore ways to reduce the number of clutch and pan actions.

Given our observation of multiple zoom-in/zoom-out and pan operations, a first question to ask is whether there exists some technique akin to cursor acceleration that could be applied to pinch-to-zoom operations to reduce clutching. Figure 5 depicts an analysis of zoom and pan speed data, aggregated across all single-handed trials (blocks 3-4 only, to reduce learning effects). Zoom and pan gestures both exhibit a ballistic pattern, with an initial high-speed movement to resize or reposition the target. For zoom actions, an initial ballistic movement peaking at 20% of the total duration, and is followed by a longer, low-speed tail beginning at about 40% of the duration. Pan movements exhibit this same ballistic profile, but without the longer, low-speed tail.

Considering screen location data for both of our studies, panning was not required, but was a high-frequency operation. This suggests that participants were deliberately repositioning content on the display. To understand why pan operations were occurring, we look at the final location of target and dock to determine why participants reposition content. At task completion, the mean distance between the target/dock and the center of the screen is 248.9 px (SD 193.7). Histogram data for distance from the center of the screen is shown in Figure 7. In a scatter plot of the final location of dock and target shown in Figure 7, we can see that target locations are grouped around the center of the display and that locations near the edges are avoided. The slight bias to the right-of-center in Figure 7 may be due to handedness of participants, but more data is needed to determine if there is any significant bias.

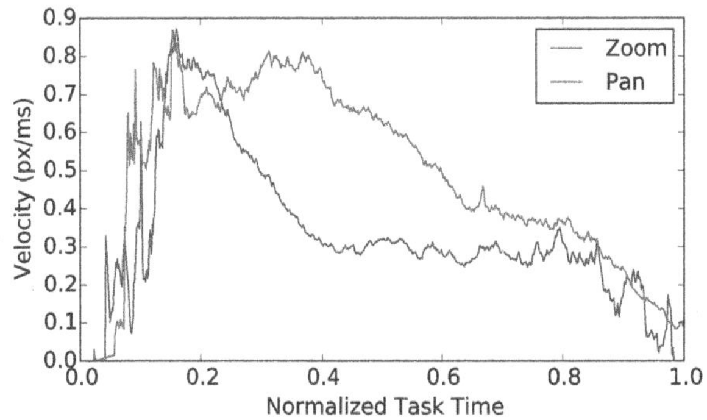

Figure 5: Mean pan and zoom velocity profiles for docking tasks with duration between 2681 ms to 7005 ms (mean time +/- 1 SD, normalized time for zoom-in, blocks 3 and 4 only).

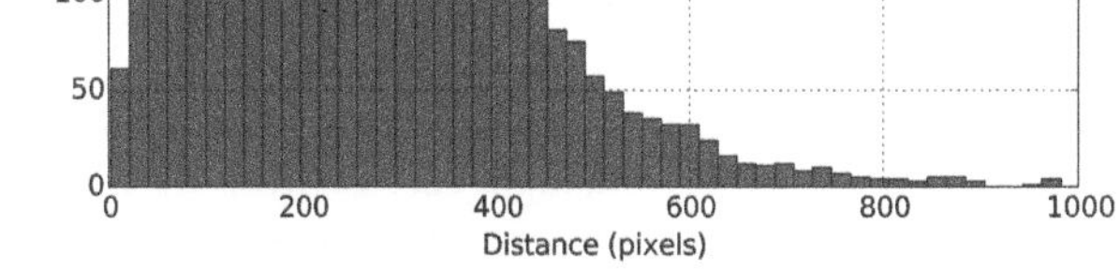

Figure 6: Distances from the final target to the center of the screen, measured in pixels.

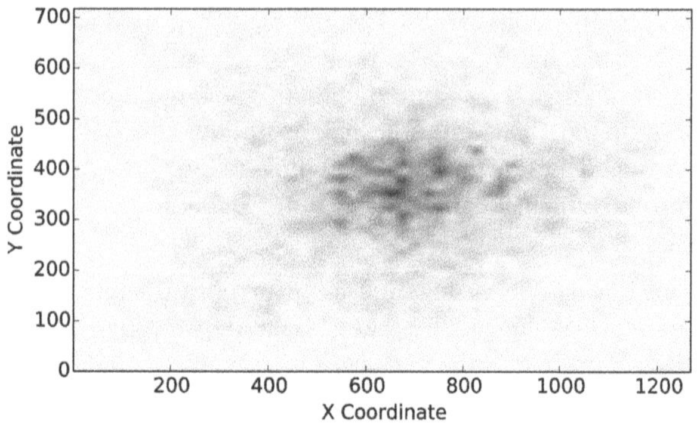

Figure 7: Heat map showing screen coordinates of completed experiment 2 docking and drawing tasks, demonstrating that users tend to pan the target to the center of the display.

We leverage these study insights regarding balistic velocity profiles when clutching, and the tendancy to pan content to the centre when zooming, to design an enhanced pinch-to-zoom technique.

PINCH-TO-ZOOM-PLUS (PZP)

PZP is designed to reduce the need to clutch and pan while zooming. To accomplish this, we incorporate two distinct augmentations to pinch-to-zoom. Zoom acceleration is a zoom transfer function that increases the relative zoom factor during rapid spreading or pinching movements. Pan-to-center is an automatic translation that moves the zoom target toward the center of the display.

Zoom Acceleration

With standard pinch-to-zoom, two contact points are positioned on the screen near the area of interest, and spread apart to zoom-in, or pinched together to zoom-out. This results in a linear zoom scale change proportional to the change in distance between the two contact points.

However, velocity data from Study 2 shows the gesture is not performed at constant speed: pinch-to-zoom behaviour exhibits an early ballistic pattern, where the user uses an initial high-speed movement to perform larger scale manipulations, followed by a corrective phase for final positioning (Figure 5). This speed profile is similar to other aimed mouse movement [3].

To reinforce this behaviour, we designed a pinch-to-zoom acceleration function to dynamically adjust a zoom scale multiplier based on the velocity of pinch and spread movement. With high velocity, the zoom scale multiplier increases the rate of zoom beyond the standard pinch-to-zoom rate. With slow velocity, the standard pinch-to-zoom zoom is used. Note that Jellinek and Card [11] found that mouse acceleration functions do not provide performance benefits, although recent work has been more encouraging [3,8]. More relevant to us, Casiez et al. [3] show that mouse acceleration functions can reduce clutching. An acceleration function will let people adjust the zoom scale more quickly, and we expect that this will decrease clutching.

Our acceleration function is not only motivated by the results of the formative studies, but uses study results to tune the function parameters. Figure 9 provides pseudo code for the acceleration function. Two thresholds, min and max, are calculated using the average pinch and spread velocity and standard deviation (SD) from study 2. Min is equal to mean velocity minus 1 SD, and max is set equal to mean velocity plus 1 SD. Study 2 yields a mean velocity of 1260 px/ms (SD 1190), creating a min threshold of 70 px/ms and a max threshold of 2450 px/ms. Using these thresholds and the current velocity of pinch or spread movement, we calculate a scale multiplier to increase the standard linear zoom scale change (or decrease it when zooming out):

- If current velocity is below min, scale multiplier = 1.0.
- If velocity is between min and max, the scale multiplier is in [1.0, 2.0], linearly interpolated by current velocity.
- If velocity is above max, scale multiplier = 2.0.

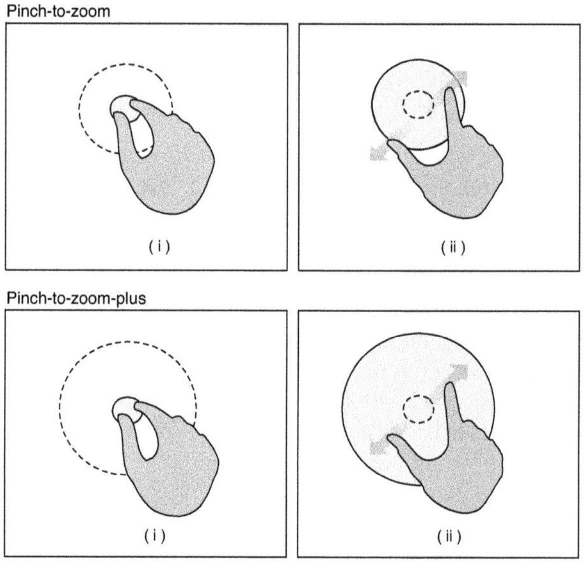

Figure 8: Zoom acceleration. Standard pinch-to-zoom (i) pinch and (ii) spread. PZP (iii) pinch and (iv) spread magnify the effects of these movements.

```
// lower and upper bounds based on mean from experiment 2
min = MEAN_VELOCITY - 1 SD
max = MEAN_VELOCITY + 1 SD

// return a multiplier from 1.0 to 2.0
if (current_velocity > min)
    return max( 1.0 + (current_velocity - min / max - min), 2.0 )
else
    return 1.0
```

Figure 9: Function to return the scale multiplier, which returns a value of 1.0 to 2.0 based on the current velocity

This change to the control-gain function results in acceleration at the start of the pinch-to-zoom gesture, which smoothly changes to standard linear movement during the low-speed tail of movement. This behaviour is similar to existing mouse pointer acceleration techniques [3].

Pan-to-Centre

Zooming requires that the user place their fingers directly over the area of interest, which can cause target occlusion [16]. We observed in our initial studies, particularly in study 2, that users typically panned this area of interest to the center of the screen before or during the zoom operation. Our goal is to partially automate this pan operation during a pinch-to-zoom gesture by moving the content of interest to the central area of the display (Figure 11).

Looking at the pan velocity in Figure 6, we note that pan follows a ballistic profile, but without the longer, low-speed tail found in zoom operations. This ballistic profile is more similar to un-aimed movements of the kind characterized by Flash and Hogan [5]. This indicates that participants panned toward the center of the display without a precise goal for the final content position. They simply wished to avoid the edge of the display. The scatterplot in Figure 7 supports this characterization of behaviour.

Pan-to-center is expressed as a translation applied directly to the pinch-to-zoom gesture. In study 2, we found that the mean distance from the target to the center of the screen at task end was 247.8 px, SD 193.7 (Figure 6). We use a similar threshold for pan-to-center, specifically mean plus 1 SD, or 441.6 px, which represents 65% of the distance to the center of the screen. In particular, if we examine Figure 7, we see that only a band around the edge of the display is avoided. This band that participants avoid represents approximately 35% of the distance from the edge of the display to the center. Our pan-to-center approximates movement into this center-region.

The pan-to-center algorithm is shown in (Figure 10). It performs as follows:

- A user places their fingers on the display, yielding a point of interest calculated as the mid-point between the user's fingers [14]. This point's coordinates are (center_x, center_y).
- The algorithm calculates a circular region in the center of the display, as described in the previous paragraph. This is the target region for the pan.
- Next, the algorithm calculates a distance remaining between the midpoint and target (lines 7 and 8).
- The algorithm gradually pans to the center of the display. The translation is attenuated such that the pan to center is gradual (less than $1/6^{th}$ of the remaining distance) and stops once the target point has moved into the center region of the display (lines 11 – 16 in Figure 10). The $1/6^{th}$ distance attenuation in our algorithm was an empirically determined value found to smooth the movement. During a pilot of this technique, we found that users preferred a gradual movement over a quick "snap" to the final target.

The goal of our design was to allow a 13x scale using a single clutch, but in general users still need to clutch. To support multiple clutches, the starting midpoint (center_x, center_y) is saved and re-used for each subsequent clutch operation. In this way, the initial target location, defined as the initial midpoint between finger contact points [14], is panned toward the center of the display (Figure 11). If no contact is made for a period of time (682 ms, the mean clutch time from study 1 plus 2 SD), the midpoint resets.

```
1  // mean target distance derived from experiment 2
2  // defines a target region around center of screen
3  // auto-pan to this region, then stop panning
4  center_radius = MEAN_TARGET_DISTANCE - 1 SD
5
6  // remaining distance from midpoint to display center
7  remaining_x = (center_x - current_x)
8  remaining_y = (center_y - curent_y)
9
10 // move distance of a single clutch
11 dx = min(remaining_x / 6, remaining_x * center_radius)
12 dy = min(remaining_y / 6, remaining_x * center_radius)
13
14 // adjust signs so that (dx, dy) properly translate
15 if current_x > center_x then dx = -dx
16 if current_y > center_y then dy = -dy
17
18 return dx, dy
```

Figure 10. Pan distance calculation.

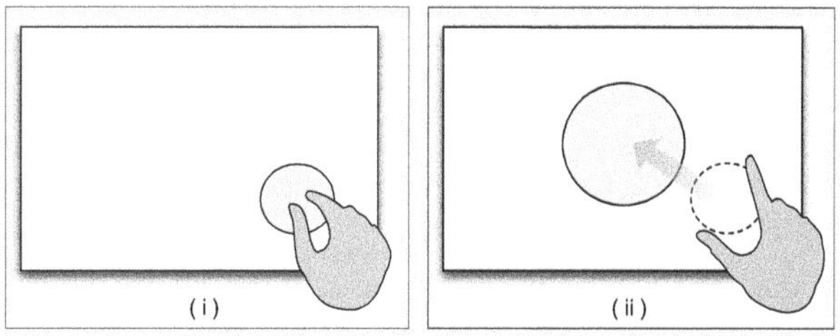

Figure 11: Pan-to-center. Zooming on a target near the edge (i) causes it to be scaled and translated to the center (ii).

EVALUATION

We performed a controlled experiment to evaluate the performance of PZP compared to standard pinch-to-zoom. Our hypothesis is that PZP will reduce task effort, measured as the number of clutches and pans required to complete the experimental task.

Task and Apparatus

We use the drawing task from study 2 (Figure 4) with the initial circular target placed at one of eight locations around the perimeter of the screen. The task is complete after the user draws a circle within the indicated region, and the zoom-level and pan are automatically reset for the next task. The same tablet from the formative studies was also used for this experiment. As in the formative studies, an overhead video camera recorded the experiment to capture additional user behaviours.

Participants

We recruited 24 participants, 16 male (15 right-handed, 1 left-handed) and 8 female (6 right-handed and 2 left-handed) with an average age of 26.0 (SD 4.7). Participants were asked about their smartphone or tablet usage, and self-reported a mean usage of 15.3 hours per week (SD 13.8). When recruiting participants, we asked for people who were "regularly used" a smartphone or tablet. Based on this filter, and the self-reported usage, we consider these users to be proficient with pinch-to-zoom. A $10 voucher was offered as remuneration.

Design

The experiment was a mixed between-subjects and within-subjects design. Within-subject factors were 2 technique conditions (Pinch-to-Zoom-Plus PZP and standard pinch-to-zoom PZ), 3 zoom levels (7x, 13x, 19x), one zoom direction (zoom-in), one tolerance (7 mm), and 8 positions along the perimeter of the screen (top-left, top-center, top-right, middle-left, middle-right, bottom-left, bottom-center, bottom-right). Hand condition (unimanual versus bimanual) was treated as a between-subject factor, with participants being randomly assigned to either the unimanual or bimanual condition. Hand condition ensures that PZP works for both unimanual and bimanual pinch-to-zoom gestures.

Technique conditions were fully crossed and presented in a randomly ordered block of trials, to balance potential learning effects. Four repetitions of each task were presented, to provide adequate time to learn the technique. Practice blocks of 12 tasks were presented at the start of each block. Not counting practice tasks, the experiment had 192 tasks per participant.

At the end of the experiment, we conducted a short interview to record participants' subjective impressions of the two techniques. The experiment took 45 minutes.

Pre-Processing

Excluding practice blocks, a total of 4632 tasks were performed across 24 participants. 140 tasks with an elapsed time of more than two standard deviations from the mean were excluded, which reduced the total tasks to 4492. Excessive time per trial was chosen for filtering data, as it presented the best indication of abnormal performance when completing a task (e.g. a participant stopping to ask a question mid-task, answering their mobile phone, etc.).

Results

Two-factor ANOVA and Bonferroni-Dunn correction were used for pairwise comparisons including the effects of handedness, acceleration and zoom level. Dependent measures were zoom-count, pan-count and elapsed time for each task (to determine the potential effects of the changes on task duration).

Zoom and Pan Actions

The mean number of zoom actions was 3.01 (i.e. 2.01 clutches). PZP reduced the number of zoom actions by 21% (a 43% reduction in clutches). Tasks completed without acceleration required a mean of 3.36 zoom actions (SD 2.26), but tasks completed with the accelerated technique only required a mean of 2.65 zoom actions (SD 1.45). This was a significant effect ($F_{1,23}$ = 11.63, $p < 0.01$), indicating a reduction in zoom clutch actions. There was no observed learning effect for zoom actions on block ($F_{1,23}$ = 0.89, ns).

PZP also reduced the amount of panning required by 14%: tasks completed without acceleration required a mean of 7.1 pans (SD 2.64), while tasks completed with acceleration required a mean 6.1 pans (SD 2.42). This was a significant effect ($F_{1,23}$ = 13.80, $p < 0.01$). There was no panning learning effect on block ($F_{1,23}$ = 0.28, ns).

Other variables (hand condition, zoom level, position) had no significant effect on zoom or pan actions.

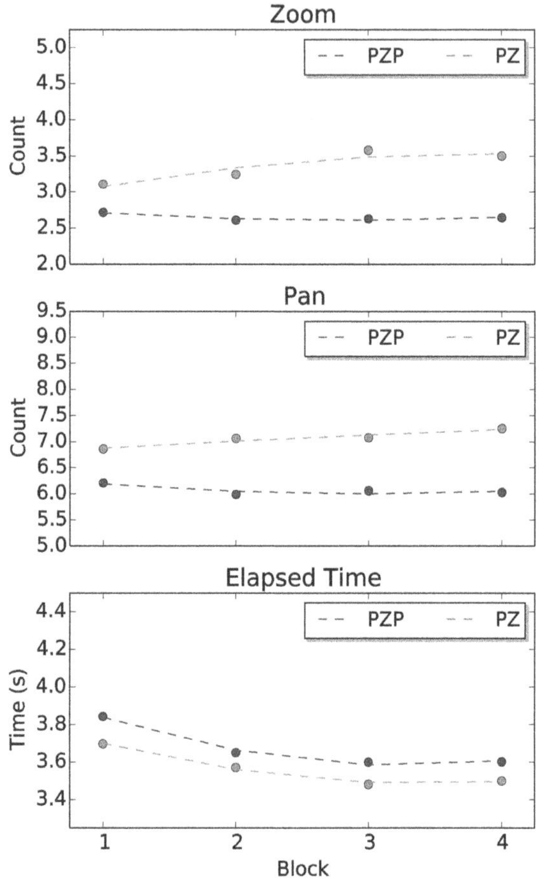

Figure 12: Measures by Block. PZP required far fewer zoom actions and pans than standard pinch-to-zoom, with comparable times required to complete the task.

Task Time

Mean task completion time was 3.62s (SD 1.25). Zoom-level, as expected, directly correlated to completion time: 7x scale tasks took 3.06s, 13x took 3.65s and 19x took 4.16s to complete, a significant effect ($F_{1,23}$ = 118.45, $p < 0.01$). Position of the target had no significant impact on task completion time ($F_{1,23}$ = 4.95, ns). Technique (PZP vs. PZ) had no statistically significant effect on time (F_{23} = 1.56, ns). Presentation order of PZP vs. PZ conditions was not significant ($F_{1,23}$ = 1.25, ns) suggesting no technique carry-over effect.

There was a significant learning effect for elapsed time, where time improved across blocks. Mean times for all tasks (PZ and PZP) were 3.77s, 3.61s, 3.54s and 3.55s for blocks 1 through 4 ($F_{1,23} = 8.76$, $p < 0.01$).

User Feedback

Participants seemed quick to grasp the PZP technique. Several participants indicated that it was a fairly seamless change from current pinch-to-zoom behaviour. P2 "couldn't see a difference" between PZP and PZ behaviour. P6 also indicated that she "couldn't really tell the difference between [PZP] and [PZ] behaviour".

Those that noticed the difference seemed to like PZP, but did not always find it easy to adjust to using it. P1 said "For single-handed operation, the [PZP] technique was much better… because the automatic movement was taken care of." P4 said "I think the [PZP] case is better when I need to move the target to the center, like Google Maps." However, P5 commented, "I feel like I'm fighting [PZP], but I'm getting used to it".

Discussion

PZP had a significant impact on the number of clutch and pan actions. The number of clutches was reduced by 21% and the number of pans reduced by 14%. This demonstrates that PZP achieved its primary goals. We did not see a significant time saving associated with the reduced clutch and pan behaviours. However, we did see a persistent learning effect with decreasing time, and when observing our participants, we noted that their ingrained behaviour with standard pinch-to-zoom may have reduced the benefit from PZP. Many of our participants used multi-touch smartphones and tablets extensively prior to this study, and had high familiarity with the expected behavior of standard pinch-to-zoom. The "fighting" comment from P5 above is a fair description of participants who struggled to adapt to PZP. For these reasons, we conducted a follow-up longitudinal study.

LONGITUDINAL STUDY

To assess whether additional practice is needed to acclimatize to the behaviour of the PZP technique, we conducted a small longitudinal study. Using the same hardware and task as the controlled experiment, participants performed zooming tasks for five consecutive days using PZP. We recruited 5 participants, 2 male (both right-handed) and 3 female (1 right and 2 left-handed) with an average age of 23.0 (SD 5.1). The tasks included 3 zoom levels (7x, 13x, 19x), one zoom direction (zoom-in), one tolerance (7 mm), and 8 positions around the perimeter of the display (top-left, top-center, top-right, middle-left, middle-right, bottom-left, bottom-center, bottom-right). All tasks were performed unimanually using the participants preferred hand. Practice blocks of 12 tasks were presented at the start of each block. Six task repetitions were presented each day, providing time to learn the technique. Task and zoom/pan actions were recorded.

Results

Excluding practice blocks, a total of 720 tasks were performed across 5 participants. Zoom action count across days had little variance: mean values were 2.48 on day 1 and 2.50 on day 5 (Figure 13 top). Pan action count across days also had little variance: mean values were 5.97 on day 1 and 5.89 on day 5 (Figure 13 middle). This suggests PZP's efficacy for consistent reduction of clutch and pan actions. In addition, task time decreased significantly ($F_{1,4} = 6.4$, $p < 0.01$). Over the course of 5 days, time improved by 27.1% (Figure 13 bottom). Mean task time fell from 3.51s on day 1 to 2.56s on day 5.

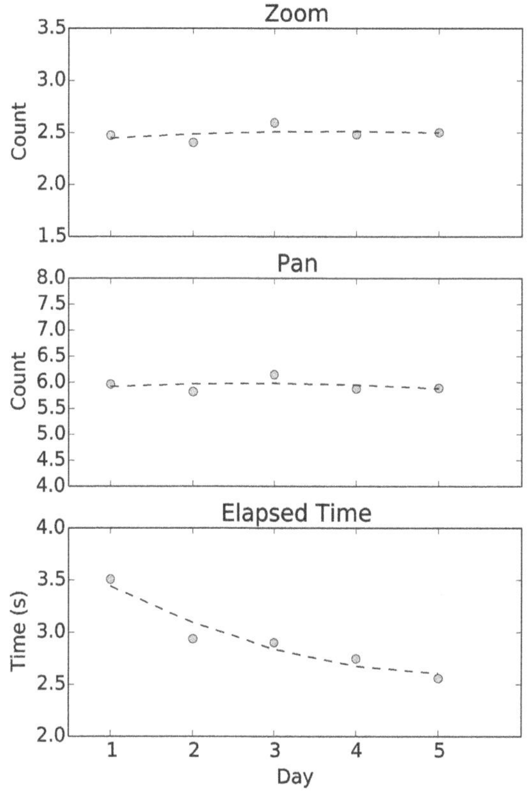

Figure 13: PZP mean action counts and task times over 5 days. Zoom and pan actions remain constant, but task time is significantly reduced over the 5 days.

DISCUSSION

We are optimistic about the results that we have achieved, but there are caveats: zoom acceleration was designed to reduce effort - specifically the number of pans and clutches - and not necessarily task time. As Casiez et al. and others point out [3,11], accelerated CD gain functions may not always reduce task time. With that in mind, our evaluation results are encouraging.

The longitudinal study was introduced to determine the "upper-bounds" of our technique, and see if task-time improvements may be possible for advanced pinch-to-zoom users. The results of the longitudinal study suggest that PZP performance may improve with additional training. Performance continued to improve over a 5-day period, so lengthy training may be necessary to see the effect. Overall, we were impressed that expert users were able to overcome their ingrained knowledge of standard pinch-to-zoom to harness the benefits of PZP enhancements.

In general, the PZP automatic pan assumes user always wish to keep a single point of interest visible by moving it near the center of the screen. However, this may not be a universally applicable strategy, since not all tasks have a well-defined single point of interest. Some map navigation tasks, such as route finding, require zooming two or more points. Users can initiate PZP at the centroid of multiple points of interest and still gain a benefit, but this may not be intuitive. A technique to selectively disable automatic panning may be a useful future refinement for PZP.

CONCLUSIONS AND FUTURE WORK

Since its inception pinch-to-zoom has become an effective, usable technique for enlarging content on multi-touch displays. However, as content increases in size and displays increase in resolution, the need to support ever-larger scale factors has resulted in inefficiencies.

In this paper, we analyze two of those inefficiencies: the performance of multiple sequential clutch operations while zooming to attain a desired scaling of content; and the performance of multiple panning translations to ensure content remains within the field of view on the display. First, we show that zoom and pan actions are quite common, even with relatively modest scale factors. Next, leveraging the kinematics and positional data associated with zoom and pan actions, we design PZP, a modified form of pinch-to-zoom that seeks to reduce these operations. Finally, through a controlled study and a longitudinal study, we show that PZP can significantly reduce the number of zoom and pan operations.

Future work will include a longitudinal study comparing the performance of PZP with standard PZ, to determine if the long-term performance gains translate into improved temporal performance. Regardless of a significant reduction in time, PZP has the potential to make zooming easier for everyone. PZP does not require specialized hardware, does not have complex algorithms, and remains backward compatible with standard pinch-to-zoom and all other multi-touch gestures. This enhanced pinch-to-zoom can be added to all multi-touch operating systems.

ACKNOWLEDGEMENTS

Research funding provided by the Natural Science and Engineering Council (NSERC), GRAND Networks of Centres of Excellence, and the Ontario Research Fund for Research Excellence.

REFERENCES

1. Albinsson, P.A. and Zhai, S. High precision touch screen interaction. *CHI '03* (2003), 105.
2. Buxton, B. Multi-touch systems that i have known and loved. *Microsoft Research*, (2007).
3. Casiez, G., Vogel, D., Balakrishnan, R., and Cockburn, A. The Impact of Control-Display Gain on User Performance in Pointing Tasks. *Human-Computer Interaction 23*, 3 (2008), 215.
4. Cockburn, A., Karlson, A., and Bederson, B.B. A review of overview+ detail, zooming, and focus+ context interfaces. *ACM Computing Surveys 41*, 1 (2008), 2.
5. Flash, T. and Hogan, N. The coordination of arm movements: an experimentally confirmed mathematical model. *The journal of Neuroscience*, (1985).
6. Forlines, C. and Shen, C. DTLens: multi-user tabletop spatial data exploration. *UIST'05*, (2005), 119.
7. Hinckley, K. and Song, H. Sensor synaesthesia. *CHI '11* (2011), 801.
8. Hinckley, K., Cutrell, E., Bathiche, S., and Muss, T. Quantitative analysis of scrolling techniques. *CHI '02* (2002).
9. Hinckley, K., Czerwinski, M., and Sinclair, M. Interaction and modeling techniques for desktop two-handed input. *UIST '98*, (1998), 49.
10. Hoggan, E., Nacenta, M., Kristensson, P.O., Williamson, J., Oulasvirta, A., Lehtiö, A. Multi-touch pinch gestures: performance and ergonomics. *ITS '13* (2013), 219.
11. Jellinek, H.D. and Card, S.K. Powermice and user performance. *CHI '90* (1990).
12. Käser, D.P., Agrawala, M., and Pauly, M. FingerGlass: Efficient multiscale interaction on multitouch screens. *CHI '11* (2011), 1601.
13. Lank, E. and Phan, S. *Focus+Context sketching on a pocket PC. CHI EA '04* (2004).
14. Malacria, S., Lecolinet, E., and Guiard, Y. Clutch-free panning and integrated pan-zoom control on touch-sensitive surfaces: the cyclostar approach. *CHI '10* (2010).
15. Negulescu, M., Ruiz, J., and Lank, E. ZoomPointing revisited: supporting mixed-resolution gesturing on interactive surfaces. *ITS '11* (2011), 150.
16. Sears, A. and Shneiderman, B. High precision touchscreens: design strategies and comparisons with a mouse. *International Journal of Man-Machine Studies 34*, 4 (1991), 593.
17. Tran, J.J., Trewin, S., Swart, C., John, B.E., and Thomas, J.C. Exploring pinch and spread gestures on mobile devices. *MobileHCI '13* (2013), 151.
18. Wellner, P. The DigitalDesk calculator: tangible manipulation on a desktop display. *UIST '91*, (1991), 27.
19. Wellner, P. Digital Desk. (1991).

Sensing Techniques for Tablet+Stylus Interaction

Ken Hinckley[1], Michel Pahud[1], Hrvoje Benko[1], Pourang Irani[1,2], Francois Guimbretiere[1,3], Marcel Gavriliu[1], Xiang 'Anthony' Chen[1], Fabrice Matulic[1], Bill Buxton[1], & Andy Wilson[1]

[1]Microsoft Research, Redmond, WA {kenh, benko, mpahud, bibuxton, awilson}@microsoft.com

[2]University of Manitoba, Dept. of Comp. Sci., Winnipeg, MB, Canada, irani@cs.umanitoba.ca

[3]Cornell University, Information Science Department, Ithaca, NY francois@cs.cornell.edu

ABSTRACT
We explore *grip* and *motion* sensing to afford new techniques that leverage how users naturally manipulate tablet and stylus devices during pen + touch interaction. We can detect whether the user holds the pen in a writing grip or tucked between his fingers. We can distinguish bare-handed inputs, such as drag and pinch gestures produced by the nonpreferred hand, from touch gestures produced by the hand holding the pen, which necessarily impart a detectable motion signal to the stylus. We can sense which hand grips the tablet, and determine the screen's relative orientation to the pen. By selectively combining these signals and using them to complement one another, we can tailor interaction to the context, such as by ignoring unintentional touch inputs while writing, or supporting contextually-appropriate tools such as a magnifier for detailed stroke work that appears when the user pinches with the pen tucked between his fingers. These and other techniques can be used to impart new, previously unanticipated subtleties to pen + touch interaction on tablets.

Author Keywords
Sensing; pen+touch; motion; grip; tablet; bimanual input

ACM Classification Keywords
H.5.2 [Information Interfaces and Presentation]: Input

INTRODUCTION
In the modern context of multi-touch tablets, pen input has received renewed interest, particularly when used as a distinct modality in tandem with touch [21,34,55]. However, many problems and ambiguities arise because the system can't easily determine whether the user intends to interact with the pen, with touch, or with the two in combination. As one example, systems employ various heuristics to ignore *unintentional* touch inputs associated with resting the palm on the screen while writing, but typically these come at the expense of limiting simultaneous *intentional* touches produced by the nonpreferred hand [1,2,42].

UIST '14, October 05 - 08 2014, Honolulu, HI, USA

ACM 978-1-4503-3069-5/14/10…$15.00
http://dx.doi.org/10.1145/2642918.2647379

As witnessed by the proliferation in mobile sensing [7,12,19,23,24,39], there is great potential to resolve such ambiguities using sensors, rather than foisting complexity on the user to establish the missing context [6]. As sensors and computation migrate into tiny mobile devices, pens no longer need to be conceived primarily as passive intermediaries without a life once they move away from the display.

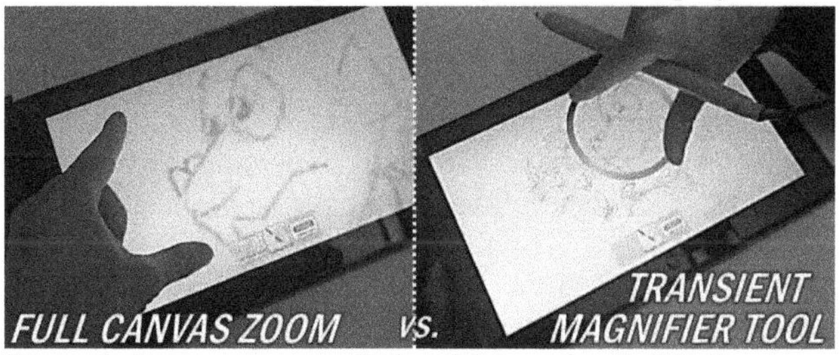

Figure 1. Our sensors can distinguish bare-handed (*left*) vs. pen-in-hand (*right*) inputs to evoke contextually-appropriate tools.

To extend this perspective, we show novel ways of evoking contextually-appropriate tools. For example, if the user tucks the pen while performing a pinch gesture (*Figure 1, right*), this brings up a magnifying tool particularly well suited to detail work with the pen. This is sensed by detecting the *Tuck* grip in combination with a hard-contact motion signal on the pen *at the same time* the hand holding it contacts the touchscreen. Performing a bare-handed pinch gesture with the other hand, however, does not produce this pattern and can therefore invoke a distinct behavior (*Figure 1, left*).

We also report observations of a rich vocabulary of naturally occurring behaviors, including *tuck* vs. *palm* grips for stowing the pen, as well as a new class of finger *extension grips* (from the hand holding the pen) for touchscreen manipulation. That such behaviors have gone largely unnoticed, much less actively sensed by pens and tablets, reflects the opportunities for contextual adaptation and fresh nuances of expression afforded by adding a few new sensors.

Overall, our contributions include the following:

- Observations of natural grips and usage patterns that arise when using pen and touch together on a tablet.
- Novel hardware / software solutions that sense grip and motion to capture the full context of stylus and tablet use.
- Using sensors to *mitigate unintentional touch* (from the palm, or from the thumb when picking up the tablet), but also to *promote intentional touch* by the nonpreferred hand, or via extension grips to interleave pen and touch.
- Novel contextually-appropriate tools that combine grip, motion, and touchscreen contact, including distinct tools

for bare-handed input, pinch input while tucking the pen, and drafting tools that the user can summon with the nonpreferred hand when the pen is poised for writing.
- Preliminary observations and user reactions arising from initial user experience with these tools and techniques.

Collectively, these observations and novel techniques illustrate how contextual sensors on modern stylus and tablet devices have the potential to ameliorate ambiguities inherent in simultaneous pen+touch interaction, while also affording a broad design space of novel interactions.

RELATED WORK

Our research threads together themes from mobile sensing, sensor-augmented pens, grip sensing, and pen + touch input.

Mobile Sensing on Handhelds

Tilt, pressure, and proximity sensing on mobiles enables contextual adaptations such as detecting handedness [14], portrait/landscape detection [19], or walking vs. stationary usage [40]. Grip sensing allows a mobile to detect how the user holds it [53], or to use grasp to automatically engage functions [49] such as placing a call, taking a picture, or watching a video [24]. We adopt this perspective of sensing natural user behavior, but bring it to pen and tablet interaction, where the behaviors to sense—and the new possibilities for pen+touch—remain largely unexplored.

Multi-touch input and inertial sensors (IMU's with 3-axis gyroscopes, accelerometers, and magnetometers) afford new possibilities for mobiles to discern user intent based on grasp and motion dynamics [3]. Devices can distinguish if the user touches the screen with the thumb vs. the index finger [12], or use grip sensing to avoid accidental screen auto-rotation [7]. Whacking [23] or jerking motions [39] offer out-of-band signals distinct from incidental handling of a device. We illustrate new techniques that leverage these types of motion sensing, grip sensing, and multi-touch inputs when they are distributed across separate pen and tablet devices.

Grips and Sensing for Tablets

Lightweight tablets afford many new grips, movements, and sensing techniques. BiTouch and BiPad [52] demonstrates bimanual interactions that take natural tablet grips into account. Sensing tablet grips affords bringing up a touchscreen keyboard in a contextually-appropriate location [8]. GroupTogether [32] senses clusters of co-located users to support lightweight exchange of information by subtly orienting a tablet towards another user with micro-mobility gestures [29]. Our system is the first to implement full grip sensing and motion sensing—on both tablet and stylus at the same time—for pen + touch interaction.

Palm Detection and Unintentional Touch Handling

Palm contact can cause false activations during pen + touch interaction [1,2,42]. For example, many iPad note-taking applications include palm-blocking (e.g. [11,35,36]), but details of these heuristics are unpublished and vary widely; they often appear to rely on application-specific assumptions about how and where the user will write. Other palm-rejection techniques require the user to bring the pen tip on or near the screen before setting the palm down, which requires users to modify their natural movements (e.g. [55], or Microsoft Windows tablets, which turn off touch when the pen comes in range). Our approach uses sensors to detect when a touchscreen contact is associated with the hand holding the pen, thus showing that the problem can be framed as one of sensing appropriate contextual information.

Sensor-Augmented and Multi-DOF Stylus Input

Auxiliary tilt, roll, and other stylus degrees-of-freedom can be combined [15] to call up menus [50] or trigger mode switches [4] without necessarily disrupting natural use [54]. Conte [51] explores a tilt-sensitive "digital Conte crayon" for pen + touch interaction on a tabletop. In particular, Conte explores interactions where the user orients or holds or the crayon on the display, while other fingers from the same hand reach out and touch the screen to pick colors or choose modes. We consider similar capabilities where the user can extend one or more fingers while tucking the stylus. We also sense distinct contexts with separate functions, even when the user holds the pen away from the screen.

Pens can be augmented with motion [17,48], grip [46,47], and near-surface range sensing [28]. MTPen [46] uses grip sensing to detect a tripod writing grip, or to invoke different brushes. Sun et al. [47] use an integrated IMU on the pen to assist grip recognition, an approach which we adopt here, and also sense the orientation of the tablet (e.g. horizontal vs. drafting table). Context sensing examples have also been proposed, such as sensing if the user forgets the pen [17]. Lee et al. [26] employ an orientation-sensing stylus to reduce occlusion problems. Our work goes beyond these efforts; compared to the most closely related work (i.e. MTPen [46], FlexAura [28], and [17,21]), the main things that distinguish our contribution are our behavioral observations, the holistic pen and tablet sensing platform, and application of new techniques to well-considered UI challenges.

Synchronous Gestures and Cross-Channel Inputs

The literature shows examples of distributed sensing techniques such as bumping two tablets together [16] or tapping a mobile phone against a multi-touch tabletop [41]. Synchronous events or correlations across input channels can also enable new types of gestures. The 1Line keyboard [9] uses a bezel thump as a spacebar by noting that normal keystrokes produce a bump at the same time as the touch-down event, whereas a bezel thump arrives without a corresponding touch event. Smart-Its Friends [22] pairs two devices when the user shakes them together. *Are You With Me?* [27] uses motion signal similarities to sense if two mobile devices are being carried by the same person, while *Your Phone or Mine?* [38] correlates mobile phone motions with depth image patches. Sensor Synaesthesia [20] and GripSense [12] combine touchscreen and motion signals. Our research contributes cross-device and cross-channel inputs for a distributed tablet–stylus sensing system to detect unique contexts and behaviors that arise in pen+touch input.

OBSERVATIONS OF PEN & TABLET BEHAVIORS

Several papers identify distinct grips for tasks such as writing and brushing [46,47], or holding tablets [8,52]. But the literature still lacks an inventory of pen grips and postures while interacting on a tablet with pen + touch. We therefore sought to enumerate common grips that arise in digital pen-and-tablet tasks, and particularly touchscreen interactions articulated while the pen is in hand. Our task thus spans note-taking with a pen, as well as a secondary task (web browsing) that primarily employs touch. We chose web browsing for this secondary task because writing side-by-side with reading the web offers a compelling scenario from the literature for digital ink (e.g. [18,44]).

Nine people (4 female, 1 left-handed) participated in the observational study. Users interacted with a 10" Windows 8 tablet, with multi-touch and an electromagnetic pen digitizer, using OneNote to jot notes and Internet Explorer to browse the web. We observed a wide variety of behaviors (B1-B12) that helped inform our designs, as well as many previously unrecognized pen grips, as illustrated in Figure 2 (some are drawn from the literature). At present, we focus on behaviors of right-handers; left-handers are known to exhibit a variety of additional grips and accommodations (e.g. [13]).

B1. Stowing the pen during touch. Users often stowed the pen [21,46] when performing touch gestures. Users only put the pen down when they anticipated they wouldn't need it again for a prolonged time, or if they encountered a task that they felt was too awkward to perform with the pen in-hand, such as typing a lot of text using the on-screen keyboard.

B2. Tuck vs. Palm for stowing the pen. Unlike previous studies, we observed two distinct grips that users employ to stow the pen. All users exhibited the *Tuck* grip (pen laced between fingers), but many also employed a *Palm* grip (with fingers wrapped lightly around the barrel) to stow the pen during pauses or to afford touch interactions.

B3. Preferred pen stowing grip depends on task context. For users that employed both *Tuck* and *Palm* grips, *Tuck* afforded quick, transient touch interactions, while *Palm* was primarily used if the user anticipated a longer sequence of touch interactions. Other users always used *Tuck* to stow the pen.

B4. Grip vs. Pose. For each *grip* we observed a range of *poses*, often by wrist supination (turning the palm upward). Grasping motions with a pen therefore encompass the pattern of hand contact on the barrel, as well as the 3D orientation of the pen. We observed full palmar supination for *Tuck* and *Palm*, but only half-supination for the *Writing* grip.

B5. Extension Grips. We observed many grips where users extended one or more fingers while holding the pen to touch the screen, from both the *Tuck* and the *Palm* grips. However, not all extensions were observed from each grip; in particular, we did not observe any extension grips from the *Writing* grip, and the common *Tuck–Middle Extension Grip* did not occur with the *Palm* grip. (The 4-5 finger grips are logical, but our touch gestures required two fingers at most.)

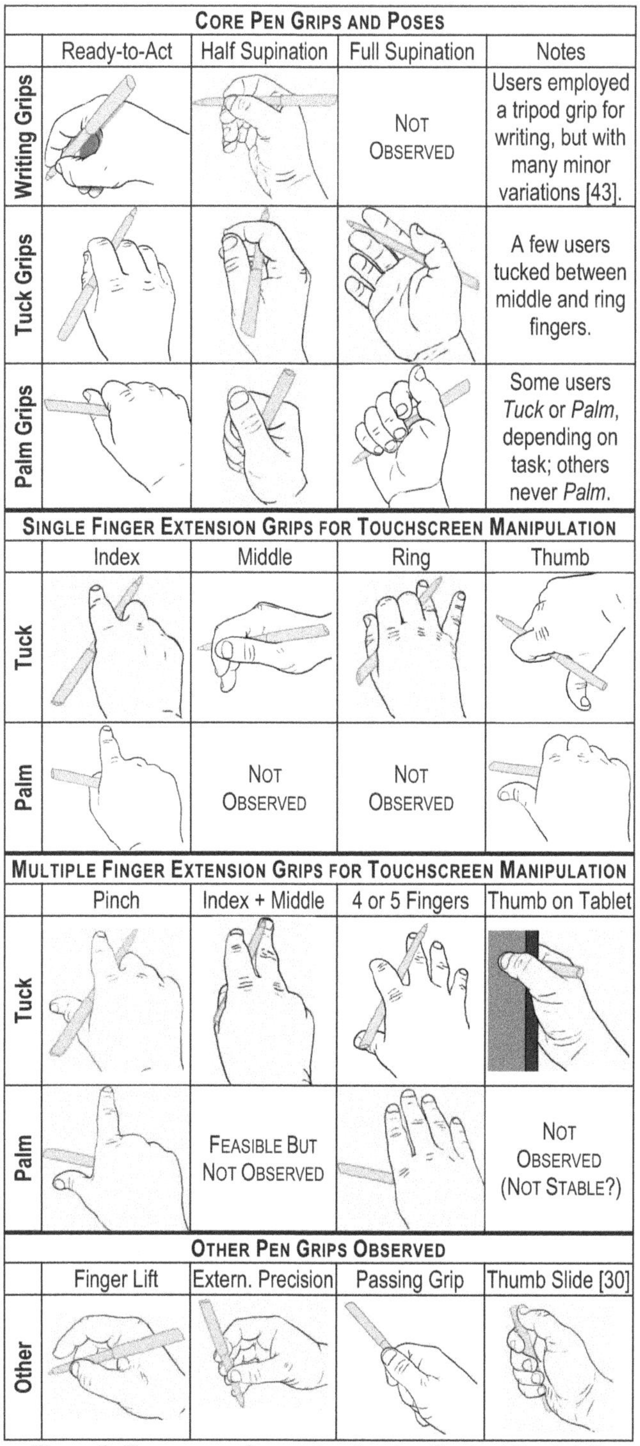

Figure 2. Taxonomy of pen + touch grips. See text for details.

B6. Variation in pen grips. Users exhibited many variations in the tripod grip for writing (see also [43]), leading to corresponding variations in users' resulting *Tuck* and *Palm* grips, such as one user's tendency to favor her ring finger for single-touch (Figure 2, *Tuck–Ring Finger Extension Grip*).

B7. Re-gripping. An implicit theme of observations B1-B6 is that users shift between a variety of grips. Furthermore, users often exhibited subtle adjustments to their grasp while writing and handling the pen. These naturally occurring *re-gripping behaviors* appeared to be motivated by comfort, fatigue, and functional considerations (such as reaching out a finger during an extension grip, as in B5).

B8. Consistency in grips. Each user consistently applied the same core pen grips in the same situations. Users also tended to maintain whatever grip required the least effort, until a perceived interaction barrier such as fatigue or inefficiency gave them an incentive to shift grips. Users switched tablet grips more often when sitting than standing, perhaps because there are few effective ways to hold a tablet while standing.

B9. Touchscreen avoidance behaviors. Users often adopted pen grips and hand postures, such as floating the palm above the screen while writing, or splaying out their fingers in a crab-like posture, to avoid incidental contact with the screen. Another form of touchscreen avoidance was perching the thumb along the outside rim of the tablet bezel, rather than letting it stray too close to the touchscreen when picking up the tablet with one hand. These unnatural and potentially fatiguing accomodations reflect the system's inability to distinguish the context of intentional vs. unintentional touch.

B10. Finger Lift for activating pen controls. Users activated the pen barrel button from the *Writing* grip, and then only with the index finger. Users held the pen still when tapping the button. The thumb is also potentially available for controls from the *Thumb Slide* grip, as noted by [30].

B11. External Precision Grip. Users employed this grip, with the pen held toward the fingertips [30] and perpendicular to the writing surface, for precise pointing at small targets, such as the web links in our web browsing task.

B12. Passing Grip. We also observed passing prehension [33] when participants passed the pen and tablet back to the experimenter. Users tended to hold the device securely, in more of a power grip, and extended it from their body while keeping it level, so that their intent was clear and so that the other person could grab it from the far side.

Having observed these natural behaviors, we now turn our attention to stylus + tablet hardware that can sense them. Note that it is not our intention to recognize all of these grips, or to leverage all of these behaviors, but rather to inform our approach and help shape many of our design decisions.

REALIZING GRIP+MOTION SENSING FOR PEN/TABLET

To support the range of context sensing techniques that we envisioned, we designed custom hardware to augment the stylus and tablet with inertial sensors and capacitive grip sensing, as well custom software to handle simultaneous pen + touch events from the touchscreen.

Pen Hardware Design

A flexible capacitive grid consisting of 7×30 sensing elements covers the entire barrel of the pen, which we wrap in heat-shrink tubing to protect the sensor and to provide a smooth and easy-to-grip cylindrical surface for sensing. The interior of the pen consists of a 3D-printed case that holds a miniature Wacom electromagnetic pen, a AAAA battery, and our custom circuitry. For inertial sensing we use the STMicroelectronics L3G4200D MEMS gyroscope as well as a LSM303DLHC accelerometer / magnetometer module. The capacitive grip sensor consists of a copper grid custom-printed on a flexible Kapton substrate, connected to a Cypress CY8CTMA463-60BUI touch controller. We stream data to a host using the 2.4GHz Nordic Semiconductor nRF24L01 transceiver operating at 2Mbps. An Atmel XMEGA 32A4U microcontroller runs our firmware.

We stream all inertial sensors off the pen at 130Hz, and the 7×30 capacitance map (Figure 3) at 30Hz. We designed our pen to be wireless; however, it proved difficult to change the battery without damaging the grip sensor, so we had to add a cable for power. The pen is 19cm long × 14mm diameter.

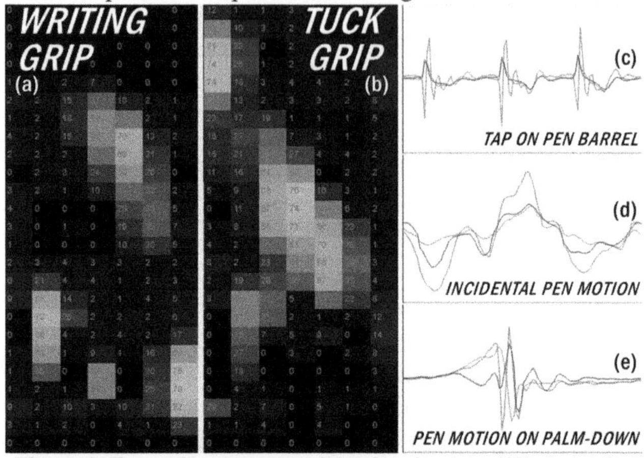

Figure 3. Example pen sensor data showing two different grips (a,b) and three example gyro signals (c,d,e). See text for details.

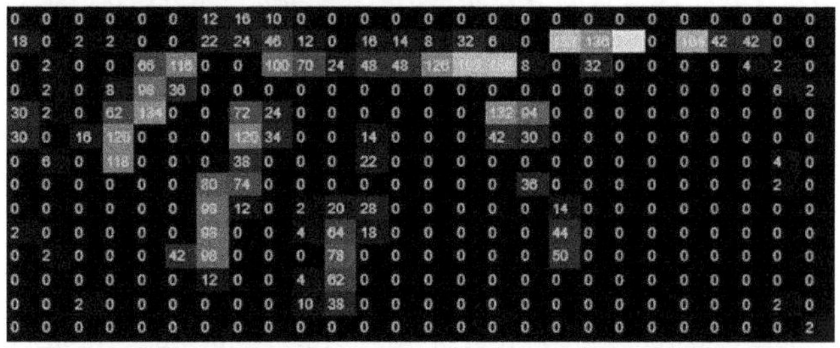

Figure 4. Example tablet case grip sensor data showing four fingers reaching in from the top to grasp the tablet.

Tablet Hardware Design

The tablet case (Figure 4) covers the entire back surface and sides of the tablet. The rigid case is constructed from printed circuit boards consisting of 44×26 capacitive sensing elements. There is a small insensitive area (in the middle of the case on the back side) where the integrated circuits are mounted. The case includes the same sensor components as the pen, except there are four touch controllers for different parts of the capacitive grid. We stream the tablet sensor data via USB, with the tablet's inertial sensors sampled at 100Hz and the tablet's 44×26 capacitance map sampled at 25Hz.

Simultaneous Pen and Touch from the Touchscreen

Because by default Windows deactivates touch when the pen comes in range (as a palm-rejection technique), we employ the Windows *Raw Input* API to capture multi-touch and pen events directly from the HID controller. Using this approach the *Samsung Series 7 Slate* we use for our prototype can report up to 8 touch contacts simultaneously with pen input.

Software Design

We time-stamp the pen / tablet sensor data on an external PC, compute grips, and then dispatch events to the tablet for presentation in the UI. Thus our implementaton consists of a distributed system with four cooperating components: the stylus, the tablet case, the tablet itself, and the external PC.

Inertial Sensor Fusion

We combine the accelerometer, gyro, and magnetometer using a direct cosine matrix algorithm ([31,37]). This produces stable yaw, pitch, and roll values in an east-north-up Earth coordinate frame, yielding the stylus orientation in a consistent reference frame relative to the tablet.

Stylus Grip Classification

At present we recognize four distinct grips: *Writing*, *Tuck*, *Palm*, and *No Grip* (for when the stylus is not held). Per observed behavior B4 (*Grip vs. Pose*), the grip recognition considers the pattern of hand contact (capacitive grip sensing) as well as the pose (orientation) of the stylus. We processed the incoming data to extract salient features and then trained a multi-class classifier to extract the stylus grips. We performed a multi-class classification of the stylus grip patterns by using a set of one-vs-all learners, where each learner was a Support Vector Machine (SVM) classifier. The result is a probability distribution over all four grips.

We selected features for grip classification that carefully considered the cylindrical symmetry of the stylus form-factor. Sensed grips should be agnostic to the roll angle of the pen; likewise, the size of the user's hand, or a grip higher or lower on the pen barrel, should not affect classification. Thus we compute a *normalized image* invariant with respect to grip height and roll angle. From the raw 7×30 capacitance map, we fit the non-zero capacitance values into a 7×10 normalized image. We shift the capacitance map in the y-dimension so that the first row of lit pixels corresponds to the bottom of the normalized image, and then scale the non-zero capacitance pixels to fit in the 10 rows of the normalized image. The features employed for grip classification therefore include the stylus yaw and pitch angles, the normalized grip image, as well as the normalized grip histogram in the x and y dimensions. We also include features for the number of lit (non-zero) pixels, and the pixel sum of all 7×30 capacitance values from the raw capacitance map.

Grip Training Dataset Collection

We recruited nine right-handed participants (4 female), all with prior exposure to pen/tablet use, to generate the training dataset. Per observation B7, grip classification must account for transitions between grips, grasp modification during extension grips (B5), and naturally occurring re-gripping behaviors. With this in mind, we designed our procedure to elicit such transitions. Our training data therefore incorporates common transitions between grips, as well as any re-gripping behaviors that users exhibited.

To collect all of the main grips for each user, we led users through a script illustrating specific grips and actions to perform in each grip. These included stowing the pen using touch (per observation B1) from both the Tuck and Palm grips (B2). We also included different sequences of tasks to capture the various common transitions between grips (B3). We led users through the full range of supination for each grip (B4) and included transitions between *Writing* and the single-finger and two-finger extension grips (B5), with articulation of direct-manipulation gestures such as tapping, dragging, and pinching. However, for writing tasks we did not specify any particlar tripod grip to use, but rather let users hold the pen naturally so that our dataset would capture cross-user variations in *Writing* grips (per B6). The data collection lasted approximately 15 minutes per user, with a total of 1200 samples for each user, per grip, yielding a total training dataset of 1200 × 3 grips × 9 users = 32400 samples.

Stylus Grip Recognition Accuracy

A10-fold cross-validation using the collected grip training dataset yielded an overall accuracy of 88% for the user-independent model. We also conducted a separate follow-up study with nine additional right-handed users, none of whom contributed to the training dataset. The task required users to write as well as perform specified touch gestures (tap, drag, and pinch) while holding the pen in the *Tuck* and *Palm* grips (i.e. it did not employ the same protocol used to collect the training dataset, to provide greater ecological validity). We assessed 8100 total samples (9 users × 3 grips × 300 samples at 250ms intervals) from the new users. This yielded user-independent grip recognition accuracy of 93% for the *Writing* grip, 93% for *Tuck*, and 77% for *Palm*. The relatively low recognition rate for the *Palm* grip appeared to stem from several users' tendency to hold the pen very lightly in this grip, resulting in a somewhat inconsistent pattern of contact sensed by the capacitive grip array. However, the system was still able to distinguish *Writing* vs. non-writing grips (i.e. Tuck *or* Palm) with 97% accuracy. Since the interaction techniques described below do not depend on any distinction between the *Tuck* vs. *Palm* grips, we proceeded with this user-independent grip model, which works well enough even without collecting training data for newly-encountered users.

GRIP + MOTION INTERACTION TECHNIQUES

Building on the behaviors we observed and the grip-recognition capability detailed above, our goal was to explore the design space of sensing techniques for tablet + stylus interaction. We explicitly sought to investigate techniques in the foreground of attention, such as new gestures made possible by additional degrees-of-freedom, as well as background sensing techniques that use context to automatically sense natural user behavior [6].

We pursued these goals in the context of a simple sketching application because we felt this would best showcase our ideas. Although sketching is a different scenario than the *writing side-by-side with reading the web* task used to generate observations B1-B12, we felt that the converse—

conducting behavioral observations on an already-existing sketching application—would not have yielded the same richness of observations. The behavioral study thus served as a point of departure, with insights that we now apply to our sketching application. It includes annotation, panning, and zooming capabilities representing a broad sample of popular pen-based applications (such as Microsoft OneNote, or Paper by FiftyThree [11]), and thereby provides various examples that illustrate the utility of our approach.

Pen Orientation Sensed Relative to the Tablet

Our inertial sensor fusion allows us to maintain a common reference frame relative to the tablet. We employ this tablet-relative orientation at the grip-recognition phase, as well as in the interpretation of the pen motion (such as for the airbrush tool, described later). It is important to emphasize here that we only can sense the *orientation* of the stylus relative to the tablet. Inertial sensing cannot reliabily determine the (x,y) translation or z-altitude of the pen without resort to some other absolute external reference.

PALM 'REJECTION' AS A PROBLEM OF CONTEXT

Sensing unintentional palm contact is a difficult problem because, at the onset of touch, there is often insufficient information to distinguish what type of touch is occuring. A palm *might* be recognizalbe as a touch with a large contact area, but such contacts always start small and may take a while to pass a certain size threshold. Also, some unintentional touches (such as contact produced by the knuckles) may never turn into a "large" contact. This strategy therefore necessitates delays (introduces lag) in processing touch events, and still may fail to detect many contacts [1,2].

Recently, Schwarz et al. demonstrated probabilistic palm rejection using the touch events after the palm makes contact with the screen [42]. Our approach is complementary because its cues (that the pen is held in a *Writing* grip or not) arrive before the hand touches down, or coincident with hand contact (in the form of the 'bump' motion signal).

To increase stability and avoid fatigue, users naturally rest their hand on the writing surface, but (per behavior B9), current tablet users are forced to adopt touchscreen avoidance behaviors. Simply sensing that the user is holding the pen is not sufficient to address this problem because people stow the pen while using touch (B1) and employ various extension grips to touch the screen (B5). Stylus orientation is also insufficient because each grip can be associated with a range of wrist supinations (B4) and because users hold the pen in a variety of ways (B6).

However, since unintentional touch primarily occurs incident to writing, sensing the *Writing* grip itself is a powerful cue, particularly because the user typically adopts a writing grip prior to resting his hand on the display. Hence, a highly conservative palm-rejection algorithm could simply reject any touch that occurs when the pen is held in the *Writing* grip. This, however, would preclude *intentional* touches made by the nonpreferred hand whenever the pen is held in the writing grip, which eliminantes many desirable scenarios (e.g. panning and zooming with the nonpreferred hand), as well as simultaneous pen + touch gestures [21].

With our sensors, we noticed that when the user plants his hand on the screen, it simultaneously induces a corresponding signal on the pen's motion sensors. (The tablet's motion sensors also pick up some of this motion, but at present we do not rely on this signal because it is damped somewhat by the greater mass of the tablet.)

The stylus motion exhibits a characteristic hard-contact profile similar to that seen with bump, whack, and thump gestures in other contexts ([9,16,23,41]). We look for a peak (using the second order finite difference [9] on the three combined axes of the accelerometer or gyro) that exceeds a minimum threshold within a 10-sample window. We also know exactly when to look for this signal because the palm produces a bump at the same time that the touchscreen detects the new contact. We can identify this peak within a maximum of 56ms after the touch-down event in the worst case (including all network delays).

This allows us to employ a resonable movement threshold for the bump signal, while also trivially rejecting other motion signals that do not occur coincident to a new touchscreen contact. However, our approach can and will miss subtle contacts, such as accidentally brushing the screen with a pinky, or if the user tries to fool the sensors by setting his hand down gently, for example. Nonetheless, we find our detection scheme works well for most normal pen interactions during writing.

For as long as the detected palm contact persists, we flag any new touches as a "palm" if they land within a 300 pixel radius. We found it helpful to provide feedback of the initial palm detection by playing a brief "radar circle" animation, centered on the palm-down location, that fades as it expands. This provides non-distracting feedback that confirms to the user that the palm contact was successfully detected. Without this feedback, the user may be left with a nagging uncertainty as to whether or not their palm has triggered an undesired action (such as calling up a menu, or leaving behind an ink trace) that is currently occluded by the hand.

Note that the *Paper* app by FiftyThree provides a *Pencil* hardware accessory [11] that activates a palm-blocking feature. However, the user must explicitly provide the context that the *Pencil* is in use by holding it on the screen to pair it. *Paper's* palm blocking further appears to only operate when the *Pencil* tip is actually in contact with the screen, which prevents it from sensing natural palm contact as the hand approaches. Hence, our context-sensing approach works very differently and can detect many types of palm contact that *Paper* and other related approaches [42] cannot.

Permitting Intentional Touch

Of course, the whole point of this approach is to permit simultaneous intentional touches, even when the palm is resting on the screen. With the above criteria, any new touch that occurs away from the palm (which is not accompanied by a bump on the pen) represents a true intentional touch. Our current implementation uses the first two additional touches that are not flagged as a palm contact to support the standard pinch-to-zoom gesture. Palm contact is ignored and does not interfere with pan/zoom, even if the palm moves.

However, because we still track the palm—rather than outright 'rejecting' it per se—our approach also can support techniques that use the palm location as an input, such as to help correctly orient menus [5] or to anchor objects [45].

DIFFERENTIATING PEN-IN-HAND VS. BARE HAND INPUT

The Magnifier Tool vs. Full Canvas Zoom

The functionality of our Magnifier Tool (Figure 1) was inspired by FiftyThree's *Paper* application [10]. *Paper* invokes a focus-plus-context magnifier (known as the "loupe") which is especially well suited to sketching tasks where the user wants to make a few detailed strokes without losing the overall context of the workspace. Unlike *Paper*, we support both the Magnifier *and* Full-Canvas Zooming by sensing how the user is interacting with the pen and tablet.

When the user stows the pen (via *Tuck* or *Palm*, per B2), we recognize this grip. If the user then brings two fingers into contact with the display, we check the stylus for a corresponding "bump" that occurs at the same time as the touch. When we see this combined stylus bump + two-finger touch, it brings up the Magnifier Tool. Users found the appearance of the tool in this context natural and appealing.

If we see a two-finger touch without any corresponding bump on the stylus, we instead infer that the user made the touch with their other (nonpreferred) hand, which is not holding the pen. This then triggers the standard two-finger pan and zoom interaction to allow full canvas zoom (rather than the focus-plus-context Magnifier Tool).

The Magnifier zooms only the region of the canvas under the circular tool. The magnifier interactively resizes itself according to the spread between the user's two fingers. The user may also touch down a finger on the border of the Magnifier to drag it to a new location. A single finger tap, or pen stroke, anywhere outside of the Magnifier dismisses it, leaving the canvas undisturbed at its original zoom level.

Note that, since we employ a minimum motion threshold to detect the bump signal, if the user touches their fingers down very lightly the stylus may not detect a motion signal sufficient to exceed this threshold. Nonetheless, our current thresholds are sufficient to detect the motions produced when users naturally bring their fingers to the screen with the pen stowed. Yet the way the sensing works thus affords an explicit work-around, by touching lightly, a noteworth point that crops up again in the informal evaluation reported near the end of this paper.

The Pen Controls

As another example, a single-finger tap while the pen is stowed brings up a small in-place palette containing the *Pen Controls*, allowing the user to change modes, or to modifiy the pen color and stroke thickness, without making a round-trip to a toolbar docked at the edge of the workspace. This example again takes advantage of the bump generated on the stylus when the user taps the touchscreen from an extension grip, using any single finger to make touchscreen contact (per B5). The tools appear next to the finger. The user may then interact with the radial menus using either pen or touch, as studies have consistently found that users expect pen and touch to be interchangable for UI controls [21,34].

FURTHER DIFFERENTIATING INPUTS BY PEN GRIP

The Drafting Tools

Our inspiration for the Drafting Tools arose from the observation that users often maintain the Writing grip between bursts of writing activity. For example, during pauses users often rotate the wrist away from the screen, to bring the pen into the *Writing–Half Supination* pose (B4). We reasoned, therefore, that the Writing grip itself represents an interesting context that might be explicitly supported by providing various Drafting Tools that take into account that the user is holding the pen in a ready-to-write posture.

The user calls up the drafting tools explicitly, by touching down a single finger of the nonpreferred hand (recognized by a single touch without a corresponding bump signal on the stylus). If the pen is held in the Writing grip, this brings up a small palette that currently offers two pen + touch tool modes, an *Airbrush* and a *Compass*, although we envision placing additional tools here (such as a straightedge, a french curve [25], pen + touch tape drawing [21], and so forth).

The current Drafting Tool is invoked as soon as the user touches down his finger; currently, the Airbrush is the initial default mode. The user can then tap on another tool (such as the Compass) to change modes. All drafting tools are implemented as spring-loaded modes; the mode is maintained only so long as the user holds down his finger.

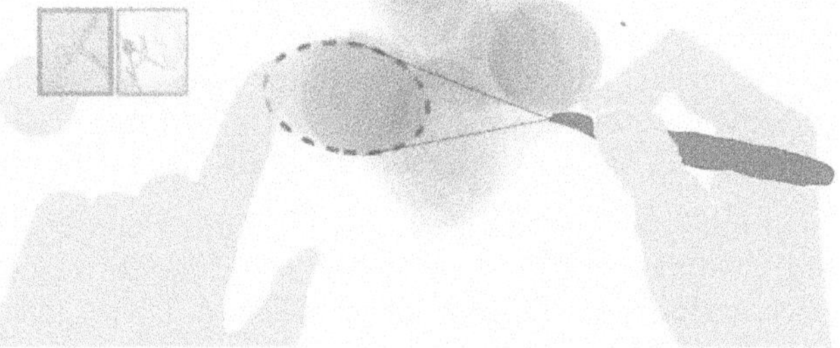

Figure 5. Airbrush tool. The nonpreferred hand indicates where to spray, while the pen orientation defines the conic section. The drafting tools palette (upper left) indicates the current mode.

Airbrush Tool

The Airbrush initially shows cursor feedback, as a gray dashed ellipse, of where the airbrush will spray if the user starts the paint flow. The user indicates where the airbrush tool should spray by the position of the (nonpreferred hand) finger. This is necessary because (as noted previously) inertial sensing cannot determine the absolute *(x,y,z)* location of the pen tip above the tablet, only a 3D orientation relative to the tablet. The relative sensing of the stylus orientation can be demonstrated by rotating the tablet, rather than the stylus, as shown in the accompanying video figure.

The user controls the spray ellipse by changing the azimuth and elevation angles of the pen with respect to the tablet surface. The user can hold the pen well above the tablet screen, making it easy to angle the pen as desired, unlike a previous exploration of an airbrush-like tool [47] which did not employ the stylus tilt angles, likely because it is difficult to reorient the pen while also keeping it within the limited ~15mm proximity sensing range of the tablet.

The user turns the paint flow on and off by tapping their index finger on the barrel of the pen (further detailed below). When the user activates the spray, the feedback changes to a bold red dashed ellipse to give clear feedback of the shape of the spray being produced. In our current prototype, we then "spray" highly transparent ellipses onto the canvas, which is sufficient for our proof-of-concept implementation.

Compass Tool

The Drafting Tools palette also includes a Compass, which supports a pen + touch mode where the pen is constrained to draw circular arcs centered about the current location of the finger (again of the nonpreferred hand). None of the extra degrees-of-freedom of the stylus are required by this mode.

Single-Tap Virtual Pen Barrel Button

Mechanical pen barrel buttons are convenient for menus and switching modes, but they force the user to hold the stylus in a particular grip [46] so that the finger can reach the button. They also can suffer from problems of accidental activation if the user mistakenly presses the button while writing.

To address these problems Song et al. [46] implement a virtual pen barrel button based on double-tap or finger slide motions, sensed through capacitive grip on the pen barrel. It is difficult to support single-tap interactions using capacitive grip alone, because many false single-touch contacts can be generated when the user shifts grips on the pen. Our system overcomes this limitation and successfully supports single-tap activation of a virtual barrel button by strategically combining all of the stylus sensing channels.

To identify candidate tap events, we look for a bump signal from the finger tap (*Figure 3c*) at the same time that a new touch contact appears on the capacitance image map. However, this cannot filter out all false positives produced by re-gripping the pen, because shifting grips can also produce bump signals coincident with new finger contacts.

To filter these out, we rely on our observation that users hold the pen still to maintain a stable tripod grasp when they lift the index finger to tap on the barrel (per observation B10). We therefore look at the ongoing accelerometer and gyro signals and compute a simple time-decaying motion signal similar to that employed by Hinckley et al. [19] to determine whether a mobile device is moving or held still. We then only accept candidate tap events that occur when the stylus is *not moving*, which effectively filters out any false contacts.

Note that the stylus must remain in a new moving (or not moving) state for at least 100ms. Otherwise, the pen barrel tap itself can trigger brief activation of a "moving" signal, which of course would thwart recognition of the barrel tap.

TABLET GRIP DETECTION TECHNIQUES

We use capacitive grip sensing on the back and sides of the tablet case to detect a number of additional contexts.

Thumb Menu and Handedness Detection

While we have so far focused on interactions involving the pen, there are many instances where the user picks up and holds a tablet with both hands, making the pen unavailable. We use grip to sense which hand the user is holding the tablet with. We then use this to summon a Thumb Menu at the appropriate side of the tablet, which allows the user to activate various buttons and menus directly with the thumb. If the user grasps the tablet with a second hand, we leave the Thumb Menu visible at the side where it first appeared.

If we observe the user grasping the pen while holding the tablet with one hand, we can immediately infer the user's handedness, although we do not yet use this to customize how menus appear, since our grip recognition is currently only trained for right-handed users.

Detecting Unintentional Thumb Contact

When the Thumb Menu first appears, it fades in over a 1.5 second interval; if the user lets go of the tablet it fades out after 350ms. The purpose of this animation feedback is to present the Thumb Menu in a tentative state, so that if the user's thumb strays onto the touchscreen while picking up the tablet, the menu can be ignored. We infer that a thumb is an unintentional touch if it occurs coincident with a new hand grip on the corresponding back portion of the tablet case. We then detect the thumb as an unintentional contact, and freeze the fade-in of the Thumb Menu if the unintentional thumb contact overlaps it. This feedback indicates to the user that the thumb contact has been recognized, but intercepted to prevent accidental activation of the menu. The user can then intentionally interact with the Thumb Menu, if desired, simply by lifting the thumb and bringing it back down on the menu. The fade-in animation then completes.

If the user does not place the thumb on the screen when picking up the tablet, the fade-in also serves as secondary cue that the Thumb Menu is fully ready for use. Since accidental activation mainly tends to occur when the user first grasps the tablet, after a few seconds elapse we assume that any hand contact with the screen was intentional. This therefore illustrates how our detection scheme blocks unintentional touch, while also allowing intention touches to get through, unlike the simple thumb-blocking heuristics on the iPad Mini, for example, which ignore any hand contact near the edge of the screen in certain applications.

Tablet Handoff: Passing the Tablet to Another User

We explored one final interaction, that of passing a tablet to another user as a way to offer an alternative, more physical semantic of sharing content with another user [18], much as observed during device micro-mobility [29,32]. Studies of passing prehension [33] and our observations (B12) indicate a characteristic sequence of motions. A user extends the object to offer it, while holding it level. He maintains his grip until the other person has firmly grasped the object. The person passing the object then lets go.

We employ our sensors to detect these states, using the tablet case grip sensing to determine when each user is grasping the device, and the tablet orientation to determine if the tablet is level. When these conditions are met, a special annotation layer peels over the tablet, as if a transparency or a sheet of vellum had been dropped over the display. The other user is then free to annotate the content, but not to make digital copies or navigate to other documents or files. This is a very different and much more limited form of sharing than the digital transfer of information supported by other cross-device information transfer techniques (e.g. [32]). We do not trigger Tablet Handoff when a single user holds the display up with two hands; during such interactions, users angle the tablet towards themselves, and thus it is not level.

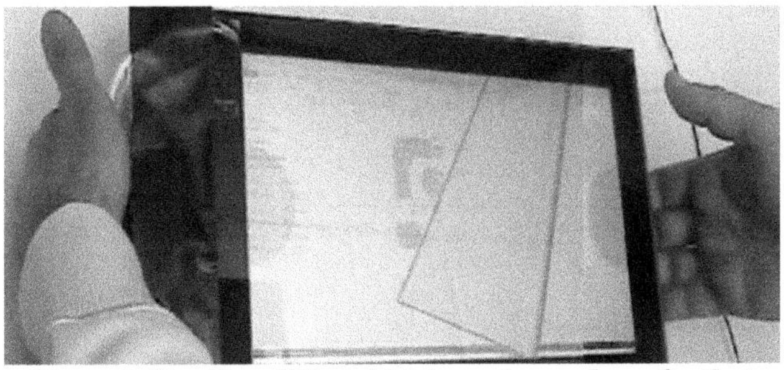

Figure 6. Handing off the tablet drops down a layer for that user's annotations (shown by a page curl animation).

PRELIMINARY USER EVALUATION

We ran an informal study with 8 people (3 female, all right-handed, 23-51 years old, mean 37). All participants were office workers with previous experience on pen-operated devices with touch. To focus on preliminary user reactions, rather than how the techniques should reveal themselves, the experimenter demonstrated each technique, after which test users tried it themselves. Each session lasted 60-90 minutes.

Detecting Unintentional Palm Contact: The sensors detected many instances of palm contact that would not be picked up by approaches that require proximity of the pen tip to the display. However, there were still instances where the user brushed the screen or touched down lightly (e.g. with a pinky finger) that the sensors were not able to detect. Users were excited about the technique because many had suffered false touch inputs. One user commented he would easily get in the habit of landing with a "heavy" palm to ensure the sensors could always pick up motion. Users also appreciated the ability to pinch-to-zoom with the nonpreferred hand when the palm was already resting on the display.

Magnifier Tool: Users quickly understood the Magnifier, and were able to easily call it up. A couple of users performed an initial interaction with a light touch that the system could not detect, but they quickly adapted to making a more deliberate gesture that could be sensed. This suggests an opportunity to improve the detection by making it more sensitive to fine motions, but on the other hand users sometimes leveraged this range of expression to *intentionally* bypass the Magnifier. For example, one user stated he could employ this when using his tablet one-handed to selectively call up the Magnifier, or instead invoke pinch-to-zoom.

Pen Controls: Users were easily able to call up the pen controls by tapping with the pen tucked. However, users commented that depending on what they were doing with the pen, this could sometimes require them to change grips just to call up the tools. Several users proposed bringing up the pen controls using the virtual pen barrel button instead. We find this an interesting suggestion, but it is unclear *where* to bring up the menu if the pen is out of range when tapped.

Drafting Tools and the Airbrush: Users found the basic idea of calling up pen-specific drafting tools when they were holding the pen ready-to-write to be intuitive. Users found using the airbrush fun and exciting, but several commented that tapping the pen barrel to turn it on and off would disturb the location of the spray ellipse. Users also had a mixed reaction to the need to indicate where to spray by holding down a finger, because "your non-dominant had is doing the drawing, which is a little odd" as one participant commented.

Thumb Menu / Detecting Unintentional Thumb Contact: These capabilities resonated particularly well with our test users, and many felt strongly that it was natural to bring up a menu near to the thumb while also guarding against unintended thumb contact. Several users suggested improving the technique by using the location of the sensed grip to position the Thumb Menu closer to the thumb.

Overall Reactions: On the whole test users were excited by the system (commenting "it's like magic" and "this system is very cool, hopefully someday I can use it.") Users found the palm detection to be the most useful capability, as all had previously experienced this problem firsthand. The virtual barrel button was the lowest ranked feature, perhaps because its only demonstrated use was to turn on / off the Airbrush.

CONCLUSION: CHALLENGES, LIMITS, & FUTURE WORK

Although the present research makes considerable progress on many issues in sensing for stylus+tablet interaction, a number of challenges and limitations remain to be addressed:

- The thickness and length of our stylus prototype, as well as the presence of a tether for power, limit our ability to deploy it for truly mobile use and to observe a wider range of naturally-occurring behaviors with pen and tablet.
- Our current techniques for sensing pen-in-hand interactions require detecting some minimum force motion-signal threshold on the accelerometer and/or stylus. With more sophisticated signal-processing

techniques, or by combining the signal from the tablet's motion sensors as well, it may be possible to make the system more sensitive, but very soft touches likely represent an inherent challenge for this type of approach.

- Our observations and techniques need to be extended for left-hand users, to situational impairments such as mobility (i.e. walking) and one-handed interaction, and in general to a wide variety of other human accessibility concerns that our system does not yet address adequately.

Nonetheless, we have contributed a number of techniques that demonstrate how stylus and tablet sensing allows us to tailor pen+touch interaction to the context, such as by ameliorating unintentional palm contact while writing, yet still allowing full articulation of intentional touches by the nonpreferred hand. We can also combine these modalities to support contextually-appropriate tools, such as the Magnifier Tool, Drafting Tools (e.g. airbrush), and the Thumb Menu, all depending on how the user holds the tablet and pen.

A common theme in our techniques is the many ways that motion sensing, grip sensing, and multi-touch from the touchscreen can be combined to reinforce one another, both to avoid false positives as well as to help extract specific signals that would otherwise be difficult to isolate from a single sensing modality. Collectively, these techniques illustrate some of the compelling ways that grip and motion sensing afford contextual awareness in pen computing, and thereby open up the potential for a rich new space of expression for tablets using natural pen + touch interaction.

REFERENCES

1. Annett, M., et al. The Pen is Mightier: Understanding Stylus Behaviour While Inking on Tablets. *Graphics Interface (GI 2014)*.
2. Annett, M., et al. Is it Intended or Unintended? Palm Rejection during Direct Pen Interaction. (Currently submitted for review), 2014.
3. Becchio, C., et al. Grasping intentions: from thought experiments to emprical evidence. Frontiers in Human Neuroscience, 2012. **6**(117).
4. Bi, X., et al. An Exploration of Pen Rolling. *UIST'08*.
5. Brandl, P., et al. Occlusion-aware menu design for digital tabletops. *CHI'09 Extended Abstracts*.
6. Buxton, W. Integrating the Periphery and Context: A New Taxonomy of Telematics. *Proc. Graphics Interface '95*.
7. Cheng, L.-P., et al. iRotate grasp: automatic screen rotation based on grasp of mobile devices. *UIST Adjunct Proc. '12*.
8. Cheng, L.-P., et al. iGrasp: grasp-based adaptive keyboard for mobile devices. *CHI '13 Extended Abstracts*.
9. Chun Yat Li, F., et al. The 1Line Keyboard: A QWERTY Layout in a Single Line. *UIST'11*.
10. FiftyThree, I. *A closer look at zoom*. http://tinyurl.com/mxqdshz.
11. FiftyThree, I. *Pencil (for Paper)*. http://www.fiftythree.com/pencil.
12. Goel, M., et al. GripSense: Using Built-In Sensors to Detect Hand Posture and Pressure on Commodity Mobile Phones. *UIST'12*.
13. Guiard, Y., Millerat, F., Writing Postures in Left-Handers: Inverters are Hand-Crossers. Neuropsychologia, 1984. **22**(5): p. 535-538.
14. Harrison, B., et al. Squeeze me, hold me, tilt me! An exploration of manipulative user interfaces. *CHI'98*.
15. Hasan, K., et al. A-coord input: coordinating auxiliary input streams for augmenting contextual pen-based interactions. *CHI '12*.
16. Hinckley, K. Synchronous Gestures for Multiple Users and Computers. *UIST'03*.
17. Hinckley, K., et al. Motion and Context Sensing Techniques for Pen Computing. *Proc. Graphics Interface 2013 (GI'13)*.
18. Hinckley, K., et al. Codex: A Dual-Screen Tablet Computer. *CHI'09*.
19. Hinckley, K., Pierce, J., Sinclair, M., Horvitz, E. Sensing techniques for mobile interaction. *UIST 2000*.
20. Hinckley, K., Song, H. Sensor Synaesthesia: Touch in Motion, and Motion in Touch. *CHI 2011*.
21. Hinckley, K., et al. Pen + Touch = New Tools. *UIST 2010*.
22. Holmquist, L., et al. Smart-Its Friends: A Technique for Users to Easily Establish Connections between Smart Artefacts. *Ubicomp'01*.
23. Hudson, S., et al. Whack Gestures: Inexact and Inattentive Interaction with Mobile Devices. *TEI 2010*.
24. Kim, K.-E., et al. Hand Grip Pattern Recognition for Mobile User Interfaces. *Proceedings of AAAI/IAAI-2006: Innovative Appl.*
25. Kurtenbach, G., et al. The design of a GUI paradigm based on tablets, two-hands, and transparency. *CHI'97*.
26. Lee, D., et al. PhantomPen: virtualization of pen head for digital drawing free from pen occlusion & visual parallax. *UIST'12*.
27. Lester, J., et al. Are You With Me? Using Accelerometers to Determine if Two Devices are Carried. *Pervasive'04*.
28. Liu, S., Guimbretiere, F. FlexAura: A Flexible Near-Surface Range Sensor. *UIST '12*.
29. Luff, P., Heath, C. Mobility in collaboration. *CSCW '98*.
30. Mackenzie, C., Iberall, T., *The Grasping Hand*. Advances in Psychology 104. 1994, Amsterdam: North Holland.
31. Mahoney, R., Nonlinear Complementary Filters on the Special Orthogonal Group. IEEE Trans. on Automatic Control, 2008. **53**(5).
32. Marquardt, N., et al. Cross-Device Interaction via Micro-mobility and F-formations. *UIST '12*. 2012. Cambridge, MA.
33. Mason, A., MacKenzie, C., Grip forces when passing an object to a partner. Exp. Brain Res, 2005(163): p. 173-187.
34. Matulic, F., Norrie, M. Supporting active reading on pen and touch-operated tabletops. *Proc. Int'l Working Conf. on Advanced Visual Interfaces (AVI'12)*. 2012. Capri Island, Italy.
35. Moleskine Journal (iPad app). 2014. http://tinyurl.com/kqhtomz.
36. Penultimate by Evernote (iPad app). 2014. http://tinyurl.com/kx82c8a.
37. Premerlani, W., Bizard, P. *Direction Cosine Matrix IMU: Theory*. 2009. http://gentlenav.googlecode.com/files/DCMDraft2.pdf.
38. Rofouei, M., et al. Your Phone or Mine? Fusing Body, Touch and Device Sensing for MultiUser Device-Display Interaction. *CHI 2012*.
39. Roudaut, A., et al. TimeTilt: Using Sensor-Based Gestures to Travel through Multiple Applications on a Mobile Device. *Interact '09*.
40. Schmidt, A., et al. Advanced interaction in context. *Handheld and Ubiquitous Computing (HUC'99)*.
41. Schmidt, D., et al. PhoneTouch: A Technique for Direct Phone Interaction on Surfaces. *UIST'10*.
42. Schwarz, J., et al. Probabilistic Palm Rejection Using Spatiotemporal Touch Features and Iterative Classification. *CHI'14*.
43. Selin, A., *Pencil Grip: A descriptive Model and Four Empirical Studies*. 2003: Akademi University Press.
44. Sellen, A., Shaw., K. How Knowledge Workers Use the Web. *CHI'02*.
45. Siio, I., Tsujita, H. Mobile interaction using paperweight metaphor. *UIST '06*.
46. Song, H., et al. Grips and Gestures on a Multi-Touch Pen. *CHI'11*.
47. Sun, M., et al. Enhancing Naturalness of Pen-and-Tablet Drawing through Context Sensing. *Interactive Tabletops and Surfaces (ITS '11)*.
48. Suzuki, Y., et al. Stylus Enhancement to Enrich Interaction with Computers. *HCII 2007, Part II*. 2007: Springer-Verlag.
49. Taylor, B., Bove Jr., V. Graspables: Grasp-Recognition as a User Interface. *CHI'09*.
50. Tian, F., et al. Tilt Menu: Using the 3D Orientation Information of Pen Devices to Extend the Selection Capability. *CHI'08*.
51. Vogel, D., Casiez, G. Conte: Multimodal Input Inspired by an Artist's Crayon. *UIST 2011*.
52. Wagner, J., et al. BiTouch and BiPad: Designing Bimanual Interaction for Hand-held Tablets. *CHI'12*.
53. Wimmer, R., Boring, S. HandSense - Discriminating Different Ways of Grasping and Holding a Tangible User Interface. *TEI '09*.
54. Xin, Y., et al. Natural Use Profiles for the Pen: An Empirical Exploration of Pressure, Tilt, and Azimuth. *CHI'12*.
55. Yoon, D., Chen, N., Guimbretiere, F. TextTearing: Expanding Whitespace for Digital Ink Annotation. *UIST'13*.

Swipeboard: A Text Entry Technique for Ultra-Small Interfaces That Supports Novice to Expert Transitions

Xiang 'Anthony' Chen[12], Tovi Grossman[1], George Fitzmaurice[1]

[1]User Interface Group
Autodesk Research
{firstname.lastname}@autodesk.com

[2]HCI Institute
Carnegie Mellon University
xiangchen@acm.org

ABSTRACT

Ultra-small smart devices, such as smart watches, have become increasingly popular in recent years. Most of these devices rely on touch as the primary input modality, which makes tasks such as text entry increasingly difficult as the devices continue to shrink. In the sole pursuit of entry speed, the ultimate solution is a shorthand technique (e.g., Morse code) that sequences tokens of input (e.g., key, tap, swipe) into unique representations of each character. However, learning such techniques is hard, as it often resorts to rote memory. Our technique, Swipeboard, leverages our spatial memory of a QWERTY keyboard to learn, and eventually master a shorthand, eyes-free text entry method designed for ultra-small interfaces. Characters are entered with two swipes; the first swipe specifies the region where the character is located, and the second swipe specifies the character within that region. Our study showed that with less than two hours' training, Tested on a reduced word set, Swipeboard users achieved 19.58 words per minute (WPM), 15% faster than an existing baseline technique.

Author Keywords

Text entry, input technique, mobile device, Swipeboard.

ACM Classification Keywords

H.5.2 [Information interfaces and presentation]: User Interfaces - Graphical user interfaces; Input devices and strategies.

INTRODUCTION

Typing is an important part of our digital activities, either with a desktop computer or other smart devices. For smart devices, soft keyboards have become the dominant text entry modality. However, as smart devices become miniaturized, it is increasingly difficult to type on a soft keyboard, due to the 'fat finger' problem [13].

To mitigate this problem, prior work has proposed various text entry solutions, that may involve new gestures [12,18,19] or additional sensors [11,15]. However, not all of these techniques can be adapted to ultra-small interfaces, and those that can usually have a limited entry speed well below 20 WPM [10].

In contrast, shorthand techniques (e.g., Morse code) promises a much faster entry speed (reportedly, the world's fastest Morse code entry is 140 WPM [4]). While such techniques can be easily adapted to an ultra-small interface, learning them is hard, as it often resorts to rote memory. This creates a dilemma: techniques palatable to users only give incremental improvements, while shorthand techniques can go significantly faster but create a high barrier for user learning and acceptance.

In this paper, we present Swipeboard, a technique that supports fast text entry on ultra-small interfaces. Swipeboard divides the keyboard into nine regions (Figure 1a). Entering any character requires two swipes: the first swipe specifies the region where the character is located, and the second swipe specifies the character within that region (Figure 1b). This technique leverages our spatial memory of a QWERTY keyboard to ease novice learning, while an expert can perform efficient, eyes-free, shorthand input. Further, the technique is *target agnostic*, requiring no knowledge of target locations or dimensions [17].

We present a performance model and a user study to demonstrate how Swipeboard users' behavior will transition from novice to experts, and how their performance can increase through learning and practice: in less than two hours, participants transcribing from a reduced word set achieved 19.58 WPM on a 12mm x 12mm interface, 15% faster than an existing baseline technique.

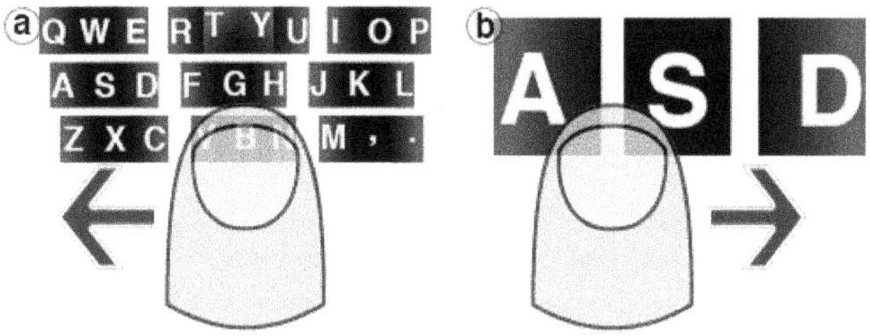

Figure 1. Swipeboard: the first swipe specifies one of the nine regions subdivided from a QWERTY keyboard; the second swipe specifies the character. For example, swiping left goes from (a) to (b), then swiping right types 'D'.

UIST '14, October 05 - 08 2014, Honolulu, HI, USA
Copyright 2014 ACM 978-1-4503-3069-5/14/10···$15.00.
http://dx.doi.org/10.1145/2642918.2647354

RELATED WORK

The miniaturization of ultra-small interfaces limits the use of conventional numeric keypads, keyboards, and touch input. Wigdor and Balakrishnan designed a chord input to improve the traditional *Multitap* on the few and small phone keys [16]. The use of a touch screen inspires other possibilities. *MultiWidget* uses a dialing gesture along the watch's edges to specify a numeric value [1]. This suggests a watch's tangibility could ease the input. *Zoomboard* uses iterative zooming for enlarging and acquiring keys on a soft keyboard [10]. This mitigates the 'fat finger' problem, but still requires a fair amount of visual attention and motor skills.

In contrast, shorthand text entry techniques are potentially eyes-free with high entry speed, especially for expert users. Two approaches for designing such techniques have been explored. A *continuous* approach, such as *EdgeWrite*, maps a word to a continuous stroke [18]. A *discrete* approach, such as *H4-Writer*, uses a base-4 Huffman coding to generate unique key sequences for each letter [8]. *Quikwriting* uses grouping to map characters to a base-9 encoding [12]. Unfortunately, such techniques usually require extensive learning and reference character maps, making them impractical for broad adoption.

What would be more desirable is a system that guides novices "*to perform like experts*" [2]. For example, Kurtenbach's marking menus provide *self-revelation* to help novices navigate and select an item, while *guidance* and *rehearsal* further train novices towards using the menu like experts [7]. Kristensson and Zhai also articulate this idea in building the text entry system *Shark*^{2} [5]. With *Shark*^{2}, novices simply trace a word by searching and inking through its constituent letters, experts eventually can memorize and execute this process as one single stroke, and the system accommodates users' behavior between these two 'extremes'. Unfortunately the technique may not scale well to ultra-small interfaces.

In summary, existing approaches that are based on the QWERTY layout either plateau at limited WPM, or are impractical on ultra-small interfaces; in contrast, shorthand techniques that rely on non-conventional layouts or gestures can achieve faster entry but are usually difficult to learn. In this paper, our goal is to design a text entry technique that supports novice to expert behaviors, and gradually scales users' performance to achieve a high entry speed.

SWIPEBOARD

To achieve this goal, we design Swipeboard – a text entry technique that leverages our spatial memory of a QWERTY keyboard layout to encode each alphabetic character into two touch actions that navigate to the key of that character. From a motor perspective, this makes the technique similar to the two-level simple marking menu technique [6]. Learning from Zhao and Balakrishnan's work [20], we also used simple, discrete actions, which are more suitable for ultra-small interfaces, rather than requiring compound, continuous strokes.

Swipeboard divides a QWERTY keyboard into nine regions (Figure 1a); the first swipe specifies the region where the character is located, e.g., swiping left goes to "ASD" (Figure 1b), or swiping up goes to "RTYU", and a tap, anywhere on the interface, brings up "FGH". A second swipe (or tap) specifies the character within the first region: in the cases of three keys (e.g., Figure 1b), swiping left selects the key on the left, tapping anywhere selects the key on the center, and swiping right selects the key on the right; in the one case of four keys ("RTYU"), swiping left selects 'R', up-left selects 'T', up-right selects 'Y' and right selects 'U'. If the first swipe (or tap) is incorrect, a swipe down, or a 2-second timeout, restores the keyboard to the top level (Figure 1a). Other combinations of swipes are reserved for additional functions. A double-swipe down-left deletes a character, double-swipe down-right enters a space, and a double-swipe up switches to symbols and numbers.

Swipeboard has several beneficial features. First the technique is *target agnostic*: the actions can occur anywhere on the display, and no spatial target selection is required. This supports use on ultra-small interfaces even when visual cues might be illegible to human eyes. Second, the gestures are based on the familiar QWERTY layout, supporting novice use. Finally, the technique should allow an expert to chunk a single character entry into an efficient and eyes-free double swipe (or tap), dispensing with reliance on the visuals, thus supporting fast text entry.

We have found the technique can be used at very small sizes, with the limiting factor being the legibility of the keyboard (for novices' learning), not the input area (our study participants were able to use Swipeboard as small as 12 mm by 12 mm). In general, this technique can be used on smart watches (Figure 2a), and potentially smart eyewear, with an input area on the side (Figure 2b).

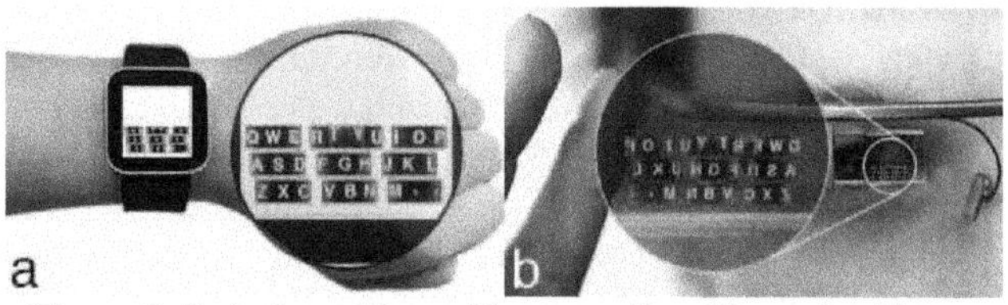

Figure 2. Swipeboard is usable as small as 12 mm by 12 mm, supporting potential usage on (a) smart watches or (b) smart eyewear.

PERFORMANCE MODEL

Swipeboard encodes each character with a first swipe (or tap) to locate the key on the keyboard, and a second swipe (or tap) to specify the key. We call a swipe (or tap) an *action*. Users will begin in a novice phase, where they must identify the gesture for a target before each action, while the finger is up. We call this process *up*. Text entry in this novice phase will be perceived and carried out as two separate *units of interaction* that consists of a total of four steps (1st up, 1st action, 2nd up, and 2nd action).

Essentially, novices will rely on the visuals of the keyboard, as well as their spatial memory of a QWERTY keyboard, to specify a key. This mechanism allows them to learn and rehearse each character entry. Gradually, they will transition towards an expert phase by trying to associate two actions for a given character. The time for the *up* actions will gradually decrease as less reliance on visual search cuts the decision making time. When reaching the expert phase, each character entry will be chunked into a single unit of interaction that consists of two consecutive actions, dispensing with deliberate searching steps. In particular, we predict Swipeboard performance to be:

$$T = T_{u1} + T_{a1+} + T_{u2} + T_{a2},$$

where the total time T is the sum of two *up* steps (T_{u1}, T_{u2}) and two *action* steps (T_{a1}, T_{a2}). Based on research on gesture performance modeling, we expect a stroke or tap time to be approximately 100 ms [3]. Thus, for a novice, we have a character entry time, T_{nov}:

$$T_{nov} = T_{u1} + 100 + T_{u2} + 100$$

To model optimal expert use, we make two assumptions. First, their initial reaction time is optimal, so we assign a value of 200ms to T_{u1} as an approximate human limit [14]. Second, we assume the expert will chunk the two swipes into a single action, reducing T_{u2} to the time taken to lift the finger between the two swipes. Mackenzie has found that it takes approximately 127ms to lift up *and* tap in place [9]. When repeating such action the finger would be up approximately half of the time, therefore we estimate our *up* time T_{u2} as half of that, 64ms. As such, we predict optimal upper limit character entry time, T_{opt} as:

$$T_{opt} = 200 + 100 + 64 + 100$$

This equates to 464ms per character, or 25.87 WPM. The model shows that the difference between Swipeboard novices and experts lie in the time while the finger is up. The novice must determine the correct swipe at each level mostly through visual search, while an expert immediately performs the actions upon recalling what actions are associated to the desired key. Below, we present a study that provides data to support our model.

USER STUDY

The goal of our study is to measure the effectiveness of Swipeboard for entering text on an ultra-small interface. Specifically, we compared our technique with Zoomboard – a state-of-the-art text entry method for miniaturized devices [10]. Our study observes how Swipeboard users' behavior transitions from novice to expert, and how the performance increases through learning and practice.

Design

The study consisted of a series of text entry trials. To accelerate the learning elicited within the timeframe of our lab study, each trial consisted of a single four letter word, with each word consisting of four characters from the set: E, T, A, N and S, such as 'EATS', 'SEAT', 'NEST'. Our goal of choosing this reduced word set is *not* to replace a regular text entry study, but rather to develop a way to quickly test the novice-expert performance growth by artificially accelerating the learning of the techniques focusing on a small word set. This would help provide insights into Swipeboard's optimal entry time from a motor skill perspective. The character set was chosen so that a broad range of the possible swipe directions would be required.

To prevent the transfer effects between techniques inherent in within-subjects designs, we employed a repeated measures between-subjects factorial design. The independent variable was *Technique* (ZoomBoard vs. Swipeboard). Participants were randomly assigned to one of the two groups. They were asked to complete two sessions of trials on separate days with one day in between. Each session contained 4 blocks of trials. For each block, participants were asked to enter 108 words, (nine consecutive sets, each containing 12 distinct words). In summary, the experimental design was:

2 Techniques x
8 participants per Technique x
2 sessions per participant x
4 blocks per session x
108 words per block
= 13824 data points.

Apparatus

We implemented both SwipeBoard and ZoomBoard with iOS, deployed on an Apple iPad tablet device – a platform that was also used in Oney et al.'s study [10]. At development time, this served as a simulation platform for rapidly prototyping and experimenting with different input and output resolutions, and more importantly, with full touch capability, which was unavailable on most commercial ultra-small interfaces at the time we conducted the study. Note that the design of Swipeboard, however, is not restricted to this platform; it can be generalized and transferred to other miniaturized interfaces, e.g., ring-sized, wrist-worn, or head-mounted devices.

We used a keyboard dimension of 12 mm by 12 mm (about ¼ the size of a regular smart watch) on the iPad display wherein we enabled and used native iOS touch events to implement the two text entry techniques. All input events outside of this zone were ignored. We measured the completion time for each word (from tapping the 'start' button to the complete and correct entry of a word), counted the errors, and, for each character, logged the time for each *up* and *action* events. Two sizes were used to render each key on each text entry step, based on Zoomboard's original paper [10] – small size: 1.5mm x 1.5mm and large size: 4.4mm x 4.4mm. For Zoomboard, small size was used before zooming and large size afterwards. For Swipeboard, small and large sizes were used before and after the first swipe (or tap), respectively.

Participants

We recruited 16 participants from a local university. They were between 21 to 26 years old, 9 female and 7 male. One of them was mixed-handed and two left-handed. All were smart phone users. All but one typed with a soft keyboard on a daily basis.

Task and Stimuli

Each participant was asked to finish a series of text transcribing tasks using our selected word set.

At the beginning of each task, a word prompted the participants. They were asked to read and memorize the presented word, then to press the 'start' button after which the word was removed and a technique was activated for transcribing that word. Timing started when the 'start' button was pressed, and stopped when the entire word is transcribed correctly. When an erroneous character was entered, the display highlighted it with red, and the word will re-appear. The time for correcting errors was counted into the total completion time. Upon finishing a word, the system automatically advanced to the next one.

The two groups of participants used ZoomBoard and SwipeBoard, respectively, as described below:

ZoomBoard. To enter a character, a user will tap a corresponding key on the keyboard. This first tap will not select the key, but will only zoom the keyboard into the tapped region. Then the user will perform a second tap on the desired key in order to select it. The user can also swipe down to zoom out from the current region. The keyboard will also zoom out to the original size after the second tap or a two-second timeout of no user actions. At any time, the user can swipe left to delete an entered character, and swipe right to enter a 'space'.

SwipeBoard. To enter a character, a user will firstly swipe to select one of the nine regions where the corresponding key is located (Figure 1): upper-left, up, upper-right, right, lower-right, down, lower-left, left; except for the central region, where a tap anywhere within the interface is used for selection. After the first swipe or tap, the interface will show the selected region of three or four keys. In the cases of three keys (Figure 1), the user will swipe left to select the left key, right for the right key, and tap anywhere for the key at the center. In the only case of four keys ("RTYU"), the user will swipe left for 'R', up-left for 'T', up-right for 'Y' and right for 'U'. At this step, the user can also swipe down to return to the full keyboard view. At any time, swiping lower-left twice deletes an entered character, and swiping low-right twice enters a 'space'.

Results and Analysis

In this section we discuss the results based on text entry speed and error rates. We then relate the data to our performance model.

Text Entry Speed

Figure 3 shows the aggregated WPM results (including error correction time). Although Swipeboard did not start faster (9.09 WPM) than Zoomboard (10.76 WPM), participants were able to quickly learn the technique and, as shown in Figure 3, achieve a higher entry speed than Zoomboard's from the third block of the study onwards (after about 35 to 45 minutes' of usage time). As the study went on, Swipeboard continued to accelerate. By the end of the study (the 8th block performed in the 2nd session), Swipeboard's WPM was 19.58, 15% faster than Zoomboard (17.08 WPM).

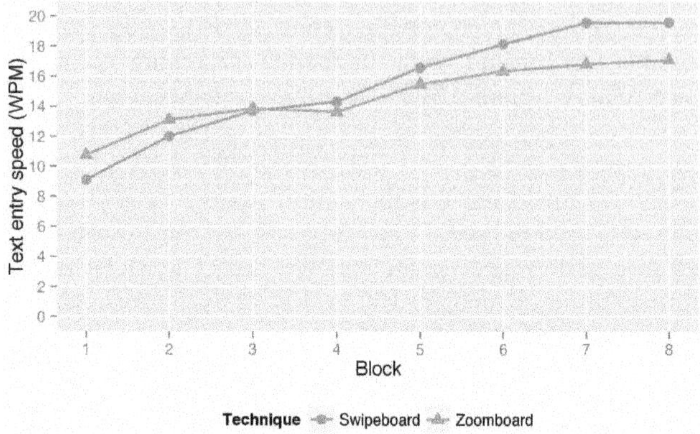

Figure 3. With less than two hours' training, Swipeboard users achieved 19.58 words per minute (WPM) entering text on a 12mm x 12mm interface, 15% faster than Zoomboard [10].

The overall effect of technique was significant ($F_{1, 14}$ = 6.503, p = .0112). The effect of block ($F_{7, 105}$ = 52.99, p < .0001), and the interaction between technique and block ($F_{7, 98}$ = 3.952, p = .0004) were also significant. This indicates that there was a learning effect in both technique and the Swipeboard produced a faster learning curve, as well as a higher text entry speed compared to Zoomboard.

Error Rate

As both techniques require two steps for entering a character, we recorded two types of errors inherent to this design:

- *Soft error*: error made in the first step of entering a character, such as, for Zoomboard, zooming into the wrong area of the keyboard, and for Swipeboard, swiping or tapping to the wrong regions of keys.
- *Hard error*: error made in the second step of entering a character, such as, for Zoomboard tapping the wrong key on the zoomed in area, and for Swipeboard, swiping or tapping for the wrong character within a region of key.

Essentially, soft errors reflected the difficulty of making the first step. Overall, the soft error rates were 4.183% for Swipeboard and 4.739% for Zoomboard. The difference was not significant ($F_{1, 14}$ = .9764, p = .3237). Hard errors are errors that resulted in a mistyped character. The hard error rates were 13.30% for Swipeboard and 14.90% for Zoomboard and the difference was significant ($F_{1, 14}$ = 3.933, p = .0481). Figure 4 shows the two error rates of both techniques.

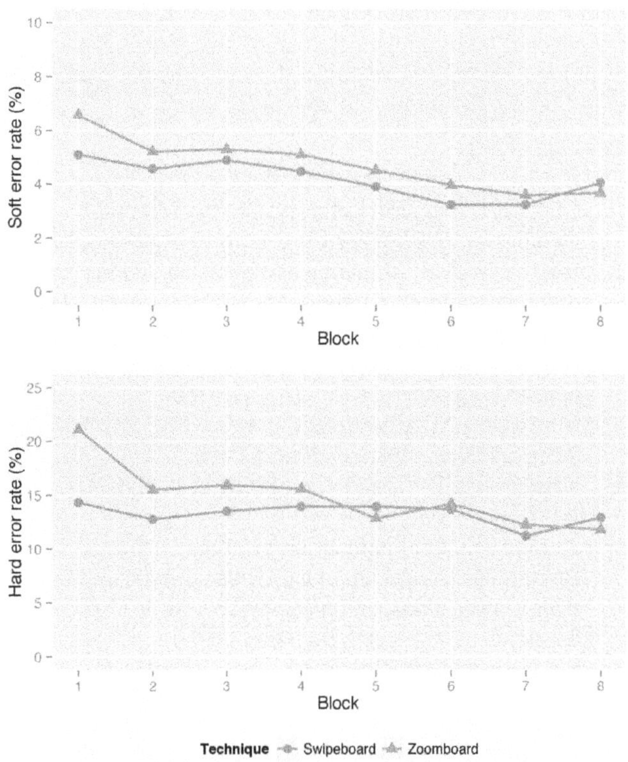

Figure 4. Soft and hard error rates of Swipeboard and Zoomboard: soft errors are made in the first step; hard errors in the second step and result in mistyped characters.

Performance Model

Figure 5 shows a breakdown associated with our model of the two techniques' completion time, plotted across all blocks in the study. As the time for both *actions* was almost always constant, we focused on the *up* time – the portion that actually contributed to the difference in the two techniques' entry speed.

For the 1st *up*, Swipeboard participants started much slower than Zoomboard. However, through learning and practice, the time rapidly dropped and the gap between the two techniques greatly decreased. In the second half of the study, the difference had been reduced to about 65 ms. As Swipeboard users transitioned from novices to experts, they relied less on visually searching the keyboard but instead gradually memorized the association between characters and the swipes/taps, resulting in a shorter reaction time in this initial interaction. For the 2nd up, Swipeboard participants also demonstrated a similar learning curve: from novices to experts, their reaction time continuously became shorter, whereas Zoomboard's time only had a minor decrease. Zoomboard's second tap suffers from the 'fat finger' problem, where there is an upper bound as to how fast a user can select a small target. Swipeboard, on the other hand, is target agnostic, providing users with a larger room for improvement.

LIMITATIONS, TRADE-OFFS AND FUTURE WORK

We discuss existing limitations and trade-offs of our work and point to possible future research directions.

Expanding the word set. Our study used a reduced word set. The five letters were selected to strike a balance between high usage frequency and a variety of swipes/taps when using Swipeboard as the entry technique. Although this five-letter set already covers 43% of all letter frequency occurrences in English, a full letter set (and perhaps including some symbols) is still needed if we are to reflect the learning curve of a user typing in day-to-day scenarios.

Extending to more platforms. Swipeboard can benefit a variety of interactive platforms, such as smart rings, smart watches, and smart eyewear. Our study in this paper is very basic and cannot address each of these devices individually. More testing is required to study ergonomic issues, e.g., devices' orientations and placements. Modalities other than touch can also be included into comparison.

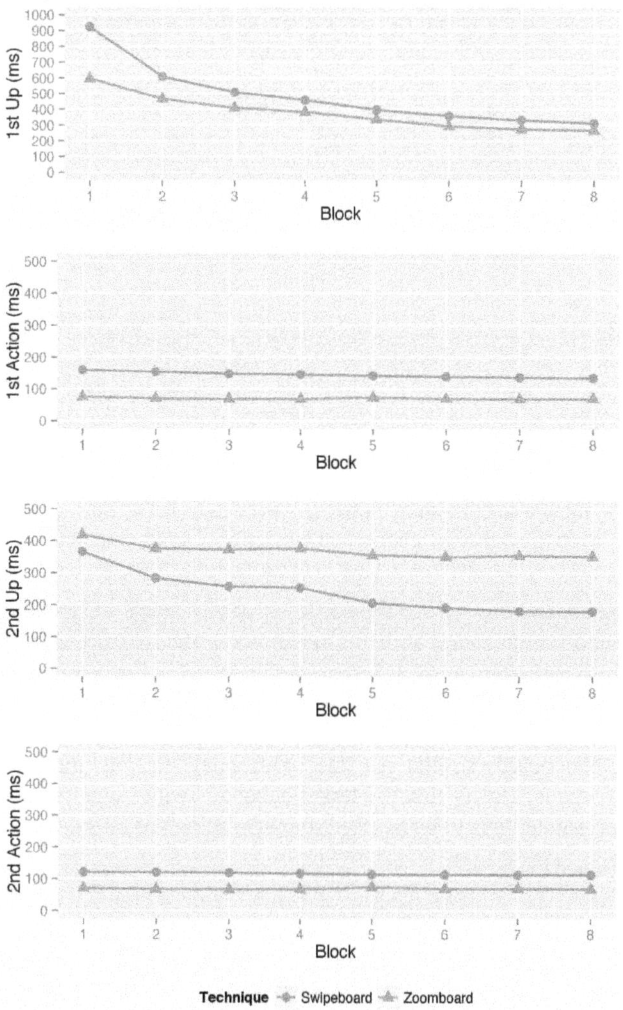

Figure 5. In error-free trials, a break-down of the techniques' completion time shows that as Swipeboard users transitioned from novices to experts, they spent less time deciding on each swipe actions.

Observing more training. Based on our performance model, there is still room for improvement in participants' Swipeboard performance. Anecdotally, the first author trained about a total of four hours of Swipeboard practice and can achieve an entry speed of 32.9 WPM.

Considering individual character entry. Swipeboard users transition from novices to experts by trying to memorize the association between the swipes/taps and the characters. Our data shows that some character entries, however, seemed easier to memorize and execute than the others. Figure 6 shows the aggregated character entry time in our study. There was a difference in per character difficulties, especially for novices (see how first block participants entered 'A' much faster than 'N' – the former character requires two identical and consecutive swipe-left); however, as participants got better in using the technique, the gaps became smaller. This suggests that with Swipeboard, not all the character entries are created equal. Future work should address this by, for example, providing more training on harder character entries, or adjusting the recognizer to learn how users would enter the more difficult characters.

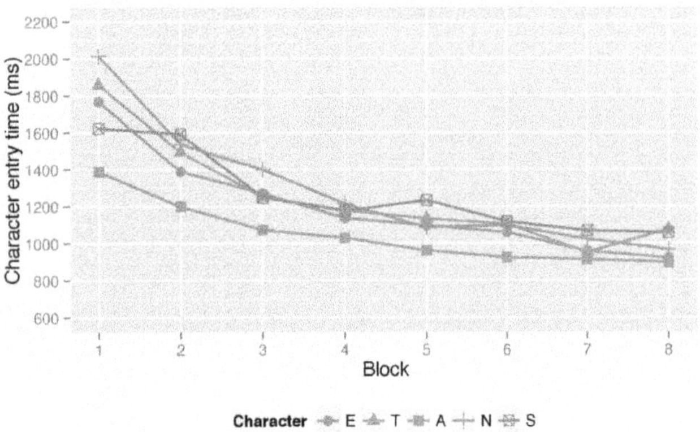

Figure 6. Individual character entry time shows that with Swipeboard some characters entries are easier to memorize and execute; such difference is most notable at the novice level.

Incorporating other models. Future work can also incorporate a probabilistic model when recognizing entries of characters with different usage frequencies. Language models can also be used where only the first swipes or taps are needed to specify a word – this interestingly makes Swipeboard similar to the traditional T9 on numeric keypads, except that the target agnostic swipes/taps require no actual keys to be devised or rendered on the interface.

CONCLUSION

With the miniaturization of smart devices, typing on an ultra-small interface is becoming a pressing design challenge. Our technique leverages people's spatial memory of a QWERTY keyboard to learn, use, and master a shorthand text entry method that is otherwise hard to learn and be accepted by general users. Swipeboard's design accommodates a wide range of user behavior, from novices to experts, and allowed users, with less than two hours' training, to achieve an entry speed of 19.58 WPM when typing a reduced word set on a 12mm x 12mm interface. Swipeboard's target agnostic nature also makes it a useful technique for small wearable devices where visual cues might be illegible or unavailable to the users.

REFERENCES

1. Blasko, G. and Feiner, S. Evaluation of an Eyes-Free Cursorless Numeric Entry System for Wearable Computers. *IEEE Wearable Computers*, (2006), 21–28.
2. Buxton, W.A.S. Chunking and phrasing and the design of human-computer dialogues. *IFIP Congress* (1995), 494–499.
3. Cao, X. and Zhai, S. Modeling human performance of pen stroke gestures. *CHI '07*, 1495-1504.
4. Cornwell, J.M. Morse Code at 140 WPM. *The National Association for Amateur Radio*, 2008.
5. Kristensson, P.-O. and Zhai, S. SHARK 2. *ACM UIST '04*, 43-52.
6. Kurtenbach, G., Fitzmaurice, G., Baudel, T., and Buxton, B. The design of a GUI paradigm based on tablets, two-hands, and transparency. *ACM CHI '97*, 35–42.
7. Kurtenbach, G.P. The design and evaluation of marking menus. Diss., University of Toronto, 1993.
8. MacKenzie, I.S., Soukoreff, R.W., and Helga, J. 1 thumb, 4 buttons, 20 words per minute. *ACM UIST '11*, 471-480.
9. MacKenzie, I.S. and Zhang, S.X. The design and evaluation of a high-performance soft keyboard. *ACM CHI '99*, 25–31.
10. Oney, S., Harrison, C., Ogan, A., and Wiese, J. ZoomBoard. *ACM CHI '13*, 2799-2802.
11. Partridge, K., Chatterjee, S., Sazawal, V., Borriello, G., and Want, R. TiltType. *ACM UIST* (2002), 201-204.
12. Perlin, K. Quikwriting. *ACM UIST '98*, 215–216.
13. Siek, K.A., Rogers, Y., and Connelly, K.H. Fat finger worries: how older and younger users physically interact with PDAs. *INTERACT 2005*. 267–280.
14. Welford, A.T. Reaction time, speed of performance, and age. *Annals of the New York Academy of Sciences 515*, 1 (1988), 1–17.
15. Wigdor, D. and Balakrishnan, R. TiltText. *ACM UIST* , 81–90.
16. Wigdor, D. and Balakrishnan, R. A comparison of consecutive and concurrent input text entry techniques for mobile phones. *ACM CHI '04*, 81–88.
17. Wobbrock, J.O., Fogarty, J., Liu, S.-Y.S., Kimuro, S., and Harada, S. The angle mouse. *ACM CHI '09*, 1401–1410.
18. Wobbrock, J.O., Myers, B.A., and Kembel, J.A. EdgeWrite. *ACM UIST '03,* 61–70.
19. Zhai, S. and Kristensson, P.-O. Shorthand writing on stylus keyboard. *ACM CHI '03*, 97-104.
20. Zhao, S., and Balakrishnan, R. Simple vs. compound mark hierarchical marking menus. *ACM UIST '04*. 33-42).

Improvements to Keyboard Optimization with Integer Programming

Andreas Karrenbauer[1], **Antti Oulasvirta**[1,2,3]
[1]Max Planck Institute for Informatics, [2]Saarland University, [3]Aalto University

ABSTRACT

Keyboard optimization is concerned with the design of keyboards for different terminals, languages, user groups, and tasks. Previous work in HCI has used random search based methods, such as simulated annealing. These "black box" approaches are convenient, because good solutions are found quickly and no assumption must be made about the objective function. This paper contributes by developing integer programming (IP) as a complementary approach. To this end, we present IP formulations for the letter assignment problem and solve them by branch-and-bound. Although computationally expensive, we show that IP offers two strong benefits. First, its structured non-random search approach improves the outcomes. Second, it guarantees bounds, which increases the designer's confidence over the quality of results. We report improvements to three keyboard optimization cases.

Author Keywords

User interface optimization; Integer programming; Keyboard layouts; Branch-and-bound; Random search methods.

ACM Classification Keywords

D.2.2. Software: Design tools and techniques: UIs

INTRODUCTION

This paper advances the optimization of text entry methods for human performance. In particular, we look at the letter assignment problem, or the problem of keyboard layouts. This problem is known to be NP-complete [6] and computational solutions have received increasing attention. Active research areas include the optimization of keyboards for various terminals, languages, and user groups (e.g., [4, 9, 20, 2, 8, 25]).

Given the amount of interest, it is important to try to find improvements to optimization methods. Although UI optimization is presently focusing on keyboards, advances in the keyboard design case can be useful more generally to UI design problems concerned with layouts. Examples of layout optimization include menus [2] and widgets [10].

This paper addresses a significant limitation of the presently used class of methods. So far only *random search* methods have been used. They iteratively sample the solution space [22] and consult a model of users' performance weighted by a frequency distribution of their actions. Common methods include local search and simulated annealing. This "black box" approach is convenient, because good solutions can be found quickly and no assumption must be made about the objective function. The drawback is that such methods offer no guarantee for finding the global optimum, nor do they inform distance to it. Even *if* the global optimum was found, the designer can never know this for sure. Moreover, designers have no objective criterion for stopping the optimization and no confidence that the best-found design cannot be beaten.

UIST 2014, October 5–8, 2014, Honolulu, HI, USA.

ACM 978-1-4503-3069-5/14/10 ...$15.00.
http://dx.doi.org/10.1145/2642918.2647382

This paper contributes by studying *exact methods* as a complementary approach. They use a structured (non-random) search approach that guarantees the optimal solution in finite time. Identifying the globally optimal design is desirable particularly for commonly used UIs where even small changes can have a large impact. Moreover, during search, exact methods estimate bounds. In other words, they inform the designer that the best-found solution is within a certain percent from the optimum. This increases confidence and pre-empts fruitless search.

Given these benefits, why were exact methods not previously used in HCI? Until a decade ago it was easy to ignore them because global optimization of assignment problems with more than 20 items was held impossible. The simplest formulation of the virtual keyboard problem with 26 keyslots has a search space of $4 * 10^{26}$. However, efficiency has improved from 1988 to 2004 by a factor of 5,280,000 [5]. It is thus now possible to solve more meaningful problems also in HCI.

The present paper is a proof-of-concept study targeting keyboard design. Although our longer-term goal is to develop exact methods for a wider class of UI design tasks, keyboards offer a solid starting point for our research. It is the most extensively studied case of UI optimization and allows benchmarking the benefits. Moreover, even slight improvements in keyboard layouts not only improve productivity [4] but can also enhance ergonomics and learnability [17]. Furthermore, the case is analytically favorable, because the task and the objective function involved are relatively well-understood and straightforward.

We formulate various letter assignment tasks as *integer programming* (IP) problems [24]. Since there is no unique formulation, we investigate a few models w.r.t. trade-offs such as computational efficiency, memory requirements, and the strength of bound. To solve them, we build on a standard solution called *branch-and-bound*. Here the idea is to structure the search space as a tree and construct an "oracle" that provides bounds that tell which subtrees (branches) to disregard (prune). We show techniques for branching and bounding that are sufficiently efficient to improve over the state-of-the-art in keyboard optimization. We then demonstrate these capabilities across three keyboard optimization cases from previous literature. Our approach is directly usable in the available IP solvers such as CPLEX and Gurobi.

BACKGROUND: THE LETTER ASSIGNMENT PROBLEM

Given n letters and n keyslots, the task of the letter assignment problem is to minimize the average cost $c_{k\ell}$ of selecting letter ℓ after k weighted by the bigram probability $p_{k\ell}$:

$$\min \sum_k \sum_\ell p_{k\ell} \cdot c_{k\ell} \quad (1)$$

It is an instance of the Koopmans-Beckman Problem [15, 6], which is NP-hard. As we will see later, this problem can be modeled with a quadratic function on binary variables. Thus, it belongs to a broad class of problems called *quadratic assignment problem* (QAP) where the goal is to minimize the total pair-wise interaction cost [22, 24].

Except for a few papers using heuristic cost functions (e.g., [9]), the *Fitts-bigram energy* is used (see also [4]). Here, the probabilities $p_{\ell k}$ are given by a bigram distribution of representative corpus of text. The cost $c_{\ell k}$ is given by Fitts' law (e.g., [19]):

$$MT = a + b \log_2 \left(\frac{D_{k\ell}}{W_\ell} + 1 \right), \quad (2)$$

where $D_{\ell k}$ is distance between the two keys containing ℓ and k, and W_ℓ is the width of the button that contains ℓ. Fitts law is best understood as an estimate of movement performance achievable by skilled users. The cost for repeating the same letter is assumed to be constant, i.e. $c_{\ell\ell} = c$. Since the optimum assignment is not affected by the choice of a, b, c, the task collapses to distance minimization [25]. We later also consider a task that is not about distance minimization: touch typing with ten fingers on a physical keyboard.

Previous Work Using Random Search Methods

Previous work has exclusively used random search methods to solve this problem. These methods iteratively randomly sample the neighborhood of a given solution. The variants differ in sampling strategy and update procedure.

1) *Local search* starts from a random position in the search space and randomly samples its neighborhood. A recent example is the 26 letter trapezoidal keyboard of Dunlop et al. [8]. **2)** *Metropolis–Hastings algorithm* is a variant of local search that uses a probabilistic decision criterion that allows it to escape from local minima. A known example is the hexagonal keyboard of Zhai et al. optimized for stylus tapping on PDAs [25]. **3)** *Simulated annealing* is an adaptation of the Metropolis–Hastings algorithm that uses a cooling schedule that is an analogue with thermodynamic free energy. A recent example is the split keyboard of Oulasvirta et al. optimized for two-thumb typing performance [20]. **4)** *Genetic algorithms* represent layouts as "genotypes" that are competitively evolved by mutations and cross-overs. A recent example is the physical keyboard layout of Goettl et al. optimized using a heuristic cost model [11]. **5)** *Ant colony optimization* is based on a biological metaphor of an ant colony cooperatively foraging for food. The method was recently used to improve the hexagonal keyboard of Zhai et al. [2].

OVERVIEW OF THE APPROACH

We formulate the QAP as an integer programming (IP) problem in order to then study it using a standard solution: branch-and-bound. The QAP has been studied extensively in the discrete optimization community. The letter assignment problem was among the earliest problems studied within this context [21]. We here provide an overview of the approach and present technical details of our solution in the next section. A detailed review of the work is beyond the scope of this paper. The interested reader is referred to the survey of Loiola et al. [18].

The basic idea of IP is to describe the design space by *equations and inequalities*, also called constraints. The task of an Integer Programming Problem is to decide whether there is a solution that satisfies all constraints and that assigns only integers to the variables. This problem is also called Integer Feasibility Problem. Already the restriction to linear constraints and moreover to binary variables is NP-complete.[1] Though this sounds discouraging, it also shows the great modeling power that comes with IP: there are IP models for every problem in NP. Moreover, there are efficient solvers that solve integer programs much faster than a brute force search in practice. A key concept is a divide-and-conquer strategy called *branch-and-bound*, which we will briefly discuss after modeling the letter assignment problem as an IP. To this end, we present how to model keypress times as a quadratic function.

Formulation of the QAP as IP

The letter assignment problem can be reformulated as an IP problem with a quadratic objective function [6]. Let $x_{\ell j}$ be a binary variable which is 1 if letter ℓ is assigned to keyslot j and 0 otherwise. Hence, we obtain $c_{k\ell} = \sum_i \sum_j t_{ij} \cdot x_{ki} \cdot x_{\ell j}$, where t_{ij} represents the movement time from key i to key j, e.g. as in Eq. (2). By substituting $c_{k\ell}$ in Eq. (1), the goal becomes to find the

$$\min \sum_{i=1}^{n} \sum_{j=1}^{n} \sum_{k=1}^{n} \sum_{\ell=1}^{n} p_{k\ell} t_{ij} x_{ki} x_{\ell j} \quad (3)$$

subject to

$$\sum_{\ell=1}^{n} x_{\ell j} = 1 \qquad \forall j \in \{1, \ldots, n\} \quad (4)$$

$$\sum_{j=1}^{n} x_{\ell j} = 1 \qquad \forall \ell \in \{1, \ldots, n\} \quad (5)$$

$$x_{\ell j} \in \{0, 1\} \qquad \forall \ell, j \in \{1, \ldots, n\} \quad (6)$$

[1] Note that the keyboard optimization problem is trivially feasible: The hardness comes in when we ask whether there is a layout of at most a certain cost.

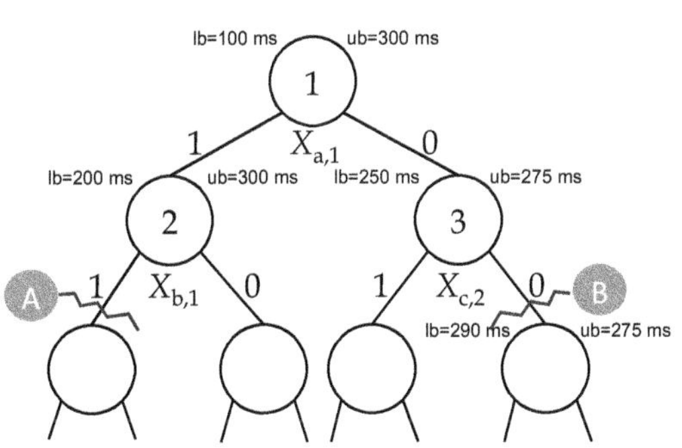

Figure 1: Branch-and-bound divides the search space (all keyboard layouts) into a tree (branch) that can be pruned based on (A) infeasibility of solutions and (B) bounds. lb and ub refer to the best known lower and upper bounds for the subtree rooted at the corresponding node.

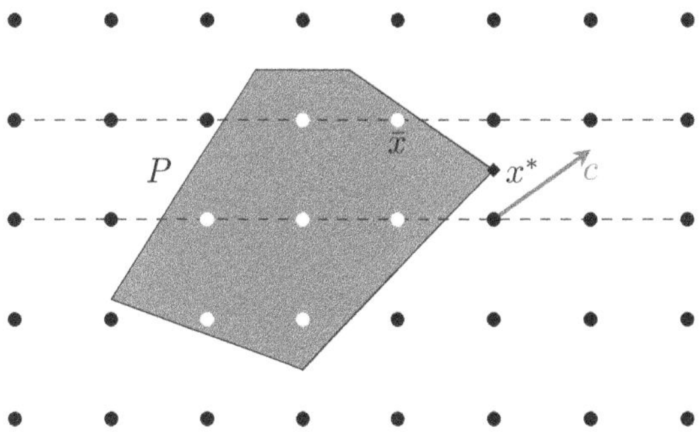

Figure 2: The gray area together with its boundary shows the linear relaxation, which contains the feasible integral solutions (white). x^* is the optimum solution over the relaxation w.r.t. the linear objective function $c^T x$, whereas $\bar{x}$ is the optimum among all integral solutions.

In other words, each slot must contain exactly one letter due to the constraints (4) and each letter must be assigned to exactly one slot because of the constraints (5). The so-called *integrality constraints* (6) reflect the restriction to binary solutions as required at the beginning of this subsection.

Branch-and-Bound

Branch-and-bound solves the QAP by performing an *implicit* exhaustive search. We imagine the search as a tree, where we make a decision at each node to partition the search space. Figure 1 provides an overview.

For the sake of presentation, we first describe a simple branching strategy, which fixes one variable in each iteration. At each node of the tree, we select a letter and assign it to an empty slot, e.g. letter 'a' to slot 1 at node 1 in Fig. 1. Such a decision is represented by one of the two children of a node, whereas the other child means the opposite, i.e. we forbid this letter-slot-combination for the corresponding subtree.

Suppose that we have already found a feasible binary solution with an objective value of z, for example by a random assignment of the letters to the keyslots, by some heuristics, or by branching down to a leave of the tree. If we now had an "oracle" that told us at some node that all feasible integral solutions in the subtree rooted at this node have objective values of *at least* z, then we could simply discard this entire subtree because it will not offer an improvement. This leads to two kinds of pruning that can be done: 1) based on infeasibility, e.g., two letters cannot be assigned to the same slot as shown in case A in Fig. 1, and 2) on bounds, e.g., as illustrated in case B in Fig. 1 where the lower bound is worse than the objective value of the incumbent.

It remains to show that there are effective methods to compute good lower bounds for the integer solutions in a subtree.

Relaxation

There is a systematic approach to obtain lower bounds for an IP when the objective function and all constraints are linear. Before we show how to obtain such a setting in our case, we illustrate its benefits for branch and bound.

A system of linear constraints describes a closed convex set, which is bounded in our case (illustrated by the gray area in Fig. 2). The integral points are shown as small disks, which are white when they satisfy the linear constraints and thus correspond to feasible solutions for the IP. Since the set of feasible IP solutions is contained in the set of points that satisfy the linear constraints, the latter is called *Linear Programming relaxation* or LP relaxation. Moreover, this overestimation of the feasible solutions implies that the minimum of a function over the IP solutions is at least the minimum taken over the relaxation. Hence, an optimum solution over the relaxation yields a mathematical guarantee for the objective value of any IP solution. The difference between the optimum objective value of the IP and of the LP relaxation is called *integrality gap*.

Finding an optimum of the LP relaxation is a convex optimization problem, which can be solved efficiently, e.g. by Interior Point Methods (cf. Chapter 9 in [3]). If a variable of an optimum LP solution, say $x^*_\bullet$, is not integer, it can be used for branching, which splits the problem into two independent subproblems. That is, the set of feasible solutions is divided into disjoint pieces. In the example of Fig. 2, these are the parts on and below the bottom dashed line, on and above the top dashed line, and the strip between the two dashed lines, where the latter does not contain integer points in its interior and thus can be discarded in the search. This yields two new child nodes in the branching tree with the new constraints $x_\bullet \leq \lfloor x^*_\bullet \rfloor$ and $x_\bullet \geq \lceil x^*_\bullet \rceil$, respectively. If all variables are constrained between 0 and 1 as in the QAP, this amounts to setting the branching variable to either 0 or 1 in the respective subproblems. The interested reader is referred to the textbook [24] for further details about this method.

LINEARIZATIONS

We present two linear formulations that are equivalent to the QAP. However, they differ when the integrality constraints $x_{\ell j} \in \{0, 1\}$ are relaxed to $0 \leq x_{\ell j} \leq 1$.

In a nutshell, the first formulation yields stronger lower bounds, but requires much more space and takes longer to solve in each node of the branch-and-bound tree. The second one is much smaller and quicker to solve, but the lower bounds are very weak. We propose to solve both IPs in parallel to use the former to obtain good lower bounds, and the latter one to quickly explore the search space allowing the solver's built-in heuristics to improve the upper bound rapidly.

Reformulation-Linearization Technique

The basic idea is to substitute all non-linear terms by new variables and thus obtain a linear objective function. That is, we introduce $y_{ijk\ell} := x_{ki} \cdot x_{\ell j}$. To obtain linear constraints, Adam and Johnson [1] observed that $\sum_k y_{ijk\ell} = x_{\ell j} \cdot \sum_k x_{ki} = x_{\ell j}$. The intuition behind these additional constraints is based on the following observations. If $x_{\ell j} = 0$ then all products that contain $x_{\ell j}$ and thus all the corresponding y-variables must be 0 as well. Since slot i contains exactly one letter, $y_{ijk\ell}$ is 1 for exactly one k and 0 otherwise, provided that $x_{\ell j} = 1$. A similar arguments holds for the sum over all slots i. Moreover, the products $x_{ki} \cdot x_{\ell j}$ are non-negative and commutative. This yields the IP formulation

$$\min \sum_{i=1}^{n} \sum_{j=1}^{n} \sum_{k=1}^{n} \sum_{\ell=1}^{n} p_{k\ell} t_{ij} y_{ijk\ell} \tag{7}$$

subject to

$$\sum_{\ell=1}^{n} x_{\ell j} = 1 \qquad \forall j \in \{1, \dots, n\} \tag{8}$$

$$\sum_{j=1}^{n} x_{\ell j} = 1 \qquad \forall \ell \in \{1, \dots, n\} \tag{9}$$

$$x_{\ell j} \in \{0, 1\} \qquad \forall \ell, j \in \{1, \dots, n\} \tag{10}$$

$$\sum_{k=1}^{n} y_{ijk\ell} = x_{\ell j} \qquad \forall i, j, \ell \in \{1, \dots, n\} \tag{11}$$

$$\sum_{i=1}^{n} y_{ijk\ell} = x_{\ell j} \qquad \forall j, k, \ell \in \{1, \dots, n\} \tag{12}$$

$$0 \leq y_{ijk\ell} = y_{ji\ell k} \qquad \forall i, j, k, \ell \in \{1, \dots, n\} \tag{13}$$

such that all binary solutions are feasible assignments and their cost is the same as in the quadratic case. It is also called level-1 *Reformulation-Linearization Technique* (RLT1). As the name suggests there are also higher levels of this techniques considered in literature (up to 3), but their size grows with a higher polynomial in n. Thus their memory requirements are much more demanding and as of yet impractical for $n > 27$ [12]. Since even the size of RLT1 is quite challenging for optimizing layouts with $n = 34$ characters, we do not yet consider RLT2 and RLT3 in this work.

Kaufman-Broeckx Linearization

We also investigate a formulation by Kaufman and Broeckx [14] that is minimal in terms of new variables. That is, instead of the n^4 variables $y_{ki\ell j}$ only n^2 variables

$$w_{\ell j} = x_{\ell j} \sum_{k=1}^{n} \sum_{i=1}^{n} p_{k\ell} t_{ij} x_{ki}$$

are introduced. Thus the objective function becomes

$$\min \sum_{\ell=1}^{n} \sum_{j=1}^{n} w_{ij}.$$

If $x_{\ell j} = 1$, then the contribution of $w_{\ell j}$ to the objective is a linear function, and it is 0 if $x_{\ell j} = 0$. Hence, it suffices to add the constraints

$$w_{\ell j} \geq 0$$

$$w_{\ell j} \geq \sum_{k=1}^{n} \sum_{i=1}^{n} p_{k\ell} t_{ij} x_{ki} - a_{ij} \cdot (1 - x_{\ell j})$$

with $a_{\ell j} = \sum_{k=1}^{n} \sum_{i=1}^{n} p_{k\ell} t_{ij}$. In fact, any upper bound on $\sum_{k=1}^{n} \sum_{i=1}^{n} p_{k\ell} t_{ij}$ will do for $a_{\ell j}$ such that the right-hand side is at most 0 whenever $x_{\ell j} = 0$ because in any optimum solution $w_{\ell j}$ will be tight at the maximum of both right-hand sides.

This formulation is much smaller in size and thus much easier to solve than RLT1, but the achieved lower bounds are much weaker. It can be strengthened by replacing the non-negativity constraints with the Gilmore-Lawler Bound [16].

Case: Symmetric Cost Function

We start by considering the Fitts-bigram energy case given in Eq. 1. It covers virtual keyboards operated by moving a single end-effector (e.g., stylus, finger, mouse) (e.g., [4, 8, 19, 25]). In this case, the instance becomes entirely symmetric by replacing the probabilities with $p'_{k\ell} := (p_{k\ell} + p_{\ell k})/2$. We thereby obtain a symmetric quadratic form as objective function. This symmetry can be exploited to reduce the size of the formulations by a constant factor.

Case: Non-symmetric Cost Function

We encounter a non-symmetric cost function in cases where the time cost of returning from slot ℓ to k is not equivalent to that from k to ℓ. An example that we later examine is the ten-finger typing case. Here, typing "F" after "I" receives a different predicted movement time than typing "I" after "F." In these cases, we use the formulations as described above.

RESULTS

To evaluate the approach, we consider three previously studied cases of keyboard optimization. Our goal is not to "compete" against random search. Rather the studies should be understood as proofs-of-concept for the two main advantages of IP: improved chance of finding the global optimum and the estimation of bounds.

Figure 3 shows the winner layouts and provides an overview of the optimization tasks. The cases differ in 1) keyboard layout, 2) the size of search space, 3) objective function, and 4) the existence of previous optimized layouts. In all cases, we minimize movement time and assume constant button width and no whitespace between buttons. Two of the keyboard types (a, c) are actually in use by billions of users.

For each case, we used one computer with 32 Intel Xeon 2.70Ghz processors (16 physical, 32 virtual cores) and 256GB RAM. Both formulations for a case were solved in parallel as proposed. Gurobi 5.6 was used with the Interior Point Method to solve the root relaxation. The results reported here were obtained within two days.

Case 1: 26 Letter Trapezoid Layout for Touchscreens

This case considers the trapezoid-shaped virtual keyboard common on smartphones with touchscreens. The search space is 4×10^{26}. A previous case of this layout is given in the multi-objective case of Dunlop and Levine [8].

Our objective function uses the Zhai-Hunter-Smith variant of Fitts' law [25] ($a = 0.0, b = 0.084, c = 0.127$). The bigram distribution updates previously used distributions. We combined two distributions representative of modern text entry with smartphones, weighed 50/50: the mobile email set [23] and the NUS SMS corpus [7]. We assume that the spacebar is fixed to the elongated key on the bottom. The baselines are Qwerty (33.65 wpm) and the Dvorak Simplified Keyboard (DSK) (33.97 wpm). Computation was carried out using the symmetric case described above.

The winner keyboard, presented in Figure 3 was computed within 34 hours. The predicted wpm for the winner keyboard is 43.10, which is within 4% of the global optimum. It is an improvement of 28% over Qwerty.

Case 2: The Zhai-Hunter-Smith Hexagonal Layout

Our second case considers the hexagonal layout familiar from the work of Zhai et al. [25]. The search space is 9×10^{30}. This is a keyboard operated on PDAs by using a stylus.

In our task, 29 characters are considered as shown in Figure 3. For direct comparison of results, we use the same objective function of Zhai et al. It was also used in a follow-up paper by Bailly et al. that found the improved Justhci layout [2]. The alphabetical, Metropolis [25], and Justhci [2] keyboards achieve predicted rates of 32.37, 42.02, and 42.38 wpm, respectively. For IP solution, we use the symmetric case described above.

The winner keyboard, presented in Figure 3 was computed within 15 hours and lies within 7% of the global optimum. Unlike in Justhci and Metropolis, the spacebar is not in the middle. In comparison to Metropolis, not only letters E, A , I, but also O, is close to the spacebar. The predicted wpm is 42.65. It is an improvement of 0.6% over justhci, 1.5% over metropolis, and 32 % over the alphabetical layout.

Case 3: 3-Row Physical Keyboard for Ten-Finger Typing

Our third case considers the full 34 character 3-row physical keyboard. The case is motivated as there are aspirations to challenge Qwerty and optimize layouts for different languages [9]. Our task involves the 26 letters and the 8 most frequent characters in our corpus. The search space is 3×10^{38}.

As the movement model, we use a previously ignored regression model of ten-finger typing [13]. The Hiraga model considers various effects of expert touch typists: finger and hand differences, and effects of moving fingers up/down on the key columns. More precisely, it predicts movement time t_{ij} (msec) from keyslot i to j as

$$t_{ij} = 185.8 - 40h + 18.3r - 11.0f + 0.154R + 1.07F, \quad (14)$$

where h, r, f, are parameters describing hand transition, row transition, and finger transition, respectively, and R and F are weights for row and fingers. See the original paper for values. The caveat of this model is that the parameters were obtained based on a single expert typist. However, its predictions for the difference between Qwerty and DSK matches well with empirical literature [17]. We are not aware of validating evidence for the existing heuristic models (e.g., [9, 11]).

As the frequency distribution, we use a selection of chat room data, mobile email, newspaper English, SMS data, and Tweets, with uniform weighing[2]. Our baselines are the alphabetical, Qwerty, and DSK layouts, which receive 74.49, 73.21, and 76.59 wpm, respectively. For solution, we used the non-symmetric approach described above.

The winner keyboard, presented in Figure 3, was found within 7 minutes. The predicted wpm for the keyboard is 78.36. It is an improvement of 7.0% over Qwerty, and 2.3% over DSK. This is computed to within 0.95% of the global optimum. We consider this a significant achievement given the size of the search space. The layout has a prominent DSK-like feature: the letters on the middle row have a large overlap with those in DSK. Another interesting feature is that spacebar and period are next to each other.

DISCUSSION

Our long-term goal is a general framework for using IP in UI optimization together with random search methods. The challenge is that although IP is already a general optimization approach, performance is heavily dependent on the modeling of case-specific properties and the choice of methods. The results presented in this paper for keyboards are promising. Our techniques allowed for solving the "classic" 26 letter Fitts-bigram case to a (guaranteed) 4 % range from optimality and approaching optimality to a 1 % in the case of physical keyboards, even if the search space was much larger. To our knowledge, this is the first time that optimality bounds have been presented in user interface optimization in HCI.

In the future, IP should be extended to cover other important factors in keyboard optimization. One of them is error correction: Here the task is to make the local neighborhood of a key as statistically unambigous as possible [8]. Another is predictive text entry: Here the task is to assign letters on a reduced-key grid in order to minimize the number of keypresses per character. The third challenge is to consider how users at various level of expertise should be taken into account. In contrast, existing cost functions consider only expert performance. The fourth is the varying size of keys. Here the challenge is to optimize not only the positions of letters but also their individual size [25]. We presently see no reason why IP could not be extended to cover these problems. However, success will depend analytical work to find efficient models for IP solvers.

We support further research efforts by offering instructions on our project homepage for further cases in keyboard optimization. The page informs how to replicate our results and

[2] All distributions and case data are released on the project hompage.

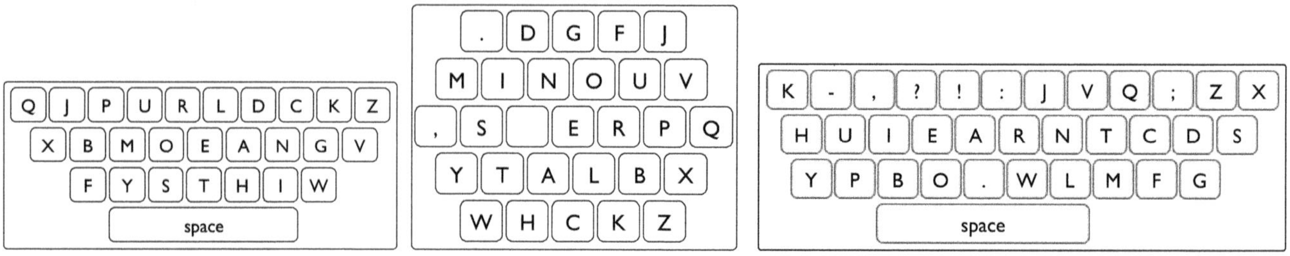

(a) Virtual trapezoidal: Pred. 43.10 wpm (b) Virtual hexagonal: Pred. 42.65 wpm (c) Physical 3-row standard: Pred 78.36 wpm

Figure 3: The best keyboard designs identified for three keyboard optimization tasks.

extend the models to other problems by using familiar logical terms and clauses.

CONCLUSION

Because keyboard design problems often include enormous search spaces, it is important to research efficient and appropriate optimization methods. This paper has presented an integer programming (IP) approach and applied it to three cases of keyboard layout optimization. The results are favorable, showing clear improvements achieved over previous baselines. Moreover, IP can inform the designer on how far from the optimum a given design is, or how much a particular decision is going to cost. Our results show that some very large problems can be computed to a 1% margin from optimality. We emphasize that IP is complementary to other approaches. That is, we may run them in parallel and layouts might be injected as new incumbents in the branch-and-bound process. Moreover, standard solvers like CPLEX and Gurobi offer APIs to interact with the search via callbacks. In turn, heuristic approaches benefit from IP because the latter reports a guarantee for the quality of the solution. In the future, we aim to extend this approach to other layout problems in HCI.

ACKNOWLEDGEMENTS

This research was funded by the Max Planck Center for Visual Computing and Communication and the Cluster of Excellence for Multimodal Computing and Interaction at Saarland University. Code and data are released on the project homepage at http://resources.mpi-inf.mpg.de/keyboardoptimization/.

REFERENCES

1. Adams, W. P., and Johnson, T. A. Improved linear programming-based lower bounds for the quadratic assignment problem. *DIMACS 16* (1994), 43–75.
2. Bailly, G., et al. Menuoptimizer: Interactive optimization of menu systems. In *Proc. UIST*, ACM (2013), 331–342.
3. Bertsimas, D., and Tsitsiklis, J. *Introduction to Linear Optimization*, 1st ed. Athena Scientific, 1997.
4. Bi, X., Smith, B. A., and Zhai, S. Multilingual touchscreen keyboard design and optimization. *Human–Computer Interaction 27*, 4 (2012), 352–382.
5. Bixby, R., and Rothberg, E. Progress in computational mixed integer programming. *Annals of Operations Research 149*, 1 (2007), 37–41.
6. Burkard, R. E., and Offermann, D. M. J. Entwurf von schreibmaschinentastaturen mittels quadratischer zuordnungsprobleme. *Zeitschrift für Operations Research 21*, 4 (1977), B121–B132.
7. Chen, T., and Kan, M.-Y. Creating a live, public short message service corpus: The nus sms corpus. *Language Resources and Evaluation 47*, 2 (2013), 299–335.
8. Dunlop, M., and Levine, J. Multidimensional pareto optimization of touchscreen keyboards for speed, familiarity and improved spell checking. In *Proc. CHI*, ACM (2012), 2669–2678.
9. Eggers, J., et al. Optimization of the keyboard arrangement problem using an ant colony algorithm. *European Journal of Operational Research 148*, 3 (2003), 672–686.
10. Gajos, K., and Weld, D. S. Supple: automatically generating user interfaces. In *Proc. IUI*, ACM (2004), 93–100.
11. Goettl, J. S., Brugh, A. W., and Julstrom, B. A. Call me e-mail: arranging the keyboard with a permutation-coded genetic algorithm. In *Proc. Applied Computing*, ACM (2005), 947–951.
12. Hahn, P. M., et al. A level-3 reformulation-linearization technique-based bound for the quadratic assignment problem. *INFORMS J. on Computing 24*, 2 (Apr. 2012), 202–209.
13. Hiraga, Y., et al. An assignment of key-codes for a japanese character keyboard. In *Proc. Computational Linguistics*, ACL (1980), 249–256.
14. Kaufman, L., and Broeckx, F. An algorithm for the quadratic assignment problem using bender's decomposition. *European Journal of Operational Research 2*, 3 (1978), 207–211.
15. Koopmans, T. C., and Beckmann, M. Assignment problems and the location of economic activities. *Econometrica: Journal of the Econometric Society* (1957), 53–76.
16. Lawler, E. L., and Wood, D. E. Branch-and-bound methods: A survey. *Operations research 14*, 4 (1966), 699–719.
17. Lewis, J., Potosnak, K., and Magyar, R. Keys and keyboards. *Handbook of Human-Computer Interaction* (1997), 1285–1315.
18. Loiola, E. M., de Abreu, N. M. M., Boaventura-Netto, P. O., Hahn, P., and Querido, T. A survey for the quadratic assignment problem (2007). 657–690.
19. MacKenzie, I. S., and Zhang, S. X. The design and evaluation of a high-performance soft keyboard. In *Proc. CHI*, ACM (1999), 25–31.
20. Oulasvirta, A., et al. Improving two-thumb text entry on touchscreen devices. In *Proc. CHI*, ACM (2013), 2765–2774.
21. Pollatschek, M., Gershoni, N., and Radday, Y. Optimization of the typewritter keyboard by computer simulation. *Angewandte Informatik 10* (1976), 438–439.
22. Rao, S. S. *Engineering optimization*. John Wiley & Sons, 2009.
23. Vertanen, K., and Kristensson, P. O. A versatile dataset for text entry evaluations based on genuine mobile emails. In *Proc. MobileHCI'11*, ACM (2011), 295–298.
24. Wolsey, L. A. *Integer Programming*, vol. 42. Wiley New York, 1998.
25. Zhai, S., Hunter, M., and Smith, B. A. Performance optimization of virtual keyboards. *Human–Computer Interaction 17*, 2-3 (2002), 229–269.

Designer's Augmented Reality Toolkit, Ten Years Later: Implications for New Media Authoring Tools

Maribeth Gandy, Blair MacIntyre
Georgia Institute of Technology
85 5th St NW, Atlanta, GA 30308
maribeth@imtc.gatech.edu, blair@cc.gatech.edu

ABSTRACT
The Designer's Augmented Reality Toolkit (DART) was an augmented (AR) and mixed reality (MR) authoring tool targeted at new media designers. It was released in 2003 and was heavily used by a diverse population of creators for the next several years [31]. Ten years later, we approached a group of users to collect reflections on their use of DART, the artifacts they produced, their subsequent AR/MR authoring, their thoughts on the challenges of AR/MR authoring in general, and the state of modern tools. In this paper we present the findings from in-depth interviews with these DART developers and other AR experts. Their reflections provide insights on how to successfully engage non-technologists with new media and the challenges they face during authoring, the unique requirements of new media authoring, and how modern tools are still not meeting the needs of this type of author, highlighting where additional research is needed.

Author Keywords
Augmented Reality; Mixed Reality; Authoring Tools; Evaluation; Practitioners

ACM Classification Keywords
I.3.7 [Computer Graphics]: Three-Dimensional Graphics and Realism—Virtual Reality; H.5.2 [Information Interfaces and Presentation]: Multimedia Information Systems—Evaluation/methodology

INTRODUCTION
The Designer's Augmented Reality Toolkit (DART) was an augmented (AR) and mixed reality (MR) authoring tool designed for use by designers/non-technologists that was first released in 2003 and was heavily used by a diverse population of creators for the next several years. The inspiration for DART was our work creating AR experiences in collaboration with non-technologists in the late 1990s and early 2000s, which highlighted the need for authoring tools focused on the workflows and expertise of those outside the AR research field. DART was designed at a time when we and others in the AR research community were moving from working with "AR as technology" to thinking about "AR as new medium."

Because we were interested in supporting new media designers, DART was created as an authoring tool on top of Macromedia Director, a popular multimedia authoring environment at the time [18]. While creating DART, we first included the nuts-and-bolts technical components to support AR (e.g., live video, vision and sensor-based tracking). We also designed features that were AR workflow focused (e.g., sketch-based prototyping [37], capture/playback [14], and Wizard-of-Oz (WoZ) support [13]). The main contributions of this work were the identification of the unique requirements for AR development and the creation of guidelines for future AR authoring tools. DART manifested these guidelines via a set of design process focused components that we developed over the four years of DART development.

The principal paper on DART was published at UIST 2004 [31]. The paper discussed these key process-based features and presented early applications, authored internally, that exercised DART features and explored their utility.

While reflecting on projects done internally was valuable, the most significant feedback regarding DART would come later from our large community of external developers. There were three major releases of the toolkit, and we recorded 11,573 downloads by 4,280 unique users by November 2011. Although the last release of Director was in 2008, people are still downloading, and possibly actively using DART. Even in 2011, there were 377 downloads and we still receive the occasional support request on our developer mailing list. We have anecdotal evidence that DART was used by a significant number of people for a large number of successful projects. Our mailing list activity shows hundreds of posts with developers asking for help and requesting features. Web and YouTube searches revealed DART projects that we never knew existed.

However, these statistics and anecdotes do not provide the insights on DART that could inform the design of future authoring tools. In 2012, we approached a group of DART users to collect reflections on their use of DART and their

UIST '14, October 05 - 08 2014, Honolulu, HI, USA

http://dx.doi.org/10.1145/2642918.2647369

experiences with AR/MR authoring. In this paper we present the findings from in-depth interviews with eight external DART developers (see Table 1). They worked with the tool from our alpha version in 2003 until the present day. The majority of their projects were developed from 2004-2008. We also interviewed three AR experts that did not use DART, but who have a depth of experience that provides perspectives on AR authoring. Overall these participants were chosen to represent the full range of AR creators from those focused heavily on technology contributions to artists using AR as one of many tools in their exploration of media.

While we collected extensive feedback on the specific features of our tool, our goal was not to validate DART itself. This paper concentrates on the feedback that specifically sheds light on the needs of non-technologists in AR/MR authoring, their strategies and approaches when building complex software systems for all stages of process (from ideation to deployment), their thoughts on DART in the context of modern authoring/tools and the current state of AR. We have synthesized their reflections to highlight the requirements for authoring tools in general, many of which are not specific to AR. The insights gleaned from this study are meaningful to any type of new media authoring that utilizes physical space, location, tangible interfaces, sophisticated hardware devices, or display via head-mount or projection. Notably, some of the projects the interviewees built are not purely AR, including a tangible user interface (TUI) installation [4], virtual reality, and live video effects for performance [34].

Contributions

In the research community, it is rare to reflect on long-term use of a research toolkit, and contextualize it relative to next-generation tools. We are fortunate that DART was in use as AR technology matured and that many in the DART community transitioned from these early tools to more modern technology. While some of our findings many not seem earthshattering, we hope our study serves as inspiration for more researchers to revisit and reflect on their toolkits and developer communities after long-term use. The following are the contributions made by this paper

- Insights on how to successfully engage non-technologists with new media.
- Reflections into the unique requirements of AR authoring, which have implications for toolkits designed for other types of new technologies/media (e.g. TUIs, VR, ubicomp, and wearable computing).
- Information on how modern tools are still not meeting the needs of this type of author, highlighting where additional research is needed.

RELATED WORK

In this section we present a short survey of the most influential related work in the categories of AR authoring, other new media authoring tools, and authoring tool evaluation

AR Authoring Tools

Over the past twenty-five years there have been a large number of AR authoring tools. Projects such as Studierstube [44] the ARToolkit [7], Tinmith [35], Coterie [30], and DWARF [32] required the application developer to work at a fairly low level, with languages like C or C++. Studierstube leveraged OpenTracker, which eased requirements for hardware access. Coterie was used to create some of the early AR applications such as the Touring Machine. The ARToolkit was also combined with existing tools such as Touch Designer [5] and Adobe Flash [17] to make a tool accessible to designers. COMPOSAR was a rapid prototyping tool built using the ARToolkit that supported visual programming [46].

Subsequent projects confronted authoring from the other end of the spectrum, creating environments to simplify the creation of AR systems with minimal programming, which were more accessible to non-technologists. Examples include APRIL [26], AMIRE [1], CATOMIR [48], ImageTclAR [36], and MARS [20]. More recently, researchers and companies have begun leveraging game engines such as Unity3D for their AR authoring [33][38].

Authoring Tools for Other Domains

Other relevant authoring work can be found outside the AR community. The Context Toolkit provided developers with easy access to contextual information and operations to manage it [11]. The Phidget toolkit [19] was aimed at making tangible devices available to designers. Alice [9] was focused on lowering the threshold of entry into the world of 3D graphics and VR programming. The Designer's Outpost project found that web designers often used pens, paper, walls, and tables during the early phases of design [22]. The motivation for our use of sketch-based content for early user experience testing also comes from the work of Landay and his collaborators (Landay & Myers, 2001). The Wizard of Oz components in DART were inspired by "Suede," which supported informal prototyping of speech interface [23] and by Li et al.'s WoZ prototyping of location-based applications [27].

Evaluating Authoring Tools

In "Stuck in the Middle", Edwards et al. discuss the challenges of evaluating infrastructure software [16]. The evaluation of end-user applications is a well-explored field, but different approaches are required when measuring the value of toolkits. While a toolkit can be assessed by its technical capabilities, ultimately, what matters is the value to the end-users. They describe the evaluation of toolkits indirectly through the context of use and through applications built with the tool. Other toolkits have been evaluated by studying their use by target developers. Some were used in the classroom setting and the resulting student projects were evaluated [11,19,21]. Others, such as Designer's Outpost and Denim, were used by their target professionals (e.g., web developers) [28,22]. Some were released, like DART, to the wider community [11,19,21].

DART Background

The DART system is composed of a set of Lingo scripts (i.e., the scripting language of Director) and an Xtra plug-in (that provided low level device access) that extended Macromedia Director to support the development of MR applications. DART provided programmers with pre-built scripting components in the Lingo scripting language that could be used as-is, modified, or extended by the developer. There were "actors" which represented the content/augmentations for an application (e.g., video, 3D models, sounds, HUD elements etc.). The development of a DART application progressed by placing components on the Director score (see Fig. 1), editing/creating Lingo scripts, and/or extending the Xtra. More detailed information can be found in various publications [18,31] or on the DART website [10].

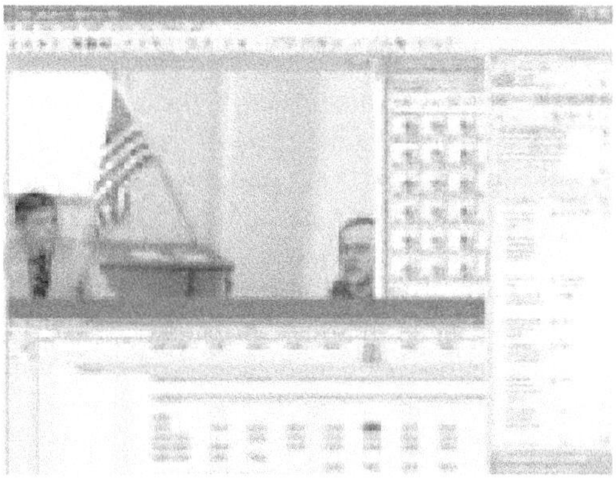

Figure 1. An example work session in DART (Four Angry Men [29]). The entire score for FAM is visible at the bottom, including nine scenes comprised of "actors" (each scene is a column in the score). The "stage" (live application) is visible, as is the content "cast" for a video actor, and a property page for a script.

THE USER STUDY

Over the period of several months we searched through our mailing list archives as well as the web to identify a set of DART users to approach. We then performed in-depth interviews with eight external DART developers ("external" is defined as users that were not part of the DART team. Two participants have or had a connection to our university. Four were affiliated with a major research team at a university in Canada. Two had no linkage to either institution). They worked with the tool from our alpha version in 2003 till present day. The majority of their projects were developed from 2004-2008. We also interviewed three AR experts that did not use DART, but who have a depth of experience that provides additional perspectives on AR authoring. Overall these eleven participants represent the full range of AR creators from those focused heavily on technology and computer science

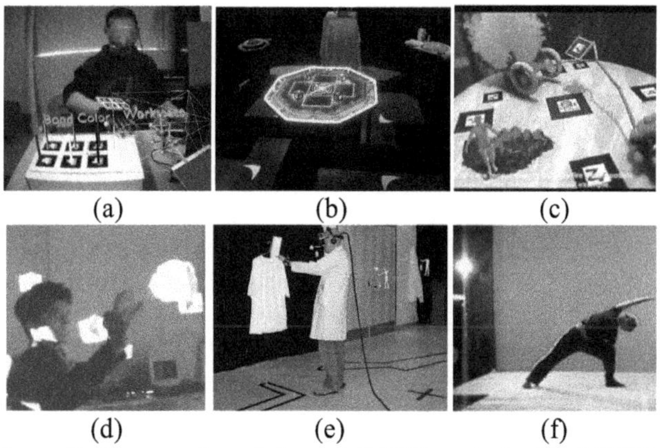

Figure 2. Images of participants' DART projects (a) (TECH) Experimental platform. Co-located collaboration from the builder's view (b) (NOVICE) A view of the installation with the center TUI table and (c) an AR view of the Greek age "Prometheus" kiosk (d) (ARTIST) A "Multi- Sequential Poetry" user reaches for an augmented cube (e) (DIRECTOR) A visitor interacting and (f) a dancer performs as Woyzek on the stage

contributions to artists using AR as one of many tools in their exploration of media (see Table 1).

In the interviews, participants were asked questions in the following categories: choosing DART, MR projects they built (with or without DART), feedback on DART (if used), and reflections on the state of current AR authoring tools. Their comments were then coded and categorized to identify common themes. Note that although pseudonyms are used for readability, the participants consented to identifying information being revealed.

The Participants

The Computer Scientist

TECH is an example of a technologist and *a power user of DART*. A computer scientist, he used DART for a series of HCI experiments exploring collaboration in AR via a molecular modeling tool [8]. He is an example of a developer who extended DART via the Xtra (Fig. 2 (a)).

The AR Novice

NOVICE was an AR neophyte who viewed the technology as *a tool to accomplish his creative goals*. He had some computing background, but his goals are not computer science related. He created an art installation called "Apollo Beyond" that consisted of multiple AR kiosks and a TUI command center (Fig 2. (b)(c)) [3,4].

The Artist and The Researcher

ARTIST is a professor of digital culture, who investigates the future of narrative through interactive storytelling and interactive cinema. She utilized DART in her research and courses over a three-year period. She collaborated on these projects with the technology manager of her lab (referred to as RESEARCHER). Both are *artists, educators, and researchers*. She did not have experience with AR prior to DART, but both were experienced with Director. She founded a research lab in 2005 exploring the future of cinema, of which DART was a core technology. This group created the greatest quantity of projects built with DART between their research and student projects (e.g., DART was used in at least three classes with 15-16 students per over a 3 year period) (Fig 2. (d)).

The Theater Director and the Software Developer

DIRECTOR is on the opposite end of the spectrum from TECH. Her background in theater is as a *director and playwright.* She uses AR to explore digital technologies in story-based theater. As a graduate student of ARTIST she created one of the most ambitious DART experiences, an AR version of the play "Woyzek" (Fig 2. (e)(f)) [42,43]. Her collaborator, DEVELOPER, who had Director experience, handled the DART programming. The team also included a composer, a choreographer, a film lighting expert, singers, dancers, and a documentarian.

Additional Participants

Additional feedback gleaned from interviews with two other DART developers (RENAISSANCE, a very technically proficient *digital media artist*, and MUSICIAN, an experienced AR designer with limited programming skills who has built *interactive AR music* applications). The insights regarding general AR authoring and workflow are also drawn from interviews with three AR experts. PROFESSOR has worked in AR *media theory and humanities* research at our university for over a decade. STUDENT was a graduate student in Human Centered Computing at our university, researching *AR authoring and multi-scale design*. He also collaborated on an AR art installation, "Inbox" [2]. Lastly, MANAGER was the producer of an AR project the band Duran Duran used during their live performances [34].

REFLECTIONS ON DART AND AR AUTHORING

At a basic level, all participants appreciated the fact that DART made their AR project possible. It was striking how often the interviewees uttered the exact phrase, "it was amazing it [the project] worked". The developers appreciated the lower barrier to entry and rapid development provided by DART. It was used successfully to run a range of large systems for trade shows, user studies, and art installations. Many interviewees expressed a desire for DART features in modern tools. RESEARCHER and MUSICIAN acknowledged DART for informing their own authoring tools. However, their early experiences with AR authoring and DART also provided a mechanism through which the participants could reflect on authoring challenges, tool design choices, and the affordances and constraints of AR in general. It is those insights is what we present in the next section.

Key Findings

From the interview data we have identified three topics that are particularly meaningful to many kinds of new media authoring toolkits: *the impact of existing workflows and expectations, the challenge of debugging, and the underutilization of advanced prototyping tools.*

The impact of workflows and expectations

ARTIST and RESEARCHER developed processes for AR design and to manage the obstacles they faced due to the backgrounds and existing workflows of their students. They found that those who worked in time-based media (e.g., film) struggled more with understanding the possibilities of AR. Surprisingly, theoretical students had less trouble due to their lack of preconceptions about the technology. ARTIST explained that often film students initially made projects that were focused on presenting 2D content in squares (i.e., "Using [AR] like a television") as "they couldn't think in terms of the physical world." She found that it was crucial for the students to develop their own simple AR application as soon as possible, to foster the development of a correct mental model of how AR worked.

To support this need, they created a tool that distilled the authoring process down to placing a video texture on a single marker [41]. They found that the act of creating this very basic application helped the students understand AR. This exposed the film students to a feature of AR that is diametrically opposed to film, the fact that the creator loses control over the viewer's POV, and thus cannot completely control the experience through editing. Much of the work that went on in the classes was to help the student explore what aspects of cinema could be leveraged in an AR experience and which could not. In some cases, they found that the "perfectionist" tendencies of film students, accustomed to absolute control over the user experience, would negatively affect their AR designs.

NOVICE's reflections on creating the Apollo Beyond installation revealed unanticipated uses of DART features. He interpreted DART concepts to align with his inexperienced mental model of AR and computing technologies. For example, the capture/playback functionality (meant for prototyping) was used for controlling content in the live experience. He also heavily utilized video "actors", in some cases placing them in multiple layers as a simple way to create visual effects. NOVICE also leveraged the Director score to debug the five networked kiosks because he could watch the execution flow visually. Most surprising is the fact that networked communication between the kiosks was achieved by using the DART WoZ component. NOVICE explained that it was a method of setting up networked communication that he understood.

This phenomenon was echoed by PROFESSOR who observed that his students author in a way they understand, even though it is also "wrong." He explained that for his students authoring "doesn't have to be easy, it just has to be possible." Artists are familiar with developing a workflow, even if it is tedious, and then focusing on exploring and refining a creative concept. However, he has seen that this can have negative effects on the experience (e.g. slow performance, unexpected behavior, non-ideal interfaces, etc.) and the student developers do not understand that their approach is to blame. Therefore, there is a tension between letting them author in whatever way works for their workflow, and keeping them from "creating a subpar artifact through this hackery." Similar phenomena were observed in the Papier Mache project where developers had "the lingering impression that the system must be broken, when in fact the system was just being slow because [they] were pushing the limits of computation speed" [21].

These problems could have been ameliorated through additional documentation. Those unfamiliar with the domain struggled with understanding the affordances of AR. MUSICIAN, ARTIST, RESEARCHER, RENAISSANCE, and DIRECTOR commented that they would have preferred much more complex applications to refer to rather than the small templates we provided (e.g., DIRECTOR commented that she only knew her vision for "Woyzek" was possible because of having seen the Three Angry Men project [29]). We had assumed that "bite-sized" examples would efficiently convey the relevant syntax, but the developers were unfamiliar with the medium of AR and were unsure how to change their workflow and ideation processes appropriately.

The problem of debugging

Many of our users' challenges were related to debugging technology problems. Specifically, they struggled to determine whether an application was not working as expected due to hardware problems with their sensors, a failure of the transport mechanism for sensor updates, a bug in DART, or a developer error in the DART project. RESEARCHER summed it up as "not enough high level access to low level debug information." He admits that at times frustration over unexpected behavior would be blamed on DART, when it fact it was due to hardware failure or developer error. For example, they struggled with confusing tracker errors until a knowledgeable visitor noticed that the tracker hardware was broken. DART did not provide enough transparency about all elements of the system that would have helped them *identify the source of errors*. This aligns with results from Papier Mache, where they observed developers becoming confused by sensing errors that were "mysterious" from their perspective [21].

The interviewees noted DART's lack of support for debugging the larger system outside of the software, the "quagmire of tediousness" referred to by Greenberg & Fitchett [19]. DART had components that helped the developers debug the 3D scene and replay tracker data, but these assumed that elements outside of the DART environment were working correctly. Therefore, when hardware, such as cameras or trackers, were not behaving as expected or when 3D models imported incorrectly there was little high-level trouble-shooting support. Developers were expected to devise their own tests via scripts, refer to debugging statements sent to the console, or investigate via external programs for those systems.

The DART components were built with a *computational thinker's debugging strategy* in mind, but more research is needed to create debugging constructs that are appropriate for a designer's expertise and development approach.

Underutilized prototyping tools

The interviews revealed that DART was used for prototyping. NOVICE, ARTIST, and RESEARCHER indicated that DART was often the *first step in an AR project*. ARTIST and RESEARCHER commented that students continued to create early versions of experiences in DART before implementing them fully in different tools. NOVICE commented that he still occasionally uses DART to rapidly demonstrate AR concepts to potential clients.

However, when asked about their use of the DART features intended to ameliorate the AR specific authoring challenges related to physical space, prototyping, and debugging, ARTIST explained they "got in a habit of not using them" because their applications "were not sophisticated enough to need them." This is an interesting comment considering how complex many of their DART applications were. She explained that they chose to "just build…and then try it."

The concept of providing methods for simulating sensor input to aid in prototyping were present in other toolkits including Phidgets [19] and the Context Toolkit [11]. However, similar DART components were under-utilized by external developers. Internally, we used these components extensively. For example, WoZ features were utilized in the Voices of Oakland project for evaluation as well as a replacement for GPS in the deployed version [12]. However, the interviews reveal that, while they liked the concept (e.g., MUSICIAN attempted to include similar features in his own tools), the external developers were not used to having this functionality in an authoring tool. They recognized that using these features could have benefits, but assumed there would be a steep learning curve and felt it was more efficient to use traditional methods. As the Designer's Outpost team found previously, it is necessary to minimize extra effort required by users in order for them to integrate a new tool into their workflow [23].

We did not do an adequate job of demonstrating the value of these components to our community. DART was informed heavily by rapid prototyping research. We implicitly assumed that our users would be aware of this research (e.g., the value of informal content for early experience testing and the potential of transforming early ideation artifacts into prototypes) and that they would be familiar with the unique challenges of AR authoring (e.g., the need for *in situ* prototyping and the challenges of debugging). Therefore, we only provided low-level examples of capture/playback and WoZ components, thinking that developers would only need guidance in syntax. However, our target users were, by design, AR novices and had little large-scale software development experience. Upon reflection it is clear they required guidance regarding the AR development process and that we should have also disseminated sophisticated example projects to illustrate the value of the features.

IMPLICATIONS FOR FUTURE AUTHORING TOOLS

We collected reflections from the interviewees regarding the challenges of AR authoring and on what is needed in an ideal tool informed by their experiences with DART. The comments fall into the categories of *access*, *layered authoring*, *collaboration with diverse teams*, *making the process less painful*, and *the importance of community*.

Access

ARTIST commented on a continuing "hunger for tools" among AR designers. A common theme amongst all interviewees was a feeling that, while there are far more tools for AR authoring than there were ten years ago, these tools are designed to support applications that are less sophisticated in many ways than those supported by DART. This is a population of researchers and artists interested in exploring the future of AR, technologically and creatively. They want to focus their efforts on design rather than on developing their own tool chain or working at a very low level with hardware and software. Interviewees who had previously worked with non-vision based tracking, HMDs, or custom interaction devices commented that current tools provide few, if any, features to support working with these components. However, they also noted the need for more than hardware support. In general the less technologically expert developers expressed a desire for "a lower barrier to entry" to AR in general.

Layered Authoring

Regardless of technical proficiency, interviewees consistently expressed a desire for a tool to support prototyping without coding. TECH described his need for a system that let him tag physical objects for later content placement. ARTIST expressed a desire to identify physical locations by moving through the space or interacting with a 2D map. RESEARCHER created a custom authoring tool to allow his students to link video to markers with no programming. However, the answer is not an authoring tool without scripting. Instead, they need a layered environment, allowing them to engage at an appropriate level of complexity, where lower level access requires technical sophistication but also allows for greater flexibility.

Other toolkits have provided layered authoring. For example, ComposAR allows the developer to author with direct manipulation and tangible interactions or extend the tool via Python [46]. And the applications demonstrated by our group of interviewees illustrate the value of layered authoring tools in DART. TECH added support at a low level for shared video streaming, NOVICE created a low-cost tabletop tangible user interface and implemented a networked application despite his lack of experience, and film students were able to create artistic AR installations without any previous programming experience. The layered approach supports a range of developer abilities and foci. This is particularly important on large projects such as "Woyzek" where some contributors barely interacted with the AR aspects of the project and yet effective and efficient collaboration was critical.

STUDENT described his AR art installation project built for a mobile platform using C++ tools for development [2]. He discussed the workflow he and his non-technical collaborator developed during the project. Germane to the discussion of layered authoring, he wished there had been a mechanism to allow the designer to participate in lightweight technical work such as auditioning content. However, their tools were totally inaccessible to the collaborator even for simple tasks. When asked what the ideal tool would have been for their project, he jokingly responded "a drag and drop tool for creating shipping container art installations." However, this comment points to a possible future direction for layered authoring tools. DIRECTOR made a similar comment about wanting a personalized 2D tool for tagging locations in the "Woyzek" experience. Perhaps what are needed are *meta-tools* that let teams begin a project by coopting or building their own simple authoring environment.

Collaborations with Diverse Teams

Projects like "Woyzek" show that diverse teams are often required for ambitious AR projects. There was an agreement among many of the interviewees that, as AR projects become more sophisticated and commercial, we will see a *movement toward specialization* among contributors, a process that plays out in other media such as film. When developing the requirements for AR authoring tools, then, it is necessary to consider to what extent each contributor will understand and participate in all aspects of the AR design and development process. The interviewees presented contrasting views on the roles of collaborators. DIRECTOR commented that she prefers to "focus on making art" and is not interested in developing advanced programming expertise, while others like ARTIST feel that AR authoring requires all contributors to possess a wide range of expertise, including the technical. STUDENT shared his opinion that it is important for the workflow to support a hierarchy of collaborators with a variety of skills.

MUSICIAN described his experience as a technical novice attempting to work with technical collaborators to create his AR music experiences. As they were using ARToolkit, MUSICIAN could not contribute directly to the technical components of the project. He explained "the feeling was like that of a painter who was not allowed to touch the paintbrush but, rather, had to relay instructions to someone else who would then go to another room, apply the paint, then bring the work-in-progress back for the painter to see and suggest corrections. This breaks the traditional dialogue with one's materials that is an essential part of the creative process." He commented, "the attraction of tools like DART was that I could actually do it myself and stay up all night if necessary rather than keep some poor programmer up all night then change my mind the next day."

PROFESSOR described his view on diverse teams in the context of film. He pointed out that screenwriters do not engage with technology and they are not typically special effects experts, but they have clearly internalized the capabilities of film such that they can write scenes appropriate for the technology and budget of the film. He also commented that it is "built into their DNA what movies look like." On traditional mainstream movies the roles are very defined and compartmentalized, but "everyone involved from the sound designers to the costumer knows how the medium works."

However, AR lacks standard design and development approaches. Few people working on projects have AR "built into their DNA" yet. Therefore, the workflow, which includes domain specific authoring tools as well as established media software such as Adobe Photoshop, must consider the expertise and goals of various contributors (e.g. developer, artist, camera operator etc.) and allow them to explore the medium together, guiding them into appropriate design choices.

Making the process less painful

The interviews revealed that many developers such as DIRECTOR, NOVICE, STUDENT, and MANAGER felt overwhelmed and exhausted by their ambitious AR projects. For example, both NOVICE and STUDENT temporarily vowed to never work with AR again at the end of their projects. While these types of novel applications help us understand the potential of a medium like AR, the work requires a diverse set of expertise that caused the interviewees to feel frustrated and fatigued.

NOVICE kept a blog tracing the development of "Apollo and Beyond" [3]. It detailed his confusion with choosing appropriate camera lenses, configuring a wireless video system for the handheld viewers, and building the tangible projection table. They had to investigate "a lot of things we never thought we'd have to deal with." Similarly, in DIRECTOR's "making of" documentary for "Woyzek" we see her constructing a stage, experimenting with stage lighting, directing the dancers, and working on musical lyrics with the composer [39]. She commented in the interview "every step, there was so much more to learn and so much to do."

Some of these struggles are inherent to all ambitious projects such as staging a play, shooting a film, or building a video game. However, it is valuable for those researching new media authoring tools to consider these elements of the process that exist outside the bounds of the software. While adding additional features to an authoring environment could have relieved some of the aforementioned struggles (e.g. utilities to help novices determine camera specifications, hardware prototyping support, or pre-visualization support for those filming augmentation videos) some low-tech resources such as approachable guides on camera calibration might have helped as well. In more established media such as film there are workflows and a vast array of resources, software, and equipment designed to make production as efficient as possible. As AR matures we must craft similar solutions to make it less painful to create large-scale experiences.

The importance of community

One reason for the wide adoption of the ARToolkit was the active developer community. Their mailing list was often the resource used by novices to help them overcome the initial learning curve. A lesson learned via our interviews was the importance of community to the success of DART as well. The interviewees as well as posts to our DART mailing list revealed that many attributed their success with DART to the mailing list and the availability of the development team to answer questions. NOVICE's comment that "if you guys hadn't had that mailing list we wouldn't have gotten off the ground," echoed the analysis of our mailing list, which showed that early help overcoming common initial problems (e.g. getting DART to access their camera, errors with 3D model loading, and a blank screen caused by Director not using the OpenGL renderer) was critical to getting new users acclimated to DART. The importance of responsive technical support to the interviewees' projects and the level to which they cited the mailing list as an invaluable resource was surprising. We also theorize that our responsiveness to user questions and an active online community gave the project a sense of permanence. Perhaps these were signals to developers that this was an active project that would not suddenly go dormant. The lesson is that the value of these low-tech components of a tool ecosystem should not be overlooked.

THE WAY FORWARD

The main goal of this paper is to motivate fellow researchers to make tools for non-technologists. The findings of this paper apply to many new technology paradigms besides AR. A motivating example lies with projection mapping technology. Although there are many impressive and compelling projection mapping papers and research demos spanning the last decade, the tools are not released by the researchers. As a result the exploration of this technology by developers, artists, and others has been relatively modest due to the effort and domain knowledge required to build such systems. We want to encourage researchers of these types of new technologies to consider making them available in an approachable way.

The feedback from our participants revealed their "hunger for tools." Existing AR authoring tools, although numerous (e.g. Qualcomm's Vuforia, Metaio's Junaio, Aurasma's

Studio etc.), are not meeting all the user needs. These tools, and DART, have much in common with standard UI toolkits. The advent of toolkits, such at the Macintosh Toolbox helped users quickly develop with what became the standard building block of GUIs, scrollbars, dialogs, and buttons, without extensive programming. These toolkits caused an explosion of GUI applications with a consistent interface. However, these tools also serve as a disincentive to explore other types of interfaces that were not supported by the toolkit, such as two-handed input [25]. Similarly, modern AR tools are approachable, yet their architecture guides users to create specific types of AR experiences (e.g., 3D virtual worlds rendered on top of printed markers and GPS-based points-of-interest mobile apps). Our main critiques of many modern tools are the limited functionality (e.g. low level or no layered authoring, tied to particular tracking technology), the lack of support for multiple heterogeneous sensors or easy switching of technology (which is critical in such a rapidly evolving domain), and the focus on building for deployment rather than ideation and prototyping.

In the original DART paper ten years ago we made a set of claims regarding AR authoring needs. They centered around the tension between a requirement for power and the need to make a new medium accessible to new types of creators, as well as the unique AR-specific challenges of authoring for and in the physical world. Our subsequent reflections on these claims ten years later bear out our early hypotheses that design tools should be predictable and powerful (but not necessarily easy to use) to be useful, and that providing abstractions to unify multiple unrelated technologies is extremely important. But we also found that some functionality intended to ameliorate the challenges of designing and debugging were under-used because they were too novel and not well documented (e.g., WoZ support and capture/playback). We argue that the key lessons from this research are the value of integrating new technology into trusted existing tools (in a way that lets developers appropriate and extend it) and fostering a rapidly responsive developer community.

CONCLUSION

We know that DART was used for many projects ranging from simple prototypes to deployed systems. However, reducing the friction of use to attract a robust user base made it much harder to evaluate. DART was released freely to the community without a formal mechanism, beyond the mailing list, for monitoring the developers and its use. A shortcoming of this qualitative study is that it was performed years after the final release of DART, making it challenging to locate developers. Also, the recruitment strategy, of finding developers that built DART systems, meant that our results reflect the experiences of those who found DART useful. There are undoubtedly many others that got no value from DART, but it was difficult to identify and locate such people years later.

However, the elapsed time since DART's release also provides benefits. For example, ARTIST & RESEARCHER used the tool for years in a variety of ways. They were able to comment on DART from the perspective of having used it for a long period of time in a vast number of projects and from then building their own DART-influenced tools. All the participants were able to provide feedback on DART in the context of other modern tools and technology. We believe the participants' feedback on DART has more significance since it is tempered by the passage of time and the advancement of the AR medium.

Our participants utilized DART throughout the AR design process. They created applications where the physical world was a key to the experience. They successfully collaborated with diverse teams and took advantage of the layered access of DART. Their feedback, as well as our own experiences, showed that current new media tools are overlooking some specific authoring needs. For example, they should support a greater range of hardware access, help users identify the source of application errors in complex systems, lower the effort required to engage with advanced prototyping tools, convey the affordances & constraints of the medium, acknowledge and accommodate existing workflows, and support collaborations among diverse teams.

ACKNOWLEDGMENTS

The authors would like to thank all the contributors to DART over the years, both developers and users. This work was supported by a seed grant from the GVU Center at Georgia Tech and by NSF CAREER Grant 0347712.

REFERENCES

1. Abawi, D., Dorner, R., Haller, M., & Zauner, J. (2004, March 15). *Efficient Mixed Reality Application Development.* 1st European Conference on Visual Media Production, London, England.
2. Barba, E., Rouse, R., Bolter, J. D., & MacIntyre, B. (2010). *Thinking Inside the Box: Meaning Making in a Handheld Augmented Reality Experience.* The 9th IEEE International Symposium on Mixed and Augmented Reality (ISMAR 2010), Seoul, Korea.
3. Barker, S. (2006a). Retrieved from http://apollobeyond1.blogspot.com/
4. Barker, S. (2006b). Apollo Beyond Interactive Exhibit | Digital Frontiers Media, Retrieved May 16, 2012, 2012, from http://digitalfrontiersmedia.com/apollo-beyond-interactive-exhibit
5. Berry, R., Oikawa, M., Prasad, J., Unterberg, J., Liu, W., Cheok, A. D., & Kato, H. (2008). *Augmented Reality for Artists and Designers.* ACM SIGGRAPH ASIA 2008: emerging technologies.
6. Billinghurst, M., Bowskill, J., Jessop, M., & Morphett, J. (1998, October 19-20). *A Wearable Spatial Conferencing Space.* The International Symposium on Wearable Computing, Pittsburgh, Pennsylvania.

7. Billinghurst, M., Weghorst, S., & Furness, T. A. I. (1998). Shared Space: An Augmented Reality Approach for Computer Supported Collaborative Work. *Virtual Reality, 3*, 25-36.
8. Chastine, J., & Zhu, Y. (2008). *The Cost of Supporting References in Collaborative Augmented Reality.* Graphics Interface (GI).
9. Conway, M., Audia, S., Burnette, T., Cosgrove, D., Christiansen, K., Deline, R., . . . Pausch, R. (2000). *Alice: Lessons Learned from Building a 3D System for Novices.* CHI, The Hague, The Netherlands.
10. DART website (2014), from http://ael.gatech.edu/dart/.
11. Dey, A. K., Salber, D., & Abowd, G. D. (2001). A Conceptual Framework and a Toolkit for Supporting the Rapid Prototyping of Context-Aware Applications. *Human Computer Interaction*(2), 97-166.
12. Dow, S., Lee, J., Oezbek, C., MacIntyre, B., Bolter, J. D., & Gandy, M. (2005a, Jun 15-17). *Exploring Spatial Narratives and Mixed Reality Experiences in Oakland Cemetery.* ACM SIGCHI Conference on Advances in Computer Entertainment (ACE '05), Valencia, Spain.
13. Dow, S., Lee, J., Oezbek, C., MacIntyre, B., Bolter, J. D., & Gandy, M. (2005b). *Wizard of Oz interfaces for mixed reality applications.* CHI '05 extended abstracts on Human factors in computing systems (CHI EA '05), Portland, Oregon.
14. Dow, S., MacIntyre, B., Gandy, M., & Bolter, J. D. (2004). *Prototyping Applications for the Physical World Using Integrated Capture/Playback Facilities.* In Extended Abstracts of Conference on Ubiquitous Computing (UBICOMP04), Nottingham, U.K.
15. Dunser, A., Grasset, R., & Billinghurst, M. (2008). *A Survey of Evaluation Techniques Used in Augmented Reality Studies.* The International Conference on Computer Graphics and Interactive Techniques, Singapore.
16. Edwards, K., Bellotti, V., Dey, A. K., & Newman, M. W. (2003). *Stuck in the Middle: The Challenges of User-centered Design and Evaluation for Infrastructure.* SIGCHI conference on Human factors in computing systems (CHI '03).
17. FLARToolkit. (2011). Retrieved Aug 24, 2011, http://www.libspark.org/wiki/saqoosha/FLARToolKit/en
18. Gandy, M., MacIntyre, B., Dow, S., & Bolter, J. D. (2006). Supporting Early Design Activities for AR Experiences. In M. Haller, M. Billinghurst & B. Thomas (Eds.), *Emerging Technologies of Augmented Reality: Interfaces and Design* (Vol. 1, pp. 160-180): IGI Global.
19. Greenberg, S., & Fitchett, C. (2001, November 11-14). *Phidgets: Easy Development of Physical Interfaces through Physical Widgets.* The 14th Annual ACM Symposium on User Interface Software and Technology, Orlando, Florida.
20. Guven, S., & Feiner, S. (2003, October 21-23). *Authoring 3D Hypermedia for Wearable Augmented and Virtual Reality.* The International Symposium on Wearable Computers, White Plains, New York.
21. Klemmer, S. R., Li, J., Lin, J., & Landay, J. (2004). *Papier-Mache: Toolkit Support for Tangible Input.* The ACM Conference on Human Factors in Computing Systems (CHI '04).
22. Klemmer, S. R., Newman, M. W., Farrell, R., Bilezikjian, M., & Landay, J. (2001). *The Designer's Outpost: A Tangible Interface for Collaborative Web Site Design.* ACM Symposium on User Interface Software and Technology (UIST).
23. Klemmer, S. R., Sinha, A. K., Chen, J., Landay, J., Aboobaker, N., & Wang, A. (2000). *Suede: A Wizard of Oz Prototyping Tool for Speech User Interfaces.* ACM Symposium on User Interface Software and Technology
24. Landay, J., & Myers, B. A. (2001). Sketching Interfaces: Toward a More Human Interface Design. *IEEE Computer, 34*(3), 56-64.
25. Latulipe, C., Mann, S., Kaplan, C. S., & Clarke, C. L. A. (2006). *symSpline: Symmetric two-handed spline manipulation.* Paper presented at the Proceedings of the SIGCHI conference on Human Factors in computing systems, Montreal, Quebec, Canada.
26. Ledermann, F. (2011). APRIL - Augmented Presentation and Interaction Authoring Language Retrieved September 2, 2011, from http://studierstube.icg.tugraz.at/april/
27. Li, Y., Hong, J. I., & Landay, J. (2007). Design Challenges and Principles for Wizard of Oz Testing of Location-Enhanced Applications. *IEEE Pervasive Computing, 6*(2), 70-75.
28. Lin, J., Hong, J. I., & Landay, J. (2001). *DENIM: An Informal Tool for Early Stage Web Site Design.* CHI '01 extended abstracts on Human factors in computing systems, Seattle, Washington.
29. MacIntyre, B., Bolter, J. D., Vaughn, J., Hannigan, B., Gandy, M., Moreno, E., . . . Voida, S. (2003). *Three Angry Men: An Augmented-Reality Experiment in Point-of-View Drama.* The International Conference on Technologies for Interactive Digital Storytelling and Entertainment, Darmstadt, Germany.
30. MacIntyre, B., & Feiner, S. (1998, July 19-24). *A Distributed 3D Graphics Library.* SIGGRAPH, Orlando, Florida.
31. MacIntyre, B., Gandy, M., Dow, S., & Bolter, J. D. (2004, October 24-27). *DART: A Toolkit for Rapid Design Exploration of Augmented Reality Experiences.* The 17th annual ACM symposium on User interface software and technology (UIST '04), Santa Fe, NM.
32. MacWilliams, A., Reicher, T., Klinker, G., & Bruegge, B. (2004). *Design Patterns for Augmented Reality*

Systems. The International Workshop Exploring the Design and Engineering of Mixed Reality Systems, Funchal, Madeira.

33. Oda, O., Lister, L., & Feiner, S. (2008, January 8-10). *Developing an Augmented Reality Racing Game.* Paper The International ICST Conference on Intelligent Technologies for Interactive Entertainment, Mexico.

34. Pair, J., Chastine, J., & Gandy, M. (2002). *The Duran Duran Project: The Augmented Reality Toolkit in Live Performance.* The International Workshop on Augmented Reality Toolkit.

35. Piekarski, W., & Thomas, B. (2003, October 7-10). *An Object-Oriented Software Architecture for 3D Mixed Reality Applications.* International Symposium on Mixed and Augmented Reality, Tokyo, Japan.

36. Owen, C., Tang, A., & Xiao, F. (2003). *ImageTclAR: A Blended Script and Compile Code Development System for Augmented Reality.* The International Workshop on Software Technology.

37. Presti, P., Gandy, M., MacIntyre, B., & Dow, S. (2005). *A Sketch Interface to Support Storyboarding of Augmented Reality Experiences.* The Conference on Computer Graphics and Interactive Techniques, Los Angeles, California.

38. Qualcomm Augmented Reality SDK. (2011). 2011, from developer.qualcomm.com/dev/augmented-reality

39. Quinsland, K. (Writer). (2007). The Making of Woyzeck.

40. Reitmayr, G., & Schmalstieg, D. (2001). *An open software architecture for virtual reality interaction.* The Proceedings of the ACM symposium on Virtual reality software and technology, Banff, Alberta, Canada.

41. Roth, A. (2011). *The Arlab and Cave libraries: On authoring augmented reality and virtual reality experiences using a graphical programming language.* The 2011 IEEE International Symposium on Mixed and Augmented Reality - Arts, Media, and Humanities.

42. Rouse, R. (2007). *Woyzek: Augmented Reality Performance Installation and Master's Project.* MA in Communication & Culture. Retrieved from http://www.rebeccarouse.com/uploads/5/7/8/1/5781195/woyzeckfinal_-_abcd.pdf

43. Rouse, R., Lee, M. M., Padgett, B., & Shepard, K. (2007). Woyzek: Augmented Reality Performance Installation, An Augmented Reality installation presenting an adaptation of "Woyzek"). Toronto, ON

44. Schmalstieg, D., Fuhrmann, A., Hesina, G., Szalavari, Z., Encarnacao, L. M., Gervautz, M., & Purgathofer, W. (2002). The Studierstube Augmented Reality Project. *PRESENCE- Teleoperators and Virtual Environments, 11*(1), 32-54

45. Schmalstieg, D., & Wagner, D. (2007, November 13-16). *Experiences with Handheld Augmented Reality.* The International Symposium on Mixed and Augmented Reality, Nara, Japan

46. Seichter, H., Looser, J., & Billinghurst, M. (2008, 15-18 Sept. 2008). *ComposAR: An intuitive tool for authoring AR applications.* The 7th IEEE/ACM International Symposium on Mixed and Augmented Reality, 2008.

47. Warne, P., & Wozniewski, M. (2011). Farrago: AR Funkit for iPhone and iPod Touch: Hololabs Studio. Retrieved from http://farragoapp.com/

48. Zauner, J., & Haller, M. (2004, June). *Authoring of Mixed Reality Applications Including Multi-Marker Calibration for Mobile Devices.* The 10th Eurographics Symposium on Virtual Environments.

Participants	TECH	MANAGER	STUDENT	NOVICE	RENAISSANCE
Description	A computer scientist completing a PhD. in AR who extended DART	A computer professional, experienced with AR, who led the AR project for Duran Duran	A PhD student in Human Centered Computing who focused on AR research	A MS student with some software development experience who was inexperienced with AR	A Digital Media graduate student, with skills in 3D modeling and programming, who explores the medium of video games
Used DART?	Yes	No	No	Yes	Yes
Projects	A molecular modeling prototype and 3 experiment applications	AR system for a live performance. Collaborated with a team that included computer scientists, musicians, and crew	An AR installation set in a shipping container using handheld devices. Worked with a non-technologist collaborator.	An AR installation comprised of 4 AR puzzle kiosks and a center table that was a TUI. Collaborated with 3D artist.	An AR "toy" with a virtual dog and an AR art project where animated silhouettes in physical pictures frames would respond to each other.

Participants	MUSICIAN	PROFESSOR	ARTIST & RESEARCHER	DIRECTOR & DEVELOPER
Description	A researcher and artist who has built AR applications and AR authoring tools	A professor of digital media with extensive experience in the medium of AR	A professor and the technology manager of her lab focused on future cinema research and AR.	A theater director and the software developer that programmed in DART
Used DART?	Yes	No	Yes	Yes
Projects	Previously built music focused AR applications using the ARToolkit (and later TouchDesigner). He experimented with DART but did not use it for a full-fledged experience.	His students have built a variety of artistic AR experiences, often focused on historic tours	The research lab was originally built around DART. They used DART in multiple offerings of courses (used by ~45 students) and they built dozens of research projects/art installations using DART.	Designed, developed, and exhibited an AR version of a play

Table 1. The Interviewees

RoomAlive: Magical Experiences Enabled by Scalable, Adaptive Projector-Camera Units

Brett Jones[1,2], Rajinder Sodhi[1,2], Michael Murdock[1,3], Ravish Mehra[1,4], Hrvoje Benko[1], Andrew D. Wilson[1], Eyal Ofek[1], Blair MacIntyre[1,5], Nikunj Raghuvanshi[1], Lior Shapira[1]
[1]Microsoft Research, Redmond [2]University of Illinois at Urbana-Champaign
[3]University of Southern California [4]UNC Chapel Hill [5]Georgia Tech

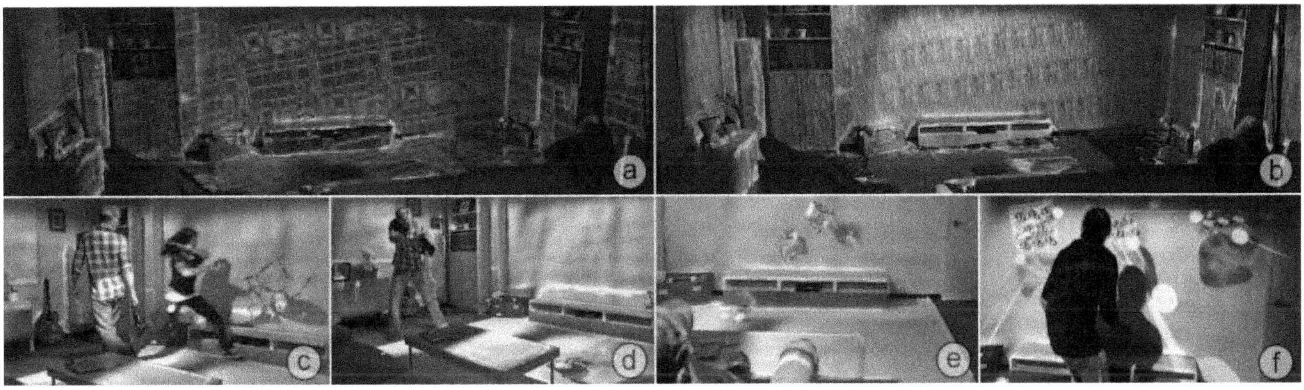

Figure 1. *RoomAlive* is a proof-of-concept system that transforms any room into an immersive, augmented gaming experience. E.g. *RoomAlive* can change the room's appearance to be (a) *Tron* themed, or (b) a swampy river. In an example *Whack-A-Mole* game, players physically (c) whack or (d) shoot moles popping out of their floor, walls and couch. (e) Players control a robot running around the room and shoot enemy robots using a video game controller. (f) An adventure game where players avoid deadly blow dart traps with physical body movement. (*All images in the paper were captured live; with the real-time working prototype*).

ABSTRACT
RoomAlive is a proof-of-concept prototype that transforms any room into an immersive, augmented entertainment experience. Our system enables new interactive projection mapping experiences that dynamically adapts content to any room. Users can touch, shoot, stomp, dodge and steer projected content that seamlessly co-exists with their existing physical environment. The basic building blocks of *RoomAlive* are projector-depth camera units, which can be combined through a scalable, distributed framework. The projector-depth camera units are individually auto-calibrating, self-localizing, and create a unified model of the room with no user intervention. We investigate the design space of gaming experiences that are possible with *RoomAlive* and explore methods for dynamically mapping content based on room layout and user position. Finally we showcase four experience prototypes that demonstrate the novel interactive experiences that are possible with *RoomAlive* and discuss the design challenges of adapting any game to any room.

UIST 2014, October 5–8, 2014, Honolulu, HI, USA.

ACM 978-1-4503-3069-5/14/10...$15.00.
http://dx.doi.org/10.1145/2642918.2647383

Author Keywords
Projection mapping; spatial augmented reality; projector-camera system

ACM Classification Keywords
H.5.2 User Interfaces: Graphical user interfaces, Input devices and strategies, Interaction styles.

INTRODUCTION
In recent years the way people play video games changed. We can now interact more naturally with the game world by moving our body (i.e., Nintendo Wiimote, Microsoft Kinect and PlayStation Move). Coupled with new display technologies (e.g., Oculus Rift), we can now feel more *"in the game"* than ever before. However, despite these advances, the game world is still distinctly separate from our real world. We may feel more present in the game world, but the game is not present in our world.

This paper makes a system contribution by demonstrating a novel distributed system that enables a unique set of augmented reality experiences in any room. Our proof-of-concept prototype, *RoomAlive,* transforms any room into an immersive, augmented entertainment experience and enables users to naturally interact with augmented content in their everyday physical environment. RoomAlive builds on a wide array of research fields. Although each individual component of RoomAlive could be improved, the unified system demonstrates the immersive, augmented gaming experiences that might be possible when games can adapt to our room.

Figure 2. Each projector + depth camera unit (a procam unit) consists of a commodity wide field-of-view projector, depth camera and computer.

The basic building block of *RoomAlive* is a combination of a projector and a depth camera (Figure 2), or *procam* unit [28]. By tiling and overlapping multiple procam units, *RoomAlive* is able to cover the room's walls and furniture with input/output pixels. *RoomAlive* tracks users' movements and dynamically adapts the gaming content to the room. Users can touch, shoot, dodge and steer virtual content that seamlessly co-exists with the existing physical environment.

RoomAlive captures and analyses a unified 3D model of the appearance and geometry of the room, identifying planar surfaces like walls and the floor. This is used to adapt the augmented content to the particular room, for instance spawning enemy robots only on the floor of the room. The content also reacts to the user's movement. *RoomAlive* uses a distributed framework for tracking body movement and touch detection using optical-flow based particle tracking [4,15], and pointing using an infrared gun [19].

To demonstrate the scalability of our prototype system, six procam units were used to cover the floor, walls and furniture of a large living room. We explore the design space of whole-room, augmented interactive experiences and the authoring process for these experiences. Through our exploration, we showcase four example experiences that demonstrate the rich and immersive experiences that are possible with *RoomAlive*. Finally, we discuss design guidelines and system limitations for future game designers who wish to create adaptive interactive projection mapped games.

MOTIVATING SCENARIO

Imagine playing a video game in your living room without a television. Instead, the game happens *in* the room, all around you. When the game starts, the room magically transforms into an ancient castle, the walls turn to stone, and flaming torches emerge from the walls casting flickering shadows onto the furniture. Out of the corner of your eye, you see a glowing idol appear on your couch. You walk towards the idol when suddenly, a trap opens on the wall next to you, exposing blow darts ready to fire. You leap out of the way, only to land on the floor face-to-face with a giant cockroach. You quickly get up and jump on the roach. You reach the idol successfully, and a scoreboard drops down showing that you have just scored the best time for the adventure course. This is just one of many interaction scenarios that are made possible by *RoomAlive*.

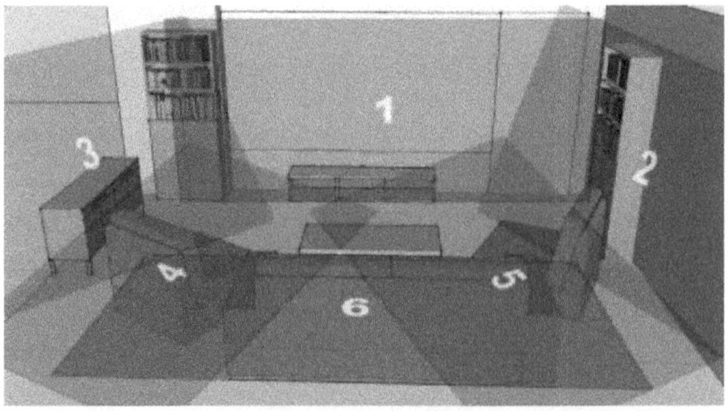

Figure 3. We have installed *RoomAlive* in a large (18 ft x 12 ft) living room using six overlapping *procam* units, with three units pointed towards the three walls of the room, and another three are pointed downwards to cover the floor.

RELATED WORK

Immersive Displays

With gaming experiences, bigger is often better. A larger display has a wider field of view, which makes the user feel more immersed and more present in the experience [16,30]. CAVE systems [10] and tiled displays [7,33] surround the user in visuals, but require special blank projection surfaces. Head mounted displays (HMDs) [26], enable users to be completely immersed in virtual environments, but require each user to wear a device. Optically opaque displays like the Oculus Rift block out the physical environment, and even see-through HMDs often limit the user's field of view (the frame of the glasses). HMDs can also increase the chance of simulator sickness by downgrading the user's perception to the resolution, frame-rate and latency of the display. *RoomAlive* provides unencumbered shared, augmented experience that adapts to the physical environment.

Spatial Augmented Reality

Spatial Augmented Reality (SAR) uses projected light to alter the appearance of physical objects (e.g. [3,5,34,35,36]). Previous work has explored SAR in mobile form factors [14,31,41], steerable projector systems [27,42], and even for novel gaming experiences: e.g. racing a car across a desktop [6], playing chess [44], or playing miniature golf on top of wooden blocks [19]. By using real-time depth sensors, previous work has enabled physical interactions using similar *procam* units [4,43,45].

Most closely related to our work is *IllumiRoom* [18], where a single projector was used to surround a traditional television with projected light to enhance gaming experiences. *IllumiRoom* explored focus plus context visualizations anchored by traditional screen based gaming experiences. *RoomAlive* explores gaming completely untethered from a screen, in a unified, scalable multi-projector system that dynamically adapts gaming content to the room and explores additional methods for physical interaction in the environment.

Commercially, SAR is known as 'projection mapping' and has recently exploded in popularity [22,29]. Projection mapping can create stunning visuals for outdoor advertising, theater, theme parks, museums and art galleries. However, the projected content is usually passive, and must be laboriously created specifically to the underlying surface. In contrast, with *RoomAlive* users can physically interact with projected content that adapts to any living room environment.

ROOMALIVE SYSTEM

The *RoomAlive* system is comprised of multiple projector-depth camera units or "procam" units. Each unit contains a depth-camera (which includes a color camera, infrared (IR) camera and IR emitter), a commodity wide field-of-view projector, and a computer. A single unit can be used in isolation to create a set-up like IllumiRoom [18], or multiple units can be combined to canvas an entire living room in I/O pixels.

Our current proof-of-concept prototype demonstrates the *RoomAlive* concept in a large living room (18 ft x 12 ft), with six procam units overlapping to cover three walls, the floor and all the furniture in the room (see Figure 3). *RoomAlive* is implemented as a plug-in to the Unity3D commercial game engine. Unity3D enables designers to easily author game content using an intuitive 3D editor and an interactive development environment.

With *RoomAlive* procam units are connected through a distributed client-server model. Each client node is responsible for tracking the players and the room geometry within the view of its own local depth sensor. The clients are also responsible for any un-synchronized local game state (e.g. intensive physics simulations) and for rendering their local view of the global scene, including view dependent rendering. The master server node synchronizes game state and user tracking state across units. The master server node also acts as a client, handling its own game state and rendering.

Procam Hardware

To demonstrate the flexibility of the approach, the procam units are built using a variety of commodity wide field of view projectors (InFocus IN1126, BenQ W770ST, BenQ W1080ST). Each unit also contains a Microsoft Kinect for Windows v1 sensor.

In our prototype, each unit is connected to its own personal computer with a high-end consumer grade graphics card (e.g., NVidia GTX 660 Ti). We use high-end personal computers to explore rich, computationally intensive interactions (e.g., GPU based optical flow) that will be possible in smaller form factors in the future. All procam units are currently mounted to the ceiling of the living room. Procams could also be mounted on the ceiling, tripod or placed on a bookshelf or a coffee table, or generally any location that maximizes coverage and minimizes occlusions.

Automatic Calibration

The *RoomAlive* calibration process is completely automatic, requiring no user intervention and is distributed across multiple procam units. Installers simply mount the procam

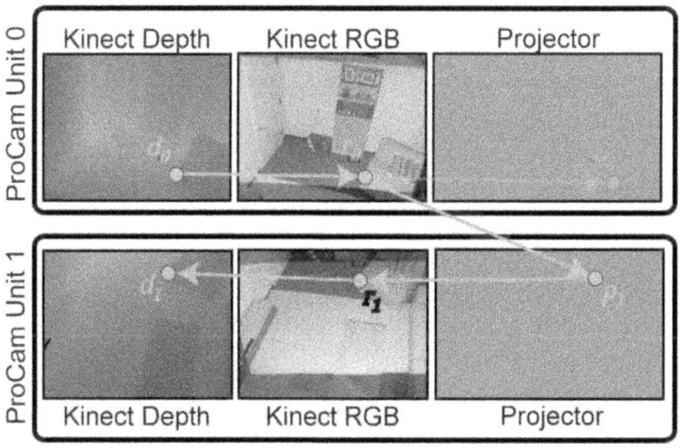

Figure 4. To compute correspondences between two units (*Unit 0* and *Unit 1*), we map a depth pixel in *Unit 0* (d_0), to an RGB pixel in *Unit 0* (r_0). Next, we look up the corresponding projector pixel in *Unit 1* (p_1), via the decoded Gray codes. We then invert the Gray code correspondences to look up the RGB pixel in *Unit 1* (r_1). Finally, we invert the Kinect's transfer map resulting in depth pixel (d_1).

units with some overlap (~10%) between units. Each procam unit displays a Gray code sequence [2], while all other procam units observe and decode the sequences. This establishes dense correspondences between each projector pixel and all Kinect cameras that can observe that point.

Each correspondence is transformed into the Kinect's depth image via the Kinect SDK, resulting in 2D to 3D point correspondences. Using these correspondences, we solve for the intrinsics and extrinsics of each unit using OpenCV's calibrateCamera function. To increase robustness we embed this in a RANSAC procedure [11]. This process only works for non-planar scenes. A procam unit viewing a planar surface may be temporarily rotated to view a non-planar scene for internal calibration.

To establish global extrinsics (rotation and translation) between units, we chain together correspondences (see Figure 4). A rigid transform is estimated between each pair of procam units using a singular value decomposition, and is refined via pairwise iterative closest point [24]. These transforms are chained together using a maximal spanning tree with weights using the number of inliers for each pairwise transform. The global coordinate system is centered at the first unit to connect to the system, and it is adjusted so gravity points downwards (via the Kinect's accelerometer).

Automatic Scene Analysis

A unified 3D model of the room is formed by combining the depth maps from each unit (on the master node). This model is analyzed, finding continuous planar surfaces (walls, floor) across units and labeling these surfaces. This process must be repeated when the system performs a new scan of the environment, e.g., recalibration or when objects are moved.

The system uses recent techniques in plane and scene model analysis [23]. To find planes, the surface normal is calculated using principal component analysis. The Hough transform [17] is used to select a finite set of planes. Each 3D point and its surface normal votes for a plane equation parameterized by its azimuth, elevation, and distance from the origin. A greedy strategy is used for associating scene points with planes. Unassigned 3D points that lie in the vicinity of each candidate plane (up to ~10 cm), and has compatible normal direction, are associated with the plane (~0.1° angle). Planes are categorized into 'vertical', 'horizontal' or 'other' based on their orientation with respect to gravity. The 'floor' is identified as the lowest 'horizontal' plane. Within each plane, points that are close together are converted into polygons using the outer hull of the set. Texture coordinates are assigned according to gravity and the principal component axis.

Authoring Augmented Content

RoomAlive makes use of Unity3D's modular plugin framework and scripting interface (Figure 5). Game designers only need to add a single game object to their scene to load the *RoomAlive* plugin. The game designer then has access to the API of *RoomAlive* directly within the scripting interface of Unity3D. *RoomAlive* uses a high resolution 3D model of the room as seen from the current procam unit, and uses Unity3D to render the virtual objects from the projector's point of view. Alternatively, designers could use a stored room model for testing purposes.

Game art assets can be easily imported from external content authoring software and positioned relative to the augmented environment and previewed in situ. Behaviors can then be applied to a game object using a C# scripting interface, e.g., how to react to gun fire. These scripts have access to the *RoomAlive* API, enabling queries regarding scene semantics (e.g., "On floor?") or players' touch collision events.

Mapping Content

One of the key technical challenges in making a projection based experience work in any living room is the placement of virtual game elements. Unlike traditional game design where elements like the game terrain are known *a priori*, *RoomAlive* experiences must operate in multitude of rooms.

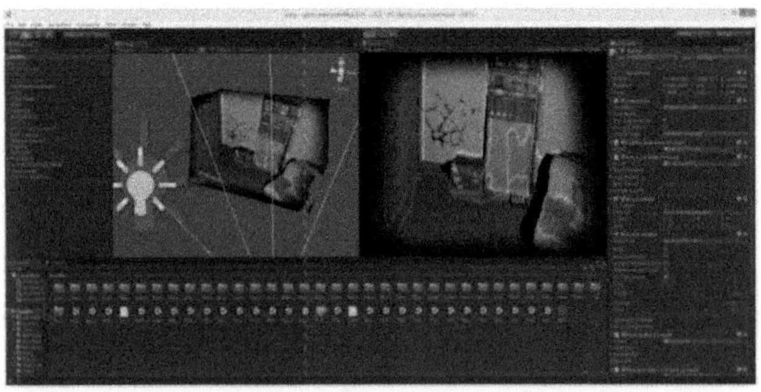

Figure 5. In the Unity3D editor's *Play* mode (debug mode), a high resolution model of the current living room is automatically instantiated, along with virtual cameras (with correct intrinsics/extrinsics) for all the procam units in the scene. On the left is the scene view where artists can drag and drop game assets and view the game from any arbitrary viewpoint. On the right is a live-preview of the image that the projector will display.

The mapping of game elements to a physical environment must be done in real time. Content must be mapped procedurally based on a set of rules that combine the goals of the game designer with the structure of the physical space, which can be significantly complex [39]. While we do not offer a complete solution to this problem, *RoomAlive* employs four techniques for mapping:

- *Random mapping* maps content in a uniformly random way. For example, targets presented to the user can be mapped to random positions around the room.
- *Semantic Mapping* leverages additional semantic information recovered from the scene to map content. For instance, grass and rock game objects could be mapped to only appear in locations on the floor of the room. To accomplish this, the game script queries the *RoomAlive* API on start-up to supply a list of points that belong to the floor of the room, which can then be sampled to instantiate game content.
- *User-constrained mapping* places content based on the current location of the user or user state. For example, a cannon that shoots at a user can be dynamically placed at a location in the room that offers a clear view of the user.
- *User-driven mapping* relies on users to interactively arrange content in the room, spawning content during a gaming experience by touching a physical surface or pointing with a gun at surfaces in the room. This enables users to level-edit or re-decorate their game room.

Tracking User Interaction

RoomAlive supports interacting with augmented content by whole body movement, touching, stomping, pointing/shooting and traditional controller input. For computational efficiency, processing is done locally on each client procam unit, and only resulting changes in game state are synchronized across units.

Proxy Particle Representation

To enable interaction through body movement, touching and stomping, we use the captured depth map along with a real-time physics simulation. Using a similar approach as [4,15], moving objects (e.g., players) in the room are represented by a cloud of spherical *'proxy particles'*, that are capable of exerting frictional forces. This enables physically realistic interactions with virtual game objects. For instance, a collision event can be triggered by the proxy particles when the user touches or stomps the physical environment.

The proxy particles are tracked using a depth-aware optical flow algorithm. The 3D flow field pipeline uses a GPU implementation of Brox's algorithm [8] to compute optical flow on the captured 2D depth video, updating the proxy particles to follow moving objects. While flow is typically computed on the RGB image, we do not use the color video, as projected content can lead to incorrect flow results. The computed 2D flow field is re-projected onto the depth data to generate the 3D displacements of the proxy particles.

Gun/Pointing Input

To support pointing at a distance, *RoomAlive* supports a pointing/gun controller. The gun controller uses an integrated IR LED matching the Kinect's infrared band-pass filter. Optics within the gun focus the light, generating a light spot when the player presses the trigger. The light is observed by the IR camera and the target 3D location is recovered.

Traditional Controller Input

In addition to natural user interactions, *RoomAlive* also supports traditional physical game controllers, such as a Microsoft Wireless Xbox controller. This allows users to interact with whole room augmented games using the same input affordances as traditional television gaming experiences. The controller is connected to the server, which distributes user interaction to the clients.

Rendering

Projection mapped content can only physically appear where there is a physical surface. However, virtual content can appear to be at any arbitrary 3D location, by displaying a perspective rendering of the virtual content on the surface, from the view direction of the player.

RoomAlive tracks the player's head position and renders all virtual content with a two-pass *view dependent rendering* [5] (see Figure 6). Content that is aligned with the physical environment can be rendered realistically without a need for view dependent rendering. A unique challenge is the possible presence of multiple users. While multi-user viewpoint rendering remains an open problem [38], RoomAlive uses a simple approach by averaging users' head positions. In practice, 3D scene geometry that strays farther than existing physical surfaces makes *RoomAlive* a single-viewer experience. For scenes where the virtual content is near the physical surfaces, rendering with the average head position offers a good working solution [13].

Another challenge arises from the use of existing room furniture as projection surfaces which may contain a non-white surface albedo. To overcome this problem, a radiometric compensation [32] is applied to compensate the projected image for the color of the surface. This process is limited by the brightness, dynamic range and color space of the projector and some desired surface colors maybe unachievable. For example, a solid red object in our physical environment cannot be made to appear completely green.

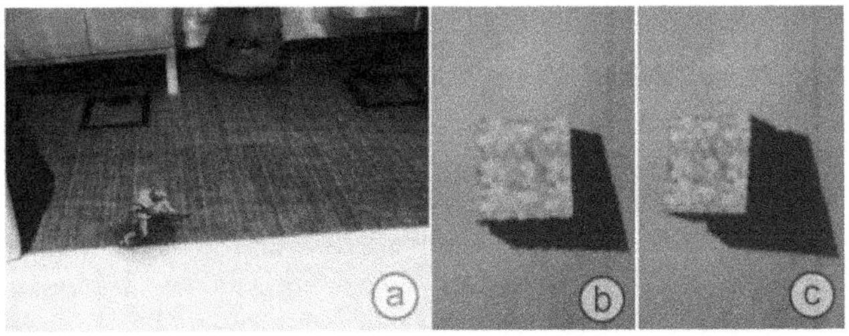

Figure 6. (a) Virtual objects that exist off-surface like this game character are rendered in a view dependent manner with radiometric compensation. (b) A virtual cube placed in front of a wall and viewed straight on. (c) The same cube viewed from a more oblique angle to the right.

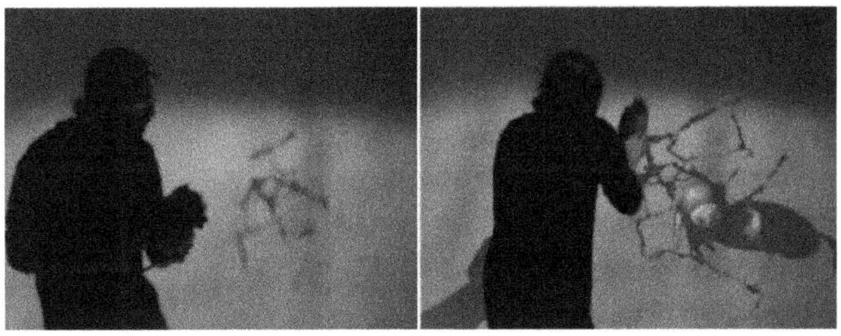

Figure 7. Playing room adaptive *Whack-A-Mole* with an IR gun. First, a crack appears to draw the user's attention.

EXAMPLE EXPERIENCES

We envision the *RoomAlive* system supporting a diverse range of applications, limited only by the imagination of game designers. Four example applications were prototyped to demonstrate the potential of whole-room augmented experiences. These experiences were developed in partnership with a game designer, and illustrate the interactive capabilities of the system. These experiences represent a limited survey and are not an exhaustive list. An accompanying video showcases the experiences.

Whack-A-Mole

The *Whack-A-Mole* experience demonstrates a combination of whole body movement, touch and gun/pointing input. Similar to the popular arcade game, in *Whack-A-Mole,* users race to whack, stomp, and shoot moles that randomly appear in the living room. The moles are generated uniformly across the entire room. First, a crack appears on a surface in the room (see Figure 7). Then an audio clip plays, "*I'm over here*", attracting the user's attention followed by a 3D animated mole that emerges from the crack. The mole is rendered from the player's viewpoint and casts appropriate shadows onto the physical room. Figure 1c-d shows a player whacking and shooting a mole on a wall and floor. A virtual scoreboard on the wall counts the player's achievements.

Robot Attack

RoomAlive also supports non-physically realistic gaming mechanics that create entirely new experiences in the living room. *Robot Attack* (based on Unity3D's *Angry Bots*) allows a user to control a virtual character that can run across the walls, floor, chair, etc. (see Figure 8 and Figure 1e). The character is entirely constrained to the surfaces of the living room. The character can move forwards, backwards, left,

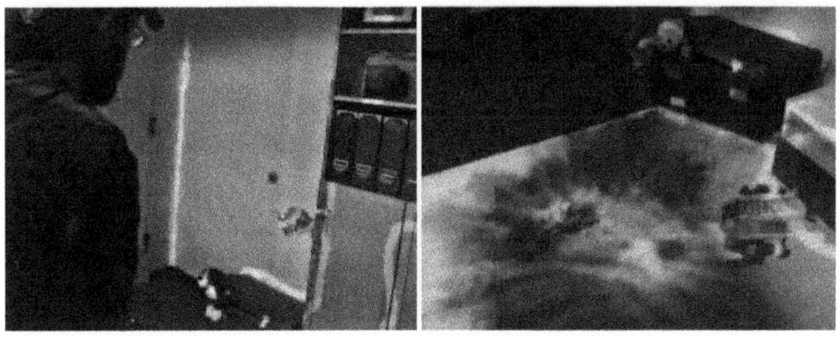

Figure 8. (left) A virtual character runs up the side of a bookshelf. (right) A virtual character fights a robot tank.

right on the surface, but not off of the surface. As the character moves around the living room, surface constrained enemy robots appear, tracking and firing weapons at the virtual character. The character must defend and shoot back against the robots. The surface constrained nature of the experience enables the game characters to walk up walls, adapting their orientation to the normal vector of the surface. Weapons also follow a similar behavior, where 'bullets' remain surface constrained going up and around objects rather than bouncing away. The control of the game is done using a traditional game controller.

Traps

While the previous experiences demonstrate virtual objects near a physical surface, virtual objects can also appear unattached to a physical surface. In *Traps*, a user is surrounded by virtual traps and must navigate the physical environment to avoid being hit by virtual darts. This experience is inspired by many adventure games where players must run, dodge and advance through complex obstacles. If a user navigates through a trigger volume, darts are emitted and collide with physics-enabled proxy particles that represent the user and any dynamically moving object. Because the darts move through open space, they are rendered in view dependent fashion. If the user is hit, blood particles are emitted at the collision location, which follows the user based on proxy particle tracking (see Figure 9).

Setting the Stage

Imagine being able to instantly transform your entire room to match the environment of a video game or film. *RoomAlive* can use projected light to automatically augment the appearance of the entire room, procedurally changing the surface color of objects in the room environment. Figure 1 (a-b) shows two examples of procedurally generated environments. Any Unity3D material, including procedural materials, can be easily assigned to a part of the room geometry with a few clicks. The automatically generated texture coordinates are used for each room polygon. Game designers can specify semantic groups to be given a texture (e.g., *vertical* surfaces). We demonstrate special effects that use 3D scene information, such as rain, or animated insects crawling over floors and tables (Figure 14).

DESIGN CONSIDERATIONS

In order to create experiences for *RoomAlive*, game designers must consider the unique benefits and challenges associated

Figure 9. Blow dart traps pop out of the wall, forcing the user to dodge. If the user is hit, battle damage shows on their body.

Figure 10. The room is transformed (via the extracted polygons and texture coordinates) into: (a) a cockroach infestation and (b) a futuristic style game room.

with interactive, adaptive, projection-mapped game content. Four critical aspects should be considered when designing room sized augmented experiences.

Input Choice Tradeoffs

RoomAlive supports a variety of input techniques. Some, such as touching or stomping, can enable physical interactions, which move users around the room. However, certain parts of a living room environment may be less suitable for touch-based experiences. For example, an expensive vase or painting may be inappropriate for direct contact. Particularly for children's games, designers may want to limit touch interaction to the floor and walls (large vertical planes). Users could also tag fragile objects removing them from areas of play. Alternatively, the experiences could rely solely on whole body movement, pointing and shooting, or traditional controller input. Pointing and controller input are ideal for controlling objects at a distance, such as a virtual car driving across a wall. We generally found that experiences were most enjoyable when all forms of input were available to users.

Capturing User Attention

When the display surface consists of a large living room environment, directing a user's attention becomes a critical aspect of designing the experience. If a user is on one side of the living room, they may not realize that their attention is needed on the opposite end of the room. Surround sound may be used to direct the user's attention to an approximate location in the room. Also the designer can incorporate a *warm-up* animation into the game design, for instance in *Whack-A-Mole,* a large crack appears seconds before the mole pops out, attracting the user's attention by appearing in their peripheral vision (Figure 7).

Selecting Game Physics

Living room projected experiences enable game designers to create unique interactions that may not be physically realistic. The concept of gravity can be applied globally to all virtual objects in an experience, as is done traditionally in a typical game. Alternatively, gravity can also be applied locally to a virtual object, constraining the object to a surface [19]. For example, a ball rolling on a surface can bounce off the wall or continue rolling up the wall depending on the experience. A local surface adherence model requires a local coordinate system, where each virtual object's local "floor plane" lies tangent to a surface. For instance, a virtual

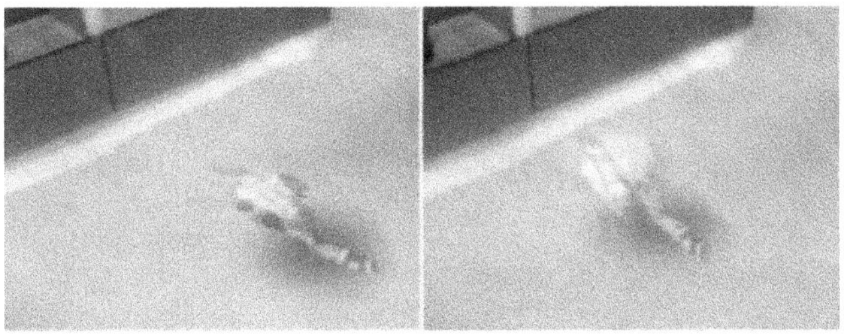

Figure 11. Calibration errors between units result in ghosting artifacts in projector overlapping regions. (*left*) The character in a single projector, and (*right*) in an overlapping region.

character's "up" direction would be the normal perpendicular to the tangent plane on the surface (see *Robot Attack*).

Controlling Player Movement

In traditional video games, the user is represented as an avatar in a virtual world. The game designer has explicit control over the actions that are possible in the virtual world, including where the user's avatar can walk, what objects they can interact with, etc. In a *RoomAlive* experience, a player's movement and actions are completely controlled by the user, and therefore uncontrollable by the game designer. Imagine a game that involves building physical pillow forts for a virtual snow fight. The game designer cannot stop a user from knocking over another user's pillow fort. A game designer cannot control where a user walks or the surfaces they interact with. Everything is fair game. Therefore, the designer must take care to handle edge cases and ensure that the game mechanics guide the user into a desirable behavior.

SYSTEM LIMITATIONS

While *RoomAlive* enables new and exciting interaction possibilities in the living room, there are several challenges with the current implementation. Foremost are calibration errors caused by non-metric distortions in the raw Kinect data and by deviations from factory calibration settings in the Kinect's own internal calibration. This results in visual errors that causes virtual content to appear *ghosted* in overlapping projector regions (see Figure 11). In practice the overlap regions are small, and we smoothly blend between projector images, so visual artifacts are not as noticeable. In the future, more precise depth estimates of the Microsoft Kinect V2 should reduce the sensing noise and ensure better calibration between procam units. More advanced calibration techniques [1,20,21,37] could also be used to correct for imperfections in calibration.

Interaction with real-time projector camera systems is always impacted by system latency. Off-the-shelf projectors have significant latency, and when combined with latency due to the depth-camera, graphics card and processing, can lead to image ghosting effects where fast moving objects trail behind. Recent research has demonstrated hardware solutions to virtually eliminate latency [25]. In the meantime, designers must balance creating a compelling game without allowing latency to affect the illusion.

Finally, a key challenge in supporting a wide variety of interactions is handling tracking issues that arise from overlapping Kinect sensors. We found the tracking results from the skeleton tracker to be relatively unreliable in overlapping regions, and therefore used the optical flow proxy particle tracking approach. Existing structured light depth cameras can be mechanically augmented to improve noise [9]. New time-of-flight depth sensors (e.g., Microsoft Kinect v2) may have less noise in overlapping regions. Advanced approaches for pose and dynamic object tracking can also be used to improve the *RoomAlive* tracking system [12,40].

CONCLUSION & FUTURE WORK

We have presented *RoomAlive*, a novel system for transforming a room environment into an interactive display. By calibrating and unifying multiple uniquely situated projector camera units, we demonstrate how a distributed rendering approach can be used to seamlessly merge our physical and virtual worlds. Through the development of a range of example experiences, we have shown wide and varied interaction possibilities where *RoomAlive* can be applied in the real world to create truly new experiences.

In the future we will explore approaches and experiences that involve multiple users and multi-user viewpoint rendering. We will also explore new ways to increase immersion with spatialized sound. *RoomAlive* provides a glimpse of how a scalable multi-projector system can transform any room into an immersive augmented gaming experience. Many new and exciting possibilities remain to be explored.

REFERENCES

1. Aliaga, D., Yeung, Y., and Law, A. Fast high-resolution appearance editing using superimposed projections. *ACM TOG*, (2012).
2. Batlle, J., Mouaddib, E., and Salvi, J. Recent progress in coded structured light as a technique to solve correspondence problem: A survey. *Pattern Recognition 31*, 7 (1998), 963–982.
3. Behringer, R. Placing Artificial Objects in Real Scenes. *Proc. of IWAR*, (1998).
4. Benko, H., Jota, R., and Wilson, A. MirageTable: freehand interaction on a projected augmented reality tabletop. *ACM CHI*, (2012).
5. Bimber, O. and Raskar, R. *Spatial augmented reality: Merging real and virtual worlds*. AK Peters Ltd, 2005.
6. Bimber, O. PlayReal: SAR Games. http://140.78.90.140/medien/ar/research.php. 2008.
7. Brown, M., Majumder, A., and Yang, R. Camera-based calibration techniques for seamless multiprojector displays. *IEEE Visualization and Computer Graphics*, (2005).
8. Brox, T., Papenberg, N., and Weickert, J. High Accuracy Optical Flow Estimation Based on a Theory for Warping. *IEEE ECCV*, (2004).
9. Butler, A., Izadi, S., Hilliges, O., Molyneaux, D., Hodges, S., and Kim, D. Shake ' n ' Sense : Reducing Interference for Overlapping Structured Light Depth Cameras. *ACM CHI*, (2012), 1933–1936.

10. Cruz-Neira, C., Sandin, D., and DeFanti, T. Surround-screen projection-based virtual reality: the design and implementation of the CAVE. *ACM SIGGRAPH*, (1993).
11. Fischler, M.A. and Bolles, R.C. Random sample consensus. *Communications of the ACM 24*, 6 (1981), 381–395.
12. Fuchs, H. and Frahm, J.-M. Scanning and tracking dynamic objects with commodity depth cameras. *IEEE ISMAR*, (2013).
13. Hancock, M., Nacenta, M., Gutwin, C., and Carpendale, S. The effects of changing projection geometry on the interpretation of 3D orientation on tabletops. *Proc. of ITS*, (2009).
14. Harrison, C., Benko, H., Wilson, A.D., and Way, O.M. OmniTouch : Wearable multitouch interaction everywhere. *ACM UIST*, (2011).
15. Hilliges, O., Kim, D., Izadi, S., Weiss, M., and Wilson, A. HoloDesk: direct 3d interactions with a situated see-through display. *ACM CHI*, (2012).
16. Hou, J., Nam, Y., Peng, W., and Lee, K.M. Effects of screen size, viewing angle, and players' immersion tendencies on game experience. *Computers in Human Behavior 28*, 2 (2012), 617–623.
17. Illingworth, J. and Kittler, J. A survey of the hough transform. *Computer Vision, Graphics, and Image Processing 44*, 1 (1988), 87–116.
18. Jones, B.R., Benko, H., Ofek, E., and Wilson, A.D. IllumiRoom: peripheral projected illusions for interactive experiences. *ACM CHI*, (2013).
19. Jones, B.R., Sodhi, R., Campbell, R.H., Garnett, G., and Bailey, B.P. Build your world and play in it: Interacting with surface particles on complex objects. *IEEE ISMAR*, (2010).
20. Kainz, B., Hauswiesner, S., Reitmayr, G., et al. OmniKinect : Real-Time Dense Volumetric Data Acquisition and Applications. *IEEE VR*, (2012).
21. Lee, J.C., Dietz, P.H., Maynes-Aminzade, D., Raskar, R., and Hudson, S.E. Automatic projector calibration with embedded light sensors. *ACM UIST*, (2004).
22. Mine, M., Rose, D., Yang, B., Jeroen van Baar, and Grundhöfer, A. Projection-Based Augmented Reality in Disney Theme Parks. *IEEE Computer 45*, 7 (2012), 32–40.
23. Nathan Silberman, Lior Shapira, Ran Gal, P.K. A Contour Completion Model for Augmenting Surface Reconstructions. *ECCV*, (2014).
24. Newcombe, R.A., Davison, A.J., Izadi, S., et al. KinectFusion: Real-time dense surface mapping and tracking. *IEEE ISMAR*, (2011).
25. Ng, A., Lepinski, J., Wigdor, D., Sanders, S., and Dietz, P. Designing for Low-Latency Direct-Touch Input. *ACM UIST*, (2012).
26. OculusVR. http://www.oculusvr.com. 2014.
27. Pinhanez, C. The Everywhere Displays Projector: A Device to create ubiquitous graphical interfaces. *Proc. UbiComp*, (2001), 315–331.
28. ProCams. http://www.procams.org. 2007.
29. Projection Mapping Central. Projection Mapping Central. *http://projection-mapping.org*, 2014.
30. R. Sekular, R.B. Perception 2nd Edition. (1990).
31. Raskar, R., van Baar, J., Beardsley, P., Willwacher, T., Rao, S., and Forlines, C. iLamps: geometrically aware and self-configuring projectors. *ACM TOG 223*, (2003).
32. Raskar, R. and Beardsley, P. A self-correcting projector. *IEEE CVPR*, (2001).
33. Raskar, R., Brown, M.S., Welch, G., Towles, H., Scales, B., and Fuchs, H. Multi-projector displays using camera-based registration. *IEEE Visualization*, (1999).
34. Raskar, R., Welch, G., Cutts, M., Lake, A., Stesin, L., and Fuchs, H. The office of the future: A unified approach to image-based modeling and spatially immersive displays. *ACM SIGGRAPH*, (1998).
35. Raskar, R., Welch, G., and Fuchs, H. Spatially augmented reality. *IWAR*, (1998).
36. Raskar, R., Welch, G., Low, K.L., and Bandyopadhyay, D. Shader lamps: Animating real objects with image-based illumination. *Proc. Eurographics*, (2001).
37. Sajadi, B., Member, S., and Majumder, A. Auto-Calibration of Multi-Projector CAVE-like Immersive Environments. *ACM TOG 17*, 1 (2011), 1–13.
38. Schulze, J.P., Acevedo, D., Mangan, J., Prudhomme, A., Nguyen, P., and Weber, P. Democratizing rendering for multiple viewers in surround VR systems. *IEEE 3DUI*, (2012).
39. Smith, G., Othenin-girard, A., Whitehead, J., and Wardrip-fruin, N. PCG-Based Game Design : Creating Endless Web. *In Proc. of Foundations of Digital Games*, (2012).
40. Straka, M., Hauswiesner, S., Ruther, M., and Bischof, H. Rapid Skin: Estimating the 3D Human Pose and Shape in Real-Time. *IEEE 3DIMPVT*, (2012).
41. Willis, K.D.D., Poupyrev, I., Hudson, S.E., and Mahler, M. SideBySide: Ad-hoc Multi-user Interaction with Handheld Projectors. *ACM CHI*, (2011).
42. Wilson, A., Benko, H., Izadi, S., and Hilliges, O. Steerable augmented reality with the beamatron. *ACM UIST*, (2012).
43. Wilson, A.D. and Benko, H. Combining multiple depth cameras and projectors for interactions on, above and between surfaces. *ACM UIST*, (2010), 273–282.
44. Wilson, A.D. PlayAnywhere: a compact interactive tabletop projection-vision system. *ACM UIST*, (2005).
45. Xiao, R. and Hudson, S.E. WorldKit : Rapid and Easy Creation of Ad-hoc Interactive Applications on Everyday Surfaces. *ACM CHI*, (2013).

Dyadic Projected Spatial Augmented Reality

Hrvoje Benko
Microsoft Research
Redmond, WA, USA
benko@microsoft.com

Andrew D. Wilson
Microsoft Research
Redmond, WA, USA
awilson@microsoft.com

Federico Zannier
Microsoft
Redmond, WA, USA
fzannier@microsoft.com

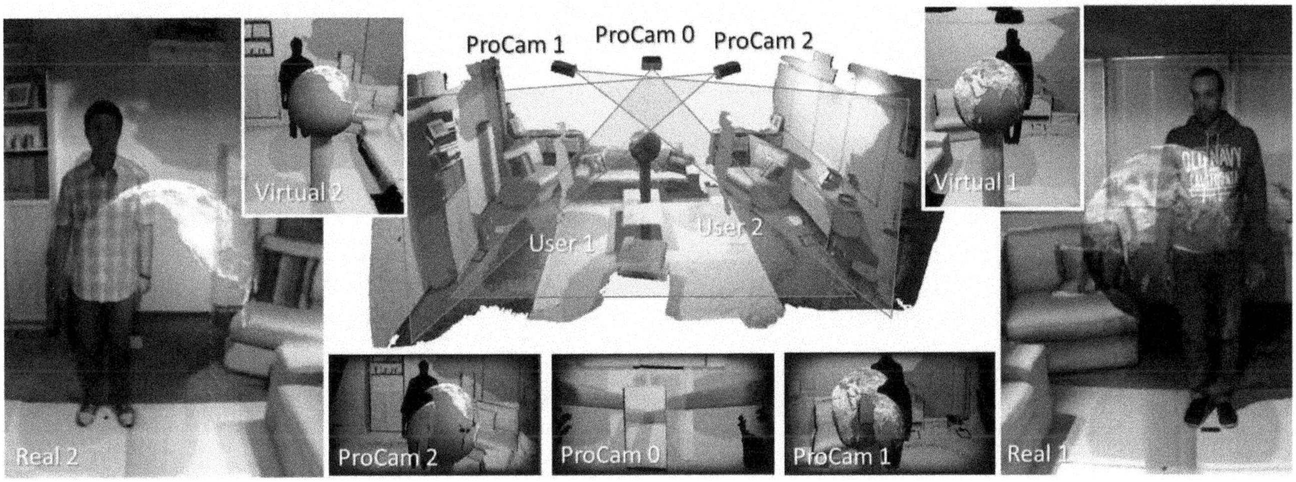

Figure 1. Dyadic projected spatial augmented reality enables two users to interact with a shared virtual scene and each other in a face to face arrangement. Center: Room geometry, user geometry and projector camera pairs are illustrated. Virtual 1 & 2: The desired view for each user is rendered offscreen. ProCam 0, 1 & 2: Projected graphics are warped to account for surface geometry, including the other user. Real 1 & 2: Each user's resulting view compares well with the desired view (Virtual 1 & 2).

ABSTRACT
Mano-a-Mano is a unique spatial augmented reality system that combines dynamic projection mapping, multiple perspective views and device-less interaction to support face to face, or dyadic, interaction with 3D virtual objects. Its main advantage over more traditional AR approaches, such as handheld devices with composited graphics or see-through head worn displays, is that users are able to interact with 3D virtual objects and each other without cumbersome devices that obstruct face to face interaction. We detail our prototype system and a number of interactive experiences. We present an initial user experiment that shows that participants are able to deduce the size and distance of a virtual projected object. A second experiment shows that participants are able to infer which of a number of targets the other user indicates by pointing.

Author Keywords
Augmented reality; projector camera system; depth cameras

UIST '14, October 05 - 08 2014, Honolulu, HI, USA
Copyright 2014 ACM 978-1-4503-3069-5/14/10...$15.00.
http://dx.doi.org/10.1145/2642918.2647402

ACM Classification Keywords
H.5.2 [Information Interfaces and Presentation]: User Interfaces - Graphical user interfaces;

INTRODUCTION
"Spatial Augmented Reality" (SAR) [26] techniques create augmented reality experiences by changing the look of the physical environment with projected light [4, 25, 35]. Whereas many augmented reality approaches involve rendering graphics over a live video feed on hand held or head worn devices, SAR places the augmenting graphics over the physical object itself and so does not divert the users' attention from the real world. "See-through" head worn displays can achieve similar effects, but presently support a limited field of view and require wearing bulky equipment that can hinder face to face interaction among users.

Under the right circumstances SAR systems can change the surface appearance of an object to make it appear as if it is made of a different material. For example, a carpeted floor can be made to look like a mossy bog. With the knowledge of the user's head position SAR systems can project light over the physical environment so that a virtual 3D object appears correctly over the real world. In both cases it is necessary to have a precise geometric model of the physical environment. Intuitively, this model is used to alter the projected graphics to account for the distortion of the projected image caused by variation in the real world surface geometry. When the physical environment includes moving objects (e.g., people), this model must be updated in real time. Commodity depth cameras such as the Microsoft Kinect now make it relatively easy to compute geometric models of dynamic indoor environments. Because it can be used to render virtual 3D objects and scenes, SAR may seem like a practical, available alternative to holographic video. However, in comparison to true holographic techniques, SAR appears very limiting, since by its use of view-dependent rendering it seems to support a single view and therefore only a single user. However, when using projection techniques in larger environments (e.g., throughout a room) there may be configurations where what is visible to one user is not visible to another, thus creating the possibility for multiple simultaneous views.

In this paper we explore one such configuration that is particularly useful: face to face, or dyadic, interaction. We demonstrate *Mano-a-Mano*, a projected SAR system which supports separate perspective views for two users when they are arranged face to face in a room with several feet of space between them. *Mano-a-Mano* renders virtual 3D objects as if they are hovering in the space between the two users. Moreover, various interactions with these objects are supported. For example, in a combat-style game, a player can summon a fireball to their raised hand and throw it at the other player. Both players see the appropriate view of the action.

The dyad configuration of *Mano-a-Mano* allows for multiple simultaneous views by assuming that each user is largely unaware of graphics projected on the wall behind them, or on their own bodies. Instead, those graphics are intended for the other user. For example, an object held in front of the body by one user is rendered twice: first on the far wall to give that user the view of the object in their hand, and second on their body so that the other user also sees the object in the first user's hand (Figure 5a).

We envision *Mano-a-Mano* to be useful in a variety of dyadic interactions. We anticipate collaborative scenarios that rely on the shared understanding of the 3D layout and motion of virtual objects, such that if one user points at an object, the other user sees them pointing at that object. Of further interest is to what extent *Mano-a-Mano* gives users the impression of *object presence* [11]: that is, whether virtual objects appear to be the correct size and distance, even when a number of familiar depth cues are absent or in conflict (e.g., stereoscopy). In short, we would like to know if users "buy" the effect. We make the following contributions:

- A room-scale SAR system supporting dyadic interactions, including a number of early demonstrations.
- A study which tests users' ability to correctly perceive the distance and size of 3D virtual objects rendered in projected SAR.
- A study which tests users' ability to determine which of several objects is indicated by the other user's pointing gesture.

After reviewing related work, we detail the *Mano-a-Mano* system, describe a number of demonstration interactions, present the two user studies and lastly discuss a variety of issues regarding dyadic projected SAR.

RELATED WORK

Providing large-scale immersive experiences is a major thread of virtual reality research. A larger display enables a larger field of view to the user, which induces a more powerful sense of presence and immersion in the experience (which can also induce simulator sickness) [15, 30]. CAVE [8] has been a popular method of creating large virtual reality experiences by projecting content on three to six walls of a cube shaped empty room. In contrast to CAVE which completely surrounds and isolates the user, our system builds on the concept of Spatial Augmented Reality (SAR) [4] to envelop a pair of users in a shared projector-augmented experience, enabling them to interact with virtual objects in a normal room without the use of special glasses and equipment.

Our approach also differs from previous efforts to support computer-aided face-to-face interactions employing transparent screens [14, 15, 17] or "immaterial" fog screens [22] between users. For example, ClearBoard [17] uses a window metaphor for face-to-face collaboration between two remote users.

Spatial Augmented Reality

Raskar et al. [25, 26, 27] first demonstrated a working implementation of SAR by registering a virtual 3D model with the underlying 3D physical object in order to overlay virtual content. This was followed by Underkoffler et al.'s concept of an I/O Bulb [35], a projector-camera pair capable of both sensing and providing computational illumination (i.e., augmentation). This I/O Bulb vision has been further developed with room [18, 28, 37], tabletop [3, 36], mobile [12, 24] and steerable form factors [23, 38].

With the emergence of widely available Microsoft Kinect depth cameras, research into larger scale SAR interactions has accelerated [3, 19, 36, 37, 38]. Our work draws inspiration from our earlier project, called LightSpace [37], which first demonstrated a system which combines three projector and depth camera pairs to augment the surfaces in the environment. The augmentations and interactions in LightSpace were constrained to the available surfaces and no perspective views were available.

Availability of real-time depth capture enables a new generation of SAR systems which can compensate for moving projection surfaces as well as provide correct perspective views [3, 34, 38]. For example, MirageTable [3] offers a perspective stereoscopic view to a single user working on a projected SAR tabletop by compensating the projection for the user's hands and any other physical objects on the table. Our work extends the state of the art by both addressing the entire room and by providing multiple simultaneous perspective views to two users.

Immersive Displays with Multiple Perspective Views

Providing multiple people with personal perspective views in augmented or virtual environments has traditionally been achieved through head-worn displays [7], where each user has their own view on their own personal display. In practice, the obstruction of the face with such displays and their narrow field of view can lead to unnatural face-to-face interactions. Our solution avoids this difficulty. Alternatively, projection-bases systems rely on either *time-* or *space-multiplexing* the projected images to show multiple independent views. Agrawala et al. [2] demonstrates a time-multiplexed approach with synchronized shutter glasses to enable two stereoscopic user perspectives on an interactive tabletop. While conceptually simple, this approach tends to suffer from low image brightness and sometimes perceivable flicker since each eye only gets a small slice of the available light in each frame.

In contrast, Bimber et al.'s Virtual Showcase [5] uses multi-plane beam combiners to enable up to four independent perspectives on a spatially-multiplexed tabletop: each view appears at a different location of the display and is optically combined with four mirrors. Similarly, IllusionHole [21] uses spatial-multiplexing to provide multiple participants correct perspective views around the tabletop. Their display greatly reduces the visible display area for each user to ensure minimal image overlap. Our work also employs spatial multiplexing approach to support multiple views. In contrast, we exploit the fact that in the face-to-face arrangement, most of the surfaces that each person sees are on their partner's body or in their partner's background. These surfaces are good for projections of individual views, as they are not easily perceived by their partner.

Depth Perception and Object Presence

The ability of our system to provide two users with a sense of spatial presence in a room-scale augmented reality hinges on the human ability to perceive depth from a perspective view without binocular cues. Conventional measures of person- and object-presence have mostly been defined for virtual environment displays that surround and isolate the user [31]. Stevens and colleagues found that the users can experience a measurable sense of object-presence with projection-augmented models [33]. However, their questionnaire-based study examined only planar projections and not perspective views.

The relative importance of various depth cues in perception of virtual objects [9] is an important consideration for our system since we do not offer stereoscopic vision. Sollenberger and Milgram [32] showed a large improvement of head-coupled stereo over static non-head-coupled non-stereo displays while Arthur et al.'s experiments [1] showed that users greatly preferred head coupling without stereo to stereo head-coupled displays in fish-tank VR. How such results apply to perspective SAR configurations remains unclear. The most closely related work in this space is the depth perception study of MirageTable [3] which showed substantial accuracy in users' estimates of depth on a SAR tabletop with head-coupled stereo view. Also related is a pilot experiment reported by Broecker et al. [6] who investigated a variety of cues affecting depth perception in a view-dependent near-field SAR, but found no statistically significant results.

While focusing on projected tabletops, Hancock et al. [11] evaluated people's ability to judge object orientation under different projection conditions. Their work highlights the importance of correct perspective on judgment of objects' spatial presence especially in multi-user scenarios. There is also a long line of related research in cognitive psychology on understanding the relative importance of different cues for depth perception (e.g., [9, 10, 30]). The complete review of this work is beyond the scope of this paper, but the three volume book by Howard [16] offers the definitive summary of knowledge on the topic.

SYSTEM DESCRIPTION

We describe our prototype dyadic SAR system, including hardware configuration, scene modeling, dynamic projection mapping and support for multiple simultaneous views. Technical contributions of our work include: a particular configuration of pro-cam units to support dyadic interaction, a graphics pipeline that blends views from two simultaneous perspectives while supporting projection onto dynamic depth maps (e.g., people), and the design of interactions and experiences that showcase these capabilities.

Hardware Configuration

Our prototype dyadic SAR system employs three HD video projectors (BenQ W1080ST), each paired with a Kinect for Windows v2 sensor. Their mounting was chosen to both display and sense around two users that are approximately facing each other in a large room. Two of the projector and camera pairs are mounted on the ceiling, about two feet above the heads of each of the two users. These are oriented so that they approximately face one another, covering the opposite walls and part of the floor (Figure 1). Roughly speaking, each user's view is rendered by the projector above them. The precise surface geometry necessary for dynamic projection mapping for a user's view is provided by the Kinect paired with the projector above them. Meanwhile, body tracking of that user is supported by the opposite facing Kinect camera. While mounted significantly higher than in most applications, Kinect body tracking works well in this configuration. This symmetric arrangement of projectors and cameras follows the symmetric nature of dyadic interaction. The third projector and camera pair is mounted on the ceiling, facing downwards, to cover the area between the areas covered by the first two projectors.

Our current implementation is primarily hosted on a single PC which drives all three projectors. As the current Kinect for Windows v2 SDK can support only one camera per PC, we have three additional PCs which send the Kinect depth images and other image processing results (e.g., body tracking, optical flow) to the main PC via network. All depth data is merged into a single scene in Unity 3D (http://unity3d.com). Unity provides a convenient overview of all sensed geometry and virtual objects in the room, and can be used to quickly script new interactive applications. Furthermore, a variety of Unity surface shaders such as lighting, shadows and procedural texturing methods are available to make virtual objects appear more realistic.

Calibration and Scene Model

Precise dynamic projection mapping requires the pose, focal length and optical center of each projector and Kinect camera. Our prototype system recovers this information in an offline automatic procedure whereby each projector in turn displays a series of Gray code patterns. These patterns are observed by the color camera of the paired Kinect sensor. Given the coordinate mapping functions of the Kinect SDK, this Gray code pattern is used to establish the precise mapping from a 3D point in the Kinect camera's coordinate frame to the corresponding point in the projector's image.

The relative pose of each projector camera pair is established by having all Kinect color cameras additionally observe the Gray code patterns of all other projectors, noting regions where the other projectors overlap with the camera's own paired projector, and computing the transform that brings corresponding 3D points of overlapping regions into alignment. This process results in a world coordinate system for all projectors and cameras. The calibration procedure is further described in [19].

Dynamic projection mapping also requires the precise surface geometry of the physical environment. The Kinect for Window v2 sensor includes a time-of-flight depth camera which generally produces more precise depth maps than the original Kinect sensor. In particular, the precision of depth data for the v2 camera is approximately constant over the range of depth (0.5m-4.5m), whereas the depth precision of the original Kinect sensor degrades with distance [20].

As with related projects [37, 3] moving objects such as user's bodies are handled separately from the static geometry of the room. This is primarily for two reasons: first, the system may project onto regions of the room that are otherwise occluded by moving objects. Second, static geometries support various offline analysis and optimization procedures that are difficult to perform on dynamic geometry. Furthermore, this model of the environment is pre-processed to provide detailed collision geometry used in rigid body physics simulations.

Dynamic Projection Mapping

Given the parameters of all projectors and depth cameras, as well as the geometry of the room, it is relatively straightforward to render graphics that change the surface appearance of physical objects in the room [27, 37]. This can be implemented as a single vertex shader which employs the mapping from 3D world coordinate point to the 2D point in a projector's image, as computed from calibration.

Rendering a virtual 3D object so that it appears correct from a given user's viewpoint is more complex and can be implemented as a multi-pass rendering process, whereby the virtual objects and real physical geometry are rendered offscreen from the desired viewpoint (see Figure 1 Virtual images). This offscreen rendering is then combined with the surface geometry and projector parameters in a standard projective texturing procedure, where only the physical geometry is rendered. We use a process similar to that described in [3]. The user's viewpoint is set to follow the head position determined by Kinect body tracking.

Supporting Multiple Views

The placement of the two opposite facing projectors was chosen so that each projector primarily displays the view corresponding to the user standing under it. A virtual object placed several feet above the ground and between the users, for example, is rendered twice, once for each user. Because the users are looking in opposite directions, one user is unlikely to see the graphics intended for the other user, because it will appear on the wall behind them, or on their own bodies. In this work we do not consider configurations with more than two users, or where users are not arranged face to face. In these more complex configurations, it is likely that one user will see the projection intended for another user. We speculate that such visual "cross-talk" may be disruptive to users, depending greatly on the task and configuration.

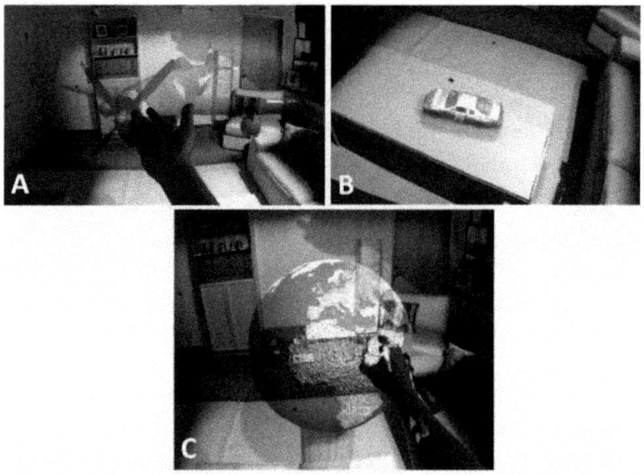

Figure 2. Examining virtual objects: a) airplane model in hand, b) race car on the table, c) hand spinning the globe. Note that while the objects are projected over diverse physical geometry, they appear correct to the user.

When the virtual object is placed nearer the ground between the users, the view of the object intended for one user may be seen by the other. Our rendering procedure models the view of each user as a standard perspective graphics camera. Where the physical surfaces addressed by each view overlap, the renderings are blended so that both are ultimately visible. For example, two views of the same object may appear on the floor. In the case when the object is placed on the ground, the two renderings of the object will overlap and meet at the ground. The impact of this "double rendering" may depend greatly on the application and is a matter of future research.

In some cases it may be more appropriate to render the object only once from a neutral viewpoint above and between the users as suggested by Hancock et al. [11].

Interactions

In addition to seeing virtual 3D objects rendered correctly, users may also interact with them in various ways. We have explored a number of simple interactions supported by Kinect body tracking and lower-level features derived from depth and infrared images. For example, "touching" a virtual object can be implemented by intersecting either the tracked hand position or points taken from the user's depth map, with the geometry of the virtual object.

An important and compelling interaction is the ability for the user to hold a virtual object in their hand (Figure 2a). The virtual object may be scripted to follow a point just above the hand as it is tracked in 3D by Kinect. The multi-view rendering described above renders the object once for each user's view, as described above. As the user holds their hand up in front of their body, their view will generate a large projection at the far surface of the room, possibly spanning the other user's body. Meanwhile, that second user's view will generate a small projection of the object, possibly over the first user's torso (see example in Figure 1).

Held objects can be dropped or thrown by meeting some conditions for release. For example, a held ball may be thrown if the velocity or acceleration of the hand exceeds some threshold. At the moment of release, the ball might take the velocity of throwing hand. Catching or "picking up" might be implemented by simply testing when an object is sufficiently close to the tracked hand.

Some applications may benefit from detecting the collision of virtual objects with the room or the user, leading to a realistic collision response. Our prototype uses pre-computed collision geometries for the static parts of the room, and approximates the shape of moving objects such as the user with a number of sphere colliders [3] (Figure 3).

Figure 3. A Unity view showing sphere collider proxies used to determine run-time collisions between game objects (e.g., the incoming fireball) and dynamic surface geometry (e.g., users).

While with our rendering pipeline it is straightforward to apply a texture to a static part of the room, applying a texture to a moving object such as the user requires real time tracking of the projection surface. We have experimented with using low level motion features such as optical flow with encouraging results. Real time optical flow is computed from the Kinect infrared video. A texture can be applied to moving objects by determining an initial placement of the texture and then following the surface over many frames using the motion estimated by optical flow (Figure 4c).

EXPERIENCES

In this section we describe a number of initial interactive *Mano-a-Mano* experiences. The accompanying video includes shots taken from the user's point of view.

Rendering Virtual Objects

As an initial demonstration of dynamic projection mapping, we placed a number of static models above the coffee table in the middle of the room. For example, a model of an airplane, a racecar or a globe is shown in Figure 2. While both users can get a good sense of the airplane, the globe is more challenging because each user views different sides. We incorporated a rudimentary ability to spin the globe by "touching" or intersecting with the globe.

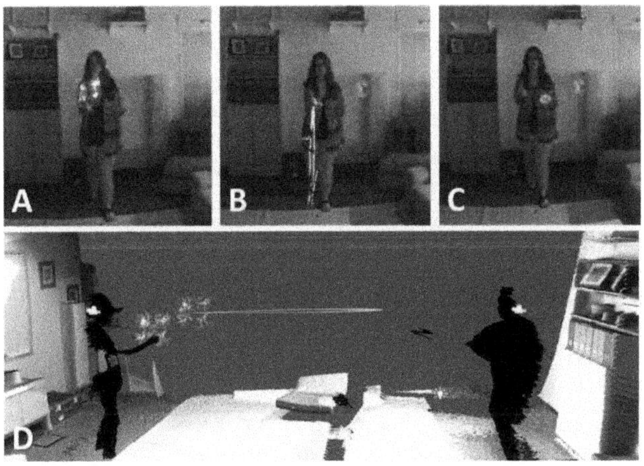

Figure 4. Fireball game: a) the user sees their partner holding a fireball; b) partner throws the fireball, the trail is visible; c) when the partner is hit, blood damage sticks to their body and its position gets updated with optical flow; d) Unity view showing flying and held fireballs.

Fireball

To test the ability to hold a virtual object and throw it accurately, we created a fun, fast-paced combat-style game where players summon a fireball by raising their hand. The fireball appears to hover over the hand a few inches. The player can quickly throw the fireball at the opposing player. If it hits the wall, damage is temporarily rendered at the point of collision. If it strikes the user, a blood texture is applied to the user. This visual effect tracks the projection surface on the player using optical flow as described above, and the attacking player scores a point (Figure 4). Release of the fireball is triggered by exceeding a threshold on the velocity of the hand holding the fireball. The direction is determined by computing the ray from the tracked head position through the hand. With a little practice, players can accurately direct their shot.

Catch

Two users can play catch with a virtual tennis ball (Figure 5). This experience extends the previous example by adding a rudimentary means to catch the ball: if the ball is sufficiently close to the hand, it is considered "caught" and is placed in the hand. The player may then throw it back to the other player.

If the player is unable to catch the ball, it may collide with the user or other objects in the room. In this case the ball will bounce and roll in a physically plausible way. The ability of the player to catch the ball hinges directly on their ability to perceive the virtual object in space.

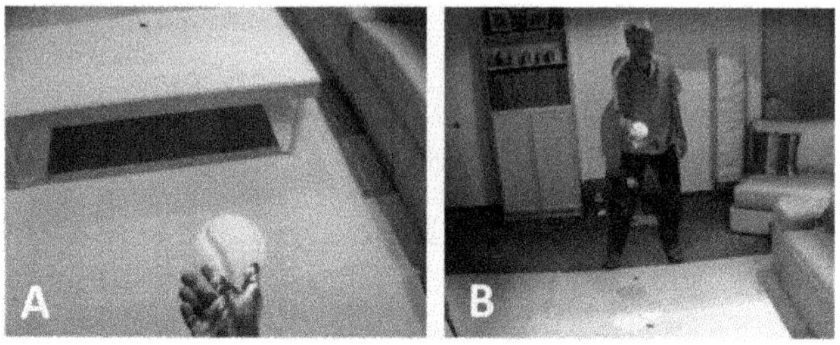

Figure 5. Playing catch with a virtual ball in *Mano-a-Mano*: a) ball in player's hand, b) ball in partner's hand. Note: from the partner's viewpoint the ball is rendered on the table in front.

USER EXPERIMENTS

To evaluate the effectiveness of our dyadic projected SAR system, we conducted two user experiments that focus on the most relevant aspects of a dyadic SAR system: first, can users correctly perceive virtual objects, and second, can users understand their collaborators' interactions with virtual objects?

Our studies offer initial support to the claim that dyadic SAR can support effective interaction with virtual objects between two face-to-face participants.

The first experiment focuses on examining the effectiveness of a single-user monoscopic perspective view to convey the sense of the virtual object's spatial presence. In particular, we examine whether the participants can perceive projected virtual objects as *spatial* rather than appearing only at the projection surface (*projected)*, and what factors affect their perception. The second study quantifies how well two collaborators understand each other's pointing references when discussing virtual objects between them in a face-to-face scenario.

We recruited 11 participants from our organization (5 female, mean age 36 years, std. dev. = 10 years). The participants performed both experiments in order and then completed a questionnaire to gather subjective feedback. The participants were compensated with a $10 coupon and the total session took approximately 30 minutes to complete.

Experiment 1: Object Presence

While previous SAR research [3] demonstrates that users can perceive perspective-projected virtual objects as *spatial*, rather than *projected*, those experiments were done with stereoscopic projections and virtual objects were always close to the projection surface. In our room-scale environment, it is unclear whether the users will perceive the spatial characteristics of virtual objects when they are projected without stereo and far away from the projection surface. This ability to perceive virtual object's presence in mid-air is crucial for any view-dependent larger-scale SAR scenario.

Experiment Design

As a measure of the virtual object presence, we asked the participants to rate the distance to and size of projected virtual objects (similar to [3]). The projected test object was a green cube of three different sizes (small=10cm, medium=15cm and large=20cm edge) and virtually positioned at three different distances from the participant (near=1.5m, middle=2.5m, and far=3.5m). From the participant's point of view, the image of the virtual object was always projected on the back wall of the room (approximately 3.75m away from the user) (Figure 6).

It is important to note that the object's sizes were highly confusable across our tested distances (this was intentional). In fact, when projected at the nearest location the smallest object subtended roughly the same visual angle as the largest object at the farthest distance.

In addition to varying size and distance, we introduced two different conditions for performing this task: with and without physical markers. The *with markers* condition included three black poles placed exactly at the location where the virtual object could appear, while the *no markers* condition had those poles removed (Figure 6). If observed correctly, the virtual object would appear to sit on the physical marker. Our goal was not to tell the participant where the object is with the physical marker, but rather to aid them by giving them a real-world physical anchor that they can compare to the virtual object. The participants were still required to determine which of the three markers the virtual object is attached to. In addition to our main hypothesis that the participants are able to correctly understand the spatial placement of projected virtual objects (*H1*), we hypothesized that having a physical object marking the possible location of the virtual object makes the rating task simpler (*H2*). This was motivated by our observations that virtual objects projected in the collaborator's hand always seemed a bit more spatial and real, than the objects purely placed in mid-air. The physical markers in our experiment served as a controlled proxy for the user's hand.

Lastly, we hypothesized that participants are more accurate in rating objects closer to the projection surface (*H3*), i.e., further away from the participant, since the real world and the virtual object's location are in closer agreement in such cases. This is contrary to the real world behavior where humans are better in rating closer objects as objects further away form a smaller visual angle and are therefore harder to see [10].

In summary, our experiment design was: Size (3) x Distance (3) x Condition (2). The participants performed 4 ratings for each of these combinations resulting in a total of 72 ratings per participant. We recorded the participant's rating of both size and distance of the object as well as their response time.

Figure 6. Experiment 1: a) participant performing the "with markers" condition, where black poles serve as physical markers for the location of the virtual cubes; b) Unity view showing the virtual object at the far distance; c) three real-word cubes sit on the table in front of the participant for comparison.

Procedure

Each participant was first given a brief introduction to our system, and then asked to stand facing the side of the room where their perspective projected view would be shown. In front of them was a short coffee table on top of which we place three physical models of the three cubes. Those physical cubes precisely matched the scale of projected virtual cubes. The three possible locations where the virtual object would appear were marked on the floor with a number (1-near, 2-mid, 3-far).

We asked the participants to verbally rate each object's size (indicating "small", "medium", or "large") and distance (indicating "1", "2", or "3", corresponding to the marked floor location). The coordinator recorded their ratings and advanced to the next trial. To ensure the same amount of stimulus across all participants, the object was projected for exactly 5 seconds, after which it disappeared. The participants were instructed to give their ratings as soon as they felt confident, and their response time was recorded as the time from the object's appearance to the time of coordinator's entry. For evaluation simplicity, the trials were grouped by condition since setup of physical markers required time and would render collection of large dataset difficult. The presentation of size and distance trials was randomized within each condition block, and the order of conditions was counterbalanced across users to reduce the effects of ordering. Before each condition, the participants were given a practice session where they were shown each object at each size and distance combination (without the 5 second limit) and the study coordinators gave them feedback on their ratings.

The participants were initially positioned such that the objects appeared at the same physical location on the back wall. They were explicitly told that they could move around if that helped them make a decision, but were asked to remain roughly within a step away from the initial position marked on the floor. While the projection was monoscopic, participants could use other depth cues including shading, perspective, shadows, size, and motion parallax.

Results

Overall, participants were more accurate in rating Distance (88.8%) than Size of virtual objects (70.7%). When considering both Distance and Size, they provided a correct rating in 66.5% of trials, which is significantly better than chance (1 out of 9 combinations). These findings support our *H1* hypothesis that users can and do perceive virtual objects as having spatial presence in a perspective SAR scenario.

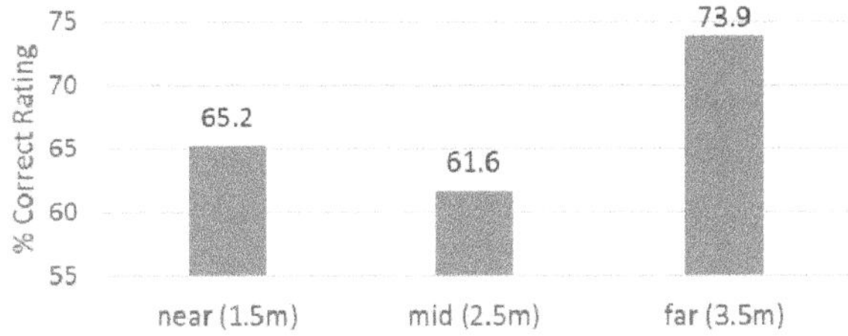

Figure 7. Effect of Distance on the participant's overall ratings of objects depth placement and size.

Out of 792 total trials, only 9 ratings were more than one option away from the ground truth in either size or distance (e.g., mistaking a "small" size for "large") and those could be considered outliers. Given only three possible options in each category, this is not surprising, but this effectively means that the participants were either right on target ("correct") or one target off ("incorrect").

We therefore coded the participant's responses into a binary variable ("correct" or "incorrect") for each of the size, distance, as well as size and distance combined rating. Given such binary responses, standard linear regression models or analysis of variance (ANOVA) are not appropriate since they assume scalar responses drawn from a normal distribution. The appropriate method of statistical analysis for correctness of user's ratings is *repeated measures logistic regression* [40]. We used IBM SPSS v.21 to calculate our statistics. In our case, logistic regression computed the correlation between the varied factors (e.g., different sizes, distances, or conditions) and a binary outcome ("correct" or "incorrect"). The significance metric for logistic regression is Wald Chi-Square (χ^2).

We ran our analysis on the model containing the following factors: Condition, Size, and Distance. When analyzing the overall correctness (i.e., correct for both size and distance), we found significant effects for Distance ($\chi^2 = 11.746$, df = 2, p = .003; a p-value <=0.05 shows a statistically significant effect), but not for Size or Condition. Distance had a strong effect on the ratings with *far* distance (3.5m away) being significantly more accurate than *near* and *mid* (Figure 7). This result runs contrary to the real-world behavior where closer objects tend to be easier to rate, but it confirms our *H3* hypothesis, that being closer to the projection surface makes it easier for the user to correctly perceive the spatial characteristics of the projected 3D virtual object. In our experiment, the *far* distance was only 25cm away from the back wall where the object was being projected.

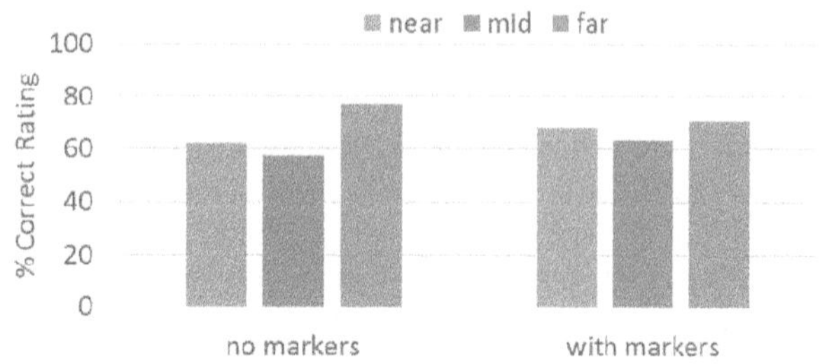

Figure 8. Participants' performance across different Conditions at different Distances.

While participants were more correct in the condition with physical markers (67.4%) versus no markers (65.6%), Condition was not found to have a statistically significant effect. This result failed to confirm our hypothesis *H2*. We further analyzed our results to understand why. Presence of markers improved participants' ratings on average 6% when objects were far away from the projection surface (at *near* and *mid* distances), but actually hurt their performance in the *far* distance (Figure 8). This might be explained by the fact that at the *far* location, participants already had a large physical reference, the projection wall itself, to help them judge distance and were potentially just distracted by the presence of multiple poles in front of the projected object. We speculate that when the virtual object was further away from the projection surface, the presence of physical markers may have been beneficial.

Furthermore, interaction of Size*Distance had a highly significant effect ($\chi^2 = 47.482$, df = 4, $p < .001$). This was not surprising, since some of the combinations were easily identifiable (e.g., the small cube at the far distance was the smallest projected object) while some were highly confusable (e.g., the medium cube at the near position is easily confused with the large cube at mid position).

We also identified an effect of gender on our results ($\chi^2 = 6.524$, df = 1, p = .011) with males outperforming female participants by 12%. While this agrees with results of other experiments that evaluate spatial ability (e.g., Mental Rotation Test [29]), note that our sample size is rather small (5 female and 6 males) and therefore it is difficult to draw gender conclusions from our experiment.

Response time includes the time for the coordinator to log the result and advance the trial (approximately 1 second). The average response time was 6.47s (std. dev. = 2.27s). We performed repeated measures ANOVA on the response time and found that it closely correlates with our rating analysis: *participants were significantly faster in responding to conditions where they were also found to be more accurate.* This indicates that our results do not fall under a speed-accuracy tradeoff common to many targeting experiments. Since these results are closely correlated and exhibit similar statistically significant effects, we omit detailed analysis of the response time.

Subjective Feedback

While our quantitative data does not show statistically significant benefits to the presence of physical markers in the first experiment, 9 out of 11 participants stated that having physical markers helped them complete the task.

Our questionnaire captured the participants' feedback on the statement "I could tell where the objects were in space" as the average rating of 3.81 (with markers) vs. 3.0 (without markers) (t-test p<0.005) on a 5 point Likert scale (5 indicating agreement). The responses for "I am confident that my guesses are correct", yielded similar responses on the same scale: average rating of 3.09 (with markers) vs. 2.54 (without markers) (t-test p<0.007). Participants were asked to comment on any strategies they used to complete the trials. While most of the participants reported using movement and size to rate the objects, 5 out of 11 participants self-reported relying heavily on the position of virtual shadows as well.

Experiment 2: Understanding Collaborator's Spatial References in a Dyad

The main purpose of our SAR system is to allow two people to interact in an unobstructed face-to-face manner (e.g., see our *Fireball* or *Catch* experiences above). The effectiveness of that experience hinges on the user's ability to understand what their partners are doing, so that they may respond appropriately. We designed the second experiment to explore how well the user understands the actions and intentions of their collaborator when discussing virtual objects in a face-to-face scenario in Dyadic SAR.

Experiment Design

We designed a task in which the participant observed their *partner* (one of the study coordinators) raise a short pole to their eye level and point at one of 16 spheres that appeared between the participant and the coordinator. Participants verbally indicated which sphere they believed their partner was pointing at. The spheres were arranged in a 4x4 grid and were clearly numbered (Figure 9). In this configuration, the spheres in the grid were projected partially on the human bodies in space and partially on the walls behind them.

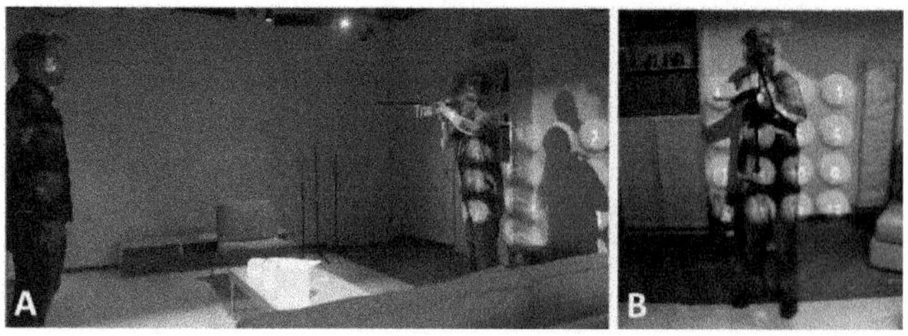

Figure 9. Experiment 2: a) side view of the participant and their partner pointing at a target; b) participant's perspective (recorded with a helmet camera).

Each sphere in the grid was 10cm in diameter and the spheres were 11 cm apart (center to center). The grid floated 1.5 meters above the floor. This particular arrangement of targets was found in our pilot experiment to be dense enough to be potentially confusable while offering enough spatial resolution to mimic the requirements in many real world face-to-face tasks (e.g., two people discussing an architectural model between them). While targeting with a rifle-like aiming gesture is not a natural pointing style, we chose this pose to avoid the ambiguity of individual person's pointing style. We are not interested in understanding how well can the participants understand pointing gestures in general, but rather how well can they understand a particular spatial reference when performed with respect to a virtual object in front of them. In our pilot experiments, this targeting style was selected as the least ambiguous.

Rather than comparing targeting performance among multiple conditions, this experiment was designed to quantify the overall accuracy of participant's understanding of their partner's references. We therefore measured the error (in meters) in their estimate as the distance from the sphere they indicated to the actual targeted sphere.

Procedure

The same group of participants from the first experiment participated in this experiment. Each participant stood at the same location as in the first experiment. Their collaborator stood on the other side of the room (~2.5m away). At the start of the trial, the collaborator was silently prompted by the system to point at a specific numbered ball in the grid. The participant then verbally indicated which sphere they believe their collaborator was pointing at. The trial was not time limited, but participants were instructed to respond as soon as they felt confident in their rating. One of the study coordinators entered their response to conclude the trial. The collaborator returned to a neutral pose (non-targeting) between each trial. Before running the experiment, each participant was given a set of 15 practice trials during which they were given feedback on their performance.

We randomized the order of presentation of target spheres and each participant gave two ratings for each sphere condition for a total of 32 ratings.

Results

Participants identified the correct target in 54.5% of 352 total trials. While this might appear low, it is significantly higher than chance (1 out of 16) and is more impressive when one considers the distance between the selected target and the true target. Averaged over all trials this spatial error was 0.056m (std. dev. = 0.063m). This low value indicates that when participants selected the incorrect target, they overwhelmingly indicated one of the nearest neighbor targets (the targets themselves were 0.11m away). Errors were not uniformly distributed. For example, the lower right target exhibited more than twice the error compared to targets in the upper right corner (Figure 10); however, our data does not offer any explanation for this effect.

The angular difference in targeting two adjacent target spheres was approximately 4.5°. That participants could tell the target reference to within a 12cm radius is impressive and provides evidence that our system is capable of presenting virtual information between the two unencumbered users in a way that enables mutual spatial understanding.

4 0.0638	3 0.0492	2 0.0409	1 0.065
8 0.0483	7 0.0516	6 0.0425	5 0.0454
12 0.052	11 0.0736	10 0.0635	9 0.065
16 0.0824	15 0.0582	14 0.0482	13 0.0524

Figure 10. The 4x4 target grid (left) is shown from the participant's perspective (Unity3D view). The table (right) with average amount of error (in meters) for the participant's rating of each of the spheres in a grid. The numbers are color-coded to indicate performance (green=best, red=worst).

DISCUSSION

The figures in this paper and the accompanying video demonstrate that the dynamic projective texturing process is accurate enough to generate good monocular views of virtual objects for each user.

Less clear is to what extent, and under what circumstances, users of our system have a good sense of the virtual object's presence at the correct distance and size. While the first user experiment demonstrates that users are able to perform much better than chance on determining object size and distance in a controlled setting, subjects clearly performed worse at this task than if real objects were presented. Stereo projection would likely enhance the correct perception of size and distance (as in [3]). However, today's stereo projection technologies generally require wearing glasses, obstructing the face and impinging on the fluidity of face to fact interaction.

In practice, the sense of object presence may depend on a number of factors which are not considered in the user experiments [9]. For example, an object of familiar size and shape such as a tennis ball may be easier to correctly perceive than an abstract, featureless cube. Our own experience with the *Fireball* and *Catch* application examples suggest that interacting directly with a virtual object lends a stronger sense of the position and size of the object. For example, when holding a virtual object, it seems as if the higher level, cognitive realization that the object is being held in the hand helps in seeing the virtual object in the hand. This effect may be similar to that of "visual capture" studied in psychology, whereby, for example, a ventriloquist's voice appears to be coming from a dummy's mouth. Note that this cue may be stronger than the markers provided in the first experiment: in that task, participants determined which of three physical references indicated the distance of the object. When holding an object, the hand is the one possible physical reference.

While holding and moving a virtual object gives a stronger sense of object presence, it is also our experience that watching the other user hold the object similarly helps. In fact, the effect is often stronger, since the projection of the held object may lie on the other user's body, placing its projection closer to the object's simulated position. As shown in the first experiment participants found the task easier when the object was nearer the projection surface.

Participant's success in the second experiment indicates a rudimentary shared understanding of the layout of virtual objects between them, and thereby a basis for more advanced collaborative interactions. As with the first experiment, our experience pointing and gesturing towards virtual objects may be rather different than that of the experiment, as the context of the task and arrangement of objects can have a great impact, as well as the various ways in which people gesture in more natural tasks.

CONCLUSION

Mano-a-Mano is a unique spatial augmented reality system that combines dynamic projection mapping, multiple perspective views and device-less interaction to support dyadic interaction with virtual 3D objects. We show a few initial interactive experiences with the system that demonstrate some fundamental interactions, but clearly there is the potential to investigate applications that go beyond gaming. Of particular interest are those that leverage the system's unique capabilities to support collaboration and co-reference of 3D virtual objects, especially where uninterrupted face to face interaction is valuable.

ACKNOWLEDGMENTS

We would like to thank Brett Jones, Rajinder Sodhi, Michael Murdock, Eyal Ofek, Ravish Mehra, Blair MacIntyre and Nikunj Raghuvanshi for their foundational work on the RoomAlive system which enabled this project.

REFERENCES

1. Arthur, K., Booth, K.S., and Ware, C. 1993. Evaluating 3D Task Performance for Fish Tank Virtual Worlds. In *ACM Trans. on Information Systems,* 11(3). 239–265.
2. Agrawala, M., Beers, A.C., McDowall, I., Fröhlich, B., Bolas, M., and Hanrahan. P. 1997. The two-user Responsive Workbench: support for collaboration through individual views of a shared space. In *Proc. of ACM SIGGRAPH '97.* 327–332.
3. Benko, H., Jota, R. and Wilson, A. D. 2012. MirageTable: Freehand Interaction on a Projected Augmented Reality Tabletop. In *Proc. of ACM CHI '12.* 199–208.
4. Bimber, O. and Raskar, R. 2005. Spatial Augmented Reality: Merging Real and Virtual Worlds. A. K. Peters, Ltd., Natick, MA, USA.
5. Bimber, O., Fröhlich, B., Schmalstieg, D., and Encarnacao, L. M. 2002. The Virtual Showcase. *IEEE Comput. Graph. Appl.,* 21(6) (November 2001). 48-55.
6. Broecker, M., Smith, R.T., and Thomas, B. 2014. Depth Perception in View-Dependent Near-Field Spatial AR. *Australasian User Interface Conf. (AUIC '14).* (poster).
7. Cakmakci, O., Member, S., Rolland, J., and Member, A. 2006. Head-Worn Displays: A Review. *IEEE Journal of Display Technology.*
8. Cruz-Neira, C., Sandin, D.J., and DeFanti, T.A. 1993. Surround-screen projection-based virtual reality: The design and implementation of the CAVE. In *Proc. of ACM SIGGRAPH '93.* 135–142.
9. Cutting, J.E., and Vishton, P.M. 1995. Perceiving layout and knowing distances: The integration, relative potency, and contextual use of different information about depth. In W. Epstein and S. Rogers (eds). *Handbook of perception of space and motion,* 69–117.
10. Gilinsky, A.S. 1951. Perceived Size and Distance in Visual Space. *Psychological Review,* 58, 460–480.
11. Hancock, M., Nacenta, M., Gutwin, C., and Carpendale, S. 2009. The effects of changing projection geometry on the interpretation of 3D orientation on tabletops. In *Proc. of ACM ITS '09.* 175–182.
12. Harrison, C., Benko, H., and Wilson, A.D. 2011. OmniTouch: Wearable Multitouch Interaction Everywhere. In *Proc. of ACM UIST '11.* 441–450.
13. Heo, H., Park, H.K., Kim, S., Chung, J., Lee, G. and Lee, W. 2014. Transwall: a transparent double-sided touch display facilitating co-located face-to-face interactions. In *CHI '14 Extended Abstracts.* 435–438.
14. Hirakawa, M. and Koike, S. 2004. A Collaborative Augmented Reality System Using Transparent Display. In *Proc. of the IEEE Int. Symposium on Multimedia Software Engineering* (ISMSE '04). 410–416.
15. Hou, J., Nam, Y., Peng, W., and Lee, K.M. 2012. Effects of screen size, viewing angle, and players' immersion tendencies on game experience. *Comp. in Human Behavior,* 28(2). 617–623.
16. Howard, I. 2012. Perceiving in Depth. New York: Oxford University Press. ISBN 978-0-199-76414-3.
17. Ishii, H. and Kobayashi, M. 1992. ClearBoard: a seamless medium for shared drawing and conversation with eye contact. In *Proc. of ACM CHI '92.* 525–532.
18. Jones, B., Benko, H., Ofek, E., and Wilson, A. D. 2013. IllumiRoom: Peripheral Projected Illusions for Interactive Experiences. In *Proc. of ACM CHI '13.*
19. Jones, B., Sodhi, R., Murdock, M., Mehra, R., Benko, H., Wilson, A., Ofek, E., MacIntyre, B., Raghuvanshi, N., Shapira, L. 2014. Roomalive: Magical Experiences Enabled by Scalable Adaptive Projector Camera Units. In Proc. of *ACM UIST '14.*
20. Khoshelham, K. 2012. Accuracy Analysis of Kinect Depth Data. In *Proc. Of Int. Achieves of Photogrammetry, Remote Sensing and SI Sciences.* Aug.
21. Kitamura, Y., Konishi, T., Masaki, T. and Kishino, F. 2001. IllusionHole: A Stereoscopic Display for Multiple Observers. In *Proc. SPIE vol. 4297, Stereoscopic Displays and Virtual Reality Systems VIII.*

22. Olwal, A., DiVerdi, S., Candussi, N., Rakkolainen, I., and Hollerer, T. 2006. An Immaterial, Dual-sided Display System with 3D Interaction. In Proc. of IEEE Conference on Virtual Reality (VR '06). 279–280.

23. Pinhanez, C. S. 2001. The Everywhere Displays Projector: A Device to Create Ubiquitous Graphical Interfaces. In *Proc. of ACM UBICOMP '01*. 315–331.

24. Raskar, R., van Baar, J., Beardsley, P., Willwacher, T., Rao, S., and Forlines, C. 2003. iLamps: Geometrically aware and self-configuring projectors. *ACM TOG 223,* 809–818.

25. Raskar, R., Welch, G., Cutts, M., Lake, A., Stesin, L. and Fuchs, H. 1998. The office of the future: a unified approach to image-based modeling and spatially immersive displays. In *Proc. of ACM SIGGRAPH '98.* 179-188.

26. Raskar, R., Welch, G. and Fuchs, H. 1998. Spatially Augmented Reality. In *Proc. of IEEE Workshop on Augmented Reality (IWAR'98).*

27. Raskar, R., Welch, G., Low, K.-L., and Bandyopadhyay, D. 2001. Shader Lamps: Animating Real Objects with Image-Based Illumination. In *Proc. of the Eurographics Workshop on Rendering Techniques*. 89-102.

28. Rekimoto, J. and Saitoh, M. 1999. Augmented Surfaces: A Spatially Continuous Work Space for Hybrid Computing Environments. In *Proc. of ACM SIGCHI '99.* 378–385.

29. Richardson, J.T.E. 1994. Gender differences in mental rotation. *Perceptual and Motor Skills*, 78. 435-448.

30. Sekular, R.B. Perception. 2nd Edition. (1990).

31. Sheridan, T.B. 1992. Musings on telepresence and virtual presence. *Presence: Teleoperators and Virtual Environments,* 1(1). 120-125.

32. Sollenberger, R.L. and Milgram, P. 1991. A comparative study of rotational and stereoscopic computer graphics depth cues. In *Proc. of Human Factors Society 35th Annual Meeting.* 1452–1456.

33. Stevens, B. Jerrams-Smith, J., Heathcote, D. and Callear, D. 2002. Putting the Virtual into Reality: Assessing Object-Presence with Projection-Augmented Models. *Presence,* 11(1). 79–92.

34. Tang, Y., Lam, B., Stavness, I., and Fels, S. 2011. Kinect-based augmented reality projection with perspective correction. In *ACM SIGGRAPH '11.* (poster).

35. Underkoffler, J., Ullmer, B., and Ishii, H. 1999. Emancipated pixels: Real-world graphics in the luminous room. In *Proc. of ACM SIGGRAPH '99.* 385–392.

36. Wilson, A. 2007. Depth-Sensing Video Cameras for 3D Tangible Tabletop Interaction. In *Proc. of IEEE International Workshop on Horizontal Interactive Human-Computer Systems (TABLETOP '07).* 201–204.

37. Wilson A. and Benko H. 2010. Combining multiple depth cameras and projectors for interactions on, above and between surfaces. In *Proc. of ACM UIST'10.* 273-282.

38. Wilson, A. D., Benko, H., Izadi, S., and Hilliges, O. 2012. Steerable Augmented Reality with the Beamatron. In *Proc. of ACM UIST '12.* 413-422.

39. Wilson, A. D., Izadi, S., Hilliges, O., Garcia-Mendoza, A., and Kirk, D. 2008. Bringing physics to the surface. In *Proc. of ACM UIST '08.* 67-76.

40. Winer, B.J., Brown, D. and Michels, K. 1991. Statistical Principles in Experimental Design, 3rd Ed. New York, NY. McGraw-Hill.

Tracs: Transparency Control for See-through Displays

David Lindlbauer[1], Toru Aoki[2], Robert Walter[1], Yuji UEMA[2], Anita Höchtl[3], Michael Haller[3], Masahiko Inami[2], Jörg Müller[1,4]
[1]Quality and Usability Lab, Telekom Innovation Laboratories, TU Berlin, Germany
[2]Keio University, Yokohama City, Kanagawa, Japan
[3]Media Interaction Lab, University of Applied Sciences Upper Austria, Hagenberg, Austria
[4]Alexander von Humboldt Institute for Internet and Society, Berlin, Germany

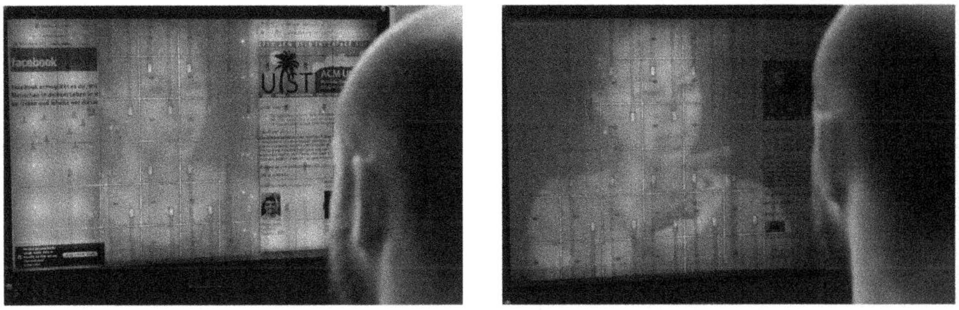

Figure 1. Tracs is a dual-sided transparency-controlled see-through display system to avoid visual interference on transparent displays and to support fast switching between personal work and collaboration. Users can control the transparency of specific parts of the display (*left*) or overall (*right*).

ABSTRACT
We present Tracs, a dual-sided see-through display system with controllable transparency. Traditional displays are a constant visual and communication barrier, hindering fast and efficient collaboration of spatially close or facing co-workers. Transparent displays could potentially remove these barriers, but introduce new issues of personal privacy, screen content privacy and visual interference. We therefore propose a solution with controllable transparency to overcome these problems. Tracs consists of two see-through displays, with a transparency-control layer, a backlight layer and a polarization adjustment layer in-between. The transparency-control layer is built as a grid of individually addressable transparency-controlled patches, allowing users to control the transparency overall or just locally. Additionally, the locally switchable backlight layer improves the contrast of LCD screen content. Tracs allows users to switch between personal and collaborative work fast and easily and gives them full control of transparent regions on their display.

Author Keywords
Transparent display; transparency-controlled display;

ACM Classification Keywords
H.5.m. Information Interfaces and Presentation (e.g. HCI): Miscellaneous

INTRODUCTION
Traditional displays are dominating our office environments. They provide crystal-clear images on the one side, but block the view on the environment behind the display. Consequently, these displays are a constant visual barrier and thus also a communication barrier. Additionally, they do not allow for face-to-face communication while seeing screen content, one of the main affordances of transparent displays [18].

Transparent displays offer the ability to see screen content as well as the environment behind the display. They have been explored for co-located collaboration [10, 18, 19, 21, 22], exposing beneficial features like workspace awareness. However, traditional (non-transparent) displays still are ubiquitous. We believe this is because transparent displays lack basic features of traditional displays such as shielding from visual disturbances from the environment behind the display. In order to make see-through display devices more usable, we believe it is important to allow users to change the transparency of their display on-demand. This way, visual interference can be decreased and users can regain privacy by turning the display opaque.

In this paper, we present Tracs (TRAnsparency Controlled Screens), a dual-sided transparency-controlled display system. With Tracs, users can control the transparency of individual areas of their display (see Figure 1). It consists of two see-through displays enclosing a transparency-control layer, a backlight layer, and a polarization adjustment layer.

The transparency-control layer is a grid of transparency-controllable patches and is created from a single piece of PDLC (Polymer Dispersed Liquid Crystal) switchable diffuser with additional pieces of transparent ITO (Indium Tin Oxide) film for controlling the individual patches.

The transparency of the PDLC diffuser is controlled by adjusting the voltage supplied to it. Tracs' backlight layer, a LED matrix mounted on transparent ITO, improves the contrast of the see-through display. The polarization adjustment layer is added to enable users to see through the LCDs.

RELATED WORK

Transparent Displays

Using transparent displays for co-located collaboration and using their features like face-to-face communication and gaze-awareness has been proposed by Tang and Minnemann with VideoDraw [21] and VideoWhiteboard [22] as well as by Ishii and Kobayashi with Clearboard-0 [10]. They emphasized the importance of integrating content directly into the communication channel to allow users to switch focus and task smoothly. Hirakawa et al. [8] used a see-through display as collaborative working environment in combination with augmented reality. Olwal et al. [19] used an interactive dual-sided FogScreen for multi-user face-to-face collaboration, giving users the ability to collaborate closely while being able to see and interact with screen content. With MUSTARD [12] and PiVOT [13], Karnik et al. explored the possiblity to target contents at specific users, giving them the ability to see contents collaboratively or exclusively. HoloDesk [7] and SpaceTop [17] use an optical see-through display for 2D and 3D spatial interactions behind the display. In Transwall, Heo et al. [6] display equal content on both sides of a transparent display for facilitating interpersonal communication, mostly through gaming. Li et al. [18] used a dual-sided projected transparent display for collaborative work. They discuss the affordances and possibility of such setups, with enhancements in workspace awareness being fundamental advantages of transparent displays over traditional displays.

With Tracs, we focus on controlling the transparency and the ability to see or hide the environment behind the display. Prior systems could control transparency only by overlaying the environment behind the display with screen content. Tracs' transparency-control layer offers the unique ability to control transparency independent of screen content, thus allowing users to avoid visual interference and to switch seamlessly between personal (opaque) and collaborative (transparent) usage on demand.

Transparency and Visual Interference

Insights from research on interface transparency evaluations (e.g., [1, 3, 4]) show decreased performance of task execution (e.g., selection or menu interaction) with transparent user interfaces. For transparent displays, Laramee and Ware [16] showed that visual rivalry between screen content and background leads to decreased performance and readability. With Tracs, users control the transparency of our see-through displays and can therefore avoid potential visual rivalry.

Switchable diffuser in HCI

For our transparency-control matrix, we used PDLC switchable diffuser, a material normally employed in architecture (e.g., meeting rooms, trains) that has also been used in HCI before. Prior systems mostly used switchable diffuser for camera see-through systems (e.g., [2, 14]) or for projecting through surfaces [11]. For Squama, Rekimoto [20] used a large-scale grid of switchable diffusers as programmable physical architecture and for dynamic shadow creation. He focused on making use of the interplay between transparency and opacity, also by conveying information with the diffuser themselves, without additional devices or displays (except camera tracking). In contrast to this, our work focuses on creating a dual-sided see-through display system which uses the property of adjustable transparency. Tracs should enhance the user experience when working with transparent displays.

TRACS

Tracs gives users the ability to toggle the transparency of individual areas on the display through its transparency-control layer (see Figure 1). These areas support more fine-grained adjustments for users and to cover a broader range of use-cases and applications, e.g., to allow users to create collaborative (transparent) and personal (opaque) regions on their display simultaneously (see Figure 8). Additionally, this enables users to block visual interference locally without having to turn the whole display opaque.

Hardware Components

Tracs consists of a stack of five hardware components (see Figure 2). We use two transparent 22" LCDs (Samsung LTI220MT02[1]) as a basis for displaying content. In-between the two displays, Tracs includes a transparency-control layer which allows users to manually control the transparency of the displays. Furthermore, we included a backlight layer to increase the contrast of the LCDs and a polarisation adjustment layer to improve the transparency of the displays.

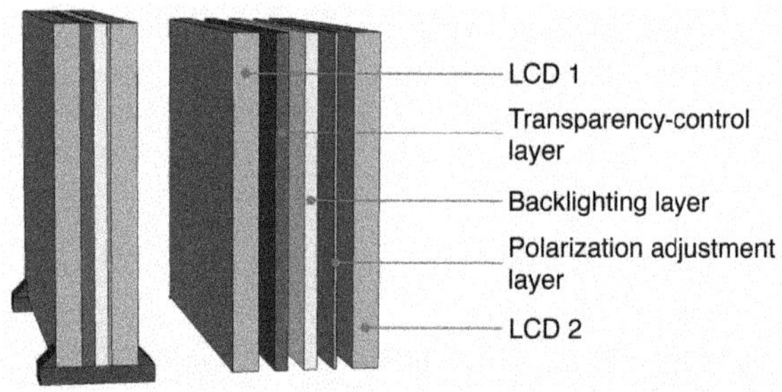

Figure 2. Schematic of the dual-sided screen system, consisting of two transparent LCDs, a transparency-control layer, a transparent backlight and a half-wave retardation film for adjusting polarization.

Transparent displays

Transparent LCDs rely on ambient light for displaying screen content. They are transparent when turned off or displaying non-black content. Since they do not emit light, contrast is limited compared to e.g., transparent OLEDs (not commercially available yet). We chose displays over projection to make Tracs self-contained and to cover a broad range of co-located collaborative use cases (e.g., office context with workers facing each other). Since we used transparent LCDs in our setup, we equipped Tracs with an additional backlight and polarisation adjustment layer.

[1]Each display offers a transparency of about 15% according to the specification.

Transparency-control layer

Our current prototype consists of a 9×6 matrix of individually controllable patches, each with a size of 5 cm $\times$ 5 cm. We constructed the matrix from a single piece of PDLC switchable diffuser (see Figure 3). This material is composed of two layers of ITO and one layer of polymer dispersed liquid crystals. The conductive sides of the ITO layers are facing each other, with the crystals in between. When no voltage is applied, the material is diffuse (60% VLT[2], 90% haze), and becomes clear (80% VLT, 10% haze) when voltage is applied (60 volts). One ITO layer serves as anode (*layer A*), the other as cathode (*layer C*). Our transparency-control matrix is a passive matrix layout with a common anode.

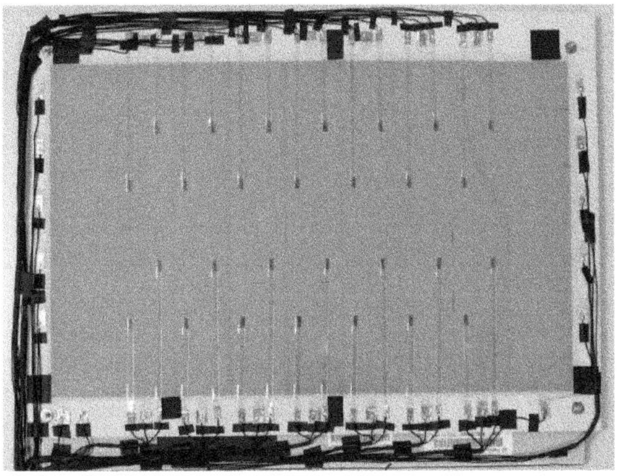

Figure 3. Our current 22" prototype of the transparency-control matrix. Each of the 54 patches can be controlled individually.

We first laser engrave *layer C* of ITO in a grid-like manner to create the individual patches (see Figure 4, cuts are dashed red lines *right*, resulting patches *left*). Note that in order to disconnect the individual patches from each other, each line consists of two cuts (distance 1 mm). The ITO between the two cuts is removed manually to avoid current from flowing. The cuts only go through *layer C*, *layer A* is left intact (see Figure 4, *center*). Damaging the conductive coating of *layer A* side would not allow us to use it as a common anode.

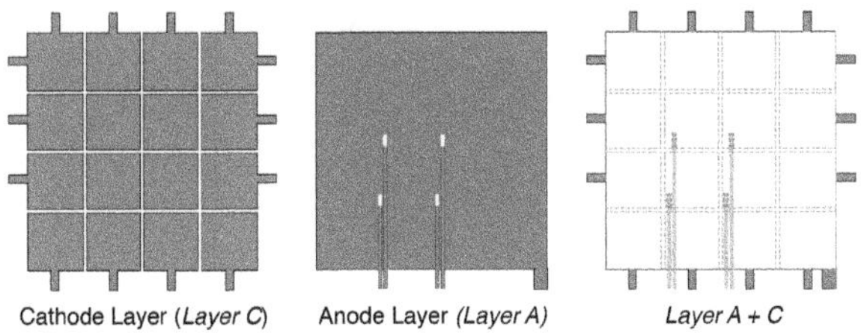

Figure 4. Schematic of a 4×4 transparency-control matrix: cathode layer (*layer C, left*) with individual patches, common anode layer (*layer A, center*) and *A* and *C* combined (*right*). Both layers have connectors for the wiring (areas outside of grid). We added additional strips of ITO on top of the anode layer (*center*, light green) to connect inner patches.

For controlling the patches in *layer C* individually, we connect them to the cables running at the outside. Therefore, we laser engrave 5 mm $\times$ 10 mm holes into *layer A* (see Figure 4, *right*). Subsequently, we applied thin separate strips of ITO from the outside to the holes and connect the strips with the holes, *layer C* respectively[3]. Patches at the edges are connected with small additional areas on the outside to avoid cutting holes. These transparent ITO connections in combination with the common anode from *layer A* allow us to control the transparency of each patch individually. The patches are controlled with 8 Texas Instruments TPIC6B595 high voltage 8-Bit shift registers, which can handle load up to 60 volts, connected to a microcontroller.

Backlight layer

We constructed the Tracs backlight matrix by mounting LEDs on top of a piece of ITO (80% VLT, 2% haze) using wire glue. In order to being able to control the LEDs individually, we used a passive matrix addressing scheme, with individually addressable rows and columns. All lines for anodes and cathodes were engraved into ITO (Figure 5, red lines) to construct the matrix from a single layer of transparent material.

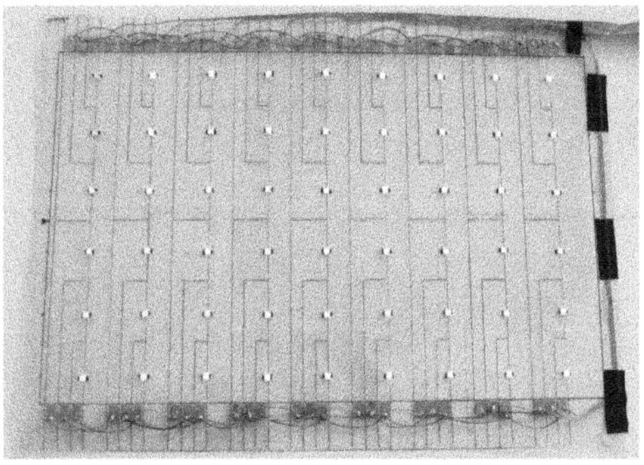

Figure 5. Tracs' backlight matrix is composed of LEDs mounted on ITO and controlled via a passive matrix addressing scheme. The red lines highlight the engraving in the ITO and are not visible for users.

Polarization adjustment layer

Each LCD used for Tracs has a linear polarizer film (orientation 45°) applied to their front- and backside in order for them to work. Since the two LCDs are polarized orthogonally once positioned back-to-back, the displays would be completely opaque. In order to overcome this issue, we included an additional layer of transparent half-wave retardation film[4] (see Figure 6) in-between the two displays. The film acts as a polarization rotator by shifting the phase of the input light by π, rotating the incoming linearly polarized light by 90°, respectively, cf. Figure 2 [5].

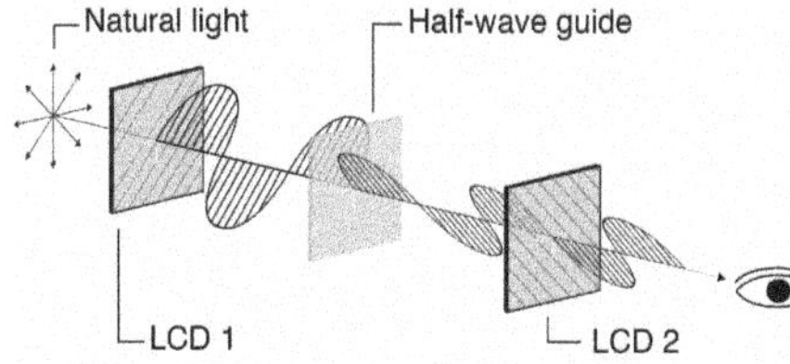

Figure 6. The polarization is adjusted using a half-wave retardation film positioned between the screens. Without the film, users could not see through the display, since the displays are polarized orthogonally.

---

[2]VLT = visible light transmission

[3]We used 3M™Z-Axis Electrically Conductive Tape 9703 for connecting the two layers of ITO.

[4]We used an American Polarizers APHW92-003-PC-280NM half wave retardation film (92% VLT)

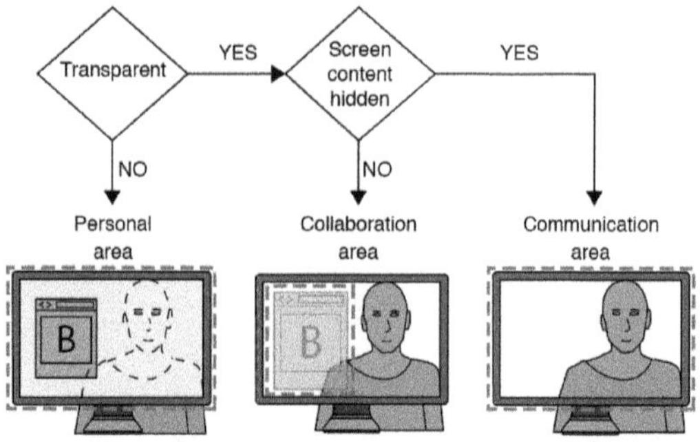

Figure 7. Tracs' three states: personal (opaque, *left*), collaboration (transparent, screen content visible, *center*), and communication (transparent, screen content hidden, *left*).

USAGE AND APPLICATIONS

Tracs offers users with three basic usage states, which are (1) personal, (2) collaboration and (3) communication (see Figure 7). Each state is possible on either the full display or on a specific area (see Figure 8). In personal state, Tracs acts like a regular display, preventing visual interference and privacy. During collaboration, the display is transparent and the screen content visible. This way, users can relate to items visible on the screen just by looking at them and establish a shared focus. During the communication state, the display is transparent and no screen content visible, allowing users to communicate freely. Tracs' custom control software allows users to implicitly select the different states through controlling the transparency of patches and screen content.

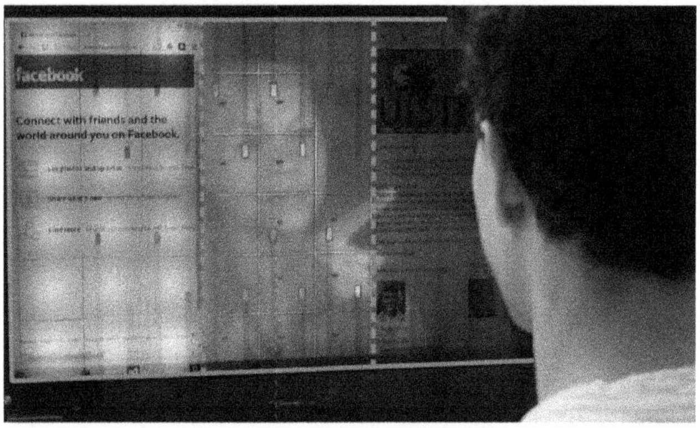

Figure 8. Tracs' states combined on a single display, personal (*left*), communication (*center*), collaboration (*right*).

DISCUSSION

We believe that by being able to control transparency, thus privacy, and visual interference, those limitations of see-through displays can be overcome and new ways of collaboration be opened. Transparent displays could bring together benefits from shoulder-to-shoulder collaboration (shared perspective on screen content) and face-to-face collaboration (eye-contact) [9, 18]. Like reducing spatial distance can increase collaboration [15], we believe that removing the barrier introduced by traditional displays can make collaboration more instant and effective. However, we believe users need to be able to choose between transparent and opaque to increase to usability and acceptance of transparent displays.

Quality and Transparency

Currently, Tracs uses transparent LCDs, which require additional environmental light to provide a good view through the display. Otherwise transparency would be limited. Transparent OLED displays do not suffer from such limitations, but their commercial availability is limited. Tracs is designed in a way to work with many types of see-through displays because of its flexible layering. The transparency-control layer can applied to an OLED to equip it with controllable transparency. The most influential factor for the Tracs' transparency are the LCDs, which give it a approximate overall transparency of 10%. This is a limiting factor for potential deployment and needs to be resolved.

Our current backlight emits light only at one side, and, while PDLC diffusely reflects the backlight also to the same side, there is a decrease in brightness and some minor reflections. To improve contrast from both sides, a second backlight layer could be added or a transparent electroluminescence display emitting light at both sides could serve as backlight.

Currently, the LCDs are 5 cm apart, so the LEDs illuminate the correct area and the switchable diffuser is not directly on the display, which results in a parallax effects. While in our experience this does not decrease Tracs' practical usability (e.g., when pointing), showing overlapping contents on both displays is currently not supported. In terms of ergonomics, our displays have to be positioned in a way that users are able to see through them without having any edges within their view. Feedback we received also addressed the possibility to tilt the display for a more comfortable viewing angle. Both points are important for transparent displays in general and need to be taken into account.

Switching and Symmetry

While Tracs gives users the possibility to switch between transparent and opaque states, it is yet unclear, which one users prefer. Users might only switch to transparent mode in case of actual collaboration and not during daily work, therefore decreasing workspace awareness. However, we believe that by making switching effortlessly, users would be encouraged to collaborate more frequently. Since users can switch to transparent state all the time, these switches could occur in moments not wanted for one of the users. Switching is currently negotiated verbally by users. Being able to prevent unwanted switches, especially to transparent mode, is important for systems like Tracs.

FUTURE WORK

For future work, we plan to increase the efficiency and resolution of the transparency-control matrix design to support more fine grained control over the transparency. Additionally, working with components of higher transparency, e.g., transparent OLEDs, would give us the opportunity for evolving our setup. Furthermore, applying our concept of transparency-control to more device class (e.g., smartphones, tablet) is an interesting point for future research. Finally, the negotiation process between collaborators, whether or when to change transparency, introduces an interesting challenge, which we will look into.

CONCLUSION

In this paper, we presented Tracs, a transparency-controlled see-through display system. With Tracs, users can control the transparency of individual areas of a display. Tracs includes a locally switchable backlight, increasing the contrast of transparent LCDs. We proposed using transparency-controlled see-through displays for fostering on-demand collaboration while retaining a personal space, which is not possible with conventional see-through displays. We believe that this mechanism is substantial for improving the usability of see-through displays and that it allows us to resolve issues regarding personal privacy, screen content privacy, and visual interference.

ACKNOWLEDGMENTS

We want to thank Constantin Schmidt and Dieter Eberle for hardware support, Ines Ben Said and Andreas Fender for the video, and Alexandra Ion for extensive discussion and feedback. This work was supported by the ICT Labs of the European Institute of Innovation and Technology. The eGlasses consortium receives the funding support of NCBiR, FWF, SNSF, ANR, and FNR in the framework of the ERA-NET CHIST-ERA II. This research was supported by the Singapore National Research Foundation under its International Research Center Keio-NUS CUTE Center @ Singapore Funding Initiative and administered by the IDM Program Office.

REFERENCES

1. Baudisch, P., and Gutwin, C. Multiblending: displaying overlapping windows simultaneously without the drawbacks of alpha blending. In *Proc. CHI '04* (2004), 367–374.
2. Gross, M., Würmlin, S., Naef, M., Lamboray, E., Spagno, C., Kunz, A., Koller-Meier, E., Svoboda, T., Gool, L. V., Lang, S., Strehlke, K., Moere, A. V., and Staadt, O. blue-c: a spatially immersive display and 3D video portal for telepresence. *Proc. Siggraph '03* (2003), 819–827.
3. Gutwin, C., Dyck, J., and Fedak, C. The Effects of Dynamic Transparency on Targeting Performance. In *Proc. GI '03* (2003), 105–112.
4. Harrison, B. L., Ishii, H., Vicente, K. J., and Buxton, W. A. S. Transparent Layered User Interfaces : An Evaluation of a Display Design to Enhance Focused and Divided Attention. In *Proc. CHI '95* (1995), 317–324.
5. Hecht, E. *Optics*, 4th international edition ed. Pearson Education Limited, 2013.
6. Heo, H., Park, H., Kim, S., Chung, J., Lee, G., and Lee, W. TransWall. In *Proc. CHI EA '14* (2014), 435–438.
7. Hilliges, O., Kim, D., Izadi, S., Weiss, M., and Wilson, A. D. HoloDesk: Direct 3D Interactions with a Situated See-Through Display. In *Proc. CHI '12* (2012), 2421–2430.
8. Hirakawa, M., and Koike, S. A Collaborative Augmented Reality System using Transparent Display. In *Proc. ISMSE '04* (2004), 410–416.
9. Inkpen, K., Hawkey, K., Kellar, M., Mandryk, R., Parker, K., Reilly, D., Scott, S., and Whalen, T. Exploring Display Factors that Influence Co-Located Collaboration: Angle, Size, Number, and User Arrangement. In *Proc. HCI International '05* (2005).
10. Ishii, H., and Kobayashi, M. ClearBoard: A Seamless Medium for Shared Drawing and Conversation with Eye Contact. In *Proc. CHI '92* (1992), 525–532.
11. Izadi, S., Hodges, S., Taylor, S., Rosenfeld, D., Villar, N., Butler, A., and Westhues, J. Going Beyond the Display: A Surface Technology with an Electronically Switchable Diffuser. In *Proc. UIST '08* (2008), 269–278.
12. Karnik, A., Mayol-Cuevas, W., and Subramanian, S. MUSTARD : A Multi User See Through AR Display. In *Proc. CHI '12* (2012), 2541–2550.
13. Karnik, A., Plasencia, D. M., Mayol-Cuevas, W., and Subramanian, S. PiVOT : Personalized View-Overlays for Tabletops. In *Proc. UIST '12* (2012), 271–280.
14. Kollarits, R. I., Woodworth, C., Ribera, J. E., and Gitlin, R. D. An Eye-Contact Camera Display System for Video Phone Applications. *SID Digest* (1995).
15. Kraut, R., Egido, C., and Galegher, J. Patterns of Contact and Communication in Scientific Research Collaboration. In *Proc. CSCW '88* (1988), 1–12.
16. Laramee, R. S., and Ware, C. Rivalry and interference with a head-mounted display. *ACM TOCHI 9*, 3 (2002), 238–251.
17. Lee, J., Olwal, A., Ishii, H., and Boulanger, C. SpaceTop: integrating 2D and spatial 3D interactions in a see-through desktop environment. In *Proc. CHI '13* (2013), 189–192.
18. Li, J., Greenberg, S., Sharlin, E., and Jorge, J. Interactive Two-Sided Transparent Displays: Designing for Collaboration. In *Proc. DIS '14* (2014), 395–404.
19. Olwal, A., DiVerdi, S., Rakkolainen, I., and Höllerer, T. Consigalo : Multi-user Face-to-face Interaction on Immaterial Displays. In *Proc. INTETAIN '08* (2008).
20. Rekimoto, J. Squama: modular visibility control of walls and windows for programmable physical architectures. In *Proc. AVI '12* (2012), 168–171.
21. Tang, J. C., and Minneman, S. L. VideoDraw : A Video Interface For Collaborative Drawing. In *Proc. CHI '90* (1990), 313–320.
22. Tang, J. C., and Minneman, S. L. VideoWhiteboard : Video Shadows to Support Remote Collaboration. In *Proc. CHI '91* (1991), 315–322.

HaptoMime: Mid-Air Haptic Interaction with a Floating Virtual Screen

Yasuaki Monnai, Keisuke Hasegawa, Masahiro Fujiwara, Kazuma Yoshino, Seki Inoue, Hiroyuki Shinoda
Graduate School of Frontier Science, The University of Tokyo, Japan
{Yasuaki_Monnai, Keisuke_Hasegawa, Masahiro_Fujiwara, Kazuma_Yoshino, Seki_Inoue}@ipc.i.u-tokyo.ac.jp, Hiroyuki_Shinoda@k.u-tokyo.ac.jp

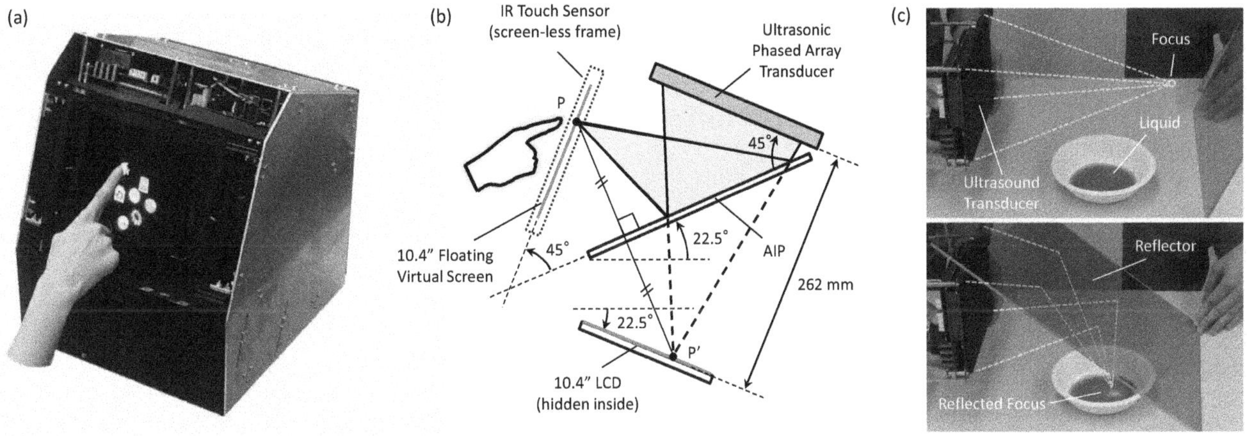

Figure 1: HaptoMime enables interaction with floating images in the presence of ultrasonic tactile feedback. (a) System appearance. (b) System configuration. (c) Redirection of an acoustic radiation pressure by ultrasonic reflection.

ABSTRACT

We present HaptoMime, a mid-air interaction system that allows users to touch a floating virtual screen with hands-free tactile feedback. Floating images formed by tailored light beams are inherently lacking in tactile feedback. Here we propose a method to superpose hands-free tactile feedback on such a floating image using ultrasound. By tracking a fingertip with an electronically steerable ultrasonic beam, the fingertip encounters a mechanical force consistent with the floating image. We demonstrate and characterize the proposed transmission scheme and discuss promising applications with an emphasis that it helps us 'pantomime' in mid-air.

Author Keywords

Mid-air interaction; tactile feedback; aerial imaging.

UIST '14, October 05 - 08 2014, Honolulu, HI, USA
Copyright 2014 ACM 978-1-4503-3069-5/14/10...$15.00.
http://dx.doi.org/10.1145/2642918.2647407

ACM Classification Keywords

H.5.2. User Interfaces, Haptic I/O

INTRODUCTION

The dream of interacting with mid-air projected 3D images has fascinated people and driven a variety of relevant researches thus far [18]. Although its practical implementation is still challenging, a breakthrough of 2D mid-air projection has been attained recently by the invention of a transmissive mirror [17,13,22]. It allows us to observe a screen floating in front of the mirror which is actually placed behind the mirror. Since all the visual effects such as binocular parallax and motion parallax are inherited to the floating screen, we cannot distinguish it from a real screen until we touch it. Combined with a sensor that detects our finger motion, it can be used as a virtual touch screen [14].

The interaction in mid-air, however, is inherently lacking in tactile feedback [6,4,3,8]. Although other modalities such as audio-visual effects can be employed to indicate touch events [6,1,12], they do not work directly on a fingertip. The indirect indication makes it hard to perceive just the depth of the fingertip. Consequently, users tend to insert the fingertip deeply into the floating image [6]. It not only makes the finger stroke long, but also involves a contradictory optical occlusion in which the floating image supposed to appear in front of the finger is occluded by the finger.

In this paper, we propose a method to superpose hands-free tactile feedback onto a floating virtual screen using a system shown in Figure 1 (a). The presence of tactile feedback assists natural and precise touch interaction with the virtual screen. As a means of the tactile feedback, we employ acoustic radiation pressure generated by intense ultrasound [11,9,10,16,7,5,21]. An ultrasonic phased array transducer delivers focused ultrasound onto the fingertip so that it encounters a mechanical force at a position and timing consistent with the floating image. In order to ensure visual and mechanical consistency, the acoustic radiation pressure ought to be superposed perpendicularly to the floating image. However, the overlap of the propagation axes of the optical rays and ultrasonic beams involves a geometric collision between the optical and ultrasonic apparatuses. Here we solve this problem by delivering the ultrasound via specular reflection at the flat and stiff surface of the transmissive mirror as illustrated in Figure 1 (b) and (c). We experimentally characterize the ultrasonic beam steering performance of the system. We then describe a guideline for tactile rendering and aerial graphic design, and discuss promising applications with an emphasis that it helps us 'pantomime' in mid-air.

RELATED WORK

Floating Imaging

The invention of a transmissive mirror has paved the way for high quality floating imaging using a compact and low-cost setup as compared to conventional techniques such as using a concave mirror [18]. The transmissive mirrors have been implemented with a tiny corner-reflector array [17,13] or a combination of a half-mirror and a retro-reflector [22]. In either case, the essential trick is that an angle of emergence of light beams becomes equal to that of incidence [17]. Consequently, a depth-inverted 3D image of an object placed behind the mirror appears on the other side of the mirror, i.e. mid-air. When the object is 2D, the identical image appears in mid-air. In this paper, we employ a commercial product based on the corner-reflector array, an Aerial Imaging Plate (AIP) developed by ASUKANET co. ltd [2], for our system.

Interaction with Floating Images

Several pioneering works have explored direct interaction with floating images using a transmissive mirror [14], a Fresnel lens [6], and a concave mirror [4]. In addition, interaction with pseudo-floating images has also been implemented with a see-through screen [8] or a stereo projector [3]. Despite the feasibility of rich Augmented Reality experiences, those methods are lacking in tactile feedback. The interaction inaccuracy involved by the lack of tactile feedback appears in such a way that the fingertip is inserted deeply beyond the floating image [6]. An attempt to use a mechanical device to present tactile feedback has been proposed recently [15]. Still, hands-free implementation is preferable.

Hands-Free Tactile Feedback

The demand for hands-free tactile feedback has driven researches on air jet flow [20], vortex ring [19], and acoustic radiation pressure [11]. To manage high-speed and high-resolution tactile feedback at a relatively long distance, the acoustic radiation pressure is attractive. A sharp mechanical force localized within a 1cm spot can be generated by focused intense ultrasound of 40 kHz at a distance of 25 cm [11]. The focal spot is steerable in mid-air using a phased array transducer. By optimizing the distribution of an amplitude and phase of the array, sophisticated beam shaping such as side-lobe suppression and multiple-foci formation can be attained [5]. Since ultrasound travels at a speed of 340 m/s and can be modulated with a 1 kHz bandwidth in a normal indoor environment [10], tactile feedback with a short delay and high frame-rate is feasible.

To combine visual and tactile feedbacks, the use of an acoustically transparent optical screen has been explored [23,5]. However, the visual and tactile feedbacks have been spatially separated in those implementations. An attempt to superpose tactile feedback directly on a floating image has been presented in [9]. There, a 2D floating image was generated by a concave mirror-based system. Users were requested to put a tracking marker on a finger, and turn their palm upward and place it at the same depth as the floating image. Focused ultrasound then impinged upon the palm along the image plane. Since the mechanical force was oriented in parallel with the image plane, visual and mechanical consistency was ensured only for such a situation as touching falling droplets.

IMPLEMENTATION

System Configuration

The proposed system consists of four key components, the AIP, a liquid crystal display (LCD), an infrared (IR) touch sensor, and an ultrasonic phased array transducer. The cross-sectional geometry is illustrated in Figure 1 (b). The floating virtual screen is generated by reflecting the LCD through the AIP. The virtual screen is overlaid with the IR touch sensor to detect finger insertion. According to the touch data, the ultrasonic phased array transducer delivers focused ultrasound onto the fingertip. For the ultrasound transmission, we employ an indirect path reflected at the surface of the AIP so that the ultrasound impinges on the virtual screen perpendicularly. The brightness of the floating image becomes highest when a user sees the AIP at an angle of 45°. Here we place the AIP at 22.5° from the horizontal plane so that a user facing the system naturally sees the AIP at about 45°. The floating virtual screen consequently appears at 67.5°. When seen at a large azimuthal angle, single-reflection appears as a ghost image [13]. To avoid this, users should face the system within the angular width of about 30°.

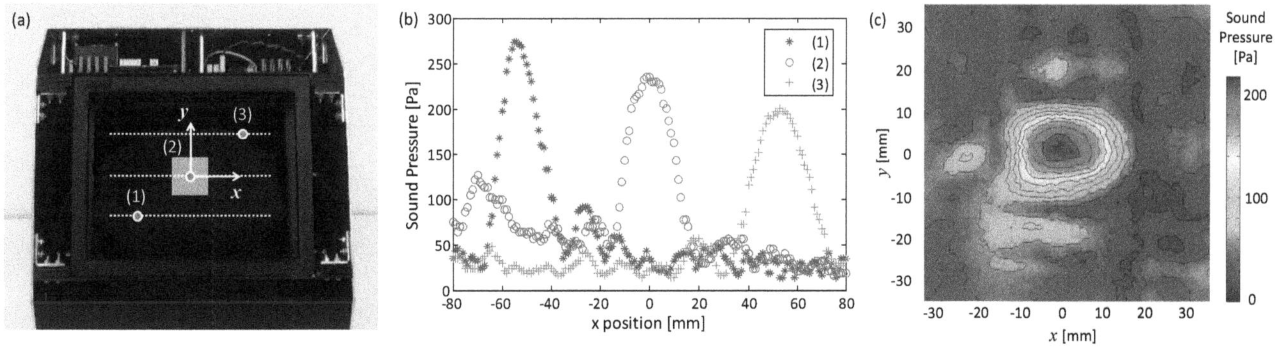

Figure 2: Characterization of ultrasound focus steering on the virtual screen. (a) The focus position is switched between: (1) (-53 mm, -40 mm), (2) (0 mm, 0 mm), and (3) (53 mm, 40 mm) for characterization. (b) Comparison of the beam shapes between the three positions. (c) Sound pressure distribution around the focus at (2). The scanned area is indicated by the white rectangle in (a).

The entire system is controlled by a Windows 7 computer (Endeavor NB50E, Epson) running on AMD E-450 APU (1.65 GHz). It drives the LCD and the ultrasonic transducer based on the data acquired from the IR touch sensor. The LCD (DLH1068, Litemax) is 10.4 inch with the brightness of 1600 cd/m^2 and the resolution of 800×600 (SVGA). The IR touch sensor (RE1300G010S, IRTOUCH Systems) detects finger insertion with spatial and temporal resolutions of 1.5 mm and 15 ms, respectively. The ultrasonic phased array transducer consists of 498 pieces of transducers (T4010A, Nippon Ceramic). It is controlled by a custom-made driver board incorporating FPGAs (EP3C16Q240, Altera). Each transducer has a diameter of 10 mm and is aligned in a square grid of 280 mm by 180 mm. The transducer is driven at the resonant frequency of 40 kHz with a peak-to-peak voltage of 24 V. The driver board controls the phase and amplitude of each transducer independently. Furthermore, it modulates the ultrasound waveform. While the former contributes to beam steering, the latter contributes to tactile rendering as explained in the following sections. The ultrasonic focus can be refreshed in every 4 ms (0.25 kHz). There, 3 ms accounts for a serial communication between the main computer and the driver board while the other 1 ms for the wave propagation from the transducer to the fingertip (0.3 m).

Steering of Reflected Ultrasound

When focused ultrasound is specularly reflected, the focus is accordingly transferred to the mirror symmetric position as illustrated in Figure 1 (c). Hence, as in Figure 1 (b), the transducer is able to form a focus at a point P on the floating image by simply aiming at the symmetric point P' on the LCD located straight ahead of the transducer. To confirm this principle, we measured the sound pressure distribution around a focus formed at three different positions defined in Figure 2 (a). The signal was recorded with a standard microphone (Brüel&Kjær Type 4138) mounted on an automated stage and connected to a pre-amplifier (Brüel&Kjær Type 2670). Beam profiles scanned in the x direction at each y position are plotted in Figure 2 (b). A clear focus is observed at the predefined position in all cases. The beam widths (3dB) are (1) 17 mm, (2) 21 mm, and (3) 26 mm, respectively. They are narrow enough to selectively hit a fingertip. We consider that the slight difference of the beam shapes between (1) and (3) is attributed to different multi-path interferences involved by the asymmetric structure inside the system. Although the structure is symmetric with respect to the x-axis, it is asymmetric in y because the AIP is inclined. Figure 2 (c) shows a 2D scan of the sound pressure distribution around the focus at (2). A clear focal spot is observed in the middle. We thus confirm the ultrasound focus steering via the reflective indirect path.

Ultrasonic Tactile Rendering

The feeling of the tactile feedback can be designed by modulating the acoustic radiation pressure. According to a literature [10], the amount of a mechanical force generated by focused ultrasound is 1.6 gram force using 324 pieces of transducers of the same type as our system. Although such a weak force is hard to perceive on a skin as a static force, a modulation of the ultrasonic waveform can clearly stimulate human tactile receptors [5]. There exist several types of tactile receptors with different spatio-temporal responses on a skin. When using ultrasound of 40 kHz, the size of a focal spot is mostly not smaller than 8.5 mm (one wavelength). As it is close to the fingertip size, the acoustic radiation pressure impinges on the fingertip uniformly. Among the tactile receptors, Merkel cells and Meissner corpuscles, which are located near the skin surface, are not reactive against such a uniform force. On the other hand, deeply located Pacinian corpuscles are reactive against such a uniform force. To stimulate the Pacinian corpuscles with the acoustic radiation pressure, the waveform should be modulated with frequencies higher than 100 Hz. To this end, we select three typical vibratory waveforms from an audio percussion sound library. Figure 3 shows three waveforms we found useful. The abscissa and ordinate show a time sequence and normalized radiation pressure, respectively. Subjective descriptions of the perceived tactile feeling of those waveforms are (a) stiff and light, (b) air flow burst, and (c) vibratory.

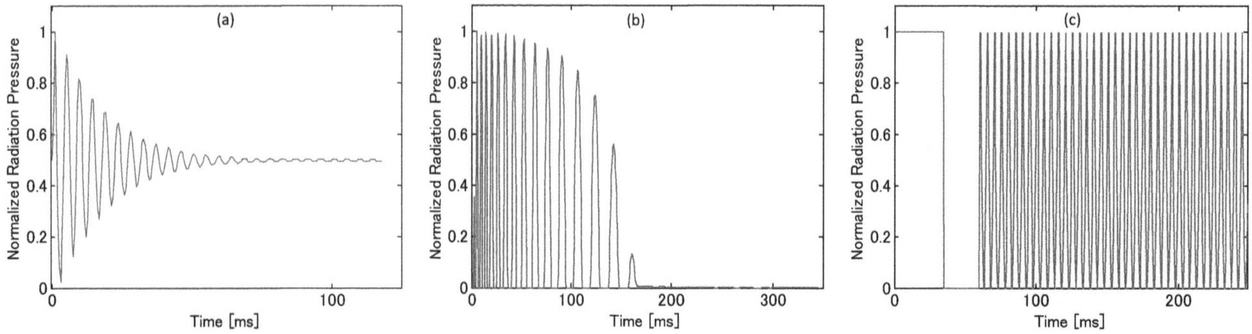

Figure 3: Waveforms of the ultrasonic tactile feedback. Audio percussion sounds with frequency components of several hundred Hz are employed to modulate the 40 kHz ultrasound.

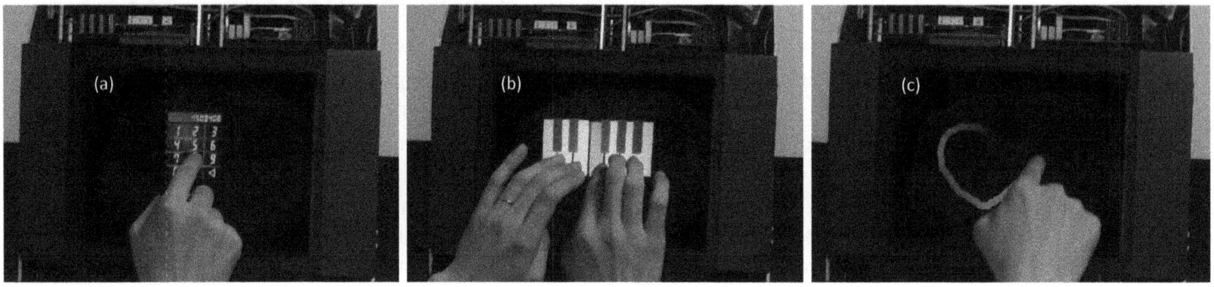

Figure 4: Applications of the system. (a) A floating virtual touch panel allows users to input keys in mid-air without leaving fingerprints. (b) Rhythmical input in mid-air is assisted by the tactile feedback. (c) Users can draw graphics in mid-air by constraining the finger trace onto the virtual 2D canvas.

Aerial Graphic Design

We set three guidelines for graphic design that enhances the interaction experience with the floating virtual screen. Firstly, the boundary of the AIP ought to be obscured under the darkness because otherwise it involves a visual discontinuity between the sights in and outside the AIP. Thus, the space above the AIP needs to be shaded to sink in black. Likewise, the background of the floating screen must be colored as dark as possible. For this reason, the LCD must hold high contrast.

Secondly, objects displayed on the floating screen must be located in the middle of the AIP, as far away from the boundary as possible. In this way, floating images always stay inside the AIP even when motion parallax is introduced. If only a fraction of the image reaches the boundary and partially occluded, users get confused by the discrepancy between the two eye images.

Thirdly, objects on the floating screen ought to disappear immediately when a finger is inserted deeper than the image plane. In such a situation, the objects supposed to appear in front of the finger are occluded by the finger. To avoid this visual contradiction, the objects must black out temporally during the finger insertion. Yet, it can be instantaneous as the tactile feedback suppresses deep finger insertion by physically inducing the bounce or extraction of the finger when the stroke reaches the image plane.

APPLICATION

Liberation from a physical screen will enable comfortable and secure use of computers. As an example, the implementation of a floating touch panel is presented in Figure 4 (a). It enables natural and precise key input in mid-air with the help of the tactile feedback. This technology, for instance, allows users to enjoy web-browsing even when their hands are wet or dirty during cooking. In a public situation, a risk of contagion by sharing a touch screen with multiple unidentified users can be reduced. Furthermore, there remains no fingerprint on a virtual screen, which is desirable for secure key input. The tactile feedback also assists rhythmical key input in mid-air by physically indicating the end of a touch stroke as represented in Figure 4 (b).

The tactile feedback provides us with clues to guide our motion in mid-air. For example, users can draw graphics by constraining the finger trace onto the virtual 2D canvas as shown in Figure 4 (c). In the real world, the perception of surface constraint is provided via tactile feedback in the form of normal and friction forces. Hence, the artificial reconstruction of such tactile cues helps us perform tasks in a 3D space as if we pantomime. It is also worth mentioning that intuitive handling will always take place via surfaces, irrespective of the form of an interface, whether it deals with 3D virtual objects or 2D virtual screen layers. Such surfaces can be equipped with tactile feedback with the proposed transmission scheme.

CONCLUSION

In this paper, we presented HaptoMime, a system that enables us to interact with a floating virtual screen in the presence of hands-free tactile feedback. We proposed an ultrasound transmission scheme via an indirect reflective path that superposes tactile sensation on a floating image consistently. We experimentally demonstrated the ultrasonic beam steering on the image plane. Using an IR touch sensor, we implemented a mid-air touch interface with tactile feedback. We then discussed promising applications of the system. Liberation from a physical screen will enable comfortable and secure use of computers. The tactile feedback allows users to perform natural and precise inputs in mid-air.

ACKNOWLEDGMENT

We thank Nobuaki Takanashi, NEC Corporation who advised the alignment of the ultrasound transducers using a visual display surface as a sound reflector in 2010. We also thank Yasutoshi Makino for the naming of HaptoMime for our system. This work was partly supported by JSPS KAKENHI Grant Number 25240032.

REFERENCES

1. Annett, M., Grossman, T., Wigdor, D., and Fitzmaurice, G. Medusa: A Proximity-Aware Multi-touch Tabletop. *Proc. UIST*, (2011), 337-346.
2. ASUKANET co. ltd. http://www.asukanet.co.jp
3. Benko, H., Jota, R., and Wilson, A.D. MirageTable: Freehand Interaction on a Projected Augmented Reality Tabletop. *Proc. CHI*, (2012), 199-208.
4. Butler, A., Hilliges, O., Izadi, S., Hodges, S., Molyneaux, D., Kim, D., and Kong, D. Vermeer: direct interaction with a 360° viewable 3D display. *Proc. UIST*, (2011), 569-579.
5. Carter, T., Seah, S.A., Long, B., Drinkwater, B., and Subramanian, S. UltraHaptics: multi-point mid-air haptic feedback for touch surfaces. *Proc. UIST*, (2013), 505-514.
6. Chan, L.W., Kao, H.S., Chen, M.Y., Lee, M.S., Hsu, J., and Hung, Y.P. Touching the Void: Direct-Touch Interaction for Intangible Displays. *Proc. CHI*, (2010), 2625-2634.
7. Hasegawa, K. and Shinoda, H. Aerial Display of Vibrotactile Sensation with High Spatial-Temporal Resolution using Large-Aperture Airborne Ultrasound Phased Array, *Proc. IEEE World Haptics Conference*, (2013), 31-36.
8. Hilliges, O., Kim, D., Izadi, S., Weiss, M., and Wilson, A.D. HoloDesk: direct 3d interactions with a situated see-through display. *Proc. CHI*, (2012), 2421-2430.
9. Hoshi, T., Takahashi, M., Nakatsuma, K., and Shinoda, H. Touchable holography. *SIGGRAPH E-Tech*, (2009), 23:1.
10. Hoshi, T., Takahashi, M., Iwamoto, T., and Shinoda, H. Noncontact tactile display based on radiation pressure of airborne ultrasound. *IEEE Transactions on Haptics* 3, 3 (2010), 155 –165.
11. Iwamoto, T., Tatezono, M., and Shinoda, H. Non-contact method for producing tactile sensation using airborne ultrasound. *Proc. EuroHaptics*, Springer-Verlag (2008), 504–513.
12. Kane, S.K., Morris, M.R., Perkins, A.Z., Wigdor, D., Ladner, R.E., and Wobbrock, J.O. Access overlays: improving non-visual access to large touch screens for blind users. *Proc. UIST*, (2011), 273-282.
13. Maekawa, S., Nitta, K., and Matoba, O. Transmissive Optical Imaging Device with Micromirror Array. *Proc. SPIE* 6392 (2006), 63920E.
14. Maekawa, S. Floating touch display. *2nd Int. Symp. on Universal Communication.*, (2008).
15. Markon, S., Maekawa, S., Onat, A., Zhibo, Z., and Miyake, H. Improved interaction methods for medical visualization with floating images, *Proc. ICME*, (2013), 462-466.
16. Marshall, M.T., Carter, T., Alexander, J., and Subramanian, S. Ultra-tangibles: creating movable tangible objects on interactive tables. *Proc. CHI*, (2012), 2185-2188.
17. Otsubo, M. Jpn. Unexamined Patent Publication No. 1997-5503 (1997).
18. Rakkolainen, I. How Feasible Are Star Wars Mid-air Displays? *Proc. Int. Conf. Information Visualization* (2007), 935-942.
19. Sodhi, R., Poupyrev, I., Glisson, M., and Israr, A. AIREAL: Interactive Tactile Experiences in Free Air. *Proc. SIGGRAPH*, (2013), 134:1-10.
20. Suzuki, Y. and Kobayashi, M. Air Jet Driven Force Feedback in Virtual Reality. *IEEE Comp. Graphics and Applications*, 25, (2005), 44-47.
21. Wilson, G., Carter, T., Subramanian, S., and Brewster, S. Perception of Ultrasonic Haptic Feedback on the Hand: Localisation and Apparent Motion, *Proc. CHI*, (2014), 1133-1142.
22. Yamamoto, H. and Suyama, S. Aerial 3D LED displayby use of retroreflective sheeting, *Proc SPIE* 8648, (2013), 86480Q.
23. Yoshino, K. and Shinoda, H. Visio-Acoustic Screen for Contactless Touch Interface with Tactile Sensation, *Proc. IEEE World Haptics Conference*, (2013), 419-423.

Declarative Interaction Design for Data Visualization

Arvind Satyanarayan
Stanford University
arvindsatya@cs.stanford.edu

Kanit Wongsuphasawat
University of Washington
kanitw@uw.edu

Jeffrey Heer
University of Washington
jheer@uw.edu

ABSTRACT
Declarative visualization grammars can accelerate development, facilitate retargeting across platforms, and allow language-level optimizations. However, existing declarative visualization languages are primarily concerned with visual encoding, and rely on imperative event handlers for interactive behaviors. In response, we introduce a model of declarative interaction design for data visualizations. Adopting methods from reactive programming, we model low-level events as composable data *streams* from which we form higher-level semantic *signals*. Signals feed *predicates* and *scale inversions*, which allow us to generalize interactive selections at the level of item geometry (pixels) into interactive queries over the data domain. *Production rules* then use these queries to manipulate the visualization's appearance. To facilitate reuse and sharing, these constructs can be encapsulated as named *interactors*: standalone, purely declarative specifications of interaction techniques. We assess our model's feasibility and expressivity by instantiating it with extensions to the Vega visualization grammar. Through a diverse range of examples, we demonstrate coverage over an established taxonomy of visualization interaction techniques.

Author Keywords
Visualization; interaction design; toolkits; declarative design.

ACM Classification Keywords
D.2.2 Software Engineering: Design Tools and Techniques; I.3.6 Methodology and Techniques: Interaction Techniques

INTRODUCTION
Declarative languages decouple specification (the *what*) from execution (the *how*). Popular in domains ranging from web design (e.g., HTML/CSS) to database queries (e.g., SQL), declarative languages are now widely used to design custom data visualizations as well. Designers describe mappings between data values and properties of graphical primitives; a language runtime then determines appropriate control flows for data processing, rendering, and animation [5, 6, 40]. This decoupling lets users focus on visual encoding decisions, leaving the runtime to unobtrusively optimize processing [17]. Declarative design also simplifies retargeting, for instance allowing a visualization specification to be rendered in a browser using HTML5 Canvas or Scalable Vector Graphics (SVG), or as a static image for print-based media [36].

UIST 2014, October 5–8, 2014, Honolulu, HI, USA.

ACM 978-1-4503-3069-5/14/10...$15.00.
http://dx.doi.org/10.1145/2642918.2647360

However, these languages provide little support for declarative design of *interactions*. Some tools [5, 6] offer a predefined palette of interaction techniques (brushing, zooming, etc.) that can be declaratively applied. However, these "interactor typologies" artificially restrict designers' options and typically support customization of only a limited set of parameters. For custom interactions, designers must instead author *imperative* event handling callbacks. These callbacks undo the benefits of declarative design by exposing execution details, forcing users to manually maintain state [8] and coordinate interleavings — a complex and error-prone task colloquially referred to as "callback hell" [12].

In this paper, we introduce a model of declarative interaction design for data visualizations with expressiveness comparable to imperative approaches. We first model interactive input events as composable *streams* of data. Input event streams are treated as first-class data sets, and thus are subject to the full range of applicable data processing operators, including filtering, aggregation and summary statistics. Interactions can also be composed into arbitrary reactive expressions [38] called *signals*. When a new event enters a stream, it propagates to dependent signals and the expressions are automatically re-evaluated. This approach, modeled on Functional Reactive Programming (FRP) [3], defers the complexity of coordinating event-driven state changes to the language.

By default, interactions occur at the visual (pixel) level. However, with visualizations, this is often insufficient. Instead, to maximize reuse and expressivity, interactions must be lifted to the data level [16]. Under our model, signals can be used to construct intensional and extensional *predicates* that define membership in an interactive selection. By passing signals through *scale inversions* [11, 16] that map visual values to corresponding data values, predicates can also express dynamic queries over data. Predicates can then be used to modify visual encodings using declarative *production rules*.

Our model also facilitates reusing interactions both within and across designs. Interaction specifications (streams, signals, predicates, and rules) can be encapsulated as named *interactors*: standalone declarative specifications that provide a file format for interaction techniques. Moreover, streams and signals are named to decouple low-level event processing from application-level semantic events. Downstream interaction logic is defined in terms of these named, semantic properties and not low-level input events. For example, when combining two conflicting interactions or to retarget interactions across form factors, we can simply rebind signals to different low-level input events without any downstream modification.

We instantiate this model through reactive extensions to Vega, a JSON-based visualization grammar [36]; an example Vega visualization is shown in Figure 1. Although our model could be implemented within other frameworks, Vega's JSON environment allows us to assess the extent to which our model enables *declarative* interaction design, and evaluate its expressivity. We construct a diverse range of examples which demonstrate substantial coverage of an existing taxonomy of interaction techniques for data visualization [42], including brushing & linking, panning, zooming, and filtering with control widgets. These examples show that, through composition, reuse, and repurposing of interaction techniques, our model promotes the accretive design of richer interactions.

RELATED WORK

Our declarative interaction model extends prior work on visualization systems, reactive programming and UI toolkits.

Interaction Support in Visualization Toolkits

Interaction is an important component of effective data visualization [25, 32], and most existing tools support a set of common interaction techniques. Prefuse [18] provides controls for focus, hover, drag, and tooltips, along with a predicate language to express dynamic queries. Improvise [39] introduces *live properties* — active variables that parameterize a visualization and can be bound to control widgets. Live properties take part in *coordinated queries* for linked brushing or synchronized scrolling across multiple views.

Our model shares some conceptual underpinnings with these systems. Improvise's live properties provide a basic form of reactivity, while coordinated queries and prefuse's predicates lift interactions to the data domain. However, both systems take a monolithic approach to interaction design. Interactors must be defined within a rigid class hierarchy, and subclassed to be customized or composed. This approach complicates interaction design and reduces flexibility, requiring entirely new imperative code to modify input event handling or to target new platforms (e.g., from mouse to touch input).

Declarative tools such as Protovis [5] and D3 [6] similarly offer a palette of standard interaction techniques, with black-boxed event processing and limited customization via exposed parameters. Custom interaction designs require imperative event handling callbacks, imposing different specification styles on visual design and interaction design [4]. These callbacks can stymie the benefits of declarative design by exposing execution details and requiring increased development effort. Other declarative models, such as Wilkinson's Grammar of Graphics [41] and Wickham's ggplot2 [40] do not include support for interaction.

Stencil [9] is a visualization language that models data using streaming semantics. When a data value changes, it is automatically propagated to visual glyphs, and the visualization re-renders. Stencil's authors note that user input can be modeled as a data stream, but they do not close the loop and extend their language to support interaction design. Stencil lacks constructs necessary to generate interactive selections and generalize them to dynamic queries [16].

Similarly, Quadrigram [33] (née Impure [30]) constructs visualization applications using dataflow semantics. However, the visualization components themselves are "black boxed" into a chart typology with built-in selection interactions. As it does not expose raw input events nor consider user interaction as a data source, Quadrigram's expressivity is restricted.

Constraint Programming

Imperative event callbacks often present development hurdles [28]. Callbacks registered outside the visualization specification allow users to externally manipulate visualization state and manually update dependencies [8]. This approach breaks encapsulation and necessitates the introduction of side-effects: external calls to maintain state [7]. Callback execution order can also be unpredictable, requiring users to coordinate interleaved calls [12]. As a result, callbacks can make it difficult to reason about the current state of the visualization, which is now the product of both the original specification and the side-effects of interaction callbacks.

One alternative to callback-oriented imperative programming is constraint-based specification. Systems like Gilt [28] and μconstraints [21] implement one-way constraints: when the value of a constrained interface is modified, its dependents are automatically affected. Other systems, like Cassowary [2], implement two-way constraints using more complex constraint solvers. Recently, ConstraintJS [29] and Bret Victor's prototype for drawing data visualizations [37] have shown that constraint programming is suitable for authoring web applications and data visualizations, respectively.

While constraint systems remove many of the obstacles introduced by callbacks, they do not involve general consideration of event handling, a crucial element for interaction design. In fact, the authors of ConstraintJS intend for their system to complement event architectures [29].

Functional Reactive Programming

Functional Reactive Programming (FRP) [13] formalizes semantics similar to one-way constraints. Drawing from dataflow programming [24], FRP recasts mutable states as

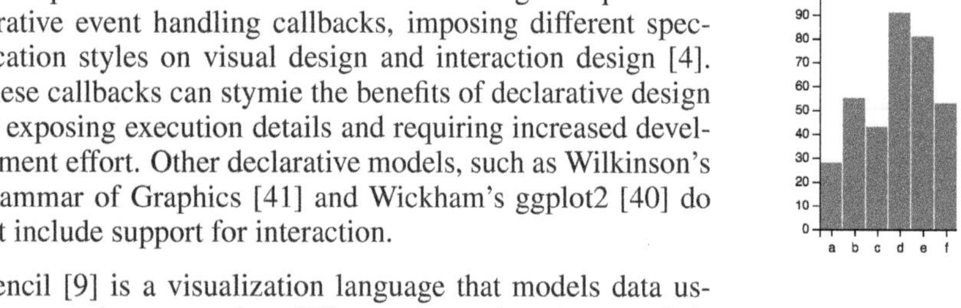


```
{ "data": [{"name": "table", "url": "data/letter_counts.json"}],

  "scales": [{
      "name": "x", "type": "ordinal", "range": "width",
      "domain": {"data": "table", "field": "data.letter"}
    }, {
      "name": "y", "type": "linear", "range": "height",
      "domain": {"data": "table", "field": "data.count"}
  }],

  "axes": [{"type": "x", "scale": "x"}, {"type": "y", "scale": "y"}],

  "marks": [{
    "type": "rect", "from": {"data": "table"},
    "properties": { "update": {
        "x": {"scale": "x", "field": "data.letter"},
        "width": {"scale": "x", "band": true, "offset": -1},
        "y": {"scale": "y", "field": "data.count"},
        "y2": {"scale": "y", "value": 0},
        "fill": {"value": "steelblue"}
      }
    }
}]}
```

Figure 1. A JSON specification for a bar chart, demonstrating Vega's [36] existing abstractions. Data is imported from a URL. Scales are defined to transform data values to visual values. Properties of graphical marks (in this case rectangles) are determined by scale mappings. Guides (here, axes) can be instantiated as well.

time-varying streams of values. Among FRP variants [3], we focus on Event-Driven FRP (E-FRP), in which values change only in response to discrete events [38]. E-FRP models value changes with two constructs: *streams*, which are potentially infinite sequences of events, and *signals*, defined as the most recent event from a stream. Signals are akin to variables and can be composed into expressions. Runtimes for reactive languages construct a dataflow dependency graph; when a new event fires, the event enters the appropriate streams and propagates to any dependent signals, for which any dependent expressions are automatically re- evaluated. Languages like Flapjax [26] and ELM [10] demonstrate how E-FRP semantics can be used to author interactive web applications.

However, existing instantiations of E-FRP lack primitives critical for developing interactive *data visualizations*. By default, they only consider interaction events over the visual or geometric space of a browser window. For data visualization, it is important to be able to generalize selections to the data domain [11, 16, 39]. Our model adopts the semantics of E-FRP and extends it with primitives necessary to perform interactions at both the visual and data levels.

Reusable Interactions

Myers et al.'s Garnet system introduces *Interactors* [27]: a scheme for encapsulating interactive behaviors that enables reuse by decoupling input events from application logic. Our notion of interactors extends this work. In addition to endowing interactors with reactive semantics, in our model interactors expose their constituent components (signals, predicates, and rules); a visualization can choose to use an entire interactor or chosen subsets. Compared to Garnet, whose interactors can only be generalized through provided parameters, our interactors allow more granular reuse and repurposing.

DECLARATIVE INTERACTION MODEL DESIGN

With our model, we contribute a declarative grammar of interaction design for data visualization. It extends and seamlessly integrates with existing grammars of graphics, offering a lower-level compositional approach to interaction design. As we later demonstrate, our model facilitates development, enables richer customization, and allows greater reuse of interaction techniques without an undue loss of expressivity.

Event Streams and Signals

Our model adopts the semantics of Event-Driven Functional Reactive Programming (E-FRP) [38]. Low-level input events (e.g., mouse events and keystrokes) are captured through *streams*, rather than event callbacks. Abstracting event handling as streams reduces the burden of combining and sequencing events — operations that would require callbacks to coordinate external states. To this end, we introduce a syntax for selecting and composing event streams, as shown in Figure 2. While prior work has formulated regex-based symbols for event selection [23], we instead draw inspiration from CSS selectors. As a result, our syntax operators are likely to be more familiar to visualization designers.

An event stream is denoted using an event name (e.g., `mousemove`), optionally prepended with a mark type

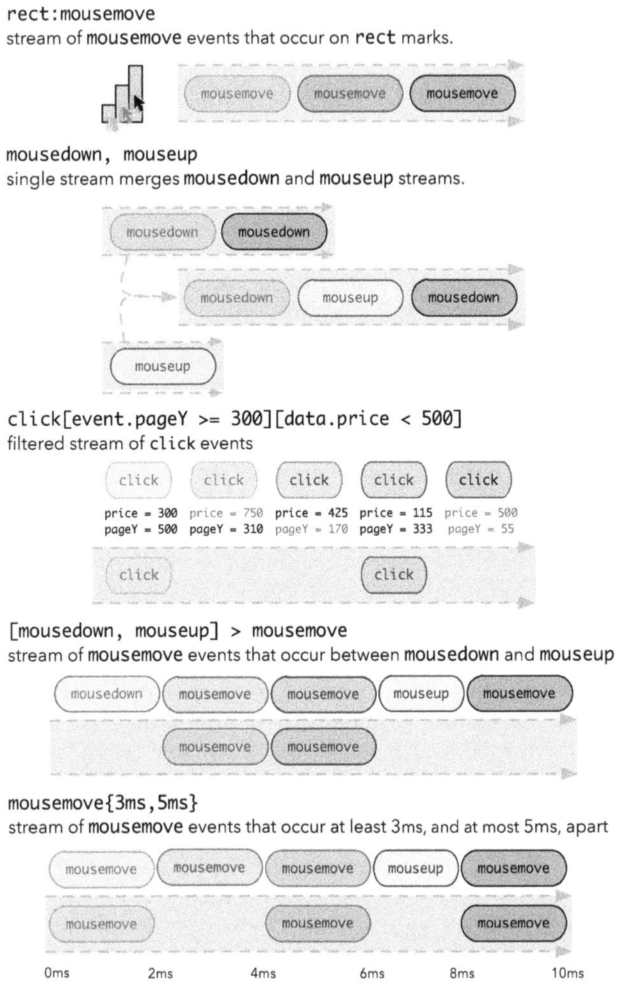

Figure 2. Event streams can be instantiated, composed, filtered, and sequenced using a syntax inspired by CSS3 selectors and regular expressions. This determines which events are captured by a particular stream (denoted by the dashed grey rectangles).

(e.g., `rect:`, or `symbol:`). The comma operator (`,`) merges streams to produce a single stream with interleaved events. Square brackets (`[]`) filter events based on their properties. When followed by the right-combinator (>), square brackets also define bounding events for the stream, serving as a "pre-filter" with the right-combinator selecting "children." Curly braces ({}) denote minimum and maximum time intervals between events. These operators are composable: `[mousedown, mousemove] > [keydown, keyup] > mousemove{5ms,10ms}` is a stream of `mousemove` events occurring at least 5ms apart and at most 10ms apart, between `keydown` and `keyup` events, which in turn occur between `mousedown` and `mouseup` events.

Critically, our model treats events as first-class data sources. Not only can data transformations (e.g., statistical calculations) be run over event streams, but events can also be composed into arbitrary reactive expressions as *signals*. By default, signals return the most recent event from a stream. However, by drawing from multiple event streams, they can

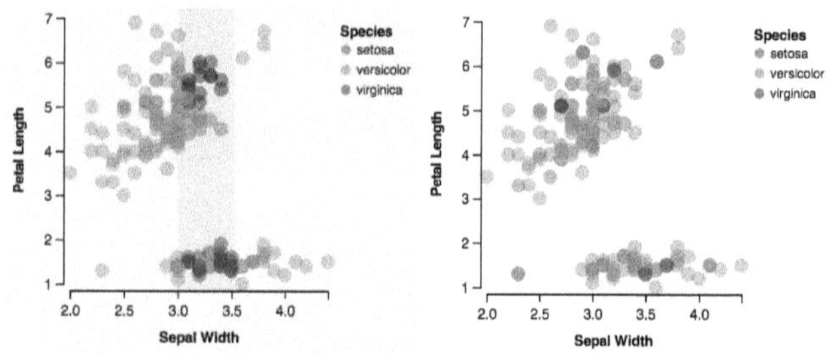

Figure 3. Points are highlighted using an intensional predicate to select points where `3.0 < data.sepalWidth < 3.5` (left) or with an extensional predicate to select points `#56, #110, #79, #95, #40, #120, ...` (right).

define finite-state machines — each stream triggering a transition between states, for example. By virtue of being modeled as data sources, signals can serve as input to visual encoding primitives (scales, guides, and marks) thereby endowing them with reactive semantics. When an event fires, it enters appropriate streams and is propagated to corresponding signals; signals are re-evaluated and dependent visual encodings re-calculated and re-rendered automatically.

Upon definition, streams and signals must be given unique names. These named entities are then used to define the rest of an interaction technique. This separation decouples input events from downstream application logic. Thus, an interaction can be triggered by a different set of events by simply rebinding stream and signal declarations. As we later demonstrate, rebinding is particularly useful for retargeting interactions or for combining otherwise conflicting interactions.

Predicates and Scale Inversion

Selection is a fundamental operation in interactive visualization design: subsequent operators are applied to selected items to manipulate them. For visual design, it can be sufficient to make a predetermined selection for example, "select all rectangles." With interaction design, however, selections are driven by user input. For instance, a user may brush over points of interest, or adjust a slider to filter data.

To express interactive selections, we introduce reactive *predicates*. *Intensional* predicates specify conditions over the properties of members while *extensional* predicates explicitly enumerate all members of the selection set [16]; this difference is shown in Figure 3. Predicates can be combined using logical `AND` or `OR`. They may be defined inline to toggle the properties of visual encodings but, if defined once at the top-level with a name and parameterized operands, can be reused.

Predicate operands are typically signals and, as signals are drawn from streams of input events, predicates express interactive selections at the visual level by default. However, pixel-level selection is often insufficient, as a single visualization may have multiple distinct visual spaces. In such cases, it is necessary to generalize an interactive selection into a query over the data domain [16]. For example, consider a simple overview+detail setup (Figure 4), in which the constituent plots have distinct coordinate spaces but shared data domains.

Scale functions are a critical first-class component in visualization design [41] as they transform data values into visual values such as pixels or colors. By applying an *inverted* scale function to predicate operands, we can lift a predicate to the data domain [11]. However, naïve application of scale inversion can breakdown when trying to express a range selection as a query. The semantics of quantitative scales allow a scale inversion of range extents to naturally transform pixel-level values to data values. The semantics of inverting discrete categorical or ordinal scales, however, are more complex.

To mask this complexity from the user, our model provides a special *range* predicate. This predicate calculates range extents in pixel space using either constants or signal values and, if a scale inversion is specified, produces a corresponding query: intensional for quantitative scales, extensional for categorical data. Figure 4 illustrates how range predicates and scale inversion allow brushing in the coordinate space of the overview plot to filter points displayed in the detail plot.

Production Rules

When predicates are applied directly to visual encoding properties, they serve as toggles. However, for more complex behaviors, our model provides *production rules*, an established design pattern [15] that we endow with reactive semantics. A rule defines the outcomes of evaluating a sequence of predicates (an `if-elseif-else` chain) to set property values. For example, a rule might set a mark's fill color to green if predicate `A` is true, use a scale-transformed data value if `B` is true, or otherwise set the color grey by default. Rules can be defined inline with visual encoding properties, or can be reused if defined at the top-level with a unique name and parameterized outcome branches.

User-Defined Functions

During our design process, we encountered visualizations in which interactions trigger custom data transforms. For exam-

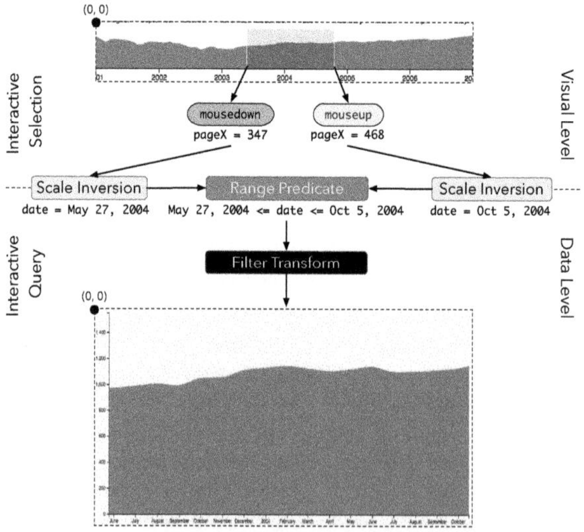

Figure 4. *Predicates* use signal values to define interactive selections of elements. Using *scale inversion*, predicates can be generalized to define interactive queries, and thus operate across different coordinate spaces in the same visualization: context (top) and focus (bottom).

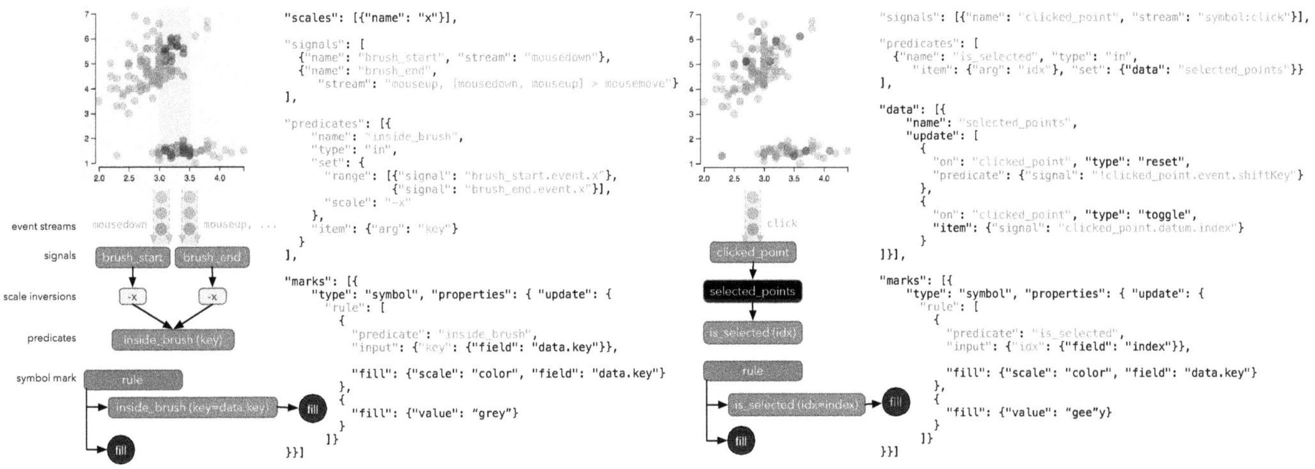

Figure 5. Expressing the selections in Figure 3 with our extensions to Vega: (left) brushing (only one dimension shown); (right) click/shift-click selection. Signal definitions and usage are in blue, event streams in orange, predicate definition and application in purple, rules in red, and names in green.

ple, sorting a co-occurrence matrix by frequency or applying a clustering algorithm to place similar rows and columns in close proximity. It is not feasible for a declarative language to natively support all possible functions, yet custom operations must still be expressible. Following the precedent of languages such as SQL, we provide *user-defined functions*. These functions can be declaratively invoked within the specification, akin to applying predicates, but must be registered and defined at runtime. User-defined functions ensure that the language remains concise and domain-specific, while ensuring extensibility to idiosyncratic operations.

Encapsulated Interactors

To allow reuse of custom interaction techniques, our model's primitives can be parameterized and encapsulated as named *interactors*. Interactors can subsequently be applied to containers or groups, or the top-level visualization, and function like mixins. An interactor's specification is merged into the host specification and, to prevent conflicts, its components are addressable only under its namespace.

When applied to the top-level visualization, only one instance of the interactor (and its primitives) is created. When applied to groups, however, the interactor is scoped to the group and thus multiple instances of the interactor may exist (one per group instance). In such cases, the signals and predicates of an interactor instance may be referenced using the corresponding group's key. However, it is often more useful to be able to automatically aggregate across instances. To facilitate this, when referencing an interactor's predicate, `latest`, `any`, or `all` flags use the most recently activated interactor, or perform logical `OR` or `AND` aggregates over all interactor instances, respectively.

Figure 6 illustrates how a brush interactor, extracted from Figure 5, can be applied to create a scatterplot matrix. Six instances of the brush interactor exist, one for each cell. The `latest` flag ensures that the `inside_brush` predicate is taken from the most recently used interactor, as determined by which cell the interaction occurs in. If we wished to allow multiple brushes, we would use the `all` flag instead.

IMPLEMENTATION

We implemented our model through reactive extensions to the Vega visualization grammar [36]. While our model can be instantiated under other visualization toolkits (e.g., D3 [6]), we chose Vega as its visualizations are purely declarative JSON specifications. As a result, reactive extensions to Vega allow us to assess the extent to which our model enables *declarative* interaction design. It is important to note that, by implementing our model, we seek to evaluate its feasability and expressivity (rather than the effectiveness of specific Vega syntax).

In Vega, the properties of graphical *marks* such as bars, lines, arcs, and text labels are bound to the attributes of backing data objects. Data sets can be specified inline or imported from a URL. The grammar includes data transformation operations, including common statistical summaries and visual layout algorithms such as force-directed layout, treemaps, and cartographic projections. Following the Grammar of Graphics [41], scales and guides (i.e., axes and legends) are provided as first-class objects. A JavaScript runtime parses JSON Vega specifications into web-based components rendered using HTML5 Canvas or SVG. Vega specifications can also be rendered server-side to produce static PNG or SVG files. Figure 1 illustrates how these abstractions are used to create a bar chart in Vega.

Vega uses a multi-stage pipeline for constructing visualizations, similar to Protovis [5]. A Vega JSON specification is parsed into a `View` object that manages data sets, data transformation pipelines, and visual encoding functions that determine the properties of graphical marks. In the build phase, an abstract *scenegraph* of marks is constructed with one node for each datum per mark; encoder functions then modify node properties. Finally, the abstract scenegraph is rendered, for example to an HTML5 Canvas.

We augment the parser to support our model's primitives and construct the necessary dataflow graph. Event listeners are registered to capture input events, and serve as source nodes in this graph. The `View` object is the sole sink. The remaining nodes in the graph are signals: either named signals from the specification, or anonymous signals automatically constructed when a signal is used in the specification of another primitive, for example within a predicate or mark property.

Events are propagated using a push-based model [3]. When a source node receives an event, it pushes the event to all dependents. When a signal value changes, corresponding encoders are re-evaluated in a localized update to the visualization scenegraph. If a signal value triggers a change in a data set (for example, a signal feeds a predicate used in a filter transform), the corresponding transform pipeline and implicated scengraph branches are updated. To prevent wasteful computation and momentary inconsistencies — known as reactive *glitches* [8] — updates execute in topological order: a signal changes only when all of its parents are up-to-date.

Vega features an extensible data transformation pipeline; we reuse this feature to implement user-defined functions (UDFs). UDFs are named JavaScript functions that are registered with the Vega runtime, and can then be declaratively referenced in the specification, like built-in transformations.

We leave performance optimization to future work. However, all example visualizations render without visible lags using Google Chrome 34 on an Apple MacBook Pro with a 2.3 GHz Intel Core i7 processor and 8 GB of RAM.

EXAMPLE INTERACTIVE VISUALIZATIONS

To evaluate the expressivity of our language, we present a range of examples and demonstrate coverage over Yi et al.'s interaction taxonomy [42]. Yi et al. identify seven categories based on user intent: *select*, to mark items of interest; *explore*, to examine a different subset of data; *reconfigure*, to show a different arrangement of data; *encode*, to use a different visual encoding; *abstract/elaborate*, to show more or less detail; *filter*, to show something conditionally; and, *connect*, to show related items. It is important to note that these categories are not mutually exclusive, and an interaction technique can be classified under several categories. We choose example interactive visualizations to demonstrate that our model can express interactions across all seven categories and how, through composition of its primitives, supports the accretive design of richer interactions.

Select: Brushing and Click/Shift-Click

Figure 3 demonstrates two interaction techniques for selecting points. The first allows a user to brush over a region, and highlights points that lie within the brush extents. Signals are registered to capture the start and end positions of the brush, by default `mousedown` and `[mousedown, mouseup] > mousemove`, respectively. A range predicate uses scale inversion to test whether a point's data value falls within the specified horizontal and vertical data ranges. Figure 5 (left) illustrates how a one-dimensional version of this interaction can be expressed in Vega JSON.

The second selection technique allows the user to select individual points of interest. A signal over clicked points feeds data transforms that add or toggle points in a new "selected" data source. A predicate checks if the `shiftKey` is set and, if not, clears the data source before adding points. Another predicate is then used to highlight points that exist within the data source. Figure 5 (right) contains the Vega JSON for this interaction. Both selection techniques use a production rule to set the fill color of selected points.

Connect: Brushing & Linking

We can extend the previous example to create an encapsulated interactor for brushing and linking. We can then apply the interactor to add brushing to the scatterplot matrix shown in Figure 6. Each cell of the matrix is an instance of a group mark with its own coordinate space. The plotting symbol, and necessary spatial scale functions, are specified within this group. To brush within a cell of the matrix, we apply the brush interactor to the group's specification, and pass in the

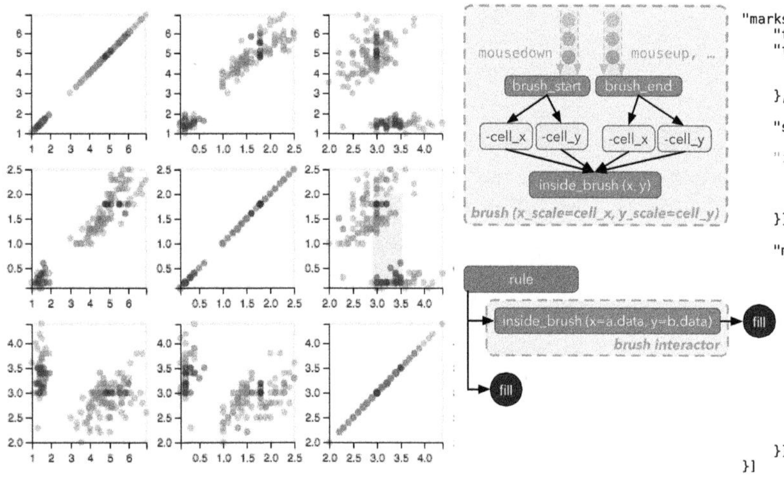


```
"marks": [{
    "type": "group",
    "from": {
      "data": "fields",
      "transform": [{"type": "cross"}]
    },

    "scales": [{"name": "cell_x", ...}, {"name": "cell_y", ...}],

    "interactors": [{
        "name": "brush",
        "url": "http://full/linkto/brush.json",
        "input": {"x_scale": "cell_x", "y_scale": "cell_y"}
    }],

    "marks": [{
      "type": "symbol", "properties": { "update": {
        "rule": [
          {
            "predicate": "brush:inside_brush", "latest": 1
            "input": {"x": {"field": {"group": "a.data"}},
                      "y": {"field": {"group": "b.data"}}},

            "fill": {"scale": "color", "field": "data.key"},
          },
          {"fill": {"value": "grey"}}
        ]}
      }, ...
    }]
}]
```

Figure 6. We can extract and parameterize the brushing interaction into an interactor, and apply it to the groups that define each cell of the scatterplot matrix. Primitives within the interactor can be referenced under its namespace.

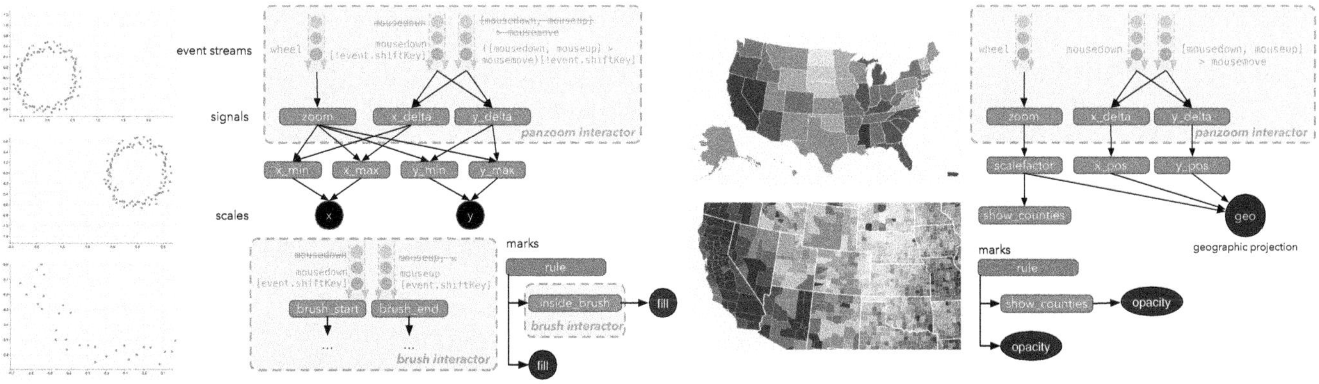

Figure 7. (left) Panning & zooming a scatterplot. Brushing can be added accretively by including the `brush` interactor, and rebinding event streams (indicated with strikethroughs). By extracting pan & zoom interactions to an interactor, we can repurpose it to perform semantic zooming on a geographic map (right). A map of the United States shows a choropleth of state-level unemployment. Once the map is zoomed past a threshold, states break up into counties, and show a choropleth of county-level unemployment.

appropriate scales. Signals and predicates defined within the interactor are addressable under its namespace.

Had the interactor predicates defined selections over pixel space, the production rule would only highlight points within the same cell as the brush (as each cell has a different coordinate space). However, as shown in Fig. 5 (left), the interactor predicates use scale inversion to lift the selection into the data domain. Thus, the production rule correctly performs the linking operation across scatter plots.

Abstract/Elaborate: Overview+Detail

With our brush interactor, we can also create the overview + detail visualization shown in Figure 4. In this case, brushing is restricted to the horizontal dimension. In our visualization, we override the `height` property of the visual brush added by the interactor, and ignore the vertical range predicates it populates. We use the horizontal range predicate with a filter transformation, to filter points for display in the detail plot. As a user draws a brush, signals update the horizontal range predicate, which in turn reactively filters points in the data source, updates scale functions and re-renders the detail view.

Explore and Encode: Panning & Zooming

Figure 7 (left) shows pan and zoom interactions for a scatter plot. By default, scale functions calculate their domain automatically from a data source. For this interaction, however, we must parameterize the domain using reactive signals. For panning, a `start` signal captures an initial `(x,y)` position, and subsequent `pan` signals calculate a delta. This delta is used to offset the scale domains. Similarly, a `zoom` signal applies a scale factor to the domains depending on the zoom direction. By default, these signals are mapped to `mousedown`, `[mousedown, mouseup] > mousemove` and `mousewheel`, respectively.

When adding a brushing interaction to this visualization, the brush signals may conflict with the signals for panning: on drag, both interactions might fire. One option to resolve this conflict is to begin brushing only when the `shiftKey` is depressed. If we try combining these interactions using D3 [6], which offers brushing and panning as part of its interactor typology, the process can be onerous. Additional callbacks must be registered that either instantiate or destroy a particular interaction depending on the `shiftKey` state.

In our model, the brush and pan signals can be rebound without modifying the interactor's definition. Instead, we provide alternate source event streams when instantiating the interactor. For example, `mousedown[event.shiftKey]` can drive the brush start signal, while the pan start signal can be triggered by `mousedown[!event.shiftKey]`. Similarly, the signals could be rebound to support touch interaction: one-finger drag to brush, two-finger drag to pan, and pinch to zoom.

We can also extract the pan & zoom definitions into their own interactor, and apply it to instead trigger semantic zooming [31], an *encoding* interaction technique shown in Figure 7 (right). At the top-level, the visualization shows a choropleth map of state-level unemployment. After crossing a specified zoom threshold, states subdivide to show a choropleth map of country-level unemployment. Here, the pan signals drive the geographic projection's translation and the zoom signals drive the projection's scale parameter. By default, both maps are drawn with states overlaying counties. A production rule uses a predicate to test whether the zoom signal is above a specified threshold; if it is, the state-level map is rendered transparently, displaying the county-level map underneath it.

Reconfigure: Index Chart

Figure 8 (left) shows an index chart: a line chart that interactively normalizes time series to show percentage change based on the current index point. To calculate the index point, we construct a signal over `mousemove` events and then drive the `x` coordinate through a scale inversion. As it is a quantitative scale, scale inversion results in a value from a continuous domain (i.e., any date/time from Jan 1 2000–Dec 31 2010). However, our dataset only contains stock prices for the start of every month, with the line interpolating between these points. To use scale inversion for an index point, we need to find the nearest data value. We build predicates that, for each time series, find a point that falls within a 2-week window on either side of the inverted point and use this as our index point. Using Vega's data transformations, we join the index point

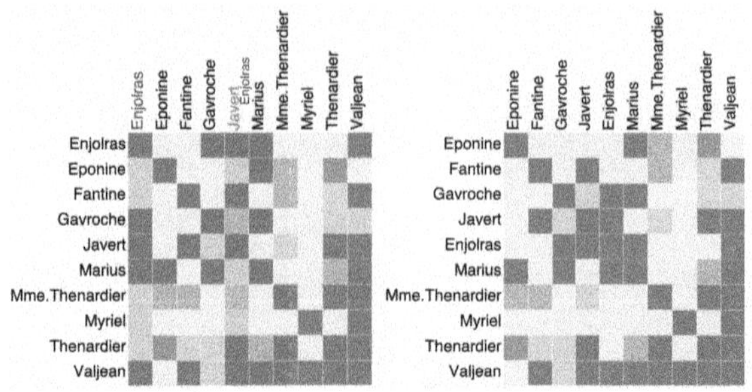

Figure 9. Re-arranging the columns of a co-occurrence matrix. The blue-headed column, Enjolras, is being dragged (left) and dropped over the red-headed column, Javert (right).

against the original data set and normalize the data values. Scale functions are defined in terms of the normalized data.

As a user moves their mouse across the index chart, the signal and scale inversion automatically update, data transforms find a new index point and normalize the data, scale functions update, and the visualization is re-rendered. This example demonstrates how interaction can be used in a feedback loop to provide data values that drive the visualization.

Reconfigure: Reordering Columns of a Matrix

Figure 9 shows a co-occurrence matrix of Les Misérables characters. To reorder the columns of the matrix, we first construct a data source that models the sort order of characters and initialize it to an alphabetical ordering. A signal on `.col_label:mousedown` captures the source column to be reordered, while a signal on `[.col_label:mousedown, mouseup] > mousemove` updates the target column location. On `mouseup`, the data source is updated using a UDF to remove the source column, and reinsert it at the target column's index.

Filter: Control Widgets

Figure 8 (right) shows the Job Voyager [19] visualization with control widgets to filter the visualized data. A textbox allows users to enter search terms to filter job titles, while the radio buttons allow users to filter by gender. We bind signals to the value of these control widgets, and then construct predicates attached to filter data transformations. For the textbox signal, a match predicate tests search terms against job titles, while an equality predicate filters by gender based on the radio button signal. This example illustrates how external query widgets can easily be bound into our reactive interaction model.

DISCUSSION: COGNITIVE DIMENSIONS OF NOTATION

The example interactive visualizations in the previous section demonstrate our model's expressiveness. Here, we seek to evaluate our model from a designer's standpoint. We use the Cognitive Dimensions of Notation [4], which provides a set of heuristics for evaluating the efficacy of notational systems such as programming languages and interfaces. Of the 14 dimensions, we evaluate our model against a relevant subset, and primarily compare it against common practices: declarative specification of visual encoding using D3 [6] and imperative event handling callbacks for interaction.

Abstractions (types and availability of abstraction mechanisms) and *Viscosity* (resistance to change). Streams and signals abstract the low-level events that trigger interactions and decouple them from downstream logic. This approach can facilitate rapid iteration: the result of an interaction can be designed (for example, highlighting points), and then a variety of different event triggers can be prototyped by simply rebinding the appropriate signals. As our examples demonstrate, binding signals reduces the burden for resolving conflicting interactions or retargeting to different platforms. By comparison, iterating with event callbacks can be more difficult. For example, a specific sequence of events may require a specific ordering of callbacks, and coordinating the visualization state across these various sequences falls to the designer.

Premature Commitment (constraints on the order of doing things). Abstracting streams and signals does impose a premature commitment. Users must create them before they are able to use any lower-level events to trigger state changes. This requirement could be relaxed: users could use low-level streams and signals inline, for example in a predicate definition. However, we believe inline reference to low-level events streams is a poor design pattern, as it makes an interaction technique dependent on a specific set of events, a common problem with existing interactor typologies. This pattern re-

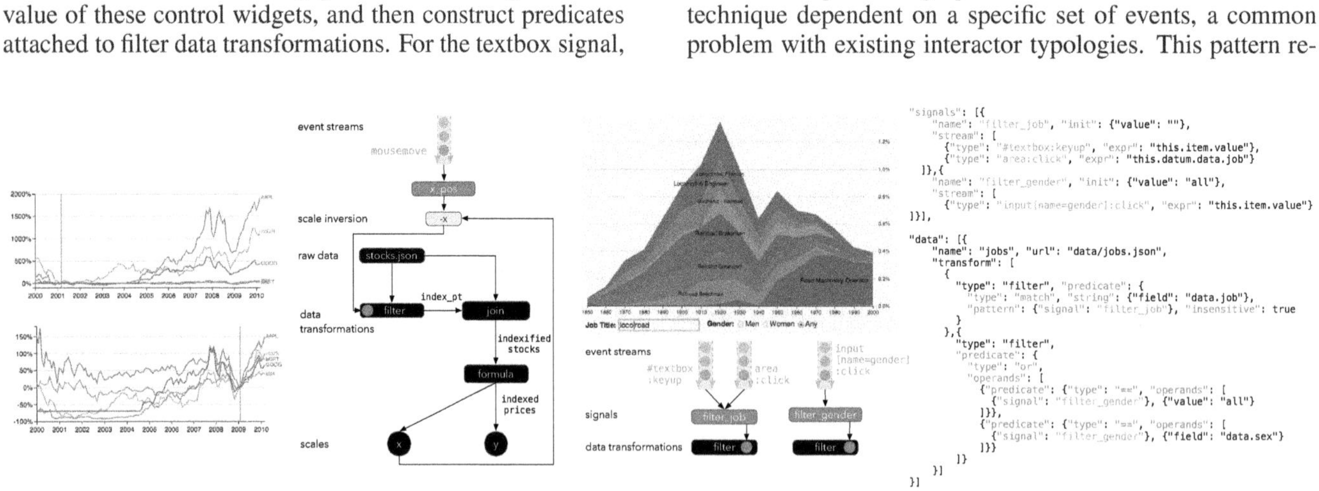

Figure 8. (left) An index chart that shows the percentage changes for a collection of time-series. The index point (red vertical line) is determined by the x position of a `mousemove` signal. (right) The job voyager can be filtered using signals bound to the state of control widgets. A textbox allows for pattern-based filtering of job titles while radio buttons allow gender-based filtering.

duces reusability, making it more difficult to resolve conflicting interactions (e.g., brushing vs. panning) or retarget interactions across input modalities.

Hidden Dependencies (important links between entities are not visible). Abstracting streams and signals also introduces hidden dependencies, as they obscure which input events are triggering a particular visual state change. However, we believe that the viscosity advantages outweigh the complexities of added hidden dependencies, which can be alleviated by naming the abstractions appropriately. Furthermore, as our code examples illustrate, under our model all the factors that directly affect a particular state are captured within a single specification. For example, a signal definition specifies all events or signals that may affect its value; similarly, a visual property may use a rule which enumerates all the values it may take. With D3, the visual specification may not completely define all visualization states. Instead, the user must trace a flow through event callbacks, a process further exacerbated by unpredictable execution order. The user is forced to coordinate interleaved callbacks, introducing *hard mental operations* and *error-proneness*.

Consistency (similar semantics are expressed in similar syntactic forms). Our interaction model is best suited for systems that declaratively specify visual encodings, and would feel foreign in imperative systems. However, given the widespread adoption of D3, and Vega's increasing integration in systems [14, 22, 34] we believe this is not a significant liability. By contrast, registering event callbacks on D3 visualizations breaks consistency: visual design is declarative while interaction design is imperative. It requires users to think in terms of different notational systems, and exposes underlying implementation and execution concerns.

Visibility (ability to view components easily). One of the primarily advantages of using D3, and registering event callbacks, is being able to debug code directly within a web browser [6]: the generated visualization can be inspected, while the JavaScript console can be used to interactively debug event callbacks. However, this is more difficult with Vega: its runtime environment, which parses and renders a specification, introduces its own stack of runtime abstractions. It is important to note that this is a limitation of the current implementation of our model, rather than an inherent limitation in the model itself. For example, our model might also be used to implement extensions to D3, thus gaining the advantages of declarative interaction design without losing debugging capabilities.

In summary, our model introduces some hidden dependencies and decreases visibility. However, we believe these are outweighed by the increase in specification consistency of visual encoding and interaction, and the decrease in viscosity by supporting abstraction mechanisms.

CONCLUSION

Our model contributes a substantive step towards enabling declarative interaction design for data visualization. An important next step is to assess the language's accessibility through user evaluations. Are new users able to learn this model? Can experts accustomed to callback-driven programming quickly transition to a reactive model? Our work here primarily focuses on the design of model primitives, and we only implemented cursory optimizations of our reactive dataflow graph. While existing performance is adequate for many common visualization scenarios, more extensive performance optimization is possible. For example, insights from the streaming data literature [1] might be applied to optimize interactive queries.

Vega's declarative format has facilitated integration into a variety of systems, including graphical design tools [34], statistical packages [14], and computational environments [22]. We anticipate that our model's declarative approach, and the ability to package reusable techniques as interactors, will facilitate similar integration opportunities. We intend to contribute our extensions back into the public Vega project. By reducing the burden for programmatic generation of interactions, we also hope to spur study into alternate, non-textual, ways of specifying interactions; for example, interaction design through demonstration or by direct manipulation.

Learning and adapting examples is an important part of the design process [20, 35]. Designers can use our notion of encapsulated, standalone interactors, to share, reuse, and learn from the design of others. Corpora of interaction designs could be created — similar to `bl.ocks.org` with D3 [6] visualizations — allowing users to browse through designs for inspiration, or adapt them for their own visualizations.

ACKNOWLEDGMENTS

This work was supported by an SAP Stanford Graduate Fellowship, the Intel ISTC for Big Data, and DARPA XDATA.

REFERENCES

1. Arasu, A., Babcock, B., Babu, S., Cieslewicz, J., Datar, M., Ito, K., Motwani, R., Srivastava, U., and Widom, J. Stream: The stanford data stream management system. *Book chapter* (2004).
2. Badros, G. J., Borning, A., and Stuckey, P. J. The cassowary linear arithmetic constraint solving algorithm. *ACM Trans. on Computer-Human Interaction (TOCHI) 8*, 4 (2001), 267–306.
3. Bainomugisha, E., Carreton, A. L., Cutsem, T. v., Mostinckx, S., and Meuter, W. d. A survey on reactive programming. *ACM Computing Surveys (CSUR) 45*, 4 (2013), 52.
4. Blackwell, A. F., Britton, C., Cox, A., Green, T. R., Gurr, C., Kadoda, G., Kutar, M., Loomes, M., Nehaniv, C. L., Petre, M., et al. Cognitive dimensions of notations: Design tools for cognitive technology. In *Cognitive Technology: Instruments of Mind*. Springer, 2001, 325–341.
5. Bostock, M., and Heer, J. Protovis: A graphical toolkit for visualization. *IEEE Trans. Visualization & Comp. Graphics 15*, 6 (2009), 1121–1128.
6. Bostock, M., Ogievetsky, V., and Heer, J. D3: Data-Driven Documents. *IEEE Trans. Visualization & Comp. Graphics 17*, 12 (2011), 2301–2309.

7. Cooper, G. H. *Integrating dataflow evaluation into a practical higher-order call-by-value language*. PhD thesis, Brown University, 2008.
8. Cooper, G. H., and Krishnamurthi, S. Embedding dynamic dataflow in a call-by-value language. In *Programming Languages and Systems*. Springer, 2006, 294–308.
9. Cottam, J., and Lumsdaine, A. Stencil: a conceptual model for representation and interaction. In *Information Visualisation*, IEEE (2008), 51–56.
10. Czaplicki, E., and Chong, S. Asynchronous functional reactive programming for guis. In *Proc. ACM SIGPLAN*, ACM (2013), 411–422.
11. Derthick, M., Kolojejchick, J., and Roth, S. F. An interactive visual query environment for exploring data. In *Proc. ACM UIST*, ACM (1997), 189–198.
12. Edwards, J. Coherent reaction. In *Proc. ACM SIGPLAN*, ACM (2009), 925–932.
13. Elliott, C., and Hudak, P. Functional reactive animation. In *ACM SIGPLAN Notices*, vol. 32, ACM (1997), 263–273.
14. ggvis: Interactive grammar of graphics for R. `http://ggvis.rstudio.com/`, April 2014.
15. Heer, J., and Agrawala, M. Software design patterns for information visualization. *IEEE Trans. Visualization & Comp. Graphics 12*, 5 (2006), 853–860.
16. Heer, J., Agrawala, M., and Willett, W. Generalized selection via interactive query relaxation. In *Proc. ACM CHI*, ACM (2008), 959–968.
17. Heer, J., and Bostock, M. Declarative language design for interactive visualization. *IEEE Trans. Visualization & Comp. Graphics 16*, 6 (2010), 1149–1156.
18. Heer, J., Card, S. K., and Landay, J. A. Prefuse: a toolkit for interactive information visualization. In *Proc. ACM CHI*, ACM (2005), 421–430.
19. Heer, J., Viégas, F. B., and Wattenberg, M. Voyagers and voyeurs: supporting asynchronous collaborative information visualization. In *Proc. ACM CHI*, ACM (2007), 1029–1038.
20. Herring, S. R., Chang, C.-C., Krantzler, J., and Bailey, B. P. Getting inspired!: understanding how and why examples are used in creative design practice. In *Proc. ACM CHI*, ACM (2009), 87–96.
21. Hudson, S. E., and Smith, I. Ultra-lightweight constraints. In *Proceedings of the 9th annual ACM symposium on User interface software and technology*, ACM (1996), 147 -155.
22. The IPython Notebook. `http://ipython.org/notebook.html`, April 2014.
23. Kin, K., Hartmann, B., DeRose, T., and Agrawala, M. Proton++: a customizable declarative multitouch framework. In *Proc. ACM UIST*, ACM (2012), 477–486.
24. Lee, E. A., and Messerschmitt, D. G. Synchronous data flow. *IEEE Proc. 75*, 9 (1987), 1235–1245.
25. Liu, Z., and Stasko, J. T. Mental models, visual reasoning and interaction in information visualization: A top-down perspective. *IEEE Trans. Visualization & Comp. Graphics 16*, 6 (2010), 999–1008.
26. Meyerovich, L. A., Guha, A., Baskin, J., Cooper, G. H., Greenberg, M., Bromfield, A., and Krishnamurthi, S. Flapjax: a programming language for ajax applications. In *ACM SIGPLAN Notices*, vol. 44, ACM (2009), 1–20.
27. Myers, B. A. A new model for handling input. *ACM Trans. on Information Systems (TOIS) 8*, 3 (1990), 289–320.
28. Myers, B. A. Separating application code from toolkits: eliminating the spaghetti of call-backs. In *Proc. ACM UIST*, ACM (1991), 211–220.
29. Oney, S., Myers, B., and Brandt, J. Constraintjs: programming interactive behaviors for the web by integrating constraints and states. In *Proc. ACM UIST*, ACM (2012), 229–238.
30. Ortiz, S., and Cid, V. P. Use cases of impure, an information interface, 2010.
31. Perlin, K., and Fox, D. Pad: an alternative approach to the computer interface. In *Proc. Comp. Graphics & Interactive Techniques*, ACM (1993), 57–64.
32. Pike, W. A., Stasko, J., Chang, R., and O'Connell, T. A. The science of interaction. *Information Visualization 8*, 4 (2009), 263–274.
33. Quadrigram. `http://www.quadrigram.com/`, April 2014.
34. Satyanarayan, A., and Heer, J. Lyra: An interactive visualization design environment. *Computer Graphics Forum (Proc. EuroVis)* (2014).
35. Schön, D. A. *The reflective practitioner: How professionals think in action*, vol. 5126. Basic books, 1983.
36. Vega: A Visualization Grammar. `http://trifacta.github.io/vega`, April 2014.
37. Victor, B. Drawing Dynamic Visualizations. `http://vimeo.com/66085662`, February 2013.
38. Wan, Z., Taha, W., and Hudak, P. Event-driven FRP. In *Practical Aspects of Declarative Languages*. Springer, 2002, 155–172.
39. Weaver, C. Building highly-coordinated visualizations in Improvise. In *Proc. IEEE Information Visualization* (2004), 159–166.
40. Wickham, H. *ggplot2: Elegant Graphics for Data Analysis*. Springer, 2009.
41. Wilkinson, L. *The Grammar of Graphics*. Springer, 2005.
42. Yi, J. S., ah Kang, Y., Stasko, J. T., and Jacko, J. A. Toward a deeper understanding of the role of interaction in information visualization. *Visualization and Computer Graphics, IEEE Transactions on 13*, 6 (2007), 1224–1231.

Laevo: A Temporal Desktop Interface for Integrated Knowledge Work

Steven Jeuris, Steven Houben, Jakob Bardram
The Pervasive Interaction Technology Laboratory
IT University of Copenhagen, Rued Langgaardsvej 7, DK-2300 Copenhagen, DK
{sjeu, shou, bardram}@itu.dk

ABSTRACT
Prior studies show that knowledge work is characterized by highly interlinked practices, including *task, file and window management*. However, existing personal information management tools primarily focus on a limited subset of knowledge work, forcing users to perform additional manual configuration work to integrate the different tools they use. In order to understand *tool usage*, we review literature on how users' activities are created and evolve over time as part of knowledge worker practices. From this we derive the *activity life cycle*, a conceptual framework describing the different states and transitions of an activity. The life cycle is used to inform the design of Laevo, a *temporal activity-centric* desktop interface for personal knowledge work. Laevo allows users to structure work within dedicated workspaces, managed on a timeline. Through a *centralized notification system* which doubles as a to-do list, incoming interruptions can be handled. Our field study indicates how highlighting the temporal nature of activities results in lightweight scalable activity management, while making users more aware about their ongoing and planned work.

Author Keywords
Personal information management; knowledge work; tool integration; activity-centric computing

ACM Classification Keywords
H.5.2 Information interfaces and presentation (e.g., HCI): User Interfaces – Graphical user interfaces (GUI)

INTRODUCTION
Knowledge work includes producing, transforming, consuming and communicating large amounts of diverse information. Traditionally, the digital artifacts associated with this work are managed using different personal information management (PIM) tools, each specializing in a particular task. Examples include calendars, to-do lists, email clients, file managers and web browsers. While a wide range of specialized tools allows users to select those most suited for their work, it also introduces *information fragmentation*: for each tool information items are stored, managed and viewed within a separate application-specific collection [7]. Studies have shown that information is often organized within hierarchies reflecting the users' projects or tasks [7, 8, 16]. Because a single project can make use of several tools, it is left to the user to associate the different related information items and maintain consistency across the separate project hierarchies. Moreover, information items are meaningful beyond the context of the tool which manages them. For example email has been shown to be the primary source of new events entered in a calendar, which in turn is not only used for planning, but also for reporting purposes and recording memorable events [37]; folder hierarchies can act as kind of project plans [20]; action-oriented items like emails or temporary files are used as reminders [39].

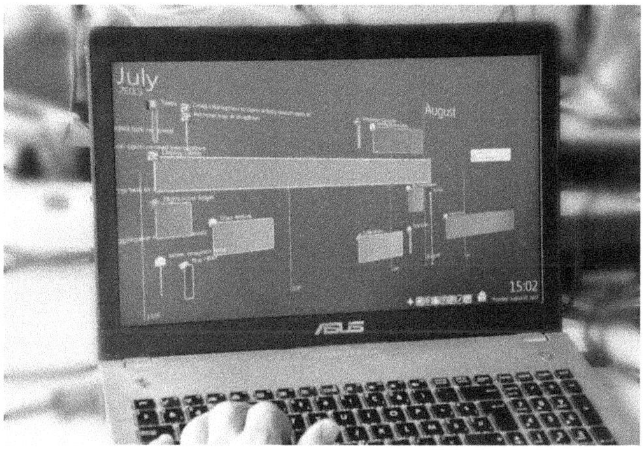

Figure 1. Laevo is an *activity-centric* desktop interface that supports (i) persisting, restoring and managing window configurations and files within *dedicated workspaces* which are managed on a timeline; (ii) handling *interruptions* and to-do items through a centralized notification system, in place or by redirecting them to new or existing workspaces.

Improving *tool integration* could overcome the significant overhead of manually having to configure and exchange information items. Prior research has proposed the concept of activity as a structuring mechanism, organizing information items [4, 30, 38], communication and collaboration [17, 29] within the context of actual higher-level knowledge work. Existing *activity-centric* systems however, primarily focus on the ad hoc construction of activities, often neglecting the importance of other knowledge worker practices integral to their work, such as interruption handling, archiving and planning.

UIST 2014, October 5–8, 2014, Honolulu, HI, USA.

ACM 978-1-4503-3069-5/14/10 ...$15.00.
http://dx.doi.org/10.1145/2642918.2647391

Task, window and file management, usually supported by separate tools, occur at different points in time throughout the life cycle of an activity. In order to analyze the emergence and evolution of activities over time we review prior research. Based on this review we derive a temporal conceptual framework for knowledge work, *the activity life cycle*. It depicts the different states and transitions of an activity over time. Informed by this conceptual framework, we designed and implemented *Laevo*, a *temporal activity-centric* desktop interface specifically designed for knowledge work on a single personal computer within an office setting. It is capable of persisting, restoring and managing window configurations and files within dedicated workspaces which are managed on a timeline and a to-do list. The to-do list doubles as a *centralized notification system* through which incoming interruptions, like emails, can be handled, in place or by redirecting them to new or existing workspaces.

In this paper we (i) introduce a temporal conceptual framework for knowledge work, *the activity life cycle*, (ii) describe the design and implementation of an activity-centric computing system based on this framework, addressing challenges reported in prior literature, and (iii) report on a *field study* during which 6 participants used the system on their personal computers during a period of two weeks.

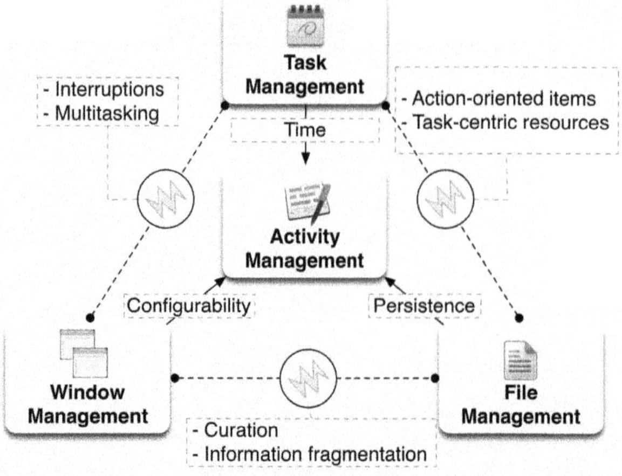

Figure 2. Overview of task, window and file management, highlighting conflicts between them.

LITERATURE REVIEW

Task, window and file management are an integral part of knowledge work. Widespread PIM tools primarily focus on supporting the management of only one of these. As a result, the user is required to coordinate tool use and pass information around. Prior research has explored tool integration to some extent, but often neglects at least one part of knowledge work. In this section, we review literature from different perspectives to gain insight in the commonalities and conflicts between them. By relating them to existing *activity-centric* computing systems we describe opportunities to further improve tool integration. An overview is given in Figure 2.

Knowledge Work Practices

Window Management

Window managers are tools that allow users to handle an increasing number of windows by allowing them to be spatially grouped together, thus leveraging human spatial memory. Switching between these separate window groups facilitates *multitasking*. Many modern window managers (such as those of Windows XP up to Windows 8) automatically support *application grouping* in which windows from the same application are grouped together under one item on the taskbar. Extending on this idea, GroupBar [35] gives the user more control by allowing them to group arbitrary windows together manually. Overall, existing window managers focus on similar lightweight *task management*. The Rooms system [15] was one of the earliest to provide such functionality, using *virtual desktops*. Work is distributed across several different desktop environments, each of which are *dedicated workspaces* only showing the windows open on that particular desktop. More recent window managers have explored alternate visualizations. One such example is Scalable Fabric [32], in which windows shrink in size when moving them into the periphery, allowing to organize them in labeled groups. WindowScape [36] offers implicit task management by storing snapshots of short-lived window groupings which can be returned to at later moment in time. Elastic Windows [21] allows organizing windows *hierarchically* and window operations can be performed on window groups, e.g. collapsing of entire window hierarchies. Spatial arrangement doesn't need to be restricted to 2D space, e.g. BumpTop [2] allows dragging and tossing around objects in 3D space, taking the desktop metaphor even further. However, long term task management like planning and reporting is not supported in any of these systems.

Task Management

We define a *task* as a set of actions which need to be performed in order to achieve a certain goal. In a desktop environment, one task is usually associated with several applications and documents. *Window management* helps out in organizing these during an ongoing multitasking session, but window configurations are lost once work is discontinued. In order to more easily re-initialize a working context users often aggregate related documents in task-specific folders [7, 8, 16]. Several systems explore integrating *task-centric resources* within existing applications. Taskmaster [6], e.g., recasts email as task management. Task Gallery [33] allows users to organize windows and files in tasks which are represented in a 3D desktop environment. Mylyn [23] is an extension for the Eclipse programming environment which allows switching between programming tasks and automatically builds up their context. These approaches however are application-specific, and only support aggregating a limited set of document types. TAGtivity [30] allows tagging any resource within a PC environment. While tags don't necessarily need to represent tasks, they were shown to be used in such a way, allowing to maintain multiple working contexts. TaskTracer [10] monitors user's interaction on a computer and associates them with tasks. A user interface provides an overview of the created task context. What many of these tools neglect is that *planning* tasks plays a crucial role in knowledge work as well. The user needs to be able to prepare, structure and reflect on future work. The widespread adoption of electronic calendars and to-do lists indicate their value in task management. However, these tools are intrinsically disconnected from the actual resources needed to start work on them [37].

File Management

Whittaker describes three *information curation processes*: keeping, management and exploitation [39]. People preserve large quantities of emails, bookmarks and personal files and organize them in ways that will promote future retrieval. However, information items are stored, managed and viewed from within application-specific collections, causing *information fragmentation* [7]. Not all information items are purely informative. Some are *action-oriented*, like emails. They require the recipient to do something, possibly before a certain date. They are generally kept around as a reminder. In order to alleviate the overhead of organizing files, time-based organization has been brought forward in previous research. Lifestreams [11] was the first to do so, providing a simple stream of documents over time. TimeScape [31] extends on this by integrating with the desktop interface. Time travel allows going to past and future states of the desktop. Only those documents used or placed at a certain point in time show up. Other approaches, like Haystack [1], offer the ability to construct individualized information collections by creating relations between separate information items. To simplify file retrieval, Leyline [13] offers information about the creation, use and sharing of documents and their context – *provenance*. Despite support for simplified access to the underlying file hierarchies, in essence files are a remnant of the original desktop metaphor. Users are forced to mentally connect window representations to the files they represent. When restoring window configurations users are still confronted with finding all the related files.

Integrated Knowledge Work

It is clear that task, window and file management are three practices intrinsically linked to each other. As depicted in Figure 2 supporting the three practices separately causes conflicts once they overlap. Window managers support lightweight *multitasking* but are unaware of the specified tasks in traditional task management tools. *Interruptions* often lead to new tasks or revisitation of old ones [19]. Handling them requires opening up the relevant windows. *Task-centric resources* are often grouped together in the file system. Folder hierarchies sometimes act as kind of project plans [20]. *Action-oriented* items like emails or temporary files are used as reminders [39]. Additionally, email has been shown to be the primary source of new events entered in a calendar, which in its turn is not only used for planning, but also for reporting purposes and recording memorable events [37]. Lastly, information *curation* is handled differently per application, causing *information fragmentation*.

What unifies these different practices is the actual work they set out to support. Studies have shown people organize their work in higher-level thematically connected units of work, often referred to in literature as *tasks* or *activities* [3, 9, 14]. By constructing tool integration around computational representations of activities, *meta-work* can be offloaded to a centralized *activity management* system. Such a system needs to integrate with the core aspects of task, window and file management; activities evolve over time, should be easily configurable and should be persisted so their context is not lost.

Activity-Centric Systems

Prior systems have incorporated *activity management* into the desktop interface. Within these systems, files, applications, communication and collaboration are structured within computational representations of activities. Activity-centric systems allow the user to switch between different ongoing activities by suspending and resuming them, thus facilitating multitasking. ABC [4], e.g., replaced the Windows Taskbar with an Activity Bar, showing the current list of activities and allowing to easily switch between them. Integrating with Apple OS X, Giornata [38] follows a similar approach, informed by activity theory. Additionally, activities can also be annotated with optional freeform tags. Other activity-centric systems such as Activity explorer [12] and co-Activity Manager [17] have explored how communication alerts can be tied to the activities from which they arise, automatically linking notifications to the right context. Some systems have extended the scope of managing activity contexts to some degree including other practices like planning in UMEA [22] or automated archival over time in TimeSpace [25]. However, most of these systems provide little or no support for the entire *activity life cycle*: the source of an activity, transitions and interrelations with other activities.

The core contribution of this paper to activity-centric systems research is a temporal activity-based computing system which is specifically designed to mitigate challenges reported in prior literature [4, 5, 17, 38]. Specifically, *Laevo* addresses the challenges of: (i) scalability when using an activity-centric system over longer periods of time; (ii) difficulty for users to easily identify and express the intent of an activity; and (iii) supporting different types and scopes of activities. Our approach differs from prior work as we introduce a new activity model that embraces the entire life cycle of complex knowledge work, focusing on all the practices that influence it over time. These include short- and long-term planning, archiving, multitasking and interruption handling. Without providing support for these practices, the benefits of activity-centric systems are potentially lost since low-level application and document configuration problems are simply replaced with higher-level activity management challenges. The interactions as part of our introduced 'temporal activity management' provide support for these practices and allow activities to go through different states, preserving and updating their context accordingly.

THE ACTIVITY LIFE CYCLE

Prior research has mainly focused on which information and which services the activity *context* is comprised of, based on theories of cognition and observations of real-world practice. However, knowledge work is evolutionary by nature [24]. Based on our literature review we conclude that it is equally important to investigate the transience of information; where does it come from, how is it passed from one tool to another

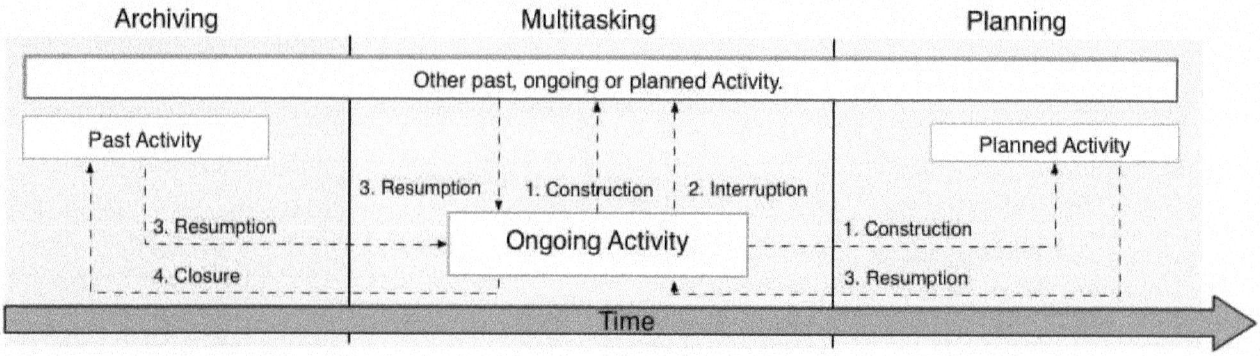

Figure 3. Modern knowledge work consists of archiving, multitasking and planning. Four fundamental practices, related to these processes, determine how an activity evolves over time.

and when is it no longer needed. Within the context of activities this means investigating how the activity context is created, used and changes over time. As concluded in the evaluation of Giornata *"[this] raises further research questions about how individuals think about the stages in an activity's lifecycle"* [38]. In this section we describe *the activity life cycle* (Figure 3), a conceptual framework representing four fundamental practices that influence the state of activities over time and frame them within three fundamental processes of knowledge work: *archiving*, *multitasking* and *planning*. These processes largely correspond to file, window and task management respectively, covering the majority of PIM tools.

Knowledge Work Processes

Multitasking is a common process which involves switching between, and managing a large number of windows, files and other resources that are associated with different activity contexts [9, 14, 19]. Within activity-centric computing this is supported by allowing the user to aggregate the related resources into meaningful structures reflecting the ongoing parallel activities and providing support to easily switch between them. Restoring the entire work context is automated, minimizing reconfiguration work the user otherwise has to do manually. Malone identified two important *archiving* practices of how office workers physically organize their information in their desks and offices: filing and piling [28]. Structuring work within labeled activities allows for systematic ordering, which could be seen as filing. In contrast, when working on a particular activity, documents can easily be piled within the open activity context without too much consideration. Following 'overview first, zoom and filter, then details-on-demand' [34], users can search through filed activities, and retrieve the activity context piles on demand. Lastly, short- and long-term *planning* are essential parts of knowledge work which shape future activities. When planning activities, a context can already be built up to be exploited once work on the activity starts.

Activity States and Transitions

Activities can be in three different states: *ongoing* when part of the current multitasking session, *past* when work has been discontinued and *planned* when intending to work on them at a later time. We identified four practices that influence the activity life cycle, and thus cause the activity state to change:

1. *Construction*– Construction is the practice of defining the context of an ongoing or planned activity. During this practice, users gradually build up and modify the content, thus refining the scope of the activity. Because there are no clear borders that fully define activities up front, the overhead of constructing, updating and moving resources in between activities should be minimized, supporting ad hoc and post hoc activity creation. Improving general activity awareness can reduce occasions where activities become intertwined.
2. *Interruption*– External and self-interruptions are events which often carry context that elicits the user to reconstruct or resume a different past, ongoing or planned activity. By providing a central interruption mechanism, the context of incoming interruptions can be easily incorporated into new or existing activities, supporting *construction*. Additionally, coupling interruption handling to activity construction also improves activity awareness, as users are encouraged to actively pair incoming interruptions to their corresponding activities.
3. *Resumption*– Resumption is the practice of restoring the content and context of a previously *constructed* past, ongoing or planned activity. When resuming an activity, ideally its context should reflect the user's mental model before the activity was interrupted. This facilitates quicker resumption, essential for efficient multitasking. Although activities can become irrelevant, they might need to be revisited shortly, or even restored at a later point in time.
4. *Closure*– When an ongoing activity loses its temporal relevance during *multitasking*, its content and context are removed from the set of parallel activities. Rather than deconstructing the activity, the entire constructed context and content should be preserved in such a way to allow for easy resumption at a later time. Archiving should be instant, and reversible.

LAEVO

Laevo is a *temporal activity-centric* desktop interface for Windows 7 and 8. It is designed for personal use on a single computer in support of office work. Going back to the seminal work of Rooms [15], *Laevo* allows users to structure work (applications and files) within *dedicated workspaces*. Similar to other activity-centric systems [4, 17, 38], each workspace can be used to reflect a separate activity. Where previous activity-centric systems focused mainly on providing functionality within these workspaces, Laevo focuses on all practices which influence activities over time. The entire *activity life cycle* is supported by introducing workspaces for to-do items, planned activities and providing support for interruptions and easy transitions between different activity states. When working within a workspace, Laevo's user interface is kept to a bare minimum; no new interface elements are introduced except for a system tray icon through which the user is notified of incoming *interruptions*. Only when opening the activity overview, the user is presented with a touch-enabled full screen user interface through which activities and interruptions can be accessed and managed.

Dedicated Activity Workspace

When working on a particular activity, only the relevant activity context is visible, which helps reducing information overload and keeping focus. This is achieved by setting up a virtual desktop per activity, thus still supporting all the existing tools the user is used to (Figure 4). The context of the activity automatically arises from the user working within the desktop workspace; windows which are opened within the workspace are assigned to the activity it represents (*construction*), but the underlying resources remain unmodified. When the user switches to a different workspace, all open windows of that context are restored (*resumption*). In order to organize files within activities, each activity has access to an *activity context library* (Figure 4A). This is a standard Windows library, similar to "Pictures" or "My Documents", which is always accessible from the side menu in Windows Explorer. It aggregates files from a specified set of paths. The content of the library is contextualized as it only shows paths assigned to the specific activity. The files are physically located in a folder which is automatically created for each activity (*construction*), reflecting its date and name, e.g. "3-11-2014 UIST 2014 paper". This supports the common file management practice of structuring files within folders representing tasks [16]. Users can still use their existing folder hierarchies by adding new folder locations to the library. There are no clear-cut borders in between activities: while working on one activity the users might have started work on another. Therefore the system provides a flexible mechanism by which windows can be moved in between different workspaces (*construction*). Similarly to how files are cut and pasted, shortcut keys can perform these operations on application windows once they have focus. Cut windows disappear immediately and are reassigned to the workspace in which they are pasted. Several cut operations can be performed in a row, placing them on a stack until a paste operation processes them all. Other shortcut keys allow quick access to the activity context library, creating new empty activities, closing the current activity or switching between the last two accessed ones.

Users can always see at a glance whether something requires their attention; Laevo's system tray icon lights up yellow when new *interruptions* arrive (Figure 4B). The visualization is intentionally kept to a minimum in order not to disrupt the flow of the user. Users decide for themselves when they want to address interruptions, which they can do by opening up the activity overview.

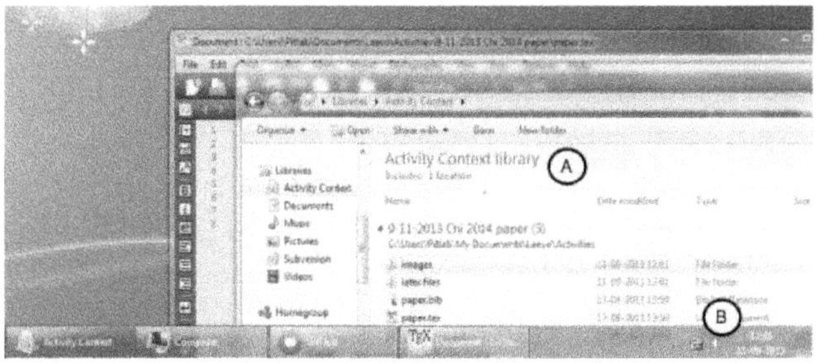

Figure 4. The activity context library (A) and tray icon (B) within a dedicated activity workspace.

Activity Overview

We provide an overview of activities in *time* and space, highlighting the *activity life cycle* (Figure 5). At a glance users can see when activities were open or are *planned*, while spatial organization, colors and icons can be used to identify activities or indicate relationships between them. This can be a powerful cue for recall by invoking episodic memory [26], facilitating *resumption* of old activities. A full screen representation hides the low-level details of the work the user was working on, and is intended to help users reason on a higher abstraction, contrasting the ongoing activity with surrounding ones. The timeline is the "heart" of the application, and can be accessed at any point in time using a re-appropriated keyboard button, CAPS LOCK [1], which allows quick access to other activities (*resumption*). It also acts as a modifier key to access all other shortcut keys. Alternatively the user can double-click the tray icon to access the overview. The granularity of activities can vary drastically; some lasting weeks, others mere minutes. Therefore, the timeline supports continuous touch-enabled panning and zooming in order to show any arbitrary time interval. Depending on the zoom level, the semantically most meaningful labels are shown (e.g. months or days). A one-dimensional representation of time, as opposed to a more traditional calendar layout, emphasizes the concurrency of activities. Lastly, applying a perspective transformation has two advantages. It saves screen estate without hampering readability too much [27], and it strengthens the presentation of time following the common conceptual metaphor of expressing time as a physical path in space. E.g."approaching the end of the year", or "leaving days behind".

Figure 5 highlights the different components on the overview screen, as well as the different *states* activities can be in. An activity can either be *open* to represent ongoing work (Figure 5A), *closed* when finished in the past and now *archived* in time (Figure 5B) or *planned* when a time slot has been assigned for it in the future (Figure 5C). Activities are represented by rectangular areas which stretch along the timeline horizontally, indicating when the working context was open. Only one workspace can be *active* at any given time (highlighted with a yellow border on the timeline), but several can be open simultaneously, allowing for *multitasking*. An activity is made active simply by clicking on it, after which the overview is hidden and its dedicated workspace shows up. Yellow lines along the bottom of a workspace

[1] an idea borrowed from humanized.com/enso

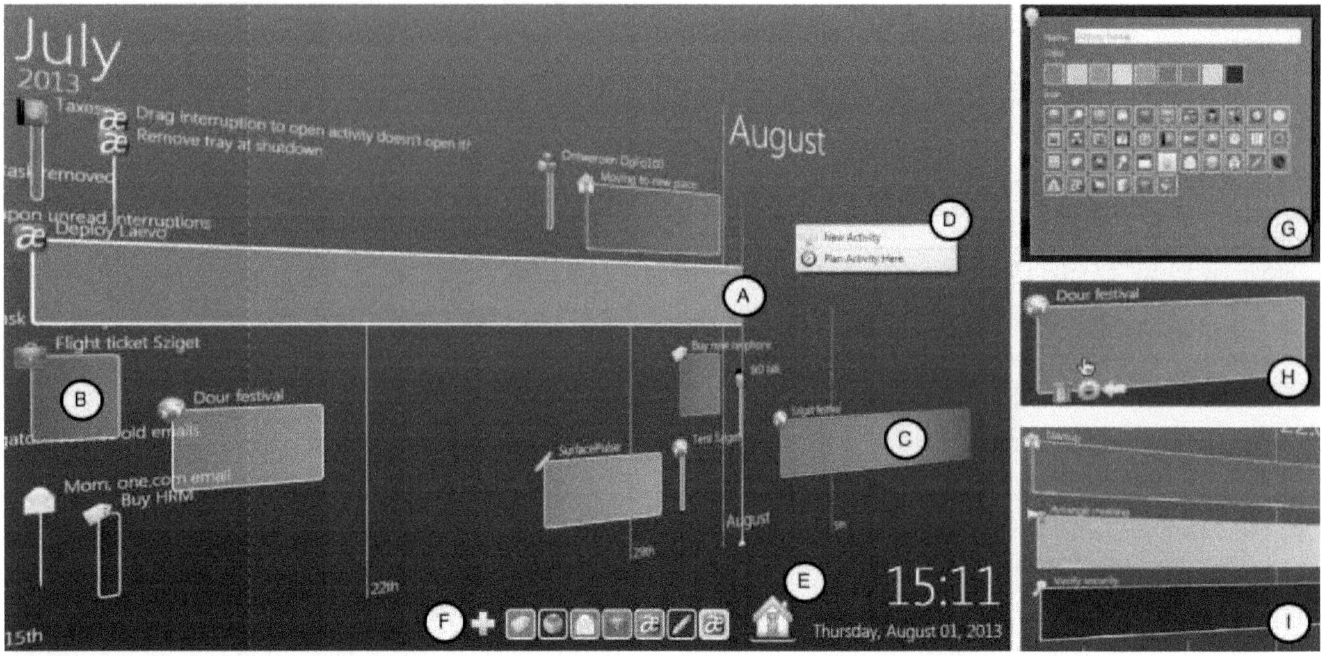

Figure 5. The activity overview through which activities are accessed and managed. It displays open ongoing activities (A), archived activities (B), planned activities (C), a context menu through which new activities can be created (D), the home activity (E) and to-do list (F). The three detailed images show the popup menu to edit activities (G), action buttons when hovering over an activity (H) and attention span lines (I).

indicate when they were active (Figure 5I), but this visualization can be disabled when deemed too distracting. Users need to change activity states themselves, which increases their awareness about them. Closed and planned activities can be opened through a hover menu, positioned near the mouse (Figure 5H). Doing so brings the activity into the current multitasking session, visually represented by stretching the rectangle up to a line which indicates the current time. Activating an activity does not open it, so it can be inspected without changing its state. The same menu is used to edit and remove activities, although removing them is discouraged. Instead, the system encourages *archival* over *time* by simply *closing* activities. To reinforce this, an ongoing activity can only be removed after it has been closed, and when it does not contain any open windows. Past activities that do have windows open in them are displayed with an orange border. The user can adjust the name, icon and color of each activity in a pop up menu (Figure 5G) which is opened from the hover menu. As the activity is edited, changes are reflected immediately in the pop up menu as well; its background color and icon in the top left changes. From the timeline, activities can be dragged up and down, allowing to organize them vertically. This combined with the *temporal* dimension in which they are displayed gives plenty of possible visual cues to identify them, following the redundancy gain principle. To allow for easy *construction* the activity names can be changed directly from the timeline as well; the labels act like ordinary input boxes.

When starting Laevo, all windows previously not associated to an activity are assigned to a permanent *home activity* (Figure 5E). It can be used as a workspace for smaller, less important tasks which aren't immediately recognized as an activity, or aren't activity-specific.

To-Do List and Interruptions

Although future activities can be *planned* accurately on the timeline, there is also a need for less structured *task management*. Laevo allows the user to create *to-do items* which behave the same way as activities, except that they are always visible on the overview screen (Figure 5F). Only their icons and colors are shown to save space. However, hovering over them shows their name, as well as a menu to edit or remove them (Figure 6A). Simple drag operations allow users to rearrange to-do items to reflect their priority.

Once a user decides to start working on, or plan an activity, the to-do item can be dragged to the timeline. Dropping it in front of the current time opens it, while dropping it behind plans it at that particular position (Figure 6B). Alternatively to-do items can be dragged to existing activities, merging their contents. This includes merging the associated windows, as well as the set up activity context library paths, including the automatically created activity folder.

Laevo features a centralized notification system for *interruptions*, well integrated with the rest of the system. It does so by equating interruptions with to-do items. They are added to the to-do list but can be distinguished by their flashing yellow border (Figure 6A). When within a workspace, the tray icon lights up as long as there are unattended interruptions. Opening them for the first time opens up their context with the appropriate application. E.g. when an email is received it shows up in the to-do list with the subject as name; clicking on it opens up the email message. Using the normal to-do list functionality this allows users to either handle interruptions in place (from within its workspace), merge them with existing activities, open, remove or plan them. This simplifies activity *construction*.

Figure 6. Interruptions, e.g. emails (A), arrive in the to-do list and are highlighted. To-do items can be dragged to the time line to start work on them or plan them (B).

TECHNICAL IMPLEMENTATION

In order to integrate with Windows 7 and 8, we designed a generic infrastructure through which Laevo interfaces. This component-based *Activity-Based Computing (ABC) infrastructure* handles common functionality, expected from an activity-centric computing system. It's comprised of a *virtual desktop manager (VDM)* which relieves Laevo from having to do custom window management; an *interruption handler* which aggregates interruptions received by applications; and *activity services* which expose operations in an application-agnostic way. It serves as a basis to build new activity-centric systems on; no direct interfacing with the operating system is required. The components provide extension points in order to integrate applications which are unaware about the activity-centric system. Both the infrastructure and Laevo are written in .NET. Laevo uses Windows Presentation Foundation (WPF) for its front end, and the infrastructure uses P/Invoke to communicate with the operating system.

The VDM offers a very minimalistic API. Through a virtual desktop manager an infinite amount of virtual desktops can be created. Besides switching between and merging desktops, the API also supports cut and paste operations on windows. To allow restarting activity-centric applications without losing window configurations, the state of the VDM can be persisted. All open windows previously handled by the VDM are reassigned to the correct desktops upon restarting. Through configuration files application-specific behavior can be defined, e.g. which windows should be cut during cut and paste operations. Lastly, a debug client which communicates with the VDM through Inter Process Communication can be used to see details about the managed windows, useful when setting up application-specific behaviors.

The interruption handler allows applications to publish interruptions which will be integrated into the activity-centric system. .NET's Managed Extensibility Framework (MEF) is used to provide an extension point for application plugins. Besides publishing interruptions these plugins also define how the related context should be opened once the user decides to look at them, e.g. opening up an email. A plugin was written which regularly checks Gmail's Atom feed for unread emails. Using the activity services from the infrastructure, the email is opened in a new tab in the default web browser when opening the interruption.

FIELD STUDY

After verifying the usability and stability in a one day in situ field study including 12 participants, we deployed Laevo during a two-week field study. The goal of this second study was to assess the short- and mid-term feasibility of using the system and explore the perceived impact of Laevo on the work practices of users.

Experimental Setup

6 participants (age ranging from 28 to 59 – 1 female) were recruited to participate in the experiment. Participants were recruited from a broad range of backgrounds, including consulting and software development, to represent different types of knowledge work. We required participants to have experience with either Windows 7 or 8. Similar to the pilot study, the experiment was conducted in situ, meaning that the system was deployed on their personal computer, used in their own work environment. Two out of 12 users from the pilot study participated in this second long term study. The other 4 participants used Laevo for the first time.

Method

Users were sent a link to a blog post containing an installer and a complete manual of Laevo. Participants were requested to use the system over a period of 14 days during their day-to-day work. During this period, they were asked to keep a diary, in which they had to add an entry once each day. The entry was based on a number of predefined questions on how and if they used the system that day, with a particular focus on any special events. Additionally, usage data from the system was automatically collected throughout the experiment. At the end of the experiment participants were requested to anonymize any sensitive information before submitting their data and diary. From this data, a local representation of their timeline could be reconstructed for analysis. Finally, after the experiment was completed, participants were invited for a semi-structured interview in which their experiences with the system were discussed. Initial questions were individually outlined beforehand based on their diaries.

Results

All participants experienced benefits by structuring their work within the context of activities, confirming prior findings of in situ field studies which have evaluated activity-centric systems. Once activities are set up, people like having only those things for the task at hand visible as it helps them in keeping *focus*. Participants experienced losing less time when switching between parallel tasks since the right folders and files were still open. Without Laevo, extreme *filers* (P1, P2, P4) ordinarily closed windows in order to coordinate many parallel tasks.

> *"I'm getting used to not having a cluttered desktop. I made an activity for something that only took about one hour, but this allowed me to focus on the task at hand." – P1*

When asked to elaborate on where this focus came from it became clear that Laevo made participants more aware about their activities. The activity overview played an important role in this. Participants argued that each time they switched between activities they were exposed 'at a glance' to all ongoing and planned work, which P5 stated as being an advantage over a to-do list on paper which can easily be ignored. This allowed them to make more conscious decisions about which activities to prioritize. As mentioned by one user:

> *"By explicitly defining your activity, you are [...] forced to reflect on what is your current active 'task', [which] seems to make you less distracted. When you do switch to something else, it becomes a very conscious choice."* – *P6*

Analyzing the participants' timelines indicated that for all users except one (P3) the majority of activities were concrete instantiations aimed towards a certain goal, as opposed to 'types' of activities like 'programming'. Noteworthy, two users (P2, P3) who were using Outlook instead of Gmail, and thus weren't receiving email interruptions, created long-running 'check email' activities.

> *"Using other [VDMs] I structured my work according to [type of work]. What distinguishes Laevo from other [VDMs] is it is inviting to organize [work] as concrete activities."* – *P6*

The activity model provided by Laevo was appropriated by users to support different activity *scopes*, ranging from only having short hour-based tasks (P2, P6), to long term projects that lasted several weeks (P3, P4), to a combination of both (P1, P5) (Figure 7).

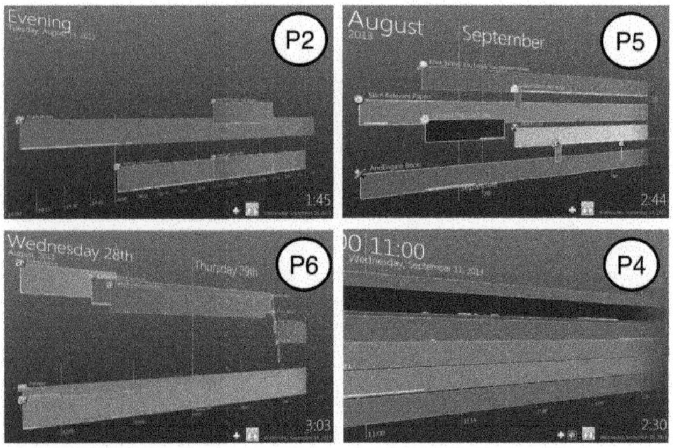

Figure 7. Different activity scopes, depicted by the timelines of participants P2, P4, P5 and P6.

One user (P5) created a number of short tasks at the start of each day, meticulously planning which work needed to be done. As the day progressed he used the activity timeline to check whether he was still on schedule, reprioritizing activities where needed. Another user (P4), however, argued that activities only made sense to him for long term projects. As part of his work, he created activities for each of the clients he was working with. For all smaller tasks he used the home activity, or simply handled them inside the currently open one. In general, all participants saw the home activity as a catch all environment, often used for quick and dirty work or private activities, thus keeping actual work separated from 'daily clutter'.

All participants that eventually created short-term activities mentioned a *'learning curve'* they had to go through when using Laevo. After a while, P1 and P2 adopted a 'nothing ventured, nothing gained' attitude towards creating activities. The up-front configuration work initially seems like an overhead, but over time users start to see several advantages when doing so: *less clutter*, increased *focus*, *productivity* and *efficiency*.

> *"[...] the more separate activities I start in Laevo, the less I'm tempted to quickly do another activity within an existing one, the more fluently and efficient I can work. You have to 'learn to use' Laevo – as is the case with everything."* – *P2*

Participants incorporated the system to varying degrees into their existing work practices, depending on how much overlap there was with the other tools they used. Before using Laevo, P2 used to write to-do items on a piece of paper. She first experimented with planning activities in the future in order to remind her of them, but afterwards started using the built-in to-do list instead. P1 opened up entire projects within to-do items as placeholders for side-projects he wanted to start working on when he had some spare time. Another participant (P5) preferred Google's task list since he could easily access it from his mobile phone. However, at the start of each day he manually transferred the to-do items with the highest priority to Laevo's timeline, planning his day. He preferred Laevo's overview over Google's task list. Lastly, P6 did not use the to-do list nor the incoming email interruptions since he kept an elaborate to-do list on paper, which he divided in different zones by priority.

Similarly, participants used different approaches to construct activities. P5 had set up emails to arrive in his to-do list. A request to update his daily report of Laevo lead to opening it up as a new activity, while a reminder email by Google was dragged to the corresponding time on the timeline. Another participant (P4) who had not set up email interruptions manually cut and pasted email windows to the corresponding activities, effectively using them as reminders within his long-running projects. P2 manually introduced to-do's, which lead to the creation of activities the next day. Analysing the timelines of all participants (e.g. Figure 7), it was clear that users applied a wide variety of color schemes and physical layouts.

Laevo currently provides limited support for the revisitation of past activities. Previously closed activities that are reopened are shown on the timeline as a continuous visualization which most participants found to be an incorrect representation. The original design rationale behind this feature was to create a connection between the two points in time the activity was used. The yellow lines indicate when the activity was active. The users, however, argued that it should not be represented as a continuum but rather as *multiple instances* of that particular activity.

Three out of six participants (P2, P5, P6) continued using the system after the two week study. Two other users mentioned they would continue using Laevo in case stability issues would be resolved (P1 and P4) and in case integration with Outlook would be provided (P4).

DISCUSSION AND CONCLUSION

The contributions presented in this paper are twofold. On the one hand, we presented a conceptual framework—the activity life cycle—that, through the temporal unfolding of activities in PIM, highlights open challenges reported in prior activity-centric systems research (e.g., [4, 5, 17, 38]). The framework describes the constant and interleaved construction, interruption, resumption and closure of activities which needs to be addressed in the design of activity-centric computing systems. On the other hand, we introduced and evaluated a personal activity-centric system based on the conceptual framework—Laevo—able to support integrated task, window and file management using a temporal user interface. In the remainder of the section, we relate the results of the evaluation to the open challenges driving our design, outline how this work could evolve to support activities spanning multiple devices and users, and finally our proposal for a rethinking of PIM.

Scalability, Activity Scopes and Human Intent

The introduced temporal dimension provides a lightweight *scalable* solution, capable of visualizing activities of *varying scope* (from long-term projects to ad hoc tasks) in parallel. One of the open questions in activity-centric computing is who should define the *intent* of an activity, when and how? Laevo follows Kidd's recommendation; we should not try to predict what users want to do with the represented information since *"the marks are on the knowledge worker"*. Rather we should provide users with *"structures which are both flexible in their semantics and generative in nature"* [24]. Laevo allows users to externalize ongoing and planned work while automatically storing the marks they make for future reference able to facilitate users' recollection. This rich information visualization incorporates most of the required task types to easily access information [34], reducing information overload; participants reported being more *focused*, *productive* and *efficient* during our evaluation. The explicit full screen interface made users more *aware* about their ongoing and planned activities, empowering them to make conscious decisions on how to structure and organize their work. Structuring work within the context of activities, and providing strong provenance cues of their life cycle and interrelations with other activities, is how we envision to support what Whittaker refers to as *the curation lifecycle* [39]. Although these results provide an initial validation of the activity life cycle framework, a long-term study is still needed in order to assess to which degree a user's activity history will be able to inform later activity construction and/or resumption.

Multi-device and Collaboration

While Laevo focuses entirely on single device PIM, activity-centric computing has traditionally incorporated support for cross-device and collaborative activities (e.g. [5]). Ongoing and future work on Laevo seeks to incorporate support for multi-device activity management by allowing to share activity definitions and their content across devices. Technically, this can be achieved by using the activity model to distribute, share and synchronize resources (e.g. files) [18]. Within an ecology of devices, Laevo is specifically designed to act as a master device (e.g. desktop computer), providing rich support for the creation of content. This allows for mobile devices, which are optimized for information consumption, to easily access and extend on the distributed activity-centric information *while* the activities take place. E.g., during a meeting planned through Laevo, meeting notes could be shared.

Integrated Knowledge Work

One of the design goals of Laevo is to provide a full integration of *task, window and file management*. The current implementation demonstrates several interaction techniques working towards this goal. For example, the window cut and paste operations allow users to more easily create and reconfigure activities, without having to move underlying resources around. It narrows the gap between window and file management, raising interesting questions for further research on how window management can be re-designed to outgrow its original purpose. Further research on Laevo is therefore to increasingly move away from files, as their main intent of persisting information could be replaced by persisting *window configurations*, represented as activities.

ACKNOWLEDGMENTS

This research has been funded by the Danish Agency for Science, Technology and Innovation under the project "Next Generation Technology for Global Software Development", #10-092313 and the EU Marie Curie Network iCareNet under grant number 264738.

REFERENCES

1. Adar, E., Karger, D., and Stein, L. A. Haystack: Per-user information environments. In *Proc. CIKM '99*, ACM (1999), 413–422.
2. Agarawala, A., and Balakrishnan, R. Keepin' it real: Pushing the desktop metaphor with physics, piles and the pen. In *Proc. CHI '06*, ACM (2006), 1283–1292.
3. Bannon, L., Cypher, A., Greenspan, S., and Monty, M. L. Evaluation and analysis of users' activity organization. In *Proc. CHI '83*, ACM (1983), 54–57.
4. Bardram, J., Bunde-Pedersen, J., and Soegaard, M. Support for activity-based computing in a personal computing operating system. In *Proc. CHI '06*, ACM (2006), 211–220.
5. Bardram, J. E. Activity-based computing for medical work in hospitals. *ACM Trans. Comput.-Hum. Interact. 16*, 2 (June 2009), 10:1–10:36.
6. Bellotti, V., Ducheneaut, N., Howard, M., and Smith, I. Taking email to task: The design and evaluation of a task management centered email tool. In *Proc. CHI '03*, ACM (2003), 345–352.
7. Bergman, O., Beyth-Marom, R., and Nachmias, R. The project fragmentation problem in personal information management. In *Proc. CHI '06*, ACM (2006), 271–274.
8. Boardman, R., and Sasse, M. A. "stuff goes into the computer and doesn't come out": A cross-tool study of personal information management. In *Proc. CHI '04*, ACM (2004), 583–590.

9. Czerwinski, M., Horvitz, E., and Wilhite, S. A diary study of task switching and interruptions. In *Proc. CHI '04*, ACM (2004), 175–182.
10. Dragunov, A. N., Dietterich, T. G., Johnsrude, K., McLaughlin, M., Li, L., and Herlocker, J. L. Tasktracer: A desktop environment to support multi-tasking knowledge workers. In *Proc. IUI '05*, ACM (2005), 75–82.
11. Freeman, E., and Gelernter, D. Lifestreams: A storage model for personal data. *SIGMOD Rec. 25*, 1 (Mar. 1996), 80–86.
12. Geyer, W., Muller, M. J., Moore, M. T., Wilcox, E., Cheng, L.-T., Brownholtz, B., Hill, C., and Millen, D. R. Activity explorer: activity-centric collaboration from research to product. *IBM Systems Journal 45*, 4 (2006), 713–738.
13. Ghorashi, S., and Jensen, C. Leyline: Provenance-based search using a graphical sketchpad. In *Proc. HCIR '12*, ACM (2012), 2:1–2:10.
14. González, V. M., and Mark, G. "constant, constant, multi-tasking craziness": Managing multiple working spheres. In *Proc. CHI '04*, ACM (2004), 113–120.
15. Henderson, Jr., D. A., and Card, S. Rooms: The use of multiple virtual workspaces to reduce space contention in a window-based graphical user interface. *ACM Trans. Graph. 5*, 3 (July 1986), 211–243.
16. Henderson, S. Genre, task, topic and time: Facets of personal digital document management. In *Proc. CHINZ '05*, ACM (2005), 75–82.
17. Houben, S., Bardram, J. E., Vermeulen, J., Luyten, K., and Coninx, K. Activity-centric support for ad hoc knowledge work: A case study of co-activity manager. In *Proc. CHI '13*, ACM (2013), 2263–2272.
18. Houben, S., Nielsen, S., Esbensen, M., and Bardram, J. E. Noosphere: An activity-centric infrastructure for distributed interaction. In *Proc. MUM '13*, ACM (2013), 13:1–13:10.
19. Jin, J., and Dabbish, L. A. Self-interruption on the computer: A typology of discretionary task interleaving. In *Proc. CHI '09*, ACM (2009), 1799–1808.
20. Jones, W., Phuwanartnurak, A. J., Gill, R., and Bruce, H. Don't take my folders away!: Organizing personal information to get things done. In *Ext. Abstracts CHI '05*, ACM (2005), 1505–1508.
21. Kandogan, E., and Shneiderman, B. Elastic windows: Evaluation of multi-window operations. In *Proc. CHI '97*, ACM (1997), 250–257.
22. Kaptelinin, V. Umea: Translating interaction histories into project contexts. In *Proc. CHI '03*, ACM (2003), 353–360.
23. Kersten, M., and Murphy, G. C. Using task context to improve programmer productivity. In *Proc. SIGSOFT '06/FSE-14*, ACM (2006), 1–11.
24. Kidd, A. The marks are on the knowledge worker. In *Proc. CHI '94*, ACM (1994), 186–191.
25. Krishnan, A., and Jones, S. Timespace: Activity-based temporal visualisation of personal information spaces. *Personal Ubiquitous Comput. 9*, 1 (Jan. 2005), 46–65.
26. Lamming, M., and Flynn, M. Forget-me-not: Intimate computing in support of human memory. In *Proc. FRIEND21, '94 Int. Symp. on Next Generation Human Interface*, Citeseer (1994), 4.
27. Larson, K., van Dantzich, M., Czerwinski, M., and Robertson, G. Text in 3d: Some legibility results. In *Ext. Abstracts CHI '00*, ACM (2000), 145–146.
28. Malone, T. W. How do people organize their desks?: Implications for the design of office information systems. *ACM Trans. Inf. Syst. 1*, 1 (Jan. 1983), 99–112.
29. Muller, M. J., Geyer, W., Brownholtz, B., Wilcox, E., and Millen, D. R. One-hundred days in an activity-centric collaboration environment based on shared objects. In *Proc. CHI '04*, ACM (2004), 375–382.
30. Oleksik, G., Wilson, M. L., Tashman, C., Mendes Rodrigues, E., Kazai, G., Smyth, G., Milic-Frayling, N., and Jones, R. Lightweight tagging expands information and activity management practices. In *Proc. CHI '09*, ACM (2009), 279–288.
31. Rekimoto, J. Timescape: A time machine for the desktop environment. In *Ext. Abstracts CHI '99*, ACM (1999), 180–181.
32. Robertson, G., Horvitz, E., Czerwinski, M., Baudisch, P., Hutchings, D. R., Meyers, B., Robbins, D., and Smith, G. Scalable fabric: Flexible task management. In *Proc. AVI '04*, ACM (2004), 85–89.
33. Robertson, G., van Dantzich, M., Robbins, D., Czerwinski, M., Hinckley, K., Risden, K., Thiel, D., and Gorokhovsky, V. The task gallery: A 3d window manager. In *Proc. CHI '00*, ACM (2000), 494–501.
34. Shneiderman, B. The eyes have it: a task by data type taxonomy for information visualizations. In *Proc. VL '96*, IEEE (Sep 1996), 336–343.
35. Smith, G., Baudisch, P., Robertson, G., Czerwinski, M., Meyers, B., Robbins, D., Horvitz, E., and Andrews, D. Groupbar: The taskbar evolved. In *Proc. OZCHI '03* (2003), 34–43.
36. Tashman, C. Windowscape: A task oriented window manager. In *Proc. UIST '06*, ACM (2006), 77–80.
37. Tungare, M., Perez-Quinones, M., and Sams, A. An exploratory study of calendar use. *arXiv preprint arXiv:0809.3447* (2008).
38. Voida, S., and Mynatt, E. D. It feels better than filing: Everyday work experiences in an activity-based computing system. In *Proc. CHI '09*, ACM (2009), 259–268.
39. Whittaker, S. Personal information management: from information consumption to curation. *Annual review of information science and technology 45*, 1 (2011), 1–62.

Reflection: Enabling Event Prediction As an On-Device Service for Mobile Interaction

Yang Li
Google Research
yangli@acm.org

ABSTRACT
By knowing which upcoming action a user might perform, a mobile application can optimize its user interface for accomplishing the task. However, it is technically challenging for developers to implement event prediction in their own application. We created Reflection, an on-device service that answers queries from a mobile application regarding which actions the user is likely to perform at a given time. Any application can register itself and communicate with Reflection via a simple API. Reflection continuously learns a prediction model for each application based on its evolving event history. It employs a novel method for prediction by 1) combining multiple well-designed predictors with an online learning method, and 2) capturing event patterns not only within but also across registered applications—only possible as an infrastructure solution. We evaluated Reflection with two sets of large-scale, in situ mobile event logs, which showed our infrastructure approach is feasible.

Author Keywords
Event prediction; mobile computing; online learning; passive aggressive; infrastructure; API; probabilistic model.

INTRODUCTION
Predictive or adaptive user interfaces dynamically optimize the interaction flow or UI layout for specific actions that a user is likely to perform, e.g., [2, 6, 8, 10-14, 17, 20-24]. They promise to reduce the amount of user effort needed for carrying out an interaction task, which is crucial for mobile devices as they offer a sheer number of functionalities that can only be accessed via a limited interaction bandwidth. One simple example of predictive UIs is a recency list that has been used by many applications such as a phone dialer. This approach assumes a recently performed action is likely to be performed again, so presenting a recent item at a top position in a list potentially reduces the user effort for searching the list.

UIST '14, October 05 - 08 2014, Honolulu, HI, USA

ACM 978-1-4503-3069-5/14/10···$15.00.
http://dx.doi.org/10.1145/2642918.2647355

Apparently, such an optimization is only possible when user actions—more generally interaction events—can be accurately predicted. However, it is technically challenging for developers to implement an effective prediction method in their application, which often requires a significant amount of engineering effort and high levels of technical expertise such as signal processing and machine learning.

Previous work has investigated methods for predicting interaction events for several specific domains, such as app launches [20, 23], local business searches [24], phone calls [11] and web browsing [6, 13]. Prior work has also contributed useful datasets and conceptual understandings about user behaviors on popular mobile platforms such as Android [1] and iPhones [19].

However, there lacks a general method and infrastructure support for developers to easily enable event prediction in their application. Prior methods were mostly tuned for predicting specific types of behavior in their domain, e.g., app invocations in a Launcher (often the Home screen on a mobile device) [20]. To predict interaction events in an arbitrary application, a prediction method needs to be easily customizable and dynamically adaptable for unexpected behaviors that might occur in the application.

Thus, our goal is to create an infrastructure for developers to easily incorporate event prediction into their mobile applications. Such an infrastructure frees application developers from repetitive effort of creating their own prediction component in each application. It saves scarce mobile computing resources by sharing the same data management and prediction components across applications. In addition, an infrastructure solution enables an untapped opportunity for making more accurate prediction because as a central service it sees events across applications.

In this paper, we present Reflection, an on-device infrastructure that provides event prediction as a service for mobile applications. An application can send its interaction events to Reflection via a simple API and the application can then query Reflection for how likely each of the events would occur at a given time. These events can be arbitrary and only meaningful to the application, e.g., they can be app names for a launcher, phone numbers dialed for a dialer or search queries entered in a search box. An application can then optimize its user interface based on the predicted results, e.g., sorting a list of options based on their prediction scores. We here focus on the support for enabling event prediction, rather than how to leverage prediction results for interface optimization, which is beyond the scope of this paper.

Because Reflection, as an infrastructure, is designed to serve arbitrary applications, its prediction model cannot be trained offline—a distinction with prior work. Reflection employs an online learning approach, based on [4], to combine multiple event prediction mechanisms that each has proven useful for predicting certain behaviors. It continuously refines a prediction model for each application as it receives events from the application. Reflection also learns how the events from a target application relate to those from other applications, because interaction behaviors in an application might be situated in a larger context. Utilizing events across applications effectively addresses the sparsity of events for each single application, which has been a challenge for learning prediction models.

To our knowledge, Reflection is the first mobile infrastructure that provides event prediction as a general service to applications. The paper offers the following contributions.

- A general method for event prediction that combines a set of well-designed prediction mechanisms via an online learning framework. Such a method is essential to an infrastructure for enabling event prediction for an arbitrary application.
- A carefully engineered mobile on-device infrastructure that provides event prediction as a service to applications, which an application can communicate through a concise set of APIs. The infrastructure consumes negligible CPU time and battery, which is crucial for mobile platforms.
- A thorough evaluation of Reflection based on two large-scale datasets that shows such an infrastructure approach is feasible. Reflection achieved reasonable accuracy when the semantics and underlying distribution of target events are unknown—a challenge that a general infrastructure faces.
- A deep analysis that revealed how such an infrastructure system evolves over time, and the benefit of leveraging events across applications for prediction—a unique advantage of our infrastructure approach. These findings are useful for designing future event prediction systems.

RELATED WORK

We discuss how Reflection relates to previous work on mobile event analyses, predictive user interfaces as well as prediction methods.

Mobile Event Collection & Analyses

The design of event prediction methods can benefit from a solid understanding of mobile user behaviors. With the wide adoption of mobile devices, it is possible to collect event logs about interaction behaviors at a large scale. Shepard et al. developed LiveLab [19], a logging infrastructure for measuring smartphone (iPhone) usage such as app launches and phone calls longitudinally. In particular, they deployed LiveLab to 25 users for one year that generated a useful dataset for the research community. We evaluated Reflection based on the dataset. Meanwhile, Böhmer et al. developed AppSensor, an event logger for Android-powered devices and collected data from over four thousand users [1]. In experimenting with Reflection, we employed a similar approach for collecting event logs from Android devices. These previous studies contributed useful findings for understanding mobile behaviors.

Predictive User Interfaces

Developing interfaces that can reduce or eliminate the need for user input by predicting user actions has been an important research topic, e.g., [2, 6, 8, 10-14, 17, 20-24]. Prior work has used event prediction for optimizing interaction tasks in a traditional PC environment, such as menu selection [17], file accesses, website visits, window switches as well as command lines [6, 7, 14]. Recently, as mobile apps flourish, extensive work has been devoted to predicting app launches—which application the user is likely to invoke, to reduce user effort in searching for a target application or accelerate a launch by prefetching the content of a target app (e.g., [10, 12, 13, 20, 23]). Previous work has also investigated prediction-based UI optimization for other mobile interaction tasks, such as ranking phone calls [11, 13], recommending web or local searches [13, 24] and inducing shortcuts [2].

Compared to these previous systems, which mostly focused on specific applications of event prediction, we enabled event prediction as a general service that can be directly used by any application. This type of support is lacking in previous work. Our effort resonates with early work for providing infrastructure support for context-aware applications (e.g., [5, 9]), although we addressed different challenges and focused on prediction methods in addition to infrastructure design in this work.

Event Prediction Methods

The methods of Most Recently Used (MRU) and Most Frequently Used (MFU) items are often employed in the previous literature, e.g., [6, 17], and existing commercial products. These heuristics-based methods are easy to implement and their behaviors are well-understood by users. MRU and MFU have also been frequently used as baseline methods in previous work. Similarly, we also compared our approach against these methods.

Previous work revealed the regularity of event transitions in mobile use, formally a Markov chain, especially in app launches. Böhmer et al. characterized this regularity with a transition probability matrix based on a dataset collected from over 4,000 users [1]. Yan et al. used event transitions as a "triggers and followers" feature in their decision process [23]; Shin et al. used "last-used app" as a random variable in their Naïve Bayesian model [20]; Fitchett and Cockburn also combined event transition probabilities with other features in their work [6]. Rahmati et al. further discovered that prediction accuracy drops when using more history beyond the last event [13]. In Reflection, we employ two types of transition probabilities: one for event transitions within a target application and one for transitions cross applications. This factorization turns out to be effective.

The temporal pattern of event occurrences is frequently used for event prediction [6, 10-13, 20, 23]. Specific hours of a day or days of a week might be more likely for certain events to occur than other times, e.g., a user might always use a Flashlight app at night. A typical approach for utilizing temporal patterns is to derive a probabilistic distribution based on how often a target event occurs in a given time window. We also used the hour of a day and the day of the week when an event occurs as features.

Likewise, previous work has also studied spatial patterns of events. Cell tower IDs only give a coarse estimate about the user's location, but has proven useful in event prediction (e.g., [20]). In contrast, GPS localization that gives much more precise location information of the user does not significantly improve prediction accuracy [13]. In addition, the excessive battery consumption of GPS is prohibitive for mobile devices. Thus, we decided not to use energy hungry signals such as GPS in our work. Reflection does not perform any active sensing and entirely relies on events contributed by applications.

To combine individual prediction features, a number of inference models have been used previously, e.g., a sequential decision process [23] or a Naïve Bayesian model [13, 20]. Typically, these models either need to be predetermined or require a dedicated training phase. In contrast, we designed our learning method based on online passive-aggressive algorithms [4], which can learn from events as they occur.

PROGRAMMING WITH REFLECTION

We here illustrate how mobile developers can enable event prediction in their application using Reflection. Reflection is currently implemented as an Android service, which runs in the background only in response to an application request. Although programming details here are specific to Java and Android, the design of the Reflection system can be generalized beyond the specific programming language and mobile platform we are using.

Assume Ben is developing a Phone Dialer application. To save the user's effort of searching a desired contact, he wants the application to automatically recommend a list of contacts that the user is likely to call when the user opens the app. To do so, Ben first registers his application to use Reflection (see Figure 1). Here appContext is the Java Interface (from the Android SDK) to global information about an application environment—equivalents can be found on other mobile platforms—by which Reflection can perform operations such as invoking a background service (process). Because Reflection runs in a separate background process rather than in the application's own process, all the API calls to Reflection are asynchronous and the return results have to be received through a callback listener.

```
Reflection reflection = new Reflection(appContext);
reflection.register(new RegisterListener() {
  @Override
  public void onRegistered(int key) {
    dialerAppKey = key;
    // Save the key permanently for future communication
    // with Reflection
  }
});
```

Figure 1. Registering an application for using Reflection.

Once registered, the application receives a randomly generated unique integer key, e.g., dialerAppKey. Internally, Reflection creates a prediction model that can be uniquely identified by the key. The application can store the key persistently for future communication with Reflection, for both contributing events and querying for prediction. The key is private to the application such that other applications cannot access the application's event data. Every time the user accesses a contact, such as "Ann", the Phone Dialer application sends an event, e.g., the name of the accessed contact, to Reflection (see Figure 2). In general, an application only sends events that it wants Reflection to predict in the future.

```
reflection.send(dialerAppKey, "Ann", new SendListener() {
  @Override
  public void onEventAdded(int success) {
    if (success == 1) {
      // The event has been successfully added to Reflection
    }
  }
});
```

Figure 2. Sending an application-specific event to Reflection.

Once Reflection receives an event, it updates the prediction model referred by the key in the send request. The developer can add additional semantics to the event using hierarchies, e.g., prefixing "Ann" with "family" delimited by "/" to indicate Ann belongs to the contact group of family members.

```
reflection.send(dialerAppKey, "family / Ann");
```

Reflection extracts multiple sub-events from an event that has hierarchies for updating prediction models. For example, the event "family / Ann" will generate two sub-events: "family / Ann" and "family". The event hierarchy allows Reflection to capture more commonality across events, e.g., "family / Carl" will also generate the "family" sub-event.

```
reflection.query(dialerAppKey, new QueryListener() {
  @Override
  public void onQueryProcessed(List<Prediction> items) {
    // Populate the recent call list with the prediction results
    for (Prediction prediction : items) {
      String contactName = prediction.event;
      float score = prediction.score;
      addItem(contactName, score);
    }
  }
});
```

Figure 3. Querying Reflection for upcoming events.

To show a list of contacts when the user opens the Phone Dialer application, the application queries Reflection for contacts that the user is likely to access (see Figure 3).

Reflection computes a score for each unique event that has been committed by the application, and returns a list of contacts sorted based on their scores in an asynchronous callback listener. The scores can be useful for further inference in the application or more detailed UI optimization, e.g., enlarging items based on their scores for easy acquisition.

Reflection allows an application to use a filter in a query. For example, the following query will only return the sub-events of "family".

```
reflection.query(dialerAppKey, "family/", queryListener);
```

Independently, another mobile developer, Karen, is developing a mobile Ordering application for a pizza restaurant. To better personalize customers' ordering experience, Karen uses Reflection to help optimize dish recommendations. To do so, whenever the user makes an order, the Ordering application sends the order name as an event to Reflection.

```
reflection.send(orderAppKey, "seafood deluxe");
```

The Ordering application can query Reflection for the dishes that the user might want to order at a given time. Reflection captures event patterns both within the same application (e.g., the user might often order "seafood deluxe" with "buffalo wings") and across different applications (e.g., ordering "seafood deluxe" might often co-occur with calling "Ann"). Leveraging cross-application patterns is possible because Reflection receives events from various applications. Each application developer does not have to be aware of interaction behaviors in other applications. All the complexity for capturing event patterns is transparent to developers and they only need to communicate with Reflection via these simple APIs.

THE PREDICTION ENGINE

Our approach for event prediction combines a set of well-behaved primitive predictors, as features, using an online learning method. We first describe each of these primitive event predictors and then discuss how we combine them.

Event Prediction Features

Probabilistic Recency. As mentioned earlier, the recency of an event is a simple but effective indicator for whether the event is going to reoccur. It is easy to update recency rankings of each event by always moving a newly occurred event to the top of a ranking list. Recency has been widely used in the research literature and commercial products such as a recent call list or recently opened files.

However, a recency ranking—the position of an item in the ranking list—does not indicate how likely an event would occur. Because we intend to use recency as a feature that contributes to the final prediction, it is desirable for the numerical value of recency to be proportional to how likely an event would occur. Thus, we derived a power function that outputs the probability of an event, e_i, given its recency ranking, r_i, based on Equation 1. We use e_i to denote the ith event of all unique events in the target application throughout the paper.

$$P(e_i|r_i) = \alpha r_i^{-\beta} \tag{1}$$

where α and β are coefficients that are acquired by fitting a power function over the distribution of recency rankings of a pilot dataset. We chose a power function because empirically we found it fits the recency distribution better than other functions such as exponential functions.

Frequency. Another simple measure that has been widely used is the frequency of visited items, i.e., more frequently used items are more likely to be revisited. Because frequency counts can be widely spread, it is difficult to derive a probability function as we did for recency rankings. Instead, given the frequency count, f_i, of an event, e_i, we acquire a score based on the following procedure for $f_i > 0$ (see Equation 2).

$$P(e_i|f_i) \approx 1 - \frac{1}{f_i} + \epsilon \tag{2}$$

where ϵ is an arbitrarily small positive value. Although the score is not probabilistically justified, it is in a range of 0 to 1 that is comparable with the value range of other features. This property is important for us to weigh these individual features appropriately for yielding the final prediction.

Conjunct Markov Chain. Previous work has shown that the last event, e_l, often signals how likely an event, e_i, is about to occur. Formally, this feature measures the transition probability, $P(e_i|e_l)$, between two adjacent events in the sequence—a first-order Markov chain [16]. The transition probability distribution can be easily updated as each event arrives (see Equation 3). We apply Laplace smoothing here to give unobserved transitions a non-zero probability.

$$P(e_i|e_l) = \frac{|e_l e_i| + dP(e_i)}{|e_l| + d} \tag{3}$$

$|e_l e_i|$ is the number of occurrences of the transition from e_l to e_i, and $|e_l|$ is the number of observations of e_l. $P(e_i)$ is the prior probability of e_i and d is an estimate of the total number of unique events.

A first-order Markov chain only relies on the immediately preceding event, which can be unreliable. However, looking at a longer event sequence in the past—a higher order Markov chain—would require more observations to train and can be sensitive to noise as well. Instead, we can consider all the unique events in the temporal proximity T of the last event as "preceding" events, denoted as E_l^T. We then combine these transitions using Equation 4, which essentially takes the average of the log probabilities of these first-order Markov chains.

$$P(e_i|E_l^T) = \left(\prod_{e_r \in E_l^T} P(e_i|e_r)\right)^{1/|E_l^T|} \tag{4}$$

In our current implementation, we set T to be 0 to only consider the most recent concurring events, e.g., multiple sub-events from an event hierarchy.

Cross-Application Conjunct Markov Chain. In addition to event transitions within a target application, we consider how the last event from other applications predicts the event occurrence in the target application. Leveraging other applications' events allows Reflection to capture more event correlations that can potentially boost the prediction accuracy of each application. The calculation of this feature is similar to Equations 3 and 4 except that E_l^T is the last occurred events in non-target applications. We also want to look at a larger time window T for the past events, i.e., one minute, to be more robust to noise from other applications.

Previous work tends to look at event transitions within a single application behavior, e.g., app launching, without leveraging event transitions outside of the target application. It is worth mentioning that by factorizing Markov chains as two separate features—within and cross-application Markov, we effectively reduce the state space of transition probabilities and address the sparsity of events.

Temporal & Spatial Regularity. Many mobile interaction behaviors have a strong spatiotemporal pattern, e.g., calling someone on weekends or checking emails only at work. Unlike signals such as motion acceleration or GPS locations, time can be acquired for free. In particular, we use the probability for an event to occur in a specific hour of the day, $P(e_i|h_j)$, or on a specific day of the week, $P(e_i|d_j)$. For locations, we use the cell tower ID and its Geo code as a coarse measure of the user's location because it can be easily acquired on a device such as a smartphone. Similar to Markov probabilities, we use Laplace smoothing to give unobserved hours, days, cell tower IDs and Geo codes a non-zero probability.

Poisson. Lastly, we look at the frequency pattern of events—how often an event is supposed to occur in a given time interval based on its expected occurrence frequency. For example, Ben calls Angela about twice a week and these calls can occur on any day of the week. This can be modeled with a Poisson distribution that outputs the probability of a given number of events to occur in a predefined time interval (e.g., a day) (see Equation 5).

$$P(e_i|c_i\lambda_i) = \frac{\lambda_i^{(c_i+1)}e^{-\lambda_i}}{(c_i+1)!} \quad (5)$$

Given that the event, e_i, has occurred in the day c_i times and its expected rate of occurrence for a day, λ_i, Equation 5 computes the probability for the event to occur again. λ_i is incrementally calculated for each day.

We can potentially add more situational factors here, such as GPS locations or motion signals. However, previous work suggested this additional information adds little to overall prediction accuracy, because these dimensions are often correlated with event time that can already be acquired for free. These extra signals may also incur significant battery consumption and computational cost that are undesirable for a mobile infrastructure. In total, we investigate nine features and their combination. These features are Recency, Frequency, Markov, Cross-Markov, Hour, Day, Cell-Tower, Cell-Geo and Poisson.

Combining Features with Online Learning

Each of these features predicts the occurrence of an event based on a specific aspect of event patterns. Intuitively, an event could depend more on some of the features but less on the rest. For example, a user might use Music Player more often at certain hours of the day (Hour), e.g., when she commutes, but visits a stock portfolio website only when her investment advisor calls (Cross-Markov). The occurrence of an event often depends on multiple features.

To generate a prediction score based on multiple features, a typical approach is to linearly combine them with a set of weights. Formally, let us use ϕ_j to refer the jth feature, $1 \leq j \leq 9$, which gives a score for each event at time t, denoted as $\phi_j(t,i)$. By concatenating the outcome of each feature, we acquire a feature vector for e_i at time t, $\Phi(t,i) = (\phi_1(t,i), \cdots, \phi_9(t,i))$. We can score each event based on the dot product of its weight vector, $\boldsymbol{w}_i$, and feature vector $\Phi(t,i)$ (see Equation 6). Events with a higher score are more likely to occur than those with a lower score.

$$Score(e_i, t) = \boldsymbol{w}_i \cdot \Phi(t,i) \quad (6)$$

Note that $\boldsymbol{w}_i$ is specific to each event (as denoted by its subscript) because the dependency on these features is often different from event to event. However, it would be difficult or impossible to determine, in advance, which feature an event relies on and how much it does so. Instead, it is only feasible to learn these weights from event occurrences as user behaviors unfold.

Such a learning task is often framed as online learning in which a prediction engine needs to continuously update itself as event instances are observed in a sequential manner. Probably one of the earliest and most well-known online learning algorithms is Perceptron that updates its weights only when its prediction is inconsistent with an observation [15]. We here use Passive Aggressive algorithms [4], a class of online learning algorithms that enhances Perceptron by applying additional constraints when updating the weights: 1) minimizing the change to the weights so as to be conservative when seeing a single observation, and 2) enforcing a minimum margin between the scores of the target event and the rest events (similar to SVM [3] but only using a single event instance).

Upon receiving each event, we use it as the target event (i.e., a labeled example) and see how our prediction is consistent with it. We update the weight vector of events whose prediction score violates the required minimum margin with respect to the target event's, by increasing the weights of the target event and decreasing the weights of the violated non-target events. Crammer et al. derived a closed form solution for updating the weights of a violated event [4], which we adapted for our situation where both the weight vector and the feature vector vary for each event. Briefly, we denote the index of the target event as r, and the index of a violated non-target event as s, $r \neq s$. We decrease the weights of the violated event e_s according to Equation 7.

$$w_s^{t+1} = w_s^t - \tau^t \Phi(t,s) \quad (7)$$

where $\tau^t = \frac{1-Score(e_r,t)+Score(e_s,t)}{\|\Phi(t,r)\|^2+\|\Phi(t,s)\|^2}$, i.e., the margin between the violated event and the target event divided by the sum of their L2 Norm squares. We increase the weights of the target event, e_r, for the same rate, according to Equation 8.

$$w_r^{t+1} = w_r^t + \tau^t \Phi(t,r) \quad (8)$$

Overall, we see the prediction score for each event is generated independently (Equation 6), but the algorithm calibrates the weights of different events during learning by ensuring the target event's score is sufficiently larger than non-target ones'. Reflection continuously retrains these individual features and refines the feature dependency of each event—the weights—as each event is observed.

IMPLEMENTATION

We implemented Reflection in Java, using Android SDK. The prediction engine of Reflection does not use any Android-specific API calls and is platform independent. Reflection consists of two components: the *service* and the *client library*. The service is implemented as an Android Service running in a separate process in the background. It hosts the prediction engine, by receiving requests from applications and passing them to the prediction engine, and sending responses (results) back to applications. The service exits itself when it processes all the requests. The client library runs in the application's process and implements the asynchronous API calls that we described earlier. The library encapsulates the details for communicating with the service, which is implemented based on Android's Service Binding and the Messenger Handler mechanism. All the computation takes place locally on the device.

EXPERIMENTS

The API of Reflection is straightforward to use as shown in previous examples. We here concentrate on how well Reflection can predict events of interest and how it adapts itself for addressing different types of interaction behaviors. In this experiment, we chose three popular mobile applications as clients of Reflection, i.e., the App *Launcher* (i.e., the Home Screen on Android and iPhone), the Phone *Dialer* and the *Browser*.

Experimental Datasets

We evaluated Reflection with two large-scale sets of in situ event logs: one was collected by us on Android-powered devices and the other was collected from iPhones by prior work [13]. For the Android dataset, we instrumented a logger that runs quietly in the background on an Android device and captures interaction events such as applications being launched, phone call events, web URLs (including search queries) being issued and device status, e.g. docking. All privacy-sensitive information such as phone numbers and web queries were stored locally on the user's device and only their index IDs were collected, e.g., we can identify if two phone calls are made to the same number but cannot recover the number. The logger used a similar approach to previous work for capturing events [1]. We deployed the logger to over one hundred Android participants, and found they used a variety of Android devices including both smartphones and tablets such as Google Nexus devices and the Amazon Kindle Fire.

Filtering Datasets

To simulate the target input of Reflection, namely a series of events contributed by applications, we filtered both the Android and iPhone datasets to only include events of the three applications mentioned. We consider an app usage as an event that Launcher would send to Reflection only if the app usage immediately follows the invocation of Launcher in the collected log trace, which is chronologically stored. In contrast, if an app usage is recorded when a user clicks on the Back button, it is not considered an event from Launcher.

For our analysis, we excluded users who only used their devices occasionally during data collection. In particular, we selected users whose log traces were longer than one month. We also required that each of the three behaviors had at least 20 unique events that occurred during the course of data collection for each user, to ensure a lower bound of event prediction complexity—the more unique events there are the more difficult it is for prediction.

Based on these selection criteria, we acquired the log traces of 57 users from our Android volunteers, which involved 141,196 events generated over one to three months (Median=39 days, Min=33, Max=106). We acquired 478,029 events from 23 iPhone users, which were generated roughly over one year (Median=367 days, Min=279, Max=480).

To understand the complexity of the datasets, we analyzed the number of unique events in each of these behaviors (see Figure 4). There is much variation in the number of unique events per user and per behavior. For the Android dataset, the number of unique apps that a user invoked in Launcher obeys an exponential distribution (Median=47, Min=22, Max=116). Both the number of unique phone calls and the number of unique URLs for each user seem to obey a power law distribution (Dialer: Median=40, Min=20, Max=115, and Browser: Median=40, Min=20, Max=227).

For the iPhone dataset, the medians of the number of unique events for app launching, phone calling and web

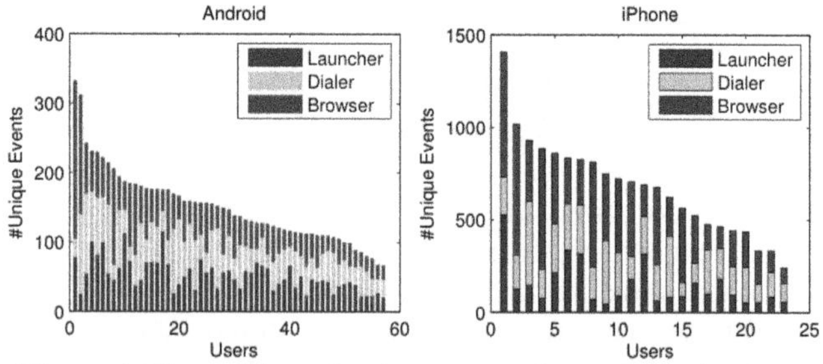

Figure 4. The number of unique events for each application of each user for the Android (Left) and iPhone (Right) dataset.

browsing are 96 (Min=46, Max=527), 189 (Min=73, Max=452) and 257 (Min=83, Max=708), respectively. It is understandable that the iPhone dataset has significantly more unique events per user because it was collected over a much longer time period than the Android dataset.

In addition to the number of unique targets that an event predictor has to choose from, the prediction complexity is also affected by how often an event occurs. Intuitively, the more an event occurs, the better chance a predictor can learn from it. We found the number of occurrences of an event in each target application for each user strongly obeys a power law distribution, with a few events occurring very often and the rest occurring rarely (see Figure 5).

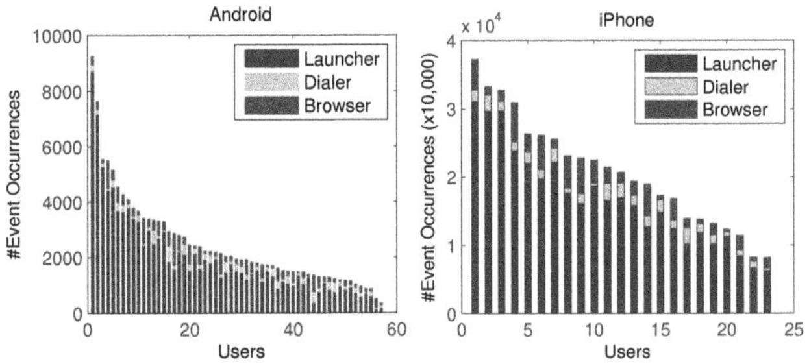

Figure 5. The number of event occurrences in each application of each user for the Android (Left) and iPhone (Right) dataset.

For the Android dataset, the mean length of each user's log trace—the number of events in the trace—is 2,477 events (SD=1,676). In particular, app launches accounted for the dominant portion of a trace (Mean=75%, SD=15%), which is followed by browser events (Mean=15%, SD=12%) and calling events (Mean=10%, SD=7%). For the iPhone dataset, the mean length of each user's log trace is 20,688 events (SD=8,061), and similar to the Android dataset, app usage accounted for the dominant portion of a trace (Mean=80%, SD=7%), followed by browser events (Mean=12%, SD=7%) and calling events (Mean=8%, SD=3%).

Experimental Procedures

Based on the two datasets, we evaluated the performance of each of the nine features as a standalone predictor (referred to as a component predictor) and their combination (referred to as Reflection) as well as in comparison with Naïve Bayesian models.

We fed a prediction method with an event stream (a log trace in a dataset) in an online fashion—event by event. We let the method predict an event if the event has been observed at least once, using the timestamp of the event as the query time. For the iPhone dataset that has Cell information collected, we also used Cell-Tower and Cell-Geo at query time. We record the ranking of the target event to calculate how often it is ranked as the top choice. We then let the prediction method learn from the event, and repeat the process for each event in the stream. Our evaluation methodology is significantly different from prior work that used a dedicated training dataset, e.g., Shin et al. used a *10*-fold cross-validation scheme in their work [20].

Prediction Accuracy

As expected, the accuracy of each prediction method generally increases as more event occurrences are observed (see Figure 6). Reflection consistently outperformed its component predictors across both datasets, which indicated that our combination of these predictors resulted in better accuracy than using each of them alone.

Comparing with Component Predictors

On average, after an app launch event has occurred 40 times, Reflection can predict it as a top guess with 44% accuracy compared to 41% accuracy by Frequency, $\chi^2_1=7.8$, $p<0.01$, the strongest component predictor for Launcher for the Android dataset. We see more significant improvement in several other situations. For example, Reflection improved the Browser behavior prediction for iPhone and Android by 15% and 7% respectively, and the iPhone Dialer prediction by 7%, compared to the strongest component predictor in each of these target behaviors.

The strongest component predictor for each behavior tends to vary. For example, in the iPhone dataset, Markov appears to be the most accurate component predictor for Launcher, which is similar to previous findings [13, 20]. However, Cell-Geo seems to be a strong predictor for Dialer.

Across all the behaviors, Frequency seemed to perform better for the Android dataset than for the iPhone dataset. This is probably because the data collection for the Android dataset was performed over a relatively short duration so the accuracy of frequently occurred events dominates the overall performance. Poisson performed poorly for Launcher and Browser, but seemed to be a useful predictor for Dialer whose events occur more regularly in a given time interval, e.g., the number of calls to someone per day. We also observed that although Recency performed well when there were few event occurrences—especially for Dialer and Browser, its rate of improvement as more events became observed seems noticeably slower than other features or quickly plateaued.

Analyzing the Contribution of the Component Predictors

Additionally, we want to understand how each component predictor contributes to the overall accuracy of Reflection when they are combined and how their weights evolve over time. By analyzing the weight vector of each event that is learned by Reflection, we found the dependency on these features varies from event to event. To give an aggregated analysis of feature dependencies in each application, upon learning from each event occurrence, we averaged the weight vectors across all the events in the application. Here we discuss our analysis for the Android dataset (Figure 7).

Overall, we found that Recency tends to be a dominant feature initially but became less so as more event occurrences were observed, which is consistent when it is used as a standalone predictor. Day and Hour are more useful for Launcher (Figure 7-a) than for Browser prediction (Figure 7-c).

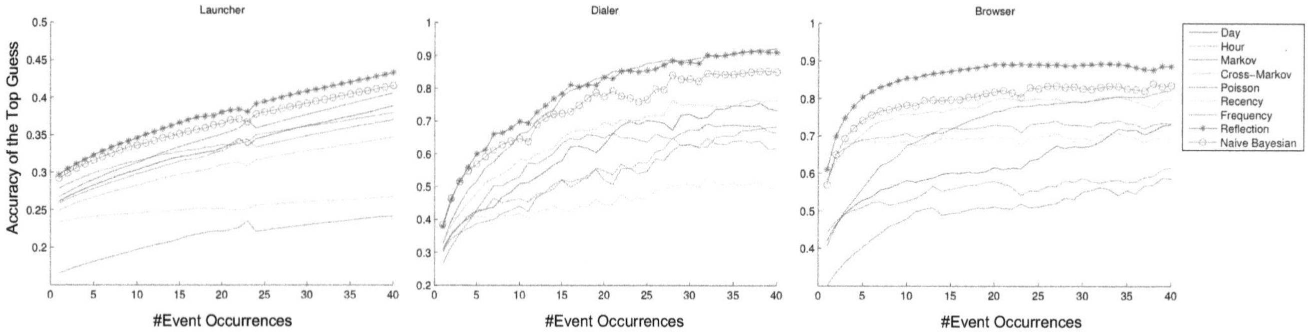

a) The accuracy of each predictor versus the number of occurrences for each event for the Android dataset.

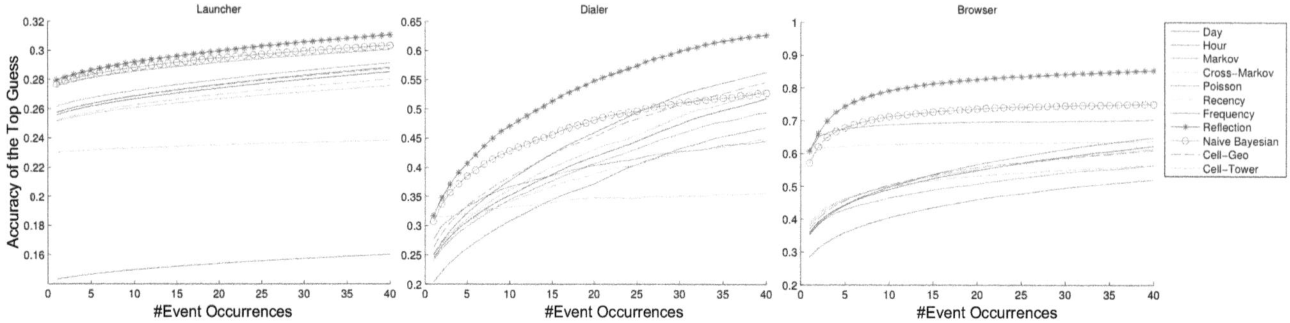

b) The accuracy of each predictor versus the number of occurrences for each event for the iPhone dataset.

Figure 6. The accuracy of each predictor overall increases as more event occurrences are observed. The accuracy is calculated based on how often the top guess of a predictor is correct, after a target event has been observed for a given number of times.

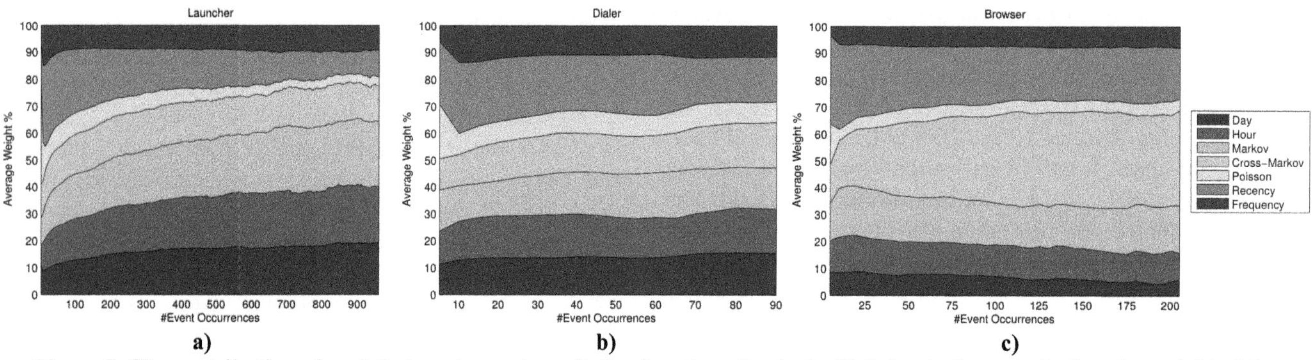

Figure 7. The contribution of each feature to event prediction based on the Android dataset, characterized as the weight of the feature, evolves as events are observed. The weights are normalized and then averaged across all the target events in each behavior.

The contribution of Frequency seems moderate across all the applications, which at a quick glance seems contradictory to our previous analysis in Figure 6. This is because frequently occurred events tend to dominate the overall accuracy in Figure 6-a, while here we are observing how weights are allocated to each feature across events, using normalized weight vectors.

Markov and Cross-Markov are generally useful features across all the application behaviors. In particular, Cross-Markov grew into a dominant feature for predicting Browser behaviors as more occurrences are observed. We analyzed how Reflection behaves with or without Cross-Markov. We found Cross-Markov in many cases improved the performance of Reflection, and it tremendously improved prediction accuracy for Browser.

Finally, Poisson had the lowest prediction power compared to other features although it seemed to be more useful to Dialer than other behaviors. Overall, although each application has several champion features, other features still contributed to the overall performance in a non-trivial way.

Comparing with Naïve Bayesian Models

To gain an understanding of how Reflection performs in comparison with previous methods, we compared Reflection with a Naïve Bayesian model, which has been used in previous work [13, 20]. We explored a variety of feature combinations, and found using many features in a Naïve Bayesian model—that is more vulnerable for overfitting—generally hurts its performance based on our dataset (see Figure 8).

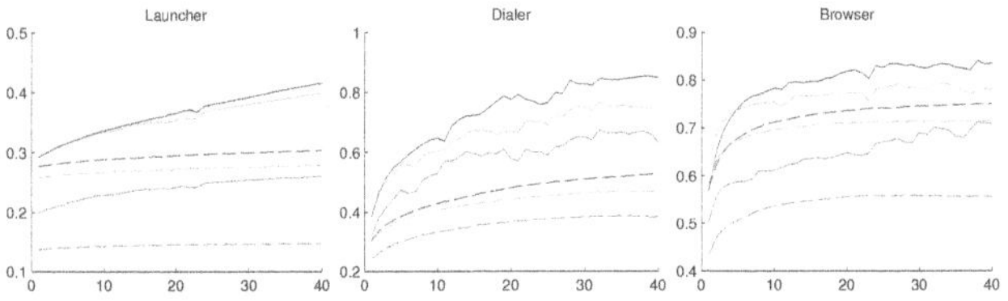

Figure 8. The performance of Naïve Bayesian Models with three different feature combinations: all 9 features (red), 8 features—excluding Poisson (green) and 3 features—Markov+Hour+Cell-Tower (blue), for the Android (solid) and the iPhone (dashed) datasets.

We found a Naïve Bayesian model that uses Markov, Hour and Cell-Tower (the blue plots in Figure 8) gives good overall accuracy across the three behaviors, which has also shown effective in previous work (e.g., [20]). Thus, we compared the performance of this Naïve Bayesian model with Reflection. Overall, Reflection outperformed the Naïve Bayesian model for all the testing conditions across both datasets (see Figure 6).

Although it is difficult to directly compare our results with previously reported results due to different datasets and experimental procedures, these results give a useful understanding of how Reflection behaves in comparison with a Naïve Bayesian approach in an online learning situation. A Naïve Bayesian model assumes conditional independency between features and relies on features giving probability scores, which can be inaccurate especially with limited observations. In contrast, Reflection has little requirements for features and is more flexible in combining them.

TIME PERFORMANCE & BATTERY USAGE

To understand how fast Reflection can predict and learn and how the time cost varies as the complexity increases, we evaluated our current implementation of Reflection on a Google Nexus 5 smartphone, running Android™ 4.4 (KitKat), with a Qualcomm Snapdragon™ 800, 2.26GHz processor. We tested Reflection with 31,077 predictions and training cases on the device.

The overall time complexity for both prediction and learning is linearithmic, $O(N \log N)$, in the number of unique events N. Asymptotically, the expensive part for prediction involves sorting all the events to generate a ranking list while for learning it is sorting the margins between the target and non-target events [18]. However, empirically, we found the most time-consuming component is actually generating the feature vector for each event.

In practice, we can limit the number of possible events for each application. For example, when we chose 100 unique events per application as an upper bound, it took roughly 4ms to either learn from an observation or make a prediction. When we allowed 200 unique events per application—a reasonably large size for many applications, it took about 10ms for either learning or prediction. We can further improve the speed performance by caching featurization results and profiling our implementation. We measured Reflection's energy overhead using a Mosoon power meter. A "query" or "send" request takes about 3 μAh of battery capacity to process and Reflection does not consume battery at other times.

DISCUSSION

Reflection is the first infrastructure that enables event prediction as a general service on mobile devices. We here discuss our findings, limitations and plans for future work.

Cross-Application Markov

A unique design of Reflection is to capture first-order Markov chains of events that occur across different applications as a distinct feature for prediction. Our experiments revealed the non-trivial contribution that Cross-Markov can bring to the overall performance, especially sparsely occurred events such as Browser and Dialer behaviors. Although we can alternatively use event transitions without the distinction of within and cross-application transitions, factorizing event transitions as two separate features allows each of these signals to have many fewer parameters to learn which eases training, and gives Reflection's ensemble predictor the flexibility to weigh each type of transition on its own. Leveraging cross-application event transitions is only feasible in an infrastructure, because it would be impossible for an application to access events of other applications due to security constraints. An important issue to study in the future is how events from obscure applications might affect Cross-Markov. We currently use multiple preceding events from a previous time window (see Equation 4). It is worth investigating how to take into account the applications that issue these events.

Limitations of Our Experiments

We have experimented with Reflection based on three types of behaviors across two popular mobile platforms. We chose these behaviors as target applications mainly because they are typical interaction behaviors on mobile devices. Their logs are easy to collect at a large scale or existing datasets for them are already available. However, our current evaluation has limitations. First, our dataset is an approximation of the three target behaviors. It might miss or over-count certain events due to imperfect logging and filtering mechanisms. Second, our offline evaluation does not examine how prediction ultimately affects users, which is likely affected by application specific factors, e.g. how predictions are presented. We plan to experiment with Reflection for more target behaviors and when it is in use by real applications and users, e.g., suggesting destinations in a Maps application or improving the language model for text entry.

Generality Versus Specificity

As a general infrastructure, Reflection does not assume specific semantics and underlying distributions of target events. In contrast, prior work was largely optimized for its target domain. For example, Shin et al. selected features that are most predictive based on a fixed dataset using an offline feature selection process [20]. Yan et al. used a predefined decision process that performs optimally for predicting app launches [23]. Fitchett and Cockburn combined features based on predetermined coefficients [6]. These approaches would not be feasible for an infrastructure that needs to serve applications whose behaviors can be unexpected. In contrast, Reflection learns the importance of each feature over time, which allows additional features to be easily added. For example, we can add a content-based predictor that predicts based on textual content an application contributes along an event. Because each feature is trained on its own, adding a feature has little impacts on the architecture of the infrastructure.

However, the weakness of Reflection's nature as a general service is the lack of support for leveraging application specific features. High-level event-specific patterns can be tremendously useful for improving prediction accuracy that would otherwise be difficult to learn just from data. For example, temporal bursts have been shown highly useful for predicting app usages such as games [23]. As a first step, we weighed simplicity over comprehensiveness. In future work, we intend to explore support for applications to specify unique event patterns they might have. This is analogous to the general methodology of combining learning with declarative information.

CONCLUSIONS

We presented Reflection, an on-device infrastructure that provides event prediction as a service to mobile applications. We investigated a set of features and their combination based on an online learning framework, which adapts a prediction model to specific interaction behaviors dynamically as events occur. Our experiments based on two datasets indicated that Reflection achieves reasonable accuracy by only relying on application-contributed events, without expensive sensing or knowledge of the underlying distribution of target events.

ACKNOWLEDGMENTS

I would like to thank Samy Bengio and Yoram Singer for their insightful advice on online learning, Zhiwei Guan, Matei Negulescu and Hubert Pham for their generous help, and anonymous reviewers for their useful feedback.

REFERENCES

1. Böhmer, M., Hecht, B., Schöning, J., Krüger, A., and Bauer, G. Falling asleep with Angry Birds, Facebook and Kindle: a large scale study on mobile application usage. MobileHCI'11. 47-56.
2. Bridle, R. and McCreath, E. Inducing shortcuts on a mobile phone interface. IUI'06. 327-329.
3. Cortes, C. and Vapnik, V., *Support-Vector Networks.* Mach. Learn., 1995. **20**(3): 273-297.
4. Crammer, K., Dekel, O., Keshet, J., Shalev-Shwartz, S., and Singer, Y., *Online Passive-Aggressive Algorithms.* The Journal of Machine Learning Research, 2006: 551-585.
5. Dey, A.K., Salber, D., and Abowd, G.D., *A Conceptual Framework and a Toolkit for Supporting the Rapid Prototyping of Context-Aware Applications.* Human-Computer Interaction, 2001. **16**(2-3): 97-166.
6. Fitchett, S. and Cockburn, A. AccessRank: predicting what users will do next. CHI'12. 2239-2242.
7. Fitchett, S., Cockburn, A., and Gutwin, C. Improving navigation-based file retrieval. CHI'13. 2329-2338.
8. Fukazawa, Y., Hara, M., Onogi, M., and Ueno, H. Automatic mobile menu customization based on user operation history. MobileHCI'09. 1-4.
9. Hong, J.I. and Landay, J.A. An Architecture for Privacy-Sensitive Ubiquitous Computing. Mobisys'04. 177-189.
10. Lee, H., Choi, Y.S., and Kim, Y.-J., *An adaptive user interface based on spatiotemporal structure learning, IEEE Communications,* 2011. 118-124.
11. Lee, S., Seo, J., and Lee, G. An adaptive speed-call list algorithm and its evaluation with ESM. CHI'10.2019-2022.
12. Parate, A., Böhmer, M., Chu, D., Ganesan, D., and Marlin, B.M. Practical prediction and prefetch for faster access to applications on mobile phones. Ubicomp'13. 275-284.
13. Rahmati, A., Shepard, C., Tossell, C., Kortum, P., and Zhong, L., *Practical context awareness: measuring and utilizing the context dependency of mobile usage*, in *Technical Report 2012-08-31*2012, Rice University.
14. Rattenbury, T. and Canny, J. CAAD: An Automatic Task Support System. CHI'07. 687-696.
15. Rosenblatt, F., *The Perceptron--a perceiving and recognizing automaton*, 1957, Cornell Aeronautical Lab.
16. Russell, S. and Norvig, P., *Artificial Intelligence: A Modern Approach*. 2 ed. 2003.
17. Sears, A. and Shneiderman, B., *Split menus: effectively using selection frequency to organize menus.* TOCHI, 1994. **1**(1): 27-51.
18. Shalev-Shwartz, S. and Singer, Y., *Efficient Learning of Label Ranking by Soft Projections onto Polyhedra.* J. Mach. Learn. Res., 2006. **7**: 1567-1599.
19. Shepard, C., Rahmati, A., Tossell, C., Zhong, L., and Kortum, P., *LiveLab: measuring wireless networks and smartphone users in the field.* SIGMETRICS Perform. Eval. Rev., 2011. **38**(3): 15-20.
20. Shin, C., Hong, J.-H., and Dey, A.K. Understanding and prediction of mobile application usage for smart phones. UbiComp'12. 173-182.
21. Vetek, A., Flanagan, J.A., Colley, A., and Keränen, T. SmartActions: Context-Aware Mobile Phone Shortcuts. INTERACT'09. 796-799.
22. Weld, D.S., Anderson, C., Domingos, P., Etzioni, O., Gajos, K., Lau, T., and Wolfman, S. Automatically personalizing user interfaces. IJCAI'03. 1613-1619.
23. Yan, T., Chu, D., Ganesan, D., Kansal, A., and Liu, J. Fast app launching for mobile devices using predictive user context. MobiSys'12. 113-126.
24. Zhuang, J., Mei, T., Hoi, S.C.H., Xu, Y.-Q., and Li, S. When recommendation meets mobile: contextual and personalized recommendation on the go. Ubicomp'11. 153-162.

Humane Representation of Thought: A Trail Map for the 21ST Century

Bret Victor
worrydream.com
bret@worrydream.com

ABSTRACT

New representations of thought — written language, mathematical notation, information graphics, etc — have been responsible for some of the most significant leaps in the progress of civilization, by expanding humanity's collectively-thinkable territory.

But at debilitating cost. These representations, having been invented for static media such as paper, tap into a small subset of human capabilities and neglect the rest. Knowledge work means sitting at a desk, interpreting and manipulating symbols. The human body is reduced to an eye staring at tiny rectangles and fingers on a pen or keyboard.

Like any severely unbalanced way of living, this is crippling to mind and body. But less obviously, and more importantly, it is enormously wasteful of the vast human potential. Human beings naturally have many powerful modes of thinking and understanding. Most are incompatible with static media. In a culture that has contorted itself around the limitations of marks on paper, these modes are undeveloped, unrecognized, or scorned.

We are now seeing the start of a dynamic medium. To a large extent, people today are using this medium merely to emulate and extend static representations from the era of paper, and to further constrain the ways in which the human body can interact with external representations of thought.

But the dynamic medium offers the opportunity to deliberately invent *a humane and empowering form of knowledge work.* We can design dynamic representations which draw on the entire range of human capabilities — all senses, all forms of movement, all forms of understanding — instead of straining a few and atrophying the rest.

This talk suggests how each of the human activities in which thought is externalized (conversing, presenting, reading, writing, etc) can be redesigned around such representations.

Author Keywords

Dynamic representations

ACM Classification Keywords

H.5.0 [Information Interfaces and Presentation]: General

BIO

Bret Victor has designed experimental UI concepts at Apple, interactive data graphics for Al Gore, and musical instruments at Alesis. He's responsible for "Inventing on Principle", "Learnable Programming", "Media for Thinking the Unthinkable", "Up and Down the Ladder of Abstraction", and everything else at worrydream.com. He holds a BSEE from Caltech and MSEE from UC Berkeley.

UIST'14, October 5-8, 2014, Honolulu, HI, USA.
ACM 978-1-4503-3069-5/14/10.
http://dx.doi.org/10.1145/2642918.2642920

Author Index

www.ingramcontent.com/pod-product-compliance
Ingram Content Group UK Ltd.
Pitfield, Milton Keynes, MK11 3LW, UK
UKHW051420290926
15471UKWH00009B/1694

9 781450 333702